FIGHTERS OVER ISRAEL

FIGHTERS OVER ISRAEL

LON NORDEEN

ILLUSTRATIONS BY KEN KOTIK

GUILD PUBLISHING
LONDON · NEW YORK · SYDNEY · TORONTO

This edition published 1991
by Guild Publishing
by arrangement with Greenhill Books,
Lionel Leventhal Limited

This edition published by arrangement with Orion Books,
a division of Crown Publishers, Inc.

CN 1037

Design by Jake Victor Thomas

Printed in Great Britain by
Butler & Tanner Limited, Frome, Somerset.

Contents

Acknowledgments vii

Maps ix

Introduction 1

1 War of Independence 4

2 The Early Years 26

3 The Sinai Conflict 35

4 Modernization 53

5 The Six-Day War 66

6 War of Attrition 88

7 The Yom Kippur War 117

8 Unending Conflict 149

Appendix 189

Notes 203

Index 215

Acknowledgments

I would like to thank the following people who provided research material, photographs, and other assistance: Keith Schirmer; Michael Manahan and Priut Design; Rudy Augerten; Col. Elizer Cohen (Ret.); Lt. Col. S. Gilboa (Ret.); Lt. Col. Nori Harel (Ret.); Aharon Lapidot, editor, *Israel Air Force Magazine*; Lou Lenard; Col. N. Merchavi (Ret.); Lt. Col. Y. Offer (Ret.); Maj. Gen. Benjamin Peled (Ret.); Brig. Gen. Joshua Shani (Ret.); Col. Yallo Shavit (Ret.); Lt. Hila Yafat; Col. Aharon Yoeli (Ret.); Amir Yoeli; and many other Israel Air Force personnel who cannot be named.

Yigal and Nurit Berman were very kind and helpful, while Shirley King deserves special mention for her assistance.

Most of all, Suzy and Brad, thank you for being so patient and understanding.

Lon Nordeen

I would like to thank Dot and Erin for their sacrifice and understanding; my mother and father for teaching through example and value of hard work; and Bob Pukala, John Brooks, and Robert (Beaver) Blake for research materials used in the preparation of the illustrations.

Ken Kotik

Israel's Changing Borders

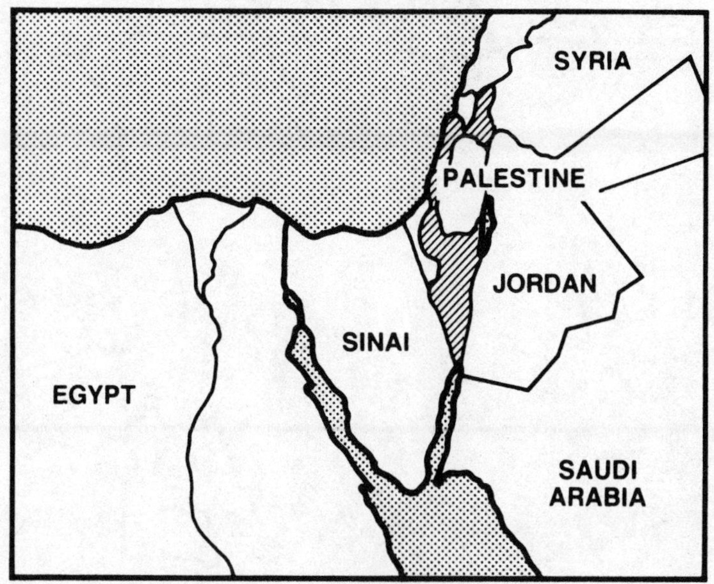
SYRIA
PALESTINE
JORDAN
SINAI
EGYPT
SAUDI
ARABIA

1947 U.N. PARTITION

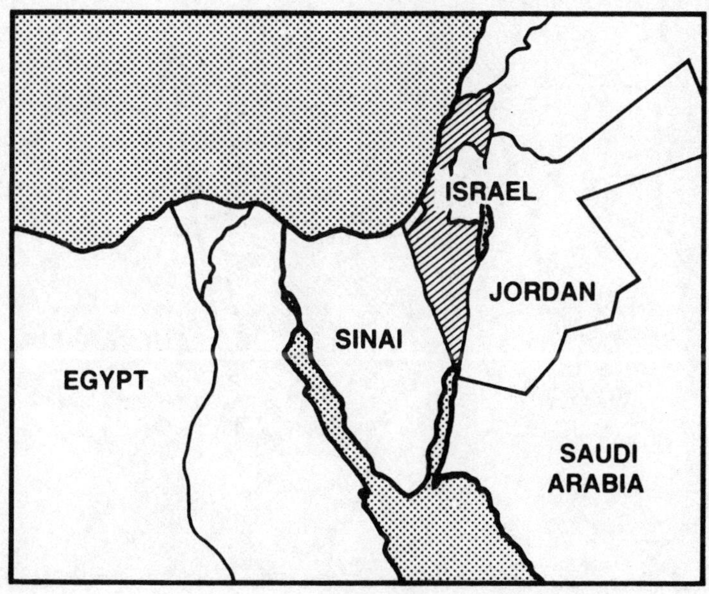
ISRAEL
JORDAN
SINAI
EGYPT
SAUDI
ARABIA

1949 ISRAELI–ARAB
ARMISTICE LINES

Operation Kadesh
1956 Conflict

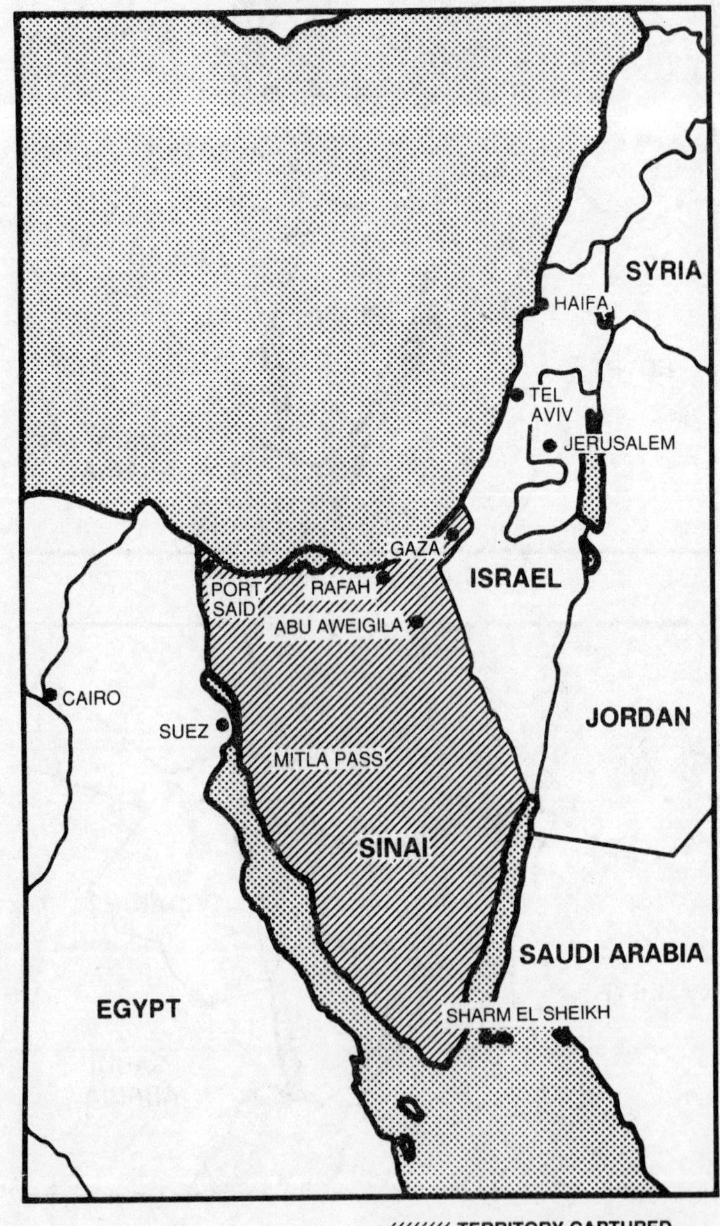

SYRIA
HAIFA
TEL AVIV
JERUSALEM
GAZA
ISRAEL
PORT SAID
RAFAH
ABU AWEIGILA
CAIRO
JORDAN
SUEZ
MITLA PASS
SINAI
SAUDI ARABIA
EGYPT
SHARM EL SHEIKH
TERRITORY CAPTURED DURING THE 1956 CONFLICT

1967 Arab Israeli War

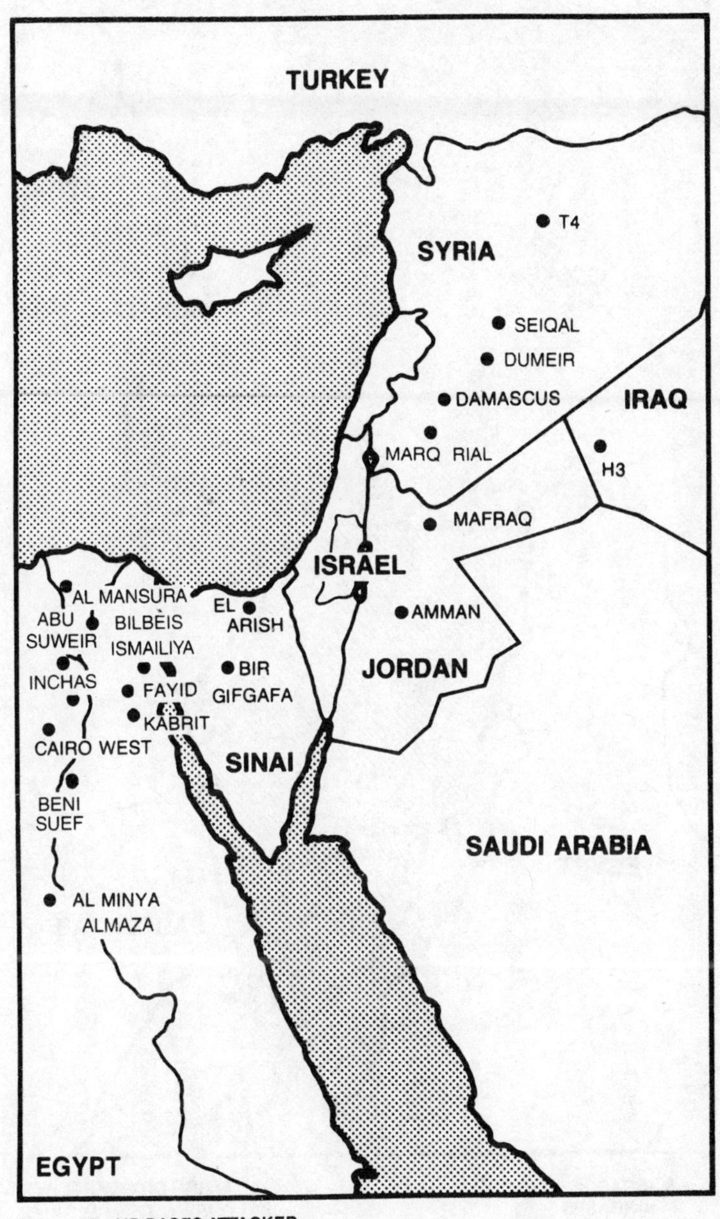

TURKEY
SYRIA
T4
SEIQAL
DUMEIR
DAMASCUS
IRAQ
MARQ RIAL
H3
MAFRAQ
ISRAEL
AL MANSURA
ABU SUWEIR
BILBEIS
ISMAILIYA
EL ARISH
AMMAN
INCHAS
FAYID
BIR GIFGAFA
JORDAN
KABRIT
CAIRO WEST
SINAI
BENI SUEF
SAUDI ARABIA
AL MINYA
ALMAZA
EGYPT
AIR BASES ATTACKED BY IAF IN 1967

Israel and Occupied Lands

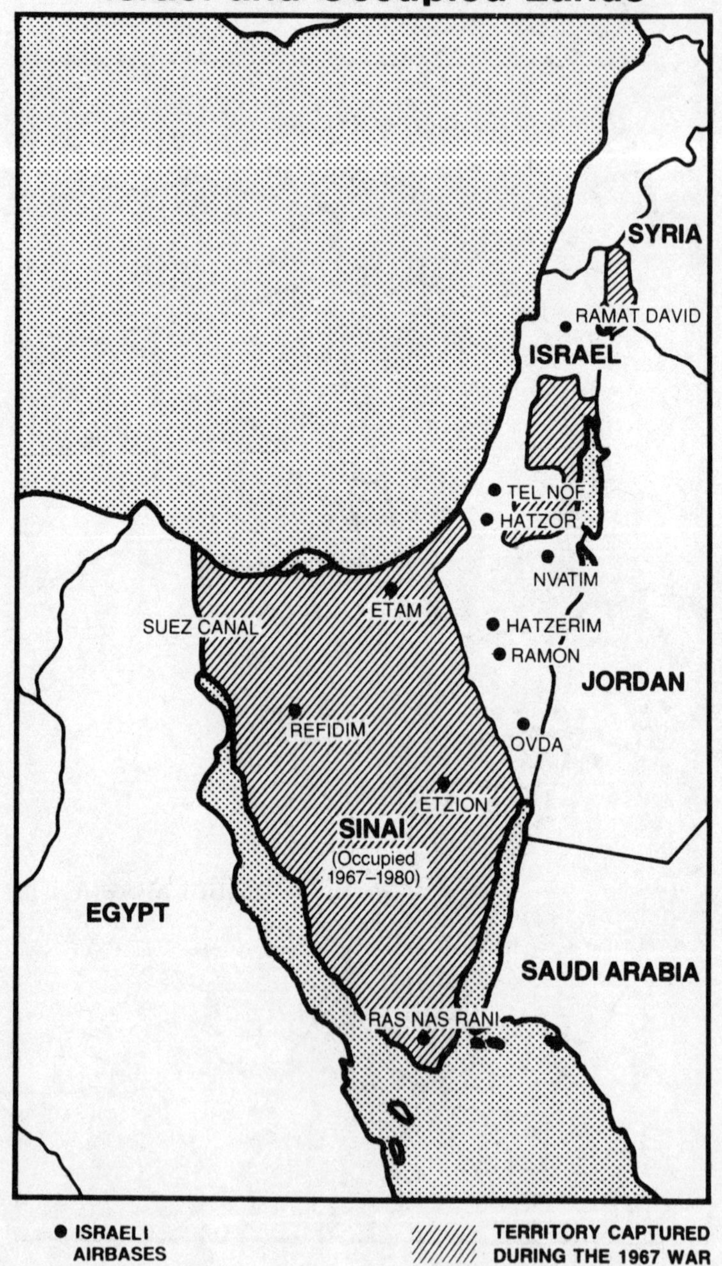
SYRIA
RAMAT DAVID
ISRAEL
TEL NOF
HATZOR
NVATIM
ETAM
SUEZ CANAL
HATZERIM
RAMON
JORDAN
REFIDIM
OVDA
ETZION
SINAI
(Occupied
1967–1980)
EGYPT
SAUDI ARABIA
RAS NAS RANI
ISRAELI
AIRBASES
TERRITORY CAPTURED
DURING THE 1967 WAR

The Entebbe Rescue Mission

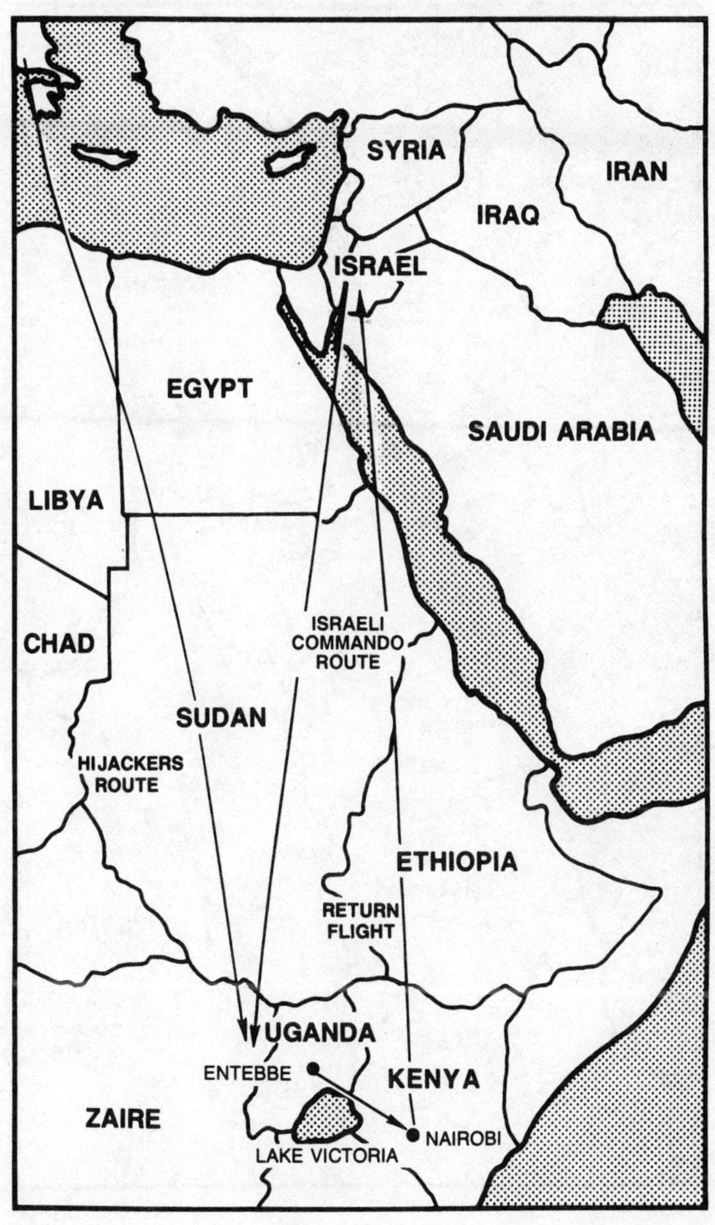
SYRIA
IRAN
IRAQ
ISRAEL
EGYPT
SAUDI ARABIA
LIBYA
ISRAELI
COMMANDO
ROUTE
CHAD
SUDAN
HIJACKERS
ROUTE
ETHIOPIA
RETURN
FLIGHT
UGANDA
ENTEBBE
KENYA
ZAIRE
NAIROBI
LAKE VICTORIA

IAF Operations in Lebanon

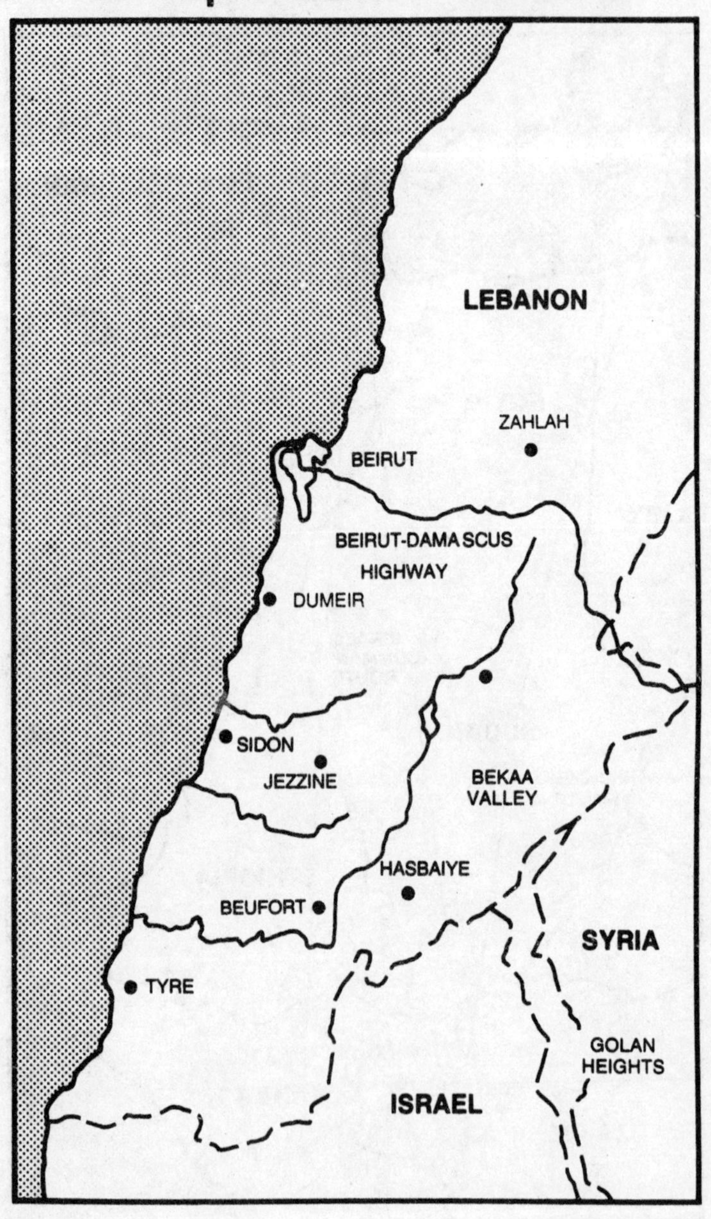

LEBANON
ZAHLAH
BEIRUT
BEIRUT-DAMASCUS
HIGHWAY
DUMEIR
SIDON
JEZZINE
BEKAA
VALLEY
HASBAIYE
BEUFORT
SYRIA
TYRE
GOLAN
HEIGHTS
ISRAEL

Introduction

Israel is a small nation surrounded by neighbors who have tried to destroy it since its birth on May 15, 1948. Arab neighbors regard the land on which Israel stands as theirs, unjustly taken from them by the British. Arab forces have repeatedly tried to undermine the Jewish state through overt hostile actions as well as through more subtle efforts. During the four plus decades that have elapsed since the creation of Israel, its citizens have fought four major wars (1948, 1956, 1967, 1973), several significant conflicts (including the War of Attrition, Operation Litani, and Operation Peace for Galilee in Lebanon), and thousands of local battles and terrorist engagements. The Israeli Air Force has played a major role in most of these military actions.

Outnumbered and surrounded by hostile Arab nations, Israel has from its inception had a critical need to develop its air force. The very day Israel's independence was declared, Arab planes bombed Tel Aviv. Even in the days of propeller-driven aircraft, Tel Aviv and other major Israeli cities were less than fifteen minutes flying time from airfields in Egypt, Jordan, and Syria. In early 1948 Israel's air fleet consisted of only two dozen light, civilian planes. Shortly after it became a nation, the air force was upgraded and by 1949 grew to over one hundred transports, fighters, and bombers. The founders of the Israeli Air Force (IAF) did not have a defensive mentality: the first fighter missions flown by the air arm on May 29, 1948, attacked an advancing Egyptian column.

Since Israel must fight outnumbered, it relies on the IAF and reserve forces to even the odds. In a conflict, the IAF is charged with defending the skies so reserve forces can mobilize. Destruction of enemy air forces on the ground, as in the 1967 war, is one way to achieve air superiority. Once air superiority is achieved, the IAF concentrates on providing support for Israeli ground and naval forces with fighter sweeps, close air support, strikes against enemy troops well behind the battle area, supply drops, casualty evacuation, scouting, air defense, and many other missions.

From its humble beginning in 1947 when the air arm comprised less than twenty worn-out light aircraft, the IAF has developed into one of the most experienced and respected air forces in the world. Israel, a country with a population of only four million, today fields an air force comparable in size to that of such major powers as Britain, France, and West Germany. In terms of experience, the IAF can match even the much larger air forces of the United States and the Soviet Union. During the past twenty-five years the IAF has claimed more than five hundred air-to-air victories against first-line Soviet-built jet fighters, flown hundreds of thousands of combat sorties, and successfully battled the densest collection of air defense weaponry ever deployed.

To upgrade the effectiveness of their forces, many countries have sought to learn the IAF's secrets of success. Israel in general and the IAF in particular are among the most security-conscious groups in the world. Despite mountains of press, accurate information on the IAF's history, structure, development, doctrine, tactics, and equipment is limited. More than a decade of research has gone into the production of this work. The author and illustrator have reviewed volumes of information on the IAF and interviewed dozens of people—including those who have served with the force and its former opponents—in search of historical information.

Our research has led us to the conclusion that people are the real secret weapon of the IAF. Recruiting concepts, such as The Good Ones Fly, have attracted the best and brightest Israeli youth to the IAF. Screening, testing, and training procedures developed over several decades along with the rigors of almost continuous combat have produced pilots, navigators, and other aircrew who are second to none. The Israelis fly their planes aggressively, and training standards are high. During the past four decades, dozens of IAF aircraft and numerous aircrew have been lost in operational accidents during realistic training. Despite these losses the IAF has continued to train aggressively following the old Roman proverb which states that, "The more you sweat in peace, the less you will bleed in war." The same tough screening and training standards have been applied to the mechanics, weapons loaders, air defense gunners, intelligence staffs, and other personnel who make up the IAF. *Fighters Over Israel* tells the story of this dynamic air force and how it accomplished the task that needed to be done.

1

War of Independence

The creation of the Israeli Air Force was a natural outgrowth of Jewish efforts to form self-defense military organizations. An air service equipped with light civilian airplanes was formed in late 1947. With the birth of Israel in 1948, this air service became part of the new Israeli military.

In 1917, the year the British took control of Palestine, approximately 85,000 Jews lived in the area. In exchange for Jewish support during World War I, Britian backed the creation of a Jewish homeland, thus opening the way for the immigration of Jews to Palestine.[1]

As Jewish immigration increased, so did the anxieties of Palestinian Arabs. The Palestinans thought the influx of Jews would threaten their rights to the land. The popular Muslim Mufti of Jerusalem, Haj Amin el Husseini, called for Arabs to resist the Jews. Disturbances between the two cultures increased and large-scale anti-Jewish riots occurred in Palestine in 1922, 1929, and 1936.

To protect themselves from persecution, Jewish community leaders established a number of defense organizations. In the 1920s the Jews established militia units collectively known as the *Haganah* (Defense) to protect Jewish settlements. In the face of continued violence, some Jews favored a more aggressive approach. The Irgun Zvai Leumi (National Military Organization), headed by Menachem Begin and Lohamei Herut Yisrael (Fighters For Israel and Freedom) struck back against the Arabs and attacked British targets.[2]

The British government attempted to smooth relations in Palestine and moved toward a policy designed to separate Arabs and Jews. The 1937 Peel Commission report concluded that it would be advisable to partition Palestine along ethnic lines: Transjordan for the Arabs, a new Jewish state, and an independent Jerusalem.

The MacDonald White Paper, released by the British government in May 1939, set tight limits on Jewish immigration. These restrictions angered the Jews and prompted members of some of the more violent Jewish military groups to strike out against the British. However, the five hundred thousands Jews in Palestine supported the British once World War II broke out in September 1939. More than forty thousand Jewish volunteers from Palestine served with British and Commonwealth forces during the war. Many Jews fought in combat, some served as members of ground crews in aviation support units, and a small number flew as pilots with the Royal Air Force (RAF) or Commonwealth air arms.

In November 1945, Ernest Bevin, the foreign secretary, announced that Britain planned to continue to follow the Jewish immigration limits established in 1939. Despite worldwide pressure to allow Holocaust victims to settle in Palestine after World War II, British forces turned back refugee ships. In response to these policies, the Jews united in action against the British. The Haganah and other military groups openly clashed with the British troops that garrisoned Palestine, while the Jewish community smuggled in thousands of illegal immigrants.

The British declared martial law and fought back against Jewish terrorism, but their determination soon faded. In February 1947, Bevin referred the "Palestine problem" to the United Nations.[3] He also announced that Britain would withdraw its forces from Palestine by mid-1948. Expecting to have to fight, Jewish community leaders began importing arms and organizing a military force for self defense.

The first Jewish effort to organize an air force took place on November 10, 1947, when military leaders formed the Haganah Sherut-Avir (Air Service). Yehoshua Eshel was named head of this new unit and Aharon Remez appointed chief of operations. A fighter pilot who flew with the RAF during World War II, Remez controlled the day-to-day operations and worked hard to expand the capabilities of the air service.

The Jews faced two major challenges in establishing an air force: finding planes and recruiting pilots. The air service initially had a complement of eleven single-engine light aircraft of the following types: Tiger Moth, R.W.D.-13, Zlin, Taylorcraft, Auster, Seabee, and Rapide.[4] Soon two Taylorcraft and six Auster Autocraft light airplanes were added to this fleet.

In January 1948, Aviron, a Jewish-owned, import company purchased the scrapped hulks of twenty-five Auster light observation aircraft from the British. The Auster was the standard British army artillery observation and liaison aircraft during World War II. The three-seat, high-wing craft could take off from short strips and carry a payload in excess of five hundred pounds.[5] By combining the parts of these surplus hulks, air service maintenance personnel produced six serviceable aircraft. These ex–British Army Austers and civilian light planes constituted the bulk of Israel's air arm until well into 1948. These aircraft were frequently the only link to outlying Jewish villages. In addition to undertaking resupply and reconnaissance missions, air service pilots fired rifles and machine guns and dropped homemade bombs on Arab forces.

Finding pilots to fly the air service planes was difficult; about forty Jewish pilots served initially. Some of these pilots had earned their wings through civilian flying clubs, while others had been trained to fly military aircraft by the RAF and Commonwealth air forces during World War II. The Haganah also used its worldwide network of contacts to recruit foreign pilots.

In November 1947, a UN commission recommended the establishment of separate Arab and Jewish states in Palestine with Jerusalem governed by a UN-sponsored international trusteeship. The plan was ratified by a UN vote on November 29, 1947.

In Palestine, fighting began almost immediately as Arabs and Jews struggled over important settlements, rail centers, and roads. During the first six months of the War of Independence (November 1947–April 1948), Jewish forces were on the defensive. The Haganah was busy organizing combat units and acquiring weapons from British depots and sources overseas. Jewish forces incurred heavy losses while trying to resupply outlying settlements. It was not until the second phase of the war (April–May 1948) that Jewish units conducted several successful offensives. The State of Israel was established on May 15, 1948.

Struggling to establish a homeland, the Jews faced powerful Arab armies. King Farouk's Egyptian Army totaled fifty-five thousand men, plus armor and artillery. The Royal Egyptian Air Force (REAF) included about forty Spitfire fighters, ten C-47 Dakota aircraft modified to carry bombs, twenty Dakota transports, and an assortment of trainer and liaison aircraft.

King Abdullah of Transjordan had one of the most effective armies in the Middle East. This Arab Legion consisted of approximately eight thousand men trained and led by British officers, with armor and artillery support, but no air force.

The eight-thousand strong Syrian army had been trained by the French and included a small element of tanks and self-propelled artillery. The Syrian air component included Harvard trainers that could carry light bombs and machine guns. The smaller four-thousand-man Lebanese army, which shared a heritage of French training and equipment, was also poised to attack Israel.

Iraq was likewise committed to preventing the creation of an independent Jewish State of Israel. The country's twenty-one-thousand-man, British-trained army was well equipped with tanks, armored cars, artillery, and aircraft. The Arab Liberation Army and Arab Home Guard troops were already fighting Jewish forces in Palestine and looked forward to support from neighboring armies.[6]

Arab invasion forces totaled about thirty thousand men with limited armor, artillery, and air support. These forces had significant advantages over Israel in both manpower and equipment, and they could attack the new nation from several directions simultaneously. However, poor communications and rivalries among Arab leaders and army commanders made it difficult to coordinate the actions of the various Arab armies. Morale was another Arab weakness; while Egyptian, Syrian, Lebanese, and other Arab troops were invading Palestine, Jewish soldiers were defending their homes. The Jews could field a force of nearly forty thousand but had weapons for less than half that number and no tanks, fighter aircraft, artillery, or heavy ordinance.[7]

David Ben Gurion, chairman of the Jewish Agency, predicted a long and bloody war would be waged to establish the state of Israel. He believed that Israel would have to fight back several Arab invasions. At a meeting of the Napoi (Labor) party in Tel Aviv in August 1947, Ben Gurion stated that the Haganah would have to "obtain heavy arms: tanks, artillery, halftracks and heavy munitions for the ground units, fighter planes for the foundation of an air force, torpedo boats and even submarines for the Navy."[8] Jewish military leaders were slow to respond, but Ben Gurion began sending agents overseas to buy weapons. In 1945 Ben Gurion had visited the United States and opened communications with Jewish leaders to raise money and secure the necessary equipment.

Yehuda Arazi was sent to New York late in 1947 to acquire aircraft and heavy weapons for the Haganah. Arazi and his associates had a difficult task: Although public opinion favored the Jewish cause, on December 5, 1947, the U.S. government announced a total embargo on arms shipments to the Middle East. Despite intense lobbying by the Jewish agency and pro-Zionist groups, the embargo was maintained.

In late 1947 Adolf (Al) W. Schwimmer, an experienced U.S. Army Air Corps crewman and TWA flight engineer, contacted Shlomo Shamir, the Haganah officer in New York, about a plan to airlift Jewish refugees into Palestine. Arazi agreed to support Schwimmer's plan, provided that aircraft could be acquired quickly. The Schwimmer Aviation Company was hastily established and a maintenance base set up at the Burbank, California, airport. The company bought ten C-46 Commando twin-engine transports and three four-engine Constellation long-range transports from war surplus stocks and reconditioned them at Burbank.[9] Schwimmer also recruited aircrews and maintenance technicians with valuable wartime experience to maintain and fly these aircraft.

The first C-46 left Teterboro, New Jersey, on March 6, 1948, for the long flight to Palestine. Flying the same route traveled by thousands of World War II transports, the C-46 stopped at Labrador, Greenland, Iceland, Ireland, and then Geneva, where the discovery of several pistols by Swiss customs led to long delays. The transport finally arrived in Palestine on May 3, 1948.

Because of U.S. restrictions on exports of aircraft, all of Schwimmer's aircraft were given Panamanian civil registration certificates. Five transports left Panama on May 8, 1948, and headed across South America, the Atlantic, and Africa to the Middle East. It was not until May 16 that the aircraft reached Israel.

Czechoslovakia was looking for foreign currency and was willing to sell arms to any country that could pay in secure Western money. The Czechs had sold rifles, machine guns, and ammunition to Syria, and arranged transport by ship. When Jewish agents reproached Czech officials for the Syrian arms deal, they were told that the sale was simply a commercial transaction and that the Czechs were also willing to sell to the Haganah.

In early 1948, Jewish leaders took the Czechs up on their offer. A DC-4 transport of Overseas Airways, a U.S. firm, left Czechoslovakia on March 31, 1948, bound for an abandoned British air base in Palestine. The aircraft carried a cargo of two hundred rifles, forty machine guns, and ammunition, all of which were distributed to Jewish troops. Although several other supply runs were completed, U.S. authorities in Prague soon put a stop to the airlift, which used U.S.-licensed carriers.

On April 23, 1948, Czechoslovakia agreed to sell ten Avia S199 fighters and provide pilot training to the Jews.[10] Disassembled and in crates, the first Avia was flown out of Zatec, Czechoslovakia, on May 20, only five days after the establishment of the State of Israel. Al Schwimmer's C-46 transports flew a relay between Czechoslovakia and Israel carrying disassembled fighter aircraft and other weapons.

The Avia S199 was not a popular aircraft, but at least it was a fighter that could counter the Egyptian Spitfires on more or less equal terms. At the end of World War II, the Avia aircraft works in Czechoslovakia was producing Messerschmitt bf 109 fighters. When the plane's Daimler Benz 605 engines were no longer available from Germany, Czech engineers substituted the 1350-horsepower Junkers Jumo 211F.

This engine was not an ideal replacement, but it was the only power plant available. The Czechs fitted this engine to the rapidly expanding backlog of airframes coming off their assembly line. The Jumo engine, with its high torque, accentuated the bf 109 fighter's poor takeoff and landing characteristics. The S199 was nicknamed the Mezec, or mule, by Czech pilots.[11]

Czech, Israeli, and Jewish volunteer mechanics reassembled the Avias upon their arrival in Israel. On May 29, 1948, the first four were turned over to the newly commissioned 101st Fighter Squadron, which was based at Eqron near Tel Aviv.[12] Of the five pilots who could fly the Avias, two were Israelis—squadron commander Modi Alon and Ezer Weizman—and three were foreign volunteers, Eddie Cohen from South Africa, and Cy Rubenfield and Lou Lenart, both from the United States.

With the establishment of the State of Israel, the war predicted by Ben Gurion became a reality. Syria and Iraq advanced from the north, Egypt attached from the south, and the Arab Legion invaded Jerusalem. Checking these attacks came at considerable cost to the Israelis, who suffered hundreds of casualties and had to evacuate a number of kibbutzim and towns, including the old city of Jerusalem. Egyptian Spitfires attacked the new nation on its first day as an independent state. In the ensuing weeks, Dakota bombers, escorted by Spitfires, roamed over Israel at will. During one raid, Egyptian bombers hit the central Tel Aviv bus station, killing more than forty people and wounding more than one hundred.

With the founding of Israel, Yisrael Amiv took over the IAF, which was composed of three squadrons, some twenty operational planes and thirty-eight pilots. Amiv's tenure lasted only several weeks and, in late May, Aharon Remez was promoted to commander in chief of the IAF.

Israel's small fleet of light aircraft did what it could to help in the fighting. The existing force had been divided into three squadrons: the Galilee stationed at Yavnell, the Tel Aviv located at Sde Dov, and the Negev based at Dorot and Niram. Often the light planes performed attack missions using hand-dropped bombs and machine guns. One Jewish pilot, known simply as Pinchas, described how he readied his Auster for an attack:

> I asked the settlers to get me a machine gunner. One of the boys of the village offered to be my machine gunner. I took on a load of grenades. Then I ripped off both doors of my plane to give my gunner, whom I strapped into his seat, room to maneuver. I set up the gun so the propellers would not interfere with its action. Then we took off. A few minutes later we were flying over the Nvatim region where the Arab bands were attacking. We opened fire with great success; before long the enemy was in flight.[13]

These nuisance raiders had little impact on the course of battle but continued to chip away at the morale of the enemy.

Lou Lenart, an American pilot who flew some of the first fighter missions of the Israel Air Force, described the events:

> We knew the Egyptians had over forty aircraft, mostly Spitfire fighters. We also knew that at the beginning we had only four aircraft . . . what could we do to have an impact?
>
> We got to Israel along with the aircraft, and the mechanics worked to reassemble the fighters inside two hangars. As luck would have it, one day the Egyptians bombed the other hangar, the one which did not contain our planes, but several people were killed. We worked feverishly to get the planes together to commit them as soon as possible. The plan was to attack El Arish at first light as soon as we were ready. The first flight was to be a test flight and a combat mission at the same time. However, at about five o'clock in the evening on May twenty-ninth the commander of the Givati Brigade came up. They had blown the bridge at Isdud—and they were desperate because between the Egyptian army of ten thousand men with several hundred vehicles and Tel Aviv stood only about 250 Israeli soldiers. The Egyptians were so confident of victory that they were lined up bumper to bumper behind the bridge. We were told that it was a matter of life and death that we fly *right now.* I wasn't sure where Isdud was—I had only been in the country a few days, but I knew it was very close.
>
> So we climbed into the airplanes and there was a great amount of excitement—it was the culmination of all we had worked for and a chance for us to strike back.
>
> At a signal the doors opened, engines started, and we did a fast taxi out to the head of the runway. It was a runway heading west toward the sea. I looked back and saw the other aircraft taxiing behind me. At the head of the runway I pushed the throttle and kept my fingers crossed. Would it take off? You never knew. I took off and did a pass around the field at 30 or 40 feet. Eddie Cohen was still on the ground with engine trouble. I did

> two circuits with Modi Alon and we took off since we couldn't wait. We climbed up to about 6,000 feet over the sea and I looked down and saw, like ants, the Egyptian column. By that time Eddie Cohen and Ezer Weizman were catching up with us.
>
> I couldn't wait since the ack-ack had started and hanging around just invited fire, so I pushed the nose down and attacked with Modi on my left. I dropped my two bombs in the square of this village (Isdud). The surprising thing for me was the amount of ack-ack. I saw a lot of ground fire over Japan, but never like this. I don't know how we got out of it. So I made four or five passes and then flew around looking for everybody. It turned out I was the first to take off and the last to land.
>
> I don't know how much damage we caused, but the psychological shock of attack by fighter planes shook them up. It was an exhilarating moment and also a sad time because we lost one aircraft, 25 percent of our air force, but worse than that, Eddie Cohen was killed. We were like brothers and I felt very bad that he was lost on that first mission.[14]

The fighter flown by Lou Lenart and the other pilots was the Avia S199. As a result of the British arms embargo, the Czechoslovakian-built derivative of the Messershmitt bf 109 was the only aircraft that Israel was able to acquire.

At 5:30 A.M. on May 30, Ezer Weizman, later to become commander of the IAF, and Cy Rubenfield, an American volunteer, bombed the Tulkarm railway station and strafed a column of Iraqi and Jordanian troops advancing into Israel. Rubenfield's Avia was hit by antiaircraft fire, but he successfully bailed out and came down near a Jewish village.

Flying alone, Modi Alon, commander of the 101st Fighter Squadron—the first Israeli fighter squadron and the only one ever officially identified—attacked an advancing Arab column near Latrun the following day.

Since the outbreak of widespread fighting on May 15, 1948, Egyptian Spitfire fighters and C-47 Dakota transports that had been converted into bombers had made repeated attacks against Israeli targets. On the afternoon of June 3, two Egyptian C-47

Dakota bombers, escorted by several Spitfires, swept in from the sea to bomb Tel Aviv. Modi Alon, piloting the only serviceable Avia fighter, attacked one of the Egyptian C-47s. Damaged by cannon and machine-gun fire, the Dakota crashed into the sea south of Tel Aviv. A head-on pass against the second Dakota sent it, too, hurtling to earth. Ignoring the air raid sirens, many inhabitants of Tel Aviv ran out into the streets to watch the battle. The twenty-seven-year-old former RAF flight lieutenant chalked up the first air combat victories of the Israel Air Force.

The sizable South African Jewish community included a number of experienced pilots, aircrew, and technicians who were sympathetic to the Israeli cause. Boris Senior, a former lieutenant in the South African Air Force, acquired nearly a squadron of surplus P-40 fighters, which had been sold as scrap in South Africa, with the intent of supplying them to the Haganah in Palestine. When he was not able to secure export rights for these fighters, he set up the Pan African Air Charter Company. Senior used this company to acquire aircraft and hire aircrew to transport civilian aircraft to Palestine. Senior and his associates flew a Beechcraft, Rapide, and several other aircraft to Israel.

On June 4, 1948, Israeli light planes, including Senior's Beechcraft and Rapide and a Fairchild, bombed and strafed an Egyptian ship convoy that was ferrying troops north from Gaza. The aircraft repeatedly attacked the Egyptian convoy, using handheld bombs and machine guns. Although the Israeli planes scored only a single hit and the Egyptian shot down the Fairchild, the convoy retreated.

Additional aircraft from Piper Cubs to large transports and Avia fighters were beginning to arrive in Israel in a steady stream, thanks to both legal and clandestine purchasing efforts by Jews in Europe, the United States, and other countries. The C-47 Dakota transports that arrived in May were quickly pressed into service. While most transports carried cargo and troops to outlying settlements, some were converted into makeshift bombers. On June 10 three C-47s dumped over 4,500 pounds of bombs on the Transjordan capital of Amman during a nocturnal attack.[15]

While the arms and aircraft-buying efforts of the worldwide Haganah organization made newspaper headlines, this same network was busy collecting funds, disseminating information about events in Palestine, and recruiting volunteers. The Haganah especially sought World War II veterans who could contribute their military knowledge and experience. Pilots, aircrew, and skilled mechanics were very much sought after. Some were Jewish and wanted to help Israel, many were bored with their postwar life and wanted to see action, while others joined for the money. Salaries for a pilot with combat experience were as high as $600 per month. Volunteers from the United States, Canada, South Africa, Great Britain, and other countries numbered in the hundreds. Named the *Mahal* (volunteers from abroad) by the Israelis, this group formed the backbone of the air force during the War of Independence. Because of the large representation of English-speaking volunteers, English became the main language of the Israel Air Force.

A UN-sponsored cease-fire began on June 11, 1948. During this period, both sides rearmed and reorganized. It was a critical break for Israel; although the new nation had managed to hold off the combined Arab armies, it had suffered over fifteen hundred men killed and several thousand wounded and had to give up considerable territory.

By late June the C-46 flights from Czechoslovakia, which were known as Operation Bolak, had transported nearly a dozen Avia fighters to Israel, where they were assembled by technicians. After a successful attack by Egyptian aircraft, the 101st Fighter Squadron was moved to a strip in Herzalia, where the aircraft could be camouflaged among the trees of an orange grove. The squadron settled into its new facilities and continued training activities for its pilots.

In June, the Israeli purchasing team in Czechoslovakia concluded an important agreement. The Czech government wished to dispose of some seventy-five Spitfires that had been flown home from England by Czech pilots at the end of World War II. Israel agreed to purchase fifty of the aircraft, all Spitfire Mk 9 models, and the spares and equipment necessary to maintain them.[16] The sale of Spitfires was a great step forward for the Israelis. However, almost three months would pass before any of the fighters reached Israel, because the planes had to be overhauled, payment terms arranged, and transportation worked out.

Back in the United States, Al Schwimmer's export of C-46s

and Constellations had aroused considerable consternation. The FBI was examining Schwimmer's activities, and customs officials limited the export of transport and surplus military aircraft. However, Schwimmer found four B-17 four-engine heavy bombers, and four A-20 twin-engine medium bombers and purchased them through a dummy corporation.

Only three of the B-17s could be quickly overhauled and put into shape for shipment to Israel. The three B-17s left Miami airport for Puerto Rico on June 12, 1948. The next day they flew across the Atlantic to the Azores. After filing flight plans listing Corsica as their final destination, the B-17s flew across the Mediterranean. Following a brief refueling stop in Corsica, the B-17s flew on to Zatec, Czechoslovakia. Here the B-17s were armed with machine guns and bombs.

Once U.S. authorities discovered that the B-17s had flown to Czechoslovakia, a country allied with the Soviet Union, the crackdown on arms exports to Israel was intensified. Despite efforts to stop them, aircraft and volunteer pilots continued to make their way to Israel, often by very circuitous paths.

In early July the cease-fire broke down and widespread fighting started in the north of Israel, around Jerusalem, and on the Egyptian front. On July 9, four Avia of the 101st Fighter Squadron were assigned to attack the Egyptian airfield at El Arish. One Avia crashed on takeoff and the others, after failing to locate El Arish because of dense clouds, bombed and strafed Egyptian troops near Gaza. During the attacks, one of the Avias piloted by Robert Vickerman, a volunteer from the United States, was lost. That night IAF Dakota bombers and light aircraft flew bombing and harassment raids against several Arab targets.

Syrian infantry, supported by artillery and tanks, staged a major counterattack on July 10 against the Israelis, who had achieved gains the previous night. Harvard trainers, armed with machine guns and light bombs, supported the Syrian offensive by attacking Israeli troops. Few Israeli Avias were serviceable and those available were engaged on the Egyptian front. The Syrian pilots made the most of their air superiority, chasing Israeli vehicles up and down roads and harassing them with machine-gun fire. Later in the day, two Israeli Avias engaged the Syrian planes. One Harvard was shot down by Maurice Mann.

Lionel Bloch, a South African who piloted the other Avia, chased a fleeing Harvard as it withdrew over the Golan Heights. His aircraft failed to return.

Because of the heavy fighting, the Israelis intensified the airlift of weapons and supplies from Czechoslovakia. Transports also flew night attack sorties but not always with positive results. Some aircraft attacked friendly territory while others hit empty fields or dumped their bombs into the sea. A night attack of Syrian positions on July 13 by a Dakota nearly ended in disaster. The crew successfully pushed six bombs out the side cargo door, but a seventh caught on the door as it was released, ripping off the door, and damaging the Dakota's tail assembly. The pilot was able to fly back to Ramat David airfield, but the C-47 was out of service for a considerable period of time.

The three B-17s that had been smuggled out of the United States to Czechoslovakia in June left Zatec airfield on July 14 for Israel. On the way, the three delivered calling cards—500-pound bombs dropped on Cairo, Gaza, and El Arish. These aircraft were immediately pressed into service. C-47s and light planes flew night bombing raids against Arab targets while the B-17s conducted both daylight and nocturnal attacks. The pace of operations was intense and the arrival of the B-17s added considerably to the available firepower. Although the number of attack sorties flown by the IAF from July 8 to 14 nearly equaled those performed July 15 to 18, the weight of the bombs delivered during the latter period was five times greater.[17]

The Arab air forces reacted vigorously to these attacks. On July 11, Jerusalem suffered its first air attack. Before it was driven off by antiaircraft fire, an Iraqi trainer dropped several small bombs on Ramat David airfield. The loss of a Harvard to an Israeli Avia sharply curtailed Syrian air attacks.

Egyptian fighters repeatedly attacked Israeli settlements near the battle zone, using hit-and-run tactics in order to minimize the possibility of interception by Israeli fighters. One Jewish settlement suffered seven air attacks on a single day. In retaliation for Israeli B-17 raids, Egyptian fighters also bombed and strafed Tel Aviv on several occasions.

In the spring of 1948, Rudolph Augarten, an American pilot who had flown fighters with the U.S. Army Air Corps in Europe during World War II, volunteered to fly for Israel. He trained on

Arrado trainers and Avia fighters in Czechoslovakia and arrived in Israel in July 1948. He served as a pilot, director of operations of the 101st Fighter Squadron, and a base commander with the IAF.

Augarten commented on his first mission:

> My turn to fly came up on July 18 and a truce was to take effect that evening at 6:00 P.M. Our flight took off at about 5:30 and we were to fly down to a town just south of Beersheba named Beerasluge to bomb and strafe an Egyptian column. Modi Alon led the flight. The second pilot was Sid Anteim from Boston and I was the third pilot to take off. We found the convoy and they bombed, but I only had guns so I ran up and down strafing. Then I joined the other two and we headed back to base. Modi was in the lead, I was on the left and Sid Anteim was on the right. Sid radioed, "Hey Rudy, there is something on your left." I gave it gas and came up right behind two Spits with Egyptian Roundels. I put my gunsight on one, pulled the trigger, and nothing happened. I said, on the radio, "For Christ sake, I'm out of ammunition," so I put my nose down to get out of the way and Modi came in and shot down one Spit.[18]

After ten days of heavy fighting, a cease-fire came into effect on July 18, providing an opportunity for the IAF to repair and overhaul aircraft and to resupply. The many volunteer pilots, aircrews, maintenance personnel, and Israeli conscripts who made up the air force intensified their training efforts.

With fighting expected to resume at any time, collecting additional aircraft weapons and spare parts was vital. American pressure and a change in attitude in Prague led to the announcement in late July that Israeli facilities at Zatec airfield in Czechoslovakia were to be closed, shutting off the aerial pipeline that had provided Israel with its only fighters and tons of other weapons. Transport crews flew to the point of exhaustion to move spare parts, weapons, and equipment to Israel before the base was closed. Between August 6 and 12 they lifted out forty tons of supplies.

Secret procurement efforts by Jewish agents in other countries continued to bear fruit. In early 1948 a dummy film production company was established in England and four Bristol Beaufighters were purchased, allegedly for use in a film about the exploits of New Zealand fliers during World War II. The four Beaufighters were flown to Israel. One of them was cannibalized for spare parts and the remaining three flew operational missions from Ramat David airfield throughout the summer.

The IAF's first Spitfire did not come from Czechoslovakia but from Egypt and England! On the new nation's first day, Israeli machine gunners hit an attacking Egyptian Spitfire. Its pilot crash-landed on the beach near Tel Aviv and was captured. Parts of the damaged Spitfire were used along with other plane parts taken from dumps at several former RAF air bases to produce a serviceable aircraft. This Spitfire first flew on July 23, 1948, containing the fuselage of a photo reconnaissance model and the wing of an Mk 9 fighter. Later a second Spitfire was constructed using parts obtained from the various abandoned RAF bases.[19]

Having decided to focus its efforts on defeating Egyptian forces in the south, the Israeli high command prepared to move men and supplies into position for the offensive. Since truck convoys would be easily detected and subject to attack, Prime Minister Ben Gurion asked the Air Transport Command, the logistics arm of the air force, to transfer the necessary men and supplies. Using a tractor and a bulldozer, Jewish settlers and Israeli troops created a 4,000-foot dirt runway on a relatively flat section of the Negev Desert. To maintain secrecy and escape marauding Egyptian Spitfires, the transports flew at night, unloaded their cargo, and flew out by dawn. Finding the single poorly lit strip was a challenge since the Israelis had no navigation aids. Takeoffs and landings created large dust clouds, which gave the resupply effort its name—Operation Dust.

Between August 18 and September 9, C-46s of the Air Transport Command flew hundreds of sorties to the Negev airstrip. Fewer than ten aircraft were available, and usually only five to eight planes were serviceable. Pilots, maintenance crews, and logistics personnel pushed themselves to the limit. On the night of September 7, transport aircrews flew thirteen trips to the airstrip, delivering eighty-one tons of supplies. By September 9, the transport crews had flown 170 sorties, delivering more than one thousand tons of supplies and moving nearly twenty-four hundred people.

The combination of pressure by Israeli officials to maintain the dangerous missions, the punishing pace of operations, and the poor condition of the aircraft, led to morale problems among the foreign volunteers. Many transport crews were made up of foreign volunteers who had come to Israel expecting to help form a new Israeli airline. When the transport crews learned that the semi-independent Air Transport Command was to be integrated into the air force, they went on strike, grounding all aircraft. Although flying operations resumed after a few days, a few disgruntled individuals quit and left Israel. In spite of these problems the remaining aircrews resumed Operation Dust in early October and additional supplies and troops were flown into the Negev.[20]

Since July, when Czechoslovakia agreed to supply Spitfire fighters, a group of Israeli agents had been busy coordinating the selection, overhaul, and delivery of the aircraft. By the fall of 1948 the changing political climate in Czechoslovakia caused a chill in its relations with the new state of Israel. As a result, an increasing number of obstacles slowed the delivery schedule for the Spitfires. Because the fighters were needed immediately, Israeli officials decided that the Spitfires would be flown to Israel. Weaponry and support equipment for the fighters could be shipped to Israel in transport aircraft and by ship. The Czech Spitfires had a ferry range of only about 950 miles, so Israeli engineers had to modify the fuel system of the fighters to include new internal fuel tanks and a 90-gallon external tank to make the 1,300-mile flight to Israel.[21]

On September 22, six modified Spitfires left Czechoslovakia for the Yugoslav airfield at Podgorica. All six Spitfires made it to Podgorica but one was damaged beyond repair when Tuxie Blou, a South African volunteer, was forced to make a wheels-up landing because his gear would not come down.

The remaining five Spitfires and a C-54 escort left for Israel on September 27. Two of the aircraft developed fuel problems and had to land at Maritza airfield on the island of Rhodes where they were interned. The three remaining Spitfires and the C-54 flew on to Israel. With the delivery of the Spitfires, the IAF finally had a fighter plane that allowed the volunteer pilots to engage the enemy confidently.

In late September the IAF fighter force received another boost. Four disassembled and crated P-51 Mustang fighters arrived in Israel from the United States. It was several weeks before these aircraft became operational with the 101st Fighter Squadron because they had to be reassembled and fitted with weapons.

By the fall of 1948, the IAF had grown to nearly one hundred aircraft, including about ten bombers, twenty-five fighters, fifteen multiengined transports, and nearly fifty light planes of various types. However, at any one time a lack of spare parts kept perhaps a third of these aircraft out of service.[22]

On October 15 Israeli forces began a new offensive in the south. Aerial operations started in the evening with an attack on the Egyptian air base at El Arish and strikes against targets near the towns of Gaza and Majdal. Israeli B-17 bombers and C-46 and C-47 transports armed with bombs flew nocturnal attacks against Egyptian targets.

Despite Israeli efforts, the Royal Egyptian Air Force (REAF) continued to fly attack missions over the battle area. Most Egyptian fighter sorties were flown from the air base at El Arish, which was home for a Spitfire squadron that was supported by a detachment of Italian-built Fiat G55 fighters. The IAF specifically targeted Egyptian frontline positions and the El Arish air base for attack during the October 15 offensive. During seven days of intense operations, IAF aircraft flew several hundred sorties, dropped more than two hundred tons of bombs, and downed three Egyptian fighters in air combat. Rudolph Augarten later described his experiences flying during this period:

> The first kill I had was on a patrol mission over Faluja on October 16. I ran into a couple of Spitfires. I went after one and shot him down and he crashed just north of Gaza. I was flying a Messerschmitt that had a profile similar to a Spitfire. Usually we went on patrols with only two or three aircraft so if you saw a plane, you could almost be assured that it was the enemy. So you did not have to hesitate—if you used aggressive tactics you had a good chance of knocking someone down

> because they generally did not show very much willingness to fight.[23]

During the summer and fall of 1948, accidents and Egyptian antiaircraft fire claimed the lives of more than a dozen Israeli and volunteer pilots and crewmen. Modi Alon, commander of the 101st Fighter Squadron who had three air combat victories to this credit, was killed on October 16 when his damaged aircraft crashed while approaching Herzalia. During an attack on the Egyptian fort at Iraq Suqeiden on October 20, Arab antiaircraft fire downed a Beaufighter, killing three crew members. On October 24, an engine fire caused a C-47 to crash while approaching Eqron airfield, killing the crew of four.

While Egyptian forces at El Arish suffered many casualties and lost several aircraft to Israel air attacks, the airfield was never put out of action. Egyptian aircraft based at El Arish and at other Sinai airfields continued to strike back against the Israelis. Egyptian Spitfires bombed and strafed Israeli ground troops on numerous occasions and on October 19 they attacked and heavily damaged two Israeli ships in the Mediterranean.

While Israel was beginning to seize the initiative from the Arabs, losses had been heavy. Hoping to buy time to gather more arms and prepare for a new offensive, Israeli military commanders supported a cease-fire. On October 22, a UN-arranged cease-fire came into effect on the southern front, yet sniping, artillery fire, raids, and attacks continued. The pace of Israeli air operations slowed, but transport and reconnaissance missions continued to be flown.

Rudolph Augarten described the events of November 4, 1948:

> We flew down over El Arish to see what was happening, Boris Senior and I. We saw this Dakota. Boris went after the plane. He pulled up and didn't hit it. On an impulse I decided to go after it, so I went down and really shot up that plane and it crashed on the runway. . . . By the fall our squadron had ME109s (Avias), Spitfires, and two P-51s and I flew all three. The Spitfire was the plane I preferred because of its handling qualities. The big advantage of the P-51 was its armament (six 0.5-inch machine guns) and better range. I was able to get kills

> with the ME109 (Avia), the Spitfire, and the P-51. This was very typical of what we were doing then—everybody flew whatever aircraft that was available.[24]

Despite the cease-fire, Israeli fighters and bombers repeatedly attacked the Faluja pocket, a salient that contained four thousand Egyptian troops that had been surrounded by Israeli ground forces. During the day Israeli B-17s and fighters struck and at night bomb-armed transports dumped bombs on the defenders. But the defenders held on and fought back with heavy antiaircraft fire. The Egyptians held these strong defensive positions until the armistice in 1949.[25]

Although heavy ground combat operations had ceased temporarily in the south, fighting between Syrian, Lebanese, and Israeli forces continued on the northern front. IAF aircraft struck at Arab convoys and staging bases behind the front lines.

During the fall of 1948, the RAF flew reconnaissance sorties over Israel with high-flying Mosquito aircraft. Israeli Air Force pilots often attempted to intercept the Mosquitos, but were unable to climb quickly enough to catch them. On November 20, the pilots of the 101st Fighter Squadron were alerted to one of the RAF snoopers. Wayne Peake, a non-Jewish volunteer from the United States, rushed to one of the squadron's few P-51 Mustang fighters and took off. Climbing as rapidly as possible, Peake closed on the Mosquito. But a fault in his oxygen system blurred his vision at the higher altitude. Recovering his senses, Peake flew into firing position behind the Mosquito and opened fire. Almost immediately his 0.5-inch machine guns stopped firing because he had exhausted his ammunition supply. Dejected by his failure, Peake spiraled down and returned to the base. However, it turned out that his machine-gun fire had hit home. Observers on the ground saw the Mosquito catch fire and explode over the Mediterranean. British forces conducted an air-and-sea search after the Mosquito did not return, but they never found a trace of the aircraft. As a result of the loss, RAF reconnaissance flights over Israel were suspended.[26]

During the fall, the REAF stepped up its efforts against Israel. Egyptian pilot training was intensified and several alternative airfields were established in the Sinai. The air force had received additional aircraft, including Spitfires, and Sterling four-engine bombers from England, and several dozen Fiat G55 and Aeromacchi C205 Veltro fighters from Italy.

The IAF continued to receive reinforcements through its international network of agents. Harvard trainers, bought and shipped in crates from Canada and the United States, entered service. This was the same aircraft used successfully by Syrian forces against Israeli troops early in the war. These trainer aircraft were armed with machine guns and light bombs and served as dive bombers.

Twelve more Czech Spitfires set out on December 18, but two crashed when they encountered a severe snowstorm in Czechoslovakia. The pilots were killed. The remaining Spitfires arrived in Israel on December 22.

On December 22, Israeli troops launched Operation Horev, an all-out offensive against Egyptian forces. The objective of the Israeli offensive was to cut off the supply route to Gaza. To weaken Egyptian forces southwest of Gaza, Israeli troops made a diversionary attack against the city itself. Israeli aircraft attacked the El Arish airfield southwest of Gaza on December 22, and also bombed and strafed Egyptian troops in the area.

Rudy Augerten described a mission he flew over the Egyptian airfield:

> Although I didn't claim it as a kill, I shot and damaged a Fiat that had his wheels down and was in the landing pattern at El Arish. That was our first encounter with the Fiat. I was flying a reconnaissance mission in a Spitfire with Doyle over El Arish and I saw this plane in the landing pattern. By the time I caught him he had his wheels down and was on final approach. I shot him and he crashed off the runway. There was a tremendous amount of flak coming up so I stayed close to the ground until I was five or six miles away from the airfield.[27]

Egyptian armed forces, reacting to the threat to their rear, counterattacked vigorously, but Israeli troops tightened their grip on Gaza. The REAF strongly defended El Arish and struck at the Israeli columns advancing into the Sinai near Gaza. Angered by the Israelis' success, Egyptian pilots bombed targets in Israel including the Mishmar Haemak kibbutz, Allenbay bridge, and the town of Jericho. Air combat was also heavy: On December 28, Israeli Spitfires downed three Egyptian Fiat fighters. On December 31 and January 5, 1949, volunteer pilots flying for Israel shot down additional Egyptian fighters.

With Gaza surrounded and Egyptian forces in retreat, Egypt asked England to intercede. Evoking the 1936 Anglo-Egyptian Treaty, the British called for an Israeli withdrawal from Egyptian territory. The British government made it clear that it was prepared to enter the conflict to support Egyptian sovereignty.

On January 6, Egypt indicated that it would like to initiate a cease-fire leading to discussions for an armistice agreement. The fighting was to end the following day at 2:00 P.M.

Royal Air Force aircraft stationed near the Suez Canal flew early morning reconnaissance sorties near the Israeli border to monitor the situation. The first flight consisted of a Mosquito escorted by four Tempest fighters. A second group of four Spitfires overflew an Israeli roadblock in Egyptian territory and was greeted by antiaircraft fire. One Spitfire was hit and its pilot bailed out. The three remaining RAF Spitfires circled and watched their comrade as he parachuted to earth.

Two IAF Spitfires, piloted by 101st Fighter Squadron volunteers Slick Goodlin and John McElroy, attacked the circling RAF fighters and shot down all three. One of the RAF pilots was killed while the other two parachuted to safety.[28] Goodlin and McElroy stated that they did not notice the RAF markings on the Spitfires.

When the four RAF Spitfires did not return, the British sent Spitfire reconnaissance planes, with an escort of Tempest fighters, to search for the missing aircraft. A patrol of Israeli Spitfires engaged and shot down several of these RAF aircraft.[29] However, Britain protested its losses through diplomatic channels and threatened to retaliate against further Israeli aggression.

The fighting between Israel and the Arabs ended at 2:00 P.M. on January 7, 1949. With the cease-fire between Egypt and Israel, Transjordan, Lebanon, and Iraq decided to suspend military operations. Israel's first and bloodiest war was over. The new nation had suffered six thousand men and women killed and twelve thousand wounded, but it had established a Jewish homeland.

From a small group of light planes, the IAF had grown to over one hundred aircraft, including more than fifty fighters and bombers, by the end of the War of Independence. Aircraft acquired from around the world, including the fighters from Czechoslovakia, were forged into a fighting force that wrestled the initiative from the REAF and contributed significantly to the outcome of the war. The IAF had downed twenty-three Egyptian, Syrian, and British aircraft in air combat. Israeli aircraft losses totaled about fifteen aircraft but many of these were lost in accidents rather than in combat.

The 660 volunteer pilots, aircrew members, and skilled maintenance personnel who fought during the war formed the backbone of the air force. Twenty Mahal foreign volunteers died in the fighting. After the war, Prime Minister David Ben Gurion paid tribute to these men: "In spite of the contribution made by Israeli boys, Israel would not have been able to build up an air force and operate it without the assistance extended by the volunteers from abroad, who had acquired their experience in the service of the allied power during World War II."[30]

2

The Early Years

The fighting between Israel and its Arab neighbors ended early in 1949. Protracted negotations led to armistice agreements between Israel and Egypt—February 24, Lebanon—March 23, Transjordan—April 3, and Syria—July 20. No agreement was reached with Iraq. These agreements ended the fighting but were not formal peace treaties because the Arab countries refused to recognize the State of Israel. Following the Israeli victory, thousands of Palestinian Arabs who had not fled the country during the fighting packed up and left. Many left with little more than the clothes on their backs. These refugees were placed in large camps established by Egypt, Transjordan (now called simply Jordan), Syria, and Lebanon near the Israeli border. They rarely were able to obtain jobs and had little opportunity to integrate into the social and economic hierarchy of their new land. The refugee camps became filled with disenchanted people who saw little hope for the future. Egypt, Syria, and Jordan recruited many young men from these camps and sent them to special commando training camps to continue the war against Israel. These commandos became known as the *fedayeen* (those who sacrifice themselves). Terrorist groups organized during this period later became a major factor in the continuing Arab opposition to Israel.

Arab countries also employed all the economic and diplomatic means at their disposal to isolate Israel. By 1950 Israel had demobilized most of the troops who had fought in the War of Independence and was struggling to organize its infrastructure, establish a stable political system, and deal with serious economic problems. It was an austere time.

With the armistice, the air force faced many problems. Most of the foreign volunteers returned to their home countries, leaving the service short of pilots and skilled ground crews. Although the air force had more than one hundred aircraft, many were damaged or worn out. Many planes were cannibalized to keep others in flyable condition.

Aharon Remez, commander of the IAF, set up a pilot-training course and set about upgrading the air force. He wanted to create a powerful, independent air force that could defeat the enemy in any future war. Remez's plans and ambitions did not sit well with Prime Minister Ben Gurion and the senior officers of the Israeli high command, who were concentrating on strengthening the ground forces.

The IAF received the remainder of the fifty Spitfires purchased from Czechoslovakia in early 1949. These Spitfires and a few P-51 Mustangs served to protect Israeli airspace. The attack element of the air force included the B-17s that had been spirited out of the United States by Al Schwimmer's organization. More than twenty-five types of transport, liaison, and utility aircraft were in service including Curtis C-46, Douglas C-47, Douglas C-54/DC-5, Lockheed Hudson, Lockheed Constellation, de Havilland Rapide, Norduyn Norseman, and a diversity of smaller aircraft.

As pilot-training efforts expanded, so did the IAF trainer force. Israel purchased twenty surplus Boeing PT-17 biplane trainers from the United States, forty Fokker S.11 trainers from the Netherlands, and twenty-five Harvard (T-6) advanced trainer aircraft from France. Following 40–60 hours of flying in the PT-17 or S.11 primary trainers, Israeli cadets flew an additional 150 hours in the Harvard. Students training to fly fighters were assigned to Spitfires or P-51s at an operational training unit. Transport and bomber pilot candidates continued their instruction in twin-engine Anson or Consul aircraft.

In 1950, Maj. Gen. Aharon Remez resigned his commission and retired from military service. Although Remez had made improvements during his two years as commander, he was disappointed at the low priority and limited funding the Israel Defense Force High Command afforded the air force. Shlomo Shamir, a naval officer, took over the top position in the air force. His tenure as commander was short and within less than a year he was succeeded by Maj. Gen. Chaim Laskov, an infantry officer. During Laskov's administration, the IAF acquired a large number of secondhand and war surplus piston-engined fighters and fighter-bombers. Contacts in the United States purchased two PBY Catalina amphibious patrol aircraft. Through extensive lobbying, Israel acquired an export license for these aircraft plus their spare parts and support equipment.

In 1950 France agreed to supply Israel with surplus Mosquito fighter-bombers. The twin-engine aircraft had a fine record. During and after World War II, it had served as a night fighter, fighter-bomber, and reconnaissance aircraft with the RAF. The Mosquito was built primarily of pressure-bonded plywood, a material that was easy to obtain. Most of the French Mosquitos were in poor shape, but were available at very low prices. Between June 1951 and May 1952, sixty Mosquitos were reconditioned by Israeli technicians with the help of Nord Aviation personnel and flown to Israel.[1] These aircraft served as the backbone of the IAF attack force into the mid-1950s.

Italian authorities indicated a willingness to supply Israel with surplus Spitfire fighters, extra engines, and spare parts. Following a prolonged series of negotiations, in early 1953 Italy sold Israel thirty aircraft. Sweden, which likewise was modernizing its fighter fleet with jets, had a supply of P-51 Mustangs available. These Mustangs were in first-class condition. The Swedish government responded favorably to an Israeli inquiry concerning purchase of the aircraft. During the winter and spring of 1953, Swedish Air Force pilots flew twenty-five P-51s to Israel.[2] Israel also purchased a dozen P-51 fighters from Italian arms dealers, and these were delivered in 1955.

An intensified pilot-training program continued to produce results. Israeli students began attending RAF flying schools to complete their intermediate and advanced training or to acquire instructor pilot status. These candidates often encountered pilot trainees from Arab countries who were also attending the RAF programs. Egypt, Iraq, Syria, Jordan, and several other Arab countries were building up their air arms by expanding their pilot-training efforts and acquiring advanced equipment.

Although the acquisition of Spitfires, Mosquitos, and Mustangs along with the increased number of pilots considerably expanded the IAF, the Israelis faced a new problem: Piston engine fighters were becoming obsolete. The Royal Egyptian Air Force had received its first British-built jet fighter, the Gloster

Meteor, in late 1949. Shortly thereafter, Egypt acquired twenty single-engine Vampire FB5 fighter-bombers.

The Korean conflict, which was raging at this time, demonstrated that piston engine aircraft were no match for the latest jet fighters in air combat. While Mosquitos, Spitfires, and Mustangs were useful for ground attack, the IAF needed jets to protect its skies.

In 1950 Israeli representatives approached U.S. and British officials about the possibility of acquiring jet fighters to counter Egypt's, but were turned down. France was supplying the Mosquitos and was willing to consider the Israeli request for the Ouragon, its first indigenously designed and built jet fighter. However, approval was stymied by political wrangling. Dassault in France and Macchi in Italy were producing versions of the British Vampire fighter under license and Israeli representatives contacted these firms. But the British government would not allow export of these aircraft.

Eventually, however, as a way to maintain the balance of power in the Middle East, Britain agreed to supply Israel with Meteor jet fighters and resumed deliveries of jets to Arab countries; Egypt received Meteors and Vampires, Syria was supplied with Meteors, while Jordan was given Vampire fighters. On February 10, 1953, Israel ordered eleven Meteor F Mk 8 fighters and four T.7 trainers from Gloster Aircraft, Ltd. The IAF joined the jet age on June 17, 1953, with the delivery of the first two T.7 Meteor trainers. Meteor deliveries continued into 1954.

In 1953 Dan Tolkovsky, a South African and former RAF officer, was given command of the IAF. Tolkovsky instituted many reforms that improved the air force. Since Israel could not hope to match its neighbors numerically, quality, efficiency, and professionalism became the new goals. People were the key. Highly motivated, superbly trained pilots, ground crew, and support personnel equipped with good multipurpose aircraft, Tolkovsky believed, could defeat a numerically superior adversary. He established high standards for dress, behavior, training, maintenance, flying skills, and many other areas. Pilot-training standards were set extremely high and a majority of those who started flight training did not complete it. Only the best graduated. Officers were sent overseas to France and Britain to attend command and staff schools, test pilot training, and other top military courses. Air force personnel at all levels examined their functions, established new standards of performance, and set up training schedules to maintain their proficiency.

Tolkovsky maintained that the air force could have a significant impact on the outcome of the ground battle. Fighters would be used first to destroy enemy aircraft in the air and on the ground. Once air superiority was achieved, aircraft could then concentrate on providing support for ground forces.

Tolkovsky knew that Israel could not afford to purchase and maintain a large air force; aircraft must be capable of performing multiple missions. The small size of Israel itself and its armed forces required that the battles be fought over and on enemy territory.[3]

To help the air force maintain its new jet fighters and keep all aircraft in peak condition, Israeli officials formed Bedek Aircraft, Ltd. The company was headed by Al Schwimmer, the American engineer who had led the team that acquired C-46, Constellation transports, and B-17s for Israel. Bedek maintenance personnel and technicians overhauled IAF aircraft and modified and upgraded them to improve their performance. Over the years Bedek developed into Israel Aircraft Industries, which by the 1980s had produced hundreds of combat aircraft, transports, and executive jets and employed over five thousand people.[4]

The armistice agreements signed in 1949 were considered only a temporary truce by the Arab countries. Raids against civilian targets and artillery attacks continued on a limited scale along Israel's borders. In late 1954 and early 1955 Israeli troops repeatedly attacked targets in the Gaza Strip and the Sinai in retaliation against guerrilla activity. In response, Egyptian President Nasser increased the strength of his forces along the Israeli border and set out to expand his military force structure. Nasser sought to obtain more weapons, including Meteor and Vampire jet fighters from Great Britain. When additional arms were not immediately delivered, Nasser began negotiations with a new source of weaponry—Czechoslovakia. A mere seven years before, this country had provided Israel with its first fighter aircraft. Soviet leaders gave Czechoslovakia permission to supply Egypt with the latest military hardware—including MiG-15 fighters and IL-28 jet bombers.

To match this threat, Israel needed a new supply of up-to-date combat aircraft. Air combat in Korea had demonstrated that the Meteor was no match for the MiG-15. The F-86 Sabre was the only Western fighter aircraft that had proven itself capable of countering the MiG-15. While the United States would not sell the F-86 to Israel, Canada indicated a willingness to consider the sale of the Canadian-built Sabre Mk 6. This aircraft combined a late-model Sabre airframe with the high-thrust Orenda jet engine. Israel ordered twenty-four Sabres and Canada produced the aircraft, but U.S. intervention prevented delivery of the jets.[5]

Sweden at this time was introducing a new jet fighter into its inventory, the SAAB J-29. Israel approached SAAB and the Swedish government, which agreed to sell its planes to the new nation. The J-29 was evaluated and judged to be a good fighter, but its limited ground attack capability was a disadvantage.[6]

For the first time, the French government indicated a willingness to supply advanced fighter aircraft to Israel. France was deeply involved in the civil war in Algeria and President Nasser had supplied arms, training, and political assistance to Algerian resistance fighters. French leaders felt that a strong Israel would keep Nasser's attention focused on the Middle East. The French firm Dassault was developing the Mystere II, an advanced, swept-wing interceptor. Israeli test pilots flew both the J-29 and Mystere II and judged the French aircraft to be superior. In late 1954 France agreed to supply Israel with thirty Dassault Ouragon and twenty-four Mystere II fighters. The first French-designed jet fighter, the Ouragon, was rapidly approaching obsolescence, but it was a better combat aircraft than the Meteor. Highly maneuverable and easy to fly, the 35-foot-long Ouragon could reach a speed of over 550 miles per hour. The 15,000-pound fighter-bomber was armed with four 20-mm cannons and could carry an underwing load of bombs or rockets.[7]

When the Mystere II encountered development problems, Israel canceled its order for the aircraft and chose instead the much improved Mystere IVA. The IAF would have to wait a year for delivery of the advanced fighter and to bridge the gap Israel ordered an additional supply of Ouragons. The first Dassault

Ouragon fighters were delivered to Israel in November 1955. Eventually Israel received seventy-five Ouragons—twenty-four of these were new jets and fifty-one were refurbished aircraft that had seen service with the French Air Force (Armee de l'Air).

The Dassault Mystere IVA was the French Air Force's premier fighter during the mid-1950s. Powered by a 7,710-pound-thrust Hispano Suiza Verdon turbojet engine, the Mystere IVA had a length of 42.1 feet, a 36.5-foot wingspan, and a maximum takeoff weight of 20,000 pounds.[8] Capable of performing both fighter and attack missions, the aircraft was armed with two 30-mm DEFA cannons and a variety of external ordinance including bombs, rocket pods, and fuel tanks. Faster, better armed, and more advanced than the Ouragon, the Mystere IVA ideally fulfilled Israeli requirements; it could beat the MiG-15 in air combat and effectively attack ground targets with cannon fire, bombs, and rockets.

During the mid-1950s tensions were heightened in the Middle East. Egypt, Syria, Jordan, Iraq, and Israel strengthened their arsenals and *fedayeen* guerrillas based in Egypt stepped up their raids into Israel. As casualties mounted, Israeli army units struck back. Eventually the air arms became involved. Israeli and Arab aircraft flew regular reconnaissance missions along each others' borders. Occasionally these planes flew past their respective borders to gather information and test their adversary's response time. On August 31, 1955, IAF Meteor fighters and Egyptian Vampires fought the first jet air battle in the Middle East.

Retired IAF Col. Aharon Yoeli recalled the event:

> At seven o'clock in the morning, a standby of four airplanes, Meteor 8s, were ready. I was not a standby pilot, but I am an early riser and bang—the siren goes off. The two duty guys are brushing their eyes and by that time Sedan and I are in the aircraft and we made contact with the controller who said, "Take off heading southwest, fly to 7,000 feet." It was a cloudy day and the sun was only ten to fifteen degrees above the horizon. We took off headed south and were told that there was a bogey consisting of two airplanes flying southbound below us at two to three o'clock. I made a left turn so

> they couldn't see me because I would be in the sun and two minutes later my number two said, "I see them," and I turned my head and I saw them.
>
> We simply pulled up and started to come down behind them. The closing speed was, say, 150 miles per hour. Number two was behind me. My sight was on night brightness, and since I was slowly closing in, I had no time to mess with it. I saw one aircraft at about five hundred yards range, opened the safety cover, and slowly closed line astern behind the Vampire. At 200 to 250 yards, I opened fire. My tracers moved from the left to the wing, and I simply shifted them to the center and I didn't finish until I saw the bubble explode. We were at about 3,000 feet and I was flying at about 460 knots. Bang, the airplane broke up but didn't explode and I pulled up to the left.
>
> Number two was following; he warned me that the Egyptian number two was behind me. Then I saw him. The second Vampire turned southbound and started to dive toward a sandy area at 1,000 feet. When I was straight behind him, he started to roll with his nose down, and I thought that damn son of a gun will hit the ground before I can shoot him. So I missed a chance to shoot him. He made another roll and I closed in. I headed the gun sight up front as I used to do when shooting targets in training, and I said, "This is the right deflection angle and the right range." I pulled the trigger and hit the cockpit—bang—unbelievable—the airplane exploded right there! That was that! The two other bogeys had already crossed the border so I went back, made two victory rolls over the base, and I landed.[9]

In August 1955, President Nasser signed a major arms deal with Czechoslovakia. By early 1956 large numbers of Soviet-built MiG-15s had entered service with the EAF. The Egyptian army and navy were also receiving a significant quantity of new weaponry. The new arms and support enhanced Nasser's position. He ordered the withdrawal of British troops who were protecting the Suez Canal, increased the forces along the Israeli border, and pressured King Hussein of Jordan into expanding the number of *fedayeen* guerrilla bases in his country. Guerrilla raids, artillery duels, and attacks intensified along the Egyptian border and occurred with increasing frequency along the borders with Syria and Jordan. On April 12, 1956, an Egyptian Vampire was shot down over Israeli territory by an IAF Ouragon, marking the first victory for the French-built fighter.[10]

Israel was compelled to procure new, up-to-date weaponry in order to meet the Arab buildup, and France was one of the only countries willing to supply Israel with advanced weaponry, especially jet fighter aircraft. In April 1956 the first French-built Mystere IVA fighters arrived in Israel. The IAF intensified its training efforts in order to increase the number of combat-ready pilots and support personnel and to bring the new Ouragon and Mystere IVA squadrons to full operational status.

Low-scale conflict with Israel continued during the summer of 1956 and Egypt's relations with Britain, France, and the United States were severely strained. Nasser made a fateful decision on July 26, 1956, when he announced his intention to nationalize the Suez Canal. This was the first step toward a coalition war involving Israel, Great Britain, and France against Egypt.

3

The Sinai Conflict

The sixteen C-47 Dakota transports, each carrying some two dozen paratroops of the Israeli 890 Airborne Battalion, sped above the sand and rock of the Sinai Desert, flying at only 500 feet to evade radar detection. Ten Meteor fighters flew at low altitude with the Dakotas in order to protect them against interception by Egyptian fighters. Mystere fighters took turns patrolling along the Suez Canal and Great Bitter Lake, a position from which they could detect any Egyptian fighters taking off from their bases. Although the Mystere pilots could observe fighters being towed around on the taxiways, they were under strict orders not to take action unless the MiGs rose to engage.

The IAF plan called for its transport aircraft to drop paratroops near Mitla Pass and then keep this force and other advancing units resupplied. Fighters were to provide air cover for Israeli forces and refrain from engaging Egyptian aircraft unless they struck first. The IAF planners hoped that if Israel refrained from striking Egyptian cities or airfields, then the Egyptians might also select not to attack Israel.

At 4:30 P.M. on October 29, 1956, the sixteen Israeli C-47s ascended to 1,500 feet and the paratroopers began to jump.[1] The 395 paratroopers landed several miles east of the entrance to Mitla Pass and marched to the mouth of the pass where they set up defensive fortifications. This assault interdicted the major transit route from the Suez Canal to Egyptian positions in the central Sinai. Mitla Pass is only 45 miles from the canal and 155 miles from Israel. The Egyptians were surprised by the paratroop assault and the full-scale invasion of the Sinai, which began the following day. The Israeli campaign was timed to coincide with the British and French offensive against Egypt.

In Israel the conflict was known as Operation Kadesh. Israel's intention was threefold: (1) to eliminate *fedayeen* bases in the Sinai and the area surrounding Gaza, (2) to disrupt the Egyptian war-making capability in order to prevent an attack on Israel, and (3) to open the Gulf of Eilat to Israeli shipping.

The fighting between Israel and Egypt continued for eight days. The action was divided into three phases: the opening assault (October 29–30), heavy fighting (October 31–November 1), and exploitation (November 2–5), during which Israel took control of the Sinai. The action ended with the cease-fire.

The two primary causes that led to the 1956 conflict were the alignment of Egypt with the Soviet Union and the nationalization of the Suez Canal. Israel sought to acquire a reliable supply of weapons to balance the Soviet equipment provided to Egypt, while France saw Israel as a potential ally in efforts to regain control of the Suez Canal and reduce President Nasser's influence in the ongoing conflict in Algeria. Initial discussions between France and Israel led to the sale of French tanks, plus Ouragon and Mystere IVA fighters, to Israel.

In September 1956, Israeli representatives met with French officials in Paris to initiate plans for coordinated military action.[2] Britain and France were already beginning to move forces into position for Operation Musketeer, an effort to regain control of the Suez Canal. On October 24, after a series of meetings, Israeli Prime Minister Ben Gurion agreed to initiate limited military actions in the Sinai if British and French forces would strike at Egyptian airfields no later than thirty-six hours after the start of the Israeli incursion. Ben Gurion was particularly worried about the threat of attack by Egyptian IL-28 medium bombers against Tel Aviv, Jerusalem, and other Israeli cities. The French agreed to provide French Air Force fighters and pilots to help protect Israel from air attack. If Egypt struck Israeli targets, the IAF planned to begin immediately an all-out air offensive against the EAF and expected to rely on the French for air defense. After several days of fighting, Anglo-French attacks against Egyptian airfields were expected to eliminate the air threat to Israel. Then the IAF could apply the full weight of its aerial firepower against Egyptian ground forces in the Sinai in order to assist advancing Israeli units.

The French also flew a last-minute supply of weapons and ammunition to Israel and provided transport aircraft to help move material to the Sinai battlefield. Moshe Dayan later commented on the importance of this cooperation: "If it were not for the Anglo-French operation, it is doubtful whether Israel would have launched her campaign; and if she had, its character, both militarily and politically, would have been different."[3]

The 1956 conflict between Israeli and Egyptian forces took place in the Sinai Peninsula, a parched piece of land shaped like an inverted triangle. The southern part of the Sinai is hilly, with mountains reaching as high as 8,000 feet. A force of about two thousand Egyptian troops was stationed in the Sharm el Sheikh region at the southern tip of the Sinai. Armed with coastal artillery and a sizable number of antiaircraft guns and supported by several Egyptian naval vessels, this garrison interdicted shipping bound for the Israeli port of Eilat.[4]

The northern Sinai is a relatively flat coastal plain along the Mediterranean but south of this is a region of desert and mountainous terrain. Only three major roads cross the central Sinai: one parallels a rail line along the coast, a second skirts the mountains from Abu Awergila to Bir Gifgafa, and the final road is located south of the central hilly region cutting through Mitla Pass.

Most of Egypt's thirty-thousand-man force in the Sinai was located in the north, parallel to the Israeli border, and in the Gaza Strip. Egyptian troops were deployed in well-fortified defensive positions and supported by a considerable amount of artillery, tanks, and antitank guns.

Until 1955 the EAF had a close relationship with the RAF. As a result, the EAF was organized into wings like the RAF, relied upon British training concepts, and flew mostly English aircraft, including the Meteor and Vampire fighters and Lancaster bombers. In late 1955 the first Soviet-built MiG-15s began arriving in Egypt and with them came a large number of Czech and Soviet advisors and technicians. These foreign advisors reassembled the crated MiGs, trained Egyptians to fly and maintain the aircraft, and initiated programs to instill Soviet tactical philosophy and organization. The EAF could not easily absorb the more than eighty MiG-15 fighters, thirty to forty IL-28 bombers, and twenty IL-14 transports, MiG-15 UTI, and Yak-11 trainers that were delivered over a ten-month period. The Czech and Russian advisors hurriedly conducted training courses and assisted with maintenance, but it would take time to develop an experienced, capable cadre of support personnel.[5]

A shortage of skilled pilots and aircrews compounded the Egyptians' plight. The Egyptian Air Force Academy, located at Bilbeis, expanded its program, adding Yak-11s to its fleet of Gomhoria and Harvard trainers. However, as with skilled maintenance personnel, it took time to train combat-capable pilots. While the EAF had some five hundred pilots in October 1956, only about three hundred were capable of flying operationally, and the number rated on MiG-15s and IL-28s must have been less than one hundred.[6]

On the eve of the 1956 conflict, the EAF had a total strength of about sixty-four hundred, comprising four hundred officers, three thousand enlisted personnel, and three thousand civilians. Air Vice-Marshall Mohamed Sodky had at his disposal a force of about 255 aircraft organized into the following squadrons: three MiG-15s (fighters), three Vampires (fighter-bombers), two Meteors (fighters), three IL-28s (bombers), plus two transports and one liaison. Israeli intelligence sources identified as fully operational only two squadrons of MiG-15s, two of transports, and one squadron each of Vampires, Meteors, and IL-28s.[7]

Egypt had at its disposal over two dozen airfields. Many of these had been built by the British during World War II, although several had been recently upgraded by Egypt to accommodate the new Russian-built jets. Most of the major Egyptian airfields were located in the Cairo–Suez Canal area. These included Abu Suweir, Fayid, Inchas, Almaza, Cairo West, and Bilbeis. In the Sinai the EAF had operational airfields at El Arish, Bir Hamma, and Bir Gifgafa.

Normal peacetime strength of the IAF was about three thousand men, including over three hundred pilots. However, wartime mobilization expanded the force to more than ten thousand.[8] The IAF was commanded by Brig. Gen. Dan Tolkovsky. A former pilot with the RAF, General Tolkovsky considerably upgraded the capability of the IAF after he assumed command three years earlier.

At the outbreak of hostilities, the IAF had three operational jet fighter squadrons, which included some sixty Mystere IVA, Ouragon, and Meteor jets. Three fighter-bomber squadrons operated about sixteen Mosquito and thirty P-51 aircraft, while two B-17 bombers and twenty-one Harvard trainers could also be used on attack missions. The IAF transport force included sixteen C-47 Dakota and four Noratlas transports.[9] This considerable force was supported by French fighter squadrons whose mission was to protect Israeli cities from Egyptian attack. On October 23 more than two dozen French Air Force Mystere IVA fighters, including most of the 2 Escadre based at St. Dizier, left for Israel's Ramat David air base. Among these aircraft were Mystere IVA fighters from both 1/2 Cigonge and 3/2 Alsace units. Two days later the French deployed eighteen F-84F fighter-bombers of 1 Escadre from the 1/1 Corse, 2/1 Morvan, and 3/1 Argonne units, along with their maintenance personnel, from Dijon to Lod, the civil airport near Tel Aviv. The French also loaned several C-47 Dakota transports to the IAF for the conflict.[10]

Israel had eight major airfields available for use, with Ramat David, Hatzor, and Eqron being the most important. In addition, Lod could be used.

To conquer the Sinai, Israel deployed nine brigades totaling nearly forty-five thousand men along its southern border.[11] The largest force was to engage and defeat the Egyptian forces in the northern Sinai, which were concentrated in the triangle formed by Rafah, El Arish, and Abu Aweigila. Following the defeat of this Egyptian concentration, Israeli units planned to follow the coastal and central roads across the Sinai. The Israeli 202nd Airborne Brigade was assigned the mission of seizing Mitla Pass. Elements of the brigade not used in the paratroop assault were reinforced with artillery, half-tracks, and light tanks and given the task of linking up with the troops in Mitla Pass under the command of Col. Ariel Sharon. Another brigade was assigned the task of defeating Egyptian forces in the southern Sinai and capturing the fortifications at Sharm el Sheikh.

The conflict began with the paratroop drop into Mitla Pass. While the paratroopers dug in to prepare for an Egyptian counterattack, Sharon's convoy of airborne troops began their drive toward Mitla Pass. Sharon's paratroopers quickly captured an Egyptian frontier outpost at Kuntilla and, after a night march, engaged and defeated an Egyptian force entrenched near the town of Thamed. Israeli Piper Cubs landed in the desert to fly out the wounded and, at 7:00 A.M., several IAF transports delivered supplies and ammunition via parachute to the column. Suddenly six Egyptian MiGs swept in from the east at low altitude and caught Sharon's column by surprise. The Egyptian fighters bombed and strafed the Israeli convoy, destroying several vehicles and wounding six soldiers. Seeing that his men were tired and demoralized by the surprise air attack, Sharon ordered a rest. However, his force was again subjected to air attack at 11:00 A.M. by four Vampire fighters.

Entrenched at the north of Mitla Pass, Colonel Eiton's paratroopers were attacked by Egyptian troops at dawn on October 30. At about 7:30 A.M. two MiG-15 fighters strafed the entrenched paratroopers and destroyed a Piper Cub aircraft that was parked nearby in the desert. Within an hour four more Egyptian Vampire fighter-bombers strafed the Israeli paratroopers. The Vampires, which had flown from nearby Fayid airfield, were escorted by two MiG-15 fighters. Lieutenant Colonel Eiton, the Israeli paratroop commander, put in an urgent call for air cover.[12]

In the afternoon, the IAF began to fly patrols over the battle area and started attacking Egyptian convoys that were moving into the Sinai with reinforcements. Portions of the Egyptian 2nd Brigade, which was moving up from the Suez Canal to the western entrance of Mitla Pass, were repeatedly bombed, rocketed, and strafed by Israeli aircraft. In the late afternoon on October 30, six Israeli Mystere IVA fighters battled with six MiG-15 jets over Kabrit, an Egyptian air base near the Suez Canal. Lieutenant Yosef Tsuk, an Israeli Mystere pilot, shot down one of the MiG-15s. The surviving MiGs counterattacked. Tsuk's Mystere was hit by cannon fire, but he was able to return safely to his base.[13] This was the first air combat victory credited to the recently delivered Mystere IVA jet fighter. The dogfight proved that an aggressive pilot in the larger and heavier French-built fighter could engage and defeat the MiG-15, which had earned a reputation for its agility during combat in the skies over North Korea.

While Sharon's and Eiton's paratroopers were engaged in operations in the central Sinai, other Israeli units went into action in the north. Early on October 30, an infantry brigade led by Col. Joseph Harpaz advanced on foot across desert terrain that was impassable to vehicles and seized Egyptian fortifications surrounding the road junction of Queisima. Israeli forces converged on the heavily fortified Egyptian positions at Abu Aweigila.

The Israeli invasion of the Sinai began in earnest on the morning of October 30, and by late in the day Colonel Sharon's column had linked up with Lieutenant Colonel Eiton's paratroops at Mitla Pass.

On the first full day of the Sinai conflict, October 30, Israeli aircraft flew several hundred sorties. IAF fighters downed one Egyptian MiG-15 over Kabrit air base and performed over one hundred successful ground attack missions. It took time for Egypt to react to the Mitla Pass assault, and as a result, the EAF aircraft flew only about fifty combat sorties on October 30. However, the EAF conducted several effective ground attack missions against Israeli forces.

Late on October 30, British and French authorities issued an ultimatum calling for Israel and Egypt to stay ten miles away from the Suez Canal and to end the fighting in the Sinai within twelve hours. If these conditions were not met, Britain and France threatened to assault the Suez Canal and occupy its key positions.[14] Israel accepted the ultimatum, but Egypt rejected it.

The residents of Haifa, Israel, were awakened at 3:30 A.M. the following morning by gunfire from an Egyptian destroyer. The *Ibrahim Al Awwal* fired more than two hundred shells into the town before it was attacked and driven off by the French destroyer *Crescent.* About two hours later, two Israeli destroyers, the *Eilat* and the *Jaffa,* intercepted the *Ibrahim Al Awwat* and engaged her with gunfire. At dawn, two Israeli Ouragon fighters attacked and damaged the Egyptian vessel with rockets.[15]

With no hope of escaping—thanks to the air attack damage and continuing gunfire from the nearby Israeli destroyers—the captain of the ship ran up the white flag at 7:10 A.M. The ship was boarded, captured, and towed into Haifa harbor.

In the early morning hours, Israeli transports air-dropped supplies to the 202nd Paratroop Brigade near Mitla Pass. Colonel Sharon awakened suddenly with a 600-pound bundle of supplies landed within three feet of his head.[16]

The paratroopers received a wake-up call at 5:45 A.M. from four Egyptian Vampire fighter-bombers. Yallo Shavit, an IAF pilot who was patrolling over Mitla Pass in a Mystere fighter that morning, described his battle with these Egyptian jets:

> We got a panic call from the ground controller who gave the microphone to Colonel Eiton, who knew me personally. He said. "We are not well protected so try to be here as soon as possible. I know that you are short of fuel, but try to do whatever you can." When we heard his call, immediately we went into a split S and dived 90 degrees down to get over the area in the shortest time. While we were doing this, I saw four points glittering like mirrors from the sun. Four Egyptian Vampires had taken off from a base near the Suez Canal and were flying at 1,500 feet, which was above the morning clouds. I saw them and said to number one, "You be number two because once I lose eyesight, we are going to lose them." So we changed positions and I kept my eyes on these points. We crossed the speed of sound and we put the engines on idle and put the speed brakes out. We leveled off at about 2,000 feet and I recall to this day our speed was about 550 knots, which with a Mystere is a very high speed.
>
> They were flying like 250 knots so the closing speed, wow, it was like a missile. . . . I picked up one and put the cross on him and he was flying into the sun, but it was not too bright yet. I saw the cross on him and saw the bullets miss him. So I took a deflection, fired a short burst and one or two bullets hit him. Immediately he got inverted with smoke. I pulled up and went up to 10,000 feet with my speed. Number two did an S turn and got one and then I saw him shooting at another. The fourth one ran away, and I got him with a short burst as he ran toward the Suez Canal and he exploded in the air. Meanwhile number one started shouting fuel, fuel. . . . We climbed up to 36,000 feet in order to save fuel and headed back to base. We were so short of fuel. . . . I landed first and cleared the runway and he landed and his engine cut off at the end of the landing. . . . Both of us landed with zero fuel—just a miracle.
>
> The main point was that we were well trained to look

> around to find aircraft. Secondly, we learned how to use the cannons in air-to-air by doing many dogfights: Mystere against Ouragon, Mystere against Meteor, Mystere against Mustang. Even though we were pilots young in age, we had a lot of experience.[17]

Shortly after noon, a heavy task force of Israeli paratroopers, reinforced with armor, moved into Mitla Pass. This task force was trapped when heavy fire destroyed the lead vehicles. The remainder of the paratroop force was drawn into the action. Egyptian fighter-bombers supported their troops in the pass with several attacks. A particularly effective air strike occurred at about 4:00 P.M. when four Meteor fighter-bombers and six MiG-15s strafed the Israeli vehicles that were stalled on the road and then with rockets attacked the troops encamped at the east end of the pass. Two Israeli Ouragon fighters engaged and drove off the MiGs, but the Meteors returned again to strafe the paratroopers. These attacks destroyed several vehicles and caused over a dozen casualties.[18]

A night assault by the paratroopers resulted in the capture of the Egyptian positions in Mitla Pass. However, the hand-to-hand combat required to dislodge the well-entrenched Egyptian defenders cost Israel 34 killed and 102 wounded. Israeli transports landed in the desert during the night to bring in additional supplies and to carry out casualties.

Israeli forces assaulted Abu Aweigila and outflanked Egyptian defensive positions in the central Sinai. Determined Egyptian resistance slowed Israeli forces and IAF fighter-bombers were called in to blast the defenders and restrict the flow of Egyptian reinforcements. Propeller-driven Mustang and Mosquito fighter-bombers and Ouragon jets set upon Egyptian convoys and blasted positions with bombs, rockets, and machine-gun fire.

Eliezer (Cheetah) Cohen, a P-51 pilot who later retired with the rank of colonel, described his attacks against Egyptian forces:

> In 1956 my first mission was to attack a convoy of Egyptian tanks that was strolling along the Sinai. We met them with six P-51s and we destroyed twelve tanks

and twenty-five to thirty vehicles. We hit this convoy badly and as we left, we sent the Ouragons and Mosquitos in and they hit this convoy more and more.

We would put the tank on the centerline of our nose, fly very low at the level of the tank, and at the last moment, when you felt you had to pull up to not hit the tank, you released the napalm bomb and then pulled up, and the bomb hit the tank. We always attacked from 90 degrees and dropped only one bomb at a time so each Mustang, which carried two napalm bombs, six 5-inch rockets, and several hundred 0.5 rounds for the six machine guns, could do a hell of a job. The rockets were huge but not very accurate. But when they hit a tank, they destroyed it. On my second mission, I was attacking Egyptians near Aba Aweigila. On my first run, I attacked a self-propelled gun, like a tank but with a big cannon, and as I ran in, I saw an Egyptian soldier sitting on the tank shooting a machine gun at me. My angle of attack toward him made me a steady target, no angle of deflection. He hit me. You could really hear it and here comes all the oil from my engine radiator and it covered my windscreen. I was blacked out. I told myself, "Oh my god, I am in trouble. I will have to parachute over enemy positions." The engine slipped, but I made 4,000 feet before the propeller stopped. . . . I decided to fly south to open the space between Abu Aweigila before I went down. I knew from briefings that an Israeli armored division was coming behind the Egyptians. I could force land near these forces, which were coming from the south. I manually threw off the napalm and the rockets and landed. It was really easy. I was in the middle of the desert. Now I had to walk. I saw many retreating Egyptian soldiers and at first I hid, but my coveralls looked like theirs and, because my skin is dark since my parents were from Turkey, I fit right in. After hours of walking, I reached a road, and I saw Egyptian vehicles. I though, "Jesus Christ, now I am in big trouble because I am still behind enemy lines and our forces are not in yet." I found a small bridge, covered myself with stones so no one could see me and waited. Then I heard

> someone speaking Hebrew. He said, "Moshe, give me a Coca Cola." And then I understood that Israeli soldiers were using Egyptian vehicles. I came out, but they though I was an Egyptian and they ran off. They came back with a tank and you can't imagine who commanded this tank—my cousin! He recognized me and he yelled, "What are you doing here?" I got a car and drove back to my plane and took my parachute, radio, maps, and everything. When I got back to my base, they were very surprised.[19]

Late in the afternoon, Mystere fighters, patrolling along the northern coast road over El Arish, engaged a flight of Egyptian MiGs. The brief dogfight that ensued saw the destruction of two MiG-15 fighters.

On October 31 there was intense air and ground action in the Sinai. The IAF flew several hundred ground attack and interdiction missions in support of advancing Israeli troops and these missions destroyed or disabled many Egyptian vehicles. French F-84F fighter-bombers also flew attack sorties against targets in the Sinai with considerable success.[20] Mystere patrols fought air engagements with several Egyptian aircraft and downed four Vampire fighter-bombers and two MiG-15s.[21] Israeli transports flew dozens of resupply missions in support of advancing Israeli units. The EAF flew more than one hundred sorties over the Sinai during the day. Egyptian pilots conducted a number of successful air strikes against Israeli forces and top-cover MiGs intercepted and drove off several flights of Israel fighter-bombers. IAF fighters, however, were beginning to win the air-superiority battle over the Sinai.

British and French forces entered the war against Egypt during the night on October 31. Starting at about 10:30 P.M. Canberra and Valiant bombers of the RAF began bombing Egyptian airfields. Because of the threat of interception by EAF MiG-15, Meteor, and Vampire fighters, the RAF aircraft bombed their targets at night, from an altitude of 40,000 feet. EAF airfields at Almaza, Inchas, Abu Suweir, Kabrit, and Cairo International were struck by RAF bombers, which dropped both contact and delayed-action bombs. These initial raids damaged the airfields but destroyed only fourteen aircraft.[22] In response to these attacks, Egyptian, Czech, and Soviet pilots immediately began ferrying EAF aircraft to remote airfields or to locations out of the country. At first, light Royal Navy fighter-bombers from the aircraft carriers HMS *Albion*, HMS *Bulwork*, and HMS *Eagle* plus land-based French and British fighters operating from Cyprus continued to pound Egyptian airfields. During the first twenty-four hours of their involvement, British and French aircraft flew over five hundred sorties, attacked over a dozen Egyptian airfields, and destroyed more than one hundred Egyptian aircraft.[23]

On November 1, Israeli forces began their assault on Rafah, the heavily fortified Egyptian town at the end of the Gaza Strip. When concentrated Egyptian fire stalled the initial assault, Israeli artillery and aircraft were called in. Mosquito fighter-bombers struck with rockets, bombs, and cannons, while artillery and naval gunfire from Israeli destroyers and a French cruiser pounded the Egyptian defenses.[24] Intense fighting continued until mid-morning, when the Egyptian forces began to withdraw. Retreating Egyptian forces fought back vigorously despite being harried by Israeli armor and repeatedly attacked by IAF fighter-bombers.

Egyptian troops fought stubbornly in the defense of the Sinai but Israeli forces were gaining the upper hand through rapid maneuvers, surprise, and heavy close air support. Interdiction attacks by the IAF inhibited the movement of Egyptian forces. The British and French attacks against Egyptian airfields contributed to the defeat of the Sinai defenders by eliminating their air cover and bringing the focus of the conflict back to the Suez Canal.

President Nasser, on November 1, urged his troops in the Sinai to disengage from Israeli units and fall back to the Suez Canal to protect it from attack by an expected Anglo-French invasion force. By late afternoon, many EAF aircraft had been dispersed to airfields in Saudi Arabia, Syria, or southern Egypt. Those that remained in Egypt were under concentrated attack by British and French fighter-bombers. As a result, the IAF had complete air superiority over the Sinai, and, with some assistance from three French squadrons stationed in Israel, provided unhindered close air support, resupply, and reconnaissance efforts for advancing Israeli columns.

On November 2, Israeli troops drove into El Arish; Egyptian troops had evacuated the airfield and supply depot during the previous night. The fall of Rafah and El Arish cut off the two brigades of Egyptian and Palestinian troops in the Gaza Strip. While the Egyptians held strong defensive positions, the city of Gaza was rapidly taken by Israeli forces. After several hours of fighting, General Digany, the Egyptian commander, surrendered the city to minimize civilian casualties.

The final phase of the war in the Sinai began on November 2 as Israeli units began to close on the Suez Canal and Sharm el Sheikh. Egyptian troops fortified at the southern end of the Sinai were able to halt ships traveling through the Gulf of Aqaba toward the Israeli port of Eilat. After crossing the border on October 30, Col. Avraham Yoffe's 9th Israeli Brigade began to move south along the Gulf of Aqaba early on the morning of November 2. The going was slow because the desert road was uphill and covered with drifting sand.

Israeli Chief of Staff Gen. Moshe Dayan was concerned about the 9th Brigade's capability to move rapidly south across the rugged Sinai terrain and seize Sharm el Sheikh. The United Nations was calling for an end of the fighting between Israel and Egypt and an immediate suspension of the Anglo-French attacks against Egyptian targets.

To increase the force in the southern Sinai, Dayan ordered Colonel Sharon, whose paratroopers were still holding Mitla Pass, to send a detachment south along the Gulf of Suez road toward Sharm el Sheikh.[25] Two companies of paratroopers were also dropped near the town of El Tur in order to secure the western route to Sharm el Sheikh. Following the capture of the airfield at El Tur, IAF transports flew in an additional battalion of troops, vehicles, ammunition, and supplies. Israeli fighter-bombers bombed and strafed the Egyptian positions at Sharm el Sheikh and one of the Mysteres was shot down by antiaircraft fire. Major Benjamin Peled, commander of a Mystere squadron, ejected successfully but landed near the Egyptian position. Despite an injured leg, he was able to take refuge in hilly terrain near the outpost. A Piper Cub pilot spotted Major Peled, landed on a flat stretch of ground, and picked him up, right under the noses of the Egyptian defenders.

By the end of November 2 those Egyptian forces that had not

been cut off had largely withdrawn from the Sinai to positions along the Suez Canal. British and French aircraft from Cyprus, Malta, and aircraft carriers in the Mediterranean continued to strike at Egyptian airfields and began to hit army positions near Port Said and adjacent to the Suez Canal. Eight French Air Force F-84F fighter-bombers, flown from an Israeli airfield, attacked and destroyed about twenty IL-28 bombers located at Luxor air base in central Egypt.[26]

Israeli troops assaulted the remaining Egyptian defensive positions in the Gaza Strip and central Sinai on November 3. With assistance from artillery and IAF close support strikes, Israeli troops forced the surrender of the last Egyptian defensive positions in the Gaza Strip and northern Sinai by late in the day.

Israeli aircraft intensified their assault against fortifications near Sharm el Sheikh beginning at dawn on November 3.[27] Egyptian troops at Sharm el Sheikh were without air cover but fought back courageously. Their antiaircraft fire continued to claim victims; many IAF aircraft were damaged and several Mustangs were shot down in the course of these air attacks.

The final Israeli assault against Sharm el Sheikh began about 3:30 A.M. on November 5. The heavy Egyptian fire initially stalled the assault and caused dozens of casualties. At the first light, with the assistance of heavy mortar fire plus repeated air strikes by IAF aircraft using napalm, rockets, and gunfire, the Israelis regained the initiative. They overran Egyptian positions one by one, and by 9:00 A.M. the fighting in the Sinai was over.

On the same day that Egyptian forces were defeated at Sharm el Sheikh (November 5), British paratroops were assaulting Egyptian positions on the Suez Canal near Port Said and French troops were landing near Port Fuad. The following morning British and French troops landed on the beach at Port Said. Royal Marine Commando Unit No. 45 was flown into action from the assault carriers HMS *Theseus* and HMS *Ocean* via helicopters, marking the first time in warfare that a large-scale amphibious assault was conducted using helicopters.

British and French forces moved south along the Suez Canal and made significant gains against the defending Egyptian troops with assistance from tanks and fighter-bombers. Following Egypt's request on November 2 for a cease-fire, the United States, Soviet Union, and other UN members pressured Britain and France until the two nations finally agreed to end their invasion in the early hours of November 7.

In a little more than one hundred hours of fighting, Israel had achieved Operation Kadesh's objectives: almost the whole Sinai Peninsula had been captured, Egyptian forces defeated, guerrilla bases in the Gaza Strip destroyed, and the blockade of the Strait of Tiran broken. Israeli forces, in the process, suffered 181 killed, 800 wounded, and 4 captured. Egyptian combat losses in the Sinai included about 1,000 killed, 4,000 wounded, and 6,000 captured. Egyptian war material captured by Israeli forces included 100 tanks, 1,000 vehicles, and 200 artillery pieces. Fewer than 100 Israeli tanks, half-tracks, and other pieces of heavy equipment were destroyed in the fighting.[28]

It is important to place in perspective the Anglo-French involvement in the 1956 conflict. After the war, Moshe Dayan admitted that Israel might not have agreed to invade the Sinai at all in the absence of English and French assistance. Britain and France committed 90,000 men, 130 warships and support vessels including two French and five British aircraft carriers, plus 500 aircraft to the operation. Combat aircraft, transports, and helicopters of the RAF, Royal Navy, French Air Force, and French Naval air arm units flew several thousand sorties during their seven-day involvement. Britain and France claimed to have destroyed about 200 Egyptian aircraft on the ground and provided effective support for their ground forces. Anglo/French troops seized Port Said, Port Fuad, and the northern portion of the Suez Canal. In the process, British forces suffered 16 dead, 96 wounded, and lost 8 aircraft (one Canberra bomber, one Venom, two Sea Hawks, two Wyvern fighter-bombers, and two Whirlwind helicopters), while French losses included 10 dead, 33 wounded, and 2 aircraft (one Corsair and one F-84F fighter-bomber). Egyptian losses in combat with British and French forces are estimated to be 650 dead, 900 wounded, and included more than 200 aircraft of all types.[29] The English and French took few risks in their battles with the Egyptians. The slow pace of military action and the intensity of political opposition were disastrous for Britain and France. Any hopes the two nations had of regaining control of the Suez Canal were dashed when the United Nations forced their troops to withdraw following the cease-fire.

After the war the United States and the Soviet Union exerted tremendous pressure on Israel to evacuate its forces from the Sinai. Reluctantly Israel agreed to withdraw and, in exchange, the United Nations created a peacekeeping force that took control of Sharm el Sheikh and the Gaza Strip. Although the Gaza Strip quickly came under Egyptian domination, guerrilla activity did not begin again for many years.

The IAF began the Suez conflict bound by its own tight restrictions. Initially Israeli aircraft did not strike at airfields for two reasons: Israel did not want to be viewed as the aggressor and it hoped the Egyptians would think along the same lines. When Egyptian fighter-bombers struck at advancing Israeli columns and paratroop positions near Mitla Pass on October 30, the IAF stepped up its air cover over the ground forces and began attacking Egyptian units. The IAF was able to defend its units in the Sinai from air attack and simultaneously perform ground attack missions because three squadrons of French fighters were on hand to defend Israeli airspace against Egyptian air attacks. In addition, the IAF did not have to allocate attack sorties against Egyptian air bases because the British and French performed this mission.

The IAF relied on its small force of recently introduced Mystere IVA fighters to achieve superiority in the air over the Sinai. Of seven Egyptian aircraft downed by the Israelis, all fell to Mystere IVA pilots, many of whom had little experience with their new aircraft. Ouragon and Meteor fighters also flew fighter patrol missions but were used more often in the ground attack role.[30]

The air superiority contest over the Sinai only lasted five days. Egypt did not react to the October 29 paratroop assault on Mitla Pass, but it did strike back beginning at dawn the following day. Egyptian MiG-15s, Meteors, and Vampires flew effective ground attack missions and clashed with Israeli aircraft on more than a dozen occasions. Although Egyptian pilots damaged several Israeli planes, their only air combat victory during the 1956 conflict was to down a Piper Cub. British and

One of the first aircraft to serve with the Air Service of the Haganah, the foundation of the Israeli Air Force, was the British-built Auster.

The Czech-built Avia S199 combined the Messerschmit Bf 109G airframe and the Jumo bomber engine. It was an unpleasant aircraft to take off and land because of the high torque of the engine and its narrow-track landing gear. While it was not a popular aircraft, in the hands of a capable pilot it could counter the Spitfire, its principal adversary.

An Israeli photographer captured the image of the first air battle over the new state of Israel on June 3, 1948. Modi Alon, commander of the first IAF fighter squadron, intercepted and shot down two Egyptian C-47 Dakota transports that were dropping bombs on Tel Aviv.

IAF transports, such as this C-47, were sometimes used as bombers at night. However, bringing arms to Israel and moving troops and weaponry to the battlefield were their primary missions.

2163

On June 17, 1953, the IAF joined the jet age with the delivery of two Meteor T.7 trainers. Israeli Prime Minister David Ben Gurion, who addressed the crowd at the delivery ceremony, named the aircraft *Gale* and *Tempest*.

The IAF acquired the Mystere IVA fighter in 1956 and the aircraft served until the early 1970s. This swept-wing jet performed both fighter and attack missions. During the 1956 conflict, Israeli Mystere IVA pilots downed seven Egyptian MiGs and Vampires over the Sinai while French-flown Mystere IVAs patrolled over Israel to protect against Arab attacks.

Israeli C-47 and Noratlas unloading supplies in the Sinai. IAF transports delivered Israeli paratroops to Mitla Pass and moved fuel and ammunition into the Sinai to help maintain the advance of armored columns during the 1956 Sinai Conflict.

The Dassault Supere Mystere B2 was the first European combat aircraft capable of supersonic speed in level flight. Israel procured a squadron-sized force of these highly capable aircraft, the first of which was delivered in 1959.

To modernize the pilot training program and upgrade the capabilities of the Israeli aviation industry, Israel put into service the Fouga Magister jet trainer.

An IAF Mirage IIIC prepares to take off with a heavy load of bombs and external fuel tanks. Almost the entire IAF fighter force was committed to the initial series of strikes against Arab airfields on the morning of June 5, 1967.

The Arab air forces were not totally out of action in 1967. A pair of Egyptian MiG-17 fighter-bombers strafed an Israeli supply convoy, destroying several vehicles and causing numerous casualties.

An IAF Mirage on a reconnaissance mission captures the image of the remains of five MiG-21 fighters at an Arab airfield.

The A-4 was an ideal replacement for the IAF's aging inventory of French-built aircraft. The Skyhawk could carry a heavy weapons load, was easy to fly, and was relatively cheap to buy and operate. The A-4 was the first new American-built aircraft to serve with the IAF.

Israeli commandos jump from a UH-1D transport helicopter. These light, turbine-powered helicopters were used extensively in the anti-terrorist role.

French air strikes, which began on the night of October 31, eliminated the EAF as a factor in the Sinai fighting.

Ground attack was the focus of the IAF during the last five days of the Sinai campaign. The harsh desert terrain kept the Egyptian convoys on the few main roads, with little or no cover for escape. Beginning on October 30, IAF aircraft harassed Egyptian columns that were moving across the Sinai to engage Israeli forces. The fighter-bombers also attacked Egyptian fortifications to weaken them for armor and infantry assault. Close air support missions helped Israeli combat troops overcome strong Egyptian fortifications in several Sinai battles.

During the conflict, all IAF combat aircraft were pressed into service to fly ground attack missions, including the Mystere IVA, Ouragon, and Meteor jet fighters, and Mustang, Mosquito, and even Harvard (trainer) propeller-driven aircraft. Antiquated B-17 bombers also flew operational missions, striking the Egyptians at Sharm el Sheikh and flying maritime patrol sorties over the Mediterranean and Gulf of Aqaba. Ground attack aircraft blasted Egyptian targets with bombs, rockets, and napalm, plus cannon and machine-gun fire. Egyptian antiaircraft fire was frequently intense. Thirteen of the fifteen Israeli losses were to antiaircraft fire, including ten P-51 Mustangs.[31] On the plus side, IAF attack sorties disabled an Egyptian destroyer, blasted dozens of defensive positions, and destroyed more than two hundred tanks and vehicles in the Sinai. Israeli ground commanders stated after the conflict that interdiction and close air support operations hastened the Israeli advance, reduced casualties, and shortened the campaign. While the outcome would probably have been the same, the conflict would have taken a few days longer without support from Israeli air strikes, and more casualties would have been suffered to defeat Egyptian forces in the Sinai.

Beginning on October 31, Israeli-based French F-84F fighter-bombers flew attack missions against Egyptian forces in the Sinai. One aircraft was lost in the course of operations, but the pilot successfully ejected and landed in the Sinai Desert.[32]

IAF scout planes and transports helped ensure the Israeli victory in the Sinai campaign. Piper Cubs performed vital scouting and liaison missions, which aided the ground commanders in understanding the situation on the battlefield. The pilots of these small aircraft frequently landed on rough desert terrain to evacuate casualties and rescue downed IAF pilots. One Piper Cub was destroyed in an air attack and another was shot down by EAF fighters. The IAF transport force made possible the opening move of the Sinai campaign—the interdiction of Mitla Pass by Israeli paratroopers. This innovative strike into the Egyptian-held Sinai came as a complete surprise. Israeli Dakota and Noratlas transports delivered supplies to advancing Israeli columns, resupplied the paratroops at the Mitla Pass, and aided in the capture of Sharm el Sheikh through the rapid deployment of additional forces into the Sinai.

The forces involved in the Sinai fighting were fairly evenly matched in numbers of aircraft, troops, tanks, armored vehicles, and artillery. It was the confidence, initiative, spirit, and leadership of Israeli personnel in the air and on the ground, along with Anglo-French intervention that overcame the Egyptian forces. Aggressive maneuvers on the ground were supported by initiatives in the air. Brig. Gen. Dan Tolkovsky, commander of the air force, stated after the conflict that peacetime training and preparations were the biggest contributors to the efficiency of the IAF in battle. Intense training, the calling up of the reserves, and good maintenance enabled the IAF to fly four missions a day with their Mystere and Ouragon jets and more than two sorties a day with their older Mustangs and Mosquitos. Combat-damaged aircraft were quickly repaired and Israel had almost two pilots available to fly each aircraft. All of these factors combined to enable the IAF to support a rigorous flying schedule. During the war, the IAF flew 1,986 sorties, almost 500 of which were ground attack missions in support of advancing troops in the Sinai.[33] The successful Sinai campaign prompted senior Israeli leaders to reorganize their military force and strengthen the armor and the jet fighter components.

4

Modernization

Within weeks of the end of the 1956 Sinai conflict, political pressure from the United Nations forced Israel to pull its troops out of the Sinai. Israeli political and military leaders vowed that this would not happen again. During the next decade the Israeli army, navy, and air force were strengthened. In the event of a future conflict, Israel planned to strike a powerful opening blow, carry the fight to the enemy, and quickly achieve victory. This doctrine would allow Israel to maximize the effectiveness of its mostly reserve army, reduce losses to a minimum, and force the conclusion of the conflict before significant enemy reinforcements and political intervention could affect the outcome of the war.

Israeli leaders understood that, in the event of war, they could not rely on external assistance like that provided by France and Great Britain in the 1956 conflict. The security of the country required a powerful army and an air force composed of fighters capable of performing both air-to-air and attack missions.

The Israelis developed an offensive doctrine that called for fast-moving armored columns (composed primarily of tanks) and a strong air force to spearhead a preemptive attack. Since areas where the fighting was most likely to occur—the Sinai Desert, the Golan Heights, and the Jordan River Valley—afforded little or no cover from air attack, Israeli air superiority was vital to the success of this concept of war. The doctrine called for the destruction of enemy air forces early in the war. Direct attacks against enemy airfields would destroy aircraft on the ground, before they could get into battle. Once enemy air forces had been eliminated and air superiority achieved, the IAF would concentrate on providing support for advancing Israeli ground forces.

Even though Egypt lost the 1956 war in the eyes of the world, the Arab nations considered the "Suez War" a victory because they perceived that President Nasser had overcome Britain, France, and Israel in a political sense. Following the 1956 war, the Soviet Union rapidly resupplied Egypt with new aircraft and weapons to replace those destroyed during the conflict. Scores of advisors were sent to Egypt to train the EAF and large numbers of Egyptian pilots and support personnel traveled to the Soviet Union for military training. By late 1957, the EAF had been rearmed with new Soviet-built aircraft and the air forces of Syria, Jordan, and Iraq had been considerably strengthened.

To meet this threat and support the new offensive doctrine, Israel expanded the IAF. The piston-engined Mustang, Mosquito, and B-17 combat aircraft and Harvard trainers were phased out as quickly as possible and replaced by modern jets. Since the relationship between Israel and France remained strong after the 1956 conflict, the IAF turned to France for these new aircraft.

While not equal in performance to the Soviet-built MiG-15/17, the Ouragon jet fighter had proven itself in action during the 1956 conflict and was immediately available. Israel placed an order in late 1956 for an additional supply of Ouragon jets and France delivered the first of these in 1957. Forty-five ex–French Air Force Ouragon fighters were supplied to Israel. With this second purchase, the Israeli Ouragon force grew to two squadrons and more than seventy aircraft.

Israel also procured additional Mystere IVA fighters from France to make up for combat and operational losses and to expand the frontline fighter force. By the late 1950s, the IAF had received in excess of sixty Mystere IVA fighters. During the late 1950s and early 1960s, the two Mystere IVA squadrons were responsible for the air defense of Israel.

In 1957 Israel purchased eighteen Vautour IIA aircraft to form a fighter-bomber squadron to replace aging Mosquito and B-17 bombers. A large, twin-engine, swept-wing aircraft, the Vautour IIA was armed with four 30-mm cannons. The aircraft could also carry more than 4,000 pounds of weaponry in its internal bomb bay and on underwing pylons. Produced by the French firm Sud Aviation, the French Air Force operated several versions of the Vautour, including fighter-bomber, reconnaissance, and radar-equipped fighter models. The Vautour could fly at nearly 700 miles per hour and had a radius of action in excess of 750 miles.

Satisfied with the performance of the attack version, the IAF purchased seven two-seat Vautour IIN all-weather fighters. These specialized jets served with the remaining NF-13 Meteors in the single IAF night/all-weather fighter squadron. This special unit had the responsibility for night and bad weather air defense of Israeli airspace. Later the IAF purchased four two-seat Vautour IIBR aircraft with a glazed nose and internally mounted sensor pallet in the weapons bay. These planes were used on reconnaissance missions. About thirty Vautour aircraft were eventually delivered to the IAF. Until mid-1958 their existence in Israel was a matter of utmost secrecy.[1]

After purchasing all of these planes and upgrading the role of the air force, Brig. Gen. Dan Tolkovsky had achieved his goal of priority status for the air force. The air arm was first in line for the allocation of defense funds and also received the best Israeli manpower.

Becoming a fighter pilot became the ultimate goal of young Israeli males. The IAF pilot-training pilot program was the most rigorous in the world—nearly 90 percent of the applicants selected for the program were eventually rejected. Extremely high standards were established because the Israelis knew that only an air force with top-quality pilots could fight outnumbered and win.

Israeli youth seeking to be pilots first had to pass a demanding series of preliminary tests and character analyses. Pilot candidates began their training immediately after secondary school. This contrasts with most air forces, which require pilot trainees first to complete their college education. The twenty-month course began with about ten hours of flight training on Piper Super Cub aircraft. This first course was intended more to identify those with flight aptitude than to be a real instructional phase. Students who successfully completed this part of the training then attended intensified classes on applied mathematics, physics, aeronautics, meterology, electronics, navigation, and other subjects. Following the classroom phase, pilot candidates took a demanding infantry-training course to test their physical abilities and become familiar with the missions of the ground forces.

General and aerobatic flight instruction comprised the next part of the IAF pilot-training course. In the late 1950s, pilot trainees flew the Boeing PT-17 biplane and then graduated to the T-6 Harvard training aircraft. Advanced flight training used piston-engined Mustang and jet-powered Meteor fighters. In the early 1960s the Israelis changed the training syllabus so that pilot trainees proceeded from the Piper Super Cub directly into a new jet trainer, the Air Fouga Magister. The new training cycle introduced Israeli pilot candidates to jet aircraft at an earlier stage, better preparing them for the advanced jet fighters that were entering service with the IAF in large numbers.[2]

This new generation of jet aircraft and weaponry demanded skilled aircraft mechanics and electronics technicians. The IAF considerably expanded its maintenance and support staff to ensure that the new jet aircraft were always ready to fly. Conscripts received intense training while skilled personnel were encouraged to reenlist or serve in civilian positions with the air force or aviation firms.

In July 1958, Ezer Weizman became the new commander of the IAF. The thirty-four-year-old brigadier general was determined to expand the capability and effectiveness of the air force. A former pilot with the RAF, Weizman had served with the first IAF fighter squadron in the 1948 War of Independence and held high-ranking positions, including deputy to Dan Tolkovsky.

Weizman continued to strengthen the air force and worked to give it greater independence and esprit de corps. Weizman is best characterized by his statement "Israel's best defense is in the skies of Cairo."[3] Air force personnel focused on his operational plan to attack enemy aircraft on the ground and destroy any aircraft that made it into the air.

Massive Soviet resupply and training efforts strengthened the air arms of Egypt, Syria, and Iraq. Jordan, Lebanon, and Iraq received Hawker Hunter fighters and training assistance from the United Kingdom. The EAF, in particular, worried Israeli planners. In the late 1950s, the EAF received hundreds of MiG-15 and MiG-17 fighters and IL-28 jet bombers. In addition to Soviet assistance, Egypt enlisted the support of German scientists and technicians in an attempt to provide a domestic aircraft and guided missile industrial base. A team of designers was hard at work developing the lightweight HA-300 supersonic fighter, while a group of engineers worked to produce advanced guided missiles.[4]

In 1958 the IAF ordered the supersonic Super Mystere B2 fighter from France. The first European fighter capable of sustained supersonic flight, the aircraft was an evolutionary improvement of the Dassault Mystere IVA. The Super Mystere featured new systems, a thinner wing, and a more powerful SNECMA Atar 101G afterburning turbojet engine that produced a maximum thrust of 9,800 pounds. The aircraft had a maximum takeoff weight of 22,000 pounds, was armed with two 30-mm DEFA cannons and could carry up to 2,000 pounds of external ordnance. Since it could perform both fighter and attack missions, the Super Mystere fulfilled IAF multirole requirements. The first Super Mysteres entered service with the IAF in 1959, and the new fighter squadron was operational within less than a year.[5]

In the late 1950s the Israeli firm Bedek Aircraft, Ltd. (now Israel Aircraft Industries) entered into an agreement with the French company Air Fouga to produce the Magister jet trainer in Israel. The 6,500-pound aircraft was propelled by two 880-pound-thrust Turbomecca Marbore turbojet engines, and was capable of full aerobatics. The Magister could be used as a trainer and as a light strike aircraft, using rockets, light bombs, and two internal machine guns. Israel purchased a small number of these trainers from Air Fouga, the parent company, but most IAF models were assembled by Bedek using a mixture of Israeli-built and imported components. The Israeli version of the aircraft differed from the standard Magister in having larger, unpowered ailerons and strengthened wings that could accommodate external weaponry.

To upgrade the IAF further, Israel again turned to France. Dassault, producer of the Ouragon, Mystere IVA, and Super Mystere, began the design of a small delta-wing fighter in the early 1950s in response to NATO and French Air Force requirements. Promising test results with several prototypes prompted the French Air Force to order ten Mirage IIIA preproduction models and place an option for one hundred production versions in 1958. The Mirage IIIC fighter was developed to defend French airspace from attack by Soviet nuclear-armed bombers. With its Mach 2 speed and ability to climb to over 50,000 feet in less than five minutes, the 20,000-pound Mirage IIIC was expected to make quick work of high-flying enemy bombers. Normal armament for the high-altitude intercept mission was a single radar-guided Matra 511 or 530 air-to-air missile. The Mirage IIIC's Cyrano 1 radar and semiactive radar-homing air-to-air missile allowed the pilot to intercept targets at night and in poor weather. For daytime air combat the aircraft could be armed with two 30-mm DEFA cannons and two American-built AIM-9B Sidewinder infrared-homing air-to-air missiles. Most French air force Mirage IIICs carried only missile armament, since the fuel tanks for the rocket used to boost rate of climb displaced the cannons and their supply of ammunition. For ground attack missions, the Mirage IIIC could accommodate bombs, air-to-surface guided missiles, and fuel tanks in addition to the aircraft's internal cannons.

IAF officials closely followed the development of the Mirage fighter. In 1959 Ezer Weizman, commander of the IAF, traveled to France with Danny Shapira, the IAF's chief test pilot, to evaluate the fighter. Shapira put one of the early Mirages through a demanding flight evaluation, including supersonic flight. At a time when Mach 2 flight was the realm of an exclusive group, Shapira became only the twelfth pilot in France to reach that speed. The IAF's command was very impressed with the aircraft. Following discussions with the ministry of defense, Israeli officials placed an order for twenty-four of the fighters. Like the French fighters, IAF Mirages were equipped with the Cyrano 1 radar. Even though Israel later purchased a limited supply of Matra 530 air-to-air missiles, the IAF continued to rely on the potent DEFA 30-mm cannon as the primary air combat weapon of the Mirage IIIC fighter.

The Mirage IIIC fighter entered service with the IAF on April 7, 1962, and by 1967 the Mirage fleet had expanded to seventy-two aircraft, which comprised three fighter squadrons. Three Mirage IIIB two-seat trainers were also purchased to ease pilot-training efforts.[6]

Air operations in the 1956 conflict underscored the importance of the IAF transport fleet. The C-47 Dakota contributed significantly to Israel's 1956 victory, and, even in the 1960s, a dozen of these aircraft remained in service. Worn and tired C-47s that were acquired during the 1948 War of Independence were retired and replaced by later models purchased from civilian sources and the French air force.

The only Israeli transport that could deliver the large loads needed to support the ground forces during the 1956 conflict was the Noratlas. Satisfied with its performance, the IAF bought more of these capable aircraft and by the mid-1960s about twenty Noratlases were in service. Half of these aircraft were purchased from France and the remainder were supplied by West Germany.

To transport heavy loads beyond the capacity of the Noratlas, the IAF purchased several four-engined Boeing Stratocruisers secondhand from civilian and military sources during the 1960s. Israel Aircraft Industries engineers and technicians combined the airframes of several former Pan American Airways Stratocruisers with the aft fuselages of ex-USAF C-97 aircraft to come up with aircraft that could air-drop heavy payloads, haul cargo, transport troops, and refuel in the air. At least five of these transports were available on the eve of the 1967 war.[7]

After a several-year flight evaluation of helicopters, IAF planners decided to purchase a substantial force of vertical-lift aircraft. In late 1956, the first of six Sikorsky S-55 utility transport helicopters entered service with the IAF. Used for air and sea rescue and coastal patrol, as well as for airborne ambulances, these relatively low-powered helicopters were limited by the high temperatures common in Israel. Israel had better luck with the five-seat, turbine-powered Sud Aviation Alouette II helicopter. Developed to be used in hot, high-altitude environments, these helicopters operated with considerable success. Larger Sikorsky S-58 helicopters purchased from the United States in 1958 performed successfully and an additional supply of these aircraft were bought from West Germany. Slightly larger than the S-55, the S-58 had nearly twice the horsepower of its predecessor, which resulted in a dramatic performance improvement in the heat. The S-58 could carry eighteen troops, a ton of cargo, or eight stretchers to a range of more than 200 miles. The IAF force of more than thirty S-58 medium-lift helicopters was used to transport airborne troops on border patrol and to perform commando operations.

The lift capability of the helicopter force was considerably expanded in the mid-1960s with the introduction of the French-built Super Frelon helicopter. Nine of these aircraft had entered service by the 1967 war. The Super Frelon made possible new combat tactics because it was capable of carrying thirty troops, or jeeps, light artillery, or heavy equipment. Super Frelon and S-58 helicopter crews trained with airborne troops and conducted large-scale airlift exercises to refine combat tactics. Helicopter crews were also taught special techniques to evade enemy interceptors. IAF helicopter pilot training was conducted using Bell 47 and Alouette light helicopters and was as intense as that experienced by fighter-pilot trainees.[8]

During the 1960s the IAF's fleet of basic trainer and liaison aircraft was modernized. Older light planes were taken out of service and replaced by new Piper Super Cub and Cessna 185 Skywagon aircraft. A small number of specialized aircraft like the Dornier DO 27 and Pilatus Turbo-porter short-take-off-and-landing liaison planes were also put into service.

The years following the 1956 conflict were relatively peaceful for Israel. Although no formal peace treaties had been signed to end Arab/Israeli conflict, UN forces located in the Sinai helped guarantee safe passage for Israeli shipping and also helped keep the peace. During the next several years, internal unrest in Lebanon, Jordan, Iraq, and Syria forced these nations to focus their attention on domestic problems. Still, sporadic terrorist attacks did not cease with the Israel/Syria border area being the most embattled area.

Air confrontations continued between Israel and its neighbors as planes crossed borders to test reaction times. On December 20, 1958, an Egyptian MiG-17 was shot down by an Israeli pilot flying a Mystere IVA. The Super Mystere B2 achieved its first combat victory on April 28, 1961, when a patrol of two Super Mystere fighters intercepted a pair of Egyptian MiG-17s. One of the MiGs escaped, but the pilot of the other lost control of his jet and bailed out.[9] In the fall of 1962 four IAF Super Mystere fighters clashed with four Syrian MiG-17 fighters over the Golan Heights. During the air battle one Israeli jet was heavily damaged and no MiGs were hit.

During the arms race between Israel and its Arab neighbors in the early 1960s, Egypt rapidly developed a powerful air force and gained considerable combat experience through participation in the civil war in North Yemen. Israeli defense planners were particularly worried about the threat of attack by the thirty TU-16 medium and forty IL-28 light bombers of the EAF, which could deliver over 350 tons of bombs against Israeli targets in a single raid. The Iraqi Air Force also operated both of these bombers, while the air arm of Syria had a small contingent of IL-28s. A coordinated Arab air strike, protected by fighter escort, was a possibility that Israel had to face. No less important was the threat of air attack by the hundreds of fighter-bombers in service with the air arms of Egypt, Syria, Jordan, Iraq, Lebanon, and other Arab countries. By the mid-1960s, this force outnumbered the IAF by more than three to one and included over 250 supersonic MiG-19/21 fighters and 350 MiG-15/17, SU-7, and Hawker Hunter fighter-bombers.[10]

To even the odds, Israel planned to strike the first blow in a future conflict. Titled the "operational plan," this offensive doctrine called for a simultaneous surprise attack of Arab airfields. The Israelis calculated the number of sorties that would be required to deliver enough bombs, rockets, and cannon shells to destroy a majority of the Arab aircraft on the ground. Even if all IAF aircraft reached their targets and performed successfully, the air arm was not large enough, nor could the IAF carry a large enough payload to complete the job in a single wave. Because most of the frontline IAF aircraft were designed to perform air-to-air combat rather than ground attack, the useful ordnance payload that most IAF fighters could carry per sortie against typical target airfields was limited (Vautour—4,000 pounds; Mirage IIIC—2,000 pounds; Super Mystere B2—2,000 pounds; Mystere IVA—1,000 pounds; and Ouragon—500 pounds). In figuring the chances for a successful preemptive attack, Israeli planners had to account for aircraft lost due to enemy fire, maintenance problems, and pilot error. A preemptive attack would only succeed if the exact location of enemy aircraft could be determined. To maximize the number of effective sorties, IAF ground crews would rapidly have to refuel, rearm, and return to service the aircraft that had completed their mission. A conveyor belt-like system would be necessary in order to destroy all the potential targets.[11]

The airfields targeted for initial attack housed Egyptian TU-16 and IL-28 bombers and MiG-19/21 fighters. To protect Israeli cities and minimize the risk to the heavily laden Israeli fighter-bombers, it was imperative that the first wave of Israeli planes either destroy or damage these Egyptian aircraft. Subsequent waves of attacking aircraft could eliminate crippled jets, blast lower priority targets, and hit the main base of other Arab air forces. To make this plan work, almost all IAF aircraft had to be committed to the attack, with less than one squadron of fighters to be held in reserve to provide air defense. This offensive plan also counted on surprise and confusion among the Egyptians and their Arab allies. A confused enemy would not be able to react quickly to the strikes, and the enemy's aircraft would be destroyed before an effective defense or counterattack could be organized.

The operational plan was tested often by the Israelis. Pilots constantly practiced ground attack techniques, navigation, and air-to-air tactics. Model target airfields, constructed in the Negev Desert, gave pilots a chance to practice and hone their skills. Large-scale mock attacks helped train pilots and give ground crews experience in dealing with rapid servicing, rearming, and refueling.

Any Arab aircraft that made it into the air during the planned offensive were to be engaged immediately and shot down. Israeli pilots flew mock dogfights and air-to-air exercises. The defection of two Arab pilots with their aircraft in 1965 and 1966 gave the IAF an opportunity to evaluate and fly simulated combat against their principal adversaries' frontline fighters—the MiG-17 and MiG-21. These tactical insights, plus rigorous training, tempered the IAF into a force that had air combat skills unmatched anywhere in the world.

Tension between Israel and Syria increased in the early 1960s as terrorist raids and shellings intensified along Israel's northern borders. In 1964, Syria began efforts to divert the Jordan River to deprive Israel of its primary source of irrigation water. Fighting erupted on the Golan Heights in November 1964 with artillery, tanks, and aircraft trading fire.

A high state of unrest continued into the summer of 1966, when Syrian and Israeli fighters engaged in several dogfights. The Israelis scored the first Mirage air combat victory on July 14, 1966. A strike force of Mystere IVA fighter-bombers, attacking Syrian artillery batteries in response to heavy shelling, was threatened by a flight of Syrian MiG-21 fighters. A top-cover flight of Mirages tangled with the MiGs.

Capt. Yoram Agmon was the first to spot the Syrian MiG-21s:

> I suddenly noticed something shining on my left, at very low altitude. It was moving in a southeasterly direction towards the confluence of the Jordan and the Yarmuk. I radioed to the lead that I had made eye contact with the plane. I did everything without taking my eyes off that shining spot. I was flying low, about 500 feet off the ground, at high speed, and, at about 2,000 meters, I identified a pair of MiG-21s. I was getting closer when they were warned of my presence and turned sharply to the left. Although I knew that the MiG-21 maneuvered well, I was surprised at the extraordinary angle of the turn. I lost sight of the right-hand MiG, but pulled sharply upwards to try to slow down and close in on the left-hand one. At about 350 meters I got alongside him and shot off a short round, though with no result. I maneuvered again quickly, and reduced the distance between us to 250 meters. I aimed the second round carefully and was immediately rewarded with a powerful explosion in his right wing, which was torn off at the fuselage. The plane began to spin downward; I passed alongside and saw the pilot bail out. I took my way westward and joined the formation near the Sea of Galilee.[12]

A month later a second Mirage pilot claimed another Syrian MiG-21 that was strafing an Israeli patrol boat in the Sea of Galilee.

In response to increasing terrorist attacks along the Jordanian/Israeli border, on November 13, 1966, Israeli armored columns moved into Jordanian territory to attack guerrilla bases. Jordanian troops counterattacked this Israeli force and two Royal Jordanian Air Force Hunters took part in the engagement. These aircraft made several successful strafing passes, but were subsequently intercepted by a flight of Israeli Mirage fighters. After a prolonged dogfight, one of the Hunters was shot down. Israeli raids against targets in both Jordan and Syria experienced heavy opposition from antiaircraft fire, and several IAF aircraft were damaged or lost.

Two weeks after the air battle over Jordan, Israeli aircraft fought with Egyptian MiGs over the Negev Desert and scored additional victories. An Israeli Piper Cub, which was flying a reconnaissance mission along the Israeli/Egyptian border, was suddenly attacked by two EAF MiG-19 fighters. Diving to the deck, the Cub pilot turned and twisted low over the desert to escape and radioed for help. The two MiGs were toying with the Piper Cub and did not notice the two delta-wing Mirage fighters that lined up on them. One of the Israeli Mirage pilots tracked a MiG on his radar and locked onto it. When a light on the Mirage pilot's instrument panel came on, indicating that his Matra 530 air-to-air missile was seeking its target, the Israeli pilot fired the weapon. The missile quickly covered the mile and a half to the MiG and its 60-pound warhead ignited the MiG-19's fuel tanks, causing a massive explosion. The second Mirage pilot swept in and raked the other MiG with cannon fire, quickly shooting it down. This dogfight, which took place on November 28, 1966, saw the first successful use of air-to-air guided missiles in Middle East combat.[13]

During 1966 Gen. Mordechai Hod replaced Ezer Weizman as the commander of the IAF. A fighter pilot in the 1948 war, Hod led the IAF's only Ouragon squadron in the 1956 conflict and served as the assistant to General Weizman during the early 1960s.

In the decade between the end of the 1956 conflict and the 1967 war, the IAF had enlarged its inventory, introduced Mach 2 fighters, and substantially improved its pilot cadre, tactical doctrine, and operational effectiveness. By 1967, the IAF operated almost 100 supersonic fighters, nearly 150 subsonic fighter-bombers, 60 combat-capable jet trainers, and a sizable complement of transports, helicopters, and light aircraft.[14]

The spring of 1967 saw an increasing number of clashes along the northern border between Syria and Israel. The largest air battle fought in the Middle East since the 1956 conflict occurred on April 7, 1967, when a heavy Syrian artillery barrage led to a sizable Israeli air strike. Syrian MiG-21s intercepted the attack and a large air battle ensued, resulting in the loss of six Syrian aircraft.[15]

Tensions increased as Egyptian President Nasser, in support of Syria, mobilized additional troops and strengthened Egyptian positions in the Sinai. On May 18, President Nasser ordered UN forces to withdraw from Sharm el Sheikh and positions in the Sinai along the Egyptian/Israeli border. Two days later, Israel responded by mobilizing a number of reserve units and putting the IAF on a state of full alert. Egyptian forces subsequently blockaded the Straits of Tiran, halting shipping to the Israeli port of Eilat. Although neither Egypt nor Israel appeared to want war, events were out of control.

5

The Six-Day War

At about 8:45 A.M. on June 5, 1967, Israeli fighter-bombers simultaneously attacked the major EAF bases at El Arish, Jebel Libni, Bir Thamada, Bir Gifgafa, Kabrit, Inchas, Cairo West, Abu Suweir, and Fayid. They blasted the runways of these bases with bombs and then swept back and forth to strafe parked aircraft, control towers, hangars, and antiaircraft positions.

The attacks came as a complete surprise, and the Israeli fighter-bombers left dozens of flaming Egyptian aircraft and damaged facilities in their wake. Within minutes, additional groups of attackers appeared and the cycle of destruction continued. Despite the surprise, about a dozen EAF fighters made it into the air and fought back. Egyptian MiGs shot down Israeli aircraft near Abu Suweir and Cairo West air bases, while antiaircraft fire claimed victims at several other airfields. A total of eight IAF aircraft were lost during the first series of strikes. Four Israeli planes were shot down by Egyptian fighters and four were lost to antiaircraft fire. However, the EAF lost more than one hundred planes during the first in a series of Israeli air strikes, which lasted about forty-five minutes. Most of these aircraft were destroyed on the ground, but ten were shot down by IAF fighters, a few others were destroyed while trying to land on damaged runways, and some ran out of fuel.

By 9:30 A.M., the IAF launched a second series of strikes against Egyptian airfields. Israeli fighter bombers that had returned from the initial attacks were refueled, rearmed, and sent back into the air in ten minutes or less. Repair crews worked furiously on battle-damaged fighters, quickly returning them to operational status. The 115 sorties of the second wave reattacked some airfields hit earlier and also struck new targets, including Mansura, Helwan, El Minya, Almaza, Luxor, Deversoir, Hurghada, and Bilbeis air bases. This series of raids destroyed about one hundred EAF aircraft, with the loss of only a single Israeli aircraft.

By 1:00 P.M., the repeated Israeli air strikes had eliminated half of the EAF. Nearly three hundred Egyptian aircraft had been destroyed, including most of the TU-16 and IL-28 bombers that posed a threat to Israel, and many of the advanced MiG-21 and MiG-19 fighter aircraft. The EAF also suffered significant personnel losses and damage to air base facilities.[1]

During the late morning and early afternoon, Jordanian and Syrian aircraft struck back at Israel. Jordanian Hawker Hunters attacked Kfar Surkin and Netania airfields, destroying a transport. Syrian MiGs bombed an oil refinery at Haifa and strafed Megiddo airfield. IAF fighters were in action against Egypt and did not intercept these raids.

When artillery shells began to hit near Ramat David airfield and Jordanian ground troops attacked Israeli forces near Jerusalem, IAF fighter-bombers went into action against Jordan. The Royal Jordanian Air Force bases at Mafraq and Amman were hit beginning at about 12:45 P.M. Eighteen Hawker Hunters, most on the ground, were destroyed in the attacks, but one was shot down in air combat. Several Jordanian transports and helicopters were also hit, and airfield facilities were damaged. The Jordanian radar site at Ajlun was bombed and destroyed. A single IAF Mystere was lost in air combat with the Jordanian Hunters.

Israeli fighter-bombers struck Syrian airfields at Damascus, Marj Riyal, Damyr, and Seiqal at about 1:00 P.M. A more remote airfield, T-4, was hit just after 4:00 P.M. During these air strikes, a total of sixty-one Syrian aircraft were damaged or destroyed on the ground, while seven MiG-21s and three MiG-17s were shot down in air combat. Since the element of surprise had been lost, the attacking IAF fighter-bombers had to brave fierce antiaircraft fire and numerous MiGs, which were airborne over their bases. Two Mysteres were lost to antiaircraft fire over Damascus. Another Mystere pilot was surprised by a flight of four MiG-17s while strafing ground targets and was shot down. A total of four IAF aircraft were lost to the Syrian defenses.[2]

In retaliation for a 2:00 P.M. Iraqi air strike that hit a factory at Netania, three Vautour fighter-bombers were dispatched to attack an airfield in Iraq. The aircraft flew across Jordan and struck the Iraqi airfield at H-3. While the air base sustained damage, defending Iraqi MiG-21 and Hawker Hunter fighters forced the Israeli pilots to withdraw.

Throughout the afternoon and early evening, IAF fighter-bombers continued to strike at Arab airfields. Delayed-action bombs were employed in order to disrupt runway repair efforts. Egyptian radar sites also were hit; all sixteen in the Sinai were put out of action and many west of the Suez Canal were also destroyed.

Yallo Shavit discussed his role in the Israeli air attacks on June 5:

> In 1967 I was commander of the one Super Mystere squadron. It was like two squadrons as we had almost forty aircraft. French aircraft were at Bedek IAI for depot overhaul and we used them during the war. . . . They didn't like it but it was war.
>
> We had excellent pilots because this was the channel of supply for pilots for the Mirage squadrons. We were caught in 1967 with a bunch of good pilots who were about to graduate.
>
> The armament which won the 1967 war was the cannon, no doubt about it. We just went down to low level, got in close, and shot one target after the other. We spent hours at the ranges. If you didn't hit the target of 4 by 4 by 4 [feet] in the middle, it didn't count. It was the same with the air-to-air gunnery, so the tough rules of the training paid for themselves later in war.
>
> The first day was a tough one. . . . We got up at about 3:00 A.M. The briefing started at 5:00 A.M. We went to the aircraft at about 6:15 A.M. and took off around 7:00 A.M. It took us some forty minutes to reach Inchas. I was there at 7:55 A.M., ten minutes after the first raid of four Mirages. We bombed and hit the runways and strafed the aircraft on the ground. My number three was hit or made a mistake and crashed into the ground. We did five passes and on the last one, I was hit by 12.7-mm antiaircraft fire. It was a mistake to make so many passes, but there were so many MiGs. They hit my

auxiliary hydraulic system and the air brakes were caught out, and I got a warning that one of the undercarriage doors might be open. So I kept my speed below 250 knots. Can you imagine flying back at 250 knots and seeing all the war around you? I saw a MiG taking off from Inchas after I was hit. I asked my number two and three—they were youngsters—to fly next to me to protect me in case the MiGs attacked. Out of the blue came one of the MiGs and I pulled up and fired at him. He pulled down and disappeared at low level.

When I came back for a landing, it was tough because many aircraft were hit on the first mission. We had a lot of casualities on the first mission because of our inexperience and their heavy defenses.

A lot of other aircraft were also damaged, so there was a problem where to land. Bene Peled, my wing commander at Hatzor, told me to bail out as he was afraid that I would block the runway. I told him, "Not me, I will circle around and then get in." I crossed the intersection so I would not block the runway, and landed. I finished the runway on the overrun. The aircraft survived with minimum damage. The ground crew took the aircraft and prepared it for flight the next day.

I went to the brief, changed aircraft, and flew to Mansura, again with bombs and cannon. I came back and then attacked Mafraq, Jordan. The antiaircraft fire there was tough, but no big thing—you get hit, this is war. Three missions by 2:00 P.M.

In the afternoon I flew to Seiqal, a base in Syria on the edge of the Iraqi desert. . . . MiG-21s were flying top cover over the air base. We had four aircraft. My number three got hit by a bullet as we flew over the West Bank. He was hit in the external fuel tank and was low on gas. I ordered him to follow me, drop his bombs, and then climb up to look for MiGs. So we went into bombing, the four of us.

After the attack, I turned left and saw a long train—two of them (MiG-21s) were sitting on us. I asked number two to follow me, number three to go up, and number four to turn the other way. I saw number four and the two MiGs coming out of the turn, and I told number four to take a left so that we can sandwich them. But their number two saw me and he pulled up. I asked my number two to take him, and I continued with their number one. I had experience fighting with the MiG-21 because I was one of those who did the dogfights with the MiG-21 brought by the defecting pilot from Iraq that arrived in 1966. We flew the Super Mystere against the MiG-21, and I knew exactly the position where he sees me and does not see me. What their number one did when he saw me was level off, gain speed, and climb. I knew that I couldn't follow his tactic because I would be on my back and he would come down and shoot me. So what I did was drop my fuel tanks, and played a little trick on him. When he pulled out, I went to a position where he could see me and I showed him my belly. He saw me and said, "Ah, ha!" and put his nose down to 60 or 70 degrees, diving toward me. I knew from training that if a MiG-21 and Super Mystere crossed the horizon going down at the same time, it would take the MiG more time to recover from the dive because the Super Mystere was more agile.

I came into a barrel roll and I got him with his nose down. It was at low altitude, about 2,000 feet. He went into a tight turn, and I almost lost him because he had a lot of energy, but he made a mistake by changing direction. When he did this, I got into firing position. Then my number three said over the radio, "Number one, with all due respect, you are doing OK."

I said, "Shut up, I'm in the middle of a dogfight." I got the MiG at very low speed—150 knots—300 feet over the hangars. He did a turn and I fired. He exploded and fell right into the hangars in the middle of the base. I went down to minimum altitude, below 100 feet and gained some speed. One of my guys shot the other MiG, and I saw the wing of the MiG-21 separate above me at about 4,000 feet, and the pilot bailed out. We met and flew back to Hatzor and landed in the dark.

> At 8:30 P.M. we were back in the air with bombs. My number one had flares and we were attacking Jordanian artillery, which was shelling Jerusalem. We reloaded and went back around 10:00 P.M. and came back at 11:00 P.M. It was a full day of six missions.
>
> Early the next morning on the first mission, we lost a Super Mystere shot air-to-air by rockets or missiles from a MiG. He was flying over the Sinai like he was over Tel Aviv on Independence Day, and they got him.[3]

Operation Focus, the preemptive attack of Arab air forces that had been practiced for years, succeeded beyond all expectations. By the evening of June 5, twenty-five Arab airfields had been attacked with some 350 Arab aircraft damaged or destroyed. Most were hit on the ground but over two dozen had been shot down in air combat.

Surprise was the key to this victory. For years the IAF had made a habit of scrambling a large number of training sorties at dawn, which flew west over the Mediterranean, as if toward Egypt. The EAF responded by flying patrols over the northern Sinai, which usually took off just after sunrise. So the actual Israeli air strikes were timed to arrive over Egyptian airfields when the Egyptian morning patrols had landed and at a time when senior officers would be in transit from their home to work. Israeli aircraft took off according to a precise schedule that enabled them to arrive simultaneously over their respective targets at 8:45 A.M. Cairo time. The aircraft flew at low level, below radar coverage, and maintained complete radio silence.

Israel used various means to deceive and confuse enemy radars. Prior to and during the attacks, C-47 transports flew back and forth along the Israeli/Egyptian frontier, dispensing chaff. Other electronic countermeasures also were employed to disrupt Egyptian radar and radio communications and to deny electronic intelligence to the many other forces monitoring the Middle East.[4]

The Israeli attacks had been so successful that Arab leaders speculated that the IAF must have received assistance from the USAF and RAF. Other analysts suggested that the precise nature of the attacks and destruction of hundreds of parked aircraft must have been the result of the use of a new air-to-ground guided missile. The real secret of the success was the years of planning and training and the willingness of Israel to risk an all-or-nothing surprise assault with nearly all of its available aircraft. The IAF committed all but a dozen aircraft to the initial series of raids, and sequenced the sorties so that the targeted airfields were under almost constant attack. Rapid turnaround ensured that this cycle of attacks was maintained for several hours.

During the initial air strikes the IAF introduced a new weapon designed to maximize damage to enemy runways known as the "dibber" bomb. Low-level attacks against runways with conventional bombs did not prove to be a very effective tactic because the weapons frequently would bounce back into the air, causing only limited runway damage and creating a hazard to the attacking aircraft. High-angle dive-bombing tactics would have solved this problem, but attacking fighter-bombers would have been exposed to enemy defenses. Instead, Israeli fighter-bombers used runway destruction bombs—the product of the state-owned ordnance firm Israel Military Industries. These bombs could be released safely from low altitude and at high speed, and still cause considerable damage to runways. When released, a parachute opened to ensure separation from the aircraft and orient the weapon perpendicular to the ground. After two or three seconds, a booster rocket fired that drove the hard-nosed bomb deep into the runway, where its explosion would cause a much larger crater than would conventional bombs.[5]

On the initial series of airfield strikes, Mirage III and Mystere IVA aircraft carried two special antirunway bombs plus fuel tanks. Vautours were armed with four 1,000-pound bombs, while Super Mysteres carried two 500-pound bombs and external fuel tanks. Even the aging Ouragon was used on the first strike. The Ouragons were armed with four 200-pound bombs or rockets. Once pilots had delivered their bombs or rockets, they made several low-level strafing passes with their cannons.

The primary targets of the initial strike were the EAF TU-16 and IL-28 bombers, which could threaten Israeli cities and airfields. Located at Cairo West and Beni Sueif airfields, the TU-16 bombers were parked in concrete revetments. Accurate cannon fire destroyed these aircraft in their revetments.[6] Abu Suweir, home of an IL-28 light-bomber regiment, was repeatedly attacked and most of those aircraft destroyed. Also targeted and destroyed in the initial raids were MiG fighters, Sukhoi fighter-bombers, transports, and helicopters.[7]

The vital element of surprise was nearly lost on the morning of June 5. At about 8:05 A.M., an IL-14 transport carrying General Amer, the Egyptian chief of staff, General Sidki, the EAF commander, and a Soviet air force general took off and headed into the Sinai Peninsula. After several minutes, the IL-14 headed south toward Sharm el Sheikh. If the aircraft had turned north toward Gaza, the crew might have been able to spot the large number of Israeli aircraft that were heading east to attack Egyptian airfields. In the end, however, the flight of this transport also aided Israel. Egyptian antiaircraft gunners were warned not to fire on any planes at that hour lest they hit these senior officers. Once the attack began, the chief of staff and air force commander were out of the action since they could not find a safe place to land.[8]

Also that morning, Jordanian radar operators at the mountain top station at Ajlun noticed considerable activity over Israeli air bases. At 8:38 A.M. they sent a message to Egyptian War Minister Shams al Din Badran regarding this activity. But a recent directive had forbidden direct communication between Jordanian and Egyptian forces, so the message was not relayed from the war minister's office to frontline commanders in time.[9]

While the bulk of the IAF was striking Egyptian airfields, Israeli armor was pouring over the border at several different points into the Sinai. An *ugda* (roughly a division) led by Brig. Gen. Israel Tal crossed the border into the Gaza strip and attacked Egyptian forces at Khan Yunis on the Mediterranean, while a supporting brigade moved into Gaza. This force fought a tough battle at Rafah and then moved west along the northern coast to the outskirts of El Arish. The Suez Canal was Tal's *ugda*'s ultimate goal. A similar-size force under the command of Brig. Gen. Avraham Yoffe moved across the desert and engaged Egyptian forces on the route toward the important Giddi and Mitla Passes in the central Sinai. Brig. Gen. Ariel Sharon's division was charged with the destruction of the strong Egyptian defenses in the central Sinai near Abu Aweigila. The Israeli attack force included two armored divisions, one mechanized division, and several supporting brigades with more than 70,000 men and 750 tanks.

Egyptian forces in the Sinai totaled about 90,000 men and over 900 tanks organized into five infantry and two armored divisions.[10] Most of these forces were located in the central and northern Sinai behind a strong network of fortifications.

While most IAF sorties flown on June 5 were directed against Arab airfields, fighter-bombers and armed trainers also flew numerous interdiction and attack missions in support of advancing Israeli troops. Beginning at about 8:00 A.M., IAF Fouga Magister armed trainers flew close support sorties.

IAF transports delivered supplies and ammunition to mobile columns in the Sinai from the outset of hostilities. Helicopters were used to rescue downed pilots, evacuate wounded from the battlefield, and ferry troops and supplies. After nightfall on June 5, IAF S-58 and Super Frelon helicopters transported paratroopers behind the positions at Abu Aweigila for a surprise assault. The paratroopers defeated Egyptian artillery units that had been holding up the Israeli advance.

Eliezer Cohen led the helicopter squadron used in this operation:

> There is a saying that comes from the Bible that says you have to use some tricks and fight with your brain to win a war. The story was that we were to be involved to achieve air superiority. When we entered the war, I was standing by to take paratroopers to attack airfields in the Sinai. But the results of the fighter attacks in the first two or three hours—you know how good it was. At 10:00 o'clock the head of operations of the Israel Air Force called me on the phone and said, "Listen, you are out of a job because we destroyed all the airfields and the airplanes." Now General Sharon is in trouble trying to penetrate with his division in the Sinai because the Egyptians installed twenty-five batteries of 122-mm and 130-mm cannon and they were hitting our troops badly. . . . General Sharon was already planning this helicopter movement behind enemy lines the day before. . . . At 2:00 P.M. I went to a briefing with General Sharon and he told me and Danny Matt, the paratroop commander,

> to take the paratroopers behind enemy lines and to attack the three or four batteries in the center with grenades and Uzis.
>
> I saw that I had no time to prepare. Darkness came at 5:30 P.M. and I had to start flying before then to drop the pathfinders who will set up lights and radio devices. When we left the general, it was 2:30 P.M. and we had to take off at 4:30 P.M. . . . At the time all the helicopters were out searching for pilots who had ejected during the attacks against enemy airfields. . . . When I went to meet Sharon, I had only seven helicopters. At the time we had thirty S-58s. Now in a very short time, I had to prepare the paratroops into groups and ready the aircraft. We didn't have enough time, so everything was made highly simple. Danny Matt said, "Your group, go with these helicopters." He was just pointing with his fingers. . . . The pathfinders took off and got into position. I climbed to 5,000 feet and got on the radio and told all my pilots to switch to squadron channel. I told them in plain language, "Listen, we are going to start a big operation. Stop whatever you are doing. Everyone come to me." We started the operation with seven helicopters but the second round was with fifteen. By the third round, we had twenty, and the fourth we did with twenty-four helicopters.
>
> We dropped five hundred paratroopers behind the artillery, returned, and waited for their attack. When a big cannon is firing, it is like daylight. Dozens of them were shooting in the distance, and it was daylight. The paratroopers came with Uzis and hand grenades, and they hit four batteries in the center, and all the others stopped. They started that attack at ten before midnight and at 12:15 it was total darkness, and we knew that we did it.[11]

The Israelis had hoped that they would not have to go to war with Jordan or Syria, since Egypt was the primary threat and Israeli military planners did not want to fight a multifront war. The Jordanians had concentrated nine brigades of troops, mostly infantry units but with sizable armor and artillery support, on the West Bank after the initiation of the Jordanian, Egyptian, and Syrian pact of May 30. Brig. Gen. Uzi Narkiss, commander of the six brigades of Israel's central command, was promised two additional brigades plus support from troops of the northern command (whose troops were to defend the Israeli/Syrian border) in the event of war with Jordan.

Israeli troops expected limited action, but when shells started hitting near Ramat David airfield and falling on the suburbs of Tel Aviv and serious fighting began in and around Jerusalem, offensive plans were put into action. The urban terrain of Jerusalem and its historic nature forced the Israelis to rely on infantry, with support from armor, artillery, and limited air power. Early in the afternoon of June 5, Israeli troops began to assault Jordanian positions in Jerusalem. IAF fighter-bombers went into action against Jordanian artillery and Jordanian army units, which were moving forward toward the front line. The air strikes made a significant contribution by silencing Jordanian artillery and hampering the movement of support forces.

On the first day of the 1967 war, the IAF paid a high price for its success. The air force suffered the loss of nineteen aircraft: two Mirage IIIC, four Super Mystere B2, four Mystere IVA, four Ouragon, one Vautour, and four Fouga Magister planes. Aircrew losses on June 5 were eight killed and eleven missing.[12]

During the night of June 5, Egyptian, Syrian, and Iraqi military commanders dispersed their surviving aircraft to remote bases and began repairing damaged runways and facilities. While badly hurt, Arab air forces were not completely out of action. At dawn on June 6, the Arab air arms began to strike back at the Israelis. Two Egyptian SU-7 fighter-bombers swept and attacked an element of Tal's *ugda* in the northern Sinai. However these fighter-bombers were intercepted by a flight of Mirages and sent rapidly crashing to earth. A number of Egyptian air strikes successfully hit their targets later in the day, causing some Israeli casualties.

Early on June 6, an Iraqi TU-16 Badger bomber penetrated Israeli airspace and dropped three bombs that caused several casualties in the town of Netania. The aircraft then tried to bomb Ramat David air base but was intercepted by an Israeli Mirage III that damaged the TU-16 with a missile. The damaged bomber overflew an Israeli convoy as it headed east toward Iraq and was shot down by antiaircraft fire. At about 9:00 A.M. two Hawker Hunter fighters of the Lebanese Air Force flew into Israeli airspace. Israeli Mirages intercepted the intruders, shooting down one of the Hunters and driving the other off.

During the first twenty-four hours of fighting, Israeli forces in the Sinai had taken El Arish and had overcome strong defensive positions in the northern Sinai at Abu Ameigila. Egyptian defenders had fought with courage and caused considerable Israeli casualties, but the defenses had been penetrated. Heavy air support could now be brought into play to restrict the mobility of the Egyptian army and assist Israeli ground forces. Israeli aircraft went into action against Egyptian columns in the Sinai at dawn on the morning of June 6. Mirage IIIJ, Super Mystere, Mystere IVA, Ouragon, Vautour, and Fouga Magister fighter-bombers attacked Egyptian convoys on the roads from Egypt to the Sinai.

On the second day of fighting, Gen. Hakin Amer, Egyptian commander-in-chief, ordered the commanders of units in the Sinai to pull back to the Suez Canal. However, Israeli fighter-bombers disrupted the flow of Egyptian forces from the Sinai toward Egypt proper. With the northern coast road blocked at El Arish, Egyptian forces had only three paths to take west toward their homeland: the Ismailiya road, the road through Giddi Pass, and the highway through Mitla Pass. Aircraft pounded retreating convoys from the west while Israeli armor harassed them from the east. The forces under the command of Generals Tal, Yoffe, and Sharon fought several battles against counterattacking Egyptian units as they continued their advance across the Sinai. During the day, Israeli infantry and paratroops assaulted Gaza with support from tanks and IAF aircraft and artillery. Heavy fighting continued throughout the day, but by evening the town had fallen into Israeli hands.

IAF aircraft continued to attack Arab airfields sporadically throughout the day. In retaliation for the TU-16 attack against Israel, the IAF staged an air strike against the Iraqi airfield at H-3. The IAF sent a flight of four Vautours with an escort of two Mirages to strike the airfield. Like the attack flown on the previous day against H-3, the strike force ran into intense Iraqi fighter opposition. The Iraqi fighters aggressively defended their base but the Israelis shot down two Hunters and a MiG-21, destroyed ten aircraft on the ground, and damaged the runways. Ben-Zion Zohar, a Vautour pilot, downed one of the Hunters while a Mirage pilot claimed two victories.[13]

On the Jordanian front, heavy fighting continued in Jerusalem and on the West Bank, with Israeli paratroopers and infantry bearing the brunt of the fighting. The troops of the Jordanian army fought tenaciously and ground was given at considerable cost to both sides. Brig. Gen. David Elazar, the officer in charge of the northern command, sent a reinforced armored brigade into action to assist in the capture of Jordanian territory on the West Bank. Jordanian forces fought back aggressively and several counterattacks hit Israeli armor by surprise, causing heavy casualties. Israeli commanders called for close air support, and these air strikes damaged and destroyed many Jordanian vehicles. Iraqi units also suffered from Israeli air strikes. A brigade of Iraqi armor moving up to support Jordanian troops on the West Bank was repeatedly hit by IAF fighter-bombers and suffered many casualties.

On the second day of the 1967 war, the IAF had concentrated on supporting advancing ground troops on the Egyptian and Jordanian fronts. However, a sizable number of attack sorties were flown against Arab airfields. The IAF admitted that seven aircraft had been lost in action on June 6, the second day of the conflict. Israeli losses in two days of fighting thus totaled twenty-six aircraft.[14]

Heavy fighting continued in the Sinai on June 7, the third day of the conflict, as advancing Israeli forces met retreating Egyptian forces on the few available roads. Using flares, IAF fighter-bombers attacked several Egyptian convoys at night, but with the dawn, concentrated air strikes began. An Israeli column of paratroopers and armor advancing on the northern coast road was attacked several times by Egyptian fighter-bombers, causing numerous casualties. The EAF continued to fly attack sorties against the Israelis in the Sinai with the small number of aircraft that had survived the initial air strikes.

An Israeli armored brigade moved forward against heavy opposition in order to seal off Mitla Pass, while another force headed for the Giddi Pass. Late on June 7, a small group of Israeli tanks blocked Mitla Pass. This force ambushed several Egyptian convoys and was nearly overrun itself by the Egyptians. Air strikes against Egyptian vehicles helped save this small Israeli force. Continued air and ground attacks turned Mitla Pass into a graveyard of burned-out tanks and armored vehicles.

Elements of the Tal *ugda* fought a major battle with rearguard Egyptian armor near Bir Gifgafa on June 7. After six hours of heavy fighting, Israeli tanks, with heavy support from IAF fighter-bombers, succeeded in routing an element of the defending Egyptian 4th Armored Division. The Israelis also captured the large air base near Bir Gifgafa that was the EAF's headquarters in the Sinai. Later that night, Egyptian T-55 tanks, using night vision systems, attacked and drove back an Israeli armored unit in the central Sinai. The Egyptian counterattack was stopped when an Israeli relief force of Centurion tanks supported by flare-dropping Vautour fighter-bombers came to the rescue.

Israeli torpedo boats fired on the Egyptian positions at Sharm el Sheikh on June 7. When the boats did not receive return fire, a force of paratroopers was dispatched by helicopter to find out why. These troops took control of the airfield and found the Sharm el Sheikh defenses to be deserted. Additional paratroops were subsequently flown in by transport aircraft.

June 7 was also a day of heavy fighting on the Jordanian front. Israeli paratroopers attacked Jordanian positions around Jerusalem just after dawn and pushed into the old city. The IAF's aircraft attacked and scattered a Jordanian column that was moving up to reinforce units in Jerusalem. By late in the day, Jerusalem was totally in the hands of Israeli forces.

Israeli armor repeatedly attacked the Jordanian 40th Armored Brigade on the West Bank near the town of Qabatiya. After a four-hour battle, Jordanian troops began to withdraw. Israeli armored units overran Bethlehem, Hebron, Jericho, and other towns, completing the capture of Samaria, Judea, and the West Bank. Israel and Jordan agreed to a UN-sponsored ceasefire in the afternoon and the fighting ended at 8:00 P.M. on June 7. Jordanian forces had fought hard, but the Israelis had nevertheless seized control of the West Bank territory. In three days of heavy fighting, Jordan suffered some 3,000 casualties and lost 187 tanks, hundreds of other vehicles, and over 20 aircraft. Israeli losses on the Jordanian front were 550 killed and 2,400 wounded, while 112 tanks, dozens of vehicles, and several aircraft were destroyed.[15]

During the third day of fighting, the IAF flew hundreds of close air support, interdiction, and fighter patrol sorties against Jordanian, Egyptian, and Iraqi forces. For the first time SA-2 surface-to-air missile (SAM) sites in Egypt near the Suez Canal were attacked. Mirage fighters fought several air battles and shot down seven Arab aircraft. By the end of the day, the IAF had claimed that more than four hundred Arab aircraft had been destroyed—most on the ground, but nearly fifty had been shot down in dogfights.[16] Israeli aircraft raided a number of airfields in Egypt, Syria, and Iraq during the day. However, an attack on the H-3 air base in Iraq did not go according to plan.

Colonel S, an IAF wing commander during the 1967 war, recalled this tough mission against the Iraqi H-3 airfield:

> In the 1967 war, most of my sorties were with the Mirage, but then one sortie I remember I did with the Vautour. It was an attack on H-3, the Iraqi airfield, the third attack with Vautours on the third day of the war. On the second day, there was an attack with Vautours on H-3 with no casualties. Now on this sortie, I was number two because I didn't have enough knowledge on the Vautour then. There was a formation leader: I was his number two, and then there were numbers three and four. We were escorted by four Mirage fighters. These planes carried bombs, and they intended to use them in case there was no opposition, or to drop them and protect us in case we met enemy fighters. The first plan was to go alone, only Vautours, but I knew that we might meet Hunters so I demanded an escort of Mirages. OK, low-level flight, we reached the target, and then about two or three kilometers before the airfield, we saw that there were Hunters in the air. We didn't know how many, but more than four, six, or eight. The Mirage flight started to get speed, dropped their bombs, and we had to do our job.
>
> At that time, the leader lost communication. Everything continued as planned. We bombed the runway. The Vautour is very tricky—you had bombs in

the bomb bay and when you have the bombs outside of the bomb bay, you cannot do more than one-and-a-half *gs* with the aircraft. After you drop the bombs, until you get the bomb rack inside, you cannot do more than one-and-a-half *gs*. So you have got to fly very smoothly and it takes about twenty seconds until the bomb bay closes. So you drop the bombs and then continue more or less smoothly. During the attack, I got shot at by ground cannon. When the bomb bay had closed—at the same second—I got a warning that a Hunter was very near behind me. So I started to turn in order to save my life. At that time, I couldn't see my number one because we split during the attack. Until now I don't know who warned me. I was in a very difficult position because I lost all my speed, all my height, and the Hunter was closing. When he was very near, I changed the direction of the maneuver and I saw him going out. During those maneuvers, I saw that two aircraft were shot down, just flames in the sky, and I didn't know at the time whose planes they were. Now I know it was one Hunter and one Mirage that were shot down over the airfield. So I started to gather speed because I was very slow and had the flaps down. By that time the attack was over, and I heard the remaining aircraft reorganize for the return. I gathered speed headed home.

What happened was, number one was lost at the beginning. Nobody knows when and why he went down. At the end, he was found some kilometers away from the airfield, crashed. The pilot and navigator were dead. He was flying a glazed-nose Vautour and the rest of us had single seaters. Now number three finished his first attack and went back for another strafing run. On this second attack, they got him and he bailed out. Number four did the mission, was left alone, and he came back home. The Mirage flight did their best; they shot down two Hunters. One of them was shot down himself and he bailed out. So we had two prisoners in Iraq—number three of the Vautours and one of the Mirages. . . . It was a very tough mission because of the Hunters. Nobody anticipated that we would meet so many aircraft in the

> air. . . . Some say they were Iraqis; some say they were Jordanians. We don't know for sure. They were flying from Baghdad to H-3 and, by surprise, they found us. I tend to think it was an accident, because they were not flying in a way to cover the airfield. They were coming toward final from the other side, so we just collided. They found themselves in the air with Vautours, a big aircraft, as their target. So this attack, it was not a very big success, but, as a matter of fact, from then on we didn't have any more attacks from the Iraqis or Jordanians.[17]

June 8, the fourth day of the 1967 conflict, saw Israeli forces consolidate their hold on the Sinai Peninsula. An element of the Tal *ugda* on the northern coast road overcame Egyptian defenses and reached the Suez Canal at Qantara, while other Israeli forces drew near the canal. Advancing Israeli units continued to suffer losses to Egyptian ambushes and attacks by EAF aircraft. Patrolling Mirages intercepted some of the attacking fighter-bombers and downed three in air combat.

On the afternoon of June 8, Israeli aircraft detected a ship off the Sinai coast, and military commanders decided to send the IAF into action against the vessel. Mirage III and Mystere IV fighter-bombers made multiple attacks and hit the ship with rockets, napalm, and cannon fire. A motor torpedo boat of the Israeli navy then intercepted the damaged ship and attacked it with torpedoes and gunfire. Despite the heavy damage caused by these attacks, the USS *Liberty*, a U.S. Navy intelligence-gathering vessel, was able to limp away and eventually reach Malta. Thirty-four of the crew of the USS *Liberty* were killed and 164 wounded by the Israeli assault. The reason for the attack has never been fully explained but probably had to do with the ship's ability to gather intelligence about Israeli military activities.

The fighting in the Sinai ended on the early morning of June 9, when both sides agreed to the United Nations' call for a cease-fire. After the cease-fire, Egyptian troops continued to move west in an attempt to cross the canal to safety. They left behind about 700 tanks, 500 artillery pieces, and 10,000 trucks and other vehicles. Egyptian forces suffered over 10,000 killed and wounded and another 5,500 were captured. Israeli losses on the Sinai front totaled about 300 killed and more than 1,000 wounded.[18]

During the first four days of the 1967 war, Syrian forces participated in the conflict in only a limited way: Syrian aircraft struck targets in Israel on June 5, several limited ground attacks were made against four Israeli border settlements, and Syrian artillery sporadically shelled Israeli targets. On the first day of the conflict, the IAF attacked several Syrian airfields, destroying over sixty aircraft. Subsequently, numerous air strikes were flown against Syrian artillery positions on the Golan Heights in an attempt to end the shelling. Israeli military leaders refrained from large-scale attacks on the Golan Heights because ground troops and air support were committed in the Sinai and on the Jordanian front. However, once the fighting on these fronts was successfully concluded, Israel turned its attention to Syria. While the United Nations was pushing for a total cease-fire, Israel elected to settle an old score with its northern neighbor.

The Israel/Syrian border in 1967 ran from the Sea of Galilee to the Lebanon border near Mount Hermon and had a length of some 50 miles. The border included the Sea of Galilee and the steep hills of the Golan Heights, ideal defensive positions for the Syrians. Since the War of Independence in 1948, the Syrians had fortified the border area with mine fields, barbed-wire fences, and concrete bunkers. These fortifications were manned by over thirty thousand Syrian troops, who were supported by several hundred tanks and artillery pieces.

On June 8, the IAF initiated a blistering series of raids against Syrian positions on the Golan Heights. During the next two days, the IAF flew hundreds of ground support sorties over the Golan Heights, more than were flown on any other front. Syrian antiaircraft fire was intense and several Israeli aircraft were lost during these attacks. While these air attacks and artillery fire disrupted efforts to reinforce Syrian frontline defenses during daylight hours, they had little impact on the concrete-reinforced fortifications.

An Israeli force, composed of two armored brigades, a mechanized brigade, the Golani Infantry Brigade, and supporting units, was given the task of seizing the Golan Heights. This force of about 20,000 men and 250 tanks, under the command of Brig. Gen. David Elazar, assaulted the Syrians beginning at about 7:00 A.M. on June 9, the fifth day of the conflict.[19] The main thrust was made by the Golani Brigade and the two armored brigades. These units assaulted the tough terrain of the Golan Heights with the objective of seizing the town of Quneitra, the site of the headquarters of Syrian forces on the Golan Heights.

Additional Israeli units struck into Syrian territory in the central and southern parts of the Golan Heights to support the main effort in the north. The steep terrain, mines, and heavy Syrian fire slowed the assault and Israeli forces suffered dozens of casualties despite support from artillery and air strikes. Syrian defensive positions were only overrun after costly hand-to-hand fighting which resulted in heavy casualties on both sides. Syrian counterattacks slowed the Israeli advance but the timely arrival of IAF fighter-bombers and additional troops stopped the Syrian assault. During the night a renewed Israeli attack breached the Syrian line in a number of positions and penetrated onto the Golan Heights.

Israeli units continued the offensive on June 10 despite heavy Syrian resistance and the United Nations' call for an immediate cease-fire. Syrian resolve slackened late in the morning and troops began to pull back from defensive positions around Quneitra. Taking advantage of this withdrawl, IAF helicopters ferried paratroopers into positions behind Syrian lines to capture important road junctions and speed the advance of Israeli armored forces. The IAF's fighter-bombers continued to hit retreating Syrian columns with bombs and cannon fire. By late afternoon, Israeli units had advanced to within 40 miles of Damascus. At 6:30 P.M., Israel finally agreed to end the fighting and a UN-sponsored cease-fire came into effect. During the fighting with Syria, Israel suffered the loss of 127 killed and 625 wounded, plus 160 tanks, dozens of vehicles, and several aircraft destroyed. However, Israel had captured the Golan Heights. Syrian forces suffered about 600 killed, 700 wounded, and were forced to give up valuable terrain to Israel.

In the 1967 war, the Israel Defense Forces won a significant victory. In six days of heavy fighting, the armed forces of its principal adversaries—Egypt, Jordan, and Syria—were battered. Israel had captured the Sinai Peninsula, the West Bank territory, and the Golan Heights. While the war was won on the ground, Israeli aircraft made a significant contribution to the victory.

The IAF quickly achieved air superiority over its Arab opponents through a surprise first assault and air-to-air combat. The air force then assisted the army in winning the ground battle by flying thousands of ground attack sorties, by moving supplies to advancing troops, and by using helicopters to transport paratroopers into enemy rear area positions, evacuate wounded, rescue downed pilots, and conduct reconnaissance sorties.

What were the ingredients of the successful IAF air campaign? The first ingredient was the successful achievement of a surprise attack. For years the IAF had prepared for this one mission. The force was developed, trained, armed, and equipped to perform the surprise assault. Accurate intelligence efforts enabled aircraft to be dispatched to the right targets. For the second ingredient, nearly all IAF fighter-bombers were committed to the surprise attack. This almost total concentration of force on the primary objective was a big risk but it payed off. And for the third ingredient, Arab aircraft were not housed in protective shelters and most airfields were not heavily defended. This made the task of destroying the Arab air forces on the ground much easier.

The successful preemptive assault had both real and perceived effects on the outcome of the conflict. The destruction of Egyptian, Jordanian, and Syrian air power disrupted battle plans, damaged Arab morale, and almost totally eliminated the air threat to Israel and its advancing armies. Without defending fighter cover, Arab armies could only rely on antiaircraft fire for defense against Israeli air strikes. Once it achieved air superiority, the IAF was able to reduce the number of air combat patrol sorties to a minimum and concentrate on flying ground attack missions. Air superiority also meant that IAF transports, helicopters, reconnaissance, and liaison aircraft were able to perform their important missions with minimal interference from Arab fighters.

The IAF flew 3,279 fighter-bomber sorties during the conflict. Reportedly 469 Arab aircraft were destroyed during the War: 391 on the ground, 60 in air-to-air combat, 3 shot down by

Israeli antiaircraft fire, and 15 lost due to fuel exhaustion or flying into the ground.[21]

The IAF admitted the loss of forty-six aircraft, with twenty-three more heavily damaged. Aircrew casualties included twenty-four pilots killed, eighteen wounded, and seven taken prisoner. In six days of fighting, more than 20 percent of the IAF's frontline tactical aircraft had been destroyed and 8.4 percent of its pilots killed.[22]

Mirage IIIC, Super Mystere B2, Vautour, Mystere IVA, and even aging Ouragon fighter-bombers were used on the initial assault against Arab airfields. After the first pass to deliver special antirunway weapons, conventional high-explosive bombs, or rockets, these fighter-bombers made several strafing passes against aircraft or airport facilities. Later these aircraft joined Fouga Magister trainers in the ground support and road interdiction roles. High-explosive and napalm bombs, rockets, and cannon fire were used with telling effect against Arab vehicles, defensive positions, and troop concentrations. Hundreds of Arab vehicles were destroyed in the Sinai, on the Jordanian front, and on the Golan heights. Attacking aircraft regularly faced heavy antiaircraft fire, which destroyed most of the Israeli aircraft lost during the war.

The Six-Day War saw IAF aircraft in dozens of air combat engagements with Arab aircraft. Many battles were fought over Arab airfields during the initial air strikes, and dogfights occurred on each day of the conflict as Israeli fighters met Egyptian, Syrian, Jordanian, or Iraqi aircraft that flew in support of their forces. Despite Israeli air cover, numerous successful Arab air strikes were flown. However, many Arab attacks were intercepted by IAF fighters and sixty Arab aircraft were shot down in air combat. Mirage pilots achieved over 80 percent of the air-to-air victories, but flyers of older IAF jets also shot down Arab aircraft: Supere Mystere pilots downed five planes, Mystere IV pilots three, while Vautour and Ouragon aviators each hit a single Arab jet. Aircraft cannon were used to achieve all of these victories.[23]

According to official releases, only three or four IAF aircraft were lost to Arab fighters. However, a high-ranking IAF officer later disclosed that in fact ten aircraft had been "bounced" by enemy fighters and shot down.[24]

The IAF transport force of C-47 and Nordatlas aircraft moved thousands of tons of supplies to the front and air-dropped food, fuel, and ammunition to advancing columns. Captured Arab airfields and desert strips were used by the transports to deliver troops and supplies and to evacuate wounded.

Helicopters were used extensively in the 1967 conflict to carry troops, rescue downed pilots, and move casualties rapidly to forward field hospitals. Super Frelon and S-58 transport helicopters delivered paratroops into position on numerous occasions to assault Arab defenses from behind or capture important road junctions.

During the 1967 war, the IAF proved that it could have a dramatic impact on the course of battle in the Middle East. Israeli airpower had reigned supreme. However, Arab forces had learned a bitter lesson and immediately began to take steps to change the status quo.

6

War of Attrition

Less than a month after the cease-fire that ended the Six-Day War, Egyptian and Israeli troops fought a two-week series of bitter battles around Port Fuad at the northern end of the Suez Canal. Both sides committed aircraft to the fighting: Egyptian forces lost a MiG-17 to antiaircraft fire on July 4, 1967, while an SU-7 EAF fighter-bomber was shot down by an Israeli Mirage on July 8. Another major battle erupted along the Suez Canal on July 15, during which five Egyptian jets and a single Israeli aircraft were shot down.

Israel, flush with victory, had hoped that Egypt, Jordan, and Syria would enter into negotiations for a peace treaty that would bring an end to the hostilities that had continued since the birth of Israel in 1948. General Dayan stated that he was expecting a call from Cairo or Amman at any time. However, instead of a phone call, the Arabs responded with military and political action.

An Arab summit conference held in Khartoum in August and September 1967 dashed any Israeli hope for peace. Participants in the conference stated that there would be no recognition of Israel and agreed upon a strategy of confrontation that included economic boycott, political efforts, terrori. m, and military confrontation. Evidence of Arab resolve to fight back came on October 21, 1967, when the Israeli destroyer *Eilat* was hit and sunk by several Styx antiship missiles. Forty-seven Israeli sailors were killed and ninety-one wounded in the attack. In retaliation, Israeli aircraft bombed Egyptian naval facilities at Alexandria and Port Said and Israeli artillery batteries severely damaged the Egyptian oil refinery near the city of Suez.

The United Nations, continuing its efforts to prevent renewed conflict, passed Resolution 242 on November 22, 1967. It called for Israel to pull back to its pre-1967 borders in exchange for Arab recognition of the State of Israel, establishment of demilitarized zones between Israel and Arab countries, and discussions regarding the fate of Palestinian refugees. Neither side accepted this resolution. The territories acquired in the Six-Day War considerably strengthened Israel's strategic situation: Egyptian forces now had to cross the Suez Canal and Sinai Peninsula to threaten Israel, while in the east, capture of the Jordan River Valley and Golan Heights gave Israel much more defensible borders.

However, Israel now had to administer the nearly one million Arab civilians who lived in the captured territories of the West Bank and Gaza Strip. And immediately after the 1967 war, Egyptian and Syrian forces received hundreds of tactical aircraft, tanks, and other military systems from the Soviet Union, which also sent scores of "advisors," whose arrival forced Israel to increase its preparations for renewed conflict.

Israel needed new fighters to replace the forty-eight jets lost in action during the Six-Day War. The IAF inventory after the 1967 conflict included approximately three squadrons of Mirage IIIC fighters (about sixty-five aircraft), one Super Mystere squadron (twenty-five aircraft), one Vautour squadron (fifteen aircraft), two Mystere IVA (thirty-five planes), and two Ouragon squadrons (thirty aircraft). The subsonic Vautour, Mystere IVA, and Ouragon aircraft had been delivered in the late 1950s and were reaching the end of their service lives. In an emergency, the IAF could press into service two squadrons of Magister trainers (eighty aircraft), but this aircraft suffered heavy losses during operations in the 1967 war. Support services were provided by two squadrons of transports, one flying C-47s and the other Noratlas aircraft, and a composite wing of S-58, Super Frelon, Alouette, and Bell 47G helicopters.[1]

Prior to the 1967 conflict, the IAF had worked closely with the French aircraft manufacturer Dassault to develop an upgraded version of the Mirage IIIC fighter. An order for fifty of these improved aircraft, designated the Mirage V, had been placed in 1966 and the jets were already on the assembly line. The IAF planned to purchase at least one hundred Mirage Vs and intended to evaluate the then-new Mirage F1 fighter. These jets were never delivered to the IAF because President Charles de Gaulle of France imposed an arms embargo against Israel.

As a result of the embargo, Israel Aircraft Industries, with the assistance of numerous Israeli and foreign firms, set out to establish a production line for an aircraft essentially identical to the Mirage V. Israeli firms had gained experience by overhauling and modifying French combat aircraft, producing the Fouga Magister trainer, developing the Arava transport, and upgrading the Westwind Business Jet. The plans for the Mirage and its Altar 9C turbojet engine were provided by Alfred Frouenknech, a Swiss engineer who later served a two-year jail term for his part in the transfer of these documents. Israeli engineers worked around the clock to develop and produce the new Nesher (Eagle) fighter.[2]

In the early 1960s, Israeli officials tried to purchase U.S. combat aircraft in an attempt to find another source of supply for the IAF. While the initial answer was negative, the U.S. government agreed to supply Israel with defensive weapons such as the Hawk surface-to-air missile system. A delegation headed by the IAF commander, Gen. Ezer Weizman, visited Washington, D.C., in late 1965 to ask the United States to sell Israel fighter aircraft. The delegation was successful and a contract for the sale of the first U.S.-built jets, forty-eight A-4 Skyhawk fighter-bombers, was signed in late 1966. However, Israeli requests for F-4 Phantom or A-6 Intruder aircraft were turned down. Senior U.S. leaders felt that these advanced jets would upset the balance of power in the Middle East, and the aircraft were needed by U.S. forces to support air operations in Viet Nam.

The IAF wanted to buy a high-performance fighter, like the Mirage V or F-4 Phantom, that could perform both air combat and attack missions. However, the U.S. agreement to sell combat aircraft to Israel was a major breakthrough, and the Skyhawk fighter-bomber had good range, could carry a sizable weapons load, and cost only about two-thirds as much as a new Mirage. The IAF eventually received more than three hundred Skyhawks of eight variants, making it the most widely used combat aircraft in the history of Israel's air force.

The A-4 Skyhawk is a small attack jet capable of operating from an aircraft carrier. The Israeli version of the Skyhawk, the A-4H, differed from U.S. Navy versions in having 30-mm cannon armament, a rear-mounted brake parachute, a larger square-tipped tail, and minor avionic changes.[3] With the Skyhawk came American training, maintenance concepts, and weaponry. The first Skyhawk was delivered in the fall of 1967 and all forty-eight aircraft were in service by late 1968.

Terrorist activities intensified along the Syrian and Jordanian borders in late 1967 and early 1968. These confrontations were the prelude to a prolonged struggle. Large training camps located in Jordan and Lebanon generated a steady supply of Palestinians who were ready and willing to fight to the death to hit back at Israel. Jordanian troops and Iraqi forces that were stationed in Jordan collaborated with these guerrilla groups and often supported their efforts with artillery fire and logistical assistance. Terrorists directed their attacks against civilian targets like settlements, schools, and public places in an attempt to undermine personal security and erode public confidence. Israeli efforts against these attacks were constrained by political restrictions that limited action in the occupied West Bank and prevented the launching of full-scale assaults against guerrilla bases in Jordan, Syria, and Lebanon. Israeli forces heavily patrolled the border and terrorists who crossed the border were pursued or ambushed. However, the Israelis used air attacks, surprise commando assaults, and artillery fire to hit terrorist base camps and staging areas to disrupt their operations. The IAF's tactical aircraft flew hundreds of fighter-bomber sorties against terrorist positions in Jordan in 1968 and 1969. Helicopters such as the S-58 and the new UH-ID Huey were used to assist Israeli troops in their battle against terrorists in the Jordan River Valley.

Russian resupply and training efforts quickly rebuilt the Egyptian and Syrian armed forces. By mid-1968, the Egyptian army had regained most of its pre-1967 war strength and thousands of Russian advisors assisted in training efforts. Nearly 150,000 Egyptian troops were well entrenched in positions along the Suez Canal. These men were supported by almost one thousand artillery pieces, plus more than five hundred tanks. The EAF was strengthened and Russian advisors drilled it in their training concepts. The EAF in late 1968 included 110 MiG-21 and 80 MiG-19 fighters, 120 MiG-15/17 and 40 SU-7 fighter-bombers, and 40 IL-28 and 10 TU-16 bombers. New airfields were built to accommodate the additional air force units and concrete shelters were constructed to protect aircraft and vital support equipment. In 1968 an independent Egyptian Air Defense Force was established to protect Egypt and its forces from air attack. A network of radars, SA-2 surface-to-air missile batteries, and antiaircraft guns was set up to protect Cairo and important military and industrial positions.[4]

The Syrian Air Force also benefited from Russian resupply and intensified training efforts. By late 1968 the force had a strength of sixty MIG-21 fighters and seventy MIG-15/17 and twenty SU-7 fighter-bombers. The Royal Jordanian Air Force had received a dozen Hawker Hunter fighter-bombers and was in the process of acquiring a squadron of supersonic F-104A fighters from the United States.[5]

The IAF had taken over several former Egyptian air bases in the Sinai and deployed a sizable number of aircraft to these new airfields. Major air bases, headquarters, and logistics centers were hardened against attack and were protected by antiaircraft guns. Several Hawk surface-to-air missile batteries were also positioned to defend Sinai positions.

Israeli ground forces manned a limited number of observation posts located along the Suez Canal in order to monitor Egyptian activities. Held back, out of range of artillery fire, was a force of about ten thousand men organized into two armored brigades and supporting units. These Israeli troops in the Sinai had many tanks and armored vehicles, but only a limited amount of artillery. In the event of an Egyptian attack, these units were to move forward and destroy any bridgehead across the canal.

On September 8, 1968, a massive artillery barrage was launched by Egyptian forces all along the Suez Canal. During the six-hour-long barrage, over ten thousand shells landed; ten Israeli troops were killed and eighteen were wounded. Israel retaliated by shelling the cities of Suez and Ismailiya and the oil refinery near Suez. To demonstrate its determination, Egypt staged another intensified artillery attack on October 26, which killed thirteen Israeli soldiers. In addition, civilians living in Suez, Ismailiya, and other towns near the Suez Canal were evacuated by Egyptian authorities.

As a deterrent to future artillery attacks, on October 31 Israeli paratroops, carried deep into Egypt by IAF helicopters, sabotaged a dam, destroyed two bridges spanning the Nile, and damaged a power transformer substation near the town of Naj Hammadi.

Eliezer (Cheetah) Cohen, then chief of operations for the IAF, discussed these operations:

> We started to do special helicopter operations and they didn't have an answer for it. We did it as a deterrent. When you put a small bomb on a dam on the Nile you are giving a message: Next time we will come with a bigger bomb. We released the bombs from the helicopters. Using the cargo sling, the helicopter hovered over the dam and we put the bomb—a special-shaped charge, one like those used to attack tanks—next to the wall and destroyed the dam. There are many dams on the Nile. Once we came and destroyed a small dam, we demonstrated that we had the ability to hit targets well behind the front lines. This sent a message. They thought about it and stopped fighting along the Suez Canal for a few weeks because they knew that we could do terrible things to them . . . We showed that we could cut their electricity, break the dams, and flood their fields.[6]

These raids startled the Egyptians and their Soviet advisors, resulting in the strengthening of air and ground defenses around vital rear-area Egyptian assets. Except for small-scale artillery attacks and reconnaissance sorties, the Suez Canal front remained quiet into 1969.

Israeli forces used this quiet period to their advantage and constructed a series of concrete-and-steel-reinforced fortifications along the Suez Canal. Each of these positions included two or three tanks and several squads of troops. The positions were to serve only as lookout posts to deter the Egyptians from crossing the Suez Canal. Concrete, sand, and steel protected the troops of the so-called Bar Lev line from artillery fire, but defense of the Sinai still rested with Israeli armored forces. Aside from an air battle near the Suez Canal on December 12, 1968, which resulted in the destruction of a single EAF MiG-17, air action on the Sinai front was limited during this period.

Throughout 1968 the IAF flew attack missions against guerrilla camps in Lebanon, Syria, and Jordan, as well as Jordanian and Syrian army artillery batteries that continued to shell Israeli settlements. Hundreds of helicopter missions supported border patrols and antiterrorist commando raids. Pilots of the new A-4 Skyhawk squadrons flew most of their missions in support of these antiterrorist operations.

A successful attack carried out against an EL AL airliner at Athens Airport on December 25, 1968, prompted the Israeli government to take action. Guerrilla groups based in Beirut were identified as being responsible for this and earlier assaults against EL AL aircraft.

At 9:30 P.M. on the night of December 28, four IAF Super Frelon helicopters landed on the main runway of Beirut International Airport and a large number of heavily armed paratroopers disembarked. Moving swiftly, the paratroopers seized control of the main terminal. Passengers on aircraft belonging to Arab airlines were escorted off the planes and into the terminal. Once the aircraft were emptied, demolition charges were placed aboard and, one by one, fourteen airliners were blown up. A fifth helicopter landed next to the main highway that linked the airport to Beirut. Paratroopers from this helicopter blocked the highway, preventing police or the Lebanese army from interfering with the operation. Within an hour the paratroopers had left, leaving behind fourteen destroyed airliners but no civilian or military casualties.[7] This raid was staged to serve notice that Israel could and would strike out against those who supported terrorism. The political repercussions from this raid were high, though, as it prompted the French to impose a total arms embargo against Israel and generated widespread criticism.

Tensions along the Israeli/Syrian border intensified early in 1969 and on February 12 the first air battle between Israel and Syria in nearly two years occurred. Syrian fighters contested IAF aircraft again on February 24, during an Israeli raid against a terrorist camp near Damascus. Israel claimed to have downed three Syrian MiGs and to have suffered no losses in these air battles.

A new, more dangerous phase of the confrontation on the Suez front began on March 8, 1969. Just before noon, a flight of Egyptian MiG-21 fighters penetrated into the Sinai near Great Bitter Lake. Israeli Mirages intercepted this patrol and one

Egyptian jet was shot down. Six hours later, Egyptian forces initiated a massive artillery barrage against Israeli fortifications all along the Suez Canal. The same day President Nasser announced the start of a "War of Attrition" against Israel. Using artillery and commando raids, Egyptian forces hoped to destroy Israeli fortifications near the Suez Canal and inflict heavy casualties. Israeli artillery responded in kind to these attacks. On March 9, the Egyptian chief of staff, Gen. Abdul Moneim Riadh, and some of his staff who were observing the action from forward positions near Ismailiya were killed by Israeli artillery fire.

Heavy shelling continued for days, and in early April, Egyptian forces staged a number of successful commando raids against Israeli patrols, supply convoys, and fortifications. Egypt took advantage of its superiority in artillery firepower, numerical strength, and willingness to accept a moderate level of casualties.

Israel regularly struck back in response to attacks along its borders, but increasing tension and rising casualties created a serious concern. At an April 17, 1969, news conference, Defense Minister Moshe Dayan stated that Israel had suffered sixteen hundred casualties in the nearly continuous border clashes that had taken place in the twenty-two months since the end of the 1967 war. By way of contrast, he pointed out that there had been thirty-six hundred Israeli casualties in the Six-Day War. Dayan said that Arab claims of success were greatly exaggerated. Commenting on Israeli and Arab aircraft losses, he stated, "We have lost seven jets and one Piper Cub since the [1967] War, all downed by ground fire. The Egyptians have lost fifteen jets and the Syrians three."[8]

While military action along the Suez Canal continued at a high level in the spring of 1969, there was no reduction in counterterrorist operations along the Jordanian, Syrian, and Lebanese borders. Terrorist bases and several radar stations in Jordan were bombed on April 22, and one of the attacking Israeli aircraft was lost to antiaircraft fire. Arab confrontations, including terrorist attacks and shelling, continued and Israeli forces responded with commando raids and air attacks.

In May, heavy fighting broke out along the Israeli/Syrian border, and on May 29, a Syrian MiG-21 was shot down by a missile fired from an IAF Mirage. Syria moved additional troops, tanks, and artillery up to the border and shelling continued. A major air battle erupted over the Golan Heights on July 8, and Israeli Mirage fighters downed seven MiG-21 aircraft. This was the biggest Israeli/Syrian aerial confrontation since the 1967 war.

Throughout the spring of 1969 the United Nations attempted to mediate a total cease-fire in the Middle East. While many meetings were held and many proposals put forward, none of the warring factions were willing to end the fighting.

Almost daily shelling and commando activity occurred along the Suez Canal and air activity intensified. Egyptian fighter-bombers flew a heavy series of raids against Israeli targets in the Sinai on May 21. However, Israeli defenses were ready—three EAF MiG-21s were shot down by Israeli Mirages and a single MiG fell to a Hawk surface-to-air missile. On June 17, two Israeli Mirages flew at supersonic speed over President Nasser's home at Heliopolis, producing a loud sonic boom that shattered windows and caused considerable unrest. This "attack" prompted Nasser to replace the EAF commander, Air Vice-Marshall Musstafa Shalaby el-Hennawy, and the chief of air defenses, Maj. Gen. Hassan Kemal. President Nasser also responded by ordering an increase in the number of commando raids, artillery barrages, and EAF air strikes against Israeli positions in the Sinai. Air battles, which occurred on several occasions in late June and early July 1969, resulted in the loss of nine Egyptian jets. However, Egyptian shelling, commando raids, and air strikes increased the Israeli casualty toll to 106 dead and wounded in July.

Israel responded to this worsening situation along the Suez Canal by changing its tactics. On July 19, a force of naval commandos stormed Green Island, an Egyptian fortress located at the southern end of the Suez Canal. The raiders captured the fortress and set demolition charges that destroyed the structure. The following day, the IAF flew a massive series of air strikes against Egyptian military positions all along the Suez Canal. This was the first time that the IAF had flown a large-scale air offensive against Egyptian forces since the end of the 1967 War.

The EAF contested these air strikes and flew raids into the

Sinai, resulting in several large air battles. Israeli authorities claimed their forces shot down five Egyptian jets, including two SU-7 and two MiG-17 fighter-bombers and a single MiG-21 fighter, on July 20. During the battles, two Israeli aircraft were lost, including a Mirage that was shot down in a dogfight with Egyptian MiG-21s. This was the first Israeli admissions of the loss of an aircraft in air combat since the 1967 war.[9]

The military objective of Israel's new air offensive was the suppression of Egyptian forces along the Suez Canal at a minimum cost to Israel. Israeli air strikes continued for several weeks. Egyptian fighters rose to challenge the Israeli attackers while EAF fighter-bombers frequently struck Israeli positions in the Sinai. During several large air battles on July 24, Israeli forces claimed six Egyptian MiGs and an SU-7. Israeli raids against Egyptian positions continued almost daily and on August 19, the IAF pounded numerous Egyptian artillery positions for several hours. However, during the day a Skyhawk fighter-bomber fell to Egyptian antiaircraft fire.

S. Gilboa, a former Mystere squadron commander, commented about his flying experience during this period:

> As a reserve officer in 1969, I continued to fly Mysteres. I remember bombing some cannon sites very near the Suez Canal. We were in formations one behind the other, a difference of three minutes. It was very simple. On some days we used to make four sorties. We used to pick one or two targets and hit them and hit them like a hammer until they would go down. It was a way of delivering a message. At that time, the missiles were not in the area and the antiaircraft fire was not very accurate. We came in at 8,000 feet, roll in, drop, and out—no strafing, just one or two bombing runs and then back home. Formation after formation, we hit the targets. For a time we didn't think it had an impact but later on we found out it affected them very strongly. We knew this due to two facts: an Egyptian soldier who swam to our side told us about the situation, and one day our aircraft took a photograph of a graveyard. We started to take pictures every two or three days and to count. We saw that they were digging graves at a higher

> rate, and we understood that they were suffering heavy casualties.[10]

During September 1969, conflict along the Suez Canal intensified to the highest level since the 1967 war. During the night of September 7, Israeli naval commandos blew up several Egyptian patrol boats at their anchorage at Ras el Sadat in the Gulf of Suez. This opened the way for Israeli landing craft to cross the gulf and bring ashore a sizable raiding party of armored vehicles. To achieve surprise in the assault, the Israelis used Russian-built tanks and armored vehicles captured in the 1967 war. Dozens of Egyptian vehicles and defensive positions were destroyed during the raid. Israeli aircraft bombed and strafed several Egyptian SA-2 batteries and other military positions in support of this attack. One Israeli aircraft was hit by antiaircraft fire during these air strikes and its pilot was lost after ejecting into the Gulf of Suez.

After the raid, the IAF continued to plaster the Egyptian positions with bombs. Israeli aircraft attacked a radar site near the Gulf of Suez on September 9 and an SA-2 battery near the Suez Canal on September 10. In the six weeks since the initiation of intensified air strikes against Egyptian forces along the Suez Canal, the IAF had flown over one thousand sorties and Israeli forces had shot down twenty-one Egyptian planes for the loss of only three aircraft.

On September 11, the EAF sought revenge for the Israeli assault across the Gulf of Suez. Three separate air raids totaling sixty to seventy sorties penetrated into the Sinai and struck at Israeli positions. Israeli officials stated that eight Egyptian aircraft had been brought down by IAF fighters, three by antiaircraft fire, and two by Hawk missiles.[11] This was the biggest one-day Israeli claim since the first day of the 1967 war. Late in the afternoon, Israeli aircraft flew a series of raids into Egypt and a Mirage fighter was lost to antiaircraft fire.

At a September 13 press conference, Defense Minister Moshe Dayan stated that the recent armored raid and air attacks were undertaken to force the Egyptians to "think twice" about their strategy along the Suez Canal. Dayan added that Nasser should know "that his front is wide open in the Gulf region." The defense minister said, "We have opted for selected response, and

IAF Spitfire Mk 9 and EAF Fiat G55 were adversaries in the 1948 War of Independence.

IAF Meteor and EAF Vampire were the principal front-line fighters of the two air arms during the mid–1950s.

The EAF MiG-15 and IAF Mystere IVA met in action over the Sinai during the 1956 conflict.

N
708
708

Front-line fighters of the Middle East in the early 1960s included the Israeli Super Mystere, Jordanian Hawker Hunter and Egyptian MiG-19.

The A-4 and the SU-7 were the primary attack aircraft employed by the Israeli and Arab air forces during the War of Attrition.

Adversaries in the 1973 War included the Egyptian MiG-21 fighter and the Israeli F-4E Phantom.

669

The IAF F-15 Eagle fought the SAF MiG-25 Foxbat in the skies over Lebanon in 1982.

The IAF F-16A and SAF MiG-23 met in action over Lebanon during the 1982 conflict.

we maintain the right to choose the targets, the weapons, and the magnitude of the blow."[12]

It was not a hollow threat. In late 1968 the U.S. government had agreed to supply Israel with fifty F-4E Phantom aircraft as a result of the intensification of fighting in the Middle East and increased Soviet involvement in Egypt and Syria. The first of these supersonic fighter-bombers, which the IAF nicknamed the Kurnass (heavy hammer), arrived in Israel on September 5, 1969. A single F-4E Phantom could carry the same number of bombs as eight Mirage or Mystere fighters. With its speed, range, payload, and capability to perform both the fighter and attack missions, the Phantom was the perfect airplane for the IAF's offensive-oriented tactics. A second batch of forty-two A-4H Skyhawks, which had been ordered in early 1968, also began to arrive in Israel during the fall of 1969.

The Egyptians struck at Israeli targets in the Sinai on October 6 and the raid was intercepted by Israeli forces. Three MiG-21 fighters were shot down in air combat and a MiG-17 fighter-bomber fell to a Hawk missile. While many EAF aircraft were downed or damaged, Egyptian pilots continued to brave the Israeli defenses and many strikes hit home. This added to Israeli casualties caused by Egyptian artillery barrages, commando raids, and tank fire. In retaliation, the IAF continued to bomb Egyptian SAM sites and stepped up its attacks against positions further inland. On October 22, IAF F-4 Phantom crews flew their first combat missions against an SA-2 surface-to-air missile site at Abu Suweir, Egypt. Each of the Phantoms in the two-plane raid carried eleven bombs. They "crossed the Canal north of Quneitra" and, according to one of the pilots, "We were doing 540 knots, turned south and pulled up to 20,000 (feet). We came in long and let go. We hit well, and could see lots of smoke coming from the target."[13] Early on November 4, Phantoms woke up Cairo with a sonic boom that broke windows, and on November 11, the first air combat victory was achieved by an F-4. An Egyptian MiG-21 was shot down over Jebel Ataka by a missile from a Phantom. Two other Egyptian MiGs were shot down on this day by Mirage fighters.

Most of the Egyptian SAM positions near the Suez Canal had been knocked out by November 1969, and the IAF had gained a high degree of air superiority over the Suez Canal area. The

Israeli chief of staff, Lt. Gen. Haim Bar Lev, commented about the Egyptian air raids into the Sinai during a November 1969 interview:

> Their planes attack, but they do not hit anything. They don't take time to get a proper angle of attack. They get rid of their bombs all at once, as soon as possible. They do everything to be over our territory as short a time as possible.
>
> Today, for instance, we were bombing on their side. And we have been hurting Nasser, so for the first time in two months the Egyptians sent up their MiGs—eight MiGs. We shot down two by cannon and one by an air-to-air missile. We prefer to use cannon because with a missile you have to have certain conditions. You have to be at a proper distance. And if the other pilot sees the missile, he can avoid it. With cannon, you go the way he goes and follow him. We use missiles when the conditions are right for them. But mostly, we use cannon.[14]

The IAF Mirage IIIC fighter could carry the French Matra 530, American AIM-9B/D Sidewinder, or the Israeli-developed Shafrir air-to-air missiles. These weapons all utilize infrared-homing guidance, which requires the attacking aircraft to approach a target from the rear, where the missile seeker can "see" the hot jet-engine exhaust. The Shafrir was developed by the Israeli RAFAEL Armament Development Agency. The IAF F-4 Phantoms carried both the infrared-homing Sidewinder and the longer-range, radar-guided AIM-7 Sparrow air-to-air missile. This weapon could be used at night and could hit a target head-on or from the side, but its complicated firing procedures reduced the likelihood of a successful attack in the swirling dogfights that were common in the Middle East. Cannons and missiles were complementary weapons: The range of the cannon was from zero to 4,000 feet, while missiles were effective from 2,500 feet to over 5 miles, depending upon target speed and altitude. Not all the Egyptian aircraft shot down fell to Israeli fighters. Between May and November 1969, fifty-one Egyptian aircraft were downed: thirty-four in air battles, nine by antiaircraft fire, and eight by Hawk surface-to-air missiles.[15]

During the fall of 1969, the IAF also flew hundreds of sorties in support of antiterrorist activities along the Lebanese, Syrian, and Jordanian borders. The IAF aircraft rocketed, bombed, and strafed terrorist training camps and Jordanian and Iraqi artillery batteries. Yallo Shavit, a retired IAF brigadier general, commented about the antiterrorist role of the air force during this period:

> During the War of Attrition I was deputy wing commander of Base One. We had Mirages, Skyhawks, and Phantoms. As the wing commander and deputy were allowed to fly with any squadron, I might fly a Skyhawk in the morning, then a Mirage, and then a Phantom late in the day. The Skyhawk was easy: You take the book, learn the emergency procedures, and fly the plane. We flew many missions against Jordanian targets. I believe that the first time the Israeli government used the air force to stop the shelling of Israel was in the Jordan Valley. Listen, we hit them below the belt so badly that up until today it is quiet there. The people there know what we can do. You know Irbid Heights, it is between Mafraq and the Jordan Valley, south of the Golan Heights. They were shelling targets in Israel from there. So we took off with eighteen Mk.81 [250-pound] bombs on a Skyhawk and eight aircraft—144 bombs—and we would drop them in the middle of the village next to the artillery battery firing at Israel. It went on like this for two or three weeks and then the firing stopped. It was a tough war, they were shelling our kibbutzim day and night. With each of our missions a Jordanian village would disappear. It hurt and they learned a lesson.[16]

On November 17, the IAF flew dozens of strike sorties against radar sites and artillery positions in Jordan. During an air strike against a radar site near Mazar, one of the attacking Israeli aircraft was downed by Jordanian antiaircraft fire. This was the seventh Israeli fighter-bomber to be lost over Jordan since the 1967 war. An IAF spokesman stated that "the Jordan figures were high because they occurred shortly after the war when pilots were going into their targets on a wartime basis, taking more risks. We had to tell the pilots to be more cautious and we rethought our tactics."[17] An IAF base commander also commented on IAF losses over Jordanian targets: "When we bombed artillery, antiaircraft sites, or El Fatah camps, the batteries were heavily defended. We made mistakes: we used the wrong weapons sometimes; we used the wrong tactics. But we learned a lot since July 20, 1969, when the current Suez War of Attrition began from the Israeli side."[18]

The morale of Egyptian forces had declined to a low point by mid-December 1969. Vice-President Sadat and Defense Minister General Fawzi made an urgent visit to Moscow to appeal for assistance. In fighting with Israel, more than sixty Egyptian aircraft and several dozen pilots had been lost and almost all of the air defense network near the Suez Canal had been put out of action. Although Egyptian forces struck back and inflicted casualties on the Israelis, each success caused an intensification of the Israeli air attacks.

With Soviet assistance, the Egyptians began to reconstruct their air defenses. Missile batteries, radar systems, and antiaircraft guns were placed near the Suez Canal and fortified with sand and concrete. Israeli reconnaissance aircraft detected this buildup. On December 25, in an unprecedented eight-and-one-half-hour series of heavy air strikes, the IAF hit every major air defense position from Suez City to Qantara. The following day a second series of intense raids blasted the Egyptian defenses.

That night Israeli commandos staged a raid that snatched a whole Soviet-built radar warning system from Egyptian territory. Soviet advisors had installed an advanced P-12 Spoonrest surveillance radar near Ras Gharib to upgrade Egyptian radar coverage along the Gulf of Suez. A specially trained group of commandos was landed by helicopter near the radar site after sunset on December 26. Israeli fighter-bombers and artillery struck at positions surrounding the site to divert the attention of nearby Egyptian army units. The commandos quickly overpowered the guards and dismantled the radar van and antenna into two loads that could be lifted out by helicopter. Two Sikorsky CH-53D heavy-lift helicopters came in and carried out the equipment. This was the first major success of the American-built CH-53D helicopter, which had only been in service with the IAF for a short time. Israeli technicians were able to evaluate the performance of this advanced radar system and shared this information with the United States.

Since Israel had the upper hand in the ongoing conflict with Egypt, senior Israeli government officials had no incentive to make the compromises that would have been necessary to reach a negotiated settlement to end the fighting. The Israeli leadership decided to use the air force as a bludgeon in an attempt to force Egypt to seek peace. On January 7, 1970, IAF fighter-bombers initiated a strategic bombing campaign by attacking three military bases within thirty-five miles of Cairo.

On the following day, dozens of Egyptian aircraft penetrated into the Sinai to hit back in response to the new Israeli deep-strike raids. Egyptian fighter-bombers successfully hit several targets, causing casualties and moderate damage. However, two SU-7 aircraft were lost to Israeli ground fire.

Israeli interdiction missions were resumed on January 13, when a supply depot of El Khanka, fifteen miles northeast of Cairo, was hit. Three separate targets around Cairo were bombed on January 10. However, one of the Israeli jets was shot down by Egyptian antiaircraft fire. The goal of the new air offensive was to relieve pressure along the Suez Canal and Disrupt Egyptian military preparations. Golda Meir, Premier of Israel, stated, "Nasser is not happy. The war has been brought home to him. . . . He can't fool his people anymore. Maybe that is the most important thing that has happened. You can't lie anymore when people hear planes right over Cairo."[19]

Israeli deep-strike attacks and commando raids battered Egyptian forces to the point that President Nasser made an urgent trip to Moscow on January 22. During four days of meetings in the Soviet Union, the Egyptian president acknowledged that his forces were unable to deal with the Israeli attacks. Nasser requested that Egypt be supplied with advanced attack aircraft that would be used to strike back at Israel. Soviet leaders would not supply offensive weapons, but did agree to upgrade the Egyptian air defense capability rapidly.

Soviet Premier Kosygin sent a personal note to President Nixon on January 31, stating that Israel was attacking Egypt at will and that if the United States would not restrain Israel, the Soviet Union would be forced to come to the assistance of Egypt.[20] A massive Soviet airlift of war materiel to Egypt began almost immediately. While Soviet and Egyptian consultations continued, Israeli jets struck targets near Cairo on January 23 and 28. President Nixon replied to Premier Kosygin on February 4. His note denied responsibility for the current situation but Nixon agreed to work toward a cease-fire.

On February 6, President Nixon said he was seriously considering the sale to Israel of an additional twenty-five F-4 Phantom II and eighty A-4 Skyhawk aircraft along with other war materiel. This sale was discussed to let the Soviet Union know that the United States planned to support Israel to help maintain the balance of power in light of the Soviet assistance that was being provided to Egypt and Syria. These airplanes would come from the production lines and thus could not be delivered until 1971.

On February 8, Egyptian fighters clashed with Israeli jets flying a deep-strike raid and two MiG-21 aircraft were shot down by IAF fighters. This was the first time that Egyptian fighters challenged IAF aircraft during one of the air strikes over the Nile delta. Egyptian fighter-bombers struck back, flying several successful raids against Israeli positions in the Sinai on February 9. When Israeli fighters jumped the Egyptian fighter-bombers, they were engaged by top-cover MiG-21s and one Israeli Mirage was shot down. Israel acknowledged this loss as the second aircraft to be shot down in air combat, while eight others had been lost to antiaircraft fire on the Egyptian front since the 1967 war.

During a television interview aired in the United States on February 8, 1970, President Nasser stated, "The Israelis think they are strong—all right, they are strong. They know they have air superiority." He added, "The problem is not the airplanes really. The problem which we feel here in the Arab countries—not only here in Egypt—is the problem of pilots. We have more planes than pilots; the Israelis have two pilots for every airplane; so the Israelis have air security and air supremacy." President Nasser said that in its recent raids against targets near Cairo, Israel demonstrated "the arrogance of power."[21]

A deep-strike raid by Israeli aircraft near Cairo on February 12 mistakenly hit the Abu Zohal concrete factory, killing sixty-eight civilians and wounding ninety-eight. This strike intensified Egyptian and Soviet resolve. By late February, massive quantities of Soviet equipment were arriving in Egypt. Thousands of Soviet advisors were helping to reestablish an air-defense network to protect vital targets in Egypt.

On March 18, the United States disclosed that Soviet forces had deployed dozens of new SA-2 and SA-3 air-defense missile batteries around Cairo, Alexandria, the Aswan Dam, and other vital rear-area locations. A senior Israeli military officer said that these new air defenses were a threat and would be attacked, "because they represent a new obstacle to attacking aircraft." According to the officer, the SA-3 had never been used in combat, "not even in Vietnam." He added that the missile had a range of about twelve miles and was thought to be much more effective than the earlier SA-2.[22]

A massive series of Israeli raids were flown in late March 1970 to destroy new air defense sites being deployed along the Suez Canal. Egyptian fighters aggressively challenged these raids, and numerous air battles occurred, resulting in the loss of nine Egyptian aircraft in less than a week. An Israeli spokesman stated that the nine Egyptian jets shot down were all MiG-21 fighters and that fifty-four of this type of aircraft had been downed since the 1967 war.[23]

Israeli aircraft continued to bomb Egyptian positions in central Egypt. However, Israel refrained from striking locations known to be protected by Soviet troops. A flight of IAF fighter-bombers heading for a target in the Nile valley was called back on April 17, when Israeli ground controllers discovered that they were headed for an intercept with a formation of MiG-21 fighters flown by Soviet pilots. The Soviets controlled several airfields and had been flying fighter patrols over Egypt. Israel was not ready intentionally to engage in combat with Soviet pilots. Israel ended its deep-penetration attacks against rear-area targets in Egypt because of the threat of direct conflict with Soviet military personnel. Since January 1970, the IAF had flown 3,300 sorties over Egyptian territory and delivered more than 8,000 tons of bombs.

The northern borders of Israel were also the scene of considerable action during late 1969 and spring of 1970. Israeli commando raids and air strikes conducted against guerrilla positions in southern Lebanon led Israeli and Syrian forces along the Golan

Heights to trade artillery and tank fire. Both sides committed aircraft to the fighting, and on December 11, 1969, the Syrians lost three planes to Israeli Mirages. Another air battle took place over the Golan Heights on January 8, 1970, resulting in the destruction of three Syrian MiGs. These battles raised the total of Syrian aircraft losses since the 1967 war to seventeen. Ground action, including artillery and tank fire, did not let up along the Israeli/Syrian border and on January 23, a Syrian MiG-21 overflew the city of Haifa at supersonic speed, smashing windows. Later in the day, IAF Phantoms reciprocated by "booming" Damascus and several other Syrian cities. Border fighting continued and on February 2, an Israeli Mirage on a reconnaissance mission was lost to Syrian antiaircraft fire over the Golan Heights.

While the Egyptian front was the focus of IAF activity during the spring of 1970, terrorist attacks were answered with air strikes along the Lebanese, Syrian, and Jordanian borders. Israeli forces initiated large-scale attacks against Syria on April 2, in response to repeated cease-fire violations. "If the Syrians are not impressed by one blow, then we shall deal them a second," said Lt. Gen. Haim Bar Lev. He added, "If the cease-fire line ceases to be quiet, our blows will grow harder." Israeli planes pounded Syrian positions all along the Golan Heights and shot down three MiG-21 fighters in air combat. However, Israel admitted the loss of one aircraft, thought to be an F-4 Phantom, to Syrian antiaircraft fire.[24]

During a strike flown by ten Skyhawks against terrorist camps near Mt. Hermon on May 12, a pair of IAF Skyhawk fighter-bombers was attacked by Syrian MiG-17s. Lt. Col. Ezra Dotan, a Skyhawk squadron commander, heard his number two shouting into the radio: "MiGs! MiGs!" "Are you sure?" he asked him, "I don't see any aircraft!" "Affirmative," came number two's reply. "Get them!" he commanded.

Dotan continues his story:

> I still didn't see them, and I wasn't 100 percent sure that they were really MiGs. But the instant I broke, I saw them—MiG-17s. By then, my number two was inside their formation, threatening one of the MiGs. However, at that time, the IAF Skyhawks weren't equipped with

air-to-air gunsights, and my number two had to estimate the range. As a result, he started firing from too far away.

I saw he didn't have a chance to succeed, and I decided to go in after him. Quickly, I climbed to high altitude and rolled left, into the Syrian formation. I acted so fast, they didn't have time to react. Right out of the roll, I went after their number two. While I was diving, he turned left, then straightened out. But it didn't help—I came out of my dive only 130 meters behind him!

I closed in on him as close as possible and thought fast. What could I fire at him? I decided to use . . . my AT rockets! I fired two clusters; they passed underneath his tail. The Syrian pilot didn't even notice he was being fired on. But I didn't give up—I still had plenty of rockets. I fired two more clusters, estimated range from my air-to-ground gunsight, pulled the Skyhawk's nose up—just like an air-to-ground attack—and fired two more clusters. The Syrian's craft was ripped to shreds; trailing black smoke, he fell at the foot of Mount Hermon.

"Break! MiGs after you!" my number two shouted into the radio. A glance at my mirror confirmed the warning: a MiG was firing on me at that very moment, his tracers slipping past my right wing, and another pair of MiGs was on my tail. Later it turned out that I'd been in the middle of eight MiGs.

I slowed down and let one of the pair pass me. I could have got him—but I realized that if I tried, his wingmen would wipe me out. So I decided to save my skin and my Skyhawk, broke left and down. It surprised the MiGs, and they were ahead of me before they realized what was happening. One of them used his afterburner and streaked away—I realized this meant he was using up valuable fuel, which put him at a disadvantage. So I jettisoned my heavy rocket clusters and streaked right after him.

The Syrian realized I was closing in and dipped close to the ground. That was when I thanked Heaven for my

> Skyhawk—its fantastic maneuverability let me keep chasing after him, in and out of streambeds, between hills. At one point, there were so many trees and rocks streaming past my cockpit, I couldn't follow the MiG by line of sight! I climbed a bit higher, then spotted him below and ahead of me. I closed in on him as fast as I could—my Skyhawk was faster than his MiG, and I almost passed him. I slowed down, but couldn't get my nose down far enough to hit him with my guns.
>
> If the Syrian had had the sense to keep flying straight, he might have got away. But he decided to break suddenly, which meant he had to climb a bit. That was when he got into my sights. I dropped down a bit—by then he was filling my entire windscreen—and fired at the base of his wing. The wing flew off, and the MiG plummeted to the ground.
>
> Then I climbed to join my number two, who had been covering me from above, and we returned to base together. The whole base saw our victory roll![25]

On the Suez front, air action had increased because of Egyptian attacks. Since Soviet pilots were responsible for flying protective patrols over Egypt, the EAF was free to concentrate its operations against Israeli targets. During the period April 18–24, 1970, EAF aircraft flew several major air raids against Israeli positions in the Sinai, causing considerable casualties and damage. Israeli fighters and antiaircraft defenses downed several SU-7 and MiG-17 fighter-bombers and two IL-28 bombers that had penetrated 125 miles into the Sinai to attack targets near El Arish. In concert with these air attacks Egyptian forces intensified shelling, damaging Israeli positions along the Suez Canal. On May 2, President Nasser remarked, "A change has taken place. Our armed forces have regained the initiative with bold military operations in the air and on land."[26]

In early May, Egyptian and Soviet troops began to reconstruct the air defense network parallel to the Suez Canal. New SA-2 and SA-3 sites, protected by antiaircraft guns, were installed from Port Said on the Mediterranean Sea to as far south as the Aswan Dam. At the same time, heavy Egyptian air attacks hit Israeli positions almost every day. Israeli defenses claimed seven Egyptian aircraft during the May 14–16 period. On May 14, Egyptian commandos destroyed an Israeli patrol boat at the port of Eilat and the Egyptian navy sank an Israeli fishing boat in the Mediterranean. In retaliation for these assaults, Israeli Phantoms bombed an Egyptian destroyer and a missile boat in the Red Sea.

Beginning on May 30, an intensified series of Israeli air raids began. Within a week more than four thousand bombs fell on Egyptian fortifications. The strike capacity of the IAF had expanded considerably with the introduction of the Skyhawks and Phantoms. At times the pace of operations was so intense that the air force ran short of bombs.

In the summer of 1970, the IAF had in service two F-4 Phantom squadrons (about forty aircraft), three Mirage squadrons (about sixty aircraft), three A-4 Skyhawk squadrons (about eighty aircraft), one Super Mystere squadron (about twenty aircraft), one Vautour squadron (about ten aircraft), and one Mystere IV squadron (about twenty aircraft). Ouragon and Fouga Magister aircraft were used in the operational-training role. Support services were provided by about forty Noratlas, Stratocruiser, and Dakota transports. The vertical-lift component included about twelve Super Frelon, ten Sikorsky CH-53, twenty-five Bell 205, and twenty Alouette light helicopters.[27] To combat Soviet-built surface-to-air missiles, the United States supplied Israel with jamming pods. These advanced electronic countermeasure (ECM) systems had been used successfully by U.S. forces against the SA-2 radar in Vietnam. Several two-seat Vautour aircraft were also equipped with ECM equipment to jam or deceive Egyptian air defense systems.

In June, U.S. Secretary of State William Rogers announced a renewed effort to bring peace to the Middle East. Israel, Egypt, and Jordan indicated a willingness to consider a cease-fire, but each faction made final efforts to ensure it had a strong bargaining position. For Israel this meant concentrated attacks against the rapidly expanding network of Egyptian air defenses along the Suez Canal.

In June, Egyptian troops, with assistance from the Soviets, began moving their air defense network closer to the Suez Canal. Israeli fighter-bombers hammered the new defenses despite the knowledge that Soviet troops were operating some of the missile sites. Egyptian aircraft provided cover for their ground forces and frequently attacked Israeli positions. In the process, about ten planes were lost to Israeli defenses in June.

During the night of June 29, the Egyptians, with Soviet assistance, moved twelve SA-2 batteries, several SA-3 batteries, and protective antiaircraft guns forward to form a missile screen parallel to the Suez Canal. The following morning a patrol of Israeli Phantoms was ambushed by these new sites and two of the F-4s were shot down. Israeli fighter-bombers aggressively hammered at the air defense batteries, but the Egyptians rapidly repaired battle-damaged sites and fought back with heavy missile and antiaircraft fire. During the next week, seven of the missile batteries were destroyed or damaged by Israeli raids. However, another Phantom jet was lost. Maj. Gen. Haim Bar Lev, Israeli chief of staff, commented that the new Egyptian air defense screen was intended to "drive us from our freedom of air operation along the canal and to enable the Egyptians to concentrate and intensify their offensive ability along the Canal." He added, "In the whole system we feel the Russian hand—in planning, directing, and operating the whole system."[28]

According to Major General Bar Lev, the missiles were more effective because the sites were located close enough to protect each other. Also, ripple fire tactics were used—whereby all the missiles of a battery were fired at a target—making it difficult for the aircraft to escape. The SA-2 batteries used in the June 30 ambush were described as improved models having greater performance, better computers, and optical-tracking capability. A typical SA-2 battery had six ready-to-launch missiles, a central tracking and guidance radar, and a number of antiaircraft guns for close-in protection. The SA-2 was effective against aircraft flying at medium and high altitudes, to a range of 20 miles. Major General Bar Lev was most concerned with the SA-3s because they were effective against low-flying aircraft and were manned by Soviet crews. A typical SA-3 battery consisted of a detection and guidance radar (known by the NATO code name of Low Blow) and four two-round missile launchers. The SA-3 missile had a maximum range of 13 miles and could hit targets below 500 feet.

Israeli fighter-bombers flew hundreds of strike missions against the missile sites and Egyptian frontline positions along the canal. On July 10, IAF fighters shot down three Egyptian MiG-21s that interfered with one of these raids. However, on July 18, a Phantom was shot down by an SA-3 missile and another F-4 was damaged. Despite the intense bombing, the Israelis were not able to eliminate the Egyptian air defenses along the Suez Canal.

Israeli planners began talking of a ground offensive across the Suez Canal to destroy the new air defense network, and the possibility of a direct confrontation with Soviet troops appeared a distinct possibility. Brig. Gen. Mordechai Hod, commander of the IAF, stated that the new threat was a "Russian fist covered by an Egyptian glove."[29]

In concert with the new ground-based air defense network, Soviet fighters began patrolling closer to the Suez Canal. On July 25 a Soviet pilot flying a MiG-21 attacked an Israeli Skyhawk and damaged its wings and tail with an Atoll heat-seeking air-to-air missile. The identity of the MiG-21 pilots was determined by Israeli intelligence units that monitored radio communications between the aircraft and their ground controllers.[30] The next day Israeli fighters shot down two Egyptian MiG-17s that crossed into the Sinai. Senior Israeli government and military personnel debated the next move and decided that the Russians should be taught a lesson. On the afternoon of July 30, a flight of Israeli Mirages flew a reconnaissance patrol into Egyptian air space to bait the Soviet pilots into action. More than a squadron of Soviet MiG-21s scrambled after the decoy and they were met by flights of Mirage and Phantom fighters.

One of the Israeli pilots who participated in the air battle described the situation:

> I was number two of a pair of Phantoms; we and two Mirages were up against about ten MiGs. It was a little unsettling to see so many aircraft at once, so many fuel tanks being jettisoned all over the place. I didn't care about numerical superiority—I was just afraid someone might bump into my aircraft!
>
> One of the Mirages fired an air-to-air missile seconds after the battle began. The missile hit a MiG and set it on fire. The pilot bailed out; the aircraft went into a spin and dropped like a stone from 30,000 feet. The Russian

pilot's parachute opened right away—it's not supposed to: chutes are designed to open automatically at 10,000 feet, so their wearers don't freeze or suffocate at high altitudes. But this pilot used the manual apparatus and opened the chute himself! Maybe he didn't want to be taken alive . . . or maybe he just didn't know any better.

Now some more of our aircraft had joined the battle; the Russians no longer had numerical superiority. I started looking for a MiG to kill. Finally I found one—its pilot was making a right turn, trying to close in on my number one. I broke to the right—the MiG left my number one and started chasing me! We stuck together for a while, dropping to about 15,000 feet; at that point he was only about 150 meters from me. I could see the pilot's helmet clearly.

By this time I'd realized the Russian pilot was inexperienced; he didn't know how to handle his aircraft in a combat situation. At 15,000 feet he proved this fact by trying to escape in a steep dive to 7,000 feet. All we had to do was follow him and lock our radar onto him—and fire a missile. There was a tremendous explosion—but the MiG came out of the cloud of smoke apparently unharmed. That made me mad and I fired a second missile—which turned out to be unnecessary. The Russian aircraft had, in fact, been severely damaged by the first missile; suddenly it burst into flames and fell apart. By the time the second missile reached it, it wasn't there any more.[31]

Israeli Phantom and Mirage pilots shot down five Russian jets in the short dogfight with no loss to themselves.

Heavy fighting continued along the Suez Canal, but Israeli, Soviet, U.S., and Arab representatives began to make serious headway toward a cease-fire. On August 3, 1970, Israel admitted that another Phantom had been lost during attacks against air defense positions near the Suez Canal. This plane was acknowledged to be the sixteenth aircraft lost in action with Egyptian forces and the twenty-sixth plane lost in combat on all fronts since the 1967 war.

Israeli warplanes continued to strike at targets in Egypt, Jordan, and Lebanon right up until the cease-fire took effect on August 8. The cease-fire terms called for both sides to freeze the number of ground forces, air defense systems, and other weapons deployed near the Suez Canal.

During the 1,141 days that had elapsed since the end of the 1967 war, the IAF flew thousands of combat sorties. During these missions, hundreds of thousands of pounds of ordnance were delivered against targets in Egypt, Syria, Jordan, and Lebanon. A total of 113 Egyptian, Syrian, and Soviet aircraft were shot down in air combat during the period while another 25 fell to Israeli Hawk missile and antiaircraft fire.[32] During the War of Attrition, the IAF had modernized much of its force structure, replacing older French aircraft with new American systems. The IAF inventory of helicopters was cxpanded, and those vehicles played a vital role in defeating terrorist raids, evacuating wounded, and moving troops involved in commando raids. Transport, liaison, and training aircraft provided necessary support and assistance.

However, the IAF was stressed almost to the breaking point during the period that ran from mid-1969 to the cease-fire of 1970. The strain of sustained combat operations on multiple fronts, training and maintenance requirements, and the introduction of new sophisticated systems (such as the A-4 Skyhawk, F-4 Phantom, and electronic-warfare systems) took their toll. Toward the end of the War of Attrition, the IAF faced off against a Soviet-developed air defense network that was one of the most advanced in the world. The system in place along the Suez Canal surpassed even the defenses around Moscow in density and depth. Israeli air attacks damaged this air defense network but were unable to destroy it. The massive Soviet and Egyptian investment in weapons and troops plus the commitment to prevail, no matter what the cost, fundamentally changed the balance of power along the Suez Canal. Because of this new air defense network, the IAF could no longer provide large-scale close air support for Israeli ground troops with an acceptable loss rate, as it had in the 1967 war.

Immediately before the August 8 cease-fire, Egyptian and Soviet forces moved additional SAM batteries and antiaircraft guns to forward positions near the Suez Canal. During the fall of 1970, additional missile batteries were positioned along the waterway. These new systems extended missile coverage into the Israeli-held Sinai and strengthened the already formidable Egyptian air defense shield.

Israel vigorously protested these cease-fire violations and threatened to renew hostilities unless the new missile sites were pulled back. However, Egypt ignored these threats. The United States delivered advanced ECM pods, Shrike antiradar missiles, and other weapons to Israel and promised to supply additional F-4 Phantom and A-4 Skyhawk aircraft to strengthen Israel and maintain a balance of power between the two countries.

Meanwhile Israel Aircraft Industries and other Israeli firms were in the process of refurbishing and upgrading IAF aircraft. Mirage IIIC fighters were reworked to extend their service life, while Super Mystere B-2 aircraft were fitted with a new American engine—the Pratt & Whitney J52 turbojet—and new electronic systems. Even the relatively new Phantoms and Skyhawks were upgraded. IAF A-4E/H Skyhawks were fitted with a computerized weapons delivery system that considerably improved the air-to-ground weapons delivery capability of the Israeli Skyhawk. This new system allowed IAF pilots to bomb more accurately, thus reducing the number of sorties necessary to hit a given target.

IAF officials liked the Skyhawk so much that they bought a new version of the jet that was custom designed to meet their requirements. Known as the A-4N, this new airplane combined the sophisticated attack system installed on other IAF Skyhawks with the airframe that was developed for the U.S. Marine Corps. With its increased power, speed, payload capacity, and accuracy, the A-4N was, at the time of its delivery in 1972, one of the most effective attack aircraft in the world. Israel also improved its F-4 Phantoms by fitting them with leading-edge flaps to improve their maneuverability and by adding new systems and weapons.

One of the biggest IAF programs involved the production of the Nesher, a copy of the embargoed Mirage V, in Israel. The prototype Nesher first flew in late 1969, and by the early 1970s deliveries were underway. Even as the first versions of the Nesher were being assembled, IAF engineers were working to integrate a new engine into the airframe to improve performance. The General Electric J79 jet engine, used in the F-4 Phantom, had greater thrust, better fuel consumption, and was much more reliable than the French-designed Attar turbojet that propelled the Mirage III and the Nesher. After successful flight tests in a Mirage IIIB two-seat trainer, Israeli Aircraft Industries began the difficult task of producing a new aircraft that combined the J79 turbojet, a revised Nesher airframe, and an advanced weapon-delivery system. The prototype Kfir fighter reportedly flew for the first time in June 1973.[33]

Despite tension over the cease-fire violations, the Suez Canal front remained relatively quiet until September 11, 1971, when an EAF SU-7 was downed over the Sinai. A week later Egyptian missile batteries shot down an Israeli Stratocruiser transport that was flying over the Sinai, fourteen miles back from the Suez Canal. Israel and Egypt traded artillery fire along the waterway for more than a week after this incident. During late 1971 and early 1972, Soviet-piloted MiG-25 reconnaissance aircraft overflew the Sinai on numerous occasions. The MiG-25 flew at a speed of more than Mach 2 and an altitude of over 70,000 feet, which was above the reach of Israeli Mirage and Phantom interceptors. Israel responded to the MiG-25 overflights by sending Teledyne Ryan Firebee reconnaissance drones over Egyptian territory. On June 13, 1972, Israeli and Egyptian fighters fought over the Mediterranean Sea and two EAF MiG-21 aircraft were shot down.

In late 1970 and early 1971, Jordanian troops fought a bloody series of battles and expelled terrorist groups that had contested the throne of King Hussein. Once the terrorist groups were expelled, the border between the Israeli-held West Bank and Jordan became quiet. However, the guerrillas did not give up. They moved to Syria and Lebanon. During the next several years, hundreds of air strikes were flown over Lebanon to hit these guerrilla camps.

The Israeli/Syrian border remained relatively calm until the fall of 1972. Intensified terrorist activity and shelling was answered by Israeli air strikes. In August 1972, four Syrian aircraft were shot down over the Golan Heights. Eight more Syrian fighters were destroyed during several large air engagements in November 1972. In January and again in September 1973, the

IAF fought large-scale air battles with the Syrian air force, resulting in the destruction of twenty Syrian fighters for the loss of a single Israeli aircraft.

By 1973 the IAF had grown to a strength of 120 F-4E Phantom, 160 A-4E/H/N Skyhawk, 70 Mirage III/Nesher, and 16 Super Mystere combat aircraft. Support types included 6 RF-4E reconnaissance aircraft, 86 Magister trainers, and 10 Stratocruiser, 20 Noratlas, 10 C-47, and 2 C-130E transports. The helicopter component of the IAF included 12 Super Frelon, 12 CH-53, 45 AB-205, and 5 Alouette II helicopters. In 1971, antiaircraft defense weapons were officially transferred from the army artillery branch to the air force. The IAF thus gained functional control over 10 Hawk surface-to-air missile batteries and more than 300 20–40-mm antiaircraft guns.[34]

7

The Yom Kippur War

After the War of Attrition, Israel continued to hold the Sinai Peninsula, Golan Heights, and Jordanian territory that had been captured during the 1967 war. Israel showed no willingness to negotiate a peace treaty and return the territory, so Arab leaders began planning for war. Egypt and Syria secretly prepared for a simultaneous attack against Israeli forces on the Golan Heights and an invasion across the Suez Canal into the Sinai Peninsula. Egyptian President Sadat (who became president after the death of Nasser in 1970) and Syrian Premier Assad hoped to overwhelm the Israeli defenses, capture terrain, and then call for a cease-fire before the Israeli reserves could counter attack.

Egyptian and Syrian efforts to disguise their preparations for war had been highly successful. Israeli leaders misjudged Arab intentions and discounted the possibility of war. However, evidence of a massive shift of Arab forces to forward positions late on October 6, 1973, prompted Israel to mobilize the army hurriedly and prepare the air force for action. Within hours the IAF was ready to fly a massive series of preemptive air strikes similar in concept to the operation staged in 1967. However, Prime Minister Golda Meir refused to authorize the air attacks so as not to appear to have started the conflict. As a result of both the political decision not to strike first and the late mobilization, regular army units on the Golan Heights and in the Sinai and the air force had to bear the brunt of the initial Arab assault. IAF pilots flew attack missions against the well-defended advancing Arab armies in an attempt to slow this advance and buy time for the Israeli reserve forces to move to the battlefield. Israeli air and ground forces fought with determination and the massive Arab invasion was halted, but at a great cost to Israel. At the end of the conflict, Syrian forces had been driven back from the

Golan Heights and the Egyptian army was held in check in the Sinai. However, it was a pyrrhic victory because of the shock caused by the surprise Arab attack, and the heavy casualties and loss of materiel suffered by Israel.

The fifth major Arab–Israeli conflict began on October 6, 1973, the Yom Kippur Jewish holiday. Since it was the major holiday of the year, Israeli forces were at a reduced level of readiness. The war, which lasted for almost three weeks, can be divided into three phases. The Arab assault took place from October 6 to 9. An Israeli offensive on the Golan Heights and holding actions in the Sinai were the major actions of the second phase, which lasted from October 10 to 14. An Israeli invasion into Egypt and continued fighting on the Golan Heights constituted the final stage, which ran from October 15 to 25. The IAF played a significant role in the war.

Egyptian, Syrian, and Iraqi fighter-bombers spearheaded Operation Badr, the Arab assault, and were active throughout the war. In mid-1973 EAF had a strength of over 400 Soviet-built combat aircraft, including 210 MiG-21 fighters, 100 MiG-17 and 80 SU-7 fighter-bombers, and IL-28 and 16 TU-16 bombers. Several hundred helicopters, and transport, training, and liaison aircraft were also in service.[1] Egyptian forces were augmented during the conflict by a squadron of Algerian SU-7 fighter-bombers, an Iraqi Hawker Hunter unit, and two squadrons of Libyan Mirage aircraft.[2]

The Syrian Arab Air Force in 1973 had a total inventory of more than 500 aircraft, including some 200 MiG-21 fighters, and 120 MiG-17 and 45 SU-7 fighter-bombers.[3] Syrian aviation units were supported by squadron-sized detachments of Iraqi Hawker Hunter and MiG-21 aircraft.

The Arab invasion began at about 2:00 P.M. on October 6, when Egyptian, Syrian, and Iraqi fighter-bombers conducted a coordinated attack on dozens of Israeli targets. Over two hundred Egyptian aircraft penetrated into the Sinai and bombed three Israeli airfields, several Hawk missile batteries, two artillery positions, a number of radar and ECM sites, plus several military headquarters. Kelt air-to-surface missiles fired from Egyptian TU-16 bombers also hit several Israeli targets.

Captain N was a pilot on alert at an air base in the southern

Sinai near Sharm el Sheikh on the afternoon of October 6:

> I decided to take off—the controller was screaming that there were orders not to take off. However, I decided that the orders were from 400 kilometers away and they didn't know what was going on. I cranked the engines and told my number two to do the same and to scramble as quickly as possible. Standby is very close to the runway so we cranked the engines, went to the runway, and took off. I looked back to see that number two was airborne and that everything was okay, and I saw smoke plumes on the runway, like cotton balls. And I didn't understand. I told my navigator, "Look! What do you make of this?" He said, "They are bombing the runways, this must be war!"
>
> Then we saw a glimpse of a MiG that was shining in the sun—it was far away, perhaps four miles. There were a lot of them. From then on I don't remember everything. It is just a collection of still pictures. I remember telling number two that there is an attack on the field and nearby facilities and that he should split from me and work on his own to cover the navy base to the south.
>
> First he shot down a MiG-21 right over Sharm el Sheikh, I saw it go down.
>
> My navigator was experienced, he had participated in the battle against the Syrians over the sea on the thirteenth of September 1973, when we shot down thirteen Syrian MiGs and lost only one Mirage. . . . This was my first battle. He said, "Hey, you didn't punch your external tanks!" So I jettisoned them. Then we rushed into what looked like a mass of hornets, there were so many MiGs together. Very quickly I found myself in some maneuvers with two MiG-17s. I was turning after one and the other was at my six o'clock. The one behind us was shooting rockets at me. I saw them missing and I thought, "Don't look back, look forward." Then I shouted to my navigator, "Lock the radar up, I want to shoot the MiG-17 with a radar

missile." It didn't work because we were too low, my navigator shouted that it wouldn't lock on because there was too much clutter. So I selected a heat missile, an AIM-9D Sidewinder. I pushed the button and nothing happened. The one-second delay time seemed like eternity. I almost fired another missile. Then the Sidewinder went out and boom, a big explosion. And I thought, well, I shot down an aircraft! It was a black-and-red ball of fire and I kept staring at it. My navigator yelled, "Leave it, there are others."

There were two MiGs making a pop-up maneuver on my left so I turned after them. They saw me and broke very hard so we went into a sort of a scissors maneuver. One MiG-17 turned too sharp for a Phantom and I could not stay with him in the turn so I went into the vertical, looked, and came very close to gun range. The MiG was jinking very sharply and he tried to shake me away. The Phantom is very heavy and not very agile. . . . We went into a pass and I fired. I saw the bullets hitting his wings but he didn't explode, so I left him. He was smoking but there were so many MiGs and I saw another one coming.

I went into a scissors with another MiG who was jinking in an attempt to escape. I shot a missile from a very short range and boom! I saw the missile go in the jet pipe and there was a huge explosion.

Of course you get lost in such a battle and I saw that we were south over the coast. I saw two MiGs strafing the Hawk battery that was there. I came in to interfere with their attacks and they saw me. They split toward me and I made a hard turn down toward one. I passed him head on and went after the other and started shooting the gun at him. My bullets hit him but he didn't explode. That MiG-17 is a tough aircraft. Then I started sinking. The MiG-17 was flying straight and level and opening from me—I couldn't understand what was happening. I looked at the instruments and saw that one engine was out. I got stall stagnation when I shot the gun. Here we are at 1,000 feet. I told my navigator that we have a slight problem and that we have to restart the engine. I shut it down, lit it, and it started. By that time the MiG was at about one mile. He was running very low along the coast. We opened both burners and within 15 seconds we were within range and we shot a Sidewinder missile at him. It hit and he exploded over the water.

All this time I had heard my number two shouting about his fight. After my battle I turned around and saw a Phantom chasing a MiG-21. They were flying so low that you could see shock waves behind both aircraft on the water. I yelled to number two to be careful because he was too close to the water. He said, "I know, I know," but kept chasing the bouncing MiG.

I took off north and came upon a couple of MiGs which were attacking our airfield. I flew straight into them. They saw me and started turning, but I was experienced now! I took the rear one and nailed him with my last Sidewinder. He exploded over the ground. The other one I engaged with the gun and hit him. I fired again, then silence—I was out of ammunition and too low for a radar missile so he got away.

It was quiet. I circled around and saw several smoke plumes from the ground. I called my number two. He said that he was okay and that he had shot down two MiG-17s and one MiG-21. I told him that I had shot at six MiGs and was sure that four had exploded. We went in to land because we were out of weapons and low on fuel. We saw a hole in the middle of the runway and another in the middle of the taxiway. Then four Neshers came from up north and they shouted, "What's going on, where are the MiGs?" They caped [flew a protective patrol over the airfield] and we called the tower, but there was no answer. We picked 04 runway and landed hard, right on the end like on a carrier, and stood on the brakes. We stopped just short of a hole which was more like a hill. When I looked at it I was amazed because it was such a big pile of debris.[4]

The Israeli airfield at Refidim in the central Sinai was taken by surprise and put out of action by several flights of Egyptian

SU-7 fighter-bombers; many other positions suffered damage from these Egyptian air strikes. On the Golan Heights, over one hundred Syrian aircraft conducted similar attacks that caused damage to many Israeli positions. Because of the element of surprise and the use of low-altitude tactics, only one Syrian aircraft was lost to Israeli defenses during these attacks. Syrian Mi-8 helicopters lifted commandos to the top of Mount Hermon and the Israeli outpost on top of the mountain was captured following a brief battle. This was a serious loss for Israel because the position was an important observation post.

While the Syrian air strikes were underway, the ground assault began. Five Syrian divisions with more than 75,000 men and 1,200 tanks attacked two Israeli armored brigades with a combined strength of only 8,000 men and 170 tanks. The Syrian force received heavy fire support from 1,000 guns and mortars while Israel had only 60 self-propelled cannons on the whole northern front.

In the Sinai, the Egyptian fighter-bombers continued to pound Israeli positions. Israeli fighters, Hawk surface-to-air missile batteries, and antiaircraft fire downed ten of the attackers. In concert with the air strikes, Egyptian artillery blasted Israeli fortifications with over 2,000 guns. More than 10,500 shells hit Israeli targets in the first minute of firing. As this barrage continued, thousands of Egyptian infantry crossed the Suez Canal in small boats and engineers established pontoon bridges across the waterway to allow armored vehicles and artillery to cross.

Israeli defenses in the Sinai relied upon sixteen fortified outposts of the so-called Bar Lev line that ran the length of the canal from near Port Said to the town of Suez. Manned by a total of only 450 reservists, many of these positions fell to the Egyptians on the first day of fighting. Held back from the Suez Canal were three Israeli armored brigades with a total strength of about 10,000 men and 280 tanks. These units initiated immediate counterattacks against the Egyptian bridgeheads and attempted to link up with the battered Bar Lev strong points. While some Israeli tanks made it to the Suez Canal, dozens were knocked out by tank, rocket, and cannon fire from attacking Egyptian forces.

In the late afternoon on October 6, some thirty Mi-8 transport helicopters flew into the Sinai to deliver Egyptian commandos. However, Israeli fighters and antiaircraft guns downed over a dozen of the Egyptian troop-carrying helicopters. The troops that made it into the Sinai assaulted Israeli command posts and struck at Israeli convoys that were moving to the front.

On both the Sinai and Golan fronts, the hard-pressed defenders called for reinforcements, artillery, and air support to stem the relentless Arab assault. However, the Egyptian and Syrian invasion planners took into account Israeli superiority in the air. The simultaneous attack on two fronts prevented the Israelis from concentrating their efforts. The IAF was forced simultaneously to fly air defense missions over the Sinai and northern Israel, to defend against Arab air strikes, and to strike advancing Egyptian and Syrian units. Cries from battered Israeli ground forces for close air support often could not be fulfilled. The IAF aircraft that flew over the battlefield ran into a barrage of missiles and gunfire. The Egyptian air defense shield, which proved to be such a difficult adversary during the electronic summer of 1970, had been considerably strengthened. The Egyptian Air Defense Force concentrated more than 60 of its 150 SAM batteries along the Suez Canal.[5] These missile batteries were positioned in an overlapping manner so that they could protect each another, and thousands of antiaircraft guns were situated near the missile sites for close-in protection. The effectiveness of the Egyptian air defense screen was further enhanced by a comprehensive command-and-control network that tied together visual spotters, dozens of search radars, and the weapons themselves. Many dummy missile sites were set up and both real and camouflage batteries were protected by sand-and-concrete fortifications.

Since the War of Attrition, large numbers of new, Soviet-supplied weapons were introduced into the Egyptian Air Defense Force. The SA-6 surface-to-air missile system consisted of a radar/fire control vehicle and four transporter/launcher units, each of which held three missiles. The SA-6 system was highly mobile since it was mounted on a tank chassis. After firing, the battery could immediately move to a new position to minimize the chance of a successful counterattack. The SA-6 system was effective against low-flying aircraft, had a high rate of fire, and was immune to Israeli ECM equipment. Capable of hitting targets at a range of over 17 miles, the missile was hard to evade because it was very fast.[6]

Another new Soviet-supplied weapon was the ZSU-23-4 radar-guided antiaircraft cannon, which used the same tank chassis as the SA-6 system. The ZSU-23-4 had a fire control radar and optical-tracking system that enabled the gunner to detect and fire at aircraft flying at low altitudes and high speeds. Because of its high firepower and effective range of over 2 miles, the ZSU-23-4 was a dangerous foe.[7] A third new system to see service with Arab forces was the SA-7 Grail antiaircraft missile. This infrared-homing weapon was first used by the North Vietnamese in 1972 and proved surprisingly effective against helicopters and slow-flying aircraft. Similar in appearance to a bazooka antitank weapon, the shoulder-fired missile traveled at a speed of Mach 1.5 and had an effective range of about 2 miles.[8]

A similar lethal network of air defense systems was established by the Syrian forces on the Golan Heights. Most of the thirty-four Syrian SA-2, SA-3, and SA-6 missile batteries were concentrated in the area between the Golan Heights and Damascus, but others protected important positions in central Syria. As on the Sinai front, hundreds of antiaircraft guns and SA-7 missiles accompanied advancing armored units to defend against Israeli fighter-bombers.

Following the air assault that initiated the 1973 war, the Arab air forces continued to fly attack strikes against Israeli targets on the Golan Heights and in the Sinai. However, a large percentage of the Arab fighter force was held back to protect rear-area positions. Defense against Israeli air strikes near the front lines rested primarily with the Arab air defense forces.

Israeli fighter-bombers began to fly close support missions and strike Arab targets within an hour of the attack, but the results of these initial air strikes were limited. On October 6, the first day of the Yom Kippur War, six Israeli aircraft were lost—four on the Egyptian front and two on the Golan Heights, with four of the aircrew being killed.[9] Egyptian authorities admitted that fifteen aircraft had been shot down, while the Syrians suffered only five losses to Israeli fighters and antiaircraft weapons. During the first day of fighting, Arab forces had made considerable gains on the ground and were moving up their air defense screen to check Israeli air strikes.

The second day of the conflict saw intense IAF activity as Israeli jets attempted to assist the ground forces in holding the line against the Arab assault. Just after dawn on October 7, dozens of IAF aircraft penetrated into Egypt and bombed seven airfields. These attacks caused damage, but the lasting impact was limited because Egyptian aircraft were protected by shelters and runway damage was rapidly repaired. During the attacks, Israeli fighters fought with defending fighters and many Egyptian planes were shot down. However, about five Israeli jets were lost to Egyptian defenses. Israeli jets also struck at the Egyptian bridges that spanned the Suez Canal and advancing armor, but they suffered heavy losses to missile and antiaircraft fire. Egyptian fighter-bombers flew a number of successful attack missions against targets in the Sinai on the second day of the war, but several EAF planes were shot down by Israeli fighters and antiaircraft fire.

For Israel, the situation on the Golan Heights was desperate. Syrian units had continued their assault throughout the hours of darkness using Soviet-supplied night vision equipment. While Israeli defenses in the northern part of the Golan Heights held, Syrian tanks in the south overran the Israeli 188th Armored Brigade. By morning this unit had been almost completely destroyed. Reserve tanks and infantry were shoved into the breach to stem the Syrian assault. The IAF was forced to ignore the enemy air defenses and fly attack missions against advancing Syrian columns. Later in the morning, Phantom fighter-bombers flew dozens of strikes against Syrian missile batteries. However, limited intelligence information, poor weather, and heavy opposition resulted in the loss of five F-4 Phantoms for the destruction of only a small number of air defense sites.

Col. Yallo Shavit, who was an air base commander during the 1973 war, discussed the problem that the IAF faced:

> The entire situation was very vague during the beginning. On Sunday, the second day of the war, they started in the north to clean the missile sites. It takes

> time, this operation—six, seven, eight hours—you start with the decoys and the AAA [antiaircraft guns] and then the missiles. In the midst of the operation we were told, "Disaster on the Egyptian front, attack there." So in order to start there you had to take on the missiles. We had to start the same operation again. Meanwhile we paid the casualties on the Golan without results. We went to Egypt and paid the price with limited results. And then Sunday afternoon we went back to Syria because they almost took the Golan Heights. The air force was moved like a platoon—you cannot do that—the air force suffered casualties without getting their rewards. When you go to clean SAMs, the price was about one aircraft per battery—these were the statistics. But we paid more than that because we kept switching back and forth from the Syrian to the Egyptian to the Syrian front. But we were the only element which could help on the Golan Heights at that time so we did it.[10]

Syrian and Iraqi jets were also active on the second day of the war. IAF fighters and air defense units engaged these attackers and over a dozen Arab fighters and helicopters were shot down during the day on the northern front. However, the IAF suffered its highest losses of any single day of the war on Sunday, October 7, when twenty-two Israeli planes were shot down by the Syrian and Egyptian defenses.[11]

On the third day of the war, Israeli reinforcements halted the Syrian assault on the Golan Heights. At great cost to themselves, defending Israeli tanks, troops, and jets had destroyed hundreds of Syrian tanks and other armored vehicles. IAF fighter-bombers blasted convoys that were moving reinforcements, fuel, and ammunition to sustain the Syrian advance. As a result of heavy losses, the Syrians ceased their advance and began to dig in. Syrian units fought hard to hold the ground they had captured and struck back against the advancing Israelis with tank fire, air attacks, and artillery. The IAF flew dozens of fighter patrol missions on the northern front and shot down more than twenty Arab aircraft. Dozens of IAF attack sorties hit Syrian targets, including a series of raids against airfields. However, the Syrian defenses were ready and losses on the attacks against the Syrian airfields were heavy, totaling four F-4 Phantoms.

In the Sinai, Egyptian fighter-bombers struck at Israeli positions but Israeli jets intervened, resulting in several major air battles. Israeli armored columns rolled forward to hit the Egyptian bridgehead into the Sinai but the attacks achieved little, and heavy losses were suffered. Egypt had moved over seventy thousand men, five hundred tanks, and thousands of antiaircraft weapons into the Sinai. Expecting Israeli counterattacks, the defenders had dug in and protected their positions with mines, cannons, and missiles. In the afternoon the IAF flew nearly one hundred sorties against four SAM batteries that defended Port Said and was successful in putting these units out of action.

IAF air defense, helicopter, and transport elements were deeply involved in Israeli battle plans. Hawk batteries and antiaircraft units in the Sinai and on the Golan Heights were the target of dozens of Arab air strikes. Reserve antiaircraft units moved up to the battlefield and provided protective firepower with their 20- and 40-mm cannons. Noratlas, C-47 and C-130 transports flew around the clock in order to move men and material into the Sinai or to northern Israel to support combat operations. On many return flights these aircraft evacuated casualties for treatment at Israeli hospitals. Helicopters of the IAF were heavily involved in supporting the mobilization and rescuing aircrew shot down by Arab antiaircraft fire. These helicopters played a vital role in saving lives by moving the wounded rapidly to medical trauma centers. Maintenance and support personnel worked to exhaustion in order to ensure that combat and transport aircraft were ready for action.

By the fourth day of the war, a sizable number of reserve units had reached the northern front and Israeli forces began to push back the Syrians. However, the Syrians fell back in good order and frequently ambushed advancing Israeli units. Syrian forces began firing FROG-7 surface-to-surface missiles into Israeli territory with the hope of hitting Ramat David air base and the headquarters of the northern command. About a dozen of the Soviet-supplied missiles hit near civilian settlements that surrounded the air base and headquarters. In retaliation for these missile attacks, the IAF heavily bombed a number of strategic targets in Syria, including the air force headquarters near Damascus and the Homs oil storage facility. Israeli jets also bombed an Iraqi convoy moving through central Syria toward the front, a radar site in Lebanon, and several Syrian positions near the battlefield. Israeli fighters and air defenses claimed the destruction of ten Arab aircraft on the Golan Heights during the fourth day of the war.

On October 9, Egyptian tanks raced out from their defensive positions along the Suez Canal and struck south toward Ras el Sudr. This advance was stopped by Israeli armor and air attacks. Israeli units continued to arrive in the Sinai but, except for local attacks, these forces refrained from battle. Israeli army commanders were still moving troops into the Sinai and examining battle plans. The IAF flew over four hundred fighter patrol and strike sorties on the Egyptian front on October 9. Israeli jets struck at Egyptian bridges crossing the Suez Canal and military concentrations on both sides of the waterway. Egyptian airfields at Katamia and Mansura were hit, and air defense positions near Port Said were again blasted. Six Egyptian aircraft were said to have been downed during the day, although Egyptian fighters and antiaircraft fire probably claimed a similar number of the attacking Israeli aircraft.

By the end of the fourth day of fighting, the Israelis had halted the Syrian invasion of the Golan Heights and stabilized the situation in the Sinai. The desperate defense that halted the Arab advance cost Israel more than one thousand casualties and the loss of three hundred tanks and other armored vehicles. The strong Arab air defenses also took a heavy toll of Israeli aircraft; more than fifty were shot down during the first four days of fighting and dozens more were damaged. More than 20 percent of the IAF's frontline combat aircraft had been shot down or put out of action during these four days of intense fighting, and pilot losses were also heavy. Most of the aircraft downed during this period were hit while flying ground support or interdiction missions.

N. Merchavi, a pilot who flew both A-4 Skyhawk and F-4 Phantom aircraft during the conflict, commented on the situation:

> We played the game by our rules and suddenly we didn't know the new rules or how to play. Until 1970 we had

> total air superiority. We were good at air-to-air missions and could attack any point in the Middle East without any chance to be interrupted. But then came the SAMs, the SA-2, improved SA-2, the SA-3, and then in 1973 the SA-6. When you look at the statistics you see that we didn't lose all that many aircraft to the missile threat. . . . What the missile threat did was to take away the capability of the pilot to search and find targets. During the Yom Kippur War the systems that were supposed to support the pilot and help him do his job didn't exist. These were the ECM and intelligence systems. We came in to fight like we did in 1967 but the conditions were different. So it took us about seven days to overcome the uncertainness and understand how to do the job properly.[12]

Pilots on ground support missions had to find and identify their targets while flying at high speeds and low altitudes. At the same time they had to watch out for missiles, gunfire, and enemy fighters while accurately delivering their bombs and rockets. Targeting and intelligence data were generally many hours old, and it was not always possible to talk with ground controllers because of the changing tactical situation and communications jamming. As a result of this situation, many pilots were forced to make multiple passes and were hit or shot down in the process of searching for and attacking their targets.

The Israelis tried different tactics and used a variety of countermeasures in an attempt to reduce their losses. Missions were flown against preplanned targets or battlefield positions that could be marked by smoke from artillery. High-speed, low-level flight profiles were flown and strike aircraft made a single pass, popping up only to deliver their weapons. Several aircraft hit a single target from different directions, while helicopters, low-flying aircraft, or ground observers provided warning of SAMs, antiaircraft fire, or the approach of enemy fighters. To hit targets behind the front lines, flights of aircraft would penetrate at medium altitude, which placed them above the effective altitude of most antiaircraft fire. Shrike radar-homing missiles were fired to force Arab air defense radars to shut down or face destruction. Stand-off jammers were employed to disrupt Arab radars. Strike aircraft carried their own jamming pods and dispensed decoy flares and chaff during the attack in order to confuse the defenses. Aircraft fired upon by missiles made violent maneuvers in order to escape.[13]

The Israelis also used remotely piloted vehicles (RPVs) to perform dangerous reconnaissance missions over the battlefield and as decoys to distract and confuse the Arab air defenses. Drones built in the United States and supplied to Israel in the early 1970s flew these dangerous missions.[14]

Pilots flying interdiction missions against rear-area targets such as airfields, bridges, or oil storage facilities, used indirect flight paths in order to skirt battlefield defenses and achieve surprise. These new tactics and techniques, plus improved intelligence and targeting selection, considerably reduced the Israeli loss rate during strike operations.

During the second phase of the conflict, which lasted from October 10 to 14, the Israelis cleared the Syrians from the Golan Heights and reached a stalemate in the Sinai. At an October 10 news conference, Maj. Gen. Aaron Yariv, advisor to the chief of staff, stated, "It is not going to be a short war. The people of Israel can expect no early and elegant victories. We will have to do a lot of fighting." He added, "I don't want to say that the Syrians have been broken but we have dealt them a severe blow." On the Sinai front the general said that Israel had done no more than "redress the situation" caused by Egyptian numerical superiority. General Yariv acknowledged that "quite a number of our aircraft have been lost" due to the Arab air defenses. But he added that in air power, "the balance is very heavy in our favor."[15]

During the next several days (October 10–12) the IAF staged an intense series of interdiction raids against Syrian targets including airfields, military headquarters, power plants, and the oil storage facility at Homs. These attacks were hotly contested. The following interview with an Israeli Phantom pilot tells the story of one of these missions:

> Four attacking Damascus International Airport. Early morning. All is calm. As we drop from the mountains toward Damascus, we notice a cloud of black smoke from burning fuel tanks. Flying low we pass underneath

> the cloud. Poor visibility. Terrible AA smoke rising toward us.
>
> One minute to climb. The first pair climbs and so do we. The airfield is beneath us. Two long runways. Impossible to miss. I aim and press the bomb button. Bombs released, the aircraft shudders—almost sighs with relief. Beneath us Damascus Valley seems to be boiling and steaming; missiles are flying through the air and AA shells are everywhere. Two minutes later the first pair breaks away. They're on to us. Jettison tanks. Full afterburner. Break left as hard as I can. Everything is happening so fast! To the west I see a Phantom breaking left, with a MiG on its tail. I get behind them. If the MiG straightens its wings, I tell myself, I'll launch a missile at it. The MiGs wings straighten, I launch.
>
> My earphones crackle with S's voice: "Break you son-of-a-bitch! Break!" Another MiG, some 600 meters behind S and me, is firing its gun like a madman. "He won't hit us," I assured S. "We're out of range." The MiG I fired on explodes—and in that instant, we're hit in the right wing. The Syrian has crept up behind us into range. Formation leader says to break contact. "Number four aircraft stuck with MiGs," I reply. Number three flies over us and begins to fire his gun. Amazingly, it helps: the MiGs scatter.
>
> We limp back to the rendezvous point. I report to the formation leader: the aircraft is skidding out of control, right engine temperature is shaky and we're low on fuel. Nevertheless I manage to land. Ground crews swarm all over the aircraft. A hole as big as a bucket in the right wingtip.
>
> Mission score: four good hits on the target, one MiG killed, landed safely home.[16]

While a number of IAF jets were lost during this series of interdiction missions, many Syrian and Iraqi fighters were shot down in dogfights. The Syrians also pulled a number of their missile batteries back from the front lines in order to defend against these attacks. In addition to these deep attack missions,

IAF aircraft continued to fly a large number of ground support and fighter patrol missions over the Golan Heights each day.

As Israeli forces advanced across the Golan Heights, the Syrian leadership began to call for help from Arab allies and the Soviet Union. The Syrian Air Force stepped up its ground attack efforts, while Iraq committed additional forces and aircraft to the northern front. Sizable air battles occurred over the Golan Heights; IAF fighters and air defense systems claimed thirty-six victories on the northern front during the period October 10–12.

In response to Arab requests for assistance, the Soviet Union began flying replacement aircraft and military equipment to Syria and Egypt. Dozens of Soviet transport planes arrived daily and additional materiel was dispatched via cargo ships. An Iraqi armored division arrived in Syria, and Jordan sent an armored brigade into battle. During the night of October 12, Israel staged a dramatic commando raid against an Iraqi column that was moving toward the front on the Baghdad–Damascus Highway. A squad of troops was lifted into position above the highway by a CH-53 transport helicopter. The paratroopers destroyed a bridge, planted mines, and waited for the arrival of the Iraqi convoy. The paratroopers destroyed the lead vehicles of the convoy and then withdrew to the helicopter pickup point. Israeli Phantoms then swept in and blasted the stalled convoy, with bombs destroying many additional vehicles.[17]

The war on the Golan Heights was still being fought with considerable intensity. N. Merchavi commented:

> Israeli ground forces came and took the territory occupied by the Syrians back and moved into Syria to Tel Sharms, which is about five miles east of the green border [1967 cease-fire line]. But the missile sites were further back so the Syrian air defense system, at about a week after the war started, was still very good. On the twelfth of October I got a mission from the headquarters to attack with four Skyhawks fully loaded with weapons and fuel and go to the Damascus area at 6:00 o'clock in the morning to hit SAM sites. The mission plan from headquarters said that we should go in at about 14,000

feet, which makes the aircraft in our loaded condition able to fly at about 280 knots at maximum power. . . .

We had the E model with the fixed gunsight, without RWR [radar warning receiver], and the old [8,600-pound-thrust Pratt & Whitney J52 turbojet] engine. So I decided not to go to the Damascus area directly from our border at 14,000 feet. I preferred to go to the north because there I leaned on Mount Hermon, and then I at least had one side clear from the missile sites. To make a long story short, we tried to attack several times. On our initial attack I entered first and put numbers three and four three miles behind to warm me about missile launches. I got close to a fixed SA-2 site, rolled in to bomb it, then I saw about twenty launches of SA-6s! At the time we knew all about missiles and how to identify them because we saw many. I was very surprised to see the simultaneous launching of so many missiles. None of us were shot down during the ambush because we all maneuvered like crazy. But I saw my number two release his bombs, start to recover, and then I saw a missile pass by me and I warned him to break. He turned and I saw an explosion and the aircraft come out of the orange smoke of the SA-6. He got out of it without serious damage and we got back to Mount Hermon. We tried to come back two more times but had to leave because the defenses were alerted.[18]

On the Golan Heights, Syrian and Iraqi armor, supported by aircraft, made several serious counterattacks, but Israeli units held the line and continued their slow advance. By October 15, fighting on the Golan Heights had reached a stalemate. During the previous three days the IAF had flown almost two hundred strike sorties against Syrian airfields, fuel dumps, and battlefield targets. Many Arab aircraft were engaged during Israeli fighter patrol and strike sorties, and over two dozen were shot down during October 13–15. Israeli aircraft losses were relatively light, but heavy Syrian tank and artillery fire and air strikes caused dozens of casualties among the ground forces.

There was a lull in ground action on the Sinai front during October 10–13 as both sides built up their forces for renewed offensive action. However, Israeli and Egyptian units continued to make frequent small-scale probes and trade artillery fire. The Egyptians held a narrow strip of territory, running the entire 102-mile length of the Suez Canal, that varied in width from two to nine miles. Opposing them was an Israeli force of about five divisions, which included more than sixty thousand men and six hundred tanks.

Despite the relative lull on the ground, heavy air action continued. The IAF struck at battlefield targets, including bridges across the Suez Canal, armored formations, and air defense sites. Many counter-air missions were flown against Egyptian airfields, but since aircraft were protected by shelters and runway damage was rapidly repaired, most airstrips were back in operation within several hours. Egyptian radars and observers detected most of the approaching Israeli strikes so the defenses were ready for the attackers. As a result, Israeli fighter-bombers suffered losses to the strong missile and gun defenses that protected Egyptian air bases. Attacking Israeli jets also had to contend with formations of MiG fighters that hovered over their home airfields. The following account describes the outcome of one of these deep strike missions:

> There were four of us. We felt really good; we kept singing into the radio. The attack was successful and we knew it. We could see the explosions, right on the target—a good feeling.
>
> We formed up again and headed for home. We kept looking around for MiGs, but there was nothing there. Total silence—and suddenly, total uproar. The aircraft next to us had climbed slightly—and there were two MiGs after him. Then I felt a blow to the aircraft. I thought H—my pilot—had jettisoned the fuel tanks. But it was a MiG firing behind us. I shouted for H to break left. Meanwhile, I saw another MiG firing on a Phantom from our formation. The Phantom was seriously damaged: flames streamed out its left-hand engine. The first MiG was still on our tail, closing to 400 meters and firing. I told H to break away; the burst missed us. But the MiG kept closing on us and firing; we were losing speed and the aircraft was sluggish. I had a feeling that

> the next burst would run right through the cockpit and it would be all over.
>
> The MiG got within 150 meters of us—and we were hit. The whole aircraft shook with the blow; the rear fuselage and wings burst into flames. I don't remember hearing anything over the radio from that point on—maybe because I was shouting myself. The entire aircraft was now in flames. I shouted to H to jump and pulled my ejection handle. I watched the fight continue on my way down; MiGs were firing all over the place, and another Phantom's crew bailed out. I saw H land safely—and then I was too busy with my own landing to see anything else.[19]

IAF Phantoms engaged and downed many MiGs in dogfights that broke out during the deep-strike raids, but they also suffered their share of losses to Egyptian fighters and ground defenses.

At dawn on October 14, the Egyptians made their long-awaited breakout from their defensive positions along the Suez Canal. Columns of Egyptian tanks attacked toward the Mitla and Giddi Passes, moved west along the Tasa road, and north into central Sinai. The attack was preceded by a massive artillery barrage and air strikes flown by dozens of Arab fighter-bombers. Algerian SU-7s and Libyan Mirages flown by Egyptian and Pakistani pilots participated in these strikes. North Korean pilots were also supporting the Arab effort by flying MiG-21 patrol missions over central Egypt.[20]

Israeli tanks engaged the advancing Egyptian columns from prepared, hull-down positions that gave them a considerable tactical advantage. The ensuing tank battle was the largest to be fought since World War II. Israeli tank fire, artillery, and dozens of air strikes repulsed the Egyptian attack. Over 220 Egyptian tanks and other armored vehicles were knocked out and 10 Arab aircraft shot down, while Israeli forces suffered only limited losses.

The IAF flew many sorties in support of Isareli ground forces and also staged dozens of attacks against Egyptian missile batteries and airfields. Captain N, the pilot who fought with Egyptian MiGs over Sharm el Sheikh at the start of the war, participated in one of these missions:

> On October fourteenth I took part in an attack against Tanta [an Egyptian airfield], which was where the Mirages were operating from. My squadron leader led the attack and I brought up the rear. On our way in to bomb the air base we flew at low level and high speed. Over the Nile Delta a MiG-21 made a quarter pass at my aircraft with his cannon, but he didn't lead me enough and missed. I looked out and saw a MiG lined up with my wingman at 400 yards and firing—a great flame was jumping out from his cannon. I yelled for him to break right and he did. I cleaned up my plane by dumping my bombs and fuel tanks and broke with the MiG. I yelled to my wingman to turn so that I could fire my missile out at the MiG and he did. The Sidewinder guided to the right, I thought it was going for my wingman, but it came back and hit the MiG, blowing him up.
>
> After this I called my leader and he said that we should head for home. Now, I had no bombs or missiles left. Separate from my wingman, we headed northeast at high speed flying very low and passing out of Egypt over the Mediterranean.
>
> I was very low on fuel and I started to climb to save gas for the flight back. All of a sudden a missile flashed by! I looked back and saw a MiG-21. I went up and the MiG climbed with me and he came within 100 meters. I could see him clearly—he was wearing a leather flight helmet. We were so close I could see the instruments in his cockpit. I thought to myself, so this is how it will end—no missiles, almost no fuel, over the cold water and this guy seems to be good. Up we went. But I had one trick left. At 250 knots I engaged the afterburners and nosed over. He tried to follow me down but evidently lost control because he started spinning and flew right into the water with a big splash!
>
> I had made it but was now in real fuel trouble. I climbed to 35,000 feet, put one engine in idle, and got on the radio. I finally made it to El Arish, where I landed.

> Just after I turned off the runway onto the taxiway the engines flamed out. What a mission![21]

On October 15, the United States publicly disclosed that it was supplying Israel with military assistance. Heavy losses and much greater than anticipated ammunition consumption prompted Israel to ask for support from the United States beginning on the second day of the conflict. The United States provided some vital supplies right away and these were transported to Israel on EL AL aircraft. Once the extent of the Soviet air-and-sea resupply effort and Israeli losses were learned, the United States initiated a massive operation. Some of the American aid was carried to Israel on U.S. Air Force C-141 and C-5 cargo aircraft, but additional material was organized for transport by ship. In addition to munitions, dozens of F-4 Phantom and A-4 Skyhawk fighter-bombers were flown directly to Israel. These aircraft were taken directly from U.S. Air Force, Navy, and Marine Corps squadrons and training units. A variety of advanced equipment was also provided to Israel including ECM systems and specialized laser, electro-optical guided weapons, Shrike antiradar missiles, and other high-technology munitions.[22]

On October 15, Egyptian forces again made a series of probing attacks into the Sinai, but the assault failed. The defeat of the Sinai offensive and the serious losses suffered by armored units forced Egypt to reconsider its tactics. This defeat reduced the Egyptian numerical superiority on the southern front and prompted Israel to begin its long-planned counteroffensive against Egyptian forces.

On October 15, the IAF flew hundreds of attack sorties against Egyptian battlefield and rear-area targets, while Israeli ground forces redeployed for a surprise attack. During the night, Israeli armor and infantry units forced their way to the Suez Canal at a point just north of Great Bitter Lake, which was the junction of the Egyptian 2nd and 3rd Armies. Tanks and other Israeli vehicles moved across the canal during the night and the troops established a bridgehead in Egyptian territory. Once across, Israeli forces fanned out and destroyed a number of SAM sites and defensive positions. These ground attacks opened a hole in the Egyptian air defense shield and allowed the IAF to operate with greater safety and effectiveness in the area. Egyptian commanders were initially unaware of the Israeli assault across the Suez Canal. They thought that the attacks on their positions in the central Sinai were an attempt to roll back their bridgehead. Egyptian units fought a fierce battle to push back the Israelis. On several occasions, strong Egyptian attacks closed the road to the Israeli crossing site. Israeli troops at the Suez Canal crossing site and on the west bank of the canal were surrounded. A determined assault by Israeli tanks and paratroopers reopened the road to the Israeli bridgehead.

Frantic calls for help from air defense sites and supply depots located in Egyptian territory alerted the Egyptian high command that Israeli forces had crossed the Suez Canal. Late on October 16, Egyptian forces began blasting the Israeli crossing site with artillery and air strikes. Israeli fighters hovered over the bridgehead and intercepted the Egyptian jets that came in to bomb the crossing site. The IAF downed ten Egyptian aircraft with its fighters and antiaircraft fire during one big battle on the afternoon of October 16. Egyptian tank attacks against the Israeli crossing site were also defeated. A pontoon bridge was established across the Suez Canal on the afternoon of October 17, and dozens of Israeli tanks poured into Egypt. While the bridgehead was still the focus of ground action, the IAF flew dozens of strike missions against missile batteries near Port Said, Qantara, Suez City, and several airfields.

Israeli forces pushed into Egypt; General Sharon's tanks moved north toward Ismailiya; General Adan's armor struck south toward the town of Suez. Taking advantage of the ever-expanding hole in the air defense screen, the Israeli jets pounded Egyptian forces near the Suez Canal, on the west bank of the canal, and flew nonstop fighter patrols to protect the advancing armor from Egyptian air strikes.

Optimism was high that this new offensive would turn the tide in favor of Israel and end the war. Defense Minister Moshe Dayan said, "I don't think this war is going to drag on." General Shlomo Gazit told reporters on October 18, that more than ten SAM batteries had been destroyed in the day's fighting and that Israeli planes were now, "completely free" to operate behind Egyptian lines in this sector. The general added that some missile batteries were captured intact and, "We have some things to bring back." He said, "Egyptian planes made repeated forays in the area and 25 were shot down."[23] Because of the destruction of its air defense shield, Egypt was forced to send in the air force to plug the gap and strike at Israeli ground forces. Egyptian MiG-21s engaged IAF Mirages in swirling dogfights over the Suez Canal while MiG-17, SU-7, and Mirage fighter-bombers flew in at low altitude to bomb, rocket, and strafe the bridges and advancing Israeli armor. Egypt sent in L-29 Delfin jet trainers and even Mi-8 helicopters to blast the Israelis. Barrels of napalm, rolled from the door of an Mi-8 transport helicopter, almost hit Defense Minister Moshe Dayan, who was visiting the Suez Canal crossing site. Israeli fighters and heavy ground fire took a heavy toll of the attacking Arab aircraft.

Thousands of additional Israeli troops and hundreds of tanks and other armored vehicles crossed the Suez Canal into Egypt on October 19 and 20 to support the invasion of Egypt. On October 20, there were in excess of ten thousand men and over three hundred tanks operating in Egyptian territory. This force was moving on a north–south axis, with the objective of cutting off the Egyptian 3rd Army. The ground offensive received considerable assistance from the IAF now that the Egyptian air defenses in the area had been neutralized. In addition, the IAF continued to hit rear-area targets and blast missile sites near the battle zone.

Egypt moved forces back from the Sinai to cut off any Israeli thrust toward Cairo and fought back with fierce determination. Scores of Arab aircraft struck at the crossing site and Israeli armor in the expanding bridgehead. Air action was intense and Israel authorities estimated that by October 20, over 110 Egyptian aircraft had been shot down.

Israeli forces had found a weakness, crossed the Suez Canal, and destroyed the air defenses and resupply units that supported the Egyptian invasion force in the Sinai. Airpower and armor, the most powerful Israeli military assets, could now be fully utilized in the battle against Egypt. Lt. Gen. David Elazar, Israeli chief of staff, commented to reporters, "The objective is to win the war and destroy the Egyptian armed forces."[24] Fearful that the gains of the early part of the war would be lost to the Israeli counteroffensive, Egypt began pressing for a cease-fire.

The Israeli offensive on the northern front had pushed the

Syrians off the Golan Heights and penetrated into Syria on the northern sector of the front. However, the Israeli assault into Syria had stalled just outside Sassa. The massive Soviet resupply effort strengthened the Arab armies, and counterattacks by Syrian, Iraqi, and Jordanian units halted the Israeli drive. Syrian artillery was especially active but Israeli forces returned the favor by using long-range 175-mm cannon to shell military targets in the suburbs of Damascus. On October 16 and 17, most of the IAF's sorties were flown on the southern front, but Israeli jets struck bridges in northern Syria, the Mount Hermon position, the Syrian Latakia naval base, and several battlefield targets. Syrian fighters contested these raids and conducted their own strikes against Israeli positions. Israeli fighters and antiaircraft weapons claimed fifteen Arab aircraft on the northern front during the two days of heavy fighting.

On October 18, the IAF was fully committed to support the drive against Egyptian forces in the Sinai and did not see action on the Golan Heights. Several Israeli army units were withdrawn from the Syrian front and sent to the Sinai to support the invasion into Egypt. Syrian, Iraqi, and Jordanian forces staged a series of counterattacks on October 19 and 20, but Israeli units were well entrenched and the Arab attacks failed to gain any ground. Arab aircraft supported these attacks and four were reportedly shot down by Israeli fighters.

Realizing that a cease-fire was near, on October 21, the Israeli army made an all-out effort to recapture Mount Hermon. While IAF fighter-bombers made diversionary raids against targets near Damascus, CH-53 transport helicopters swept in and dropped Israeli paratroops near the summit. A column of Golani infantry and armor assaulted the hill from below, using the road that led up to the position. Both attacks stalled because of heavy Syrian fire, and Israeli units suffered many casualties. The Syrians flew in reinforcements but three of the Mi-8 transport helicopters were shot down by Israeli jets. Syrian fighters swept in to protect the helicopters and a big dogfight occurred, with both sides suffering losses. The Israeli ground assault continued throughout the night, and, by the morning of October 22, the outpost on the summit of Mount Hermon was in Israeli hands. On October 22, the IAF blasted Syrian armor that was attempting to move up to Mount Hermon, hit other battlefield targets, and fought several air battles with Syrian aircraft. Early on October 23, a major Israeli air strike hit a fuel storage depot northeast of Damascus. Two formations of fighters challenged the attackers, and nine Syrian jets were shot down by Israeli Mirages and Phantoms. A UN cease-fire came into effect on the evening of October 23, and the Yom Kippur War ended on the northern front.

In the Sinai, air and ground action continued with considerable intensity, and on October 20 and 21, Israeli forces captured hundreds of square miles of Egyptian territory. Air action was also heavy as IAF fighter-bombers blasted targets in the battle area. Israeli fighters achieved air superiority in the area of the Israeli invasion into Egypt, which enabled IAF transports to operate out of the captured air base at Fayid.

Early on October 22, the United Nations announced that a cease-fire would come into effect that evening. Prior to the cease-fire, Israeli forces made fierce attacks north toward Ismailiya and south near the town of Suez in an attempt to complete the encirclement of the Egyptian 3rd Army, which held positions in the Sinai running from the Gulf of Suez to Great Bitter Lake. During the day, over five hundred ground attack and patrol sorties were flown by the IAF in support of these Israeli attacks.

On October 18, the IAF initiated a five-day series of defense suppression raids that hit Egyptian missile sites all along the Suez Canal, from Port Said to the Gulf of Suez. Working in conjunction with ground forces, these efforts severely damaged the Egyptian air defense network. While Israeli army units hit SAM sites with artillery and tank fire, and captured many intact, the IAF plastered others with bombs and guided missiles. Shrike antiradar missiles were used with good effect, and the IAF also used recently introduced ECM systems to suppress surviving radar sites.

N. Merachavi, cited earlier in this chapter, participated in these raids:

> On October twenty-second our squadron of F-4s had the mission to destroy six SA-2 and SA-3 missile sites near the town of Suez. It was a very smooth mission. We came in at close to 0.95 Mach with a full load of Mk 117

> [750-pound] bombs with very good cover of ECM. We flew in at about 14,000 feet and after three or four minutes, all the sites were destroyed and none of us were hurt. . . . By the end of the war we had many calm and comfortable missions, the way you thought they should go. I think that we learned what to do and how to do it. If you look, you can get the impression that the air-to-air mission was the glory of this war, but I don't think so. Most of the real dirty work was done by the attackers, who mostly did a good job.[25]

The October 22 cease-fire broke down almost immediately as both Israeli and Egyptian forces continued to trade artillery fire. At dawn, Israeli units continued their attacks and by late on October 23, the Egyptian 3rd Army's supply line had been cut. Early on October 24, Israeli armored columns moved into the town of Suez in an attempt to capture it before a second cease-fire took effect. Egyptian commandos ambushed the Israeli columns and heavy fighting continued until well after sundown. Israeli forces were forced to pull out of Suez after suffering serious losses.

The IAF maintained a heavy pace of operations on the Sinai front during the last two days of fighting: Over six hundred sorties were flown, more than twenty Egyptian aircraft were shot down, and tons of supplies were moved to the west bank of the canal to support the ground offensive. Late on October 24, a second cease-fire ended the fighting between Israel and Egypt, and the Yom Kippur War came to an end.

After suffering heavy casualties due to the surprise Arab attack on two fronts, Israeli ground, naval, and air forces pushed back the Syrians and outflanked the Egyptians. In the course of nineteen days of fighting, Israel suffered 2,812 killed, and over 7,500 wounded, and lost 103 aircraft, 6 helicopters, 1 naval vessel, and more than 400 tanks and 500 other armored vehicles. Arab casualties totaled more than 8,000 killed and 19,000 wounded, and equipment losses included some 2,000 tanks, 1,000 other armored vehicles, 500 artillery pieces, 392 aircraft, 55 helicopters, and 15 naval vessels.[26]

The cease-fire of October 24 ended the fighting, but for some time Egypt, Syria, and Israel continued to maintain the positions they had captured during the conflict. Israeli troops held the Golan Heights and a sizable segment of Syrian and Egyptian territory. Egyptian forces were in possession of a large segment of the Sinai along the Suez Canal.

Skirmishes and air attacks continued on the southern front for some time after the cease-fire agreement. On December 6, an air battle occurred near the Suez Canal that resulted in the loss of an Egyptian MiG-21. It was not until January 18, 1974, that Israel and Egypt agreed upon terms to pull their respective armies back to prewar positions.

Disengagement on the northern front took even longer. Artillery fire and sniping continued along the cease-fire line, but on January 26, Syria intensified its shelling. Syrian authorities admitted that it was conducting a war of attrition to force Israel to continue its costly mobilization. United States Secretary of State Henry Kissinger established a dialogue between Israel and Syria in February 1974 in order to bring about a lasting peace. His efforts began to make progress but on April 13, 1974, Syrian forces attempted to capture the Israeli outpost on Mount Hermon. Heavy fighting continued daily into May and the air forces of both sides became involved. Kissinger's diplomatic efforts finally bore fruit on May 31, when a peace treaty was signed. Both Syria and Israel had suffered heavy casualties and lost many tanks, aircraft, and other weapons during eighty-one days of continuous fighting in the spring of 1974.

In order to review the activities of the IAF during the 1973 war, it is important to first identify the missions of the force: (1) to protect Israeli airspace, (2) to achieve air superiority over the battle zone, (3) to support ground and sea operations, (4) to fulfill IDF transportation, reconnaissance, communications, and intelligence needs.

The IAF clearly achieved its first mission, the defense of Israeli airspace. However, it can be added that the Arab air forces made only a few attempts to strike targets in Israel. Egyptian fighter-bombers hit targets in the eastern Sinai, while several Syrian strikes attempted to hit the oil refinery near Haifa. Israeli fighters intercepted and turned back most of these raids. The IAF was unable to intercept or interfere with the Syrian surface-to-surface missile attacks using FROG-7s, which caused minor damage to Ramat David air base and several surrounding civilian settlements. IAF fighter-bombers blasted oil storage tanks at the Homs refinery, hit electrical power plants, and struck other targets in Syria in response to these missile attacks.

In the 1967 war, Israel had achieved air superiority by destroying enemy aircraft on the ground. During the War of Attrition, the IAF shot down or drove off many of the Arab jets that penetrated into the Sinai or Golan Heights to interfere with Israeli operations. The IAF used fighters, strike aircraft, and air defense weapons to fight the air superiority battle during the 1973 war. The IAF aircraft capable of performing this air superiority role included about 75 Mirage/Nesher and 120 F-4E Phantom II fighters. Israeli air defense systems included ten Hawk missile batteries and several hundred 20- and 40-mm antiaircraft guns.[27] Toward the end of the war, Israel received several Chapparal air defense systems from the United States. Hawk batteries were positioned in hardened sites in the Sinai, on the Golan Heights, and in Israeli territory in order to defend Israeli positions. Antiaircraft guns were used to protect airfields, Hawk sites, and ground forces. Israeli jets and antiaircraft weapons fought hundreds of engagements and shot down more than three hundred Arab aircraft. Since Arab fighter-bombers generally employed high-speed, low-level attack profiles, many penetrated into the battle area and were able to hit Israeli frontline units and defensive positions. IAF fighters were able to achieve a high degree of air superiority over Israeli airspace and the areas near the front lines. But the Arab air defense screen prevented Israel from securing air superiority over the entire battle zone, as had been achieved during the latter part of the 1967 war.

Israeli aircraft flew 3,961 top-cover, escort, air defense, and reconnaissance missions during the 1973 conflict. Fighter aircraft were involved in 117 air engagements (65 on the Syrian front and 52 on the southern front), which included over 450 aircraft. The IAF has stated that its pilots downed 334 Arab aircraft for the loss of only 3 Israeli planes.[28] Other sources list 277 Israeli air combat victories during the 1973 conflict.[29] Air combat usually took place over Arab territory following strike operations, or else over the battle area. The most common scenario involved groups of two or four Israeli fighters in engagements with four or more Arab aircraft near the battlefield. The Mirage/Nesher fighters, which carried two Shafrir infrared-homing air-to-air missiles and their 30-mm cannons, accounted for about two-thirds of the Israeli air combat victories. F-4 Phantom aircraft were used mostly in the ground attack role, but they also performed hundreds of patrol and intercept missions. Phantoms struck many rear-area targets such as airfields, oil storage facilities, and other strategic positions that were protected by Arab fighters. After delivering their bombs, Phantom crews frequently took on Arab fighters, attacking them with Sidewinder and Sparrow missiles or 20-mm cannons. One-third of the Israeli air combat victories were claimed by Phantom crews. About two-thirds of the Israeli air combat victories were achieved with air-to-air missiles, most of which were infrared-guided air-to-air missiles, but ten planes were shot down with Sparrow radar-homing missiles. The remaining one-third of the kills were made with cannon fire.[30]

While the IAF claims that only three of its aircraft were lost in air combat, some officers admitted that many of the Israeli aircraft losses placed in the unknown category probably were downed by Arab fighters. Some sources list twenty-one IAF air combat losses while the USAF estimated Israeli air-to-air casualties at 10 percent of the total. If the USAF estimate of eleven air combat losses is accurate, Israeli pilots achieved a kill/loss ratio of about 25 to 1. Even if the IAF had lost twenty-one jets to Arab fighters, the Israeli exchange ratio would be 13 to 1. By way of contrast, during the Korean War, U.S. F-86 Sabre jet pilots achieved a 6-to-1 kill ratio against the MiG-15. In Viet nam combat, the overall U.S. kill/loss ratio was less than 3 to 1 in favor of U.S. pilots. In the heat of battle Israeli forces accidently shot down two of their own aircraft. Since Arab air forces were flying Mirage aircraft, it is easy to understand how this could occur.

The IAF's antiaircraft weapons played an important part in the 1973 war. Even after mobilization, the Israeli inventory of air defense weapons totaled less than 10 percent of those in service with Egyptian and Syrian forces. These systems destroyed, damaged, or degraded the effectiveness of Arab aircraft that had evaded IAF fighters or penetrated below-radar surveillance coverage. During the 1973 war, Israeli Hawk and Chaparal missiles shot down thirteen Arab planes, while antiaircraft guns and small-arms fire downed thirty aircraft.[31]

Israeli fighters and air defense weapons engaged many of the attackers and took a heavy toll of Arab aircraft. However, Egyptian, Syrian, Iraqi, and Libyan aircraft did penetrate the defenses on many occasions, causing casualties and damage to Israeli forces.

During the conflict, IAF fixed-wing aircraft flew a total of 11,233 sorties, some 60 percent of which (7,272) were ground attack missions. The IAF flew 1,830 attack missions on the Syrian front and 5,442 strike sorties against the Egyptians.[32] For the first few days of the war, IAF fighter-bombers had to ignore enemy air defenses and concentrate on pounding the advancing Arab columns in order to assist the hard-pressed Israeli ground forces. During the October 6–9 period, more than fifty IAF aircraft were shot down by the Arab air defenses. Pilots of A-4

Israeli Air Force
October 1973 War
Daily Loss Summary

			Daily Sorties		
Day	*Date*	*A/C Lost*	*Egypt*	*Syria*	*Remarks*
1	Oct 6	6	197	25	Yom Kippur
2	7	22	241	247	
3	8	9	434	188	
4	9	17	442	168	
5	10	3	296	230	
6	11	10	69	353	
7	12	5	172	197	
8	13	6	96	133	
9	14	2	229	48	Second Egyptian offensive
10	15	3	246	62	
11	16	2	283	30	Sharon's counterattack
12	17	5	213	18	
13	18	6	263	0	
14	19	0	375	2	Fayid air base falls
15	20	3	376	4	
16	21	3	327	55	
17	22	0	532	24	
18	23	0	354	42	
19	24	0	315	4	Cease-fire

Used with permission from John F. Kreis, *Air Warfare and Air Base Defense 1914–1973* (Washington, DC:, Special Studies, Office of Air Force History, USAF, 1988) 338.

Skyhawk and Super Mystere aircraft performed most of these dangerous missions. During the war, sixty aircraft were downed while flying ground support missions—thirty-three of these were lost on the Egyptian front and twenty-seven over the Golan Heights. IAF casualties were heavy—thirty-one aircrew were killed, fourteen were captured, and many other Israeli pilots and navigators suffered injuries.[33]

The IAF fighter-bombers delivered the full range of conventional air-to-ground munitions: high-explosive bombs, cluster bombs, and rockets. These weapons were delivered using low-level-attack, loft, or dive techniques. The U.S. resupply effort enabled the IAF to use large numbers of guided weapons, including guided bombs plus Shrike and Maverick missiles.

In attacks near the battlefield, IAF strike aircraft damaged or destroyed hundreds of Arab vehicles, positions, and fortifications. While hundreds of sorties were flown against Egyptian and Syrian airfields, these raids only destroyed twenty-two aircraft, because most planes were housed in protective shelters, but many bases suffered heavy damage to runways and facilities. The IAF also conducted a successful series of strategic attacks against Syrian command centers, fuel and oil storage sites, electrical power plants, and harbor facilities.

Arab SA-2, SA-3, and SA-6 batteries fired several thousand missiles at Israeli planes and shot down forty-one of them. Antiaircraft fire was responsible for the destruction of thirty-one Israeli planes while three were lost to both SAM and antiaircraft fire. Shoulder-launched SA-7 missiles hit and damaged many aircraft, but only three fell to this weapon; a further three were lost to a combination of SA-7 and antiaircraft fire.[34] The Arab air defenses reportedly shot down fifty-eight of their own aircraft, because many Arab jets did not have an IFF system, a system to identify friend from foe. Missile and gun crews also tended to shoot first and ask questions later. Israeli losses during the 1973 war included thirty-three F-4 Phantoms, fifty-three A-4 Skyhawks, eleven Mirage/Nesher aircraft, six Super Mysteres, and six helicopters.[35] Several other aircraft were lost in action during the fighting that continued on the Syrian front well into 1974.

A total of 236 IAF aircraft suffered damage during the war, and 215 of these were repaired and placed back into service within one week.[36] These statistics call attention to the maintenance personnel of the IAF who, with the assistance of workers from Israeli companies, were able to repair hundreds of battle-damaged aircraft rapidly. Munitions handlers and personnel who conducted routine maintenance and resupply also deserve credit for their tireless efforts.

The helicopter and transport aircraft of the IAF flew thousands of sorties in support of Israeli operations. Helicopters conducted rescue, medical-evacuation, scout, assault, reconnaissance, and liaison missions near and beyond the front lines. Transport aircraft moved men and vital supplies to the front and even operated from captured airfields on the west bank of the Suez Canal.

Although the Arab air forces (Egyptian, Syrian, Iraqi, Algerian, and Libyan) had a numerical advantage at the start of the war, they flew fewer sorties than the IAF. Together, the Arab air units flew about 10,000 sorties during the conflict: about 7,000 were flown on the Egyptian front and 3,000 from Syrian bases. Over 60 percent of this total were fighter patrol and air defense missions, with the remainder attack and reconnaissance sorties. Total Arab losses were estimated to be: EAF, 225 aircraft and 42 helicopters; Syrian Air Force, 121 aircraft and 13 helicopters; Iraqi Air Force, 21 aircraft; while Algeria and Libya lost about 30 aircraft.[37]

Following the 1973 war many theorists declared that the Arab air defenses had caused such heavy losses that the fighter-bomber was obsolete. The IAF did suffer heavy losses during the first few days of the conflict, when pilots braved enemy fire to blunt the Arab attacks in the Sinai and on the Golan Heights. However, the total Israeli loss rate dropped significantly as the war progressed, because of the use of better tactics, widespread use of ECM, and effects of the ground offensive. During the conflict more than 550 Arab and Israeli aircraft were lost to all causes. Ground-based air defense weapons were responsible for the destruction of about 200 aircraft and helicopters. However, nearly 350 were shot down by other aircraft in air combat—the IAF was the victor in the vast majority of these engagements. After the conflict, the IAF set its sights on overcoming the challenge of surface-to-air missile and gun systems.

8

Unending Conflict

Following the 1973 conflict, there was no sense of celebration in Israel even though the country's army, navy, and air force had halted the Arab assault and defeated their combined adversaries on the battlefield. The surprise attack, bitter fighting, and heavy losses had shattered public confidence. After the war the Israeli government and military forces went through a period of recrimination and self-examination. The Israeli government appointed a committee, headed by Shimon Agronat, president of the Supreme Court, to examine the events leading up to the war and the political and military decisions made during the conflict.

The Agronat Report's conclusions and recommendations were classified as secret. However, the little information released revealed that the committee identified a number of errors and incorrect assumptions made by the intelligence branch and senior military and civilian leadership. Overconfidence concerning the ability of the regular army and air force to blunt a massive Arab assault delayed the call for mobilization and contributed to the early Israeli setbacks. The Arab armies staged a coordinated surprise attack, took advantage of their numerical superiority, and employed oil embargos and other political and economic leverage against countries that provided assistance to Israel.

After the Yom Kippur War, Israelis were forced to accept the facts that their military forces were not invincible and that many changes had to be made to ensure future security. These security investments included the expansion and reorganization of Israel's armed forces and negotiation, which led to a peace treaty with Egypt. Despite these changes, Israeli forces were soon involved in continuing conflict with terrorists along the Israel/Lebanon border.

The Israeli military leadership examined the lessons of the

1973 war and debated the future role of the army, air force, and navy. Military systems, such as aircraft, tanks, and ships, had proved to be very vulnerable to missiles, rockets, artillery, and other modern weapons. The high loss rate experienced in the 1973 war forced the Israelis to increase the number of weapons and combat units and to maintain larger stockpiles of hardware and ammunition. To rearm rapidly, Israel bought many new aircraft, tanks, missiles, and advanced systems from the United States. However, Israel also instituted a long-term program to encourage domestic industries to produce equipment, supplies, and ammunition, and thereby reduce the country's dependence on foreign sources. Israel's intelligence organization was reorganized and surveillance capabilities upgraded to prevent military surprises.

During the 1970s, the army and air force were expanded and new tactical doctrines tested. The new Israeli blitzkrieg tactics called for combat forces to operate as an integrated team: fighter aircraft, helicopters, tanks, armored personnel carriers, mobile artillery, and airborne forces would work together to overcome the enemy and achieve victory with reduced losses.

Maj. Gen. Benjamin Peled commanded the IAF during the 1973 war and continued to serve in this capacity for several years after the conflict. He strengthened the air arm and revised its missions and tactics to reflect the new Israeli combat doctrine. Following the war, General Peled acknowledged that aircraft losses in 1973 were two and one-half times the number suffered in the 1967 conflict. Peled pointed out that the Yom Kippur War lasted three times as long as the earlier conflict. He added that, even though enemy defenses were more formidable in 1973, Israeli pilots flew more missions per aircraft lost than in 1967. At the International Symposium on Military Aspects of the Arab–Israeli Conflict, which was held in Jerusalem in 1975, General Peled identified a number of lessons learned from the Yom Kippur War. He cited the need for rapid intelligence collection and dissemination, improved communications, better army and air force command and control, and better weapons. But people, he said, remain the dominant component of air warfare. "Psychological factors, skill, motivation, and pilot training are more important than any material consideration," he added. He listed air force mission priorities as (1) air superiority, (2) strategic, (3) deep interdiction, and (4) close support. Peled stated, "World War II–type close air support is not possible in a modern real war," and added that it is a waste of airpower to assist ground forces in accomplishing what they should be able to achieve on their own.[1]

In the years following the 1973 war, the Israeli army purchased hundreds of additional self-propelled guns, surface-to-surface rockets, and other advanced artillery systems. To increase army firepower, Israel deployed large numbers of multiple-rocket launchers. Although not as accurate or long-ranging as cannon, a barrage from only one multiple-rocket launcher equals the firepower of a battery of guns or of an air strike.

The Israeli army also purchased dozens of U.S.-built Lance surface-to-surface missiles. This 50-mile-range missile is armed with a warhead that contains 836 grenade-like bomblets. It can blast an area more than a quarter of a mile in diameter and is ideal for suppressing enemy surface-to-air missile sites.

The shock of combat had produced a tough, experienced air force. By the end of 1973, U.S. resupply efforts had nearly restored the air force's numerical strength to its prewar level. However, the Phantoms, Skyhawks, transports, helicopters, and other aircraft delivered to Israel were quite different from those in service. Air force and Israeli industry personnel worked at a feverish pace to repair battle-damaged aircraft and reconfigure newly supplied planes with common systems, radios, and other equipment. Major modification programs upgraded the navigation, attack, and ECM systems of Israeli combat aircraft. Israeli Skyhawk jets were fitted with a tail cone extension to minimize their infrared signature and reduce their vulnerability to the SA-7 shoulder-fired antiaircraft missile.

The IAF purchased large numbers of guided missiles, smart bombs, and advanced weapons in order to increase the ability of Israeli pilots to destroy point targets. Aircraft, weapon, and ECM upgrades and the use of modified tactics enabled IAF aircrews to reduce their exposure to enemy defenses and still perform their missions effectively. It took several years for the IAF to make up for the aircrew losses suffered during the Yom Kippur conflict. Intensified training programs replaced aircrew losses and created a larger pool of pilots, navigators, and aircrews. Performance standards were raised to ensure that IAF aircrews maintained combat capability.

The air force ordered additional A-4N Skyhawk and F-4E Phantom aircraft from the United States and increased the production rate of jets made in Israel. On April 14, 1975, the IAF received its first Israeli-built Kfir fighter. Produced by Israel Aircraft Industries, the new fighter-bomber integrated the General Electric J79 engine that powers the Phantom, an upgraded Mirage/Nesher airframe, and electronics and systems developed in Israel. This program demonstrated the Israeli resolve to produce high-technology weapons domestically in order to ensure a source of supply in times of tension. The supersonic Kfir fighter, which could perform both fighter and attack missions, first entered service with the IAF's premier fighter squadron in 1975 and subsequently replaced Skyhawks in other units.[2]

The air superiority capability of the IAF was significantly improved by the introduction of F-15 Eagles, the first of which arrived in Israel on October 10, 1976. Israel was the first foreign country to receive this new fighter. The premier air superiority fighter of the USAF, the supersonic F-15 featured a pulse Doppler radar capable of detecting low-flying aircraft and an armament of eight air-to-air missiles and a 20-mm cannon. In late 1977, Israel announced it had ordered seventy-five F-16 Fighting Falcon jets to replace aging Skyhawks. The F-16 could perform both fighter and ground attack missions.

While the IAF reduced its responsibility in the close support role following the Yom Kippur War, the air arm's commitment to assist the Israeli ground forces remained a high priority. New tactics called for Phantom, Skyhawk, and Kfir fighter-bombers to concentrate on the interdiction mission. These attacks hit targets behind the front lines with the goal of slowing the advance of enemy reinforcements. If enemy air defenses could be suppressed, Israeli fighter-bombers could blast targets near the front lines.

In 1974, the IAF purchased six AH-1 Cobra missile-armed attack helicopters to test new concepts for their use as a reaction force to support army units in repelling an unexpected attack. Following successful trials, the IAF ordered thirty more AH-1 Cobras and thirty 500M Defender helicopters armed with TOW antitank missiles.

Calls from the army for vertical-lift support during the Yom Kippur War underscored the need for an enlarged helicopter force. Following the 1973 conflict, Israel upgraded its fleet of Super Frelon transport helicopters through the addition of more powerful and reliable U.S.-built turbine engines and other improvements. In addition, older Bell 205 helicopters were sold and replaced by more capable Bell 212 utility transports. The IAF also bought additional Bell 206 scout helicopters and heavy-lift Sikorsky CH-53s.

During the 1973 war, the USAF gave Israel twelve C-130E Hercules transport planes. Following the conflict, the lift capacity of the IAF was expanded considerably by the Israeli purchase of an additional ten C-130H Hercules aircraft. Two of these aircraft were fitted with aerial refueling systems to extend the strike range of Israeli Phantoms and Skyhawks.

The IAF air defense force was also strengthened following the 1973 war. The Hawk surface-to-air missile was replaced by the much more advanced Improved Hawk Systems. Air defense units received mobile Chapparal missiles, Vulcan 20-mm guns, and Russian-built 23-mm cannons that had been captured from Arab forces. Modern air defense radars, command and control systems, and shoulder-fired Redeye missiles also improved the capability of Israeli forces to protect themselves against air attack.

Coordination between the air force and army was increased during the 1970s. Through closer communications, the leaders of Israeli air and ground forces developed a better appreciation of each others' strengths and weaknesses and a better awareness of how best to conduct combined operations. Organizational changes and streamlined command and control procedures improved the flow of intelligence information between the air and ground services. Tactical air control parties were assigned to army division headquarters and forward air control groups were located at brigade headquarters to coordinate fighter, helicopter, transport, and air defense activities.

Israel learned in 1973 that wars are won or lost on the basis of available information. During the late 1970s, the intelligence collection and dissemination capabilities of Israeli ground and air forces were improved. New intelligence collection platforms such as the E-2C Hawkeye radar early warning aircraft, OV-ID

Mohawk reconnaissance plane, and a variety of unmanned, remotely-piloted vehicles entered service. These new systems were used to monitor Arab military activities. Israeli military leaders vowed that they would not be surprised again.

Once Israel's defense against Syria and Egypt had been strengthened, combating terrorism became the prime security focus of the Israel Defense Forces. After Syria, Jordan, and Egypt had suppressed the PLO and other Palestinian groups, members of these organizations began to operate primarily from Lebanon. Well-funded terrorist organizations attracted a considerable following and expanded their power and influence in Lebanon at the expense of the central government and the Maronite Christian community. During 1974, terrorist groups stepped up their activities. Terrorists massacred several families in Galilee in April, killed dozens of children at a school in Maalot in May, and exploded bombs at theaters and public places throughout the year. In 1975, guerrillas began regularly to fire rockets at Israeli communities along the Lebanese border. In March 1975, the seaside Savoy Hotel in Tel Aviv was captured by PLO terrorists who came ashore in rubber boats. In retaliation for these raids and international terrorist attacks, Israeli forces strengthened their patrols along the border and began striking back. Israeli jets blasted known guerrilla bases in southern Lebanon and many terrorist camps were assaulted by helicopter-borne commandos.

The Lebanese civil war, which broke out in early 1975, pitted the Muslims and the various guerrilla groups against the ruling Christian community. This conflict disrupted the central government, destroying much of Beirut and killing more than sixty thousand people. While the attention of the PLO and other groups was focused internally on Lebanon, terrorism against Israel was reduced. In June 1976, Syrian forces moved into Lebanon, changing the balance of power there. In response to the civil war and Syrian intervention, Israel began to supply Christian armies in southern Lebanon with weapons, training, and support.

A dramatic hijacking triggered the first Israeli anti-terrorist operation to be conducted outside the Middle East. IAF C-130 Hercules and a Boeing 707 transport aircraft played a major role in this mission. On June 27, 1976, four gunmen, two from the German Baader-Meinhof gang and two from the Popular Front for the Liberation of Palestine, hijacked Air France flight 139, which was flying from Tel Aviv to Paris via Athens. After the takeover, the crew of 12 and the 246 passengers flew to Benghazi, Libya, for refueling and then on to Entebbe airport in Uganda. The hijackers took the passengers and crew off the plane and held them in the airport terminal with the blessing of Ugandan leader Idi Amin Dada. Non-Jewish hostages were released, but the 105 Israeli and Jewish passengers were threatened with death unless 53 prisoners held by Israel, Switzerland, France, Kenya, and West Germany were released.

The Israeli government refused to give in, but agreed to negotiate to buy time and gather information on the unfolding events. At the same time, Israeli military leaders began planning a rescue operation. Maj. Gen. Benjamin Peled, air force commander, directed logistics and Brig. Gen. Dan Shamron, chief paratroop and infantry officer, conceived the rescue plans in concert with many other senior Israeli officers.

Operation Thunderball, a daring rescue operation, involved an elite group of Israeli paratroops and commandos. Led by Lt. Col. Yonni Netanyahu, these troops repeatedly rehearsed the actual rescue operation.

Brig. Gen. (Ret.) Joshua Shani was the commander of the IAF's C-130 squadron in 1976. He was involved in planning logistics for the operation and flew the lead aircraft on the rescue mission. Shani recalled:

> We started to do some planning on the first day, without anyone even approaching us, because, looking at the map, we knew that the only aircraft that could fly to Uganda and do the mission was the C-130. Although no one dreamed that we would conduct a military operation, my deputies and I studied the maps to see the distance, guess at payload, fuel requirements, navigation problems, and other needs. We did this to save time in case we were approached—then we would already have some answers.
>
> The hijacking took place on Sunday, June 27, 1976, and we started our planning on Monday. On Tuesday evening, we were officially asked by air force

headquarters to come and give some answers about our capabilities. I was at a wedding in Haifa, and it was very unusual to get a telephone call like that. I went to the headquarters from the wedding and we started to work on our plan. First we talked among ourselves, air force guys, then we met and coordinated with the army and we came up with a plan which we never executed—it was a bad plan. This plan was to drop paratroopers from two C-130s into Lake Victoria in the middle of the night. These troops would get into rubber boats and sneak in very quietly up to the airport and storm the terminal and free the hostages in Uganda, then tell Idi Amin, "Everyone is free, no terrorists, now let us go."

We didn't trust Idi Amin. We also knew that we might have to fight his troops, plus the drop into Lake Victoria was dangerous enough, and then we found out it was filled with crocodiles. Technically it was difficult to fly the C-130 round-trip. We went through two full rehearsals of this first mission. One was successful and the other not very good.

Eventually we came to our senses and just made it simple. To land was the only way to do the mission. We and the army people came to the same conclusion at the same time. After the second failed rehearsal, we met and agreed to take three airplanes, to land on the main runway, and do the job. Later we decided we needed four planes. Of course, what we wanted to do was land only one aircraft in the first ten minutes—maximum surprise, minimum noise. Only after we got rid of the terrorists would the other three C-130s come in.

We made one-and-a-half rehearsals for the actual operation. One was a demonstration that I made for the chief of staff of the army, General Gur, the chief of staff of the air force, General Peled, and chief of operations of the air force, Colonel Ben-Nun, now air force chief of staff, on how I could land on a runway without lights. They wanted to see it with their own eyes. We came in at night and landed at Sharm el Sheikh. It wasn't perfect but good enough. We knew that at Entebbe it would be easier because there was more contrast between the water and the runway than at Sharm el Sheikh. That same night we did a full rehearsal with four airplanes, the special forces, the black Mercedes, Landrover jeeps, and even a building like the terminal. The minister of defense and lots of officials watched the rehearsal and it was very successful.

Early the next morning, Saturday [July 3, 1976], we held a big briefing at my squadron with all the forces involved. At this big show business briefing, we used big maps. The *real* briefing came later when we sat with the troops and crews and talked details. There was no way to cover everything with less than two days of planning and rehearsal. So we left lots of things for improvisation and common sense.

We took off at early afternoon using five airplanes—one was a spare. We landed at Sharm el Sheikh so that we could take off from the most southern airport and have more fuel to maneuver. We didn't have fuel for the round-trip. We planned to refuel either at Entebbe or Nairobi, Kenya, on the way back. We waited for the government to make a decision about when to execute the mission. We had to take off, to keep our time schedule, and if the government decided to cancel, they were to call us on the radio and say to come back. We took off at a temperature of 105 degrees Fahrenheit at over 180,000 pounds, which was more than 10,000 pounds heavier than the wartime maximum takeoff weight of the C-130. Maximum power, brakes off, taxi, and the aircraft did not accelerate, but there was no force in the world that could make us abort this mission. We prayed for every knot and took off just a few knots above stall speed. It was very difficult even to make the turn toward our course. We were a formation of four flying south in the middle of the Red Sea in full radio silence, one after the other. I didn't know if they were still behind me since I couldn't use the radio. Maybe number four hit the water because we flew just a few feet above the water to avoid radar detection by the

Saudi and Egyptian radars. The other pilots understood the problem and, from time to time, they overtook me, showed themselves, and then went back to their position. We flew this way until Ethiopia. Then we climbed to 20,000 feet into the darkness. We flew in a loose formation and used the radar to see each other and avoid huge thunderstorms which were along the way.

We continued until the border of Kenya and Uganda and then began to look for a bay which showed up well on radar. It was here that we planned to have the three airplanes hold for seven minutes while my plane continued on. Unfortunately, over the bay, which was our final navigation point, there was a huge African thunderstorm with rain up to 50,000 feet or so. We had to penetrate it in formation and it was hell inside—hail, lots of lighting, noise, and wind. I just crossed it in five minutes or so, but the other planes stayed in a holding pattern in this terrible storm. This was one of the most difficult parts of the mission. Remember, we were overloaded, people and vehicles weren't strapped down. It wasn't very pleasant.

I left them and pressed on. I saw the runway from maybe twenty miles, light rain, overcast, but quite good visibility below the clouds. I landed, of course, completely dark, no external lights. I stopped the plane in the middle of the runway and the doors were opened. A few soldiers jumped from both side doors with portable runway lights to mark the way for the other three airplanes. We knew that once the shooting started, the lights would go off. The job of these troops was to take the control tower. I continued toward where the hostages were and stopped. The other troops came out with the Mercedes and the two Landrovers. They drove to the terminal and ran in shouting in Hebrew and English, "Everyone lie on the floor," and after a short bit of fighting, all the terrorists were dead. Two of the hostages were wounded also in the crossfire.

The other three aircraft came in to land and I stayed on the side waiting, watching, in constant communication. Then I heard that Yoni, commander of the special forces, was hit outside of the terminal after the rescue. He was hit by a Ugandian soldier who was up in the old tower with a machine gun.

Number two landed without any problem; but when number three was just over the threshold, the Ugandians switched off the lights. He found that there was no runway beneath him so he flew on and made a hard landing on another runway about a mile ahead. Number four landed on the short runway with our portable lights. Then we were all on the ground, the terrorists were dead, and the Ugandians were shooting with tracers, not well aimed but a dangerous situation. We were trying to get some fuel from the tanks using an adapter we had brought with us to connect with their lines. The operation was successful, the hostages ready to go, the soldiers began to withdraw and return to the planes. Since the refueling process would take about an hour and the Ugandians were shooting in the area, we decided not to refuel and take any unnecessary risks. We taxied out onto the runway and one by one took off, heading toward Nairobi.

Before takeoff, the troops from my airplane shot up the Ugandian MiGs that were parked not far from the old terminal because there was a theoretical chance that they could chase us. We all knew that it was only a small possibility because they were MiG-17 day fighters and their level of training in night interception was low, but we took no chances. Anyway, Idi Amin was an S.O.B. and we hated MiGs as you know, so we eliminated them.

We taxied out onto the runway and one by one took off toward Nairobi. They let us land, the four of us. We got fuel and being on the ground was the first time we had time to go and see the hostages, which was a very emotional moment. It was a thing you remember forever, of course—some of them were shocked, some hysterical, laughter, none of them wanted to leave the airplane. They said we'll stay here until you bring us to Tel Aviv. The troops had their first chance to relax also. Eventually we got our fuel and took off for an eight-hour flight to Tel Aviv. About four hours before we landed,

> everyone in our country knew of the rescue because it was officially announced. Halfway up the Red Sea, we got an escort of F-4 Phantoms. It was a good feeling. And then landing, a short briefing, parties, and behaving wild. It was a great evening, but I didn't remember much because I hadn't slept well for six days.[3]

During the civil war in Lebanon, a sizable PLO force moved south to escape Christian and Syrian forces that were entrenched around Beirut. PLO units routinely clashed with Christian, Druze, and Shiite Muslim forces in southern Lebanon. Israel armed the Christian and Druze armies that contested the PLO infiltration.

In late 1977, Israel began to attack PLO positions with aircraft, artillery, ships, and ground troops to drive them away from the border area. Following a PLO rocket attack against Nahariya that killed three civilians in November, the IAF went into action. Israeli Phantom, Skyhawk, and—for the first time—Kfir fighter-bombers plastered over a dozen suspected PLO positions in southern Lebanon. This heavy series of retaliatory raids destroyed many PLO bases, but also caused numerous civilian casualties and generated an international public outcry.

In a bold move, in November 1977, Egyptian President Sadat called for a peace conference between Egypt and Israel. Prime Minister Begin welcomed the overture and invited Sadat to Israel. President Sadat traveled to Jerusalem and met with Prime Minister Begin and addressed the Israeli parliament. This set the stage for a peace initiative that after thirty years of hostility, ultimately led to an Egyptian/Israeli peace treaty.

David Ivry replaced Benjamin Peled as commander of the IAF in 1977. A quiet, cool fighter pilot, Lieutenant General Ivry inherited a force that had recovered from the 1973 conflict and was in the process of introducing a wide variety of advanced weaponry. The new air force commander soon had an opportunity to test many of these new systems in the skies over Lebanon.

The Egyptian/Israeli peace plan angered the PLO and the leaders of other Arab states, because Syrian and Jordanian territory captured in the 1967 war was still in Israeli hands and the

Palestinian question was still unresolved. As a result, terrorist attacks against Israel dramatically increased and Syria boosted its troop strength in Lebanon to more than thirty thousand. On March 11, 1978, a PLO terrorist team came ashore on the Israeli coast and captured a bus on the Tel Aviv–Haifa highway. Israeli forces assaulted the bus and killed the terrorists, but thirty-four civilians, including many women and children, were killed in the process. In response to this attack Israel launched Operation Latani. More than twenty-five thousand Israeli troops, supported by armor, artillery, and air strikes, assaulted Lebanon on March 15, 1978, with the goal of destroying PLO bases and driving out the terrorists. Israeli armored columns quickly moved north beyond the Litani River, killing more than 250 terrorists and capturing hundreds more.

During the operation, Israeli strike aircraft blasted dozens of suspected terrorist targets while fighters flew many patrol missions to deter Syrian planes. Reconnaissance aircraft, scout helicopters, and unmanned drones monitored the Israeli advance and identified the location of terrorist units and the activities of Syrian forces. The IAF's transport aircraft and helicopters contributed to the success of the operation through the movement of men and supplies and the evacuation of wounded Israeli troops.

Amir Yoeli, an Israeli pilot, commented on his participation in Operation Litani:

> I was flying the A-4 Skyhawk at the time and was still, as we say, "in my diapers." Pinpointing the targets was the most difficult part of the missions. At the time I was a junior member of the squadron so I had less of a responsibility in running the show up there but could concentrate on finding the target while the leader took care of the rest. Lebanon is a very beautiful country and flying over it gave me a feeling of tranquillity. The sights of our soldiers in there, the understanding of the guerillas, and their methods kept my targets at top priority. On one occasion I was given an artillery battery to locate and wipe out. We had prepared the flight very carefully and studied the target to the last detail. The leader questioned us until we started mumbling the

description. The planes were ready and we took off at 12:55 and the target was only twenty-eight minutes away.

All went well until we reached Sidon. A batch of clouds was serving as an anti-identification screen. The sun was behind us and the winds, according to the I.N.S. [inertial navigation system] were at 35 knots. It meant a long wait before some clearing up would enable us to locate the targets. After some radio discussions, we were given an alternate target—after all that work. The new target was a group of small-caliber antiaircraft guns. We spotted the site and headed for the drop. All my armament was ready and red ARM lights were on. Number one dove in and I followed close behind. As I was taking my eyes off him, I spotted black puffs ahead. We were both diving right into them. The dust from the ground identified the exact location of the guns and I was fixed onto the place where the dust was created. Sure enough, number one dropped his bombs and I mine. As we pulled out we looked back to see the hits, and they were on the money. The air pollution caused by the battery was gone and there was a warm feeling that there was one less antiaircraft site to worry about. As we headed back, we crossed a formation flying towards our initial target, we could see it clearly now, but it was their turn to play hide and seek. Our missions were far apart because it was a small area and everybody wanted a piece of the action.[4]

Israeli forces continued to hold a portion of southern Lebanon until June 1978, when a UN force took over. After Israeli units withdrew, the area near the border was controlled by a group of Christian militia armies. One led by Major Saad Haddad received considerable training and weaponry from Israel. Despite Israeli aid, the Christian armies were unable to halt PLO infiltration into southern Lebanon totally.

The United States fostered the peace negotiations between Egypt and Israel, and by late 1978 the two sides agreed to meet and work out the final details. President Sadat and Prime Minister Begin met with U.S. President Jimmy Carter at Camp David,

In the fall of 1969 the IAF received its first F-4E Phantom II. This aircraft could carry the same weapons load as four or more of the earlier aircraft then in service, and it could also defeat the latest MiGs in air combat.

A Mirage IIIC of the 101st Squadron lands after a mission. Note the empty air-to-air missile-launch rails under the wings. During the War of Attrition IAF fighter pilots increasingly used air-to-air missiles, like this Israeli-built Shafrir. Cannon and missiles each had their unique advantages; cannon were close-in weapons, up to 5,000 feet, while missiles had an effective range of 2,000 feet to 3 miles but had to be fired at the target aircraft's hot engine exhaust.

The strike camera of an IAF Phantom pilot took this unique photograph of his wingman chasing an Egyptian MiG-17 low over the Sinai desert. Seconds after this photograph was taken, the MiG was shot down.

Wounded Israeli troops being evacuated by a UH-1 helicopter. Hundreds of Israeli soldiers were saved by helicopters, which rapidly transported them to trauma centers.

An A-4 Skyhawk overflies a column of Israeli infantry while returning from a strike on the Golan Heights.

An Arab airfield under attack by IAF Phantoms. Heavy anti-aircraft defenses and Arab fighter patrols made this a dangerous mission. The results of these attacks were limited because aircraft and important facilities were protected by sand and concrete shelters.

IAF air-defense troops pose in front of a Hawk surface-to-air missile launcher in the Sinai. Air force controlled Hawk air-defense missiles and anti-aircraft guns protected army units during the 1973 War and downed more than forty Arab aircraft.

4X-FBJ
305

IAF Hercules C-130 transports played a vital part in the famous Entebbe hostage rescue mission. The C-130 is the IAF principal heavy-lift tactical transport, but the Hercules is also used to air-refuel F-4 Phantoms and A-4 Skyhawks.

IAF F-15 squadrons have the mission of defending Israeli airspace and achieving air superiority. Eagle pilots achieved more than sixty air-combat victories against Syrian aircraft in the skies over Lebanon.

An IAF F-16A Fighting Falcon. The F-16 was used by the IAF to bomb the Iraqi nuclear reactor near Baghdad in June 1981. The aircraft also engaged in air combat against Syrian aircraft and achieved more than forty victories.

107

The IAF used the Model 500 Defender attack helicopter in action during the Lebanon conflict.

In 1978 the IAF placed into service its first squadron of Kfir fighters. Built in Israel, these aircraft combined the J-79 turbo-jet engine from the Phantom with an upgraded Nesher (Mirage copy) airframe and Israeli-developed avionics. Israel aircraft industries produced over 200 Kfir aircraft and the fighter was used extensively during the Lebanon conflict.

A major contributor to the lopsided Israeli air combat kill ration was the E-2C Hawkeye command and control aircraft. Radar operators could detect incoming Syrian aircraft and vector IAF fighters to surprise them.

Maryland, in September 1978, to set an agenda for peace. Egypt agreed to recognize the State of Israel and sign a peace treaty, while Israel returned the Sinai to Egyptian control. Egypt, Israel, and other Middle East nations were offered military and economic aid in exchange for their support of the new peace initiatives. In June 1978, the U.S. Congress ratified a plan to supply sixty F-15 Eagle fighters to Saudi Arabia and fifty F-5E Tiger fighter-bombers to Egypt. Subsequently, Egypt received thirty-five F-4E Phantoms and forty F-16s in place of the F-5E fighters promised in the Camp David accords. The United States also agreed to provide Jordan with F-5E fighters, improved Hawk surface-to-air missiles, and other American weaponry.

Israeli military planners were concerned that modern Western tactical aircraft being supplied to Arab countries could upset the airpower balance in the Middle East. Maj. Gen. David Ivry, the IAF commander in 1978, stated, "We train all the time, but in every war we also train those who fly against us. And while we could afford adverse ratios of one to three, four, or even five when the Arabs were flying MiGs, we cannot accept those ratios when they fly the F-5E, much less the F-15."[5] As part of the peace plan, the United States agreed to provide an additional seventy-five F-16 fighter-bombers and fifteen F-15 fighters to Israel.

Terrorist attacks subsided for a time after Operation Latani. However, in the spring of 1979, the PLO intensified its efforts. In response to a particularly damaging attack at Nahariya on April 22, Israel changed its tactics from retaliating against terrorist attacks to preventing them. The IAF began flying regular reconnaissance missions over Lebanon, including the portions of the country under Syrian control. Terrorist training bases, headquarters, and artillery positions were blasted with bombs and naval gunfire or raided by commando units.

Israel unofficially agreed to refrain from directly confronting Syrian forces in Lebanon so long as they stayed in the northern part of the country and did not interfere with IAF reconnaissance and antiterrorist missions. However, aggressive Israeli air strikes against the terrorists prompted the Syrians to take action to support the PLO. On June 27, 1979, two flights of Syrian MiGs challenged an Israeli raid over Lebanon. Five Syrian MiG-21 fighters were shot down—four claimed by F-15 pilots and one destroyed by a Kfir pilot. This was the first air combat victory for both the F-15 and the Kfir and the most serious Israeli/Syrian air engagement since April 24, 1974.

The F-15 squadron leader tells the story of the combat:

> We took off, fully armed for air-to-air combat, to cover the attacking aircraft. We linked up with the Kfirs on the way and climbed to 20,000 feet. Up there, the air is clear and there's no condensation. We patrolled the length and breadth of the "Battle Triangle," knowing all the time that we could run into MiGs at any moment. Over Sidon, we received orders to head north because enemy aircraft were heading for us at 15,000 feet.
>
> The radar showed two MiG formations advancing on us—one attacking, one covering. The MiGs were no more than ten miles from our strike aircraft. Hitting the afterburners, we swooped down on them. They tried to break away when they saw what we were up to—but they never had much chance to do so: we had already locked onto most of them, splitting them up among us like wolves dividing their prey. "My" MiG was one of the second formation. The F-15 pilots hit the MiGs the moment they came within range. I wanted to make sure of my MiG and closed in, not waiting for him to approach me. By the time I got within firing range, three of the MiGs were already spiralling down. I slowed down, aimed, and fired a missile, and climbed above it—so my aircraft wouldn't be inadvertently damaged. My number two confirmed my kill. The fifth MiG was downed by a lone Kfir, which had finally joined us.[6]

This story recounts the Kfir pilot's part in the dogfight:

> Captain S, a Kfir C-2 pilot, went into his first aerial combat with mixed feelings. He had been ordered on a combat patrol to cover attacking Phantoms on strike missions against PLO encampments in southern Lebanon; leading his number two at 12,000 feet at a speed of 400 knots, he received orders to engage Syrian Air Force MiGs approaching from the east with combat

> intentions. Releasing their drop tanks, the Kfirs vectored onto the Syrians.
>
> But the faster F-15 Eagles were already engaging the MiGs, identified as MiG-21 PFMA(J)s, and one of them was already falling vertically, leaving a smoke steamer as it spun out of control, with the pilot ejecting. Another MiG had an Eagle sitting on its tail.
>
> Captain S—covered by his wingman—maneuvered his Kfir onto two Syrian MiGs. Without hesitation, the young captain launched a Shafrir AAM [air-to-air missile] which exploded close to the number one of the Syrian Pair. Surprisingly, they maintained formation. S closed in and broke away to move himself into position once more. As he neared, he watched the Syrian MiG start ejecting white smoke and, immediately after, the pilot blew off his hood and bailed out. Without wasting time, the Kfir pilots closed in on the remaining MiG but, before they could open fire, the aircraft flew into a cloud bank and contact was lost.[7]

Israel continued to fly sorties over Lebanon, and on September 19, 1979, Syrian MiG-23 fighters attacked and fired on an IAF RF-4 but failed to hit it with their air-to-air missiles. Syrian aircraft again challenged Israeli air operations on September 24, and in the ensuing series of dogfights, IAF F-15s shot down four MiG-21 fighters. Tension between Israel and Syria remained high as a result of the air battles over Lebanon.

By late 1980, the IAF was receiving a steady stream of advanced F-15, F-16, and Kfir fighters and had a force of over forty Cobra and Defender attack helicopters. Aircraft such as the F-15, Kfir, E-2C Hawkeye, and prototype remotely piloted vehicles like the IAI Scout and Tadiran Mastiff had proven their utility in action over Lebanon. The IAF was also having several ex-airline Boeing 707 transports reworked into aerial-refueling tankers to support long-range attack operations. The withdrawal from the Sinai, which was agreed to in the Camp David Accord, had a dramatic impact on the IAF and its operations. Almost one-third of the operational strength of the force had been stationed in the Sinai. These aircraft were rapidly relocated to Israel. While the United States had agreed to build three new airfields in southern Israel, these bases would not be ready until the early 1980s. Particularly distressing was the loss of training airspace over the sparsely populated Sinai. Fixed-wing and helicopter training flights were increasingly flown over the Mediterranean Sea and the Negev Desert region.

Despite Syrian aerial opposition, Israeli forces continued to raid terrorist targets in Lebanon. During 1980 and early 1981 several air battles took place: four Syrian MiG-21 fighters were shot down, while no Israeli planes were lost. On April 28, 1981, the Syrians used transport helicopters to move troops into position to help the PLO defeat a Christian militia force fighting near Zahal, a town on the Beirut–Damascus highway. Prime Minister Begin authorized a strike against the helicopters to demonstrate his support for the Christian faction, which was fighting both the PLO and the Syrians in Lebanon. Israeli F-16 fighters attacked and shot down two Syrian Mi-8 helicopters.

Syria retaliated for this action by moving a number of SA-6 SAM batteries into the Bekaa Valley. Israel vigorously reacted to this escalation and threatened to attack the missile sites unless they were withdrawn. Dozens of drone aircraft were flown over the Bekaa Valley to test the defenses and collect intelligence. Several of these drones were shot down by the Syrians.

Terrorist raids and heavy shelling of Israeli border villages continued, and in April 1981, PLO raiders even tried to infiltrate Israel using a hot-air balloon. In response to terrorist attacks and Israeli frustration concerning the new Syrian SAMs in the Bekaa Valley, the IAF conducted an intense series of strikes against PLO targets in southern Lebanon. These attacks were soon answered by guerrilla artillery fire that hit towns and villages in northern Israel. As the cycle continued, Israel intensified its blows.

Then on June 7, 1981, Israel shocked the world when it announced that the IAF had bombed and destroyed the Iraqi Osirak nuclear reactor. If the Osirak reactor were to become operational, it would produce radioactive by-products that could be made into nuclear bombs or missile warheads. Israel was determined to prevent the reactor from coming into service.

The IAF had carefully planned and practiced the attack. Known as Operation Babylon, the risky raid was performed by fourteen hand-picked pilots, eight of whom flew F-16 fighter-bombers while the remaining six escorted the attackers in F-15s. Plans for the secret mission had been set well over a year earlier, after diplomatic efforts had failed to halt the construction of the Iraqi nuclear reactor. On two occasions the attack had been postponed. At 3:00 P.M. on June 7, 1981, the strike force took off from Etzion Air Base in the Sinai and headed toward Baghdad. The aircraft flew at low altitude on a path that skirted Arab military bases and villages and evaded Jordanian, Saudi, and Iraqi search radars. As the warplanes sped toward the target, they made several brief radio transmissions to report on their progress. Just prior to reaching the target, the F-15s broke into three groups and climbed to 25,000 feet to patrol near the important Iraqi fighter bases that surrounded Baghdad. One by one, the F-16s popped up, dived on the reactor complex, and released their bombs. After the bomb release, the Falcon pilots made a hard turn, dived to a lower altitude, and raced back toward Israel. Iraqi antiaircraft fire rose to meet the last few Israeli attackers but none were hit.

Sixteen bombs hit the target, and all but one of them exploded. The reactor dome was shattered and the building was reduced to smoking rubble. One French technician who was working late at the complex was killed.

In order to conserve fuel, the eight F-16s and six F-15s climbed to high altitude as they exited Iraqi territory. No fighters or missiles challenged the returning Israeli aircraft despite the fact they flew at high altitude over Saudi Arabia and Jordan. On the way home, they broke radio silence in order to inform headquarters of the successful mission and zero losses. Ninety minutes after the attack, the F-16 pilots were landing at Etzion, while the F-15 crews touched down at their home base.[8]

Operation Babylon destroyed the unfueled reactor and eliminated the Iraqi nuclear threat to Israel. The IAF had again demonstrated its capability to perform a surprise attack.

In response to continued shelling and raids from Lebanon, during June and July 1981, the IAF flew an intense series of air strikes against terrorist training bases, headquarters, and artillery positions throughout southern Lebanon. The PLO headquarters in Beirut was shattered by bombs on July 17 and hundreds of people were killed and wounded. The PLO responded with artillery, which grew so intense that Israel was forced to evacuate several border settlements. The U.S. special envoy Philip Habib arranged a cease-fire that took effect on July 24, 1981. Both sides honored the truce, but tension along the Israel/Lebanon border remained at a high level.

Israel refrained from striking Lebanese terrorist targets following the cease-fire but flew reconnaissance sorties to monitor Syrian and PLO activities. Syrian aircraft challenged these patrols on several occasions. In the dogfights that resulted, Syria lost a MiG-25 Foxbat on July 29, 1981, two MiG-23 Floggers in a battle on April 21, 1982, and two MiG-21s to IAF F-16s on May 26, 1982.

Terrorist activity against Israel's northern villages intensified during the spring of 1982—in May there were twenty-six separate incidents. Sustained shelling and the attempt on the life of Shalmo Argov, the Israeli ambassador in London, prompted Israel to conduct a series of air strikes against terrorist positions in Beirut and southern Lebanon. When the PLO responded with heavy artillery fire, Israel initiated an invasion of Lebanon that had long been planned by Defense Minister Ariel Sharon and other members of the Israeli government. The goal of this invasion, dubbed Peace for Galilee, was the elimination of the PLO and other terrorist groups that inhabited southern Labanon and the punishment of Syrian units.

The IAF played a major role in the Peace for Galilee operation. In a carefully orchestrated series of attacks, Israeli forces demolished the Syrian air defense network in the Bekaa Valley and scored a resounding aerial victory over the Syrians. When the Syrians threw their fighters into the fray, Israeli jets ambushed them. The result was some of the largest air battles ever witnessed in the Middle East. Over a four-day period, Israeli pilots shot down eighty-five Syrian aircraft and reportedly did not lose a single plane in air combat.

Some forty thousand troops with more than five hundred tanks and nearly one thousand other armored vehicles moved into Lebanon on June 6, 1982. Three division-sized task forces advanced north on different routes with the aim of quickly overrunning terrorist units before they could flee. Israeli landing craft put tanks and troops ashore south of Sidon to block the coast road escape route. Artillery, helicopter gunships, and aircraft blasted guerilla defenders.

Because of the surprise nature of the attack and the rapid advance, Israeli air and ground losses were small during the first few days of fighting. Aharon Ahiaz, a reserve pilot of a Skyhawk flying close air support for the invasion, had the misfortune of overflying a PLO antiaircraft training camp. His A-4 was hit by several SA-7 missiles and he spent seventy-five days as the prisoner of the PLO in Beirut before he was released. An IAF Cobra helicopter was also lost in action on the second day of fighting.[9]

Israeli pilots scored their first air combat victory of the Peace for Galilee operation on June 7 when a single Syrian MiG-23 was shot down. Israeli troops captured many terrorist camps and engaged in ground combat for the first time with Syrian forces near Jezzin on the second day of the invasion. On June 8, Israeli forces continued to drive north and met with heavy resistance from retreating PLO and Syrian commandos. Several air battles occurred over Lebanon when Syrian aircraft challenged Israeli planes, and seven MiGs were shot down.

One of the Israeli pilots gave his view of the action:

> "During a sortie in which I was providing cover for our forces this morning [June 8], I received a message that two Syrian planes were closing in on us. Almost immediately, I spotted them on my screen. Judging by the MiGs' speed and direction, it was clear they had taken off on an attack mission," said the 25-year-old pilot who downed one of the two Syrian MiGs in a brief dogfight southeast of Beirut. The tall, slim captain said that this had been his first combat experience against enemy planes. "I attacked the MiG closest to me, while my partner, who flew the other plane that was with me on that mission, attacked the second MiG. I acted according to our combat doctrine, aware of the specific performance of my plane. I hit the MiG, it went into a spin, dropped and crashed. I did not see what happened to the pilots of the two MiGs," he added, "whether or not they managed to bail out after we hit their planes. We saw no parachutes."[10]

Worried by the quick Israeli capture of Southern Lebanon and the heavy losses suffered by PLO and Syrian units, President Assad ordered more SAM batteries to deploy into the Bekaa Valley and additional armored units to cross the border into Lebanon. Israeli air reconnaissance detected this buildup, and the IAF was given the authorization to attack the SAM defenses in the Bekaa Valley and to bomb the Syrian reinforcements. At dawn on June 9, Israeli tanks began moving north to flank the Syrians and drive directly into the Bekaa Valley. The IAF's CH-53 helicopters lifted troops into the Shouf mountains to block the Syrian retreat. Syrian and Israeli tanks fought several major battles during the day. The Syrians were forced to fall back, but both sides suffered heavy losses.

The events that led up to the Israeli air attacks in the Bekaa Valley were described by Brigadier General B, an IAF officer, who was unidentified for security reasons:

> As background, it was important to note that the missile batteries enabled the terrorists to fire at us from the Lebanese Bekaa Valley. The Syrians provided the terrorists with aircover and missile protection, which enabled them to operate freely. Two days prior to the IAF attack, Syrian missiles were launched from the Bekaa at our aircraft. These attempts to engage our forces could have hindered the IDF ground advance. Therefore, the Government of Israel decided that it would not be possible to simply shrug off the launching of missiles at our planes.[11]

The Syrians had moved an extensive air defense network into the Bekaa Valley in order to provide protection for their ground troops in Lebanon. This air defense shield included fifteen SA-6, two SA-3, and two SA-2 missile batteries with over two hundred ready-to-fire missiles and more than four hundred antiaircraft guns.

"The destruction of the missile batteries was the greatest test which the IAF has ever encountered," an IAF Colonel admitted. "Our aircraft had to face an advanced and concentrated array of missiles which were reinforced by the most sophisticated fighter aircraft in the eastern bloc. Moreover, strategic surprise was impossible under the circumstances. The Syrians were waiting for us."[12]

Lt. Gen. Rafael Eitan, Israeli chief of staff during the 1982 assault into Lebanon, explained how the Syrian SAM sites were destroyed:

> From the operational point of view I can say that we used the mini-RPVs, long before the war, to identify and locate all the Syrian missile batteries. We then used superior electronic devices which enabled us to "blind" or neutralize the missile sites' ground-to-air radar. We rendered them ineffective to take reliable fixes on our aircraft aloft. But in advance of direct aerial attacks, we used long-range artillery.[13]

Brigadier General B. continued his description of the attack against the SAMs in the Bekaa Valley on June 9:

> The incoming fire from all directions created confusion among Syrian ranks. The brunt of the operation called for a direct air attack upon the missile batteries. Most of the batteries were destroyed by iron bombs. The bulk of the Syrian deployment contained SA-6 missiles which, because of their mobility, are not dug in and were therefore relatively easy to identify. The remaining missiles were of the SA-2 and SA-3 type. The Syrians tried to hide the missiles beneath a smoke-screen. Yet, in spite of the smoke, or perhaps because of it, our pilots were able to detect all the targets. IAF planes swept in low and launched their Shrike missile at the Syrian batteries after target acquisition had been achieved. The Shrike anti-radiation, air-to-surface missile (which had been adapted and improved by Israeli technicians) homed in on the electromagnetic radiation emitted by the Soviet-built air defense radars. Diversionary devices were also camouflaged to resemble overflying aircraft in order to distract and confuse Syrian ground radar. Within a short span of time, the entire Syrian missile deployment began to crumble.[14]

"The operation lasted two hours," added Brigadeer General B.

> Our attacking planes encountered about one hundred MiG-21 and MiG-23 [Syrian] aircraft, which swooped into the area, wave after wave. The MiG aircraft were ostensibly dispatched to the area in order to protect the missiles against IAF attack. This was an absurdity! Why was it necessary to protect antiaircraft missile batteries? The raison d'etre of the missile batteries is to down aircraft.[15]

Captain G, an IAF pilot, recalled his part in the operation:

> We were in the air at the climax of the large-scale attack on the missile batteries; the air was filled with tension due to the large number of enemy aircraft flying about the area. We had to differentiate between our aircraft and those of the enemy. We waited until we achieved positive identification of the target while simultaneously approaching two enemy aircraft, painted brown and light yellow. We gave chase and when the aircraft reached a routine launch mode, I fired and was able to see the hit; immediately I turned to go for the other aircraft but I was too slow. My number two had already shot him down.[16]

With the IAF attack on the Syrian missile batteries in full swing, Maj. R flew in a foursome of F-15s sent to cover the attacking planes.

> I will never forget that flight as long as I live. We were flying over the Bakaa Valley, and the sun was sinking into the sea. The radar caught sight of two MiG-21s although we had trouble seeing them because the setting sun was in our eyes.
>
> Both Number Four and I launched missiles, but suddenly we found ourselves in an inferno of AA tracer fire and rockets from the ground. I saw the approaching rockets, and yelled to Number Three to get out.
>
> Meanwhile he downed one of the two MiGs. I followed

the second one northwards, and then I noticed something yellow under my left wing. I remember thinking, "Another MiG!"

The MiG I was chasing passed some 200 meters ahead of me. I looked at the pilot and he looked at me. I remember his white helmet clearly. He cut suddenly in an amazing turn that I would estimate at something like 8.5 G. He was getting in behind me. We were both flying very fast. I had to do something. At 800 meters I shot a missile and missed him. I shot a second and this time hit his tail. He continued flying and only gradually, gently crashed into the fields below.

I was hypnotized by the crash; suddenly the urgent command, "Cut! Cut!" was shouted over the radio. I had begun to cut when a great crash shook the plane. A missile had hit squarely on the exhaust of my right engine, and my tail was aflame.

"I will not bail out in Syrian territory," was the one thought that kept flashing through my mind. I had turned off my right engine and was rapidly losing power. If I could only make it out of AA fire range and cross the mountains. Meanwhile the other planes of my formation got in behind to cover me. Slowly, excruciatingly, I managed to climb and just barely scraped over the mountain ridges. I thought of flying out over the sea, where at least our navy was there to pick me up.

It took an enormous load off my mind that the other planes were covering for me. I had nothing to worry about except for the actual flying, which was difficult enough under the circumstances.

With each mile my mind became easier. I felt that I would be able to make it to an IAF base after all. My tail was still burning and only one engine was operational, but I did get to the Ramat David airfield. Landing was a tricky business, but somehow I got through it safely. The other planes had been behind me in the fullest sense of the word, ready to help out with suggestions and excellent flying advice.

I had always known that the F-15 was a dependable plane, but I had never before realized quite to what

> extent. Not only was my tail completely burnt and my right engine incapacitated, afterwards I saw that there had been a massive fuel leak, damage to the thermostat, and no fewer than four hundred bullet holes in the body of the plane. With all this, I managed to fly for twenty minutes after being hit and to land safely. If I had been flying any other type of plane, I don't think I would have come out of this alive.[17]

Lieutenant General Eitan discussed the Syrian response to the Israeli strikes:

> The first reaction of the Syrians when we attacked their missiles was to scramble their air forces . . . any [Syrian fighter pilots] who crossed an imaginary line in the direction of our forces was destroyed, shot down. The imaginary line was actually the range of the missile batteries in Syria proper. The basic tactic of the Syrian air force is to take to the air and to cross this imaginary line, which brings them outside the protective range of their home-based missiles. They do what they can, then run back for cover.[18]

An IAF Phantom squadron commander summed up the operation: "The success of the operation was not only in that the mission was accomplished in the best possible manner, but that all our pilots returned home safely. . . . From an aviation and military viewpoint, we made history. I am certain that this operation will have broad repercussions upon all the world's air forces."[19]

Certainly the Soviet Union, supplier of the Syrian-manned SAM batteries and MiG fighters, took notice. Col. Gen. Yensery S. Yuvarov, deputy commander of the Soviet Air Defense Force, and a team of Russian military experts were promptly dispatched to Syria to investigate what had happened.

Of the nineteen Syrian SAM sights in the Bekaa Valley, ten were put out of action almost immediately and seventeen had been damaged or destroyed by the end of the day. The IAF had studied the lessons of the 1973 war and was now well prepared to deal with air defense systems. First, the search and fire control radars of the Syrian air defense network were jammed and many drones and decoys were flown over the Bekaa Valley in order to confuse the defenses. Then Israeli artillery, rockets, Shrike antiradar missiles, and other weapons blasted the Syrian command centers and radars, blinding the defenses. Dozens of F-16s, Phantoms, Kfirs, and Skyhawks then rolled in and bombed the Syrian SA-2 and SA-3 missile sites, SA-6 vehicles, and antiaircraft guns. Israeli jets delivered their bombs from medium altitude so that they remained above the effective range of light antiaircraft fire. The attacking aircraft also spewed out hundreds of flares, which confused and neutralized the seekers of SA-7 infrared-homing missiles.

The IAF had E-2C airborne warning and control aircraft in the air using their long-range radar to scan Syrian airspace for warning of an attack by Syrian fighter aircraft. Israeli RPVs were probably circling over the major Syrian fighter bases, giving the Israelis warning that Syrian MiGs were moving to take off. The Israelis undoubtedly jammed the radio and data link communications between aircraft and control centers, depriving the Syrian pilots of an accurate picture of the tactical situation. Flights of F-15s and F-16s were vectored in to ambush each successive wave of Syrian fighters. At one point during the operation, there were reportedly ninety Israeli aircraft and sixty Syrian jets airborne over the battle area. This was one of the biggest aerial confrontations since World War II. With the advantages of accurate situation awareness and better aircraft, weapons, and pilots, it is easy to understand how Israeli pilots were able to shoot down dozens of Syrian jets.

On June 10, Israeli armed columns continued their drive north toward Beirut and into central Lebanon, resulting in several major ground battles between Israeli, Syrian, and PLO forces. Israeli fighter-bombers again bombed SAM batteries in the Bekaa Valley and hit Syrian reinforcements that were moving into Lebanon. A series of major air battles erupted as waves of Syrian Air Force aircraft few into Lebanon to challenge Israeli jets and ground forces. Syrian fighters and Gazelle attack helicopters armed with HOT antitank missiles hit a number of Israeli vehicles and caused many casualties. However, the Syrians paid a heavy price: twenty-six Syrian fighters and three helicopters were shot down by a combination of Israeli jets and antiaircraft fire during this fifth day of Peace for Galilee.[20]

Maj. Gen. David Ivry, the IAF commander in 1982, summarized the air situation during a press conference held just after the war on the celebration of the thirty-fourth Israeli Air Force Day:

> It took them [the Syrians] time to evaluate what was happening in the air battles. By Friday morning [June 11] they already understood the situation. We had already shot down 60 of their aircraft. Nevertheless, they continued to scramble them. I believe that what happened then was already the result of a psychological pressure of "let's make a last effort to shoot down several Israeli aircraft." And this was already a reaction of impulse and less of consideration. I cannot say for certain that this is what happened. This is a feeling. What is interesting is that when we began to attack on Friday, June 4, the Syrians did not react despite the fact that we were attacking Beirut, and, as a rule in the past, when we attacked terrorist targets in the Beirut area, the Syrians would react. In my opinion, the cumulative effect of the last three years was a factor here. In the three years before the war we became a significant deterrent factor in the air. We had shot down 24 Syrian planes [including 2 Mi-8 helicopters] without losing a single aircraft. On Monday, June 7, 1982, they began to intercept us. In the beginning they thought twice. On Monday a MiG-23 was shot down. On Tuesday [June 8] a few more began to come. Seven were shot down. And with the attack on the missiles there began a massive intercept effort.[21]

By June 11, the sixth day of the conflict, Israeli forces reached the outskirts of Beirut and threatened to cut off the main road between the city and the Bekaa Valley. Israeli armored units rushed forward and called for heavy air support in order to capture additional terrain before a UN-arranged cease-fire took effect at noon.

Amir Yoeli, an IAF pilot who served with a Kfir C2 squadron, flew a ground attack mission in support of this battle:

> I was given a ground support mission to hit a target near the road that led east from Beirut. We came in from the east because we wanted the sun behind us, and since there was very little SAM activity at the time, there wasn't a problem. As we approached our target, we communicated with our forces on the ground and tried to get the exact location of their vehicles. The sky was constantly disturbed by black puffs at about 10,000 feet, but the forces underneath were living through a shelling attack. It was very hard to get an exact location from them. We circled around the approximate point but could not identify any of our troops. At last I spotted some heavy artillery with help from a guiding voice of an officer on the ground. All systems were go and we dove for a positive identification of the target. After verifying with some local groups that we are not going against our own troops, we went in. I dropped first, and my wingman a few seconds after me. It was a hit. Another pair of Kfirs joined in on the channel and I directed them to another battery a bit west of the one we had just hit. Since there were explosions still going on the ground, it was easy for them to come in after us and destroy their target. It did not take more than thirty seconds before we heard the ground forces cheer on the radio. Whether or not both batteries were aiming at our troops or only one, I still don't know, but it doesn't make much of a difference. Our targets were always difficult and we had to use extreme caution being most of the time over hostile territory.[22]

On June 11, 1982, large numbers of Syrian aircraft again took to the air and tried to attack Israeli jets and ground forces. Israeli fighters pounced on the attackers and eighteen Syrian aircraft were shot down by the Israelis. The cease-fire brought the fighting to an end late in the day on June 11. During a week of heavy fighting, the IAF had shot down more than eighty Syrian aircraft, knocked out twenty SAM batteries in the Bekaa

Valley, and destroyed hundreds of Syrian and terrorist vehicles and fortifications. Terrorist groups and Syrian units fought back aggressively against the massive Israeli ground assault and caused many casualties. However, the weight of numbers, air superiority, and the mobility and firepower of Israeli forces overwhelmed the defenders.

The cease-fire broke down on June 13, and heavy fighting resumed between Israeli, Syrian, and terrorist units. Israeli forces continued their drive north in an attempt to link up with the Christian Phalangists to trap PLO and Syrian units in Beirut. By late June, the Israelis had indeed linked up with the Christian forces and had closed the trap. Fighter-bombers pounded terrorist and Syrian positions blocking the path of the Israeli advance and hammered resupply convoys.

Israeli and Syrian fighters again clashed on June 24 and two MiG-23 aircraft were shot down in a brief dogfight. Syrian forces pushed additional SA-6 batteries into the Bekaa Valley to rebuild their defenses. Israeli reconnaissance patrols quickly detected this move. Air strikes put one battery out of action on June 24 and blasted several other Syrian air defense units in the Bekaa Valley two days later.

Israeli forces began the siege of Beirut on July 1 with a massive overflight of fighters at dusk. The IAF jets made mock bombing runs and blasted the city with sonic booms from high-speed passes. Ground forces clashed daily, and heavy artillery fire chewed up the city. Initially the IAF played only a limited role in the siege. However, in response to a heavy PLO counter-attack on July 22, Israeli tanks, artillery, and fighter-bombers hammered guerrilla strongpoints throughout Beirut. These were the first direct strikes made against Syrian fortifications since June 25. The Syrians moved a battery of SA-8 mobile SAMs into the Bekaa Valley during the night of July 24. The latest Soviet-built tactical air defense weapon, the radar-guided SA-8 missile, could hit aircraft from a range of more than six miles and reach an altitude of over four miles. Israeli reconnaissance spotted this deployment, and fighter-bombers destroyed three of the four vehicles of the battery. The remaining SA-8 launcher exacted revenge late in the afternoon of July 25 by shooting down an Israeli F-4 Phantom.

The IAF played a major role in Peace for Galilee and the siege of Beirut. During the initial period of action, which lasted from June 6 to 11, IAF aircraft flew more than two thousand sorties. Israeli jets, helicopters, and transports flew several thousand sorties in support of later operations.

In air-to-air combat, the IAF accounted for eighty-five Syrian aircraft. Some forty-four of these fell to pilots flying the F-16 Falcon, while F-15 crews were credited with forty victories. One Syrian aircraft was downed by an F-4 Phantom crew. Most Syrian losses were MiG-21 and MiG-23 fighters, but some SU-22 fighter-bombers and helicopters were also shot down.[23] Most of these victories were attributed to short-range infrared-guided missiles, including the late-model AIM-9L, earlier versions of the Sidewinder, the Rafael Shafrir 2 and the new Rafael Python. A number of Syrian jets were destroyed by AIM-7F missiles fired from IAF F-15s but only about six aircraft fell to Israeli aircraft cannons. The need for positive visual identification—because of the crowded skies—prompted Israeli pilots to rely primarily on short-range dogfight missiles.

An IAF F-16 pilot who fought during the 1982 conflict commented, "The weapons system has shortened the duration of air battles." He added, "Once we used to shoot them down with guns at a range of 100–300 meters from behind. To reach such relatively short range, you need time—several minutes. The improvement of the weapons systems permits shooting them down at a longer range, and reduces the risk."[24]

The pilot continued, "The Syrian pilots in some instances showed greater boldness than usual, and they tried to fight. . . . One should bear in mind that Syrian pilots had combat experience from battles they fought with us in the past, and they did apply some of the things they had learned. But the gap is still wide."[25] He concluded, "While the downing of many MiGs brought great satisfaction and honor, the attack on the missiles is one of the great achievements of the air force and will be long remembered."[26]

During the Lebanon conflict, the IAF demonstrated that it had integrated the hard lessons of the 1973 war through its destruction of the Syrian air defense umbrella in the Bekaa Valley. Israeli pilots then concentrated their attention on stopping Syrian reinforcements from reaching the battle area and on destroying PLO strongpoints and fortifications. Accurate intelligence, the advanced weapons delivery systems fitted to Israeli fighter-bombers, and intensified training enabled Israeli pilots to bomb targets with pinpoint accuracy. Israeli aircrew and aircraft losses were kept to a minimum through the heavy use of ECM, decoy flares, and weapons delivery tactics that kept aircraft above the range of most antiaircraft fire.

"The war of the helicopters," said Major General Irvy, "was extremely dangerous this time. They flew over an area where it was difficult to determine the location of the concealed danger. At times, an area at the front was already mopped up, but in the rear of the front line there were still terrorists who fired at the helicopters."[27]

Helicopters and transport aircraft played a vital role in helping to ensure the success of Israeli operations in Lebanon. Transport and helicopter crews braved heavy fire to evacuate wounded troops and move vital supplies to the front line. Transport helicopters evacuated more than one thousand wounded to hospitals in Israel. During the assault of Beaufort Castle, a helicopter flew up to the fort and evacuated wounded even as the battle raged. A Bell 212 helicopter was shot down in the process of flying one of these important medical rescue missions. Also, C-130 transports served to evacuate injured soldiers. Fixed- and rotor-wing transports brought ammunition, food, and supplies to the front line and moved captured PLO war materiel back to Israel.

The IAF AH-1 Cobras and MD-500 Defenders flew hundreds of scout and attack sorties during the conflict. In attacks against Syrian and PLO forces, attack helicopters fired 137 TOW wire-guided missiles. Ninety-nine of these hit home, resulting in the destruction of twenty-nine tanks, fifty-six other vehicles, four radar sites, one Syrian Gazelle helicopter, and several additional targets.[28]

Four Israeli helicopters were lost in action, two of which were shot down by friendly antiaircraft fire.[29] Several effective attacks by Syrian Gazelle attack helicopters scared Israeli ground troops, and, as a result, army units sometimes fired on IAF helicopters. The IAF has the responsibility of providing air defense for the Israeli army. During the Lebanon conflict, IAF antiaircraft units worked closely with the army. Their antiaircraft systems downed several Syrian aircraft and helicopters with gun and missile fire. Army commanders liked the Vulcan air defense system because the cannon was also highly effective against ground targets.

The success of the IAF in the 1982 Lebanon conflict can be attributed to effective equipment, well-trained personnel, and a flexible tactical doctrine that coordinated air force, army, and navy operations. Israeli battle commanders benefited from the efficient command and control network that was developed following the 1973 war. This system could integrate information from many sources, including real-time intelligence from RPVs and AWACS aircraft.

The Israeli siege of Beirut ended in late August. As part of the cease-fire agreement, a multinational force composed of soldiers from the United States, France, Italy, and Great Britain took control of Beirut to oversee the withdrawal of PLO forces. Even after the multinational force took control of Beirut, a large force of Israeli troops continued to garrison southern Lebanon. The IAF provided support for this occupation force. Helicopters and transports flew in and out of Lebanon with supplies, while reconnaissance and fighter aircraft patrolled over the northern part of the country to keep tabs on the Syrians and Lebanese factions.

Following the Lebanon war, Israel continued to strengthen the IAF. An additional seventy-five F-16 Falcon fighter-bombers were ordered. These new jets were improved versions of the F-16C/D Fighting Falcons, which featured the high-thrust General Electric F110 turbofan engine and a significant amount of Israeli-built avionics equipment. At the same time, Israeli companies initiated development of a new home-built fighter. Known as the Lavi, this new jet was to succeed the Kfir on the Israel Aircraft Industries assembly line. In 1982, Lt. Gen. Amos Lapidot, Lavi program manager, assumed command of the IAF.

In January 1983, Israel disclosed that the Soviet Union had supplied Syria with several batteries of long-range SA-5 antiaircraft missiles. With a range of over 150 miles against high-flying targets, the SA-5 could threaten IAF aircraft over Lebanon and much of northern Israel. Israeli planners viewed the SA-5 deployment as a provocative act. However, since the missile sites were located on Syrian territory and none were fired at

Israeli planes, only diplomatic efforts were used to challenge the new threat.

Israel continued its reconnaissance missions over Lebanon, and when buildups of terrorist forces were detected, Israeli aircraft bombed their positions. On November 20, 1983, a Kfir was lost to antiaircraft fire during a strike against targets in the Shouf mountains of Lebanon. An IAF pilot described the situation:

> We easily found the area—it was already covered with smoke and debris from previous attacks, with bomb craters clearly visible in the dark ground. We entered the attack, but were immediately faced by dense antiaircraft fire; the gunners were expecting us. On releasing my bombs, I saw the aircraft of my companion leaving behind white trails of fuel. He reported over the radio that he had been hit. I tried to locate and report on the damage, but he said that he was having difficulty in controlling the Kfir. I told him to try and keep altitude in order to gain distance, but he entered into a wide spin pointing toward the ground. He ejected at the last moment, his parachute opening just before the Kfir hit the ground.[30] The Israeli pilot was rescued by Lebanese Christian forces and returned to Israel.

The UN peacekeeping forces in Lebanon used their airpower on several occasions to hit back at Syrian and Lebanese artillery. In September, October, and November 1983, French Navy Super Etendard fighter-bombers blasted Druze gun batteries and other positions. On December 4, U.S. Navy carrier-based A-6 and A-7 attack aircraft bombed gun positions that had been pounding the U.S. Marine positions around the Beirut airport. During the series of strikes, an A-6 and an A-7 were lost to missile fire. The skies of Lebanon were dangerous because of the presence of the Syrians and the various Lebanese factions, which were armed with a variety of advanced Soviet-supplied antiaircraft weapons.

Israel continued to occupy a portion of southern Lebanon until 1985. After the Israeli withdrawal from Lebanon, the IAF assumed prime responsibility for reconnaissance and attack of terrorist targets.

After the PLO withdrawal from Lebanon in 1982, its members settled in several Arab countries. A major PLO base was set up in Tunis, Tunisia, and from here many international terrorist activities were coordinated. In response to a terrorist attack against a yacht in Cyprus that left three Israelis dead, the IAF was again called into action. On October 1, 1985, IAF F-15s flew 1,500 miles across the Mediterranean Sea and bombed the PLO headquarters in Tunisia. The raid destroyed several buildings and killed seventy-three people. An Israeli pilot who flew on the attack said,

> After I pulled out of the dive, I saw the bombs hitting the target accurately. A lot of smoke curled up. From the bird's view you don't see much detail. The picture is not as you see it afterwards on television. You only see that you hit those houses you wanted to hit. We assembled again and started on our way home. After this there is the release of tension which is huge. I myself gave an enormous shout in the cockpit to get rid of the tension. The feeling is mixed: you see the huge destruction you left behind, but with the knowledge that we carried out the task perfectly, just as we wanted to do it.[31]

The IAF F-15 Eagle fighter-bombers that performed the mission flew a five-hour round-trip mission and refueled several times from Boeing 707 tankers. While several aircraft swooped in to deliver their bombs, other F-15s patrolled overhead to defend against air attack by Tunisian fighters. An E-2C Hawkeye radar-warning plane escorted the strike group. Israeli Defense Minister Yitzak Rabin said that the raid was flown to demonstrate to the PLO that "the long arm of Israeli retribution will reach them wherever they are."[32]

Following the Israeli raid on Tunisia, Syrian planes began challenging Israeli reconnaissance missions over Lebanon. On November 20, 1985, IAF F-15 Eagle fighters engaged and shot down two Syrian MiG-23s that had attempted to ambush an Israeli reconnaissance plane. The IAF's commander, Maj. Gen. Amos Lapidot, commented about the event in an interview:

> They are not very happy about us carrying out routine reconnaissance over Lebanon, and they attempt to interfere with us from time to time. During the past weeks they stepped up these actions and have provoked dangerous situations. There were several occasions in the past weeks when we were forced to abort our missions in order not to heat up the situation too much.
>
> Today a situation developed to which we could not avoid reacting. Their approach was made in such a threatening posture and at such a range that we were forced to abort the patrol. We had to defend our reconnaissance planes with additional combat aircraft that were there for that purpose.
>
> We operate with the intention of keeping the Syrian planes at arm's length and not provoking a confrontation, so that we can carry out our reconnaissance as usual.
>
> Today, for some reason, the Syrians continued threatening our planes, reaching such close range that we were forced to engage them.
>
> One has to remember that modern combat aircraft are armed with missiles that have ranges of 20 kilometers or more. Therefore the danger to our planes begins when the Syrian planes are still in their own airspace. And when we react, we can do so while still in Lebanese airspace.[33]

This was the first Israeli–Syrian dogfight since 1983. The IAF had flown many sorties over Lebanon and struck targets thirteen times since the 1982 conflict, but Syrian aircraft stayed well clear of those bombing missions.

In spite of the Syrian challenge, the IAF continued its reconnaissance and bombing attacks in Lebanon. In October 1986, and IAF F-4E Phantom was lost near Sidon, Lebanon, during an attack against a terrorist base. The pilot and navigator of the Phantom successfully ejected. The pilot of the aircraft clung to the skid of an IAF Cobra attack helicopter and was carried through heavy antiaircraft fire to safety, but the navigator was captured by a Lebanese military force. The IAF has routinely flown reconnaissance aircraft and unmanned RPV drones over

Lebanon to monitor Syrian and terrorist activities. Terrorist targets detected by these reconnaissance operations have been struck on a frequent basis.

As the IAF moved into its fourth decade, the air arm had to face a new set of economic, political, and military challenges. The IAF inventory now included a large force of F-15, F-16, F-4, Kfir, and A-4 tactical aircraft, plus hundreds of support systems ranging from advanced radar networks to trainers. All of the famed Mirage/Nesher fighters were gone, having been sold to Argentina or retired, and A-4 Skyhawks were also rapidly being retired from service. Early-model Kfir jets were also gone, having been placed in storage or sold. For several years, two dozen Kfirs were leased to the U.S. Navy and Marine Corps and used as adversary aircraft to simulate enemy jets. During the early 1980s, the Israeli government supported the development of a new Israeli-built fighter. Known as the Lavi, this new aircraft was to be the replacement for aging Israeli Skyhawk, Kfir, and Phantom fighter-bombers. The Lavi was also to serve as the IAF's new advanced trainer aircraft. Israel Aircraft Industries had already refurbished the IAF's fleet of Fouga Magister primary jet trainers.

The IAF flies many specialized surveillance aircraft, including E-2C Hawkeye radar planes and (according to the U.S. Congressional Record) Boeing 707, OV-1D Mohawk, and Beech RU-21 aircraft fitted with specialized sensors. The air force has over two dozen Boeing 707 and C-130 aircraft, and these transports serve in both refueling and logistics roles. The famous C-47 Dakotas still fly with the IAF, and small numbers of Israeli-built Arava transports are in use. The helicopter component was upgraded through the addition of a small number of Aerospatiale SA-366 Dauphin helicopters. The IAF plans to purchase AH-64 Apache attack helicopters, and UH-60 Blackhawk transport helicopters.

Israeli air superiority was challenged by a number of developments in the late 1980s. First, the air arms of its potential opponents were receiving an infusion of advanced aircraft. Syria now has the Soviet-built MiG-29, which is similar to the West's latest fighters; Saudi Arabia has purchased dozens of Tornado and F-15 fighters; while Jordan has bought the French

Mirage 2000. The qualitative improvement in Arab aircraft, weapons, and pilot experience has diminished Israel's margin of superiority.

The introduction of advanced short- and medium-range surface-to-surface missiles into the armed forces of Syria, Iraq, Saudi Arabia, and other neighboring Arab countries has created a new threat to Israel. The fighters and Hawk surface-to-air missiles of the IAF have almost no capability to intercept these high-speed weapons. This is not a new threat. During the 1973 war, Syria fired a number of FROG rockets at Israeli targets, but the weapon had limited range and poor accuracy. Modern Soviet- and Chinese-produced SS-12, SS-21, CSS2 and similar western-designed missiles have much greater reach, improved accuracy, and can be armed with conventional, chemical, or even nuclear warheads. These missiles could damage and/or destroy Israeli airfields and army formations, and threaten civilian population centers as well. The Israeli military and civilian leadership has made it known that it would not tolerate an attack by surface-to-surface missiles and would retaliate with all means at its disposal, including the use of special weapons if necessary. At the same time, Israel has initiated a sizable civil defense effort and a program to develop and field air defense missiles capable of shooting down tactical ballistic missiles. The selection of several Israeli firms to participate in the U.S. Strategic Defense Initiative (Star Wars) indicates that progress has been made toward this goal. In addition, Israel demonstrated its capability to produce long range ballistic missiles on September 21, 1988, with the launching of Offeq (Horizon) 1, the country's first satellite. This launch made Israel the eighth nation to place a satellite in space.

The peace treaty with Egypt and budget cutbacks have had a significant impact on the IAF. In August 1987, the Israeli cabinet decided to cancel the Lavi fighter. In addition, the IAF has been forced to streamline its operations in order to save money. Major General Lapidot transferred command of the IAF to Maj. Gen. Avihu Ben-Nun in September 1987. Major General Ben-Nun was the commander of one of the IAF's first Phantom squadrons, commander of two air bases, and head of military planning.

As the IAF moves into the 1990s, it will increasingly need to focus on quality rather than quantity. In the wake of the Lavi cancellation, additional F-16s have been ordered. These new fighters will be supported by Phantoms, which are being upgraded by Israel Aircraft Industries, and declining numbers of Skyhawks and Kfirs. Advanced avionics and ECM systems developed for the Lavi will be fitted to IAF aircraft and new stand-off weapons and guided missiles put into service. Innovative doctrine and tactics, developed through thousands of hours of combat and training, would be used by IAF personnel should they have to fight. Intensified training and higher standards have been instituted to ensure that all IAF personnel remain ready for action. This is a vital necessity because with each passing year more combat-experienced pilots, maintenance personnel, ordnance handlers, and other veterans retire from the force. Speaking about air force strategy, Major General Ben-Nun has stated, "We must keep the balance of quality in our favor. We don't have an answer to everything. Avionics and advanced weapons are only one kind of answer. Keeping and attracting good people is our single biggest problem—though we still do it better than anyone else."[34]

The IAF has a proud heritage. In the event of a future call to action, the personnel of the force will do their best to ensure victory. Members of the IAF, the fighter pilots, the mechanics, and the air defense missile battery commanders know that they are Israel's first line of defense and that the safety of the country rests in their hands.

Appendix

IAF Aircraft

Aircraft	Crew	Wing Span (ft.)	Length (ft.)	Loaded Weight (lb.)	Engines	Engine Thrust (HP or lb.)	Maximum Speed (MPH)	Range (mi.)	Ceiling (ft.)	Weapons
Airspeed Consul	2	53.4	35.4	8,300	2 Armstrong Siddeley Cheetah	365 HP each	190	900	19,000	—
Auster AOP5	2/3	36	22.4	1,990	1 Lycoming 0-290	130 HP	130	250	15,000	Grenades & bombs
Avia S199	1	32.5	29.7	7,700	1 Junkers Jumo 211F	1,350 HP	367	528	31,000	2 20-mm cannons 2 13-mm machine guns
Avro Anson	2	56.5	42.2	9,770	2 Armstong Siddeley Cheetah	420 HP	190	700	19,200	—
Beechcraft Bonanza, Model 35	4	32.8	25.2	2,650	1 Continental E185	185 HP	184	750	17,000	Bombs, 1 machine gun
Beechcraft Queen Air	2	50.2	35.5	8,800	2 Lycoming 1-650-540	380 HP each	248	1,560	26,800	—
Beechcraft RU-21	2/4	45.9	35.5	9,650	2 Pratt & Whitney T74CP	550 HP each	249	1,170	25,500	ECM equipment
Boeing B-17G	10	103.7	74.4	44,560	4 Wright R-1820	1200 HP each	287	1,800	35,000	13 12.7-mm machine guns
Boeing C-97 Strato-cruiser	4	141.2	110.3	153,000	4 Pratt & Whitney R4360	3500 HP each	375	4,300	35,000	—
Boeing Stearman PT-17	2	32.1	25	2,717	1 Continental W670	220 HP	124	505	11,300	

Boeing 707-320	3/5	145.7	152.9	328,000	4 Pratt & Whitney JT3D	18,000 lb. each	615	5,735	39,000	—
Bristol Beau-fighter	2	57.9	42.8	21,000	2 Bristol Hercules	1670 HP each	312	1,480	26,000	4 20-mm cannons, 6 0.303-in. machine guns
Britten-Norman Islander	2	49	39.5	6,300	2 Lycoming 0-540-54C5	260 HP each	170	1,263	14,600	—
Cessna Skywagon	1	36	25.9	2,800	1 Teledyne Continental 0-47OU	230 HP	170	1,163	17,700	—
Cessna Super Skywagon	1	36.6	27.6	3,300	1 Teledyne Continental	285 HP	173	1,275	16,100	
Consolidated PBY-5 Catalina	2	104	63.9	34,000	2 Pratt & Whitney R1820	1200 HP each	196	2,520	15,800	—
Curtis C-46 Commando	2	108.1	76.4	45,000	2 Pratt & Whitney R2800	2,000 HP each	234	1,200	24,500	—
Dassault Ouragon	1	40.2	35.2	13,646	1 Hispano Suiza Nene 104B	5,000 lb.	584	520	42,500	4 20-mm cannons, 2,000 lb. of weapons
Dassault Mirage IIIC	1	26.9	38.4	18,600	1 Snecma ATAR B	9,370 lb., 13,378 lb. afterburner	386	400	59,000	2 30-mm cannons, 2,000 lb. of weapons, 2 AAMs
Dassault Mystere IVA	1	36.5	42.1	16,530	1 Hispano Suiza Verdon 350	7,716 lb.	696	572	49,200	2 30-mm cannons, 2,000 lb. of weapons

IAF Aircraft *(continued)*

Aircraft	Crew	Wing Span (ft.)	Length (ft.)	Loaded Weight (lb.)	Engines	Engine Thrust (HP or lb.)	Maximum Speed (MPH)	Range (mi.)	Ceiling (ft.)	Weapons
Dassault Super Mystere B2	1	34.5	46.1	19,840	1 Snecma ATAR 101G	7,495 dry, 9,920 afterburner	783	540	55,700	2 30-mm cannons, 2,000 lb. of weapons
De Havilland Tiger Moth	2	29.4	23.9	1,770	1 De Havilland Gypsy	130 HP	109	201	13,600	—
De Havilland Dragon Rapide	2	48	34.5	6,000	2 De Havilland Gypsy	200 HP each	150	520	16,000	—
De Havilland Chipmunk	2	34.4	25.4	2,000	1 Bristol Siddeley Gypsy Major	140 HP	138	300	16,000	—
De Havilland Mosquito FB6	2	54.1	40.5	22,300	2 Rolls Royce Merlin	1,230 HP each	380	1,200	36,000	4 20-mm cannons, 4 0.303-in. machine guns, bombs, rockets
Dornier DO27	1	39.4	31.6	4,000	1 Lycoming 650-480	274 HP	174	685	20,800	—
Dornier DO28	2	51.9	37.5	8,000	2 Lycoming 10,540	290 HP each	184	768	19,400	—
Douglas C-47 Dakota	2	95	64.5	26,000	2 Pratt & Whitney R1830	1,200 HP each	229	1,500	23,000	Bombs
Douglas C-54	3	117.5	93.9	7,300	4 Pratt & Whitney R2000	1,350 HP each	274	3,300	22,500	—

Douglas DC-5	3	78	62.2	20,000	2 Wright GR-1320	900 HP each	230	1,600	23,700	—
Fairchild F-24	1	36.3	24.9	2,500	1 Ranger G-410B2	165 HP	132	640	16,800	Bombs, machine gun
Fokker S11	2	36.1	26.8	2,425	1 Lycoming 0435	190 HP	130	400	12,630	—
Fouga Magister	2	37	33.6	6,978	2 Turbomeca Marbore	836 lb. each	440	576	40,000	2 machine guns, rockets, bombs
General Dynamics F-16A/B	1/2	31	49.5	24,000	1 Pratt & Whitney F100	14,670 dry 23,800 afterburner	1,350	500	50,000	1 20-mm cannon, 6 AAMs 12,000 lb. of weapons
General Dynamics F-16C/D	1/2	31	49.5	27,000	1 General Electric F110	16,000 dry 27,000 afterburner	1,360	600	50,000	1 20-mm cannon, 6 AAMs 12,000 lb. of weapons
Gloster Meteor F.8	1	37.1	44.6	15.700	2 Rolls Royce Derwent	3,500 lb. each	592	600	40,000	4 20-mm cannons, rockets, bombs
Grumman E-2C	5	80.7	57.6	50,000	2 Allison T-56	4,900 HP each	374	1,600	30,000	—
Grumman OV-1D	2	48	41	18,000	2 Avco Lycoming T56	1,160 HP each	285	900	25,000	—
Grumman Widgeon	2	40	31.1	4,528	2 Ranger L-440	200 HP each	153	920	14,600	—
IAI Arava	2	68.5	42.5	15,000	1 Pratt & Whitney PT-6	780 HP	203	650	24,000	3 machine guns
IAI Nesher	1	26.9	49.2	20,000	1 Snecma ATAR 9C	9,500 lb. dry, 14,110 lb. afterburner	1,320	650	45,000	2 30-mm cannons, 2 AAMs, 4,000 lb. of weapons

IAF Aircraft *(continued)*

Aircraft	Crew	Wing Span (ft.)	Length (ft.)	Loaded Weight (lb.)	Engines	Engine Thrust (HP or lb.)	Maximum Speed (MPH)	Range (mi.)	Ceiling (ft.)	Weapons
IAI Kfir	1	26.9	50.8	23,000	1 General Electric J79	11,870 lb. dry, 17,900 lb. afterburner	1,320	650	50,000	2 30-mm cannons, 6,000 lb. of weapons
IAI Westwind	2	44.8	52.1	20,000	2 General Electric CJ 010	3,100 lb. each	541	2,120	45,000	—
Lockheed C-130 H	4	132.6	97.7	155,000	4 Allison T-56	4,050 HP each	384	4,700	23,000	—
Lockheed Hudson	2	65.5	44.3	18,500	2 Wright Cyclone	1,200 HP each	250	2,160	24,500	—
Lockheed Lode Star	3	65.5	49.8	18,500	2 Wright Cyclone	1,200 HP each	271	1,600	3,000	—
Lockheed Constellation	3	123	95.1	72,000	4 Wright R 3350	2,200 HP each	330	2,400	25,000	—
McDonnell Douglas A-4H Skyhawk	1	27.5	40.3	18,000	1 Pratt & Whitney J-52 P8	9,300 lb.	675	600	47,000	2 30-mm cannons, 6,000 lb. of weapons
McDonnell Douglas A-4N Skyhawk	1	27.5	42.6	20,000	1 Pratt & Whitney J52 P408	11,200 lb.	685	606	47,000	2 30-mm cannons, 8,200 lb. of weapons
McDonnell Douglas F-4E Phantom	2	38.2	62.9	56,000	2 General Electric J79-GE-17	11,820 dry, 17,900 afterburner	1,500	800	58,700	1 20-mm cannon, 8 AAMs, 12,000 lb. of weapons

McDonnell Douglas F-15A Eagle	1	42.7	63.8	42,000	2 Pratt & Whitney F100	14,670 dry, 23,800 afterburner	1,650	800	60,000	1 20-mm cannon, 8 AAMs, 12,000 lb. of weapons
Miles Gemini	2	50	36	5,300	2 Cirrus Blackburn	100 HP each	145	820	13,500	—
Norduyn Norseman	2	51.7	32.4	7,400	1 Pratt & Whitney WASP	600 HP	155	442	17,000	—
Nord Morecrin	2	33.6	23.6	2,300	1 Regnier 460	135 HP	174	560	16,400	—
Nord Noratlas	4 4	106.8	72.1	45,400	2 Bristol 1738	2,040 HP	252	1,740	28,200	—
North American AT-6	2	42	29.5	5,000	1 Pratt & Whitney R1340	550 HP	210	630	24,000	Machine guns, bombs
North American P-51D Mustang	1	37	32.2	11,600	1 Packard V 1650	1,450 HP	437	950	41,900	6 12.7-mm machine guns, rockets, bombs
Pilatus PC-6	1 1	49.9	36.1	4,400	1 Turbo Mecca Astazov	532 HP	174	500	28,000	—
Piper Cub	2	35.2	22	1,400	1 Lycoming	125 HP	110	500	9,500	Bombs
Republic Seabee	2	37.6	27.9	3,000	1 Franklin 6A8-215	215 HP	120	560	11,700	—
RWD-13	1	37.7	25.6	1,958	PZI Junior	120 HP	135	500	19,500	—
Socata Ralley E	1	31.3	22.7	1,874	Continental 0-300	145 HP	136	550	11,800	—
Sud Aviation Vautour IIA	1	49.5	54.1	33,000	2 Snecma ATAR 101	7,716 HP each	690	1,000	49,000	4 30-mm cannons, 5,300 lb. of weapons

IAF Aircraft *(continued)*

Aircraft	Crew	Wing Span (ft.)	Length (ft.)	Loaded Weight (lb.)	Engines	Engine Thrust (HP or lb.)	Maximum Speed (MPH)	Range (mi.)	Ceiling (ft.)	Weapons
Supermarine Spitfire Mk 9	1	36.9	31.2	7,300	1 Rolls Royce Merlin	1,710 HP	404	434	42,000	2 20-mm cannons, 4 0.303-in. machine guns, 1,000 lb. of weapons
Taylor-craft C	1	36	22	1,200	1 Lycoming 0-145	55 HP	105	275	17,000	—
Temco Buckaroo	1	29.1	21.7	1,840	1 Continental C145	145 HP	160	400	14,000	—
Vultee BT-13	2	42	28.6	3,981	1 Pratt & Whitney T2B2	450 HP	182	800	21,000	—

IAF Helicopters

Aircraft	Crew	Rotor Diameter (in.)	Length (ft.)	Loaded Weight (lb.)	Engines	Engine Thrust (HP)	Maximum Speed (MPH)	Range (mi.)	Ceiling (ft.)	Weapons
Aero-spatiale Frelon SA 321K	2	62	63.6	27,550	3 Turbo-mecca Turmo	1,550 each	149	404	7,300	—

Bell AH-IS Cobra	2	44	44.4	9,500	1 Avco Lycoming T55	1,800	172	357	11,400	1 20-mm cannon, 8 TOW missiles, 38 rockets
Bell 476	2	37.1	32.5	2,850	1 Lycoming VO 435	270	105	250	17,600	—
Bell 206 Set Ranger	2	33.3	31.1	3,000	1 Allison 250-C18	317	133	362	18,500	—
Bell UH-1D (Augusta 205)	2	48	41.9	9,500	1 Avco Lycoming T53	1,250	138	360	11,000	—
Bell 212	2	48.1	57.2	11,200	1 Pratt & Whitney PT 6T	1,800	161	261	14,200	—
Hiller VH-12E	2	35.4	27.9	2,700	1 Franklin 6V4	200	95	500	5,200	
McDonnell Douglas Model 500	2	26.3	23	2,550	1 Allison 250-C20	420	152	366	14,400	Guns, 4 TOW missiles
McDonnell Douglas AH-64	2	48	58.2	16,000	2 6E T700	1,800	185	400	18,000	1 30-mm cannon, 16 Hellfire rockets
Sikorsky S-55	2	53	42.2	7,900	1 Wright R-1300	800	112	360	8,600	—
Sikorsky S-58	2	56	56.8	13,000	1 Wright Cyclone	1,525	122	248	9,100	—
Sikorsky CH-53	2	72.2	67.1	42,000	3 General Electric T64	3,925 each	196	251	21,000	—
Sikorsky UH-60	2	53.6	64.9	18,000	2 6E T700	1,800	155	400	18,000	

IAF Helicopters *(continued)*

Aircraft	Crew	Wing Span (ft.)	Length (ft.)	Loaded Weight (lb.)	Engines	Engine Thrust (HP or lb.)	Maximum Speed (MPH)	Range (mi.)	Ceiling (ft.)	Weapons
Black Hawk										
Sud Aviation Alouette	2	33.4	31.9	3,527	1 Turbo-Artouste IIC	530	115	350	7,050	—

IAF/Arab Air Forces Exchange Ratio

	Total Arab losses	Aircraft Loss Breakdown: In air combat	On the ground	From air defense weapons	Unknown, fracticide and maneuvering suicide	IAF combat losses (ACM losses)
1948	57	23	30	4	2	8 (2)
1948–56	3	3				0 (0)
1956	9	7			2	15 (1)
1956–67	13	12			1	0 (0)
June 1967 War	451	60	378	3	10	48 (10)
War of attrition (June 1967–August 1970)	150	113	—	25	12	38 (4)
August 1970–October 1973	39	34	—	4	1	8 (2)
Yom Kippur War October 1973	447	277	22	43	105	109 (11)

November 1973–June 1979	6	6	—	—	—	2 (0)
June 1979–June 1982	25	22	—	—	3	0 (0)
Lebanon, June 1982	95	85	—	7	3	6 (0)
Since June 1982	5	3	—	1	1	2 (0)
Total	1300	644	430	87	140	236 (30)

Overall exchange ratio in air-to-air combat: 21.5 to 1; overall conflict exchange ratio: 5.5 to 1. The IAF does not recognize "ace" status. However, many pilots have achieved more than five air-to-air victories and one individual has seventeen kills to his credit.

Table prepared from IAFs sources; Dick Pawloski, "Changes in Soviet Air Combat Doctrine and Force Structure," *General Dynamics Publication* (July 1987): II–129; and material from numerous books and periodicals.

IAF Air-to-Air Victories

1948 Total: 23 Cannon: 100%
15 Spitfire
6 Avia
2 Mustang (est.)

1948–56 Total: 3 Cannon: 100%
2 Meteor
1 Ouragon

1956 Total: 7 Cannon: 100%
7 Mystere IV

1956–67 Total: 12 Cannon: 93% Missile: 7%
1 Mystere IV
11 Mirage

1967 Total: 60 Cannon: 100%
50 Mirage
5 Super Mystere
3 Mystere IV
1 Ouragon
1 Vautour

War of Attrition Total: 113 Cannon: 70% Missile: 30%
105 Mirage
5 Phantom
2 Skyhawk

1970–73 Total: 34 Cannon: 70% Missile: 30%
14 Mirage/Nesher
20 Phantom (est.)

Yom Kippur War Total: 277 Cannon: 30% Missile: 70%
183 Mirage/Nesher
94 Phantom (est.)

1973–79 Total: 6 Cannon: 20% Missile: 80%
3 Phantom
3 Mirage/Nesher (est.)

1979–82 Total: 22 Cannon: 10% Missile: 90%
14 F-15
7 F-16
1 Kfir

Lebanon, 1982 Total: 85 Cannon: 7% Missile: 93%
40 F-15
44 F-16
1 Phantom

Since June 1982 Total: 3 Missile: 100%
3 F-15
Total: 644

Breakdown of IAF Victories by Fighter Type

	Approximate Victories	Percent of Totals
Mirage, Nesher, Kfir	367	56.99
F-4 Phantom	123	19.10
F-15 Eagle	57	8.85
F-16 Falcon	51	7.92
Spitfire	15	2.33
Mystere IV	11	1.70
Avia	6	0.93
Super Mystere B2	5	0.78
Meteor	2	0.31
Ouragon	2	0.31
A-4 Skyhawk	2	0.31
P-51 Mustang	2	0.31
Vautour	1	0.16
Totals	644	100.00

Approximate breakdown of victories by weapon type

Cannon	(20-mm, 30-mm)	45
Missile	(AIM-9 Sidewinder, Shafrir, Python, Matra 530, AIM-7 Sparrow)	55

Notes

Chapter 1. War of Independence

1. J. N. Westwood, *The History of the Middle East Wars* (Greenwich, CT: Bison Books, 1984), 8.

2. Ze'ev Schiff, *A History of the Israeli Army* (New York: Macmillan, 1985), 15.

3. Westwood, *History of Middle East Wars,* 10.

4. "A Short History of the Israeli Air Force," *Aerospace Historian* (March 1972): 11.

5. William Gunston, *An Illustrated Guide to the Israeli Air Force* (New York: Arco Books, 1982), 16–17.

6. Trevor N. Dupuy, *Elusive Victory: The Arab-Israeli Wars, 1947–1974,* (New York: Harper & Row, 1978) 12–19.

7. Westwood, *History of Middle East Wars,* 13.

8. David J. Bercuson, *The Secret Army* (New York: Stein & Day, 1984), 20–21.

9. Richard Goldman and Murray Rubenstein, *Shield of David* (Englewood Cliffs, NJ: Prentice-Hall, 1978), 29.

10. Robert Jackson, *The Israel Air Force Story* (London: Tandem Books, 1970), 31.

11. Gunston, *Illustrated Guide,* 34–38.

12. Goldman and Rubenstein, *Shield of David,* 42–43.

13. Benjamin Kegan, *The Secret Battle for Israel* (Cleveland, OH: World, 1966), 55.

14. Lou Lenart, interview with author, Los Angeles, May 22, 1988.

15. Bercuson, *Secret Army,* 130.

16. Gunston, *Illustrated Guide,* 38–39.

17. Nathaniel Linch, *Edge of the Sword* (New York: Putnam, 1962), 316.

18. Rudolph Augarten, interview with author, Los Angeles, June 22, 1988.

19. Bercuson, *Secret Army*, 188.

20. Jackson, *Israel Air Force Story*, 43.

21. Goldman and Rubenstein, *Shield of David*, 47.

22. Ibid., 50.

23. Rudolph Augarten, interview with author, Los Angeles, June 22, 1988.

24. Ibid.

25. Linch, *Edge of the Sword*, 364–65.

26. "Mosquito," *Born in Battle Magazine*, #19 (Eshel Dramit, Ltd., 1981): 26–28.

27. Rudolph Augarten, interview with author, Los Angeles, June 22, 1988.

28. Goldman and Rubenstein, *Shield of David*, 54–55.

29. Ezer Weizman, *On Eagles' Wings* (New York: Macmillan, 1976), 80–82.

30. "A Short History of the Israel Air Force," *Aerospace Historian* (March 1972): 13.

Chapter 2. The Early Years

1. Benjamin Kegan, *The Secret Battle for Israel* (Cleveland, OH: World, 1966), 179–82.

2. William Gunston, *An Illustrated Guide to the Israeli Air Force* (New York: Arco Books, 1982), 42–43.

3. "Expansion to 1956," *Born in Battle Magazine* #2 (Eshel Dramit, Ltd., 1978): 18–19.

4. Robert Jackson, *The Israel Air Force Story* (London: Tandem Books, 1970), 65–68.

5. Ibid., 65.

6. Kegan, *Secret Battle*, 204.

7. Kenneth Munson, *Dassault MP 450 Ouragon* (Windsor: Profile Publications Ltd., 1979), 132–145.

8. Gunston, *Illustrated Guide*, 62–63.

9. Aharon Yoeli, interview with author, Tel Aviv, November 17, 1988.

10. Richard Goldman and Murray Rubenstein, *Shield of David* (Englewood Cliffs, NJ: Prentice-Hall, 1978), 72.

Chapter 3. The Sinai Conflict

1. S.L.A. Marshall, *Sinai Victory* (Nashville, TN: Battery Press, 1968), 33.

2. J. N. Westwood, *The History of the Middle East Wars* (Greenwich, CT: Bison Books, 1984), 35.

3. Moshe Dayan, *Diary of the Sinai Campaign* (New York: Harper & Row, 1966), 33.

4. Trevor N. Dupuy, *Elusive Victory: The Arab-Israeli Wars, 1947–1974* (New York: Harper & Row, 1978), 138–43.

5. Ibid., 146–47.

6. Sidney Bisk and David Larcombe, "We Trained Nasser's Air Force," *Royal Air Force Flying Review* (January 1957): 25–26.

7. Alfred Goldberg, "*Air Operations in the Sinai Campaign*" (Maxwell Air Force Base, AL: Air War College, Air University, November, 1959), 5.

8. Dayan, *Diary*, 218.

9. Goldberg, *Sinai Campaign*, 5–7.

10. Patrick Falcon, "Thirty Years Later—Review of the French Air Force Contribution to the Suez Victory," *Air Fan* (November 1986): 68–77.

11. Chaim Herzog, *The Arab-Israeli Wars* (New York: Random House, 1982), 118–20.

12. Marshall, *Sinai Victory*, 45.

13. Guy Rimon, "Pride of Place," *Israel Air Force Magazine* (1989) 58.

14. Vic Flintman, "The Suez Campaign 1956," *Scale Aircraft Modeling* (November 1986): 54–75.

15. "History of the IAF 101 Squadron," *Born In Battle Defense Update* #75 (September 1986): 42–45.

16. Marshall, *Sinai Victory*, 69.

17. Yallo Shavit, interview with author, Tel Aviv, Israel, November 17, 1987.

18. Robert Henriques, *One Hundred Hours to the Suez* (New York: Collins, 1957), 196–99.

19. Eliezer Cohen, interview with author, Tel Aviv, Israel, November 15, 1987.

20. Charles Christienne and Pierre Lissarague, *The History of French Military Aviation* (Washington, DC: Smithsonian Institution Press, 1986), 473.

21. "IAF 101 Squadron," p. 44.

22. Glen Ashley, "Suez Crisis," *Scale Models International* (September 1984): 493.

23. Flintman, *Suez Campaign 1956*, 59.

24. Dupuy, *Elusive Victory*, 211.

25. Marshall, *Sinai Victory*, 141–165.

26. Alan W. Hall, "Republic F-84 Thunderstreak," *Scale Aircraft Modeling*, (March 1987): 250–83.

27. Vic Flintman, "Suez 1956, a Lesson in Airpower," *Air Pictorial* (August–September 1965): 270.

28. Dupuy, *Elusive Victory*, 212.

29. Flintman, *Suez Campaign, 1956*, 66.

30. Ze'ev Schiff, *A History of the Israeli Army* (New York: Macmillan, 149.

31. Ibid.

32. Christienne and Lissarague, *French Military Aviation*, 473.

33. Schiff, *Israeli Army*, 149.

Chapter 4. Modernization

1. William Gunston, *An Illustrated Guide to the Israeli Air Force* (New York: Arco Books, 1982) 60–65.

2. J. A. Cook, *Quantity or Quality? An Analysis of Current UPT Philosophy*, Professional Study No. 4544 (Maxwell Air Force Base, AL: Air War College, Air University, January, 1972). This study provides an overview of the Israeli pilot training philosophy.

3. Ezer Weizman, *On Eagles' Wings* (New York: Macmillan, 1976), 173–98.

4. "Egypt's Aviation Industry," *Interavia* (November 1966): 1796–98.

5. Gunston, *Illustrated Guide*, 72–73.

6. "Dassault Mirage III," *Born in Battle Magazine* #13 (Eshel Dramit, Ltd., 1981): 4–5.

7. Richard Goldman and Murray Rubenstein, *Shield of David* (Englewood Cliffs, NJ: Prentice-Hall, 1978), 78.

8. Thomas J. Marshall, "Israeli Helicopter Forces, Organization and Tactics," *Military Review* (May 1972): 94–99.

9. Robert Jackson, *The Israel Air Force Story* (London: Tandem Books, 1970), 127.

10. Edward Luttwak and David Horowitz, *The Israeli Army* (New York: A. Lane Publishers, 1975), 223.

11. Ibid., 187.

12. Guy Rimon, "Pride of Place," *Israel Air Force Magazine* (1989 Annual Edition): 59.

13. "Dassault Mirage III," 24.

14. A. J. Barker, *Six-Day War* (New York: Ballantine Books, 1974), 39.

15. Gunther E. Rothenberg, *The Anatomy of the Israeli Army* (New York: Hippocrene Books, 1979), 132.

Chapter 5. The Six Day War

1. Ze'ev Schiff, *A History of the Israeli Army* (New York: Macmillan, 1985), 155.

2. "The Six-Day War," *Born in Battle Magazine* #6 (Eshel Dramit, Ltd., 1979): 22.

3. Yallo Shavit, interview with author, Tel Aviv, November 17, 1987.

4. Edgar O'Ballance, *The Third Arab-Israeli War* (Hamden, CT: Anchor Books, 1970), 70.

5. "Airfield Attack, Lessons of Middle East Wars," *Born in Battle Magazine* #37 (Eshel Dramit, Ltd., 1984): 13.

6. Warren Wetmore, "Israelis' Air Punch Major Factor in War," *Aviation Week & Space Technology* (July 3, 1967): 18–23.

7. David Horowitz and Edward Luttwak, *The Israeli Army* (1975), 227.

8. David Eshel and Stanley M. Ulanoff, *The Fighting Israeli Air Force* (New York: Arco Books, 1985), 54–60.

9. D. K. Palit, *Return to the Sinai* (New Delhi: Palit & Palit, 1974), 23.

10. Chaim Herzog, *The Arab-Israeli Wars*, (New York: Random House, 1982), 197.

11. Eliezer Cohen, interview with author, Tel Aviv, November 15, 1987.

12. Wetmore, "Israelis' Air Punch," 19.

13. Guy Rimon, "Pride of Place," *Israel Air Force Magazine* (1989 Annual Edition): 60.

14. Wetmore, "Israelis' Air Punch," 23.

15. Trevor Dupuy, *Elusive Victory: The Arab-Israeli Wars, 1947–1974* (New York: Harper & Row, 1978), 315.

16. "Massive Resupply Narrows Israeli Margin," *Aviation Week & Space Technology* (June 19, 1967): 16.

17. A retired senior IAF officer, interview with author, Tel Aviv, November 17, 1987.

18. Dupuy, *Elusive Victory*, 279.

19. Gunther E. Rothenberg, *The Anatomy of the Israeli Army* (New York: Hippocrene Books, 1979), 146–47.

20. Dupuy, *Elusive Victory*, 326.

21. Schiff, *Israeli Army*, 156.

22. Ibid.

23. "Six-Day War," 21.

24. Major General B. Peled (Ret.), interview with author, Tel Aviv, June 18, 1978.

Chapter 6. The War of Attrition

1. *Military Balance* (London: International Institute for Strategic Studies, 1968–69), 45.

2. D. Eshel, Ed., "From Mirage to Kfir," *War Data*, No. 2 (Eshel-Dramit, Ltd., 1979): 10.

3. Kenneth Munson, "Skyhawk," *War Data,* No. 7 (Eshel Dramit, Ltd., 1980): 12.

4. *Military Balance*, 44.

5. Ibid., 46.

6. Eliezer Cohen, interview with author, Tel Aviv, November 1987.

7. "Airborne & Commando Raids," *Born in Battle,* #5 (Eshel Dramit, Ltd., 1979): 56.

8. James Feron, "Dayan Ridicules Claims of Arabs on Israeli Toll," *The New York Times* (April 18, 1969): 7.

9. James Feron, "Israeli Jets Attack UAR" *The New York Times* (July 21, 1969): 1.

10. S. Gilboa, interview with author, Tel Aviv, November 17, 1987.

11. James Feron, "Israeli Reports Downing 11 Jets in Suez Clashes," *The New York Times* (September 12, 1969): 1.

12. James Feron, "Israelis Maintain Pressure on UAR in New Airstrike," *The New York Times* (September 14, 1969): 1.

13. Hirsh Goodman, "Reliable Veteran," *The Jerusalem Post Magazine* (October 19, 1984): 4–5.

14. "A Talk with General Bar Lev," *Newsweek* (November 24, 1969): 52.

15. John Bentley, "Inside Israel's Air Force," *Flight International* (March 19, 1970): 427.

16. Yallo Shavit, interview with author, Tel Aviv, November 17, 1987.

17. John Bentley, "Inside Israel's Air Force Part 2—The Enemy We Face," *Flight International* (April 23, 1970): 669.

18. Ibid., 668.

19. "Mrs. Meir Declares Israeli Air Raids Show that Nasser Is a Failure," *The New York Times* (February 6, 1970): 11.

20. Edgar O'Ballance, *The Electronic War in the Middle East: 1968–70* (London: Faber & Faber, 1974), 107.

21. Peter Grosse, "Nasser Concedes that Israelis Have Air Superiority in Mideast," *The New York Times* (February 8, 1970): 6.

22. "Israeli Planes Seek to Thwart SAM-3s," *The New York Times* (March 25, 1970): 8.

23. James Feron, "Israelis Report Downing 5 MiGs Over Suez Canal," *The New York Times* (March 28, 1970): 4.

24. "Middle East: Other Fronts," *Newsweek* (April 13, 1970): 39.

25. Munson, "Skyhawk," 38–40.

26. Lawrence Whetlen, "June 1967–June 1971: Four Years of Canal War Reconsidered," *New Middle East* (June 1971): 19.

27. *Military Balance*, 32.

28. Richard Eder, "Israelis Report Russians Fire Rockets," *The New York Times* (July, 1970): 6.

29. O'Ballance, *Electronic War in the Middle East*, 114.

30. "The Air War in the Middle East: Israel's Air Force," *Born In Battle Magazine*, #2 (Eshel Dramit, Ltd., 1978): 50.

31. Ibid.

32. Ze'ev Schiff, "The Israel Air Force," *Air Force Magazine* (August 1976): 36.

33. Eshel, "From Mirage to Kfir," 12–13.

34. *Military Balance* (London: International Institute for Strategic Studies, 1971–1972): 29.

Chapter 7. The Yom Kippur War

1. *Military Balance* (London: International Institute of Strategic Studies, 1973–74), 33.

2. "Yom Kippur Arab-Israeli War," *Warplane* #93 (1983): 1841–45.

3. *Military Balance*, 36.

4. IAF Wing Commander, interview with author, Ramat David Air Base, Israel, November 15, 1987.

5. "Air Defense—Evolution of the Air Defense Missile Threat," *Born in Battle* #78 (Eshel Dramit, Ltd., December 1986): 18–29.

6. James M. Loop and Steven J. Zaloga, *Soviet Tanks and Combat Vehicles 1946–The Present* (Dorset: Arms & Armour Press, 1988), 216–21.

7. Ibid., 201–8.

8. Major A.J.C. Cavalle, ed., *Airpower and the Spring*, (Washing-

ton, DC: Invasion USAF Southeast Asia Monogram Series (1982), 44.

9. "The War in the Air," *Born in Battle Defense Update* #42, Yom Kippur Special (Eshel Dramit, Ltd., 1983): 18.

10. Yallo Shavit, interview with author, Tel Aviv, November 17, 1987.

11. John F. Kreis, *Air Warfare and Air Base Defense*, USAF Special Studies (Washington, DC: Office of Air Force History, 1988), 338.

12. N. Merchavi, interview with author, Tel Aviv, November 19, 1987.

13. Senate Committee of Armed Services, Subcommittee on Tactical Air Power, Hearings, March 11–21, 1974, 4306–18.

14. Mike Gaines, "Pilotless over the Battlefield," *Flight International* (December 1979): 1837.

15. "The War of the Day of Judgment," *Newsweek* (October 22, 1973): 28–29.

16. "Israel's Phantoms," *Born in Battle*, F-4 Phantom II Special Issue (Eshel Dramit, Ltd., 1981): 45.

17. "Selected Readings in Tactics," *The 1973 Middle East War*, U.S. Army Command and General Staff College Publication RB 100-2 (Ft. Leavenworth, KS: August 1976), 5–9.

18. N. Merchavi, interview.

19. "Israel's Phantoms," 44.

20. Ze'ev Schiff, *A History of the Israeli Army* (New York: Macmillan, 1985), 161.

21. IAF Wing Commander, interview.

22. Senate Committee of Armed Services, Hearings, Department of Defense Appropriations Fiscal Year 1977, Book 5, 440.

23. Terrance Smith, "Tel Aviv Says Attack Destroys Artillery and Missile Sites," *The New York Times* (October 19, 1973): 1.

24. Henry Kamm, "Two Top Generals Foresee Sinai Triumph," *The New York Times* (October 21, 1973): 6.

25. N. Merchavi, interview.

26. Trevor Dupuy, *Elusive Victory: The Arab-Israeli Wars, 1947–1974* (New York: Harper & Row, 1978), 609.

27. *Military Balance* (London: International Institute of Strategic Studies, 1972–73), 33.

28. Charles W. Corddry, "The Yom Kippur War Lessons New and Old," *National Defense* (May–June 1974): 509.

29. "The War in The Air," 22.

30. Senate Committee of Armed Services, 4249.

31. "Air Defense Equipment in Israel," *Born in Battle* #23, (Eshel Dramit, Ltd., 1982): 23.

32. Corddry, "Yom Kippur War," 508.

33. "The War in the Air," 19–20.

34. Corddry, "Yom Kippur War," 508.

35. Ibid.

36. Dupuy, *Elusive Victory*, 609.

37. "Yom Kippur War," 1845.

Chapter 8. Unending Conflict

1. Benjamin Peled, Notes from the International Symposium on Military Aspects of the Arab–Israeli Conflict, October 12–17, 1975, Jerusalem.

2. "From Kfir to Lavi," *Defense Update* #55 (Eshel Dramit, Ltd., 1984): 20.

3. Brigadier General Joshua Shani, interview with author, Washington, DC, May 13, 1988.

4. Amir Yoeli, interview with author, New York, January 20, 1988.

5. Bonner Day, "New Role for the Israeli Air Force" *Air Force Magazine* (August 1978): 35.

6. "Eagle vs. MiG," *Born in Battle Magazine* #13 (Eshel Dramit, Ltd., 1980): 37.

7. "Kfir in Combat," *Born in Battle Magazine* #14, (Eshel Dramit, Ltd., 1980): 37.

8. Dan McKinnon, *Bullseye One Reactor* (San Diego, CA: House of Hits Publishing, 1987), 108–175.

9. "Interview with Captured Pilot," *The Jerusalem Post* (July 4–10, 1982): 7.

10. Major Moshe Fogel, "The Syrian Missiles, Peace for Galilee Combat Reports," *IDF Journal* (December 1982): 43.

11. Ibid.

12. Ibid.

13. Paul S. Cutler, " 'We Learned both Tactical and Strategic Lessons in Lebanon,' Lt. Gen. Rafael Eitan," *Military Electronics Countermeasures* (February 1983): 100.

14. Fogel, "Syrian Missiles," 43.

15. Ibid.

16. Ibid.

17. Guy Rimon, "My F-15 Was on Fire," *Israel Air Force Magazine* (October 1988): 13.

18. Cutler, "We Learned Lessons," 100.

19. Fogel, "Syrian Missiles," 43.

20. "Israel Reveals Lebanon War Victories," *Flight International* (April 9, 1983): 979.

21. Yoram Inspector, "Complete Air Superiority," *Bamahane (Hebrew)* #42 (July 21, 1982): 10–11.

22. Yoeli interview.

23. "U.S. Arms Used in Lebanon War Outstrip Soviets," *Wall Street Journal* (August 5, 1982): 4.

24. Tzvi Gutman, "The Magic Formula of the F-16 Pilots," *Bita 'on Heyl Ha' Avir* (Hebrew) #28 (July 1982): 6.

25. Ibid.

26. Ibid.

27. Inspector, "Complete Air Superiority," 10–11.

28. Karl Schnell, "Experiences of the Lebanon War," *Military Technology* (July 1984): 30.

29. Ibid.

30. "From Kfir to Lavi," 20.

31. "Bombing Raid at the Heart of the PLO," *Israel Air Force Magazine* (November 1985): 12–13.

32. "Targeting the PLO," *Newsweek* (October 14, 1985): 52.

33. "Syrian Air Force Much More Aggressive: Interview with IAF Commander Lapidot," *The Jerusalem Post* (November 21, 1985): 19.

34. Merov Halperin, "General Avihu Ben-Nun, Incoming IAF Commander," *Israel Air Force Magazine* (September 1987): 46.

Index

A-4 Skyhawk fighter-bombers, 90, 91, 94, 97, 99, 104, 106–108, 109, 114, 116, 132–133, 137, 146–147, 151, 152, 160, 175, 185, 187
Abu Aweigila, 37, 39, 41, 43, 44, 73, 74
Abu Suweir airfield, 38, 45, 66, 72–73, 99
Abu Zohal, 104
Adan, General, 138
Agmon, Yoram, 63
Agronat, Shimon, 149
Agronat Report, 149
AH-1 Cobra attack helicopters, 152, 165, 180
Ahiaz, Aharon, 169
AIM-7 Sparrow air-to-air missiles, 100, 145, 179
AIM-9 Sidewinder missiles, 100, 120, 121, 136, 145, 179
AIM-9L short-range infrared missiles, 179
air defenses:
  Egyptian, 109–110, 112, 113–114, 123–124, 126, 134, 137, 139, 141
  Israeli, 132, 144–145, 153, 187
  Syrian, 124, 126, 132, 168, 170–175, 178, 181
Air Fouga, 57
Air France flight, 139, 155
Ajlun radar site, 67, 73
Alexandria, 88, 105
Almaza airfield, 38, 45, 66
Alon, Modi, 10, 12, 13, 17, 21
Alouette light helicopter, 59, 89, 109, 116
Amer, Hakin, 73, 77
Amiv, Yisrael, 10
Amman, 13, 67
Anglo-Egyptian Treaty (1936), 24
Anteim, Sid, 17
Arab Home Guard, 7
Arab Legion, 7, 10
Arab Liberation Army, 7
Arava transports, 90, 185
Arazi, Yehuda, 8
Argov, Shalmo, 168
arms embargoes, 8, 9, 12, 15, 89, 94
Assad, Hafez al-, 117, 170
Aswan Dam, 105, 108
Augarten, Rudolph, 16–17, 20–22, 23
Auster Autocraft light airplanes, 6, 10
Avia aircraft works, 9
Avia S199 fighters, 9, 12, 14, 15–16, 21–22

B, Brigadier General, 170, 171–172
B-17 heavy bombers, 15, 16, 20, 22, 27, 38, 51, 54
Badran, Shams al Din, 73
Baghdad, 167
Bar Lev, Haim, 100, 106, 110
Bar Lev line, 93, 122
Beaufort Castle, 180
Bedek Aircraft, Ltd., *see* Israel Aircraft Industries
Begin, Menachem, 4, 160, 162, 166
Beirut, 154, 167, 168, 169, 176, 177, 178, 181

Beirut International Airport, 94, 182
Bekaa Valley, 166, 168, 170, 172, 174, 175, 176, 177–178, 179
Bell 205 helicopters, 109, 116, 153
Bell 206 scout helicopter, 153
Bell 212 transport helicopters, 153, 180
Ben Gurion, David, 7–8, 18, 25, 27, 36
Beni Sueif airfield, 72
Ben-Nun, Avihu, 156, 186, 187
Bevin, Ernest, 5
Bilbeis, 38, 66
Bir Gifgafa airfield, 37, 38, 66, 79
Bloch, Lionel, 16
Boeing PT-17 trainers, 27, 56
Boeing 707 transports, 154, 165, 183, 185
Boeing Stratocruiser transports, 59, 109, 115, 116
Bristol Beaufighters, 18, 21

C-46 Commando twin-engine transports, 8, 9, 14–15, 18, 20
C-47 Dakota transports, 7, 10, 12–13, 15, 16, 20, 21, 27, 35, 39, 52, 58, 71, 89, 109, 116, 127, 185
C-130 Hercules transports, 116, 127, 153, 154, 155, 156, 180, 185
Cairo, 16, 92, 99, 103, 104, 105
Cairo West airfield, 38, 66, 72
Camp David Accords, 163, 165
Canada, 14, 23, 31
Carter, Jimmy, 162
cease-fires, 24, 96, 104, 109, 112, 117
  in Operation Peace for Galilee, 168, 176, 177–178
  in Sinai Conflict, 36, 49
  in Six-Day War, 79, 82, 83, 84
  violations of, 106, 114, 115
  in War of Attrition, 113
  in War of Independence, 14, 15, 17, 21, 22, 24
  in Yom Kippur War, 139, 140, 141, 142–143
Chapparal missiles, 144, 145, 153
Cohen, Eddie, 10, 11, 12
Cohen, Eliezer (Cheetah), 43–45, 74–75, 93
Commonwealth air forces, 5, 6
Czechoslovakia, 9, 14, 15, 16, 17, 19, 30–31, 33

Damascus, 67, 94, 106, 124, 127–128, 140–141
Damascus International Airport, 130
Dassault, 29, 31, 57, 89
Dayan, Moshe, 36–37, 47, 49, 88, 95, 98–99, 138, 139
de Gaulle, Charles, 89
de Havilland Rapide aircraft, 6, 13, 27
Digany, General, 47
Dotan, Ezra, 106–108

E-2C Hawkeye radar early warning aircraft, 153, 165, 175, 183, 185
EAF, *see* Egyptian Air Force
ECM (electronic countermeasure) systems, 109, 114, 118, 123, 129, 130, 137, 141, 142, 148, 151, 180, 187
Egypt:
  air defenses of, 109–110, 112, 113–114, 123–124, 126, 134, 137, 139, 141
  in border conflicts, 32, 64, 65, 71

British support for, 24, 29, 53–54
fedayeen in, 26, 32–33, 35
France and, 34, 35, 36, 41, 45, 46, 48–51
in peace initiatives, 88, 143, 160, 162–163, 186
Soviet aid to, 33, 36, 54, 56, 89, 102, 103–104, 105, 108, 109–110, 111, 113, 132, 137, 140
Syrian cooperation with, 117–118, 154
war losses of, 49, 66, 67, 82–83, 95, 96, 102, 105, 110, 113, 124, 125, 135, 137, 138, 139, 143, 147, 148
see also specific conflicts
Egyptian Air Force (EAF), 7, 22–25, 28–29, 37–38, 61
in 1948 attacks on Israel, 10, 13, 16, 20, 21, 22–24, 25
in Sinai Conflict, 38, 40, 41–43, 45, 46, 50–51
in Six-Day War, 66–67, 68–69, 71, 76, 78, 82, 85, 86
Soviet advisors to, 37, 54, 89, 91, 93, 102, 105
in War of Attrition, 88, 96–100, 103–105, 108–109, 111, 115
in Yom Kippur War, 118–125, 127, 134, 138, 139, 143, 146, 148
Egyptian Air Force Academy, 38
Eilat, 37, 47, 65, 109
Eilat, 41, 88
Eitan, Rafael, 171, 174
Eiton, Colonel, 40–41, 42
EL AL, 94, 137
El Arish, 11, 15, 16, 20, 21, 23, 38, 39, 45, 47, 66, 73, 77, 108, 136
Elazar, David, 78, 84, 139
El Khanka, 103
engines, aircraft, 9, 57, 90, 114–115, 133, 152, 181
Entebbe hijacking, 154–160
Eqron airfield, 9, 21, 39
Eshel, Yehoshua, 5
Etzion Air Base, 167

F-4 Phantoms, 99, 100, 104, 109, 110, 111–112, 114, 116, 120, 125, 135, 137, 141, 144, 145, 147, 152, 160, 174, 175, 178, 179, 185, 187
F-15 Eagles, 152, 164–165, 167, 172, 175, 179, 183, 185
F-16 Fighting Falcons, 152, 167, 168, 175, 179, 181, 185, 187
F-84F fighter-bombers, 39, 45, 48, 49, 51
Faluja, 20, 22
Fatah, El, 102
Fawzi, General, 102
Fayid airfield, 38, 40, 66, 141
FBI (Federal Bureau of Investigation), 15
fedayeen, 26, 32–34, 35
see also terrorists, Palestinian
Fiat G55 fighters, 20, 23, 24
Fouga Magister trainers, 56, 57, 74, 77, 86, 89, 90, 109, 116, 185
France, 27, 28, 29, 30, 31, 34, 53, 54, 181
in Sinai Conflict, 34, 35, 36, 41, 45, 46, 48–51
French Air Force (Armee de l'Air), 32, 36, 39, 46, 49, 54, 57
FROG surface-to-surface missiles, 127, 143, 186
Frouenknech, Alfred, 90

G, Captain, 172
Gaza, 13, 15, 16, 20, 23, 24, 47, 73

Gaza Strip, 30, 37, 46, 47, 48, 49, 50, 73, 89
Gazelle attack helicopters, 175, 180
Gazit, Shlomo, 138–139
Giddi Pass, 73, 135
Gilboa, S., 97–98
Gloster Meteor fighters, 28–29, 32, 35, 37, 38, 43, 50, 51, 55, 56
Gloster Meteor T.7 trainers, 29
Golan Heights, 16, 53, 60, 62, 83–84, 85, 88, 96, 101, 105–108, 115, 117–118, 122, 123, 124, 125–126, 127, 128, 130, 132–133, 139–141, 143
Golani Infantry Brigade, 83–84
Goodlin, Slick, 24
Great Bitter Lake, 35, 94, 137, 141
Great Britain, 5, 14, 24, 29–30, 53, 54, 181
  in Sinai Conflict, 34, 35, 36, 41, 45, 46, 48–51
Green Island fortress, 96
Gulf of Aqaba, 47, 51
Gulf of Eilat, 36
Gulf of Suez, 47, 98, 102, 141
Gur, General, 156

H-3 airfield, 68, 77, 80–82
Habib, Philip, 168
Haddad, Saad, 162
Haganah, 4, 5, 7–10
  arms and aircraft bought by, 6, 8–10, 13–15, 17–18, 19–20, 23
  volunteers recruited by, 6, 8, 14
Haganah Sherut-Avir (Air Service), 5
Haifa, 41, 67, 106, 143
Harpaz, Joseph, 40
Harvard T-6 advanced trainers, 51, 54, 56
Harvard trainers, 7, 15–16, 23, 27, 38
Hatzor airfield, 39, 69, 70
Hawker Hunter fighter-bombers, 56, 61, 63, 67, 68, 77, 80–81, 92, 118
Hawk surface-to-air missiles, 90, 92, 96, 98, 99, 101, 113, 116, 118, 122, 144, 145, 153, 186
Heliopolis, 96
Hennawy, Mustafa Shalaby el-, 96
Herzalia, 14, 21
Hod, Mordechai, 64, 111
Homs refinery, 128, 130, 144
Husseini, Haj Amin el, 4

IAF, *see* Israeli Air Force
IAI Lavi advanced trainers, 181, 185, 186, 187
IAI Scout RPV, 165
Ibrahim Al Awwal, 41
IL-28 light bombers, 31, 36, 37, 38, 48, 56, 61, 67, 73, 91, 118
Inchas airfield, 38, 45, 66, 68, 69
International Symposium on Military Aspects of the Arab-Israeli Conflict (1975), 150
Iraq, 7, 26, 60
  in combined Arab front, 10, 12, 24, 128, 132–133, 140
  military expansion in, 28, 32, 54, 91
  nuclear reactor in, 166–167
Iraqi Air Force, 16, 54, 56, 61
  in Six-Day War, 67–68, 76, 77–78, 86
  in Yom Kippur War, 118, 126, 132, 133, 146, 148
Irbid Heights, 101
Irgun Zvai Leumi, 4
Isdud, 11, 12
Ismailiya, 92, 95, 138, 141
Israel:

in alliance with Britain and France, 34–52, 53, 54
statehood established by, 1, 4, 6, 25
U.S. aid to, 137, 147, 150, 151
see also specific conflicts
Israel Aircraft Industries (IAI), 30, 57, 59, 68, 89–90, 114–115, 152, 165, 181, 185, 186, 187
Israel Defense Forces, 154–168
in counterterrorist activities, 154–160, 161–162, 163–165, 166, 167, 168
high command of, 18, 27
Israeli Air Force (IAF):
air superiority of, 1–2, 30, 50, 53, 74, 85, 99, 104, 129, 141, 143, 144, 150, 185
antiterrorist actions of, 35, 101, 105, 106, 115, 154–160, 161–162, 163–165, 166, 167, 168, 178, 179, 182, 183, 184–185
first fighter mission of, 11–12
foreign volunteers in, 9, 10, 12, 14, 16–17, 19, 20, 21, 22, 24, 25, 26
formation and supply of, 2, 4, 5–6, 8–10, 13–15, 16, 19–20, 23
helicopter force of, 59–60, 74–75, 84, 87, 92, 93, 94, 113, 116, 127, 148, 153, 161, 179, 180, 181
maintenance and support staff in, 56, 61, 62, 66, 127, 148, 187
offensive doctrine ("operational plan") of, 53, 61–62
pilot training in, 27, 28, 29–30, 34, 42–43, 52, 55–56, 58, 60, 62, 68, 150, 151–152, 166, 180, 187
post-Independence expansion of, 27–30
post-Sinai-Conflict expansion of, 54–60, 64
preemptive strikes by, 66–73, 85, 117
in pre-Six-Day-War attacks, 62–64
in Sinai Conflict, 35, 39, 40, 41, 42–45, 46, 47, 48, 50–52
in Six-Day War, 66–71, 76–78, 80–87
support role of, 1–2, 30, 35, 39, 41, 43, 45, 46, 47, 48, 51–52, 53, 74, 76, 77, 78, 85, 89, 109, 113, 127, 128, 129, 135, 143, 146, 151, 152, 179, 181
transport force of, 52, 59, 74, 79, 87, 89, 127, 140, 143, 148, 161, 179, 180, 181
in War of Attrition, 88, 91, 92, 93–116
in War of Independence, 1, 4–25
in Yom Kippur War, 117–148
Israel Military Industries, 72
Italy, 28, 29, 181
Ivry, David, 160, 163, 176, 180

Jaffa, 41
Jebel Ataka, 99
Jerusalem, 4, 6, 10, 16, 76, 79, 160
Jewish Agency, 7, 8
Jezzin, 169
Jordan (Transjordan), 1, 4, 7, 12, 13, 115, 132
in cease-fires, 24, 26, 88, 109, 113
in combined Arab front, 12, 24, 132–133, 140
military expansion in, 28–29, 32, 34, 54, 56, 75–76, 91, 93–94, 115, 185–186

PLO and, 154, 160
Soviet aid to, 54, 56
see also specific conflicts
Jordanian Air Force, 54, 56, 61, 63, 67, 85, 86, 92
Jordanian/Israeli border, 63, 91, 95, 101, 106, 115
Jordan River Valley, 53, 62, 89, 101

Kabrit air base, 40, 41, 45, 66
Kelt air-to-surface missiles, 118
Kemal, Hassan, 96
Kfir fighters, 115, 152, 160, 164–165, 175, 181, 182, 185, 187
Khan Yunis, 73
kibbutzim, 10, 24, 101
Kissinger, Henry, 143
Kosygin, Aleksei, 103, 104
Kuntilla, 39

L-29 Delfin trainers, 139
Lance surface-to-surface missiles, 151
Lapidot, Amos, 181, 183–184, 186
Laskov, Chaim, 27
Latakia naval base, 140
Lebanese Air Force, 56, 61, 77
Lebanese/Israeli border, 95, 101, 106, 149, 168
Lebanon, 1, 167–186
civil war in, 154, 160
in combined Arab front, 24, 26
domestic problems in, 60, 154, 160–165, 167–186
guerrillas in, 91, 93, 105–106, 115
Israeli invasion of, 113, 168–183
PLO and, 154, 160–170, 178, 180–181
see also Operation Peace for Galilee
Lenart, Lou, 10, 11–12
Libyan Air Force, 135, 148
Litani River, 161
Lockheed Constellation transports, 8, 15, 27
Lohamei Herut Yisrael, 4

MacDonald White Paper (1939), 5
Mafraq air base, 67, 69, 101
Mahal, 14, 25
Mann, Maurice, 15
Mansura airfield, 66, 69, 128
Matra air-to-air missiles, 58, 64, 100
Matt, Danny, 74, 75
Mazar, 101
McElroy, John, 24
MD-500/500M Defender helicopters, 152, 180
Meir, Golda, 103, 117
Merchavi, N., 128–129, 132–133, 141–142
Messerschmitt bf 109 fighters, 9, 12, 20
Mi-8 transport helicopters, 122, 139, 140
MiG-15 fighters, 31, 32, 33, 35, 37, 38, 39–40, 41, 43, 45, 50, 54, 56, 91, 92
MiG-17 fighters, 54, 56, 60, 62, 67, 88, 91, 92, 93, 97, 99, 106–108, 118, 119–121, 139
MiG-19 fighters, 61, 62, 64, 67, 68–70, 72, 73, 91
MiG-21 fighters, 62, 63, 64, 67, 68, 77, 91, 92, 94, 95, 96, 99, 100, 104, 106, 111-112, 115, 118, 119, 121, 136, 139, 164–165, 168, 179
MiG-23 Flogger fighters, 165, 168, 169, 179, 183
MiG-25 Foxbat fighters, 168
MiG-29 fighters, 185
Mirage IIIB trainers, 58

Mirage IIIC fighters, 57–58, 61, 62, 63, 64, 68, 72, 76, 77, 80–81, 82, 86, 88, 89, 94, 96, 99, 100, 104, 111–112, 114, 116, 118, 139
Mirage V fighters, 89, 90
Mitla Pass, 35, 37, 39, 40, 41, 42, 43, 50, 52, 73, 78–79, 135
Mosquito reconnaissance aircraft, 22, 24
Mosquito fighter-bombers, 28, 38, 43, 44, 46, 51, 52, 54
Mount Hermon, 83, 106–107, 122, 133, 140, 143
Mystere IVA fighters, 31, 32, 34, 35, 36, 38, 39, 40, 42–43, 45, 47, 50, 51, 52, 54, 60, 61, 62, 67, 72, 77, 82, 86, 89, 97, 109

N, Captain, 118–121, 135–137
Nahariya, 160, 163
Napoi (Labor) party, 7
Narkiss, Uzi, 76
Nasser, Gamal Abdul, 30, 31, 33–34, 36, 46, 54, 64–65, 95, 96, 98, 103, 104, 108, 117
Negev Desert, 18, 19, 62, 64, 166
Nesher (Mirage/Nesher) fighters, 90, 114, 116, 144–145, 147, 185
Netania, 67, 76
Netanyahu, Yonni, 155, 158–159
Netherlands, 27
Nixon, Richard, 103, 104
Noratlas transports, 39, 52, 59, 87, 89, 109, 116, 127
Nord Aviation, 28

101st Fighter Squadron (IAF), 9–10, 12, 14, 15, 17, 20, 21, 22, 24
Offeq (Horizon) I satellite, 186
Operation Babylon, 166–167
Operation Badr, 118
Operation Bolak, 14
Operation Dust, 18–19
Operation Focus, 71
Operation Horev, 23
Operation Kadesh, *see* Sinai Conflict
Operation Litani, 161–162, 163
Operation Musketeer, 36
Operation Peace for Galilee, 168–183
  antiterrorist operations in, 168, 178, 179, 182, 183
  attack on Syrian air defenses in, 170–175, 179
  Israeli forces in, 168–181
  Israeli losses in, 169, 170, 176, 180
  siege of Beirut in, 178–181
  Syrian forces in, 168–181
  Syrian losses in, 168, 170, 176, 177–178, 179, 180
Operation Thunderball, 155–160
Osirak nuclear reactor, 166, 167
Ouragon fighters, 29, 31, 32, 34, 36, 38, 41, 43, 44, 50, 51, 52, 54, 61, 72, 77, 86, 89, 109
OV-ID Mohawk reconnaissance, 153–154, 185

P-51 Mustang fighters, 20, 21–22, 27, 28, 38, 43, 48, 51, 52, 54, 56
Palestine, 4–14
  British control of, 4–5
  Jewish immigration to, 4–5
Palestine Liberation Organization, *see* PLO
Palestinian terrorists, *see* terrorists, Palestinian
Pan African Air Charter Company, 13
paratroops, British, 48
paratroops, Israeli, 39–41, 47, 50, 52, 74–75

202nd Airborne Brigade, 39–40, 41, 47
890 Airborne Battalion, 35
in Mitla Pass interdiction, 35, 39–40, 41, 43
in Six-Day War, 74–75, 78, 79, 83–84, 85, 87
in War of Attrition, 92–93, 94
in Yom Kippur War, 132, 138, 140
peacekeeping forces, UN, 50, 60, 65
peace treaties, 143, 149, 186
Peake, Wayne, 22
Peel Commission report (1937), 4
Peled, Benjamin (Bene), 47, 69, 150–151, 155, 156, 160
pilot training, IAF, 27, 28, 29–30, 34, 42–43, 52, 55–56, 58, 60, 62, 68, 150, 166, 151–152, 166, 180, 187
Pinchas (pilot), 10
Piper Cubs, 13, 39, 40, 50, 51–52, 64, 95
Piper Super Cubs, 55, 56, 60
PLO (Palestine Liberation Organization), 154, 160, 161, 162, 163, 164, 166, 167–168, 169, 170, 175, 178, 179, 181, 183
Popular Front for the Liberation of Palestine, 155
Port Fuad, 48, 49, 88
Port Said, 48, 49, 88, 108, 122, 127, 128, 138

Qabatiya, 79
Qantara, 82, 102, 138
Quneitra, 84, 99

R, Major, 172–174
Rabin, Yitzhak, 183
RAFAEL Armament Development Agency, 100
Rafael Shafrir air-to-air missiles, 100, 144–145, 165, 179
Rafah, 39, 46, 47, 73
Ramat David air base, 16, 18, 39, 67, 76, 127, 143, 173
Ras el Sudr, 128
Ras Gharib, 102
Red Sea, 109, 160
Refidim airfield, 121
refugees, Palestinian, 26, 89
Remez, Aharon, 5, 10, 27
Resolution 242, UN, 88–89
RF-4 reconnaissance aircraft, 116, 165
Riadh, Abdul Moneim, 95
Rogers, William, 109
Royal Air Force (RAF), 5, 6, 22, 24, 28, 37, 45–46, 49
Royal Egyptian Air Force, *see* Egyptian Air Force
Royal Jordanian Air Force, *see* Jordanian Air Force
RPVs (remotely piloted vehicles), 115, 130, 165, 171, 175, 184
Rubenfield, Cy, 10, 12

S, Captain, 164–165
SA-2 surface-to-air missiles, 80, 92, 98, 99, 105, 110, 124, 129, 141, 147, 170, 171, 175
SA-3 surface-to-air missiles, 105, 110, 124, 129, 141, 147, 170, 171, 175
SA-6 surface-to-air missiles, 123, 124, 129, 133, 147, 170, 171, 175
SA-7 Grail homing missiles, 124, 151, 169, 175
Sadat, Anwar, 102, 117, 160, 162
SAF, *see* Syrian Air Force
Sassa, 140
Saudi Arabia, 185, 186
Schwimmer, Adolf (Al) W., 8, 14–15, 30
Schwimmer Aviation Company, 8
Sea of Galilee, 63, 83
Seiqal airfield, 67, 69

Senior, Boris, 13, 21
Shafrir air-to-air missiles, 100, 144–145, 165, 179
Shamir, Shlomo, 8, 27
Shamron, Dan, 155
Shani, Joshua, 155–160
Shapira, Danny, 58
Sharm el Sheikh, 37, 39, 47, 48, 50, 51, 52, 65, 79, 119, 156, 157
Sharon, Ariel, 39, 40–41, 47, 73, 74, 75, 77, 138, 168
Shavit, Yallo, 41–43, 68–71, 101, 125–126
Shouf mountains, 170, 182
Shrike radar-homing missiles, 114, 129, 137, 141, 147, 171, 175
Sidki, General, 73
Sidon, 162, 164, 168, 184
Sikorsky CH-53 heavy-lift helicopters, 102–103, 109, 116, 132, 140, 153, 170
Sikorsky S-58 medium-lift helicopters, 59, 60, 74, 87, 89, 91
Sinai, 35–52, 73, 92
  UN forces in, 60, 64–65
  War of Attrition and, 89, 92, 97, 99, 100, 103, 108
  Yom Kippur War and, 117, 118, 123, 124, 127, 128, 130, 133–139, 141, 143
Sinai Conflict (1956), 35–52
  British and French forces in, 33, 34, 35, 36, 41, 45, 46, 48–52
  causes of, 36–38
  cease-fires in, 36, 49
  EAF in, 38, 40, 41–43, 45, 46, 50–51
  Egyptian armed forces in, 37–38, 40–50
  final phase of, 36, 47–49
  IAF in, 35, 39, 40, 41, 42–45, 46, 47, 48, 50–52
  Israeli losses in, 43, 49, 51
  phase 1 of, 35, 36, 38–45
  phase 2 of, 36, 45–46
  political results of, 53–54
Six-Day War, 66–87
  first day of, 66–67
  second day of, 77–78
  third day of, 78–82
  fourth day of, 82, 83
  fifth day of, 82–84
  sixth day of, 84
  cease-fires in, 79, 82, 83, 84
  EAF in, 66–67, 68–69, 71, 74–79, 82, 85, 86
  Egyptian armed forces in, 74, 77, 78–79, 82–83, 84
  Egyptian losses in, 66, 67, 82–83
  IAF in, 66–71, 76–78, 80–87
  Iraqi Air Force in, 67–68, 76, 77–78, 86
  Israeli armed forces in, 73–74, 76, 77, 78–80, 82, 83–84
  Israeli losses in, 66, 67, 76, 78, 79–80, 83, 84, 89, 95
  Jordan in, 67, 71, 75–76, 78, 79, 84, 85, 86
  Syrian forces in, 67, 69–70, 83–86
Sodky, Mohamed, 38
South Africa, 13, 14
Soviet Air Defense Force, 174
Soviet Union, 36, 50, 54, 89, 102, 103–104, 132, 174, 181
  advisors and technicians from, 37, 54, 89, 91, 93, 102, 105
  aid to Egypt from, 33, 36, 37–38, 54, 56, 89, 102, 103–104, 105, 108, 109–110, 111, 113, 132, 137, 140
  aid to Syria from, 56, 89, 132, 140, 181, 185
  War of Attrition and, 105, 108, 109, 111–112, 113, 115
Spitfire fighters, 7, 9, 10, 12, 14, 17–24, 27, 28

Sterling bombers, 22–23
Straits of Tiran, 49, 65
Stratocruiser transports, 59, 109, 115, 116
SU-7 fighter-bombers, 76, 88, 91, 92, 97, 103, 115, 118, 139
SU-22 fighter-bombers, 179
Sud Aviation, 54, 59
Suez, 88, 92, 102, 122, 138, 141, 142
Suez Canal, 33–35, 49–50, 117
  War of Attrition and, 88, 91–99, 102, 103, 105, 108–113, 115
  Yom Kippur War and, 117, 122, 125, 128, 134–135, 137–138, 139, 141, 143
  see also Sinai Conflict
Super Frelon transport
helicopters, 59–60, 74, 87, 89, 94, 109, 116, 153
Super Mystere fighters, 57, 60, 61, 68–71, 72, 77, 86, 89, 109, 114, 116, 147
Sweden, 28, 31
Syria, 7, 10, 15–16
  air defenses of, 124, 126, 132, 168, 170–175, 178, 181
  in cease-fires, 26, 88, 142–143
  in combined Arab front, 10, 22
  domestic problems in, 60, 154, 160, 161, 163–165
  Israeli invasion of, 75, 83–84, 95–96, 117
  in Lebanese domestic conflict, 154, 160, 161, 163–165, 181, 182, 186
  military expansion in, 28, 29, 32, 34, 91, 93–94, 105–106, 115
  Soviet aid to, 104, 105–106, 115, 132
  see also specific conflicts
Syrian Air Force (SAF), 54, 56, 61, 62, 64, 161, 163–165, 166, 168, 183–186
  in Six-Day War, 67, 69–70, 83–86
  in War of Attrition, 106–108, 115–116
  in Yom Kippur War, 118, 122, 126, 127, 132, 133, 140–141, 143, 146, 148
Syrian/Israeli border, 60, 64, 83, 91, 94, 95, 101, 106, 115–116

T-4 airfield, 67
Tadiran Mastiff RPV, 165
Tal, Israel, 73, 74, 77
Tanta airfield, 136
Tel Aviv, 1, 7, 10, 11, 13, 76, 159
Teledyne Ryan Firebee reconnaissance drones, 115, 130
Tel Sharms, 132
terrorists, Palestinian, 154, 155, 178, 180, 185
  in attacks on Israel, 32–34, 60, 62, 63, 106, 115, 154, 166, 168, 170, 180
  camps and bases of, 26, 32, 91, 93, 94, 95, 101, 106, 115, 154, 163, 164, 169, 184
  IAF attacks on, 32–34, 101, 105, 106, 115, 154–160, 161–162, 163–165, 166, 167, 168, 178, 179, 182, 183, 184–185
Tolkovsky, Dan, 29–30, 38, 52, 55, 56
Transjordan, *see* Jordan
Tsuk, Yosef, 40
TU-16 Badger medium bombers, 61, 67, 72, 76, 91, 118
Tunisia, 183

United Nations (UN), 5, 6, 47, 49, 50, 53, 79, 82, 83, 84, 88, 96, 141, 162
  peacekeeping forces of, 50, 60, 65, 162, 182
  Resolution 242 of, 88–89

United States, 13, 14, 23, 27, 31, 50, 103–104, 114, 137, 150, 151, 152, 162–163, 165, 181
  aid to Israel from, 137, 147, 150, 151
United States Air Force (USAF), 137, 145
United States Navy, 182, 185

Vampire fighter-bombers, 29, 32, 33, 34, 37, 38, 39, 41–43, 45, 50
Vautour fighter-bombers, 54–55, 67–68, 72, 77, 79, 80–82, 86 89, 109
Vickerman, Robert, 15

War of Attrition, 88–116
  cease-fires in, 113
  EAF in, 88, 96–100, 103–105, 108–109, 111, 115
  Egyptian armed forces in, 89, 92, 95, 108, 109–110, 113
  Egyptian losses in, 95, 96, 102, 105, 110, 113
  IAF in, 88, 91, 92, 93–116
  Iraqi forces in, 91
  Israeli armed forces in, 88, 89, 91, 92, 105–106, 115
  Israeli counterterrorist actions in, 91, 94, 95, 101, 105–106, 115
  Israeli losses in, 95, 96, 97, 101–102, 104, 112, 116
  SAF in, 106–108, 115–116
  Soviet forces in, 105, 108, 109, 111–112, 113, 115
  Syrian losses in, 95, 106, 113, 115–116
  War of Independence, 6–7, 10–25
  Arab invasion forces in, 7–8, 10
  armistice agreement in, 22, 24, 26, 30
  cease-fires in, 14, 15, 17, 21, 22, 24
  Egypt in, 6–7, 11–13, 16, 20–21, 22, 23–24
  IAF in, 1, 4–25
  Operation Dust in, 18–19
  Operation Horev in, 23–24
  Syrian forces in, 15–16, 22
Weizman, Ezer, 10, 12, 56, 58, 64, 90
West Bank, 63, 69, 79, 85, 89, 91, 95, 101, 106, 115

Yak-II trainers, 37, 38
Yariv, Aaron, 130
Yoeli, Aharon, 32–33
Yoeli, Amir, 161–162, 177
Yoffe, Avraham, 47, 73, 77
Yom Kippur, 118
Yom Kippur War, 118–148
  Agronat Report on, 149
  cease-fires in, 139, 140, 141, 142–143
  combined Arab forces in, 118, 124, 125, 126, 127, 133, 135, 139, 140, 142, 143, 144, 145, 146, 148
  EAF in, 118–125, 127, 134, 138, 139, 143, 146, 148
  Egyptian armed forces in, 118, 122–123, 127, 134, 137–139, 141, 142, 143
  Egyptian losses in, 124, 125, 135, 137, 138, 139, 143, 147, 148
  final phase of, 118, 137–142
  first phase of, 118–130
  IAF in, 117–148
  invasion of Egypt in, 137–139, 141
  Iraqi Air Force in, 118, 126, 132, 133, 146, 148
  Iraqi losses in, 148
  Israeli armed forces in, 117, 122–123, 125–128, 130, 132–134, 135, 137–143

Israeli losses in, 122, 124, 125, 126–127, 128, 131, 133, 134, 135, 140, 142, 143, 145, 147, 148, 150
Israeli paratroops in, 132, 138, 140
lessons learned from, 149–151, 153, 174, 179
SAF in, 118, 122, 126, 127, 132, 133, 140–141, 143, 146, 148
second phase of, 118, 130–137
Syrian armed forces in, 117–118, 122, 123, 125, 126, 127, 133, 140, 143
Syrian losses in, 124, 126, 131, 140, 141, 143, 147, 148
Yuvarov, Yensery S., 174

Zohar, Ben-Zion, 78

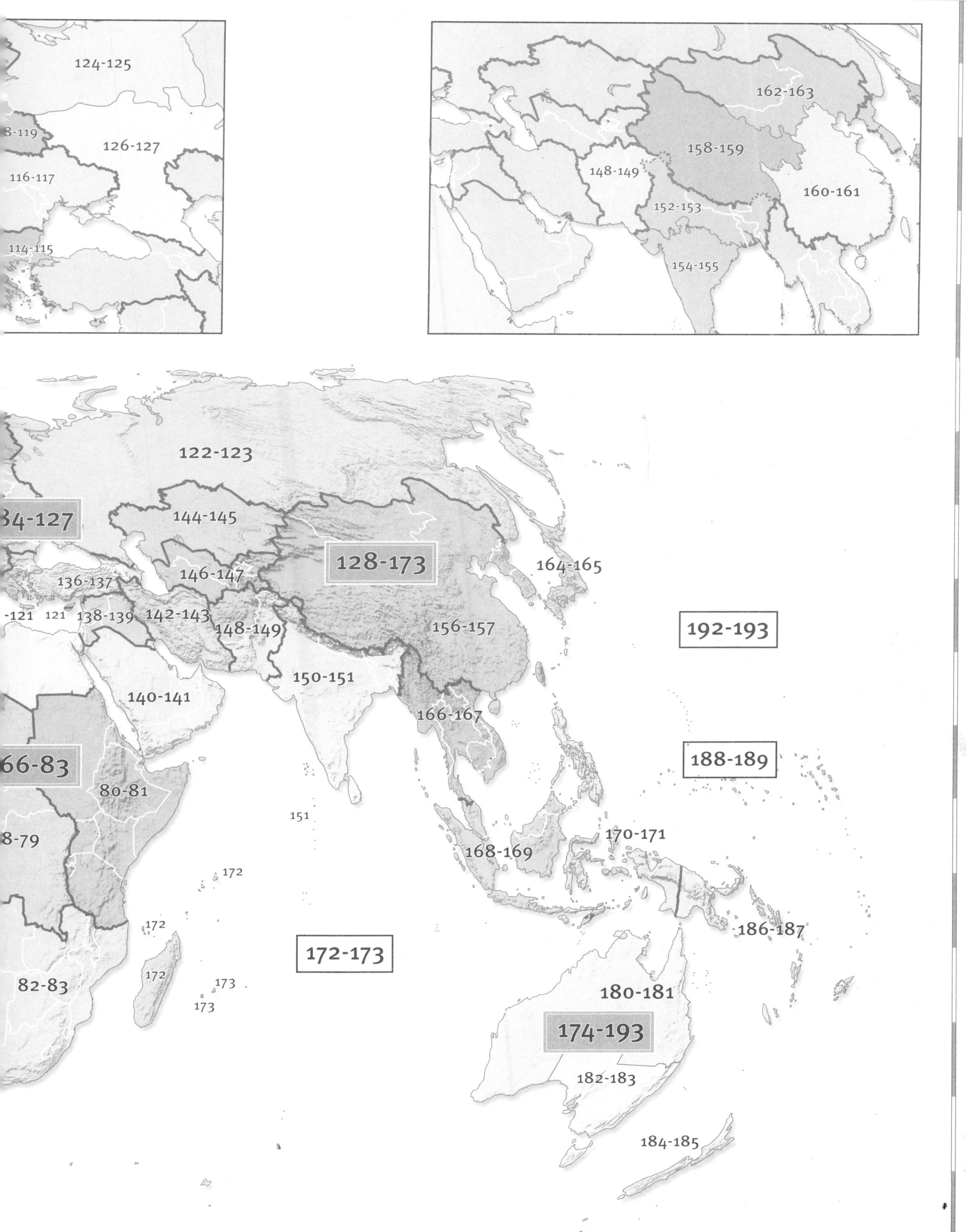
124-125
126-127
116-117
114-115
162-163
158-159
148-149
160-161
152-153
154-155
122-123
144-145
128-173
164-165
146-147
136-137
121
138-139
142-143
148-149
156-157
192-193
150-151
140-141
166-167
188-189
80-81
151
170-171
168-169
172
172
186-187
172-173
172
173
173
180-181
82-83
174-193
182-183
184-185

DORLING KINDERSLEY

TRAVELLER'S ATLAS

DK

A Dorling Kindersley Book

LONDON, NEW YORK, MUNICH, MELBOURNE, DELHI

FOR THE FIRST EDITION

WRITTEN AND EDITED BY
Cambridge International Reference on Current Affairs (CIRCA)

PROJECT MANAGER
Catherine Jagger

EDITORS
Roger East • Chris Jagger

RESEARCH AND EDITORIAL TEAM
John Coggins • Lawrence Joffe • Richard Naisby •
Carina O'Reilly • Carolyn Postgate • Elizabeth Postgate • Richard J Thomas

TEXT LAYOUT
Elizabeth Postgate

DESIGN
Nicola Liddiard

PICTURE RESEARCH
Louise Thomas

DORLING KINDERSLEY CARTOGRAPHY

EDITOR-IN-CHIEF
Andrew Heritage

SENIOR CARTOGRAPHIC MANAGER
David Roberts

CARTOGRAPHERS
Roger Bullen • Simon Mumford • Rob Stokes • Iorwerth Watkins

SENIOR DIGITAL CARTOGRAPHER
Phil Rowles

PRODUCTION
Wendy Penn

First published in Great Britain in 2005 by Dorling Kindersley Limited, 80 Strand, London WC2R 0RL.

see our complete catalogue at
www.dk.com

A CIP catalogue record for this book is available from the British Library.
ISBN-13: 978-1-4053-1253-0
ISBN-10: 1-4053-1253-X

Printed and bound by Star Standard in Singapore.

INTRODUCTION

Travel, whether for work, or pleasure, or sheer adventure (and often a mixture of all three) is the fastest-growing industry on our planet. Information about travel, how to get there, destinations, sights, activities and detailed listings of recommended restaurants, shops and hotels cascade daily out of our newspapers, mobile phones and on-line accounts. But very few of these information providers set the experience and opportunities of travel in an informative and illuminating global context. Only an atlas can achieve this.

The travel industry has transformed our world in many ways, for good or ill in equal balance. In providing wealth to developing countries it has sometimes eroded what is special or unique about them. In the developed world it has frequently transformed the domain of the few into the playground of the undiscriminating many. Nevertheless, we are all more mobile, and seek to explore our world – and are enabled to do it – in a way unenvisioned by our forebears.

The DK Traveller's Atlas combines two innovative aspects of DK's publishing catalogue in recent years – the unprecedented success of the DK Eyewitness Travel Guides with their winning formula, "The Guides That Show You What Others Only Tell You", and the DK World Atlas range, products which have broken the traditional atlas publishing mould by turning mere books of maps into colourful geographical experiences, books which show you what a place is like, rather than just where it is.

Detailed mapping drawn from DK's authoritative databases provides unparalled reference for planning any holiday or excursion from Yorkshire to the Yucatán, and is complemented by stunning photography and a range of suggested activities for destinations as varied as New England and the New Hebrides. While all the information and recommendations are made in good faith from a range of seasoned travellers and exploration experts, we must stress that the DK Traveller's Atlas is designed as a planning resource only – it is not a replacement for more detailed research once a choice of destination has been made. Although today none of our maps say "Here be dragons", hazards there may be.

Nevertheless, our World is our home, and it is there for us to enjoy.

Bon Voyage

Contents

Introduction ... v

Contents & Key to Regional Maps ... vi–vii

The Physical World ... viii–ix

The Global Climate ... x–xi

The Political World ... xii–xiii

Flags of the World ... xiv–xv

Health Precautions ... xvi–xvii

Atlas of the World

North America

North America ... xviii–1

Physical North America ... 2–3

Political North America ... 4–5

North American Activities ... 6–7

Canada ... 8–9

Canada: Western Provinces ... 10–11
Alberta, British Columbia, Manitoba, Saskatchewan, Yukon

Canada: Eastern Provinces ... 12–13
New Brunswick, Newfoundland & Labrador, Nova Scotia, Ontario, Prince Edward Island, Québec, St Pierre & Miquelon

Southeastern Canada ... 14–15
Southern Ontario, Southern Québec

United States of America ... 16–17

USA: Northeastern States ... 18–19
Connecticut, Maine, Massachussetts, New Hampshire, New Jersey, New York, Pennsylvania, Rhode Island, Vermont

USA: Mid-Eastern States ... 20–21
Delaware, District of Columbia, Kentucky, Maryland, North Carolina, South Carolina, Tennessee, Virginia, West Virginia

USA: Southern States ... 22–23
Alabama, Florida, Georgia, Louisiana, Mississippi

USA: Texas ... 24–25

USA: South Midwestern States ... 26–27
Arkansas, Kansas, Missouri, Oklahoma

USA: North Midwestern States ... 28–29
Iowa, Minnesota, Nebraska, North Dakota, South Dakota

USA: Great Lakes States ... 30–31
Illinois, Indiana, Michigan, Ohio, Wisconsin

USA: North Mountain States ... 32–33
Idaho, Montana, Oregon, Washington, Wyoming

USA: California & Nevada ... 34–35

USA: South Mountain States ... 36–37
Arizona, Colorado, New Mexico, Utah

USA: Hawai'i & Alaska ... 38–39

Mexico ... 40–41

Central America ... 42–43
Belize, Costa Rica, El Salvador, Guatemala, Honduras, Nicaragua, Panama

The Caribbean ... 44–45
Anguilla, Antigua & Barbuda, Aruba, Bahamas, Barbados, British Virgin Islands, Cayman Islands, Cuba, Dominica, Dominican Republic, Grenada, Guadeloupe, Haiti, Jamaica, Martinique, Montserrat, Navassa Island, Netherlands Antilles, Puerto Rico, St Kitts & Nevis, St Lucia, St Vincent & the Grenadines, Trinidad & Tobago, Turks & Caicos Islands, Virgin Islands (US)

South America

South America ... 46–47

Physical South America ... 48–49

Political South America ... 50–51

South American Activities ... 52–53

Northern South America ... 54–55
Colombia, French Guiana, Guyana, Surinam, Venezuela

Western South America ... 56–57
Bolivia, Ecuador, Peru

Brazil ... 58–59

Eastern South America ... 60–61
Southeast Brazil, Northeast Argentina, Uruguay

Southern South America ... 62–63
Argentina, Chile, Paraguay

The Atlantic Ocean ... 64–65

Africa

Africa ... 66–67

Physical Africa ... 68–69

Political Africa ... 70–71

African Activities ... 72–73

North Africa ... 74–75
Algeria, Egypt, Libya, Morocco, Tunisia, Western Sahara

West Africa ... 76–77
Benin, Burkina, Cape Verde, Gambia, Ghana, Guinea, Guinea-Bissau, Ivory Coast, Liberia, Mali, Mauritania, Niger, Nigeria, Senegal, Sierra Leone, Togo

Central Africa ... 78–79
Cameroon, Central African Republic, Chad, Congo, Dem. Rep. Congo, Equatorial Guinea, Gabon, Sao Tome & Principe

East Africa ... 80–81
Burundi, Djibouti, Eritrea, Ethiopia, Kenya, Rwanda, Somalia, Sudan, Tanzania, Uganda

Southern Africa ... 82–83
Angola, Botswana, Lesotho, Malawi, Mozambique, Namibia, South Africa, Swaziland, Zambia, Zimbabwe

Europe

Europe ... 84–85

Physical Europe ... 86–87

Political Europe ... 88–89

European Activities ... 90–91

Scandinavia, Finland & Iceland ... 92–93
Denmark, Finland, Iceland, Norway, Svalbard, Sweden

Southern Scandinavia ... 94–95
Denmark, Faeroe Islands, Southern Norway, Southern Sweden

The British Isles ... 96–97
Channel Islands, Isle of Man, Ireland, United Kingdom

The Low Countries ... 98–99
Belgium, Luxembourg, Netherlands

Germany ... 100–101

France ... 102–103
France, Monaco

The Iberian Peninsula ... 104–105
Andorra, Gibraltar, Portugal, Spain

The Italian Peninsula ... 106–107
Italy, San Marino, Vatican City

The Alpine States ... 108–109
Austria, Liechtenstein, Slovenia, Switzerland

Central Europe ... 110–111
Czech Republic, Hungary, Poland, Slovakia

Southeast Europe ... 112–113
Albania, Bosnia & Herzegovina, Croatia, Macedonia, Serbia & Montenegro (Yugoslavia)

Bulgaria & Greece ... 114–115
(including European Turkey)

Romania, Moldova & Ukraine ... 116–117

The Baltic States & Belarus 118–119
Belarus, Estonia, Latvia, Lithuania, Kaliningrad

The Mediterranean 120–121

The Russian Federation 122–123

Northern European Russia 124–125

Southern European Russia 126–127

Asia

Asia 128–129

Physical Asia 130–131

Political Asia 132–133

Asian Activities 134–135

Turkey & the Caucasus 136–137
Armenia, Azerbaijan, Georgia, Turkey

The Near East 138–139
Iraq, Israel, Jordan, Lebanon, Syria

The Arabian Peninsula 140–141
Bahrain, Kuwait, Oman, Qatar, Saudi Arabia, United Arab Emirates, Yemen

Iran & the Gulf States 142–143
Bahrain, Iran, Kuwait, Qatar, United Arab Emirates

Kazakhstan 144–145

Central Asia 146–147
Kyrgyzstan, Tajikistan, Turkmenistan, Uzbekistan

Afghanistan & Pakistan 148–149

South Asia 150–151
Bangladesh, Bhutan, India, Maldives, Nepal, Pakistan, Sri Lanka

Northern India & the Himalayan States 152–153
Bangladesh, Bhutan, Nepal, Northern India

Southern India & Sri Lanka 154–155

Mainland East Asia 156–157
China, Mongolia, North Korea, South Korea, Taiwan

Western China 158–159

Eastern China 160–161
Eastern China, Taiwan

Northeastern China, Mongolia & Korea 162–163
Mongolia, Northeastern China, North Korea, South Korea

Japan 164–165

Mainland Southeast Asia 166–167
Burma, Cambodia, Laos, Paracel Islands, Philippines, Spratly Islands, Thailand, Vietnam

Western Maritime Southeast Asia 168–169
Brunei, Indonesia, Malaysia, Singapore

Eastern Maritime Southeast Asia 170–171
East Timor, Indonesia, Philippines

The Indian Ocean 172–173

Australasia & Oceania

Australasia & Oceania 174–175

Political Australasia & Oceania .. 176–177

Australasian & Oceanian Activities 178–179

Australia 180–181

Southeast Australia 182–183
New South Wales, South Australia, Tasmania, Victoria

New Zealand 184–185

Melanesia 186–187
Papua New Guinea, Fiji, Solomon Islands, Vanuatu, New Caledonia

Micronesia 188–189
Guam, Marshall Islands, Micronesia, Nauru, Northern Mariana Islands, Palau, Wake Island

Polynesia 190–191
Cook Islands, Easter Island, French Polynesia, Kiribati, Niue, Pitcairn Islands, Tokelau, Tuvalu, Wallis & Futuna

The Pacific Ocean 192–193

Antarctica 194–195

The Arctic 196–197

Index–Gazetteer

The Time Zones/World Languages & Religions 198–199

Factfile 200–209

Vaccination Chart 210–211

Index 212–349

Credits/Acknowledgements 350

Key to Regional Maps

Physical Features

ELEVATION

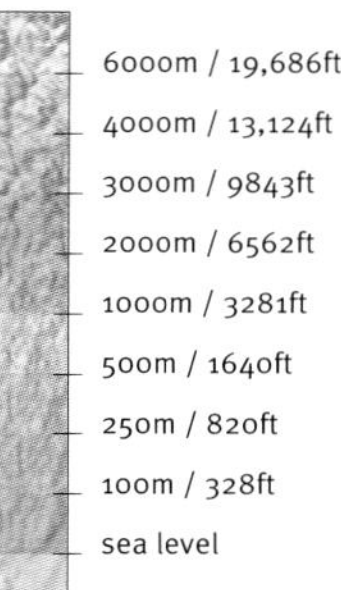
6000m / 19,686ft
4000m / 13,124ft
3000m / 9843ft
2000m / 6562ft
1000m / 3281ft
500m / 1640ft
250m / 820ft
100m / 328ft
sea level
below sea level

- elevation above sea level (mountain height)
- volcano
- pass
- elevation below sea level (depression depth)

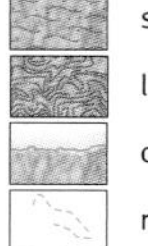

- sand desert
- lava flow
- coastline
- reef
- atoll

SEA DEPTH

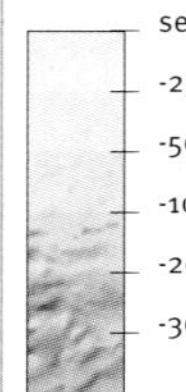
sea level
-250m / -820ft
-500m / -1640ft
-1000m / -3281ft
-2000m / -6562ft
-3000m / -9843ft

- seamount / guyot symbol
- undersea spot depth

Drainage Features

- main river
- secondary river
- tertiary river
- minor river
- main seasonal river
- secondary seasonal river
- canal
- waterfall
- rapids
- dam
- perennial lake
- seasonal lake
- perennial salt lake
- seasonal salt lake
- reservoir
- salt flat / salt pan
- marsh / salt marsh
- mangrove
- wadi
- spring / waterhole / oasis

Ice Features

- ice cap / sheet
- ice shelf
- glacier / snowfield
- summer pack ice limit
- winter pack ice limit

Communications

- motorway / highway
- motorway / highway (under construction)
- major road
- minor road
- tunnel (road)
- main line
- minor line
- tunnel (rail)
- international airport

Borders

- full international border
- undefined international border
- disputed de facto border
- disputed territorial claim border
- indication of country extent (Pacific only)
- indication of dependent territory extent (Pacific only)
- demarcation/ cease fire line
- autonomous / federal region border
- 2nd order internal administrative border
- 3rd order internal administrative border

Settlements

- built up area

settlement population symbols

- more than 5 million
- 1 million to 5 million
- 500,000 to 1 million
- 100,000 to 500,000
- 50,000 to 100,000
- 10,000 to 50,000
- fewer than 10,000
- country/dependent territory capital city
- autonomous / federal region / 2nd order internal administrative centre
- 3rd order internal administrative centre

Miscellaneous Features

- ancient wall
- site of interest
- scientific station

Graticule Features

- lines of latitude and longitude / Equator
- Tropics / Polar circles
- degrees of longitude / latitude

The Physical World

The Earth's surface is constantly being transformed: it is uplifted, folded and faulted by tectonic forces; weathered and eroded by wind, water and ice. Sometimes change is dramatic, the spectacular results of earthquakes or floods. More often it is a slow process lasting millions of years. A physical map of the world represents a snapshot of the ever-evolving architecture of the Earth. This terrain map shows the whole surface of the Earth, both above and below the sea.

Longest Rivers

Nile (NE Africa)	4,160 miles	(6,695 km)
Amazon (South America)	4,049 miles	(6,516 km)
Yangtze (China)	3,915 miles	(6,299 km)
Mississippi/Missouri (USA)	3,710 miles	(5,969 km)
Ob'-Irtysh (Russian Federation)	3,461 miles	(5,570 km)
Yellow River (China)	3,395 miles	(5,464 km)
Congo (Central Africa)	2,900 miles	(4,667 km)
Mekong (Southeast Asia)	2,749 miles	(4,425 km)
Lena (Russian Federation)	2,734 miles	(4,400 km)
Mackenzie (Canada)	2,640 miles	(4,250 km)
Yenisey (Russian Federation)	2,541 miles	(4,090 km)

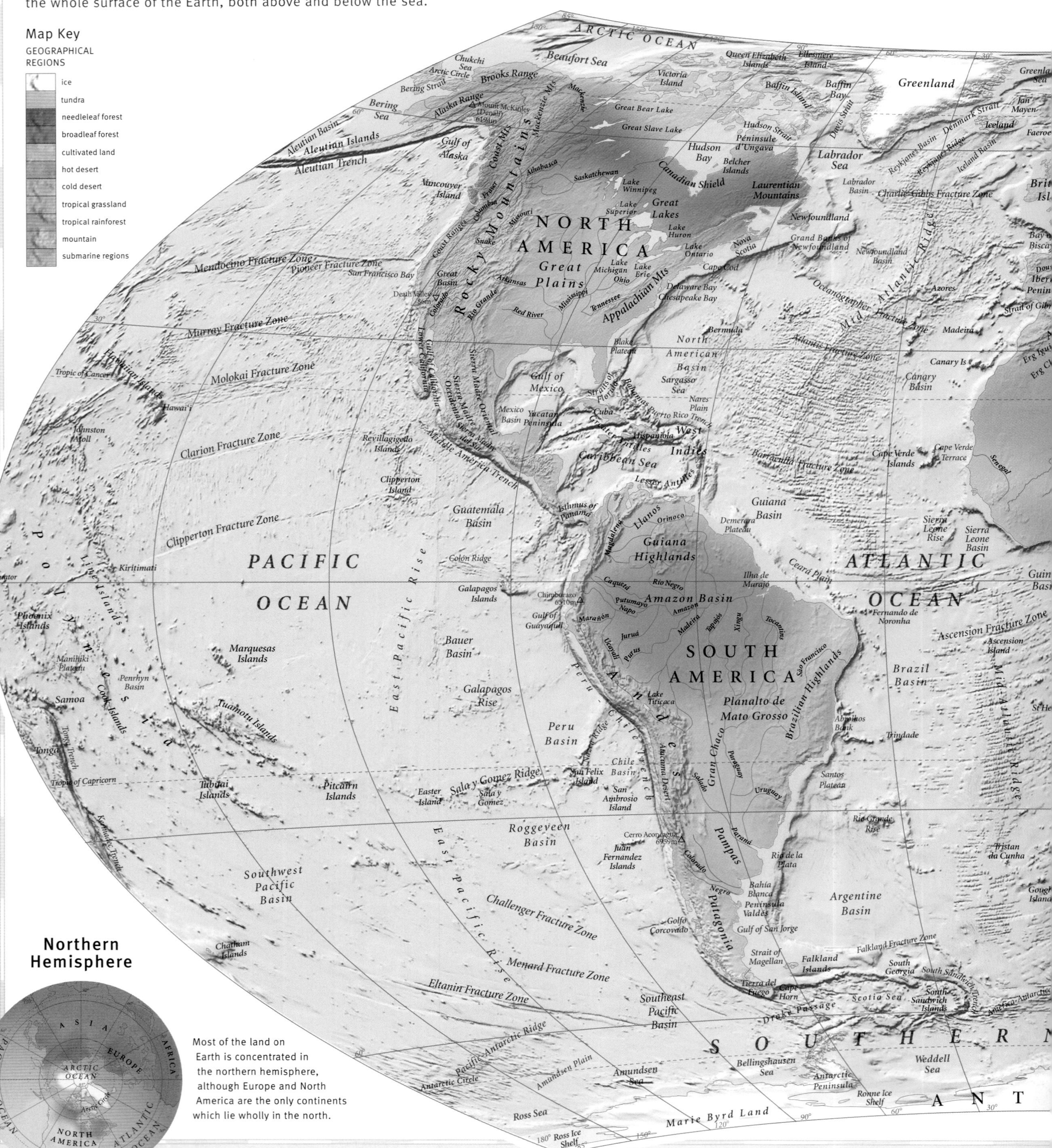
Map Key
GEOGRAPHICAL REGIONS
ice
tundra
needleleaf forest
broadleaf forest
cultivated land
hot desert
cold desert
tropical grassland
tropical rainforest
mountain
submarine regions
ARCTIC OCEAN
Beaufort Sea
Chukchi Sea
Arctic Circle
Brooks Range
Bering Strait
Bering Sea
Alaska Range
Aleutian Basin
Aleutian Islands
Aleutian Trench
Gulf of Alaska
Victoria Island
Queen Elizabeth Islands
Ellesmere Island
Baffin Island
Baffin Bay
Davis Strait
Greenland
Greenland Sea
Jan Mayen
Denmark Strait
Iceland
Great Bear Lake
Great Slave Lake
Hudson Strait
Hudson Bay
Belcher Islands
Canadian Shield
Laurentian Mountains
Labrador Sea
Labrador Basin
Reykjanes Basin
Reykjanes Ridge
Iceland Basin
Charlie-Gibbs Fracture Zone
Vancouver Island
Coast Mts
Rocky Mountains
Mackenzie Mts
Athabasca
Saskatchewan
Lake Winnipeg
Lake Superior
Great Lakes
Lake Huron
Lake Michigan
Lake Erie
Lake Ontario
NORTH AMERICA
Great Plains
Newfoundland
Nova Scotia
Grand Banks of Newfoundland
Newfoundland Basin
Cape Cod
Appalachian Mts
Delaware Bay
Chesapeake Bay
Mendocino Fracture Zone
Pioneer Fracture Zone
San Francisco Bay
Great Basin
Death Valley
Arkansas
Red River
Mississippi
Tennessee
Rio Grande
Colorado
Murray Fracture Zone
Bermuda
North American Basin
Blake Plateau
Sargasso Sea
Nares Plain
Mid-Atlantic Ridge
Oceanographer Fracture Zone
Atlantis Fracture Zone
Azores
Madeira
Canary Is
Canary Basin
Tropic of Cancer
Hawaiian Islands
Hawai'i
Molokai Fracture Zone
Gulf of California
Sierra Madre Occidental
Sierra Madre Oriental
Gulf of Mexico
Mexico Basin
Yucatan Peninsula
Straits of Florida
Bahamas
Cuba
Puerto Rico Trench
Hispaniola
West Indies
Greater Antilles
Caribbean Sea
Lesser Antilles
Johnston Atoll
Clarion Fracture Zone
Revillagigedo Islands
Middle America Trench
Clipperton Island
Barracuda Fracture Zone
Cape Verde Islands
Cape Verde Terrace
Senegal
Clipperton Fracture Zone
Guatemala Basin
Isthmus of Panama
Llanos
Orinoco
Guiana Highlands
Demerara Plateau
Guiana Basin
Sierra Leone Rise
Sierra Leone Basin
Kiritimati
Line Islands
Equator
PACIFIC OCEAN
Colon Ridge
Galapagos Islands
Chimborazo 6310m
Gulf of Guayaquil
Caqueta
Rio Negro
Putumayo
Napo
Amazon Basin
Amazon
Marañon
Ilha de Marajo
Ceara Plain
ATLANTIC OCEAN
Fernando de Noronha
Ascension Fracture Zone
Ascension Island
Phoenix Islands
Manihiki Plateau
Marquesas Islands
Bauer Basin
East Pacific Rise
Juruá
Purus
Madeira
Tapajós
Xingu
Tocantins
São Francisco
SOUTH AMERICA
Brazilian Highlands
Brazil Basin
Penrhyn Basin
Samoa
Cook Islands
Polynesia
Tuamotu Islands
Galapagos Rise
Peru Basin
Peru-Chile Trench
Andes
Lake Titicaca
Planalto de Mato Grosso
Abrolhos Bank
Trindade
Tonga
Tonga Trench
Tropic of Capricorn
Tubuai Islands
Pitcairn Islands
Easter Island
Sala y Gomez Ridge
San Felix Island
Chile Basin
San Ambrosio Island
Atacama Desert
Gran Chaco
Paraguay
Salado
Uruguay
Santos Plateau
Rio Grande Rise
Kermadec Trench
Roggeveen Basin
Cerro Aconcagua 6959m
Juan Fernandez Islands
Pampas
Paraná
Rio de la Plata
Tristan da Cunha
Colorado
Southwest Pacific Basin
Negro
Bahía Blanca
Península Valdés
Patagonia
Argentine Basin
Gough Island
Challenger Fracture Zone
Golfo Corcovado
Gulf of San Jorge
Chatham Islands
Menard Fracture Zone
Strait of Magellan
Falkland Islands
Falkland Fracture Zone
South Georgia
Eltanin Fracture Zone
Tierra del Fuego
Cape Horn
Drake Passage
Scotia Sea
South Sandwich Islands
South Sandwich Trench
Southeast Pacific Basin
Pacific-Antarctic Ridge
SOUTHERN
Antarctic Circle
Amundsen Plain
Amundsen Sea
Bellingshausen Sea
Antarctic Peninsula
Weddell Sea
Ronne Ice Shelf
ANT
Ross Sea
Ross Ice Shelf
Marie Byrd Land
Northern Hemisphere
ASIA
EUROPE
AFRICA
ARCTIC OCEAN
Arctic Circle
PACIFIC OCEAN
ATLANTIC OCEAN
NORTH AMERICA
Tropic of Cancer

Most of the land on Earth is concentrated in the northern hemisphere, although Europe and North America are the only continents which lie wholly in the north.

Highest Waterfalls

Angel (Venezuela)	3,212 ft	(979 m)
Tugela (South Africa)	3,110 ft	(948 m)
Utigard (Norway)	2,625 ft	(800 m)
Mongefossen (Norway)	2,539 ft	(774 m)
Mtarazi (Zimbabwe)	2,500 ft	(762 m)
Yosemite (USA)	2,425 ft	(739 m)
Ostre Mardola Foss (Norway)	2,156 ft	(657 m)
Tyssestrengane (Norway)	2,119 ft	(646 m)
***Cuquenan** (Venezuela)	2,001 ft	(610 m)
Sutherland (New Zealand)	1,903 ft	(580 m)
***Kjellfossen** (Norway)	1,841 ft	(561 m)

** indicates that the total height is a single leap*

Highest Mountains
(HEIGHT ABOVE SEA LEVEL)

Everest	29,035 ft	(8,850 m)
K2	28,253 ft	(8,611 m)
Kanchenjunga I	28,210 ft	(8,598 m)
Makalu I	27,767 ft	(8,463 m)
Cho Oyu	26,907 ft	(8,201 m)
Dhaulagiri I	26,796 ft	(8,167 m)
Manaslu I	26,783 ft	(8,163 m)
Nanga Parbat I	26,661 ft	(8,126 m)
Annapurna I	26,547 ft	(8,091 m)
Gasherbrum I	26,471 ft	(8,068 m)

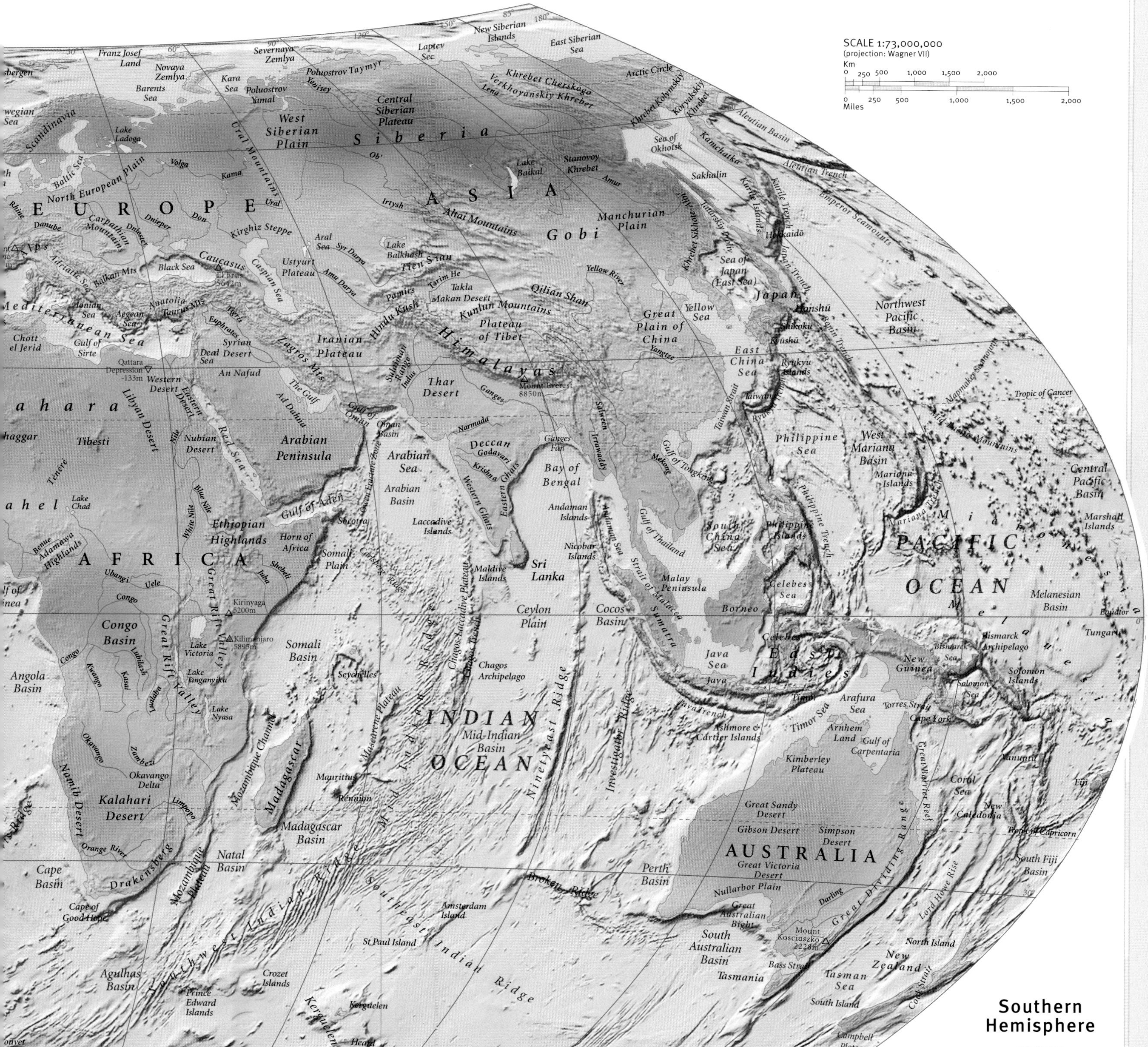

SCALE 1:73,000,000
(projection: Wagner VII)

Southern Hemisphere

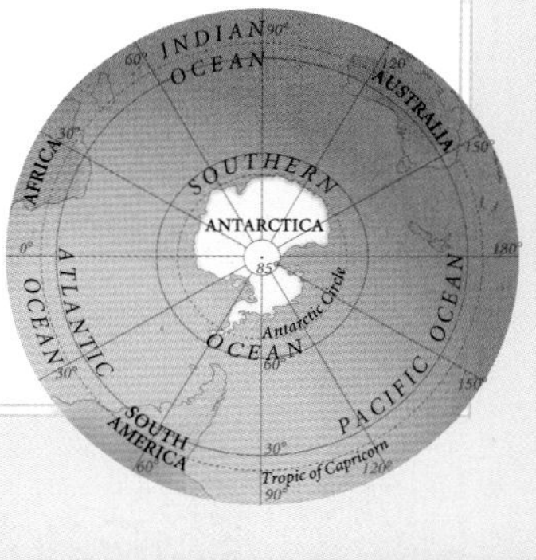

Oceans dominate the southern hemisphere. Australia and Antarctica are the only continental landmasses which lie entirely in the south.

The Global Climate

The Earth's climatic types consist of stable patterns of weather conditions averaged out over a long period of time. Different climates are categorized according to particular combinations of temperature and humidity. By contrast, weather consists of short-term fluctuations in wind, temperature and humidity conditions. Different climates are determined by latitude, altitude, the prevailing wind and circulation of ocean currents. Longer-term changes in climate, such as global warming or the onset of ice ages, are punctuated by shorter-term events which comprise the day-to-day weather of a region, such as frontal depressions, hurricanes and blizzards.

The Earth is currently in a warm phase between ice ages. Warmer temperatures result in higher sea levels as more of the polar ice caps melt. Most of the world's population lives near coasts, so any changes which might cause sea levels to rise, could have a potentially disastrous impact.

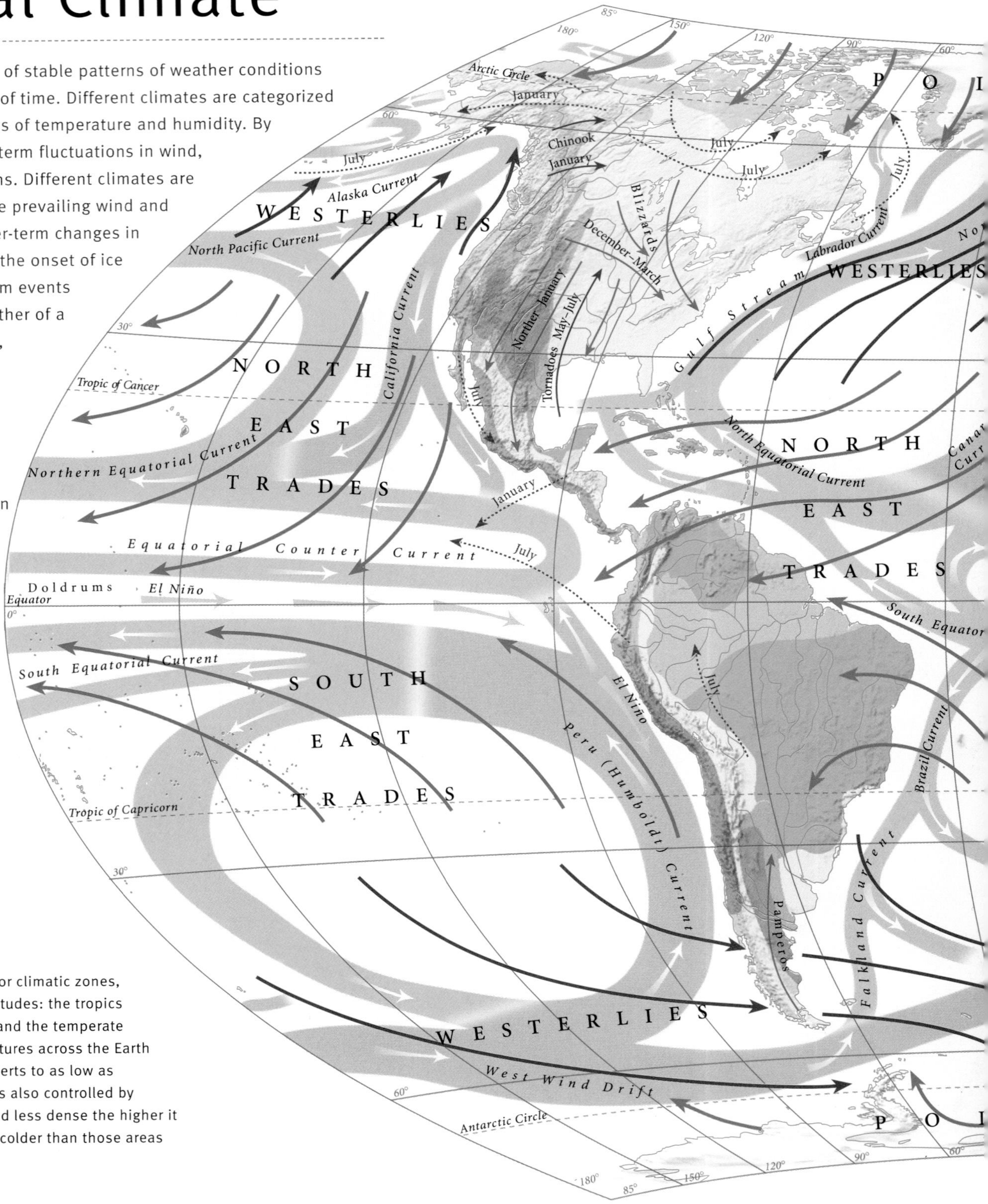

Temperature

The world can be divided into three major climatic zones, stretching like large belts across the latitudes: the tropics which are warm; the cold polar regions and the temperate zones which lie between them. Temperatures across the Earth range from above 30°C (86°F) in the deserts to as low as -55°C (-70°F) at the poles. Temperature is also controlled by altitude; because air becomes cooler and less dense the higher it gets, mountainous regions are typically colder than those areas which are at, or close to, sea level.

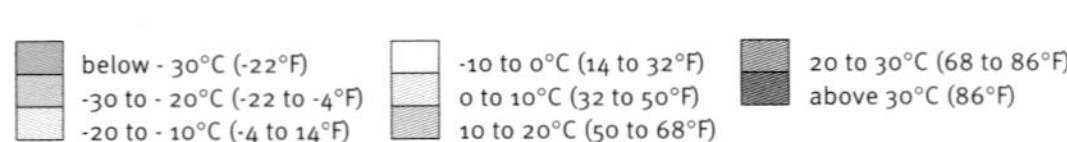
below - 30°C (-22°F)
-30 to - 20°C (-22 to -4°F)
-20 to - 10°C (-4 to 14°F)
-10 to 0°C (14 to 32°F)
0 to 10°C (32 to 50°F)
10 to 20°C (50 to 68°F)
20 to 30°C (68 to 86°F)
above 30°C (86°F)

Average January temperatures

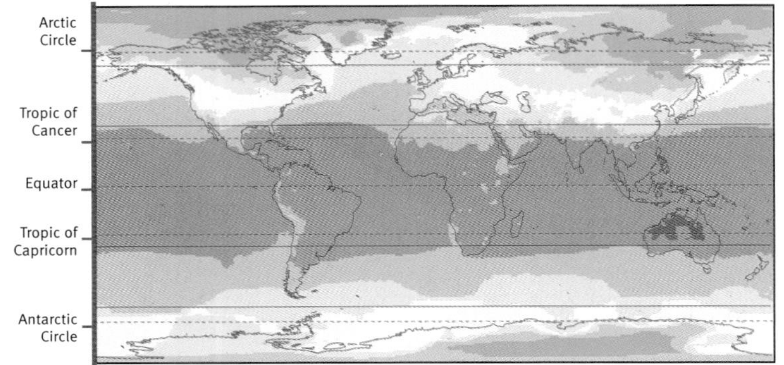
Arctic Circle
Tropic of Cancer
Equator
Tropic of Capricorn
Antarctic Circle

Average July temperatures

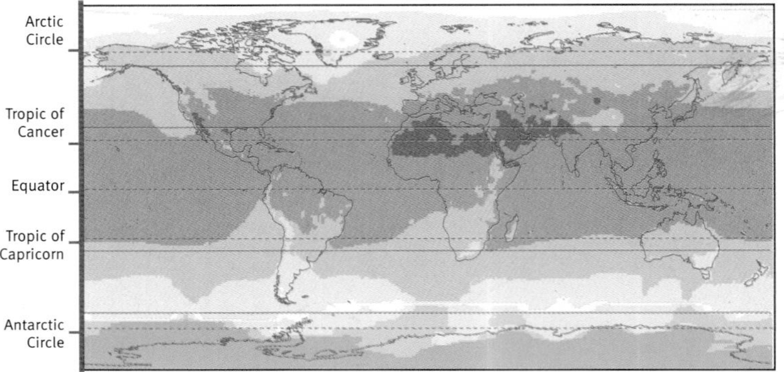
Arctic Circle
Tropic of Cancer
Equator
Tropic of Capricorn
Antarctic Circle

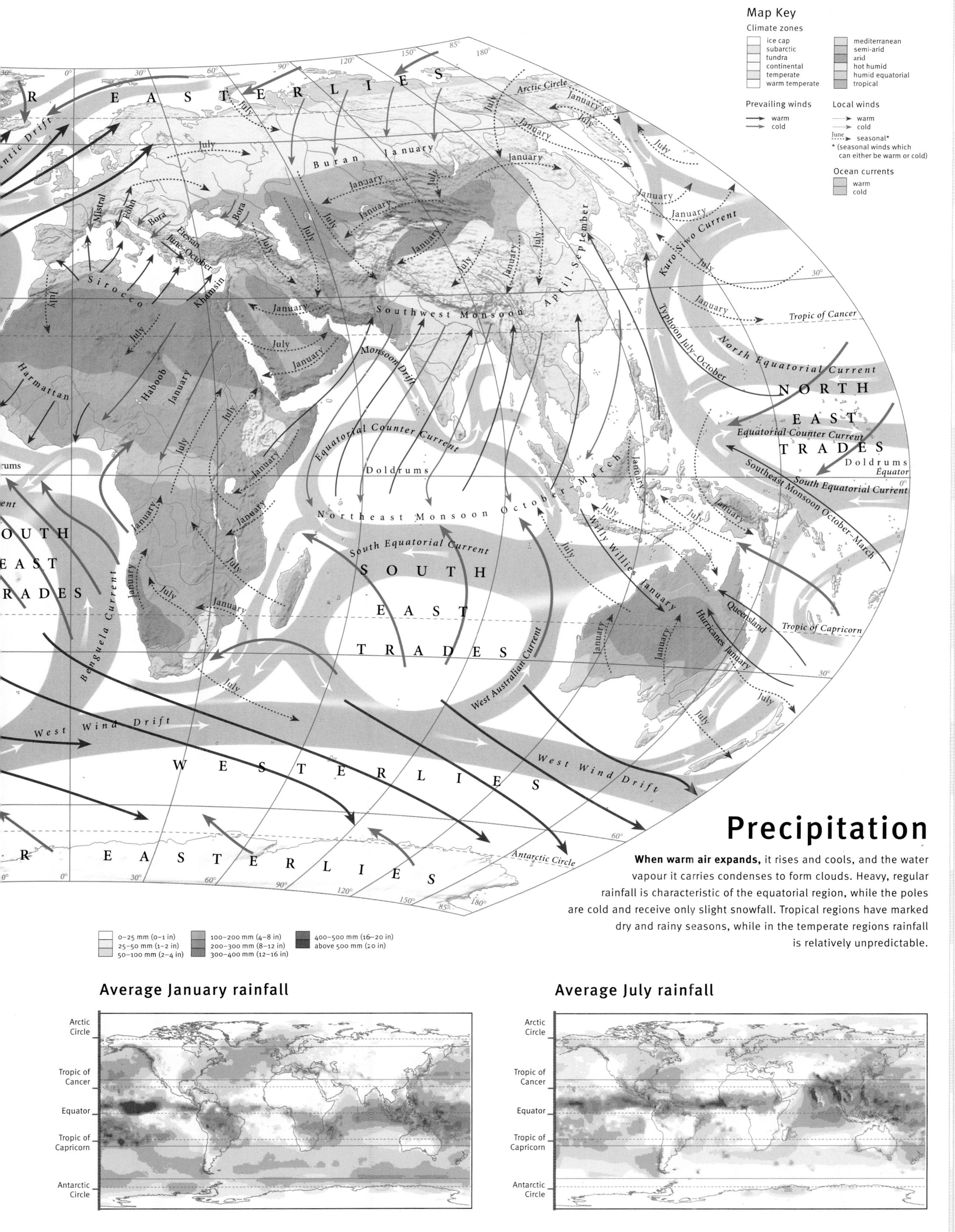
Map Key
Climate zones
ice cap
subarctic
tundra
continental
temperate
warm temperate
mediterranean
semi-arid
arid
hot humid
humid equatorial
tropical
Prevailing winds
warm
cold
Local winds
warm
cold
June seasonal*
* (seasonal winds which can either be warm or cold)
Ocean currents
warm
cold
Arctic Circle
Tropic of Cancer
Equator
Tropic of Capricorn
Antarctic Circle
E A S T E R L I E S
W E S T E R L I E S
N O R T H E A S T T R A D E S
S O U T H E A S T T R A D E S
Buran January
Mistral
Föhn
Bora
Etesian June–October
Sirocco
Khamsin
Harmattan
Haboob
Southwest Monsoon
Northeast Monsoon October–March
Monsoon Drift
Equatorial Counter Current
South Equatorial Current
North Equatorial Current
Kuro Siwo Current
Typhoon July–October
April–September
Doldrums
Southeast Monsoon October–March
Willy Willies January
Hurricanes January
Queensland
West Australian Current
Benguela Current
West Wind Drift

Precipitation

When warm air expands, it rises and cools, and the water vapour it carries condenses to form clouds. Heavy, regular rainfall is characteristic of the equatorial region, while the poles are cold and receive only slight snowfall. Tropical regions have marked dry and rainy seasons, while in the temperate regions rainfall is relatively unpredictable.

0–25 mm (0–1 in)
25–50 mm (1–2 in)
50–100 mm (2–4 in)
100–200 mm (4–8 in)
200–300 mm (8–12 in)
300–400 mm (12–16 in)
400–500 mm (16–20 in)
above 500 mm (20 in)

Average January rainfall

Arctic Circle
Tropic of Cancer
Equator
Tropic of Capricorn
Antarctic Circle

Average July rainfall

Arctic Circle
Tropic of Cancer
Equator
Tropic of Capricorn
Antarctic Circle

The Political World

There are 193 independent countries in the world today. With the exception of Antarctica, where territorial claims have been deferred by international treaty, every land area of the Earth's surface either belongs to, or is claimed by, one country or another. The largest country in the world is the Russian Federation, the smallest is Vatican City. Some 60 overseas dependent territories remain, administered variously by France, Australia, Denmark, New Zealand, Norway, Portugal, the UK, the USA and the Netherlands.

International Borders

The map shows three main types of boundary between states. Full borders represent internationally agreed and recognized territorial boundaries. Undefined borders exist where no fixed boundary between states has been demarcated; the boundaries indicated in this way show approximate areas of sovereignty. A disputed border is indicated where a de facto territorial boundary exists, which is not agreed or is subject to arbitration.

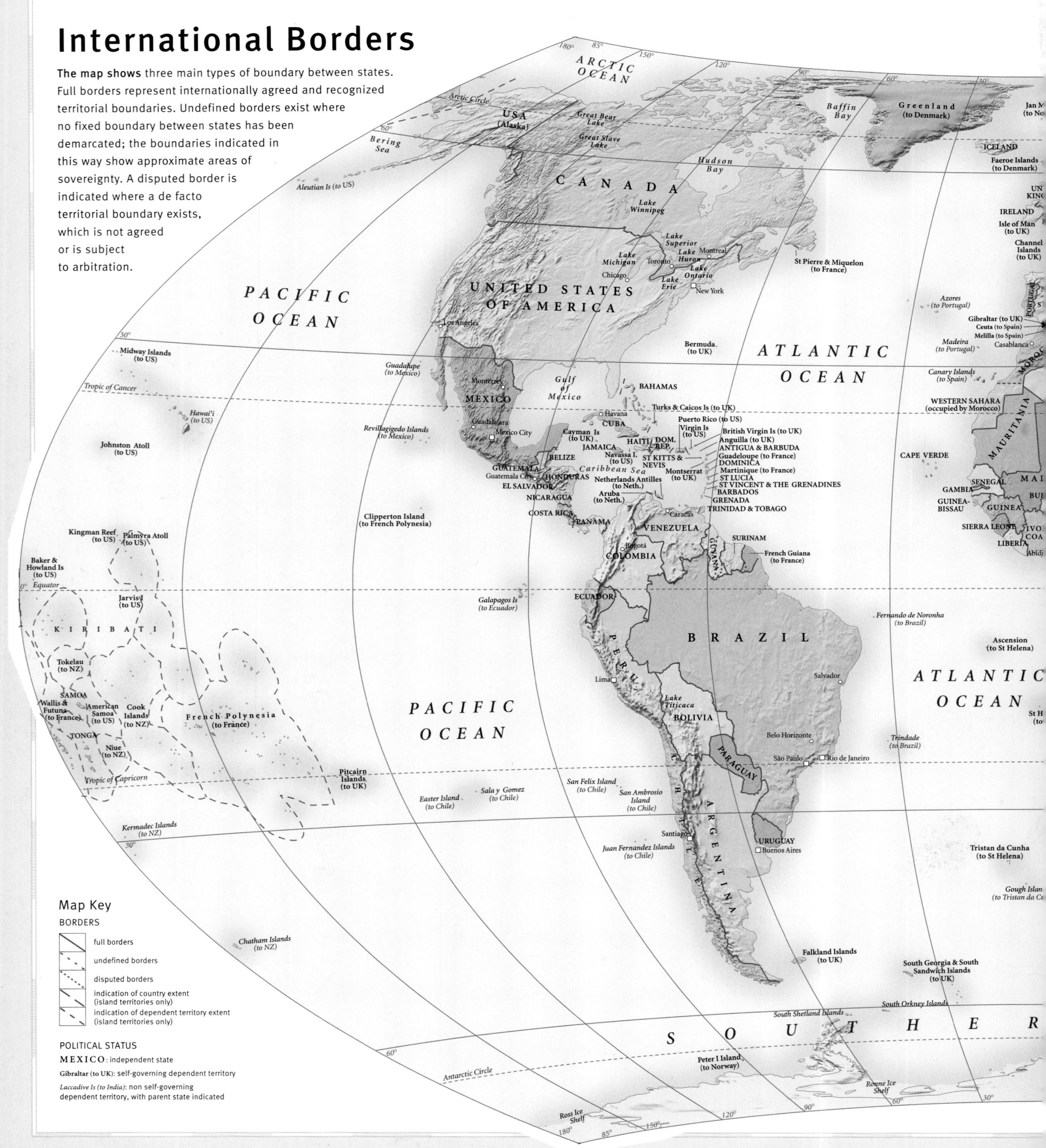
ARCTIC OCEAN
Arctic Circle
USA (Alaska)
Bering Sea
Aleutian Is (to US)
Great Bear Lake
Great Slave Lake
Baffin Bay
Greenland (to Denmark)
ICELAND
Faeroe Islands (to Denmark)
IRELAND
Isle of Man (to UK)
Channel Islands (to UK)
Hudson Bay
CANADA
Lake Winnipeg
Lake Superior
Lake Michigan
Lake Huron
Lake Ontario
Lake Erie
Montreal
Toronto
Chicago
New York
St Pierre & Miquelon (to France)
UNITED STATES OF AMERICA
Los Angeles
PACIFIC OCEAN
Midway Islands (to US)
Tropic of Cancer
Hawai'i (to US)
Johnston Atoll (to US)
Bermuda (to UK)
ATLANTIC OCEAN
Azores (to Portugal)
Gibraltar (to UK)
Ceuta (to Spain)
Melilla (to Spain)
Casablanca
Madeira (to Portugal)
Canary Islands (to Spain)
WESTERN SAHARA (occupied by Morocco)
MAURITANIA
CAPE VERDE
SENEGAL
GAMBIA
GUINEA-BISSAU
GUINEA
SIERRA LEONE
LIBERIA
Guadalupe (to Mexico)
Gulf of Mexico
Monterrey
MEXICO
Guadalajara
Mexico City
Revillagigedo Islands (to Mexico)
BAHAMAS
Turks & Caicos Is (to UK)
Havana
CUBA
Cayman Is (to UK)
JAMAICA
HAITI
DOM. REP.
Puerto Rico (to US)
Virgin Is (to US)
British Virgin Is (to UK)
Anguilla (to UK)
ANTIGUA & BARBUDA
Guadeloupe (to France)
DOMINICA
Martinique (to France)
ST LUCIA
ST VINCENT & THE GRENADINES
BARBADOS
GRENADA
TRINIDAD & TOBAGO
Navassa I. (to US)
ST KITTS & NEVIS
Montserrat (to UK)
Netherlands Antilles (to Neth.)
Aruba (to Neth.)
Caribbean Sea
BELIZE
GUATEMALA
Guatemala City
HONDURAS
EL SALVADOR
NICARAGUA
COSTA RICA
PANAMA
Caracas
VENEZUELA
SURINAM
GUYANA
French Guiana (to France)
Bogotá
COLOMBIA
Clipperton Island (to French Polynesia)
Kingman Reef (to US)
Palmyra Atoll (to US)
Baker & Howland Is (to US)
Equator
Jarvis I (to US)
KIRIBATI
Galapagos Is (to Ecuador)
ECUADOR
Fernando de Noronha (to Brazil)
Ascension (to St Helena)
BRAZIL
PERU
Lima
Salvador
Tokelau (to NZ)
SAMOA
Wallis & Futuna (to France)
American Samoa (to US)
Cook Islands (to NZ)
TONGA
Niue (to NZ)
French Polynesia (to France)
Tropic of Capricorn
Pitcairn Islands (to UK)
Lake Titicaca
BOLIVIA
Belo Horizonte
Trindade (to Brazil)
PARAGUAY
São Paulo
Rio de Janeiro
Easter Island (to Chile)
Sala y Gomez (to Chile)
San Felix Island (to Chile)
San Ambrosio Island (to Chile)
Kermadec Islands (to NZ)
CHILE
Santiago
ARGENTINA
URUGUAY
Buenos Aires
Juan Fernandez Islands (to Chile)
Tristan da Cunha (to St Helena)
Chatham Islands (to NZ)
Falkland Islands (to UK)
South Georgia & South Sandwich Islands (to UK)
South Orkney Islands
South Shetland Islands
SOUTHER
Peter I Island (to Norway)
Antarctic Circle
Ronne Ice Shelf
Ross Ice Shelf
Map Key
BORDERS
full borders
undefined borders
disputed borders
indication of country extent (island territories only)
indication of dependent territory extent (island territories only)
POLITICAL STATUS
MEXICO: independent state
Gibraltar (to UK): self-governing dependent territory
Laccadive Is (to India): non self-governing dependent territory, with parent state indicated

Population and Settlement

The Earth's population is projected to rise from its current level of about 6.4 billion to reach some 10 billion by 2025. The global distribution of this rapidly growing population is very uneven, and is dictated by climate, terrain and natural and economic resources. The great majority of the Earth's people live in coastal zones, and along river valleys. It is estimated that over half of the world's population live in cities – most of them in Asia – as a result of mass migration from rural areas in search of jobs, resulting in the growth of huge sprawling camps on the edge of many Third World cities. Many of these people live in the so-called 'megacities', some with populations as great as 40 million.

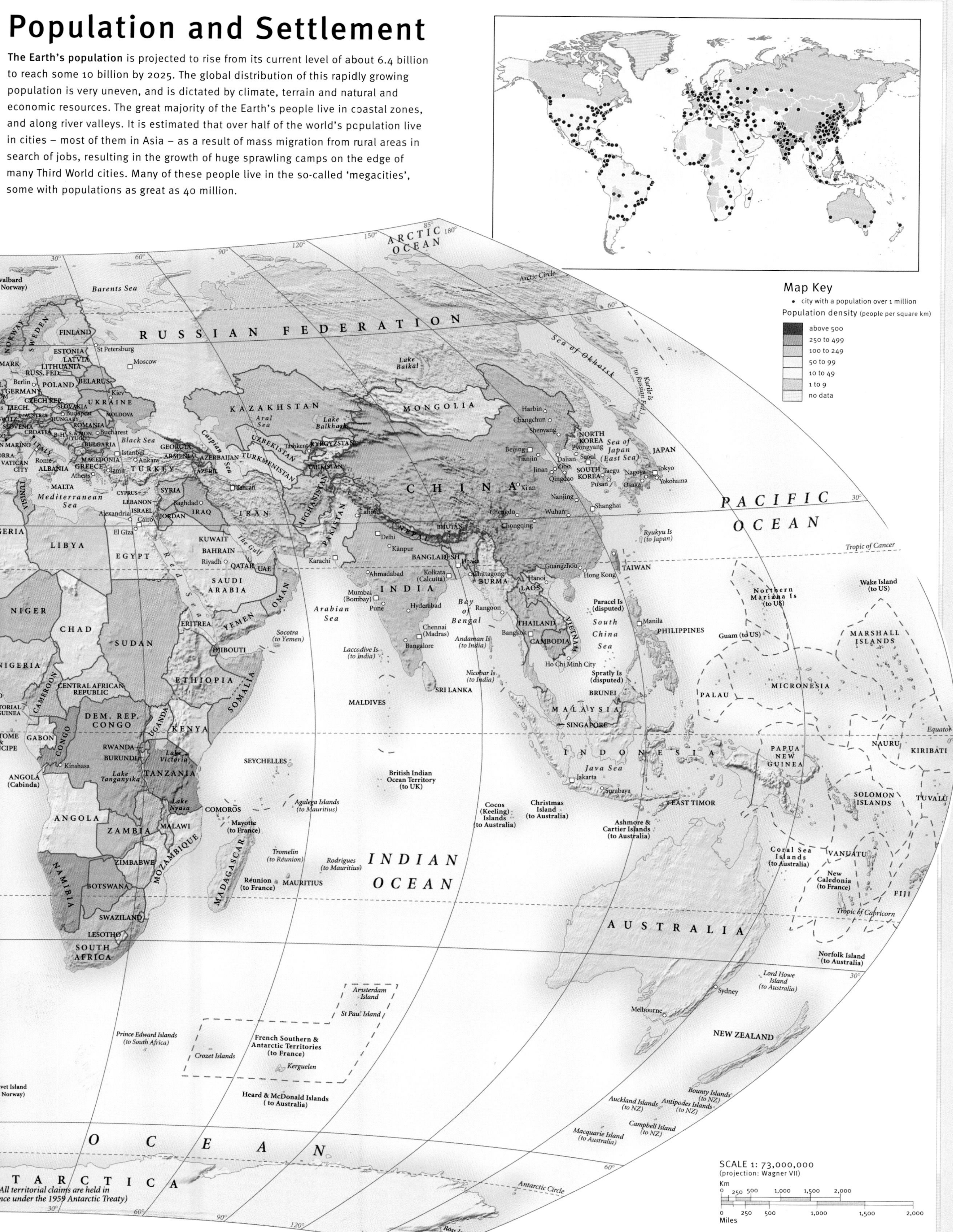

Map Key
city with a population over 1 million
Population density (people per square km)
above 500
250 to 499
100 to 249
50 to 99
10 to 49
1 to 9
no data
SCALE 1: 73,000,000
(projection: Wagner VII)
Km
0 250 500 1,000 1,500 2,000
0 250 500 1,000 1,500 2,000
Miles
ARCTIC OCEAN
Arctic Circle
Barents Sea
RUSSIAN FEDERATION
FINLAND
NORWAY
SWEDEN
ESTONIA
LATVIA
LITHUANIA
RUSS. FED.
St Petersburg
Moscow
Berlin
POLAND
BELARUS
Kiev
UKRAINE
MOLDOVA
CZECH REP.
SLOVAKIA
AUSTRIA
HUNGARY
Budapest
ROMANIA
Bucharest
SLOVENIA
CROATIA
BULGARIA
Istanbul
Black Sea
Rome
ALBANIA
MACEDONIA
GREECE
Athens
Izmir
Ankara
TURKEY
MALTA
Mediterranean Sea
CYPRUS
LEBANON
SYRIA
ISRAEL
JORDAN
Cairo
Alexandria
El Giza
Baghdad
IRAQ
IRAN
Tehran
GEORGIA
ARMENIA
AZERBAIJAN
Caspian Sea
KAZAKHSTAN
Aral Sea
UZBEKISTAN
TURKMENISTAN
Tashkent
KYRGYZSTAN
TAJIKISTAN
AFGHANISTAN
PAKISTAN
Lahore
Karachi
Lake Balkhash
Lake Baikal
MONGOLIA
CHINA
Harbin
Changchun
Shenyang
Beijing
Tianjin
Jinan
Dalian
Qingdao
Xi'an
Nanjing
Shanghai
Wuhan
Chengdu
Chongqing
Guangzhou
Hong Kong
TAIWAN
NORTH KOREA
Pyongyang
Seoul
SOUTH KOREA
Taegu
Pusan
Sea of Japan (East Sea)
JAPAN
Tokyo
Yokohama
Nagoya
Osaka
Sea of Okhotsk
Kurile Is (to Russian Fed.)
Ryukyu Is (to Japan)
PACIFIC OCEAN
Tropic of Cancer
Delhi
Kanpur
NEPAL
BHUTAN
BANGLADESH
Dhaka
Chittagong
Kolkata (Calcutta)
Ahmadabad
INDIA
Mumbai (Bombay)
Pune
Hyderabad
Chennai (Madras)
Bangalore
SRI LANKA
MALDIVES
Arabian Sea
Bay of Bengal
Laccadive Is (to India)
Andaman Is (to India)
Nicobar Is (to India)
BURMA
Rangoon
LAOS
Hanoi
THAILAND
Bangkok
CAMBODIA
VIETNAM
Ho Chi Minh City
Paracel Is (disputed)
South China Sea
Spratly Is (disputed)
Manila
PHILIPPINES
BRUNEI
MALAYSIA
SINGAPORE
INDONESIA
Java Sea
Jakarta
Surabaya
EAST TIMOR
PAPUA NEW GUINEA
PALAU
MICRONESIA
Northern Mariana Is (to US)
Guam (to US)
Wake Island (to US)
MARSHALL ISLANDS
NAURU
KIRIBATI
Equator
SOLOMON ISLANDS
TUVALU
VANUATU
New Caledonia (to France)
FIJI
Coral Sea Islands (to Australia)
Tropic of Capricorn
Norfolk Island (to Australia)
Lord Howe Island (to Australia)
AUSTRALIA
Sydney
Melbourne
NEW ZEALAND
Ashmore & Cartier Islands (to Australia)
Christmas Island (to Australia)
Cocos (Keeling) Islands (to Australia)
British Indian Ocean Territory (to UK)
INDIAN OCEAN
KUWAIT
BAHRAIN
Riyadh
QATAR
UAE
The Gulf
SAUDI ARABIA
OMAN
YEMEN
Red Sea
Socotra (to Yemen)
ERITREA
DJIBOUTI
ETHIOPIA
SOMALIA
LIBYA
EGYPT
SUDAN
CHAD
NIGER
NIGERIA
CAMEROON
CENTRAL AFRICAN REPUBLIC
GABON
CONGO
DEM. REP. CONGO
Kinshasa
UGANDA
KENYA
RWANDA
BURUNDI
Lake Victoria
Lake Tanganyika
TANZANIA
Lake Nyasa
ANGOLA
ANGOLA (Cabinda)
ZAMBIA
MALAWI
MOZAMBIQUE
ZIMBABWE
NAMIBIA
BOTSWANA
SWAZILAND
LESOTHO
SOUTH AFRICA
SEYCHELLES
COMOROS
Mayotte (to France)
Agalega Islands (to Mauritius)
MADAGASCAR
Tromelin (to Réunion)
Réunion (to France)
MAURITIUS
Rodrigues (to Mauritius)
Amsterdam Island
St Paul Island
French Southern & Antarctic Territories (to France)
Crozet Islands
Kerguelen
Prince Edward Islands (to South Africa)
Heard & McDonald Islands (to Australia)
Bouvet Island (to Norway)
Svalbard (to Norway)
Bounty Islands (to NZ)
Auckland Islands (to NZ)
Antipodes Islands (to NZ)
Campbell Island (to NZ)
Macquarie Island (to Australia)
OCEAN
ANTARCTICA
(All territorial claims are held in abeyance under the 1959 Antarctic Treaty)
Antarctic Circle
Ross Ice Shelf

Flags of the World

NORTH AMERICA

CANADA
PAGES 8–15

UNITED STATES OF AMERICA
PAGES 16–39

MEXICO
PAGES 40–41

BELIZE
PAGES 42–43

COSTA RICA
PAGES 42–43

EL SALVADOR
PAGES 42–43

GUATEMALA
PAGES 42–43

HONDURAS
PAGES 42–43

GRENADA
PAGES 44–45

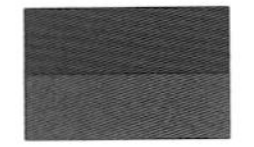
HAITI
PAGES 44–45

JAMAICA
PAGES 44–45

ST KITTS & NEVIS
PAGES 44–45

ST LUCIA
PAGES 44–45

ST VINCENT & THE GRENADINES
PAGES 44–45

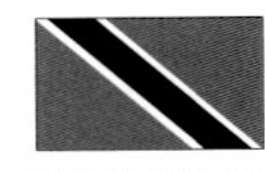
TRINIDAD & TOBAGO
PAGES 44–45

SOUTH AMERICA

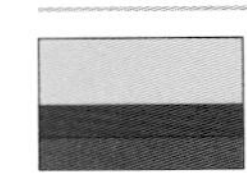
COLOMBIA
PAGES 54–55

URUGUAY
PAGES 60–61

CHILE
PAGES 62–63

PARAGUAY
PAGES 62–63

AFRICA

ALGERIA
PAGES 74–75

EGYPT
PAGES 74–75

LIBYA
PAGES 74–75

MOROCCO
PAGES 74–75

TUNISIA
PAGES 74–75

LIBERIA
PAGES 76–77

MALI
PAGES 76–77

MAURITANIA
PAGES 76–77

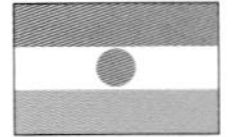
NIGER
PAGES 76–77

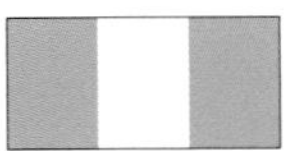
NIGERIA
PAGES 76–77

SENEGAL
PAGES 76–77

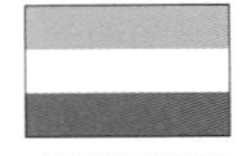
SIERRA LEONE
PAGES 76–77

TOGO
PAGES 76–77

BURUNDI
PAGES 80–81

DJIBOUTI
PAGES 80–81

ERITREA
PAGES 80–81

ETHIOPIA
PAGES 80–81

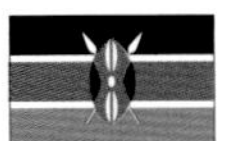
KENYA
PAGES 80–81

RWANDA
PAGES 80–81

SOMALIA
PAGES 80–81

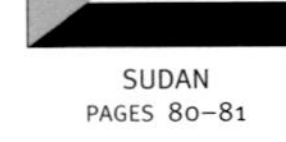
SUDAN
PAGES 80–81

SOUTH AFRICA
PAGES 82–83

SWAZILAND
PAGES 82–83

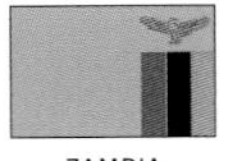
ZAMBIA
PAGES 82–83

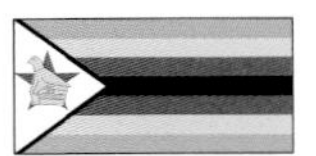
ZIMBABWE
PAGES 82–83

EUROPE

DENMARK
PAGES 92–93

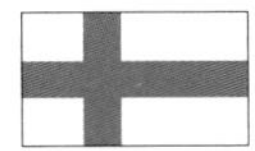
FINLAND
PAGES 92–93

ICELAND
PAGES 92–93

NORWAY
PAGES 92–95

MONACO
PAGES 102–103

ANDORRA
PAGES 104–105

PORTUGAL
PAGES 104–105

SPAIN
PAGES 104–105

ITALY
PAGES 106–107

SAN MARINO
PAGES 106–107

VATICAN CITY
PAGES 106–107

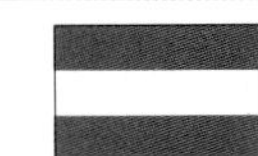
AUSTRIA
PAGES 108–109

BOSNIA &
HERZEGOVINA
PAGES 112–113

CROATIA
PAGES 112–113

MACEDONIA
PAGES 112–113

SERBIA & MONTENEGRO
(YUGOSLAVIA)
PAGES 112–113

BULGARIA
PAGES 114–115

GREECE
PAGES 114–115

MOLDOVA
PAGES 116–117

ROMANIA
PAGES 116–117

ASIA

ARMENIA
PAGES 136–137

AZERBAIJAN
PAGES 136–137

GEORGIA
PAGES 136–137

TURKEY
PAGES 136–137/114–115

IRAQ
PAGES 138–139

ISRAEL
PAGES 138–139

JORDAN
PAGES 138–139

LEBANON
PAGES 138–139

IRAN
PAGES 142–143

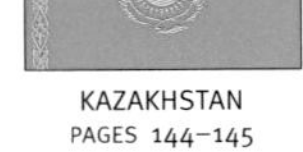
KAZAKHSTAN
PAGES 144–145

KYRGYZSTAN
PAGES 146–147

TAJIKISTAN
PAGES 146–147

TURKMENISTAN
PAGES 146–147

UZBEKISTAN
PAGES 146–147

AFGHANISTAN
PAGES 148–149

PAKISTAN
PAGES 148–151

TAIWAN
PAGES 160–161

JAPAN
PAGES 164–165

BURMA
PAGES 166–167

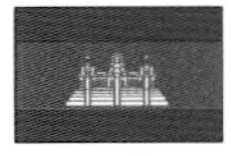
CAMBODIA
PAGES 166–167

LAOS
PAGES 166–167

PHILIPPINES
PAGES 166–167

THAILAND
PAGES 166–167

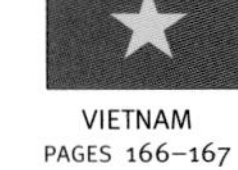
VIETNAM
PAGES 166–167

MAURITIUS
PAGES 172–173

SEYCHELLES
PAGES 172–173

AUSTRALASIA & OCEANIA

AUSTRALIA
PAGES 180–183

NEW ZEALAND
PAGES 184–185

PAPUA NEW GUINEA
PAGES 186–187

FIJI
PAGES 186–187

SOLOMON ISLANDS
PAGES 186–187

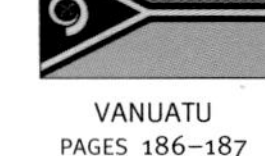
VANUATU
PAGES 186–187

NICARAGUA
PAGES 42–43

PANAMA
PAGES 42–43

ANTIGUA & BARBUDA
PAGES 44–45

BAHAMAS
PAGES 44–45

BARBADOS
PAGES 44–45

CUBA
PAGES 44–45

DOMINICA
PAGES 44–45

DOMINICAN REPUBLIC
PAGES 44–45

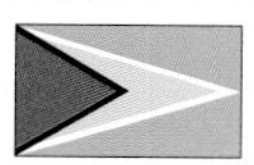
GUYANA
PAGES 54–55

SURINAM
PAGES 54–55

VENEZUELA
PAGES 54–55

BOLIVIA
PAGES 56–57

ECUADOR
PAGES 56–57

PERU
PAGES 56–57

BRAZIL
PAGES 58–59

ARGENTINA
PAGES 60–61

BENIN
PAGES 76–77

BURKINA
PAGES 76–77

CAPE VERDE
PAGES 76–77

GAMBIA
PAGES 76–77

GHANA
PAGES 76–77

GUINEA
PAGES 76–77

GUINEA-BISSAU
PAGES 76–77

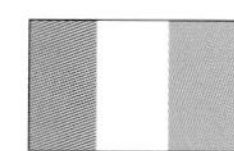
IVORY COAST
PAGES 76–77

CAMEROON
PAGES 78–79

CENTRAL AFRICAN REPUBLIC
PAGES 78–79

CHAD
PAGES 78–79

CONGO
PAGES 78–79

DEM. REP. CONGO
PAGES 78–79

EQUATORIAL GUINEA
PAGES 78–79

GABON
PAGES 78–79

SAO TOME & PRINCIPE
PAGES 78–79

TANZANIA
PAGES 80–81

UGANDA
PAGES 80–81

ANGOLA
PAGES 82–83

BOTSWANA
PAGES 82–83

LESOTHO
PAGES 82–83

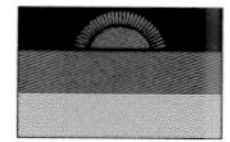
MALAWI
PAGES 82–83

MOZAMBIQUE
PAGES 82–83

NAMIBIA
PAGES 82–83

SWEDEN
PAGES 92–95

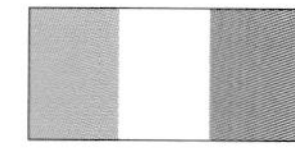
REPUBLIC OF IRELAND
PAGES 96–97

UNITED KINGDOM
PAGES 96–97

BELGIUM
PAGES 98–99

LUXEMBOURG
PAGES 98–99

NETHERLANDS
PAGES 98–99

GERMANY
PAGES 100–101

FRANCE
PAGES 102–103

LIECHTENSTEIN
PAGES 108–109

SLOVENIA
PAGES 108–109

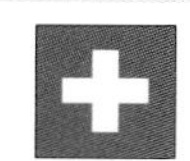
SWITZERLAND
PAGES 108–109

CZECH REPUBLIC
PAGES 110–111

HUNGARY
PAGES 110–111

POLAND
PAGES 110–111

SLOVAKIA
PAGES 110–111

ALBANIA
PAGES 112–113

UKRAINE
PAGES 116–117

BELARUS
PAGES 118–119

ESTONIA
PAGES 118–119

LATVIA
PAGES 118–119

LITHUANIA
PAGES 118–119

CYPRUS
PAGES 120–121

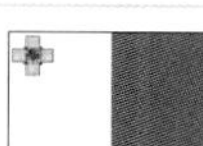
MALTA
PAGES 120–121

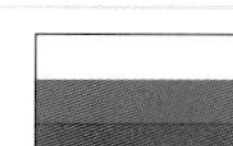
RUSSIAN FEDERATION
PAGES 122–127

SYRIA
PAGES 138–139

BAHRAIN
PAGES 140–143

KUWAIT
PAGES 140–143

OMAN
PAGES 140–141

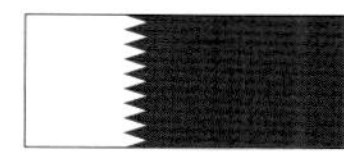
QATAR
PAGES 140–143

SAUDI ARABIA
PAGES 140–141

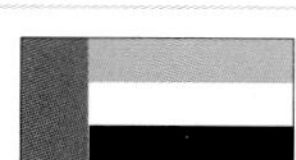
UNITED ARAB EMIRATES
PAGES 140–143

YEMEN
PAGES 140–141

BANGLADESH
PAGES 150–153

BHUTAN
PAGES 150–153

INDIA
PAGES 150–155

NEPAL
PAGES 150–153

SRI LANKA
PAGES 150–151/154–155

CHINA
PAGES 158–163

MONGOLIA
PAGES 156–157/162–163

NORTH KOREA
PAGES 156–157/162–163

SOUTH KOREA
PAGES 156–157/162–163

BRUNEI
PAGES 168–169

INDONESIA
PAGES 168–171

EAST TIMOR
PAGES 170–171

MALAYSIA
PAGES 168–169

SINGAPORE
PAGES 168–169

COMOROS
PAGES 172–173

MADAGASCAR
PAGES 172–173

MALDIVES
PAGES 172–173

MARSHALL ISLANDS
PAGES 188–189

MICRONESIA
PAGES 188–189

NAURU
PAGES 188–189

PALAU
PAGES 188–189

KIRIBATI
PAGES 190–191

TUVALU
PAGES 190–191

TONGA
PAGES 192–193

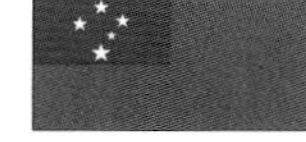
SAMOA
PAGES 192–193

Health Precautions

It is routine for travellers to be immunized against diphtheria, tetanus, whooping cough, hepatitis B, measles and polio. Other diseases that could require precautions are cholera, dengue fever, influenza, hepatitis A, Japanese encephalitis, Lyme disease, meningitis, pneumococcal disease, rabies, tick-borne encephalitis, tuberculosis (TB), typhoid and yellow fever.

Travellers should arrange suitable health insurance before departure and take a basic medical kit. Visiting a travel clinic or doctor at least 4–6 weeks prior to departure is advisable for vaccinations and current medical advice, which will vary depending on destination, length and type of stay, health status, age and intended activities. A vaccination chart has been included on pp210–211 for guidance.

Once abroad, the most common health problem for travellers is diarrhoea, caused by bacteria in food and drink. Simple safety precautions such as only drinking bottled or boiled water, eating well-cooked food and avoiding ice, salads and fruit will reduce the risk of a spoiled holiday.

Malaria

Malaria is endemic in over 100 tropical and subtropical countries. Risk of infection is greatest in low-lying rural areas and at the end of the rainy season. The disease is transmitted by mosquito bites, so simple precautions of using mosquito nets and avoiding exposure to bites, especially between dusk and dawn, will help to reduce the risk. Various anti-malarial drugs are available, usually taken over several weeks prior to, during and after visiting a malaria zone. Medical advice will specify which drugs are suitable for protection against the mosquitoes in a particular region and warn of side effects, which can be highly serious. Fever is the main symptom of malaria – a high temperature within three months of visiting an affected area requires immediate medical attention.

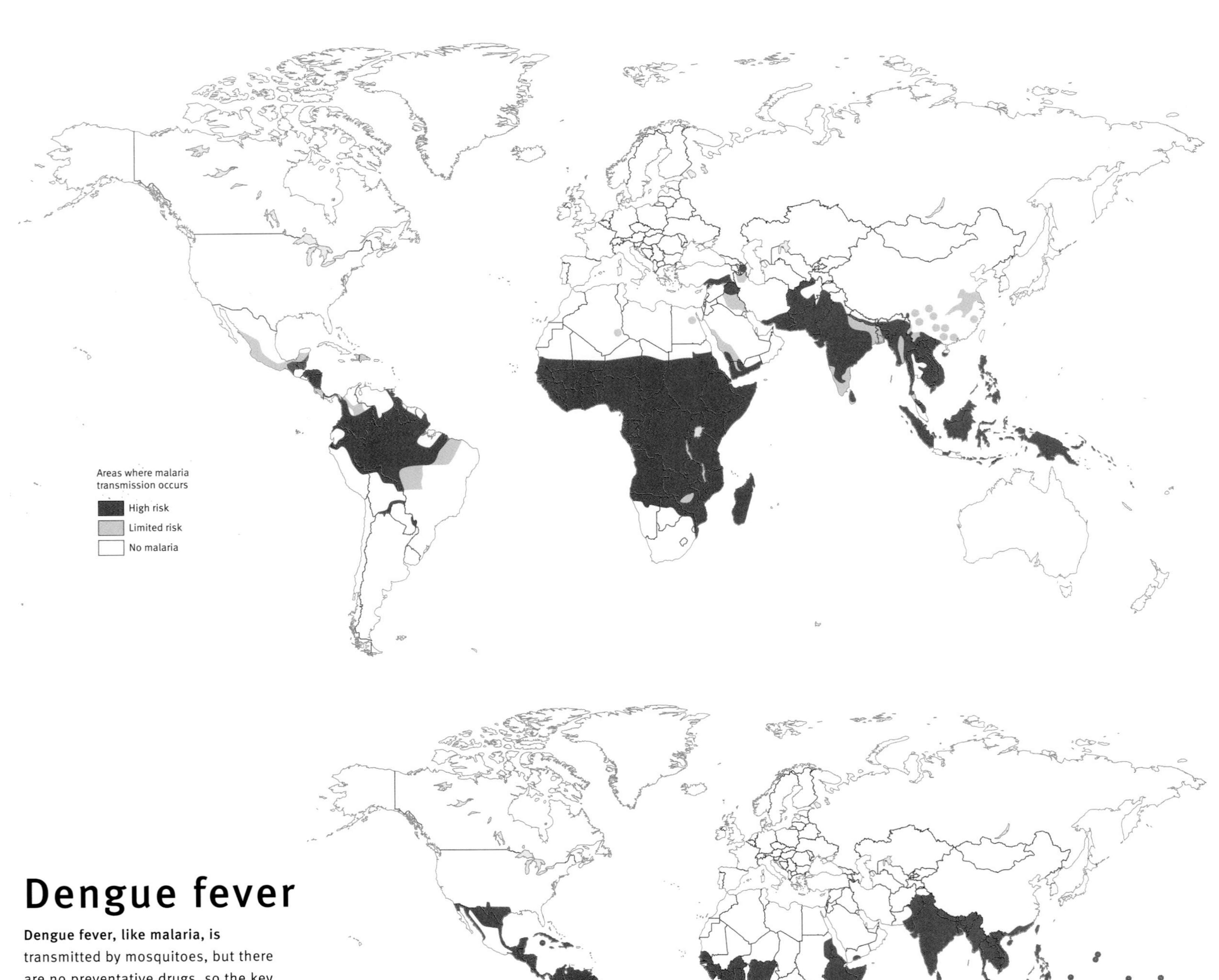
Areas where malaria transmission occurs
High risk
Limited risk
No malaria

Dengue fever

Dengue fever, like malaria, is transmitted by mosquitoes, but there are no preventative drugs, so the key is to avoid being bitten by wearing long-sleeved clothing during the day and sleeping under mosquito nets at night. The disease only occurs in tropical low-lying areas below 600 m (2,000 ft). Symptoms are a sudden onset of fever, sometimes accompanied by a rash and deep muscular pains.

Countries / areas with a risk of transmission

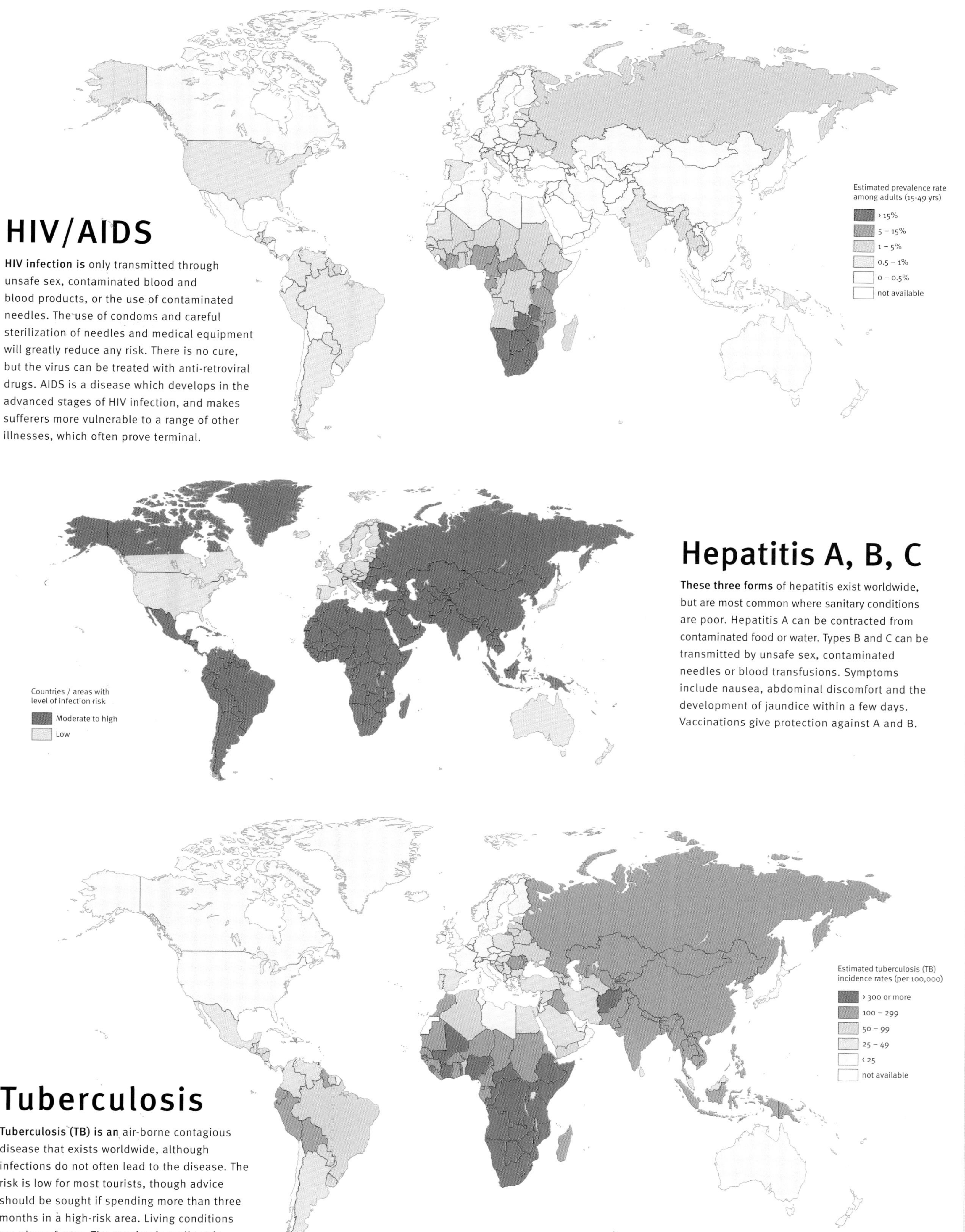
Estimated prevalence rate among adults (15-49 yrs)
› 15%
5 – 15%
1 – 5%
0.5 – 1%
0 – 0.5%
not available
Countries / areas with level of infection risk
Moderate to high
Low
Estimated tuberculosis (TB) incidence rates (per 100,000)
› 300 or more
100 – 299
50 – 99
25 – 49
‹ 25
not available

HIV/AIDS

HIV infection is only transmitted through unsafe sex, contaminated blood and blood products, or the use of contaminated needles. The use of condoms and careful sterilization of needles and medical equipment will greatly reduce any risk. There is no cure, but the virus can be treated with anti-retroviral drugs. AIDS is a disease which develops in the advanced stages of HIV infection, and makes sufferers more vulnerable to a range of other illnesses, which often prove terminal.

Hepatitis A, B, C

These three forms of hepatitis exist worldwide, but are most common where sanitary conditions are poor. Hepatitis A can be contracted from contaminated food or water. Types B and C can be transmitted by unsafe sex, contaminated needles or blood transfusions. Symptoms include nausea, abdominal discomfort and the development of jaundice within a few days. Vaccinations give protection against A and B.

Tuberculosis

Tuberculosis (TB) is an air-borne contagious disease that exists worldwide, although infections do not often lead to the disease. The risk is low for most tourists, though advice should be sought if spending more than three months in a high-risk area. Living conditions are also a factor. The vaccine is really only effective for babies under six months.

Source for all maps: WHO, 2004

North America

"Catch the Detroit Lightnin' out of Santa Fe,
the Great Northern out of Cheyenne, from sea to shining sea."

ROBERT HUNTER, b.1923

Physical North America

North America offers a spectacular variety of landscape, from the great mountain ranges of the west that stretch from the Bering Strait to the sunny Gulf of California, to vast prairies with open sky in every direction to the horizon. The fertile central lowlands of the Midwest give way to the river delta of the Mississippi and Missouri to the south, while in the east the Appalachians, among the oldest mountains in the world, separate the cities of the eastern seaboard from the rest of the continent. The Canadian Shield in the north of the continent is a huge region where repeated glaciation has left a landscape of hillocks and plains and the basins and islands of the far north stretch off into the Arctic Circle. To the south the continent is tropical, from Florida to the islands of the Caribbean and south into Central America.

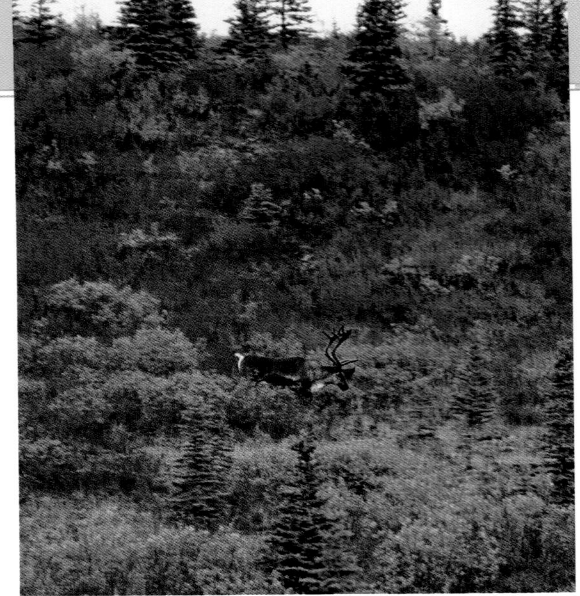

Tundra

Barren tundra covers a large part of North America and though it supports few human inhabitants, it is home to a wide variety of animal life, including caribou and polar bears. The ecosystem is fragile and highly vulnerable to overhunting, climate change and development such as mining or drilling for oil.

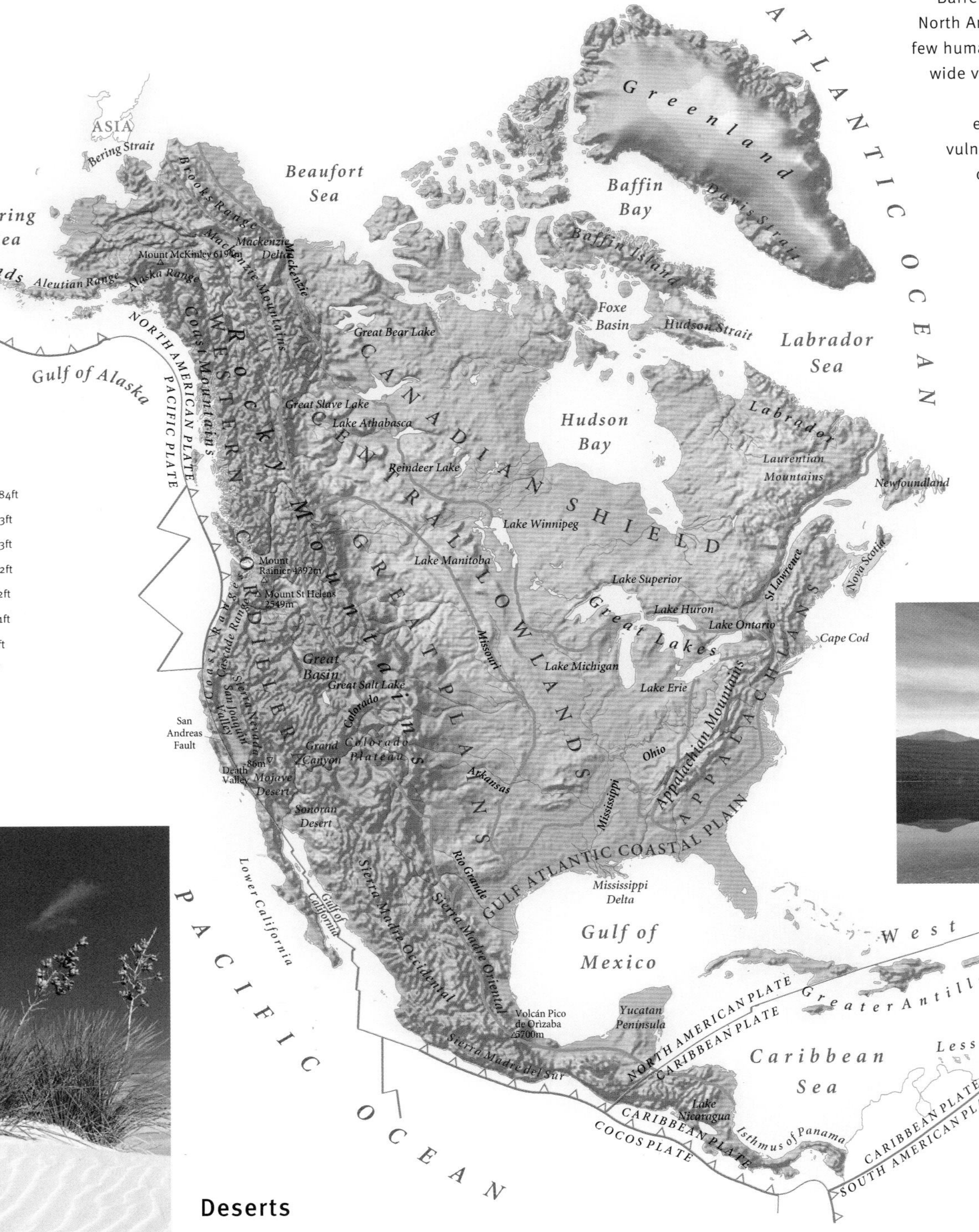

Mountains

The spectacular Rocky Mountains, which run from the north to the south of the continent, offer opportunities for exhilarating hiking and varied winter sports.

Map Key

ELEVATION

- 3500m / 11,484ft
- 3000m / 9843ft
- 2500m / 8203ft
- 2000m / 6562ft
- 1500m / 4922ft
- 1000m / 3281ft
- 500m / 1640ft
- 250m / 820ft
- 100m / 328ft
- sea level

Deserts

Some of North America's largest cities sit at the edge of deserts. The open expanses of white sands in New Mexico contrast with eerie landscapes like California's Death Valley. These deserts are home to a surprising number of animals including coyotes, snakes and roadrunners.

SCALE 1:46,600,000
(projection: Lambert Azimuthal Equal Area)

Km 0 200 400 600 800 1000

Miles 0 200 400 600 800 1000

PLATE MARGINS

- constructive
- destructive
- conservative
- uncertain
- physiographic regions

Climate

A continent as varied as North America has a similarly diverse climate, with extremes ranging from the heat and dust of the southwestern desert, to the lush, tropical conditions of Florida and the Caribbean, the notoriously persistent rain of the northwestern seaboard and the Arctic conditions of the far north. Parts of North America also suffer extreme storms – tornadoes can carve swathes of destruction and lift houses off the ground, while hurricanes regularly batter southern coastal areas and the islands of the Caribbean.

Tornadoes: The USA experiences more "twisters" than any other country, especially in the south and Midwest (known as Tornado Alley). They can last from a few seconds to an hour.

Arctic Circle
Nome
Fairbanks
Aklavik
Eismitte
Resolute
Kugluktuk
Haines Junction
Iqaluit
Juneau
Fort Vermillon
Fort St John
Churchill
Happy Valley - Goose Bay
Torbay
Vancouver
Medicine Hat
Winnipeg
Montréal
Toronto
Boise
Sioux City
New York
Salt Lake City
San Francisco
Denver
Las Vegas
Los Angeles
Phoenix
Little Rock
Atlanta
Cape Hatteras
Guaymas
Houston
Chihuahua
New Orleans
Miami
Nassau
Tropic of Cancer
Santo Domingo
Fort-de-France
Mérida
Kingston
Acapulco
San Salvador
San José

Climate

- ice cap
- tundra
- subarctic
- cool continental
- warm humid
- semi-arid
- arid
- humid equatorial
- tropical
- daily hours of sunshine, January
- daily hours of sunshine, July
- direction of hurricanes
- tornado zones

Temperature

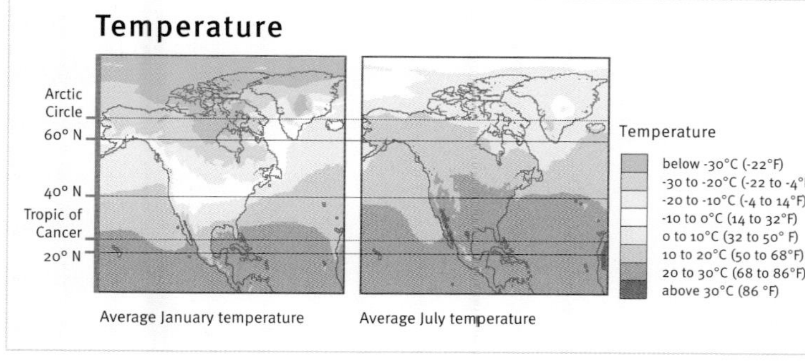
Arctic Circle
60° N
40° N
Tropic of Cancer
20° N

Average January temperature

Average July temperature

Temperature

- below -30°C (-22°F)
- -30 to -20°C (-22 to -4°F)
- -20 to -10°C (-4 to 14°F)
- -10 to 0°C (14 to 32°F)
- 0 to 10°C (32 to 50°F)
- 10 to 20°C (50 to 68°F)
- 20 to 30°C (68 to 86°F)
- above 30°C (86 °F)

Rainfall

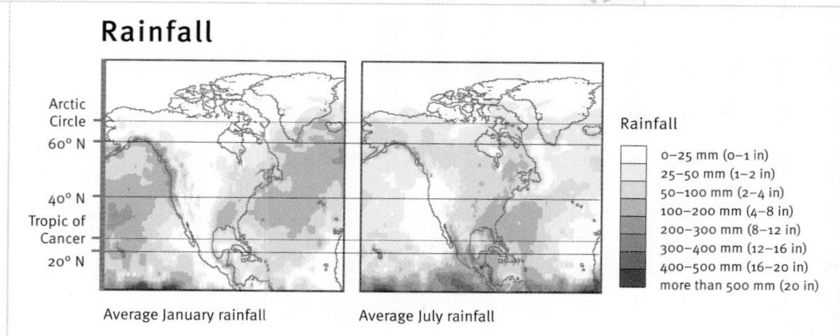
Arctic Circle
60° N
40° N
Tropic of Cancer
20° N

Average January rainfall

Average July rainfall

Rainfall

- 0–25 mm (0–1 in)
- 25–50 mm (1–2 in)
- 50–100 mm (2–4 in)
- 100–200 mm (4–8 in)
- 200–300 mm (8–12 in)
- 300–400 mm (12–16 in)
- 400–500 mm (16–20 in)
- more than 500 mm (20 in)

ARCTIC OCEAN
Greenland
Bering Strait
Brooks Range
Beaufort Sea
Baffin Bay
Bering Sea
Aleutian Range
Mackenzie Mountains
Mackenzie
Gulf of Alaska
Labrador Sea
Hudson Strait
Hudson Bay
PACIFIC OCEAN
Rocky Mountains
Great Plains
Edmonton
Newfoundland
Vancouver
Calgary
Winnipeg
St Lawrence
Great Lakes
Seattle
Québec
Montréal
Portland
Ottawa
Boston
Cape Cod
Minneapolis
Toronto
Buffalo
New York
Detroit
Chicago
Philadelphia
Sacramento
Pittsburgh
Baltimore
San Francisco
Oakland
Denver
Washington D.C.
San José
Indianapolis
Cincinnati
Saint Louis
Appalachian Mountains
Colorado
Los Angeles
Albuquerque
Tulsa
Nashville
Charlotte
San Diego
Phoenix
Oklahoma City
Atlanta
Tucson
El Paso
Dallas
Jacksonville
Lower California
Austin
Houston
Rio Grande
Tampa
San Antonio
Miami
ATLANTIC OCEAN
Monterrey
Gulf of Mexico
Havana
San Juan
Guadalajara
Yucatán Peninsula
Santo Domingo
Mexico City
Caribbean Sea
Guatemala City
Managua

Using the Land and Sea

- cropland
- forest
- ice cap
- mountain region
- pasture
- tundra
- wetland
- desert
- major conurbations
- cattle
- goats
- pigs
- poultry
- reindeer
- sheep
- bananas
- citrus fruits
- coffee
- corn (maize)
- cotton
- fishing
- fruit
- maple syrup
- peanuts
- rice
- shellfish
- soya beans
- sugar cane
- timber
- tobacco
- vineyards
- wheat

Using Land and Sea

Vast tracts of North America cannot sustain farming, particularly in the far north, where snow cover precludes agriculture. In the central belt cereals are grown on massive farms, along with corn and soya. The southern USA produces much citrus fruit and wineries have sprung up across California to take advantage of the dry climate. Many Caribbean countries depend on crops such as bananas and sugar cane – market volatility has led several of them to try to diversify while developing tourism as their main industry.

Prairies: The central belt, from the Canadian prairies to Texas, is the breadbasket of the continent. Corn and wheat are grown throughout this region, often in fields so vast that no boundary is visible.

Political North America

The USA has identified itself with the political values of the "free world" since the founding fathers drew up its constitution in the 18th century. Universal suffrage came more gradually, with the extension of the vote beyond the property-owning classes and eventually (in the early 20th century) to women too. The US secular democratic model balances a strong executive and separately elected legislature with a judiciary devoted to upholding constitutional rights. Individual states jealously defend their areas of independence from federal government encroachment. Canada's democracy must likewise cope with the demands of provincial autonomy within a federal system. In Central America, authoritarian regimes have recently given way to governments elected on the US model. Haiti stands out as the most unstable of Caribbean countries.

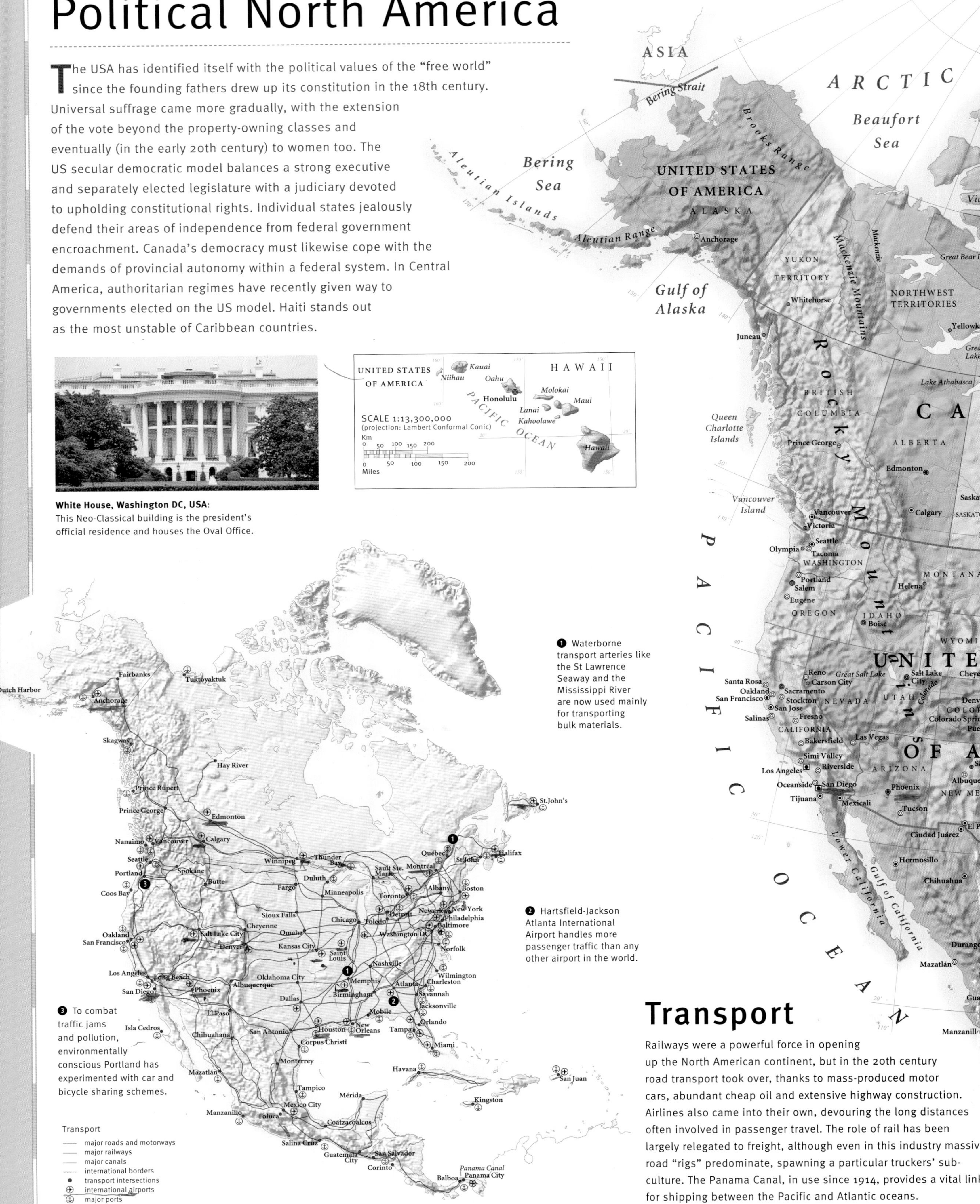

UNITED STATES OF AMERICA
HAWAII
Kauai
Niihau
Oahu
Honolulu
Molokai
Maui
Lanai
Kahoolawe
Hawaii
PACIFIC OCEAN
SCALE 1:13,300,000
(projection: Lambert Conformal Conic)
Km
Miles
ASIA
Bering Strait
ARCTIC
Beaufort Sea
Brooks Range
Bering Sea
Aleutian Islands
UNITED STATES OF AMERICA
ALASKA
Aleutian Range
Anchorage
YUKON TERRITORY
Whitehorse
Mackenzie Mountains
NORTHWEST TERRITORIES
Great Bear Lake
Yellowknife
Gulf of Alaska
Juneau
Rocky Mountains
BRITISH COLUMBIA
Queen Charlotte Islands
Prince George
ALBERTA
Edmonton
Calgary
Vancouver Island
Vancouver
Victoria
Seattle
Olympia
Tacoma
WASHINGTON
MONTANA
Helena
Portland
Salem
Eugene
OREGON
IDAHO
Boise
PACIFIC OCEAN
Reno
Great Salt Lake
Salt Lake City
Santa Rosa
Carson City
Oakland
Sacramento
San Francisco
Stockton
NEVADA
UTAH
San Jose
Salinas
Fresno
CALIFORNIA
Bakersfield
Las Vegas
Simi Valley
Los Angeles
Riverside
ARIZONA
Oceanside
San Diego
Phoenix
Tijuana
Mexicali
Tucson
Ciudad Juárez
Hermosillo
Chihuahua
Lower California
Gulf of California
Durango
Mazatlán
Manzanillo
1 Waterborne transport arteries like the St Lawrence Seaway and the Mississippi River are now used mainly for transporting bulk materials.
2 Hartsfield-Jackson Atlanta International Airport handles more passenger traffic than any other airport in the world.
3 To combat traffic jams and pollution, environmentally conscious Portland has experimented with car and bicycle sharing schemes.
Transport
major roads and motorways
major railways
major canals
international borders
transport intersections
international airports
major ports

White House, Washington DC, USA: This Neo-Classical building is the president's official residence and houses the Oval Office.

Transport

Railways were a powerful force in opening up the North American continent, but in the 20th century road transport took over, thanks to mass-produced motor cars, abundant cheap oil and extensive highway construction. Airlines also came into their own, devouring the long distances often involved in passenger travel. The role of rail has been largely relegated to freight, although even in this industry massive road "rigs" predominate, spawning a particular truckers' sub-culture. The Panama Canal, in use since 1914, provides a vital link for shipping between the Pacific and Atlantic oceans.

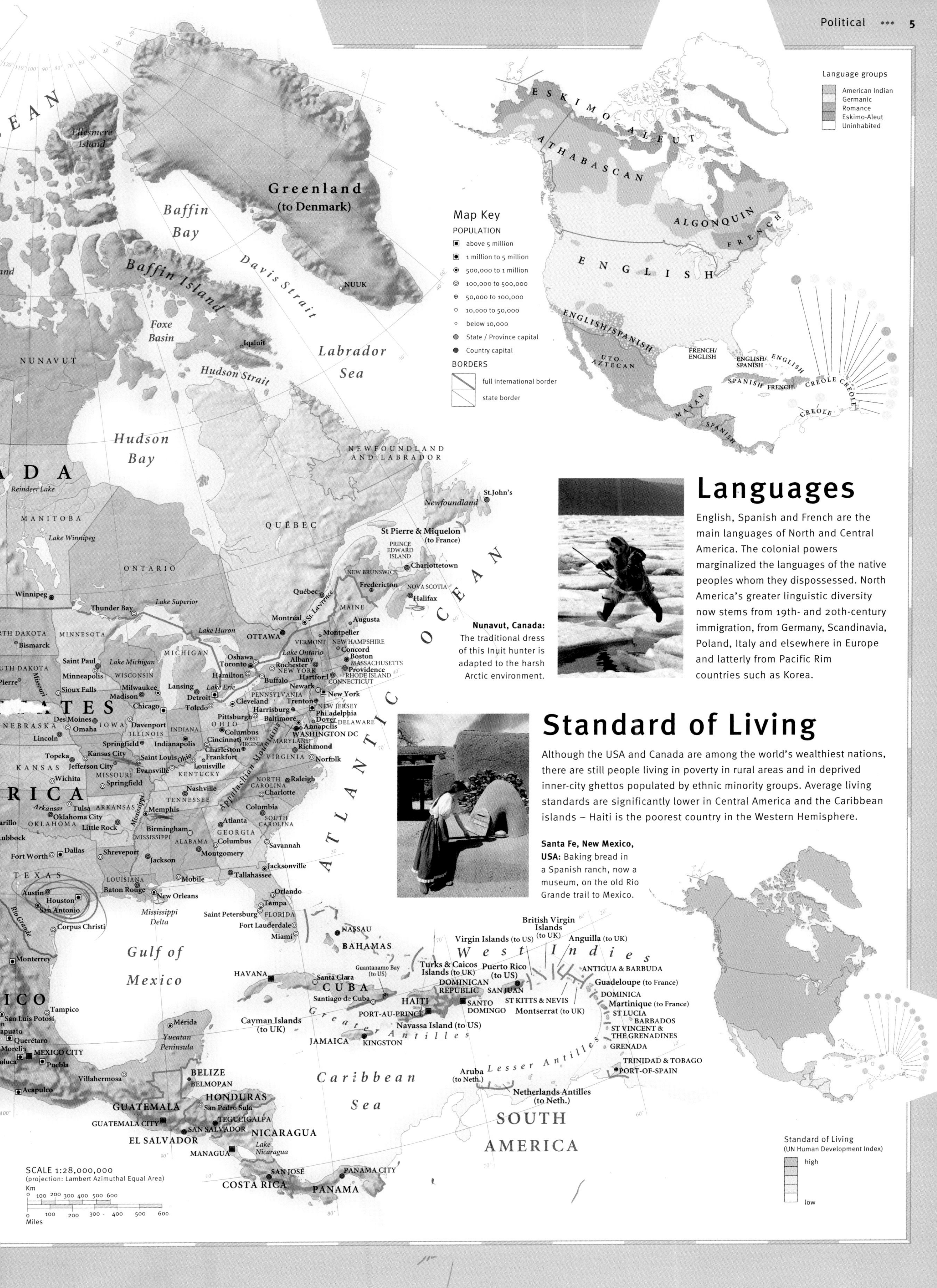
Greenland
(to Denmark)
Ellesmere Island
Baffin Bay
Baffin Island
Davis Strait
NUUK
Foxe Basin
Iqaluit
NUNAVUT
Hudson Strait
Labrador Sea
Hudson Bay
NEWFOUNDLAND AND LABRADOR
Newfoundland
St.John's
QUÉBEC
St Pierre & Miquelon (to France)
PRINCE EDWARD ISLAND
Charlottetown
NEW BRUNSWICK
Fredericton
NOVA SCOTIA
Halifax
MANITOBA
Lake Winnipeg
ONTARIO
Winnipeg
Thunder Bay
Lake Superior
Québec
Montréal
OTTAWA
MAINE
Augusta
Lake Huron
MINNESOTA
MICHIGAN
Lake Michigan
WISCONSIN
Lake Ontario
Lake Erie
Toronto
Boston
New York
WASHINGTON DC
ATLANTIC OCEAN
Appalachian Mountains
Mississippi
Gulf of Mexico
Mississippi Delta
Yucatan Peninsula
MEXICO CITY
NASSAU
BAHAMAS
HAVANA
CUBA
HAITI
PORT-AU-PRINCE
DOMINICAN REPUBLIC
SANTO DOMINGO
Puerto Rico (to US)
SAN JUAN
JAMAICA
KINGSTON
West Indies
Greater Antilles
Lesser Antilles
Caribbean Sea
BELIZE
BELMOPAN
HONDURAS
TEGUCIGALPA
GUATEMALA
GUATEMALA CITY
EL SALVADOR
SAN SALVADOR
NICARAGUA
MANAGUA
COSTA RICA
SAN JOSÉ
PANAMA
PANAMA CITY
SOUTH AMERICA
TRINIDAD & TOBAGO
PORT-OF-SPAIN
Map Key
POPULATION
above 5 million
1 million to 5 million
500,000 to 1 million
100,000 to 500,000
50,000 to 100,000
10,000 to 50,000
below 10,000
State / Province capital
Country capital
BORDERS
full international border
state border
SCALE 1:28,000,000
(projection: Lambert Azimuthal Equal Area)
Km
0 100 200 300 400 500 600
0 100 200 300 400 500 600
Miles
Language groups
American Indian
Germanic
Romance
Eskimo-Aleut
Uninhabited
ESKIMO-ALEUT
ATHABASCAN
ALGONQUIN
FRENCH
ENGLISH
ENGLISH/SPANISH
UTO-AZTECAN
FRENCH/ENGLISH
ENGLISH/SPANISH
ENGLISH
SPANISH
FRENCH
CREOLE
MAYAN
Standard of Living
(UN Human Development Index)
high
low

Languages

English, Spanish and French are the main languages of North and Central America. The colonial powers marginalized the languages of the native peoples whom they dispossessed. North America's greater linguistic diversity now stems from 19th- and 20th-century immigration, from Germany, Scandinavia, Poland, Italy and elsewhere in Europe and latterly from Pacific Rim countries such as Korea.

Nunavut, Canada: The traditional dress of this Inuit hunter is adapted to the harsh Arctic environment.

Standard of Living

Although the USA and Canada are among the world's wealthiest nations, there are still people living in poverty in rural areas and in deprived inner-city ghettos populated by ethnic minority groups. Average living standards are significantly lower in Central America and the Caribbean islands – Haiti is the poorest country in the Western Hemisphere.

Santa Fe, New Mexico, USA: Baking bread in a Spanish ranch, now a museum, on the old Rio Grande trail to Mexico.

Banff National Park, Canada

Seattle, USA

New Mexico, USA

Vancouver, Canada

Pico de Orizaba, Mexico

Activities

The USA caters for entertainment on the grand scale. The theme parks of the sunshine states of Florida and California attract visitors from all over the world. Millions of fans hungrily lap up the big national sports – American football, baseball, basketball and ice hockey – not just on TV but in state-of-the-art stadiums, supercharged with a highly partisan atmosphere. In Mexico and Central America soccer stirs the sporting passions, along with wrestling, bullfighting and the rodeo.

Cities such as San Francisco and New York fizz with cosmopolitan atmosphere, great shopping, high-energy nightlife and cultural attractions. Love them or hate them, America's huge shopping malls and drive-thru fast food restaurants are also part of the experience. Mexico's colourful festivals, beach resorts and spectacular scenery always reward visitors. Surfers head for the Pacific coast and Hawai'i, while Florida's beaches are for diving, boating and soaking up the sun. Further south, Belize and Honduras share the second-largest coral reef on earth. North America's national parks have trekking, whitewater rafting and canoeing opportunities aplenty. Top Rocky Mountain ski resorts include Aspen in Colorado and Whistler in British Columbia, which also caters for snowmobiling, heli-skiing and dog-sledding.

What to Do

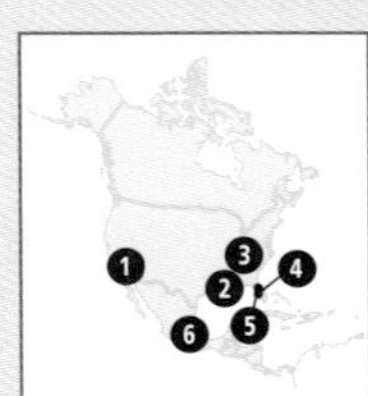

❶ Las Vegas, Nevada, USA
Beat the bank in this city's glitzy casinos

❷ Mardi Gras, New Orleans, USA
Carnival, masked balls, and exuberant parades

❸ Kentucky Derby, Louisville, USA
The jewel in the triple crown of thoroughbred horseracing's calendar

❹ Disney World®, Florida, USA
Meet Mickey Mouse and other cartoon favourites at the world's largest theme park

❺ Universal Studios, Florida, USA
The film sets, stunts, and special effects that made the American movie industry famous

❻ Charreria, Mexico City, Mexico
Displays of daring horsemanship and machismo

Natural Sights

The USA boasts the most extensive national park system in the world. Yellowstone, its first and still best-loved park, opened in 1872. The landscapes of Arizona, Utah and New Mexico offer amazing canyons, Bryce National Park's colourful amphitheatres, striking rock formations in Arches National Park and exquisitely varied desert scenery – White Sands National Monument, the Painted Desert, Monument Valley and many more. California has the oldest, largest and tallest trees on earth, while northwestern USA and southwestern Canada are known for their beautiful Rocky Mountain glaciers and lakes. Much of the rest of Canada and Alaska are untouched wildernesses, with coastal areas accessible for spectacular sea trips and whalewatching.

Mexico and Central America play host to unspoiled rainforests and myriad birdlife, as well as several active volcanoes on the Pacific's "Ring of Fire". The West Indies are blessed with many idyllic beaches, making these island states a popular choice for sun-seekers.

Glacier National Park, Montana, USA: Winding across the park, past St Mary Lake and through awe-inspiring mountain scenery, the 92 km (57 mile) Going-to-the-Sun road is one of America's most beautiful drives.

What to See

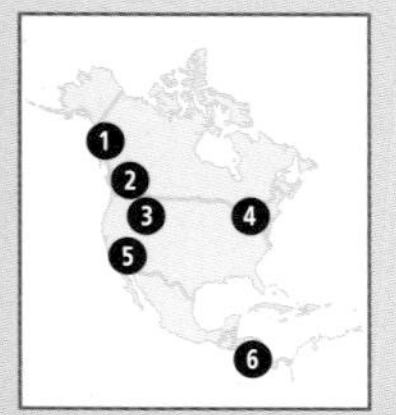

❶ Glacier Bay, Alaska
Spot humpback, gray and minke whales among the icebergs

❷ Banff National Park, Alberta, Canada
Serene turquoise lakes amid the jagged peaks of the Rocky Mountains

❸ Yellowstone National Park, Wyoming, USA
Huge volcanic caldera of colourful hot springs, geysers and wildlife

❹ Niagara Falls, Canada/USA
These immense, powerful waterfalls make a breathtaking, natural spectacle

❺ Grand Canyon, Arizona, USA
The world's most impressive canyon, crafted through the ages by the Colorado River

❻ Corcovado National Park, Costa Rica
Coastal rainforest with tapirs, anteaters, peccaries and jaguars

Small
sugar

Pumpkins at Thanksgiving, USA

Whale-spotting, Northeast USA

Les Pitons, St Lucia

Cancún, Mexico

San Bernardino, USA

Xalapa, Mexico: One of a superb collection of colossal Olmec heads in Xalapa's Museo Antropologia. Often called Mesoamerica's first civilization, Olmec society began around 1200 BCE.

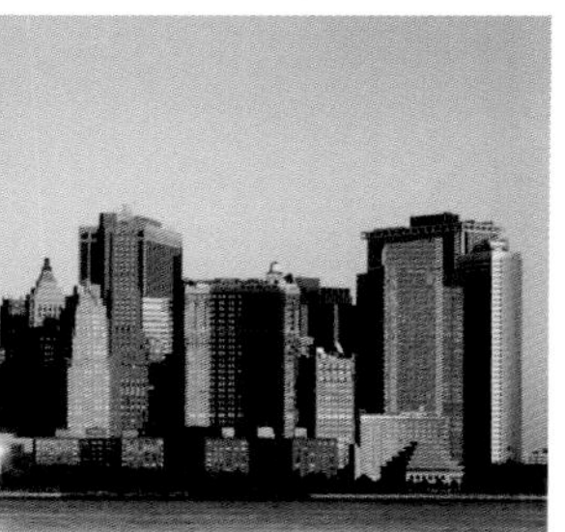

Manhattan: New York's most famous borough has a distinctive skyline, mixing Art Deco pinnacles with high-tech glassy blocks. Starkly missing are the iconic twin towers of the World Trade Center, destroyed on 9/11.

Cultural Sights

The great cultures that flourished prior to the arrival of European settlers have left impressive traces, above all in Mexico's Yucatan Peninsula and in Central America, centres for the Aztec and Mayan empires. In New Mexico, Arizona and Colorado, well-preserved ruins of the Anasazi, dating back 1,400 years, can be seen at Mesa Verde. For those interested in more recent history, museums and memorials to pioneers, politicians, technological triumphs and legendary musicians are something of an American speciality, while many cities, particularly along the west and northeast coasts, have a wealth of world-class art collections. New York's Broadway is a great centre of theatre. Gleaming, modern Canadian cities like Montréal mix French and English traditions, and Mexico City, one of the world's largest cities, is a thriving throng of ancient sights, colonial buildings and vibrant markets.

What to See

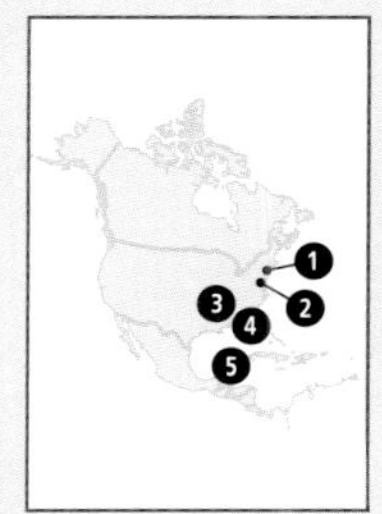

❶ Metropolitan Museum of Art, New York, USA
World art and culture from the pharoahs to Jackson Pollock

❷ White House, Washington DC, USA
Pomp and power at the president's world-famous residence

❸ Graceland, Tennessee, USA
Elvis Presley's home, full of memorabilia

❹ Kennedy Space Center, Florida, USA
Re-live the moon missions and try a simulated space flight

❺ Chichén Itzá, Mexico
Still-mysterious, Mayan pyramid

Great North American Journeys

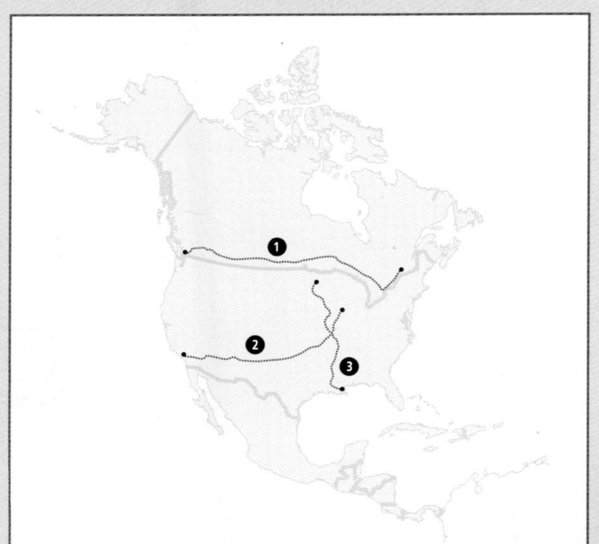

❶ Canadian Pacific Railroad
Montréal – Vancouver
3,200 km (2,000 miles)
The link that made Canada a truly continental nation. On the dramatic stretch through the Rocky Mountains to the west coast, the Rocky Mountaineer runs excursions in luxurious style, with a special domed carriage for unrivalled views.

❷ Route 66
Chicago – Los Angeles
3,620 km (2,250 miles)
Get your kicks on Route 66 – a classic road, first charted in 1926, the stretch from Oklahoma was immortalized as the "mother road" in John Steinbeck's novel *The Grapes of Wrath,* set during the dustbowl years of the 1930s. Now modern interstate highways run parallel to the historic road.

❸ Highway 61
New Orleans – Minnesota
2,735 km (1,700 miles)
A historical pilgrimage rather than a scenic drive, the "freedom road" led African-Americans north in search of rights and opportunities in the 1940s and 1950s. With them they brought the blues music of the Mississippi delta that lies at the heart of rock.

Journeys

In tune with its long love affair with the car, the USA is best toured by road. The dramatic Pacific Coast Highway from Los Angeles ends in beautiful Oregon. The Great River Road tracks the Mississippi from its source in Minnesota to the Gulf of Mexico. In the east, the modern Blue Ridge Parkway traverses the Great Smoky Mountains and Shenandoah National Park, Route 100 presents vistas of Vermont's fantastic autumn colours and the Florida Keys are connected by the magnificent Overseas Highway. Prior to the motor age, half a million settlers once drove their wagons west along the Oregon Trail, 3,200 km (2,000 miles) from Missouri. Interpretative centres and monuments now mark the route. The railroads too, though long eclipsed by the car, still offer some fabulous options, such as Mexico's breathtaking 13-hour Copper Canyon ride from Los Mochis on the coast to Chihuahua, or Canada's Rocky Mountaineer. An ocean cruise from Seattle to Glacier Bay in Alaska can't be beaten for scenery, but Caribbean cruises offer an alternative for lovers of luxury.

66
DINER

Albuquerque, New Mexico, USA: A 1950s design classic, this Route 66 diner takes you back to that era, with memorabilia covering the walls and staff in period costume who serve classic burgers and thick milkshakes, to the sound of a period juke box.

Canada

Canada is enormous, second only to Russia in size, but nine-tenths of it is uninhabited; most of the population lives along the long southern border with the USA. For the visitor this means that a great deal of the country to the north, much of it with superb scenery, is remote and inaccessible. Forays into the wilderness, however, can be arranged from the more frequented and tourism-oriented areas in both the western and eastern provinces.

Vancouver, a go-ahead Pacific coastal city with much to offer the visitor in its own right, is a great starting point. Mountain and whitewater adventures beckon the intrepid traveller north from here, deeper into British Columbia or even further, to the Mackenzie Mountains of Yukon Territory, with the added lure of seeing the best of Canadian wildlife.

No less scenic options are the parks of the Rocky Mountains, whose great facilities for winter sports (and climbing in summer) ensure there is no lack of thrills on offer. In the east, the Toronto–Québec axis holds more historic and cultural attractions but also has Canada's top natural wonder, the mighty Niagara Falls.

Activities

View the Northern Lights (*aurora borealis)* in **Yukon, Nunavut** and the **Northwest Territories** (September–October is best)
Stay up all night **north of the Arctic Circle** to enjoy the midnight sun (June–July)
Greet the first sunrise for 30 days at the Sunrise Festival in **Inuvik**, Northwest Territories, plus dog races and fireworks (early January)
Lodge in the annually reconstructed Ice Hotel near the city of **Québec** (winter only)
Cheer the Blue Jays baseball team in the Rogers Centre, **Toronto's** sports stadium
Heli-ski in **Yukon's** northern peaks (skiers are lifted by helicopter to pristine slopes)

Whistler, British Columbia: Canada's most famous winter sport destination is also known for its year-round range of activities. Kayaking – a kayak is the Inuit word for a canoe – is a popular and particularly suitable way to get around in this region of many lakes and rivers.

196

Parry Channel
Viscount Melville Sound
Banks Island
Victoria Island
Prince Albert Peninsula

38

BRITISH COLUMBIA
ALBERTA
SASKATCHEWAN
Edmonton
Calgary
Saskatoon
Vancouver
Victoria
Prince George
ROCKY MOUNTAINS
UNITED STATES

192

Horseshoe Falls, Niagara: These are 800 m (2,625 ft) wide and 50 m (164 ft) high. A series of rocky tunnels takes visitors on a *Journey Behind the Falls*, where the wall of water is so thick it blocks out the view.

SCALE 1:14,700,000
(projection: Lambert Azimuthal Equal Area)

16

Baffin Bay
Baffin Island
Davis Strait
Foxe Basin
Hudson Strait
LABRADOR SEA
Hudson Bay
James Bay
Gulf of St. Lawrence
ATLANTIC OCEAN
Great Lakes
Lake Superior
Lake Huron
Lake Michigan
Lake Ontario
Lake Erie
Laurentian Mountains
NEWFOUNDLAND & LABRADOR
NEW BRUNSWICK
NOVA SCOTIA
PRINCE EDWARD ISLAND
QUÉBEC
ONTARIO
MANITOBA
NUNAVUT
GREENLAND (to Denmark)
Ellesmere Island
Devon Island
Southampton Island
Toronto
Ottawa
Montréal
Québec
Winnipeg
Thunder Bay
Halifax
St John's
Iqaluit
196
16
64

Iqaluit, Baffin Island: This little town, with its mainly Inuit population, is the gateway to Baffin Island. Spectacular fjords and knife-edged mountains offer unbeatable kayaking, glacier walks, dog-sledding and exhilarating snowmobiling.

What to See

❶ Auyuittuq National Park (on Baffin Island) Offers one of the few hiking trails north of the Arctic Circle

❷ Mackenzie Mountains Spectacular mountains cut through by deep canyons forged by the South Nahanni river

❸ Wood Buffalo National Park (near Fort Smith) Canada's largest park is home to a huge herd of free-roaming bison

❹ Vancouver Beautiful mountains frame the glass towers and copper-topped skyscrapers

❺ Rocky Mountain National Parks Banff and Jasper – Canada's first national parks – have striking scenery, turquoise lakes, impressive canyons and glaciers

❻ Valley of the Dinosaurs (near Drumheller) Rich in dinosaur finds and dramatic features such as Horseshoe Canyon

❼ Tunnels of Moose Jaw Lavish recreation of gangster Al Capone's hideout and how Chinese immigrants lived in this underworld

❽ Toronto Canada's largest city and financial and commercial hub, home of the world's tallest free-standing structure, the CN Tower

❾ Niagara Falls The thundering Horseshoe (or Canadian) Falls are one of the world's great natural wonders

❿ Ottawa Compromise choice of capital, now known for its Gothic parliament and first-rate museums

⓫ Montréal Bilingual city of splendid churches, notably the Basilique Notre-Dame-de-Montréal

⓬ Québec Former Iroquois village, this rare North American example of a walled city is now the heart of French-speaking Canada

Map Key

POPULATION	ELEVATION
■ 1 million to 5 million	6000m / 19,686ft
● 500,000 to 1 million	4000m / 13,124ft
◎ 100,000 to 500,000	3000m / 9843ft
⊕ 50,000 to 100,000	2000m / 6562ft
○ 10,000 to 50,000	1000m / 3281ft
○ below 10,000	500m / 1640ft
	250m / 820ft
	100m / 328ft
	sea level

Canada: Western Provinces

Alberta, British Columbia, Manitoba, Saskatchewan, Yukon Territory

British Columbia is a land of dramatic scenery and a magnet for outdoor sports enthusiasts. The western Coast Mountains run north into Alaska, and the Rocky Mountains further inland stretch into Yukon Territory, a relatively unspoiled wilderness which is home to a significant number of Native American people, many maintaining traditional lifestyles. A sharp descent eastwards unveils the vast, flat expanses of Alberta, Saskatchewan and Manitoba, the prairie provinces which first attracted settlers with the promise of empty lands and fertile soils. The descendants of early European immigrants still make up much of the population.

Tourism is largely concentrated on the southern half of British Columbia (it is the second-biggest industry in the province, after timber). Vancouver is a favourite city for many. Modern and wealthy, it nestles in a fantastic location, looking across to Vancouver Island. The island itself is a big tourist destination, offering dramatic landscapes and excellent opportunities for viewing whales and other marine wildlife. Banff and Jasper National Parks, famous worldwide for their majestic Rocky Mountain scenery, are great focal points for a wide range of outdoor activities in both summer and winter.

Vancouver: British Columbia's largest city enjoys a great rivalry with its US neighbour Seattle. Both are lively and comfortable cities, with fabulous countryside nearby, thriving waterfronts overlooking offshore islands and noted for their abundant marine wildlife.

Activities

Brave a bungee jump at **Nanaimo** on Vancouver Island	Go whale watching at **Pacific Rim National Park Reserve**, Vancouver Island, known for killer and gray whales
See polar bears safely from a Tundra Buggy®, **Churchill** (October–November)	Snocoach onto the Athabasca Glacier in **Jasper National Park**, Alberta
Attend the ten-day **Calgary Stampede** festival of all things cowboy, including the Half-Million Dollar Rodeo (July)	Go whitewater rafting along the Maligne River in **Jasper National Park**
Cheer on the Edmonton Oilers at an ice hockey game in the **Skyreach Center**, Edmonton, Alberta (October–April)	Hike around **Banff**, Alberta – the Banff National Park has numerous trails through breathtaking scenery, ranging from half-day to five-day hikes
Take the Rocky Mountaineer, a luxury rail trip across the **Rocky Mountains** from Vancouver to Calgary	Rock climb – **Banff National Park** is a favourite destination among many of the world's best climbers
Ski in **Whistler**, Canada's largest ski resort, near Vancouver, perfect for both alpine and cross-country skiing – some runs stay open most of the year	Admire the wildernesses of the **Saint Elias Mountains**, Yukon Territory, in a light aircraft flight from Haines Junction

Map Key

POPULATION

- 500,000 to 1 million
- 100,000 to 500,000
- 50,000 to 100,000
- 10,000 to 50,000
- below 10,000

ELEVATION

- 6000m / 19,686ft
- 4000m / 13,124ft
- 3000m / 9843ft
- 2000m / 6562ft
- 1000m / 3281ft
- 500m / 1640ft
- 250m / 820ft
- 100m / 328ft
- sea level

38
8
192

Moraine Lake, Banff National Park: The shimmering waters of Banff's lakes have enchanted visitors for centuries, especially since the creation in 1885 of Canada's first national park. Moraine Lake lies in the Valley of the Ten Peaks.

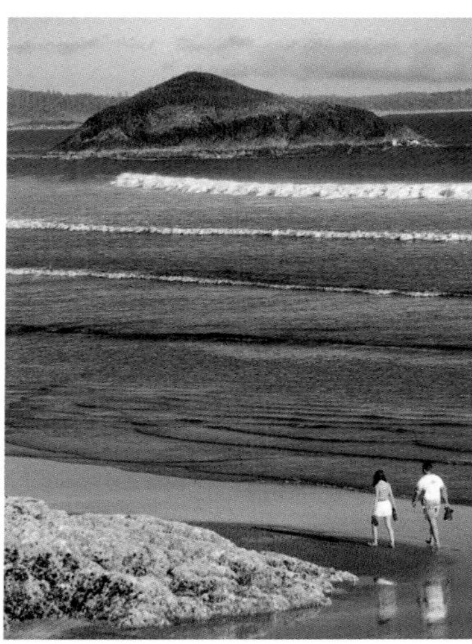

Long Beach, Vancouver Island: The windswept sands of Long Beach in Pacific Rim National Park Reserve are renowned for their beauty, with crashing Pacific rollers. More than 20 species of whale can be spotted offshore and there are daily viewing trips from March to August.

What to See

Valley of the Dinosaurs, Vancouver
see pp8–9

❶ Dawson
A living museum of the gold-rush days, on the confluence of the Yukon and Klondike Rivers

❷ Vancouver Island
The Pacific Rim National Park Reserve, home to Canada's best whale watching and the tough West Coast Trail

❸ University of British Columbia Museum of Anthropology
This outstanding museum in Vancouver houses a remarkable collection of Native American art from totem poles to canoes

❹ Columbia Icefield
The peaks and valleys of Jasper National Park lie under glaciers up to 900 m (3000 ft) thick

❺ Yoho National Park
(near Golden)
The Takakkaw Falls, rock towers at Hoodoo Creek and glacial lakes make up Yoho, meaning "awe and wonder"

❻ Banff National Park
(around Banff)
Renowned for sparkling lakes and rugged mountains, Banff is home to bears and elk

❼ Marble Canyon
(near Banff)
Limestone formations and the nearby ochre Paint Pot pools are top sights in Kootenay National Park

❽ Royal Tyrrell Museum of Palaeontology
(in Drumheller)
This excellent museum uses high-tech interactive computers and 3-D dioramas to recreate prehistoric landscapes and bring dinosaurs to life

❾ Wanuskewin Heritage Park
(near Saskatoon)
Reveals the Plains Indians culture and the area's archaeology, including local digs of 6,000-year-old hunter settlements

❿ Little Manitou Lake
(near Watrous)
Known for its healing properties and 13 times more salty than the Dead Sea

⓫ Regina
See the drills of Royal Canadian Mounted Police at their Academy

⓬ Big Muddy Badlands
(near Minton)
Glacially formed, bizarre landscape of buttes and ravines, once a hideout for Butch Cassidy

⓭ Winnipeg
City at the east-west halfway point of Canada, plus the Manitoba Museum of Man and Nature

⓮ Churchill
The "polar bear capital of the world" is also good for seeing beluga whales and the Northern Lights

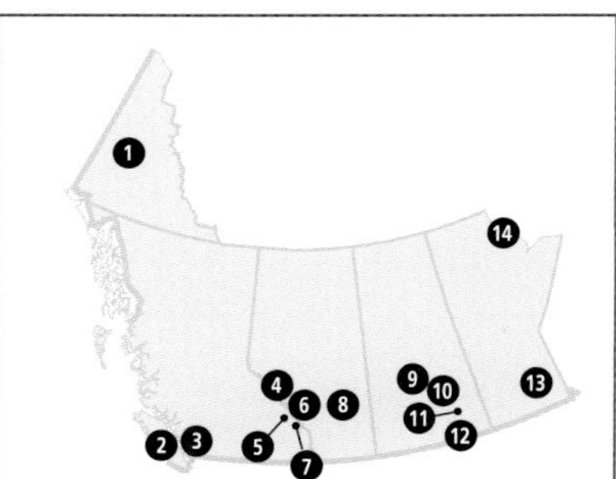

1
14
4
6
8
9
10
11
12
13
2
3
5
7

SCALE 1:8,250,000
(projection: Lambert Conformal Conic)
Km 0 25 50 100 150 200 250
Miles 0 25 50 100 150 200 250

8
12
16

Canada: Eastern Provinces

New Brunswick, Newfoundland & Labrador, Nova Scotia, Ontario, Prince Edward Island, Québec, *St Pierre & Miquelon* (to France)

Colonized by both the French and the British during the 17th century, Canada's eastern provinces are still marked – and enlivened – by their dual influences. French is one of Canada's two official languages, alongside English – and Québec is the largest French-speaking territory in the world. The region also contains the last fragment of once-sizable French territories, the islands of St Pierre and Miquelon.

Most of the area's man-made attractions are to be found in the south, particularly along the border with the USA, where the main settlements developed and where most of the people still live. Away from the cities, Ontario, Québec and the Atlantic provinces also have much magnificent scenery and plentiful wildlife. The north of this region, around Hudson Bay, remains snow-covered almost all year round and the indigenous Inuit people make up the bulk of its sparse population.

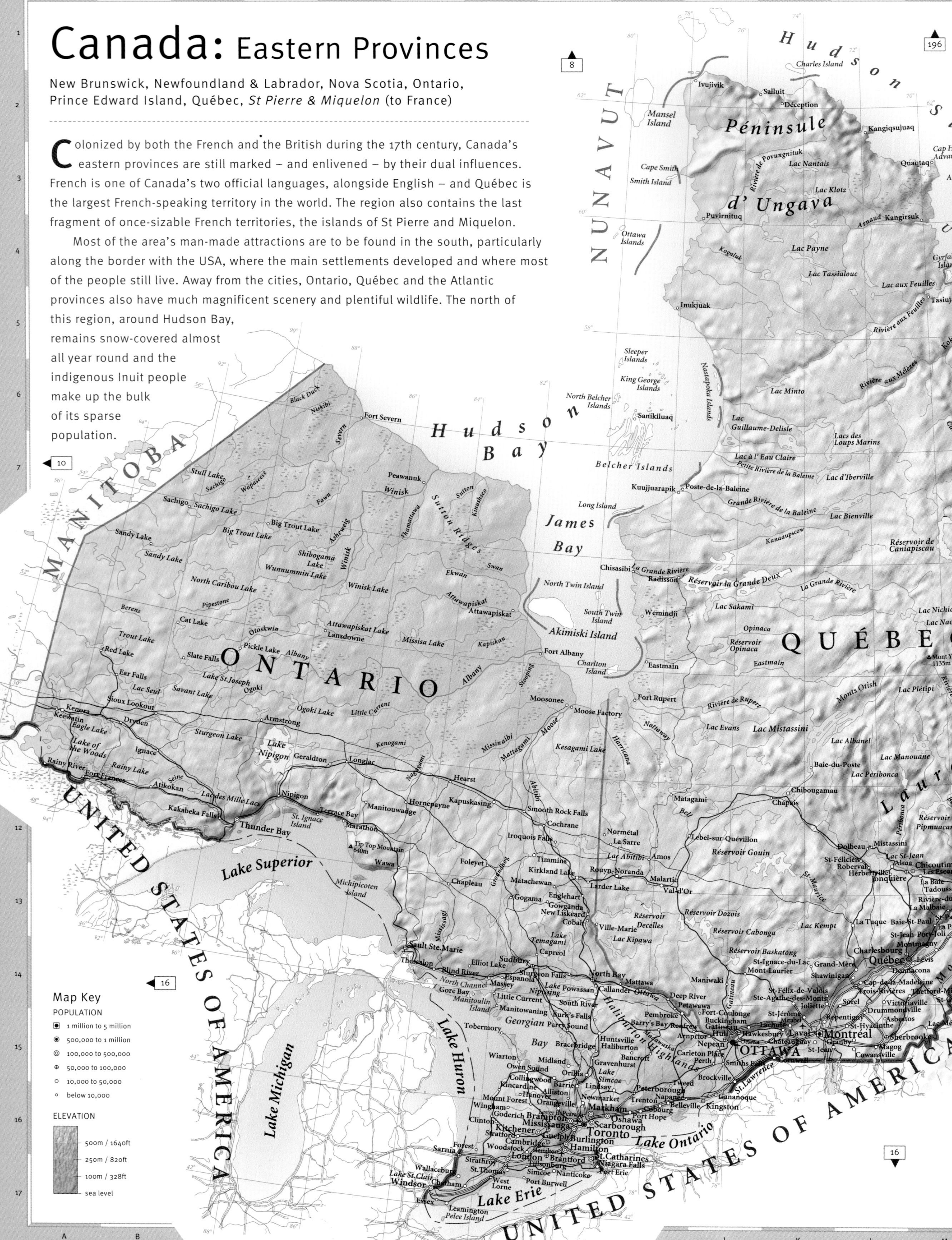
8
196
10
16
16
Hudson Strait
Péninsule d' Ungava
NUNAVUT
Hudson Bay
James Bay
MANITOBA
ONTARIO
QUÉBEC
UNITED STATES OF AMERICA
Lake Superior
Lake Michigan
Lake Huron
Georgian Bay
Lake Erie
Lake Ontario
Belcher Islands
Akimiski Island
Mansel Island
Charles Island
Ivujivik
Salluit
Déception
Kangiqsujuaq
Quaqtaq
Puvirnituq
Kangirsuk
Inukjuak
Sanikiluaq
Kuujjuarapik
Poste-de-la-Baleine
Chisasibi
Radisson
Wemindji
Eastmain
Fort Rupert
Moosonee
Moose Factory
Fort Albany
Attawapiskat
Fort Severn
Peawanuk
Big Trout Lake
Sandy Lake
Sachigo
Pickle Lake
Sioux Lookout
Kenora
Dryden
Fort Frances
Atikokan
Thunder Bay
Nipigon
Geraldton
Longlac
Hearst
Kapuskasing
Cochrane
Timmins
Kirkland Lake
Rouyn-Noranda
Val-d'Or
Amos
Chibougamau
Matagami
Wawa
Sault Ste.Marie
Sudbury
North Bay
Ottawa
Pembroke
Kingston
Belleville
Peterborough
Barrie
Toronto
Mississauga
Scarborough
Hamilton
Oshawa
Brampton
Kitchener
Guelph
London
Sarnia
Windsor
St.Catharines
Niagara Falls
Fort Erie
Montréal
Laval
Québec
Lévis
Trois-Rivières
Sherbrooke
Drummondville
Chicoutimi
Jonquière
Dolbeau
La Tuque
Shawinigan
Réservoir Gouin
Réservoir Cabonga
Réservoir Baskatong
Lac Mistassini
Lac Abitibi
Lake Nipigon
Lake of the Woods
Lac Seul
Mont Yapeitso 1135m
Tip Top Mountain 640m
Map Key
POPULATION
1 million to 5 million
500,000 to 1 million
100,000 to 500,000
50,000 to 100,000
10,000 to 50,000
below 10,000
ELEVATION
500m / 1640ft
250m / 820ft
100m / 328ft
sea level

N O P Q R S T U V W X Y Z

L'Anse-aux-Meadows, Newfoundland: Visitors to the site of what is believed to be the first European settlement in North America can get hands-on experience of the Viking way of life in the reconstructed encampment of eight wood and earth buildings.

What to See

Montreal, Niagara Falls, Ottawa, Québec, Toronto *see* pp8–9

❶ Point Pelee
Spit extending 20 km (12 miles) into Lake Erie, Canada's most southerly point, famous for birdwatching

❷ Maid of the Mist
A close-up view of Niagara Falls from this intrepid boat is a great way to feel their force

❸ Royal Ontario Museum (Toronto)
This vast collection features an imperial Ming tomb from China

❹ Algonquin Provincial Park (in the Haliburton Highlands)
Full of bears, moose, and beavers, with good fishing and canoeing

❺ National Gallery of Canada (Ottawa)
A significant collection of Canadian and international art is displayed in this modern gallery

❻ Musée des Beaux Arts (Montréal)
Art gallery displaying European paintings from medieval times onwards

❼ The Citadel (Québec)
This magnificent fort, was built by both the British and French armies, to defend against an American attack that never came

❽ Sainte-Anne-de-Beaupré
(near Québec) 20th-century basilica on the site of a church built by sailors who survived a shipwreck in 1658

❾ Bay of Fundy
Spectacular eroded cliffs and sea stacks caused by the world's highest tides, which attract many whales

❿ Prince Edward Island
Noted for its richly coloured panoramas and for Cavendish Beach, the location of the house made famous in L. M. Montgomery's *Anne of Green Gables*

⓫ Cape Breton Island
Rugged island at the northern end of Nova Scotia, renowned for its scenic highway, the Cabot Trail, which circles the island

⓬ Gros Morne National Park
Magnificent mountains, fjords and waterfalls, with moose and caribou roaming wild, part of Newfoundland's north peninsula

⓭ L'Anse-aux-Meadows
(near St.Anthony)
First Viking settlement in North America, dating from 1000 CE

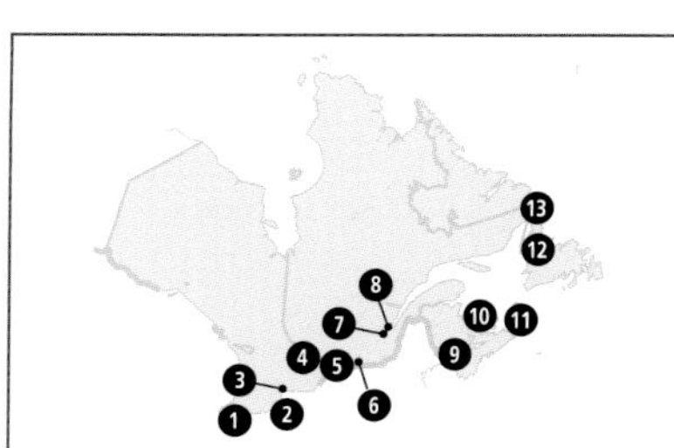

Toronto: The city's skyline is dominated by the 553 m (1,815 ft) CN Tower, which houses the world's largest revolving restaurant and the longest inside staircase – thankfully, there are also glass-fronted elevators to whizz sightseers up to the observation lookouts in under a minute.

Activities

Canoe in the lakes of the **Haliburton Highlands**, Ontario

Imitate a wolf howl in **Algonquin Provincial Park**, Ontario – a nightly organized exercise in August, attempting to elicit responses from real animals

Cycle the **Route Verte**, 2,400 km (1,500 miles) of bike trails across Québec

Go sea-kayaking at **St John's**, Newfoundland, with the chance of spotting whales

Practise your golf on **Prince Edward Island**, home to an amazing concentration of Canada's best courses

Play ice hockey in **Windsor**, Ontario, which claims to have invented the game in 1800

Dance in a *ceilidh* on **Prince Edward Island**, proud of its Celtic heritage

Discover the history of humankind at the **Royal Ontario Museum** in Toronto, Canada's largest museum

SCALE 1:7,750,000
(projection: Lambert Conformal Conic)
Km 0 25 50 100 150 200 250
Miles 0 25 50 100 150 200 250

Button Islands
Port Burwell
LABRADOR SEA
Torngat Mountains
Saglek Bay
Hebron
Kangiqsualujjuaq
Cod Island
Okak Islands
George
Rivière à la Baleine
South Aulatsivik Island
Nain
Tunungayualok Island
Kogaluk
Lac Champdoré
Labrador
Hopedale
Makkovik
Cape Harrison
Lac aux Goélands
Attikamagen Lake
Kanairiktok
Schefferville
Petitsikapau Lake
Rigolet
Lake Melville
Hamilton Inlet
Mealy Mountains
Eagle
Cartwright
Smallwood Reservoir
Churchill Falls
North West River
Happy Valley-Goose Bay
NEWFOUNDLAND & LABRADOR
Port Hope Simpson
Shabogamo Lake
Churchill
Lake Joseph
Atikonak Lac
Belle Isle
Labrador City
Mont Wright 899m
Ashuanipi Lake
Little Mecatina
Red Bay
Cape Bauld
Forteau
St.Anthony
Rivière-St-Paul
St-Augustin
Strait of Belle Isle
Petit Lac Manicouagan
Monts Groulx
Moisie
Natashquan
Roddickton
Grey Islands
Réservoir Manicouagan
Mountains
La Tabatière
Port Saunders
Harrington Harbour
White Bay
Romaine
Long Range Mountains
Baie Verte
Fogo Island
Notre Dame Bay
Lac-Allard
Mingan
Natashquan
Sally's Cove
Gros Morne 806m
Sept-Îles
Longue-Pointe
Havre-St-Pierre
Moisie
Détroit de Jacques-Cartier
Île d'Anticosti
Gander
Bonavista Bay
Bonavista
Deer Lake
Grand Lake
Grand Falls
Port-Cartier
Port-Menier
Buchans
Red Indian Lake
Corner Brook
Honguedo Passage
Clarenville
Baie-Trinité
Newfoundland
Stephenville
Trinity Bay
Carbonear
St.John's
Godbout
Mont-Louis
Grande-Vallée
Gulf of St. Lawrence
Cape St.George
Meelpaeg Lake
Baie-Comeau
Ste-Anne-des-Monts
Murdochville
Hauterive
Cap-Chat
Mont Jacques-Cartier 1268m
Gaspé
St. George's Bay
Matane
Percé
Rocher Percé
Burgeo
Placentia
Péninsule de Gaspé
Grande-Rivière
Mont-Joli
Chandler
Table Mountain 587m
Harbour Breton
Avalon Peninsula
Amqui
New-Richmond
Cape Ray
Channel-Port aux Basques
Marystown
Placentia Bay
Cape Race
Dalhousie
Îles de la Madeleine
Grand Bank
Campbellton
Caraquet
Shippagan
Chaleur Bay
Cabot Strait
Tracadie
Bathurst
Kedgwick
ST PIERRE & MIQUELON (to France)
Cape North
Edmundston
Neguac
PRINCE EDWARD ISLAND
St-Léonard
Mount Carleton 820m
Chatham
Tignish
Ingonish Beach
Grand Falls
Newcastle
Chéticamp
Cape Breton Island
Plaster Rock
Sydney Mines
NEW BRUNSWICK
Prince Edward Island
Glace Bay
Souris
Sydney
Richibucto
Doaktown
Kensington
Summerside
Charlottetown
Inverness
Shediac
Northumberland Strait
Hartland
Woodstock
Minto
Moncton
Riverview
Sackville
Port Hawkesbury
Amherst
New Glasgow
Antigonish
Chedabucto Bay
Canso
Fredericton
Oromocto
Sussex
Springhill
McAdam
Truro
Hampton
Minas Basin
St.Stephen
Saint John
Kentville
Sheet Harbour
NOVA SCOTIA
Grand Manan Island
Windsor
Halifax
Middleton
Dartmouth
Bay of Fundy
Digby
Lunenburg
Bridgewater
Lake Rossignol
Sable Island
Liverpool
Shelburne
Yarmouth
Cape Sable
ATLANTIC OCEAN

64 ▶

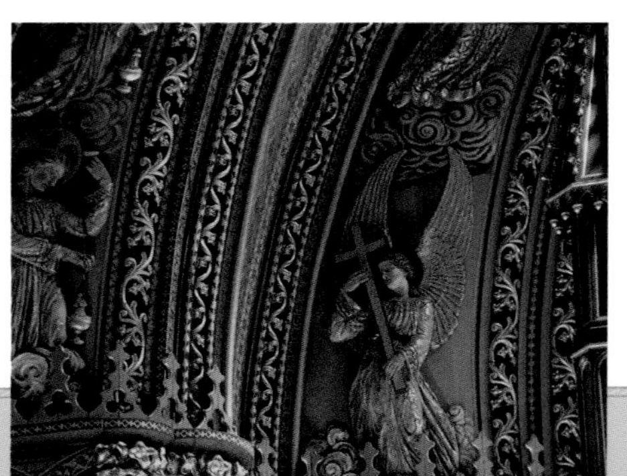

Basilique Notre-Dame-de-Montréal: Richly decorated, this 1829 Catholic showpiece in Montréal is one of North America's most eye-catching churches.

N O P Q R S W X Y Z

Southeastern Canada

Southern Ontario, Southern Québec

Southern Ontario and Québec are richly endowed with attractive lakes, hills and forests. Half of Canada's population lives here, but urban development is concentrated in the strip around the Great Lakes and their principal outlet, the St Lawrence river, notably in four main cities. Toronto, the largest, is a thriving commercial and financial centre. Further east, but still on the Ontario side of the border with Québec, is Canada's federal capital, Ottawa. Chosen as a compromise between the competing claims of Toronto and Montréal, it is worth visiting for its excellent museums. Bilingual Montréal has a lively cultural atmosphere amid a mix of modern skyscrapers and characterful older buildings, while the traditional walled city of Québec takes the prize for picturesque charm. On the Niagara river, flowing from Lake Erie to Lake Ontario, lies one of North America's most famous sights, Niagara Falls, which attracts a staggering 14 million visitors each year.

CLUB DE HOCKEY CANADIEN

Hockey Hall of Fame, Toronto: This replica dressing room is part of a lavish exhibition and tribute to Canada's most popular sport, ice hockey. Originating in Canada, the game had its beginnings on frozen lakes and ponds. It now ignites Canadian passions like nothing else.

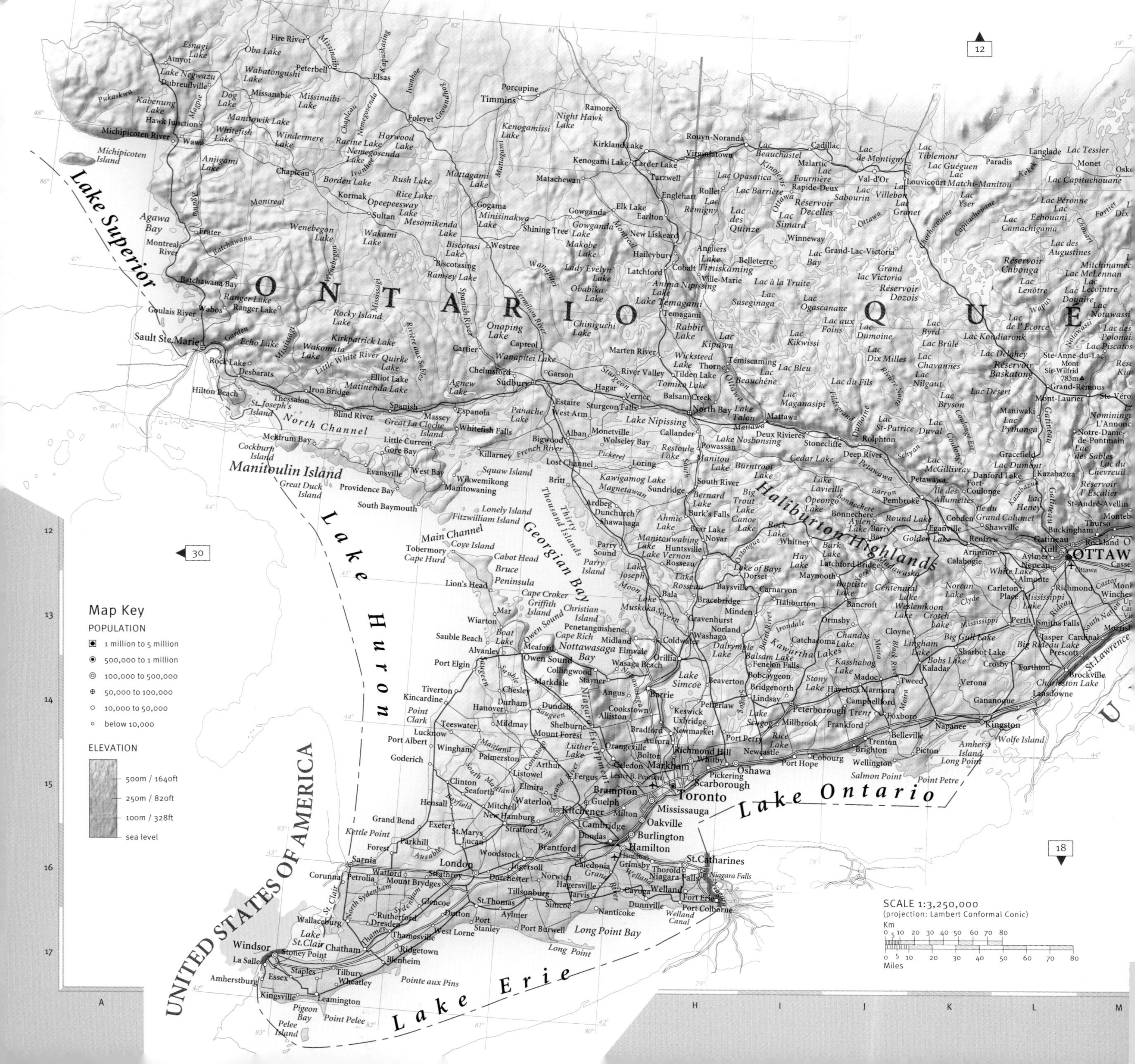

12

30

18

Map Key

POPULATION

- 1 million to 5 million
- 500,000 to 1 million
- 100,000 to 500,000
- 50,000 to 100,000
- 10,000 to 50,000
- below 10,000

ELEVATION

- 500m / 1640ft
- 250m / 820ft
- 100m / 328ft
- sea level

SCALE 1:3,250,000
(projection: Lambert Conformal Conic)
Km 0 5 10 20 30 40 50 60 70 80
Miles 0 5 10 20 30 40 50 60 70 80

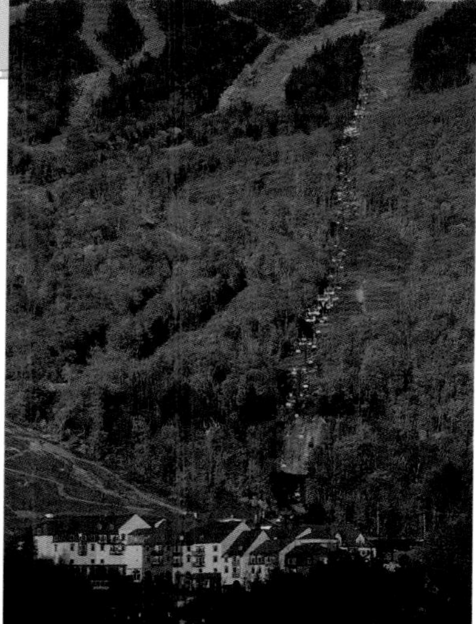

St-Jovite: A typical village in the wooded valleys of the Laurentian Mountains, with colourful old French-style buildings, St-Jovite is best seen in autumn. The area has winter ski runs and is a popular getaway frcm nearby Ottawa and Montréal.

Château Frontenac, Québec: The steep green copper-roofed landmark that dominates the skyline of old Québec is a luxury hotel overlooking the St Lawrence river. It is designed like a French-style château with 600 rooms.

12

What to See

Montréal, Niagara Falls, Ottawa, Québec, Toronto *see* pp8–9

Algonquin Provincial Park, Point Pelee, Sainte-Anne-de-Beaupré *see* pp12–13

❶ Sudbury Basin
Meteor crater, 190 km (120 miles) across, formed two billion years ago, creating a lake, and now a mining complex

❷ Flowerpot Island
Just off Tobermory in Lake Huron, noted for its coastal rock columns

❸ Sainte-Marie among the Hurons
(near Midland) Reconstructed settlement of 1639, half European, half Huron, where the Jesuits attempted to convert the Hurons to Christianity

❹ Casa Loma
(in Toronto) Medieval-style castle-cum-mansion with 98 rooms, built in 1911 by Sir Henry Pellatt, who made his fortune harnessing Niagara Falls for electricity

❺ Serpent Mounds
(beside Rice Lake) A grove of oak trees encloses nine burial mounds dating back 2,000 years ago that are still sacred to Native Americans

❻ Canadian Museum of Civilization
(in Hull) This modern museum is devoted to the progress of the Canadian people from Viking times through to the present day

❼ Laurentian Mountains
Beautiful mountains and lakes, perfect for fishing, hiking, cycling, skiing and sledding

❽ Lac St-Jean
Set amid spruce-covered wilderness, this tranquil lake, ideal for sailing and swimming, is fed by tiny rivers tumbling over the crater walls

❾ Montmorency Falls
(near Québec) Created by the Montmorency river emptying into the St Lawrence. The suspension bridge across the falls gives the best views – but is not for the faint-hearted!

❿ Peninsule de Gaspé
Soaring cliffs and wilderness, including dense pine forests and a variety of wildlife, plus good salmon fishing and the world's tallest windmill

Activities

Birdwatch at **Point Pelee**, on Lake Erie, the southern tip of Canada, noted as a stopping point for bird migration	Sip wine at the Niagara Grape and Wine Festival in **St Catharines**, Ontario (September)
Bungee jump at **Wakefield** near Ottawa	Dress up for the theatre at **Stratford**, Ontario, seeing a play at the Shakespeare Festival (May to early November)
Watch the Changing of the Guard at the **Citadel** in Québec	Go whale watching at **Tadoussac**, Québec. The estuary has beluga whales year-round, plus minke, fin and blue whales in summer
Fish in **Algonquin Provincial Park**, Ontario	

The United States of America

Coterminous USA (for Alaska and Hawaii see pages 38–39)

The sheer size of the USA lends something epic to a transcontinental journey by road, surely the most appropriate way to appreciate how much of its popular culture revolves around the motor car. The sense of reliving so many movies and songs lends enchantment to the view even across huge stretches of flat Midwest prairie landscape. By contrast, there's almost too much for any tourist to absorb in the great cities of the west and northeast coasts and the breathtaking national parks, many of which are in a broad band in the west, stretching over to the east side of the Rocky Mountains. Florida's own bid for the tourist limelight rests partly on its claim to be the "Sunshine State", but equally on the development of huge theme parks, above all Disney World®.

8
192
192
40
CANADA
UNITED STATES
MEXICO
PACIFIC OCEAN
GULF
WASHINGTON
OREGON
CALIFORNIA
NEVADA
IDAHO
MONTANA
WYOMING
UTAH
ARIZONA
COLORADO
NEW MEXICO
NORTH DAKOTA
SOUTH DAKOTA
NEBRASKA
KANSAS
OKLAHOMA
TEXAS
ROCKY MOUNTAINS
GREAT PLAINS
Great Basin
Colorado Plateau
Mojave Desert
Sonoran Desert
Seattle
Portland
San Francisco
Los Angeles
San Diego
Sacramento
Las Vegas
Salt Lake City
Phoenix
Tucson
Denver
Albuquerque
El Paso
Dallas
Houston
San Antonio
Austin
Oklahoma City
Wichita
Boise
Spokane
Cheyenne
Map Key
POPULATION
above 5 million
1 million to 5 million
500,000 to 1 million
100,000 to 500,000
50,000 to 100,000
10,000 to 50,000
below 10,000
ELEVATION
4000m / 13,124ft
3000m / 9843ft
2000m / 6562ft
1000m / 3281ft
500m / 1640ft
250m / 820ft
100m / 328ft
sea level

Yellowstone National Park, Wyoming: Amid dramatic volcanic landscapes, the highlight for many visitors is the park's wildlife, be it bison walking along the road, elk or moose wandering the hillside. Care should be taken when encountering any animals, especially black or grizzly bears.

What to See

❶ Seattle
Interlaced with lakes and creeks, the thriving home of Boeing, Microsoft, and Starbucks is one of the USA's most popular cities

❷ Yellowstone National Park
America's first and best-loved national park is rich in spectacular natural features – notably the Old Faithful geyser, plus plentiful and varied wildlife

❸ San Francisco
Many people's favourite US city, a multicultural centre renowned for its many skyscrapers, gay scene, trams, Alcatraz and the magnificent Golden Gate Bridge

❹ Los Angeles
Entertainment centre of the world, this sprawling metropolis contains Hollywood, Universal Studios, Disneyland ® and the Getty Museum

❺ Las Vegas
World-famous for gambling and showbiz, "The Strip" is alive with themed hotel/casinos

❻ Grand Canyon
The most famous of all canyons, up to 29 km (18 miles) wide. Book well ahead for activities and accommodation

❼ Graceland
(in Memphis) You don't have to be an Elvis Presley fan to marvel at his house, tomb, cars, and private jets

❽ Niagara Falls
Arguably the world's two most spectacular waterfalls: Canada's Horseshoe Falls and the smaller American Falls

❾ New York
Cultural and financial centre of the USA, with iconic landmarks such as the Empire State Building, Central Park and Broadway

❿ Washington DC
Devoid of skyscrapers, the city built to be the US capital offers top-class museums and visits to the nation's political institutions

⓫ Disney World®
(near Orlando) The world's most famous theme park, dominated by its Cinderella Castle; other huge attractions nearby are Sea World and Universal Studios

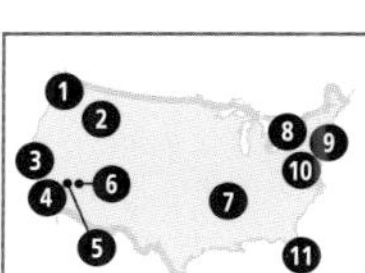

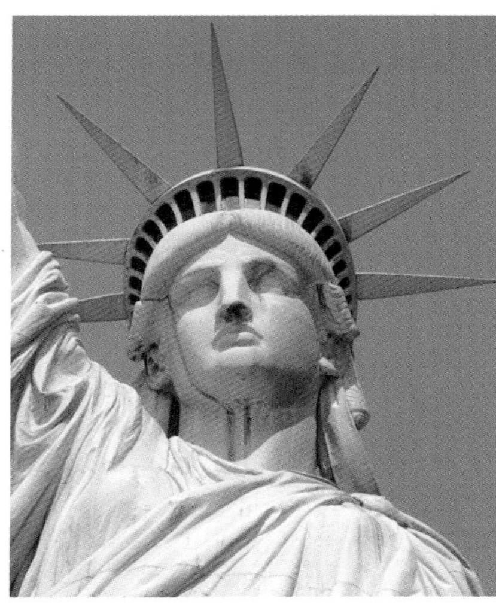

Statue of Liberty, New York: A gift from the French to mark the US centennial in 1876, "Liberty Enlightening the World" is an icon of freedom and democracy, with the rays of her crown representing the seven seas and seven continents. Ferries take tourists across the harbour to Liberty Island for a close up view.

Activities

- Drive across America – from **Chicago** to **California** on the classic Route 66
- Observe bears, moose, cougars and other wildlife in the **Rocky Mountains**
- Stroll down **Sunset Strip**, Los Angeles past the shops and cafes and with luck you may spot a celebrity
- Soak up the sport and razzmatazz of a top baseball or American football match
- See the lovely colours of **New England** in autumn (September–October)
- Enjoy the thrill of **Kingda Ka**, the world's most exciting roller coaster, in Jackson, New Jersey
- Hike in the great open wildernesses of **Yellowstone National Park**
- Simulate a space flight at **Kennedy Space Center**, Florida
- Climb challenging rockfaces in the **Sierra Nevada**

8

64

44

44

SCALE 1: 12,700,000
(projection: Lambert Azimuthal Equal Area)

Grand Canyon, Arizona: Prepare to be overwhelmed by the sheer scale of one of the world's truly breathtaking sights. The chasm carved by the Colorado River is 349 km (217 miles) long and up to 1,500 m (5,000 ft) deep.

USA: Northeastern States

Connecticut, Maine, Massachusetts, New Hampshire, New Jersey, New York, Pennsylvania, Rhode Island, Vermont

Along the indented coast and in the vast woodlands of the northeastern states, the arrival of the early European settlers in the 17th century is commemorated at various sites, as are other historical episodes and milestones in the development of the USA and its assertion of independence in 1776.

The region is bordered by the Great Lakes in the west, famed for the huge Niagara Falls, which straddle the border with Canada. The Appalachian Mountains cut through New York and Pennsylvania states and culminate in the rounded hills of Maine, the most northerly of the six states of New England. This region is well-known for its beautiful autumn leaf colours and its rustic character which has prevailed since the early 17th century. Long Island has been the holiday playground for generations of urbanites with enough money to exchange the city stresses for a seaside idyll. By contrast, the great cities of the Atlantic seaboard now form an almost continuous urban region. For all New England's charms, the bulk of the region's tourism is concentrated around these cities. New York claims to be the world's most visited city, a buzzing, frenetic metropolis crammed full of must-see sights from the Metropolitan Museum of Art to the Statue of Liberty. Boston, the country's pre-eminent centre of learning and Philadelphia, noted for its associations with the War of Independence, are also big destinations both for Americans and foreign travellers.

Three Brothers Mountain, Adirondack Mountains: A riot of deep rich colour in the autumn, the Adirondacks encompass various ecosystems, hundreds of lakes and rivers, and span almost a quarter of New York state.

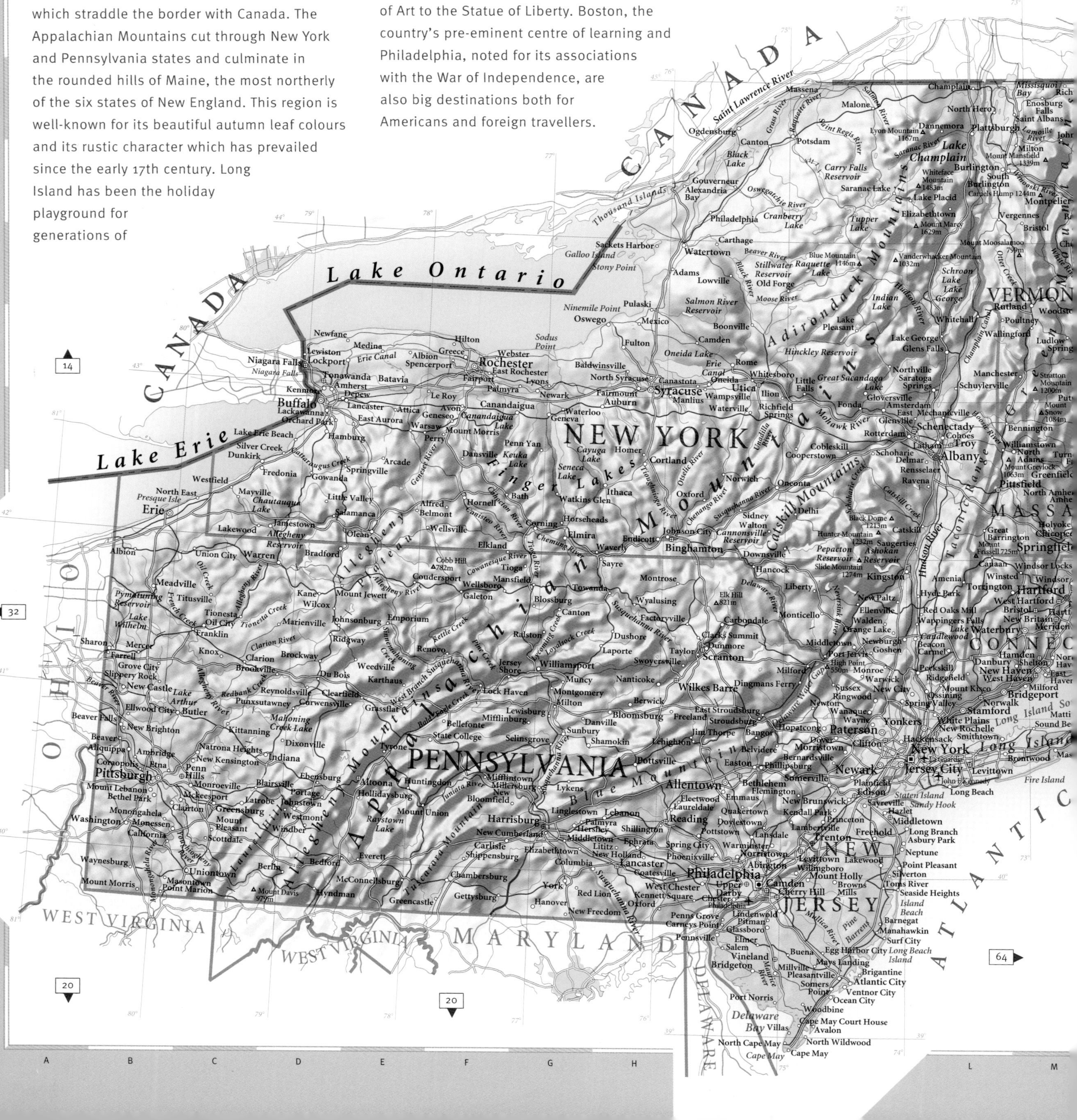

14

32

20

20

64

CANADA
MAINE
Appalachian Mountains
Gulf of Maine
Casco Bay
Bay of Fundy
Massachusetts Bay
Cape Cod Bay
Buzzards Bay
Rhode Island Sound
Block Island Sound
Nantucket Sound
NEW HAMPSHIRE
RHODE ISLAND
OCEAN
Saint John River
Allagash River
Aroostook River
Machias River
Penobscot River
Kennebec River
Androscoggin River
Saco River
Connecticut River
Saint Croix River
Grand Manan Channel
Madawaska
Fort Kent
Van Buren
Long Lake
Bear Lake
Dickey
Eagle Lake
Fish River Lake
Limestone
Caribou
Washburn
Presque Isle
Fort Fairfield
Squa Pan Mountain
Ashland 451m
Mars Hill
Saddleback Mountain 517m
Churchill Lake
Eagle Lake
Chamberlain Lake
Mount Chase 744m
Houlton
Island Falls
Patten
Mount Katahdin 1605m
Mattawamkeag Lake
Sherman Mills
Chiputneticook Lakes
Seboomook Lake
Chesuncook Lake
Moosehead Lake
Millinocket Lake
Boundary Bald Mountain 1109m
Jackman
Millinocket
Pemadumcook Lake
Danforth
Vanceboro
Big Squaw Mountain 974m
White Cap Mountain 1111m
Greenville
Mattawamkeag
Coburn Mountain 1133m
Moose River
Brownville Junction
Sebec Lake
Milo
Lincoln
West Grand Lake
Woodland
Calais
Flagstaff Lake
Bigelow Mountain 1265m
Guilford
Big Lake
Aziscohos Lake
Stratton
Bingham
Sugarloaf Mountain 1291m
Saddleback Mountain 1255m
Rangeley
Sebasticook Lake
Old Town
Milford
Eastport
Lubec
Lead Mountain 466m
Gardner Lake
Mooselookmeguntic Lake
Madison
Pittsfield
Bangor
Brewer
Hampden
Graham Lake
Machias
Skowhegan
Farmington
Bucksport
Milbridge
Cross Island
Jonesport
Great Wass Island
Old Speck Mountain 1274m
Wilton
Oakland
Winslow
Searsport
Ellsworth
Blue Hill
Petit Manan Point
Bar Harbor
Mount Desert Island
Rumford
Livermore Falls
China Lake
Belfast
Penobscot Bay
Augusta
Bethel
Deer Isle
Swans Island
Mount Washington 1917m
Norway
South Paris
Gardiner
Camden
Rockland
Thomaston
Isle au Haut
Vinalhaven Island
Lewiston
Auburn
Waldoboro
Wiscasset
Matinicus Island
Seal Island
Ragged Island
Bridgton
Sebago Lake
Lisbon Falls
Bath
Brunswick
Boothbay Harbor
North Windham
Westbrook
Gorham
Portland
South Portland
Cape Elizabeth
Saco
Biddeford
Kennebunk
Sanford
Alfred
Wolfeboro
Lake Winnipesaukee
Rochester
Somersworth
Dover
York Harbor
Kittery
Portsmouth
Hampton
Newburyport
Plum Island
Cape Ann
Gloucester
Beverly
Salem
Lynn
Malden
Boston
Logan International
Quincy
Weymouth
Marshfield
Race Point
Provincetown
Kingston
Plymouth
Cape Cod
Orleans
Nauset Beach
Barnstable
Yarmouth
Monomoy Island
Hyannis
Falmouth
East Falmouth
New Bedford
Fairhaven
Fall River
Taunton
Brockton
Providence
Cranston
Warwick
Newport
Kingston
Westerly
Block Island
Martha's Vineyard
Edgartown
Oak Bluffs
Nantucket
Nantucket Island
Great Point
Montauk
Montauk Point
Concord
Manchester
Nashua
Lowell
Lawrence
Haverhill
Worcester
Cambridge
Framingham
Fitchburg
Leominster
Woonsocket
Sag Harbor
Lake Memphremagog
Colebrook
Berlin
Lancaster
Groveton
Littleton
Lyndonville
Guildhall
Woodsville
Conway
North Conway
Squam Lake
Plymouth
Meredith
Laconia
Newport
Sunapee Lake
Keene
Peterborough
Milford
Goffstown

12 ▶

14 ▲

Cape Neddick Lighthouse, York, Maine: Nicknamed "The Nubble", Maine's southernmost and most visited lighthouse was built in 1871. With more than 8,050 km (5,000 miles) of inlets, bays and harbours, Maine's coastline is dotted with lighthouses that have for centuries been guiding mariners to safety.

64 ▶

Activities

- Float across the mountains at the **Adirondack Balloon Festival** (September)
- Ski at **Lake Placid**, New York state, venue for the Winter Olympics in 1932 and 1980
- Race a yacht off **Newport**, Rhode Island, a favourite resort for wealthy Americans
- Eat your fill at **Hershey's Chocolate World**, near Philadelphia. The *Hershey Bar* is so popular in the US that Americans are amazed how few foreigners know of it!
- Visit the **New York Metropolitan Opera**, at one of the world's great opera houses
- Take in a show on **Broadway**, New York
- Play the slot machines in gambling halls, such as the Indian-style Taj Mahal casino, in **Atlantic City**, New Jersey
- Hike in **Acadia National Park**, Maine
- Take the steep cog railway in the **White Mountains**, New Hampshire, to the top of Mount Washington, where wind speeds of 372 km/h (231 mph) have been recorded

64 ▶

Times Square, Manhattan: At the heart of New York city's theatre district old-world Broadway glamour rubs shoulders with modernity; this famous intersection is home to MTV's studios and E Walk – a vast entertainment and retail complex.

What to See

New York, Niagara Falls
see pp16–17

❶ Pittsburgh
Former industrial city that has cleaned up its image. Home of the fascinating Carnegie museums of Art and Natural History

❷ Gettysburg
Site of a pivotal battle of the Civil War, and of Abraham Lincoln's famous Gettysburg Address, setting out his vision for the nation

❸ Hershey's Chocolate World
(near Harrisburg) Celebrates America's love affair with the *Hershey Bar*

❹ Lancaster County
Settled by the Amish people, who live simply without most modern aids

❺ Philadelphia
The "birthplace of the USA", best known for its Liberty Bell and Independence Hall, site of the first reading of the Declaration of Independence in 1776

❻ Atlantic City
This gambling city is known as "Las Vegas of the East"

❼ Princeton
Small town centred on its Ivy League university and research institutes; Albert Einstein worked at the Institute for Advanced Study

❽ Manhattan
Colonial churches and early US monuments stand in the shadow of skyscrapers, old and new, along famous roads like Wall Street and Broadway

❾ Metropolitan Museum of Art
World's third-largest art collection, spanning 300,000 years of world culture, including a whole Egyptian temple

❿ Newport
Exclusive Rhode Island summer resort, with sumptuous residences, and the International Tennis Hall of Fame

⓫ Cape Cod
Popular holiday resort in an area of great beauty, where the Pilgrim Fathers landed the *Mayflower* in 1620

⓬ Boston
One of the oldest and most distinguished US cities, a commercial, intellectual and cultural centre, with the world-renowned Harvard University and Massachusetts Institute of Technology

⓭ Salem
Made famous by Arthur Miller's *The Crucible*, Salem has a museum on the notorious witch trials of 1692, plus the broader, historical Essex Institute

⓮ White Mountains National Forest
Popular outdoor recreation area

⓯ Acadia National Park
Rocky coasts, forests, streams, and lakes, offering a wide range of outdoor activities

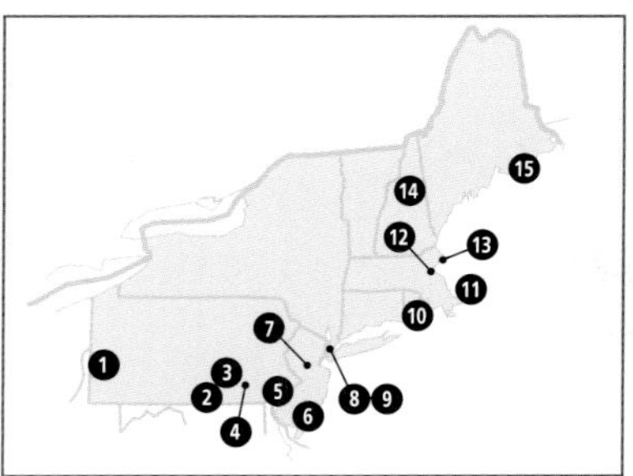
1
2
3
4
5
6
7
8
9
10
11
12
13
14
15

SCALE 1:3,000,000
(projection: Lambert Conformal Conic)
Km 0 5 10 20 30 40 50 60 70 80 90 100
Miles 0 5 10 20 30 40 50 60 70 80 90 100

Map Key

POPULATION
- ▣ above 5 million
- ◙ 1 million to 5 million
- ◉ 500,000 to 1 million
- ◎ 100,000 to 500,000
- ⊕ 50,000 to 100,000
- ○ 10,000 to 50,000
- ∘ below 10,000

ELEVATION

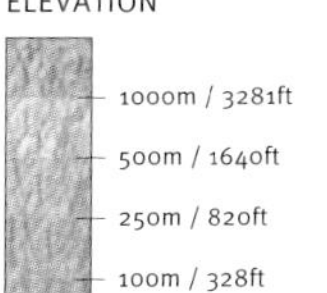

- 1000m / 3281ft
- 500m / 1640ft
- 250m / 820ft
- 100m / 328ft
- sea level

USA: Mid-Eastern States

Delaware, District of Columbia, Kentucky, Maryland, North Carolina, South Carolina, Tennessee, Virginia, West Virginia

The attractions of the Mid-Eastern states come in several distinct forms. Kentucky – known for its Bluegrass plains – and much of Tennessee are cotton-growing country, where tourism is largely focused on Mammoth Cave and Elvis Presley's former home Graceland, in Memphis, as well as the famous horse races of Louisville, Kentucky.

East Tennessee and West Virginia have some very attractive scenery, dominated by the southern Appalachian Mountains, which include the Great Smoky and Shenandoah ranges, providing excellent hiking amid forests and waterfalls. The Blue Ridge Parkway runs for 346 km (215 miles) along the crest of the ranges. It is a lovely route in spring for the blossoming meadows and autumn for the turning foliage.

East of the Appalachian Mountains, in the large, fertile coastal plain, the Carolinas in the south draw visitors to their historic mansions and towns like Charleston, evoking the pre-Civil War plantation days. Further north, Baltimore epitomizes the rich maritime heritage of Maryland, while the federal capital Washington DC is a must for anyone interested in the architectural symbols of government and spacious town planning.

Virginia's main source of income is tourism, based on its rich history and its importance in the 1861–1865 Civil War, when its capital, Richmond, was the seat of the Confederacy.

Kentucky Horse Racing: Kentucky is famous for its thoroughbred breeding and racing, centred on Lexington with its Kentucky Horse Park, a world-famous equestrian theme park, housing the International Museum of the Horse.

30

26

22

Activities

- Enjoy a concert by the world-class **Baltimore** Symphony Orchestra
- Hike in the **Great Smoky Mountains**
- Play golf at **Hilton Head Island**, a fashionable and wealthy resort off the coast of South Carolina
- See **Louisville**'s Kentucky Derby, a July racing calendar highlight
- Sail at **Annapolis** the sailing capital of the USA (near Baltimore)
- Sip bourbon at the traditional **Labrot and Graham Distillery** in Woodford County, Kentucky
- Go whitewater rafting on the **New River**, West Virginia

Great Smoky Mountains on the Tennessee-North Carolina border: The view from Clingmans Dome, Tennessee's highest peak. This national park has over 800 miles (1,300 km) of trails, scenic waterfalls and 1,500 species of flowering plants.

What to See

Graceland, Washington DC
see pp16–17

1 Nashville
The capital of country music, heard nationwide on the *Grand Ole Opry* radio programme. Also has a complete reconstruction of the Parthenon from Athens

2 Mammoth Cave
(near Brownsville) The world's longest cave system has various short and full-day tours

3 Lexington
At the heart of Bluegrass Country, this town is a world-famous horse-breeding centre

4 Cumberland Gap
An important passage through the hills of southeast Kentucky, the national park includes the Daniel Boone Forest and its attractive natural bridge

5 Great Smoky Mountains
The most visited US national park, named because of the mist and cloud that rise out of valleys like smoke signals

6 New River Gorge
One of the world's longest and highest steel arch bridges spans this 1,000 ft (300 m) deep gorge, which offers whitewater rafting and magnificent views

7 Shenandoah National Park
Taking in the Blue Ridge Mountains, Shenandoah is famed for its autumn colouring

8 Monticello
(near Charlottesville) President Thomas Jefferson's Palladian mansion was designed by him and has various inventions to ease domestic life

9 Baltimore
Maryland's largest city is a major industrial seaport and cultural centre, with universities, museums and a world-class orchestra

10 National Aquarium
(in Baltimore) One of the best aquariums in the world, with excellent rainforest, sea cliff and coral displays

11 Baltimore and Ohio Railroad Museum
A wide range of trains, old railway buildings and memorabilia make this Baltimore's top museum, as well as a mecca for trainspotters

12 Colonial Williamsburg
Open-air living museum of the town in 1633, with over 100 restored and reconstructed buildings. Costumed "residents" informatively recreate the lives of the period for visitors

13 Outer Banks
A chain of unspoiled, scenic narrow islands, with a monument to the Wright brothers at the site of their first historic flight in 1903

14 Charleston
Retaining some of the feel of plantation days, a historic town still full of Georgian mansions

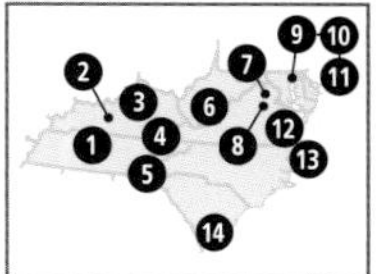
1
2
3
4
5
6
7
8
9
10
11
12
13
14

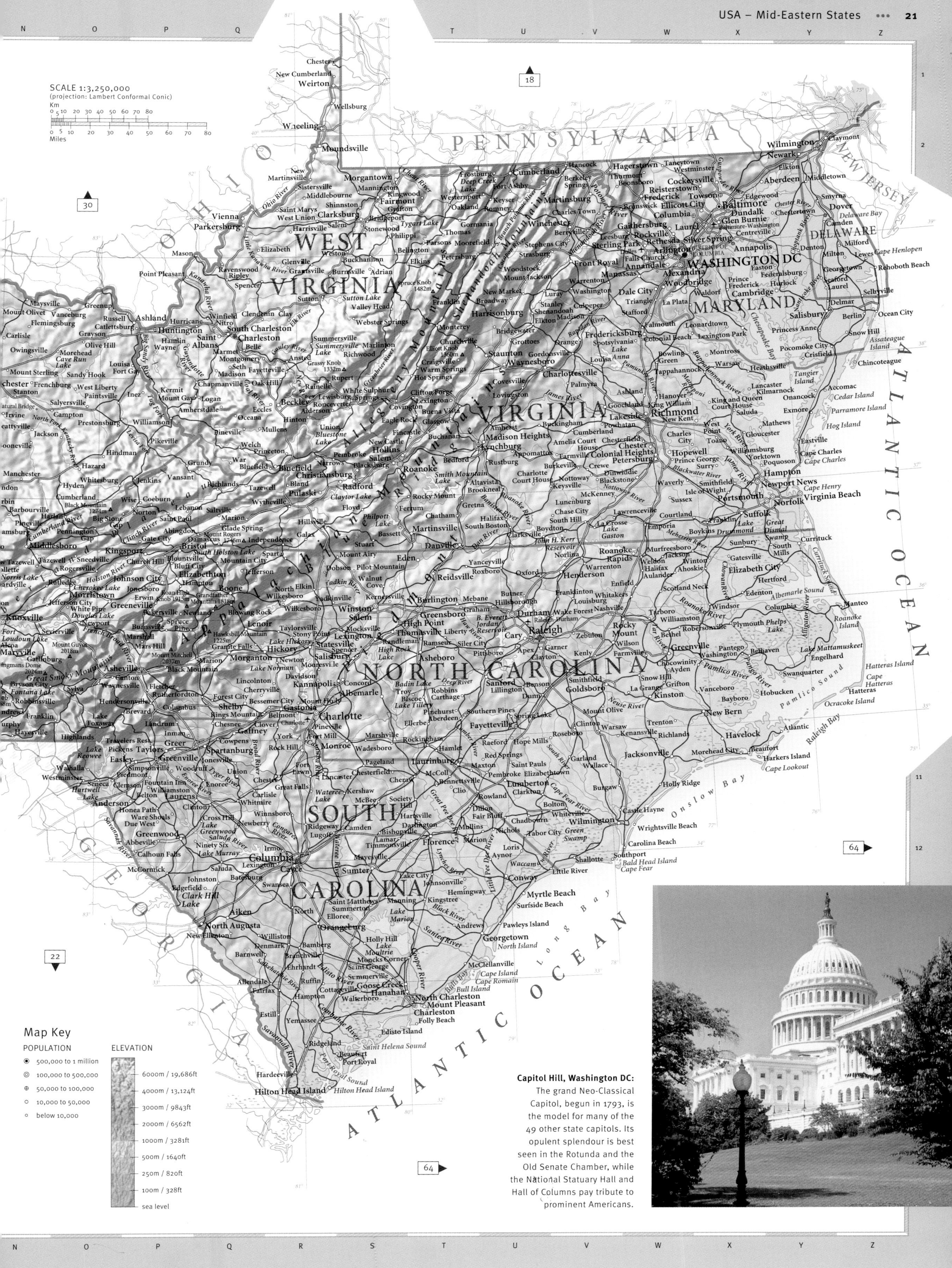
SCALE 1:3,250,000
(projection: Lambert Conformal Conic)
Km
Miles
PENNSYLVANIA
WEST VIRGINIA
VIRGINIA
MARYLAND
DELAWARE
NEW JERSEY
NORTH CAROLINA
SOUTH CAROLINA
OHIO
GEORGIA
ATLANTIC OCEAN
WASHINGTON DC
Appalachian Mountains
Blue Ridge
Allegheny Mountains
Shenandoah Mountains
Piedmont
Map Key
POPULATION
500,000 to 1 million
100,000 to 500,000
50,000 to 100,000
10,000 to 50,000
below 10,000
ELEVATION
6000m / 19,686ft
4000m / 13,124ft
3000m / 9843ft
2000m / 6562ft
1000m / 3281ft
500m / 1640ft
250m / 820ft
100m / 328ft
sea level
18
30
22
64
64

Capitol Hill, Washington DC: The grand Neo-Classical Capitol, begun in 1793, is the model for many of the 49 other state capitols. Its opulent splendour is best seen in the Rotunda and the Old Senate Chamber, while the National Statuary Hall and Hall of Columns pay tribute to prominent Americans.

USA: Southern States

Alabama, Florida, Georgia, Louisiana, Mississippi

Go south to experience the sense of separate identity that this region draws from its history. Defeat in the American Civil War (1861–1865) brought chronic poverty to the Confederate states, while the freeing of four million black slaves led to a struggle over racial segregation reaching its peak with the Civil Rights movement of the 1960s. French influences also come through strongly in the culinary heritage, especially in Louisiana, where the French language is still spoken in Cajun communities near the coast.

Florida, the "Sunshine State", has become the biggest tourist destination in the region – and indeed in America – due to its excellent climate, fine beaches and a determined effort to entertain. There are numerous theme parks around Tampa and Orlando and many attractions in the large coastal conurbation around Miami. Another place in the region competing for the tourists' attention is New Orleans, the cosmopolitan city whose annual Mardi Gras carnival sees the streets entirely given over to exuberant celebration.

ARKANSAS
MISSISSIPPI
LOUISIANA
TEXAS
Shreveport
Bossier City
Monroe
Vicksburg
Jackson
Alexandria
Lake Charles
Lafayette
Baton Rouge
New Orleans
Natchez
Greenville
Hattiesburg
Gulfport
Houma
Mississippi River
Red River
Atchafalaya Bay
Chandeleur Sound
Breton Sound
Lake Pontchartrain
Marsh Island
Isles Dernieres
Timbalier Island

26

24

40

Everglades National Park, Florida: These low-lying wetlands are a paradise for wildlife. American crocodiles and alligators congregate at the "Gator Hole", hollowed out by the alligators in the dry season to reach the water below. Best visited in March–April.

What to See

Disney World®
see pp16–17

❶ New Orleans
A multicultural mix of French, Spanish, Cajun and Creole plus a charming historic centre give the birthplace of jazz a unique buzz

❷ Baton Rouge
Louisiana's capital is known for its historic buildings, lively nightlife and varied culture

❸ Natchez
Small town founded in 1716, an important port in the days of the cotton trade, with many Grand Revival-style houses

❹ Atlanta
Birthplace of civil rights campaigner Martin Luther King and author of *Gone with the Wind* Margaret Mitchell. The home of Coca-Cola and the CNN Center can be visited

❺ Okefenokee Swamp
Known to Native Americans as "Land of the Quaking Earth" because of its floating islands, this peat bog supports whole forests and numerous alligators

❻ Saint Augustine
Settled in 1565, the oldest European town in North America, with a refurbished Spanish colonial-style old town

❼ Kennedy Space Center
The US Air Force's largest rocket-testing and launch area, with fascinating exhibits and films about space travel Visitors can experience the life of an astronaut and attend launch days

❽ Orlando Odditorium
Ripley's Believe it or Not weird exhibits include the world's tallest man and a Rolls-Royce made entirely of matchsticks

❾ Universal Studios
(in Orlando) Experience 3-D special effects and thrilling rides in a theme park of Universal's most famous movies

❿ Sea World
(in Orlando) Watching trained killer whales and feeding the dolphins head an extensive line up of aquatic treats

⓫ Fantasy of Flight
(near Lakeland) Rare and vintage aircraft, with a flight simulator and daily flypast

⓬ Busch Gardens
Zoo-cum-theme park in Tampa, known for breeding endangered species such as the black rhinoceros

⓭ Salvador Dali Museum
Large collection of works by the Catalan Surrealist painter, in Saint Petersburg, which is famed for its "perpetual" sunshine

⓮ Everglades National Park
Fascinating area of swamp and marshland occupying the whole southern tip of Florida

⓯ Fort Lauderdale
The "Venice of the USA", crammed with artificial waterways, is now a major resort

⓰ Miami
Huge centre for business and leisure, its most unusual attraction is a 12th-century church imported from Spain by William Randolph Hearst

⓱ Florida Keys
Chain of idyllic coral islands ending at Key West, once home of writers Tennessee Williams and Ernest Hemingway

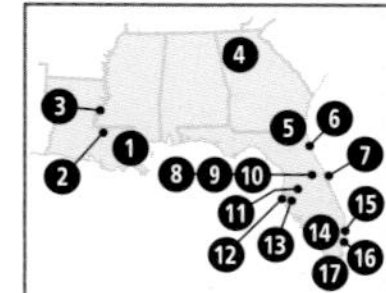
1
2
3
4
5
6
7
8
9
10
11
12
13
14
15
16
17

A beach on the Florida panhandle: Some of the state's most beautiful beaches lie in northwest Florida between Pensacola and Panama City, offering brilliant quartz sand, water sports and amusement parks, as well as more secluded spots. The winter sunshine makes Florida a year-round destination.

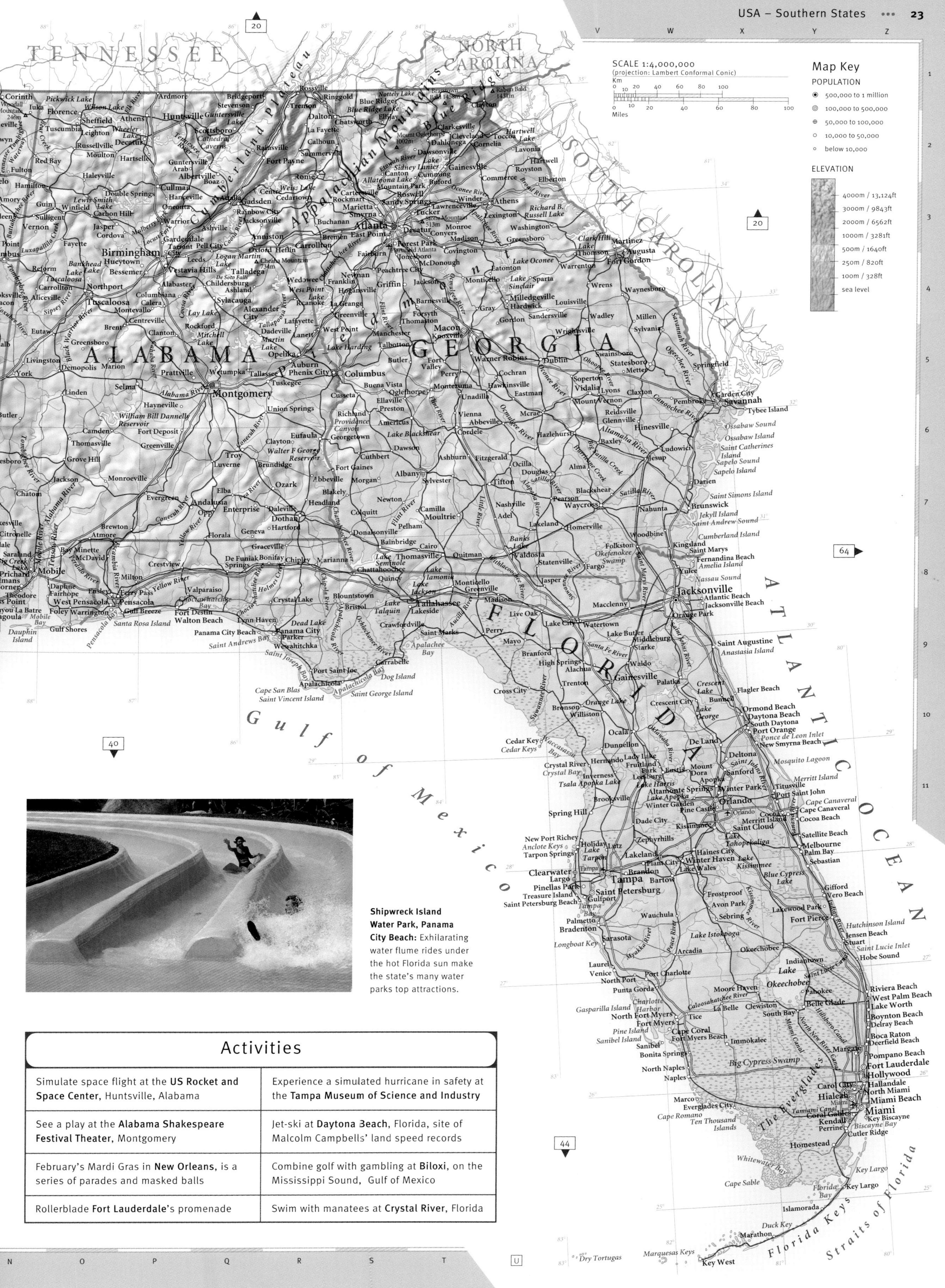
TENNESSEE
NORTH CAROLINA
SOUTH CAROLINA
ALABAMA
GEORGIA
FLORIDA
ATLANTIC OCEAN
Gulf of Mexico
Straits of Florida
Florida Keys
Cumberland Plateau
Appalachian Mountains
Blue Ridge
Piedmont
The Everglades
Lake Okeechobee
Big Cypress Swamp
Okefenokee Swamp
SCALE 1:4,000,000
(projection: Lambert Conformal Conic)
Km
Miles
Map Key
POPULATION
500,000 to 1 million
100,000 to 500,000
50,000 to 100,000
10,000 to 50,000
below 10,000
ELEVATION
4000m / 13,124ft
3000m / 9843ft
2000m / 6562ft
1000m / 3281ft
500m / 1640ft
250m / 820ft
100m / 328ft
sea level
Atlanta
Birmingham
Montgomery
Mobile
Huntsville
Columbus
Macon
Augusta
Savannah
Tallahassee
Jacksonville
Orlando
Tampa
Saint Petersburg
Miami
Fort Lauderdale
Key West

Shipwreck Island Water Park, Panama City Beach: Exhilarating water flume rides under the hot Florida sun make the state's many water parks top attractions.

Activities

Simulate space flight at the **US Rocket and Space Center**, Huntsville, Alabama	Experience a simulated hurricane in safety at the **Tampa Museum of Science and Industry**
See a play at the **Alabama Shakespeare Festival Theater**, Montgomery	Jet-ski at **Daytona Beach**, Florida, site of Malcolm Campbells' land speed records
February's Mardi Gras in **New Orleans**, is a series of parades and masked balls	Combine golf with gambling at **Biloxi**, on the Mississippi Sound, Gulf of Mexico
Rollerblade **Fort Lauderdale**'s promenade	Swim with manatees at **Crystal River**, Florida

USA: Texas

Explored in the 16th century by Spaniards moving north from Mexico in search of gold, Texas proudly remembers the war which secured its independence from Mexico in 1836, although the site that is now the major attraction of this heritage industry – the Alamo fort – was actually the scene of a heroic defeat.

The Wild West days of the 19th century, when abundant land drew migrants to raise cattle in Texas, are more widely evoked for tourists than the pioneering oil years of the early 20th century, whose successes still form the basis of the state's wealth.

Texas is not only the largest US state apart from Alaska, it also prides itself on having everything bigger and better than elsewhere. The eastern side, from futuristic Dallas down to the Gulf coast, including Houston – the "oil city" – packs in most of the state's tourist attractions, ranging from theme parks such as Sea World and the famous Fort Worth Zoo, to Houston's Lyndon B. Johnson Space Center and Dallas' commemorations of President John F. Kennedy's assassination there in 1963.

Outside the big cities, the Hispanic influences that enliven Texan cuisine are particularly strong, especially in the south and west. A vast, flat plateau dominates the centre of the state, extending all the way to New Mexico. The border with Mexico along the Rio Grande, running from El Paso in the far west to the Gulf of Mexico, encompasses hugely scenic areas, including Texas' most famous natural sight, Big Bend National Park.

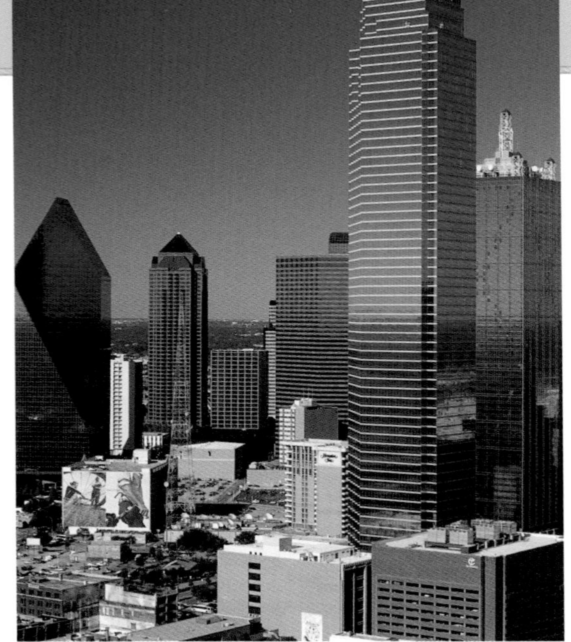

Dallas: Sparkling glass and steel office towers – including the city's tallest building, the 72-storey Bank of America Tower – dominate the view from the neighbouring 50-storey Reunion Tower.

NEW MEXICO
MEXICO
36
40
El Paso
Canutillo
San Elizario
Clint
Fabens
Tornillo
Fort Hancock
McNary
Esperanza
Sierra Blanca
Dell City
Salt Basin
Salt Flat
Guadalupe Mountains
Guadalupe Peak 2667m
Red Bluff Reservoir
Orla
Pecos River
Hueco Mountains
Sierra Diablo
Delaware Mountains
Apache Mountains
Rio Grande
Sierra Vieja
Van Horn
Kent
Toyah
Pecos
Barstow
Saragosa
Balmorhea
Davis Mountains
Mount Livermore 2554m
Valentine
Fort Davis
Marfa
Alpine
Fort Stockton
Stockton Plateau
Glass Mountains
Marathon
Cathedral Mountain 2093m
Candelaria
Ruidosa
Chinati Mountains
Shafter
Casa Piedra
Presidio
Redford
Terlingua
Santiago Mountains
Emory Peak 2385m
Big Bend National Park
Kermit
Wink
Mentone
Wickett
Monahans
Penwell
Royalty
Grandfalls
Imperial
McCamey
Girvin
Goldsmith
Andrews
Seminole
Seagraves
Wellman
Denver City
Plains
Tokio
Sulphur Springs
Whiteface
Levelland
Morton
Enochs
Sudan
Muleshoe
Earth
Springlake
Farwell
Bovina
Friona
Hereford
Dimmitt
Adrian
Canadian River
Channing
Hartley
Dalhart
Texline
Running Water Draw
Sulphur Draw
Mustang Draw
Coyanosa Draw
Alamito Creek
Terlingua Creek
Maravillas Creek

Big Bend National Park: Situated on the Mexican frontier, this park is one of the wildest and most isolated corners of the USA, taking its name from the 90° turn in the Rio Grande. Roadrunners, javelinas and coyote can be spotted among the wild flowers and cacti.

Activities

- Hike in the river canyons and pine forests of **Big Bend National Park**
- Eat a giant, 2 kg (4.5 lb) steak for free – provided you can manage it all in an hour – at the **Big Texan Steak Ranch**, Amarillo
- Relive the American Wild West, from rodeos to train robberies, in Fort Worth's **Stockyards National Historic District**
- Experience the fiery delights of Tex-Mex, the Texan take on Mexican cuisine
- Cheer on the Texas Rangers baseball team, who play at **Arlington**, near Dallas

What to See

❶ Palo Duro Canyon (near Canyon) This deep, red and yellow gorge cuts through the Texas panhandle

❷ Guadalupe Mountains National Park West Texas' rugged wilderness is rich in wildlife and was once home to the Apaches

❸ Big Bend National Park On the great bend in the Rio Grande, the park includes the Chihuahuan desert, the Rio Grande valley, and the Chisos Mountains

❹ Fort Worth Zoo One of the USA's top zoos has natural habitat settings including Raptor Canyon, the Koala Outback and Asian Falls

❺ Dallas Futuristic city of glass skyscrapers, on the banks of the Trinity River

❻ Sixth Floor Museum (in Dallas) The site of the sniper's nest, found after JFK's assassination, documents the shooting and the president's life

❼ Sea World (near San Antonio) One of the chain of marine entertainment centres, with trained killer whales

❽ The Alamo This famous 16th-century mission is where 187 men died in a heroic defence against the Mexican army

❾ Natural Bridge Caverns (near San Antonio) Water-formed caverns hold Texas' largest stalactite caves

❿ Austin The state capital's most unusual summer draw is when millions of Mexican free-tailed bats emerge from their roost under Congress Avenue Bridge

⓫ George Bush Sr. Presidential Library (in College Station) Interesting memorabilia and information about the first President Bush

⓬ Houston The fourth-largest city in the USA and Texas' oil-processing centre; the Menil Collection houses superb Cubist paintings by Picasso and Braque

⓭ Lyndon B. Johnson Space Center (near Houston) Mission Control has an excellent visitor centre featuring all aspects of the space programme

⓮ Padre Island National Seashore A long barrier island with beautiful beaches. The rippling dunes are ideal for birdwatching

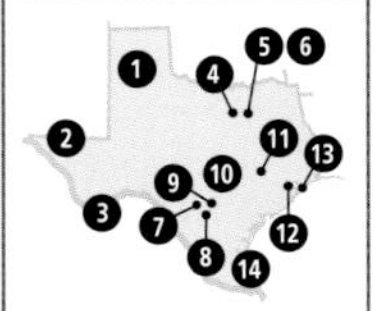

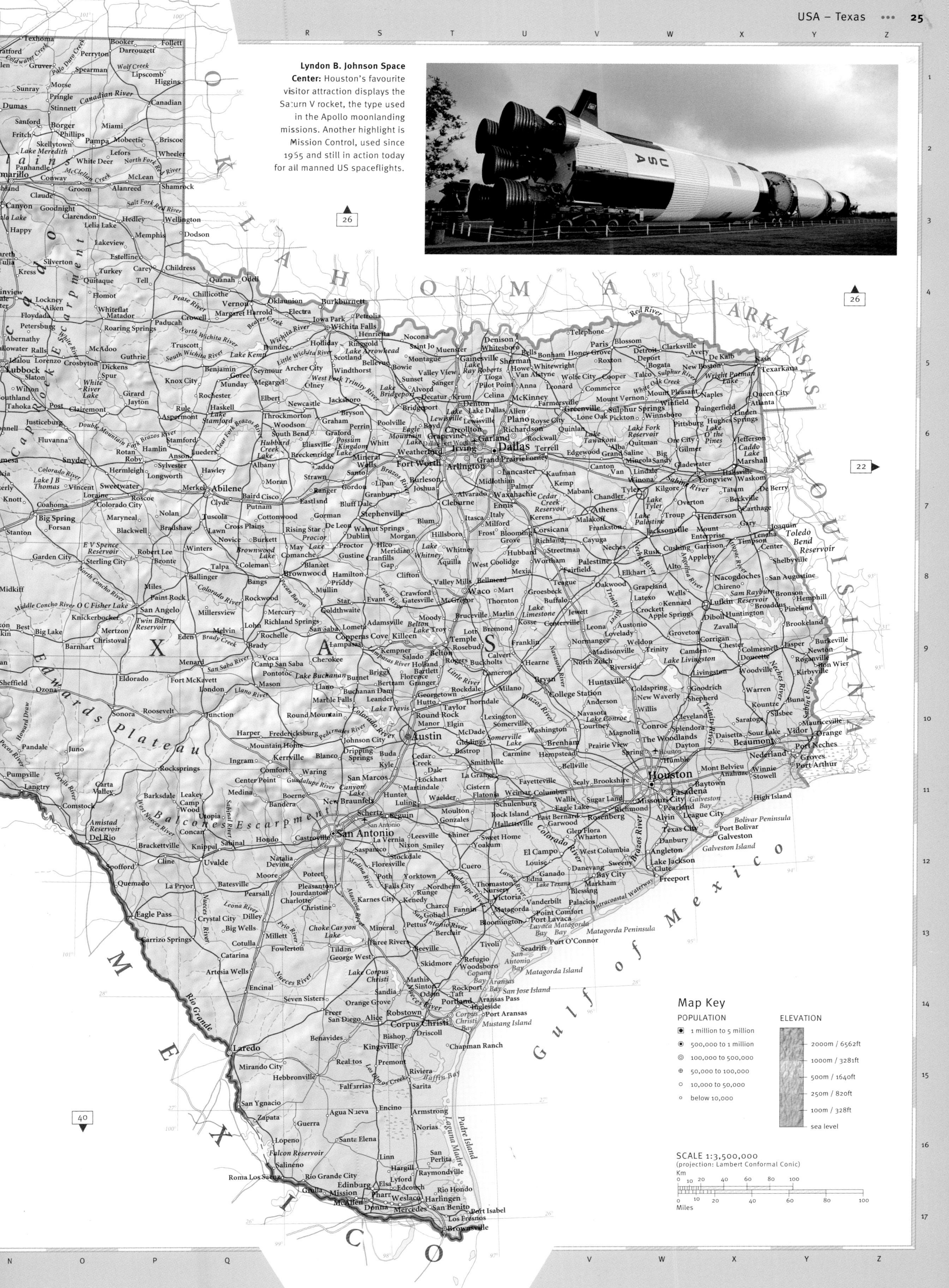
R S T U V W X Y Z
1 2 3 4 5 6 7 8 9 10 11 12 13 14 15 16 17
N O P Q V W X Y Z
OKLAHOMA
ARKANSAS
LOUISIANA
TEXAS
MEXICO
Gulf of Mexico
Edwards Plateau
Balcones Escarpment
Map Key
POPULATION
1 million to 5 million
500,000 to 1 million
100,000 to 500,000
50,000 to 100,000
10,000 to 50,000
below 10,000
ELEVATION
2000m / 6562ft
1000m / 3281ft
500m / 1640ft
250m / 820ft
100m / 328ft
sea level
SCALE 1:3,500,000
(projection: Lambert Conformal Conic)
Km
0 10 20 40 60 80 100
0 10 20 40 60 80 100
Miles

Lyndon B. Johnson Space Center: Houston's favourite visitor attraction displays the Saturn V rocket, the type used in the Apollo moonlanding missions. Another highlight is Mission Control, used since 1965 and still in action today for all manned US spaceflights.

26
26
22
40

USA: South Midwestern States

Arkansas, Kansas, Missouri, Oklahoma

The south Midwest is the least-visited part of the USA; early explorers spoke of these lands as the "great American Desert". The settlers who spread across here in the mid-19th century, from the confluence of the Missouri and Mississippi rivers up onto the treeless expanse of the Great Plains, turned it into one of the world's richest agricultural regions, until over-intensive farming and periodic droughts provoked the "Dustbowl" soil erosion of the 1930s, the abandonment of many farms and a mass exodus to the west coast, famously depicted in John Steinbeck's novel *The Grapes of Wrath*.

Now it is farming country once again, its vast fields dotted with giant machines at planting and harvest times, and patrolled between times by crop-spraying aircraft. Visitors to Saint Louis, Kansas City and Oklahoma City can also experience first hand the products of the beer and meat industries and learn about the development of jazz.

The wooded Ozark Plateau, straddling Arkansas and Missouri, is the best scenic attraction, offering peace and tranquillity. This region is noted for its religious fervour and for Little Rock, political hometown of former president Bill Clinton.

28

36

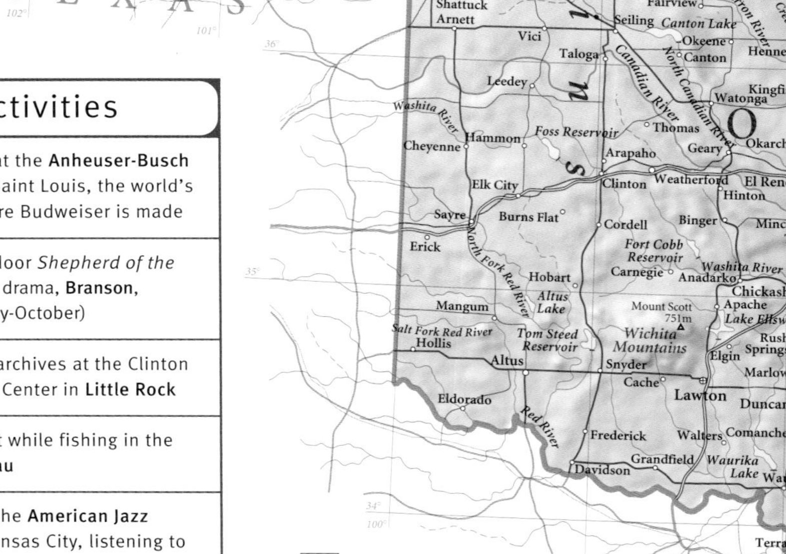

NEBRASKA
KANSAS
COLORADO
NEW MEXICO
TEXAS
Great Plains
Smoky Hills
Red Hills
Saint Francis
Atwood
Oberlin
Norton
Phillipsburg
Goodland
Colby
Hoxie
Stockton
Hill City
Plainville
Oakley
Wa Keeney
Ellis
Hays
Sharon Springs
Tribune
Leoti
Scott City
Dighton
Ness City
La Crosse
Great Bend
Syracuse
Lakin
Garden City
Jetmore
Larned
Kinsley
Cimarron
Dodge City
Johnson
Ulysses
Montezuma
Bucklin
Greensburg
Pratt
Sublette
Satanta
Meade
Minneola
Coldwater
Ashland
Hugoton
Liberal
Elkhart
Boise City
Keyes
Guymon
Hooker
Beaver
Forgan
Buffalo
Texhoma
Goodwell
Laverne
Elmwood
Fort Supply
Woodward
Shattuck
Arnett
Vici
Taloga
Leedey
Cheyenne
Hammon
Elk City
Sayre
Erick
Burns Flat
Clinton
Cordell
Hobart
Mangum
Hollis
Altus
Eldorado
Frederick
Lawton
Anadarko
Wichita Mountains
Canadian River
Cimarron River
Arkansas River
Red River

American Jazz Museum: Kansas City's top attraction recreates the swinging jazz era of its heyday in the 1930s.

Activities

Take a tour at the **Anheuser-Busch Brewery** in Saint Louis, the world's largest, where Budweiser is made

See the outdoor *Shepherd of the Hills* pioneer drama, **Branson,** Missouri (May-October)

Browse the archives at the Clinton Presidential Center in **Little Rock**

Catch a trout while fishing in the **Ozark Plateau**

Chill out at the **American Jazz Museum,** Kansas City, listening to local hero Charlie Parker's jazz sax

24

What to See

❶ Dodge City
Notorious Wild West town famous for its outlaws and buffalo hunters. Reconstructions of saloons and other buildings line Historic Front Street

❷ Kansas City
The "barbecue capital" is famous for steak and jazz (Charlie Parker invented bebop here)

❸ Hannibal
Mark Twain's boyhood home. Much of *Tom Sawyer* was set here – visit Becky Thatcher's home and other sites from the book

❹ Saint Louis
Dominated by the magnificent Gateway Arch, Saint Louis' attractions include the house of ragtime composer Scott Joplin, a hands-on science centre and a top zoo

❺ Silver Dollar City
(near Branson) High-tech roller coasters and water rides set in a pioneer theme

❻ Buffalo River
Scenic recreation area in northern Arkansas, which is popular for float fishing

❼ Ozark Plateau
A protected national forest, encompassing lakes, waterfalls, gorges and hills offering magnificent views and a folk art centre

❽ Little Rock
Capital of Arkansas, featuring the Old Mill on the north side of the river, where scenes in *Gone with the Wind* were shot

❾ Hot Springs
Popular resort for enjoying the healing thermal waters. The old Fordyce Bathhouse gives an impression of spa life in former times

❿ Crater of Diamonds
(near Murfreesboro) This source of natural diamonds is a state park open to the public

⓫ Oklahoma City
Founded and built on April 22, 1889 as part of the great land rush. Main sights include the National Cowboy Museum and the National Stockyards

⓬ Woolaroc Wildlife Preserve
(near Bartlesville) Drive-through ranch, roamed by bison and longhorn cattle, plus a world-class display of Colt guns

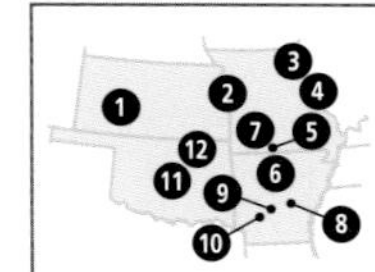

1
2
3
4
5
6
7
8
9
10
11
12

Gateway Arch, Saint Louis: Designed by Eero Saarinen, the striking stainless steel arch symbolizes the city's role as a commercial and cultural gateway between the eastern US and the wide open lands to the west.

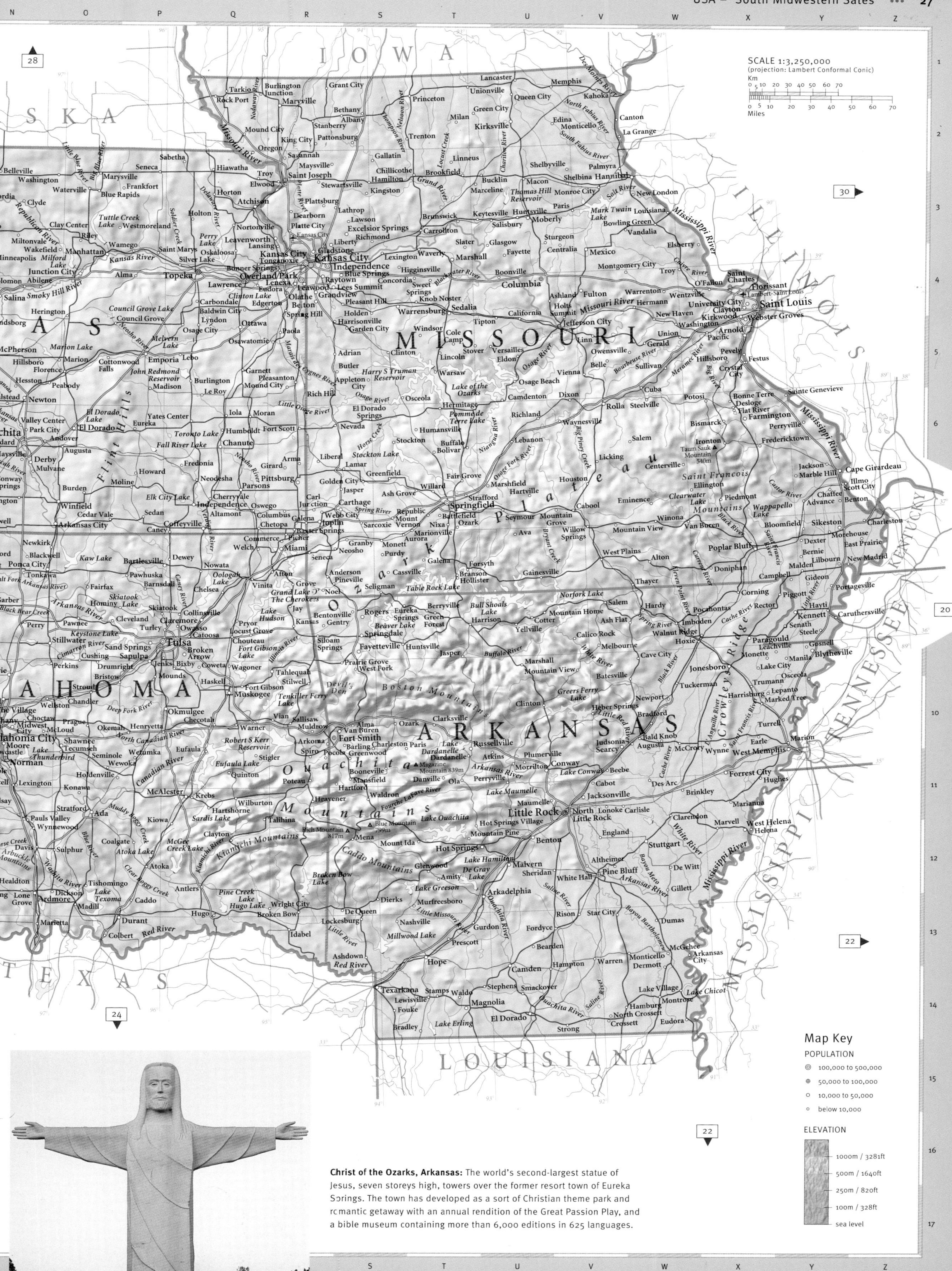
IOWA
MISSOURI
ARKANSAS
ILLINOIS
KENTUCKY
TENNESSEE
MISSISSIPPI
LOUISIANA
TEXAS
OKLAHOMA
Ozark Plateau
Ouachita Mountains
Boston Mountains
Saint Francois Mountains
Crowley's Ridge
Flint Hills
Kansas City
Saint Louis
Springfield
Columbia
Jefferson City
Little Rock
Fort Smith
Tulsa
Mississippi River
Missouri River
SCALE 1:3,250,000
(projection: Lambert Conformal Conic)
Km
Miles
Map Key
POPULATION
100,000 to 500,000
50,000 to 100,000
10,000 to 50,000
below 10,000
ELEVATION
1000m / 3281ft
500m / 1640ft
250m / 820ft
100m / 328ft
sea level

Christ of the Ozarks, Arkansas: The world's second-largest statue of Jesus, seven storeys high, towers over the former resort town of Eureka Springs. The town has developed as a sort of Christian theme park and romantic getaway with an annual rendition of the Great Passion Play, and a bible museum containing more than 6,000 editions in 625 languages.

USA: North Midwestern States

Iowa, Minnesota, Nebraska, North Dakota, South Dakota

By far the top destination in the region is southwest South Dakota, which includes Mount Rushmore – an enormous carving of four US presidents – in the Black Hills and the gaunt yet colourful landscape of Badlands National Park as well as a host of smaller attractions, making it an excellent base for tourists.

Nebraska and Iowa offer visitors the prospect of huge fields of corn stretching to the horizon, crossed by mile after mile of flat interstate freeway perhaps best seen beneath a full prairie moon. The whole region is mainly rural save for parts of Minnesota, whose major urban centres are the gleaming twin cities of Minneapolis and Saint Paul, on either side of the Mississippi. These cities have most for the visitor in terms of culture and modernity. Further north, however, the region towards the border with Canada has some of the best lakeland holiday country.

The Mammoth Site, Hot Springs, South Dakota: Sinbad the Mammoth is one of the many fantastic mammoth fossils discovered in 1974 in a prehistoric spring-fed sinkhole.

Chimney Rock, Nebraska: A landmark for pioneers on the Oregon Trail as they headed west, this unusual rock formation rises 500 ft (152 m) above the grassy plains.

Activities

- Watch the nightly Wild West play *The Trial of Jack McCall* in **Deadwood**, South Dakota
- Fly a Mustang simulator, ride a roller coaster, rub noses with a shark, and shop in Minneapolis' futuristic **Mall of America**
- Canoe in the **Superior National Forest**, near Ely, in northeast Minnesota
- Pan for gold at the fascinating Black Hills Mining Museum in **Lead**, South Dakota
- Take to the skies at the **National Balloon Classic, Indianola**, Iowa
- Enter the **Iowa State Fair**'s hog-calling contest at Des Moines in mid-August

What to See

1 Needles Highway Intriguing rock pinnacles line this magnificent mountain road through the Black Hills

2 Mount Rushmore Hewn from the cliff, these huge carvings of US presidents were featured in Hitchcock's film *North by Northwest*

3 Rapid City The gateway to the Black Hills has a Dinosaur Park and Reptile Gardens

4 Wind Cave (near Hot Springs) One of the world's longest and most beautiful cave systems has bison grazing on the prairie above it

5 Badlands Colourful prairie plateau furrowed by erosion, with bizarre rock formations

6 Agate Fossil Beds (near Harrison) Fossil remains from 20 million years ago

7 Oregon Trail (near Scottsbluff) Pioneers' wagon tracks are still visible at Chimney Rock

8 Voyageurs National Park (near International Falls) Wilderness of lakes and swamps, excellent for sailing and fishing and one of the USA's largest wolf sanctuaries

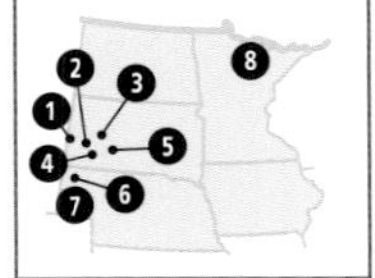
1
2
3
4
5
6
7
8

MONTANA
WYOMING
COLORADO
NO
SOUT
N E
Williston
Dickinson
Belle Fourche
Spearfish
Lead
Deadwood
Sturgis
Black Hills
Rapid City
Mount Rushmore 1745m
Custer
Hot Springs
Badlands
Scottsbluff
Chimney Rock
Harrison
Sand Hills
North Platte River
Lake C. W. McConaughy

32

36

Mount Rushmore, South Dakota: Presidents Washington, Jefferson, Theodore Roosevelt and Lincoln each 60 ft (18 m) tall, are a national monument. The nearby Crazy Horse, commemorating the great Sioux warrior, will be the world's largest sculpture when finished.

CANADA
NORTH DAKOTA
SOUTH DAKOTA
NEBRASKA
KANSAS
MINNESOTA
IOWA
WISCONSIN
ILLINOIS
MISSOURI
Lake of the Woods
Rainy Lake
Lake Superior
Upper Red Lake
Lower Red Lake
Mille Lacs Lake
Lake Francis Case
Lake Sharpe
Lewis And Clark Lake
Red River
Missouri River
Mississippi River
Minneapolis
Saint Paul
Duluth
Fargo
Sioux Falls
Omaha
Lincoln
Des Moines
Cedar Rapids
Davenport
Rochester
Sioux City
Council Bluffs
Map Key
POPULATION
100,000 to 500,000
50,000 to 100,000
10,000 to 50,000
below 10,000
ELEVATION
2000m / 6562ft
1000m / 3281ft
500m / 1640ft
250m / 820ft
100m / 328ft
sea level
SCALE 1:3,500,000
(projection: Lambert Conformal Conic)
Km
0 10 20 40 60 80 100 120
0 10 20 40 60 80 100 120
Miles
10
12
30
26

USA: Great Lakes States

Illinois, Indiana, Michigan, Ohio, Wisconsin

Sometimes given the unwanted name of the "Rust Belt", the industrial region bordering the Great Lakes has few scenic attractions on dry land, but legacy of its world-beating engineering prowess has endowed it with some major tourist sites, linked to the development of the motor industry and air flight a century or more ago.

Detroit and Dayton in Ohio may epitomize this history, but the region's biggest destination for visitors is undoubtedly Chicago. The USA's second city has long since shed its association with gangsters and is now a thriving commercial and cultural centre renowned for just about everything, even its windy weather. Milwaukee, too, with a strong German settler heritage and self-styled as the beer capital of the world has a touch of class. A long-serving mayor with unusual vision can take credit for the removal of an inner-city flyover as part of a regeneration scheme that has made the Milwaukee downtown riverfront an attractive and desirable area.

Chicago: Its dramatic skyline, seen across Lake Michigan, features the Sears Tower on the left, currently the world's third tallest building at 527 m (1,729 ft). After a devastating fire in 1871, Chicago built the world's first skyscraper in 1885 and later developed the Prairie School of architecture under Frank Lloyd Wright.

What to See

1 Mackinac Fort
(near Saint Ignace)
18th-century fort built by the British to guard the Straits of Mackinac which links Lake Huron and Lake Michigan

2 Milwaukee
The Miller Brewing Company Tour showcases the history of the second largest brewery in the US

3 Chicago
The "Windy City" has awe-inspiring architecture and plays host to top-quality art, music and sport

4 Cahokia Mounds State Historic Site
(near Collinsville)
The archaeological remains of a significant pre-Columbian Native American settlement

5 Cincinnati
The former industrial city has reinvented itself as a lively centre for dining and shopping

6 Dayton
The Wright brothers' home town has sights connected to the aviation pioneers

7 Amish Country
(near Strasburg) The Amish community live a "plain" life, using few modern inventions

8 Detroit
Home of the US motor industry, "Motor City" has interesting museums celebrating the car and holds lively summer festivals

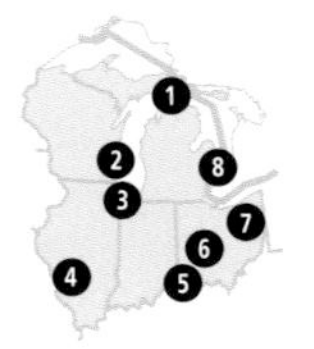

ROCK AND ROLL HALL OF FAME AND MUSEUM

Rock 'n' Roll Hall of Fame, Cleveland: Displaying the history of popular music and memorabilia, from blues through to the modern day, in I. M. Pei's astonishing triangular building.

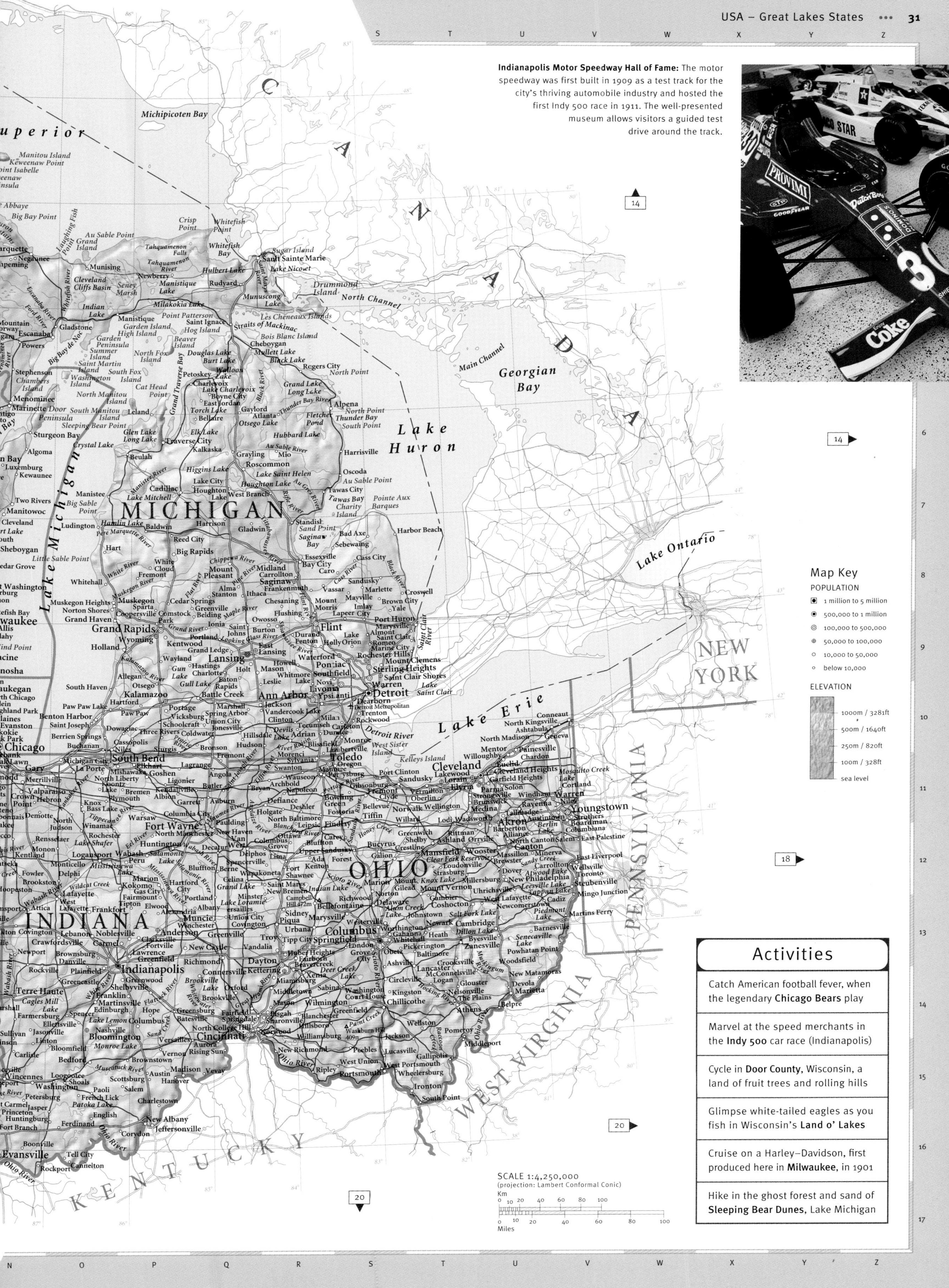
CANADA
MICHIGAN
INDIANA
OHIO
NEW YORK
PENNSYLVANIA
WEST VIRGINIA
KENTUCKY
Lake Superior
Lake Michigan
Lake Huron
Georgian Bay
Lake Erie
Lake Ontario
Detroit
Chicago
Cleveland
Toledo
Columbus
Indianapolis
Cincinnati
Grand Rapids
Lansing
Flint
Fort Wayne
Dayton
Akron
Youngstown
Evansville
South Bend
Map Key
POPULATION
1 million to 5 million
500,000 to 1 million
100,000 to 500,000
50,000 to 100,000
10,000 to 50,000
below 10,000
ELEVATION
1000m / 3281ft
500m / 1640ft
250m / 820ft
100m / 328ft
sea level
SCALE 1:4,250,000
(projection: Lambert Conformal Conic)
Km
Miles

Indianapolis Motor Speedway Hall of Fame: The motor speedway was first built in 1909 as a test track for the city's thriving automobile industry and hosted the first Indy 500 race in 1911. The well-presented museum allows visitors a guided test drive around the track.

Activities

- Catch American football fever, when the legendary **Chicago Bears** play
- Marvel at the speed merchants in the **Indy 500** car race (Indianapolis)
- Cycle in **Door County,** Wisconsin, a land of fruit trees and rolling hills
- Glimpse white-tailed eagles as you fish in Wisconsin's **Land o' Lakes**
- Cruise on a Harley–Davidson, first produced here in **Milwaukee,** in 1901
- Hike in the ghost forest and sand of **Sleeping Bear Dunes,** Lake Michigan

USA: North Mountain States

Idaho, Montana, Oregon, Washington, Wyoming

The northwestern states, which can only be reached overland from the east by crossing some intractable terrain, were among the last to be settled by Europeans in the 19th century. Fur-trappers and gold prospectors arrived first, following the Snake River westwards as it wound its way through the Rocky Mountains. Today it is the combination of dramatic landscapes and modern cities that strikes the 21st-century visitor.

The USA's first national park, which opened at Yellowstone in 1872, is an example of the emphasis on conservation for which the northwest has set something of a national standard. It is now one of the country's major tourist attractions.

Across the region the visitor will encounter a wide range of scenery, and no shortage of cultural interest. Mount Saint Helens' devastating eruption in 1980 has created a fascinating new landscape in southern Washington State, while to the north is the much-loved city of Seattle, famous for its coffee houses, set on the beautiful Puget Sound and with three major national parks nearby.

Old Faithful Geyser, Yellowstone National Park: So called because of the regular 90-minute intervals between its eruptions, Old Faithful Geyser is the park's icon. Its steaming plume shoots up to 55 m (180 ft) into the air, spurting nearly 32,000 litres (8,400 gallons) of water in 2–5 minutes.

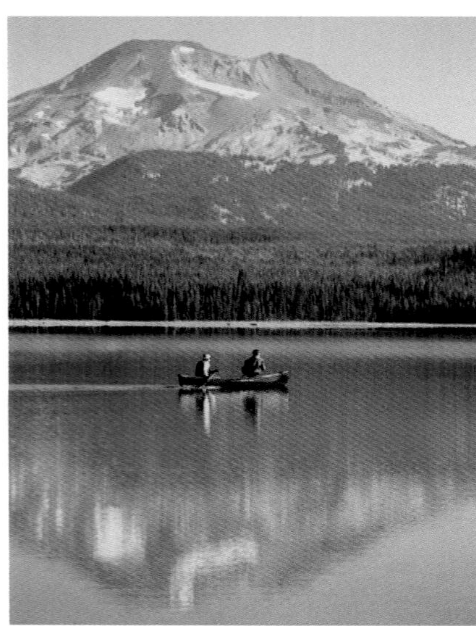

Elk Lake, Oregon: Popular for fishing, windsurfing and sailing, this hidden gem lies in the South Cascade Mountains. The Cascade Lakes Highway also takes in Mount Bachelor and the Devil's Garden lava flow.

Activities

- Sandboard at the **Oregon Dunes National Recreation Area** on the coast
- Watch a summer rodeo in **Cody**, Wyoming
- Enjoy a play during **Ashland's** Oregon Shakespeare Festival (February–October)
- Support the Mariners, **Seattle's** top-quality baseball team
- Revolve slowly as you dine at the top of Seattle's landmark **Space Needle**
- Fish, canoe or hike in Wyoming's mountainous **Grand Teton National Park**
- Watch for orcas (killer whales) swimming past – **Puget Sound**, Seattle
- View Seattle from **Mount Rainier** – a cone volcano with striking glaciers
- Sip a Pumpkin Spice Crème in **Seattle**, home of the first Starbucks coffee house

10

192

SCALE 1:4,250,000
(projection: Lambert Conformal Conic)

Km 0 10 20 40 60 80 100

Miles 0 10 20 40 60 80 100

34

N O P Q R S T U V W X Y Z

Map Key

POPULATION

- 500,000 to 1 million
- 100,000 to 500,000
- 50,000 to 100,000
- 10,000 to 50,000
- below 10,000

ELEVATION

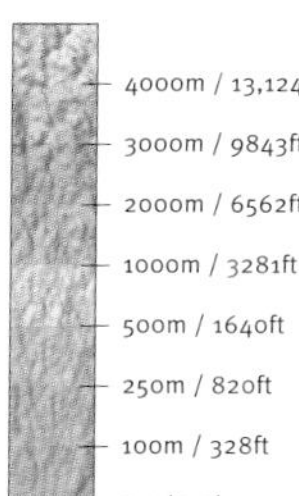
4000m / 13,124ft
3000m / 9843ft
2000m / 6562ft
1000m / 3281ft
500m / 1640ft
250m / 820ft
100m / 328ft
sea level

10

What to See

Seattle, Yellowstone National Park
see pp16–17

❶ Olympic Peninsula
Many rare species roam a beautiful land of snowcapped mountains and rainforests

❷ Boeing Construction Facility
(near Seattle) Inside the world's largest building, see Boeing making its 747, 767, and 777 planes

❸ Mount Saint Helens
On 18 May 1980 this huge volcano erupted. As the forests begin to regenerate, marvel at the bleak evidence of the raw power of nature

❹ Portland
The attractively modern "City of Roses" has Far Eastern and Victorian influences and several exquisite parks, set against a backdrop of Mount Hood

❺ Columbia River Gorge
Separating Oregon and Washington, the mighty river has many spectacular waterfalls, such as Multnomah Falls 186m (620 ft)

❻ Crater Lake
Famed for its Pinnacles and rim drive, the deepest lake in the USA was created 7,700 years ago by volcanic eruption

❼ Boise
Capital of Idaho, the charming, compact desert town is named after its many trees

❽ Craters of the Moon
Volcanic eruptions have formed a surreal lunar landscape of fascinating patterns which illustrate the diverse lava types

❾ Devil's Tower
Featured in *Close Encounters of the Third Kind*, this landmark basaltic lava pillar is an impressive sight and a must for rock climbers

❿ Little Bighorn
(near Billings) Scene of General Custer's doomed last stand against the combined forces of the Sioux and the Cheyenne

⓫ Waterton-Glacier International Peace Park (north of Kalispell)
This US–Canadian park is a majestic, untouched mountain wilderness

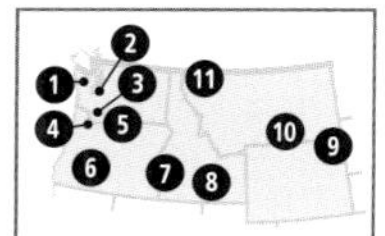
1 2 3 4 5 6 7 8 9 10 11

Seattle: The futuristic Space Needle with its revolving restaurant dominates the skyline of this attractive city. Mount Rainier – known for its excellent hiking to the beautiful, permanently snow-capped summit – is one of three national parks nearby.

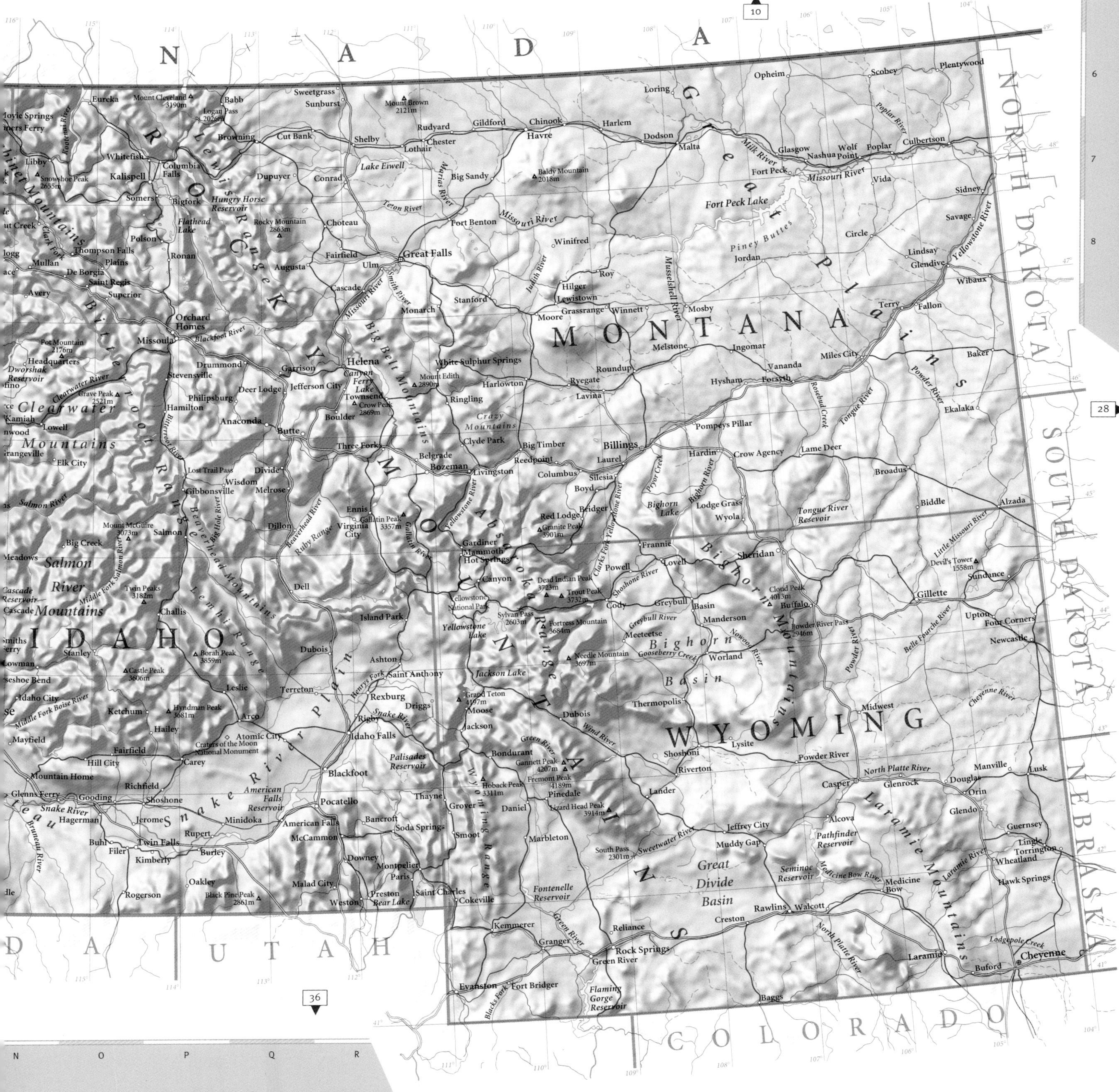

USA: California & Nevada

California's great climate, beautiful scenery and dynamic economy, bound up in the legend of Hollywood, continue to attract immigrants and tourists alike. The vast conurbations of Los Angeles, San Francisco, and San Diego offer world-class museums and huge entertainment parks. The coast has great wildlife, gorgeous vistas and a string of 300-year-old Spanish missions. Inland, the wide variety of landscapes in the many national parks ranges from the Mojave and Sonoran deserts of the south and Death Valley, one of the hottest and driest places on earth, to the alpine meadows and stunning glacial valleys of Yosemite. Other parks can boast the oldest, largest and tallest trees in the world. Nevada's main claim to fame is the glitz of its great gambling centres, Las Vegas and Reno.

Death Valley: Native Americans called it "the land where the ground is on fire", an apt name for the hottest, driest and lowest point in the USA. It earned its current name in the pioneer age.

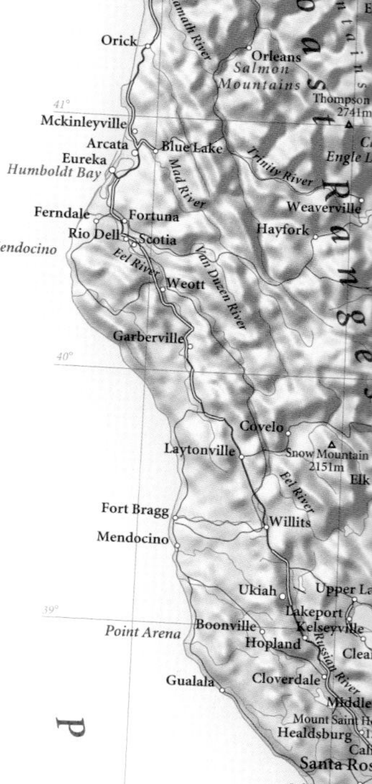
Smith River
Crescent City
Siskiyou Mountains
Happy Camp
Klamath
Klamath River
Orick
Orleans
Salmon Mountains
Thompson 2741m
Mckinleyville
Arcata
Eureka
Humboldt Bay
Blue Lake
Mad River
Trinity River
Weaverville
Hayfork
Ferndale
Rio Dell
Fortuna
Scotia
Cape Mendocino
Eel River
Weott
Van Duzen River
Garberville
Covelo
Laytonville
Snow Mountain 2151m
Willits
Fort Bragg
Mendocino
Ukiah
Lakeport
Kelseyville
Point Arena
Boonville
Hopland
Gualala
Cloverdale
Healdsburg
Sebastopol
Bodega Head
Point Reyes
192

Golden Gate Bridge, San Francisco: One of the world's longest suspension bridges, the Golden Gate was a marvel of engineering when it was built in the 1930s. Carrying 118,000 vehicles a day, it offers breathtaking views across San Francisco and its bay.

Map Key

POPULATION	ELEVATION
1 million to 5 million	4000m / 13,124ft
500,000 to 1 million	3000m / 9843ft
100,000 to 500,000	2000m / 6562ft
50,000 to 100,000	1000m / 3281ft
10,000 to 50,000	500m / 1640ft
below 10,000	250m / 820ft
	100m / 328ft
	sea level

What to See

Las Vegas, Los Angeles, San Francisco *see* pp16–17

❶ Lava Beds National Monument
(near Tulelake) Over 200 caves created by lava flows in an eerie volcanic landscape

❷ Lake Tahoe
Known for its good climate and offering a huge range of activities, including winter sports. You can tell when you reach the Nevada border – you'll see a casino!

❸ San Andreas Fault
At Point Reyes National Seashore there are signs of the 40-second 1906 earthquake, which reduced San Francisco to rubble and triggered theories about the causes of earthquakes

❹ Alcatraz
(off San Francisco) Originally an island fort, Alcatraz became a high-security prison, housing criminals such as Al Capone

❺ Yosemite
A national park since 1890, its wonderful scenery includes the elegant Yosemite Falls, the towering Half Dome, and sheer granite cliffs

❻ Mono Lake
Three times saltier than the ocean, with startling tufa towers rising from its waters; the lake has a fishless ecosystem

❼ Big Sur
Spectacular rugged shoreline running south of San Francisco, with cypress trees, pretty bays, and sea otters

❽ Hearst Castle™
(near Morro Bay) This lavish castle was built using strangely juxtaposed antiquities for newspaper magnate William Randolph Hearst, who inspired the film *Citizen Kane*

❾ Sequoia and King's Canyon National Parks
Breathtaking mountain scenery and giant trees. The sequoia General Sherman is the earth's largest living organism: 9 m (30 ft) in diameter and 84 m (276 ft) tall

❿ Death Valley National Park
Vast expanse of vivid desert colours, canyons and mountains, with salt flats reaching 86 m (282 ft) below sea level

⓫ Getty Center
(in Los Angeles) An outstanding collection covering the past 12 centuries of Western art. Its Roman villa is modelled after one from Italy's Herculaneum and displays antiquities

⓬ Universal Studios
(in Los Angeles) A functioning film studio and amusement park, with thrilling special effect demonstrations – experience earthquakes and avalanches

⓭ San Diego
Close to Mexico, California's oldest city has a desert climate and fabulous beaches. The world-famous San Diego Zoo is renowned for its research, breeding projects and natural settings

⓮ Great Basin National Park
(near Connor's Pass) This desert region of limestone caves and windswept rocks has no natural outflows for rainwater, which simply evaporates

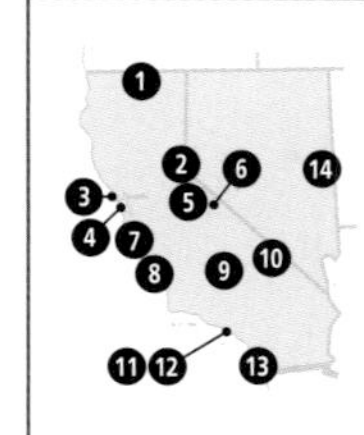
1
2
3
4
5
6
7
8
9
10
11
12
13
14

Activities

Taste wine at the **Napa Valley**'s classic wineries, such as Domaine Chandon or Robert Mondavi	Wonder at the splendour of giant trees, in the "Avenue of Giants" in **Redwood National Park**, north California
Take a ride on **San Francisco's** cable car up and down the city's slopes	Ski at **Lake Tahoe** on the California–Nevada border (November–April)
Catch a wave, surfing at the **north Californian beaches**	Pan for gold the old way in **Jamestown**, in the Sierra Nevada
Ride mountain torrents, whitewater rafting on the **Kern River**, north of Los Angeles (April–September)	Tread in the footprints of screen legends, outside **Mann's Chinese Theatre**, Hollywood Boulevard, Los Angeles

Las Vegas: The sparkling vista of neon along "The Strip" is chock-a-block with lavishly themed hotel and casinos. The Paris casino boasts a replica of the Eiffel Tower; Luxor has a pyramid and sphinx; and the Mirage has an artificial volcano that erupts every 15 minutes.

OREGON
IDAHO
UTAH
ARIZONA
MEXICO
NEVADA
CALIFORNIA
Great Basin
OCEAN

Dorris
Lower Klamath Lake
Tulelake
Goose Lake
Montague
Clear Lake Reservoir
Fort Bidwell
Upper Lake
Alkali Lake
Massacre Lake
Catnip Mountain 2223m
Trident Peak 2558m
McDermitt
Owyhee
Mountain City
Jackpot
Matterhorn 3304m
Duffer Peak 2864m
Granite Peak 2966m
Santa Rosa Range
McAfee Peak 3182m
Independence Mountains
Mount Shasta 4316m
Mount Shasta
Mccloud
Dunsmuir
Cedarville
Middle Alkali Lake
Alturas
Canby
Pit River
Warner Mountains
Eagle Peak 3015m
Big Mountain 2593m
Paradise Valley
Montello
Tuscarora
Lower Lake
King Lear Peak 2720m
Black Rock Desert
Little Humboldt River
Rock Creek
Big Valley Mountains
Adin
Bieber
Madeline
Fox Mountain 2494m
Wells
Hole in the Mountain Peak 3437m
Oasis
McCloud River
Fall River Mills
Burney
Winnemucca
Golconda
Halleck
Observation Peak 2427m
Sonoma Peak 2864m
Humboldt River
Elko
Lamoille
Spring Creek
Snow Water Lake
Severn Troughs Range
Carlin
Eagle Lake
Central Valley
Redding
Gerlach
Rye Patch Reservoir
Imlay
Battle Mountain
Emigrant Pass 1864m
Ruby Dome 3471m
Spruce Mountain 3128m
Lassen Peak 3187m
Susanville
Hot Springs Peak 2341m
Empire
Humboldt
Star Peak 2997m
Mount Tobin 2979m
Beowawe
Pine Creek
Huntington Creek
Ruby Mountains
Smoke Creek Desert
Kumiva Peak 2511m
Mount Lewis 2950m
Chester
Fredonyer Pass 1759m
Westwood
Lake Almanor
Honey Lake
Winnemucca Lake
Trinity Peak 2236m
Franklin Lake
Bluff
Herlong
Lovelock
Reese River
Ruby Lake
Los Molinos
Trinity Range
Alkali Flat
Becky Peak 2840m
Corning
Doyle
Pyramid Lake
Humboldt Lake
Stillwater Range
Carson Sink
Humboldt Salt Marsh
Roberts Creek Mountain 3089m
Quincy
Nixon
Orland
Chico
Paradise
Portola
Virginia Peak 2550m
Wadsworth
Newark Lake
Mount Callaghan 3105m
Schell Creek Range
Loyalton
Reno
Sparks
Fernley
Diamond Peak 3235m
Lake Oroville
Downieville
Sierra City
Hazen
Eureka
Willows
Oroville
Biggs
Gridley
Truckee River
Reno-Cannon
Fallon
Austin
McGill
North Schell Peak 3622m
Mount Lola 2787m
Truckee
Virginia City
Lahontan Reservoir
Summit Mountain 3189m
Ruth
Ely
Mount Moriah 3673m
Live Oak
Colusa
Yuba City
Grass Valley
Nevada City
Donner Pass 2160m
Kings Beach
Carson River
North Shoshone Peak 3143m
Bunker Hill 3497m
Mount Hamilton 3275m
Egan Range
Snake Range
Marysville
Olivehurst
Lake Tahoe
Tahoe City
Carson City
Fairview Peak 2531m
Shoshone Mountains
Toiyabe Range
Wheeler Peak 3981m
Arbuckle
Feather River
Sacramento River
North Fork American River
South Lake Tahoe
Minden
Gardnerville
Walker River
Yerington
Connors Pass 2354m
Lincoln
Roseville
Auburn
Rocklin
Citrus Heights
Knights Landing
Woodland
North Highlands
Folsom
Carmichael
South Fork American River
Camino
Placerville
Freel Peak 3317m
Echo Summit 2249m
Markleeville
East Walker River
West Walker River
Schurz
Gabbs
Arc Dome 3588m
Mount Jefferson 3642m
Currant Mountain 3509m
Currant
Lund
Lake Berryessa
Sacramento
Davis
Wellington
Walker Lake
Round Mountain
Morey Peak 3123m
Monitor Range
Hot Creek Range
Pancake Range
Big Smoky Valley
Vacaville
Dixon
Cosumnes River
Sutter Creek
Mokelumne River
Ione
Jackson
Mount Patterson 3558m
Mount Grant 3425m
Luning
Hawthorne
Mina
Troy Peak 3443m
Grant Range
Wilson Creek Range
Napa
Fairfield
Vallejo
Rio Vista
Galt
Camanche Reservoir
West Point
Arnold
Devils Gate 2292m
Bridgeport
Warm Springs
Lodi
San Andreas
Murphys
Columbia
Sonora
Eagle Peak 3610m
Matterhorn Peak 3738m
Mono Lake
Columbus Salt Marsh
Concord
Walnut Creek
Stockton
Martinez
Mount Diablo 1173m
Calaveras River
Angels Camp
Jamestown
Yosemite National Park
Lee Vining
Montgomery Pass 2185m
Lone Mountain 2776m
Tonopah
Kawich Peak 2866m
Worthington Peak 2697m
Pioche
Panaca
Oakland
Metropolitan Oakland
Tracy
Manteca
Stanislaus River
Oakdale
Don Pedro Reservoir
Tioga Pass 3031m
Mount Dana 3979m
El Capitan 2483m
Half Dome 2900m
June Lake
Boundary Peak 4005m
Goldfield
Cactus Peak 2281m
Kawich Range
Caliente
Livermore
Riverbank
Modesto
Coulterville
El Portal
Owens River
Mount Ritter 4010m
Lake Crowley
White Mountains
Silver Peak Range
Mount Irish 2664m
Pahranagat Range
Hayward
Fremont
Redwood City
Tuolumne River
Lake McClure
Mariposa
Merced Peak 3574m
Turlock
Merced River
Patterson
Milpitas
Santa Clara
San Jose
San Joaquin River
Livingston
Atwater
Merced
Le Grand
Bishop
Mount Humphreys 4263m
Alamo
Elgin
Groom Lake
Pahute Mesa
Los Gatos
Gustine
Chowchilla
Big Pine
North Palisade 4341m
Morgan Hill
Gilroy
Los Banos
San Luis Reservoir
Dos Palos
Madera
Friant
Pine Flat Lake
Inyo Mountains
Owens River
Meadow Valley Wash
Mormon Peak 2260m
Mesquite
Watsonville
Hollister
Castroville
San Juan Bautista
Marina
Salinas
Mendota
Fresno
Clovis
Independence
Beatty
Daylight Pass 1316m
Hayford Peak 3021m
Indian Springs
Sheep Range
Virgin River
Logandale
Overton
Monterey
Carmel
Seaside
Gonzales
Soledad
Salinas River
California Aqueduct
Fowler
Selma
Kingsburg
Sanger
Reedley
Dinuba
Lone Pine
Mount Whitney 4418m
Towne Pass 1511m
Death Valley
Panamint Range
Amargosa Range
Spring Mountains
Muddy Peak 1635m
Echo Bay
Jumbo Peak 1757m
Point Sur
Greenfield
King City
San Benito Mountain 1597m
Lemoore
Hanford
Kings River
Visalia
Exeter
Woodlake
Owens Lake
Olancha Peak 3695m
Olancha
Badwater Basin -86m
Charleston Peak 3632m
Las Vegas
North Las Vegas
Lake Mead
Stratford
Tulare
Lindsay
Strathmore
Haiwee Reservoir
Telescope Peak 3368m
Pahrump
Paradise
McCarran
East Las Vegas
Henderson
Hoover Dam
Boulder City
Coalinga
Corcoran
Tipton
Pixley
Porterville
Sequoia National Park
Tulare Lake Bed
Avenal
Sloan
Santa Lucia Range
Alpaugh
Earlimart
Johnsondale
Tecopa
San Miguel
Delano
Trona
Jean
Colorado River
Paso Robles
McFarland
Kernville
South Fork Kern River
Inyokern
Ridgecrest
Kingston Peak 2232m
Ivanpah Lake
Cambria
Lost Hills
Wasco
Isabella Lake
Clark Mountain 2417m
Atascadero
Shafter
Oildale
Kern River
Piute Peak 2570m
Mountain Pass 1455m
Searchlight
Lake Mohave
Morro Bay
San Luis Obispo
Black Mountain 1104m
Buttonwillow
Bakersfield
Johannesburg
Baker
New York Mountains
Lamont
Arvin
Tehachapi
Soda Lake
Devils Playground
Pismo Beach
Grover City
Arroyo Grande
Nipomo
Ford City
Taft
Taft Heights
Buena Vista Lake Bed
Maricopa
Los Angeles Aqueduct
California City
Mojave
Boron
Harper Lake
Mojave Desert
Providence Mountains
Guadalupe
Santa Maria
Tehachapi Mountains
Lebec
Rogers Lake
Barstow
Yermo
Mojave River
Needles
Mount Pinos 2692m
Tejon Pass 1273m
Rosamond
Rosamond Lake
Lancaster
San Rafael Mountains
Los Alamos
Ludlow
Ord Mountain 1923m
Lompoc
Santa Ynez River
Big Pine Mountain 2081m
Palmdale
Oro Grande
Victorville
Apple Valley
Amboy
Lake Havasu
Point Arguello
Point Conception
Santa Barbara
Ojai
Carpinteria
Fillmore
Hesperia
Bristol Lake
Cadiz Lake
Danby Lake
Parker Dam
Goleta
Ventura
Santa Paula
Simi Valley
Wrightwood
Mount San Antonio 3067m
Santa Barbara Channel
Oxnard
San Fernando
Burbank
Glendale
Pasadena
San Bernardino
San Gorgonio Mountain 3505m
Twentynine Palms
Colorado River
Thousand Oaks
Beverly Hills
Los Angeles
Alhambra
Ontario
Redlands
Yucca Valley
Joshua Tree
San Miguel Island
Santa Cruz Island
Santa Monica
Whittier
Pomona
Riverside
Banning
Desert Hot Springs
Inglewood
Fullerton
Santa Rosa Island
Torrance
Anaheim
Corona
San Jacinto Peak 3293m
Palm Springs
Colorado River Aqueduct
Desert Center
Palen Dry Lake
Long Beach
Santa Ana
San Jacinto
Hemet
Cathedral City
Indio
Coachella
Blythe
Huntington Beach
Mecca
Chocolate Mountains
Channel Islands
San Pedro Channel
Laguna Beach
Temecula
Toro Peak 2657m
Santa Rosa Mountains
Coachella Canal
Palo Verde
Santa Barbara Island
Santa Catalina Island
Avalon
San Clemente
Fallbrook
Salton Sea
San Nicolas Island
Outer Santa Barbara Passage
Gulf of Santa Catalina
Oceanside
Carlsbad
Vista
Escondido
Niland
Calipatria
Sonoran Desert
Julian
Ramona
Encinitas
Poway
Westmorland
Brawley
Imperial Dam
Laguna Dam
San Clemente Island
Santee
Lakeside
Laguna Mountains
Imperial
El Centro
Holtville
La Mesa
El Cajon
San Diego
National City
Chula Vista
Coronado
Calexico

SCALE 1:3,250,000
(projection: Lambert Conformal Conic)
Km
0 5 10 20 30 40 50 60 70 80
0 5 10 20 30 40 50 60 70 80
Miles

32
36
36
192
40

N O P Q R S T U V W X Y Z
1 2 3 4 5 6 7 8 9 10 11 12 13 14 15 16 17

USA: South Mountain States

Arizona, Colorado, New Mexico, Utah

Tourists are drawn to the south mountain states by the natural wonders – vast canyons, exotic desert colours and rock formations, great salt plains in the north and the dramatic Rocky Mountains of Colorado. There is rich variety too in the patterns of human settlement. The ruins of cliff dwellings built a thousand years ago are all that remain of the Anasazi people, but Native Americans own one-third of the land in Arizona, while Spanish and Mexican conquest and settlement have left a strong Hispanic presence. North Utah is dominated by the Mormons, among the earliest Anglo-American settlers when they came to the Great Salt Lake in 1847 seeking religious freedom.

What to See

Grand Canyon
see pp16–17

1 Salt Lake City
Founded by the Mormons in 1847, and still dominated by them, this unusual city is well-planned and clean

2 Dinosaur National Monument
(near Canyon of Lodore) Quarry where numerous fossilized dinosaur remains have been found

3 Rocky Mountain National Park
Alpine meadows, deep valleys and shimmering lakes make the Continental Divide popular for sightseeing and winter sports

4 Arches National Park (near Moab)
Hundreds of magnificent sandstone arches formed by the wind and weather

5 Canyonlands National Park
(near Moab) Coloured canyons with sweeping bends and a profusion of rock pinnacles, a fantastic hiking area

6 Mesa Verde
(near Cortez) Anasazi multistoreyed ruins built into the cliff face, dating from 600 to 1400 CE

7 Bryce Canyon
One of the highlights among the USA's national parks, its orange and white amphitheatre contains thousands of bizarre rock needles

8 Zion National Park
(near Hurricane)
A fantastic landscape of rock formations and sheer-sided gorges

9 Meteor Crater
This crater enabled scientists to establish the nature of meteors, and that they did indeed fall from the sky

10 Petrified Forest
Colourful fossilized trees dot the landscape of the Painted Desert

11 Monument Valley
Iconic landscape of huge sandstone formations in a red desert, symbolizing the American West

12 Davis-Monthan Air Force Base
(near Tucson) Graveyard for thousands of fighter planes, dating from World War II onwards

13 White Sands National Monument
(near Alamogordo)
Constantly changing landscape of white sand dunes in the midst of a vast missile-testing area

14 Carlsbad Caverns
Impressive cave system, with superb formations, massive chambers, and a quarter of a million bats

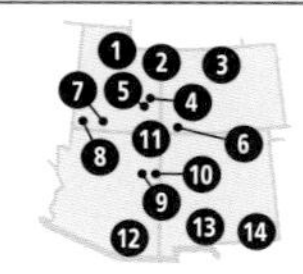

34

Gunfight at the OK Corral, Tombstone: Arguments still rage over the rights and wrongs of the feuds between the Earps and the Clantons, which came to a head in the infamous shootout of 1881 that is re-enacted daily in southern Arizona.

Activities

- Join the rich and famous on the ski slopes of **Aspen**, Colorado
- Fly over the **Grand Canyon** to get a true idea of its vastness
- Immerse yourself in Native American culture in the reservations of **Arizona** and **New Mexico**
- Hire a boat on **Lake Powell**, a man-made recreation area on the Utah–Arizona border, and see the 90 m (295 ft) high Rainbow Bridge
- Take the dramatic cable car ride to **Sandia Peak**, near Albuquerque
- Attend the UFO Festival in **Roswell**, New Mexico (beginning of July)

40

Monument Valley: Famous buttes and mesas soar up from the seemingly endless desert, providing a backdrop for a string of Hollywood movies, from John Ford's *Stagecoach* to the science-fiction *Back to the Future*.

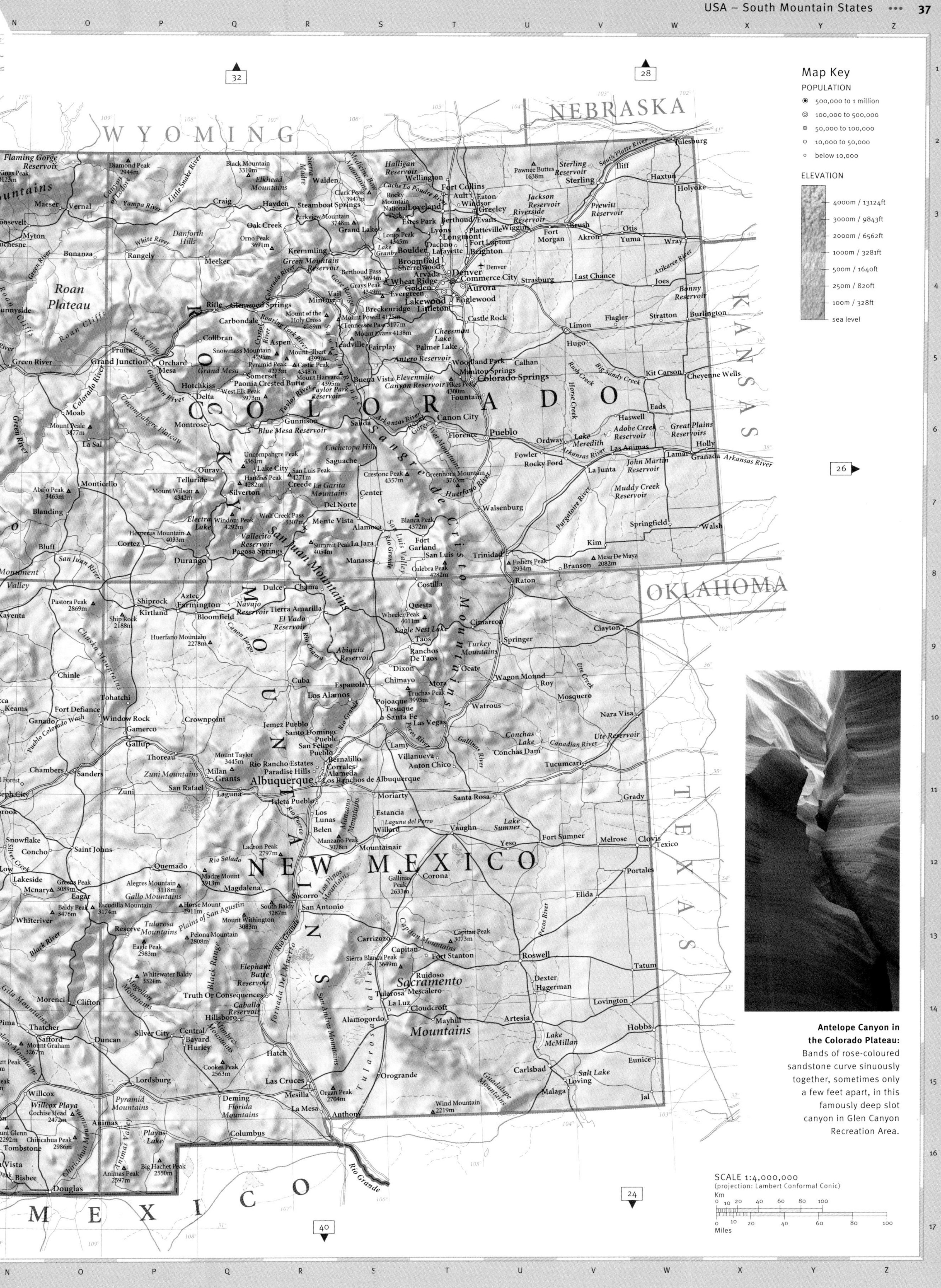

N O P Q R S T U V W X Y Z
1 2 3 4 5 6 7 8 9 10 11 12 13 14 15 16 17
32
28
26
24
40
Map Key
POPULATION
500,000 to 1 million
100,000 to 500,000
50,000 to 100,000
10,000 to 50,000
below 10,000
ELEVATION
4000m / 13124ft
3000m / 9843ft
2000m / 6562ft
1000m / 3281ft
500m / 1640ft
250m / 820ft
100m / 328ft
sea level
SCALE 1:4,000,000
(projection: Lambert Conformal Conic)
Km
0 10 20 40 60 80 100
0 10 20 40 60 80 100
Miles
WYOMING
NEBRASKA
KANSAS
OKLAHOMA
TEXAS
COLORADO
NEW MEXICO
MEXICO
ROCKY MOUNTAINS
Denver
Aurora
Colorado Springs
Pueblo
Albuquerque
Santa Fe
Las Cruces
Grand Junction
Fort Collins
Boulder
Roswell
Farmington

Antelope Canyon in the Colorado Plateau: Bands of rose-coloured sandstone curve sinuously together, sometimes only a few feet apart, in this famously deep slot canyon in Glen Canyon Recreation Area.

USA: Hawai‘i

Exotic Hawai‘i belongs with the USA since it became the 50th state of the union in 1959, but to go there is to visit a world apart – perhaps not surprisingly since it's a 4,300 km (2,400 mile) flight from California. Part of Polynesia, its 122 islands are the peaks of the world's largest volcanoes, rising from the floor of the Pacific Ocean. The eight largest islands have lush tropical vegetation and excellent beaches and are actively volcanic, making them the most reliable place in the world to see lava flowing. The year-round good climate has also helped Hawai‘i become a favourite destination for holidaymakers in search of sun, sea and surf.

The "Aloha State" is famed for its hospitality and Polynesian culture, from traditional crafts of woven baskets or flower and feather garlands to the distinctive music and chanting and the ritualistic hula dance.

Activities

- See surfers tackle **O‘ahu's** "Banzai Pipeline", an awesome, tubed surfing break
- Fly over **Kilauea** on Hawai‘i to watch the red-hot lava blacken as it flows into the sea
- Go whale-watching from the former whaling station of **Lahaina,** Maui
- Watch the hula dance festival at **Papohaku Beach Park,** Moloka‘i
- Learn about tsunamis in the Pacific Tsunami Museum at **Hilo,** itself destroyed several times by tsunami (on Hawai‘i)

What to See

❶ Mount McKinley
North America's highest mountain is home to grizzly bears, wolves and caribou

❷ Anchorage
A good base for scenic attractions, with moose wandering the streets

❸ Kenai Peninsula
A dazzling array of glaciers and fjords, reminiscent of the west coast of Norway

❹ Wrangell–St Elias (near McCarthy)
A grandiose mountain region with numerous glaciers, lakes, wild rivers and a rich variety of wildlife

❺ Glacier Bay
An inlet between two promontories where 16 glaciers reach the sea

❻ Totem Bight State Historical Park (near Ketchikan) An imposing number of Native totem poles

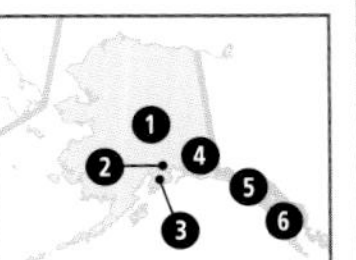

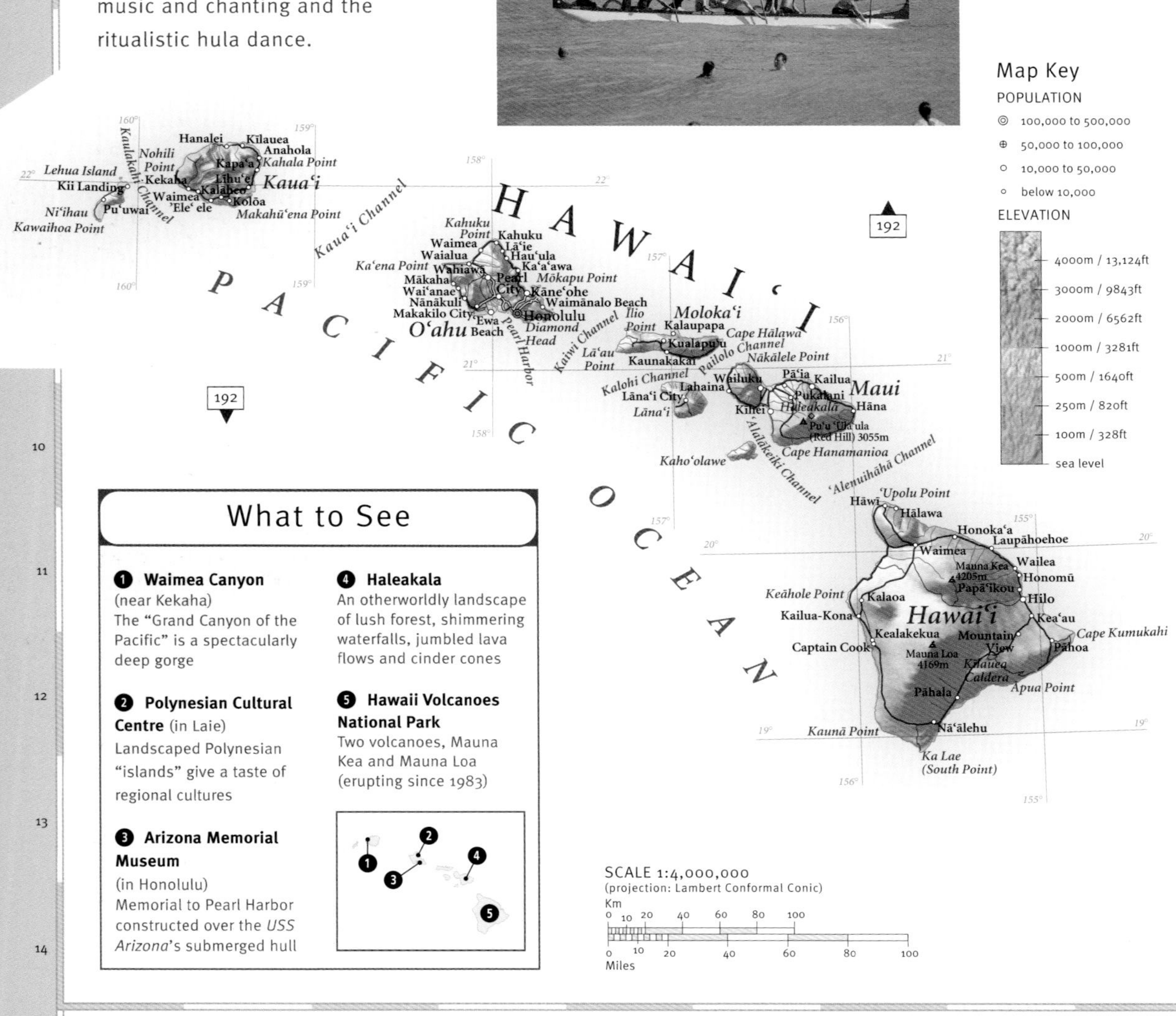

HAWAI‘I
PACIFIC OCEAN
Kaua‘i
Ni‘ihau
O‘ahu
Honolulu
Moloka‘i
Lāna‘i
Maui
Kaho‘olawe
Hawai‘i
Kaua‘i Channel
Kaiwi Channel
Kalohi Channel
Pailolo Channel
‘Alenuihāhā Channel
Hilo
Kailua-Kona
Lahaina
Mauna Kea 4205m
Mauna Loa 4169m
Ka Lae (South Point)

Waikiki Beach, O‘ahu: The golden beaches and sheltered waters make Waikiki Beach a year-round mecca for sunlovers, set against a backdrop of Diamond Head Crater.

Map Key

POPULATION
- ◎ 100,000 to 500,000
- ⊕ 50,000 to 100,000
- ○ 10,000 to 50,000
- ○ below 10,000

ELEVATION
- 4000m / 13,124ft
- 3000m / 9843ft
- 2000m / 6562ft
- 1000m / 3281ft
- 500m / 1640ft
- 250m / 820ft
- 100m / 328ft
- sea level

192

What to See

❶ Waimea Canyon
(near Kekaha)
The "Grand Canyon of the Pacific" is a spectacularly deep gorge

❷ Polynesian Cultural Centre (in Laie)
Landscaped Polynesian "islands" give a taste of regional cultures

❸ Arizona Memorial Museum
(in Honolulu)
Memorial to Pearl Harbor constructed over the *USS Arizona*'s submerged hull

❹ Haleakala
An otherworldly landscape of lush forest, shimmering waterfalls, jumbled lava flows and cinder cones

❺ Hawaii Volcanoes National Park
Two volcanoes, Mauna Kea and Mauna Loa (erupting since 1983)

SCALE 1:4,000,000
(projection: Lambert Conformal Conic)
Km 0 10 20 40 60 80 100
Miles 0 10 20 40 60 80 100

196

122

CHUKCHI SEA
RUSSIAN FEDERATION
Bering Strait
BERING SEA
Saint Lawrence Island
Pribilof Islands
Aleutian Islands
Near Islands
Rat Islands
Andreanof Islands
Islands of Four Mountains
Fox Islands
PACIFIC OCEAN

Map Key

POPULATION
- ◎ 100,000 to 500,000
- ⊕ 50,000 to 100,000
- ○ 10,000 to 50,000
- ○ below 10,000

ELEVATION
- 4000m / 13,124ft
- 3000m / 9843ft
- 2000m / 6562ft
- 1000m / 3281ft
- 500m / 1640ft
- 250m / 820ft
- 100m / 328ft
- sea level

192

Portage Glacier, SE of Anchorage: A boat ride takes tourists past blue and white floating icebergs to the tip of the retreating glacier.

196

USA: Alaska

Alaska is a land of ice, forest, mountains and plains, twice the size of Texas. With two-thirds of the state under permafrost and the southwest coastline lying on the volcanic "Ring of Fire", America's "Last Frontier" is a harsh but very rewarding place for tourists in search of dreamlike images of pristine wildernesses, towering snow-capped peaks and grizzly bears. A popular way to visit is by taking a cruise up the Canadian coast from Vancouver, which offers excellent whale-watching opportunities en route.

Alaska was purchased from Russia in 1867, 30 years before the discovery of gold in the Yukon River brought a surge of prospectors to the Klondike, just across the border in Canada. Its prosperity is now bound up with oil, which was first discovered here in 1968. From this stems a dilemma of which visitors cannot help but become aware – one of the USA's great contemporary debates. The drive to extract more oil is powerful, but should it override the preservation of a virgin environment and the protection of traditional livelihoods of indigenous peoples such as the Aleuts and Inupiaq?

Denali National Park: View en route to Wonder Lake of snow-clad Mount McKinley, which was originally called Denali, "the Great One", by the Athabascans.

10

Activities

- Pan for gold in the spruce forests of **Moose River**, home to moose, bears and bald eagles (near Anchorage)
- Cruise to **Glacier Bay**, southeast Alaska, for fantastic coastal scenery and whale-watching opportunities
- Ski at **Mount Alyeska**, near Anchorage
- View the **Northern Lights**, a cosmic night spectacular
- Hike the 53 km (33 miles) **Chilkoot Trail**, from Skagway , a memorial to the Klondike gold rush
- Catch a stage of the **Iditarod dog-sled race** from Anchorage to Nome on the west coast

192

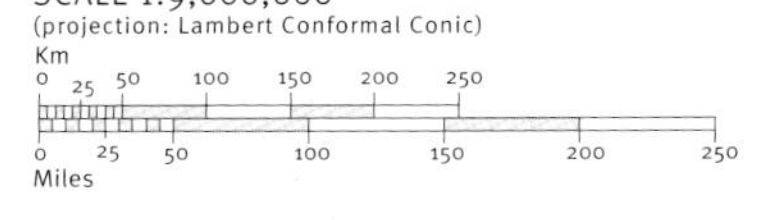

SCALE 1:9,000,000
(projection: Lambert Conformal Conic)

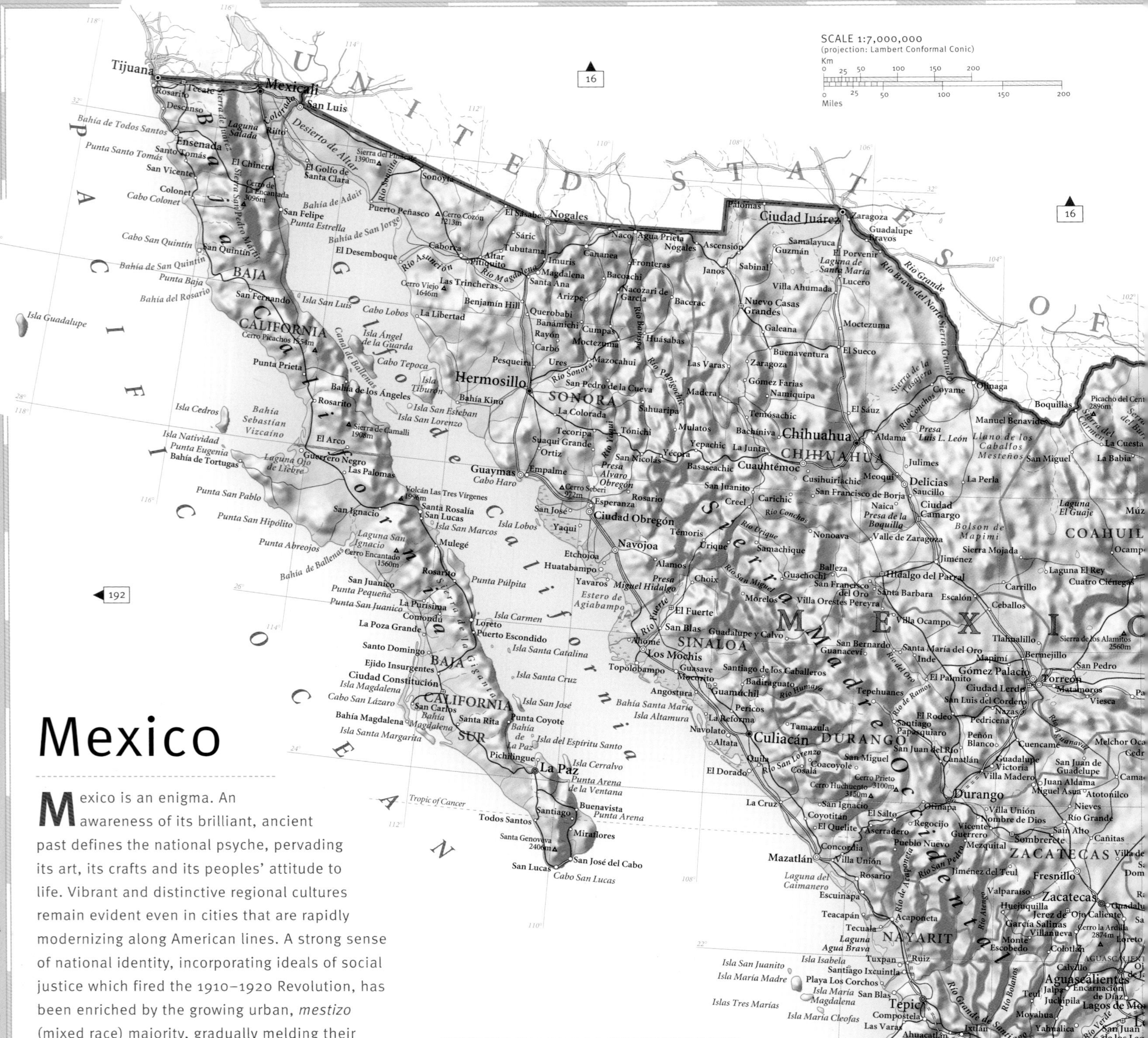

Mexico

Mexico is an enigma. An awareness of its brilliant, ancient past defines the national psyche, pervading its art, its crafts and its peoples' attitude to life. Vibrant and distinctive regional cultures remain evident even in cities that are rapidly modernizing along American lines. A strong sense of national identity, incorporating ideals of social justice which fired the 1910–1920 Revolution, has been enriched by the growing urban, *mestizo* (mixed race) majority, gradually melding their distinctive native heritages with those of colonial Spain. Yet its many indigenous peoples remain marginalized in rural poverty.

Contrasts are everywhere – mysterious semi-ruined cities of the Olmec, Toltec, Aztec, Maya and other great civilizations range over deserts, semi-arid volcanic tablelands, lush rainforest and tropical coastal plains each with their distinctive flora and fauna. Extremes of wealth coincide with absolute poverty – bustling Amerindian markets do business in the shadow of elaborate colonial churches, glitzy resorts are a stroll along white beaches from simple fishing villages while heaving industrialized cities are never far from sleepy towns little changed since the Spanish conquest. Fiestas are commonplace, inviting visitors to immerse themselves in local spectacle, colour and music.

Zócalo, Mexico City: Indigenous dancers daily recall their ancestors on the city's central plaza at what was formerly the heart of the great Aztec capital of Tenochtitlán. Nearby are the remains of the Templo Mayor (Great Temple), the sacred centre of the Aztec universe.

Mexico: Administrative Regions

Ⓓ DISTRITO FEDERAL

Map Key

POPULATION

- above 5 million
- 1 million to 5 million
- 500,000 to 1 million
- 100,000 to 500,000
- 50,000 to 100,000
- 10,000 to 50,000
- below 10,000

ELEVATION

- 4000m / 13,124ft
- 3000m / 9843ft
- 2000m / 6562ft
- 1000m / 3281ft
- 500m / 1640ft
- 250m / 820ft
- 100m / 328ft
- sea level

What to See

❶ Baja California
This 1,287 km (800 mile) tongue of land is loved primarily for its desert and mountain wildernesses, lonely beaches and wildlife

❷ Copper Canyon
(near Creel) This amazing gorge is 229 m (750 ft) deeper and four times bigger than the USA's Grand Canyon

❸ Zacatecas
On a desert plain, its colonial centre is a warren of lanes and has excellent museums

❹ Guadalajara
Mexico's second-largest city retains its provincial ambience and extensive colonial charm

❺ Guanajuato
Pastel façades, crooked cobbled alleyways and colonial architecture have earned this vibrant city a UNESCO World Heritage site listing

❻ Mexico City
An intoxicating mega-city with colonial serenity amid the raucous modernity

❼ Teotihuacán
The civilization that created this awesome city remains a mystery. Climb the huge Pyramid of the Sun

❽ Taxco
This time-warped maze of a town, clinging to a hillside, is famous for its silverware

❾ Cholula
The grass-covered pyramid with a church on top offers views of Popocatépetl volcano

❿ Acapulco
This one-time jet-set resort has aged gracefully, its balmy climate attracting visitors to its beaches and legendary nightlife

⓫ Monte Albán
The ancient Zapotec capital is a gem of archaeology – near the colonial city of Oaxaca

⓬ Palenque
Set in tropical rainforest this classic Mayan site is the most hauntingly beautiful in Mexico

⓭ Chichén Itzá
The Temple of the Warriors, the ball court, Great Pyramid and platform of the skulls are highlights in this Toltec-Maya capital

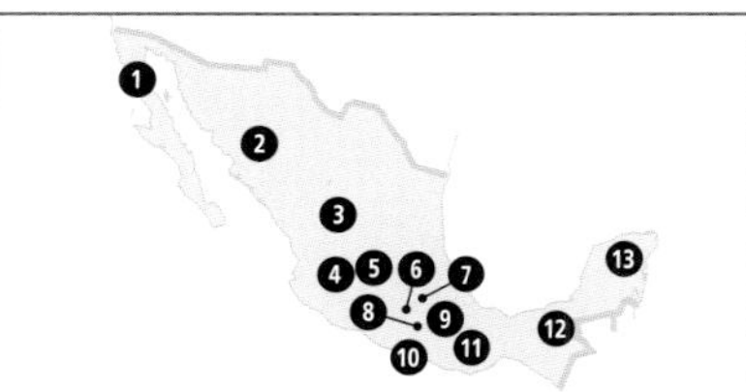
1
2
3
4
5
6
7
8
9
10
11
12
13

Xel-Ha, Yucatan Peninsula: Time lingers here, where nature reserves and eco-tourism seek to protect this magical region. Once settled by the Maya civilization, it abounds in flora, fauna and marine life. Snorkellers and divers value the crystal clear waters of the lagoons and coral reefs, while far-sighted visitors opt for the peace of remoter white beaches backing onto jungle.

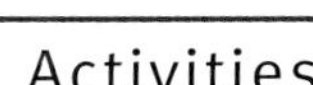

Activities

- Enjoy first class whale watching, birdwatching and sport fishing in **Baja California**
- Scuba dive or snorkel on magnificent coral reefs off **Yucatan's** beaches
- Observe Mexicans celebrating their ancestors on the **Day of the Dead** (1–2 November)
- Hike around the delightful wilderness scenery of **Veracruz-Llave** and **Morelos** states
- Savour the spectacle of a major football match at Mexico City's magnificent **Azteca Stadium**

Mexico City: The Catedral Metropolitana took 250 years to complete and now represents an unusual combination of many architectural styles. Built on a lake bed like the rest of the city, it needs frequent reinforcements to prevent further sinkage into the loose subsoil.

16
Villa Acuña
Piedras Negras
Nava
Villa Unión
Nueva Rosita
Sabinas
Hidalgo
Juárez
Nuevo Laredo
Anáhuac
Lampazos
La Gloria
Presa Falcón
Nueva Ciudad Guerrera
Mier
Ciudad Miguel Alemán
Reynosa
Camargo
Cerralvo
NUEVO LEÓN
Monterrey
China
General Bravo
Río Bravo
Matamoros
Valle Hermoso
Cándido Aguilar
Cadereyta
Allende
Montemorelos
General Terán
Laguna Madre
Linares
Burgos
San Fernando
San Carlos
Villa Mainero
Villagrán
TAMAULIPAS
Jiménez
Abasolo
Soto la Marina
La Pesca
Ciudad Victoria
Tropic of Cancer
Aldama
Xicoténcatl
González
Ciudad Mante
Antiguo Morelos
Altamira
Ciudad Madero
Tampico
Laguna de Pueblo Viejo
Ébano
SAN LUIS POTOSÍ
San Luis Potosí
Cerritos
Ciudad del Maíz
Cárdenas
Rayón
Río Verde
Ciudad Valles
Pánuco
Tamuín
Higos
Tanquián
Tempoal
Laguna de Tamiahua
Cabo Rojo
Naranjos
Tamazunchale
Tantoyuca
Tamiahua
Tuxpán
Dolores Hidalgo
Guanajuato
San Miguel de Allende
QUERÉTARO
Querétaro
Celaya
Poza Rica
Gutiérrez Zamora
Papantla
Nautla
Martínez de La Torre
HIDALGO
Pachuca
Tula
San Juan del Río
Acámbaro
Tulancingo
Teziutlán
Altotonga
VERACRUZ-LLAVE
Xalapa
Veracruz
Morelia
Zitácuaro
MÉXICO
MEXICO (MEXICO CITY)
Toluca
Tlaxcala
TLAXCALA
Puebla
Huamantla
Orizaba
Córdoba
Boca del Río
Alvarado
Punta Roca Partida
Bahía de Campeche
Cuernavaca
Cuautla
MORELOS
PUEBLA
Tehuacán
Tierra Blanca
San Andrés Tuxtla
Catemaco
Coatzacoalcos
Cosamaloapan
Minatitlán
Taxco
Iguala
Tuxtepec
Chilpancingo
Guerrero
Sierra Madre del Sur
Acapulco
Oaxaca
OAXACA
Istmo de Tehuantepec
Matías Romero
Juchitán
Salina Cruz
Tehuantepec
Puerto Escondido
Pochutla
Puerto Ángel
Golfo de Tehuantepec
Punta Maldonado
Pinotepa Nacional
PACIFIC OCEAN

44
Yucatan Channel
Río Lagartos
Cabo Catoche
Isla Mujeres
Chiquilá
Cancún
Puerto Juárez
Puerto Morelos
Progreso
Dzilam de Bravo
Tizimín
Mérida
Motul
Izamal
Espita
Valladolid
Playa del Carmen
Cozumel
Isla Cozumel
Hunucmá
YUCATÁN
Celestún
Maxcanú
Ticul
Oxkutzcab
Peto
Yucatan Peninsula
Tekax
Hecelchakán
Tenabo
Campeche
Seybaplaya
Champotón
Hopelchén
Felipe Carrillo Puerto
Bahía de la Ascensión
Bahía del Espíritu Santo
Punta Herrero
QUINTANA ROO
CAMPECHE
Xpujil
Chetumal
Bacalar
Majahual
Banco Chinchorro
Sabancuy
Laguna de Términos
Carmen
Francisco Escárcega
Candelaria
Nuevo Coahuila
Frontera
Paraíso
TABASCO
Villahermosa
Macuspana
Emiliano Zapata
Tenosique
Palenque
Comalcalco
Cárdenas
BELIZE
GUATEMALA
Teapa
Pichucalco
Simojovel
Ocosingo
San Cristóbal de Las Casas
CHIAPAS
Tuxtla Gutiérrez
Cintalapa
Comitán
Venustiano Carranza
Las Margaritas
Arriaga
Tonalá
Pijijiapan
Mapastepec
Escuintla
Huixtla
Tapachula
Ciudad Hidalgo
Puerto Madero
Motozintla de Mendoza
Volcán Tacaná
42

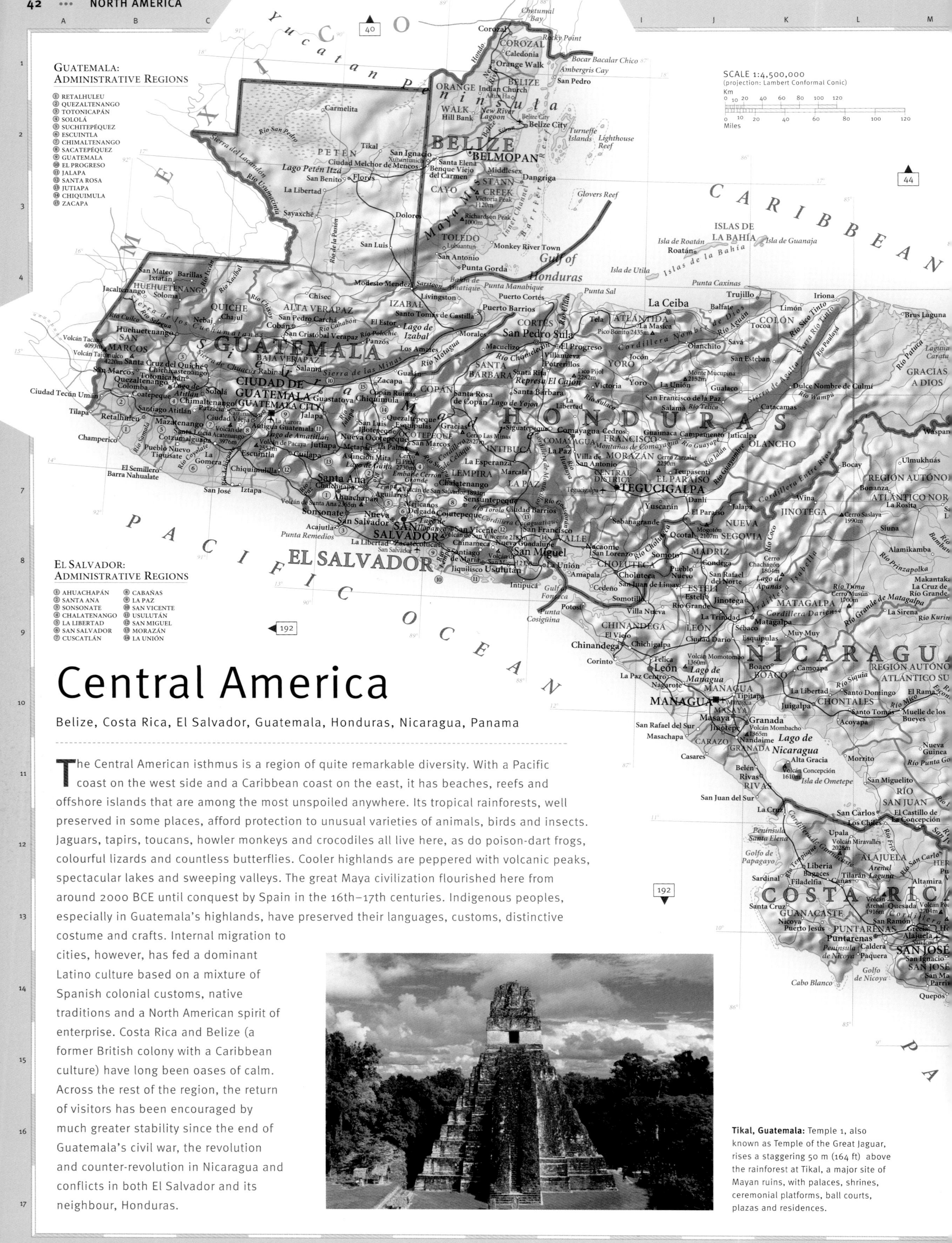

GUATEMALA: ADMINISTRATIVE REGIONS
① RETALHULEU
② QUEZALTENANGO
③ TOTONICAPÁN
④ SOLOLÁ
⑤ SUCHITEPÉQUEZ
⑥ ESCUINTLA
⑦ CHIMALTENANGO
⑧ SACATEPÉQUEZ
⑨ GUATEMALA
⑩ EL PROGRESO
⑪ JALAPA
⑫ SANTA ROSA
⑬ JUTIAPA
⑭ CHIQUIMULA
⑮ ZACAPA
EL SALVADOR: ADMINISTRATIVE REGIONS
① AHUACHAPÁN
② SANTA ANA
③ SONSONATE
④ CHALATENANGO
⑤ LA LIBERTAD
⑥ SAN SALVADOR
⑦ CUSCATLÁN
⑧ CABAÑAS
⑨ LA PAZ
⑩ SAN VICENTE
⑪ USULUTÁN
⑫ SAN MIGUEL
⑬ MORAZÁN
⑭ LA UNIÓN
SCALE 1:4,500,000
(projection: Lambert Conformal Conic)
Km
Miles
MEXICO
Yucatan Peninsula
BELIZE
BELMOPAN
GUATEMALA
CIUDAD DE GUATEMALA (GUATEMALA CITY)
EL SALVADOR
SAN SALVADOR
HONDURAS
TEGUCIGALPA
NICARAGUA
MANAGUA
COSTA RICA
SAN JOSÉ
CARIBBEAN
PACIFIC OCEAN
Gulf of Honduras
Lago de Nicaragua
Lago de Izabal
Lago Petén Itzá
40
44
192
192

Central America

Belize, Costa Rica, El Salvador, Guatemala, Honduras, Nicaragua, Panama

The Central American isthmus is a region of quite remarkable diversity. With a Pacific coast on the west side and a Caribbean coast on the east, it has beaches, reefs and offshore islands that are among the most unspoiled anywhere. Its tropical rainforests, well preserved in some places, afford protection to unusual varieties of animals, birds and insects. Jaguars, tapirs, toucans, howler monkeys and crocodiles all live here, as do poison-dart frogs, colourful lizards and countless butterflies. Cooler highlands are peppered with volcanic peaks, spectacular lakes and sweeping valleys. The great Maya civilization flourished here from around 2000 BCE until conquest by Spain in the 16th–17th centuries. Indigenous peoples, especially in Guatemala's highlands, have preserved their languages, customs, distinctive costume and crafts. Internal migration to cities, however, has fed a dominant Latino culture based on a mixture of Spanish colonial customs, native traditions and a North American spirit of enterprise. Costa Rica and Belize (a former British colony with a Caribbean culture) have long been oases of calm. Across the rest of the region, the return of visitors has been encouraged by much greater stability since the end of Guatemala's civil war, the revolution and counter-revolution in Nicaragua and conflicts in both El Salvador and its neighbour, Honduras.

Tikal, Guatemala: Temple 1, also known as Temple of the Great Jaguar, rises a staggering 50 m (164 ft) above the rainforest at Tikal, a major site of Mayan ruins, with palaces, shrines, ceremonial platforms, ball courts, plazas and residences.

Chichicastenango, Guatemala: Women sell flowers on the steps of the 400-year old church of Santo Tomás, location for the country's liveliest and most colourful market. Copal incense fills the air as thousands of indigenous people mix religious observance with business and large crowds of visitors shop for local handicrafts.

What to See

1 Tikal
Of the great cities of the Maya period (250 BCE–900 CE) none matched the majesty and power of Tikal whose temples rise mysteriously out of the rainforest

2 Barrier Reef
An ecological wonder, Belize's barrier reef is the world's second-largest. Its cayes (small islands) have coral reefs teeming with exotic sea life

3 Chichicastenango
Famous Amerindian handicraft market centred on the charming, 400-year-old Santo Tomás church in this little Guatemalan hill town

4 Lago de Atitlán
Native Guatemalan communities with their own language and dress are dotted around this large lake, fabled for its dramatic setting beneath towering volcanoes

5 Antigua Guatemala
Once capital of Spanish colonial Guatemala. With cobbled streets, churches, convents and grand residences

6 Copán
Set in jungle, Honduras' important Maya site has a collection of reliefs depicting Copán's kings carved on the 63-step Hieroglyphic Stairway

7 Lago de Ilopango
El Salvador's largest freshwater lake, formed in a giant volcano, is an ideal place for fishing, boating and picnicking

8 Laguna de Alegria
(near Usulután) An emerald green lagoon in the dormant Tecapa volcano, provides a rare chance to crater dive

9 León Cathedral
Central America's largest cathedral contains grand colonial religious art and the tombs of Nicaragua's most famous citizens

10 Islas del Maíz
Remote, beautiful and unspoiled, these Nicaraguan islands are largely undiscovered Caribbean gems

11 Parque Nacional Volcán Arenal
Costa Rica is dotted with wildlife reserves. This one has the added drama of a continuously active volcano

12 Panama Canal
Linking the Atlantic and Pacific was one of the greatest ever feats of engineering. Ships use a series of locks to cross the 80 km (50 mile) isthmus

13 Darien National Park
Guided tours allow travel deep into rainforests revealing rich flora and fauna

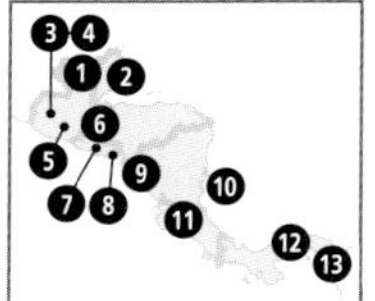

Activities

Scuba and snorkel in crystal clear waters off **Belize's** cayes
Take out a kayak to experience the full grandeur of **Lago de Atitlán**, Guatemala
Zip through Costa Rica's **Monteverde Cloud Forest** on an aerial tram
Hike around **Lago de Nicaragua**, with its awesome twin volcanoes forming Isla de Ometepe
Go whitewater rafting on **Rio Congrejal's** scary rapids near La Ceiba, Honduras
Take your binoculars for a spot of birdwatching in **Panama's** national parks, where around 1,000 species can be found
Surf the Pacific rollers at the new surf resort of **La Libertad**, El Salvador

Barrier reef off Belize: Often referred to as one of the "Seven Underwater Wonders of the World", Belize's famous barrier reef of corals and spectacular underwater gardens teems with sea life in waters averaging 26–29°C – a paradise for scuba divers and snorkellers.

Map Key

POPULATION	ELEVATION
500,000 to 1 million	4000m / 13,124ft
100,000 to 500,000	3000m / 9843ft
50,000 to 100,000	2000m / 6562ft
10,000 to 50,000	1000m / 3281ft
below 10,000	500m / 1640ft
	250m / 820ft
	100m / 328ft
	sea level

44 ▶
▲ 44 
54 ▶
192 ▼

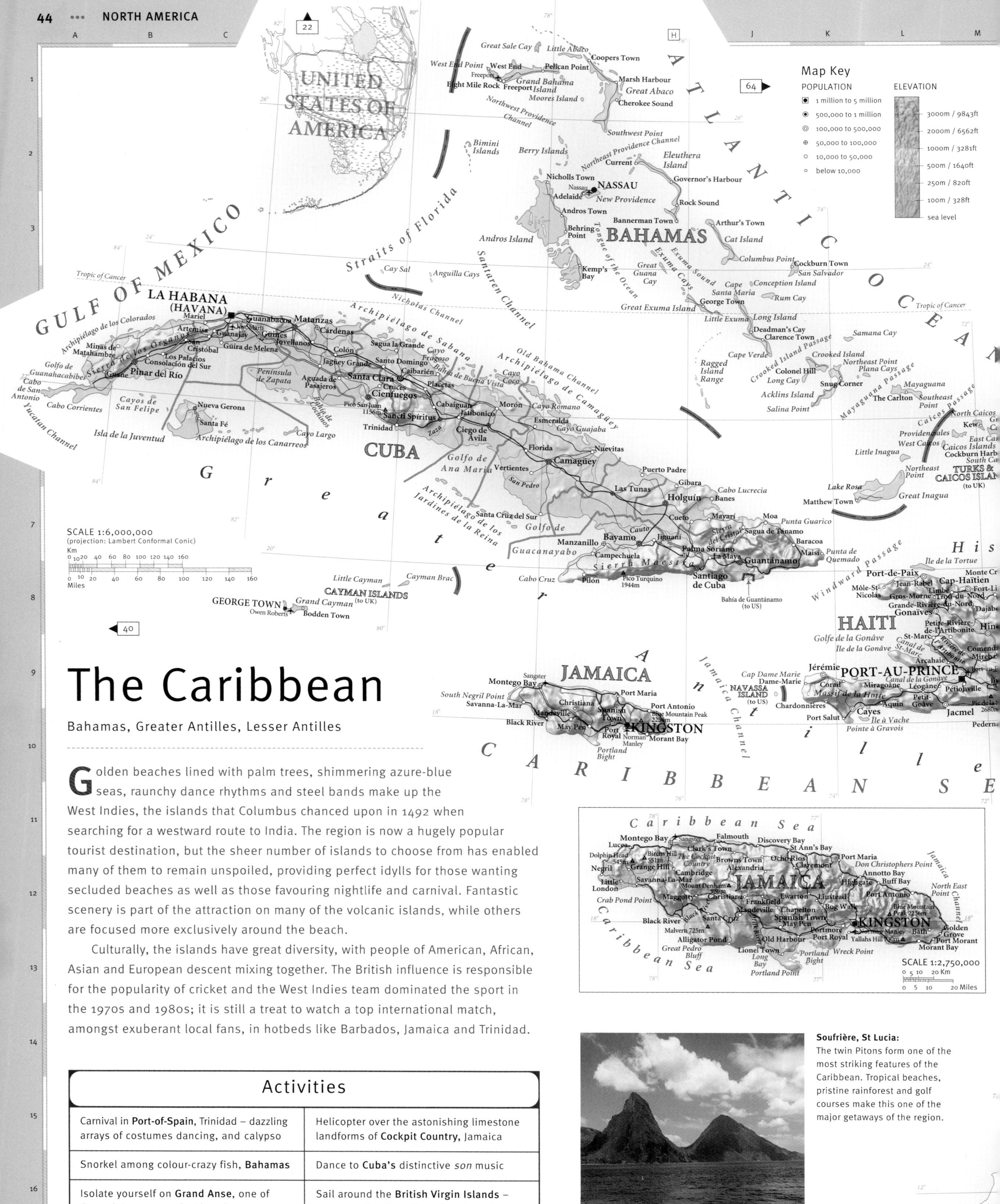
22
64
40
Map Key
POPULATION
1 million to 5 million
500,000 to 1 million
100,000 to 500,000
50,000 to 100,000
10,000 to 50,000
below 10,000
ELEVATION
3000m / 9843ft
2000m / 6562ft
1000m / 3281ft
500m / 1640ft
250m / 820ft
100m / 328ft
sea level
UNITED STATES OF AMERICA
GULF OF MEXICO
ATLANTIC OCEAN
Straits of Florida
BAHAMAS
NASSAU
New Providence
Grand Bahama
Freeport
Great Abaco
Marsh Harbour
Eleuthera Island
Andros Island
Cat Island
Great Exuma Island
Long Island
Crooked Island
Acklins Island
Mayaguana
Great Inagua
Little Inagua
TURKS & CAICOS ISLANDS (to UK)
Cockburn Town
Tropic of Cancer
LA HABANA (HAVANA)
Matanzas
Pinar del Río
Santa Clara
Cienfuegos
Sancti Spíritus
Ciego de Ávila
Camagüey
Las Tunas
Holguín
Bayamo
Manzanillo
Santiago de Cuba
Guantánamo
Bahía de Guantánamo (to US)
Pico Turquino 1944m
Sierra Maestra
Isla de la Juventud
Nueva Gerona
CUBA
Yucatan Channel
Windward Passage
CAYMAN ISLANDS (to UK)
GEORGE TOWN
Grand Cayman
Little Cayman
Cayman Brac
SCALE 1:6,000,000
(projection: Lambert Conformal Conic)
JAMAICA
KINGSTON
Montego Bay
Port Antonio
Jamaica Channel
NAVASSA ISLAND (to US)
HAITI
PORT-AU-PRINCE
Cap-Haïtien
Gonaïves
Jérémie
Jacmel
Île de la Gonâve
Golfe de la Gonâve
CARIBBEAN SEA
Greater Antilles
Caribbean Sea
Falmouth
Discovery Bay
St Ann's Bay
Ocho Rios
Port Maria
Mandeville
Spanish Town
Portmore
Port Royal
Morant Bay
Black River
Savanna-La-Mar
Negril
Blue Mountain Peak 2256m
SCALE 1:2,750,000
COLOMBIA

The Caribbean

Bahamas, Greater Antilles, Lesser Antilles

Golden beaches lined with palm trees, shimmering azure-blue seas, raunchy dance rhythms and steel bands make up the West Indies, the islands that Columbus chanced upon in 1492 when searching for a westward route to India. The region is now a hugely popular tourist destination, but the sheer number of islands to choose from has enabled many of them to remain unspoiled, providing perfect idylls for those wanting secluded beaches as well as those favouring nightlife and carnival. Fantastic scenery is part of the attraction on many of the volcanic islands, while others are focused more exclusively around the beach.

Culturally, the islands have great diversity, with people of American, African, Asian and European descent mixing together. The British influence is responsible for the popularity of cricket and the West Indies team dominated the sport in the 1970s and 1980s; it is still a treat to watch a top international match, amongst exuberant local fans, in hotbeds like Barbados, Jamaica and Trinidad.

Activities

Carnival in **Port-of-Spain**, Trinidad – dazzling arrays of costumes dancing, and calypso	Helicopter over the astonishing limestone landforms of **Cockpit Country,** Jamaica
Snorkel among colour-crazy fish, **Bahamas**	Dance to **Cuba's** distinctive *son* music
Isolate yourself on **Grand Anse**, one of Grenada's many perfect beaches	Sail around the **British Virgin Islands** – craggy peaks of mostly underwater volcanoes
Tee off at **Teeth of the Dogs,** a world-class golf course in the Dominican Republic	Scuba dive off **Grand Cayman** for some of the region's best reefs and marine life

Soufrière, St Lucia: The twin Pitons form one of the most striking features of the Caribbean. Tropical beaches, pristine rainforest and golf courses make this one of the major getaways of the region.

Museo del Carnival, Santiago de Cuba: This religious festival involves music, brightly-coloured masks and dancing – the conga being one of the more popular ways to parade the streets.

What to See

❶ Bahamas
Pink sands, dolphins, diving and fishing have made these islands hugely popular. Those keen on sailing and windsurfing are also well-catered for

❷ Cuba
Island of Latin rhythms and stylish buildings that inspired Hemingway's *The Old Man and the Sea*

❸ Puerto Rico
Spanish colonial architecture of the captal, San Juan, contrasts with the tropical forests of El Yunque National Park

❹ Morne Trois Pitons
Dominica's best national park, a World Heritage Site, has lush rainforest, hot springs and waterfalls

❺ St Lucia
A relaxing island, where two pyramidal mountains soar out of the sea

❻ Barbados
Known for its perfect beaches, historic towns and attractive walks and of course – cricket!

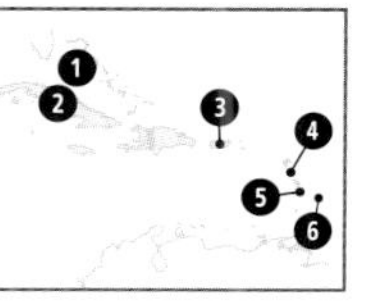
1
2
3
4
5
6

Tobago: Verdant landscapes, gorgeously clean, white, sandy beaches and calm turquoise seas – filled with excellent marine life and suitable for a wide range of sporting activities.

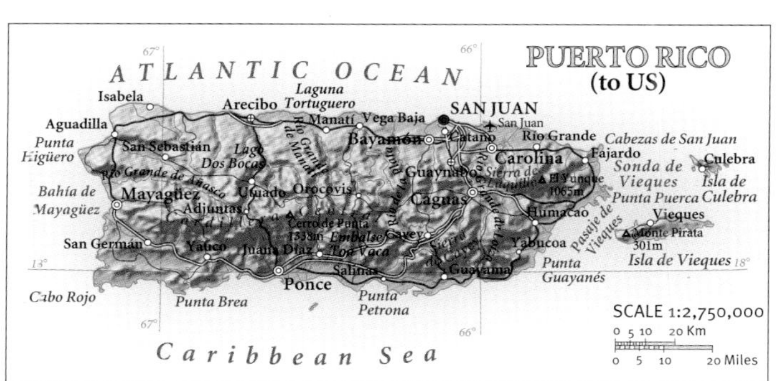
ATLANTIC OCEAN
PUERTO RICO
(to US)
SAN JUAN
Aguadilla
Arecibo
Mayagüez
Ponce
Caguas
Carolina
Fajardo
Culebra
Vieques
Isla de Vieques
Caribbean Sea
SCALE 1:2,750,000

GUADELOUPE
(to France)
ATLANTIC OCEAN
Caribbean Sea
Grande Terre
Basse Terre
BASSE-TERRE
Pointe-à-Pitre
Le Moule
Capesterre-Belle-Eau
SCALE 1:2,750,000

64

DOMINICAN REPUBLIC
SANTO DOMINGO
PUERTO RICO
(to US)
SAN JUAN
BRITISH VIRGIN ISLANDS
(to UK)
ROAD TOWN
CHARLOTTE AMALIE
VIRGIN ISLANDS
(to US)
ANGUILLA
(to UK)
THE VALLEY
NETHERLANDS ANTILLES
(to Netherlands)
ST KITTS & NEVIS
BASSETERRE
ANTIGUA & BARBUDA
ST JOHN'S
PLYMOUTH
MONTSERRAT
(to UK)
GUADELOUPE
(to France)
BASSE-TERRE
DOMINICA
ROSEAU
MARTINIQUE
(to France)
FORT-DE-FRANCE
ST LUCIA
CASTRIES
BARBADOS
BRIDGETOWN
ST VINCENT & THE GRENADINES
KINGSTOWN
GRENADA
ST GEORGE'S
TRINIDAD & TOBAGO
PORT-OF-SPAIN
Leeward Islands
Lesser Antilles
Windward Islands
Lesser Antilles
ARUBA
(to Netherlands)
ORANJESTAD
NETHERLANDS ANTILLES
(to Netherlands)
WILLEMSTAD
VENEZUELA

64

DOMINICA
ROSEAU
ATLANTIC OCEAN
Caribbean Sea
SCALE 1:2,250,000

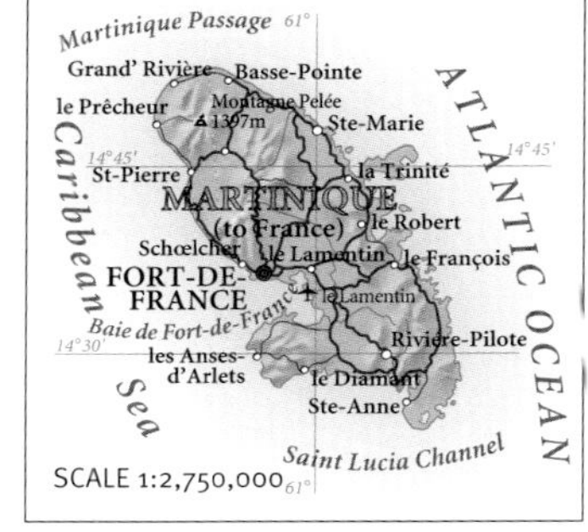
MARTINIQUE
(to France)
FORT-DE-FRANCE
ATLANTIC OCEAN
Caribbean Sea
SCALE 1:2,750,000

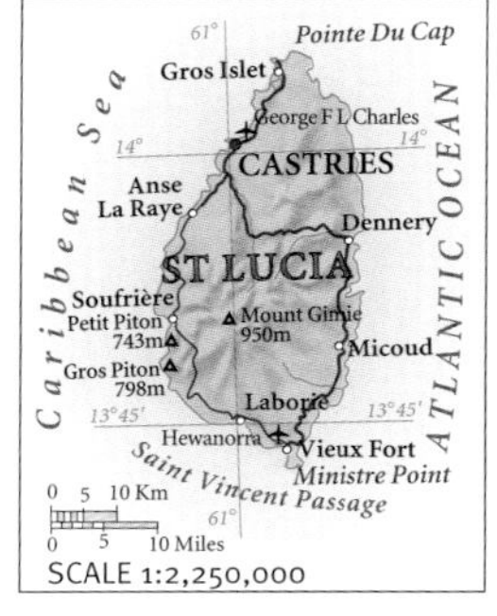
ST LUCIA
CASTRIES
ATLANTIC OCEAN
Caribbean Sea
SCALE 1:2,250,000

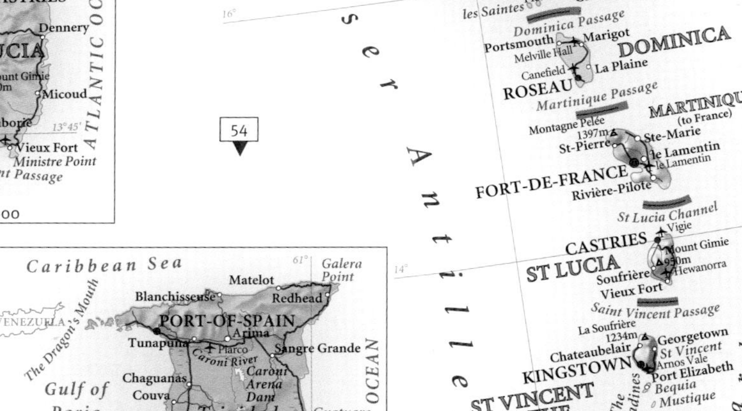

54

ATLANTIC OCEAN
BARBADOS
BRIDGETOWN
SCALE 1:2,250,000

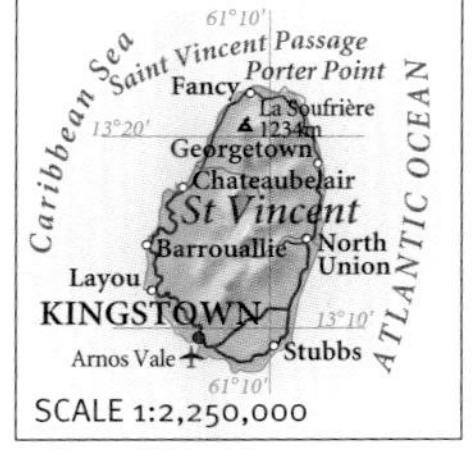
St Vincent
KINGSTOWN
ATLANTIC OCEAN
Caribbean Sea
SCALE 1:2,250,000

GRENADA
ST.GEORGE'S
ATLANTIC OCEAN
Caribbean Sea
SCALE 1:2,250,000

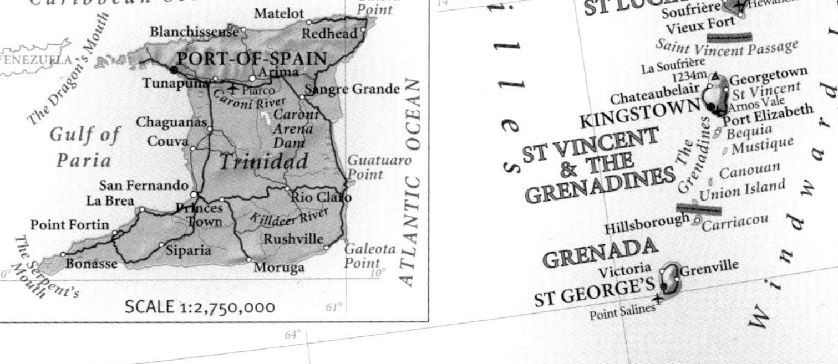
Caribbean Sea
PORT-OF-SPAIN
Trinidad
Gulf of Paria
San Fernando
ATLANTIC OCEAN
SCALE 1:2,750,000

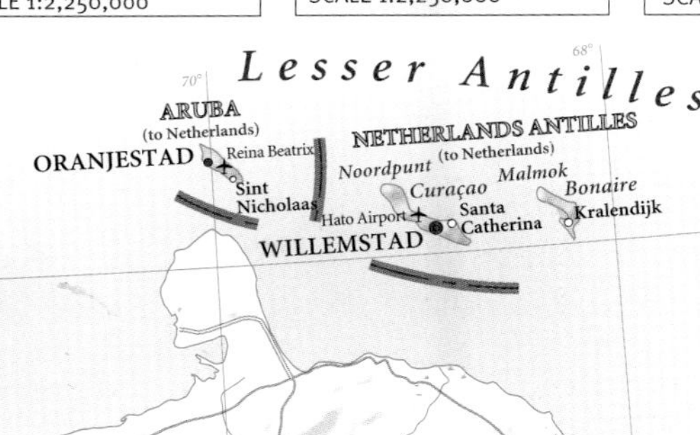

54

South America

"My poetry was born between the hill and the river, it took its voice from the rain, and like the timber, it steeped itself in the forests." PABLO NERUDA, 1904-1973

Physical South America

South America, stretching from the Caribbean Sea to the Southern Ocean, covers three main physical regions. In the west, the vast mountain range of the Andes marches through seven countries. The Andean mountains are harsh and unforgiving, containing some of the world's largest volcanoes. Lake Titicaca lies in a dormant crater. It is, at 3,800 m (12,500 ft), the highest significant body of water in the world and the largest lake in South America. In the east, the Brazilian and Guyana shields are ancient mountain formations, far more eroded than the much younger Andes. Between these two are the huge, tropically rainforested, river basins of the Amazon and the Orinoco, the broad grassland expanses of pampas and *llanos* and the Gran Chaco lowland plain.

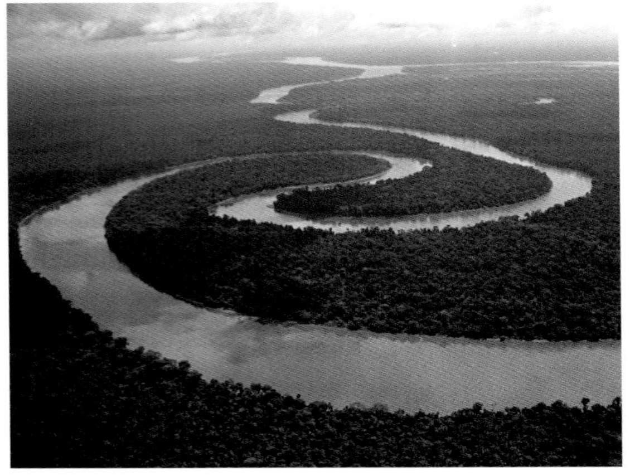

Amazon

The Amazon Basin, the world's largest, covers half of Brazil. Its extraordinary fecundity is the result of extremely high rainfall and the rich silt carried by the Amazon and its many tributaries. The rainforests host a profusion of animals and plants. Commercial extraction of hardwood is a major cause of damage to the fragile ecosystem.

SCALE 1:33,900,000
(projection: Lambert Azimuthal Equal Area)
Km 0 100 200 400 600 800
Miles 0 100 200 400 600 800

Map Key

ELEVATION

6000m / 19,686ft
4000m / 13,124ft
3000m / 9843ft
2000m / 6562ft
1500m / 4922ft
1000m / 3281ft
500m / 1640ft
250m / 820ft
100m / 328ft
sea level

PLATE MARGINS

constructive
destructive
conservative
uncertain
physiographic regions

Punta Gallinas
Gulf of Venezuela
Lake Maracaibo
Gulf of Darien
Gulf of Panama
Cauca
Magdalena
Cordillera Occidental
Cordillera Central
Cordillera Oriental
Llanos
Orinoco
Pakaraima Mountains
GUYANA SHIELD
Guiana Highlands
Tumuc-Humac Mountains
Rio Negro
Branco
Japurá
COCOS PLATE
NAZCA PLATE
Cotopaxi 5897m
Chimborazo 6310m
Cordillera Real
Putumayo
Amazon
Amazon Basin
Represa Balbina
Ilha de Marajó
ATLANTIC OCEAN
Gulf of Guayaquil
Marañón
Juruá
Purus
Madeira
Tapajós
Xingu
Tocantins
Serra do Carajás
Serra do Cachimbo
Cabo de São Roque
Planalto da Borborema
Punta Negra
SOUTH AMERICAN PLATE
NAZCA PLATE
Ucayali
Nevado Huascarán 6768m
ANDEAN
SUB-ANDEAN SYSTEM
Araguaia
Tocantins
BRAZILIAN SHIELD
Represa de Sobradinho
Chapada dos Parecis
Guaporé
Planalto de Mato Grosso
Serra Formosa
Serra do Roncador
Serra Dourada
São Francisco
Brazilian Highlands
Serra do Espinhaço
PACIFIC OCEAN
Madre de Dios
Lake Titicaca
Lago Poopó
Andes
Altiplano
Pantanal
Serra do Caiapó
Serra de Maracajú
Paraná
Serra da Mantiqueira
Atacama Desert
Pilcomayo
Gran Chaco
Paraguay
SISTEM MESETA
Cerro Ojos del Salado 6880m
Serra Geral
Serra do Mar
Uruguay
Mesopotamia
Paraná
Lagoa dos Patos
Mirim Lagoon
Cerro Aconcagua 6959m
Salado
Pampas
Río de la Plat
NAZCA PLATE
SOUTH AMERICAN PLATE
PATAGONIAN SHIELD
Patagonia
Colorado
Río Negro
Península Valdés
Isla de Chiloé
Chico
Lago Colhué Huapí
Gulf of San Jorge
Deseado
Golfo de Penas
ANTARCTIC PLATE
Bahía Grande
Falkland Islands
Strait of Magellan
Tierra del Fuego
SOUTH AMERICAN PLATE
SCOTIA PLATE
Cape Horn

Andes

The Andes form a natural border between Argentina and Chile in the south of the continent, leaving a thin strip of coast to the west that contains the Atacama Desert, one of the driest places on the planet – some areas have never recorded any rainfall. Within the mountains, the Altiplano – a flat plateau at 3,800 m (12,500 ft) – covers Bolivia and parts of Peru.

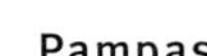

Pampas

Wide plains of pampas grass are typical of Argentina and Paraguay, supporting massive herds of cattle to produce meat, hides and milk. The word "pampas" comes from an Amerindian term meaning "flat surface".

Climate

In the tropical northeast of the continent, high rainfall and temperatures feed the lush vegetation. These tropical conditions are found over half the continent of South America. In the west, the Andes barrier creates a rainshadow – an area in the lee of the mountains with less rain and cloud cover. As one travels south to the pampas plains of Paraguay and Argentina, the tropical conditions give way to mild winters and cool summers. Finally, in the deep south of Patagonia, Antarctic conditions creep in – the ferocity of the winds off Cape Horn makes it one of the world's most dangerous areas for shipping.

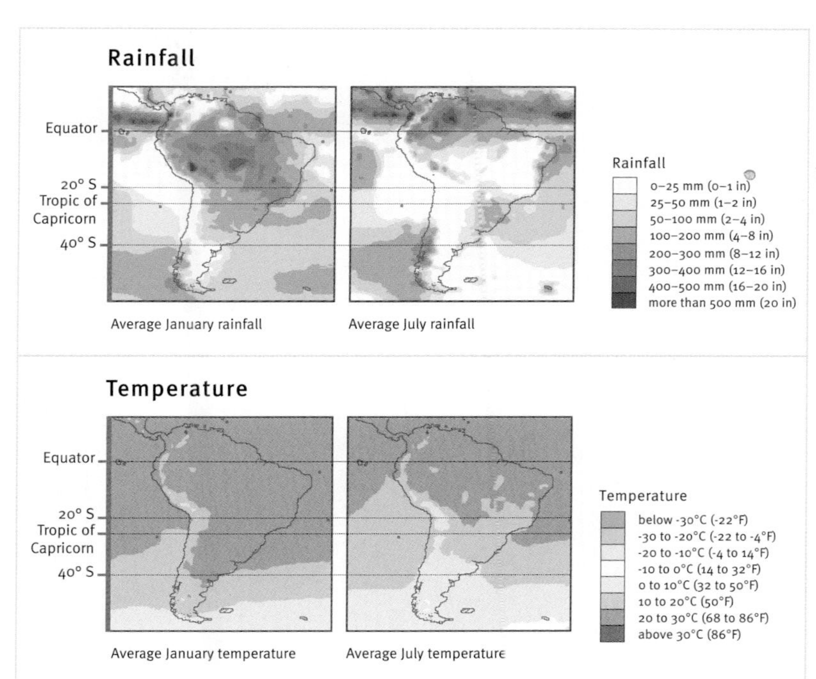

Rainfall
Equator
20° S
Tropic of Capricorn
40° S
Average January rainfall
Average July rainfall
Rainfall
0–25 mm (0–1 in)
25–50 mm (1–2 in)
50–100 mm (2–4 in)
100–200 mm (4–8 in)
200–300 mm (8–12 in)
300–400 mm (12–16 in)
400–500 mm (16–20 in)
more than 500 mm (20 in)
Temperature
Equator
20° S
Tropic of Capricorn
40° S
Average January temperature
Average July temperature
Temperature
below -30°C (-22°F)
-30 to -20°C (-22 to -4°F)
-20 to -10°C (-4 to 14°F)
-10 to 0°C (14 to 32°F)
0 to 10°C (32 to 50°F)
10 to 20°C (50°F)
20 to 30°C (68 to 86°F)
above 30°C (86°F)

Maracaibo
Caracas
Georgetown
Cayenne
Bogotá
Equator
Quito
Belém
Manaus
Altos
Recife
Lima
La Paz
Santa Cruz
Brasília
Belo Horizonte
La Quiaca
Rio de Janeiro
Tropic of Capricorn
Antofagasta
Asunción
Cordoba
Porto Alegre
Santiago
Buenos Aires
Montevideo
Concepción
Pamperos
Stanley
Climate
tundra
cool continental
warm humid
semi-arid
arid
humid equatorial
tropical
daily hours of sunshine, January
daily hours of sunshine, July
cold wind

Guiana Highlands, Brazil: Early morning mist masks the canopy of the rainforest in the Amazon Basin.

Caribbean Sea
ATLANTIC OCEAN
PACIFIC OCEAN
Barranquilla
Gulf of Darien
Gulf of Panama
Medellín
Maracaibo
Caracas
Llanos
Orinoco
Bogotá
Cali
Guiana Highlands
Rio Negro
Amazon Basin
Putumayo
Amazon
Manaus
Ilha de Marajó
Belém
Tocantins
Xingu
Tapajós
Madeira
Purus
Juruá
Gulf of Guayaquil
Marañón
Fortaleza
Recife
Araguaia
Andes
Lima
Planalto de Mato Grosso
Brasília
São Francisco
Brazilian Highlands
Salvador
Belo Horizonte
Pilcomayo
Gran Chaco
Paraguay
Paraná
Rio de Janeiro
São Paulo
Curitiba
Uruguay
Porto Alegre
Córdoba
Rosario
Santiago
Pampas
Buenos Aires
Montevideo
Colorado
Rio Negro
Patagonia
Chico
Gulf of San Jorge
Bahia Grande
Tierra del Fuego
Cape Horn
Using the Land and Sea
barren land
cropland
desert
forest
mountain region
pasture
major conurbations
cattle
pigs
sheep
bananas
corn (maize)
citrus fruits
cocoa
cotton
coffee
fishing
oil palms
peanuts
rubber
shellfish
soya beans
sugar cane
vineyards
wheat

Using Land and Sea

The southern pampas is good for cereal growing and cattle ranching, while Chile's central valley supports vineyards and farms producing fruit and walnuts. Soya is widely grown in Uruguay and Brazil, often for use in animal feed. Brazil is the world's largest coffee grower and also a major producer of oranges and sugar. In the west, the higher regions are grazed by alpacas and llamas as well as sheep and cattle, while coastal regions support the production of cash crops such as rice and bananas. In the north, particularly in Colombia, many farmers are put off by big fluctuations in prices for cash crops and opt to grow more lucrative narcotics, especially coca, instead.

Colca Canyon, Peru: Steep mountainsides are packed with terraces to maximize crop-growing space in the deep valleys of the Andes mountains.

Political South America

Populated originally by a number of Amerindian tribes, brought together in the west by the Incas of Peru, South America was colonized from the 16th century by Spanish and Portuguese adventurers. The states that emerged sought independence in the 19th century under the inspirational leadership of Simon de Bolívar. Today almost all have long-established political systems based on a strong presidency. Most underwent periods of right-wing and military leadership in the 1970s, but the general trend now is for more left-wing governments and usually more democratic transfers of power. Alongside these republics sits the largest remaining overseas colony in the world – French Guiana, legally part of the European Union.

San Francisco Church, Lima, Peru: South America's cities showcase elaborate churches, monasteries and convents, built by the Spanish and Portuguese colonial settlers.

Transport

Tarmac highways, though usually confined to the more densely inhabited coastal regions, carry huge juggernaut lorries between cities and are now also starting to slice through once unsullied rainforests – conservationists agonize over the effect of this intrusion on delicate ecologies. Argentina has the world's largest private road system. Railways burgeoned in the 19th century, while a system of internal air corridors is now well established, though sometimes unreliable.

Transport
- major roads and motorways
- major railways
- international borders
- transport intersections
- international airports
- major ports

Matses Indians hunting on the Amazon: Over 300 different tribes live in the Amazon Basin, speaking at least 170 languages and dialects.

❶ Peru Highway 1 is part of the Pan-American Highway which runs the entire length of the Americas from Alaska to southern Chile.

❷ The great plains of the Gran Chaco are best crossed on horseback in the company of local gauchos.

❸ Many of the towns and villages deep within the Amazon Basin are best accessed by light aircraft or river ferries. To reach further up the smaller tributaries you still need to travel by canoe or dinghy.

SPANISH
ENGLISH
DUTCH
FRENCH
CARIBAN
ARAWAKAN
QUECHUA
AYMARA
GUARANI
PORTUGUESE
GERMAN
GERMAN
GERMAN
SPANISH
Language groups
American Indian
Germanic
Romance

Languages

South America is dominated by Spanish, spoken in all but four countries. The main exception is Brazil, the largest Portuguese-speaking nation in the world – the others are Guyana (English), Surinam (Dutch) and French Guiana (French). These colonial languages overlaid Amerindian indigenous languages, which survive most strongly in Bolivia where Aymara and Quechua are joint official languages with Spanish.

Inti Raimi, Peru: This Inca festival to the sun god is still held at the temple of Sacsayhuaman in Cusco each year on the winter solstice in June.

Standard of Living

Rich mineral resources and pastureland have generated considerable wealth, but the grand town houses and vast ranches of the elite contrast sharply with enormous problem slum areas such as the *favelas* of Brazil. The indigenous peoples remain at the bottom of the social hierarchy, often only living at subsistence level.

Standard of Living
(UN Human Development Index)
low
high

SCALE 1:24,000,000
(projection: Lambert Azimuthal Equal Area)

Map Key

POPULATION
- above 5 million
- 1 million to 5 million
- 500,000 to 1 million
- 100,000 to 500,000
- 50,000 to 100,000
- 10,000 to 50,000
- below 10,000
- Country capital
- State capital

BORDERS
- full international border
- disputed de facto border
- disputed territorial claim border
- state border

Angel Falls, Venezuela

Wine maker, Argentina

The Cathedral, Paracas, Peru

La Paz, Bolivia

Tierra del Fuego, Argentina/Chile

Tierradentro, Colombia: South American bus journeys are character-forming. Many passengers ride on the roof as the drivers negotiate winding, pot-holed mountain roads, avoiding the occasional mudslide.

Journeys

The South American continent has the least-developed road network in the world. Many parts of the jungle are either completely or seasonally inaccessible, except by plane or riverboat. The former are quick and reasonably priced, although somewhat unreliable; the latter, mainly used by local inhabitants, can take weeks because of the enormous distances. Time permitting, they are ideal for a closer view of the region. The Andes have a surprising number of railways, which provide a great way to get around – they are not quick, but the scenery is superb. Some of the most spectacular journeys, using switchback trains, are the Riobamba Express through Ecuador, the train to Machu Picchu and the classic route into the Cordillera Blanca, also in Peru. There are several excellent cruises available, the most famous being around the Galapagos Islands, while those from Chile and southern Argentina sail among fantastic fjords and glaciers.

Great South American Journeys

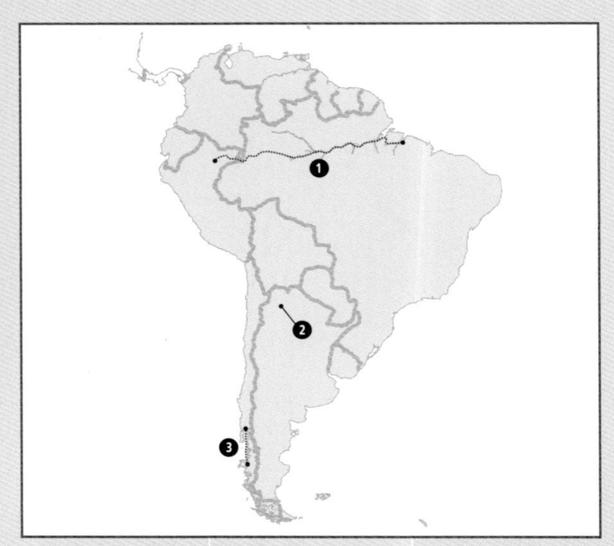

❶ Riverboat Cruise in the Amazon Basin
Belém, Brazil – Iquitos, Peru
3,800 km (2,400 miles)
The best way to enjoy the Amazon river, stopping off frequently, seeing incomparable wildlife and meeting local cultures.

❷ Train to the Clouds, Argentina
Salta – San Antonio de los Cobres
210 km (130 miles)
Day trip that climbs 3,900 m (13,000 ft) in the Andes, via switchbacks and tunnels and crosses the Polvorilla Canyon.

❸ Chile Cruise
Puerto Montt – San Rafael Glacier
1,600 km (1,000 miles)
This challenging cruise explores the remote islands off the unspoiled Chilean coast on its way down to the 300,000-year-old San Rafael Glacier.

Natural Sights

The western coast is partly made up of arid desert, forming a thin strip between the Pacific and the Andes, including dramatic features such as the Atacama Desert, the driest place on earth, and other stark desert landscapes. The Andes, the world's second-greatest mountain range, rise up to 6,959 m (22,831 ft) at Cerro Aconcagua in Argentina, with many other peaks approaching this height. At the southern end of the continent are fantastic glacial landscapes, and the famed Torres del Paine National Park with its huge towers of rock. Much of the rest of the continent is covered with Amazon rainforest, which, despite serious environmental concerns, is still being cleared at an astonishing rate – something like the area of Switzerland is lost every year. This region is sparsely populated and includes many tourist centres, as well as some sights which are extremely challenging to reach, like the breathtaking Angel Falls, the highest waterfall in the world. However, those making a special effort are always well rewarded.

What to See

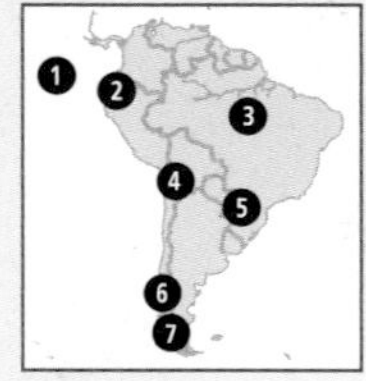

❶ Galapagos Islands
Cruise around these wildlife havens made famous by Darwin

❷ Avenue of the Volcanoes, Ecuador
Highlight of the jagged Andes mountains

❸ Amazon Basin
The world's largest rainforest has a huge variety of wildlife

❹ Salar de Uyuni, Bolivia
A vast shimmering lake of salt

❺ Iguaçu Falls
On the Argentina-Brazil border, these dramatic falls are one of the world's wonders

❻ Lake District, Chile
A land of towering peaks, lakes, rivers and volcanoes

❼ Glaciers National Park, Argentina
Vast icy landscapes, including the majestic Perito Moreno glacier

Marine iguanas, Galapagos Islands: These Ecuadorian islands have a unique ecosystem with endemic species, such as marine iguanas, lava lizards, rice rats and giant tortoises.

Atacama Desert, Chile

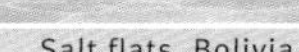

Salt flats, Bolivia

Amazon, Brazil

Rio de Janeiro, Brazil

Waterfall, Guyana

Machu Picchu, Peru: The mystery may never be solved as to whether this Inca city was a royal palace, a high temple of the "Virgins of the Sun", or just a small town. It was never found by the Spanish *conquistadores* and so is remarkably well preserved.

Cultural Sights

Inca sights dominate the popular image of this continent, especially those of the magnificent Inca capital, Cusco, whose empire extended into Bolivia and Ecuador. However, there are also significant remains of numerous other cultures, notably at Tiahuanaco in Bolivia, and the Sipan tombs of northern Peru. The lack of written record of these comparatively modern pre-colonial civilizations has tantalized and excited visitors, and in spite of many remains, surprisingly little is known about them. Striking throughout much of the continent is the wealth of excellent Spanish colonial architecture. Particularly well preserved are Quito, Sucre, Cartagena and Arequipa, which also boasts the extensive Santa Catalina Convent. Argentina is well known for its huge cattle ranches, called *estancias*, some of which can be visited and may even provide accommodation.

What to See

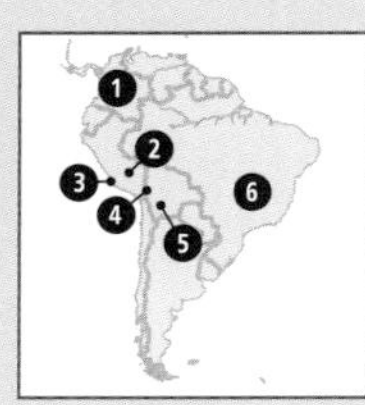

❶ Gold Museum, Bogotá, Colombia
Showcasing golden masterpieces of past civilizations

❷ Machu Picchu, Peru
The lost city of the great Inca empire

❸ Nazca Lines, Peru
Mysterious pictures drawn in the sand over 1,000 years ago and only visible from the air

❹ Uros Islands, Peru/Bolivia
Floating islands made of reeds on Lake Titicaca. Home of the Aymara Amerindians

❺ Silver Mines, Potosí, Bolivia
The once-great mines that fed the Spanish *conquistadores*' thirst for the precious metal

❻ Brasília, Brazil
A startling collection of buildings – Brasília embodies the principles of Modern architecture

Activities

Amazonian forest lodges and treetop walkways provide visitors with first-hand experience of the jungle's diversity of wildlife while limiting their impact on the environment. The astonishing variety of the Galapagos Islands is worth the trip, although some species that live there can also be seen on the mainland Pacific coast. There are excellent opportunities for mountaineering and hiking, particularly in the Andes, where Andean condors (amongst the world's largest flying birds) soar through the deep, terraced Colca Canyon. Mendoza in Argentina has the continent's top ski resort, and has views of its highest mountain, Cerro Aconcagua. Football dominates the sporting scene and national teams arouse passionate support – repaid in the World Cup, which has been won by a South American nation more often than not.

What to Do

❶ Canopy Walkway, Iquitos, Peru
View the jungle wildlife from the treetops

❷ Inca Trail, Peru
Hike 48 km (30 miles) along the Inca route to Machu Picchu

❸ Amazon, Brazil
Take a fascinating night boat ride searching for caymans with glinting red eyes

❹ Witchcraft Market, La Paz, Bolivia
Search for traditional health remedies as concocted by the Callawaya culture

❺ Carnival, Rio de Janeiro, Brazil
Live the carnival atmosphere amid the colourful samba-dancing throng

❻ Tango in Buenos Aires, Argentina
Watch the tango the way it should be and try it yourself

Sugarloaf Mountain at night, Rio de Janeiro, Brazil: Rio nightlife is festive all year round, with something for everyone – from tasty restaurant meals, to lively bars, samba halls and dance clubs.

Northern South America

Colombia, Guyana, Surinam, Venezuela, *French Guiana* (to France)

SCALE 1:7,250,000
(projection: Lambert Azimuthal Equal Area)
Km 0 25 50 100 150 200
Miles 0 25 50 100 150 200

Pristine natural environments – Andean mountains, waterfalls, tropical jungles, grasslands, seas, coasts – teem with exotic species of plant, animal and marine life. Turbulent histories have produced complex fusions of pre-colonial, Spanish and African cultures. Venezuela and Colombia, the latter unsafe in parts for visitors, can be fascinating and extremely rewarding experiences. In Guyana, the British colonial legacy is interwoven with rich Afro-Caribbean and south Asian cultures. Surinam, a former Dutch colony, also draws on African, Amerindian and Asian backgrounds for its demographic mix.

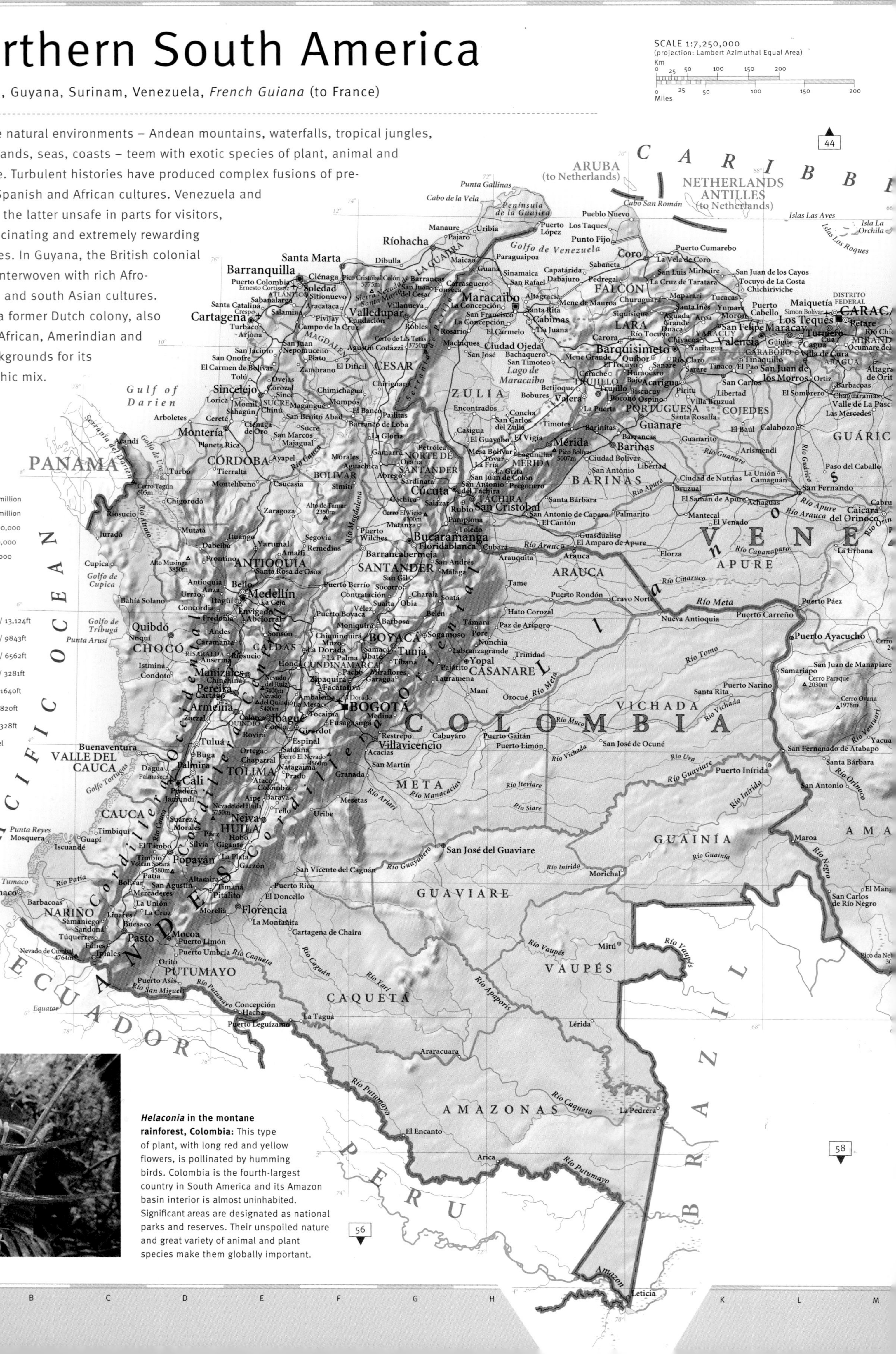

Map Key

POPULATION
- 1 million to 5 million
- 500,000 to 1 million
- 100,000 to 500,000
- 50,000 to 100,000
- 10,000 to 50,000
- below 10,000

ELEVATION
- 4000m / 13,124ft
- 3000m / 9843ft
- 2000m / 6562ft
- 1000m / 3281ft
- 500m / 1640ft
- 250m / 820ft
- 100m / 328ft
- sea level

***Helaconia* in the montane rainforest, Colombia:** This type of plant, with long red and yellow flowers, is pollinated by humming birds. Colombia is the fourth-largest country in South America and its Amazon basin interior is almost uninhabited. Significant areas are designated as national parks and reserves. Their unspoiled nature and great variety of animal and plant species make them globally important.

Cayenne, French Guiana: One of South America's most appealing cities, ethnically diverse Cayenne combines tropical ambience with French colonial style.

Activities

Observe leatherback turtles near **Mana** in French Guiana, April–September	Spot whales and dolphins off **Buenaventura**, Colombia
Ride or hike across the tree-scattered plains of **Rupununi Savannah**, Guyana	Ride the world's longest cable car from **Mérida** high into Venezuela's Andes
Tour of **Brownberg Nature Park**, Surinam overlooking an enormous reservoir	Study the artefacts and crafts of local cultures in **Puerto Ayacucho**, Venezuela
Snorkel and dive at the great coral reefs of the **Islas del Rosario**, off Cartagena, Colombia	Visit a cave-dwelling nocturnal bird colony at **Cueva del Guácharo** near Cumaná, Venezuela

Angel Falls (Salto Ángel), Venezuela: Water plummets from so high, 979 m (3,212 ft) that the torrent can evaporate into mist during the dry season. Situated above remote jungle in Canaima National Park, the falls were chanced on in 1935 by US pilot Jimmy Angel, whose name they bear.

64

58

58

What to See

❶ Cartagena
Cartagena's churches, plazas and atmospheric grand mansions are a Spanish colonial legacy. In addition it offers a lively nightlife and numerous other nearby attractions

❷ Ciudad Perdida
(near Santa Marta) Ancient ruined city of the Tayrona people – reached by a tough five-day hike through a beautiful national park

❸ Bogotá
Skyscrapers, colonial churches, top museums and expensive shops coincide with shocking poverty but Colombia's capital beats to a vibrant rhythm

❹ Gold Museum
(in Bogotá) One of Latin America's most important museums contains pre-Hispanic treasures and artefacts from Colombia's indigenous cultures

❺ Islas los Roques
This collection of Venezuelan reef islands, tidal islets and reefs has glistening, white sands broken up by stretches of green mangrove swamps

❻ Angel Falls (Salto Ángel)
The highest falls in the world at 979 m (3,212 ft) pour down from a plateau with its own eco-system to dense jungle below. Making the trek up on foot is an unforgettable experience

❼ La Gran Sabana
A vast region of high savannah features abruptly rising mesas, riverbeds strewn with jasper and a plethora of wildlife and plants, including rare orchids

❽ Kaieteur Falls
At their most dramatic during the wet season (January to August), Guyana's great falls, set in rainforest, are 226 m (741 ft) high

❾ Georgetown
Set amid flowering trees, Guyana's capital retains its British colonial charm and claims the world's largest wooden Gothic cathedral

❿ Voltzberg Nature Reserve
(on Coppename River) Climb Voltzberg peak at sunrise for remarkable views through rising mists of the Surinam's reawakening rainforest

⓫ Paramaribo
A capital of colourful markets, with a bustling waterfront, Catholic cathedral, Hindu temples, synagogues, mosques and colonial Dutch buildings

⓬ Centre Spatial Guyanais (near Kourou)
A high-tech enclave, France's premier space centre has free guided tours. Invitations are needed to spectate at one of the official *Ariane* rocket launches

⓭ Îles du Salut
Three small islands, including Île du Diable (Devil's Island), France's notorious 19th-20th-century penal colony

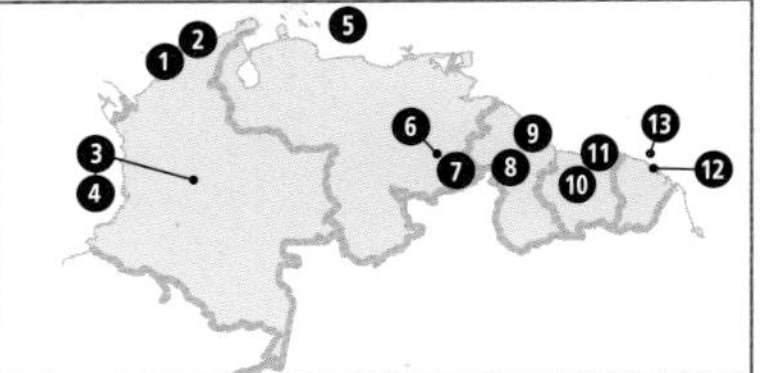

Western South America

Bolivia, Ecuador, Peru

The dramatic Inca citadel of Machu Picchu has done more than anything to put western South America on the global tourist map. The region, which stretches from the Equator down to the Argentine border, can also offer dramatic Andean scenery, fine Spanish colonial buildings, and the remains of cultures long predating the Incas, whose own extensive empire crumbled almost without resistance in face of the arrival of the Spanish *conquistadores* in 1532. The high Andes, a volcanic area with many peaks over 6,100 m (20,000 ft) high, descends abruptly to the east into the Amazon basin, inaccessible by land transport. Most of the population is concentrated in the arid coastal strip west of the Andes, while some 960 km (600 miles) off the Pacific coast lie the Galapagos Islands, a naturalist's paradise made famous by Charles Darwin. Ecuador, Bolivia, and Peru share much common history, including their struggle for independence from Spain in the early 19th century.

Turbulent through much of the 20th century, their recent relative stability, together with many top-class attractions, has helped the region establish itself as an important destination.

What to See

1 Galapagos Islands
Famous for the wildlife that inspired Darwin's theory of evolution, and now a world-renowned conservation area, most easily reached by air from Quito

2 Quito
A colonial-style city nestled between mountain peaks. A mix of old and new, known for its churches, monasteries, and convents

3 Cotopaxi
Snow-capped, perfectly symmetrical, 5,897 m (19,347 ft) volcano that until 1904 was erupting every 20 years. In the Avenue of Volcanoes, it is a popular climb in the *paramo* (high-altitude grassland)

4 Laguna Quilotoa
(near Latacunga)
Emerald green lake in a steep-walled caldera, which was formed by a now-extinct volcano

5 Cuenca
Former Inca town that was almost completely destroyed and rebuilt by the Spanish, with gleaming white churches, monasteries and cobbled streets

6 Tucume
(near Lambayeque)
Complex of 26 adobe pyramids from 1000 CE, once a religious centre

7 Royal Sipan Tombs
(near Chiclayo) The Americas' answer to Tutankhamun, the Lord of Sipan was buried with all his finery around 300 BCE, and only uncovered in 1987 when grave robbers started to plunder the site

8 Manu Biosphere Reserve
(in Madre de Dios)
Largely unspoiled part of the Amazon jungle, offering the chance to see endangered giant river otter, caiman, capybara, and the occasional jaguar

9 Machu Picchu
Dramatic Inca citadel rediscovered in 1911 by Hiram Bingham, reached by hiking the Inca trail or taking a scenic train ride

10 Cusco
Once capital of the Inca empire, with Spanish colonial architecture built over extensive Inca palaces and temples. In nearby Sacred Valley are the Pisac citadel and Ollantaytambo temple

11 Nazca
Mysterious drawings in the desert – such as the hummingbird, 171 m (560 ft) long – perhaps 1,500 years old and only visible from the air

12 Rio Colca Canyon
Arguably the world's deepest canyon, terraced extensively by the Incas, it is the best place to see the world's largest flying bird, the Andean condor

13 Lake Titicaca
The world's highest navigable lake, astride the Peru-Bolivia border. From the Peruvian town of Puno, visit the Uros Islands – floating reed islands, home to Aymara Indians

14 Tiahuanaco
(near La Paz)
Centre of the region's most significant pre-Inca civilization, which flourished widely for two millennia from 1000 BCE

15 La Paz
The highest capital in the world, at 3,500 m (10,700 ft), situated in a canyon and renowned for its festivals

16 Cal Orko Dinosaur Footprints
(near Sucre) A sheer rock face inlaid with 5,000 footprints from 150 types of dinosaur (up to a metre across, in the case of Apatosaurus)

17 Potosí
Silver mining at nearby Cerro Rico caused a 17th-century boom in this city, renowned for its Spanish architecture

18 Salar de Uyuni
The world's largest salt lake is a flat expanse of white, which becomes a huge mirror of the mountains during the rainy season (December–April)

Map Key

POPULATION
- above 5 million
- 1 million to 5 million
- 500,000 to 1 million
- 100,000 to 500,000
- 50,000 to 100,000
- 10,000 to 50,000
- below 10,000

ELEVATION
- 6000m / 19,686ft
- 4000m / 13,124ft
- 3000m / 9843ft
- 2000m / 6562ft
- 1000m / 3281ft
- 500m / 1640ft
- 250m / 820ft
- 100m / 328ft
- sea level

ECUADOREAN ADMINISTRATIVE REGIONS
1 CARCHI
2 TUNGURAHUA
3 BOLÍVAR
4 CHIMBORAZO
5 ZAMORA CHINCHIPE

192
54
58

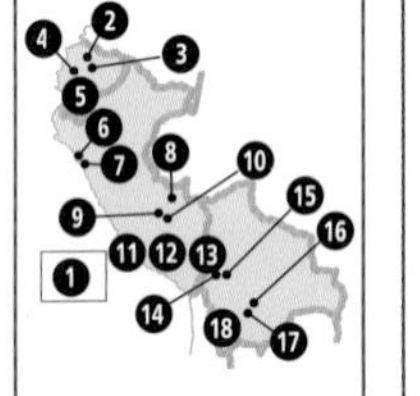

Salar de Coipasa: Bolivia's second-largest salt flat is known as the "Mirror of Heaven". It is roamed by llamas and alpacas, two of the four types of camelid found in South America. Llamas are used as beasts of burden, but cannot carry the weight of a human being.

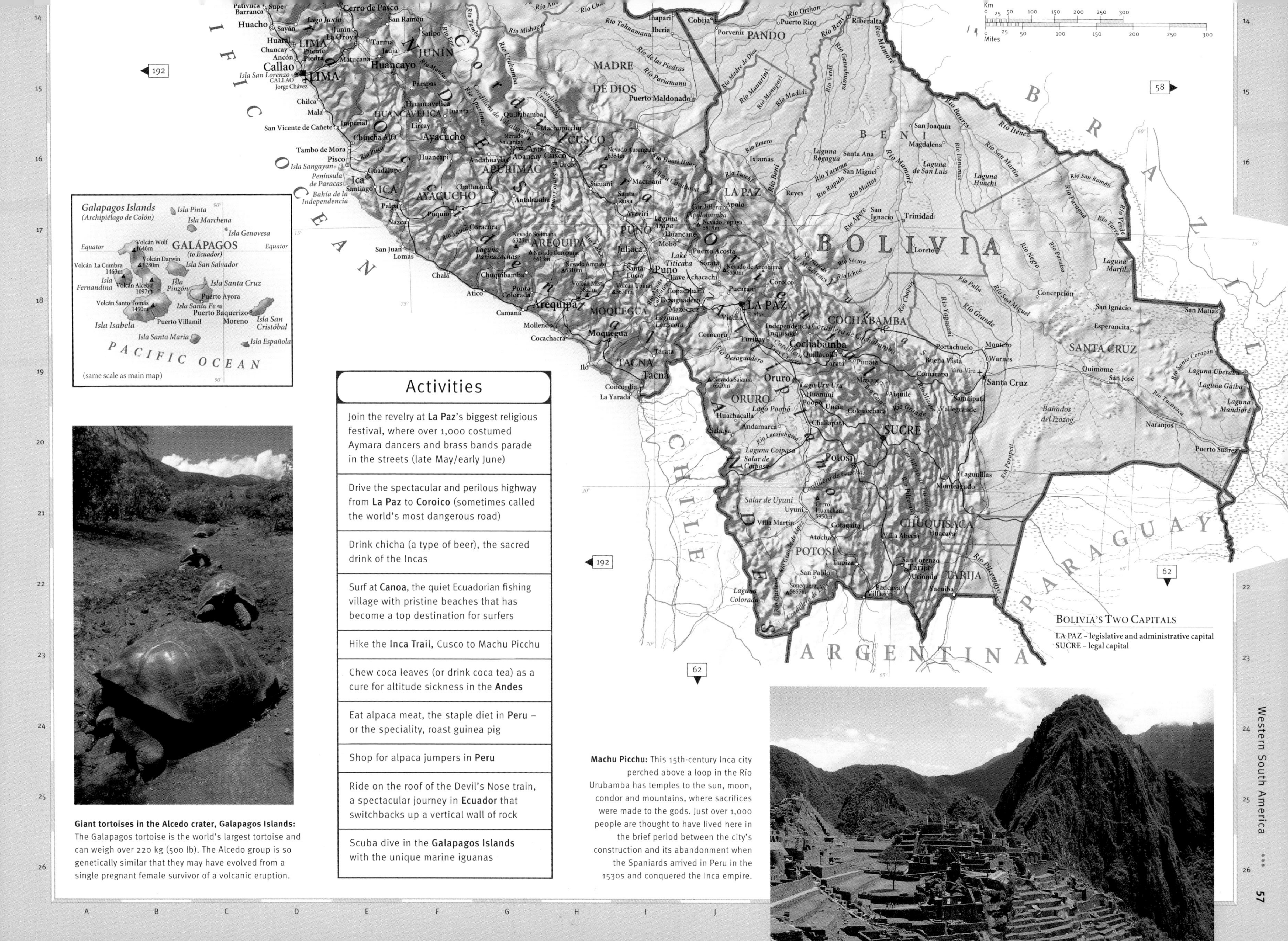

BOLIVIA
PERU
BRAZIL
PARAGUAY
ARGENTINA
CHILE
PACIFIC OCEAN
Cordillera Occidental
Altiplano
ANDES
PANDO
BENI
LA PAZ
COCHABAMBA
SANTA CRUZ
ORURO
POTOSÍ
CHUQUISACA
TARIJA
MADRE DE DIOS
CUSCO
PUNO
AREQUIPA
MOQUEGUA
TACNA
APURÍMAC
AYACUCHO
HUANCAVELICA
JUNÍN
LIMA
ICA
LA PAZ
SUCRE
Lima
Callao
Cusco
Arequipa
Puno
Oruro
Cochabamba
Potosí
Santa Cruz
Trinidad
Tarija
Lake Titicaca
Salar de Uyuni
Machupicchu
Galapagos Islands
(Archipiélago de Colón)
GALÁPAGOS
(to Ecuador)
Isla Pinta
Isla Marchena
Isla Genovesa
Isla San Salvador
Isla Santa Cruz
Isla Isabela
Isla Fernandina
Isla San Cristóbal
Isla Española
Isla Santa María
Isla Santa Fe
Puerto Ayora
Puerto Baquerizo Moreno
Puerto Villamil
Equator
PACIFIC OCEAN
(same scale as main map)
Km
Miles

192
58
62
192
62

Bolivia's Two Capitals

LA PAZ – legislative and administrative capital
SUCRE – legal capital

Activities

- Join the revelry at **La Paz**'s biggest religious festival, where over 1,000 costumed Aymara dancers and brass bands parade in the streets (late May/early June)
- Drive the spectacular and perilous highway from **La Paz** to **Coroico** (sometimes called the world's most dangerous road)
- Drink chicha (a type of beer), the sacred drink of the Incas
- Surf at **Canoa**, the quiet Ecuadorian fishing village with pristine beaches that has become a top destination for surfers
- Hike the **Inca Trail**, Cusco to Machu Picchu
- Chew coca leaves (or drink coca tea) as a cure for altitude sickness in the **Andes**
- Eat alpaca meat, the staple diet in **Peru** – or the speciality, roast guinea pig
- Shop for alpaca jumpers in **Peru**
- Ride on the roof of the Devil's Nose train, a spectacular journey in **Ecuador** that switchbacks up a vertical wall of rock
- Scuba dive in the **Galapagos Islands** with the unique marine iguanas

Giant tortoises in the Alcedo crater, Galapagos Islands: The Galapagos tortoise is the world's largest tortoise and can weigh over 220 kg (500 lb). The Alcedo group is so genetically similar that they may have evolved from a single pregnant female survivor of a volcanic eruption.

Machu Picchu: This 15th-century Inca city perched above a loop in the Río Urubamba has temples to the sun, moon, condor and mountains, where sacrifices were made to the gods. Just over 1,000 people are thought to have lived here in the brief period between the city's construction and its abandonment when the Spaniards arrived in Peru in the 1530s and conquered the Inca empire.

Brazil

The biggest country in South America by far, the continent's only Portuguese-speaking nation can be seen at its most flamboyant in its most famous cities, names synonymous with Latin temperament and tropical fun – Rio de Janeiro, São Paulo, Brasília, Salvador. By contrast the Amazon rainforest, covering vast areas of the interior, displays life at an altogether more peaceful tempo. Preservation of this important natural treasure from the advance of logging and ranching is vital for its role as the world's prime converter of carbon dioxide and its enormous, and often unique, collection of biological species. The people living deep within the Amazon Basin, isolated but not entirely cut off from the rest of the world, have lived in sympathy with their environment for thousands of years. However, this way of life is increasingly threatened by the demands of, and contacts with, the outside world.

Although many grasp the opportunity to explore the Amazon jungle, visitors to so large a country would do better to focus on a specific place. Choices include the magnificent Iguaçu Falls, unique Pantanal wetlands, massive sand dunes of Natal, colonial history of Olinda, African-Brazilian culture of Salvador, architectural majesty of Brasília and the big city splendour of Rio and São Paulo. However, nowhere are Brazil's notoriously enormous wealth disparities more evident than in Rio where the grandeur of beachside villas and high-rise city life is fringed by the appalling conditions of the slum *favelas*.

A walkway in the treetop Ariau Amazon Towers Hotel, near Manaus: The Ariau claims to be the only treetop hotel in the Amazon, giving guests an arboreal view of the world's most famous jungle. Its a fantastic base for exploring the river and its rainforest.

What to See

1 Manaus
Fascinating city in the jungle and a favoured central base for expeditions into the Amazon. Also, home to the famous opera house

2 Porto Velho
From this town at the very edge of "tamed" Brazil you can experience a modern frontier lifestyle

3 Natal
A popular destination for sun-seekers and a base for dune buggying on nearby beaches

4 Olinda
This coastal city shows off the best of the country's colonial past with several good examples of 16th- and 17th century Portuguese architecture

5 Salvador
The "African" capital of Bahia state is a great place to catch a display of *capoeira* – a lively mix of martial arts, acrobatics and dance

6 Lençóis
Escape from the heat of the coast to this little town in Chapada Diamintina highlands. Explore the waterfalls, views and caves

7 Ilha do Bananal
The world's largest river island, so named because of the many banana trees found here. Part of Araguaia National Park

8 Brasília
Brazil's purpose-built capital, dominated by Oscar Niemeyer's striking architecture

9 Pantanal
Set off from Corumbá to explore this wetland, arguably one of the world's most important environmental sites

10 Emas National Park
(near Mineiros) A great place to glimpse jaguars and tapirs

11 Abrolhos
(near Caravelas) Find tranquillity amid reefs, whales and seabirds at Brazil's premier marine national park

12 Búzios
(near Rio de Janeiro) The beach paradise made famous by Bridget Bardot in the 1960s

13 Rio de Janeiro
With Copacabana Beach and the statue of Christ, the home of carnival is a stimulating, scenic and hedonistic mix

14 São Paulo
Brazil's cosmopolitan economic centre where Avenida Paulista is the place to window shop

15 Vale do Ribeiro
(near São Paulo)Caves as big as cathedrals – not to be missed

16 Florianópolis
The place to go for a typical "Brazilian" holiday experience and great for surfing

17 Caxias do Sul
This is the heart of the Brazilian wine country

A margay in the eastern Amazon forest: There are thought to be many millions of animal and plant species as yet undiscovered in the depths of the Amazon Basin.

BRAZIL
PERU
BOLIVIA
PARAGUAY
ARGENTINA
URUGUAY
ATLANTIC OCEAN
ACRE
RONDÔNIA
MATO GROSSO
MATO GROSSO DO SUL
TOCANTINS
PIAUÍ
BAHIA
GOIÁS
DISTRITO FEDERAL
MINAS GERAIS
ESPÍRITO SANTO
RIO DE JANEIRO
SÃO PAULO
PARANÁ
SANTA CATARINA
RIO GRANDE DO SUL
SERGIPE
ALAGOAS
PERNAMBUCO
PARAÍBA
RIO GRANDE DO NORTE
BRASÍLIA
Planalto Central (Brazilian Highlands)
Planalto de Mato Grosso
Pantanal
Tropic of Capricorn
56
62
64
Map Key
POPULATION
above 5 million
1 million to 5 million
500,000 to 1 million
100,000 to 500,000
50,000 to 100,000
10,000 to 50,000
below 10,000
ELEVATION
3000m / 9843ft
2000m / 6562ft
1000m / 3281ft
500m / 1640ft
250m / 820ft
100m / 328ft
sea level
SCALE 1:14,250,000
(projection: Lambert Azimuthal Equal Area)

Christ the Redeemer, Rio de Janeiro: Completed in 1931, the statue (Cristo Redentor, or just Cristo, in Portuguese) gazing down from Corcovado Hill has come to symbolize Rio and to a certain degree Brazil. It conveys the welcoming attitude of the Brazilian people to all visitors.

Activities

Watch whales at **Praia da Rosa**, Santa Catarina state, southern Brazil	Admire the beautiful game (football) and the beautiful bodies on **Rio's** Ipanema and Copacabana beaches
Scramble over mountainous sand dunes in a dune buggy from **Natal**	Tipple at the Grape Festival in **Caxias do Sul**, north of Porto Alegre
Dance to the samba beat in samba-capital **Salvador**, Bahia	Join the ultimate party at **Rio's** carnival
Catch the scenic railway across the **Serra do Mar** from Paranaguá inland to the Paraná state capital of Curitiba	Attend the opera in the midst of the Amazon jungle, at the astonishing opera house in **Manaus**

Eastern South America

Uruguay, Northeast Argentina, Southeast Brazil

At the centre of this region's appeal is the blend of lively urban atmosphere in some of South America's most exciting cities – Rio de Janeiro, São Paulo, and Buenos Aires – juxtaposed against the powerful draw of the wide open spaces. The *gaucho*, the self-reliant cowboy living by his own austere code of honour, has almost mythical status here.

Among the many superlative sights are the spectacular waterfall on the Iguaçu river and one of the world's largest man-made structures – the Itaipú Dam. The Uruguay and Paraná rivers join together north of Buenos Aires to emerge between Argentina and Uruguay at the head of the great estuary of the River Plate (Río de la Plata).

Uruguay, a less well-known destination, encapsulates the region in a single country – a metropolitan centre in Montevideo and acres of *gaucho* territory fringed by glorious beaches along the Atlantic coast.

Northeastern Argentina encompasses Mesopotamia, with centuries of colonial history and majestic natural parks, and west of the Paraná river, the grasslands of the Pampas. The European-style Buenos Aires is its major city highlight.

Iguaçu Falls (Cataratas del Iguazú): This awe-inspiring system of cataracts on the border of Brazil and Argentina, is one of the world's largest falls by volume. Wooden walkways extend up to the edge of the action so that visitors can experience their full power.

Activities

- Observe the basking sea lions on **Isla dos Lobos**, Uruguay's Atlantic marine reserve
- Cruise the **Paraná** river from the charming waterfront at Rosario, Argentina or keep time to the beat of the *chamamé* (accordion music) at Corrientes
- Enjoy the sunshine at Uruguay's top beach resort, **Punta del Este**, east of Montevideo
- Taste the juicy, apricot-flavoured fruit of the *butía* palm (jelly palm), a delicacy in **Aguas Dulces**, near Cabo Polonio, Uruguay
- Get into the party spirit with a gourd of *mate* in **Buenos Aires**, then twirl to the tango and lose yourself in the intoxicating beat
- Gaze up at the balcony of the **Casa Rosada** (presidential palace, in Plaza de Mayo, Buenos Aires), and imagine yourself in an ecstatic crowd acclaiming the victorious Juan and Eva Perón in 1946

Carnival time, Rio de Janeiro: The party in Rio during the week leading up to Lent surpasses all others as the most famous and flamboyant carnival in the world. The samba parade, in particular, brings the city to a peak of exuberance with outlandish costumes and throbbing music filling the streets.

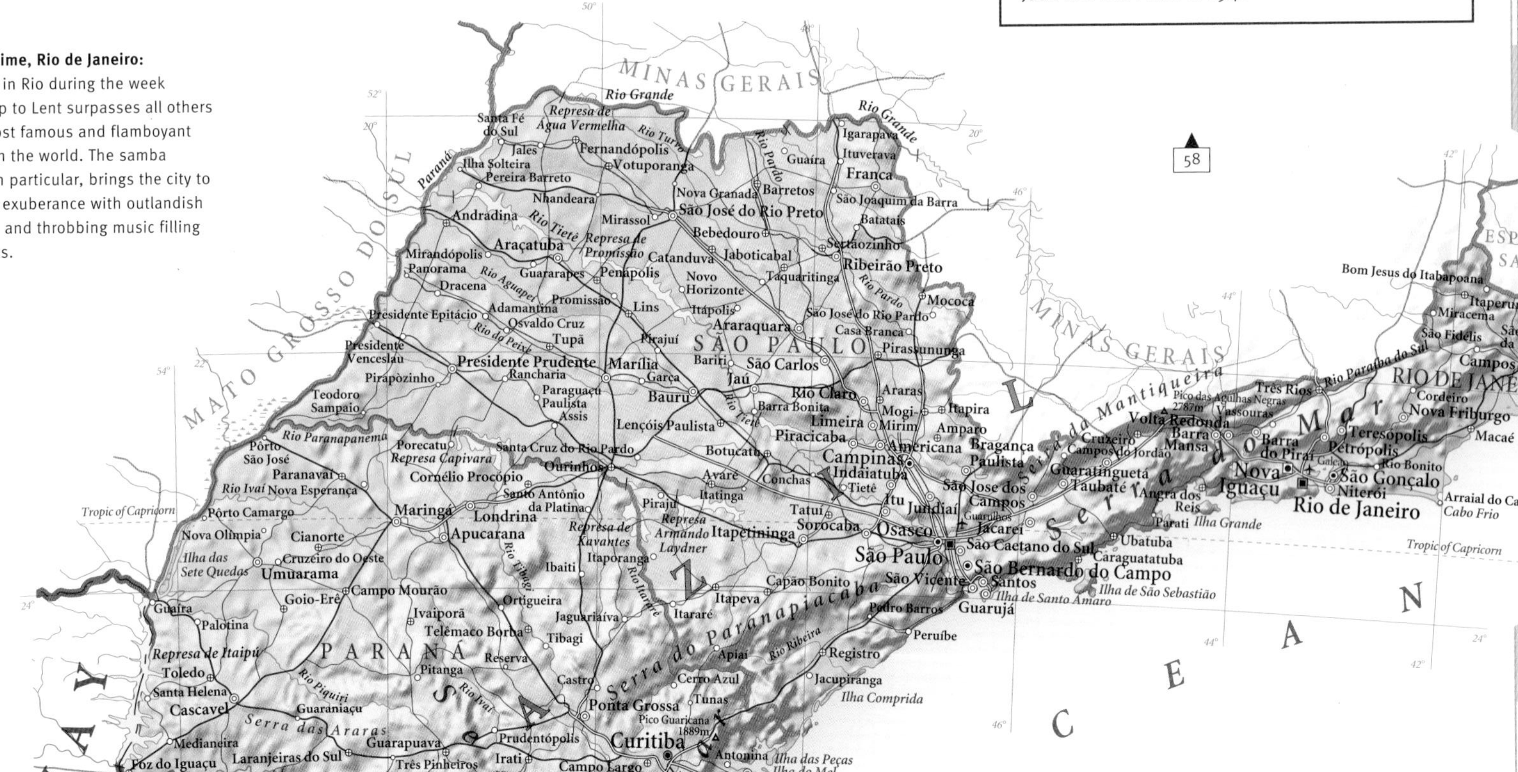
MINAS GERAIS
MATO GROSSO DO SUL
SÃO PAULO
PARANÁ
RIO DE JANEIRO
ESPÍRITO SANTO
PARAGUAY
OCEAN
São Paulo
Rio de Janeiro
Curitiba
Campinas
Santos
Niterói
São Gonçalo
Nova Iguaçu
Petrópolis
Teresópolis
Nova Friburgo
Volta Redonda
São José dos Campos
Taubaté
Sorocaba
Jundiaí
Osasco
São Bernardo do Campo
Guarujá
Ribeirão Preto
São José do Rio Preto
Araçatuba
Presidente Prudente
Marília
Bauru
Londrina
Maringá
Apucarana
Ponta Grossa
Cascavel
Foz do Iguaçu
Guaíra
Paranaguá
Joinville
Blumenau
Ilha Grande
Ilha de São Sebastião
Tropic of Capricorn
Serra da Mantiqueira
Serra do Mar
Rio Paranapanema
Rio Tietê
Rio Grande
58
62
64

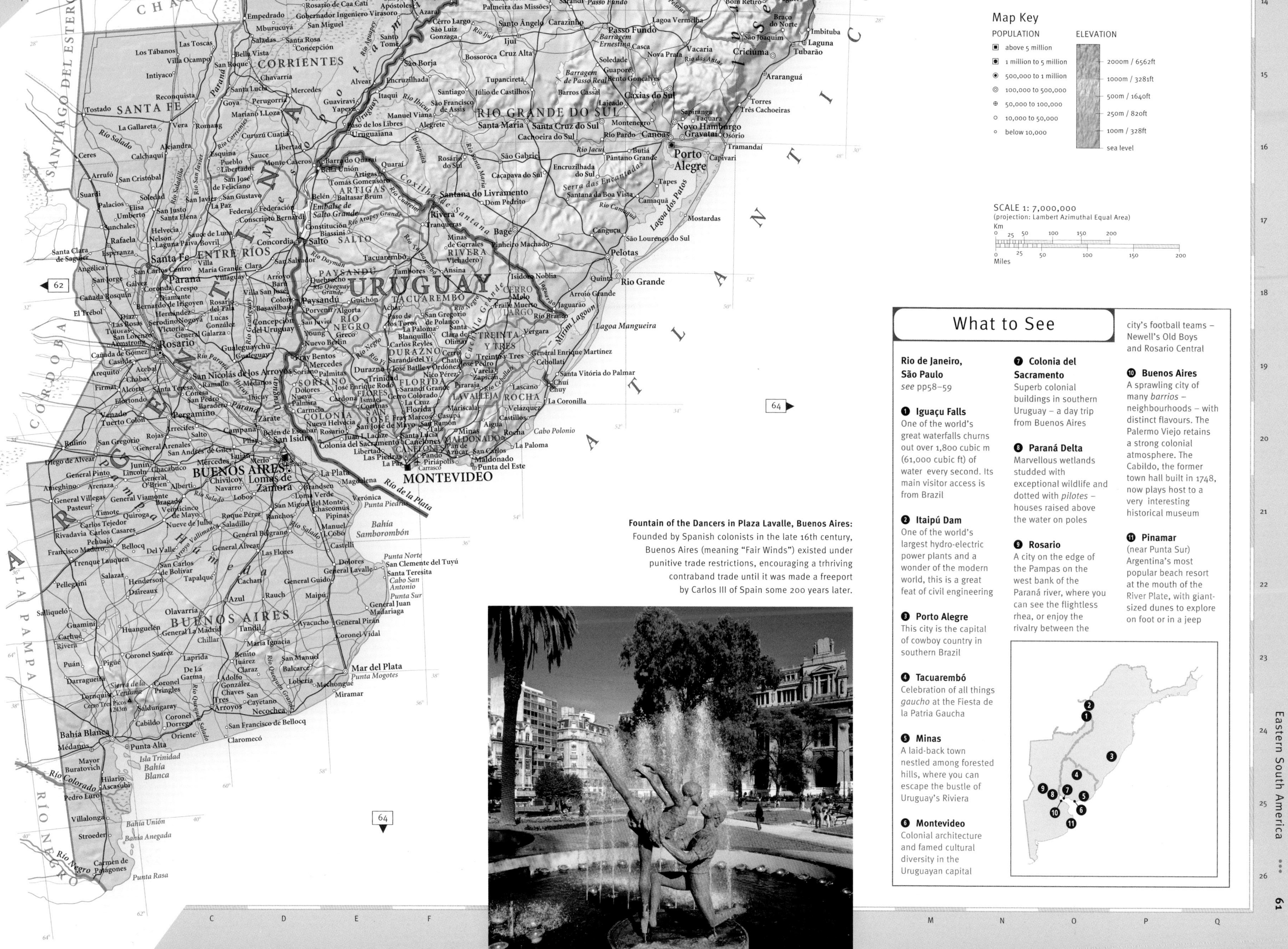
Map Key
POPULATION
above 5 million
1 million to 5 million
500,000 to 1 million
100,000 to 500,000
50,000 to 100,000
10,000 to 50,000
below 10,000
ELEVATION
2000m / 6562ft
1000m / 3281ft
500m / 1640ft
250m / 820ft
100m / 328ft
sea level
SCALE 1: 7,000,000
(projection: Lambert Azimuthal Equal Area)
Km
0 25 50 100 150 200
0 25 50 100 150 200
Miles
URUGUAY
BUENOS AIRES
MONTEVIDEO
RIO GRANDE DO SUL
SANTA FE
CORRIENTES
ENTRE RÍOS
Porto Alegre
Florianópolis
Mar del Plata
Río de la Plata
Bahía Blanca
62
64
64

What to See

Rio de Janeiro, São Paulo
see pp58–59

❶ Iguaçu Falls
One of the world's great waterfalls churns out over 1,800 cubic m (61,000 cubic ft) of water every second. Its main visitor access is from Brazil

❷ Itaipú Dam
One of the world's largest hydro-electric power plants and a wonder of the modern world, this is a great feat of civil engineering

❸ Porto Alegre
This city is the capital of cowboy country in southern Brazil

❹ Tacuarembó
Celebration of all things *gaucho* at the Fiesta de la Patria Gaucha

❺ Minas
A laid-back town nestled among forested hills, where you can escape the bustle of Uruguay's Riviera

❻ Montevideo
Colonial architecture and famed cultural diversity in the Uruguayan capital

❼ Colonia del Sacramento
Superb colonial buildings in southern Uruguay – a day trip from Buenos Aires

❽ Paraná Delta
Marvellous wetlands studded with exceptional wildlife and dotted with *pilotes* – houses raised above the water on poles

❾ Rosario
A city on the edge of the Pampas on the west bank of the Paraná river, where you can see the flightless rhea, or enjoy the rivalry between the city's football teams – Newell's Old Boys and Rosario Central

❿ Buenos Aires
A sprawling city of many *barrios* – neighbourhoods – with distinct flavours. The Palermo Viejo retains a strong colonial atmosphere. The Cabildo, the former town hall built in 1748, now plays host to a very interesting historical museum

⓫ Pinamar
(near Punta Sur)
Argentina's most popular beach resort at the mouth of the River Plate, with giant-sized dunes to explore on foot or in a jeep

Fountain of the Dancers in Plaza Lavalle, Buenos Aires: Founded by Spanish colonists in the late 16th century, Buenos Aires (meaning "Fair Winds") existed under punitive trade restrictions, encouraging a trhriving contraband trade until it was made a freeport by Carlos III of Spain some 200 years later.

Southern South America

Argentina, Chile, Paraguay

On the southern half of South America, the states of Paraguay, Chile and Argentina differ markedly from the tropical nations of the north. Divided by the southern Andes, all three have a noticeably "European" atmosphere, with Spanish and Italian heritage most apparent, though strongly influenced by Amerindian cultures. These societies are predominantly urban, with the population concentrated in the three capitals – Buenos Aires, Santiago and Asunción. Each city sports plenty of colonial architecture and great nightlife. Those seeking outdoor adventure will find plenty of opportunity in the region with natural features on a grand scale and many memorable activities. The mighty Andean spine offers skiing and mountaineering while for strange beauty explore northern Chile's arid Atacama Desert (*Desierto de Atacama*) and the open expanses of the Gran Chaco plain. Argentina boasts the vast, flat Pampas, home to rugged ranch life and the windswept reaches of Patagonia, and further south, Tierra del Fuego is a wild island of forests and glaciers.

Tatio Geysers in the Atacama Desert (*Desierto de Atacama*): This strip of desert is one of the most arid places in the world. Whole years, sometimes decades, can go by without a drop of rain; it is 50 times drier than the USA's Death Valley. Consequently, only the hardiest lifeforms, such as bacteria, survive here.

56
58
192
60
192

Map Key

POPULATION

- 1 million to 5 million
- 500,000 to 1 million
- 100,000 to 500,000
- 50,000 to 100,000
- 10,000 to 50,000
- below 10,000

ELEVATION

- 6000m / 19,686ft
- 4000m / 13,124ft
- 3000m / 9843ft
- 2000m / 6562ft
- 1000m / 3281ft
- 500m / 1640ft
- 250m / 820ft
- 100m / 328ft
- sea level

What to See

1 Calama
City in the Atacama Desert, amid the enormous copper mines that still power Chile's economy. Base for desert and Tatio geysers visits

2 Le Paige Museum
(in San Pedro de Atacama) Exhibits of ancient human remains and tools – preserved in harsh, desert conditions

3 Salta
A beautiful colonial city amongst soaring Andean landscapes

4 Parque Nacional Rio Pilcomayo
(N Argentina) Important wetlands – offering wildlife tours and camping

5 Gran Chaco
An enormous flat plain that covers most of Paraguay – home to ranchers and native Amerindians

6 Asunción
Spanish colonial "Mother of Cities" – one of the oldest in South America and capital of Paraguay

7 Caacupé
A religious centre for Catholic Paraguayans and a destination for local pilgrims

8 Manzana Jesuitica (in Córdoba)
17th-century church, college and university found in second city of Argentina

9 Pampas
Sweeping grasslands, stetching across central Argentina with unique animal species

10 Santiago
Chile's European-influenced capital, close to skiing and Maipo vineyards

11 Valparaíso
A delightful and lively port city just to west of Santiago

12 Lake District
Snow-topped volcanic peaks are mirrored in clear-watered lakes in this characteristically Chilean landscape

13 Isla de Chiloé
Known for superb wood carving and its blend of indigenous and colonial traditions

14 Tierra del Fuego
Wilderness island at southern tip of South America with lakes, forests and glaciers

15 Ushuaia
The southernmost city in the world and home to the "end of the world" train

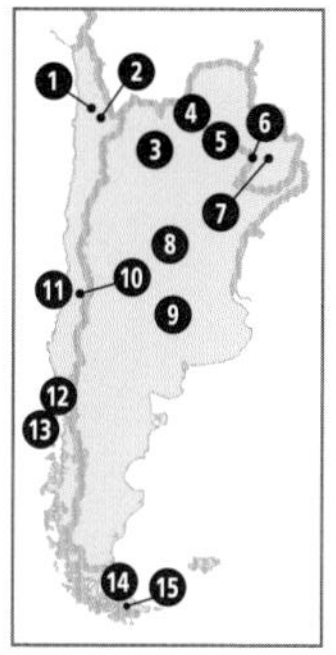

192

Torres del Paine National Park, Puerto Natales: Sheer granite peaks soar above the windswept grasslands and blue-green lakes of southern Chile. Flightless rheas (*ñandu*) and llama-like *guanaco* live here, plus aptly named torrent ducks swim against the fast flowing rivers.

64

Southern right whale off Península Valdés, Argentina: Every year, between May and December, around 500 southern right whales come to raise their calves off the coast of Argentina, where they have become a major tourist attraction.

194

SCALE 1:9,750,000
(projection: Lambert Azimuthal Equal Area)

Activities

Help out with farm chores as a ranch hand on an *estancia* in **El Calafate**, Patagonia

Explore the high **Andes** on horseback from Pucón, south of Santiago

Paddle in the healing waters of **Lago Ypacaraí**, Asunción

Taste some of the world's most delicious beef at a gaucho barbecue on Argentina's **Pampas**

The Atlantic Ocean

The Atlantic Ocean contains far-flung islands of varying climates. Spain's subtropical Canary Islands, just off Africa, have mass tourist appeal for European visitors seeking guaranteed sun, beaches and lively nightlife, amid beautiful scenery. There are also secluded spots on the islands, as there are on Portugal's Azores and Madeira. To the west, the UK's Bermuda has a similar appeal for Americans and claims one of the highest densities of golf courses in the world. The more distant, colder islands in the Atlantic's southern reaches have a mix of exhilarating scenery and wildlife.

Madeira: These triangular, thatched houses are typical of Santana on the north coast of Madeira, where traditional agriculture and crafts are still an important way of life.

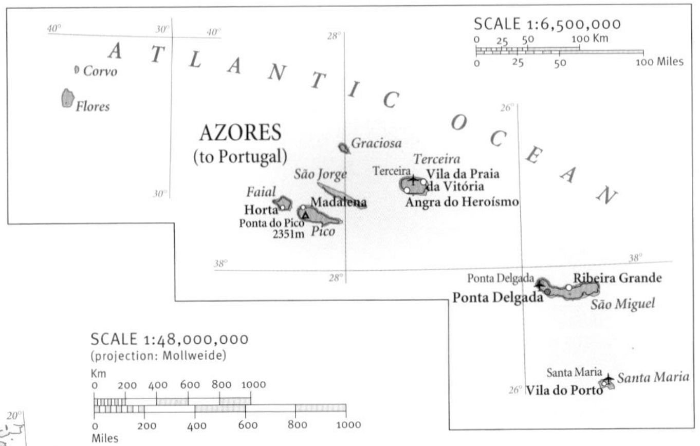

Activities

- Laze on the **Canary Islands'** beaches, surf in the afternoon and party the night away
- Brave the bull-running on **Terceira** in the Azores, where the bull is attached to a rope held by teams of men
- Play a round of golf on **Bermuda**
- Observe the abundant South Atlantic wildlife, such as penguins, sea-lions and elephant seals on the windy **Falkland Islands**
- Sip madeira on **Madeira**, home of this famous fortified wine
- Set out to sea to watch for marine life at **Faial** in the Azores (sperm and pilot whales, dolphins and loggerhead turtles)

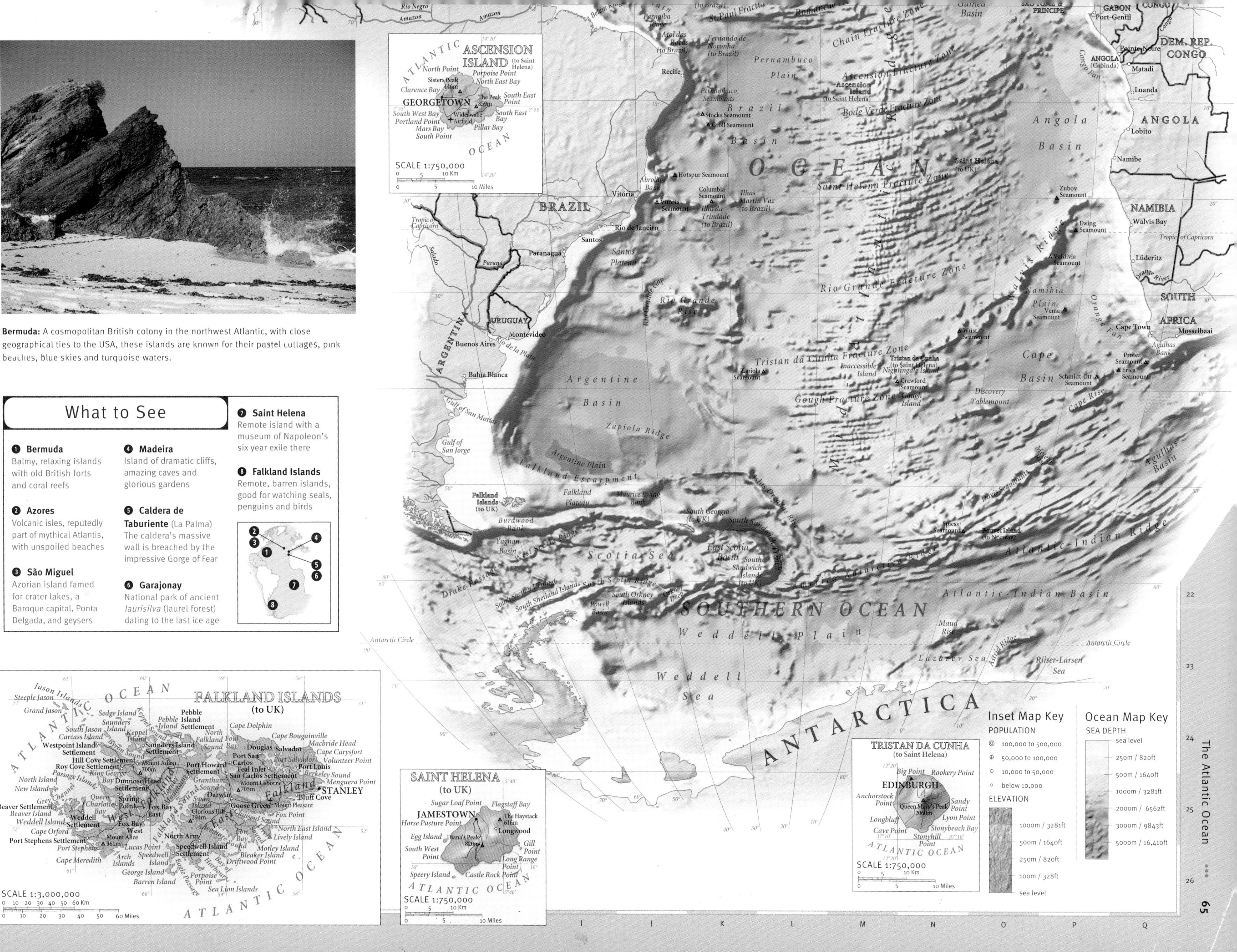
ASCENSION ISLAND (to Saint Helena)
GEORGETOWN
North Point
Sisters Peak
Porpoise Point
North East Bay
Clarence Bay
The Peak 859m
South East Point
South West Bay
Portland Point
Mars Bay
South Point
Pillar Bay
ATLANTIC OCEAN
SCALE 1:750,000
BRAZIL
URUGUAY
ARGENTINA
Montevideo
Buenos Aires
Bahía Blanca
Rio de Janeiro
Santos
Paranaguá
Vitória
Recife
Amazon
Rio Negro
Paraná
Salado
Tropic of Capricorn
Gulf of San Matías
Gulf of San Jorge
Río de la Plata
Falkland Islands (to UK)
Argentine Basin
Argentine Plain
Zapiola Ridge
Falkland Escarpment
Falkland Plateau
Rio Grande Rise
Rio Grande Fracture Zone
Santos Plateau
Brazil Basin
Pernambuco Plain
Fernando de Noronha (to Brazil)
Atol das Rocas (to Brazil)
Ascension Fracture Zone
Chain Fracture Zone
Bode Verde Fracture Zone
Saint Helena Fracture Zone
Saint Helena (to UK)
Tristan da Cunha Fracture Zone
Gough Fracture Zone
Ilhas Martin Vaz (to Brazil)
Ilha da Trindade (to Brazil)
Hotspur Seamount
OCEAN
Angola Basin
Cape Basin
Walvis Ridge
Namibia Plain
Cape Rise
Agulhas Basin
Discovery Tablemount
ANGOLA
NAMIBIA
SOUTH AFRICA
DEM. REP. CONGO
GABON
Port-Gentil
Luanda
Lobito
Namibe
Walvis Bay
Lüderitz
Cape Town
Mosselbaai
Orange River
Drake Passage
Scotia Sea
East Scotia Basin
South Sandwich Islands (to UK)
South Georgia (to UK)
South Orkney Islands
South Shetland Islands
Burdwood Bank
Yaghan Basin
Powell Basin
SOUTHERN OCEAN
Weddell Plain
Weddell Sea
Atlantic-Indian Ridge
Atlantic-Indian Basin
Bouvet Island (to Norway)
Maud Rise
Lazarev Sea
Riiser-Larsen Sea
Antarctic Circle
ANTARCTICA
FALKLAND ISLANDS (to UK)
STANLEY
West Falkland
East Falkland
Falkland Sound
SCALE 1:3,000,000
SAINT HELENA (to UK)
JAMESTOWN
Diana's Peak 820m
Longwood
Flagstaff Bay
Sugar Loaf Point
Horse Pasture Point
Egg Island
South West Point
Speery Island
Castle Rock Point
Long Range Point
Gill Point
The Haystack 616m
TRISTAN DA CUNHA (to Saint Helena)
EDINBURGH
Queen Mary's Peak 2060m
Big Point
Rookery Point
Anchorstock Point
Sandy Point
Longbluff
Lyon Point
Cave Point
Stonyhill Point
Stonybeach Bay
Inset Map Key
POPULATION
100,000 to 500,000
50,000 to 100,000
10,000 to 50,000
below 10,000
ELEVATION
1000m / 3281ft
500m / 1640ft
250m / 820ft
100m / 328ft
sea level
Ocean Map Key
SEA DEPTH
sea level
250m / 820ft
500m / 1640ft
1000m / 3281ft
2000m / 6562ft
3000m / 9843ft
5000m / 16,410ft

Bermuda: A cosmopolitan British colony in the northwest Atlantic, with close geographical ties to the USA, these islands are known for their pastel cottages, pink beaches, blue skies and turquoise waters.

What to See

❶ Bermuda
Balmy, relaxing islands with old British forts and coral reefs

❷ Azores
Volcanic isles, reputedly part of mythical Atlantis, with unspoiled beaches

❸ São Miguel
Azorian island famed for crater lakes, a Baroque capital, Ponta Delgada, and geysers

❹ Madeira
Island of dramatic cliffs, amazing caves and glorious gardens

❺ Caldera de Taburiente (La Palma)
The caldera's massive wall is breached by the impressive Gorge of Fear

❻ Garajonay
National park of ancient *laurisilva* (laurel forest) dating to the last ice age

❼ Saint Helena
Remote island with a museum of Napoleon's six year exile there

❽ Falkland Islands
Remote, barren islands, good for watching seals, penguins and birds

Africa

"Copper sun or scarlet sea,
jungle star or jungle track...
where the birds of Eden sing" COUNTEE CULLEN, 1903-1946

Physical Africa

Africa's vast expanses of desert and jungle fill visitors with a real sense of adventure. The Great Rift Valley, running down the eastern side of the continent, creates dramatic scenery in Kenya and Ethiopia that is only rivalled by the rugged mountains and canyons of South Africa. But it is the mighty rivers that are the lifeblood of this continent, and are still vital for travel and industry. The Nile, the world's longest river, runs north through Sudan and Egypt, while the great Congo Basin covers much of central Africa, the Niger and its tributaries dominate the west and the Zambezi in the south offers the greatest spectacle – the Victoria Falls.

Desert

The landscapes of the vast Sahara vary from the bare volcanic uplands of the Tibesti and Ahaggar plateaus to barren, gravelly basins or classic sand dunes in Morocco. In southern Africa, the thin strip of Namib Desert, lying in a rainshadow, has fantastic dunes at Sossuvlei, while the Kalahari is rich in wildlife.

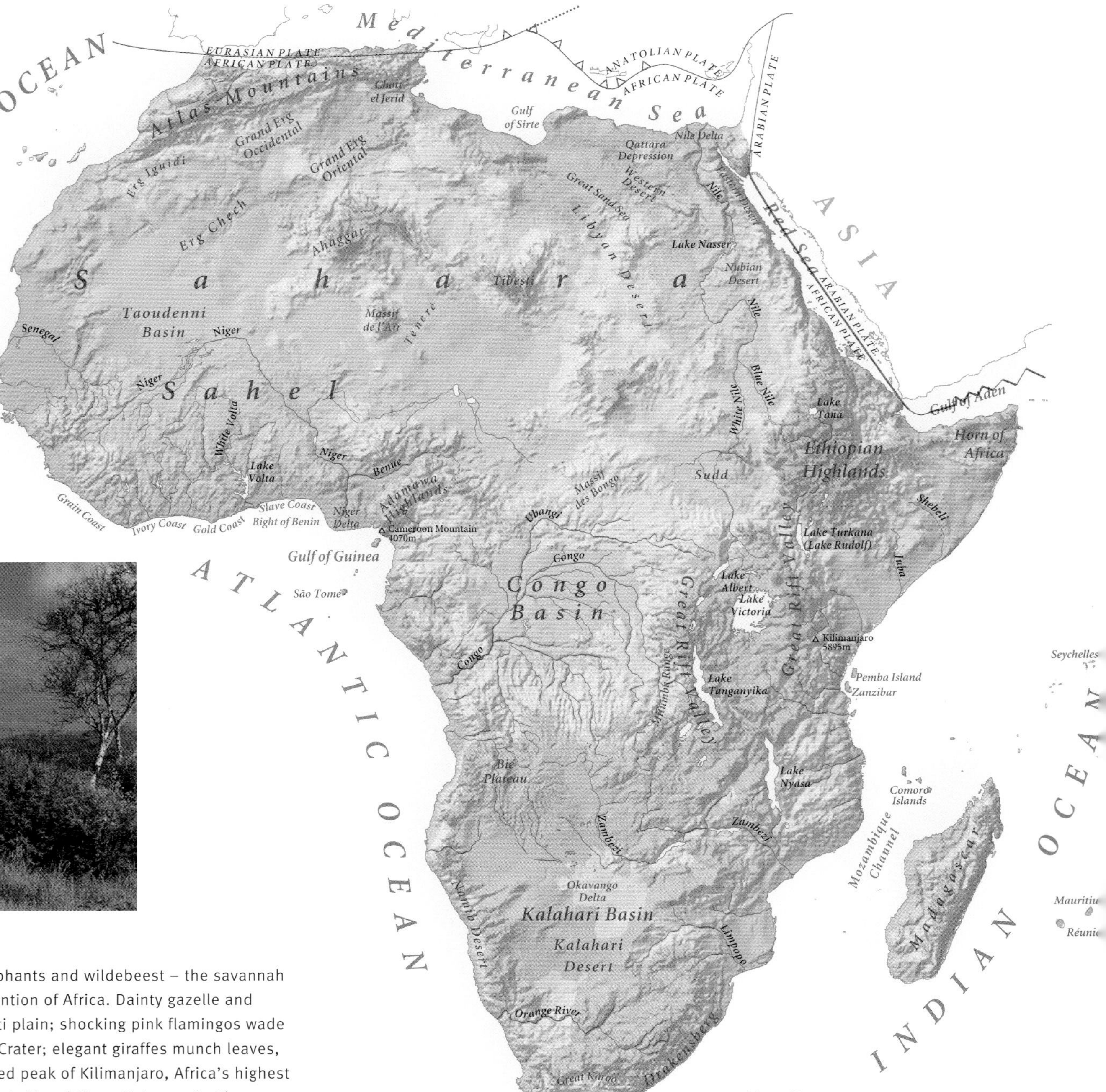

SCALE 1:40,000,000
(projection: Lambert Azimuthal Equal Area)
Km 0 100 200 400 600 800
0 100 200 400 600 800 Miles

Savannah

Grassy plains roamed by lions, elephants and wildebeest – the savannah is the first image evoked by the mention of Africa. Dainty gazelle and antelope graze Tanzania's Serengeti plain; shocking pink flamingos wade in the wetlands of the Ngorongoro Crater; elegant giraffes munch leaves, silhouetted against the snow-capped peak of Kilimanjaro, Africa's highest mountain. For wildlife safaris, Kenya's Masai Mara, Botswana's Okavango Delta or South Africa's Kruger National Park stand out.

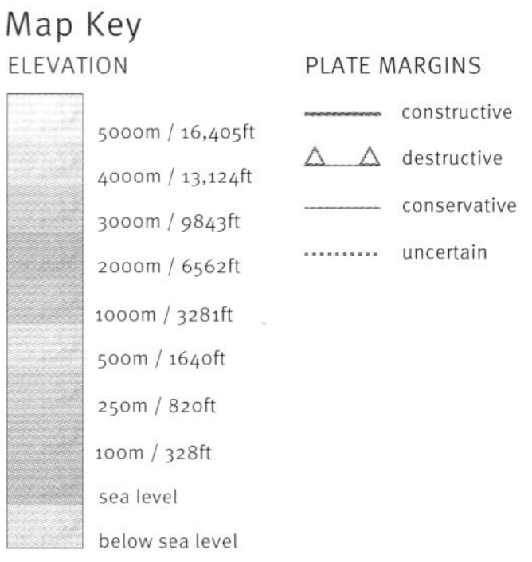

Jungle

The rainforests along the equator hold a treasure trove of birds and animals – colourful parakeets, dangerous crocodiles, chattering monkeys and bathing hippos. National parks make some of this region easily accessible. The highlands of Rwanda and Uganda are the last preserve of the world's largest primate – the gorilla.

Map Key

ELEVATION
5000m / 16,405ft
4000m / 13,124ft
3000m / 9843ft
2000m / 6562ft
1000m / 3281ft
500m / 1640ft
250m / 820ft
100m / 328ft
sea level
below sea level

PLATE MARGINS
constructive
destructive
conservative
uncertain

Climate

Almost the whole continent lies within the Tropics, so temperatures are hot all year, but it is rainfall patterns that define Africa's biogeographic zones. Rising air over the tropics causes deserts, while sinking air over equatorial regions leads to heavy rainfall and the dense jungles of the Congo, Niger and Volta river basins. In between lie savannah grasslands and the Sahel, a fragile ecosystem of near-desert grassland. The Mediterranean-style climates of the most northern and southern coasts make great beach resorts – Tunisia is a major package destination for Europeans and Zanzibar a popular tropical paradise. Unpleasant dusty winds blow out of the Sahara to the north in March–April and south in November–March.

Climate
arid
humid equatorial
mediterranean
semi-arid
tropical
warm humid
daily hours of sunshine, January
daily hours of sunshine, July
cold wind
hot wind

Rainfall

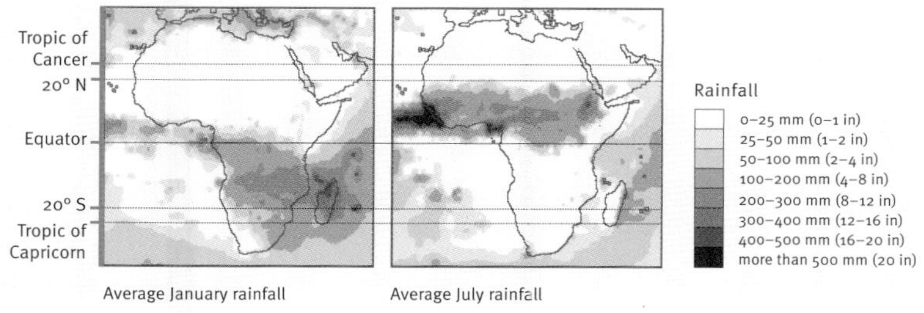

Tropic of Cancer
20° N
Equator
20° S
Tropic of Capricorn

Average January rainfall

Average July rainfall

Rainfall
0–25 mm (0–1 in)
25–50 mm (1–2 in)
50–100 mm (2–4 in)
100–200 mm (4–8 in)
200–300 mm (8–12 in)
300–400 mm (12–16 in)
400–500 mm (16–20 in)
more than 500 mm (20 in)

Temperature

Tropic of Cancer
20° N
Equator
20° S
Tropic of Capricorn

Average January temperature

Average July temperature

Temperature
0 to 10°C (32 to 50° F)
10 to 20°C (50 to 68°F)
20 to 30°C (68 to 86°F)
above 30°C (86°F)

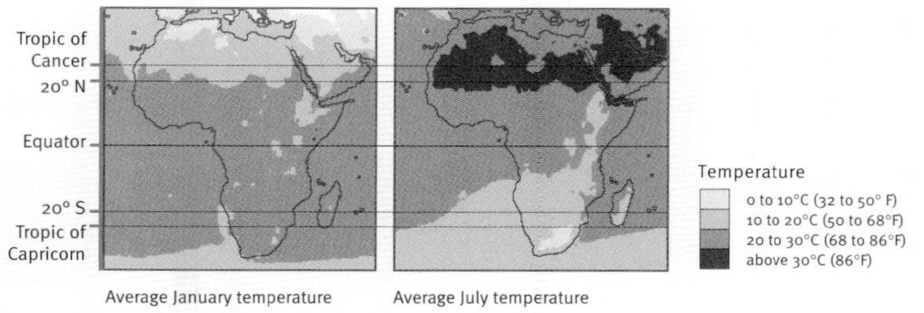

Zagora, Morocco: The dunes of the Sahara are continuously moving, encroaching on cultivated land. Barriers made of palm fronds are the most successful means of preventing the relentless incursion of wind-blown sand.

Using Land and Sea

Kenya, Ethiopia, Rwanda, Uganda and Burundi benefit from fertile volcanic soils to grow tea and coffee, while Lake Victoria and Lake Nyasa support substantial fishing industries. The green Nile valley stands out as a ribbon of life through the surrounding desert, sustaining five millennia of civilization and date groves are widespread across the north. The equatorial west coast is plantation country – rubber, cocoa, bananas, peanuts – and the coastal waters are rich in fish, heavily exploited by boats from Europe. South Africa has Mediterranean-style vineyards, citrus orchards and other fruit-growing areas. Much of the rest of Africa is pasture for grazing cattle and goats, the traditional way of life for nomadic herders.

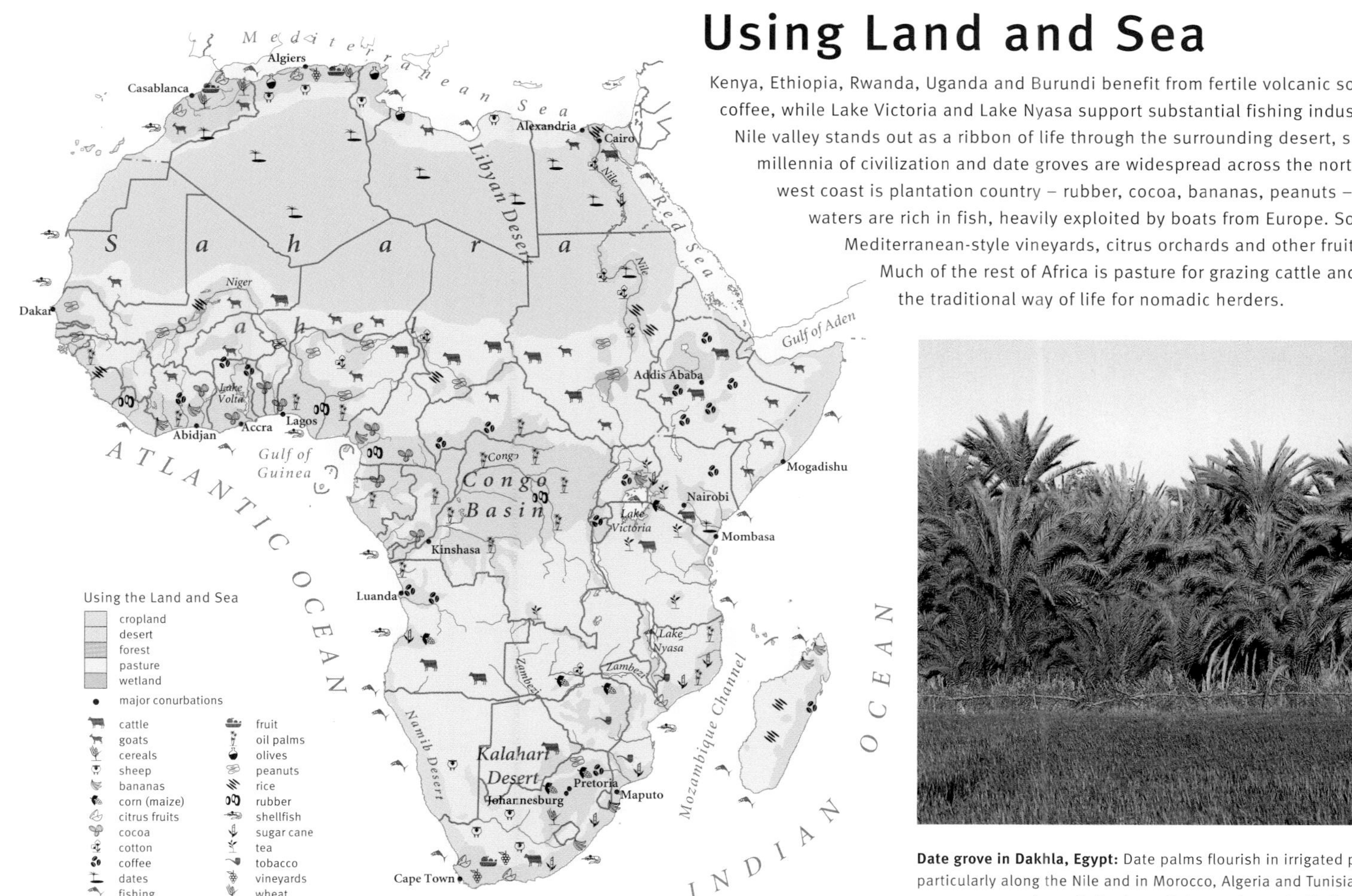
Mediterranean Sea
Atlantic Ocean
Indian Ocean
Sahara
Sahel
Libyan Desert
Congo Basin
Kalahari Desert
Namib Desert
Gulf of Guinea
Gulf of Aden
Red Sea
Mozambique Channel
Using the Land and Sea
cropland
desert
forest
pasture
wetland
major conurbations
cattle
goats
cereals
sheep
bananas
corn (maize)
citrus fruits
cocoa
cotton
coffee
dates
fishing
fruit
oil palms
olives
peanuts
rice
rubber
shellfish
sugar cane
tea
tobacco
vineyards
wheat

Date grove in Dakhla, Egypt: Date palms flourish in irrigated plantations, particularly along the Nile and in Morocco, Algeria and Tunisia. A variety of other crops are grown beneath the trees. Dates are harvested in September and October.

Political Africa

Within one lifetime the political map of Africa has changed completely. Its only independent states in 1950 were Egypt (then a monarchy), the proud empire of Ethiopia, the republic founded by freed American slaves in Liberia and white-ruled apartheid South Africa. Since then, not only have those four countries been transformed – in miraculously peaceful fashion in South Africa, under Nelson Mandela's leadership – but nearly 50 more independent states have emerged from the dismantling of the British, French and Portuguese colonial empires. Most are now republics – many have experienced great turbulence, often to the degree of civil war or the ravages of inter-ethnic violence, a prime example being Rwanda in 1994. Despotic regimes have mostly given way to multiparty systems, without always bringing genuine political freedom.

Languages

Some 1,300 African languages fall into four main groups, of which the Niger–Congo is the largest (including 500 languages within the Bantu sub-group alone). Others, such as Zulu and Xhosa or the Shona languages, are linguistically similar, but most have fewer than a million speakers. This favours use of a common *lingua franca* (Swahili in the east, Arabic in the north) and the former colonial languages, which dominate education and government.

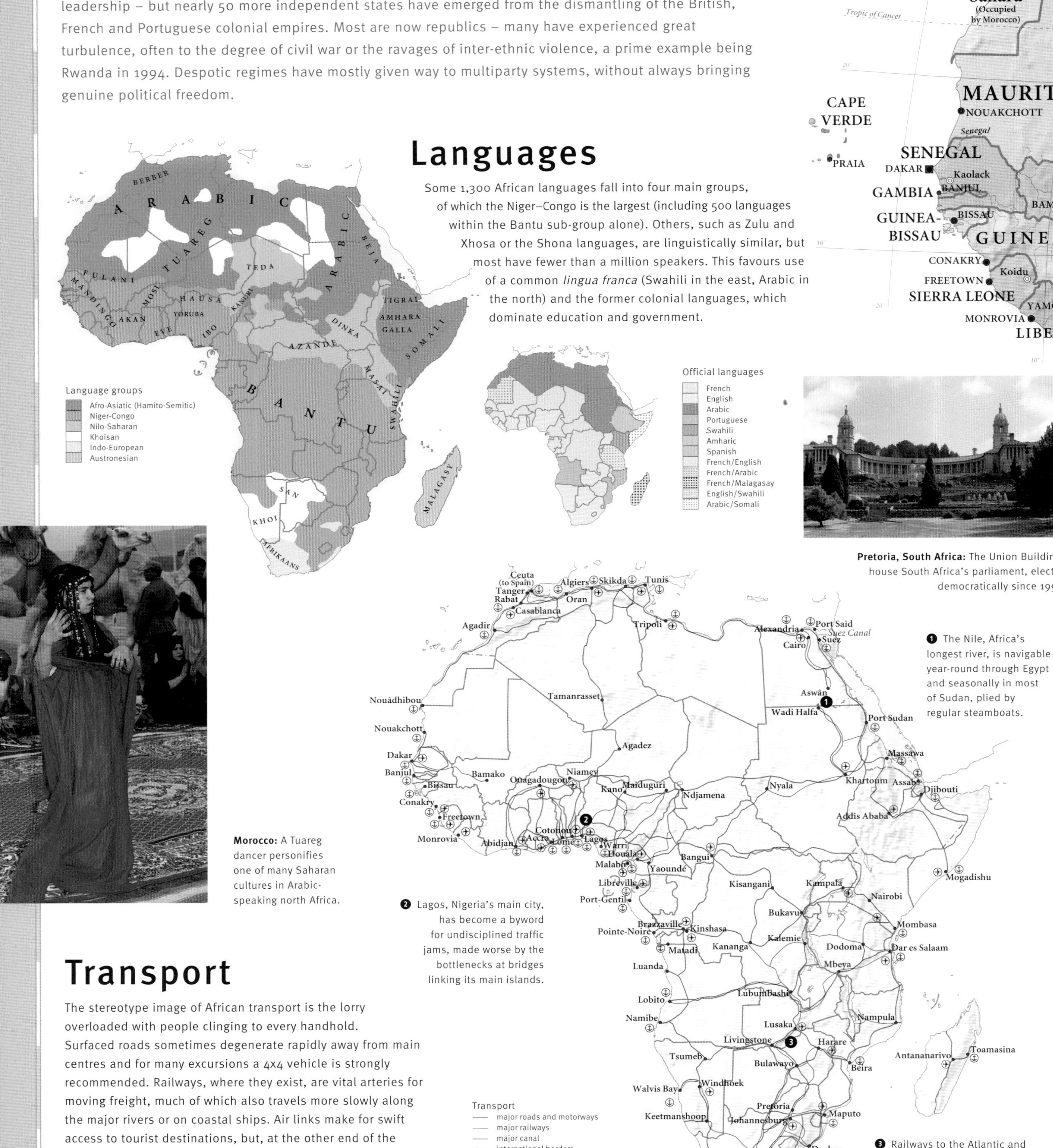
Language groups
Afro-Asiatic (Hamito-Semitic)
Niger-Congo
Nilo-Saharan
Khoisan
Indo-European
Austronesian
ARABIC
BANTU
Official languages
French
English
Arabic
Portuguese
Swahili
Amharic
Spanish
French/English
French/Arabic
French/Malagasay
English/Swahili
Arabic/Somali
Transport
major roads and motorways
major railways
major canal
international borders
transport intersections
international airports
major ports

Pretoria, South Africa: The Union Buildings house South Africa's parliament, elected democratically since 1994.

Morocco: A Tuareg dancer personifies one of many Saharan cultures in Arabic-speaking north Africa.

❶ The Nile, Africa's longest river, is navigable year-round through Egypt and seasonally in most of Sudan, plied by regular steamboats.

❷ Lagos, Nigeria's main city, has become a byword for undisciplined traffic jams, made worse by the bottlenecks at bridges linking its main islands.

❸ Railways to the Atlantic and Indian Ocean ports are crucial for landlocked Zambia and Zimbabwe.

Transport

The stereotype image of African transport is the lorry overloaded with people clinging to every handhold. Surfaced roads sometimes degenerate rapidly away from main centres and for many excursions a 4x4 vehicle is strongly recommended. Railways, where they exist, are vital arteries for moving freight, much of which also travels more slowly along the major rivers or on coastal ships. Air links make for swift access to tourist destinations, but, at the other end of the transport spectrum, it is remarkable how far people routinely walk in rural Africa.

SCALE 1:30,500,000
(projection: Lambert Azimuthal Equal Area)

Km 0 100 200 400 600 800 1000

Miles 0 50 100 200 300 400 500 600 700 800 900 1000

Map Key

POPULATION

- above 5 million
- 1 million to 5 million
- 500,000 to 1 million
- 100,000 to 500,000
- 50,000 to 100,000
- 10,000 to 50,000
- Country capital

BORDERS

- full international border
- disputed de facto border
- ceasefire line

Standard of Living

Although mineral resources create pockets of wealth, many African communities suffer destitution unparalleled elsewhere, made worse by war and the devastating spread of HIV/AIDS. Life expectancy in Sierra Leone and Zambia is as low as 37 years. Local economies need well-targeted international assistance to break out of poverty.

Standard of Living
(UN Human Development Index)

high

low

Zulu dancer, South Africa: The post-apartheid "Rainbow Nation" embraces the varied traditions of its peoples.

Lake Tangrela, Burkina

Burchell's zebras, African savannah

Cape Town, South Africa

Serengeti, Tanzania

Pyramids at Giza, Egypt

Great African Journeys

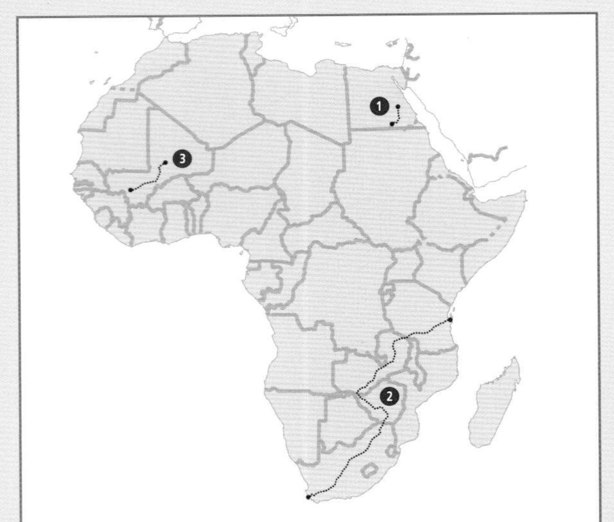

❶ Nile Cruise, Egypt
Luxor – Abu Simbel
480 km (300 miles)
The classic cruise starts at the famed ancient capital of Thebes (near Luxor), continues past the Aswan Dam, and along Lake Nasser to Ramses II's intimidating temple of Abu Simbel. The whole temple was moved stone by stone before the site was flooded by the lake.

❷ Edwardian Train Safari
Cape Town, South Africa – Dar es Salaam, Tanzania
6,100 km (3,800 miles)
This epic and luxurious train journey takes a fortnight to visit the southern highlights – Kruger National Park, Bulawayo, Victoria Falls, Kilimanjaro, Ngorongoro Crater, and the Serengeti.

❸ The Road to Timbuktu, Mali
Bamako – Gao – Timbuktu (Tombouctou)
1,600 km (1,000 miles)
The elusive, mysterious and once-great city can be reached by a fascinating journey following the course of the Niger river from Mali's capital, Bamako, and taking in Djenné's huge mud-brick mosque on the way.

Journeys

Since the epic feats of exploration by 19th-century Europeans, this continent has continued to present challenges to travel and navigation by visitors, whether they have to contend with the great desert of the Sahara, the huge central rainforests or the swamplands of the Okavango. Don't be put off by poor infrastructure – the extensive rail networks and roads built in colonial times may cost too much to maintain, but there are still luxury rail journeys to be had along the South African Garden Route or evocative trips on the Marrakech Express. For the adventurous, other remarkable routes to take by car, train or boat include various options from Kenya down to South Africa through Botswana, Zimbabwe or Mozambique, trips through the West African coast countries or travelling the fascinating and Arab-influenced north coast. Overland safaris offer tourists multi-country journeys, camping out in game reserves and getting a closer view of the continent's unspoiled expanses. For desert lovers the vast expanses of the Sahara can be seen by camel treks in Sudan or Morocco, offering an insight into nomadic life.

Nile river, Egypt: *Feluccas* (traditional sailboats) have been used for millennia as the main form of transport for goods and people along the Nile.

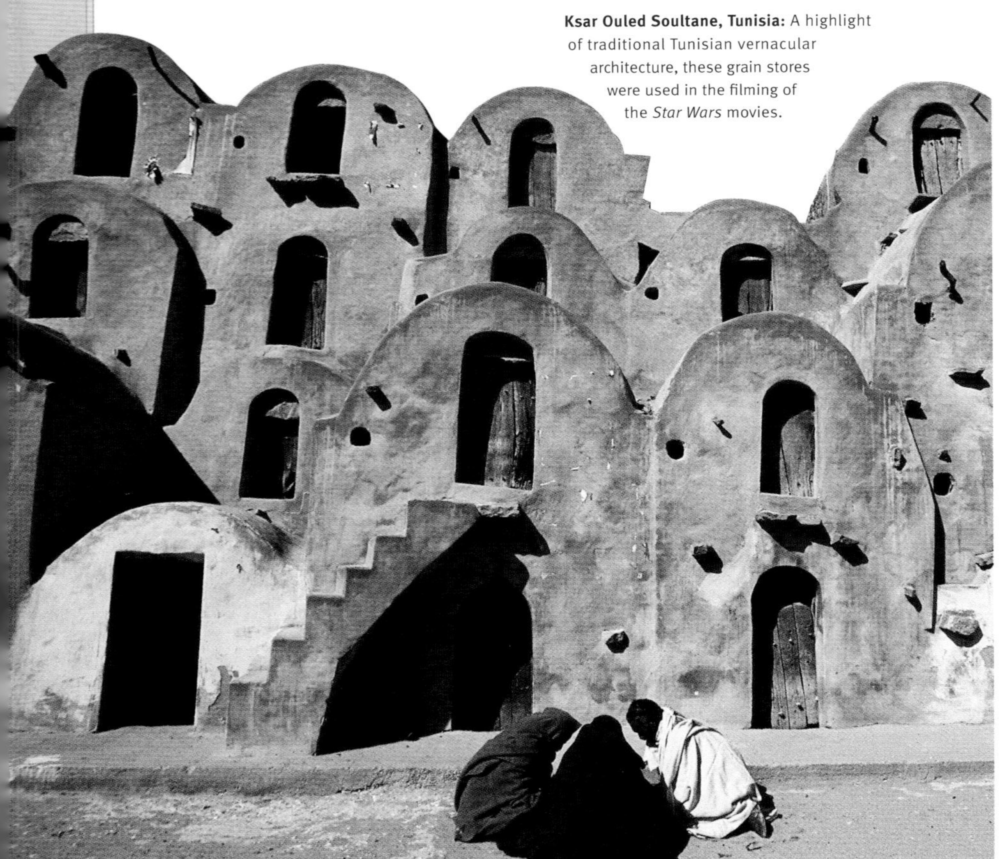
Ksar Ouled Soultane, Tunisia: A highlight of traditional Tunisian vernacular architecture, these grain stores were used in the filming of the *Star Wars* movies.

Cultural Sights

Africa's early history is dominated by the amazing legacy of the ancient Egyptians, a fascinating 5,000-year-old culture that left monuments, huge temples and beautiful tombs of immense wealth. Millions of tourists take idyllic cruises down the Nile or stay in Cairo, the continent's largest city, for a visit to the pyramids and the treasure-filled Cairo Museum. Even older pyramids can be found in the Sudan and there are numerous other remains such as the mysterious ruins of Great Zimbabwe. The Mediterranean coast has a number of impressive Roman sites, as well as many photogenic medieval *kasbahs* and *souqs*. Across the continent are a multitude of different cultures, with indigenous tribes, busy markets and local cuisine. In some places, such as Lesotho, it is even possible to meet and stay with people living true to traditional ways.

What to See

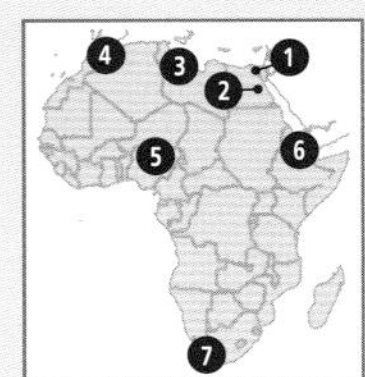

❶ Pyramids of Giza, Egypt
Visit the only survivor of the "Seven Wonders of the Ancient World"

❷ Karnak, Egypt
Immense temple complex from the ancient civilization

❸ Leptis Magna, Libya
A whole Roman city – one of the empire's grandest – in the desert

❹ Fès, Morocco
Medieval *medina* (town) with *souqs* and massive walls

❺ Durbar at Kano, Nigeria
Charging horsemen, muscular wrestlers, lute players and horn blowers, celebrating the end of Ramadan

❻ Lalibela, Ethiopia
Eleven 12th-century churches carved from solid rock

❼ Cape Town, South Africa
A vibrant concoction of Dutch, British and Cape Malay influences

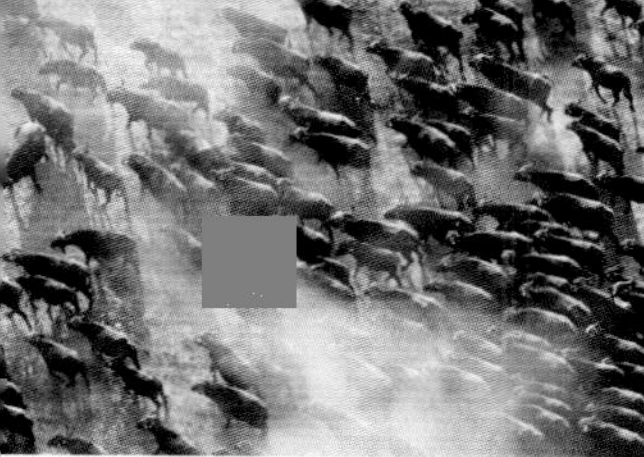
African buffalo herd, Botswana

Ouarzazate, Morocco

Congo river, Dem. Rep. Congo

Pottery jars, Djerba, Tunisia

Skeleton Coast, Namibia

Activities

Big game hunting can still be done in Africa, but most visitors nowadays shoot only pictures, a better way of preserving the potential of the vast savannahs and deep forests teeming with wildlife. Taking a *pirogue* (dugout canoe) up Gabon's Ogooue river or a *mekoro* along Okavango's waterways, is a good way to spot a hippopotamus. There are hiking opportunities too – vast deserts to explore, beautiful swamplands and rainforests. For beaches, Tunisia leads the way as a Mediterranean destination with excellent weather, facilities and a variety of cultural sights at a fraction of the price of other resorts. The Red Sea states are renowned for their coral and have world-class diving centres, while the Indian Ocean attractions of Zanzibar rate highly.

What to Do

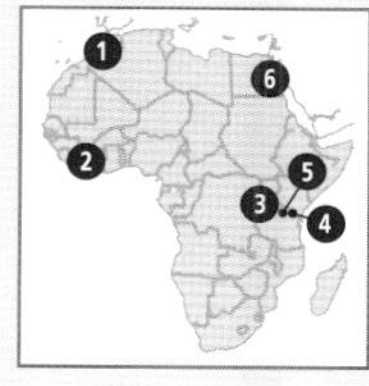

❶ **Atlas Mountains, Morocco**
Superb trekking past picturesque *kasbahs*

❷ **Man, Ivory Coast**
Revel at the exciting local masked-dancing festivals

❸ **Rwanda**
Visit the Virunga National Park to see how these most human of apes live in the wild

❺ **Kilimanjaro, Tanzania**
Climb Africa's tallest mountain at 5,895 m (19,340 ft) overlooking the savannah plains

❹ **Olduvai Gorge, Tanzania**
Discover the story of our earliest human ancestors from the fossilized remains found in this valley

❻ **Hurghada, Egypt**
Dive in the Red Sea among tropical fish and coral

Masai Mara National Reserve, Kenya: Tours deep into the Masai Mara can reward visitors with sightings of cheetahs, elephants, kudu, flamingos, wildebeest and zebras in their natural habitat.

Natural Sights

The Sahara desert stretches across most of north Africa, from the foothills of the Atlas Mountains to the Nile valley, from the coastal delights of Tunisia to Timbuktu on the Niger river. This vast, mostly uninhabited expanse is noted for the enchanting sand dunes of the Grand Erg Oriental and the beautiful oasis towns. Further to the south lie the great jungles and rivers of central Africa, some of them probably off-limits for most travellers due to regional instability. The west and south are dominated by the Great Rift Valley, which runs all the way down the continent from the Dead Sea in Jordan. Essential wonders include the animal-rich Ngorongoro Crater, majestic Kilimanjaro and the two great waterfalls, Victoria and Murchison. But even better known are the great wildlife parks where big game still roam the plains – Serengeti, Kruger and Masai Mara to name but a few.

What to See

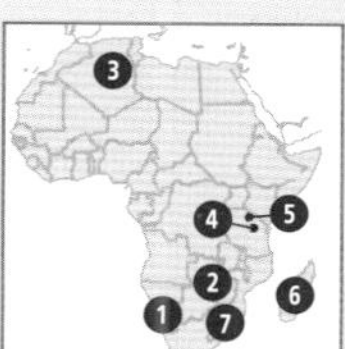

❶ **Sossusvlei Sand Dunes, Namibia**
Beautiful haunting desert scenery

❷ **Victoria Falls, Zambia/Zimbabwe**
The thunderous roar can be heard for miles

❸ **Grand Erg Oriental**
Part of the vast Sahara desert, noted for its spectacular sands

❹ **Ngorongoro Crater, Tanzania**
Spy a rare black rhino or black-maned lion

❺ **Serengeti, Tanzania**
Witness the great wildebeest migration at the end of May

❻ **Madagascar**
Lush rainforests with their own distinctive species of animals

❼ **Kruger National Park, South Africa**
Lions, giraffes, elands, zebras and rhinos – the continent's top safari experience

Victoria Falls, Zambia/Zimbabwe:
The spray from the turbulent waters of the Zambezi river rushing over the edge of the gorge gives the falls its native name Musi-O-Tunya – "the smoke that thunders".

North Africa

Algeria, Egypt, Libya, Morocco, Tunisia, Western Sahara

Egypt's ancient dynasties, going back almost 5,000 years and representing the height of civilization at that time, have left some of the most amazing archaeological sites on earth. The great temples and tombs along the Nile Valley, and the 50 or more pyramids in the north, were already considered well worth visiting in Roman times. Cairo, Egypt's modern capital, combines fascinating museums and characterful hotels with teeming streets and lively markets.

Further west, the north African desert has preserved many Roman sites and the *kasbahs* (fortresses) and *medinas* (old quarters) of cities linked to the trans-Saharan trading caravan routes give them an exotic feel, appreciated by travellers and film directors alike. Tunisia has latterly become a major beach destination for Europeans, while Morocco attracts visitors not only to seaside resorts but inland to Marrakech, Fès and other historic cities. Libya, and particularly Algeria, lag behind due to less favourable political conditions.

Leptis Magna, Libya: This major Roman city, near present-day Tripoli, has an unequalled range of well-preserved buildings, from this fantastic theatre, to the Severan Forum and the extensive Hadrianic baths.

104
120
64

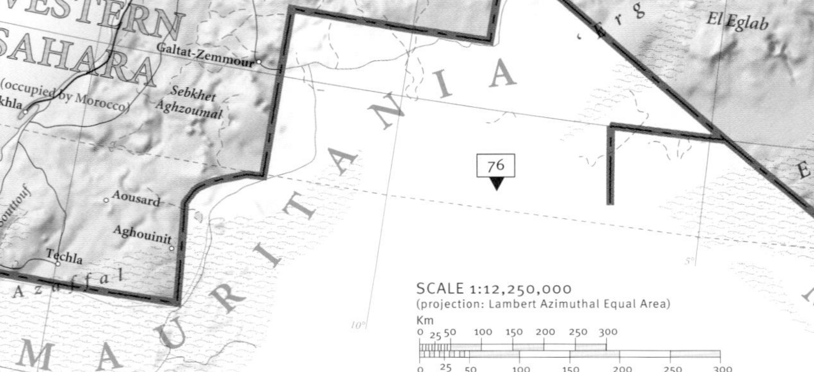

PORTUGAL
SPAIN
GIBRALTAR
Strait of Gibraltar
Tanger
Ceuta (to Spain)
Tétouan
Melilla (to Spain)
ALGER (ALGIERS)
Oran
Mostaganem
Tizi Ouzou
Béjaïa
Skikda
Annaba
Constantine
Sétif
Blida
Chlef
Tlemcen
Sidi Bel Abbès
Oujda
RABAT
Mohammedia
Casablanca
El-Jadida
Safi
Essaouira
Marrakech
Agadir
Fès
Meknès
Kénitra
Larache
Ouarzazate
Taroudannt
MOROCCO
Tiznit
Sidi-Ifni
Guelmime
Tan-Tan
Cap Juby
Tarfaya
LAÂYOUNE
Boujdour
Smara
Bou Craa
WESTERN SAHARA (occupied by Morocco)
Ad Dakhla
Tropic of Cancer
Cap Barbas
Bir-Gandouz
Lagouira
ATLANTIC OCEAN
MAURITANIA
MALI
ALGERIA
Grand Erg Occidental
Grand Erg Oriental
Hamada du Dra
Erg Iguidi
Erg Chech
Tanezrouft
Ahaggar
Tamanrasset
Ghardaïa
Ouargla
Hassi Messaoud
Touggourt
Biskra
Laghouat
Béchar
Tindouf
Adrar
Timimoun
El Goléa
In-Salah
Reggane
I-n-Guezzam
Illizi
Djanet
Atlas Saharien
Hauts Plateaux
Haut Atlas
Anti Atlas
SCALE 1:12,250,000
(projection: Lambert Azimuthal Equal Area)
Km 0 25 50 100 150 200 250 300
Miles 0 25 50 100 150 200 250 300

76
76

Erg Chebbi Dunes, Morocco: Camel processions cross the spectacular 40 km (25 mile) stretch of classic Sahara dunes, near Merzouga, on their way to the famous Date Festival which is held every October in Erfoud. Traditional music and dancing accompany the date tasting.

Map Key

POPULATION
- above 5 million
- 1 million to 5 million
- 500,000 to 1 million
- 100,000 to 500,000
- 50,000 to 100,000
- 10,000 to 50,000
- below 10,000

ELEVATION

4000m / 13,124ft
3000m / 9843ft
2000m / 6562ft
1000m / 3281ft
500m / 1640ft
250m / 820ft
100m / 328ft
sea level

What to See

❶ Jbel Toubkal
The highest peak in north Africa, dominating the Atlas Mountains at 4,165 m (13,664 ft), has superb trekking

❷ Marrakech
Within the pink-plastered walls of the old town, the Jemaa el-Fna (Square of the Dead) is a bustling plaza, leading off to a labyrinth of *souqs*

❸ Casablanca
Morocco's largest city, a creation of the European colonial era, has a lively, commercial feel and is home to the Hassan II Mosque, one of the world's largest

❹ Fès
Spiritual and cultural centre, and former capital of Morocco, this superbly preserved medieval town has a huge *medina*, extensive *souqs* and impressive walls

❺ Tlemcen
Arab imperial city whose heyday was during the 12th–16th centuries, now noteworthy for its Grand Mosque, Mansourah Fortress and Almohad Ramparts

❻ Djemila
(near Sétif) This remarkably intact Roman garrison town is not the largest such site in north Africa, but has fine buildings, mosaics and marble statues

❼ Dougga
(near Béja) Probably occupied since the 2nd millennium BCE, the extensive ruins include a well-preserved capitol, a brothel and a fine pre-Roman mausoleum

❽ Tunis
A rich Islamic trading centre during the 12th–16th centuries, now known for its old *medina*, the antiquities in the Bardo Museum and Carthage's ruins

❾ Matmata
(near Tataouine)
Its underground houses, a tradition dating back over 400 years, were used as the troglodyte dwellings in the filming of *Star Wars*

❿ Tripoli
Seafront capital with an architectural mix of Roman and Turkish buildings, whitewashed alleys and the classical Jamahiriyah Museum

⓫ Leptis Magna
(near Al Khums) One of the best-preserved Roman cities in the world, an extravaganza of marble

⓬ Acacus Mountains
Bewitching desert, dramatic rock formations and prehistoric art dating to at least 8000 BCE, near the oasis town of Ghat

⓭ Cairo
Africa's largest city, founded in 969 CE, with bustling streets and historic buildings

⓮ Egyptian Museum
(in Cairo) Staggering displays of antiquities including Tutankhamun's treasure and the Royal Mummy Room's pharoahs

⓯ Pyramids of Giza
The only survivor of the "Seven Wonders of the Ancient World", the pyramids and sphinx date from around 2500 BCE

⓰ St Catherine's Monastery
(near Gebel Musa) Built in the 6th century CE, this fortress-cum-monastery lies at the foot of Mount Sinai, where Moses is said to have received the Ten Commandments

⓱ Valley of the Kings
Long, inclined corridors descend to decorated, pillared halls each ending in a burial chamber (Tutankhamun's is among the least impressive). Nearby, Queen Nefertari's tomb has been restored to all its dazzling colour

⓲ Temple of Karnak
(in Luxor) The greatest temple complex of them all, a massive site whose Great Hypostyle Hall of 134 huge columns covers 6,000 sq m (64,600 sq ft)

⓳ Abu Simbel
Guarded by four colossal statues of Ramses II, this amazing temple served as an impressive warning of the pharoah's power to those coming into Egypt from the south

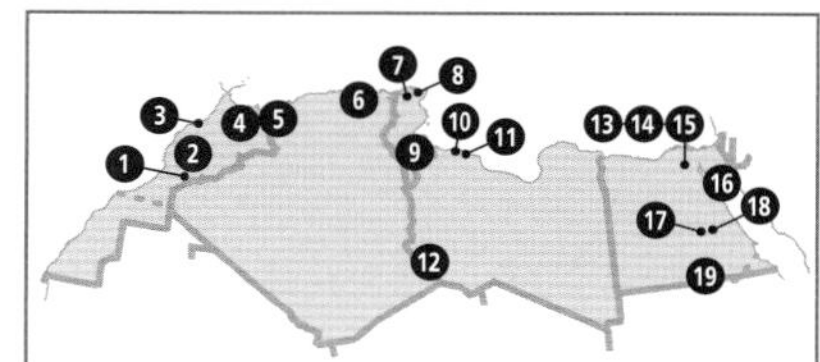

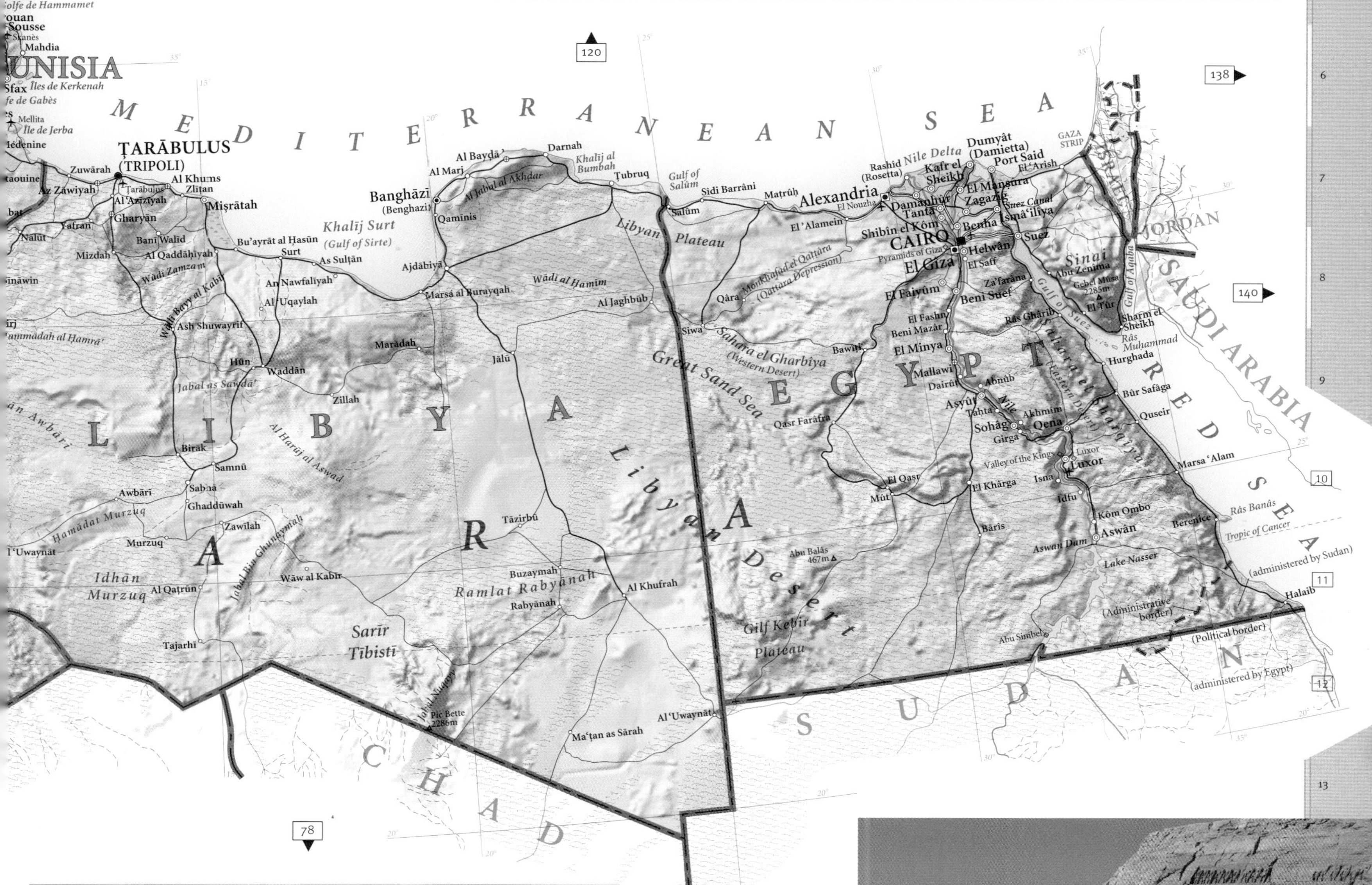

Activities

Observe traditional Berber courtship rituals at the **Imilchil** Betrothal Fair, Morocco (early September)	Windsurf at **Ras Sudr** on the Gulf of Suez
Trek in the **Haut Atlas** mountains	Attend the sound and light shows that bring life to **Karnak's** Egyptian history
Soak up the sun at **Hammamet**, one of Tunisia's many popular beach resorts	Glimpse the penetrating sun at the Ascension of Ramses II (22nd February) at **Abu Simbel**, Egypt, when the sun's rays reach through to the inner sanctuary
Visit the pyramids at **Giza** to see the empty tombs of the pharaohs, long ago plundered by grave robbers (Cairo)	Dive at **Hurghada**, Red Sea to see the best coral reefs in the world

Abu Simbel: The colossal Temple of Ramses II and the nearby Temple of Nefertari, his wife, were raised in a mammoth engineering project led by UNESCO between 1964 and 1968 to save them from the rising waters of Lake Nasser following the completion of the Aswan Dam.

West Africa

Benin, Burkina, Cape Verde, Gambia, Ghana, Guinea, Guinea-Bissau, Ivory Coast, Liberia, Mali, Mauritania, Niger, Nigeria, Senegal, Sierra Leone, Togo

Pristine beaches, dazzling wildlife, delicious food, Benin bronzes, Ashanti gold and the tallest cathedral in Christendom – west Africa has variety aplenty. Many layers of history enrich local cultures. Lively north Nigerian pageants and Mali's fabled Timbuktu (Tombouctou) testify to the impact of Islam. Further south and west you find older customs – Ivory Coast strongmen who juggle young girls, the talking drums of the Ewe or the mask ceremonies of the Dan, Baga, Bobo and Mossi tribes.

Nature is equally diverse with savannah, forest and flamingo-rich deltas, best seen on cruises down the arterial rivers of Gambia, Senegal and Niger. Tourists can scuba dive off Cape Verde, sip sun-downers in coastal Ghana, Sierra Leone or Togo and meet hospitable locals at lively markets. Fascinating forts and museums recall a more shameful Atlantic legacy – slavery.

Corruption, instability and conflict still blight the hopes of postcolonial independence – despite its diamonds, oil and cocoa, this is a predominantly poor region. Yet improved air links are attracting increasing numbers seeking an affordable and exciting vacation.

Ségou, Mali: Three women chat in a market abounding in carvings, textiles, jewellery and pottery. This town of broad French colonial boulevards is also a traditional departure point for a journey up the Niger river. Visitors can watch the sun set from a waterfront pavement, or travel 9 km (6 miles) upstream to little Ségou Koro, once capital of the Bambara Kingdom and site of enchanting mosques and historic architecture.

74

74

64

Map Key

POPULATION
- 1 million to 5 million
- 500,000 to 1 million
- 100,000 to 500,000
- 50,000 to 100,000
- 10,000 to 50,000
- below 10,000

ELEVATION
- 2000m / 6562ft
- 1000m / 3281ft
- 500m / 1640ft
- 250m / 820ft
- 100m / 328ft
- sea level

CAPE VERDE (same scale as main map)

SCALE 1:10,000,000
(projection: Lambert Azimuth Equal Area)
Km 0 25 50 100 150 200 250
Miles 0 25 50 100 150 200 250

What to See

1 Parc National du Banc d'Arguin
(near Nouâdhibou) Perhaps the continent's finest bird sanctuary

2 Île de Gorée
(near Dakar) With its slave-trading past, this peaceful retreat is historically fascinating

3 Dakar
A chaotic, cosmopolitan city with lively nightlife. Its modern African music clubs showcase hip-hop and local talent

4 Gambia
A perfect introduction to Africa with spirited markets, birdwatching and languid river scenery

5 Arquipélago dos Bijagós
Idyllic islands of turtles, beaches, seafood and faded colonial charm

6 Fouta Djallon
With its rolling hills and refreshingly cooler climate, this area is a true hiker's delight

7 The Great Mosque
(in Djenné) A dramatic focal point for this bustling, ancient town

8 Basilique de Nôtre Dame de la Paix
(in Yamoussoukro) The world's tallest church at 149 m (489 ft) is the most prominent feature of Ivory Coast's capital

9 Cotonou
You can buy anything from raloes and fast food to monkeys' testicles at the city's Grand Marché

10 The Durbar at Kano
End-Ramadan festivities in northern Nigeria's main city are a spectacle of Fulanis on charging horses and colourfully attired horn-blowers

11 Yankari
(near Bauchi) Elephants, lions and hippos inhabit this vast national game reserve, with relaxing warm springs at Wikki

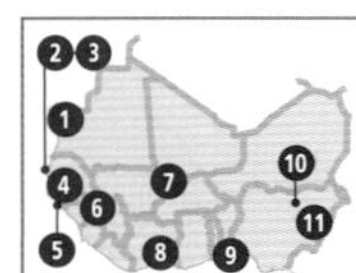

La Cascade de Man, Ivory Coast: This spectacular waterfall in a bamboo forest is also home to many butterflies. Visitors can take a quick dip in the frothing pool at its base during the wetter months of August to November.

Activities

Enjoy African cinema at the Fespaco Pan-African Film Festival in **Ouagadougou**
Shop for authentic *kente* cloth, traditional stools or gold jewellery at **Kumasi**, Ghana's bustling epicentre of Ashanti culture
See Wodaabe warriors, in ochre face-paint and ostrich plumes, flashing teeth and dancing at the Geerewol ceremony, **Niger**
Understand voodoo culture at **Ouidah**, a historic port in Benin
Thrash about with net-wielding fishermen in northwest Nigeria's **Rima river**, during the Argungu Fishing & Cultural Festival (March)
Enter the world of the mask-making Dogon people of **Bandiagara**, Mali
Taste camel cheese in **Mauritania** – similar to goat cheese apparently

Great Mosque at Djenné, Mali: This five-storey structure is the largest mud-brick building on earth. Constructed in 1907, it incorporates the sophisticated design of a now-destroyed original of 1280.

74

78

78

Central Africa

Cameroon, Central African Republic, Chad, Congo, Dem. Rep. Congo, Equatorial Guinea, Gabon, São Tomé & Príncipe

Many hail Cameroon as Africa's new jewel destination. This nation of 280 ethnic groups is bilingual in English and French, with fine cuisine, superb beaches around Kribi and nine excellent nature reserves. Tourists can sleep in rainforests, shop for wonderful sculptures, listen to Bafut's expert xylophone-players or watch festive stilt-walkers. Manu Dibango's infectious music epitomizes Cameroon's *joie de vivre* and regular flights from Europe encourage predictions of 500,000 visitors annually. Elsewhere, the region is afflicted by sporadic crime, corruption and instability. The Democratic Republic of the Congo (DRC), formerly Zaire, is a vast country scarred by decades of corrupt rule and a still-simmering civil war, reinforcing its image from Joseph Conrad's novel *Heart of Darkness*. The DRC's sophisticated capital, Kinshasa, is worth visiting, but little remains of the 14th–17th century Kongo kingdom and hazards prevent eco-tourism in the DRC's Congo river basin, eastern jungles and southern savannahs. In Gabon, oil wealth has spawned new hotels, while in Congo (Brazzaville) travellers can explore luxuriant mangroves skirting a network of rivers. Mix caution with common sense, escape humidity by visiting during November to February, and you may discover pleasant surprises in central Africa.

Map Key

POPULATION

- 1 million to 5 million
- 500,000 to 1 million
- 100,000 to 500,000
- 50,000 to 100,000
- 10,000 to 50,000
- below 10,000

ELEVATION

- 4000m / 13,124ft
- 3000m / 9843ft
- 2000m / 6562ft
- 1000m / 3281ft
- 500m / 1640ft
- 250m / 820ft
- 100m / 328ft
- sea level

74

76

80

What to See

1 Neolithic Rock Art in the Ennedi
Hidden between red sandstone canyons and cathedral-like outcrops are some astonishing examples of 8,000-year-old rock art

2 Parc National du Waza, Cameroon (near Maroua) Elephants gather in their hundreds around the park's main watering hole

3 St Floris Park
All the major species live in CAR's main national park, though numbers are depleted

4 Cameroon Mountain
Allocate two days for an invigorating 27 km (17 mile) hike through tropical forest to the icy zenith of central Africa's highest peak

5 Foumban
This Muslim town has the amazing 14th-century Bamoun sultan's palace and a colourful market

6 Yaoundé
The Benedictine Monastery's small Musée d'Art Camerounais displays fabulous masks, bowls and bronze pipes

7 Isla de Bioco
Spectacular mountain vistas open out in this tropical paradise island belonging to Equatorial Guinea – Africa's only Spanish-speaking nation

8 Sao Tome & Principe
These islands have attractive, lush scenery and bizarre remnants of extinct volcanoes

9 Lambaréné
The picturesque hospital where Albert Schweitzer won a Nobel Prize for his pioneering medical philanthropy still functions at this river port and trading nexus

10 Loufoulakari Falls
(near Brazzaville) Tour these remarkable falls and visit the nearby Poto Poto painting school

11 Kinshasa
The DRC's capital city is renowned for the swaying rhythms of *soukous* music

Congo river, Democratic Republic of the Congo: A fisherman handles a net as the other moors their traditional pirogue to the water's edge. Fishermen along this mighty river navigate perilous rapids and need strength and balance – skills honed over generations – to land their carp, tilapia or highly-prized capitaine.

Rumsiki Mountains, Extrême-Nord, Cameroon: Erosion has left these tremendous basaltic pillars – cores of ancient volcanoes – towering above the landscape. Tourists can see traditional ways of life at the nearby Rumsiki village and craft centre – don't miss a visit to the witch doctor who uses a crab in a clay pot to tell fortunes.

SCALE 1:10,500,000
(projection: Lambert Azimuthal Equal Area)

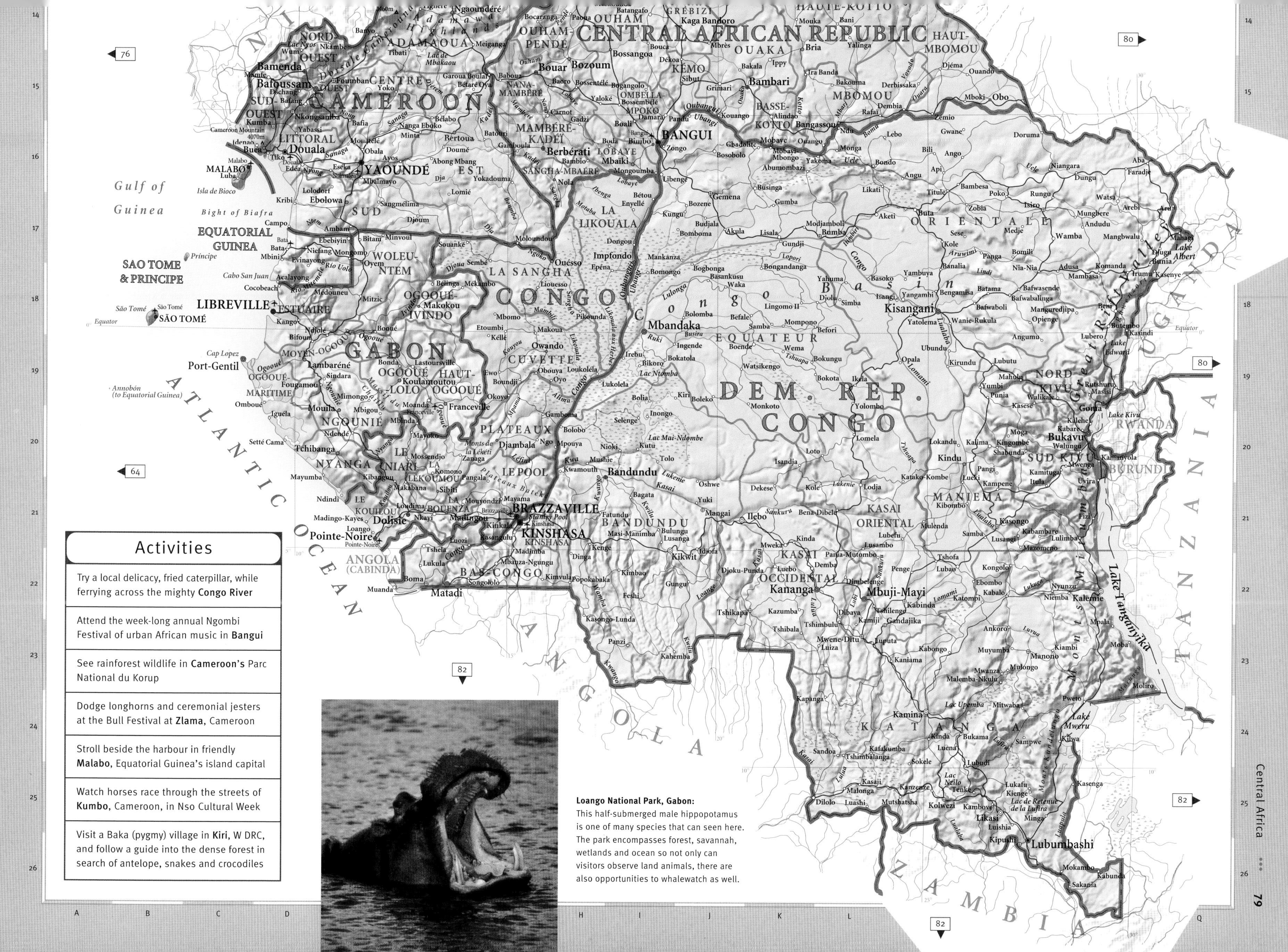
CAMEROON
CENTRAL AFRICAN REPUBLIC
EQUATORIAL GUINEA
SAO TOME & PRINCIPE
GABON
CONGO
DEM. REP. CONGO
ANGOLA
ZAMBIA
TANZANIA
UGANDA
RWANDA
BURUNDI
ANGOLA (CABINDA)
ATLANTIC OCEAN
Gulf of Guinea
Bight of Biafra
YAOUNDÉ
BANGUI
MALABO
LIBREVILLE
SÃO TOMÉ
BRAZZAVILLE
KINSHASA
Douala
Port-Gentil
Pointe-Noire
Kisangani
Mbandaka
Lubumbashi
Mbuji-Mayi
Kananga
Bukavu
Goma
Matadi
Lake Tanganyika
Lake Kivu
Lake Albert
76
80
64
82

Activities

Try a local delicacy, fried caterpillar, while ferrying across the mighty **Congo River**
Attend the week-long annual Ngombi Festival of urban African music in **Bangui**
See rainforest wildlife in **Cameroon's** Parc National du Korup
Dodge longhorns and ceremonial jesters at the Bull Festival at **Zlama**, Cameroon
Stroll beside the harbour in friendly **Malabo**, Equatorial Guinea's island capital
Watch horses race through the streets of **Kumbo**, Cameroon, in Nso Cultural Week
Visit a Baka (pygmy) village in **Kiri**, W DRC, and follow a guide into the dense forest in search of antelope, snakes and crocodiles

Loango National Park, Gabon: This half-submerged male hippopotamus is one of many species that can seen here. The park encompasses forest, savannah, wetlands and ocean so not only can visitors observe land animals, there are also opportunities to whalewatch as well.

East Africa

Burundi, Djibouti, Eritrea, Ethiopia, Kenya, Rwanda, Somalia, Sudan, Tanzania, Uganda

If any region deserves the title "birthplace of mankind", it is probably east Africa. Three million years ago early human beings lived in the Great Rift Valley. In the 3rd century BCE the Nubian empire flourished in Sudan. Axum in Ethiopia was arguably the world's first Christian kingdom, with awe-inspiring ancient churches and mountain-top monasteries. Southern Ethiopia, by contrast, is largely Muslim – witness the 99 mosques of 16th-century Harer. East Africa's vast lakes feed the mighty Nile and nourish a kaleidoscope of animals. The region is replete with picturesque beaches, offering many hidden gems for the intrepid, although much of it has been fraught with political turmoil and recurrent famine. More stable Kenya and Tanzania offer safari holidays in their great game parks and the ascent of Kilimanjaro is becoming something of a rite of passage for trekkers celebrating their 50th birthdays.

What to See

1 Nubian Pyramids (near Kabushiya) More ancient than their Egyptian cousins, the great pyramids recall the civilization of Meroe

2 Gonder Dubbed the "Camelot of Africa", this 17th-century castle has a church with dazzling murals

3 Lalibela Eleven beautiful and still-operative Axumite churches hewn from rock

4 Danakil Desert This volcanic depression attracts the more daring traveller to its steaming lava lakes

5 Balho (near Yoboki, Djibouti) Nomad village, offering insights into a way of life that is fast eroding

6 Burundi Despite local instability, Tutsi royal master drummers and Twa pottery are worth seeing

7 Lake Victoria Straddling Uganda, Kenya and Tanzania, the world's third largest lake is an outstanding natural feature/

8 Masai Mara National Reserve Package tours allow thousands to buy pretty soapstone sculptures, snap elephants and rhino, visit local villages and see the famous Masai jumping dancers

9 Olduvai Gorge (in the Serengeti Plain) Follow in the footsteps of the great palaeontologists to rediscover the sites of our earliest ancestors

10 Ngorongoro Crater Few places offer such a diversity of flora, fauna and dramatic, volcanic savannah scenery

11 Kilimanjaro Tanzania's perpetually snow-capped peak is the tallest in Africa – best visited in the dry months, June–October

12 Mombasa Brilliant white beaches, sophisticated nightlife, majestic views of the serene Indian Ocean and a unique blend of Arab, African and Portuguese culture

13 Zanzibar Long ruled by Arabs and Persians, with distinctive architecture, quaint alleyways and the pleasantly ubiquitous smell of cloves

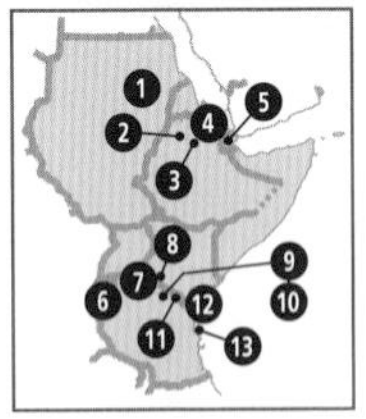

Ngorongoro Conservation Area, Tanzania: Like some surrealistic vision, a flamingo colony wades through shallow water in one of the soda-rich volcanic crater lakes of the Great Rift Valley. Blessed by plentiful rain from March to May, these lakes attract birds in droves. The Ngorongoro Crater forms the southeastern corner of the Serengeti National Park, a vast park of 14,763 sq km (5,700 sq miles) in area.

74

78

140

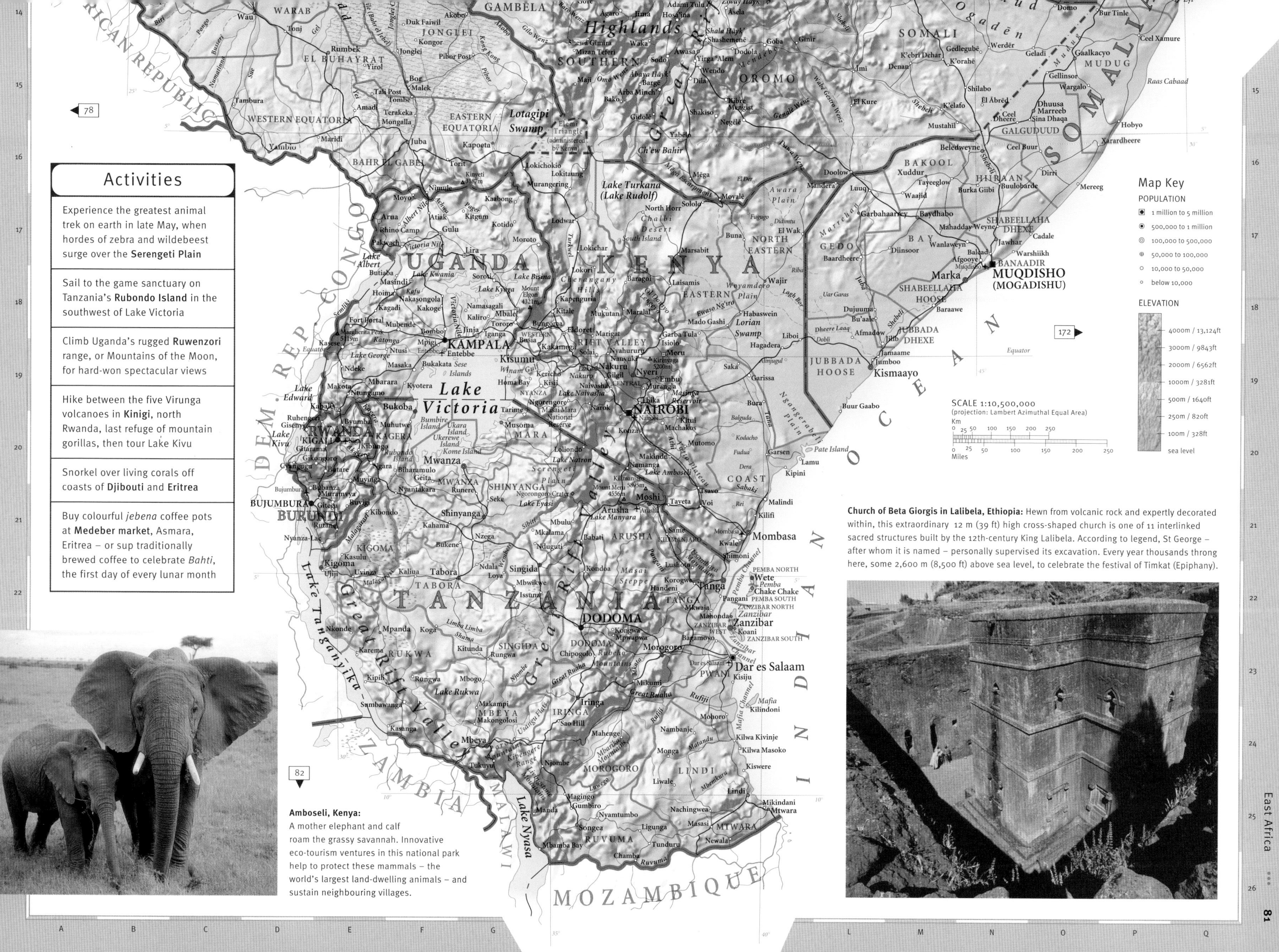
Map Key
POPULATION
1 million to 5 million
500,000 to 1 million
100,000 to 500,000
50,000 to 100,000
10,000 to 50,000
below 10,000
ELEVATION
4000m / 13,124ft
3000m / 9843ft
2000m / 6562ft
1000m / 3281ft
500m / 1640ft
250m / 820ft
100m / 328ft
sea level
SCALE 1:10,500,000
(projection: Lambert Azimuthal Equal Area)
Km
Miles
KENYA
UGANDA
TANZANIA
SOMALIA
INDIAN OCEAN
DEM. REP. CONGO
ZAMBIA
MALAWI
MOZAMBIQUE
RWANDA
BURUNDI
Lake Victoria
Lake Turkana (Lake Rudolf)
Lake Tanganyika
Lake Nyasa
NAIROBI
KAMPALA
DODOMA
MUQDISHO (MOGADISHU)
Mombasa
Dar es Salaam
Zanzibar
Kismaayo
Great Rift Valley
Equator

78

172

82

Activities

Experience the greatest animal trek on earth in late May, when hordes of zebra and wildebeest surge over the **Serengeti Plain**

Sail to the game sanctuary on Tanzania's **Rubondo Island** in the southwest of Lake Victoria

Climb Uganda's rugged **Ruwenzori** range, or Mountains of the Moon, for hard-won spectacular views

Hike between the five Virunga volcanoes in **Kinigi**, north Rwanda, last refuge of mountain gorillas, then tour Lake Kivu

Snorkel over living corals off coasts of **Djibouti** and **Eritrea**

Buy colourful *jebena* coffee pots at **Medeber market**, Asmara, Eritrea – or sup traditionally brewed coffee to celebrate *Bahti*, the first day of every lunar month

Amboseli, Kenya: A mother elephant and calf roam the grassy savannah. Innovative eco-tourism ventures in this national park help to protect these mammals – the world's largest land-dwelling animals – and sustain neighbouring villages.

Church of Beta Giorgis in Lalibela, Ethiopia: Hewn from volcanic rock and expertly decorated within, this extraordinary 12 m (39 ft) high cross-shaped church is one of 11 interlinked sacred structures built by the 12th-century King Lalibela. According to legend, St George – after whom it is named – personally supervised its excavation. Every year thousands throng here, some 2,600 m (8,500 ft) above sea level, to celebrate the festival of Timkat (Epiphany).

Southern Africa

Angola, Botswana, Lesotho, Malawi, Mozambique, Namibia, South Africa, Swaziland, Zambia, Zimbabwe

Freed from its pariah status during the apartheid years, South Africa has blossomed into a world-beating tourist destination, mixing mountains, great rivers, vineyards, beaches and game reserves with desert, forest and arid savannah. The Cape's Mediterranean flora and fauna contrast with a humid subtropical zone around Kwazulu/Natal. South Africa's music, cuisine and sport are justly famous. Architecture ranges from gracious, 18th-century, Cape Dutch farmsteads to dazzling, contemporary, Ndebele homes. For nightlife, gold-fuelled Johannesburg vies with Cape Town's old-world charm. The years of racial division and exploitation are sensitively evoked. In Cape Town this is done both at museums like Robben Island and Old Slave Lodge, and through gestures like hanging the once-banned painting "Black Christ" in the National Gallery.

Visitors are assured excellent infrastructure and easy transport to attractive, neighbouring states. Consider the breathtaking alpine vistas of the inland kingdoms of Lesotho and Swaziland, the watery charms of Malawi or those underexplored former Portuguese colonies, Angola and Mozambique. Namibia boasts the dramatic springtime blooming of the Kalahari Desert. Botswana is famed for its San (Bushmen) settlements and teeming flamingos and pelicans. While political strife largely precludes visitors enjoying Zimbabwe, adjoining Zambia abounds with animal and birdlife.

What to See

1 Lake Nyasa
Africa's third largest lake hosts diverse wildlife and water sports

2 Etosha
Virtually every regional species is found in this national park – most numerous are springbok

3 Spitzkoppe
(near Swakopmund)
A hikers' paradise known for its jewellery, black marble, rocky outcrops, yellow Butter Trees and San (Bushmen) rock art

4 Okakarara village
Herero male elders still communicate with ancestors over an eternal flame by night

5 Okavango Delta
Wild dogs, giraffe, zebra, wildebeest and a myriad of antelope populate the world's largest inland delta

6 Victoria Falls
Known locally as Musi-O-Tunya (The Smoke That Thunders), this majestic spectacle is best viewed from the Zambian side of the border with Zimbabwe

7 Lake Kariba
The man-made lake on the Zambezi offers bungee jumping, fishing and scuba diving, plus whitewater rafting downstream from the Victoria Falls

8 Matobo Hills
(near Bulawayo)
Rock forms used as Stone Age dwellings, and as a spiritual focus

9 Great Zimbabwe Ruins (near Masvingo)
The mysterious stone complex built by an indigenous civilization of great sophistication

10 Kruger National Park
This vast park features fantastic wildlife safaris alongside landscape attractions like the Blyde River Canyon and Pilgrim's Rest

11 Maputo
This irrepressible capital city is fast becoming a tourism magnet and luxury conference venue

12 Kwazulu/Natal
In the shade of the Drakensberg mountains, expert Zulu craftswomen sell their wares and show visitors the skills of grass-weaving (*uhasha*) or threading exquisite bead designs

13 Hluhluwe Umfolozi Park (near St. Lucia)
Eco-tourists may spot rare white rhino, or explore the nearby St Lucia Wetland Park

14 Wild Coast
(near Port St. Johns)
Africa untrammelled reveals itself in the rolling hills of the Eastern Cape – pipe-smoking women, distinctive red blankets, clicking Xhosa language and haunting music

15 Port Elizabeth
An eccentric reminder of Britain in South Africa, the "windy city" has fine beaches, a pyramid and an Oceanarium

16 Karoo National Park
(near Beaufort West)
The dinosaur skeleton park of this arid region attracts palaeontologists

17 Stellenbosch
This beautiful Afrikaner university town of whitewashed walls and gables is set in world-famous wine country

18 Cape Town
South Africa's "mother city" has the renovated Victoria and Albert Docks, 17th-century pentagonal castle and the Parade's flower-sellers

19 District Six Museum (in Cape Town)
Homage to a once thriving, racially mixed community, destroyed under apartheid

20 Robben Island
(off Cape Town) Nelson Mandela's prison cell draws many to the once-forbidden island, with views of Table Mountain. It holds curiosities like a Muslim *kramat (shrine)*, leper church, and governor's house

Blyde River Canyon, South Africa: An intrepid hiker surveys the canyon carved by the Blyde River over the ages through shale and quartzite. Located at the centre of South Africa's huge Kruger National Park, this lookout point offers magnificent views.

Activities

- Roll the dice at casinos in **Swaziland**
- Canoe down Zambia's **Zambezi** river
- Fish off Angola's coast at **Palmeirinhas**
- Take a township tour in **Soweto**
- Swim with Jackass penguins at sheltered **Boulders Beach,** near Cape Town
- Ride an ostrich in South Africa's **Little Karoo**
- Groove to jazz, hip-hop and *kwaito* at **Cape Town's** North Sea Music Festival
- Shop for spices and curios in **Durban**
- Hike the five-day Otter Trail in **Tsitsikamma National Park,** South Africa

SCALE 1:10,500,000
(projection: Lambert Azimuthal Equal Area)
Km 0 25 50 100 150 200 250 300
Miles 0 25 50 100 150 200 250 300

78
80
64
12
13

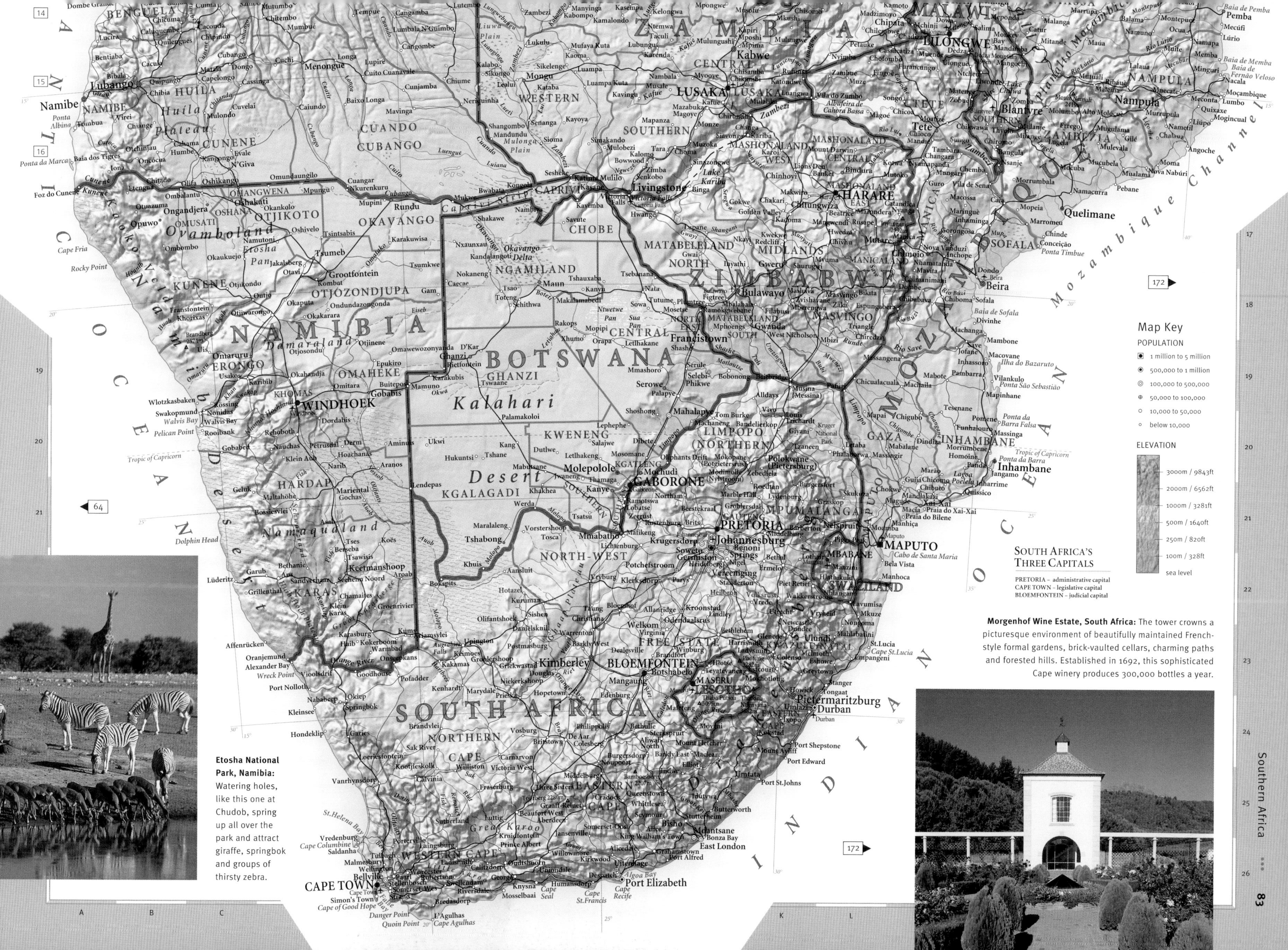
Map Key
POPULATION
1 million to 5 million
500,000 to 1 million
100,000 to 500,000
50,000 to 100,000
10,000 to 50,000
below 10,000
ELEVATION
3000m / 9843ft
2000m / 6562ft
1000m / 3281ft
500m / 1640ft
250m / 820ft
100m / 328ft
sea level
SOUTH AFRICA'S THREE CAPITALS
PRETORIA – administrative capital
CAPE TOWN – legislative capital
BLOEMFONTEIN – judicial capital
ZAMBIA
MALAWI
MOZAMBIQUE
ZIMBABWE
BOTSWANA
NAMIBIA
SOUTH AFRICA
LESOTHO
SWAZILAND
ATLANTIC OCEAN
INDIAN OCEAN
Mozambique Channel
Kalahari Desert
Namib Desert
LUSAKA
HARARE
LILONGWE
WINDHOEK
GABORONE
PRETORIA
MAPUTO
MASERU
MBABANE
BLOEMFONTEIN
CAPE TOWN
Johannesburg
Durban
Port Elizabeth
East London
Beira
Bulawayo
Livingstone
Tropic of Capricorn
172
64
172

Etosha National Park, Namibia: Watering holes, like this one at Chudob, spring up all over the park and attract giraffe, springbok and groups of thirsty zebra.

Morgenhof Wine Estate, South Africa: The tower crowns a picturesque environment of beautifully maintained French-style formal gardens, brick-vaulted cellars, charming paths and forested hills. Established in 1692, this sophisticated Cape winery produces 300,000 bottles a year.

Europe

"If you live in Europe...things change...
but continuity never seems to break.
You don't have to throw the past away." NADINE GORDIMER, b.1923

Physical Europe

Europe may be relatively small – dwarfed by Asia, Africa and the Americas in terms of land mass – but it is a continent of considerable physical diversity. To the south lie the young peaks of the Alpine uplands, which include the Pyrenees, the Alps and the Carpathian Mountains, as well as the Apennines and the Dinaric Alps. Stretching from the Fens of eastern England to the Ural Mountains in Russia is the fertile North European Plain, much of it, especially in the east, covered in woodland. North of this, the Atlantic Highlands include the Cairngorms of Scotland and the Scandinavian mountain ranges. The glaciation that shaped much of the far north has left distinctive marks, such as the fjords of Norway and the shallow lakes of Finland.

Mountains

The Alps, stretching across France, Italy, Switzerland, Germany, Austria, Liechtenstein, and Slovenia, have for many years been a centre for winter sports. The increase in temperature following global warming is causing consternation that the season is shortening due to lack of snow.

Rivers

The rivers of Europe resonate with the history of war and empire. The Thames was once the centre of a global empire built on the back of British naval strength. The Rhine, flowing from Switzerland to the North Sea, formed the northern border of the Roman Empire. The Danube, rising nearby but flowing east to the Black Sea, saw the ebb and flow of Christendom and Muslim Turkish rule.

Map Key
ELEVATION

4000m / 13,124ft
3000m / 9843ft
2000m / 6562ft
1000m / 3281ft
500m / 1640ft
250m / 820ft
100m / 328ft
sea level

PLATE MARGINS

constructive
destructive
conservative
uncertain

physiographic regions

SCALE 1:25,500,000
(projection: Lambert Azimuthal Equal Area)

Km 0 100 200 400 600

0 50 100 200 300 400 500 600 Miles

Forests

Forests stretch across much of Germany and eastern Europe, often framing turreted castles on towering crags. European forest cover is expanding by half a million hectares a year.

Climate

Europe's climate is generally mild. It experiences few extremes in temperature, apart from the far north and the sun-baked south, making it ideal for agriculture. Rain falls in moderate quantities, although visitors to Ireland or Wales may find it can last a long time. The warm air coming from the North Atlantic Drift allows western Europe to experience much gentler weather than would otherwise be possible at such a latitude; the Mediterranean flora of western Ireland are one sign of this. In the east and north, winters can be harsh and heavy snows are common.

Jura mountains, Switzerland: Evergreen fir forests that cover much of the mountainous regions of Europe are well suited to survive the winter snows.

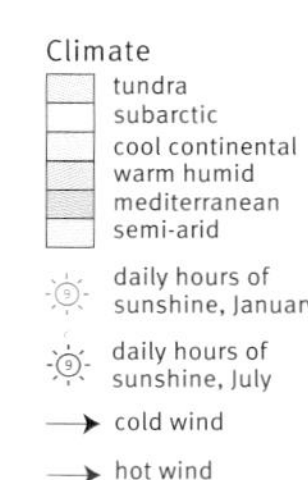
Climate
tundra
subarctic
cool continental
warm humid
mediterranean
semi-arid
daily hours of sunshine, January
daily hours of sunshine, July
cold wind
hot wind

Arctic Circle
Reykjavík
Karasjok
Murmansk
Pechora
Bodø
Pajala
Hoyvík
Kajaani
Archangel
Härnösand
Sveg
Bergen
Oslo
Helsinki
St Petersburg
Kirov
Ufa
Malin Head
Dundee
Stockholm
Tallinn
Vestervig
Gothenburg
Shannon
Morecambe
Riga
Moscow
Malmö
Hamburg
Exeter
London
Minsk
Brussels
Berlin
Warsaw
Paris
Kharkiv
Prague
Astrakhan'
A Coruña
Bordeaux
Zürich
Munich
Rostov-na-Donu
Lyon
Vienna
Bratislava
Toulouse
Zagreb
Simferopol'
Milan
Lisbon
Madrid
Monaco
Belgrade
Bucharest
Sarajevo
Sofia
Constanța
Barcelona
Gibraltar
Palma
Naples
Tirana
İstanbul
Cagliari
Salonica
Messina
Athens
Mistral
Bora
Sirocco

Temperature

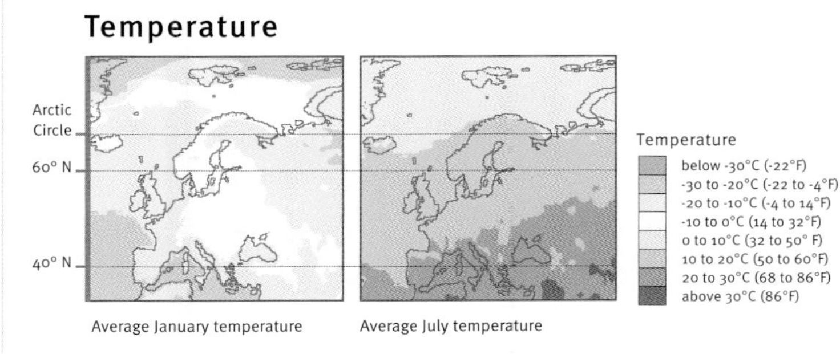
Arctic Circle
60° N
40° N
Temperature
below -30°C (-22°F)
-30 to -20°C (-22 to -4°F)
-20 to -10°C (-4 to 14°F)
-10 to 0°C (14 to 32°F)
0 to 10°C (32 to 50° F)
10 to 20°C (50 to 60°F)
20 to 30°C (68 to 86°F)
above 30°C (86°F)

Average January temperature

Average July temperature

Rainfall

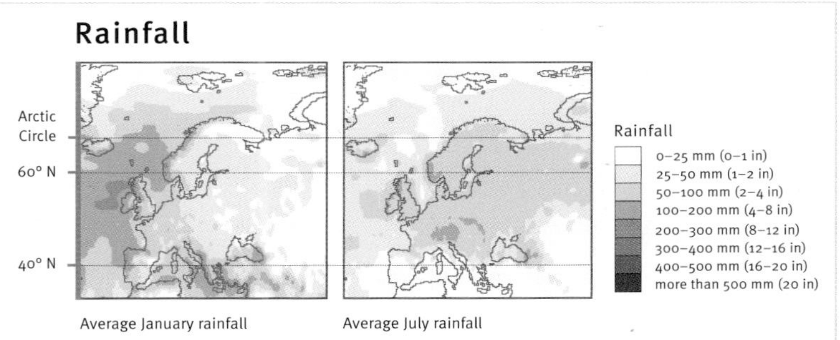
Arctic Circle
60° N
40° N
Rainfall
0–25 mm (0–1 in)
25–50 mm (1–2 in)
50–100 mm (2–4 in)
100–200 mm (4–8 in)
200–300 mm (8–12 in)
300–400 mm (12–16 in)
400–500 mm (16–20 in)
more than 500 mm (20 in)

Average January rainfall

Average July rainfall

Using Land and Sea

Despite urbanization and high population density, over half of Europe's land is still agricultural. France is western Europe's leading agricultural producer. Large subsidies for Europe's farmers have come under attack as too costly, wasteful and unfair, denying market access to much poorer producers in developing countries. Some communities that depend heavily on fishing face a serious crisis, many stocks having been brought to the edge of extinction by overexploitation.

Using the Land and Sea
cropland
forest
ice cap
mountain region
pasture
tundra
wetland
major conurbations
cattle
goats
pigs
poultry
reindeer
sheep
cereals
citrus fruits
cotton
fishing
fodder
fruit
olive oil
potatoes
rice
root crops
roses
shellfish
sunflowers
timber
tobacco
vineyards
ATLANTIC OCEAN
North Sea
Baltic Sea
Black Sea
Mediterranean Sea
Pechora
Ural Mountains
Northern Dvina
Perm'
Kazan'
Ufa
Samara
Volga
Oslo
Stockholm
St Petersburg
Nizhniy Novgorod
Moscow
Glasgow
Dublin
Leeds
Liverpool
Manchester
Birmingham
Copenhagen
Hamburg
London
The Hague
Amsterdam
Rotterdam
Berlin
Minsk
Brussels
Essen
Elbe
Vistula
Warsaw
Paris
Loire
Seine
Rhine
Frankfurt am Main
Prague
Kiev
Dnieper
Kharkiv
Don
Dnipropetrovs'k
Donets'k
Stuttgart
Danube
Munich
Vienna
Dniester
Lyon
Rhône
Milan
Budapest
Odesa
Turin
Po
Caucasus
Tagus
Madrid
Ebro
Pyrenees
Marseille
Barcelona
Bucharest
Rome
Sofia
İstanbul
Athens

Alentejo plains, Portugal: A patchwork of cork oak and olive tree plantations alternate with wheatfields to maximize land productivity.

Political Europe

Rooted in the ideas and learning of ancient Greece and Rome, Western civilization as it developed from the Renaissance to the present day reflects the overwhelming ascendancy of European powers. Its imprint spread throughout the "known world", reaching ever further across the oceans through European discovery and colonization. Democracy, a concept born in Athens, reignited by the French Revolution and given durable parliamentary form in the United Kingdom, has taken hold everywhere on the continent since the defeat of fascism (in 1945) and the collapse of communism (since 1989). Nationalism has fragmented the Balkans and fuelled regionalism in Belgium, Spain and elsewhere, but the drive towards integration is manifest in the expanding membership of the European Union.

Houses of Parliament, London, UK: Overlooking the River Thames, Big Ben towers above the 19th-century Palace of Westminster, home of the UK's so-called "mother of parliaments".

Standard of Living

Standard of Living
(UN Human Development Index)
low
high

The countries of northern and western Europe enjoy some of the highest living standards in the world, with Norway and Switzerland among the most prosperous. Further east people are much poorer, particularly in the Balkans, but nowhere else on the continent comes close to Moldova for grinding rural poverty.

Map Key

POPULATION

- above 5 million
- 1 million to 5 million
- 500,000 to 1 million
- 100,000 to 500,000
- 50,000 to 100,000
- 10,000 to 50,000
- Country capital

BORDERS

- full international border

SCALE 1:17,250,000
(projection: Lambert Azimuthal Equal Area)

Km 0 50 100 200 300 400 500 600 700 800 900 1000

Miles 0 50 100 200 300 400 500 600 700

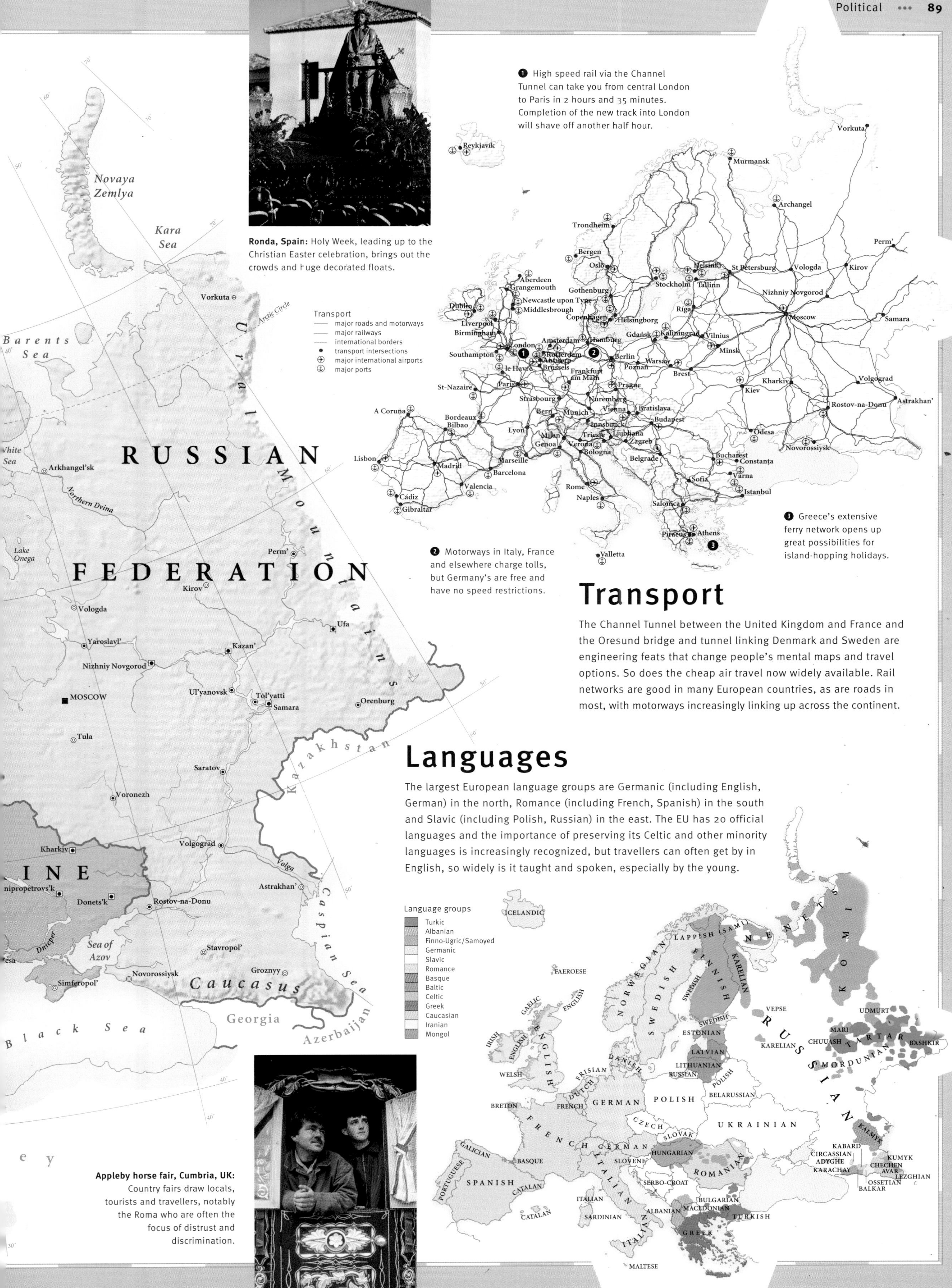
Transport
major roads and motorways
major railways
international borders
transport intersections
major international airports
major ports
Language groups
Turkic
Albanian
Finno-Ugric/Samoyed
Germanic
Slavic
Romance
Basque
Baltic
Celtic
Greek
Caucasian
Iranian
Mongol
RUSSIAN FEDERATION
Ural Mountains
Kazakhstan
Caspian Sea
Black Sea
Caucasus
Georgia
Azerbaijan

Ronda, Spain: Holy Week, leading up to the Christian Easter celebration, brings out the crowds and huge decorated floats.

❶ High speed rail via the Channel Tunnel can take you from central London to Paris in 2 hours and 35 minutes. Completion of the new track into London will shave off another half hour.

❷ Motorways in Italy, France and elsewhere charge tolls, but Germany's are free and have no speed restrictions.

❸ Greece's extensive ferry network opens up great possibilities for island-hopping holidays.

Transport

The Channel Tunnel between the United Kingdom and France and the Oresund bridge and tunnel linking Denmark and Sweden are engineering feats that change people's mental maps and travel options. So does the cheap air travel now widely available. Rail networks are good in many European countries, as are roads in most, with motorways increasingly linking up across the continent.

Languages

The largest European language groups are Germanic (including English, German) in the north, Romance (including French, Spanish) in the south and Slavic (including Polish, Russian) in the east. The EU has 20 official languages and the importance of preserving its Celtic and other minority languages is increasingly recognized, but travellers can often get by in English, so widely is it taught and spoken, especially by the young.

Appleby horse fair, Cumbria, UK: Country fairs draw locals, tourists and travellers, notably the Roma who are often the focus of distrust and discrimination.

Mont St-Michel, France

Lake District, England

Riga, Latvia

Puffins, Iceland

Kassopi, Greece

Journeys

Many European countries pride themselves on excellent rail networks, making this a fine way to reach the continent's many great historic cities. Unlimited travel on "Inter Rail" tickets, pre-paid for specified periods, is especially popular among students. The recent revolution in the cost of short-haul air travel, with the rapid growth of budget airlines, has brought a boom in short "city breaks" and "fly-drive" holidays, where the flexibility of a hire car makes a whole region easily accessible. Motorists will find numerous scenic drives throughout the continent, such as the renowned Amalfi drive along the coast of central Italy. Cruises are both popular and relaxing, whether by sea (particularly in the Baltic and the Mediterranean) or down one of the great rivers (the Danube is second to none). A canal holiday, along France's famous Canal du Midi for example, offers an even more leisurely pace. At the other extreme, choose the excitement of an icebreaker trip to the Arctic.

Budapest, Hungary: The waters of the Danube river reflect the Neo-Gothic parliament building. Winding its way through 2,740 km (1,700 miles) of European heartland, from the Black Forest to the Black Sea, the Danube forms a natural border between several countries.

Great European Journeys

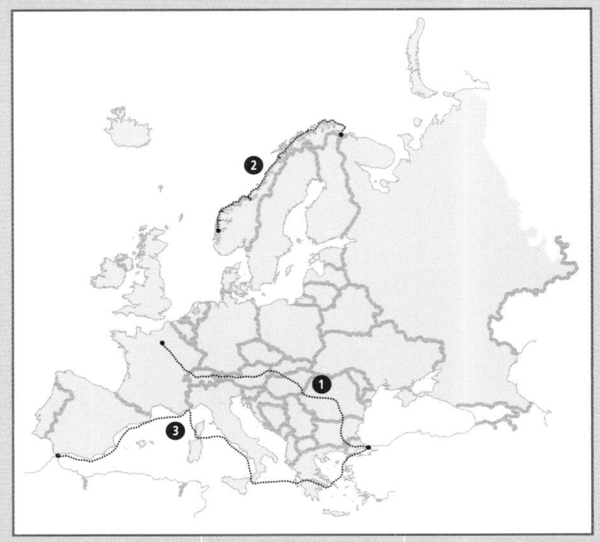

❶ Orient Express
Paris, France – Istanbul, Turkey
2,900 km (1,800 miles)
The original route of Europe's most famous and luxurious train ride is once again available, a six-day trip from the French capital across the Alps to Budapest then Bucharest and on to Turkey. Other options include London and Venice.

❷ Fjord Cruise, Norway
Bergen – Kirkenes
2,334 km (1,450 miles)
Sailed by the Vikings 1,000 years ago, this "North Way" takes you along the spectacular, rugged coastline of Norway's famous fjords, steep-sided inlets with hanging waterfalls and on into the Arctic Circle, almost to Russia.

❸ Mediterranean Cruise
Strait of Gibraltar – Istanbul, Turkey
4,000 km (2,500 miles)
A glorious way to see the key cities of the Mediterranean while basking in the sun and enjoying the relaxed lifestyle of the idyllic islands. Many shorter routes are available, but for those with time, enjoy the full trip.

Natural Sights

Northwestern Europe's green Atlantic coastlines, in the light of long summer days, have a powerful appeal for visitors to Ireland, Scotland and Norway. In a continent that can seem bursting with people, these remote locations are a great way to get away, offering scenic and generally quite straightforward hiking possibilities – even the chance of rainy weather does not dampen most people's enthusiasm. The Alps form the dramatic backbone of central Europe, with picturesque lakes and valleys that have enchanted hikers for generations. Some of the world's most challenging slopes and rock faces occur in the Alps and the Pyrenees also attract ardent skiers and climbers. The forests of Germany and Poland have their own distinctive atmosphere, while the fantastic coastlines of the Mediterranean are especially loved by holiday-makers.

What to See

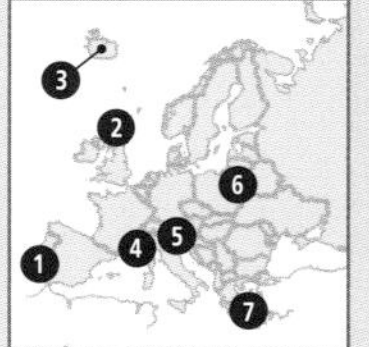

❶ Algarve, Portugal
Portugal's southern coastline is known for its popular beaches and colourful cliffs

❷ Scottish Highlands
Explore the haunting beauty of the valleys, mountains and lochs

❸ Iceland
Volcanic wonderland of hot springs, vast glaciers and waterfalls

❹ Camargue, France
Rich wetlands famous for flamingos and wild white horses

❺ Alps
Dramatic beauty of jagged outcrops in Europe's highest mountain range

❻ Bialowieza Forest, Poland
Unique lowland forest roamed by endangered European bison

❼ Greek Islands
Dotted liberally across the waters of the Aegean Sea these offer sandy beaches, ancient ruins and hot nightlife

Godafoss falls, Iceland: These impressive horseshoe falls, whose name means "Waterfall of the Gods", are in the north of Iceland. The island's relative youth in geological terms has created a raw and evolving landscape rife with waterfalls and volcanic activity.

Geiranger Fjord, Norway

Kremlin, Moscow, Russia

Amsterdam, Netherlands

Tallinn, Estonia

Lauterbrunnen, Switzerland

Activities

Football is Europe's biggest sport, with passions running high. It attracts far more fans than golf or tennis and tickets are red hot for matches between top clubs like Manchester United, Inter Milan and Real Madrid. The region's most popular outdoor pursuits are walking and skiing. For evening entertainment, London is renowned for its West End theatre, Vienna and Milan for opera, Berlin and Barcelona for nightlife and Rome and Paris for overall ambience. Music festivals bring other cities to the fore – Salzburg (Austria) in July, or Bayreuth (Germany) in August for the music of Wagner. The Edinburgh Festival, also in August, featuring alternative music, dance and drama, is famous as a springboard for new talent. Pop and rock festivals attract huge numbers of young people to venues such as Glastonbury in England and Roskilde in Denmark.

What to Do

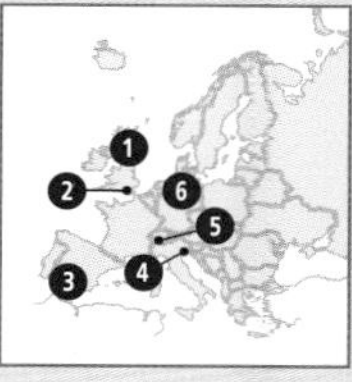

1
2
6
5
3
4

1 Golf, St Andrews, Scotland
Play on golf's oldest and most famous courses

2 West End, London, UK
Take in a show at one of around 50 theatres

3 Bullfights, Seville, Spain
The Feria de Abril is a high point – the season runs from Easter through the summer

4 Venice, Italy
A gondola is the best (and most expensive) way to glide around the enchanting canals

5 Matterhorn, Switzerland
A unique exhilarating climbing challenge for the suitably fit, with great skiing nearby

6 Berlin Philharmonic Orchestra, Germany
Attend a concert by Europe's top classical orchestra

Casa Batlló, Barcelona, Spain: The organic forms of Antoni Gaudí's architecture are dotted throughout Barcelona, giving it a unique and magical feel.

Cultural Sights

Impressive ancient remains are a striking feature throughout Europe, from prehistoric cave dwellings, earthworks and standing stones such as Stonehenge, to the architectural magnificence of Greek and Roman temples, palaces and amphitheatres, concentrated in but not limited to the Mediterranean area. The impact of Islam is strongest in Spain's Moorish heritage, while the shifting fortunes of European countries as leading world powers is reflected in the wealth of medieval cities from Spain, Portugal and France to the Low Countries and the UK as much as through the treasures of their superb museums. The surviving palaces and awesome religious buildings of Sweden, Poland, European Russia and central Europe testify to their periods of regional power. The finest flowering of the Renaissance, however, in art and architecture alike, can be found in Italy, the legacy of the rivalry between its once great city states.

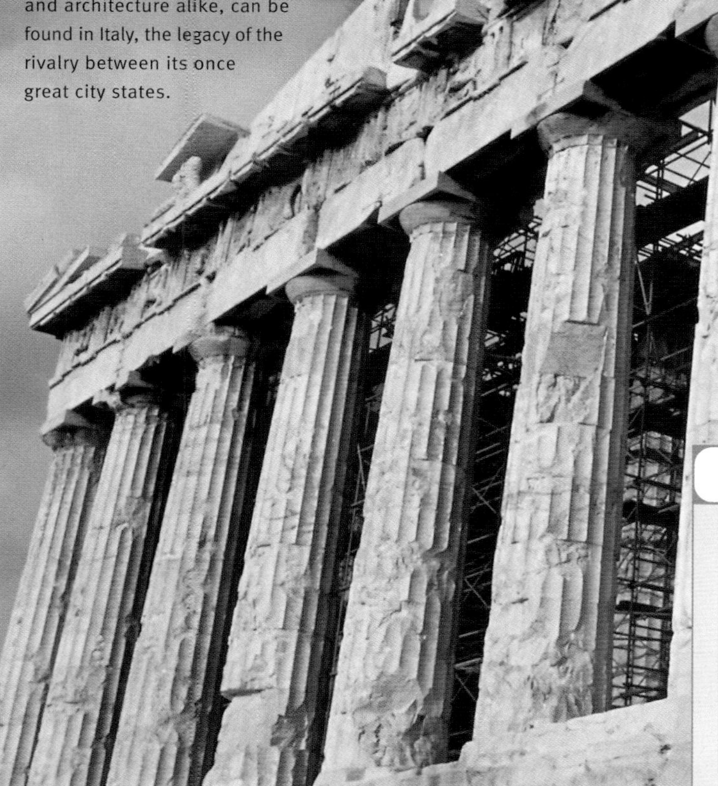
The Parthenon, Athens, Greece: This huge symbol of the might of ancient Greece, built 2,500 years ago, is a masterpiece of refined architectural design, based on the careful calculation of perfect proportions, with gently tapered columns and slightly curved horizontal planes. This all combines to make it supremely pleasing to the eye.

What to See

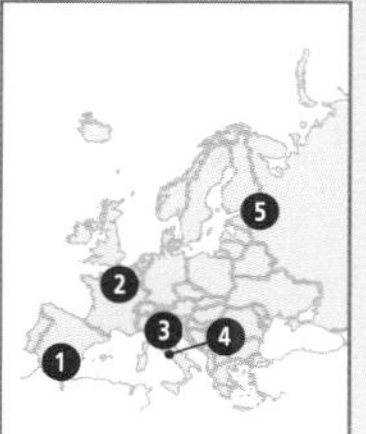

5
2
1
3
4

1 Alhambra, Granada, Spain
This Moorish palace justifies the inscription "Nothing in life could be more cruel than to be blind in Granada"

2 Louvre, Paris, France
The world's largest art museum, most famous for its Renaissance masterpieces such as Leonardo da Vinci's enigmatic *Mona Lisa* and classical treasures like the *Venus de Milo*

3 Duomo, Florence, Italy
Brunelleschi's vast octagonal dome and Giotto's bell tower make this beautiful cathedral the crowning achievement of Florentine architecture

4 Colosseum, Rome, Italy
The imperial Roman capital's atmospheric amphitheatre hosted bloody gladiator battles

5 Petrodvorets, Saint Petersburg, Russia
Peter the Great's Grand Palace is a dazzling display of interior opulence and magnificent gardens

Scandinavia, Finland & Iceland

Denmark, Norway, Sweden, Finland, Iceland

Jutting into the Arctic Circle, this northern swathe of Europe has some of the continent's harshest environments, but also some of its most magnificent scenery. Iceland, sitting on the Mid-Atlantic Ridge, is an actively volcanic wonderland of waterfalls and glaciers, but in terms of landscape Norway is perhaps most famous, above all for the magnificent steep-sided fjords along its west coast. A boat trip north from Bergen or Trondheim is a fine way to enjoy this coastline, as well as giving an appreciation of the rigours faced by generations of fishermen. Norway is also a departure point for expeditions to the North Pole.

Standards of living are high, making the region expensive for tourists. Norwegians, Icelanders, Danes and Swedes speak closely related languages, whereas Finnish is quite distinct, brought from the east by its early settlers. The Lapps, or Sami, maintain their traditional, reindeer-herding way of life in the northern regions of Norway, Sweden, and Finland.

What to See

Southern Scandinavia
see pp94–95

1 Myvatn
Beautiful lake and hot springs. Nearby are the still-smouldering Krafla volcano and Namaskard sulphurous mudpools

2 Geysir
Home on the eponymous "geyser", now sadly dormant, a superheated jet bursts skyward from the Strokkur geyser, its near neighbour, every five minutes

3 Gulfoss
(near Geysir) In an island of impressive waterfalls, Gulfoss, meaning "golden falls", is the most scenic

4 Glacier Lagoon
(near Hofn)
Awesome lagoon of floating blue and white icebergs, used as a location in several James Bond movies

5 Norwegian Fjords
Stretching from Stavanger to North Cape, these long, narrow inlets, cut into the mountains by glaciers, are among the world's most dramatic landscape formations

6 Icehotel
(in Jukkasjarvi) This unusual complex is built every October from thousands of tons of ice. Inside, a chilly -5°C, it is well insulated from the -20 to -30°C outside

7 Savonlinna Castle
Perched on an island in Finland's scenic Lake Region and built in 1475, Scandinavia's best-preserved medieval castle has several interesting architectural quirks

8 Helsinki
Modelled on Saint Petersburg, the Finnish capital has museums focusing on its culture.

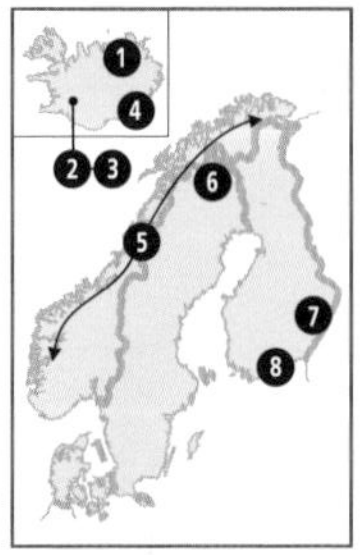

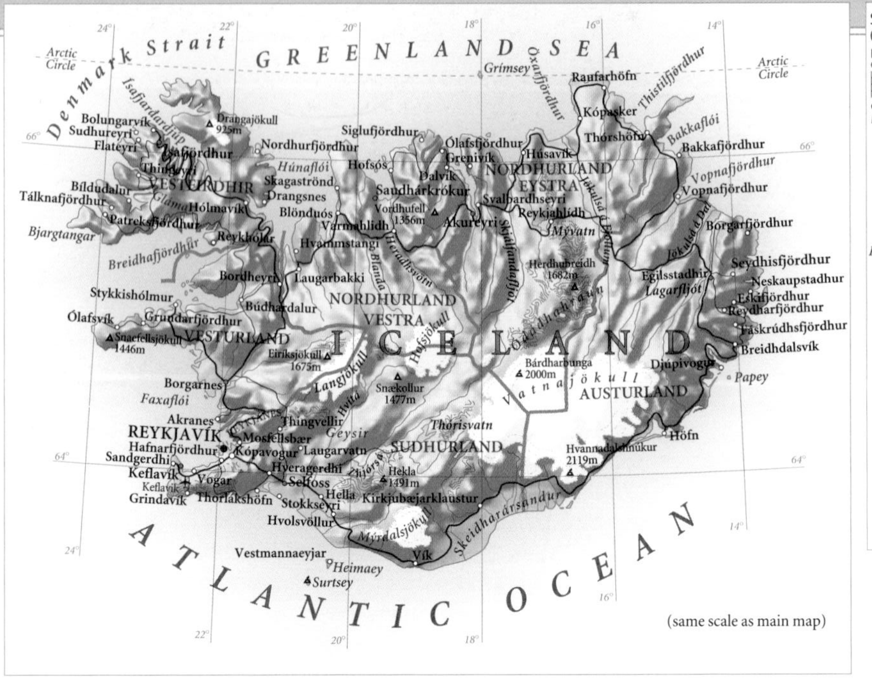

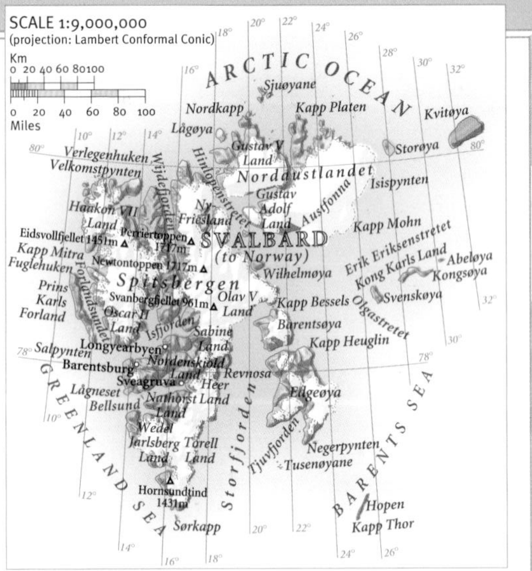

Svartifoss, Iceland: Black hexagonal basalt columns frame this fabulous waterfall in Iceland's Skaftafell National Park.

Uspenski Cathedral, Helsinki: This red-brick cathedral, built in the 1860s, has 13 gold onion domes representing Jesus Christ and his disciples.

(same scale as main map)

SCALE 1:9,000,000
(projection: Lambert Conformal Conic)

196

124

Map Key

POPULATION
- 500,000 to 1 million
- 100,000 to 500,000
- 50,000 to 100,000
- 10,000 to 50,000
- below 10,000

ELEVATION
- 2000m / 6562ft
- 1000m / 3281ft
- 500m / 1640ft
- 250m / 820ft
- 100m / 328ft
- sea level

SCALE 1:5,500,000
(projection: Lambert Conformal Conic)
Km
Miles
NORWEGIAN SEA
NORTH SEA
Skagerrak
Kattegat
BALTIC SEA
Gulf of Bothnia
Gulf of Finland
NORWAY
SWEDEN
FINLAND
DENMARK
GERMANY
OSLO
STOCKHOLM
HELSINKI
KØBENHAVN
ÅLAND
Gotland
Öland
Bornholm
64
100
118
124

Geiranger Fjord: Norway's fjords are renowned for their dramatic scenery – and many people think Geiranger is the best. Cruises take tourists past sparkling waterfalls that appear to hang from the steep mountainsides.

Activities

- Go whale watching off **Olafsvik**, Iceland and see humpback, minke or blue whales
- Plaster on a natural mudpack and relax in the hot waters of the **Blue Lagoon**, Iceland
- Snowmobile on **Vatnajokull**, Iceland, the largest glacier in Europe
- Enjoy the midnight sun at Norway's **North Cape**, in June–July, and Northern Lights (*aurora borealis*) in the winter
- Try Finland's largest woodsmoke sauna, plus the traditional practise of patting oneself with birch twigs, at **Kuopio**
- Send your Christmas cards from **Santa Claus Village** (near Rovaniemi), Finland
- See the world wife-carrying championships in **Sonkajarvi**, Finland (Saturday, early July)
- Take an icebreaker cruise from **Kemi** on the northern tip of the Gulf of Bothnia

Southern Scandinavia

Southern Norway, Southern Sweden, Denmark

The southern region of Scandinavia is the more easily habitable and accessible part, so not surprisingly it is also the economic and political hub. Norway, Sweden and Denmark have a closely interwoven history and enjoy a high degree of cultural unity, in both literature and art. Intricately carved woodwork is a distinctive feature of many buildings, whether residential or ecclesiastical and fine intact examples can still be found of the traditional wooden stave churches. Denmark, with less to boast of in the landscape department than its Scandinavian neighbours, can claim instead to have one of Europe's most vibrant and socially innovative cities, Copenhagen, as its capital. Swedes, on the other hand, would certainly advance the rival claims of Stockholm on this score.

Scandinavian summers can be surprisingly warm, if relatively brief, and outdoor holidays are popular, making the best of opportunities not only to walk in the wonderful countryside but to sail, swim or just mess around on the many lakes. The excellent winter sports facilities, particularly for cross-country skiing, are an even bigger draw for visitors to the Scandinavian mainland. Norway has the best ski resorts. Its capital, Oslo, even has facilities for quite extensive ski-touring – and summer hiking – within its boundaries, as well as fine museums reflecting a distinguished history of seagoing exploration, going back some 1,500 years to early Viking times.

Borgund stave church, Norway: This church in Sogn og Fjordane, built around 1200 CE, is one of the best examples of a wooden stave church – where wall timbers are placed vertically and the roof is supported by free-standing columns.

What to See

1 Nidaros Cathedral (in Trondheim) Dating back over 1,000 years, Scandinavia's largest Gothic church was, until 1908, the crowning place of Norway's kings

2 Norway in a Nutshell ® (from Bergen) A round trip by train and boat, showcasing some of the country's best scenery

3 Bygdoy Museum Island (in Oslo) The island's museums chronicle seafaring craft, the country's folk traditions, architecture and its pre-eminent playwright Henrik Ibsen

4 Drottningholm (near Stockholm) The royal palace's dazzling interior and gardens are likened to Versailles

5 Stockholm Sweden's capital links 14 islands offering a mix of elegant buildings, parks and museums

6 Kalmar Castle In a dramatic island setting, this 12th-century castle was remodelled as a Renaissance palace

7 Nimis (near Molle) Bizarre stairway and tower structure made entirely of driftwood

8 Kronborg Castle (in Helsingor) This grand 16th-century Danish castle is the setting for Shakespeare's *Hamlet*

9 Copenhagen Cosmopolitan capital, with fine museums and palaces amid charming canals and streets

10 Odense The birthplace of much-loved storyteller Hans Christian Andersen is a pleasant university town

11 Legoland (in Billund) Plastic Brick heaven, in the country of origin of this toy phenomenon, with many elaborate buildings such as Titania's palace

12 Arhus Charming, narrow, medieval streets lead to interesting churches and museums in this cultural capital

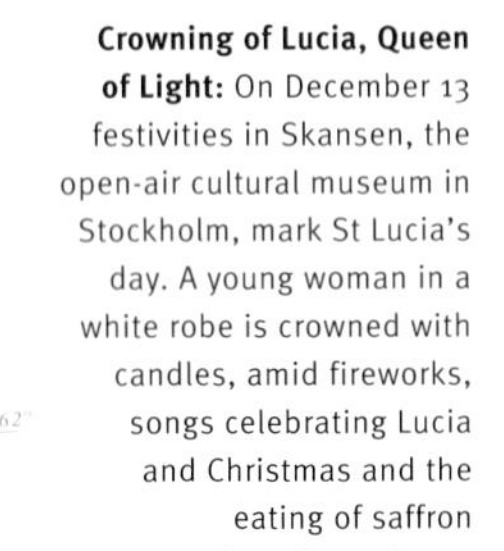

Crowning of Lucia, Queen of Light: On December 13 festivities in Skansen, the open-air cultural museum in Stockholm, mark St Lucia's day. A young woman in a white robe is crowned with candles, amid fireworks, songs celebrating Lucia and Christmas and the eating of saffron *lussekatter* buns.

92

96

Map Key
POPULATION
500,000 to 1 million
100,000 to 500,000
50,000 to 100,000
10,000 to 50,000
below 10,000
ELEVATION
2000m / 6562ft
1000m / 3281ft
500m / 1640ft
250m / 820ft
100m / 328ft
sea level
FAEROE ISLANDS (to Denmark)
TÓRSHAVN
ATLANTIC OCEAN
(same scale as main map)
SCALE 1:3,250,000
(projection: Lambert Conformal Conic)
Km
Miles
NORTH SEA
Skagerrak
Kattegat
BALTIC SEA
SWEDEN
DENMARK
GERMANY
FINLAND
Ålands Hav
OSLO
STOCKHOLM
KØBENHAVN (COPENHAGEN)
Göteborg (Gothenburg)
Malmö
Gotland
Öland
Bornholm
Jylland
Sjælland
118
96
100
110

Activities

Take in the four-day rock event – an extravaganza of live music known throughout Europe – at **Roskilde,** Denmark (end of June)

Watch the fireworks at the Fire Festival Regatta in **Silkeborg,** central Denmark (start of August)

Ski in **Lillehammer,** Norway, beautiful location of the 1994 Winter Olympics and suitable for all forms of skiing (mid-November to April)

Attend **Gotland's** Medieval Week. Islanders dress in medieval garb, tend market stalls and stage around 100 medieval events (in August)

Attend an opera – complete with original 18th-century scenery – at the unique Court Theatre in **Drottningholm Palace,** Stockholm

Copenhagen: The narrow Nyhavn (New Harbour) Canal is flanked by bustling pavement cafés on a broad promenade, lined with brightly coloured houses, three of which were lived in by Hans Christian Andersen.

The British Isles

United Kingdom, Ireland

A collection of nations sharing centuries of constantly intertwining history reside on these islands. England prides itself on its heritage. Its stately homes, castles, cities, engineering feats, countryside and constantly groundbreaking popular culture convey the wealth of ideas and self-confidence of its people over the centuries. London is one of the world's most visited cities, for its theatre, historic buildings, museums, galleries and royal pageantry.

Scotland has fine mountain scenery, memorable castles and the flavour of its peerless malt whiskys. Wales also has its imposing castles, often left by the English, and a cultural richness embodied in the annual Eisteddfod festival of poetry and music.

Northern Ireland is emerging from troubled times and boasts the unique Giant's Causeway and the ancestral beginnings of several US presidents. Its independent, prosperous neighbour, Ireland, has a rich Christian heritage with many artefacts and ruins from its heyday, during the 3rd-5th centuries, as one of the faith's leading centres.

Activities

- Walk the **Pennine Way**, from Edale in the Peak District 400 km (250 miles) to Kirk Yetholm by the Scottish border
- Shop at London's inimitable **Harrods**, then adjourn to the **Ritz** for tea
- Take the scenic railway to the top of **Snowdon**, Wales's highest peak
- Search for the fabled monster on Scotland's famous **Loch Ness**
- Attend the **Braemar Highland Games** and witness the best in Scottish pipe and drum bands, dancing and caber-tossing
- Try oysters, a local delicacy, at the **Galway Oyster Festival** (September)
- Kiss the Blarney Stone at **Blarney Castle**, near Cork, and get the gift of the gab – but beware of falling off the battlements!

Tobermory, Scotland: Small towns and beautiful castles dot the remote and mountainous Hebridean isles of Scotland, ideal for those wanting to get away from urban stress for hiking or fishing. In some places the Scots Gaelic tongue is still the main language.

Map Key

POPULATION
- above 5 million
- 1 million to 5 million
- 500,000 to 1 million
- 100,000 to 500,000
- 50,000 to 100,000
- 10,000 to 50,000
- below 10,000

ELEVATION
- 1000m / 3281ft
- 500m / 1640ft
- 250m / 820ft
- 100m / 328ft
- sea level

92

64

What to See

1 Scottish Highlands Spectacular mountains, glens, lochs and rivers, form the British Isles' most unspoiled and dramatic landscapes

2 Edinburgh Scotland's capital is known for its imposing castle and its August Festival of music, drama and entertainment

3 Lake District Stark mountains and shimmering lakes that have inspired writers as diverse as William Wordsworth and Beatrix Potter

4 York This fascinating walled city, well served by museums revealing its Roman and Viking past, has a medieval web of narrow streets

5 Caernarfon Castle Constructed in 1282 to subdue the Welsh, arguably the greatest of Edward I's castles

6 Blenheim Palace (near Oxford) Marking his defeat of the French in 1704, this lavish Baroque palace was given to the Duke of Marlborough. Winston Churchill was born here

7 Bath Famed before Roman times for its therapeutic waters and since the 18th century for its Georgian buildings

8 Stonehenge On an already ancient site, this massive stone circle was completed around 1500 BCE. Its purpose is still unclear

9 London Pageantry combines with history and culture in this great city. The Tower of London, British Museum and London Eye are highlights

10 Dublin James Joyce's city, as famous for its pubs as for Trinity College and the Book of Kells

11 Giant's Causeway According to legend, this extraordinary expanse of hexagonal stone columns was the work of giants

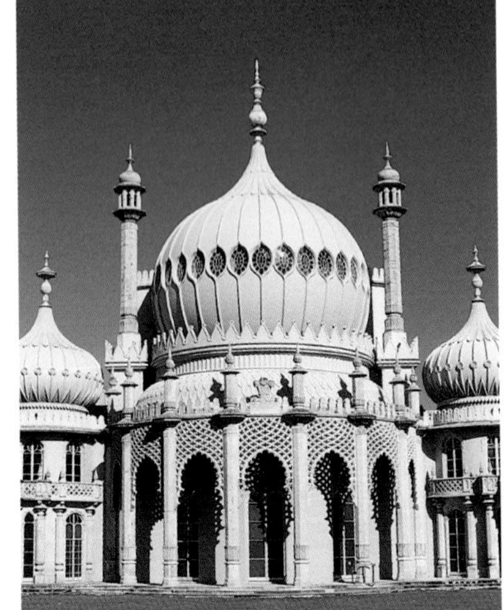

Brighton Pavilion, southern England: The Prince Regent built this exuberant oriental-style palace in the 1800s in the fashionable seaside resort of Brighton. Still popular with visitors today, for its fun-loving charm and great nightlife, the city is also noted for its gay scene.

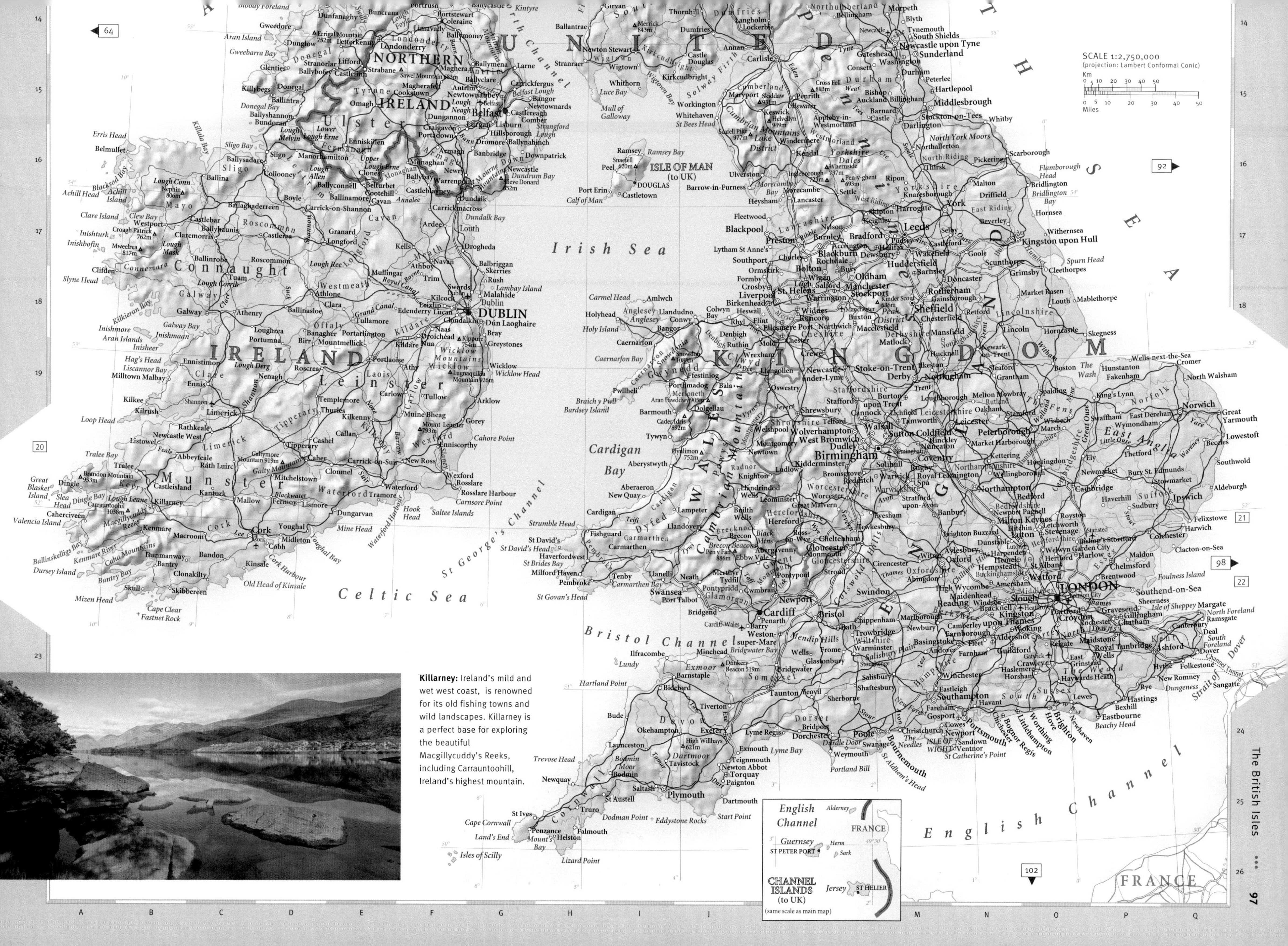
SCALE 1:2,750,000
(projection: Lambert Conformal Conic)
NORTH SEA
UNITED KINGDOM
ENGLAND
WALES
NORTHERN IRELAND
IRELAND
FRANCE
Irish Sea
Celtic Sea
English Channel
Bristol Channel
St George's Channel
North Channel
Cardigan Bay
ISLE OF MAN (to UK)
CHANNEL ISLANDS (to UK)
(same scale as main map)
LONDON
DUBLIN
Birmingham
Manchester
Liverpool
Cardiff
Belfast
Cork
Connaught
Munster
Leinster
Ulster
Cambrian Mountains
Pennines
Isles of Scilly

Killarney: Ireland's mild and wet west coast, is renowned for its old fishing towns and wild landscapes. Killarney is a perfect base for exploring the beautiful Macgillycuddy's Reeks, including Carrauntoohill, Ireland's highest mountain.

The Low Countries

Belgium, Luxembourg, Netherlands

The splendid old buildings of Bruges and Brussels reflect an extraordinary period of wealth in the 14th and early 15th centuries, when this region stood in the very forefront of world trade, science and culture. Its great seafaring traditions built up Rotterdam's position as the world's largest port and helped establish Antwerp, a 16th-century jewel, as the centre of the diamond trade. Amsterdam too has fine architecture, an intricate network of canals and a reputation for liberality. The heavy footprint of two World Wars across the region is marked by memorials and interpretative displays at key sites.

Many visitors seek out the great museums displaying the work of world-famous Flemish artists, including Rubens in Antwerp, Rembrandt, Vermeer and other 17th-century masters in Amsterdam and The Hague and the 19th-century impressionist Van Gogh, also in Amsterdam. Other delights include colourful fields of tulips in spring and landscapes dotted with traditional water-pumping windmills. These are part of the perpetual effort to preserve the extensive areas that lie below sea level and also include an impressive network of dams and dykes to protect them from flooding.

Alkmaar's market: This traditional Dutch cheese-making town still has Gouda and Edam laid out in the market on Friday mornings to be carried off on sledges by porters to the 500-year-old Weigh House on the left.

What to See

❶ **Amsterdam**
Great cultural centre, famous for its network of canals, fabulous art museums and coffee houses where smoking marijuana is accepted – and legal

❷ **The Anne Frank House** (in Amsterdam)
Where the daughter of a Jewish family, in hiding from the Nazis, kept her poignant diary until discovered and sent to Bergen-Belsen

❸ **Hoge Veluwe National Park**
(near Otterlo) Strange mix of forests and woods, shifting sands, and heathland, plus the Kröller-Müller Museum noted for its modern art collection

❹ **The Hague**
The Dutch political capital has fine parliament buildings and museums, built around the castle of the counts of Holland

❺ **Delft**
Charming 17th-century town with quaint canals and bridges, home of Vermeer and the famed blue and white pottery

❻ **Bruges**
Much of the historic city dates back some 700 years, and oversaw a flowering of Flemish art

❼ **Antwerp**
Rubens' former home town Traditionally a great intellectual and diamond centre. Large Gothic cathedral

❽ **Brussels**
Capital of Belgium and the European Union, known for fine food and its central Grand Place

❾ **Waterloo**
Scene of Wellington's defeat of Napoleon in 1815, with fascinating battle exhibits

❿ **Luxembourg**
Historic hilltop city with excellent location and interesting buildings, often overlooked by travellers

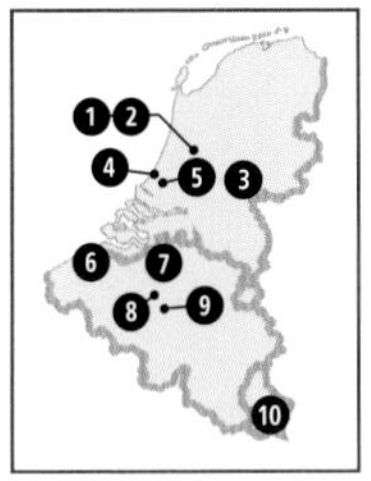

Map Key

POPULATION
- 500,000 to 1 million
- 100,000 to 500,000
- 50,000 to 100,000
- 10,000 to 50,000
- below 10,000

ELEVATION
- 500m / 1640ft
- 250m / 820ft
- 100m / 328ft
- sea level

◀ 96

100 ▶

100 ▶

NETHERLANDS' TWO CAPITALS

AMSTERDAM – capital
THE HAGUE – seat of government

NORTH SEA
GERMANY
FRANCE
BELGIUM
LUXEMBOURG
ZEELAND
NOORD-BRABANT
LIMBURG
WEST-VLAANDEREN
OOST-VLAANDEREN
ANTWERPEN
VLAAMS BRABANT
BRABANT WALLON
HAINAUT
NAMUR
LIÈGE
DIEKIRCH
GREVENMACHER
Flanders
Famenne
Fagne
Ardennes
Hautes Fagnes
Middelburg
Vlissingen
Breda
Tilburg
's-Hertogenbosch
Eindhoven
Helmond
Roosendaal
Bergen op Zoom
Oosterhout
Venlo
Roermond
Maastricht
Heerlen
Kerkrade
Oostende (Ostend)
Brugge (Bruges)
Knokke-Heist
Zeebrugge
Blankenberge
Middelkerke
De Panne
Ieper
Kortrijk
Roeselare
Mouscron
Tournai
Gent (Ghent)
Aalst
Dendermonde
Sint-Niklaas
Antwerpen (Antwerp)
Mechelen
Turnhout
Leuven
Hasselt
Genk
BRUSSEL/BRUXELLES (BRUSSELS)
Waterloo
Wavre
Mons
La Louvière
Charleroi
Namur
Liège
Verviers
Spa
Dinant
Bastogne
Arlon
Luxembourg
Esch-sur-Alzette
Diekirch
Grevenmacher
Botrange 694m
Baraque Michel 675m
Baraque de Fraiture 651m
Meuse
Scheldt
Sambre
Semois
Moselle
Albertkanaal
100
102
102
102
102
SCALE 1:1,100,000
(projection: Lambert Conformal Conic)
Km 0 5 10 20 30 40
Miles 0 5 10 20 30 40

Activities

- Overindulge in **Belgium's** distinctive beers and fine chocolates
- Take a boat along **Amsterdam's** canals – a great way to see the city
- Boogie the nights away at the North Sea Jazz Festival, in **The Hague**
- Canoe through interesting waterways in the hilly, wooded **Ardennes**, Belgium
- Observe one of **Antwerp's** fascinating diamond-cutting demonstrations
- Soak up the classical sounds of **Amsterdam's** prolific and famous Concertgebouw Orchestra
- Devour a huge plate of mussels in the streets off **Brussels'** Grand Place
- Rent bikes and cruise the network of Dutch cycleways

River Leie, Ghent: Medieval town made prosperous by the cloth trade, with many historic buildings bordering the river, as well as an impressive cathedral and town hall, adorned with many fine works of art.

Atomium, Brussels: Representing an atom of iron magnified 165 billion times, the Atomium towers over the theme park Mini-Europe, which features miniatures of 300 of Europe's major sights.

Germany

A kaleidoscope of high culture, folk tradition, scenic beauty and sheer variety – not, perhaps, the first image conjured up by the name Germany. Of course the country bears the marks of its recent history – the ruthless pursuit of power up to 1945, the drive to rebuild prosperity on the ruins of defeat and the division of communist East from more economically successful West until reunification in 1990. The visitor may still see signs of that East-West division, but will become aware too of the older one between protestant north and mainly Catholic Bavaria. There are also physical transitions from the dune-lined northern coasts to the wide German plain, then the southern hills and Alpine mountains. If Berlin and Munich stand out as the most magnetic cities, the rich heritage of other provincial centres and smaller cities is bound to impress – the legacy of their role as capitals of the kingdoms, dukedoms and princely states, which gradually came together as one nation in the 19th century.

Brandenburg Gate, Berlin: The broad avenue of Unter den Linden was blocked off here by the Berlin Wall until 1989.

What to See

❶ Hamburg
This Hanseatic City is Europe's second-largest port, but younger people come for the pulsing life along the Reeperbahn

❷ Berlin
Germany's reunified capital is its liveliest city, amid reminders of its turbulent history such as the imposing Brandenburg Gate, the glorious new Reichstag, and the dignified Holocaust Memorial

❸ Potsdam
The historic heart of Prussia's erstwhile capital is a World Heritage Site and the Rococo Sans Souci palace its crowning romantic glory

❹ Dresden
The 18th-century Baroque masterpiece, the Zwinger Palace, has been restored since the 1945 Allied bombing of the city. Hosting several museums, Raphael's *Sistine Madonna* is its most prized treasure

❺ Weimar
Charming but unassuming town, home of Goethe and Schiller, and briefly German capital in 1919

❻ Cologne (Köln)
Overshadowed by its great Gothic cathedral, the city has plentiful reminders of its Roman origins, from sturdy city walls to the exquisite Dionysus mosaic

❼ Mosel Valley
Vineyards and romantic riverside castles between Trier and Koblenz make a perfect cycle tour

❽ Trier
Fine Roman remains like the Porta Nigra grace the picturesque town where Karl Marx was born and Mosel wine is made

❾ Heidelberg
A medieval town of pink sandstone, whose vibrant university is Germany's oldest, founded in 1386

❿ Black Forest (Schwarzwald)
Well established as a favourite German holiday region, with wooded walks and vigorous climbs set amid charming timber-built villages

⓫ Konstanz
The centre for relaxing lakeside indulgence, gentle boating or more strenuous water sports

⓬ Neuschwanstein
(near Füssen)
Mad King Ludwig of Bavaria's extravagant lakeside fairytale castle

⓭ Munich
Technology explained in the Deutsche Museum, swimming places along the Isar river and beer gardens for summer evening relaxation

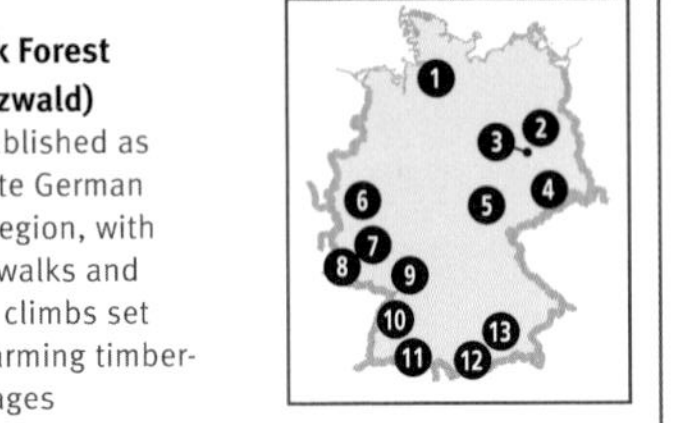

1
2
3
4
5
6
7
8
9
10
11
12
13

Heidelberg: The Alte Brücke needs nine stone spans to cross the broad river Neckar. Also known as the Karl-Theodor Brücke after its 18th-century architect, it is adorned with his statue and that of the Greek goddess Athene – inkeeping with the vainglorious image of the town that made student duels famous.

SCALE 1:2,500,000
(projection: Lambert Conformal Conic)

94
96
110
98

Map Key
POPULATION
1 million to 5 million
500,000 to 1 million
100,000 to 500,000
50,000 to 100,000
10,000 to 50,000
below 10,000
ELEVATION
2000m / 6562ft
1000m / 3281ft
500m / 1640ft
250m / 820ft
100m / 328ft
sea level
GERMANY
NORDRHEIN-WESTFALEN
HESSEN
THÜRINGEN
SACHSEN
RHEINLAND-PFALZ
SAARLAND
BADEN-WÜRTTEMBERG
BAYERN
BELGIUM
LUXEMBOURG
FRANCE
SWITZERLAND
AUSTRIA
CZECH REPUBLIC
Lake Constance
Bavarian Alps
Köln (Cologne)
Düsseldorf
Dortmund
Essen
Bonn
Frankfurt am Main
Stuttgart
Nürnberg (Nuremberg)
München (Munich)
Dresden
Leipzig
Chemnitz
Erfurt
Regensburg
Augsburg
Würzburg
102
108
110

Bavarian Alps: The area around Berchtesgaden is famous for its dramatically sited buildings, like this charming church.

Activities

- Enjoy magnificent views from the cable car as it climbs **Zugspitze**, Germany's highest peak
- Indulge your fancy dress fantasies and make fun of the political establishment at **Cologne's** irreverent annual carnival parade
- Take the traditional New Year walk around peaceful car-free **Baltrum** in the Ostfriesische Inseln, lit up by fireworks from the mainland
- Look down on debates through the glass dome of Berlin's rebuilt **Reichstag**, designed to make a point about "transparency" in political life
- Soak up the beer, pretzels and oompah bands among Bavarians in *dirndl* and *lederhosen* at **Munich's** Oktoberfest

France

France, Monaco

More tourists choose France than anywhere else. Partly it's the romantic allure of Paris in the springtime or the glamorous Côte d'Azur, Impressionist paintings, café culture, *haute cuisine* and fine wine or the simpler pleasures of village markets, distinctive cheeses and *patisseries* (cake shops). Also, it's the ease of access for visitors from countries with less sun, less space and less sense of style. The scenery can charm or inspire, as vineyards cling to terraced hillsides, woodland gives way to the Pyrenees or the Alps and great rivers cut through the Massif Central, flowing west to the Atlantic coast. Cathedrals, châteaux, fine manor houses and self-confident modern architecture all testify to the wealth this land has produced.

Avignon: The festival in July–August dominates the calendar for top musicians, ballet and drama. Historic buildings provide fine backdrops for open-air performances, while the streets are enlivened by informal music, theatre and circus acts.

96

Saumur, Loire valley: Of the many beautiful châteaux of the Loire, Saumur with its lofty white stone walls, turrets and battlements has most credibility as a fortress. Others are out-and-out Renaissance pleasure palaces like lovely Chenonceau or Chambord, which was originally designed by Leonardo da Vinci.

64

What to See

1 Bayeux Tapestry
11th-century historical masterpiece depicting the Norman conquest of England at the Battle of Hastings in 1066

2 Mont St-Michel
Benedictine monastery sitting dramatically on a steep-sided island, reached by a causeway

3 Carnac
(near Auray) Breton seaside town famous for its prehistoric standing stones arranged in linear patterns 6,000 years ago

4 Abbaye de Fontevraud
(near Chinon) France's largest abbey, dating from 1101, is now a concert venue. Its church contains the tombs of English kings Henry II and Richard the Lionheart

5 Loire Valley
This broad river runs through the very heart of France, lined by beautiful châteaux and historic cities, from Orléans to Tours and lively maritime Nantes

6 World War I Battlefields
Humbling reminders of the carnage of the Somme trenches

7 Versailles
Louis XIV's magnificent 17th-century palace, set in sumptuous grounds with ornamental lakes, fountains and the fake farm village where Marie Antoinette frolicked as the Revolution loomed

8 Paris
The Eiffel Tower, as well as the Nôtre Dame and Sacré Coeur cathedrals, presides over a welter of monuments, museums, art galleries, exclusive shops and literary cafés

9 Reims
French kings were once crowned in this Champagne city's 13th-century cathedral, superb enough to rival Chartres

10 Annecy
Alpine lakeside town with a well-preserved medieval quarter threaded by canals

11 Lascaux
(near Montignac) Cave art from the Palaeolithic era that so impressed Picasso. Now protected from public view, but you can visit an exact replica

12 Carcassonne
Perfectly restored walled medieval citadel, captured in 1209 in a crusade against the heretical Cathar sect

13 Arles
A rival to Nîmes as Provence's finest Roman city, with the added attractions of 12th-century churches and memories of the painter Vincent van Gogh

14 Aix-en-Provence
Elegant old university town, overlooked by Cézanne's beloved Mont St-Victoire. The café-lined Cours Mirabeau is the place to be seen on an early evening promenade

15 Bonifacio
Picturesque walled port at the southern tip of Corsica

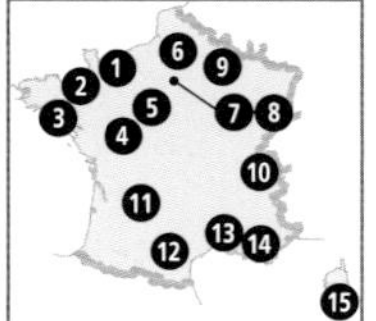

104

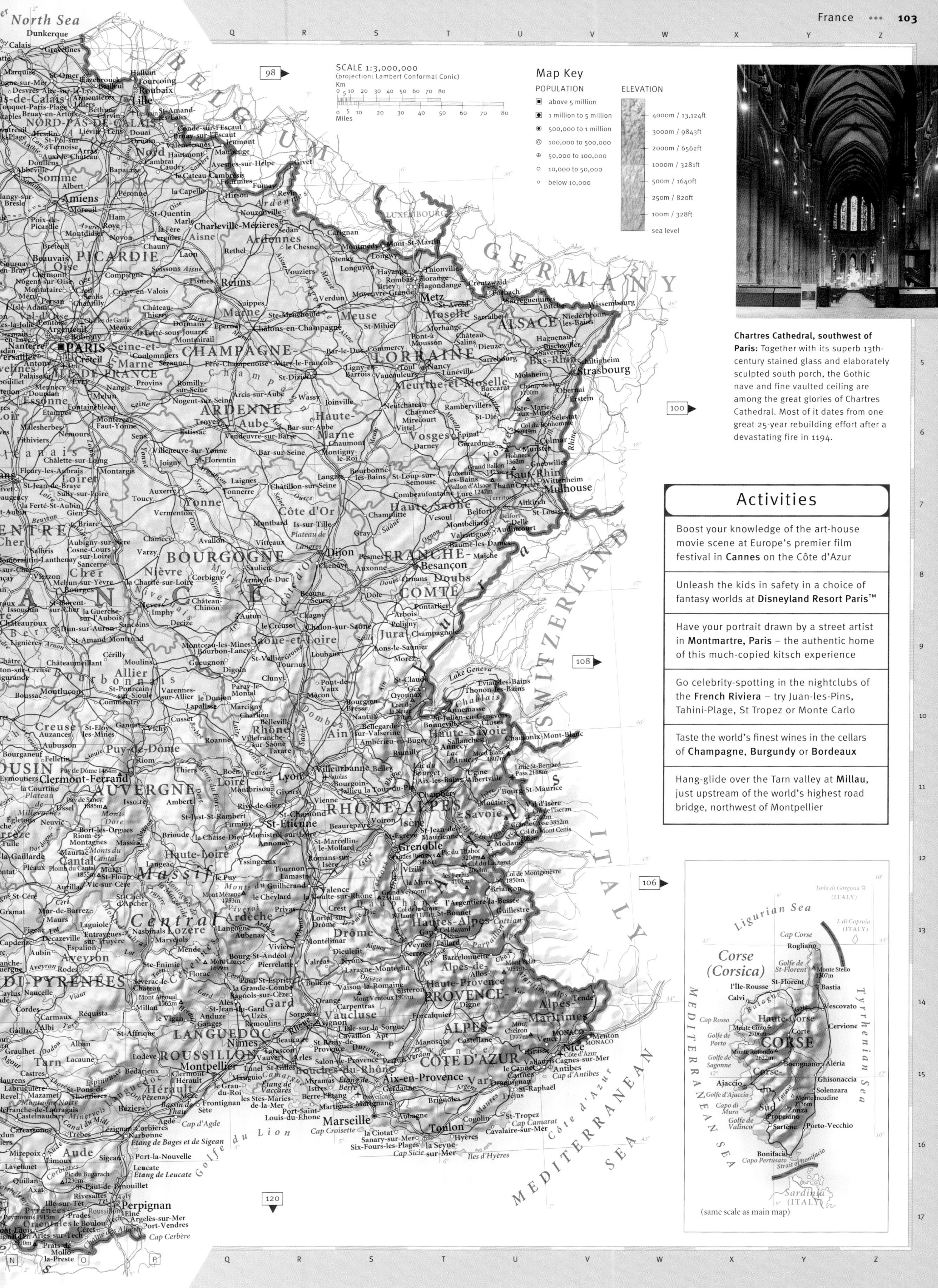
SCALE 1:3,000,000
(projection: Lambert Conformal Conic)
Km
Miles
Map Key
POPULATION
above 5 million
1 million to 5 million
500,000 to 1 million
100,000 to 500,000
50,000 to 100,000
10,000 to 50,000
below 10,000
ELEVATION
4000m / 13,124ft
3000m / 9843ft
2000m / 6562ft
1000m / 3281ft
500m / 1640ft
250m / 820ft
100m / 328ft
sea level
North Sea
BELGIUM
GERMANY
LUXEMBOURG
SWITZERLAND
ITALY
MEDITERRANEAN SEA
Golfe du Lion
PARIS
Lyon
Marseille
Strasbourg
Dijon
Grenoble
Montpellier
Nice
Toulon
Reims
Metz
Lille
Corse (Corsica)
Ligurian Sea
Tyrrhenian Sea
(same scale as main map)

Chartres Cathedral, southwest of Paris: Together with its superb 13th-century stained glass and elaborately sculpted south porch, the Gothic nave and fine vaulted ceiling are among the great glories of Chartres Cathedral. Most of it dates from one great 25-year rebuilding effort after a devastating fire in 1194.

Activities

Boost your knowledge of the art-house movie scene at Europe's premier film festival in **Cannes** on the Côte d'Azur

Unleash the kids in safety in a choice of fantasy worlds at **Disneyland Resort Paris™**

Have your portrait drawn by a street artist in **Montmartre, Paris** – the authentic home of this much-copied kitsch experience

Go celebrity-spotting in the nightclubs of the **French Riviera** – try Juan-les-Pins, Tahini-Plage, St Tropez or Monte Carlo

Taste the world's finest wines in the cellars of **Champagne, Burgundy** or **Bordeaux**

Hang-glide over the Tarn valley at **Millau**, just upstream of the world's highest road bridge, northwest of Montpellier

The Iberian Peninsula

Andorra, Gibraltar, Portugal, Spain
(Azores, Canary Islands, Madeira on pp64)

The Iberian peninsula stretches from the Pyrenees to within sight of Africa across the Strait of Gibraltar, and from Portugal's temperate Atlantic coast to the holiday brochure beach resorts of the Costa del Sol, Costa Blanca, and Costa Brava. Invading Greeks, Carthaginians, Romans, Visigoths and Moors left an exotic legacy even before the rise of the great Spanish and Portuguese empires, which carved up the New World in the 16th-century Age of Discovery. History and Catholicism contribute to a culture steeped in the rich and violent pageantry of flamenco and the bullfight, while sunshine encourages the famous afternoon siesta. Moorish and medieval architectural glories are increasingly being joined by modern masterpieces, such as the extraordinary buildings of Antoni Gaudí in Barcelona and the futuristic Guggenheim museum in Bilbao.

Map Key

POPULATION

- 1 million to 5 million
- 500,000 to 1 million
- 100,000 to 500,000
- 50,000 to 100,000
- 10,000 to 50,000
- below 10,000

ELEVATION

- 3000m / 9843ft
- 2000m / 6562ft
- 1000m / 3281ft
- 500m / 1640ft
- 250m / 820ft
- 100m / 328ft
- sea level

Activities

- Sample the wide range of port – from white to tawny and ruby – in the wine lodges of the **Douro valley**, near Oporto
- Follow in the footsteps of a sauropod at the **Dinosaur Footprints Park**, near Coimbra
- Celebrate at Las Fallas, when **Valencia** erupts in fire and fireworks for this popular Spanish fiesta (12–19 March)
- Take a pilgrimage to visually stunning **Santiago** de Compostela, which for centuries has received pilgrims from all over Europe
- Watch a bullfight at **Ronda**, the dramatically scenic home of the sport in Andalucía
- Hike in the **Ordesa valley** to enjoy the magnificent Pyrenees mountains
- Ski at **Berat** in the Pyrenees
- Tour **Mini Hollywood**, near the Costa del Sol, to see the sets of *For a Few Dollars More* and other spaghetti westerns

64

74

Estoril, Portugal: This spa town on the Atlantic Riviera became an enclave for exiled European monarchs in the mid-20th century. Still a popular beach resort, within easy reach of Lisbon and Sintra, it has seven golf courses and the largest casino in Europe, but is slightly cooler and wetter than the southern coastal strip of the Algarve.

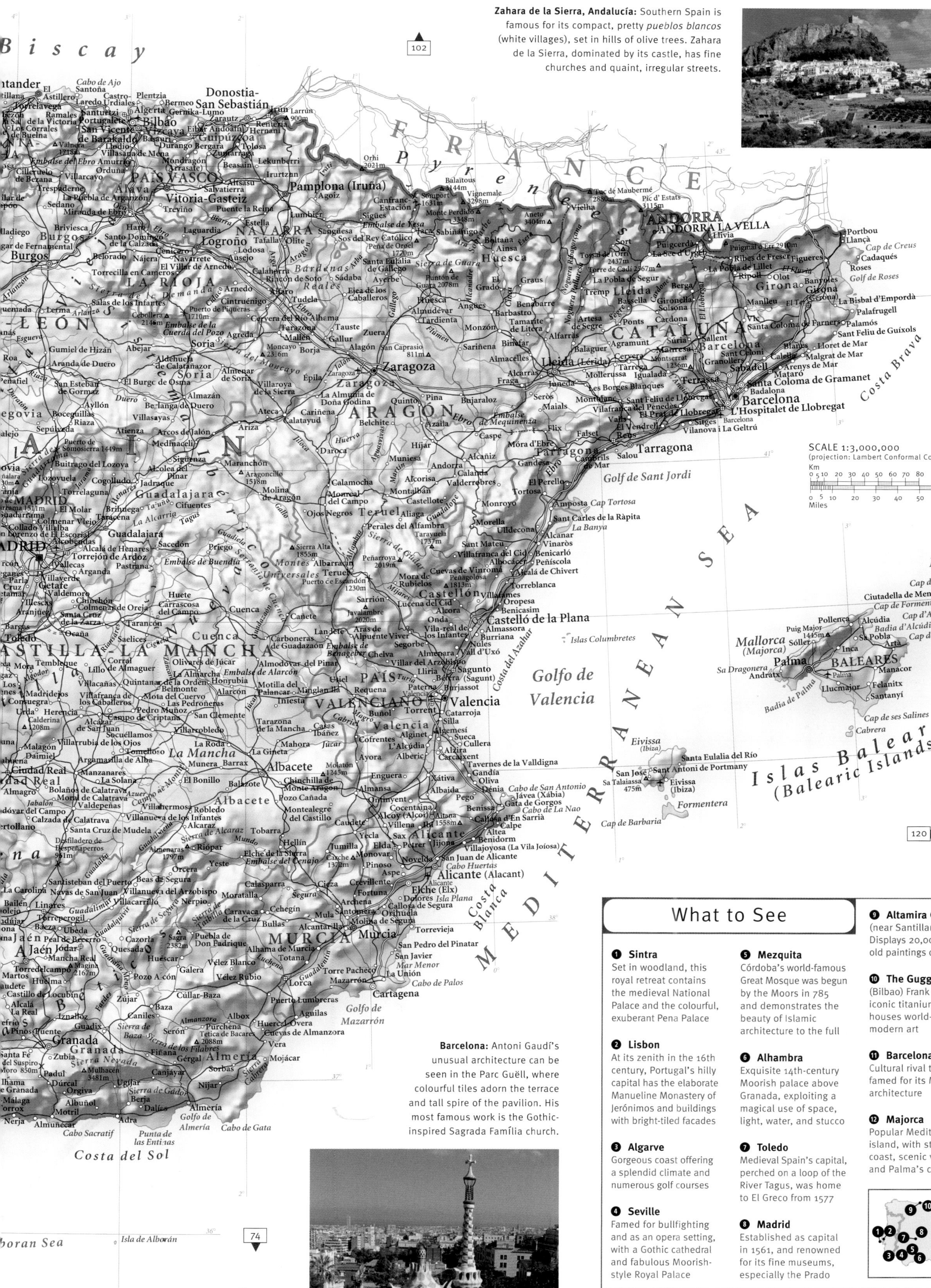

Biscay
FRANCE
Pyrenees
ANDORRA
ANDORRA LA VELLA
Santander
Bilbao
Donostia-San Sebastián
PAÍS VASCO
Vitoria-Gasteiz
Pamplona (Iruña)
NAVARRA
Logroño
LA RIOJA
Burgos
LEÓN
Soria
Zaragoza
ARAGÓN
Huesca
Lleida (Lérida)
CATALUÑA
Girona
Barcelona
L'Hospitalet de Llobregat
Sabadell
Terrassa
Santa Coloma de Gramanet
Tarragona
Costa Brava
Golf de Sant Jordi
MADRID
Guadalajara
Teruel
Cuenca
CASTILLA-LA MANCHA
Toledo
Castellón de la Plana
PAÍS VALENCIANO
Valencia
Golfo de Valencia
Albacete
Alicante (Alacant)
Costa Blanca
Murcia
MURCIA
Cartagena
Jaén
Granada
Almería
Costa del Sol
MEDITERRANEAN SEA
Islas Baleares (Balearic Islands)
Mallorca (Majorca)
Palma
Menorca (Minorca)
Eivissa (Ibiza)
Formentera
Islas Columbretes
Alboran Sea
Isla de Alborán
Melilla (to Spain)
Islas Chafarinas (to Spain)
Peñon de Alhucemas (to Spain)
SCALE 1:3,000,000
(projection: Lambert Conformal Conic)
102
120
74

Zahara de la Sierra, Andalucía: Southern Spain is famous for its compact, pretty *pueblos blancos* (white villages), set in hills of olive trees. Zahara de la Sierra, dominated by its castle, has fine churches and quaint, irregular streets.

Barcelona: Antoni Gaudí's unusual architecture can be seen in the Parc Güell, where colourful tiles adorn the terrace and tall spire of the pavilion. His most famous work is the Gothic-inspired Sagrada Família church.

What to See

1 Sintra
Set in woodland, this royal retreat contains the medieval National Palace and the colourful, exuberant Pena Palace

2 Lisbon
At its zenith in the 16th century, Portugal's hilly capital has the elaborate Manueline Monastery of Jerónimos and buildings with bright-tiled facades

3 Algarve
Gorgeous coast offering a splendid climate and numerous golf courses

4 Seville
Famed for bullfighting and as an opera setting, with a Gothic cathedral and fabulous Moorish-style Royal Palace

5 Mezquita
Córdoba's world-famous Great Mosque was begun by the Moors in 785 and demonstrates the beauty of Islamic architecture to the full

6 Alhambra
Exquisite 14th-century Moorish palace above Granada, exploiting a magical use of space, light, water, and stucco

7 Toledo
Medieval Spain's capital, perched on a loop of the River Tagus, was home to El Greco from 1577

8 Madrid
Established as capital in 1561, and renowned for its fine museums, especially the Prado

9 Altamira Caves
(near Santillana) Displays 20,000-year-old paintings of bison

10 The Guggenheim
(Bilbao) Frank O. Gehry's iconic titanium building houses world-class modern art

11 Barcelona
Cultural rival to Madrid, famed for its Modernist architecture

12 Majorca
Popular Mediterranean island, with stunning coast, scenic villages, and Palma's cathedral

The Italian Peninsula

Italy, San Marino, Vatican City

While Italy's Roman remains are plentiful and compelling, much of its unrivalled architectural and artistic heritage stems from the trading pre-eminence of its city states during the Renaissance period (from the 14th-century). No cultural itinerary can do full justice to these glories – magnificent Rome, Florence and Venice, gems such as Perugia and Orvieto in Umbria, Urbino and Ravenna further north and Pisa, Siena and the Tuscan hill towns. North Italy, bounded by the Alps, has beautiful mountain and lake scenery, while the south is another world, more savage in its beauty. The teeming city of Naples lies near Vesuvius, one of Italy's two famous volcanoes. The other, Etna, is on the island of Sicily, which has many historic reminders of its strategic Mediterranean location.

Santa Maria in Trastevere, Rome: Originally built in the 2nd or 3rd century CE, it was possibly the first church in Rome where Christian Mass was celebrated openly. The present-day basilica, begun in the 12th century, is decorated with golden mosaics of saints and biblical stories, a feature that adorns many churches throughout Italy.

108
108
112
102

SCALE 1:2,750,000
(projection: Lambert Conformal Conic)

What to See

❶ Milan
Italy's economic and fashion hub, this sophisticated city has an elaborate, late-Gothic cathedral with superb views from the roof. Recently refurbished, the prestigious La Scala opera house claims Europe's largest stage

❷ Lago di Garda
Italy's most popular lake, hemmed in by the craggy Alps to the north, has excellent hiking possibilities, plus the Peninsula of Sermione with its Scaligero Castle

❸ Venice
This once great maritime republic with its canals and romantic alleyways – uncluttered by cars – shines with the mercantile wealth of its palazzos and churches, none grander than St Mark's Basilica

❹ Ravenna
Lavish golden mosaics adorn Ravenna's fine churches, dating from its heyday in the 5th–8th centuries CE, as capital of the Western Roman Empire and the region's main trading link with Byzantium. The great Florentine poet Dante Alighieri was buried here in 1321

❺ Florence
Renaissance home of the Medici family and the artist Michelangelo, distinctive for its iconic white, green and pink-marbled cathedral. The Uffizi Gallery and other acclaimed museums house a wealth of great art treasures

❻ Cinque Terre
Just west of La Spezia, Italy's famous five – Monterosso, Vernazza, Corniglia, Manarola, and Riomaggiore – are scenic coastal villages

❼ Vatican City
The seat of the papacy and the world's smallest independent state is dominated by the huge, domed St Peter's Basilica. Michelangelo's vast masterpiece – the frescoed ceiling of the Sistine Chapel – was completed nearly 500 years ago

❽ Rome
The "Eternal City" throbs with modern life amid its remarkable Roman remains, Renaissance churches, elegant piazzas and fountains

❾ Capri
This small, pretty island remains an enchanting destination with beautiful sea caves, such as the Blue Grotto, and the ruins of Emperor Tiberius's villa

❿ Pompei
Pliny's famous letters describing the eruption of Vesuvius in 79 CE that buried Pompei have put the town on the map forever, the extensive ruins giving a graphic insight into typical Roman life

⓫ Matera
This troglodyte town consisted of many *sassi* – buildings half-constructed, half-bored into the rock, which had no electricity, water or sewerage until well into the 20th century

⓬ Etna
Europe's largest and most active volcano towers 3,350 m (11,200 ft) over eastern Sicily, with dramatic scenery and good hiking. Craters are sometimes roped off due to the volcano's unpredictability

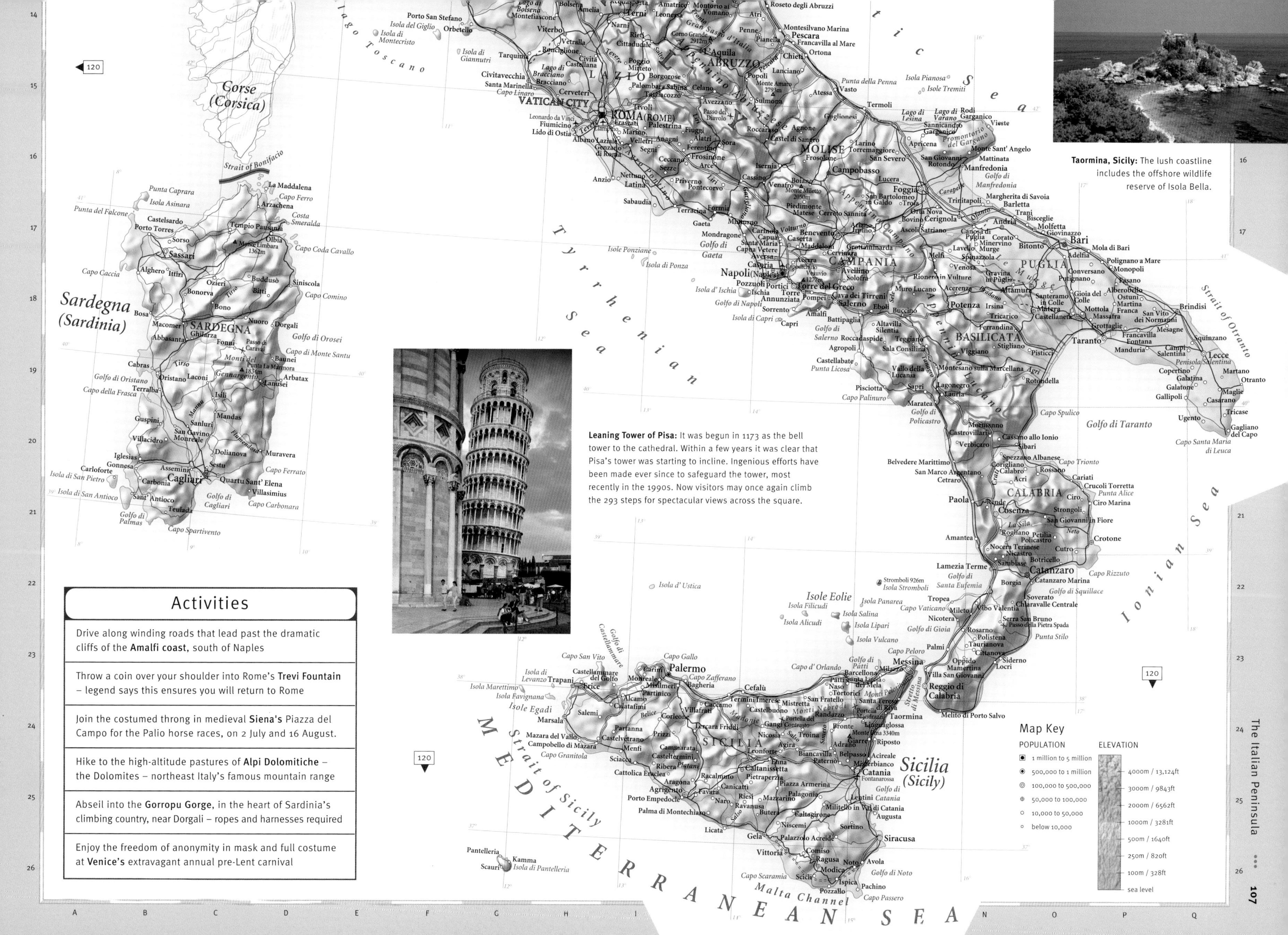
Map Key
POPULATION
1 million to 5 million
500,000 to 1 million
100,000 to 500,000
50,000 to 100,000
10,000 to 50,000
below 10,000
ELEVATION
4000m / 13,124ft
3000m / 9843ft
2000m / 6562ft
1000m / 3281ft
500m / 1640ft
250m / 820ft
100m / 328ft
sea level
Tyrrhenian Sea
Ionian Sea
Mediterranean Sea
Strait of Sicily
Strait of Otranto
Strait of Bonifacio
Malta Channel
Sardegna (Sardinia)
Sicilia (Sicily)
Corse (Corsica)

Taormina, Sicily: The lush coastline includes the offshore wildlife reserve of Isola Bella.

Leaning Tower of Pisa: It was begun in 1173 as the bell tower to the cathedral. Within a few years it was clear that Pisa's tower was starting to incline. Ingenious efforts have been made ever since to safeguard the tower, most recently in the 1990s. Now visitors may once again climb the 293 steps for spectacular views across the square.

Activities

- Drive along winding roads that lead past the dramatic cliffs of the **Amalfi coast**, south of Naples
- Throw a coin over your shoulder into Rome's **Trevi Fountain** – legend says this ensures you will return to Rome
- Join the costumed throng in medieval **Siena's** Piazza del Campo for the Palio horse races, on 2 July and 16 August.
- Hike to the high-altitude pastures of **Alpi Dolomitiche** – the Dolomites – northeast Italy's famous mountain range
- Abseil into the **Gorropu Gorge**, in the heart of Sardinia's climbing country, near Dorgali – ropes and harnesses required
- Enjoy the freedom of anonymity in mask and full costume at **Venice's** extravagant annual pre-Lent carnival

The Alpine States

Austria, Liechtenstein, Slovenia, Switzerland

The birthplace of modern skiing and mountaineering, Switzerland and Austria are the core of a scenically spectacular Alpine region in central Europe that extends south into Slovenia and includes tiny Liechtenstein.

Switzerland's fantastic setting and profusion of winter sports have attracted successive generations of holidaymakers. The sources of the Rhône and Rhine lie in its mountains, which are dotted with picturesque meadows, chalets and lakes.

Austria once stood at the heart of the Habsburg Empire, with Vienna as its capital and the Danube its artery to the east. It remains an international centre of culture and music, taking pride in its links with many of the great composers.

Slovenia, part of the Austro-Hungarian Empire until 1919 and also influenced culturally by nearby Italy, is the most westernized of the former communist Yugoslav states. Its sparkling lakes and magnificent cave systems are gradually being discovered by tourists.

Triple Bridge, Ljubljana: Preseren Square is the lively heart of Slovenia's capital, dominated by its distinctive Triple Bridge and the pink Franciscan Church. The city's architecture is an intriguing mix of Baroque, Art Nouveau, postmodernist and communist styles.

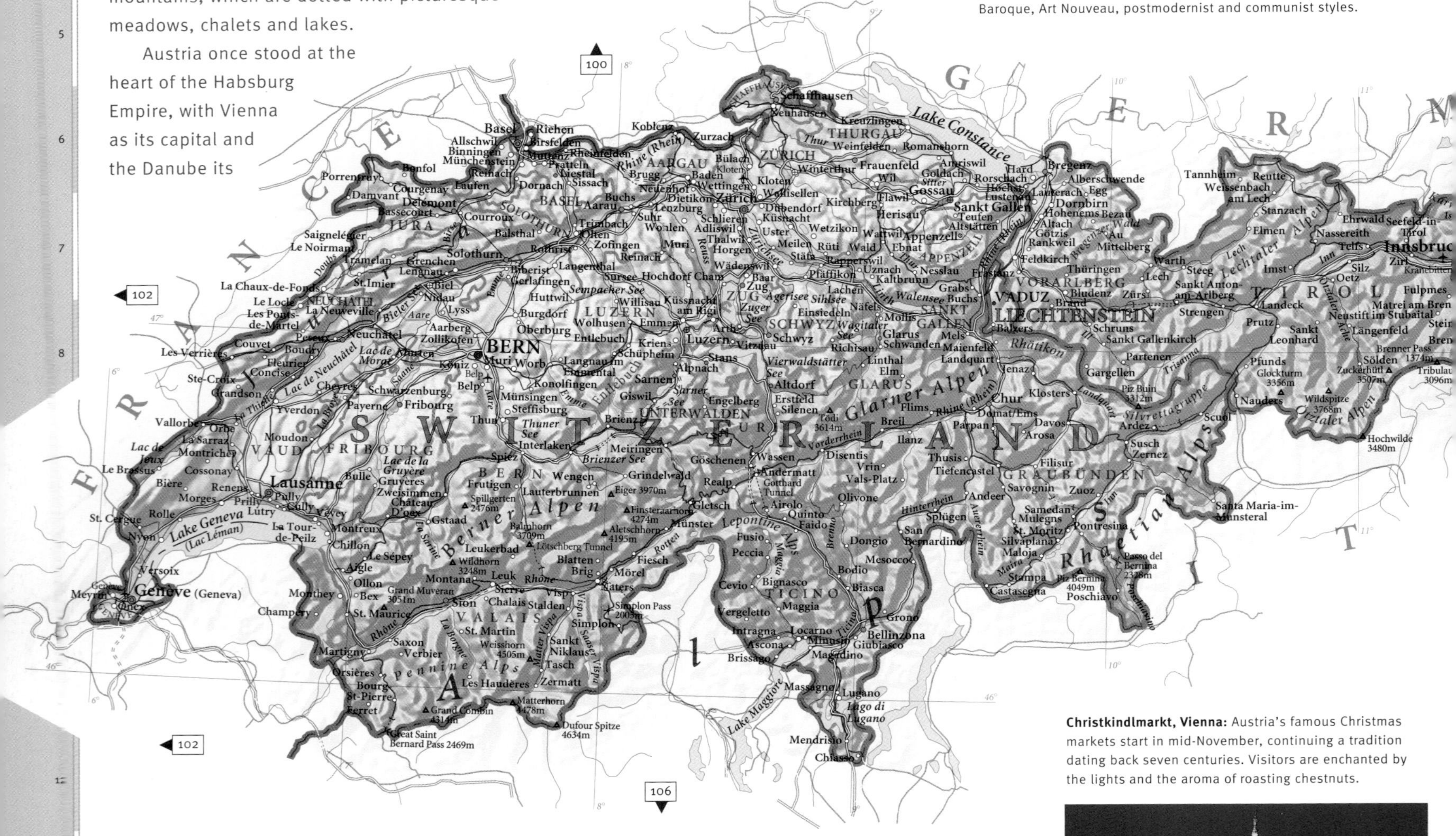

Christkindlmarkt, Vienna: Austria's famous Christmas markets start in mid-November, continuing a tradition dating back seven centuries. Visitors are enchanted by the lights and the aroma of roasting chestnuts.

What to See

1 Geneva
On Lake Geneva, the UN's second headquarters city has fine mansions and the best Swiss museums

2 Basel
Old town and industrial centre, noted for Gothic buildings, a world-class zoo, and art gallery

3 Luzern
Museums celebrating Pablo Picasso and Richard Wagner and a summer music festival

4 Zermatt
Charming Swiss village, at the foot of the Matterhorn, a centre for skiing and climbing

5 Lugano
Attractive town of villas and elegant piazzas, set beside Lake Lugano

6 Innsbruck
Host of two Winter Olympics – a good base to explore the enchanting Tyrol and enjoy its skiing

7 Salzburg
Baroque spires decorate the hilly city of Mozart's birth, which holds a famous music festival

8 Hohe Tauern National Park
Austria's best scenery, plus Grossglockner (its highest peak)

9 Dachstein Caves
(near Hallstatt)
The Giant Ice Cave and Werfen Ice Cave are equally amazing but also very cold, even in the midst of summer

10 Melk Abbey
Huge fortified Baroque monastery perching above the Danube

11 Vienna
Great intellectual and musical centre, with sumptuous Habsburg palaces and the Kunsthistorisches museum

12 Graz
Once home to Holy Roman Emperor Friedrich III, this old city bears many signs of his motto "Austria rules the World"

13 Hochosterwitz
(near Klagenfurt)
Dramatic medieval castle perched on a rock, which inspired Walt Disney's *Snow White* castle

14 Lake Bled
Stunning lake in the Julian Alps with a fairytale island Church of the Assumption, with its wishing bell, and cliff-top castle. Also an important rowing centre

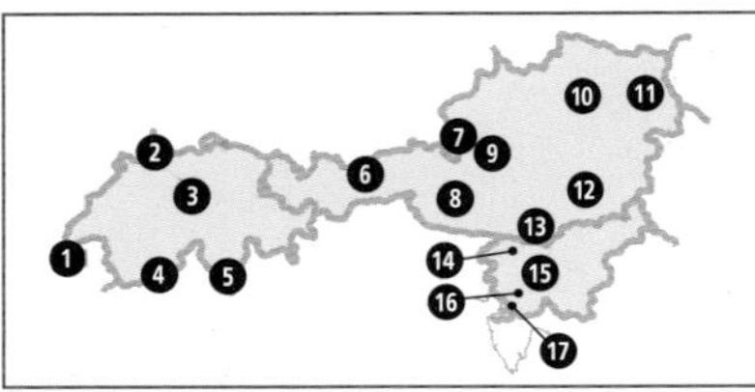

15 Ljubljana
Pastel-coloured Baroque and Habsburg buildings and lively riverside cafés

16 Predjama Castle
(near Vrhnika) Set into a cliff, this 12th-century castle has many secret passages and caves

17 Skocjan Caves
(near Divaca)
A natural bridge spans the world's largest underground canyon

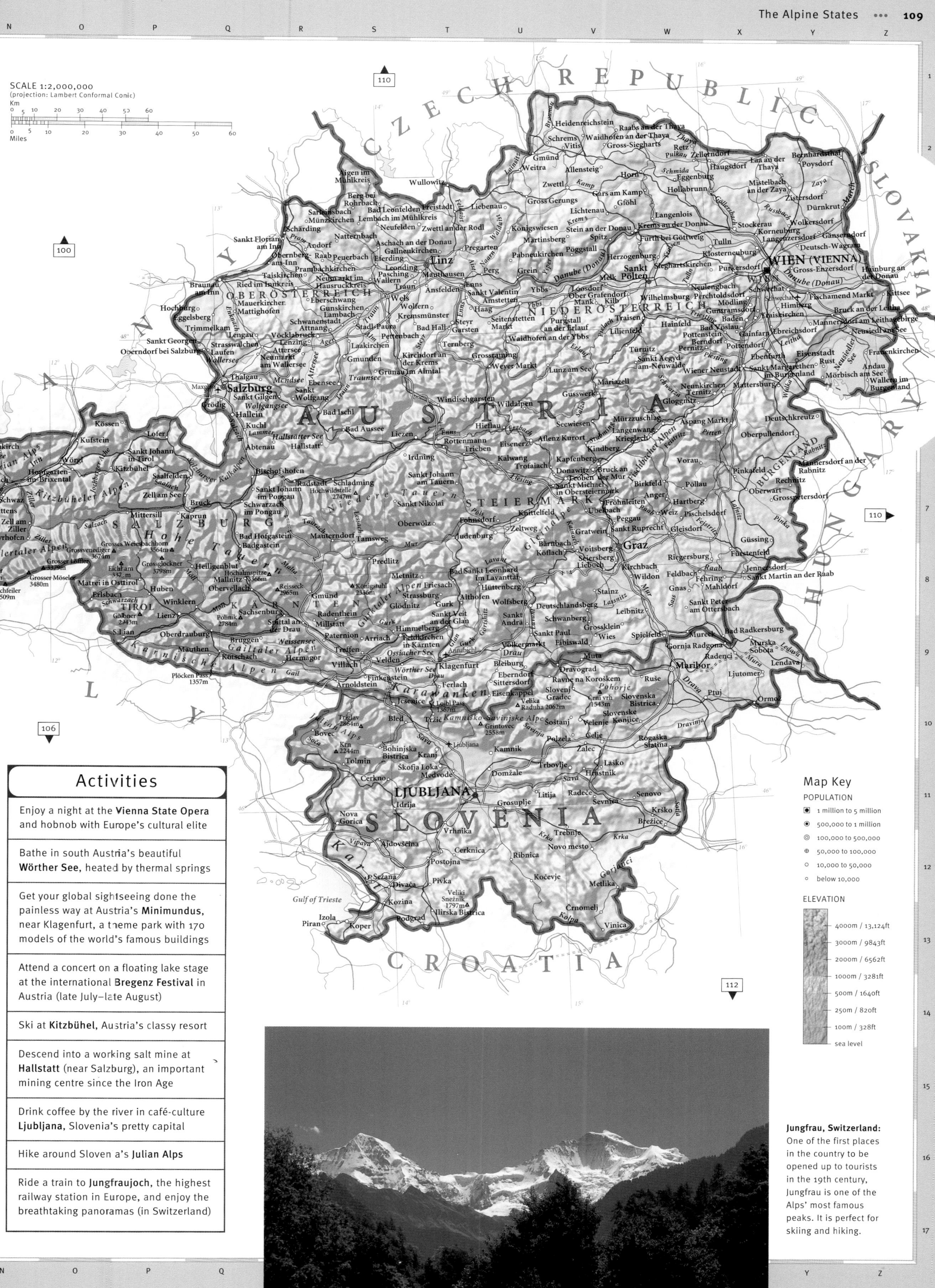
SCALE 1:2,000,000
(projection: Lambert Conformal Conic)
Km
Miles
CZECH REPUBLIC
SLOVAKIA
HUNGARY
AUSTRIA
SLOVENIA
CROATIA
ITALY
GERMANY
OBERÖSTERREICH
NIEDERÖSTERREICH
STEIERMARK
SALZBURG
KÄRNTEN
TIROL
BURGENLAND
WIEN (VIENNA)
Linz
Salzburg
Graz
Innsbruck
Klagenfurt
LJUBLJANA
Maribor
Gulf of Trieste
Map Key
POPULATION
1 million to 5 million
500,000 to 1 million
100,000 to 500,000
50,000 to 100,000
10,000 to 50,000
below 10,000
ELEVATION
4000m / 13,124ft
3000m / 9843ft
2000m / 6562ft
1000m / 3281ft
500m / 1640ft
250m / 820ft
100m / 328ft
sea level

Activities

- Enjoy a night at the **Vienna State Opera** and hobnob with Europe's cultural elite
- Bathe in south Austria's beautiful **Wörther See**, heated by thermal springs
- Get your global sightseeing done the painless way at Austria's **Minimundus**, near Klagenfurt, a theme park with 170 models of the world's famous buildings
- Attend a concert on a floating lake stage at the international **Bregenz Festival** in Austria (late July–late August)
- Ski at **Kitzbühel**, Austria's classy resort
- Descend into a working salt mine at **Hallstatt** (near Salzburg), an important mining centre since the Iron Age
- Drink coffee by the river in café-culture **Ljubljana**, Slovenia's pretty capital
- Hike around Slovenia's **Julian Alps**
- Ride a train to **Jungfraujoch**, the highest railway station in Europe, and enjoy the breathtaking panoramas (in Switzerland)

Jungfrau, Switzerland: One of the first places in the country to be opened up to tourists in the 19th century, Jungfrau is one of the Alps' most famous peaks. It is perfect for skiing and hiking.

Central Europe

Czech Republic, Hungary, Poland, Slovakia

A turbulent history has bequeathed central Europe a rich cultural heritage, widely shared around the world through the works of its many great writers and composers, and celebrated in particular in its vibrant and historic capital cities – Prague, and the almost equally popular Budapest, are the main focus for tourists.

Slovakia, with the Tatra Mountains, has most to offer in the region in the way of spectacular scenery, and its capital, Bratislava, while somewhat put in the shade by the greater glories of Prague, is a delightful old city that is being discovered by more and more visitors.

Poland has huge swathes of forest, many fine castles and several historically interesting cities, in addition to the capital Warsaw, such as the Baltic port of Gdansk and medieval Krakow. For many visitors the most moving experience is a visit to the site of the Nazi concentration camps at Auschwitz.

The scattering of Bohemian castles and pretty towns set amid a lush landscape give visitors to the Czech Republic a strong reason to find some time to spend away from Prague. Hungary, too, has both historical and natural attractions outside its capital, notably its "seaside" around Lake Balaton with sandy beaches and mineral spas.

Pieskowa Castle, Poland: This 14th-century castle was built to protect the trade route between Krakow and Wroclaw. Extended in a profusion of styles, it now houses part of the royal collection from Wawel Castle in Krakow.

What to See

1 Slowinski National Park
(near Leba) Beautiful stretch of wildlife-rich coast with unusual, high, shifting dunes

2 Gdansk
The former Hanseatic trading hub and port of Danzig has a legacy of fine buildings and some fascinating museums

3 Warsaw
Systematically destroyed by the retreating Nazis, the historic old town has been meticulously reconstructed. Also, Elegant shops line Nowy Swiat street and the vast Culture Palace is a relic of the Communist era

4 Auschwitz (Oswiecim)
A chilling witness to the Nazi holocaust, the Birkenau concentration camp complex is where over a million people were exterminated

5 Krakow
Krakow's magnificent centre was spared major destruction during World War II. Its huge square is overlooked by the cathedral and royal palace on Wawel Hill

6 Wieliczka Salt Mine
Seven hundred years of mining have left a labyrinth of tunnels, lakes and a chapel, carved entirely from salt

7 Tatra Mountains
Straddling the border of Poland and Slovakia, central Europe's top wildlife destination has fabulous mountains, waterfalls and lakes

8 Budapest
Separated from broad-boulevarded Pest by the Danube, Habsburg Buda is dominated by its great castle and palace

9 Lake Balaton
Hungary's "seaside" is packed with fashionable resorts. Convenient vineyards aid the year-round festivities

10 Esterhazy Palace
(near Kapuvar) Stunning rococo court complex, where Haydn was once director of music

11 Sopron
Out of reach of Mongol and Turk invaders, this city has fine unspoiled medieval buildings

12 Prague
Prague's stately castle watches over this elegant cultural city, also loved for its beer

13 Karlstejn Castle
(near Beroun)With lavish rooms built to house relics of the Holy Roman Empire

118 ▶

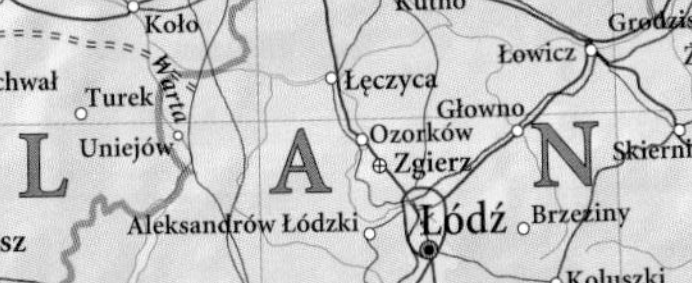
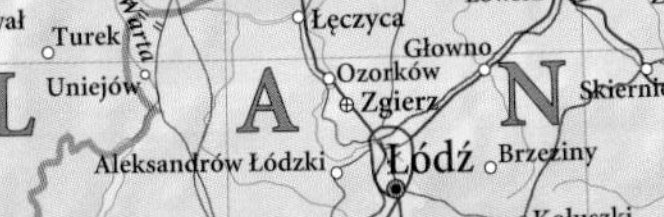

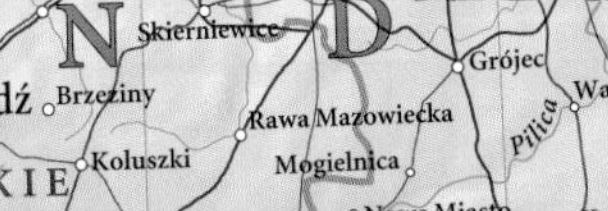

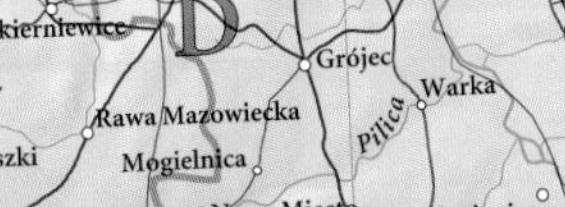

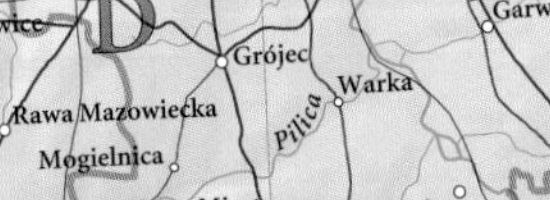
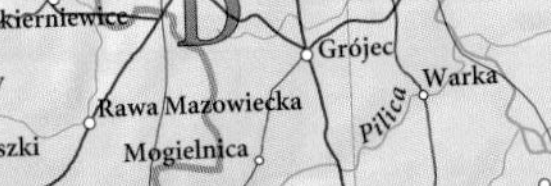
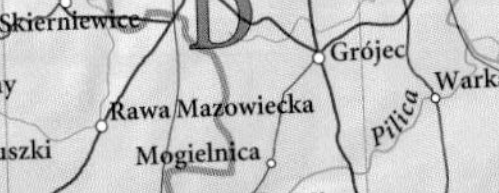

BALTIC SEA
Gulf of Danzig
Pomeranian Bay
RUSSIAN FEDERATION (Kaliningrad)
LITHUANIA
BELARUS
POLAND
POMORSKIE
ZACHODNIO-POMORSKIE
WARMIŃSKO-MAZURSKIE
PODLASKIE
KUJAWSKO-POMORSKIE
MAZOWIECKIE
WIELKOPOLSKIE
LUBUSKIE
ŁÓDZKIE
LUBELSKIE
WARSZAWA (WARSAW)
Gdańsk
Gdynia
Sopot
Szczecin
Koszalin
Słupsk
Elbląg
Olsztyn
Białystok
Bydgoszcz
Toruń
Poznań
Łódź
Płock
Włocławek
Gorzów Wielkopolski
Kalisz
Zielona Góra

Tyn Church, Prague: Dominating one side of the Old Town Square, this Gothic church with fine Baroque interior was founded in 1385, with characteristic asymmetrical spires to represent both masculine and feminine sides of the world.

Activities
Escape bustling streets in Budapest's period-piece **Gerbeaud** coffee house
Get a taste for Hungary's most distinctive cooking ingredient at the **Paprika Museum** in Kalocsa, Hungary
Immerse yourself in a classical concert in the **Aggtelek caves**, Hungary
Take the waters in the scenic spa town of **Karlovy Vary**, Czech Republic
Settle down to a Sunday morning summer concert at Chopin's birthplace of **Zelazowa Wola**, west of Warsaw
Visit the museum of Copernicus, famous for proposing the heliocentric theory of the solar system, at his birthplace in Gothic **Torun**, Poland,
Cycle through the Slovakian **Tatra Mountains** on a network of trails
SCALE 1:2,750,000
(projection: Lambert Conformal Conic)
Km
Miles
Map Key
POPULATION
1 million to 5 million
500,000 to 1 million
100,000 to 500,000
50,000 to 100,000
10,000 to 50,000
below 10,000
ELEVATION
2000m / 6562ft
1000m / 3281ft
500m / 1640ft
250m / 820ft
100m / 328ft
sea level
100
108
112
116
CZECH REPUBLIC
SLOVAKIA
HUNGARY
AUSTRIA
UKRAINE
ROMANIA
CROATIA
SLOVENIA
SERB. & MON. (YUGOSLAVIA)
PRAHA (PRAGUE)
BRATISLAVA
BUDAPEST
Carpathian Mountains
Great Hungarian Plain
Little Alföld
Bohemian Forest

Babolna Stud Farm, Hungary: This famous stud farm was set up by Emperor Joseph II in 1789, and developed the elegant Shagya-Arabian horse, ideal for driving carriages and riding.

Southeast Europe

Albania, Bosnia & Herzegovina, Croatia, Macedonia, Serbia & Montenegro (Yugoslavia)

For tourists, Croatia stands out among the successor states created from the break-up of communist Yugoslavia in the 1990s. Its beautiful Dalmatian coast, bordering the Adriatic Sea, has a Mediterranean climate so well suited to beach holidays in the sun that it can rival the Spanish Costas. In addition, it is studded with historic towns, of which Dubrovnik is the crowning glory, the architectural styles of the Balkans combining with influences from neighbouring Italy.

Elsewhere, though currently less visited, the other countries of this region have plenty of attractions for the discerning and curious traveller. There is beautiful countryside, great for hiking in the summer and skiing in the winter, plus a rich historical legacy from the last 2,500 years – the power of Alexander the Great's kingdom of Macedon peaked in the 4th century BCE, its fortunes superceding those of ancient Greece in previous centuries. Further influences from the Roman era can be traced in fine architectural remains, notably the immense palace at Split. Byzantine influences are also strong. In medieval times the ebb and flow of contending Ottoman and Austro-Hungarian armies up and down the Danube left Croatia endowed with a string of impressive castles and the lands to the south marked by Ottoman Muslim traditions.

Dubrovnik, Croatia: This architecturally unique city arose in the 12th century when the sea channel between the islet settlement of Ragusa and the mainland was filled in to become the marble-paved main street, Placa Stradun. At that time the city's walls were begun in order to defend against any attacks, from sea or from land.

Jajce: Due to its period under the Muslim Ottoman empire, Bosnia & Herzegovina has many mosques, such as those in the charming medieval town of Jajce.

108
110
116

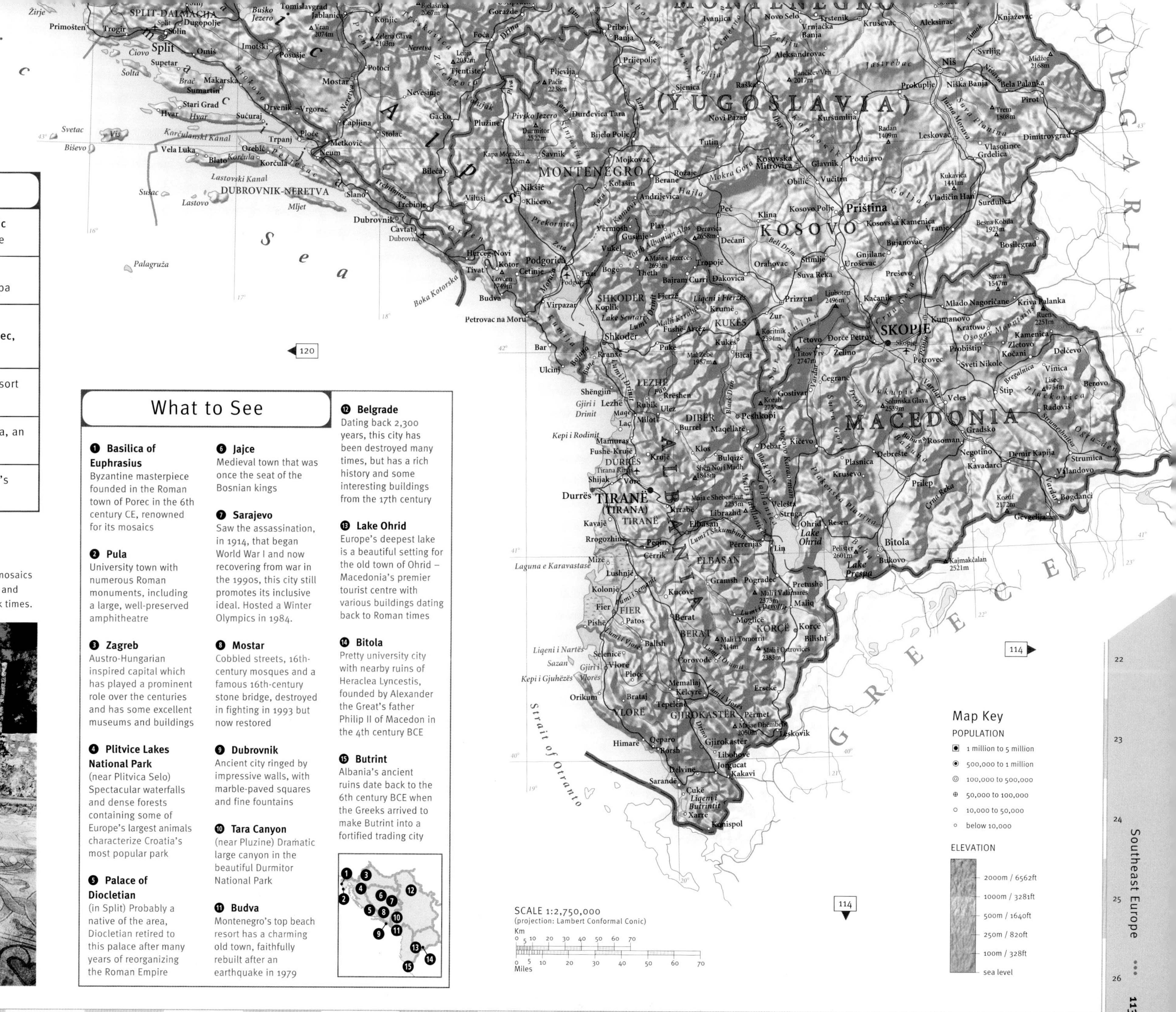

Adriatic Sea
(YUGOSLAVIA)
MONTENEGRO
KOSOVO
MACEDONIA
ALBANIA
BULGARIA
GREECE
Dinaric Alps
SPLIT-DALMACIJA
DUBROVNIK-NERETVA
Split
Dubrovnik
Podgorica
Priština
SKOPJE
TIRANË (TIRANA)
Durrës
Bitola
Lake Ohrid
Lake Prespa
Strait of Otranto
Map Key
POPULATION
1 million to 5 million
500,000 to 1 million
100,000 to 500,000
50,000 to 100,000
10,000 to 50,000
below 10,000
ELEVATION
2000m / 6562ft
1000m / 3281ft
500m / 1640ft
250m / 820ft
100m / 328ft
sea level
SCALE 1:2,750,000
(projection: Lambert Conformal Conic)

106
120
114
114

Activities

Bathe on the beaches on the **"Adriatic Riviera"**, Dalmatia's popular coastline

Hike around Macedonia's **Pelister National Park**, overlooking Lake Prespa

Visit the castles of north Croatia, such as **Veliki Tabor**, **Varazdin**, **Cakovec**, and **Trakoscan**

Ski in **Kapaonik**, the largest winter resort in Serbia

Wander through the ruins of Apollonia, an ancient Greek city in **Albania**

Raft down the Neretva river in Bosnia's new **Prenj National Park**

Butrint: Albania's ancient remains have fine mosaics from the late Roman era in the 5th century CE and other earlier sites date back to classical Greek times.

What to See

1 Basilica of Euphrasius
Byzantine masterpiece founded in the Roman town of Porec in the 6th century CE, renowned for its mosaics

2 Pula
University town with numerous Roman monuments, including a large, well-preserved amphitheatre

3 Zagreb
Austro-Hungarian inspired capital which has played a prominent role over the centuries and has some excellent museums and buildings

4 Plitvice Lakes National Park
(near Plitvica Selo) Spectacular waterfalls and dense forests containing some of Europe's largest animals characterize Croatia's most popular park

5 Palace of Diocletian
(in Split) Probably a native of the area, Diocletian retired to this palace after many years of reorganizing the Roman Empire

6 Jajce
Medieval town that was once the seat of the Bosnian kings

7 Sarajevo
Saw the assassination, in 1914, that began World War I and now recovering from war in the 1990s, this city still promotes its inclusive ideal. Hosted a Winter Olympics in 1984.

8 Mostar
Cobbled streets, 16th-century mosques and a famous 16th-century stone bridge, destroyed in fighting in 1993 but now restored

9 Dubrovnik
Ancient city ringed by impressive walls, with marble-paved squares and fine fountains

10 Tara Canyon
(near Pluzine) Dramatic large canyon in the beautiful Durmitor National Park

11 Budva
Montenegro's top beach resort has a charming old town, faithfully rebuilt after an earthquake in 1979

12 Belgrade
Dating back 2,300 years, this city has been destroyed many times, but has a rich history and some interesting buildings from the 17th century

13 Lake Ohrid
Europe's deepest lake is a beautiful setting for the old town of Ohrid – Macedonia's premier tourist centre with various buildings dating back to Roman times

14 Bitola
Pretty university city with nearby ruins of Heraclea Lyncestis, founded by Alexander the Great's father Philip II of Macedon in the 4th century BCE

15 Butrint
Albania's ancient ruins date back to the 6th century BCE when the Greeks arrived to make Butrint into a fortified trading city

Bulgaria & Greece

Including European Turkey

Greece is acclaimed as the original heart of Western civilization. Amid its rugged terrain and numerous islands, a golden age of philosophy and the arts flourished in the 5th and 4th centuries BCE. The farming and seafaring skills on which this glory was built are still evident today, but the rapid urbanization of the past 50 years has left more than half the population now living in the capital, Athens, and in the northern city of Salonica. The country has an extraordinary wealth of internationally renowned ancient sights, as well as many fine monasteries set in fabulous mountain scenery picturesque villages, dramatic gorges and secluded coves. The idyllic islands are popular destinations, mixing sun, sea, scenery and sights with nightlife ranging from the relaxed to the hectic.

Bulgaria, which like Greece was dominated for centuries by the Ottoman Turks, became part of the Soviet bloc after World War II but has gradually emerged since 1989 on a path towards European integration. Its tourist industry, once mainly based around good-value skiing and Black Sea beach resorts, is now attracting a growing number of visitors fascinated by its heritage, including fine Roman remains, Byzantine churches and beautiful monasteries.

What to See

1 Plovdiv
Bulgaria's second city has a charming old town, Byzantine churches, Turkish mosques and a Roman amphitheatre only uncovered during a freak landslide in 1972

2 Koprivshtitsa
(near Pirdop) Carefully preserved village in the Sredna Gora mountains, with cobblestone streets and over 400 restored historic buildings

3 Sofia
City of fine churches at the foot of Mount Vitosha, part of a national park including the serene 1345 Dragalevtsi Monastery

4 Rila Monastery
(near Blagoevgrad) Bulgaria's largest and most famous religious centre, set in the scenic Rila mountains, was founded in 927 CE

5 Meteora
Extraordinary medieval monasteries perched on almost inaccessible pinnacles of rock

6 Mount Athos
Women are debarred from entering the peninsula, a preserve of monasticism since the 5th century CE. Its 20 monasteries are of great architectural and artistic interest, set amid superb coastal scenery

7 Delphi
(at Delfoi) Believed by the ancients to be the centre of the earth, the site of the oracle includes the temple and theatre of Apollo

8 Athens
Pericles oversaw from 447 BCE the building of the Parthenon and Acropolis, now among many treasures in the ancient city

9 Mycenae
(near Argos) Imposing Lion Gate and city ruins discovered in 1874 by Heinrich Schliemann in his quest for a factual basis for Homer's epics

10 Kardamaina
(on Kos) Golden sands and swinging nightlife

11 Mykonos
A sun-seeker's paradise: tavernas, discos, family and nudist beaches and water sports

12 Knossos Palace
(near Irakleio) The largest Minoan palace, vividly coloured home of the legendary King Minos and the minotaur, reached its zenith over 3,500 years ago

Istanbul *see* pp136–137

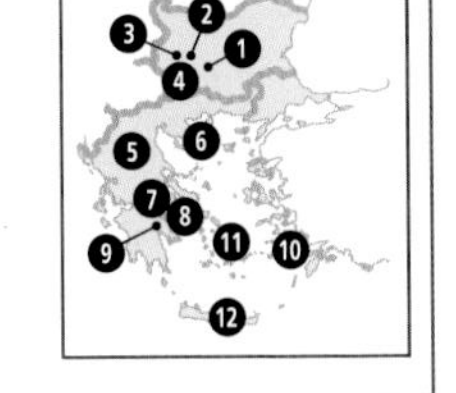
3
2
1
4
5
6
7
8
9
11
10
12

Activities

Take the day trek down Crete's famous **Samaria Gorge** to the village of Agia Roumeli, then enjoy the unusually cool water at the beach

Give "martinitsas" (small red and white thread dolls) to mark spring in Bulgaria

Take the dramatic **Dhiakofto** to **Kalavryta** train via the Vouraikos Gorge, near Patra

Watch the endangered loggerhead turtles at **Laganas** on Zakynthos, Ionian Islands

Hike to the summit of **Mount Olympus**, believed by the ancient Greeks to be the home of the gods

Attend the **Festival of Roses**, Kazanluk, Bulgaria – petals are picked for perfume

Corfu: Naturalist Gerald Durrell's childhood home, and setting for several of his books, is a top destination for sun-seekers. It is one of the beautiful Ionian Islands, the largest of which, Kefallinia, was the setting for another bestseller, *Captain Corelli's Mandolin* by Louis de Bernières.

ROMANIA
BULGARIA
BLACK SEA
TURKEY
SERBIA & MONTENEGRO (YUGOSLAVIA)
MACEDONIA
Sofia
Plovdiv
Varna
Burgas
Ruse
Istanbul
Map Key
POPULATION
above 5 million
1 million to 5 million
500,000 to 1 million
100,000 to 500,000
50,000 to 100,000
10,000 to 50,000
below 10,000
ELEVATION
3000m / 9843ft
2000m / 6562ft
1000m / 3281ft
500m / 1640ft
250m / 820ft
100m / 328ft
sea level

116
112

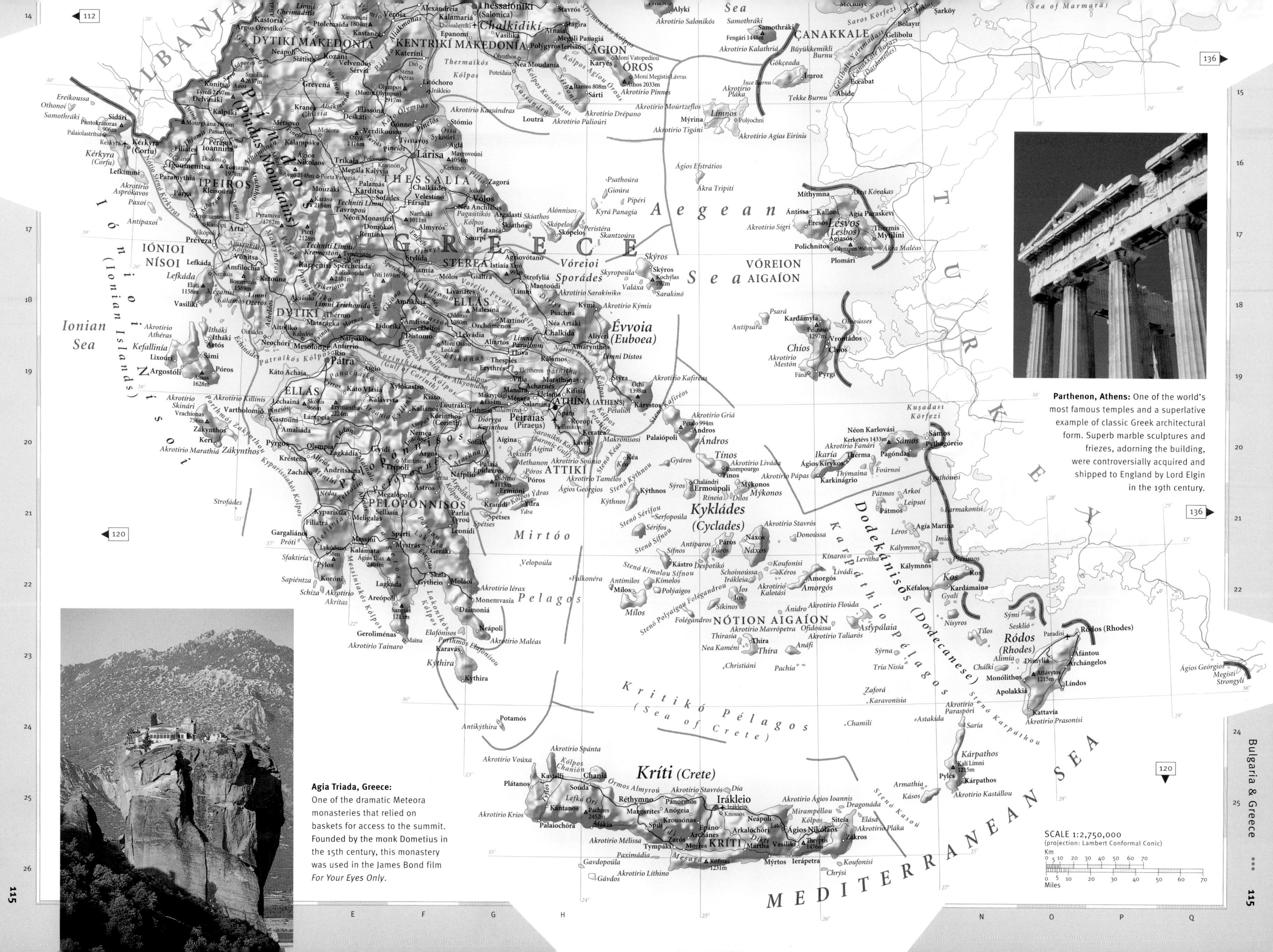
GREECE
TURKEY
ALBANIA
Aegean Sea
MEDITERRANEAN SEA
Ionian Sea
Iónioi Nísoi (Ionian Islands)
Píndos (Pindus Mountains)
Kykládes (Cyclades)
Dodekánisos (Dodecanese)
Kríti (Crete)
Kritikó Pélagos (Sea of Crete)
Karpáthio Pélagos
Mirtóo Pelagos
Vóreioi Sporádes
VÓREION AIGAÍON
NÓTION AIGAÍON
PELOPÓNNISOS
ATTIKÍ
STEREÁ ELLÁS
THESSALÍA
ÍPEIROS
KENTRIKÍ MAKEDONÍA
DYTIKÍ MAKEDONÍA
DYTIKÍ ELLÁS
IÓNIOI NÍSOI
ÁGION ÓROS
ÇANAKKALE
Athína (Athens)
Peiraías (Piraeus)
Thessaloníki (Salonica)
Irákleio
Ródos (Rhodes)
Évvoia (Euboea)
Lésvos (Lesbos)
Chíos
Sámos
Kos
Kárpathos
Kýthira
SCALE 1:2,750,000
(projection: Lambert Conformal Conic)
Km
Miles

Parthenon, Athens: One of the world's most famous temples and a superlative example of classic Greek architectural form. Superb marble sculptures and friezes, adorning the building, were controversially acquired and shipped to England by Lord Elgin in the 19th century.

Agia Triada, Greece: One of the dramatic Meteora monasteries that relied on baskets for access to the summit. Founded by the monk Dometius in the 15th century, this monastery was used in the James Bond film *For Your Eyes Only*.

Romania, Moldova & Ukraine

Bridging the divide between central Europe and Russia are a trio of under-visited countries – Romania, its former Soviet neighbour Moldova and the far larger Ukraine. The very cultures of the region can entice visitors keen to experience another, transitional, side of Europe, en route from the dark and mysterious forests of Transylvania, through the acres of vineyards in Moldova's central Codru wine region and on into the plains and ancient cities of Ukraine.

Romania and Moldova are close cousins, speaking a language which is recognizably Latin in origin and sharing a heritage which prides itself on its ties to the West. However, these countries still remain intriguingly "eastern European". In Ukraine you can find a real eagerness to embrace Europe, yet much of the population (particularly in the east) is Russian-speaking and there are close ties with the country's long-dominant eastern neighbour.

Fresco at the Voronet Monastery, Romania: This detail of the Last Judgement is from the Voronet Monastery, one of the finest examples of the painted churches in the northeastern Bukovina region. The monastery was built in 1488 to celebrate the defeat of the Turks by the Romanian prince, Stephen.

Activities

- Explore the tunnels and taste the wine of the underground winery at **Cricova Cellars**, near Chisinau
- Bask in the sun and paddle at the **Black Sea** resorts of Romania and the Crimea
- Discover the fact and fiction surrounding legend on a dedicated "Dracula" tour of **Transylvania**
- Promenade along the Black Sea waterfront at **Yalta**
- Hike around the wonderful, forest-covered mountains of the **Ukrainian Carpathians**
- Cool your feet in the fountain in Kiev's **Independence Square** after a hard day's sightseeing
- Attend a church service among the Christian Turks of **Gagauzia** in southern Moldova

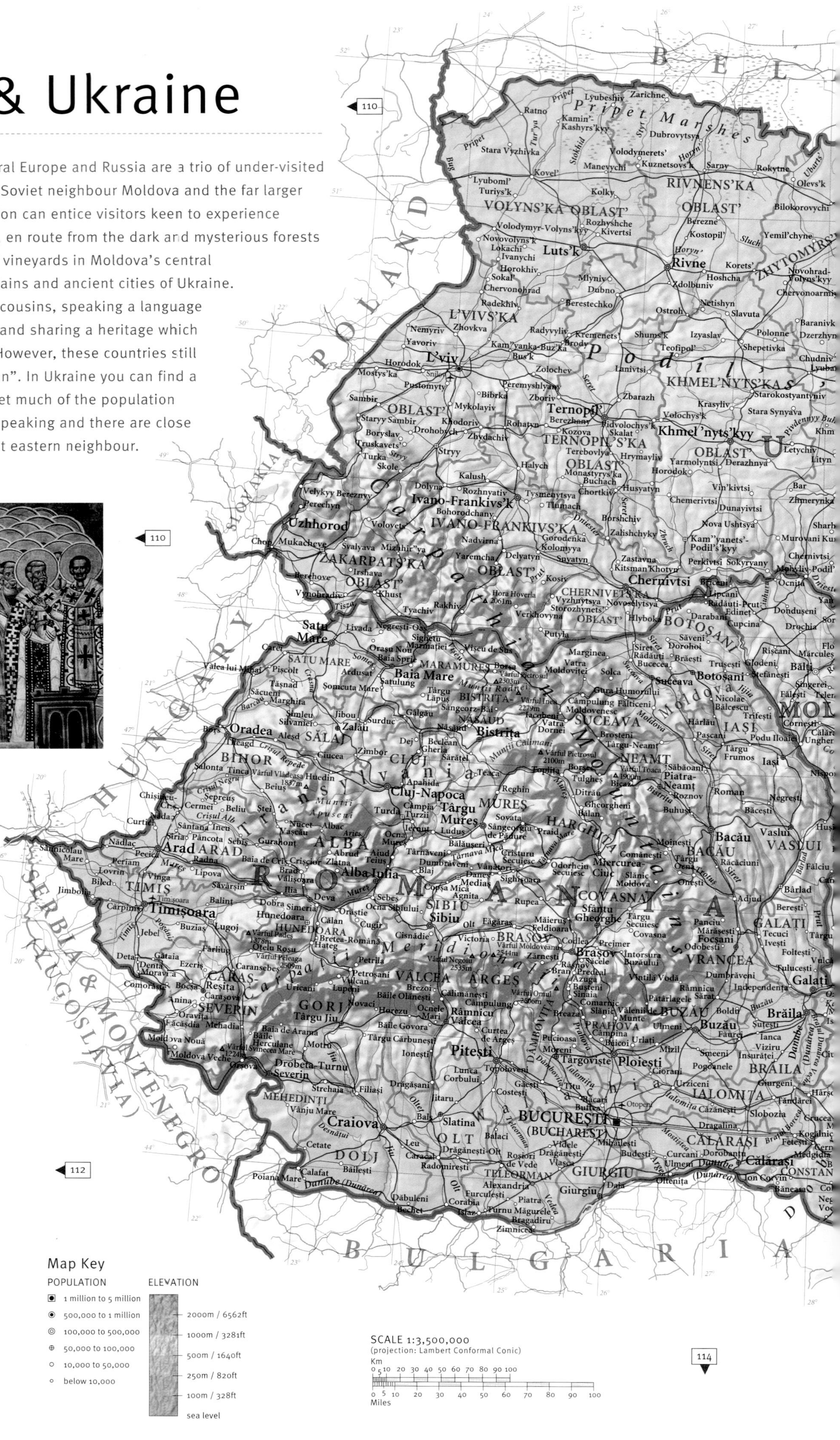

110
110
112
114

Map Key

POPULATION
- 1 million to 5 million
- 500,000 to 1 million
- 100,000 to 500,000
- 50,000 to 100,000
- 10,000 to 50,000
- below 10,000

ELEVATION
- 2000m / 6562ft
- 1000m / 3281ft
- 500m / 1640ft
- 250m / 820ft
- 100m / 328ft
- sea level

SCALE 1:3,500,000
(projection: Lambert Conformal Conic)
Km 0 5 10 20 30 40 50 60 70 80 90 100
Miles 0 5 10 20 30 40 50 60 70 80 90 100

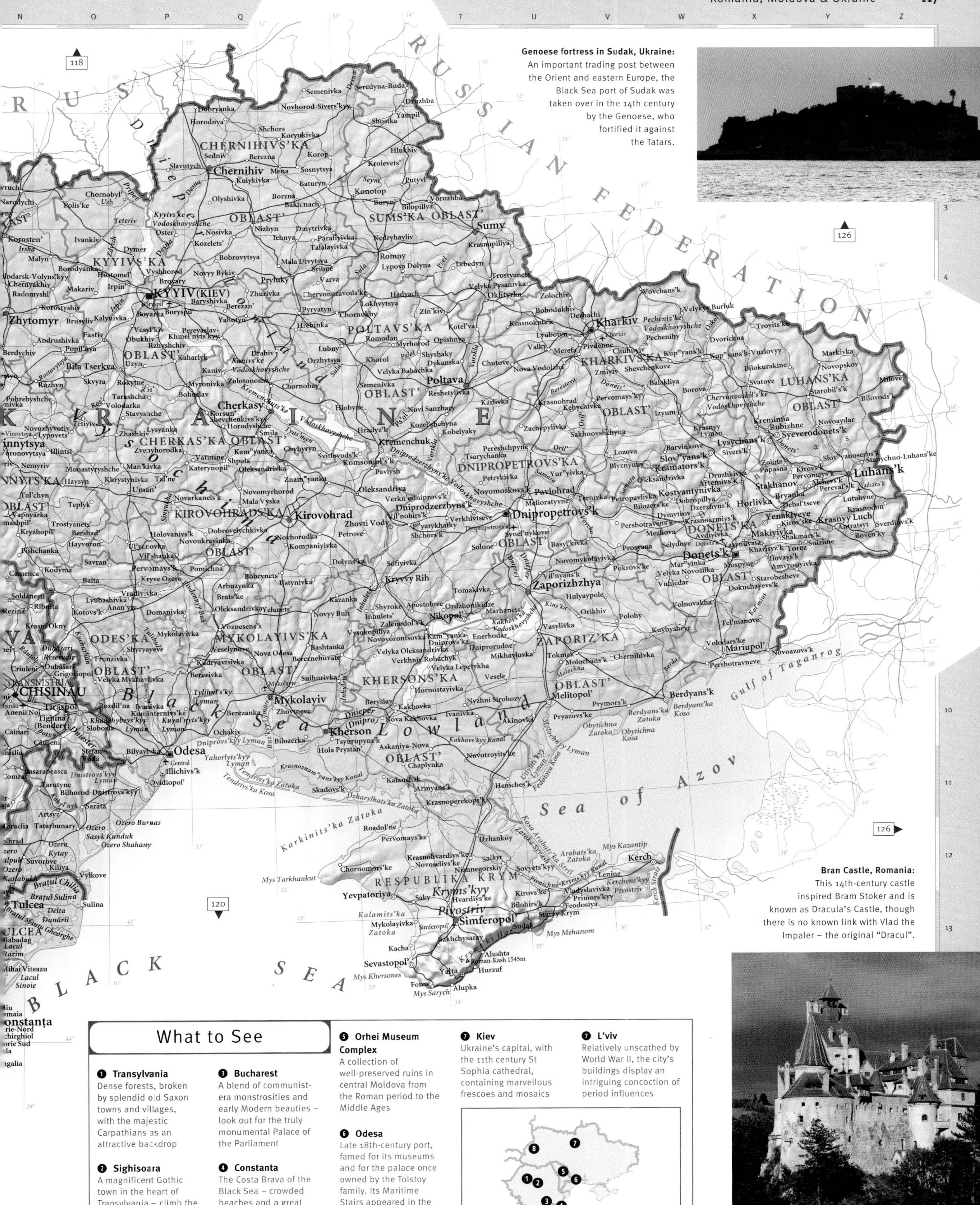
RUSSIAN FEDERATION
UKRAINE
BLACK SEA
Sea of Azov
Gulf of Taganrog
Dnieper Lowland
Black Sea Lowland
CHERNIHIVS'KA OBLAST'
SUMS'KA OBLAST'
KYYIVS'KA OBLAST'
POLTAVS'KA OBLAST'
KHARKIVS'KA OBLAST'
LUHANS'KA OBLAST'
CHERKAS'KA OBLAST'
KIROVOHRADS'KA OBLAST'
DNIPROPETROVS'KA OBLAST'
DONETS'KA OBLAST'
ODES'KA OBLAST'
MYKOLAYIVS'KA OBLAST'
KHERSONS'KA OBLAST'
ZAPORIZ'KA OBLAST'
RESPUBLIKA KRYM
KYYIV (KIEV)
Chernihiv
Sumy
Kharkiv
Poltava
Cherkasy
Kirovohrad
Kremenchuk
Dnipropetrovs'k
Donets'k
Luhans'k
Zaporizhzhya
Kryvyy Rih
Mykolayiv
Kherson
Odesa
CHISINAU
Simferopol'
Sevastopol'
Yevpatoriya
Kerch
Melitopol'
Berdyans'k
Mariupol'
Zhytomyr
Vinnytsya
118
126
120

Genoese fortress in Sudak, Ukraine: An important trading post between the Orient and eastern Europe, the Black Sea port of Sudak was taken over in the 14th century by the Genoese, who fortified it against the Tatars.

Bran Castle, Romania: This 14th-century castle inspired Bram Stoker and is known as Dracula's Castle, though there is no known link with Vlad the Impaler – the original "Dracul".

What to See

❶ Transylvania
Dense forests, broken by splendid old Saxon towns and villages, with the majestic Carpathians as an attractive backdrop

❷ Sighisoara
A magnificent Gothic town in the heart of Transylvania – climb the tower for unrivalled views

❸ Bucharest
A blend of communist-era monstrosities and early Modern beauties – look out for the truly monumental Palace of the Parliament

❹ Constanta
The Costa Brava of the Black Sea – crowded beaches and a great party atmosphere

❺ Orhei Museum Complex
A collection of well-preserved ruins in central Moldova from the Roman period to the Middle Ages

❻ Odesa
Late 18th-century port, famed for its museums and for the palace once owned by the Tolstoy family. Its Maritime Stairs appeared in the film *Battleship Potemkin*

❼ Kiev
Ukraine's capital, with the 11th century St Sophia cathedral, containing marvellous frescoes and mosaics

❼ L'viv
Relatively unscathed by World War II, the city's buildings display an intriguing concoction of period influences

The Baltic States & Belarus

Belarus, Estonia, Latvia, Lithuania, Kaliningrad

Estonia's walled and cobble-streeted capital, Tallinn, has become a particular favourite for lovers of the picturesque. Indeed, what Estonia, Latvia and Lithuania may lack in major tourist highlights, they make up for in charm. Their towns and landscapes have been attracting an increasing flow of visitors since they won back independence from the old Soviet Union in the early 1990s. The many museums reflect local pride in national traditions, with strong European roots in the dominant Lutheran religion and a powerful musical tradition. Belarus is an enigmatic country covered with forests and marshes. Its cities are dominated by communist-era buildings.

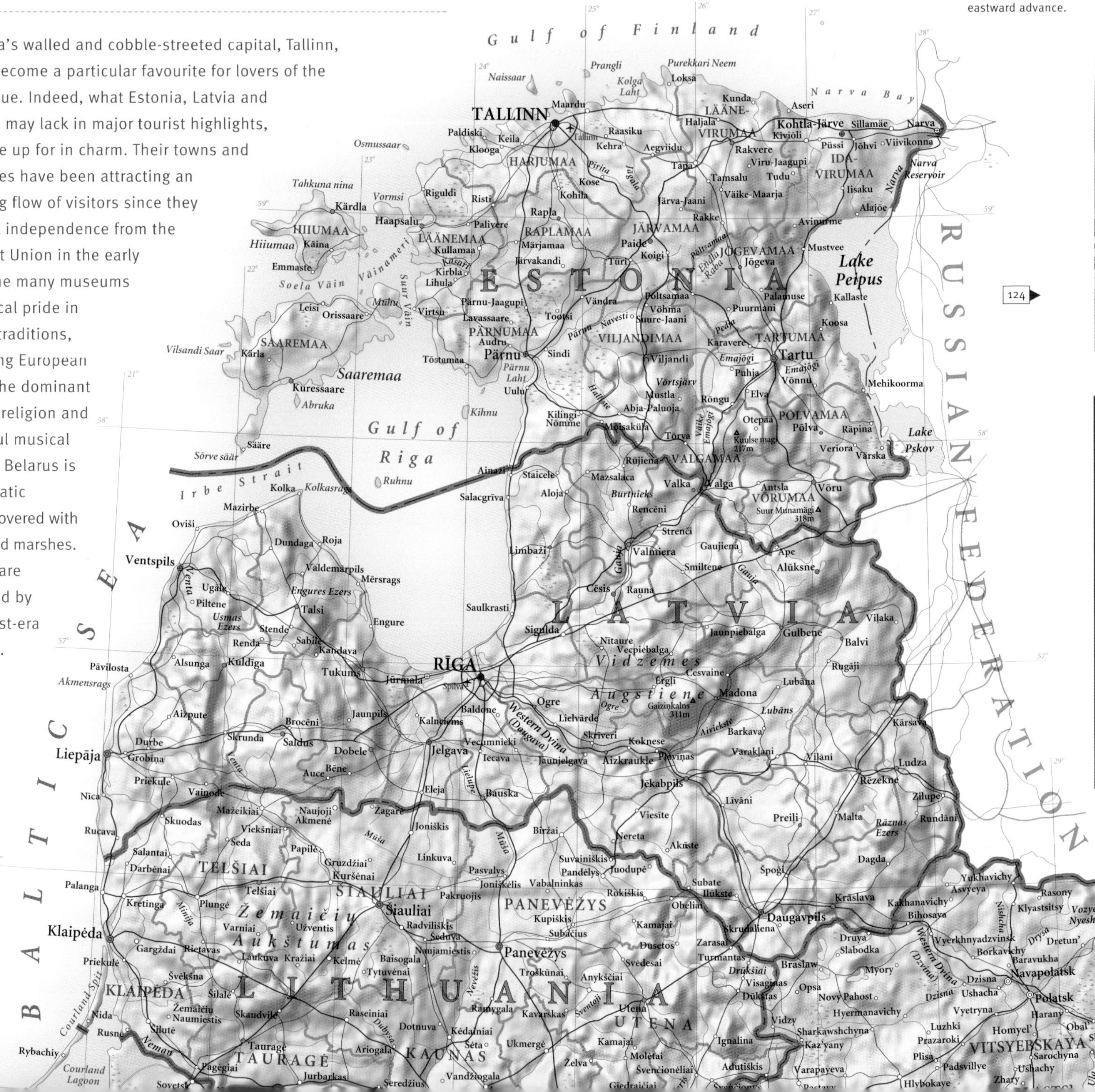

Alexander Nevsky Cathedral, Tallinn: This richly decorated Orthodox church was built in 1900 by an architect from Saint Petersburg. It is dedicated to the Prince of Novgorod, who led the Ice Battle on Lake Peipus in 1242 and halted the Germans' eastward advance.

Activities

- Ride horses in the **Gouja National Park**, Latvia
- Enjoy **Tallinn's** musical delights – from street choirs, brass bands and string quartets to the Estonian National Opera
- Drink coffee in café-culture **Tartu**, Estonia's renowned university town
- Prove it is not possible to "walk the seven bridges of Königsberg" (**Kaliningrad**) without crossing your own path – a renowned 18th-century mathematical problem
- Watch a performance of world champions of Latin American Formation Dancing in **Klaipeda**, Lithuania
- Visit Belarus's working farm and reconstructed 19th-century living museum village at **Dudutki**

▲ 92
124 ▶
126 ▶

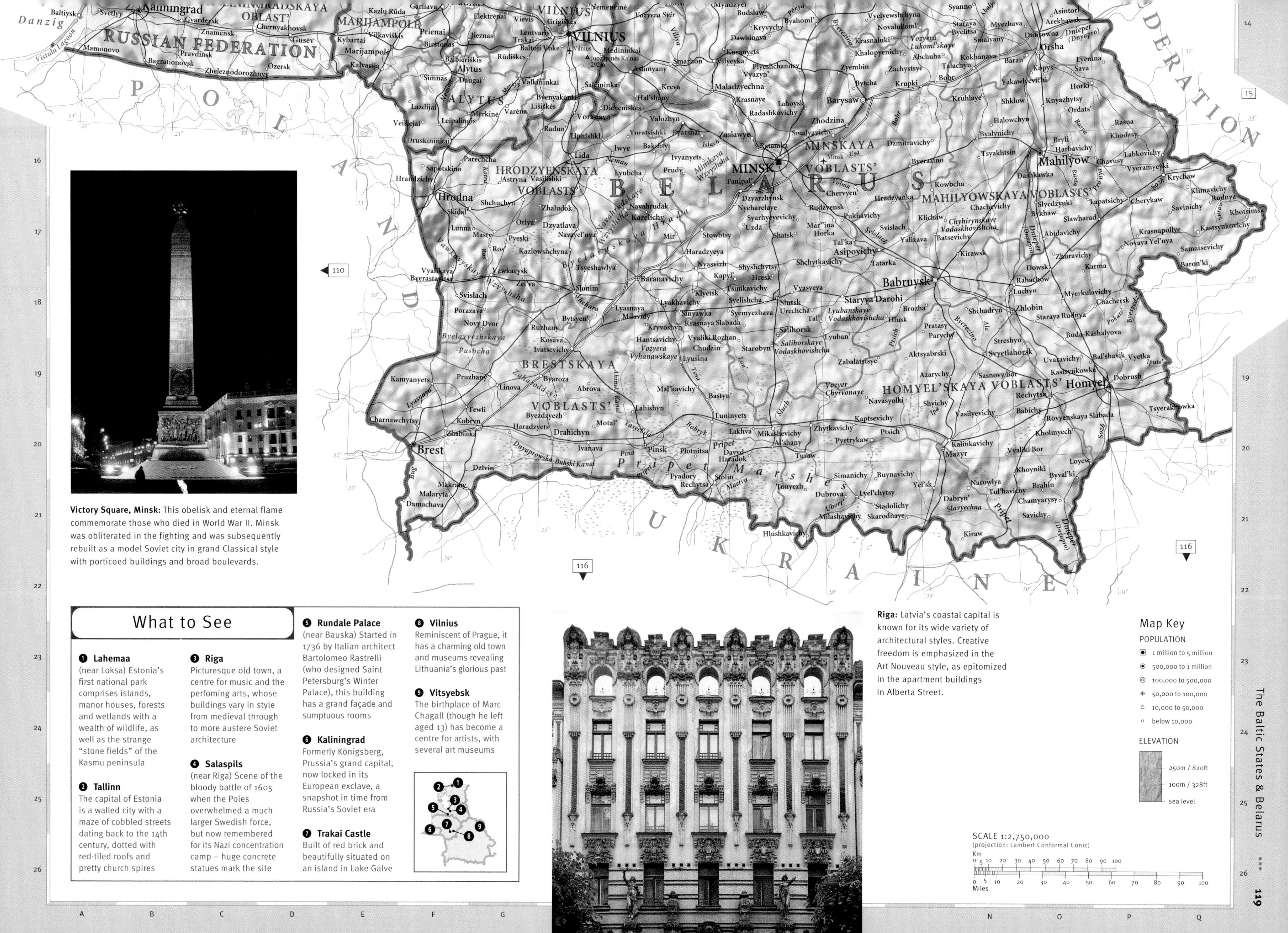

RUSSIAN FEDERATION
POLAND
BELARUS
UKRAINE
VILNIUS
MINSK
HRODZYENSKAYA VOBLASTS'
MINSKAYA VOBLASTS'
MAHILYOWSKAYA VOBLASTS'
BRESTSKAYA VOBLASTS'
HOMYEL'SKAYA VOBLASTS'
Kaliningrad
Hrodna
Brest
Baranavichy
Babruysk
Mahilyow
Homyel'
Pinsk
Mazyr
Barysaw
Orsha
Pripet Marshes
Dnieper (Dnyapro)
110
116
116
15

Victory Square, Minsk: This obelisk and eternal flame commemorate those who died in World War II. Minsk was obliterated in the fighting and was subsequently rebuilt as a model Soviet city in grand Classical style with porticoed buildings and broad boulevards.

What to See

❶ Lahemaa
(near Loksa) Estonia's first national park comprises islands, manor houses, forests and wetlands with a wealth of wildlife, as well as the strange "stone fields" of the Kasmu peninsula

❷ Tallinn
The capital of Estonia is a walled city with a maze of cobbled streets dating back to the 14th century, dotted with red-tiled roofs and pretty church spires

❸ Riga
Picturesque old town, a centre for music and the perfoming arts, whose buildings vary in style from medieval through to more austere Soviet architecture

❹ Salaspils
(near Riga) Scene of the bloody battle of 1605 when the Poles overwhelmed a much larger Swedish force, but now remembered for its Nazi concentration camp – huge concrete statues mark the site

❺ Rundale Palace
(near Bauska) Started in 1736 by Italian architect Bartolomeo Rastrelli (who designed Saint Petersburg's Winter Palace), this building has a grand façade and sumptuous rooms

❻ Kaliningrad
Formerly Königsberg, Prussia's grand capital, now locked in its European exclave, a snapshot in time from Russia's Soviet era

❼ Trakai Castle
Built of red brick and beautifully situated on an island in Lake Galve

❽ Vilnius
Reminiscent of Prague, it has a charming old town and museums revealing Lithuania's glorious past

❾ Vitsyebsk
The birthplace of Marc Chagall (though he left aged 13) has become a centre for artists, with several art museums

Riga: Latvia's coastal capital is known for its wide variety of architectural styles. Creative freedom is emphasized in the Art Nouveau style, as epitomized in the apartment buildings in Alberta Street.

Map Key

POPULATION
- 1 million to 5 million
- 500,000 to 1 million
- 100,000 to 500,000
- 50,000 to 100,000
- 10,000 to 50,000
- below 10,000

ELEVATION
- 250m / 820ft
- 100m / 328ft
- sea level

SCALE 1:2,750,000
(projection: Lambert Conformal Conic)

The Mediterranean

The warm, sunny climate and beautiful beaches of the Mediterranean would themselves be enough to make it a highly attractive holiday region, but it is the cultural legacy that makes it truly irresistible. Throughout history this virtually landlocked sea, stretching from Gibraltar to the coast of the Near East, has been crisscrossed by traders and conquerors, leaving behind them great Greek temples in Turkey and Italy, Roman cities in north Africa, Moorish palaces in Spain and imposing fortifications at strategic locations. A way to make sense of all the connections is a themed cruise around the sea.

Mandraki harbour, Rhodes: This beautiful Greek island is also one of its most popular, dominated by its ancient walled city, begun in 408 BCE.

SCALE 1:10,100,000
(projection: Lambert Conformal Conic)
Km
0 25 50 100 150 200 250 300
0 25 50 100 150 200 250 300
Miles
ATLANTIC OCEAN
PORTUGAL
SPAIN
FRANCE
ANDORRA
MONACO
SWITZERLAND
SAN MARINO
VATICAN CITY
MOROCCO
ALGERIA
TUNISIA
MEDITERRANEAN
Bay of Biscay
Golfe du Lion
Ligurian Sea
Tyrrhenian Sea
Tyrrhenian Basin
Algerian Basin
Alboran Sea
Strait of Gibraltar
Strait of Bonifacio
Strait of Sicily
Islas Baleares (Balearic Islands)
Mallorca (Majorca)
Menorca (Minorca)
Eivissa (Ibiza)
Formentera
Corse (Corsica) (to France)
Sardegna (Sardinia) (to Italy)
Sicilia (Sicily)
Isole Pelagie (to Italy)
Isola di Pantelleria (to Italy)
GIBRALTAR (to UK)
Ceuta (part of Spain)
Melilla (part of Spain)
Cabo Ortegal
A Coruña
Cabo Fisterra
Gijón (Xixón)
Oviedo
Santander
Donostia-San Sebastián
Bilbao
Vitoria-Gasteiz
Pamplona (Iruña)
Logroño
Burgos
León
Ourense
Vigo
Porto
Vila Nova de Gaia
Cabo Mondego
Cabo Carvoeiro
LISBOA (LISBON)
Cabo da Roca
Setúbal
Cabo de São Vicente
Salamanca
Valladolid
Zaragoza
Lleida
Tarragona
Barcelona
Mataró
Sabadell
Costa Brava
MADRID
Getafe
Badajoz
Sierra Morena
Córdoba
Jaén
Sevilla (Seville)
Huelva
Golfo de Cádiz
Cádiz
Algeciras
Málaga
Granada
Sierra Nevada
Almería
Cabo de Gata
Costa del Sol
Cartagena
Cabo de Palos
Murcia
Elche
Alicante
Benidorm
Albacete
Valencia
Golfo de Valencia
Castelló de la Plana
Palma
Bordeaux
Toulouse
Montpellier
Nîmes
Perpignan
Marseille
Toulon
Cannes
Nice
Aix-en-Provence
Lyon
St-Étienne
Grenoble
Villeurbanne
Côte d'Azur
Ajaccio
Torino (Turin)
Milano (Milan)
Genova (Genoa)
Golfo di Genova
Bergamo
Brescia
Verona
Venezia (Venice)
Padova
Bologna
Firenze (Florence)
Pisa
Livorno
Perugia
Ravenna
Rimini
Ancona
ROMA (ROME)
Civitavecchia
Napoli (Naples)
Salerno
Palermo
Agrigento
Catania
Sassari
Cagliari
VALLETTA
Malta
Tanger
Kénitra
RABAT
Salé
Casablanca
Mohammedia
Meknès
Fès
Oujda
Safi
Marrakech
Haut Atlas
Moyen Atlas
Tlemcen
Oran
Mostaganem
Chlef
Sidi Bel Abbès
ALGER (ALGIERS)
Tizi Ouzou
Blida
Béjaïa
Skikda
Constantine
Sétif
Annaba
Batna
Atlas Tellien
Atlas Saharien
Hauts Plateaux
Chott El Hodna
Bizerte
TUNIS
Golfe de Hammamet
Sousse
Sfax
Gabès
Île de Jerba
Îles de Kerkenah
Médenine
ṬARĀBULUS (TRIPOLI)
Zuwārah
Al 'Azīzīyah
Gharyān
Al Khums
Miṣrātah

64
102
108
74

Activities

See the Barbary apes living on the **Rock of Gibraltar**, a British outpost on the Mediterranean	Trace the history of the Knights of St John, founded to guard the Holy Sepulchre, who resided in **Jerusalem**, **Cyprus**, **Rhodes** and finally **Malta**
Live it up in **Ibiza** (Balearic Islands) – the Mediterranean's wildest nightlife	Brush up on the ancient Greeks, throughout **Greece** and **Turkey**
Spot the celebrities on the **Côte d'Azur** at the Cannes film festival	Snorkel off volcanic **Thira** and relax on the Greek islands
Enjoy the thrills of the Grand Prix in the streets of **Monaco**, and gamble away in the Monte Carlo Casino	Watch loggerhead turtles nesting on beaches at **Pafos**, Cyprus (summer)
Visit Napoleon's birthplace in **Ajaccio**, on Corsica	Follow in Aeneas' footsteps around the Mediterranean to **Carthage**, Tunisia
Stop off at **Rome, Florence**, and **Venice** for the greatest art and architecture	Soak up the atmosphere of the **north African** *souqs*
Savour a cheesecake-like *pastizzi*, **Malta's** traditional snack	Explore north Africa's Roman sites: **Leptis Magna, Dougga** and **Djemila**

Majorca, Balearic Islands: The Coves d'Arta on the east coast have been hollowed out by the sea. Majorca's mild climate and lovely beaches attract hordes of visitors each year.

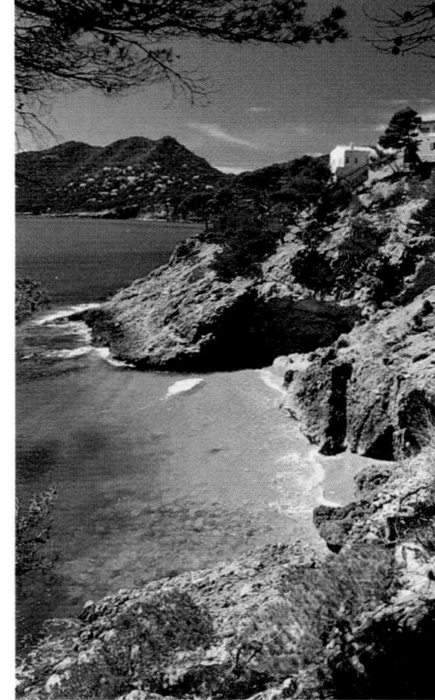

What to See – Malta

❶ **Ggantija**
(near Victoria) Temples of huge stone blocks begun in 3500 BCE

❷ **St Paul's Cathedral**
(near Rabat) Baroque cathedral crowning the ancient capital of Mdina

❸ **Valletta**
"City of Stairs". Visit St John's Co-Cathedral and Grand Master's Palace

❹ **Tarxien Temples**
(near Valletta) Three Megalithic temples, up to 6,000 years old, and the Hypogeum temple-cum-burial place – one of the world's major archaeological sites

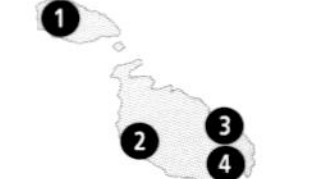

1
2
3
4

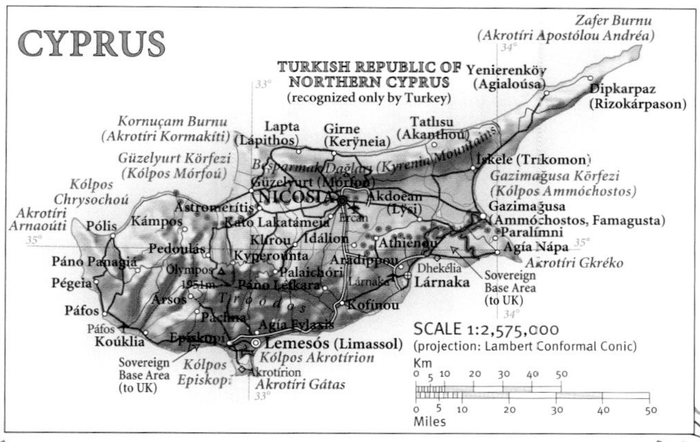

What to See – Cyprus

1 Cyprus Museum
(in Nicosia) Archaeological artefacts from all periods

2 Avakas Gorge
(near Pegeia) Trek in the wild Akamas peninsula

3 Pafos
Beautiful resort, plus ruins with fine mosaics

4 Palea Enklistra
(near Kouklia) This Byzantine cave-hermitage from around 1439 has an unusual frescoed ceiling

5 Kourian
(near Episkopi) Dating back to 1300 BCE, though most of its fabulous remains are later, this glorious city overlooking the sea has magnificent mosaics and a theatre

6 Troodos Mountains
Forested trails around Mount Olympos lead to monasteries and churches

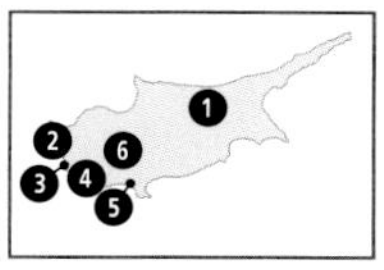

CYPRUS

TURKISH REPUBLIC OF NORTHERN CYPRUS (recognized only by Turkey)

SCALE 1:2,575,000
(projection: Lambert Conformal Conic)

In 1974 Turkey occupied the northern part of Cyprus while Greek Cypriots remained in control of the south. Cyprus was effectively partitioned and a UN buffer zone currently divides the two areas. In 1983 the north of the island proclaimed itself the Turkish Republic of North Cyprus. It was only recognized by Turkey.

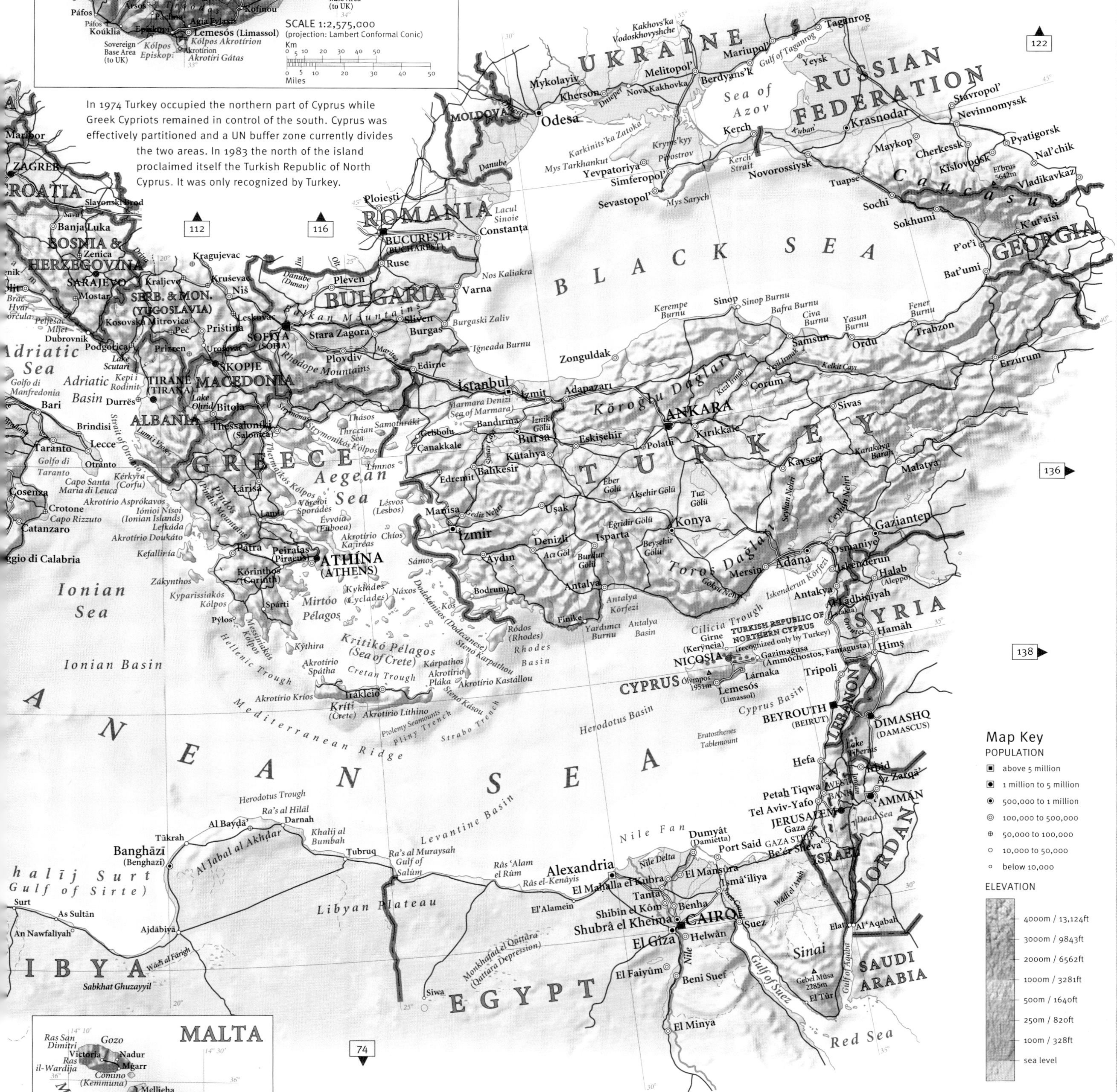

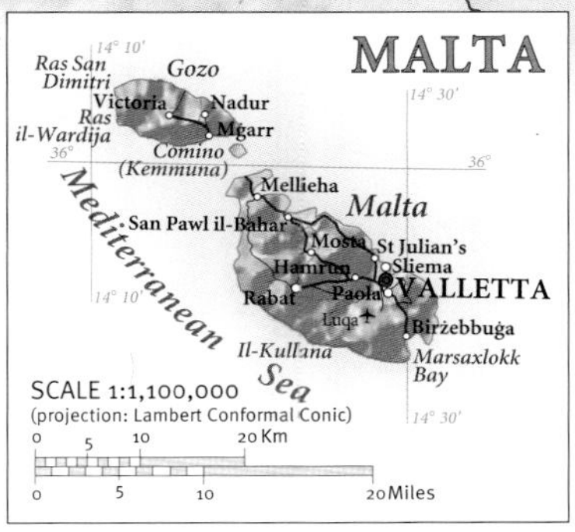

112
116
122
136
138
74

MALTA

SCALE 1:1,100,000
(projection: Lambert Conformal Conic)

Valletta, Malta: The Knights of St John lived on Malta from 1530 to 1798. After the defeat by the Turks in 1565, a new capital – Valletta – was planned as a massively fortified city.

Map Key

POPULATION
- above 5 million
- 1 million to 5 million
- 500,000 to 1 million
- 100,000 to 500,000
- 50,000 to 100,000
- 10,000 to 50,000
- below 10,000

ELEVATION
- 4000m / 13,124ft
- 3000m / 9843ft
- 2000m / 6562ft
- 1000m / 3281ft
- 500m / 1640ft
- 250m / 820ft
- 100m / 328ft
- sea level

SEA DEPTH
- sea level
- 250m / 820ft
- 500m / 1640ft
- 1000m / 3281ft
- 2000m / 6562ft
- 3000m / 9843ft

The Russian Federation

Throne Room, Petrodvorets, Saint Petersburg: The Petrodvorets palace, also known as Peterhof, was begun in 1714 as a summer residence for Peter the Great on the outskirts of the new capital. His daughter Elizabeth commissioned Italian architect Bartolomeo Rastrelli to rebuild the Great Palace in the Baroque style, creating the grand exterior seen today. In the 1770s, however, many rooms were redecorated in Classical style under Catherine the Great, including the richly gilded Throne Room.

Building on its history and its vast open spaces, Russia has a lot to entice the adventurous tourist and since the collapse of communism in 1991 it has stretched its arms wide to visitors. The great cities of Moscow and Saint Petersburg dominate European Russia. Both national capitals in their time, they are packed full of museums, galleries and palaces. Beautiful Tsarist architecture and the arresting onion-domed Orthodox cathedrals compete along skylines with the grandiose Soviet-era constructions, ranging from the austere concrete apartment blocks of the Moscow suburbs to Stalin's splendid Neo-Gothic wedding-cake seven sisters.

The Russian countryside remains a bigger draw to Russians than overseas visitors. Nonetheless, an excellent choice of climatic zones presents itself, extending from the "White Nights" of the Arctic Circle to the warmth of the Black Sea coast. Russia's vastness covers many landscapes – dark taiga forests, awesome mountain ranges and dramatic coastlines.

SCALE 1:20,850,000
(projection: Lambert Conformal Conic)

What to See

❶ Saint Petersburg
This pastel city of canals dazzles with its exquisite architecture and famous Hermitage Museum

❷ Velikiy Novgorod
A wonderful collection of architectural treasures dating to the 12th century

❸ Moscow
Vibrant capital with fine galleries, museums and excellent nightlife

❹ Golden Ring
"Open air museums" – small ancient towns that showcase Russia's medieval past, such as Yaroslavl' and Vladimir

❺ Sochi
Black Sea resort with splendid *dachas* and a Caucasus backdrop

❻ El'brus
Europe's highest peak soars 5,642 m (18,510 ft)

❼ Yekaterinburg
A cultural centre east of the Urals, scene of the murder of the last Tsar Nicholas II and his family in July 1918

❽ Yakutiya
Understand the culture of the hardy Evenk nomads who have adapted to life in this harsh Siberian region

❾ Lake Baikal
Nestled in mountains, a beautiful body of water with lakeside activities

❿ Vladivostok
Russia's San Francisco, with hilltop Pacific views

⓫ Lazovsky Nature Reserve
(near Vladivostock) Home of the elusive Amur tiger

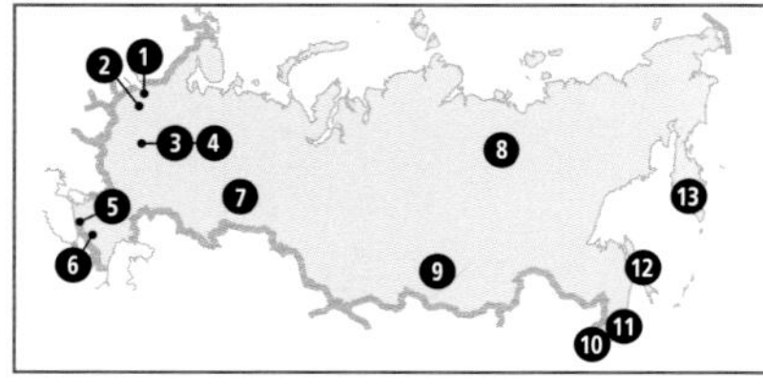

⓬ Sakhalin
A picturesque, peaceful Pacific wilderness

⓭ Kamchatka
Mountainous and forested frontier province – permits are required

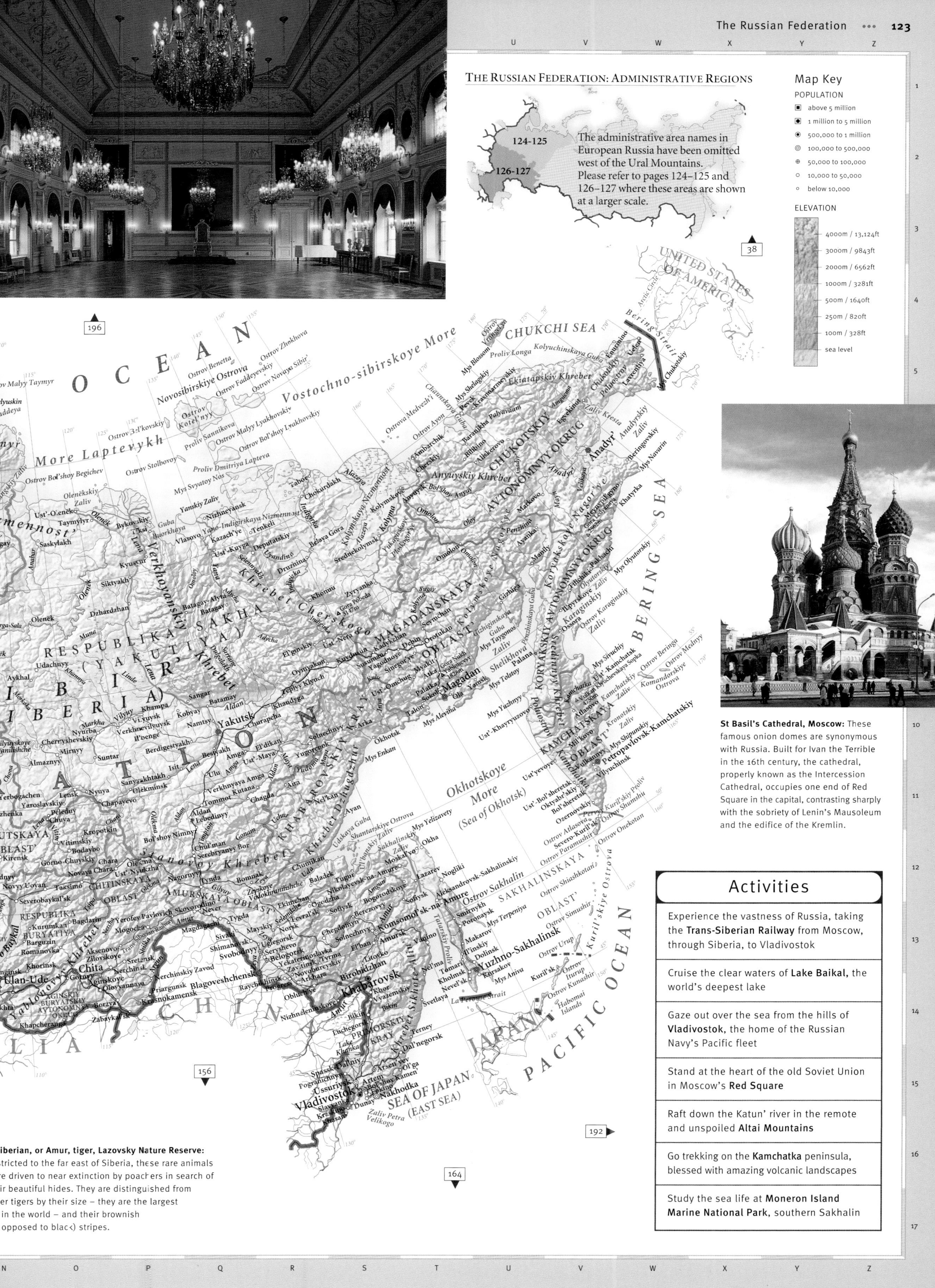
THE RUSSIAN FEDERATION: ADMINISTRATIVE REGIONS
124-125
126-127
The administrative area names in European Russia have been omitted west of the Ural Mountains. Please refer to pages 124–125 and 126–127 where these areas are shown at a larger scale.
38
Map Key
POPULATION
above 5 million
1 million to 5 million
500,000 to 1 million
100,000 to 500,000
50,000 to 100,000
10,000 to 50,000
below 10,000
ELEVATION
4000m / 13,124ft
3000m / 9843ft
2000m / 6562ft
1000m / 3281ft
500m / 1640ft
250m / 820ft
100m / 328ft
sea level
196
156
164
192
UNITED STATES OF AMERICA
OCEAN
CHUKCHI SEA
Vostochno-sibirskoye More
More Laptevykh
Novosibirskiye Ostrova
CHUKOTSKIY AVTONOMNYY OKRUG
KORYAKSKIY AVTONOMNYY OKRUG
MAGADANSKAYA OBLAST'
KAMCHATSKAYA OBLAST'
RESPUBLIKA SAKHA (YAKUTIYA)
KHABAROVSKIY KRAY
SAKHALINSKAYA OBLAST'
PRIMORSKIY KRAY
AMURSKAYA OBLAST'
CHITINSKAYA OBLAST'
BERING SEA
Bering Strait
Okhotskoye More (Sea of Okhotsk)
SEA OF JAPAN (EAST SEA)
PACIFIC OCEAN
JAPAN
CHINA
Yakutsk
Magadan
Anadyr'
Petropavlovsk-Kamchatskiy
Yuzhno-Sakhalinsk
Khabarovsk
Blagoveshchensk
Vladivostok
Nakhodka
Chita
Ulan-Ude
Komsomol'sk-na-Amure
Verkhoyanskiy Khrebet
Khrebet Cherskogo
Stanovoy Khrebet
La Perouse Strait
Tatarskiy Proliv

St Basil's Cathedral, Moscow: These famous onion domes are synonymous with Russia. Built for Ivan the Terrible in the 16th century, the cathedral, properly known as the Intercession Cathedral, occupies one end of Red Square in the capital, contrasting sharply with the sobriety of Lenin's Mausoleum and the edifice of the Kremlin.

A Siberian, or Amur, tiger, Lazovsky Nature Reserve: Restricted to the far east of Siberia, these rare animals were driven to near extinction by poachers in search of their beautiful hides. They are distinguished from other tigers by their size – they are the largest cat in the world – and their brownish (as opposed to black) stripes.

Activities

- Experience the vastness of Russia, taking the **Trans-Siberian Railway** from Moscow, through Siberia, to Vladivostok
- Cruise the clear waters of **Lake Baikal,** the world's deepest lake
- Gaze out over the sea from the hills of **Vladivostok**, the home of the Russian Navy's Pacific fleet
- Stand at the heart of the old Soviet Union in Moscow's **Red Square**
- Raft down the Katun' river in the remote and unspoiled **Altai Mountains**
- Go trekking on the **Kamchatka** peninsula, blessed with amazing volcanic landscapes
- Study the sea life at **Moneron Island Marine National Park**, southern Sakhalin

Northern European Russia

Bounded by the icy Arctic Ocean, the forested mountains of the northern Urals (Ural'skiye Gory) and the political borders of eastern Europe, northern European Russia contains much of what is considered essentially Russian – freezing winters, vast expanses of featureless plain, glorious lakes, the dense forests of the taiga and the glories of Saint Petersburg.

Once Petrograd, then Leningrad, this "Northern Venice" is rightfully famed as a jewel on the Baltic, with fine architecture and some of the country's most significant historical sights, including the Winter Palace and the St Peter and Paul Fortress.

In its hinterland are the ancient Russian cities of Velikiy Novgorod and the "Golden Ring", all steeped in centuries of Slavic history and bordered by forests and plains. Just east of Saint Petersburg sits Europe's largest lake, Ladoga (*Ladozhskoye Ozero*), while to the north lies the frozen tundra which sweeps down to the White Sea. Intrepid visitors can stare at the bleak Soviet industrial landscape or experience the latest Russian pastime of skidooing.

What to See

Golden Ring, Saint Petersburg
see pp122–123

1 Murmansk
Totally dark in the depths of winter, the largest city inside the Arctic Circle is a perfect base for skidooing

2 Solovki (Solovetskiye Ostrova)
Home for almost 600 years to a beautiful monastery, the Solovki archipelago also has a monument to a local gulag prison

3 Malye Karely Open Air Museum (near Archangel) Wooden buildings from all ages and areas of Russia

4 Valaam Islands
A haven of tranquillity in the north of the striking Lake Ladoga (*Ladozhskoye Ozero*) and home to a 10th-century monastery

5 Petrozavodsk
The cultural and economic centre of Karelia, a Russian city by Lake Onega, with more than a hint of its Finnish connections

6 Vyborg
One of Europe's oldest cities with an imposing medieval castle, this Baltic port has noticeably retained some of its Scandinavian heritage in its eclectic architecture and among its quiet streets

7 Pskov
One of Russia's oldest cities and with many medieval churches

8 Velikiy Novgorod
One of the chief glories of the old Kremlin of this splendid city is the incomparable 11th-century Byzantine Cathedral of St Sophia

9 Perm' 36
(near Chusovoy)
Appreciate the hardship of a gulag existence at the preserved prison camps in the foothills of the Urals

The cruiser *Aurora*, Saint Petersburg: The *Aurora* became a potent symbol of the Russian Revolution of 1917. A single shot from the ship was the signal for the start of the storming of the Winter Palace.

Malye Karely Open Air Museum, near Archangel: Combining different styles and forms, the collection of wooden architecture includes windmills and bell towers – the bells are chimed on religious holidays. There are also traditional wooden bathhouses (saunas) in a nearby hotel complex.

196
92
118
126

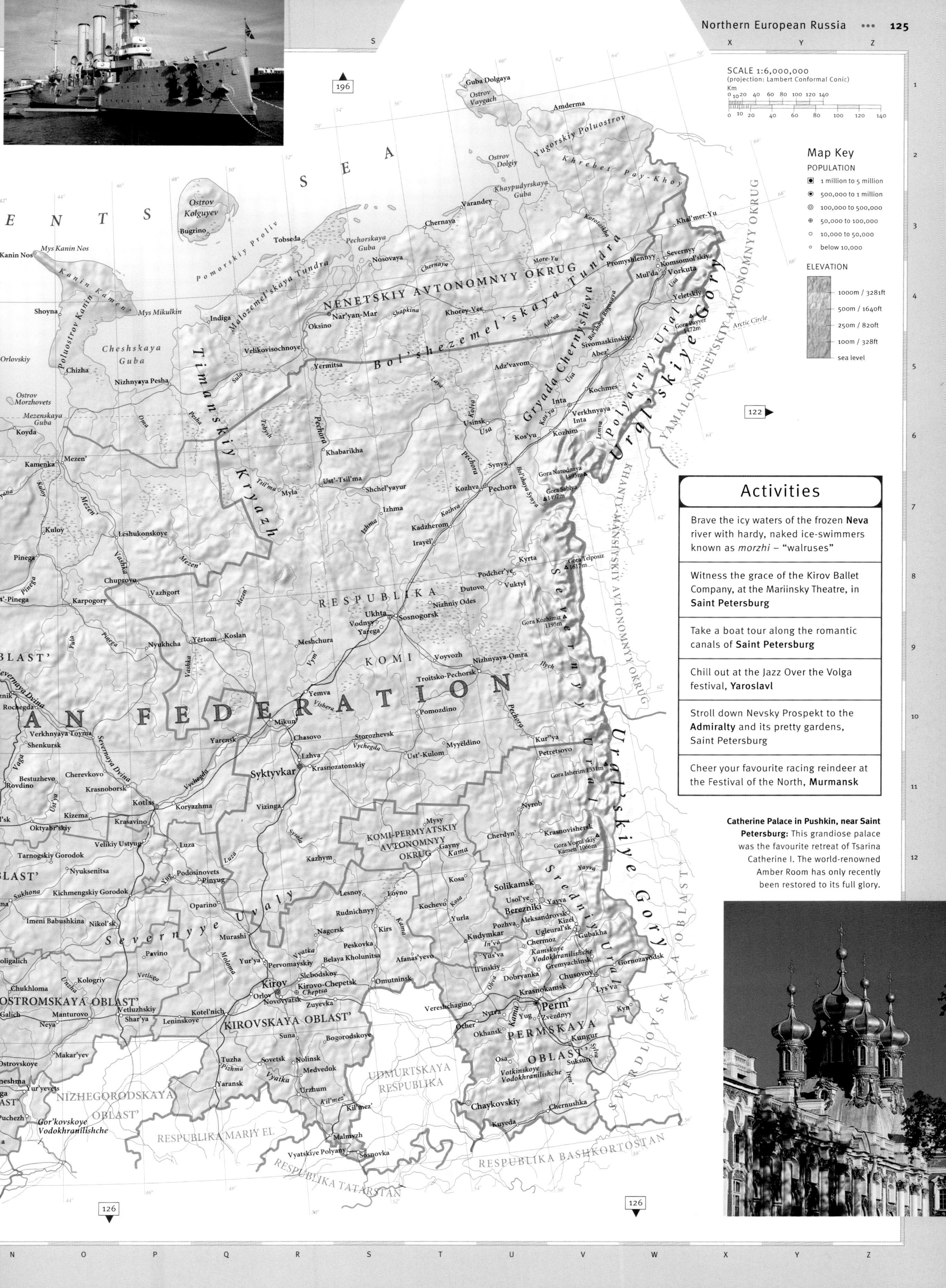
SCALE 1:6,000,000
(projection: Lambert Conformal Conic)
Km 0 10 20 40 60 80 100 120 140
0 10 20 40 60 80 100 120 140
Map Key
POPULATION
1 million to 5 million
500,000 to 1 million
100,000 to 500,000
50,000 to 100,000
10,000 to 50,000
below 10,000
ELEVATION
1000m / 3281ft
500m / 1640ft
250m / 820ft
100m / 328ft
sea level
196
122
126
126
BARENTS SEA
Ostrov Kolguyev
Ostrov Vaygach
Yugorskiy Poluostrov
Khrebet Pay-Khoy
NENETSKIY AVTONOMNYY OKRUG
Bol'shezemel'skaya Tundra
Malozemel'skaya Tundra
Timanskiy Kryazh
Cheshskaya Guba
Poluostrov Kanin
Nar'yan-Mar
Vorkuta
Inta
Usinsk
Pechora
Ukhta
Sosnogorsk
REPUBLIKA KOMI
RUSSIAN FEDERATION
Syktyvkar
Kotlas
KOMI-PERMYATSKIY AVTONOMNYY OKRUG
Severnyye Uvaly
Kirov
KIROVSKAYA OBLAST'
Perm'
PERMSKAYA OBLAST'
Solikamsk
Berezniki
Polyarnyy Ural
Ural'skiye Gory
Severnyy Ural
Sredniy Ural
YAMALO-NENETSKIY AVTONOMNYY OKRUG
KHANTY-MANSIYSKIY AVTONOMNYY OKRUG
SVERDLOVSKAYA OBLAST'
UDMURTSKAYA RESPUBLIKA
RESPUBLIKA MARIY EL
RESPUBLIKA TATARSTAN
RESPUBLIKA BASHKORTOSTAN
NIZHEGORODSKAYA OBLAST'
KOSTROMSKAYA OBLAST'
Arctic Circle
Gora Narodnaya 1895m
Gora Telposiz 1617m
Chaykovskiy

Activities

Brave the icy waters of the frozen **Neva** river with hardy, naked ice-swimmers known as *morzhi* – "walruses"

Witness the grace of the Kirov Ballet Company, at the Mariinsky Theatre, in **Saint Petersburg**

Take a boat tour along the romantic canals of **Saint Petersburg**

Chill out at the Jazz Over the Volga festival, **Yaroslavl**

Stroll down Nevsky Prospekt to the **Admiralty** and its pretty gardens, Saint Petersburg

Cheer your favourite racing reindeer at the Festival of the North, **Murmansk**

Catherine Palace in Pushkin, near Saint Petersburg: This grandiose palace was the favourite retreat of Tsarina Catherine I. The world-renowned Amber Room has only recently been restored to its full glory.

SCALE 1:6,000,000
(projection: Lambert Conformal Conic)
Km 0 10 20 40 60 80 100 120 140
Miles 0 10 20 40 60 80 100 120 140

Southern European Russia

The southern half of European Russia is where the continent of Europe both physically and culturally collides with Asia. Dominated politically by Moscow, this clash is both the region's greatest asset and its darkest flaw. Along with the great Russian cities of Moscow and Volgograd can be found the Turkic centre of Kazan', Europe's only Buddhist capital, Elista, and the remains of Groznyy in war-torn Chechnya.

The attractions of the region are unfairly neglected by foreign tourists, who tend to stick to the relative certainty of Moscow and Saint Petersburg further north. Increasingly, however, travel companies are exploiting the charms of the broad Volga River and the delights of Russia's "Costa del Sol" on the shores of the Black Sea.

Independent travel into the region is made tricky by Russian bureaucracy and the lack of a modern infrastructure for international tourists. Guided tours are available, although the tumultuous Caucasus is unlikely to be "safe" for the foreseeable future.

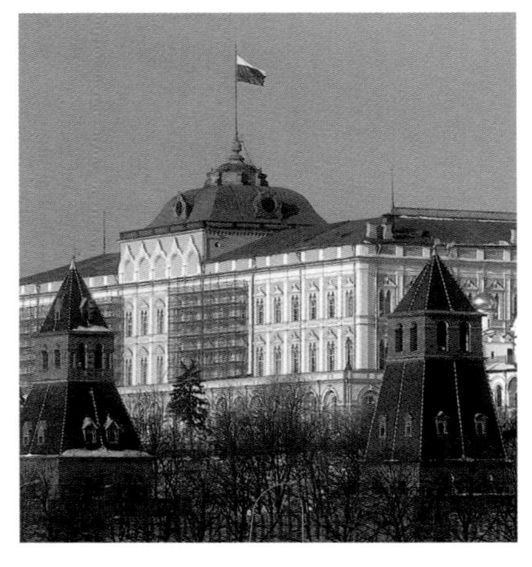

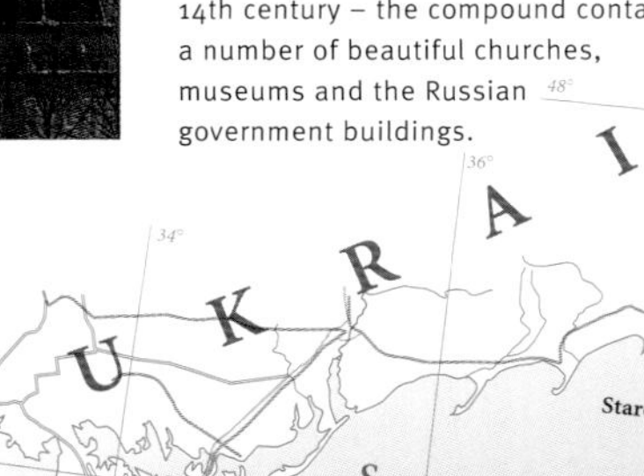

The Kremlin, Moscow: The city's original citadel dates back to the 14th century – the compound contains a number of beautiful churches, museums and the Russian government buildings.

Activities

Gaze in admiration at the defiant and colossal Soviet era statue of **Rodina (Motherland)** in Volgograd	Cruise gently down the lazy **Volga** river
	Take a sauna at Moscow's famous **Sandunov Banya** bathhouse
Eat pancakes in **Moscow** during the traditional Russian pre-Lent Maslenitsa festival, a good way to see off winter	Rejuvenate at a Black Sea spa town such as **Anapa**
Treat your tastebuds to *borshcht* (beetroot soup) with soured cream	Enjoy the inner warmth from a shot of Russia's national drink, vodka

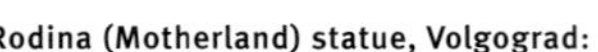

Rodina (Motherland) statue, Volgograd: One of the largest statues on earth, 52 m (171 ft) high, sits above a memorial to Russia's casualties in World War II. The Battle of Stalingrad (as Volgograd was then known) cost over one million Russian lives, but underlined the country's grim determination to repel the Nazis.

N O P Q R S T U V W X Y Z
Map Key
POPULATION
above 5 million
1 million to 5 million
500,000 to 1 million
100,000 to 500,000
50,000 to 100,000
10,000 to 50,000
below 10,000
ELEVATION
4000m / 13,124ft
3000m / 9843ft
2000m / 6562ft
1000m / 3281ft
500m / 1640ft
250m / 820ft
100m / 328ft
sea level
KIROVSKAYA OBLAST'
PERMSKAYA OBLAST'
SVERDLOVSKAYA OBLAST'
CHELYABINSKAYA OBLAST'
KOSTROMSKAYA OBLAST'
NIZHEGORODSKAYA OBLAST'
UDMURTSKAYA RESPUBLIKA
RESPUBLIKA MARIY EL
CHAVASH RESPUBLIKI
RESPUBLIKA TATARSTAN
RESPUBLIKA BASHKORTOSTAN
RESPUBLIKA MORDOVIYA
UL'YANOVSKAYA OBLAST'
PENZENSKAYA OBLAST'
SAMARSKAYA OBLAST'
ORENBURGSKAYA OBLAST'
SARATOVSKAYA OBLAST'
VOLGOGRADSKAYA OBLAST'
ASTRAKHANSKAYA OBLAST'
RESPUBLIKA KALMYKIYA
RESPUBLIKA DAGESTAN
CHECHENSKAYA RESPUBLIKA
KAZAKHSTAN
AZERBAIJAN
Caspian Sea
Caspian Depression
124
122
144
136

What to See

El'brus, Moscow, Sochi
see pp122-123

❶ Red Square
(in Moscow)
The city's famous centrepiece surrounded by the Kremlin walls, Lenin's Mausoleum, the GUM department store and St Basil's Cathedral

❷ Kolomenskoe Park
(near Moscow)
Wander among churches, fascinating museums, silver birches and recreated historical sights, while enjoying the views of Moscow

❸ Vladimir
Founded over 1,000 years ago, Vladimir was once capital of Russia, now a feature of the tourist trail for its interesting museums and elegant churches

❹ Prioksko-Terrasny Reserve
(near Serpukhov) Catch a glimpse of a massive European bison at the specialist breeding centre within the reserve

❺ Kazan'
The capital of Muslim Tatarstan, where the traditions of Central Asia come face to face with Mother Russia

❻ Penza
Five universities, galleries and theatres make Penza an ideal place to mix with the bright young things of Russia's tomorrow

❼ Volga
Enjoy the natural and architectural delights strung along the banks of Europe's longest river

❽ Samara
City on the Volga, home to an annual amateur music festival complete with floating guitar-shaped stage

❾ Saratov
The 400-year-old former capital of the lower Volga region, modern Saratov boasts Russia's oldest circus

❿ Volgograd
Formerly Stalingrad, the city is haunted by the famous battle against the Nazis in 1943 which proved to be the turning point of World War II. Come for the truly amazing monuments

⓫ Southern Ural'skiye Gory (Urals)
Join a cross-country trek on horseback through stunning mountain scenery on the very edge of Europe

⓬ Gelendzhik
A Black Sea spa town and resort with a number of ancient stone dolmen, hidden in the surrounding woodland. There are plenty of opportunities for recreation with riding and trekking in the local hills and a good beach

Holy Trinity – St Sergiy Lavra, Sergiyev Posad, near Moscow: This monastery, founded in the mid-14th century, and later heavily fortified, is a masterpiece of Russian architecture.

Asia

"And there were gardens bright with sinuous rills, where blossomed many an incense tree; and here were forests ancient as the hills, enfolding sunny spots of greenery."

SAMUEL TAYLOR COLERIDGE,
1772-1834

Physical Asia

Asia is a continent of two halves. The vast plateaus and wild plains that sweep across the northern reaches are cut off by some of the world's most dramatic mountain ranges from the great river basins of southern Asia – the Ganges, Brahmaputra, Indus, Mekong, Yangtze and Yellow River. Many of these rivers rise in the huge Plateau of Tibet, the world's highest and coldest plain, known as the "roof of the world". The Tigris and Euphrates rivers in Iraq, and the Indus in Pakistan, saw the growth of great ancient civilizations, thriving in their fertile valleys. Japan, the Philippines and much of Indonesia lie along tectonic plate boundaries, the latter alone contains one-third of the world's active volcanoes.

Mountains

The spectacular ranges of the Hindu Kush, Pamirs, Tien Shan and above all, the magnificent Himalayas throw down the gauntlet to trekkers and mountaineers. Even the base camp of Mount Everest is at over 5,500 m (18,000 ft), although its still another 3,350 m (11,000 ft) to reach the summit. These ranges have formed an almost solid wall between China and the west, but the few strategic passes through them were plied by thousands of caravans on the Silk Road.

Desert

Asia's great cold deserts – the Gobi in Mongolia, the Kara Kum in Turkmenistan, the Takla Makan in China – are landscapes of bare rocks, though rolling sand dunes occur in the Gobi near the fiery-coloured Flaming Cliffs. Further north lies semi-desert or scrubland known as steppe. The Empty Quarter of the Arabian Peninsula is the world's largest uninterrupted sand desert, drained by ephemeral watercourses known as *wadis*.

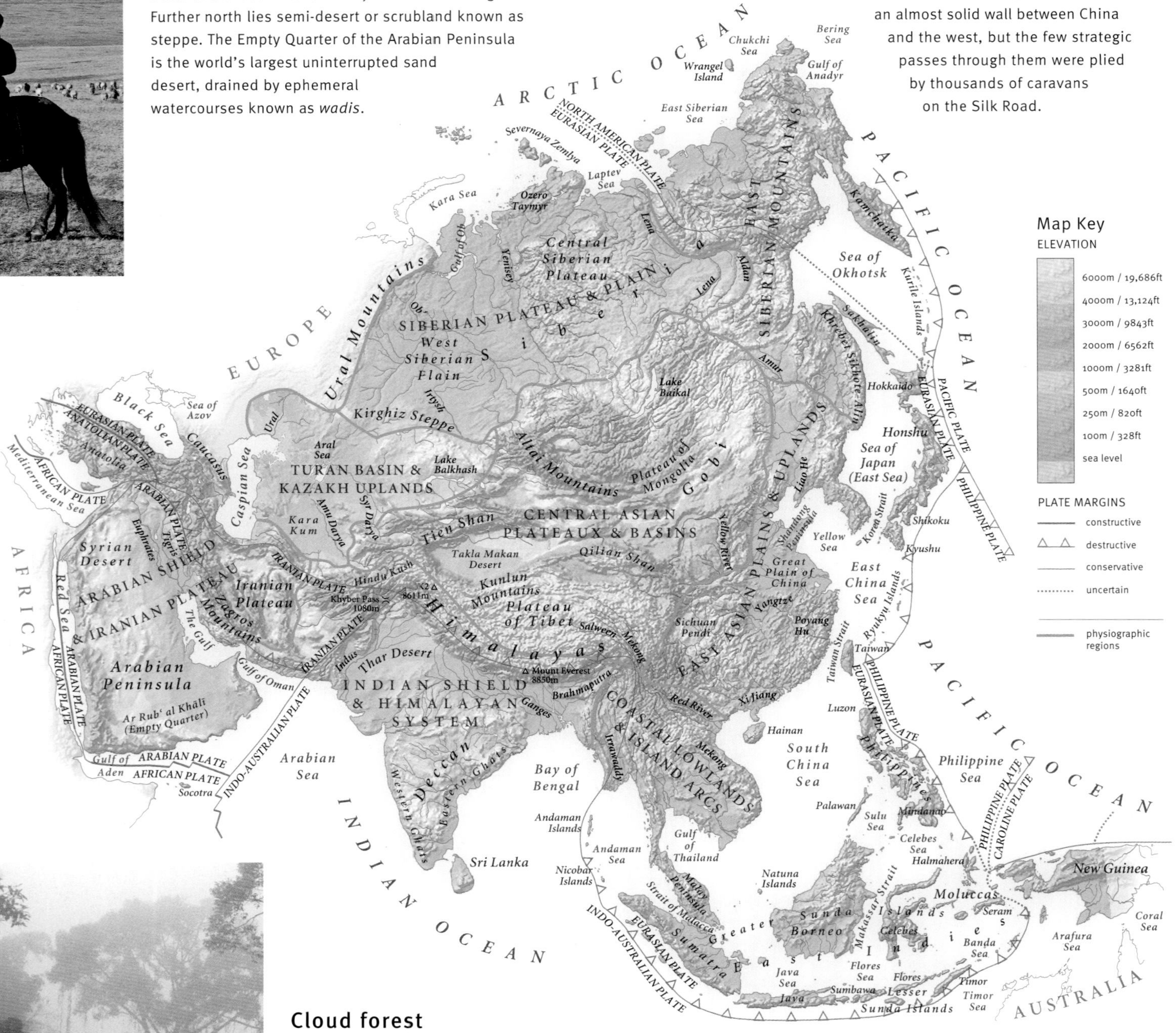

Map Key

ELEVATION

6000m / 19,686ft
4000m / 13,124ft
3000m / 9843ft
2000m / 6562ft
1000m / 3281ft
500m / 1640ft
250m / 820ft
100m / 328ft
sea level

PLATE MARGINS

constructive
destructive
conservative
uncertain

physiographic regions

Cloud forest

The equatorial regions of Southeast Asia are clad in dense and ancient rainforest, alive with wildlife. The forest on the Malay Peninsula is 130 million years old. Indonesia is famous for its endearing orang utans swinging through the branches, but many other exotic and endangered species can also be spotted here – among them the Javan rhino, Sumatran tiger, Burmese python and proboscis monkey.

SCALE 1:63,000,000
(projection: Lambert Azimuthal Equal Area)

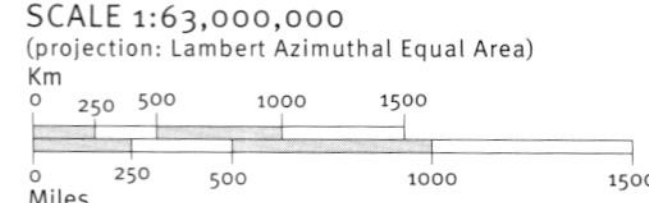
Km
0 250 500 1000 1500
0 250 500 1000 1500
Miles

Climate

In the inland desert regions, such as the Gobi, temperatures can soar to 40°C (104°F) in summer and plummet to -40°C (-40°F) in winter – one of the most extreme ranges in the world. The major event in south Asia, by contrast, is the monsoon – a wind that brings annual torrential downpours in May to September (west and central India) or June to October (southeast Asia). The major part of the year's rain falls during the monsoon period. Combined with summer increases in glacial meltwater from the Himalayas, this swells the rivers so much that flooding of plains and deltas is a fact of life in China, India and Bangladesh.

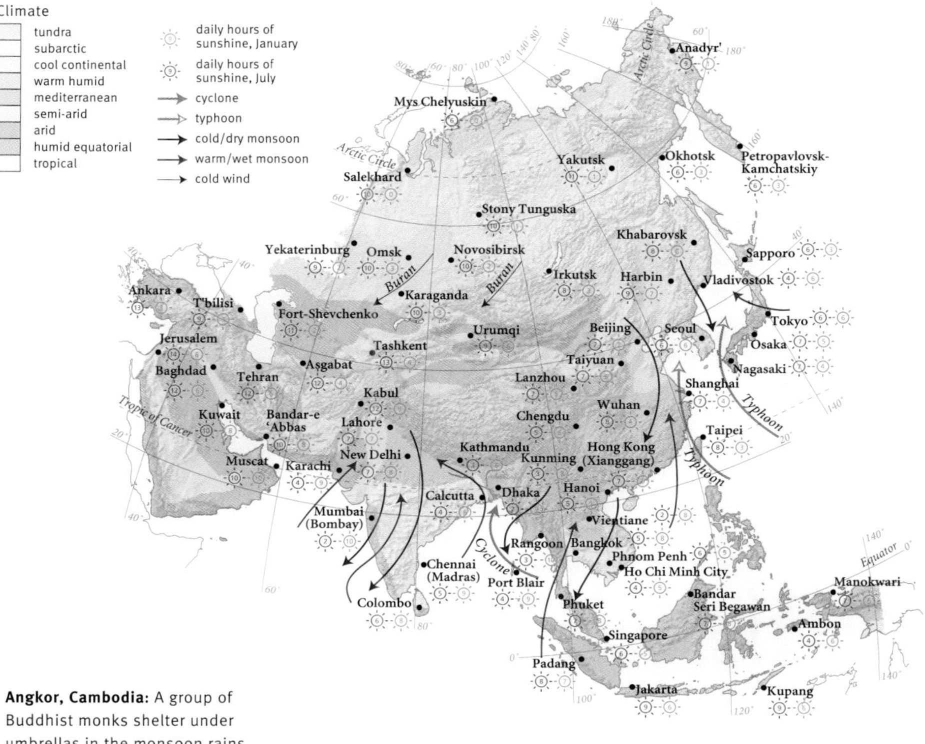

Climate
tundra
subarctic
cool continental
warm humid
mediterranean
semi-arid
arid
humid equatorial
tropical
daily hours of sunshine, January
daily hours of sunshine, July
cyclone
typhoon
cold/dry monsoon
warm/wet monsoon
cold wind
Anadyr'
Mys Chelyuskin
Arctic Circle
Salekhard
Yakutsk
Okhotsk
Petropavlovsk-Kamchatskiy
Stony Tunguska
Yekaterinburg
Omsk
Novosibirsk
Khabarovsk
Sapporo
Irkutsk
Harbin
Vladivostok
Ankara
T'bilisi
Buran
Karaganda
Fort-Shevchenko
Tokyo
Jerusalem
Urumqi
Beijing
Seoul
Osaka
Tashkent
Asgabat
Taiyuan
Nagasaki
Baghdad
Tehran
Lanzhou
Shanghai
Kabul
Tropic of Cancer
Kuwait
Bandar-e 'Abbas
Lahore
Chengdu
Wuhan
Typhoon
Taipei
New Delhi
Kathmandu
Hong Kong (Xianggang)
Muscat
Karachi
Kunming
Calcutta
Dhaka
Hanoi
Mumbai (Bombay)
Vientiane
Rangoon
Bangkok
Cyclone
Chennai (Madras)
Phnom Penh
Ho Chi Minh City
Port Blair
Colombo
Phuket
Bandar Seri Begawan
Manokwari
Equator
Singapore
Ambon
Padang
Jakarta
Kupang

Angkor, Cambodia: A group of Buddhist monks shelter under umbrellas in the monsoon rains.

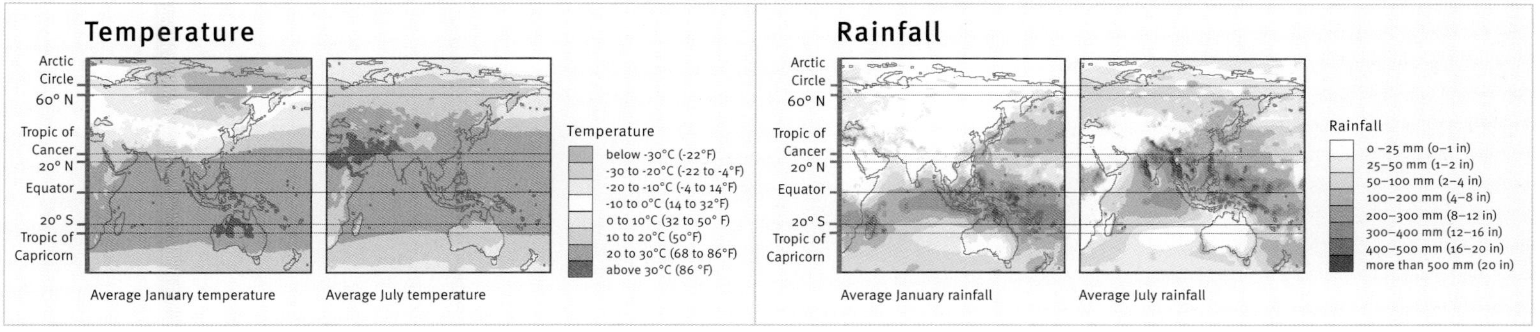

Temperature
Arctic Circle
60° N
Tropic of Cancer
20° N
Equator
20° S
Tropic of Capricorn
Average January temperature
Average July temperature
Temperature
below -30°C (-22°F)
-30 to -20°C (-22 to -4°F)
-20 to -10°C (-4 to 14°F)
-10 to 0°C (14 to 32°F)
0 to 10°C (32 to 50° F)
10 to 20°C (50°F)
20 to 30°C (68 to 86°F)
above 30°C (86 °F)
Rainfall
Arctic Circle
60° N
Tropic of Cancer
20° N
Equator
20° S
Tropic of Capricorn
Average January rainfall
Average July rainfall
Rainfall
0 –25 mm (0–1 in)
25–50 mm (1–2 in)
50–100 mm (2–4 in)
100–200 mm (4–8 in)
200–300 mm (8–12 in)
300–400 mm (12–16 in)
400–500 mm (16–20 in)
more than 500 mm (20 in)

Using Land and Sea

In a continent where so much land is barren desert or steep mountain, the pressure for farmable land has led to extensive terracing – as in the Banaue region of the Philippines – or the use of annually flooded river deltas, as in Bangladesh. Rice grown in water-filled paddy fields is the crop most associated with Asia, but wheat is more widespread. Cotton and tea are grown in China and the Indian subcontinent, while the hotter Malay Peninsula and East Indies are historically famous for their spices and rubber. The seas around these islands are rich in fish and prawn, which is central to the region's cuisine. The wealth and modernity of the cities of Saudi Arabia, Oman, and the Gulf states are based on oil.

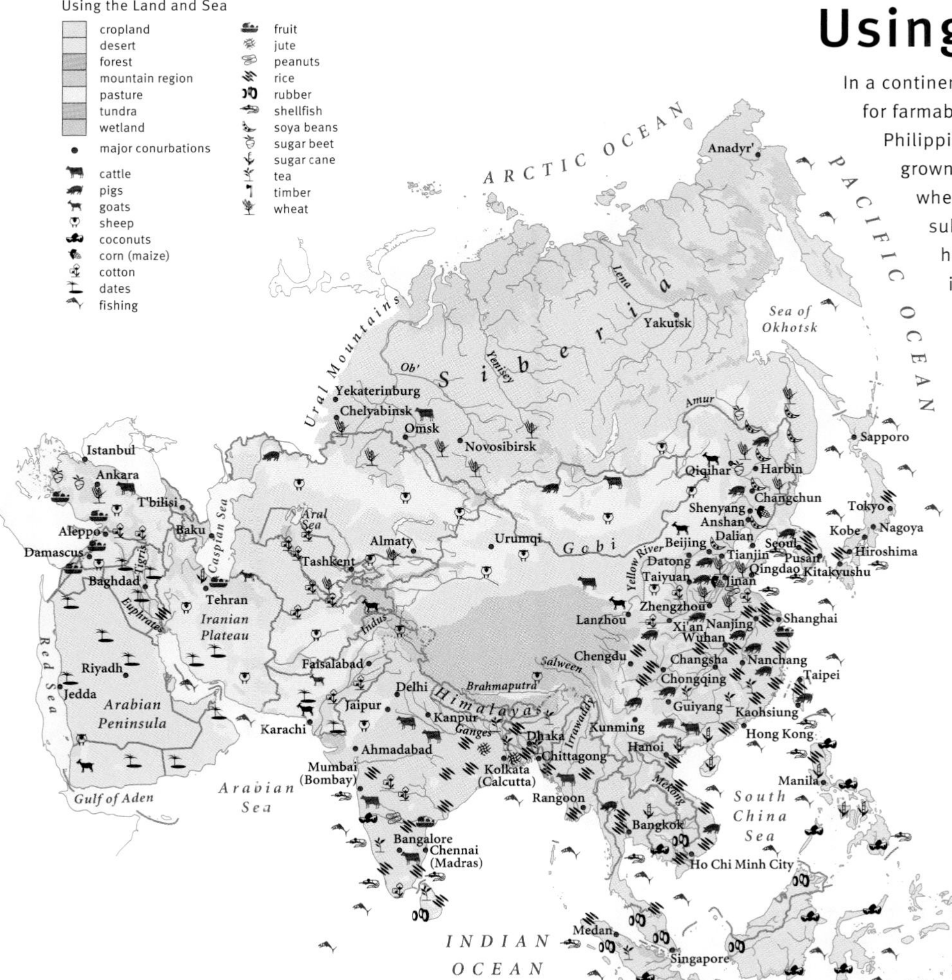

Using the Land and Sea
cropland
desert
forest
mountain region
pasture
tundra
wetland
major conurbations
cattle
pigs
goats
sheep
coconuts
corn (maize)
cotton
dates
fishing
fruit
jute
peanuts
rice
rubber
shellfish
soya beans
sugar beet
sugar cane
tea
timber
wheat
ARCTIC OCEAN
PACIFIC OCEAN
Anadyr'
Lena
Siberia
Yakutsk
Sea of Okhotsk
Ural Mountains
Ob'
Yenisey
Yekaterinburg
Chelyabinsk
Omsk
Novosibirsk
Amur
Sapporo
Istanbul
Ankara
T'bilisi
Qiqihar
Harbin
Changchun
Aleppo
Baku
Aral Sea
Caspian Sea
Shenyang
Anshan
Tokyo
Nagoya
Damascus
Tashkent
Almaty
Urumqi
Gobi
Dalian
Beijing
Kobe
Hiroshima
Seoul
Tianjin
Datong
Pusan
Qingdao
Kitakyushu
Baghdad
Tigris
Euphrates
Taiyuan
Jinan
Tehran
Yellow River
Iranian Plateau
Zhengzhou
Shanghai
Indus
Lanzhou
Xi'an
Nanjing
Wuhan
Chengdu
Salween
Changsha
Nanchang
Red Sea
Riyadh
Faisalabad
Taipei
Jedda
Arabian Peninsula
Delhi
Brahmaputra
Himalayas
Chongqing
Guiyang
Kaohsiung
Jaipur
Kanpur
Ganges
Irrawaddy
Kunming
Hong Kong
Karachi
Dhaka
Ahmadabad
Chittagong
Hanoi
Mumbai (Bombay)
Kolkata (Calcutta)
Mekong
Manila
Gulf of Aden
Arabian Sea
Rangoon
South China Sea
Bangkok
Bangalore
Chennai (Madras)
Ho Chi Minh City
INDIAN OCEAN
Medan
Singapore
Jakarta
Surabaya
Semarang

Nong Bau, Thailand: Water buffalo and banteng are used to plough the paddy fields, but the rice is planted and harvested by hand. Where rain is plentiful, three crops can be grown each year.

Political Asia

The world's largest continent, Asia is home to 60% of its people, but the political systems under which they live could hardly be more varied – from Japan's modern Western-style parliamentary government to North Korea's isolated dictatorship and Iran's Islamic theocracy. China, fast becoming an economic powerhouse, remains adherent to single-party communism, while in India, the world's largest democracy, secular principles contend with the challenge of Hindu nationalism. Indonesia is likewise secular, although its Muslim population is the world's largest. Pakistan, by contrast, was founded explicitly as an Islamic state. Nowhere is more closely identified with fundamentalist Islam than the Middle East, still mired in decades of conflict stemming from the creation of the Jewish state of Israel in 1948, yet the kingdoms of the Gulf are among the most conservative anywhere.

ARCTIC OCEAN
East Siberian Sea
Laptev Sea
Kara Sea
Arctic Circle
Noril'sk
Central Siberian Plateau
Siberia
Lower Tunguska
Yakutsk
Ural Mountains
EUROPE
RUSSIAN FEDERATION
Stony Tunguska
West Siberian Plain
Yekaterinburg
Chelyabinsk
Omsk
Tomsk
Krasnoyarsk
Lake Baikal
Novosibirsk
Novokuznetsk
Irkutsk
Rudnyy
Ural'sk
Istanbul
Black Sea
ANKARA
TURKEY
Sokhumi
GEORGIA
K'ut'aisi
T'BILISI
Bat'umi
Anatolia
ARMENIA
YEREVAN
Gäncä
AZERB.
BAKU
Adana
Gaziantep
CYPRUS
NICOSIA
Aleppo
LEBANON
Tripoli
BEIRUT
SYRIA
DAMASCUS
Haifa
Tel Aviv-Yafo
Gaza
JERUSALEM
AMMAN
ISRAEL
JORDAN
Mosul
Kirkuk
Tabriz
Caspian Sea
Aktau
KAZAKHSTAN
ASTANA
Karaganda
Semipalatinsk
Zhezkazgan
Aral Sea
Syr Darya
Kyzylorda
Balkhash
Lake Balkhash
UZBEKISTAN
Amu Darya
Dasoguz
TURKMENISTAN
ASGABAT
TEHRAN
Gorgan
BAGHDAD
Euphrates
Tigris
IRAQ
An Najaf
Basra
Qom
Mashhad
Esfahan
Ahvaz
IRAN
Iranian Plateau
KUWAIT
SAUDI ARABIA
Kerman
Shiraz
Zahedan
Bandar-e 'Abbas
MANAMA
BAHRAIN
QATAR
DOHA
ABU DHABI
UAE
The Gulf
RIYADH
JEDDA
At Ta'if
Red Sea
AFRICA
Tropic of Cancer
Arabian Peninsula
Ar Rub' al Khali (Empty Quarter)
Gulf of Oman
Ar Rustaq
MUSCAT
Sur
OMAN
SANA
YEMEN
Ta'izz
Aden
Gulf of Aden
Socotra (to Yemen)
Arabian Sea
INDIAN OCEAN
Taraz
BISHKEK
Almaty
Karakol
KYRGYZSTAN
TASHKENT
Osh
Tien Shan
DUSHANBE
TAJIKISTAN
Balkh
Herat
Qal'eh-ye Now
AFGHANISTAN
KABUL
Kandahar
Quetta
Peshawar
(line of control)
(claimed by India)
Srinagar
ISLAMABAD
Jammu
(administered by China, claimed by India)
Gujranwala
Faisalabad
Lahore
Multan
Ludhiana
PAKISTAN
Larkana
Shikarpur
Indus
Thar Desert
Karachi
Hyderabad
Delhi
NEW DELHI
Bareilly
Agra
Jaipur
Kanpur
Lucknow
Urumqi
Tarim He
Takla Makan Desert
Kunlun Mountains
Plateau of Tibet
(Much of Arunachal Pradesh is claimed by China)
Brahmaputra
Himalayas
NEPAL
KATHMANDU
THIMPHU
BHUTAN
Guwahati
Patna
Varanasi
Ganges
Rajshahi
Rangpur
BANGLADESH
Brahmanbaria
DHAKA
Khulna
Chittagong
INDIA
Ahmadabad
Vadodara
Bhopal
Indore
Narmada
Surat
Jamshedpur
Kolkata (Calcutta)
Nagpur
Bhubaneshwar
Mumbai (Bombay)
Pune
Godavari
Solapur
Hyderabad
Krishna
Vijayawada
Hubli
Bangalore
Mysore
Chennai (Madras)
Coimbatore
Cochin (Kochi)
Trivandrum
Jaffna
SRI LANKA
COLOMBO
Bay of Bengal
Andaman Islands (to India)
Andaman Sea
Nicobar Islands (to India)
Sühbaatar
Erdenet
ULAN BATOR
Choybalsan
MONGOLIA
Altai Mountains
Gobi
Inner Mongolia
BEIJING
Baotou
Datong
Yellow River
Shijiazhuang
Taiyuan
Lanzhou
Zhengzhou
Luoyang
Xi'an
CHINA
Mekong
Salween
Mianyang
Chengdu
Chongqing
Leshan
Guiyang
Kunming
Liuzhou
Nanning
BURMA
Mandalay
Taunggyi
Irrawaddy
Pakokku
Prome
Pegu
RANGOON
Bassein
Bogale
HANOI
Louangphabang
LAOS
VIENTIANE
Chiang Mai
THAILAND
Pakxe
BANGKOK
Batdambang
CAMBODIA
PHNOM PENH
Gulf of Thailand
Kota Bharu
Taiping
Medan
KUALA LUMPUR
PUTRAJAYA
SINGAPORE
Sumatra
Equator
Jambi
Padang
Palembang
JAKARTA

Standard of Living

Standard of Living
(UN Human Development Index)
low
high

Vast differences in standards of living exist between Asian states. Oil has brought massive wealth to the rulers of the Middle East and Brunei, while Afghanistan and Mongolia struggle to carve a living from barren countryside. Modern cities like Hong Kong and Tokyo contrast sharply with the poverty surrounding the sprawling cities of Manila and Mumbai.

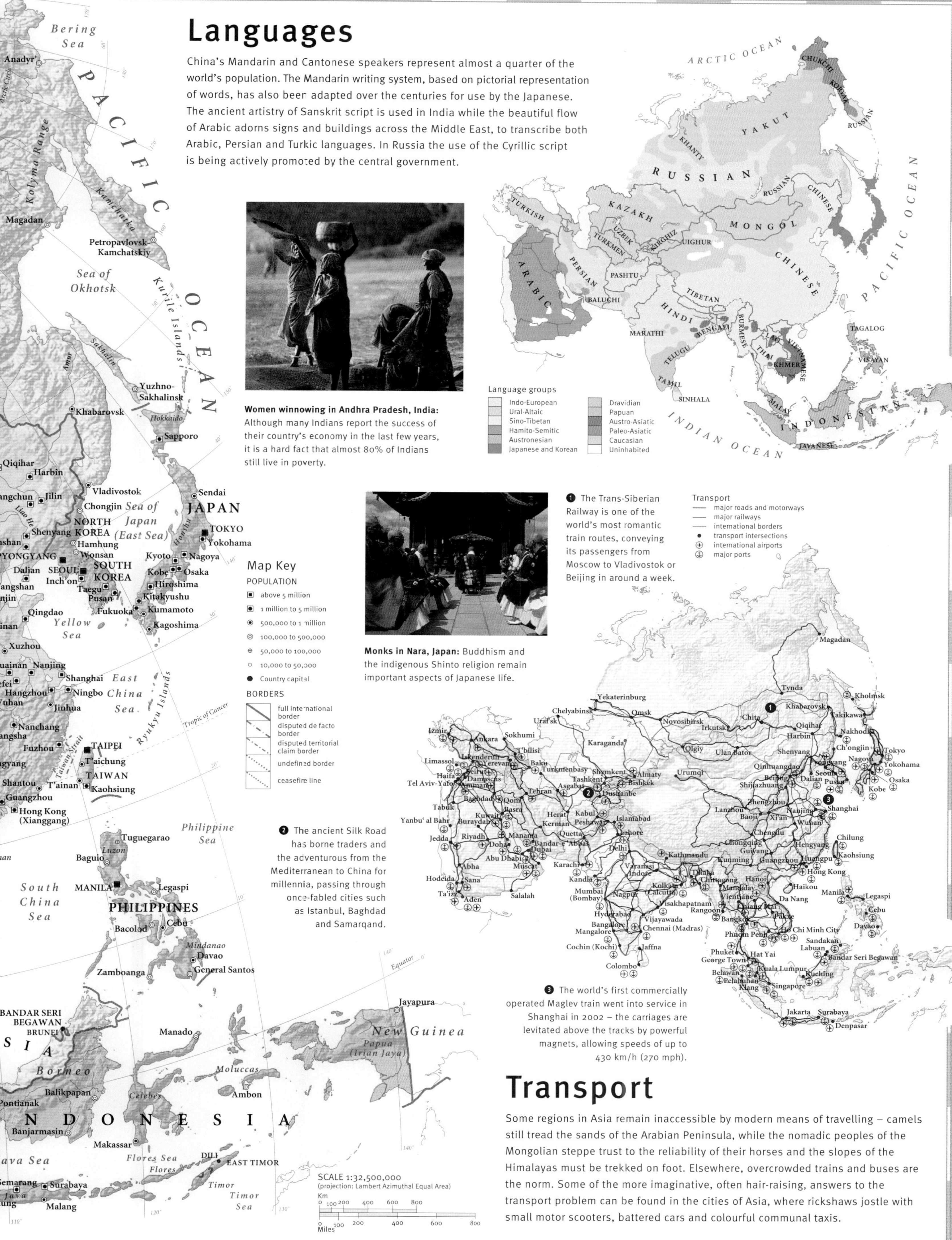

Map Key
POPULATION
above 5 million
1 million to 5 million
500,000 to 1 million
100,000 to 500,000
50,000 to 100,000
10,000 to 50,000
Country capital
BORDERS
full international border
disputed de facto border
disputed territorial claim border
undefined border
ceasefire line
Language groups
Indo-European
Ural-Altaic
Sino-Tibetan
Hamito-Semitic
Austronesian
Japanese and Korean
Dravidian
Papuan
Austro-Asiatic
Paleo-Asiatic
Caucasian
Uninhabited
Transport
major roads and motorways
major railways
international borders
transport intersections
international airports
major ports
SCALE 1:32,500,000
(projection: Lambert Azimuthal Equal Area)

Languages

China's Mandarin and Cantonese speakers represent almost a quarter of the world's population. The Mandarin writing system, based on pictorial representation of words, has also been adapted over the centuries for use by the Japanese. The ancient artistry of Sanskrit script is used in India while the beautiful flow of Arabic adorns signs and buildings across the Middle East, to transcribe both Arabic, Persian and Turkic languages. In Russia the use of the Cyrillic script is being actively promoted by the central government.

Women winnowing in Andhra Pradesh, India: Although many Indians report the success of their country's economy in the last few years, it is a hard fact that almost 80% of Indians still live in poverty.

Monks in Nara, Japan: Buddhism and the indigenous Shinto religion remain important aspects of Japanese life.

❶ The Trans-Siberian Railway is one of the world's most romantic train routes, conveying its passengers from Moscow to Vladivostok or Beijing in around a week.

❷ The ancient Silk Road has borne traders and the adventurous from the Mediterranean to China for millennia, passing through once-fabled cities such as Istanbul, Baghdad and Samarqand.

❸ The world's first commercially operated Maglev train went into service in Shanghai in 2002 – the carriages are levitated above the tracks by powerful magnets, allowing speeds of up to 430 km/h (270 mph).

Transport

Some regions in Asia remain inaccessible by modern means of travelling – camels still tread the sands of the Arabian Peninsula, while the nomadic peoples of the Mongolian steppe trust to the reliability of their horses and the slopes of the Himalayas must be trekked on foot. Elsewhere, overcrowded trains and buses are the norm. Some of the more imaginative, often hair-raising, answers to the transport problem can be found in the cities of Asia, where rickshaws jostle with small motor scooters, battered cars and colourful communal taxis.

Taj Mahal, India

Ko Chang, Thailand

Hong Kong, China

Annapurna, Nepal

Masjed-e-Emam, Esfahan, Iran

Activities

The Middle East is a place of great pilgrimages, of searching out famed biblical locations and hunting down the origins of civilization. But take time out to float in the Dead Sea, where it is impossible to sink and hard to get sunburnt thanks to the filtering effect of the salty haze. Ancient Persia (Iran) and central Asia are linked by a trading culture that extends all the way to China. Visits to silk carpet factories and other local industries are a fascinating element of travelling in this part of the world. In the Indian subcontinent, famed for its spirituality as much as for its teeming cities, a dip in the Ganges is one way to connect with the culture, while rush-hour driving in Mumbai (Bombay) is an experience that may not be enjoyed at the time, but will remain with you forever. Powerful reminders recur in Japan and Southeast Asia of the impact of modern warfare in the region, none more moving than a visit to Hiroshima where the first atomic bomb was dropped on this Japanese city.

What to Do

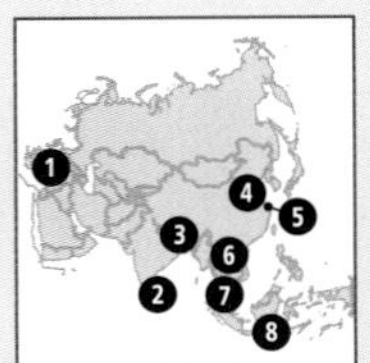

1 Turkish Baths
Steam and scrub your troubles away, before a relaxing massage

2 Sri Lankan Elephant Orphanage
Ride on an elephant or help out at feeding time

3 Mount Everest, Nepal
Trek to Base Camp; only serious mountaineers go all the way to the top

4 Great Wall, China
Take a walk along the 2,000-year-old wall

5 Shanghai Acrobats, China
Gape at their feats of contortion and balance

6 Eat Scorpion, Laos
The taste is somewhat like potato crisps

7 Ko Tao, Thailand
Learn to scuba dive in maximum water visibility – 40 m (130 ft)

8 Bali, Indonesia
Soak up the sun on black sandy beaches

Jerusalem, Israel: This holy city attracts Jewish, Muslim and Christian pilgrims to its religious sites.

Natural Sights

The three best-loved symbols of Asian wildlife are the panda, the tiger and the orang utan. China's massive reserves are trying to preserve some of the last remnants of panda habitat and more of these endearing animals survive in that country, both in captivity and in the wild, than anywhere else. India's many game reserves are fine places to see the Bengal tiger, while the orang utan, the "man of the forest", can be found in the less commercialized rainforests of Borneo and Sumatra. The rest of Southeast Asia also contains much highly diverse rainforest and swampland. The Middle East and large parts of central and northern Asia are covered by great deserts, such as the Gobi and the Empty Quarter. Here too it is possible to see some highly endangered species, notably the Przewalski horse in Mongolia and the Arabian oryx in Oman and Jordan. Both of these animals were hunted to extinction in the wild, but now exist again as small populations of reintroduced animals.

What to See

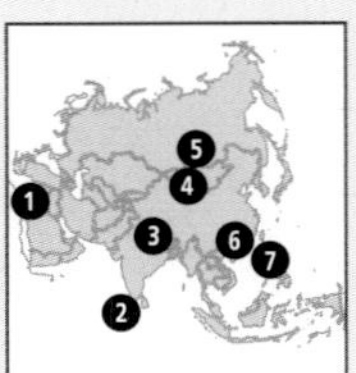

1 Wadi Rum, Jordan
Awe-inspiring silence among rocks eroded by wind and sand

2 Maldives
Idyllic resort islands of coral lagoons, beaches and huts on stilts

3 Himalayas
Take a flight over the world's greatest range

4 Flaming Cliffs, Mongolia
Deep reds and oranges colour the cliffs of the southern Gobi desert

5 Lake Baikal, Russia
The world's oldest and deepest lake, which has developed unique freshwater fauna

6 Guilin, China
Ethereal mountain peaks loom out of the mist along the Li river

7 Banaue, Philippines
Spectacular rice terraces constructed 2,000 years ago

Mount Fuji, Japan: This most beautiful and symmetrical of mountains is at the heart of the Japanese spirit and has inspired great artists, such as Katsushika Hokusai and Ando Hiroshige.

Ceremonial drummer, Indonesia

Hierapolis, Turkey

Ha Long Bay, Vietnam

Kathmandu, Nepal

Ratmanov Island, Siberia, Russia

Cultural Sights

Asia has a rich cultural legacy, encompassing the cradles of both oriental and Middle Eastern civilizations. Successive Chinese dynasties have left their mark with creations that still hold their power today – from exquisitely decorated cave temples, to the fascinating terracotta army of Xi'an and the secretive palaces of Beijing. The Middle East's rich architectural heritage ranges from prehistoric remains to Roman cities and from the holy places of Jerusalem to great Muslim centres such as Esfahan in Iran. Today, many of Asia's vast cities are more about the present than the past. Containing millions of people, they are known for their industrial prowess and business acumen, with ultra-modern buildings giving places like Dubai, Shanghai, Hong Kong and Tokyo their distinctive skylines.

Phra Boromathat Chaiya, Thailand: A row of Buddha likenesses in one of Thailand's few surviving Srivijaya-period temples.

What to See

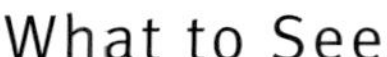

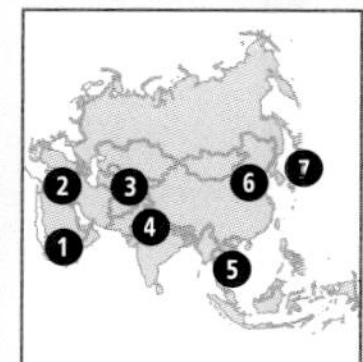

❶ Shibam, Yemen
Towering ancient mud-brick skyscrapers in this magical city

❷ Petra, Jordan
The fabled rose-red city, hewn out of the rock over 2,000 years ago

❸ Samarqand, Uzbekistan
Blue and white-tiled mosques dazzle the eye

❹ Taj Mahal, India
A gleaming 400-year-old mausoleum of marble, light and water

❺ Angkor Wat, Cambodia
Visit the tree-entwined temples of the ancient Khmer empire

❻ Forbidden City, Beijing, China
For centuries hidden from public view, it is the largest imperial palace in the world

❼ Tokyo
This stimulating, vital city is an ultra-modern cultural thrill

Journeys

Asia's sprawling mass has some fine train rides, among the most scenic being those in Thailand and the route running north–south down the length of Vietnam. In India the railway system is extraordinarily complex, a challenge to the uninitiated user but a feat of organization whose results can be highly rewarding. The Palace on Wheels, a luxury train modelled on the private railway cars of the former rulers of Rajasthan, is a good way to take in the "Golden Triangle" of Agra, Jaipur and Delhi. For more modern luxury try the bullet trains of Japan, technological wonders that remain impressive 40 years after their first introduction. One of the most famous of Asia's road routes is the Karakoram Highway. This traces a perilous path over the "roof of the world" from China ultimately to Pakistan and claimed many lives during the course of its construction. Much older is the King's Highway in Jordan, the ancient route, predating the Romans, that winds its way through the mountains and impressive *wadis* (river channels) to the east of the Dead Sea.

МСК
2000
МОСКВА-ВЛАДИВО

Trans-Siberian Railway, Russian Federation: The classic way to cross this vast country takes about five days non-stop, though stopovers can be arranged in places like Irkutsk near Lake Baikal.

Great Asian Journeys

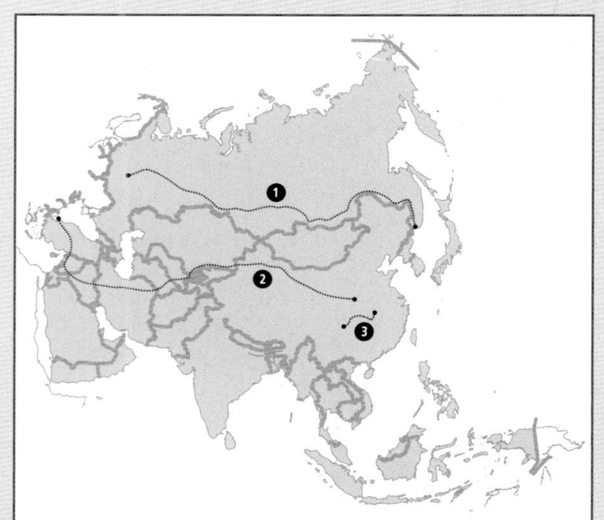

❶ Trans-Siberian Railway
Moscow – Vladivostok
9,600 km (6,000 miles)
Tsar Alexander III initiated this immense project in the 1890s. Completed in 1905, it now stretches a third of the way round the globe, crossing steppe, taiga and mountains. An alternative route visits Ulan Bator and ends in Beijing.

❷ Silk Road
Xi'an – Istanbul
12,900 km (8,000 miles)
Asia's main artery for the flow of trade, culture and ideas was already thriving 2,000 years ago. It brought prosperity to the cities through which it passed. The architecture and exotic markets of Kashi (Kashgar), Samarqand, and Buxoro (Bukhara) are legendary.

❸ Yangtze Three Gorges Cruise
Chongqing – Wuhan
880 km (550 miles)
A majestic journey, following the mighty Yangtze river through the dramatic gorges of Qutang, Wu and Xiling to reach the biggest engineering project on earth – the vast dam that will flood much of this idyllic scenery forever.

Turkey & the Caucasus

Armenia, Azerbaijan, Georgia, Turkey

Thanks to its turbulent history and location, this region provides a rich tapestry of historical interest, cultural diversity and breathtaking landscapes. It is a land of myths, legends, kingdoms and empires, fought over and ruled by many powers, each leaving their unique cultural fingerprint.

Important and fascinating archaeological sites are plentiful, ranging from the Neolithic village of Catal Huyuk to the magnificent Roman city of Ephesus. The region is also peppered with architectural marvels, from the domes and minarets of Istanbul's mosques to the wooden houses and churches of the Black Sea region and the juxtaposition of Baku's medieval walled city with its austere communist-era blocks.

Although largely mountainous, Turkey and the Caucasus have, throughout history, been a crucial transit area for trade, linking the Caspian, Black and Mediterranean seas. Ideas, technologies and the arts have been funnelled through the region and creating its vibrant culture and exciting cuisine. Turkish food conjures images of kebabs but it also offers much wider variety, from filled flat breads to filling stews, fresh fish, creamy rice pudding and rosewater-flavoured pastries.

The region's rich mix of peoples, cultures and religions has led to many periods of unrest and it is still advisable to check before travelling to certain areas of eastern Turkey and the Caucasus.

Activities

- Join in the traditional banquet toast given by a *tamada* (loosely, a toastmaster) – in the local wines of Georgia's **Kakheti province**
- Soar over the magical fairy chimneys of the **Cappadocian** landscape in a hot air balloon – from Goreme or Urgup, near Nevsehir
- Sprawl on a heated marble slab in a *hamam* (Turkish bath) as you await a rigorous massage
- Wrap up warm to watch the sun rise over the mountains around **Nemrut Dagi**, near Kahta, where huge stone heads guard a royal tumulus
- Watch one of **Istanbul's** top football teams – Besiktas, Fenerbahce or Galatasaray (usually on Saturdays or Sundays, September–May)
- Follow the Lycian Way along the **Mediterranean coast** through superb scenery (best in April, May, or October; walking boots are essential)

The Blue Mosque (Sultanahmet), Istanbul: Built between 1609 and 1616 – 66 years before work started on London's St Paul's Cathedral – this impressive mosque was designed to rival its neighbour, the great Hagia Sofia. It was seen as sacreligious in having six minarets, when at the time the only other such mosque was the great al-Haram in Mecca. Its name comes from the sumptuous blue and white tiles of the interior which were made in Iznik, world famous for its ceramic production.

114

11

12

13

114

120

Whirling Dervishes, Turkey: Founded by the Sufic mystic Celaleddin Rumi, the Konya-based Mevlevi order believe that music and dance induce an ecstatic state that liberates from the tribulations of daily life. The *sema* ritual dance is performed for visitors at the Mevlevi Lodge, Istanbul.

What to See

❶ Gallipoli (Gelibolu)
Lush countryside makes the setting for some of the bloodiest military encounters of World War I even more poignant

❷ Istanbul
The erstwhile capital of the Byzantine Empire is a grandiose city of decadent beauty where magnificent architecture intermingles with a bustling metropolis

❸ Black Sea Coast
Breathtaking valleys and summer pastures line the Black Sea. This tea-growing region is full of hidden gems

❹ Ephesus
(near Selcuk) Turkey's Mediterranean coast has a wealth of sites from Roman, Byzantine and earlier times. Among the most impressive is Ephesus but do not miss Pergamon, Aphrodisias and Termessos

❺ Pamukkale
The remains of a flourishing Roman city surround hot springs that flow over meringue-like terraces. Take a dip, but avoid midday when most tour groups arrive

❻ Turquoise Coast
Coves and lagoons with golden sandy beaches are interspersed with numerous ancient archaeological sites along the coast from Marmaris to Antalya

❼ Konya
The most fundamentally religious city in Turkey is a place of pilgrimage for Muslims and is home to the Sufic whirling Dervish sect

❽ Hattusas
(near Yozgat) Situated in a plain surrounded by rocky outcrops, this impressive walled city was once capital of the Hittite Empire

❾ Derinkuyu and Kaymakli
(near Nevsehir) Carved from soft volcanic tuff, whole cities of tunnels, rooms, churches and ventilation chimneys let imaginations run wild. Avoid if claustrophobic

❿ Ataturk Dam (Ataturk Baraji)
A masterpiece of modern engineering, this huge dam and irrigation project is enabling local farming but depriving neighbouring countries of much-needed water

⓫ Sanliurfa
The reputed birthplace of Prophet Abraham has a lively cultural mix, with a dark, sumptuous covered bazaar, leafy mosque gardens and sacred carp pools

⓬ Harran
(near Sanliurfa) Children scamper among ancient ruins in this village of beehive-shaped mud huts, which has been continuously inhabited for 6,000 years and is mentioned in the Bible

⓭ Sumela
(near Torul) Nestled into a sheer rock face, this imposing 13th-century monastery with lovely frescoes is worth the delightful but strenuous uphill woodland walk

⓮ Ishak Pasa
(near Dogubayazit) A grandiose palace that employs an eclectic mix of architectural styles to dominate the wind-swept valley below

⓯ Lake Sevan
In a stunning setting, this lake has delicious salmon and trout

⓰ Ateni Sioni
(near Gori) In beautiful surroundings, this fine example of a Georgian church is renowned for its 11th-century stone carvings and frescoes

⓱ Uplistsikhe (Fortress of God)
(near Gori) A natural cave complex, inhabited from the 6th century BCE for 2,000 years, it contains Georgia's first theatre, also dwellings, capacious wine cellars and gloomy dungeons

⓲ Baku
At the heart of the Azeri capital is the restored walled city, with narrow streets and a relaxed Middle Eastern tea-house culture

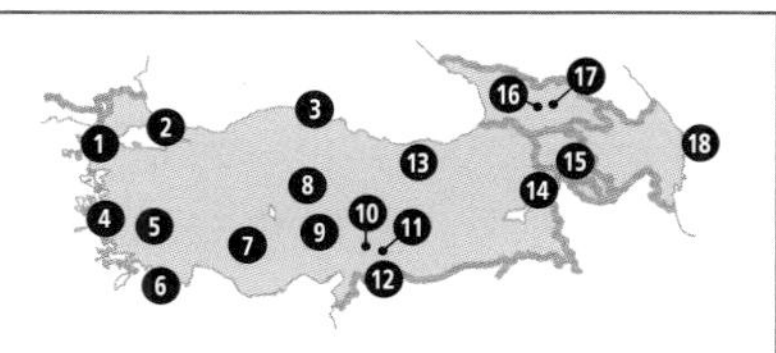

Map Key

POPULATION
- above 5 million
- 1 million to 5 million
- 500,000 to 1 million
- 100,000 to 500,000
- 50,000 to 100,000
- 10,000 to 50,000
- below 10,000

ELEVATION
- 4000m / 13,124ft
- 3000m / 9843ft
- 2000m / 6562ft
- 1000m / 3281ft
- 500m / 1640ft
- 250m / 820ft
- 100m / 328ft
- sea level

SCALE 1:4,500,000
(projection: Lambert Conformal Conic)

Black Sea Coast: Running along northern Turkey and into Georgia, this undiscovered coastline is nonetheless one of the region's loveliest and most fertile. It is famed for its cherries, tea and chestnuts.

The Near East

Iraq, Israel, Jordan, Lebanon, Syria

Some of the world's oldest civilizations developed in this region – the Fertile Crescent. It is venerated by Jews, Muslims, and Christians, but torn by competing religious, ethnic and national claims to the land. Security concerns, which have damaged tourism across the region, belie the fact that most parts are actually quite safe and give a warm welcome to visitors.

The Great Rift Valley runs from Lebanon down into East Africa, dividing Israel from Jordan and forming the Sea of Galilee, the Jordan river and the Dead Sea (the lowest point on earth). It is the setting for many of the biblical stories, with fabulous remains, interesting churches and dramatic scenery. Jericho, which dates back to 7000 BCE, is the leading contender among several in the region to being the oldest city in the world.

Mesopotamia, meaning "between two rivers" (the Tigris and Euphrates), was the cradle of great civilizations. Unfortunately, its archaeological sites, such as Hatra and Ur, within modern Iraq, are currently off limits.

Many peoples have left their mark on the region, such as the Nabataeans who built the fabled rose-red city of Petra in Jordan, but the most widespread remains are the well-preserved Roman sites and the more recent medieval Crusader castles.

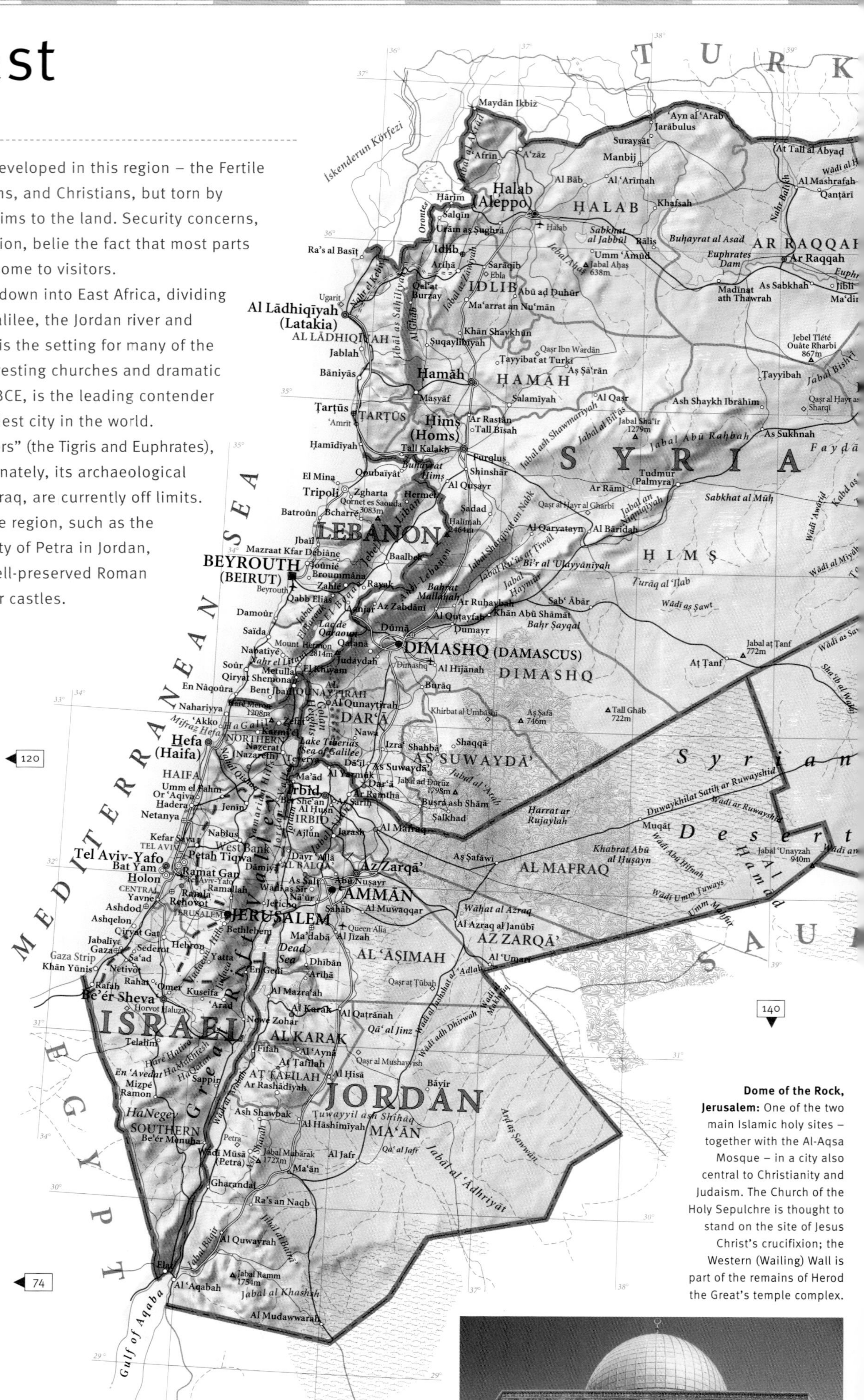

What to See

1 Crac des Chevaliers
(near Tall Kalakh)
The greatest of the Crusader castles was never breached and is remarkably intact

2 Palmyra
Huge ancient city, most of the surviving remains dating to Roman times, including the famous Temple of Bel

3 Damascus
Continuously inhabited for 7,000 years; the splendid Umayyad Mosque is famed for its golden mosaics

4 Baalbek
The "Sun City" of the Roman world, with extravagant temples and extensive ruins

5 Byblos (Jbail)
Dating back perhaps 7,000 years, this picturesque fishing town has Roman ruins and a restored Crusader castle

6 Jerusalem
Sacred for all three major monotheistic religions and home of the Dead Sea Scrolls, the oldest biblical text

7 Masada
(near En Gedi)
Dramatically located fortress, site of a mass suicide in 73 CE, and symbol of Jewish resistance to imperial Roman rule

8 Maktesh Ramon
(near Mizpe Ramon)
A 40 km (25 mile) crater, providing expansive views across a moon-like landscape

9 Petra
Reached via a narrow cleft through the rock, a fabulous hidden Nabataean city of tombs and temples carved into the valley sides

10 Ma'daba
Mosaic-making centre of the 6th century CE; the famous map of the Holy Land adorns the Greek Orthodox church

11 Jarash
One of ten cities in the Greco-Roman Decapolis; chariot races are still held in its reconstructed hippodrome

12 Qusayr Amra
(near Al Azraq al Janubi)
Small Umayyad bathhouse, painted with erotic frescoes

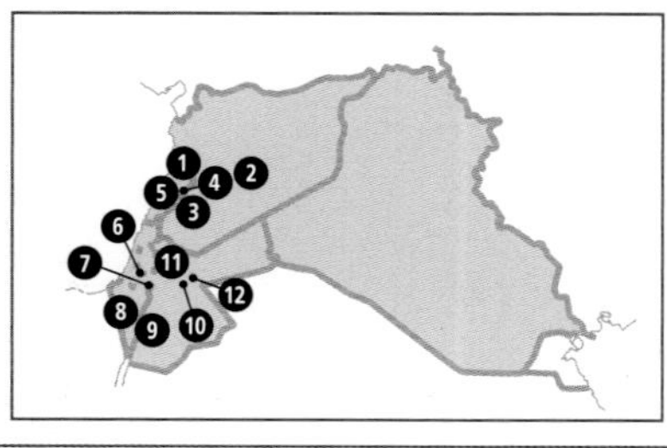

120

140

74

Dome of the Rock, Jerusalem: One of the two main Islamic holy sites – together with the Al-Aqsa Mosque – in a city also central to Christianity and Judaism. The Church of the Holy Sepulchre is thought to stand on the site of Jesus Christ's crucifixion; the Western (Wailing) Wall is part of the remains of Herod the Great's temple complex.

SCALE 1:3,500,000
(projection: Lambert Conformal Conic)
Km 0 10 20 40 60 80 100 120
Miles 0 10 20 40 60 80 100 120

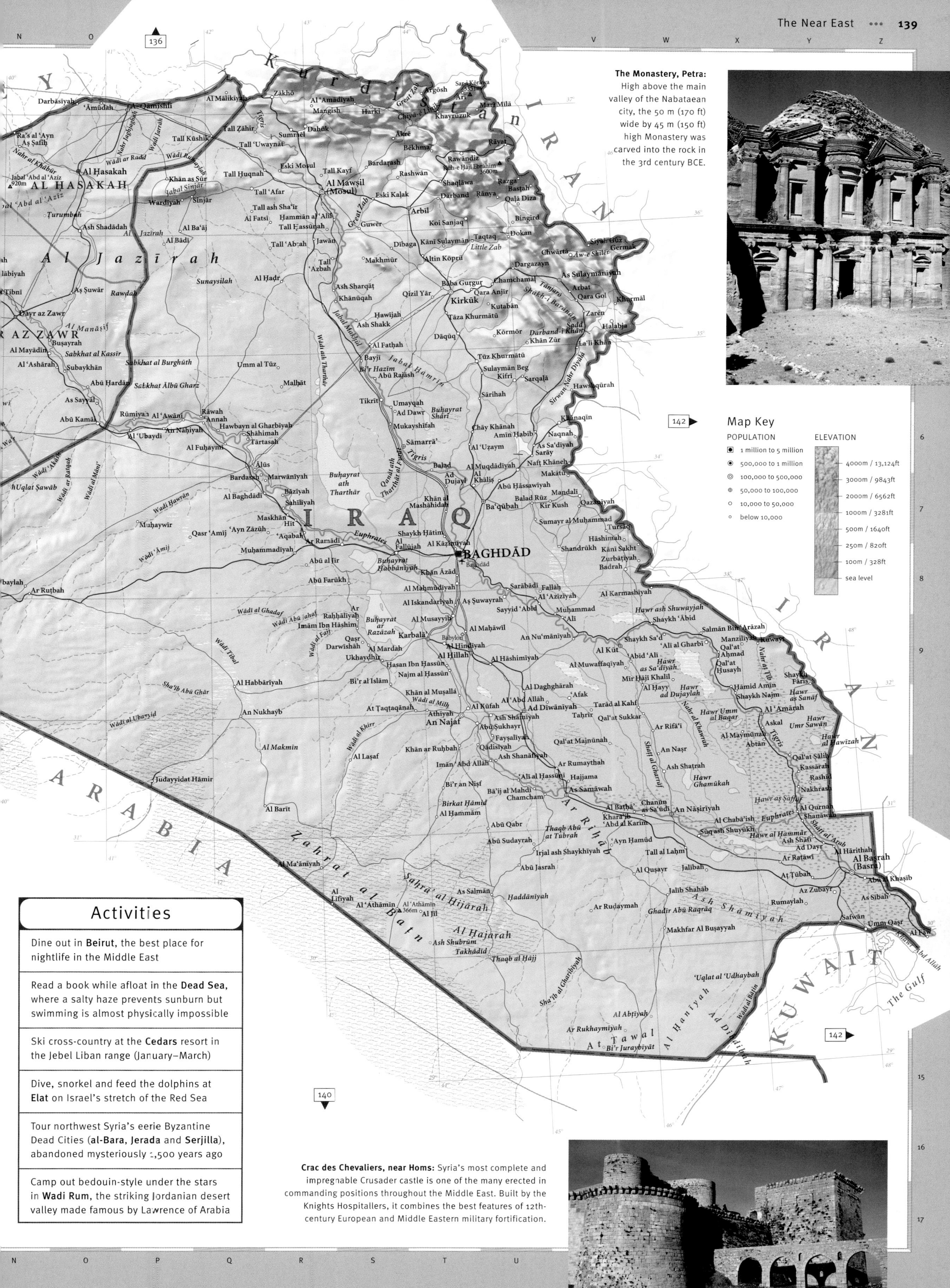

136
142
140
IRAQ
IRAN
KUWAIT
ARABIA
Kurdistan
Al Jazīrah
AL HASAKAH
BAGHDĀD
Al Mawşil (Mosul)
Kirkūk
Arbīl
As Sulaymānīyah
Tikrīt
Sāmarrā'
Ba'qūbah
Al Fallūjah
Ar Ramādī
Karbalā'
Al Ḩillah
An Najaf
Ad Dīwānīyah
Al Kūt
Al 'Amārah
An Nāşirīyah
As Samāwah
Al Başrah (Basra)
Umm Qaşr
Al Fāw
Ar Ruţbah
Tigris
Euphrates
The Gulf
Map Key
POPULATION
1 million to 5 million
500,000 to 1 million
100,000 to 500,000
50,000 to 100,000
10,000 to 50,000
below 10,000
ELEVATION
4000m / 13,124ft
3000m / 9843ft
2000m / 6562ft
1000m / 3281ft
500m / 1640ft
250m / 820ft
100m / 328ft
sea level

The Monastery, Petra: High above the main valley of the Nabataean city, the 50 m (170 ft) wide by 45 m (150 ft) high Monastery was carved into the rock in the 3rd century BCE.

Crac des Chevaliers, near Homs: Syria's most complete and impregnable Crusader castle is one of the many erected in commanding positions throughout the Middle East. Built by the Knights Hospitallers, it combines the best features of 12th-century European and Middle Eastern military fortification.

Activities

- Dine out in **Beirut**, the best place for nightlife in the Middle East
- Read a book while afloat in the **Dead Sea**, where a salty haze prevents sunburn but swimming is almost physically impossible
- Ski cross-country at the **Cedars** resort in the Jebel Liban range (January–March)
- Dive, snorkel and feed the dolphins at **Elat** on Israel's stretch of the Red Sea
- Tour northwest Syria's eerie Byzantine Dead Cities (**al-Bara**, **Jerada** and **Serjilla**), abandoned mysteriously 1,500 years ago
- Camp out bedouin-style under the stars in **Wadi Rum**, the striking Jordanian desert valley made famous by Lawrence of Arabia

The Arabian Peninsula

Bahrain, Kuwait, Oman, Qatar, Saudi Arabia, United Arab Emirates (UAE), Yemen

Bordered by the Red Sea, the Indian Ocean and The Gulf, the Arabian Peninsula has many interesting trading ports set amid rocky coastal regions. Yemen, once the home of the Queen of Saba (known in Hebrew as Sheba), has a treasure trove of dramatic walled towns and villages located along its rugged western shore. The buildings have a distinct architecture, resembling ancient multistoreyed "skyscrapers". Saudi Arabia was completely closed to tourists until 2000. Non-Muslims are still prohibited from visiting its two great Islamic holy cities, Mecca and Medina, which welcome two million pilgrims each year.

Least developed, Oman has the best sights. Its mountainous east features attractive coastlands and fascinating forts, many undergoing restoration. The United Arab Emirates (UAE) is dominated by ritzy Dubai which, with more expatriates than locals, allows a virtually unrestricted lifestyle. Massive construction projects, adding to the already large number of world-class hotels, include ambitious schemes for the world's largest tower, an underwater hotel and a man-made archipelago map of the world. Bahrain, a tiny island with a long trading history, hosts a grand prix. Qatar and Kuwait are also keen to attract visitors, but though much larger, have less to offer, especially since Kuwait's National Museum was looted and ransacked during the 1990–1991 Iraqi invasion.

Nizwa Fort, Oman: This imposing 17th-century citadel, set in a sea of lush date palms on the western side of the Hajar mountains, is the largest on the Arabian Peninsula, and served as the palace for the *imam* (religious leader) who ruled Oman's interior region.

Activities

- Witness green turtles laying eggs at **Ras al Hadd**, on the eastern tip of the Omani coastline (tours go in the evening, returning again at 5am to see the young emerge)
- Go dune-bashing in a 4WD at the **Big Red Sand Dune** near Dubai (organized tours recommended)
- Dive for pearls in the shallow waters off **Bahrain**, following a tradition that was once a lucrative industry
- Sandboard in the extensive dunes around Qatar's **Inland Sea** (Khawr al Udayd)
- Barter at the extensive gold *souq* in **Dubai**
- Watch camel-racing at **Al-Shahaniya stadium**, 60 km (37 miles) west of Doha. Cars follow the race alongside the track

What to See

1 Medain Salih
(near Al Ula) Nabataean rock tombs, Saudi's answer to Jordan's Petra, and better preserved, if less impressive

2 Jedda
Important commercial centre on the Red Sea, also known for its diving and a group of houses built entirely of coral

3 Habalah
Deserted cliff village in the Asir National Park, only reached by cable car. The original inhabitants created it as a safe haven after escaping from the Turks

4 Riyadh
Saudi Arabia's modern capital, with two huge skyscrapers dominating the skyline, is a shopper's paradise

5 Bahrain
Numerous sites of interest including 80,000 burial mounds and a 32 km (20 mile) causeway to mainland Saudi Arabia.

6 Khawr al Udayd
Qatar's Inland Sea is reached through beautiful sand dunes, with fine views across to Saudi Arabia

7 Dubai
Multicultural city of skyscrapers boasting the best of everything, known for its luxury hotels and Disneyland-style shopping malls, recreating Venice, Egypt, or traditional Arabia

8 Hatta
(near Haba) Rock pools, popular with local visitors, set among beautiful mountain scenery, close to the Omani-UAE border

9 Jabreen Fort
(near Bahla) Built in 1670 and often used as a retreat for *imams*, this superb fort has many original exquisite painted ceilings

10 Nizwa
Main centre of the Hajar range, with a fine restored fort sporting a huge round tower and picturesque mosque

11 Muscat
Omani capital set amid craggy mountains, split into many suburbs, each with its own fort

12 Shibam
The "Manhattan of the Desert", a walled village with 500 seven- or eight-storey buildings, situated in Wadi Hadramawt

13 Mar'ib
Once the capital of Saba, famed for the great dam built for irrigation in the 6th century BCE

14 Shihara
(near Huth) Fortified village with a stone bridge over a 300 m (1,000 ft) gorge

15 Sana
Supposedly founded by Noah's son Shem, Yemen's capital is known for its distinctive "tower houses" – multistoreyed buildings of rammed earth and mud brick

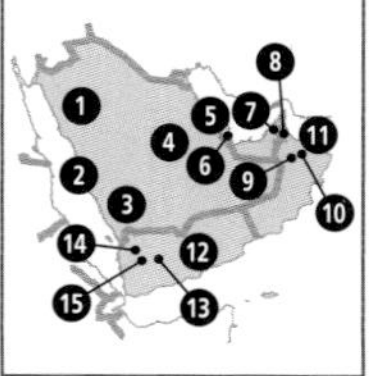

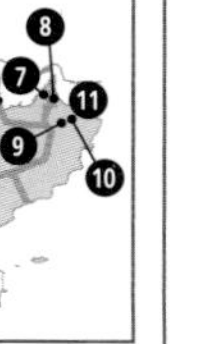

SCALE 1:8,250,000
(projection: Lambert Conformal Conic)

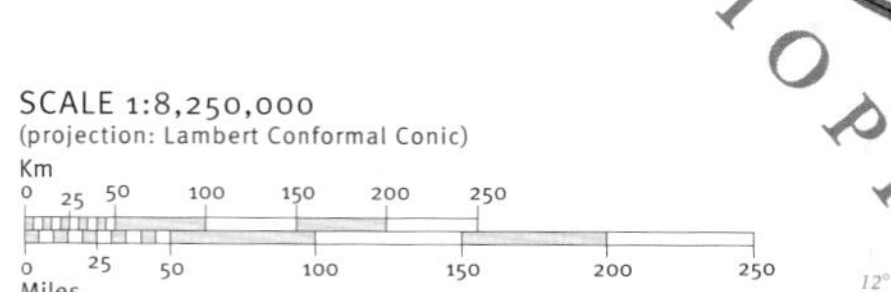
Km
0 25 50 100 150 200 250
0 25 50 100 150 200 250
Miles

74
74
80
80

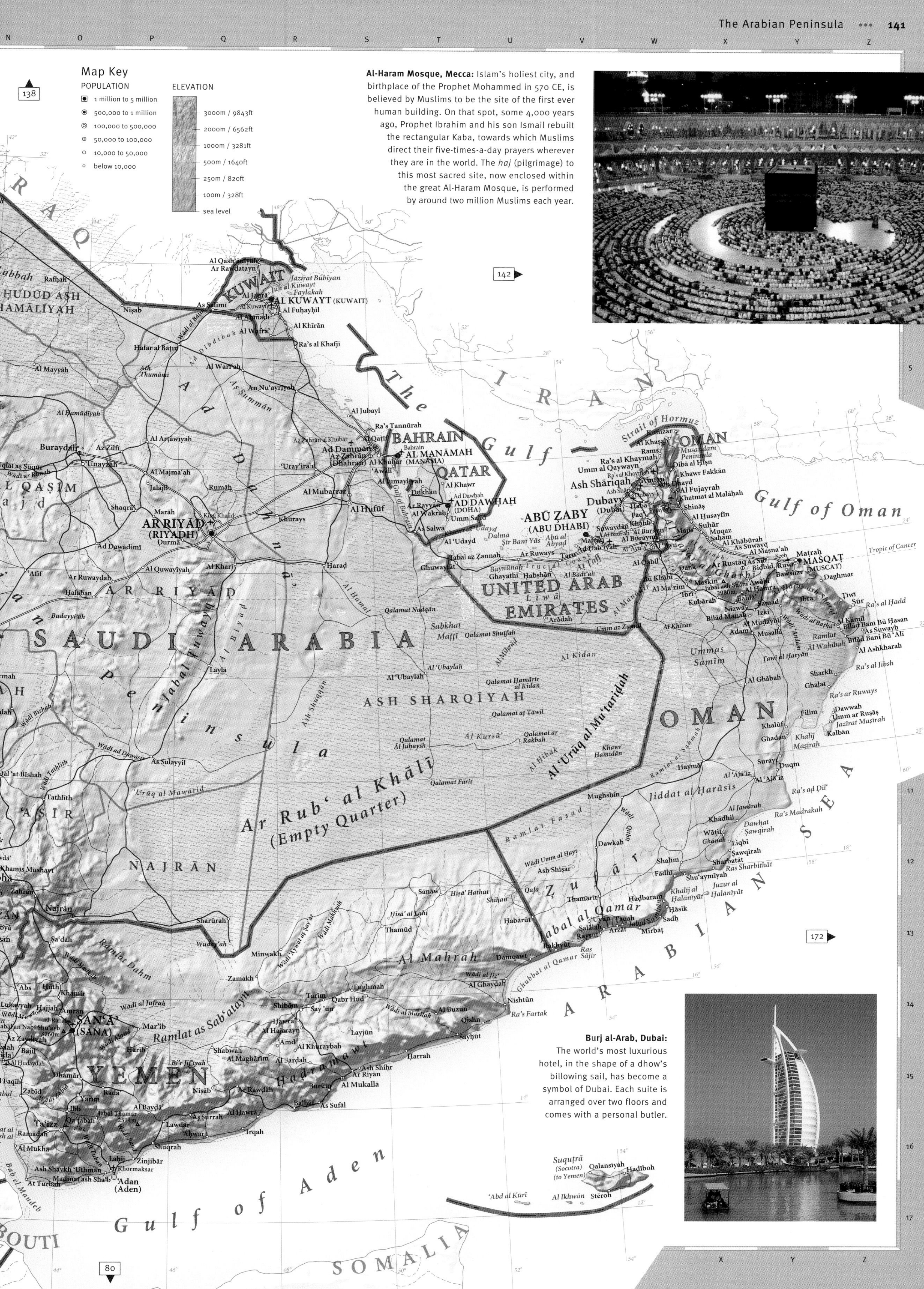
N O P Q R S T U V W X Y Z
138
Map Key
POPULATION
1 million to 5 million
500,000 to 1 million
100,000 to 500,000
50,000 to 100,000
10,000 to 50,000
below 10,000
ELEVATION
3000m / 9843ft
2000m / 6562ft
1000m / 3281ft
500m / 1640ft
250m / 820ft
100m / 328ft
sea level
142
IRAQ
KUWAIT
AL KUWAYT (KUWAIT)
Al Jahra'
Al Ahmadi
Al Wafra'
Al Khīrān
Ra's al Khafjī
Jazīrat Būbiyān
Faylakah
Al Fuḩayḩīl
Ḩafar al Bāţin
Al Mayyāh
Ath Thumāmī
Al Wari'ah
An Nu'ayrīyah
Al Jubayl
Ra's Tannūrah
Ad Dammām
Az Zahrān (Dhahran)
Al Khubar
Al Qaţīf
BAHRAIN
AL MANĀMAH (MANAMA)
QATAR
Al Khawr
Dukhān
AD DAWḨAH (DOHA)
Umm Sa'id
Ar Rayyān
Al Wakrah
Salwá
Al Hufūf
Al Mubarraz
Buraydah
'Unayzah
AL QAŞĪM
Al Majma'ah
Shaqrā'
Rumāḩ
AR RIYĀD (RIYADH)
Ad Dawādimī
Durmā
Al Kharj
Al Quwayiyah
Ḩaraḑ
AR RIYĀḐ
SAUDI ARABIA
Ad Dahnā'
Aş Şummān
Arabian Peninsula
Laylá
Al Aflāj
As Sulayyil
Wādī ad Dawāsir
'Urūq al Mawārid
Ar Rub' al Khālī (Empty Quarter)
ASH SHARQĪYAH
NAJRĀN
Najrān
Sharūrah
Abhā
Khamīs Mushayţ
'ASĪR
Jīzān
Şa'dah
Ramlat Dahm
IRAN
The Gulf
Strait of Hormuz
Musandam Peninsula
OMAN
Ra's al Khaymah
Umm al Qaywayn
Ash Shāriqah
'Ajmān
Dubayy (Dubai)
ABŪ ẒABY (ABU DHABI)
Al Fujayrah
Khawr Fakkān
Dibā al Ḩişn
Al 'Ayn
Al Buraymī
UNITED ARAB EMIRATES
Līwā
Gulf of Oman
Tropic of Cancer
MASQAŢ (MUSCAT)
Maţraḩ
Şuḩār
Al Khābūrah
Ar Rustāq
Nizwá
Ibrā
Şūr
Ra's al Ḩadd
Jabal ash Shām 2980m
Ramlat Al Wahībah
Umm as Samīm
OMAN
Al 'Urūq al Mu'tariḍah
Maşīrah
Jazīrat Maşīrah
Jiddat al Ḩarāsīs
Duqm
Ramlat Fasad
Ẓufār
Thamarīt
Şalālah
Rakhyūt
Mirbāţ
Jabal al Qamar
Ḩalāniyāt
Arabian Sea
172
YEMEN
ŞAN'Ā' (SANA)
Jabal an Nabī Shu'ayb 3760m
Mar'ib
Ramlat as Sab'atayn
Shibām
Sayūn
Tarīm
Ḩaḑramawt
Al Mahrah
Al Ghayḑah
Nishtūn
Ra's Fartak
Al Mukallā
Ash Shihr
Ta'izz
Jabal Şabir
Al Mukhā
'Adan (Aden)
Zinjibār
Bāb el Mandeb
Gulf of Aden
Suquţrā (Socotra) (to Yemen)
Ḩadībōh
'Abd al Kūrī
DJIBOUTI
SOMALIA
80
X Y Z

Al-Haram Mosque, Mecca: Islam's holiest city, and birthplace of the Prophet Mohammed in 570 CE, is believed by Muslims to be the site of the first ever human building. On that spot, some 4,000 years ago, Prophet Ibrahim and his son Ismail rebuilt the rectangular Kaba, towards which Muslims direct their five-times-a-day prayers wherever they are in the world. The *haj* (pilgrimage) to this most sacred site, now enclosed within the great Al-Haram Mosque, is performed by around two million Muslims each year.

Burj al-Arab, Dubai: The world's most luxurious hotel, in the shape of a dhow's billowing sail, has become a symbol of Dubai. Each suite is arranged over two floors and comes with a personal butler.

Iran & the Gulf States

Bahrain, Iran, Kuwait, Qatar, United Arab Emirates (UAE)

136

The exotic and mysterious land of Iran, formerly known as Persia, retains a unique culture and distinguished history. Full of enormous blue-tiled mosques, ancient ruins, old bazaars and carpets, it is now the world's largest theocracy, following the 1979 Islamic Revolution. It is an inexpensive country to visit, with top-class sights as well as many areas of interest that are still almost undiscovered by tourists. To experience local life takes time – exploring the bazaars, puffing on a *qalyan* (water pipe) in the traditional teahouses, shopping for carpets, sweating in one of the many bathhouses or, if you're lucky, getting an invitation to dine in an Iranian home.

Nowhere is better for this than Esfahan, the fabulous trad ng centre, which also has some of the country's finest architecture and historical sights. Many of its elegant, cool blue mosques and other buildings date from the time of Shah Abbas, who came to power in 1587 and set out to make Esfahan "half the world". The city today certainly merits a lengthy visit, but most visitors' itineraries will also include other great historic monuments such as ruined Persepolis and the Castles of the Assassins in the north.

138

Drying carpets on a cliff near Tehran: Washing in cold water helps to preserve the fragile natural dyes used to colour the wool. Each tribe has its own patterns and much of the weaving is still done on traditional looms in family houses.

Activities

Hike in the forests near the beautiful village of **Masuleh**, northwest Iran
Reflect on the atrocities of the Iran-Iraq War of the 1980s in the museum dedicated to that conflict in **Kerman**, central Iran
Barter for a carpet or rug – choosing from **Iran's** many regional styles with their own distinctive tribal symbols
Emerge laden with bargains from Iran's largest and oldest bazaar, in **Tabriz**, northwest Iran, the first entry point from Turkey and Azerbaijan
Support a local wrestling favourite in the ring at **Tehran**

140

What to See

Bahrain, Kuwait, Qatar, UAE
see pp140–141

❶ Throne of Soleiman
(near Zanjan) Remote fortified hilltop settlement by a lake amid rocky mountains, with ruins dating back 2,500 years

❷ Castles of the Assassins
(near Qazvin) Built by the religious cult known as the Assassins, the mostly rubble remains of seven castles are set in craggy uplands

❸ Tehran
Iran's capital is a vast metropolis with many fine museums and an immense haphazard covered bazaar

❹ Emam Khomeini Square
A huge square in central Esfahan built in 1612 with the famous blue and yellow-tiled Emam Mosque

❺ Yazd
Wedged between the northern and southern deserts, Yazd's Zoroastrian Fire Temple attracts followers of this pre-Islamic cult from all over the world

❻ Bisotun
(near Kermanshah) A vast stone panel set in the cliffs, dating from the 7th century BCE and written in three different languages

❼ Shiraz
Former Persian capital, most of its mosques, mausoleums and gardens were built in the 18th century and are being restored

❽ Persepolis
(near Shiraz) Started by Darius I in 518 BCE, this magnificent palace complex was extended over the next 200 years until it was destroyed by the Greeks

❾ Bam
Isolated in the desert, this mud-brick city with a huge fort is slowly being restored to its former glory, following its devastation by an earthquake in 2003

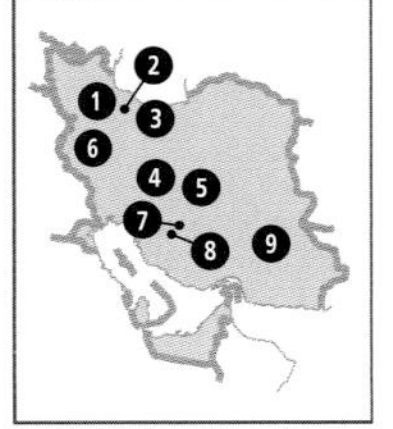

Persepolis, Fars: These impressive remains of fabulous palaces, with exquisite stone carvings, testify to the magnificence and power of the Persian Achaemenid Empire (6th–4th centuries BCE).

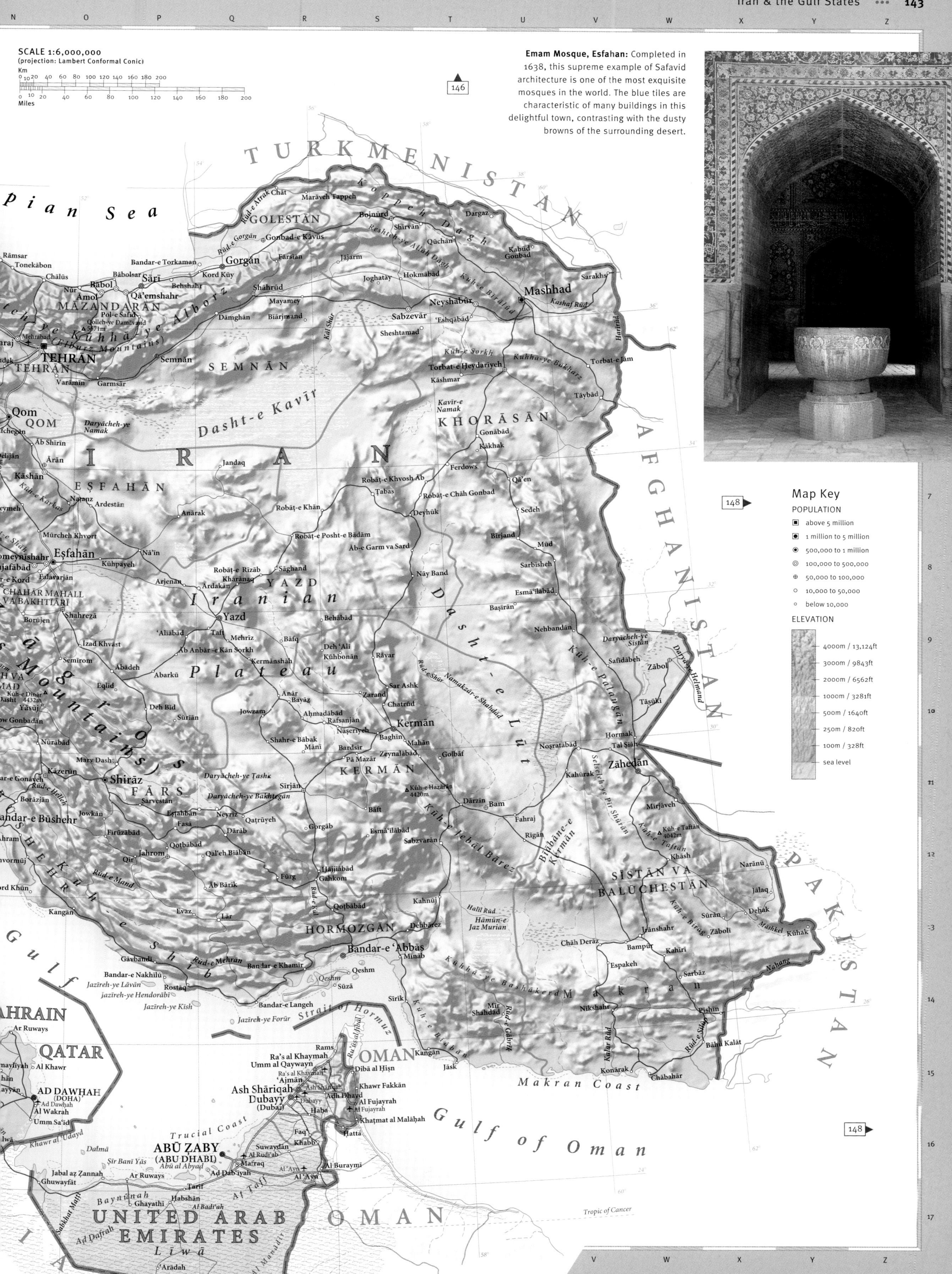
N O P Q R S T U V W X Y Z
SCALE 1:6,000,000
(projection: Lambert Conformal Conic)
Km
0 10 20 40 60 80 100 120 140 160 180 200
0 10 20 40 60 80 100 120 140 160 180 200
Miles
146
148
148
Map Key
POPULATION
above 5 million
1 million to 5 million
500,000 to 1 million
100,000 to 500,000
50,000 to 100,000
10,000 to 50,000
below 10,000
ELEVATION
4000m / 13,124ft
3000m / 9843ft
2000m / 6562ft
1000m / 3281ft
500m / 1640ft
250m / 820ft
100m / 328ft
sea level
TURKMENISTAN
AFGHANISTAN
PAKISTAN
IRAN
QATAR
BAHRAIN
OMAN
UNITED ARAB EMIRATES
Caspian Sea
Gulf of Oman
Strait of Hormuz
Makran Coast
Tropic of Cancer
TEHRĀN
Mashhad
Eşfahān
Shīrāz
Yazd
Kermān
Zāhedān
Qom
Gorgān
Sārī
Bābol
Āmol
Semnān
Kāshān
Bandar-e 'Abbās
Bandar-e Būshehr
AD DAWḤAH (DOHA)
ABŪ ẒABY (ABU DHABI)
Dubayy (Dubai)
Ash Shāriqah
Ra's al Khaymah
Al Fujayrah
GOLESTĀN
MĀZANDARĀN
SEMNĀN
KHORĀSĀN
EŞFAHĀN
YAZD
KERMĀN
FĀRS
HORMOZGĀN
SĪSTĀN VA BALŪCHESTĀN
CHAHĀR MAHALL VA BAKHTIĀRĪ
Dasht-e Kavīr
Dasht-e Lūt
Iranian Plateau
Zagros Mountains
Kūhhā-ye Alborz (Elburz Mountains)
Kopet Dagh
Makran
Emam Mosque, Esfahan: Completed in 1638, this supreme example of Safavid architecture is one of the most exquisite mosques in the world. The blue tiles are characteristic of many buildings in this delightful town, contrasting with the dusty browns of the surrounding desert.
7 8 9 10 11 12 13 14 15 16 17
V W X Y Z

Kazakhstan

Kazakhstan is a big blank on most tourist maps. For years, under Soviet rule, this huge area of steppeland between Europe and China remained inaccessible to all but the very privileged – or the very foolhardy. Here, the Soviet Union built its huge space port at Baykonyr, here too are the nuclear wastelands of the Polygon test site. With this discouraging legacy of the recent past, Kazakhstan remains a mystery to most in the West. Around the huge grasslands, though, are rich reminders of the former glories of the Silk Road, and great natural beauty in the high mountains which form the country's southwestern borders. Kazakhstan is undergoing an economic boom driven by rich oil and gas deposits. As a result, even the capital has been moved and rebuilt in modern style at Astana. The biggest city, and commercial heart of Kazakhstan, remains Almaty – the old capital – which nestles attractively at the foot of the Alatau Mountains, and it is here that most visitors will make their base. The mountains temper the harsh summer heat and provide welcome opportunities for skiing in winter.

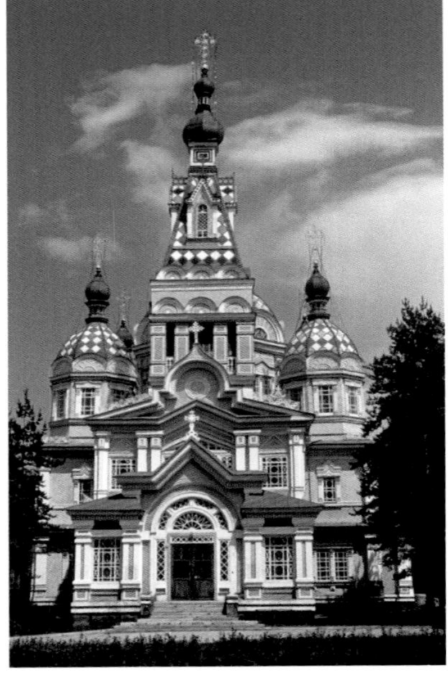

Almaty: The wooden Zenkov Cathedral in Almaty's Panfilov Park, supposedly built without the use of nails, survived the great earthquake of 1911 which levelled much of the city.

Activities

- Drink *kumiss* – the fermented mare's milk beloved of Genghis Khan and generations of nomads
- Birdwatchers can see an impressive variety of waterfowl at **Korgalzhyn** nature reserve
- Wander round the monuments and mausoleums of **Taraz**, a city that thrived on the great Silk Road
- Be pampered at a health resort in **Kokshetau**, north Kazakhstan
- Go skating on the enormous **Medeo** skating rink, set amid the mountains near Almaty
- Experienced mountaineers can tackle the Tien Shan peaks from the **Khan Tengri International Climbing Centre**, near Almaty

122

Map Key

POPULATION

- 1 million to 5 million
- 500,000 to 1 million
- 100,000 to 500,000
- 50,000 to 100,000
- 10,000 to 50,000
- below 10,000

ELEVATION

- 4000m / 13,124ft
- 3000m / 9843ft
- 2000m / 6562ft
- 1000m / 3281ft
- 500m / 1640ft
- 250m / 820ft
- 100m / 328ft
- sea level

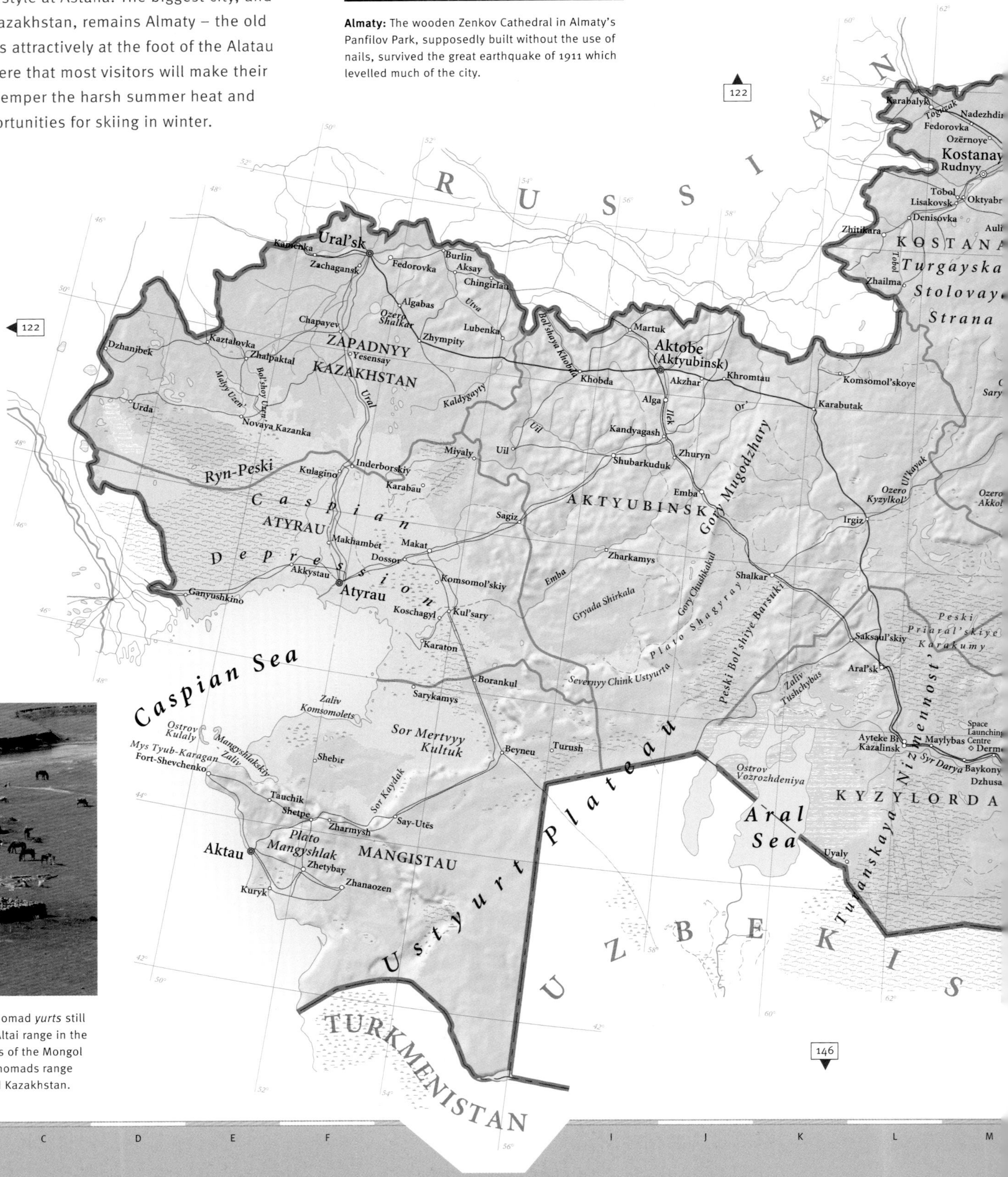

122

146

Altai Mountains: Traditional nomad *yurts* still dot the high pastures of the Altai range in the summer months. Descendants of the Mongol armies of Genghis Khan, the nomads range between Mongolia, China and Kazakhstan.

Tien Shan: These formidable mountains run through Kazakhstan's southeastern corner, topped by the 6,995 m (22,950 ft) Pik Khan Tengri.

What to See

❶ Lake Burabay
(near Borovoye) Scenic, lake with a startling rock formation, known locally as "Little Switzerland"

❷ Astana
The capital since 1997, Astana has pleasant tree-lined avenues and a relaxing, modern air

❸ Semipalatinsk
Dostoyevsky museum dedicated to his time in exile here

❹ Altai Mountains
Climbing, heli-skiing and horse trekking are all popular activities in the stunning Altai range

❺ Dzhungarian Gap
(near Dostyk) The only route though the mountains separating Central Asia and China has seen armies come and go for millennia

❻ Zenkov Cathedral
(in Almaty) One of the world's largest wooden structures and a rare survivor of pre-Soviet Christian architecture

❼ Medeo
(near Almaty) The ice rink here claims to be the world's largest

❽ Khodia Ahmed Yasavi Mausoleum
(in Turkestan) Exquisitely tiled mausoleum built by Tamerlane the Great

❾ Baykonyr
Commercial rocket launches to outer space take place from the Baykonyr cosmodrome

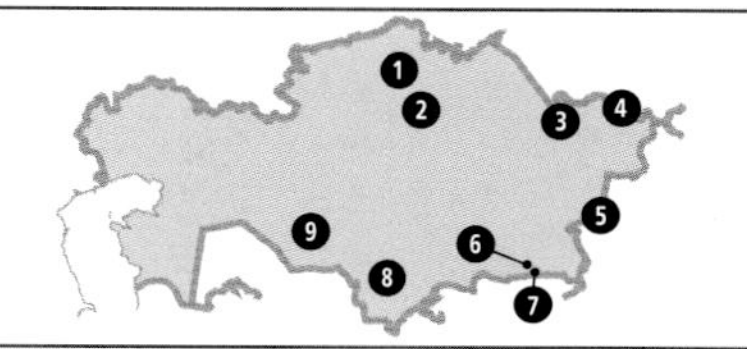

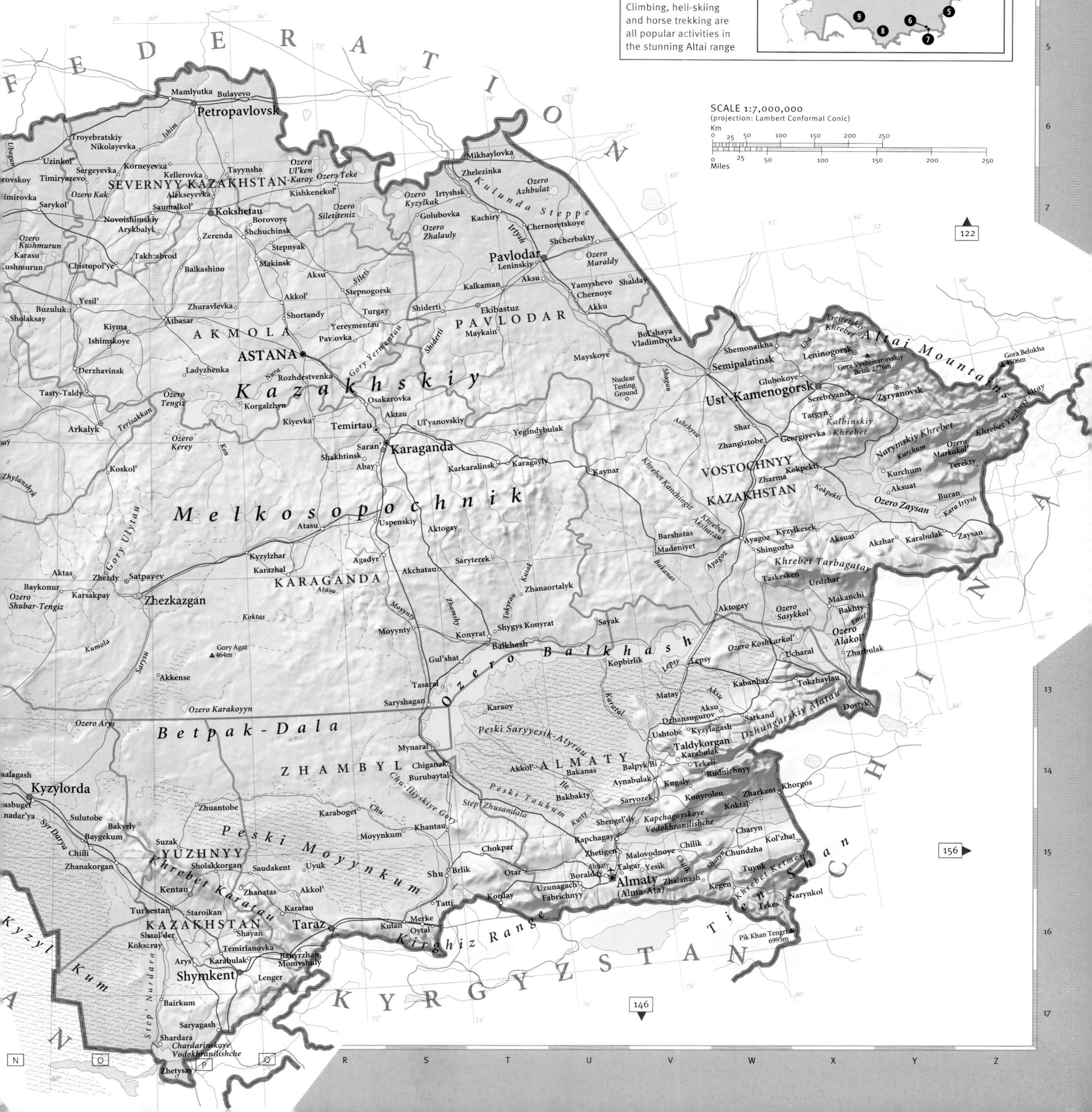

SCALE 1:7,000,000
(projection: Lambert Conformal Conic)
Km 0 25 50 100 150 200 250
Miles 0 25 50 100 150 200 250

122
156
146

Central Asia

Kyrgyzstan, Tajikistan, Turkmenistan, Uzbekistan

The fascinating crossroads countries of Central Asia span the region between the Caspian Sea and China, through which Mongol forces ebbed and flowed for centuries from the time of Genghis Khan (1206–1227 CE). Across this territory the great Silk Road brought merchants and adventurers from west and east, and even today the goods traded in its bazaars are an enticement to the traveller. The landscape changes from desert to high mountain with rich fertile river valleys. Those cities that have remained intact have some of the most spectacular architecture on earth. Independent since the break up of the Soviet Union, Kyrgyzstan, Uzbekistan and Turkmenistan have all suffered from unrest, though its possible to travel safely there. The long civil war in Tajikistan, however, places it off limits to most.

Activities

Relax in the Labi-Hauz, a plaza with a pool, amongst extravagantly robed gentlemen, **Buxoro**

Hone your haggling buying carpets in the **Tolkuchka Bazaar**, Asgabat

Stay in a *yurt* (tent) in the high mountain passes of the **Pamir** range

Ride purebred Akhal-Teke horses in the mountains west of **Asgabat**

Slap on the mud at thermal springs around **Issyk-Kul** lake, Kyrgyzstan

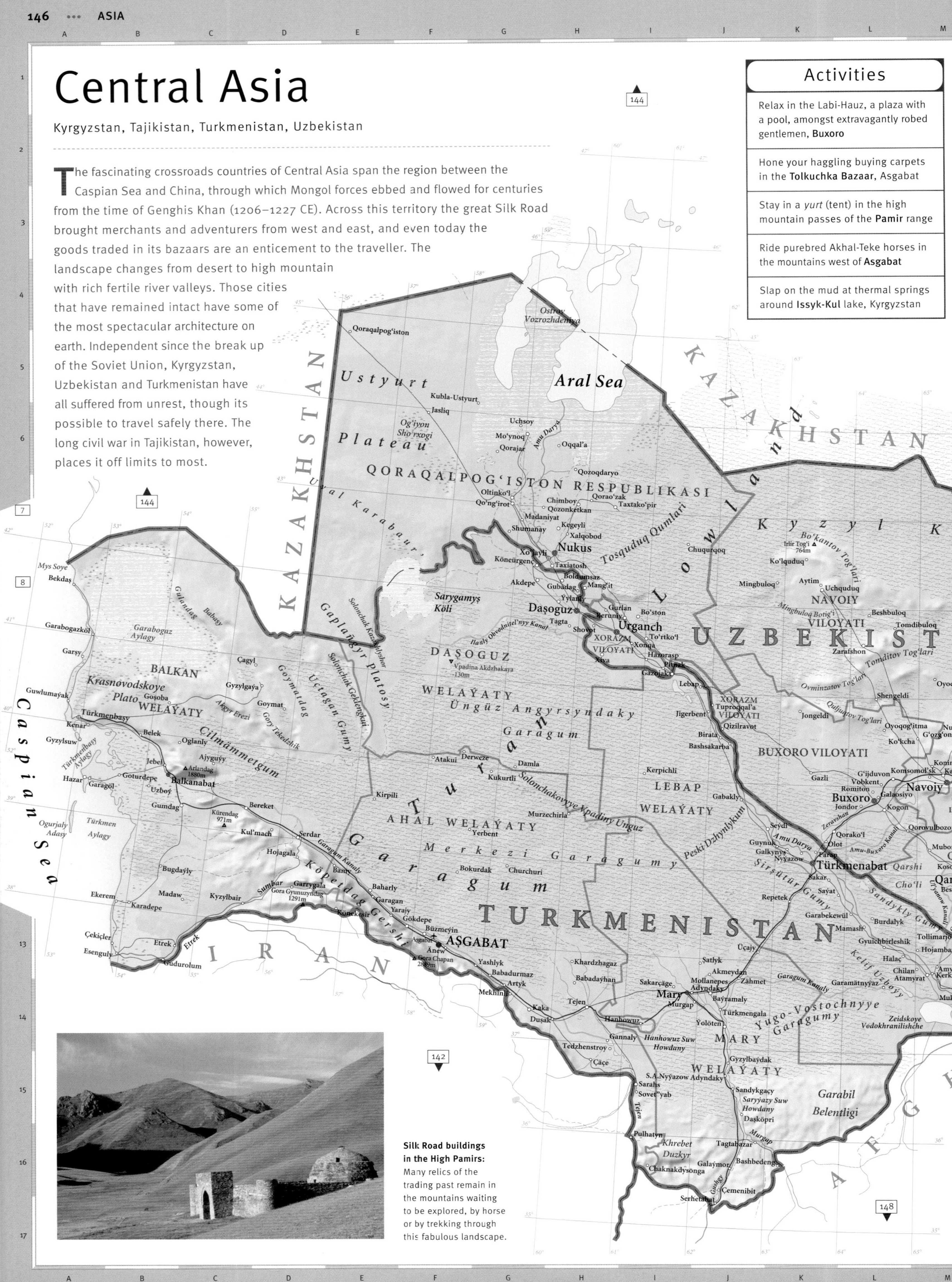

144
144
142
148
KAZAKHSTAN
UZBEKISTAN
TURKMENISTAN
IRAN
AFGH
Caspian Sea
Aral Sea
Ostrov Vozrozhdeniya
Ustyurt Plateau
QORAQALPOG'ISTON RESPUBLIKASI
Turan Lowland
Kyzyl K
Garagum
Merkezi Garagumy
Üngüz Angyrsyndaky Garagum
BALKAN WELAÝATY
DAŞOGUZ WELAÝATY
AHAL WELAÝATY
LEBAP WELAÝATY
MARY WELAÝATY
XORAZM VILOYATI
NAVOIY VILOYATI
BUXORO VILOYATI
Nukus
Daşoguz
Urganch
Xiva
Türkmenbaşy
Balkanabat
AŞGABAT
Mary
Türkmenabat
Buxoro
Navoiy
Qarshi
Garabogazköl
Krasnovodskoye Plato
Sarygamyş Köli
Köpetdag
Garagum Kanaly
Amu Darya
Tejen
Murgap
Garabil Belentligi

Silk Road buildings in the High Pamirs: Many relics of the trading past remain in the mountains waiting to be explored, by horse or by trekking through this fabulous landscape.

What to See

❶ Aral Sea
This huge inland sea is fast drying up, since the diversion of its feeder rivers. Stranded fishing boats lie over a hundred miles from the nearest water and fish canneries now have a ghostly air

❷ Xiva
This beautifully restored Silk Road city – more museum than living space – possesses some of Asia's finest tilework

❸ Asgabat
The expensively rebuilt capital's idiosyncracies are testament to the eccentric will of a post-independence president. Tolkuchka Bazaar is one of Central Asia's most fascinating

❹ Merv
(near Bayramaly) The ruins of Merv are an eerie, desolate reminder of what was an important city until it was sacked by the Mongols in 1221

❺ Buxoro
This rich trading city on the Silk Road has many mosques. The Kalan minaret impressed Genghis Khan in the 13th century

❻ Samarqand
Gorgeous architecture and rich history make Samarqand one of the jewels of the Silk Road

❼ Tashkent
Huge, urbane and metropolitan, Tashkent still retains a flavour of the east but with a thriving nightlife and westernized attitudes

❽ Fergana Valley
This lush, fertile valley, carved up into different republics by Stalin, is now a major cotton-producing centre

❾ Osh Bazaar
(in Bishkek) Ancient bazaar in the mountains where everything is available, from guns, to opium, to silks

❿ Pamir Sky Highway
A tortuous and spectacular road from Khorugh to Osh through the Pamir Mountains that, while dangerous, gives unparalleled views of mountain scenery

⓫ Lake Issyk-Kul
Vast, deep and mysterious, Lake Issyk-Kul lies hard against the Alatau Mountains. Heated by thermal springs, it never freezes and was used for secret submarine testing

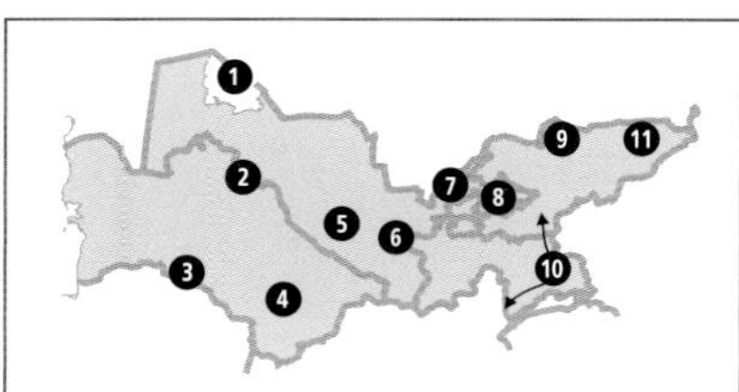

The Registan, Samarqand: Once a showpiece city for the might of the Timurid empire, Samarqand has as its focal point this magnificent square, enclosed on three sides by the beautiful tiled walls of Ulugh Beg *madrassa* – a religious school.

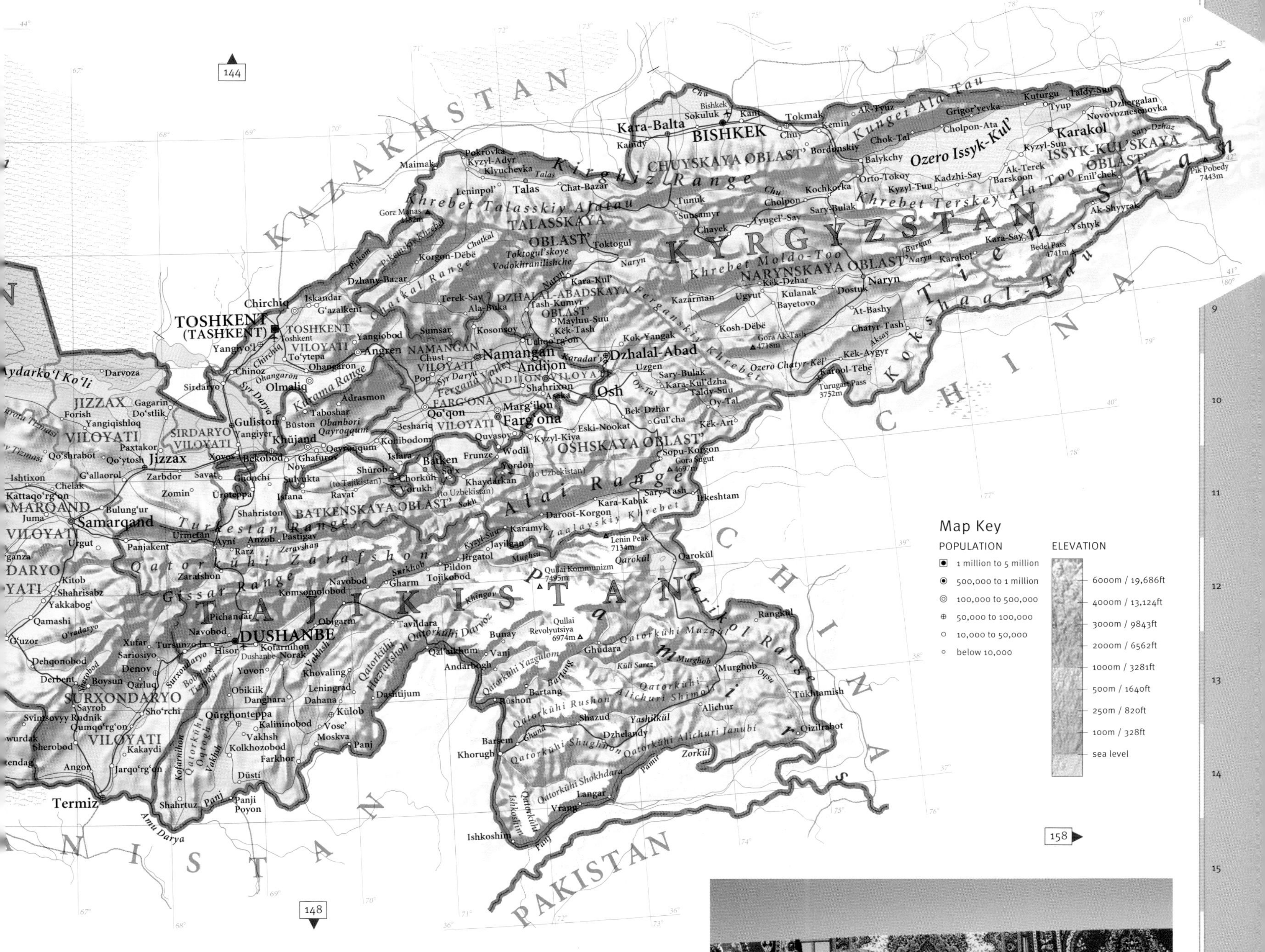

144

KAZAKHSTAN · KYRGYZSTAN · TAJIKISTAN · CHINA · PAKISTAN

BISHKEK · TOSHKENT (TASHKENT) · DUSHANBE

158

148

Map Key

POPULATION	ELEVATION
1 million to 5 million	6000m / 19,686ft
500,000 to 1 million	4000m / 13,124ft
100,000 to 500,000	3000m / 9843ft
50,000 to 100,000	2000m / 6562ft
10,000 to 50,000	1000m / 3281ft
below 10,000	500m / 1640ft
	250m / 820ft
	100m / 328ft
	sea level

SCALE 1:4,750,000
(projection: Lambert Conformal Conic)
Km 0 10 20 40 60 80 100 120
Miles 0 10 20 40 60 80 100 120

Asgabat: The carpet markets of Asgabat are a riot of colour and sound. Hand-woven carpets in traditional styles have distinctive designs that are unique to each tribe and have been traded for centuries.

Afghanistan & Pakistan

At the meeting of the three great mountain ranges – the Hindu Kush, the Karakoram and the Himalayas – rise K2 and Nanga Parbat, two of the world's highest peaks, surrounded by ruggedly beautiful mountain scenery – a paradise for trekkers and archaeological enthusiasts alike.

In the fertile plain of the Indus basin, home to the majority of the modern population, are 5,000-year-old remains indicating the presence of a highly developed people. Much later, Mughals and Greeks left their mark, and the famed Buddhist Ghandara school of sculpture had its centre in the lush green Peshawar valley. Early Islam took root in the Indus valley in the 7th century CE and there are numerous magnificent masterpieces of Muslim architecture dating from this period onwards across the region.

The Silk Road, along which trade, technologies and ideas flowed, wound through the region, giving its mountain passes enormous military and economic significance. As a result, a series of imposing strongholds and forts dominate the area.

Due to the recent war and ongoing unrest in Afghanistan, tourism to the area is currently not safe for Westerners. It has, however, much natural beauty and traces remain of its historic past, which may one day put it on the tourist trail again.

Batura Glacier: Set in the breathtaking scenery of the Karakoram Range, this immense glacier is one of the world's largest. It is a top destination for trekking from May to October, when flowers cover the surrounding valleys.

142

What to See

❶ Mazar-e Sharif
The Blue Mosque, tomb of Hazrat Ali, is the focus of this town

❷ Kabul
Discover Kabul's monuments and the nearby Garden of Babur

❸ Karakoram Highway
For unrivalled mountain scenery on the old Silk Road (Gilgit to Hunza)

❹ Nanga Parbat
The world's ninth highest peak can be viewed safely from trekking routes around its base. Treks often begin from Gilgit

❺ Swat River Valley
(Mingaora)
A historic summer retreat styled the "Switzerland of Asia", this verdant valley was an early Buddhist centre

❻ Peshawar
A riot of colour, this is a high-walled frontier town of traditional mud-brick buildings

❼ Taxila
(near Islamabad)
Archaeological sites, at the junction of three trade routes, reflect a rich cultural mix

❽ Lahore
The one-time Mogul capital is famed for its elegant pink and white architecture

❾ Multan
This Indus valley town has some of Pakistan's finest examples of early Muslim architecture

❿ Quetta
The Western Frontier's legendary stronghold is a popular summer resort, surrounded by fruit-tree-covered hills

⓫ Mohenjo-Daro
(near Larkana) At this serene archaeological site, settlement dates back 5,000 years

⓬ Thatta
(near Gharo) A ghost town with a 2,000-year history. Ruined mosques and mausoleums hint at the former greatness of the capital of three dynasties

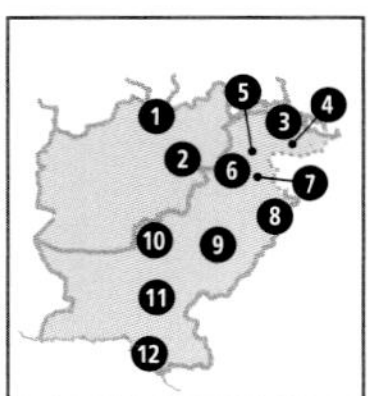

Siāhān Range
Tagas
Panjgūr
Central Makrān
IRAN
Ispikān
Nihing
Mand
Nasīrābād
Kech
Hoshāb
Kolwa
Turbat
Dasht
Suntsar
Khor Kalmat
Jīwani
Gwādar
Gwādar West Bay
Gwādar East Bay
Pasni
Astola Island
Ormāra
A R A B I A N

Rohtas Fort: Built by Sher Shah Suri in 1541 to guard the strategic Ghaan gorge in Pakistan's North-West Frontier Province. The fort complex is enclosed by more than 4 km (2.5 miles) of fortified walls, imposing bastions, and monumental gateways.

SCALE 1:5,000,000
(projection: Lambert Conformal Conic)
Km 0 10 20 40 60 80 100 120 140 160 180 200
Miles 0 10 20 40 60 80 100 120 140 160 180 200

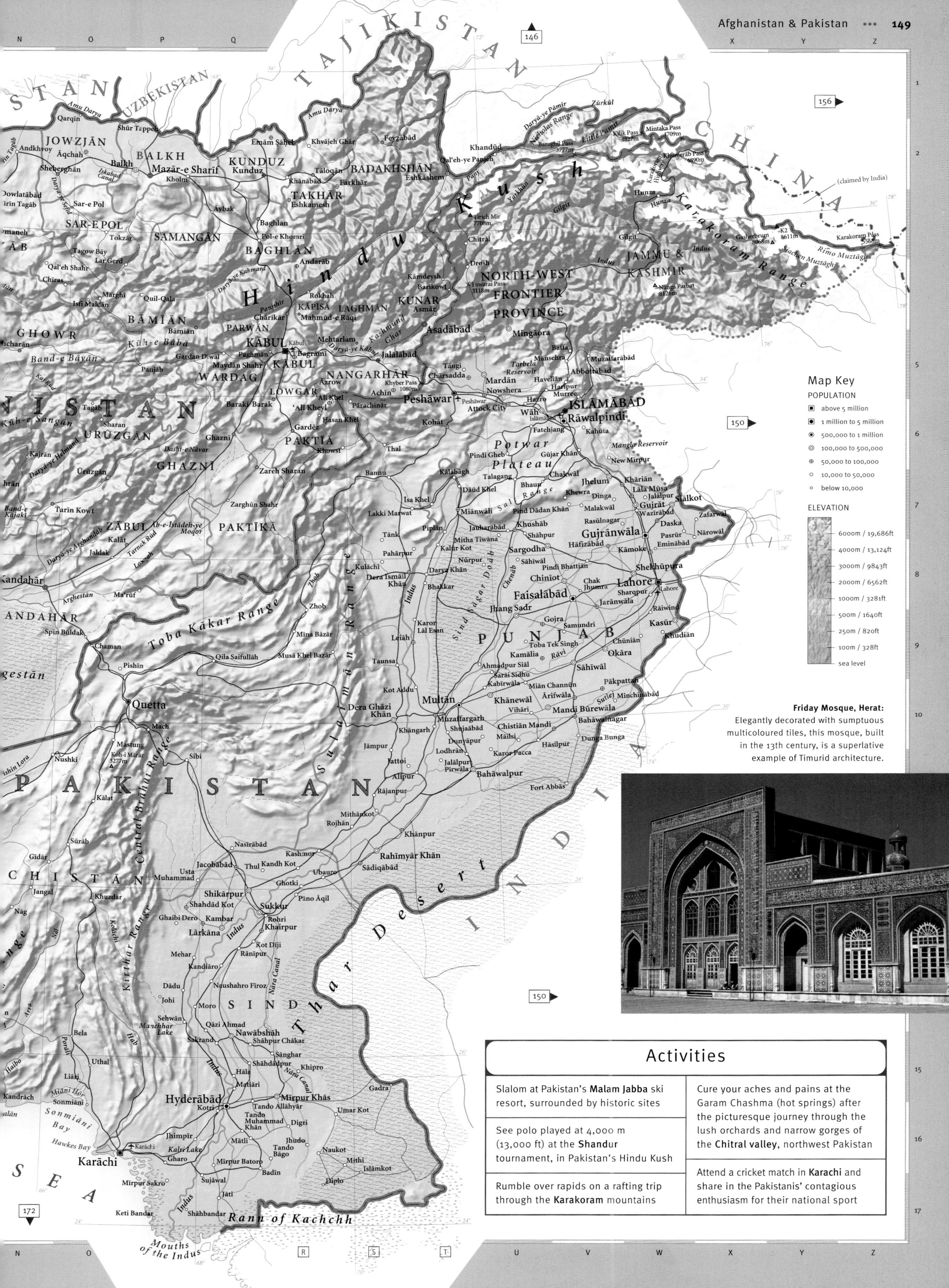
TAJIKISTAN
UZBEKISTAN
CHINA
INDIA
PAKISTAN
Hindu Kush
Karakoram Range
Toba Kākar Range
Sulaimān Range
Central Brahui Range
Kīrthar Range
Thar Desert
Potwar Plateau
Salt Range
Sind Sāgar Doab
PUNJAB
SIND
NORTH-WEST FRONTIER PROVINCE
JAMMU & KASHMIR
ISLĀMĀBĀD
Rāwalpindi
Peshāwar
Lahore
Faisalābād
Multān
Quetta
Karāchi
Hyderābād
KĀBUL
Kandahār
Mazār-e Sharīf
Rann of Kachchh
Mouths of the Indus
ARABIAN SEA
Map Key
POPULATION
above 5 million
1 million to 5 million
500,000 to 1 million
100,000 to 500,000
50,000 to 100,000
10,000 to 50,000
below 10,000
ELEVATION
6000m / 19,686ft
4000m / 13,124ft
3000m / 9843ft
2000m / 6562ft
1000m / 3281ft
500m / 1640ft
250m / 820ft
100m / 328ft
sea level
146
156
150
150
172

Friday Mosque, Herat: Elegantly decorated with sumptuous multicoloured tiles, this mosque, built in the 13th century, is a superlative example of Timurid architecture.

Activities

- Slalom at Pakistan's **Malam Jabba** ski resort, surrounded by historic sites
- See polo played at 4,000 m (13,000 ft) at the **Shandur** tournament, in Pakistan's Hindu Kush
- Rumble over rapids on a rafting trip through the **Karakoram** mountains
- Cure your aches and pains at the Garam Chashma (hot springs) after the picturesque journey through the lush orchards and narrow gorges of the **Chitral valley**, northwest Pakistan
- Attend a cricket match in **Karachi** and share in the Pakistanis' contagious enthusiasm for their national sport

South Asia

Bangladesh, Bhutan, India, Maldives, Nepal, Pakistan, Sri Lanka

In its varied climates, from hot, humid and equatorial to desert and mountain, South Asia has developed a fascinating array of ecosystems. The range of food plants and crops has given rise to some of the most exciting of the world's food traditions. Each region has its own unique style of cooking. As a general rule, the further south the hotter the spices.

The cultural sights here are often set in an amazing geographical context, all part of the region's tantalizing draw. Northern India is filled with archaeological wonders from spectacular Buddhist temples and sacred caves to magnificent Mughal architecture. In the Punjab there are also sites dating back to before 4,000 BCE from the Harappan civilization of the Indus valley. Primitive tribes still inhabit forested areas and islands in the Andamans.

The region's lowland areas mostly have a hot, humid climate and there is a long tradition of escaping to cool hill resorts. Many of these are sites of great beauty and historic interest.

The catastrophe of the 2004 tsunami affected several areas in the region, but notably left the west coast of Sri Lanka and certain islands in the Maldives unscathed. Tourism provides an invaluable source of income and even the worst-affected resorts are welcoming visitors back.

What to See

1 Indus Valley
3rd millennium BCE civilization with two-storey houses, each with a private bathroom

2 Rann of Kachchh
Onagers (wild asses) roam this scorched plain of salt flats, a haven for migratory birds

3 Gujarat
The mangrove swamps and extinct volcanoes of this extraordinary land teem with wildlife

4 Madhya Pradesh
On the Deccan plateau's northern edge two rock types meet, forming magical landscapes of cliffs and waterfalls

5 The Golden Triangle
The land between Delhi, Jaipur and Agra has some of India's finest Mughal architecture, including the Taj Mahal

6 Himalayas
In the crisp, thin air of this most dramatic and forbidding of mountain ranges lies a land of ancient mysticism

7 Kathmandu Valley
Numerous religious and archaeological sites are set against this truly spectacular backdrop

8 Sikkim
This humid region hosts a myriad of flowers, birds, and butterflies

9 Bhumthang
The rich beauty of the delightful villages and temples in Bhutan's cultural heart is best appreciated on foot

10 Ganges
India's most holy river brings life to the lowlands of northern India and Bangladesh

11 Sundarbans National Park
Lying where the Ganges and Brahmaputra deltas join the Bay of Bengal, the world's largest mangrove forest is a wildlife haven

12 Goa
Portuguese until 1961, the emerald land of Goa is a firm favorite among sun-seekers

13 Kerala
Known as "Heaven on Earth", this land of lush waterways, and cashew and coconut plantations is steeped in history

14 Sri Lanka
Among Sri Lanka's shrines, the Temple of the Sacred Tooth Relic reputedly houses four of the Lord Buddha's teeth

15 Maldives
For classic tropical island holidays. Most resorts are on their own island surrounded by fish-filled lagoons

16 Andaman and Nicobar Islands
These unique tropical rainforest islands are host to numerous bird and animal species

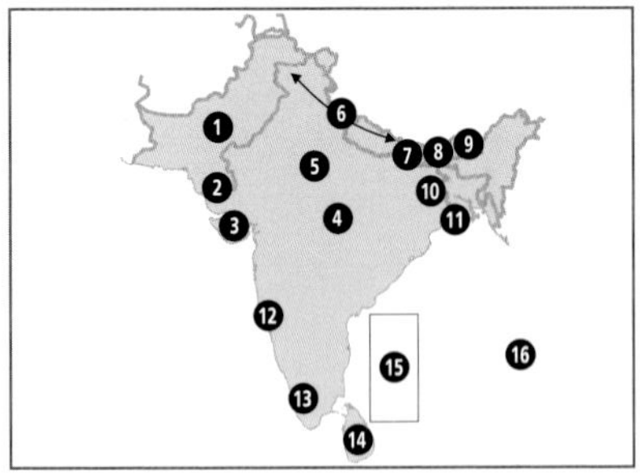

Amritsar, Punjab: Once a peaceful lake in a forest, this location has long been a centre for meditation. Today, the magnificent Golden Temple stands as a symbol of the Sikh religion and is a famous pilgrimage site.

146
148
156
142
10
11

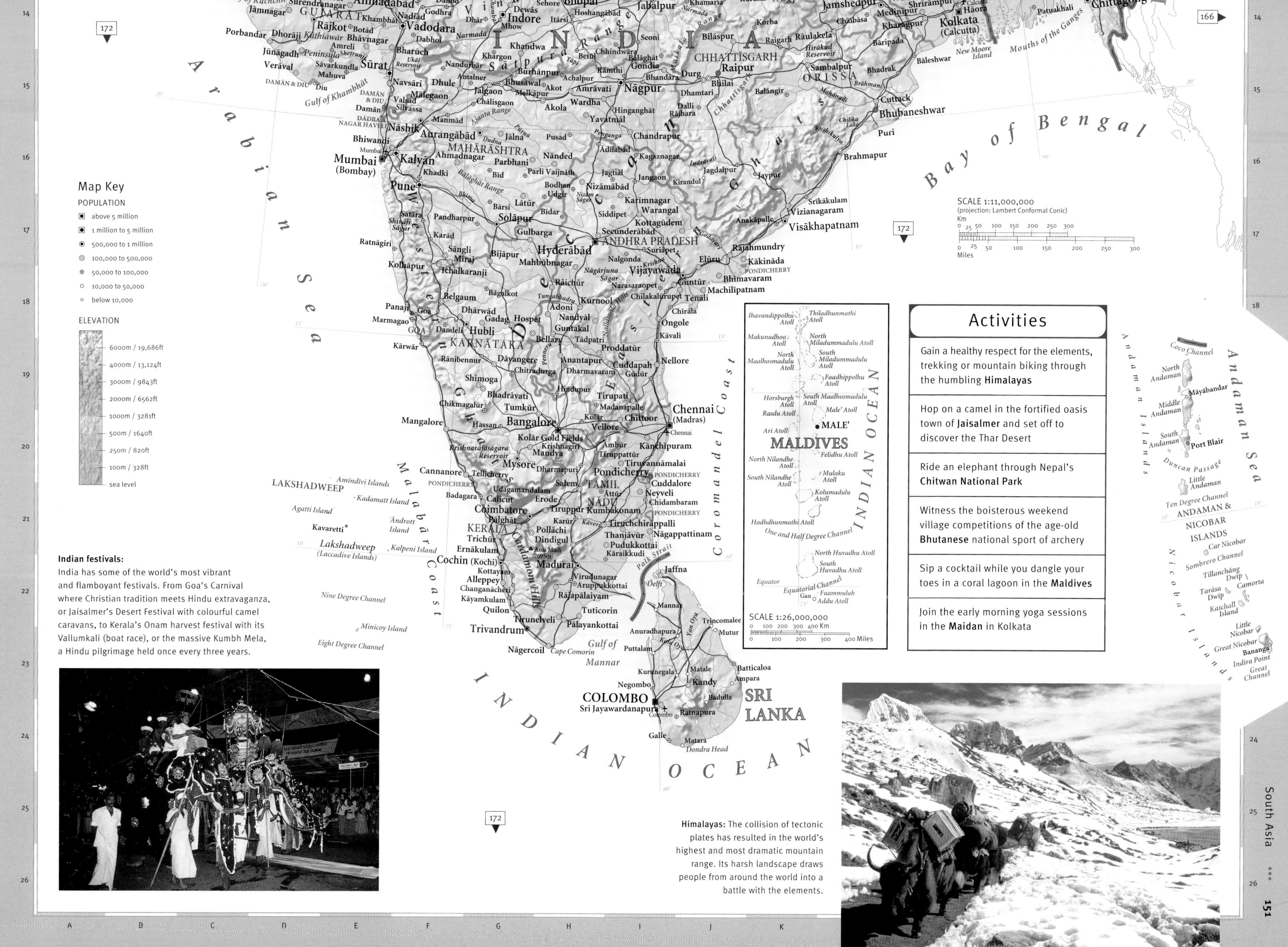
Arabian Sea
Bay of Bengal
INDIAN OCEAN
INDIA
GUJARAT
MAHARASHTRA
KARNATAKA
ANDHRA PRADESH
CHHATTISGARH
ORISSA
KERALA
TAMIL NADU
LAKSHADWEEP
SRI LANKA
COLOMBO
Sri Jayawardanapura
MALDIVES
MALE'
ANDAMAN & NICOBAR ISLANDS
Andaman Islands
Nicobar Islands
Andaman Sea
Port Blair
Mumbai (Bombay)
Kolkata (Calcutta)
Chennai (Madras)
Bangalore
Hyderabad
Malabar Coast
Coromandel Coast
Gulf of Mannar
Palk Strait
Cardamom Hills
172
166
SCALE 1:11,000,000
(projection: Lambert Conformal Conic)
SCALE 1:26,000,000

Map Key

POPULATION

- ■ above 5 million
- ◼ 1 million to 5 million
- ◉ 500,000 to 1 million
- ◎ 100,000 to 500,000
- ⊕ 50,000 to 100,000
- ○ 10,000 to 50,000
- ◦ below 10,000

ELEVATION

- 6000m / 19,686ft
- 4000m / 13,124ft
- 3000m / 9843ft
- 2000m / 6562ft
- 1000m / 3281ft
- 500m / 1640ft
- 250m / 820ft
- 100m / 328ft
- sea level

Indian festivals: India has some of the world's most vibrant and flamboyant festivals. From Goa's Carnival where Christian tradition meets Hindu extravaganza, or Jaisalmer's Desert Festival with colourful camel caravans, to Kerala's Onam harvest festival with its Vallumkali (boat race), or the massive Kumbh Mela, a Hindu pilgrimage held once every three years.

Activities

- Gain a healthy respect for the elements, trekking or mountain biking through the humbling **Himalayas**
- Hop on a camel in the fortified oasis town of **Jaisalmer** and set off to discover the Thar Desert
- Ride an elephant through Nepal's **Chitwan National Park**
- Witness the boisterous weekend village competitions of the age-old **Bhutanese** national sport of archery
- Sip a cocktail while you dangle your toes in a coral lagoon in the **Maldives**
- Join the early morning yoga sessions in the **Maidan** in Kolkata

Himalayas: The collision of tectonic plates has resulted in the world's highest and most dramatic mountain range. Its harsh landscape draws people from around the world into a battle with the elements.

Northern India & the Himalayan States

Bangladesh, Bhutan, Nepal, Arunachal Pradesh, Assam, Bihar, Chandigarh, Delhi, Haryana, Himachal Pradesh, Jammu & Kashmir, Jharkhand, Manipur, Meghalaya, Mizoram, Nagaland, Punjab, Rajasthan, Sikkim, Tripura, Uttaranchal, Uttar Pradesh, West Bengal

With the Himalayas sweeping across its northern border and the sacred Ganges and Brahmaputra river basins draining the southern portion, the region is defined by its geography. Much of the land is rich farming country, dedicated to growing cereals and rice especially in the east. Assam is famous for its tea and other regional crops include cardamom, jute and saffron.

The world's highest mountains have long been a focus for physical and spiritual journeys. Huge biodiversity in the animal and plant life of the Himalayan foothills makes the region ideal for spotting rare species. This is the domain of Bengal tigers, spotted deer, monkeys, one-horned rhinoceroses and a great variety of birdlife.

Hill stations are scattered throughout the lower fringes of the mountain ranges, providing respite from the hot, crowded, lowland cities. Archaeological and spiritual sites, set against spectacular scenery, surround ancient resort locations such as Almora in Uttaranchal.

Both beauty and adventure await in the region's forbidding mountains, verdant hills, lush jungles, glassy lakes, quiet villages, and bustling cities.

SCALE 1:6,500,000
(projection: Lambert Conformal Conic)
Km 0 10 20 40 60 80 100 120 140 160 180 200
Miles 0 10 20 40 60 80 100 120 140 160 180 200

148
158
154

Map Key

POPULATION
- 1 million to 5 million
- 500,000 to 1 million
- 100,000 to 500,000
- 50,000 to 100,000
- 10,000 to 50,000
- below 10,000

ELEVATION
- 6000m / 19,686ft
- 4000m / 13,124ft
- 3000m / 9843ft
- 2000m / 6562ft
- 1000m / 3281ft
- 500m / 1640ft
- 250m / 820ft
- 100m / 328ft
- sea level

Kala Bhairab, Thamel, Kathmandu: With a terrifying expression and a necklace of skulls, this six-armed monumental statue, carved from a single stone, represents the destructive manifestation of the God Shiva.

Activities

Get a guided tour glimpse of the endangered Bengal tiger in the **Sundarbans Park,** Bangladesh	See Hindu pilgrims perform ritual bathing in the Ganges at **Varanasi**
Trundle along the **"Toy Train"** tracks to Darjiling, West Bengal	Hang-glide through the Himalayan foothills in the **Langtang** region, north of Kathmandu

What to See

1 Jaisalmer
A jewel of the desert, this remote fortified city is known for crafts and colourful bazaars

2 Jantar Mantar
The Jaipur Observatory contains building-sized sundials, one of which is accurate to two seconds

3 Delhi
For total immersion in city life, forge your way through crowded streets to the capital's temples, forts, tombs, and parks

4 Taj Mahal
Agra's achingly beautiful example of Mughal architecture plus the imposing Red Fort

5 Kailasa (in Ellora)
Paintings and sculptures decorate the world's largest monolith temple

6 Ajanta
(near Aurangabad) The earliest of these lavishly decorated Buddhist cave temples dates to 200 BCE

7 Pokhara
Set among gentle hills and tranquil lakes, Pokhara has stunning views of the snow-capped Annapurna range

8 Kathmandu
Spectacular views from the Monkey Temple are reached after enduring steep stairs and boisterous monkeys

9 Sagarmatha
Dominated by Mount Everest, the park is home to lesser pandas and snow leopards

10 Darjiling
Deep in the heart of tea-growing country, colonial plantation houses dot the lush, verdant hills

11 Taktsang – Tiger's Lair (near Paro)
Perched vertiginously up a 900 m (3,000 ft) cliff, this hermitage can be admired by climbing to an observation point

12 Simtokha
(near Thimphu) This fortified and vibrantly decorated monastery (*dzong*) is Bhutan's oldest intact example

13 Jigme Dorji
(near Tongsa) The largest of Bhutan's protected wildlife areas is home to the red panda

14 Paharpur
(near Jaipur Hat) Ruins of the magnificent Buddhist monastery of Somapuri Vihara

15 Dhaka
17th-century capital city with Hindu temples and Mughal architecture

16 Rangamati
Tribal villages in a natural haven of waterfalls and rolling hills

17 Sitakunda
(near Chittagong) This location of Buddhist and Chandranath temples is also sacred to Hindus

18 Cox's Bazar
120 km (75 miles) of fine golden sandy beach with nearby temples, pagodas and islands

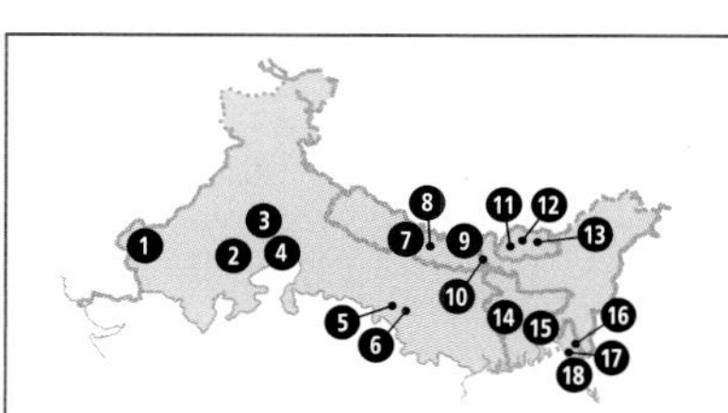

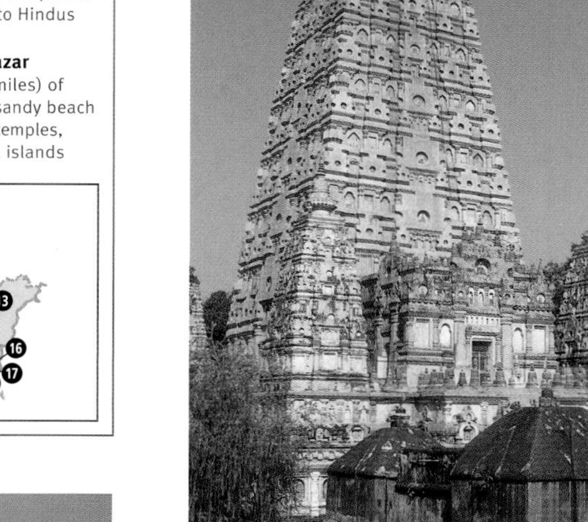

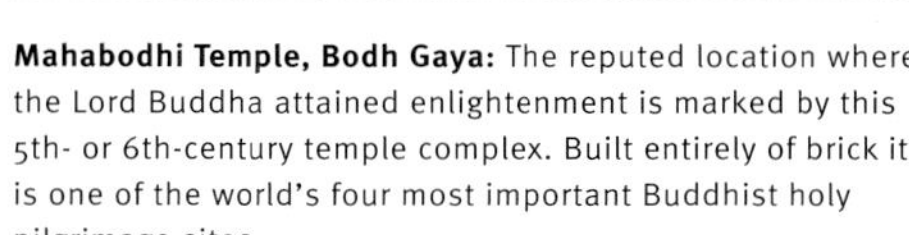

Mahabodhi Temple, Bodh Gaya: The reputed location where the Lord Buddha attained enlightenment is marked by this 5th- or 6th-century temple complex. Built entirely of brick it is one of the world's four most important Buddhist holy pilgrimage sites.

Jaswant Thanda, Jodhpur: Near the famed Red Fort, this elegant white marble memorial was built in 1899 and is dedicated to Maharaja Jaswant Singh II, who cleared the area of bandits and implemented social reforms.

Southern India & Sri Lanka

Sri Lanka, Andhra Pradesh, Chhattisgarh, Dadra & Nagar Haveli, Daman & Diu, Goa, Gujarat, Karnataka, Kerala, Lakshadweep, Madhya Pradesh, Maharashtra, Orissa, Pondicherry, Tamil Nadu

The undulating Deccan plateau, bounded by the Western and Eastern Ghats, underlies this land of vivid colour, vibrant festivals and rich spices. South of India is the teardrop-shaped island of Sri Lanka, which has a long tradition of producing high-quality tea and a dazzling array of gems including sapphires, rubies, cat's eyes and moonstones. Southern India has a very different atmosphere to the northern states, which were influenced by successive invading powers. By contrast, the native Dravidian culture and languages of peoples such as the Tamils remain pure in rural areas.

The Mughals, whose empire covered most of modern-day India and Pakistan, built some of India's most striking architecture. Immensely decorative forts, palaces, and mausoleums capture the spirit of the age. Along the coast the influence of colonial powers is strongest. Many of the ports have fine examples of Dutch, Portuguese and British architecture.

The contrasting habitats of the region and life-giving monsoon rains have led to enormous biodiversity. There are many localized species. Onagers (wild asses) roam the salt plains of Gujarat, certain frog species are unique to the Western Ghats and elephants wander the parks of Sri Lanka.

India is a country of contrasts and variety. The mountain ranges, plains, hot summers and monsoons give each locale its distinctive flavour, with varying traditions, cuisine, culture, and works of art, plus distinctive plant and animal populations. The region is at once ancient and modern, arid and verdant, rich and poor, with more than enough to absorb the visitor for many lifetimes.

What to See

1 Kajuraho
(near Chhatarpur) Surrounded by wide, immaculate, green lawns, these Jain temples are decorated with erotic scenes of deities

2 Mandu
High on a cliff, this extensive Muslim fortress overlooks a dusty backdrop of windswept wilderness

3 Mumbai (Bombay)
A hectic city whose Chhatrapati Shivaji, the former railway terminus, symbolizes the merging of cultures with its blend of grand Victorian Gothic and Indian palatial architectural themes

4 Pattadakal
(near Bijapur) The Temple of Virupaksha is one of nine magnificent Hindu temples which blend diverse Indian architectural traditions

5 Panaji
This graceful city in Goa (*see* pp150–151), with Baroque churches, convents and forts, has fascinating shops, bars and atmospheric backstreets to explore

6 Jog Falls
The Sharavathi river creates India's highest waterfall when it tumbles down a sheer rock face of over 250 m (800 ft). This thrilling spectacle is most impressive after the monsoon, which normally ends in January

7 Mysore
South India's palace city is also renowned for incense sticks, lustrous silks and sweetly scented sandalwood

8 Kanchipuram
This temple city, a major centre for religious pilgrimage, is filled with intricately carved architectural marvels that serve different Hindu sects

9 Chennai (Madras)
Cheaper than Mumbai, the bustling metropolis of Chennai is south India's fashion capital. Its Fort St George hints at a grand colonial past

10 Periyar Tiger Reserve
(Periyar Lake) In undulating grassland and forest, reaching 2,000 m (6,500 ft) above sea level, birds such as the Malabar hornbill and jungle mynah mingle with tigers, buffalo, elephants and deer

11 Sigiriya
(near Dambulla) Protruding from the jungle, this mammoth pillow-shaped monolith towers over a 1,500-year-old palace complex

12 Dambulla
An enormous recumbent Buddha statue enjoys the view from this rocky outcrop, where temple frescoes date back over 2,000 years

13 Negombo
Mercifully unscathed after the 2004 tsunami, this delightfully characteristic fishing village is renowned for its fresh seafood

14 Galle
This bustling port and provincial capital with its austere Star Fort is one of Sri Lanka's seven UNESCO World Heritage Sites

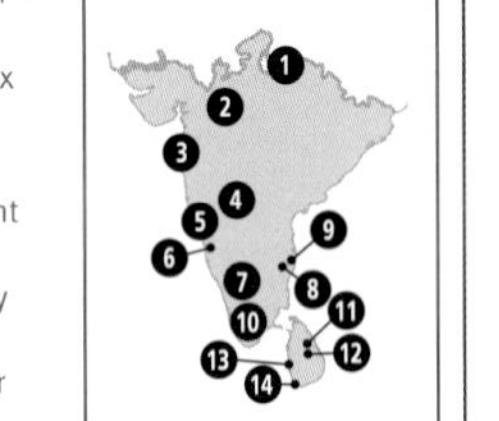
1
2
3
4
5
6
7
8
9
10
11
12
13
14

Pinnawela Elephant Orphanage, Sri Lanka: Founded in 1975, the orphanage cares for baby elephants found abandoned in the jungle. Around 60 elephants are given protection here at any one time. It is best to visit at feeding times, when the baby elephants are bottle-fed, or when the elephants go for their daily bath in the nearby river.

152
148
152

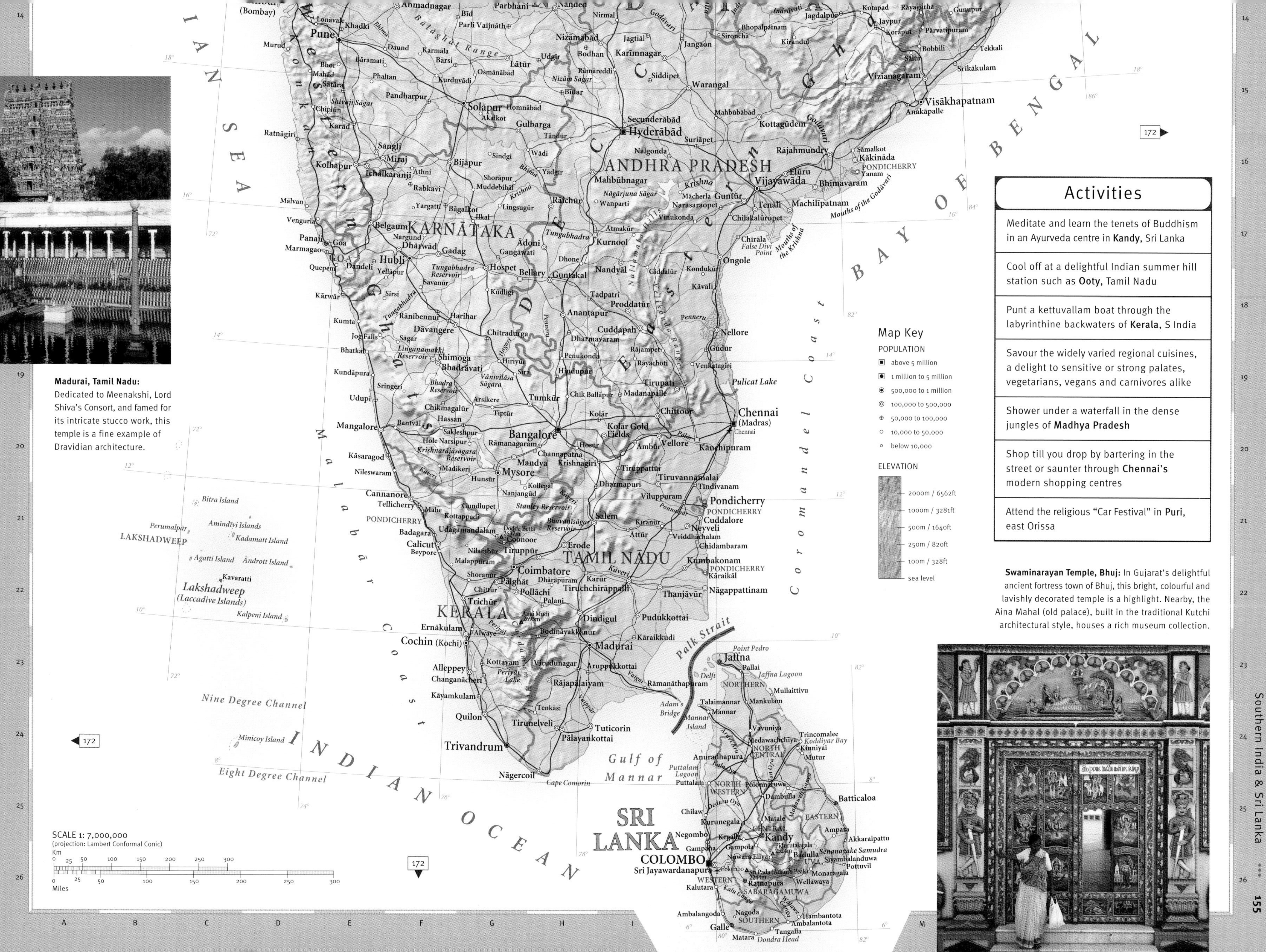

BAY OF BENGAL
ARABIAN SEA
INDIAN OCEAN
ANDHRA PRADESH
KARNĀTAKA
TAMIL NĀDU
KERALA
SRI LANKA
Western Ghats
Eastern Ghats
Deccan
Konkan
Malabar Coast
Coromandel Coast
Gulf of Mannar
Palk Strait
Nine Degree Channel
Eight Degree Channel
Lakshadweep (Laccadive Islands)
LAKSHADWEEP
Minicoy Island
Mumbai (Bombay)
Pune
Hyderābād
Secunderābād
Visākhapatnam
Chennai (Madras)
Bangalore
Mysore
Coimbatore
Madurai
Cochin (Kochi)
Trivandrum
Pondicherry
PONDICHERRY
Calicut
Mangalore
Hubli
Belgaum
Kurnool
Vijayawāda
Tirupati
Salem
Tuticorin
Nāgercoil
Cape Comorin
Jaffna
Kandy
COLOMBO
Sri Jayawardanapura
Galle
Trincomalee
Batticaloa
Adam's Bridge
172
172
172
172

Activities

- Meditate and learn the tenets of Buddhism in an Ayurveda centre in **Kandy**, Sri Lanka
- Cool off at a delightful Indian summer hill station such as **Ooty**, Tamil Nadu
- Punt a kettuvallam boat through the labyrinthine backwaters of **Kerala**, S India
- Savour the widely varied regional cuisines, a delight to sensitive or strong palates, vegetarians, vegans and carnivores alike
- Shower under a waterfall in the dense jungles of **Madhya Pradesh**
- Shop till you drop by bartering in the street or saunter through **Chennai's** modern shopping centres
- Attend the religious "Car Festival" in **Puri**, east Orissa

Map Key

POPULATION
- above 5 million
- 1 million to 5 million
- 500,000 to 1 million
- 100,000 to 500,000
- 50,000 to 100,000
- 10,000 to 50,000
- below 10,000

ELEVATION
- 2000m / 6562ft
- 1000m / 3281ft
- 500m / 1640ft
- 250m / 820ft
- 100m / 328ft
- sea level

SCALE 1: 7,000,000
(projection: Lambert Conformal Conic)
Km 0 25 50 100 150 200 250 300
Miles 0 25 50 100 150 200 250 300

Madurai, Tamil Nadu: Dedicated to Meenakshi, Lord Shiva's Consort, and famed for its intricate stucco work, this temple is a fine example of Dravidian architecture.

Swaminarayan Temple, Bhuj: In Gujarat's delightful ancient fortress town of Bhuj, this bright, colourful and lavishly decorated temple is a highlight. Nearby, the Aina Mahal (old palace), built in the traditional Kutchi architectural style, houses a rich museum collection.

Mainland East Asia

China, Mongolia, North Korea, South Korea, Taiwan

Chinese civilization traces back a continuous lineage further than any other on earth. The visible legacy of successive dynasties since the Qin of the 3rd century BCE is a major element in its attractiveness to today's traveller. The country has much magnificent and varied scenery and a well-established state tourist service transports visitors the huge distances between destinations. China's current rapid development also allows a fascinating insight into a society experiencing material and social change on a vast scale. This is most evident in huge and dynamic cities such as Shanghai, but the countryside too can conjure up striking images of the modern against a backdrop of the seemingly timeless.

Mongolia is one of the world's least populated countries and North Korea one of the most tightly controlled, whereas South Korea offers its own version of the contrast between shiny modernity and long-established patterns of life.

Shanghai: The Pudong New Area is the financial district, with some of the tallest buildings in China. Immense projects in the last 15 years mean that Shanghai now rivals Hong Kong as China's commercial centre.

What to See

1 Potala Palace
(in Lhasa) 17th-century palace of the Dalai Lama

2 Gobi
A gravel and rock wilderness where temperatures range from below -40°C to above 40°C

3 Pyongyang
North Korea's eerily quiet capital, where foreign tourism is tightly orchestrated, is a showpiece of landmarks and monuments

4 Seoul
The sprawling capital of South Korea is a mixture of skyscrapers and centuries-old royal palaces and pagodas

5 Beijing
This 3,000-year-old city holds the Ming Dynasty's inner sanctum – the 15th-century Forbidden City palace complex

6 Great Wall of China
Not actually visible from outer space, but 6,000 km (3,700 miles) long from Gansu province to the coast near Beijing

7 Yungang Caves
(near Datong) Fantastic display of 1,500-year-old Buddhist rock sculpture, 50,000 carvings survive

8 Shanghai
Flashy skyscrapers, dazzling neon lights, and the shopper's mecca of Nanjing Road

9 Terracotta Warriors
(in Xi'an) 6,000 slightly larger-than-life soldiers guard the tomb of the first Qin emperor who died in 210 BCE

10 Yangtze Gorges
China's mighty river has three spectacular gorges downstream from Chongqing. Since the completion of the Three Gorges Dam their impact has been reduced

11 Stone Forest
(near Kunming) Maze of jagged limestone pinnacles forming an eerie landscape

12 Guilin
Starting point for seeing the grand limestone peaks that rear up along the Li river

13 Hong Kong
Sometimes regarded as one giant shopping mall, this once-British colony was returned to Chinese rule in 1997

14 Taipei
Taiwan's capital, known for its frenetic pace, tasty cuisine, the Chiang Kai-Shek Memorial Hall, and Taipei 101 (the world's tallest building)

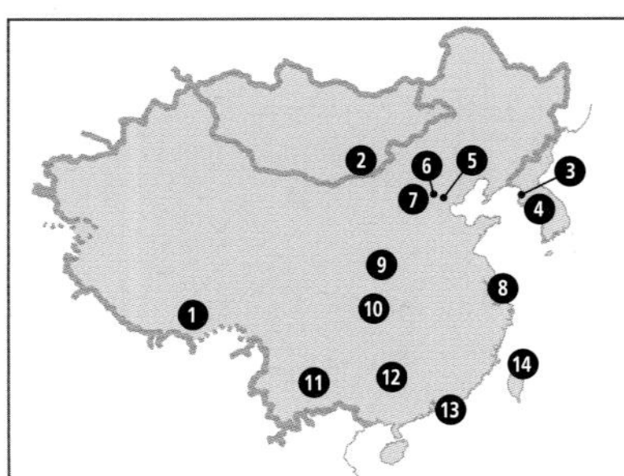

Temple of Heaven, Beijing: The Hall of Prayer for Good Harvest is the centrepiece of this allegorical Ming Dynasty temple complex.

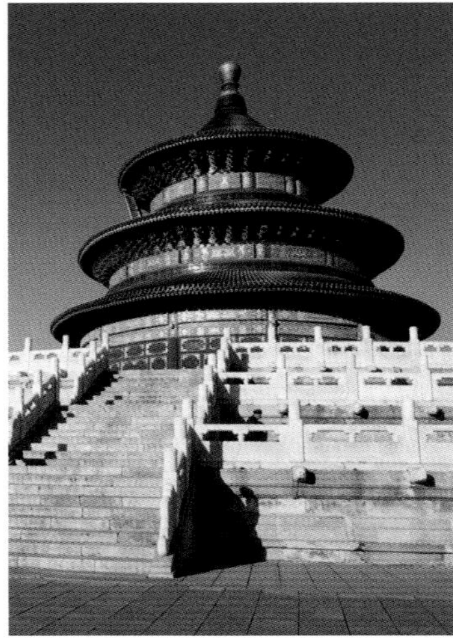

Activities

- Watch the world-famous **Shanghai** Acrobats perform unbelievable contortions and feats of balance
- Follow the Silk Road west across China, from **Xi'an** to **Kashi**
- Ride the steep Peak Tram for spectacular views over **Hong Kong**
- See how silk is made and buy silk carpets in **Suzhou**, near Shanghai
- Drink psaochung tea in **Pinglin**, Taiwan, where it is grown
- Visit Mao's mausoleum in Beijing's **Tiananmen Square**

RUSSIAN FEDERATION
MONGOLIA
CHINA
NORTH KOREA
SOUTH KOREA
JAPAN
TAIWAN
VIETNAM
LAOS
SEA OF JAPAN (EAST SEA)
Yellow Sea
EAST CHINA SEA
SOUTH CHINA SEA
Korea Bay
Bo Hai
Gulf of Tongking
Korea Strait
Taiwan Strait
Bashi Channel
Tropic of Cancer
Gobi
NEI MONGOL ZIZHIQU
INNER MONGOLIA
Da Hinggan Ling
Manchuria
HEILONGJIANG
JILIN
LIAONING
HEBEI
SHANXI
SHANDONG
HENAN
SHAANXI
NINGXIA
JIANGSU
ANHUI
HUBEI
SICHUAN
CHONGQING SHI
HUNAN
JIANGXI
ZHEJIANG
FUJIAN
GUIZHOU
YUNNAN
GUANGXI ZHUANGZU ZIZHIQU
GUANGDONG
HAINAN
Hainan Dao
ULAANBAATAR (ULAN BATOR)
BEIJING (PEKING)
P'YŎNGYANG
SOUL (SEOUL)
T'AIPEI
Shanghai
SHANGHAI SHI
Tianjin
TIANJIN SHI
Hong Kong (Xianggang)
Macao (Aomen)
Harbin
Changchun
Shenyang
Dalian
Qingdao
Jinan
Zhengzhou
Xi'an
Lanzhou
Xining
Yinchuan
Baotou
Hohhot
Datong
Taiyuan
Shijiazhuang
Nanjing
Hefei
Wuhan
Changsha
Nanchang
Hangzhou
Ningbo
Fuzhou
Xiamen
Guangzhou
Nanning
Kunming
Guiyang
Chengdu
Chongqing
Haikou
Pusan
Taegu
Inch'ŏn
Kaohsiung
Qiqihar
Jilin
Yellow River (Huang He)
Yangtze (Chang Jiang)
Amur (Heilong Jiang)
Matsu Tao (to Taiwan)
Chinmen Tao (to Taiwan)
P'enghu Liehtao (China and Taiwan claim all of each other's territory)
122
164
166
170
192
Map Key
POPULATION
above 5 million
1 million to 5 million
500,000 to 1 million
100,000 to 500,000
50,000 to 100,000
10,000 to 50,000
below 10,000
ELEVATION
6000m / 19,686ft
4000m / 13,124ft
3000m / 9843ft
2000m / 6562ft
1000m / 3281ft
500m / 1640ft
250m / 820ft
100m / 328ft
sea level
SCALE 1:14,000,000
(projection: Lambert Conformal Conic)
Km 0 25 50 100 150 200 250 300 350 400 450 500
Miles 0 25 50 100 150 200 250 300 350 400 450 500

Li river, Guilin: Buffalo are a familiar sight on the banks of the Lijiang or Li river, set against the backdrop that has made Guilin famous – its steep, almost vertical limestone peaks rising from the riverbank.

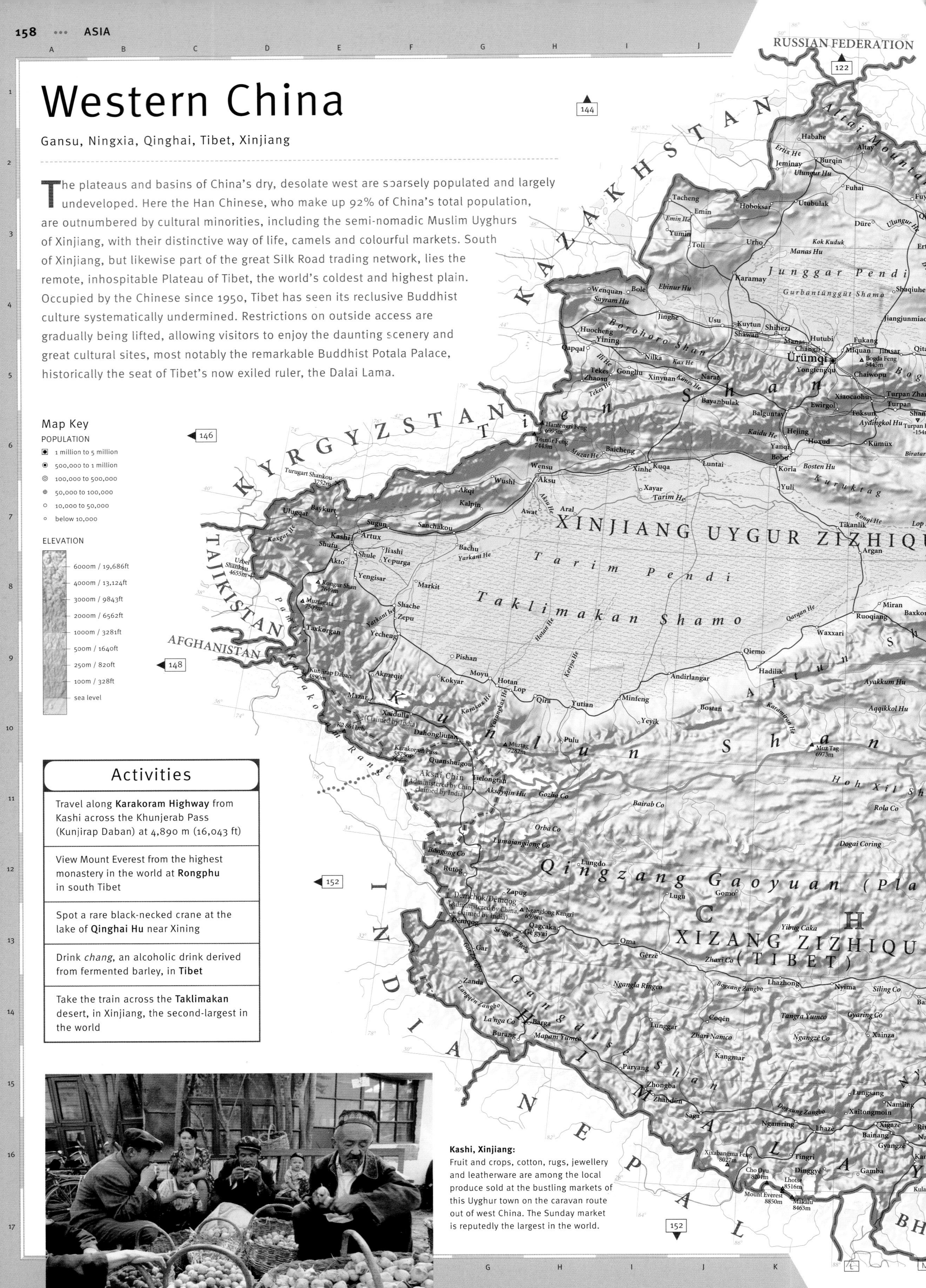
RUSSIAN FEDERATION
KAZAKHSTAN
KYRGYZSTAN
TAJIKISTAN
AFGHANISTAN
INDIA
NEPAL
XINJIANG UYGUR ZIZHIQU
Tarim Pendi
Taklimakan Shamo
Junggar Pendi
Tian Shan
Kunlun Shan
Altun Shan
Qingzang Gaoyuan (Plat
XIZANG ZIZHIQU (TIBET)
Ürümqi

Western China

Gansu, Ningxia, Qinghai, Tibet, Xinjiang

The plateaus and basins of China's dry, desolate west are sparsely populated and largely undeveloped. Here the Han Chinese, who make up 92% of China's total population, are outnumbered by cultural minorities, including the semi-nomadic Muslim Uyghurs of Xinjiang, with their distinctive way of life, camels and colourful markets. South of Xinjiang, but likewise part of the great Silk Road trading network, lies the remote, inhospitable Plateau of Tibet, the world's coldest and highest plain. Occupied by the Chinese since 1950, Tibet has seen its reclusive Buddhist culture systematically undermined. Restrictions on outside access are gradually being lifted, allowing visitors to enjoy the daunting scenery and great cultural sites, most notably the remarkable Buddhist Potala Palace, historically the seat of Tibet's now exiled ruler, the Dalai Lama.

Map Key

POPULATION

- 1 million to 5 million
- 500,000 to 1 million
- 100,000 to 500,000
- 50,000 to 100,000
- 10,000 to 50,000
- below 10,000

ELEVATION

- 6000m / 19,686ft
- 4000m / 13,124ft
- 3000m / 9843ft
- 2000m / 6562ft
- 1000m / 3281ft
- 500m / 1640ft
- 250m / 820ft
- 100m / 328ft
- sea level

Activities

Activities
Travel along **Karakoram Highway** from Kashi across the Khunjerab Pass (Kunjirap Daban) at 4,890 m (16,043 ft)
View Mount Everest from the highest monastery in the world at **Rongphu** in south Tibet
Spot a rare black-necked crane at the lake of **Qinghai Hu** near Xining
Drink *chang*, an alcoholic drink derived from fermented barley, in **Tibet**
Take the train across the **Taklimakan** desert, in Xinjiang, the second-largest in the world

Kashi, Xinjiang: Fruit and crops, cotton, rugs, jewellery and leatherware are among the local produce sold at the bustling markets of this Uyghur town on the caravan route out of west China. The Sunday market is reputedly the largest in the world.

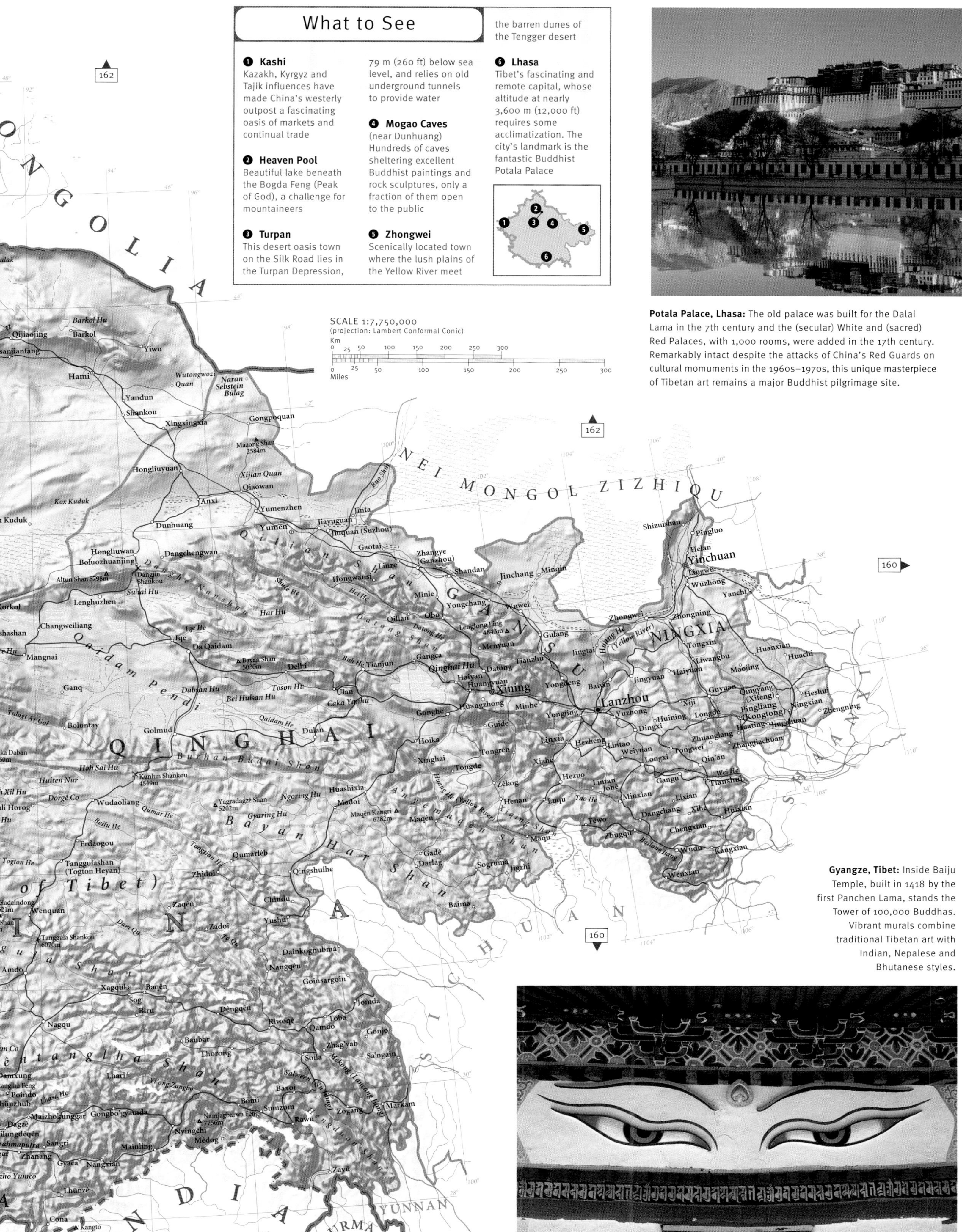

MONGOLIA
NEI MONGOL ZIZHIQU
GANSU
NINGXIA
QINGHAI
SICHUAN
SHAANXI
INDIA
BURMA
YUNNAN
Barkol Hu
Barkol
Qijiaojing
Yiwu
Hami
Wutongwozi Quan
Naran Sebstein Bulag
Yandun
Shankou
Xingxingxia
Gongpoquan
Mazong Shan 2584m
Hongliuyuan
Xijian Quan
Qiaowan
Kox Kuduk
Anxi
Yumenzhen
Dunhuang
Yumen
Jiayuguan
Jiuquan (Suzhou)
Jinta
Ruo Shui
Hongliuwan
Boluozhuanjing
Dangchengwan
Altun Shan 5798m
Su'ai Hu
Lenghuzhen
Xorkol
Changweiliang
Har Hu
Mangnai
Da Qaidam
Qaidam Pendi
Bayan Shan 5030m
Delhi
Ganq
Dabsan Hu
Toson Hu
Bei Hulsan Hu
Boluntay
Golmud
Dulan
Ulan
Caka Yanhu
Tianjun
Qinghai Hu
Gaotai
Zhangye (Ganzhou)
Linze
Shandan
Hongwansi
Jinchang
Mingin
Minle
Yongchang
Wuwei
Qilian
Obo
Lenglong Ling 4843m
Menyuan
Gulang
Datong
Haiyan
Huangyuan
Xining
Tianzhu
Jingtai
Baiyin
Yongdeng
Lanzhou
Gonghe
Huangzhong
Minhe
Yongjing
Shizuishan
Pingluo
Helan
Yinchuan
Lingwu
Wuzhong
Yanchi
Zhongwei
Zhongning
Huang He (Yellow River)
Tongxin
Haiyuan
Huanxian
Huachi
Liwangbu
Maojing
Jingyuan
Guyuan
Qingyang (Xifeng)
Pingliang (Kongtong)
Heshui
Ningxian
Zhengning
Xiji
Longde
Huating
Jingchuan
Huining
Dingxi
Yuzhong
Linxia
Hezheng
Lintao
Weiyuan
Longxi
Tongwei
Zhuanglang
Zhangjiachuan
Qin'an
Tianshui
Gangu
Wushan
Lixian
Xihe
Huixian
Dangchang
Chengxian
Kangxian
Wudu
Wenxian
Zhugqu
Têwo
Zhuoni
Lintan
Hezuo
Luqu
Maqu
Xiahe
Tongren
Tongde
Zêkog
Henan
Hoika
Xinghai
Guide
Kunlun Shankou 4849m
Burhan Budai Shan
Hoh Sai Hu
Huiten Nur
Dorgê Co
Wudaoliang
Yagradagzê Shan 5202m
Ngoring Hu
Gyaring Hu
Huashixia
Madoi
Maqên Kangri 6282m
Maqên
Bayan Har Shan
Amne Machin Shan
Erdaogou
Tanggulashan (Togton Heyan)
Togton He
Qumarlêb
Zhidoi
Qingshuihe
Gadê
Darlag
Sogruma
Jigzhi
Baima
Chindu
Yushu
Zaqên
Zadoi
Wenquan
Tanggula Shankou 6070m
Dainkognubma
Nangqên
Goinsargoin
Amdo
Xagquka
Baqên
Sog
Biru
Dêngqên
Jomda
Nagqu
Riwoqê
Qamdo
Tôba
Gonjo
Zhag'yab
Banbar
Lhorong
Soila
Sa'ngain
Lhari
Baxoi
Markam
Bomi
Sumzom
Rawu
Zogang
Namjagbarwa Feng 7756m
Nyingchi
Mêdog
Gongbo'gyamda
Maizhokunggar
Dagzê
Lhünzhub
Nyainqêntanglha Shan
Damxung
Poindo
Brahmaputra
Sangri
Mainling
Zhanang
Gyaca
Nangxian
Lhünzê
Cona
Kangto 7102m
Zayü
Hengduan Shan
Salween
Mekong (Lancang Jiang)
SCALE 1:7,750,000
(projection: Lambert Conformal Conic)
Km
0 25 50 100 150 200 250 300
0 25 50 100 150 200 250 300
Miles

162
162
160
160
152
166

What to See

❶ Kashi
Kazakh, Kyrgyz and Tajik influences have made China's westerly outpost a fascinating oasis of markets and continual trade

❷ Heaven Pool
Beautiful lake beneath the Bogda Feng (Peak of God), a challenge for mountaineers

❸ Turpan
This desert oasis town on the Silk Road lies in the Turpan Depression, 79 m (260 ft) below sea level, and relies on old underground tunnels to provide water

❹ Mogao Caves
(near Dunhuang) Hundreds of caves sheltering excellent Buddhist paintings and rock sculptures, only a fraction of them open to the public

❺ Zhongwei
Scenically located town where the lush plains of the Yellow River meet the barren dunes of the Tengger desert

❻ Lhasa
Tibet's fascinating and remote capital, whose altitude at nearly 3,600 m (12,000 ft) requires some acclimatization. The city's landmark is the fantastic Buddhist Potala Palace

Potala Palace, Lhasa: The old palace was built for the Dalai Lama in the 7th century and the (secular) White and (sacred) Red Palaces, with 1,000 rooms, were added in the 17th century. Remarkably intact despite the attacks of China's Red Guards on cultural momuments in the 1960s–1970s, this unique masterpiece of Tibetan art remains a major Buddhist pilgrimage site.

Gyangze, Tibet: Inside Baiju Temple, built in 1418 by the first Panchen Lama, stands the Tower of 100,000 Buddhas. Vibrant murals combine traditional Tibetan art with Indian, Nepalese and Bhutanese styles.

Eastern China

Taiwan, Anhui, Beijing, Fujian, Guangdong, Guangxi, Guizhou, Hainan, Hebei, Henan, Hubei, Hunan, Jiangsu, Jiangxi, Shaanxi, Shandong, Shanghai, Shanxi, Sichuan, Tianjin, Yunnan, Zhejiang

The east is China's bustling heartland, with more than 20 cities of over a million people. Essentially, it was this region that the famous Great Wall was constructed to protect from the Mongols to the north. Beijing, the capital and China's cultural and political centre since the 15th century, is rich in Buddhist temples and imperial palaces of the later dynasties, especially the Qing (Manchus) who ruled from 1644 to 1911, while a former capital city, Xi'an, houses the imperial burial complex of the Terracotta Warriors.

In contrast to these ancient sites stand modern cities with the trappings of western civilization such as Hong Kong, with its superb natural harbour, and the ultradynamic Shanghai. Less frenetically, the Li and Yangtze rivers flow through some of China's most beautiful scenic areas.

The island of Taiwan tempts visitors with mountains, fine buildings and fabulous artworks brought over from the mainland by ousted nationalists in 1949. The island is still regarded by China as a renegade province.

Each region specializes in crafts, from luscious silks and embroidery to colourful enamel *cloisonné* work or evocative Chinese paintings. Regional cuisines also vary from the easily recognized Cantonese style of the south to Beijing's steamed dumplings, noodles and hot pots, or Sichuan's hotter and spicier dishes.

Great Wall of China: First begun over 2,000 years ago, much of this extensive defensive structure was rebuilt during the Ming Dynasty (14th–17th centuries). Today, many stretches are in disrepair but several reconstructed sections can be visited near Beijing and it is possible to hike along much of the rest.

Map Key

POPULATION	ELEVATION
above 5 million	6000m / 19,686ft
1 million to 5 million	4000m / 13,124ft
500,000 to 1 million	3000m / 9843ft
100,000 to 500,000	2000m / 6562ft
50,000 to 100,000	1000m / 3281ft
10,000 to 50,000	500m / 1640ft
below 10,000	250m / 820ft
	100m / 328ft
	sea level

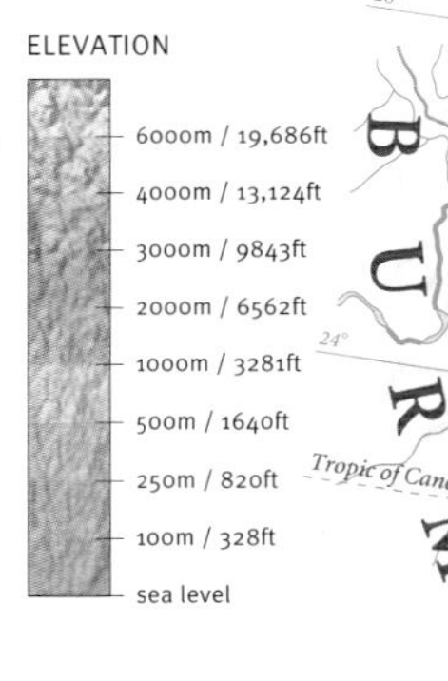

Hong Kong: This high-tech, high-rise city set around China's busiest harbour also offers first class shopping and a rich and varied nightlife – there will never be a dull moment.

Activities

Contemplate the many inscriptions on the path up **Tai Shan**, Shandong, following in the footsteps of famous Chinese from Confucius to Mao

Feast on Peking duck in **Beijing** and enjoy a night at the opera, Chinese-style, where singers in elaborate costumes and makeup bring scenes vividly to life with no props

Cruise the **Yangtze gorges** – ideally before the dam half-submerges them

Take a free lesson in *tai chi* in **Hong Kong Park** (Tuesday, Friday, and Saturday mornings)

Climb 3,000 m (10,000 ft) **Emei Shan**, Sichuan, seeing monkeys and red pandas, monasteries and temples

What to See

Beijing, Great Wall, Guilin, Hong Kong, Shanghai, Stone Forest, Terracotta Warriors, Yangtze Gorges, Yungang Caves *see* pp156–157

❶ Tiananmen Square
The world's largest public square, in the centre of Beijing, abuts the Forbidden City, the Great Hall of the People and Mao's Mausoleum.

❷ Summer Palace
(in Beijing) A serene imperial park of bridges, courtyard-style gardens and richly painted pagodas, set around a vast lake, overlooked by the spectacular Tower of Buddhist Incense on Longevity Hill

❸ Badaling
(near Beijing) The place to see restored sections of the Great Wall

❹ Shaolin Monastery
(near Luoyang) A grand religious building, famous for its martial arts and often used as a film location

❺ Xi'an
Home of the Terracotta Warriors, this thick-walled city of palaces, pagodas and pavilions was once among the greatest in the world

❻ Three Gorges Dam
The world's largest construction project will create a reservoir 500 km (300 miles) long by 2009, submerging a large part of the majestic Yangtze gorges

❼ Dazhu Stone Sculptures
Begun in the 9th century by the Tang Dynasty, hundreds of exuberant sculptures fill the narrow valley

❽ Chengdu
Prides itself on its fine temples, but famed as the giant panda capital. Its breeding centre also cares for red pandas and black-necked cranes

❾ Grand Buddha
(in Leshan) Carved into a cliff, the 71 m (240 ft) Buddha is the tallest in the world, completed 1,200 years ago

❿ Reed Flute Caves
The natural beauty of these caves close to Guilin is rivalled by the neighbouring Seven Star caves

⓫ Suzhou
The "Venice of the Orient" is famed for its traditional courtyard-style gardens

⓬ Shanghai Museum
Ultramodern museum housing a fantastic collection of bronzes

⓭ National Palace Museum (in Taipei)
The world's finest collection of Chinese art, taken from China by Chiang Kai-Shek

⓮ Taroko Gorge
(north of Hualien) Giant cliffs, marble-walled canyons, a range of different ecosystems and hidden temples

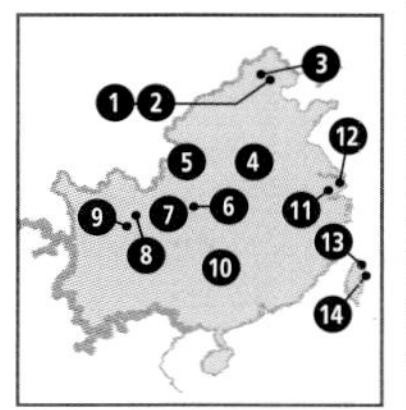

Giant panda cub, Chengdu: Of the 1,000 giant pandas in the world, more than three-quarters live in Sichuan. Chengdu has a zoo and breeding research centre dedicated to these endearing animals and other endangered species. The Wolong Panda Reserve, a three-hour drive from Chengdu, provides observation spots for pandas in their natural habitat.

SCALE 1:8,500,000
(projection: Lambert Conformal Conic)

162 ▶

192 ▶

170 ▼

Northeastern China, Mongolia, & Korea

Mongolia, North Korea, South Korea, Heilongjiang, Inner Mongolia, Jilin, Liaoning

This region of east Asia has for centuries been a domain of shifting borders and competing colonial powers. Landlocked Mongolia's most attractive features for the visitor are its amazing desert landscapes and its people's nomadic traditions, although Genghis Khan's vast Mongol empire of the 13th century left relatively few visible traces.

The dynamic spirit of Dalian makes this port one of the more interesting cities of northern China. Most visitors overlook this area in favour of the attraction-rich southeast, despite its having been home to China's last ruling dynasty, the Qing (1644–1911). North Korea is largely closed to visitors, but South Korea's capital, Seoul, is now one of the world's largest cities and holds many of the country's cultural highlights.

Map Key

POPULATION

- above 5 million
- 1 million to 5 million
- 500,000 to 1 million
- 100,000 to 500,000
- 50,000 to 100,000
- 10,000 to 50,000
- below 10,000

ELEVATION

- 4000m / 13,124ft
- 3000m / 9843ft
- 2000m / 6562ft
- 1000m / 3281ft
- 500m / 1640ft
- 250m / 820ft
- 100m / 328ft
- sea level

SCALE 1:7,750,000
(projection: Lambert Conformal Conic)
Km 0 25 50 100 150 200
Miles 0 25 50 100 150 200

122

158

158

What to See

Gobi, Pyongyang, Seoul *see* pp156–157

❶ **Flaming Cliffs**
(near Bulgan) Amazing fossils have been found in these beautiful orange-pink coloured rocks in the Gobi

❷ **Erdene Zuu Khiid**
(near Hujirt) Buddhist monastery built from the ruins of Genghis Khan's capital Karakorum

❸ **Ulan Bator**
Mongolia's only major city is home to the Gandan Monastery and museums of culture

❹ **Khustai National Park** (near Ulan Bator)
Mongolian steppe reserve for the wild Przewalski horse

❺ **Genghis Khan Mausoleum**
(near Ordos) Pilgrimage centre for Mongolians since the relocation in 1954 of the Great Khan's ashes

❻ **Hohhot**
The Xiletuzhao Temple graces Inner Mongolia's capital, which has a mix of Chinese and Mongolian traditions

❼ **Dalian**
Vibrant northern port and fashion centre, noted for its mish-mash of architecture

❽ **Seoraksan National Park** (near Sokch'o)
South Korea's most beautiful national park teems with waterfalls, hot springs, temples and forests

❾ **Kyongju**
Ancient capital of the Silla Dynasty, which flourished in the 3rd–10th centuries – a collection of ruins, caves and temples, notably Bulguksa

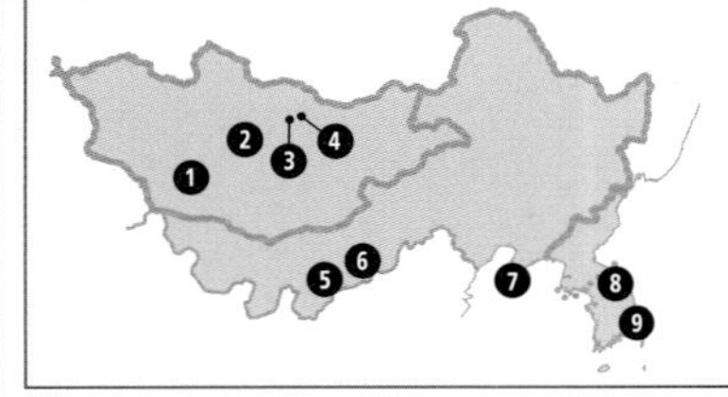

Activities

Celebrate the Ice Lantern Festival in **Harbin**, China, (January–February), with models in ice of the Great Wall and Forbidden City

Wrestle at the Naadam Festival, held in July in **Mongolia**, with archery and horse races

Appear to defy gravity on the optical illusion Mystery Road on **Cheju-do** island

Rock climb on the unusual formations of **Chiaksan National Park** in South Korea

Try a bowl of *kim chee* (pickled vegetables) – a classic Korean dish

Inside a *ger*, Mongolia: *Gers* (or *yurts*) are traditional portable houses, still in use in Mongolia and west China. They are entered forwards, but exited backwards, and it is a faux pas to step on, rather than over, the wooden threshhold. The righthand side of the tent is reserved for the women.

Changgyeong Palace, Seoul: The city was founded in 1392 by the Yi Dynasty, who ruled the "Hermit Kingdom" until 1910. They built many fine palaces, including the Changgyeong, begun in 1484, which now lies in the shadow of modern skyscrapers.

122

122

164

160

Korean dancers perform the *Buchaechum* (fan dance): In this traditional and popular dance, that celebrates the beauty of nature, women wearing colourful *hanboks*, like those once worn in the royal court, twirl and unfurl vibrant fans to represent falling flower petals. In the finale, the dancers form a swirling flower blossom.

Japan

Despite much that on the surface is recognizably westernized – fast trains, fast food, fast living – it does not take much to reveal the oriental base on which Japanese life is founded; then the culture shock really kicks in.

Magnificent mountain scenery competes with the truly staggering cityscapes of one of the world's largest cities, and certainly its busiest: Tokyo. For the tourist there is an unending supply of delights, whether visual, cultural or gastronomic, not to mention the warmth of the locals. Walking the streets of Japan's cities leaves you feeling future-shocked and mystified while simultaneously comfortable and secure.

For a break, quiet temple complexes with fascinating histories and vistas will tempt, along with the verdant hillsides of the interior and the untouched wildernesses of Hokkaido island. You could join the Japanese on holiday themselves, in the sun-drenched islands of the south, or take part in the fun of Disney, Japanese-style and marvel at a refined culture's paradoxical capacity for kitsch.

Perhaps the greatest pleasure to be had in Japan is the cu sine. Its apparent simplicity of ingredients and preparation belie a wealth of tastes and sensations. Be sure to try seafood morsels at the *sushi* bar, enjoy a skewer of barbecued chicken at a *yakitoriya,* savour the crunch of *tempura* (seafood or vegetables in batter) and embrace the hot tingle of *wasabi* paste.

Sunset over the busy streets of East Shinjuku, Tokyo: When West Shinjuku (the busy heart of commercial Tokyo) shuts down, East Shinjuku comes to life. Encompassing a red-light district, countless bars, and offering a wide choice of entertainment from movies to *pachinko* parlours, it has a long tradition of providing (mostly male) commuters with after work amusements.

What to See

1 Hokkaido
Escape to nature in Daisetsuzan National Park's mountains, at the heart of Hokkaido

2 Tokyo
Once a fishing village, Tokyo is now arguably the world's greatest metropolis – fast, lively and modern, with a sleek and efficient transport system

3 International Film Festival
Immerse yourself in the ubiquitous *manga* animations at Tokyo's annual IFF

4 Mount Fuji
See the sun rise in the east on Japan's famous, sacred peak and highest mountain. Its an almost perfect, snow-capped cone

5 Nagoya
Baseball is a national obsession. Nagoya's Chunichi Dragons are one of the best teams

6 Amanohashidate
(near Miyazu)
One of the "wonders" of Japan. Viewed with your head between your knees, the "bridge to heaven", a pine-studded sand bar, seems to float in midair

7 Kyoto
Geisha still step gracefully through the backstreets of this cultural gold mine

8 Cherry Blossom
(Kyoto) Enjoy the April floral riot along the *Tetsugaku-no-michi* (Path of Philosophy)

9 Nara
The Todai temple complex is just one of the treasures dotted around the immense park in this former imperial capital

10 Osaka
Japan's third city, Osaka typifies modern Japan: technological, fun-loving and industrious

11 Himeji
Built on a high bluff, Japan's most famous castle exemplifies elegant, feudal military architecture. It is an easy stop on the bullet train from Tokyo to Hiroshima

12 Hiroshima
A vibrant city which has much to offer beyond the remembrance of the first atomic bomb, but still more to teach the world about peace

13 Fukuoka
One of the six grand sumo tournaments is held in Fukuoka: witness the pageantry and power of a *sumo basho*

14 Kumamoto Prefecture
(on Kyushu) A good spot for *ryokan* (traditional Japanese spas), unwinding body and mind

15 Okinawa
The Ryukyu Islands offer a Pacific paradise of golden sand and soothing sunshine

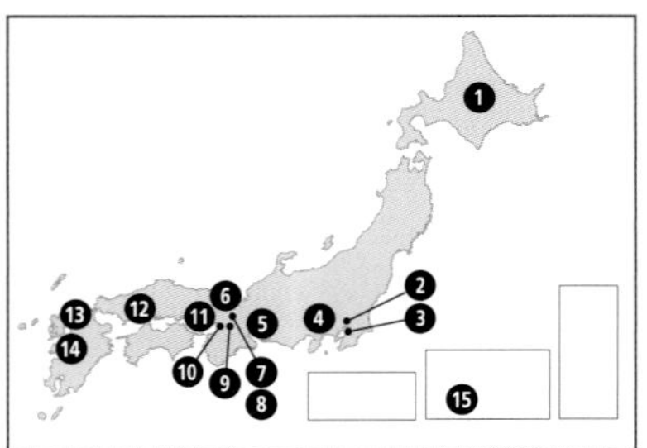

156

156

SCALE 1:4,370,000
(projection: Lambert Conformal Conic)
Km 0 10 20 40 60 80 100
Miles 0 10 20 40 60 80 100

192

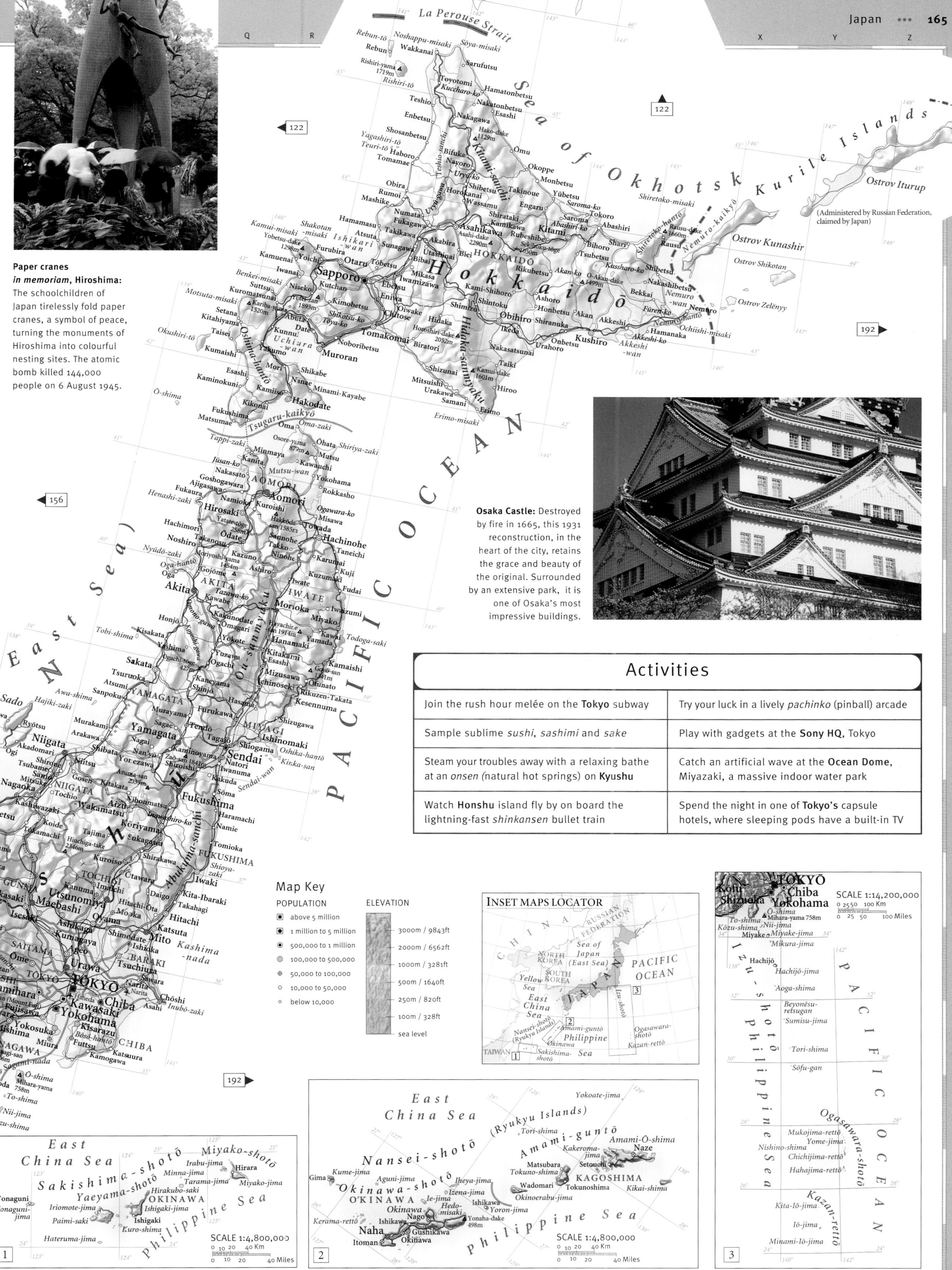
La Perouse Strait
Sea of Okhotsk
Kurile Islands
Ostrov Iturup
(Administered by Russian Federation, claimed by Japan)
Ostrov Kunashir
Ostrov Shikotan
Ostrov Zelënyy
Hokkaidō
Sapporo
Asahikawa
Hakodate
Muroran
Kushiro
Obihiro
Tsugaru-kaikyō
Aomori
Hachinohe
Akita
Morioka
Sendai
Yamagata
Fukushima
Niigata
Utsunomiya
Maebashi
Mito
Urawa
TOKYO
Chiba
Kawasaki
Yokohama
PACIFIC OCEAN
East Sea
Sado
Map Key
POPULATION
above 5 million
1 million to 5 million
500,000 to 1 million
100,000 to 500,000
50,000 to 100,000
10,000 to 50,000
below 10,000
ELEVATION
3000m / 9843ft
2000m / 6562ft
1000m / 3281ft
500m / 1640ft
250m / 820ft
100m / 328ft
sea level
INSET MAPS LOCATOR
CHINA
RUSSIAN FEDERATION
Sea of Japan (East Sea)
NORTH KOREA
SOUTH KOREA
JAPAN
PACIFIC OCEAN
Yellow Sea
East China Sea
Philippine Sea
TAIWAN
SCALE 1:14,200,000
Izu-shotō
Philippine Sea
Ogasawara-shotō
Kazan-rettō
East China Sea
Nansei-shotō (Ryukyu Islands)
Amami-guntō
Okinawa-shotō
OKINAWA
Naha
KAGOSHIMA
Philippine Sea
SCALE 1:4,800,000
Sakishima-shotō
Miyako-shotō
Yaeyama-shotō
Yonaguni
Ishigaki
SCALE 1:4,800,000

Paper cranes *in memoriam*, Hiroshima: The schoolchildren of Japan tirelessly fold paper cranes, a symbol of peace, turning the monuments of Hiroshima into colourful nesting sites. The atomic bomb killed 144,000 people on 6 August 1945.

Osaka Castle: Destroyed by fire in 1665, this 1931 reconstruction, in the heart of the city, retains the grace and beauty of the original. Surrounded by an extensive park, it is one of Osaka's most impressive buildings.

Activities

Join the rush hour melée on the **Tokyo** subway	Try your luck in a lively *pachinko* (pinball) arcade
Sample sublime *sushi*, *sashimi* and *sake*	Play with gadgets at the **Sony HQ**, Tokyo
Steam your troubles away with a relaxing bathe at an *onsen* (natural hot springs) on **Kyushu**	Catch an artificial wave at the **Ocean Dome**, Miyazaki, a massive indoor water park
Watch **Honshu** island fly by on board the lightning-fast *shinkansen* bullet train	Spend the night in one of **Tokyo's** capsule hotels, where sleeping pods have a built-in TV

Mainland Southeast Asia

Burma, Cambodia, Laos, Thailand, Vietnam

For a real sense and flavour of the Far East, head for the markets – colourful, exciting hubs of activity each with its own special feel. The people are overwhelmingly friendly and the food, famous for its quality and variety, is a true art form that will delight the adventurous. Tradition and religion feature strongly in the culture, with many flamboyant festivals and theatre, dance and puppetry performances.

Of all the ancient sites, the tree-entwined ruins of Angkor Wat are the best known. Discovered deep in the jungle by a local 16th-century ruler, they later fired the interest of European colonists in the lost Khmer kingdoms. More sites, many of them equally evocative, have been discovered in the last 100 years and travellers often find that the most alluring are those in less-visited locations – such as Thailand's Phimai and Cambodia's Prea Khan.

The typically lush landscapes change seasonally, as the growth of vegetation and cultivation follows the cycle of two contrasting monsoon winds blowing from the southwest in June–October, bringing heavy downpours, and from the northwest in November–March, bringing cool, dry conditions. Wildlife tours are popular. Atlas moths – the world's largest – are found in tropical forest highlands, Sambar deer and capped gibbons in the open forests of Thailand's central plains and endangered Irrawaddy dolphins in coastal waters and rivers. Along the coastlines of the region are beautiful golden beaches, dramatic rocks, islands and caves.

Wat Phra That Choeng Chum, Sakon Nakhon: The main *wat* of this former Khmer town is richly decorated. A *wat* is a complex of buildings – within an enclosure – functioning as a Buddhist monastery, temple and community centre. There is a long tradition of donating to your local *wat* and as a result they contain some of the region's finest architecture.

152

BANGLADESH
Bay of Bengal
Tropic of Cancer
SAGAING
CHIN STATE
MAGWE
PEGU
IRRAWADDY
Mandalay
Sagaing
Myingyan
Pakokku
Sittwe
Sinchaingbyin
Rathedaung
Buthidaung
Kyaukpyu
Ramree Island
Cheduba Island
Sandoway
Prome
Henzada
Bassein
Pegu
Maubin
Myaungmya
Moulmeingyun
Bogale
Pyapon
YANGON (RANGOON)
Mouths of the Irrawaddy
Gulf of Martaban
Preparis Island
Great Coco Island
Little Coco Island
Andaman Sea
Mergui Archipelago
Strait of Malacca
Ban Kam Phu
Ko Phra Thong
Thalang
Ko Phuket

172

Phuket, south Thailand: Known for its clear blue waters and long sandy beaches, Thailand's largest island also attracts visitors to its Phuket FantaSea theme park, smart hotels, adventure trips around Phang Nga Bay and the nightlife of Patong.

What to See

❶ Pindaya Caves
(near Taunggyi)
Stalactites hang from massive limestone caves filled with thousands of Buddha images.

❷ Yangon (Rangoon)
The city's charm is in its shady parks, lakes and boulevards of colonial architecture. A special delight is at night, when the streets fill with stalls and bustling shoppers

❸ Phuket
Recovering after the 2004 tsunami, Thailand's most visited island is packed with attractions

❹ Chiang Mai
This famous walled city was once capital of the Lanna Kingdom, and has numerous *wats* (religious compounds) dating from this period

❺ Sukhothai
The cradle of Thai civilization – a vast network of intricately carved temples, *stupas*, *wats* and water features

❻ Bangkok
Contrasting with the city's excitement is Dusit Park – a calm oasis of water features, manicured lawns, pavilions and mansions

❼ Khao Yai
(near Sara Buri)
Thailand's first national park encompasses evergreen forest and grassland habitats. It is home to the country's few remaining tigers

❽ Prasat Hin Khao Phnom Rung
(near Nang Rong)
Magnificent 10th-century Khmer temple complex

❾ Louangphabang
This once great capital city combines traditional architecture with colonial styles and is the nucleus of thriving Lao culture

❿ Pak Ou Caves
(near Louangphabang)
Thousands of Buddha statues are sheltered in caves where the Ou and Mekong rivers meet

⓫ Plain of Jars
(near Pek)
An intriguing conundrum – thousands of jars littering the landscape were possibly ancient coffins, carved from solid sandstone

⓬ Khone Pha Pheng
This vast waterfall on the Laos-Cambodia border is the largest in southeast Asia. Most impressive during the rainy season (June–October)

⓭ Angkor Wat
(near Siemreab)
Famous temple complex where the trees and intricately carved buildings have fused over time

⓮ Toul Sleng Genocide Museum
(in Phnom Penh) The museum documents atrocities committed in that very building – an overwhelming experience

⓯ Ha Noi
Noted for its many lakes and leafy boulevards lined with honey-coloured buildings

⓰ My Son Sanctuary
(near Da Nang)
In a dramatic setting, these remarkable brick tower-temples are the vestiges of the 4th–13th-century Champa Kingdom

⓱ Nha Trang
A haven for beach lovers, this resort caters for all kinds of water sport amid coves, lush islands and coral reefs

⓲ Ho Chi Minh (Saigon)
Embued with a strongly capitalist spirit, this lively city is a good base for visiting the Cu Chi Tunnels – once used to infiltrate behind US army lines – and the Cao Dai Temple at Tay Ninh. Try some of the delicious local cuisine as well

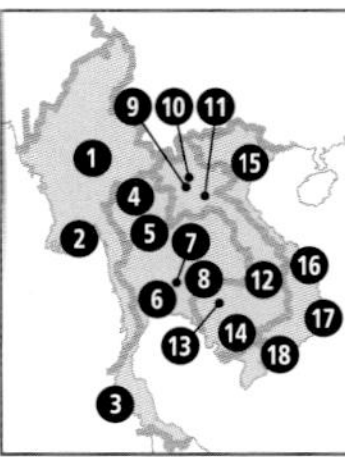
1
2
3
4
5
6
7
8
9
10
11
12
13
14
15
16
17
18

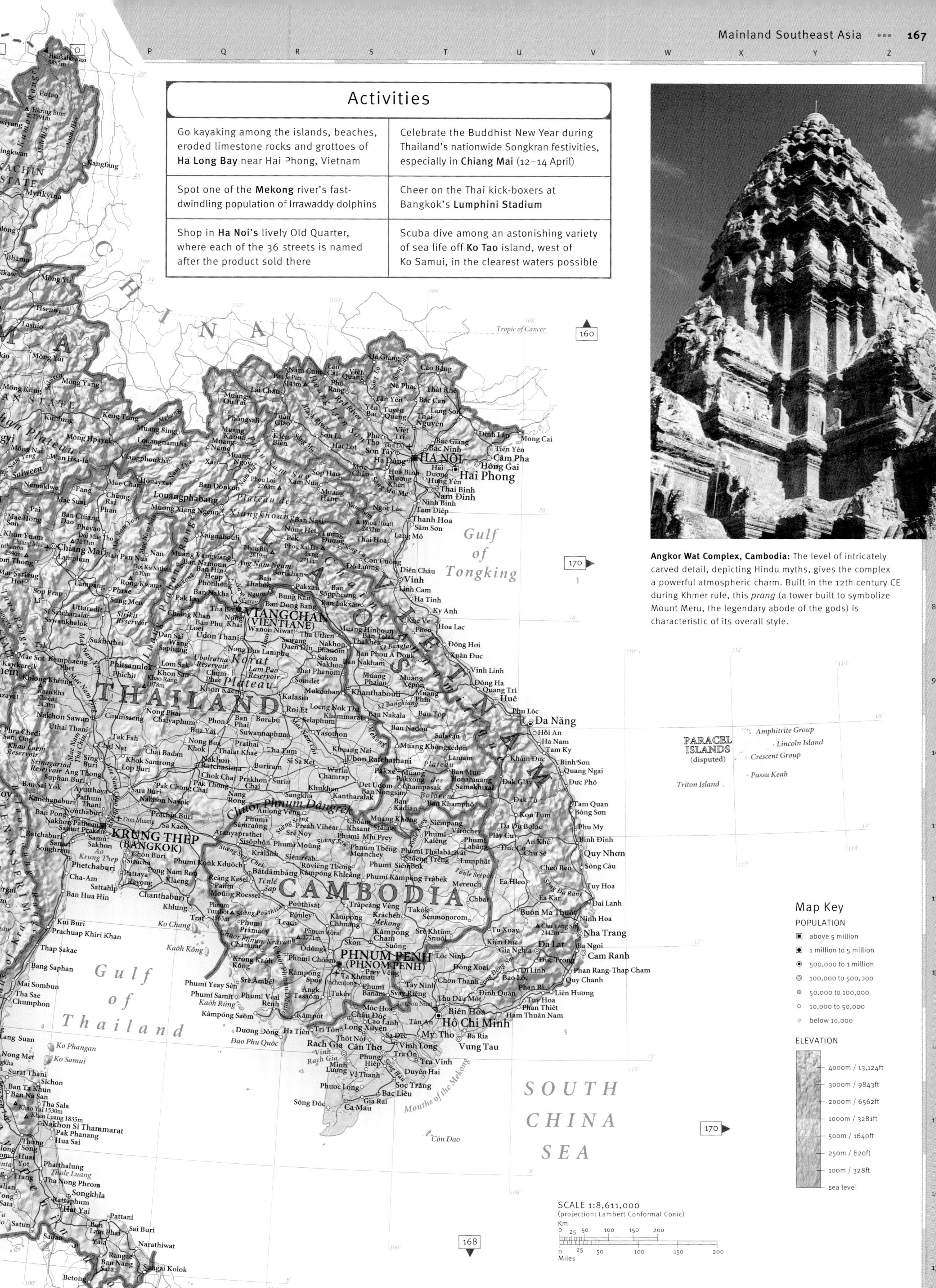
CHINA
MYANMAR
THAILAND
LAOS
VIETNAM
CAMBODIA
MALAYSIA
Gulf of Tongking
Gulf of Thailand
SOUTH CHINA SEA
PARACEL ISLANDS (disputed)
Tropic of Cancer
HA NOI
Hai Phong
VIANGCHAN (VIENTIANE)
KRUNG THEP (BANGKOK)
PHNUM PENH (PHNOM PENH)
Hô Chi Minh
Da Năng
Huê
Khorat Plateau
Mouths of the Mekong
160
170
170
168
Map Key
POPULATION
above 5 million
1 million to 5 million
500,000 to 1 million
100,000 to 500,000
50,000 to 100,000
10,000 to 50,000
below 10,000
ELEVATION
4000m / 13,124ft
3000m / 9843ft
2000m / 6562ft
1000m / 3281ft
500m / 1640ft
250m / 820ft
100m / 328ft
sea level
SCALE 1:8,611,000
(projection: Lambert Conformal Conic)

Activities

Go kayaking among the islands, beaches, eroded limestone rocks and grottoes of **Ha Long Bay** near Hai Phong, Vietnam	Celebrate the Buddhist New Year during Thailand's nationwide Songkran festivities, especially in **Chiang Mai** (12–14 April)
Spot one of the **Mekong** river's fast-dwindling population of Irrawaddy dolphins	Cheer on the Thai kick-boxers at Bangkok's **Lumphini Stadium**
Shop in **Ha Noi's** lively Old Quarter, where each of the 36 streets is named after the product sold there	Scuba dive among an astonishing variety of sea life off **Ko Tao** island, west of Ko Samui, in the clearest waters possible

Angkor Wat Complex, Cambodia: The level of intricately carved detail, depicting Hindu myths, gives the complex a powerful atmospheric charm. Built in the 12th century CE during Khmer rule, this *prang* (a tower built to symbolize Mount Meru, the legendary abode of the gods) is characteristic of its overall style.

Western Maritime Southeast Asia

Indonesia, Malaysia, Brunei, Singapore

The jungles of Malaysia are among the world's oldest, having first put down roots 130 million years ago. Their maturity has given the region great biological diversity. The world's largest flower (*Rafflesia arnoldii*) can be found here, as can the orang utan and the proboscis monkey. In the chain of volcanic mountains running along the western edge of the Indonesian islands, hill resorts offer a cool, crisp, mosquito-free retreat from the humid lowlands.

Surfing enthusiasts agree that Indonesia has some of the finest locations and best breakers in the world; Bali is particularly famous both for this and the associated party atmosphere, but some lesser-known islands, such as the Mentawai, are of equal calibre.

Although most of the region escaped damage by the 2004 tsunami, the northern Sumatran region of Aceh was one of the hardest hit areas and it will take time to recover. The tribal lifestyle is still common in Borneo, where whole villages often live in a traditional longhouse. Visitors are welcome to stay in these and suitable gifts are appreciated as payment. Ethnically the region is a diverse mix of Malays, Chinese, Javanese and other groups. Local culture is strongly influenced by this diversity, which enriches the region's music, cuisine and other art forms. Islam is the majority religion and Indonesia has the world's largest Muslim population.

Sepilok Orang Utan Sanctuary, Sabah: An orang utan (literally "man of the forest") swinging from vines through the forests of Borneo. The Sepilok Sanctuary is the largest orang utan sanctuary in the world.

166

Malaysia's Two Capitals

KUALA LUMPUR – capital
PUTRAJAYA – administrative capital

172

Singapore: The city-state welcomes visitors with the impressive sight of skyscrapers clustered together in its business district. Singapore is an excellent destination with first rate shopping and also provides a delicious focal point for several Asian cuisines.

172

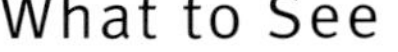

What to See

1 Danau Toba
The legacy of an ancient volcanic eruption, this tranquil lake is a cool haven from surrounding mosquito-ridden jungles

2 Pinang
"The Pearl of the Orient" with magnificent palm-fringed beaches and religious buildings is Malaysia in microcosm

3 Cameron Highlands
(near Ipoh) With a lush temperate climate and verdant landscape, this famous hill resort has a colonial elegance

4 Batu Caves
(near Kuala Lumpur) A grand staircase leads to three sacred caverns

5 Genting Highlands
(near Kuala Lumpur) A lively hill resort with a difference, Asia's Las Vegas has a man-made lake, hotels and casinos

6 Pulau Tioman
Breathtakingly beautiful volcanic island where the pace of life is slow and the deep-sea diving world-renowned

7 Singapore
An ultraclean metropolis and magnet for the shopaholic, with "one thousand malls", and a mouthwatering focal point for Asia's cuisines

8 Niah Caves
(near Miri) Accessible by boat and a 3 km (2 mile) hike, here lies evidence of 5,000-year-old human habitation

9 Sultan Omar Ali Saifuddin Mosque
(Bandar Seri Begawan) The Far East's largest mosque sits, dazzling white and gold-domed, in its own lagoon

10 Kampong Ayer
(Bandar Seri Begawan) Appearing to float on water, Brunei's vast village of stilt houses dates back 1,000 years

11 Gunung Kinabalu
Southeast Asia's highest mountain towers over a national park of giant flowers, waterfalls, caves, and hot springs

12 Ujung Kulon National Park
(near Cikawung) The reclusive single-horned Javan rhino, macaques and crocodiles inhabit this lowland rainforest

13 Borobudur
(near Yogyakarta) A magnificent 8th-century Buddhist temple, crowned with latticed, bell-shaped stupas

14 Lovina
This north coast group of resorts provides an ideal base to discover the wonders of Bali

15 Goa Lawah
(near Karangasem) Elegant temples mark the entrance to this sacred cave, home to a multitude of fruit bats

16 Sangeh Sacred Monkey Forest
(near Denpasar) With the atmospheric Pura Bukit Sari temple at its heart, the forest is home to giant nutmeg trees

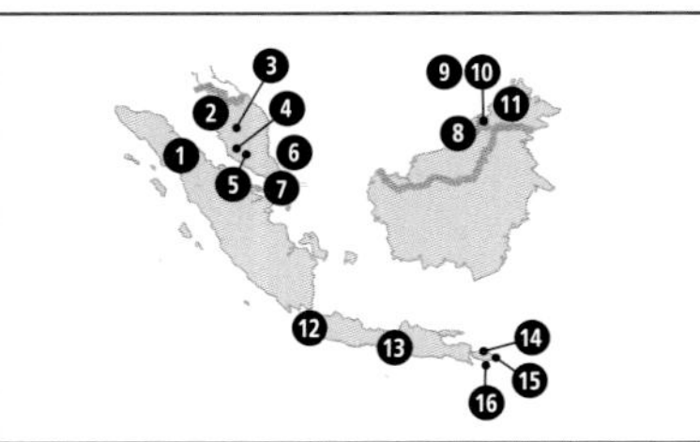
1
2
3
4
5
6
7
8
9
10
11
12
13
14
15
16

Activities

- Saunter along the world's longest canopy walkway in 130-million-year-old rainforest, **Taman Negara National Park**, Malaysia
- Have a go at *sepak takraw*, **Malaysia's** no-hands volleyball-style game
- Stand beneath and marvel at Kuala Lumpur's 452 m (1,483 ft) **Petronas Towers**, the world's second highest building
- Goggle at the lakeside antics of varied bird life in Brunei's **Tasek Merimbun National Park**
- Study the intricacies of local music and dance in lessons at the schools in **Peliatan**, Bali
- Attend a gamelan orchestra rehearsal for free at the **Indonesian Academy of Performing Arts**, Denpasar, Bali
- Trek in tea plantations up **Gunung Kerinci**, Sumatra, SE Asia's highest active volcano
- Sip colonial history with a Singapore Gin Sling at the **Raffles Hotel** Long Bar, Singapore

Batubulan, Bali: The age-old story of good versus evil is played out in the Barong Dance. Evil is represented by Rangda, a witch, and good by the half-lion Barong Keket and his followers with their *keris* (knife). Fortunately good triumphs, after the witch's magic is overpowered. This energetic ritual dance performance is a magnificent spectacle to behold.

156
170

Map Key

POPULATION
- above 5 million
- 1 million to 5 million
- 500,000 to 1 million
- 100,000 to 500,000
- 50,000 to 100,000
- 10,000 to 50,000
- below 10,000

ELEVATION
- 4000m / 13,124ft
- 3000m / 9843ft
- 2000m / 6562ft
- 1000m / 3281ft
- 500m / 1640ft
- 250m / 820ft
- 100m / 328ft
- sea level

SCALE 1:8,750,000
(projection: Mercator)
Km 0 25 50 100 150 200
Miles 0 25 50 100 150 200

170
170

Eastern Maritime Southeast Asia

Indonesia, East Timor, Philippines

Straddling the Equator is this enormous collection of islands, each with its own identity, history, and culture – often a lively blend of vibrant local tribal traditions and those of colonial conquerors. From the early 16th century the islands formed the core of the Asian spice trade with Europe attracting the Portuguese, Spanish and Dutch. Many colonial buildings were built and remain today as distinctive features of the architectural mix.

The islands are largely volcanic and run along the fault lines where five tectonic plates meet, giving the region mountainous terrain with narrow coastal strips. This active geology has created spectacular landscapes of waterfalls, caves, and even an underground river in Palawan, enticing intrepid explorers.

Most islands are thick with rainforest and are home to an array of plant and animal species, many of them endangered by loss of habitat through activities such as logging. The Tubbataha Reef, in the Sulu Sea, has a high density of marine species, birds, and turtles. The region has countless opportunities to indulge in watersports, with numerous coral reefs, lagoons and white sandy beaches.

Much of the island of New Guinea, the western half of which lies in Indonesia, remains tantalizingly unexplored and tribal warriors may still greet approaching ships. Here, the Lorentz National Park preserves a unique, continuous cross-section of ecosystems from mountain peak through forested hills and lowlands to tropical marine environments.

The boat-shaped houses of Tana Toraja, Sulawesi: According to local myth, the earliest ancestors came from the north and were stranded on Sulawesi. They used their vessels to shelter from the elements, and so began this fascinating architectural tradition of building north-facing houses resembling these ships.

What to See

❶ Vigan Founded in the 16th century, this city's architectural splendour blends Chinese, Filipino and European influences

❷ Banaue (near Bontoc) Vistas of rice terraces, which trace the contours of the land

❸ Benguet Mummies (near Bontoc) In caves around the town of Kabayan are the well-preserved, tattooed mummies of up to 30 tribal chieftains

❹ Intramuros The medieval walled city at Manila's heart mixes religious, military, domestic and colonial architecture

❺ Hidden Valley, Laguna (near Manila) A large volcanic crater encloses a forested land of mineral springs, with pools of varying temperature and cascading waterfalls

❻ Lake Taal Still active, the majestic Taal volcano rises from calm waters, enclosing a lake within a lake

❼ Puerto Princesa Surrounded by a national park of dense forest teeming with wildlife, an immense underground river leads from a lagoon to the sea

❽ Boracay (off Panay) Classic small tropical paradise island. Its White Beach is rated amongst the world's best beaches

❾ Bohol Grass on the island's surreal, molehill-shaped "Chocolate Hills" turns a deep brown at the end of the dry season, earning them their name

❿ Zamboanga The Philippines' most romantic city with hot springs, picturesque mountains, bat caves and sandy beaches lined with tropical shells and fragrant flowers

⓫ Tana Toraja (around Rantepao) Sulawesi's colourful heartland gives a taste of tribal life

⓬ Bantimurung Waterfall (near Maros) The focal point in a densely forested, magical land of limestone rocks, where butterflies flutter

⓭ Keli Mutu Most spectacular at dawn, three differently coloured crater lakes crown the volcano on Flores, Indonesia's most beautiful island

⓮ Pulau Komodo This hot, dry and austerely beautiful sun-beaten volcanic island is home to the famed giant monitor lizards... here be dragons

⓯ Gili Islands (off Lombok) A tranquil atmosphere pervades these tiny islands of magnificent coral reefs and sandy beaches, where no motorized transport is allowed

⓰ Pulau Sumba Sumba's appeal is its rich tribal atmosphere, ceremonies, colourful fabrics, monumental tombstones and blue-tongued skinks

⓱ Baliem Valley (near Ilaga) Enclosed by imposing mountains, this "Shangri La" of timeless tribal farmland was only discovered by outsiders in 1938

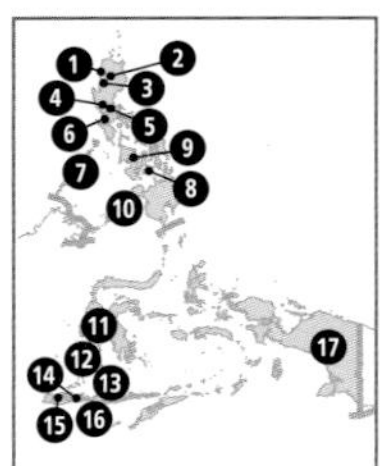
1
2
3
4
5
6
7
8
9
10
11
12
13
14
15
16
17

Map Key

POPULATION

- 1 million to 5 million
- 500,000 to 1 million
- 100,000 to 500,000
- 50,000 to 100,000
- 10,000 to 50,000
- below 10,000

ELEVATION

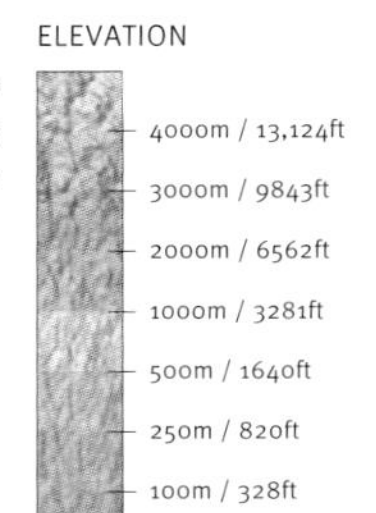
4000m / 13,124ft
3000m / 9843ft
2000m / 6562ft
1000m / 3281ft
500m / 1640ft
250m / 820ft
100m / 328ft
sea level

SCALE 1:11,800,000
(projection: Lambert Azimuthal Equal Area)

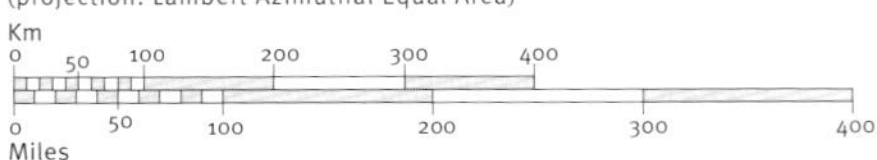
Km
0 50 100 200 300 400
0 50 100 200 300 400
Miles

Rice terraces of the Cordilleras, Banaue, Luzon: These breathtakingly spectacular rice terraces were constructed 2,000 years ago by local tribes using rudimentary tools. Now a UNESCO World Heritage Site, the terraces are valued because they exemplify the balance that can be achieved between human beings and the environment.

SOUTH
SPRATLY ISLANDS
(disputed)
CHINA
SEA
Quezon
Brooke's Point
Balabac Island
Balabac Strait
168
MALAYSI
KALIMANTAN
TIMUR
Equator
I
N
KALIMANTAN
SELATAN
Makassar
Java
Sea
NUSA TENGGA
Bayan
Gunung Tambora
Mataram
Sumbawabesar
Pulau Lombok
Taliwang
Kuta
Gunung Takan
Nusa
Lesse

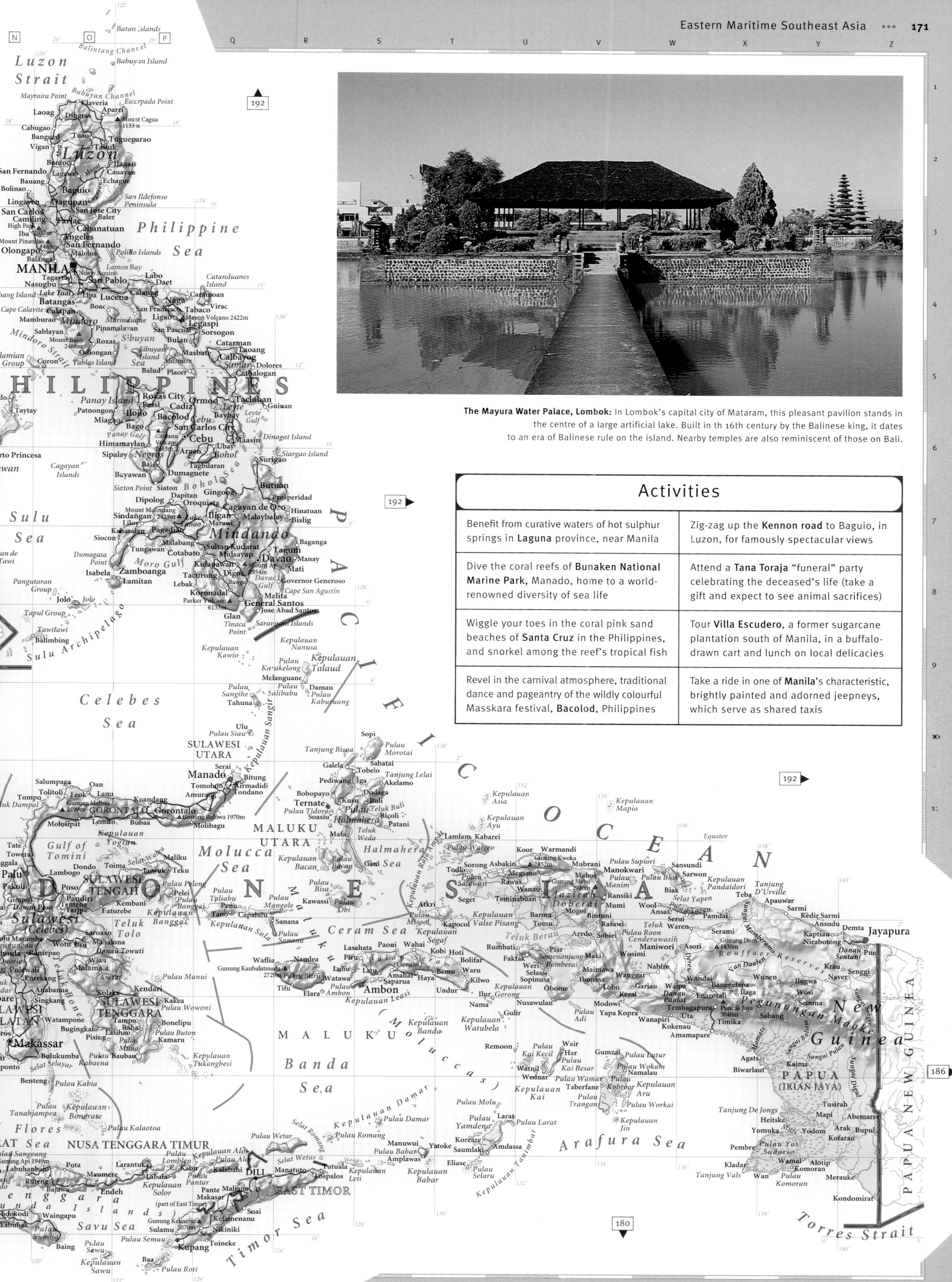
Luzon Strait
Luzon
Philippine Sea
PHILIPPINES
Mindoro
Mindanao
Sulu Sea
Celebes Sea
Sulu Archipelago
PACIFIC OCEAN
SULAWESI UTARA
MALUKU UTARA
Molucca Sea
Halmahera Sea
Ceram Sea
Banda Sea
MALUKU
Arafura Sea
Timor Sea
Savu Sea
Flores Sea
NUSA TENGGARA TIMUR
EAST TIMOR
SULAWESI TENGAH
SULAWESI TENGGARA
SULAWESI SELATAN
Gulf of Tomini
INDONESIA
PAPUA (IRIAN JAYA)
New Guinea
PAPUA NEW GUINEA
Torres Strait
192
180
186

The Mayura Water Palace, Lombok: In Lombok's capital city of Mataram, this pleasant pavilion stands in the centre of a large artificial lake. Built in th 16th century by the Balinese king, it dates to an era of Balinese rule on the island. Nearby temples are also reminiscent of those on Bali.

Activities

Benefit from curative waters of hot sulphur springs in **Laguna** province, near Manila	Zig-zag up the **Kennon road** to Baguio, in Luzon, for famously spectacular views
Dive the coral reefs of **Bunaken National Marine Park,** Manado, home to a world-renowned diversity of sea life	Attend a **Tana Toraja** "funeral" party celebrating the deceased's life (take a gift and expect to see animal sacrifices)
Wiggle your toes in the coral pink sand beaches of **Santa Cruz** in the Philippines, and snorkel among the reef's tropical fish	Tour **Villa Escudero**, a former sugarcane plantation south of Manila, in a buffalo-drawn cart and lunch on local delicacies
Revel in the carnival atmosphere, traditional dance and pageantry of the wildly colourful Masskara festival, **Bacolod**, Philippines	Take a ride in one of **Manila**'s characteristic, brightly painted and adorned jeepneys, which serve as shared taxis

The Indian Ocean

Natural beauty and fine beaches draw large numbers of tourists to Mauritius, the Seychelles and Réunion. The Comoros Islands are less frequented, largely due to political instability rather than any lack of potential attractions. Madagascar too has fine beaches, but is justly most celebrated for its distinctive wildlife. This is the product of a long history of isolation, also characteristic of other islands in the Indian Ocean, but nowhere more prolific in its consequences than in the world's fourth largest island. Under threat from deforestation, Madagascar's rainforests and unique species attract scientists and tourists alike.

In the Maldives, a cluster of hundreds of low-lying coral atolls, whole uninhabited islands have been developed as individual hotel and beach resorts. The Andaman and Nicobar Islands were badly affected by the 2004 tsunami, whose waves reached as far as the African coast. Highly dependent on tourism, all these countries place a high priority on rapidly restoring their resorts.

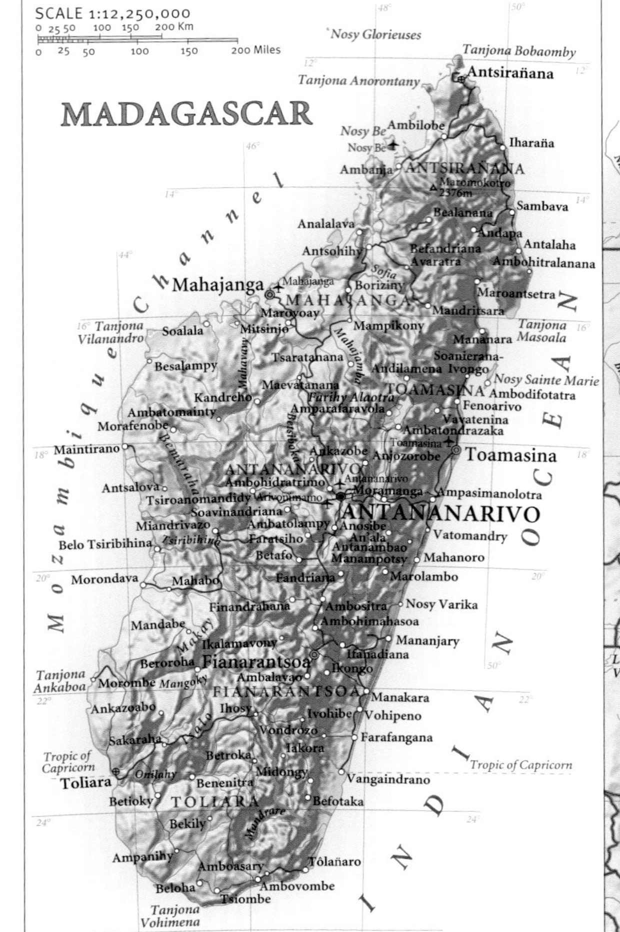

SCALE 1:12,250,000
MADAGASCAR
Antsirañana
ANTSIRANANA
Mahajanga
MAHAJANGA
TOAMASINA
Toamasina
ANTANANARIVO
FIANARANTSOA
Fianarantsoa
TOLIARA
Toliara
Mozambique Channel
INDIAN OCEAN
Tropic of Capricorn

What to See

❶ **Seychelles**
Delightful beaches, rainforests thronged with birds and coco-de-mer palms (the world's largest seed). Visit the former leper colony on Curieuse, now a fascinating marine national park

❷ **Comoros Islands**
Beautiful islands of rainforests, tumbling waterfalls, white sands and cobblestone Arab-style *medinas* (old town centres). The fossil fish *coelocanth* is found in local seas

❸ **Montagne d'Ambre**
(near Antsiranana)
Prominent volcanic massif, with numerous birds, frogs, geckoes, snakes and several bizarre chameleons

❹ **Tsingy de Bemaraha**
Incredible wildlife includes six species of lemur, plus a forest of limestone pinnacles

❺ **Réunion**
Forbidding mountains and gorges make this French destination ideal for hikers

❻ **Mauritius**
Accessible island known for its beaches, sporting activities and dramatic mountains offering short hikes

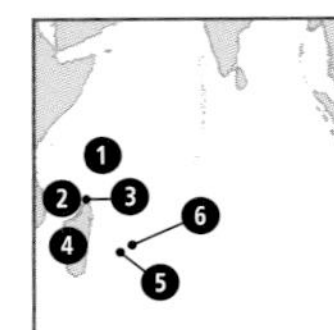

Berenty, Madagascar:
There are 15 species of lemur found on Madagascar and the Comoros, all of which are endangered. The most famous is the striking ring-tailed lemur. Nearly half the world's chameleon species live in Madagascar and numerous plants are only found here, such as the rosy periwinkle – derivatives of which are being developed as a cure for cancer.

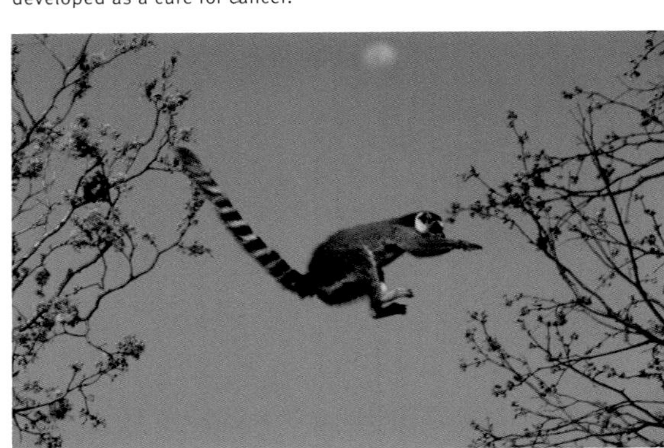

Île aux Cerfs, Mauritius:
A recent controversial addition to this paradise island is a golf course that could have a substantial negative impact on the local environment.

Activities

Tour **Aldabra Atoll**, Seychelles, home to over 200,000 giant land tortoises, as well as many seabirds, manta rays and tiger sharks

Test your two-wheeled agility by mountain biking in the rugged terrain of **Réunion**

Deep-sea fish in the waters off **Mauritius**, ideal for the serious angler, where there are healthy populations of marlin and yellowfin tuna, several species of shark and the spectacular sailfish

Walk undersea in lead boots near **Grand Baie** reef, Mauritius, or ride on La Nessee, a semi-submersible boat, for a close-up tour of the reefs without getting wet

Dive among stingray and barracuda at **Nosy Be**, Madagascar's premier resort island

Canoe down the spectacular **Manambolo** river, Madagascar

SCALE 1:47,000,000
(projection: Mollweide)
ASIA
INDIA
CHINA
INDIAN OCEAN
SOUTHERN OCEAN
AUSTRALIA
ANTARCTICA
INDONESIA
MALAYSIA
Bay of Bengal
Arabian Sea
Ninetyeast Ridge
Southeast Indian Ridge
Kerguelen Plateau
South Indian Basin
Inset Map Key
POPULATION
500,000 to 1 million
100,000 to 500,000
50,000 to 100,000
10,000 to 50,000
below 10,000
ELEVATION
Ocean Map Key
SEA DEPTH
RÉUNION (to France)
SCALE 1:2,250,000
MAURITIUS
SCALE 1:2,250,000

Australasia & Oceania

"Don't worry about the world coming to an end today.
It's already tomorrow in Australia" CHARLES M SCHULTZ, 1922-2000

Political Australasia & Oceania

Australasia, usually taken to mean the island continent of Australia and New Zealand, has a political history and culture dominated by the British colonial legacy, complete with similar Westminster-style parliamentary systems and the same monarch as ceremonial head of state. Oceania, made up of the many island states of the south Pacific, is traditionally subdivided into three areas – Melanesia, Micronesia and Polynesia. Each has its own history but the continuing importance of tribal customs is a common feature and the influence of chiefs is still greatly respected even when they do not have actual political power. Political parties exist in most countries in Oceania, but tend to be highly volatile, with distinctions based at least as much on individuals and local group allegiances as on their policies and ideologies.

Parliament House, Canberra, Australia: This new building opened in 1988, but the federal parliament has been meeting in Canberra, the country's custom-built capital, since 1927.

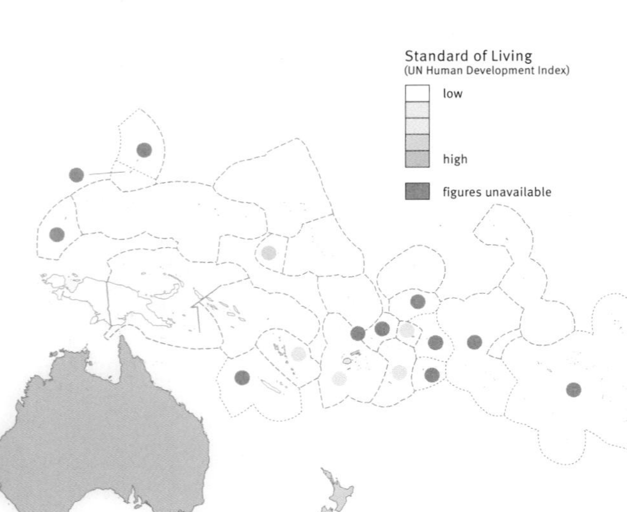

Standard of Living
(UN Human Development Index)
low
high
figures unavailable

Standard of Living

Australasia enjoys a "Western" standard of living, although unemployment and social deprivation are disproportionately high among Aborigines and Maoris, whose life expectancy is significantly below the average. Oceania has generally lower living standards, more actual poverty and more people living from subsistence farming.

Philippine Sea
Northern Mariana Islands (to US)
Mariana Islands
Saipan
Guam (to US)
HAGÅTÑA
Micronesia
Bikini Atoll
Ralik C
Yap
KOROR (OREOR)
Babeldaob
PALAU
Caroline Islands
Chuuk
Pohnpei
PALIKIR
Kosrae
MICRONESIA
Melanesia
NAURU
Equator
PAPUA NEW GUINEA
Bismarck Sea
New Ireland
Wewak
New Britain
Rabaul
New Guinea
Madang
Mount Hagen
Lae
Ubai
Arawa
Bougainville Island
Solomon Islands
Solomon Sea
Tapini
PORT MORESBY
New Georgia Islands
HONIARA
Guadalcanal
SOLOMON ISLANDS
Santa Cruz Islands
Banks Islands
VANUATU
Espiritu Santo
Malekula
Arafura Sea
Torres Strait
Coral Sea
Coral Sea Islands (to Australia)
New Caledonia (to France)
NOUMEA
Timor Sea
Darwin
Joseph Bonaparte Gulf
Arnhem Land
Katherine
Gulf of Carpentaria
Cape York Peninsula
Great Barrier Reef
Cairns
Normanton
Townsville
Wyndham
Kimberley Plateau
Derby
Broome
NORTHERN TERRITORY
Tennant Creek
Tanami Desert
Hughenden
Mount Isa
Mackay
Rockhampton
QUEENSLAND
Barcaldine
INDIAN OCEAN
Port Hedland
Great Sandy Desert
Alice Springs
Simpson Desert
Charleville
Miles
Brisbane
Toowoomba
Great Dividing Range
AUSTRALIA
Cunnamulla
Grafton
Norfolk I. (to Aus
Lord Howe Island (to Australia)
Hamersley Range
Gibson Desert
Lake Eyre North
Grey Range
Bourke
Darling
Barwon
Dubbo
Newcastle
WESTERN AUSTRALIA
SOUTH AUSTRALIA
Flinders Ranges
Wilcannia
NEW SOUTH WALES
Lake Torrens
Sydney
Wollongong
Tropic of Capricorn
Carnavon
Great Victoria Desert
Lake Everard
Lake Gairdner
Port Augusta
Campbelltown
CANBERRA
AUSTRALIAN CAPITAL TERRITORY
Mount Magnet
Ceduna
Whyalla
Murray
Wagga Wagga
Kalgoorlie
Nullarbor Plain
Great Australian Bight
Adelaide
Bendigo
Geraldton
Kangaroo Island
Horsham
VICTORIA
Ballarat
Melbourne
Tasman Sea
Mount Gambier
Geelong
Perth
Esperance
Bass Strait
Launceston
Albany
TASMANIA
Tasmania
Hobart
SOUTHERN

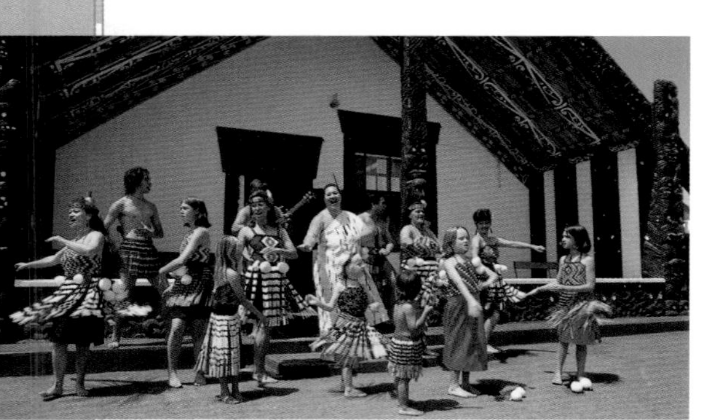

Maori meeting house, New Zealand: Maori rights are theoretically protected by the Treaty of Waitangi, although serious disputes continue.

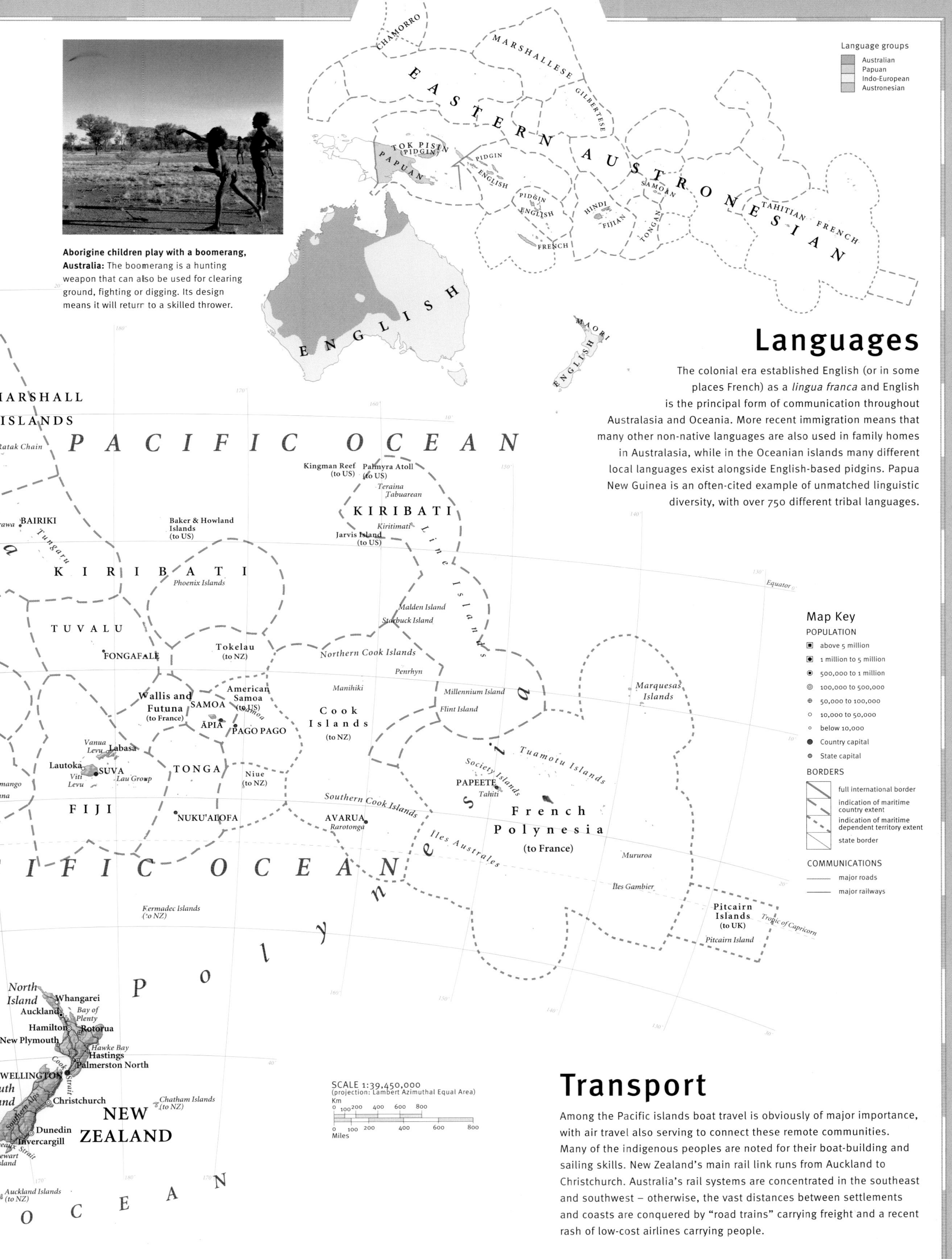
Language groups
Australian
Papuan
Indo-European
Austronesian
CHAMORRO
MARSHALLESE
GILBERTESE
EASTERN AUSTRONESIAN
TOK PISIN (PIDGIN)
PAPUAN
PIDGIN ENGLISH
PIDGIN ENGLISH
HINDI
FIJIAN
SAMOAN
TONGAN
TAHITIAN FRENCH
FRENCH
ENGLISH
MAORI
ENGLISH
MARSHALL ISLANDS
Ratak Chain
PACIFIC OCEAN
Kingman Reef (to US)
Palmyra Atoll (to US)
Teraina
Tabuarean
KIRIBATI
Kiritimati
Jarvis Island (to US)
Line Islands
BAIRIKI
Tungaru
Baker & Howland Islands (to US)
KIRIBATI
Phoenix Islands
Equator
Malden Island
Starbuck Island
TUVALU
FONGAFALE
Tokelau (to NZ)
Northern Cook Islands
Penrhyn
Manihiki
Millennium Island
Flint Island
Marquesas Islands
Wallis and Futuna (to France)
SAMOA
APIA
American Samoa (to US)
PAGO PAGO
Cook Islands (to NZ)
Vanua Levu
Labasa
Lautoka
SUVA
Viti Levu
Lau Group
TONGA
Niue (to NZ)
FIJI
NUKU'ALOFA
Southern Cook Islands
AVARUA
Rarotonga
Society Islands
PAPEETE
Tahiti
Tuamotu Islands
French Polynesia (to France)
Îles Australes
Mururoa
Îles Gambier
PACIFIC OCEAN
Kermadec Islands (to NZ)
Pitcairn Islands (to UK)
Pitcairn Island
Tropic of Capricorn
Polynesia
North Island
Whangarei
Auckland
Bay of Plenty
Hamilton
Rotorua
New Plymouth
Hawke Bay
Hastings
Palmerston North
WELLINGTON
Cook Strait
Christchurch
Southern Alps
Chatham Islands (to NZ)
NEW ZEALAND
Dunedin
Invercargill
Auckland Islands (to NZ)
OCEAN
SCALE 1:39,450,000
(projection: Lambert Azimuthal Equal Area)
Km
0 100 200 400 600 800
0 100 200 400 600 800
Miles
Map Key
POPULATION
above 5 million
1 million to 5 million
500,000 to 1 million
100,000 to 500,000
50,000 to 100,000
10,000 to 50,000
below 10,000
Country capital
State capital
BORDERS
full international border
indication of maritime country extent
indication of maritime dependent territory extent
state border
COMMUNICATIONS
major roads
major railways

Aborigine children play with a boomerang, Australia: The boomerang is a hunting weapon that can also be used for clearing ground, fighting or digging. Its design means it will return to a skilled thrower.

Languages

The colonial era established English (or in some places French) as a *lingua franca* and English is the principal form of communication throughout Australasia and Oceania. More recent immigration means that many other non-native languages are also used in family homes in Australasia, while in the Oceanian islands many different local languages exist alongside English-based pidgins. Papua New Guinea is an often-cited example of unmatched linguistic diversity, with over 750 different tribal languages.

Transport

Among the Pacific islands boat travel is obviously of major importance, with air travel also serving to connect these remote communities. Many of the indigenous peoples are noted for their boat-building and sailing skills. New Zealand's main rail link runs from Auckland to Christchurch. Australia's rail systems are concentrated in the southeast and southwest – otherwise, the vast distances between settlements and coasts are conquered by "road trains" carrying freight and a recent rash of low-cost airlines carrying people.

Ulithi Atoll, Micronesia

Blue Mountains, Australia

Marlborough, New Zealand

Great Barrier Reef, Australia

Suva, Fiji

Kangaroo road sign, Uluru-Kata Tjuta National Park, Australia: Driving across the Outback can take days in this country, comparable in size to the USA. This vast plain is punctuated by the incongruous humps of Uluru (Ayers Rock) and Kata Tjuta (the Olgas). The focus for this national park, they are of enormous ceremonial and cultural significance to Aboriginal tribes.

Journeys

Cheap internal flights are the best way to get around Australia for those wishing to see a lot in a short space of time and there are often particularly good deals for travellers on round-the-world tickets. Another good option is to travel by car or take a coach trip, following the long and varied eastern coastline from Sydney to Cairns, or even as far as the northern tip of Cape York (four-wheel drive vehicle needed). Alternatively, the coastline near Melbourne is a particularly beautiful stretch, while the long 1,600 km (1,000 mile) drive inland from Darwin to Alice Springs passes through stunning red desert. The limited rail network includes Queensland's dramatic coastal Kuranda Railway. New Zealand is a much smaller country to get around. Excellent train rides include the Trans-Alpine Express from Christchurch to Greymouth. Serene cruises tour Doubtful Sound or cross Lake Wakatipu. A great destination for hiking, New Zealand has many one-day classic trails such as the Tongarira Crossing and longer treks like the five-day Heaphy Track.

Great Australasian Journeys

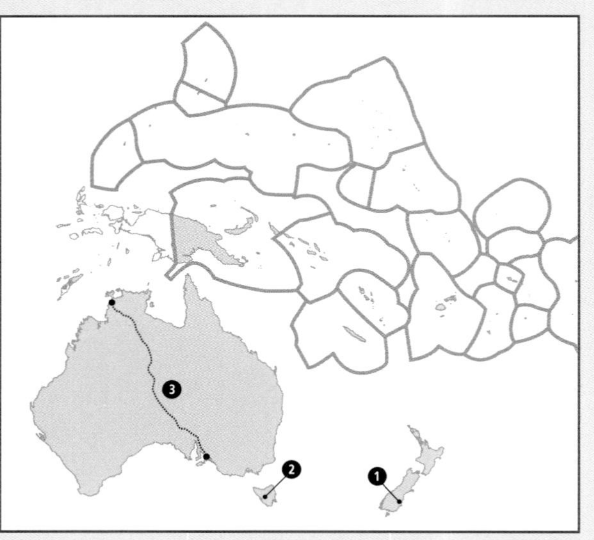

❶ Taieri Gorge Railway, New Zealand
Dunedin – Middlemarch
60 km (38 miles)
Departing from the grand, architecturally interesting Dunedin railway station, the line follows this deeply carved gorge through tunnels and over bridges and viaducts. The track penetrates the heart of South Island's mountain landscapes.

❷ Overland Track, Australia
Cradle Mountain – Lake St Clair
80 km (50 miles)
Tasmania's famous hiking trail crosses alpine moors, waterfall valleys, rainforests and buttongrass plains, through this beautiful national park. It takes five days to complete so hikers stay the night in tents or huts.

❸ The Telegraph Route, Australia
Darwin – Adelaide
3,200 km (2,000 miles)
Alice Springs grew up as a midpoint when an overland telegraph route was being planned from Adelaide to Darwin (and ultimately on to Europe). Now the car or coach journey winds through fascinating desert scenery.

Cultural Sights

Little is known of the great pre-colonial cultures of Australasia and the islands of Oceania, although there is much speculation as to their origins and the links between different groups. However, the whole region actively promotes their heritage, with fine examples of meeting houses, tribal displays and local crafts. The arrival of European settlers from the late 18th century, initially around Sydney, led to rapid and varied changes, resulting in the many dynamic cities of today, which have limited history but are pleasant places to live. Sydney has become the leading city of the continent and is an immensely attractive destination for travellers, outshining its Australian rival Melbourne. New Zealand has a more traditional flavour, with cities such as Christchurch and Dunedin harking back to English and Scottish roots.

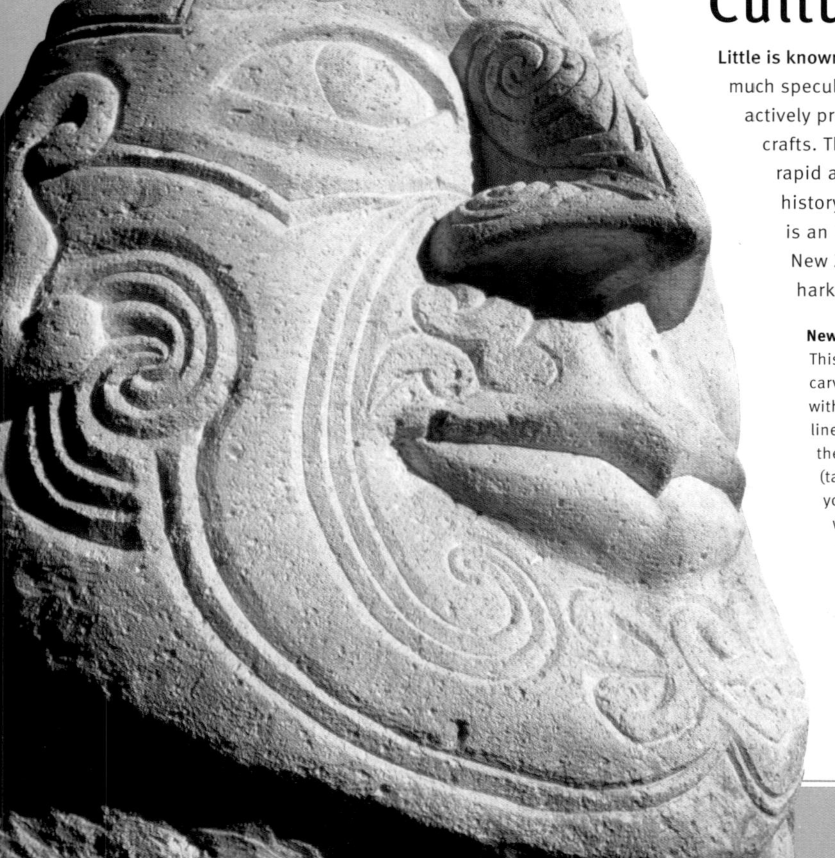

New Zealand: This Maori head is carved in white stone, with intricate curved lines representing the traditional *moko* (tattoo). Today many young Maoris still wear the *moko* with pride.

What to See

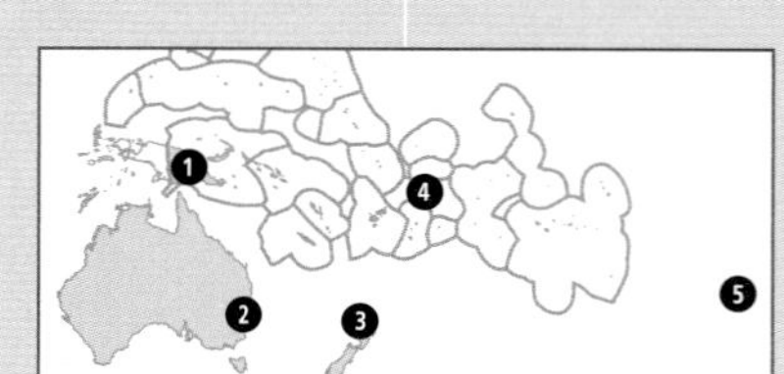

❶ Goroka, Papua New Guinea
Every September up to 40,000 painted warriors gather in a riot of colour

❷ Sydney Opera House, Australia
Its architecturally inspirational outline dominates the harbour

❸ Waitangi Meeting House, New Zealand
Learn of Maori history and their interaction with British settlers

❹ Pulemelei Mound, Samoa
Polynesia's largest ancient structure, a mysterious step pyramid in the jungle

❺ Easter Island
Ponder the cultural significance of the huge and forbidding *maui* statues

Moeraki boulders, New Zealand

Sydney, Australia

Tari, Papua New Guinea

Bungle Bungles, Australia

Tennyson Inlet, New Zealand

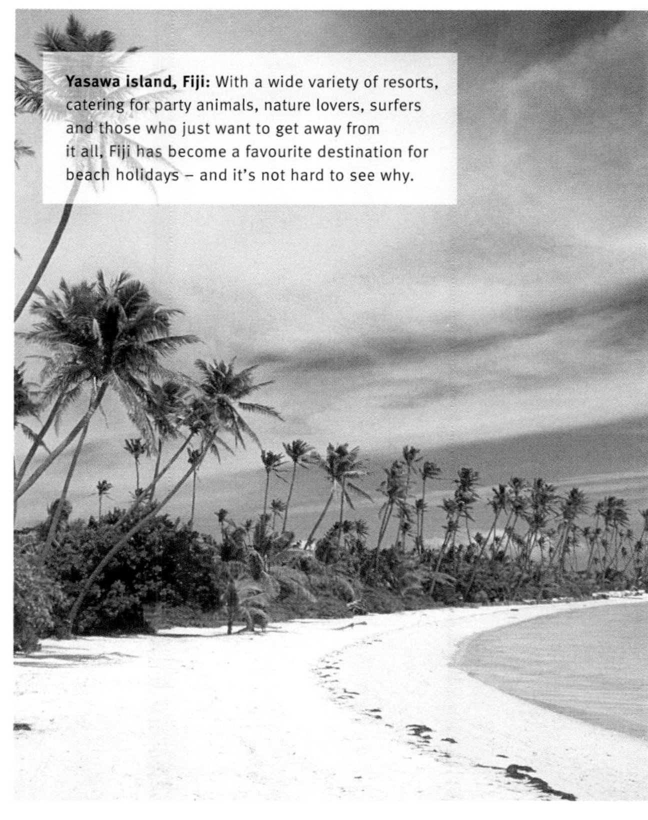
Yasawa island, Fiji: With a wide variety of resorts, catering for party animals, nature lovers, surfers and those who just want to get away from it all, Fiji has become a favourite destination for beach holidays – and it's not hard to see why.

Activities

This region has a strong claim to the title of outdoor sports centre of the world, with New Zealand especially standing out. For scuba divers, surely nowhere can rival Australia's fabulous Great Barrier Reef, with its superb opportunities for seeing a myriad of colourful fish and fascinating corals, although some access restrictions have become necessary in a bid to halt damage to the ecosystem. The chance to explore World War II wrecks off the coasts of some of the islands of the Pacific make them, too, dream destinations for the more serious diver. More generally, the whole Queensland coast is known for its water sports, while much of the rest of Australia is great for hiking and trekking on unspoiled and remote trails. New Zealand's best areas for outdoor activities are in South Island, the original home of bungee jumping and of the more recently invented sport of jetboating. Other options here include canoeing and whitewater rafting. New Zealanders also have a strong athletic tradition as runners and many beautiful areas encourage cyclists and hikers to go exploring. Australia has an unparalleled record at cricket and both Australia and New Zealand are world powers at rugby – Samoa and Fiji also compete at international level.

What to Do

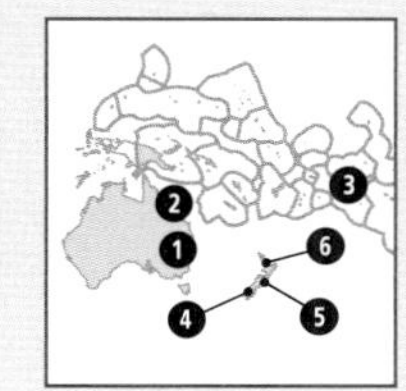

❶ **Warrumbungle Range, Australia**
Sheer cliffs and spires, a challenge for climbers

❷ **Whitsunday Islands, Australia**
Dive from a boat on the Great Barrier Reef

❸ **Cook Islands**
Gyrate your hips in the traditional dances of this Polynesian paradise

❹ **Queenstown, New Zealand**
Test your nerve at three dramatic bungee jumps, jetboating, hang-gliding and many other outdoor pursuits

❺ **Kaikoura, New Zealand**
Whale-watching capital, where sperm whales take a break on their long migrations

❻ **Waitomo Caves, New Zealand**
Abseil or raft into the cave network and see magical glowworms

Natural Sights

The natural wonders of this continent are many and varied. One can travel for hundreds of miles among great termite mounds in the Australian Outback, occasionally coming upon dramatic rock formations of which Uluru (Ayers Rock) is the most outstanding. Great national parks include Kakadu, immortalized in the filming of *Crocodile Dundee* and there are pockets of ancient virgin rainforest, such as those of northern Queensland. The Great Barrier Reef stands out as the leading attraction of the east coast, which also has many fine beaches. In New Zealand's South Island the famous fiordlands were created by the action of glaciers, of which there are still impressive examples in the high mountains. North Island is especially notable for the extensive volcanic activity of its seething mud, geysers and hot springs around Rotorua. Many of the Pacific islands still have virtually untouched beaches, often amid rocky terrain against a dramatic backdrop that testifies to their volcanic formation.

What to See

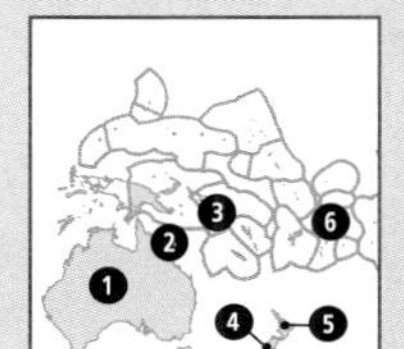

❶ **Uluru, Australia**
Gigantic red rock with spiritual meaning for the Aborigines

❷ **Great Barrier Reef**
Take a glass-bottomed boat or snorkel for a close-up view of coral and tropical fish

❸ **Rennell, Solomon Islands**
The world's largest raised coral atoll with many endemic species

❹ **Franz Josef Glacier, New Zealand**
Hike along the Waiho river to this famous glacier or go flightseeing for sweeping views

❺ **Rotorua, New Zealand**
Thermally active area with colourful pools, geysers and springs

❻ **Alofaaga Blowholes, Samoa**
Astonishing vents in the rocks that spout seawater and can toss objects high in the air

Milford Sound, New Zealand: Mitre Peak, the world's highest sea cliff, forms a dramatic landmark in the Fiordland National Park, on South Island.

Australia

Australia, the world's sixth-largest country, spans over 3,200 km (2,000 miles) north-south from the tropical rainforests of Queensland to the peaks and gorges of Tasmania. Unique marsupial mammals, including koalas and kangaroos, are attractions in their own right, along with eyecatching exotic birds. Spectacular natural features such as Uluru (Ayers Rock) stand out within the huge, arid and sparsely populated central Outback. This desert terrain holds the key to the Aboriginal people's special relationship with the land they have inhabited for millennia, powerfully reflected in their traditional art.

Most Australians live along the coast east of the Great Dividing Range, enjoying a favourable climate and within reach of magnificent beaches, even in the larger cities. Vibrant Sydney, in particular, has plenty to see and do, whether sporting, cultural or simply recreational. The Queensland coast is dominated by the Great Barrier Reef, the largest living thing on earth, attracting visitors to Cairns and similar resorts for snorkelling, diving and other outdoor activities.

What to See

1 Bungle Bungles These fragile, rounded rocks are covered with alternate bands of orange (oxide) and black (lichens and algae)

2 Kakadu National Park (near Cooinda) Beautiful wetlands, with plentiful wildlife and Aboriginal rock art, were the film location of *Crocodile Dundee*

3 Cape Tribulation Named by Captain Cook when he grounded on a coral reef here in 1770, this gorgeous coast borders an ancient Australian rainforest

4 Great Barrier Reef The world's largest reef stretches along the Queensland coast for 2,000 km (1,250 miles), offering great diving

5 Fraser Island The world's largest sand island, 120 km (75 miles) long, is ideal for swimming in the dune lakes, birdwatching or driving along the sandy tracks

6 Sydney Australia's oldest and largest city bristles with fascinating museums, galleries and varying styles of architecture

7 Alice Springs Founded for the overland telegraph line in the 1870s, a pleasant modern town set amid superb desert scenery, gorges and cliffs

8 Kings Canyon (near Hermannsburg) A spectacular gorge with steep cliffs and excellent walking trails

9 Uluru (Ayers Rock) Huge red rock rising out of the plain to a height of 340 m (1,140 ft), that changes colour at dawn and dusk. Don't climb the rock – its a spritual site for Aborigines

10 Shark Bay Where the first European landed in Australia in 1616. Now known for its fine beaches and Monkey Mia's friendly dolphins, which swim with humans and take food from the hand

11 The Pinnacles Flat sandy desert with unusual limestone pillars up to 5 m (17 ft) high (visit early in the day for best light)

12 Wave Rock (near Kondinin) Shaped like a perfect wave and 15 m (50 ft) high, but solid and multicoloured, with Aboriginal rock art and a wildlife sanctuary

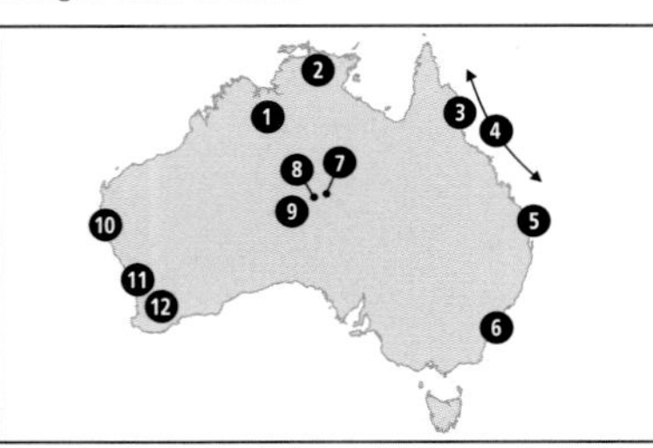

Sydney Opera House: One of the world's truly distinctive buildings, whose dramatic roof design is said to have come to architect Jørn Utzon while peeling an orange.

172

INDIAN OCEAN
WESTERN AUSTRALIA
Great Sandy Desert
Little Sandy Desert
Gibson Desert
Cape Londonderry
Cape Bougainville
Kalumburu
Bigge Island
Bonaparte Archipelago
Heywood Islands
Adele Island
Mount Hann 779m
Collier Bay
King Sound
Lombadina
Derby
Kimberley Plateau
King Leopold Range
Fitzroy Crossing
Fitzroy River
Broome
Eighty Mile Beach
De Grey River
Port Hedland
Dampier Archipelago
Dampier
Karratha
Wickham
Roebourne
Whim Creek
Marble Bar
Barrow Island
Fortescue River
Percival Lakes
Lake Dora
Lake Auld
Onslow
Wittenoom
North West Cape
Exmouth
Exmouth Gulf
Learmonth
Hamersley Range
Ashburton River
Tom Price
Mount Meharry 1251m
Paraburdoo
Newman
Lake Disappointment
Kenneth Range
Barlee Range
Coral Bay
Mount Augustus 1105m
Kumarina Roadhouse
Minilya
Tropic of Capricorn
Lake Macleod
Waldburg Range
Carnarvon Range
Gascoyne River
Gascoyne Junction
Carnarvon
Bernier Island
Dorre Island
Shark Bay
Lake Gregory
Lake Carnegie
Robinson Range
Wiluna
Lake Way
Lake Wells
Denham
Dirk Hartog Island
Meekatharra
Lake Annean
Murchison River
Lake Throssell
Lake Yeo
Lake Austin
Kalbarri
Mount Magnet
Leonara
Lake Carey
Yalgoo
Lake Ballard
Lake Barlee
Geraldton
Mongers Lake
Menzies
Lake Rebecca
Lake Moore
Wubin
Pithara
Kalgoorlie
Coolgardie
Kambalda
Kitchener
Moora
The Pinnacles
Southern Cross
Lake Lefroy
Lake Cowan
Merredin
Gingin
Wanneroo
Northam
York
Lake Johnston
Norseman
Balladonia
Perth
Fremantle
Rockingham
Mandurah
Kondinin
Lake Dundas
Brookton
Lake Hope
Lake King
Narrogin
Tower Peak 594m
Ravensthorpe
Esperance
Wagin
Katanning
Bunbury
Collie
Busselton
Bridgetown
Manjimup
Stirling Range
Margaret River
Cape Leeuwin
Augusta
Pemberton
Mount Barker
Albany

172

194

Activities

Scuba dive at the **Great Barrier Reef**	Lollop through the desert near **Alice Springs** on a camel
Learn building skills from termites, whose mounds stretch 1,600 km (1,000 miles) south from Darwin	Join the surfers at Sydney's **Bondi Beach**
	See an opera at **Sydney Opera House**
Have a laugh at the **Henley-on-Todd Regatta,** as men race bottomless boats along a dry river deep in the Outback	Sunbathe on **Cable Beach,** Australia, by the crystal waters of the Indian Ocean

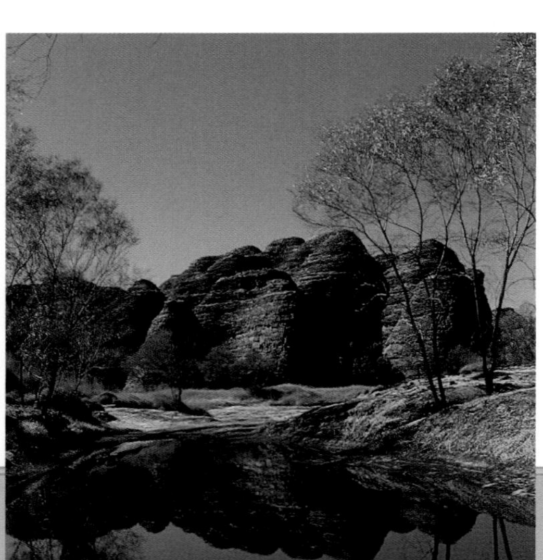

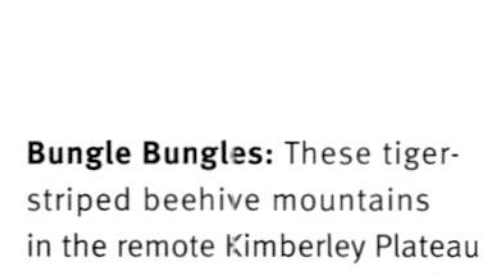

Bungle Bungles: These tiger-striped beehive mountains in the remote Kimberley Plateau region are large, weathered sandstone and conglomerate domes, set amid stunning gorges and pools.

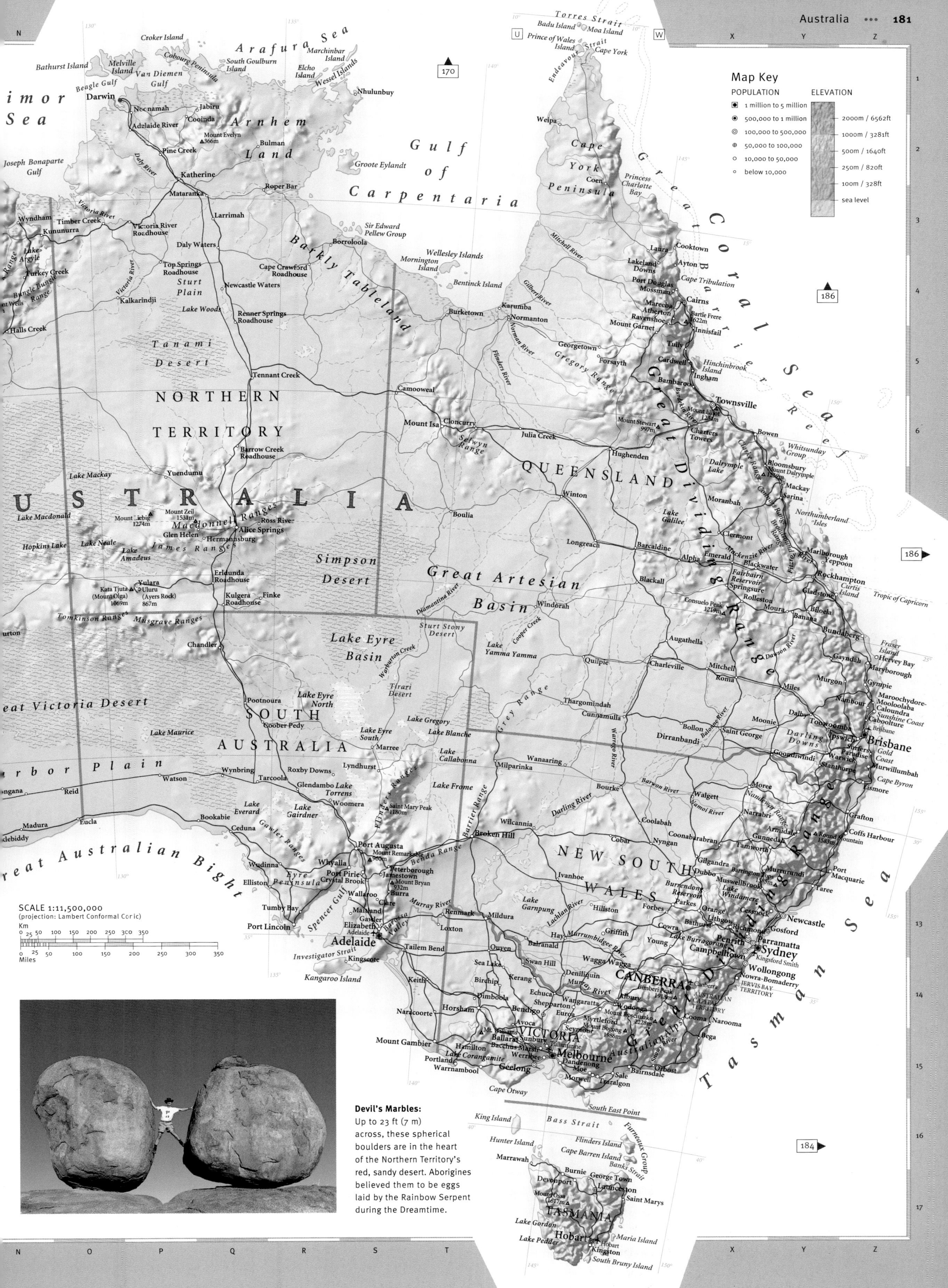
Map Key
POPULATION
1 million to 5 million
500,000 to 1 million
100,000 to 500,000
50,000 to 100,000
10,000 to 50,000
below 10,000
ELEVATION
2000m / 6562ft
1000m / 3281ft
500m / 1640ft
250m / 820ft
100m / 328ft
sea level
SCALE 1:11,500,000
(projection: Lambert Conformal Conic)
Km
Miles
AUSTRALIA
NORTHERN TERRITORY
QUEENSLAND
SOUTH AUSTRALIA
NEW SOUTH WALES
VICTORIA
TASMANIA
CANBERRA
AUSTRALIAN CAPITAL TERRITORY
JERVIS BAY TERRITORY
Arafura Sea
Timor Sea
Gulf of Carpentaria
Coral Sea
Tasman Sea
Great Australian Bight
Bass Strait
Torres Strait
Great Barrier Reef
Great Dividing Range
Great Artesian Basin
Simpson Desert
Tanami Desert
Great Victoria Desert
Nullarbor Plain
Lake Eyre Basin
Barkly Tableland
Arnhem Land
Cape York Peninsula
Darwin
Katherine
Tennant Creek
Alice Springs
Cairns
Townsville
Mackay
Rockhampton
Brisbane
Sydney
Newcastle
Wollongong
Melbourne
Geelong
Adelaide
Port Augusta
Hobart
Launceston
Broken Hill
Mount Isa
Devonport
Kangaroo Island
King Island
Flinders Island
Tropic of Capricorn
170
186
184

Devil's Marbles: Up to 23 ft (7 m) across, these spherical boulders are in the heart of the Northern Territory's red, sandy desert. Aborigines believed them to be eggs laid by the Rainbow Serpent during the Dreamtime.

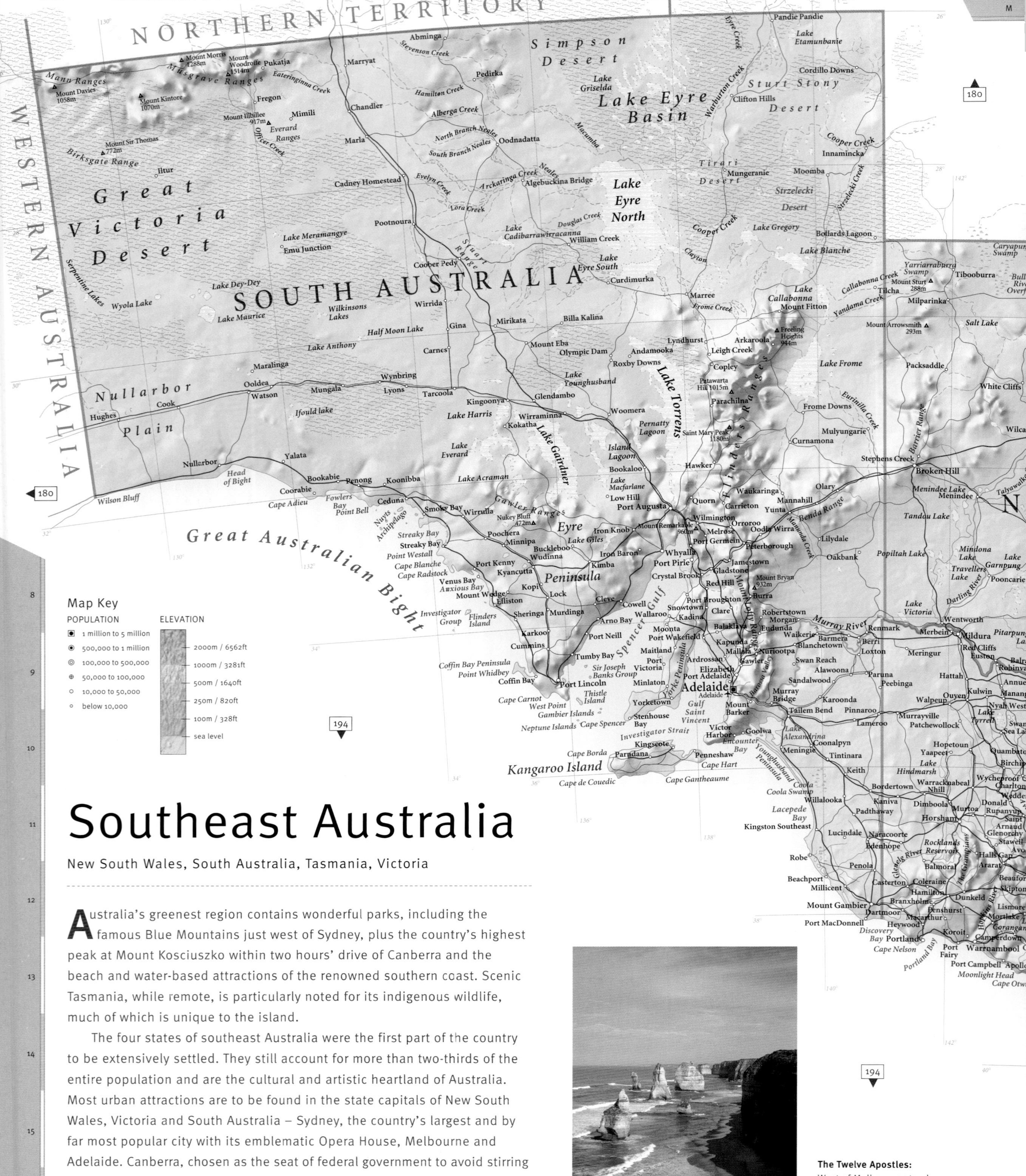
NORTHERN TERRITORY
WESTERN AUSTRALIA
SOUTH AUSTRALIA
Great Victoria Desert
Simpson Desert
Lake Eyre Basin
Sturt Stony Desert
Tirari Desert
Strzelecki Desert
Lake Eyre North
Lake Eyre South
Lake Torrens
Lake Gairdner
Lake Frome
Nullarbor Plain
Great Australian Bight
Eyre Peninsula
Spencer Gulf
Gulf Saint Vincent
Investigator Strait
Kangaroo Island
Flinders Ranges
Mount Lofty Ranges
Gawler Ranges
Musgrave Ranges
Mann Ranges
Stuart Range
Barrier Range
Murray River
Darling River
Coober Pedy
Marla
Oodnadatta
Woomera
Port Augusta
Whyalla
Port Pirie
Port Lincoln
Ceduna
Adelaide
Mount Gambier
Broken Hill
Mildura
Renmark
Murray Bridge
Victor Harbor
Kingston Southeast
Robe
Naracoorte
Portland
Warrnambool
Moonlight Head
Cape Otway
180
194
Map Key
POPULATION
1 million to 5 million
500,000 to 1 million
100,000 to 500,000
50,000 to 100,000
10,000 to 50,000
below 10,000
ELEVATION
2000m / 6562ft
1000m / 3281ft
500m / 1640ft
250m / 820ft
100m / 328ft
sea level

Southeast Australia

New South Wales, South Australia, Tasmania, Victoria

Australia's greenest region contains wonderful parks, including the famous Blue Mountains just west of Sydney, plus the country's highest peak at Mount Kosciuszko within two hours' drive of Canberra and the beach and water-based attractions of the renowned southern coast. Scenic Tasmania, while remote, is particularly noted for its indigenous wildlife, much of which is unique to the island.

The four states of southeast Australia were the first part of the country to be extensively settled. They still account for more than two-thirds of the entire population and are the cultural and artistic heartland of Australia. Most urban attractions are to be found in the state capitals of New South Wales, Victoria and South Australia – Sydney, the country's largest and by far most popular city with its emblematic Opera House, Melbourne and Adelaide. Canberra, chosen as the seat of federal government to avoid stirring up the Sydney–Melbourne rivalry, is one of the few urban centres not on the coast, although it has splendid scenery to compensate. Brisbane offers lively nightlife and a stopping-off point en route to the Great Barrier Reef. Typically modern, well-planned and clean, these cities – with the exception of Sydney – are viewed by many visitors as the gateway to the surrounding natural wonders and the multitude of outdoor activities on offer in Australia.

The Twelve Apostles: West of Melbourne stand 12 eroded limestone formations guarding the southern coast. Victoria's beautiful stretch of cliffs and beaches is thought by many to be Australia's finest coastline and Bells Beach holds an international surfing competition each Easter.

Blessing of the Fleet, Sydney: This annual festival held at Darling Harbour on Labour Day weekend is especially popular among Sydney's Italian community. Brightly decorated fishing boats are blessed for their life at sea and revellers dress in flamboyant fancy dress.

SCALE 1:6,000,000
(projection: Lambert Conformal Conic)

Activities

- Sample the delights of the **Hunter Valley** wineries, 100 km (60 miles) north of Sydney
- Walk the **Overland Track** from Tasmania's Cradle Mountain
- Watch for southern right whales at **Logans Beach**, Melbourne
- Ski on **Mount Hotham**, Victoria, for some of Australia's best snow (June–September)
- Take a boat ride in **Sydney's** large natural harbour
- Go whitewater rafting on the **Snowy River**, east Victoria
- Surf on **Sydney's** Maroubra and Narrabeen beaches
- Spot eastern grey kangaroos in the **Blue Mountains**, northwest of Sydney
- See the world's top-class Formula One drivers compete at the Australian Grand Prix, **Melbourne** (March)

184 ▶

Parliament House, Canberra: Opened in 1988, Australia's political headquarters has a gleaming and distinctive exterior with an Aboriginal mosaic on the forecourt and an entrance foyer of grey-green marble pillars, representing a eucalyptus forest. "Canberra" derives from the Aboriginal word for meeting place.

What to See

Sydney *see* pp180–181

❶ Flinders Ranges
South Australia's scenic mountain range has several species of colourful parrots among its birdlife

❷ Adelaide
Conservative and relaxed city, with lots of green parkland and naturally enclosed by sea and mountains

❸ Kangaroo Island
Australia's third-largest island has kangaroos, koalas, wallabies and fairy penguins, as well as fascinating scenery, such as the bizarre Remarkable Rocks

❹ The Twelve Apostles
(near Port Campbell) Huge stone pillars lying a short way from the cliffs, on the awe-inspiring Great Ocean Road heading west from Melbourne

❺ Goldfields Tourist Route
From Ballarat, this takes in the 19th-century gold rush centres, including the reconstructed gold-mining town Sovereign Hill and its fascinating Gold Museum

❻ Melbourne
Australia's clean and modern second city abounds with startling architecture. However, to understand its roots visit the old gaol and penal museum

❼ Cradle Mountain
Tasmania's best-known national park is a feast of spectacular mountain peaks, gorges and lakes, great for seeing wildlife and for easily accessible hiking, centred around Mount Ossa

❽ Snowy Mountains
Dramatic mountains, popular for skiing in the winter, hiking in summer and noted for the range of wild flowers and the highest peak, Mount Kosciuszko

❾ Canberra
Australia's compromise choice capital, between rivals Sydney and Melbourne, is a product of the 20th century, with a carefully planned, immaculate centre around an artificial lake

❿ Blue Mountains
Named for the blue haze of oil given off by eucalyptus trees, the magnificent bushwalks, gorges and cliffs are a good place to ride and to see wildlife such as eastern grey kangaroos

⓫ Bondi Beach
A crescent-shaped beach of golden sand, a mecca for sun-seekers and surfers in search of the perfect wave. Or try inline skating on the promenade past the trendy seafront cafés

⓬ Brisbane
Scenic Queensland city built on a meandering river, known for its lively nightlife, fine squares, skyscrapers and bridges

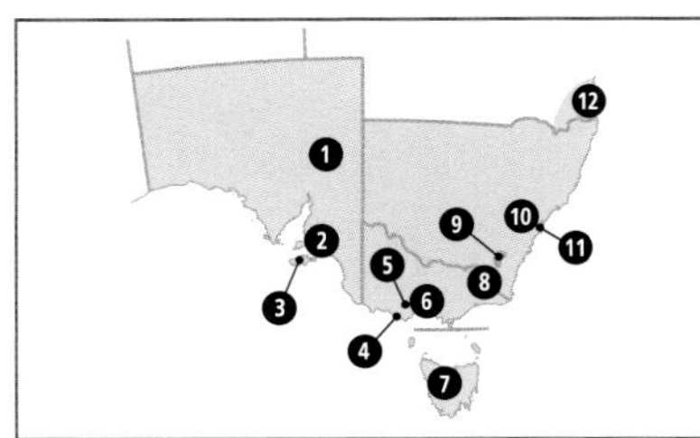

New Zealand

A country for the open-air enthusiast, from the endless beaches of the subtropical north to the rocky inlets of Fiordland in the far southwest, New Zealand can also inspire its visitors with the unforgettable sight of great whales offshore, introduce them to its unique flightless birds and other unusual wildlife and leave them pondering the place of the indigenous Maori people and their particular cultural heritage in its contemporary society.

Auckland, the largest city, has a lively atmosphere and a modern feel, as does the capital, Wellington, both on the volcanic North Island, whose extensive thermal activity is best seen at Rotorua. By contrast the country's strong historic ties with Britain are more in evidence in Christchurch and quieter Dunedin on South Island, which is dominated by the great glaciers of the Southern Alps.

Despite its small population, New Zealand is a sporting force to be reckoned with. The national rugby union team, the All Blacks, is renowned worldwide. Cricket is played during the summer months coinciding with the main tourist season, so visitors can plan an itinerary that takes in an international match. Those who prefer more instant thrills head instead for the Queenstown area in the Southern Alps, famed for its hair-raising bungee jumps, tandem skydiving, whitewater rafting and the New Zealand speciality of jetboating, which involves racing at breakneck speeds down river gorges.

Activities

- Search for traces of the *Lord of the Rings* film trilogy – made on location nationwide
- Boogie board down the steep dunes of **Ninety Mile Beach**, tip of North Island
- Hike the **Tongariro Crossing**, near Lake Taupo, over volcanic terrain, and past hot springs and craters
- Experience the ethereal light of the glowworms in **Waitomo Caves**, North Island – the blackwater rafting is optional
- Watch the All Blacks play rugby in **Auckland**, starting each match with their intimidating traditional song and dance – the *haka*
- Marvel at enormous sperm whales resting between dives at **Kaikoura**, South Island
- Trek the **Routeburn Track** 33 km (20 miles) through forested valleys rich in wildlife and waterfalls – Lake Wakatipu, South Island
- Bungee jump 134 m (450 ft) at **Nevis Highwire Bungee**, near Queenstown

Maori Meeting House, Waitangi: The meeting house, decorated with characteristic Maori wall carvings, was erected in the Waitangi Treaty Grounds in 1940. This marked the centenary of the agreement central to Maori rights campaigns today, whereby the British established their sovereignty in exchange for a promise to respect Maori land ownership.

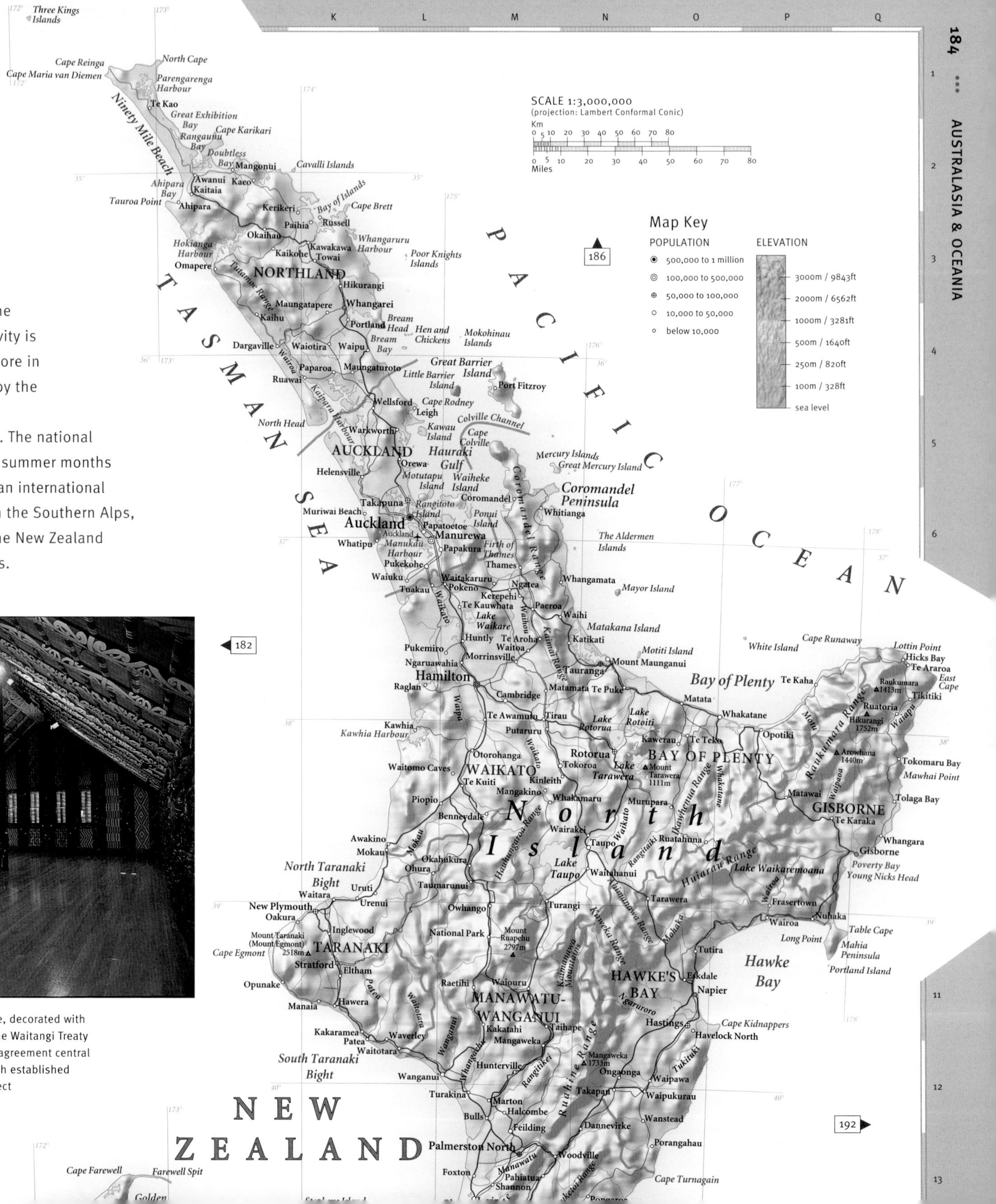

SCALE 1:3,000,000
(projection: Lambert Conformal Conic)

Map Key

POPULATION
- 500,000 to 1 million
- 100,000 to 500,000
- 50,000 to 100,000
- 10,000 to 50,000
- below 10,000

ELEVATION
- 3000m / 9843ft
- 2000m / 6562ft
- 1000m / 3281ft
- 500m / 1640ft
- 250m / 820ft
- 100m / 328ft
- sea level

186
182
192

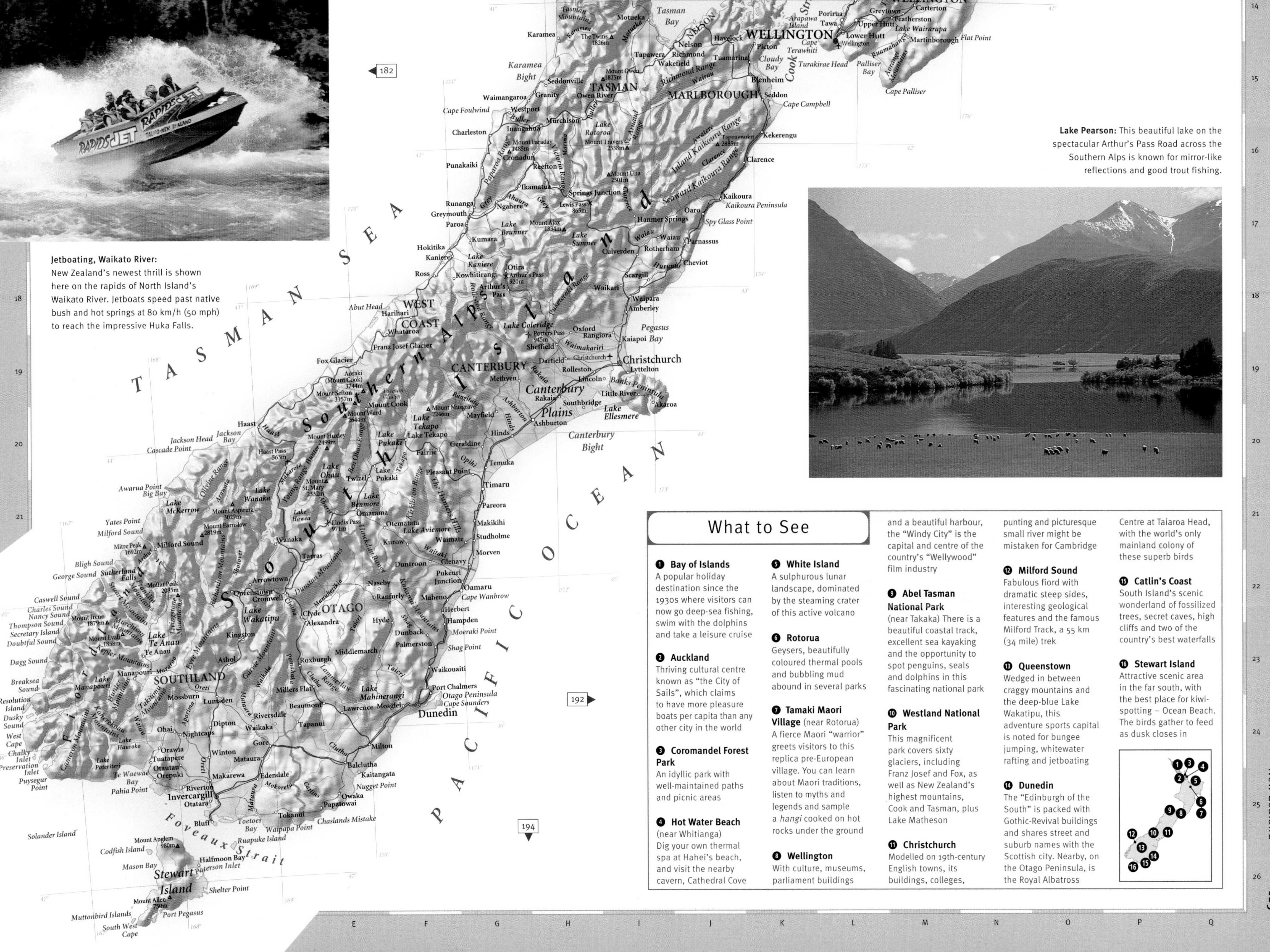
TASMAN SEA
PACIFIC OCEAN
South Island
Southern Alps
WELLINGTON
Wellington
NELSON
Nelson
TASMAN
MARLBOROUGH
WEST COAST
CANTERBURY
OTAGO
SOUTHLAND
Christchurch
Dunedin
Invercargill
Blenheim
Picton
Kaikoura
Greymouth
Hokitika
Westport
Timaru
Oamaru
Queenstown
Cromwell
Arrowtown
Wanaka
Te Anau
Milford Sound
Fiordland
Stewart Island
Foveaux Strait
Cook Strait
Canterbury Plains
Canterbury Bight
Banks Peninsula
Otago Peninsula
Lake Wakatipu
Lake Te Anau
Lake Manapouri
Lake Wanaka
Lake Tekapo
Lake Pukaki
Lake Ohau
Lake Ellesmere
Aoraki (Mount Cook) 3744m
Mount Aspiring 3027m
Arthur's Pass 920m
Haast Pass 563m
Lewis Pass 865m
Franz Josef Glacier
Fox Glacier
Cape Foulwind
Cape Campbell
Cape Palliser
Karamea Bight
Tasman Bay
Pegasus Bay
Solander Island
Codfish Island
Muttonbird Islands
South West Cape
Puysegur Point
Slope Point
Nugget Point
Chaslands Mistake
Waipapa Point

182

192

194

Jetboating, Waikato River: New Zealand's newest thrill is shown here on the rapids of North Island's Waikato River. Jetboats speed past native bush and hot springs at 80 km/h (50 mph) to reach the impressive Huka Falls.

Lake Pearson: This beautiful lake on the spectacular Arthur's Pass Road across the Southern Alps is known for mirror-like reflections and good trout fishing.

What to See

❶ Bay of Islands
A popular holiday destination since the 1930s where visitors can now go deep-sea fishing, swim with the dolphins and take a leisure cruise

❷ Auckland
Thriving cultural centre known as "the City of Sails", which claims to have more pleasure boats per capita than any other city in the world

❸ Coromandel Forest Park
An idyllic park with well-maintained paths and picnic areas

❹ Hot Water Beach (near Whitianga)
Dig your own thermal spa at Hahei's beach, and visit the nearby cavern, Cathedral Cove

❺ White Island
A sulphurous lunar landscape, dominated by the steaming crater of this active volcano

❻ Rotorua
Geysers, beautifully coloured thermal pools and bubbling mud abound in several parks

❼ Tamaki Maori Village (near Rotorua)
A fierce Maori "warrior" greets visitors to this replica pre-European village. You can learn about Maori traditions, listen to myths and legends and sample a *hangi* cooked on hot rocks under the ground

❽ Wellington
With culture, museums, parliament buildings and a beautiful harbour, the "Windy City" is the capital and centre of the country's "Wellywood" film industry

❾ Abel Tasman National Park
(near Takaka) There is a beautiful coastal track, excellent sea kayaking and the opportunity to spot penguins, seals and dolphins in this fascinating national park

❿ Westland National Park
This magnificent park covers sixty glaciers, including Franz Josef and Fox, as well as New Zealand's highest mountains, Cook and Tasman, plus Lake Matheson

⓫ Christchurch
Modelled on 19th-century English towns, its buildings, colleges, punting and picturesque small river might be mistaken for Cambridge

⓬ Milford Sound
Fabulous fiord with dramatic steep sides, interesting geological features and the famous Milford Track, a 55 km (34 mile) trek

⓭ Queenstown
Wedged in between craggy mountains and the deep-blue Lake Wakatipu, this adventure sports capital is noted for bungee jumping, whitewater rafting and jetboating

⓮ Dunedin
The "Edinburgh of the South" is packed with Gothic-Revival buildings and shares street and suburb names with the Scottish city. Nearby, on the Otago Peninsula, is the Royal Albatross Centre at Taiaroa Head, with the world's only mainland colony of these superb birds

⓯ Catlin's Coast
South Island's scenic wonderland of fossilized trees, secret caves, high cliffs and two of the country's best waterfalls

⓰ Stewart Island
Attractive scenic area in the far south, with the best place for kiwi-spotting – Ocean Beach. The birds gather to feed as dusk closes in

Melanesia

Papua New Guinea, Fiji, Solomon Islands, Vanuatu, *New Caledonia* (to France)

The differing, vibrant cultures and traditional village way of life make each island in Melanesia a unique experience for the visitor. With landscape ranging from tropical rainforests to sandy beaches, black volcanic rock formations, coral reefs and cave networks, the region is brimming with the sights and sounds of abundant vegetation and wildlife.

On the front line of the Pacific conflict during World War II, many islands have reminders of the carnage – wrecks of ships lie abandoned at the bottom of bays and crashed aeroplanes rust amid the rainforests.

Tribal traditions are still alive throughout the region and locals celebrate many colourful ceremonies and gatherings – from Fiji's fire-walking to New Ireland's shark-calling. Many areas of Melanesia are relatively undeveloped for tourism and as a result offer an attractive combination of seclusion and genuine friendliness from locals.

188
170
180

PACIFIC OCEAN
Bismarck Archipelago
Bismarck Sea
New Guinea
PAPUA NEW GUINEA
INDONESIA
AUSTRALIA
Solomon Sea
Coral Sea
Gulf of Papua
Torres Strait
Solomon Islands
SANDAUN
EAST SEPIK
MADANG
ENGA
WESTERN HIGHLANDS
SOUTHERN HIGHLANDS
EASTERN HIGHLANDS
CHIMBU
MOROBE
WESTERN
GULF
CENTRAL
NORTHERN
NATIONAL CAPITAL DISTRICT
MILNE BAY
PORT MORESBY
MANUS
NEW IRELAND
WEST NEW BRITAIN
EAST NEW BRITAIN
NORTH SOLOMONS
Bougainville Island
ISABEL
WESTERN
CENTRAL
HONIARA
Guadalcanal
New Georgia Islands
Louisiade Archipelago
D'Entrecasteaux Islands
Admiralty Islands
New Ireland
New Britain

Activities

Trek to the wreck at **Loloata**, near Port Moresby, one of the region's numerous crashed World War II planes
Savour **New Caledonia**'s traditional *bougna* – a festival dish of yam, taro and lobster baked in banana leaves
Whale watch off **Fiji** or **New Caledonia**, July–September
Mingle with thousands of painted warriors at the annual tribal gathering in **Goroka**, Papua New Guinea
Listen to Fijian serenades while sipping cocktails on the evening sugar train to **Sigatoka**
Get hitched in paradise. Many island resorts in **Vanuatu** specialize in wedding and honeymoon packages
Keep dry and admire the vividly coloured fish, shark and phosphoric coral in **Nouméa's** renowned aquarium

Spirit House (*Haus Tambaran*) in Tungimbit, Papua New Guinea: Spirit houses – where the initiated men of the tribe gather – are the focal point of villages throughout Papua New Guinea. The houses are decorated inside and out with high-quality wood-carving and masks representing the tribe's ancestors are mounted in the roof beams.

Map Key

POPULATION

◎ 100,000 to 500,000
⊕ 50,000 to 100,000
○ 10,000 to 50,000
◦ below 10,000

ELEVATION

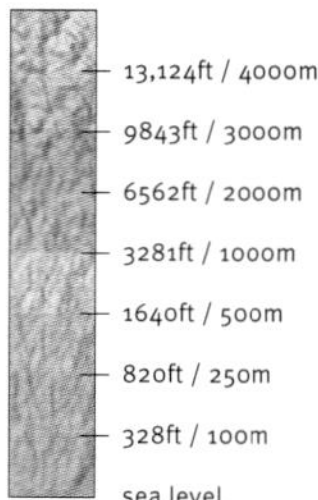
13,124ft / 4000m
9843ft / 3000m
6562ft / 2000m
3281ft / 1000m
1640ft / 500m
820ft / 250m
328ft / 100m
sea level

Huli Wigmen of Tari Valley, Papua New Guinea: One of the many tribes that inhabit secluded and remote valleys, seen here at the Sing Sing day in Sogeri in the jungle highlands near Port Moresby. Tribes from the surrounding areas come together, dressed in full, brightly coloured tribal costume for this annual competition of song and dance.

What to See

❶ Sepik River
Cuts through the heart of dense jungle, rich in varied birdlife, and lined with villages where traditional crafts flourish

❷ Mendi Valley
Cave paintings are set in a dramatic landscape inhabited by friendly tribes in lavish costume

❸ Mount Wilhelm
Papua New Guinea's highest peak is the focus of several challenging guided trekking tours

❹ Ohu Butterfly Farm
(near Madang) Rare and exquisite butterflies flutter through verdant mountainside rainforest with magnificent views

❺ Milne Bay
This site of a decisive World War II battle is ideal for snorkelling, fishing and finding uninhabited islands

❻ Savo
(near Honiara) A tiny volcanic island where megapode birds lay their eggs on scorching black volcanic sand

❼ East Rennell
The world's largest raised coral atoll is a World Heritage Site with many endemic species

❽ Vanuatu
Rugged scenery with pristine beaches, hot springs, corals and lovely lagoons

❾ Nouméa
A bustling French café atmosphere, elegant colonial buildings and lively nightlife

❿ Blue River Provincial Park
(near Yaté) Shady forest paths lead you through a land of giant trees, swimming holes, waterfalls and parakeets

⓫ Île des Pins
Beaches of powdered coral surround a landscape of densely forested volcanic rock and raised coral reef

⓬ Mamanuca Group
Collection of tiny holiday islands, to the west of Viti Levu. It is most famous for the minute party island of Beachcomber where you can dance by night and water-ski by day

⓭ Sigatoka Valley and Dunes
(near Korolevu) Fiji's "fruit and vegetable bowl" has 3,500-year-old remains and ancient cannibal villages

⓮ Tavuni Hill
(near Korolevu) This Tongan fort features a killing stone and 200-year-old ruined temple

⓯ Nadi
Highlights are the bright, finely carved Sri Siva-Subramaniya Temple and the idyllic "Sleeping Giant" orchid gardens

⓰ Viti Levu Highlands
Traditional village life remains intact, off the beaten track, in lesser-known inland Fiji

⓱ Suva
Fiji's multicultural capital with diverse religious buildings and a bustling, characterful market

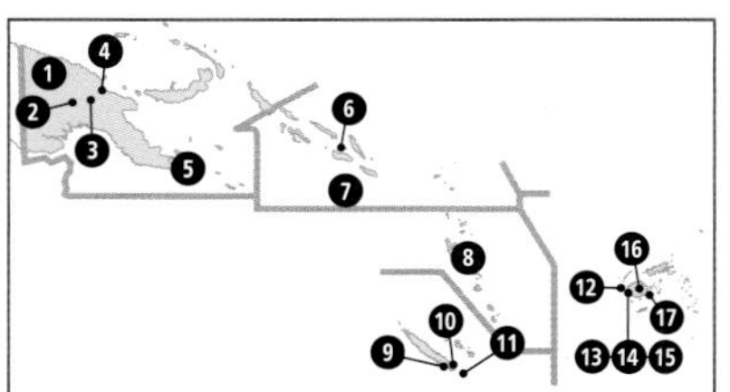

Viti Levu, Fiji: Lapped by turquoise waves, the beaches of Fiji's coral coast are covered with fine, white, powdery sand. Luxurious resorts nestle in coconut plantations and welcome tourists for a stay in a beach-front *bure*, a traditional thatched hut.

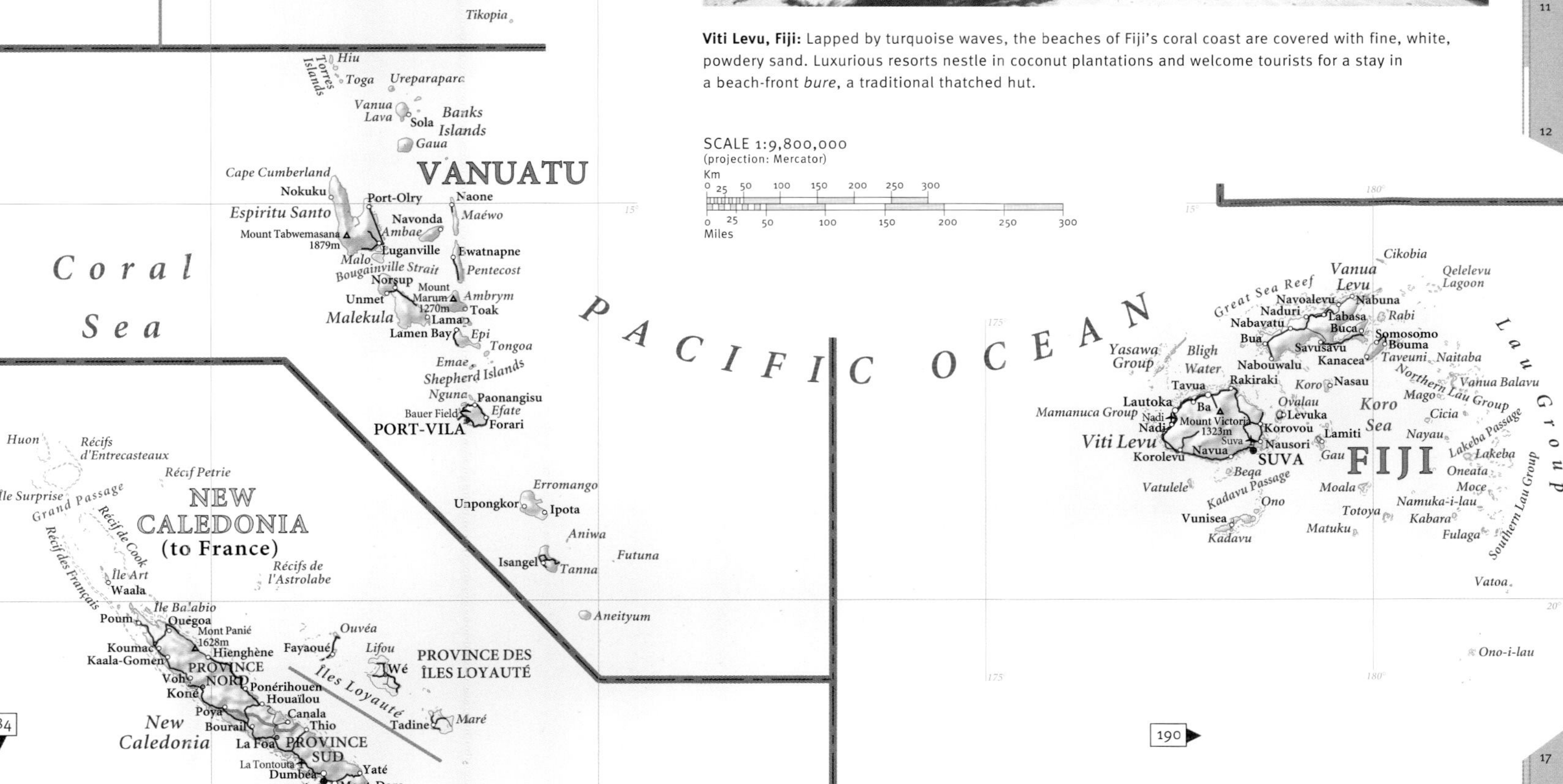
SOLOMON ISLANDS
MALAITA
Sikaiana
Ulawa Island
Three Sisters Islands
Kirakira
San Cristobal
Star Harbour
MAKIRA
Tinakula
Reef Islands
Duff Islands
TEMOTU
Nendö
Lata
Noka
Santa Cruz Islands
Utupua
Vanikolo
Anuta
Fatutaka
Tikopia
Hiu
Torres Islands
Toga
Ureparapara
Vanua Lava
Sola
Banks Islands
Gaua
VANUATU
Cape Cumberland
Nokuku
Port-Olry
Naone
Espiritu Santo
Navonda
Maéwo
Mount Tabwemasana 1879m
Ambae
Malo
Luganville
Ewatnapne
Bougainville Strait
Pentecost
Norsup
Unmet
Mount Marum 1270m
Ambrym
Toak
Malekula
Lamap
Lamen Bay
Epi
Tongoa
Emae
Shepherd Islands
Nguna
Paonangisu
Bauer Field
Efate
Forari
PORT-VILA
Erromango
Unpongkor
Ipota
Aniwa
Futuna
Isangel
Tanna
Aneityum
Coral Sea
PACIFIC OCEAN
Huon
Récifs d'Entrecasteaux
Récif Petrie
Île Surprise
Grand Passage
NEW CALEDONIA (to France)
Récif de Cook
Récif des Français
Île Art
Waala
Récifs de l'Astrolabe
Île Balabio
Pouin
Ouégoa
Mont Panié 1628m
Hienghène
Koumac
Kaala-Gomen
PROVINCE NORD
Voh
Koné
Ponérihouen
Houaïlou
Poya
Canala
Bourail
Thio
New Caledonia
La Foa
PROVINCE SUD
La Tontouta
Dumbéa
Yaté
NOUMÉA
Mont-Dore
Vao
Île des Pins
Grand Récif Sud
Ouvéa
Fayaoué
Lifou
Wé
Îles Loyauté
PROVINCE DES ÎLES LOYAUTÉ
Tadine
Maré
Île Walpole
SCALE 1:9,800,000
(projection: Mercator)
Km
Miles
0 25 50 100 150 200 250 300
Cikobia
Qelelevu Lagoon
Vanua Levu
Great Sea Reef
Navoalevu
Nabuna
Naduri
Labasa
Rabi
Nabavatu
Buca
Somosomo
Bua
Savusavu
Bouma
Yasawa Group
Bligh Water
Nabouwalu
Kanacea
Taveuni
Naitaba
Rakiraki
Northern Lau Group
Vanua Balavu
Tavua
Koro
Nasau
Mago
Lautoka
Ba
Ovalau
Koro Sea
Cicia
Mamanuca Group
Nadi
Mount Victoria 1323m
Levuka
Korovou
Lamiti
Nayau
Lakeba Passage
Viti Levu
Suva
Nausori
Navua
Korolevu
SUVA
Gau
FIJI
Lakeba
Lau Group
Beqa
Oneata
Vatulele
Kadavu Passage
Moala
Moce
Ono
Totoya
Namuka-i-lau
Vunisea
Matuku
Kabara
Kadavu
Fulaga
Southern Lau Group
Vatoa
Ono-i-lau

188
190
184
190

Micronesia

Marshall Islands, Micronesia, Nauru, Palau, Guam, Northern Mariana Islands, Wake Island

The Micronesian islands lie in the western reaches of the Pacific Ocean and are all part of the same volcanic zone. The Federated States of Micronesia is the largest group, with more than 600 atolls and forested volcanic islands across an area of 2,900 sq km (1,120 sq miles).

Visitors come to get away from it all on remote, unspoiled atolls and islands, with white sandy beaches, volcanic scenery and excellent diving, enhanced by the presence of many wrecks from World War II. It is these same features – isolation and a lack of infrastructure and resources – that have led many of the region's inhabitants to emigrate, drawn to New Zealand and Australia by the prospect of a westernized lifestyle.

Palau

Babeldaob is a densely jungled, volcanic island with fine beaches and mangrove forests. Beliliou, scene of bloody Pacific War battles, has world-class dive locations and, like the Rock Islands, an amazing variety of marine life.

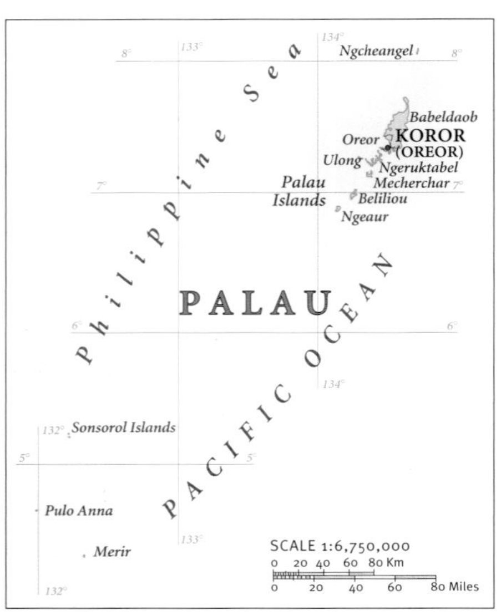

Philippine Sea
Ngcheangel
Babeldaob
Oreor
KOROR (OREOR)
Ulong
Ngeruktabel
Mecherchar
Palau Islands
Beliliou
Ngeaur
PALAU
PACIFIC OCEAN
Sonsorol Islands
Pulo Anna
Merir
SCALE 1:6,750,000
0 20 40 60 80 Km
0 20 40 60 80 Miles

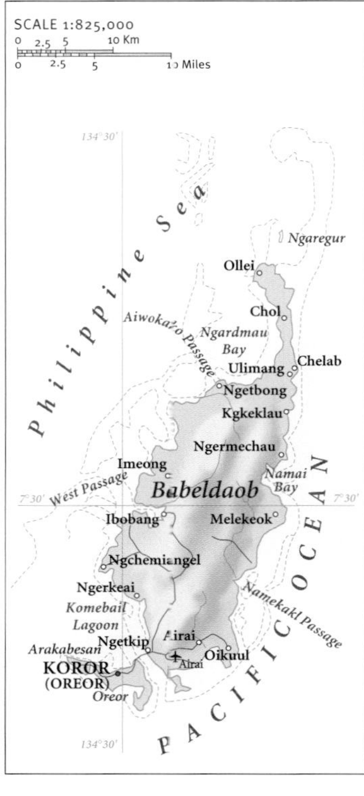

SCALE 1:825,000
0 2.5 5 10 Km
0 2.5 5 10 Miles
Philippine Sea
Ngaregur
Ollei
Chol
Aiwokako Passage
Ngardmau Bay
Ulimang
Chelab
Ngetbong
Ngkeklau
Ngermechau
Imeong
West Passage
Babeldaob
Namai Bay
Ibobang
Melekeok
Ngchemiangel
Ngerkeai
Komebail Lagoon
Arakabesan
Ngetkip
Airai
Oikuul
Nameklakl Passage
KOROR (OREOR)
Oreor
PACIFIC OCEAN

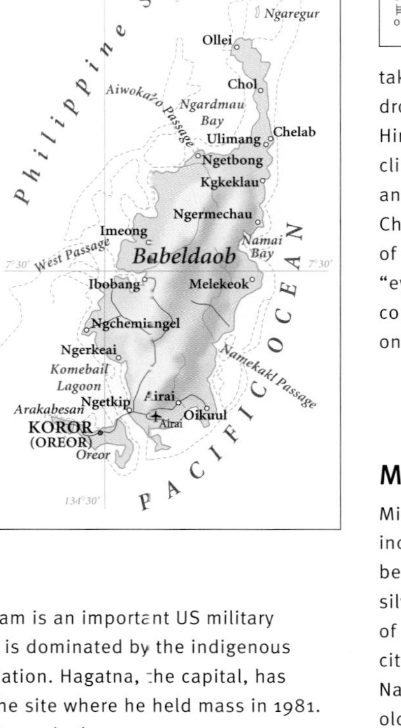

Guam (to US)

Lying at the southern end of the Mariana Islands, Guam is an important US military base and tourist destination. Social and political life is dominated by the indigenous Chamorro, who comprise just under half of the population. Hagatna, the capital, has an unusual revolving statue of Pope John Paul II on the site where he held mass in 1981. The main tourist activities are in Tumon Bay, geared towards the more expensive Japanese market and affording the opportunity at low tide to wade out to the reef. Inarajan has some of the island's richest Chamorro sights, as well as Gadao's Cave, which has ancient pictographs said to have been drawn by the mighty local chieftain, Gadao.

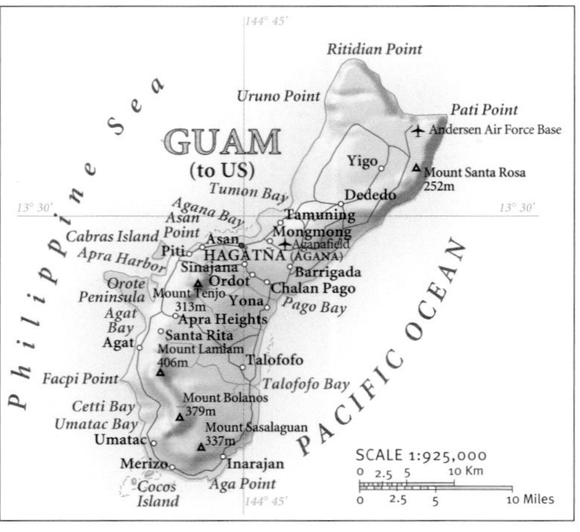

Ritidian Point
Uruno Point
Pati Point
Andersen Air Force Base
GUAM (to US)
Yigo
Mount Santa Rosa 252m
Tumon Bay
Dededo
Agana Bay
Tamuning
Asan Point
Mongmong
Cabras Island
Apra Harbor
Piti
HAGÅTÑA (AGANA)
Sinajana
Ordot
Barrigada
Orote Peninsula
Mount Tenjo 313m
Yona
Chalan Pago
Pago Bay
Agat Bay
Apra Heights
Agat
Santa Rita
Mount Lamlam 406m
Talofofo
Facpi Point
Talofofo Bay
Cetti Bay
Mount Bolanos 379m
Umatac Bay
Umatac
Mount Sasalaguan 337m
Merizo
Inarajan
Cocos Island
Aga Point
Philippine Sea
PACIFIC OCEAN
SCALE 1:925,000
0 2.5 5 10 Km
0 2.5 5 10 Miles

Northern Mariana Islands (to US)

The major centre in the Northern Mariana Islands is Saipan, which still retains some charm despite the large number of tourists, and has dramatic cliffs and rocky coasts as well as beach resorts and golf courses. Nearby Tinian is more unspoiled and also more interesting, both as the take-off site for the plane that dropped the atomic bombs on Hiroshima and Nagasaki at the climax of World War II and for its ancient Chamorro village. The Chamorro are famous for a set of facial expressions, called "eyebrow", which virtually constitutes a language on its own.

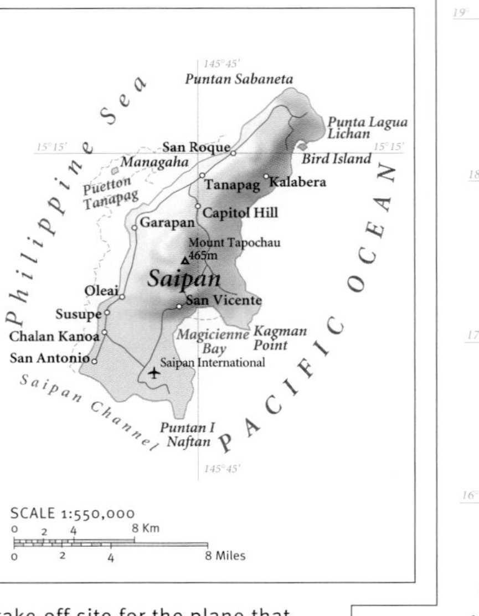

Philippine Sea
Puntan Sabaneta
Punta Lagua Lichan
San Roque
Managaha
Bird Island
Puetton Tanapag
Tanapag
Kalabera
Capitol Hill
Garapan
Mount Tapochau 465m
Saipan
Oleai
San Vicente
Susupe
Chalan Kanoa
Magicienne Bay
Kagman Point
San Antonio
Saipan International
Saipan Channel
Puntan I Naftan
PACIFIC OCEAN
SCALE 1:550,000
0 2 4 8 Km
0 2 4 8 Miles

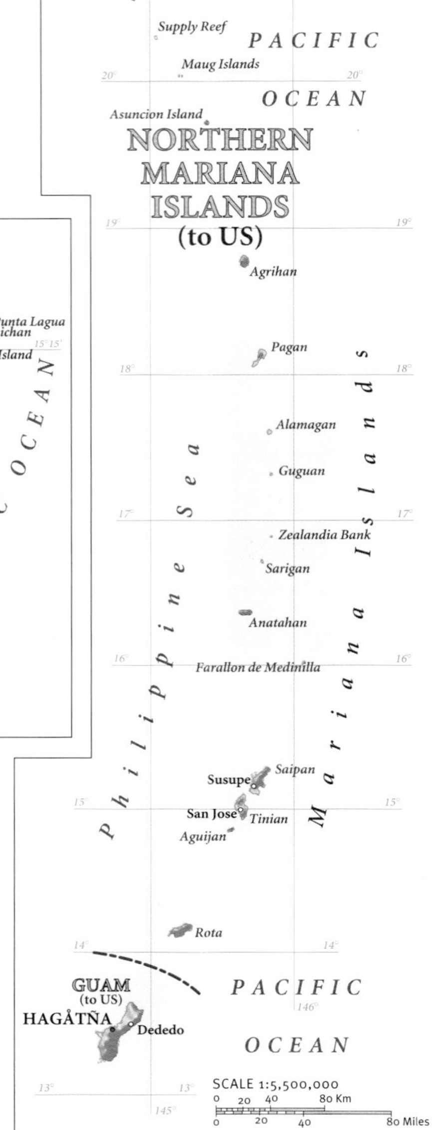

Farallon de Pajaros
Supply Reef
PACIFIC OCEAN
Maug Islands
Asuncion Island
NORTHERN MARIANA ISLANDS (to US)
Agrihan
Pagan
Alamagan
Guguan
Zealandia Bank
Sarigan
Anatahan
Farallon de Medinilla
Philippine Sea
Mariana Islands
Susupe
Saipan
San Jose
Tinian
Aguijan
Rota
GUAM (to US)
HAGÅTÑA
Dededo
PACIFIC OCEAN
SCALE 1:5,500,000
0 20 40 80 Km
0 20 40 80 Miles

Micronesia

Micronesia is a mixture of high volcanic islands and low-lying coral atolls that includes all the Caroline Islands except Palau. The Japanese fleet resting on the bed of the lagoon off Chuuk sank with everything on board from fighter planes to silverware – a fantastic site for serious divers to explore. Kosrae is a volcanic jewel of untouched rainforests and beautiful reefs, plus the 14th-century ruins of a royal city on the islet of Lelu. Pohnpei is another paradise with the ancient stone city of Nan Madol, while Yap remains one of the most traditional islands, with centuries-old stone footpaths and rolling countryside.

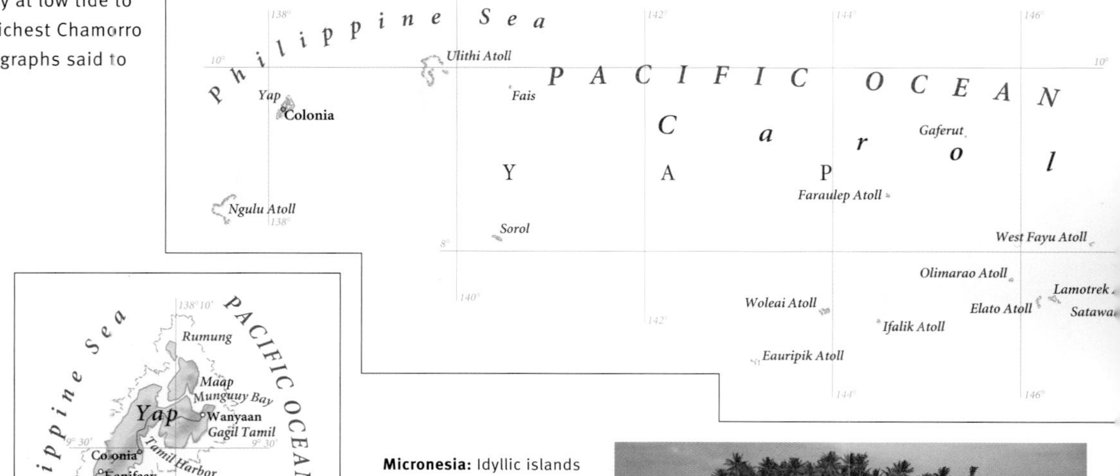

Philippine Sea
Ulithi Atoll
PACIFIC OCEAN
Yap
Colonia
Fais
Caroline
YAP
Gaferut
Ngulu Atoll
Faraulep Atoll
Sorol
West Fayu Atoll
Olimarao Atoll
Lamotrek
Woleai Atoll
Elato Atoll
Satawal
Ifalik Atoll
Eauripik Atoll
Rumung
Maap
Mungunuy Bay
Yap
Wanyaan
Gagil Tamil
Colonia
Tamil Harbor
Eanifaay
PACIFIC OCEAN
SCALE 1:925,000
0 2.5 5 10 Km
0 2.5 5 10 Miles

Micronesia: Idyllic islands with sandy beaches are surrounded by coral reefs, colourful tropical fish, and endangered green turtles.

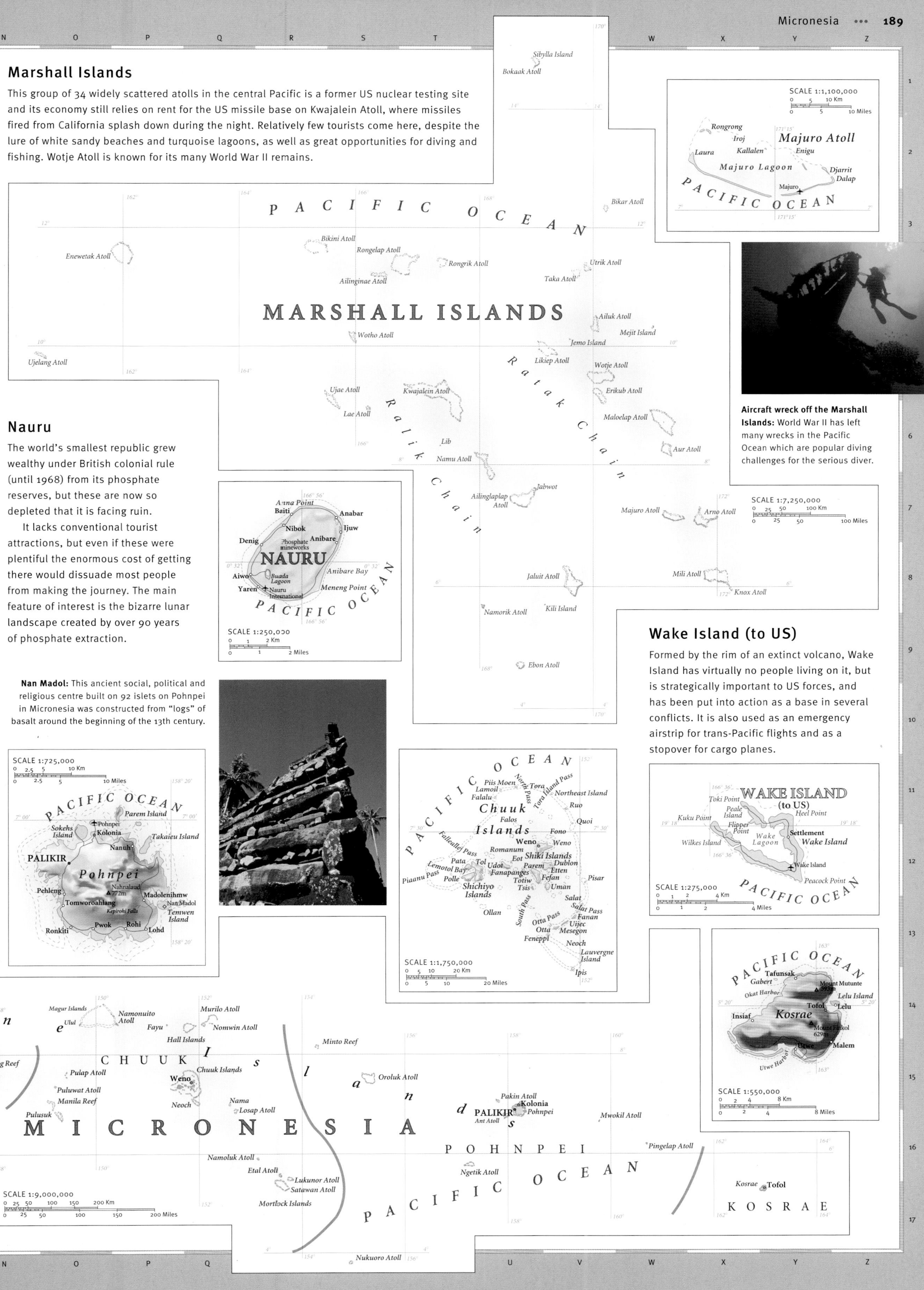

N O P Q R S T W X Y Z
1 2 3 4 5 6 7 8 9 10 11 12 13 14 15 16 17
PACIFIC OCEAN
MARSHALL ISLANDS
Sibylla Island
Bokaak Atoll
Bikar Atoll
Enewetak Atoll
Bikini Atoll
Rongelap Atoll
Rongrik Atoll
Ailinginae Atoll
Utrik Atoll
Taka Atoll
Ailuk Atoll
Mejit Island
Wotho Atoll
Jemo Island
Ujelang Atoll
Likiep Atoll
Wotje Atoll
Ratak Chain
Ujae Atoll
Kwajalein Atoll
Erikub Atoll
Lae Atoll
Maloelap Atoll
Ralik Chain
Lib
Namu Atoll
Aur Atoll
Jabwot
Ailinglaplap Atoll
Majuro Atoll
Arno Atoll
Jaluit Atoll
Mili Atoll
Knox Atoll
Namorik Atoll
Kili Island
Ebon Atoll
SCALE 1:7,250,000
SCALE 1:1,100,000
Rongrong
Iroj
Majuro Atoll
Laura
Kallalen
Enigu
Majuro Lagoon
Djarrit
Dalap
Majuro
NAURU
Anna Point
Baiti
Anabar
Nibok
Ijuw
Denig
Phosphate mineworks
Anibare
Aiwo
Buada Lagoon
Anibare Bay
Yaren
Nauru International
Meneng Point
SCALE 1:250,000
SCALE 1:725,000
Parem Island
Pohnpei
Sokehs Island
Kolonia
Takaieu Island
Nanuh
PALIKIR
Pohnpei
Nahnalaud 772m
Pehleng
Madolenihmw
Tomworoahlang
Nan Madol
Temwen Island
Kepirohi Falls
Ronkiti
Pwok
Rohi
Lohd
SCALE 1:1,750,000
Chuuk Islands
Piis Moen
Tora
North Pass
Tora Island Pass
Lamoil
Falalu
Northeast Island
Ruo
Falos
Quoi
Fono
Weno
Falealej Pass
Romanum
Shiki Islands
Eot
Pata
Tol
Udot
Parem
Dublon
Lemotol Bay
Fanapanges
Etten
Piaanu Pass
Polle
Totiw
Fefan
Pisar
Tsis
Uman
Shichiyo Islands
Salat
Salat Pass
Ollan
South Pass
Otta Pass
Fanan
Uijec
Otta
Mesegon
Feneppi
Neoch
Lauvergne Island
Ipis
WAKE ISLAND (to US)
Toki Point
Peale Island
Heel Point
Kuku Point
Flipper Point
Settlement
Wilkes Island
Wake Lagoon
Wake Island
Peacock Point
SCALE 1:275,000
Kosrae
Tafunsak
Gabert
Mount Mutunte
Okat Harbor
Lelu Island
Tofol
Lelu
Insiaf
Mount Fenkol 629m
Utwe
Malem
Utwe Harbor
SCALE 1:550,000
MICRONESIA
CHUUK
Islands
Magur Islands
Namonuito Atoll
Ulul
Murilo Atoll
Fayu
Nomwin Atoll
Hall Islands
Minto Reef
Pulap Atoll
Chuuk Islands
Weno
Oroluk Atoll
Puluwat Atoll
Manila Reef
Pakin Atoll
Kolonia
PALIKIR
Pohnpei
Ant Atoll
Nama
Losap Atoll
Mwokil Atoll
Neoch
Pulusuk
POHNPEI
Pingelap Atoll
Namoluk Atoll
Etal Atoll
Lukunor Atoll
Satawan Atoll
Ngetik Atoll
Kosrae
Tofol
Mortlock Islands
KOSRAE
Nukuoro Atoll
SCALE 1:9,000,000

Marshall Islands

This group of 34 widely scattered atolls in the central Pacific is a former US nuclear testing site and its economy still relies on rent for the US missile base on Kwajalein Atoll, where missiles fired from California splash down during the night. Relatively few tourists come here, despite the lure of white sandy beaches and turquoise lagoons, as well as great opportunities for diving and fishing. Wotje Atoll is known for its many World War II remains.

Aircraft wreck off the Marshall Islands: World War II has left many wrecks in the Pacific Ocean which are popular diving challenges for the serious diver.

Nauru

The world's smallest republic grew wealthy under British colonial rule (until 1968) from its phosphate reserves, but these are now so depleted that it is facing ruin.

It lacks conventional tourist attractions, but even if these were plentiful the enormous cost of getting there would dissuade most people from making the journey. The main feature of interest is the bizarre lunar landscape created by over 90 years of phosphate extraction.

Nan Madol: This ancient social, political and religious centre built on 92 islets on Pohnpei in Micronesia was constructed from "logs" of basalt around the beginning of the 13th century.

Wake Island (to US)

Formed by the rim of an extinct volcano, Wake Island has virtually no people living on it, but is strategically important to US forces, and has been put into action as a base in several conflicts. It is also used as an emergency airstrip for trans-Pacific flights and as a stopover for cargo planes.

Polynesia

Kiribati, Tuvalu, Cook Islands, Easter Island, French Polynesia, Niue, Pitcairn Islands, Tokelau, Wallis & Futuna

Beautiful lagoons, excellent diving around coral reefs and perfect beaches are the most evident attractions of the Polynesian islands. Scattered over a vast area in the south Pacific, some are low-lying coral atolls, often enclosing their own lagoons, whereas others are the upper parts of great volcanoes rising from the ocean floor, providing a backdrop of dramatic scenery as the terrain soars to conical volcanic peaks. French Polynesia, the Cook Islands and Easter Island – with its huge and mysterious carved figures – are the main tourist destinations. Many of the other island groups receive very few visitors indeed.

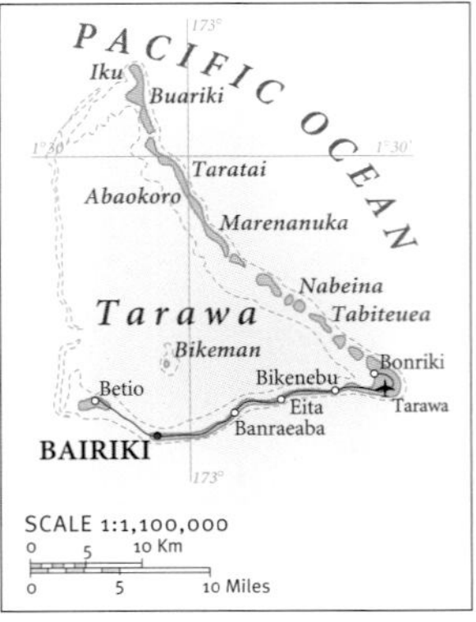
PACIFIC OCEAN
Iku
Buariki
Taratai
Abaokoro
Marenanuka
Nabeina
Tabiteuea
Tarawa
Bikeman
Bonriki
Betio
Bikenebu
Eita
Banraeaba
Tarawa
BAIRIKI
SCALE 1:1,100,000
0 5 10 Km
0 5 10 Miles

Kiribati

Pronounced "keer-ee-bus", this former British colony became independent in 1979. The islands spread over thousands of miles – the easternmost point, on Millennium Island, is the first place on earth to welcome the new year. Superb beaches, World War II wrecks and good diving characterize the islands.

Polynesian dancing: With no written language, dances were used to preserve stories and rituals, accompanied by music and chanting inspired by the sounds of the ocean, wind, and rain.

Tuvalu

One of the world's smallest states, it will be the first country to disappear if global warming causes sea levels to rise. Particularly beautiful from the air, Funafuti Atoll has a fine lagoon and a conservation area for manta rays, dolphins and green turtles.

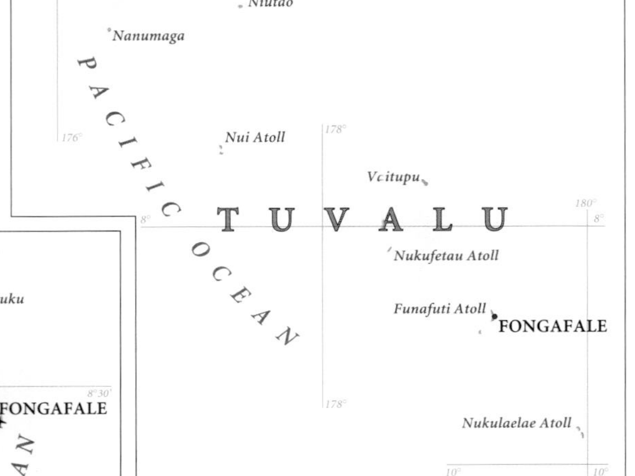
Nanumea Atoll
Niutao
Nanumaga
Nui Atoll
Vaitupu
PACIFIC OCEAN
TUVALU
Nukufetau Atoll
Funafuti Atoll
FONGAFALE
Nukulaelae Atoll
Niulakita
SCALE 1:6,750,000
0 20 40 60 80 Km
0 20 40 60 80 Miles
Fualifeke
Te Ava I Te Lape
Amatuku
Tepuka
Fualopa
Fongafale
Funafuti Atoll
FONGAFALE
Fuafatu
Funafuti
Te Ava Fuagea
Funangongo
Fatato
Vasafua
Te Ava Pua Pua
Fuagea
Falefatu
Tefala
Funafara
Teafuafou
Telele
PACIFIC OCEAN
SCALE 1:550,000
0 2 4 Km
0 2 4 Miles

Tokelau (to NZ)

These three low-lying atolls have an area under 12 sq km (5 sq miles) and a mere 500 people each. Fortnightly cargo ships from Samoa take more than a day to make the journey. Life is lived at an incredibly slow pace as there is virtually nothing to do, other than relax, dive in the lagoons and play *kilikiti*, the popular local version of cricket.

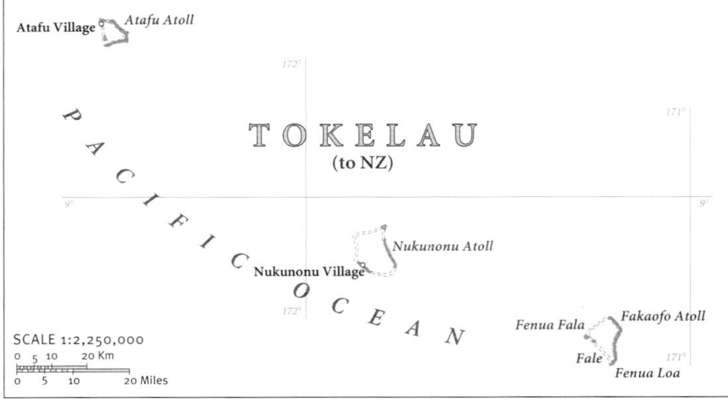
Atafu Village
Atafu Atoll
TOKELAU
(to NZ)
PACIFIC OCEAN
Nukunonu Atoll
Nukunonu Village
Fenua Fala
Fakaofo Atoll
Fale
Fenua Loa
SCALE 1:2,250,000
0 5 10 20 Km
0 5 10 20 Miles

Wallis & Futuna (to France)

Surrounded by a lagoon, Wallis has a perfectly circular crater lake, Lalolalo, and the remains of a 15th-century Tongan settlement. Futuna, 230 km (145 miles) away, has no lagoon and cultural links to Samoa rather than Tonga, with nice churches and the beautiful Alofi beaches.

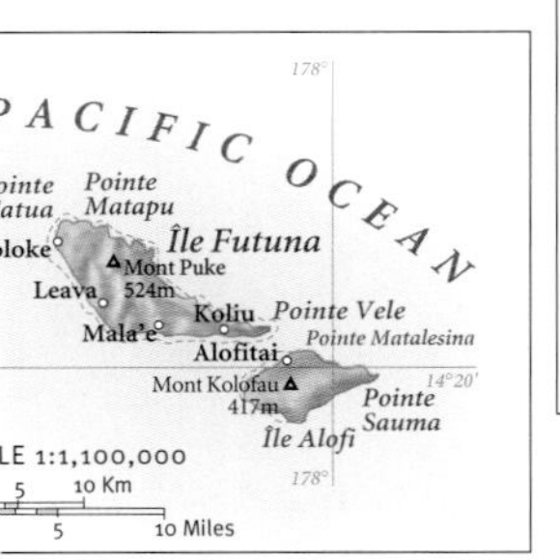
PACIFIC OCEAN
Pointe Fatua
Pointe Matapu
Toloke
Île Futuna
Mont Puke 524m
Leava
Koliu
Pointe Vele
Mala'e
Pointe Matalesina
Alofitai
Mont Kolofau 417m
Pointe Sauma
Île Alofi
SCALE 1:1,100,000
0 5 10 Km
0 5 10 Miles

Nukuloa
Nukutapu
Hihifo
Vaitupu
Îles Wallis
Baie de l'Ouest
Alele
Île Luaniva
Ahoa
Île Uvea
MATĀ'UTU
Baie de Mati'utu
Nukuhifala
Mala'atoli
Tepa
Halalo
Pointe Matala'a
Nukuatea
Île Faioa
Île Fenuafo'ou
PACIFIC OCEAN
SCALE 1:1,100,000
0 5 10 Km
0 5 10 Miles

Cook Islands (to NZ)

In this mix of coral atolls and volcanic peaks, Rarotonga is best at catering for tourists and provides regular displays of Polynesian dancing. It has a rugged, untouched centre and clean, white beaches surrounded by clear, shallow lagoons where the snorkelling is hard to beat.

Penrhyn
Rakahanga
Manihiki
Pukapuka
Nassau
Northern Cook Islands
Suwarrow
COOK ISLANDS
(to NZ)
PACIFIC OCEAN
Palmerston
Southern Cook Islands
Aitutaki
Manuae
Takutea
Mitiaro
Atiu
Mauke
Rarotonga
AVARUA
Mangaia
SCALE 1:22,250,000
0 50 100 200 300 Km
0 50 100 200 300 Miles

Niue (to NZ)

Niue is the world's largest coral island. Its coast and forests provide fine walking, including the chance to explore some dramatic caves and chasms. There is also excellent diving and snorkelling.

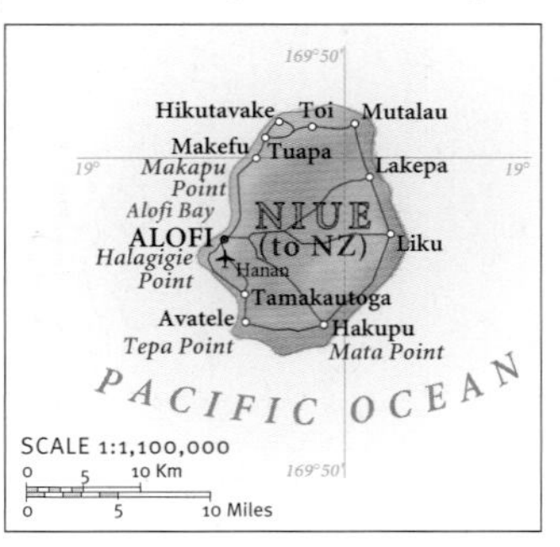
Hikutavake
Toi
Mutalau
Makefu
Tuapa
Makapu Point
Lakepa
Alofi Bay
NIUE (to NZ)
ALOFI
Halagigie Point
Hanan
Liku
Tamakautoga
Avatele
Hakupu
Tepa Point
Mata Point
PACIFIC OCEAN
SCALE 1:1,100,000
0 5 10 Km
0 5 10 Miles

Aitutaki Lagoon, Cook Islands: Often described as the pearl of the Pacific, Aitutaki is an idyll of white sand, sparkling turquoise waters and tropical coconut palms. The first European to discover it was Captain Bligh just before the infamous mutiny on HMS *Bounty*.

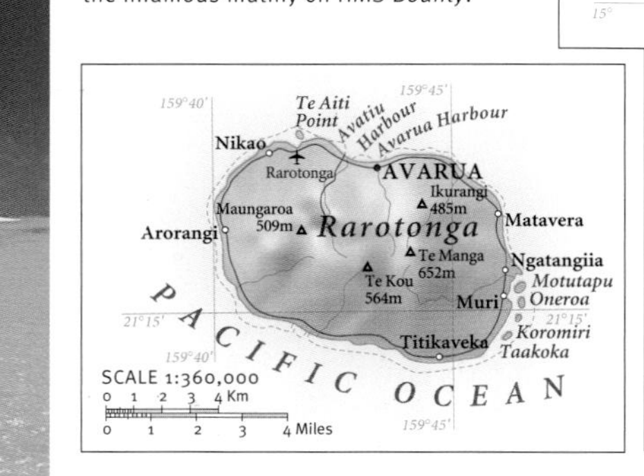
Te Aiti Point
Avatiu Harbour
Avarua Harbour
Nikao
Rarotonga
AVARUA
Ikurangi 485m
Maungaroa 509m
Arorangi
Rarotonga
Matavera
Te Manga 652m
Ngatangiia
Te Kou 564m
Motutapu
Muri
Oneroa
Koromiri
Titikaveka
Taakoka
PACIFIC OCEAN
SCALE 1:360,000
0 1 2 3 4 Km
0 1 2 3 4 Miles

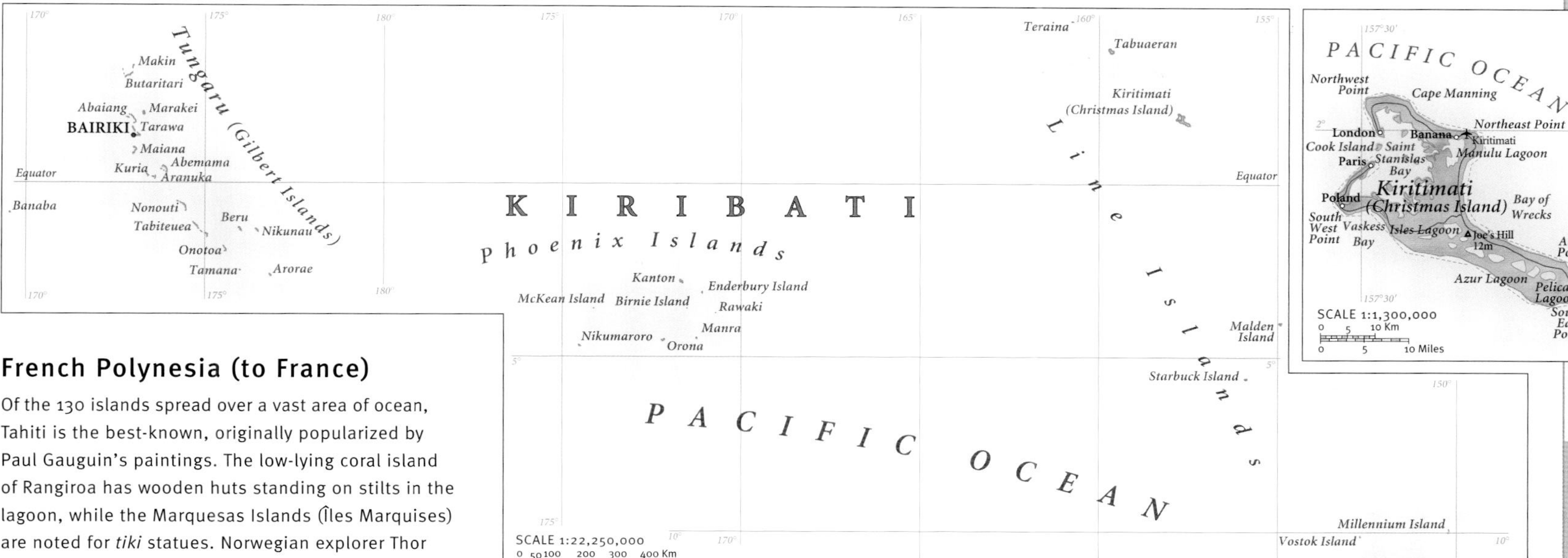

KIRIBATI
Tungaru (Gilbert Islands)
Makin
Butaritari
Abaiang
Marakei
BAIRIKI
Tarawa
Maiana
Abemama
Kuria
Aranuka
Equator
Banaba
Nonouti
Tabiteuea
Beru
Nikunau
Onotoa
Tamana
Arorae
Phoenix Islands
Kanton
Enderbury Island
McKean Island
Birnie Island
Rawaki
Manra
Nikumaroro
Orona
Teraina
Tabuaeran
Kiritimati (Christmas Island)
Line Islands
Malden Island
Starbuck Island
PACIFIC OCEAN
Millennium Island
Vostok Island
Flint Island
SCALE 1:22,250,000
0 50 100 200 300 400 Km
0 50 100 200 300 400 Miles
PACIFIC OCEAN
Northwest Point
Cape Manning
Northeast Point
London
Banana
Kiritimati
Cook Island
Saint Stanislas Bay
Paris
Manulu Lagoon
Poland
Kiritimati (Christmas Island)
Bay of Wrecks
South West Point
Vaskess Bay
Isles Lagoon
Joe's Hill 12m
Aeon Point
Azur Lagoon
Pelican Lagoon
South East Point
SCALE 1:1,300,000
0 5 10 Km
0 5 10 Miles

French Polynesia (to France)

Of the 130 islands spread over a vast area of ocean, Tahiti is the best-known, originally popularized by Paul Gauguin's paintings. The low-lying coral island of Rangiroa has wooden huts standing on stilts in the lagoon, while the Marquesas Islands (Îles Marquises) are noted for *tiki* statues. Norwegian explorer Thor Heyerdahl lived on Fatu Hiva for eight months.

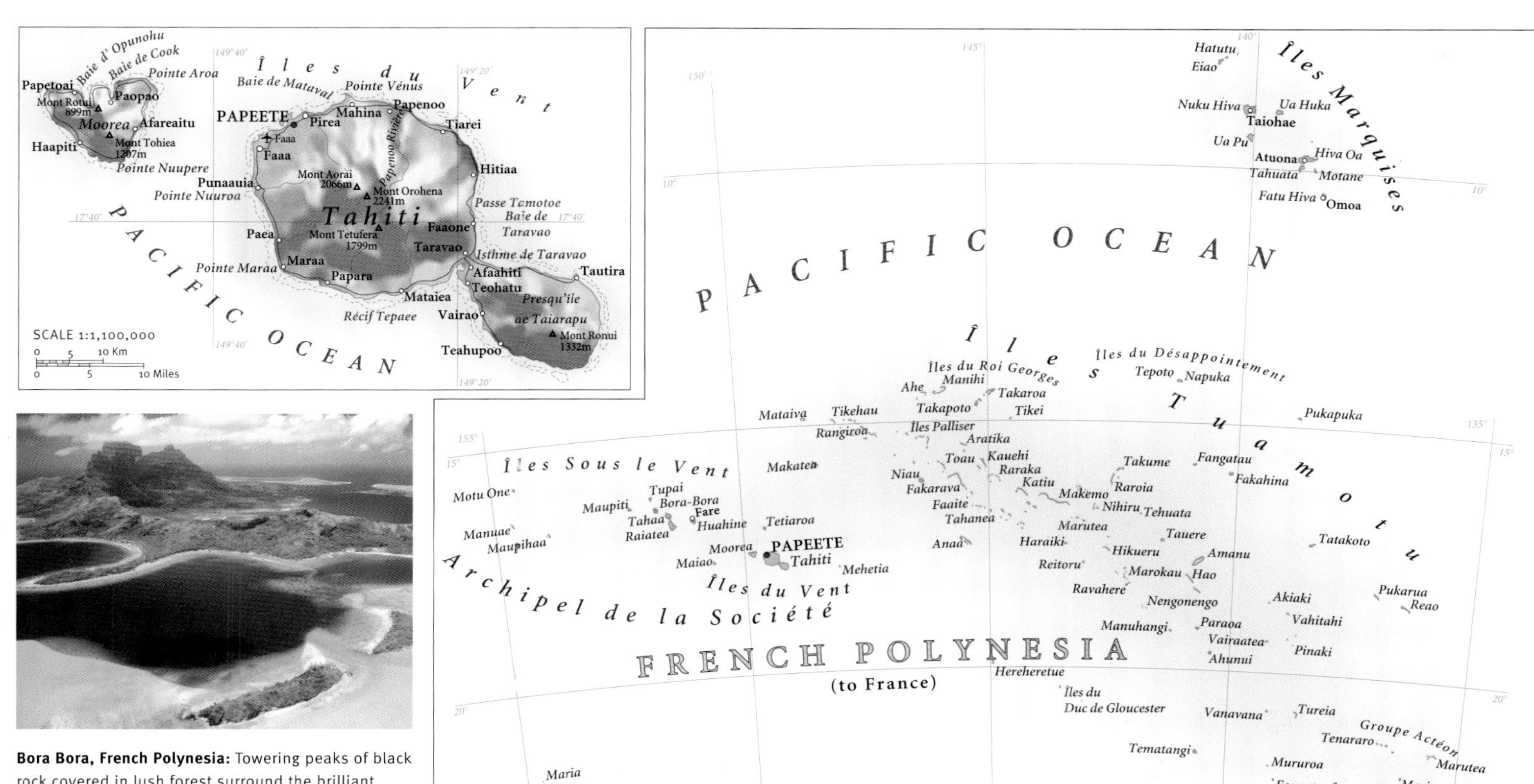

Îles du Vent
Baie d' Opunohu
Baie de Cook
Pointe Aroa
Baie de Matavai
Pointe Vénus
Papetoai
Mont Rotui 899m
Paopao
Moorea
Afareaitu
Haapiti
Mont Tohiea 1207m
Pointe Nuupere
PAPEETE
Pirea
Mahina
Papenoo
Tiarei
Faaa
Punaauia
Pointe Nuuroa
Mont Aorai 2066m
Mont Orohena 2241m
Hitiaa
Tahiti
Mont Tetufera 1799m
Passe Temotoe
Baie de Taravao
Paea
Faaone
Taravao
Isthme de Taravao
Pointe Maraa
Maraa
Papara
Afaahiti
Teohatu
Tautira
Presqu'île de Taiarapu
Mataiea
Récif Tepaee
Vairao
Mont Ronui 1332m
Teahupoo
PACIFIC OCEAN
SCALE 1:1,100,000
0 5 10 Km
0 5 10 Miles
Hatutu
Eiao
Îles Marquises
Nuku Hiva
Ua Huka
Taiohae
Ua Pu
Atuona
Hiva Oa
Tahuata
Motane
Fatu Hiva
Omoa
PACIFIC OCEAN
Îles Tuamotu
Îles du Roi Georges
Manihi
Ahe
Takaroa
Takapoto
Tikei
Îles du Désappointement
Tepoto
Napuka
Mataiva
Tikehau
Rangiroa
Îles Palliser
Aratika
Pukapuka
Îles Sous le Vent
Makatea
Toau
Kauehi
Niau
Raraka
Takume
Fangatau
Fakarava
Katiu
Raroia
Fakahina
Motu One
Tupai
Bora-Bora
Faaite
Makemo
Nihiru
Tehuata
Maupiti
Tahaa
Fare
Tahanea
Marutea
Raiatea
Huahine
Tetiaroa
Tauere
Manuae
Maupihaa
Moorea
PAPEETE
Anaa
Haraiki
Hikueru
Amanu
Tatakoto
Maiao
Tahiti
Mehetia
Reitoru
Marokau
Hao
Îles du Vent
Ravahere
Nengonengo
Akiaki
Pukarua
Reao
Archipel de la Société
Manuhangi
Paraoa
Vahitahi
Vairaatea
Ahunui
Pinaki
FRENCH POLYNESIA (to France)
Hereheretue
Îles du Duc de Gloucester
Vanavana
Tureia
Groupe Actéon
Tenararo
Tematangi
Marutea
Mururoa
Fangataufa
Maria
Maria
Rurutu
Îles Gambier
Mangareva
Rimatara
Tubuai
Temoe
Tropic of Capricorn
Raevavae
Îles Australes
Rapa Iti
Marotiri
SCALE 1:16,000,000
0 25 50 100 150 200 Km
0 25 50 100 150 200 Miles

Bora Bora, French Polynesia: Towering peaks of black rock covered in lush forest surround the brilliant turquoise lagoon, popular for windsurfing, jetskiing, swimming and scuba diving to the coral reef.

Pitcairn Islands (to UK)

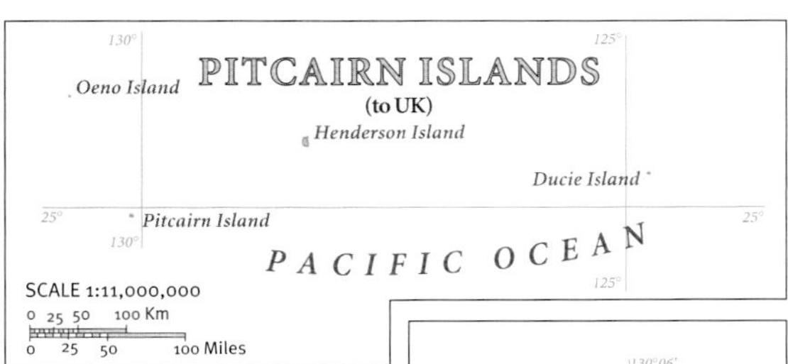

PITCAIRN ISLANDS (to UK)
Oeno Island
Henderson Island
Ducie Island
Pitcairn Island
PACIFIC OCEAN
SCALE 1:11,000,000
0 25 50 100 Km
0 25 50 100 Miles

Mutineers from *HMS Bounty* landed in 1790 on these green islands – now home to barely 50 people. Attractions include lovely lagoons and Polynesian rock art. Henderson Island is formed from coral uplifted by volcanoes. It has an untouched landscape and rare birdlife.

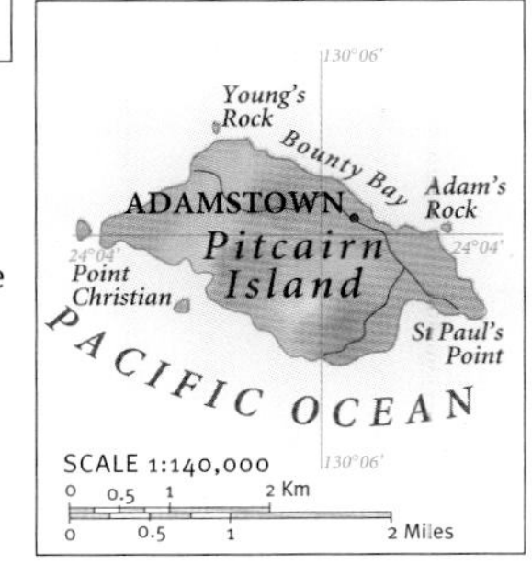

Young's Rock
Bounty Bay
Adam's Rock
ADAMSTOWN
Pitcairn Island
Point Christian
St Paul's Point
PACIFIC OCEAN
SCALE 1:140,000
0 0.5 1 2 Km
0 0.5 1 2 Miles

Easter Island (to Chile)

This remote place, 1,900 km (1,200 miles) from the next inhabited island and almost twice that far from Chile, is a big tourist destination due to its world-famous *maui* statues, up to 10 m (34 ft) high, erected some 400 to 900 years ago. Visitors can see the stone quarries, ponder why so many *maui* have been left face forward to the ground, and attempt to decipher the hieroglyphic script that developed here.

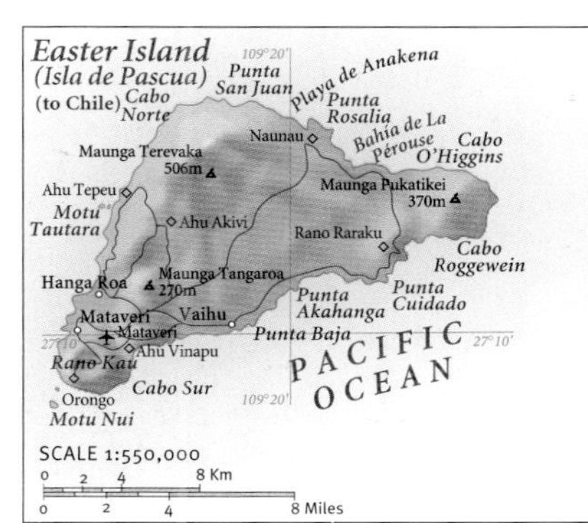

Easter Island (Isla de Pascua) (to Chile)
Punta San Juan
Playa de Anakena
Cabo Norte
Punta Rosalia
Bahía de La Pérouse
Cabo O'Higgins
Maunga Terevaka 506m
Naunau
Maunga Pukatikei 370m
Ahu Tepeu
Motu Tautara
Ahu Akivi
Rano Raraku
Cabo Roggewein
Hanga Roa
Maunga Tangaroa 270m
Punta Akahanga
Punta Cuidado
Mataveri
Vaihu
Punta Baja
Rano Kau
Ahu Vinapu
PACIFIC OCEAN
Cabo Sur
Orongo
Motu Nui
SCALE 1:550,000
0 2 4 8 Km
0 2 4 8 Miles

Ahu Tongariki, Easter Island: The *maui* statues in this row near Rano Raraku volcano are the largest on the island.

Pacific Ocean

The Pacific is the world's largest and deepest ocean, circled by active tectonic plate boundaries known as the "Ring of Fire". It surrounds islands and coral atolls whose remoteness has left them with unique wildlife and untouched landscapes. Major tourist destinations include the most volcanic islands on earth, in Hawai'i, the Galapagos Islands with the endemic wildlife that inspired Charles Darwin and Easter Island with its inscrutable stone statues. Elsewhere, exotic coral reefs and World War II wrecks are ideal for diving enthusiasts, while idyllic white sandy beaches and traditional cultures provide a great getaway from the modern world.

Activities

- Arrive in Samoa before you left Australia, by flying over the **international dateline**
- Slither down the 5 m (16 ft) **Papasee'a Sliding Rock** into the pool below, in Samoa
- Go snorkelling at **Palolo Deep National Marine Reserve**, in Samoa
- Soak up the *fa'a Samoa*, the traditional way of life that gives these islands their distinct culture
- Scan the ocean for whales, sharks and turtles at **Hufangalupe**, on the island of Tongatapu

Inset Map Key

POPULATION

○ below 10,000

ELEVATION

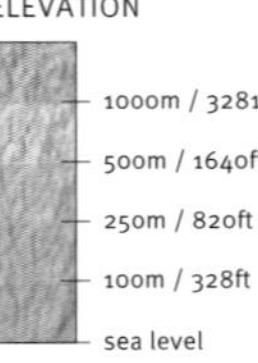
1000m / 3281ft
500m / 1640ft
250m / 820ft
100m / 328ft
sea level

Ocean Map Key

SEA DEPTH

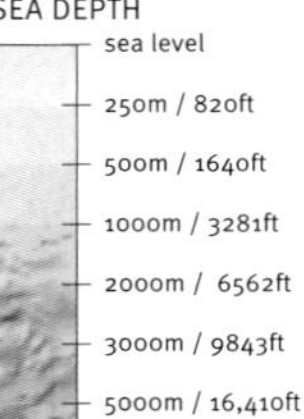
sea level
250m / 820ft
500m / 1640ft
1000m / 3281ft
2000m / 6562ft
3000m / 9843ft
5000m / 16,410ft

What to See – Samoa

❶ Falealupo Peninsula
Beautiful rainforest reserve set beside delightful beaches, with a canopy walkway

❷ Lava Field
(near Fagamalo) Moonscape created by the eruption of Mount Matavanu in 1905–1911. It is an amateur geologist's dream to see all the formations

❸ Pulemelei Mound
(near Satupaiteau) This step pyramid is Polynesia's largest ancient structure and a mystery to this day. It is set in jungle near the Olemoe Falls

❹ Alofaaga Blowholes
(near Taga) See a coconut tossed 60 m (200 ft) in the air by these blowholes

❺ Robert Louis Stevenson Museum
(in Apia) The writer spent his last years in Villa Vailima and is buried on top of nearby Mount Vaea

❻ Manua Islands
Deep valleys, dramatic soaring cliffs and exotic flora and fauna in one of the world's most scenic places

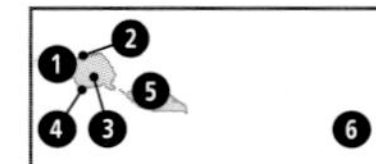

SCALE 1:3,670,000

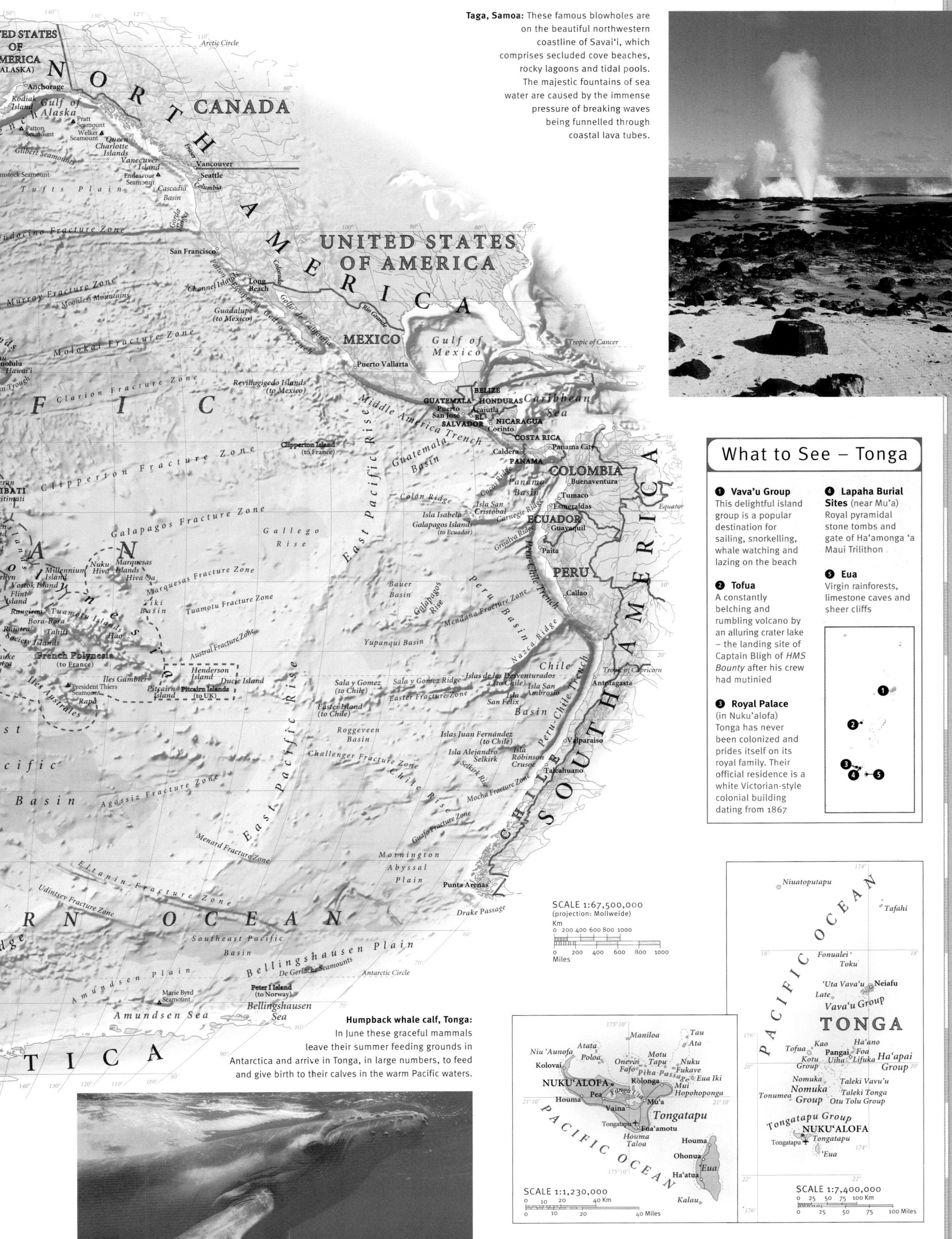

N O P Q R S T U V W X Y Z
UNITED STATES OF AMERICA (ALASKA)
Arctic Circle
Anchorage
Kodiak Island
Gulf of Alaska
Pratt Seamount
Patton Seamount
Welker Seamount
Queen Charlotte Islands
Gilbert Seamount
Vancouver Island
Endeavour Seamount
Comstock Seamount
Tufts Plain
Cascadia Basin
NORTH AMERICA
CANADA
Vancouver
Seattle
Columbia
Mendocino Fracture Zone
San Francisco
UNITED STATES OF AMERICA
Murray Fracture Zone
Moonless Mountains
Channel Islands
Long Beach
Colorado
Guadalupe (to Mexico)
Molokai Fracture Zone
Rio Grande
MEXICO
Gulf of Mexico
Tropic of Cancer
Honolulu
Hawai'i
Puerto Vallarta
Clarion Fracture Zone
Revillagigedo Islands (to Mexico)
BELIZE
GUATEMALA
HONDURAS
Caribbean Sea
Puerto San José
Acajutla
EL SALVADOR
NICARAGUA
Corinto
Middle America Trench
COSTA RICA
Clipperton Island (to France)
Caldera
Panama City
PANAMA
Clipperton Fracture Zone
Guatemala Basin
COLOMBIA
Buenaventura
Panama Basin
Tumaco
Esmeraldas
Colón Ridge
Isla San Cristobal
Isla Isabela
Galapagos Islands (to Ecuador)
ECUADOR
Guayaquil
Equator
Galapagos Fracture Zone
Gallego Rise
East Pacific Rise
Paita
Millennium Island
Nuku Hiva
Marquesas Islands
Hiva Oa
Marquesas Fracture Zone
Vostok Island
Flint Island
PERU
Callao
Peru-Chile Trench
Bauer Basin
Galapagos Rise
Peru Basin
Mendaña Fracture Zone
Rangiroa
Tuamotu Islands
Tuamotu Fracture Zone
Bora-Bora
Tahiti
Society Islands
Hao
Austral Fracture Zone
Yupanqui Basin
Nazca Ridge
French Polynesia (to France)
Henderson Island
Ducie Island
Iles Gambier
Pitcairn Island
Pitcairn Islands (to UK)
Chile Basin
Tropic of Capricorn
Antofagasta
President Thiers Seamount
Rapa
Iles Australes
Sala y Gomez (to Chile)
Sala y Gomez Ridge
Islas de los Desventurados (to Chile)
Isla San Ambrosio
Isla San Felix
Easter Fracture Zone
Easter Island (to Chile)
Roggeveen Basin
Islas Juan Fernández (to Chile)
Isla Alejandro Selkirk
Isla Róbinson Crusoe
Valparaiso
Talcahuano
Challenger Fracture Zone
Chile Rise
Selkirk Rise
Agassiz Fracture Zone
Mocha Fracture Zone
Guafo Fracture Zone
SOUTH AMERICA
CHILE
Menard Fracture Zone
Mornington Abyssal Plain
Punta Arenas
Eltanin Fracture Zone
Udintsev Fracture Zone
Drake Passage
OCEAN
Southeast Pacific Basin
Bellingshausen Plain
De Gerlache Seamounts
Antarctic Circle
Amundsen Plain
Marie Byrd Seamount
Peter I Island (to Norway)
Bellingshausen Sea
Amundsen Sea
SCALE 1:67,500,000
(projection: Mollweide)
Km 0 200 400 600 800 1000
0 200 400 600 800 1000 Miles
Niuatoputapu
Tafahi
PACIFIC OCEAN
Fonualei
Toku
'Uta Vava'u
Neiafu
Late
Vava'u Group
TONGA
Kao
Ha'ano
Tofua
Pangai
Foa
Kotu Group
Uiha
Lifuka
Ha'apai Group
Nomuka
Taleki Vava'u
Tonumea
Nomuka Group
Taleki Tonga
Otu Tolu Group
Tongatapu Group
NUKU'ALOFA
Tongatapu
'Eua
SCALE 1:7,400,000
0 25 50 75 100 Km
0 25 50 75 100 Miles
Manilo
Tau
Ata
Atata
Motu Tapu
Nuku
Niu 'Aunofa
Poloa
Onevai
Fafa
Fukave
Kolovai
Eua Iki
Kolonga
Mui Hopohoponga
NUKU'ALOFA
Pea
Mu'a
Houma
Vaina
Tongatapu
Fua'amotu
Houma Taloa
Houma
Ohonua
'Eua
Ha'atua
Kalau
PACIFIC OCEAN
SCALE 1:1,230,000
0 10 20 40 Km
0 10 20 40 Miles

Taga, Samoa: These famous blowholes are on the beautiful northwestern coastline of Savai'i, which comprises secluded cove beaches, rocky lagoons and tidal pools. The majestic fountains of sea water are caused by the immense pressure of breaking waves being funnelled through coastal lava tubes.

What to See – Tonga

❶ **Vava'u Group**
This delightful island group is a popular destination for sailing, snorkelling, whale watching and lazing on the beach

❷ **Tofua**
A constantly belching and rumbling volcano by an alluring crater lake – the landing site of Captain Bligh of *HMS Bounty* after his crew had mutinied

❸ **Royal Palace**
(in Nuku'alofa)
Tonga has never been colonized and prides itself on its royal family. Their official residence is a white Victorian-style colonial building dating from 1867

❹ **Lapaha Burial Sites** (near Mu'a)
Royal pyramidal stone tombs and gate of Ha'amonga 'a Maui Trilithon

❺ **Eua**
Virgin rainforests, limestone caves and sheer cliffs

Humpback whale calf, Tonga: In June these graceful mammals leave their summer feeding grounds in Antarctica and arrive in Tonga, in large numbers, to feed and give birth to their calves in the warm Pacific waters.

Antarctica

Antarctica is this planet's last truly untamed wilderness. Nobody lives there except for scientific research and virtually the whole continent is covered by ice, much of it over 2,000 m (6,500 ft) thick. Volcanic craters and bays form dramatic landscapes, while giant icebergs float through deep channels and may make landings impossible.

Cruises to Antarctica have become popular in recent years, for the spectacular scenery and the wildlife. Huge breeding colonies of seals and penguins make an impressive sight and visitors also have a good chance of seeing various types of whale. The scientific research stations are also fascinating to visit, performing key research about global climate and conditions. December to March is the season for short cruises, generally departing from the tip of South America for ten days or more, but a much longer period, requiring an ice-breaker cruise, is needed for a true experience of the depths of this wilderness.

◀ 192

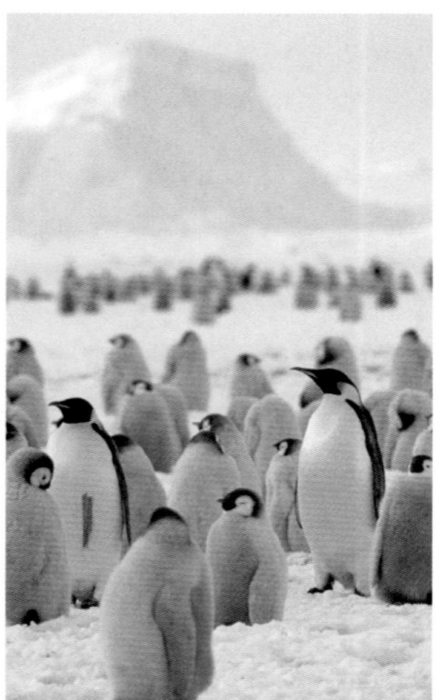

Emperor penguin rookery: The largest penguins and the only animals to winter on the Antarctic ice, emperor penguins huddle together and take turns to be on the inside of the group.

Activities

- Admire the two million chinstrap penguins, on **Zavodovski Island** during a tour of the Southern Ocean
- Send your postcards home with Antarctic stamps from **Port Lockroy**, Anvers Island and get your passport stamped
- Camp on the ice for the essential Antarctic experience
- Float in small inflatable Zodiac boats for shore excursions
- Spot whales in the **Drake Passage**, off the Antarctic Peninsula
- Embark on an icebreaker cruise through the pack ice
- Take a dip at **Deception Island**, in the South Shetland Islands, where the freezing Antarctic waters mix with steaming thermal waters of the bay

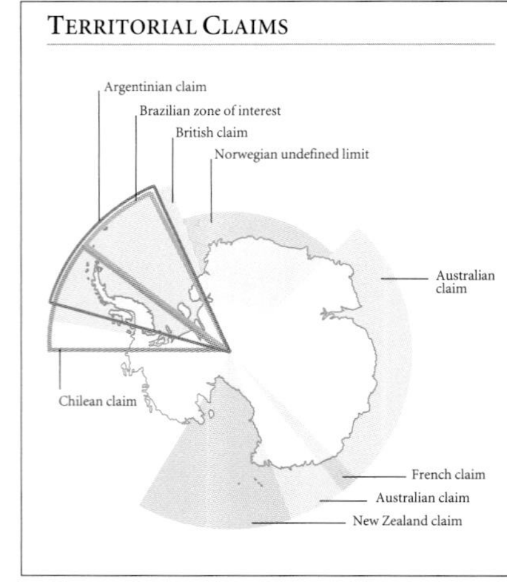

TERRITORIAL CLAIMS
Argentinian claim
Brazilian zone of interest
British claim
Norwegian undefined limit
Australian claim
Chilean claim
French claim
Australian claim
New Zealand claim

What to See

❶ South Shetland Islands
The first point to be reached from Tierra del Fuego is a wildlife haven, noted for large penguin rookeries and seal colonies

❷ Deception Island
(in the Bransfield Strait) Horseshoe-shaped, collapsed, volcanic caldera forming a safe natural harbour, despite periodic eruptions

❸ Port Lockroy
(on Anvers Island) A British naval base during World War II, reached via the dramatic Neumayer Channel

❹ Paradise Harbour
(on Foyn Coast) Popular for "Zodiac cruising" among the icebergs that calve off the glacier

❺ Lemaire Channel
(on the Loubet Coast) Enormous sheer cliffs fall straight into the sea at one of the most-visited and photogenic Antarctic channels

❻ Halley Research Station
Visit the station that discovered a hole in the ozone layer back in 1985

❼ Ross Ice Shelf
The world's largest floating ice sheet

❽ Discovery Hut
(near Scott Base) Captain Scott's 1901–04 hut from the time of his first abortive attempt to reach the South Pole is remarkably well-preserved

❾ The Dry Valleys
(in Victoria Land) No snow or rain has fallen in the desolate, ice-free valleys – Victoria, Wright and Taylor – for over two million years

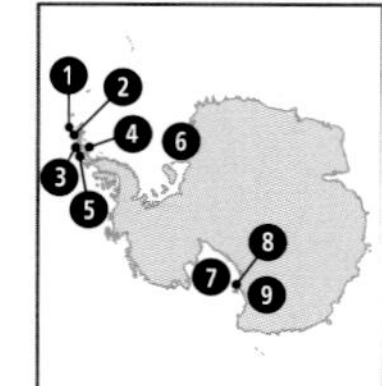

Gerlache Strait: This impressive strait on the way from Deception Island, in the South Shetland Islands, to the Lemaire Channel is noted for its deep blue ice – the deeper the blue, the less air there is trapped in it.

Map Key

ELEVATION

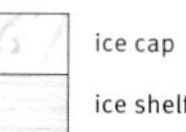

ice cap

ice shelf

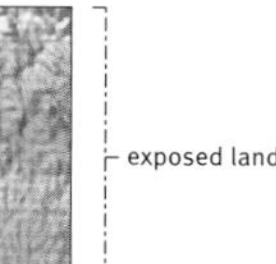

exposed land

64
SOUTHERN OCEAN
SCALE 1:16,500,000
(projection: Lambert Azimuthal Equal Area)
Km
0 50 100 150 200 250 300 350 400 450 500
Miles
0 50 100 150 200 250 300 350 400 450 500
172
192
SOUTHERN OCEAN
Antarctic Circle
Limit of summer pack ice
Georg von Neumayer (to Germany)
Sanae (to South Africa)
Fimbul Ice Shelf
Maitri (to India)
Novolazarevskaya (to Russian Federation)
Princess Astrid Kyst
Cape Norvegia
Riiser-Larsen Sea
Riiser-Larsen Ice Shelf
Kronprinsesse Märtha Kyst
Borg Massif
Mühlig-Hofmann Mountains
Wohlthat Mountains
Fimbulheimen
Prinsesse Ragnhild Kyst
Asuka (to Japan)
Sør Rondane Mountains
Dronning Maud Land
Maudheimvidda
Thorshavnheiane
Belgica Mountains
Mount Victor 2588m
Prins Harald Kyst
Riiser-Larsen Peninsula
Lützow Holmbukta
Syowa (to Japan)
Thyer Glacier
Kronprins Olav Kyst
Molodezhnaya (to Russian Federation)
Casey Bay
Amundsen Bay
Nye Mountains
Napier Mountains
Cape Batterbee
Mount Elkins 2300m
Enderby Land
Dismal Mountains
Edward VIII Gulf
Law Promontory
Kemp Land
Hansen Mountains
Mawson Coast
Mawson (to Australia)
Gustav Bull Mountains
Mac. Robertson Land
Mount Menzies 3355m
Prince Charles Mountains
Lars Christensen Coast
Cape Darnley
Lambert Glacier
Amery Ice Shelf
Gillock Island
Mackenzie Bay
Ingrid Christensen Coast
Zhongshan (to China)
Prydz Bay
Davis (to Australia)
Princess Elizabeth Land
West Ice Shelf
King Leopold and Queen Astrid Land
Mikhaylov Island
Philippi Glacier
Greater Antarctica
Wilhelm II Land
Wilhelm II Coast
Davis Sea
Mirny (to Russian Federation)
Queen Mary Coast
Masson Island
Shackleton Ice Shelf
Northcliffe Glacier
Denman Glacier
Mill Island
Scott Glacier
Bowman Island
Knox Coast
Vincennes Bay
Wilkes Land
Casey (to Australia)
Budd Coast
Cape Poinsett
Cape Waldron
Sabrina Coast
Dalton Iceberg Tongue
Banzare Coast
Cape Goodenough
Porpoise Bay
Terre Adélie
Wilkes Coast
Cape Keltie
Dibble Iceberg Tongue
George V Land
Adélie Coast
Dumont d'Urville (to France)
Cape Gray
Mertz Glacier
Ninnis Glacier
George V Coast
Cape Freshfield
Cape Hudson
Dumont d'Urville Sea
Leningradskaya (to Russian Federation)
Cape Cheetham
Oates Land
Rennick Glacier
Mount Minto 4163m
Cape Adare
Borchgrevink Coast
Coulman Island
Balleny Islands
Scott Island
Ross Sea
Drygalski Ice Tongue
Scott Coast
Victoria Land
Ross Island
Mount Erebus 3794m
Scott Base (to NZ)
McMurdo Base (to US)
Mount Lister 4026m
Hillary Coast
Mount McClintock 3492m
Byrd Glacier
Shackleton Coast
Nimrod Glacier
Mount Markham 4351m
Mount Kirkpatrick 4528m
Transantarctic Mountains
Queen Maud Mountains
Dufek Coast
Beardmore Glacier
Amundsen Coast
Gould Coast
Horlick Mountains
Watson Escarpment
Siple Coast
Ross Ice Shelf
Roosevelt Island
Shirase Coast
Edward VII Peninsula
Sulzberger Bay
South Pole
Amundsen-Scott (to US)
Vostok (to Russian Federation)
South Geomagnetic Pole
ANTARCTICA
Foundation Ice Stream
Pensacola Mountains
Support Force Glacier
Recovery Glacier
Filchner Ice Shelf
Slessor Glacier
Theron Mountains
Belgrano II (to Argentina)
Luitpold Coast
Coats Land
Halley (to UK)
Caird Coast
Brunt Ice Shelf
Stancomb-Wills Glacier
V W X Y Z
N O P Q R S T U V W X Y Z
1 2 3 4 5 13 14

Glacier in the Lemaire Channel: Noted for its trapped icebergs, it is home to minke whales, leopard seals and penguins.

The Arctic

The Arctic Ocean spans the northern waters within the Arctic Circle between Russia, Canada, Scandinavia and Greenland. In contrast to Antarctica, which is a largely empty continent surrounded by oceans, the Arctic regions have more variety of land and culture. The thrill of experiencing the harsh climate is increasingly drawing tourists and the ultimate challenge is a trip to the North Pole in one of the icebreaker cruise ships, an expensive journey with success far from guaranteed.

Alternatively, the huge granite cliffs of Greenland provide some of the most challenging mountaineering anywhere. However, the Arctic does not need to be so daunting and the beautiful glaciers and fjords of Greenland offer dramatic Arctic scenery that is more easily accessible. There is ample opportunity for hiking, skiing, dogsledding and most other winter activities and cruises take people to breathtaking glacial lagoons.

Northern Lights *(aurora borealis)*: Streamers of coloured light, caused by charged particles from the sun being attracted by the earth's magnetic field, appear in the Arctic sky throughout the year and are best seen in the early autumn and spring. Each phenomenal display lasts from a few minutes to a couple of hours.

Map Key

POPULATION	SEA DEPTH
above 5 million	sea level
1 million to 5 million	250m / 820ft
500,000 to 1 million	500m / 1640ft
100,000 to 500,000	1000m / 3281ft
50,000 to 100,000	2000m / 6562ft
10,000 to 50,000	3000m / 9843ft
below 10,000	

8

SCALE 1:23,500,000
(projection: Lambert Azimuthal Equal Area)
Km 0 100 200 300 400 500 600
Miles 0 100 200 300 400 500 600

Polar bear and cub: Around 30,000 polar bears roam the Arctic regions of northern Canada and Russia and the coastal areas of Greenland and Svalbard. The largest land carnivore, they hunt seals and are strong swimmers, with a thick layer of blubber to keep them warm in the freezing water.

Activities

- Hike the remote **Kangerlussaq** to **Sisimiut** Trek, 150 km (105 miles) across Greenland. The low route and the more challenging high route are popular with skiers too
- Freeze in the Festival of the North in **Murmansk**, Russia, (late March), where the sporting activities include reindeer races, deer-plus-ski races, and through-the-ice swimming
- Visit the **North Pole** on an icebreaker tour – using a vessel specially designed to break the pack ice (either on a diesel-powered ship, or the more flexible Russian nuclear-powered boats)
- Climb the spectacular 2,012 m (6,700 ft) granite face of **Uiluit Qaaqa**, above Tasermiut Fjord
- Take a dogsledding tour or go skidooing on **Spitsbergen**, Svalbard

What to See

1 Northeast Greenland National Park
Inhabited by muskoxen, caribou and polar bears, this vast expanse covering nearly half of Greenland is the world's largest national park

2 Uummannaq
Dominated by the colourful Uummannaq mountain, Greenland's sunniest spot hosts the bizarre World Ice Golf Championships each year in March – where the greens are white and the balls are bright orange

3 Disko Bay
(Qeqertarsuup Tunua)
This iceberg-studded expanse of water lies on Greenland's west coast

4 Nuuk
Capital of around 14,000 people whose National Museum became famous in 1977 for displaying eight 500-year-old mummies found frozen in a cave at Qilaqitsoq

5 Tasermiut Fjord
Greenland's spectacular fjord with a glacier at its head and with huge granite fells on either side enjoyed by climbers

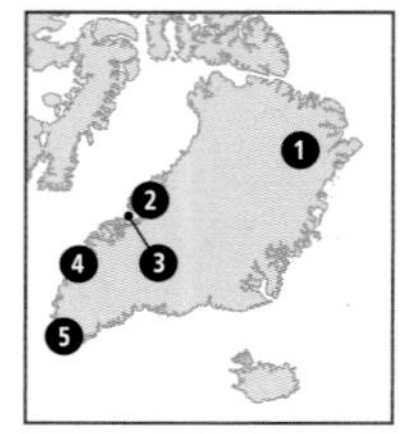

Disko Bay, Greenland: Icebergs calve from the Eqi Glacier, the most productive in the Northern Hemisphere and float into the bay, which is home to seals and the world's biggest Arctic tern colony. The town of Ilulissat, meaning "iceberg" in the Greenlandic Inuit language, is home to 4,000 people and 2,500 sled dogs.

64

ARCTIC OCEAN
Bering Sea
Aleutian Basin
Sea of Okhotsk
Chukchi Sea
East Siberian Sea
Beaufort Sea
Canada Basin
Canada Plain
Mendeleyev Ridge
Wrangel Plain
Laptev Sea
Lomonosov Ridge
Makarov Basin
Fram Basin
Nansen Cordillera
Nansen Basin
North Pole
Kara Sea
Barents Sea
Barents Plain
Greenland Sea
Norwegian Sea
Denmark Strait
Baffin Bay
Lincoln Sea
Wandel Sea
UNITED STATES OF AMERICA
ALASKA
RUSSIAN FEDERATION
Siberia
GREENLAND (to Denmark)
SVALBARD (to Norway)
ICELAND
NORWAY
SWEDEN
FINLAND
ESTONIA
LATVIA
EUROPE
Anchorage
Magadan
Noril'sk
Vorkuta
Murmansk
Archangel
REYKJAVÍK
HELSINKI
TALLINN
STOCKHOLM
OSLO
MOSCOW
RIGA
Franz Josef Land
Novaya Zemlya
Severnaya Zemlya
Ellesmere Island
Queen Elizabeth Islands
Banks Island
Limit of permanent ice cap
Limit of summer pack ice
Limit of winter pack ice

The Time Zones

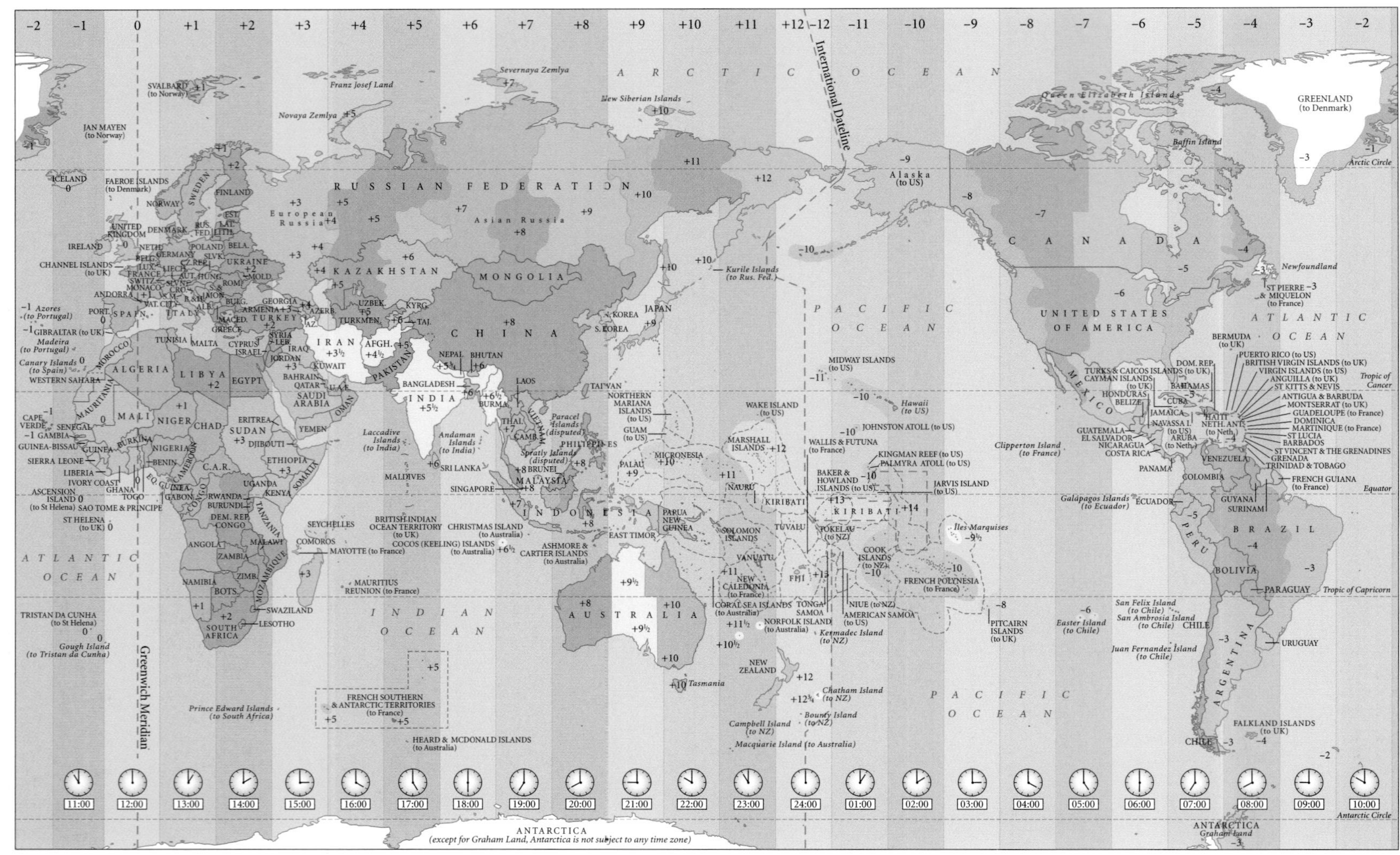
-2 -1 0 +1 +2 +3 +4 +5 +6 +7 +8 +9 +10 +11 +12 -12 -11 -10 -9 -8 -7 -6 -5 -4 -3 -2
International Dateline
Greenwich Meridian
A R C T I C O C E A N
GREENLAND (to Denmark)
R U S S I A N F E D E R A T I O N
European Russia
Asian Russia
K A Z A K H S T A N
M O N G O L I A
C H I N A
I N D I A
I R A N
C A N A D A
U N I T E D S T A T E S O F A M E R I C A
P A C I F I C O C E A N
A T L A N T I C O C E A N
I N D I A N O C E A N
A U S T R A L I A
I N D O N E S I A
K I R I B A T I
B R A Z I L
ALGERIA
LIBYA
EGYPT
SUDAN
NIGER
MALI
CHAD
SOUTH AFRICA
NEW ZEALAND
Alaska (to US)
Hawaii (to US)
Arctic Circle
Tropic of Cancer
Equator
Tropic of Capricorn
Antarctic Circle
11:00
12:00
13:00
14:00
15:00
16:00
17:00
18:00
19:00
20:00
21:00
22:00
23:00
24:00
01:00
02:00
03:00
04:00
05:00
06:00
07:00
08:00
09:00
10:00
ANTARCTICA
(except for Graham Land, Antarctica is not subject to any time zone)

The numbers at the top of the map indicate the number of hours each time zone is ahead or behind Greenwich Mean Time (GMT). The clocks and 24-hour times given at the bottom of the map show the time in each time zone when it is 12:00 hours noon GMT.

Time Zones

The present system of international timekeeping divides the world into 24 time zones by means of 24 standard meridians of longitude, each 15º apart. Time is measured in each zone as so many hours ahead or behind the time at the Greenwich Meridian (GMT). Countries, or parts of countries, falling in the vicinity of each zone, adopt its time as shown on the map above. Therefore, using the map, when it is 12:00 noon GMT, it will be 2:00 pm in Zambia; similarly, when it is 4:30 pm. GMT, it will be 11:30 am in Peru.

Greenwich Mean Time (GMT)

Greenwich Mean Time (or Universal Time, as it is more correctly called) has been the internationally accepted basis for calculating solar time – measured in relation to the Earth's rotation around the Sun – since 1884. Greenwich Mean Time is specifically the solar time at the site of the former Royal Observatory in the London Borough of Greenwich, United Kingdom. The Greenwich Meridian is an imaginary line around the world that runs through the North and South poles. It corresponds to 0º of longitude, which lies on this site at Greenwich. Time is measured around the world in relation to the official time along the Meridian.

Standard Time

Standard time is the official time, designated by law, in any specific country or region. Standard time was initiated in 1884, after it became apparent that the practice of keeping various systems of local time was causing confusion – particularly in the USA and Canada, where several railroad routes passed through scores of areas which calculated local time by different rules. The standard time of a particular region is calculated in reference to the longitudinal time zone in which it falls. In practice, these zones do not always match their longitudinal position; in some places the area of the zone has been altered in shape for the convenience of inhabitants, as can be seen in the map. For example, while Greenland occupies three time zones, the majority of the territory uses a standard time of -3 hours GMT. Similarly China, which spans five time zones, is standardized at +8 hours GMT.

The International Dateline

The International Dateline is an imaginary line that extends from pole to pole, and roughly corresponds to a line of 180º longitude for much of its length. This line is the arbitrary marker between calendar days. By moving from east to west across the line, a traveller will need to set their calendar back one day, while those travelling in the opposite direction will need to add a day. This is to compensate for the use of standard time around the world, which is based on the time at noon along the Greenwich Meridian, approximately halfway around the world. Wide deviations from 180º longitude occur through the Bering Strait – to avoid dividing Siberia into two separate calendar days – and in the Pacific Ocean – to allow certain Pacific islands the same calendar day as New Zealand. Changes were made to the International Dateline in 1995 that made Millennium Island (formerly Caroline Island) in Kiribati the first land area to witness the beginning of the year 2000.

Daylight Saving Time

Also known as summer time, daylight saving is a system of advancing clocks in order to extend the waking day during periods of later daylight hours. This normally means advancing clocks by one hour in early spring, and reverting back to standard time in early autumn. The system of daylight saving is used throughout much of Europe, the USA, Australia, and many other countries worldwide, although there are no standardized dates for the changeover to summer time due to the differences in hours of daylight at different latitudes. Daylight saving was first introduced in certain countries during the First World War, to decrease the need for artificial light and heat – the system stayed in place after the war, as it proved practical. During the Second World War, some countries went so far as to keep their clocks an hour ahead of standard time continuously, and the UK temporarily introduced 'double summer time', which advanced clocks two hours ahead of standard time during the summer months.

World Languages

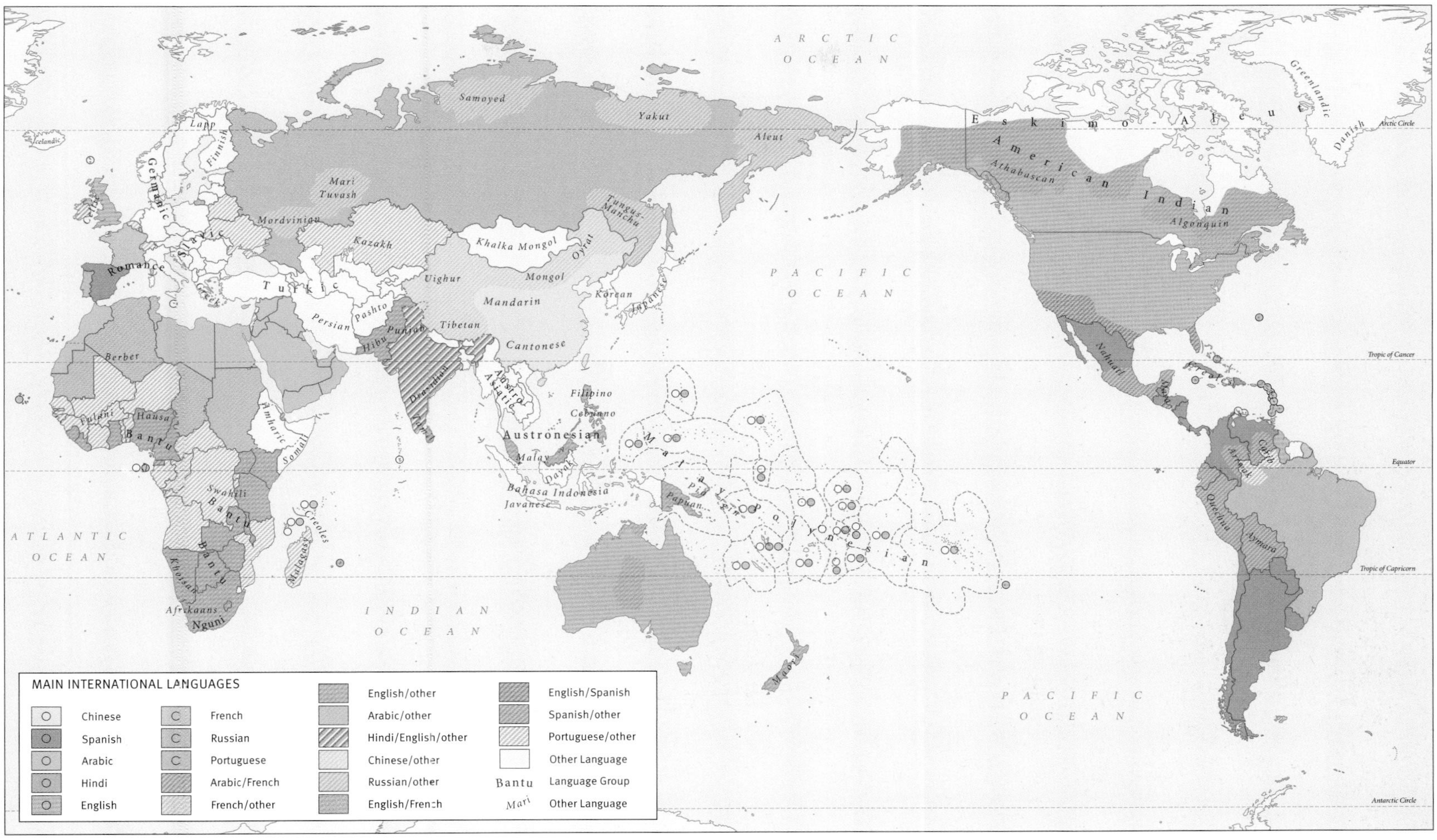

ARCTIC OCEAN

PACIFIC OCEAN

ATLANTIC OCEAN

INDIAN OCEAN

PACIFIC OCEAN

Icelandic, Lapp, Finnish, Germanic, Celtic, Slavic, Romance, Greek, Mordvinian, Mari, Tuvash, Samoyed, Yakut, Aleut, Tungus-Manchu, Kazakh, Khalka Mongol, Oyrat, Mongol, Turkic, Uighur, Mandarin, Korean, Japanese, Persian, Pashto, Punjabi, Hindi, Dravidian, Tibetan, Cantonese, Austro-Asiatic, Filipino, Cebuano, Austronesian, Malay, Bahasa Indonesia, Javanese, Dayak, Papuan, Malayo-Polynesian, Maori, Berber, Fulani, Hausa, Bantu, Amharic, Somali, Swahili, Creoles, Malagasy, Khoisan, Afrikaans, Nguni, Eskimo-Aleut, American Indian, Athabascan, Algonquin, Greenlandic, Danish, Nahuatl, Maya, Carib, Arawak, Quechua, Aymara

Arctic Circle

Tropic of Cancer

Equator

Tropic of Capricorn

Antarctic Circle

MAIN INTERNATIONAL LANGUAGES

- Chinese
- Spanish
- Arabic
- Hindi
- English
- French
- Russian
- Portuguese
- Arabic/French
- French/other
- English/other
- Arabic/other
- Hindi/English/other
- Chinese/other
- Russian/other
- English/French
- English/Spanish
- Spanish/other
- Portuguese/other
- Other Language
- Bantu — Language Group
- Mari — Other Language

World Religion

ARCTIC OCEAN

PACIFIC OCEAN

ATLANTIC OCEAN

INDIAN OCEAN

PACIFIC OCEAN

RUSSIAN FEDERATION

European Russia

Asiatic Russia

KAZAKHSTAN

MONGOLIA

CHINA

JAPAN

INDIA

INDONESIA

AUSTRALIA

NEW ZEALAND

CANADA

UNITED STATES OF AMERICA

Alaska (to US)

GREENLAND (to Denmark)

MEXICO

BRAZIL

PERU

BOLIVIA

PARAGUAY

CHILE

ARGENTINA

URUGUAY

ALGERIA

LIBYA

EGYPT

MALI

NIGER

CHAD

SUDAN

ETHIOPIA

NIGERIA

SAUDI ARABIA

IRAN

TURKEY

AFGH.

PAKISTAN

SOUTH AFRICA

Arctic Circle

Tropic of Cancer

Equator

Tropic of Capricorn

Antarctic Circle

MAIN INTERNATIONAL LANGUAGES

- Protestant Christianity
- Catholic Christianity
- Orthodox Christianity
- Shi'a Islam
- Sunni Islam
- Hinduism
- Judaism
- Theravada Buddhism
- Mahayana Buddhism
- Tibetan Buddhism
- Other
- Marxism / Maoism

STATE POLICY

- ▲ Secular ideologies governing
- ● Communist states during 20th century
- ■ Non-pluralist states

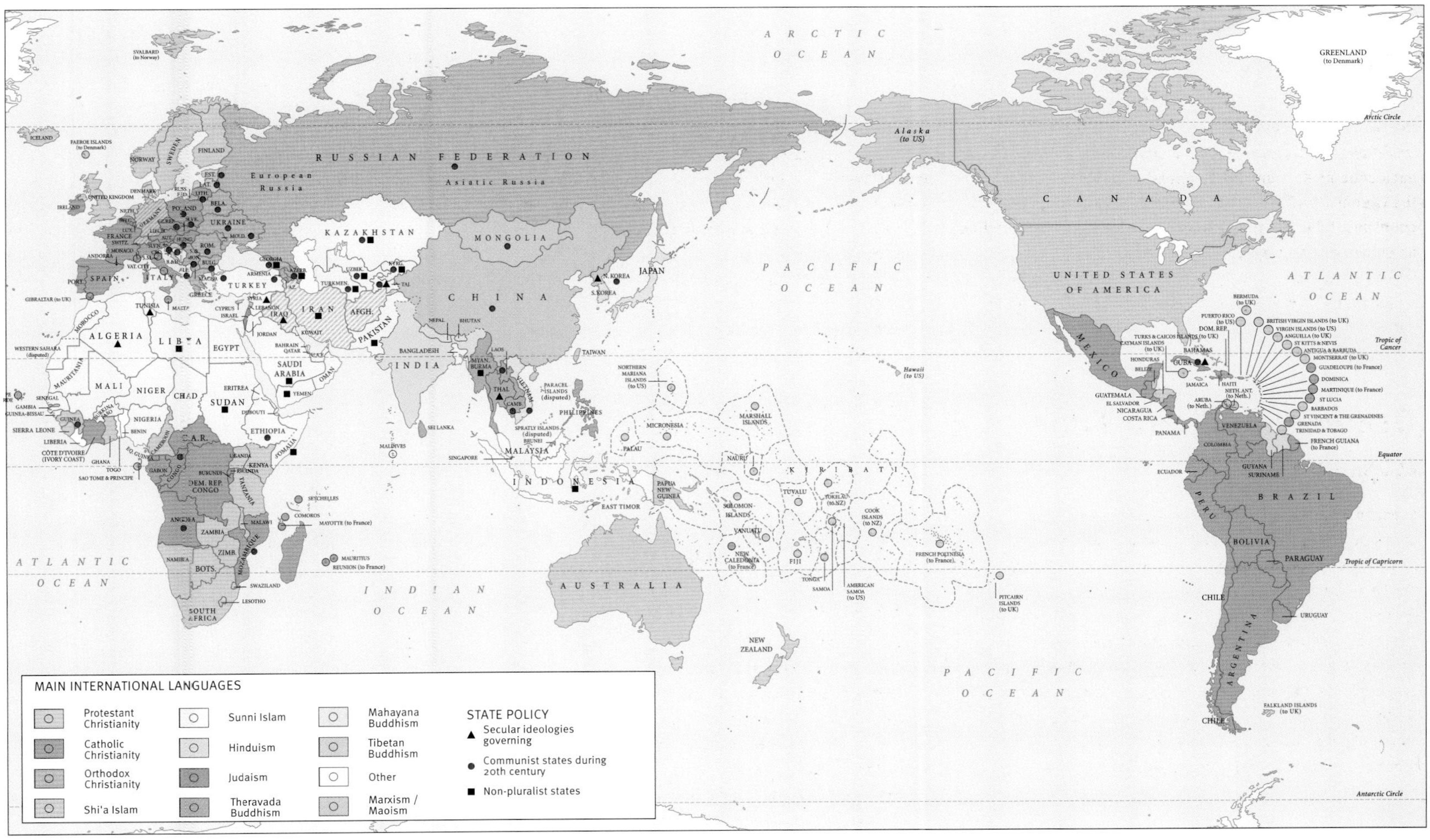

Factfile

AFGHANISTAN–COLOMBIA

Key to symbols

- Time zone
- Dialling code
- Electricity voltage
- Side of road for driving
- Internet ID code

IDP International drivers permit
Visa Refers to UK Nationals

AFGHANISTAN

+4.5 +93 220V Right .af

Area: 251,772 sq. miles (652,090 sq. km)
Population: 24.9 million
Capital: Kabul
Languages: Pashtu, Tajik, Dari, Farsi, Uzbek
Currency: New afghani = 100 puls
Banks closed: Friday
IDP required: Yes **Visa:** Yes
Tourist office: www.afghanistan-mfa.net
Climate: Mountain/cold desert

Month	J	F	M	A	M	J	J	A	S	O	N	D
Temp (ºC)	-8	-6	7	13	19	31	33	33	20	15	9	-3
Rainfall (cm)	3	4	9	10	2	1	0	0	0	2	2	1

ALBANIA

+1 +355 220V Right .al

Area: 10,579 sq. miles (27,400 sq. km)
Population: 3.2 million
Capital: Tirana
Languages: Albanian, Greek
Currency: Lek = 100 qindarka (qintars)
Banks closed: Sunday
IDP required: Yes **Visa:** No
Tourist office: www.albaniantourism.com
Climate: Mediterranean/continental

Month	J	F	M	A	M	J	J	A	S	O	N	D
Temp (ºC)	2	2	5	13	18	28	31	31	21	17	13	10
Rainfall (cm)	14	15	13	12	12	9	3	3	6	11	21	17

ALGERIA

+1 +213 220V Right .dz

Area: 919,590 sq. miles (2,381,740 sq. km)
Population: 32.3 million
Capital: Algiers
Languages: Arabic, Tamazight, French
Currency: Algerian dinar = 100 centimes
Banks closed: Friday
IDP required: Yes **Visa:** Yes
Tourist office: www.tourisme.dz
Climate: Hot desert/Mediterranean

Month	J	F	M	A	M	J	J	A	S	O	N	D
Temp (ºC)	9	9	14	17	19	22	28	29	27	20	16	11
Rainfall (cm)	11	8	7	4	5	2	0	1	4	8	13	14

ANDORRA

+1 +376 240V Right .ad

Area: 180 sq. miles (465 sq. km)
Population: 69,865
Capital: Andorra la Vella
Languages: Spanish, Catalan, French
Currency: Euro = 100 cents
Banks closed: Sunday
IDP required: No **Visa:** No
Tourist office: www.andorra.ad
Climate: Mountain

Month	J	F	M	A	M	J	J	A	S	O	N	D
Temp (ºC)	-1	-1	7	9	12	23	26	24	16	11	6	-1
Rainfall (cm)	3	4	5	6	11	7	7	10	8	7	7	7

ANGOLA

+1 +244 220V Right .ao

Area: 481,351 sq. miles (1,246,700 sq. km)
Population: 14.1 million
Capital: Luanda
Languages: Portuguese, Umbundu, Kimbundu
Currency: Readjusted kwanza = 100 lwei
Banks closed: Sunday
IDP required: Yes **Visa:** Yes
Tourist office: www.angola.org
Climate: Tropical/steppe

Month	J	F	M	A	M	J	J	A	S	O	N	D
Temp (ºC)	26	29	30	29	26	23	18	18	19	24	26	26
Rainfall (cm)	3	4	8	12	1	0	0	0	0	1	3	2

ANTARCTICA

n/a n/a n/a n/a .aq

Area: 5,366,790 sq. miles (13,900,000 sq. km)
Population: None
Capital: None
Languages: None
Currency: None
Banks closed: None
IDP required: No **Visa:** No
Tourist office: www.antarctica.ac.uk
Climate: Freezing

Month	J	F	M	A	M	J	J	A	S	O	N	D
Temp (ºC)	-27	-40	-54	-59	-57	-57	-63	-62	-62	-51	-38	-27
Rainfall (cm)	0	0	0	0	0	0	0	0	0	0	0	0

ANTIGUA & BARBUDA

-4.5 +1268 220V Left .ag

Area: 170 sq. miles (440 sq. km)
Population: 68,320
Capital: St. John's
Languages: English, English patois
Currency: Eastern Caribbean dollar = 100 cents
Banks closed: Sunday
IDP required: No **Visa:** No
Tourist office: www.antigua-barbuda.org
Climate: Tropical oceanic

Month	J	F	M	A	M	J	J	A	S	O	N	D
Temp (ºC)	18	17	21	22	23	24	28	28	27	24	23	14
Rainfall (cm)	8	5	5	8	10	10	13	13	15	15	15	13

ARGENTINA

-3 +54 220V Right .ar

Area: 1,056,636 sq. miles (2,736,690 sq. km)
Population: 38.9 million
Capital: Buenos Aires
Languages: Spanish, Italian, Amerindian
Currency: Argentine peso = 100 centavos
Banks closed: Sunday
IDP required: Yes **Visa:** No
Tourist office: www.turismo.gov.ar
Climate: Mountain/steppe/subtropical

Month	J	F	M	A	M	J	J	A	S	O	N	D
Temp (ºC)	29	28	21	17	13	5	6	6	13	16	19	28
Rainfall (cm)	8	7	11	9	8	6	6	6	8	9	8	10

ARMENIA

+4 +374 220V Right .am

Area: 11,506 sq. miles (29,800 sq. km)
Population: 3.1 million
Capital: Yerevan
Languages: Armenian, Azeri, Russian
Currency: Dram = 100 luma
Banks closed: Sunday
IDP required: Yes **Visa:** Yes
Tourist office: www.armeniainfo.am
Climate: Mountain

Month	J	F	M	A	M	J	J	A	S	O	N	D
Temp (ºC)	-8	-5	7	12	18	29	32	33	21	14	8	-2
Rainfall (cm)	3	3	3	5	5	3	1	1	2	2	2	3

AUSTRALIA

+8/+11 +61 220V Left .au

Area: 2,941,283 sq. miles (7,617,930 sq. km)
Population: 19.9 million
Capital: Canberra
Languages: English, many others
Currency: Australian dollar = 100 cents
Banks closed: Sunday
IDP required: No **Visa:** Yes
Tourist office: www.australia.com
Climate: Desert/steppe/tropical/Mediterranean

Month	J	F	M	A	M	J	J	A	S	O	N	D
Temp (ºC)	28	28	18	13	10	1	1	2	10	13	17	27
Rainfall (cm)	5	4	6	4	5	5	5	6	4	6	5	5

AUSTRIA

+1 +43 220V Right .at

Area: 31,942 sq. miles (82,730 sq. km)
Population: 8.1 million
Capital: Vienna
Languages: German, Croat, Slovene, Hungarian
Currency: Euro = 100 cents
Banks closed: Sunday
IDP required: No **Visa:** No
Tourist office: www.austria.info
Climate: Mountain/continental

Month	J	F	M	A	M	J	J	A	S	O	N	D
Temp (ºC)	-4	-3	4	11	15	23	25	24	16	11	5	-1
Rainfall (cm)	4	4	4	5	7	7	8	7	4	6	5	5

AZERBAIJAN

+4 +994 220V Right .az

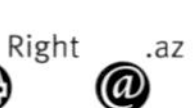

Area: 33,436 sq. miles (86,600 sq. km)
Population: 8.4 million
Capital: Baku
Languages: Azeri, Russian
Currency: Manat = 100 gopik
Banks closed: Sunday
IDP required: Yes **Visa:** Yes
Tourist office: www.mfa.gov.az
Climate: Mountain/steppe

Month	J	F	M	A	M	J	J	A	S	O	N	D
Temp (ºC)	7	8	6	11	18	26	29	29	22	17	11	10
Rainfall (cm)	2	2	2	3	2	1	1	1	2	3	3	3

BAHAMAS

-5 +1242 120V Left .bs

Area: 3865 sq. miles (10,010 sq. km)
Population: 317,000
Capital: Nassau
Languages: English, English & French Creole
Currency: Bahamian dollar = 100 cents
Banks closed: Sunday
IDP required: No **Visa:** No
Tourist office: www.bahamas.com
Climate: Tropical oceanic

Month	J	F	M	A	M	J	J	A	S	O	N	D
Temp (ºC)	18	18	23	24	26	27	31	32	31	26	24	23
Rainfall (cm)	4	4	4	6	12	16	15	14	18	17	7	3

BAHRAIN

+3 +973 230V Right .bh

Area: 273 sq. miles (706 sq. km)
Population: 739,000
Capital: Manama
Languages: Arabic
Currency: Bahraini dinar = 1,000 fils
Banks closed: Friday
IDP required: Yes **Visa:** Yes
Tourist office: www.bahraintourism.com
Climate: Hot desert

Month	J	F	M	A	M	J	J	A	S	O	N	D
Temp (ºC)	14	15	21	25	30	36	37	38	32	28	25	16
Rainfall (cm)	1	2	1	1	0	0	0	0	0	0	2	2

BANGLADESH

+6 +880 220V Left .bd

Area: 51,703 sq. miles (133,910 sq. km)
Population: 150 million
Capital: Dhaka
Languages: Bengali, Urdu, many others
Currency: Taka = 100 poisha
Banks closed: Friday
IDP required: Yes **Visa:** Yes
Tourist office: www.bangladeshtourism.org
Climate: Tropical/subtropical

Month	J	F	M	A	M	J	J	A	S	O	N	D
Temp (ºC)	12	13	33	35	34	29	29	29	29	28	24	13
Rainfall (cm)	2	3	6	10	19	32	44	31	25	17	3	0

BARBADOS

-4 +1246 110V Left .bb

Area: 166 sq. miles (430 sq. km)
Population: 271,000
Capital: Bridgetown
Languages: Bajan, English
Currency: Barbados dollar = 100 cents
Banks closed: Sunday
IDP required: Yes **Visa:** No
Tourist office: www.barmot.gov.bb
Climate: Tropical oceanic

Month	J	F	M	A	M	J	J	A	S	O	N	D
Temp (ºC)	21	21	21	26	31	31	27	31	31	27	26	25
Rainfall (cm)	7	3	3	4	6	11	15	15	17	18	21	10

BELARUS

+2 +375 220V Right .by

Area: 80,154 sq. miles (207,600 sq. km)
Population: 9.9 million
Capital: Minsk
Languages: Belarussian, Russian
Currency: Belarussian rouble = 100 kopeks
Banks closed: Sunday
IDP required: Yes **Visa:** No
Tourist office: www.belintourist.by
Climate: Continental

Month	J	F	M	A	M	J	J	A	S	O	N	D
Temp (ºC)	-13	-11	-3	6	13	22	23	22	13	7	1	-8
Rainfall (cm)	3	3	3	4	7	7	7	8	5	5	5	4

BELGIUM

+1 +32 220V Right .be

Area: 12,672 sq. miles (32,820 sq. km)
Population: 10.3 million
Capital: Brussels
Languages: Dutch, French, German
Currency: Euro = 100 cents
Banks closed: Sunday
IDP required: No **Visa:** No
Tourist office: www.belgium-tourism.net
Climate: Maritime

Month	J	F	M	A	M	J	J	A	S	O	N	D
Temp (ºC)	-1	0	6	10	13	22	23	22	16	11	6	0
Rainfall (cm)	7	6	5	6	6	8	10	8	6	8	8	9

BELIZE

-6 +501 110V Right .bz

Area: 8803 sq. miles (22,800 sq. km)
Population: 261,000
Capital: Belmopan
Languages: Creole, Spanish, English, others
Currency: Belizean dollar = 100 cents
Banks closed: Sunday
IDP required: No **Visa:** No
Tourist office: www.btia.org
Climate: Tropical equatorial

Month	J	F	M	A	M	J	J	A	S	O	N	D
Temp (ºC)	19	25	26	27	31	31	31	31	27	26	20	20
Rainfall (cm)	14	6	4	6	11	20	16	17	24	31	23	19

BENIN

+1 +229 220V Right .bj

Area: 42,710 sq. miles (110,620 sq. km)
Population: 6.9 million
Capital: Porto-Novo
Languages: Fon, Bariba, Yoruba, Adja, French
Currency: CFA franc = 100 centimes
Banks closed: Sunday
IDP required: Yes **Visa:** Yes
Tourist office: www.tourisme.gouv.bj
Climate: Tropical wet and dry

Month	J	F	M	A	M	J	J	A	S	O	N	D
Temp (°C)	25	28	28	28	26	25	25	23	25	26	26	26
Rainfall (cm)	3	3	12	13	25	37	9	4	7	14	6	1

BHUTAN

+6 +975 220V Left .bt

Area: 18,147 sq. miles (47,000 sq. km)
Population: 2.3 million
Capital: Thimphu
Languages: Dzongkha, Nepali, Assamese
Currency: Ngultrum = 100 chetrum
Banks closed: Sunday
IDP required: Yes **Visa:** Yes
Tourist office: www.kingdomofbhutan.com
Climate: Mountain/tropical monsoon

Month	J	F	M	A	M	J	J	A	S	O	N	D
Temp (°C)	2	4	16	20	30	29	29	24	24	20	15	3
Rainfall (cm)	2	4	2	6	12	25	37	35	16	4	1	0

BOLIVIA

-4 +591 220V Right .bo

Area: 418,683 sq. miles (1,084,390 sq. km)
Population: 9 million
Capitals: La Paz (admin); Sucre (judicial)
Languages: Aymara, Quechua, Spanish
Currency: Boliviano = 100 centavos
Banks closed: Sunday
IDP required: Yes **Visa:** No
Tourist office: www.turismobolivia.bo
Climate: Tropical/mountain

Month	J	F	M	A	M	J	J	A	S	O	N	D
Temp (°C)	12	12	12	11	11	1	1	2	11	19	19	18
Rainfall (cm)	11	11	7	3	1	1	1	1	3	4	5	9

BOSNIA & HERZEGOVINA

+1 +387 220V Right .ba

   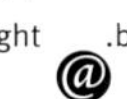

Area: 19,741 sq. miles (51,130 sq. km)
Population: 4.2 million
Capital: Sarajevo
Languages: Serbo-Croat
Currency: Marka = 100 pfeninga
Banks closed: Sunday
IDP required: Yes **Visa:** No
Tourist office: www.mvp.gov.ba
Climate: Continental

Month	J	F	M	A	M	J	J	A	S	O	N	D
Temp (°C)	-4	-3	5	10	14	24	26	27	16	11	6	-1
Rainfall (cm)	7	6	6	6	9	9	7	7	8	10	9	9

BOTSWANA

+2 +267 220V Left .bw

Area: 218,814 sq. miles (566,730 sq. km)
Population: 1.8 million
Capital: Gaborone
Languages: Setswana, English, Shona, others
Currency: Pula = 100 thebe
Banks closed: Sunday
IDP required: No **Visa:** No
Tourist office: www.botswanatourism.org
Climate: Steppe/hot desert

Month	J	F	M	A	M	J	J	A	S	O	N	D
Temp (°C)	33	32	23	20	16	3	3	5	20	23	24	32
Rainfall (cm)	8	8	7	3	2	1	1	0	1	5	6	8

BRAZIL

-3 +55 220V Right .br

Area: 3,265,059 sq. miles (8,456,510 sq. km)
Population: 181 million
Capital: Brasília
Languages: Portuguese, other languages
Currency: Real = 100 centavos
Banks closed: Sunday
IDP required: Yes **Visa:** No
Tourist office: www.embratur.gov.br
Climate: Tropical equatorial/other

Month	J	F	M	A	M	J	J	A	S	O	N	D
Temp (°C)	29	29	25	24	22	18	17	18	21	22	23	28
Rainfall (cm)	13	12	13	11	8	5	4	4	7	8	10	14

BRUNEI

+8 +673 220V Left .bn

Area: 2035 sq. miles (5270 sq. km)
Population: 366,000
Capital: Bandar Seri Begawan
Languages: Malay, English, Chinese
Currency: Brunei dollar = 100 cents
Banks closed: Friday
IDP required: Yes **Visa:** No
Tourist office: www.tourismbrunei.com
Climate: Tropical equatorial

Month	J	F	M	A	M	J	J	A	S	O	N	D
Temp (°C)	27	27	28	32	32	28	28	28	28	24	28	27
Rainfall (cm)	11	12	15	30	35	35	32	30	42	47	42	29

BULGARIA

+2 +359 230V Right .bg

Area: 42,683 sq. miles (110,550 sq. km)
Population: 7.8 million
Capital: Sofia
Languages: Bulgarian, Turkish, Romani
Currency: Lev = 100 stotinki
Banks closed: Sunday
IDP required: Yes **Visa:** No
Tourist office: www.bulgariatravel.org
Climate: Mediterranean/continental

Month	J	F	M	A	M	J	J	A	S	O	N	D
Temp (°C)	-4	-3	6	11	16	24	27	26	17	13	6	-2
Rainfall (cm)	4	3	4	6	9	7	7	6	4	7	5	5

BURKINA

0 +226 220V Right .bf

Area: 105,714 sq. miles (273,800 sq. km)
Population: 13.4 million
Capital: Ouagadougou
Languages: Mossi, Fulani, French, Tuareg
Currency: CFA franc = 100 centimes
Banks closed: Sunday
IDP required: Yes **Visa:** Yes
Tourist office: +226 5030 6396
Climate: Tropical/steppe

Month	J	F	M	A	M	J	J	A	S	O	N	D
Temp (°C)	16	29	40	39	38	30	30	27	28	29	29	17
Rainfall (cm)	0	0	1	2	8	12	20	28	15	3	0	0

BURMA (MYANMAR)

+6.5 +95 230V Right .mm

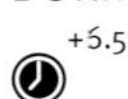   

Area: 253,876 sq. miles (657,540 sq. km)
Population: 50.1 million
Capital: Rangoon (Yangon)
Languages: Burmese, Shan, Karen, others
Currency: Kyat = 100 pyas
Banks closed: Sunday
IDP required: Yes **Visa:** Yes
Tourist office: www.myanmar-tourism.com
Climate: Tropical/mountain

Month	J	F	M	A	M	J	J	A	S	O	N	D
Temp (°C)	18	19	36	36	33	27	27	27	27	28	27	19
Rainfall (cm)	0	1	1	5	31	48	58	53	39	18	7	1

BURUNDI

+2 +257 220V Right .bi

Area: 9,903 sq. miles (25,650 sq. km)
Population: 7.1 million
Capital: Bujumbura
Languages: Kirundi, French, Kiswahili
Currency: Burundi franc = 100 centimes
Banks closed: Sunday
IDP required: No **Visa:** Yes
Tourist office: ontbur@cbinf.com
Climate: Tropical wet and dry

Month	J	F	M	A	M	J	J	A	S	O	N	D
Temp (°C)	24	24	24	24	24	18	17	30	31	30	24	24
Rainfall (cm)	9	11	12	13	6	1	1	1	4	6	10	11

CAMBODIA

+7 +855 230V Right .kh

Area: 68,154 sq. miles (176,520 sq. km)
Population: 14.5 million
Capital: Phnom Penh
Languages: Khmer, French, Chinese, others
Currency: Riel = 100 sen
Banks closed: Sunday
IDP required: No **Visa:** Yes
Tourist office: www.mot.gov.kh
Climate: Tropical monsoon

Month	J	F	M	A	M	J	J	A	S	O	N	D
Temp (°C)	21	22	34	35	34	29	28	29	28	27	27	22
Rainfall (cm)	1	1	4	8	13	16	17	16	22	26	13	5

CAMEROON

+1 +237 220V Right .cm

Area: 179,691 sq. miles (465,400 sq. km)
Population: 16.3 million
Capital: Yaoundé
Languages: Bamileke, Fang, Fulani, French
Currency: CFA franc = 100 centimes
Banks closed: Sunday
IDP required: Yes **Visa:** Yes
Tourist office: www.mintour.gov.cm
Climate: Tropical equatorial

Month	J	F	M	A	M	J	J	A	S	O	N	D
Temp (°C)	29	29	29	29	24	23	23	18	19	18	24	24
Rainfall (cm)	2	7	15	17	20	15	7	8	21	30	12	2

CANADA

-3.5/-8 +1 110V Right .ca

Area: 3,560,217 sq. miles (9,220,970 sq. km)
Population: 31.7 million
Capital: Ottawa
Languages: English, French, others
Currency: Canadian dollar = 100 cents
Banks closed: Sunday
IDP required: No **Visa:** No
Tourist office: www.canadatourism.com
Climate: Continental/subarctic/mountain

Month	J	F	M	A	M	J	J	A	S	O	N	D
Temp (°C)	-9	-9	-1	5	12	23	26	25	16	9	3	-6
Rainfall (cm)	7	6	7	6	7	7	7	7	7	6	7	7

CAPE VERDE

-1 +238 220V Right .cv

Area: 1,556 sq. miles (4,030 sq. km)
Population: 473,000
Capital: Praia
Languages: Portuguese Creole, Portuguese
Currency: Cape Verde escudo = 100 centavos
Banks closed: Sunday
IDP required: Yes **Visa:** Yes
Tourist office: www.virtualcapeverde.net
Climate: Tropical oceanic

Month	J	F	M	A	M	J	J	A	S	O	N	D
Temp (°C)	20	19	20	24	24	25	26	29	29	29	26	24
Rainfall (cm)	0	0	0	0	0	0	1	10	11	3	1	0

CENTRAL AFRICAN REPUBLIC

+1 +236 220V Right .cf

Area: 240,533 sq. miles (622,980 sq. km)
Population: 3.9 million
Capital: Bangui
Languages: Sango, Banda, Gbaya, French
Currency: CFA franc = 100 centimes
Banks closed: Sunday
IDP required: Yes **Visa:** Yes
Tourist office: +236 614566
Climate: Tropical equatorial

Month	J	F	M	A	M	J	J	A	S	O	N	D
Temp (°C)	26	34	33	33	27	26	25	25	26	26	26	19
Rainfall (cm)	3	4	13	14	19	11	23	21	15	20	13	1

CHAD

+1 +235 220V Right .td

Area: 486,177 sq. miles (1,259,200 sq. km)
Population: 8.9 million
Capital: N'Djamena
Languages: French, Sara, Arabic, Maba
Currency: CFA franc = 100 centimes
Banks closed: Sunday
IDP required: Yes **Visa:** Yes
Tourist office: +235 522303
Climate: Hot desert/steppe/tropical

Month	J	F	M	A	M	J	J	A	S	O	N	D
Temp (°C)	14	16	40	42	40	31	28	27	28	29	27	14
Rainfall (cm)	1	1	1	[illegible]	3	7	17	32	12	4	1	1

CHILE

-4 +56 220V Right .cl

Area: 289,112 sq. miles (748,800 sq. km)
Population: 16 million
Capital: Santiago
Languages: Spanish, Amerindian languages
Currency: Chilean peso = 100 centavos
Banks closed: Sunday
IDP required: Yes **Visa:** No
Tourist office: www.sernatur.cl
Climate: Desert/mountain/maritime

Month	J	F	M	A	M	J	J	A	S	O	N	D
Temp (°C)	29	29	18	15	13	3	3	4	13	15	18	28
Rainfall (cm)	0	0	1	1	6	8	8	6	3	2	1	1

CHINA

+8 +86 220V Right .cn

Area: 3,600,927 sq. miles (9,326,410 sq. km)
Population: 1.31 billion
Capital: Beijing
Languages: Mandarin, Wu, Cantonese, others
Currency: Renminbi (yuan) = 10 jiao = 100 fen
Banks closed: Sunday
IDP required: No **Visa:** Yes
Tourist office: www.cits.net
Climate: Mountain/tropical/steppe

Month	J	F	M	A	M	J	J	A	S	O	N	D
Temp (°C)	-10	-8	5	14	20	31	31	30	20	13	4	-8
Rainfall (cm)	0	1	1	2	4	8	24	14	6	2	1	0

COLOMBIA

-5 +57 110V Right .co

Area: 401,042 sq. miles (1,038,700 sq. km)
Population: 44.9 million
Capital: Bogotá
Languages: Spanish, Amerindian languages
Currency: Colombian peso = 100 centavos
Banks closed: Sunday
IDP required: Yes **Visa:** No
Tourist office: www.turismocolombia.com
Climate: Tropical/mountain

Month	J	F	M	A	M	J	J	A	S	O	N	D
Temp (°C)	9	20	15	19	19	15	14	14	14	15	15	9
Rainfall (cm)	6	7	10	15	11	6	5	6	6	16	12	7

Factfile

COMOROS–INDIA

Key to symbols

- Time zone
- Dialling code
- Electricity voltage
- Side of road for driving
- Internet ID code

IDP International drivers permit
Visa Refers to UK Nationals

COMOROS

+3 +269 220V Right .km

Area: 861 sq. miles (2230 sq. km)
Population: 790,000
Capital: Moroni
Languages: Arabic, Comoran, French
Currency: Comoros franc = 100 centimes
Banks closed: Sunday
IDP required: Yes **Visa:** Yes
Tourist office: +269 744242
Climate: Tropical oceanic

Month	J	F	M	A	M	J	J	A	S	O	N	D
Temp (ºC)	27	27	31	27	26	24	19	9	19	25	31	31
Rainfall (cm)	35	31	30	30	23	22	19	2	12	9	10	22

CONGO

+1 +242 220V Right .cg

Area: 131,853 sq. miles (341,500 sq. km)
Population: 3.8 million
Capital: Brazzaville
Languages: Kongo, Teke, Lingala, French
Currency: CFA franc = 100 centimes
Banks closed: Sunday
IDP required: Yes **Visa:** Yes
Tourist office: +242 814022
Climate: Tropical equatorial

Month	J	F	M	A	M	J	J	A	S	O	N	D
Temp (ºC)	26	27	33	33	27	18	17	18	26	27	26	26
Rainfall (cm)	16	13	19	18	11	2	0	0	6	14	29	21

CONGO, DEM. REPUBLIC

+1 +243 220V Right .zr

Area: 875,520 sq. miles (2,267,600 sq. km)
Population: 54.4 million
Capital: Kinshasa
Languages: Kiswahili, Tshiluba, French, others
Currency: Congolese franc = 100 centimes
Banks closed: Sunday
IDP required: Yes **Visa:** Yes
Tourist office: +243 12 30070
Climate: Tropical equatorial/wet and dry

Month	J	F	M	A	M	J	J	A	S	O	N	D
Temp (ºC)	26	31	32	32	27	19	18	18	26	26	27	26
Rainfall (cm)	14	15	20	20	16	1	0	0	3	12	22	14

COSTA RICA

-6 +506 120V Right .cr

Area: 19,714 sq. miles (51,060 sq. km)
Population: 4.3 million
Capital: San José
Languages: Spanish, English Creole, others
Currency: Costa Rican colón = 100 centimos
Banks closed: Sunday
IDP required: No **Visa:** No
Tourist office: www.visitcostarica.com
Climate: Tropical wet and dry

Month	J	F	M	A	M	J	J	A	S	O	N	D
Temp (ºC)	14	14	21	26	27	26	21	21	21	21	21	14
Rainfall (cm)	2	1	2	5	23	24	21	24	31	30	15	4

CROATIA

+1 +385 220V Right .hr

Area: 21,829 sq. miles (56,538 sq. km)
Population: 4.4 million
Capital: Zagreb
Languages: Croatian
Currency: Kuna = 100 lipas
Banks closed: Sunday
IDP required: No **Visa:** No
Tourist office: www.croatia.hr
Climate: Mediterranean/continental

Month	J	F	M	A	M	J	J	A	S	O	N	D
Temp (ºC)	-2	-1	7	12	17	25	27	27	18	12	7	0
Rainfall (cm)	6	5	5	6	9	10	8	7	7	9	9	7

CUBA

-5 +53 220V Right .cu

Area: 42,803 sq. miles (110,860 sq. km)
Population: 11.3 million
Capital: Havana
Languages: Spanish
Currency: Cuban peso = 100 centavos
Banks closed: Sunday
IDP required: No **Visa:** No
Tourist office: www.cubatravel.cu
Climate: Tropical oceanic

Month	J	F	M	A	M	J	J	A	S	O	N	D
Temp (ºC)	18	18	23	25	26	27	32	32	31	26	24	19
Rainfall (cm)	7	5	5	6	12	17	13	14	15	17	8	6

CYPRUS

+2 +357 240V Left .cy

Area: 3,568 sq. miles (9,240 sq. km)
Population: 808,000
Capital: Nicosia
Languages: Greek, Turkish
Currency: Cyprus pound; New Turkish lira
Banks closed: Sunday
IDP required: No **Visa:** No
Tourist office: www.visitcyprus.org.cy
Climate: Mediterranean

Month	J	F	M	A	M	J	J	A	S	O	N	D
Temp (ºC)	5	5	13	17	22	34	37	37	26	21	16	7
Rainfall (cm)	8	5	4	2	2	1	0	0	1	3	3	7

CZECH REPUBLIC

+1 +420 220V Right .cz

Area: 30,449 sq. miles (78,864 sq. km)
Population: 10.2 million
Capital: Prague
Languages: Czech, Slovak, Hungarian
Currency: Czech koruna = 100 haleru
Banks closed: Sunday
IDP required: No **Visa:** No
Tourist office: www.czechtourism.cz
Climate: Continental

Month	J	F	M	A	M	J	J	A	S	O	N	D
Temp (ºC)	-5	-4	3	8	13	21	23	22	14	9	3	-3
Rainfall (cm)	2	2	2	3	5	5	7	6	3	3	2	2

DENMARK

+1 +45 220V Right .dk

Area: 16,359 sq. miles (42,370 sq. km)
Population: 5.4 million
Capital: Copenhagen
Languages: Danish
Currency: Danish krone = 100 øre
Banks closed: Sunday
IDP required: No **Visa:** No
Tourist office: www.visitdenmark.com
Climate: Maritime

Month	J	F	M	A	M	J	J	A	S	O	N	D
Temp (ºC)	-2	-3	-1	7	12	19	22	21	15	10	5	3
Rainfall (cm)	5	4	3	4	4	5	7	7	6	6	5	5

DJIBOUTI

+3 +253 220V Right .dj

Area: 8,950 sq. miles (23,180 sq. km)
Population: 712,000
Capital: Djibouti
Languages: Somali, Afar, French, Arabic
Currency: Djibouti franc = 100 centimes
Banks closed: Friday
IDP required: Yes **Visa:** Yes
Tourist office: www.office-tourisme.dj
Climate: Hot desert

Month	J	F	M	A	M	J	J	A	S	O	N	D
Temp (ºC)	23	24	28	29	31	37	41	39	33	30	28	23
Rainfall (cm)	1	1	3	1	1	0	0	1	1	1	2	1

DOMINICA

-4 +1767 220V Left .dm

Area: 290 sq. miles (750 sq. km)
Population: 69,278
Capital: Roseau
Languages: French Creole, English
Currency: East Caribbean dollar = 100 cents
Banks closed: Sunday
IDP required: Yes **Visa:** No
Tourist office: www.dominica.dm
Climate: Tropical oceanic

Month	J	F	M	A	M	J	J	A	S	O	N	D
Temp (ºC)	20	19	20	26	27	32	27	32	32	27	27	26
Rainfall (cm)	13	7	7	6	10	20	27	26	23	20	22	16

DOMINICAN REPUBLIC

-4 +1809 110V Right .do

 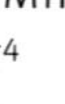     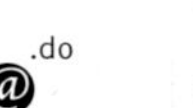

Area: 18,679 sq. miles (48,380 sq. km)
Population: 8.9 million
Capital: Santo Domingo
Languages: Spanish, French Creole
Currency: Dom. Republic peso = 100 centavos
Banks closed: Sunday
IDP required: No **Visa:** No
Tourist office: www.dominicana.com.do
Climate: Tropical equatorial/oceanic

Month	J	F	M	A	M	J	J	A	S	O	N	D
Temp (ºC)	19	19	19	25	26	31	31	31	31	31	26	19
Rainfall (cm)	6	4	5	10	17	16	16	16	19	15	12	6

EAST TIMOR

+8 +670 220V n/a .tp

Area: 5,641 sq. miles (14,609 sq. km)
Population: 820,000
Capital: Dili
Languages: Tetum Bahasa Indonesia, others
Currency: US dollar = 100 cents
Banks closed: Sunday
IDP required: No **Visa:** No
Tourist office: www.mfac.gov.tp
Climate: Tropical equatorial

Month	J	F	M	A	M	J	J	A	S	O	N	D
Temp (ºC)	27	27	27	27	26	26	25	24	25	26	27	27
Rainfall (cm)	14	13	14	8	8	5	2	1	2	2	6	14

ECUADOR

-5 +593 110V Right .ec

Area: 106,888 sq. miles (276,840 sq. km)
Population: 13.2 million
Capital: Quito
Languages: Spanish, Quechua, others
Currency: US dollar = 100 cents
Banks closed: Sunday
IDP required: No **Visa:** No
Tourist office: www.vivecuador.com
Climate: Tropical/mountain

Month	J	F	M	A	M	J	J	A	S	O	N	D
Temp (ºC)	15	15	15	15	15	7	7	23	23	15	7	15
Rainfall (cm)	10	11	14	18	14	4	2	3	7	11	10	8

EGYPT

+2 +20 220V Right .eg

Area: 384,343 sq. miles (995,450 sq. km)
Population: 73.4 million
Capital: Cairo
Languages: Arabic, French, English, Berber
Currency: Egyptian pound = 100 piastres
Banks closed: Friday
IDP required: Yes **Visa:** Yes
Tourist office: www.touregypt.net
Climate: Hot desert/Mediterranean

Month	J	F	M	A	M	J	J	A	S	O	N	D
Temp (ºC)	8	9	11	21	25	35	36	35	26	24	20	15
Rainfall (cm)	1	1	1	0	0	0	0	0	0	0	0	1

EL SALVADOR

-6 +503 110V Right .sv

Area: 8,000 sq. miles (20,720 sq. km)
Population: 6.6 million
Capital: San Salvador
Languages: Spanish
Currency: Salvadorean colón; US dollar
Banks closed: Sunday
IDP required: No **Visa:** No
Tourist office: www.elsalvadorturismo.gob.sv
Climate: Tropical wet and dry

Month	J	F	M	A	M	J	J	A	S	O	N	D
Temp (ºC)	16	16	34	34	33	25	25	26	25	25	24	16
Rainfall (cm)	1	1	1	4	20	33	29	30	31	24	4	1

EQUATORIAL GUINEA

+1 +240 220V Right .gq

Area: 10,830 sq. miles (28,050 sq. km)
Population: 507,000
Capital: Malabo
Languages: Spanish, Fang, Bubi
Currency: CFA franc = 100 centimes
Banks closed: Sunday
IDP required: No **Visa:** Yes
Tourist office: Paris Embassy +33 1 5688 5454
Climate: Tropical equatorial

Month	J	F	M	A	M	J	J	A	S	O	N	D
Temp (ºC)	19	32	26	32	31	25	25	25	26	26	26	26
Rainfall (cm)	1	3	19	16	26	30	16	11	20	23	12	2

ERITREA

+3 +291 220V Right .er

Area: 45,405 sq. miles (117,600 sq. km)
Population: 4.3 million
Capital: Asmara
Languages: Tigrinya, English, Tigre, Afar, other
Currency: Nakfa = 100 cents
Banks closed: Sunday
IDP required: Yes **Visa:** Yes
Tourist office: www.shaebia.org/mot.html
Climate: Hot desert/mountain

Month	J	F	M	A	M	J	J	A	S	O	N	D
Temp (ºC)	6	7	17	25	25	26	16	16	18	16	16	7
Rainfall (cm)	0	0	1	3	4	4	16	14	2	1	2	0

ESTONIA

+2 +372 220V Right .ee

Area: 17,423 sq. miles (45,125 sq. km)
Population: 1.3 million
Capital: Tallinn
Languages: Estonian, Russian
Currency: Kroon = 100 senti
Banks closed: Sunday
IDP required: No **Visa:** No
Tourist office: www.visitestonia.com
Climate: Continental

Month	J	F	M	A	M	J	J	A	S	O	N	D
Temp (ºC)	-10	-11	-7	4	9	19	20	20	12	7	1	-4
Rainfall (cm)	4	3	2	3	4	4	7	8	7	7	6	4

ETHIOPIA

+3 +251 220V Right .et

Area: 428,571 sq. miles (1,110,000 sq. km)
Population: 72.4 million
Capital: Addis Ababa
Languages: Amharic, Tigrinya, English, Arabic
Currency: Ethiopian birr = 100 cents
Banks closed: Sunday
IDP required: No **Visa:** Yes
Tourist office: www.tourismethiopia.org
Climate: Mountain/steppe

Month	J	F	M	A	M	J	J	A	S	O	N	D
Temp (ºC)	6	16	25	25	25	16	16	16	16	16	6	5
Rainfall (cm)	1	4	7	9	9	14	28	30	19	2	2	1

FIJI

+12 +679 240V Left .fj

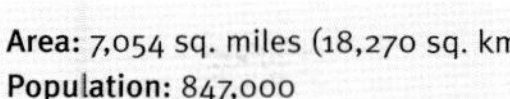

Area: 7,054 sq. miles (18,270 sq. km)
Population: 847,000
Capital: Suva
Languages: Fijian, English, Hindi, Urdu, Tamil
Currency: Fiji dollar = 100 cents
Banks closed: Sunday
IDP required: Yes **Visa:** No
Tourist office: www.bulafiji.com
Climate: Tropical oceanic

Month	J	F	M	A	M	J	J	A	S	O	N	D
Temp (ºC)	29	29	29	29	25	24	20	20	24	24	25	29
Rainfall (cm)	29	27	37	31	26	17	13	21	20	21	25	32

FINLAND

+2 +358 230V Right .fi

Area: 117,610 sq. miles (304,610 sq. km)
Population: 5.2 million
Capital: Helsinki
Languages: Finnish, Swedish, Sámi
Currency: Euro = 100 cents
Banks closed: Sunday
IDP required: No **Visa:** No
Tourist office: www.visitfinland.com
Climate: Subarctic/continental

Month	J	F	M	A	M	J	J	A	S	O	N	D
Temp (ºC)	-9	-10	-7	3	9	19	22	20	12	6	1	-3
Rainfall (cm)	6	4	4	4	4	5	7	7	7	7	7	7

FRANCE

+1 +33 220V Right .fr

Area: 212,394 sq. miles (550,100 sq. km)
Population: 60.4 million
Capital: Paris
Languages: French, Provençal, Breton, others
Currency: Euro = 100 cents
Banks closed: Sunday
IDP required: No **Visa:** No
Tourist office: www.franceguide.com
Climate: Maritime/Mediterranean/mountain

Month	J	F	M	A	M	J	J	A	S	O	N	D
Temp (ºC)	1	1	8	11	15	23	25	24	17	12	8	2
Rainfall (cm)	6	5	4	4	6	5	6	6	6	5	5	5

GABON

+1 +241 220V Right .ga

Area: 99,486 sq. miles (257,670 sq. km)
Population: 1.4 million
Capital: Libreville
Languages: Fang, French, Punu, Sira, Nzebi
Currency: CFA franc = 100 centimes
Banks closed: Sunday
IDP required: Yes **Visa:** Yes
Tourist office: www.gabontour.com
Climate: Tropical equatorial

Month	J	F	M	A	M	J	J	A	S	O	N	D
Temp (ºC)	31	27	32	32	27	21	20	21	26	26	26	27
Rainfall (cm)	25	24	34	34	24	1	0	2	10	35	37	25

GAMBIA

0 +220 220V Right .gm

Area: 3,861 sq. miles (10,000 sq. km)
Population: 1.5 million
Capital: Banjul
Languages: Mandinka, Fulani, Wolof, English
Currency: Dalasi = 100 butut
Banks closed: Sunday
IDP required: Yes **Visa:** No
Tourist office: www.visitthegambia.gm
Climate: Tropical wet and dry

Month	J	F	M	A	M	J	J	A	S	O	N	D
Temp (ºC)	15	16	34	33	26	32	27	26	27	27	25	16
Rainfall (cm)	0	0	0	0	1	6	28	50	31	11	2	0

GEORGIA

+4 +995 220V Right .ge

Area: 26,911 sq. miles (69,700 sq. km)
Population: 5.1 million
Capital: Tbilisi
Languages: Georgian, Russian, Azeri, others
Currency: Lari = 100 tetri
Banks closed: Sunday
IDP required: Yes **Visa:** Yes
Tourist office: www.tourism.gov.ge
Climate: Mountain/subtropical

Month	J	F	M	A	M	J	J	A	S	O	N	D
Temp (ºC)	-1	0	8	13	18	28	31	30	20	15	10	1
Rainfall (cm)	2	2	3	6	8	6	5	4	4	4	3	2

GERMANY

+1 +49 230V Right .de

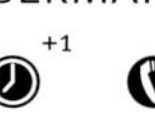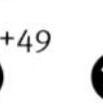

Area: 134,950 sq. miles (349,520 sq. km)
Population: 82.5 million
Capital: Berlin
Languages: German, Turkish
Currency: Euro = 100 cents
Banks closed: Sunday
IDP required: No **Visa:** No
Tourist office: www.germany-tourism.de
Climate: Continental/maritime

Month	J	F	M	A	M	J	J	A	S	O	N	D
Temp (ºC)	-3	-3	4	9	14	22	24	23	15	10	5	-1
Rainfall (cm)	5	4	3	4	5	7	7	7	5	5	5	4

GHANA

0 +233 220V Right .gh

Area: 88,810 sq. miles (230,020 sq. km)
Population: 21.4 million
Capital: Accra
Languages: Twi, Fanti, Ewe, Ga, Adangbe
Currency: Cedi = 100 psewas
Banks closed: Sunday
IDP required: Yes **Visa:** Yes
Tourist office: www.ghanatourism.gov.gh
Climate: Tropical wet and dry/equatorial

Month	J	F	M	A	M	J	J	A	S	O	N	D
Temp (ºC)	27	31	31	31	31	26	23	22	23	26	31	31
Rainfall (cm)	2	3	6	8	14	18	5	2	4	6	4	2

GREECE

+2 +30 220V Right .gr

Area: 50,521 sq. miles (130,850 sq. km)
Population: 11 million
Capital: Athens
Languages: Greek, Turkish, Macedonian
Currency: Euro = 100 cents
Banks closed: Sunday
IDP required: No **Visa:** No
Tourist office: www.gnto.gr
Climate: Mediterranean

Month	J	F	M	A	M	J	J	A	S	O	N	D
Temp (ºC)	6	7	12	16	21	30	33	33	24	20	16	8
Rainfall (cm)	6	4	4	2	2	1	1	1	2	5	6	7

GRENADA

-4 +1473 220V Left .gd

Area: 131 sq. miles (340 sq. km)
Population: 89,357
Capital: St. George's
Languages: English, English Creole
Currency: East Caribbean dollar = 100 cents
Banks closed: Sunday
IDP required: Yes **Visa:** No
Tourist office: www.grenadagrenadines.com
Climate: Tropical oceanic

Month	J	F	M	A	M	J	J	A	S	O	N	D
Temp (ºC)	21	21	25	26	31	31	31	27	27	27	26	21
Rainfall (cm)	13	6	7	6	12	9	21	22	21	23	14	17

GUATEMALA

-6 +502 110V Right .gt

Area: 41,865 sq. miles (108,430 sq. km)
Population: 12.7 million
Capital: Guatemala City
Languages: Quiché, Mam, Spanish, others
Currency: Quetzal = 100 centavos
Banks closed: Sunday
IDP required: No **Visa:** No
Tourist office: www.mayaspirit.com.gt
Climate: Tropical equatorial/wet and dry

Month	J	F	M	A	M	J	J	A	S	O	N	D
Temp (ºC)	12	12	21	28	29	27	21	21	21	20	19	13
Rainfall (cm)	1	0	1	3	15	27	20	20	23	17	2	1

GUINEA

0 +224 220V Right .gn

Area: 94,927 sq. miles (245,860 sq. km)
Population: 8.6 million
Capital: Conakry
Languages: Fulani, Malinke, Soussou, French
Currency: Guinea franc = 100 centimes
Banks closed: Sunday
IDP required: Yes **Visa:** Yes
Tourist office: www.guinee.gov.gn
Climate: Tropical monsoon

Month	J	F	M	A	M	J	J	A	S	O	N	D
Temp (ºC)	27	27	32	32	32	27	22	22	23	27	28	27
Rainfall (cm)	0	0	1	2	16	56	130	105	68	37	12	1

GUINEA-BISSAU

0 +245 220V Right .gw

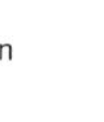

Area: 10,857 sq. miles (28,120 sq. km)
Population: 1.5 million
Capital: Bissau
Languages: Portuguese Creole, Balante, Fulani
Currency: CFA franc = 100 centimes
Banks closed: Sunday
IDP required: Yes **Visa:** Yes
Tourist office: +245 213905
Climate: Tropical monsoon

Month	J	F	M	A	M	J	J	A	S	O	N	D
Temp (ºC)	18	19	34	33	33	27	26	26	26	27	27	19
Rainfall (cm)	0	0	0	0	2	17	49	62	42	20	4	1

GUYANA

-4 +592 110V Left .gy

Area: 76,004 sq. miles (196,850 sq. km)
Population: 767,000
Capital: Georgetown
Languages: English Creole, Hindi, Tamil, other
Currency: Guyana dollar = 100 cents
Banks closed: Sunday
IDP required: No **Visa:** No
Tourist office: www.guyana-tourism.com
Climate: Tropical equatorial

Month	J	F	M	A	M	J	J	A	S	O	N	D
Temp (ºC)	23	23	27	27	27	27	27	30	31	31	30	27
Rainfall (cm)	20	11	18	14	29	30	25	18	8	8	16	29

HAITI

-5 +509 110V Right .ht

Area: 10,641 sq. miles (27,560 sq. km)
Population: 8.4 million
Capital: Port-au-Prince
Languages: French Creole, French
Currency: Gourde = 100 centimes
Banks closed: Sunday
IDP required: Yes **Visa:** No
Tourist office: www.haititourisme.org
Climate: Tropical equatorial/oceanic

Month	J	F	M	A	M	J	J	A	S	O	N	D
Temp (ºC)	20	20	27	27	27	28	34	34	28	27	27	26
Rainfall (cm)	3	6	9	16	23	10	7	15	18	17	9	3

HONDURAS

-6 +504 110V Right .hn

Area: 43,201 sq. miles (111,890 sq. km)
Population: 7.1 million
Capital: Tegucigalpa
Languages: Spanish, Garífuna, English Creole
Currency: Lempira = 100 centavos
Banks closed: Sunday
IDP required: No **Visa:** No
Tourist office: www.letsgohonduras.com
Climate: Tropical equatorial

Month	J	F	M	A	M	J	J	A	S	O	N	D
Temp (ºC)	14	21	29	30	30	23	23	23	23	22	16	15
Rainfall (cm)	1	0	0	3	18	18	7	7	15	9	4	1

HUNGARY

+1 +36 220V Right .hu

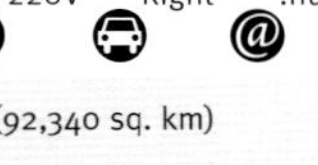

Area: 35,652 sq. miles (92,340 sq. km)
Population: 9.8 million
Capital: Budapest
Languages: Hungarian (Magyar)
Currency: Forint = 100 fillér
Banks closed: Sunday
IDP required: Yes **Visa:** No
Tourist office: www.hungary.com
Climate: Continental

Month	J	F	M	A	M	J	J	A	S	O	N	D
Temp (ºC)	-4	-2	6	12	17	26	28	27	18	12	6	-1
Rainfall (cm)	4	4	4	5	7	7	6	5	3	6	7	5

ICELAND

0 +354 220V Right .is

Area: 38,707 sq. miles (100,250 sq. km)
Population: 292,000
Capital: Reykjavík
Languages: Icelandic
Currency: Icelandic króna = 100 aurar
Banks closed: Sunday
IDP required: Yes **Visa:** No
Tourist office: www.icetourist.is
Climate: Subarctic

Month	J	F	M	A	M	J	J	A	S	O	N	D
Temp (ºC)	-2	-2	2	4	7	12	14	14	9	5	2	-2
Rainfall (cm)	9	6	6	6	4	4	5	6	7	9	8	8

INDIA

+5.5 +91 220V Left .in

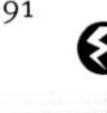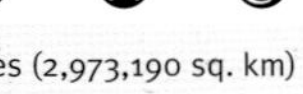

Area: 1,147,949 sq. miles (2,973,190 sq. km)
Population: 1.08 billion
Capital: New Delhi
Languages: Hindi, English, Urdu, Bengali, other
Currency: Indian rupee = 100 paise
Banks closed: Sunday
IDP required: Yes **Visa:** Yes
Tourist office: www.tourismofindia.com
Climate: Tropical/desert/mountain/monsoon

Month	J	F	M	A	M	J	J	A	S	O	N	D
Temp (ºC)	7	9	23	28	41	39	36	30	29	26	20	8
Rainfall (cm)	2	2	1	1	1	7	18	17	12	1	1	1

Factfile

INDONESIA–MONGOLIA

Key to symbols

- Time zone
- Dialling code
- Electricity voltage
- Side of road for driving
- Internet ID code

IDP International drivers permit
Visa Refers to UK Nationals

INDONESIA

+7/+9 +62 220V Left .id

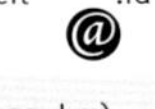

Area: 693,700 sq. miles (1,796,700 sq. km)
Population: 223 million
Capital: Jakarta
Languages: Javanese, Sundanese, Dutch, other
Currency: Rupiah = 100 sen
Banks closed: Sunday
IDP required: Yes **Visa:** Yes
Tourist office: www.budpar.go.ic
Climate: Tropical equatorial/monsoon

Month	J	F	M	A	M	J	J	A	S	O	N	D
Temp (ºC)	23	23	27	31	31	27	27	27	31	31	27	23
Rainfall (cm)	30	30	21	15	11	10	6	4	7	11	14	20

IRAN

+3.5 +98 230V Right .ir

Area: 631,660 sq. miles (1,636,000 sq. km)
Population: 69.8 million
Capital: Tehran
Languages: Farsi, Kurdish, Turkmen, Arabic
Currency: Iranian rial = 100 dinars
Banks closed: Friday
IDP required: Yes **Visa:** Yes
Tourist office: www.itto.org
Climate: Mountain/cold desert

Month	J	F	M	A	M	J	J	A	S	O	N	D
Temp (ºC)	-3	0	10	16	21	34	37	36	25	18	12	1
Rainfall (cm)	5	4	5	4	1	0	0	0	0	1	2	3

IRAQ

+3 +964 230V Right .iq

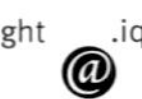

Area: 168,869 sq. miles (437,370 sq. km)
Population: 25.9 million
Capital: Baghdad
Languages: Arabic, Kurdish, Armenian, others
Currency: New Iraqi dinar = 1,000 fils
Banks closed: Friday
IDP required: Yes **Visa:** Yes
Tourist office: www.iraqiembassy.org
Climate: Hot desert/steppe

Month	J	F	M	A	M	J	J	A	S	O	N	D
Temp (ºC)	4	6	16	22	28	41	43	43	31	25	18	6
Rainfall (cm)	2	3	3	1	1	1	1	1	1	1	2	3

IRELAND

0 +353 220V Left .ie

Area: 26,598 sq. miles (68,890 sq. km)
Population: 4 million
Capital: Dublin
Languages: English, Irish Gaelic
Currency: Euro = 100 cents
Banks closed: Sunday
IDP required: No **Visa:** No
Tourist office: www.ireland.ie
Climate: Maritime

Month	J	F	M	A	M	J	J	A	S	O	N	D
Temp (ºC)	1	2	7	9	11	18	20	19	13	10	7	3
Rainfall (cm)	7	6	5	5	6	6	7	7	7	7	7	7

ISRAEL

+2 +972 230V Right .il

Area: 7,849 sq. miles (20,330 sc. km)
Population: 6.6 million
Capital: Jerusalem
Languages: Hebrew, Arabic, Yiddish,others
Currency: Shekel = 100 agorot
Banks closed: Saturday
IDP required: Yes **Visa:** No
Tourist office: www.tourism.gov.il
Climate: Hot desert/Mediterranean

Month	J	F	M	A	M	J	J	A	S	O	N	D
Temp (ºC)	5	6	13	17	21	23	31	31	29	21	17	7
Rainfall (cm)	13	13	6	3	0	0	0	0	0	1	7	9

ITALY

+1 +39 230V Right .it

Area: 113,536 sq. miles (294,060 sq. km)
Population: 57.3 million
Capital: Rome
Languages: Italian, German, French, others
Currency: Euro = 100 cents
Banks closed: Sunday
IDP required: No **Visa:** No
Tourist office: www.enit.it
Climate: Mediterranean/mountain

Month	J	F	M	A	M	J	J	A	S	O	N	D
Temp (ºC)	5	5	11	15	18	28	30	30	22	18	13	6
Rainfall (cm)	7	6	6	5	5	4	2	2	6	10	13	9

IVORY COAST

0 +225 220V Right .ci

Area: 122,780 sq. miles (318,000 sq. km)
Population: 16.9 million
Capital: Yamoussoukro
Languages: Akan, French, Kru, Voltaic
Currency: CFA franc = 100 centimes
Banks closed: Sunday
IDP required: No **Visa:** Yes
Tourist office: www.tourismeci.org
Climate: Tropical wet and dry

Month	J	F	M	A	M	J	J	A	S	O	N	D
Temp (ºC)	27	32	32	32	28	26	23	22	23	26	27	27
Rainfall (cm)	4	5	10	13	36	50	21	5	7	17	20	8

JAMAICA

-5 +1876 110V Left .jm

Area: 4,181 sq. miles (10,830 sq. km)
Population: 2.7 million
Capital: Kingston
Languages: English Creole, English
Currency: Jamaican dollar = 100 cents
Banks closed: Sunday
IDP required: No **Visa:** No
Tourist office: www.visitjamaica.com
Climate: Tropical oceanic

Month	J	F	M	A	M	J	J	A	S	O	N	D
Temp (ºC)	19	19	20	26	27	28	32	32	32	27	27	26
Rainfall (cm)	2	2	2	3	10	9	9	9	10	18	7	4

JAPAN

+9 +81 100V Left .jp

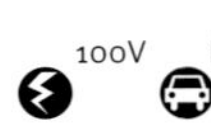

Area: 145,374 sq. miles (376,520 sq. km)
Population: 128 million
Capital: Tokyo
Languages: Japanese, Korean, Chinese
Currency: Yen = 100 sen
Banks closed: Sunday
IDP required: Yes **Visa:** No
Tourist office: www.jnto.go.jp
Climate: Continental/subtropical

Month	J	F	M	A	M	J	J	A	S	O	N	D
Temp (ºC)	-2	-1	7	13	17	21	28	30	26	17	11	1
Rainfall (cm)	5	7	11	14	15	17	14	15	23	21	10	6

JORDAN

+2 +962 230V Right .jo

Area: 34,336 sq. miles (88,930 sq. km)
Population: 5.6 million
Capital: Amman
Languages: Arabic
Currency: Jordanian dinar = 1,000 fils
Banks closed: Friday
IDP required: Yes **Visa:** Yes
Tourist office: www.tourism.jo
Climate: Hot desert/steppe/Mediterranean

Month	J	F	M	A	M	J	J	A	S	O	N	D
Temp (ºC)	21	22	34	35	34	29	28	29	28	27	27	22
Rainfall (cm)	1	1	4	8	13	16	17	16	22	26	13	5

KAZAKHSTAN

+5/+6 +7 220V Right .kz

Area: 1,049,150 sq. miles (2,717,300 sq. km)
Population: 15.4 million
Capital: Astana
Languages: Kazakh, Russian, Ukrainian, other
Currency: Tenge = 100 tiyn
Banks closed: Sunday
IDP required: Yes **Visa:** Yes
Tourist office: www.kazsport.kz
Climate: Cold desert/steppe

Month	J	F	M	A	M	J	J	A	S	O	N	D
Temp (ºC)	-14	-13	-1	8	15	24	27	27	15	8	-1	-9
Rainfall (cm)	3	2	6	10	9	7	4	3	3	5	5	3

KENYA

+3 +254 220V Left .ke

Area: 218,907 sq. miles (566,970 sq. km)
Population: 32.4 million
Capital: Nairobi
Languages: Kiswahili, English, Kikuyu, others
Currency: Kenya shilling = 100 cents
Banks closed: Sunday
IDP required: No **Visa:** Yes
Tourist office: www.ktdc.co.ke
Climate: Steppe/mountain/tropical

Month	J	F	M	A	M	J	J	A	S	O	N	D
Temp (ºC)	25	26	25	19	18	17	11	11	11	19	19	19
Rainfall (cm)	4	6	13	21	16	5	2	2	3	5	11	9

KIRIBATI

+12 +686 240V Right .ki

Area: 274 sq. miles (710 sq. km)
Population: 100,798
Capital: Bairiki (Tarawa Atoll)
Languages: English, Kiribati
Currency: Australian dollar = 100 cents
Banks closed: Sunday
IDP required: Yes **Visa:** No
Tourist office: www.tcsp.com
Climate: Tropical oceanic

Month	J	F	M	A	M	J	J	A	S	O	N	D
Temp (ºC)	28	28	28	28	28	26	25	25	32	32	32	28
Rainfall (cm)	29	20	14	20	14	12	10	20	16	7	6	32

KUWAIT

+3 +965 240V Right .kw

Area: 6,880 sq. miles (17,820 sq. km)
Population: 2.6 million
Capital: Kuwait City
Languages: Arabic, English
Currency: Kuwaiti dinar = 1,000 fils
Banks closed: Friday
IDP required: Yes **Visa:** Yes
Tourist office: www.kuwaittourism.com
Climate: Hot desert

Month	J	F	M	A	M	J	J	A	S	O	N	D
Temp (ºC)	9	11	19	24	30	33	39	40	38	28	21	12
Rainfall (cm)	2	2	3	1	0	0	0	0	0	0	2	3

KYRGYZSTAN

+6 +996 220V Right .kg

Area: 76,641 sq. miles (198,500 sq. km)
Population: 5.2 million
Capital: Bishkek
Languages: Kyrgyz, Russian, Uzbek, Tatar
Currency: Som = 100 tyyn
Banks closed: Sunday
IDP required: Yes **Visa:** Yes
Tourist office: gatiskr@bishkek.gov.kg
Climate: Mountain

Month	J	F	M	A	M	J	J	A	S	O	N	D
Temp (ºC)	-10	-7	4	11	17	25	30	29	17	10	2	-6
Rainfall (cm)	2	2	5	6	6	4	2	1	2	3	3	3

LAOS

+7 +856 230V Right .la

Area: 89,112 sq. miles (230,800 sq. km)
Population: 5.8 million
Capital: Vientiane
Languages: Lao, Vietnamese, Chinese, French
Currency: New kip = 100 at
Banks closed: Sunday
IDP required: Yes **Visa:** Yes
Tourist office: www.visit-mekong.com/laos
Climate: Tropical monsoon

Month	J	F	M	A	M	J	J	A	S	O	N	D
Temp (ºC)	14	17	33	34	32	28	28	28	28	26	24	16
Rainfall (cm)	1	2	4	10	27	30	27	29	30	11	2	0

LATVIA

+2 +371 220V Right .lv

Area: 24,938 sq. miles (64,589 sq. km)
Population: 2.3 million
Capital: Riga
Languages: Latvian, Russian
Currency: Lats = 100 santims
Banks closed: Sunday
IDP required: Yes **Visa:** No
Tourist office: www.latviatourism.lv
Climate: Continental

Month	J	F	M	A	M	J	J	A	S	O	N	D
Temp (ºC)	-10	-10	-3	6	11	21	22	21	13	8	2	-7
Rainfall (cm)	3	3	3	3	4	5	5	7	6	6	6	5

LEBANON

+2 +961 230V Right .lb

Area: 3,950 sq. miles (10,230 sq. km)
Population: 3.7 million
Capital: Beirut
Languages: Arabic, French, Armenian, others
Currency: Lebanese pound = 100 piastres
Banks closed: Sunday
IDP required: Yes **Visa:** Yes
Tourist office: www.destinationlebanon.com
Climate: Mediterranean/mountain

Month	J	F	M	A	M	J	J	A	S	O	N	D
Temp (ºC)	11	11	12	18	22	25	31	32	30	24	20	16
Rainfall (cm)	19	16	9	6	2	0	0	0	1	5	13	19

LESOTHO

+2 +266 220V Left .ls

Area: 11,718 sq. miles (30,350 sq. km)
Population: 1.8 million
Capital: Maseru
Languages: English, Sesotho, isiZulu
Currency: Loti = 100 lisente
Banks closed: Sunday
IDP required: Yes **Visa:** No
Tourist office: www.lesotho.gov.ls
Climate: Mountain

Month	J	F	M	A	M	J	J	A	S	O	N	D
Temp (ºC)	28	27	19	15	11	0	-1	2	14	17	19	28
Rainfall (cm)	11	9	10	7	3	1	1	2	2	6	8	9

LIBERIA

0 +231 110V Right .lr

Area: 37,189 sq. miles (96,320 sq. km)
Population: 3.5 million
Capital: Monrovia
Languages: Kpelle, Vai, Bassa, English, others
Currency: Liberian dollar = 100 cents
Banks closed: Sunday
IDP required: Yes **Visa:** Yes
Tourist office: +231 226269
Climate: Tropical equatorial

Month	J	F	M	A	M	J	J	A	S	O	N	D
Temp (ºC)	27	26	31	31	26	25	22	25	22	25	26	27
Rainfall (cm)	3	6	10	22	52	97	100	37	74	77	24	13

LIBYA

+1 +218 220V Right .ly

Area: 679,358 sq. miles (1,759,540 sq. km)
Population: 5.7 million
Capital: Tripoli
Languages: Arabic, Tuareg
Currency: Libyan dinar = 1,000 dirhams
Banks closed: Friday
IDP required: No **Visa:** Yes
Tourist office: www.arabtours.co.uk
Climate: Hot desert

Month	J	F	M	A	M	J	J	A	S	O	N	D
Temp (ºC)	8	9	15	18	20	23	29	30	29	23	19	9
Rainfall (cm)	8	5	3	1	1	0	0	0	1	4	7	9

LIECHTENSTEIN

+1 +423 230V Right .li

Area: 62 sq. miles (160 sq. km)
Population: 33,436
Capital: Vaduz
Languages: German, Alemannish, Italian
Currency: Swiss franc = 100 rappen/centimes
Banks closed: Sunday
IDP required: No **Visa:** No
Tourist office: www.tourismus.li
Climate: Mountain

Month	J	F	M	A	M	J	J	A	S	O	N	D
Temp (ºC)	-3	-1	6	10	14	23	25	24	16	10	5	-1
Rainfall (cm)	7	7	7	8	10	13	14	12	10	8	7	6

LITHUANIA

+2 +370 220V Right .lt

Area: 25,174 sq. miles (65,200 sq. km)
Population: 3.4 million
Capital: Vilnius
Languages: Lithuanian, Russian
Currency: Litas = 100 centu; Euro = 100 cents
Banks closed: Sunday
IDP required: No **Visa:** No
Tourist office: www.tourism.lt
Climate: Continental

Month	J	F	M	A	M	J	J	A	S	O	N	D
Temp (ºC)	-11	-10	-3	7	13	21	23	22	13	7	2	-7
Rainfall (cm)	3	4	4	4	9	7	5	10	6	5	7	4

LUXEMBOURG

+1 +352 220V Right .lu

Area: 998 sq. miles (2585 sq. km)
Population: 459,000
Capital: Luxembourg-Ville
Languages: Luxembourgish, German, French
Currency: Euro = 100 cents
Banks closed: Sunday
IDP required: No **Visa:** No
Tourist office: www.ont.lu
Climate: Maritime

Month	J	F	M	A	M	J	J	A	S	O	N	D
Temp (ºC)	-1	-1	1	9	13	21	23	22	15	10	5	0
Rainfall (cm)	6	7	4	5	6	6	6	8	7	5	7	8

MACEDONIA

+1 +389 220V Right .mk

Area: 9,929 sq. miles (25,715 sq. km)
Population: 2.1 million
Capital: Skopje
Languages: Macedonian, Albanian, Serbo-Croat
Currency: Macedonian denar = 100 deni
Banks closed: Sunday
IDP required: No **Visa:** No
Tourist office: +389 2 3118 498
Climate: Continental

Month	J	F	M	A	M	J	J	A	S	O	N	D
Temp (ºC)	-3	-3	6	12	17	28	31	31	19	12	7	-1
Rainfall (cm)	4	3	4	4	5	5	3	3	4	6	6	5

MADAGASCAR

+3 +261 220V Right .mg

Area: 224,533 sq. miles (581,540 sq. km)
Population: 17.9 million
Capital: Antananarivo
Languages: Malagasy, French
Currency: Ariary = 5 iraimbilanja
Banks closed: Sunday
IDP required: No **Visa:** Yes
Tourist office: www.tourisme.gov.mg
Climate: Tropical

Month	J	F	M	A	M	J	J	A	S	O	N	D
Temp (ºC)	21	21	21	19	18	10	9	9	17	27	27	27
Rainfall (cm)	30	28	18	5	2	1	1	1	2	6	14	29

MALAWI

+2 +265 230V Left .mw

Area: 36,324 sq. miles (94,080 sq. km)
Population: 12.3 million
Capital: Lilongwe
Languages: Chewa, Lomwe, English, others
Currency: Malawi kwacha = 100 tambala
Banks closed: Sunday
IDP required: Yes **Visa:** No
Tourist office: www.tourismmalawi.com
Climate: Tropical wet and dry

Month	J	F	M	A	M	J	J	A	S	O	N	D
Temp (ºC)	22	22	22	21	18	8	7	8	20	30	29	28
Rainfall (cm)	21	22	13	4	0	0	0	0	0	0	5	13

MALAYSIA

+8 +60 240V Left .my

Area: 126,853 sq. miles (328,550 sq. km)
Population: 24.9 million
Capital: Kuala Lumpur; Putrajaya (admin)
Languages: Malay, Chinese, Tamil, English
Currency: Ringgit = 100 sen
Banks closed: Sunday
IDP required: Yes **Visa:** No
Tourist office: www.tourism.gov.my
Climate: Tropical equatorial

Month	J	F	M	A	M	J	J	A	S	O	N	D
Temp (ºC)	22	33	33	28	28	28	28	28	28	28	28	22
Rainfall (cm)	16	20	26	29	22	13	10	16	22	25	26	19

MALDIVES

+5 +960 230V Left .mv

Area: 116 sq. miles (300 sq. km)
Population: 328,000
Capital: Male
Languages: Dhivehi, Sinhala, Tamil, Arabic
Currency: Rufiyaa = 100 lari
Banks closed: Friday
IDP required: No **Visa:** Yes
Tourist office: www.visitmaldives.com.mv
Climate: Tropical oceanic

Month	J	F	M	A	M	J	J	A	S	O	N	D
Temp (ºC)	27	26	27	33	34	34	27	21	22	27	27	20
Rainfall (cm)	5	3	3	6	19	31	24	21	17	18	17	9

MALI

0 +223 220V Right .ml

Area: 471,115 sq. miles (1,220,190 sq. km)
Population: 13.4 million
Capital: Bamako
Languages: Bambara, Fulani, Senufo, French
Currency: CFA franc = 100 centimes
Banks closed: Sunday
IDP required: Yes **Visa:** Yes
Tourist office: www.malitourisme.com
Climate: Hot desert/steppe

Month	J	F	M	A	M	J	J	A	S	O	N	D
Temp (ºC)	16	28	39	39	39	29	27	27	27	28	18	17
Rainfall (cm)	0	0	0	2	7	14	28	35	21	4	2	0

MALTA

+1 +356 240V Left .mt

Area: 124 sq. miles (320 sq. km)
Population: 396,000
Capital: Valletta
Languages: Maltese, English
Currency: Maltese lira = 100 cents
Banks closed: Sunday
IDP required: Yes **Visa:** No
Tourist office: www.visitmalta.com
Climate: Mediterranean

Month	J	F	M	A	M	J	J	A	S	O	N	D
Temp (ºC)	10	10	11	16	19	23	29	29	27	22	18	14
Rainfall (cm)	9	6	4	2	1	0	0	1	3	6	9	11

MARSHALL ISLANDS

+12 +692 110V Right .mh

Area: 70 sq. miles (181 sq. km)
Population: 57,738
Capital: Majuro
Languages: Marshallese, English, Japanese
Currency: US dollar = 100 cents
Banks closed: Sunday
IDP required: No **Visa:** Yes
Tourist office: www.visitmarshallislands.com
Climate: Tropical oceanic

Month	J	F	M	A	M	J	J	A	S	O	N	D
Temp (ºC)	25	27	26	28	28	27	27	31	31	31	27	26
Rainfall (cm)	26	14	22	23	26	30	32	26	36	35	33	31

MAURITANIA

0 +222 220V Right .mr

Area: 395,953 sq. miles (1,025,520 sq. km)
Population: 3 million
Capital: Nouakchott
Languages: Hassaniyah Arabic, Wolof, French
Currency: Ouguiya = 5 khoums
Banks closed: Friday
IDP required: Yes **Visa:** Yes
Tourist office: +222 525 3572
Climate: Hot desert

Month	J	F	M	A	M	J	J	A	S	O	N	D
Temp (ºC)	14	15	25	25	34	28	28	28	34	33	25	13
Rainfall (cm)	0	0	0	0	0	0	1	10	2	1	0	0

MAURITIUS

+4 +230 220V Left .mu

Area: 718 sq. miles (1,860 sq. km)
Population: 1.2 million
Capital: Port Louis
Languages: French Creole, Hindi, Urdu, others
Currency: Mauritian rupee = 100 cents
Banks closed: Sunday
IDP required: Yes **Visa:** No
Tourist office: www.mauritius.net
Climate: Tropical oceanic

Month	J	F	M	A	M	J	J	A	S	O	N	D
Temp (ºC)	30	29	29	25	23	17	17	17	21	23	24	29
Rainfall (cm)	22	20	22	13	10	7	6	6	4	4	5	12

MEXICO

-6 +52 110V Right .mx

Area: 736,945 sq. miles (1,908,690 sq. km)
Population: 105 million
Capital: Mexico City
Languages: Spanish, Nahuatl, Mayan, others
Currency: Mexican peso = 100 centavos
Banks closed: Sunday
IDP required: Yes **Visa:** No
Tourist office: www.sectur.gob.mx
Climate: Tropical/mountain/desert

Month	J	F	M	A	M	J	J	A	S	O	N	D
Temp (ºC)	6	6	11	25	26	24	18	18	18	16	14	6
Rainfall (cm)	1	1	1	2	5	12	17	15	13	5	2	1

MICRONESIA

+10/+11 +691 120V Right .fm

Area: 271 sq. miles (702 sq. km)
Population: 108,155
Capital: Palikir (Pohnpei Island)
Languages: Trukese, Pohnpeian, English, other
Currency: US dollar = 100 cents
Banks closed: Sunday
IDP required: No **Visa:** No
Tourist office: www.visit-fsm.org
Climate: Tropical oceanic

Month	J	F	M	A	M	J	J	A	S	O	N	D
Temp (ºC)	27	27	27	27	27	26	23	30	23	30	26	26
Rainfall (cm)	31	23	33	44	52	46	43	40	41	41	40	52

MOLDOVA

+2 +373 220V Right .md

Area: 13,012 sq. miles (33,700 sq. km)
Population: 4.3 million
Capital: Chisinau
Languages: Moldovan, Ukrainian, Russian
Currency: Moldovan leu = 100 bani
Banks closed: Sunday
IDP required: Yes **Visa:** Yes
Tourist office: www.turism.md
Climate: Continental

Month	J	F	M	A	M	J	J	A	S	O	N	D
Temp (ºC)	-5	-5	2	11	17	26	27	27	17	12	6	-4
Rainfall (cm)	6	5	4	4	3	7	7	4	5	2	4	5

MONACO

+1 +377 220V Right .mc

   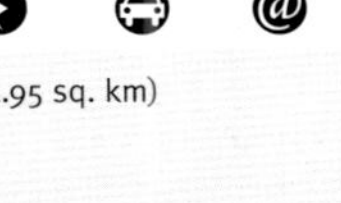

Area: 0.75 sq. miles (1.95 sq. km)
Population: 32,270
Capital: Monaco-Ville
Languages: French, Italian, Monégasque
Currency: Euro = 100 cents
Banks closed: Sunday
IDP required: No **Visa:** No
Tourist office: www.monaco-tourisme.com
Climate: Mediterranenan

Month	J	F	M	A	M	J	J	A	S	O	N	D
Temp (ºC)	8	8	12	14	17	21	22	22	20	18	14	12
Rainfall (cm)	6	6	7	7	6	3	2	2	7	11	12	10

MONGOLIA

+8 +976 230V Right .mn

   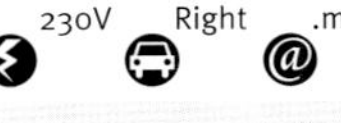

Area: 604,247 sq. miles (1,565,000 sq. km)
Population: 2.6 million
Capital: Ulan Bator
Languages: Khalkha, Kazakh, Chinese, Russian
Currency: Tugrik = 100 möngö
Banks closed: Sunday
IDP required: Yes **Visa:** Yes
Tourist office: www.travelmongolia.org
Climate: Mountain/cold desert/steppe

Month	J	F	M	A	M	J	J	A	S	O	N	D
Temp (ºC)	-32	-29	-13	-1	6	21	22	21	8	-1	-13	-28
Rainfall (cm)	0	0	0	1	1	3	8	5	2	1	1	0

Factfile

MOROCCO–SLOVAKIA

Key to symbols

- Time zone
- Dialling code
- Electricity voltage
- Side of road for driving
- Internet ID code

IDP International drivers permit
Visa Refers to UK Nationals

MOROCCO

0 +212 220V Right .ma

Area: 172,316 sq. miles (446,300 sq. km)
Population: 31.1 million
Capital: Rabat
Languages: Arabic, Berber, French, others
Currency: Moroccan dirham = 100 centimes
Banks closed: Sunday
IDP required: No **Visa:** No
Tourist office: www.visitmorocco.com
Climate: Hot desert/mountain/Mediterranean

Month	J	F	M	A	M	J	J	A	S	O	N	D
Temp (ºC)	8	8	15	17	18	21	28	28	27	20	17	9
Rainfall (cm)	7	6	7	4	3	1	0	0	1	5	8	9

MOZAMBIQUE

+2 +258 220V Left .mz

Area: 302,737 sq. miles (784,090 sq. km)
Population: 19.2 million
Capital: Maputo
Languages: Makua, Xitsonga, Portuguese
Currency: Metical = 100 centavos
Banks closed: Sunday
IDP required: Yes **Visa:** Yes
Tourist office: +258 1 310 755
Climate: Tropical wet and dry

Month	J	F	M	A	M	J	J	A	S	O	N	D
Temp (ºC)	30	31	29	24	22	13	13	14	22	23	24	25
Rainfall (cm)	13	13	13	5	3	2	1	1	3	5	8	10

NAMIBIA

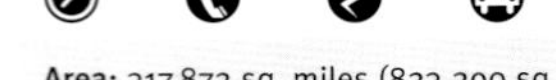

+2 +264 220V Left .na

Area: 317,872 sq. miles (823,290 sq. km)
Population: 2 million
Capital: Windhoek
Languages: Ovambo, German, Afrikaans
Currency: Namibian dollar = 100 cents
Banks closed: Sunday
IDP required: Yes **Visa:** No
Tourist office: www.namibiatourism.com.na
Climate: Hot desert/steppe

Month	J	F	M	A	M	J	J	A	S	O	N	D
Temp (ºC)	29	22	21	19	16	7	6	16	19	22	22	30
Rainfall (cm)	8	7	8	4	1	0	0	0	0	1	2	5

NAURU

+12 +674 240V Left .nr

Area: 8.1 sq. miles (21 sq. km)
Population: 12,809
Capital: None
Languages: Nauruan, Kiribati, Chinese, English
Currency: Australian dollar = 100 cents
Banks closed: Sunday
IDP required: No **Visa:** Yes
Tourist office: www.spto.org
Climate: Tropical oceanic

Month	J	F	M	A	M	J	J	A	S	O	N	D
Temp (ºC)	23	28	32	32	32	28	28	28	32	28	28	28
Rainfall (cm)	32	21	18	9	5	10	16	19	12	10	15	24

NEPAL

+5.75 +977 230V Left .np

Area: 52,818 sq. miles (136,800 sq. km)
Population: 25.7 million
Capital: Kathmandu
Languages: Nepali, Maithili, Bhojpuri
Currency: Nepalese rupee = 100 paise
Banks closed: Saturday
IDP required: Yes **Visa:** Yes
Tourist office: www.welcomenepal.com
Climate: Mountain/subtropical

Month	J	F	M	A	M	J	J	A	S	O	N	D
Temp (ºC)	2	4	16	20	30	29	29	24	24	20	15	3
Rainfall (cm)	2	4	2	6	12	25	37	35	16	4	1	0

NETHERLANDS

+1 +31 230V Right .nl

Area: 13,097 sq. miles (33,920 sq. km)
Population: 16.2 million
Capital: Amsterdam; The Hague (admin)
Languages: Dutch, Frisian
Currency: Euro = 100 cents
Banks closed: Sunday
IDP required: No **Visa:** No
Tourist office: www.holland.com
Climate: Maritime

Month	J	F	M	A	M	J	J	A	S	O	N	D
Temp (ºC)	-1	-1	6	9	13	21	22	22	15	11	6	1
Rainfall (cm)	7	5	4	5	5	6	8	9	7	7	7	6

NEW ZEALAND

+12 +64 230V Left .nz

Area: 103,733 sq. miles (268,670 sq. km)
Population: 3.9 million
Capital: Wellington
Languages: English, Maori
Currency: New Zealand dollar = 100 cents
Banks closed: Sunday
IDP required: No **Visa:** No
Tourist office: www.newzealand.com
Climate: Maritime/subtropical

Month	J	F	M	A	M	J	J	A	S	O	N	D
Temp (ºC)	21	21	19	14	11	7	6	6	11	13	14	16
Rainfall (cm)	8	8	8	10	12	12	14	12	10	10	9	9

NICARAGUA

-6 +505 120V Right .ni

Area: 45,849 sq. miles (118,750 sq. km)
Population: 5.6 million
Capital: Managua
Languages: Spanish, English Creole, Miskito
Currency: Córdoba oro = 100 centavos
Banks closed: Sunday
IDP required: No **Visa:** No
Tourist office: www.visit-nicaragua.com
Climate: Tropical equatorial/wet and dry

Month	J	F	M	A	M	J	J	A	S	O	N	D
Temp (ºC)	20	27	34	34	34	27	27	27	27	27	21	20
Rainfall (cm)	1	0	1	1	8	30	13	13	18	24	6	1

NIGER

+1 +227 220V Right .ne

Area: 489,073 sq. miles (1,266,700 sq. km)
Population: 12.4 million
Capital: Niamey
Languages: Hausa, Djerma, Fulani, French
Currency: CFA franc = 100 centimes
Banks closed: Sunday
IDP required: Yes **Visa:** Yes
Tourist office: +227 732 447
Climate: Hot desert/steppe

Month	J	F	M	A	M	J	J	A	S	O	N	D
Temp (ºC)	14	18	41	42	41	32	29	28	29	31	28	15
Rainfall (cm)	0	0	1	1	3	8	13	19	9	1	0	0

NIGERIA

+1 +234 240V Right .ng

Area: 351,648 sq. miles (910,770 sq. km)
Population: 127 million
Capital: Abuja
Languages: Hausa, English, Yoruba, Ibo
Currency: Naira = 100 kobo
Banks closed: Sunday
IDP required: Yes **Visa:** Yes
Tourist office: +234 9 234 2727
Climate: Tropical/steppe

Month	J	F	M	A	M	J	J	A	S	O	N	D
Temp (ºC)	27	32	32	32	28	26	23	23	23	26	28	28
Rainfall (cm)	3	5	10	15	27	46	28	6	14	21	7	3

NORTH KOREA

+9 +850 110V Right .kp

Area: 46,490 sq. miles (120,410 sq. km)
Population: 22.8 million
Capital: Pyongyang
Languages: Korean
Currency: North Korean won = 100 chon
Banks closed: Sunday
IDP required: No **Visa:** Yes
Tourist office: nta@silibank.com
Climate: Continental

Month	J	F	M	A	M	J	J	A	S	O	N	D
Temp (ºC)	-13	-10	2	10	16	26	29	29	19	12	4	-10
Rainfall (cm)	2	1	3	5	7	8	24	23	11	5	4	2

NORWAY

    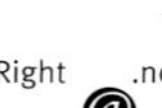

+1 +47 220V Right .no

Area: 118,467 sq. miles (306,830 sq. km)
Population: 4.6 million
Capital: Oslo
Languages: Norwegian, Sámi
Currency: Norwegian krone = 100 øre
Banks closed: Sunday
IDP required: No **Visa:** No
Tourist office: www.visitnorway.com
Climate: Maritime/subarctic

Month	J	F	M	A	M	J	J	A	S	O	N	D
Temp (ºC)	-7	-7	0	6	11	20	22	21	12	6	1	-4
Rainfall (cm)	5	4	3	4	4	7	8	10	8	7	7	6

OMAN

+4 +968 220V Right .om

Area: 82,031 sq. miles (212,460 sq. km)
Population: 2.9 million
Capital: Muscat
Languages: Arabic, Baluchi, Farsi, Hindi, other
Currency: Omani rial = 1,000 baizas
Banks closed: Friday
IDP required: No **Visa:** Yes
Tourist office: www.omantourism.gov.om
Climate: Hot desert

Month	J	F	M	A	M	J	J	A	S	O	N	D
Temp (ºC)	19	19	25	29	37	38	36	31	31	31	24	20
Rainfall (cm)	3	2	1	1	0	0	0	0	0	0	1	2

PAKISTAN

+5 +92 220V Left .pk

Area: 297,637 sq. miles (770,880 sq. km)
Population: 157 million
Capital: Islamabad
Languages: Punjabi, Sindhi, Pashtu, others
Currency: Pakistani rupee = 100 paisa
Banks closed: Sunday
IDP required: No **Visa:** Yes
Tourist office: www.tourism.gov.pk
Climate: Mountain/steppe/hot desert

Month	J	F	M	A	M	J	J	A	S	O	N	D
Temp (ºC)	13	14	24	28	34	34	33	29	28	28	25	14
Rainfall (cm)	1	1	1	0	0	2	8	4	1	0	0	1

PALAU

+9 +680 115V Right .pw

Area: 196 sq. miles (508 sq. km)
Population: 20,016
Capital: Koror
Languages: Palauan, English, Japanese, other
Currency: US dollar = 100 cents
Banks closed: Sunday
IDP required: No **Visa:** No
Tourist office: www.visit-palau.com
Climate: Tropical oceanic

Month	J	F	M	A	M	J	J	A	S	O	N	D
Temp (ºC)	29	29	29	29	29	28	24	28	24	33	33	29
Rainfall (cm)	41	45	40	28	19	27	26	29	35	36	31	44

PANAMA

-5 +507 120V Right .pa

Area: 29,340 sq. miles (75,990 sq. km)
Population: 3.2 million
Capital: Panama City
Languages: English Creole, Spanish, others
Currency: Balboa = 100 centesimos
Banks closed: Sunday
IDP required: No **Visa:** No
Tourist office: www.visitpanama.com
Climate: Tropical wet and dry

Month	J	F	M	A	M	J	J	A	S	O	N	D
Temp (ºC)	22	27	32	27	27	27	27	27	26	26	26	27
Rainfall (cm)	3	1	2	7	20	21	18	20	21	26	26	12

PAPUA NEW GUINEA

+10 +675 240V Left .pg

Area: 174,849 sq. miles (452,860 sq. km)
Population: 5.8 million
Capital: Port Moresby
Languages: Pidgin English, Papuan, others
Currency: Kina = 100 toeas
Banks closed: Sunday
IDP required: No **Visa:** Yes
Tourist office: www.pngtourism.org.pg
Climate: Tropical equatorial/monsoon

Month	J	F	M	A	M	J	J	A	S	O	N	D
Temp (ºC)	32	28	28	28	27	26	23	23	26	27	28	32
Rainfall (cm)	18	19	17	11	6	3	3	2	3	4	5	11

PARAGUAY

-4 +595 220V Right .py

Area: 153,398 sq. miles (397,300 sq. km)
Population: 6 million
Capital: Asunción
Languages: Guaraní, Spanish, German
Currency: Guaraní = 100 centimos
Banks closed: Sunday
IDP required: No **Visa:** No
Tourist office: www.senatur.gov.py
Climate: Tropical/subtropical

Month	J	F	M	A	M	J	J	A	S	O	N	D
Temp (ºC)	35	34	27	24	14	12	12	20	22	24	25	34
Rainfall (cm)	14	13	11	13	12	7	6	4	8	14	15	16

PERU

-5 +51 220V Right .pe

Area: 494,208 sq. miles (1,280,000 sq. km)
Population: 27.6 million
Capital: Lima
Languages: Spanish, Quechua, Aymara
Currency: New sol = 100 centimos
Banks closed: Sunday
IDP required: No **Visa:** No
Tourist office: www.go2peru.com
Climate: Tropical/mountain/desert

Month	J	F	M	A	M	J	J	A	S	O	N	D
Temp (ºC)	28	28	28	22	20	14	14	13	17	18	20	22
Rainfall (cm)	0	0	0	0	1	1	1	1	1	0	0	0

PHILIPPINES

+8 +63 220V Right .ph

Area: 115,123 sq. miles (298,170 sq. km)
Population: 81.4 million
Capital: Manila
Languages: Filipino, English, Tagalog, others
Currency: Philippine peso = 100 centavos
Banks closed: Sunday
IDP required: Yes **Visa:** No
Tourist office: www.wowphilippines.com.ph
Climate: Tropical monsoon/equatorial

Month	J	F	M	A	M	J	J	A	S	O	N	D
Temp (ºC)	21	21	28	34	34	33	28	28	28	27	27	21
Rainfall (cm)	2	1	2	3	13	25	43	42	36	19	15	7

POLAND

+1 +48 220V Right .pl

Area: 117,552 sq. miles (304,460 sq. km)
Population: 38.6 million
Capital: Warsaw
Languages: Polish
Currency: Zloty = 100 groszy
Banks closed: Sunday
IDP required: Yes **Visa:** No
Tourist office: www.pot.gov.pl
Climate: Continental

Month	J	F	M	A	M	J	J	A	S	O	N	D
Temp (ºC)	-6	-6	2	8	15	23	24	23	15	9	4	-3
Rainfall (cm)	3	3	3	4	5	7	10	7	4	4	3	4

PORTUGAL

0 +351 220V Right .pt

Area: 35,502 sq. miles (91,950 sq. km)
Population: 10.1 million
Capital: Lisbon
Languages: Portuguese
Currency: Euro = 100 cents
Banks closed: Sunday
IDP required: No **Visa:** No
Tourist office: www.visitportugal.pt
Climate: Mediterranean/maritime

Month	J	F	M	A	M	J	J	A	S	O	N	D
Temp (ºC)	8	8	14	16	17	20	27	28	26	18	14	9
Rainfall (cm)	11	8	11	5	4	2	0	0	3	6	9	10

QATAR

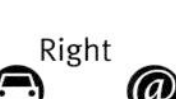
+3 +974 240V Right .qa

Area: 4,247 sq. miles (11,000 sq. km)
Population: 619,000
Capital: Doha
Languages: Arabic
Currency: Qatar riyal = 100 dirhams
Banks closed: Friday
IDP required: Yes **Visa:** Yes
Tourist office: www.experienceqatar.com
Climate: Hot desert

Month	J	F	M	A	M	J	J	A	S	O	N	D
Temp (ºC)	14	15	22	27	32	38	39	39	33	30	25	16
Rainfall (cm)	5	20	34	5	0	0	0	0	0	0	1	10

ROMANIA

+2 +40 220V Right .ro

Area: 88,934 sq. miles (230,340 sq. km)
Population: 22.3 million
Capital: Bucharest
Languages: Romanian, Hungarian, German
Currency: Romanian leu = 100 bani
Banks closed: Sunday
IDP required: No **Visa:** No
Tourist office: www.romaniatourism.com
Climate: Continental

Month	J	F	M	A	M	J	J	A	S	O	N	D
Temp (ºC)	-7	-5	5	12	17	27	30	30	18	12	6	-3
Rainfall (cm)	5	3	3	6	8	12	5	5	5	3	4	3

RUSSIAN FEDERATION

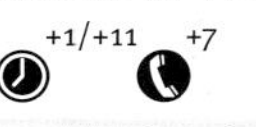
+1/+11 +7 220V Right .ru

Area: 6,562,100 sq. miles (16,995,800 sq. km)
Population: 142 million
Capital: Moscow
Languages: Russian, Tatar, Ukrainian, others
Currency: Russian rouble = 100 kopeks
Banks closed: Sunday
IDP required: Yes **Visa:** Yes
Tourist office: www.russia-tourism.ru
Climate: Subarctic/mountain/steppe

Month	J	F	M	A	M	J	J	A	S	O	N	D
Temp (ºC)	-16	-14	-4	5	14	21	23	22	12	6	-1	-10
Rainfall (cm)	4	4	4	4	5	6	9	7	6	5	5	5

RWANDA

+2 +250 220V Right .rw

Area: 9,633 sq. miles (24,950 sq. km)
Population: 8.5 million
Capital: Kigali
Languages: Kinyarwanda, French, Kiswahili
Currency: Rwanda franc = 100 centimes
Banks closed: Sunday
IDP required: Yes **Visa:** Yes
Tourist office: www.rwandatourism.com
Climate: Tropical wet and dry

aMonth	J	F	M	A	M	J	J	A	S	O	N	D
Temp (ºC)	21	21	21	20	20	15	14	27	27	21	20	20
Rainfall (cm)	10	8	10	18	13	2	1	3	6	11	11	9

ST KITTS & NEVIS

-4 +1869 230V Left .kn

Area: 139 sq. miles (360 sq. km)
Population: 38,836
Capital: Basseterre
Languages: English, English Creole
Currency: East Caribbean dollar = 100 cents
Banks closed: Sunday
IDP required: No **Visa:** No
Tourist office: www.stkittstourism.kn
Climate: Tropical oceanic

Month	J	F	M	A	M	J	J	A	S	O	N	D
Temp (ºC)	21	26	21	27	28	32	27	32	32	28	27	21
Rainfall (cm)	12	9	11	9	10	11	16	18	17	20	18	14

ST LUCIA

-4 +1758 220V Left .lc

Area: 236 sq. miles (610 sq. km)
Population: 164,213
Capital: Castries
Languages: English, French Creole
Currency: East Caribbean dollar = 100 cents
Banks closed: Sunday
IDP required: No **Visa:** No
Tourist office: www.stlucia.org
Climate: Tropical oceanic

Month	J	F	M	A	M	J	J	A	S	O	N	D
Temp (ºC)	21	21	24	27	31	31	31	27	27	27	26	21
Rainfall (cm)	14	9	10	9	15	22	24	27	25	24	23	20

ST VINCENT & THE GRENADINES

-4 +1784 220V Left .vc

Area: 131 sq. miles (340 sq. km)
Population: 117,193
Capital: Kingstown
Languages: English, English Creole
Currency: East Caribbean dollar = 100 cents
Banks closed: Sunday
IDP required: No **Visa:** No
Tourist office: www.svgtourism.com
Climate: Tropical oceanic

Month	J	F	M	A	M	J	J	A	S	O	N	D
Temp (ºC)	17	17	18	26	27	27	33	33	33	27	26	25
Rainfall (cm)	13	10	10	8	15	23	23	28	25	23	23	20

SAMOA

-11 +685 240V Right .ws

Area: 1,093 sq. miles (2,830 sq. km)
Population: 180,000
Capital: Apia
Languages: Samoan, English
Currency: Tala = 100 sene
Banks closed: Sunday
IDP required: No **Visa:** No
Tourist office: www.visitsamoa.ws
Climate: Tropical oceanic

Month	J	F	M	A	M	J	J	A	S	O	N	D
Temp (ºC)	27	27	27	27	26	26	26	27	26	27	27	26
Rainfall (cm)	46	39	36	25	16	13	8	9	13	17	27	37

SAN MARINO

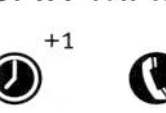
+1 +378 220V Right .sm

Area: 24 sq. miles (61 sq. km)
Population: 28,503
Capital: San Marino
Languages: Italian
Currency: Euro = 100 cents
Banks closed: Sunday
IDP required: No **Visa:** No
Tourist office: www.visitsanmarino.com
Climate: Mediterranean

Month	J	F	M	A	M	J	J	A	S	O	N	D
Temp (ºC)	2	2	8	12	16	25	28	28	20	15	10	4
Rainfall (cm)	7	7	7	7	6	7	5	6	9	10	11	9

SAO TOME & PRINCIPE

0 +239 220V Right .st

Area: 371 sq. miles (960 sq. km)
Population: 181,565
Capital: São Tomé
Languages: Portuguese Creole, Portuguese
Currency: Dobra = 100 centimos
Banks closed: Sunday
IDP required: Yes **Visa:** Yes
Tourist office: +239 2 21542
Climate: Tropical equatorial

Month	J	F	M	A	M	J	J	A	S	O	N	D
Temp (ºC)	30	30	31	30	26	25	21	21	21	25	25	25
Rainfall (cm)	8	11	15	13	14	3	0	0	2	11	12	9

SAUDI ARABIA

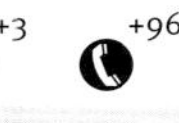
+3 +966 125V Right .sa

Area: 816,480 sq. miles (2,114,690 sq. km)
Population: 24.9 million
Capital: Riyadh; Jiddah (administrative)
Languages: Arabic
Currency: Saudi riyal = 100 halalat
Banks closed: Friday
IDP required: No **Visa:** Yes
Tourist office: www.mofa.gov.sa
Climate: Hot desert

Month	J	F	M	A	M	J	J	A	S	O	N	D
Temp (ºC)	8	9	21	25	30	42	42	42	31	25	21	9
Rainfall (cm)	1	2	2	3	1	1	1	1	1	1	1	1

SENEGAL

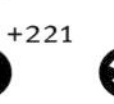
0 +221 230V Right .sn

Area: 74,336 sq. miles (192,530 sq. km)
Population: 10.3 million
Capital: Dakar
Languages: Wolof, Pulaar, Serer, French, other
Currency: CFA franc = 100 centimes
Banks closed: Sunday
IDP required: Yes **Visa:** No
Tourist office: +221 821 1126
Climate: Steppe/tropical

Month	J	F	M	A	M	J	J	A	S	O	N	D
Temp (ºC)	18	17	23	23	25	27	28	28	32	32	27	23
Rainfall (cm)	0	0	0	0	0	2	9	25	13	4	0	1

SERBIA & MONTENEGRO

+1 +381 220V Right .yu

Area: 39,449 sq. miles (102,173 sq. km)
Population: 10.5 million
Capital: Belgrade
Languages: Serbo-Croat, Albanian, Hungarian
Currency: Dinar (Serbia); euro (Montenegro)
Banks closed: Sunday
IDP required: No **Visa:** No
Tourist office: www.belgradetourism.org.yu
Climate: Continental

Month	J	F	M	A	M	J	J	A	S	O	N	D
Temp (ºC)	0	2	7	13	18	21	23	23	19	13	8	3
Rainfall (cm)	5	5	5	5	7	10	6	6	5	6	6	6

SEYCHELLES

+4 +248 240V Left .sc

Area: 104 sq. miles (270 sq. km)
Population: 80,832
Capital: Victoria
Languages: French Creole, English, French
Currency: Seychelles rupee = 100 cents
Banks closed: Sunday
IDP required: No **Visa:** No
Tourist office: www.seychelles.com
Climate: Tropical oceanic

Month	J	F	M	A	M	J	J	A	S	O	N	D
Temp (ºC)	26	29	29	30	29	27	24	24	26	26	26	26
Rainfall (cm)	39	27	23	18	17	10	8	7	13	16	23	34

SIERRA LEONE

0 +232 220V Right .sl

Area: 27,652 sq. miles (71,620 sq. km)
Population: 5.2 million
Capital: Freetown
Languages: Mende, Temne, Krio, English
Currency: Leone = 100 cents
Banks closed: Sunday
IDP required: Yes **Visa:** Yes
Tourist office: ntbslinfo@yahoo.com
Climate: Tropical equatorial/monsoon

Month	J	F	M	A	M	J	J	A	S	O	N	D
Temp (ºC)	27	27	30	31	30	27	23	23	23	26	27	27
Rainfall (cm)	1	0	1	6	16	30	89	90	61	31	13	4

SINGAPORE

+8 +65 220V Left .sg

Area: 236 sq. miles (610 sq. km)
Population: 4.3 million
Capital: Singapore
Languages: Mandarin, Malay, Tamil, English
Currency: Singapore dollar = 100 cents
Banks closed: Sunday
IDP required: No **Visa:** No
Tourist office: www.stb.com.sg
Climate: Tropical equatorial

Month	J	F	M	A	M	J	J	A	S	O	N	D
Temp (ºC)	23	27	28	28	32	28	28	28	28	27	27	27
Rainfall (cm)	25	17	19	19	17	17	17	20	18	21	25	26

SLOVAKIA

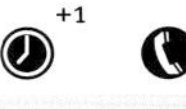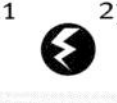
+1 +421 230V Right .sk

Area: 18,933 sq. miles (49,036 sq. km)
Population: 5.4 million
Capital: Bratislava
Languages: Slovak, Hungarian, Czech
Currency: Slovak koruna = 100 halierov
Banks closed: Sunday
IDP required: Yes **Visa:** No
Tourist office: www.slovakiatourism.sk
Climate: Continental

Month	J	F	M	A	M	J	J	A	S	O	N	D
Temp (ºC)	-3	-2	5	11	16	24	26	26	17	11	6	0
Rainfall (cm)	4	5	4	4	6	6	7	7	4	5	6	6

Factfile

SLOVENIA–ZIMBABWE

Key to symbols

- Time zone
- Dialling code
- Electricity voltage
- Side of road for driving
- Internet ID code

IDP International drivers permit
Visa Refers to UK Nationals

SLOVENIA

+1 · +386 · 220V · Right · .si

Area: 7,819 sq. miles (20,250 sq. km)
Population: 2 million
Capital: Ljubljana
Languages: Slovene, Serbo-Croat
Currency: Tolar = 100 stotinov
Banks closed: Sunday
IDP required: No **Visa:** No
Tourist office: www.slovenia-tourism.si
Climate: Continental/Mediterranean

Month	J	F	M	A	M	J	J	A	S	O	N	D
Temp (°C)	-4	-4	5	10	15	24	27	26	17	11	5	-1
Rainfall (cm)	9	9	8	10	12	13	11	13	14	15	13	11

SOLOMON ISLANDS

+11 · +677 · 240V · Left · .sb

Area: 10,806 sq. miles (27,990 sq. km)
Population: 491,000
Capital: Honiara
Languages: English, Pidgin English, other
Currency: Solomon Islands dollar = 100 cents
Banks closed: Sunday
IDP required: No **Visa:** No
Tourist office: www.visitsolomons.com.sb
Climate: Tropical equatorial

Month	J	F	M	A	M	J	J	A	S	O	N	D
Temp (°C)	31	27	27	27	31	27	22	22	22	31	27	27
Rainfall (cm)	28	29	36	21	14	10	10	9	10	15	14	22

SOMALIA

+3 · +252 · 220V · Left · .so

Area: 242,216 sq. miles (627,340 sq. km)
Population: 10.3 million
Capital: Mogadishu
Languages: Somali, Arabic, English, Italian
Currency: Somali shilling = 100 centesimi
Banks closed: Friday
IDP required: Yes **Visa:** Yes
Tourist office: www.unsomalia.net
Climate: Hot desert/steppe

Month	J	F	M	A	M	J	J	A	S	O	N	D
Temp (°C)	27	27	28	32	32	26	23	23	23	27	31	27
Rainfall (cm)	0	0	0	6	6	10	6	5	3	2	4	1

SOUTH AFRICA

+2 · +27 · 220V · Left · .za

Area: 471,444 sq. miles (1,221,040 sq. km)
Population: 45.2 million
Capital: Pretoria; Cape Town; Bloemfontein
Languages: English, isiZulu, Afrikaans, others
Currency: Rand = 100 cents
Banks closed: Sunday
IDP required: Yes **Visa:** No
Tourist office: www.southafrica.net
Climate: Desert/subtropical/mediterranean

Month	J	F	M	A	M	J	J	A	S	O	N	D
Temp (°C)	27	27	20	17	6	3	3	14	17	20	21	28
Rainfall (cm)	13	11	11	4	2	2	1	1	2	6	13	13

SOUTH KOREA

+9 · +82 · 220V · Right · .kr

Area: 38,120 sq. miles (98,730 sq. km)
Population: 48 million
Capital: Seoul
Languages: Korean
Currency: South Korean won = 100 chon
Banks closed: Sunday
IDP required: Yes **Visa:** No
Tourist office: www.tour2korea.com
Climate: Continental

Month	J	F	M	A	M	J	J	A	S	O	N	D
Temp (°C)	-9	-7	3	11	17	27	29	31	21	13	6	-7
Rainfall (cm)	3	2	4	8	8	13	38	27	12	4	5	3

SPAIN

+1 · +34 · 220V · Right · .es

Area: 192,834 sq. miles (499,440 sq. km)
Population: 41.1 million
Capital: Madrid
Languages: Spanish, Catalan, Galician, Basque
Currency: Euro = 100 cents
Banks closed: Sunday
IDP required: No **Visa:** No
Tourist office: www.spain.info
Climate: Mediterranean/maritime/mountain

Month	J	F	M	A	M	J	J	A	S	O	N	D
Temp (°C)	2	2	10	13	16	27	31	30	20	15	9	2
Rainfall (cm)	4	3	4	5	5	3	1	2	3	5	5	5

SRI LANKA

+5.5 · +94 · 230V · Left · .lk

Area: 24,996 sq. miles (64,740 sq. km)
Population: 19.2 million
Capital: Colombo
Languages: Sinhala, Tamil, English
Currency: Sri Lanka rupee = 100 cents
Banks closed: Sunday
IDP required: Yes **Visa:** No
Tourist office: www.srilankatourism.org
Climate: Tropical monsoon/equatorial

Month	J	F	M	A	M	J	J	A	S	O	N	D
Temp (°C)	22	22	31	31	31	27	27	27	27	27	26	22
Rainfall (cm)	9	7	15	23	37	22	14	11	16	35	32	15

SUDAN

+2 · +249 · 240V · Right · .sd

Area: 967,500 sq. miles (2,506,000 sq. km)
Population: 34.3 million
Capital: Khartoum
Languages: Arabic, Dinka, Nuer, Nubia, others
Currency: Sudanese pound = 100 piastres
Banks closed: Friday
IDP required: Yes **Visa:** Yes
Tourist office: +249 183 472 604
Climate: Hot desert/steppe/tropical

Month	J	F	M	A	M	J	J	A	S	O	N	D
Temp (°C)	15	16	29	41	42	41	32	31	32	32	28	17
Rainfall (cm)	0	0	0	0	0	1	5	7	2	1	0	0

SURINAM

-3 · +597 · 127V · Left · .sr

Area: 62,344 sq. miles (161,470 sq. km)
Population: 439,000
Capital: Paramaribo
Languages: Creole, Dutch, Javanese, others
Currency: Suriname dollar = 100 cents
Banks closed: Sunday
IDP required: Yes **Visa:** Yes
Tourist office: www.suriname-tourism.com
Climate: Tropical equatorial

Month	J	F	M	A	M	J	J	A	S	O	N	D
Temp (°C)	22	22	22	27	27	27	27	28	33	33	32	26
Rainfall (cm)	21	17	20	23	31	30	23	16	8	8	13	22

SWAZILAND

+2 · +268 · 220V · Left · .sz

Area: 6,641 sq. miles (17,200 sq. km)
Population: 1.1 million
Capital: Mbabane
Languages: English, siSwati, isiZulu, Xitsonga
Currency: Lilangeni = 100 cents
Banks closed: Sunday
IDP required: Yes **Visa:** No
Tourist office: www.mintour.gov.sz
Climate: Subtropical

Month	J	F	M	A	M	J	J	A	S	O	N	D
Temp (°C)	25	25	19	18	15	6	6	7	16	18	19	25
Rainfall (cm)	25	21	19	7	3	2	2	3	6	13	17	21

SWEDEN

+1 · +46 · 230V · Right · .se

Area: 158,926 sq. miles (411,620 sq. km)
Population: 8.9 million
Capital: Stockholm
Languages: Swedish, Finnish, Sámi
Currency: Swedish krona = 100 öre
Banks closed: Sunday
IDP required: No **Visa:** No
Tourist office: www.visit-sweden.com
Climate: Subarctic/continental

Month	J	F	M	A	M	J	J	A	S	O	N	D
Temp (°C)	-5	-5	-4	5	10	19	22	20	12	7	3	0
Rainfall (cm)	4	3	3	3	3	5	6	8	6	5	5	5

SWITZERLAND

+1 · +41 · 220V · Right · .ch

Area: 15,355 sq. miles (39,770 sq. km)
Population: 7.2 million
Capital: Bern
Languages: German, French, Italian, Romansch
Currency: Swiss franc = 100 rappen/centimes
Banks closed: Sunday
IDP required: No **Visa:** No
Tourist office: www.myswitzerland.com
Climate: Mountain/continental

Month	J	F	M	A	M	J	J	A	S	O	N	D
Temp (°C)	-4	-3	5	9	13	21	23	22	15	9	4	-2
Rainfall (cm)	6	5	6	7	9	12	12	12	10	7	7	5

SYRIA

+2 · +963 · 220V · Right · .sy

Area: 71,066 sq. miles (184,060 sq. km)
Population: 18.2 million
Capital: Damascus
Languages: Arabic, French, Kurdish, others
Currency: Syrian pound = 100 piastres
Banks closed: Friday
IDP required: Yes **Visa:** Yes
Tourist office: www.syriatourism.org
Climate: Steppe/hot desert/Mediterranean

Month	J	F	M	A	M	J	J	A	S	O	N	D
Temp (°C)	2	4	12	17	21	33	36	37	25	20	14	4
Rainfall (cm)	4	4	1	1	0	0	0	0	2	1	4	4

TAIWAN

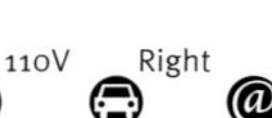

+8 · +886 · 110V · Right · .tw

Area: 12,456 sq. miles (32,260 sq. km)
Population: 22.8 million
Capital: Taipei
Languages: Amoy Chinese, Mandarin Chinese
Currency: Taiwan dollar = 100 cents
Banks closed: Sunday
IDP required: Yes **Visa:** No
Tourist office: www.tva.org.tw
Climate: Tropical monsoon

Month	J	F	M	A	M	J	J	A	S	O	N	D
Temp (°C)	12	12	18	21	25	32	33	33	27	23	21	14
Rainfall (cm)	9	14	18	17	23	29	23	31	24	12	7	7

TAJIKISTAN

+5 · +992 · 220V · Right · .tj

Area: 55,251 sq. miles (143,100 sq. km)
Population: 6.3 million
Capital: Dushanbe
Languages: Tajik, Uzbek, Russian
Currency: Somoni = 100 diram
Banks closed: Sunday
IDP required: Yes **Visa:** Yes
Tourist office: mfart@tajik.net
Climate: Mountain

Month	J	F	M	A	M	J	J	A	S	O	N	D
Temp (°C)	-4	-2	9	15	20	33	37	36	22	15	10	0
Rainfall (cm)	8	7	11	11	7	2	0	0	0	2	5	7

TANZANIA

+3 · +255 · 230V · Left · .tz

Area: 342,100 sq. miles (886,040 sq. km)
Population: 37.7 million
Capital: Dodoma
Languages: Kiswahili, Sukuma, English, others
Currency: Tanzanian shilling = 100 cents
Banks closed: Sunday
IDP required: Yes **Visa:** Yes
Tourist office: www.tanzaniatouristboard.com
Climate: Tropical/mountain

Month	J	F	M	A	M	J	J	A	S	O	N	D
Temp (°C)	31	31	28	27	26	25	19	19	19	25	26	28
Rainfall (cm)	7	7	13	29	19	3	3	3	3	4	7	9

THAILAND

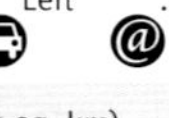

+7 · +66 · 220V · Left · .th

Area: 197,255 sq. miles (510,890 sq. km)
Population: 63.5 million
Capital: Bangkok
Languages: Thai, Chinese, Malay, Khmer, other
Currency: Baht = 100 stang
Banks closed: Sunday
IDP required: Yes **Visa:** No
Tourist office: www.tourismthailand.org
Climate: Tropical equatorial/monsoon

Month	J	F	M	A	M	J	J	A	S	O	N	D
Temp (°C)	20	28	34	35	34	29	28	28	28	28	22	20
Rainfall (cm)	1	2	4	6	20	16	16	18	31	21	7	1

TOGO

0 · +228 · 220V · Right · .tg

Area: 21,000 sq. miles (54,390 sq. km)
Population: 5 million
Capital: Lomé
Languages: Ewe, Kabye, Gurma, French
Currency: CFA franc = 100 centimes
Banks closed: Sunday
IDP required: Yes **Visa:** Yes
Tourist office: +228 2 214 313
Climate: Tropical equatorial/wet and dry

Month	J	F	M	A	M	J	J	A	S	O	N	D
Temp (°C)	27	32	32	32	27	26	22	22	22	26	27	27
Rainfall (cm)	2	2	7	11	15	27	9	3	4	11	3	1

TONGA

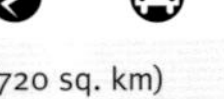

+12 · +676 · 240V · Left · .to

Area: 278 sq. miles (720 sq. km)
Population: 110,237
Capital: Nuku'alofa
Languages: English, Tongan
Currency: Pa'anga (Tongan dollar) = 100 seniti
Banks closed: Sunday
IDP required: No **Visa:** No
Tourist office: www.tongaholiday.com
Climate: Tropical oceanic

Month	J	F	M	A	M	J	J	A	S	O	N	D
Temp (°C)	29	29	29	25	23	22	18	18	18	23	24	24
Rainfall (cm)	14	19	22	13	14	11	11	14	11	10	10	13

TRINIDAD & TOBAGO

-4 +1868 110V Left .tt

Area: 1,981 sq. miles (5,130 sq. km)
Population: 1.3 million
Capital: Port-of-Spain
Languages: Creole, English, Hindi, French
Currency: Trinidad & Tobago dollar = 100 cents
Banks closed: Sunday
IDP required: Yes **Visa:** No
Tourist office: www.visittnt.com
Climate: Tropical oceanic

Month	J	F	M	A	M	J	J	A	S	O	N	D
Temp (°C)	21	20	20	32	32	32	26	26	27	27	27	26
Rainfall (cm)	7	4	5	5	9	19	22	24	19	17	18	12

TUNISIA

+1 +216 220V Right .tn

Area: 59,984 sq. miles (155,360 sq. km)
Population: 9.9 million
Capital: Tunis
Languages: Arabic, French
Currency: Tunisian dinar = 1,000 millimes
Banks closed: Sunday
IDP required: No **Visa:** No
Tourist office: www.tourismtunisia.com
Climate: Mediterranean/hot desert

Month	J	F	M	A	M	J	J	A	S	O	N	D
Temp (°C)	6	7	13	16	19	23	32	33	31	20	16	7
Rainfall (cm)	6	5	4	4	2	1	0	1	3	5	5	6

TURKEY

+2 +90 220V Right .tr

Area: 297,154 sq. miles (769,630 sq. km)
Population: 72.3 million
Capital: Ankara
Languages: Turkish, Kurdish, Arabic, others
Currency: New Turkish lira = 100 kurus
Banks closed: Sunday
IDP required: No **Visa:** Yes
Tourist office: www.turizm.gov.tr
Climate: Mountain/Mediterranean

Month	J	F	M	A	M	J	J	A	S	O	N	D
Temp (°C)	0	3	10	11	16	19	23	23	19	14	9	2
Rainfall (cm)	3	3	3	3	5	3	1	1	2	2	3	5

TURKMENISTAN

+5 +993 220V Right .tm

Area: 188,455 sq. miles (488,100 sq. km)
Population: 4.9 million
Capital: Ashgabat
Languages: Turkmen, Uzbek, Russian, Kazakh
Currency: Manat = 100 tenga
Banks closed: Sunday
IDP required: Yes **Visa:** Yes
Tourist office: www.tourism-sport.gov.tm
Climate: Desert/steppe

Month	J	F	M	A	M	J	J	A	S	O	N	D
Temp (°C)	-1	7	9	15	20	26	29	27	22	15	9	4
Rainfall (cm)	3	2	5	4	3	1	0	0	0	1	2	2

TUVALU

+12 +688 240V Right .tv

Area: 10 sq. miles (26 sq. km)
Population: 11,468
Capital: Fongafale, on Funafuti Atoll
Languages: Tuvaluan, Kiribati, English
Currency: Australian and Tuvaluan dollar
Banks closed: Sunday
IDP required: No **Visa:** No
Tourist office: www.timelesstuvalu.com
Climate: Tropical oceanic

Month	J	F	M	A	M	J	J	A	S	O	N	D
Temp (°C)	29	29	29	29	29	28	24	28	24	33	33	29
Rainfall (cm)	41	45	40	28	19	27	26	29	35	36	31	44

UGANDA

+3 +256 240V Left .ug

  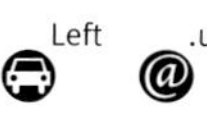

Area: 77,046 sq. miles (199,550 sq. km)
Population: 26.7 million
Capital: Kampala
Languages: Luganda, Nkole, English, others
Currency: New Uganda shilling = 100 cents
Banks closed: Sunday
IDP required: Yes **Visa:** Yes
Tourist office: +256 41 343 947
Climate: Tropical wet and dry

Month	J	F	M	A	M	J	J	A	S	O	N	D
Temp (°C)	28	28	27	22	21	17	17	16	22	22	22	22
Rainfall (cm)	5	6	13	18	15	7	5	9	9	10	12	10

UKRAINE

+2 +380 220V Right .ua

Area: 233,089 sq. miles (603,700 sq. km)
Population: 48.2 million
Capital: Kiev
Languages: Ukrainian, Russian, Tatar
Currency: Hryvna = 100 kopiykas
Banks closed: Sunday
IDP required: Yes **Visa:** Yes
Tourist office: www.intouristuk.com
Climate: Continental/steppe/Mediterranean

Month	J	F	M	A	M	J	J	A	S	O	N	D
Temp (°C)	-10	-8	-1	10	16	24	25	24	15	10	3	-6
Rainfall (cm)	6	6	5	5	5	6	9	9	3	3	6	6

UNITED ARAB EMIRATES

+4 +971 220V Right .ae

Area: 32,278 sq. miles (83,600 sq. km)
Population: 3.1 million
Capital: Abu Dhabi
Languages: Arabic, Farsi, English, others
Currency: UAE dirham = 100 fils
Banks closed: Friday
IDP required: Yes **Visa:** No
Tourist office: www.dubaitourism.ae
Climate: Hot desert

Month	J	F	M	A	M	J	J	A	S	O	N	D
Temp (°C)	14	15	23	27	31	33	40	41	39	29	25	16
Rainfall (cm)	1	1	1	1	0	0	0	0	0	0	0	0

UNITED KINGDOM

0 +44 240V Left .uk

Area: 93,282 sq. miles (241,600 sq. km)
Population: 59.4 million
Capital: London
Languages: English, Welsh, Gaelic
Currency: Pound sterling = 100 pence
Banks closed: Sunday
IDP required: No **Visa:** No
Tourist office: www.visitbritain.com
Climate: Maritime

Month	J	F	M	A	M	J	J	A	S	O	N	D
Temp (°C)	2	2	3	10	13	20	22	21	15	11	8	6
Rainfall (cm)	5	4	4	4	5	5	6	6	5	6	6	5

UNITED STATES

-5/-11 +1 110V Right n/a

Area: 3,539,224 sq. miles (9,166,600 sq. km)
Population: 297 million
Capital: Washington D.C.
Languages: English, Spanish, Chinese, others
Currency: US dollar = 100 cents
Banks closed: Sunday
IDP required: Yes **Visa:** No
Tourist office: www.tinet.ita.doc.gov
Climate: Subtropical/mountain/desert

Month	J	F	M	A	M	J	J	A	S	O	N	D
Temp (°C)	-3	-2	7	13	18	28	31	29	21	14	8	-2
Rainfall (cm)	9	8	9	8	9	10	11	11	9	7	7	8

URUGUAY

-3 +598 220V Right .uy

Area: 67,494 sq. miles (174,810 sq. km)
Population: 3.4 million
Capital: Montevideo
Languages: Spanish
Currency: Uruguayan peso = 100 centésimos
Banks closed: Sunday
IDP required: Yes **Visa:** No
Tourist office: www.mintur.gub.uy
Climate: Subtropical

Month	J	F	M	A	M	J	J	A	S	O	N	D
Temp (°C)	28	28	21	17	14	6	6	6	13	15	18	26
Rainfall (cm)	7	7	10	10	8	8	7	8	8	7	7	8

UZBEKISTAN

+5/+6 +998 220V Right .uz

Area: 172,741 sq. miles (447,400 sq. km)
Population: 26.5 million
Capital: Tashkent
Languages: Uzbek, Russian, Tajik, Kazakh
Currency: Som = 100 tiyin
Banks closed: Sunday
IDP required: Yes **Visa:** Yes
Tourist office: www.uzbektourism.uz
Climate: Desert/mountain

Month	J	F	M	A	M	J	J	A	S	O	N	D
Temp (°C)	-6	-3	8	13	20	31	33	32	19	12	7	-2
Rainfall (cm)	5	3	7	6	4	1	1	0	0	3	4	4

VANUATU

+11 +678 240V Right .vu

     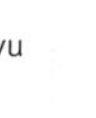

Area: 4707 sq. miles (12,190 sq. km)
Population: 217,000
Capital: Port Vila
Languages: Bislama, English, French, others
Currency: Vatu = 100 centimes
Banks closed: Sunday
IDP required: No **Visa:** No
Tourist office: www.vanuatutourism.com
Climate: Tropical oceanic

Month	J	F	M	A	M	J	J	A	S	O	N	D
Temp (°C)	31	31	27	26	25	24	19	19	20	25	25	31
Rainfall (cm)	26	28	30	24	14	12	97	89	97	12	17	18

VATICAN CITY

+1 +39 220V Right .va

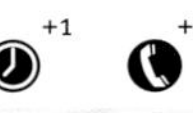   

Area: 0.17 sq. miles (0.44 sq. km)
Population: 921
Capital: Vatican City
Languages: Italian, Latin
Currency: Euro = 100 cents
Banks closed: Sunday
IDP required: No **Visa:** No
Tourist office: www.vatican.va
Climate: Mediterranean

Month	J	F	M	A	M	J	J	A	S	O	N	D
Temp (°C)	5	5	11	15	18	28	30	30	22	18	13	6
Rainfall (cm)	7	6	6	5	5	4	2	2	6	10	13	9

VENEZUELA

-4 +58 110V Right .ve

Area: 340,560 sq. miles (882,050 sq. km)
Population: 26.2 million
Capital: Caracas
Languages: Spanish, Amerindian languages
Currency: Bolívar = 100 centimos
Banks closed: Sunday
IDP required: No **Visa:** No
Tourist office: www.think-venezuela.net
Climate: Tropical wet and dry/equatorial

Month	J	F	M	A	M	J	J	A	S	O	N	D
Temp (°C)	13	13	20	27	27	22	21	21	22	21	21	20
Rainfall (cm)	2	1	2	3	8	10	11	11	11	11	9	5

VIETNAM

+7 +84 220V Right .vn

Area: 125,621 sq. miles (325,360 sq. km)
Population: 82.5 million
Capital: Hanoi
Languages: Vietnamese, Chinese, Thai, others
Currency: Dông = 10 hao = 100 xu
Banks closed: Sunday
IDP required: Yes **Visa:** Yes
Tourist office: www.vn-tourism.com
Climate: Tropical monsoon

Month	J	F	M	A	M	J	J	A	S	O	N	D
Temp (°C)	13	14	20	24	28	33	33	32	28	26	22	15
Rainfall (cm)	2	3	4	8	20	24	32	34	25	10	4	2

YEMEN

+3 +967 220V Right .ye

   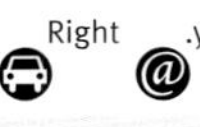

Area: 217,362 sq. miles (562,970 sq. km)
Population: 20.7 million
Capital: Sana
Languages: Arabic
Currency: Yemeni rial = 100 sene
Banks closed: Friday
IDP required: Yes **Visa:** Yes
Tourist office: www.yementourism.com
Climate: Hot desert/mountain

Month	J	F	M	A	M	J	J	A	S	O	N	D
Temp (°C)	0	8	16	17	18	28	28	27	18	14	4	2
Rainfall (cm)	0	0	1	7	1	0	5	5	0	0	0	0

ZAMBIA

+2 +260 230V Left .zm

Area: 285,992 sq. miles (740,720 sq. km)
Population: 10.9 million
Capital: Lusaka
Languages: Bemba, Tonga, English, others
Currency: Zambian kwacha = 100 ngwee
Banks closed: Sunday
IDP required: Yes **Visa:** Yes
Tourist office: www.zambiatourism.com
Climate: Tropical wet and dry

Month	J	F	M	A	M	J	J	A	S	O	N	D
Temp (°C)	22	22	22	21	19	10	9	12	29	31	29	22
Rainfall (cm)	23	19	14	2	0	0	0	0	0	1	9	15

ZIMBABWE

+2 +263 220V Left .zw

Area: 149,293 sq. miles (386,670 sq. km)
Population: 12.9 million
Capital: Harare
Languages: Shona, isiNdebele, English
Currency: Zimbabwe dollar = 100 cents
Banks closed: Sunday
IDP required: No **Visa:** Yes
Tourist office: www.zimbabwetourism.co.zw
Climate: Tropical wet and dry/steppe

Month	J	F	M	A	M	J	J	A	S	O	N	D
Temp (°C)	21	21	20	20	16	7	7	8	19	28	27	26
Rainfall (cm)	20	18	12	3	1	0	0	0	1	3	10	16

Factfile

SLOVENIA–ZIMBABWE

Key to symbols

- Time zone
- Dialling code
- Electricity voltage
- Side of road for driving
- Internet ID code

IDP International drivers permit
Visa Refers to UK Nationals

Vaccination Chart

Diphtheria, poliomyelitis, and tetanus immunization are recommended for all travel. This table shows recommendations by country for hepatitis A, typhoid, malaria, yellow fever, and meningitis as of April 2005. It does not cover pregnant women and infants.

Vaccination requirements are constantly being revised by the relevant health authorities. Travellers should always seek up-to-date medical advice.

Key to symbols

- ● Immunization is an essential requirement for entry to the country concerned and you will require a certificate; this may depend on whether you are arriving from or will be departing to an infected area
- ❍ Immunization or tablets are recommended
- ▲ Depends on the area visited
- ◆ Depends on the season
- ❑ Meningitis, depending on the area visited and the season
- ■ Meningitis ACWY, required for those visiting Saudi Arabia for the *haj* or *umra*

Country	Hep. A, Typhoid	Malaria	Yellow Fever	Meningitis ACWY
AFGHANISTAN	❍	❍ ▲ ◆	●	
ALBANIA	❍		●	
ALGERIA	❍		●	
ANDORRA				
ANGOLA	❍	❍	● ❍	❑
ANTARCTICA				
ANTIGUA & BARBUDA	❍		●	
ARGENTINA	❍	❍ ▲		
ARMENIA	❍	❍ ◆		
AUSTRALIA			●	
AUSTRIA				
AZERBAIJAN	❍	❍ ▲ ◆		
BAHAMAS	❍		●	
BAHRAIN	❍			
BANGLADESH	❍	❍	●	
BARBADOS	❍		●	
BELARUS	❍			
BELGIUM				
BELIZE	❍	❍	●	
BENIN	❍	❍	● ❍	❑
BHUTAN	❍	❍ ▲	●	❑
BOLIVIA	❍	❍ ▲	● ❍ ▲	
BOSNIA & HERZEGOVINA	❍			
BOTSWANA	❍	❍ ▲ ◆	●	
BRAZIL	❍	❍ ▲	● ❍ ▲	
BRUNEI	❍		●	
BULGARIA	❍			
BURKINA	❍	❍	● ❍	❑
BURMA (MYANMAR)	❍	❍	●	
BURUNDI	❍	❍	● ❍	❑
CAMBODIA	❍	❍	●	
CAMEROON	❍	❍	● ❍	❑
CANADA				
CAPE VERDE	❍		●	
CENTRAL AFRICAN REPUBLIC	❍	❍	● ❍	❑
CHAD	❍	❍	❍ ▲	❑
CHILE	❍		●	
CHINA	❍	❍ ▲	●	

Country	Hep. A, Typhoid	Malaria	Yellow Fever	Meningitis ACWY
COLOMBIA	❍	❍ ▲	❍	
COMOROS	❍	❍		
CONGO	❍	❍	● ❍	
CONGO, DEM. REPUBLIC	❍	❍	● ❍	❑
COSTA RICA	❍	❍ ▲		
CROATIA	❍			
CUBA	❍			
CYPRUS				
CZECH REPUBLIC	❍			
DENMARK				
DJIBOUTI	❍	❍	●	
DOMINICA	❍		●	
DOMINICAN REPUBLIC	❍	❍		
EAST TIMOR	❍	❍		
ECUADOR	❍	❍ ▲	● ❍ ▲	
EGYPT	❍	▲ ◆	●	
EL SALVADOR	❍	❍ ▲	●	
EQUATORIAL GUINEA	❍	❍	● ❍	
ERITREA	❍	❍	●	❑
ESTONIA				
ETHIOPIA	❍	❍ ▲	● ❍	❑
FIJI	❍		●	
FINLAND				
FRANCE				
GABON	❍	❍	● ❍	
GAMBIA	❍	❍	● ❍	❑
GEORGIA	❍			
GERMANY				
GHANA	❍	❍	● ❍	❑
GREECE			●	
GRENADA	❍		●	
GUATEMALA	❍	❍ ▲	●	
GUINEA	❍	❍	● ❍	❑
GUINEA-BISSAU	❍	❍	● ❍	❑
GUYANA	❍	❍	● ❍	
HAITI	❍	❍	●	
HONDURAS	❍	❍	●	
HUNGARY				
ICELAND				
INDIA	❍	❍	●	
INDONESIA	❍	❍ ▲	●	
IRAN	❍	❍		
IRAQ	❍	❍ ▲ ◆	●	
IRELAND				
ISRAEL	❍			
ITALY				
IVORY COAST	❍	❍	● ❍	❑
JAMAICA	❍		●	
JAPAN	❍			
JORDAN	❍		●	
KAZAKHSTAN	❍		●	
KENYA	❍	❍	● ❍	❑

Country	Hep. A, Typhoid	Malaria	Yellow Fever	Meningitis ACWY
KIRIBATI	❍		●	
KUWAIT	❍			
KYRGYZSTAN	❍			
LAOS	❍	❍	●	
LATVIA				
LEBANON	❍		●	
LESOTHO	❍		●	
LIBERIA	❍	❍	● ❍	
LIBYA	❍		●	
LIECHTENSTEIN				
LITHUANIA				
LUXEMBOURG				
MACEDONIA	❍			
MADAGASCAR	❍	❍		
MALAWI	❍	❍	●	
MALAYSIA	❍	❍ ▲	●	
MALDIVES	❍		●	
MALI	❍	❍	❍ ● ▲	❑
MALTA			●	
MARSHALL ISLANDS	❍			
MAURITANIA	❍	❍	●	
MAURITIUS	❍	❍ ▲	●	
MEXICO	❍	❍ ▲		
MICRONESIA	❍			
MOLDOVA	❍			
MONACO				
MONGOLIA	❍			
MOROCCO	❍			
MOZAMBIQUE	❍	❍	●	❑
NAMIBIA	❍	❍ ▲	●	❑
NAURU	❍		●	
NEPAL	❍	❍ ▲	●	
NETHERLANDS				
NEW ZEALAND				
NICARAGUA	❍	❍	●	
NIGER	❍	❍	❍ ● ▲	❑
NIGERIA	❍	❍	● ❍	❑
NORTH KOREA	❍			
NORWAY				
OMAN	❍	❍ ▲	●	
PAKISTAN	❍	❍	●	
PALAU	❍		●	
PANAMA	❍	❍	❍ ▲	
PAPUA NEW GUINEA	❍	❍ ▲	●	
PARAGUAY	❍	❍ ▲	●	
PERU	❍	❍ ▲	● ❍ ▲	
PHILIPPINES	❍	❍ ▲	●	
POLAND				
PORTUGAL			● ▲	
QATAR	❍			
ROMANIA	❍			
RUSSIAN FEDERATION	❍ ▲			

Country	Hep. A, Typhoid	Malaria	Yellow Fever	Meningitis ACWY
RWANDA	❍	❍	● ❍	❑
ST KITTS & NEVIS	❍		●	
ST LUCIA	❍		●	
ST VINCENT & GRENADINES	❍		●	
SAMOA	❍		●	
SAN MARINO				
SAO TOME & PRINCIPE	❍	❍	● ❍	
SAUDI ARABIA	❍	❍ ▲	●	■
SENEGAL	❍	❍	● ❍	❑
SERBIA & MONTENEGRO	❍ ▲			
SEYCHELLES	❍		●	
SIERRA LEONE	❍	❍	● ❍	❑
SINGAPORE	❍		●	
SLOVAKIA	❍			
SLOVENIA	❍			
SOLOMON ISLANDS	❍	❍	●	
SOMALIA	❍	❍	● ❍	❑
SOUTH AFRICA	❍	❍ ▲	●	
SOUTH KOREA	❍			
SPAIN				
SRI LANKA	❍	❍	●	
SUDAN	❍	❍	● ❍ ▲	❑
SURINAM	❍	❍	● ❍	
SWAZILAND	❍	❍	●	
SWEDEN				
SWITZERLAND				
SYRIA	❍	❍ ▲ ◆	●	
TAIWAN	❍			
TAJIKISTAN	❍	❍ ▲ ◆		
TANZANIA	❍	❍	● ❍	❑
THAILAND	❍	❍ ▲	●	
TOGO	❍	❍	● ❍	❑
TONGA	❍		●	
TRINIDAD & TOBAGO	❍		● ❍ ▲	
TUNISIA	❍		●	
TURKEY	❍	❍ ▲ ◆		
TURKMENISTAN	❍	❍ ▲ ◆		
TUVALU	❍			
UGANDA	❍	❍	● ❍	❑
UKRAINE	❍			
UNITED ARAB EMIRATES	❍			
UNITED KINGDOM				
UNITED STATES				
URUGUAY	❍			
UZBEKISTAN	❍			
VANUATU	❍	❍		
VATICAN CITY				
VENEZUELA	❍	❍	❍	
VIETNAM	❍	❍ ▲	●	
YEMEN	❍	❍	●	
ZAMBIA	❍	❍	❍ ▲	❑
ZIMBABWE	❍	❍ ▲ ◆	●	

INDEX

GLOSSARY OF ABBREVIATIONS

This glossary provides a comprehensive guide to the abbreviations used in this Atlas, and in the Index.

A
abbrev. abbreviated
AD Anno Domini
Afr. Afrikaans
Alb. Albanian
Amh. Amharic
anc. ancient
approx. approximately
Ar. Arabic
Arm. Armenian
ASEAN Association of South East Asian Nations
ASSR Autonomous Soviet Socialist Republic
Aust. Australian
Az. Azerbaijani
Azerb. Azerbaijan

B
Basq. Basque
BC before Christ
Bel. Belarussian
Ben. Bengali
Ber. Berber
B-H Bosnia-Herzegovina
bn billion (one thousand million)
BP British Petroleum
Bret. Breton
Brit. British
Bul. Bulgarian
Bur. Burmese

C
C central
C. Cape
°C degrees Centigrade
CACM Central America Common Market
Cam. Cambodian
Cant. Cantonese
CAR Central African Republic
Cast. Castilian
Cat. Catalan
CEEAC Central America Common Market
Chin. Chinese
CIS Commonwealth of Independent States
cm centimetre(s)
Cro. Croat
Cz. Czech
Czech Rep. Czech Republic

D
Dan. Danish
Div. Divehi
Dom. Rep. Dominican Republic
Dut. Dutch

E
E east
EC *see* EU
EEC *see* EU
ECOWAS Economic Community of West African States
ECU European Currency Unit
EMS European Monetary System
Eng. English
est estimated
Est. Estonian
EU European Union (previously European Community [EC], European Economic Community [EEC])

F
°F degrees Fahrenheit
Faer. Faeroese
Fij. Fijian
Fin. Finnish
Fr. French
Fris. Frisian
ft foot/feet
FYROM Former Yugoslav Republic of Macedonia

G
g gram(s)
Gael. Gaelic
Gal. Galician
GDP Gross Domestic Product (the total value of goods and services produced by a country excluding income from foreign countries)
Geor. Georgian
Ger. German
Gk Greek
GNP Gross National Product (the total value of goods and services produced by a country)

H
Heb. Hebrew
HEP hydro-electric power
Hind. Hindi
hist. historical
Hung. Hungarian

I
I. Island
Icel. Icelandic
in inch(es)
In. Inuit (Eskimo)
Ind. Indonesian
Intl International
Ir. Irish
Is Islands
It. Italian

J
Jap. Japanese

K
Kaz. Kazakh
kg kilogram(s)
Kir. Kirghiz
km kilometre(s)
km² square kilometre (singular)
Kor. Korean
Kurd. Kurdish

L
L. Lake
LAIA Latin American Integration Association
Lao. Laotian
Lapp. Lappish
Lat. Latin
Latv. Latvian
Liech. Liechtenstein
Lith. Lithuanian
Lus. Lusatian
Lux. Luxembourg

M
m million/metre(s)
Mac. Macedonian
Maced. Macedonia
Mal. Malay
Malg. Malagasy
Malt. Maltese
mi. mile(s)
Mong. Mongolian
Mt. Mountain
Mts Mountains

N
N north
NAFTA North American Free Trade Agreement
Nep. Nepali
Neth. Netherlands
Nic. Nicaraguan
Nor. Norwegian
NZ New Zealand

P
Pash. Pashtu
PNG Papua New Guinea
Pol. Polish
Poly. Polynesian
Port. Portuguese
prev. previously

R
Rep. Republic
Res. Reservoir
Rmsch Romansch
Rom. Romanian
Rus. Russian
Russ. Fed. Russian Federation

S
S south
SADC Southern Africa Development Community
SCr. Serbian/Croatian
Sinh. Sinhala
Slvk Slovak
Slvn. Slovene
Som. Somali
Sp. Spanish
St., St Saint
Strs Straits
Swa. Swahili
Swe. Swedish
Switz. Switzerland

T
Taj. Tajik
Th. Thai
Thai. Thailand
Tib. Tibetan
Turk. Turkish
Turkm. Turkmenistan

U
UAE United Arab Emirates
Uigh. Uighur
UK United Kingdom
Ukr. Ukrainian
UN United Nations
Urd. Urdu
US/USA United States of America
USSR Union of Soviet Socialist Republics
Uzb. Uzbek

V
var. variant
Vdkhr. Vodokhranilishche (Russian for reservoir)
Vdskh. Vodoskhovyshche (Ukrainian for reservoir)
Vtn. Vietnamese

W
W west
Wel. Welsh

Y
Yugo. Yugoslavia

THIS INDEX LISTS all the placenames and features shown on the regional and continental maps in this Atlas. Placenames are referenced to the largest scale map on which they appear. The policy followed throughout the Atlas is to use the local spelling or local name at regional level; commonly-used English language names may occasionally be added (in parentheses) where this is an aid to identification e.g. Firenze (Florence). English names, where they exist, have been used for all international features e.g. oceans and country names; they are also used on the continental maps and in the introductory section; these are then fully cross-referenced to the local names found on the regional maps. The index also contains commonly-found alternative names and variant spellings, which are also fully cross-referenced.

All main entry names are those of settlements unless otherwise indicated by the use of italicized definitions or representative symbols, which are keyed at the foot of each page.

1

25 de Mayo *see* Veinticinco de Mayo
137 *Y13* **26 Bakı Komissarı** ***Rus.*** Imeni 26 Bakinskikh Komissarov. SE Azerbaijan
26 Baku Komissarlary Adyndaky *see* Uzboý
10 *M16* **100 Mile House** ***var.*** Hundred Mile House. British Columbia, SW Canada

A

Aa *see* Gauja
95 *G24* **Aabenraa** ***var.*** Åbenrå, ***Ger.*** Apenrade. Sønderjylland, SW Denmark
95 *G20* **Aabybro** ***var.*** Åbybro. Nordjylland, N Denmark
101 *C16* **Aachen** ***Dut.*** Aken, ***Fr.*** Aix-la-Chapelle; ***anc.*** Aquae Grani, Aquisgranum. Nordrhein-Westfalen, W Germany
Aaiún *see* Laâyoune
95 *M24* **Aakirkeby** ***var.*** Åkirkeby. Bornholm, E Denmark
Āak Nông *see* Gia Nghia
95 *G20* **Aalborg** ***var.*** Ålborg, Ålborg-Nørresundby; ***anc.*** Alburgum. Nordjylland, N Denmark
Aalborg Bugt *see* Ålborg Bugt
101 *J21* **Aalen** Baden-Württemberg, S Germany
95 *G21* **Aalestrup** ***var.*** Ålestrup. Viborg, NW Denmark
98 *I11* **Aalsmeer** Noord-Holland, C Netherlands
99 *F18* **Aalst** ***Fr.*** Alost. Oost-Vlaanderen, C Belgium
99 *K18* **Aalst** Noord-Brabant, S Netherlands
98 *O12* **Aalten** Gelderland, E Netherlands
99 *D17* **Aalter** Oost-Vlaanderen, NW Belgium
Aanaar *see* Inari
Aanaarjävri *see* Inarijärvi
93 *M17* **Äänekoski** Länsi-Suomi, W Finland
138 *H7* **Aanjar** ***var.*** 'Anjar. C Lebanon
83 *G21* **Aansluit** Northern Cape, N South Africa
Aar *see* Aare
108 *F7* **Aarau** Aargau, N Switzerland
108 *D8* **Aarberg** Bern, W Switzerland
99 *D16* **Aardenburg** Zeeland, SW Netherlands
108 *D8* **Aare** ***var.*** Aar. ≈ W Switzerland
108 *F7* **Aargau** ***Fr.*** Argovie. ◈ *canton* N Switzerland
Aarhus *see* Århus
Aarlen *see* Arlon
95 *G21* **Aars** ***var.*** Års. Nordjylland, N Denmark
99 *I17* **Aarschot** Vlaams Brabant, C Belgium
Aassi, Nahr el *see* Orontes
Aat *see* Ath
160 *G7* **Aba** ***prev.*** Ngawa. Sichuan, C China
77 *V17* **Aba** Abia, S Nigeria
79 *P16* **Aba** Orientale, NE Dem. Rep. Congo
140 *J6* **Abā al Qazāz, Bi'r** *well* NW Saudi Arabia
Abā as Su'ūd *see* Najrān
59 *G14* **Abacaxis, Rio** ≈ NW Brazil
Abaco Island *see* Great Abaco/Little Abaco
Abaco Island *see* Great Abaco, N Bahamas
142 *K10* **Ābādān** Khūzestān, SW Iran
143 *O10* **Ābādeh** Fārs, C Iran
74 *H8* **Abadla** W Algeria
59 *M20* **Abaeté** Minas Gerais, SE Brazil
Abag Qi *see* Xin Hot
62 *P7* **Abaí** Caazapá, S Paraguay
191 *O2* **Abaiang** ***var.*** Apia; ***prev.*** Charlotte Island. *atoll* Tungaru, W Kiribati
Abaj *see* Abay
77 *U15* **Abaji** Federal Capital District, C Nigeria
37 *O7* **Abajo Peak** ▲ Utah, W USA
77 *V16* **Abakaliki** Ebonyi, SE Nigeria
122 *K13* **Abakan** Respublika Khakasiya, S Russian Federation
77 *S11* **Abala** Tillabéri, SW Niger
77 *U11* **Abalak** Tahoua, C Niger
119 *N14* **Abalyanka** ***Rus.*** Obolyanka. ≈ N Belarus
122 *L12* **Aban** Krasnoyarskiy Kray, S Russian Federation
143 *P9* **Āb Anbār-e Kān Sorkh** Yazd, C Iran
57 *G16* **Abancay** Apurímac, SE Peru
190 *H2* **Abaokoro** *atoll* Tungaru, W Kiribati
Abariringa *see* Kanton
143 *P10* **Abarkū** Yazd, C Iran
165 *V3* **Abashiri** ***var.*** Abasiri. Hokkaidō, NE Japan
165 *U3* **Abashiri-ko** ◎ Hokkaidō, NE Japan
Abasiri *see* Abashiri
41 *P10* **Abasolo** Tamaulipas, C Mexico
186 *F9* **Abau** Central, S PNG
145 *R10* **Abay** ***var.*** Abaj. Karaganda, C Kazakhstan
81 *I15* **Ābaya Hāyk'** ***Eng.*** Lake Margherita, ***It.*** Abbaia. ◎ SW Ethiopia
Ābay Wenz *see* Blue Nile
122 *K13* **Abaza** Respublika Khakasiya, S Russian Federation
Abbaia *see* Ābaya Hāyk'
143 *Q13* **Āb Bārīk** Fārs, S Iran
107 *C18* **Abbasanta** Sardegna, Italy, C Mediterranean Sea
Abbatis Villa *see* Abbeville
30 *M3* **Abbaye, Point** *headland* Michigan, N USA
Abbazia *see* Opatija
Abbé, Lake *see* Abhe, Lake
103 *N2* **Abbeville** ***anc.*** Abbatis Villa. Somme, N France
23 *R7* **Abbeville** Alabama, S USA
23 *U6* **Abbeville** Georgia, SE USA
22 *I9* **Abbeville** Louisiana, S USA
21 *P12* **Abbeville** South Carolina, SE USA
97 *B20* **Abbeyfeale** ***Ir.*** Mainistir na Féile. SW Ireland
106 *D8* **Abbiategrasso** Lombardia, NW Italy
93 *I14* **Abborrträsk** Norrbotten, N Sweden
194 *J9* **Abbot Ice Shelf** *ice shelf* Antarctica
10 *M17* **Abbotsford** British Columbia, SW Canada
30 *K6* **Abbotsford** Wisconsin, N USA
149 *U5* **Abbottābād** North-West Frontier Province, NW Pakistan
119 *M14* **Abchuha** ***Rus.*** Obchuga. Minskaya Voblasts', NW Belarus
98 *I10* **Abcoude** Utrecht, C Netherlands
139 *N2* **'Abd al 'Azīz, Jabal** ▲▲ NE Syria
141 *U17* **'Abd al Kūrī** *island* SE Yemen
139 *Z13* **'Abd Allāh, Khawr** *bay* Iraq/Kuwait
127 *U6* **Abdulino** Orenburgskaya Oblast', W Russian Federation
78 *J10* **Abéché** ***var.*** Abécher, Abeshr. Ouaddaï, SE Chad
Abécher *see* Abéché
143 *S8* **Āb-e Garm va Sard** Yazd, E Iran
77 *R8* **Abeïbara** Kidal, NE Mali
105 *P5* **Abejar** Castilla-León, N Spain
54 *E9* **Abejorral** Antioquia, W Colombia
Abela *see* Ávila
Abellinum *see* Avellino
92 *Q2* **Abeløya** *island* Kong Karls Land, E Svalbard
80 *I13* **Ābeltī** Oromo, C Ethiopia
191 *O2* **Abemama** ***var.*** Apamama; ***prev.*** Roger Simpson Island. *atoll* Tungaru, W Kiribati
171 *Y15* **Abemaree** ***var.*** Abemarre. Papua, E Indonesia
77 *O16* **Abengourou** E Ivory Coast
Åbenrå *see* Aabenraa
101 *L22* **Abens** ≈ SE Germany
77 *S16* **Abeokuta** Ogun, SW Nigeria
97 *I20* **Aberaeron** SW Wales, UK
Aberbrothock *see* Arbroath
Abercorn *see* Mbala
29 *R6* **Abercrombie** North Dakota, N USA
183 *T7* **Aberdeen** New South Wales, SE Australia
11 *T15* **Aberdeen** Saskatchewan, S Canada
83 *H25* **Aberdeen** Eastern Cape, S South Africa
96 *L9* **Aberdeen** ***anc.*** Devana. NE Scotland, UK
21 *X2* **Aberdeen** Maryland, NE USA
23 *N3* **Aberdeen** Mississippi, S USA
21 *T10* **Aberdeen** North Carolina, SE USA
29 *P8* **Aberdeen** South Dakota, N USA
32 *F8* **Aberdeen** Washington, NW USA
96 *K9* **Aberdeen** *cultural region* NE Scotland, UK
8 *L8* **Aberdeen Lake** ◎ Nunavut, NE Canada
96 *J10* **Aberfeldy** C Scotland, UK
97 *K21* **Abergavenny** ***anc.*** Gobannium. SE Wales, UK
Abergwaun *see* Fishguard
Abermarre *see* Abemaree
25 *N5* **Abernathy** Texas, SW USA
Abersee *see* Wolfgangsee
Abertawe *see* Swansea
Aberteifi *see* Cardigan
32 *I15* **Abert, Lake** ◎ Oregon, NW USA
97 *I20* **Aberystwyth** W Wales, UK
Abeshr *see* Abéché
Ábeskovvu *see* Abisko
106 *F10* **Abetone** Toscana, C Italy
125 *V5* **Abez'** Respublika Komi, NW Russian Federation
142 *M5* **Āb Garm** Qazvīn, N Iran
141 *N12* **Abhā** 'Asīr, SW Saudi Arabia
142 *M5* **Abhar** Zanjān, NW Iran
Abhé Bad/Ābhē Bid Hāyk' *see* Abhe, Lake
80 *K12* **Abhe, Lake** ***var.*** Lake Abbé, ***Amh.*** Ābhē Bid Hāyk', ***Som.*** Abhé Bad. ◎ Djibouti/Ethiopia
77 *V17* **Abia** ◈ *state* SE Nigeria
139 *V9* **'Abīd 'Alī** E Iraq
119 *O17* **Abidavichy** ***Rus.*** Obidovichi. Mahilyowskaya Voblasts', E Belarus
115 *L15* **Abide** Çanakkale, NW Turkey
77 *N17* **Abidjan** S Ivory Coast
Āb-i-Istāda *see* Īstādeh-ye Moqor, Āb-e-
27 *N4* **Abilene** Kansas, C USA
25 *Q7* **Abilene** Texas, SW USA
Abindonia *see* Abingdon
97 *M21* **Abingdon** ***anc.*** Abindonia. S England, UK
30 *K12* **Abingdon** Illinois, N USA
21 *P8* **Abingdon** Virginia, NE USA
Abingdon *see* Pinta, Isla
18 *J15* **Abington** Pennsylvania, NE USA
126 *K14* **Abinsk** Krasnodarskiy Kray, SW Russian Federation
37 *R9* **Abiquiu Reservoir** ▣ New Mexico, SW USA
92 *I10* **Abisko** ***Lapp.*** Ábeskovvu. Norrbotten, N Sweden
12 *G12* **Abitibi** ≈ Ontario, S Canada
12 *H12* **Abitibi, Lac** ◎ Ontario /Québec, S Canada
80 *J10* **Ābīy Ādī** Tigray, N Ethiopia
118 *H6* **Abja-Paluoja** Viljandimaa, S Estonia
137 *Q8* **Abkhazia** ◈ *autonomous republic* NW Georgia
182 *F1* **Abminga** South Australia
75 *W9* **Abnûb** C Egypt
Åbo *see* Turku
152 *G9* **Abohar** Punjab, N India
77 *O17* **Aboisso** SE Ivory Coast
78 *H5* **Abo, Massif d'** ▲▲ NW Chad
77 *R16* **Abomey** S Benin
79 *F16* **Abong Mbang** Est, SE Cameroon
111 *L23* **Abony** Pest, C Hungary
78 *J11* **Abou-Déïa** Salamat, SE Chad
Aboudouhour *see* Abū aḍ Ḍuhūr
Abou Kémal *see* Abū Kamāl
Abou Simbel *see* Abu Simbel
137 *T12* **Abovyan** C Armenia
171 *O2* **Abra** ≈ Luzon, N Philippines
141 *P15* **Abrād, Wādī** *seasonal river* W Yemen
Abraham Bay *see* The Carlton
104 *G10* **Abrantes** ***var.*** Abrántes. Santarém, C Portugal
62 *J4* **Abra Pampa** Jujuy, N Argentina
Abrashlare *see* Brezovo
54 *G7* **Abrego** Norte de Santander, N Colombia
Abrene *see* Pytalovo
40 *C7* **Abreojos, Punta** *headland* W Mexico
65 *J16* **Abrolhos Bank** *undersea feature* W Atlantic Ocean
119 *H19* **Abrova** ***Rus.*** Obrovo. Brestskaya Voblasts', SW Belarus
116 *G11* **Abrud** ***Ger.*** Gross-Schlatten, ***Hung.*** Abrudbánya. Alba, SW Romania
Abrudbánya *see* Abrud
118 *E6* **Abruka** *island* SW Estonia
107 *J15* **Abruzzese, Appennino** ▲▲ C Italy
107 *J14* **Abruzzo** ◈ *region* C Italy
141 *N14* **'Abs** ***var.*** Sūq 'Abs. W Yemen
33 *T12* **Absaroka Range** ▲▲ Montana/Wyoming, NW USA
137 *Z11* **Abşeron Yarımadası** ***Rus.*** Apsheronskiy Poluostrov. *peninsula* E Azerbaijan
143 *N6* **Āb Shīrīn** Eşfahān, C Iran
139 *X10* **Abtān** SE Iraq
109 *R6* **Abtenau** Salzburg, NW Austria
164 *E12* **Abu** Yamaguchi, Honshū, SW Japan
152 *E14* **Ābu** Rājasthān, N India
138 *I4* **Abū aḍ Ḍuhūr** ***Fr.*** Aboudouhour. Idlib, NW Syria
143 *P17* **Abū al Abyaḍ** *island* C UAE
138 *K10* **Abū al Ḥuşayn, Khabrat** ◎ N Jordan
139 *R8* **Abū al Jīr** C Iraq
139 *Y12* **Abū al Khaşīb** ***var.*** Abul Khasib. SE Iraq
139 *U12* **Abū at Tubrah, Thaqb** *well* S Iraq
75 *V11* **Abu Balâs** ▲ SW Egypt
Abu Dhabi *see* Abū Ẓaby
139 *R8* **Abū Farūkh** C Iraq
80 *C12* **Abu Gabra** Southern Darfur, W Sudan
139 *P10* **Abū Ghār, Sha'īb** *dry watercourse* S Iraq
80 *G7* **Abu Hamed** River Nile, N Sudan
139 *O5* **Abū Ḥardān** ***var.*** Hajîne. Dayr az Zawr, E Syria
139 *T7* **Abū Ḥāssawīyah** E Iraq
138 *K10* **Abū Ḥifnah, Wādī** *dry watercourse* N Jordan
77 *V15* **Abuja** ● (Nigeria) Federal Capital District, C Nigeria
139 *R9* **Abū Jahaf, Wādī** *dry watercourse* C Iraq
56 *F12* **Abujao, Río** ≈ E Peru
139 *U12* **Abū Jasrah** S Iraq
139 *O6* **Abū Kamāl** ***Fr.*** Abou Kémal. Dayr az Zawr, E Syria
165 *P12* **Abukuma-sanchi** ▲▲ Honshū, C Japan
Abula *see* Ávila
Abul Khasib *see* Abū al Khaşīb
79 *K16* **Abumombazi** ***var.*** Abumonbazi. Equateur, N Dem. Rep. Congo
Abumonbazi *see* Abumombazi
59 *D15* **Abunã** Rondônia, W Brazil
56 *K13* **Abunã, Rio** ***var.*** Río Abuná. ≈ Bolivia/Brazil
138 *G10* **Abū Nuşayr** ***var.*** Abu Nuseir. 'Al Āşimah, W Jordan

◆ COUNTRY
● COUNTRY CAPITAL
◇ DEPENDENT TERRITORY
○ DEPENDENT TERRITORY CAPITAL
◈ ADMINISTRATIVE REGION
✕ INTERNATIONAL AIRPORT
▲ MOUNTAIN
▲▲ MOUNTAIN RANGE
⩕ VOLCANO
≈ RIVER
◎ LAKE
▣ RESERVOIR

Abu Nuseir see Abū Nuşayr
139 T12 Abū Qabr S Iraq
138 K5 Abū Raḩbah, Jabal ▲ C Syria
139 S5 Abū Rajāsh N Iraq
139 W13 Abū Raqrāq, Ghadīr well S Iraq
152 E14 Ābu Road Rājasthān, N India
80 I6 Abu Shagara, Ras headland NE Sudan
75 W12 Abu Simbel var. Abou Simbel, Abū Sunbul. ancient monument S Egypt
139 U12 Abū Sudayrah S Iraq
139 T10 Abū Şukhayr S Iraq
Abū Sunbul see Abu Simbel
165 R4 Abuta Hokkaidō, NE Japan
185 E18 Abut Head headland South Island, NZ
80 E9 Abu 'Urug Northern Kordofan, C Sudan
80 K12 Ābuyē Mēda ▲ C Ethiopia
80 D11 Abu Zabad Western Kordofan, C Sudan
Abū Ẓabī see Abū Ẓaby
143 P16 Abū Ẓaby var. Abū Ẓabī, Eng. Abu Dhabi. ● (UAE) Abū Ẓaby, C UAE
75 X8 Abu Zenīma E Egypt
95 N17 Åby Östergötland, S Sweden
Abyaḑ, Al Baḩr al see White Nile
Åbybro see Aabybro
80 D13 Abyei Western Kordofan, S Sudan
Abyla see Ávila
Abymes see les Abymes
Abyssinia see Ethiopia
Açāba see Assaba
54 F11 Acacías Meta, C Colombia
58 L13 Açailandia Maranhão, E Brazil
Acaill see Achill Island
42 E8 Acajutla Sonsonate, W El Salvador
79 D17 Acalayong SW Equatorial Guinea
41 N13 Acámbaro Guanajuato, C Mexico
54 C6 Acandí Chocó, NW Colombia
104 H4 A Cañiza var. La Cañiza. Galicia, NW Spain
40 J11 Acaponeta Nayarit, C Mexico
40 J11 Acaponeta, Río de ↝ C Mexico
41 O16 Acapulco var. Acapulco de Juárez. Guerrero, S Mexico
Acapulco de Juárez see Acapulco
55 T13 Acarai Mountains Sp. Serra Acaraí. ⛰ Brazil/Guyana
Acaraí, Serra see Acarai Mountains
58 O13 Acaraú Ceará, NE Brazil
54 J6 Acarigua Portuguesa, N Venezuela
42 C6 Acatenango, Volcán de ✱ S Guatemala
41 Q15 Acatlán var. Acatlán de Osorio. Puebla, S Mexico
Acatlán de Osorio see Acatlán
41 S15 Acayucan var. Acayucán. Veracruz-Llave, E Mexico
Accho see 'Akko
21 Y5 Accomac Virginia, NE USA
77 Q17 Accra ● (Ghana) SE Ghana
97 L17 Accrington NW England, UK
61 B19 Acebal Santa Fe, C Argentina
168 H8 Aceh off. Daerah Istimewa Aceh, var. Acheen, Achin, Atchin, Atjeh. ◈ autonomous district NW Indonesia
107 M18 Acerenza Basilicata, S Italy
107 K17 Acerra anc. Acerrae. Campania, S Italy
Acerrae see Acerra
Ach'asar Lerr see Achkasar
57 J17 Achacachi La Paz, W Bolivia
54 K7 Achaguas Apure, C Venezuela
154 H12 Achalpur prev. Elichpur, Ellichpur. Mahārāshtra, C India
61 F18 Achar Tacuarembó, C Uruguay
115 H19 Acharnés var. Aharnes; prev. Akharnaí. Attikí, C Greece
Acheen see Aceh
99 K16 Achel Limburg, NE Belgium
115 D16 Achelóos var. Akhelóös, Aspropótamos; anc. Achelous. ↝ W Greece
Achelous see Achelóos
163 W8 Acheng Heilongjiang, NE China
109 N6 Achenkirch Tirol, W Austria
101 L24 Achenpass pass Austria/Germany
109 N7 Achensee ◎ W Austria
101 F22 Achern Baden-Württemberg, SW Germany
115 C16 Acherón ↝ W Greece
77 W11 Achétinamou ↝ S Niger
152 J12 Achhnera Uttar Pradesh, N India
42 C7 Achiguate, Río ↝ S Guatemala
97 A16 Achill Head Ir. Ceann Acla. headland W Ireland
97 A16 Achill Island Ir. Acaill. island W Ireland
100 H11 Achim Niedersachsen, NW Germany
149 S5 Achīn Nangarhār, E Afghanistan
Achin see Aceh
122 K12 Achinsk Krasnoyarskiy Kray, S Russian Federation
162 E5 Achit Nuur ◎ NW Mongolia
137 T11 Achkasar Arm. Ach'asar Lerr. ▲ Armenia/Georgia
126 K13 Achuyevo Krasnodarskiy Kray, SW Russian Federation
81 F16 Achwa var. Aswa. ↝ N Uganda
136 E15 Acıgöl salt lake SW Turkey
107 L24 Acireale Sicilia, Italy, C Mediterranean Sea
Aciris see Agri
25 N7 Ackerly Texas, SW USA
22 M4 Ackerman Mississippi, S USA
29 W13 Ackley Iowa, C USA
44 J5 Acklins Island island SE Bahamas
Acla, Ceann see Achill Head
62 H11 Aconcagua, Cerro ▲ W Argentina
Açores/Açores, Arquipélago dos/Açores, Ilhas dos see Azores
104 G2 A Coruña Cast. La Coruña ◈ province Galicia, NW Spain
104 H2 A Coruña Cast. La Coruña, Eng. Corunna; anc. Caronium. Galicia, NW Spain
42 L10 Acoyapa Chontales, S Nicaragua
106 H13 Acquapendente Lazio, C Italy
106 J13 Acquasanta Terme Marche, C Italy
106 I13 Acquasparta Lazio, C Italy
106 C9 Acqui Terme Piemonte, NW Italy
Acrae see Palazzolo Acreide
182 F7 Acraman, Lake salt lake South Australia
59 A15 Acre off. Estado do Acre. ◈ state W Brazil
Acre see 'Akko
59 C16 Acre, Rio ↝ W Brazil
107 N20 Acri Calabria, SW Italy
Acte see Ágion Óros
191 Y12 Actéon, Groupe island group Îles Tuamotu, SE French Polynesia
15 P12 Acton-Vale Québec, SE Canada
41 P13 Actopan var. Actopán. Hidalgo, C Mexico
59 P14 Açu var. Assu. Rio Grande do Norte, E Brazil
Acunum Acusio see Montélimar
77 Q17 Ada SE Ghana
29 R5 Ada Minnesota, N USA
31 R12 Ada Ohio, N USA
27 O12 Ada Oklahoma, C USA
112 L8 Ada Serbia, N Serbia and Montenegro (Yugo.)
Ada Bazar see Adapazarı
40 D3 Adair, Bahía de bay NW Mexico
104 M7 Adaja ↝ N Spain
38 H17 Adak Island island Aleutian Islands, Alaska, USA
Adalia see Antalya
Adalia, Gulf of see Antalya Körfezi
141 X9 Adam N Oman
Adama see Nazrēt
60 I8 Adamantina São Paulo, S Brazil
79 E14 Adamaoua Eng. Adamawa. ◈ province N Cameroon
77 Y14 Adamawa ◈ state E Nigeria
Adamawa see Adamaoua
106 F6 Adamello ▲ N Italy
81 J14 Ādamī Tulu Oromo, C Ethiopia
63 M23 Adam, Mount var. Monte Independencia. ▲ West Falkland, Falkland Islands
29 R16 Adams Nebraska, C USA
18 H8 Adams New York, NE USA
29 Q3 Adams North Dakota, N USA
155 I23 Adam's Bridge chain of shoals NW Sri Lanka
32 H10 Adams, Mount ▲ Washington, NW USA
Adam's Peak see Sri Pada
191 R16 Adam's Rock island Pitcairn Island, Pitcairn Islands
191 P16 Adamstown ○ (Pitcairn Islands) Pitcairn Island, Pitcairn Islands
20 G10 Adamsville Tennessee, S USA
25 S9 Adamsville Texas, SW USA
141 O17 'Adan Eng. Aden. SW Yemen
136 K16 Adana var. Seyhan. Adana, S Turkey
136 K16 Adana var. Seyhan. ◈ province S Turkey
Adâncata see Horlivka
169 V12 Adang, Teluk bay Borneo, C Indonesia
136 F11 Adapazarı prev. Ada Bazar. Sakarya, NW Turkey
80 H8 Adarama River Nile, NE Sudan
195 Q16 Adare, Cape headland Antarctica
106 E6 Adda anc. Addua. ↝ N Italy
80 A13 Adda ↝ W Sudan
143 Q17 Aḑ Ḑab'īyah Abū Ẓaby, C UAE
143 O18 Aḑ Ḑafrah desert S UAE
141 Q6 Ad Dahnā' desert E Saudi Arabia
74 A11 Ad Dakhla var. Dakhla. SW Western Sahara
Ad Dalanj see Dilling
Ad Damar see Ed Damer
Ad Damazīn see Ed Damazin
Ad Dāmir see Ed Damer
173 N2 Ad Dammām desert NE Saudi Arabia
141 R6 Ad Dammān var. Dammām. Ash Sharqīyah, NE Saudi Arabia
Ad Dāmūr see Damoûr
140 K5 Ad Dār al Ḩamrā' Tabūk, NW Saudi Arabia
140 M13 Ad Darb Jīzān, SW Saudi Arabia
141 O8 Ad Dawādimī Ar Riyāḑ, C Saudi Arabia
143 N16 Ad Dawḩah Eng. Doha. ● (Qatar) C Qatar
143 N16 Ad Dawḩah Eng. Doha. × C Qatar
139 S6 Ad Dawr N Iraq
139 Y12 Ad Dayr var. Dayr, Shahbān. E Iraq
Addi Arkay see Ādī Ārk'ay
139 X15 Ad Dibdibah physical region Iraq/Kuwait
Aḑ Ḑiffah see Libyan Plateau
Addis Ababa see Ādīs Ābeba
Addison see Webster Springs
139 U10 Ad Dīwānīyah var. Diwaniyah. C Iraq
Addua see Adda
151 K22 Addu Atoll atoll S Maldives
Ad Dujail see Ad Dujayl
139 T7 Ad Dujayl var. Ad Dujail. N Iraq
Ad Duwaym/Ad Duwēm see Ed Dueim
99 D16 Adegem Oost-Vlaanderen, NW Belgium
23 U7 Adel Georgia, SE USA
29 U14 Adel Iowa, C USA
182 I9 Adelaide state capital South Australia
44 H2 Adelaide New Providence, N Bahamas
182 I9 Adelaide × South Australia
194 H6 Adelaide Island island Antarctica
181 P2 Adelaide River Northern Territory, N Australia
76 M10 'Adel Bagrou Hodh ech Chargui, SE Mauritania
186 D6 Adelbert Range ⛰ N PNG
180 K3 Adele Island island Western Australia
107 O17 Adelfia Puglia, SE Italy
195 V16 Adélie Coast physical region Antarctica
195 V14 Adélie, Terre physical region Antarctica
Adelnau see Odolanów
Adelsberg see Postojna
Aden see 'Adan
141 Q17 Aden, Gulf of gulf SW Arabian Sea
77 V10 Aderbissinat Agadez, C Niger
Adhaim see Al 'Uẓaym
143 R16 Adh Dhayd var. Al Dhaid. Ash Shāriqah, NE UAE
140 M4 'Adhfā' spring/well NW Saudi Arabia
138 I13 'Ādhriyāt, Jabāl al ▲ S Jordan
80 I10 Ādī Ārk'ay var. Addi Arkay. Amhara, N Ethiopia
182 C7 Adieu, Cape headland South Australia
106 H8 Adige Ger. Etsch. ↝ N Italy
80 J10 Ādīgrat Tigray, N Ethiopia
154 I13 Ādilābād var. Ādilābād. Andhra Pradesh, C India
35 P2 Adin California, W USA
171 V14 Adi, Pulau island E Indonesia
18 K8 Adirondack Mountains ⛰ New York, NE USA
80 J13 Ādīs Ābeba Eng. Addis Ababa. ● (Ethiopia) Ādīs Ābeba, C Ethiopia
80 J13 Ādīs Ābeba × Ādīs Ābeba, C Ethiopia
80 I11 Ādīs Zemen Amhara, N Ethiopia
Adi Ugri see Mendefera
137 N15 Adıyaman Adıyaman, SE Turkey
137 N15 Adıyaman ◈ province S Turkey
116 L11 Adjud Vrancea, E Romania
45 T6 Adjuntas C Puerto Rico
Adjuntas, Presa de las see Vicente Guerrero, Presa
Ādkup see Erikub Atoll
126 L15 Adler Krasnodarskiy Kray, SW Russian Federation
Adler see Orlice
108 G7 Adliswil Zürich, NW Switzerland
32 G7 Admiralty Inlet inlet Washington, NW USA
39 X13 Admiralty Island island Alexander Archipelago, Alaska, USA
186 E5 Admiralty Islands island group N PNG
136 B14 Adnan Menderes × (İzmir) İzmir, W Turkey
37 V6 Adobe Creek Reservoir ▣ Colorado, C USA
77 T16 Ado-Ekiti Ekiti, SW Nigeria
Adola see Kibre Mengist
61 C23 Adolfo González Chaues Buenos Aires, E Argentina
155 H17 Ādoni Andhra Pradesh, C India
102 K15 Adour anc. Aturus. ↝ SW France
Adowa see Ādwa
105 O15 Adra Andalucía, S Spain
107 L24 Adrano Sicilia, Italy, C Mediterranean Sea
74 I9 Adrar C Algeria
76 K7 Adrar ◈ region C Mauritania
74 L11 Adrar ⛰ SE Algeria
74 A12 Adrar Souttouf ⛰ SW Western Sahara
Adrasman see Adrasmon
147 Q10 Adrasmon Rus. Adrasman. NW Tajikistan
78 K10 Adré Ouaddaï, E Chad
106 H9 Adria anc. Atria, Hadria, Hatria. Veneto, NE Italy
31 R10 Adrian Michigan, N USA
29 S11 Adrian Minnesota, N USA
27 R5 Adrian Missouri, C USA
24 M2 Adrian Texas, SW USA
21 S4 Adrian West Virginia, NE USA
Adrianople/Adrianopolis see Edirne
121 P7 Adriatic Basin undersea feature Adriatic Sea, N Mediterranean Sea
Adriatico, Mare see Adriatic Sea
106 L13 Adriatic Sea Alb. Deti Adriatik, It. Mare Adriatico, SCr. Jadransko More, Slvn. Jadransko Morje. sea N Mediterranean Sea
Adriatik, Deti see Adriatic Sea
Adua see Ādwa
Aduana del Sásabe see El Sásabe
79 O17 Adusa Orientale, NE Dem. Rep. Congo
118 J13 Adutiškis Vilnius, E Lithuania
27 Y7 Advance Missouri, USA
65 D25 Adventure Sound bay East Falkland, Falkland Islands
80 J10 Ādwa var. Adowa, It. Adua. Tigray, N Ethiopia
123 Q8 Adycha ↝ NE Russian Federation
126 L14 Adygeya, Respublika ◈ autonomous republic SW Russian Federation
Adzhikui see Ajyguýy
77 N17 Adzopé SE Ivory Coast
127 U4 Adz'va ↝ NW Russian Federation
125 U5 Adz'vavom Respublika Komi, NW Russian Federation
Ædua see Autun
115 K19 Aegean Islands island group Greece/Turkey
Aegean North see Vóreion Aigaíon
115 I17 Aegean Sea Gk. Aigaíon Pélagos, Aigaío Pélagos, Turk. Ege Denizi. sea NE Mediterranean Sea
Aegean South see Nótion Aigaíon
118 H3 Aegviidu Ger. Charlottenhof. Harjumaa, NW Estonia
Aegyptus see Egypt
Aelana see Al 'Aqabah
Aelok see Ailuk Atoll
Aelōninae see Ailinginae Atoll
Aeļōņļapļap see Ailinglaplap Atoll
Æmilia see Emilia-Romagna
Æmilianum see Millau
Aemona see Ljubljana
Aenaria see Ischia
Aeolian Islands see Eolie, Isole
191 Z3 Aeon Point headland Kiritimati, NE Kiribati
95 G24 Ærø Ger. Arrö. island C Denmark
95 H24 Ærøskøbing Fyn, C Denmark
Æsernia see Isernia
104 G3 A Estrada Galicia, NW Spain
115 C18 Aetós Itháki, Iónioi Nísoi, Greece, C Mediterranean Sea
191 Q8 Afaahiti Tahiti, W French Polynesia
139 U10 'Afak C Iraq
Afanasjevo see Afanas'yevo
125 T14 Afanas'yevo var. Afanasjevo. Kirovskaya Oblast', NW Russian Federation
Afándou see Afántou
115 O23 Afántou var. Afándou. Ródos, Dodekánisos, Greece, Aegean Sea
Afar Depression see Danakil Desert
80 K11 Afar ◈ region NE Ethiopia
191 O7 Afareaitu Moorea, W French Polynesia
140 L7 'Afariyah, Bi'r al well NW Saudi Arabia
Afars et des Issas, Territoire Français des see Djibouti
83 D22 Affenrücken Karas, SW Namibia
Afghānestān, Dowlat-e Eslāmī-ye see Afghanistan
148 M6 Afghanistan off. Islamic State of Afghanistan, Per. Dowlat-e Eslāmī-ye Afghānestān; prev. Republic of Afghanistan. ◆ Islamic state C Asia
Afgoi see Afgooye
81 N17 Afgooye It. Afgoi. Shabeellaha Hoose, S Somalia
141 N8 'Afīf Ar Riyāḑ, C Saudi Arabia
77 V17 Afikpo Ebonyi, SE Nigeria
Afiun Karahissar see Afyon
Åfjord see Åi Åfjord
109 V6 Aflenz Kurort Steiermark, E Austria
74 J6 Aflou N Algeria
81 L18 Afmadow Jubbada Hoose, S Somalia
39 Q14 Afognak Island island Alaska, USA
104 J2 A Fonsagrada Galicia, NW Spain
186 E9 Afore Northern, S PNG
59 O15 Afrânio Pernambuco, E Brazil
68-73 Africa continent
172 K11 Africana Seamount undersea feature SW Indian Ocean
138 I2 'Afrīn Ḩalab, N Syria
136 M15 Afşin Kahramanmaraş, C Turkey
98 J7 Afsluitdijk dam N Netherlands
29 U15 Afton Iowa, C USA
29 W9 Afton Minnesota, N USA
27 R8 Afton Oklahoma, C USA
136 F14 Afyon prev. Afyonkarahisar. Afyon, W Turkey
136 F14 Afyon var. Afiun Karahisar, Afyonkarahisar. ◈ province W Turkey
Afyonkarahisar see Afyon
Agadès see Agadez
77 V10 Agadez prev. Agadès. Agadez, C Niger
77 W8 Agadez ◈ department N Niger
74 E8 Agadir SW Morocco
64 M9 Agadir Canyon undersea feature SE Atlantic Ocean
145 R12 Agadyr' Karaganda, C Kazakhstan
173 O7 Agalega Islands island group N Mauritius
42 K6 Agalta, Sierra de ⛰ E Honduras
122 I10 Agan ↝ C Russian Federation
Agana/Agaña see Hagåtña
188 B15 Agana Bay bay NW Guam
188 C16 Agana Field × (Agana) C Guam
171 Kk13 Agano-gawa ↝ Honshū, C Japan
188 B17 Aga Point headland S Guam
154 G9 Agar Madhya Pradesh, C India
81 I14 Āgaro Oromo, C Ethiopia
153 V15 Agartala Tripura, NE India
194 I5 Agassiz, Cape headland Antarctica
9 N2 Agassiz Ice Cap ice feature Nunavut, N Canada
175 V13 Agassiz Fracture Zone tectonic feature S Pacific Ocean
188 B16 Agat W Guam
188 B16 Agat Bay bay W Guam
145 P13 Agat, Gory hill C Kazakhstan
Agatha see Agde
115 M20 Agathónisi island Dodekánisos, Greece, Aegean Sea
171 X14 Agats Papua, E Indonesia
155 C21 Agatti Island island Lakshadweep, India, N Indian Ocean
38 D16 Agattu Island island Aleutian Islands, Alaska, USA
38 D16 Agattu Strait strait Aleutian Islands, Alaska, USA
14 B8 Agawa ↝ Ontario, S Canada
14 B8 Agawa Bay lake bay Ontario, S Canada
77 N17 Agboville SE Ivory Coast
137 V12 Ağdam Rus. Agdam. SW Azerbaijan
103 P16 Agde anc. Agatha. Hérault, S France
103 P16 Agde, Cap d' headland S France
Agedabia see Ajdābiyā
102 L14 Agen anc. Aginnum. Lot-et-Garonne, SW France
Agendicum see Sens
165 O13 Ageo Saitama, Honshū, S Japan
109 R5 Ager ↝ N Austria
Agere Hiywet see Hāgere Hiywet
108 G8 Ägerisee ◎ W Switzerland
142 M10 Āghā Jārī Khūzestān, SW Iran
39 P15 Aghiyuk Island island Alaska, USA
74 B12 Aghouinit SE Western Sahara
Aghri Dagh see Büyükağrı Dağı
74 B10 Aghzoumal, Sebkhet var. Sebjet Agsumal. salt lake E Western Sahara
115 F15 Agiá var. Ayiá. Thessalía, C Greece
40 G7 Agiabampo, Estero de estuary NW Mexico
121 P3 Agía Fýlaxis var. Ayia Phyla. S Cyprus
Agialoúsa see Yenierenköy
115 M21 Agía Marína Léros, Dodekánisos, Greece, Aegean Sea
121 Q2 Agía Nápa var. Ayia Napa. E Cyprus
115 L16 Agía Paraskeví Lésvos, E Greece
115 J15 Agías Eirínis, Akrotírio headland Límnos, E Greece
115 L17 Agiasós var. Ayiásos, Ayiássos. Lésvos, E Greece
Aginnum see Agen
123 O14 Aginskiy Buryatskiy Avtonomnyy Okrug ◈ autonomous district S Russian Federation
123 O14 Aginskoye Aginskiy Buryatskiy Avtonomnyy Okrug, S Russian Federation
115 I14 Ágion Óros Eng. Mount Athos. ◈ monastic republic NE Greece
115 H14 Ágion Óros var. Akte, Aktí; anc. Acte. peninsula NE Greece
114 D13 Ágios Achílleios religious building Dytikí Makedonía, N Greece
115 J16 Ágios Efstrátios var. Áyios Evstrátios, Hagios Evstrátios. island E Greece
115 H20 Ágios Geórgios island Kykládes, Greece, Aegean Sea
115 Q23 Ágios Geórgios island SE Greece
115 E21 Ágios Ilías ▲ S Greece
115 K25 Ágios Ioánnis, Akrotírio headland Kríti, Greece, E Mediterranean Sea
115 L20 Ágios Kírykos var. Áyios Kírikos. Ikaría, Dodekánisos, Greece, Aegean Sea
115 D16 Ágios Nikólaos Thessalía, C Greece
115 K25 Ágios Nikólaos var. Áyios Nikólaos. Kríti, Greece, E Mediterranean Sea
115 H14 Agíou Órous, Kólpos gulf N Greece
107 K24 Agira anc. Agyrium. Sicilia, Italy, C Mediterranean Sea
115 G20 Agkístri island S Greece
114 G12 Ágkistro var. Angistro. ▲ NE Greece
103 O17 Agly ↝ S France
Agnetheln see Agnita
14 E10 Agnew Lake ◎ Ontario, S Canada
77 O16 Agnibilékrou E Ivory Coast
116 I11 Agnita Ger. Agnetheln, Hung. Szentágota. Sibiu, SW Romania
107 K15 Agnone Molise, C Italy
164 K14 Ago Mie, Honshū, SW Japan
106 C8 Agogna ↝ N Italy
Agoitz see Agoiz
105 R3 Agoiz var. Agoitz, Aoiz. Navarra, N Spain
77 P17 Agona Swedru var. Swedru. SE Ghana
Agordat see Akurdet
Agosta see Augusta
103 N15 Agout ↝ S France
152 J12 Agra Uttar Pradesh, N India
Agra and Oudh, United Provinces of see Uttar Pradesh
Agram see Zagreb
105 U5 Agramunt Cataluña, NE Spain
105 Q5 Agreda Castilla-León, N Spain
137 S13 Ağrı var. Karaköse; prev. Karakılısse. Ağrı, NE Turkey
137 S13 Ağrı ◈ province NE Turkey
107 N19 Agri anc. Aciris. ↝ S Italy
Agri Dagi see Büyükağrı Dağı
107 J24 Agrigento Gk. Akragas; prev. Girgenti. Sicilia, Italy, C Mediterranean Sea
188 K4 Agrihan island N Northern Mariana Islands
115 D18 Agrínio prev. Agrinion. Dytikí Ellás, W Greece
Agrinion see Agrínio
115 G17 Agriovótano Évvoia, C Greece
107 L18 Agropoli Campania, S Italy
127 T3 Agryz Udmurtskaya Respublika, NW Russian Federation
137 U11 Ağstafa Rus. Akstafa. NW Azerbaijan
137 X11 Ağsu Rus. Akhsu. C Azerbaijan
Agsumal, Sebjet see Aghzoumal, Sebkhet
40 J11 Agua Brava, Laguna lagoon W Mexico
54 F7 Aguachica Cesar, N Colombia
59 J20 Água Clara Mato Grosso do Sul, SW Brazil
44 D5 Aguada de Pasajeros Cienfuegos, C Cuba
54 J5 Aguada Grande Lara, N Venezuela
45 S5 Aguadilla W Puerto Rico
43 S16 Aguadulce Coclé, S Panama
104 L14 Aguadulce Andalucía, S Spain
41 O8 Agualeguas Nuevo León, NE Mexico
40 L9 Aguanaval, Río ↝ C Mexico
42 J5 Aguán, Río ↝ N Honduras
25 R16 Agua Nueva Texas, SW USA
60 J8 Aguapeí, Rio ↝ S Brazil
61 E14 Aguapey, Río ↝ NE Argentina
40 G3 Agua Prieta Sonora, NW Mexico
104 G5 A Guarda var. A Guardia, Laguardia, La Guardia. Galicia, NW Spain
A Guardia see A Guarda
56 E6 Aguarico, Río ↝ Ecuador/Peru
55 O6 Aguasay Monagas, NE Venezuela
40 M12 Aguascalientes Aguascalientes, C Mexico
40 L12 Aguascalientes ◈ state C Mexico
57 I18 Aguas Calientes, Río ↝ S Peru
105 R7 Aguasvivas ↝ NE Spain
60 J7 Água Vermelha, Represa de ▣ S Brazil
56 E12 Aguaytía Ucayali, C Peru
104 I5 A Gudiña var. La Gudiña. Galicia, NW Spain
104 G7 Águeda Aveiro, N Portugal
104 J8 Águeda ↝ Portugal/Spain
77 Q8 Aguelhok Kidal, NE Mali
77 V12 Aguié Maradi, S Niger
188 K8 Aguijan island S Northern Mariana Islands
104 M14 Aguilar var. Aguilar de la Frontera. Andalucía, S Spain
104 M3 Aguilar de Campóo Castilla-León, N Spain
Aguilar de la Frontera see Aguilar
42 F7 Aguilares San Salvador, C El Salvador
105 Q14 Aguilas Murcia, SE Spain
40 L15 Aguililla Michoacán de Ocampo, SW Mexico
Agulhas see L'Agulhas
172 J11 Agulhas Bank undersea feature SW Indian Ocean
172 K11 Agulhas Basin undersea feature SW Indian Ocean
83 F26 Agulhas, Cape Afr. Kaap Agulhas. headland SW South Africa
Agulhas, Kaap see Agulhas, Cape
60 O9 Agulhas Negras, Pico das ▲ SE Brazil
172 K11 Agulhas Plateau undersea feature SW Indian Ocean
165 S16 Aguni-jima island Nansei-shotō, SW Japan
Agurain see Salvatierra
54 G5 Agustín Codazzi var. Codazzi. Cesar, N Colombia
Agyrium see Agira
74 L12 Ahaggar high plateau region SE Algeria
146 E12 Ahal Welaýaty Rus. Akhalskiy Velayat. ◈ province C Turkmenistan
142 K2 Ahar Āzarbāyjān-e Khāvarī, NW Iran
Aharnes see Acharnés
138 J3 Aḩaş, Jabal ▲ NW Syria
138 J3 Aḩaş, Jebal ▲ W Syria
185 G16 Ahaura ↝ South Island, NZ
100 E13 Ahaus Nordrhein-Westfalen, NW Germany
191 U9 Ahe atoll Îles Tuamotu, C French Polynesia
184 N10 Ahimanawa Range ⛰ North Island, NZ
119 I19 Ahinski Kanal Rus. Oginskiy Kanal. canal SW Belarus
186 G10 Ahioma SE PNG
184 I2 Ahipara Northland, North Island, NZ
184 I2 Ahipara Bay bay SE Tasman Sea
Áhkká see Akka
39 N13 Ahklun Mountains ⛰ Alaska, USA
137 R14 Ahlat Bitlis, E Turkey
101 F14 Ahlen Nordrhein-Westfalen, W Germany
154 D10 Ahmadābād var. Ahmedabad. Gujarāt, W India
143 R10 Ahmadābād Kermān, C Iran
Ahmadi see Al Aḩmadī
Ahmad Khel see Ḩasan Khēl
155 F14 Ahmadnagar var. Ahmednagar. Mahārāshtra, W India
149 T9 Ahmadpur Siāl Punjab, E Pakistan
77 N5 Aḩmar, 'Erg el desert N Mali
80 K13 Ahmar Mountains ⛰ C Ethiopia
Ahmedabad see Ahmadābād
Ahmednagar see Ahmadnagar
114 N12 Ahmetbey Kırklareli, NW Turkey
14 H12 Ahmic Lake ◎ Ontario, S Canada
190 G12 Ahoa Île Uvea, E Wallis and Futuna
40 G8 Ahomé Sinaloa, C Mexico
21 X8 Ahoskie North Carolina, SE USA
101 D17 Ahr ↝ W Germany
143 N12 Ahram var. Ahrom. Būshehr, S Iran
100 J9 Ahrensburg Schleswig-Holstein, N Germany
Ahrom see Ahram
93 L17 Ähtäri Länsi-Suomi, W Finland
40 K12 Ahuacatlán Nayarit, C Mexico
42 E7 Ahuachapán Ahuachapán, W El Salvador
42 A9 Ahuachapán ◈ department W El Salvador

◆ Country ● Country Capital ◇ Dependent Territory ○ Dependent Territory Capital ◈ Administrative Region × International Airport ▲ Mountain ⛰ Mountain Range ✱ Volcano ↝ River ◎ Lake ▣ Reservoir

191 V16 **Ahu Akivi** *var.* Siete Moai. *ancient monument* Easter Island, Chile, E Pacific Ocean
191 W11 **Ahunui** *atoll* Îles Tuamotu, C French Polynesia
185 E20 **Ahuriri** South Island, NZ
95 L22 **Åhus** Skåne, S Sweden
Ahu Tahira *see* Ahu Vinapu
191 V16 **Ahu Tepeu** *ancient monument* Easter Island, Chile, E Pacific Ocean
191 V17 **Ahu Vinapu** *var.* Ahu Tahira. *ancient monument* Easter Island, Chile, E Pacific Ocean
142 L9 **Ahvāz** *var.* Ahwāz; *prev.* Nāsiri. Khūzestān, SW Iran
Ahvenanmaa *see* Åland
141 Q16 **Aḥwar** SW Yemen
Ahwāz *see* Ahvāz
94 H7 **Åi Åfjord** *var.* Åfjord, Årnes. Sør-Trondelag, C Norway
Aibak *see* Āybak
101 K22 **Aichach** Bayern, SE Germany
164 L14 **Aichi** *off.* Aichi-ken, *var.* Aiti. ◆ *prefecture* Honshū, SW Japan
Aïdin *see* Aydın
Aidussina *see* Ajdovščina
Aifir, Clochán an *see* Giant's Causeway
Aigaíon Pélagos/Aigaío Pélagos *see* Aegean Sea
109 S3 **Aigen im Mülkreis** Oberösterreich, N Austria
115 G20 **Aígina** *var.* Aíyina, Egina. Aígina, C Greece
115 G20 **Aígina** *island* S Greece
115 E18 **Aígio** *var.* Egio; *prev.* Aíyion. Dytikí Ellás, S Greece
108 C10 **Aigle** Vaud, SW Switzerland
103 P14 **Aigoual, Mont** ▲ S France
173 O16 **Aigrettes, Pointe des** *headland* W Réunion
61 G19 **Aiguá** *var.* Aigua. Maldonado, S Uruguay
103 S13 **Aigues** SE France
103 N10 **Aigurande** Indre, C France
Ai-hun *see* Heihe
165 N10 **Aikawa** Niigata, Sado, C Japan
21 Q13 **Aiken** South Carolina, SE USA
25 N4 **Aiken** Texas, SW USA
160 F13 **Ailao Shan** ▲ SW China
43 W14 **Ailigandí** San Blas, NE Panama
189 R4 **Ailinginae Atoll** *var.* Aelōninae. *atoll* Ralik Chain, SW Marshall Islands
189 T7 **Ailinglaplap Atoll** *var.* Aelōnlaplap. *atoll* Ralik Chain, S Marshall Islands
Aillionn, Loch *see* Allen, Lough
96 H13 **Ailsa Craig** *island* SW Scotland, UK
189 V5 **Ailuk Atoll** *var.* Aelok. *atoll* Ratak Chain, NE Marshall Islands
123 R11 **Aim** Khabarovskiy Kray, E Russian Federation
103 R11 **Ain** ◆ *department* E France
103 S10 **Ain** E France
118 G7 **Ainaži** *Est.* Heinaste, *Ger.* Hainasch. Limbaži, N Latvia
74 L6 **Aïn Beïda** NE Algeria
76 K4 **'Aïn Ben Tili** Tiris Zemmour, N Mauritania
74 J5 **Aïn Defla** *var.* Aïn Eddefla. N Algeria
Aïn Eddefla *see* Aïn Defla
74 L5 **Aïn El Bey** × (Constantine) NE Algeria
115 C19 **Aínos** ▲ Kefallinía, Iónioi Nísoi, Greece, C Mediterranean Sea
105 T4 **Ainsa** Aragón, NE Spain
74 I7 **Aïn Sefra** NW Algeria
29 N13 **Ainsworth** Nebraska, C USA
Aintab *see* Gaziantep
74 H5 **Aïn Témouchent** N Algeria
186 C6 **Aiome** Madang, N PNG
Aïoun el Atrous/Aïoun el Atroûss *see* 'Ayoûn el 'Atroûs
54 E11 **Aipe** Huila, C Colombia
56 D9 **Aipena, Río** N Peru
57 L19 **Aiquile** Cochabamba, C Bolivia
Aïr *see* Aïr, Massif de l'
188 E10 **Airai** Babeldaob, C Palau
188 E10 **Airai** × (Oreor) Babeldaob, N Palau
168 I11 **Airbangis** Sumatera, NW Indonesia
11 Q16 **Airdrie** Alberta, SW Canada
96 I12 **Airdrie** S Scotland, UK
Air du Azbine *see* Aïr, Massif de l'
97 M17 **Aire** N England, UK
102 K15 **Aire-sur-l'Adour** Landes, SW France
103 O1 **Aire-sur-la-Lys** Pas-de-Calais, N France
9 Q6 **Air Force Island** *island* Baffin Island, Nunavut, NE Canada
169 Q13 **Airhitam, Teluk** *bay* Borneo, C Indonesia
171 Q11 **Airmadidi** Sulawesi, N Indonesia
77 V8 **Aïr, Massif de l'** *var.* Aïr, Air du Azbine, Asben. ▲ N Niger
108 G10 **Airolo** Ticino, S Switzerland
102 K9 **Airvault** Deux-Sèvres, W France
101 K19 **Aisch** S Germany
63 G20 **Aisén** *off.* Región Aisén del General Carlos Ibañez del Campo, *var.* Aysen. ◆ *region* S Chile
10 H7 **Aishihik Lake** ◎ Yukon Territory, W Canada
103 P3 **Aisne** ◆ *department* N France
103 R4 **Aisne** NE France
109 T4 **Aist** N Austria
114 K13 **Aisými** Anatolikí Makedonía kai Thráki, NE Greece
105 S11 **Aitana** ▲ E Spain
186 B5 **Aitape** *var.* Eitape. Sandaun, NW PNG
Aiti *see* Aichi
29 V6 **Aitkin** Minnesota, N USA
115 D18 **Aitolikó** *var.* Etoliko; *prev.* Aitolikón. Dytikí Ellás, C Greece
Aitolikón *see* Aitolikó
190 L15 **Aitutaki** *island* S Cook Islands
116 H11 **Aiud** *Ger.* Strassburg, *Hung.* Nagyenyed; *prev.* Engeten. Alba, SW Romania
118 I9 **Aiviekste** C Latvia
189 Q8 **Aiwo** SW Nauru
188 E8 **Aiwokako Passage** *passage* Babeldaob, N Palau
Aix *see* Aix-en-Provence
103 S15 **Aix-en-Provence** *var.* Aix; *anc.* Aquae Sextiae. Bouches-du-Rhône, SE France
Aix-la-Chapelle *see* Aachen
103 T11 **Aix-les-Bains** Savoie, E France
186 A6 **Aiyang, Mount** ▲ NW PNG
Aíyina *see* Aígina
Aíyion *see* Aígio
153 W15 **Āīzawl** Mizoram, NE India
118 H9 **Aizkraukle** Aizkraukle, S Latvia
118 C9 **Aizpute** Liepāja, W Latvia
165 O11 **Aizu-Wakamatsu** *var.* Aizuwakamatu. Fukushima, Honshū, C Japan
Aizuwakamatu *see* Aizu-Wakamatsu
103 X15 **Ajaccio** Corse, France, C Mediterranean Sea
103 X15 **Ajaccio, Golfe d'** *gulf* Corse, France, C Mediterranean Sea
41 Q15 **Ajalpán** Puebla, S Mexico
154 F13 **Ajanta Range** ▲ C India
137 R10 **Ajaria** ◆ *autonomous republic* SW Georgia
Ajastan *see* Armenia
93 G14 **Ajaureforsen** Västerbotten, N Sweden
185 H17 **Ajax, Mount** ▲ South Island, NZ
162 F9 **Aj Bogd Uul** ▲ SW Mongolia
75 R8 **Ajdābiyā** *var.* Agedabia, Ajdābiyah. NE Libya
Ajdābiyah *see* Ajdābiyā
109 S12 **Ajdovščina** *Ger.* Haidenschaft, *It.* Aidussina. W Slovenia
165 Q7 **Ajigasawa** Aomori, Honshū, C Japan
Ajjinena *see* El Geneina
111 H23 **Ajka** Veszprém, W Hungary
138 G9 **'Ajlūn** Irbid, N Jordan
138 H9 **'Ajlūn, Jabal** ▲ W Jordan
Ajluokta *see* Drag
143 R15 **'Ajmān** *var.* Ajman, 'Ujmān. 'Ajmān, NE UAE
152 G12 **Ajmer** *var.* Ajmere. Rājasthān, N India
36 J15 **Ajo** Arizona, SW USA
105 N2 **Ajo, Cabo de** *headland* N Spain
36 J16 **Ajo Range** ▲ Arizona, SW USA
146 C14 **Ajyguyy** *Rus.* Adzhikui. Balkan Welaýaty, W Turkmenistan
Akaba *see* Al 'Aqabah
165 T3 **Akabira** Hokkaidō, NE Japan
165 N10 **Akadomari** Niigata, Sado, C Japan
81 E20 **Akagera** *var.* Kagera. Rwanda/Tanzania **see also** Kagera
191 W16 **Akahanga, Punta** *headland* Easter Island, Chile, E Pacific Ocean
80 J13 **Āk'ak'i** Oromo, C Ethiopia
155 G15 **Akalkot** Mahārāshtra, W India
Akamagaseki *see* Shimonoseki
165 U4 **Akan** Hokkaidō, NE Japan
165 U4 **Akan-ko** ◎ Hokkaidō, NE Japan
Akanthoú *see* Tatlısu
185 I19 **Akaroa** Canterbury, South Island, NZ
80 E6 **Akasha** Northern, N Sudan
164 I13 **Akashi** *var.* Akasi. Hyōgo, Honshū, SW Japan
139 N7 **'Akāsh, Wādī** *var.* Wādī 'Ukash. *dry watercourse* W Iraq
Akasi *see* Akashi
92 K11 **Äkäsjokisuu** Lappi, N Finland
137 S11 **Akbaba Dağı** ▲ Armenia/Turkey
Akbük Limanı *see* Güllük Körfezi
127 V8 **Akbulak** Orenburgskaya Oblast', W Russian Federation
137 O11 **Akçaabat** Trabzon, NE Turkey
137 N15 **Akçadağ** Malatya, C Turkey
136 G11 **Akçakoca** Bolu, NW Turkey
Akchakaya, Vpadina *see* Akdzhakaya, Vpadina
76 H7 **Akchâr** *desert* W Mauritania
145 S12 **Akchatau** *Kaz.* Aqshataū. Karaganda, C Kazakhstan
136 L13 **Akdağlar** ▲ C Turkey
136 E17 **Ak Dağları** ▲ SW Turkey
136 K13 **Akdağmadeni** Yozgat, C Turkey
146 G8 **Akdepe** *prev.* Ak-Tepe, Leninsk, *Turkm.* Lenin. Daşoguz Welaýaty, N Turkmenistan
Ak-Dere *see* Byala
121 P2 **Akdoğan** *Gk.* Lýsi. C Cyprus
122 J14 **Ak-Dovurak** Respublika Tyva, S Russian Federation
146 F9 **Akdzhakaya, Vpadina** *var.* Vpadina Akchakaya. *depression* N Turkmenistan
171 S11 **Akelamo** Pulau Halmahera, E Indonesia
Aken *see* Aachen
Akermanceaster *see* Bath
95 P15 **Åkersberga** Stockholm, C Sweden
95 H15 **Akershus** ◆ *county* S Norway
79 L16 **Aketi** Orientale, N Dem. Rep. Congo
146 C10 **Akgyr Erezi** *Rus.* Gryada Akkyr. *hill range* NW Turkmenistan
Akhalskiy Velayat *see* Ahal Welaýaty
137 S10 **Akhalts'ikhe** SW Georgia
Akhangaran *see* Ohangaron
Akharnaí *see* Acharnés
75 R7 **Akhḍar, Al Jabal al** *hill range* NE Libya
Akhelóös *see* Achelóos
39 Q15 **Akhiok** Kodiak Island, Alaska, USA
136 C13 **Akhisar** Manisa, W Turkey
75 X10 **Akhmîm** *anc.* Panopolis. C Egypt
152 H6 **Akhnūr** Jammu and Kashmir, NW India
Akhsu *see* Ağsu
127 P11 **Akhtuba** SW Russian Federation
127 P11 **Akhtubinsk** Astrakhanskaya Oblast', SW Russian Federation
Akhtyrka *see* Okhtyrka
164 H14 **Aki** Kōchi, Shikoku, SW Japan
39 N12 **Akiachak** Alaska, USA
39 N12 **Akiak** Alaska, USA
191 X11 **Akiaki** *atoll* Îles Tuamotu, E French Polynesia
12 H9 **Akimiski Island** *island* Nunavut, C Canada
136 K17 **Akıncı Burnu** *headland* S Turkey
Akıncılar *see* Selçuk
117 U10 **Akinovka** Zaporiz'ka Oblast', S Ukraine
Åkirkeby *see* Aakirkeby
165 P8 **Akita** Akita, Honshū, C Japan
165 Q8 **Akita** *off.* Akita-ken. ◆ *prefecture* Honshū, C Japan
76 H8 **Akjoujt** *prev.* Fort-Repoux. Inchiri, W Mauritania
92 H11 **Akka** ▲ *Lapp.* Áhkká. N Sweden
92 H11 **Akkajaure** ◎ N Sweden
Akkala *see* Oqqal'a
155 L25 **Akkaraipattu** Eastern Province, E Sri Lanka
145 P13 **Akkense** Karaganda, C Kazakhstan
Akkerman *see* Bilhorod-Dnistrovs'kyy
127 W8 **Akkermanovka** Orenburgskaya Oblast', W Russian Federation
165 V4 **Akkeshi** Hokkaidō, NE Japan
165 V4 **Akkeshi-ko** ◎ Hokkaidō, NE Japan
165 V5 **Akkeshi-wan** *bay* NW Pacific Ocean
138 F8 **'Akko** *Eng.* Acre, *Fr.* Saint-Jean-d'Acre; *Bibl.* Accho, Ptolemaïs. Northern, N Israel
145 Q8 **Akkol'** *Kaz.* Aqköl; *prev.* Alekseyevka, *Kaz.* Alekseevka. Akmola, C Kazakhstan
145 T14 **Akkol'** *Kaz.* Aqköl. Almaty, SE Kazakhstan
145 Q16 **Akkol'** *Kaz.* Aqköl. Zhambyl, S Kazakhstan
144 M11 **Akkol', Ozero** *prev.* Ozero Zhaman-Akkol'. ◎ C Kazakhstan
98 L6 **Akkrum** Friesland, N Netherlands
145 U8 **Akku** *prev.* Lebyazh'ye. Pavlodar, NE Kazakhstan
144 F12 **Akkystau** *Kaz.* Aqqystaū. Atyrau, SW Kazakhstan
8 G6 **Aklavik** Northwest Territories, NW Canada
Akmenrags *see* Akmensrags
118 B9 **Akmensrags** *prev.* Akmenrags. *headland* W Latvia
158 E9 **Akmeqit** Xinjiang Uygur Zizhiqu, NW China
146 J14 **Akmeydan** Mary Welaýaty, C Turkmenistan
Akmola *see* Astana
145 P9 **Akmola** *off.* Akmolinskaya Oblast', *Kaz.* Aqmola Oblysy; *prev.* Tselinogradskaya Oblast. ◆ *province* C Kazakhstan
Akmolinsk *see* Astana
Akmolinskaya Oblast' *see* Akmola
Aknavásár *see* Târgu Ocna
118 I11 **Aknīste** Jēkabpils, S Latvia
81 G14 **Akobo** Jonglei, SE Sudan
81 G14 **Akobo** *var.* Akobowenz. Ethiopia/Sudan
Akobowenz *see* Akobo
154 H12 **Akola** Mahārāshtra, C India
Akordat *see* Akurdet
77 Q16 **Akosombo Dam** *dam* SE Ghana
154 H12 **Akot** Mahārāshtra, C India
77 N16 **Akoupé** SE Ivory Coast
12 M3 **Akpatok Island** *island* Nunavut, E Canada
158 G7 **Akqi** Xinjiang Uygur Zizhiqu, NW China
138 I2 **Akrād, Jabal al** ▲ N Syria
Akragas *see* Agrigento
92 H3 **Akranes** Vesturland, W Iceland
139 S2 **Ākrē** *Ar.* 'Aqrah. N Iraq
95 C16 **Åkrehamn** Rogaland, S Norway
77 V9 **Akréréb** Agadez, C Niger
115 D22 **Akrítas, Akrotírio** *headland* S Greece
37 V3 **Akron** Colorado, C USA
29 R12 **Akron** Iowa, C USA
31 U12 **Akron** Ohio, N USA
Akrotiri *see* Akrotírion
Akrotiri Bay *see* Akrotírion, Kólpos
121 P3 **Akrotírion** *var.* Akrotiri. *UK air base* S Cyprus
121 P3 **Akrotírion, Kólpos** *var.* Akrotiri Bay. *bay* S Cyprus
121 O3 **Akrotiri Sovereign Base Area** *UK military installation* S Cyprus
158 F11 **Aksai Chin** *Chin.* Aksayqin. *disputed region* China/India
Aksaj *see* Aksay
136 I15 **Aksaray** Aksaray, C Turkey
136 I15 **Aksaray** ◆ *province* C Turkey
144 G8 **Aksay** *var.* Aksaj, *Kaz.* Aqsay. Zapadnyy Kazakhstan, NW Kazakhstan
127 O11 **Aksay** Volgogradskaya Oblast', SW Russian Federation
147 W10 **Aksay** *var.* Toxkan He. China/Kyrgyzstan
Aksay/Aksay Kazakzu Zizhixian *see* Boluozhuanjing/Hongliuwan
Aksayqin *see* Aksai Chin
158 G11 **Aksayqin Hu** ◎ NW China
136 G14 **Akşehir** Konya, W Turkey
136 G14 **Akşehir Gölü** ◎ C Turkey
136 G16 **Akseki** Antalya, SW Turkey
123 P13 **Aksenovo-Zilovskoye** Chitinskaya Oblast', S Russian Federation
145 V11 **Akshatau, Khrebet** ▲ E Kazakhstan
147 Y8 **Ak-Shyyrak** Issyk-Kul'skaya Oblast', E Kyrgyzstan
Akstafa *see* Ağstafa
158 H7 **Aksu** Xinjiang Uygur Zizhiqu, NW China
145 R8 **Aksu** *Kaz.* Aqsū. Akmola, N Kazakhstan
145 T8 **Aksu** *var.* Jermak, *Kaz.* Ermak; *prev.* Yermak. Pavlodar, NE Kazakhstan
145 W13 **Aksu** *Kaz.* Aqsū. Almaty, SE Kazakhstan
145 V13 **Aksu** *Kaz.* Aqsū. SE Kazakhstan
145 X11 **Aksuat** *Kaz.* Aqsūat. Vostochnyy Kazakhstan, E Kazakhstan
145 Y11 **Aksuat** *Kaz.* Aqsūat. Vostochnyy Kazakhstan, SE Kazakhstan
127 S4 **Aksubayevo** Respublika Tatarstan, W Russian Federation
158 H7 **Aksu He** *Rus.* Sary-Dzhaz. China/Kyrgyzstan **see also** Sary-Dzhaz
80 J10 **Āksum** Tigray, N Ethiopia
145 O12 **Aktas** *Kaz.* Aqtas. Karaganda, C Kazakhstan
Aktash *see* Oqtosh
147 V9 **Ak-Tash, Gora** ▲ C Kyrgyzstan
145 R10 **Aktau** *Kaz.* Aqtaū. Karaganda, C Kazakhstan
144 E11 **Aktau** *Kaz.* Aqtaū; *prev.* Shevchenko. Mangistau, W Kazakhstan
Aktau, Khrebet *see* Oqtogh, SW Tajikistan
Aktau, Khrebet *see* Oqtow Tizmasi, C Uzbekistan
Akte *see* Ágion Óros
Ak-Tepe *see* Akdepe
147 X7 **Ak-Terek** Issyk-Kul'skaya Oblast', E Kyrgyzstan
Aktí *see* Ágion Óros
158 E8 **Akto** Xinjiang Uygur Zizhiqu, NW China
144 I10 **Aktobe** *Kaz.* Aqtöbe. *prev.* Aktyubinsk. Aktyubinsk, NW Kazakhstan
145 V12 **Aktogay** *Kaz.* Aqtoghay. Vostochnyy Kazakhstan, E Kazakhstan
119 M18 **Aktsyabrski** *Rus.* Oktyabr'skiy; *prev.* Karpilovka. Homyel'skaya Voblasts', SE Belarus
Aktyubinsk *see* Aktobe
144 H11 **Aktyubinsk** *off.* Aktyubinskaya Oblast', *Kaz.* Aqtöbe Oblysy. ◆ *province* W Kazakhstan
Aktyubinsk *see* Aktobe
147 W7 **Ak-Tyuz** *var.* Aktyuz. Chuyskaya Oblast', N Kyrgyzstan
79 J17 **Akula** Equateur, NW Dem. Rep. Congo
164 C15 **Akune** Kagoshima, Kyūshū, SW Japan
38 L16 **Akun Island** *island* Aleutian Islands, Alaska, USA
80 J9 **Akurdet** *var.* Agordat, Akordat. C Eritrea
77 T16 **Akure** Ondo, SW Nigeria
92 J2 **Akureyri** Nordhurland Eystra, N Iceland
38 L17 **Akutan** Akutan Island, Alaska, USA
38 K17 **Akutan Island** *island* Aleutian Islands, Alaska, USA
77 V17 **Akwa Ibom** ◆ *state* SE Nigeria
Akyab *see* Sittwe
127 W7 **Ak"yar** Respublika Bashkortostan, W Russian Federation
144 J10 **Akzhar** *prev.* Novorossiyskiy, Novorossiyskoye. Aktyubinsk, NW Kazakhstan
145 Y11 **Akzhar** *Kaz.* Aqzhar. Vostochnyy Kazakhstan, E Kazakhstan
94 F13 **Ål** Buskerud, S Norway
119 N18 **Ala** *Rus.* Ola. SE Belarus
20 H11 **Alabama** *off.* State of Alabama; also known as Camellia State, Heart of Dixie, The Cotton State, Yellowhammer State. ◆ *state* S USA
23 P6 **Alabama River** Alabama, S USA
23 P4 **Alabaster** Alabama, S USA
139 U10 **Al 'Abd Allāh** *var.* Al Abdullah. S Iraq
Al Abdullah *see* Al 'Abd Allāh
139 W14 **Al Abṭīyah** *well* S Iraq
147 S9 **Ala-Buka** Dzhalal-Abadskaya Oblast', W Kyrgyzstan
136 J12 **Alaca** Çorum, N Turkey
136 K10 **Alaçam** Samsun, N Turkey
Alacant *see* Alicante
23 V9 **Alachua** Florida, SE USA
137 S13 **Aladağlar** ▲ W Turkey
136 K15 **Ala Dağları** ▲ C Turkey
127 O16 **Alagir** Respublika Severnaya Osetiya, SW Russian Federation
106 B6 **Alagna Valsesia** Valle d'Aosta, NW Italy
103 P12 **Alagnon** C France
59 P16 **Alagoas** *off.* Estado de Alagoas. ◆ *state* E Brazil
59 P17 **Alagoinhas** Bahia, E Brazil
105 R5 **Alagón** Aragón, NE Spain
104 J9 **Alagón** W Spain
93 K16 **Alahärmä** Länsi-Suomi, W Finland
al Ahdar *see* Al Akhḍar
Álaheaieatnu *see* Altaelva
142 K12 **Al Aḥmadī** *var.* Ahmadi. E Kuwait
Al Ain *see* Al 'Ayn
105 Z8 **Alaior** *prev.* Alayor. Menorca, Spain, W Mediterranean Sea
147 T11 **Alai Range** *Rus.* Alayskiy Khrebet. ▲ Kyrgyzstan/Tajikistan
Alais *see* Alès
141 X11 **Al 'Ajā'iz** E Oman
141 X11 **Al 'Ajā'iz** *oasis* SE Oman
93 L16 **Alajärvi** Länsi-Suomi, W Finland
118 K4 **Alajõe** Ida-Virumaa, NE Estonia
42 M13 **Alajuela** Alajuela, C Costa Rica
42 L12 **Alajuela** *off.* Provincia de Alajuela. ◆ *province* N Costa Rica
43 T14 **Alajuela, Lago** ◎ C Panama
38 M11 **Alakanuk** Alaska, USA
140 K5 **Al Akhḍar** *var.* al Ahdar. Tabūk, NW Saudi Arabia
Alaköl *see* Alakol', Ozero
145 X13 **Alakol', Ozero** *Kaz.* Alaköl. ◎ SE Kazakhstan
124 I5 **Alakurtti** Murmanskaya Oblast', NW Russian Federation
38 F10 **'Alalākeiki Channel** *var.* Alalakeiki Channel. *channel* Hawai'i, USA, C Pacific Ocean
Al 'Alamayn *see* El 'Alamein
139 R1 **Al 'Amādīyah** N Iraq
188 K5 **Alamagan** *island* C Northern Mariana Islands
139 X10 **Al 'Amārah** *var.* Amara. E Iraq
80 J11 **Ālamat'ā** Tigray, N Ethiopia
37 R11 **Alameda** New Mexico, SW USA
121 T13 **'Alam el Rûm, Râs** *headland* N Egypt
Alamícamba *see* Alamikamba
42 M8 **Alamikamba** *var.* Alamícamba. Región Autónoma Atlántico Norte, NE Nicaragua
24 K11 **Alamito Creek** Texas, SW USA
40 M8 **Alamitos, Sierra de los** ▲ NE Mexico
35 X9 **Alamo** Nevada, W USA
20 F9 **Alamo** Tennessee, S USA
41 Q12 **Álamo** Veracruz-Llave, C Mexico
37 S14 **Alamogordo** New Mexico, SW USA
36 J12 **Alamo Lake** ⊠ Arizona, SW USA
40 H7 **Alamos** Sonora, NW Mexico
37 S7 **Alamosa** Colorado, C USA
93 J20 **Åland** *var.* Aland Islands, *Fin.* Ahvenanmaa. ◆ *province* SW Finland
93 J19 **Åland** *Fin.* Ahvenanmaa. *island* SW Finland
93 J20 **Åland** *var.* Aland Islands, *Fin.* Ahvenanmaa. *island group* SW Finland
Aland Islands *see* Åland
Aland Sea *see* Ålands Hav
95 Q14 **Ålands Hav** *var.* Aland Sea. *strait* Baltic Sea/Gulf of Bothnia
43 P16 **Alanje** Chiriquí, SW Panama
25 O2 **Alanreed** Texas, SW USA
136 G17 **Alanya** Antalya, S Turkey
23 U7 **Alapaha River** Florida/Georgia, SE USA
122 G10 **Alapayevsk** Sverdlovskaya Oblast', C Russian Federation
Alappuzha *see* Alleppey
138 F14 **Al 'Aqabah** *var.* Akaba, Aqaba, 'Aqaba; *anc.* Aelana, Elath. Ma'ān, SW Jordan
Al 'Arabīyah as Su'ūdīyah *see* Saudi Arabia
al Araïch *see* Larache
105 Q10 **Alarcón** Castilla-La Mancha, C Spain
105 Q9 **Alarcón, Embalse de** ⊠ C Spain
138 J2 **Al 'Arīmah** *Fr.* Arime. Ḥalab, N Syria
Al 'Arīsh *see* El 'Arîsh
141 P6 **Al Arṭāwīyah** Ar Riyāḍ, N Saudi Arabia
Alasca, Golfo de *see* Alaska, Gulf of
136 D14 **Alaşehir** Manisa, W Turkey
139 N5 **Al 'Asharah** *var.* Ashara. Dayr az Zawr, E Syria
138 H10 **'Al 'Āṣimah** *off.* Muḥāfaẓat 'Al Āṣhimah. *prev.* 'Ammān ◆ *governorate* NW Jordan
Al Ashkhara *see* Al Ashkharah
141 Z9 **Al Ashkharah** *var.* Al Ashkhara. NE Oman
39 P8 **Alaska** *off.* State of Alaska; also known as Land of the Midnight Sun, The Last Frontier, Seward's Folly; *prev.* Russian America. ◆ *state* NW USA
39 T13 **Alaska, Gulf of** *var.* Golfo de Alasca. *gulf* Canada/USA
39 O15 **Alaska Peninsula** *peninsula* Alaska, USA
39 Q11 **Alaska Range** ▲ Alaska, USA
Al-Asnam *see* Chlef
106 B10 **Alassio** Liguria, NW Italy
Alat *see* Olot
137 Y12 **Älät** *Rus.* Alyat; *prev.* Alyaty-Pristan'. SE Azerbaijan
139 S13 **Al 'Athāmīn** S Iraq
39 P7 **Alatna River** Alaska, USA
107 J15 **Alatri** Lazio, C Italy
Alattio *see* Alta
127 P5 **Alatyr'** Chuvashskaya Respublika, W Russian Federation
56 C7 **Alausí** Chimborazo, C Ecuador
105 O3 **Álava** *Basq.* Araba. ◆ *province* País Vasco, N Spain
137 T11 **Alaverdi** N Armenia
Alavo *see* Alavus
93 N14 **Ala-Vuokki** Oulu, E Finland
93 K17 **Alavus** *Swe.* Alavo. Länsi-Suomi, W Finland
Al 'Awābī *see* Awābī
139 P6 **Al 'Awānī** W Iraq
Al Awaynāt *see* Al 'Uwaynāt
182 K9 **Alawoona** South Australia
Alaykel'/Alay-Kuu *see* Këk-Art
143 R17 **Al 'Ayn** *var.* Al Ain. Abū Ẓaby, E UAE
143 R17 **Al 'Ayn** *var.* Al Ain. × Abū Ẓaby, E UAE
138 G12 **Al 'Aynā** Al Karak, W Jordan
Alayor *see* Alaior
Alayskiy Khrebet *see* Alai Range
123 S6 **Alazeya** NE Russian Federation
139 U8 **Al 'Azīzīyah** *var.* Aziziya. E Iraq
120 M12 **Al 'Azīzīyah** NW Libya
138 I10 **Al Azraq al Janūbī** Az Zarqā', N Jordan
106 B9 **Alba** *anc.* Alba Pompeia. Piemonte, NW Italy
25 V6 **Alba** Texas, SW USA
116 G11 **Alba** ◆ *county* W Romania
139 P3 **Al Ba'āj** N Iraq
138 J2 **Al Bāb** Ḥalab, N Syria
116 G10 **Albac** *Hung.* Fehérvölgy; *prev.* Álbák. Alba, SW Romania
105 Q11 **Albacete** Castilla-La Mancha, C Spain
105 P11 **Albacete** ◆ *province* Castilla-La Mancha, C Spain
140 I4 **Al Bad'** Tabūk, NW Saudi Arabia
104 L7 **Alba de Tormes** Castilla-León, N Spain
139 P3 **Al Bādī** N Iraq
141 V8 **Al Badī'ah** × (Abū Ẓaby) Abū Ẓaby, C UAE
143 P17 **Al Badī'ah** *var.* Al Bedei'ah. *spring/well* C UAE
139 Q7 **Al Baghdādī** *var.* Khān al Baghdādī. SW Iraq
Al Bāha *see* Al Bāḥah
140 M11 **Al Bāḥah** *var.* Al Bāha. Al Bāḥah, SW Saudi Arabia
140 M11 **Al Bāḥah** *off.* Minṭaqat al Bāḥah. ◆ *province* W Saudi Arabia
Al Baḥrayn *see* Bahrain
105 S11 **Albaida** País Valenciano, E Spain
116 H11 **Alba Iulia** *Ger.* Weissenburg, *Hung.* Gyulafehérvár; *prev.* Bălgrad, Karlsburg, Károly-Fehérvár. Alba, W Romania
Álbák *see* Albac
138 G10 **Al Balqā'** *off.* Muḥāfaẓat al Balqā', *var.* Balqā'. ◆ *governorate* NW Jordan
14 F11 **Alban** Ontario, S Canada
103 O15 **Alban** Tarn, S France
12 K11 **Albanel, Lac** ◎ Québec, SE Canada
113 L20 **Albania** *off.* Republic of Albania, *Alb.* Republika e Shqipërisë, Shqipëria; *prev.* People's Socialist Republic of Albania. ◆ *republic* SE Europe
Albania *see* Aubagne
107 H15 **Albano Laziale** Lazio, C Italy
180 J14 **Albany** Western Australia
23 S7 **Albany** Georgia, SE USA
31 P13 **Albany** Indiana, N USA
20 L8 **Albany** Kentucky, S USA
29 U7 **Albany** Minnesota, N USA
27 R2 **Albany** Missouri, C USA
18 L10 **Albany** *state capital* New York, NE USA
32 G12 **Albany** Oregon, NW USA
25 Q6 **Albany** Texas, SW USA
12 F10 **Albany** Ontario, S Canada
Alba Pompeia *see* Alba
Alba Regia *see* Székesfehérvár
138 J6 **Al Bāridah** *var.* Bāridah. Ḥimṣ, C Syria
139 Q11 **Al Barīt** S Iraq
105 R8 **Albarracín** Aragón, NE Spain
139 Y12 **Al Baṣrah** *Eng.* Basra; *hist.* Busra, Bussora. SE Iraq
139 V11 **Al Baṭḥā'** SE Iraq
141 X8 **Al Bāṭinah** *var.* Batinah. *coastal region* N Oman
Al Batrūn *see* Batroûn
121 Q12 **Al Bayḍā'** *var.* Beida. NE Libya
141 P16 **Al Bayḍā'** *var.* Al Beida. SW Yemen
Al Bedei'ah *see* Al Badī'ah
Al Beida *see* Al Bayḍā'
21 S10 **Albemarle** *var.* Albermarle. North Carolina, SE USA
Albemarle Island *see* Isabela, Isla
21 N8 **Albemarle Sound** *inlet* W Atlantic Ocean
106 B10 **Albenga** Liguria, NW Italy
104 L8 **Alberche** C Spain
103 O17 **Albères, Chaîne des** *var.* les Albères, Montes Albères. ▲ France/Spain
Albères, Montes *see* Albères, Chaîne des
182 F2 **Alberga Creek** *seasonal river* South Australia
104 G7 **Albergaria-a-Velha** Aveiro, N Portugal
105 S10 **Alberic** País Valenciano, E Spain
Albermarle *see* Albemarle
107 P18 **Alberobello** Puglia, SE Italy
108 J7 **Alberschwende** Vorarlberg, W Austria
103 O3 **Albert** Somme, N France
11 O12 **Alberta** ◆ *province* SW Canada
Albert Edward Nyanza *see* Edward, Lake
61 C20 **Alberti** Buenos Aires, E Argentina
111 K23 **Albertirsa** Pest, C Hungary
99 I16 **Albertkanaal** *canal* N Belgium
79 P17 **Albert, Lake** *var.* Albert Nyanza, Lac Mobutu Sese Seko. ◎ Uganda/Dem. Rep. Congo
29 V11 **Albert Lea** Minnesota, N USA
81 F16 **Albert Nile** NW Uganda
Albert Nyanza *see* Albert, Lake
103 T11 **Albertville** Savoie, E France
23 Q2 **Albertville** Alabama, S USA
Albertville *see* Kalemie
103 N15 **Albi** *anc.* Albiga. Tarn, S France
29 W15 **Albia** Iowa, C USA
Albiga *see* Albi
55 X9 **Albina** Marowijne, NE Surinam
83 A15 **Albina, Ponta** *headland* SW Angola
30 M16 **Albion** Illinois, N USA
31 P11 **Albion** Indiana, N USA

◆ Country ◇ Dependent Territory ◆ Administrative Region ▲ Mountain ▲ Volcano ◎ Lake
● Country Capital ○ Dependent Territory Capital × International Airport ▲ Mountain Range River ⊠ Reservoir

29 P14 **Albion** Nebraska, C USA
18 E9 **Albion** New York, NE USA
18 B12 **Albion** Pennsylvania, NE USA
Al Biqā' *see* El Beqaa
140 J4 **Al Bi'r** *var.* Bi'r Ibn Hirmās. Tabūk, NW Saudi Arabia
140 M12 **Al Birk** Makkah, SW Saudi Arabia
141 Q9 **Al Biyāḍ** *desert* C Saudi Arabia
98 H13 **Alblasserdam** Zuid-Holland, SW Netherlands
105 T8 **Albocácer** *var.* Albocasser. País Valenciano, E Spain
Albocasser *see* Albocácer
95 H19 **Ålbæk** Nordjylland, N Denmark
Albona *see* Labin
105 O17 **Alborán, Isla de** *island* S Spain
Alborán, Mar de *see* Alboran Sea
105 N17 **Alboran Sea** *Sp.* Mar de Alborán. *sea* SW Mediterranean Sea
Ålborg *see* Aalborg
95 H21 **Ålborg Bugt** *var.* Aalborg Bugt. *bay* N Denmark
Ålborg-Nørresundby *see* Aalborg
143 O5 **Alborz, Reshteh-ye Kūhhā-ye** *Eng.* Elburz Mountains. ▲ N Iran
105 Q14 **Albox** Andalucía, S Spain
101 H23 **Albstadt** Baden-Württemberg, SW Germany
104 G14 **Albufeira** Beja, S Portugal
139 P5 **Ālbū Gharz, Sabkhat** ◎ W Iraq
105 O15 **Albuñol** Andalucía, S Spain
37 Q11 **Albuquerque** New Mexico, SW USA
141 W8 **Al Buraymī** *var.* Buraimi. N Oman
143 R17 **Al Buraymī** *var.* Buraimi. *spring/well* Oman/UAE
Al Burayqah *see* Marsá al Burayqah
Alburgum *see* Aalborg
104 I10 **Alburquerque** Extremadura, W Spain
181 V14 **Albury** New South Wales, SE Australia
141 T14 **Al Buzūn** SE Yemen
93 G17 **Alby** Västernorrland, C Sweden
Albyn, Glen *see* Mor, Glen
104 G12 **Alcácer do Sal** Setúbal, W Portugal
Alcalá de Chisvert *see* Alcalá de Chivert
105 T8 **Alcalá de Chivert** *var.* Alcalá de Chisvert. País Valenciano, E Spain
104 K14 **Alcalá de Guadaira** Andalucía, S Spain
105 O8 **Alcalá de Henares** *Ar.* Alkal'a; *anc.* Complutum. Madrid, C Spain
104 K16 **Alcalá de los Gazules** Andalucía, S Spain
105 N14 **Alcalá La Real** Andalucía, S Spain
107 I23 **Alcamo** Sicilia, Italy, C Mediterranean Sea
105 T4 **Alcanadre** ∽ NE Spain
105 T8 **Alcanar** Cataluña, NE Spain
104 J5 **Alcañices** Castilla-León, N Spain
105 T7 **Alcañiz** Aragón, NE Spain
104 J9 **Alcántara** Extremadura, W Spain
104 J9 **Alcántara, Embalse de** ⊟ W Spain
105 R13 **Alcantarilla** Murcia, SE Spain
105 P11 **Alcaraz** Castilla-La Mancha, C Spain
105 P12 **Alcaraz, Sierra de** ▲ C Spain
104 I12 **Alcarrache** ∽ SW Spain
105 T6 **Alcarràs** Cataluña, NE Spain
105 N14 **Alcaudete** Andalucía, S Spain
Alcázar *see* Ksar-el-Kebir
105 O10 **Alcázar de San Juan** *anc* Alce. Castilla-La Mancha, C Spain
Alcazarquivir *see* Ksar-el-Kebir
Alce *see* Alcázar de San Juan
57 B17 **Alcebo, Volcán** ⛰ Galapagos Islands, Ecuador, E Pacific Ocean
139 X12 **Al Chabā'ish** *var.* Al Kaba'ish. SE Iraq
117 Y7 **Alchevs'k** *prev.* Kommunarsk, Voroshilovsk. Luhans'ka Oblast', E Ukraine
Alcira *see* Alzira
21 N9 **Alcoa** Tennessee, S USA
104 F9 **Alcobaça** Leiria, C Portugal
105 N8 **Alcobendas** Madrid, C Spain
Alcoi *see* Alcoy
105 P7 **Alcolea del Pinar** Castilla-La Mancha, C Spain
104 I11 **Alconchel** Extremadura, W Spain
105 S9 **Alcora** País Valenciano, E Spain
105 N8 **Alcorcón** Madrid, C Spain
105 S7 **Alcorisa** Aragón, NE Spain
61 B19 **Alcorta** Santa Fe, C Argentina
104 H14 **Alcoutim** Faro, S Portugal
33 W15 **Alcova** Wyoming, C USA
105 S11 **Alcoy** *Cat.* Alcoi. País Valenciano, E Spain
105 Y9 **Alcúdia, Badia d'** *bay* Mallorca, Spain, W Mediterranean Sea
172 M7 **Aldabra Group** *island group* SW Seychelles
139 U10 **Al Daghghārah** C Iraq
40 J5 **Aldama** Chihuahua, N Mexico
41 P11 **Aldama** Tamaulipas, C Mexico
123 Q11 **Aldan** Respublika Sakha (Yakutiya), NE Russian Federation
123 Q10 **Aldan** ∽ NE Russian Federation
162 G7 **Aldar** Dzavhan, W Mongolia
al Dar al Baida *see* Rabat
97 Q20 **Aldeburgh** E England, UK
105 P5 **Aldehuela de Calatañazor** Castilla-León, N Spain
Aldeia Nova *see* Aldeia Nova de São Bento
104 H13 **Aldeia Nova de São Bento** *var.* Aldeia Nova. Beja, S Portugal
29 V11 **Alden** Minnesota, N USA
184 N6 **Aldermen Islands, The** *island group* N NZ
97 L25 **Alderney** *island* Channel Islands
97 N22 **Aldershot** S England, UK
21 R6 **Alderson** West Virginia, NE USA
Al Dhaid *see* Adh Dhayd
30 J11 **Aledo** Illinois, N USA
76 H9 **Aleg** Brakna, SW Mauritania
64 Q10 **Alegranza** *island* Islas Canarias, Spain, NE Atlantic Ocean
37 P12 **Alegres Mountain** ▲ New Mexico, SW USA
61 F15 **Alegrete** Rio Grande do Sul, S Brazil
61 C16 **Alejandra** Santa Fe, C Argentina
193 T11 **Alejandro Selkirk, Isla** *island* Islas Juan Fernández, Chile, E Pacific Ocean
124 I12 **Alekhovshchina** Leningradskaya Oblast', NW Russian Federation
39 O13 **Aleknagik** Alaska, USA
Aleksandriya *see* Oleksandriya
Aleksandropol' *see* Gyumri
126 L3 **Aleksandrov** Vladimirskaya Oblast', W Russian Federation
113 N14 **Aleksandrovac** Serbia, C Serbia and Montenegro (Yugo.)
127 R9 **Aleksandrov Gay** Saratovskaya Oblast', W Russian Federation
127 U6 **Aleksandrovka** Orenburgskaya Oblast', W Russian Federation
Aleksandrovka *see* Oleksandrivka
114 J8 **Aleksandrovo** Lovech, N Bulgaria
125 V13 **Aleksandrovsk** Permskaya Oblast', NW Russian Federation
Aleksandrovsk *see* Zaporizhzhya
127 N14 **Aleksandrovskoye** Stavropol'skiy Kray, SW Russian Federation
123 T12 **Aleksandrovsk-Sakhalinskiy** Ostrov Sakhalin, Sakhalinskaya Oblast', SE Russian Federation
110 J10 **Aleksandrów Kujawski** Kujawsko-pomorskie, C Poland
110 K12 **Aleksandrów Łódzki** Łódzkie, C Poland
Alekseevka *see* Terekty
126 L9 **Alekseyevka** Belgorodskaya Oblast', W Russian Federation
145 P7 **Alekseyevka** *Kaz.* Alekseevka. Akmola, N Kazakhstan
127 S7 **Alekseyevka** Samarskaya Oblast', W Russian Federation
Alekseyevka *see* Akkol', Akmola, Kazakhstan
Alekseyevka *see* Terekty, Vostochnyy Kazakhstan, Kazakhstan
127 R4 **Alekseyevskoye** Respublika Tatarstan, W Russian Federation
126 K5 **Aleksin** Tul'skaya Oblast', W Russian Federation
113 O14 **Aleksinac** Serbia, SE Serbia and Montenegro (Yugo.)
190 G11 **Alele** Île Uvea, E Wallis and Futuna
95 N20 **Ålem** Kalmar, S Sweden
102 L6 **Alençon** Orne, N France
58 I12 **Alenquer** Pará, NE Brazil
38 G10 **'Alenuihaha Channel** *var.* Alenuihaha Channel. *channel* Hawai'i, USA, C Pacific Ocean
Alep/Aleppo *see* Ḥalab
103 Y15 **Aléria** Corse, France, C Mediterranean Sea
197 Q11 **Alert** Ellesmere Island, Nunavut, N Canada
103 Q14 **Alès** *prev.* Alais. Gard, S France
116 G9 **Aleşd** *Hung.* Élesd. Bihor, SW Romania
106 C9 **Alessandria** *Fr.* Alexandrie. Piemonte, N Italy
Ålestrup *see* Aalestrup
94 D9 **Ålesund** Møre og Romsdal, S Norway
108 E10 **Aletschhorn** ▲ SW Switzerland
197 S1 **Aleutian Basin** *undersea feature* Bering Sea
38 H17 **Aleutian Islands** *island group* Alaska, USA
39 F14 **Aleutian Range** ▲ Alaska, USA
192 L3 **Aleutian Trench** *undersea feature* S Bering Sea
123 T10 **Alevina, Mys** *headland* E Russian Federation
15 Q6 **Alex** ∽ Québec, SE Canada
28 J3 **Alexander** North Dakota, N USA
39 W14 **Alexander Archipelago** *island group* Alaska, USA
Alexanderbaai *see* Alexander Bay
83 D23 **Alexander Bay** *Afr.* Alexanderbaai. Northern Cape, W South Africa
23 Q5 **Alexander City** Alabama, S USA
194 J6 **Alexander Island** *island* Antarctica
Alexander Range *see* Kirghiz Range
183 O12 **Alexandra** Victoria, SE Australia
185 D22 **Alexandra** Otago, South Island, NZ
115 F14 **Alexándreia** *var.* Alexándria. Kentrikí Makedonía, N Greece
Alexandretta *see* İskenderun
Alexandretta, Gulf of *see* İskenderun Körfezi
15 N13 **Alexandria** Ontario, SE Canada
121 U13 **Alexandria** *Ar.* Al Iskandarīyah. N Egypt
44 I12 **Alexandria** C Jamaica
116 I15 **Alexandria** Teleorman, S Romania
31 P13 **Alexandria** Indiana, N USA
20 M4 **Alexandria** Kentucky, S USA
22 H7 **Alexandria** Louisiana, S USA
29 T7 **Alexandria** Minnesota, N USA
29 Q11 **Alexandria** South Dakota, N USA
21 W4 **Alexandria** Virginia, NE USA
Alexándria *see* Alexándreia
18 I7 **Alexandria Bay** New York, NE USA
Alexandrie *see* Alessandria
182 J10 **Alexandrina, Lake** ◎ South Australia
114 K13 **Alexandroúpoli** *var.* Alexandroúpolis, *Turk.* Dedeagaç, Dedeagach. Anatolikí Makedonía kai Thráki, NE Greece
Alexandroúpolis *see* Alexandroúpoli
10 L15 **Alexis Creek** British Columbia, SW Canada
122 I13 **Aleysk** Altayskiy Kray, S Russian Federation
10 L15 **Alexis Creek** British Columbia, SW Canada
122 I13 **Aleysk** Altayskiy Kray, S Russian Federation
139 S8 **Al Fallūjah** *var.* Falluja. C Iraq
105 R8 **Alfambra** ∽ E Spain
Al Faqa *see* Faq'
141 R15 **Al Farḍah** C Yemen
105 Q4 **Alfaro** La Rioja, N Spain
105 U5 **Alfarràs** Cataluña, NE Spain
Al Fāshir *see* El Fasher
Al Fashn *see* El Fashn
114 M7 **Alfatar** Silistra, NE Bulgaria
139 S5 **Al Fatḥah** C Iraq
139 Q3 **Al Fatsī** N Iraq
139 Z13 **Al Fāw** *var.* Fao. SE Iraq
Al Fayyūm *see* El Faiyûm
115 D20 **Alfeiós** *prev.* Alfiós, *anc.* Alpheius, Alpheus. ∽ S Greece
100 I13 **Alfeld** Niedersachsen, C Germany
Alfiós *see* Alfeiós
Alföld *see* Great Hungarian Plain
94 C11 **Ålfotbreen** *glacier* S Norway
19 P9 **Alfred** Maine, NE USA
18 F11 **Alfred** New York, NE USA
61 K14 **Alfredo Vagner** Santa Catarina, S Brazil
94 M12 **Alfta** Gävleborg, C Sweden
140 K12 **Al Fuḥayḥīl** *var.* Fahaheel. SE Kuwait
139 Q6 **Al Fuḥaymī** C Iraq
143 S16 **Al Fujayrah** *Eng.* Fujairah. Al Fujayrah, NE UAE
143 S16 **Al Fujayrah** *Eng.* Fujairah. ✕ Al Fujayrah, NE UAE
Al Furāt *see* Euphrates
144 I10 **Alga** *Kaz.* Algha. Aktyubinsk, NW Kazakhstan
144 G9 **Algabas** Zapadnyy Kazakhstan, NW Kazakhstan
95 C17 **Ålgård** Rogaland, S Norway
104 G14 **Algarve** *cultural region* S Portugal
182 G3 **Algebuckina Bridge** South Australia
104 K16 **Algeciras** Andalucía, SW Spain
105 S10 **Algemesí** País Valenciano, E Spain
Al-Genain *see* El Geneina
120 F9 **Alger** *var.* Algiers, El Djazaïr, Al Jazair. ● (Algeria) N Algeria
74 H9 **Algeria** *off.* Democratic and Popular Republic of Algeria. ◆ *republic* N Africa
120 J8 **Algerian Basin** *var.* Balearic Plain. *undersea feature* W Mediterranean Sea
Algha *see* Alga
138 I4 **Al Ghāb** ◎ NW Syria
141 X10 **Al Ghābah** *var.* Ghaba. C Oman
141 U14 **Al Ghayḍah** E Yemen
140 M6 **Al Ghazālah** Ḥā'il, NW Saudi Arabia
107 B17 **Alghero** Sardegna, Italy, C Mediterranean Sea
95 M20 **Älghult** Kronoberg, S Sweden
Al Ghurdaqah *see* Hurghada
Algiers *see* Alger
105 S10 **Alginet** País Valenciano, E Spain
83 I26 **Algoa Bay** *bay* S South Africa
104 L15 **Algodonales** Andalucía, S Spain
105 N9 **Algodor** ∽ C Spain
Al Golea *see* El Goléa
31 N6 **Algoma** Wisconsin, N USA
29 U12 **Algona** Iowa, C USA
20 L8 **Algood** Tennessee, S USA
105 O2 **Algorta** País Vasco, N Spain
61 E18 **Algorta** Río Negro, W Uruguay
Al Haba *see* Haba
139 Q10 **Al Habbārīyah** S Iraq
Al Hadhar *see* Al Ḥaḍr
139 Q4 **Al Ḥaḍr** *var.* Al Hadhar; *anc.* Hatra. NW Iraq
139 T13 **Al Ḥajarah** *desert* S Iraq
141 W8 **Al Ḥajar al Gharbī** ▲ N Oman
141 Y8 **Al Ḥajar ash Sharqī** ▲ NE Oman
141 R15 **Al Ḥajarayn** C Yemen
138 L10 **Al Ḥamād** *desert* Jordan/Saudi Arabia
Al Hamad *see* Syrian Desert
75 N9 **Al Ḥamādah al Ḥamrā'** *var.* Al Ḥamrā'. *desert* NW Libya
105 N15 **Alhama de Granada** Andalucía, S Spain
105 R13 **Alhama de Murcia** Murcia, SE Spain
35 T15 **Alhambra** California, W USA
139 T12 **Al Ḥammām** S Iraq
141 X8 **Al Ḥamrā'** NE Oman
Al Ḥamrā' *see* Al Ḥamādah al Ḥamrā'
141 O6 **Al Ḥamūdīyah** *spring/well* N Saudi Arabia
140 M7 **Al Ḥanākīyah** Al Madīnah, W Saudi Arabia
139 W14 **Al Ḥanīyah** *escarpment* Iraq/Saudi Arabia
139 Y12 **Al Ḥārithah** SE Iraq
140 L3 **Al Ḥarrah** *desert* NW Saudi Arabia
75 Q10 **Al Harūj al Aswad** *desert* C Libya
Al Hasaifin *see* Al Ḥusayfīn
139 N2 **Al Ḥasakah** *var.* Al Hasijah, El Haseke, *Fr.* Hassetché. Al Ḥasakah, NE Syria
139 O2 **Al Ḥasakah** *off.* Muḥāfaẓat al Ḥasakah, *var.* Al Hasakah, Āl Hasakah, Hasakah, Hassakeh. ◐ *governorate* NE Syria
139 T9 **Al Hāshimīyah** C Iraq
138 G13 **Al Hāshimīyah** Ma'ān, S Jordan
Al Hasijah *see* Al Ḥasakah
104 M15 **Alhaurín el Grande** Andalucía, S Spain
141 Q16 **Al Ḥawrā** S Yemen
139 V10 **Al Ḥayy** *var.* Kut al Hai, Kūt al Ḥayy. E Iraq
141 U11 **Al Ḥibāk** *desert* E Saudi Arabia
138 H8 **Al Hījānah** *var.* Hejanah, Hijanah. Dimashq, W Syria
140 K7 **Al Ḥijāz** *Eng.* Hejaz. *physical region* NW Saudi Arabia
Al Hilbeh *see* 'Ulayyānīyah, Bi'r al
139 T9 **Al Ḥillah** *var.* Hilla. C Iraq
139 T9 **Al Hindīyah** *var.* Hindiya. C Iraq
138 G12 **Al Ḥisā** Aṭ Ṭafīlah, W Jordan
74 G5 **Al-Hoceïma** *var.* al Hoceima, Al-Hoceima, Alhucemas; *prev.* Villa Sanjurjo. N Morocco
Alhucemas *see* Al-Hoceïma
105 N17 **Alhucemas, Peñon de** *island group* S Spain
141 N15 **Al Ḥudaydah** *Eng.* Hodeida. W Yemen
141 N15 **Al Ḥudaydah** *Eng.* Hodeida. ✕ W Yemen
140 M4 **Al Ḥudūd ash Shamālīyah** *var.* Minṭaqat al Ḥudūd ash Shamālīyah, *Eng.* Northern Border Region. ◐ *province* N Saudi Arabia
141 S7 **Al Hufūf** *var.* Hofuf. Ash Sharqīyah, NE Saudi Arabia
al-Hurma *see* Al Khurmah
141 X7 **Al Ḥusayfīn** *var.* Al Hasaifin. N Oman
138 G9 **Al Ḥuṣn** *var.* Husn. Irbid, N Jordan
139 U9 **'Alī** E Iraq
104 L10 **Alia** Extremadura, W Spain
143 P9 **'Alīābād** Yazd, C Iran
'Alīābād *see* Qā'emshahr
105 S7 **Aliaga** Aragón, NE Spain
136 B13 **Aliağa** İzmir, W Turkey
Aliákmon *see* Aliákmonas
115 F14 **Aliákmonas** *prev.* Aliákmon, *anc.* Haliacmon. ∽ N Greece
139 W9 **'Alī al Gharbī** E Iraq
139 U11 **'Alī al Ḥassūnī** S Iraq
115 G18 **Alíartos** Stereá Ellás, C Greece
137 Y12 **Äli-Bayramlı** *Rus.* Ali-Bayramly. SE Azerbaijan
Ali-Bayramly *see* Äli-Bayramlı
114 P12 **Alibey Barajı** ⊟ NW Turkey
77 S13 **Alibori** ∽ N Benin
112 M10 **Alibunar** Serbia, NE Serbia and Montenegro (Yugo.)
105 S12 **Alicante** *Cat.* Alacant; *Lat.* Lucentum. País Valenciano, SE Spain
105 S12 **Alicante** ◐ *province* País Valenciano, SE Spain
105 S12 **Alicante** ✕ Murcia, E Spain
83 I25 **Alice** Eastern Cape, S South Africa
25 S14 **Alice** Texas, SW USA
83 I25 **Alicedale** Eastern Cape, S South Africa
65 B25 **Alice, Mount** *hill* West Falkland, Falkland Islands
107 P20 **Alice, Punta** *headland* S Italy
181 Q7 **Alice Springs** Northern Territory, C Australia
23 N4 **Aliceville** Alabama, S USA
147 U13 **Alichur** SE Tajikistan
147 U14 **Alichuri Janubí, Qatorkŭhi** *Rus.* Yuzhno-Alichurskiy Khrebet. ▲ SE Tajikistan
147 U13 **Alichuri Shimolí, Qatorkŭhi** *Rus.* Severo-Alichurskiy Khrebet. ▲ SE Tajikistan
107 K22 **Alicudi, Isola** *island* Isole Eolie, S Italy
152 J11 **Aligarh** Uttar Pradesh, N India
142 M7 **Alīgūdarz** Lorestān, W Iran
163 U5 **Alihe** *var.* Oroqen Zizhiqi. Nei Mongol Zizhiqu, N China
149 R6 **'Alī Kbel** *Pash.* 'Alī Khēl. Paktīkā, E Afghanistan
Ali Khel *see* 'Alī Kheyl, Paktīā, Afghanistan
'Alī Khēl *see* 'Alī Kbel, Paktīkā, Afghanistan
149 R6 **'Alī Kheyl** *var.* Ali Khel, Jajı. Paktīā, SE Afghanistan
141 V17 **Al Ikhwān** *island group* SE Yemen
Aliki *see* Alykí
79 H19 **Alima** ∽ C Congo
Al Imārāt al 'Arabīyah al Muttaḥidah *see* United Arab Emirates
115 N23 **Alimía** *island* Dodekánisos, Greece, Aegean Sea
55 V12 **Alimimuni Piek** ▲ S Surinam
79 K15 **Alindao** Basse-Kotto, S Central African Republic
95 J18 **Alingsås** Västra Götaland, S Sweden
81 K18 **Alinjugul** *spring/well* E Kenya
149 S11 **Alīpur** Punjab, E Pakistan
153 T12 **Alīpur Duār** West Bengal, NE India
18 B14 **Aliquippa** Pennsylvania, NE USA
80 L12 **'Ali Sabieh** *var.* 'Alī Sabīḥ. S Djibouti
'Alī Sabīḥ *see* 'Ali Sabieh
140 K3 **Al 'Isāwīyah** Al Jawf, NW Saudi Arabia
104 J10 **Aliseda** Extremadura, W Spain
139 T8 **Al Iskandarīyah** C Iraq
Al Iskandarīyah *see* Alexandria
123 T6 **Aliskerovo** Chukotskiy Avtonomnyy Okrug, NE Russian Federation
114 H13 **Alistráti** Kentrikí Makedonía, NE Greece
39 P15 **Alitak Bay** *bay* Kodiak Island, Alaska, USA
Al Ittiḥād *see* Madīnat ash Sha'b
115 H18 **Alivéri** *var.* Alivérion. Évvoia, C Greece
Alivérion *see* Alivéri
Aliwal-Noord *see* Aliwal North
83 I24 **Aliwal North** *Afr.* Aliwal-Noord. Eastern Cape, SE South Africa
121 Q13 **Al Jabal al Akhḍar** ▲ NE Libya
138 H13 **Al Jafr** Ma'ān, S Jordan
75 T8 **Al Jaghbūb** NE Libya
142 K11 **Al Jahrā'** *var.* Al Jahrah, Jahra. C Kuwait
Al Jahrah *see* Al Jahrā'
Al Jamāhīrīyah al 'Arabīyah al Lībīyah ash Sha'bīyah al Ishtirākīy *see* Libya
140 K3 **Al Jarāwī** *spring/well* NW Saudi Arabia
141 X11 **Al Jawārah** *oasis* SE Oman
140 L3 **Al Jawf** *var.* Jauf. Al Jawf, NW Saudi Arabia
140 L4 **Al Jawf** *off.* Minṭaqat al Jawf. ◐ *province* N Saudi Arabia
Al Jawlān *see* Golan Heights
Al Jazair *see* Alger
139 N4 **Al Jazīrah** *physical region* Iraq/Syria
104 F14 **Aljezur** Faro, S Portugal
139 S13 **Al Jil** S Iraq
138 G11 **Al Jīzah** *var.* Jiza. 'Al Āşimah, N Jordan
Al Jīzah *see* El Gîza
Al Jubail *see* Al Jubayl
141 S6 **Al Jubayl** *var.* Al Jubail. Ash Sharqīyah, NE Saudi Arabia
141 T10 **Āl Juḥaysh, Qalamat** *well* SE Saudi Arabia
143 N15 **Al Jumaylīyah** N Qatar
Al Junaynah *see* El Geneina
104 G13 **Aljustrel** Beja, S Portugal
Al Kaba'ish *see* Al Chabā'ish
Al-Kadhimain *see* Al Kāẓimīyah
Al Kāf *see* El Kef
Alkal'a *see* Alcalá de Henares
35 W4 **Alkali Flat** *salt flat* Nevada, W USA
35 Q1 **Alkali Lake** ◎ Nevada, W USA
141 Z9 **Al Kāmil** NE Oman
138 G11 **Al Karak** *var.* El Kerak, Karak, Kerak; *anc.* Kir Moab, Kir of Moab. Al Karak, W Jordan
138 G12 **Al Karak** *off.* Muḥāfaẓat al Karak. ◐ *governorate* W Jordan
139 W8 **Al Karmashīyah** E Iraq
Al-Kashaniya *see* Al Qash'ānīyah
Al-Kasr al-Kebir *see* Ksar-el-Kebir
139 T8 **Al Kāẓimīyah** *var.* Al-Kadhimain, Kadhimain. C Iraq
99 J18 **Alken** Limburg, NE Belgium
141 X8 **Al Khābūrah** *var.* Khabura. N Oman
Al Khalīl *see* Hebron
139 T7 **Al Khāliş** C Iraq
Al Khaluf *see* Khalūf
Al Khārijah *see* El Khârga
141 Q8 **Al Kharj** Ar Riyāḍ, C Saudi Arabia
141 W6 **Al Khaşab** *var.* Khasab. N Oman
Al Khaur *see* Al Khawr
143 N15 **Al Khawr** *var.* Al Khaur, Al Khor. N Qatar
142 K12 **Al Khīrān** *var.* Al Khiran. SE Kuwait
141 W9 **Al Khīrān** *spring/well* NW Oman
Al Khiyām *see* El Khiyam
Al-Khobar *see* Al Khubar
Al Khor *see* Al Khawr
141 S6 **Al Khubar** *var.* Al-Khobar. Ash Sharqīyah, NE Saudi Arabia
75 T11 **Al Khufrah** SE Libya
120 M12 **Al Khums** *var.* Homs, Khoms, Khums. NW Libya
141 R15 **Al Khuraybah** C Yemen
140 M9 **Al Khurmah** *var.* al-Hurma. Makkah, W Saudi Arabia
141 V9 **Al Kidan** *desert* NE Saudi Arabia
127 V4 **Alkino-2** Respublika Bashkortostan, W Russian Federation
98 H9 **Alkmaar** Noord-Holland, NW Netherlands
139 T10 **Al Kūfah** *var.* Kufa. S Iraq
141 T10 **Al Kursū'** *desert* E Saudi Arabia
139 V9 **Al Kūt** *var.* Kūt al 'Amārah, Kut al Imara. E Iraq
Al-Kuwait *see* Al Kuwayt
Al Kuwayr *see* Guwēr
142 K11 **Al Kuwayt** *var.* Al-Kuwait, *Eng.* Kuwait, Kuwait City; *prev.* Qurein. ● (Kuwait) E Kuwait
142 K11 **Al Kuwayt** ✕ C Kuwait
115 G19 **Alkyonidón, Kólpos** *gulf* C Greece
141 N4 **Al Labbah** *physical region* N Saudi Arabia
138 G4 **Al Lādhiqīyah** *Eng.* Latakia, *Fr.* Lattaquié; *anc.* Laodicea, Laodicea ad Mare. Al Lādhiqīyah, W Syria
138 H4 **Al Lādhiqīyah** *off.* Muḥāfaẓat al Lādhiqīyah, *var.* Al Lathqiyah, Latakia, Lattakia. ◐ *governorate* W Syria
19 R2 **Allagash River** ∽ Maine, NE USA
152 M13 **Allahābād** Uttar Pradesh, N India
143 S3 **Allāh Dāgh, Reshteh-ye** ▲ NE Iran
39 Q8 **Allakaket** Alaska, USA
11 T15 **Allan** Saskatchewan, S Canada
166 L6 **Allanmyo** Magwe, C Burma
83 I22 **Allanridge** Free State, C South Africa
104 H4 **Allariz** Galicia, NW Spain
139 R11 **Al Laşaf** *var.* Al Lussuf. S Iraq
Al Lathqiyah *see* Al Lādhiqīyah
23 S2 **Allatoona Lake** ⊟ Georgia, SE USA
83 J19 **Alldays** Limpopo, NE South Africa
Alle *see* Łyna
31 P10 **Allegan** Michigan, N USA
18 E14 **Allegheny Mountains** ▲ NE USA
18 E12 **Allegheny Plateau** ▲ New York/Pennsylvania, NE USA
18 D11 **Allegheny Reservoir** ⊟ New York/Pennsylvania, NE USA
18 E12 **Allegheny River** ∽ New York/Pennsylvania, NE USA
22 K9 **Allemands, Lac des** ◎ Louisiana, S USA
25 U6 **Allen** Texas, SW USA
21 R14 **Allendale** South Carolina, SE USA
41 N6 **Allende** Coahuila de Zaragoza, NE Mexico
41 O9 **Allende** Nuevo León, NE Mexico
97 D16 **Allen, Lough** *Ir.* Loch Aillionn. ◎ NW Ireland
185 B26 **Allen, Mount** ▲ Stewart Island, Southland, SW NZ
109 V2 **Allensteig** Niederösterreich, N Austria
Allenstein *see* Olsztyn
18 I14 **Allentown** Pennsylvania, NE USA
155 G23 **Alleppey** *var.* Alappuzha; *prev.* Alleppi. Kerala, SW India
Alleppi *see* Alleppey
100 J12 **Aller** ∽ NW Germany
29 V16 **Allerton** Iowa, C USA
99 K19 **Alleur** Liège, E Belgium
101 J25 **Allgäuer Alpen** ▲ Austria/Germany
28 J13 **Alliance** Nebraska, C USA
31 U12 **Alliance** Ohio, N USA
103 O10 **Allier** ◐ *department* N France
139 R13 **Al Līfīyah** S Iraq
44 J13 **Alligator Pond** C Jamaica
21 Y9 **Alligator River** ∽ North Carolina, SE USA
29 W12 **Allison** Iowa, C USA
14 G14 **Alliston** Ontario, S Canada
140 L11 **Al Līth** Makkah, SW Saudi Arabia
Al Liwā' *see* Līwā
96 J12 **Alloa** C Scotland, UK
103 U14 **Allos** Alpes-de-Haute-Provence, SE France
108 D6 **Allschwil** Basel-Land, NW Switzerland
Al Lubnān *see* Lebanon
141 N14 **Al Luḥayyah** W Yemen
14 K12 **Allumettes, Île des** *island* Québec, SE Canada
Al Lussuf *see* Al Laşaf
109 S5 **Alm** ∽ N Austria
15 Q7 **Alma** Québec, SE Canada
27 S10 **Alma** Arkansas, C USA
23 V7 **Alma** Georgia, SE USA
27 P4 **Alma** Kansas, C USA
31 Q8 **Alma** Michigan, N USA
29 O17 **Alma** Nebraska, C USA
30 I7 **Alma** Wisconsin, N USA
139 R12 **Al Ma'ānīyah** S Iraq
Alma-Ata *see* Almaty
Alma-Atinskaya Oblast' *see* Almaty
Almacellas *see* Almacelles
105 T5 **Almacelles** *var.* Almacellas. Cataluña, NE Spain
104 F11 **Almada** Setúbal, W Portugal
104 L11 **Almadén** Castilla-La Mancha, C Spain
140 L7 **Al Madīnah** *Eng.* Medina. Al Madīnah, W Saudi Arabia
140 L7 **Al Madīnah** *off.* Minṭaqat al Madīnah. ◐ *province* W Saudi Arabia
138 H9 **Al Mafraq** *var.* Mafraq. Al Mafraq, N Jordan
138 J10 **Al Mafraq** *off.* Muḥāfaẓat al Mafraq. ◐ *governorate* NW Jordan
141 R15 **Al Maghārim** C Yemen
105 N11 **Almagro** Castilla-La Mancha, C Spain
Al Maḥallah al Kubrá *see* El Maḥalla el Kubra
139 T9 **Al Maḥāwīl** *var.* Khān al Maḥāwīl. C Iraq
Al Mahdīyah *see* Mahdia
139 T8 **Al Maḥmūdīyah** *var.* Mahmudiya. C Iraq
141 T14 **Al Mahrah** ▲ E Yemen
141 P7 **Al Majma'ah** Ar Riyāḍ, C Saudi Arabia
139 Q11 **Al Makmin** *well* S Iraq
139 Q1 **Al Mālikīyah** *var.* Malkiye. Al Ḥasakah, N Syria
Almalyk *see* Olmaliq
Al Mamlakah al Urdunīyah al Hāshimīyah *see* Jordan
Al Mamlakah *see* Morocco
143 Q18 **Al Manādir** *var.* Al Manadir. *desert* Oman/UAE
142 L15 **Al Manāmah** *Eng.* Manama. ● (Bahrain) N Bahrain
139 O5 **Al Manāşif** ▲ E Syria
35 O4 **Almanor, Lake** ⊟ California, W USA
105 R11 **Almansa** Castilla-La Mancha, C Spain
Al Manşūrah *see* El Manşûra
104 L3 **Almanza** Castilla-León, N Spain
104 L8 **Almanzor** ▲ W Spain
105 P14 **Almanzora** ∽ SE Spain
139 S9 **Al Mardah** C Iraq
Al-Mariyya *see* Almería
75 R7 **Al Marj** *var.* Barka, *It.* Barce. NE Libya
138 L2 **Al Mashrafah** Ar Raqqah, N Syria
141 X8 **Al Maşna'ah** *var.* Al Muşana'a. NE Oman
105 T9 **Almassora** País Valenciano, E Spain
Almatinskaya Oblast' *see* Almaty
145 U15 **Almaty** *var.* Alma-Ata. Almaty, SE Kazakhstan

◆ Country ◇ Dependent Territory ◐ Administrative Region ▲ Mountain ⛰ Volcano ◎ Lake
● Country Capital ○ Dependent Territory Capital ✕ International Airport ▲ Mountain Range ∽ River ⊟ Reservoir

145 S14 **Almaty** *off.* Almatinskaya Oblast', *Kaz.* Almaty Oblysy; *prev.* Alma-Atinskaya Oblast'. ◆ *province* SE Kazakhstan
145 U15 **Almaty** ✕ Almaty, SE Kazakhstan
Almaty Oblysy *see* Almaty
al-Mawailih *see* Al Muwayliḥ
139 R3 **Al Mawṣil** *Eng.* Mosul. N Iraq
139 N5 **Al Mayādīn** *var.* Mayadin, *Fr.* Meyadine. Dayr az Zawr, E Syria
139 X10 **Al Maymūnah** *var.* Maimuna. SE Iraq
141 N5 **Al Mayyāh** Ḥā'il, N Saudi Arabia
Al Ma'zam *see* Al Ma'zim
105 P6 **Almazán** Castilla-León, N Spain
141 W8 **Al Ma'zim** *var.* Al Ma'zam. NW Oman
123 N11 **Almaznyy** Respublika Sakha (Yakutiya), NE Russian Federation
Al Mazra' *see* Al Mazra'ah
138 G11 **Al Mazra'ah** *var.* Al Mazra', Mazra'a. Al Karak, W Jordan
101 G15 **Alme** ⤳ W Germany
104 I7 **Almeida** Guarda, N Portugal
104 G10 **Almeirim** Santarém, C Portugal
98 O10 **Almelo** Overijssel, E Netherlands
105 S9 **Almenara** País Valenciano, E Spain
105 P12 **Almenaras** ▲ S Spain
105 P5 **Almenar de Soria** Castilla-León, N Spain
104 J6 **Almendra, Embalse de** ⊡ Castilla-León, NW Spain
104 J11 **Almendralejo** Extremadura, W Spain
98 J10 **Almere** *var.* Almere-stad. Flevoland, C Netherlands
98 J10 **Almere-Buiten** Flevoland, C Netherlands
98 J10 **Almere-Haven** Flevoland, C Netherlands
Almere-stad *see* Almere
105 P15 **Almería** *Ar.* Al-Mariyya; *anc.* Unci, *Lat.* Portus Magnus. Andalucía, S Spain
105 P14 **Almería** ◆ *province* Andalucía, S Spain
105 P15 **Almería, Golfo de** *gulf* S Spain
127 S5 **Al'met'yevsk** Respublika Tatarstan, W Russian Federation
95 L21 **Älmhult** Kronoberg, S Sweden
141 U9 **Al Miḥrāḍ** *desert* NE Saudi Arabia
Al Mīnā' *see* El Mina
104 L17 **Almina, Punta** *headland* Ceuta, Spain, N Africa
Al Minyā *see* El Minya
Al Miqdādīyah *see* Al Muqdādīyah
43 P14 **Almirante** Bocas del Toro, NW Panama
Almirós *see* Almyrós
140 M9 **Al Mislaḥ** *spring/well* W Saudi Arabia
Almissa *see* Omiš
104 G13 **Almodôvar** *var.* Almodóvar. Beja, S Portugal
104 M11 **Almodóvar del Campo** Castilla-La Mancha, C Spain
105 Q9 **Almodóvar del Pinar** Castilla-La Mancha, C Spain
31 S9 **Almont** Michigan, N USA
14 L13 **Almonte** Ontario, SE Canada
104 J14 **Almonte** Andalucía, S Spain
104 K9 **Almonte** ⤳ W Spain
152 K9 **Almora** Uttaranchal, N India
104 M8 **Almorox** Castilla-La Mancha, C Spain
141 S7 **Al Mubarraz** Ash Sharqīyah, E Saudi Arabia
Al Muḍaibī *see* Al Muḍaybī
138 G15 **Al Mudawwarah** Ma'ān, SW Jordan
141 Y9 **Al Muḍaybī** *var.* Al Muḍaibī. NE Oman
Almudébar *see* Almudévar
105 S5 **Almudévar** *var.* Almudébar. Aragón, NE Spain
141 S15 **Al Mukallā** *var.* Mukalla. SE Yemen
141 N16 **Al Mukhā** *Eng.* Mocha. SW Yemen
105 N15 **Almuñécar** Andalucía, S Spain
139 U7 **Al Muqdādīyah** *var.* Al Miqdādīyah. C Iraq
140 L3 **Al Murayr** *spring/well* NW Saudi Arabia
136 M12 **Almus** Tokat, N Turkey
Al Muṣana'a *see* Al Maṣna'ah
139 T9 **Al Musayyib** *var.* Musaiyib. C Iraq
139 V9 **Al Muwaffaqīyah** S Iraq
138 H10 **Al Muwaqqar** *var.* El Muwaqqar. 'Al Āṣimah, W Jordan
140 J5 **Al Muwayliḥ** *var.* al-Mawailih. Tabūk, NW Saudi Arabia
115 F17 **Almyrós** *var.* Almirós. Thessalía, C Greece
115 I24 **Almyroú, Órmos** *bay* Kríti, Greece, E Mediterranean Sea
Al Nūwfalīyah *see* An Nawfalīyah
96 L13 **Alnwick** N England, UK
Al Obayyid *see* El Obeid
Al Odaid *see* Al 'Udayd
190 B16 **Alofi** ○ (Niue) W Niue
190 A16 **Alofi Bay** *bay* W Niue, C Pacific Ocean
190 E13 **Alofi, Île** *island* S Wallis and Futuna
190 E13 **Alofitai** Île Alofi, W Wallis and Futuna
Aloha State *see* Hawaii
118 G7 **Aloja** Limbaži, N Latvia
153 X10 **Along** Arunāchel Pradesh, NE India
115 H16 **Alónnisos** *island* Vóreioi Sporádes, Greece, Aegean Sea
104 M15 **Álora** Andalucía, S Spain
171 Q16 **Alor, Kepulauan** *island group* E Indonesia
171 Q16 **Alor, Pulau** *prev.* Ombai. *island* Kepulauan Alor, E Indonesia
168 I7 **Alor Setar** *var.* Alor Star, Alur Setar. Kedah, Peninsular Malaysia
Alost *see* Aalst
154 F9 **Ālot** Madhya Pradesh, C India
186 G10 **Alotau** Milne Bay, SE PNG
171 Y16 **Alotip** Papua, E Indonesia
Al Oued *see* El Oued
35 R12 **Alpaugh** California, W USA
Alpen *see* Alps
31 R6 **Alpena** Michigan, N USA
Alpes *see* Alps
103 S14 **Alpes-de-Haute-Provence** ◆ *department* SE France
103 U14 **Alpes-Maritimes** ◆ *department* SE France
181 W8 **Alpha** Queensland, E Australia
197 R9 **Alpha Cordillera** *var.* Alpha Ridge. *undersea feature* Arctic Ocean
Alpha Ridge *see* Alpha Cordillera
Alpheius *see* Alfeiós
99 I15 **Alphen** Noord-Brabant, S Netherlands
98 H11 **Alphen aan den Rijn** *var.* Alphen. Zuid-Holland, C Netherlands
Alpheus *see* Alfeiós
Alpi *see* Alps
104 G10 **Alpiarça** Santarém, C Portugal
24 K10 **Alpine** Texas, SW USA
108 F8 **Alpnach** Unterwalden, W Switzerland
108 D11 **Alps** *Fr.* Alpes, *Ger.* Alpen, *It.* Alpi. ▲ C Europe
141 W8 **Al Qābil** *var.* Qabil. N Oman
Al Qaḍārif *see* Gedaref
75 P8 **Al Qaddāḥīyah** N Libya
Al Qāhirah *see* Cairo
140 K4 **Al Qalībah** Tabūk, NW Saudi Arabia
139 O1 **Al Qāmishlī** *var.* Kamishli, Qamishly. Al Ḥasakah, NE Syria
138 I6 **Al Qaryatayn** *var.* Qaryatayn, *Fr.* Qariateïne. Ḥimṣ, C Syria
142 K11 **Al Qash'ānīyah** *var.* Al-Kashaniya. NE Kuwait
141 N7 **Al Qaṣīm** *off.* Minṭaqat Qaṣīm, Qassim. ◆ *province* C Saudi Arabia
138 J5 **Al Qaṣr** Ḥimṣ, C Syria
Al Qaṣr *see* El Qaṣr
Al Qaṣrayn *see* Kasserine
141 S6 **Al Qaṭīf** Ash Sharqīyah, NE Saudi Arabia
138 G11 **Al Qaṭrānah** *var.* El Qatrani, Qatrana. Al Karak, W Jordan
75 P11 **Al Qaṭrūn** SW Libya
Al Qayrawān *see* Kairouan
Al-Qsar al-Kbir *see* Ksar-el-Kebir
Al Qubayyāt *see* Qoubaïyât
Al Quds/Al Quds ash Sharīf *see* Jerusalem
104 H12 **Alqueva, Barragem do** ⊡ Portugal/Spain
138 G8 **Al Qunayṭirah** *var.* El Kuneitra, El Quneitra, Kuneitra, Qunaytra. Al Qunayṭirah, SW Syria
138 G8 **Al Qunayṭirah** *off.* Muḥāfaẓat al Qunayṭirah, *var.* El Q'unayṭirah, Qunaytirah, *Fr.* Kuneitra. ◆ *governorate* SW Syria
140 M11 **Al Qunfudhah** Makkah, SW Saudi Arabia
140 K2 **Al Qurayyāt** Al Jawf, NW Saudi Arabia
139 Y11 **Al Qurnah** *var.* Kurna. SE Iraq
139 V12 **Al Quṣayr** S Iraq
138 I6 **Al Quṣayr** *var.* El Quseir, Quṣayr, *Fr.* Kousseir. Ḥimṣ, W Syria
Al Quṣayr *see* Quseir
138 H7 **Al Quṭayfah** *var.* Quṭayfah, Qutayfe, Quteife, *Fr.* Kouteifé. Dimashq, W Syria
141 P8 **Al Quwayīyah** Ar Riyāḍ, C Saudi Arabia
Al Qūwayr *see* Guwêr
138 F14 **Al Quwayrah** *var.* El Quweira. Ma'ān, SW Jordan
Al Rayyan *see* Ar Rayyān
Al Ruweis *see* Ar Ruways
95 G24 **Als** *Ger.* Alsen. *island* SW Denmark
103 U5 **Alsace** *Ger.* Elsass; *anc.* Alsatia. ◆ *region* NE France
11 R16 **Alsask** Saskatchewan, S Canada
Alsasua *see* Altsasu
Alsatia *see* Alsace
101 C16 **Alsdorf** Nordrhein-Westfalen, W Germany
10 G8 **Alsek** ⤳ Canada/USA
Alsen *see* Als
101 F19 **Alsenz** ⤳ W Germany
101 H17 **Alsfeld** Hessen, C Germany
119 K20 **Al'shany** *Rus.* Ol'shany. Brestskaya Voblasts', SW Belarus
Alsókubin *see* Dolný Kubín
118 C9 **Alsunga** Kuldīga, W Latvia
Alt *see* Olt
92 K9 **Alta** *Fin.* Alattio. Finnmark, N Norway
29 T12 **Alta** Iowa, C USA
108 I7 **Altach** Vorarlberg, W Austria
92 K9 **Altaelva** *Lapp.* Álaheaieatnu. ⤳ N Norway
92 J8 **Altafjorden** *fjord* NE Norwegian Sea
62 K10 **Alta Gracia** Córdoba, C Argentina
42 K11 **Alta Gracia** Rivas, SW Nicaragua
54 H4 **Altagracia** Zulia, NW Venezuela
54 M5 **Altagracia de Orituco** Guárico, N Venezuela
Altai *see* Altai Mountains
122 J14 **Altai Mountains** *var.* Altai, *Chin.* Altay Shan, *Rus.* Altay. ▲ Asia/Europe
23 V6 **Altamaha River** ⤳ Georgia, SE USA
58 J13 **Altamira** Pará, NE Brazil
54 D12 **Altamira** Huila, S Colombia
42 M13 **Altamira** Alajuela, N Costa Rica
41 Q11 **Altamira** Tamaulipas, C Mexico
30 L15 **Altamont** Illinois, N USA
27 Q7 **Altamont** Kansas, C USA
32 H16 **Altamont** Oregon, NW USA
20 K10 **Altamont** Tennessee, S USA
23 X11 **Altamonte Springs** Florida, SE USA
107 O17 **Altamura** *anc.* Lupatia. Puglia, SE Italy
40 H9 **Altamura, Isla** *island* C Mexico
162 G7 **Altan** Dzavhan, W Mongolia
162 G6 **Altanbulag** Dzavhan, N Mongolia
163 Q7 **Altan Emel** *var.* Xin Barag Youqi. Nei Mongol Zizhiqu, N China
162 J8 **Altan-Ovoo** Arhangay, C Mongolia
162 E7 **Altanteel** Hovd, W Mongolia
40 F3 **Altar** Sonora, NW Mexico
40 D2 **Altar, Desierto de** *var.* Sonoran Desert. *desert* Mexico/USA **see also** Sonoran Desert
105 Q8 **Alta, Sierra** ▲ N Spain
40 H9 **Altata** Sinaloa, C Mexico
42 D4 **Alta Verapaz** *off.* Departamento de Alta Verapaz. ◆ *department* C Guatemala
107 L18 **Altavilla Silentia** Campania, S Italy
21 T7 **Altavista** Virginia, NE USA
158 L2 **Altay** Xinjiang Uygur Zizhiqu, NW China
162 G5 **Altay** Dzavhan, N Mongolia
162 G8 **Altay** *prev.* Yösönbulag. Govĭ-Altay, W Mongolia
Altay *see* Altai Mountains
122 J14 **Altay, Respublika** *var.* Gornyy Altay; *prev.* Gorno-Altayskaya Respublika. ◆ *autonomous republic* S Russian Federation
Altay Shan *see* Altai Mountains
123 I13 **Altayskiy Kray** ◆ *territory* S Russian Federation
Altbetsche *see* Bečej
101 L20 **Altdorf** Bayern, SE Germany
108 G8 **Altdorf** *var.* Altorf. Uri, C Switzerland
105 T11 **Altea** País Valenciano, E Spain
100 L10 **Alte Elde** ⤳ N Germany
101 M16 **Altenburg** Thüringen, E Germany
Altenburg *see* Bucureşti, Romania
Altenburg *see* Baia de Criş, Romania
100 P12 **Alte Oder** ⤳ NE Germany
104 H10 **Alter do Chão** Portalegre, C Portugal
92 I10 **Altevatnet** *Lapp.* Álttesjávri. ⊚ N Norway
27 V12 **Altheimer** Arkansas, C USA
109 T9 **Althofen** Kärnten, S Austria
114 H7 **Altimir** Vratsa, NW Bulgaria
136 K11 **Altınkaya Barajı** ⊡ N Turkey
139 S3 **Altin Köprü** *var.* Altun Kupri. N Iraq
136 E13 **Altıntaş** Kütahya, W Turkey
57 K18 **Altiplano** *physical region* W South America
Altkanischa *see* Kanjiža
103 U7 **Altkirch** Haut-Rhin, NE France
Altlublau *see* Stará L'ubovňa
100 L12 **Altmark** *cultural region* N Germany
Altmoldowa *see* Moldova Veche
25 W8 **Alto** Texas, SW USA
104 H11 **Alto Alentejo** *physical region* S Portugal
59 I19 **Alto Araguaia** Mato Grosso, C Brazil
58 L12 **Alto Bonito** Pará, NE Brazil
83 O15 **Alto Molócuè** Zambézia, NE Mozambique
30 K15 **Alton** Illinois, N USA
27 W8 **Alton** Missouri, C USA
11 X17 **Altona** Manitoba, S Canada
18 E14 **Altoona** Pennsylvania, NE USA
30 J6 **Altoona** Wisconsin, N USA
62 N3 **Alto Paraguay** *off.* Departamento del Alto Paraguay. ◆ *department* N Paraguay
59 L17 **Alto Paraíso de Goiás** Goiás, S Brazil
62 P6 **Alto Paraná** *off.* Departamento del Alto Paraná. ◆ *department* E Paraguay
Alto Paraná *see* Paraná
59 L15 **Alto Parnaíba** Maranhão, E Brazil
56 H13 **Alto Purús, Río** ⤳ E Peru
Altorf *see* Altdorf
63 H19 **Alto Río Senguer** *var.* Alto Río Senguerr. Chubut, S Argentina
41 Q13 **Altotonga** Veracruz-Llave, E Mexico
101 N23 **Altötting** Bayern, SE Germany
Altpasua *see* Stara Pazova
162 I5 **Altraga** Hövsgöl, N Mongolia
Alt-Schwanenburg *see* Gulbene
105 P3 **Altsasu** *Cast.* Alsasua. Navarra, N Spain
Altsohl *see* Zvolen
108 I7 **Altstätten** Sankt Gallen, NE Switzerland
Álttesjávri *see* Altevatnet
42 G1 **Altun Ha** *ruins* Belize, N Belize
Altun Kupri *see* Altin Köprü
158 D8 **Altun Shan** ▲ C China
158 L9 **Altun Shan** *var.* Altyn Tagh. ▲ NW China
35 P2 **Alturas** California, W USA
26 K12 **Altus** Oklahoma, C USA
26 K11 **Altus Lake** ⊡ Oklahoma, C USA
Altvater *see* Praděd
Altyn Tagh *see* Altun Shan
Alu *see* Shortland Island
al-'Ubaila *see* Al 'Ubaylah
139 O6 **Al 'Ubaydī** W Iraq
141 T9 **Al 'Ubaylah** *var.* al-'Ubaila. Ash Sharqīyah, E Saudi Arabia
141 T9 **Al 'Ubaylah** *spring/well* E Saudi Arabia
Al Ubayyiḍ *see* El Obeid
141 T7 **Al 'Udayd** *var.* Al Odaid. Abū Ẓaby, W UAE
118 J8 **Alūksne** *Ger.* Marienburg. Alūksne, NE Latvia
140 K6 **Al 'Ulā** Al Madīnah, NW Saudi Arabia
173 N4 **Alula-Fartak Trench** *var.* Illaue Fartak Trench. *undersea feature* W Indian Ocean
138 I11 **Al 'Umarī** 'Al Āṣimah, E Jordan
31 S13 **Alum Creek Lake** ⊡ Ohio, N USA
63 H15 **Aluminé** Neuquén, C Argentina
95 O14 **Alunda** Uppsala, C Sweden
117 T14 **Alupka** Respublika Krym, S Ukraine
75 P8 **Al 'Uqaylah** N Libya
Al Uqṣur *see* Luxor
Al Urdunn *see* Jordan
168 J9 **Alur Panal** *bay* Sumatera, W Indonesia
141 V10 **Al 'Urūq al Mu'tariḍah** *salt lake* SE Saudi Arabia
139 Q7 **Ālūs** C Iraq
117 T13 **Alushta** Respublika Krym, S Ukraine
75 U12 **Al 'Uwaynāt** SE Libya
75 N11 **Al 'Uwaynāt** *var.* Al Awaynāt. SW Libya
139 T6 **Al 'Uzaym** *var.* Adhaim. E Iraq
26 L8 **Alva** Oklahoma, C USA
104 H8 **Alva** ⤳ N Portugal
95 J18 **Älvängen** Västra Götaland, S Sweden
14 F14 **Alvanley** Ontario, S Canada
41 S14 **Alvarado** Veracruz-Llave, E Mexico
25 T7 **Alvarado** Texas, SW USA
58 D13 **Alvarães** Amazonas, NW Brazil
40 G6 **Alvaro Obregón, Presa** ⊡ W Mexico
94 H10 **Alvdal** Hedmark, S Norway
94 K12 **Älvdalen** Dalarna, C Sweden
61 E15 **Alvear** Corrientes, NE Argentina
104 F10 **Alverca do Ribatejo** Lisboa, C Portugal
95 L20 **Alvesta** Kronoberg, S Sweden
25 W12 **Alvin** Texas, SW USA
94 O13 **Älvkarleby** Uppsala, C Sweden
25 S5 **Alvord** Texas, SW USA
93 G18 **Älvros** Jämtland, C Sweden
92 J13 **Älvsbyn** Norrbotten, N Sweden
142 K12 **Al Wafrā'** SE Kuwait
140 J6 **Al Wajh** Tabūk, NW Saudi Arabia
143 N16 **Al Wakrah** *var.* Wakra. C Qatar
138 M8 **al Walaj, Sha'īb** *dry watercourse* W Iraq
152 I11 **Alwar** Rājasthān, N India
141 Q5 **Al Wari'ah** Ash Sharqīyah, N Saudi Arabia
155 G22 **Alwaye** Kerala, SW India
Alxa Zuoqi *see* Bayan Hot
Alx Youqi *see* Ehen Hudag
Al Yaman *see* Yemen
138 G9 **Al Yarmūk** Irbid, N Jordan
Alyat/Alyaty-Pristan' *see* Ələt
115 I14 **Alykí** *var.* Aliki. Thásos, N Greece
119 F14 **Alytus** *Pol.* Olita. Alytus, S Lithuania
119 F15 **Alytus** ◆ *province* S Lithuania
101 N23 **Alz** ⤳ SE Germany
33 Y11 **Alzada** Montana, NW USA
122 L12 **Alzamay** Irkutskaya Oblast', S Russian Federation
99 M25 **Alzette** ⤳ S Luxembourg
105 S10 **Alzira** *var.* Alcira; *anc.* Saetabicula, Suero. País Valenciano, E Spain
Al Zubair *see* Az Zubayr
181 O8 **Amadeus, Lake** *seasonal lake* Northern Territory, C Australia
81 E15 **Amadi** Western Equatoria, SW Sudan
9 R7 **Amadjuak Lake** ⊚ Baffin Island, Nunavut, N Canada
95 J23 **Amager** *island* E Denmark
165 N14 **Amagi-san** ▲ Honshū, S Japan
171 S13 **Amahai** *var.* Masohi. Pulau Seram, E Indonesia
38 M16 **Amak Island** *island* Alaska, USA
164 B14 **Amakusa-nada** *gulf* Kyūshū, SW Japan
95 J16 **Åmål** Västra Götaland, S Sweden
54 E8 **Amalfi** Antioquia, N Colombia
107 L18 **Amalfi** Campania, S Italy
115 D19 **Amaliáda** *var.* Amaliás. Dytikí Ellás, S Greece
Amaliás *see* Amaliáda
154 F12 **Amalner** Mahārāshtra, C India
171 W14 **Amamapare** Papua, E Indonesia
59 H21 **Amambaí, Serra de** *var.* Cordillera de Amambay, Serra de Amambay. ▲ Brazil/Paraguay **see also** Amambay, Cordillera de
62 P4 **Amambay** *off.* Departamento del Amambay. ◆ *department* E Paraguay
62 P5 **Amambay, Cordillera de** *var.* Serra de Amambaí, Serra de Amambay. ▲ Brazil/Paraguay **see also** Amambaí, Serra de
Amambay, Serra de *see* Amambaí, Serra de/Amambay, Cordillera de
165 U16 **Amami-guntō** *island group* SW Japan
165 V15 **Amami-Ō-shima** *island* S Japan
186 A5 **Amanab** Sandaun, NW PNG
106 J13 **Amandola** Marche, C Italy
107 N21 **Amantea** Calabria, SW Italy
191 W10 **Amanu** *island* Îles Tuamotu, C French Polynesia
58 J10 **Amapá** Amapá, NE Brazil
58 J11 **Amapá** *off.* Estado de Amapá; *prev.* Território de Amapá. ◆ *state* NE Brazil
42 H8 **Amapala** Valle, S Honduras
Amara *see* Al 'Amārah
104 H6 **Amarante** Porto, N Portugal
166 M5 **Amarapura** Mandalay, C Burma
162 L9 **Amardalay** Dundgovĭ, C Mongolia
104 I12 **Amareleja** Beja, S Portugal
35 V11 **Amargosa Range** ▲ California, W USA
25 N2 **Amarillo** Texas, SW USA
Amarinthos *see* Amárynthos
107 K15 **Amaro, Monte** ▲ C Italy
115 H18 **Amárynthos** *var.* Amarinthos. Évvoia, C Greece
Amasia *see* Amasya
136 K12 **Amasya** *anc.* Amasia. Amasya, N Turkey
136 K11 **Amasya** ◆ *province* N Turkey
42 F4 **Amatique, Bahía de** *bay* Gulf of Honduras, W Caribbean Sea
42 D6 **Amatitlán, Lago de** ⊚ S Guatemala
107 J14 **Amatrice** Lazio, C Italy
190 C8 **Amatuku** *atoll* C Tuvalu
99 J20 **Amay** Liège, E Belgium
58 I12 **Amazon** *Sp.* Amazonas. ⤳ Brazil/Peru
59 C14 **Amazonas** *off.* Estado do Amazonas. ◆ *state* N Brazil
54 G15 **Amazonas** *off.* Comisaria del Amazonas. ◆ *province* SE Colombia
56 C10 **Amazonas** *off.* Departamento de Amazonas. ◆ *department* N Peru
54 M12 **Amazonas** *off.* Territorio Amazonas. ◆ *federal territory* S Venezuela
Amazonas *see* Amazon
58 F13 **Amazon Basin** *basin* N South America
64 I13 **Amazon Fan** *undersea feature* W Atlantic Ocean
58 K11 **Amazon, Mouths of the** *delta* NE Brazil
187 R13 **Ambae** *var.* Aoba, Omba. *island* C Vanuatu
152 I9 **Ambāla** Haryāna, NW India
155 J26 **Ambalangoda** Southern Province, SW Sri Lanka
155 K26 **Ambalantota** Southern Province, S Sri Lanka
172 I6 **Ambalavao** Fianarantsoa, C Madagascar
54 E10 **Ambalema** Tolima, C Colombia
79 E17 **Ambam** Sud, S Cameroon
172 J2 **Ambanja** Antsiranana, N Madagascar
123 T6 **Ambarchik** Respublika Sakha (Yakutiya), NE Russian Federation
62 K9 **Ambargasta, Salinas de** *salt lake* C Argentina
124 J6 **Ambarnyy** Respublika Kareliya, NW Russian Federation
56 C7 **Ambato** Tungurahua, C Ecuador
172 I5 **Ambatolampy** Antananarivo, C Madagascar
172 H4 **Ambatomainty** Mahajanga, W Madagascar
172 J4 **Ambatondrazaka** Toamasina, C Madagascar
101 L20 **Amberg** *var.* Amberg in der Oberpfalz. Bayern, SE Germany
Amberg in der Oberpfalz *see* Amberg
42 H1 **Ambergris Cay** *island* NE Belize
103 S11 **Ambérieu-en-Bugey** Ain, E France
185 I18 **Amberley** Canterbury, South Island, NZ
103 P11 **Ambert** Puy-de-Dôme, C France
Ambianum *see* Amiens
76 J11 **Ambidédi** Kayes, SW Mali
154 M10 **Ambikāpur** Chhattīsgarh, C India
172 J2 **Ambilobe** Antsiranana, N Madagascar
39 O7 **Ambler** Alaska, USA
Amblève *see* Amel
Ambo *see* Hägere Hiywet
172 I8 **Amboasary** Toliara, S Madagascar
172 J4 **Ambodifotatra** *var.* Ambodifototra. Toamasina, E Madagascar
Amboenten *see* Ambunten
172 I5 **Ambohidratrimo** Antananarivo, C Madagascar
172 I6 **Ambohimahasoa** Fianarantsoa, SE Madagascar
172 K3 **Ambohitralanana** Antsiranana, NE Madagascar
Amboina *see* Ambon
102 M8 **Amboise** Indre-et-Loire, C France
171 S13 **Ambon** *prev.* Amboina, Amboyna. Pulau Ambon, E Indonesia
171 S13 **Ambon, Pulau** *island* E Indonesia
81 I20 **Amboseli, Lake** ⊚ Kenya/Tanzania
172 I6 **Ambositra** Fianarantsoa, SE Madagascar
172 I8 **Ambovombe** Toliara, S Madagascar
35 W14 **Amboy** California, W USA
30 L11 **Amboy** Illinois, N USA
Amboyna *see* Ambon
Ambracia *see* Árta
18 B14 **Ambridge** Pennsylvania, NE USA
Ambrim *see* Ambrym
Ambrizete *see* N'Zeto
187 R13 **Ambrym** *var.* Ambrim. *island* C Vanuatu
8 K3 **Amund Ringnes Island** *island Nunavut, N Canada*
169 T16 **Ambunten** *prev.* Amboenten. Pulau Madura, E Indonesia
186 B6 **Ambunti** East Sepik, NW PNG
155 I20 **Āmbūr** Tamil Nādu, SE India
38 E17 **Amchitka Island** *island* Aleutian Islands, Alaska, USA
38 F17 **Amchitka Pass** *strait* Aleutian Islands, Alaska, USA
141 R15 **'Amd** C Yemen
78 J10 **Am Dam** Ouaddaï, E Chad
171 U16 **Amdassa** Pulau Yamdena, E Indonesia
125 U1 **Amderma** Nenetskiy Avtonomnyy Okrug, NW Russian Federation
159 N14 **Amdo** Xizang Zizhiqu, W China
40 K13 **Ameca** Jalisco, SW Mexico
41 P14 **Amecameca** *var.* Amecameca de Juárez. México, C Mexico
Amecameca de Juárez *see* Amecameca
61 A20 **Ameghino** Buenos Aires, E Argentina
99 M21 **Amel** *Fr.* Amblève. Liège, E Belgium
98 K4 **Ameland** *Fris.* It Amelân. *island* Waddeneilanden, N Netherlands
Amelân, It *see* Ameland
107 H14 **Amelia** Umbria, C Italy
21 V6 **Amelia Court House** Virginia, NE USA
23 W8 **Amelia Island** *island* Florida, SE USA
18 L12 **Amenia** New York, NE USA
America *see* United States of America
65 M21 **America-Antarctica Ridge** *undersea feature* S Atlantic Ocean
America in Miniature *see* Maryland
60 L9 **Americana** São Paulo, S Brazil
33 Q15 **American Falls** Idaho, NW USA
33 Q15 **American Falls Reservoir** ⊡ Idaho, NW USA
36 L3 **American Fork** Utah, W USA
192 K16 **American Samoa** ◇ *US unincorporated territory* W Polynesia
23 S6 **Americus** Georgia, SE USA
98 K12 **Amerongen** Utrecht, C Netherlands
98 K11 **Amersfoort** Utrecht, C Netherlands
97 N21 **Amersham** SE England, UK
30 I5 **Amery** Wisconsin, N USA
195 W6 **Amery Ice Shelf** *ice shelf* Antarctica
29 V13 **Ames** Iowa, C USA
19 P10 **Amesbury** Massachusetts, NE USA
Amestratus *see* Mistretta
115 F18 **Amfíkleia** *var.* Amfíklia. Stereá Ellás, C Greece
Amfíklia *see* Amfíkleia
115 D17 **Amfilochía** *var.* Amfilokhía. Dytikí Ellás, C Greece
Amfilokhía *see* Amfilochía
114 H13 **Amfípoli** *anc.* Amphipolis. *site of ancient city* Kentrikí Makedonía, NE Greece
115 F18 **Ámfissa** Stereá Ellás, C Greece
123 Q10 **Amga** Respublika Sakha (Yakutiya), NE Russian Federation
123 Q11 **Amga** ⤳ NE Russian Federation
163 R7 **Amgalang** *var.* Xin Barag Zuoqi. Nei Mongol Zizhiqu, N China
123 V5 **Amguema** ⤳ NE Russian Federation
123 S12 **Amgun'** ⤳ SE Russian Federation
80 J12 **Amhara** ◆ *region* N Ethiopia
13 P15 **Amherst** Nova Scotia, SE Canada
18 M11 **Amherst** Massachusetts, NE USA
18 D10 **Amherst** New York, NE USA
24 M4 **Amherst** Texas, SW USA
21 U6 **Amherst** Virginia, NE USA
Amherst *see* Kyaikkami
14 C18 **Amherstburg** Ontario, S Canada
21 Q6 **Amherstdale** West Virginia, NE USA
14 K15 **Amherst Island** *island* Ontario, SE Canada
Amida *see* Diyarbakır
28 J6 **Amidon** North Dakota, N USA
103 O3 **Amiens** *anc.* Ambianum, Samarobriva. Somme, N France
139 P8 **'Āmij, Wādī** *var.* Wadi 'Amiq. *dry watercourse* W Iraq
136 L17 **Amik Ovası** ⊚ S Turkey
76 E9 **Amilcar Cabral** ✕ Sal, NE Cape Verde
Amilḥayt, Wādī *see* Umm al Ḥayt, Wādī
Amíndaion/Amindeo *see* Amýntaio
155 C21 **Amindivi Islands** *island group* Lakshadweep, India, N Indian Ocean
139 U6 **Amīn Ḥabīb** E Iraq
83 E20 **Aminuis** Omaheke, E Namibia
'Amiq, Wadi *see* 'Āmij, Wādī
142 J7 **Amīrābād** Īlām, NW Iran
Amirante Bank *see* Amirante Ridge
173 N6 **Amirante Basin** *undersea feature* W Indian Ocean
173 N6 **Amirante Islands** *var.* Amirantes Group. *island group* C Seychelles
173 N7 **Amirante Ridge** *var.* Amirante Bank. *undersea feature* W Indian Ocean
Amirantes Group *see* Amirante Islands
173 N7 **Amirante Trench** *undersea feature* W Indian Ocean
11 U13 **Amisk Lake** ⊚ Saskatchewan, C Canada
Amistad, Presa de la *see* Amistad Reservoir
25 O12 **Amistad Reservoir** *var.* Presa de la Amistad. ⊡ Mexico/USA
Amisus *see* Samsun
22 K8 **Amite** *var.* Amite City. Louisiana, S USA
Amite City *see* Amite
27 T12 **Amity** Arkansas, C USA

◆ Country ◇ Dependent Territory ◆ Administrative Region ▲ Mountain ☒ Volcano ⊚ Lake
● Country Capital ○ Dependent Territory Capital ✕ International Airport ▲ Mountain Range ⤳ River ⊡ Reservoir

154 H11 **Amla** *prev.* Amulla. Madhya Pradesh, C India
38 I17 **Amlia Island** *island* Aleutian Islands, Alaska, USA
97 I18 **Amlwch** NW Wales, UK
Ammaia *see* Portalegre
138 H10 **'Ammān** *var.* Amman; *anc.* Philadelphia, *Bibl.* Rabbah Ammon, Rabbath Ammon. ● (Jordan) 'Al Āṣimah, NW Jordan
'Ammān *see* 'Al Āṣimah
93 N14 **Ämmänsaari** Oulu, E Finland
92 H13 **Ammarnäs** Västerbotten, N Sweden
197 O15 **Ammassalik** *var.* Angmagssalik. Tunu, S Greenland
101 K24 **Ammer** ~ SE Germany
101 K24 **Ammersee** ◎ SE Germany
98 J13 **Ammerzoden** Gelderland, C Netherlands
Ammóchostos *see* Gazimağusa
Ammóchostos, Kólpos *see* Gazimağusa Körfezi
Amnok-kang *see* Yalu
Amoea *see* Portalegre
Amoentai *see* Amuntai
Amoerang *see* Amurang
143 O4 **Āmol** *var.* Amul. Māzandarān, N Iran
115 K21 **Amorgós** Amorgós, Kykládes, Greece, Aegean Sea
115 K22 **Amorgós** *island* Kykládes, Greece, Aegean Sea
23 N3 **Amory** Mississippi, S USA
12 I13 **Amos** Québec, SE Canada
95 G15 **Åmot** Buskerud, S Norway
95 E15 **Åmot** Telemark, S Norway
95 J15 **Åmotfors** Värmland, C Sweden
76 L10 **Amourj** Hodh ech Chargui, SE Mauritania
Amoy *see* Xiamen
172 H7 **Ampanihy** Toliara, SW Madagascar
155 L25 **Ampara** *var.* Amparai. Eastern Province, E Sri Lanka
172 J4 **Amparafaravola** Toamasina, E Madagascar
Amparai *see* Ampara
60 M9 **Amparo** São Paulo, S Brazil
172 J5 **Ampasimanolotra** Toamasina, E Madagascar
57 H17 **Ampato, Nevado** ▲ S Peru
101 L23 **Amper** ~ SE Germany
64 M9 **Ampère Seamount** *undersea feature* E Atlantic Ocean
Amphipolis *see* Amfípoli
167 X10 **Amphitrite Group** *island group* N Paracel Islands
171 T16 **Amplawas** *var.* Emplawas. Pulau Babar, E Indonesia
105 U7 **Amposta** Cataluña, NE Spain
15 V7 **Amqui** Québec, SE Canada
141 O14 **'Amrān** W Yemen
Amraoti *see* Amrāvati
154 H12 **Amrāvati** *prev.* Amraoti. Mahārāshtra, C India
154 C11 **Amreli** Gujarāt, W India
108 H6 **Amriswil** Thurgau, NE Switzerland
138 H5 **'Amrīt** *ruins* Ṭarṭūs, W Syria
152 H7 **Amritsar** Punjab, N India
152 J10 **Amroha** Uttar Pradesh, N India
100 G7 **Amrum** *island* NW Germany
93 I15 **Åmsele** Västerbotten, N Sweden
98 I10 **Amstelveen** Noord-Holland, C Netherlands
98 I10 **Amsterdam** ● (Netherlands) Noord-Holland, C Netherlands
18 K10 **Amsterdam** New York, NE USA
173 Q11 **Amsterdam Fracture Zone** *tectonic feature* S Indian Ocean
173 R11 **Amsterdam Island** *island* NE French Southern and Antarctic Territories
109 U4 **Amstetten** Niederösterreich, N Austria
78 J11 **Am Timan** Salamat, SE Chad
146 L12 **Amu-Buxoro Kanali** *var.* Aral-Bukhorskiy Kanal. *canal* C Uzbekistan
139 O1 **'Āmūdah** *var.* Amude. Al Ḥasakah, N Syria
147 O15 **Amu Darya** *Rus.* Amudar'ya, *Taj.* Dar"yoi Amu, *Turkm.* Amyderya, *Uzb.* Amudaryo; *anc.* Oxus. ~ C Asia
Amu-Dar'ya *see* Amyderýa
Amudar'ya/Amudaryo/Amu, Dar"yoi *see* Amu Darya
Amude *see* 'Āmūdah
140 L3 **'Amūd, Jabal al** ▲ NW Saudi Arabia
38 J17 **Amukta Island** *island* Aleutian Islands, Alaska, USA
38 J17 **Amukta Pass** *strait* Aleutian Islands, Alaska, USA
Amul *see* Āmol
Amulla *see* Amla
Amundsen Basin *see* Fram Basin
195 X3 **Amundsen Bay** *bay* Antarctica
195 P10 **Amundsen Coast** *physical region* Antarctica
8 I6 **Amundsen Gulf** *gulf* Northwest Territories, N Canada
193 O14 **Amundsen Plain** *undersea feature* S Pacific Ocean
195 Q9 **Amundsen-Scott** *US research station* Antarctica
194 J11 **Amundsen Sea** *sea* S Pacific Ocean
94 M12 **Amungen** ◎ C Sweden
169 U13 **Amuntai** *prev.* Amoentai. Borneo, C Indonesia
123 R14 **Amur** *Chin.* Heilong Jiang. ~ China/Russian Federation
171 Q11 **Amurang** *prev.* Amoerang. Sulawesi, C Indonesia
105 O3 **Amurrio** País Vasco, N Spain
123 S13 **Amursk** Khabarovskiy Kray, SE Russian Federation
123 Q12 **Amurskaya Oblast'** ◐ *province* SE Russian Federation
80 G7 **'Amur, Wadi** ~ NE Sudan
115 C17 **Amvrakikós Kólpos** *gulf* W Greece
Amvrosiyevka *see* Amvrosiyivka
117 X8 **Amvrosiyivka** *Rus.* Amvrosiyevka. Donets'ka Oblast', SE Ukraine
146 M14 **Amyderýa** *Rus.* Amu-Dar'ya. Lebap Welaýaty, NE Turkmenistan
Amyderya *see* Amu Darya
114 E13 **Amýntaio** *var.* Amindeo; *prev.* Amíndaion. Dytikí Makedonía, N Greece
14 B6 **Amyot** Ontario, S Canada
191 U10 **Anaa** *atoll* Îles Tuamotu, C French Polynesia
Anabanoea *see* Anabanua
171 N14 **Anabanua** *prev.* Anabanoea. Sulawesi, C Indonesia
189 R8 **Anabar** NE Nauru
123 N8 **Anabar** ~ NE Russian Federation
An Abhainn Mhór *see* Blackwater
55 O6 **Anaco** Anzoátegui, NE Venezuela
33 Q10 **Anaconda** Montana, NW USA
32 H7 **Anacortes** Washington, NW USA
26 M11 **Anadarko** Oklahoma, C USA
114 N12 **Ana Dere** ~ NW Turkey
104 G8 **Anadia** Aveiro, N Portugal
Anadolu Dağları *see* Doğu Karadeniz Dağları
123 V6 **Anadyr'** Chukotskiy Avtonomnyy Okrug, NE Russian Federation
123 V6 **Anadyr'** ~ NE Russian Federation
Anadyr, Gulf of *see* Anadyrskiy Zaliv
123 W6 **Anadyrskiy Zaliv** *Eng.* Gulf of Anadyr. *gulf* NE Russian Federation
115 K22 **Anáfi** *anc.* Anaphe. *island* Kykládes, Greece, Aegean Sea
107 J15 **Anagni** Lazio, C Italy
'Ānah *see* 'Annah
35 T15 **Anaheim** California, W USA
10 L15 **Anahim Lake** British Columbia, SW Canada
38 B8 **Anahola** Kaua'i, Hawai'i, USA, C Pacific Ocean
25 X11 **Anahuac** Texas, SW USA
41 O7 **Anáhuac** Nuevo León, NE Mexico
155 G22 **Anai Mudi** ▲ S India
Anaiza *see* 'Unayzah
155 M15 **Anakāpalle** Andhra Pradesh, E India
191 W15 **Anakena, Playa de** *beach* Easter Island, Chile, E Pacific Ocean
39 Q7 **Anaktuvuk Pass** Alaska, USA
39 Q6 **Anaktuvuk River** ~ Alaska, USA
172 J3 **Analalava** Mahajanga, NW Madagascar
44 F6 **Ana María, Golfo de** *gulf* C Cuba
Anambas Islands *see* Anambas, Kepulauan
169 N8 **Anambas, Kepulauan** *var.* Anambas Islands. *island group* W Indonesia
77 U17 **Anambra** ◐ *state* SE Nigeria
29 N4 **Anamoose** North Dakota, N USA
29 Y13 **Anamosa** Iowa, C USA
136 H17 **Anamur** İçel, S Turkey
136 H17 **Anamur Burnu** *headland* S Turkey
154 O12 **Ānandapur** Orissa, E India
155 H18 **Anantapur** Andhra Pradesh, S India
152 H5 **Anantnāg** *var.* Islamabad. Jammu and Kashmir, NW India
Ananyev *see* Anan'yiv
117 O9 **Anan'yiv** *Rus.* Ananyev. Odes'ka Oblast', SW Ukraine
126 J14 **Anapa** Krasnodarskiy Kray, SW Russian Federation
Anaphe *see* Anáfi
59 K18 **Anápolis** Goiás, C Brazil
143 R10 **Anār** Kermān, C Iran
Anār *see* Inari
143 P7 **Anārak** Eşfahān, C Iran
Anar Dara *see* Anār Darreh
148 J7 **Anār Darreh** *var.* Anar Dara. Farāh, W Afghanistan
Anárjohka *see* Inarijoki
23 X9 **Anastasia Island** *island* Florida, SE USA
188 K7 **Anatahan** *island* C Northern Mariana Islands
136 H14 **Anatolia** *plateau* C Turkey
114 H13 **Anatolikí Makedonía kai Thráki** *Eng.* Macedonia East and Thrace. ◐ *region* NE Greece
Anatom *see* Aneityum
62 L8 **Añatuya** Santiago del Estero, N Argentina
An Baile Meánach *see* Ballymena
An Bhearú *see* Barrow
An Bhóinn *see* Boyne
An Blascaod Mór *see* Great Blasket Island
An Cabhán *see* Cavan
An Caisleán Nua *see* Newcastle
An Caisleán Riabhach *see* Castlereagh, Northern Ireland, UK
An Caisleán Riabhach *see* Castlerea, Ireland
56 C13 **Ancash** *off.* Departamento de Ancash. ◐ *department* W Peru
An Cathair *see* Caher
102 J8 **Ancenis** Loire-Atlantique, NW France
An Chanáil Ríoga *see* Royal Canal
An Cheacha *see* Caha Mountains
39 R11 **Anchorage** Alaska, USA
39 R12 **Anchorage** ✕ Alaska, USA
39 Q13 **Anchor Point** Alaska, USA
An Chorr Chríochach *see* Cookstown
65 M24 **Anchorstack Point** *headland* W Tristan da Cunha
An Clár *see* Clare
An Clochán *see* Clifden
An Clochán Liath *see* Dunglow
23 U12 **Anclote Keys** *island group* Florida, SE USA
An Cóbh *see* Cobh
57 J17 **Ancohuma, Nevado de** ▲ W Bolivia
An Comar *see* Comber
57 D14 **Ancón** Lima, W Peru
106 J12 **Ancona** Marche, C Italy
Ancuabe *see* Ancuabi
82 Q13 **Ancuabi** *var.* Ancuabe. Cabo Delgado, NE Mozambique
63 F17 **Ancud** *prev.* San Carlos de Ancud. Los Lagos, S Chile
63 G17 **Ancud, Golfo de** *gulf* S Chile
Ancyra *see* Ankara
163 V8 **Anda** Heilongjiang, NE China
57 G16 **Andahuaylas** Apurímac, S Peru
An Daingean *see* Dingle
153 R15 **Andāl** West Bengal, NE India
94 E9 **Åndalsnes** Møre og Romsdal, S Norway
104 K13 **Andalucía** *Eng.* Andalusia. ◐ *autonomous community* S Spain
23 P7 **Andalusia** Alabama, S USA
Andalusia *see* Andalucía
151 Q21 **Andaman and Nicobar Islands** *var.* Andamans and Nicobars. ◐ *union territory* India, NE Indian Ocean
173 T4 **Andaman Basin** *undersea feature* NE Indian Ocean
151 P19 **Andaman Islands** *island group* India, NE Indian Ocean
173 T4 **Andaman Sea** *sea* NE Indian Ocean
57 K19 **Andamarca** Oruro, C Bolivia
182 H5 **Andamooka** South Australia
141 Y9 **'Andām, Wādī** *seasonal river* NE Oman
172 J3 **Andapa** Antsirañana, NE Madagascar
149 R4 **Andarāb** *var.* Banow. Baghlān, NE Afghanistan
Andarbag *see* Andarbogh
147 S13 **Andarbogh** *Rus.* Andarbag, Anderbak. S Tajikistan
109 Z5 **Andau** Burgenland, E Austria
108 I10 **Andeer** Graubünden, S Switzerland
92 H9 **Andenes** Nordland, C Norway
99 J20 **Andenne** Namur, SE Belgium
77 S11 **Andéramboukane** Gao, E Mali
Anderbak *see* Andarbogh
99 G18 **Anderlecht** Brussels, C Belgium
99 G21 **Anderlues** Hainaut, S Belgium
108 G9 **Andermatt** Uri, C Switzerland
101 E17 **Andernach** *anc.* Antunnacum. Rheinland-Pfalz, SW Germany
188 D15 **Andersen Air Force Base** *air base* NE Guam
39 R9 **Anderson** Alaska, USA
35 N4 **Anderson** California, W USA
31 P13 **Anderson** Indiana, N USA
27 R8 **Anderson** Missouri, C USA
21 P11 **Anderson** South Carolina, SE USA
25 V10 **Anderson** Texas, SW USA
95 K20 **Anderstorp** Jönköping, S Sweden
54 D9 **Andes** Antioquia, W Colombia
57 D14 **Andes** ▲▲ W South America
29 P12 **Andes, Lake** ◎ South Dakota, N USA
92 H9 **Andfjorden** *fjord* E Norwegian Sea
155 H16 **Andhra Pradesh** ◐ *state* E India
98 J8 **Andijk** Noord-Holland, NW Netherlands
147 S10 **Andijon** *Rus.* Andizhan. Andijon Viloyati, E Uzbekistan
147 S10 **Andijon Viloyati** *Rus.* Andizhanskaya Oblast'. ◐ *province* E Uzbekistan
Andikíthira *see* Antikýthira
172 J4 **Andilamena** Toamasina, C Madagascar
142 L8 **Andīmeshk** *var.* Andimishk; *prev.* Salehābād. Khūzestān, SW Iran
Andimishk *see* Andīmeshk
Andipáros *see* Antíparos
Andipaxi *see* Antípaxoi
Andípsara *see* Antípsara
136 L16 **Andırın** Kahramanmaraş, S Turkey
158 J8 **Andirlangar** Xinjiang Uygur Zizhiqu, NW China
Andírrion *see* Antírrio
Ándissa *see* Ántissa
Andizhan *see* Andijon
Andizhanskaya Oblast' *see* Andijon Viloyati
149 N2 **Andkhvoy** Fāryāb, N Afghanistan
105 Q2 **Andoain** País Vasco, N Spain
163 Y15 **Andong** *Jap.* Antō. E South Korea
109 R4 **Andorf** Oberösterreich, N Austria
105 S7 **Andorra** Aragón, NE Spain
105 V4 **Andorra** *off.* Principality of Andorra, *Cat.* Valls d'Andorra, *Fr.* Vallée d'Andorre. ◆ *monarchy* SW Europe
Andorra *see* Andorra la Vella
105 V4 **Andorra la Vella** *var.* Andorra, *Fr.* Andorre la Vielle, *Sp.* Andorra la Vieja. ● (Andorra) C Andorra
Andorra la Vieja *see* Andorra la Vella
Andorra, Valls d'/Andorre, Vallée d' *see* Andorra
Andorre la Vielle *see* Andorra la Vella
97 M22 **Andover** S England, UK
27 N6 **Andover** Kansas, C USA
92 G10 **Andøya** *island* C Norway
60 I8 **Andradina** São Paulo, S Brazil
39 N10 **Andreafsky River** ~ Alaska, USA
38 H17 **Andreanof Islands** *island group* Aleutian Islands, Alaska, USA
124 H16 **Andreapol'** Tverskaya Oblast', W Russian Federation
Andreas, Cape *see* Zafer Burnu
Andreevka *see* Kabanbay
21 N10 **Andrews** North Carolina, SE USA
21 T13 **Andrews** South Carolina, SE USA
24 M7 **Andrews** Texas, SW USA
173 N5 **Andrew Tablemount** *var.* Gora Andryu. *undersea feature* W Indian Ocean
Andreyevka *see* Kabanbay
107 N17 **Andria** Puglia, SE Italy
113 K16 **Andrijevica** Montenegro, SW Serbia and Montenegro (Yugo.)
115 E20 **Andrítsaina** Pelopónnisos, S Greece
An Droichead Nua *see* Newbridge
Andropov *see* Rybinsk
115 J19 **Ándros** Ándros, Kykládes, Greece, Aegean Sea
115 J20 **Ándros** *island* Kykládes, Greece, Aegean Sea
19 O7 **Androscoggin River** ~ Maine/New Hampshire, NE USA
44 F3 **Andros Island** *island* NW Bahamas
127 R7 **Androsovka** Samarskaya Oblast', W Russian Federation
44 G3 **Andros Town** Andros Island, NW Bahamas
155 D21 **Āndrott Island** *island* Lakshadweep, India, N Indian Ocean
117 N5 **Andrushivka** Zhytomyrs'ka Oblast', N Ukraine
111 K17 **Andrychów** Małopolskie, S Poland
Andryu, Gora *see* Andrew Tablemount
92 I10 **Andselv** Troms, N Norway
79 O17 **Andudu** Orientale, NE Dem. Rep. Congo
105 N13 **Andújar** *anc.* Illiturgis. Andalucía, SW Spain
82 C12 **Andulo** Bié, W Angola
103 Q14 **Anduze** Gard, S France
An Earagail *see* Errigal Mountain
95 L19 **Aneby** Jönköping, S Sweden
Anécho *see* Aného
77 Q9 **Anéfis** Kidal, NE Mali
45 U8 **Anegada** *island* NE British Virgin Islands
61 B25 **Anegada, Bahía** *bay* E Argentina
45 U9 **Anegada Passage** *passage* Anguilla/British Virgin Islands
77 R17 **Aného** *var.* Anécho; *prev.* Petit-Popo. S Togo
197 D17 **Aneityum** *var.* Anatom; *prev.* Kéamu. *island* S Vanuatu
117 N10 **Anenii Noi** *Rus.* Novyye Aneny. C Moldova
186 F7 **Anepmete** New Britain, E PNG
105 U4 **Aneto** ▲ NE Spain
146 F13 **Änew** *Rus.* Annau. Ahal Welaýaty, C Turkmenistan
Änewetak *see* Enewetak Atoll
77 Y8 **Aney** Agadez, NE Niger
An Fheoir *see* Nore
122 L12 **Angara** ~ C Russian Federation
122 M13 **Angarsk** Irkutskaya Oblast', S Russian Federation
93 G17 **Ånge** Västernorrland, C Sweden
Angel *see* Úhlava
40 D4 **Ángel de la Guarda, Isla** *island* NW Mexico
171 O3 **Angeles** *off.* Angeles City. Luzon, N Philippines
Angeles City *see* Angeles
Angel Falls *see* Ángel, Salto
95 J22 **Ängelholm** Skåne, S Sweden
61 A17 **Angélica** Santa Fe, C Argentina
25 W8 **Angelina River** ~ Texas, SW USA
55 Q9 **Ángel, Salto** *Eng.* Angel Falls. *waterfall* E Venezuela
95 M15 **Ängelsberg** Västmanland, C Sweden
35 P8 **Angels Camp** California, W USA
109 W7 **Anger** Steiermark, SE Austria
Angerapp *see* Ozersk
Angerburg *see* Węgorzewo
93 H15 **Ångermanälven** ~ N Sweden
100 P11 **Angermünde** Brandenburg, NE Germany
102 K7 **Angers** *anc.* Juliomagus. Maine-et-Loire, NW France
15 W7 **Angers** ~ Québec, SE Canada
93 J16 **Ängesön** *island* N Sweden
Angistro *see* Ágkistro
114 H13 **Angítis** ~ NE Greece
167 R13 **Ângk Tasaôm** *prev.* Angtassom. Takêv, S Cambodia
185 C25 **Anglem, Mount** ▲ Stewart Island, Southland, SW NZ
97 I18 **Anglesey** *cultural region* NW Wales, UK
97 I18 **Anglesey** *island* NW Wales, UK
102 I15 **Anglet** Pyrénées-Atlantiques, SW France
25 W12 **Angleton** Texas, SW USA
Anglia *see* England
14 H9 **Angliers** Québec, SE Canada
Anglo-Egyptian Sudan *see* Sudan
Angmagssalik *see* Ammassalik
167 Q7 **Ang Nam Ngum** ◎ C Laos
79 N16 **Ango** Orientale, N Dem. Rep. Congo
83 Q15 **Angoche** Nampula, E Mozambique
63 G14 **Angol** Araucanía, C Chile
31 Q11 **Angola** Indiana, N USA
82 A9 **Angola** *off.* Republic of Angola; *prev.* People's Republic of Angola, Portuguese West Africa. ◆ *republic* SW Africa
65 P15 **Angola Basin** *undersea feature* E Atlantic Ocean
39 X13 **Angoon** Admiralty Island, Alaska, USA
147 O14 **Angor** Surkhondaryo Wiloyati, S Uzbekistan
Angora *see* Ankara
186 C6 **Angoram** East Sepik, NW PNG
40 H8 **Angostura** Sinaloa, C Mexico
Angostura *see* Ciudad Bolívar
41 U17 **Angostura, Presa de la** ⊡ SE Mexico
28 J11 **Angostura Reservoir** ⊡ South Dakota, N USA
102 L11 **Angoulême** *anc.* Iculisma. Charente, W France
102 K11 **Angoumois** *cultural region* W France
64 O2 **Angra do Heroísmo** Terceira, Azores, Portugal, NE Atlantic Ocean
60 O10 **Angra dos Reis** Rio de Janeiro, SE Brazil
Angra Pequena *see* Lüderitz
147 Q10 **Angren** Toshkent Viloyati, E Uzbekistan
Angtassom *see* Ângk Tasaôm
167 O10 **Ang Thong** *var.* Angthong. Ang Thong, C Thailand
79 M16 **Angu** Orientale, N Dem. Rep. Congo
105 S5 **Angües** Aragón, NE Spain
45 U9 **Anguilla** ◇ *UK dependent territory* E West Indies
45 V9 **Anguilla** *island* E West Indies
44 F4 **Anguilla Cays** *islets* SW Bahamas
Angul *see* Anugul
161 N1 **Anguli Nur** ◎ E China
79 O18 **Angumu** Orientale, E Dem. Rep. Congo
14 G14 **Angus** Ontario, S Canada
96 J10 **Angus** *cultural region* E Scotland, UK
59 K19 **Anhangüera** Goiás, S Brazil
99 I21 **Anhée** Namur, S Belgium
95 I21 **Anholt** *island* C Denmark
160 M11 **Anhua** *var.* Dongping. Hunan, S China
161 P8 **Anhui** *var.* Anhui Sheng, Anhwei, Wan. ◐ *province* E China
Anhui Sheng/Anhwei *see* Anhui
39 O11 **Aniak** Alaska, USA
39 O12 **Aniak River** ~ Alaska, USA
An Iarmhí *see* Westmeath
189 R8 **Anibare** E Nauru
189 R8 **Anibare Bay** *bay* E Nauru, W Pacific Ocean
Anicium *see* le Puy
115 K22 **Ánidro** *island* Kykládes, Greece, Aegean Sea
77 R15 **Anié** C Togo
77 Q15 **Anié** ~ C Togo
102 J16 **Anie, Pic d'** ▲ SW France
127 Y7 **Anikhovka** Orenburgskaya Oblast', W Russian Federation
14 G9 **Anima Nipissing Lake** ◎ Ontario, S Canada
37 O16 **Animas** New Mexico, SW USA
37 P16 **Animas Peak** ▲ New Mexico, SW USA
37 P16 **Animas Valley** *valley* New Mexico, SW USA
116 F13 **Anina** *Ger.* Steierdorf, *Hung.* Stájerlakanina; *prev.* Ştaierdorf-Anina, Steierdorf-Anina, Steyerlak-Anina. Caraş-Severin, SW Romania
29 U14 **Anita** Iowa, C USA
123 U14 **Aniva, Mys** *headland* Ostrov Sakhalin, SE Russian Federation
187 S15 **Aniwa** *island* S Vanuatu
93 M19 **Anjalankoski** Etelä-Suomi, S Finland
'Anjar *see* Aanjar
Anjiangying *see* Luanping
14 B8 **Anjigami Lake** ◎ Ontario, S Canada
164 K14 **Anjō** *var.* Anzyô. Aichi, Honshū, SW Japan
102 J8 **Anjou** *cultural region* NW France
172 I13 **Anjouan** *var.* Nzwani, Johanna Island. *island* SE Comoros
172 J4 **Anjozorobe** Antananarivo, C Madagascar
163 W13 **Anju** W North Korea
98 M5 **Anjum** *Fris.* Eanjum. Friesland, N Netherlands
172 G6 **Ankaboa, Tanjona** *headland* W Madagascar
160 L7 **Ankang** *prev.* Xing'an. Shaanxi, C China
136 I12 **Ankara** *prev.* Angora, *anc.* Ancyra. ● (Turkey) Ankara, C Turkey
136 H12 **Ankara** ◐ *province* C Turkey
95 N19 **Ankarsrum** Kalmar, S Sweden
172 H6 **Ankazoabo** Toliara, SW Madagascar
172 I4 **Ankazobe** Antananarivo, C Madagascar
29 V14 **Ankeny** Iowa, C USA
167 U11 **An Khê** Gia Lai, C Vietnam
100 O9 **Anklam** Mecklenburg-Vorpommern, NE Germany
80 K13 **Ānkober** Amhara, N Ethiopia
77 O17 **Ankobra** ~ S Ghana
79 N22 **Ankoro** Katanga, SE Dem. Rep. Congo
99 L24 **Anlier, Forêt d'** *forest* SE Belgium
160 I13 **Anlong** Guizhou, S China
An Longfort *see* Longford
167 R11 **Ânlong Vêng** Siĕmréab, NW Cambodia
An Lorgain *see* Lurgan
161 N8 **Anlu** Hubei, C China
An Mhí *see* Meath
An Mhuir Cheilteach *see* Celtic Sea
An Muileann gCearr *see* Mullingar
93 F16 **Ann** Jämtland, C Sweden
126 M8 **Anna** Voronezhskaya Oblast', W Russian Federation
30 L17 **Anna** Illinois, N USA
25 U5 **Anna** Texas, SW USA
74 L5 **Annaba** *prev.* Bône. NE Algeria
An Nabatīyah at Taḥtā *see* Nabatîyé
101 N17 **Annaberg-Buchholz** Sachsen, E Germany
109 T9 **Annabichl** ✕ (Klagenfurt) Kärnten, S Austria
140 M5 **An Nafūd** *desert* NW Saudi Arabia
139 P6 **'Annah** *var.* 'Ānah. NW Iraq
139 P6 **An Nāḥiyah** W Iraq
139 T10 **An Najaf** *var.* Najaf. S Iraq
21 V5 **Anna, Lake** ⊡ Virginia, NE USA
97 F16 **Annalee** ~ N Ireland
167 S9 **Annamitique, Chaîne** ▲▲ C Laos
97 J14 **Annan** S Scotland, UK
29 U8 **Annandale** Minnesota, N USA
21 W4 **Annandale** Virginia, NE USA
189 Q7 **Anna Point** *headland* N Nauru
21 X3 **Annapolis** *state capital* Maryland, NE USA
188 A10 **Anna, Pulo** *island* S Palau
153 O10 **Annapurna** ▲ C Nepal
An Nāqūrah *see* En Nâqoûra
31 R10 **Ann Arbor** Michigan, N USA
An Nás *see* Naas
139 W12 **An Nāşirīyah** *var.* Nasiriya. SE Iraq
139 W11 **An Naşr** E Iraq
Annau *see* Änew
121 O13 **An Nawfalīyah** *var.* Al Nūwfalīyah. N Libya
19 P10 **Ann, Cape** *headland* Massachusetts, NE USA
180 I10 **Annean, Lake** ◎ Western Australia
Anneciacum *see* Annecy
103 T11 **Annecy** *anc.* Anneciacum. Haute-Savoie, E France
103 T11 **Annecy, Lac d'** ◎ E France
103 T10 **Annemasse** Haute-Savoie, E France
39 Z14 **Annette Island** *island* Alexander Archipelago, Alaska, USA
An Nhon *see* Binh Đinh
An Nīl al Abyaḍ *see* White Nile
An Nīl al Azraq *see* Blue Nile
23 Q3 **Anniston** Alabama, S USA
79 A19 **Annobón** *island* W Equatorial Guinea
103 R12 **Annonay** Ardèche, E France
44 K12 **Annotto Bay** C Jamaica
141 R5 **An Nu'ayrīyah** *var.* Narıya. Ash Sharqīyah, NE Saudi Arabia
182 M9 **Annuello** Victoria, SE Australia
139 Q10 **An Nukhayb** S Iraq
139 U9 **An Nu'mānīyah** E Iraq
Áno Arkhánai *see* Epáno Archánes
115 J25 **Anógeia** *var.* Anogia, Anóyia. Kríti, Greece, E Mediterranean Sea
Anogia *see* Anógeia
29 V8 **Anoka** Minnesota, N USA
An Ómaigh *see* Omagh
172 I1 **Anorontany, Tanjona** *headland* N Madagascar
172 J5 **Anosibe An'Ala** Toamasina, E Madagascar
Anóyia *see* Anógeia
An Pointe *see* Warrenpoint
161 P9 **Anqing** Anhui, E China
161 Q5 **Anqiu** Shandong, E China
An Ráth *see* Ráth Luirc
An Ribhéar *see* Kenmare River
An Ros *see* Rush
99 K19 **Ans** Liège, E Belgium
Anşāb *see* Nişāb
171 W12 **Ansas** Papua, E Indonesia
101 J20 **Ansbach** Bayern, SE Germany
An Sciobairín *see* Skibbereen
An Scoil *see* Skull
An Seancheann *see* Old Head of Kinsale
45 Y5 **Anse-Bertrand** Grande Terre, N Guadeloupe
172 H17 **Anse Boileau** Mahé, NE Seychelles
45 S11 **Anse La Raye** NW Saint Lucia
54 D9 **Anserma** Caldas, W Colombia
109 T4 **Ansfelden** Oberösterreich, N Austria
163 U12 **Anshan** Liaoning, NE China
160 J12 **Anshun** Guizhou, S China
61 F17 **Ansina** Tacuarembó, C Uruguay
29 O15 **Ansley** Nebraska, C USA
25 P6 **Anson** Texas, SW USA
77 Q10 **Ansongo** Gao, E Mali
An Srath Bán *see* Strabane
21 R5 **Ansted** West Virginia, NE USA
171 Y13 **Ansudu** Papua, E Indonesia
57 G15 **Anta** Cusco, S Peru
57 G16 **Antabamba** Apurímac, C Peru
Antafalva *see* Kovačica
136 L17 **Antakya** *anc.* Antioch, Antiochia. Hatay, S Turkey
172 K3 **Antalaha** Antsirañana, NE Madagascar
136 F17 **Antalya** *prev.* Adalia, *anc.* Attaleia, *Bibl.* Attalia. Antalya, SW Turkey
136 F17 **Antalya** ◐ *province* SW Turkey
136 F16 **Antalya** ✕ Antalya, SW Turkey
121 U10 **Antalya Basin** *undersea feature* E Mediterranean Sea
Antalya, Gulf of *see* Antalya Körfezi
136 F16 **Antalya Körfezi** *var.* Gulf of Adalia, *Eng.* Gulf of Antalya. *gulf* SW Turkey

172 J5 **Antanambao Manampotsy** Toamasina, E Madagascar
172 I5 **Antananarivo *prev.*** Tananarive. ● (Madagascar) Antananarivo, C Madagascar
172 I4 **Antananarivo** ◈ *province* C Madagascar
172 J5 **Antananarivo** ✕ Antananarivo, C Madagascar
An tAonach *see* Nenagh
204-205 **Antarctica** *continent*
194 I5 **Antarctic Peninsula** *peninsula* Antarctica
61 J15 **Antas, Rio das** ≈ S Brazil
189 U16 **Ant Atoll** *atoll* Caroline Islands, E Micronesia
An Teampall Mór *see* Templemore
Antep *see* Gaziantep
104 M15 **Antequera *anc.*** Anticaria, Antiquaria. Andalucía, S Spain
Antequera *see* Oaxaca
37 S5 **Antero Reservoir** ▣ Colorado, C USA
26 M7 **Anthony** Kansas, C USA
37 R16 **Anthony** New Mexico, SW USA
182 D5 **Anthony, Lake** *salt lake* South Australia
74 E8 **Anti-Atlas** ⛰ SW Morocco
103 U15 **Antibes *anc.*** Antipolis. Alpes-Maritimes, SE France
103 U15 **Antibes, Cap d'** *headland* SE France
Anticaria *see* Antequera
13 Q11 **Anticosti, Île d' *Eng.*** Anticosti Island. *island* Québec, E Canada
Anticosti Island *see* Anticosti, Île d'
102 K3 **Antifer, Cap d'** *headland* N France
30 L6 **Antigo** Wisconsin, N USA
13 Q15 **Antigonish** Nova Scotia, SE Canada
64 P11 **Antigua** Fuerteventura, Islas Canarias, NE Atlantic Ocean
45 X10 **Antigua** *island* S Antigua and Barbuda, Leeward Islands
Antigua *see* Antigua Guatemala
45 W9 **Antigua and Barbuda** ◆ *commonwealth republic* E West Indies
42 C6 **Antigua Guatemala *var.*** Antigua. Sacatepéquez, SW Guatemala
41 P11 **Antiguo Morelos *var.*** Antiguo-Morelos. Tamaulipas, C Mexico
115 F19 **Antíkyras, Kólpos** *gulf* C Greece
115 G24 **Antikýthira *var.*** Andikíthira. *island* S Greece
138 I7 **Anti-Lebanon *var.*** Jebel esh Sharqi, ***Ar.*** Al Jabal ash Sharqī, ***Fr.*** Anti-Liban. ⛰ Lebanon/Syria
Anti-Liban *see* Anti-Lebanon
115 I22 **Antímilos** *island* Kykládes, Greece, Aegean Sea
36 L6 **Antimony** Utah, W USA
An tInbhear Mór *see* Arklow
30 M10 **Antioch** Illinois, N USA
Antioch *see* Antakya
102 I10 **Antioche, Pertuis d'** *inlet* W France
Antiochia *see* Antakya
54 D8 **Antioquia** Antioquia, C Colombia
54 E8 **Antioquia *off.*** Departamento de Antioquia. ◈ *province* C Colombia
115 J21 **Antíparos *var.*** Andipáros. *island* Kykládes, Greece, Aegean Sea
115 B17 **Antípaxoi *var.*** Andipaxi. *island* Iónioi Nísoi, Greece, C Mediterranean Sea
122 J8 **Antipayuta** Yamalo-Nenetskiy Avtonomnyy Okrug, N Russian Federation
192 L12 **Antipodes Islands** *island group* S NZ
Antipolis *see* Antibes
115 J18 **Antípsara *var.*** Andípsara. *island* E Greece
Antiquaria *see* Antequera
15 N10 **Antique, Lac** ◎ Québec, SE Canada
115 E18 **Antírrio *var.*** Andírrion. Dytikí Ellás, C Greece
115 K16 **Ántissa *var.*** Ándissa. Lésvos, E Greece
An tIúr *see* Newry
Antivari *see* Bar
56 C6 **Antizana** ▲ N Ecuador
27 Q13 **Antlers** Oklahoma, C USA
93 J14 **Antnäs** Norrbotten, N Sweden
Antō *see* Andong
62 G5 **Antofagasta** Antofagasta, N Chile
62 G6 **Antofagasta *off.*** Región de Antofagasta. ◈ *region* N Chile
62 I7 **Antofalla, Salar de** *salt lake* NW Argentina
99 D20 **Antoing** Hainaut, SW Belgium
24 M5 **Anton** Texas, SW USA
43 S16 **Antón** Coclé, C Panama
37 T11 **Anton Chico** New Mexico, SW USA
60 K12 **Antonina** Paraná, S Brazil
103 O5 **Antony** Hauts-de-Seine, N France
Antratsit *see* Antratsyt
117 Y8 **Antratsyt *Rus.*** Antratsit. Luhans'ka Oblast', E Ukraine
97 G15 **Antrim *Ir.*** Aontroim. NE Northern Ireland, UK
97 G14 **Antrim *Ir.*** Aontroim. *cultural region* NE Northern Ireland, UK
97 G14 **Antrim Mountains** ⛰ NE Northern Ireland, UK
172 H5 **Antsalova** Mahajanga, W Madagascar
Antserana *see* Antsirañana
An tSionainn *see* Shannon
172 J2 **Antsirañana *var.*** Antserana; ***prev.*** Antsirane, Diégo-Suarez. Antsirañana, N Madagascar
172 J2 **Antsirañana** ◈ *province* N Madagascar
Antsirane *see* Antsirañana
An tSiúir *see* Suir
118 I7 **Antsla *Ger.*** Anzen. Võrumaa, SE Estonia
An tSláine *see* Slaney
172 J3 **Antsohihy** Mahajanga, NW Madagascar
63 G14 **Antuco, Volcán** ▲ C Chile
169 W10 **Antu, Gunung** ▲ Borneo, N Indonesia
An Tullach *see* Tullow
An-tung *see* Dandong
Antunnacum *see* Andernach
Antwerp *see* Antwerpen
99 G16 **Antwerpen *Eng.*** Antwerp, ***Fr.*** Anvers. Antwerpen, N Belgium
99 H16 **Antwerpen *Eng.*** Antwerp. ◈ *province* N Belgium
An Uaimh *see* Navan
154 N12 **Anugul *var.*** Angul. Orissa, E India
152 F9 **Anūpgarh** Rājasthān, NW India
154 K10 **Anūppur** Madhya Pradesh, C India
155 K24 **Anuradhapura** North Central Province, C Sri Lanka
187 S11 **Anuta** *island*, E Solomon Islands
Anvers *see* Antwerpen
194 G4 **Anvers Island** *island* Antarctica
39 N11 **Anvik** Alaska, USA
39 N10 **Anvik River** ≈ Alaska, USA
38 F17 **Anvil Peak** ▲ Semisopochnoi Island, Alaska, USA
159 P7 **Anxi *var.*** Yuanquan. Gansu, N China
182 F8 **Anxious Bay** *bay* South Australia
161 O5 **Anyang** Henan, C China
159 S11 **A'nyêmaqên Shan** ⛰ C China
118 H12 **Anykščiai** Utena, E Lithuania
161 P13 **Anyuan *var.*** Xinshan. Jiangxi, S China
123 T7 **Anyuysk** Chukotskiy Avtonomnyy Okrug, NE Russian Federation
123 T7 **Anyuyskiy Khrebet** ⛰ NE Russian Federation
54 D8 **Anza** Antioquia, C Colombia
Anzen *see* Antsla
107 I16 **Anzio** Lazio, C Italy
55 O6 **Anzoátegui *off.*** Estado Anzoátegui. ◈ *state* NE Venezuela
147 P12 **Anzob** W Tajikistan
Anzyô *see* Anjō
165 X13 **Aoga-shima** *island* Izu-shotō, SE Japan
Aohan Qi *see* Xinhui
Aoiz *see* Agoiz
186 M9 **Aola *var.*** Tenaghau. Guadalcanal, C Solomon Islands
166 M15 **Ao Luk Nua** Krabi, SW Thailand
Aomen *see* Macao
172 N8 **Aomori** Aomori, Honshū, C Japan
165 Q6 **Aomori *off.*** Aomori-ken. ◈ *prefecture* Honshū, C Japan
Aontroim *see* Antrim
117 C15 **Aóos *var.*** Vijosa, Vijosë, ***Alb.*** Lumi i Vjosës,. ≈ Albania/Greece ***see also*** Vjosës, Lumi i
191 Q7 **Aorai, Mont** ※ Tahiti, W French Polynesia
185 E19 **Aoraki *prev.*** Aorangi, Mount Cook. ▲ South Island, NZ
167 R13 **Aôral, Phnum *prev.*** Phnom Aural. ▲ W Cambodia
Aorangi *see* Aoraki
185 L15 **Aorangi Mountains** ⛰ North Island, NZ
184 H13 **Aorere** ≈ South Island, NZ
106 A7 **Aosta *anc.*** Augusta Praetoria. Valle d'Aosta, NW Italy
77 O11 **Aougoundou, Lac** ◎ S Mali
76 K9 **Aoukâr *var.*** Aouker. *plateau* C Mauritania
78 J13 **Aouk, Bahr** ≈ Central African Republic/Chad
Aouker *see* Aoukâr
74 B11 **Aousard** SE Western Sahara
164 H12 **Aoya** Tottori, Honshū, SW Japan
Aoyang *see* Shanggao
78 H5 **Aozou** Borkou-Ennedi-Tibesti, N Chad
26 M11 **Apache** Oklahoma, C USA
36 L14 **Apache Junction** Arizona, SW USA
24 J9 **Apache Mountains** ⛰ Texas, SW USA
36 M16 **Apache Peak** ▲ Arizona, SW USA
116 H10 **Apahida** Cluj, NW Romania
23 T9 **Apalachee Bay** *bay* Florida, SE USA
23 T3 **Apalachee River** ≈ Georgia, SE USA
23 S10 **Apalachicola** Florida, SE USA
23 S10 **Apalachicola Bay** *bay* Florida, SE USA
23 R9 **Apalachicola River** ≈ Florida, SE USA
Apam *see* Apan
Apamama *see* Abemama
41 P14 **Apan *var.*** Apam. Hidalgo, C Mexico
42 J8 **Apanás, Lago de** ◎ NW Nicaragua
54 H14 **Apaporis, Río** ≈ Brazil/Colombia
185 C23 **Aparima** ≈ South Island, NZ
171 O1 **Aparri** Luzon, N Philippines
112 J9 **Apatin** Serbia, NW Serbia and Montenegro (Yugo.)
124 J4 **Apatity** Murmanskaya Oblast', NW Russian Federation
55 X9 **Apatou** NW French Guiana
40 M14 **Apatzingán *var.*** Apatzingán de la Constitución. Michoacán de Ocampo, SW Mexico
171 X12 **Apauwar** Papua, E Indonesia
Apaxtla *see* Apaxtla de Castrejón
41 O15 **Apaxtla de Castrejón *var.*** Apaxtla. Guerrero, S Mexico
118 J7 **Ape** Alūksne, NE Latvia
98 L11 **Apeldoorn** Gelderland, E Netherlands
Apennines *see* Appennino
Apenrade *see* Aabenraa
57 L17 **Apere, Río** ≈ C Bolivia
55 W11 **Apetina** Sipaliwini, SE Surinam
21 U9 **Apex** North Carolina, SE USA
79 M16 **Api** Orientale, N Dem. Rep. Congo
152 M9 **Api** ▲ NW Nepal
Apia *see* Abaiang
192 H16 **Āpia** ● (Samoa) Upolu, SE Samoa
60 K11 **Apiaí** São Paulo, S Brazil
170 M16 **Api, Gunung** ▲ Pulau Sangeang, S Indonesia
187 N9 **Apio** Maramasike Island, N Solomon Islands
41 O15 **Apipilulco** Guerrero, S Mexico
41 P14 **Apizaco** Tlaxcala, S Mexico
104 I4 **A Pobla de Trives *Cast.*** Puebla de Trives. Galicia, NW Spain
55 U9 **Apoera** Sipaliwini, NW Surinam
115 O23 **Apolakkiá** Ródos, Dodekánisos, Greece, Aegean Sea
101 L16 **Apolda** Thüringen, C Germany
192 H16 **Apolima Strait** *strait* C Pacific Ocean
182 M13 **Apollo Bay** Victoria, SE Australia
Apollonia *see* Sozopol
57 J16 **Apolo** La Paz, W Bolivia
57 J16 **Apolobamba, Cordillera** ⛰ Bolivia/Peru
171 Q8 **Apo, Mount** ※ Mindanao, S Philippines
23 W11 **Apopka** Florida, SE USA
23 W11 **Apopka, Lake** ◎ Florida, SE USA
59 J19 **Aporé, Rio** ≈ SW Brazil
30 K2 **Apostle Islands** *island group* Wisconsin, N USA
Apostolas Andreas, Cape *see* Zafer Burnu
61 F14 **Apóstoles** Misiones, NE Argentina
Apostólou Andréa, Akrotíri *see* Zafer Burnu
117 S9 **Apostolove *Rus.*** Apostolovo. Dnipropetrovs'ka Oblast', E Ukraine
Apostolovo *see* Apostolove
17 S10 **Appalachian Mountains** ⛰ E USA
95 K14 **Äppelbo** Dalarna, C Sweden
98 N7 **Appelscha *Fris.*** Appelskea. Friesland, N Netherlands
Appelskea *see* Appelscha
106 G11 **Appennino *Eng.*** Apennines. ⛰ Italy/San Marino
107 L17 **Appennino Campano** ⛰ C Italy
108 I7 **Appenzell** Appenzell, NW Switzerland
108 H7 **Appenzell** ◈ *canton* NE Switzerland
55 V12 **Appikalo** Sipaliwini, S Surinam
98 O5 **Appingedam** Groningen, NE Netherlands
25 X8 **Appleby** Texas, SW USA
97 L15 **Appleby-in-Westmorland** NW England, UK
30 K10 **Apple River** ≈ Illinois, N USA
30 I5 **Apple River** ≈ Wisconsin, N USA
25 W9 **Apple Springs** Texas, SW USA
29 S8 **Appleton** Minnesota, N USA
30 M7 **Appleton** Wisconsin, N USA
27 S5 **Appleton City** Missouri, C USA
35 U14 **Apple Valley** California, W USA
29 V9 **Apple Valley** Minnesota, N USA
21 U6 **Appomattox** Virginia, NE USA
188 B16 **Apra Harbour** *harbour* W Guam
188 B16 **Apra Heights** W Guam
106 F6 **Aprica, Passo dell'** *pass* N Italy
107 M15 **Apricena *anc.*** Hadria Picena. Puglia, SE Italy
126 L14 **Apsheronsk** Krasnodarskiy Kray, SW Russian Federation
Apsheronskiy Poluostrov *see* Abşeron Yarımadası
103 S15 **Apt *anc.*** Apta Julia. Vaucluse, SE France
Apta Julia *see* Apt
38 H12 **'Āpua Point *var.*** Apua Point *headland* Hawai'i, USA, C Pacific Ocean
60 I10 **Apucarana** Paraná, S Brazil
Apulia *see* Puglia
54 K8 **Apure *off.*** Estado Apure. ◈ *state* C Venezuela
54 J7 **Apure, Río** ≈ W Venezuela
57 F16 **Apurímac *off.*** Departamento de Apurímac. ◈ *department* C Peru
57 F15 **Apurímac, Río** ≈ S Peru
116 G10 **Apuseni, Munții** ⛰ W Romania
Aqaba/'Aqaba *see* Al 'Aqabah
138 F15 **Aqaba, Gulf of *var.*** Gulf of Elat, ***Ar.*** Khalīj al 'Aqabah; ***anc.*** Sinus Aelaniticus. *gulf* NE Red Sea
139 R7 **'Aqabah** C Iraq
'Aqabah, Khalīj al *see* Aqaba, Gulf of
149 O2 **Āqchah *var.*** Āqcheh. Jowzjān, N Afghanistan
Āqcheh *see* Āqchah
Aqköl *see* Akkol'
Aqmola *see* Astana
Aqmola Oblysy *see* Akmola
158 L10 **Aqqikkol Hu** ◎ NW China
Aqqystaū *see* Akkystau
'Aqrah *see* Ākrē
Aqsay *see* Aksay
Aqshataū *see* Akchatau
Aqsū *see* Aksu
Aqsūat *see* Aksuat
Aqtas *see* Aktas
Aqtaū *see* Aktau
Aqtöbe/Aqtöbe Oblysy *see* Aktobe
Aqtoghay *see* Aktogay
Aquae Augustae *see* Dax
Aquae Calidae *see* Bath
Aquae Flaviae *see* Chaves
Aquae Grani *see* Aachen
Aquae Panoniae *see* Baden
Aquae Sextiae *see* Aix-en-Provence
Aquae Solis *see* Bath
Aquae Tarbelicae *see* Dax
36 J11 **Aquarius Mountains** ⛰ Arizona, SW USA
62 O5 **Aquidabán, Río** ≈ E Paraguay
59 H20 **Aquidauana** Mato Grosso do Sul, S Brazil
40 L15 **Aquila** Michoacán de Ocampo, S Mexico
Aquila/Aquila degli Abruzzi *see* L'Aquila
25 T8 **Aquilla** Texas, SW USA
44 L9 **Aquin** S Haiti
Aquisgranum *see* Aachen
102 J13 **Aquitaine** ◈ *region* SW France
Aqzhar *see* Akzhar
153 P13 **Āra *prev.*** Arrah. Bihār, N India
105 S4 **Ara** ≈ NE Spain
23 P2 **Arab** Alabama, S USA
Araba *see* Álava
138 G12 **'Arabah, Wādī al *Heb.*** Ha'Arava. *dry watercourse* Israel/Jordan
117 U12 **Arabats'ka Strilka, Kosa** *spit* S Ukraine
117 U12 **Arabats'ka Zatoka** *gulf* S Ukraine
'Arab, Baḩr al *see* Arab, Bahr el
80 C12 **Arab, Bahr el *var.*** Baḩr al 'Arab. ≈ S Sudan
56 E7 **Arabela, Río** ≈ N Peru
173 O4 **Arabian Basin** *undersea feature* N Arabian Sea
Arabian Desert *see* Sahara el Sharqîya
141 N9 **Arabian Peninsula** *peninsula* SW Asia
141 W14 **Arabian Sea** *sea* NW Indian Ocean
Arabicus, Sinus *see* Red Sea
'Arabī, Khalīj al *see* Gulf, The
Arabistan *see* Khūzestān
'Arabīyah as Su'ūdīyah, Al Mamlakah al *see* Saudi Arabia
'Arabīyah Jumhūrīyah, Mişr al *see* Egypt
138 I9 **'Arab, Jabal al** ⛰ S Syria
Arab Republic of Egypt *see* Egypt
Arabs Gulf *see* 'Arab, Khalîg el
139 Y12 **'Arab, Shaṭṭ al *Eng.*** Shatt al Arab, ***Per.*** Arvand Rūd. ≈ Iran/Iraq
136 I11 **Araç** Kastamonu, N Turkey
59 P16 **Aracaju** *state capital* Sergipe, E Brazil
54 F5 **Aracataca** Magdalena, N Colombia
58 P13 **Aracati** Ceará, E Brazil
60 J8 **Araçatuba** São Paulo, S Brazil
104 J13 **Aracena** Andalucía, S Spain
115 F20 **Arachnaío** ⛰ S Greece
115 D16 **Árachthos *var.*** Arta; ***prev.*** Árakhthos, ***anc.*** Arachthus. ≈ W Greece
Arachthus *see* Árachthos
59 N19 **Araçuai** Minas Gerais, SE Brazil
136 I11 **Araç Çayı** ≈ N Turkey
138 F11 **'Arad** Southern, S Israel
116 F11 **Arad** Arad, W Romania
116 F11 **Arad** ◈ *county* W Romania
78 J9 **Arada** Biltine, NE Chad
143 P18 **'Arādah** Abū Ẓaby, S UAE
Aradhippou *see* Aradíppou
121 Q3 **Aradíppou *var.*** Aradhippou. SE Cyprus
174 K6 **Arafura Sea *Ind.*** Laut Arafuru. *sea* W Pacific Ocean
174 L6 **Arafura Shelf** *undersea feature* C Arafura Sea
Arafuru, Laut *see* Arafura Sea
59 J18 **Aragarças** Goiás, C Brazil
Aragats, Gora *see* Aragats Lerr
137 T12 **Aragats Lerr *Rus.*** Gora Aragats. ▲ W Armenia
32 E14 **Arago, Cape** *headland* Oregon, NW USA
105 R6 **Aragón** ◈ *autonomous community* E Spain
105 Q4 **Aragón** ≈ NE Spain
107 I24 **Aragona** Sicilia, Italy, C Mediterranean Sea
105 Q7 **Aragoncillo** ▲ C Spain
54 L5 **Aragua *off.*** Estado Aragua. ◈ *state* N Venezuela
55 N6 **Aragua de Barcelona** Anzoátegui, NE Venezuela
55 O5 **Aragua de Maturín** Monagas, NE Venezuela
59 K15 **Araguaia, Río *var.*** Araguaya. ≈ C Brazil
59 K19 **Araguari** Minas Gerais, SE Brazil
58 J11 **Araguari, Rio** ≈ SW Brazil
Araguaya *see* Araguaia, Río
104 K14 **Arahal** Andalucía, S Spain
165 N11 **Arai** Niigata, Honshū, C Japan
Árainn *see* Inishmore
Árainn Mhór *see* Aran Island
Ara Jovis *see* Aranjuez
74 J11 **Arak** C Algeria
171 Y15 **Arak** Papua, E Indonesia
142 M7 **Arāk *prev.*** Sultānābād. Markazī, W Iran
188 D10 **Arakabesan** *island* Palau Islands, N Palau
55 S7 **Arakaka** NW Guyana
166 K6 **Arakan State *var.*** Rakhine State. ◈ *state* W Burma
166 K5 **Arakan Yoma** ⛰ W Burma
165 O10 **Arakawa** Niigata, Honshū, C Japan
Árakhthos *see* Árachthos
Araks/Arak's *see* Aras
158 H7 **Aral** Xinjiang Uygur Zizhiqu, NW China
Aral *see* Aral'sk, Kazakhstan
Aral *see* Vose', Tajikistan
Aral-Bukhorskiy Kanal *see* Amu-Buxoro Kanali
137 T12 **Aralik** Iğdır, E Turkey
146 H5 **Aral Sea *Kaz.*** Aral Tengizi, ***Rus.*** Aral'skoye More, ***Uzb.*** Orol Dengizi. *inland sea* Kazakhstan/Uzbekistan
144 L13 **Aral'sk *Kaz.*** Aral. Kzylorda, SW Kazakhstan
Aral'skoye More/Aral Tengizi *see* Aral Sea
41 O10 **Aramberri** Nuevo León, NE Mexico
186 B8 **Aramia** ≈ SW PNG
143 N6 **Ārān *var.*** Golārā. Eşfahān, C Iran
105 N5 **Aranda de Duero** Castilla-León, N Spain
112 M12 **Aranđelovac *prev.*** Arandjelovac. Serbia, C Serbia and Montenegro (Yugo.)
Arandjelovac *see* Aranđelovac
97 J19 **Aran Fawddwy** ▲ NW Wales, UK
97 C14 **Aran Island *Ir.*** Árainn Mhór. *island* NW Ireland
97 A18 **Aran Islands** *island group* W Ireland
105 N9 **Aranjuez *anc.*** Ara Jovis. Madrid, C Spain
83 E20 **Aranos** Hardap, SE Namibia
25 U14 **Aransas Bay** *inlet* Texas, SW USA
25 T14 **Aransas Pass** Texas, SW USA
191 O3 **Aranuka *prev.*** Nanouki. *atoll* Tungaru, W Kiribati
167 Q11 **Aranyaprathet** Prachin Buri, S Thailand
Aranyosasztal *see* Zlatý Stôl
Aranyosgyéres *see* Câmpia Turzii
Aranyosmarót *see* Zlaté Moravce
164 C14 **Arao** Kumamoto, Kyūshū, SW Japan
77 O8 **Araouane** Tombouctou, N Mali
26 L10 **Arapaho** Oklahoma, C USA
29 N16 **Arapahoe** Nebraska, C USA
57 I16 **Arapa, Laguna** ◎ SE Peru
185 K14 **Arapawa Island** *island* C NZ
61 E17 **Arapey Grande, Río** ≈ N Uruguay
59 P16 **Arapiraca** Alagoas, E Brazil
140 M3 **'Ar'ar** Al Ḥudūd ash Shamālīyah, NW Saudi Arabia
54 G15 **Araracuara** Caquetá, S Colombia
61 K15 **Araranguá** Santa Catarina, S Brazil
60 L8 **Araraquara** São Paulo, S Brazil
59 O13 **Araras** Ceará, E Brazil
58 I14 **Araras** Pará, N Brazil
60 L9 **Araras** São Paulo, S Brazil
60 H11 **Araras, Serra das** ⛰ S Brazil
137 U12 **Ararat** S Armenia
182 M12 **Ararat** Victoria, SE Australia
Ararat, Mount *see* Büyükağrı Dağı
140 M3 **'Ar'ar, Wādī** *dry watercourse* Iraq/Saudi Arabia
142 L1 **Aras *Arm.*** Arak's, ***Az.*** Araz Nehri, ***Per.*** Rūd-e Aras, ***Rus.*** Araks; ***prev.*** Araxes. ≈ SW Asia
105 R9 **Aras de Alpuente** País Valenciano, E Spain
137 S13 **Aras Güneyi Dağları** ⛰ NE Turkey
Aras, Rūd-e *see* Aras
191 U9 **Aratika** *atoll* Îles Tuamotu, C French Polynesia
Aratürük *see* Yiwu
54 I8 **Arauca** Arauca, NE Colombia
54 I8 **Arauca *off.*** Intendencia de Arauca. ◈ *province* NE Colombia
63 G15 **Araucanía *off.*** Región de la Araucanía. ◈ *region* C Chile
54 L7 **Arauca, Río** ≈ Colombia/Venezuela
63 F14 **Arauco** Bío Bío, C Chile
63 F14 **Arauco, Golfo de** *gulf* S Chile
54 H8 **Arauquita** Arauca, C Colombia
Arausio *see* Orange
152 F13 **Arāvali Range** ⛰ N India
186 J7 **Arawa** Bougainville Island, NE PNG
185 C20 **Arawata** ≈ South Island, NZ
186 F7 **Arawe Islands** *island group* E PNG
59 L20 **Araxá** Minas Gerais, SE Brazil
Araxes *see* Aras
55 O5 **Araya** Sucre, N Venezuela
105 R4 **Arba** ≈ N Spain
81 I15 **Ārba Minch'** Southern, S Ethiopia
139 U4 **Arbat** NE Iraq
107 D19 **Arbatax** Sardegna, Italy, C Mediterranean Sea
Arbe *see* Rab
Arbela *see* Arbīl
139 S3 **Arbīl *var.*** Erbil, Irbīl, ***Kurd.*** Hawlēr; ***anc.*** Arbela. N Iraq
95 M16 **Arboga** Västmanland, C Sweden
95 M16 **Arbogaån** ≈ C Sweden
103 S9 **Arbois** Jura, E France
54 D6 **Arboletes** Antioquia, NW Colombia
11 X15 **Arborg** Manitoba, S Canada
94 N12 **Arbrå** Gävleborg, C Sweden
96 K10 **Arbroath *anc.*** Aberbrothock. E Scotland, UK
35 N6 **Arbuckle** California, W USA
27 N12 **Arbuckle Mountains** ⛰ Oklahoma, C USA
Arbuzinka *see* Arbyzynka
117 Q8 **Arbyzynka *Rus.*** Arbuzinka. Mykolayivs'ka Oblast', S Ukraine
103 U12 **Arc** ≈ E France
102 J13 **Arcachon** Gironde, SW France
102 J13 **Arcachon, Bassin d'** *inlet* SW France
18 E10 **Arcade** New York, NE USA
23 W14 **Arcadia** Florida, SE USA
22 H5 **Arcadia** Louisiana, S USA
30 J7 **Arcadia** Wisconsin, N USA
Arcae Remorum *see* Châlons-en-Champagne
44 L9 **Arcahaie** C Haiti
34 K3 **Arcata** California, W USA
35 U6 **Arc Dome** ▲ Nevada, W USA
107 J16 **Arce** Lazio, C Italy
41 O15 **Arcelia** Guerrero, S Mexico
99 M15 **Arcen** Limburg, SE Netherlands
Archangel *see* Arkhangel'sk
Archangel Bay *see* Chëshskaya Guba
115 O23 **Archángelos *var.*** Arhangelos, Arkhángelos. Ródos, Dodekánisos, Greece, Aegean Sea
114 F7 **Archar** ≈ NW Bulgaria
31 R11 **Archbold** Ohio, N USA
105 R12 **Archena** Murcia, SE Spain
25 R5 **Archer City** Texas, SW USA
104 M14 **Archidona** Andalucía, S Spain
65 B25 **Arch Islands** *island group* SW Falkland Islands
106 G13 **Arcidosso** Toscana, C Italy
103 Q5 **Arcis-sur-Aube** Aube, N France
182 F3 **Arckaringa Creek** *seasonal river* South Australia
106 G7 **Arco** Trentino-Alto Adige, N Italy
33 Q14 **Arco** Idaho, NW USA
30 M14 **Arcola** Illinois, N USA
105 P6 **Arcos de Jalón** Castilla-León, N Spain
104 K15 **Arcos de la Frontera** Andalucía, S Spain
104 G5 **Arcos de Valdevez** Viana do Castelo, N Portugal
59 P15 **Arcoverde** Pernambuco, E Brazil
102 H5 **Arcovest, Pointe de l'** *headland* NW France
Arctic-Mid Oceanic Ridge *see* Nansen Cordillera
197 R8 **Arctic Ocean** *ocean*
8 G7 **Arctic Red River** ≈ Northwest Territories /Yukon Territory, NW Canada
Arctic Red River *see* Tsiigehtchic
39 S6 **Arctic Village** Alaska, USA
194 H1 **Arctowski** *Polish research station* South Shetland Islands, Antarctica
114 I12 **Arda *var.*** Ardhas, ***Gk.*** Ardas. ≈ Bulgaria/Greece ***see also*** Ardas
142 L2 **Ardabīl *var.*** Ardebil. Ardabīl, NW Iran
142 L2 **Ardabīl *off.*** Ostān-e Ardabīl. ◈ *province* NW Iran
137 R11 **Ardahan** Ardahan, NE Turkey
137 S11 **Ardahan** ◈ *province* NE Turkey
143 P8 **Ardakān** Yazd, C Iran
94 E12 **Årdalstangen** Sogn og Fjordane, S Norway
137 R11 **Ardanuç** Artvin, NE Turkey
114 L12 **Ardas *var.*** Ardhas, ***Bul.*** Arda. ≈ Bulgaria/Greece ***see also*** Arda
138 I13 **Arḑ aş Şawwān *var.*** Ardh es Suwwān. *plain* S Jordan
127 P5 **Ardatov** Respublika Mordoviya, W Russian Federation
14 G12 **Ardbeg** Ontario, S Canada
Ardeal *see* Transylvania
Ardebil *see* Ardabīl
103 Q13 **Ardèche** ≈ C France
103 Q13 **Ardèche** ◈ *department* E France
97 F17 **Ardee *Ir.*** Baile Átha Fhirdhia. NE Ireland
103 Q3 **Ardennes** ◈ *department* NE France
99 J23 **Ardennes** *physical region* Belgium/France
137 Q11 **Ardeşen** Rize, NE Turkey
143 O7 **Ardestān *var.*** Ardistan. Eşfahān, C Iran
108 J9 **Ardez** Graubünden, SE Switzerland
Ardhas *see* Arda/Ardas
Ardh es Suwwān *see* Arḑ aş Şawwān
104 I12 **Ardila, Ribeira de *Sp.*** Ardilla. ≈ Portugal/Spain ***see also*** Ardilla
11 T17 **Ardill** Saskatchewan, S Canada
104 I12 **Ardilla *Port.*** Ribeira de Ardila. ≈ Portugal/Spain ***see also*** Ardila, Ribeira de
40 M11 **Ardilla, Cerro la** ▲ C Mexico
114 J12 **Ardino** Kŭrdzhali, S Bulgaria
Ardistan *see* Ardestān
183 P9 **Ardlethan** New South Wales, SE Australia
Ard Mhacha *see* Armagh
23 P1 **Ardmore** Alabama, S USA
27 N13 **Ardmore** Oklahoma, C USA
20 J10 **Ardmore** Tennessee, S USA
96 G10 **Ardnamurchan, Point of** *headland* N Scotland, UK
Árdni *see* Arnøya
99 C17 **Ardooie** West-Vlaanderen, W Belgium
182 I9 **Ardrossan** South Australia
116 H9 **Ardusat *Hung.*** Erdőszáda. Maramureş, N Romania
93 F16 **Åre** Jämtland, C Sweden
79 P16 **Arebi** Orientale, NE Dem. Rep. Congo
45 T5 **Arecibo** C Puerto Rico
171 V13 **Aredo** Papua, E Indonesia
59 P14 **Areia Branca** Rio Grande do Norte, E Brazil
119 O14 **Arekhawsk *Rus.*** Orekhovsk. Vitsyebskaya Voblasts', N Belarus
Arel *see* Arlon
Arelas/Arelate *see* Arles
Arenal, Embalse de *see* Arenal Laguna
42 L12 **Arenal Laguna *var.*** Embalse de Arenal. ◎ NW Costa Rica
42 L13 **Arenal, Volcán** ※ NW Costa Rica
34 K6 **Arena, Point** *headland* California, W USA
59 H17 **Arenápolis** Mato Grosso, W Brazil

◆ COUNTRY ● COUNTRY CAPITAL ◇ DEPENDENT TERRITORY ○ DEPENDENT TERRITORY CAPITAL ◈ ADMINISTRATIVE REGION ✕ INTERNATIONAL AIRPORT ▲ MOUNTAIN ⛰ MOUNTAIN RANGE ※ VOLCANO ≈ RIVER ◎ LAKE ▣ RESERVOIR

40 G10 **Arena, Punta** *headland* W Mexico
104 L8 **Arenas de San Pedro** Castilla-León, N Spain
63 I24 **Arenas, Punta de** *headland* S Argentina
61 B20 **Arenaza** Buenos Aires, E Argentina
95 F17 **Arendal** Aust-Agder, S Norway
99 J16 **Arendonk** Antwerpen, N Belgium
43 T15 **Arenosa** Panamá, N Panama
Arensburg *see* Kuressaare
105 W5 **Arenys de Mar** Cataluña, NE Spain
106 C9 **Arenzano** Liguria, NW Italy
115 F22 **Areópoli** *prev.* Areópolis. Pelopónnisos, S Greece
Areópolis *see* Areópoli
57 H18 **Arequipa** Arequipa, SE Peru
57 G17 **Arequipa** *off.* Departamento de Arequipa. ⬖ *department* SW Peru
61 B19 **Arequito** Santa Fe, C Argentina
104 M7 **Arévalo** Castilla-León, N Spain
106 H12 **Arezzo** *anc.* Arretium. Toscana, C Italy
105 Q4 **Arga** ≈ N Spain
Argaeus *see* Erciyes Dağı
115 G17 **Argalastí** Thessalía, C Greece
105 O10 **Argamasilla de Alba** Castilla-La Mancha, C Spain
158 L8 **Argan** Xinjiang Uygur Zizhiqu, NW China
105 O8 **Arganda** Madrid, C Spain
104 H8 **Arganil** Coimbra, N Portugal
171 P6 **Argao** Cebu, C Philippines
153 V15 **Argartala** Tripura, NE India
123 N9 **Arga-Sala** ≈ NE Russian Federation
103 P17 **Argelès-sur-Mer** Pyrénées-Orientales, S France
103 T15 **Argens** ≈ SE France
106 H9 **Argenta** Emilia-Romagna, N Italy
102 K5 **Argentan** Orne, N France
103 N12 **Argentat** Corrèze, C France
106 A9 **Argentera** Piemonte, NE Italy
103 N5 **Argenteuil** Val-d'Oise, N France
62 K13 **Argentina** *off.* Republic of Argentina. ◆ *republic* S South America
Argentina Basin *see* Argentine Basin
Argentine Abyssal Plain *see* Argentine Plain
65 I19 **Argentine Basin** *var.* Argentina Basin. *undersea feature* SW Atlantic Ocean
65 I20 **Argentine Plain** *var.* Argentine Abyssal Plain. *undersea feature* SW Atlantic Ocean
Argentine Rise *see* Falkland Plateau
63 H22 **Argentino, Lago** ◎ S Argentina
102 K8 **Argenton-Château** Deux-Sèvres, W France
102 M9 **Argenton-sur-Creuse** Indre, C France
Argentoratum *see* Strasbourg
116 I12 **Argeș** ⬖ *county* S Romania
116 K14 **Argeș** ≈ S Romania
149 O8 **Arghandāb, Daryā-ye** ≈ SE Afghanistan
Arghastān *see* Arghestān
149 O8 **Arghestān** *Pash.* Arghastān. ≈ SE Afghanistan
Argirocastro *see* Gjirokastër
80 E7 **Argo** Northern, N Sudan
173 P7 **Argo Fracture Zone** *tectonic feature* C Indian Ocean
115 F20 **Argolikós Kólpos** *gulf* S Greece
103 R4 **Argonne** *physical region* NE France
115 F20 **Árgos** Pelopónnisos, S Greece
139 S1 **Argōsh** N Iraq
115 D14 **Árgos Orestikó** Dytikí Makedonía, N Greece
115 B19 **Argostóli** *var.* Argostólion. Kefallinía, Iónioi Nísoi, Greece, C Mediterranean Sea
Argostólion *see* Argostóli
Argovie *see* Aargau
35 O14 **Arguello, Point** *headland* California, W USA
127 P16 **Argun** Chechenskaya Respublika, SW Russian Federation
157 T2 **Argun** *Chin.* Ergun He, *Rus.* Argun'. ≈ China/Russian Federation
77 T12 **Argungu** Kebbi, NW Nigeria
162 J9 **Arguut** Övörhangay, C Mongolia
181 N3 **Argyle, Lake** *salt lake* Western Australia
96 G12 **Argyll** *cultural region* W Scotland, UK
Argyrokastron *see* Gjirokastër
162 I7 **Arhangay** ⬖ *province* C Mongolia
Arhangelos *see* Archángelos
95 P14 **Arholma** Stockholm, C Sweden
95 G22 **Århus** *var.* Aarhus. Århus, C Denmark
95 G22 **Århus** ⬖ *county* C Denmark
139 T1 **Āri** E Iraq
Aria *see* Herāt
83 F22 **Ariamsvlei** Karas, SE Namibia
107 L17 **Ariano Irpino** Campania, S Italy
54 F11 **Ariari, Río** ≈ C Colombia
151 K19 **Ari Atoll** *atoll* C Maldives
77 P11 **Aribinda** N Burkina
62 G2 **Arica** *hist.* San Marcos de Arica. Tarapacá, N Chile
54 H16 **Arica** Amazonas, S Colombia
62 G2 **Arica** × Tarapacá, N Chile
114 E13 **Aridaía** *var.* Aridea, Aridhaía. Dytikí Makedonía, N Greece
Aridea *see* Aridaía
172 I15 **Aride, Île** *island* Inner Islands, NE Seychelles
Aridhaía *see* Aridaía
103 N17 **Ariège** ⬖ *department* S France
102 M16 **Ariège** *var.* la Riege. ≈ Andorra/France
116 H11 **Arieș** ≈ W Romania
149 U10 **Ārifwāla** Punjab, E Pakistan
Ariguaní *see* El Difícil
138 G11 **Arīḩā** Al Karak, W Jordan
138 I3 **Arīḩā** *var.* Arīhā. Idlib, W Syria
Arīḩā *see* Jericho
37 W4 **Arikaree River** ≈ Colorado/Nebraska, C USA
164 B14 **Arikawa** Nagasaki, Nakadōri-jima, SW Japan
112 L13 **Arilje** Serbia, W Serbia and Montenegro (Yugo.)
45 U14 **Arima** Trinidad, Trinidad and Tobago
Arime *see* Al 'Arīmah
Ariminum *see* Rimini
59 H16 **Arinos, Rio** ≈ W Brazil
40 M14 **Ario de Rosales** *var.* Ario de Rosáles. Michoacán de Ocampo, SW Mexico
118 F12 **Ariogala** Kaunas, C Lithuania
59 E15 **Ariquemes** Rondônia, W Brazil
121 W13 **'Arîsh, Wâdi el** ≈ NE Egypt
54 K6 **Arismendi** Barinas, C Venezuela
10 J14 **Aristazabal Island** *island* SW Canada
60 F13 **Aristóbulo del Valle** Misiones, NE Argentina
172 I5 **Arivonimamo** × (Antananarivo) Antananarivo, C Madagascar
Arixang *see* Wenquan
105 Q6 **Ariza** Aragón, NE Spain
62 I6 **Arizaro, Salar de** *salt lake* NW Argentina
62 K13 **Arizona** San Luis, C Argentina
36 J12 **Arizona** *off.* State of Arizona; also known as Copper State, Grand Canyon State. ⬖ *state* SW USA
40 G4 **Arizpe** Sonora, NW Mexico
95 J16 **Arjäng** Värmland, C Sweden
143 P8 **Arjenān** Yazd, C Iran
92 I13 **Arjeplog** Norrbotten, N Sweden
54 E5 **Arjona** Bolívar, N Colombia
105 N13 **Arjona** Andalucía, S Spain
123 S10 **Arka** Khabarovskiy Kray, E Russian Federation
22 L2 **Arkabutla Lake** ⊠ Mississippi, S USA
127 O7 **Arkadak** Saratovskaya Oblast', W Russian Federation
27 T13 **Arkadelphia** Arkansas, C USA
115 J25 **Arkalochóri** *prev.* Arkalohori, Arkalokhórion. Kríti, Greece, E Mediterranean Sea
Arkalohori/Arkalokhórion *see* Arkalochóri
145 O10 **Arkalyk** *Kaz.* Arqalyq. Kostanay, N Kazakhstan
27 U10 **Arkansas** *off.* State of Arkansas; also known as The Land of Opportunity. ⬖ *state* S USA
27 W14 **Arkansas City** Arkansas, C USA
27 O7 **Arkansas City** Kansas, C USA
16 K11 **Arkansas River** ≈ C USA
182 J5 **Arkaroola** South Australia
Arkhángelos *see* Archángelos
124 L8 **Arkhangel'sk** *Eng.* Archangel. Arkhangel'skaya Oblast', NW Russian Federation
124 L9 **Arkhangel'skaya Oblast'** ⬖ *province* NW Russian Federation
127 O14 **Arkhangel'skoye** Stavropol'skiy Kray, SW Russian Federation
123 R14 **Arkhara** Amurskaya Oblast', S Russian Federation
97 G19 **Arklow** *Ir.* An tInbhear Mór. SE Ireland
115 M20 **Arkoí** *island* Dodekánisos, Greece, Aegean Sea
27 R11 **Arkoma** Oklahoma, C USA
100 O7 **Arkona, Kap** *headland* NE Germany
95 N17 **Arkösund** Östergötland, S Sweden
122 J6 **Arkticheskogo Instituta, Ostrova** *island* N Russian Federation
95 C15 **Arlanda** × (Stockholm) Stockholm, C Sweden
146 C11 **Arlandag** *Rus.* Gora Arlan. ▲ W Turkmenistan
Arlan, Gora *see* Arlandag
105 O5 **Arlanza** ≈ N Spain
105 N5 **Arlanzón** ≈ N Spain
103 R15 **Arles** *var.* Arles-sur-Rhône; *anc.* Arelas, Arelate. Bouches-du-Rhône, SE France
Arles-sur-Rhône *see* Arles
103 O17 **Arles-sur-Tech** Pyrénées-Orientales, S France
29 U9 **Arlington** Minnesota, N USA
29 R15 **Arlington** Nebraska, C USA
32 J11 **Arlington** Oregon, NW USA
29 R10 **Arlington** South Dakota, N USA
20 F10 **Arlington** Tennessee, S USA
25 T6 **Arlington** Texas, SW USA
21 W4 **Arlington** Virginia, NE USA
32 H7 **Arlington** Washington, NW USA
30 M10 **Arlington Heights** Illinois, N USA
77 U8 **Arlit** Agadez, C Niger
99 L24 **Arlon** *Dut.* Aarlen, *Ger.* Arel; *Lat.* Orolaunum. Luxembourg, SE Belgium
27 R7 **Arma** Kansas, C USA
97 F16 **Armagh** *Ir.* Ard Mhacha. S Northern Ireland, UK
97 F16 **Armagh** *cultural region* S Northern Ireland, UK
102 K15 **Armagnac** *cultural region* S France
103 Q7 **Armançon** ≈ C France
60 K10 **Armando Laydner, Represa** ⊠ S Brazil
115 M24 **Armathía** *island* SE Greece
126 M14 **Armavir** Krasnodarskiy Kray, SW Russian Federation
137 T12 **Armavir** *Rus.* Oktemberyan. *prev.* Hoktemberyan. SW Armenia
54 E10 **Armenia** Quindío, W Colombia
137 T12 **Armenia** *off.* Republic of Armenia, *var.* Ajastan, *Arm.* Hayastani Hanrapetut'yun; *prev.* Armenian Soviet Socialist Republic. ◆ *republic* SW Asia
Armenierstadt *see* Gherla
103 O1 **Armentières** Nord, N France
40 K14 **Armería** Colima, SW Mexico
183 T5 **Armidale** New South Wales, SE Australia
29 P11 **Armour** South Dakota, N USA
61 B18 **Armstrong** Santa Fe, C Argentina
11 N16 **Armstrong** British Columbia, SW Canada
12 D11 **Armstrong** Ontario, S Canada
29 U11 **Armstrong** Iowa, C USA
25 S16 **Armstrong** Texas, SW USA
117 S11 **Armyans'k** *Rus.* Armyansk. Respublika Krym, S Ukraine
115 H14 **Arnaía** *var.* Arnea. Kentrikí Makedonía, N Greece
121 N2 **Arnaoúti, Akrotíri** *var.* Arnaoútis, Cape Arnaouti. *headland* W Cyprus
Arnaouti, Cape/Arnaoútis *see* Arnaoúti, Akrotíri
12 L4 **Arnaud** ≈ Québec, E Canada
103 Q8 **Arnay-le-Duc** Côte d'Or, C France
Arnea *see* Arnaía
105 Q4 **Arnedo** La Rioja, N Spain
95 I14 **Årnes** Akershus, S Norway
Årnes *see* Åi Åfjord
26 K9 **Arnett** Oklahoma, C USA
98 L12 **Arnhem** Gelderland, SE Netherlands
181 Q2 **Arnhem Land** *physical region* Northern Territory, N Australia
106 F11 **Arno** ≈ C Italy
Arno *see* Arno Atoll
189 W7 **Arno Atoll** *var.* Arno. *atoll* Ratak Chain, NE Marshall Islands
182 H8 **Arno Bay** South Australia
35 Q8 **Arnold** California, W USA
27 X5 **Arnold** Missouri, C USA
29 N15 **Arnold** Nebraska, C USA
109 R10 **Arnoldstein** *Slvn.* Pod Klošter. Kärnten, S Austria
103 N9 **Arnon** ≈ C France
45 P14 **Arnos Vale** × (Kingstown) Saint Vincent, SE Saint Vincent and the Grenadines
92 I8 **Arnøya** *Lapp.* Árdni *island* N Norway
14 L12 **Arnprior** Ontario, SE Canada
101 G15 **Arnsberg** Nordrhein-Westfalen, W Germany
101 K16 **Arnstadt** Thüringen, C Germany
Arnswalde *see* Choszczno
54 K5 **Aroa** Yaracuy, N Venezuela
83 E21 **Aroab** Karas, SE Namibia
115 E19 **Ároania** ▲ S Greece
191 O6 **Aroa, Pointe** *headland* Moorea, W French Polynesia
Aroe Islands *see* Aru, Kepulauan
101 H15 **Arolsen** Niedersachsen, C Germany
106 C7 **Arona** Piemonte, NE Italy
19 R3 **Aroostook River** ≈ Canada/USA
Arop Island *see* Long Island
38 M12 **Aropuk Lake** ◎ Alaska, USA
191 P4 **Arorae** *atoll* Tungaru, W Kiribati
190 G16 **Arorangi** Rarotonga, S Cook Islands
108 I9 **Arosa** Graubünden, S Switzerland
104 F4 **Arousa, Ría de** *estuary* E Atlantic Ocean
184 P8 **Arowhana** ▲ North Island, NZ
137 V12 **Arp'a** *Az.* Arpaçay. ≈ Armenia/Azerbaijan
137 S11 **Arpaçay** Kars, NE Turkey
Arpaçay *see* Arp'a
Arqalyq *see* Arkalyk
149 N14 **Arra** ≈ SW Pakistan
Arrabona *see* Győr
Arrah *see* Āra
Ar Rahad *see* Er Rahad
139 R9 **Ar Raḩḩālīyah** C Iraq
60 Q10 **Arraial do Cabo** Rio de Janeiro, SE Brazil
104 H11 **Arraiolos** Évora, S Portugal
139 R8 **Ar Ramādī** *var.* Ramadi, Rumadiya. SW Iraq
138 J6 **Ar Rāmī** Ḩimş, C Syria
Ar Rams *see* Rams
138 H9 **Ar Ramthā** *var.* Ramtha. Irbid, N Jordan
96 H13 **Arran, Isle of** *island* SW Scotland, UK
138 L3 **Ar Raqqah** *var.* Rakka; *anc.* Nicephorium. Ar Raqqah, N Syria
138 L3 **Ar Raqqah** *off.* Muḩāfaẓat al Raqqah, *var.* Raqqah, *Fr.* Rakka. ⬖ *governorate* N Syria
103 O2 **Arras** *anc.* Nemetocenna. Pas-de-Calais, N France
Arrasate *see* Mondragón
138 G12 **Ar Rashādīyah** Aṭ Ṭafīlah, W Jordan
138 I5 **Ar Rastān** *var.* Rastâne. Ḩimş, W Syria
139 X12 **Ar Raṭāwī** E Iraq
102 L15 **Arrats** ≈ S France
141 N10 **Ar Rawḑah** Makkah, S Saudi Arabia
141 Q15 **Ar Rawḑah** S Yemen
142 K11 **Ar Rawḑatayn** *var.* Raudhatain. N Kuwait
143 N16 **Ar Rayyān** *var.* Al Rayyan. C Qatar
102 L17 **Arreau** Hautes-Pyrénées, S France
64 Q11 **Arrecife** *var.* Arrecife de Lanzarote, Puerto Arrecife. Lanzarote, Islas Canarias, NE Atlantic Ocean
Arrecife de Lanzarote *see* Arrecife
43 P6 **Arrecife Edinburgh** *reef* NE Nicaragua
61 C19 **Arrecifes** Buenos Aires, E Argentina
102 F6 **Arrée, Monts d'** ▲ NW France
Ar Refa'i *see* Ar Rifā'ī
Arretium *see* Arezzo
Arriaca *see* Guadalajara
109 S9 **Arriach** Kärnten, S Austria
41 T16 **Arriaga** Chiapas, SE Mexico
41 N12 **Arriaga** San Luis Potosí, C Mexico
139 W10 **Ar Rifā'ī** *var.* Ar Refa'i. SE Iraq
139 V12 **Ar Riḩāb** *salt flat* S Iraq
104 L2 **Arriondas** Asturias, N Spain
141 Q7 **Ar Riyāḑ** *Eng.* Riyadh. ● (Saudi Arabia) Ar Riyāḑ, C Saudi Arabia
141 O8 **Ar Riyāḑ** *off.* Minṭaqat ar Riyāḑ. ⬖ *province* C Saudi Arabia
141 S15 **Ar Riyān** S Yemen
Arrö *see* Ærø
61 H18 **Arroio Grande** Rio Grande do Sul, S Brazil
102 K15 **Arros** ≈ S France
103 Q9 **Arroux** ≈ C France
25 R5 **Arrowhead, Lake** ⊠ Texas, SW USA
182 L5 **Arrowsmith, Mount** *hill* New South Wales, SE Australia
185 D21 **Arrowtown** Otago, South Island, NZ
61 D17 **Arroyo Barú** Entre Ríos, E Argentina
104 J10 **Arroyo de la Luz** Extremadura, W Spain
63 J16 **Arroyo de la Ventana** Río Negro, SE Argentina
35 P13 **Arroyo Grande** California, W USA
Ar Ru'ays *see* Ar Ruways
141 R11 **Ar Rub' al Khālī** *Eng.* Empty Quarter, Great Sandy Desert. *desert* SW Asia
139 V13 **Ar Ruḑaymah** S Iraq
61 A16 **Arrufó** Santa Fe, C Argentina
138 I7 **Ar Ruḩaybah** *var.* Ruhaybeh, *Fr.* Rouhaïbé. Dimashq, W Syria
139 V15 **Ar Rukhaymīyah** *well* S Iraq
139 U11 **Ar Rumaythah** *var.* Rumaitha. S Iraq
141 X8 **Ar Rustāq** *var.* Rostak, Rustaq. N Oman
139 N8 **Ar Ruṭbah** *var.* Rutba. SW Iraq
140 M3 **Ar Rūthīyah** *spring/well* NW Saudi Arabia
ar-Ruwaida *see* Ar Ruwayḑah
141 O8 **Ar Ruwayḑah** *var.* ar-Ruwaida. Jīzān, C Saudi Arabia
143 N15 **Ar Ruways** *var.* Al Ruweis, Ar Ru'ays, Ruwais. N Qatar
143 O17 **Ar Ruways** *var.* Ar Ru'ays, Ruwaisv. Abū Ẓaby, W UAE
Ārs *see* Aars
Arsanias *see* Murat Nehri
123 S15 **Arsen'yev** Primorskiy Kray, SE Russian Federation
155 G19 **Arsikere** Karnātaka, W India
127 R3 **Arsk** Respublika Tatarstan, W Russian Federation
94 N10 **Årskogen** Gävleborg, C Sweden
121 O3 **Ársos** C Cyprus
94 N13 **Årsunda** Gävleborg, C Sweden
Arta *see* Árachthos
115 C17 **Árta** *anc.* Ambracia. Ípeiros, W Greece
137 T12 **Artashat** S Armenia
40 M15 **Arteaga** Michoacán de Ocampo, SW Mexico
123 S15 **Artem** Primorskiy Kray, SE Russian Federation
44 C4 **Artemisa** La Habana, W Cuba
117 W7 **Artemivs'k** Donets'ka Oblast', E Ukraine
122 K13 **Artemovsk** Krasnoyarskiy Kray, S Russian Federation
105 U5 **Artesa de Segre** Cataluña, NE Spain
37 U14 **Artesia** New Mexico, SW USA
25 Q14 **Artesia Wells** Texas, SW USA
108 G8 **Arth** Schwyz, C Switzerland
14 F15 **Arthur** Ontario, S Canada
30 M14 **Arthur** Illinois, N USA
28 L14 **Arthur** Nebraska, C USA
29 Q5 **Arthur** North Dakota, N USA
185 B21 **Arthur** ≈ South Island, NZ
18 B13 **Arthur, Lake** ⊠ Pennsylvania, NE USA
183 N15 **Arthur River** ≈ Tasmania, SE Australia
185 G18 **Arthur's Pass** Canterbury, South Island, NZ
185 G17 **Arthur's Pass** *pass* South Island, NZ
44 I3 **Arthur's Town** Cat Island, C Bahamas
44 M9 **Artibonite, Rivière de l'** ≈ C Haiti
61 E16 **Artigas** *prev.* San Eugenio, San Eugenio del Cuareim. Artigas, N Uruguay
61 E16 **Artigas** ⬖ *department* N Uruguay
194 H1 **Artigas** *Uruguayan research station* Antarctica
137 T11 **Art'ik** W Armenia
187 O16 **Art, Île** *island* Îles Belep, W New Caledonia
103 O2 **Artois** *cultural region* N France
136 L12 **Artova** Tokat, N Turkey
105 Y9 **Artrutx, Cap d'** *var.* Cabo Dartuch. *headland* Menorca, Spain, W Mediterranean Sea
Artsiz *see* Artsyz
117 N11 **Artsyz** *Rus.* Artsiz. Odes'ka Oblast', SW Ukraine
158 E7 **Artux** Xinjiang Uygur Zizhiqu, NW China
137 R11 **Artvin** Artvin, NE Turkey
137 R11 **Artvin** ⬖ *province* NE Turkey
146 G14 **Artyk** Ahal Welaýaty, C Turkmenistan
79 Q16 **Aru** Orientale, NE Dem. Rep. Congo
81 E17 **Arua** NW Uganda
104 I4 **A Rúa de Valdeorras** *var.* La Rúa. Galicia, NW Spain
Aruângua *see* Luangwa
45 O15 **Aruba** *var.* Oruba. ◇ *Dutch autonomous region* S West Indies
Aru Islands *see* Aru, Kepulauan
171 W15 **Aru, Kepulauan** *Eng.* Aru Islands; *prev.* Aroe Islands. *island group* E Indonesia
153 W10 **Arunāchal Pradesh** *prev.* North East Frontier Agency, North East Frontier Agency of Assam. ⬖ *state* NE India
Arun Qi *see* Naji
155 H23 **Aruppukkottai** Tamil Nādu, SE India
81 I20 **Arusha** Arusha, N Tanzania
81 J21 **Arusha** ⬖ *region* E Tanzania
81 I20 **Arusha** × Arusha, N Tanzania
54 C9 **Arusí, Punta** *headland* NW Colombia
155 J23 **Aruvi Aru** ≈ NW Sri Lanka
79 M17 **Aruwimi** *var.* Ituri (upper course). ≈ NE Dem.Rep. Congo
Árva *see* Orava
37 T4 **Arvada** Colorado, C USA
Arvand Rūd *see* 'Arab, Shaṭṭ al
162 J8 **Arvayheer** Övörhangay, C Mongolia
9 O10 **Arviat** *prev.* Eskimo Point. Nunavut, C Canada
93 I14 **Arvidsjaur** Norrbotten, N Sweden
95 J15 **Arvika** Värmland, C Sweden
92 J8 **Årviksand** Troms, N Norway
35 S13 **Arvin** California, W USA
163 S8 **Arxan** Nei Mongol Zizhiqu, N China
145 P7 **Arykbalyk** *Kaz.* Aryqbalyq. Severnyy Kazakhstan, N Kazakhstan
Aryqbalyq *see* Arykbalyk
145 P17 **Arys'** *Kaz.* Arys. Yuzhnyy Kazakhstan, S Kazakhstan
Arys *see* Orzysz
Arys Köli *see* Arys, Ozero
145 O14 **Arys, Ozero** *Kaz.* Arys Köli. ◎ C Kazakhstan
107 D16 **Arzachena** Sardegna, Italy, C Mediterranean Sea
127 O4 **Arzamas** Nizhegorodskaya Oblast', W Russian Federation
141 V13 **Arzāt** S Oman
104 H3 **Arzúa** Galicia, NW Spain
111 A16 **Aš** *Ger.* Asch. Karlovarský Kraj, W Czech Republic
95 H15 **Ås** Akershus, S Norway
95 H20 **Asaa** *prev.* Åsa. Nordjylland, N Denmark
Aså *see* Asaa
83 E21 **Asab** Karas, S Namibia
77 U16 **Asaba** Delta, S Nigeria
149 S4 **Asadābād** *var.* Asadābād; *prev.* Chaghasarāy. Kunar, E Afghanistan
138 K3 **Asad, Buḩayrat al** ◎ N Syria
63 H20 **Asador, Pampa del** *plain* S Argentina
165 P14 **Asahi** Chiba, Honshū, S Japan
164 M11 **Asahi** Toyama, Honshū, SW Japan
165 T3 **Asahi-dake** ▲ Hokkaidō, N Japan
165 T3 **Asahikawa** Hokkaidō, N Japan
147 S10 **Asaka** *Rus.* Assake; *prev.* Leninsk. Andijon Viloyati, E Uzbekistan
77 P17 **Asamankese** SE Ghana
188 B15 **Asan** W Guam
188 B15 **Asan Point** *headland* W Guam
153 R15 **Āsānsol** West Bengal, NE India
80 K12 **Āsayita** Afar, NE Ethiopia
171 T12 **Asbakin** Papua, E Indonesia
Asben *see* Aïr, Massif de l'
15 Q12 **Asbestos** Québec, SE Canada
29 Y13 **Asbury** Iowa, C USA
18 K15 **Asbury Park** New Jersey, NE USA
41 Z12 **Ascención, Bahiá de la** *bay* NW Caribbean Sea
40 I3 **Ascensión** Chihuahua, N Mexico
65 M14 **Ascension Fracture Zone** *tectonic feature* C Atlantic Ocean
65 G14 **Ascension Island** ◇ *dependency of St. Helena* C Atlantic Ocean
65 N16 **Ascension Island** *island* C Atlantic Ocean
Asch *see* Aš
109 S3 **Aschach an der Donau** Oberösterreich, N Austria
101 H18 **Aschaffenburg** Bayern, SW Germany
101 F14 **Ascheberg** Nordrhein-Westfalen, W Germany
101 L14 **Aschersleben** Sachsen-Anhalt, C Germany
106 G12 **Asciano** Toscana, C Italy
106 J13 **Ascoli Piceno** *anc.* Asculum Picenum. Marche, C Italy
107 M17 **Ascoli Satriano** *anc.* Asculub, Asculum Apulum. Puglia, SE Italy
108 G11 **Ascona** Ticino, S Switzerland
Asculub *see* Ascoli Satriano
Asculum Picenum *see* Ascoli Piceno
80 L11 **Āseb** *var.* Assab, *Amh.* Āseb. SE Eritrea
95 M20 **Åseda** Kronoberg, S Sweden
127 T6 **Asekeyevo** Orenburgskaya Oblast', W Russian Federation
81 J14 **Āsela** *var.* Asella, Aselle, Asselle. Oromo, C Ethiopia
93 H15 **Åsele** Västerbotten, N Sweden
Asella/Aselle *see* Āsela
94 K12 **Åsen** Dalarna, C Sweden
114 J11 **Asenovgrad** *prev.* Stanimaka. Plovdiv, C Bulgaria
171 O13 **Asera** Sulawesi, C Indonesia
95 E17 **Åseral** Vest-Agder, S Norway
118 J3 **Aseri** *var.* Asserien, *Ger.* Asserin. Ida-Virumaa, NE Estonia
40 J10 **Aserradero** Durango, W Mexico
146 F13 **Aşgabat** *prev.* Ashgabat, Ashkhabad, Poltoratsk. ● (Turkmenistan) Ahal Welaýaty, C Turkmenistan
146 F13 **Aşgabat** × Ahal Welaýaty, C Turkmenistan
95 H16 **Åsgårdstrand** Vestfold, S Norway
Ashara *see* Al 'Ashārah
23 T6 **Ashburn** Georgia, SE USA
185 G19 **Ashburton** Canterbury, South Island, NZ
185 G19 **Ashburton** ≈ South Island, NZ
180 H8 **Ashburton River** ≈ Western Australia
145 V10 **Ashchysu** ≈ E Kazakhstan
10 M16 **Ashcroft** British Columbia, SW Canada
138 E10 **Ashdod** *anc.* Azotos, *Lat.* Azotus. Central, W Israel
27 S14 **Ashdown** Arkansas, C USA
21 T9 **Asheboro** North Carolina, SE USA
11 X15 **Ashern** Manitoba, S Canada
21 P10 **Asheville** North Carolina, SE USA
12 E8 **Asheweig** ≈ Ontario, C Canada
27 V9 **Ash Flat** Arkansas, C USA
183 T4 **Ashford** New South Wales, SE Australia
97 P22 **Ashford** SE England, UK
36 K11 **Ash Fork** Arizona, SW USA
Ashgabat *see* Aşgabat
27 T7 **Ash Grove** Missouri, C USA
165 O12 **Ashikaga** *var.* Asikaga. Tochigi, Honshū, S Japan
165 Q8 **Ashiro** Iwate, Honshū, C Japan
164 F15 **Ashizuri-misaki** *headland* Shikoku, SW Japan
Ashkelon *see* Ashqelon
Ashkhabad *see* Aşgabat
23 Q4 **Ashland** Alabama, S USA
26 K7 **Ashland** Kansas, C USA
21 P5 **Ashland** Kentucky, S USA
19 S2 **Ashland** Maine, NE USA
22 M1 **Ashland** Mississippi, S USA
27 U4 **Ashland** Missouri, C USA
29 S15 **Ashland** Nebraska, C USA
31 T12 **Ashland** Ohio, N USA
32 G15 **Ashland** Oregon, NW USA
21 W6 **Ashland** Virginia, NE USA
30 K3 **Ashland** Wisconsin, N USA
20 I8 **Ashland City** Tennessee, S USA
183 S4 **Ashley** New South Wales, SE Australia
29 O7 **Ashley** North Dakota, N USA
173 W7 **Ashmore and Cartier Islands** ◇ *Australian external territory* E Indian Ocean
119 I14 **Ashmyany** *Rus.* Oshmyany. Hrodzyenskaya Voblasts', W Belarus
18 K12 **Ashokan Reservoir** ⊠ New York, NE USA
165 U4 **Ashoro** Hokkaidō, NE Japan
138 E10 **Ashqelon** *var.* Ashkelon. Southern, C Israel
Ashraf *see* Behshahr
139 O3 **Ash Shadādah** *var.* Ash Shaddādah, Jisr ash Shadadi, Shaddādī, Shedadi, Tell Shedadi. Al Ḩasakah, NE Syria
Ash Shaddādah *see* Ash Shadādah
139 Y12 **Ash Shāfī** E Iraq
139 R4 **Ash Shakk** *var.* Shaykh. C Iraq
Ash Sham/Ash Shām *see* Dimashq
139 T10 **Ash Shāmīyah** *var.* Shamiya. C Iraq
139 Y13 **Ash Shāmīyah** *var.* Al Bādiyah al Janūbīyah. *desert* S Iraq
139 T11 **Ash Shanāfīyah** *var.* Ash Shināfiyah. S Iraq
138 G13 **Ash Sharāh** *var.* Esh Sharā. ▲ W Jordan
143 R16 **Ash Shāriqah** *Eng.* Sharjah. Ash Shāriqah, NE UAE
143 R16 **Ash Shāriqah** *var.* Sharjah. × Ash Shāriqah, NE UAE
140 I4 **Ash Sharmah** *var.* Šarma. Tabūk, NW Saudi Arabia
139 R4 **Ash Sharqāṭ** NW Iraq
141 S10 **Ash Sharqīyah** *off.* Al Minṭaqah ash Sharqīyah, *Eng.* Eastern Region. ⬖ *province* E Saudi Arabia
139 W11 **Ash Shaṭrah** *var.* Shatra. SE Iraq
138 G13 **Ash Shawbak** Ma'ān, W Jordan
138 L5 **Ash Shaykh Ibrāhīm** Ḩimş, C Syria
141 O17 **Ash Shaykh 'Uthmān** SW Yemen
141 S15 **Ash Shiḩr** SE Yemen
Ash Shināfiyah *see* Ash Shanāfīyah
141 V12 **Ash Shişar** *var.* Shisur. SW Oman
139 S13 **Ash Shubrūm** *well* S Iraq
141 R10 **Ash Shuqqān** *desert* E Saudi Arabia
75 O9 **Ash Shuwayrif** *var.* Ash Shwayrif. N Libya
Ash Shwayrif *see* Ash Shuwayrif
31 U10 **Ashtabula** Ohio, N USA
29 Q5 **Ashtabula, Lake** ⊠ North Dakota, N USA
137 T12 **Ashtarak** W Armenia
142 M6 **Āshtīān** *var.* Āshtiyān. Markazī, W Iran
Āshtiyān *see* Āshtīān
33 R13 **Ashton** Idaho, NW USA
13 O10 **Ashuanipi Lake** ◎ Newfoundland and Labrador, E Canada
15 P6 **Ashuapmushuan** ≈ Québec, SE Canada
23 Q3 **Ashville** Alabama, S USA
31 S14 **Ashville** Ohio, N USA

◆ Country ◇ Dependent Territory ⬖ Administrative Region ▲ Mountain ⩚ Volcano ◎ Lake
● Country Capital ○ Dependent Territory Capital × International Airport ▲ Mountain Range ≈ River ⊠ Reservoir

30 K3 **Ashwabay, Mount** *hill* Wisconsin, N USA
171 T11 **Asia, Kepulauan** *island group* E Indonesia
154 N13 **Āsika** Orissa, E India
Asikaga *see* Ashikaga
93 M18 **Asikkala** *var.* Vääksy. Etelä-Suomi, S Finland
74 G5 **Asilah** N Morocco
'Aṣī, Nahr al *see* Orontes
107 B16 **Asinara, Isola** *island* W Italy
122 J12 **Asino** Tomskaya Oblast', C Russian Federation
119 O14 **Asintorf** *Rus.* Osintorf. Vitsyebskaya Voblasts', N Belarus
119 L17 **Asipovichy** *Rus.* Osipovichi. Mahilyowskaya Voblasts', C Belarus
141 N12 **'Asīr** *off.* Minṭaqat 'Asīr. ◐ *province* SW Saudi Arabia
140 M11 **'Asīr** *Eng.* Asir. ⛰ SW Saudi Arabia
139 X10 **Askal** E Iraq
137 P13 **Aşkale** Erzurum, NE Turkey
117 T11 **Askaniya-Nova** Khersons'ka Oblast', S Ukraine
95 H15 **Asker** Akershus, S Norway
95 L17 **Askersund** Örebro, C Sweden
Askī Kalak *see* Eski Kaļak
95 I15 **Askim** Østfold, S Norway
127 V3 **Askino** Respublika Bashkortostan, W Russian Federation
115 D14 **Áskio** ⛰ N Greece
152 L9 **Askot** Uttaranchal, N India
94 C12 **Askvoll** Sogn og Fjordane, S Norway
136 A13 **Aslan Burnu** *headland* W Turkey
136 L16 **Aslantaş Barajı** ⊟ S Turkey
149 S4 **Asmār** *var.* Bar Kunar. Kunar, E Afghanistan
80 I9 **Asmara** *Amh.* Āsmera. ● (Eritrea) C Eritrea
Āsmera *see* Asmara
95 L21 **Åsnen** ◎ S Sweden
115 F19 **Asopós** ≈ S Greece
171 W13 **Asori** Papua, E Indonesia
80 G12 **Āsosa** Benishangul, W Ethiopia
32 M10 **Asotin** Washington, NW USA
Aspadana *see* Eşfahān
Aspang *see* Aspang Markt
109 X6 **Aspang Markt** *var.* Aspang. Niederösterreich, E Austria
105 S12 **Aspe** País Valenciano, E Spain
37 R5 **Aspen** Colorado, C USA
25 P6 **Aspermont** Texas, SW USA
Asphaltites, Lacus *see* Dead Sea
Aspinwall *see* Colón
185 C20 **Aspiring, Mount** ▲ South Island, NZ
115 B16 **Asprókavos, Akrotírio** *headland* Kérkyra, Iónioi Nísoi, Greece, C Mediterranean Sea
Aspropótamos *see* Achelóos
Assab *see* Aseb
76 J10 **Assaba** *var.* Açâba. ◐ *region* S Mauritania
138 L4 **As Sabkhah** *var.* Sabkha. Ar Raqqah, NE Syria
139 U6 **As Sa'dīyah** E Iraq
Assad, Lake *see* Asad, Buḩayrat al
138 I8 **Aş Şafā** ▲ S Syria
138 I10 **Aş Şafāwī** Al Mafraq, N Jordan
Aş Şaff *see* El Şaff
139 N2 **Aş Şafīḩ** Al Ḩasakah, N Syria
Aş Şaḩrā' al Gharbīyah *see* Sahara el Gharbîya
Aş Şaḩrā' ash Sharqīyah *see* Sahara el Sharqîya
Assake *see* Asaka
As Salamīyah *see* Salamīyah
141 Q4 **As Sālimī** *var.* Salemy. SW Kuwait
As Sallūm *see* Salûm
139 T13 **As Salmān** S Iraq
138 G10 **As Salṭ** *var.* Salt. Al Balqā', NW Jordan
142 M16 **As Salwā** *var.* Salwa, Salwah. S Qatar
153 V12 **Assam** ◐ *state* NE India
Assamaka *see* Assamakka
77 T8 **Assamakka** *var.* Assamaka. Agadez, NW Niger
139 U11 **As Samāwah** *var.* Samawa. S Iraq
As Saqia al Hamra *see* Saguia al Hamra
138 J4 **Aş Şā'rān** Ḩamāh, C Syria
138 G9 **Aş Şarīḩ** Irbid, N Jordan
21 Z5 **Assateague Island** *island* Maryland, NE USA
139 O6 **As Sayyāl** *var.* Sayyāl. Dayr az Zawr, E Syria
99 G18 **Asse** Vlaams Brabant, C Belgium
99 D16 **Assebroek** West-Vlaanderen, NW Belgium
Asselle *see* Āsela
107 C20 **Assemini** Sardegna, Italy, C Mediterranean Sea
98 N7 **Assen** Drenthe, NE Netherlands
99 E16 **Assenede** Oost-Vlaanderen, NW Belgium
95 G24 **Assens** Fyn, C Denmark
Asserien/Asserin *see* Aseri
99 I21 **Assesse** Namur, SE Belgium
141 Y8 **As Sīb** *var.* Seeb. NE Oman
139 Z13 **As Sībah** *var.* Sibah. SE Iraq
11 T17 **Assiniboia** Saskatchewan, S Canada
11 V15 **Assiniboine** ≈ Manitoba, S Canada
11 P16 **Assiniboine, Mount** ▲ Alberta/British Columbia, SW Canada
Assiout *see* Asyūt
60 J9 **Assis** São Paulo, S Brazil
106 I13 **Assisi** Umbria, C Italy
Assiut *see* Asyūt
Assling *see* Jesenice
Assouan *see* Aswân
Assu *see* Açu
Assuan *see* Aswân
142 K12 **Aş Şubayḩīyah** *var.* Subiyah. S Kuwait
141 R16 **As Sufāl** S Yemen
138 L5 **As Sukhnah** *var.* Sukhne, *Fr.* Soukhné. Ḩimş, C Syria
139 U4 **As Sulaymānīyah** *var.* Sulaimaniya, *Kurd.* Slēmānī. NE Iraq
141 P11 **As Sulayyil** Ar Riyāḍ, S Saudi Arabia
121 O13 **As Sulṭān** N Libya
141 Q5 **Aş Şummān** *desert* N Saudi Arabia
141 Q16 **Aş Şurrah** SW Yemen
139 N4 **Aş Şuwār** *var.* Şuwār. Dayr az Zawr, E Syria
138 H9 **As Suwaydā'** *var.* El Suweida, Es Suweida, Suweida, *Fr.* Soueida. As Suwaydā', SW Syria
138 H9 **As Suwaydā'** *off.* Muḩāfaẓat as Suwaydā', *var.* As Suwaydā, Suwaydā, Suweida, *Fr.* Soueida. ◐ *governorate* S Syria
141 Z9 **As Suwayḩ** NE Oman
141 X8 **As Suwayq** *var.* Suwaik. N Oman
139 T8 **Aş Şuwayrah** *var.* Suwaira. E Iraq
As Suways *see* Suez
Asta Colonia *see* Asti
Astacus *see* İzmit
115 M23 **Astakída** *island* SE Greece
145 Q9 **Astana** *prev.* Akmola, Akmolinsk, Tselinograd, Aqmola. ● (Kazakhstan) Akmola, N Kazakhstan
142 M3 **Āstāneh** Gīlān, NW Iran
Asta Pompeia *see* Asti
137 Y14 **Astara** S Azerbaijan
Astarabad *see* Gorgān
99 L15 **Asten** Noord-Brabant, SE Netherlands
Asterābād *see* Gorgān
106 C8 **Asti** *anc.* Asta Colonia, Asta Pompeia, Hasta Colonia, Hasta Pompeia. Piemonte, NW Italy
Astigi *see* Ecija
Astipálaia *see* Astypálaia
148 L16 **Astola Island** *island* SW Pakistan
152 H4 **Astor** Jammu and Kashmir, NW India
104 K4 **Astorga** *anc.* Asturica Augusta. Castilla-León, N Spain
32 F10 **Astoria** Oregon, NW USA
95 J22 **Åstorp** Skåne, S Sweden
Astrabad *see* Gorgān
127 Q13 **Astrakhan'** Astrakhanskaya Oblast', SW Russian Federation
Astrakhan-Bazar *see* Cälilabad
127 Q11 **Astrakhanskaya Oblast'** ◐ *province* SW Russian Federation
93 J15 **Åsträsk** Västerbotten, N Sweden
Astrida *see* Butare
65 O22 **Astrid Ridge** *undersea feature* S Atlantic Ocean
187 P15 **Astrolabe, Récifs de l'** *reef* C New Caledonia
121 P2 **Astromerítis** N Cyprus
115 F20 **Ástros** Pelopónnisos, S Greece
119 G16 **Astryna** *Rus.* Ostryna. Hrodzyenskaya Voblasts', W Belarus
104 J2 **Asturias** ◐ *autonomous community* NW Spain
Asturias *see* Oviedo
Asturica Augusta *see* Astorga
115 L22 **Astypálaia** *var.* Astipálaia, *It.* Stampalia. *island* Kykládes, Greece, Aegean Sea
192 G16 **Asuisui, Cape** *headland* Savai'i, W Samoa
195 S2 **Asuka** *Japanese research station* Antarctica
62 O6 **Asunción** ● (Paraguay) Central, S Paraguay
62 O6 **Asunción** × Central, S Paraguay
188 K3 **Asuncion Island** *island* N Northern Mariana Islands
42 E6 **Asunción Mita** Jutiapa, SE Guatemala
Asunción Nochixtlán *see* Nochixtlán
40 E3 **Asunción, Río** ≈ NW Mexico
95 M18 **Åsunden** ◎ S Sweden
118 K11 **Asvyeya** *Rus.* Osveya. Vitsyebskaya Voblasts', N Belarus
Aswa *see* Achwa
75 X11 **Aswân** *var.* Assouan, Assuan; *anc.* Syene. SE Egypt
75 X11 **Aswan High Dam** *dam* SE Egypt
75 W9 **Asyût** *var.* Assiout, Assiut, Siut; *anc.* Lycopolis. C Egypt
193 W15 **Ata** *island* Tongatapu Group, SW Tonga
62 G8 **Atacama** *off.* Región de Atacama. ◐ *region* C Chile
Atacama Desert *see* Atacama, Desierto de
62 H4 **Atacama, Desierto de** *Eng.* Atacama Desert. *desert* N Chile
62 I6 **Atacama, Puna de** ⛰ NW Argentina
62 I5 **Atacama, Salar de** *salt lake* N Chile
54 E11 **Ataco** Tolima, C Colombia
190 H8 **Atafu Atoll** *island* NW Tokelau
190 H8 **Atafu Village** Atafu Atoll, NW Tokelau
74 K12 **Atakor** ⛰ SE Algeria
77 R14 **Atakora, Chaîne de l'** *var* Atakora Mountains. ⛰ N Benin
Atakora Mountains *see* Atakora, Chaîne de l'
77 R16 **Atakpamé** C Togo
146 F11 **Atakui** Ahal Welaýaty, C Turkmenistan
58 B13 **Atalaia do Norte** Amazonas, N Brazil
146 M14 **Atamyrat** *prev.* Kerki. Lebap Welaýaty, E Turkmenistan
76 J7 **Aṭâr** Adrar, W Mauritania
162 G10 **Atas Bogd** ▲ SW Mongolia
35 P12 **Atascadero** California, W USA
25 S13 **Atascosa River** ≈ Texas, SW USA
145 R11 **Atasu** Karaganda, C Kazakhstan
145 R12 **Atasu** ≈ C Kazakhstan
193 V15 **Atata** *island* Tongatapu Group, S Tonga
136 H10 **Atatürk** × (İstanbul) İstanbul, NW Turkey
137 N16 **Atatürk Barajı** ⊟ S Turkey
Atax *see* Aude
80 G8 **Atbara** *var.* 'Aṭbāra. River Nile, NE Sudan
80 H8 **Atbara** *var.* Nahr 'Aṭbarah. ≈ Eritrea/Sudan
'Aṭbārah/'Aṭbarah, Nahr *see* Atbara
145 P9 **Atbasar** Akmola, N Kazakhstan
At-Bashi *see* At-Bashy
147 W9 **At-Bashy** *var.* At-Bashi. Narynskaya Oblast', C Kyrgyzstan
22 I10 **Atchafalaya Bay** *bay* Louisiana, S USA
22 I8 **Atchafalaya River** ≈ Louisiana, S USA
Atchin *see* Aceh
27 Q3 **Atchison** Kansas, C USA
77 P16 **Atebubu** C Ghana
105 Q6 **Ateca** Aragón, NE Spain
40 K11 **Atengo, Río** ≈ C Mexico
Aternum *see* Pescara
107 K15 **Atessa** Abruzzo, C Italy
Ateste *see* Este
99 E19 **Ath** *var.* Aat. Hainaut, SW Belgium
11 Q13 **Athabasca** Alberta, SW Canada
11 Q12 **Athabasca** *var.* Athabaska. ≈ Alberta, SW Canada
11 R10 **Athabasca, Lake** ◎ Alberta/Saskatchewan, SW Canada
Athabaska *see* Athabasca
115 C16 **Athamánon** ⛰ C Greece
97 F17 **Athboy** *Ir.* Baile Átha Buí. E Ireland
Athenae *see* Athína
97 C18 **Athenry** *Ir.* Baile Átha an Rí. W Ireland
23 P2 **Athens** Alabama, S USA
23 T3 **Athens** Georgia, SE USA
31 T14 **Athens** Ohio, N USA
20 M10 **Athens** Tennessee, S USA
25 V7 **Athens** Texas, SW USA
Athens *see* Athína
115 B18 **Athéras, Akrotírio** *headland* Kefallinía, Iónioi Nísoi, Greece, C Mediterranean Sea
181 W4 **Atherton** Queensland, NE Australia
81 I19 **Athi** ≈ S Kenya
121 Q2 **Athíenou** SE Cyprus
115 H19 **Athína** *Eng.* Athens; *prev.* Athínai, *anc.* Athenae. ● (Greece) Attikí, C Greece
Athínai *see* Athína
139 S10 **Athīyah** C Iraq
97 D18 **Athlone** *Ir.* Baile Átha Luain. C Ireland
155 F16 **Athni** Karnātaka, W India
185 C23 **Athol** Southland, South Island, NZ
19 N11 **Athol** Massachusetts, NE USA
115 I15 **Áthos** ▲ NE Greece
Athos, Mount *see* Ágion Óros
Ath Thawrah *see* Madīnat ath Thawrah
141 P5 **Ath Thumāmī** *spring/well* N Saudi Arabia
99 L25 **Athus** Luxembourg, SE Belgium
97 E19 **Athy** *Ir.* Baile Átha Í. C Ireland
78 I10 **Ati** Batha, C Chad
81 F16 **Atiak** NW Uganda
57 G17 **Atico** Arequipa, SW Peru
105 O6 **Atienza** Castilla-La Mancha, C Spain
39 Q6 **Atigun Pass** *pass* Alaska, USA
12 B12 **Atikokan** Ontario, S Canada
13 O9 **Atikonak Lac** ◎ Newfoundland and Labrador, E Canada
42 C6 **Atitlán, Lago de** ◎ W Guatemala
190 L16 **Atiu** *island* S Cook Islands
Atjeh *see* Aceh
123 T9 **Atka** Magadanskaya Oblast', E Russian Federation
38 H17 **Atka** Atka Island, Alaska, USA
38 H17 **Atka Island** *island* Aleutian Islands, Alaska, USA
127 O7 **Atkarsk** Saratovskaya Oblast', W Russian Federation
27 U11 **Atkins** Arkansas, C USA
29 O13 **Atkinson** Nebraska, C USA
171 T12 **Atkri** Papua, E Indonesia
41 O13 **Atlacomulco** *var.* Atlacomulco de Fabela. México, C Mexico
Atlacomulco de Fabela *see* Atlacomulco
23 S3 **Atlanta** *state capital* Georgia, SE USA
31 R6 **Atlanta** Michigan, N USA
25 X6 **Atlanta** Texas, SW USA
29 T15 **Atlantic** Iowa, C USA
21 Y10 **Atlantic** North Carolina, SE USA
23 W8 **Atlantic Beach** Florida, SE USA
18 J17 **Atlantic City** New Jersey, NE USA
172 L14 **Atlantic-Indian Basin** *undersea feature* SW Indian Ocean
172 K13 **Atlantic-Indian Ridge** *undersea feature* SW Indian Ocean
54 E4 **Atlántico** *off.* Departamento del Atlántico. ◐ *province* NW Colombia
64-65 **Atlantic Ocean** *ocean*
42 K7 **Atlántico Norte, Región Autónoma** *prev.* Zelaya Norte. ◐ *autonomous region* NE Nicaragua
42 L10 **Atlántico Sur, Región Autónoma** *prev.* Zelaya *Sur.* ◐ *autonomous region* SE Nicaragua
42 I5 **Atlántida** ◐ *department* N Honduras
77 Y15 **Atlantika Mountains** ⛰ E Nigeria
64 J10 **Atlantis Fracture Zone** *tectonic feature* NW Atlantic Ocean
74 H7 **Atlas Mountains** ⛰ NW Africa
123 V11 **Atlasova, Ostrov** *island* SE Russian Federation
123 V10 **Atlasovo** Kamchatskaya Oblast', E Russian Federation
120 G11 **Atlas Saharien** *var.* Saharan Atlas. ⛰ Algeria/Morocco
Atlas, Tell *see* Atlas Tellien
120 H10 **Atlas Tellien** *Eng.* Tell Atlas. ⛰ N Algeria
10 I9 **Atlin** British Columbia, W Canada
10 I9 **Atlin Lake** ◎ British Columbia, W Canada
41 P14 **Atlixco** Puebla, S Mexico
94 B11 **Atløyna** *island* S Norway
155 I17 **Ātmakūr** Andhra Pradesh, C India
23 O8 **Atmore** Alabama, S USA
101 J20 **Atmühl** ≈ S Germany
94 H11 **Atna** ≈ S Norway
164 E13 **Atō** Yamaguchi, Honshū, SW Japan
57 L21 **Atocha** Potosí, S Bolivia
27 P12 **Atoka** Oklahoma, C USA
27 O12 **Atoka Lake** *var.* Atoka Reservoir. ⊟ Oklahoma, C USA
Atoka Reservoir *see* Atoka Lake
33 Q14 **Atomic City** Idaho, NW USA
40 L10 **Atotonilco** Zacatecas, C Mexico
40 M13 **Atotonilco el Alto** *var.* Atotonilco. Jalisco, SW Mexico
77 N7 **Atouila, 'Erg** *desert* N Mali
41 N16 **Atoyac** *var.* Atoyac de Alvarez. Guerrero, S Mexico
Atoyac de Alvarez *see* Atoyac
41 P15 **Atoyac, Río** ≈ S Mexico
39 O5 **Atqasuk** Alaska, USA
Atrak/Atrak, Rūd-e *see* Etrek
95 J20 **Ätran** ≈ S Sweden
54 C7 **Atrato, Río** ≈ NW Colombia
Atrek *see* Etrek
107 K14 **Atri** Abruzzo, C Italy
Atria *see* Adria
165 P9 **Atsumi** Yamagata, Honshū, C Japan
165 S3 **Atsuta** Hokkaidō, NE Japan
143 Q17 **Aṭ Ṭaff** *desert* C UAE
138 G12 **Aṭ Ṭafīlah** *var.* Et Tafila, Tafila. Aṭ Ṭafīlah, W Jordan
138 G12 **Aṭ Ṭafīlah** *off.* Muḩāfaẓat aṭ Ṭafīlah. ◐ *governorate* W Jordan
140 L10 **Aṭ Ṭā'if** Makkah, W Saudi Arabia
Attaleia/Attalia *see* Antalya
23 Q3 **Attalla** Alabama, S USA
138 L2 **At Tall al Abyaḑ** *var.* Tall al Abyaḑ, Tell Abyad, *Fr.* Tell Abiad. Ar Raqqah, N Syria
138 L7 **Aṭ Ṭanf** Ḩimş, S Syria
Attapu *see* Samakhixai
139 S10 **At Ṭaqṭaqānah** C Iraq
115 O23 **Attávytos** ▲ Ródos, Dodekánisos, Greece, Aegean Sea
139 V15 **At Tawal** *desert* Iraq/Saudi Arabia
12 G9 **Attawapiskat** Ontario, C Canada
12 F9 **Attawapiskat** ≈ Ontario, S Canada
12 D9 **Attawapiskat Lake** ◎ Ontario, C Canada
At Taybé *see* Ṭayyibah
101 F16 **Attendorn** Nordrhein-Westfalen, W Germany
109 R5 **Attersee** Salzburg, NW Austria
109 R5 **Attersee** ◎ N Austria
99 L24 **Attert** Luxembourg, SE Belgium
138 M4 **At Tibnī** *var.* Tibnī. Dayr az Zawr, NE Syria
31 N13 **Attica** Indiana, N USA
18 E10 **Attica** New York, NE USA
Attica *see* Attikí
13 N7 **Attikamagen Lake** ◎ Newfoundland and Labrador, E Canada
115 H20 **Attikí** *Eng.* Attica. ◐ *region* C Greece
19 O12 **Attleboro** Massachusetts, NE USA
109 R5 **Attnang** Oberösterreich, N Austria
149 U6 **Attock City** Punjab, E Pakistan
Attopeu *see* Samakhixai
25 X8 **Attoyac River** ≈ Texas, SW USA
38 D16 **Attu** Attu Island, Alaska, USA
139 Y12 **Aṭ Ṭūbah** E Iraq
140 K4 **Aṭ Ṭubayq** *plain* Jordan/Saudi Arabia
38 C16 **Attu Island** *island* Aleutian Islands, Alaska, USA
Aṭ Ṭūr *see* El Ṭûr
155 I21 **Āttūr** Tamil Nādu, SE India
141 N17 **At Turbah** SW Yemen
62 I12 **Atuel, Río** ≈ C Argentina
Atugi *see* Atsugi
191 X7 **Atuona** Hiva Oa, NE French Polynesia
Aturus *see* Adour
95 M18 **Åtvidaberg** Östergötland, S Sweden
35 P9 **Atwater** California, W USA
29 T8 **Atwater** Minnesota, N USA
26 I2 **Atwood** Kansas, C USA
31 U12 **Atwood Lake** ⊟ Ohio, N USA
127 P5 **Atyashevo** Respublika Mordoviya, W Russian Federation
144 F12 **Atyrau** *prev.* Gur'yev. Atyrau, W Kazakhstan
144 E11 **Atyrau** *off.* Atyrauskaya Oblast', *var. Kaz.* Atyraū Oblysy; *prev.* Gur'yevskaya Oblast'. ◐ *province* W Kazakhstan
Atyraū Oblysy/Atyrauskaya Oblast' *see* Atyrau
108 I7 **Au** Vorarlberg, NW Austria
186 B4 **Aua Island** *island* NW PNG
103 S16 **Aubagne** *anc.* Albania. Bouches-du-Rhône, SE France
99 L25 **Aubange** Luxembourg, SE Belgium
103 Q6 **Aube** ◐ *department* N France
103 R6 **Aube** ≈ N France
99 L19 **Aubel** Liège, E Belgium
103 Q13 **Aubenas** Ardèche, E France
103 O8 **Aubigny-sur-Nère** Cher, C France
103 O13 **Aubin** Aveyron, S France
103 O13 **Aubrac, Monts d'** ⛰ S France
36 J10 **Aubrey Cliffs** *cliff* Arizona, SW USA
23 R5 **Auburn** Alabama, S USA
35 P6 **Auburn** California, W USA
30 K14 **Auburn** Illinois, N USA
31 Q11 **Auburn** Indiana, N USA
20 J7 **Auburn** Kentucky, S USA
19 P8 **Auburn** Maine, NE USA
19 N11 **Auburn** Massachusetts, NE USA
29 S16 **Auburn** Nebraska, C USA
18 H10 **Auburn** New York, NE USA
32 H8 **Auburn** Washington, NW USA
103 N11 **Aubusson** Creuse, C France
118 E10 **Auce** *Ger.* Autz. Dobele, SW Latvia
102 L15 **Auch** *Lat.* Augusta Auscorum, Elimberrum. Gers, S France
77 U16 **Auchi** Edo, S Nigeria
23 T9 **Aucilla River** ≈ Florida/Georgia, SE USA
184 L6 **Auckland** Auckland, North Island, NZ
184 K5 **Auckland** *off.* Auckland Region. ◐ *region* North Island, NZ
184 L6 **Auckland** × Auckland, North Island, NZ
192 J12 **Auckland Islands** *island group* S NZ
103 O16 **Aude** ◐ *department* S France
103 N16 **Aude** *anc.* Atax. ≈ S France
Audenarde *see* Oudenaarde
Audern *see* Audru
102 E6 **Audierne** Finistère, NW France
102 E6 **Audierne, Baie d'** *bay* NW France
103 U7 **Audincourt** Doubs, E France
118 G5 **Audru** *Ger.* Audern. Pärnumaa, SW Estonia
29 T14 **Audubon** Iowa, C USA
101 N17 **Aue** Sachsen, E Germany
100 H12 **Aue** ≈ NW Germany
100 L9 **Auerbach** Bayern, SE Germany
101 M17 **Auerbach** Sachsen, E Germany
108 I10 **Auererrhein** ≈ SW Switzerland
101 N17 **Auersberg** ▲ E Germany
181 W9 **Augathella** Queensland, E Australia
31 Q12 **Auglaize River** ≈ Ohio, N USA
83 F22 **Augrabies Falls** *waterfall* W South Africa
31 R7 **Au Gres River** ≈ Michigan, N USA
Augsbourg *see* Augsburg
101 K22 **Augsburg** *Fr.* Augsbourg; *anc.* Augusta Vindelicorum. Bayern, S Germany
180 I14 **Augusta** Western Australia
107 L25 **Augusta** *It.* Agosta. Sicilia, Italy, C Mediterranean Sea
27 W11 **Augusta** Arkansas, C USA
23 V3 **Augusta** Georgia, SE USA
27 O6 **Augusta** Kansas, C USA
19 Q7 **Augusta** *state capital* Maine, NE USA
33 Q8 **Augusta** Montana, NW USA
Augusta *see* London
Augusta Auscorum *see* Auch
Augusta Emerita *see* Mérida
Augusta Praetoria *see* Aosta
Augusta Suessionum *see* Soissons
Augusta Trajana *see* Stara Zagora
Augusta Treverorum *see* Trier
Augusta Vangionum *see* Worms
Augusta Vindelicorum *see* Augsburg
95 G24 **Augustenborg** *Ger.* Augustenburg. Sønderjylland, SW Denmark
Augustenburg *see* Augustenborg
39 Q13 **Augustine Island** *island* Alaska, USA
14 L9 **Augustines, Lac des** ◎ Québec, SE Canada
Augustobona Tricassium *see* Troyes
Augustodunum *see* Autun
Augustodurum *see* Bayeux
Augustoritum Lemovicensium *see* Limoges
110 O8 **Augustów** *Rus.* Avgustov. Podlaskie, NE Poland
Augustow Canal *see* Augustowski, Kanał
110 O8 **Augustowski, Kanał** *Eng.* Augustow Canal, *Rus.* Avgustovskiy Kanal. *canal* NE Poland
180 I9 **Augustus, Mount** ▲ Western Australia
186 M9 **Auki** Malaita, N Solomon Islands
21 W8 **Aulander** North Carolina, SE USA
180 L7 **Auld, Lake** *salt lake* Western Australia
Aulie Ata/Auliye-Ata *see* Taraz
144 M8 **Auliyekol'** *prev.* Semiozernoye. Kostanay, N Kazakhstan
106 E10 **Aulla** Toscana, C Italy
102 F6 **Aulne** ≈ NW France
Aulong *see* Ulong
37 T3 **Ault** Colorado, C USA
Avlum *see* Aulum
103 N3 **Aumale** Seine-Maritime, N France
Auminzatau, Gory *see* Owminzatovo-Toshi
77 T14 **Auna** Niger, W Nigeria
95 H21 **Auning** Århus, C Denmark
192 K17 **Aunu'u Island** *island* W American Samoa
83 E20 **Auob** *var.* Oup. ≈ Namibia/South Africa
93 K19 **Aura** Länsi-Suomi, W Finland
109 R5 **Aurach** ≈ N Austria
Aural, Phnom *see* Aôral, Phnum
153 O14 **Aurangābād** Bihār, N India
154 F13 **Aurangābād** Mahārāshtra, C India
189 V7 **Aur Atoll** *atoll* E Marshall Islands
102 G7 **Auray** Morbihan, NW France
94 G13 **Aurdal** Oppland, S Norway
94 F8 **Aure** Møre og Romsdal, S Norway
29 T12 **Aurelia** Iowa, C USA
Aurelia Aquensis *see* Baden-Baden
Aurelianum *see* Orléans
120 J10 **Aurès, Massif de l'** ⛰ NE Algeria
100 F10 **Aurich** Niedersachsen, NW Germany
103 O13 **Aurillac** Cantal, C France
Aurine, Alpi *see* Zillertaler Alpen
Aurium *see* Ourense
14 H15 **Aurora** Ontario, S Canada
55 S8 **Aurora** NW Guyana
37 T4 **Aurora** Colorado, C USA
30 M11 **Aurora** Illinois, N USA
31 Q15 **Aurora** Indiana, N USA
29 W4 **Aurora** Minnesota, N USA
27 S8 **Aurora** Missouri, C USA
29 P16 **Aurora** Nebraska, C USA
36 J5 **Aurora** Utah, W USA
Aurora *see* Maéwo, Vanuatu
Aurora *see* San Francisco, Philippines
94 F10 **Aursjøen** ◎ S Norway
94 I8 **Aursunden** ◎ S Norway
83 D21 **Aus** Karas, SW Namibia
Ausa *see* Vic
14 E16 **Ausable** ≈ Ontario, S Canada
31 O3 **Au Sable Point** *headland* Michigan, N USA
31 S7 **Au Sable Point** *headland* Michigan, N USA
31 R6 **Au Sable River** ≈ Michigan, N USA
57 H16 **Ausangate, Nevado** ▲ C Peru
Auschwitz *see* Oświęcim
Ausculum Apulum *see* Ascoli Satriano
105 Q4 **Ausejo** La Rioja, N Spain
Aussig *see* Ústí nad Labem
95 F17 **Aust-Agder** ◐ *county* S Norway
92 P2 **Austfonna** *glacier* NE Svalbard
31 P15 **Austin** Indiana, N USA
29 W11 **Austin** Minnesota, N USA
35 U5 **Austin** Nevada, W USA
25 S10 **Austin** *state capital* Texas, S USA
180 J10 **Austin, Lake** *salt lake* Western Australia
31 V11 **Austintown** Ohio, N USA
25 V9 **Austonio** Texas, SW USA
Australes, Archipel des *see* Australes, Îles
Australes et Antarctiques Françaises, Terres *see* French Southern and Antarctic Territories
191 T14 **Australes, Îles** *var.* Archipel des Australes, Îles Tubuai, Tubuai Islands, *Eng.* Austral Islands. *island group* SW French Polynesia
175 Y11 **Austral Fracture Zone** *tectonic feature* S Pacific Ocean
181 O7 **Australia** *off.* Commonwealth of Australia. ◆ *commonwealth republic*
174 M8 **Australia** *continent*
183 Q12 **Australian Alps** ⛰ SE Australia
183 R11 **Australian Capital Territory** *prev.* Federal Capital Territory. ◐ *territory* SE Australia
Australie, Bassin Nord de l' *see* North Australian Basin
Austral Islands *see* Australes, Îles
Austrava *see* Ostrov
109 T6 **Austria** *off.* Republic of Austria, *Ger.* Österreich. ◆ *republic* C Europe
92 K3 **Austurland** ◐ *region* SE Iceland
92 G10 **Austvågøya** *island* C Norway
Ausuituq *see* Grise Fiord
58 G13 **Autazes** Amazonas, N Brazil
102 M16 **Auterive** Haute-Garonne, S France
Autesiodorum *see* Auxerre
103 N2 **Authie** ≈ N France
Autissiodorum *see* Auxerre
40 K14 **Autlán** *var.* Autlán de Navarro. Jalisco, SW Mexico
Autlán de Navarro *see* Autlán
Autricum *see* Chartres
103 Q9 **Autun** *anc.* Ædua, Augustodunum. Saône-et-Loire, C France
Autz *see* Auce
99 H20 **Auvelais** Namur, S Belgium
103 P11 **Auvergne** ◐ *region* C France
102 M12 **Auvézère** ≈ W France
103 P7 **Auxerre** *anc.* Autesiodorum, Autissiodorum. Yonne, C France
103 N2 **Auxi-le-Château** Pas-de-Calais, N France
103 S8 **Auxonne** Côte d'Or, C France
55 P9 **Auyan Tebuy** ▲ SE Venezuela
103 O10 **Auzances** Creuse, C France
27 U8 **Ava** Missouri, C USA
142 M5 **Āvaj** Qazvīn, N Iran
95 C15 **Avaldsnes** Rogaland, S Norway
103 Q8 **Avallon** Yonne, C France
102 K6 **Avaloirs, Mont des** ▲ NW France
35 S16 **Avalon** Santa Catalina Island, California, W USA
18 J17 **Avalon** New Jersey, NE USA
13 V13 **Avalon Peninsula** *peninsula* Newfoundland and Labrador, E Canada
197 Q11 **Avannaarsua** ◐ *province* N Greenland
60 K10 **Avaré** São Paulo, S Brazil
Avaricum *see* Bourges
190 H16 **Avarua** ○ (Cook Islands) Rarotonga, S Cook Islands
190 H16 **Avarua Harbour** *harbour* Rarotonga, S Cook Islands
Avasfelsőfalu *see* Negreşti-Oaş
38 L17 **Avatanak Island** *island* Aleutian Islands, Alaska, USA
190 B16 **Avatele** S Niue

◆ Country ● Country Capital ◇ Dependent Territory ○ Dependent Territory Capital ◐ Administrative Region × International Airport ▲ Mountain ⛰ Mountain Range Volcano ≈ River ◎ Lake ⊟ Reservoir

190 H16 **Avatiu** Rarotonga, S Cook Islands
190 H15 **Avatiu Harbour** *harbour* Rarotonga, S Cook Islands
Avdeyevka *see* Avdiyivka
114 J13 **Ávdira** Anatolikí Makedonía kai Thráki, NE Greece
117 X8 **Avdiyivka** *Rus.* Avdeyevka. Donets'ka Oblast', SE Ukraine
162 K7 **Avdzaga** C Mongolia
104 G6 **Ave** ≈ N Portugal
104 G7 **Aveiro** *anc.* Talabriga. Aveiro, W Portugal
104 G7 **Aveiro** ◐ *district* N Portugal
Avela *see* Ávila
99 D18 **Avelgem** West-Vlaanderen, W Belgium
61 D20 **Avellaneda** Buenos Aires, E Argentina
107 L17 **Avellino** *anc.* Abellinum. Campania, S Italy
35 Q12 **Avenal** California, W USA
Avenio *see* Avignon
94 E8 **Averoya** *island* S Norway
107 K17 **Aversa** Campania, S Italy
33 N9 **Avery** Idaho, NW USA
25 W5 **Avery** Texas, SW USA
Aves, Islas de *see* Las Aves, Islas
Avesnes *see* Avesnes-sur-Helpe
103 Q2 **Avesnes-sur-Helpe** *var.* Avesnes. Nord, N France
64 G12 **Aves Ridge** *undersea feature* SE Caribbean Sea
95 M14 **Avesta** Dalarna, C Sweden
103 O14 **Aveyron** ◐ *department* S France
103 N14 **Aveyron** ≈ S France
107 J15 **Avezzano** Abruzzo, C Italy
115 D16 **Avgó** ▲ C Greece
Avgustov *see* Augustów
Avgustovskiy Kanal *see* Augustowski, Kanał
96 J9 **Aviemore** N Scotland, UK
185 F21 **Aviemore, Lake** ◎ South Island, NZ
103 R15 **Avignon** *anc.* Avenio. Vaucluse, SE France
104 M7 **Ávila** *var.* Avila; *anc.* Abela, Abula, Abyla, Avela. Castilla-León, C Spain
104 L8 **Ávila** ◐ *province* Castilla-León, C Spain
104 K2 **Avilés** Asturias, NW Spain
118 J4 **Avinurme** *Ger.* Awwinorm. Ida-Virumaa, NE Estonia
104 H10 **Avis** Portalegre, C Portugal
95 F22 **Avlum** Ringkøbing, C Denmark
182 M11 **Avoca** Victoria, SE Australia
29 T14 **Avoca** Iowa, C USA
182 M11 **Avoca River** ≈ Victoria, SE Australia
107 L25 **Avola** Sicilia, Italy, C Mediterranean Sea
18 F10 **Avon** New York, NE USA
29 P12 **Avon** South Dakota, N USA
97 M23 **Avon** ≈ S England, UK
97 L20 **Avon** ≈ C England, UK
36 K13 **Avondale** Arizona, SW USA
23 X13 **Avon Park** Florida, SE USA
102 J5 **Avranches** Manche, N France
103 O3 **Avre** ≈ N France
186 M6 **Avuavu** *var.* Kolotambu. Guadalcanal, C Solomon Islands
Avveel *see* Ivalo, Finland
Avveel *see* Ivalojoki, Finland
Avvil *see* Ivalo
77 O17 **Awaaso** *var.* Awaso. SW Ghana
141 X8 **Awābī** *var.* Al 'Awābī. NE Oman
184 L9 **Awakino** Waikato, North Island, NZ
142 M15 **'Awālī** C Bahrain
99 K19 **Awans** Liège, E Belgium
184 I2 **Awanui** Northland, North Island, NZ
148 M14 **Awārān** Baluchistān, SW Pakistan
81 K16 **Awara Plain** *plain* NE Kenya
80 M13 **Āwarē** Somali, E Ethiopia
138 M6 **'Awāriḍ, Wādī** *dry watercourse* E Syria
185 B20 **Awarua Point** *headland* South Island, NZ
81 J14 **Āwasa** Southern, S Ethiopia
80 K13 **Āwash** Afar, NE Ethiopia
80 K12 **Āwash** *var.* Hawash. ≈ C Ethiopia
Awaso *see* Awaaso
158 H7 **Awat** Xinjiang Uygur Zizhiqu, NW China
185 J15 **Awatere** ≈ South Island, NZ
75 O10 **Awbārī** SW Libya
75 N9 **Awbāri, Idhān** *var.* Edeyen d'Oubari. *desert* Algeria/Libya
80 C13 **Aweil** Northern Bahr el Ghazal, SW Sudan
96 H11 **Awe, Loch** ◎ W Scotland, UK
77 U16 **Awka** Anambra, SW Nigeria
39 O6 **Awuna River** ≈ Alaska, USA
Awwinorm *see* Avinurme
Ax *see* Dax
Axarfjördhur *see* Öxarfjördhur
103 N17 **Axat** Aude, S France
99 F16 **Axel** Zeeland, SW Netherlands
8 M2 **Axel Heiberg Island** *var.* Axel Heiburg. *island* Nunavut, N Canada
Axel Heiburg *see* Axel Heiberg Island
77 O17 **Axim** S Ghana
114 F13 **Axiós** *var.* Vardar. ≈ Greece/FYR Macedonia *see also* Vardar
103 N17 **Ax-les-Thermes** Ariège, S France
120 D11 **Ayachi, Jbel** ▲ C Morocco
61 D22 **Ayacucho** Buenos Aires, E Argentina
57 F15 **Ayacucho** Ayacucho, S Peru
57 E16 **Ayacucho** *off.* Departamento de Ayacucho. ◐ *department* SW Peru
145 W11 **Ayagoz** *var.* Ayaguz, *Kaz.* Ayaköz; *prev.* Sergiopol. Vostochnyy Kazakhstan, E Kazakhstan
145 V12 **Ayagoz** *var.* Ayaguz, *Kaz.* Ayaköz. ≈ E Kazakhstan
Ayaguz *see* Ayagoz
Ayakagytma *see* Oyoqig'itma
Ayakkuduk *see* Oyoqquduq
158 L10 **Ayakkum Hu** ◎ NW China
Ayaköz *see* Ayagoz
104 H14 **Ayamonte** Andalucía, S Spain
123 S11 **Ayan** Khabarovskiy Kray, E Russian Federation
136 J10 **Ayancık** Sinop, N Turkey
55 S9 **Ayanganna Mountain** ▲ C Guyana
77 U16 **Ayangba** Kogi, C Nigeria
123 U7 **Ayanka** Koryakskiy Avtonomnyy Okrug, E Russian Federation
54 E7 **Ayapel** Córdoba, NW Colombia
136 H12 **Ayaş** Ankara, N Turkey
57 I16 **Ayaviri** Puno, S Peru
149 P3 **Āybak** *var.* Aibak, Haibak; *prev.* Samangān. Samangān, NE Afghanistan
147 N10 **Aydarko'l Ko'li** *Rus.* Ozero Aydarkul'. ◎ C Uzbekistan
Aydarkul', Ozero *see* Aydarko'l Ko'li
21 W10 **Ayden** North Carolina, SE USA
136 C15 **Aydın** *var.* Aïdin; *anc.* Tralles. Aydın, SW Turkey
136 C15 **Aydın** *var.* Aïdin. ◐ *province* SW Turkey
136 I17 **Aydıncık** İçel, S Turkey
136 C15 **Aydın Dağları** ⛰ W Turkey
158 L6 **Aydingkol Hu** ◎ NW China
127 X7 **Aydyrlinskiy** Orenburgskaya Oblast', W Russian Federation
105 S4 **Ayerbe** Aragón, NE Spain
Ayers Rock *see* Uluru
Ayeyarwady *see* Irrawaddy
Ayiá *see* Agiá
Ayia Napa *see* Agía Nápa
Ayia Phyla *see* Agía Fýlaxis
Ayiásos/Ayiássos *see* Agiasós
Áyios Evstrátios *see* Ágios Efstrátios
Áyios Kírikos *see* Ágios Kírykos
Áyios Nikólaos *see* Ágios Nikólaos
Ayios Seryios *see* Yeniboğaziçi
80 I11 **Āykel** Amhara, N Ethiopia
123 N9 **Aykhal** Respublika Sakha (Yakutiya), NE Russian Federation
14 J12 **Aylen Lake** ◎ Ontario, SE Canada
97 N21 **Aylesbury** SE England, UK
105 O6 **Ayllón** Castilla-León, N Spain
14 F17 **Aylmer** Ontario, S Canada
14 L12 **Aylmer** Québec, SE Canada
15 R12 **Aylmer, Lac** ◎ Québec, SE Canada
8 L9 **Aylmer Lake** ◎ Northwest Territories, NW Canada
145 V14 **Aynabulak** Almaty, SE Kazakhstan
138 K2 **'Ayn al 'Arab** Ḥalab, N Syria
Aynayn *see* 'Aynīn
139 V12 **'Ayn Ḥamūd** S Iraq
147 P12 **Ayní** *prev. Rus.* Varzimanor Ayni. W Tajikistan
140 M10 **'Aynīn** *var.* Aynayn. *spring/well* SW Saudi Arabia
21 U12 **Aynor** South Carolina, SE USA
139 Q7 **'Ayn Zāzūh** C Iraq
153 N12 **Ayodhya** Uttar Pradesh, N India
123 S6 **Ayon, Ostrov** *island* NE Russian Federation
105 R11 **Ayora** País Valenciano, E Spain
77 Q11 **Ayorou** Tillabéri, W Niger
79 E16 **Ayos** Centre, S Cameroon
76 L5 **'Ayoûn 'Abd el Mâlek** *well* N Mauritania
76 K10 **'Ayoûn el 'Atroûs** *var.* Aïoun el Atrous, Aïoun el Atroûss. Hodh el Gharbi, SE Mauritania
96 I13 **Ayr** W Scotland, UK
96 I13 **Ayr** ≈ W Scotland, UK
96 I13 **Ayrshire** *cultural region* SW Scotland, UK
Aysen *see* Aisén
80 L12 **Āysha** Somali, E Ethiopia
144 L14 **Ayteke Bi** *Kaz.* Zhangaqazaly *prev.* Novokazalinsk. Kyzylorda, SW Kazakhstan
146 K8 **Aytim** Navoiy Viloyati, N Uzbekistan
181 W4 **Ayton** Queensland, NE Australia
114 M9 **Aytos** Burgas, E Bulgaria
171 T11 **Ayu, Kepulauan** *island group* E Indonesia
A Yun Pa *see* Cheo Reo
169 V11 **Ayu, Tanjung** *headland* Borneo, N Indonesia
40 K13 **Ayutla** Jalisco, C Mexico
41 P16 **Ayutla** *var.* Ayutla de los Libres. Guerrero, S Mexico
Ayutla de los Libres *see* Ayutlá
167 O11 **Ayutthaya** *var.* Phra Nakhon Si Ayutthaya. Phra Nakhon Si Ayutthaya, C Thailand
136 B13 **Ayvalık** Balıkesir, W Turkey
99 L20 **Aywaille** Liège, E Belgium
141 R13 **'Aywat aş Şay'ar, Wādī** *seasonal river* N Yemen
Azaffal *see* Azeffâl
105 T9 **Azahar, Costa del** *coastal region* E Spain
105 S6 **Azaila** Aragón, NE Spain
104 F10 **Azambuja** Lisboa, C Portugal
153 N13 **Āzamgarh** Uttar Pradesh, N India
77 O9 **Azaouâd** *desert* C Mali
77 S10 **Azaouagh, Vallée de l'** *var.* Azaouak. ≈ W Niger
Azaouak *see* Azaouagh, Vallée de l'
61 F14 **Azara** Misiones, NE Argentina
142 K3 **Āzarān** Āžarbāyjān-e Khāvarī, N Iran
Azärbaycan/Azärbaycan Respublikası *see* Azerbaijan
Āžarbāyjān-e Bākhtarī *see* Āžarbāyjān-e Gharbī
142 I4 **Āžarbāyjān-e Gharbī** *off.* Ostān-e Āžarbāyjān-e Gharbī; *Eng.* West Azerbaijan; *prev.* Āžarbāyjān-e Bākhtarī. ◐ *province* NW Iran
Āžarbāyjān-e Khāvarī *see* Āžarbāyjān-e Sharqī
142 J3 **Āžarbāyjān-e Sharqī** *off.* Ostān-e Āžarbāyjān-e Sharqī, *Eng.* East Azerbaijan; *prev.* Āžarbāyjān-e Sharqī. ◐ *province* NW Iran
77 W13 **Azare** Bauchi, N Nigeria
119 M19 **Azarychy** *Rus.* Ozarichi. Homyel'skaya Voblasts', SE Belarus
102 L8 **Azay-le-Rideau** Indre-et-Loire, C France
138 I2 **A'zāz** Ḥalab, NW Syria
76 H7 **Azeffâl** *var.* Azaffal. *desert* Mauritania/Western Sahara
137 V12 **Azerbaijan** *off.* Azerbaijani Republic, *Az.* Azärbaycan, Azärbaycan Respublikası; *prev.* Azerbaijan SSR. ◆ *republic* SE Asia
145 T7 **Azhbulat, Ozero** ◎ NE Kazakhstan
74 F7 **Azilal** C Morocco
Azimabad *see* Patna
19 O6 **Aziscohos Lake** ⊠ Maine, NE USA
Azizbekov *see* Vayk'
Azizie *see* Telish
Aziziya *see* Al 'Azīzīyah
127 T4 **Aznakayevo** Respublika Tatarstan, W Russian Federation
56 C8 **Azogues** Cañar, S Ecuador
64 N2 **Azores** *var.* Açores, Ilhas dos Açores, *Port.* Arquipélago dos Açores. *island group* Portugal, NE Atlantic Ocean
64 L8 **Azores-Biscay Rise** *undersea feature* E Atlantic Ocean
Azotos/Azotus *see* Ashdod
78 K11 **Azoum, Bahr** *seasonal river* SE Chad
126 L12 **Azov** Rostovskaya Oblast', SW Russian Federation
126 J13 **Azov, Sea of** *Rus.* Azovskoye More, *Ukr.* Azovs'ke More. *sea* NE Black Sea
Azovs'ke More/Azovskoye More *see* Azov, Sea of
138 I10 **Azraq, Wāḥat al** *oasis* N Jordan
Āzro *see* Āzrow
74 G6 **Azrou** C Morocco
149 R5 **Āzrow** *var.* Āzro. Lowgar, E Afghanistan
37 P8 **Aztec** New Mexico, SW USA
36 M13 **Aztec Peak** ▲ Arizona, SW USA
45 N9 **Azua** *var.* Azua de Compostela. S Dominican Republic
Azua de Compostela *see* Azua
104 K12 **Azuaga** Extremadura, W Spain
56 B8 **Azuay** ◐ *province* W Ecuador
164 C13 **Azuchi-Ō-shima** *island* SW Japan
105 O11 **Azuer** ≈ C Spain
43 S17 **Azuero, Península de** *peninsula* S Panama
62 I6 **Azufre, Volcán** *var.* Volcán Lastarria. ▲ N Chile
116 J12 **Azuga** Prahova, SE Romania
61 C22 **Azul** Buenos Aires, E Argentina
62 I8 **Azul, Cerro** ▲ NW Argentina
56 E12 **Azul, Cordillera** ⛰ C Peru
165 P11 **Azuma-san** ▲ Honshū, C Japan
103 V15 **Azur, Côte d'** *coastal region* SE France
191 Z3 **Azur Lagoon** ◎ Kiritimati, E Kiribati
'Azza *see* Gaza
Az Zāb al Kabīr *see* Great Zab
138 H7 **Az Zabdānī** *var.* Zabadani. Dimashq, W Syria
141 W8 **Az Ẓāhirah** *desert* NW Oman
141 S6 **Az Ẓahrān** *Eng.* Dhahran. Ash Sharqīyah, NE Saudi Arabia
141 R6 **Az Ẓahrān al Khubar** *var.* Dhahran Al Khobar. × Ash Sharqīyah, NE Saudi Arabia
Az Zaqāzīq *see* Zagazig
138 H10 **Az Zarqā'** *var.* Zarqa. Az Zarqā', NW Jordan
138 I11 **Az Zarqā'** *off.* Muḥāfaẓat az Zarqā', *var.* Zarqa. ◐ *governorate* N Jordan
75 O7 **Az Zāwiyah** *var.* Zawia. NW Libya
141 N15 **Az Zaydīyah** W Yemen
74 I11 **Azzel Matti, Sebkha** *var.* Sebkra Azz el Matti. *salt flat* C Algeria
141 P6 **Az Zilfī** Ar Riyāḍ, N Saudi Arabia
139 Y13 **Az Zubayr** *var.* Al Zubair. SE Iraq
Az Zuqur *see* Jabal Zuuqar, Jazīrat

B

187 X15 **Ba** *prev.* Mba. Viti Levu, W Fiji
Ba *see* Đa Răng
171 P17 **Baa** Pulau Rote, C Indonesia
138 H7 **Baalbek** *var.* Ba'labakk; *anc.* Heliopolis. E Lebanon
108 G8 **Baar** Zug, N Switzerland
81 L17 **Baardheere** *var.* Bardere, *It.* Bardera. Gedo, SW Somalia
80 Q12 **Baargaal** Bari, NE Somalia
99 I15 **Baarle-Hertog** Antwerpen, N Belgium
99 I15 **Baarle-Nassau** Noord-Brabant, S Netherlands
98 J11 **Baarn** Utrecht, C Netherlands
114 D13 **Baba** *var.* Buševa, *Gk.* Varnoús. ⛰ FYR Macedonia/Greece
76 H10 **Bababé** Brakna, W Mauritania
136 G10 **Baba Burnu** *headland* NW Turkey
117 N13 **Babadag** Tulcea, SE Romania
137 X10 **Babadağ Dağı** ▲ NE Azerbaijan
146 H14 **Babadaýhan** *Rus.* Babadaykhan; *prev.* Kirovsk. Ahal Welaýaty, C Turkmenistan
Babadaykhan *see* Babadaýhan
146 G14 **Babadurmaz** Ahal Welaýaty, C Turkmenistan
114 M12 **Babaeski** Kırklareli, NW Turkey
139 T4 **Bāba Gurgur** N Iraq
56 B7 **Babahoyo** *prev.* Bodegas. Los Ríos, C Ecuador
149 P5 **Bābā, Kūh-e** ⛰ C Afghanistan
171 N12 **Babana** Sulawesi, C Indonesia
Babao *see* Qilian
171 Q12 **Babar, Kepulauan** *island group* E Indonesia
171 T12 **Babar, Pulau** *island* Kepulauan Babar, E Indonesia
152 G4 **Bābāsar Pass** *pass* India/Pakistan
Babashy, Gory *see* Babaşy
146 C9 **Babaşy** *Rus.* Gory Babashy. ⛰ W Turkmenistan
168 M13 **Babat** Sumatera, W Indonesia
Babatag, Khrebet *see* Bobotogh, Qatorkŭhi
81 H21 **Babati** Arusha, NE Tanzania
124 J13 **Babayevo** Vologodskaya Oblast', NW Russian Federation
127 Q15 **Babayurt** Respublika Dagestan, SW Russian Federation
33 P6 **Babb** Montana, NW USA
29 X4 **Babbitt** Minnesota, N USA
188 E9 **Babeldaob** *var.* Babeldaop, Babelthuap. *island* N Palau
Babeldaop *see* Babeldaob
141 N17 **Bab el Mandeb** *strait* Gulf of Aden/Red Sea
Babelthuap *see* Babeldaob
111 K17 **Babia Góra** *var.* Babia Hora. ▲ Slovakia/Poland
Babia Hora *see* Babia Góra
Babian Jiang *see* Black River
Babichi *see* Babichy
119 N19 **Babichy** *Rus.* Babichi. Homyel'skaya Voblasts', SE Belarus
112 I10 **Babina Greda** Vukovar-Srijem, E Croatia
10 K13 **Babine Lake** ◎ British Columbia, SW Canada
143 O4 **Bābol** *var.* Babul, Balfrush, Barfrush; *prev.* Barfurush. Māzandarān, N Iran
143 O4 **Bābolsar** *var.* Babulsar; *prev.* Meshed-i-Sar. Māzandarān, N Iran
36 L16 **Baboquivari Peak** ▲ Arizona, SW USA
79 G15 **Baboua** Nana-Mambéré, W Central African Republic
119 M17 **Babruysk** *Rus.* Bobruysk. Mahilyowskaya Voblasts', E Belarus
Babu *see* Hezhou
Babul *see* Bābol
Babulsar *see* Bābolsar
113 O19 **Babuna** ▲ C FYR Macedonia
113 O19 **Babuna** ⛰ C FYR Macedonia
148 K7 **Bābūs, Dasht-e** *Pash.* Bebas, Dasht-i. ⛰ W Afghanistan
171 O1 **Babuyan Channel** *channel* N Philippines
171 O1 **Babuyan Island** *island* N Philippines
139 T9 **Babylon** *site of ancient city* C Iraq
112 J9 **Bač** *Ger.* Batsch. Serbia, NW Serbia and Montenegro (Yugo.)
58 M13 **Bacabal** Maranhão, E Brazil
41 Y14 **Bacalar** Quintana Roo, SE Mexico
41 Y14 **Bacalar Chico, Boca** *strait* SE Mexico
171 Q12 **Bacan, Kepulauan** *island group* E Indonesia
171 S12 **Bacan, Pulau** *prev.* Batjan. *island* Maluku, E Indonesia
116 L10 **Bacău** *Hung.* Bákó. Bacău, NE Romania
116 K11 **Bacău** ◐ *county* E Romania
Bắc Bộ, Vịnh *see* Tongking, Gulf of
167 T5 **Bắc Can** Bắc Thai, N Vietnam
103 T5 **Baccarat** Meurthe-et-Moselle, NE France
183 N12 **Bacchus Marsh** Victoria, SE Australia
40 H4 **Bacerac** Sonora, NW Mexico
116 L10 **Băceşti** Vaslui, E Romania
167 T6 **Bắc Giang** Ha Bắc, N Vietnam
54 I5 **Bachaquero** Zulia, NW Venezuela
Bacher *see* Pohorje
118 M13 **Bacheykava** *Rus.* Bocheykovo. Vitsyebskaya Voblasts', N Belarus
40 I5 **Bachíniva** Chihuahua, N Mexico
158 G8 **Bachu** Xinjiang Uygur Zizhiqu, NW China
9 N8 **Back** ≈ Nunavut, N Canada
112 K10 **Bačka Palanka** *prev.* Palanka. Serbia, NW Serbia and Montenegro (Yugo.)
112 K8 **Bačka Topola** *Hung.* Topolya; *prev. Hung.* Bácstopolya. Serbia, N Serbia and Montenegro (Yugo.)
95 J17 **Bäckefors** Västra Götaland, S Sweden
Bäckermühle Schulzenmühle *see* Żywiec
95 L16 **Bäckhammar** Värmland, C Sweden
112 K9 **Bački Petrovac** *Hung.* Petrőcz; *prev.* Petrovac, Petrovácz. Serbia, NW Serbia and Montenegro (Yugo.)
101 I21 **Backnang** Baden-Württemberg, SW Germany
167 S15 **Bac Liêu** *var.* Vinh Loi. Minh Hai, S Vietnam
167 T6 **Bắc Ninh** Ha Bắc, N Vietnam
40 G4 **Bacoachi** Sonora, NW Mexico
171 P6 **Bacolod** *off.* Bacolod City. Negros, C Philippines
171 O4 **Baco, Mount** ▲ Mindoro, N Philippines
111 K25 **Bácsalmás** Bács-Kiskun, S Hungary
Bácsjózseffalva *see* Žednik
111 J24 **Bács-Kiskun** *off.* Bács-Kiskun Megye. ◐ *county* S Hungary
Bácsszenttamás *see* Srbobran
Bácstopolya *see* Bačka Topola
Bactra *see* Balkh
Bada *see* Xilin
155 F21 **Badagara** Kerala, SW India
101 M24 **Bad Aibling** Bayern, SE Germany
162 I13 **Badain Jaran Shamo** *desert* N China
104 I11 **Badajoz** *anc.* Pax Augusta. Extremadura, W Spain
104 J11 **Badajoz** ◐ *province* Extremadura, W Spain
149 S2 **Badakhshān** ◐ *province* NE Afghanistan
105 W6 **Badalona** *anc.* Baetulo. Cataluña, E Spain
154 O11 **Bādāmapāhārh** Orissa, E India
152 K8 **Badarīnāth** ▲ N India
169 O10 **Badas, Kepulauan** *island group* W Indonesia
109 S6 **Bad Aussee** Salzburg, E Austria
31 S8 **Bad Axe** Michigan, N USA
101 G16 **Bad Berleburg** Nordrhein-Westfalen, W Germany
101 L17 **Bad Blankenburg** Thüringen, C Germany
Bad Borseck *see* Borsec
101 G18 **Bad Camberg** Hessen, W Germany
100 L8 **Bad Doberan** Mecklenburg-Vorpommern, N Germany
101 N14 **Bad Düben** Sachsen, E Germany
109 X4 **Baden** *var.* Baden bei Wien; *anc.* Aquae Panoniae, Thermae Pannonicae. Niederösterreich, NE Austria
108 F9 **Baden** Aargau, N Switzerland
101 G21 **Baden-Baden** *anc.* Aurelia Aquensis. Baden-Württemberg, SW Germany
Baden bei Wien *see* Baden
101 G22 **Baden-Württemberg** *Fr.* Bade-Wurtemberg. ◐ *state* SW Germany
112 A10 **Baderna** Istra, NW Croatia
Bade-Wurtemberg *see* Baden-Württemberg
101 H20 **Bad Fredrichshall** Baden-Württemberg, S Germany
100 P11 **Bad Freienwalde** Brandenburg, NE Germany
109 Q8 **Badgastein** *var.* Gastein. Salzburg, NW Austria
Badger State *see* Wisconsin
148 L4 **Bādghīs** ◐ *province* NW Afghanistan
109 T5 **Bad Hall** Oberösterreich, N Austria
101 J14 **Bad Harzburg** Niedersachsen, C Germany
101 I16 **Bad Hersfeld** Hessen, C Germany
98 I10 **Badhoevedorp** Noord-Holland, C Netherlands
109 Q8 **Bad Hofgastein** Salzburg, NW Austria
Bad Homburg *see* Bad Homburg vor der Höhe
101 G18 **Bad Homburg vor der Höhe** *var.* Bad Homburg. Hessen, W Germany
101 E17 **Bad Honnef** Nordrhein-Westfalen, W Germany
149 Q17 **Badīn** Sind, SE Pakistan
21 S10 **Badin Lake** ⊠ North Carolina, SE USA
40 I8 **Badiraguato** Sinaloa, C Mexico
109 R6 **Bad Ischl** Oberösterreich, N Austria
Badjawa *see* Bajawa
Badje-Sohppar *see* Övre Soppero
101 J18 **Bad Kissingen** Bayern, SE Germany
Bad Königswart *see* Lázně Kynžvart
101 F19 **Bad Kreuznach** Rheinland-Pfalz, SW Germany
101 F24 **Bad Krozingen** Baden-Württemberg, SW Germany
101 G16 **Bad Laasphe** Nordrhein-Westfalen, W Germany
28 J6 **Badlands** *physical region* North Dakota, N USA
101 K16 **Bad Langensalza** Thüringen, C Germany
109 T3 **Bad Leonfelden** Oberösterreich, N Austria
101 I20 **Bad Mergentheim** Baden-Württemberg, SW Germany
101 H17 **Bad Nauheim** Hessen, W Germany
101 E17 **Bad Neuenahr-Ahrweiler** Rheinland-Pfalz, W Germany
Bad Neustadt *see* Bad Neustadt an der Saale
101 J18 **Bad Neustadt an der Saale** *var.* Bad Neustadt. Berlin, C Germany
Badnur *see* Betūl
100 H13 **Bad Oeynhausen** Nordrhein-Westfalen, NW Germany
100 J9 **Bad Oldesloe** Schleswig-Holstein, N Germany
77 Q16 **Badou** C Togo
Bad Polzin *see* Połczyn-Zdrój
100 H13 **Bad Pyrmont** Niedersachsen, C Germany
109 X9 **Bad Radkersburg** Steiermark, SE Austria
139 V8 **Badrah** E Iraq
162 J6 **Badrah** Hövsgöl, N Mongolia
101 N24 **Bad Reichenhall** Bayern, SE Germany
140 K8 **Badr Ḥunayn** Al Madīnah, W Saudi Arabia
28 M10 **Bad River** ≈ South Dakota, N USA
30 K4 **Bad River** ≈ Wisconsin, N USA
100 H13 **Bad Salzuflen** Nordrhein-Westfalen, NW Germany
101 J16 **Bad Salzungen** Thüringen, C Germany
109 V8 **Bad Sankt Leonhard im Lavanttal** Kärnten, S Austria
100 K9 **Bad Schwartau** Schleswig-Holstein, N Germany
101 L24 **Bad Tölz** Bayern, SE Germany
181 U1 **Badu Island** *island* Queensland, NE Australia
155 K25 **Badulla** Uva Province, C Sri Lanka
109 X5 **Bad Vöslau** Niederösterreich, NE Austria
101 I24 **Bad Waldsee** Baden-Württemberg, S Germany
35 U11 **Badwater Basin** *depression* California, W USA
101 J20 **Bad Windsheim** Bayern, C Germany
101 J23 **Bad Wörishofen** Bayern, S Germany
100 G10 **Bad Zwischenahn** Niedersachsen, NW Germany
104 M13 **Baena** Andalucía, S Spain
Baeterrae/Baeterrae Septimanorum *see* Béziers
Baetic Cordillera/Baetic Mountains *see* Béticos, Sistemas
Baetulo *see* Badalona
57 K18 **Baeza** Napo, NE Ecuador
105 N13 **Baeza** Andalucía, S Spain
79 D15 **Bafang** Ouest, W Cameroon
76 H12 **Bafatá** C Guinea-Bissau
149 U5 **Baffa** North-West Frontier Province, NW Pakistan
197 O11 **Baffin Basin** *undersea feature* N Labrador Sea
197 N12 **Baffin Bay** *bay* Canada/Greenland
25 T15 **Baffin Bay** *inlet* Texas, SW USA
196 M12 **Baffin Island** *island* Nunavut, NE Canada
79 E15 **Bafia** Centre, C Cameroon
77 R14 **Bafilo** NE Togo
76 J12 **Bafing** ≈ W Africa
76 J12 **Bafoulabé** Kayes, W Mali
79 D15 **Bafoussam** Ouest, W Cameroon
143 R9 **Bāfq** Yazd, C Iran
136 L10 **Bafra** Samsun, N Turkey
136 L10 **Bafra Burnu** *headland* N Turkey
143 S12 **Bāft** Kermān, S Iran
79 N18 **Bafwabalinga** Orientale, NE Dem. Rep. Congo
79 N18 **Bafwaboli** Orientale, NE Dem. Rep. Congo
79 N17 **Bafwasende** Orientale, NE Dem. Rep. Congo
42 K13 **Bagaces** Guanacaste, NW Costa Rica
153 O12 **Bagaha** Bihār, N India
155 F16 **Bāgalkot** Karnātaka, W India
81 J22 **Bagamoyo** Pwani, E Tanzania
168 J8 **Bagan Datuk** *var.* Bagan Datok. Perak, Peninsular Malaysia
171 R7 **Baganga** Mindanao, S Philippines
168 J9 **Bagansiapiapi** *var.* Pasirpangarayan. Sumatera, W Indonesia
162 M8 **Baga Nuur** *var.* Nüürst. Töv, C Mongolia
Bagaria *see* Bagheria
77 T11 **Bagaroua** Tahoua, W Niger
79 I20 **Bagata** Bandundu, W Dem. Rep. Congo
Bagdad *see* Baghdād
123 O13 **Bagdarin** Respublika Buryatiya, S Russian Federation
61 G17 **Bagé** Rio Grande do Sul, S Brazil
Bagenalstown *see* Muine Bheag
Bagerhat *see* Bagherhat
103 P16 **Bages et de Sigean, Étang de** ◎ S France
33 W17 **Baggs** Wyoming, C USA
154 F11 **Bāgh** Madhya Pradesh, C India
139 T8 **Baghdād** *var.* Bagdad, *Eng.* Baghdad. ● (Iraq) C Iraq
139 T8 **Baghdād** × C Iraq
153 T16 **Bagherhat** *var.* Bagerhat. Khulna, S Bangladesh
107 J23 **Bagheria** *var.* Bagaria. Sicilia, Italy, C Mediterranean Sea
143 S10 **Bāghīn** Kermān, C Iran
149 Q3 **Baghlān** Baghlān, NE Afghanistan
149 Q3 **Baghlān** *var.* Bāghlān. ◐ *province* NE Afghanistan
148 M7 **Bāghrān** Helmand, S Afghanistan
29 T4 **Bagley** Minnesota, N USA
106 H10 **Bagnacavallo** Emilia-Romagna, C Italy
102 K16 **Bagnères-de-Bigorre** Hautes-Pyrénées, S France
102 L17 **Bagnères-de-Luchon** Hautes-Pyrénées, S France
106 F11 **Bagni di Lucca** Toscana, C Italy
106 H11 **Bagno di Romagna** Emilia-Romagna, C Italy
103 R14 **Bagnols-sur-Cèze** Gard, S France
162 M14 **Bag Nur** ◎ N China
171 P6 **Bago** *off.* Bago City. Negros, C Philippines
Bago *see* Pegu
76 M13 **Bagoé** ≈ Ivory Coast/Mali
Bagrāmē *see* Bagrāmī
149 R5 **Bagrāmī** *var.* Bagrāmē. Kābul, E Afghanistan
119 B14 **Bagrationovsk** *Ger.* Preussisch Eylau. Kaliningradskaya Oblast', W Russian Federation
Bagrax *see* Bohu
Bagrax Hu *see* Bosten Hu
56 C10 **Bagua** Amazonas, NE Peru
171 O2 **Baguio** *off.* Baguio City. Luzon, N Philippines
77 V9 **Bagzane, Monts** ▲ N Niger
Bāḥah, Minṭaqat al *see* Al Bāḥah

44 H3 **Bahamas** *off.* Commonwealth of the Bahamas. ◆ *commonwealth republic* N West Indies
153 S15 **Baharampur** *prev.* Berhampore. West Bengal, NE India
146 E12 **Baharly** *var.* Bäherden, *Rus.* Bakharden; *prev.* Bakherden. Ahal Welaýaty, C Turkmenistan
149 U10 **Bahāwalnagar** Punjab, E Pakistan
149 T11 **Bahāwalpur** Punjab, E Pakistan
136 L16 **Bahçe** Osmaniye, S Turkey
160 J8 **Ba He** ∽ C China
Bäherden *see* Baharly
59 N16 **Bahia** *off.* Estado da Bahia. ◐ *state* E Brazil
61 B24 **Bahía Blanca** Buenos Aires, E Argentina
40 L15 **Bahía Bufadero** Michoacán de Ocampo, SW Mexico
63 J19 **Bahía Bustamante** Chubut, SE Argentina
40 D5 **Bahía de los Ángeles** Baja California, NW Mexico
40 C6 **Bahía de Tortugas** Baja California Sur, W Mexico
42 J4 **Bahía, Islas de la** *Eng.* Bay Islands. *island group* N Honduras
40 E5 **Bahía Kino** Sonora, NW Mexico
40 E9 **Bahía Magdalena** *var.* Puerto Magdalena. Baja California Sur, W Mexico
54 C8 **Bahía Solano** *var.* Ciudad Mutis, Solano. Chocó, W Colombia
80 I11 **Bahir Dar** *var.* Bahr Dar, Bahrdar Giyorgis. Amhara, N Ethiopia
141 X8 **Bahlā'** *var.* Bahlah, Bahlat. NW Oman
Bāhla *see* Bālān
Bahlah/Bahlat *see* Bahlā'
152 M11 **Bahraich** Uttar Pradesh, N India
143 M14 **Bahrain** *off.* State of Bahrain, Dawlat al Bahrayn, *Ar.* Al Baḩrayn; *prev.* Bahrein, *anc.* Tylos or Tyros. ◆ *monarchy* SW Asia
142 M14 **Bahrain** ✕ C Bahrain
142 M15 **Bahrain, Gulf of** *gulf* Persian Gulf, NW Arabian Sea
138 I7 **Baḩrat Mallāḩah** ◎ W Syria
Bahrayn, Dawlat al *see* Bahrain
Bahr Dar/Bahrdar Giyorgis *see* Bahir Dar
Bahrein *see* Bahrain
81 E16 **Bahr el Gabel** ◐ *state* S Sudan
80 E13 **Bahr ez Zaref** ∽ C Sudan
Bahr Tabariya, Sea of *see* Tiberias, Lake
143 W15 **Bāhū Kalāt** Sīstān va Balūchestān, SE Iran
118 N13 **Bahushewsk** *Rus.* Bogushëvsk. Vitsyebskaya Voblasts', NE Belarus
Bai *see* Tagow Bāy
116 G13 **Baia de Aramă** Mehedinţi, SW Romania
116 G11 **Baia de Criş** *Ger.* Altenburg, *Hung.* Körösbánya. Hunedoara, SW Romania
83 A16 **Baia dos Tigres** Namibe, SW Angola
82 A13 **Baia Farta** Benguela, W Angola
116 H9 **Baia Mare** *Ger.* Frauenbach, *Hung.* Nagybánya; *prev.* Neustadt. Maramureş, NW Romania
116 H8 **Baia Sprie** *Ger.* Mittelstadt, *Hung.* Felsőbánya. Maramureş, NW Romania
78 G13 **Baïbokoum** Logone-Oriental, SW Chad
160 F12 **Baicao Ling** ⛰ SW China
163 U9 **Baicheng** *var.* Pai-ch'eng; *prev.* T'aon-an. Jilin, NE China
158 I6 **Baicheng** *var.* Bay. Xinjiang Uygur Zizhiqu, NW China
116 J13 **Băicoi** Prahova, SE Romania
Baidoa *see* Baydhabo
15 U6 **Baie-Comeau** Québec, SE Canada
15 T7 **Baie-des-Bacon** Québec, SE Canada
15 S8 **Baie-des-Rochers** Québec, SE Canada
15 U6 **Baie-des-Sables** Québec, SE Canada
12 K11 **Baie-du-Poste** Québec, SE Canada
172 H17 **Baie Lazare** Mahé, NE Seychelles
45 Y5 **Baie-Mahault** Basse Terre, C Guadeloupe
15 R9 **Baie-St-Paul** Québec, SE Canada
15 V5 **Baie-Trinité** Québec, SE Canada
13 T11 **Baie Verte** Newfoundland and Labrador, SE Canada
163 X11 **Baihe** *prev.* Erdaobaihe. Jilin, NE China
Baiguan *see* Shangyu
139 U11 **Bā'ij al Mahdī** S Iraq
Baiji *see* Bayjī
Baikal, Lake *see* Baykal, Ozero
Bailādila *see* Kirandul
Baile an Chaistil *see* Ballycastle
Baile an Róba *see* Ballinrobe
Baile an tSratha *see* Ballintra
Baile Átha an Rí *see* Athenry
Baile Átha Buí *see* Athboy
Baile Átha Cliath *see* Dublin
Baile Átha Fhirdhia *see* Ardee
Baile Átha Í *see* Athy
Baile Átha Luain *see* Athlone
Baile Átha Troim *see* Trim
Baile Brigín *see* Balbriggan
Baile Easa Dara *see* Ballysadare
116 I13 **Băile Govora** Vâlcea, SW Romania
116 F13 **Băile Herculane** *Ger.* Herkulesbad, *Hung.* Herkulesfürdő. Caraş-Severin, SW Romania
Baile Locha Riach *see* Loughrea
Baile Mhistéala *see* Mitchelstown
Baile Monaidh *see* Ballymoney
105 N12 **Bailén** Andalucía, S Spain
Baile na hInse *see* Ballynahinch
Baile na Lorgan *see* Castleblayney
Baile na Mainistreach *see* Newtownabbey
Baile Nua na hArda *see* Newtownards
116 I12 **Băile Olăneşti** Vâlcea, SW Romania
116 H14 **Băileşti** Dolj, SW Romania
163 N12 **Bailingmiao** *var.* Darhan Muminggan Lianheqi. Nei Mongol Zizhiqu, N China
58 K11 **Bailique, Ilha** *island* NE Brazil
103 O1 **Bailleul** Nord, N France
78 H12 **Ba Illi** Chari-Baguirmi, SW Chad
159 V12 **Bailong Jiang** ∽ C China
82 C13 **Bailundo** *Port.* Vila Teixeira da Silva. Huambo, C Angola
159 T13 **Baima** *var.* Sêraitang. Qinghai, C China
Baima *see* Baxoi
186 C8 **Baimuru** Gulf, S PNG
158 M16 **Bainang** Xizang Zizhiqu, W China
23 S8 **Bainbridge** Georgia, SE USA
171 O17 **Baing** Pulau Sumba, SE Indonesia
158 M14 **Baingoin** Xizang Zizhiqu, W China
104 G2 **Baio Grande** Galicia, NW Spain
104 G4 **Baiona** Galicia, NW Spain
163 V7 **Baiquan** Heilongjiang, NE China
Bā'ir *see* Bāyir
158 I11 **Bairab Co** ◎ W China
25 Q7 **Baird** Texas, SW USA
39 N7 **Baird Mountains** ⛰ Alaska, USA
Baireuth *see* Bayreuth
190 H3 **Bairiki** ● (Kiribati) Tarawa, NW Kiribati
Bairin Youqi *see* Daban
Bairin Zuoqi *see* Lindong
145 P17 **Bairkum** *Kaz.* Bayyrqum. Yuzhnyy Kazakhstan, S Kazakhstan
183 P12 **Bairnsdale** Victoria, SE Australia
171 P6 **Bais** Negros, S Philippines
102 L15 **Baïse** *var.* Baise. ∽ S France
163 W11 **Baishan** *prev.* Hunjiang. Jilin, NE China
Baishan *see* Mashan
118 F12 **Baisogala** Šiauliai, C Lithuania
189 Q7 **Baiti** N Nauru
104 G13 **Baixo Alentejo** *physical region* S Portugal
64 P5 **Baixo, Ilhéu de** *island* Madeira, Portugal, NE Atlantic Ocean
83 E15 **Baixo Longa** Cuando Cubango, SE Angola
159 V10 **Baiyin** Gansu, C China
160 E8 **Baiyü** *var.* Jianshe. Sichuan, C China
161 N14 **Baiyun** ✕ (Guangzhou) Guangdong, S China
160 K4 **Baiyu Shan** ⛰ C China
111 J25 **Baja** Bács-Kiskun, S Hungary
40 C4 **Baja California** ◐ *state* NW Mexico
40 C4 **Baja California** *Eng.* Lower California. *peninsula* NW Mexico
40 E9 **Baja California Sur** ◐ *state* W Mexico
Bājah *see* Béja
Bajan *see* Bayan
191 V16 **Baja, Punta** *headland* Easter Island, Chile, E Pacific Ocean
40 B4 **Baja, Punta** *headland* NW Mexico
55 R5 **Baja, Punta** *headland* NE Venezuela
42 D5 **Baja Verapaz** *off.* Departamento de Baja Verapaz. ◐ *department* C Guatemala
171 N16 **Bajawa** *prev.* Badjawa. Flores, S Indonesia
153 S16 **Baj Baj** *prev.* Budge-Budge. West Bengal, E India
141 N15 **Bājil** W Yemen
183 U4 **Bajimba, Mount** ▲ New South Wales, SE Australia
112 K13 **Bajina Bašta** Serbia, W Serbia and Montenegro (Yugo.)
153 U14 **Bajitpur** Dhaka, E Bangladesh
112 K8 **Bajmok** Serbia, NW Serbia and Montenegro (Yugo.)
Bajo Boquete *see* Boquete
113 L17 **Bajram Curri** Kukës, N Albania
79 J14 **Bakala** Ouaka, C Central African Republic
127 T4 **Bakaly** Respublika Bashkortostan, W Russian Federation
Bakan *see* Shimonoseki
145 U14 **Bakanas** *Kaz.* Baqanas. Almaty, SE Kazakhstan
145 V12 **Bakanas** *Kaz.* Baqanas. ∽ E Kazakhstan
145 U14 **Bakbakty** *Kaz.* Baqbaqty. Almaty, SE Kazakhstan
122 J12 **Bakchar** Tomskaya Oblast', C Russian Federation
76 I11 **Bakel** E Senegal
35 W13 **Baker** California, W USA
22 J8 **Baker** Louisiana, S USA
33 Y9 **Baker** Montana, NW USA
32 L12 **Baker** Oregon, NW USA
192 L7 **Baker and Howland Islands** ◇ *US unincorporated territory* W Polynesia
36 L12 **Baker Butte** ▲ Arizona, SW USA
39 X15 **Baker Island** *island* Alexander Archipelago, Alaska, USA
9 N9 **Baker Lake** Nunavut, N Canada
9 N9 **Baker Lake** ◎ Nunavut, N Canada
32 H6 **Baker, Mount** ▲ Washington, NW USA
35 R13 **Bakersfield** California, W USA
24 M9 **Bakersfield** Texas, SW USA
21 P9 **Bakersville** North Carolina, SE USA
Bākhābī *see* Bū Khābī
Bakharden *see* Baharly
Bakhardok *see* Bokurdak
143 U5 **Bākharz, Kuhhā-ye** ⛰ NE Iran
152 D13 **Bākhāsar** Rājasthān, NW India
Bakhchisaray *see* Bakhchysaray
117 T13 **Bakhchysaray** *Rus.* Bakhchisaray. Respublika Krym, S Ukraine
Bakherden *see* Baharly
117 R3 **Bakhmach** Chernihivs'ka Oblast', N Ukraine
Bākhtarān *see* Kermānshāh
143 Q11 **Bakhtegān, Daryācheh-ye** ◎ C Iran
145 X12 **Bakhty** Vostochnyy Kazakhstan, E Kazakhstan
137 Z11 **Bakı** *Eng.* Baku. ● (Azerbaijan) E Azerbaijan
137 Z11 **Bakı** ✕ E Azerbaijan
136 C13 **Bakır Çayı** ∽ W Turkey
92 L1 **Bakkafjördhur** Austurland, NE Iceland
92 L1 **Bakkaflói** *sea area* W Norwegian Sea
81 I15 **Bako** Southern, S Ethiopia
76 L15 **Bako** NW Ivory Coast
Bákó *see* Bacău
111 H23 **Bakony** *Eng.* Bakony Mountains, *Ger.* Bakonywald. ⛰ W Hungary
Bakony Mountains/ Bakonywald *see* Bakony
81 M16 **Bakool** *off.* Gobolka Bakool. ◐ *region* W Somalia
79 L15 **Bakouma** Mbomou, SE Central African Republic
127 N15 **Baksan** Kabardino-Balkarskaya Respublika, SW Russian Federation
119 I16 **Bakshty** Hrodzyenskaya Voblasts', W Belarus
Baku *see* Bakı
194 K12 **Bakutis Coast** *physical region* Antarctica
Bakwanga *see* Mbuji-Mayi
145 O15 **Bakyrly** Yuzhnyy Kazakhstan, S Kazakhstan
14 H13 **Bala** Ontario, S Canada
97 J19 **Bala** NW Wales, UK
136 I13 **Balâ** Ankara, C Turkey
170 L7 **Balabac Island** *island* W Philippines
Balabac, Selat *see* Balabac Strait
169 V5 **Balabac Strait** *var.* Selat Balabac. *strait* Malaysia/Philippines
Ba'labakk *see* Baalbek
187 P16 **Balabio, Île** *island* Province Nord, W New Caledonia
116 I14 **Balaci** Teleorman, S Romania
139 R7 **Balad** N Iraq
123 R12 **Baladek** Khabarovskiy Kray, SE Russian Federation
139 U7 **Balad Rūz** E Iraq
154 J11 **Bālāghāt** Madhya Pradesh, C India
155 F14 **Bālāghāt Range** ⛰ W India
103 X14 **Balagne** *physical region* Corse, France, C Mediterranean Sea
105 U5 **Balaguer** Cataluña, NE Spain
105 S3 **Balaïtous** *var.* Pic de Balaïtous. ▲ France/Spain
Balaïtous, Pic de *see* Balaïtous
Balák *see* Ballangen
127 O3 **Balakhna** Nizhegorodskaya Oblast', W Russian Federation
122 L12 **Balakhta** Krasnoyarskiy Kray, S Russian Federation
182 I9 **Balaklava** South Australia
Balakleya *see* Balakliya
117 V6 **Balakliya** *Rus.* Balakleya. Kharkivs'ka Oblast', E Ukraine
127 Q7 **Balakovo** Saratovskaya Oblast', W Russian Federation
83 P14 **Balama** Cabo Delgado, N Mozambique
169 U6 **Balambangan, Pulau** *island* East Malaysia
148 L3 **Bālā Morghāb** Laghmān, NW Afghanistan
152 E11 **Bālān** *prev.* Bāhla. Rājasthān, NW India
116 J10 **Bălan** *Hung.* Balánbánya. Harghita, C Romania
Balánbánya *see* Bălan
171 O3 **Balanga** Luzon, N Philippines
154 M12 **Bālāngir** *prev.* Bolangir. Orissa, E India
127 N8 **Balashov** Saratovskaya Oblast', W Russian Federation
Balasore *see* Bāleshwar
111 K21 **Balassagyarmat** Nógrád, N Hungary
29 S10 **Balaton** Minnesota, N USA
11 H24 **Balaton** *var.* Lake Balaton, *Ger.* Plattensee. ◎ W Hungary
111 I23 **Balatonfüred** *var.* Füred. Veszprém, W Hungary
Balaton, Lake *see* Balaton
116 I11 **Bălăuşeri** *Ger.* Bladenmarkt, *Hung.* Balavásár. Mureş, C Romania
Balavásár *see* Bălăuşeri
105 Q11 **Balazote** Castilla-La Mancha, C Spain
Balázsfalva *see* Blaj
119 F14 **Balbieriškis** Kaunas, S Lithuania
186 J7 **Balbi, Mount** ▲ Bougainville Island, NE PNG
58 F11 **Balbina, Represa** ⊡ NW Brazil
43 T15 **Balboa** Panamá, C Panama
97 G17 **Balbriggan** *Ir.* Baile Brigín. E Ireland
Balbunar *see* Kubrat
81 N17 **Balcad** Shabeellaha Dhexe, C Somalia
61 D23 **Balcarce** Buenos Aires, E Argentina
11 U16 **Balcarres** Saskatchewan, S Canada
114 O8 **Balchik** Dobrich, NE Bulgaria
185 E24 **Balclutha** Otago, South Island, NZ
25 Q2 **Balcones Escarpment** *escarpment* Texas, SW USA
18 F14 **Bald Eagle Creek** ∽ Pennsylvania, NE USA
Baldenburg *see* Biały Bór
21 V12 **Bald Head Island** *island* North Carolina, SE USA
27 W10 **Bald Knob** Arkansas, C USA
30 K17 **Bald Knob** *hill* Illinois, N USA
Baldohn *see* Baldone
118 G9 **Baldone** *Ger.* Baldohn. Rīga, W Latvia
22 I9 **Baldwin** Louisiana, S USA
31 P7 **Baldwin** Michigan, N USA
27 Q4 **Baldwin City** Kansas, C USA
39 N8 **Baldwin Peninsula** *headland* Alaska, USA
18 H9 **Baldwinsville** New York, NE USA
23 N2 **Baldwyn** Mississippi, S USA
11 W15 **Baldy Mountain** ▲ Manitoba, S Canada
33 T7 **Baldy Mountain** ▲ Montana, NW USA
37 O13 **Baldy Peak** ▲ Arizona, SW USA
Bâle *see* Basel
105 X9 **Baleares** ◐ *autonomous community* E Spain
105 X11 **Baleares, Islas** *Eng.* Balearic Islands. *island group* Spain, W Mediterranean Sea
Baleares Major *see* Mallorca
Balearic Islands *see* Baleares, Islas
Balearic Plain *see* Algerian Basin
Balearis Minor *see* Menorca
169 S9 **Baleh, Batang** ∽ East Malaysia
12 J8 **Baleine, Grande Rivière de la** ∽ Québec, E Canada
12 K7 **Baleine, Petite Rivière de la** ∽ Québec, SE Canada
13 N6 **Baleine, Rivière à la** ∽ Québec, E Canada
99 J16 **Balen** Antwerpen, N Belgium
171 O3 **Baler** Luzon, N Philippines
154 P11 **Bāleshwar** *prev.* Balasore. Orissa, E India
77 S12 **Baléyara** Tillabéri, W Niger
127 T1 **Balezino** Udmurtskaya Respublika, NW Russian Federation
42 J4 **Balfate** Colón, N Honduras
11 O17 **Balfour** British Columbia, SW Canada
29 N3 **Balfour** North Dakota, N USA
Balfrush *see* Bābol
122 L14 **Balgazyn** Respublika Tyva, S Russian Federation
11 U16 **Balgonie** Saskatchewan, S Canada
Bălgrad *see* Alba Iulia
81 J19 **Balguda** *spring/well* S Kenya
158 K6 **Balguntay** Xinjiang Uygur Zizhiqu, NW China
141 R16 **Balḩāf** S Yemen
152 F13 **Bāli** Rājasthān, N India
169 U17 **Bali** ◐ *province* S Indonesia
169 T17 **Bali** *island* C Indonesia
111 K16 **Balice** ✕ (Kraków) Małopolskie, S Poland
171 Y14 **Baliem, Sungai** ∽ Papua, E Indonesia
136 C12 **Balıkesir** Balıkesir, W Turkey
136 C12 **Balıkesir** ◐ *province* NW Turkey
138 L3 **Balīkh, Nahr** ∽ N Syria
169 V12 **Balikpapan** Borneo, C Indonesia
Bali, Laut *see* Bali Sea
171 N9 **Balimbing** Tawitawi, SW Philippines
186 B8 **Balimo** Western, SW PNG
Bálinc *see* Balinţ
101 H23 **Balingen** Baden-Württemberg, SW Germany
116 F11 **Balinţ** *Hung.* Bálinc. Timiş, W Romania
171 O1 **Balintang Channel** *channel* N Philippines
138 K3 **Bālis** Ḩalab, N Syria
169 T16 **Bali Sea** *Ind.* Laut Bali. *sea* C Indonesia
98 K7 **Balk** Friesland, N Netherlands
146 B11 **Balkanabat** *Rus.* Nebitdag. Balkan Welaýaty, W Turkmenistan
121 R6 **Balkan Mountains** *Bul./SCr.* Stara Planina. ⛰ Bulgaria/Serbia and Montenegro (Yugo.)
Balkanskiy Velayat *see* Balkan Welaýaty
146 B9 **Balkan Welaýaty** *Rus.* Balkanskiy Velayat. ◐ *province* W Turkmenistan
145 P8 **Balkashino** Akmola, N Kazakhstan
149 O2 **Balkh** *anc.* Bactra. Balkh, N Afghanistan
149 P2 **Balkh** ◐ *province* N Afghanistan
145 T13 **Balkhash** *Kaz.* Balqash. Karaganda, SE Kazakhstan
Balkhash, Lake *see* Balkhash, Ozero
145 T13 **Balkhash, Ozero** *Eng.* Lake Balkhash, *Kaz.* Balqash. ◎ SE Kazakhstan
Balla Balla *see* Mbalabala
96 H10 **Ballachulish** N Scotland, UK
180 M12 **Balladonia** Western Australia
97 C16 **Ballaghaderreen** *Ir.* Bealach an Doirín. C Ireland
92 H10 **Ballangen** *Lapp.* Bálák. Nordland, NW Norway
97 H14 **Ballantrae** W Scotland, UK
183 N12 **Ballarat** Victoria, SE Australia
180 K11 **Ballard, Lake** *salt lake* Western Australia
Ballari *see* Bellary
76 L11 **Ballé** Koulikoro, W Mali
40 D7 **Ballenas, Bahía de** *bay* W Mexico
40 D5 **Ballenas, Canal de** *channel* NW Mexico
195 R17 **Balleny Islands** *island group* Antarctica
40 J7 **Balleza** *var.* San Pablo Balleza. Chihuahua, N Mexico
114 M13 **Ballı** Tekirdağ, NW Turkey
153 O13 **Ballia** Uttar Pradesh, N India
183 V4 **Ballina** New South Wales, SE Australia
97 C16 **Ballina** *Ir.* Béal an Átha. W Ireland
97 D16 **Ballinamore** *Ir.* Béal an Átha Móir. NW Ireland
97 D18 **Ballinasloe** *Ir.* Béal Átha na Sluaighe. W Ireland
25 P8 **Ballinger** Texas, SW USA
97 C17 **Ballinrobe** *Ir.* Baile an Róba. W Ireland
97 A21 **Ballinskelligs Bay** *Ir.* Bá na Scealg. *inlet* SW Ireland
97 D15 **Ballintra** *Ir.* Baile an tSratha. NW Ireland
103 T7 **Ballon d'Alsace** ▲ NE France
Ballon de Guebwiller *see* Grand Ballon
113 K21 **Ballsh** *var.* Ballshi. Fier, SW Albania
Ballshi *see* Ballsh
98 K4 **Ballum** Friesland, N Netherlands
97 F16 **Ballybay** *Ir.* Béal Átha Beithe. N Ireland
97 E14 **Ballybofey** *Ir.* Bealach Féich. NW Ireland
97 G14 **Ballycastle** *Ir.* Baile an Chaistil. N Northern Ireland, UK
97 G15 **Ballyclare** *Ir.* Bealach Cláir. E Northern Ireland, UK
97 E16 **Ballyconnell** *Ir.* Béal Átha Conaill. N Ireland
97 C17 **Ballyhaunis** *Ir.* Beál Átha hAmhnais. W Ireland
97 G14 **Ballymena** *Ir.* An Baile Meánach. NE Northern Ireland, UK
97 F14 **Ballymoney** *Ir.* Baile Monaidh. NE Northern Ireland, UK
97 G15 **Ballynahinch** *Ir.* Baile na hInse. SE Northern Ireland, UK
97 D16 **Ballysadare** *Ir.* Baile Easa Dara. NW Ireland
97 D15 **Ballyshannon** *Ir.* Béal Átha Seanaidh. NW Ireland
63 H19 **Balmaceda** Aisén, S Chile
63 G23 **Balmaceda, Cerro** ▲ S Chile
111 N22 **Balmazújváros** Hajdú-Bihar, E Hungary
108 E10 **Balmhorn** ▲ SW Switzerland
182 L12 **Balmoral** Victoria, SE Australia
24 K9 **Balmorhea** Texas, SW USA
Balneario Claromecó *see* Claromecó
Balochistān *see* Baluchistān
82 B13 **Balombo** *Port.* Norton de Matos, Vila Norton de Matos. Benguela, W Angola
82 B13 **Balombo** ∽ W Angola
181 X10 **Balonne River** ∽ Queensland, E Australia
152 E13 **Bālotra** Rājasthān, N India
145 V14 **Balpyk Bi** *prev.* Kirovskiy *Kaz.* Kīrov. Almaty, SE Kazakhstan
Balqā'/Balqā', Muḩāfaẓat al *see* Al Balqā'
Balqash *see* Balkhash/Balkhash, Ozero
152 M12 **Balrāmpur** Uttar Pradesh, N India
182 M9 **Balranald** New South Wales, SE Australia
116 H14 **Balş** Olt, S Romania
14 H11 **Balsam Creek** Ontario, S Canada
30 I5 **Balsam Lake** Wisconsin, N USA
14 I14 **Balsam Lake** ◎ Ontario, SE Canada
59 M14 **Balsas** Maranhão, E Brazil
40 M15 **Balsas, Río** *var.* Río Mexcala. ∽ S Mexico
43 W16 **Balsas, Río** ∽ SE Panama
119 O18 **Bal'shavik** *Rus.* Bol'shevik. Homyel'skaya Voblasts', SE Belarus
95 O15 **Bålsta** Uppsala, C Sweden
108 E7 **Balsthal** Solothurn, NW Switzerland
117 O8 **Balta** Odes'ka Oblast', SW Ukraine
105 N5 **Baltanás** Castilla-León, N Spain
61 E16 **Baltasar Brum** Artigas, N Uruguay
116 M9 **Bălţi** *Rus.* Bel'tsy. N Moldova
Baltic Port *see* Paldiski
118 B10 **Baltic Sea** *Ger.* Ostee, *Rus.* Baltiskoye More. *sea* N Europe
21 X3 **Baltimore** Maryland, NE USA
31 T13 **Baltimore** Ohio, N USA
21 X3 **Baltimore-Washington** ✕ Maryland, E USA
Baltischport/Baltiski *see* Paldiski
Baltiskoye More *see* Baltic Sea
119 A14 **Baltiysk** *Ger.* Pillau. Kaliningradskaya Oblast', W Russian Federation
Baltkrievija *see* Belarus
119 H14 **Baltoji Vokė** Vilnius, SE Lithuania
Balūchestān va Sīstān *see* Sīstān va Balūchestān
148 M12 **Baluchistān** *var.* Balochistān, Beluchistan. ◐ *province* SW Pakistan
171 P5 **Balud** Masbate, N Philippines
169 T9 **Balui, Batang** ∽ East Malaysia
153 S13 **Bālurghat** West Bengal, NE India
118 J8 **Balvi** Balvi, NE Latvia
147 W7 **Balykchy** *Kir.* Ysyk-Köl; *prev.* Issyk-Kul', Rybach'ye. Issyk-Kul'skaya Oblast', NE Kyrgyzstan
56 B7 **Balzar** Guayas, W Ecuador
108 I8 **Balzers** S Liechtenstein
143 T12 **Bam** Kermān, SE Iran
77 Y13 **Bama** Borno, NE Nigeria
76 L12 **Bamako** ● (Mali) Capital District, SW Mali
77 P10 **Bamba** Gao, C Mali
42 M8 **Bambana, Río** ∽ NE Nicaragua
79 J15 **Bambari** Ouaka, C Central African Republic
181 W5 **Bambaroo** Queensland, NE Australia
101 K19 **Bamberg** Bayern, SE Germany
21 R14 **Bamberg** South Carolina, SE USA
79 M16 **Bambesa** Orientale, N Dem. Rep. Congo
76 G11 **Bambey** W Senegal
79 H16 **Bambio** Sangha-Mbaéré, SW Central African Republic
83 I24 **Bamboesberge** ▲ S South Africa
79 D14 **Bamenda** Nord-Ouest, W Cameroon
10 K17 **Bamfield** Vancouver Island, British Columbia, SW Canada
Bami *see* Bamy
149 P4 **Bāmīān** *var.* Bāmiān. Bāmīān, NE Afghanistan
149 O4 **Bāmīān** ◐ *province* C Afghanistan
79 J14 **Bamingui** Bamingui-Bangoran, C Central African Republic
78 J13 **Bamingui** ∽ N Central African Republic
78 J13 **Bamingui-Bangoran** ◐ *prefecture* N Central African Republic
143 V13 **Bampūr** Sīstān va Balūchestān, SE Iran
186 C8 **Bamu** ∽ SW PNG
146 E12 **Bamy** *Rus.* Bami. Ahal Welaýaty, C Turkmenistan
Bán *see* Bánovce nad Bebravou
81 N17 **Banaadir** *off.* Gobolka Banaadir. ◐ *region* S Somalia
191 N3 **Banaba** *var.* Ocean Island. *island* Tungaru, W Kiribati
59 O14 **Banabuiú, Açude** ⊡ NE Brazil
57 O19 **Bañados del Izozog** *salt lake* SE Bolivia
97 D18 **Banagher** *Ir.* Beannchar. C Ireland
79 M17 **Banalia** Orientale, N Dem. Rep. Congo
76 L12 **Banamba** Koulikoro, W Mali
40 G4 **Banámichi** Sonora, NW Mexico
181 Y9 **Banana** Queensland, E Australia
191 Z2 **Banana** *prev.* Main Camp. Kiritimati, E Kiribati
59 K16 **Bananal, Ilha do** *island* C Brazil
23 Y12 **Banana River** *lagoon* Florida, SE USA
151 Q22 **Bananga** Andaman and Nicobar Islands, India, NE Indian Ocean
Banaras *see* Vārānasi
114 N13 **Banarlı** Tekirdağ, NW Turkey
152 H12 **Banās** ∽ N India
75 Z11 **Banās, Rås** *headland* E Egypt
112 N10 **Banatski Karlovac** Serbia, NE Serbia and Montenegro (Yugo.)
141 P16 **Banā, Wādī** *dry watercourse* SW Yemen
136 E14 **Banaz** Uşak, W Turkey
136 E14 **Banaz Çayı** ∽ W Turkey
159 P14 **Banbar** *var.* Coka. Xizang Zizhiqu, W China
97 G15 **Banbridge** *Ir.* Droichead na Banna. SE Northern Ireland, UK
Ban Bua Yai *see* Bua Yai
97 M21 **Banbury** S England, UK
167 O7 **Ban Chiang Dao** Chiang Mai, NW Thailand
96 K9 **Banchory** NE Scotland, UK
14 J13 **Bancroft** Ontario, SE Canada
33 R15 **Bancroft** Idaho, NW USA
29 U11 **Bancroft** Iowa, C USA
154 I9 **Banda** Madhya Pradesh, C India
152 L13 **Bānda** Uttar Pradesh, N India
168 F7 **Bandaaceh** *var.* Banda Atjeh; *prev.* Koetaradja, Kutaradja, Kutaraja. Sumatera, W Indonesia
Banda Atjeh *see* Bandaaceh
171 S14 **Banda, Kepulauan** *island group* E Indonesia
Banda, Laut *see* Banda Sea
77 N17 **Bandama** *var.* Bandama Fleuve. ∽ S Ivory Coast
77 N15 **Bandama Blanc** ∽ C Ivory Coast
Bandama Fleuve *see* Bandama
Bandar 'Abbās *see* Bandar-e 'Abbās
153 W16 **Bandarban** Chittagong, SE Bangladesh
80 Q13 **Bandarbeyla** *var.* Bender Beila, Bender Beyla. Bari, NE Somalia
143 R14 **Bandar-e 'Abbās** *var.* Bandar 'Abbās; *prev.* Gombroon. Hormozgān, S Iran
142 M3 **Bandar-e Anzalī** Gīlān, NW Iran
143 N12 **Bandar-e Būshehr** *var.* Būshehr, *Eng.* Bushire. Būshehr, S Iran
142 M11 **Bandar-e Gonāveh** *var.* Ganāveh; *prev.* Gonāveh. Būshehr, SW Iran
143 R14 **Bandar-e Khamīr** Hormozgān, S Iran
143 Q14 **Bandar-e Langeh** *var.* Bandar-e Lengeh, Lingeh. Hormozgān, S Iran
Bandar-e Lengeh *see* Bandar-e Langeh
142 L10 **Bandar-e Māhshahr** *var.* Māh-Shahr; *prev.* Bandar-e Ma'shūr. Khūzestān, SW Iran
Bandar-e Ma'shūr *see* Bandar-e Māhshahr
143 O14 **Bandar-e Nakhīlū** Hormozgān, S Iran
Bandar-e Shāh *see* Bandar-e Torkaman
143 P4 **Bandar-e Torkaman** *var.* Bandar-e Torkeman, Bandar-e Torkman; *prev.* Bandar-e Shāh. Golestān, N Iran
Bandar-e Torkeman/Bandar-e Torkman *see* Bandar-e Torkaman

Bandar Kassim *see* Boosaaso
168 M15 **Bandarlampung** *prev.* Tanjungkarang, Teloekbetoeng, Telukbetung. Sumatera, W Indonesia
Bandar Maharani *see* Muar
Bandar Masulipatnam *see* Machilīpatnam
Bandar Penggaram *see* Batu Pahat
169 T7 **Bandar Seri Begawan** *prev.* Brunei Town. ● (Brunei) N Brunei
169 T7 **Bandar Seri Begawan** ✕ N Brunei
171 R15 **Banda Sea** *var.* Laut Banda. *sea* E Indonesia
104 H5 **Bande** Galicia, NW Spain
59 G15 **Bandeirantes** Mato Grosso, W Brazil
59 N20 **Bandeira, Pico da** ▲ SE Brazil
83 K19 **Bandelierkop** Limpopo, NE South Africa
62 L8 **Bandera** Santiago del Estero, N Argentina
25 Q11 **Bandera** Texas, SW USA
40 J13 **Banderas, Bahía de** *bay* W Mexico
77 O11 **Bandiagara** Mopti, C Mali
152 I12 **Bāndīkūi** Rājasthān, N India
136 C11 **Bandırma** *var.* Penderma. Balıkesir, NW Turkey
Bandjarmasin *see* Banjarmasin
Bandoeng *see* Bandung
97 C21 **Bandon** *Ir.* Droicheadna Bandan. SW Ireland
32 E14 **Bandon** Oregon, NW USA
167 R8 **Ban Dong Bang** Nong Khai, E Thailand
167 Q6 **Ban Donkon** Oudômxai, N Laos
172 J14 **Bandrélé** SE Mayotte
79 H20 **Bandundu** *prev.* Banningville. Bandundu, W Dem. Rep. Congo
79 I21 **Bandundu** *off.* Région de Bandundu. ◈ *region* W Dem. Rep. Congo
169 O16 **Bandung** *prev.* Bandoeng. Jawa, C Indonesia
116 L15 **Băneasa** Constanța, SW Romania
142 J4 **Bāneh** Kordestān, N Iran
44 I7 **Banes** Holguín, E Cuba
11 P16 **Banff** Alberta, SW Canada
96 K8 **Banff** NE Scotland, UK
96 K8 **Banff** *cultural region* NE Scotland, UK
Bánffyhunyad *see* Huedin
77 N14 **Banfora** SW Burkina
155 H19 **Bangalore** Karnātaka, S India
153 S16 **Bangaon** West Bengal, NE India
79 L15 **Bangassou** Mbomou, SE Central African Republic
186 D7 **Bangeta, Mount** ▲ C PNG
171 P12 **Banggai, Kepulauan** *island group* C Indonesia
171 Q12 **Banggai, Pulau** *island* Kepulauan Banggai, N Indonesia
171 X13 **Banggelapa** Papua, E Indonesia
Banggi *see* Banggi, Pulau
169 V6 **Banggi, Pulau** *var.* Banggi. *island* East Malaysia
121 P13 **Banghāzī** *Eng.* Bengazi, Benghazi, *It.* Bengasi. NE Libya
Bang Hieng *see* Xé Banghiang
169 O13 **Bangka-Belitung** *off.* Propinsi Bangka-Belitung. ◈ *province* W Indonesia
169 P11 **Bangkai, Tanjung** *var.* Bankai. *headland* Borneo, N Indonesia
169 S16 **Bangkalan** Pulau Madura, C Indonesia
169 N12 **Bangka, Pulau** *island* W Indonesia
169 N13 **Bangka, Selat** *strait* Sumatera, W Indonesia
168 J11 **Bangkinang** Sumatera, W Indonesia
168 K12 **Bangko** Sumatera, W Indonesia
Bangkok *see* Krung Thep
Bangkok, Bight of *see* Krung Thep, Ao
153 T14 **Bangladesh** *off.* People's Republic of Bangladesh; *prev.* East Pakistan. ◆ *republic* S Asia
167 V13 **Ba Ngoi** Khanh Hoa, S Vietnam
152 K5 **Bangong Co** *var.* Pangong Tso. ◎ China/India *see also* Pangong Tso
97 G15 **Bangor** *Ir.* Beannchar. E Northern Ireland, UK
97 I18 **Bangor** NW Wales, UK
19 R6 **Bangor** Maine, NE USA
18 I14 **Bangor** Pennsylvania, NE USA
Bang Phra *see* Trat
Bang Pla Soi *see* Chon Buri
25 Q8 **Bangs** Texas, SW USA
167 N13 **Bang Saphan** *var.* Bang Saphan Yai. Prachuap Khiri Khan, SW Thailand
Bang Saphan Yai *see* Bang Saphan
36 I8 **Bangs, Mount** ▲ Arizona, SW USA
93 E15 **Bangsund** Nord-Trøndelag, C Norway
171 O2 **Bangued** Luzon, N Philippines
79 I15 **Bangui** ● (Central African Republic) Ombella-Mpoko, SW Central African Republic
79 I15 **Bangui** ✕ Ombella-Mpoko, SW Central African Republic
83 N16 **Bangula** Southern, S Malawi
Bangwaketse *see* Southern
82 K12 **Bangweulu, Lake** *var.* Lake Bengweulu. ◎ N Zambia
Banhā *see* Benha
Ban Hat Yai *see* Hat Yai
167 Q7 **Ban Hin Heup** Viangchan, C Laos
Ban Houayxay/Ban Houei Sai *see* Houayxay
167 O12 **Ban Hua Hin** *var.* Hua Hin. Prachuap Khiri Khan, SW Thailand
79 L14 **Bani** Haute-Kotto, E Central African Republic
77 N12 **Bani** ≈ S Mali
45 O9 **Baní** S Dominican Republic
Banias *see* Bāniyās
77 S11 **Bani Bangou** Tillabéri, SW Niger
76 M12 **Banifing** *var.* Ngorolaka. ≈ Burkina/Mali
77 R13 **Banikoara** N Benin
Banī Mazār *see* Beni Mazâr
114 K8 **Baniski Lom** ≈ N Bulgaria
21 U7 **Banister River** ≈ Virginia, NE USA
Banī Suwayf *see* Beni Suef
75 O8 **Banī Walīd** NW Libya
138 H5 **Bāniyās** *var.* Banias, Baniyas, Paneas. Tarṭūs, W Syria
113 K14 **Banja** Serbia, W Serbia and Montenegro (Yugo.)
Banjak, Kepulauan *see* Banyak, Kepulauan
112 J12 **Banja Koviljača** Serbia, W Serbia and Montenegro (Yugo.)
112 G11 **Banja Luka** Republika Srpska, NW Bosnia and Herzegovina
169 T13 **Banjarmasin** *prev.* Bandjarmasin. Borneo, C Indonesia
76 F11 **Banjul** *prev.* Bathurst. ● (Gambia) W Gambia
76 F11 **Banjul** ✕ W Gambia
Bank *see* Bankä
137 Y13 **Bankä** *Rus.* Bank. SE Azerbaijan
167 S11 **Ban Kadian** *var.* Ban Kadiene. Champasak, S Laos
Ban Kadiene *see* Ban Kadian
Bankai *see* Bangkai, Tanjung
166 M14 **Ban Kam Phuam** Phangnga, SW Thailand
Ban Kantang *see* Kantang
77 O11 **Bankass** Mopti, S Mali
95 L19 **Bankeryd** Jönköping, S Sweden
83 K16 **Banket** Mashonaland West, N Zimbabwe
167 T11 **Ban Khamphô** Attapu, S Laos
23 O4 **Bankhead Lake** ▣ Alabama, S USA
77 Q11 **Bankilaré** Tillabéri, SW Niger
Banks, Îles *see* Banks Islands
10 I14 **Banks Island** *island* British Columbia, SW Canada
187 R12 **Banks Islands** *Fr.* Îles Banks. *island group* N Vanuatu
23 U8 **Banks Lake** ◎ Georgia, SE USA
32 K8 **Banks Lake** ▣ Washington, NW USA
185 I19 **Banks Peninsula** *peninsula* South Island, NZ
183 Q15 **Banks Strait** *strait* SW Tasman Sea
Ban Kui Nua *see* Kui Buri
153 R16 **Bānkura** West Bengal, NE India
167 S8 **Ban Lakxao** *var.* Lak Sao. Bolikhamxai, C Laos
167 O16 **Ban Lam Phai** Songkhla, SW Thailand
Ban Mae Sot *see* Mae Sot
Ban Mae Suai *see* Mae Suai
Ban Mak Khaeng *see* Udon Thani
166 M3 **Banmauk** Sagaing, N Burma
Banmo *see* Bhamo
167 T10 **Ban Mun-Houamuang** S Laos
97 F14 **Bann** *var.* Lower Bann, Upper Bann. ≈ N Northern Ireland, UK
167 S10 **Ban Nadou** Salavan, S Laos
167 S9 **Ban Nakala** Savannakhét, S Laos
167 Q8 **Ban Nakha** Viangchan, C Laos
167 S9 **Ban Nakham** Khammouan, S Laos
167 P7 **Ban Namoun** Xaignabouli, N Laos
167 O17 **Ban Nang Sata** Yala, SW Thailand
167 N15 **Ban Na San** Surat Thani, SW Thailand
167 R7 **Ban Nasi** Xiangkhoang, N Laos
44 I3 **Bannerman Town** Eleuthera Island, C Bahamas
35 V15 **Banning** California, W USA
Banningville *see* Bandundu
167 S11 **Ban Nongsim** Champasak, S Laos
149 S7 **Bannu** *prev.* Edwardesabad. North-West Frontier Province, NW Pakistan
Bañolas *see* Banyoles
56 C7 **Baños** Tungurahua, C Ecuador
Bánovce *see* Bánovce nad Bebravou
111 I19 **Bánovce nad Bebravou** *var.* Bánovce, *Hung.* Bán. Trenčiansky Kraj, W Slovakia
112 I12 **Banovići** Federacija Bosna I Hercegovina, E Bosnia and Herzegovina
Banow *see* Andarāb
Ban Pak Phanang *see* Pak Phanang
167 O7 **Ban Pan Nua** Lampang, NW Thailand
167 Q9 **Ban Phai** Khon Kaen, E Thailand
167 T9 **Ban Phou A Douk** Khammouan, C Laos
167 Q8 **Ban Phu** Uthai Thani, W Thailand
167 O11 **Ban Pong** Ratchaburi, W Thailand
190 I3 **Banraeaba** Tarawa, W Kiribati
167 N10 **Ban Sai Yok** Kanchanaburi, W Thailand
Ban Sattahip/Ban Sattahipp *see* Sattahip
Ban Sichon *see* Sichon
Ban Si Racha *see* Siracha
111 J19 **Banská Bystrica** *Ger.* Neusohl, *Hung.* Besztercebánya. Banskobystrický Kraj, C Slovakia
111 K20 **Banskobystrický Kraj** ◈ *region* C Slovakia
167 R8 **Ban Sôppheung** Bolikhamxai, C Laos
Ban Sop Prap *see* Sop Prap
152 G15 **Bānswāra** Rājasthān, N India
167 N15 **Ban Ta Khun** Surat Thani, SW Thailand
Ban Takua Pa *see* Takua Pa
167 S8 **Ban Talak** Khammouan, C Laos
77 R15 **Bantè** W Benin
169 N16 **Banten** *off.* Propinsi Banten. ◈ *province* W Indonesia
167 Q8 **Ban Thabôk** Bolikhamxai, C Laos
167 T9 **Ban Tôp** Savannakhét, S Laos
97 B21 **Bantry** *Ir.* Beanntraí. SW Ireland
97 A21 **Bantry Bay** *Ir.* Bá Bheanntraí. *bay* SW Ireland
155 F19 **Bantvāl** *var.* Bantwāl. Karnātaka, E India
Bantwāl *see* Bantvāl
114 N9 **Banya** Burgas, E Bulgaria
168 G10 **Banyak, Kepulauan** *prev.* Kepulauan Banjak. *island group* NW Indonesia
105 U8 **Banya, La** *headland* E Spain
79 E14 **Banyo** Adamaoua, NW Cameroon
105 X4 **Banyoles** *var.* Bañolas. Cataluña, NE Spain
167 N16 **Ban Yong Sata** Trang, SW Thailand
195 X14 **Banzare Coast** *physical region* Antarctica
173 Q14 **Banzare Seamounts** *undersea feature* S Indian Ocean
Banzart *see* Bizerte
163 Q12 **Baochang** *var.* Taibus Qi. Nei Mongol Zizhiqu, N China
161 O3 **Baoding** *var.* Pao-ting; *prev.* Tsingyuan. Hebei, E China
Baoebaoe *see* Baubau
Baoi, Oileán *see* Dursey Island
160 J6 **Baoji** *var.* Pao-chi, Paoki. Shaanxi, C China
163 U9 **Baokang** *var.* Hoqin Zuoyi Zhongji. Nei Mongol Zizhiqu, N China
186 L8 **Baolo** Santa Isabel, N Solomon Islands
157 U13 **Bao Lôc** Lâm Đông, S Vietnam
153 Z7 **Baoqing** Heilongjiang, NE China
Baoqing *see* Shaoyang
79 H15 **Baoro** Nana-Mambéré, W Central African Republic
160 E12 **Baoshan** *var.* Pao-shan. Yunnan, SW China
163 N13 **Baotou** *var.* Pao-t'ou, Paotow. Nei Mongol Zizhiqu, N China
76 L14 **Baoulé** ≈ S Mali
76 K12 **Baoulé** ≈ W Mali
103 O2 **Bapaume** Pas-de-Calais, N France
14 J13 **Baptiste Lake** ◎ Ontario, SE Canada
Bapu *see* Meigu
Baqanas *see* Bakanas
Baqbaqty *see* Bakbakty
159 P14 **Baqên** *var.* Dartang. Xizang Zizhiqu, W China
138 F14 **Bāqir, Jabal** ⛰ S Jordan
139 T7 **Ba'qūbah** *var.* Qubba. C Iraq
62 H5 **Baquedano** Antofagasta, N Chile
116 M6 **Bar** Vinnyts'ka Oblast', C Ukraine
113 J18 **Bar** *It.* Antivari. Montenegro, SW Serbia and Montenegro (Yugo.)
80 E10 **Bara** Northern Kordofan, C Sudan
81 M18 **Baraawe** *It.* Brava. Shabeellaha Hoose, S Somalia
152 M12 **Bāra Banki** Uttar Pradesh, N India
30 L8 **Baraboo** Wisconsin, N USA
30 K8 **Baraboo Range** *hill range* Wisconsin, N USA
Baracaldo *see* San Vicente de Barakaldo
15 Y6 **Barachois** Québec, SE Canada
44 J7 **Baracoa** Guantánamo, E Cuba
61 C19 **Baradero** Buenos Aires, E Argentina
183 R6 **Baradine** New South Wales, SE Australia
Baraf Daja Islands *see* Damar, Kepulauan
154 M12 **Baragarh** Orissa, E India
81 I17 **Baragoi** Rift Valley, W Kenya
45 N9 **Barahona** SW Dominican Republic
153 W13 **Barail Range** ⛰ NE India
80 I9 **Baraka** *var.* Barka, *Ar.* Khawr Barakah. *seasonal river* Eritrea/Sudan
80 G10 **Barakat** Gezira, C Sudan
Barakī *see* Barakī Barak
149 Q6 **Barakī Barak** *var.* Barakī, Baraki Rajan. Lowgar, E Afghanistan
Baraki Rajan *see* Barakī Barak
154 N11 **Bārākot** Orissa, E India
55 S7 **Barama River** ≈ N Guyana
155 E14 **Bārāmati** Mahārāshtra, W India
152 H5 **Bārāmūla** Jammu and Kashmir, NW India
119 N14 **Baran'** Vitsyebskaya Voblasts', NE Belarus
152 I14 **Bārān** Rājasthān, N India
139 U4 **Barānān, Shākh-i** ⛰ E Iraq
119 I17 **Baranavichy** *Pol.* Baranowicze, *Rus.* Baranovichi. Brestskaya Voblasts', SW Belarus
123 T6 **Baranikha** Chukotskiy Avtonomnyy Okrug, NE Russian Federation
116 M4 **Baranivka** Zhytomyrs'ka Oblast', N Ukraine
39 W14 **Baranof Island** *island* Alexander Archipelago, Alaska, USA
Baranovichi/Baranowicze *see* Baranavichy
111 N15 **Baranów Sandomierski** Podkarpackie, SE Poland
111 I26 **Baranya** *off.* Baranya Megye. ◈ *county* S Hungary
153 R13 **Barāri** Bihār, NE India
22 L10 **Barataria Bay** *bay* Louisiana, S USA
Barat Daya, Kepulauan *see* Damar, Kepulauan
118 L12 **Baravukha** *Rus.* Borovukha. Vitsyebskaya Voblasts', N Belarus
54 E11 **Baraya** Huila, C Colombia
59 M21 **Barbacena** Minas Gerais, SE Brazil
54 B13 **Barbacoas** Nariño, SW Colombia
54 L6 **Barbacoas** Aragua, N Venezuela
45 Z13 **Barbados** ◆ *commonwealth republic* SE West Indies
105 U11 **Barbaria, Cap de** *var.* Cabo de Berberia. *headland* Formentera, E Spain
114 N13 **Barbaros** Tekirdağ, NW Turkey
74 A11 **Barbas, Cap** *headland* S Western Sahara
105 T5 **Barbastro** Aragón, NE Spain
104 K16 **Barbate** ≈ SW Spain
104 K16 **Barbate de Franco** Andalucía, S Spain
9 N1 **Barbeau Peak** ▲ Nunavut, N Canada
83 K21 **Barberton** Mpumalanga, NE South Africa
31 U12 **Barberton** Ohio, N USA
102 K12 **Barbezieux-St-Hilaire** Charente, W France
54 G9 **Barbosa** Boyacá, C Colombia
21 N7 **Barbourville** Kentucky, S USA
45 W9 **Barbuda** *island* N Antigua and Barbuda
181 W8 **Barcaldine** Queensland, E Australia
Barcarozsnyó *see* Râşnov
104 I11 **Barcarrota** Extremadura, W Spain
Barcău *see* Berettyó
Barce *see* Al Marj
107 L23 **Barcellona** *var.* Barcellona Pozzo di Gotto. Sicilia, Italy, C Mediterranean Sea
Barcellona Pozzo di Gotto *see* Barcellona
105 W6 **Barcelona** *anc.* Barcino, Barcinona. Cataluña, E Spain
55 N5 **Barcelona** Anzoátegui, NE Venezuela
105 S5 **Barcelona** ◈ *province* Cataluña, NE Spain
105 W6 **Barcelona** ✕ Cataluña, E Spain
103 U14 **Barcelonnette** Alpes-de-Haute-Provence, SE France
58 E12 **Barcelos** Amazonas, N Brazil
104 G5 **Barcelos** Braga, N Portugal
110 I10 **Barcin** *Ger.* Bartschin. Kujawski-pomorskie, C Poland
Barcino/Barcinona *see* Barcelona
Barcoo *see* Cooper Creek
111 H26 **Barcs** Somogy, SW Hungary
137 W11 **Bärdä** *Rus.* Barda. C Azerbaijan
78 H5 **Bardaï** Borkou-Ennedi-Tibesti, N Chad
139 R2 **Bardaṛash** N Iraq
139 Q7 **Bardasah** SW Iraq
153 S16 **Barddhamān** West Bengal, NE India
111 N18 **Bardejov** *Ger.* Bartfeld, *Hung.* Bártfa. Prešovský Kraj, E Slovakia
105 R4 **Bárdenas Reales** *physical region* N Spain
Bardera/Bardere *see* Baardheere
Bardesīr *see* Bardsīr
92 K3 **Bárdharbunga** ▲ C Iceland
Bardhë, Drini i *see* Beli Drim
106 E9 **Bardi** Emilia-Romagna, C Italy
106 A8 **Bardonecchia** Piemonte, W Italy
97 H19 **Bardsey Island** *island* NW Wales, UK
143 S11 **Bardsīr** *var.* Bardesīr, Mashīz. Kermān, C Iran
20 L6 **Bardstown** Kentucky, S USA
Barduli *see* Barletta
20 G7 **Bardwell** Kentucky, S USA
152 K11 **Bareilly** *var.* Bareli. Uttar Pradesh, N India
Bareli *see* Bareilly
98 H13 **Barendrecht** Zuid-Holland, SW Netherlands
102 M3 **Barentin** Seine-Maritime, N France
92 N3 **Barentsburg** Spitsbergen, W Svalbard
Barentsevo More/Barents Havet *see* Barents Sea
92 O3 **Barentsøya** *island* E Svalbard
197 T11 **Barents Plain** *undersea feature* N Barents Sea
127 P3 **Barents Sea** *Nor.* Barents Havet, *Rus.* Barentsevo More. *sea* Arctic Ocean
197 U14 **Barents Trough** *undersea feature* SW Barents Sea
80 I9 **Barentu** W Eritrea
102 J3 **Barfleur** Manche, N France
102 J3 **Barfleur, Pointe de** *headland* N France
Barfrush/Barfurush *see* Bābol
158 H14 **Barga** Xizang Zizhiqu, W China
105 N9 **Bargas** Castilla-La Mancha, C Spain
81 I15 **Bargē** Southern, S Ethiopia
106 A9 **Barge** Piemonte, NE Italy
153 U16 **Barguna** Khulna, S Bangladesh
Bärguşad *see* Vorotan
123 N13 **Barguzin** Respublika Buryatiya, S Russian Federation
153 O13 **Barhaj** Uttar Pradesh, N India
183 N10 **Barham** New South Wales, SE Australia
152 J12 **Barhan** Uttar Pradesh, N India
19 S7 **Bar Harbor** Mount Desert Island, Maine, NE USA
153 R14 **Barharwa** Jhārkhand, NE India
153 P15 **Barhi** Jhārkhand, N India
107 O17 **Bari** *var.* Bari delle Puglie; *anc.* Barium. Puglia, SE Italy
80 P12 **Bari** *off.* Gobolka Bari. ◈ *region* NE Somalia
167 T14 **Ba Ria** Ba Ria-Vung Tau, S Vietnam
Bāridah *see* Al Bāridah
Bari delle Puglie *see* Bari
Barikot *see* Barīkowṭ
149 T4 **Barīkowṭ** *var.* Barikot. Kunar, NE Afghanistan
42 C4 **Barillas** *var.* Santa Cruz Barillas. Huehuetenango, NW Guatemala
54 J6 **Barinas** Barinas, W Venezuela
54 I7 **Barinas** *off.* Estado Barinas; *prev.* Zamora. ◈ *state* C Venezuela
54 I6 **Barinitas** Barinas, NW Venezuela
154 P11 **Bāripada** Orissa, E India
60 K9 **Bariri** São Paulo, S Brazil
75 W11 **Bârîs** S Egypt
152 G14 **Bari Sādri** Rājasthān, N India
153 U16 **Barisal** Khulna, S Bangladesh
168 I10 **Barisan, Pegunungan** ⛰ Sumatera, W Indonesia
169 T12 **Barito, Sungai** ≈ Borneo, C Indonesia
Barium *see* Bari
Bårjås *see* Porjus
Barka *see* Baraka
Barka *see* Al Marj
160 H8 **Barkam** Sichuan, C China
118 J9 **Barkava** Madona, C Latvia
10 M15 **Barkerville** British Columbia, SW Canada
14 J12 **Bark Lake** ◎ Ontario, SE Canada
20 H7 **Barkley, Lake** ▣ Kentucky/Tennessee, S USA
10 K17 **Barkley Sound** *inlet* British Columbia, W Canada
83 J24 **Barkly East** *Afr.* Barkly-Oos. Eastern Cape, SE South Africa
Barkly-Oos *see* Barkly East
181 S4 **Barkly Tableland** *plateau* Northern Territory/Queensland, N Australia
Barkly-Wes *see* Barkly West
83 H22 **Barkly West** *Afr.* Barkly-Wes. Northern Cape, N South Africa
159 O5 **Barkol** *var.* Barkol Kazak Zizhixian. Xinjiang Uygur Zizhiqu, NW China
159 O5 **Barkol Hu** ◎ NW China
Barkol Kazak Zizhixian *see* Barkol
30 J3 **Bark Point** *headland* Wisconsin, N USA
25 P11 **Barksdale** Texas, SW USA
Bar Kunar *see* Asmār
116 L11 **Bârlad** *prev.* Bîrlad. Vaslui, E Romania
116 M11 **Bârlad** *prev.* Bîrlad. ≈ E Romania
76 D9 **Barlavento, Ilhas de** *var.* Windward Islands. *island group* N Cape Verde
103 R5 **Bar-le-Duc** *var.* Bar-sur-Ornain. Meuse, NE France
180 K11 **Barlee, Lake** ◎ Western Australia
180 H8 **Barlee Range** ⛰ Western Australia
107 N16 **Barletta** *anc.* Barduli. Puglia, SE Italy
110 E10 **Barlinek** *Ger.* Berlinchen. Zachodnio-pomorskie, NW Poland
27 S11 **Barling** Arkansas, C USA
171 U12 **Barma** Papua, E Indonesia
183 Q9 **Barmedman** New South Wales, SE Australia
Barmen-Elberfeld *see* Wuppertal
152 D12 **Bārmer** Rājasthān, NW India
182 K9 **Barmera** South Australia
97 I19 **Barmouth** NW Wales, UK
154 F10 **Barnagar** Madhya Pradesh, C India
152 H9 **Barnāla** Punjab, NW India
97 L15 **Barnard Castle** N England, UK
183 O6 **Barnato** New South Wales, SE Australia
122 I13 **Barnaul** Altayskiy Kray, C Russian Federation
109 V8 **Bärnbach** Steiermark, SE Austria
18 K16 **Barnegat** New Jersey, NE USA
23 S4 **Barnesville** Georgia, SE USA
29 R6 **Barnesville** Minnesota, N USA
31 U13 **Barnesville** Ohio, N USA
98 K11 **Barneveld** *var.* Barnveld. Gelderland, C Netherlands
25 O9 **Barnhart** Texas, SW USA
27 P8 **Barnsdall** Oklahoma, C USA
97 M17 **Barnsley** N England, UK
19 Q12 **Barnstable** Massachusetts, NE USA
97 I23 **Barnstaple** SW England, UK
Barnveld *see* Barneveld
21 Q14 **Barnwell** South Carolina, SE USA
77 U15 **Baro** Niger, C Nigeria
Baro *see* Baro Wenz
Baroda *see* Vadodara
149 U2 **Baroghil Pass** *var.* Kowtal-e Barowghīl. *pass* Afghanistan/Pakistan
119 Q17 **Baron'ki** *Rus.* Boron'ki. Mahilyowskaya Voblasts', E Belarus
182 J9 **Barossa Valley** *valley* South Australia
Baroui *see* Salisbury
81 H14 **Baro Wenz** *var.* Baro, Nahr Barū. ≈ Ethiopia/Sudan
153 U12 **Barpeta** Assam, NE India
31 S7 **Barques, Pointe Aux** *headland* Michigan, N USA
54 I5 **Barquisimeto** Lara, NW Venezuela
59 N16 **Barra** Bahia, E Brazil
96 E9 **Barra** *island* NW Scotland, UK
183 T5 **Barraba** New South Wales, SE Australia
60 L9 **Barra Bonita** São Paulo, S Brazil
64 J12 **Barracuda Fracture Zone** *var.* Fifteen Twenty Fracture Zone. *tectonic feature* SW Atlantic Ocean
64 G11 **Barracuda Ridge** *undersea feature* N Atlantic Ocean
43 N12 **Barra del Colorado** Limón, NE Costa Rica
43 N9 **Barra de Río Grande** Región Autónoma Atlántico Sur, E Nicaragua
82 A11 **Barra do Cuanza** Luanda, NW Angola
60 O9 **Barra do Piraí** Rio de Janeiro, SE Brazil
61 D16 **Barra do Quaraí** Rio Grande do Sul, SE Brazil
59 G14 **Barra do São Manuel** Pará, N Brazil
83 N19 **Barra Falsa, Ponta da** *headland* S Mozambique
96 E10 **Barra Head** *headland* NW Scotland, UK
Barram *see* Baram, Batang
60 O9 **Barra Mansa** Rio de Janeiro, SE Brazil
57 D14 **Barranca** Lima, W Peru
54 F8 **Barrancabermeja** Santander, N Colombia
54 H4 **Barrancas** La Guajira, N Colombia
54 J6 **Barrancas** Barinas, NW Venezuela
55 Q6 **Barrancas** Monagas, NE Venezuela
54 F6 **Barranco de Loba** Bolívar, N Colombia
104 I12 **Barrancos** Beja, S Portugal
62 N7 **Barranqueras** Chaco, N Argentina
54 E4 **Barranquilla** Atlántico, N Colombia
83 N20 **Barra, Ponta da** *headland* S Mozambique
105 P11 **Barrax** Castilla-La Mancha, C Spain
19 N11 **Barre** Massachusetts, NE USA
18 M7 **Barre** Vermont, NE USA
59 M17 **Barreiras** Bahia, E Brazil
104 F11 **Barreiro** Setúbal, W Portugal
65 C26 **Barren Island** *island* S Falkland Islands
20 K7 **Barren River Lake** ▣ Kentucky, S USA
60 L7 **Barretos** São Paulo, S Brazil
11 P14 **Barrhead** Alberta, SW Canada
14 G14 **Barrie** Ontario, S Canada
11 N16 **Barrière** British Columbia, SW Canada
14 H8 **Barrière, Lac** ◎ Québec, SE Canada
182 L6 **Barrier Range** *hill range* New South Wales, SE Australia
42 G3 **Barrier Reef** *reef* E Belize
188 C16 **Barrigada** C Guam
Barrington Island *see* Santa Fe, Isla
183 T7 **Barrington Tops** ▲ New South Wales, SE Australia
183 O4 **Barringun** New South Wales, SE Australia
59 K18 **Barro Alto** Goiás, S Brazil
59 N14 **Barro Duro** Piauí, NE Brazil
30 I5 **Barron** Wisconsin, N USA
14 J12 **Barron** ≈ Ontario, SE Canada
61 H15 **Barros Cassal** Rio Grande do Sul, S Brazil
45 P14 **Barrouallie** Saint Vincent, W Saint Vincent and the Grenadines
39 O4 **Barrow** Alaska, USA
97 E20 **Barrow** *Ir.* An Bhearú. ≈ SE Ireland
181 Q6 **Barrow Creek Roadhouse** Northern Territory, N Australia
97 J16 **Barrow-in-Furness** NW England, UK
180 G7 **Barrow Island** *island* Western Australia
39 O4 **Barrow, Point** *headland* Alaska, USA
11 V14 **Barrows** Manitoba, S Canada
97 J22 **Barry** S Wales, UK
14 J12 **Barry's Bay** Ontario, SE Canada
144 K14 **Barsakel'mes, Ostrov** *island* SW Kazakhstan
Baršć Łužyca *see* Forst
147 S14 **Barsem** S Tajikistan
145 V11 **Barshatas** Vostochnyy Kazakhstan, E Kazakhstan
155 F14 **Bārsi** Mahārāshtra, W India
100 I13 **Barsinghausen** Niedersachsen, C Germany
147 X8 **Barskoon** Issyk-Kul'skaya Oblast', E Kyrgyzstan
100 F10 **Barssel** Niedersachsen, NW Germany
35 U14 **Barstow** California, W USA
24 L8 **Barstow** Texas, SW USA
103 R6 **Bar-sur-Aube** Aube, NE France
Bar-sur-Ornain *see* Bar-le-Duc
103 Q6 **Bar-sur-Seine** Aube, N France
147 S13 **Bartang** S Tajikistan
147 T13 **Bartang** ≈ SE Tajikistan
Bartenstein *see* Bartoszyce
Bártfa/Bartfeld *see* Bardejov
100 N7 **Barth** Mecklenburg-Vorpommern, NE Germany
27 W13 **Bartholomew, Bayou** ≈ Arkansas/Louisiana, S USA
55 T8 **Bartica** N Guyana
136 H10 **Bartın** Bartin, NW Turkey
136 H10 **Bartın** ◈ *province* NW Turkey
181 W4 **Bartle Frere** ▲ Queensland, E Australia
27 P8 **Bartlesville** Oklahoma, C USA
29 P14 **Bartlett** Nebraska, C USA
20 E10 **Bartlett** Tennessee, S USA
25 T9 **Bartlett** Texas, SW USA
36 L13 **Bartlett Reservoir** ▣ Arizona, SW USA
19 N6 **Barton** Vermont, NE USA
110 L7 **Bartoszyce** *Ger.* Bartenstein. Warmińsko-Mazurskie, NE Poland
23 W12 **Bartow** Florida, SE USA
Bartschin *see* Barcin

168 J10 Barumun, Sungai ≈ Sumatera, W Indonesia
Barū, Nahr see Baro Wenz
169 S17 Barung, Nusa island S Indonesia
168 H9 Barus Sumatera, NW Indonesia
162 L10 Baruunsuu Ömnögovĭ, S Mongolia
163 P8 Baruun-Urt Sühbaatar, E Mongolia
43 P15 Barú, Volcán var. Volcán de Chiriquí. ✻ W Panama
99 K21 Barvaux Luxembourg, SE Belgium
42 M13 Barva, Volcán ✻ NW Costa Rica
117 W6 Barvinkove Kharkivs'ka Oblast', E Ukraine
154 G11 Barwāh Madhya Pradesh, C India
Bärwalde Neumark see Mieszkowice
154 F11 Barwāni Madhya Pradesh, C India
183 P5 Barwon River ≈ New South Wales, SE Australia
119 L15 Barysaw Rus. Borisov. Minskaya Voblasts', NE Belarus
127 Q6 Barysh Ul'yanovskaya Oblast', W Russian Federation
117 Q4 Baryshivka Kyyivs'ka Oblast', N Ukraine
79 J17 Basankusu Equateur, NW Dem. Rep. Congo
117 N11 Basarabeasca Rus. Bessarabka. SE Moldova
116 M14 Basarabi Constanța, SW Romania
40 H6 Basaseachic Chihuahua, NW Mexico
105 O2 Basauri País Vasco, N Spain
61 D18 Basavilbaso Entre Ríos, E Argentina
79 F21 Bas-Congo off. Région du Bas-Congo; prev. Bas-Zaïre. ◈ region SW Dem. Rep. Congo
108 E6 Basel Eng. Basle, Fr. Bâle. Basel-Stadt, NW Switzerland
108 E7 Basel Eng. Basle, Fr. Bâle. ◈ canton NW Switzerland
143 T14 Bashākerd, Kūhhā-ye ⛰ SE Iran
11 Q15 Bashaw Alberta, SW Canada
146 K16 Bashbedeng Mary Welaýaty, S Turkmenistan
161 T15 Bashi Channel Chin. Pa-shih Hai-hsia. channel Philippines/Taiwan
Bashkiria see Bashkortostan, Respublika
122 F11 Bashkortostan, Respublika prev. Bashkiria. ◈ autonomous republic W Russian Federation
127 N6 Bashmakovo Penzenskaya Oblast', W Russian Federation
146 J10 Bashsakarba Lebap Welaýaty, NE Turkmenistan
117 R9 Bashtanka Mykolayivs'ka Oblast', S Ukraine
22 H8 Basile Louisiana, S USA
107 M18 Basilicata ◈ region S Italy
33 V13 Basin Wyoming, C USA
97 N22 Basingstoke S England, UK
143 U8 Başīrān Khorāsān, E Iran
112 B10 Baška It. Bescanuova. Primorje-Gorski Kotar, NW Croatia
137 T15 Başkale Van, SE Turkey
14 L10 Baskatong, Réservoir ▣ Québec, SE Canada
137 O14 Baskil Elazığ, E Turkey
Basle see Basel
154 H9 Bāsoda Madhya Pradesh, C India
79 L17 Basoko Orientale, N Dem. Rep. Congo
Basque Country, The see País Vasco
Basra see Al Başrah
103 U5 Bas-Rhin ◈ department NE France
Bassam see Grand-Bassam
11 Q16 Bassano Alberta, SW Canada
106 H7 Bassano del Grappa Veneto, NE Italy
77 Q15 Bassar var. Bassari. NW Togo
Bassari see Bassar
172 L9 Bassas da India island group W Madagascar
108 D7 Bassecourt Jura, W Switzerland
166 K8 Bassein var. Pathein. Irrawaddy, SW Burma
79 J15 Basse-Kotto ◈ prefecture S Central African Republic
105 V5 Bassella Cataluña, NE Spain
102 J5 Basse-Normandie Eng. Lower Normandy. ◈ region N France
45 Q11 Basse-Pointe N Martinique
76 H12 Basse Santa Su E Gambia
Basse-Saxe see Niedersachsen
45 X6 Basse-Terre ○ (Guadeloupe) Basse Terre, SW Guadeloupe
45 X6 Basse Terre island W Guadeloupe
45 V10 Basseterre ● (Saint Kitts and Nevis) Saint Kitts, Saint Kitts and Nevis
29 O13 Bassett Nebraska, C USA
21 S7 Bassett Virginia, NE USA
37 N15 Bassett Peak ▲ Arizona, SW USA
76 M10 Bassikounou Hodh ech Chargui, SE Mauritania
77 R15 Bassila W Benin
Bass, Îlots de see Marotiri
31 O11 Bass Lake Indiana, N USA
183 O14 Bass Strait strait SE Australia
100 H11 Bassum Niedersachsen, NW Germany
29 X3 Basswood Lake ◎ Canada/USA
95 J21 Båstad Skåne, S Sweden
139 U2 Baṣṭah E Iraq
153 N12 Basti Uttar Pradesh, N India
103 X14 Bastia Corse, France, C Mediterranean Sea
99 L23 Bastogne Luxembourg, SE Belgium
22 I5 Bastrop Louisiana, S USA
25 T11 Bastrop Texas, SW USA
93 J15 Bastuträsk Västerbotten, N Sweden
119 J19 Bastyn' Rus. Bostyn'. Brestskaya Voblasts', SW Belarus
Basuo see Dongfang
Basutoland see Lesotho
119 O15 Basya ≈ E Belarus
117 V8 Basyl'kivka Dnipropetrovs'ka Oblast', E Ukraine
79 D17 Bata NW Equatorial Guinea
79 D17 Bata ✕ S Equatorial Guinea
Batae Coritanorum see Leicester
123 Q8 Batagay Respublika Sakha (Yakutiya), NE Russian Federation
123 P8 Batagay-Alyta Respublika Sakha (Yakutiya), NE Russian Federation
112 L10 Batajnica Serbia, N Serbia and Montenegro (Yugo.)
136 H15 Bataklık Gölü ◎ S Turkey
114 H11 Batak, Yazovir ▣ SW Bulgaria
152 H7 Batāla Punjab, N India
104 F9 Batalha Leiria, C Portugal
79 N17 Batama Orientale, NE Dem. Rep. Congo
123 Q10 Batamay Respublika Sakha (Yakutiya), NE Russian Federation
160 F9 Batang var. Bazhong. Sichuan, C China
79 I14 Batangafo Ouham, NW Central African Republic
171 P8 Batangas off. Batangas City. Luzon, N Philippines
Bătania see Battonya
171 Q10 Batan Islands island group N Philippines
60 L8 Batatais São Paulo, S Brazil
18 E10 Batavia New York, NE USA
Batavia see Jakarta
173 T9 Batavia Seamount undersea feature E Indian Ocean
126 L12 Bataysk Rostovskaya Oblast', SW Russian Federation
14 B9 Batchawana ≈ Ontario, S Canada
14 B9 Batchawana Bay Ontario, S Canada
167 Q12 Bătdâmbâng prev. Battambang. Bătdâmbâng, NW Cambodia
79 G20 Batéké, Plateaux plateau S Congo
183 S11 Batemans Bay New South Wales, SE Australia
21 Q13 Batesburg South Carolina, SE USA
28 K12 Batesland South Dakota, N USA
27 V10 Batesville Arkansas, C USA
31 Q14 Batesville Indiana, N USA
22 L2 Batesville Mississippi, S USA
25 Q13 Batesville Texas, SW USA
44 L13 Bath E Jamaica
97 L22 Bath hist. Akermanceaster, anc. Aquae Calidae, Aquae Solis. SW England, UK
19 Q8 Bath Maine, NE USA
18 F11 Bath New York, NE USA
Bath see Berkeley Springs
78 I10 Batha off. Préfecture du Batha. ◈ prefecture C Chad
78 I10 Batha seasonal river C Chad
141 Y8 Baṭḥā', Wādī al dry watercourse NE Oman
152 H9 Bathinda Punjab, NW India
98 M11 Bathmen Overijssel, E Netherlands
45 Z14 Bathsheba E Barbados
183 R8 Bathurst New South Wales, SE Australia
13 O13 Bathurst New Brunswick, SE Canada
Bathurst see Banjul
8 H6 Bathurst, Cape headland Northwest Territories, NW Canada
196 L8 Bathurst Inlet Nunavut, N Canada
8 M4 Bathurst Inlet inlet Nunavut, N Canada
181 O1 Bathurst Island island Northern Territory, N Australia
197 O9 Bathurst Island island Parry Islands, Nunavut, N Canada
77 O14 Batié SW Burkina
Batinah see Al Bāṭinah
141 Y9 Bāṭin, Wādī al dry watercourse SW Asia
15 P9 Batiscan ≈ Québec, SE Canada
136 F16 Batı Toroslar ⛰ SW Turkey
Batjan see Bacan, Pulau
147 R11 Batken Batkenskaya Oblast', SW Kyrgyzstan
Batken Oblasty see Batkenskaya Oblast'
147 Q11 Batkenskaya Oblast' Kir. Batken Oblasty. ◈ province SW Kyrgyzstan
Batlle y Ordóñez see José Batlle y Ordóñez
183 Q10 Batlow New South Wales, SE Australia
137 Q15 Batman var. Iluh. Batman, SE Turkey
137 Q15 Batman ◈ province SE Turkey
74 L6 Batna NE Algeria
Batoe see Batu, Kepulauan
162 K7 Bat-Öldziyt Töv, C Mongolia
22 J8 Baton Rouge state capital Louisiana, S USA
79 G15 Batouri Est, E Cameroon
138 G14 Baṭrā', Jibāl al ⛰ S Jordan
138 G6 Batroûn var. Al Batrūn. N Lebanon
Batsch see Bač
Batsevichi see Batsevichy
119 M17 Batsevichy Rus. Batsevichi. Mahilyowskaya Voblasts', E Belarus
92 M7 Båtsfjord Finnmark, N Norway
Battambang see Bătdâmbâng
195 X3 Batterbee, Cape headland Antarctica
155 L24 Batticaloa Eastern Province, E Sri Lanka
99 L19 Battice Liège, E Belgium
107 L18 Battipaglia Campania, S Italy
11 R15 Battle ≈ Alberta /Saskatchewan, SW Canada
Battle Born State see Nevada
31 Q10 Battle Creek Michigan, N USA
27 T7 Battlefield Missouri, C USA
11 S15 Battleford Saskatchewan, S Canada
29 S6 Battle Lake Minnesota, N USA
35 U3 Battle Mountain Nevada, W USA
111 M25 Battonya Rom. Bătania. Békés, SE Hungary
168 D11 Batu, Kepulauan prev. Batoe. island group W Indonesia
137 Q10 Bat'umi W Georgia
168 K10 Batu Pahat prev. Bandar Penggaram. Johor, Peninsular Malaysia
171 O12 Baturebe Sulawesi, N Indonesia
122 J12 Baturino Tomskaya Oblast', C Russian Federation
117 R3 Baturyn Chernihivs'ka Oblast', N Ukraine
138 F10 Bat Yam Tel Aviv, C Israel
127 Q4 Batyrevo Chuvashskaya Respublika, W Russian Federation
Batys Qazaqstan Oblysy see Zapadnyy Kazakhstan
102 F5 Batz, Île de island NW France
169 Q10 Bau Sarawak, East Malaysia
171 N2 Bauang Luzon, N Philippines
171 P14 Baubau var. Baoebaoe. Pulau Buton, C Indonesia
77 W14 Bauchi Bauchi, NE Nigeria
77 W14 Bauchi ◈ state C Nigeria
102 H7 Baud Morbihan, NW France
29 T2 Baudette Minnesota, N USA
193 S9 Bauer Basin undersea feature E Pacific Ocean
187 R14 Bauer Field var. Port Vila. ✕ (Port-Vila) Éfaté, C Vanuatu
13 T9 Bauld, Cape headland Newfoundland and Labrador, E Canada
103 T8 Baume-les-Dames Doubs, E France
101 I15 Baunatal Hessen, C Germany
107 D18 Baunei Sardegna, Italy, C Mediterranean Sea
57 M15 Baures, Río ≈ N Bolivia
60 K9 Bauru São Paulo, S Brazil
Baushar see Bawshar
118 G10 Bauska Ger. Bauske. Bauska, S Latvia
Bauske see Bauska
101 Q15 Bautzen Lus. Budyšin. Sachsen, E Germany
145 Q16 Bauyrzhan Momyshuly Kaz. Baüyrzhan Momyshuly; prev. Burnoye. Zhambyl, S Kazakhstan
Bauzanum see Bolzano
Bavaria see Bayern
109 N7 Bavarian Alps Ger. Bayrische Alpen. ⛰ Austria/Germany
Bavière see Bayern
40 H4 Bavispe, Río ≈ NW Mexico
127 T5 Bavly Respublika Tatarstan, W Russian Federation
169 P13 Bawal, Pulau island N Indonesia
169 T12 Bawan Borneo, C Indonesia
183 O12 Baw Baw, Mount ▲ Victoria, SE Australia
169 S15 Bawean, Pulau island S Indonesia
75 V9 Bawīṭī N Egypt
77 Q13 Bawku N Ghana
167 N7 Bawlakè Kayah State, C Burma
169 H11 Bawo Ofuloa Pulau Tanahmasa, W Indonesia
141 Y8 Bawshar var. Baushar. NE Oman
Ba Xian see Bazhou
158 M8 Baxkorgan Xinjiang Uygur Zizhiqu, W China
23 V6 Baxley Georgia, SE USA
159 R15 Baxoi var. Baima. Xizang Zizhiqu, W China
29 W14 Baxter Iowa, C USA
29 U6 Baxter Minnesota, N USA
27 R8 Baxter Springs Kansas, C USA
81 M17 Bay off. Gobolka Bay. ◈ region SW Somalia
Bay see Baicheng
44 H7 Bayamo Granma, E Cuba
45 U5 Bayamón E Puerto Rico
163 W8 Bayan Heilongjiang, NE China
170 L16 Bayan prev. Bajan. Pulau Lombok, C Indonesia
162 I6 Bayan Arhangay, C Mongolia
163 P7 Bayan Dornod, E Mongolia
163 N9 Bayan Dornogovĭ, SE Mongolia
162 F7 Bayan Govĭ-Altay, W Mongolia
163 O8 Bayan Hentiy, C Mongolia
152 I12 Bayāna Rājasthān, N India
149 N5 Bāyān, Band-e ⛰ C Afghanistan
162 H8 Bayanbulag Bayanhongor, C Mongolia
163 N7 Bayanbulag Hentiy, C Mongolia
158 J5 Bayanbulak Xinjiang Uygur Zizhiqu, W China
Bayan Gol see Dengkou
162 F8 Bayangol Govĭ-Altay, SW Mongolia
159 R12 Bayan Har Shan var. Bayan Khar. ⛰ C China
162 I8 Bayanhongor Bayanhongor, C Mongolia
162 H9 Bayanhongor ◈ province C Mongolia
162 K14 Bayan Hot var. Alxa Zuoqi. Nei Mongol Zizhiqu, N China
163 T9 Bayan Huxu var. Horqin Zuoyi Zhongji. Nei Mongol Zizhiqu, N China
Bayan Khar see Bayan Har Shan
168 J7 Bayan Lepas ✕ (George Town) Pinang, Peninsular Malaysia
162 K13 Bayan Mod Nei Mongol Zizhiqu, N China
Bayan Nuru see Xar Burd
163 N12 Bayan Obo Nei Mongol Zizhiqu, N China
43 V15 Bayano, Lago ◎ E Panama
162 C5 Bayan-Ölgiy ◈ province NW Mongolia
162 F9 Bayan-Ovoo Govĭ-Altay, SW Mongolia
162 H9 Bayansayr Bayanhongor, C Mongolia
159 Q9 Bayan Shan ▲ C China
162 J9 Bayanteeg Övörhangay, C Mongolia
162 L8 Bayantöhöm Töv, C Mongolia
Bayan Tumen see Choybalsan
162 H6 Bayan-Uhaa Dzavhan, C Mongolia
163 R10 Bayan Ul var. Xi Ujimqin Qi. Nei Mongol Zizhiqu, N China
162 J8 Bayan-Ulaan Övörhangay, C Mongolia
28 J14 Bayard Nebraska, C USA
37 P15 Bayard New Mexico, SW USA
103 T13 Bayard, Col pass SE France
163 O8 Bayasgalant Sühbaatar, E Mongolia
136 J12 Bayat Çorum, N Turkey
171 P6 Bayawan Negros, C Philippines
143 R10 Bayāẕ Kermān, C Iran
171 Q6 Baybay Leyte, C Philippines
21 X10 Bayboro North Carolina, SE USA
137 P12 Bayburt Bayburt, NE Turkey
137 P12 Bayburt ◈ province NE Turkey
31 R8 Bay City Michigan, N USA
25 V12 Bay City Texas, SW USA
122 I7 Baydaratskaya Guba var. Baydarata Bay. bay N Russian Federation
81 M16 Baydhabo var. Baydhowa, Isha Baydhabo, It. Baidoa. Bay, SW Somalia
Baydhowa see Baydhabo
101 N21 Bayerischer Wald ⛰ SE Germany
101 K21 Bayern Eng. Bavaria, Fr. Bavière. ◈ state SE Germany
147 V9 Bayetovo Narynskaya Oblast', C Kyrgyzstan
102 K4 Bayeux anc. Augustodurum. Calvados, N France
14 E15 Bayfield ≈ Ontario, S Canada
145 O15 Baygekum Kaz. Bäygequm. Kzylorda, S Kazakhstan
Bäygequm see Baygekum
136 C14 Bayındır İzmir, SW Turkey
138 H12 Bāyir var. Bā'ir. Ma'ān, S Jordan
Bay Islands see Bahía, Islas de la
139 R5 Bayjī var. Baiji. N Iraq
Baykadam see Saudakent
123 N13 Baykal, Ozero Eng. Lake Baikal. ◎ S Russian Federation
123 M14 Baykal'sk Irkutskaya Oblast', S Russian Federation
137 R15 Baykan Siirt, SE Turkey
123 L11 Baykit Evenkiyskiy Avtonomnyy Okrug, C Russian Federation
145 N12 Baykonur var. Baykonyr. Karaganda, C Kazakhstan
144 M14 Baykonyr var. Baykonur Kaz. Bayqongyr; prev. Leninsk. Kyzylorda, S Kazakhstan
Baykonyr see Baykonur
158 E7 Baykurt Xinjiang Uygur Zizhiqu, W China
14 I9 Bay, Lac ◎ Québec, SE Canada
127 W6 Baymak Respublika Bashkortostan, W Russian Federation
23 O8 Bay Minette Alabama, S USA
143 O17 Baynūnah desert W UAE
184 O8 Bay of Plenty off. Bay of Plenty Region. ◈ region North Island, NZ
191 Z3 Bay of Wrecks bay Kiritimati, E Kiribati
102 I15 Bayonne anc. Lapurdum. Pyrénées-Atlantiques, SW France
22 H4 Bayou D'Arbonne Lake ▣ Louisiana, S USA
23 N9 Bayou La Batre Alabama, S USA
Bayou State see Mississippi
Bayqadam see Saudakent
Bayqongyr see Baykonyr
Bayram-Ali see Baýramaly
146 J14 Baýramaly var. Bayramaly; prev. Bayram-Ali. Mary Welaýaty, S Turkmenistan
101 L19 Bayreuth var. Baireuth. Bayern, SE Germany
Bayrische Alpen see Bavarian Alps
Bayrūt see Beyrouth
22 L9 Bay Saint Louis Mississippi, S USA
Baysān see Bet She'an
162 L8 Bayshint Töv, C Mongolia
14 H13 Bays, Lake of ◎ Ontario, S Canada
22 M6 Bay Springs Mississippi, S USA
Bay State see Massachusetts
Baysun see Boysun
14 H13 Baysville Ontario, S Canada
141 N15 Bayt al Faqīh W Yemen
158 M4 Baytik Shan ⛰ China/Mongolia
Bayt Laḥm see Bethlehem
25 W11 Baytown Texas, SW USA
169 V11 Bayur, Tanjung headland Borneo, N Indonesia
121 N14 Bayy al Kabīr, Wādī dry watercourse NW Libya
Bayyrqum see Bairkum
105 P14 Baza Andalucía, S Spain
137 X10 Bazardüzü Dağı Rus. Gora Bazardyuzyu. ▲ N Azerbaijan
Bazardyuzyu, Gora see Bazardüzü Dağı
Bazargic see Dobrich
83 N18 Bazaruto, Ilha do island SE Mozambique
102 K14 Bazas Gironde, SW France
105 O14 Baza, Sierra de ⛰ S Spain
160 J8 Bazhong Sichuan, C China
Bazhong see Batang
161 P3 Bazhou prev. Baxian, Ba Xian. Hebei, E China
14 M9 Bazin ≈ Québec, SE Canada
Bazin see Pezinok
139 Q7 Bāzīyah C Iraq
138 H6 Bcharré var. Bcharreh, Bsharrī, Bsherri. NE Lebanon
Bcharreh see Bcharré
28 J5 Beach North Dakota, N USA
182 K12 Beachport South Australia
97 O23 Beachy Head headland SE England, UK
18 K13 Beacon New York, NE USA
63 J25 Beagle Channel channel Argentina/Chile
181 O1 Beagle Gulf gulf Northern Territory, N Australia
Bealach an Doirín see Ballaghaderreen
Bealach Cláir see Ballyclare
Bealach Féich see Ballybofey
172 J3 Bealanana Mahajanga, NE Madagascar
Béal an Átha see Ballina
Béal an Átha Móir see Ballinamore
Béal an Mhuirhead see Belmullet
Béal Átha Beithe see Ballybay
Béal Átha Conaill see Ballyconnell
Béal Átha hAmhnais see Ballyhaunis
Béal Átha na Sluaighe see Ballinasloe
Béal Átha Seanaidh see Ballyshannon
Bealdovuopmi see Peltovuoma
Béal Feirste see Belfast
Béal Tairbirt see Belturbet
Beanna Boirche see Mourne Mountains
Beannchar see Banagher, Ireland
Beannchar see Bangor, Northern Ireland, UK
Beanntraí see Bantry
Bearalváhki see Berlevåg
23 N2 Bear Creek ≈ Alabama/Mississippi, S USA
30 J13 Bear Creek ≈ Illinois, N USA
27 U13 Bearden Arkansas, C USA
195 Q10 Beardmore Glacier glacier Antarctica
30 K13 Beardstown Illinois, N USA
28 L14 Bear Hill ▲ Nebraska, C USA
Bear Island see Bjørnøya
14 H12 Bear Lake Ontario, S Canada
36 M1 Bear Lake ◎ Idaho/Utah, NW USA
39 U11 Bear, Mount ▲ Alaska, USA
102 J16 Béarn cultural region SW France
194 J11 Bear Peninsula peninsula Antarctica
152 I7 Beās ≈ India/Pakistan
105 P3 Beasain País Vasco, N Spain
105 O12 Beas de Segura Andalucía, S Spain
45 N10 Beata, Cabo headland SW Dominican Republic
45 N10 Beata, Isla island SW Dominican Republic
64 F11 Beata Ridge undersea feature N Caribbean Sea
29 R17 Beatrice Nebraska, C USA
83 L16 Beatrice Mashonaland East, NE Zimbabwe
11 N11 Beatton ≈ British Columbia, W Canada
11 N11 Beatton River British Columbia, W Canada
35 V10 Beatty Nevada, W USA
21 N6 Beattyville Kentucky, S USA
173 X16 Beau Bassin W Mauritius
103 R15 Beaucaire Gard, S France
14 I8 Beauchastel, Lac ◎ Québec, SE Canada
14 I10 Beauchêne, Lac ◎ Québec, SE Canada
183 V3 Beaudesert Queensland, E Australia
182 M12 Beaufort Victoria, SE Australia
21 X11 Beaufort North Carolina, SE USA
21 R15 Beaufort South Carolina, SE USA
38 M11 Beaufort Sea sea Arctic Ocean
Beaufort-Wes see Beaufort West
83 G25 Beaufort West Afr. Beaufort-Wes. Western Cape, SW South Africa
103 N7 Beaugency Loiret, C France
19 R1 Beau Lake ▣ Maine, NE USA
96 I8 Beauly N Scotland, UK
99 G21 Beaumont Hainaut, S Belgium
185 E23 Beaumont Otago, South Island, NZ
22 M7 Beaumont Mississippi, S USA
25 X10 Beaumont Texas, SW USA
102 M15 Beaumont-de-Lomagne Tarn-et-Garonne, S France
102 L6 Beaumont-sur-Sarthe Sarthe, NW France
103 R8 Beaune Côte d'Or, C France
15 R9 Beaupré Québec, SE Canada
102 J8 Beaupréau Maine-et-Loire, NW France
99 I22 Beauraing Namur, SE Belgium
103 R12 Beaurepaire Isère, E France
11 Y16 Beausejour Manitoba, S Canada
103 N4 Beauvais anc. Bellovacum, Caesaromagus. Oise, N France
11 S13 Beauval Saskatchewan, C Canada
102 I9 Beauvoir-sur-Mer Vendée, NW France
39 R8 Beaver Alaska, USA
26 J8 Beaver Oklahoma, C USA
18 B14 Beaver Pennsylvania, NE USA
36 K6 Beaver Utah, W USA
10 L9 Beaver ≈ British Columbia/Yukon Territory, W Canada
11 S13 Beaver ≈ Saskatchewan, C Canada
29 N17 Beaver City Nebraska, C USA
10 G6 Beaver Creek Yukon Territory, W Canada
31 R14 Beavercreek Ohio, N USA
39 S8 Beaver Creek ≈ Alaska, USA
26 H3 Beaver Creek ≈ Kansas/Nebraska, C USA
28 J5 Beaver Creek ≈ Montana/North Dakota, N USA
29 Q14 Beaver Creek ≈ Nebraska, C USA
25 Q4 Beaver Creek ≈ Texas, SW USA
30 M8 Beaver Dam Wisconsin, N USA
30 M8 Beaver Dam Lake ◎ Wisconsin, N USA
18 B14 Beaver Falls Pennsylvania, NE USA
33 P12 Beaverhead Mountains ⛰ Idaho/Montana, NW USA
33 Q12 Beaverhead River ≈ Montana, NW USA
65 A25 Beaver Island island W Falkland Islands
31 P5 Beaver Island island Michigan, N USA
27 S9 Beaver Lake ▣ Arkansas, C USA
11 N13 Beaverlodge Alberta, W Canada
18 I8 Beaver River ≈ New York, NE USA
26 J8 Beaver River ≈ Oklahoma, C USA
18 B13 Beaver River ≈ Pennsylvania, NE USA
65 A25 Beaver Settlement Beaver Island, W Falkland Islands
Beaver State see Oregon
14 H14 Beaverton Ontario, S Canada
32 G11 Beaverton Oregon, NW USA
152 G12 Beāwar Rājasthān, N India
Bebas, Dasht-i see Bābūs, Dasht-e
60 L8 Bebedouro São Paulo, S Brazil
101 I16 Bebra Hessen, C Germany
41 W12 Becal Campeche, SE Mexico
15 Q11 Bécancour ≈ Québec, SE Canada
97 Q19 Beccles E England, UK
112 L9 Bečej Ger. Altbetsche, Hung. Óbecse, Rácz-Becse; prev. Magyar-Becse, Stari Bečej. Serbia, N Serbia and Montenegro (Yugo.)
104 I3 Becerreá Galicia, NW Spain
74 H7 Béchar prev. Colomb-Béchar. W Algeria
39 O14 Becharof Lake ◎ Alaska, USA
116 H15 Bechet var. Bechetu. Dolj, SW Romania
Bechetu see Bechet
21 R6 Beckley West Virginia, NE USA
101 G14 Beckum Nordrhein-Westfalen, W Germany
25 X7 Beckville Texas, SW USA
35 X4 Becky Peak ▲ Nevada, W USA
116 I9 Beclean Hung. Bethlen; prev. Betlen. Bistrița-Năsăud, N Romania
Bécs see Wien
111 H18 Bečva Ger. Betschau, Pol. Beczwa. ≈ E Czech Republic
Beczwa see Bečva
103 P15 Bédarieux Hérault, S France
120 B10 Beddouza, Cap headland W Morocco
80 I13 Bedelē Oromo, C Ethiopia
147 Y8 Bedel Pass Rus. Pereval Bedel. pass China/Kyrgyzstan
Bedel, Pereval see Bedel Pass
95 H22 Beder Århus, C Denmark
97 N20 Bedford E England, UK
31 O15 Bedford Indiana, N USA
29 U16 Bedford Iowa, C USA
20 L4 Bedford Kentucky, S USA
18 D15 Bedford Pennsylvania, NE USA
21 T6 Bedford Virginia, NE USA
97 N20 Bedfordshire cultural region E England, UK
127 N5 Bednodem'yanovsk Penzenskaya Oblast', W Russian Federation
98 N5 Bedum Groningen, NE Netherlands
27 V11 Beebe Arkansas, C USA
45 T9 Beef Island ✕ (Road Town) Tortola, E British Virgin Islands
Beehive State see Utah
99 L18 Beek Limburg, SE Netherlands
99 L18 Beek ✕ (Maastricht) Limburg, SE Netherlands
99 K14 Beek-en-Donk Noord-Brabant, S Netherlands
138 F13 Be'ér Menuḥa var. Be'er Menukha. Southern, S Israel
Be'er Menukha see Be'ér Menuḥa
99 D16 Beernem West-Vlaanderen, NW Belgium
99 I16 Beerse Antwerpen, N Belgium
Beersheba see Be'ér Sheva'
138 E11 Be'ér Sheva' var. Beersheba, Ar. Bir es Saba. Southern, S Israel
98 J13 Beesd Gelderland, C Netherlands
99 M16 Beesel Limburg, SE Netherlands
83 J21 Beestekraal North-West, N South Africa
194 J7 Beethoven Peninsula peninsula Alexander Island, Antarctica
Beetstersweach see Beetsterzwaag
98 M6 Beetsterzwaag Fris. Beetstersweach. Friesland, N Netherlands
25 S13 Beeville Texas, SW USA
79 J18 Befale Equateur, NW Dem. Rep. Congo
Befandriana see Befandriana Avaratra
172 J3 Befandriana Avaratra var. Befandriana, Befandriana Nord. Mahajanga, NW Madagascar
Befandriana Nord see Befandriana Avaratra
79 K18 Befori Equateur, N Dem. Rep. Congo

172 I7 **Befotaka** Fianarantsoa, S Madagascar
183 R11 **Bega** New South Wales, SE Australia
102 G5 **Bégard** Côtes d'Armor, NW France
112 M9 **Begejski Kanal** *canal* NE Serbia and Montenegro (Yugo.)
94 G13 **Begna** ≈ S Norway
Begoml' *see* Byahoml'
Begovat *see* Bekobod
153 Q13 **Begusarāi** Bihār, NE India
143 R9 **Behābād** Yazd, C Iran
Behagle *see* Laï
55 Z10 **Béhague, Pointe** *headland* E French Guiana
Behar *see* Bihār
142 M10 **Behbahān** *var.* Behbehān. Khūzestān, SW Iran
Behbehān *see* Behbahān
44 G3 **Behring Point** Andros Island, W Bahamas
143 P4 **Behshahr** *prev.* Ashraf. Māzandarān, N Iran
163 V6 **Bei'an** Heilongjiang, NE China
Beibunar *see* Sredishte
Beibu Wan *see* Tongking, Gulf of
Beida *see* Al Bayḍā'
80 H13 **Beigi** Oromo, C Ethiopia
160 L16 **Beihai** Guangxi Zhuangzu Zizhiqu, S China
159 Q10 **Bei Hulsan Hu** ◎ C China
161 N13 **Bei Jiang** ≈ S China
161 O2 **Beijing** *var.* Pei-ching, *Eng.* Peking; *prev.* Pei-p'ing. *country/municipality capital* (China) Beijing Shi, E China
161 P2 **Beijing** × Beijing Shi, E China
Beijing *see* Beijing Shi
161 O2 **Beijing Shi** *var.* Beijing, Jing, Pei-ching, *Eng.* Peking; *prev.* Pei-p'ing. ◈ *municipality* E China
76 G8 **Beïla** Trarza, W Mauritania
98 N7 **Beilen** Drenthe, NE Netherlands
160 L15 **Beiliu** Guangxi Zhuangzu Zizhiqu, S China
159 O12 **Beilu He** ≈ W China
Beilul *see* Beylul
163 U12 **Beining** *prev.* Beizhen. Liaoning, NE China
96 H8 **Beinn Dearg** ▲ N Scotland, UK
Beinn MacDuibh *see* Ben Macdui
160 I12 **Beipan Jiang** ≈ S China
163 T12 **Beipiao** Liaoning, NE China
83 N17 **Beira** Sofala, C Mozambique
83 N17 **Beira** × Sofala, C Mozambique
104 I7 **Beira Alta** *former province* N Portugal
104 H9 **Beira Baixa** *former province* C Portugal
104 G8 **Beira Litoral** *former province* N Portugal
Beirut *see* Beyrouth
Beisān *see* Bet She'an
11 Q16 **Beiseker** Alberta, SW Canada
Beitai Ding *see* Wutai Shan
83 K19 **Beitbridge** Matabeleland South, S Zimbabwe
116 G10 **Beiuş** *Hung.* Belényes. Bihor, NW Romania
Beizhen *see* Beining
104 H12 **Beja** *anc.* Pax Julia. Beja, SE Portugal
104 G13 **Beja** ◈ *district* S Portugal
74 M5 **Béja** *var.* Bājah. N Tunisia
120 I9 **Béjaïa** *var.* Bejaïa, *Fr.* Bougie; *anc.* Saldae. NE Algeria
104 K8 **Béjar** Castilla-León, N Spain
Bejraburi *see* Phetchaburi
Bekaa Valley *see* El Beqaa
Bekabad *see* Bekobod
Békás *see* Bicaz
169 O15 **Bekasi** Jawa, C Indonesia
Bek-Budi *see* Qarshi
146 A8 **Bekdaş** *Rus.* Bekdash. Balkan Welaýaty, NW Turkmenistan
Bekdash *see* Bekdaş
147 T10 **Bek-Dzhar** Oshskaya Oblast', SW Kyrgyzstan
111 N24 **Békés** *Rom.* Bichiş. Békés, SE Hungary
111 M24 **Békés** *off.* Békés Megye. ◈ *county* SE Hungary
111 M24 **Békéscsaba** *Rom.* Bichiş-Ciaba. Békés, SE Hungary
139 S2 **Bēkhma** E Iraq
172 H7 **Bekily** Toliara, S Madagascar
165 W4 **Bekkai** Hokkaidō, NE Japan
147 Q11 **Bekobod** *Rus.* Bekabad; *prev.* Begovat. Toshkent Viloyati, E Uzbekistan
127 O7 **Bekovo** Penzenskaya Oblast', W Russian Federation
Bél *see* Beliu
152 M13 **Bela** Uttar Pradesh, N India
149 N15 **Bela** Baluchistān, SW Pakistan
79 F15 **Bélabo** Est, C Cameroon
112 N10 **Bela Crkva** *Ger.* Weisskirchen, *Hung.* Fehértemplom. Serbia, W Serbia and Montenegro (Yugo.)
173 Y16 **Bel Air** *var.* Rivière Sèche. E Mauritius
104 L12 **Belalcázar** Andalucía, S Spain
113 P15 **Bela Palanka** Serbia, SE Serbia and Montenegro (Yugo.)
119 H16 **Belarus** *off.* Republic of Belarus, *var.* Belorussia, *Latv.* Baltkrievija; *prev.* Belorussian SSR, *Rus.* Belorusskaya SSR. ◆ *republic* E Europe
Belau *see* Palau
59 H21 **Bela Vista** Mato Grosso do Sul, SW Brazil
83 L21 **Bela Vista** Maputo, S Mozambique
168 I8 **Belawan** Sumatera, W Indonesia
Běla Woda *see* Weisswasser
127 U4 **Belaya** ≈ W Russian Federation
123 R7 **Belaya Gora** Respublika Sakha (Yakutiya), NE Russian Federation
126 M11 **Belaya Kalitva** Rostovskaya Oblast', SW Russian Federation
125 R14 **Belaya Kholunitsa** Kirovskaya Oblast', NW Russian Federation
Belaya Tserkov' *see* Bila Tserkva
77 V11 **Belbédji** Zinder, S Niger
110 K13 **Bełchatów** *var.* Belchatow. Łodzkie, C Poland
Belcher, Îles *see* Belcher Islands
12 H7 **Belcher Islands** *Fr.* Îles Belcher. *island group* Nunavut, SE Canada
105 S6 **Belchite** Aragón, NE Spain
29 O2 **Belcourt** North Dakota, N USA
31 P9 **Belding** Michigan, N USA
127 U5 **Belebey** Respublika Bashkortostan, W Russian Federation
81 N16 **Beledweyne** *var.* Belet Huen, *It.* Belet Uen. Hiiraan, C Somalia
146 B10 **Belek** Balkan Welaýaty, W Turkmenistan
58 L12 **Belém** *var.* Pará. *state capital* Pará, N Brazil
65 I14 **Belém Ridge** *undersea feature* C Atlantic Ocean
37 R12 **Belen** New Mexico, SW USA
62 I7 **Belén** Catamarca, NW Argentina
54 G9 **Belén** Boyacá, C Colombia
42 J11 **Belén** Rivas, SW Nicaragua
62 O5 **Belén** Concepción, C Paraguay
61 D16 **Belén** Salto, N Uruguay
61 D20 **Belén de Escobar** Buenos Aires, E Argentina
114 J7 **Belene** Pleven, N Bulgaria
114 J7 **Belene, Ostrov** *island* N Bulgaria
43 R15 **Belén, Río** ≈ C Panama
Belényes *see* Beiuş
Belesar, Embalse de *see* Belesar, Encoro de
104 H3 **Belesar, Encoro de** *Sp.* Embalse de Belesar. ⊡ NW Spain
Belet Huen/Belet Uen *see* Beledweyne
126 J5 **Belëv** Tul'skaya Oblast', W Russian Federation
97 G15 **Belfast** *Ir.* Béal Feirste. ◐ E Northern Ireland, UK
19 R7 **Belfast** Maine, NE USA
97 G15 **Belfast** × E Northern Ireland, UK
97 G15 **Belfast Lough** *Ir.* Loch Lao *inlet* E Northern Ireland, UK
28 K5 **Belfield** North Dakota, N USA
103 U7 **Belfort** Territoire-de-Belfort, E France
Belgard *see* Białogard
155 E17 **Belgaum** Karnātaka, W India
Belgian Congo *see* Congo (Democratic Republic of)
195 T3 **Belgica Mountains** ⛰ Antarctica
België/Belgique *see* Belgium
99 F20 **Belgium** *off.* Kingdom of Belgium, *Dut.* België, *Fr.* Belgique. ◆ *monarchy* NW Europe
126 J8 **Belgorod** Belgorodskaya Oblast', W Russian Federation
Belgorod-Dnestrovskiy *see* Bilhorod-Dnistrovs'kyy
126 J8 **Belgorodskaya Oblast'** ◈ *province* W Russian Federation
Belgrad *see* Beograd
29 T8 **Belgrade** Minnesota, N USA
33 S11 **Belgrade** Montana, NW USA
Belgrade *see* Beograd
195 N5 **Belgrano II** *Argentinian research station* Antarctica
Belgrano, Cabo *see* Meredith, Cape
21 X9 **Belhaven** North Carolina, SE USA
107 I23 **Belice** *anc.* Hypsas. ≈ Sicilia, Italy, C Mediterranean Sea
Belice *see* Belize/Belize City
113 M16 **Beli Drim** *Alb.* Drini i Bardhë. ≈ Albania/Serbia and Montenegro (Yugo.)
Beligrad *see* Berat
188 C8 **Beliliou** *prev.* Peleliu. *island* S Palau
114 L8 **Beli Lom, Yazovir** ⊡ NE Bulgaria
112 I8 **Beli Manastir** *Hung.* Pélmonostor; *prev.* Monostor. Osijek-Baranja, NE Croatia
102 J13 **Bélin-Béliet** Gironde, SW France
79 F17 **Bélinga** Ogooué-Ivindo, NE Gabon
21 S4 **Belington** West Virginia, NE USA
127 O6 **Belinskiy** Penzenskaya Oblast', W Russian Federation
169 N12 **Belinyu** Pulau Bangka, W Indonesia
169 O13 **Belitung, Pulau** *island* W Indonesia
116 F10 **Beliu** *Hung.* Bél. Arad, W Romania
114 I9 **Beli Vit** ≈ NW Bulgaria
42 G2 **Belize** *Sp.* Belice; *prev.* British Honduras, Colony of Belize. ◆ *commonwealth republic* Central America
42 F2 **Belize** *Sp.* Belice. ◈ *district* NE Belize
42 G2 **Belize** ≈ Belize/Guatemala
Belize *see* Belize City
42 G2 **Belize City** *var.* Belize, *Sp.* Belice. Belize, NE Belize
42 G2 **Belize City** × Belize, NE Belize
Beljak *see* Villach
39 N16 **Belkofski** Alaska, USA
123 O6 **Bel'kovskiy, Ostrov** *island* Novosibirskiye Ostrova, NE Russian Federation
14 J8 **Bell** ≈ Québec, SE Canada
10 J15 **Bella Bella** British Columbia, SW Canada
102 M10 **Bellac** Haute-Vienne, C France
10 K15 **Bella Coola** British Columbia, SW Canada
106 D6 **Bellagio** Lombardia, N Italy
31 P6 **Bellaire** Michigan, N USA
106 D6 **Bellano** Lombardia, N Italy
155 G17 **Bellary** *var.* Ballari. Karnātaka, S India
183 S5 **Bellata** New South Wales, SE Australia
61 D16 **Bella Unión** Artigas, N Uruguay
61 C14 **Bella Vista** Corrientes, NE Argentina
62 J7 **Bella Vista** Tucumán, N Argentina
62 P4 **Bella Vista** Amambay, C Paraguay
56 B10 **Bellavista** Cajamarca, N Peru
56 D11 **Bellavista** San Martín, N Peru
183 U6 **Bellbrook** New South Wales, SE Australia
27 V5 **Belle** Missouri, C USA
21 Q5 **Belle** West Virginia, NE USA
31 R13 **Bellefontaine** Ohio, N USA
18 F14 **Bellefonte** Pennsylvania, NE USA
28 J9 **Belle Fourche** South Dakota, N USA
28 J9 **Belle Fourche Reservoir** ⊡ South Dakota, N USA
28 K9 **Belle Fourche River** ≈ South Dakota/Wyoming, N USA
103 S10 **Bellegarde-sur-Valserine** Ain, E France
23 Y14 **Belle Glade** Florida, SE USA
102 G8 **Belle Île** *island* NW France
13 T9 **Belle Isle** *island* Belle Isle, Newfoundland and Labrador, E Canada
13 S10 **Belle Isle, Strait of** *strait* Newfoundland and Labrador, E Canada
Bellenz *see* Bellinzona
29 W14 **Belle Plaine** Iowa, C USA
29 V9 **Belle Plaine** Minnesota, N USA
14 I9 **Belleterre** Québec, SE Canada
14 J15 **Belleville** Ontario, SE Canada
103 R10 **Belleville** Rhône, E France
30 K15 **Belleville** Illinois, N USA
27 N3 **Belleville** Kansas, C USA
29 Z13 **Bellevue** Iowa, C USA
29 S15 **Bellevue** Nebraska, C USA
31 S11 **Bellevue** Ohio, N USA
25 S5 **Bellevue** Texas, SW USA
32 H8 **Bellevue** Washington, NW USA
55 Y11 **Bellevue de l'Inini, Montagnes** ⛰ S French Guiana
103 S11 **Belley** Ain, E France
Bellin *see* Kangirsuk
183 V6 **Bellingen** New South Wales, SE Australia
97 L14 **Bellingham** N England, UK
32 H6 **Bellingham** Washington, NW USA
Belling Hausen Mulde *see* Southeast Pacific Basin
194 H2 **Bellingshausen** *Russian research station* South Shetland Islands, Antarctica
Bellingshausen *see* Motu One
Bellingshausen Abyssal Plain *see* Bellingshausen Plain
196 R14 **Bellingshausen Plain** *var.* Bellingshausen Abyssal Plain. *undersea feature* SE Pacific Ocean
194 I8 **Bellingshausen Sea** *sea* Antarctica
98 P6 **Bellingwolde** Groningen, NE Netherlands
108 H11 **Bellinzona** *Ger.* Bellenz. Ticino, S Switzerland
25 T8 **Bellmead** Texas, SW USA
54 E8 **Bello** Antioquia, W Colombia
61 B21 **Bellocq** Buenos Aires, E Argentina
Bello Horizonte *see* Belo Horizonte
186 L10 **Bellona** *var.* Mungiki. *island* S Solomon Islands
Bellovacum *see* Beauvais
182 D7 **Bell, Point** *headland* South Australia
20 F9 **Bells** Tennessee, S USA
25 U5 **Bells** Texas, SW USA
92 N3 **Bellsund** *inlet* SW Svalbard
106 H6 **Belluno** Veneto, NE Italy
62 L11 **Bell Ville** Córdoba, C Argentina
83 E26 **Bellville** Western Cape, SW South Africa
25 U11 **Bellville** Texas, SW USA
104 L12 **Belmez** Andalucía, S Spain
29 V12 **Belmond** Iowa, C USA
18 E11 **Belmont** New York, NE USA
21 R10 **Belmont** North Carolina, SE USA
59 O18 **Belmonte** Bahia, E Brazil
104 I8 **Belmonte** Castelo Branco, C Portugal
105 P10 **Belmonte** Castilla-La Mancha, C Spain
42 G2 **Belmopan** ● (Belize) Cayo, C Belize
97 B16 **Belmullet** *Ir.* Béal an Mhuirhead. W Ireland
123 R13 **Belogorsk** Amurskaya Oblast', SE Russian Federation
Belogorsk *see* Bilohirs'k
114 F7 **Belogradchik** Vidin, NW Bulgaria
172 H8 **Beloha** Toliara, S Madagascar
59 M20 **Belo Horizonte** *prev.* Bello Horizonte. *state capital* Minas Gerais, SE Brazil
26 M3 **Beloit** Kansas, C USA
30 L9 **Beloit** Wisconsin, N USA
Belokorovichi *see* Bilokorovychi
126 I8 **Belomorsk** Respublika Kareliya, NW Russian Federation
126 J8 **Belomorsko-Baltiyskiy Kanal** *Eng.* White Sea-Baltic Canal, White Sea Canal. *canal* NW Russian Federation
153 V15 **Belonia** Tripura, NE India
Belopol'ye *see* Bilopillya
105 O4 **Belorado** Castilla-León, N Spain
126 L14 **Belorechensk** Krasnodarskiy Kray, SW Russian Federation
127 W5 **Beloretsk** Respublika Bashkortostan, W Russian Federation
Belorussia/Belorussian SSR *see* Belarus
Belorusskaya Gryada *see* Byelaruskaya Hrada
Belorusskaya SSR *see* Belarus
Beloshchel'ye *see* Nar'yan-Mar
114 N8 **Beloslav** Varna, E Bulgaria
Belostok *see* Białystok
172 H5 **Belo Tsiribihina** *var.* Belo-sur-Tsiribihina. Toliara, W Madagascar
Belovár *see* Bjelovar
Belovezhskaya Pushcha *see* Białowieska, Puszcza/Byelavyezhskaya Pushcha
114 H10 **Belovo** Pazardzhik, C Bulgaria
Belovodsk *see* Bilovods'k
122 H9 **Beloyarskiy** Khanty-Mansiyskiy Avtonomnyy Okrug, N Russian Federation
124 K7 **Beloye More** *Eng.* White Sea. *sea* NW Russian Federation
124 K13 **Beloye, Ozero** ◎ NW Russian Federation
114 J10 **Belozem** Plovdiv, C Bulgaria
124 K13 **Belozërsk** Vologodskaya Oblast', NW Russian Federation
99 E20 **Belœil** Hainaut, SW Belgium
108 D8 **Belp** Bern, W Switzerland
108 D8 **Belp** × (Bern) Bern, C Switzerland
107 L24 **Belpasso** Sicilia, Italy, C Mediterranean Sea
31 U14 **Belpre** Ohio, N USA
98 M8 **Belterwijde** ◎ N Netherlands
27 R4 **Belton** Missouri, C USA
21 P11 **Belton** South Carolina, SE USA
25 T9 **Belton** Texas, SW USA
25 S9 **Belton Lake** ⊡ Texas, SW USA
Bel'tsy *see* Bălţi
97 E16 **Belturbet** *Ir.* Béal Tairbirt. N Ireland
Beluchistan *see* Baluchistān
145 Z9 **Belukha, Gora** ▲ Kazakhstan/Russian Federation
107 M20 **Belvedere Marittimo** Calabria, SW Italy
30 L10 **Belvidere** Illinois, N USA
18 J14 **Belvidere** New Jersey, NE USA
Bely *see* Belyy
127 V8 **Belyayevka** Orenburgskaya Oblast', W Russian Federation
Belynichi *see* Byalynichy
124 H17 **Belyy** *var.* Bely, Beyj. Tverskaya Oblast', W Russian Federation
126 I6 **Belyye Berega** Bryanskaya Oblast', W Russian Federation
122 J6 **Belyy, Ostrov** *island* N Russian Federation
122 J11 **Belyy Yar** Tomskaya Oblast', C Russian Federation
100 N13 **Belzig** Brandenburg, NE Germany
22 K4 **Belzoni** Mississippi, S USA
172 H4 **Bemaraha** *var.* Plateau du Bemaraha. ⛰ W Madagascar
82 B10 **Bembe** Uíge, NW Angola
77 S14 **Bembèrèkè** *var.* Bimbéréké. N Benin
104 K12 **Bembézar** ≈ SW Spain
104 J3 **Bembibre** Castilla-León, N Spain
29 T4 **Bemidji** Minnesota, N USA
98 L12 **Bemmel** Gelderland, SE Netherlands
171 T13 **Bemu** Pulau Seram, E Indonesia
Benāb *see* Bonāb
105 T5 **Benabarre** *var.* Benavarn. Aragón, NE Spain
Benaco *see* Garda, Lago di
79 L20 **Bena-Dibele** Kasai Oriental, C Dem. Rep. Congo
105 R9 **Benageber, Embalse de** ⊡ E Spain
183 O11 **Benalla** Victoria, SE Australia
104 M14 **Benamejí** Andalucía, S Spain
Benares *see* Vārānasi
Benavarn *see* Benabarre
104 F10 **Benavente** Santarém, C Portugal
104 K5 **Benavente** Castilla-León, N Spain
25 S15 **Benavides** Texas, SW USA
96 F8 **Benbecula** *island* NW Scotland, UK
Bencovazzo *see* Benkovac
32 H13 **Bend** Oregon, NW USA
182 K7 **Benda Range** ⛰ South Australia
183 T6 **Bendemeer** New South Wales, SE Australia
Bender *see* Tighina
Bender Beila/Bender Beyla *see* Bandarbeyla
Bender Cassim/Bender Qaasim *see* Boosaaso
Bendery *see* Tighina
183 N11 **Bendigo** Victoria, SE Australia
118 E10 **Bēne** Dobele, SW Latvia
98 K13 **Beneden-Leeuwen** Gelderland, C Netherlands
101 L24 **Benediktenwand** ▲ S Germany
Benemérita de San Cristóbal *see* San Cristóbal
77 N12 **Bénéna** Ségou, S Mali
172 I7 **Benenitra** Toliara, S Madagascar
Beneschau *see* Benešov
Beneški Zaliv *see* Venice, Gulf of
111 D17 **Benešov** *Ger.* Beneschau. Středočeský Kraj, W Czech Republic
123 Q5 **Benetta, Ostrov** *island* Novosibirskiye Ostrova, NE Russian Federation
107 L17 **Benevento** *anc.* Beneventum, Malventum. Campania, S Italy
Beneventum *see* Benevento
173 S3 **Bengal, Bay of** *bay* N Indian Ocean
79 M17 **Bengamisa** Orientale, N Dem. Rep. Congo
Bengasi *see* Banghāzī
Bengazi *see* Banghāzī
161 P7 **Bengbu** *var.* Peng-pu. Anhui, E China
32 L9 **Benge** Washington, NW USA
Benghazi *see* Banghāzī
168 K10 **Bengkalis** Pulau Bengkalis, W Indonesia
168 K10 **Bengkalis, Pulau** *island* W Indonesia
169 Q10 **Bengkayang** Borneo, C Indonesia
Bengkoelen/Bengkoeloe *see* Bengkulu
168 K14 **Bengkulu** *prev.* Bengkoeloe, Benkoelen, Benkulen. Sumatera, W Indonesia
168 J13 **Bengkulu** *off.* Propinsi Bengkulu; *prev.* Bengkoelen, Benkoelen, Benkulen. ◈ *province* W Indonesia
82 A11 **Bengo** ◈ *province* W Angola
95 J16 **Bengtsfors** Västra Götaland, S Sweden
82 B13 **Benguela** *var.* Benguella. Benguela, W Angola
83 A14 **Benguela** ◈ *province* W Angola
Benguella *see* Benguela
Bengweulu, Lake *see* Bangweulu, Lake
121 V13 **Benha** *var.* Banhā. N Egypt
192 F6 **Benham Seamount** *undersea feature* W Philippine Sea
96 H6 **Ben Hope** ▲ N Scotland, UK
79 P18 **Beni** Nord Kivu, NE Dem. Rep. Congo
57 L15 **Beni** *var.* El Beni. ◈ *department* N Bolivia
74 H8 **Beni Abbès** W Algeria
105 T8 **Benicarló** País Valenciano, E Spain
105 T9 **Benicasim** País Valenciano, E Spain
105 T12 **Benidorm** País Valenciano, SE Spain
75 W9 **Beni Mazâr** *var.* Banī Mazār. C Egypt
120 C11 **Beni-Mellal** C Morocco
77 R14 **Benin** *off.* Republic of Benin; *prev.* Dahomey. ◆ *republic* W Africa
77 S17 **Benin, Bight of** *gulf* W Africa
77 U16 **Benin City** Edo, SW Nigeria
57 K16 **Beni, Río** ≈ N Bolivia
120 F10 **Beni Saf** *var.* Beni-Saf. NW Algeria
80 H12 **Benishangul** ◈ *region* W Ethiopia
105 T11 **Benissa** País Valenciano, E Spain
121 V14 **Beni Suef** *var.* Banī Suwayf. N Egypt
11 V15 **Benito** Manitoba, S Canada
Benito *see* Uolo, Río
61 C23 **Benito Juárez** Buenos Aires, E Argentina
41 P14 **Benito Juaréz Internacional** × (México) México, S Mexico
25 P5 **Benjamin** Texas, SW USA
58 B13 **Benjamin Constant** Amazonas, N Brazil
40 F4 **Benjamín Hill** Sonora, NW Mexico
63 F19 **Benjamín, Isla** *island* Archipiélago de los Chonos, S Chile
165 Q4 **Benkei-misaki** *headland* Hokkaidō, NE Japan
28 L17 **Benkelman** Nebraska, C USA
96 I7 **Ben Klibreck** ▲ N Scotland, UK
Benkoelen *see* Bengkulu
112 D13 **Benkovac** *It.* Bencovazzo. Zadar, SW Croatia
Benkulen *see* Bengkulu
96 I11 **Ben Lawers** ▲ C Scotland, UK
96 J9 **Ben Macdui** *var.* Beinn MacDuibh. ▲ C Scotland, UK
96 G11 **Ben More** ▲ W Scotland, UK
96 I11 **Ben More** ▲ C Scotland, UK
96 H7 **Ben More Assynt** ▲ N Scotland, UK
185 E20 **Benmore, Lake** ◎ South Island, NZ
98 L12 **Bennekom** Gelderland, SE Netherlands
21 T11 **Bennettsville** South Carolina, SE USA
96 H10 **Ben Nevis** ▲ N Scotland, UK
184 M9 **Benneydale** Waikato, North Island, NZ
Bennichab *see* Bennichchâb
76 H8 **Bennichchâb** *var.* Bennichab. Inchiri, W Mauritania
18 L10 **Bennington** Vermont, NE USA
185 E20 **Ben Ohau Range** ⛰ South Island, NZ
83 J21 **Benoni** Gauteng, NE South Africa
172 J2 **Be, Nosy** *var.* Nossi-Bé. *island* NW Madagascar
Bénoué *see* Benue
42 F2 **Benque Viejo del Carmen** Cayo, W Belize
101 G19 **Bensheim** Hessen, W Germany
37 N16 **Benson** Arizona, SW USA
29 S8 **Benson** Minnesota, N USA
21 U10 **Benson** North Carolina, SE USA
171 N15 **Benteng** Pulau Selayar, C Indonesia
83 A14 **Bentiaba** Namibe, SW Angola
181 T4 **Bentinck Island** *island* Wellesley Islands, Queensland, N Australia
80 E13 **Bentiu** Wahda, S Sudan
138 G8 **Bent Jbaïl** *var.* Bint Jubayl. S Lebanon
11 Q15 **Bentley** Alberta, SW Canada
61 I15 **Bento Gonçalves** Rio Grande do Sul, S Brazil
27 U12 **Benton** Arkansas, C USA
30 L16 **Benton** Illinois, N USA
20 H7 **Benton** Kentucky, S USA
22 G5 **Benton** Louisiana, S USA
27 Y7 **Benton** Missouri, C USA
20 M10 **Benton** Tennessee, S USA
31 O10 **Benton Harbor** Michigan, N USA
27 S9 **Bentonville** Arkansas, C USA
77 V16 **Benue** ◈ *state* SE Nigeria
78 F13 **Benue** *Fr.* Bénoué. ≈ Cameroon/Nigeria
163 V12 **Benxi** *prev.* Pen-ch'i, Penhsihu, Penki. Liaoning, NE China
Benyakoni *see* Byenyakoni
112 K10 **Beočin** Serbia, N Serbia and Montenegro (Yugo.)
Beodericsworth *see* Bury St Edmunds
112 M11 **Beograd** *Eng.* Belgrade, *Ger.* Belgrad; *anc.* Singidunum. ● (Serbia and Montenegro (Yugo.)) Serbia, N Serbia and Montenegro (Yugo.)
112 L11 **Beograd** *Eng.* Belgrade. × Serbia, N Serbia and Montenegro (Yugo.)
76 M16 **Béoumi** C Ivory Coast
35 V3 **Beowawe** Nevada, W USA
164 E14 **Beppu** Ōita, Kyūshū, SW Japan
187 X15 **Beqa** *prev.* Mbengga. *island* W Fiji
Beqa Barrier Reef *see* Kavukavu Reef
45 Y14 **Bequia** *island* C Saint Vincent and the Grenadines
113 L16 **Berane** *prev.* Ivangrad. Montenegro, SW Serbia and Montenegro (Yugo.)
113 L21 **Berat** *var.* Berati, *SCr.* Beligrad. Berat, C Albania
113 L21 **Berat** ◈ *district* C Albania
Berătău *see* Berettyó
Berati *see* Berat
Beraun *see* Berounka, Czech Republic
Beraun *see* Beroun, Czech Republic
171 U13 **Berau, Teluk** *var.* MacCluer Gulf. *bay* Papua, E Indonesia
80 G8 **Berber** River Nile, NE Sudan
80 N12 **Berbera** Woqooyi Galbeed, NW Somalia
79 H16 **Berbérati** Mambéré-Kadéï, SW Central African Republic
Berberia, Cabo de *see* Barbaria, Cap de
55 T9 **Berbice River** ≈ NE Guyana
Berchid *see* Berrechid
103 N2 **Berck-Plage** Pas-de-Calais, N France
25 T13 **Berclair** Texas, SW USA
117 W10 **Berda** ≈ SE Ukraine
Berdichev *see* Berdychiv
123 P10 **Berdigestyakh** Respublika Sakha (Yakutiya), NE Russian Federation
122 J12 **Berdsk** Novosibirskaya Oblast', C Russian Federation
117 W10 **Berdyans'k** *Rus.* Berdyansk; *prev.* Osipenko. Zaporiz'ka Oblast', SE Ukraine
117 W10 **Berdyans'ka Kosa** *spit* SE Ukraine
117 V10 **Berdyans'ka Zatoka** *gulf* S Ukraine
117 N5 **Berdychiv** *Rus.* Berdichev. Zhytomyrs'ka Oblast', N Ukraine
20 M6 **Berea** Kentucky, S USA
Beregovo/Beregszász *see* Berehove
116 G8 **Berehove** *Cz.* Berehovo, *Hung.* Beregszász, *Rus.* Beregovo. Zakarpats'ka Oblast', W Ukraine
Berehovo *see* Berehove
186 D9 **Bereina** Central, S PNG
146 C11 **Bereket** *prev. Rus.* Gazandzhyk, Kazandzhik, *Turkm.* Gazanjyk. Balkan Welaýaty, W Turkmenistan
45 O12 **Berekua** S Dominica
77 O16 **Berekum** W Ghana
75 Y11 **Berenice** *var.* Mînâ Baranîs. SE Egypt
9 O14 **Berens** ≈ Manitoba/Ontario, C Canada
11 X14 **Berens River** Manitoba, C Canada
29 R12 **Beresford** South Dakota, N USA
116 J4 **Berestechko** Volyns'ka Oblast', NW Ukraine
116 M11 **Bereşti** Galaţi, E Romania
117 U6 **Berestova** ≈ E Ukraine
Beretău *see* Berettyó
111 N23 **Berettyó** *Rom.* Barcău; *prev.* Berătău, Beretău. ≈ Hungary/Romania
111 N23 **Berettyóújfalu** Hajdú-Bihar, E Hungary
Berëza/Bereza Kartuska *see* Byaroza
117 Q4 **Berezan'** Kyyivs'ka Oblast', N Ukraine
117 Q10 **Berezanka** Mykolayivs'ka Oblast', S Ukraine
116 I6 **Berezhany** *Pol.* Brzeżany. Ternopil's'ka Oblast', W Ukraine
Berezina *see* Byerezino
Berezino *see* Byerazino
117 P10 **Berezivka** *Rus.* Berezovka. Odes'ka Oblast', SW Ukraine
117 Q2 **Berezna** Chernihivs'ka Oblast', NE Ukraine
116 L3 **Berezne** Rivnens'ka Oblast', NW Ukraine
117 R9 **Bereznehuvate** Mykolayivs'ka Oblast', S Ukraine
125 N10 **Bereznik** Arkhangel'skaya Oblast', NW Russian Federation
125 U13 **Berezniki** Permskaya Oblast', NW Russian Federation
Berezovka *see* Berezivka
122 H9 **Berezovo** Khanty-Mansiyskiy Avtonomnyy Okrug, N Russian Federation
127 O9 **Berezovskaya** Volgogradskaya Oblast', SW Russian Federation
123 S13 **Berezovyy** Khabarovskiy Kray, E Russian Federation
83 E25 **Berg** ≈ W South Africa
Berg *see* Berg bei Rohrbach
105 V4 **Berga** Cataluña, NE Spain
95 N20 **Berga** Kalmar, S Sweden
136 B13 **Bergama** İzmir, W Turkey

◆ Country ● Country Capital ◇ Dependent Territory ○ Dependent Territory Capital ◈ Administrative Region × International Airport ▲ Mountain ⛰ Mountain Range Volcano ≈ River ◎ Lake ⊡ Reservoir

106 E7 **Bergamo** *anc.* Bergomum. Lombardia, N Italy
105 P3 **Bergara** País Vasco, N Spain
109 S3 **Berg bei Rohrbach** *var.* Berg. Oberösterreich, N Austria
100 O6 **Bergen** Mecklenburg-Vorpommern, NE Germany
100 I11 **Bergen** Niedersachsen, NW Germany
98 H8 **Bergen** Noord-Holland, NW Netherlands
94 C13 **Bergen** Hordaland, S Norway
Bergen *see* Mons
55 W9 **Berg en Dal** Brokopondo, C Surinam
99 G15 **Bergen op Zoom** Noord-Brabant, S Netherlands
102 L13 **Bergerac** Dordogne, SW France
99 J16 **Bergeyk** Noord-Brabant, S Netherlands
101 D16 **Bergheim** Nordrhein-Westfalen, W Germany
55 X10 **Bergi** Sipaliwini, E Surinam
101 E16 **Bergisch Gladbach** Nordrhein-Westfalen, W Germany
101 F14 **Bergkamen** Nordrhein-Westfalen, W Germany
95 N21 **Bergkvara** Kalmar, S Sweden
Bergomum *see* Bergamo
98 K13 **Bergse Maas** ≈ S Netherlands
95 P15 **Bergshamra** Stockholm, C Sweden
94 N10 **Bergsjö** Gävleborg, C Sweden
93 J14 **Bergsviken** Norrbotten, N Sweden
98 L6 **Bergum** *Fris.* Burgum. Friesland, N Netherlands
98 M6 **Bergumer Meer** ◎ N Netherlands
94 N12 **Bergviken** ◎ C Sweden
168 M11 **Berhala, Selat** *strait* Sumatera, W Indonesia
Berhampore *see* Baharampur
123 W9 **Beringa, Ostrov** *island* E Russian Federation
99 J17 **Beringen** Limburg, NE Belgium
39 T12 **Bering Glacier** *glacier* Alaska, USA
Beringov Proliv *see* Bering Strait
123 W6 **Beringovskiy** Chukotskiy Avtonomnyy Okrug, NE Russian Federation
192 L2 **Bering Sea** *sea* N Pacific Ocean
38 L9 **Bering Strait** *Rus.* Beringov Proliv. *strait* Bering Sea/Chukchi Sea
Berislav *see* Beryslav
105 O15 **Berja** Andalucía, S Spain
94 H9 **Berkåk** Sør-Trøndelag, S Norway
98 N11 **Berkel** ≈ Germany/Netherlands
35 N8 **Berkeley** California, W USA
65 E24 **Berkeley Sound** *sound* NE Falkland Islands
21 V2 **Berkeley Springs** *var.* Bath. West Virginia, NE USA
195 N6 **Berkner Island** *island* Antarctica
114 G8 **Berkovitsa** Montana, NW Bulgaria
97 M22 **Berkshire** *cultural region* S England, UK
99 H17 **Berlaar** Antwerpen, N Belgium
Berlanga *see* Berlanga de Duero
105 P6 **Berlanga de Duero** *var.* Berlanga. Castilla-León, N Spain
99 F17 **Berlare** Oost-Vlaanderen, NW Belgium
104 E9 **Berlenga, Ilha da** *island* C Portugal
92 M7 **Berlevåg** *Lapp.* Bearalváhki. Finnmark, N Norway
100 O12 **Berlin** ● (Germany) Berlin, NE Germany
21 Z4 **Berlin** Maryland, NE USA
19 O7 **Berlin** New Hampshire, NE USA
18 D16 **Berlin** Pennsylvania, NE USA
30 L7 **Berlin** Wisconsin, N USA
100 O12 **Berlin** ◈ *state* NE Germany
Berlinchen *see* Barlinek
31 U12 **Berlin Lake** ⊡ Ohio, N USA
183 R11 **Bermagui** New South Wales, SE Australia
40 L8 **Bermejillo** Durango, C Mexico
62 M6 **Bermejo (viejo), Río** ≈ N Argentina
62 L5 **Bermejo, Río** ≈ N Argentina
62 I10 **Bermejo, Río** ≈ W Argentina
105 P2 **Bermeo** País Vasco, N Spain
104 K6 **Bermillo de Sayago** Castilla-León, N Spain
106 E6 **Bermina, Pizzo** *Rmsch.* Piz Bernina. ▲ Italy/Switzerland *see also* Bernina, Piz
64 A12 **Bermuda** *var.* Bermuda Islands, Bermudas; *prev.* Somers Islands. ◇ *UK crown colony* NW Atlantic Ocean
Bermuda Islands *see* Bermuda
Bermuda-New England Seamount Arc *see* New England Seamounts
64 G10 **Bermuda Rise** *undersea feature* C Sargasso Sea
Bermudas *see* Bermuda
108 D8 **Bern** *Fr.* Berne. ● (Switzerland) Bern, W Switzerland
108 D9 **Bern** *Fr.* Berne. ◈ *canton* W Switzerland
37 R11 **Bernalillo** New Mexico, SW USA
14 H12 **Bernard Lake** ◎ Ontario, S Canada
61 B18 **Bernardo de Irigoyen** Santa Fe, NE Argentina
18 J14 **Bernardsville** New Jersey, NE USA
63 K14 **Bernasconi** La Pampa, C Argentina
100 O12 **Bernau** Brandenburg, NE Germany
102 L4 **Bernay** Eure, N France
101 L14 **Bernburg** Sachsen-Anhalt, C Germany
109 X5 **Berndorf** Niederösterreich, NE Austria
31 Q12 **Berne** Indiana, N USA
Berne *see* Bern
108 D10 **Berner Alpen** *var.* Berner Oberland, *Eng.* Bernese Oberland. ▲ SW Switzerland
Berner Oberland/Bernese Oberland *see* Berner Alpen
109 Y2 **Bernhardsthal** Niederösterreich, N Austria
22 H4 **Bernice** Louisiana, S USA
27 Y8 **Bernie** Missouri, C USA
180 G9 **Bernier Island** *island* Western Australia
Bernina Pass *see* Bernina, Passo del
108 J10 **Bernina, Passo del** *Eng.* Bernina Pass. *pass* SE Switzerland
108 J10 **Bernina, Piz** *It.* Pizzo Bermina. ▲ Italy/Switzerland *see also* Bermina, Pizzo
99 E20 **Bernissart** Hainaut, SW Belgium
101 E18 **Bernkastel-Kues** Rheinland-Pfalz, W Germany
Beroea *see* Ḩalab
172 H6 **Beroroha** Toliara, SW Madagascar
Béroubouay *see* Gbéroubouè
111 C17 **Beroun** *Ger.* Beraun. Středočeský Kraj, W Czech Republic
111 C16 **Berounka** *Ger.* Beraun. ≈ W Czech Republic
113 Q18 **Berovo** E FYR Macedonia
74 F6 **Berrechid** *var.* Berchid. W Morocco
103 R15 **Berre, Étang de** ◎ SE France
103 S15 **Berre-l'Étang** Bouches-du-Rhône, SE France
182 K9 **Berri** South Australia
31 O10 **Berrien Springs** Michigan, N USA
183 O10 **Berrigan** New South Wales, SE Australia
103 N9 **Berry** *cultural region* C France
35 N7 **Berryessa, Lake** ◎ California, W USA
44 G2 **Berry Islands** *island group* N Bahamas
27 T9 **Berryville** Arkansas, C USA
21 V3 **Berryville** Virginia, NE USA
83 D21 **Berseba** Karas, S Namibia
117 O8 **Bershad'** Vinnyts'ka Oblast', C Ukraine
28 L3 **Berthold** North Dakota, N USA
37 T3 **Berthoud** Colorado, C USA
37 S4 **Berthoud Pass** *pass* Colorado, C USA
79 F15 **Bertoua** Est, E Cameroon
25 S10 **Bertram** Texas, SW USA
63 G22 **Bertrand, Cerro** ▲ S Argentina
99 J23 **Bertrix** Luxembourg, SE Belgium
191 P3 **Beru** *var.* Peru. *atoll* Tungaru, W Kiribati
Beruni *see* Beruniy
146 I9 **Beruniy** *var.* Biruni, *Rus.* Beruni. Qoraqalpog'iston Respublikasi, W Uzbekistan
58 F13 **Beruri** Amazonas, NW Brazil
18 H14 **Berwick** Pennsylvania, NE USA
96 K12 **Berwick** *cultural region* SE Scotland, UK
96 L12 **Berwick-upon-Tweed** N England, UK
117 S10 **Beryslav** *Rus.* Berislav. Khersons'ka Oblast', S Ukraine
Berytus *see* Beyrouth
172 H4 **Besalampy** Mahajanga, W Madagascar
103 T8 **Besançon** *anc.* Besontium, Vesontio. Doubs, E France
103 P10 **Besbre** ≈ C France
Bescanuova *see* Baška
Besdan *see* Bezdan
Besed' *see* Byesyedz'
147 R10 **Beshariq** *Rus.* Besharyk; *prev.* Kirovo. Farg'ona Viloyati, E Uzbekistan
Besharyk *see* Beshariq
146 L9 **Beshbuloq** *Rus.* Beshulak. Navoiy Viloyati, N Uzbekistan
Beshenkovichi *see* Byeshankovichy
146 M13 **Beshkent** Qashqadaryo Viloyati, S Uzbekistan
Beshulak *see* Beshbuloq
112 L10 **Beška** Serbia, N Serbia and Montenegro (Yugo.)
Beskra *see* Biskra
127 O16 **Beslan** Respublika Severnaya Osetiya, SW Russian Federation
113 P16 **Besna Kobila** ▲ SE Serbia and Montenegro (Yugo.)
137 N16 **Besni** Adıyaman, S Turkey
Besontium *see* Besançon
121 Q2 **Beşparmak Dağları** *Eng.* Kyrenia Mountains. ▲ N Cyprus
Bessarabka *see* Basarabeasca
92 O2 **Bessels, Kapp** *headland* C Svalbard
23 P4 **Bessemer** Alabama, S USA
30 K3 **Bessemer** Michigan, N USA
21 Q10 **Bessemer City** North Carolina, SE USA
102 M10 **Bessines-sur-Gartempe** Haute-Vienne, C France
99 K15 **Best** Noord-Brabant, S Netherlands
25 N9 **Best** Texas, SW USA
125 O11 **Bestuzhevo** Arkhangel'skaya Oblast', NW Russian Federation
123 M11 **Bestyakh** Respublika Sakha (Yakutiya), NE Russian Federation
Beszterce *see* Bistriṭa
Besztercebánya *see* Banská Bystrica
172 I5 **Betafo** Antananarivo, C Madagascar
104 H2 **Betanzos** Galicia, NW Spain
104 G2 **Betanzos, Ría de** *estuary* NW Spain
79 G15 **Bétaré Oya** Est, E Cameroon
105 S9 **Bétera** País Valenciano, E Spain
77 R15 **Bétérou** C Benin
83 K21 **Bethal** Mpumalanga, NE South Africa
30 K15 **Bethalto** Illinois, N USA
83 D21 **Bethanie** *var.* Bethanien, Bethany. Karas, S Namibia
Bethanien *see* Bethanie
27 S2 **Bethany** Missouri, C USA
27 N10 **Bethany** Oklahoma, C USA
Bethany *see* Bethanie
39 N12 **Bethel** Alaska, USA
19 P7 **Bethel** Maine, NE USA
21 W9 **Bethel** North Carolina, SE USA
18 B15 **Bethel Park** Pennsylvania, NE USA
21 W3 **Bethesda** Maryland, NE USA
83 J22 **Bethlehem** Free State, C South Africa
18 I14 **Bethlehem** Pennsylvania, NE USA
138 F10 **Bethlehem** *Ar.* Bayt Laḩm, *Heb.* Bet Leḩem. C West Bank
Bethlen *see* Beclean
83 I24 **Bethulie** Free State, C South Africa
103 O1 **Béthune** Pas-de-Calais, N France
102 M3 **Béthune** ≈ N France
104 M14 **Béticos, Sistemas** *var.* Sistema Penibético, *Eng.* Baetic Cordillera, Baetic Mountains. ▲ S Spain
54 I6 **Betijoque** Trujillo, NW Venezuela
59 M20 **Betim** Minas Gerais, SE Brazil
190 H3 **Betio** Tarawa, W Kiribati
172 H7 **Betioky** Toliara, S Madagascar
Bet Leḩem *see* Bethlehem
Betlen *see* Beclean
167 O17 **Betong** Yala, SW Thailand
79 I16 **Bétou** La Likouala, N Congo
145 P14 **Betpak-Dala** *Kaz.* Betpaqdala. *plateau* S Kazakhstan
Betpaqdala *see* Betpak-Dala
172 H7 **Betroka** Toliara, S Madagascar
Betschau *see* Bečva
138 G9 **Bet She'an** *Ar.* Baysān, Beisān; *anc.* Scythopolis. Northern, N Israel
15 T6 **Betsiamites** Québec, SE Canada
15 T6 **Betsiamites** ≈ Québec, SE Canada
172 I4 **Betsiboka** ≈ N Madagascar
99 M25 **Bettembourg** Luxembourg, S Luxembourg
99 M23 **Bettendorf** Diekirch, NE Luxembourg
29 Z14 **Bettendorf** Iowa, C USA
75 R13 **Bette, Pic** *var.* Bikkū Bīttī, *It.* Picco Bette. ▲ S Libya
Bette, Picco *see* Bette, Pic
153 P12 **Bettiah** Bihār, N India
39 Q7 **Bettles** Alaska, USA
95 N17 **Bettna** Södermanland, C Sweden
154 H11 **Betūl** *prev.* Badnur. Madhya Pradesh, C India
154 H9 **Betwa** ≈ C India
101 F16 **Betzdorf** Rheinland-Pfalz, W Germany
82 C9 **Béu** Uíge, NW Angola
31 P6 **Beulah** Michigan, N USA
28 L5 **Beulah** North Dakota, N USA
98 M8 **Beulakerwijde** ◎ N Netherlands
98 L13 **Beuningen** Gelderland, SE Netherlands
Beuthen *see* Bytom
103 N7 **Beuvron** ≈ C France
99 F16 **Beveren** Oost-Vlaanderen, N Belgium
21 T9 **B.Everett Jordan Reservoir** *var.* Jordan Lake. ⊡ North Carolina, SE USA
97 N17 **Beverley** E England, UK
Beverley *see* Beverly
99 J17 **Beverlo** Limburg, NE Belgium
19 P11 **Beverly** Massachusetts, NE USA
32 J9 **Beverly** *var.* Beverley. Washington, NW USA
35 S15 **Beverly Hills** California, W USA
101 I14 **Beverungen** Nordrhein-Westfalen, C Germany
98 H9 **Beverwijk** Noord-Holland, W Netherlands
108 C10 **Bex** Vaud, W Switzerland
97 P23 **Bexhill** *var.* Bexhill-on-Sea. SE England, UK
Bexhill-on-Sea *see* Bexhill
136 E17 **Bey Dağları** ▲ SW Turkey
Beyj *see* Belyy
136 E10 **Beykoz** İstanbul, NW Turkey
76 K15 **Beyla** Guinée-Forestière, SE Guinea
137 X12 **Beyläqan** *prev.* Zhdanov. SW Azerbaijan
80 L10 **Beylul** *var.* Beilul. SE Eritrea
144 H14 **Beyneu** *Kaz.* Beyneū. Mangistau, SW Kazakhstan
Beyneū *see* Beyneu
165 X14 **Beyonēsu-retsugan** *Eng.* Bayonnaise Rocks. *island group* SE Japan
136 G12 **Beypazarı** Ankara, NW Turkey
155 F21 **Beypore** Kerala, SW India
138 G7 **Beyrouth** *var.* Bayrūt, *Eng.* Beirut; *anc.* Berytus. ● (Lebanon) W Lebanon
138 G7 **Beyrouth** ✖ W Lebanon
136 G15 **Beyşehir** Konya, SW Turkey
136 G15 **Beyşehir Gölü** ◎ C Turkey
108 J7 **Bezau** Vorarlberg, NW Austria
112 J8 **Bezdan** *Ger.* Besdan, *Hung.* Bezdán. Serbia, NW Serbia and Montenegro (Yugo.)
Bezdezh *see* Byezdzyezh
124 G15 **Bezhanitsy** Pskovskaya Oblast', W Russian Federation
124 K15 **Bezhetsk** Tverskaya Oblast', W Russian Federation
103 P16 **Béziers** *anc.* Baeterrae, Baeterrae Septimanorum, Julia Beterrae. Hérault, S France
Bezmein *see* Büzmeýin
Bezwada *see* Vijayawāda
154 P12 **Bhadrak** *var.* Bhadrakh. Orissa, E India
Bhadrakh *see* Bhadrak
155 F19 **Bhadra Reservoir** ⊡ SW India
155 F18 **Bhadrāvati** Karnātaka, SW India
153 R14 **Bhāgalpur** Bihār, NE India
Bhairab *see* Bhairab Bazar
153 U14 **Bhairab Bazar** *var.* Bhairab. Dhaka, C Bangladesh
153 O11 **Bhairahawa** Western, S Nepal
149 S8 **Bhakkar** Punjab, E Pakistan
153 P11 **Bhaktapur** Central, C Nepal
167 N3 **Bhamo** *var.* Banmo. Kachin State, N Burma
Bhāmragad *see* Bhāmragarh
154 K13 **Bhāmragarh** *var.* Bhāmragad. Mahārāshtra, C India
154 J12 **Bhandāra** Mahārāshtra, C India
Bhārat *see* India
152 J12 **Bharatpur** *prev.* Bhurtpore. Rājasthān, N India
154 D11 **Bharūch** Gujarāt, W India
155 E18 **Bhatkal** Karnātaka, W India
153 O13 **Bhatni** *var.* Bhatni Junction. Uttar Pradesh, N India
Bhatni Junction *see* Bhatni
153 S16 **Bhātpāra** West Bengal, NE India
149 U7 **Bhaun** Punjab, E Pakistan
Bhaunagar *see* Bhāvnagar
154 M13 **Bhavānīpātna** Orissa, E India
155 H21 **Bhavānīsāgar Reservoir** ⊡ S India
154 D11 **Bhāvnagar** *prev.* Bhaunagar. Gujarāt, W India
Bheanntraí, Bá *see* Bantry Bay
Bheara, Béal an *see* Gweebarra Bay
154 K12 **Bhilai** Chhattīsgarh, C India
152 G13 **Bhīlwāra** Rājasthān, N India
155 E14 **Bhīma** ≈ S India
155 K16 **Bhīmavaram** Andhra Pradesh, E India
154 I7 **Bhind** Madhya Pradesh, C India
152 E13 **Bhīnmāl** Rājasthān, N India
Bhir *see* Bīd
154 D13 **Bhiwandi** Mahārāshtra, W India
152 H10 **Bhiwāni** Haryāna, N India
152 L13 **Bhognīpur** Uttar Pradesh, N India
153 U16 **Bhola** Khulna, S Bangladesh
154 H10 **Bhopāl** Madhya Pradesh, C India
155 J14 **Bhopālpatnam** Chhattīsgarh, C India
155 E14 **Bhor** Mahārāshtra, W India
154 O12 **Bhubaneshwar** *prev.* Bhubaneswar, Bhuvaneshwar. Orissa, E India
Bhubaneswar *see* Bhubaneshwar
154 B9 **Bhuj** Gujarāt, W India
Bhuket *see* Phuket
Bhurtpore *see* Bharatpur
Bhusaval *see* Bhusāwal
154 G12 **Bhusāwal** *prev.* Bhusaval. Mahārāshtra, C India
153 T12 **Bhutan** *off.* Kingdom of Bhutan, *var.* Druk-yul. ◆ *monarchy* S Asia
Bhuvaneshwar *see* Bhubaneshwar
143 T15 **Bīābān, Kūh-e** ▲ S Iran
77 V18 **Biafra, Bight of** *var.* Bight of Bonny. *bay* W Africa
171 W12 **Biak** Papua, E Indonesia
171 W12 **Biak, Pulau** *island* E Indonesia
110 P12 **Biała Podlaska** Lubelskie, E Poland
110 F7 **Białogard** *Ger.* Belgard. Zachodnio-pomorskie, NW Poland
110 P10 **Białowieska, Puszcza** *Bel.* Byelavyezhskaya Pushcha, *Rus.* Belovezhskaya Pushcha. *physical region* Belarus/Poland *see also* Byelavyezhskaya Pushcha
110 G8 **Biały Bór** *Ger.* Baldenburg. Zachodnio-pomorskie, NW Poland
110 P9 **Białystok** *Rus.* Belostok, Bielostok. Podlaskie, NE Poland
107 L24 **Biancavilla** *prev.* Inessa. Sicilia, Italy, C Mediterranean Sea
Bianco, Monte *see* Blanc, Mont
76 L15 **Biankouma** W Ivory Coast
167 R7 **Bia, Phou** *var.* Pou Bia. ▲ C Laos
Bia, Pou *see* Bia, Phou
143 R5 **Biārjmand** Semnān, N Iran
105 P4 **Biarra** ≈ NE Spain
102 I15 **Biarritz** Pyrénées-Atlantiques, SW France
108 H10 **Biasca** Ticino, S Switzerland
61 E17 **Biassini** Salto, N Uruguay
165 S3 **Bibai** Hokkaidō, NE Japan
83 B15 **Bibala** *Port.* Vila Arriaga. Namibe, SW Angola
104 I4 **Bibéi** ≈ NW Spain
Biberach *see* Biberach an der Riss
101 I23 **Biberach an der Riss** *var.* Biberach, *Ger.* Biberach an der Riß. Baden-Württemberg, S Germany
108 E7 **Biberist** Solothurn, NW Switzerland
77 O16 **Bibiani** SW Ghana
112 C13 **Bibinje** Zadar, SW Croatia
Biblical Gebal *see* Jbaïl
116 I5 **Bibrka** *Pol.* Bóbrka, *Rus.* Bobrka. L'vivs'ka Oblast', NW Ukraine
117 N10 **Bic** ≈ S Moldova
113 M18 **Bicaj** Kukës, NE Albania
116 K10 **Bicaz** *Hung.* Békás. Neamṭ, NE Romania
183 Q16 **Bicheno** Tasmania, SE Australia
Bichiş *see* Békés
Bichiş-Ciaba *see* Békéscsaba
Bichitra *see* Phichit
137 P8 **Bichvint'a** *Rus.* Pitsunda. NW Georgia
15 T7 **Bic, Île du** *island* Québec, SE Canada
32 J10 **Bickleton** Washington, NW USA
36 L6 **Bicknell** Utah, W USA
171 S11 **Bicoli** Pulau Halmahera, E Indonesia
111 J22 **Bicske** Fejér, C Hungary
155 F14 **Bīd** *prev.* Bhir. Mahārāshtra, W India
77 U15 **Bida** Niger, C Nigeria
155 H15 **Bīdar** Karnātaka, C India
141 Y8 **Bidbid** NE Oman
19 P9 **Biddeford** Maine, NE USA
98 L9 **Biddinghuizen** Flevoland, C Netherlands
33 X11 **Biddle** Montana, NW USA
97 J23 **Bideford** SW England, UK
82 D13 **Bié** ◈ *province* C Angola
35 O2 **Bieber** California, W USA
110 O9 **Biebrza** ≈ NE Poland
165 T3 **Biei** Hokkaidō, NE Japan
108 D8 **Biel** *Fr.* Bienne. Bern, W Switzerland
100 G13 **Bielefeld** Nordrhein-Westfalen, NW Germany
108 D8 **Bieler See** *Fr.* Lac de Bienne. ◎ W Switzerland
Bielitz/Bielitz-Biala *see* Bielsko-Biała
106 C7 **Biella** Piemonte, N Italy
Bielostok *see* Białystok
111 J17 **Bielsko-Biała** *Ger.* Bielitz, Bielitz-Biala. Śląskie, S Poland
110 P10 **Bielsk Podlaski** Białystok, E Poland
Bien Bien *see* Điên Biên
Biên Đông *see* South China Sea
11 V17 **Bienfait** Saskatchewan, S Canada
167 T14 **Biên Hoa** Đông Nai, S Vietnam
Bienne *see* Biel
Bienne, Lac de *see* Bieler See
12 K8 **Bienville, Lac** ◎ Québec, C Canada
82 D13 **Bié, Planalto do** *var.* Bié Plateau. *plateau* C Angola
Bié Plateau *see* Bié, Planalto do
108 B9 **Bière** Vaud, W Switzerland
98 O4 **Bierum** Groningen, NE Netherlands
98 I13 **Biesbos** *var.* Biesbosch. *wetland* S Netherlands
Biesbosch *see* Biesbos
99 H21 **Biesme** Namur, S Belgium
101 H21 **Bietigheim-Bissingen** Baden-Württemberg, SW Germany
99 I23 **Bièvre** Namur, SE Belgium
79 D18 **Bifoun** Moyen-Ogooué, NW Gabon
165 T2 **Bifuka** Hokkaidō, NE Japan
136 C11 **Biga** Çanakkale, NW Turkey
136 C13 **Bigadiç** Balıkesir, W Turkey
26 J7 **Big Basin** *basin* Kansas, C USA
185 B20 **Big Bay** *bay* South Island, NZ
31 O5 **Big Bay de Noc** ◎ Michigan, N USA
31 N3 **Big Bay Point** *headland* Michigan, N USA
33 R10 **Big Belt Mountains** ▲ Montana, NW USA
29 N10 **Big Bend Dam** *dam* South Dakota, N USA
24 K12 **Big Bend National Park** *national park* Texas, S USA
22 K5 **Big Black River** ≈ Mississippi, S USA
27 O3 **Big Blue River** ≈ Kansas/Nebraska, C USA
24 M10 **Big Canyon** ≈ Texas, SW USA
33 N12 **Big Creek** Idaho, NW USA
23 N8 **Big Creek Lake** ⊡ Alabama, S USA
23 X15 **Big Cypress Swamp** *wetland* Florida, SE USA
39 S9 **Big Delta** Alaska, USA
30 K6 **Big Eau Pleine Reservoir** ⊡ Wisconsin, N USA
19 P5 **Bigelow Mountain** ▲ Maine, NE USA
29 U3 **Big Falls** Minnesota, N USA
33 P8 **Bigfork** Montana, NW USA
29 U3 **Big Fork River** ≈ Minnesota, N USA
11 S15 **Biggar** Saskatchewan, S Canada
180 L3 **Bigge Island** *island* Western Australia
35 O5 **Biggs** California, W USA
32 I11 **Biggs** Oregon, NW USA
14 K13 **Big Gull Lake** ◎ Ontario, SE Canada
37 P16 **Big Hachet Peak** ▲ New Mexico, SW USA
33 P11 **Big Hole River** ≈ Montana, NW USA
33 V13 **Bighorn Basin** *basin* Wyoming, C USA
33 U11 **Bighorn Lake** ◎ Montana /Wyoming, N USA
33 W13 **Bighorn Mountains** ▲ Wyoming, C USA
36 J13 **Big Horn Peak** ▲ Arizona, SW USA
33 V11 **Bighorn River** ≈ Montana/Wyoming, NW USA
9 S7 **Big Island** *island* Nunavut, NE Canada
39 O16 **Big Koniuji Island** *island* Shumagin Islands, Alaska, USA
25 N9 **Big Lake** Texas, SW USA
19 T5 **Big Lake** ◎ Maine, NE USA
30 I3 **Big Manitou Falls** *waterfall* Wisconsin, N USA
35 R2 **Big Mountain** ▲ Nevada, W USA
108 G10 **Bignasco** Ticino, S Switzerland
29 R16 **Big Nemaha River** ≈ Nebraska, C USA
76 G12 **Bignona** SW Senegal
Bigorra *see* Tarbes
Bigosovo *see* Bihosava
35 S10 **Big Pine** California, W USA
35 Q14 **Big Pine Mountain** ▲ California, W USA
27 V6 **Big Piney Creek** ≈ Missouri, C USA
65 M24 **Big Point** *headland* N Tristan da Cunha
31 P8 **Big Rapids** Michigan, N USA
30 K6 **Big Rib River** ≈ Wisconsin, N USA
14 L14 **Big Rideau Lake** ◎ Ontario, SE Canada
11 T14 **Big River** Saskatchewan, C Canada
27 X5 **Big River** ≈ Missouri, C USA
31 N7 **Big Sable Point** *headland* Michigan, N USA
33 S7 **Big Sandy** Montana, NW USA
25 W6 **Big Sandy** Texas, SW USA
37 V5 **Big Sandy Creek** ≈ Colorado, C USA
29 Q16 **Big Sandy Creek** ≈ Nebraska, C USA
29 V5 **Big Sandy Lake** ◎ Minnesota, N USA
36 J11 **Big Sandy River** ≈ Arizona, SW USA
21 P5 **Big Sandy River** ≈ S USA
23 V6 **Big Satilla Creek** ≈ Georgia, SE USA
29 R12 **Big Sioux River** ≈ Iowa/South Dakota, N USA
35 U7 **Big Smoky Valley** *valley* Nevada, W USA
25 N7 **Big Spring** Texas, SW USA
19 Q5 **Big Squaw Mountain** ▲ Maine, NE USA
21 O7 **Big Stone Gap** Virginia, NE USA
29 Q8 **Big Stone Lake** ◎ Minnesota/South Dakota, N USA
22 K4 **Big Sunflower River** ≈ Mississippi, S USA
33 T11 **Big Timber** Montana, NW USA
12 D8 **Big Trout Lake** Ontario, C Canada
14 I12 **Big Trout Lake** ◎ Ontario, SE Canada
35 O2 **Big Valley Mountains** ▲ California, W USA
25 Q13 **Big Wells** Texas, SW USA
14 F11 **Bigwood** Ontario, S Canada
112 D11 **Bihać** Federacija Bosna I Hercegovina, NW Bosnia and Herzegovina
153 P13 **Bihār** *prev.* Behar. ◈ *state* N India
Bihār *see* Bihār Sharīf
81 F20 **Biharamulo** Kagera, NW Tanzania
153 R13 **Bihārīganj** Bihār, NE India
153 P14 **Bihār Sharīf** *var.* Bihār. Bihār, N India
116 F10 **Bihor** ◈ *county* NW Romania
165 V3 **Bihoro** Hokkaidō, NE Japan
118 K11 **Bihosava** *Rus.* Bigosovo. Vitsyebskaya Voblasts', NW Belarus
Bijagos Archipelago *see* Bijagós, Arquipélago dos
76 G13 **Bijagós, Arquipélago dos** *var.* Bijagos Archipelago. *island group* W Guinea-Bissau
155 F16 **Bijāpur** Karnātaka, C India
142 K5 **Bījār** Kordestān, W Iran
112 J11 **Bijeljina** Republika Srpska, NE Bosnia and Herzegovina
113 K15 **Bijelo Polje** Montenegro, SW Serbia and Montenegro (Yugo.)
160 I11 **Bijie** Guizhou, S China
152 J10 **Bijnor** Uttar Pradesh, N India
152 F11 **Bīkāner** Rājasthān, NW India
189 V3 **Bikar Atoll** *var.* Pikaar. *atoll* Ratak Chain, N Marshall Islands
190 H3 **Bikeman** *atoll* Tungaru, W Kiribati
190 I3 **Bikenebu** Tarawa, W Kiribati
123 S14 **Bikin** Khabarovskiy Kray, SE Russian Federation
123 S14 **Bikin** ≈ SE Russian Federation
189 R3 **Bikini Atoll** *var.* Pikinni. *atoll* Ralik Chain, NW Marshall Islands
83 L17 **Bikita** Masvingo, E Zimbabwe
Bīkkū Bīttī *see* Bette, Pic
79 I19 **Bikoro** Equateur, W Dem. Rep. Congo
141 Z9 **Bilād Banī Bū 'Alī** NE Oman
141 Z9 **Bilād Banī Bū Ḩasan** NE Oman
141 X9 **Bilād Manaḩ** *var.* Manaḩ. NE Oman
77 Q12 **Bilanga** C Burkina
152 F12 **Bilāra** Rājasthān, N India
152 K10 **Bilāri** Uttar Pradesh, N India
138 J5 **Bil'ās, Jabal al** ▲ C Syria
154 L11 **Bilāspur** Chhattīsgarh, C India
152 I8 **Bilāspur** Himāchal Pradesh, N India
168 J9 **Bila, Sungai** ≈ Sumatera, W Indonesia
137 Y13 **Biläsuvar** *Rus.* Bilyasuvar; *prev.* Pushkino. SE Azerbaijan
117 O5 **Bila Tserkva** *Rus.* Belaya Tserkov'. Kyyivs'ka Oblast', N Ukraine
167 N11 **Bilauktaung Range** *var.* Thanintari Taungdan. ▲ Burma/Thailand
105 O2 **Bilbao** *Basq.* Bilbo. País Vasco, N Spain
Bilbo *see* Bilbao
92 H2 **Bíldudalur** Vestfirdhir, NW Iceland
113 I16 **Bileća** Republika Srpska, S Bosnia and Herzegovina
136 E12 **Bilecik** Bilecik, NW Turkey
136 F12 **Bilecik** ◈ *province* NW Turkey
116 E11 **Biled** *Ger.* Billed, *Hung.* Billéd. Timiş, W Romania
111 O15 **Biłgoraj** Lubelskie, E Poland
117 P11 **Bilhorod-Dnistrovs'kyy** *Rus.* Belgorod-Dnestrovskiy, *Rom.* Cetatea Albă; *prev.* Akkerman, *anc.* Tyras. Odes'ka Oblast', SW Ukraine

◆ Country ● Country Capital ◇ Dependent Territory ○ Dependent Territory Capital ◈ Administrative Region ✖ International Airport ▲ Mountain ▲ Mountain Range Volcano ≈ River ◎ Lake ⊡ Reservoir

79 M16 Bili Orientale, N Dem. Rep. Congo
123 T6 Bilibino Chukotskiy Avtonomnyy Okrug, NE Russian Federation
166 M8 Bilin Mon State, S Burma
113 N21 Bilisht var. Bilishti. Korçë, SE Albania
Bilishti see Bilisht
183 N10 Billabong Creek var. Moulamein Creek. seasonal river New South Wales, SE Australia
182 G4 Billa Kalina South Australia
197 Q17 Bill Baileys Bank undersea feature N Atlantic Ocean
Billed/Billéd see Biled
153 N14 Billi Uttar Pradesh, N India
97 M15 Billingham N England, UK
33 U11 Billings Montana, NW USA
95 J16 Billingsfors Västra Götaland, S Sweden
Bill of Cape Clear, The see Clear, Cape
28 L9 Billsburg South Dakota, N USA
95 F23 Billund Ribe, W Denmark
36 L11 Bill Williams Mountain ▲ Arizona, SW USA
36 I12 Bill Williams River ≈ Arizona, SW USA
77 Y8 Bilma Agadez, NE Niger
77 Y8 Bilma, Grand Erg de desert NE Niger
181 Y9 Biloela Queensland, E Australia
112 G8 Bilo Gora ⛰ N Croatia
117 U13 Bilohirs'k Rus. Belogorsk; prev. Karasubazar. Respublika Krym, S Ukraine
116 M3 Bilokorovychi Rus. Belokorovichi. Zhytomyrs'ka Oblast', N Ukraine
117 X5 Bilokurakine Luhans'ka Oblast', E Ukraine
117 T3 Bilopillya Rus. Belopol'ye. Sums'ka Oblast', NE Ukraine
117 Y6 Bilovods'k Rus. Belovodsk. Luhans'ka Oblast', E Ukraine
22 M9 Biloxi Mississippi, S USA
117 R10 Bilozerka Khersons'ka Oblast', S Ukraine
117 W7 Bilozers'ke Donets'ka Oblast', E Ukraine
98 J11 Bilthoven Utrecht, C Netherlands
78 K9 Biltine Biltine, E Chad
78 J9 Biltine off. Préfecture de Biltine. ◈ prefecture E Chad
162 D5 Bilüü Bayan-Ölgiy, W Mongolia
Bilwi see Puerto Cabezas
Bilyasuvar see Biläsuvar
117 O11 Bilyayivka Odes'ka Oblast', SW Ukraine
99 K18 Bilzen Limburg, NE Belgium
Bimbéréké see Bembèrèkè
183 R10 Bimberi Peak ▲ New South Wales, SE Australia
77 Q15 Bimbila E Ghana
79 I15 Bimbo Ombella-Mpoko, SW Central African Republic
44 F2 Bimini Islands island group W Bahamas
154 I9 Bīna Madhya Pradesh, C India
143 T4 Bīnālūd, Kūh-e ⛰ NE Iran
99 F20 Binche Hainaut, S Belgium
Bindloe Island see Marchena, Isla
83 L16 Bindura Mashonaland Central, NE Zimbabwe
105 T5 Binefar Aragón, NE Spain
83 J16 Binga Matabeleland North, W Zimbabwe
183 T5 Bingara New South Wales, SE Australia
101 F18 Bingen am Rhein Rheinland-Pfalz, SW Germany
26 M11 Binger Oklahoma, C USA
Bingerau see Węgrów
Bin Ghalfān, Jazā'ir see Ḥalāniyāt, Juzur al
19 Q6 Bingham Maine, NE USA
18 H11 Binghamton New York, NE USA
Bin Ghanīmah, Jabal see Bin Ghunaymah, Jabal
75 P11 Bin Ghunaymah, Jabal var. Jabal Bin Ghanīmah. ⛰ C Libya
139 U3 Bingird NE Iraq
Bingmei see Congjiang
137 P14 Bingöl Bingöl, E Turkey
137 P14 Bingöl ◈ province E Turkey
161 R6 Binhai var. Binhai Xian. Dongkan. Jiangsu, E China
Binhai Xian see Binhai
167 V11 Binh Đinh var. An Nhon. Binh Đinh, C Vietnam
167 U10 Binh Sơn var. Châu Ô. Quang Ngai, C Vietnam
Binimani see Bintimani
168 I8 Binjai Sumatera, W Indonesia
183 R6 Binnaway New South Wales, SE Australia
108 E6 Binningen Basel-Land, NW Switzerland
168 J8 Bintang, Banjaran ⛰ Peninsular Malaysia
168 M10 Bintan, Pulau island Kepulauan Riau, W Indonesia
76 J14 Bintimani var. Binimani. ▲ NE Sierra Leone
Bint Jubayl see Bent Jbaïl
169 S9 Bintulu Sarawak, East Malaysia
171 V12 Bintuni prev. Steenkool. Papua, E Indonesia
163 W8 Binxian Heilongjiang, NE China
160 K14 Binyang var. Binzhou. Guangxi Zhuangzu Zizhiqu, S China
161 Q4 Binzhou Shandong, E China
Binzhou see Binyang
63 G14 Bío Bío off. Región del Bío Bío. ◈ region C Chile
63 G14 Bío Bío, Río ≈ C Chile
79 C16 Bioco, Isla de var. Bioko, Eng. Fernando Po, Sp. Fernando Póo; prev. Macías Nguema Biyogo. island NW Equatorial Guinea
112 D13 Biograd na Moru It. Zaravecchia. Zadar, SW Croatia
Bioko see Bioco, Isla de
113 F14 Biokovo ⛰ S Croatia
Biorra see Birr
Bipontium see Zweibrücken
143 W13 Bīrag, Kūh-e ⛰ SE Iran
75 O10 Birāk var. Brak. C Libya
139 S10 Bi'r al Islām C Iraq
154 N11 Biramitrapur Orissa, E India
139 T11 Bi'r an Niṣf S Iraq
78 L12 Birao Vakaga, NE Central African Republic
146 J10 Birata Rus. Darganata, Dargan-Ata. Lebap Welaýaty, NE Turkmenistan
158 M6 Biratar Bulak well NW China
153 R12 Biratnagar Eastern, SE Nepal
165 R5 Biratori Hokkaidō, NE Japan
39 S8 Birch Creek Alaska, USA
38 M11 Birch Creek ≈ Alaska, USA
11 T14 Birch Hills Saskatchewan, S Canada
182 M10 Birchip Victoria, SE Australia
29 X4 Birch Lake ◎ Minnesota, N USA
11 Q11 Birch Mountains ⛰ Alberta, W Canada
11 V15 Birch River Manitoba, S Canada
44 H12 Birchs Hill hill W Jamaica
39 R11 Birchwood Alaska, USA
188 I5 Bird Island island S Northern Mariana Islands
137 N16 Birecik Şanlıurfa, S Turkey
152 M10 Birendranagar var. Surkhet. Mid Western, W Nepal
Bir es Saba see Be'ér Sheva'
74 A12 Bir-Gandouz SW Western Sahara
153 P12 Birganj Central, C Nepal
81 B14 Biri ≈ W Sudan
Bi'r Ibn Hirmās see Al Bi'r
143 U8 Bīrjand Khorāsān, E Iran
139 T11 Birkat Ḥāmid well S Iraq
95 F18 Birkeland Aust-Agder, S Norway
101 E19 Birkenfeld Rheinland-Pfalz, SW Germany
97 K18 Birkenhead NW England, UK
109 W7 Birkfeld Steiermark, SE Austria
182 A2 Birksgate Range ⛰ South Australia
Birlad see Bârlad
97 K20 Birmingham C England, UK
23 P4 Birmingham Alabama, S USA
97 M20 Birmingham ✕ C England, UK
Bir Moghrein see Bîr Mogreïn
76 J4 Bîr Mogreïn var. Bir Moghrein; prev. Fort-Trinquet. Tiris Zemmour, N Mauritania
191 S4 Birnie Island atoll Phoenix Islands, C Kiribati
Birni-Ngaouré see Birnin Gaouré
77 S12 Birnin Gaouré var. Birni-Ngaouré. Dosso, SW Niger
77 S12 Birnin Kebbi Kebbi, NW Nigeria
Birni-Nkonni see Birnin Konni
77 T12 Birnin Konni var. Birni-Nkonni. Tahoua, SW Niger
77 W13 Birnin Kudu Jigawa, N Nigeria
123 S16 Birobidzhan Yevreyskaya Avtonomnaya Oblast', SE Russian Federation
97 D18 Birr var. Parsonstown, Ir. Biorra. C Ireland
183 P4 Birrie River ≈ New South Wales/Queensland, SE Australia
108 D7 Birse ≈ NW Switzerland
Birsen see Biržai
108 E6 Birsfelden Basel-Land, NW Switzerland
127 U4 Birsk Respublika Bashkortostan, W Russian Federation
119 F14 Birštonas Kaunas, C Lithuania
159 P14 Biru Xinjiang Uygur Zizhiqu, W China
Biruni see Beruniy
122 L12 Biryusa ≈ C Russian Federation
122 L12 Biryusinsk Irkutskaya Oblast', C Russian Federation
118 G10 Biržai Ger. Birsen. Panevėžys, NE Lithuania
121 P16 Birżebbuġa SE Malta
Bisanthe see Tekirdağ
171 R12 Bisa, Pulau island Maluku, E Indonesia
37 N17 Bisbee Arizona, SW USA
29 O2 Bisbee North Dakota, N USA
Biscaia, Baía de see Biscay, Bay of
102 I13 Biscarrosse et de Parentis, Étang de ◎ SW France
104 M1 Biscay, Bay of Sp. Golfo de Vizcaya, Port. Baía de Biscaia. bay France/Spain
23 Z16 Biscayne Bay bay Florida, SE USA
64 M7 Biscay Plain undersea feature SE Bay of Biscay
107 N17 Bisceglie Puglia, SE Italy
Bischoflack see Škofja Loka
Bischofsburg see Biskupiec
109 Q7 Bischofshofen Salzburg, NW Austria
101 P15 Bischofswerda Sachsen, E Germany
103 V5 Bischwiller Bas-Rhin, NE France
21 T10 Biscoe North Carolina, SE USA
194 G5 Biscoe Islands island group Antarctica
14 E9 Biscotasi Lake ◎ Ontario, S Canada
14 E9 Biscotasing Ontario, S Canada
54 J6 Biscucuy Portuguesa, NW Venezuela
114 K11 Biser Khaskovo, S Bulgaria
113 D15 Biševo It. Busi. island SW Croatia
141 N12 Bīshah, Wādī dry watercourse C Saudi Arabia
147 U7 Bishkek var. Pishpek; prev. Frunze. ● (Kyrgyzstan) Chuyskaya Oblast', N Kyrgyzstan
147 U7 Bishkek ✕ Chuyskaya Oblast', N Kyrgyzstan
153 R16 Bishnupur West Bengal, NE India
83 J25 Bisho Eastern Cape, S South Africa
35 S9 Bishop California, W USA
25 S15 Bishop Texas, SW USA
97 L15 Bishop Auckland N England, UK
Bishop's Lynn see King's Lynn
97 O21 Bishop's Stortford E England, UK
21 S12 Bishopville South Carolina, SE USA
138 M5 Bishrī, Jabal ⛰ E Syria
163 U4 Bishui Heilongjiang, NE China
81 G17 Bisina, Lake prev. Lake Salisbury. ◎ E Uganda
Biskara see Biskra
74 L6 Biskra var. Beskra, Biskara. NE Algeria
110 M8 Biskupiec Ger. Bischofsburg. Warmińsko-Mazurskie, NE Poland
171 R7 Bislig Mindanao, S Philippines
27 X6 Bismarck Missouri, C USA
28 M5 Bismarck state capital North Dakota, N USA
186 D5 Bismarck Archipelago island group NE PNG
186 D7 Bismarck Range ⛰ N PNG
186 E6 Bismarck Sea sea W Pacific Ocean
137 P15 Bismil Diyarbakır, SE Turkey
43 N6 Bismuna, Laguna lagoon NE Nicaragua
Bisnulok see Phitsanulok
171 R10 Bisoa, Tanjung headland Pulau Halmahera, N Indonesia
28 K7 Bison South Dakota, N USA
93 H17 Bispfors Jämtland, C Sweden
76 G13 Bissau ● (Guinea-Bissau) W Guinea-Bissau
76 G13 Bissau ✕ W Guinea-Bissau
99 M24 Bissen Luxembourg, C Luxembourg
Bissojohka see Børselv
76 G12 Bissorã W Guinea-Bissau
11 O10 Bistcho Lake ◎ Alberta, W Canada
22 G5 Bistineau, Lake ▣ Louisiana, S USA
Bistrica see Ilirska Bistrica
116 I9 Bistrița Ger. Bistritz, Hung. Beszterce; prev. Nösen. Bistrița-Năsăud, N Romania
116 K10 Bistrița Ger. Bistritz. ≈ NE Romania
116 I9 Bistrița-Năsăud ◈ county N Romania
Bistritz see Bistrița
Bistritz ober Pernstein see Bystřice nad Pernštejnem
152 L11 Biswān Uttar Pradesh, N India
110 M7 Bisztynek Warmińsko-Mazurskie, NE Poland
79 E17 Bitam Woleu-Ntem, N Gabon
101 D18 Bitburg Rheinland-Pfalz, SW Germany
103 U4 Bitche Moselle, NE France
78 I11 Bitkine Guéra, C Chad
137 R15 Bitlis Bitlis, SE Turkey
137 R14 Bitlis ◈ province E Turkey
Bitoeng see Bitung
113 N20 Bitola Turk. Monastir; prev. Bitolj. S FYR Macedonia
Bitolj see Bitola
107 O17 Bitonto anc. Butuntum. Puglia, SE Italy
77 Q13 Bitou var. Bittou. SE Burkina
155 C20 Bitra Island island Lakshadweep, India, N Indian Ocean
101 M14 Bitterfeld Sachsen-Anhalt, E Germany
32 O9 Bitterroot Range ⛰ Idaho/Montana, NW USA
33 P10 Bitterroot River ≈ Montana, NW USA
107 D18 Bitti Sardegna, Italy, C Mediterranean Sea
Bittou see Bitou
171 Q11 Bitung prev. Bitoeng. Sulawesi, C Indonesia
60 I12 Bituruna Paraná, S Brazil
77 Y13 Biu Borno, E Nigeria
Biumba see Byumba
164 J13 Biwa-ko ◎ Honshū, SW Japan
171 X14 Biwarlaut Papua, E Indonesia
27 P10 Bixby Oklahoma, C USA
122 J13 Biya ≈ S Russian Federation
Biy-Khem see Bol'shoy Yenisey
122 J13 Biysk Altayskiy Kray, S Russian Federation
164 H13 Bizen Okayama, Honshū, SW Japan
Bizerta see Bizerte
120 K10 Bizerte Ar. Banzart, Eng. Bizerta. N Tunisia
Bizkaia see Vizcaya
92 G2 Bjargtangar headland W Iceland
Bjärnå see Perniö
95 K22 Bjärnum Skåne, S Sweden
93 I16 Bjästa Västernorrland, C Sweden
113 I14 Bjelašnica ▲ SE Bosnia and Herzegovina
112 C10 Bjelolasica ▲ NW Croatia
112 F8 Bjelovar Hung. Belovár. Bjelovar-Bilogora, N Croatia
112 F8 Bjelovar-Bilogora off. Bjelovarsko-Bilogorska Županija. ◈ province NE Croatia
Bjelovarsko-Bilogorska Županija see Bjelovar-Bilogora
92 H10 Bjerkvik Nordland, C Norway
95 G21 Bjerringbro Viborg, NW Denmark
Bjeshkët e Namuna see North Albanian Alps
95 L14 Björbo Dalarna, C Sweden
95 I15 Bjørkelangen Akershus, S Norway
95 O14 Björklinge Uppsala, C Sweden
93 I14 Björksele Västerbotten, N Sweden
93 I16 Björna Västernorrland, C Sweden
95 C14 Bjørnafjorden fjord S Norway
95 L16 Björneborg Värmland, C Sweden
Björneborg see Pori
95 E14 Bjørnesfjorden ◎ S Norway
92 M9 Bjørnevatn Finnmark, N Norway
197 T13 Bjørnøya Eng. Bear Island. island N Norway
93 I15 Bjurholm Västerbotten, N Sweden
95 J22 Bjuv Skåne, S Sweden
76 M12 Bla Ségou, W Mali
181 W8 Blackall Queensland, E Australia
29 V2 Black Bay lake bay Minnesota, N USA
27 N9 Black Bear Creek ≈ Oklahoma, C USA
97 K17 Blackburn NW England, UK
45 W10 Blackburne ✕ (Plymouth) E Montserrat
39 T11 Blackburn, Mount ▲ Alaska, USA
35 N5 Black Butte Lake ▣ California, W USA
194 J5 Black Coast physical region Antarctica
11 Q16 Black Diamond Alberta, SW Canada
18 K11 Black Dome ▲ New York, NE USA
113 L18 Black Drin Alb. Lumi i Drinit të Zi, SCr. Crni Drim. ≈ Albania/FYR Macedonia
12 D6 Black Duck ≈ Ontario, C Canada
29 U4 Blackduck Minnesota, N USA
33 R14 Blackfoot Idaho, NW USA
33 P9 Blackfoot River ≈ Montana, NW USA
Black Forest see Schwarzwald
28 J10 Blackhawk South Dakota, N USA
28 I10 Black Hills ⛰ South Dakota/Wyoming, N USA
11 T10 Black Lake ◎ Saskatchewan, C Canada
31 Q5 Black Lake ◎ Michigan, N USA
18 I7 Black Lake ◎ New York, NE USA
22 G6 Black Lake ▣ Louisiana, S USA
26 F7 Black Mesa ▲ Oklahoma, C USA
21 P10 Black Mountain North Carolina, SE USA
35 P13 Black Mountain ▲ California, W USA
37 Q2 Black Mountain ▲ Colorado, C USA
21 O7 Black Mountain ▲ Kentucky, E USA
96 K1 Black Mountains ⛰ SE Wales, UK
36 H10 Black Mountains ⛰ Arizona, SW USA
33 Q16 Black Pine Peak ▲ Idaho, NW USA
97 K17 Blackpool NW England, UK
37 Q14 Black Range ⛰ New Mexico, SW USA
44 I12 Black River W Jamaica
14 J14 Black River ≈ Ontario, SE Canada
167 R6 Black River Chin. Babian Jiang, Lixian Jiang, Fr. Rivière Noire, Vtn. Sông Đa. ≈ China/Vietnam
44 I12 Black River ≈ W Jamaica
39 T7 Black River ≈ Alaska, USA
37 N13 Black River ≈ Arizona, SW USA
27 X7 Black River ≈ Arkansas/Missouri, C USA
22 I7 Black River ≈ Louisiana, S USA
31 S8 Black River ≈ Michigan, N USA
31 Q5 Black River ≈ Michigan, N USA
18 I8 Black River ≈ New York, NE USA
21 T13 Black River ≈ South Carolina, SE USA
30 J7 Black River ≈ Wisconsin, N USA
30 J7 Black River Falls Wisconsin, N USA
35 R3 Black Rock Desert desert Nevada, W USA
Black Sand Desert see Garagum
21 S7 Blacksburg Virginia, NE USA
136 H10 Black Sea var. Euxine Sea, Bul. Cherno More, Rom. Marea Neagră, Rus. Chernoye More, Turk. Karadeniz, Ukr. Chorne More. sea Asia/Europe
117 Q10 Black Sea Lowland Ukr. Prychornomors'ka Nyzovyna. depression SE Europe
33 S17 Blacks Fork ≈ Wyoming, C USA
23 V7 Blackshear Georgia, SE USA
23 S6 Blackshear, Lake ▣ Georgia, SE USA
97 A16 Blacksod Bay Ir. Cuan an Fhóid Duibh. inlet W Ireland
21 V7 Blackstone Virginia, NE USA
77 O14 Black Volta var. Borongo, Mouhoun, Moun Hou, Fr. Volta Noire. ≈ W Africa
23 O5 Black Warrior River ≈ Alabama, S USA
181 X8 Blackwater Queensland, E Australia
97 D20 Blackwater Ir. An Abhainn Mhór. ≈ S Ireland
27 T4 Blackwater River ≈ Missouri, C USA
21 W7 Blackwater River ≈ Virginia, NE USA
Blackwater State see Nebraska
27 N8 Blackwell Oklahoma, C USA
25 P7 Blackwell Texas, SW USA
99 J15 Bladel Noord-Brabant, S Netherlands
Bladenmarkt see Bălăuşeri
114 G11 Blagoevgrad prev. Gorna Dzhumaya. Blagoevgrad, SW Bulgaria
114 G11 Blagoevgrad ◈ province SW Bulgaria
123 Q14 Blagoveshchensk Amurskaya Oblast', SE Russian Federation
127 V4 Blagoveshchensk Respublika Bashkortostan, W Russian Federation
102 I7 Blain Loire-Atlantique, NW France
29 V8 Blaine Minnesota, N USA
32 H6 Blaine Washington, NW USA
11 T15 Blaine Lake Saskatchewan, S Canada
29 S14 Blair Nebraska, C USA
96 J10 Blairgowrie C Scotland, UK
18 C15 Blairsville Pennsylvania, NE USA
116 H11 Blaj Ger. Blasendorf, Hung. Balázsfalva. Alba, SW Romania
64 F9 Blake-Bahama Ridge undersea feature W Atlantic Ocean
23 S7 Blakely Georgia, SE USA
64 E10 Blake Plateau var. Blake Terrace. undersea feature W Atlantic Ocean
30 M1 Blake Point headland Michigan, N USA
Blake Terrace see Blake Plateau
61 B24 Blanca, Bahía bay E Argentina
56 C12 Blanca, Cordillera ⛰ W Peru
105 T12 Blanca, Costa physical region SE Spain
37 S7 Blanca Peak ▲ Colorado, C USA
24 I9 Blanca, Sierra ▲ Texas, SW USA
120 K9 Blanc, Cap headland N Tunisia
Blanc, Cap see Nouâdhibou, Râs
31 R12 Blanchard River ≈ Ohio, N USA
182 E8 Blanche, Cape headland South Australia
182 J4 Blanche, Lake ◎ South Australia
31 R14 Blanchester Ohio, N USA
182 J9 Blanchetown South Australia
45 U13 Blanchisseuse Trinidad, Trinidad and Tobago
103 T11 Blanc, Mont It. Monte Bianco. ▲ France/Italy
25 R11 Blanco Texas, SW USA
42 K14 Blanco, Cabo headland NW Costa Rica
32 D14 Blanco, Cape headland Oregon, NW USA
62 H10 Blanco, Río ≈ W Argentina
56 F10 Blanco, Río ≈ NE Peru
15 O9 Blanc, Réservoir ▣ Québec, SE Canada
21 R7 Bland Virginia, NE USA
92 I2 Blanda ≈ N Iceland
37 O7 Blanding Utah, W USA
105 X5 Blanes Cataluña, NE Spain
103 N3 Blangy-sur-Bresle Seine-Maritime, N France
111 C18 Blanice Ger. Blanitz. ≈ SE Czech Republic
Blanitz see Blanice
99 C16 Blankenberge West-Vlaanderen, NW Belgium
101 D17 Blankenheim Nordrhein-Westfalen, W Germany
25 R8 Blanket Texas, SW USA
55 O3 Blanquilla, Isla var. La Blanquilla. island N Venezuela
Blanquilla, La see Blanquilla, Isla
61 F18 Blanquillo Durazno, C Uruguay
111 G18 Blansko Ger. Blanz. Jihomoravský Kraj, SE Czech Republic
83 N15 Blantyre var. Blantyre-Limbe. Southern, S Malawi
83 N15 Blantyre ✕ Southern, S Malawi
Blantyre-Limbe see Blantyre
Blanz see Blansko
98 J10 Blaricum Noord-Holland, C Netherlands
Blasendorf see Blaj
Blatnitsa see Durankulak
113 F15 Blato It. Blatta. Dubrovnik-Neretva, S Croatia
Blatta see Blato
108 E10 Blatten Valais, SW Switzerland
101 J20 Blaufelden Baden-Württemberg, SW Germany
95 E23 Blåvands Huk headland W Denmark
102 G6 Blavet ≈ NW France
102 J12 Blaye Gironde, SW France
183 R8 Blayney New South Wales, SE Australia
65 D25 Bleaker Island island SE Falkland Islands
109 T10 Bled Ger. Veldes. NW Slovenia
99 D20 Bléharies Hainaut, SW Belgium
109 U9 Bleiburg Slvn. Pliberk. Kärnten, S Austria
101 L17 Bleiloch-Stausee ▣ C Germany
98 H12 Bleiswijk Zuid-Holland, W Netherlands
95 L22 Blekinge ◈ county S Sweden
14 D17 Blenheim Ontario, S Canada
185 K15 Blenheim Marlborough, South Island, NZ
99 M15 Blerick Limburg, SE Netherlands
Blesae see Blois
25 V13 Blessing Texas, SW USA
14 I10 Bleu, Lac ◎ Québec, SE Canada
Blibba see Blitta
120 H10 Blida var. El Boulaida, El Boulaïda. N Algeria
95 P15 Blidö Stockholm, C Sweden
95 K18 Blidsberg Västra Götaland, S Sweden
185 A21 Bligh Sound sound South Island, NZ
187 X14 Bligh Water strait NW Fiji
14 D11 Blind River Ontario, S Canada
31 R11 Blissfield Michigan, N USA
77 R15 Blitta prev. Blibba. C Togo
19 O13 Block Island island Rhode Island, NE USA
19 O13 Block Island Sound sound Rhode Island, NE USA
98 H10 Bloemendaal Noord-Holland, W Netherlands
83 H23 Bloemfontein var. Mangaung. ● (South Africa-judicial capital) Free State, C South Africa
83 I22 Bloemhof North-West, NW South Africa
102 M7 Blois anc. Blesae. Loir-et-Cher, C France
98 L8 Blokzijl Overijssel, N Netherlands
95 N20 Blomstermåla Kalmar, S Sweden
92 I2 Blönduós Nordhurland Vestra, N Iceland
110 L11 Błonie Mazowieckie, C Poland
97 C14 Bloody Foreland Ir. Cnoc Fola. headland NW Ireland
31 N15 Bloomfield Indiana, N USA
29 X16 Bloomfield Iowa, C USA
27 Y8 Bloomfield Missouri, C USA
37 P9 Bloomfield New Mexico, SW USA
25 U7 Blooming Grove Texas, SW USA
29 W10 Blooming Prairie Minnesota, N USA
30 L13 Bloomington Illinois, N USA
31 O15 Bloomington Indiana, N USA
29 V9 Bloomington Minnesota, N USA
25 U13 Bloomington Texas, SW USA
18 H14 Bloomsburg Pennsylvania, NE USA
181 X7 Bloomsbury Queensland, NE Australia
169 R16 Blora Jawa, C Indonesia
18 G12 Blossburg Pennsylvania, NE USA
25 V5 Blossom Texas, SW USA
123 T5 Blossom, Mys headland Ostrov Vrangelya, NE Russian Federation
23 R8 Blountstown Florida, SE USA
21 P8 Blountville Tennessee, S USA
21 Q9 Blowing Rock North Carolina, SE USA
108 J8 Bludenz Vorarlberg, W Austria
36 L6 Blue Bell Knoll ▲ Utah, W USA
23 Y12 Blue Cypress Lake ◎ Florida, SE USA
29 U11 Blue Earth Minnesota, N USA
21 Q7 Bluefield Virginia, NE USA
21 R7 Bluefield West Virginia, NE USA
43 N10 Bluefields Región Autónoma Atlántico Sur, SE Nicaragua
43 N10 Bluefields, Bahía de bay W Caribbean Sea
29 Z14 Blue Grass Iowa, C USA
Bluegrass State see Kentucky
Blue Hen State see Delaware
19 S7 Blue Hill Maine, NE USA
29 P16 Blue Hill Nebraska, C USA
30 J5 Blue Hills hill range Wisconsin, N USA
34 L3 Blue Lake California, W USA
Blue Law State see Connecticut
37 Q6 Blue Mesa Reservoir ▣ Colorado, C USA
27 S12 Blue Mountain ▲ Arkansas, C USA
19 O6 Blue Mountain ▲ New Hampshire, NE USA
18 K8 Blue Mountain ▲ New York, NE USA
18 H15 Blue Mountain ridge Pennsylvania, NE USA
44 H10 Blue Mountain Peak ▲ E Jamaica
183 S8 Blue Mountains ⛰ New South Wales, SE Australia
32 L11 Blue Mountains ⛰ Oregon/Washington, NW USA
80 G12 Blue Nile ◈ state E Sudan
80 H12 Blue Nile var. Abai, Bahr el Azraq, Amh. Ābay Wenz, Ar. An Nīl al Azraq. ≈ Ethiopia/Sudan
8 J7 Bluenose Lake ◎ Nunavut, NW Canada
27 O3 Blue Rapids Kansas, C USA
23 S1 Blue Ridge Georgia, SE USA
17 S11 Blue Ridge var. Blue Ridge Mountains. ⛰ North Carolina/Virginia, E USA
23 S1 Blue Ridge Lake ▣ Georgia, SE USA
Blue Ridge Mountains see Blue Ridge
11 N15 Blue River British Columbia, SW Canada
27 O12 Blue River ≈ Oklahoma, C USA
27 R4 Blue Springs Missouri, C USA
21 R6 Bluestone Lake ▣ West Virginia, NE USA
185 C25 Bluff Southland, South Island, NZ
37 O8 Bluff Utah, W USA
21 P8 Bluff City Tennessee, S USA
65 E24 Bluff Cove East Falkland, Falkland Islands
25 S7 Bluff Dale Texas, SW USA
183 N15 Bluff Hill Point headland Tasmania, SE Australia
31 Q12 Bluffton Indiana, N USA
31 R12 Bluffton Ohio, N USA
25 T7 Blum Texas, SW USA
101 G24 Blumberg Baden-Württemberg, SW Germany
60 K13 Blumenau Santa Catarina, S Brazil
29 N9 Blunt South Dakota, N USA
32 H15 Bly Oregon, NW USA
39 R13 Blying Sound sound Alaska, USA
97 M14 Blyth N England, UK
35 Y16 Blythe California, W USA
27 Y9 Blytheville Arkansas, C USA

◆ Country ● Country Capital ◇ Dependent Territory ○ Dependent Territory Capital ◈ Administrative Region ✕ International Airport ▲ Mountain ⛰ Mountain Range ⩚ Volcano ≈ River ◎ Lake ▣ Reservoir

117 V7 **Blyznyuky** Kharkivs'ka Oblast', E Ukraine
76 I15 **Bo** S Sierra Leone
95 G16 **Bø** Telemark, S Norway
171 O4 **Boac** Marinduque, N Philippines
42 K10 **Boaco** Boaco, S Nicaragua
42 J10 **Boaco** ◈ *department* C Nicaragua
79 I15 **Boali** Ombella-Mpoko, SW Central African Republic
Boalsert *see* Bolsward
31 V12 **Boardman** Ohio, N USA
32 J11 **Boardman** Oregon, NW USA
14 F13 **Boat Lake** ◎ Ontario, S Canada
58 F10 **Boa Vista** *state capital* Roraima, NW Brazil
76 D9 **Boa Vista** *island* Ilhas de Barlavento, E Cape Verde
23 Q2 **Boaz** Alabama, S USA
160 L15 **Bobai** Guangxi Zhuangzu Zizhiqu, S China
172 J1 **Bobaomby, Tanjona** *Fr.* Cap d'Ambre. *headland* N Madagascar
155 M14 **Bobbili** Andhra Pradesh, E India
106 D9 **Bobbio** Emilia-Romagna, C Italy
14 I14 **Bobcaygeon** Ontario, SE Canada
Bober *see* Bóbr
103 O5 **Bobigny** Seine-St-Denis, N France
77 N13 **Bobo-Dioulasso** SW Burkina
110 G8 **Bobolice** *Ger.* Bublitz. Zachodnio-pomorskie, NW Poland
83 J19 **Bobonong** Central, E Botswana
171 R11 **Bobopayo** Pulau Halmahera, E Indonesia
147 P13 **Bobotogh, Qatorkŭhi** *Rus.* Khrebet Babatag. ⛰ Tajikistan/Uzbekistan
114 G10 **Bobovdol** Kyustendil, W Bulgaria
119 M15 **Bobr** Minskaya Voblasts', NW Belarus
119 M15 **Bobr** ≈ C Belarus
111 E14 **Bóbr** *Eng.* Bobrawa, *Ger.* Bober. ≈ SW Poland
Bobrawa *see* Bóbr
Bobrik *see* Bobryk
Bobrinets *see* Bobrynets'
Bobrka/Bóbrka *see* Bibrka
126 L8 **Bobrov** Voronezhskaya Oblast', W Russian Federation
117 Q4 **Bobrovytsya** Chernihivs'ka Oblast', N Ukraine
Bobruysk *see* Babruysk
119 J19 **Bobryk** *Rus.* Bobrik. ≈ SW Belarus
117 Q8 **Bobrynets'** *Rus.* Bobrinets. Kirovohrads'ka Oblast', C Ukraine
14 K14 **Bobs Lake** ◎ Ontario, SE Canada
54 I6 **Bobures** Zulia, NW Venezuela
42 H1 **Boca Bacalar Chico** *headland* N Belize
112 G11 **Bočac** Republika Srpska, NW Bosnia and Herzegovina
41 R14 **Boca del Río** Veracruz-Llave, S Mexico
55 O4 **Boca de Pozo** Nueva Esparta, NE Venezuela
59 C15 **Boca do Acre** Amazonas, N Brazil
55 N12 **Boca Mavaca** Amazonas, S Venezuela
79 G14 **Bocaranga** Ouham-Pendé, W Central African Republic
23 Z15 **Boca Raton** Florida, SE USA
43 P14 **Bocas del Toro** Bocas del Toro, NW Panama
43 P15 **Bocas del Toro** *off.* Provincia de Bocas del Toro. ◈ *province* NW Panama
43 P15 **Bocas del Toro, Archipiélago de** *island group* NW Panama
42 L7 **Bocay** Jinotega, N Nicaragua
105 N6 **Boceguillas** Castilla-León, N Spain
Bocheykovo *see* Bacheykava
111 L17 **Bochnia** Małopolskie, SE Poland
99 K16 **Bocholt** Limburg, NE Belgium
101 D14 **Bocholt** Nordrhein-Westfalen, W Germany
101 E15 **Bochum** Nordrhein-Westfalen, W Germany
103 Y15 **Bocognano** Corse, France, C Mediterranean Sea
54 I6 **Boconó** Trujillo, NW Venezuela
116 F12 **Bocşa** *Ger.* Bokschen, *Hung.* Boksánbánya. Caraş-Severin, SW Romania
79 H15 **Boda** Lobaye, SW Central African Republic
94 L12 **Boda** Dalarna, C Sweden
95 O20 **Böda** Kalmar, S Sweden
95 L19 **Bodafors** Jönköping, S Sweden
123 O12 **Bodaybo** Irkutskaya Oblast', E Russian Federation
22 G5 **Bodcau, Bayou** *var.* Bodcau Creek. ≈ Louisiana, S USA
Bodcau Creek *see* Bodcau, Bayou
44 D8 **Bodden Town** *var.* Boddentown. Grand Cayman, SW Cayman Islands
101 K14 **Bode** ≈ C Germany
34 L7 **Bodega Head** *headland* California, W USA
Bodegas *see* Babahoyo
98 H11 **Bodegraven** Zuid-Holland, C Netherlands
78 H8 **Bodélé** *depression* W Chad
92 J13 **Boden** Norrbotten, N Sweden
Bodensee *see* Constance, Lake, C Europe
65 M15 **Bode Verde Fracture Zone** *tectonic feature* E Atlantic Ocean
155 H14 **Bodhan** Andhra Pradesh, C India
162 I9 **Bodĭ** Bayanhongor, C Mongolia
155 H22 **Bodināyakkanūr** Tamil Nādu, SE India
108 H10 **Bodio** Ticino, S Switzerland
97 I24 **Bodmin** SW England, UK
97 I24 **Bodmin Moor** *moorland* SW England, UK
92 G12 **Bodø** Nordland, C Norway
59 H20 **Bodoquena, Serra da** ⛰ SW Brazil
136 B16 **Bodrum** Muğla, SW Turkey
Bodzafordulő *see* Întorsura Buzăului
99 L14 **Boekel** Noord-Brabant, SE Netherlands
Boeloekoemba *see* Bulukumba
103 Q11 **Boën** Loire, E France
79 K18 **Boende** Equateur, C Dem. Rep. Congo
25 R11 **Boerne** Texas, SW USA
Boeroe *see* Buru, Pulau
Boetoeng *see* Buton, Pulau
22 I5 **Boeuf River** ≈ Arkansas/Louisiana, S USA
76 H14 **Boffa** Guinée-Maritime, W Guinea
Bó Finne, Inis *see* Inishbofin
Boga *see* Bogë
166 L9 **Bogale** Irrawaddy, SW Burma
22 L8 **Bogalusa** Louisiana, S USA
77 Q12 **Bogandé** C Burkina
79 I15 **Bogangolo** Ombella-Mpoko, C Central African Republic
183 Q7 **Bogan River** ≈ New South Wales, SE Australia
25 W5 **Bogata** Texas, SW USA
111 D14 **Bogatynia** *Ger.* Reichenau. Dolnośląskie, SW Poland
136 K13 **Boğazlıyan** Yozgat, C Turkey
79 J17 **Bogbonga** Equateur, NW Dem. Rep. Congo
158 J14 **Bogcang Zangbo** ≈ W China
158 L5 **Bogda Feng** ▲ NW China
114 I9 **Bogdan** ▲ C Bulgaria
113 Q20 **Bogdanci** SE FYR Macedonia
158 M5 **Bogda Shan** *var.* Po-ko-to Shan. ⛰ NW China
113 K17 **Bogë** *var.* Boga. Shkodër, N Albania
Bogendorf *see* Łuków
95 G23 **Bogense** Fyn, C Denmark
183 T3 **Boggabilla** New South Wales, SE Australia
183 S6 **Boggabri** New South Wales, SE Australia
186 D6 **Bogia** Madang, N PNG
97 N23 **Bognor Regis** SE England, UK
Bogodukhov *see* Bohodukhiv
181 V15 **Bogong, Mount** ▲ Victoria, SE Australia
169 O16 **Bogor** *Dut.* Buitenzorg. Jawa, C Indonesia
126 L5 **Bogoroditsk** Tul'skaya Oblast', W Russian Federation
127 O3 **Bogorodsk** Nizhegorodskaya Oblast', W Russian Federation
Bogorodskoje *see* Bogorodskoye
123 S12 **Bogorodskoye** Khabarovskiy Kray, SE Russian Federation
125 R15 **Bogorodskoye** *var.* Bogorodskoje. Kirovskaya Oblast', NW Russian Federation
54 F10 **Bogotá** *prev.* Santa Fe, Santa Fe de Bogotá. ● (Colombia) Cundinamarca, C Colombia
153 T14 **Bogra** Rajshahi, N Bangladesh
Bogschan *see* Boldu
122 L12 **Boguchany** Krasnoyarskiy Kray, C Russian Federation
126 M9 **Boguchar** Voronezhskaya Oblast', W Russian Federation
76 H10 **Bogué** Brakna, SW Mauritania
22 K8 **Bogue Chitto** ≈ Louisiana/Mississippi, S USA
Bogushëvsk *see* Bahushewsk
Boguslav *see* Bohuslav
44 K12 **Bog Walk** C Jamaica
161 Q3 **Bo Hai** *var.* Gulf of Chihli. *gulf* NE China
161 R3 **Bohai Haixia** *strait* NE China
161 Q3 **Bohai Wan** *bay* NE China
111 C17 **Bohemia** *Cz.* Čechy, *Ger.* Böhmen. *cultural and historical region* W Czech Republic
111 B18 **Bohemian Forest** *Cz.* Ceský Les, Šumava, *Ger.* Böhmerwald. ⛰ C Europe
Bohemian-Moravian Highlands *see* Českomoravská Vrchovina
77 R16 **Bohicon** S Benin
109 S11 **Bohinjska Bistrica** *Ger.* Wocheiner Feistritz. NW Slovenia
Bohkká *see* Pokka
Böhmen *see* Bohemia
Böhmerwald *see* Bohemian Forest
Böhmisch-Krumau *see* Český Krumlov
Böhmisch-Leipa *see* Česká Lípa
Böhmisch-Mährische Höhe *see* Českomoravská Vrchovina
Böhmisch-Trübau *see* Česká Třebová
117 U5 **Bohodukhiv** *Rus.* Bogodukhov. Kharkivs'ka Oblast', E Ukraine
171 Q6 **Bohol** *island* C Philippines
171 Q7 **Bohol Sea** *var.* Mindanao Sea. *sea* S Philippines
116 I7 **Bohorodchany** Ivano-Frankivs'ka Oblast', W Ukraine
162 M9 **Böhöt** Dundgovĭ, C Mongolia
158 K6 **Bohu** *var.* Bagrax. Xinjiang Uygur Zizhiqu, NW China
111 I17 **Bohumín** *Ger.* Oderberg; *prev.* Neuoderberg, Nový Bohumín. Moravskoslezský Kraj, E Czech Republic
117 P6 **Bohuslav** *Rus.* Boguslav. Kyyivs'ka Oblast', N Ukraine
58 F11 **Boiaçu** Roraima, N Brazil
107 K16 **Boiano** Molise, C Italy
15 R8 **Boilleau** Québec, SE Canada
59 O17 **Boipeba, Ilha de** *island* SE Brazil
104 G3 **Boiro** Galicia, NW Spain
31 Q5 **Bois Blanc Island** *island* Michigan, N USA
29 R7 **Bois de Sioux River** ≈ Minnesota, N USA
33 N14 **Boise** *var.* Boise City. *state capital* Idaho, NW USA
26 G8 **Boise City** Oklahoma, C USA
33 N14 **Boise River, Middle Fork** ≈ Idaho, NW USA
Bois, Lac des *see* Woods, Lake of the
Bois-le-Duc *see* 's-Hertogenbosch
11 W17 **Boissevain** Manitoba, S Canada
15 T7 **Boisvert, Pointe au** *headland* Québec, SE Canada
100 K10 **Boizenburg** Mecklenburg-Vorpommern, N Germany
Bojador *see* Boujdour
113 K18 **Bojana** *Alb.* Bunë. ≈ Albania/Serbia and Montenegro (Yugo.) *see also* Bunë
143 S3 **Bojnūrd** *var.* Bujnurd. Khorāsān, N Iran
169 R16 **Bojonegoro** *prev.* Bodjonegoro. Jawa, C Indonesia
189 T1 **Bokaak Atoll** *var.* Bokak, Taongi. *atoll* Ratak Chain, NE Marshall Islands
Bokak *see* Bokaak Atoll
146 K8 **Bo'kantov-Tog'lari** *Rus.* Gory Bukantau. ⛰ N Uzbekistan
153 Q15 **Bokāro** Jhārkhand, N India
79 I18 **Bokatola** Equateur, NW Dem. Rep. Congo
76 H13 **Boké** Guinée-Maritime, W Guinea
Bokhara *see* Buxoro
183 Q4 **Bokharra River** ≈ New South Wales/Queensland, SE Australia
95 C16 **Boknafjorden** *fjord* S Norway
78 H11 **Bokoro** Chari-Baguirmi, W Chad
79 K19 **Bokota** Equateur, NW Dem. Rep. Congo
167 N13 **Bokpyin** Tenasserim, S Burma
Boksánbánya/Bokschen *see* Bocşa
83 F21 **Bokspits** Kgalagadi, SW Botswana
79 K18 **Bokungu** Equateur, C Dem. Rep. Congo
146 F12 **Bokurdak** *Rus.* Bakhardok. Ahal Welaýaty, C Turkmenistan
78 G10 **Bol** Lac, W Chad
76 G13 **Bolama** SW Guinea-Bissau
Bolangir *see* Balāngīr
Bolanos *see* Bolanos, Mount, Guam
Bolaños *see* Bolaños de Calatrava, Spain
105 N11 **Bolaños de Calatrava** *var.* Bolaños. Castilla-La Mancha, C Spain
188 B17 **Bolanos, Mount** *var.* Bolanos. ▲ S Guam
40 L12 **Bolaños, Río** ≈ C Mexico
115 M14 **Bolayır** Çanakkale, NW Turkey
102 L3 **Bolbec** Seine-Maritime, N France
116 L13 **Boldu** *var.* Bogschan. Buzău, SE Romania
146 H8 **Boldumsaz** *prev.* Kalinin, Kalininsk, Porsy. Daşoguz Welaýaty, N Turkmenistan
158 I4 **Bole** *var.* Bortala. Xinjiang Uygur Zizhiqu, NW China
77 O15 **Bole** NW Ghana
79 J19 **Boleko** Equateur, W Dem. Rep. Congo
111 E14 **Bolesławiec** *Ger.* Bunzlau. Dolnośląskie, SW Poland
127 R4 **Bolgar** *prev.* Kuybyshev. Respublika Tatarstan, W Russian Federation
77 P14 **Bolgatanga** N Ghana
Bolgrad *see* Bolhrad
117 N12 **Bolhrad** *Rus.* Bolgrad. Odes'ka Oblast', SW Ukraine
163 Y8 **Boli** Heilongjiang, NE China
79 I19 **Bolia** Bandundu, W Dem. Rep. Congo
93 J14 **Boliden** Västerbotten, N Sweden
171 T13 **Bolifar** Pulau Seram, E Indonesia
171 N2 **Bolinao** Luzon, N Philippines
27 T6 **Bolivar** Missouri, C USA
20 F10 **Bolivar** Tennessee, S USA
54 C12 **Bolívar** Cauca, SW Colombia
54 F7 **Bolívar** *off.* Departmento de Bolívar. ◈ *province* N Colombia
56 A13 **Bolívar** ◈ *province* C Ecuador
55 N9 **Bolívar** *off.* Estado Bolívar. ◈ *state* SE Venezuela
25 X12 **Bolivar Peninsula** *headland* Texas, SW USA
54 I6 **Bolívar, Pico** ▲ W Venezuela
57 K17 **Bolivia** *off.* Republic of Bolivia. ◆ *republic* W South America
112 O13 **Boljevac** Serbia, E Serbia and Montenegro (Yugo.)
Bolkenhain *see* Bolków
126 J5 **Bolkhov** Orlovskaya Oblast', W Russian Federation
111 F14 **Bolków** *Ger.* Bolkenhain. Dolnośląskie, SW Poland
182 K3 **Bollards Lagoon** South Australia
103 R14 **Bollène** Vaucluse, SE France
94 N12 **Bollnäs** Gävleborg, C Sweden
181 W10 **Bollon** Queensland, C Australia
192 L12 **Bollons Tablemount** *undersea feature* S Pacific Ocean
93 H17 **Bollstabruk** Västernorrland, C Sweden
Bolluilos de Par del Condado *see* Bollullos Par del Condado
104 J14 **Bollullos Par del Condado** *var.* Bolluilos de Par del Condado. Andalucía, S Spain
95 K21 **Bolmen** ◎ S Sweden
137 T10 **Bolnisi** S Georgia
79 H19 **Bolobo** Bandundu, W Dem. Rep. Congo
106 G10 **Bologna** Emilia-Romagna, N Italy
124 I15 **Bologoye** Tverskaya Oblast', W Russian Federation
79 J18 **Bolomba** Equateur, NW Dem. Rep. Congo
41 X13 **Bolonchén de Rejón** *var.* Bolonchén de Rejón. Campeche, SE Mexico
114 J13 **Boloústra, Akrotírio** *headland* NE Greece
167 L8 **Bolovens, Plateau des** *plateau* S Laos
107 H13 **Bolsena** Lazio, C Italy
107 G14 **Bolsena, Lago di** ◎ C Italy
126 B3 **Bol'shakovo** *Ger.* Kreuzingen; *prev.* Gross-Skaisgirren. Kaliningradskaya Oblast', W Russian Federation
Bol'shaya Berëstovitsa *see* Vyalikaya Byerastavitsa
127 S7 **Bol'shaya Chernigovka** Samarskaya Oblast', W Russian Federation
127 S7 **Bol'shaya Glushitsa** Samarskaya Oblast', W Russian Federation
144 H9 **Bol'shaya Khobda** *Kaz.* Ülkenqobda. ≈ Kazakhstan/Russian Federation
126 M12 **Bol'shaya Martynovka** Rostovskaya Oblast', SW Russian Federation
122 K12 **Bol'shaya Murta** Krasnoyarskiy Kray, C Russian Federation
127 V4 **Bol'shaya Rogovaya** ≈ NW Russian Federation
127 U7 **Bol'shaya Synya** ≈ NW Russian Federation
145 V9 **Bol'shaya Vladimirovka** Vostochnyy Kazakhstan, E Kazakhstan
123 V11 **Bol'sheretsk** Kamchatskaya Oblast', E Russian Federation
127 W3 **Bol'sheust'ikinskoye** Respublika Bashkortostan, W Russian Federation
Bol'shevik *see* Bal'shavik
122 L5 **Bol'shevik, Ostrov** *island* Severnaya Zemlya, N Russian Federation
127 U4 **Bol'shezemel'skaya Tundra** *physical region* NW Russian Federation
144 J13 **Bol'shiye Barsuki, Peski** *desert* SW Kazakhstan
123 T7 **Bol'shoy Anyuy** ≈ NE Russian Federation
123 N7 **Bol'shoy Begichev, Ostrov** *island* NE Russian Federation
123 S15 **Bol'shoy Kamen'** Primorskiy Kray, SE Russian Federation
127 O4 **Bol'shoye Murashkino** Nizhegorodskaya Oblast', W Russian Federation
127 W4 **Bol'shoy Iremel'** ▲ W Russian Federation
127 R7 **Bol'shoy Irgiz** ≈ W Russian Federation
123 Q6 **Bol'shoy Lyakhovskiy, Ostrov** *island* NE Russian Federation
123 Q11 **Bol'shoy Nimnyr** Respublika Sakha (Yakutiya), NE Russian Federation
Bol'shoy Rozhan *see* Vyaliki Rozhan
144 E10 **Bol'shoy Uzen'** *Kaz.* Ülkenözen. ≈ Kazakhstan/Russian Federation
40 K6 **Bolson de Mapimi** ⛰ NW Mexico
98 K6 **Bolsward** *Fris.* Boalsert. Friesland, N Netherlands
105 T4 **Boltaña** Aragón, NE Spain
14 G15 **Bolton** Ontario, S Canada
97 K17 **Bolton** *prev.* Bolton-le-Moors. NW England, UK
21 V12 **Bolton** North Carolina, SE USA
Bolton-le-Moors *see* Bolton
136 G11 **Bolu** Bolu, NW Turkey
136 G11 **Bolu** ◈ *province* NW Turkey
186 G9 **Bolubolu** Goodenough Island, S PNG
92 H1 **Bolungarvík** Vestfirdhir, NW Iceland
159 O10 **Boluntay** Qinghai, W China
159 P8 **Boluozhuanjing** *var.* Aksay, Aksay Kazakzu Zizhixian. Gansu, N China
136 F14 **Bolvadin** Afyon, W Turkey
114 M10 **Bolyarovo** *prev.* Pashkeni. Yambol, E Bulgaria
106 G6 **Bolzano** *Ger.* Bozen; *anc.* Bauzanum. Trentino-Alto Adige, N Italy
79 F22 **Boma** Bas-Congo, W Dem. Rep. Congo
183 R12 **Bombala** New South Wales, SE Australia
104 F10 **Bombarral** Leiria, C Portugal
Bombay *see* Mumbai
171 U13 **Bomberai, Semenanjung** *headland* Papua, E Indonesia
81 F18 **Bombo** S Uganda
79 I17 **Bomboma** Equateur, NW Dem. Rep. Congo
59 I14 **Bom Futuro** Pará, N Brazil
159 Q15 **Bomi** *var.* Bowo, Zhamo. Xizang Zizhiqu, W China
79 N17 **Bomili** Orientale, NE Dem. Rep. Congo
59 N17 **Bom Jesus da Lapa** Bahia, E Brazil
60 Q8 **Bom Jesus do Itabapoana** Rio de Janeiro, SE Brazil
95 C15 **Bømlafjorden** *fjord* S Norway
95 B15 **Bømlo** *island* S Norway
123 Q12 **Bomnak** Amurskaya Oblast', SE Russian Federation
79 I17 **Bomongo** Equateur, NW Dem. Rep. Congo
61 K14 **Bom Retiro** Santa Catarina, S Brazil
79 L15 **Bomu** *var.* Mbomou, Mbomu, M'Bomu. ≈ Central African Republic/Dem. Rep. Congo
142 J3 **Bonāb** *var.* Benāb, Bunab. Āzarbāyjān-e Khāvarī, N Iran
45 Q16 **Bonaire** *island* E Netherlands Antilles
39 U11 **Bona, Mount** ▲ Alaska, USA
183 Q12 **Bonang** Victoria, SE Australia
42 L7 **Bonanza** Región Autónoma Atlántico Norte, NE Nicaragua
37 O4 **Bonanza** Utah, W USA
45 O9 **Bonao** C Dominican Republic
180 L3 **Bonaparte Archipelago** *island group* Western Australia
32 K6 **Bonaparte, Mount** ▲ Washington, NW USA
39 N11 **Bonasila Dome** ▲ Alaska, USA
92 H11 **Bonåsjøen** Nordland, C Norway
45 T15 **Bonasse** Trinidad, Trinidad and Tobago
15 X7 **Bonaventure** Québec, SE Canada
15 X7 **Bonaventure** ≈ Québec, SE Canada
13 V11 **Bonavista** Newfoundland and Labrador, SE Canada
13 U11 **Bonavista Bay** *inlet* NW Atlantic Ocean
79 E19 **Bonda** Ogooué-Lolo, C Gabon
127 N6 **Bondari** Tambovskaya Oblast', W Russian Federation
106 G9 **Bondeno** Emilia-Romagna, C Italy
30 L4 **Bond Falls Flowage** ◎ Michigan, N USA
79 L16 **Bondo** Orientale, N Dem. Rep. Congo
171 N17 **Bondokodi** Pulau Sumba, S Indonesia
77 O15 **Bondoukou** E Ivory Coast
Bondoukui/Bondoukuy *see* Boundoukui
169 T17 **Bondowoso** Jawa, C Indonesia
33 S14 **Bondurant** Wyoming, C USA
Bone *see* Watampone, Indonesia
Bône *see* Annaba, Algeria
30 I5 **Bone Lake** ◎ Wisconsin, N USA
171 P14 **Bonelipu** Pulau Buton, C Indonesia
171 O15 **Bonerate, Kepulauan** *var.* Macan. *island group* C Indonesia
29 O12 **Bonesteel** South Dakota, N USA
62 I8 **Bonete, Cerro** ▲ N Argentina
171 O14 **Bone, Teluk** *bay* Sulawesi, C Indonesia
108 D6 **Bonfol** Jura, NW Switzerland
153 U12 **Bongaigaon** Assam, NE India
79 K17 **Bongandanga** Equateur, NW Dem. Rep. Congo
78 L13 **Bongo, Massif des** *var.* Chaîne des Mongos. ⛰ NE Central African Republic
78 G12 **Bongor** Mayo-Kébbi, SW Chad
77 N16 **Bongouanou** E Ivory Coast
167 V11 **Bông Sơn** *var.* Hoai Nhơn. Binh Đinh, C Vietnam
25 U5 **Bonham** Texas, SW USA
Bonhard *see* Bonyhád
103 U6 **Bonhomme, Col du** *pass* NE France
103 Y16 **Bonifacio** Corse, France, C Mediterranean Sea
Bonifacio, Bocche de/Bonifacio, Bouches de *see* Bonifacio, Strait of
103 Y16 **Bonifacio, Strait of** *Fr.* Bouches de Bonifacio, *It.* Bocche de Bonifacio. *strait* C Mediterranean Sea
23 Q8 **Bonifay** Florida, SE USA
Bonin Islands *see* Ogasawara-shotō
192 H5 **Bonin Trench** *undersea feature* NW Pacific Ocean
23 W15 **Bonita Springs** Florida, SE USA
42 I5 **Bonito, Pico** ▲ N Honduras
101 E17 **Bonn** Nordrhein-Westfalen, W Germany
14 J12 **Bonnechere** Ontario, SE Canada
14 J12 **Bonnechere** ≈ Ontario, SE Canada
33 N7 **Bonners Ferry** Idaho, NW USA
27 R4 **Bonner Springs** Kansas, C USA
102 L6 **Bonnétable** Sarthe, NW France
27 X6 **Bonne Terre** Missouri, C USA
10 J5 **Bonnet Plume** ≈ Yukon Territory, NW Canada
102 M6 **Bonneval** Eure-et-Loir, C France
103 T10 **Bonneville** Haute-Savoie, E France
36 J3 **Bonneville Salt Flats** *salt flat* Utah, W USA
77 U18 **Bonny** Rivers, S Nigeria
Bonny, Bight of *see* Biafra, Bight of
37 W4 **Bonny Reservoir** ▣ Colorado, C USA
11 R14 **Bonnyville** Alberta, SW Canada
107 C18 **Bono** Sardegna, Italy, C Mediterranean Sea
Bononia *see* Vidin, Bulgaria
Bononia *see* Boulogne-sur-Mer, France
107 B18 **Bonorva** Sardegna, Italy, C Mediterranean Sea
30 M15 **Bonpas Creek** ≈ Illinois, N USA
190 I3 **Bonriki** Tarawa, W Kiribati
183 T4 **Bonshaw** New South Wales, SE Australia
76 I16 **Bonthe** SW Sierra Leone
171 N2 **Bontoc** Luzon, N Philippines
25 Y9 **Bon Wier** Texas, SW USA
111 J25 **Bonyhád** *Ger.* Bonhard. Tolna, S Hungary
Bonzabaai *see* Bonza Bay
83 J25 **Bonza Bay** *Afr.* Bonzabaai. Eastern Cape, S South Africa
182 D7 **Bookabie** South Australia
182 H6 **Bookaloo** South Australia
37 P5 **Book Cliffs** *cliff* Colorado/Utah, W USA
25 P1 **Booker** Texas, SW USA
76 K15 **Boola** Guinée-Forestière, SE Guinea
183 O8 **Booligal** New South Wales, SE Australia
99 G17 **Boom** Antwerpen, N Belgium
43 N6 **Boom** *var.* Boon. Región Autónoma Atlántico Norte, NE Nicaragua
183 S3 **Boomi** New South Wales, SE Australia
Boon *see* Boom
29 V13 **Boone** Iowa, C USA
21 Q8 **Boone** North Carolina, SE USA
27 S11 **Booneville** Arkansas, C USA
21 N6 **Booneville** Kentucky, S USA
23 N2 **Booneville** Mississippi, S USA
21 V3 **Boonsboro** Maryland, NE USA
162 H9 **Böön Tsagaan Nuur** ◎ S Mongolia
34 L6 **Boonville** California, W USA
31 N16 **Boonville** Indiana, N USA
27 U4 **Boonville** Missouri, C USA
18 I9 **Boonville** New York, NE USA
80 M12 **Boorama** Woqooyi Galbeed, NW Somalia
183 O6 **Booroondarra, Mount** *hill* New South Wales, SE Australia
183 N9 **Booroorban** New South Wales, SE Australia
183 R9 **Boorowa** New South Wales, SE Australia
99 H17 **Boortmeerbeek** Vlaams Brabant, C Belgium
80 P11 **Boosaaso** *var.* Bandar Kassim, Bender Qaasim, Bosaso, *It.* Bender Cassim. Bari, N Somalia
19 Q8 **Boothbay Harbor** Maine, NE USA
Boothia Felix *see* Boothia Peninsula
9 N6 **Boothia, Gulf of** *gulf* Nunavut, NE Canada
8 M6 **Boothia Peninsula** *prev.* Boothia Felix. *peninsula* Nunavut, NE Canada
79 E18 **Booué** Ogooué-Ivindo, NE Gabon
101 J21 **Bopfingen** Baden-Württemberg, S Germany
101 F18 **Boppard** Rheinland-Pfalz, W Germany
62 M4 **Boquerón** *off.* Departamento de Boquerón. ◈ *department* W Paraguay
43 P15 **Boquete** *var.* Bajo Boquete. Chiriquí, W Panama
40 J6 **Boquilla, Presa de la** ▣ N Mexico
40 L5 **Boquillas** *var.* Boquillas del Carmen. Coahuila de Zaragoza, NE Mexico
Boquillas del Carmen *see* Boquillas
81 F15 **Bor** Jonglei, S Sudan
95 L20 **Bor** Jönköping, S Sweden
136 J15 **Bor** Niğde, S Turkey
112 P12 **Bor** Serbia, E Serbia and Montenegro (Yugo.)
191 S10 **Bora-Bora** *island* Îles Sous le Vent, W French Polynesia
167 Q9 **Borabu** Maha Sarakham, E Thailand
33 P13 **Borah Peak** ▲ Idaho, NW USA
145 G13 **Boralday** *prev.* Burunday. Almaty, SE Kazakhstan
144 G13 **Borankul** *prev.* Opornyy. Mangistau, SW Kazakhstan
95 J19 **Borås** Västra Götaland, S Sweden
145 U15 **Boralday** *prev.* Burunday. Almaty, SE Kazakhstan
143 N11 **Borāzjān** *var.* Borazjān. Būshehr, S Iran
Borazjān *see* Borāzjān
58 G13 **Borba** Amazonas, N Brazil
104 H11 **Borba** Évora, S Portugal
Borbetomagus *see* Worms
55 O7 **Borbón** Bolívar, E Venezuela
59 Q15 **Borborema, Planalto da** *plateau* NE Brazil
116 M14 **Borcea, Braţul** ≈ S Romania
Borchalo *see* Marneuli
195 R15 **Borchgrevink Coast** *physical region* Antarctica
137 Q11 **Borçka** Artvin, NE Turkey
98 N11 **Borculo** Gelderland, E Netherlands
182 G10 **Borda, Cape** *headland* South Australia
102 K13 **Bordeaux** *anc.* Burdigala. Gironde, SW France
11 T15 **Borden** Saskatchewan, S Canada
14 D8 **Borden Lake** ◎ Ontario, S Canada
9 N4 **Borden Peninsula** *peninsula* Baffin Island, Nunavut, NE Canada
182 K11 **Bordertown** South Australia
92 H2 **Bordheyri** Vestfirdhir, NW Iceland
95 B18 **Bordhoy** *Dan.* Bordø *Island* Faeroe Islands
106 B11 **Bordighera** Liguria, NW Italy
74 K5 **Bordj-Bou-Arreridj** *var.* Bordj Bou Arreridj, Bordj Bou Arréridj. N Algeria
74 L10 **Bordj Omar Driss** E Algeria
143 N13 **Bord Khūn** Hormozgān, S Iran
147 V7 **Bordunskiy** Chuyskaya Oblast', N Kyrgyzstan
95 M17 **Borensberg** Östergötland, S Sweden
Borgå *see* Porvoo
92 L2 **Borgarfjördhur** Austurland, NE Iceland
92 H3 **Borgarnes** Vesturland, W Iceland
93 G14 **Børgefjell** ▲ C Norway
98 O7 **Borger** Drenthe, NE Netherlands
25 N2 **Borger** Texas, SW USA
95 N20 **Borgholm** Kalmar, S Sweden
107 N22 **Borgia** Calabria, SW Italy

◆ Country ● Country Capital ◇ Dependent Territory ○ Dependent Territory Capital ◈ Administrative Region ✕ International Airport ▲ Mountain ⛰ Mountain Range Volcano ≈ River ◎ Lake ▣ Reservoir

99 J18 **Borgloon** Limburg, NE Belgium
195 P2 **Borg Massif** ▲ Antarctica
22 L9 **Borgne, Lake** ◎ Louisiana, S USA
106 C7 **Borgomanero** Piemonte, NE Italy
106 G10 **Borgo Panigale** ✕ (Bologna) Emilia-Romagna, N Italy
107 J15 **Borgorose** Lazio, C Italy
106 A9 **Borgo San Dalmazzo** Piemonte, N Italy
106 G11 **Borgo San Lorenzo** Toscana, C Italy
106 C7 **Borgosesia** Piemonte, NE Italy
106 E9 **Borgo Val di Taro** Emilia-Romagna, C Italy
106 G6 **Borgo Valsugana** Trentino-Alto Adige, N Italy
163 O11 **Borhoyn Tal** Dornogovĭ, SE Mongolia
167 R8 **Borikhan** *var.* Borikhane. Bolikhamxai, C Laos
Borikhane *see* Borikhan
Borislav *see* Boryslav
127 N8 **Borisoglebsk** Voronezhskaya Oblast', W Russian Federation
Borisov *see* Barysaw
Borisovgrad *see* Pŭrvomay
Borispol' *see* Boryspil'
172 I3 **Boriziny** Mahajanga, NW Madagascar
105 Q5 **Borja** Aragón, NE Spain
Borjas Blancas *see* Les Borges Blanques
137 S10 **Borjomi** *Rus.* Borzhomi. C Georgia
118 L12 **Borkavichy** *Rus.* Borkovichi. Vitsyebskaya Voblasts', N Belarus
101 H16 **Borken** Hessen, C Germany
101 E14 **Borken** Nordrhein-Westfalen, W Germany
92 H10 **Borkenes** Troms, N Norway
78 H7 **Borkou-Ennedi-Tibesti** *off.* Préfecture du Borkou-Ennedi-Tibesti. ◈ *prefecture* N Chad
Borkovichi *see* Borkavichy
100 E9 **Borkum** *island* NW Germany
81 K17 **Bor, Lagh** *var.* Lak Bor. *dry watercourse* NE Kenya
Bor, Lak *see* Bor, Lagh
95 M14 **Borlänge** Dalarna, C Sweden
106 C9 **Bormida** ≈ NW Italy
106 F6 **Bormio** Lombardia, N Italy
101 M16 **Borna** Sachsen, E Germany
98 O10 **Borne** Overijssel, E Netherlands
99 F17 **Bornem** Antwerpen, N Belgium
169 S10 **Borneo** *island* Brunei/Indonesia/Malaysia
101 E16 **Bornheim** Nordrhein-Westfalen, W Germany
95 L24 **Bornholm** ◈ *county* E Denmark
95 L24 **Bornholm** *island* E Denmark
77 Y13 **Borno** ◈ *state* NE Nigeria
104 K15 **Bornos** Andalucía, S Spain
162 L7 **Bornuur** Töv, C Mongolia
117 O4 **Borodyanka** Kyyivs'ka Oblast', N Ukraine
158 I5 **Borohoro Shan** ▲ NW China
77 O13 **Boromo** SW Burkina
35 T13 **Boron** California, W USA
Borongo *see* Black Volta
Boron'ki *see* Baron'ki
Borosjenő *see* Ineu
Borossebes *see* Sebiş
76 L15 **Borotou** NW Ivory Coast
117 W6 **Borova** Kharkivs'ka Oblast', E Ukraine
114 H8 **Borovan** Vratsa, NW Bulgaria
124 I14 **Borovichi** Novgorodskaya Oblast', W Russian Federation
Borovlje *see* Ferlach
112 J9 **Borovo** Vukovar-Srijem, NE Croatia
145 Q7 **Borovoye** *Kaz.* Būrabay. Akmola, N Kazakhstan
126 K4 **Borovsk** Kaluzhskaya Oblast', W Russian Federation
145 N7 **Borovskoy** Kostanay, N Kazakhstan
Borovukha *see* Baravukha
95 L23 **Borrby** Skåne, S Sweden
181 R3 **Borroloola** Northern Territory, N Australia
116 F9 **Borş** Bihor, NW Romania
116 I9 **Borşa** *Hung.* Borsa. Maramureş, N Romania
116 J10 **Borsec** *Ger.* Bad Borseck, *Hung.* Borszék. Harghita, C Romania
92 K8 **Børselv** *Lapp.* Bissojohka. Finnmark, N Norway
113 L23 **Borsh** *var.* Borshi. Vlorë, S Albania
Borshchev *see* Borshchiv
116 K7 **Borshchiv** *Pol.* Borszczów, *Rus.* Borshchev. Ternopil's'ka Oblast', W Ukraine
Borshi *see* Borsh
111 L20 **Borsod-Abaúj-Zemplén** *off.* Borsod-Abaúj-Zemplén Megye. ◈ *county* NE Hungary
99 E15 **Borssele** Zeeland, SW Netherlands
Borszczów *see* Borshchiv
Borszék *see* Borsec
Bortala *see* Bole
103 O12 **Bort-les-Orgues** Corrèze, C France
Bor u České Lípy *see* Nový Bor
162 E8 **Bor-Udzüür** Hovd, W Mongolia
143 N9 **Borūjen** Chahār Maḩall va Bakhtīārī, C Iran
142 L7 **Borūjerd** *var.* Burujird. Lorestān, W Iran
116 H6 **Boryslav** *Pol.* Borysław, *Rus.* Borislav. L'vivs'ka Oblast', NW Ukraine
Borysław *see* Boryslav
117 P4 **Boryspil'** *Rus.* Borispol'. Kyyivs'ka Oblast', N Ukraine
117 P4 **Boryspil'** *Rus.* Borispol'. ✕ (Kyyiv) Kyyivs'ka Oblast', N Ukraine
Borzhomi *see* Borjomi
117 R3 **Borzna** Chernihivs'ka Oblast', NE Ukraine
123 O14 **Borzya** Chitinskaya Oblast', S Russian Federation
107 B18 **Bosa** Sardegna, Italy, C Mediterranean Sea
112 F10 **Bosanska Dubica** *var.* Kozarska Dubica. Republika Srpska, NW Bosnia and Herzegovina
112 G10 **Bosanska Gradiška** *var.* Gradiška. Republika Srpska, N Bosnia and Herzegovina
112 F10 **Bosanska Kostajnica** *var.* Srpska Kostajnica. Republika Srpska, NW Bosnia and Herzegovina
112 E11 **Bosanska Krupa** *var.* Krupa, Krupa na Uni. Federacija Bosna I Hercegovina, NW Bosnia and Herzegovina
112 H10 **Bosanski Brod** *var.* Srpski Brod. Republika Srpska, N Bosnia and Herzegovina
112 E10 **Bosanski Novi** *var.* Novi Grad. Republika Srpska, NW Bosnia and Herzegovina
112 E11 **Bosanski Petrovac** *var.* Petrovac. Federacija Bosna I Hercegovina, NW Bosnia and Herzegovina
112 N12 **Bosanski Petrovac** Serbia, E Serbia and Montenegro (Yugo.)
112 I10 **Bosanski Šamac** *var.* Šamac. Republika Srpska, N Bosnia and Herzegovina
112 E12 **Bosansko Grahovo** *var.* Grahovo, Hrvatsko Grahovo. Federacija Bosna I Hercegovina, W Bosnia and Herzegovina
Bosaso *see* Boosaaso
186 B7 **Bosavi, Mount** ⛰ W PNG
160 J14 **Bose** Guangxi Zhuangzu Zizhiqu, S China
161 Q5 **Boshan** Shandong, E China
113 P16 **Bosilegrad** *prev.* Bosiljgrad. Serbia, SE Serbia and Montenegro (Yugo.)
Bosiljgrad *see* Bosilegrad
Bösing *see* Pezinok
98 H12 **Boskoop** Zuid-Holland, C Netherlands
111 G18 **Boskovice** *Ger.* Boskowitz. Jihomoravský Kraj, SE Czech Republic
Boskowitz *see* Boskovice
112 I10 **Bosna** ≈ N Bosnia and Herzegovina
113 G14 **Bosna I Hercegovina, Federacija** ◈ *republic* Bosnia and Herzegovina
112 H12 **Bosnia and Herzegovina** *off.* Republic of Bosnia and Herzegovina. ◆ *republic* SE Europe
79 J16 **Bosobolo** Equateur, NW Dem. Rep. Congo
165 O14 **Bōsō-hantō** *peninsula* Honshū, S Japan
Bosora *see* Buşrá ash Shām
Bosphorus/Bosporus *see* İstanbul Boğazı
Bosporus Cimmerius *see* Kerch Strait
Bosporus Thracius *see* İstanbul Boğazı
Bosra *see* Buşrá ash Shām
79 H14 **Bossangoa** Ouham, C Central African Republic
Bossé Bangou *see* Bossey Bangou
79 I15 **Bossembélé** Ombella-Mpoko, C Central African Republic
79 H15 **Bossentélé** Ouham-Pendé, W Central African Republic
77 R12 **Bossey Bangou** *var.* Bossé Bangou. Tillabéri, SW Niger
22 G5 **Bossier City** Louisiana, S USA
83 D20 **Bossiesvlei** Hardap, S Namibia
77 Y11 **Bosso** Diffa, SE Niger
61 F15 **Bossoroca** Rio Grande do Sul, S Brazil
158 J10 **Bostan** Xinjiang Uygur Zizhiqu, W China
142 K3 **Bostānābād** Āžarbāyjān-e Khāvarī, N Iran
158 K6 **Bosten Hu** *var.* Bagrax Hu. ◎ NW China
97 O18 **Boston** *prev.* St.Botolph's Town. E England, UK
19 O11 **Boston** *state capital* Massachusetts, NE USA
146 I9 **Bo'ston** *Rus.* Bustan. Qoraqalpog'iston Respublikasi, W Uzbekistan
10 M17 **Boston Bar** British Columbia, SW Canada
27 T10 **Boston Mountains** ▲ Arkansas, C USA
15 P8 **Bostonnais** ≈ Québec, SE Canada
Bostyn' *see* Bastyn'
112 J10 **Bosut** ≈ E Croatia
154 C11 **Botād** Gujarāt, W India
183 T9 **Botany Bay** *inlet* New South Wales, SE Australia
83 G18 **Boteti** *var.* Botletle. ≈ N Botswana
114 J9 **Botev** ▲ C Bulgaria
114 H9 **Botevgrad** *prev.* Orkhaniye. Sofiya, W Bulgaria
93 J16 **Bothnia, Gulf of** *Fin.* Pohjanlahti, *Swe.* Bottniska Viken. *gulf* N Baltic Sea
183 P17 **Bothwell** Tasmania, SE Australia
104 H5 **Boticas** Vila Real, N Portugal
55 W10 **Boti-Pasi** Sipaliwini, C Surinam
Botletle *see* Boteti
127 P16 **Botlikh** Chechenskaya Respublika, SW Russian Federation
117 N10 **Botna** ≈ E Moldova
116 I9 **Botoşani** *Hung.* Botosány. Botoşani, NE Romania
116 K8 **Botoşani** ◈ *county* NE Romania
Botosány *see* Botoşani
161 P4 **Botou** *prev.* Bozhen. Hebei, E China
99 M20 **Botrange** ▲ E Belgium
107 O21 **Botricello** Calabria, SW Italy
83 I23 **Botshabelo** Free State, C South Africa
93 J15 **Botsmark** Västerbotten, N Sweden
83 G19 **Botswana** *off.* Republic of Botswana. ◆ *republic* S Africa
29 N2 **Bottineau** North Dakota, N USA
Bottniska Viken *see* Bothnia, Gulf of
60 L9 **Botucatu** São Paulo, S Brazil
76 M16 **Bouaflé** C Ivory Coast
77 N16 **Bouaké** *var.* Bwake. C Ivory Coast
79 G14 **Bouar** Nana-Mambéré, W Central African Republic
74 H7 **Bouarfa** NE Morocco
111 B19 **Boubín** ▲ SW Czech Republic
79 I14 **Bouca** Ouham, W Central African Republic
15 T5 **Boucher** ≈ Québec, SE Canada
103 R15 **Bouches-du-Rhône** ◈ *department* SE France
74 C9 **Bou Craa** *var.* Bu Craa. NW Western Sahara
77 O9 **Boû Djébéha** *oasis* C Mali
108 C8 **Boudry** Neuchâtel, W Switzerland
180 L2 **Bougainville, Cape** *headland* Western Australia
65 E24 **Bougainville, Cape** *headland* East Falkland, Falkland Islands
Bougainville, Détroit de *see* Bougainville Strait, Vanuatu
186 J7 **Bougainville Island** *island* NE PNG
186 I8 **Bougainville Strait** *strait* N Solomon Islands
187 Q13 **Bougainville Strait** *Fr.* Détroit de Bougainville. *strait* C Vanuatu
120 I9 **Bougaroun, Cap** *headland* NE Algeria
77 R8 **Boughessa** Kidal, NE Mali
Bougie *see* Béjaïa
76 L13 **Bougouni** Sikasso, SW Mali
99 J24 **Bouillon** Luxembourg, SE Belgium
74 K5 **Bouira** *var.* Bouïra. N Algeria
74 D8 **Bou-Izakarn** SW Morocco
74 B9 **Boujdour** *var.* Bojador. W Western Sahara
74 G5 **Boukhalef** ✕ (Tanger) N Morocco
Boukombé *see* Boukoumbé
77 R14 **Boukoumbé** *var.* Boukombé. C Benin
76 G6 **Boû Lanouâr** Dakhlet Nouâdhibou, W Mauritania
37 T4 **Boulder** Colorado, C USA
33 R10 **Boulder** Montana, NW USA
35 X12 **Boulder City** Nevada, W USA
181 T7 **Boulia** Queensland, C Australia
15 N10 **Boullé** ≈ Québec, SE Canada
102 J9 **Boulogne** ≈ NW France
Boulogne *see* Boulogne-sur-Mer
102 L16 **Boulogne-sur-Gesse** Haute-Garonne, S France
103 N1 **Boulogne-sur-Mer** *var.* Boulogne; *anc.* Bononia, Gesoriacum, Gessoriacum. Pas-de-Calais, N France
77 Q12 **Boulsa** C Burkina
77 W11 **Boultoum** Zinder, C Niger
187 Y14 **Bouma** Taveuni, N Fiji
79 G16 **Boumba** ≈ SE Cameroon
76 J9 **Boûmdeïd** *var.* Boumdeït. Assaba, S Mauritania
Boumdeït *see* Boûmdeïd
115 C17 **Boumistós** ▲ W Greece
77 O15 **Bouna** NE Ivory Coast
19 P4 **Boundary Bald Mountain** ▲ Maine, NE USA
35 S8 **Boundary Peak** ▲ Nevada, W USA
76 M14 **Boundiali** N Ivory Coast
79 G19 **Boundji** Cuvette, C Congo
77 O13 **Boundoukui** *var.* Bondoukui, Bondoukuy. W Burkina
36 L2 **Bountiful** Utah, W USA
Bounty Basin *see* Bounty Trough
191 Q16 **Bounty Bay** *bay* Pitcairn Island, C Pacific Ocean
192 L12 **Bounty Islands** *island group* S NZ
175 Q13 **Bounty Trough** *var.* Bounty Basin. *undersea feature* S Pacific Ocean
187 P17 **Bourail** Province Sud, C New Caledonia
27 V5 **Bourbeuse River** ≈ Missouri, C USA
103 Q9 **Bourbon-Lancy** Saône-et-Loire, C France
31 N11 **Bourbonnais** Illinois, N USA
103 O10 **Bourbonnais** *cultural region* C France
103 S7 **Bourbonne-les-Bains** Haute-Marne, N France
Bourbon Vendée *see* la Roche-sur-Yon
74 M8 **Bourdj Messaouda** E Algeria
77 Q10 **Bourem** Gao, C Mali
Bourg *see* Bourg-en-Bresse
103 N11 **Bourganeuf** Creuse, C France
Bourgas *see* Burgas
Bourge-en-Bresse *see* Bourg-en-Bresse
103 S10 **Bourg-en-Bresse** *var.* Bourg, Bourge-en-Bresse. Ain, E France
103 O8 **Bourges** *anc.* Avaricum. Cher, C France
103 T11 **Bourget, Lac du** ◎ E France
103 P8 **Bourgogne** *Eng.* Burgundy. ◈ *region* E France
103 S11 **Bourgoin-Jallieu** Isère, E France
103 R14 **Bourg-St-Andéol** Ardèche, E France
103 U11 **Bourg-St-Maurice** Savoie, E France
108 C11 **Bourg St.Pierre** Valais, SW Switzerland
76 H8 **Boû Rjeïmât** *well* W Mauritania
183 P5 **Bourke** New South Wales, SE Australia
97 M24 **Bournemouth** S England, UK
99 M23 **Bourscheid** Diekirch, NE Luxembourg
74 K6 **Bou Saâda** *var.* Bou Saada. N Algeria
36 I13 **Bouse Wash** ≈ Arizona, SW USA
103 N10 **Boussac** Creuse, C France
102 M16 **Boussens** Haute-Garonne, S France
78 H12 **Bousso** *prev.* Fort-Bretonnet. Chari-Baguirmi, S Chad
76 H9 **Boutilimit** Trarza, SW Mauritania
65 D21 **Bouvet Island** ◇ *Norwegian dependency* S Atlantic Ocean
77 U11 **Bouza** Tahoua, SW Niger
109 R10 **Bovec** *Ger.* Flitsch, *It.* Plezzo. NW Slovenia
98 J8 **Bovenkarspel** Noord-Holland, NW Netherlands
29 V5 **Bovey** Minnesota, N USA
32 M9 **Bovill** Idaho, NW USA
24 L4 **Bovina** Texas, SW USA
107 M17 **Bovino** Puglia, SE Italy
61 C17 **Bovril** Entre Ríos, E Argentina
28 L2 **Bowbells** North Dakota, N USA
11 Q16 **Bow City** Alberta, SW Canada
29 O8 **Bowdle** South Dakota, N USA
181 X6 **Bowen** Queensland, NE Australia
192 L2 **Bowers Ridge** *undersea feature* S Bering Sea
25 S5 **Bowie** Texas, SW USA
11 R17 **Bow Island** Alberta, SW Canada
Bowkān *see* Būkān
20 J7 **Bowling Green** Kentucky, S USA
27 V3 **Bowling Green** Missouri, C USA
31 R11 **Bowling Green** Ohio, N USA
21 W5 **Bowling Green** Virginia, NE USA
28 J6 **Bowman** North Dakota, N USA
9 Q7 **Bowman Bay** *bay* NW Atlantic Ocean
194 I5 **Bowman Coast** *physical region* Antarctica
28 J7 **Bowman-Haley Lake** ⊠ North Dakota, N USA
195 Z11 **Bowman Island** *island* Antarctica
Bowo *see* Bomi
183 S9 **Bowral** New South Wales, SE Australia
186 E8 **Bowutu Mountains** ▲ C PNG
83 I16 **Bowwood** Southern, S Zambia
28 I12 **Box Butte Reservoir** ⊠ Nebraska, C USA
28 J10 **Box Elder** South Dakota, N USA
95 M18 **Boxholm** Östergötland, S Sweden
Bo Xian/Boxian *see* Bozhou
161 Q4 **Boxing** Shandong, E China
99 L14 **Boxmeer** Noord-Brabant, SE Netherlands
99 J14 **Boxtel** Noord-Brabant, S Netherlands
136 J10 **Boyabat** Sinop, N Turkey
54 F9 **Boyacá** *off.* Departamento de Boyacá. ◈ *province* C Colombia
117 O4 **Boyarka** Kyyivs'ka Oblast', N Ukraine
22 H7 **Boyce** Louisiana, S USA
33 U11 **Boyd** Montana, NW USA
25 S6 **Boyd** Texas, SW USA
21 V8 **Boydton** Virginia, NE USA
Boyer Ahmadī va Kohkīlūyeh *see* Kohgīlūyeh va Būyer Aḩmad
29 T13 **Boyer River** ≈ Iowa, C USA
21 W8 **Boykins** Virginia, NE USA
11 Q13 **Boyle** Alberta, SW Canada
97 D16 **Boyle** *Ir.* Mainistirna Búille. C Ireland
97 F17 **Boyne** *Ir.* An Bhóinn. ≈ E Ireland
31 Q5 **Boyne City** Michigan, N USA
23 Z14 **Boynton Beach** Florida, SE USA
147 O13 **Boysun** *Rus.* Baysun. Surkhondaryo Wiloyati, S Uzbekistan
Bozau *see* Întorsura Buzăului
136 B12 **Bozcaada** *island* Çanakkale, NW Turkey
136 C14 **Boz Dağları** ▲ W Turkey
33 S11 **Bozeman** Montana, NW USA
Bozen *see* Bolzano
79 J16 **Bozene** Equateur, NW Dem. Rep. Congo
161 P7 **Bozhou** *var.* Boxian, Bo Xian. Anhui, E China
136 H16 **Bozkır** Konya, S Turkey
136 K13 **Bozok Yaylası** *plateau* C Turkey
79 H14 **Bozoum** Ouham-Pendé, W Central African Republic
137 N16 **Bozova** Sanlıurfa, S Turkey
Bozrah *see* Buşrá ash Shām
136 E12 **Bozüyük** Bilecik, NW Turkey
106 B9 **Bra** Piemonte, NW Italy
194 G4 **Brabant Island** *island* Antarctica
99 I20 **Brabant Wallon** ◈ *province* C Belgium
113 F15 **Brač** *var.* Brach, *It.* Brazza; *anc.* Brattia. *island* S Croatia
Bracara Augusta *see* Braga
107 H15 **Bracciano** Lazio, C Italy
107 H14 **Bracciano, Lago di** ◎ C Italy
14 H13 **Bracebridge** Ontario, S Canada
Brach *see* Brač
93 G17 **Bräcke** Jämtland, C Sweden
25 P12 **Brackettville** Texas, SW USA
97 N22 **Bracknell** S England, UK
61 K14 **Braço do Norte** Santa Catarina, S Brazil
116 G11 **Brad** *Hung.* Brád. Hunedoara, SW Romania
107 N18 **Bradano** ≈ S Italy
23 V13 **Bradenton** Florida, SE USA
14 H14 **Bradford** Ontario, S Canada
97 L17 **Bradford** N England, UK
27 W10 **Bradford** Arkansas, C USA
18 D12 **Bradford** Pennsylvania, NE USA
27 T15 **Bradley** Arkansas, C USA
25 P7 **Bradshaw** Texas, SW USA
25 Q9 **Brady** Texas, SW USA
25 Q9 **Brady Creek** ≈ Texas, SW USA
96 J10 **Braemar** NE Scotland, UK
116 K8 **Brăeşti** Botoşani, NW Romania
104 G5 **Braga** *anc.* Bracara Augusta. Braga, NW Portugal
104 G5 **Braga** ◈ *district* N Portugal
116 J15 **Bragadiru** Teleorman, S Romania
61 C20 **Bragado** Buenos Aires, E Argentina
104 J5 **Bragança** *Eng.* Braganza; *anc.* Julio Briga. Bragança, NE Portugal
104 I5 **Bragança** ◈ *district* N Portugal
60 N9 **Bragança Paulista** São Paulo, S Brazil
Braganza *see* Bragança
Bragin *see* Brahin
29 V7 **Braham** Minnesota, N USA
Brahe *see* Brda
Brahestad *see* Raahe
119 O20 **Brahin** *Rus.* Bragin. Homyel'skaya Voblasts', SE Belarus
153 U15 **Brahmanbaria** Chittagong, E Bangladesh
154 O12 **Brāhmani** ≈ E India
154 N13 **Brahmapur** Orissa, E India
150 O12 **Brahmaputra** *var.* Padma, Tsangpo, *Ben.* Jamuna, *Chin.* Yarlung Zangbo Jiang, *Ind.* Bramaputra, Dihang, Siang. ≈ S Asia
97 H19 **Braich y Pwll** *headland* NW Wales, UK
183 R10 **Braidwood** New South Wales, SE Australia
30 M11 **Braidwood** Illinois, N USA
116 M13 **Brăila** Brăila, E Romania
116 L13 **Brăila** ◈ *county* SE Romania
99 G19 **Braine-l'Alleud** Brabant Wallon, C Belgium
99 F19 **Braine-le-Comte** Hainaut, SW Belgium
29 U6 **Brainerd** Minnesota, N USA
99 J19 **Braives** Liège, E Belgium
83 H23 **Brak** ≈ C South Africa
Brak *see* Birāk
99 E18 **Brakel** Oost-Vlaanderen, SW Belgium
98 J13 **Brakel** Gelderland, C Netherlands
76 H9 **Brakna** ◈ *region* S Mauritania
95 J17 **Brålanda** Västra Götaland, S Sweden
Bramaputra *see* Brahmaputra
95 F23 **Bramming** Ribe, W Denmark
14 G15 **Brampton** Ontario, S Canada
100 F12 **Bramsche** Niedersachsen, NW Germany
116 J12 **Bran** *Ger.* Törzburg, *Hung.* Törcsvár. Braşov, S Romania
29 W8 **Branch** Minnesota, N USA
21 R14 **Branchville** South Carolina, SE USA
58 F11 **Branco, Rio** ≈ N Brazil
108 J8 **Brand** Vorarlberg, W Austria
83 B18 **Brandberg** ▲ NW Namibia
95 H14 **Brandbu** Oppland, S Norway
95 F22 **Brande** Ringkøbing, W Denmark
Brandebourg *see* Brandenburg
100 M12 **Brandenburg** *var.* Brandenburg an der Havel. Brandenburg, NE Germany
20 K5 **Brandenburg** Kentucky, S USA
100 N12 **Brandenburg** *off.* Freie und Hansestadt Hamburg, *Fr.* Brandebourg. ◈ *state* NE Germany
Brandenburg an der Havel *see* Brandenburg
83 I23 **Brandfort** Free State, C South Africa
11 W16 **Brandon** Manitoba, S Canada
23 V12 **Brandon** Florida, SE USA
22 L6 **Brandon** Mississippi, S USA
97 A20 **Brandon Mountain** *Ir.* Cnoc Bréanainn. ▲ SW Ireland
Brandsen *see* Coronel Brandsen
95 I14 **Brandval** Hedmark, S Norway
83 F24 **Brandvlei** Northern Cape, W South Africa
23 U9 **Branford** Florida, SE USA
110 K7 **Braniewo** *Ger.* Braunsberg. Warmińsko-Mazurskie, NE Poland
194 H3 **Bransfield Strait** *strait* Antarctica
37 U8 **Branson** Colorado, C USA
27 T8 **Branson** Missouri, C USA
14 G16 **Brantford** Ontario, S Canada
102 L12 **Brantôme** Dordogne, SW France
182 L12 **Branxholme** Victoria, SE Australia
Brasil *see* Brazil
59 C16 **Brasiléia** Acre, W Brazil
59 K18 **Brasília** ● (Brazil) Distrito Federal, C Brazil
Braslav *see* Braslaw
118 J12 **Braslaw** *Pol.* Brasław, *Rus.* Braslav. Vitsyebskaya Voblasts', N Belarus
116 J12 **Braşov** *Ger.* Kronstadt, *Hung.* Brassó; *prev.* Oraşul Stalin. Braşov, C Romania
116 I12 **Braşov** ◈ *county* C Romania
77 U18 **Brass** Bayelsa, S Nigeria
99 H16 **Brasschaat** *var.* Brasschaet. Antwerpen, N Belgium
Brasschaet *see* Brasschaat
169 V8 **Brassey, Banjaran** *var.* Brassey Range. ▲ East Malaysia
Brassey Range *see* Brassey, Banjaran
Brassó *see* Braşov
23 T1 **Brasstown Bald** ▲ Georgia, SE USA
113 K22 **Brataj** Vlorë, SW Albania
114 J10 **Bratan** *var.* Morozov. ▲ C Bulgaria
111 F21 **Bratislava** *Ger.* Pressburg, *Hung.* Pozsony. ● (Slovakia) Bratislavský Kraj, W Slovakia
111 H21 **Bratislavský Kraj** ◈ *region* W Slovakia
114 H10 **Bratiya** ▲ C Bulgaria
122 M12 **Bratsk** Irkutskaya Oblast', C Russian Federation
117 Q8 **Brats'ke** Mykolayivs'ka Oblast', S Ukraine
122 M13 **Bratskoye Vodokhranilishche** *Eng.* Bratsk Reservoir. ⊠ S Russian Federation
Bratsk Reservoir *see* Bratskoye Vodokhranilishche
Brattia *see* Brač
94 D9 **Brattvåg** Møre og Romsdal, S Norway
112 K12 **Bratunac** Republika Srpska, E Bosnia and Herzegovina
114 J10 **Bratya Daskalovi** *prev.* Grozdovo. Stara Zagora, C Bulgaria
109 U2 **Braunau** ≈ N Austria
Braunau *see* Braunau am Inn
109 Q4 **Braunau am Inn** *var.* Braunau. Oberösterreich, N Austria
Braunsberg *see* Braniewo
100 J13 **Braunschweig** *Eng./Fr.* Brunswick. Niedersachsen, N Germany
Brava *see* Baraawe
105 Y6 **Brava, Costa** *coastal region* NE Spain
43 V16 **Brava, Punta** *headland* E Panama
95 N17 **Bråviken** *inlet* S Sweden
56 B10 **Bravo, Cerro** ▲ N Peru
Bravo del Norte, Río/Bravo, Río *see* Grande, Rio
35 X17 **Brawley** California, W USA
97 G18 **Bray** *Ir.* Bré. E Ireland
59 G16 **Brazil** *off.* Federative Republic of Brazil, *Port.* República Federativa do Brasil, *Sp.* Brasil; *prev.* United States of Brazil. ◆ *federal republic* South America
65 K15 **Brazil Basin** *var.* Brazilian Basin, Brazil'skaya Kotlovina. *undersea feature* W Atlantic Ocean
Brazilian Basin *see* Brazil Basin
Brazilian Highlands *see* Central, Planalto
Brazil'skaya Kotlovina *see* Brazil Basin
25 U10 **Brazos River** ≈ Texas, SW USA
Brazza *see* Brač
79 G21 **Brazzaville** ● (Congo) Capital District, S Congo
79 G21 **Brazzaville** ✕ Le Pool, S Congo
112 J11 **Brčko** Republika Srpska, NE Bosnia and Herzegovina
110 H8 **Brda** *Ger.* Brahe. ≈ N Poland
Bré *see* Bray
185 A23 **Breaksea Sound** *sound* South Island, NZ
184 L4 **Bream Bay** *bay* North Island, NZ
184 L4 **Bream Head** *headland* North Island, NZ
Bréanainn, Cnoc *see* Brandon Mountain
45 S6 **Brea, Punta** *headland* W Puerto Rico
22 I9 **Breaux Bridge** Louisiana, S USA
116 J13 **Breaza** Prahova, SE Romania
169 P16 **Brebes** Jawa, C Indonesia
96 K10 **Brechin** E Scotland, UK
99 H15 **Brecht** Antwerpen, N Belgium
37 S4 **Breckenridge** Colorado, C USA
29 R6 **Breckenridge** Minnesota, N USA
25 R6 **Breckenridge** Texas, SW USA
97 J21 **Brecknock** *cultural region* SE Wales, UK
63 G25 **Brecknock, Península** *headland* S Chile
111 G19 **Břeclav** *Ger.* Lundenburg. Jihomoravský Kraj, SE Czech Republic
97 J21 **Brecon** E Wales, UK
97 J21 **Brecon Beacons** ▲ S Wales, UK
99 I14 **Breda** Noord-Brabant, S Netherlands
95 K20 **Bredaryd** Jönköping, S Sweden
83 F26 **Bredasdorp** Western Cape, SW South Africa
93 H16 **Bredbyn** Västernorrland, N Sweden
122 F11 **Bredy** Chelyabinskaya Oblast', C Russian Federation
99 K17 **Bree** Limburg, NE Belgium
98 I7 **Breezand** Noord-Holland, NW Netherlands
113 P18 **Bregalnica** ≈ E FYR Macedonia
108 I6 **Bregenz** *anc.* Brigantium. Vorarlberg, W Austria
108 J7 **Bregenzer Wald** ▲ W Austria
114 F6 **Bregovo** Vidin, NW Bulgaria
102 H5 **Bréhat, Île de** *island* NW France
92 H2 **Breidhafjördhur** *bay* W Iceland
92 L3 **Breidhdalsvík** Austurland, E Iceland
108 H9 **Breil** *Ger.* Brigels. Graubünden, S Switzerland
92 J8 **Breivikbotn** Finnmark, N Norway
94 I9 **Brekken** Sør-Trøndelag, S Norway
94 G7 **Brekstad** Sør-Trøndelag, S Norway
94 B10 **Bremangerlandet** *island* S Norway
Brême *see* Bremen
100 H11 **Bremen** *Fr.* Brême. Bremen, NW Germany
23 R3 **Bremen** Georgia, SE USA
31 O11 **Bremen** Indiana, N USA
100 H10 **Bremen** *off.* Freie Hansestadt Bremen, *Fr.* Brême. ◈ *state* N Germany
100 G9 **Bremerhaven** Bremen, NW Germany
Bremersdorp *see* Manzini
32 G8 **Bremerton** Washington, NW USA
100 H10 **Bremervörde** Niedersachsen, NW Germany
25 U9 **Bremond** Texas, SW USA

25 U10 **Brenham** Texas, SW USA
108 M8 **Brenner** Tirol, W Austria
Brenner, Col du/Brennero, Passo del see Brenner Pass
108 M8 **Brenner Pass** var. Brenner Sattel, Fr. Col du Brenner, Ger. Brennerpass, It. Passo del Brennero. pass Austria/Italy
Brenner Sattel see Brenner Pass
108 G10 **Brenno** ≈ SW Switzerland
106 F7 **Breno** Lombardia, N Italy
23 O5 **Brent** Alabama, S USA
106 H7 **Brenta** ≈ NE Italy
97 P21 **Brentwood** E England, UK
18 L14 **Brentwood** Long Island, New York, NE USA
106 F7 **Brescia** anc. Brixia. Lombardia, N Italy
99 D15 **Breskens** Zeeland, SW Netherlands
Breslau see Dolnośląskie
106 H5 **Bressanone** Ger. Brixen. Trentino-Alto Adige, N Italy
96 M2 **Bressay** island NE Scotland, UK
102 K9 **Bressuire** Deux-Sèvres, W France
119 F20 **Brest** Pol. Brześć nad Bugiem, Rus. Brest-Litovsk; prev. Brześć Litewski. Brestskaya Voblasts', SW Belarus
102 F5 **Brest** Finistère, NW France
Brest-Litovsk see Brest
112 A10 **Brestova** Istra, NW Croatia
Brestskaya Oblast' see Brestskaya Voblasts'
119 G19 **Brestskaya Voblasts'** prev. Rus. Brestskaya Oblast'. ◈ province SW Belarus
102 G6 **Bretagne** Eng. Brittany; Lat. Britannia Minor. ◈ region NW France
116 G12 **Bretea-Română** Hung. Oláhbrettye; prev. Bretea-Romînă. Hunedoara, W Romania
Bretea-Romînă see Bretea-Română
103 O3 **Breteuil** Oise, N France
102 I10 **Breton, Pertuis** inlet W France
22 L10 **Breton Sound** sound Louisiana, S USA
184 K2 **Brett, Cape** headland North Island, NZ
101 G21 **Bretten** Baden-Württemberg, SW Germany
99 K15 **Breugel** Noord-Brabant, S Netherlands
106 B6 **Breuil-Cervinia** It. Cervinia. Valle d'Aosta, NW Italy
98 I11 **Breukelen** Utrecht, C Netherlands
21 P10 **Brevard** North Carolina, SE USA
38 L9 **Brevig Mission** Alaska, USA
95 G16 **Brevik** Telemark, S Norway
183 P5 **Brewarrina** New South Wales, SE Australia
19 R6 **Brewer** Maine, NE USA
29 T11 **Brewster** Minnesota, N USA
29 N14 **Brewster** Nebraska, C USA
31 U12 **Brewster** Ohio, N USA
183 O8 **Brewster, Lake** ◎ New South Wales, SE Australia
23 P7 **Brewton** Alabama, S USA
Brezhnev see Naberezhnyye Chelny
109 W12 **Brežice** Ger. Rann. E Slovenia
114 G9 **Breznik** Pernik, W Bulgaria
111 K19 **Brezno** Ger. Bries, Briesen, Hung. Breznóbánya; prev. Brezno nad Hronom. Banskobystrický Kraj, C Slovakia
Breznóbánya/Brezno nad Hronom see Brezno
116 I12 **Brezoi** Vâlcea, SW Romania
114 J10 **Brezovo** prev. Abrashlare. Plovdiv, C Bulgaria
79 K14 **Bria** Haute-Kotto, C Central African Republic
103 U13 **Briançon** anc. Brigantio. Hautes-Alpes, SE France
36 K7 **Brian Head** ▲ Utah, W USA
103 O7 **Briare** Loiret, C France
183 V2 **Bribie Island** island Queensland, E Australia
43 O14 **Bribrí** Limón, E Costa Rica
116 L8 **Briceni** var. Brinceni, Rus. Brichany. N Moldova
Bricgstow see Bristol
Brichany see Briceni
99 M24 **Bridel** Luxembourg, C Luxembourg
97 J22 **Bridgend** S Wales, UK
14 I14 **Bridgenorth** Ontario, SE Canada
23 Q1 **Bridgeport** Alabama, S USA
35 R8 **Bridgeport** California, W USA
18 L13 **Bridgeport** Connecticut, NE USA
31 N15 **Bridgeport** Illinois, N USA
28 J14 **Bridgeport** Nebraska, C USA
25 S6 **Bridgeport** Texas, SW USA
21 S3 **Bridgeport** West Virginia, NE USA
25 S5 **Bridgeport, Lake** ▣ Texas, SW USA
33 U11 **Bridger** Montana, NW USA
18 I17 **Bridgeton** New Jersey, NE USA
180 J14 **Bridgetown** Western Australia
45 Y14 **Bridgetown** ● (Barbados) SW Barbados
183 P17 **Bridgewater** Tasmania, SE Australia
13 P16 **Bridgewater** Nova Scotia, SE Canada
19 P12 **Bridgewater** Massachusetts, NE USA
29 Q11 **Bridgewater** South Dakota, N USA
21 U5 **Bridgewater** Virginia, NE USA
19 P8 **Bridgton** Maine, NE USA
97 K23 **Bridgwater** SW England, UK
97 K22 **Bridgwater Bay** bay SW England, UK
97 O16 **Bridlington** E England, UK
97 O16 **Bridlington Bay** bay E England, UK
183 P15 **Bridport** Tasmania, SE Australia
97 K24 **Bridport** S England, UK
103 O5 **Brie** cultural region N France
Brieg see Brzeg
Briel see Brielle
98 G12 **Brielle** var. Briel, Bril, Eng. The Brill. Zuid-Holland, SW Netherlands
108 E9 **Brienz** Bern, C Switzerland
108 E9 **Brienzer See** ◎ SW Switzerland
Bries/Briesen see Brezno
Brietzig see Brzesko
103 S4 **Briey** Meurthe-et-Moselle, NE France
108 E10 **Brig** Fr. Brigue, It. Briga. Valais, SW Switzerland
Briga see Brig
101 G24 **Brigach** ≈ S Germany
18 K17 **Brigantine** New Jersey, NE USA
Brigantio see Briançon
Brigantium see Bregenz
Brigels see Breil
25 S9 **Briggs** Texas, SW USA
36 L1 **Brigham City** Utah, W USA
14 J15 **Brighton** Ontario, SE Canada
97 O23 **Brighton** SE England, UK
37 T4 **Brighton** Colorado, C USA
30 K15 **Brighton** Illinois, N USA
103 T16 **Brignoles** Var, SE France
Brigue see Brig
105 O7 **Brihuega** Castilla-La Mancha, C Spain
112 A10 **Brijuni** It. Brioni. island group NW Croatia
76 G12 **Brikama** W Gambia
Bril see Brielle
Brill, The see Brielle
101 G15 **Brilon** Nordrhein-Westfalen, W Germany
Brinceni see Briceni
107 Q18 **Brindisi** anc. Brundisium, Brundusium. Puglia, SE Italy
27 W11 **Brinkley** Arkansas, C USA
Brioni see Brijuni
103 P12 **Brioude** anc. Brivas. Haute-Loire, C France
Briovera see St-Lô
183 U2 **Brisbane** state capital Queensland, E Australia
183 V2 **Brisbane** ✕ Queensland, E Australia
25 P2 **Briscoe** Texas, SW USA
106 H10 **Brisighella** Emilia-Romagna, C Italy
108 G11 **Brissago** Ticino, S Switzerland
97 K22 **Bristol** anc. Bricgstow. SW England, UK
18 M12 **Bristol** Connecticut, NE USA
23 R9 **Bristol** Florida, SE USA
19 N9 **Bristol** New Hampshire, NE USA
29 Q8 **Bristol** South Dakota, N USA
21 P8 **Bristol** Tennessee, S USA
18 M8 **Bristol** Vermont, NE USA
39 N14 **Bristol Bay** bay Alaska, USA
97 I22 **Bristol Channel** inlet England/Wales, UK
35 W14 **Bristol Lake** ◎ California, W USA
27 P10 **Bristow** Oklahoma, C USA
Britannia Minor see Bretagne
10 L12 **British Columbia** Fr. Colombie-Britannique. ◈ province SW Canada
British Guiana see Guyana
British Honduras see Belize
173 Q7 **British Indian Ocean Territory** ◇ UK dependent territory C Indian Ocean
10 I1 **British Mountains** ▲▲ Yukon Territory, NW Canada
British North Borneo see Sabah
British Solomon Islands Protectorate see Solomon Islands
45 S8 **British Virgin Islands** var. Virgin Islands. ◇ UK dependent territory E West Indies
83 J21 **Brits** North-West, N South Africa
83 H24 **Britstown** Northern Cape, W South Africa
14 F12 **Britt** Ontario, S Canada
29 V12 **Britt** Iowa, C USA
Brittany see Bretagne
29 Q7 **Britton** South Dakota, N USA
Briva Curretia see Brive-la-Gaillarde
Briva Isarae see Pontoise
Brivas see Brioude
Brive see Brive-la-Gaillarde
102 M12 **Brive-la-Gaillarde** prev. Brive, anc. Briva Curretia. Corrèze, C France
105 O4 **Briviesca** Castilla-León, N Spain
Brixen see Bressanone
Brixia see Brescia
145 S15 **Brlik** prev. Novotroickoje, Novotroitskoye. Zhambyl, SE Kazakhstan
Brněnský Kraj see Jihomoravský Kraj
111 G18 **Brno** Ger. Brünn. Jihomoravský Kraj, SE Czech Republic
96 G7 **Broad Bay** bay NW Scotland, UK
25 X8 **Broaddus** Texas, SW USA
183 O12 **Broadford** Victoria, SE Australia
96 G9 **Broadford** N Scotland, UK
96 J13 **Broad Law** ▲ S Scotland, UK
23 U3 **Broad River** ≈ Georgia, SE USA
21 N8 **Broad River** ≈ North Carolina/South Carolina, SE USA
181 Y8 **Broadsound Range** ▲▲ Queensland, E Australia
33 X11 **Broadus** Montana, NW USA
21 U4 **Broadway** Virginia, NE USA
118 E9 **Brocēni** Saldus, SW Latvia
11 U11 **Brochet** Manitoba, C Canada
11 U10 **Brochet, Lac** ◎ Manitoba, C Canada
15 S5 **Brochet, Lac au** ◎ Québec, SE Canada
101 K14 **Brocken** ▲ C Germany
19 O12 **Brockton** Massachusetts, NE USA
14 L14 **Brockville** Ontario, SE Canada
18 D13 **Brockway** Pennsylvania, NE USA
Brod/Bród see Slavonski Brod
9 N5 **Brodeur Peninsula** peninsula Baffin Island, Nunavut, NE Canada
96 H13 **Brodick** W Scotland, UK
Brod na Savi see Slavonski Brod
110 K9 **Brodnica** Ger. Buddenbrock. Kujawski-pomorskie, C Poland
112 G10 **Brod-Posavina** off. Brodsko-Posavska Županija. ◈ province NE Croatia
116 J5 **Brody** L'vivs'ka Oblast', NW Ukraine
95 G22 **Brædstrup** Vejle, C Denmark
98 I10 **Broek-in-Waterland** Noord-Holland, C Netherlands
32 L13 **Brogan** Oregon, NW USA
110 N10 **Brok** Mazowieckie, C Poland
27 P9 **Broken Arrow** Oklahoma, C USA
183 T9 **Broken Bay** bay New South Wales, SE Australia
29 N15 **Broken Bow** Nebraska, C USA
27 R13 **Broken Bow** Oklahoma, C USA
27 R12 **Broken Bow Lake** ▣ Oklahoma, C USA
182 L6 **Broken Hill** New South Wales, SE Australia
173 S10 **Broken Ridge** undersea feature S Indian Ocean
186 C6 **Broken Water Bay** bay W Bismarck Sea
55 W10 **Brokopondo** Brokopondo, NE Surinam
55 W10 **Brokopondo** ◈ district C Surinam
Bromberg see Bydgoszcz
95 L22 **Bromölla** Skåne, S Sweden
97 L20 **Bromsgrove** W England, UK
95 G20 **Brønderslev** Nordjylland, N Denmark
106 D8 **Broni** Lombardia, N Italy
10 K11 **Bronlund Peak** ▲ British Columbia, W Canada
93 F14 **Brønnøysund** Nordland, C Norway
23 V10 **Bronson** Florida, SE USA
31 Q11 **Bronson** Michigan, N USA
25 X8 **Bronson** Texas, SW USA
107 L24 **Bronte** Sicilia, Italy, C Mediterranean Sea
25 P8 **Bronte** Texas, SW USA
25 Y9 **Brookeland** Texas, SW USA
170 M7 **Brooke's Point** Palawan, W Philippines
27 T3 **Brookfield** Missouri, C USA
22 K7 **Brookhaven** Mississippi, S USA
32 E16 **Brookings** Oregon, NW USA
29 R10 **Brookings** South Dakota, N USA
29 W14 **Brooklyn** Iowa, C USA
29 U8 **Brooklyn Park** Minnesota, N USA
21 U7 **Brookneal** Virginia, NE USA
11 R16 **Brooks** Alberta, SW Canada
25 V11 **Brookshire** Texas, SW USA
38 L8 **Brooks Mountain** ▲ Alaska, USA
38 M11 **Brooks Range** ▲▲ Alaska, USA
31 O12 **Brookston** Indiana, N USA
23 V11 **Brooksville** Florida, SE USA
23 N4 **Brooksville** Mississippi, S USA
180 J13 **Brookton** Western Australia
31 Q14 **Brookville** Indiana, N USA
18 D13 **Brookville** Pennsylvania, NE USA
31 Q14 **Brookville Lake** ▣ Indiana, N USA
180 K5 **Broome** Western Australia
37 S4 **Broomfield** Colorado, C USA
Broos see Orăștie
96 J7 **Brora** N Scotland, UK
96 I7 **Brora** ≈ N Scotland, UK
95 F23 **Brørup** Ribe, W Denmark
95 L23 **Brösarp** Skåne, S Sweden
116 J9 **Broșteni** Suceava, NE Romania
102 M6 **Brou** Eure-et-Loir, C France
Broucsella see Brussel/Bruxelles
Broughton Bay see Tongjosŏn-man
9 R5 **Broughton Island** Nunavut, NE Canada
138 G7 **Broummâna** C Lebanon
22 I9 **Broussard** Louisiana, S USA
98 E13 **Brouwersdam** dam SW Netherlands
98 E13 **Brouwershaven** Zeeland, SW Netherlands
117 P4 **Brovary** Kyyivs'ka Oblast', N Ukraine
95 G20 **Brovst** Nordjylland, N Denmark
31 S8 **Brown City** Michigan, N USA
24 M6 **Brownfield** Texas, SW USA
33 Q7 **Browning** Montana, NW USA
33 R6 **Brown, Mount** ▲ Montana, NW USA
31 O14 **Brownsburg** Indiana, N USA
18 J16 **Browns Mills** New Jersey, NE USA
44 J12 **Browns Town** C Jamaica
31 P15 **Brownstown** Indiana, N USA
29 R8 **Browns Valley** Minnesota, N USA
20 K7 **Brownsville** Kentucky, S USA
20 F9 **Brownsville** Tennessee, S USA
25 T17 **Brownsville** Texas, SW USA
55 W10 **Brownsweg** Brokopondo, C Surinam
29 U9 **Brownton** Minnesota, N USA
19 R5 **Brownville Junction** Maine, NE USA
25 R8 **Brownwood** Texas, SW USA
25 R8 **Brownwood Lake** ▣ Texas, SW USA
104 I9 **Brozas** Extremadura, W Spain
119 M18 **Brozha** Mahilyowskaya Voblasts', E Belarus
103 O2 **Bruay-en-Artois** Pas-de-Calais, N France
103 P2 **Bruay-sur-l'Escaut** Nord, N France
14 F13 **Bruce Peninsula** peninsula Ontario, S Canada
20 H9 **Bruceton** Tennessee, S USA
25 T9 **Bruceville** Texas, SW USA
101 G21 **Bruchsal** Baden-Württemberg, SW Germany
109 Q7 **Bruck** Salzburg, NW Austria
Bruck see Bruck an der Mur
109 Y4 **Bruck an der Leitha** Niederösterreich, NE Austria
109 V7 **Bruck an der Mur** var. Bruck. Steiermark, C Austria
101 M24 **Bruckmühl** Bayern, SE Germany
168 E7 **Brueuh, Pulau** island NW Indonesia
Bruges see Brugge
108 F6 **Brugg** Aargau, NW Switzerland
99 C16 **Brugge** Fr. Bruges. West-Vlaanderen, NW Belgium
109 R9 **Bruggen** Kärnten, S Austria
101 E16 **Brühl** Nordrhein-Westfalen, W Germany
99 F14 **Bruinisse** Zeeland, SW Netherlands
169 R9 **Bruit, Pulau** island East Malaysia
14 K10 **Brûlé, Lac** ◎ Québec, SE Canada
30 M4 **Brule River** ≈ Michigan/Wisconsin, N USA
99 H23 **Brûly** Namur, S Belgium
59 N17 **Brumado** Bahia, E Brazil
98 M11 **Brummen** Gelderland, E Netherlands
94 H13 **Brumunddal** Hedmark, S Norway
23 Q6 **Brundidge** Alabama, S USA
Brundisium/Brundusium see Brindisi
33 N15 **Bruneau River** ≈ Idaho, NW USA
Bruneck see Brunico
169 T8 **Brunei** off. Sultanate of Brunei, Mal. Negara Brunei Darussalam. ◆ monarchy SE Asia
169 T7 **Brunei Bay** var. Teluk Brunei. bay N Brunei
Brunei, Teluk see Brunei Bay
Brunei Town see Bandar Seri Begawan
106 H5 **Brunico** Ger. Bruneck. Trentino-Alto Adige, N Italy
Brünn see Brno
185 G17 **Brunner, Lake** ◎ South Island, NZ
99 M18 **Brunssum** Limburg, SE Netherlands
23 W7 **Brunswick** Georgia, SE USA
19 Q8 **Brunswick** Maine, NE USA
21 V3 **Brunswick** Maryland, NE USA
27 T3 **Brunswick** Missouri, C USA
31 T11 **Brunswick** Ohio, N USA
Brunswick see Braunschweig
63 H24 **Brunswick, Península** headland S Chile
111 H17 **Bruntál** Ger. Freudenthal. Moravskoslezský Kraj, E Czech Republic
195 N3 **Brunt Ice Shelf** ice shelf Antarctica
Brusa see Bursa
37 U3 **Brush** Colorado, C USA
42 M5 **Brus Laguna** Gracias a Dios, E Honduras
60 K13 **Brusque** Santa Catarina, S Brazil
Brussa see Bursa
99 E18 **Brussel** var. Brussels, Fr. Bruxelles, Ger. Brüssel; anc. Broucsella. ● (Belgium) Brussels, C Belgium see also Bruxelles
Brüssel/Brussels see Brussel/Bruxelles
117 O5 **Brusyliv** Zhytomyrs'ka Oblast', N Ukraine
183 Q12 **Bruthen** Victoria, SE Australia
Bruttium see Calabria
Brüx see Most
99 E18 **Bruxelles** var. Brussels, Dut. Brussel, Ger. Brüssel; anc. Broucsella. ● (Belgium) Brussels, C Belgium see also Brussel
54 J7 **Bruzual** Apure, W Venezuela
31 Q11 **Bryan** Ohio, N USA
25 U10 **Bryan** Texas, SW USA
194 J4 **Bryan Coast** physical region Antarctica
122 L11 **Bryanka** Krasnoyarskiy Kray, C Russian Federation
117 Y7 **Bryanka** Luhans'ka Oblast', E Ukraine
182 J8 **Bryan, Mount** ▲ South Australia
126 I6 **Bryansk** Bryanskaya Oblast', W Russian Federation
126 H6 **Bryanskaya Oblast'** ◈ province W Russian Federation
194 J5 **Bryant, Cape** headland Antarctica
27 U8 **Bryant Creek** ≈ Missouri, C USA
36 K8 **Bryce Canyon** canyon Utah, W USA
119 O15 **Bryli** Rus. Bryli. Mahilyowskaya Voblasts', E Belarus
95 C17 **Bryne** Rogaland, S Norway
25 R6 **Bryson** Texas, SW USA
21 N10 **Bryson City** North Carolina, SE USA
14 K11 **Bryson, Lac** ◎ Québec, SE Canada
126 K13 **Bryukhovetskaya** Krasnodarskiy Kray, SW Russian Federation
111 H15 **Brzeg** Ger. Brieg; anc. Civitas Altae Ripae. Opolskie, S Poland
111 G14 **Brzeg Dolny** Ger. Dyhernfurth. Dolnośląskie, SW Poland
Brześć Litewski/Brześć nad Bugiem see Brest
111 L17 **Brzesko** Ger. Brietzig. Małopolskie, S Poland
Brzeżany see Berezhany
110 K12 **Brzeziny** Łódzkie, C Poland
Brzostowica Wielka see Vyalikaya Byerastavitsa
111 O17 **Brzozów** Podkarpackie, SE Poland
Bsharri/Bsherri see Bcharré
187 X14 **Bua** Vanua Levu, N Fiji
95 J20 **Bua** Halland, S Sweden
82 M13 **Bua** ≈ C Malawi
Bua see Čiovo
81 L18 **Bu'aale** It. Buale. Jubbada Dhexe, SW Somalia
189 Q8 **Buada Lagoon** lagoon Nauru, C Pacific Ocean
186 M8 **Buala** Santa Isabel, E Solomon Islands
Buale see Bu'aale
190 H1 **Buariki** atoll Tungaru, W Kiribati
167 Q10 **Bua Yai** var. Ban Bua Yai. Nakhon Ratchasima, E Thailand
75 P8 **Bu'ayrāt al Ḥasūn** var. Buwayrat al Hasūn. C Libya
76 H13 **Buba** S Guinea-Bissau
171 P11 **Bubaa** Sulawesi, N Indonesia
81 D20 **Bubanza** NW Burundi
83 K18 **Bubi** prev. Bubye. ≈ S Zimbabwe
142 L11 **Būbīyan, Jazīrat** island E Kuwait
Bublitz see Bobolice
Bubye see Bubi
187 Y13 **Buca** prev. Mbutha. Vanua Levu, N Fiji
136 F16 **Bucak** Burdur, SW Turkey
54 G8 **Bucaramanga** Santander, N Colombia
107 M18 **Buccino** Campania, S Italy
116 K9 **Bucecea** Botoșani, NE Romania
116 J6 **Buchach** Pol. Buczacz. Ternopil's'ka Oblast', W Ukraine
183 Q12 **Buchan** Victoria, SE Australia
76 J17 **Buchanan** prev. Grand Bassa. SW Liberia
23 R3 **Buchanan** Georgia, SE USA
31 O11 **Buchanan** Michigan, N USA
21 T6 **Buchanan** Virginia, NE USA
25 R10 **Buchanan Dam** Texas, SW USA
25 R10 **Buchanan, Lake** ▣ Texas, SW USA
96 L8 **Buchan Ness** headland NE Scotland, UK
13 T12 **Buchans** Newfoundland and Labrador, SE Canada
Bucharest see București
101 H20 **Buchen** Baden-Württemberg, SW Germany
100 I10 **Buchholz in der Nordheide** Niedersachsen, NW Germany
108 F7 **Buchs** Aargau, N Switzerland
108 I8 **Buchs** Sankt Gallen, NE Switzerland
100 H13 **Bückeburg** Niedersachsen, NW Germany
36 K14 **Buckeye** Arizona, SW USA
Buckeye State see Ohio
21 S4 **Buckhannon** West Virginia, NE USA
25 T9 **Buckholts** Texas, SW USA
96 K8 **Buckie** NE Scotland, UK
14 M12 **Buckingham** Québec, SE Canada
21 U6 **Buckingham** Virginia, NE USA
97 N21 **Buckinghamshire** cultural region SE England, UK
39 N8 **Buckland** Alaska, USA
182 G7 **Buckleboo** South Australia
26 K7 **Bucklin** Kansas, C USA
27 T3 **Bucklin** Missouri, C USA
36 I12 **Buckskin Mountains** ▲▲ Arizona, SW USA
19 R7 **Bucksport** Maine, NE USA
82 A9 **Buco Zau** Cabinda, NW Angola
Bu Craa see Bou Craa
116 K14 **București** Eng. Bucharest, Ger. Bukarest; prev. Altenburg, anc. Cetatea Damboviței. ● (Romania) București, S Romania
31 S12 **Bucyrus** Ohio, N USA
Buczacz see Buchach
94 E9 **Bud** Møre og Romsdal, S Norway
25 S11 **Buda** Texas, SW USA
119 O18 **Buda-Kashalyova** Rus. Buda-Koshelëvo. Homyel'skaya Voblasts', SE Belarus
Buda-Koshelëvo see Buda-Kashalyova
166 L4 **Budalin** Sagaing, C Burma
111 J22 **Budapest** off. Budapest Főváros, SCr. Budimpešta. ● (Hungary) Pest, N Hungary
152 K11 **Budaun** Uttar Pradesh, N India
141 O9 **Budayyi'ah** oasis C Saudi Arabia
195 Y12 **Budd Coast** physical region Antarctica
Buddenbrock see Brodnica
107 C17 **Buddusò** Sardegna, Italy, C Mediterranean Sea
97 I23 **Bude** SW England, UK
22 J7 **Bude** Mississippi, S USA
Budějovický Kraj see Jihočeský Kraj
99 K16 **Budel** Noord-Brabant, SE Netherlands
100 I8 **Büdelsdorf** Schleswig-Holstein, N Germany
127 O14 **Budënnovsk** Stavropol'skiy Kray, SW Russian Federation
116 K14 **Budești** Călărași, SE Romania
Budgewoi see Budgewoi Lake
183 T8 **Budgewoi Lake** var. Budgewoi. New South Wales, SE Australia
92 I2 **Búdhardalur** Vesturland, W Iceland
Budimpešta see Budapest
79 J16 **Budjala** Equateur, NW Dem. Rep. Congo
106 G10 **Budrio** Emilia-Romagna, C Italy
Budslav see Budslaw
119 K14 **Budslaw** Rus. Budslav. Minskaya Voblasts', N Belarus
Budua see Budva
169 R9 **Budu, Tanjung** headland East Malaysia
113 J17 **Budva** It. Budua. Montenegro, SW Serbia and Montenegro (Yugo.)
Budweis see České Budějovice
Budyšin see Bautzen
79 D16 **Buea** Sud-Ouest, SW Cameroon
103 S13 **Buëch** ≈ SE France
18 J17 **Buena** New Jersey, NE USA
62 K12 **Buena Esperanza** San Luis, C Argentina
54 C11 **Buenaventura** Valle del Cauca, W Colombia
40 I4 **Buenaventura** Chihuahua, N Mexico
57 M18 **Buena Vista** Santa Cruz, C Bolivia
40 G10 **Buenavista** Baja California Sur, W Mexico
37 S5 **Buena Vista** Colorado, C USA
23 S5 **Buena Vista** Georgia, SE USA
21 T6 **Buena Vista** Virginia, NE USA
44 F5 **Buena Vista, Bahia de** bay N Cuba
35 R13 **Buena Vista Lake Bed** ◎ California, W USA
105 P8 **Buendía, Embalse de** ▣ C Spain
63 F16 **Bueno, Río** ≈ S Chile
62 N12 **Buenos Aires** hist. Santa Maria del Buen Aire. ● (Argentina) Buenos Aires, E Argentina
43 O15 **Buenos Aires** Puntarenas, SE Costa Rica
61 C20 **Buenos Aires** off. Provincia de Buenos Aires. ◈ province E Argentina
63 H19 **Buenos Aires, Lago** var. Lago General Carrera. ◎ Argentina/Chile
54 C13 **Buesaco** Nariño, SW Colombia
29 U8 **Buffalo** Minnesota, N USA
27 T6 **Buffalo** Missouri, C USA
18 D10 **Buffalo** New York, NE USA
27 K8 **Buffalo** Oklahoma, C USA
28 J7 **Buffalo** South Dakota, N USA
25 V8 **Buffalo** Texas, SW USA
33 W12 **Buffalo** Wyoming, C USA
29 U11 **Buffalo Center** Iowa, C USA
24 M3 **Buffalo Lake** ▣ Texas, SW USA
30 K7 **Buffalo Lake** ▣ Wisconsin, N USA
11 S12 **Buffalo Narrows** Saskatchewan, C Canada
27 U9 **Buffalo River** ≈ Arkansas, C USA
29 R5 **Buffalo River** ≈ Minnesota, N USA
20 I10 **Buffalo River** ≈ Tennessee, S USA
30 J6 **Buffalo River** ≈ Wisconsin, N USA
44 L12 **Buff Bay** E Jamaica
23 T3 **Buford** Georgia, SE USA
28 J3 **Buford** North Dakota, N USA
33 Y17 **Buford** Wyoming, C USA
116 J14 **Buftea** București, S Romania
119 F21 **Bug** Bel. Zakhodni Buh, Eng. Western Bug, Rus. Zapadnyy Bug, Ukr. Zakhidnyy Buh. ≈ E Europe
54 D11 **Buga** Valle del Cauca, W Colombia
162 F7 **Buga** Dzavhan, W Mongolia
103 O17 **Bugarach, Pic du** ▲ S France
146 B12 **Bugdaýly** Rus. Bugdayly. Balkan Welaýaty, W Turkmenistan
Buggs Island Lake see John H.Kerr Reservoir
Bughotu see Santa Isabel
171 O14 **Bugingkalo** Sulawesi, C Indonesia
64 P6 **Bugio** island Madeira, Portugal, NE Atlantic Ocean
92 M8 **Bugøynes** Finnmark, N Norway
125 Q3 **Bugrino** Nenetskiy Avtonomnyy Okrug, NW Russian Federation
127 T5 **Bugul'ma** Respublika Tatarstan, W Russian Federation
Bügür see Luntai
127 T6 **Buguruslan** Orenburgskaya Oblast', W Russian Federation
159 R9 **Buh He** ≈ C China
33 O15 **Buhl** Idaho, NW USA
101 F22 **Bühl** Baden-Württemberg, SW Germany
116 K10 **Buhuși** Bacău, E Romania
Buie d'Istria see Buje
97 J20 **Builth Wells** E Wales, UK
186 J8 **Buin** Bougainville Island, NE PNG
108 J9 **Buin, Piz** ▲ Austria/Switzerland
127 Q4 **Buinsk** Chuvashskaya Respublika, W Russian Federation
127 Q4 **Buinsk** Respublika Tatarstan, W Russian Federation
163 R8 **Buir Nur** Mong. Buyr Nuur. ◎ China/Mongolia see also Buyr Nuur
98 M5 **Buitenpost** Fris. Bûtenpost. Friesland, N Netherlands

◆ Country
● Country Capital
◇ Dependent Territory
○ Dependent Territory Capital
◈ Administrative Region
✕ International Airport
▲ Mountain
▲▲ Mountain Range
※ Volcano
≈ River
◎ Lake
▣ Reservoir

Buitenzorg see Bogor
83 F19 **Buitepos** Omaheke, E Namibia
105 N7 **Buitrago del Lozoya** Madrid, C Spain
Buj see Buy
104 M13 **Bujalance** Andalucía, S Spain
113 O17 **Bujanovac** Serbia, SE Serbia and Montenegro (Yugo.)
105 S6 **Bujaraloz** Aragón, NE Spain
112 A9 **Buje** *It.* Buie d'Istria. Istra, NW Croatia
Bujnurd see Bojnūrd
81 D21 **Bujumbura** *prev.* Usumbura. ● (Burundi) W Burundi
81 D20 **Bujumbura** ✕ W Burundi
159 N11 **Buka Daban** *var.* Bkadaban Feng. ▲ C China
Bukadaban Feng see Buka Daban
186 J6 **Buka Island** island NE PNG
81 F18 **Bukakata** S Uganda
79 N24 **Bukama** Katanga, SE Dem. Rep. Congo
142 J4 **Būkān** *var.* Bowkān. Āżarbāyjān-e Bākhtarī, NW Iran
Bukantau, Gory see Bo'kantov Tog'lari
Bukarest see București
79 O19 **Bukavu** *prev.* Costermansville. Sud Kivu, E Dem. Rep. Congo
81 F21 **Bukene** Tabora, NW Tanzania
141 W8 **Bū Khābī** *var.* Bakhābī. NW Oman
Bukhara see Buxoro
Bukharskaya Oblast' see Buxoro Viloyati
146 J11 **Buxoro Viloyati** *Rus.* Bukharskaya Oblast'. ◈ province C Uzbekistan
168 M14 **Bukitkemuning** Sumatera, W Indonesia
168 I11 **Bukittinggi** *prev.* Fort de Kock. Sumatera, W Indonesia
111 L21 **Bükk** ▲ NE Hungary
81 F19 **Bukoba** Kagera, NW Tanzania
113 N20 **Bukovo** S FYR Macedonia
108 G6 **Bülach** Zürich, NW Switzerland
Būlaevo see Bulayevo
162 I6 **Bulag** Hövsgöl, N Mongolia
162 M7 **Bulag** Töv, C Mongolia
162 I8 **Bulagiyn Denj** Arhangay, C Mongolia
183 U7 **Bulahdelah** New South Wales, SE Australia
171 P4 **Bulan** Luzon, N Philippines
137 N11 **Bulancak** Giresun, N Turkey
152 J10 **Bulandshahr** Uttar Pradesh, N India
137 R14 **Bulanık** Muş, E Turkey
127 V7 **Bulanovo** Orenburgskaya Oblast', W Russian Federation
83 J17 **Bulawayo** *var.* Buluwayo. Matabeleland North, SW Zimbabwe
83 J17 **Bulawayo** ✕ Matabeleland North, SW Zimbabwe
145 Q6 **Bulayevo** *Kaz.* Bülaevo. Severnyy Kazakhstan, N Kazakhstan
136 D15 **Buldan** Denizli, SW Turkey
154 G12 **Buldāna** Mahārāshtra, C India
38 E16 **Buldir Island** island Aleutian Islands, Alaska, USA
Buldur see Burdur
162 H9 **Bulgan** Bayanhongor, C Mongolia
162 K6 **Bulgan** Bulgan, N Mongolia
162 F7 **Bulgan** Hovd, W Mongolia
162 J5 **Bulgan** Hövsgöl, N Mongolia
162 J10 **Bulgan** Ömnögovĭ, S Mongolia
162 J7 **Bulgan** ◈ province N Mongolia
114 H10 **Bulgaria** *off.* Republic of Bulgaria, *Bul.* Bŭlgariya; *prev.* People's Republic of Bulgaria. ◆ republic SE Europe
Bŭlgariya see Bulgaria
114 L9 **Bŭlgarka** ▲ E Bulgaria
171 S11 **Buli** Pulau Halmahera, E Indonesia
171 S11 **Buli, Teluk** bay Pulau Halmahera, E Indonesia
160 J13 **Buliu He** ≈ S China
Bullange see Büllingen
Bulla, Ostrov see Xärä Zirä Adası
104 M11 **Bullaque** ≈ C Spain
105 Q13 **Bullas** Murcia, SE Spain
80 M12 **Bullaxaar** Woqooyi Galbeed, NW Somalia
108 C9 **Bulle** Fribourg, SW Switzerland
185 G15 **Buller** ≈ South Island, NZ
183 P12 **Buller, Mount** ▲ Victoria, SE Australia
36 H11 **Bullhead City** Arizona, SW USA
99 N21 **Büllingen** *Fr.* Bullange. Liège, E Belgium
Bullion State see Missouri
21 T14 **Bull Island** island South Carolina, SE USA
182 M4 **Bulloo River Overflow** wetland New South Wales, SE Australia
184 M12 **Bulls** Manawatu-Wanganui, North Island, NZ
21 T14 **Bulls Bay** bay South Carolina, SE USA
27 U9 **Bull Shoals Lake** ▣ Arkansas/Missouri, C USA
181 Q2 **Bulman** Northern Territory, N Australia
162 I6 **Bulnayn Nuruu** ▲▲ N Mongolia
171 O11 **Bulowa, Gunung** ▲ Sulawesi, N Indonesia
Bulqiza see Bulqizë
113 L19 **Bulqizë** *var.* Bulqiza. Dibër, C Albania
Bulsar see Valsād
171 N14 **Bulukumba** *prev.* Boeloekoemba. Sulawesi, C Indonesia
79 I21 **Bulungu** Bandundu, SW Dem. Rep. Congo
Bulungur see Bulung'ur
147 O11 **Bulung'ur** *Rus.* Bulungur; *prev.* Krasnogvardeysk. Samarqand Viloyati, C Uzbekistan
Buluwayo see Bulawayo
79 K17 **Bumba** Equateur, N Dem. Rep. Congo
121 R12 **Bumbah, Khalīj al** gulf N Libya
162 K8 **Bumbat** Övörhangay, C Mongolia
81 F19 **Bumbire Island** island N Tanzania
169 V8 **Bum Bun, Pulau** island East Malaysia
81 J17 **Buna** North Eastern, NE Kenya
25 Y10 **Buna** Texas, SW USA
Bunab see Bonāb
Bunai see M'bunai
147 S13 **Bunay** S Tajikistan
180 I13 **Bunbury** Western Australia
97 E14 **Buncrana** *Ir.* Bun Cranncha. NW Ireland
Bun Cranncha see Buncrana
181 Z9 **Bundaberg** Queensland, E Australia
183 T5 **Bundarra** New South Wales, SE Australia
100 G13 **Bünde** Nordrhein-Westfalen, NW Germany
152 H13 **Būndi** Rājasthān, N India
Bun Dobhráin see Bundoran
97 D15 **Bundoran** *Ir.* Bun Dobhráin. NW Ireland
113 K18 **Bunë** *SCr.* Bojana. ≈ Albania/Serbia and Montenegro (Yugo.) see also Bojana
171 Q8 **Bunga** ≈ Mindanao, S Philippines
168 I12 **Bungalaut, Selat** strait W Indonesia
167 R8 **Bung Kan** Nong Khai, E Thailand
181 N4 **Bungle Bungle Range** ▲▲ Western Australia
82 C10 **Bungo** Uíge, NW Angola
81 G18 **Bungoma** Western, W Kenya
164 F15 **Bungo-suidō** strait SW Japan
164 E14 **Bungo-Takada** Ōita, Kyūshū, SW Japan
100 K8 **Bungsberg** hill N Germany
Bungur see Bunyu
79 P17 **Bunia** Orientale, NE Dem. Rep. Congo
35 U6 **Bunker Hill** ▲ Nevada, W USA
22 I7 **Bunkie** Louisiana, S USA
23 X10 **Bunnell** Florida, SE USA
105 S10 **Buñol** País Valenciano, E Spain
98 K11 **Bunschoten** Utrecht, C Netherlands
136 K14 **Bünyan** Kayseri, C Turkey
169 W8 **Bunyu** *var.* Bungur. Borneo, N Indonesia
169 W8 **Bunyu, Pulau** island N Indonesia
Bunzlau see Bolesławiec
Buoddobohki see Patoniva
123 P7 **Buorkhaya Guba** bay N Russian Federation
171 Z15 **Bupul** Papua, E Indonesia
81 J20 **Bura** Coast, SE Kenya
80 P12 **Buraan** Sanaag, N Somalia
Būrabay see Borovoye
Buraida see Buraydah
Buraimi see Al Buraymī
145 Y11 **Buran** Vostochnyy Kazakhstan, E Kazakhstan
158 G15 **Burang** Xizang Zizhiqu, W China
Burao see Burco
138 H8 **Burāq** Dar'ā, S Syria
141 O6 **Buraydah** *var.* Buraida. Al Qaşīm, N Saudi Arabia
35 S15 **Burbank** California, W USA
31 N11 **Burbank** Illinois, N USA
183 Q8 **Burcher** New South Wales, SE Australia
80 N13 **Burco** *var.* Burao, Bur'o. Togdheer, NW Somalia
146 L13 **Burdalyk** Lebap Welaýaty, E Turkmenistan
181 W6 **Burdekin River** ≈ Queensland, NE Australia
27 O7 **Burden** Kansas, C USA
Burdigala see Bordeaux
136 E15 **Burdur** *var.* Buldur. Burdur, SW Turkey
136 E15 **Burdur** *var.* Buldur. ◈ province SW Turkey
136 E15 **Burdur Gölü** salt lake SW Turkey
65 H21 **Burdwood Bank** undersea feature SW Atlantic Ocean
80 I12 **Burē** Amhara, N Ethiopia
80 H13 **Burē** Oromo, C Ethiopia
93 J15 **Bureå** Västerbotten, N Sweden
101 G14 **Büren** Nordrhein-Westfalen, W Germany
162 K6 **Bürengiyn Nuruu** ▲▲ N Mongolia
162 E8 **Bürenhayrhan** Hovd, W Mongolia
Bürewāla see Mandi Būrewāla
92 J9 **Burfjord** Troms, N Norway
100 L13 **Burg** *var.* Burg an der Ihle, Burg bei Magdeburg. Sachsen-Anhalt, C Germany
Burg an der Ihle see Burg
114 N10 **Burgas** *var.* Bourgas. Burgas, E Bulgaria
114 N9 **Burgas** ✕ Burgas, E Bulgaria
114 M10 **Burgas** ◈ province E Bulgaria
114 N10 **Burgaski Zaliv** gulf E Bulgaria
114 M10 **Burgasko Ezero** lagoon E Bulgaria
21 V11 **Burgaw** North Carolina, SE USA
Burg bei Magdeburg see Burg
108 E8 **Burgdorf** Bern, NW Switzerland
109 Y7 **Burgenland** *off.* Land Burgenland. ◈ state SE Austria
13 S13 **Burgeo** Newfoundland and Labrador, SE Canada
83 I24 **Burgersdorp** Eastern Cape, SE South Africa
83 K20 **Burgersfort** Mpumalanga, NE South Africa
101 N23 **Burghausen** Bayern, SE Germany
139 O5 **Burghūth, Sabkhat al** ⊚ E Syria
101 M20 **Burglengenfeld** Bayern, SE Germany
41 P9 **Burgos** Tamaulipas, C Mexico
105 N4 **Burgos** Castilla-León, N Spain
105 N4 **Burgos** ◈ province Castilla-León, N Spain
Burgstadlberg see Hradiště
95 P20 **Burgsvik** Gotland, SE Sweden
Burgum see Bergum
Burgundy see Bourgogne
159 Q11 **Burhan Budai Shan** ▲▲ C China
136 B12 **Burhaniye** Balıkesir, W Turkey
154 G12 **Burhānpur** Madhya Pradesh, C India
127 W7 **Buribay** Respublika Bashkortostan, W Russian Federation
43 O17 **Burica, Punta** headland Costa Rica/Panama
167 Q10 **Buriram** *var.* Buri Ram, Puriramya. Buri Ram, E Thailand
105 S10 **Burjassot** País Valenciano, E Spain
81 N16 **Burka Giibi** Hiiraan, C Somalia
147 X8 **Burkan** ≈ E Kyrgyzstan
25 R4 **Burkburnett** Texas, SW USA
29 O12 **Burke** South Dakota, N USA
10 K15 **Burke Channel** channel British Columbia, W Canada
194 J10 **Burke Island** island Antarctica
20 L7 **Burkesville** Kentucky, S USA
181 T4 **Burketown** Queensland, NE Australia
25 Q8 **Burkett** Texas, SW USA
25 Y9 **Burkeville** Texas, SW USA
21 V7 **Burkeville** Virginia, NE USA
77 O12 **Burkina** *off.* Burkina Faso; *prev.* Upper Volta. ◆ republic W Africa
Burkina Faso see Burkina
194 L13 **Burks, Cape** headland Antarctica
14 H12 **Burk's Falls** Ontario, S Canada
101 H23 **Burladingen** Baden-Württemberg, S Germany
25 T7 **Burleson** Texas, SW USA
33 P15 **Burley** Idaho, NW USA
144 G8 **Burlin** Zapadnyy Kazakhstan, NW Kazakhstan
14 G16 **Burlington** Ontario, S Canada
37 W4 **Burlington** Colorado, C USA
29 Y15 **Burlington** Iowa, C USA
27 P5 **Burlington** Kansas, C USA
21 T9 **Burlington** North Carolina, SE USA
28 M3 **Burlington** North Dakota, N USA
18 L7 **Burlington** Vermont, NE USA
30 M9 **Burlington** Wisconsin, N USA
27 Q1 **Burlington Junction** Missouri, C USA
166 M4 **Burma** *off.* Union of Myanmar ◆ military dictatorship SE Asia
10 L17 **Burnaby** British Columbia, SW Canada
117 O12 **Burnas, Ozero** ⊚ SW Ukraine
25 S10 **Burnet** Texas, SW USA
35 O3 **Burney** California, W USA
183 O16 **Burnie** Tasmania, SE Australia
97 L17 **Burnley** NW England, UK
Burnoye see Bauyrzhan Momyshuly
153 R15 **Burnpur** West Bengal, NE India
32 K14 **Burns** Oregon, NW USA
26 K11 **Burns Flat** Oklahoma, C USA
20 M7 **Burnside** Kentucky, S USA
8 K8 **Burnside** ≈ Nunavut, NW Canada
32 L15 **Burns Junction** Oregon, NW USA
10 L13 **Burns Lake** British Columbia, SW Canada
29 V9 **Burnsville** Minnesota, N USA
21 P9 **Burnsville** North Carolina, SE USA
21 R4 **Burnsville** West Virginia, NE USA
14 I13 **Burnt River** ≈ Ontario, SE Canada
14 I11 **Burntroot Lake** ⊚ Ontario, SE Canada
11 W12 **Burntwood** ≈ Manitoba, C Canada
Bur'o see Burco
158 L2 **Burqin** Xinjiang Uygur Zizhiqu, NW China
182 J8 **Burra** South Australia
183 S9 **Burragorang, Lake** ▣ New South Wales, SE Australia
96 K5 **Burray** island NE Scotland, UK
113 L19 **Burrel** *var.* Burreli. Dibër, C Albania
Burreli see Burrel
183 R8 **Burrendong Reservoir** ▣ New South Wales, SE Australia
183 R5 **Burren Junction** New South Wales, SE Australia
105 T9 **Burriana** País Valenciano, E Spain
183 R10 **Burrinjuck Reservoir** ▣ New South Wales, SE Australia
36 J12 **Burro Creek** ≈ Arizona, SW USA
40 M5 **Burro, Serranías del** ▲▲ NW Mexico
62 K7 **Burruyacú** Tucumán, N Argentina
136 E12 **Bursa** *var.* Brussa; *prev.* Brusa, *anc.* Prusa. Bursa, NW Turkey
136 D12 **Bursa** *var.* Brusa, Brussa. ◈ province NW Turkey
75 Y9 **Bûr Safâga** *var.* Būr Safājah. E Egypt
Būr Safājah see Bûr Safâga
Bûr Sa'îd see Port Said
81 O14 **Bur Tinle** Mudug, C Somalia
31 Q5 **Burt Lake** ⊚ Michigan, N USA
118 H7 **Burtnieks** *var.* Burtnieks Ezers. ⊚ N Latvia
Burtnieku Ezers see Burtnieks
31 Q9 **Burton** Michigan, N USA
Burton on Trent see Burton upon Trent
97 M19 **Burton upon Trent** *var.* Burton on Trent, Burton-upon-Trent. C England, UK
93 J15 **Burträsk** Västerbotten, N Sweden
145 S14 **Burubaytal** *prev.* Burylbaytal. Zhambyl, SE Kazakhstan
Burujird see Borūjerd
Burultokay see Fuhai
141 R15 **Burūm** SE Yemen
Burunday see Boralday
81 D21 **Burundi** *off.* Republic of Burundi; *prev.* Kingdom of Burundi, Urundi. ◆ republic C Africa
171 R13 **Buru, Pulau** *prev.* Boeroe. island E Indonesia
77 T17 **Burutu** Delta, S Nigeria
10 G7 **Burwash Landing** Yukon Territory, W Canada
29 O14 **Burwell** Nebraska, C USA
97 L17 **Bury** NW England, UK
123 N13 **Buryatiya, Respublika** *prev.* Buryatskaya ASSR. ◈ autonomous republic S Russian Federation
Buryatskaya ASSR see Buryatiya, Respublika
Burylbaytal see Burubaytal
117 S3 **Buryn'** Sums'ka Oblast', NE Ukraine
97 P20 **Bury St Edmunds** *hist.* Beodericsworth. E England, UK
114 G8 **Bŭrziya** ≈ NW Bulgaria
106 D9 **Busalla** Liguria, NW Italy
139 N5 **Buşayrah** Dayr az Zawr, E Syria
Buševa see Baba
143 N12 **Būshehr** *off.* Ostān-e Būshehr. ◈ province SW Iran
Būshehr/Bushire see Bandar-e Būshehr
25 N2 **Bushland** Texas, SW USA
30 J12 **Bushnell** Illinois, N USA
Busi see Biševo
81 G18 **Busia** SE Uganda
Busiasch see Buziaş
79 K16 **Businga** Equateur, NW Dem. Rep. Congo
79 J18 **Busira** ≈ NW Dem. Rep. Congo
116 I5 **Bus'k** *Rus.* Busk. L'vivs'ka Oblast', W Ukraine
95 E14 **Buskerud** ◈ county S Norway
113 F14 **Buško Jezero** ▣ SW Bosnia and Herzegovina
111 M15 **Busko-Zdrój** Świętokrzyskie, C Poland
Busra see Al Başrah, Iraq
Buşrá see Buşrá ash Shām, Syria
138 H9 **Buşrá ash Shām** *var.* Bosora, Bosra, Bozrah, Buşrá. Dar'ā, S Syria
180 I13 **Busselton** Western Australia
81 C14 **Busseri** ≈ W Sudan
106 E9 **Busseto** Emilia-Romagna, C Italy
106 A8 **Bussoleno** Piemonte, NE Italy
Bussora see Al Başrah
98 J10 **Bussum** Noord-Holland, C Netherlands
41 N7 **Bustamante** Nuevo León, NE Mexico
63 I23 **Bustamante, Punta** headland S Argentina
Bustan see Bŭston
116 J12 **Buşteni** Prahova, SE Romania
106 D7 **Busto Arsizio** Lombardia, N Italy
147 Q10 **Bŭston** *Rus.* Buston. NW Tajikistan
100 H8 **Büsum** Schleswig-Holstein, N Germany
79 M16 **Buta** Orientale, N Dem. Rep. Congo
81 E20 **Butare** *prev.* Astrida. S Rwanda
191 O2 **Butaritari** atoll Tungaru, W Kiribati
Butawal see Butwal
96 H13 **Bute** cultural region SW Scotland, UK
162 K6 **Büteeliyn Nuruu** ▲▲ N Mongolia
10 L16 **Bute Inlet** fjord British Columbia, W Canada
96 H12 **Bute, Island of** island SW Scotland, UK
79 P18 **Butembo** Nord Kivu, NE Dem. Rep. Congo
Bûtenpost see Buitenpost
107 K25 **Butera** Sicilia, Italy, C Mediterranean Sea
99 M20 **Bütgenbach** Liège, E Belgium
Butha Qi see Zalantun
166 J5 **Buthidaung** Arakan State, W Burma
61 I16 **Butiá** Rio Grande do Sul, S Brazil
81 F17 **Butiaba** NW Uganda
23 N6 **Butler** Alabama, S USA
23 S5 **Butler** Georgia, SE USA
31 Q11 **Butler** Indiana, N USA
27 R5 **Butler** Missouri, C USA
18 B14 **Butler** Pennsylvania, NE USA
194 K5 **Butler Island** island Antarctica
21 U8 **Butner** North Carolina, SE USA
171 P14 **Buton, Pulau** *var.* Pulau Butung; *prev.* Boetoeng. island C Indonesia
Bütow see Bytów
113 L23 **Butrintit, Liqeni i** ⊚ S Albania
23 N3 **Buttahatchee River** ≈ Alabama/Mississippi, S USA
33 Q10 **Butte** Montana, NW USA
29 O12 **Butte** Nebraska, C USA
168 J7 **Butterworth** Pinang, Peninsular Malaysia
83 J25 **Butterworth** *var.* Gcuwa. Eastern Cape, SE South Africa
13 O3 **Button Islands** island group Nunavut, NE Canada
35 R13 **Buttonwillow** California, W USA
171 Q7 **Butuan** *off.* Butuan City. Mindanao, S Philippines
Butung, Pulau see Buton, Pulau
Butuntum see Bitonto
126 M8 **Buturlinovka** Voronezhskaya Oblast', W Russian Federation
153 O11 **Butwal** *var.* Butawal. Western, C Nepal
101 G17 **Butzbach** Hessen, W Germany
100 L9 **Bützow** Mecklenburg-Vorpommern, N Germany
80 N13 **Buuhoodle** Togdheer, N Somalia
81 N16 **Buulobarde** *var.* Buulo Berde. Hiiraan, C Somalia Africa
Buulo Berde see Buulobarde
80 P12 **Buuraha Cal Miskaat** ▲▲ NE Somalia
81 L19 **Buur Gaabo** Jubbada Hoose, S Somalia
99 M22 **Buurgplaatz** ▲ N Luxembourg
Buwayrāt al Hasūn see Bu'ayrāt al Ḥasūn
146 L11 **Buxoro** *var.* Bokhara, *Rus.* Bukhara. Buxhoro Viloyati, C Uzbekistan
100 I10 **Buxtehude** Niedersachsen, NW Germany
97 L18 **Buxton** C England, UK
124 M14 **Buy** *var.* Buj. Kostromskaya Oblast', NW Russian Federation
162 G7 **Buyanbat** Govĭ-Altay, W Mongolia
162 H8 **Buyant** Bayanhongor, C Mongolia
162 D6 **Buyant** Bayan-Ölgiy, W Mongolia
162 H7 **Buyant** Dzavhan, C Mongolia
163 N9 **Buyant** Hentiy, C Mongolia
163 N10 **Buyant-Uhaa** Dornogovĭ, SE Mongolia
162 M7 **Buyant Ukha** ✕ (Ulaanbaatar) Töv, N Mongolia
127 Q16 **Buynaksk** Respublika Dagestan, SW Russian Federation
119 L20 **Buynavichy** *Rus.* Buynovichi. Homyel'skaya Voblasts', SE Belarus
Buynovichi see Buynavichy
76 L16 **Buyo** SW Ivory Coast
76 L16 **Buyo, Lac de** ▣ W Ivory Coast
163 R7 **Buyr Nuur** *var.* Buir Nur. ⊚ China/Mongolia see also Buir Nur
137 T13 **Büyükağrı Dağı** *var.* Aghri Dagh, Agri Dagi, Koh I Noh, Masis, *Eng.* Great Ararat, Mount Ararat. ▲ E Turkey
137 R15 **Büyük Çayı** ≈ NE Turkey
114 O13 **Büyük Çekmece** İstanbul, NW Turkey
114 N12 **Büyükkarıştıran** Kırklareli, NW Turkey
115 L14 **Büyükkemikli Burnu** headland NW Turkey
136 E15 **Büyükmenderes Nehri** ≈ SW Turkey
Büyükzap Suyu see Great Zab
102 M9 **Buzançais** Indre, C France
116 K13 **Buzău** Buzău, SE Romania
116 K13 **Buzău** ◈ county SE Romania
116 L12 **Buzău** ≈ E Romania
75 S11 **Buzaymah** *var.* Bzīmah. SE Libya
164 E13 **Buzen** Fukuoka, Kyūshū, SW Japan
116 F12 **Buziaş** *Ger.* Busiasch, *Hung.* Buziásfürdő; *prev.* Buziás. Timiş, W Romania
Buziásfürdő see Buziaş
83 M18 **Búzi, Rio** ≈ C Mozambique
117 Q10 **Buz'kyy Lyman** bay S Ukraine
146 F13 **Būzmeýin** *Rus.* Byuzmeyin; *prev.* Bezmein. Ahal Welaýaty, C Turkmenistan
145 O8 **Buzuluk** Akmola, C Kazakhstan
127 T6 **Buzuluk** Orenburgskaya Oblast', W Russian Federation
127 N8 **Buzuluk** ≈ SW Russian Federation
19 P12 **Buzzards Bay** Massachusetts, NE USA
19 P13 **Buzzards Bay** bay Massachusetts, NE USA
83 G16 **Bwabata** Caprivi, NE Namibia
186 H10 **Bwagaoia** Misima Island, SE PNG
Bwake see Bouaké
187 R13 **Bwatnapne** Pentecost, C Vanuatu
119 K14 **Byahoml'** *Rus.* Begoml'. Vitsyebskaya Voblasts', N Belarus
114 J8 **Byala** Ruse, N Bulgaria
114 N9 **Byala** *prev.* Ak-Dere. Varna, E Bulgaria
Byala Reka see Erydropótamos
114 H8 **Byala Slatina** Vratsa, NW Bulgaria
119 N15 **Byalynichy** *Rus.* Belynichi. Mahilyowskaya Voblasts', E Belarus
119 G19 **Byaroza** *Pol.* Bereza Kartuska, *Rus.* Berëza. Brestskaya Voblasts', SW Belarus
Bybles see Jbaïl
111 O14 **Bychawa** Lubelskie, SE Poland
Bychikha see Bychykha
118 N11 **Bychykha** *Rus.* Bychikha. Vitsyebskaya Voblasts', NE Belarus
111 I14 **Byczyna** *Ger.* Pitschen. Opolskie, S Poland
110 I10 **Bydgoszcz** *Ger.* Bromberg. Kujawski-pomorskie, C Poland
119 I17 **Byelaruskaya Hrada** *Rus.* Belorusskaya Gryada. ridge N Belarus
119 G18 **Byelavyezhskaya Pushcha** *Pol.* Puszcza Białowieska, *Rus.* Belovezhskaya Pushcha. forest Belarus/Poland see also Białowieska, Puszcza
119 H15 **Byenyakoni** *Rus.* Benyakoni. Hrodzyenskaya Voblasts', W Belarus
119 M16 **Byerazino** *Rus.* Berezino. Minskaya Voblasts', C Belarus
118 L13 **Byerazino** *Rus.* Berezino. Vitsyebskaya Voblasts', N Belarus
119 L14 **Byerezino** *Rus.* Berezina. ≈ C Belarus
118 M13 **Byeshankovichy** *Rus.* Beshenkovichi. Vitsyebskaya Voblasts', N Belarus
31 U13 **Byesville** Ohio, N USA
119 P18 **Byesyedz'** *Rus.* Besed'. ≈ SE Belarus
119 H19 **Byezdzyezh** *Rus.* Bezdezh. Brestskaya Voblasts', SW Belarus
93 J15 **Bygdeå** Västerbotten, N Sweden
94 F12 **Bygdin** ⊚ S Norway
93 J15 **Bygdsiljum** Västerbotten, N Sweden
95 E17 **Bygland** Aust-Agder, S Norway
95 E17 **Byglandsfjord** Aust-Agder, S Norway
119 N16 **Bykhaw** *Rus.* Bykhov. Mahilyowskaya Voblasts', E Belarus
Bykhov see Bykhaw
127 P9 **Bykovo** Volgogradskaya Oblast', SW Russian Federation
123 P7 **Bykovskiy** Respublika Sakha (Yakutiya), NE Russian Federation
195 R12 **Byrd Glacier** glacier Antarctica
14 K10 **Byrd, Lac** ⊚ Québec, SE Canada
183 P5 **Byrock** New South Wales, SE Australia
30 L10 **Byron** Illinois, N USA
183 V4 **Byron Bay** New South Wales, SE Australia
183 V4 **Byron, Cape** headland New South Wales, E Australia
63 F21 **Byron, Isla** island S Chile
Byron Island see Nikunau
65 B24 **Byron Sound** sound NW Falkland Islands
122 M6 **Byrranga, Gora** ▲▲ N Russian Federation
93 J14 **Byske** Västerbotten, N Sweden
111 K18 **Bystrá** ▲ N Slovakia
111 F18 **Bystřice nad Pernštejnem** *Ger.* Bistritz ober Pernstein. Vysočina, C Czech Republic
Bystrovka see Kemin
111 G16 **Bystrzyca Kłodzka** *Ger.* Habelschwerdt. Wałbrzych, SW Poland
111 I18 **Bytča** Žilinský Kraj, N Slovakia
119 L15 **Bytcha** *Rus.* Bytcha. Minskaya Voblasts', NE Belarus
Byteń/Byten' see Bytsyen'
111 J16 **Bytom** *Ger.* Beuthen. Śląskie, S Poland
110 H7 **Bytów** *Ger.* Bütow. Pomorskie, N Poland
119 H18 **Bytsyen'** *Pol.* Byteń, *Rus.* Byten'. Brestskaya Voblasts', SW Belarus
81 E19 **Byumba** *var.* Biumba. N Rwanda
Byuzmeyin see Būzmeýin
119 O20 **Byval'ki** Homyel'skaya Voblasts', SE Belarus
95 O20 **Byxelkrok** Kalmar, S Sweden
Byzantium see İstanbul
Bzīmah see Buzaymah

C

62 O6 **Caacupé** Cordillera, S Paraguay
62 P6 **Caaguazú** *off.* Departamento de Caaguazú. ◈ department C Paraguay
82 C13 **Caála** *var.* Kaala, Robert Williams, *Port.* Vila Robert Williams. Huambo, C Angola
62 P7 **Caazapá** Caazapá, S Paraguay
62 P7 **Caazapá** *off.* Departamento de Caazapá. ◈ department SE Paraguay
81 P15 **Cabaad, Raas** headland C Somalia
55 N10 **Cabadisocaña** Amazonas, S Venezuela
44 F5 **Cabaiguán** Sancti Spíritus, C Cuba
Caballeria, Cabo see Cavalleria, Cap de
37 Q14 **Caballo Reservoir** ▣ New Mexico, SW USA
40 L6 **Caballos Mesteños, Llano de los** plain N Mexico
104 L2 **Cabañaquinta** Asturias, N Spain
42 B9 **Cabañas** ◈ department E El Salvador
171 O3 **Cabanatuan** *off.* Cabanatuan City. Luzon, N Philippines
15 T8 **Cabano** Québec, SE Canada
104 L11 **Cabeza del Buey** Extremadura, W Spain
45 V5 **Cabezas de San Juan** headland E Puerto Rico
105 N2 **Cabezón de la Sal** Cantabria, N Spain
Cabhán see Cavan
61 B23 **Cabildo** Buenos Aires, E Argentina
Cabillonum see Chalon-sur-Saône
54 H5 **Cabimas** Zulia, NW Venezuela
82 A9 **Cabinda** *var.* Kabinda. Cabinda, NW Angola
82 A9 **Cabinda** *var.* Kabinda. ◈ province NW Angola
33 N7 **Cabinet Mountains** ▲▲ Idaho/Montana, NW USA
82 B11 **Cabiri** Bengo, NW Angola
63 J20 **Cabo Blanco** Santa Cruz, SE Argentina
82 P13 **Cabo Delgado** *off.* Província de Capo Delgado. ◈ province NE Mozambique
14 L9 **Cabonga, Réservoir** ▣ Québec, SE Canada
27 V7 **Cabool** Missouri, C USA
183 V2 **Caboolture** Queensland, E Australia
Cabora Bassa, Lake see Cahora Bassa, Albufeira de

◆ Country ● Country Capital ◇ Dependent Territory ○ Dependent Territory Capital ◈ Administrative Region ✕ International Airport ▲ Mountain ▲▲ Mountain Range Volcano ≈ River ⊚ Lake ▣ Reservoir

40 F3 **Caborca** Sonora, NW Mexico
Cabo San Lucas *see* San Lucas
27 V11 **Cabot** Arkansas, C USA
14 F12 **Cabot Head** *headland* Ontario, S Canada
13 R13 **Cabot Strait** *strait* E Canada
Cabo Verde, Ilhas do *see* Cape Verde
104 M14 **Cabra** Andalucía, S Spain
107 B19 **Cabras** Sardegna, Italy, C Mediterranean Sea
188 A15 **Cabras Island** *island* W Guam
45 O8 **Cabrera** N Dominican Republic
105 X10 **Cabrera** *anc.* Capraria. *island* Islas Baleares, Spain, W Mediterranean Sea
104 J4 **Cabrera** ≈ NW Spain
105 Q15 **Cabrera, Sierra** ▲ S Spain
11 S16 **Cabri** Saskatchewan, S Canada
105 R10 **Cabriel** ≈ E Spain
54 M7 **Cabruta** Guárico, C Venezuela
171 N2 **Cabugao** Luzon, N Philippines
54 G10 **Cabuyaro** Meta, C Colombia
60 I13 **Caçador** Santa Catarina, S Brazil
42 G8 **Cacaguatique, Cordillera** *var.* Cordillera. ▲ NE El Salvador
112 L13 **Čačak** Serbia, C Serbia and Montenegro (Yugo.)
55 Y10 **Cacao** NE French Guiana
61 H16 **Caçapava do Sul** Rio Grande do Sul, S Brazil
21 U3 **Cacapon River** ≈ West Virginia, NE USA
107 J23 **Caccamo** Sicilia, Italy, C Mediterranean Sea
107 A17 **Caccia, Capo** *headland* Sardegna, Italy, C Mediterranean Sea
146 H15 **Çäçe** *var.* Chäche, *Rus.* Chaacha. Ahal Welaýaty, S Turkmenistan
59 G18 **Cáceres** Mato Grosso, W Brazil
104 J10 **Cáceres** *Ar.* Qazris. Extremadura, W Spain
104 J9 **Cáceres** ◈ *province* Extremadura, W Spain
Cachacrou *see* Scotts Head Village
61 C21 **Cacharí** Buenos Aires, E Argentina
26 L12 **Cache** Oklahoma, C USA
10 M16 **Cache Creek** British Columbia, SW Canada
35 N6 **Cache Creek** ≈ California, W USA
37 S3 **Cache La Poudre River** ≈ Colorado, C USA
Cacheo *see* Cacheu
27 W11 **Cache River** ≈ Arkansas, C USA
30 L17 **Cache River** ≈ Illinois, N USA
76 G12 **Cacheu** *var.* Cacheo. W Guinea-Bissau
59 I15 **Cachimbo** Pará, NE Brazil
59 H15 **Cachimbo, Serra do** ▲ C Brazil
82 D13 **Cachingues** Bié, C Angola
54 G7 **Cáchira** Norte de Santander, N Colombia
61 H16 **Cachoeira do Sul** Rio Grande do Sul, S Brazil
59 O20 **Cachoeiro de Itapemirim** Espírito Santo, SE Brazil
82 E12 **Cacolo** Lunda Sul, NE Angola
83 C14 **Caconda** Huíla, C Angola
82 A9 **Cacongo** Cabinda, NW Angola
35 U9 **Cactus Peak** ▲ Nevada, W USA
82 A11 **Cacuaco** Luanda, NW Angola
83 B14 **Cacula** Huíla, SW Angola
59 O19 **Caçumba, Ilha** *island* SE Brazil
55 N10 **Cacuri** Amazonas, S Venezuela
81 N17 **Cadale** Shabeellaha Dhexe, E Somalia
105 X4 **Cadaqués** Cataluña, NE Spain
111 J18 **Čadca** *Hung.* Csaca. Žilinský Kraj, N Slovakia
27 P13 **Caddo** Oklahoma, C USA
25 R6 **Caddo** Texas, SW USA
25 X6 **Caddo Lake** ⊠ Louisiana/Texas, SW USA
27 S12 **Caddo Mountains** ▲ Arkansas, C USA
41 O8 **Cadereyta** Nuevo León, NE Mexico
97 J19 **Cader Idris** ▲ NW Wales, United Kingdom
182 F3 **Cadibarrawirracanna, Lake** *salt lake* South Australia
14 I7 **Cadillac** Québec, SE Canada
11 T17 **Cadillac** Saskatchewan, S Canada
102 K13 **Cadillac** Gironde, SW France
31 P7 **Cadillac** Michigan, N USA
105 V4 **Cadí, Torre de** ▲ NE Spain
171 P5 **Cadiz** *off.* Cadiz City. Negros, C Philippines
20 H7 **Cadiz** Kentucky, S USA
31 U13 **Cadiz** Ohio, N USA
104 J15 **Cádiz** *anc.* Gades, Gadier, Gadir, Gadire. Andalucía, SW Spain
104 K15 **Cádiz** ◈ *province* Andalucía, SW Spain
104 I15 **Cadiz, Bahía de** *bay* SW Spain
Cadiz City *see* Cadiz
104 H15 **Cádiz, Golfo de** *Eng.* Gulf of Cadiz. *gulf* Portugal/Spain
Cadiz, Gulf of *see* Cádiz, Golfo de
35 X14 **Cadiz Lake** ◎ California, W USA
182 E2 **Cadney Homestead** South Australia
Cadurcum *see* Cahors
83 F17 **Caecae** Ngamiland, NW Botswana
102 K4 **Caen** Calvados, N France
Caene/Caenepolis *see* Qena
Caerdydd *see* Cardiff
Caer Glou *see* Gloucester
Caer Gybi *see* Holyhead
Caerleon *see* Chester
Caer Luel *see* Carlisle
97 I18 **Caernarfon** *var.* Caernarvon, Carnarvon. NW Wales, UK
97 H18 **Caernarfon Bay** *bay* NW Wales, UK
97 I19 **Caernarvon** *cultural region* NW Wales, UK
Caernarvon *see* Caernarfon
Caesaraugusta *see* Zaragoza
Caesarea Mazaca *see* Kayseri
Caesarobriga *see* Talavera de la Reina
Caesarodunum *see* Tours
Caesaromagus *see* Beauvais
Caesena *see* Cesena
59 N17 **Caetité** Bahia, E Brazil
62 J6 **Cafayate** Salta, N Argentina
171 O2 **Cagayan** ≈ Luzon, N Philippines
171 Q7 **Cagayan de Oro** *off.* Cagayan de Oro City. Mindanao, S Philippines
170 M8 **Cagayan de Tawi Tawi** *island* S Philippines
171 N6 **Cagayan Islands** *island group* C Philippines
31 O14 **Cagles Mill Lake** ⊠ Indiana, N USA
106 I12 **Cagli** Marche, C Italy
107 C20 **Cagliari** *anc.* Caralis. Sardegna, Italy, C Mediterranean Sea
107 C20 **Cagliari, Golfo di** *gulf* Sardegna, Italy, C Mediterranean Sea
103 U15 **Cagnes-sur-Mer** Alpes-Maritimes, SE France
54 L5 **Cagua** Aragua, N Venezuela
171 O1 **Cagua, Mount** ▲ Luzon, N Philippines
54 F13 **Caguán, Río** ≈ SW Colombia
45 U6 **Caguas** E Puerto Rico
146 C9 **Çagyl** *Rus.* Chagyl. Balkan Welaýaty, NW Turkmenistan
23 P5 **Cahaba River** ≈ Alabama, S USA
42 E5 **Cahabón, Río** ≈ C Guatemala
83 B15 **Cahama** Cunene, SW Angola
97 B21 **Caha Mountains** *Ir.* An Cheacha. ▲ SW Ireland
97 D20 **Caher** *Ir.* An Cathair. S Ireland
97 A21 **Cahersiveen** *Ir.* Cathair Saidhbhín. SW Ireland
30 K15 **Cahokia** Illinois, N USA
83 L15 **Cahora Bassa, Albufeira de** *var.* Lake Cabora Bassa. ⊠ NW Mozambique
97 G20 **Cahore Point** *Ir.* Rinn Chathóir. *headland* SE Ireland
102 M14 **Cahors** *anc.* Cadurcum. Lot, S France
56 D9 **Cahuapanas, Río** ≈ N Peru
116 M12 **Cahul** *Rus.* Kagul. S Moldova
Cahul, Lacul *see* Kahul, Ozero
83 N16 **Caia** Sofala, C Mozambique
59 J19 **Caiapó, Serra do** ▲ C Brazil
44 F5 **Caibarién** Villa Clara, C Cuba
55 O5 **Caicara** Monagas, NE Venezuela
54 L5 **Caicara del Orinoco** Bolívar, C Venezuela
59 P14 **Caicó** Rio Grande do Norte, E Brazil
44 M6 **Caicos Islands** *island group* W Turks and Caicos Islands
44 L5 **Caicos Passage** *strait* Bahamas/Turks and Caicos Islands
161 O9 **Caidian** *prev.* Hanyang. Hubei, C China
Caiffa *see* Ḥefa
180 M12 **Caiguna** Western Australia
Caillí, Ceann *see* Hag's Head
40 J11 **Caimanero, Laguna del** *var.* Laguna del Camaronero. *lagoon* E Pacific Ocean
117 N10 **Căinari** *Rus.* Kaynary. C Moldova
57 L19 **Caine, Río** ≈ C Bolivia
Caiphas *see* Ḥefa
195 N4 **Caird Coast** *physical region* Antarctica
96 J9 **Cairn Gorm** ▲ C Scotland, UK
96 J9 **Cairngorm Mountains** ▲ C Scotland, UK
39 P12 **Cairn Mountain** ▲ Alaska, USA
181 W4 **Cairns** Queensland, NE Australia
121 V13 **Cairo** *Ar.* Al Qāhirah, *var.* El Qâhira. ● (Egypt) N Egypt
23 T8 **Cairo** Georgia, SE USA
30 L17 **Cairo** Illinois, N USA
75 V8 **Cairo** × C Egypt
Caiseal *see* Cashel
Caisleán an Bharraigh *see* Castlebar
Caisleán na Finne *see* Castlefinn
96 J6 **Caithness** *cultural region* N Scotland, UK
83 D15 **Caiundo** Cuando Cubango, S Angola
56 C11 **Cajamarca** *prev.* Caxamarca. Cajamarca, NW Peru
56 B11 **Cajamarca** *off.* Departamento de Cajamarca. ◈ *department* N Peru
103 N14 **Cajarc** Lot, S France
42 G6 **Cajón, Represa El** ⊠ NW Honduras
58 N12 **Caju, Ilha do** *island* NE Brazil
Cakaubalavu Reef *see* Kavukavu Reef
159 R10 **Caka Yanhu** ◎ C China
112 E7 **Čakovec** *Ger.* Csakathurn, *Hung.* Csáktornya; *prev. Ger.* Tschakathurn. Medimurje, N Croatia
77 V17 **Calabar** Cross River, S Nigeria
14 K13 **Calabogie** Ontario, SE Canada
54 L6 **Calabozo** Guárico, C Venezuela
107 N20 **Calabria** *anc.* Bruttium. ◈ *region* SW Italy
104 M16 **Calaburra, Punta de** *headland* S Spain
116 G14 **Calafat** Dolj, SW Romania
Calafate *see* El Calafate
105 Q4 **Calahorra** La Rioja, N Spain
103 N1 **Calais** Pas-de-Calais, N France
19 T5 **Calais** Maine, NE USA
Calais, Pas de *see* Dover, Strait of
Calalen *see* Kallalen
62 H4 **Calama** Antofagasta, N Chile
Calamianes *see* Calamian Group
170 M5 **Calamian Group** *var.* Calamianes. *island group* W Philippines
105 R7 **Calamocha** Aragón, NE Spain
29 N14 **Calamus River** ≈ Nebraska, C USA
116 G12 **Călan** *Ger.* Kalan, *Hung.* Pusztakalán. Hunedoara, SW Romania
105 S7 **Calanda** Aragón, NE Spain
168 F9 **Calang** Sumatera, W Indonesia
171 N4 **Calapan** Mindoro, N Philippines
Călăras *see* Călărași
116 M9 **Călărași** *var.* Călăras, *Rus.* Kalarash. C Moldova
116 L14 **Călărași** Călărași, SE Romania
116 K14 **Călărași** ◈ *county* SE Romania
54 E10 **Calarca** Quindío, W Colombia
105 Q12 **Calasparra** Murcia, SE Spain
107 I23 **Calatafimi** Sicilia, Italy, C Mediterranean Sea
105 Q6 **Calatayud** Aragón, NE Spain
171 O4 **Calauag** Luzon, N Philippines
35 P8 **Calaveras River** ≈ California, W USA
171 N4 **Calavite, Cape** *headland* Mindoro, N Philippines
171 Q8 **Calbayog** *off.* Calbayog City. Samar, C Philippines
22 G9 **Calcasieu Lake** ◎ Louisiana, S USA
22 H8 **Calcasieu River** ≈ Louisiana, S USA
56 B6 **Calceta** Manabí, W Ecuador
61 B16 **Calchaquí** Santa Fe, C Argentina
62 J6 **Calchaquí, Río** ≈ NW Argentina
58 J10 **Calçoene** Amapá, NE Brazil
153 S16 **Calcutta** West Bengal, NE India
153 S16 **Calcutta** × West Bengal, N India
54 E9 **Caldas** *off.* Departamento de Caldas. ◈ *province* W Colombia
104 F10 **Caldas da Rainha** Leiria, W Portugal
104 G3 **Caldas de Reis** *var.* Caldas de Reyes. Galicia, NW Spain
Caldas de Reyes *see* Caldas de Reis
58 F13 **Caldeirão** Amazonas, NW Brazil
62 G7 **Caldera** Atacama, N Chile
42 L14 **Caldera** Puntarenas, W Costa Rica
105 N10 **Calderina** ▲ C Spain
137 T13 **Çaldıran** Van, E Turkey
32 M14 **Caldwell** Idaho, NW USA
27 N8 **Caldwell** Kansas, C USA
14 G15 **Caledon** Ontario, S Canada
83 I23 **Caledon** *var.* Mohokare. ≈ Lesotho/South Africa
42 G1 **Caledonia** Corozal, N Belize
14 G16 **Caledonia** Ontario, S Canada
29 X11 **Caledonia** Minnesota, N USA
105 X5 **Calella** *var.* Calella de la Costa. Cataluña, NE Spain
Calella de la Costa *see* Calella
23 P4 **Calera** Alabama, S USA
63 I19 **Caleta Olivia** Santa Cruz, SE Argentina
35 X17 **Calexico** California, W USA
97 H16 **Calf of Man** *island* SW Isle of Man
11 Q16 **Calgary** Alberta, SW Canada
11 Q16 **Calgary** × Alberta, SW Canada
37 U5 **Calhan** Colorado, C USA
64 O5 **Calheta** Madeira, Portugal, NE Atlantic Ocean
23 R2 **Calhoun** Georgia, SE USA
20 I6 **Calhoun** Kentucky, S USA
22 M3 **Calhoun City** Mississippi, S USA
21 P12 **Calhoun Falls** South Carolina, SE USA
54 D11 **Cali** Valle del Cauca, W Colombia
27 V9 **Calico Rock** Arkansas, C USA
155 F21 **Calicut** *var.* Kozhikode. Kerala, SW India
35 Y9 **Caliente** Nevada, W USA
27 U5 **California** Missouri, C USA
18 B15 **California** Pennsylvania, NE USA
35 Q12 **California** *off.* State of California; also known as El Dorado, The Golden State. ◈ *state* W USA
35 P11 **California Aqueduct** *aqueduct* California, W USA
35 T13 **California City** California, W USA
40 F6 **California, Golfo de** *Eng.* Gulf of California; *prev.* Sea of Cortez. *gulf* W Mexico
California, Gulf of *see* California, Golfo de
137 Y13 **Cälilabad** *Rus.* Dzhalilabad; *prev.* Astrakhan-Bazar. S Azerbaijan
116 I12 **Călimănești** Vâlcea, SW Romania
116 J9 **Călimani, Munții** ▲ N Romania
Calinisc *see* Cupcina
35 X17 **Calipatria** California, W USA
Calisia *see* Kalisz
34 M7 **Calistoga** California, W USA
83 G25 **Calitzdorp** Western Cape, SW South Africa
41 W12 **Calkiní** Campeche, E Mexico
182 K4 **Callabonna Creek** *var.* Tilcha Creek. *seasonal river* New South Wales/South Australia
182 J4 **Callabonna, Lake** ◎ South Australia
102 G5 **Callac** Côtes d'Armor, NW France
35 U5 **Callaghan, Mount** ▲ Nevada, W USA
Callain *see* Callan
97 E19 **Callan** *Ir.* Callain. S Ireland
14 H11 **Callander** Ontario, S Canada
96 I11 **Callander** C Scotland, UK
98 H7 **Callantsoog** Noord-Holland, NW Netherlands
57 D14 **Callao** Callao, W Peru
57 D15 **Callao** *off.* Departamento del Callao. ◈ *constitutional province* W Peru
56 F11 **Callaria, Río** ≈ E Peru
Callatis *see* Mangalia
11 Q13 **Calling Lake** Alberta, W Canada
Callosa de Ensarriá *see* Callosa d'En Sarrià
105 T11 **Callosa d'En Sarrià** *var.* Callosa de Ensarriá. País Valenciano, E Spain
105 S12 **Callosa de Segura** País Valenciano, E Spain
29 X11 **Calmar** Iowa, C USA
Calmar *see* Kalmar
43 R16 **Calobre** Veraguas, C Panama
23 X14 **Caloosahatchee River** ≈ Florida, SE USA
183 V2 **Caloundra** Queensland, E Australia
Calp *see* Calpe
105 T11 **Calpe** *Cat.* Calp. País Valenciano, E Spain
41 P14 **Calpulalpan** Tlaxcala, S Mexico
107 K25 **Caltagirone** Sicilia, Italy, C Mediterranean Sea
107 J24 **Caltanissetta** Sicilia, Italy, C Mediterranean Sea
82 E11 **Caluango** Lunda Norte, NE Angola
82 C12 **Calucinga** Bié, W Angola
82 B12 **Calulo** Cuanza Sul, NW Angola
83 B14 **Caluquembe** Huíla, W Angola
80 Q11 **Caluula** Bari, NE Somalia
102 K4 **Calvados** ◈ *department* N France
186 I10 **Calvados Chain, The** *island group* SE PNG
25 U9 **Calvert** Texas, SW USA
20 H7 **Calvert City** Kentucky, S USA
103 X14 **Calvi** Corse, France, C Mediterranean Sea
40 L12 **Calvillo** Aguascalientes, C Mexico
83 F24 **Calvinia** Northern Cape, W South Africa
104 K8 **Calvitero** ▲ W Spain
101 G22 **Calw** Baden-Württemberg, SW Germany
Calydon *see* Kalydón
105 N11 **Calzada de Calatrava** Castilla-La Mancha, C Spain
Cama *see* Kama
82 C11 **Camabatela** Cuanza Norte, NW Angola
64 Q5 **Camacha** Porto Santo, Madeira, Portugal, NE Atlantic Ocean
14 L8 **Camachigama, Lac** ◎ Québec, SE Canada
40 M9 **Camacho** Zacatecas, C Mexico
82 D13 **Camacupa** *var.* General Machado, *Port.* Vila General Machado. Bié, C Angola
54 L7 **Camaguán** Guárico, C Venezuela
44 G6 **Camagüey** *prev.* Puerto Príncipe. Camagüey, C Cuba
44 G5 **Camagüey, Archipiélago de** *island group* C Cuba
40 D5 **Camalli, Sierra de** ▲ NW Mexico
57 G18 **Camana** *var.* Camaná. Arequipa, SW Peru
29 Z14 **Camanche** Iowa, C USA
35 P8 **Camanche Reservoir** ⊠ California, W USA
61 I16 **Camaquã** Rio Grande do Sul, S Brazil
61 H16 **Camaquã, Rio** ≈ S Brazil
64 P6 **Câmara de Lobos** Madeira, Portugal, NE Atlantic Ocean
103 U16 **Camarat, Cap** *headland* SE France
41 O8 **Camargo** Tamaulipas, C Mexico
103 R15 **Camargue** *physical region* SE France
104 F2 **Camariñas** Galicia, NW Spain
Camaronero, Laguna del *see* Caimanero, Laguna del
63 J18 **Camarones** Chaco, S Argentina
63 J18 **Camarones, Bahía** *bay* S Argentina
104 J14 **Camas** Andalucía, S Spain
167 S15 **Ca Mau** *prev.* Quan Long. Minh Hai, S Vietnam
82 E11 **Camaxilo** Lunda Norte, NE Angola
104 G3 **Cambados** Galicia, NW Spain
Cambay, Gulf of *see* Khambhāt, Gulf of
Camberia *see* Chambéry
97 N22 **Camberley** SE England, UK
167 R12 **Cambodia** *off.* Kingdom of Cambodia, *var.* Democratic Kampuchea, Roat Kampuchea, *Cam.* Kampuchea; *prev.* People's Democratic Republic of Kampuchea. ◆ *republic* SE Asia
102 I16 **Cambo-les-Bains** Pyrénées-Atlantiques, SW France
103 P2 **Cambrai** *Flem.* Kambryk; *prev.* Cambray, *anc.* Cameracum. Nord, N France
Cambray *see* Cambrai
104 H2 **Cambre** Galicia, NW Spain
35 O12 **Cambria** California, W USA
97 J20 **Cambrian Mountains** ▲ C Wales, UK
14 G16 **Cambridge** Ontario, S Canada
44 I12 **Cambridge** W Jamaica
184 M8 **Cambridge** Waikato, North Island, NZ
97 O20 **Cambridge** *Lat.* Cantabrigia. E England, UK
32 M12 **Cambridge** Idaho, NW USA
30 K11 **Cambridge** Illinois, N USA
21 Y4 **Cambridge** Maryland, NE USA
19 O11 **Cambridge** Massachusetts, NE USA
29 V7 **Cambridge** Minnesota, N USA
29 N16 **Cambridge** Nebraska, C USA
31 U13 **Cambridge** Ohio, NE USA
8 L7 **Cambridge Bay** Victoria Island, Nunavut, NW Canada
97 O20 **Cambridgeshire** *cultural region* E England, UK
105 U6 **Cambrils de Mar** Cataluña, NE Spain
Cambundi-Catembo *see* Nova Gaia
137 N11 **Çam Burnu** *headland* N Turkey
183 S9 **Camden** New South Wales, SE Australia
23 O6 **Camden** Alabama, S USA
27 U14 **Camden** Arkansas, C USA
21 Y3 **Camden** Delaware, NE USA
19 R7 **Camden** Maine, NE USA
18 I16 **Camden** New Jersey, NE USA
18 I9 **Camden** New York, NE USA
21 R12 **Camden** South Carolina, SE USA
20 H8 **Camden** Tennessee, S USA
25 X9 **Camden** Texas, SW USA
39 S5 **Camden Bay** *bay* S Beaufort Sea
27 U6 **Camdenton** Missouri, C USA
Camellia State *see* Alabama
18 M7 **Camels Hump** ▲ Vermont, NE USA
117 N8 **Camenca** *Rus.* Kamenka. N Moldova
Cameracum *see* Cambrai
22 G9 **Cameron** Louisiana, S USA
25 T9 **Cameron** Texas, SW USA
30 J5 **Cameron** Wisconsin, N USA
10 M12 **Cameron** ≈ British Columbia, W Canada
185 A24 **Cameron Mountains** ▲ South Island, NZ
79 D15 **Cameroon** *off.* Republic of Cameroon, *Fr.* Cameroun. ◆ *republic* W Africa
79 D15 **Cameroon Mountain** ▲ SW Cameroon
Cameroon Ridge *see* Camerounaise, Dorsale
Cameroun *see* Cameroon
79 E14 **Camerounaise, Dorsale** *Eng.* Cameroon Ridge. *ridge* NW Cameroon
171 N3 **Camiling** Luzon, N Philippines
23 T7 **Camilla** Georgia, SE USA
104 G5 **Caminha** Viana do Castelo, N Portugal
35 P7 **Camino** California, W USA
136 B15 **Çamiçi Gölü** ◎ SW Turkey
107 J24 **Cammarata** Sicilia, Italy, C Mediterranean Sea
42 K10 **Camoapa** Boaco, S Nicaragua
58 O13 **Camocim** Ceará, E Brazil
106 D10 **Camogli** Liguria, NW Italy
181 S5 **Camooweal** Queensland, C Australia
55 Y11 **Camopi** E French Guiana
151 Q22 **Camorta** *island* Nicobar Islands, India, NE Indian Ocean
42 I6 **Campamento** Olancho, C Honduras
61 D19 **Campana** Buenos Aires, E Argentina
63 F21 **Campana, Isla** *island* S Chile
104 K11 **Campanario** Extremadura, W Spain
107 L17 **Campania** *Eng.* Champagne. ◈ *region* S Italy
27 Y8 **Campbell** Missouri, C USA
185 K15 **Campbell, Cape** *headland* South Island, NZ
14 J14 **Campbellford** Ontario, SE Canada
31 R13 **Campbell Hill** *hill* Ohio, N USA
192 K13 **Campbell Island** *island* S NZ
175 P13 **Campbell Plateau** *undersea feature* SW Pacific Ocean
10 K17 **Campbell River** Vancouver Island, British Columbia, SW Canada
20 L6 **Campbellsville** Kentucky, S USA
13 O13 **Campbellton** New Brunswick, SE Canada
183 P16 **Campbell Town** Tasmania, SE Australia
183 S9 **Campbelltown** New South Wales, SE Australia
96 G13 **Campbeltown** W Scotland, UK
41 W13 **Campeche** Campeche, SE Mexico
41 W14 **Campeche** ◈ *state* SE Mexico
41 T14 **Campeche, Bahía de** *Eng.* Bay of Campeche. *bay* E Mexico
Campeche, Banco de *see* Campeche Bank
64 C11 **Campeche Bank** *Sp.* Banco de Campeche, Sonda de Campeche. *undersea feature* S Gulf of Mexico
Campeche, Bay of *see* Campeche, Bahía de
Campeche, Sonda de *see* Campeche Bank
44 H7 **Campechuela** Granma, E Cuba
182 M13 **Camperdown** Victoria, SE Australia
167 U6 **Câm Pha** Quang Ninh, N Vietnam
116 H10 **Câmpia Turzii** *Ger.* Jerischmarkt, *Hung.* Aranyosgyéres; *prev.* Cîmpia Turzii, Ghiriș, Gyéres. Cluj, NW Romania
104 K12 **Campillo de Llerena** Extremadura, W Spain
104 L15 **Campillos** Andalucía, S Spain
116 J13 **Câmpina** *prev.* Cîmpina. Prahova, SE Romania
59 Q15 **Campina Grande** Paraíba, E Brazil
60 L9 **Campinas** São Paulo, S Brazil
38 L10 **Camp Kulowiye** Saint Lawrence Island, Alaska, USA
79 D17 **Campo** *var.* Kampo. Sud, SW Cameroon
Campo *see* Ntem
59 N15 **Campo Alegre de Lourdes** Bahia, E Brazil
107 L16 **Campobasso** Molise, C Italy
107 H24 **Campobello di Mazara** Sicilia, Italy, C Mediterranean Sea
Campo Criptana *see* Campo de Criptana
105 O10 **Campo de Criptana** *var.* Campo Criptana. Castilla-La Mancha, C Spain
59 I16 **Campo de Diauarum** *var.* Pôsto Diuarum. Mato Grosso, W Brazil
54 E5 **Campo de la Cruz** Atlántico, N Colombia
105 P11 **Campo de Montiel** *physical region* C Spain
Campo dos Goitacazes *see* Campos
60 H12 **Campo Erê** Santa Catarina, S Brazil
62 L7 **Campo Gallo** Santiago del Estero, N Argentina
59 I20 **Campo Grande** *state capital* Mato Grosso do Sul, SW Brazil
60 K12 **Campo Largo** Paraná, S Brazil
58 N13 **Campo Maior** Piauí, E Brazil
104 I10 **Campo Maior** Portalegre, C Portugal
60 H10 **Campo Mourão** Paraná, S Brazil
60 Q9 **Campos** *var.* Campo dos Goitacazes. Rio de Janeiro, SE Brazil
59 L17 **Campos Belos** Goiás, S Brazil
60 N9 **Campos do Jordão** São Paulo, S Brazil
60 I13 **Campos Novos** Santa Catarina, S Brazil
59 O14 **Campos Sales** Ceará, E Brazil
25 Q9 **Camp San Saba** Texas, SW USA
21 N6 **Campton** Kentucky, S USA
116 I13 **Câmpulung** *prev.* Câmpulung-Mușcel, Cîmpulung. Argeș, S Romania
116 J9 **Câmpulung Moldovenesc** *var.* Cîmpulung Moldovenesc, *Ger.* Kimpolung, *Hung.* Hosszúmezjő. Suceava, NE Romania
Câmpulung-Mușcel *see* Câmpulung
Campus Stellae *see* Santiago
36 L12 **Camp Verde** Arizona, SW USA
25 P11 **Camp Wood** Texas, SW USA
167 V13 **Cam Ranh** Khanh Hoa, S Vietnam
11 Q15 **Camrose** Alberta, SW Canada
Camulodunum *see* Colchester
136 B12 **Çan** Çanakkale, NW Turkey
18 L12 **Canaan** Connecticut, NE USA
9 O13 **Canada** ◆ *commonwealth republic* N North America
197 P6 **Canada Basin** *undersea feature* Arctic Ocean
61 B18 **Cañada de Gómez** Santa Fe, C Argentina
197 P6 **Canada Plain** *undersea feature* Arctic Ocean
61 A18 **Cañada Rosquín** Santa Fe, C Argentina
25 P1 **Canadian** Texas, SW USA
16 K12 **Canadian River** ≈ SW USA
8 L12 **Canadian Shield** *physical region* Canada
63 I18 **Cañadón Grande, Sierra** ▲ S Argentina
55 P9 **Canaima** Bolívar, SE Venezuela
136 B11 **Çanakkale** *var.* Dardanelli; *prev.* Chanak, Kale Sultanie. Çanakkale, W Turkey
136 B12 **Çanakkale** ◈ *province* NW Turkey
136 B11 **Çanakkale Boğazı** *Eng.* Dardanelles. *strait* NW Turkey
187 Q17 **Canala** Province Nord, C New Caledonia
59 A15 **Canamari** Amazonas, W Brazil
18 G10 **Canandaigua** New York, NE USA
18 F10 **Canandaigua Lake** ◎ New York, NE USA
40 G3 **Cananea** Sonora, NW Mexico
56 B8 **Cañar** ◈ *province* C Ecuador
64 N10 **Canarias, Islas** *Eng.* Canary Islands. ◈ *autonomous community* Spain, NE Atlantic Ocean
44 C6 **Canarreos, Archipiélago de los** *island group* W Cuba
Canary Islands *see* Canarias, Islas
42 L13 **Cañas** Guanacaste, NW Costa Rica
18 I10 **Canastota** New York, NE USA
40 K9 **Canatlán** Durango, C Mexico
104 J9 **Cañaveral** Extremadura, W Spain

◆ Country ◇ Dependent Territory ◈ Administrative Region ▲ Mountain ⩓ Volcano ◎ Lake
● Country Capital ○ Dependent Territory Capital × International Airport ▲ Mountain Range ≈ River ⊠ Reservoir

23 *Y11* **Canaveral, Cape** *headland* Florida, SE USA
59 *O18* **Canavieiras** Bahia, E Brazil
43 *R16* **Cañazas** Veraguas, W Panama
106 *H6* **Canazei** Trentino-Alto Adige, N Italy
183 *P6* **Canbelego** New South Wales, SE Australia
183 *R10* **Canberra** ● (Australia) Australian Capital Territory, SE Australia
183 *R10* **Canberra** ✕ Australian Capital Territory, SE Australia
35 *P2* **Canby** California, W USA
29 *S9* **Canby** Minnesota, N USA
103 *N2* **Canche** ≈ N France
102 *L13* **Cancon** Lot-et-Garonne, SW France
41 *Z11* **Cancún** Quintana Roo, SE Mexico
104 *K2* **Candás** Asturias, N Spain
102 *J7* **Cande** Maine-et-Loire, NW France
41 *W14* **Candelaria** Campeche, SE Mexico
24 *J11* **Candelaria** Texas, SW USA
41 *W15* **Candelaria, Río** ≈ Guatemala/Mexico
104 *L8* **Candeleda** Castilla-León, N Spain
Candia *see* Irákleio
41 *P8* **Cándido Aguilar** Tamaulipas, C Mexico
39 *N8* **Candle** Alaska, USA
11 *T14* **Candle Lake** Saskatchewan, C Canada
18 *L13* **Candlewood, Lake** ⊠ Connecticut, NE USA
29 *O3* **Cando** North Dakota, N USA
Canea *see* Chaniá
45 *O12* **Canefield** ✕ (Roseau) SW Dominica
61 *F20* **Canelones** *prev.* Guadalupe. Canelones, S Uruguay
61 *E20* **Canelones** ◈ *department* S Uruguay
Canendiyú *see* Canindeyú
63 *F14* **Cañete** Bío Bío, C Chile
105 *Q9* **Cañete** Castilla-La Mancha, C Spain
Cañete *see* San Vicente de Cañete
27 *P8* **Caney** Kansas, C USA
27 *P8* **Caney River** ≈ Kansas/Oklahoma, C USA
105 *S3* **Canfranc-Estación** Aragón, NE Spain
83 *E14* **Cangamba** *Port.* Vila de Aljustrel. Moxico, E Angola
82 *C12* **Cangandala** Malanje, NW Angola
104 *G4* **Cangas** Galicia, NW Spain
104 *J2* **Cangas del Narcea** Asturias, N Spain
104 *L2* **Cangas de Onís** Asturias, N Spain
161 *S11* **Cangnan** *var.* Lingxi. Zhejiang, SE China
82 *C10* **Cangola** Uíge, NW Angola
83 *E14* **Cangombe** Moxico, E Angola
63 *H21* **Cangrejo, Cerro** ▲ S Argentina
61 *H17* **Canguçu** Rio Grande do Sul, S Brazil
161 *P3* **Cangzhou** Hebei, E China
12 *M7* **Caniapiscau** ≈ Québec, E Canada
12 *M8* **Caniapiscau, Réservoir de** ⊠ Québec, C Canada
107 *J24* **Canicattì** Sicilia, Italy, C Mediterranean Sea
136 *I11* **Canik Dağları** ▲ N Turkey
105 *P14* **Caniles** Andalucía, S Spain
59 *B16* **Canindé** Acre, W Brazil
62 *P6* **Canindeyú** *var.* Canendiyú, Canindiyú. ◈ *department* E Paraguay
Canindiyú *see* Canindeyú
194 *J10* **Canisteo Peninsula** *peninsula* Antarctica
18 *F11* **Canisteo River** ≈ New York, NE USA
40 *M10* **Cañitas** *var.* Cañitas de Felipe Pescador. Zacatecas, C Mexico
Cañitas de Felipe Pescador *see* Cañitas
105 *P15* **Canjáyar** Andalucía, S Spain
136 *I12* **Çankırı** *var.* Chankiri; *anc.* Gangra, Germanicopolis. Çankın, N Turkey
136 *I11* **Çankırı** *var.* Chankiri. ◈ *province* N Turkey
171 *P6* **Canlaon Volcano** ☒ Negros, C Philippines
11 *P16* **Canmore** Alberta, SW Canada
96 *F9* **Canna** *island* NW Scotland, UK
155 *F20* **Cannanore** *var.* Kananur, Kannur. Kerala, SW India
31 *O17* **Cannelton** Indiana, N USA
103 *U15* **Cannes** Alpes-Maritimes, SE France
39 *R5* **Canning River** ≈ Alaska, USA
106 *C6* **Cannobio** Piemonte, NE Italy
97 *L19* **Cannock** C England, UK
28 *M6* **Cannonball River** ≈ North Dakota, N USA
29 *W9* **Cannon Falls** Minnesota, N USA
18 *I11* **Cannonsville Reservoir** ⊠ New York, NE USA
183 *R12* **Cann River** Victoria, SE Australia
61 *I16* **Canoas** Rio Grande do Sul, S Brazil
61 *I14* **Canoas, Rio** ≈ S Brazil
14 *I12* **Canoe Lake** ◎ Ontario, SE Canada
60 *J12* **Canoinhas** Santa Catarina, S Brazil
37 *T6* **Canon City** Colorado, C USA
55 *P8* **Caño Negro** Bolívar, SE Venezuela
173 *X15* **Canonniers Point** *headland* N Mauritius
23 *W6* **Canoochee River** ≈ Georgia, SE USA
11 *V15* **Canora** Saskatchewan, S Canada
45 *Y14* **Canouan** *island* S Saint Vincent and the Grenadines
13 *R15* **Canso** Nova Scotia, SE Canada
104 *M3* **Cantabria** ◈ *autonomous community* N Spain
104 *K3* **Cantábrica, Cordillera** ▲ N Spain
Cantabrigia *see* Cambridge
103 *O12* **Cantal** ◈ *department* C France
105 *N6* **Cantalejo** Castilla-León, N Spain
103 *O12* **Cantal, Monts du** ▲ C France
104 *G8* **Cantanhede** Coimbra, C Portugal
Cantaño *see* Cataño
55 *O6* **Cantaura** Anzoátegui, NE Venezuela
116 *M11* **Cantemir** *Rus.* Kantemir. S Moldova
97 *Q22* **Canterbury** *hist.* Cantwaraburh, *anc.* Durovernum, *Lat.* Cantuaria. SE England, UK
185 *F19* **Canterbury** *off.* Canterbury Region. ◈ *region* South Island, NZ
185 *H20* **Canterbury Bight** *bight* South Island, NZ
185 *H19* **Canterbury Plains** *plain* South Island, NZ
167 *S14* **Cân Thơ** Cân Thơ, S Vietnam
104 *K13* **Cantillana** Andalucía, S Spain
59 *N15* **Canto do Buriti** Piauí, NE Brazil
23 *S2* **Canton** Georgia, SE USA
30 *K12* **Canton** Illinois, N USA
22 *L5* **Canton** Mississippi, S USA
27 *V2* **Canton** Missouri, C USA
18 *J7* **Canton** New York, NE USA
21 *O10* **Canton** North Carolina, SE USA
31 *U12* **Canton** Ohio, N USA
26 *L9* **Canton** Oklahoma, C USA
18 *G12* **Canton** Pennsylvania, NE USA
29 *R11* **Canton** South Dakota, N USA
25 *V7* **Canton** Texas, SW USA
Canton *see* Guangzhou
Canton Island *see* Kanton
26 *L9* **Canton Lake** ⊠ Oklahoma, C USA
106 *D7* **Cantù** Lombardia, N Italy
Cantuaria/Cantwaraburh *see* Canterbury
39 *R10* **Cantwell** Alaska, USA
59 *O16* **Canudos** Bahia, E Brazil
Canusium *see* Puglia, Canosa di
24 *G7* **Canutillo** Texas, SW USA
25 *N3* **Canyon** Texas, SW USA
33 *S12* **Canyon** Wyoming, C USA
32 *K13* **Canyon City** Oregon, NW USA
33 *R10* **Canyon Ferry Lake** ◎ Montana, NW USA
25 *S11* **Canyon Lake** ⊠ Texas, SW USA
167 *T5* **Cao Bằng** *var.* Caobang. Cao Bằng, N Vietnam
160 *J12* **Caodu He** ≈ S China
167 *S14* **Cao Lanh** Đông Thap, S Vietnam
82 *C11* **Caombo** Malanje, NW Angola
Caorach, Cuan na g *see* Sheep Haven
Caozhou *see* Heze
171 *Q12* **Capalulu** Pulau Mangole, E Indonesia
54 *K8* **Capanaparo, Río** ≈ Colombia/Venezuela
58 *L12* **Capanema** Pará, NE Brazil
60 *L10* **Capão Bonito** São Paulo, S Brazil
60 *I13* **Capão Doce, Morro do** ▲ S Brazil
54 *I4* **Capatárida** Falcón, N Venezuela
102 *I15* **Capbreton** Landes, SW France
Cap-Breton, Île du *see* Cape Breton Island
15 *W6* **Cap-Chat** Québec, SE Canada
15 *P11* **Cap-de-la-Madeleine** Québec, SE Canada
103 *N13* **Capdenac** Aveyron, S France
183 *Q15* **Cape Barren Island** *island* Furneaux Group, Tasmania, SE Australia
65 *O18* **Cape Basin** *undersea feature* S Atlantic Ocean
13 *R14* **Cape Breton Island** *Fr.* Île du Cap-Breton. *island* Nova Scotia, SE Canada
23 *Y11* **Cape Canaveral** Florida, SE USA
21 *Y6* **Cape Charles** Virginia, NE USA
77 *P17* **Cape Coast** *prev.* Cape Coast Castle. S Ghana
Cape Coast Castle *see* Cape Coast
19 *Q12* **Cape Cod Bay** *bay* Massachusetts, NE USA
23 *W15* **Cape Coral** Florida, SE USA
181 *R4* **Cape Crawford Roadhouse** Northern Territory, N Australia
9 *Q7* **Cape Dorset** Baffin Island, Nunavut, NE Canada
21 *N8* **Cape Fear River** ≈ North Carolina, SE USA
27 *Y7* **Cape Girardeau** Missouri, C USA
21 *T14* **Cape Island** *island* South Carolina, SE USA
186 *A6* **Capella** ▲ NW PNG
98 *H12* **Capelle aan den IJssel** Zuid-Holland, SW Netherlands
83 *C15* **Capelongo** Huíla, C Angola
18 *J17* **Cape May** New Jersey, NE USA
18 *J17* **Cape May Court House** New Jersey, NE USA
Cape Palmas *see* Harper
8 *I6* **Cape Parry** Northwest Territories, N Canada
65 *P19* **Cape Rise** *undersea feature* SW Indian Ocean
Cape Saint Jacques *see* Vung Tau
Capesterre *see* Capesterre-Belle-Eau
45 *Y6* **Capesterre-Belle-Eau** *var.* Capesterre. Basse Terre, S Guadeloupe
83 *D26* **Cape Town** *var.* Ekapa, *Afr.* Kaapstad, Kapstad. ● (South Africa-legislative capital) Western Cape, SW South Africa
83 *E26* **Cape Town** ✕ Western Cape, SW South Africa
76 *D9* **Cape Verde** *off.* Republic of Cape Verde, *Port.* Cabo Verde, Ilhas do Cabo Verde. ◆ *republic* E Atlantic Ocean
64 *L11* **Cape Verde Basin** *undersea feature* E Atlantic Ocean
64 *L10* **Cape Verde Plain** *undersea feature* E Atlantic Ocean
Cape Verde Plateau/Cape Verde Rise *see* Cape Verde Terrace
64 *L11* **Cape Verde Terrace** *var.* Cape Verde Plateau, Cape Verde Rise. *undersea feature* E Atlantic Ocean
181 *V2* **Cape York Peninsula** *peninsula* Queensland, N Australia
44 *M8* **Cap-Haïtien** *var.* Le Cap. N Haiti
43 *T15* **Capira** Panamá, C Panama
14 *K8* **Capitachouane** ≈ Québec, SE Canada
14 *L8* **Capitachouane, Lac** ◎ Québec, SE Canada
37 *T13* **Capitan** New Mexico, SW USA
194 *G3* **Capitán Arturo Prat** *Chilean research station* South Shetland Islands, Antarctica
37 *S13* **Capitan Mountains** ▲ New Mexico, SW USA
62 *M3* **Capitán Pablo Lagerenza** *var.* Mayor Pablo Lagerenza. Chaco, N Paraguay
37 *T13* **Capitan Peak** ▲ New Mexico, SW USA
188 *H5* **Capitol Hill** Saipan, S Northern Mariana Islands
60 *I9* **Capivara, Represa** ⊠ S Brazil
61 *J16* **Capivari** Rio Grande do Sul, S Brazil
113 *H15* **Čapljina** Federacija Bosna I Hercegovina, S Bosnia and Herzegovina
83 *M15* **Capoche** *var.* Kapoche. ≈ Mozambique/Zambia
Capo Delgado, Província de *see* Cabo Delgado
107 *K17* **Capodichino** ✕ (Napoli) Campania, S Italy
Capodistria *see* Koper
106 *E12* **Capraia, Isola** *island* Archipelago Toscano, C Italy
107 *B16* **Caprara, Punta** *var.* Punta dello Scorno. *headland* Isola Asinara, W Italy
Capraria, Isola di to Capraia, Isola *see* Cabrera
14 *F10* **Capreol** Ontario, S Canada
107 *K18* **Capri** Campania, S Italy
175 *S9* **Capricorn Tablemount** *undersea feature* W Pacific Ocean
107 *J18* **Capri, Isola di** *island* S Italy
83 *G16* **Caprivi** ◈ *district* NE Namibia
Caprivi Concession *see* Caprivi Strip
83 *F16* **Caprivi Strip** *Ger.* Caprivizipfel; *prev.* Caprivi Concession. *cultural region* NE Namibia
Caprivizipfel *see* Caprivi Strip
25 *O5* **Cap Rock Escarpment** *cliffs* Texas, SW USA
15 *R10* **Cap-Rouge** Québec, SE Canada
Cap Saint-Jacques *see* Vung Tau
38 *F12* **Captain Cook** Hawai'i, USA, C Pacific Ocean
183 *R10* **Captains Flat** New South Wales, SE Australia
102 *K14* **Captieux** Gironde, SW France
107 *K17* **Capua** Campania, S Italy
54 *F14* **Caquetá** *off.* Departamanto del Caquetá. ◈ *province* S Colombia
54 *E13* **Caquetá, Río** *var.* Rio Japurá, Yapurá. ≈ Brazil/Colombia *see also* Japurá, Rio
CAR *see* Central African Republic
Cara *see* Kara
57 *I16* **Carabaya, Cordillera** ▲ E Peru
54 *K5* **Carabobo** *off.* Estado Carabobo. ◈ *state* N Venezuela
116 *I14* **Caracal** Olt, S Romania
58 *F10* **Caracaraí** Rondônia, W Brazil
54 *L5* **Caracas** ● (Venezuela) Distrito Federal, N Venezuela
54 *I5* **Carache** Trujillo, N Venezuela
60 *N10* **Caraguatatuba** São Paulo, S Brazil
Caralis *see* Cagliari
54 *E9* **Caramanta** Antioquia, W Colombia
171 *P4* **Caramoan** Catanduanes Island, N Philippines
Caramurat *see* Mihail Kogălniceanu
116 *F12* **Caransebeş** *Ger.* Karansebesch, *Hung.* Karánsebes. Caraş-Severin, SW Romania
Carapella *see* Carapelle
107 *M16* **Carapelle** *var.* Carapella. ≈ SE Italy
55 *O9* **Carapo** Bolívar, SE Venezuela
13 *P13* **Caraquet** New Brunswick, SE Canada
Caras *see* Caraz
116 *F12* **Caraşova** *Hung.* Krassóvár. Caraş-Severin, SW Romania
116 *F12* **Caraş-Severin** ◈ *county* SW Romania
42 *M5* **Caratasca, Laguna de** *lagoon* NE Honduras
58 *C13* **Carauari** Amazonas, NW Brazil
Caravaca *see* Caravaca de la Cruz
105 *Q12* **Caravaca de la Cruz** *var.* Caravaca. Murcia, SE Spain
106 *E7* **Caravaggio** Lombardia, N Italy
107 *C18* **Caravai, Passo di** *pass* Sardegna, Italy, C Mediterranean Sea
59 *O19* **Caravelas** Bahia, E Brazil
56 *C12* **Caraz** *var.* Caras. Ancash, W Peru
61 *H14* **Carazinho** Rio Grande do Sul, S Brazil
42 *J11* **Carazo** ◈ *department* SW Nicaragua
Carballiño *see* O Carballiño
104 *G2* **Carballo** Galicia, NW Spain
11 *W16* **Carberry** Manitoba, S Canada
40 *F4* **Carbó** Sonora, NW Mexico
107 *C20* **Carbonara, Capo** *headland* Sardegna, Italy, C Mediterranean Sea
37 *Q5* **Carbondale** Colorado, C USA
30 *L17* **Carbondale** Illinois, N USA
27 *Q4* **Carbondale** Kansas, C USA
18 *I13* **Carbondale** Pennsylvania, NE USA
13 *V12* **Carbonear** Newfoundland and Labrador, SE Canada
105 *Q9* **Carboneras de Guadazaón** *var.* Carboneras de Guadazón. Castilla-La Mancha, C Spain
Carboneras de Guadazón *see* Carboneras de Guadazaón
23 *O3* **Carbon Hill** Alabama, S USA
107 *B20* **Carbonia** *var.* Carbonia Centro. Sardegna, Italy, C Mediterranean Sea
Carbonia Centro *see* Carbonia
105 *S10* **Carcaixent** País Valenciano, E Spain
Carcaso *see* Carcassonne
65 *B24* **Carcass Island** *island* NW Falkland Islands
103 *O16* **Carcassonne** *anc.* Carcaso. Aude, S France
105 *R12* **Carche** ▲ S Spain
56 *A13* **Carchi** ◈ *province* N Ecuador
10 *I8* **Carcross** Yukon Territory, W Canada
Cardamomes, Chaîne des *see* Krâvanh, Chuŏr Phnum
155 *G22* **Cardamom Hills** ▲ SW India
Cardamom Mountains *see* Krâvanh, Chuŏr Phnum
104 *M12* **Cardeña** Andalucía, S Spain
44 *D4* **Cárdenas** Matanzas, W Cuba
41 *O11* **Cárdenas** San Luis Potosí, C Mexico
41 *U15* **Cárdenas** Tabasco, SE Mexico
63 *H21* **Cardiel, Lago** ◎ S Argentina
97 *K22* **Cardiff** *Wel.* Caerdydd. ◐ S Wales, UK
97 *J22* **Cardiff-Wales** ✕ S Wales, UK
97 *I21* **Cardigan** *Wel.* Aberteifi. SW Wales, UK
97 *I20* **Cardigan** *cultural region* W Wales, UK
97 *I20* **Cardigan Bay** *bay* W Wales, UK
19 *N8* **Cardigan, Mount** ▲ New Hampshire, NE USA
14 *M13* **Cardinal** Ontario, SE Canada
105 *V5* **Cardona** Cataluña, NE Spain
61 *E19* **Cardona** Soriano, SW Uruguay
105 *V4* **Cardoner** ≈ NE Spain
11 *Q17* **Cardston** Alberta, SW Canada
181 *W5* **Cardwell** Queensland, NE Australia
116 *G8* **Carei** *Ger.* Gross-Karol, Karol, *Hung.* Nagykároly; *prev.* Careii-Mari. Satu Mare, NW Romania
Careii-Mari *see* Carei
58 *F13* **Careiro** Amazonas, NW Brazil
102 *J4* **Carentan** Manche, N France
104 *M2* **Cares** ≈ N Spain
33 *P14* **Carey** Idaho, NW USA
31 *S12* **Carey** Ohio, N USA
25 *P4* **Carey** Texas, SW USA
180 *L11* **Carey, Lake** ◎ Western Australia
173 *O8* **Cargados Carajos Bank** *undersea feature* C Indian Ocean
102 *G6* **Carhaix-Plouguer** Finistère, NW France
61 *A22* **Carhué** Buenos Aires, E Argentina
55 *O5* **Cariaco** Sucre, NE Venezuela
107 *O20* **Cariati** Calabria, SW Italy
44 *I11* **Caribbean Sea** *sea* W Atlantic Ocean
11 *N15* **Cariboo Mountains** ▲ British Columbia, SW Canada
11 *W9* **Caribou** Manitoba, C Canada
19 *S2* **Caribou** Maine, NE USA
11 *P10* **Caribou Mountains** ▲ Alberta, SW Canada
Caribrod *see* Dimitrovgrad
40 *I6* **Carichic** Chihuahua, N Mexico
103 *R3* **Carignan** Ardennes, N France
183 *Q5* **Carinda** New South Wales, SE Australia
105 *R6* **Cariñena** Aragón, NE Spain
107 *I23* **Carini** Sicilia, Italy, C Mediterranean Sea
107 *K17* **Carinola** Campania, S Italy
Carinthi *see* Kärnten
55 *O5* **Caripe** Monagas, NE Venezuela
55 *P5* **Caripito** Monagas, NE Venezuela
15 *W7* **Carleton** Québec, SE Canada
31 *S10* **Carleton** Michigan, N USA
13 *O14* **Carleton, Mount** ▲ New Brunswick, SE Canada
14 *L13* **Carleton Place** Ontario, SE Canada
35 *V3* **Carlin** Nevada, W USA
30 *K14* **Carlinville** Illinois, N USA
97 *K14* **Carlisle** *anc.* Caer Luel, Luguvallium, Luguvallum. NW England, UK
27 *V11* **Carlisle** Arkansas, C USA
31 *N15* **Carlisle** Indiana, N USA
29 *V14* **Carlisle** Iowa, C USA
21 *N5* **Carlisle** Kentucky, S USA
18 *F15* **Carlisle** Pennsylvania, NE USA
21 *Q11* **Carlisle** South Carolina, SE USA
38 *J17* **Carlisle Island** *island* Aleutian Islands, Alaska, USA
27 *R7* **Carl Junction** Missouri, C USA
107 *A20* **Carloforte** Sardegna, Italy, C Mediterranean Sea
Carlopago *see* Karlobag
61 *B21* **Carlos Casares** Buenos Aires, E Argentina
61 *E18* **Carlos Reyles** Durazno, C Uruguay
61 *A21* **Carlos Tejedor** Buenos Aires, E Argentina
97 *F19* **Carlow** *Ir.* Ceatharlach. SE Ireland
97 *F19* **Carlow** *Ir.* Cheatharlach. *cultural region* SE Ireland
96 *F7* **Carloway** NW Scotland, UK
Carlsbad *see* Karlovy Vary
35 *U17* **Carlsbad** California, W USA
37 *U15* **Carlsbad** New Mexico, SW USA
173 *O5* **Carlsberg Ridge** *undersea feature* S Arabian Sea
Carlsruhe *see* Karlsruhe
29 *W6* **Carlton** Minnesota, N USA
11 *V17* **Carlyle** Saskatchewan, S Canada
30 *L15* **Carlyle** Illinois, N USA
30 *L15* **Carlyle Lake** ⊠ Illinois, N USA
10 *H7* **Carmacks** Yukon Territory, W Canada
106 *B9* **Carmagnola** Piemonte, NW Italy
11 *X16* **Carman** Manitoba, S Canada
Carmana/Carmania *see* Kermān
97 *I21* **Carmarthen** SW Wales, UK
97 *I21* **Carmarthen** *cultural region* SW Wales, UK
97 *I22* **Carmarthen Bay** *inlet* SW Wales, UK
103 *N14* **Carmaux** Tarn, S France
35 *N11* **Carmel** California, W USA
31 *O13* **Carmel** Indiana, N USA
18 *L13* **Carmel** New York, NE USA
97 *H18* **Carmel Head** *headland* NW Wales, UK
42 *E2* **Carmelita** Petén, N Guatemala
61 *D19* **Carmelo** Colonia, SW Uruguay
41 *V14* **Carmen** *var.* Ciudad del Carmen. Campeche, SE Mexico
61 *A25* **Carmen de Patagones** Buenos Aires, E Argentina
40 *F8* **Carmen, Isla** *island* W Mexico
40 *M5* **Carmen, Sierra del** ▲ NW Mexico
30 *M16* **Carmi** Illinois, N USA
35 *O7* **Carmichael** California, W USA
Carmiel *see* Karmi'él
25 *U11* **Carmine** Texas, SW USA
104 *K14* **Carmona** Andalucía, S Spain
Carmona *see* Uíge
Carnaro *see* Kvarner
14 *I13* **Carnarvon** Ontario, SE Canada
83 *G24* **Carnarvon** Northern Cape, W South Africa
Carnarvon *see* Caernarfon
180 *K9* **Carnarvon Range** ▲ Western Australia
180 *G9* **Carnarvon** Western Australia
Carn Domhnach *see* Carndonagh
96 *E13* **Carndonagh** *Ir.* Carn Domhnach. NW Ireland
11 *V17* **Carnduff** Saskatchewan, S Canada
26 *L11* **Carnegie** Oklahoma, C USA
180 *L9* **Carnegie, Lake** *salt lake* Western Australia
193 *U8* **Carnegie Ridge** *undersea feature* E Pacific Ocean
96 *H9* **Carn Eige** ▲ N Scotland, UK
182 *F5* **Carnes** South Australia
194 *J12* **Carney Island** *island* Antarctica
18 *H16* **Carneys Point** New Jersey, NE USA
Carniche, Alpi *see* Karnische Alpen
151 *Q21* **Car Nicobar** *island* Nicobar Islands, India, NE Indian Ocean
79 *H15* **Carnot** Mambéré-Kadéï, W Central African Republic
182 *F10* **Carnot, Cape** *headland* South Australia
96 *K11* **Carnoustie** E Scotland, UK
97 *F20* **Carnsore Point** *Ir.* Ceann an Chairn. *headland* SE Ireland
8 *H7* **Carnwath** ≈ Northwest Territories, NW Canada
31 *R8* **Caro** Michigan, N USA
23 *Z15* **Carol City** Florida, SE USA
59 *L14* **Carolina** Maranhão, E Brazil
45 *U5* **Carolina** E Puerto Rico
21 *V12* **Carolina Beach** North Carolina, SE USA
Caroline Island *see* Millennium Island
189 *N15* **Caroline Islands** *island group* C Micronesia
192 *H7* **Caroline Ridge** *undersea feature* E Philippine Sea
Carolopois *see* Châlons-en-Champagne
45 *V14* **Caroni Arena Dam** ⊠ Trinidad, Trinidad and Tobago
Caronie, Monti *see* Nebrodi, Monti
55 *P7* **Caroní, Río** ≈ E Venezuela
45 *U14* **Caroni River** ≈ Trinidad, Trinidad and Tobago
Caronium *see* A Coruña
54 *J5* **Carora** Lara, N Venezuela
116 *J9* **Carpathian Mountains** *var.* Carpathians, *Cz./Pol.* Karpaty, *Ger.* Karpaten. ▲ E Europe
Carpathians *see* Carpathian Mountains
Carpathos/Carpathus *see* Kárpathos
116 *H12* **Carpaţii Meridionali** *var.* Alpi Transilvaniei, Carpaţii Sudici, *Eng.* South Carpathians, Transylvanian Alps, *Ger.* Südkarpaten, Transsylvanische Alpen, *Hung.* Déli-Kárpátok, Erdélyi-Havasok. ▲ C Romania
Carpaţii Sudici *see* Carpaţii Meridionali
181 *T2* **Carpentaria, Gulf of** *gulf* N Australia
Carpentoracte *see* Carpentras
103 *R14* **Carpentras** *anc.* Carpentoracte. Vaucluse, SE France
106 *F9* **Carpi** Emilia-Romagna, N Italy
116 *E11* **Cărpiniş** *Hung.* Gyertyámos. Timiş, W Romania
35 *R14* **Carpinteria** California, W USA
23 *S9* **Carrabelle** Florida, SE USA
Carraig Aonair *see* Fastnet Rock
Carraig Fhearghais *see* Carrickfergus
Carraig Mhachaire Rois *see* Carrickmacross
Carraig na Siúire *see* Carrick-on-Suir
Carrantual *see* Carrauntoohil
106 *E10* **Carrara** Toscana, C Italy
61 *F20* **Carrasco** ✕ (Montevideo) Canelones, S Uruguay
105 *P9* **Carrascosa del Campo** Castilla-La Mancha, C Spain
54 *H4* **Carrasquero** Zulia, NW Venezuela
183 *O9* **Carrathool** New South Wales, SE Australia
Carrauntohil *see* Carrauntoohil
97 *B21* **Carrauntoohil** *Ir.* Carrantual, Carrauntohil, Corrán Tuathail. ▲ SW Ireland
45 *Y15* **Carriacou** *island* N Grenada
97 *G15* **Carrickfergus** *Ir.* Carraig Fhearghais. NE Northern Ireland, UK
97 *F16* **Carrickmacross** *Ir.* Carraig Mhachaire Rois. N Ireland
97 *D16* **Carrick-on-Shannon** *Ir.* Cora Droma Rúisc. NW Ireland
97 *E20* **Carrick-on-Suir** *Ir.* Carraig na Siúire. S Ireland
182 *I7* **Carrieton** South Australia
40 *L7* **Carrillo** Chihuahua, N Mexico
29 *O4* **Carrington** North Dakota, N USA
104 *M4* **Carrión** ≈ N Spain
104 *M4* **Carrión de los Condes** Castilla-León, N Spain
25 *P13* **Carrizo Springs** Texas, SW USA
37 *S13* **Carrizozo** New Mexico, SW USA
29 *T13* **Carroll** Iowa, C USA
23 *N4* **Carrollton** Alabama, S USA
23 *R3* **Carrollton** Georgia, SE USA
30 *K14* **Carrollton** Illinois, N USA
20 *L4* **Carrollton** Kentucky, S USA
31 *R8* **Carrollton** Michigan, N USA
27 *T3* **Carrollton** Missouri, C USA
31 *U12* **Carrollton** Ohio, N USA
25 *T6* **Carrollton** Texas, SW USA
11 *U14* **Carrot** ≈ Saskatchewan, S Canada
11 *U14* **Carrot River** Saskatchewan, C Canada
18 *J7* **Carry Falls Reservoir** ⊠ New York, NE USA
136 *L11* **Çarşamba** Samsun, N Turkey
28 *L6* **Carson** North Dakota, N USA
35 *Q6* **Carson City** *state capital* Nevada, W USA
35 *R6* **Carson River** ≈ Nevada, W USA
35 *S5* **Carson Sink** *salt flat* Nevada, W USA
11 *Q16* **Carstairs** Alberta, SW Canada
Carstensz, Puntjak *see* Jaya, Puncak
54 *E5* **Cartagena** *var.* Cartagena de los Indes. Bolívar, NW Colombia
105 *R13* **Cartagena** *anc.* Carthago Nova. Murcia, SE Spain
54 *E13* **Cartagena de Chaira** Caquetá, S Colombia
Cartagena de los Indes *see* Cartagena
54 *D10* **Cartago** Valle del Cauca, W Colombia
43 *N14* **Cartago** Cartago, C Costa Rica
42 *M14* **Cartago** *off.* Provincia de Cartago. ◈ *province* C Costa Rica
25 *O11* **Carta Valley** Texas, SW USA
104 *F10* **Cartaxo** Santarém, C Portugal
104 *I14* **Cartaya** Andalucía, S Spain
Carteret Islands *see* Tulun Islands
29 *S15* **Carter Lake** Iowa, C USA
23 *S3* **Cartersville** Georgia, SE USA
185 *M14* **Carterton** Wellington, North Island, NZ
30 *J13* **Carthage** Illinois, N USA
22 *L5* **Carthage** Mississippi, S USA
27 *R7* **Carthage** Missouri, C USA
18 *I8* **Carthage** New York, NE USA
21 *T10* **Carthage** North Carolina, SE USA
20 *K8* **Carthage** Tennessee, S USA
25 *X7* **Carthage** Texas, SW USA
74 *M5* **Carthage** ✕ (Tunis) N Tunisia
Carthago Nova *see* Cartagena
14 *E10* **Cartier** Ontario, S Canada

13 S8 **Cartwright** Newfoundland and Labrador, E Canada
55 P9 **Caruana de Montaña** Bolívar, SE Venezuela
59 Q15 **Caruaru** Pernambuco, E Brazil
55 P5 **Carúpano** Sucre, NE Venezuela
Carusbur see Cherbourg
58 M12 **Carutapera** Maranhão, E Brazil
27 Y9 **Caruthersville** Missouri, C USA
103 O1 **Carvin** Pas-de-Calais, N France
58 E12 **Carvoeiro** Amazonas, NW Brazil
104 E10 **Carvoeiro, Cabo** *headland* C Portugal
21 U9 **Cary** North Carolina, SE USA
182 M3 **Caryapundy Swamp** *wetland* New South Wales/Queensland, SE Australia
65 E24 **Carysfort, Cape** *headland* East Falkland, Falkland Islands
74 F6 **Casablanca** *Ar.* Dar-el-Beida. NW Morocco
60 M8 **Casa Branca** São Paulo, S Brazil
36 L14 **Casa Grande** Arizona, SW USA
106 C8 **Casale Monferrato** Piemonte, NW Italy
106 E8 **Casalpusterlengo** Lombardia, N Italy
54 H10 **Casanare** *off.* Intendencia de Casanare. ◈ *province* C Colombia
55 P5 **Casanay** Sucre, NE Venezuela
24 K11 **Casa Piedra** Texas, SW USA
107 Q19 **Casarano** Puglia, SE Italy
42 J11 **Casares** Carazo, W Nicaragua
105 R10 **Casas Ibáñez** Castilla-La Mancha, C Spain
61 I14 **Casca** Rio Grande do Sul, S Brazil
172 I17 **Cascade** Mahé, NE Seychelles
33 N13 **Cascade** Idaho, NW USA
29 Y13 **Cascade** Iowa, C USA
33 R9 **Cascade** Montana, NW USA
185 B20 **Cascade Point** *headland* South Island, NZ
32 G13 **Cascade Range** ⛰ Oregon/Washington, NW USA
33 N12 **Cascade Reservoir** ⊞ Idaho, NW USA
193 P3 **Cascadia Basin** *undersea feature* NE Pacific Ocean
104 E11 **Cascais** Lisboa, C Portugal
15 W7 **Cascapédia** ⁓ Québec, SE Canada
59 I22 **Cascavel** Ceará, E Brazil
60 G11 **Cascavel** Paraná, S Brazil
106 I13 **Cascia** Umbria, C Italy
106 F11 **Cascina** Toscana, C Italy
19 Q8 **Casco Bay** *bay* Maine, NE USA
194 J7 **Case Island** *island* Antarctica
106 B8 **Caselle** ✕ (Torino) Piemonte, NW Italy
107 K17 **Caserta** Campania, S Italy
15 N8 **Casey** Québec, SE Canada
30 M14 **Casey** Illinois, N USA
195 Y12 **Casey** *Australian research station* Antarctica
195 W3 **Casey Bay** *bay* Antarctica
80 Q11 **Caseyr, Raas** *headland* NE Somalia
97 D20 **Cashel** *Ir.* Caiseal. S Ireland
54 G6 **Casigua** Zulia, W Venezuela
61 B19 **Casilda** Santa Fe, C Argentina
Casim see General Toshevo
183 V4 **Casino** New South Wales, SE Australia
Casinum see Cassino
111 E17 **Čáslav** *Ger.* Tschaslau. Střední Čechy, C Czech Republic
56 C13 **Casma** Ancash, C Peru
167 S7 **Ca, Sông** ⁓ N Vietnam
107 K17 **Casoria** Campania, S Italy
105 T6 **Caspe** Aragón, NE Spain
33 X15 **Casper** Wyoming, C USA
127 P13 **Caspian Depression** *Kaz.* Kaspiy Mangy Oypaty, *Rus.* Prikaspiyskaya Nizmennost'. *depression* Kazakhstan/Russian Federation
138 Kk9 **Caspian Sea** *Az.* Xäzär Dänizi, *Kaz.* Kaspiy Tengizi, *Per.* Baḩr-e Khazar, Daryā-ye Khazar, *Rus.* Kaspiyskoye More. *inland sea* Asia/Europe
83 L14 **Cassacatiza** Tete, NW Mozambique
Cassai see Kasai
82 F13 **Cassamba** Moxico, E Angola
107 N20 **Cassano allo Ionio** Calabria, SE Italy
31 S8 **Cass City** Michigan, N USA
Cassel see Kassel
14 M13 **Casselman** Ontario, SE Canada
29 R5 **Casselton** North Dakota, N USA
59 M16 **Cássia** *var.* Santa Rita de Cassia. Bahia, E Brazil
10 J9 **Cassiar** British Columbia, W Canada
10 K10 **Cassiar Mountains** ⛰ British Columbia, W Canada
83 C15 **Cassinga** Huíla, SW Angola
107 J16 **Cassino** *prev.* San Germano; *anc.* Casinum. Lazio, C Italy
29 T4 **Cass Lake** Minnesota, N USA
29 T4 **Cass Lake** ◎ Minnesota, N USA
31 P10 **Cassopolis** Michigan, N USA
31 S8 **Cass River** ⁓ Michigan, N USA
27 S8 **Cassville** Missouri, C USA
Castamoni see Kastamonu
58 L12 **Castanhal** Pará, NE Brazil
104 G8 **Castanheira de Pêra** Leiria, C Portugal
41 N7 **Castaños** Coahuila de Zaragoza, NE Mexico
108 I10 **Castasegna** Graubünden, SE Switzerland
106 D8 **Casteggio** Lombardia, N Italy
107 K23 **Castelbuono** Sicilia, Italy, C Mediterranean Sea
107 K15 **Castel di Sangro** Abruzzo, C Italy
106 H7 **Castelfranco Veneto** Veneto, NE Italy
102 K14 **Casteljaloux** Lot-et-Garonne, SW France
107 L18 **Castellabate** *var.* Santa Maria di Castellabate. Campania, S Italy
107 I23 **Castellammare del Golfo** Sicilia, Italy, C Mediterranean Sea
107 H22 **Castellammare, Golfo di** *gulf* Sicilia, Italy, C Mediterranean Sea
103 U15 **Castellane** Alpes-de-Haute-Provence, SE France
107 O18 **Castellaneta** Puglia, SE Italy
106 E9 **Castel l'Arquato** Emilia-Romagna, C Italy
61 E21 **Castelli** Buenos Aires, E Argentina
105 T9 **Castelló de la Plana** *var.* Castellón. País Valenciano, E Spain
105 S8 **Castellón** ◈ *province* País Valenciano, E Spain
Castellón see Castelló de la Plana
105 S7 **Castellote** Aragón, NE Spain
103 N16 **Castelnaudary** Aude, S France
102 L16 **Castelnau-Magnoac** Hautes-Pyrénées, S France
106 F10 **Castelnovo ne' Monti** Emilia-Romagna, C Italy
Castelnuovo see Herceg-Novi
104 H9 **Castelo Branco** Castelo Branco, C Portugal
104 H8 **Castelo Branco** ◈ *district* C Portugal
104 I10 **Castelo de Vide** Portalegre, C Portugal
104 G9 **Castelo do Bode, Barragem do** ⊞ C Portugal
106 G10 **Castel San Pietro Terme** Emilia-Romagna, C Italy
107 B17 **Castelsardo** Sardegna, Italy, C Mediterranean Sea
102 M14 **Castelsarrasin** Tarn-et-Garonne, S France
107 I24 **Casteltermini** Sicilia, Italy, C Mediterranean Sea
107 H24 **Castelvetrano** Sicilia, Italy, C Mediterranean Sea
182 L12 **Casterton** Victoria, SE Australia
102 J15 **Castets** Landes, SW France
106 H12 **Castiglione del Lago** Umbria, C Italy
106 F13 **Castiglione della Pescaia** Toscana, C Italy
106 F8 **Castiglione delle Stiviere** Lombardia, N Italy
104 M9 **Castilla-La Mancha** ◈ *autonomous community* NE Spain
104 L5 **Castilla-León** *var.* Castillia y Leon. ◈ *autonomous community* NW Spain
105 N10 **Castilla Nueva** *cultural region* C Spain
105 N6 **Castilla Vieja** *cultural region* N Spain
Castillia y Leon see Castilla-León
Castillo de Locubim see Castillo de Locubín
105 N14 **Castillo de Locubín** *var.* Castillo de Locubim. Andalucía, S Spain
102 K13 **Castillon-la-Bataille** Gironde, SW France
63 I19 **Castillo, Pampa del** *plain* S Argentina
61 G19 **Castillos** Rocha, SE Uruguay
97 B16 **Castlebar** *Ir.* Caisleán an Bharraigh. W Ireland
97 F16 **Castleblayney** *Ir.* Baile na Lorgan. N Ireland
45 O11 **Castle Bruce** E Dominica
36 M5 **Castle Dale** Utah, W USA
36 I14 **Castle Dome Peak** ▲ Arizona, SW USA
97 J14 **Castle Douglas** S Scotland, UK
97 E14 **Castlefinn** *Ir.* Caisleán na Finne. NW Ireland
97 M17 **Castleford** N England, UK
11 O17 **Castlegar** British Columbia, SW Canada
64 B12 **Castle Harbour** *inlet* Bermuda, NW Atlantic Ocean
21 V12 **Castle Hayne** North Carolina, SE USA
97 B20 **Castleisland** *Ir.* Oileán Ciarral. SW Ireland
183 N12 **Castlemaine** Victoria, SE Australia
37 R5 **Castle Peak** ▲ Colorado, C USA
33 O13 **Castle Peak** ▲ Idaho, NW USA
184 N13 **Castlepoint** Wellington, North Island, NZ
97 D17 **Castlerea** *Ir.* An Caisleán Riabhach. W Ireland
97 G15 **Castlereagh** *Ir.* An Caisleán Riabhach. N Northern Ireland, UK
183 R6 **Castlereagh River** ⁓ New South Wales, SE Australia
37 T5 **Castle Rock** Colorado, C USA
30 K7 **Castle Rock Lake** ⊞ Wisconsin, N USA
65 G25 **Castle Rock Point** *headland* S Saint Helena
97 I16 **Castletown** SE Isle of Man
29 R9 **Castlewood** South Dakota, N USA
11 R15 **Castor** Alberta, SW Canada
14 M13 **Castor** ⁓ Ontario, SE Canada
27 X7 **Castor River** ⁓ Missouri, C USA
Castra Albiensium see Castres
Castra Regina see Regensburg
103 N15 **Castres** *anc.* Castra Albiensium. Tarn, S France
98 H9 **Castricum** Noord-Holland, W Netherlands
45 S11 **Castries** ● (Saint Lucia) N Saint Lucia
60 J11 **Castro** Paraná, S Brazil
63 F17 **Castro** Los Lagos, W Chile
104 H7 **Castro Daire** Viseu, N Portugal
104 M13 **Castro del Río** Andalucía, S Spain
Castrogiovanni see Enna
104 H14 **Castro Marim** Faro, S Portugal
104 J2 **Castropol** Asturias, N Spain
105 O2 **Castro-Urdiales** *var.* Castro Urdiales. Cantabria, N Spain
104 G13 **Castro Verde** Beja, S Portugal
107 N19 **Castrovillari** Calabria, SW Italy
35 N10 **Castroville** California, W USA
25 R12 **Castroville** Texas, SW USA
104 K11 **Castuera** Extremadura, W Spain
61 F19 **Casupá** Florida, S Uruguay
185 A22 **Caswell Sound** *sound* South Island, NZ
137 Q13 **Çat** Erzurum, NE Turkey
42 K6 **Catacamas** Olancho, C Honduras
56 A10 **Catacaos** Piura, NW Peru
22 I7 **Catahoula Lake** ◎ Louisiana, S USA
137 S15 **Çatak** Van, SE Turkey
137 S15 **Çatak Çayi** ⁓ SE Turkey
114 O12 **Çatalca** İstanbul, NW Turkey
114 O12 **Çatalca Yarımadası** *physical region* NW Turkey
62 H6 **Catalina** Antofagasta, N Chile
Catalonia see Cataluña
105 U5 **Cataluña** *Cat.* Catalunya; *Eng.* Catalonia. ◈ *autonomous community* N Spain
Catalunya see Cataluña
62 I7 **Catamarca** *off.* Provincia de Catamarca. ◈ *province* NW Argentina
Catamarca see San Fernando del Valle de Catamarca
83 M16 **Catandica** Manica, C Mozambique
171 P4 **Catanduanes Island** *island* N Philippines
60 K8 **Catanduva** São Paulo, S Brazil
107 L24 **Catania** Sicilia, Italy, C Mediterranean Sea
107 M24 **Catania, Golfo di** *gulf* Sicilia, Italy, C Mediterranean Sea
45 U5 **Cataño** *var.* Cantaño. E Puerto Rico
107 O21 **Catanzaro** Calabria, SW Italy
107 O22 **Catanzaro Marina** *var.* Marina di Catanzaro. Calabria, S Italy
25 Q14 **Catarina** Texas, SW USA
171 Q5 **Catarman** Samar, C Philippines
105 S10 **Catarroja** País Valenciano, E Spain
21 R11 **Catawba River** ⁓ North Carolina/South Carolina, SE USA
171 Q5 **Catbalogan** Samar, C Philippines
14 I14 **Catchacoma** Ontario, SE Canada
41 S15 **Catemaco** Veracruz-Llave, SE Mexico
Cathair na Mart see Westport
Cathair Saidhbhín see Cahersiveen
31 P5 **Cat Head Point** *headland* Michigan, N USA
23 Q2 **Cathedral Caverns** *cave* Alabama, S USA
35 V16 **Cathedral City** California, W USA
24 K10 **Cathedral Mountain** ▲ Texas, SW USA
32 G10 **Cathlamet** Washington, NW USA
76 G13 **Catió** S Guinea-Bissau
55 O10 **Catisimiña** Bolívar, SE Venezuela
44 J3 **Cat Island** *island* C Bahamas
12 B9 **Cat Lake** Ontario, S Canada
21 P5 **Catlettsburg** Kentucky, S USA
185 D24 **Catlins** ⁓ South Island, NZ
35 R1 **Catnip Mountain** ▲ Nevada, W USA
41 Z11 **Catoche, Cabo** *headland* SE Mexico
27 P9 **Catoosa** Oklahoma, C USA
41 N10 **Catorce** San Luis Potosí, C Mexico
63 I14 **Catriel** Río Negro, C Argentina
62 K13 **Catriló** La Pampa, C Argentina
58 F11 **Catrimani** Roraima, N Brazil
58 E10 **Catrimani, Rio** ⁓ N Brazil
18 K11 **Catskill** New York, NE USA
18 K11 **Catskill Creek** ⁓ New York, NE USA
18 J11 **Catskill Mountains** ⛰ New York, NE USA
18 D11 **Cattaraugus Creek** ⁓ New York, NE USA
Cattaro see Kotor
Cattaro, Bocche di see Kotorska, Boka
107 I24 **Cattolica Eraclea** Sicilia, Italy, C Mediterranean Sea
83 B14 **Catumbela** ⁓ W Angola
83 N14 **Catur** Niassa, N Mozambique
82 C10 **Cauale** ⁓ NE Angola
171 O2 **Cauayan** Luzon, N Philippines
54 C12 **Cauca** *off.* Departamento del Cauca. ◈ *province* SW Colombia
58 P13 **Caucaia** Ceará, E Brazil
54 E7 **Cauca, Río** ⁓ N Colombia
54 E7 **Caucasia** Antioquia, NW Colombia
137 Q8 **Caucasus** *Rus.* Kavkaz. ⛰ Georgia/Russian Federation
62 I10 **Caucete** San Juan, W Argentina
105 R11 **Caudete** Castilla-La Mancha, C Spain
103 P2 **Caudry** Nord, N France
82 D11 **Caungula** Lunda Norte, NE Angola
62 G13 **Cauquenes** Maule, C Chile
55 N8 **Caura, Río** ⁓ C Venezuela
15 V7 **Causapscal** Québec, SE Canada
117 N10 **Căuşeni** *Rus.* Kaushany. E Moldova
102 M14 **Caussade** Tarn-et-Garonne, S France
102 K17 **Cauterets** Hautes-Pyrénées, S France
10 J15 **Caution, Cape** *headland* British Columbia, SW Canada
44 H7 **Cauto** ⁓ E Cuba
Cauvery see Kāveri
102 L3 **Caux, Pays de** *physical region* N France
107 L18 **Cava dei Tirreni** Campania, S Italy
104 G6 **Cávado** ⁓ N Portugal
Cavaia see Kavajë
103 R15 **Cavaillon** Vaucluse, SE France
103 U16 **Cavalaire-sur-Mer** Var, SE France
106 G6 **Cavalese** *Ger.* Gablös. Trentino-Alto Adige, N Italy
29 Q2 **Cavalier** North Dakota, N USA
76 L17 **Cavalla** *var.* Cavally, Cavally Fleuve. ⁓ Ivory Coast/Liberia
105 Y8 **Cavalleria, Cap de** *var.* Cabo Caballeria. *headland* Menorca, Spain, W Mediterranean Sea
184 K2 **Cavalli Islands** *island group* N NZ
Cavally/Cavally Fleuve see Cavalla
97 E16 **Cavan** *Ir.* Cabhán. N Ireland
97 E16 **Cavan** *Ir.* An Cabhán. *cultural region* N Ireland
106 H8 **Cavarzere** Veneto, NE Italy
27 W9 **Cave City** Arkansas, C USA
20 K7 **Cave City** Kentucky, S USA
65 M25 **Cave Point** *headland* S Tristan da Cunha
21 N5 **Cave Run Lake** ⊞ Kentucky, S USA
58 K11 **Caviana de Fora, Ilha** *var.* Ilha Caviana. *island* N Brazil
Caviana, Ilha see Caviana de Fora, Ilha
113 I16 **Cavtat** *It.* Ragusavecchia. Dubrovnik-Neretva, SE Croatia
Cawnpore see Kānpur
Caxamarca see Cajamarca
58 A13 **Caxias** Amazonas, W Brazil
58 N13 **Caxias** Maranhão, E Brazil
61 I15 **Caxias do Sul** Rio Grande do Sul, S Brazil
42 J4 **Caxinas, Punta** *headland* N Honduras
82 B11 **Caxito** Bengo, NW Angola
136 F14 **Çay** Afyon, W Turkey
40 L15 **Cayacal, Punta** *var.* Punta Mongrove. *headland* S Mexico
56 C6 **Cayambe** Pichincha, N Ecuador
56 C6 **Cayambe** ▲ N Ecuador
21 R12 **Cayce** South Carolina, SE USA
55 Y10 **Cayenne** ○ (French Guiana) NE French Guiana
55 Y10 **Cayenne** ✕ NE French Guiana
44 K10 **Cayes** *var.* Les Cayes. SW Haiti
45 U6 **Cayey** C Puerto Rico
45 U6 **Cayey, Sierra de** ⛰ E Puerto Rico
103 N14 **Caylus** Tarn-et-Garonne, S France
44 E8 **Cayman Brac** *island* E Cayman Islands
44 D8 **Cayman Islands** ◇ *UK dependent territory* W West Indies
64 D11 **Cayman Trench** *undersea feature* NW Caribbean Sea
80 O13 **Caynabo** Togdheer, N Somalia
42 F3 **Cayo** ◈ *district* SW Belize
Cayo see San Ignacio
43 N9 **Cayos Guerrero** *reef* E Nicaragua
43 O9 **Cayos King** *reef* E Nicaragua
44 E4 **Cay Sal** *islet* SW Bahamas
14 G16 **Cayuga** Ontario, S Canada
25 V8 **Cayuga** Texas, SW USA
18 G10 **Cayuga Lake** ◎ New York, NE USA
104 K13 **Cazalla de la Sierra** Andalucía, S Spain
116 L14 **Căzăneşti** Ialomiţa, SE Romania
102 M16 **Cazères** Haute-Garonne, S France
112 E10 **Cazin** Federacija Bosna I Hercegovina, NW Bosnia and Herzegovina
82 G13 **Cazombo** Moxico, E Angola
105 O13 **Cazorla** Andalucía, S Spain
Cazza see Sušac
104 L4 **Cea** ⁓ NW Spain
Ceadâr-Lunga see Ciadîr-Lunga
Ceanannas see Kells
Ceann Toirc see Kanturk
58 O13 **Ceará** *off.* Estado do Ceará. ◈ *state* C Brazil
Ceará see Fortaleza
Ceara Abyssal Plain see Ceará Plain
59 Q14 **Ceará Mirim** Rio Grande do Norte, E Brazil
64 J13 **Ceará Plain** *var.* Ceara Abyssal Plain. *undersea feature* W Atlantic Ocean
64 I13 **Ceará Ridge** *undersea feature* C Atlantic Ocean
Ceatharlach see Carlow
43 Q17 **Cébaco, Isla** *island* SW Panama
40 K7 **Ceballos** Durango, C Mexico
61 G19 **Cebollatí** Rocha, E Uruguay
61 G19 **Cebollatí, Río** ⁓ E Uruguay
105 P5 **Cebollera** ▲ N Spain
104 M8 **Cebreros** Castilla-León, N Spain
171 P6 **Cebu** *off.* Cebu City. Cebu, C Philippines
171 P6 **Cebu** *island* C Philippines
107 J16 **Ceccano** Lazio, C Italy
Čechy see Bohemia
106 F12 **Cecina** Toscana, C Italy
26 K4 **Cedar Bluff Reservoir** ⊞ Kansas, C USA
30 M8 **Cedarburg** Wisconsin, N USA
36 J7 **Cedar City** Utah, W USA
25 T11 **Cedar Creek** Texas, SW USA
28 L7 **Cedar Creek** ⁓ North Dakota, N USA
25 U7 **Cedar Creek Reservoir** ⊞ Texas, SW USA
29 W13 **Cedar Falls** Iowa, C USA
31 N8 **Cedar Grove** Wisconsin, N USA
21 Y6 **Cedar Island** *island* Virginia, NE USA
23 U11 **Cedar Key** Cedar Keys, Florida, SE USA
23 U11 **Cedar Keys** *island group* Florida, SE USA
11 V14 **Cedar Lake** ◎ Manitoba, C Canada
14 I11 **Cedar Lake** ◎ Ontario, SE Canada
24 M6 **Cedar Lake** ◎ Texas, SW USA
29 X13 **Cedar Rapids** Iowa, C USA
29 X14 **Cedar River** ⁓ Iowa/Minnesota, C USA
29 O14 **Cedar River** ⁓ Nebraska, C USA
31 P8 **Cedar Springs** Michigan, N USA
23 R3 **Cedartown** Georgia, SE USA
27 O7 **Cedar Vale** Kansas, C USA
35 Q2 **Cedarville** California, W USA
104 H1 **Cedeira** Galicia, NW Spain
42 H8 **Cedeño** Choluteca, S Honduras
41 N10 **Cedral** San Luis Potosí, C Mexico
42 I6 **Cedros** Francisco Morazán, C Honduras
40 M9 **Cedros** Zacatecas, C Mexico
40 B5 **Cedros, Isla** *island* W Mexico
193 R5 **Cedros Trench** *undersea feature* E Pacific Ocean
182 F7 **Ceduna** South Australia
110 D10 **Cedynia** *Ger.* Zehden. Zachodnio-pomorskie, W Poland
80 P12 **Ceelaayo** Sanaag, N Somalia
81 O16 **Ceel Buur** *It.* El Bur; Galguduud, C Somalia
81 N15 **Ceel Dheere** *var.* Ceel Dher, *It.* El Dere. Galguduud, C Somalia
Ceel Dher see Ceel Dheere
81 P14 **Ceel Xamure** Mudug, E Somalia
80 O12 **Ceerigaabo** *var.* Erigabo, Erigavo. Sanaag, N Somalia
107 J23 **Cefalù** *anc.* Cephaloedium. Sicilia, Italy, C Mediterranean Sea
105 N6 **Cega** ⁓ N Spain
111 K23 **Cegléd** *prev.* Czegléd. Pest, C Hungary
113 N18 **Čegrane** W FYR Macedonia
105 Q13 **Cehegín** Murcia, SE Spain
136 K12 **Çekerek** Yozgat, N Turkey
146 B13 **Çekiçler** *Rus.* Chekishlyar, *Turkm.* Chekichler. Balkan Welaýaty, W Turkmenistan
107 J15 **Celano** Abruzzo, C Italy
104 H4 **Celanova** Galicia, NW Spain
42 F6 **Celaque, Cordillera de** ⛰ W Honduras
41 N13 **Celaya** Guanajuato, C Mexico
Celebes see Sulawesi
192 F7 **Celebes Basin** *undersea feature* SE South China Sea
192 F7 **Celebes Sea** *Ind.* Laut Sulawesi. *sea* Indonesia/Philippines
41 W12 **Celestún** Yucatán, E Mexico
31 Q12 **Celina** Ohio, N USA
20 L8 **Celina** Tennessee, S USA
25 U5 **Celina** Texas, SW USA
112 G11 **Čelinac Donji** Republika Srpska, N Bosnia and Herzegovina
109 V10 **Celje** *Ger.* Cilli. C Slovenia
111 G23 **Celldömölk** Vas, W Hungary
100 J12 **Celle** *var.* Zelle. Niedersachsen, N Germany
99 D19 **Celles** Hainaut, SW Belgium
104 I7 **Celorico da Beira** Guarda, N Portugal
Celovec see Klagenfurt
64 M7 **Celtic Sea** *Ir.* An Mhuir Cheilteach. *sea* SW British Isles
64 N7 **Celtic Shelf** *undersea feature* E Atlantic Ocean
114 L13 **Çeltik Gölu** ◎ NW Turkey
146 J17 **Çemenibit** *prev. Rus.* Chemenibit. Mary Welaýaty, S Turkmenistan
113 M14 **Čemerno** ▲ C Serbia and Montenegro (Yugo.)
105 Q12 **Cenajo, Embalse del** ⊞ S Spain
171 V13 **Cenderawasih, Teluk** *var.* Teluk Irian, Teluk Sarera. *bay* W Pacific Ocean
105 P4 **Cenicero** La Rioja, N Spain
106 E9 **Ceno** ⁓ NW Italy
102 K13 **Cenon** Gironde, SW France
14 K13 **Centennial Lake** ◎ Ontario, SE Canada
Centennial State see Colorado
37 S7 **Center** Colorado, C USA
29 Q13 **Center** Nebraska, C USA
28 M5 **Center** North Dakota, N USA
25 X8 **Center** Texas, SW USA
29 W8 **Center City** Minnesota, N USA
36 L5 **Centerfield** Utah, W USA
20 K9 **Center Hill Lake** ⊞ Tennessee, S USA
29 X13 **Center Point** Iowa, C USA
25 R11 **Center Point** Texas, SW USA
29 W16 **Centerville** Iowa, C USA
27 W7 **Centerville** Missouri, C USA
29 R12 **Centerville** South Dakota, N USA
20 I9 **Centerville** Tennessee, S USA
25 V9 **Centerville** Texas, SW USA
40 M5 **Centinela, Picacho del** ▲ NE Mexico
106 G9 **Cento** Emilia-Romagna, N Italy
Centrafricaine, République see Central African Republic
39 S8 **Central** Alaska, USA
37 P15 **Central** New Mexico, SW USA
83 H18 **Central** ◈ *district* E Botswana
138 E10 **Central** ◈ *district* C Israel
81 I19 **Central** ◈ *province* C Kenya
82 M13 **Central** ◈ *region* C Malawi
153 P12 **Central** ◈ *zone* C Nepal
186 E9 **Central** ◈ *province* S PNG
63 I21 **Central** ◈ *department* C Paraguay
186 M9 **Central** *off.* Central Province. ◈ *province* S Solomon Islands
83 J14 **Central** ◈ *province* C Zambia
117 P11 **Central** ✕ (Odesa) Odes'ka Oblast', SW Ukraine
Central see Centre
79 H14 **Central African Republic** *var.* République Centrafricaine, *abbrev.* CAR; *prev.* Ubangi-Shari, Oubangui-Chari, Territoire de l'Oubangui-Chari. ◆ *republic* C Africa
192 G6 **Central Basin Trough** *undersea feature* W Pacific Ocean
Central Borneo see Kalimantan Tengah
149 P12 **Central Brāhui Range** ⛰ W Pakistan
Central Celebes see Sulawesi Tengah
29 Y13 **Central City** Iowa, C USA
20 I6 **Central City** Kentucky, S USA
29 P15 **Central City** Nebraska, C USA
54 D11 **Central, Cordillera** ⛰ W Colombia
42 M13 **Central, Cordillera** ⛰ C Costa Rica
45 N9 **Central, Cordillera** ⛰ C Dominican Republic
43 R16 **Central, Cordillera** ⛰ C Panama
45 S6 **Central, Cordillera** ⛰ Puerto Rico
42 H7 **Central District** *var.* Tegucigalpa. ◈ *district* C Honduras
30 L15 **Centralia** Illinois, N USA
27 U4 **Centralia** Missouri, C USA
32 G9 **Centralia** Washington, NW USA
Central Indian Ridge see Mid-Indian Ridge
Central Java see Jawa Tengah
Central Kalimantan see Kalimantan Tengah
148 L14 **Central Makrān Range** ⛰ W Pakistan
192 K7 **Central Pacific Basin** *undersea feature* C Pacific Ocean
59 M19 **Central, Planalto** *var.* Brazilian Highlands. ⛰ E Brazil
32 F15 **Central Point** Oregon, NW USA
155 K25 **Central Province** ◈ *province* C Sri Lanka
Central Provinces and Berar see Madhya Pradesh
186 B6 **Central Range** ⛰ NW PNG
Central Russian Upland see Srednerusskaya Vozvyshennost'
Central Siberian Plateau/Central Siberian Uplands see Srednesibirskoye Ploskogor'ye
104 K8 **Central, Sistema** ⛰ C Spain
Central Sulawesi see Sulawesi Tengah
35 N3 **Central Valley** California, W USA
35 P8 **Central Valley** *valley* California, W USA
23 Q3 **Centre** Alabama, S USA
79 E15 **Centre** *Eng.* Central. ◈ *province* C Cameroon
102 M8 **Centre** ◈ *region* N France
173 Y16 **Centre de Flacq** E Mauritius
55 Y9 **Centre Spatial Guyanais** *space station* N French Guiana
23 O5 **Centreville** Alabama, S USA
21 X3 **Centreville** Maryland, NE USA
22 J7 **Centreville** Mississippi, S USA
Centum Cellae see Civitavecchia
160 M14 **Cenxi** Guangxi Zhuangzu Zizhiqu, S China
Ceos see Kéa
Cephaloedium see Cefalu
112 I9 **Čepin** *Hung.* Csepén. Osijek-Baranja, E Croatia
Ceram see Seram, Pulau
171 R13 **Ceram Sea** *Ind.* Laut Seram. *sea* E Indonesia
192 G8 **Ceram Trough** *undersea feature* W Pacific Ocean
Cerasus see Giresun
36 I10 **Cerbat Mountains** ⛰ Arizona, SW USA
103 P17 **Cerbère, Cap** *headland* S France
104 F13 **Cercal do Alentejo** Setúbal, S Portugal
111 A18 **Čerchov** *Ger.* Czerkow. ▲ W Czech Republic
103 O13 **Cère** ⁓ C France
61 A16 **Ceres** Santa Fe, C Argentina
59 K18 **Ceres** Goiás, C Brazil
Ceresio see Lugano, Lago di
103 O17 **Céret** Pyrénées-Orientales, S France
54 E6 **Cereté** Córdoba, NW Colombia
172 I17 **Cerf, Île au** *island* Inner Islands, NE Seychelles
99 G22 **Cerfontaine** Namur, S Belgium
Cergy-Pontoise see Pontoise
107 N16 **Cerignola** Puglia, SE Italy
Cerigo see Kýthira
103 O9 **Cérilly** Allier, C France

◆ Country ● Country Capital ◇ Dependent Territory ○ Dependent Territory Capital ◈ Administrative Region ✕ International Airport ▲ Mountain ⛰ Mountain Range ⚠ Volcano ⁓ River ◎ Lake ⊞ Reservoir

136 I11 **Çerkeş** Çankırı, N Turkey
136 D10 **Çerkezköy** Tekirdağ, NW Turkey
109 T12 **Cerknica** *Ger.* Zirknitz. SW Slovenia
109 S11 **Cerkno** W Slovenia
116 F10 **Cermei** *Hung.* Csermő. Arad, W Romania
137 O15 **Çermik** Diyarbakır, SE Turkey
112 I10 **Cerna** Vukovar-Srijem, E Croatia
Cernăuţi *see* Chernivtsi
116 M14 **Cernavodă** Constanţa, SW Romania
103 U7 **Cernay** Haut-Rhin, NE France
Černice *see* Schwarzach
41 O8 **Cerralvo** Nuevo León, NE Mexico
40 G9 **Cerralvo, Isla** *island* W Mexico
107 L16 **Cerreto Sannita** Campania, S Italy
113 L20 **Cërrik** *var.* Cerriku. Elbasan, C Albania
Cerriku *see* Cërrik
41 O11 **Cerritos** San Luis Potosí, C Mexico
60 K11 **Cerro Azul** Paraná, S Brazil
61 F18 **Cerro Chato** Treinta y Tres, E Uruguay
61 F19 **Cerro Colorado** Florida, S Uruguay
56 E13 **Cerro de Pasco** Pasco, C Peru
61 G18 **Cerro Largo** ◆ *department* NE Uruguay
61 G14 **Cêrro Largo** Rio Grande do Sul, S Brazil
42 E7 **Cerrón Grande, Embalse** ⊠ N El Salvador
63 I14 **Cerros Colorados, Embalse** ⊚ W Argentina
105 V5 **Cervera** Cataluña, NE Spain
104 M3 **Cervera del Pisuerga** Castilla-León, N Spain
105 Q5 **Cervera del Río Alhama** La Rioja, N Spain
107 H15 **Cerveteri** Lazio, C Italy
106 H10 **Cervia** Emilia-Romagna, N Italy
106 J7 **Cervignano del Friuli** Friuli-Venezia Giulia, NE Italy
107 L17 **Cervinara** Campania, S Italy
Cervinia *see* Breuil-Cervinia
106 B6 **Cervino, Monte** *var.* Matterhorn. ▲ Italy/Switzerland **see also** Matterhorn
103 Y14 **Cervione** Corse, France, C Mediterranean Sea
104 I1 **Cervo** Galicia, NW Spain
54 F5 **Cesar** *off.* Departamento del Cesar. ◆ *province* N Colombia
106 H10 **Cesena** *anc.* Caesena. Emilia-Romagna, N Italy
106 I10 **Cesenatico** Emilia-Romagna, N Italy
118 H8 **Cēsis** *Ger.* Wenden. Cēsis, C Latvia
111 D15 **Česká Lípa** *Ger.* Böhmisch-Leipa. Liberecký Kraj, N Czech Republic
Česká Republika *see* Czech Republic
111 F17 **Česká Třebová** *Ger.* Böhmisch-Trübau. Pardubický Kraj, C Czech Republic
111 D19 **České Budějovice** *Ger.* Budweis. Jihočeský Kraj, S Czech Republic
111 D19 **České Velenice** Jihočeský Kraj, S Czech Republic
111 E18 **Českomoravská Vrchovina** *var.* Českomoravská Vysočina, *Eng.* Bohemian-Moravian Highlands, *Ger.* Böhmisch-Mährische Höhe. ▲ S Czech Republic
Českomoravská Vysočina *see* Českomoravská Vrchovina
111 C19 **Český Krumlov** *var.* Böhmisch-Krumau, *Ger.* Krummau. Jihočeský Kraj, S Czech Republic
Český Les *see* Bohemian Forest
112 F8 **Česma** ≈ N Croatia
136 A14 **Çeşme** İzmir, W Turkey
Cess *see* Cestos
183 T8 **Cessnock** New South Wales, SE Australia
76 K17 **Cestos** *var.* Cess. ≈ S Liberia
118 I9 **Cesvaine** Madona, E Latvia
116 G14 **Cetate** Dolj, SW Romania
Cetatea Albă *see* Bilhorod-Dnistrovs'kyy
113 J17 **Cetinje** *It.* Cettigne. Montenegro, SW Serbia and Montenegro (Yugo.)
107 N20 **Cetraro** Calabria, S Italy
Cette *see* Sète
188 A17 **Cetti Bay** *bay* SW Guam
Cettigne *see* Cetinje
104 L17 **Ceuta** *var.* Sebta. Ceuta, Spain, N Africa
106 B9 **Ceva** Piemonte, NE Italy
103 P14 **Cévennes** ▲ S France
108 G10 **Cevio** Ticino, S Switzerland
136 K16 **Ceyhan** Adana, S Turkey
136 K17 **Ceyhan Nehri** ≈ S Turkey
137 P17 **Ceylanpınar** Şanlıurfa, SE Turkey
Ceylon *see* Sri Lanka
173 R6 **Ceylon Plain** *undersea feature* N Indian Ocean
Ceyre to the Caribs *see* Marie-Galante
103 Q14 **Cèze** ≈ S France
Chaacha *see* Çäçe
127 P6 **Chaadayevka** Penzenskaya Oblast', W Russian Federation
167 O12 **Cha-Am** Phetchaburi, SW Thailand
143 W15 **Chābahār** *var.* Chāh Bahār, Chahbar. Sīstān va Balūchestān, SE Iran
61 B19 **Chabas** Santa Fe, C Argentina
103 T10 **Chablais** *physical region* E France
61 B20 **Chacabuco** Buenos Aires, E Argentina
42 K8 **Chachagón, Cerro** ▲ N Nicaragua
56 C10 **Chachapoyas** Amazonas, NW Peru
Chäche *see* Çäçe
119 O18 **Chachersk** *Rus.* Chechersk. Homyel'skaya Voblasts', SE Belarus
119 N16 **Chachevichy** *Rus.* Chechevichi. Mahilyowskaya Voblasts', E Belarus
61 B14 **Chaco** *off.* Provincia de Chaco. ◆ *province* NE Argentina
Chaco *see* Gran Chaco
62 M6 **Chaco Austral** *physical region* N Argentina
62 M3 **Chaco Boreal** *physical region* N Paraguay
62 M6 **Chaco Central** *physical region* N Argentina
39 Y15 **Chacon, Cape** *headland* Prince of Wales Island, Alaska, USA
78 H9 **Chad** *off.* Republic of Chad, *Fr.* Tchad. ◆ *republic* C Africa
122 K14 **Chadan** Respublika Tyva, S Russian Federation
21 U12 **Chadbourn** North Carolina, SE USA
83 L14 **Chadiza** Eastern, E Zambia
78 F10 **Chad, Lake** *Fr.* Lac Tchad. ⊚ C Africa
28 J12 **Chadron** Nebraska, C USA
Chadyr-Lunga *see* Ciadîr-Lunga
163 W14 **Chaeryŏng** SW North Korea
105 P17 **Chafarinas, Islas** *island group* S Spain
27 Y7 **Chaffee** Missouri, C USA
148 L12 **Chāgai Hills** *var.* Chāh Gay. ▲ Afghanistan/Pakistan
123 Q11 **Chagda** Respublika Sakha (Yakutiya), NE Russian Federation
Chaghasarāy *see* Asadābād
149 N5 **Chaghcharān** *var.* Chakhcharan, Cheghcheran, Qala Āhangarān. Ghowr, C Afghanistan
103 R9 **Chagny** Saône-et-Loire, C France
173 Q7 **Chagos Archipelago** *var.* Oil Islands. *island group* British Indian Ocean Territory
173 O6 **Chagos-Laccadive Plateau** *undersea feature* N Indian Ocean
173 Q7 **Chagos Trench** *undersea feature* N Indian Ocean
43 T14 **Chagres, Río** ≈ C Panama
45 U14 **Chaguanas** Trinidad, Trinidad and Tobago
54 M6 **Chaguaramas** Guárico, N Venezuela
Chagyl *see* Çagyl
Chahārmahāl and Bakhtīyārī *see* Chahār Maḩall va Bakhtīārī
142 M9 **Chahār Maḩall va Bakhtīārī** *off.* Ostān-e Chahār Maḩall va Bakhtīārī, *var.* Chahārmahāl and Bakhtīyārī. ◆ *province* SW Iran
Chāh Bahār/Chahbar *see* Chābahār
143 V13 **Chāh Derāz** Sīstān va Balūchestān, SE Iran
Chāh Gay *see* Chāgai Hills
167 P10 **Chai Badan** Lop Buri, C Thailand
153 Q16 **Chāībāsa** Jhārkhand, N India
79 E19 **Chaillu, Massif du** ▲ C Gabon
167 O10 **Chai Nat** *var.* Chainat, Jainat, Jayanath. Chai Nat, C Thailand
65 M14 **Chain Fracture Zone** *tectonic feature* E Atlantic Ocean
173 N5 **Chain Ridge** *undersea feature* W Indian Ocean
Chairn, Ceann an *see* Carnsore Point
158 L5 **Chaiwopu** Xinjiang Uygur Zizhiqu, W China
167 Q10 **Chaiyaphum** *var.* Jayabum. Chaiyaphum, C Thailand
62 N10 **Chajarí** Entre Ríos, E Argentina
42 C5 **Chajul** Quiché, W Guatemala
83 K16 **Chakari** Mashonaland West, N Zimbabwe
148 J9 **Chakhānsūr** Nīmrūz, SW Afghanistan
Chakhānsūr *see* Nīmrūz
Chakhcharan *see* Chaghcharān
149 V8 **Chak Jhumra** *var.* Jhumra. Punjab, E Pakistan
146 I16 **Chaknakdysonga** Ahal Welaýaty, S Turkmenistan
153 P16 **Chakradharpur** Jhārkhand, N India
152 J8 **Chakrāta** Uttaranchal, N India
149 U7 **Chakwāl** Punjab, NE Pakistan
57 F17 **Chala** Arequipa, SW Peru
102 K12 **Chalais** Charente, W France
108 D10 **Chalais** Valais, SW Switzerland
115 J20 **Chalándri** *var.* Halandri; *prev.* Khalándrion. *prehistoric site* Sýros, Kykládes, Greece, Aegean Sea
188 H6 **Chalan Kanoa** Saipan, S Northern Mariana Islands
188 C16 **Chalan Pago** C Guam
Chalap Dalam/Chalap Dalan *see* Chehel Abdālān, Kūh-e
42 F7 **Chalatenango** Chalatenango, N El Salvador
42 A9 **Chalatenango** ◆ *department* NW El Salvador
83 P15 **Chalaua** Nampula, NE Mozambique
81 I16 **Chalbi Desert** *desert* N Kenya
42 D7 **Chalchuapa** Santa Ana, W El Salvador
Chalcidice *see* Chalkidikí
Chalcis *see* Chalkída
103 N6 **Châlette-sur-Loing** Loiret, C France
15 X8 **Chaleur Bay** *Fr.* Baie des Chaleurs. *bay* New Brunswick/Québec, E Canada
Chaleurs, Baie des *see* Chaleur Bay
57 G16 **Chalhuanca** Apurímac, S Peru
154 F12 **Chālisgaon** Mahārāshtra, C India
115 N23 **Chálki** *island* Dodekánisos, Greece, Aegean Sea
115 F16 **Chalkiádes** Thessalía, C Greece
115 H18 **Chalkída** *var.* Halkida; *prev.* Khalkís, *anc.* Chalcis. Evvoia, E Greece
115 G14 **Chalkidikí** *var.* Khalkidhikí; *anc.* Chalcidice. *peninsula* NE Greece
185 A24 **Chalky Inlet** *inlet* South Island, NZ
39 S7 **Chalkyitsik** Alaska, USA
102 I9 **Challans** Vendée, NW France
57 K19 **Challapata** Oruro, SW Bolivia
192 H6 **Challenger Deep** *undersea feature* W Pacific Ocean
193 S11 **Challenger Fracture Zone** *tectonic feature* SE Pacific Ocean
192 K11 **Challenger Plateau** *undersea feature* E Tasman Sea
33 P13 **Challis** Idaho, NW USA
22 L9 **Chalmette** Louisiana, S USA
124 J11 **Chalna** Respublika Kareliya, NW Russian Federation
103 Q5 **Châlons-en-Champagne** *prev.* Châlons-sur-Marne, *hist.* Arcae Remorum, *anc.* Carolopois. Marne, NE France
Châlons-sur-Marne *see* Châlons-en-Champagne
103 R9 **Chalon-sur-Saône** *anc.* Cabillonum. Saône-et-Loire, C France
Chaltel, Cerro *see* Fitzroy, Monte
143 N4 **Chālūs** Māzandarān, N Iran
102 M11 **Châlus** Haute-Vienne, C France
101 N20 **Cham** Bayern, SE Germany
108 F7 **Cham** Zug, N Switzerland
37 R8 **Chama** New Mexico, SW USA
Cha Mai *see* Thung Song
83 E22 **Chamaites** Karas, S Namibia
149 O9 **Chaman** Baluchistān, SW Pakistan
37 R9 **Chama, Rio** ≈ New Mexico, SW USA
152 I6 **Chamba** Himāchal Pradesh, N India
81 I25 **Chamba** Ruvuma, S Tanzania
150 H12 **Chambal** ≈ C India
11 U16 **Chamberlain** Saskatchewan, S Canada
29 O11 **Chamberlain** South Dakota, N USA
19 R3 **Chamberlain Lake** ⊚ Maine, NE USA
39 S5 **Chamberlin, Mount** ▲ Alaska, USA
37 O11 **Chambers** Arizona, SW USA
18 F16 **Chambersburg** Pennsylvania, NE USA
31 N5 **Chambers Island** *island* Wisconsin, N USA
103 T11 **Chambéry** *anc.* Camberia. Savoie, E France
82 L12 **Chambeshi** Northern, NE Zambia
82 L12 **Chambeshi** ≈ NE Zambia
74 M6 **Chambi, Jebel** *var.* Jabal ash Sha'nabī. ▲ W Tunisia
15 Q7 **Chambord** Québec, SE Canada
139 U11 **Chamcham** S Iraq
139 T4 **Chamchamāl** N Iraq
40 J14 **Chamela** Jalisco, SW Mexico
42 G5 **Chamelecón, Río** ≈ NW Honduras
62 J9 **Chamical** La Rioja, C Argentina
115 L23 **Chamilí** *island* Kykládes, Greece, Aegean Sea
167 Q13 **Châmnar** Kaôh Kông, SW Cambodia
152 K9 **Chamoli** Uttaranchal, N India
103 U11 **Chamonix-Mont-Blanc** Haute-Savoie, E France
154 L11 **Chāmpa** Chhattīsgarh, C India
10 H8 **Champagne** Yukon Territory, W Canada
103 Q5 **Champagne** *cultural region* N France
Champagne *see* Campania
103 Q5 **Champagne-Ardenne** ◆ *region* N France
103 S9 **Champagnole** Jura, E France
30 M13 **Champaign** Illinois, N USA
167 S10 **Champasak** Champasak, S Laos
103 U6 **Champ de Feu** ▲ NE France
13 O7 **Champdoré, Lac** ⊚ Québec, NE Canada
42 B6 **Champerico** Retalhuleu, SW Guatemala
108 C11 **Champéry** Valais, SW Switzerland
18 L6 **Champlain** New York, NE USA
18 L9 **Champlain Canal** *canal* New York, NE USA
15 P13 **Champlain, Lac** ⊚ Canada/USA **see also** Champlain, Lake
18 L7 **Champlain, Lake** ⊚ Canada/USA **see also** Champlain, Lac
103 S7 **Champlitte** Haute-Saône, E France
41 W13 **Champotón** Campeche, SE Mexico
104 G10 **Chamusca** Santarém, C Portugal
119 O20 **Chamyarysy** *Rus.* Chemerisy. Homyel'skaya Voblasts', SE Belarus
127 P5 **Chamzinka** Respublika Mordoviya, W Russian Federation
Chanáil Mhór, An *see* Grand Canal
Chanak *see* Çanakkale
64 G7 **Chañaral** Atacama, N Chile
104 H13 **Chança, Rio** *var.* Chanza. ≈ Portugal/Spain
57 D14 **Chancay** Lima, W Peru
Chan-chiang/Chanchiang *see* Zhanjiang
64 G13 **Chanco** Maule, Chile
39 R7 **Chandalar** Alaska, USA
39 R6 **Chandalar River** ≈ Alaska, USA
152 L10 **Chandan Chauki** Uttar Pradesh, N India
153 S16 **Chandannagar** *prev.* Chandernagore. West Bengal, E India
152 K10 **Chandausi** Uttar Pradesh, N India
22 M10 **Chandeleur Islands** *island group* Louisiana, S USA
22 M9 **Chandeleur Sound** *sound* N Gulf of Mexico
152 I8 **Chandīgarh** Punjab, N India
153 Q16 **Chāndil** Jhārkhand, NE India
182 D2 **Chandler** South Australia
15 Y7 **Chandler** Québec, SE Canada
36 L14 **Chandler** Arizona, SW USA
27 O10 **Chandler** Oklahoma, C USA
25 V7 **Chandler** Texas, SW USA
39 Q6 **Chandler River** ≈ Alaska, USA
56 H13 **Chandles, Río** ≈ E Peru
163 N9 **Chandmanĭ** Dornogovĭ, SE Mongolia
14 J13 **Chandos Lake** ⊚ Ontario, SE Canada
153 U15 **Chandpur** Chittagong, C Bangladesh
154 I13 **Chandrapur** Mahārāshtra, C India
83 J15 **Changa** Southern, S Zambia
Changan *see* Xi'an, Shaanxi, China
Chang'an *see* Rong'an, Guangxi Zhuangzu Zizhiqu, China
155 G23 **Changanācheri** Kerala, SW India
83 M19 **Changane** ≈ S Mozambique
83 M16 **Changara** Tete, NW Mozambique
163 X11 **Changbai** *var.* Changbai Chosenzu Zizhixian. Jilin, NE China
Changbai Chosenzu Zizhixian *see* Changbai
163 X11 **Changbai Shan** ▲ NE China
163 V10 **Changchun** *var.* Ch'angch'un, Ch'ang-ch'un; *prev.* Hsinking. Jilin, NE China
160 M10 **Changde** Hunan, S China
161 S13 **Changhua** *Jap.* Shōka. C Taiwan
168 L10 **Changi** ✕ (Singapore) E Singapore
158 L5 **Changji** Xinjiang Uygur Zizhiqu, NW China
160 L17 **Changjiang** *var.* Changjiang Lizu Zizhixian, Shiliu. Hainan, S China
157 O13 **Chang Jiang** *var.* Yangtze Kiang, *Eng.* Yangtze. ≈ C China
161 S8 **Changjiang Kou** *delta* E China
Changjiang Lizu Zizhixian *see* Changjiang
167 F12 **Chang, Ko** *island* S Thailand
161 Q2 **Changli** Hebei, E China
163 V10 **Changling** Jilin, NE China
Changning *see* Xunwu
161 N11 **Changsha** *var.* Ch'angsha, Ch'ang-sha. Hunan, S China
161 Q10 **Changshan** Zhejiang, SE China
163 V14 **Changshan Qundao** *island group* NE China
161 S8 **Changshu** *var.* Ch'ang-shu. Jiangsu, E China
163 V11 **Changtu** Liaoning, NE China
43 P14 **Changuinola** Bocas del Toro, NW Panama
159 N9 **Changweiliang** Qinghai, W China
160 K6 **Changwu** *var.* Zhaoren. Shaanxi, C China
163 U13 **Changxing Dao** *island* N China
160 M9 **Changyang** *var.* Longzhouping. Hubei, C China
163 W14 **Changyŏn** SW North Korea
161 N5 **Changzhi** Shanxi, C China
161 R8 **Changzhou** Jiangsu, E China
115 H24 **Chaniá** *var.* Hania, Khaniá, *Eng.* Canea; *anc.* Cydonia. Kríti, Greece, E Mediterranean Sea
62 J5 **Chañi, Nevado de** ▲ NW Argentina
115 H24 **Chanión, Kólpos** *gulf* Kríti, Greece, E Mediterranean Sea
Chankiri *see* Çankırı
30 M11 **Channahon** Illinois, N USA
155 H20 **Channapatna** Karnātaka, E India
97 K26 **Channel Islands** *Fr.* Îles Normandes. *island group* S English Channel
35 R16 **Channel Islands** *island group* California, W USA
13 S13 **Channel-Port aux Basques** Newfoundland and Labrador, SE Canada
Channel, The *see* English Channel
97 Q23 **Channel Tunnel** *tunnel* France/UK
24 M2 **Channing** Texas, SW USA
Chantabun/Chantaburi *see* Chanthaburi
104 H3 **Chantada** Galicia, NW Spain
167 P12 **Chanthaburi** *var.* Chantabun, Chantaburi. Chantaburi, S Thailand
103 O4 **Chantilly** Oise, N France
139 V12 **Chanūn as Sa'ūdī** S Iraq
27 Q6 **Chanute** Kansas, C USA
Chanza *see* Chança, Rio
Ch'ao-an/Chaochow *see* Chaozhou
161 P8 **Chao Hu** ⊚ E China
167 P11 **Chao Phraya, Mae Nam** ≈ C Thailand
Chaor He *see* Qulin Gol
Chaouèn *see* Chefchaouen
161 P14 **Chaoyang** Guangdong, S China
163 T12 **Chaoyang** Liaoning, NE China
Chaoyang *see* Jiayin, Heilongjiang, China
Chaoyang *see* Huinan, Jilin, China
161 Q14 **Chaozhou** *var.* Chaoan, Ch'ao-an; *prev.* Chaochow. Guangdong, SE China
58 N13 **Chapadinha** Maranhão, E Brazil
12 K12 **Chapais** Québec, SE Canada
40 L13 **Chapala** Jalisco, SW Mexico
40 L13 **Chapala, Lago de** ⊚ C Mexico
146 F13 **Chapan, Gora** ▲ C Turkmenistan
57 M18 **Chapare, Río** ≈ C Bolivia
54 E11 **Chaparral** Tolima, C Colombia
144 F9 **Chapayev** Zapadnyy Kazakhstan, NW Kazakhstan
123 O11 **Chapayevo** Respublika Sakha (Yakutiya), NE Russian Federation
127 R6 **Chapayevsk** Samarskaya Oblast', W Russian Federation
60 H13 **Chapecó** Santa Catarina, S Brazil
60 I13 **Chapecó, Rio** ≈ S Brazil
20 J9 **Chapel Hill** Tennessee, S USA
44 J12 **Chapelton** C Jamaica
14 C8 **Chapleau** Ontario, SE Canada
14 D7 **Chapleau** ≈ Ontario, S Canada
11 T16 **Chaplin** Saskatchewan, S Canada
126 M6 **Chaplygin** Lipetskaya Oblast', W Russian Federation
117 S11 **Chaplynka** Khersons'ka Oblast', S Ukraine
9 O6 **Chapman, Cape** *headland* Nunavut, NE Canada
25 T15 **Chapman Ranch** Texas, SW USA
Chapman's *see* Okwa
21 P5 **Chapmanville** West Virginia, NE USA
28 K15 **Chappell** Nebraska, C USA
Chapra *see* Chhapra
56 D9 **Chapuli, Río** ≈ N Peru
76 I6 **Châr** *well* N Mauritania
123 P12 **Chara** Chitinskaya Oblast', S Russian Federation
123 O11 **Chara** ≈ C Russian Federation
54 G8 **Charala** Santander, C Colombia
41 N10 **Charcas** San Luis Potosí, C Mexico
25 T13 **Charco** Texas, SW USA
194 H7 **Charcot Island** *island* Antarctica
64 M8 **Charcot Seamounts** *undersea feature* E Atlantic Ocean
Chardara *see* Shardara
145 P17 **Chardarinskoye Vodokhranilishche** ⊠ S Kazakhstan
31 U11 **Chardon** Ohio, N USA
44 K9 **Chardonnières** SW Haiti
Chardzhev *see* Türkmenabat
Chardzhevskaya Oblast' *see* Lebap Welaýaty
Chardzhou/Chardzhui *see* Türkmenabat
102 L11 **Charente** ◆ *department* W France
102 J11 **Charente** ≈ W France
102 J10 **Charente-Maritime** ◆ *department* W France
137 U12 **Ch'arents'avan** C Armenia
78 I12 **Chari** *var.* Shari. ≈ Central African Republic/Chad
78 G11 **Chari-Baguirmi** *off.* Préfecture du Chari-Baguirmi. ◆ *prefecture* SW Chad
149 Q4 **Chārīkār** Parwān, NE Afghanistan
29 V15 **Chariton** Iowa, C USA
27 U3 **Chariton River** ≈ Missouri, C USA
55 T7 **Charity** NW Guyana
31 R7 **Charity Island** *island* Michigan, N USA
Chärjew *see* Türkmenabat
Chärjew Oblasty *see* Lebap Welaýaty
Charkhlik/Charkhliq *see* Ruoqiang
99 G20 **Charleroi** Hainaut, S Belgium
11 V12 **Charles** Manitoba, C Canada
15 R10 **Charlesbourg** Québec, SE Canada
21 Y7 **Charles, Cape** *headland* Virginia, NE USA
29 W12 **Charles City** Iowa, C USA
21 W6 **Charles City** Virginia, NE USA
103 O5 **Charles de Gaulle** ✕ (Paris) Seine-et-Marne, N France
12 K1 **Charles Island** *island* Nunavut, NE Canada
Charles Island *see* Santa María, Isla
30 K9 **Charles Mound** *hill* Illinois, N USA
185 A22 **Charles Sound** *sound* South Island, NZ
185 G15 **Charleston** West Coast, South Island, NZ
27 S11 **Charleston** Arkansas, C USA
30 M14 **Charleston** Illinois, N USA
22 L3 **Charleston** Mississippi, S USA
27 Z7 **Charleston** Missouri, C USA
21 T15 **Charleston** South Carolina, SE USA
21 Q5 **Charleston** *state capital* West Virginia, NE USA
14 L14 **Charleston Lake** ⊚ Ontario, SE Canada
35 W11 **Charleston Peak** ▲ Nevada, W USA
45 W10 **Charlestown** Nevis, Saint Kitts and Nevis
31 P16 **Charlestown** Indiana, N USA
18 M9 **Charlestown** New Hampshire, NE USA
21 V3 **Charles Town** West Virginia, NE USA
181 W9 **Charleville** Queensland, E Australia
103 R3 **Charleville-Mézières** Ardennes, N France
31 P5 **Charlevoix** Michigan, N USA
31 Q6 **Charlevoix, Lake** ⊚ Michigan, N USA
39 T9 **Charley River** ≈ Alaska, USA
64 J6 **Charlie-Gibbs Fracture Zone** *tectonic feature* N Atlantic Ocean
103 Q10 **Charlieu** Loire, E France
31 Q9 **Charlotte** Michigan, N USA
21 R10 **Charlotte** North Carolina, SE USA
20 I8 **Charlotte** Tennessee, S USA
25 R13 **Charlotte** Texas, SW USA
21 R10 **Charlotte** ✕ North Carolina, SE USA
45 T9 **Charlotte Amalie** *prev.* Saint Thomas. ○ (Virgin Islands (US)) Saint Thomas, N Virgin Islands (US)
21 U7 **Charlotte Court House** Virginia, NE USA
23 W14 **Charlotte Harbor** *inlet* Florida, SE USA
Charlotte Island *see* Abaiang
95 J15 **Charlottenberg** Värmland, C Sweden
Charlottenhof *see* Aegviidu
21 U5 **Charlottesville** Virginia, NE USA
Charlotte Town *see* Roseau, Dominica
Charlotte Town *see* Gouyave, Grenada
13 Q14 **Charlottetown** Prince Edward Island, Prince Edward Island, SE Canada
45 Z16 **Charlotteville** Tobago, Trinidad and Tobago
182 M11 **Charlton** Victoria, SE Australia
12 H10 **Charlton Island** *island* Nunavut, C Canada
103 T6 **Charmes** Vosges, NE France
119 F19 **Charnawchytsy** *Rus.* Chernavchitsy. Brestskaya Voblasts', SW Belarus
15 R10 **Charny** Québec, SE Canada
149 T5 **Chārsadda** North-West Frontier Province, NW Pakistan
Charshanga/Charshangngy/Charshangy *see* Köýtendag
Charsk *see* Shar
181 W6 **Charters Towers** Queensland, NE Australia
15 R12 **Chartierville** Québec, SE Canada
102 M6 **Chartres** *anc.* Autricum, Civitas Carnutum. Eure-et-Loir, C France
127 P4 **Charvash Respubliki** *prev.* Chuvashskaya Respublika, *var.* Chavash Respubliki, *Eng.* Chuvashia. ◆ *autonomous republic* W Russian Federation
145 W15 **Charyn** *Kaz.* Sharyn. Almaty, SE Kazakhstan
61 D21 **Chascomús** Buenos Aires, E Argentina
11 N16 **Chase** British Columbia, SW Canada
21 U7 **Chase City** Virginia, NE USA
19 S4 **Chase, Mount** ▲ Maine, NE USA
118 M13 **Chashniki** *Rus.* Chashniki. Vitsyebskaya Voblasts', N Belarus
115 D15 **Chásia** ▲ C Greece
29 V9 **Chaska** Minnesota, N USA
185 D25 **Chaslands Mistake** *headland* South Island, NZ
125 R11 **Chasovo** Respublika Komi, NW Russian Federation
Chasovo *see* Vazhgort
124 H14 **Chastova** Novgorodskaya Oblast', NW Russian Federation
143 R3 **Chāt** Golestān, N Iran
Chatak *see* Chhatak
Chatang *see* Zhanang
39 R9 **Chatanika** Alaska, USA
39 R9 **Chatanika River** ≈ Alaska, USA
147 T8 **Chat-Bazar** Talasskaya Oblast', NW Kyrgyzstan
45 Y14 **Chateaubelair** Saint Vincent, W Saint Vincent and the Grenadines
102 J7 **Châteaubriant** Loire-Atlantique, NW France
103 Q8 **Château-Chinon** Nièvre, C France
108 C10 **Château d'Oex** Vaud, W Switzerland
102 L7 **Château-du-Loir** Sarthe, NW France
102 M6 **Châteaudun** Eure-et-Loir, C France
102 K7 **Château-Gontier** Mayenne, NW France
15 O13 **Châteauguay** Québec, SE Canada
102 F6 **Châteaulin** Finistère, NW France
103 N9 **Châteaumeillant** Cher, C France
102 K11 **Châteauneuf-sur-Charente** Charente, W France
102 M7 **Château-Renault** Indre-et-Loire, C France
103 N9 **Châteauroux** *prev.* Indreville. Indre, C France
103 T5 **Château-Salins** Moselle, NE France
103 P4 **Château-Thierry** Aisne, N France
99 H21 **Châtelet** Hainaut, S Belgium
Châtelherault *see* Châtellerault
102 L9 **Châtellerault** *var.* Châtelherault. Vienne, W France
29 X10 **Chatfield** Minnesota, N USA
13 O14 **Chatham** New Brunswick, SE Canada
14 D17 **Chatham** Ontario, S Canada
97 P22 **Chatham** SE England, UK
30 K14 **Chatham** Illinois, N USA
21 T7 **Chatham** Virginia, NE USA
63 F22 **Chatham, Isla** *island* S Chile

◆ Country ● Country Capital ◇ Dependent Territory ○ Dependent Territory Capital ◆ Administrative Region ✕ International Airport ▲ Mountain ▲ Mountain Range Volcano ≈ River ⊚ Lake ⊠ Reservoir

Chatham Island *see* San Cristóbal, Isla
Chatham Island Rise *see* Chatham Rise
192 L12 **Chatham Islands** *island group* NZ, SW Pacific Ocean
192 L12 **Chatham Rise** *var.* Chatham Island Rise. *undersea feature* S Pacific Ocean
39 X13 **Chatham Strait** *strait* Alaska, USA
Chathóir, Rinn *see* Cahore Point
102 M9 **Châtillon-sur-Indre** Indre, C France
103 Q7 **Châtillon-sur-Seine** Côte d'Or, C France
147 S8 **Chatkal** *Uzb.* Chotqol. ≈ Kyrgyzstan/Uzbekistan
147 R9 **Chatkal Range** *Rus.* Chatkal'skiy Khrebet. ▲ Kyrgyzstan/Uzbekistan
Chatkal'skiy Khrebet *see* Chatkal Range
23 N7 **Chatom** Alabama, S USA
Chatrapur *see* Chhatrapur
143 S10 **Chatrūd** Kermān, C Iran
23 S2 **Chatsworth** Georgia, SE USA
Chāttagām *see* Chittagong
23 S8 **Chattahoochee** Florida, SE USA
23 R8 **Chattahoochee River** ≈ SE USA
20 L10 **Chattanooga** Tennessee, S USA
147 V10 **Chatyr-Kël', Ozero** ◎ C Kyrgyzstan
147 W9 **Chatyr-Tash** Narynskaya Oblast', C Kyrgyzstan
15 R12 **Chaudière** ≈ Québec, SE Canada
167 S14 **Châu Đôc** *var.* Chauphu, Chau Phu. An Giang, S Vietnam
152 D13 **Chauhtan** *prev.* Chohtan. Rājasthān, NW India
115 F/5 **Chauk** Magwe, W Burma
103 R6 **Chaumont** *prev.* Chaumont-en-Bassigny. Haute-Marne, N France
Chaumont-en-Bassigny *see* Chaumont
123 T5 **Chaunskaya Guba** *bay* NE Russian Federation
103 P3 **Chauny** Aisne, N France
Châu Ô *see* Binh Sơn
Chau Phu *see* Châu Đôc
102 I5 **Chausey, Îles** *island group* N France
Chausy *see* Chavusy
18 C11 **Chautauqua Lake** ◎ New York, NE USA
102 L9 **Chauvigny** Vienne, W France
124 L6 **Chavan'ga** Murmanskaya Oblast', NW Russian Federation
14 K10 **Chavannes, Lac** ◎ Québec, SE Canada
Chavantes, Represa de *see* Xavantes, Represa de
61 D15 **Chavarría** Corrientes, NE Argentina
Chavash Respubliki *see* Charvash Respubliki
104 I5 **Chaves** *anc.* Aquae Flaviae. Vila Real, N Portugal
Chávez, Isla *see* Santa Cruz, Isla
82 G13 **Chavuma** North Western, NW Zambia
119 O16 **Chavusy** *Rus.* Chausy. Mahilyowskaya Voblasts', E Belarus
Chayan *see* Shayan
147 U8 **Chayek** Narynskaya Oblast', C Kyrgyzstan
139 T6 **Chāy Khānah** E Iraq
125 T16 **Chaykovskiy** Permskaya Oblast', NW Russian Federation
167 T12 **Chbar** Môndól Kiri, E Cambodia
23 Q4 **Cheaha Mountain** ▲ Alabama, S USA
Cheatharlach *see* Carlow
21 S2 **Cheat River** ≈ NE USA
111 A16 **Cheb** *Ger.* Eger. Karlovarský Kraj, W Czech Republic
127 Q3 **Cheboksary** Chuvashskaya Respublika, W Russian Federation
31 Q5 **Cheboygan** Michigan, N USA
Chechaouèn *see* Chefchaouen
Chechenia *see* Chechenskaya Respublika
127 O15 **Chechenskaya Respublika** *Eng.* Chechenia, Chechnia, *Rus.* Chechnya. ◈ *autonomous republic* SW Russian Federation
76 M6 **Chech, Erg** *desert* Algeria/Mali
Chechersk *see* Chachersk
Chechevichi *see* Chachevichy
Che-chiang *see* Zhejiang
Chechnia/Chechnya *see* Chechenskaya Respublika
163 Y15 **Chech'ŏn** *Jap.* Teisen. N South Korea
111 L15 **Chęciny** Świętokrzyskie, S Poland
27 Q10 **Checotah** Oklahoma, C USA
13 R15 **Chedabucto Bay** *inlet* Nova Scotia, E Canada
166 J7 **Cheduba Island** *island* W Burma
37 T5 **Cheesman Lake** ⊠ Colorado, C USA
195 S16 **Cheetham, Cape** *headland* Antarctica
74 G5 **Chefchaouen** *var.* Chaouèn, Chechaouèn, *Sp.* Xauen. N Morocco
Chefoo *see* Yantai
38 M12 **Chefornak** Alaska, USA
123 R13 **Chegdomyn** Khabarovskiy Kray, SE Russian Federation
76 M4 **Chegga** Tiris Zemmour, NE Mauritania
Cheghcheran *see* Chaghcharān
32 G9 **Chehalis** Washington, NW USA
32 G9 **Chehalis River** ≈ Washington, NW USA
148 M6 **Chehel Abdālān, Kūh-e** *var.* Chalap Dalam, *Pash.* Chalap Dalan. ▲ C Afghanistan
115 D14 **Cheimadítis, Límni** ◎ N Greece
103 U15 **Cheiron, Mont** ▲ SE France
163 X17 **Cheju** *Jap.* Saishū. S South Korea
163 Y17 **Cheju** ✕ S South Korea
163 Y17 **Cheju-do** *Jap.* Saishū; *prev.* Quelpart. *island* S South Korea
163 X17 **Cheju-haehyŏp** *strait* S South Korea
Chekiang *see* Zhejiang
Chekichler/Chekishlyar *see* Çekiçler
188 F8 **Chelab** Babeldaob, N Palau
147 N11 **Chelak** *Rus.* Chelek. Samarqand Viloyati, C Uzbekistan
32 J7 **Chelan, Lake** ⊠ Washington, NW USA
Chelek *see* Chelak
Cheleken *see* Hazar
Chélif/Chéliff *see* Chelif, Oued
74 J5 **Chelif, Oued** *var.* Chélif, Chéliff, Chellif, Shellif. ≈ N Algeria
Chelkar *see* Shalkar
Chelkar, Ozero *see* Shalkar, Ozero
Chellif *see* Chelif, Oued
111 P14 **Chełm** *Rus.* Kholm. Lubelskie, SE Poland
110 I9 **Chełmno** *Ger.* Culm, Kulm. Kujawski-pomorskie, C Poland
14 F10 **Chelmsford** Ontario, S Canada
97 P21 **Chelmsford** E England, UK
110 J9 **Chełmża** *Ger.* Culmsee, Kulmsee. Kujawski-pomorskie, C Poland
27 Q8 **Chelsea** Oklahoma, C USA
18 M8 **Chelsea** Vermont, NE USA
97 L21 **Cheltenham** C England, UK
105 R9 **Chelva** País Valenciano, E Spain
122 G11 **Chelyabinsk** Chelyabinskaya Oblast', C Russian Federation
122 F11 **Chelyabinskaya Oblast'** ◈ *province* C Russian Federation
123 N5 **Chelyuskin, Mys** *headland* N Russian Federation
41 Y12 **Chemax** Yucatán, SE Mexico
83 N16 **Chemba** Sofala, C Mozambique
82 J13 **Chembe** Luapula, NE Zambia
Chemenibit *see* Çemenibit
Chemerisy *see* Chamyarysy
116 K7 **Chemerivtsi** Khmel'nyts'ka Oblast', W Ukraine
102 J8 **Chemillé** Maine-et-Loire, NW France
173 X17 **Chemin Grenier** S Mauritius
101 N16 **Chemnitz** *prev.* Karl-Marx-Stadt. Sachsen, E Germany
Chemulpo *see* Inch'ŏn
32 H14 **Chemult** Oregon, NW USA
18 G12 **Chemung River** ≈ New York/Pennsylvania, NE USA
149 U8 **Chenāb** ≈ India/Pakistan
39 S9 **Chena Hot Springs** Alaska, USA
18 I11 **Chenango River** ≈ New York, NE USA
168 J7 **Chenderoh, Tasik** ◎ Peninsular Malaysia
15 Q11 **Chêne, Rivière du** ≈ Québec, SE Canada
32 L8 **Cheney** Washington, NW USA
26 M6 **Cheney Reservoir** ⊠ Kansas, C USA
Chengchiatun *see* Liaoyuan
Ch'eng-chou/Chengchow *see* Zhengzhou
161 P1 **Chengde** *var.* Jehol. Hebei, E China
160 I9 **Chengdu** *var.* Chengtu, Ch'eng-tu. Sichuan, C China
161 Q14 **Chenghai** Guangdong, S China
Chenghsien *see* Zhengzhou
160 H13 **Chengjiang** Yunnan, SW China
Chengjiang *see* Taihe
160 L17 **Chengmai** *var.* Jinjiang. Hainan, S China
Chengtu/Ch'eng-tu *see* Chengdu
159 W12 **Chengxian** *var.* Cheng Xian. Gansu, C China
Chengyang *see* Juxian
Chengzhong *see* Ningming
Chenkiang *see* Zhenjiang
155 J19 **Chennai** *prev.* Madras. Tamil Nādu, S India
155 J19 **Chennai** ✕ Tamil Nādu, S India
103 R8 **Chenôve** Côte d'Or, C France
Chenstokhov *see* Częstochowa
160 L11 **Chenxi** *var.* Chenyang. Hunan, S China
Chen Xian/Chenxian/Chen Xiang *see* Chenzhou
Chenyang *see* Chenxi
161 N12 **Chenzhou** *var.* Chenxian, Chen Xian, Chen Xiang. Hunan, S China
167 U12 **Cheo Reo** *var.* A Yun Pa. Gia Lai, S Vietnam
114 I11 **Chepelare** Smolyan, S Bulgaria
114 I11 **Chepelarska Reka** ≈ S Bulgaria
56 B11 **Chepén** La Libertad, C Peru
62 J10 **Chepes** La Rioja, C Argentina
161 O15 **Chep Lap Kok** ✕ (Hong Kong) S China
43 U14 **Chepo** Panamá, C Panama
Chepping Wycombe *see* High Wycombe
127 R14 **Cheptsa** ≈ NW Russian Federation
30 K3 **Chequamegon Point** *headland* Wisconsin, N USA
103 O8 **Cher** ◈ *department* C France
102 M8 **Cher** ≈ C France
Cherangani Hills *see* Cherangany Hills
81 H17 **Cherangany Hills** *var.* Cherangani Hills. ▲ W Kenya
21 S11 **Cheraw** South Carolina, SE USA
102 J3 **Cherbourg** *anc.* Carusbur. Manche, N France
127 R5 **Cherdakly** Ul'yanovskaya Oblast', W Russian Federation
125 U12 **Cherdyn'** Permskaya Oblast', NW Russian Federation
126 J14 **Cherekha** ≈ W Russian Federation
122 M13 **Cheremkhovo** Irkutskaya Oblast', S Russian Federation
Cheren *see* Keren
124 K14 **Cherepovets** Vologodskaya Oblast', NW Russian Federation
125 O11 **Cherevkovo** Arkhangel'skaya Oblast', NW Russian Federation
74 I6 **Chergui, Chott ech** *salt lake* NW Algeria
Cherikov *see* Cherykaw
117 P6 **Cherkas'ka Oblast'** *var.* Cherkasy, *Rus.* Cherkasskaya Oblast'. ◈ *province* C Ukraine
Cherkasskaya Oblast' *see* Cherkas'ka Oblast'
Cherkassy *see* Cherkasy
117 Q6 **Cherkasy** *Rus.* Cherkassy. Cherkas'ka Oblast', C Ukraine
Cherkasy *see* Cherkas'ka Oblast'
126 M15 **Cherkessk** Karachayevo-Cherkesskaya Respublika, SW Russian Federation
122 H12 **Cherlak** Omskaya Oblast', C Russian Federation
122 H12 **Cherlakskiy** Omskaya Oblast', C Russian Federation
125 U13 **Chermoz** Permskaya Oblast', NW Russian Federation
Chernavchitsy *see* Charnawchytsy
125 T3 **Chernaya** Nenetskiy Avtonomnyy Okrug, NW Russian Federation
127 T4 **Chernaya** ≈ NW Russian Federation
Chernigov *see* Chernihiv
Chernigovskaya Oblast' *see* Chernihivs'ka Oblast'
117 Q2 **Chernihiv** *Rus.* Chernigov. Chernihivs'ka Oblast', NE Ukraine
Chernihiv *see* Chernihivs'ka Oblast'
117 V9 **Chernihivka** Zaporiz'ka Oblast', SE Ukraine
117 P2 **Chernihivs'ka Oblast'** *var.* Chernihiv, *Rus.* Chernigovskaya Oblast'. ◈ *province* NE Ukraine
114 I9 **Cherni Osŭm** ≈ N Bulgaria
116 J8 **Chernivets'ka Oblast'** *var.* Chernivtsi, *Rus.* Chernovitskaya Oblast'. ◈ *province* W Ukraine
114 I9 **Cherni Vit** ≈ NW Bulgaria
114 G10 **Cherni Vrŭkh** ▲ W Bulgaria
116 K8 **Chernivtsi** *Ger.* Czernowitz, *Rom.* Cernăuţi, *Rus.* Chernovtsy. Chernivets'ka Oblast', W Ukraine
116 M7 **Chernivtsi** Vinnyts'ka Oblast', C Ukraine
Chernivtsi *see* Chernivets'ka Oblast'
Chernobyl' *see* Chornobyl'
Cherno More *see* Black Sea
Chernomorskoye *see* Chornomors'ke
145 T7 **Chernoretskoye** Pavlodar, NE Kazakhstan
Chernovitskaya Oblast' *see* Chernivets'ka Oblast'
Chernovtsy *see* Chernivtsi
145 U8 **Chernoye** Pavlodar, NE Kazakhstan
Chernoye More *see* Black Sea
125 U16 **Chernushka** Permskaya Oblast', NW Russian Federation
117 N4 **Chernyakhiv** *Rus.* Chernyakhov. Zhytomyrs'ka Oblast', N Ukraine
Chernyakhov *see* Chernyakhiv
119 C14 **Chernyakhovsk** *Ger.* Insterburg. Kaliningradskaya Oblast', W Russian Federation
126 K8 **Chernyanka** Belgorodskaya Oblast', W Russian Federation
127 V5 **Chernyshëva, Gryada** ▲ NW Russian Federation
144 J14 **Chernyshëva, Zaliv** *gulf* SW Kazakhstan
123 O10 **Chernyshevskiy** Respublika Sakha (Yakutiya), NE Russian Federation
127 P13 **Chërnyye Zemli** *plain* SW Russian Federation
Chërnyy Irtysh *see* Ertix He
127 V7 **Chernyy Otrog** Orenburgskaya Oblast', W Russian Federation
29 T12 **Cherokee** Iowa, C USA
26 M8 **Cherokee** Oklahoma, C USA
25 R9 **Cherokee** Texas, SW USA
21 O8 **Cherokee Lake** ⊠ Tennessee, S USA
Cherokees, Lake O' The *see* Grand Lake O' The Cherokees
44 H1 **Cherokee Sound** Great Abaco, N Bahamas
153 V13 **Cherrapunji** Meghālaya, NE India
28 L9 **Cherry Creek** ≈ South Dakota, N USA
18 J16 **Cherry Hill** New Jersey, NE USA
27 Q7 **Cherryvale** Kansas, C USA
21 Q10 **Cherryville** North Carolina, SE USA
Cherski Range *see* Cherskogo, Khrebet
123 T6 **Cherskiy** Respublika Sakha (Yakutiya), NE Russian Federation
123 R8 **Cherskogo, Khrebet** *var.* Cherski Range. ▲ NE Russian Federation
Cherso *see* Cres
126 L10 **Chertkovo** Rostovskaya Oblast', SW Russian Federation
Cherven' *see* Chervyen'
114 H8 **Cherven Bryag** Pleven, N Bulgaria
116 M4 **Chervonoarmiys'k** Zhytomyrs'ka Oblast', N Ukraine
Chervonograd *see* Chervonohrad
116 I4 **Chervonohrad** *Rus.* Chervonograd. L'vivs'ka Oblast', NW Ukraine
117 W6 **Chervonooskil's'ke Vodoskhovyshche** *Rus.* Krasnooskol'skoye Vodokhranilishche. ⊠ NE Ukraine
Chervonoye, Ozero *see* Chyrvonaye, Vozyera
117 S4 **Chervonozavods'ke** Poltavs'ka Oblast', C Ukraine
119 L16 **Chervyen'** *Rus.* Cherven'. Minskaya Voblasts', C Belarus
119 P16 **Cherykaw** *Rus.* Cherikov. Mahilyowskaya Voblasts', E Belarus
31 R9 **Chesaning** Michigan, N USA
21 X5 **Chesapeake Bay** *inlet* NE USA
Cheshevlya *see* Tsyeshawlya
97 K18 **Cheshire** *cultural region* C England, UK
127 P5 **Chëshskaya Guba** *var.* Archangel Bay, Chesha Bay, Dvina Bay. *bay* NW Russian Federation
14 F14 **Chesley** Ontario, S Canada
21 Q10 **Chesnee** South Carolina, SE USA
97 K18 **Chester** *Wel.* Caerleon; *hist.* Legaceaster, *Lat.* Deva, Devana Castra. C England, UK
35 O4 **Chester** California, W USA
30 K16 **Chester** Illinois, N USA
33 S7 **Chester** Montana, NW USA
18 I16 **Chester** Pennsylvania, NE USA
21 R1 **Chester** South Carolina, SE USA
25 X9 **Chester** Texas, SW USA
21 W6 **Chester** Virginia, NE USA
21 R11 **Chester** West Virginia, NE USA
97 M18 **Chesterfield** C England, UK
21 S11 **Chesterfield** South Carolina, SE USA
21 W6 **Chesterfield** Virginia, NE USA
192 J9 **Chesterfield, Îles** *island group* NW New Caledonia
9 O9 **Chesterfield Inlet** Nunavut, NW Canada
9 O9 **Chesterfield Inlet** *inlet* Nunavut, N Canada
21 Y3 **Chester River** ≈ Delaware/Maryland, NE USA
21 X3 **Chestertown** Maryland, NE USA
19 R4 **Chesuncook Lake** ◎ Maine, NE USA
30 J5 **Chetek** Wisconsin, N USA
13 R14 **Chéticamp** Nova Scotia, SE Canada
27 Q8 **Chetopa** Kansas, C USA
41 Y14 **Chetumal** *var.* Payo Obispo. Quintana Roo, SE Mexico
Chetumal, Bahia/Chetumal, Bahía de *see* Chetumal Bay
42 G1 **Chetumal Bay** *var.* Bahia Chetumal, Bahía de Chetumal. *bay* Belize/Mexico
10 M13 **Chetwynd** British Columbia, W Canada
38 M11 **Chevak** Alaska, USA
36 M12 **Chevelon Creek** ≈ Arizona, SW USA
185 J17 **Cheviot** Canterbury, South Island, NZ
96 L13 **Cheviot Hills** *hill range* England/Scotland, UK
96 L13 **Cheviot, The** ▲ NE England, UK
14 M11 **Chevreuil, Lac du** ◎ Québec, SE Canada
81 I16 **Ch'ew Bahir** *var.* Lake Stefanie. ◎ Ethiopia/Kenya
32 L7 **Chewelah** Washington, NW USA
26 K10 **Cheyenne** Oklahoma, C USA
33 Z17 **Cheyenne** *state capital* Wyoming, C USA
26 L5 **Cheyenne Bottoms** ◎ Kansas, C USA
16 J8 **Cheyenne River** ≈ South Dakota/Wyoming, N USA
37 W5 **Cheyenne Wells** Colorado, C USA
108 C9 **Cheyres** Vaud, W Switzerland
Chezdi-Oşorheiu *see* Târgu Secuiesc
153 P13 **Chhapra** *prev.* Chapra. Bihār, N India
153 V13 **Chhatak** *var.* Chatak. Chittagong, NE Bangladesh
154 J9 **Chhatarpur** Madhya Pradesh, C India
154 N13 **Chhatrapur** *prev.* Chatrapur. Orissa, E India
154 L12 **Chhattisgarh** *plain* C India
154 K12 **Chhattisgarh** ◈ *state* E India
154 I11 **Chhindwāra** Madhya Pradesh, C India
153 T12 **Chhukha** SW Bhutan
161 S14 **Chiai** *var.* Chia-i, Chiayi, Kiayi, Jiayi, *Jap.* Kagi. C Taiwan
Chia-mu-ssu *see* Jiamusi
83 B15 **Chiange** *Port.* Vila de Almoster. Huíla, SW Angola
Chiang-hsi *see* Jiangxi
161 S12 **Chiang Kai-shek** ✕ (T'aipei) N Taiwan
167 P8 **Chiang Khan** Loei, E Thailand
167 O7 **Chiang Mai** *var.* Chiangmai, Chiengmai, Kiangmai. Chiang Mai, NW Thailand
167 O7 **Chiang Mai** ✕ Chiang Mai, NW Thailand
167 O6 **Chiang Rai** *var.* Chianpai, Chienrai, Muang Chiang Rai. Chiang Rai, NW Thailand
Chiang-su *see* Jiangsu
Chianning/Chian-ning *see* Nanjing
Chianpai *see* Chiang Rai
106 G12 **Chianti** *cultural region* C Italy
Chiapa *see* Chiapa de Corzo
41 U16 **Chiapa de Corzo** *var.* Chiapa. Chiapas, SE Mexico
41 V16 **Chiapas** ◈ *state* SE Mexico
106 J12 **Chiaravalle** Marche, C Italy
107 N22 **Chiaravalle Centrale** Calabria, SW Italy
106 E7 **Chiari** Lombardia, N Italy
108 H12 **Chiasso** Ticino, S Switzerland
137 S9 **Chiat'ura** C Georgia
41 P15 **Chiautla** *var.* Chiautla de Tapia. Puebla, S Mexico
Chiautla de Tapia *see* Chiautla
106 D10 **Chiavari** Liguria, NW Italy
106 E6 **Chiavenna** Lombardia, N Italy
Chiayi *see* Chiai
Chiazza *see* Piazza Armerina
165 O13 **Chiba** *var.* Tiba. Chiba, Honshū, S Japan
165 O14 **Chiba** *off.* Chiba-ken, *var.* Tiba. ◈ *prefecture* Honshū, S Japan
83 M18 **Chibabava** Sofala, C Mozambique
161 O10 **Chibi** *prev.* Puqi. Hubei, C China
83 B15 **Chibia** *Port.* João de Almeida, Vila João de Almeida. Huíla, SW Angola
83 M18 **Chiboma** Sofala, C Mozambique
82 J12 **Chibondo** Luapula, N Zambia
82 K11 **Chibote** Luapula, NE Zambia
12 K12 **Chibougamau** Québec, SE Canada
164 H11 **Chiburi-jima** *island* Oki-shotō, SW Japan
83 M20 **Chibuto** Gaza, S Mozambique
31 N11 **Chicago** Illinois, N USA
31 N11 **Chicago Heights** Illinois, N USA
15 W6 **Chic-Chocs, Monts** *Eng.* Shickshock Mountains. ▲ Québec, SE Canada
39 W13 **Chichagof Island** *island* Alexander Archipelago, Alaska, USA
57 K20 **Chichas, Cordillera de** ▲ SW Bolivia
41 X12 **Chichén-Itzá, Ruinas** *ruins* Yucatán, SE Mexico
97 N23 **Chichester** SE England, UK
42 C5 **Chichicastenango** Quiché, W Guatemala
42 I9 **Chichigalpa** Chinandega, NW Nicaragua
Ch'i-ch'i-ha-erh *see* Qiqihar
165 X16 **Chichijima-rettō** *Eng.* Beechy Group. *island group* SE Japan
54 K4 **Chichiriviche** Falcón, N Venezuela
39 R11 **Chickaloon** Alaska, USA
20 L10 **Chickamauga Lake** ⊠ Tennessee, S USA
23 N7 **Chickasawhay River** ≈ Mississippi, S USA
26 M11 **Chickasha** Oklahoma, C USA
39 T9 **Chicken** Alaska, USA
104 J16 **Chiclana de la Frontera** Andalucía, S Spain
56 B11 **Chiclayo** Lambayeque, NW Peru
35 N5 **Chico** California, W USA
83 L15 **Chicoa** Tete, NW Mozambique
83 M20 **Chicomo** Gaza, S Mozambique
18 M11 **Chicopee** Massachusetts, NE USA
63 I19 **Chico, Río** ≈ SE Argentina
63 I21 **Chico, Río** ≈ S Argentina
27 W14 **Chicot, Lake** ◎ Arkansas, C USA
15 R7 **Chicoutimi** Québec, SE Canada
15 Q8 **Chicoutimi** ≈ Québec, SE Canada
83 L19 **Chicualacuala** Gaza, SW Mozambique
83 B14 **Chicuma** Benguela, C Angola
155 J21 **Chidambaram** Tamil Nādu, SE India
196 K13 **Chidley, Cape** *headland* Newfoundland and Labrador, E Canada
101 N24 **Chiemsee** ◎ SE Germany
Chiengmai *see* Chiang Mai
Chienrai *see* Chiang Rai
106 B8 **Chieri** Piemonte, NW Italy
106 F8 **Chiese** ≈ N Italy
107 K14 **Chieti** *var.* Teate. Abruzzo, C Italy
99 E19 **Chièvres** Hainaut, SW Belgium
163 S12 **Chifeng** *var.* Ulanhad. Nei Mongol Zizhiqu, N China
82 F13 **Chifumage** ≈ E Angola
82 M13 **Chifunda** Eastern, NE Zambia
145 S14 **Chiganak** *var.* Čiganak. Zhambyl, SE Kazakhstan
39 P15 **Chiginagak, Mount** ▲ Alaska, USA
Chigirin *see* Chyhyryn
41 P13 **Chignahuapan** Puebla, S Mexico
39 O15 **Chignik** Alaska, USA
83 M19 **Chigombe** ≈ S Mozambique
54 D7 **Chigorodó** Antioquia, NW Colombia
83 M19 **Chigubo** Gaza, S Mozambique
162 D6 **Chihertey** Bayan-Ölgiy, W Mongolia
Chih-fu *see* Yantai
Chihli *see* Hebei
Chihli, Gulf of *see* Bo Hai
40 J6 **Chihuahua** Chihuahua, NW Mexico
40 I6 **Chihuahua** ◈ *state* N Mexico
145 O15 **Chiili** Kzylorda, S Kazakhstan
26 M7 **Chikaskia River** ≈ Kansas/Oklahoma, C USA
155 H19 **Chik Ballāpur** Karnātaka, W India
124 G15 **Chikhachevo** Pskovskaya Oblast', W Russian Federation
155 F19 **Chikmagalūr** Karnātaka, W India
83 J15 **Chikumbi** Lusaka, C Zambia
82 M13 **Chikwa** Eastern, NE Zambia
Chikwana *see* Chikwawa
83 N15 **Chikwawa** *var.* Chikwana. Southern, S Malawi
155 J16 **Chilakalūrupet** Andhra Pradesh, E India
146 L14 **Chilan** Lebap Welaýaty, E Turkmenistan
Chilapa *see* Chilapa de Alvarez
41 P16 **Chilapa de Alvarez** *var.* Chilapa. Guerrero, S Mexico
155 J25 **Chilaw** North Western Province, W Sri Lanka
57 D15 **Chilca** Lima, W Peru
23 Q4 **Childersburg** Alabama, S USA
25 P4 **Childress** Texas, SW USA
63 G14 **Chile** *off.* Republic of Chile. ◆ *republic* SW South America
193 U10 **Chile Basin** *undersea feature* E Pacific Ocean
63 H20 **Chile Chico** Aisén, W Chile
62 I9 **Chilecito** La Rioja, NW Argentina
62 H12 **Chilecito** Mendoza, W Argentina
83 L14 **Chilembwe** Eastern, E Zambia
193 S11 **Chile Rise** *undersea feature* SE Pacific Ocean
117 N13 **Chilia Braţul** ≈ SE Romania
Chilia-Nouă *see* Kiliya
145 V15 **Chilik** Almaty, SE Kazakhstan
145 V15 **Chilik** ≈ SE Kazakhstan
154 O13 **Chilika Lake** *var.* Chilka Lake. ◎ E India
82 J13 **Chililabombwe** Copperbelt, C Zambia
Chi-lin *see* Jilin
Chilka Lake *see* Chilika Lake
10 H9 **Chilkoot Pass** *pass* British Columbia, W Canada
Chill Ala, Cuan *see* Killala Bay
62 G13 **Chillán** Bío Bío, C Chile
61 C22 **Chillar** Buenos Aires, E Argentina
Chill Chiaráin, Cuan *see* Kilkieran Bay
30 K12 **Chillicothe** Illinois, N USA
27 S3 **Chillicothe** Missouri, C USA
31 S14 **Chillicothe** Ohio, N USA
25 Q4 **Chillicothe** Texas, SW USA
10 M17 **Chilliwack** British Columbia, SW Canada
Chill Mhantáin, Ceann *see* Wicklow Head
Chill Mhantáin, Sléibhte *see* Wicklow Mountains
108 C10 **Chillon** Vaud, W Switzerland
Chil'mamedkum, Peski/Chilmämetgum *see* Çilmämmetgum
63 F17 **Chiloé, Isla de** *var.* Isla Grande de Chiloé. *island* W Chile
32 H15 **Chiloquin** Oregon, NW USA
41 O16 **Chilpancingo** *var.* Chilpancingo de los Bravos. Guerrero, S Mexico
Chilpancingo de los Bravos *see* Chilpancingo
97 N21 **Chiltern Hills** *hill range* S England, UK
30 M7 **Chilton** Wisconsin, N USA
82 F11 **Chiluage** Lunda Sul, NE Angola
82 N12 **Chilumba** *prev.* Deep Bay. Northern, N Malawi
161 T12 **Chilung** *var.* Keelung, *Jap.* Kirun, Kirun'; *prev. Sp.* Santissima Trinidad. N Taiwan
83 N15 **Chilwa, Lake** *var.* Lago Chirua, Lake Shirwa. ◎ SE Malawi
167 R10 **Chi, Mae Nam** ≈ E Thailand
42 C6 **Chimaltenango** Chimaltenango, C Guatemala
42 A2 **Chimaltenango** *off.* Departamento de Chimaltenango. ◈ *department* S Guatemala
43 V15 **Chimán** Panamá, E Panama
83 M17 **Chimanimani** *prev.* Mandidzudzure, Melsetter. Manicaland, E Zimbabwe
99 G22 **Chimay** Hainaut, S Belgium
37 S10 **Chimayo** New Mexico, SW USA
Chimbay *see* Chimboy
56 A13 **Chimborazo** ◈ *province* C Ecuador
56 C7 **Chimborazo** ⚶ C Ecuador
56 C12 **Chimbote** Ancash, W Peru
146 H7 **Chimboy** *Rus.* Chimbay. Qoraqalpog'iston Respublikasi, NW Uzbekistan
186 D7 **Chimbu** ◈ *province* C PNG
54 F6 **Chimichagua** Cesar, N Colombia
Chimishliya *see* Cimişlia
Chimkent *see* Shymkent
Chimkentskaya Oblast' *see* Yuzhnyy Kazakhstan
28 I14 **Chimney Rock** *rock* Nebraska, C USA
83 M17 **Chimoio** Manica, C Mozambique
82 K11 **Chimpembe** Northern, NE Zambia
41 O8 **China** Nuevo León, NE Mexico
156 M9 **China** *off.* People's Republic of China, *Chin.* Chung-hua Jen-min Kung-ho-kuo, Zhonghua Renmin Gongheguo; *prev.* Chinese Empire. ◆ *republic* E Asia
19 Q7 **China Lake** ◎ Maine, NE USA
42 F8 **Chinameca** San Miguel, E El Salvador
Chi-nan/Chinan *see* Jinan
42 H9 **Chinandega** Chinandega, NW Nicaragua
42 H9 **Chinandega** ◈ *department* NW Nicaragua
China, People's Republic of *see* China
China, Republic of *see* Taiwan

◆ Country ● Country Capital ◇ Dependent Territory ○ Dependent Territory Capital ◈ Administrative Region ✕ International Airport ▲ Mountain ▲ Mountain Range ⚶ Volcano ≈ River ◎ Lake ⊠ Reservoir

24 J11 **Chinati Mountains** ▲ Texas, SW USA
Chinaz *see* Chinoz
57 E15 **Chincha Alta** Ica, SW Peru
11 N11 **Chinchaga** ≈ Alberta, SW Canada
Chin-chiang *see* Quanzhou
Chinchilla *see* Chinchilla de Monte Aragón
105 Q11 **Chinchilla de Monte Aragón** *var.* Chinchilla. Castilla-La Mancha, C Spain
54 D10 **Chinchiná** Caldas, W Colombia
105 O8 **Chinchón** Madrid, C Spain
41 Z14 **Chinchorro, Banco** *island* SE Mexico
Chin-chou/Chinchow *see* Jinzhou
21 Z5 **Chincoteague** Assateague Island, Virginia, NE USA
83 O17 **Chinde** Zambézia, NE Mozambique
163 X17 **Chin-do** *Jap.* Chin-tō. *island* SW South Korea
159 R13 **Chindu** *var.* Chuqung. Qinghai, C China
166 M2 **Chindwin** ≈ N Burma
Chinese Empire *see* China
Ch'ing Hai *see* Qinghai Hu
Chinghai *see* Qinghai
Chingildi *see* Shengeldi
144 H9 **Chingirlau** *Kaz.* Shyngghyrlaū. Zapadnyy Kazakhstan, W Kazakhstan
82 J13 **Chingola** Copperbelt, C Zambia
Ching-Tao/Ch'ing-tao *see* Qingdao
82 C13 **Chinguar** Huambo, C Angola
76 I7 **Chinguețți** *var.* Chinguetti. Adrar, C Mauritania
163 Z16 **Chinhae** *Jap.* Chinkai. S South Korea
166 K4 **Chin Hills** ▲ W Burma
83 K16 **Chinhoyi** *prev.* Sinoia. Mashonaland West, N Zimbabwe
Chinhsien *see* Jinzhou
39 Q14 **Chiniak, Cape** *headland* Kodiak Island, Alaska, USA
14 G10 **Chiniguchi Lake** ◎ Ontario, S Canada
149 U8 **Chinīot** Punjab, NE Pakistan
163 Y16 **Chinju** *Jap.* Shinshū. S South Korea
Chinkai *see* Chinhae
78 M13 **Chinko** ≈ E Central African Republic
37 O9 **Chinle** Arizona, SW USA
161 R13 **Chinmen Tao** *var.* Jinmen Dao, Quemoy. *island* W Taiwan
Chinnchâr *see* Shinshār
Chinnereth *see* Tiberias, Lake
164 C12 **Chino** *var.* Tino. Nagano, Honshū, S Japan
102 L8 **Chinon** Indre-et-Loire, C France
33 T7 **Chinook** Montana, NW USA
Chinook State *see* Washington
192 L4 **Chinook Trough** *undersea feature* N Pacific Ocean
36 K11 **Chino Valley** Arizona, SW USA
147 P10 **Chinoz** *Rus.* Chinaz. Toshkent Viloyati, E Uzbekistan
82 L12 **Chinsali** Northern, NE Zambia
166 K5 **Chin State** ◈ *state* W Burma
Chinsura *see* Chunchura
Chin-tō *see* Chin-do
54 E6 **Chinú** Córdoba, NW Colombia
99 K24 **Chiny, Forêt de** *forest* SE Belgium
83 M15 **Chioco** Tete, NW Mozambique
106 H8 **Chioggia** *anc.* Fossa Claudia. Veneto, NE Italy
114 H12 **Chionótrypa** ▲ NE Greece
115 L18 **Chíos** *var.* Hios, Khíos, *It.* Scio, *Turk.* Sakiz-Adasi. Chíos, E Greece
115 K18 **Chíos** *var.* Khíos. *island* E Greece
83 M14 **Chipata** *prev.* Fort Jameson. Eastern, E Zambia
83 C14 **Chipindo** Huíla, C Angola
23 R8 **Chipley** Florida, SE USA
155 D15 **Chiplūn** Mahārāshtra, W India
81 H22 **Chipogolo** Dodoma, C Tanzania
23 R8 **Chipola River** ≈ Florida, SE USA
97 L22 **Chippenham** S England, UK
30 J6 **Chippewa Falls** Wisconsin, N USA
30 J4 **Chippewa, Lake** ▣ Wisconsin, N USA
31 Q8 **Chippewa River** ≈ Michigan, N USA
30 I6 **Chippewa River** ≈ Wisconsin, N USA
Chipping Wycombe *see* High Wycombe
114 G8 **Chiprovtsi** Montana, NW Bulgaria
19 T4 **Chiputneticook Lakes** *lakes* Canada/USA
56 D13 **Chiquián** Ancash, W Peru
41 Y11 **Chiquilá** Quintana Roo, SE Mexico
42 E6 **Chiquimula** Chiquimula, SE Guatemala
42 A3 **Chiquimula** *off.* Departamento de Chiquimula. ◈ *department* SE Guatemala
42 D7 **Chiquimulilla** Santa Rosa, S Guatemala
54 F9 **Chiquinquirá** Boyacá, C Colombia
155 J17 **Chīrāla** Andhra Pradesh, E India
149 N4 **Chīras** Ghowr, N Afghanistan
152 H11 **Chirāwa** Rājasthān, N India
Chirchik *see* Chirchiq
147 Q9 **Chirchiq** *Rus.* Chirchik. Toshkent Viloyati, E Uzbekistan
147 P10 **Chirchiq** ≈ E Uzbekistan
Chire *see* Shire
83 L18 **Chiredzi** Masvingo, SE Zimbabwe
25 X8 **Chireno** Texas, SW USA
77 X7 **Chirfa** Agadez, NE Niger
37 O16 **Chiricahua Mountains** ▲ Arizona, SW USA
37 O16 **Chiricahua Peak** ▲ Arizona, SW USA
54 F6 **Chiriguaná** Cesar, N Colombia
39 P15 **Chirikof Island** *island* Alaska, USA
43 P16 **Chiriquí** *off.* Provincia de Chiriquí. ◈ *province* SW Panama
43 P17 **Chiriquí, Golfo de** *Eng.* Chiriqui Gulf. *gulf* SW Panama
43 P15 **Chiriquí Grande** Bocas del Toro, W Panama
Chiriqui Gulf *see* Chiriquí, Golfo de
43 P15 **Chiriquí, Laguna de** *lagoon* NW Panama
43 O16 **Chiriquí Viejo, Río** ≈ W Panama
Chiriquí, Volcán de *see* Barú, Volcán
83 N15 **Chiromo** Southern, S Malawi
114 J10 **Chirpan** Stara Zagora, C Bulgaria
43 N14 **Chirripó Atlántico, Río** ≈ E Costa Rica
Chirripó, Cerro *see* Chirripó Grande, Cerro
43 N14 **Chirripó Grande, Cerro** *var.* Cerro Chirripó. ▲ SE Costa Rica
43 N13 **Chirripó, Río** *var.* Río Chirripó del Pacífico. ≈ NE Costa Rica
Chirua, Lago *see* Chilwa, Lake
83 J15 **Chirundu** Southern, S Zambia
29 W8 **Chisago City** Minnesota, N USA
83 J14 **Chisamba** Central, C Zambia
39 T10 **Chisana** Alaska, USA
82 I13 **Chisasa** North Western, NW Zambia
12 I9 **Chisasibi** Québec, C Canada
42 D4 **Chisec** Alta Verapaz, C Guatemala
127 U5 **Chishmy** Respublika Bashkortostan, W Russian Federation
29 V4 **Chisholm** Minnesota, N USA
160 I11 **Chishui He** ≈ C China
Chisimaio/Chisimayu *see* Kismaayo
117 N10 **Chişinău** *Rus.* Kishinev. ● (Moldova) C Moldova
117 N10 **Chişinău** × S Moldova
Chişinău-Criş *see* Chişineu-Criş
116 F10 **Chişineu-Criş** *Hung.* Kişjenő; *prev.* Chişinău-Criş. Arad, W Romania
83 K14 **Chisomo** Central, C Zambia
106 A8 **Chisone** ≈ NW Italy
24 K12 **Chisos Mountains** ▲ Texas, SW USA
149 U10 **Chistian Mandi** Punjab, E Pakistan
39 T10 **Chistochina** Alaska, USA
127 R4 **Chistopol'** Respublika Tatarstan, W Russian Federation
145 O8 **Chistopol'ye** Severnyy Kazakhstan, N Kazakhstan
123 O13 **Chita** Chitinskaya Oblast', S Russian Federation
83 B16 **Chitado** Cunene, SW Angola
Chitaldroog/Chitaldrug *see* Chitradurga
83 C15 **Chitanda** ≈ S Angola
Chitangwiza *see* Chitungwiza
82 F10 **Chitato** Lunda Norte, NE Angola
83 C14 **Chitembo** Bié, C Angola
39 T11 **Chitina** Alaska, USA
39 T11 **Chitina River** ≈ Alaska, USA
123 O12 **Chitinskaya Oblast'** ◈ *province* S Russian Federation
82 M11 **Chitipa** Northern, NW Malawi
165 S4 **Chitose** *var.* Titose. Hokkaidō, NE Japan
155 G18 **Chitradurga** *prev.* Chitaldroog, Chitaldrug. Karnātaka, W India
149 T3 **Chitrāl** North-West Frontier Province, NW Pakistan
43 S16 **Chitré** Herrera, S Panama
153 V16 **Chittagong** *Ben.* Chāttagām. Chittagong, SE Bangladesh
153 U16 **Chittagong** ◈ *division* E Bangladesh
153 Q15 **Chittaranjan** West Bengal, NE India
152 G14 **Chittaurgarh** Rājasthān, N India
155 I19 **Chittoor** Andhra Pradesh, E India
155 G21 **Chittūr** Kerala, SW India
83 K16 **Chitungwiza** *prev.* Chitangwiza. Mashonaland East, NE Zimbabwe
62 H4 **Chíuchíu** Antofagasta, N Chile
82 F12 **Chiumbe** *var.* Tshiumbe. ≈ Angola/Dem. Rep. Congo
83 F15 **Chiume** Moxico, E Angola
82 K13 **Chiundaponde** Northern, NE Zambia
106 H13 **Chiusi** Toscana, C Italy
54 J5 **Chivacoa** Yaracuy, N Venezuela
106 B8 **Chivasso** Piemonte, NW Italy
83 L17 **Chivhu** *prev.* Enkeldoorn. Midlands, C Zimbabwe
61 C20 **Chivilcoy** Buenos Aires, E Argentina
82 N12 **Chiweta** Northern, N Malawi
42 D4 **Chixoy, Río** *var.* Río Negro, Río Salinas. ≈ Guatemala/Mexico
82 H13 **Chizela** North Western, NW Zambia
125 C5 **Chizha** Nenetskiy Avtonomnyy Okrug, NW Russian Federation
161 Q9 **Chizhou** *var.* Guichi. Anhui, E China
164 I12 **Chizu** Tottori, Honshū, SW Japan
Chkalov *see* Orenburg
74 J5 **Chlef** *var.* Ech Cheliff, Ech Chleff; *prev.* Al-Asnam, El Asnam, Orléansville. NW Algeria
115 G18 **Chlómo** ▲ C Greece
111 M15 **Chmielnik** Świętokrzyskie, C Poland
167 S11 **Chŏâm Khsant** Preăh Vihéar, N Cambodia
62 G10 **Choapa, Río** *var.* Choapo. ≈ C Chile
Choapas *see* Las Choapas
Choarta *see* Chwārtā
83 H17 **Chobe** ◈ *district* NE Botswana
14 K8 **Chochocouane** ≈ Québec, SE Canada
110 E13 **Chocianów** *Ger.* Kotzenan. Dolnośląskie, SW Poland
54 C9 **Chocó** *off.* Departamento del Chocó. ◈ *province* W Colombia
35 X16 **Chocolate Mountains** ▲ California, W USA
21 W9 **Chocowinity** North Carolina, SE USA
27 N10 **Choctaw** Oklahoma, C USA
23 Q8 **Choctawhatchee Bay** *bay* Florida, SE USA
23 Q8 **Choctawhatchee River** ≈ Florida, SE USA
Chodau *see* Chodov
163 V14 **Chŏ-do** *island* SW North Korea
Chodorów *see* Khodoriv
111 A16 **Chodov** *Ger.* Chodau. Karlovarský Kraj, W Czech Republic
110 G10 **Chodzież** Wielkopolskie, C Poland
63 J15 **Choele Choel** Río Negro, C Argentina
83 L14 **Chofombo** Tete, NW Mozambique
Chohtan *see* Chauhtan
11 U14 **Choiceland** Saskatchewan, C Canada
186 K8 **Choiseul** *var.* Lauru. *island* NW Solomon Islands
63 M23 **Choiseul Sound** *sound* East Falkland, Falkland Islands
40 H7 **Choix** Sinaloa, C Mexico
110 D10 **Chojna** Zachodnio-pomorskie, W Poland
110 H8 **Chojnice** *Ger.* Konitz. Pomorskie, N Poland
111 F14 **Chojnów** *Ger.* Hainau, Haynau. Dolnośląskie, SW Poland
167 Q10 **Chok Chai** Nakhon Ratchasima, C Thailand
80 I12 **Ch'ok'ē** *var.* Choke Mountains. ▲ NW Ethiopia
25 R13 **Choke Canyon Lake** ▣ Texas, SW USA
Choke Mountains *see* Ch'ok'ē
145 T15 **Chokpar** *Kaz.* Shoqpar. Zhambyl, S Kazakhstan
147 W7 **Chok-Tal** *var.* Choktal. Issyk-Kul'skaya Oblast', E Kyrgyzstan
Chókué *see* Chokwé
123 R7 **Chokurdakh** Respublika Sakha (Yakutiya), NE Russian Federation
83 L20 **Chokwé** *var.* Chókué. Gaza, S Mozambique
188 F8 **Chol** Babeldaob, N Palau
160 E8 **Chola Shan** ▲ C China
102 J8 **Cholet** Maine-et-Loire, NW France
63 H17 **Cholila** Chubut, W Argentina
Cholo *see* Thyolo
147 V8 **Cholpon** Narynskaya Oblast', C Kyrgyzstan
147 X7 **Cholpon-Ata** Issyk-Kul'skaya Oblast', E Kyrgyzstan
41 P14 **Cholula** Puebla, S Mexico
42 I8 **Choluteca** Choluteca, S Honduras
42 H8 **Choluteca** ◈ *department* S Honduras
42 G6 **Choluteca, Río** ≈ SW Honduras
83 I15 **Choma** Southern, S Zambia
153 T11 **Chomo Lhari** ▲ NW Bhutan
167 N7 **Chom Thong** Chiang Mai, NW Thailand
111 B15 **Chomutov** *Ger.* Komotau. Ústecký Kraj, NW Czech Republic
123 N11 **Chona** ≈ C Russian Federation
163 X15 **Ch'ŏnan** *Jap.* Tenan. W South Korea
167 P11 **Chon Buri** *prev.* Bang Pla Soi. Chon Buri, S Thailand
56 B6 **Chone** Manabí, W Ecuador
163 W13 **Ch'ŏngch'ŏn-gang** ≈ W North Korea
163 Y11 **Ch'ŏngjin** NE North Korea
163 W13 **Chŏngju** W North Korea
161 S8 **Chongming Dao** *island* E China
160 J10 **Chongqing** *var.* Ch'ung-ching, Ch'ung-ch'ing, Chungking, Pahsien, Tchongking, Yuzhou. Chongqing Shi, C China
Chongup *see* Chŏnju
161 O10 **Chongyang** *var.* Tiancheng. Hubei, C China
160 J15 **Chongzuo** Guangxi Zhuangzu Zizhiqu, S China
163 Y16 **Chŏnju** *prev.* Chŏngup, *Jap.* Seiyu. SW South Korea
163 Y15 **Chŏnju** *Jap.* Zenshū. SW South Korea
Chonnacht *see* Connaught
163 Q9 **Chonogol** Sühbaatar, E Mongolia
63 F19 **Chonos, Archipiélago de los** *island group* S Chile
42 K10 **Chontales** ◈ *department* S Nicaragua
167 T13 **Chơn Thanh** Sông Be, S Vietnam
158 K17 **Cho Oyu** *var.* Qowowuyag. ▲ China/Nepal
116 G7 **Chop** *Cz.* Čop, *Hung.* Csap. Zakarpats'ka Oblast', W Ukraine
21 Y3 **Choptank River** ≈ Maryland, NE USA
Chorcaí, Cuan *see* Cork Harbour
43 P15 **Chorcha, Cerro** ▲ W Panama
Chorku *see* Chorkŭh
147 R11 **Chorkŭh** *Rus.* Chorku. N Tajikistan
97 K17 **Chorley** NW England, UK
Chorne More *see* Black Sea
117 R5 **Chornobay** Cherkas'ka Oblast', C Ukraine
117 O3 **Chornobyl'** *Rus.* Chernobyl'. Kyyivs'ka Oblast', N Ukraine
117 R12 **Chornomors'ke** *Rus.* Chernomorskoye. Respublika Krym, S Ukraine
117 R4 **Chornukhy** Poltavs'ka Oblast', C Ukraine
Chorokh/Chorokhi *see* Çoruh Nehri
110 O9 **Choroszcz** Podlaskie, NE Poland
116 K6 **Chortkiv** *Rus.* Chortkov. Ternopil's'ka Oblast', W Ukraine
Chortkov *see* Chortkiv
Chorum *see* Çorum
110 M9 **Chorzele** Mazowieckie, C Poland
111 J16 **Chorzów** *Ger.* Königshütte; *prev.* Królewska Huta. Śląskie, S Poland
163 W12 **Ch'osan** N North Korea
Chośebuz *see* Cottbus
Chōsen-kaikyō *see* Korea Strait
164 P14 **Chōshi** *var.* Tyôsi. Chiba, Honshū, S Japan
63 H14 **Chos Malal** Neuquén, W Argentina
Chosŏn-minjujuŭi-inmin-kanghwaguk *see* North Korea
110 E9 **Choszczno** *Ger.* Arnswalde. Zachodnio-pomorskie, NW Poland
153 O15 **Chota Nāgpur** *plateau* N India
33 R8 **Choteau** Montana, NW USA
Chotqol *see* Chatkal
14 M8 **Chouart** ≈ Québec, SE Canada
76 I7 **Choûm** Adrar, C Mauritania
27 Q9 **Chouteau** Oklahoma, C USA
21 X8 **Chowan River** ≈ North Carolina, SE USA
35 Q10 **Chowchilla** California, W USA
163 P7 **Choybalsan** *prev.* Bayan Tumen. Dornod, E Mongolia
162 M9 **Choyr** Govĭ Sumber, C Mongolia
185 I19 **Christchurch** Canterbury, South Island, NZ
97 M24 **Christchurch** S England, UK
185 I18 **Christchurch** × Canterbury, South Island, NZ
44 J12 **Christiana** C Jamaica
83 H22 **Christiana** Free State, C South Africa
115 J23 **Christiáni** *island* Kykládes, Greece, Aegean Sea
Christiania *see* Oslo
14 G13 **Christian Island** *island* Ontario, S Canada
191 P16 **Christian, Point** *headland* Pitcairn Island, Pitcairn Islands
38 M11 **Christian River** ≈ Alaska, USA
Christiansand *see* Kristiansand
21 S7 **Christiansburg** Virginia, NE USA
95 G23 **Christiansfeld** Sønderjylland, SW Denmark
Christianshåb *see* Qasigiannguit
39 X14 **Christian Sound** *inlet* Alaska, USA
45 T9 **Christiansted** Saint Croix, S Virgin Islands (US)
Christiansund *see* Kristiansund
25 R13 **Christine** Texas, SW USA
173 U7 **Christmas Island** ◇ *Australian external territory* E Indian Ocean
Christmas Island *see* Kiritimati
192 M7 **Christmas Ridge** *undersea feature* C Pacific Ocean
30 L16 **Christopher** Illinois, N USA
25 P9 **Christoval** Texas, SW USA
111 F17 **Chrudim** Pardubický Kraj, C Czech Republic
115 K25 **Chrýsi** *island* SE Greece
121 N2 **Chrysochoú, Kólpos** *var.* Khrysokhou Bay. *bay* E Mediterranean Sea
114 I13 **Chrysoúpoli** *var.* Hrisoupoli; *prev.* Khrisoúpolis. Anatolikí Makedonía kai Thráki, NE Greece
111 K16 **Chrzanów** *var.* Chrzanow, *Ger.* Zaumgarten. Śląskie, S Poland
145 R15 **Chu** *Kaz.* Shū. ≈ Kazakhstan/Kyrgyzstan
42 C5 **Chuacús, Sierra de** ▲ W Guatemala
153 S15 **Chuadanga** Khulna, W Bangladesh
Chuan *see* Sichuan
Ch'uan-chou *see* Quanzhou
39 O11 **Chuathbaluk** Alaska, USA
Chubek *see* Moskva
63 I17 **Chubut** *off.* Provincia de Chubut. ◈ *province* S Argentina
63 I17 **Chubut, Río** ≈ SE Argentina
43 V15 **Chucanti, Cerro** ▲ E Panama
Ch'u-chiang *see* Shaoguan
43 W15 **Chucunaque, Río** ≈ E Panama
Chudin *see* Chudzin
116 M5 **Chudniv** Zhytomyrs'ka Oblast', N Ukraine
124 H13 **Chudovo** Novgorodskaya Oblast', W Russian Federation
Chudskoye Ozero *see* Peipus, Lake
119 J18 **Chudzin** *Rus.* Chudin. Brestskaya Voblasts', SW Belarus
39 Q13 **Chugach Islands** *island group* Alaska, USA
39 S11 **Chugach Mountains** ▲ Alaska, USA
164 G12 **Chūgoku-sanchi** ▲ Honshū, SW Japan
Chugqênsumdo *see* Jigzhi
Chuguyev *see* Chuhuyiv
117 V5 **Chuhuyiv** *var.* Chuguyev. Kharkivs'ka Oblast', E Ukraine
61 H19 **Chuí** Rio Grande do Sul, S Brazil
Chuí *see* Chuy
145 S15 **Chu-Iliyskiye Gory** *Kaz.* Shū-Ile Taūlary. ▲ S Kazakhstan
Chukai *see* Cukai
Chukchi Avtonomnyy Okrug *see* Chukotskiy Avtonomnyy Okrug
Chukchi Peninsula *see* Chukotskiy Poluostrov
197 R6 **Chukchi Plain** *undersea feature* Arctic Ocean
197 R6 **Chukchi Plateau** *undersea feature* Arctic Ocean
197 R4 **Chukchi Sea** *Rus.* Chukotskoye More. *sea* Arctic Ocean
125 N14 **Chukhloma** Kostromskaya Oblast', NW Russian Federation
Chukotka *see* Chukotskiy Avtonomnyy Okrug
123 V6 **Chukotskiy Avtonomnyy Okrug** *var.* Chukchi Avtonomnyy Okrug, Chukotka. ◈ *autonomous district* NE Russian Federation
123 W5 **Chukotskiy, Mys** *headland* NE Russian Federation
123 V5 **Chukotskiy Poluostrov** *Eng.* Chukchi Peninsula. *peninsula* NE Russian Federation
Chukotskoye More *see* Chukchi Sea
Chukurkak *see* Chuqurqoq
Chulakkurgan *see* Sholakkorgan
35 U17 **Chula Vista** California, W USA
123 Q12 **Chul'man** Respublika Sakha (Yakutiya), NE Russian Federation
56 B9 **Chulucanas** Piura, NW Peru
122 J12 **Chulym** ≈ C Russian Federation
152 K6 **Chumar** Jammu and Kashmir, N India
114 K9 **Chumerna** ▲ C Bulgaria
123 R12 **Chumikan** Khabarovskiy Kray, E Russian Federation
167 Q9 **Chum Phae** Khon Kaen, C Thailand
167 N13 **Chumphon** *var.* Jumporn. Chumphon, SW Thailand
167 O9 **Chumsaeng** *var.* Chum Saeng. Nakhon Sawan, C Thailand
122 L12 **Chuna** ≈ C Russian Federation
161 R9 **Chun'an** *var.* Pailing. Zhejiang, SE China
161 S13 **Chunan** N Taiwan
163 Y14 **Ch'unch'ŏn** *Jap.* Shunsen. N South Korea
153 S16 **Chunchura** *prev.* Chinsura. West Bengal, NE India
145 W15 **Chundzha** Almaty, SE Kazakhstan
Ch'ung-ch'ing/Ch'ung-ching *see* Chongqing
Chung-hua Jen-min Kung-ho-kuo *see* China
163 Y15 **Ch'ungju** *Jap.* Chūshū. C South Korea
Chungking *see* Chongqing
161 T14 **Chungyang Shanmo** *Chin.* Taiwan Shan. ▲ C Taiwan
149 V9 **Chūniān** Punjab, E Pakistan
122 L12 **Chunskiy** Irkutskaya Oblast', S Russian Federation
122 M11 **Chunya** ≈ C Russian Federation
124 J6 **Chupa** Respublika Kareliya, NW Russian Federation
125 P8 **Chuprovo** Respublika Komi, NW Russian Federation
57 G17 **Chuquibamba** Arequipa, SW Peru
62 H4 **Chuquicamata** Antofagasta, N Chile
57 L21 **Chuquisaca** ◈ *department* S Bolivia
Chuquisaca *see* Sucre
Chuqung *see* Chindu
146 I8 **Chuqurqoq** *Rus.* Chukurkak. Qoraqalpog'iston Respublikasi, NW Uzbekistan
127 T2 **Chur** Udmurtskaya Respublika, NW Russian Federation
108 I9 **Chur** *Fr.* Coire, *It.* Coira, *Rmsch.* Cuera, Quera; *anc.* Curia Rhaetorum. Graubünden, E Switzerland
123 Q10 **Churapcha** Respublika Sakha (Yakutiya), NE Russian Federation
11 V16 **Churchbridge** Saskatchewan, S Canada
21 O8 **Church Hill** Tennessee, S USA
11 X9 **Churchill** Manitoba, C Canada
11 X10 **Churchill** ≈ Manitoba /Saskatchewan, C Canada
13 P9 **Churchill** ≈ Newfoundland and Labrador, E Canada
11 Y9 **Churchill, Cape** *headland* Manitoba, C Canada
13 P9 **Churchill Falls** Newfoundland and Labrador, E Canada
11 S12 **Churchill Lake** ◎ Saskatchewan, C Canada
19 Q3 **Churchill Lake** ◎ Maine, NE USA
194 I5 **Churchill Peninsula** *peninsula* Antarctica
22 H8 **Church Point** Louisiana, S USA
29 O3 **Churchs Ferry** North Dakota, N USA
146 G12 **Churchuri** Ahal Welaýaty, C Turkmenistan
21 T5 **Churchville** Virginia, NE USA
152 G10 **Chūru** Rājasthān, NW India
54 J4 **Churuguara** Falcón, N Venezuela
167 U11 **Chư Sê** Gia Lai, C Vietnam
144 J12 **Chushkakul, Gory** ▲ SW Kazakhstan
Chūshū *see* Ch'ungju
37 O9 **Chuska Mountains** ▲ Arizona/New Mexico, SW USA
Chu, Sông *see* Sam, Nam
125 V14 **Chusovoy** Permskaya Oblast', NW Russian Federation
147 R10 **Chust** Namangan Viloyati, E Uzbekistan
Chust *see* Khust
15 U6 **Chute-aux-Outardes** Québec, SE Canada
117 U5 **Chutove** Poltavs'ka Oblast', C Ukraine
189 O15 **Chuuk** *var.* Truk. ◈ *state* C Micronesia
189 P15 **Chuuk Islands** *var.* Hogoley Islands; *prev.* Truk Islands. *island group* Caroline Islands, C Micronesia
Chuvashia *see* charvash Respubliki
Chuvashskaya Respublika *see* charvash Respubliki
Chuwārtah *see* Chwārtā
Chu Xian/Chuxian *see* Chuzhou
160 G13 **Chuxiong** Yunnan, SW China
147 V7 **Chuy** Chuyskaya Oblast', N Kyrgyzstan
61 H19 **Chuy** *var.* Chuí. Rocha, E Uruguay
123 O11 **Chuya** Respublika Sakha (Yakutiya), NE Russian Federation
Chüy Oblasty *see* Chuyskaya Oblast'
147 U8 **Chuyskaya Oblast'** *Kir.* Chüy Oblasty. ◈ *province* N Kyrgyzstan
161 Q7 **Chuzhou** *var.* Chuxian, Chu Xian. Anhui, E China
139 U3 **Chwārtā** *var.* Choarta, Chuwārtah. NE Iraq
119 N16 **Chyhirynskaya Vodaskhovishcha** ▣ E Belarus
117 R6 **Chyhyryn** *Rus.* Chigirin. Cherkas'ka Oblast', N Ukraine
Chyrvonaya Slabada *see* Krasnaya Slabada
119 L19 **Chyrvonaye, Vozyera** *Rus.* Ozero Chervonoye. ◎ SE Belarus
117 N11 **Ciadîr-Lunga** *var.* Ceadâr-Lunga, *Rus.* Chadyr-Lunga. S Moldova
169 P16 **Ciamis** *prev.* Tjiamis. Jawa, C Indonesia
107 I16 **Ciampino** × Lazio, C Italy
169 N16 **Cianjur** *prev.* Tjiandjoer. Jawa, C Indonesia
60 H10 **Cianorte** Paraná, S Brazil
Ciarraí *see* Kerry
112 N13 **Ćićevac** Serbia, E Serbia and Montenegro (Yugo.)
187 Z14 **Cicia** *prev.* Thithia. *island* Lau Group, E Fiji
105 P4 **Cidacos** ≈ N Spain
136 I10 **Cide** Kastamonu, N Turkey
110 L10 **Ciechanów** *prev.* Zichenau. Mazowieckie, C Poland
110 O10 **Ciechanowiec** *Ger.* Rudelstadt. Podlaskie, E Poland
110 J10 **Ciechocinek** Kujawsko-pomorskie, C Poland
44 F6 **Ciego de Ávila** Ciego de Ávila, C Cuba
54 F4 **Ciénaga** Magdalena, N Colombia
54 E6 **Ciénaga de Oro** Córdoba, NW Colombia
44 E5 **Cienfuegos** Cienfuegos, C Cuba
104 F4 **Cíes, Illas** *island group* NW Spain
111 P16 **Cieszanów** Podkarpackie, SE Poland
111 J17 **Cieszyn** *Cz.* Těšín, *Ger.* Teschen. Śląskie, S Poland
105 R12 **Cieza** Murcia, SE Spain
136 F13 **Çifteler** Eskişehir, W Turkey
105 P7 **Cifuentes** Castilla-La Mancha, C Spain
Ciganak *see* Čiganak
105 P9 **Cigüela** ≈ C Spain
136 H14 **Cihanbeyli** Konya, C Turkey
136 H14 **Cihanbeyli Yaylası** *plateau* C Turkey
104 L10 **Cíjara, Embalse de** ▣ C Spain
169 P16 **Cikalong** Jawa, S Indonesia
169 N16 **Cikawung** Jawa, S Indonesia
187 Y13 **Cikobia** *prev.* Thikombia. *island* N Fiji
169 P17 **Cilacap** *prev.* Tjilatjap. Jawa, C Indonesia
173 O16 **Cilaos** C Réunion
137 S11 **Çıldır** Ardahan, NE Turkey
137 S11 **Çıldır Gölü** ◎ NE Turkey
160 M10 **Cili** Hunan, S China
121 V10 **Cilicia Trough** *undersea feature* E Mediterranean Sea
Cill Airne *see* Killarney
Cill Chainnigh *see* Kilkenny
Cill Chaoi *see* Kilkee
Cill Choca *see* Kilcock
Cill Dara *see* Kildare
105 N3 **Cilleruelo de Bezana** Castilla-León, N Spain
Cilli *see* Celje
Cill Mhantáin *see* Wicklow
Cill Rois *see* Kilrush
146 C11 **Çilmämmetgum** *Rus.* Peski Chil'mamedkum, *Turkm.* Chilmämetgum. *desert* W Turkmenistan
137 Z11 **Çiloy Adası** *Rus.* Ostrov Zhiloy. *island* E Azerbaijan
26 J6 **Cimarron** Kansas, C USA
37 T9 **Cimarron** New Mexico, SW USA
26 M9 **Cimarron River** ≈ Kansas/Oklahoma, C USA
117 N11 **Cimişlia** *Rus.* Chimishliya. S Moldova
Cimpia Turzii *see* Câmpia Turzii
Cîmpina *see* Câmpina
Cîmpulung *see* Câmpulung

◆ Country ● Country Capital ◇ Dependent Territory ○ Dependent Territory Capital ◈ Administrative Region × International Airport ▲ Mountain ▲ Mountain Range Ж Volcano ≈ River ◎ Lake ▣ Reservoir

Cîmpulung Moldovenesc *see* Câmpulung Moldovenesc
137 P15 **Çınar** Dıyarbakır, SE Turkey
54 J8 **Cinaruco, Río** ≈ Colombia/Venezuela
Cina Selatan, Laut *see* South China Sea
105 T5 **Cinca** ≈ NE Spain
112 G13 **Cincar** ▲ SW Bosnia and Herzegovina
31 Q15 **Cincinnati** Ohio, N USA
21 M4 **Cincinnati** × Kentucky, S USA
Cinco de Outubro *see* Xá-Muteba
136 C15 **Çine** Aydın, SW Turkey
99 J21 **Ciney** Namur, SE Belgium
104 H6 **Cinfães** Viseu, N Portugal
106 J12 **Cingoli** Marche, C Italy
41 U16 **Cintalapa** *var.* Cintalapa de Figueroa. Chiapas, SE Mexico
Cintalapa de Figueroa *see* Cintalapa
103 X14 **Cinto, Monte** ▲ Corse, France, C Mediterranean Sea
Cintra *see* Sintra
105 Q5 **Cintruénigo** Navarra, N Spain
Cionn tSáile *see* Kinsale
116 K13 **Ciorani** Prahova, SE Romania
113 E14 **Čiovo** *It.* Bua. *island* S Croatia
Cipiúr *see* Kippure
63 I15 **Cipolletti** Río Negro, C Argentina
120 L7 **Circeo, Capo** *headland* C Italy
39 S8 **Circle** *var.* Circle City. Alaska, USA
33 X8 **Circle** Montana, NW USA
Circle City *see* Circle
31 S14 **Circleville** Ohio, N USA
36 K6 **Circleville** Utah, W USA
169 P16 **Cirebon** *prev.* Tjirebon. Jawa, S Indonesia
97 L21 **Cirencester** *anc.* Corinium, Corinium Dobunorum. C England, UK
Cirkvenica *see* Crikvenica
107 O20 **Ciro** Calabria, SW Italy
107 O20 **Ciro Marina** Calabria, S Italy
102 K14 **Ciron** ≈ SW France
Cirquenizza *see* Crikvenica
25 R7 **Cisco** Texas, SW USA
116 I12 **Cisnădie** *Ger.* Heltau, *Hung.* Nagydisznód. Sibiu, SW Romania
63 G18 **Cisnes, Río** ≈ S Chile
25 T11 **Cistern** Texas, SW USA
104 L3 **Cistierna** Castilla-León, N Spain
Citharista *see* la Ciotat
Citlaltépetl *see* Orizaba, Volcán Pico de
55 X10 **Citron** NW French Guiana
23 N7 **Citronelle** Alabama, S USA
35 O7 **Citrus Heights** California, W USA
106 H7 **Cittadella** Veneto, NE Italy
106 H13 **Città della Pieve** Umbria, C Italy
106 H12 **Città di Castello** Umbria, C Italy
107 I14 **Cittaducale** Lazio, C Italy
107 N22 **Cittanova** Calabria, SW Italy
Cittavecchia *see* Starigrad
116 G10 **Ciucea** *Hung.* Csucsa. Cluj, NW Romania
116 M13 **Ciucurova** Tulcea, SE Romania
Ciudad Acuña *see* Villa Acuña
41 N15 **Ciudad Altamirano** Guerrero, S Mexico
42 G7 **Ciudad Barrios** San Miguel, NE El Salvador
54 I7 **Ciudad Bolívar** Barinas, NW Venezuela
55 N7 **Ciudad Bolívar** *prev.* Angostura. Bolívar, E Venezuela
40 K6 **Ciudad Camargo** Chihuahua, N Mexico
40 E8 **Ciudad Constitución** Baja California Sur, W Mexico
Ciudad Cortés *see* Cortés
41 V17 **Ciudad Cuauhtémoc** Chiapas, SE Mexico
42 J9 **Ciudad Darío** *var.* Dario. Matagalpa, W Nicaragua
Ciudad de Dolores Hidalgo *see* Dolores Hidalgo
42 C6 **Ciudad de Guatemala** *Eng.* Guatemala City; *prev.* Santiago de los Caballeros. ● (Guatemala) Guatemala, C Guatemala
Ciudad del Carmen *see* Carmen
62 Q6 **Ciudad del Este** *prev.* Cuidad Presidente Stroessner, Presidente Stroessner, Puerto Presidente Stroessner. Alto Paraná, SE Paraguay
62 K5 **Ciudad de Libertador General San Martín** *var.* Libertador General San Martín. Jujuy, C Argentina
Ciudad Delicias *see* Delicias
41 O11 **Ciudad del Maíz** San Luis Potosí, C Mexico
Ciudad de México *see* México
54 J7 **Ciudad de Nutrias** Barinas, NW Venezuela
Ciudad de Panamá *see* Panamá
55 P7 **Ciudad Guayana** *prev.* San Tomé de Guayana, Santo Tomé de Guayana. Bolívar, NE Venezuela
40 K14 **Ciudad Guzmán** Jalisco, SW Mexico
41 V17 **Ciudad Hidalgo** Chiapas, SE Mexico
41 N14 **Ciudad Hidalgo** Michoacán de Ocampo, SW Mexico
40 J3 **Ciudad Juárez** Chihuahua, N Mexico
40 L8 **Ciudad Lerdo** Durango, C Mexico
41 Q11 **Ciudad Madero** *var.* Villa Cecilia. Tamaulipas, C Mexico
41 P11 **Ciudad Mante** Tamaulipas, C Mexico
42 F2 **Ciudad Melchor de Mencos** *var.* Melchor de Mencos. Petén, NE Guatemala
41 P8 **Ciudad Miguel Alemán** Tamaulipas, C Mexico
Ciudad Mutis *see* Bahía Solano
40 G6 **Ciudad Obregón** Sonora, NW Mexico
54 I5 **Ciudad Ojeda** Zulia, NW Venezuela
55 P7 **Ciudad Piar** Bolívar, E Venezuela
Ciudad Porfirio Díaz *see* Piedras Negras
Ciudad Quesada *see* Quesada
105 N11 **Ciudad Real** Castilla-La Mancha, C Spain
105 N11 **Ciudad Real** ◈ *province* Castilla-La Mancha, C Spain
104 J7 **Ciudad-Rodrigo** Castilla-León, N Spain
42 A6 **Ciudad Tecún Umán** San Marcos, SW Guatemala
Ciudad Trujillo *see* Santo Domingo
41 P12 **Ciudad Valles** San Luis Potosí, C Mexico
41 O10 **Ciudad Victoria** Tamaulipas, C Mexico
42 C6 **Ciudad Vieja** Suchitepéquez, S Guatemala
116 L8 **Ciuhuru** *var.* Reuţel. ≈ N Moldova
Ciutadella *see* Ciutadella de Menorca
105 Z8 **Ciutadella de Menorca** *var.* Ciutadella. Menorca, Spain, W Mediterranean Sea
136 L11 **Civa Burnu** *headland* N Turkey
106 J7 **Cividale del Friuli** Friuli-Venezia Giulia, NE Italy
107 H14 **Civita Castellana** Lazio, C Italy
106 J12 **Civitanova Marche** Marche, C Italy
Civitas Altae Ripae *see* Brzeg
Civitas Carnutum *see* Chartres
Civitas Eburovicum *see* Évreux
Civitas Nemetum *see* Speyer
107 G15 **Civitavecchia** *anc.* Centum Cellae, Trajani Portus. Lazio, C Italy
102 L10 **Civray** Vienne, W France
136 E14 **Çivril** Denizli, W Turkey
161 O5 **Cixian** Hebei, E China
137 R16 **Cizre** Şırnak, SE Turkey
Clacton *see* Clacton-on-Sea
97 Q21 **Clacton-on-Sea** *var.* Clacton. E England, UK
22 H5 **Claiborne, Lake** ◎ Louisiana, S USA
102 L10 **Clain** ≈ W France
11 Q11 **Claire, Lake** ◎ Alberta, C Canada
25 O6 **Clairemont** Texas, SW USA
34 M3 **Clair Engle Lake** ⊠ California, W USA
18 B15 **Clairton** Pennsylvania, NE USA
32 F7 **Clallam Bay** Washington, NW USA
103 P8 **Clamecy** Nièvre, C France
23 P5 **Clanton** Alabama, S USA
61 D17 **Clara** Entre Ríos, E Argentina
97 E18 **Clara** *Ir.* Clóirtheach. C Ireland
29 T9 **Clara City** Minnesota, N USA
61 D23 **Claraz** Buenos Aires, E Argentina
Clár Chlainne Mhuiris *see* Claremorris
182 I8 **Clare** South Australia
97 C19 **Clare** *Ir.* An Clár. *cultural region* W Ireland
97 C18 **Clare** ≈ W Ireland
97 A16 **Clare Island** *Ir.* Cliara. *island* W Ireland
44 J12 **Claremont** C Jamaica
29 W10 **Claremont** Minnesota, N USA
19 N9 **Claremont** New Hampshire, NE USA
27 Q9 **Claremore** Oklahoma, C USA
97 C17 **Claremorris** *Ir.* Clár Chlainne Mhuiris. W Ireland
185 J16 **Clarence** Canterbury, South Island, NZ
185 J16 **Clarence** ≈ South Island, NZ
65 F15 **Clarence Bay** *bay* Ascension Island, C Atlantic Ocean
63 H25 **Clarence, Isla** *island* S Chile
194 H2 **Clarence Island** *island* South Shetland Islands, Antarctica
183 V5 **Clarence River** ≈ New South Wales, SE Australia
44 J5 **Clarence Town** Long Island, C Bahamas
27 W12 **Clarendon** Arkansas, C USA
25 O3 **Clarendon** Texas, SW USA
13 U12 **Clarenville** Newfoundland and Labrador, SE Canada
11 Q17 **Claresholm** Alberta, SW Canada
29 T16 **Clarinda** Iowa, C USA
55 N5 **Clarines** Anzoátegui, NE Venezuela
29 V12 **Clarion** Iowa, C USA
18 C13 **Clarion** Pennsylvania, NE USA
193 O6 **Clarion Fracture Zone** *tectonic feature* NE Pacific Ocean
18 D13 **Clarion River** ≈ Pennsylvania, NE USA
29 Q9 **Clark** South Dakota, N USA
36 K11 **Clarkdale** Arizona, SW USA
15 W4 **Clarke City** Québec, SE Canada
183 Q15 **Clarke Island** *island* Furneaux Group, Tasmania, SE Australia
181 X6 **Clarke Range** ▲ Queensland, E Australia
23 T2 **Clarkesville** Georgia, SE USA
29 S9 **Clarkfield** Minnesota, N USA
33 N7 **Clark Fork** Idaho, NW USA
33 N8 **Clark Fork** ≈ Idaho/Montana, NW USA
39 Q12 **Clark, Lake** ◎ Alaska, USA
35 W12 **Clark Mountain** ▲ California, W USA
37 S3 **Clark Peak** ▲ Colorado, C USA
14 D14 **Clark, Point** *headland* Ontario, S Canada
21 S3 **Clarksburg** West Virginia, NE USA
22 K2 **Clarksdale** Mississippi, S USA
33 U12 **Clarks Fork Yellowstone River** ≈ Montana/Wyoming, NW USA
21 P13 **Clark Hill Lake** *var.* J.Storm Thurmond Reservoir. ⊠ Georgia/South Carolina, SE USA
29 R14 **Clarkson** Nebraska, C USA
39 O13 **Clarks Point** Alaska, USA
18 I13 **Clarks Summit** Pennsylvania, NE USA
32 M10 **Clarkston** Washington, NW USA
44 J12 **Clark's Town** C Jamaica
27 T10 **Clarksville** Arkansas, C USA
31 P13 **Clarksville** Indiana, N USA
20 I8 **Clarksville** Tennessee, S USA
25 W5 **Clarksville** Texas, SW USA
21 U8 **Clarksville** Virginia, NE USA
21 U11 **Clarkton** North Carolina, SE USA
61 C24 **Claromecó** *var.* Balneario Claromecó. Buenos Aires, E Argentina
25 N3 **Claude** Texas, SW USA
Clausentum *see* Southampton
171 O1 **Claveria** Luzon, N Philippines
99 J20 **Clavier** Liège, E Belgium
23 W6 **Claxton** Georgia, SE USA
21 R4 **Clay** West Virginia, NE USA
27 N3 **Clay Center** Kansas, C USA
29 P16 **Clay Center** Nebraska, C USA
21 Y2 **Claymont** Delaware, NE USA
36 M14 **Claypool** Arizona, SW USA
23 R6 **Clayton** Alabama, S USA
23 T1 **Clayton** Georgia, SE USA
22 J5 **Clayton** Louisiana, S USA
27 X5 **Clayton** Missouri, C USA
37 V9 **Clayton** New Mexico, SW USA
21 V9 **Clayton** North Carolina, SE USA
27 Q12 **Clayton** Oklahoma, C USA
182 I4 **Clayton River** *seasonal river* South Australia
21 R7 **Claytor Lake** ⊠ Virginia, NE USA
27 P13 **Clear Boggy Creek** ≈ Oklahoma, C USA
97 B22 **Clear, Cape** *var.* The Bill of Cape Clear, *Ir.* Ceann Cléire. *headland* SW Ireland
36 M12 **Clear Creek** ≈ Arizona, SW USA
39 S12 **Cleare, Cape** *headland* Montague Island, Alaska, USA
18 E13 **Clearfield** Pennsylvania, NE USA
36 L2 **Clearfield** Utah, W USA
25 Q6 **Clear Fork Brazos River** ≈ Texas, SW USA
31 T12 **Clear Fork Reservoir** ⊠ Ohio, N USA
11 N12 **Clear Hills** ▲ Alberta, SW Canada
29 V12 **Clear Lake** Iowa, C USA
29 R9 **Clear Lake** South Dakota, N USA
34 M6 **Clear Lake** ◎ California, W USA
22 G6 **Clear Lake** ⊠ Louisiana, S USA
34 M6 **Clearlake** California, W USA
35 P1 **Clear Lake Reservoir** ⊠ California, W USA
11 N16 **Clearwater** British Columbia, SW Canada
23 U12 **Clearwater** Florida, SE USA
11 R12 **Clearwater** ≈ Alberta/Saskatchewan, C Canada
27 W7 **Clearwater Lake** ⊠ Missouri, C USA
33 N10 **Clearwater Mountains** ▲ Idaho, NW USA
33 N10 **Clearwater River** ≈ Idaho, NW USA
29 S4 **Clearwater River** ≈ Minnesota, N USA
25 T7 **Cleburne** Texas, SW USA
32 I9 **Cle Elum** Washington, NW USA
97 O17 **Cleethorpes** E England, UK
Cléire, Ceann *see* Clear, Cape
21 O11 **Clemson** South Carolina, SE USA
21 Q4 **Clendenin** West Virginia, NE USA
26 M9 **Cleo Springs** Oklahoma, C USA
Clerk Island *see* Onotoa
181 X8 **Clermont** Queensland, E Australia
15 S8 **Clermont** Québec, SE Canada
103 O4 **Clermont** Oise, N France
29 X12 **Clermont** Iowa, C USA
103 P11 **Clermont-Ferrand** Puy-de-Dôme, C France
103 Q15 **Clermont-l'Hérault** Hérault, S France
99 M22 **Clervaux** Diekirch, N Luxembourg
106 G6 **Cles** Trentino-Alto Adige, N Italy
182 H8 **Cleve** South Australia
Cleve *see* Kleve
23 T2 **Cleveland** Georgia, SE USA
22 K3 **Cleveland** Mississippi, S USA
31 T11 **Cleveland** Ohio, N USA
27 O9 **Cleveland** Oklahoma, C USA
20 L10 **Cleveland** Tennessee, S USA
25 W10 **Cleveland** Texas, SW USA
31 N7 **Cleveland** Wisconsin, N USA
31 O4 **Cleveland Cliffs Basin** ◎ Michigan, N USA
31 U11 **Cleveland Heights** Ohio, N USA
33 P6 **Cleveland, Mount** ▲ Montana, NW USA
Cleves *see* Kleve
97 B16 **Clew Bay** *Ir.* Cuan Mó. *inlet* W Ireland
23 Y14 **Clewiston** Florida, SE USA
Cliara *see* Clare Island
97 A17 **Clifden** *Ir.* An Clochán. W Ireland
37 O14 **Clifton** Arizona, SW USA
18 K14 **Clifton** New Jersey, NE USA
25 S8 **Clifton** Texas, SW USA
21 S6 **Clifton Forge** Virginia, NE USA
182 I1 **Clifton Hills** South Australia
11 S17 **Climax** Saskatchewan, S Canada
21 O8 **Clinch River** ≈ Tennessee /Virginia, S USA
25 P12 **Cline** Texas, SW USA
21 N10 **Clingmans Dome** ▲ North Carolina/Tennessee, SE USA
24 H8 **Clint** Texas, SW USA
10 M16 **Clinton** British Columbia, SW Canada
14 E15 **Clinton** Ontario, S Canada
27 U10 **Clinton** Arkansas, C USA
30 L10 **Clinton** Illinois, N USA
29 Z14 **Clinton** Iowa, C USA
20 G7 **Clinton** Kentucky, S USA
22 J8 **Clinton** Louisiana, S USA
19 N11 **Clinton** Massachusetts, NE USA
31 R10 **Clinton** Michigan, N USA
22 K5 **Clinton** Mississippi, S USA
27 S5 **Clinton** Missouri, C USA
21 V10 **Clinton** North Carolina, SE USA
26 L10 **Clinton** Oklahoma, C USA
21 Q12 **Clinton** South Carolina, SE USA
21 M9 **Clinton** Tennessee, S USA
8 L9 **Clinton-Colden Lake** ◎ Northwest Territories, NW Canada
10 H5 **Clinton Creek** Yukon Territory, NW Canada
30 L13 **Clinton Lake** ⊠ Illinois, N USA
27 Q4 **Clinton Lake** ⊠ Kansas, C USA
21 T11 **Clio** South Carolina, SE USA
193 O7 **Clipperton Fracture Zone** *tectonic feature* E Pacific Ocean
193 Q7 **Clipperton Island** ◇ *French dependency of French Polynesia* E Pacific Ocean
102 J8 **Clisson** Loire-Atlantique, NW France
62 K7 **Clodomira** Santiago del Estero, N Argentina
Cloich na Coillte *see* Clonakilty
Clóirtheach *see* Clara
97 C21 **Clonakilty** *Ir.* Cloich na Coillte. SW Ireland
181 T6 **Cloncurry** Queensland, C Australia
97 F18 **Clondalkin** *Ir.* Cluain Dolcáin. E Ireland
97 E16 **Clones** *Ir.* Cluain Eois. N Ireland
97 D20 **Clonmel** *Ir.* Cluain Meala. S Ireland
100 G11 **Cloppenburg** Niedersachsen, NW Germany
29 W6 **Cloquet** Minnesota, N USA
37 S14 **Cloudcroft** New Mexico, SW USA
33 W12 **Cloud Peak** ▲ Wyoming, C USA
185 K14 **Cloudy Bay** *inlet* South Island, NZ
21 R10 **Clover** South Carolina, SE USA
34 M6 **Cloverdale** California, W USA
20 J5 **Cloverport** Kentucky, S USA
35 Q10 **Clovis** California, W USA
37 W12 **Clovis** New Mexico, SW USA
14 K13 **Cloyne** Ontario, SE Canada
Cluain Dolcáin *see* Clondalkin
Cluain Eois *see* Clones
Cluainín *see* Manorhamilton
Cluain Meala *see* Clonmel
116 H10 **Cluj** ◈ *county* NW Romania
Cluj *see* Cluj-Napoca
116 H10 **Cluj-Napoca** *Ger.* Klausenburg, *Hung.* Kolozsvár; *prev.* Cluj. Cluj, NW Romania
Clunia *see* Feldkirch
103 R10 **Cluny** Saône-et-Loire, C France
103 T10 **Cluses** Haute-Savoie, E France
106 E7 **Clusone** Lombardia, N Italy
25 W12 **Clute** Texas, SW USA
185 D23 **Clutha** ≈ South Island, NZ
97 J18 **Clwyd** *cultural region* NE Wales, UK
185 D22 **Clyde** Otago, South Island, NZ
27 N3 **Clyde** Kansas, C USA
29 P2 **Clyde** North Dakota, N USA
31 S11 **Clyde** Ohio, N USA
25 Q7 **Clyde** Texas, SW USA
14 K13 **Clyde** ≈ Ontario, SE Canada
96 J13 **Clyde** ≈ W Scotland, UK
96 H12 **Clydebank** S Scotland, UK
96 H13 **Clyde, Firth of** *inlet* S Scotland, UK
33 S11 **Clyde Park** Montana, NW USA
104 I7 **Côa, Rio** ≈ N Portugal
35 W16 **Coachella** California, W USA
35 W16 **Coachella Canal** *canal* California, W USA
40 I9 **Coacoyole** Durango, C Mexico
25 N7 **Coahoma** Texas, SW USA
10 K8 **Coal** ≈ Yukon Territory, NW Canada
40 L14 **Coalcomán** *var.* Coalcomán de Matamoros. Michoacán de Ocampo, S Mexico
Coalcomán de Matamoros *see* Coalcomán
39 T8 **Coal Creek** Alaska, USA
11 Q17 **Coaldale** Alberta, SW Canada
27 P12 **Coalgate** Oklahoma, C USA
35 P11 **Coalinga** California, W USA
10 L9 **Coal River** British Columbia, W Canada
21 Q6 **Coal River** ≈ West Virginia, NE USA
36 M2 **Coalville** Utah, W USA
58 E13 **Coari** Amazonas, N Brazil
59 D14 **Coari, Rio** ≈ NW Brazil
81 J20 **Coast** ◈ *province* SE Kenya
Coast *see* Pwani
10 G12 **Coast Mountains** *Fr.* Chaîne Côtière. ▲ Canada/USA
16 C7 **Coast Ranges** ▲ W USA
96 I12 **Coatbridge** S Scotland, UK
42 B6 **Coatepeque** Quezaltenango, SW Guatemala
18 H16 **Coatesville** Pennsylvania, NE USA
15 Q13 **Coaticook** Québec, SE Canada
9 P9 **Coats Island** *island* Nunavut, NE Canada
195 O4 **Coats Land** *physical region* Antarctica
41 T14 **Coatzacoalcos** *var.* Quetzalcoalco; *prev.* Puerto México. Veracruz-Llave, E Mexico
41 S14 **Coatzacoalcos, Río** ≈ SE Mexico
116 M15 **Cobadin** Constanţa, SW Romania
14 H9 **Cobalt** Ontario, S Canada
42 D5 **Cobán** Alta Verapaz, C Guatemala
183 O6 **Cobar** New South Wales, SE Australia
18 F12 **Cobb Hill** ▲ Pennsylvania, NE USA
14 K12 **Cobden** Ontario, SE Canada
97 D21 **Cobh** *Ir.* An Cóbh; *prev.* Cove of Cork, Queenstown. SW Ireland
57 J14 **Cobija** Pando, NW Bolivia
Coblence/Coblenz *see* Koblenz
18 J10 **Cobleskill** New York, NE USA
14 I15 **Cobourg** Ontario, SE Canada
181 P1 **Cobourg Peninsula** *headland* Northern Territory, N Australia
183 O10 **Cobram** Victoria, SE Australia
82 N13 **Cóbuè** Niassa, N Mozambique
101 K18 **Coburg** Bayern, SE Germany
19 Q5 **Coburn Mountain** ▲ Maine, NE USA
Coca *see* Puerto Francisco de Orellana
57 H18 **Cocachacra** Arequipa, SW Peru
59 J17 **Cocalinho** Mato Grosso, W Brazil
Cocanada *see* Kākināda
105 S11 **Cocentaina** País Valenciano, E Spain
57 L18 **Cochabamba** *hist.* Oropeza. Cochabamba, C Bolivia
57 K18 **Cochabamba** ◈ *department* C Bolivia
57 L18 **Cochabamba, Cordillera de** ▲ C Bolivia
101 E18 **Cochem** Rheinland-Pfalz, W Germany
37 R6 **Cochetopa Hills** ▲ Colorado, C USA
155 G22 **Cochin** *var.* Kochi. Kerala, SW India
44 D5 **Cochinos, Bahía de** *Eng.* Bay of Pigs. *bay* SE Cuba
37 O16 **Cochise Head** ▲ Arizona, SW USA
23 U5 **Cochran** Georgia, SE USA
11 P16 **Cochrane** Alberta, SW Canada
12 G12 **Cochrane** Ontario, S Canada
63 G20 **Cochrane** Aisén, S Chile
11 U10 **Cochrane** ≈ Manitoba/Saskatchewan, C Canada
Cochrane, Lago *see* Pueyrredón, Lago
Cocibolca *see* Nicaragua, Lago de
Cockade State *see* Maryland
44 M6 **Cockburn Harbour** South Caicos, S Turks and Caicos Islands
14 C11 **Cockburn Island** *island* Ontario, S Canada
44 J3 **Cockburn Town** San Salvador, E Bahamas
21 X2 **Cockeysville** Maryland, NE USA
181 N12 **Cocklebiddy** Western Australia
44 I12 **Cockpit Country, The** *physical region* W Jamaica
43 S16 **Coclé** *off.* Provincia de Coclé. ◈ *province* C Panama
43 S15 **Coclé del Norte** Colón, C Panama
23 Y12 **Cocoa** Florida, SE USA
23 Y12 **Cocoa Beach** Florida, SE USA
79 D17 **Cocobeach** Estuaire, NW Gabon
44 G5 **Coco, Cayo** *island* C Cuba
151 Q19 **Coco Channel** *strait* Andaman Sea/Bay of Bengal
173 N6 **Coco-de-Mer Seamounts** *undersea feature* W Indian Ocean
36 K10 **Coconino Plateau** *plain* Arizona, SW USA
43 N6 **Coco, Río** *var.* Río Wanki, Segoviao Wangkí. ≈ Honduras/Nicaragua
173 T8 **Cocos (Keeling) Islands** ◇ *Australian external territory* E Indian Ocean
173 T7 **Cocos Basin** *undersea feature* E Indian Ocean
188 B17 **Cocos Island** *island* S Guam
Cocos Island Ridge *see* Cocos Ridge
193 T7 **Cocos Ridge** *var.* Cocos Island Ridge. *undersea feature* E Pacific Ocean
40 K13 **Cocula** Jalisco, SW Mexico
107 D17 **Coda Cavallo, Capo** *headland* Sardegna, Italy, C Mediterranean Sea
58 E13 **Codajás** Amazonas, N Brazil
Codazzi *see* Agustín Codazzi
19 Q12 **Cod, Cape** *headland* Massachusetts, NE USA
185 B25 **Codfish Island** *island* SW NZ
106 H9 **Codigoro** Emilia-Romagna, N Italy
13 P5 **Cod Island** *island* Newfoundland and Labrador, E Canada
116 J12 **Codlea** *Ger.* Zeiden, *Hung.* Feketehalom. Braşov, C Romania
58 M13 **Codó** Maranhão, E Brazil
106 E8 **Codogno** Lombardia, N Italy
116 M10 **Codrii** *hill range* C Moldova
45 W9 **Codrington** Barbuda, Antigua and Barbuda
106 J7 **Codroipo** Friuli-Venezia Giulia, NE Italy
28 M12 **Cody** Nebraska, C USA
33 U12 **Cody** Wyoming, C USA
21 P7 **Coeburn** Virginia, NE USA
54 E10 **Coello** Tolima, W Colombia
Coemba *see* Cuemba
181 V2 **Coen** Queensland, NE Australia
101 E14 **Coesfeld** Nordrhein-Westfalen, W Germany
32 M8 **Coeur d'Alene** Idaho, NW USA
32 M8 **Coeur d'Alene Lake** ⊠ Idaho, NW USA
98 O8 **Coevorden** Drenthe, NE Netherlands
10 H6 **Coffee Creek** Yukon Territory, W Canada
30 L15 **Coffeen Lake** ⊠ Illinois, N USA
22 L3 **Coffeeville** Mississippi, S USA
27 Q8 **Coffeyville** Kansas, C USA
182 G9 **Coffin Bay** South Australia
182 F9 **Coffin Bay Peninsula** *peninsula* South Australia
183 V5 **Coffs Harbour** New South Wales, SE Australia
105 R10 **Cofrentes** País Valenciano, E Spain
Cogîlnic *see* Kohyl'nyk
102 K11 **Cognac** *anc.* Compniacum. Charente, W France
106 B7 **Cogne** Valle d'Aosta, NW Italy
103 U16 **Cogolin** Var, SE France
105 O7 **Cogolludo** Castilla-La Mancha, C Spain
Cohalm *see* Rupea
92 L8 **Čohkarášša** *var.* Cuokkarašša. ▲ N Norway
Čohkkiras *see* Jukkasjärvi
F11 **Cohocton River** ≈ New York, NE USA
18 L10 **Cohoes** New York, NE USA
183 N10 **Cohuna** Victoria, SE Australia
43 P17 **Coiba, Isla de** *island* SW Panama
63 H23 **Coig, Río** ≈ S Argentina
63 G19 **Coihaique** *var.* Coyhaique. Aisén, S Chile
155 G21 **Coimbatore** Tamil Nādu, S India
104 G8 **Coimbra** *anc.* Conimbria, Conimbriga. Coimbra, W Portugal
104 G8 **Coimbra** ◈ *district* N Portugal
104 L15 **Coín** Andalucía, S Spain
57 J20 **Coipasa, Laguna** ◎ W Bolivia
57 J20 **Coipasa, Salar de** *salt lake* W Bolivia
Coira/Coire *see* Chur
Coirib, Loch *see* Corrib, Lough
54 K6 **Cojedes** *off.* Estado Cojedes. ◈ *state* N Venezuela
42 F7 **Cojutepeque** Cuscatlán, C El Salvador
Coka *see* Banbar
33 S16 **Cokeville** Wyoming, C USA
182 M13 **Colac** Victoria, SE Australia
59 O20 **Colatina** Espírito Santo, SE Brazil
27 O13 **Colbert** Oklahoma, C USA
100 L12 **Colbitz-Letzinger Heide** *heathland* N Germany
26 I3 **Colby** Kansas, C USA
57 H17 **Colca, Río** ≈ SW Peru
97 P21 **Colchester** *hist.* Colneceaste, *anc.* Camulodunum. E England, UK
19 N13 **Colchester** Connecticut, NE USA
38 M16 **Cold Bay** Alaska, USA
11 R14 **Cold Lake** Alberta, SW Canada
11 R13 **Cold Lake** ◎ Alberta/Saskatchewan, S Canada
29 U8 **Cold Spring** Minnesota, N USA
25 W10 **Coldspring** Texas, SW USA
11 N17 **Coldstream** British Columbia, SW Canada
96 L13 **Coldstream** SE Scotland, UK
14 H13 **Coldwater** Ontario, S Canada
26 K7 **Coldwater** Kansas, C USA
31 Q10 **Coldwater** Michigan, N USA
25 N1 **Coldwater Creek** ≈ Oklahoma/Texas, SW USA
22 K2 **Coldwater River** ≈ Mississippi, S USA
183 O9 **Coleambally** New South Wales, SE Australia
19 O6 **Colebrook** New Hampshire, NE USA
27 T5 **Cole Camp** Missouri, C USA
39 T6 **Coleen River** ≈ Alaska, USA
11 P17 **Coleman** Alberta, SW Canada
25 Q8 **Coleman** Texas, SW USA
Çölemerik *see* Hakkâri
83 K22 **Colenso** KwaZulu/Natal, E South Africa
182 L12 **Coleraine** Victoria, SE Australia

◆ Country ● Country Capital ◇ Dependent Territory ○ Dependent Territory Capital ◈ Administrative Region × International Airport ▲ Mountain ▲ Mountain Range Volcano ≈ River ◎ Lake ⊠ Reservoir

97 *F14* **Coleraine** *Ir.* Cúil Raithin. N Northern Ireland, UK
185 *G18* **Coleridge, Lake** ◎ South Island, NZ
83 *H24* **Colesberg** Northern Cape, C South Africa
22 *H7* **Colfax** Louisiana, S USA
32 *L9* **Colfax** Washington, NW USA
30 *J6* **Colfax** Wisconsin, N USA
63 *I19* **Colhué Huapí, Lago** ◎ S Argentina
45 *Z6* **Colibris, Pointe des** *headland* Grande Terre, E Guadeloupe
106 *D6* **Colico** Lombardia, N Italy
99 *E14* **Colijnsplaat** Zeeland, SW Netherlands
40 *L14* **Colima** Colima, S Mexico
40 *K14* **Colima** ◈ *state* SW Mexico
40 *L14* **Colima, Nevado de** ✱ C Mexico
59 *M14* **Colinas** Maranhão, E Brazil
96 *F10* **Coll** *island* W Scotland, UK
105 *N7* **Collado Villalba** *var.* Villalba. Madrid, C Spain
183 *R4* **Collarenebri** New South Wales, SE Australia
37 *P5* **Collbran** Colorado, C USA
106 *G12* **Colle di Val d'Elsa** Toscana, C Italy
39 *R9* **College** Alaska, USA
32 *K10* **College Place** Washington, NW USA
25 *U10* **College Station** Texas, SW USA
183 *P4* **Collerina** New South Wales, SE Australia
180 *I13* **Collie** Western Australia
180 *L4* **Collier Bay** *bay* Western Australia
21 *F10* **Collierville** Tennessee, S USA
106 *F11* **Collina, Passo della** *pass* C Italy
14 *G14* **Collingwood** Ontario, S Canada
184 *I13* **Collingwood** Tasman, South Island, NZ
22 *L7* **Collins** Mississippi, S USA
30 *K15* **Collinsville** Illinois, N USA
27 *P9* **Collinsville** Oklahoma, C USA
20 *H10* **Collinwood** Tennessee, S USA
Collipo *see* Leiria
63 *G14* **Collipulli** Araucanía, C Chile
97 *D16* **Collooney** *Ir.* Cúil Mhuine. NW Ireland
29 *R10* **Colman** South Dakota, N USA
103 *U6* **Colmar** *Ger.* Kolmar. Haut-Rhin, NE France
104 *M15* **Colmenar** Andalucía, S Spain
Colmenar *see* Colmenar de Oreja
105 *O9* **Colmenar de Oreja** *var.* Colmenar. Madrid, C Spain
105 *N7* **Colmenar Viejo** Madrid, C Spain
25 *X9* **Colmesneil** Texas, SW USA
Cöln *see* Köln
Colneceaste *see* Colchester
40 *C3* **Colnet** Baja California, NW Mexico
59 *G15* **Colniza** Mato Grosso, W Brazil
Cologne *see* Köln
42 *B6* **Colomba** Quezaltenango, SW Guatemala
Colomb-Béchar *see* Béchar
54 *E11* **Colombia** Huila, C Colombia
54 *G10* **Colombia** *off.* Republic of Colombia. ◆ *republic* N South America
64 *E12* **Colombian Basin** *undersea feature* SW Caribbean Sea
Colombie-Britannique *see* British Columbia
15 *T6* **Colombier** Québec, SE Canada
155 *J25* **Colombo** ● (Sri Lanka) Western Province, W Sri Lanka
155 *J25* **Colombo** ✕ Western Province, SW Sri Lanka
29 *N11* **Colome** South Dakota, N USA
61 *D18* **Colon** Entre Ríos, E Argentina
61 *B19* **Colón** Buenos Aires, E Argentina
44 *D5* **Colón** Matanzas, C Cuba
43 *T14* **Colón** *prev.* Aspinwall. Colón, C Panama
42 *K5* **Colón** ◈ *department* NE Honduras
43 *S15* **Colón** *off.* Provincia de Colón. ◈ *province* N Panama
57 *A16* **Colón, Archipiélago de** *var.* Islas de los Galápagos, *Eng.* Galapagos Islands, Tortoise Islands. *island group* Ecuador, E Pacific Ocean
44 *K5* **Colonel Hill** Crooked Island, SE Bahamas
40 *B3* **Colonet, Cabo** *headland* NW Mexico
188 *G14* **Colonia** Yap, W Micronesia
61 *D19* **Colonia** ◈ *department* SW Uruguay
Colonia *see* Kolonia, Micronesia
Colonia *see* Colonia del Sacramento, Uruguay
Colonia Agrippina *see* Köln
61 *D20* **Colonia del Sacramento** *var.* Colonia. Colonia, SW Uruguay
62 *L8* **Colonia Dora** Santiago del Estero, N Argentina
Colonia Julia Fanestris *see* Fano
21 *W5* **Colonial Beach** Virginia, NE USA
21 *V6* **Colonial Heights** Virginia, NE USA
193 *S7* **Colón Ridge** *undersea feature* E Pacific Ocean
96 *F12* **Colonsay** *island* W Scotland, UK
57 *K22* **Colorada, Laguna** ◎ SW Bolivia
37 *R6* **Colorado** *off.* State of Colorado; also known as Centennial State, Silver State. ◈ *state* C USA
63 *H22* **Colorado, Cerro** ▲ S Argentina
25 *O7* **Colorado City** Texas, SW USA
36 *M7* **Colorado Plateau** *plateau* W USA
61 *A24* **Colorado, Río** ≈ E Argentina
43 *N12* **Colorado, Río** ≈ NE Costa Rica
Colorado, Río *see* Colorado River
16 *F12* **Colorado River** *var.* Río Colorado. ≈ Mexico/USA
16 *K14* **Colorado River** ≈ Texas, SW USA
35 *W15* **Colorado River Aqueduct** *aqueduct* California, W USA
44 *A4* **Colorados, Archipiélago de los** *island group* NW Cuba
62 *J9* **Colorados, Desagües de los** ◎ W Argentina
37 *T5* **Colorado Springs** Colorado, C USA
40 *L11* **Colotlán** Jalisco, SW Mexico
57 *L19* **Colquechaca** Potosí, C Bolivia
23 *S7* **Colquitt** Georgia, SE USA
29 *R11* **Colton** South Dakota, N USA
32 *M10* **Colton** Washington, NW USA
35 *P8* **Columbia** California, W USA
30 *K16* **Columbia** Illinois, N USA
20 *L7* **Columbia** Kentucky, S USA
22 *I6* **Columbia** Louisiana, S USA
21 *W3* **Columbia** Maryland, NE USA
22 *L7* **Columbia** Mississippi, S USA
27 *U4* **Columbia** Missouri, C USA
21 *Y9* **Columbia** North Carolina, SE USA
18 *G16* **Columbia** Pennsylvania, NE USA
21 *Q12* **Columbia** *state capital* South Carolina, SE USA
20 *I9* **Columbia** Tennessee, S USA
32 *J10* **Columbia** ≈ Canada/USA
32 *K9* **Columbia Basin** *basin* Washington, NW USA
197 *Q10* **Columbia, Cape** *headland* Ellesmere Island, Nunavut, NE Canada
31 *Q12* **Columbia City** Indiana, N USA
21 *W3* **Columbia, District of** ◈ *federal district* NE USA
33 *P7* **Columbia Falls** Montana, NW USA
11 *O15* **Columbia Icefield** *icefield* Alberta/British Columbia, S Canada
11 *O15* **Columbia, Mount** ▲ Alberta/British Columbia, SW Canada
11 *N15* **Columbia Mountains** ⛰ British Columbia, SW Canada
23 *P4* **Columbiana** Alabama, S USA
31 *V12* **Columbiana** Ohio, N USA
32 *M14* **Columbia Plateau** *plateau* Idaho/Oregon, NW USA
29 *P7* **Columbia Road Reservoir** ▣ South Dakota, N USA
65 *K16* **Columbia Seamount** *undersea feature* C Atlantic Ocean
83 *D25* **Columbine, Cape** *headland* SW South Africa
105 *U9* **Columbretes, Islas** *island group* E Spain
23 *R5* **Columbus** Georgia, SE USA
31 *P14* **Columbus** Indiana, N USA
27 *R7* **Columbus** Kansas, C USA
23 *N4* **Columbus** Mississippi, S USA
33 *U11* **Columbus** Montana, NW USA
29 *Q15* **Columbus** Nebraska, C USA
37 *Q16* **Columbus** New Mexico, SW USA
21 *P10* **Columbus** North Carolina, SE USA
28 *K2* **Columbus** North Dakota, N USA
31 *S13* **Columbus** *state capital* Ohio, N USA
25 *U11* **Columbus** Texas, SW USA
30 *L8* **Columbus** Wisconsin, N USA
31 *R12* **Columbus Grove** Ohio, N USA
29 *Y15* **Columbus Junction** Iowa, C USA
44 *J3* **Columbus Point** *headland* Cat Island, C Bahamas
35 *T8* **Columbus Salt Marsh** *salt marsh* Nevada, W USA
35 *N6* **Colusa** California, W USA
32 *L7* **Colville** Washington, NW USA
184 *M5* **Colville, Cape** *headland* North Island, NZ
184 *M5* **Colville Channel** *channel* North Island, NZ
39 *P6* **Colville River** ≈ Alaska, USA
97 *J18* **Colwyn Bay** N Wales, UK
106 *H9* **Comacchio** *var.* Commachio; *anc.* Comactium. Emilia-Romagna, N Italy
106 *H9* **Comacchio, Valli di** *lagoon* Adriatic Sea, N Mediterranean Sea
Comactium *see* Comacchio
41 *V17* **Comalapa** Chiapas, SE Mexico
41 *U15* **Comalcalco** Tabasco, SE Mexico
63 *H16* **Comallo** Río Negro, SW Argentina
26 *M12* **Comanche** Oklahoma, C USA
25 *R8* **Comanche** Texas, SW USA
194 *H2* **Comandante Ferraz** *Brazilian research station* Antarctica
62 *N5* **Comandante Fontana** Formosa, N Argentina
63 *I22* **Comandante Luis Peidra Buena** Santa Cruz, S Argentina
59 *O18* **Comandatuba** Bahia, SE Brazil
116 *K11* **Comănești** *Hung.* Kománfalva. Bacău, SW Romania
57 *M19* **Comarapa** Santa Cruz, C Bolivia
116 *J13* **Comarnic** Prahova, SE Romania
42 *H6* **Comayagua** Comayagua, W Honduras
42 *H6* **Comayagua** ◈ *department* W Honduras
42 *I6* **Comayagua, Montañas de** ⛰ C Honduras
21 *R15* **Combahee River** ≈ South Carolina, SE USA
62 *G10* **Combarbalá** Coquimbo, C Chile
103 *S7* **Combeaufontaine** Haute-Saône, E France
97 *G15* **Comber** *Ir.* An Comar. E Northern Ireland, UK
99 *K20* **Comblain-au-Pont** Liège, E Belgium
102 *I6* **Combourg** Ille-et-Vilaine, NW France
44 *M9* **Comendador** *prev.* Elías Piña. W Dominican Republic
Comer See *see* Como, Lago di
25 *R11* **Comfort** Texas, SW USA
153 *V15* **Comilla** *Ben.* Kumillā. Chittagong, E Bangladesh
99 *B18* **Comines** Hainaut, W Belgium
121 *O15* **Comino** *Malt.* Kemmuna. *island* C Malta
107 *D18* **Comino, Capo** *headland* Sardegna, Italy, C Mediterranean Sea
107 *K25* **Comiso** Sicilia, Italy, C Mediterranean Sea
41 *V16* **Comitán** *var.* Comitán de Domínguez. Chiapas, SE Mexico
Comitán de Domínguez *see* Comitán
Commachio *see* Comacchio
Commander Islands *see* Komandorskiye Ostrova
103 *O10* **Commentry** Allier, C France
23 *T2* **Commerce** Georgia, SE USA
27 *R8* **Commerce** Oklahoma, C USA
25 *V5* **Commerce** Texas, SW USA
37 *T4* **Commerce City** Colorado, C USA
103 *S5* **Commercy** Meuse, NE France
55 *W9* **Commewijne** *var.* Commewyne. ◈ *district* NE Surinam
Commewyne *see* Commewijne
15 *P8* **Commissaires, Lac des** ◎ Québec, SE Canada
64 *A12* **Commissioner's Point** *headland* W Bermuda
9 *O7* **Committee Bay** *bay* Nunavut, N Canada
106 *D7* **Como** *anc.* Comum. Lombardia, N Italy
63 *J19* **Comodoro Rivadavia** Chubut, SE Argentina
106 *D6* **Como, Lago di** *var.* Lario, *Eng.* Lake Como, *Ger.* Comer See. ◎ N Italy
Como, Lake *see* Como, Lago di
40 *E7* **Comondú** Baja California Sur, W Mexico
116 *F12* **Comorâște** *Hung.* Komornok. Caraș-Severin, SW Romania
Comores, République Fédérale Islamique des *see* Comoros
155 *G24* **Comorin, Cape** *headland* SE India
172 *M8* **Comoro Basin** *undersea feature* SW Indian Ocean
172 *I14* **Comoro Islands** *island group* W Indian Ocean
172 *H13* **Comoros** *off.* Federal Islamic Republic of the Comoros, *Fr.* République Fédérale Islamique des Comores. ◆ *republic* W Indian Ocean
10 *L17* **Comox** Vancouver Island, British Columbia, SW Canada
103 *O4* **Compiègne** Oise, N France
Complutum *see* Alcalá de Henares
Compniacum *see* Cognac
40 *K12* **Compostela** Nayarit, C Mexico
Compostella *see* Santiago
60 *L11* **Comprida, Ilha** *island* S Brazil
117 *N11* **Comrat** *Rus.* Komrat. S Moldova
25 *O11* **Comstock** Texas, SW USA
31 *P9* **Comstock Park** Michigan, N USA
193 *N3* **Comstock Seamount** *undersea feature* N Pacific Ocean
Comum *see* Como
159 *N17* **Cona** Xizang Zizhiqu, W China
76 *H14* **Conakry** ● (Guinea) Conakry, SW Guinea
76 *H14* **Conakry** ✕ Conakry, SW Guinea
Conamara *see* Connemara
Conca *see* Cuenca
25 *Q12* **Concan** Texas, SW USA
102 *F6* **Concarneau** Finistère, NW France
83 *O17* **Conceição** Sofala, C Mozambique
59 *K15* **Conceição do Araguaia** Pará, NE Brazil
58 *F10* **Conceição do Maú** Roraima, W Brazil
61 *D14* **Concepción** *var.* Concepcion. Corrientes, NE Argentina
62 *J8* **Concepción** Tucumán, N Argentina
57 *O17* **Concepción** Santa Cruz, E Bolivia
62 *G13* **Concepción** Bío Bío, C Chile
54 *E14* **Concepción** Putumayo, S Colombia
62 *O5* **Concepción** *var.* Villa Concepción. Concepción, C Paraguay
62 *O5* **Concepción** *off.* Departamento de Concepción. ◈ *department* E Paraguay
Concepción *see* La Concepción
Concepción de la Vega *see* La Vega
41 *N9* **Concepción del Oro** Zacatecas, C Mexico
61 *D18* **Concepción del Uruguay** Entre Ríos, E Argentina
42 *K11* **Concepción, Volcán** ✱ SW Nicaragua
44 *J4* **Conception Island** *island* C Bahamas
35 *P14* **Conception, Point** *headland* California, W USA
54 *H6* **Concha** Zulia, W Venezuela
60 *L9* **Conchas** São Paulo, S Brazil
37 *U11* **Conchas Dam** New Mexico, SW USA
37 *U10* **Conchas Lake** ▣ New Mexico, SW USA
102 *M5* **Conches-en-Ouche** Eure, N France
37 *N12* **Concho** Arizona, SW USA
40 *J5* **Conchos, Río** ≈ NW Mexico
41 *O8* **Conchos, Río** ≈ C Mexico
108 *C8* **Concise** Vaud, W Switzerland
35 *N8* **Concord** California, W USA
19 *O9* **Concord** *state capital* New Hampshire, NE USA
21 *R10* **Concord** North Carolina, SE USA
61 *D17* **Concordia** Entre Ríos, E Argentina
54 *D9* **Concordia** Antioquia, W Colombia
40 *J10* **Concordia** Sinaloa, C Mexico
57 *I19* **Concordia** Tacna, SW Peru
27 *N3* **Concordia** Kansas, C USA
27 *S4* **Concordia** Missouri, C USA
60 *I13* **Concórdia** Santa Catarina, S Brazil
167 *S7* **Con Cuông** Nghệ An, N Vietnam
167 *T15* **Côn Đao** *var.* Con Son. *island* S Vietnam
Condate *see* St-Claude, Jura, France
Condate *see* Rennes, Ille-et-Vilaine, France
Condate *see* Montereau-Faut-Yonne, Seine-St-Denis, France
29 *P8* **Conde** South Dakota, N USA
42 *J8* **Condega** Estelí, NW Nicaragua
103 *P2* **Condé-sur-l'Escaut** Nord, N France
102 *K5* **Condé-sur-Noireau** Calvados, N France
Condivincum *see* Nantes
183 *P8* **Condobolin** New South Wales, SE Australia
102 *L15* **Condom** Gers, S France
32 *J11* **Condon** Oregon, NW USA
54 *D9* **Condoto** Chocó, W Colombia
23 *P7* **Conecuh River** ≈ Alabama/Florida, SE USA
106 *H7* **Conegliano** Veneto, NE Italy
61 *C19* **Conesa** Buenos Aires, E Argentina
14 *F15* **Conestogo** ≈ Ontario, S Canada
Confluentes *see* Koblenz
102 *L10* **Confolens** Charente, W France
36 *J4* **Confusion Range** ⛰ Utah, W USA
62 *N6* **Confuso, Río** ≈ C Paraguay
21 *R12* **Congaree River** ≈ South Carolina, SE USA
Công Hoa Xa Hôi Chu Nghia Viêt Nam *see* Vietnam
160 *K12* **Congjiang** *var.* Bingmei. Guizhou, S China
79 *K19* **Congo** *off.* Democratic Republic of Congo; *prev.* Zaire, Belgian Congo, Congo (Kinshasa). ◆ *republic* C Africa
79 *G18* **Congo** *off.* Republic of the Congo, *Fr.* Moyen-Congo; *prev.* Middle Congo. ◆ *republic* C Africa
79 *H19* **Congo** *var.* Kongo, *Fr.* Zaire. ≈ C Africa
Congo *see* Zaire (province, Angola)
Congo/Congo (Kinshasa) *see* Congo (Democratic Republic of)
79 *K18* **Congo Basin** *drainage basin* W Dem. Rep. Congo
Congo Cone *see* Congo Fan
65 *P15* **Congo Fan** *var.* Congo Cone. *undersea feature* E Atlantic Ocean
Coni *see* Cuneo
63 *H18* **Cónico, Cerro** ▲ SW Argentina
Conimbria/Conimbriga *see* Coimbra
Conjeeveram *see* Kānchīpuram
11 *R13* **Conklin** Alberta, C Canada
24 *M1* **Conlen** Texas, SW USA
Con, Loch *see* Conn, Lough
Connacht *see* Connaught
97 *B17* **Connaught** *var.* Connacht, *Ir.* Chonnacht, Cúige. *cultural region* W Ireland
31 *V10* **Conneaut** Ohio, N USA
18 *L13* **Connecticut** *off.* State of Connecticut; also known as Blue Law State, Constitution State, Land of Steady Habits, Nutmeg State. ◈ *state* NE USA
19 *N8* **Connecticut** ≈ Canada/USA
19 *O6* **Connecticut Lakes** *lakes* New Hampshire, NE USA
32 *K9* **Connell** Washington, NW USA
97 *B17* **Connemara** *Ir.* Conamara. *region* W Ireland
31 *Q14* **Connersville** Indiana, N USA
97 *B16* **Conn, Lough** *Ir.* Loch Con. ◎ W Ireland
35 *X6* **Connors Pass** *pass* Nevada, W USA
181 *X7* **Connors Range** ⛰ Queensland, E Australia
56 *E7* **Cononaco, Río** ≈ E Ecuador
29 *W13* **Conrad** Iowa, C USA
33 *R7* **Conrad** Montana, NW USA
25 *W10* **Conroe** Texas, SW USA
25 *V10* **Conroe, Lake** ▣ Texas, SW USA
61 *C17* **Conscripto Bernardi** Entre Ríos, E Argentina
59 *M20* **Conselheiro Lafaiete** Minas Gerais, SE Brazil
Consentia *see* Cosenza
97 *L14* **Consett** N England, UK
44 *B5* **Consolación del Sur** Pinar del Río, W Cuba
Con Son *see* Côn Đao
11 *R15* **Consort** Alberta, SW Canada
Constance *see* Konstanz
108 *I6* **Constance, Lake** *Ger.* Bodensee. ◎ C Europe
104 *G9* **Constância** Santarém, C Portugal
117 *N14* **Constanța** *var.* Küstendje, *Eng.* Constanza, *Ger.* Konstanza, *Turk.* Küstence. Constanța, SE Romania
116 *L14* **Constanța** ◈ *county* SE Romania
Constantia *see* Coutances, France
Constantia *see* Konstanz, Germany
104 *K13* **Constantina** Andalucía, S Spain
74 *L5* **Constantine** *var.* Qacentina, *Ar.* Qoussantina. NE Algeria
39 *O14* **Constantine, Cape** *headland* Alaska, USA
Constantinople *see* İstanbul
Constantiola *see* Oltenișa
Constanz *see* Konstanz
Constanza *see* Constanța
62 *G13* **Constitución** Maule, C Chile
61 *D17* **Constitución** Salto, N Uruguay
Constitution State *see* Connecticut
105 *N10* **Consuegra** Castilla-La Mancha, C Spain
181 *X9* **Consuelo Peak** ▲ Queensland, E Australia
56 *E11* **Contamana** Loreto, N Peru
Contrasto, Colle del *see* Contrasto, Portella del
107 *K23* **Contrasto, Portella del** *var.* Colle del Contrasto. *pass* Sicilia, Italy, C Mediterranean Sea
54 *G8* **Contratación** Santander, C Colombia
102 *M8* **Contres** Loir-et-Cher, C France
107 *O17* **Conversano** Puglia, SE Italy
27 *U11* **Conway** Arkansas, C USA
19 *O8* **Conway** New Hampshire, NE USA
21 *U13* **Conway** South Carolina, SE USA
25 *N2* **Conway** Texas, SW USA
27 *U11* **Conway, Lake** ▣ Arkansas, C USA
27 *N7* **Conway Springs** Kansas, C USA
97 *J18* **Conwy** N Wales, UK
23 *T3* **Conyers** Georgia, SE USA
Coo *see* Kos
182 *F4* **Coober Pedy** South Australia
181 *P2* **Cooinda** Northern Territory, N Australia
182 *B6* **Cook** South Australia
29 *W4* **Cook** Minnesota, N USA
191 *N6* **Cook, Baie de** *bay* Moorea, W French Polynesia
10 *J16* **Cook, Cape** *headland* Vancouver Island, British Columbia, SW Canada
37 *Q15* **Cookes Peak** ▲ New Mexico, SW USA
20 *L8* **Cookeville** Tennessee, S USA
Cook, Grand Récif de *see* Cook, Récif de
39 *Q12* **Cook Inlet** *inlet* Alaska, USA
191 *X2* **Cook Island** *island* Line Islands, E Kiribati
190 *J14* **Cook Islands** ◇ *territory in free association with NZ* S Pacific Ocean
Cook, Mount *see* Aoraki
187 *O15* **Cook, Récif de** *var.* Grand Récif de Cook. *reef* S New Caledonia
14 *G14* **Cookstown** Ontario, S Canada
97 *F15* **Cookstown** *Ir.* An Chorr Chríochach. C Northern Ireland, UK
185 *K14* **Cook Strait** *var.* Raukawa. *strait* NZ
181 *W3* **Cooktown** Queensland, NE Australia
183 *P6* **Coolabah** New South Wales, SE Australia
182 *J11* **Coola Coola Swamp** *wetland* South Australia
183 *S7* **Coolah** New South Wales, SE Australia
183 *P9* **Coolamon** New South Wales, SE Australia
183 *T4* **Coolatai** New South Wales, SE Australia
180 *K12* **Coolgardie** Western Australia
36 *L14* **Coolidge** Arizona, SW USA
25 *U8* **Coolidge** Texas, SW USA
183 *Q11* **Cooma** New South Wales, SE Australia
Coomassie *see* Kumasi
183 *R6* **Coonabarabran** New South Wales, SE Australia
182 *J10* **Coonalpyn** South Australia
183 *R6* **Coonamble** New South Wales, SE Australia
Coondapoor *see* Kundāpura
155 *G21* **Coonoor** Tamil Nādu, SE India
29 *U14* **Coon Rapids** Iowa, C USA
29 *V8* **Coon Rapids** Minnesota, N USA
25 *V5* **Cooper** Texas, SW USA
181 *U9* **Cooper Creek** *var.* Barcoo, Cooper's Creek. *seasonal river* Queensland/South Australia
39 *R12* **Cooper Landing** Alaska, USA
21 *T14* **Cooper River** ≈ South Carolina, SE USA
Cooper's Creek *see* Cooper Creek
44 *H1* **Coopers Town** Great Abaco, N Bahamas
18 *J10* **Cooperstown** New York, NE USA
29 *P4* **Cooperstown** North Dakota, N USA
31 *P9* **Coopersville** Michigan, N USA
182 *D7* **Coorabie** South Australia
23 *Q3* **Coosa River** ≈ Alabama/Georgia, S USA
32 *E14* **Coos Bay** Oregon, NW USA
183 *Q9* **Cootamundra** New South Wales, SE Australia
97 *E16* **Cootehill** *Ir.* Muinchille. N Ireland
Čop *see* Chop
57 *J17* **Copacabana** La Paz, W Bolivia
63 *H14* **Copahué, Volcán** ▲ C Chile
41 *U16* **Copainalá** Chiapas, SE Mexico
32 *F8* **Copalis Beach** Washington, NW USA
42 *F6* **Copán** ◈ *department* W Honduras
Copán *see* Copán Ruinas
25 *T14* **Copano Bay** *bay* NW Gulf of Mexico
42 *F6* **Copán Ruinas** *var.* Copán. Copán, W Honduras
Copenhagen *see* København
107 *Q19* **Copertino** Puglia, SE Italy
62 *H7* **Copiapó** Atacama, N Chile
62 *G8* **Copiapó, Bahía** *bay* N Chile
62 *G7* **Copiapó, Río** ≈ N Chile
114 *M12* **Çöpköy** Edirne, NW Turkey
182 *I5* **Copley** South Australia
106 *H9* **Copparo** Emilia-Romagna, C Italy
55 *V10* **Coppename Rivier** *var.* Koppename. ≈ C Surinam
25 *S9* **Copperas Cove** Texas, SW USA
82 *J13* **Copperbelt** ◈ *province* C Zambia
39 *S11* **Copper Center** Alaska, USA
Coppermine *see* Kugluktuk
8 *K8* **Coppermine** ≈ Northwest Territories/Nunavut, N Canada
39 *T11* **Copper River** ≈ Alaska, USA
Copper State *see* Arizona
116 *I11* **Copșa Mică** *Ger.* Kleinkopisch, *Hung.* Kiskapus. Sibiu, C Romania
158 *J14* **Coqên** Xizang Zizhiqu, W China
Coquilhatville *see* Mbandaka
32 *E14* **Coquille** Oregon, NW USA
62 *G9* **Coquimbo** Coquimbo, N Chile
62 *G9* **Coquimbo** *off.* Región de Coquimbo. ◈ *region* C Chile
116 *I15* **Corabia** Olt, S Romania
57 *F17* **Coracora** Ayacucho, SW Peru
Cora Droma Rúisc *see* Carrick-on-Shannon
44 *K9* **Corail** SW Haiti
183 *V4* **Coraki** New South Wales, SE Australia
180 *G8* **Coral Bay** Western Australia
23 *Y16* **Coral Gables** Florida, SE USA
9 *P8* **Coral Harbour** Southampton Island, Northwest Territories, NE Canada
192 *I9* **Coral Sea** *sea* SW Pacific Ocean
192 *I9* **Coral Sea Basin** *undersea feature* N Coral Sea
192 *H9* **Coral Sea Islands** ◇ *Australian external territory* SW Pacific Ocean
182 *M12* **Corangamite, Lake** ◎ Victoria, SE Australia
Corantijn Rivier *see* Courantyne River
18 *B14* **Coraopolis** Pennsylvania, NE USA
107 *N17* **Corato** Puglia, SE Italy
103 *O17* **Corbières** ⛰ S France
103 *P8* **Corbigny** Nièvre, C France
21 *N7* **Corbin** Kentucky, S USA
104 *L14* **Corbones** ≈ SW Spain
Corcaigh *see* Cork
35 *R11* **Corcoran** California, W USA
63 *G18* **Corcovado, Golfo** *gulf* S Chile
63 *G18* **Corcovado, Volcán** ▲ S Chile
104 *F3* **Corcubión** Galicia, NW Spain
Corcyra Nigra *see* Korčula
60 *Q9* **Cordeiro** Rio de Janeiro, SE Brazil
23 *T6* **Cordele** Georgia, SE USA
26 *L11* **Cordell** Oklahoma, C USA
103 *N14* **Cordes** Tarn, S France
62 *O6* **Cordillera** *off.* Departamento de la Cordillera. ◈ *department* C Paraguay
182 *K1* **Cordillo Downs** South Australia
62 *K10* **Córdoba** Córdoba, C Argentina
41 *R14* **Córdoba** Veracruz-Llave, E Mexico
104 *M13* **Córdoba** *var.* Cordoba, *Eng.* Cordova; *anc.* Corduba. Andalucía, SW Spain
62 *K11* **Córdoba** *off.* Provincia de Córdoba. ◈ *province* C Argentina
54 *D7* **Córdoba** *off.* Departamento de Córdoba. ◈ *province* NW Colombia
104 *L13* **Córdoba** ◈ *province* Andalucía, S Spain
62 *K10* **Córdoba, Sierras de** ⛰ C Argentina
23 *O3* **Cordova** Alabama, S USA
39 *S12* **Cordova** Alaska, USA
Cordova/Corduba *see* Córdoba
Corentyne River *see* Courantyne River
Corfu *see* Kérkyra
104 *J9* **Coria** Extremadura, W Spain

◆ Country ● Country Capital ◇ Dependent Territory ○ Dependent Territory Capital ◈ Administrative Region ✕ International Airport ▲ Mountain ⛰ Mountain Range ✱ Volcano ≈ River ◎ Lake ▣ Reservoir

104 J14 **Coria del Río** Andalucía, S Spain
183 S8 **Coricudgy, Mount** ▲ New South Wales, SE Australia
107 N20 **Corigliano Calabro** Calabria, SW Italy
Corinium/Corinium Dobunorum see Cirencester
23 N1 **Corinth** Mississippi, S USA
Corinth see Kórinthos
Corinth Canal see Dióryga Korinthou
Corinth, Gulf of/Corinthiacus Sinus see Korinthiakós Kólpos
Corinthus see Kórinthos
42 I9 **Corinto** Chinandega, NW Nicaragua
97 C21 **Cork** Ir. Corcaigh. S Ireland
97 C21 **Cork** Ir. Corcaigh. cultural region SW Ireland
97 C21 **Cork** ✕ SW Ireland
97 D21 **Cork Harbour** Ir. Cuan Chorcaí. inlet SW Ireland
107 I23 **Corleone** Sicilia, Italy, C Mediterranean Sea
114 N13 **Çorlu** Tekirdağ, NW Turkey
114 N12 **Çorlu Çayı** ≈ NW Turkey
Cormaiore see Courmayeur
11 V13 **Cormorant** Manitoba, C Canada
23 T2 **Cornelia** Georgia, SE USA
60 J10 **Cornélio Procópio** Paraná, S Brazil
55 V9 **Corneliskondre** Sipaliwini, N Surinam
30 J5 **Cornell** Wisconsin, N USA
13 S12 **Corner Brook** Newfoundland and Labrador, E Canada
Corner Rise Seamounts see Corner Seamounts
64 I9 **Corner Seamounts** var. Corner Rise Seamounts. undersea feature NW Atlantic Ocean
116 M9 **Cornești** Rus. Korneshty. C Moldova
Corneto see Tarquinia
Cornhusker State see Nebraska
27 X8 **Corning** Arkansas, C USA
35 N5 **Corning** California, W USA
29 U15 **Corning** Iowa, C USA
18 G11 **Corning** New York, NE USA
Corn Islands see Maíz, Islas del
107 J14 **Corno Grande** ▲ C Italy
15 N13 **Cornwall** Ontario, SE Canada
97 H25 **Cornwall** cultural region SW England, UK
97 G25 **Cornwall, Cape** headland SW England, UK
54 J4 **Coro** prev. Santa Ana de Coro. Falcón, NW Venezuela
57 J18 **Corocoro** La Paz, W Bolivia
57 K17 **Coroico** La Paz, W Bolivia
184 M5 **Coromandel** Waikato, North Island, NZ
155 K20 **Coromandel Coast** coast E India
184 M5 **Coromandel Peninsula** peninsula North Island, NZ
184 M6 **Coromandel Range** ▲ North Island, NZ
171 N5 **Coron** Busuanga Island, W Philippines
35 T15 **Corona** California, W USA
37 T12 **Corona** New Mexico, SW USA
11 U17 **Coronach** Saskatchewan, S Canada
35 U17 **Coronado** California, W USA
43 N15 **Coronado, Bahía de** bay S Costa Rica
11 R15 **Coronation** Alberta, SW Canada
8 K7 **Coronation Gulf** gulf Nunavut, N Canada
194 I1 **Coronation Island** island Antarctica
39 X14 **Coronation Island** island Alexander Archipelago, Alaska, USA
61 B18 **Coronda** Santa Fe, C Argentina
63 F14 **Coronel** Bío Bío, C Chile
61 D20 **Coronel Brandsen** var. Brandsen. Buenos Aires, E Argentina
62 K4 **Coronel Cornejo** Salta, N Argentina
61 B24 **Coronel Dorrego** Buenos Aires, E Argentina
62 P6 **Coronel Oviedo** Caaguazú, SE Paraguay
61 B23 **Coronel Pringles** Buenos Aires, E Argentina
61 B23 **Coronel Suárez** Buenos Aires, E Argentina
61 E22 **Coronel Vidal** Buenos Aires, E Argentina
55 V9 **Coronie** ◈ district NW Surinam
57 G17 **Coropuna, Nevado** ▲ S Peru
Çorovoda see Çorovodë
113 L22 **Çorovodë** var. Çorovoda. Berat, S Albania
183 P11 **Corowa** New South Wales, SE Australia
42 G1 **Corozal** Corozal, N Belize
54 E6 **Corozal** Sucre, NW Colombia
42 G1 **Corozal** ◈ district N Belize
25 T14 **Corpus Christi** Texas, SW USA
25 T14 **Corpus Christi Bay** inlet Texas, SW USA
25 R14 **Corpus Christi, Lake** ⊞ Texas, SW USA
63 F16 **Corral** Los Lagos, C Chile
105 O9 **Corral de Almaguer** Castilla-La Mancha, C Spain
104 K6 **Corrales** Castilla-León, N Spain
37 R11 **Corrales** New Mexico, SW USA
Corrán Tuathail see Carrauntoohil
106 F9 **Correggio** Emilia-Romagna, C Italy
59 M16 **Corrente** Piauí, E Brazil
59 I19 **Correntes, Rio** ≈ SW Brazil
103 N12 **Corrèze** ◈ department C France
97 C17 **Corrib, Lough** Ir. Loch Coirib. ◎ W Ireland
61 C14 **Corrientes** Corrientes, NE Argentina
61 D15 **Corrientes** off. Provincia de Corrientes. ◈ province NE Argentina
44 A5 **Corrientes, Cabo** headland W Cuba
40 I13 **Corrientes, Cabo** headland SW Mexico
Corrientes, Provincia de see Corrientes
61 C16 **Corrientes, Río** ≈ NE Argentina
56 E8 **Corrientes, Río** ≈ Ecuador/Peru
25 W9 **Corrigan** Texas, SW USA
55 U9 **Corriverton** E Guyana
Corriza see Korçë
183 Q11 **Corryong** Victoria, SE Australia
103 Y12 **Corse** Eng. Corsica. ◈ region France, C Mediterranean Sea
103 X13 **Corse** Eng. Corsica. island France, C Mediterranean Sea
103 Y13 **Corse, Cap** headland Corse, France, C Mediterranean Sea
103 X15 **Corse-du-Sud** ◈ department Corse, France, C Mediterranean Sea
29 P11 **Corsica** South Dakota, N USA
Corsica see Corse
25 U7 **Corsicana** Texas, SW USA
103 Y15 **Corte** Corse, France, C Mediterranean Sea
63 G16 **Corte Alto** Los Lagos, S Chile
104 I13 **Cortegana** Andalucía, S Spain
43 N15 **Cortés** var. Ciudad Cortés. Puntarenas, SE Costa Rica
42 G5 **Cortés** ◈ department NW Honduras
37 P8 **Cortez** Colorado, C USA
Cortez, Sea of see California, Golfo de
106 H6 **Cortina d'Ampezzo** Veneto, NE Italy
18 H11 **Cortland** New York, NE USA
31 V11 **Cortland** Ohio, N USA
106 H12 **Cortona** Toscana, C Italy
76 H13 **Corubal, Rio** ≈ E Guinea-Bissau
104 G10 **Coruche** Santarém, C Portugal
Çoruh see Rize
137 R11 **Çoruh Nehri** Geor. Chorokhi, Rus. Chorokh. ≈ Georgia/Turkey
136 K12 **Çorum** var. Chorum. Çorum, N Turkey
136 J12 **Çorum** var. Chorum. ◈ province N Turkey
59 H19 **Corumbá** Mato Grosso do Sul, S Brazil
14 D16 **Corunna** Ontario, S Canada
Corunna see A Coruña
32 F12 **Corvallis** Oregon, NW USA
64 M1 **Corvo** var. Ilha do Corvo. island Azores, Portugal, NE Atlantic Ocean
Corvo, Ilha do see Corvo
31 O16 **Corydon** Indiana, N USA
29 V16 **Corydon** Iowa, C USA
Cos see Kos
40 I9 **Cosalá** Sinaloa, C Mexico
41 R15 **Cosamaloapan** var. Cosamaloapan de Carpio. Veracruz-Llave, E Mexico
Cosamaloapan de Carpio see Cosamaloapan
107 N21 **Cosenza** anc. Consentia. Calabria, SW Italy
31 T13 **Coshocton** Ohio, N USA
42 H9 **Cosigüina, Punta** headland NW Nicaragua
29 T9 **Cosmos** Minnesota, N USA
103 O8 **Cosne-sur-Loire** Nièvre, C France
108 B9 **Cossonay** Vaud, W Switzerland
Cossyra see Pantelleria
42 K13 **Costa Rica** off. Republic of Costa Rica. ◆ republic Central America
43 N15 **Costeña, Fila** ▲ S Costa Rica
Costermansville see Bukavu
116 I14 **Costești** Argeș, SW Romania
37 S8 **Costilla** New Mexico, SW USA
35 O7 **Cosumnes River** ≈ California, W USA
101 O16 **Coswig** Sachsen, E Germany
101 M14 **Coswig** Sachsen-Anhalt, E Germany
Cosyra see Pantelleria
171 Q7 **Cotabato** Mindanao, S Philippines
56 C5 **Cotacachi** ▲ N Ecuador
57 L21 **Cotagaita** Potosí, S Bolivia
103 V15 **Côte d'Azur** prev. Nice. ✕ (Nice) Alpes-Maritimes, SE France
Côte d'Ivoire see Ivory Coast
103 R8 **Côte d'Or** cultural region C France
103 R7 **Côte d'Or** ◈ department E France
Côte Française des Somalis see Djibouti
102 J4 **Cotentin** peninsula N France
102 G6 **Côtes d'Armor** prev. Côtes-du-Nord. ◈ department NW France
Côtes-du Nord see Côtes d'Armor
Cöthen see Köthen
Côtière, Chaîne see Coast Mountains
40 M13 **Cotija** var. Cotija de la Paz. Michoacán de Ocampo, SW Mexico
Cotija de la Paz see Cotija
77 R16 **Cotonou** var. Kotonu. S Benin
77 R16 **Cotonou** ✕ S Benin
56 B6 **Cotopaxi** prev. León. ◈ province C Ecuador
56 C6 **Cotopaxi** ✱ N Ecuador
Cotrone see Crotone
97 L21 **Cotswold Hills** var. Cotswolds. hill range S England, UK
Cotswolds see Cotswold Hills
32 F13 **Cottage Grove** Oregon, NW USA
21 S14 **Cottageville** South Carolina, SE USA
101 P14 **Cottbus** Lus. Chośebuz; prev. Kottbus. Brandenburg, E Germany
27 U9 **Cotter** Arkansas, C USA
106 A9 **Cottian Alps** Fr. Alpes Cottiennes, It. Alpi Cozie. ▲ France/Italy
Cottiennes, Alpes see Cottian Alps
Cotton State, The see Alabama
22 G4 **Cotton Valley** Louisiana, S USA
36 L12 **Cottonwood** Arizona, SW USA
32 M10 **Cottonwood** Idaho, NW USA
29 S9 **Cottonwood** Minnesota, N USA
25 Q7 **Cottonwood** Texas, SW USA
27 O5 **Cottonwood Falls** Kansas, C USA
36 L3 **Cottonwood Heights** Utah, W USA
29 S10 **Cottonwood River** ≈ Minnesota, N USA
45 O9 **Cotuí** C Dominican Republic
25 Q13 **Cotulla** Texas, SW USA
Cotyora see Ordu
102 I11 **Coubre, Pointe de la** headland W France
18 E12 **Coudersport** Pennsylvania, NE USA
15 S9 **Coudres, Île aux** island Québec, SE Canada
182 G11 **Couedic, Cape de** headland South Australia
Couentrey see Coventry
102 I6 **Couesnon** ≈ NW France
32 H10 **Cougar** Washington, NW USA
102 L10 **Couhé** Vienne, W France
32 K8 **Coulee City** Washington, NW USA
195 Q15 **Coulman Island** island Antarctica
103 P5 **Coulommiers** Seine-et-Marne, N France
14 K11 **Coulonge** ≈ Québec, SE Canada
14 K11 **Coulonge Est** ≈ Québec, SE Canada
35 Q9 **Coulterville** California, W USA
38 M9 **Council** Alaska, USA
32 M12 **Council** Idaho, NW USA
29 S15 **Council Bluffs** Iowa, C USA
27 O5 **Council Grove** Kansas, C USA
27 O5 **Council Grove Lake** ⊞ Kansas, C USA
32 G7 **Coupeville** Washington, NW USA
55 U12 **Courantyne River** var. Corantijn Rivier, Corentyne River. ≈ Guyana/Surinam
99 G21 **Courcelles** Hainaut, S Belgium
108 C7 **Courgenay** Jura, NW Switzerland
126 B2 **Courland Lagoon** Ger. Kurisches Haff, Rus. Kurskiy Zaliv. lagoon Lithuania/Russian Federation
118 B12 **Courland Spit** Lith. Kuršių Nerija, Rus. Kurshskaya Kosa. spit Lithuania/Russian Federation
106 A6 **Courmayeur** prev. Cormaiore. Valle d'Aosta, NW Italy
108 D7 **Courroux** Jura, NW Switzerland
10 K17 **Courtenay** Vancouver Island, British Columbia, SW Canada
21 W7 **Courtland** Virginia, NE USA
25 V10 **Courtney** Texas, SW USA
30 J4 **Court Oreilles, Lac** ◎ Wisconsin, N USA
Courtrai see Kortrijk
99 H19 **Court-Saint-Étienne** Wallon Brabant, C Belgium
22 G6 **Coushatta** Louisiana, S USA
172 I16 **Cousin** island Inner Islands, NE Seychelles
172 I16 **Cousine** island Inner Islands, NE Seychelles
102 J4 **Coutances** anc. Constantia. Manche, N France
102 K12 **Coutras** Gironde, SW France
45 U14 **Couva** Trinidad, Trinidad and Tobago
108 B8 **Couvet** Neuchâtel, W Switzerland
99 H22 **Couvin** Namur, S Belgium
116 K12 **Covasna** Ger. Kowasna, Hung. Kovászna. Covasna, E Romania
116 J11 **Covasna** ◈ county E Romania
14 E12 **Cove Island** island Ontario, S Canada
34 M5 **Covelo** California, W USA
97 M20 **Coventry** anc. Couentrey. C England, UK
Cove of Cork see Cobh
21 U5 **Covesville** Virginia, NE USA
104 I8 **Covilhã** Castelo Branco, E Portugal
23 T3 **Covington** Georgia, SE USA
31 N13 **Covington** Indiana, N USA
20 M3 **Covington** Kentucky, S USA
22 K8 **Covington** Louisiana, S USA
31 Q13 **Covington** Ohio, N USA
20 F9 **Covington** Tennessee, S USA
21 S6 **Covington** Virginia, NE USA
183 Q8 **Cowal, Lake** seasonal lake New South Wales, SE Australia
11 W15 **Cowan** Manitoba, S Canada
18 F12 **Cowanesque River** ≈ New York/Pennsylvania, NE USA
180 L12 **Cowan, Lake** ◎ Western Australia
15 P13 **Cowansville** Québec, SE Canada
182 H8 **Cowell** South Australia
97 M23 **Cowes** S England, UK
27 Q10 **Coweta** Oklahoma, C USA
32 G10 **Cowlitz River** ≈ Washington, NW USA
21 Q11 **Cowpens** South Carolina, SE USA
183 R8 **Cowra** New South Wales, SE Australia
Coxen Hole see Roatán
59 I19 **Coxim** Mato Grosso do Sul, S Brazil
59 I19 **Coxim, Rio** ≈ SW Brazil
Coxin Hole see Roatán
153 V17 **Cox's Bazar** Chittagong, S Bangladesh
76 H14 **Coyah** Conakry, W Guinea
40 K5 **Coyame** Chihuahua, N Mexico
24 L9 **Coyanosa Draw** ≈ Texas, SW USA
Coyhaique see Coihaique
42 C7 **Coyolate, Río** ≈ S Guatemala
Coyote State see South Dakota
40 I10 **Coyotitán** Sinaloa, C Mexico
41 N15 **Coyuca** var. Coyuca de Catalán. Guerrero, S Mexico
41 O16 **Coyuca** var. Coyuca de Benítez. Guerrero, S Mexico
Coyuca de Benítez/Coyuca de Catalán see Coyuca
29 N15 **Cozad** Nebraska, C USA
Cozie, Alpi see Cottian Alps
Cozmeni see Kitsman'
40 E3 **Cozón, Cerro** ▲ NW Mexico
41 Z12 **Cozumel** Quintana Roo, E Mexico
41 Z12 **Cozumel, Isla** island SE Mexico
32 K8 **Crab Creek** ≈ Washington, NW USA
44 H12 **Crab Pond Point** headland W Jamaica
Cracovia/Cracow see Małopolskie
83 I25 **Cradock** Eastern Cape, S South Africa
39 Y14 **Craig** Prince of Wales Island, Alaska, USA
37 Q3 **Craig** Colorado, C USA
97 F15 **Craigavon** C Northern Ireland, UK
21 T5 **Craigsville** Virginia, NE USA
101 J21 **Crailsheim** Baden-Württemberg, S Germany
116 H14 **Craiova** Dolj, SW Romania
10 K12 **Cranberry Junction** British Columbia, SW Canada
18 J8 **Cranberry Lake** ◎ New York, NE USA
11 V13 **Cranberry Portage** Manitoba, C Canada
11 P17 **Cranbrook** British Columbia, SW Canada
30 M5 **Crandon** Wisconsin, N USA
32 K14 **Crane** Oregon, NW USA
24 M9 **Crane** Texas, SW USA
Crane see The Crane
25 S8 **Cranfills Gap** Texas, SW USA
19 O12 **Cranston** Rhode Island, NE USA
Cranz see Zelenogradsk
59 L15 **Craolândia** Tocantins, E Brazil
102 J7 **Craon** Mayenne, NW France
195 V16 **Crary, Cape** headland Antarctica
Crasna see Kraszna
32 G14 **Crater Lake** ◎ Oregon, NW USA
33 P14 **Craters of the Moon National Monument** national park Idaho, NW USA
59 O14 **Crateús** Ceará, E Brazil
Crathis see Crati
107 N20 **Crati** anc. Crathis. ≈ S Italy
11 U16 **Craven** Saskatchewan, S Canada
54 I8 **Cravo Norte** Arauca, E Colombia
28 J12 **Crawford** Nebraska, C USA
25 T8 **Crawford** Texas, SW USA
11 O17 **Crawford Bay** British Columbia, SW Canada
65 M19 **Crawford Seamount** undersea feature S Atlantic Ocean
31 O13 **Crawfordsville** Indiana, N USA
23 S9 **Crawfordville** Florida, SE USA
97 O23 **Crawley** SE England, UK
33 S10 **Crazy Mountains** ▲ Montana, NW USA
11 T11 **Cree** ≈ Saskatchewan, C Canada
37 R7 **Creede** Colorado, C USA
40 I6 **Creel** Chihuahua, N Mexico
11 S11 **Cree Lake** ◎ Saskatchewan, C Canada
11 V13 **Creighton** Saskatchewan, C Canada
29 Q13 **Creighton** Nebraska, C USA
103 O4 **Creil** Oise, N France
106 E8 **Crema** Lombardia, N Italy
106 E8 **Cremona** Lombardia, N Italy
Creole State see Louisiana
112 M10 **Crepaja** Hung. Cserépalja. Serbia, N Serbia and Montenegro (Yugo.)
103 O4 **Crépy-en-Valois** Oise, N France
112 B10 **Cres** It. Cherso. Primorje-Gorski Kotar, NW Croatia
112 A11 **Cres** It. Cherso; anc. Crexa. island W Croatia
32 H14 **Crescent** Oregon, NW USA
34 K1 **Crescent City** California, W USA
23 W10 **Crescent City** Florida, SE USA
167 X10 **Crescent Group** island group C Paracel Islands
23 W10 **Crescent Lake** ◎ Florida, SE USA
29 X11 **Cresco** Iowa, C USA
61 B18 **Crespo** Entre Ríos, E Argentina
54 E5 **Crespo** ✕ (Cartagena) Bolívar, NW Colombia
103 R13 **Crest** Drôme, E France
37 R5 **Crested Butte** Colorado, C USA
31 S12 **Crestline** Ohio, N USA
11 O17 **Creston** British Columbia, SW Canada
29 U15 **Creston** Iowa, C USA
33 V16 **Creston** Wyoming, C USA
37 S7 **Crestone Peak** ▲ Colorado, C USA
23 P8 **Crestview** Florida, SE USA
121 R10 **Cretan Trough** undersea feature Aegean Sea, C Mediterranean Sea
29 R16 **Crete** Nebraska, C USA
Crete see Kríti
103 O5 **Créteil** Val-de-Marne, N France
Crete, Sea of/Creticum, Mare see Kritikó Pélagos
105 X4 **Creus, Cap de** headland NE Spain
103 N10 **Creuse** ◈ department C France
102 L9 **Creuse** ≈ C France
103 T4 **Creutzwald** Moselle, NE France
105 S12 **Crevillente** País Valenciano, E Spain
97 L18 **Crewe** C England, UK
21 V7 **Crewe** Virginia, NE USA
Crexa see Cres
43 Q15 **Cricamola, Río** ≈ NW Panama
61 K14 **Criciúma** Santa Catarina, S Brazil
96 J11 **Crieff** C Scotland, UK
112 B10 **Crikvenica** It. Cirquenizza; prev. Cirkvenica, Crjkvenica. Primorje-Gorski Kotar, NW Croatia
Crimea/Crimean Oblast see Krym, Respublika
101 M16 **Crimmitschau** var. Krimmitschau. Sachsen, E Germany
116 G11 **Crișcior** Hung. Kristyor. Hunedoara, W Romania
21 Y5 **Crisfield** Maryland, NE USA
31 P3 **Crisp Point** headland Michigan, N USA
59 L19 **Cristalina** Goiás, C Brazil
44 I7 **Cristal, Sierra del** ▲ E Cuba
43 T14 **Cristóbal** Colón, C Panama
54 F4 **Cristóbal Colón, Pico** ▲ N Colombia
Cristur/Cristuru Săcuiesc see Cristuru Secuiesc
116 I11 **Cristuru Secuiesc** prev. Cristur, Cristuru Săcuiesc, Sitaș Cristuru, Ger. Kreutz, Hung. Székelykeresztúr, Szitás-Keresztúr. Harghita, C Romania
116 F10 **Crișul Alb** var. Weisse Kreisch, Ger. Weisse Körös, Hung. Fehér-Körös. ≈ Hungary/Romania
116 F10 **Crișul Negru** Ger. Schwarze Körös, Hung. Fekete-Körös. ≈ Hungary/Romania
116 G10 **Crișul Repede** var. Schnelle Kreisch, Ger. Schnelle Körös, Hung. Sebes-Körös. ≈ Hungary/Romania
117 N10 **Criuleni** Rus. Kriulyany. C Moldova
Crivadia Vulcanului see Vulcan
Crjkvenica see Crikvenica
113 O17 **Crna Gora** ▲ FYR Macedonia/Serbia and Montenegro (Yugo.)
Crna Gora see Montenegro
113 O20 **Crna Reka** ≈ S FYR Macedonia
Crni Drim see Black Drin
109 V10 **Črni vrh** ▲ NE Slovenia
109 V13 **Črnomelj** Ger. Tschernembl. SE Slovenia
97 A17 **Croagh Patrick** Ir. Cruach Phádraig. ▲ W Ireland
112 D9 **Croatia** off. Republic of Croatia, Ger. Kroatien, SCr. Hrvatska. ◆ republic SE Europe
Croce, Picco di see Wilde Kreuzspitze
15 P8 **Croche** ≈ Québec, SE Canada
169 V7 **Crocker, Banjaran** var. Crocker Range. ▲ East Malaysia
Crocker Range see Crocker, Banjaran
25 V9 **Crockett** Texas, SW USA
Crocodile see Limpopo
20 I7 **Crofton** Kentucky, S USA
29 Q12 **Crofton** Nebraska, C USA
Croia see Krujë
103 R16 **Croisette, Cap** headland SE France
102 G8 **Croisic, Pointe du** headland NW France
103 S13 **Croix Haute, Col de la** pass E France
15 U5 **Croix, Pointe à la** headland Québec, SE Canada
14 F13 **Croker, Cape** headland Ontario, S Canada
181 P1 **Croker Island** island Northern Territory, N Australia
96 I8 **Cromarty** N Scotland, UK
99 M21 **Crombach** Liège, E Belgium
97 Q18 **Cromer** E England, UK
185 D22 **Cromwell** Otago, South Island, NZ
185 H16 **Cronadun** West Coast, South Island, NZ
39 O11 **Crooked Creek** Alaska, USA
44 K5 **Crooked Island** island SE Bahamas
44 J5 **Crooked Island Passage** channel SE Bahamas
32 I13 **Crooked River** ≈ Oregon, NW USA
29 R4 **Crookston** Minnesota, N USA
28 I10 **Crooks Tower** ▲ South Dakota, N USA
31 T14 **Crooksville** Ohio, N USA
183 R9 **Crookwell** New South Wales, SE Australia
14 L14 **Crosby** Ontario, SE Canada
97 K17 **Crosby** var. Great Crosby. NW England, UK
29 U6 **Crosby** Minnesota, N USA
28 K2 **Crosby** North Dakota, N USA
25 O6 **Crosbyton** Texas, SW USA
77 V16 **Cross** ≈ Cameroon/Nigeria
23 U10 **Cross City** Florida, SE USA
Crossen see Krosno Odrzańskie
27 V14 **Crossett** Arkansas, C USA
97 K15 **Cross Fell** ▲ N England, UK
11 P16 **Crossfield** Alberta, SW Canada
21 Q12 **Cross Hill** South Carolina, SE USA
19 U6 **Cross Island** island Maine, NE USA
11 X13 **Cross Lake** Manitoba, C Canada
22 F5 **Cross Lake** ⊞ Louisiana, S USA
36 I12 **Crossman Peak** ▲ Arizona, SW USA
25 Q7 **Cross Plains** Texas, SW USA
77 V17 **Cross River** ◈ state SE Nigeria
20 L9 **Crossville** Tennessee, S USA
31 S8 **Croswell** Michigan, N USA
14 K13 **Crotch Lake** ◎ Ontario, SE Canada
Croton/Crotona see Crotone
107 O21 **Crotone** var. Cotrone; anc. Croton, Crotona. Calabria, SW Italy
33 V11 **Crow Agency** Montana, NW USA
183 U7 **Crowdy Head** headland New South Wales, SE Australia
25 Q4 **Crowell** Texas, SW USA
183 O6 **Crowl Creek** seasonal river New South Wales, SE Australia
22 H9 **Crowley** Louisiana, S USA
35 S9 **Crowley, Lake** ⊞ California, W USA
27 X10 **Crowleys Ridge** hill range Arkansas, C USA
31 N11 **Crown Point** Indiana, N USA
37 P10 **Crownpoint** New Mexico, SW USA
33 R10 **Crow Peak** ▲ Montana, NW USA
11 P17 **Crowsnest Pass** pass Alberta/British Columbia, SW Canada
29 T6 **Crow Wing River** ≈ Minnesota, N USA
97 O22 **Croydon** SE England, UK
173 P11 **Crozet Basin** undersea feature S Indian Ocean
173 O12 **Crozet Islands** island group French Southern and Antarctic Territories
173 N12 **Crozet Plateau** var. Crozet Plateaus. undersea feature SW Indian Ocean
Crozet Plateaus see Crozet Plateau
102 E6 **Crozon** Finistère, NW France
Cruacha Dubha, Na see Macgillycuddy's Reeks
Cruach Phádraig see Croagh Patrick
116 M14 **Crucea** Constanța, SE Romania
44 E5 **Cruces** Cienfuegos, C Cuba
107 O20 **Crucoli Torretta** Calabria, SW Italy
41 P9 **Cruillas** Tamaulipas, C Mexico
64 K9 **Cruiser Tablemount** undersea feature E Atlantic Ocean
61 G14 **Cruz Alta** Rio Grande do Sul, S Brazil
44 G8 **Cruz, Cabo** headland S Cuba
60 N9 **Cruzeiro** São Paulo, S Brazil
60 H10 **Cruzeiro do Oeste** Paraná, S Brazil
59 A15 **Cruzeiro do Sul** Acre, W Brazil
23 U11 **Crystal Bay** bay Florida, SE USA
182 I8 **Crystal Brook** South Australia
11 X17 **Crystal City** Manitoba, S Canada
27 X5 **Crystal City** Missouri, C USA
25 P13 **Crystal City** Texas, SW USA
30 M4 **Crystal Falls** Michigan, N USA
23 Q8 **Crystal Lake** Florida, SE USA
31 O6 **Crystal Lake** ◎ Michigan, N USA
23 V11 **Crystal River** Florida, SE USA
37 Q5 **Crystal River** ≈ Colorado, C USA
22 K6 **Crystal Springs** Mississippi, S USA
Csaca see Čadca
Csakathurn/Csáktornya see Čakovec
Csap see Chop
Csepén see Čepin
Cserépalja see Crepaja
Csermő see Cermei
Csíkszereda see Miercurea-Ciuc
111 L24 **Csongrád** Csongrád, SE Hungary
111 L24 **Csongrád** off. Csongrád Megye. ◈ county SE Hungary
111 H22 **Csorna** Győr-Moson-Sopron, NW Hungary
Csucsa see Ciucea
111 G25 **Csurgó** Somogy, SW Hungary
Csurog see Čurug
54 L5 **Cúa** Miranda, N Venezuela
82 C11 **Cuale** Malanje, NW Angola
83 G16 **Cuando** var. Kwando. ≈ S Africa
83 E15 **Cuando Cubango** var. Kuando-Kubango. ◈ province SE Angola
83 E16 **Cuangar** Cuando Cubango, S Angola
82 D11 **Cuango** Lunda Norte, NE Angola
82 C10 **Cuango** Uíge, NW Angola
82 C10 **Cuango** var. Kwango. ≈ Angola/Dem. Rep. Congo see also Kwango
Cuan, Loch see Strangford Lough
82 C12 **Cuanza** var. Kwanza. ≈ C Angola
82 B11 **Cuanza Norte** var. Kuanza Norte. ◈ province NE Angola
82 B12 **Cuanza Sul** var. Kuanza Sul. ◈ province NE Angola

◆ Country ● Country Capital ◇ Dependent Territory ○ Dependent Territory Capital ◈ Administrative Region ✕ International Airport ▲ Mountain ▲ Mountain Range ✱ Volcano ≈ River ◎ Lake ⊞ Reservoir

61 E16 **Cuareim, Río** *var.* Rio Quaraí. ≈ Brazil/Uruguay *see also* Quaraí, Rio
83 D15 **Cuatir** ≈ S Angola
40 M7 **Cuatro Ciénegas** *var.* Cuatro Ciénegas de Carranza. Coahuila de Zaragoza, NE Mexico
Cuatro Ciénegas de Carranza *see* Cuatro Ciénegas
40 I6 **Cuauhtémoc** Chihuahua, N Mexico
41 P14 **Cuautla** Morelos, S Mexico
104 H12 **Cuba** Beja, S Portugal
27 W6 **Cuba** Missouri, C USA
37 R10 **Cuba** New Mexico, SW USA
44 E6 **Cuba** *off.* Republic of Cuba. ◆ *republic* W West Indies
82 B13 **Cubal** Benguela, W Angola
83 C15 **Cubango** *var.* Kuvango, *Port.* Vila Artur de Paiva, Vila da Ponte. Huíla, SW Angola
83 D16 **Cubango** *var.* Kavango, Kavengo, Kubango, Okavango, Okavanggo. ≈ S Africa *see also* Okavango
54 H8 **Cubará** Boyacá, N Colombia
136 I12 **Çubuk** Ankara, N Turkey
83 D14 **Cuchi** Cuando Cubango, C Angola
42 C5 **Cuchumatanes, Sierra de los** ⛰ W Guatemala
Cuculaya, Rio *see* Kukalaya, Rio
82 E12 **Cucumbi** *prev.* Trás-os-Montes. Lunda Sul, NE Angola
54 G7 **Cúcuta** *var.* San José de Cúcuta. Norte de Santander, N Colombia
31 N9 **Cudahy** Wisconsin, N USA
155 J21 **Cuddalore** Tamil Nādu, SE India
155 I18 **Cuddapah** Andhra Pradesh, S India
104 M6 **Cuéllar** Castilla-León, N Spain
82 D13 **Cuemba** *var.* Coemba. Bié, C Angola
56 B8 **Cuenca** Azuay, S Ecuador
105 Q9 **Cuenca** *anc.* Conca. Castilla-La Mancha, C Spain
105 P9 **Cuenca** ◈ *province* Castilla-La Mancha, C Spain
40 L9 **Cuencamé** *var.* Cuencamé de Ceniceros. Durango, C Mexico
Cuencamé de Ceniceros *see* Cuencamé
105 Q8 **Cuenca, Serrania de** ⛰ C Spain
Cuera *see* Chur
105 P5 **Cuerda del Pozo, Embalse de la** ▣ N Spain
41 O14 **Cuernavaca** Morelos, S Mexico
25 T12 **Cuero** Texas, SW USA
44 I7 **Cueto** Holguín, E Cuba
41 Q13 **Cuetzalán** *var.* Cuetzalán del Progreso. Puebla, S Mexico
Cuetzalán del Progreso *see* Cuetzalán
105 Q14 **Cuevas de Almanzora** Andalucía, S Spain
105 T8 **Cuevas de Vinromá** País Valenciano, E Spain
116 H12 **Cugir** *Hung.* Kudzsir. Alba, SW Romania
59 H18 **Cuiabá** *prev.* Cuyabá. *state capital* Mato Grosso, SW Brazil
59 H19 **Cuiabá, Rio** ≈ SW Brazil
41 R15 **Cuicatlán** *var.* San Juan Bautista Cuicatlán. Oaxaca, SE Mexico
191 W16 **Cuidado, Punta** *headland* Easter Island, Chile, E Pacific Ocean
Cuidad Presidente Stroessner *see* Ciudad del Este
Cúige *see* Connaught
Cúige Laighean *see* Leinster
Cúige Mumhan *see* Munster
Cuihua *see* Daguan
98 L13 **Cuijck** Noord-Brabant, SE Netherlands
Cúil an tSúdaire *see* Portarlington
42 D7 **Cuilapa** Santa Rosa, S Guatemala
42 B5 **Cuilco, Río** ≈ W Guatemala
Cúil Mhuine *see* Collooney
Cúil Raithin *see* Coleraine
83 C14 **Cuima** Huambo, C Angola
83 E16 **Cuito** *var.* Kwito. ≈ SE Angola
83 E15 **Cuíto Cuanavale** Cuando Cubango, E Angola
41 N14 **Cuitzeo, Lago de** ◎ C Mexico
27 W4 **Cuivre River** ≈ Missouri, C USA
Çuka *see* Çukë
168 L8 **Cukai** *var.* Chukai, Kemaman. Terengganu, Peninsular Malaysia
113 L23 **Çukë** *var.* Çuka. Vlorë, S Albania
Cularo *see* Grenoble
33 Y7 **Culbertson** Montana, NW USA
28 M16 **Culbertson** Nebraska, C USA
183 P10 **Culcairn** New South Wales, SE Australia
45 W5 **Culebra** *var.* Dewey. E Puerto Rico
45 W6 **Culebra, Isla de** *island* E Puerto Rico
37 T8 **Culebra Peak** ▲ Colorado, C USA
104 J5 **Culebra, Sierra de la** ⛰ NW Spain
98 J12 **Culemborg** Gelderland, C Netherlands
137 V14 **Culfa** *Rus.* Dzhul'fa. SW Azerbaijan
183 P4 **Culgoa River** ≈ New South Wales/Queensland, SE Australia
40 I9 **Culiacán** *var.* Culiacán Rosales, Culiacán-Rosales. Sinaloa, C Mexico
Culiacán-Rosales/Culiacán Rosales *see* Culiacán
105 P14 **Cúllar-Baza** Andalucía, S Spain
105 S10 **Cullera** País Valenciano, E Spain
23 P3 **Cullman** Alabama, S USA
108 B10 **Cully** Vaud, W Switzerland
Culm *see* Chełmno
Culmsee *see* Chełmża
21 V4 **Culpeper** Virginia, NE USA
185 I17 **Culverden** Canterbury, South Island, NZ
55 N5 **Cumaná** Sucre, NE Venezuela
55 O5 **Cumanacoa** Sucre, NE Venezuela
54 C13 **Cumbal, Nevado de** *elevation* S Colombia
21 O7 **Cumberland** Kentucky, S USA
21 U2 **Cumberland** Maryland, NE USA
21 V6 **Cumberland** Virginia, NE USA
187 P12 **Cumberland, Cape** *var.* Cape Nahoi. *headland* Espiritu Santo, N Vanuatu
11 V14 **Cumberland House** Saskatchewan, C Canada
23 W8 **Cumberland Island** *island* Georgia, SE USA
20 L7 **Cumberland, Lake** ▣ Kentucky, S USA
9 R5 **Cumberland Peninsula** *peninsula* Baffin Island, Nunavut, NE Canada
17 Q12 **Cumberland Plateau** *plateau* E USA
30 L1 **Cumberland Point** *headland* Michigan, N USA
21 O7 **Cumberland River** ≈ Kentucky/Tennessee, S USA
9 S6 **Cumberland Sound** *inlet* Baffin Island, Nunavut, NE Canada
96 I12 **Cumbernauld** S Scotland, UK
97 K15 **Cumbria** *cultural region* NW England, UK
97 K15 **Cumbrian Mountains** ⛰ NW England, UK
23 S2 **Cumming** Georgia, SE USA
Cummin in Pommern *see* Kamień Pomorski
182 G9 **Cummins** South Australia
96 I13 **Cumnock** W Scotland, UK
40 G4 **Cumpas** Sonora, NW Mexico
136 H16 **Çumra** Konya, C Turkey
63 G15 **Cunco** Araucanía, C Chile
54 E9 **Cundinamarca** *off.* Departamento de Cundinamarca. ◈ *province* C Colombia
41 U15 **Cunduacán** Tabasco, SE Mexico
83 C16 **Cunene** ◈ *province* S Angola
83 A16 **Cunene** *var.* Kunene. ≈ Angola/Namibia *see also* Kunene
106 A9 **Cuneo** *Fr.* Coni. Piemonte, NW Italy
83 E15 **Cunjamba** Cuando Cubango, E Angola
181 V10 **Cunnamulla** Queensland, E Australia
Čunusavvon *see* Junosuando
Cuokkarašša *see* Čohkarášša
106 B7 **Cuorgnè** Piemonte, NE Italy
96 K11 **Cupar** E Scotland, UK
116 L8 **Cupcina** *Rus.* Kupchino; *prev.* Calinisc, Kalinisk. N Moldova
54 C8 **Cupica** Chocó, W Colombia
54 C8 **Cupica, Golfo de** *gulf* W Colombia
112 N13 **Ćuprija** Serbia, E Serbia and Montenegro (Yugo.)
Cura *see* Villa de Cura
45 P16 **Curaçao** *island* Netherlands Antilles
56 H13 **Curanja, Río** ≈ E Peru
56 F7 **Curaray, Rio** ≈ Ecuador/Peru
116 K14 **Curcani** Călăraşi, SE Romania
182 H4 **Curdimurka** South Australia
103 P7 **Cure** ≈ C France
173 Y16 **Curepipe** C Mauritius
55 R6 **Curiapo** Delta Amacuro, NE Venezuela
Curia Rhaetorum *see* Chur
62 G12 **Curicó** Maule, C Chile
Curieta *see* Krk
172 I15 **Curieuse** *island* Inner Islands, NE Seychelles
59 C16 **Curitiba** Acre, W Brazil
60 K12 **Curitiba** *prev.* Curytiba. *state capital* Paraná, S Brazil
60 J13 **Curitibanos** Santa Catarina, S Brazil
183 S6 **Curlewis** New South Wales, SE Australia
182 J6 **Curnamona** South Australia
83 A15 **Curoca** ≈ SW Angola
183 T6 **Currabubula** New South Wales, SE Australia
59 Q14 **Currais Novos** Rio Grande do Norte, E Brazil
35 W7 **Currant** Nevada, W USA
35 W6 **Currant Mountain** ▲ Nevada, W USA
44 H2 **Current** Eleuthera Island, C Bahamas
27 W8 **Current River** ≈ Arkansas/Missouri, C USA
182 M14 **Currie** Tasmania, SE Australia
21 Y8 **Currituck** North Carolina, SE USA
21 Y8 **Currituck Sound** *sound* North Carolina, SE USA
39 R11 **Curry** Alaska, USA
Curtbunar *see* Tervel
116 I13 **Curtea de Argeş** *var.* Curtea-de-Arges. Argeş, S Romania
116 E10 **Curtici** *Ger.* Kurtitsch, *Hung.* Kürtös. Arad, W Romania
28 M16 **Curtis** Nebraska, C USA
104 H2 **Curtis-Estación** Galicia, NW Spain
183 O14 **Curtis Group** *island group* Tasmania, SE Australia
181 Y8 **Curtis Island** *island* Queensland, SE Australia
58 K11 **Curuá, Ilha do** *island* NE Brazil
59 A14 **Curuçá, Rio** ≈ NW Brazil
112 L9 **Čurug** *Hung.* Csurog. Serbia, N Serbia and Montenegro (Yugo.)
61 D16 **Curuzú Cuatiá** Corrientes, NE Argentina
59 M19 **Curvelo** Minas Gerais, SE Brazil
18 E14 **Curwensville** Pennsylvania, NE USA
30 M3 **Curwood, Mount** ▲ Michigan, N USA
Curytiba *see* Curitiba
Curzola *see* Korčula
42 A10 **Cuscatlán** ◈ *department* C El Salvador
57 H15 **Cusco** *var.* Cuzco. Cusco, C Peru
57 H15 **Cusco** *off.* Departamento de Cusco; *var.* Cuzco. ◈ *department* C Peru
27 O9 **Cushing** Oklahoma, C USA
25 W8 **Cushing** Texas, SW USA
40 I6 **Cusihuiriachic** Chihuahua, N Mexico
103 P10 **Cusset** Allier, C France
23 S6 **Cusseta** Georgia, SE USA
28 J10 **Custer** South Dakota, N USA
Cüstrin *see* Kostrzyn
33 Q7 **Cut Bank** Montana, NW USA
Cutch, Gulf of *see* Kachchh, Gulf of
23 S6 **Cuthbert** Georgia, SE USA
11 S15 **Cut Knife** Saskatchewan, S Canada
23 Y16 **Cutler Ridge** Florida, SE USA
22 K10 **Cut Off** Louisiana, S USA
63 I15 **Cutral-Có** Neuquén, C Argentina
107 O21 **Cutro** Calabria, SW Italy
183 O4 **Cuttaburra Channels** *seasonal river* New South Wales, SE Australia
154 O12 **Cuttack** Orissa, E India
83 C15 **Cuvelai** Cunene, SW Angola
79 G18 **Cuvette** *var.* Région de la Cuvette. ◈ *province* C Congo
173 V9 **Cuvier Basin** *undersea feature* E Indian Ocean
173 U9 **Cuvier Plateau** *undersea feature* E Indian Ocean
82 B12 **Cuvo** ≈ W Angola
100 H9 **Cuxhaven** Niedersachsen, NW Germany
Cuyabá *see* Cuiabá
Cuyuni, Río *see* Cuyuni River
55 S8 **Cuyuni River** *var.* Río Cuyuni. ≈ Guyana/Venezuela
Cuzco *see* Cusco
97 K22 **Cwmbran** *Wel.* Cwmbrân. SW Wales, UK
28 K15 **C.W.McConaughy, Lake** ▣ Nebraska, C USA
81 D20 **Cyangugu** SW Rwanda
110 D11 **Cybinka** *Ger.* Ziebingen. Lubuskie, W Poland
Cyclades *see* Kykládes
Cydonia *see* Chaniá
Cymru *see* Wales
20 M5 **Cynthiana** Kentucky, S USA
11 S17 **Cypress Hills** ⛰ Alberta/Saskatchewan, SW Canada
Cypro-Syrian Basin *see* Cyprus Basin
121 U11 **Cyprus** *off.* Republic of Cyprus, *Gk.* Kypros, *Turk.* Kıbrıs, Kıbrıs Cumhuriyeti. ◆ *republic* E Mediterranean Sea
121 W11 **Cyprus Basin** *var.* Cypro-Syrian Basin. *undersea feature* E Mediterranean Sea
Cythera *see* Kýthira
Cythnos *see* Kýthnos
110 F9 **Czaplinek** *Ger.* Tempelburg. Zachodnio-pomorskie, NW Poland
Czarna Woda *see* Wda
110 G8 **Czarne** Pomorskie, N Poland
110 G10 **Czarnków** Wielkopolskie, C Poland
111 E17 **Czech Republic** *Cz.* Česká Republika. ◆ *republic* C Europe
Czegléd *see* Cegléd
110 G12 **Czempiń** Wielkolpolskie, C Poland
Czenstochau *see* Częstochowa
Czerkow *see* Čerchov
Czernowitz *see* Chernivtsi
110 I8 **Czersk** Pomorskie, N Poland
111 J15 **Częstochowa** *Ger.* Czenstochau, Tschenstochau, *Rus.* Chenstokhov. Śląskie, S Poland
110 F10 **Człopa** *Ger.* Schloppe. Zachodnio-pomorskie, NW Poland
110 H8 **Człuchów** *Ger.* Schlochau. Pomorskie, NW Poland

D

163 V9 **Da'an** *var.* Dalai. Jilin, NE China
15 S10 **Daaquam** Québec, SE Canada
Daawo, Webi *see* Dawa Wenz
54 I4 **Dabajuro** Falcón, NW Venezuela
77 N15 **Dabakala** NE Ivory Coast
163 S11 **Daban** *var.* Bairin Youqi. Nei Mongol Zizhiqu, N China
111 K23 **Dabas** Pest, C Hungary
160 L8 **Daba Shan** ⛰ C China
Dabba *see* Daocheng
140 J5 **Dabbāgh, Jabal** ▲ NW Saudi Arabia
54 D8 **Dabeiba** Antioquia, NW Colombia
154 E11 **Dabhoi** Gujarāt, W India
161 P8 **Dabie Shan** ⛰ C China
76 J13 **Dabola** Haute-Guinée, C Guinea
77 N17 **Dabou** S Ivory Coast
162 M15 **Dabqig** *var.* Uxin Qi. Nei Mongol Zizhiqu, N China
110 P8 **Dąbrowa Białostocka** Podlaskie, NE Poland
111 M16 **Dąbrowa Tarnowska** Małopolskie, S Poland
119 M20 **Dabryn'** *Rus.* Dobryn'. Homyel'skaya Voblasts', SE Belarus
159 P10 **Dabsan Hu** ◎ C China
161 Q13 **Dabu** *var.* Huliao. Guangdong, S China
116 H15 **Dăbuleni** Dolj, SW Romania
Dacca *see* Dhaka
101 L23 **Dachau** Bayern, SE Germany
160 K8 **Dachuan** *prev.* Daxian, Da Xian. Sichuan, C China
Dacia Bank *see* Dacia Seamount
64 M10 **Dacia Seamount** *var.* Dacia Bank. *undersea feature* E Atlantic Ocean
37 T3 **Dacono** Colorado, C USA
Đăc Tô *see* Đak Tô
Dacura *see* Dákura
23 W12 **Dade City** Florida, SE USA
152 L10 **Dadeldhura** *var.* Dandeldhura. Far Western, W Nepal
23 Q5 **Dadeville** Alabama, S USA
Dadong *see* Donggang
103 N15 **Dadou** ≈ S France
154 D12 **Dādra and Nagar Haveli** ◈ *union territory* W India
149 P14 **Dādu** Sind, SE Pakistan
167 U11 **Da Du Boloc** Kon Tum, C Vietnam
160 G9 **Dadu He** ≈ C China
Daegu *see* Taegu
Daerah Istimewa Aceh *see* Aceh
171 P4 **Daet** Luzon, N Philippines
160 I11 **Dafang** Guizhou, S China
Dafeng *see* Shanglin
153 W11 **Dafla Hills** ⛰ NE India
11 U15 **Dafoe** Saskatchewan, S Canada
76 G10 **Dagana** N Senegal
Dagana *see* Dahana, Tajikistan
Dagana *see* Massakory, Chad
Dagcagoin *see* Zoigê
118 K11 **Dagda** Krāslava, SE Latvia
Dagden *see* Hiiumaa
Dagden-Sund *see* Soela Väin
127 P16 **Dagestan, Respublika** *prev.* Dagestanskaya ASSR, *Eng.* Daghestan. ◈ *autonomous republic* SW Russian Federation
Dagestanskaya ASSR *see* Dagestan, Respublika
127 R17 **Dagestanskiye Ogni** Respublika Dagestan, SW Russian Federation
185 A23 **Dagg Sound** *sound* South Island, NZ
Daghestan *see* Dagestan, Respublika
141 Y8 **Daghmar** NE Oman
Dağlıq Qarabağ *see* Nagorno-Karabakh
Dagö *see* Hiiumaa
54 D11 **Dagua** Valle del Cauca, W Colombia
160 H11 **Daguan** *var.* Cuihua. Yunnan, SW China
171 N3 **Dagupan** *off.* Dagupan City. Luzon, N Philippines
159 N16 **Dagzê** *var.* Dêqên. Xizang Zizhiqu, W China
147 Q13 **Dahana** *Rus.* Dagana, Dakhana. SW Tajikistan
163 V10 **Dahei Shan** ⛰ N China
163 T7 **Da Hinggan Ling** *Eng.* Great Khingan Range. ⛰ NE China
Dahlac Archipelago *see* Dahlak Archipelago
80 K9 **Dahlak Archipelago** *var.* Dahlac Archipelago. *island group* E Eritrea
23 T2 **Dahlonega** Georgia, SE USA
101 O14 **Dahme** Brandenburg, E Germany
100 O13 **Dahme** ≈ E Germany
141 O14 **Dahm, Ramlat** *desert* NW Yemen
154 E10 **Dāhod** *prev.* Dohad. Gujarāt, W India
Dahomey *see* Benin
158 G10 **Dahongliutan** Xinjiang Uygur Zizhiqu, NW China
Dahra *see* Dara
139 R2 **Dahūk** *var.* Dohuk, *Kurd.* Dihōk. N Iraq
116 J15 **Daia** Giurgiu, S Romania
165 P12 **Daigo** Ibaraki, Honshū, S Japan
163 O13 **Dai Hai** ◎ N China
Daihoku *see* T'aipei
186 M8 **Dai Island** *island* N Solomon Islands
166 M8 **Daik-u** Pegu, SW Burma
138 H9 **Dā'īl** Dar'ā, S Syria
167 U12 **Đai Lanh** Khanh Hoa, S Vietnam
161 Q13 **Daimao Shan** ⛰ SE China
105 N11 **Daimiel** Castilla-La Mancha, C Spain
115 F22 **Daimoniá** Pelopónnisos, S Greece
Dainan *see* T'ainan
25 W6 **Daingerfield** Texas, SW USA
Daingin, Bá an *see* Dingle Bay
159 R13 **Dainkognubma** Xizang Zizhiqu, W China
164 K14 **Daiō-zaki** *headland* Honshū, SW Japan
Dairbhre *see* Valencia Island
61 B22 **Daireaux** Buenos Aires, E Argentina
Dairen *see* Dalian
75 W9 **Dairûṭ** *var.* Dayrūṭ. C Egypt
25 X10 **Daisetta** Texas, SW USA
192 G5 **Daitō-jima** *island group* SW Japan
192 G5 **Daitō Ridge** *undersea feature* N Philippine Sea
161 N3 **Daixian** *var.* Dai Xian. Shanxi, C China
Daiyue *see* Shanyin
161 Q12 **Daiyun Shan** ⛰ SE China
44 M8 **Dajabón** NW Dominican Republic
160 G8 **Dajin Chuan** ≈ C China
148 J6 **Dak** ◎ W Afghanistan
76 F11 **Dakar** ● (Senegal) W Senegal
76 F11 **Dakar** × W Senegal
167 U10 **Đak Glây** Kon Tum, C Vietnam
Dakhana *see* Dahana
153 U16 **Dakhin Shahbazpur Island** *island* S Bangladesh
Dakhla *see* Ad Dakhla
76 F7 **Dakhlet Nouâdhibou** ◈ *region* NW Mauritania
Đak Lap *see* Kiên Đu'c
167 U13 **Đak Nông** Đắc Lắc, S Vietnam
77 U11 **Dakoro** Maradi, S Niger
29 U12 **Dakota City** Iowa, C USA
29 R13 **Dakota City** Nebraska, C USA
113 M17 **Đakovica** *var.* Djakovica, *Alb.* Gjakovë. Serbia, S Serbia and Montenegro (Yugo.)
112 I10 **Đakovo** *var.* Djakovo, *Hung.* Diakovár. Osijek-Baranja, E Croatia
Dakshin *see* Deccan
167 U11 **Đak Tô** *var.* Đắc Tô. Kon Tum, C Vietnam
43 N7 **Dákura** *var.* Dacura. Región Autónoma Atlántico Norte, NE Nicaragua
95 I14 **Dal** Akershus, S Norway
82 E12 **Dala** Lunda Sul, E Angola
108 J8 **Dalaas** Vorarlberg, W Austria
76 I13 **Dalaba** Moyenne-Guinée, W Guinea
Dalai *see* Da'an
162 I12 **Dalain Hob** *var.* Ejin Qi. Nei Mongol Zizhiqu, N China
Dalai Nor *see* Hulun Nur
163 Q11 **Dalai Nur** *salt lake* N China
Dala-Jarna *see* Järna
95 M14 **Dalälven** ≈ C Sweden
136 C16 **Dalaman** Muğla, SW Turkey
136 C16 **Dalaman** × Muğla, SW Turkey
136 D16 **Dalaman Çayı** ≈ SW Turkey
162 K11 **Dalandzadgad** Ömnögovĭ, S Mongolia
95 D17 **Dalane** *physical region* S Norway
189 Z2 **Dalap-Uliga-Djarrit** *var.* Delap-Uliga-Darrit, D-U-D. *island group* Ratak Chain, SE Marshall Islands
94 J12 **Dalarna** *prev.* Kopparberg ◈ *county* C Sweden
94 L13 **Dalarna** *prev. Eng.* Dalecarlia. *cultural region* C Sweden
95 P16 **Dalarö** Stockholm, C Sweden
167 U13 **Đa Lat** Lâm Đông, S Vietnam
162 J11 **Dalay** Ömnögovĭ, S Mongolia
148 L12 **Dālbandīn** *var.* Dāl Bandin. Baluchistān, SW Pakistan
95 J17 **Dalbosjön** *lake bay* S Sweden
181 Y10 **Dalby** Queensland, E Australia
94 D13 **Dale** Hordaland, S Norway
94 C12 **Dale** Sogn og Fjordane, S Norway
32 K12 **Dale** Oregon, NW USA
25 T11 **Dale** Texas, SW USA
Dalecarlia *see* Dalarna
21 W4 **Dale City** Virginia, NE USA
20 L8 **Dale Hollow Lake** ▣ Kentucky/Tennessee, S USA
98 O8 **Dalen** Drenthe, NE Netherlands
95 E15 **Dalen** Telemark, S Norway
166 K14 **Daletme** Chin State, W Burma
23 Q7 **Daleville** Alabama, S USA
98 M9 **Dalfsen** Overijssel, E Netherlands
24 M1 **Dalhart** Texas, SW USA
13 O13 **Dalhousie** New Brunswick, SE Canada
152 I6 **Dalhousie** Himāchal Pradesh, N India
160 F12 **Dali** *var.* Xiaguan. Yunnan, SW China
Dali *see* Idálion
163 U14 **Dalian** *var.* Dairen, Dalien, Lüda, Ta-lien, *Rus.* Dalny. Liaoning, NE China
105 O15 **Dalías** Andalucía, S Spain
Dalien *see* Dalian
Dalijan *see* Delījān
112 J9 **Dalj** *Hung.* Dalja. Osijek-Baranja, E Croatia
Dalja *see* Dalj
32 F12 **Dallas** Oregon, NW USA
25 U6 **Dallas** Texas, SW USA
25 T7 **Dallas-Fort Worth** × Texas, SW USA
154 K12 **Dalli Rājhara** Chhattīsgarh, C India
39 X15 **Dall Island** *island* Alexander Archipelago, Alaska, USA
38 M12 **Dall Lake** ◎ Alaska, USA
Dállogilli *see* Korpilombolo
77 S12 **Dallol Bosso** *seasonal river* W Niger
141 U7 **Dalmā** *island* W UAE
113 E14 **Dalmacija** *Eng.* Dalmatia, *Ger.* Dalmatien, *It.* Dalmazia. *cultural region* S Croatia
Dalmatia/Dalmatien/ Dalmazia *see* Dalmacija
123 S15 **Dal'negorsk** Primorskiy Kray, SE Russian Federation
Dalny *see* Dalian
76 M16 **Daloa** C Ivory Coast
160 J11 **Dalou Shan** ⛰ S China
181 X7 **Dalrymple Lake** ◎ Queensland, E Australia
14 H14 **Dalrymple Lake** ◎ Ontario, S Canada
181 X7 **Dalrymple, Mount** ▲ Queensland, E Australia
93 K20 **Dalsbruk** *Fin.* Taalintehdas. Länsi-Suomi, W Finland
95 K19 **Dalsjöfors** Västra Götaland, S Sweden
95 J17 **Dals Långed** *var.* Långed. Västra Götaland, S Sweden
153 O15 **Dāltenganj** *prev.* Daltonganj. Jhārkhand, N India
23 R2 **Dalton** Georgia, SE USA
Daltonganj *see* Dāltenganj
195 X14 **Dalton Iceberg Tongue** *ice feature* Antarctica
Dálvvadis *see* Jokkmokk
92 J1 **Dalvík** Nordhurland Eystra, N Iceland
35 N8 **Daly City** California, W USA
181 P2 **Daly River** ≈ Northern Territory, N Australia
181 Q3 **Daly Waters** Northern Territory, N Australia
119 F20 **Damachava** *var.* Damachova, *Pol.* Domaczewo, *Rus.* Domachëvo. Brestskaya Voblasts', SW Belarus
Damachova *see* Damachava
77 W11 **Damagaram Takaya** Zinder, S Niger
154 D12 **Damān** Damān and Diu, W India
154 B12 **Damān and Diu** ◈ *union territory* W India
75 V7 **Damanhûr** *anc.* Hermopolis Parva. N Egypt
Damão *see* Damān
161 O1 **Damaqun Shan** ⛰ E China
79 I15 **Damara** Ombella-Mpoko, S Central African Republic
83 D18 **Damaraland** *physical region* C Namibia
171 S15 **Damar, Kepulauan** *var.* Baraf Daja Islands, Kepulauan Barat Daya. *island group* C Indonesia
168 J8 **Damar Laut** Perak, Peninsular Malaysia
171 S15 **Damar, Pulau** *island* Maluku, E Indonesia
Damas *see* Dimashq
77 Y12 **Damasak** Borno, NE Nigeria
Damasco *see* Dimashq
21 Q8 **Damascus** Virginia, NE USA
Damascus *see* Dimashq
77 X13 **Damaturu** Yobe, NE Nigeria
171 R9 **Damau** Pulau Kaburuang, N Indonesia
143 O5 **Damāvand, Qolleh-ye** ▲ N Iran
82 B10 **Damba** Uíge, NW Angola
114 M12 **Dambaslar** Tekirdağ, NW Turkey
116 J13 **Dâmbovița** *prev.* Dîmbovița. ◈ *county* SE Romania
116 J13 **Dâmbovița** *prev.* Dîmbovița. ≈ S Romania
173 Y15 **D'Ambre, Île** *island* NE Mauritius
155 K24 **Dambulla** Central Province, C Sri Lanka
44 K9 **Dame-Marie** SW Haiti
44 J9 **Dame Marie, Cap** *headland* SW Haiti
143 Q4 **Dāmghān** Semnān, N Iran
Damietta *see* Dumyâṭ
138 G10 **Dāmiyā** Al Balqā', NW Jordan
146 G11 **Damla** Daşoguz Welaýaty, N Turkmenistan
Dammām *see* Ad Dammān
100 G12 **Damme** Niedersachsen, NW Germany
153 R15 **Dāmodar** ≈ NE India
154 J9 **Damoh** Madhya Pradesh, C India
77 P15 **Damongo** NW Ghana
138 G7 **Damour** *var.* Ad Dāmūr. W Lebanon
171 N11 **Dampal, Teluk** *bay* Sulawesi, C Indonesia
180 H7 **Dampier** Western Australia
180 H6 **Dampier Archipelago** *island group* Western Australia
141 U14 **Damqawt** *var.* Damqut. E Yemen
159 O13 **Dam Qu** ≈ C China
Damqut *see* Damqawt
167 R13 **Dâmrei, Chuŏr Phmun** *Fr.* Chaîne de l'Éléphant. ⛰ SW Cambodia
108 C7 **Damvant** Jura, NW Switzerland
Damwâld *see* Damwoude
98 L5 **Damwoude** *Fris.* Damwâld. Friesland, N Netherlands
159 N15 **Damxung** *var.* Gongtang. Xizang Zizhiqu, W China
80 K11 **Danakil Desert** *var.* Afar Depression, Danakil Plain. *desert* E Africa
Danakil Plain *see* Danakil Desert
35 R8 **Dana, Mount** ▲ California, W USA
76 L16 **Danané** W Ivory Coast
167 U10 **Đa Nâng** *prev.* Tourane. Quang Nam-Đa Nâng, C Vietnam
160 G9 **Danba** *var.* Zhanggu, *Tib.* Rongzhag. Sichuan, C China
Danborg *see* Daneborg
18 L13 **Danbury** Connecticut, NE USA
25 W12 **Danbury** Texas, SW USA
35 X15 **Danby Lake** ◎ California, W USA
194 H4 **Danco Coast** *physical region* Antarctica
82 B11 **Dande** ≈ NW Angola
Dandeldhura *see* Dadeldhura
155 E17 **Dandeli** Karnātaka, W India
183 O12 **Dandenong** Victoria, SE Australia
163 V13 **Dandong** *var.* Tan-tung; *prev.* An-tung. Liaoning, NE China
197 Q14 **Daneborg** *var.* Danborg. Tunu, N Greenland
25 V12 **Danevang** Texas, SW USA
Dänew *see* Galkynyş
Danfeng *see* Shizong
14 L12 **Danford Lake** Québec, SE Canada
19 T4 **Danforth** Maine, NE USA
37 P3 **Danforth Hills** ⛰ Colorado, C USA
Dangara *see* Danghara
159 V12 **Dangchang** Gansu, C China
159 P8 **Dangchengwan** *var.* Subei, Subei Mongolzu Zizhixian. Gansu, N China
82 B10 **Dange** Uíge, NW Angola
Dangerous Archipelago *see* Tuamotu, Îles
83 E26 **Danger Point** *headland* SW South Africa
147 Q13 **Danghara** *Rus.* Dangara. SW Tajikistan
159 P8 **Danghe Nanshan** ⛰ W China
80 I12 **Dangila** *var.* Dänglä. Amhara, NW Ethiopia

◆ Country
● Country Capital
◇ Dependent Territory
○ Dependent Territory Capital
◈ Administrative Region
× International Airport
▲ Mountain
⛰ Mountain Range
Volcano
≈ River
◎ Lake
▣ Reservoir

159 P8 **Dangjin Shankou** *pass* N China
Dangla *see* Tanggula Shan, China
Dang La *see* Tanggula Shankou, China
Dāngla *see* Dangila, Ethiopia
Dangme Chu *see* Manās
153 Y11 **Dāngori** Assam, NE India
Dang Raek, Phanom/Dangrek, Chaîne des *see* Dângrêk, Chuŏr Phnum
167 S11 **Dângrêk, Chuŏr Phnum** *var.* Phanom Dang Raek, Phanom Dong Rak, *Fr.* Chaîne des Dangrek. ▲ Cambodia/Thailand
42 G3 **Dangriga** *prev.* Stann Creek. Stann Creek, E Belize
161 P6 **Dangshan** Anhui, E China
33 T15 **Daniel** Wyoming, C USA
83 H22 **Daniëlskuil** Northern Cape, N South Africa
19 N12 **Danielson** Connecticut, NE USA
124 M15 **Danilov** Yaroslavskaya Oblast', W Russian Federation
127 O9 **Danilovka** Volgogradskaya Oblast', SW Russian Federation
Danish West Indies *see* Virgin Islands (US)
160 L7 **Dan Jiang** ↝ C China
160 M7 **Danjiangkou Shuiku** ⊞ C China
141 W8 **Ḑank** *var.* Dhank. NW Oman
152 J7 **Dankhar** Himāchal Pradesh, N India
126 L6 **Dankov** Lipetskaya Oblast', W Russian Federation
42 J7 **Danlí** El Paraíso, S Honduras
Danmark *see* Denmark
Danmarksstraedet *see* Denmark Strait
95 O14 **Dannemora** Uppsala, C Sweden
18 L6 **Dannemora** New York, NE USA
100 K11 **Dannenberg** Niedersachsen, N Germany
184 N12 **Dannevirke** Manawatu-Wanganui, North Island, NZ
21 U8 **Dan River** ↝ Virginia, NE USA
167 P8 **Dan Sai** Loei, C Thailand
18 F10 **Dansville** New York, NE USA
Dantzig *see* Gdańsk
116 G14 **Danube** *Bul.* Dunav, *Cz.* Dunaj, *Ger.* Donau, *Hung.* Duna, *Rom.* Dunărea. ↝ C Europe
Danubian Plain *see* Dunavska Ravnina
166 L8 **Danubyu** Irrawaddy, SW Burma
Danum *see* Doncaster
19 P11 **Danvers** Massachusetts, NE USA
27 T11 **Danville** Arkansas, C USA
31 N13 **Danville** Illinois, N USA
31 O14 **Danville** Indiana, N USA
29 Y15 **Danville** Iowa, C USA
20 M6 **Danville** Kentucky, S USA
18 G14 **Danville** Pennsylvania, NE USA
21 T6 **Danville** Virginia, NE USA
Danxian/Dan Xian *see* Danzhou
160 L17 **Danzhou** *prev.* Danxian, Dan Xian, Nada. Hainan, S China
Danzig *see* Gdańsk
Danziger Bucht *see* Danzig, Gulf of
110 J6 **Danzig, Gulf of** *var.* Gulf of Gdańsk, *Ger.* Danziger Bucht, *Pol.* Zakota Gdańska, *Rus.* Gdan'skaya Bukhta. *gulf* N Poland
160 F10 **Daocheng** *var.* Jinzhu, *Tib.* Dabba. Sichuan, C China
Daojiang *see* Daoxian
Daokou *see* Huaxian
104 H7 **Dão, Rio** ↝ N Portugal
Daosa *see* Dausa
77 Y7 **Dao Timmi** Agadez, NE Niger
160 M13 **Daoxian** *var.* Daojiang, Dao Xian. Hunan, S China
77 Q14 **Dapaong** N Togo
23 N8 **Daphne** Alabama, S USA
171 P7 **Dapitan** Mindanao, S Philippines
159 P9 **Da Qaidam** Qinghai, C China
163 V8 **Daqing** *var.* Sartu. Heilongjiang, NE China
163 O13 **Daqing Shan** ▲ N China
163 T11 **Daqin Tal** *var.* Naiman Qi. Nei Mongol Zizhiqu, N China
Daqm *see* Duqm
160 G8 **Da Qu** *var.* Do Qu. ↝ C China
139 T5 **Dāqūq** *var.* Tāwūq. N Iraq
76 G10 **Dara** *var.* Dahra. NW Senegal
138 H9 **Dar'ā** *var.* Der'a, *Fr.* Déraa. Dar'ā, SW Syria
138 H8 **Dar'ā** *off.* Muḩāfaẓat Dar'ā, *var.* Darā, Derá, Derrá. ◆ *governorate* S Syria
143 Q12 **Dārāb** Fārs, S Iran
116 K8 **Darabani** Botoşani, NW Romania
Daraj *see* Dirj
142 M8 **Dārān** Eşfahān, W Iran
167 U12 **Đa Răng, Sông** *var.* Ba. ↝ S Vietnam
Daraut-Kurgan *see* Daroot-Korgon
77 W13 **Darazo** Bauchi, E Nigeria
139 S3 **Darband** N Iraq
139 V4 **Darband-i Khān, Sadd** *dam* NE Iraq
139 N1 **Darbāsīyah** *var.* Derbisīye. Al Ḩasakah, N Syria
118 C11 **Darbėnai** Klaipėda, NW Lithuania
153 Q13 **Darbhanga** Bihār, N India
38 M9 **Darby, Cape** *headland* Alaska, USA
112 I9 **Darda** *Hung.* Dárda. Osijek-Baranja, E Croatia
27 T11 **Dardanelle** Arkansas, C USA
27 S11 **Dardanelle, Lake** ⊞ Arkansas, C USA
Dardanelles *see* Çanakkale Boğazı
Dardanelli *see* Çanakkale
Dardo *see* Kangding
Dar-el-Beida *see* Casablanca
136 M14 **Darende** Malatya, C Turkey
81 J22 **Dar es Salaam** Dar es Salaam, E Tanzania
81 J22 **Dar es Salaam** ✈ Pwani, E Tanzania
185 H18 **Darfield** Canterbury, South Island, NZ
106 F7 **Darfo** Lombardia, N Italy
80 B10 **Darfur** *var.* Darfur Massif. *cultural region* W Sudan
Darfur Massif *see* Darfur
Darganata/Dargan-Ata *see* Birata
143 T3 **Dargaz** *var.* Darreh Gaz; *prev.* Moḩammadābād. Khorāsān, NE Iran
139 U4 **Dargazayn** NE Iraq
183 P12 **Dargo** Victoria, SE Australia
162 K7 **Darhan** Bulgan, C Mongolia
162 L6 **Darhan** Darhan Uul, N Mongolia
163 N8 **Darhan** Hentiy, C Mongolia
Darhan Muminggan Lianheqi *see* Bailingmiao
162 L6 **Darhan Uul** ◆ *province* N Mongolia
23 W7 **Darien** Georgia, SE USA
43 W16 **Darién** *off.* Provincia del Darién. ◆ *province* SE Panama
Darién, Golfo del *see* Darien, Gulf of
43 X14 **Darien, Gulf of** *Sp.* Golfo del Darién. *gulf* S Caribbean Sea
Darien, Isthmus of *see* Panamá, Istmo de
42 K9 **Dariense, Cordillera** ▲ C Nicaragua
43 W15 **Darién, Serranía del** ▲ Colombia/Panama
Dario *see* Ciudad Darío
Dariorigum *see* Vannes
Dariv *see* Darvi
Darj *see* Dirj
Darjeeling *see* Darjiling
153 S12 **Darjiling** *prev.* Darjeeling. West Bengal, NE India
Darkehnen *see* Ozersk
159 S12 **Darlag** *var.* Gümai. Qinghai, C China
183 T3 **Darling Downs** *hill range* Queensland, E Australia
28 M2 **Darling, Lake** ⊞ North Dakota, N USA
180 I12 **Darling Range** ▲ Western Australia
182 L8 **Darling River** ↝ New South Wales, SE Australia
97 M15 **Darlington** N England, UK
21 T12 **Darlington** South Carolina, SE USA
30 K9 **Darlington** Wisconsin, N USA
110 G7 **Darłowo** Zachodnio-pomorskie, NW Poland
101 G19 **Darmstadt** Hessen, SW Germany
75 S7 **Darnah** *var.* Dérna. NE Libya
103 S6 **Darney** Vosges, NE France
182 M7 **Darnick** New South Wales, SE Australia
195 Y6 **Darnley, Cape** *headland* Antarctica
105 R7 **Daroca** Aragón, NE Spain
147 S11 **Daroot-Korgon** *var.* Daraut-Kurgan. Oshskaya Oblast', SW Kyrgyzstan
61 A23 **Darragueira** *var.* Darregueira. Buenos Aires, E Argentina
Darregueira *see* Darragueira
Darreh Gaz *see* Dargaz
142 K7 **Darreh Shahr** *var.* Darreh-ye Shahr. Īlām, W Iran
Darreh-ye Shahr *see* Darreh Shahr
32 I7 **Darrington** Washington, NW USA
25 P1 **Darrouzett** Texas, SW USA
153 S15 **Darsana** *var.* Darshana. Khulna, N Bangladesh
Darshana *see* Darsana
100 M7 **Darss** *peninsula* NE Germany
100 M7 **Darsser Ort** *headland* NE Germany
97 J24 **Dart** ↝ SW England, UK
Dartang *see* Baqên
97 P22 **Dartford** SE England, UK
182 L12 **Dartmoor** Victoria, SE Australia
97 I24 **Dartmoor** *moorland* SW England, UK
13 Q15 **Dartmouth** Nova Scotia, SE Canada
97 J24 **Dartmouth** SW England, UK
15 Y6 **Dartmouth** ↝ Québec, SE Canada
183 Q11 **Dartmouth Reservoir** ⊚ Victoria, SE Australia
Dartuch, Cabo *see* Artrutx, Cap d'
186 C9 **Daru** Western, SW PNG
112 G9 **Daruvar** *Hung.* Daruvár. Bjelovar-Bilogora, NE Croatia
Darvaza, Turkmenistan *see* Derweze
Darvaza, Uzbekistan *see* Darvoza
Darvazskiy Khrebet *see* Darvoz, Qatorkŭhi
162 F8 **Darvi** *var.* Dariv. Govĭ-Altay, W Mongolia
148 L9 **Darvīshān** *var.* Darweshan, Garmser. Helmand, S Afghanistan
147 R13 **Darvoz, Qatorkŭhi** *Rus.* Darvazskiy Khrebet. ▲ C Tajikistan
Darweshan *see* Darvīshān
63 J15 **Darwin** Río Negro, S Argentina
181 O1 **Darwin** *prev.* Palmerston, Port Darwin. *territory capital* Northern Territory, N Australia
65 D24 **Darwin** *var.* Darwin Settlement. East Falkland, Falkland Islands
62 H8 **Darwin, Cordillera** ▲ N Chile
57 B17 **Darwin, Volcán** ☼ Galapagos Islands, Ecuador, E Pacific Ocean
147 O10 **Darvoza** *Rus.* Darvaza. Jizzax Viloyati, C Uzbekistan
149 S8 **Darya Khān** Punjab, E Pakistan
145 O15 **Dar'yalyktakyr, Ravnina** *plain* S Kazakhstan
143 T11 **Dārzīn** Kermān, S Iran
Dashennongjia *see* Shennong Ding
Dashhowuz *see* Daşoguz
Dashhowuz Welayaty *see* Daşoguz Welaýaty
119 O16 **Dashkawka** *Rus.* Dashkovka. Mahilyowskaya Voblasts', E Belarus
Dashkhovuz *see* Daşoguz Welaýaty
Dashkhovuzskiy Velayat *see* Daşoguz Welaýaty
Dashköpri *see* Daşköpri
Dashkovka *see* Dashkawka
148 J15 **Dasht** ↝ SW Pakistan
Dashtidzhum *see* Dashtijum
147 R13 **Dashtijum** *Rus.* Dashtidzhum. SW Tajikistan
149 W7 **Daska** Punjab, NE Pakistan
146 J16 **Daşköpri** *var.* Dashköpri, *Rus.* Tashkepri. Mary Welaýaty, S Turkmenistan
146 H8 **Daşoguz** *Rus.* Dashkhovuz, *Turkm.* Dashhowuz; *prev.* Tashauz. Daşoguz Welaýaty, N Turkmenistan
146 E9 **Daşoguz Welaýaty** *var.* Dashhowuz Welayaty, *Rus.* Dashkhovuz, Dashkhovuzskiy Velayat. ◆ *province* N Turkmenistan
Đa, Sông *see* Black River
77 R15 **Dassa** *var.* Dassa-Zoumé. S Benin
Dassa-Zoumé *see* Dassa
29 U8 **Dassel** Minnesota, N USA
152 H3 **Dastegil Sar** *var.* Disteghil Sār. ▲ N India
136 C16 **Datça** Muğla, SW Turkey
165 R4 **Date** Hokkaidō, NE Japan
154 I8 **Datia** *prev.* Duttia. Madhya Pradesh, C India
Dătnejaevrie *see* Tunnsjøen
159 T10 **Datong** *var.* Qiaotou. Qinghai, C China
161 N2 **Datong** *var.* Tatung, Ta-t'ung. Shanxi, C China
Datong *see* Tong'an
159 S9 **Datong He** ↝ C China
159 S9 **Datong Shan** ▲ C China
169 O10 **Datu, Tanjung** *headland* Indonesia/Malaysia
Daua *see* Dawa Wenz
172 H16 **Dauban, Mount** ▲ Silhouette, NE Seychelles
149 T7 **Dāūd Khel** Punjab, E Pakistan
119 G15 **Daugai** Alytus, S Lithuania
Daugava *see* Western Dvina
118 J11 **Daugavpils** *Ger.* Dünaburg; *prev. Rus.* Dvinsk. *municipality* Daugvapils, SE Latvia
Dauka *see* Dawkah
Daulatabad *see* Malāyer
101 D18 **Daun** Rheinland-Pfalz, W Germany
155 E14 **Daund** *prev.* Dhond. Mahārāshtra, W India
166 M12 **Daung Kyun** *island* S Burma
11 W15 **Dauphin** Manitoba, S Canada
103 S13 **Dauphiné** *cultural region* E France
23 N9 **Dauphin Island** *island* Alabama, S USA
11 X15 **Dauphin River** Manitoba, S Canada
77 V12 **Daura** Katsina, N Nigeria
152 H12 **Dausa** *prev.* Daosa. Rājasthān, N India
Dauwa *see* Dawwah
137 Y10 **Däväçi** *Rus.* Divichi. NE Azerbaijan
155 F18 **Dāvangere** Karnātaka, W India
171 Q8 **Davao** *off.* Davao City. Mindanao, S Philippines
171 Q8 **Davao Gulf** *gulf* Mindanao, S Philippines
15 Q11 **Daveluyville** Québec, SE Canada
29 Z14 **Davenport** Iowa, C USA
32 L8 **Davenport** Washington, NW USA
43 P16 **David** Chiriquí, W Panama
15 O11 **David** ↝ Québec, SE Canada
29 R15 **David City** Nebraska, C USA
David-Gorodok *see* Davyd-Haradok
11 T16 **Davidson** Saskatchewan, S Canada
21 R10 **Davidson** North Carolina, SE USA
26 K12 **Davidson** Oklahoma, C USA
39 S6 **Davidson Mountains** ▲ Alaska, USA
172 M8 **Davie Ridge** *undersea feature* W Indian Ocean
182 A1 **Davies, Mount** ▲ South Australia
35 O7 **Davis** California, W USA
27 N12 **Davis** Oklahoma, C USA
195 Y7 **Davis** *Australian research station* Antarctica
194 H3 **Davis Coast** *physical region* Antarctica
18 C16 **Davis, Mount** ▲ Pennsylvania, NE USA
24 K9 **Davis Mountains** ▲ Texas, SW USA
195 Z9 **Davis Sea** *sea* Antarctica
65 O20 **Davis Seamounts** *undersea feature* S Atlantic Ocean
196 M13 **Davis Strait** *strait* Baffin Bay/Labrador Sea
127 U5 **Davlekanovo** Respublika Bashkortostan, W Russian Federation
108 J9 **Davos** *Rmsch.* Tavau. Graubünden, E Switzerland
119 J20 **Davyd-Haradok** *Pol.* Dawidgródek, *Rus.* David-Gorodok. Brestskaya Voblasts', SW Belarus
163 U12 **Dawa** Liaoning, NE China
141 O11 **Dawāsir, Wādī ad** *dry watercourse* S Saudi Arabia
81 K15 **Dawa Wenz** *var.* Daua, Webi Daawo. ↝ E Africa
Dawaymah, Birkat ad *see* Umm al Baqar, Hawr
Dawei *see* Tavoy
119 K14 **Dawhinava** *Rus.* Dolginovo. Minskaya Voblasts', N Belarus
Dawidgródek *see* Davyd-Haradok
141 V12 **Dawkah** *var.* Dauka. SW Oman
Dawlat Qaṭar *see* Qatar
24 M3 **Dawn** Texas, SW USA
Dawo *see* Maqên
140 M11 **Daws** Al Bāḩah, SW Saudi Arabia
10 H5 **Dawson** *var.* Dawson City. Yukon Territory, NW Canada
23 S6 **Dawson** Georgia, SE USA
29 S9 **Dawson** Minnesota, N USA
Dawson City *see* Dawson
11 N13 **Dawson Creek** British Columbia, W Canada
8 H7 **Dawson Range** ▲ Yukon Territory, W Canada
181 Y9 **Dawson River** ↝ Queensland, E Australia
10 J15 **Dawsons Landing** British Columbia, SW Canada
20 I7 **Dawson Springs** Kentucky, S USA
23 S2 **Dawsonville** Georgia, SE USA
160 G8 **Dawu** *var.* Xianshui. Sichuan, C China
Dawu *see* Maqên
Dawukou *see* Shizuishan
141 Y10 **Dawwah** *var.* Dauwa. W Oman
102 J15 **Dax** *var.* Ax; *anc.* Aquae Augustae, Aquae Tarbelicae. Landes, SW France
Da Xian/Daxian *see* Dachuan
Daxue *see* Wencheng
160 G9 **Daxue Shan** ▲ C China
Dayan *see* Lijiang
160 G12 **Dayao** *var.* Jinbi. Yunnan, SW China
Dayishan *see* Gaoyou
183 N12 **Daylesford** Victoria, SE Australia
35 U10 **Daylight Pass** *pass* California, W USA
61 D17 **Daymán, Río** ↝ N Uruguay
Dayr *see* Ad Dayr
138 G10 **Dayr 'Allā** *var.* Deir 'Alla. Al Balqā', N Jordan
139 N4 **Dayr az Zawr** *var.* Deir ez Zor. Dayr az Zawr, E Syria
138 M5 **Dayr az Zawr** *off.* Muḩāfaẓat Dayr az Zawr, *var.* Dayr Az-Zor. ◆ *governorate* E Syria
Dayr Az-Zor *see* Dayr az Zawr
Dayrūṭ *see* Dairûṭ
11 Q15 **Daysland** Alberta, SW Canada
31 R14 **Dayton** Ohio, N USA
20 L10 **Dayton** Tennessee, S USA
25 W11 **Dayton** Texas, SW USA
32 L10 **Dayton** Washington, NW USA
23 X10 **Daytona Beach** Florida, SE USA
169 U12 **Dayu** Borneo, C Indonesia
161 O13 **Dayu Ling** ▲ S China
161 R7 **Da Yunhe** *Eng.* Grand Canal. *canal* E China
161 S11 **Dayu Shan** *island* SE China
160 J9 **Dazhu** *var.* Zhuyang. Sichuan, C China
160 J9 **Dazu** *var.* Longgang. Chongqing Shi, C China
83 H24 **De Aar** Northern Cape, C South Africa
194 K5 **Deacon, Cape** *headland* Antarctica
39 R5 **Deadhorse** Alaska, USA
33 T12 **Dead Indian Peak** ▲ Wyoming, C USA
23 R9 **Dead Lake** ⊚ Florida, SE USA
44 J4 **Deadman's Cay** Long Island, C Bahamas
138 G11 **Dead Sea** *var.* Bahret Lut, Lacus Asphaltites, *Ar.* Al Baḩr al Mayyit, Baḩrat Lūt, *Heb.* Yam HaMelaḥ. *salt lake* Israel/Jordan
28 J9 **Deadwood** South Dakota, N USA
97 Q22 **Deal** SE England, UK
83 I22 **Dealesville** Free State, C South Africa
161 P10 **De'an** *var.* Puting. Jiangxi, S China
62 K9 **Deán Funes** Córdoba, C Argentina
194 L12 **Dean Island** *island* Antarctica
Deanuvuotna *see* Tanafjorden
31 S10 **Dearborn** Michigan, N USA
27 R3 **Dearborn** Missouri, C USA
Deargget *see* Tärendö
32 K9 **Deary** Idaho, NW USA
32 M9 **Deary** Washington, NW USA
10 J10 **Dease** ↝ British Columbia, W Canada
10 J10 **Dease Lake** British Columbia, W Canada
35 U11 **Death Valley** California, W USA
35 U11 **Death Valley** *valley* California, W USA
92 M8 **Deatnu** *Fin.* Tenojoki, *Nor.* Tana. ↝ Finland/Norway *see also* Tenojoki
102 L4 **Deauville** Calvados, N France
117 X7 **Debal'tseve** *Rus.* Debal'tsevo. Donets'ka Oblast', SE Ukraine
Debal'tsevo *see* Debal'tseve
113 M19 **Debar** *Ger.* Dibra, *Turk.* Debre. W FYR Macedonia
39 O9 **Debauch Mountain** ▲ Alaska, USA
De Behagle *see* Laï
25 X7 **De Berry** Texas, SW USA
127 T2 **Debessy** Udmurtskaya Respublika, NW Russian Federation
111 N16 **Dębica** Podkarpackie, SE Poland
De Bildt *see* De Bilt
98 J11 **De Bilt** *var.* De Bildt. Utrecht, C Netherlands
123 T9 **Debin** Magadanskaya Oblast', E Russian Federation
110 N13 **Dęblin** *Rus.* Ivangorod. Lubelskie, E Poland
110 D10 **Dębno** Zachodnio-pomorskie, NW Poland
39 S10 **Deborah, Mount** ▲ Alaska, USA
33 N8 **De Borgia** Montana, NW USA
Debra Birhan *see* Debre Birhan
Debra Marcos *see* Debre Mark'os
Debra Tabor *see* Debre Tabor
Debre *see* Debar
80 J13 **Debre Birhan** *var.* Debra Birhan. Amhara, N Ethiopia
111 N22 **Debrecen** *Ger.* Debreczin, *Rom.* Debreţin; *prev.* Debreczen. Hajdú-Bihar, E Hungary
Debreczen/Debreczin *see* Debrecen
80 I12 **Debre Mark'os** *var.* Debra Marcos. Amhara, N Ethiopia
113 N19 **Debrešte** SW FYR Macedonia
80 J11 **Debre Tabor** *var.* Debra Tabor. Amhara, N Ethiopia
Debreţin *see* Debrecen
80 J13 **Debre Zeyt** Oromo, C Ethiopia
113 L16 **Dečani** Serbia, S Serbia and Montenegro (Yugo.)
23 P2 **Decatur** Alabama, S USA
23 S3 **Decatur** Georgia, SE USA
30 L13 **Decatur** Illinois, N USA
31 Q12 **Decatur** Indiana, N USA
22 M5 **Decatur** Mississippi, S USA
29 S14 **Decatur** Nebraska, C USA
25 S6 **Decatur** Texas, SW USA
20 H9 **Decaturville** Tennessee, S USA
103 O13 **Decazeville** Aveyron, S France
155 H17 **Deccan** *Hind.* Dakshin. *plateau* C India
14 J8 **Decelles, Réservoir** ⊞ Québec, SE Canada
12 K2 **Déception** Québec, NE Canada
160 G11 **Dechang** *var.* Dezhou. Sichuan, C China
111 C15 **Děčín** *Ger.* Tetschen. Ústecký Kraj, NW Czech Republic
103 P9 **Decize** Nièvre, C France
98 I6 **De Cocksdorp** Noord-Holland, NW Netherlands
29 X11 **Decorah** Iowa, C USA
Dedeagaç/Dedeagach *see* Alexandroúpoli
188 C15 **Dededo** N Guam
98 N9 **Dedemsvaart** Overijssel, E Netherlands
19 O11 **Dedham** Massachusetts, NE USA
63 H19 **Dedo, Cerro** ▲ SW Argentina
77 O13 **Dédougou** W Burkina
124 G15 **Dedovichi** Pskovskaya Oblast', W Russian Federation
Dedu *see* Wudalianchi
155 J24 **Deduru Oya** ↝ W Sri Lanka
83 N14 **Dedza** Central, S Malawi
83 N14 **Dedza Mountain** ▲ C Malawi
97 J19 **Dee** *Wel.* Afon Dyfrdwy. ↝ England/Wales, UK
96 K9 **Dee** ↝ NE Scotland, UK
Deep Bay *see* Chilumba
21 T3 **Deep Creek Lake** ⊞ Maryland, NE USA
36 J4 **Deep Creek Range** ▲ Utah, W USA
27 P10 **Deep Fork** ↝ Oklahoma, C USA
14 J11 **Deep River** Ontario, SE Canada
21 T10 **Deep River** ↝ North Carolina, SE USA
183 U4 **Deepwater** New South Wales, SE Australia
31 S14 **Deer Creek Lake** ⊚ Ohio, N USA
23 Z15 **Deerfield Beach** Florida, SE USA
39 N8 **Deering** Alaska, USA
38 M16 **Deer Island** *island* Alaska, USA
19 S7 **Deer Isle** *island* Maine, NE USA
13 S11 **Deer Lake** Newfoundland and Labrador, SE Canada
99 D18 **Deerlijk** West-Vlaanderen, W Belgium
33 Q10 **Deer Lodge** Montana, NW USA
32 L8 **Deer Park** Washington, NW USA
29 U5 **Deer River** Minnesota, N USA
Deés *see* Dej
Defeng *see* Liping
31 R11 **Defiance** Ohio, N USA
23 Q8 **De Funiak Springs** Florida, SE USA
95 L23 **Degeberga** Skåne, S Sweden
104 H12 **Degebe, Ribeira** ↝ S Portugal
80 M13 **Degeh Bur** Somali, E Ethiopia
15 U9 **Dégelis** Québec, SE Canada
77 U17 **Degema** Rivers, S Nigeria
95 L16 **Degerfors** Örebro, C Sweden
193 R14 **De Gerlache Seamounts** *undersea feature* SE Pacific Ocean
101 N21 **Deggendorf** Bayern, SE Germany
80 I11 **Degoma** Amhara, N Ethiopia
De Gordyk *see* Gorredijk
27 T12 **De Gray Lake** ⊞ Arkansas, C USA
180 J6 **De Grey River** ↝ Western Australia
126 M10 **Degtevo** Rostovskaya Oblast', SW Russian Federation
143 X13 **Dehak** Sīstān va Balūchestān, SE Iran
143 R9 **Deh 'Alī** Kermān, C Iran
143 S13 **Dehbārez** *var.* Rūdān. Hormozgān, S Iran
143 P10 **Deh Bīd** Fārs, C Iran
142 M10 **Deh Dasht** Kohgīlūyeh va Būyer Aḩmad, SW Iran
75 N8 **Dehibat** SE Tunisia
Dehli *see* Delhi
142 K8 **Dehlorān** Īlām, W Iran
147 N13 **Dehqonobod** *Rus.* Dekhkanabad. Qashqadaryo Viloyati, S Uzbekistan
152 J9 **Dehra Dūn** Uttaranchal, N India
153 O14 **Dehri** Bihār, N India
148 K10 **Deh Shū** *var.* Deshu. Helmand, S Afghanistan
99 D17 **Deinze** Oost-Vlaanderen, NW Belgium
Deir 'Alla *see* Dayr 'Allā
Deir ez Zor *see* Dayr az Zawr
Deirgeirt, Loch *see* Derg, Lough
116 H9 **Dej** *Hung.* Dés; *prev.* Deés. Cluj, NW Romania
95 K15 **Deje** Värmland, C Sweden
171 Y15 **De Jongs, Tanjung** *headland* Papua, SE Indonesia
De Jouwer *see* Joure
30 M10 **De Kalb** Illinois, N USA
22 M5 **De Kalb** Mississippi, S USA
25 W5 **De Kalb** Texas, SW USA
Dekéleia *see* Dhekélia
79 K20 **Dekese** Kasai Occidental, C Dem. Rep. Congo
Dekhkanabad *see* Dehqonobod
79 I14 **Dékoa** Kémo, C Central African Republic
98 H6 **De Koog** Noord-Holland, NW Netherlands
30 M9 **Delafield** Wisconsin, N USA
61 C23 **De La Garma** Buenos Aires, E Argentina
14 K10 **Delahey, Lac** ⊚ Québec, SE Canada
80 E11 **Delami** Southern Kordofan, C Sudan
23 X11 **De Land** Florida, SE USA
35 R12 **Delano** California, W USA
29 V8 **Delano** Minnesota, N USA
36 K6 **Delano Peak** ▲ Utah, W USA
Delap-Uliga-Darrit *see* Dalap-Uliga-Djarrit
148 L7 **Delārām** Farāh, SW Afghanistan
38 F17 **Delarof Islands** *island group* Aleutian Islands, Alaska, USA
30 M9 **Delavan** Wisconsin, N USA
31 S13 **Delaware** Ohio, N USA
18 I17 **Delaware** *off.* State of Delaware; also known as Blue Hen State, Diamond State, First State. ◆ *state* NE USA
18 I17 **Delaware Bay** *bay* NE USA
24 J8 **Delaware Mountains** ▲ Texas, SW USA
18 I12 **Delaware River** ↝ NE USA
27 Q3 **Delaware River** ↝ Kansas C USA
18 J14 **Delaware Water Gap** *valley* New Jersey/Pennsylvania, NE USA
101 G14 **Delbrück** Nordrhein-Westfalen, W Germany
11 Q15 **Delburne** Alberta, SW Canada
172 M12 **Del Cano Rise** *undersea feature* SW Indian Ocean
113 Q18 **Delčevo** NE FYR Macedonia
Delcommune, Lac *see* Nzilo, Lac
98 O10 **Delden** Overijssel, E Netherlands
183 R12 **Delegate** New South Wales, SE Australia
De Lemmer *see* Lemmer
108 D7 **Delémont** *Ger.* Delsberg. Jura, NW Switzerland
25 R7 **De Leon** Texas, SW USA
115 F18 **Delfoí** Stereá Ellás, C Greece
98 G12 **Delft** Zuid-Holland, W Netherlands
155 J23 **Delft** *island* NW Sri Lanka
98 O5 **Delfzijl** Groningen, NE Netherlands
42 F7 **Delgado** San Salvador, SW El Salvador
82 Q12 **Delgado, Cabo** *headland* N Mozambique
80 E6 **Delgo** Northern, N Sudan
159 R10 **Delhi** *var.* Delingha. Qinghai, C China
152 I10 **Delhi** *var.* Dehli, *Hind.* Dilli; *hist.* Shahjahanabad. Delhi, N India
22 J5 **Delhi** Louisiana, S USA
18 J11 **Delhi** New York, NE USA
152 I10 **Delhi** ◆ *union territory* NW India
136 J17 **Deli Burnu** *headland* S Turkey
55 X10 **Délices** C French Guiana
136 J12 **Delice Çayı** ↝ C Turkey
40 J6 **Delicias** *var.* Ciudad Delicias. Chihuahua, N Mexico
143 N7 **Delījān** *var.* Dalijan, Dilijan. Markazī, W Iran
112 P12 **Deli Jovan** ▲ E Serbia and Montenegro (Yugo.)
Déli-Kárpátok *see* Carpaţii Meridionali
8 I8 **Délįne** *prev.* Fort Franklin. Northwest Territories, NW Canada
Delingha *see* Delhi
15 Q7 **Delisle** Québec, SE Canada
11 T15 **Delisle** Saskatchewan, S Canada
101 M15 **Delitzsch** Sachsen, E Germany
33 Q12 **Dell** Montana, NW USA
24 H8 **Dell City** Texas, SW USA
103 U7 **Delle** Territoire-de-Belfort, E France
36 J9 **Dellenbaugh, Mount** ▲ Arizona, SW USA
29 R11 **Dell Rapids** South Dakota, N USA
21 Y4 **Delmar** Maryland, NE USA
18 K11 **Delmar** New York, NE USA
100 G11 **Delmenhorst** Niedersachsen, NW Germany
112 C9 **Delnice** Primorje-Gorski Kotar, NW Croatia
37 R7 **Del Norte** Colorado, C USA
39 N6 **De Long Mountains** ▲ Alaska, USA
183 P16 **Deloraine** Tasmania, SE Australia
11 W17 **Deloraine** Manitoba, S Canada
31 O12 **Delphi** Indiana, N USA
31 Q12 **Delphos** Ohio, N USA
23 Z15 **Delray Beach** Florida, SE USA
25 O12 **Del Rio** Texas, SW USA
Delsberg *see* Delémont
94 N11 **Delsbo** Gävleborg, C Sweden

◆ Country
● Country Capital
◇ Dependent Territory
○ Dependent Territory Capital
◆ Administrative Region
✈ International Airport
▲ Mountain
▲ Mountain Range
☼ Volcano
↝ River
⊚ Lake
⊞ Reservoir

37 P6 **Delta** Colorado, C USA
36 K5 **Delta** Utah, W USA
77 T17 **Delta** ◆ state S Nigeria
55 Q6 **Delta Amacuro** *off.* Territorio Delta Amacuro. ◆ *federal district* NE Venezuela
39 S9 **Delta Junction** Alaska, USA
23 X11 **Deltona** Florida, SE USA
183 T5 **Delungra** New South Wales, SE Australia
154 C12 **Delvāda** Gujarāt, W India
61 B21 **Del Valle** Buenos Aires, E Argentina
Delvina *see* Delvinë
115 C15 **Delvináki** *var.* Dhelvinákion; *prev.* Pogónion. Ípeiros, W Greece
113 L23 **Delvinë** *var.* Delvina, *It.* Delvino. Vlorë, S Albania
Delvino *see* Delvinë
116 I7 **Delyatyn** Ivano-Frankivs'ka Oblast', W Ukraine
127 U5 **Dëma** ∿ W Russian Federation
105 O5 **Demanda, Sierra de la** ▲ W Spain
39 T5 **Demarcation Point** *headland* Alaska, USA
79 K21 **Demba** Kasai Occidental, C Dem. Rep. Congo
172 H13 **Dembéni** Grande Comore, NW Comoros
79 M15 **Dembia** Mbomou, SE Central African Republic
Dembidollo *see* Dembī Dolo
80 H13 **Dembī Dolo** *var.* Dembidollo. Oromo, C Ethiopia
152 K6 **Demchok** *var.* Dêmqog. China/India *see also* Dêmqog
152 L6 **Demchok** *var.* Dêmqog. *disputed region* China/India *see also* Dêmqog
98 I12 **De Meern** Utrecht, C Netherlands
99 I17 **Demer** ∿ C Belgium
64 H12 **Demerara Plain** *undersea feature* W Atlantic Ocean
64 H12 **Demerara Plateau** *undersea feature* W Atlantic Ocean
55 T9 **Demerara River** ∿ NE Guyana
126 H3 **Demidov** Smolenskaya Oblast', W Russian Federation
37 Q15 **Deming** New Mexico, SW USA
32 H6 **Deming** Washington, NW USA
58 E10 **Demini, Rio** ∿ NW Brazil
136 D13 **Demirci** Manisa, W Turkey
113 P19 **Demir Kapija** *prev.* Železna Vrata. SE FYR Macedonia
114 N11 **Demirköy** Kırklareli, NW Turkey
100 N9 **Demmin** Mecklenburg-Vorpommern, NE Germany
23 O5 **Demopolis** Alabama, S USA
31 N11 **Demotte** Indiana, N USA
158 F13 **Dêmqog** *var.* Demchok. China/India *see also* Demchok
152 L6 **Dêmqog** *var.* Demchok. *disputed region* China/India *see also* Demchok
171 Y13 **Demta** Papua, E Indonesia
122 H11 **Dem'yanka** ∿ C Russian Federation
124 H15 **Demyansk** Novgorodskaya Oblast', W Russian Federation
122 H10 **Dem'yanskoye** Tyumenskaya Oblast', C Russian Federation
103 P2 **Denain** Nord, N France
39 S10 **Denali** Alaska, USA
Denali *see* McKinley, Mount
81 M14 **Denan** Somali, E Ethiopia
Denau *see* Denov
97 J18 **Denbigh** *Wel.* Dinbych. NE Wales, UK
97 J18 **Denbigh** *cultural region* N Wales, UK
98 I6 **Den Burg** Noord-Holland, NW Netherlands
99 F18 **Dender** *Fr.* Dendre. ∿ W Belgium
99 F18 **Denderleeuw** Oost-Vlaanderen, NW Belgium
99 F17 **Dendermonde** *Fr.* Termonde. Oost-Vlaanderen, NW Belgium
Dendre *see* Dender
194 I9 **Dendtler Island** *island* Antarctica
98 P10 **Denekamp** Overijssel, E Netherlands
77 W12 **Dengas** Zinder, S Niger
Dêngkagoin *see* Têwo
162 L13 **Dengkou** *var.* Bayan Gol. Nei Mongol Zizhiqu, N China
159 Q14 **Dêngqên** *var.* Gyamotang. Xizang Zizhiqu, W China
Deng Xian *see* Dengzhou
160 M7 **Dengzhou** *prev.* Deng Xian. Henan, C China
Dengzhou *see* Penglai
Den Haag *see* 's-Gravenhage
98 N9 **Den Ham** Overijssel, E Netherlands
180 H10 **Denham** Western Australia
44 J12 **Denham, Mount** ▲ C Jamaica
22 J8 **Denham Springs** Louisiana, S USA
98 I7 **Den Helder** Noord-Holland, NW Netherlands
105 T11 **Dénia** País Valenciano, E Spain
189 Q8 **Denig** W Nauru
183 N10 **Deniliquin** New South Wales, SE Australia
29 T14 **Denison** Iowa, C USA
25 U5 **Denison** Texas, SW USA
144 L8 **Denisovka** *prev.* Ordzhonikidze. Kostanay, N Kazakhstan
136 D15 **Denizli** Denizli, SW Turkey
136 D15 **Denizli** ◆ *province* SW Turkey
Denjong *see* Sikkim
183 S7 **Denman** New South Wales, SE Australia
195 Y10 **Denman Glacier** *glacier* Antarctica
21 R14 **Denmark** South Carolina, SE USA
95 G23 **Denmark** *off.* Kingdom of Denmark, *Dan.* Danmark; *anc.* Hafnia. ◆ *monarchy* N Europe
92 H1 **Denmark Strait** *var.* Danmarksstraedet. *strait* Greenland/Iceland
45 T11 **Dennery** E Saint Lucia
98 I7 **Den Oever** Noord-Holland, NW Netherlands
147 O13 **Denov** *Rus.* Denau. Surxondaryo Viloyati, S Uzbekistan
169 U17 **Denpasar** *prev.* Paloe. Bali, C Indonesia
116 E12 **Denta** Timiş, W Romania
21 Y3 **Denton** Maryland, NE USA
25 T6 **Denton** Texas, SW USA
186 G9 **D'Entrecasteaux Islands** *island group* SE PNG
37 T4 **Denver** *state capital* Colorado, C USA
37 T4 **Denver** ✕ Colorado, C USA
24 L6 **Denver City** Texas, SW USA
152 J9 **Deoband** Uttar Pradesh, N India
Deoghar *see* Devghar
154 E13 **Deolāli** Mahārāshtra, W India
154 I10 **Deori** Madhya Pradesh, C India
153 O12 **Deoria** Uttar Pradesh, N India
99 A17 **De Panne** West-Vlaanderen, W Belgium
54 M5 **Dependencia Federal** *off.* Territorio Dependencia Federal. ◆ *federal dependency* N Venezuela
Dependencia Federal, Territorio *see* Dependencia Federal
30 M7 **De Pere** Wisconsin, N USA
18 D10 **Depew** New York, NE USA
99 E17 **De Pinte** Oost-Vlaanderen, NW Belgium
25 V5 **Deport** Texas, SW USA
123 Q8 **Deputatskiy** Respublika Sakha (Yakutiya), NE Russian Federation
Dêqên *see* Dagzê
27 S13 **De Queen** Arkansas, C USA
22 G8 **De Quincy** Louisiana, S USA
81 J20 **Dera** *spring/well* S Kenya
Der'a/Derá/Déraa *see* Dar'ā
149 S10 **Dera Ghāzi Khān** *var.* Dera Ghāzikhān. Punjab, C Pakistan
149 S8 **Dera Ismāīl Khān** North-West Frontier Province, C Pakistan
113 L16 **Đeravica** ▲ S Serbia and Montenegro (Yugo.)
116 L6 **Derazhnya** Khmel'nyts'ka Oblast', W Ukraine
127 R17 **Derbent** Respublika Dagestan, SW Russian Federation
147 N13 **Derbent** Surxondaryo Viloyati, S Uzbekistan
Derbisīye *see* Darbāsīyah
79 M15 **Derbissaka** Mbomou, SE Central African Republic
180 L4 **Derby** Western Australia
97 M19 **Derby** C England, UK
27 N7 **Derby** Kansas, C USA
97 L18 **Derbyshire** *cultural region* C England, UK
112 O11 **Đerdap** *physical region* E Serbia and Montenegro (Yugo.)
Dereli *see* Gónnoi
171 W13 **Derew** ∿ Papua, E Indonesia
127 R8 **Dergachi** Saratovskaya Oblast', W Russian Federation
Dergachi *see* Derhachi
97 C19 **Derg, Lough** *Ir.* Loch Deirgeirt. ⊚ W Ireland
117 V5 **Derhachi** *Rus.* Dergachi. Kharkivs'ka Oblast', E Ukraine
22 G8 **De Ridder** Louisiana, S USA
137 P16 **Derik** Mardin, SE Turkey
83 E20 **Derm** Hardap, C Namibia
144 M14 **Dermentobe** *prev.* Dyurmen'tyube. Kzylorda, S Kazakhstan
27 W14 **Dermott** Arkansas, C USA
Dérna *see* Darnah
Dernberg, Cape *see* Dolphin Head
22 J11 **Dernieres, Isles** *island group* Louisiana, S USA
Dernis *see* Drniš
102 I4 **Déroute, Passage de la** *strait* Channel Islands/France
Derrá *see* Dar'ā
Derry *see* Londonderry
Dertona *see* Tortona
Dertosa *see* Tortosa
80 H8 **Derudeb** Red Sea, NE Sudan
112 H10 **Derventa** Republika Srpska, N Bosnia and Herzegovina
183 O16 **Derwent Bridge** Tasmania, SE Australia
183 O17 **Derwent, River** ∿ Tasmania, SE Australia
146 F10 **Derweze** *Rus.* Darvaza. Ahal Welaýaty, C Turkmenistan
Deržavinsk *see* Derzhavinsk
145 O9 **Derzhavinsk** *var.* Deržavinsk. Akmola, C Kazakhstan
Dés *see* Dej
57 J18 **Desaguadero** Puno, S Peru
57 J18 **Desaguadero, Río** ∿ Bolivia/Peru
191 W9 **Désappointement, Îles du** *island group* Îles Tuamotu, C French Polynesia
27 W11 **Des Arc** Arkansas, C USA
14 C10 **Desbarats** Ontario, S Canada
62 H13 **Descabezado Grande, Volcán** ▲ C Chile
40 B2 **Descanso** Baja California, NW Mexico
102 L9 **Descartes** Indre-et-Loire, C France
11 T13 **Deschambault Lake** ⊚ Saskatchewan, C Canada
Deschnaer Koppe *see* Velká Deštná
32 I11 **Deschutes River** ∿ Oregon, NW USA
80 J12 **Desē** *var.* Desse, *It.* Dessie. Amhara, N Ethiopia
63 I20 **Deseado, Río** ∿ S Argentina
106 F3 **Desenzano del Garda** Lombardia, N Italy
36 K3 **Deseret Peak** ▲ Utah, W USA
64 F6 **Deserta Grande** *island* Madeira, Portugal, NE Atlantic Ocean
64 P6 **Desertas, Ilhas** *island group* Madeira, Portugal, NE Atlantic Ocean
35 X16 **Desert Center** California, W USA
35 V15 **Desert Hot Springs** California, W USA
14 K10 **Désert, Lac** ⊚ Québec, SE Canada
36 I2 **Desert Peak** ▲ Utah, W USA
31 R11 **Deshler** Ohio, N USA
Deshu *see* Deh Shū
Desiderii Fanum *see* St-Dizier
106 D7 **Desio** Lombardia, N Italy
115 E15 **Deskáti** *var.* Dheskáti. Dytikí Makedonía, N Greece
28 L2 **Des Lacs River** ∿ North Dakota, N USA
27 X6 **Desloge** Missouri, C USA
11 Q12 **Desmarais** Alberta, W Canada
29 Q10 **De Smet** South Dakota, N USA
29 V14 **Des Moines** *state capital* Iowa, C USA
17 N9 **Des Moines River** ∿ C USA
117 P4 **Desna** ∿ Russian Federation/Ukraine
116 G14 **Desnăţui** ∿ S Romania
63 F24 **Desolación, Isla** *island* S Chile
29 V14 **De Soto** Iowa, C USA
23 Q4 **De Soto Falls** *waterfall* Alabama, S USA
83 I25 **Despatch** Eastern Cape, S South Africa
105 N12 **Despeñaperros, Desfiladero de** *pass* S Spain
31 N10 **Des Plaines** Illinois, N USA
115 J21 **Despotikó** *island* Kykládes, Greece, Aegean Sea
112 N12 **Despotovac** Serbia, E Serbia and Montenegro (Yugo.)
101 M14 **Dessau** Sachsen-Anhalt, E Germany
Desse *see* Desē
99 J16 **Dessel** Antwerpen, N Belgium
Dessie *see* Desē
Destêrro *see* Florianópolis
23 P9 **Destin** Florida, SE USA
Deštná *see* Velká Deštná
193 T10 **Desventurados, Islas de los** *island group* W Chile
103 N1 **Desvres** Pas-de-Calais, N France
116 E12 **Deta** *Ger.* Detta. Timiş, W Romania
101 H14 **Detmold** Nordrhein-Westfalen, W Germany
31 S10 **Detroit** Michigan, N USA
25 W5 **Detroit** Texas, SW USA
31 S10 **Detroit** ∿ Canada/USA
29 S6 **Detroit Lakes** Minnesota, N USA
31 S10 **Detroit Metropolitan** ✕ Michigan, N USA
Detta *see* Deta
167 S10 **Det Udom** Ubon Ratchathani, E Thailand
111 K20 **Detva** *Hung.* Gyeva. Banskobystrický Kraj, C Slovakia
154 G13 **Deūlgaon Rāja** Mahārāshtra, C India
99 L15 **Deurne** Noord-Brabant, SE Netherlands
99 H16 **Deurne** ✕ (Antwerpen) Antwerpen, N Belgium
Deutsch-Brod *see* Havlíčkův Brod
Deutschendorf *see* Poprad
Deutsch-Eylau *see* Iława
109 Y6 **Deutschkreutz** Burgenland, E Austria
Deutsch Krone *see* Wałcz
Deutschland/Deutschland, Bundesrepublik *see* Germany
109 V9 **Deutschlandsberg** Steiermark, SE Austria
Deutsch-Südwestafrika *see* Namibia
109 Y3 **Deutsch-Wagram** Niederösterreich, E Austria
Deux-Ponts *see* Zweibrücken
14 I11 **Deux Rivieres** Ontario, SE Canada
102 K9 **Deux-Sèvres** ◆ *department* W France
116 G11 **Deva** *Ger.* Diemrich, *Hung.* Déva. Hunedoara, W Romania
Deva *see* Chester
Devana *see* Aberdeen
Devana Castra *see* Chester
Devdelija *see* Gevgelija
136 L12 **Deveci Dağları** ▲ N Turkey
137 P15 **Devegeçidi Barajı** ⊠ SE Turkey
136 K15 **Develi** Kayseri, C Turkey
98 M11 **Deventer** Overijssel, E Netherlands
15 O10 **Devenyns, Lac** ⊚ Québec, SE Canada
96 K8 **Deveron** ∿ NE Scotland, UK
153 R14 **Devghar** *prev.* Deoghar. Jhārkhand, NE India
27 R10 **Devil's Den** *plateau* Arkansas, C USA
35 R7 **Devils Gate** *pass* California, W USA
30 J2 **Devils Island** *island* Apostle Islands, Wisconsin, N USA
Devil's Island *see* Diable, Île du
29 P3 **Devils Lake** North Dakota, N USA
31 R10 **Devils Lake** ⊚ Michigan, N USA
29 O3 **Devils Lake** ⊚ North Dakota, N USA
35 W13 **Devils Playground** *desert* California, W USA
25 O11 **Devils River** ∿ Texas, SW USA
33 Y12 **Devils Tower** ▲ Wyoming, C USA
114 I11 **Devin** *prev.* Dovlen. Smolyan, SW Bulgaria
25 R12 **Devine** Texas, SW USA
152 H13 **Devli** Rājasthān, N India
Devne *see* Devnya
114 N8 **Devnya** *prev.* Devne. Varna, E Bulgaria
31 U14 **Devola** Ohio, N USA
Devoll *see* Devollit, Lumi i
113 M21 **Devollit, Lumi i** *var.* Devoll. ∿ SE Albania
11 Q14 **Devon** Alberta, SW Canada
97 I23 **Devon** *cultural region* SW England, UK
9 O4 **Devon Ice Cap** *ice feature* Nunavut, N Canada
8 N4 **Devon Island** *prev.* North Devon Island. *island* Parry Islands, Nunavut, NE Canada
183 O16 **Devonport** Tasmania, SE Australia
136 H11 **Devrek** Zonguldak, N Turkey
154 G10 **Dewās** Madhya Pradesh, C India
De Westerein *see* Zwaagwesteinde
27 P8 **Dewey** Oklahoma, C USA
Dewey *see* Culebra
98 M8 **De Wijk** Drenthe, NE Netherlands
27 W12 **De Witt** Arkansas, C USA
29 Z14 **De Witt** Iowa, C USA
29 R16 **De Witt** Nebraska, C USA
97 M17 **Dewsbury** N England, UK
161 Q10 **Dexing** Jiangxi, S China
27 Y8 **Dexter** Missouri, C USA
37 U14 **Dexter** New Mexico, SW USA
160 I8 **Deyang** Sichuan, C China
182 C4 **Dey-Dey, Lake** *salt lake* South Australia
143 S7 **Deyhūk** Yazd, E Iran
Deynau *see* Galkynyş
142 L8 **Dezfūl** *var.* Dizful. Khūzestān, SW Iran
161 P4 **Dezhou** Shandong, E China
Dezhou *see* Dechang
Dezh Shāhpūr *see* Marīvān
Dhahran *see* Aẓ Ẓahrān
Dhahran Al Khobar *see* Aẓ Ẓahrān al Khubar
153 U14 **Dhaka** *prev.* Dacca. ● (Bangladesh) Dhaka, C Bangladesh
153 T15 **Dhaka** ◆ *division* C Bangladesh
Dhali *see* Idálion
141 O15 **Dhamār** W Yemen
Dhambul *see* Taraz
154 K12 **Dhamtari** Chhattīsgarh, C India
153 Q15 **Dhanbād** Jhārkhand, NE India
152 L10 **Dhangadhi** *var.* Dhangarhi. Far Western, W Nepal
Dhangarhi *see* Dhangadhi
Dhank *see* Ḑank
153 R12 **Dhankuta** Eastern, E Nepal
152 I6 **Dhaola Dhār** ▲ NE India
154 F10 **Dhār** Madhya Pradesh, C India
153 R12 **Dharan** *var.* Dharan Bazar. Eastern, E Nepal
155 H21 **Dhārāpuram** Tamil Nādu, SE India
155 H20 **Dharmapuri** Tamil Nādu, SE India
155 H18 **Dharmavaram** Andhra Pradesh, E India
154 M11 **Dharmjaygarh** Chhattīsgarh, C India
Dharmsāla *see* Dharmshāla
152 I7 **Dharmshāla** *prev.* Dharmsāla. Himāchal Pradesh, N India
155 F17 **Dhārwād** *prev.* Dharwar. Karnātaka, SW India
Dharwar *see* Dhārwād
153 O10 **Dhaulāgiri** ▲ C Nepal
81 L18 **Dheere Laaq** *var.* Lak Dera, *It.* Lach Dera. *seasonal river* Kenya/Somalia
121 Q3 **Dhekéleia Sovereign Base Area** *UK military installation* E Cyprus
121 Q3 **Dhekélia** *Eng.* Dhekelia. *Gk.* Dekéleia. *UK air base* SE Cyprus
Dhelvinákion *see* Delvináki
113 M22 **Dhëmbelit, Majae** ▲ S Albania
154 O12 **Dhenkānāl** Orissa, E India
Dheskáti *see* Deskáti
138 G11 **Dhībān** 'Al Āṣimah, NW Jordan
Dhidhimótikhon *see* Didymóteicho
Dhíkti Ori *see* Díkti
138 I12 **Dhirwah, Wādī adh** *dry watercourse* C Jordan
Dhístomon *see* Dístomo
Dhodhekánisos *see* Dodekánisos
Dhodhóni *see* Dodóni
Dhofar *see* Ẓufār
Dhomokós *see* Domokós
Dhond *see* Daund
155 H17 **Dhone** Andhra Pradesh, C India
154 B11 **Dhorāji** Gujarāt, W India
Dhráma *see* Dráma
154 C10 **Dhrāngadhra** Gujarāt, W India
Dhrepanon, Akrotírio *see* Drépano, Akrotírio
153 T13 **Dhuburi** Assam, NE India
154 F12 **Dhule** *prev.* Dhulia. Mahārāshtra, C India
Dhulia *see* Dhule
Dhún Dealgan, Cuan *see* Dundalk Bay
Dhún Droma, Cuan *see* Dundrum Bay
Dhún na nGall, Bá *see* Donegal Bay
Dhū Shaykh *see* Qazānīyah
80 Q13 **Dhuudo** Bari, NE Somalia
81 N15 **Dhuusa Marreeb** *var.* Dusa Marreb, *It.* Dusa Mareb. Galguduud, C Somalia
115 J24 **Día** *island* SE Greece
55 Y9 **Diable, Île du** *var.* Devil's Island. *island* N French Guiana
15 N12 **Diable, Rivière du** ∿ Québec, SE Canada
35 N8 **Diablo, Mount** ▲ California, W USA
35 O9 **Diablo Range** ▲ California, W USA
24 I8 **Diablo, Sierra** ▲ Texas, SW USA
45 O11 **Diablotins, Morne** ▲ N Dominica
77 N11 **Diafarabé** Mopti, C Mali
77 N11 **Diaka** ∿ SW Mali
Diakovár *see* Đakovo
76 I12 **Dialakoto** S Senegal
61 B18 **Diamante** Entre Ríos, E Argentina
62 I12 **Diamante, Río** ∿ C Argentina
59 M19 **Diamantina** Minas Gerais, SE Brazil
59 N17 **Diamantina, Chapada** ▲ E Brazil
173 U11 **Diamantina Fracture Zone** *tectonic feature* E Indian Ocean
181 T8 **Diamantina River** ∿ Queensland/South Australia
38 D9 **Diamond Head** *headland* O'ahu, Hawai'i, USA, C Pacific Ocean
37 P2 **Diamond Peak** ▲ Colorado, C USA
35 W5 **Diamond Peak** ▲ Nevada, W USA
Diamond State *see* Delaware
76 J11 **Diamou** Kayes, SW Mali
95 I23 **Dianalund** Vestsjælland, C Denmark
65 G25 **Diana's Peak** ▲ C Saint Helena
160 M16 **Dianbai** *var.* Shuidong. Guangdong, S China
160 G13 **Dian Chi** ⊠ SW China
106 B10 **Diano Marina** Liguria, NW Italy
163 V11 **Diaobingshan** *var.* Tiefa. Liaoning, NE China
77 R13 **Diapaga** E Burkina
Diarbekr *see* Diyarbakır
107 J15 **Diavolo, Passo del** *pass* C Italy
61 B18 **Díaz** Santa Fe, C Argentina
141 W6 **Dibā al Ḥiṣn** *var.* Dibāh, Dibba. Ash Shāriqah, NE UAE
139 S3 **Dībaga** N Iraq
Dibāh *see* Dibā al Ḥiṣn
79 L22 **Dibaya** Kasai Occidental, S Dem. Rep. Congo
Dibba *see* Dibā al Ḥiṣn
195 W15 **Dibble Iceberg Tongue** *ice feature* Antarctica
113 L19 **Dibër** ◆ *district* E Albania
83 I20 **Dibete** Central, SE Botswana
25 W9 **Diboll** Texas, SW USA
Dibra *see* Debar
153 X11 **Dibrugarh** Assam, NE India
54 G4 **Dibulla** La Guajira, N Colombia
25 O5 **Dickens** Texas, SW USA
19 R2 **Dickey** Maine, NE USA
30 K9 **Dickeyville** Wisconsin, N USA
28 K5 **Dickinson** North Dakota, N USA
27 O13 **Dickson** Oklahoma, C USA
20 I9 **Dickson** Tennessee, S USA
Dicle *see* Tigris
Dicsőszentmárton *see* Târnăveni
98 M12 **Didam** Gelderland, E Netherlands
163 Y8 **Didao** Heilongjiang, NE China
76 L12 **Didiéni** Koulikoro, W Mali
Didimo *see* Dídymo
Didimotiho *see* Didymóteicho
81 K17 **Didimtu** *spring/well* NE Kenya
11 Q16 **Didsbury** Alberta, SW Canada
152 G11 **Dīdwāna** Rājasthān, N India
115 G20 **Dídymo** *var.* Didimo. ▲ S Greece
114 L12 **Didymóteicho** *var.* Dhidhimótikhon, Didimotiho. Anatolikí Makedonía kai Thráki, NE Greece
103 S13 **Die** Drôme, E France
77 O13 **Diébougou** SW Burkina
Diedenhofen *see* Thionville
11 S16 **Diefenbaker, Lake** ⊠ Saskatchewan, S Canada
62 H7 **Diego de Almagro** Atacama, N Chile
63 F23 **Diego de Almagro, Isla** *island* S Chile
61 A20 **Diego de Alvear** Santa Fe, C Argentina
173 Q7 **Diego Garcia** *island* S British Indian Ocean Territory
Diégo-Suarez *see* Antsirañana
99 M23 **Diekirch** Diekirch, C Luxembourg
99 L23 **Diekirch** ◆ *district* N Luxembourg
76 K11 **Diéma** Kayes, W Mali
101 H15 **Diemel** ∿ W Germany
98 I10 **Diemen** Noord-Holland, C Netherlands
Diemrich *see* Deva
167 R6 **Điện Biên** *var.* Bien Bien, Dien Bien Phu. Lai Châu, N Vietnam
Dien Bien Phu *see* Điện Biên
167 S7 **Diễn Châu** Nghê An, N Vietnam
99 K18 **Diepenbeek** Limburg, NE Belgium
98 N11 **Diepenheim** Overijssel, E Netherlands
98 M10 **Diepenveen** Overijssel, E Netherlands
100 G12 **Diepholz** Niedersachsen, NW Germany
102 M3 **Dieppe** Seine-Maritime, N France
98 M12 **Dieren** Gelderland, E Netherlands
27 S13 **Dierks** Arkansas, C USA
99 J17 **Diest** Vlaams Brabant, C Belgium
108 F7 **Dietikon** Zürich, NW Switzerland
103 R13 **Dieulefit** Drôme, E France
103 T5 **Dieuze** Moselle, NE France
119 H15 **Dieveniškės** Vilnius, SE Lithuania
98 N7 **Diever** Drenthe, NE Netherlands
101 F17 **Diez** Rheinland-Pfalz, W Germany
77 Y12 **Diffa** Diffa, SE Niger
77 Y10 **Diffa** ◆ *department* SE Niger
99 L25 **Differdange** Luxembourg, SW Luxembourg
13 O16 **Digby** Nova Scotia, SE Canada
26 J5 **Dighton** Kansas, C USA
Dignano d'Istria *see* Vodnjan
103 T14 **Digne** *var.* Digne-les-Bains. Alpes-de-Haute-Provence, SE France
Digne-les-Bains *see* Digne
Digoel *see* Digul, Sungai
103 Q10 **Digoin** Saône-et-Loire, C France
171 Q8 **Digos** Mindanao, S Philippines
149 Q16 **Digri** Sind, SE Pakistan
171 Y14 **Digul Barat, Sungai** ∿ Papua, E Indonesia
171 Y15 **Digul, Sungai** *prev.* Digoel. ∿ Papua, E Indonesia
171 Z14 **Digul Timur, Sungai** ∿ Papua, E Indonesia
Dihang *see* Brahmaputra
153 X10 **Dihāng** ∿ NE India
Dihōk *see* Dahūk
81 L17 **Diinsoor** Bay, S Somalia
Dijlah *see* Tigris
99 H17 **Dijle** ∿ C Belgium
103 R8 **Dijon** *anc.* Dibio. Côte d'Or, C France
93 H14 **Dikanäs** Västerbotten, N Sweden
80 L12 **Dikhil** SW Djibouti
136 B13 **Dikili** İzmir, W Turkey
99 B17 **Diksmuide** *var.* Dixmuide, *Fr.* Dixmude. West-Vlaanderen, W Belgium
122 K7 **Dikson** Taymyrskiy (Dolgano-Nenetskiy) Avtonomnyy Okrug, N Russian Federation
115 K25 **Díkti** *var.* Dhíkti Ori. ▲ Kríti, Greece, E Mediterranean Sea
77 Z13 **Dikwa** Borno, NE Nigeria
81 J15 **Dīla** Southern, S Ethiopia
99 G18 **Dilbeek** Vlaams Brabant, C Belgium
171 Q16 **Dili** *var.* Dilli, Dilly. ○ (East Timor) N East Timor
77 Y11 **Dilia** *var.* Dillia. ∿ SE Niger
Dilijan *see* Delījān
167 U13 **Di Linh** Lâm Đồng, S Vietnam
101 G16 **Dillenburg** Hessen, W Germany
25 Q13 **Dilley** Texas, SW USA
Dilli *see* Delhi, India
Dilli *see* Dili, East Timor
Dillia *see* Dilia
80 E11 **Dilling** *var.* Ad Dalanj. Southern Kordofan, C Sudan
101 D20 **Dillingen** Saarland, SW Germany
Dillingen *see* Dillingen an der Donau
101 J22 **Dillingen an der Donau** *var.* Dillingen. Bayern, S Germany
39 O13 **Dillingham** Alaska, USA
33 Q12 **Dillon** Montana, NW USA
21 T12 **Dillon** South Carolina, SE USA
31 T13 **Dillon Lake** ⊠ Ohio, N USA
Dilly *see* Dili
Dilman *see* Salmās
79 K24 **Dilolo** Katanga, S Dem. Rep. Congo
115 J20 **Dílos** *island* Kykládes, Greece, Aegean Sea
141 Y11 **Ḑil', Ra's aḑ** *headland* E Oman
29 R5 **Dilworth** Minnesota, N USA
138 H7 **Dimashq** *var.* Ash Shām, Esh Sham, *Eng.* Damascus, *Fr.* Damas, *It.* Damasco. ● (Syria) Dimashq, SW Syria
138 I8 **Dimashq** *off.* Muḩāfaẓat Dimashq, *var.* Damascus, *Ar.* Ash Sham, Ash Shām, Damasco, Esh Sham, *Fr.* Damas. ◆ *governorate* S Syria
138 I7 **Dimashq** ✕ Dimashq, S Syria
79 L21 **Dimbelenge** Kasai Occidental, C Dem. Rep. Congo
77 N16 **Dimbokro** E Ivory Coast
182 L11 **Dimboola** Victoria, SE Australia
Dîmboviţa *see* Dâmboviţa
Dimitrov *see* Dymytrov
114 K11 **Dimitrovgrad** Khaskovo, S Bulgaria
127 R5 **Dimitrovgrad** Ul'yanovskaya Oblast', W Russian Federation
113 Q15 **Dimitrovgrad** *prev.* Caribrod. Serbia, SE Serbia and Montenegro (Yugo.)
Dimitrovo *see* Pernik
Dimlang *see* Vogel Peak
24 M3 **Dimmitt** Texas, SW USA
114 F7 **Dimovo** Vidin, NW Bulgaria
59 A16 **Dimpolis** Acre, W Brazil
115 O23 **Dimyliá** Ródos, Dodekánisos, Greece, Aegean Sea
171 Q6 **Dinagat Island** *island* S Philippines
153 S13 **Dinajpur** Rajshahi, NW Bangladesh
102 I6 **Dinan** Côtes d'Armor, NW France
99 I21 **Dinant** Namur, S Belgium
136 E15 **Dinar** Afyon, SW Turkey
112 F13 **Dinara** ▲ W Croatia
Dinara *see* Dinaric Alps
102 I5 **Dinard** Ille-et-Vilaine, NW France
112 F13 **Dinaric Alps** *var.* Dinara. ▲ Bosnia and Herzegovina/Croatia
143 N10 **Dīnār, Kūh-e** ▲ C Iran
Dinbych *see* Denbigh
155 H22 **Dindigul** Tamil Nādu, SE India
83 M19 **Dindiza** Gaza, S Mozambique
149 V7 **Dinga** Punjab, E Pakistan
79 H21 **Dinga** Bandundu, SW Dem. Rep. Congo
158 L16 **Dinggyê** *var.* Gyangkar. Xizang Zizhiqu, W China
97 A20 **Dingle** *Ir.* An Daingean. SW Ireland
97 A20 **Dingle Bay** *Ir.* Bá an Daingin. *bay* SW Ireland
18 I13 **Dingmans Ferry** Pennsylvania, NE USA

◆ Country ● Country Capital ◇ Dependent Territory ○ Dependent Territory Capital ◆ Administrative Region ✕ International Airport ▲ Mountain ▲ Mountain Range ▲ Volcano ∿ River ⊚ Lake ⊠ Reservoir

101 N22 **Dingolfing** Bayern, SE Germany
171 O1 **Dingras** Luzon, N Philippines
76 J13 **Dinguiraye** Haute-Guinée, N Guinea
96 I8 **Dingwall** N Scotland, UK
159 V10 **Dingxi** Gansu, C China
161 Q7 **Dingyuan** Anhui, E China
161 O3 **Dingzhou** *prev.* Ding Xian. Hebei, E China
167 U6 **Đinh Lâp** Lang Sơn, N Vietnam
167 T13 **Đinh Quan** Đông Nai, S Vietnam
100 E13 **Dinkel** ≈ Germany/Netherlands
101 J21 **Dinkelsbühl** Bayern, S Germany
101 D14 **Dinslaken** Nordrhein-Westfalen, W Germany
35 R11 **Dinuba** California, W USA
21 W7 **Dinwiddie** Virginia, NE USA
98 N13 **Dinxperlo** Gelderland, E Netherlands
115 F14 **Dió** *anc.* Dium. *site of ancient city* Kentrikí Makedonía, N Greece
Diófás *see* Nucet
76 M12 **Dioïla** Koulikoro, W Mali
115 G19 **Dióryga Korinthou** *Eng.* Corinth Canal. *canal* S Greece
76 G12 **Diouloulou** SW Senegal
77 N11 **Dioura** Mopti, W Mali
76 G11 **Diourbel** W Senegal
152 L10 **Dipayal** Far Western, W Nepal
121 R1 **Dipkarpaz** *Gk.* Rizokarpaso, Rizokárpason. NE Cyprus
149 R17 **Diplo** Sind, SE Pakistan
171 P7 **Dipolog** *var.* Dipolog City. Mindanao, S Philippines
185 C23 **Dipton** Southland, South Island, NZ
77 O10 **Diré** Tombouctou, C Mali
80 L13 **Dirē Dawa** Dirē Dawa, E Ethiopia
Dirfis *see* Dírfys
115 H18 **Dírfys** *var.* Dirfis. ▲ Évvioa, C Greece
75 N9 **Dirj** *var.* Daraj, Darj. W Libya
180 G10 **Dirk Hartog Island** *island* Western Australia
77 Y8 **Dirkou** Agadez, NE Niger
181 X11 **Dirranbandi** Queensland, E Australia
81 O16 **Dirri** Galguduud, C Somalia
Dirschau *see* Tczew
37 N6 **Dirty Devil River** ≈ Utah, W USA
32 E10 **Disappointment, Cape** *headland* Washington, NW USA
180 L8 **Disappointment, Lake** *salt lake* Western Australia
183 R12 **Disaster Bay** *bay* New South Wales, SE Australia
44 J11 **Discovery Bay** C Jamaica
182 K13 **Discovery Bay** *inlet* SE Australia
Discovery Seamount/Discovery Seamounts *see* Discovery Tablemount
65 O19 **Discovery Tablemount** *var.* Discovery Seamount, Discovery Seamounts. *undersea feature* SW Indian Ocean
108 G9 **Disentis** *Rmsch.* Mustér. Graubünden, S Switzerland
39 O10 **Dishna River** ≈ Alaska, USA
195 X4 **Dismal Mountains** ▲ Antarctica
28 M14 **Dismal River** ≈ Nebraska, C USA
Disna *see* Dzisna
99 L19 **Dison** Liège, E Belgium
153 V12 **Dispur** Assam, NE India
15 R11 **Disraeli** Québec, SE Canada
115 F18 **Dístomo** *prev.* Dhístomon. Stereá Ellás, C Greece
115 H18 **Dístos, Límni** ⊚ Évvoia, C Greece
59 L18 **Distrito Federal** *Eng.* Federal District. ◈ *federal district* C Brazil
41 P14 **Distrito Federal** ◈ *federal district* S Mexico
54 L4 **Distrito Federal** *off.* Territorio Distrito Federal. ◈ *federal district* N Venezuela
Distrito Federal, Territorio *see* Distrito Federal
116 J10 **Ditrău** *Hung.* Ditró. Harghita, C Romania
Ditró *see* Ditrău
154 B12 **Diu** Damān and Diu, W India
Dium *see* Dió
109 S13 **Divača** SW Slovenia
102 K5 **Dives** ≈ N France
Divichi *see* Däväçi
33 Q11 **Divide** Montana, NW USA
Divin *see* Dzivin
83 N18 **Divinhe** Sofala, E Mozambique
59 L20 **Divinópolis** Minas Gerais, SE Brazil
127 N13 **Divnoye** Stavropol'skiy Kray, SW Russian Federation
76 M17 **Divo** S Ivory Coast
Divodurum Mediomatricum *see* Metz
137 N13 **Divriği** Sivas, C Turkey
Diwaniyah *see* Ad Dīwānīyah
14 J10 **Dix Milles, Lac** ⊚ Québec, SE Canada
14 M8 **Dix Milles, Lac des** ⊚ Québec, SE Canada
Dixmude/Dixmuide *see* Diksmuide
35 N7 **Dixon** California, W USA
30 L10 **Dixon** Illinois, N USA
20 I6 **Dixon** Kentucky, S USA
27 V6 **Dixon** Missouri, C USA
37 S9 **Dixon** New Mexico, SW USA
39 Y15 **Dixon Entrance** *strait* Canada/USA
18 D14 **Dixonville** Pennsylvania, NE USA
137 T13 **Diyadin** Ağrı, E Turkey
139 V5 **Diyālá, Nahr** *var.* Rudkhaneh-ye Sīrvān, Sīrwan. ≈ Iran/Iraq *see also* Sīrvān, Rudkhaneh-ye
137 P15 **Diyarbakır** *var.* Diarbekr; *anc.* Amida. Diyarbakır, SE Turkey
137 P15 **Diyarbakır** *var.* Diarbekr. ◈ *province* SE Turkey
Dizful *see* Dezfūl
79 F16 **Dja** ≈ SE Cameroon
Djadié *see* Zadié
77 X7 **Djado** Agadez, NE Niger
77 X6 **Djado, Plateau du** ▲ NE Niger
Djailolo *see* Halmahera, Pulau
Djajapura *see* Jayapura
Djakarta *see* Jakarta
Djakovica *see* Đakovica
Djakovo *see* Đakovo
79 G20 **Djambala** Plateaux, C Congo
Djambi *see* Jambi
Djambi *see* Hari, Batang, Sumatera, W Indonesia
74 M9 **Djanet** E Algeria
74 M11 **Djanet** *prev.* Fort Charlet. SE Algeria
Djatiwangi *see* Jatiwangi
Djaul *see* Dyaul Island
Djawa *see* Jawa
Djéblé *see* Jablah
78 I10 **Djédaa** Batha, C Chad
74 J6 **Djelfa** *var.* El Djelfa. N Algeria
79 M14 **Djéma** Haut-Mbomou, E Central African Republic
Djeneponto *see* Jeneponto
77 N12 **Djenné** *var.* Jenné. Mopti, C Mali
Djérablous *see* Jarābulus
Djerba *see* Jerba, Île de
79 F15 **Djérem** ≈ C Cameroon
Djevdjelija *see* Gevgelija
77 P11 **Djibo** N Burkina
80 L12 **Djibouti** *var.* Jibuti. ● (Djibouti) E Djibouti
80 L12 **Djibouti** *off.* Republic of Djibouti, *var.* Jibuti; *prev.* French Somaliland, French Territory of the Afars and Issas, *Fr.* Côte Française des Somalis, Territoire Français des Afars et des Issas. ◆ *republic* E Africa
80 L12 **Djibouti** ✕ C Djibouti
Djidjel/Djidjelli *see* Jijel
55 W10 **Djoemoe** Sipaliwini, C Surinam
Djokjakarta *see* Yogyakarta
79 K21 **Djoku-Punda** Kasai Occidental, S Dem. Rep. Congo
79 K18 **Djolu** Equateur, N Dem. Rep. Congo
Djorče Petrov *see* Đorče Petrov
79 F17 **Djoua** ≈ Congo/Gabon
77 R14 **Djougou** W Benin
79 F16 **Djoum** Sud, S Cameroon
78 I8 **Djourab, Erg du** *dunes* N Chad
79 P17 **Djugu** Orientale, NE Dem. Rep. Congo
Djumbir *see* Ďumbier
92 L3 **Djúpivogur** Austurland, SE Iceland
94 L13 **Djura** Dalarna, C Sweden
Djurdjevac *see* Đurđevac
83 G18 **D'Kar** Ghanzi, NW Botswana
197 U6 **Dmitriya Lapteva, Proliv** *strait* N Russian Federation
126 J7 **Dmitriyev-L'govskiy** Kurskaya Oblast', W Russian Federation
Dmitriyevsk *see* Makiyivka
126 K3 **Dmitrov** Moskovskaya Oblast', W Russian Federation
Dmitrovichi *see* Dzmitravichy
126 J6 **Dmitrovsk-Orlovskiy** Orlovskaya Oblast', W Russian Federation
117 R3 **Dmytrivka** Chernihivs'ka Oblast', N Ukraine
Dnepr *see* Dnieper
Dneprodzerzhinsk *see* Dniprodzerzhyns'k
Dneprodzerzhinskoye Vodokhranilishche *see* Dniprodzerzhyns'ke Vodoskhovyshche
Dnepropetrovsk *see* Dnipropetrovs'k
Dnepropetrovskaya Oblast' *see* Dnipropetrovs'ka Oblast'
Dneprorudnoye *see* Dniprorudne
Dneprovskiy Liman *see* Dniprovs'kyy Lyman
Dneprovsko-Bugskiy Kanal *see* Dnyaprowska-Buhski, Kanal
Dnestr *see* Dniester
Dnestrovskiy Liman *see* Dnistrovs'kyy Lyman
117 S10 **Dnieper** *Bel.* Dnyapro, *Rus.* Dnepr, *Ukr.* Dnipro. ≈ E Europe
117 P3 **Dnieper Lowland** *Bel.* Prydnyaprowskaya Nizina, *Ukr.* Prydniprovs'ka Nyzovyna. *lowlands* Belarus/Ukraine
116 M8 **Dniester** *Rom.* Nistru, *Rus.* Dnestr, *Ukr.* Dnister; *anc.* Tyras. ≈ Moldova/Ukraine
Dnipro *see* Dnieper
117 T7 **Dniprodzerzhyns'k** *Rus.* Dneprodzerzhinsk; *prev.* Kamenskoye. Dnipropetrovs'ka Oblast', E Ukraine
117 T7 **Dniprodzerzhyns'ke Vodoskhovyshche** *Rus.* Dneprodzerzhinskoye Vodokhranilishche. ⊞ C Ukraine
117 U7 **Dnipropetrovs'k** *Rus.* Dnepropetrovsk; *prev.* Yekaterinoslav. Dnipropetrovs'ka Oblast', E Ukraine
117 U8 **Dnipropetrovs'k** ✕ Dnipropetrovs'ka Oblast', S Ukraine
Dnipropetrovs'k *see* Dnipropetrovs'ka Oblast'
117 T7 **Dnipropetrovs'ka Oblast'** *var.* Dnipropetrovs'k, *Rus.* Dnepropetrovskaya Oblast'. ◈ *province* E Ukraine
117 U9 **Dniprorudne** *Rus.* Dneprorudnoye. Zaporiz'ka Oblast', SE Ukraine
117 Q11 **Dniprovs'kyy Lyman** *Rus.* Dneprovskiy Liman. *bay* S Ukraine
Dnister *see* Dniester
117 O11 **Dnistrovs'kyy Lyman** *Rus.* Dnestrovskiy Liman. *inlet* S Ukraine
124 G14 **Dno** Pskovskaya Oblast', W Russian Federation
Dnyapro *see* Dnieper
119 H20 **Dnyaprowska-Buhski, Kanal** *Rus.* Dneprovsko-Bugskiy Kanal. *canal* SW Belarus
13 O14 **Doaktown** New Brunswick, SE Canada
78 H13 **Doba** Logone-Oriental, S Chad
118 E9 **Dobele** *Ger.* Doblen. Dobele, W Latvia
101 N16 **Döbeln** Sachsen, E Germany
171 U12 **Doberai, Jazirah** *Dut.* Vogelkop. *peninsula* Papua, E Indonesia
110 F10 **Dobiegniew** *Ger.* Lubuskie, W Poland
Doblen *see* Dobele
81 K18 **Dobli** *spring/well* SW Somalia
112 H11 **Doboj** Republika Srpska, N Bosnia and Herzegovina
110 L8 **Dobre Miasto** *Ger.* Guttstadt. Warmińsko-Mazurskie, NE Poland
114 N7 **Dobrich** *Rom.* Bazargic; *prev.* Tolbukhin. Dobrich, NE Bulgaria
114 N7 **Dobrich** ◈ *province* NE Bulgaria
126 M8 **Dobrinka** Lipetskaya Oblast', W Russian Federation
126 M7 **Dobrinka** Volgogradskaya Oblast', SW Russian Federation
Dobrla Vas *see* Eberndorf
111 I15 **Dobrodzień** *Ger.* Guttentag. Opolskie, S Poland
Dobrogea *see* Dobruja
117 W7 **Dobropillya** *Rus.* Dobropol'ye. Donets'ka Oblast', SE Ukraine
Dobropol'ye *see* Dobropillya
117 P8 **Dobrovelychkivka** Kirovohrads'ka Oblast', C Ukraine
Dobrudja/Dobrudzha *see* Dobruja
114 O7 **Dobruja** *var.* Dobrudja, *Bul.* Dobrudzha, *Rom.* Dobrogea. *physical region* Bulgaria/Romania
119 P19 **Dobrush** Homyel'skaya Voblasts', SE Belarus
125 U14 **Dobryanka** Permskaya Oblast', NW Russian Federation
117 P2 **Dobryanka** Chernihivs'ka Oblast', N Ukraine
Dobryn' *see* Dabryn'
21 R8 **Dobson** North Carolina, SE USA
59 N20 **Doce, Rio** ≈ SE Brazil
93 I16 **Docksta** Västernorrland, C Sweden
41 N10 **Doctor Arroyo** Nuevo León, NE Mexico
62 L4 **Doctor Pedro P. Peña** Boquerón, W Paraguay
171 S11 **Dodaga** Pulau Halmahera, E Indonesia
155 G21 **Dodda Betta** ▲ S India
Dodecanese *see* Dodekánisos
115 M22 **Dodekánisos** *var.* Nóties Sporádes, *Eng.* Dodecanese; *prev.* Dhodhekánisos. *island group* SE Greece
26 J6 **Dodge City** Kansas, C USA
30 K9 **Dodgeville** Wisconsin, N USA
97 H25 **Dodman Point** *headland* SW England, UK
81 J14 **Dodola** Oromo, C Ethiopia
81 H22 **Dodoma** ● (Tanzania) Dodoma, C Tanzania
81 H22 **Dodoma** ◈ *region* C Tanzania
115 C16 **Dodóni** *var.* Dhodhóni. *site of ancient city* Ípeiros, W Greece
33 U7 **Dodson** Montana, NW USA
25 P3 **Dodson** Texas, SW USA
98 M12 **Doesburg** Gelderland, E Netherlands
98 N12 **Doetinchem** Gelderland, E Netherlands
158 L12 **Dogai Coring** *var.* Lake Montcalm. ⊚ W China
137 N15 **Doğanşehir** Malatya, C Turkey
23 S10 **Dog Island** *island* Florida, SE USA
14 C7 **Dog Lake** ⊚ Ontario, S Canada
106 B9 **Dogliani** Piemonte, NE Italy
164 H11 **Dōgo** *island* Oki-shotō, SW Japan
Do Gonbadān *see* Dow Gonbadān
77 S12 **Dogondoutchi** Dosso, SW Niger
Dogrular *see* Pravda
137 T13 **Doğubayazıt** Ağrı, E Turkey
137 P12 **Doğu Karadeniz Dağları** *var.* Anadolu Dağları. ▲ NE Turkey
158 K16 **Dogxung Zangbo** ≈ W China
Doha *see* Ad Dawḩah
Dohad *see* Dāhod
Dohuk *see* Dahūk
159 N16 **Doilungdêqên** *var.* Namka. Xizang Zizhiqu, W China
114 F12 **Doïranis, Límnis** *Bul.* Ezero Doyransko. ⊚ N Greece
Doire *see* Londonderry
99 H22 **Doische** Namur, S Belgium
59 P17 **Dois de Julho** ✕ (Salvador) Bahia, NE Brazil
60 H12 **Dois Vizinhos** Paraná, S Brazil
80 H10 **Doka** Gedaref, E Sudan
Doka *see* Kéita, Bahr
139 T3 **Dokan** *var.* Dūkān. E Iraq
94 H13 **Dokka** Oppland, S Norway
98 L5 **Dokkum** Friesland, N Netherlands
98 L5 **Dokkumer Ee** ≈ N Netherlands
76 K13 **Doko** Haute-Guinée, NE Guinea
Dokshitsy *see* Dokshytsy
118 K13 **Dokshytsy** *Rus.* Dokshitsy. Vitsyebskaya Voblasts', N Belarus
117 X8 **Dokuchayevs'k** *var.* Dokuchayevsk. Donets'ka Oblast', SE Ukraine
Dolak, Pulau *see* Yos Sudarso, Pulau
29 P9 **Doland** South Dakota, N USA
53 J18 **Dolavón** Chaco, S Argentina
15 P6 **Dolbeau** Québec, SE Canada
102 I5 **Dol-de-Bretagne** Ille-et-Vilaine, NW France
64 J13 **Doldrums Fracture Zone** *tectonic feature* W Atlantic Ocean
103 S8 **Dôle** Jura, E France
97 J19 **Dolgellau** NW Wales, UK
Dolginovo *see* Dawhinava
Dolgi, Ostrov *see* Dolgiy, Ostrov
127 U2 **Dolgiy, Ostrov** *var.* Ostrov Dolgi. *island* NW Russian Federation
162 J9 **Dölgöön** Övörhangay, C Mongolia
107 C20 **Dolianova** Sardegna, Italy, C Mediterranean Sea
Dolina *see* Dolyna
123 T13 **Dolinsk** Ostrov Sakhalin, Sakhalinskaya Oblast', SE Russian Federation
Dolinskaya *see* Dolyns'ka
79 F21 **Dolisie** *prev.* Loubomo. Le Niari, S Congo
116 G14 **Dolj** ◈ *county* SW Romania
98 P5 **Dollard** *bay* NW Germany
194 J5 **Dolleman Island** *island* Antarctica
114 I8 **Dolni Dŭbnik** Pleven, N Bulgaria
114 F8 **Dolni Lom** Vidin, NW Bulgaria
Dolnja Lendava *see* Lendava
114 K9 **Dolno Panicherevo** *var.* Panicherevo. Sliven, C Bulgaria
111 F14 **Dolnośląskie** ◈ *province* SW Poland
111 K18 **Dolný Kubín** *Hung.* Alsókubin. Žilinský Kraj, N Slovakia
106 H8 **Dolo** Veneto, NE Italy
Dolomites/Dolomiti *see* Dolomitiche, Alpi
106 H6 **Dolomitiche, Alpi** *var.* Dolomiti, *Eng.* Dolomites. ▲ NE Italy
Dolonnur *see* Duolun
162 K10 **Doloon** Ömnögovĭ, S Mongolia
61 E21 **Dolores** Buenos Aires, E Argentina
42 E3 **Dolores** Petén, N Guatemala
171 Q5 **Dolores** Samar, C Philippines
105 S12 **Dolores** País Valenciano, E Spain
61 D19 **Dolores** Soriano, SW Uruguay
41 N12 **Dolores Hidalgo** *var.* Ciudad de Dolores Hidalgo. Guanajuato, C Mexico
8 J7 **Dolphin and Union Strait** *strait* Northwest Territories / Nunavut, N Canada
65 D23 **Dolphin, Cape** *headland* East Falkland, Falkland Islands
44 H12 **Dolphin Head** *hill* W Jamaica
83 B21 **Dolphin Head** *var.* Cape Dernberg. *headland* SW Namibia
110 G12 **Dolsk** *Ger.* Dolzig. Wielkolpolskie, C Poland
167 S8 **Đô Lương** Nghê An, N Vietnam
116 I6 **Dolyna** *Rus.* Dolina. Ivano-Frankivs'ka Oblast', W Ukraine
117 R8 **Dolyns'ka** *Rus.* Dolinskaya. Kirovohrads'ka Oblast', S Ukraine
Dolzig *see* Dolsk
Domachëvo/Domaczewo *see* Damachava
117 P9 **Domanivka** Mykolayivs'ka Oblast', S Ukraine
153 S13 **Domar** Rajshahi, N Bangladesh
108 I9 **Domat/Ems** Graubünden, SE Switzerland
111 A18 **Domažlice** *Ger.* Taus. Plzeňský Kraj, W Czech Republic
127 X8 **Dombarovskiy** Orenburgskaya Oblast', W Russian Federation
94 G10 **Dombås** Oppland, S Norway
83 M17 **Dombe** Manica, C Mozambique
82 A13 **Dombe Grande** Benguela, C Angola
103 R10 **Dombes** *physical region* E France
111 I25 **Dombóvár** Tolna, S Hungary
99 D14 **Domburg** Zeeland, SW Netherlands
58 L13 **Dom Eliseu** Pará, NE Brazil
Domel Island *see* Letsôk-aw Kyun
103 O11 **Dôme, Puy de** ▲ C France
36 H13 **Dome Rock Mountains** ▲ Arizona, SW USA
Domesnes, Cape *see* Kolkasrags
62 G8 **Domeyko** Atacama, N Chile
62 H5 **Domeyko, Cordillera** ▲ N Chile
102 K5 **Domfront** Orne, N France
171 X13 **Dom, Gunung** ▲ Papua, E Indonesia
45 X11 **Dominica** *off.* Commonwealth of Dominica. ◆ *republic* E West Indies
Dominica Channel *see* Martinique Passage
43 N15 **Dominical** Puntarenas, SE Costa Rica
45 Q8 **Dominican Republic** ◆ *republic* C West Indies
45 X11 **Dominica Passage** *passage* E Caribbean Sea
99 K14 **Dommel** ≈ S Netherlands
81 O14 **Domo** Somali, E Ethiopia
126 L4 **Domodedovo** ✕ (Moskva) Moskovskaya Oblast', W Russian Federation
106 C6 **Domodossola** Piemonte, NE Italy
115 F17 **Domokós** *var.* Dhomokós. Stereá Ellás, C Greece
172 I14 **Domoni** Anjouan, SE Comoros
61 G16 **Dom Pedrito** Rio Grande do Sul, S Brazil
Dompoe *see* Dompu
170 M16 **Dompu** *prev.* Dompoe. Sumbawa, C Indonesia
Domschale *see* Domžale
62 H13 **Domuyo, Volcán** ✱ W Argentina
109 U11 **Domžale** *Ger.* Domschale. C Slovenia
127 O10 **Don** *var.* Duna, Tanais. ≈ SW Russian Federation
96 K9 **Don** ≈ NE Scotland, UK
182 M11 **Donald** Victoria, SE Australia
22 J9 **Donaldsonville** Louisiana, S USA
23 S8 **Donalsonville** Georgia, SE USA
Donau *see* Danube
101 G23 **Donaueschingen** Baden-Württemberg, SW Germany
101 K22 **Donaumoos** *wetland* S Germany
101 K22 **Donauwörth** Bayern, S Germany
109 U7 **Donawitz** Steiermark, SE Austria
117 X7 **Donbass** *industrial region* Russian Federation/Ukraine
104 K11 **Don Benito** Extremadura, W Spain
97 M17 **Doncaster** *anc.* Danum. N England, UK
44 K12 **Don Christophers Point** *headland* C Jamaica
55 V9 **Donderkamp** Sipaliwini, NW Surinam
82 B12 **Dondo** Cuanza Norte, NW Angola
171 O12 **Dondo** Sulawesi, N Indonesia
83 N17 **Dondo** Sofala, C Mozambique
155 K26 **Dondra Head** *headland* S Sri Lanka
Dondușani *see* Dondușeni
116 M8 **Dondușeni** *var.* Dondușani, *Rus.* Dondyushany. N Moldova
Dondyushany *see* Dondușeni
97 D15 **Donegal** *Ir.* Dún na nGall. NW Ireland
97 D14 **Donegal** *Ir.* Dún na nGall. *cultural region* NW Ireland
97 C15 **Donegal Bay** *Ir.* Bá Dhún na nGall. *bay* NW Ireland
117 X7 **Donets** ≈ Russian Federation/Ukraine
117 X8 **Donets'k** *Rus.* Donetsk; *prev.* Stalino. Donets'ka Oblast', E Ukraine
117 W8 **Donets'k** ✕ Donets'ka Oblast', E Ukraine
Donets'k *see* Donets'ka Oblast'
117 W8 **Donets'ka Oblast'** *var.* Donets'k, *Rus.* Donetskaya Oblast'; *prev. Rus.* Stalinskaya Oblast'. ◈ *province* SE Ukraine
Donetskaya Oblast' *see* Donets'ka Oblast'
157 O13 **Dongchuan** Yunnan, SW China
99 I14 **Dongen** Noord-Brabant, S Netherlands
160 K17 **Dongfang** *var.* Basuo. Hainan, S China
163 Z7 **Dongfanghong** Heilongjiang, NE China
163 W11 **Dongfeng** Jilin, NE China
171 N12 **Donggala** Sulawesi, C Indonesia
163 V13 **Donggang** *var.* Dadong, *prev.* Donggou. Liaoning, NE China
Donggou *see* Donggang
161 O14 **Dongguan** Guangdong, S China
167 T9 **Đông Ha** Quang Tri, C Vietnam
Dong Hai *see* East China Sea
160 M16 **Donghai Dao** *island* S China
162 I12 **Dong He** *Mong.* Narin Gol. ≈ N China
167 T9 **Đông Hơi** Quang Binh, C Vietnam
108 H10 **Dongio** Ticino, S Switzerland
Dongkan *see* Binhai
160 L11 **Dongkou** Hunan, S China
Dongliao *see* Liaoyuan
Dong-nai *see* Đông Nai, Sông
167 U13 **Đông Nai, Sông** *var.* Dong-nai, Dong Noi, Donnai. ≈ S Vietnam
161 N14 **Dongnan Qiuling** *plateau* SE China
163 Y9 **Dongning** Heilongjiang, NE China
Dong Noi *see* Đông Nai, Sông
83 C14 **Dongo** Huíla, C Angola
80 E7 **Dongola** *var.* Donqola, Dunqulah. Northern, N Sudan
79 I17 **Dongou** La Likouala, NE Congo
Đông Phu *see* Đông Xoai
Dongping *see* Anhua
Dong Rak, Phanom *see* Dângrêk, Chuŏr Phnum
161 Q14 **Dongshan Dao** *island* SE China
Dongsheng *see* Ordos
161 R7 **Dongtai** Jiangsu, E China
161 N10 **Dongting Hu** *var.* Tung-t'ing Hu. ⊚ S China
161 P10 **Dongxiang** *var.* Xiaogang. Jiangxi, S China
167 T13 **Đông Xoai** *var.* Đông Phu. Sông Be, S Vietnam
161 Q4 **Dongying** Shandong, E China
27 X8 **Doniphan** Missouri, C USA
Donja Łužyca *see* Niederlausitz
10 G7 **Donjek** ≈ Yukon Territory, W Canada
112 E11 **Donji Lapac** Lika-Senj, W Croatia
112 H8 **Donji Miholjac** Osijek-Baranja, NE Croatia
112 P12 **Donji Milanovac** Serbia, E Serbia and Montenegro (Yugo.)
112 G12 **Donji Vakuf** *var.* Srbobran, Federacija Bosna I Hercegovina, C Bosnia & Herzegovina
98 M6 **Donkerbroek** Friesland, N Netherlands
167 P11 **Don Muang** ✕ (Krung Thep) Nonthaburi, C Thailand
25 S17 **Donna** Texas, SW USA
15 Q10 **Donnacona** Québec, SE Canada
Donnai *see* Đông Nai, Sông
29 Y16 **Donnellson** Iowa, C USA
11 O13 **Donnelly** Alberta, W Canada
35 H6 **Donner Pass** *pass* California, W USA
101 F19 **Donnersberg** ▲ W Germany
Donoso *see* Miguel de la Borda
105 P2 **Donostia-San Sebastián** País Vasco, N Spain
115 K21 **Donoúsa** *island* Kykládes, Greece, Aegean Sea
35 P8 **Don Pedro Reservoir** ⊞ California, W USA
Donqola *see* Dongola
126 L5 **Donskoy** Tul'skaya Oblast', W Russian Federation
81 L16 **Doolow** Somali, E Ethiopia
39 Q7 **Doonerak, Mount** ▲ Alaska, USA
98 J12 **Doorn** Utrecht, C Netherlands
Doornik *see* Tournai
31 N6 **Door Peninsula** *peninsula* Wisconsin, N USA
80 P13 **Dooxo Nugaaleed** *var.* Nogal Valley. *valley* E Somalia
Do Qu *see* Da Qu
106 B7 **Dora Baltea** *anc.* Duria Major. ≈ NW Italy
180 K7 **Dora, Lake** *salt lake* Western Australia
106 A8 **Dora Riparia** *anc.* Duria Minor. ≈ NW Italy
Dorbiljin *see* Emin
Dorbod/Dorbod Mongolzu Zizhixian *see* Taikang
113 N18 **Đorče Petrov** *var.* Djorče Petrov, Gorče Petrov. N FYR Macedonia
14 F16 **Dorchester** Ontario, S Canada
97 L24 **Dorchester** *anc.* Durnovaria. S England, UK
9 P7 **Dorchester, Cape** *headland* Baffin Island, Nunavut, NE Canada
83 D19 **Dordabis** Khomas, C Namibia
102 L12 **Dordogne** ◈ *department* SW France
103 N12 **Dordogne** ≈ W France
98 H13 **Dordrecht** *var.* Dordt, Dort. Zuid-Holland, SW Netherlands
Dordt *see* Dordrecht
103 P11 **Dore** ≈ C France
11 S13 **Doré Lake** Saskatchewan, C Canada
103 O12 **Dore, Monts** ▲ C France
101 M23 **Dorfen** Bayern, SE Germany
107 D18 **Dorgali** Sardegna, Italy, C Mediterranean Sea
159 N11 **Dorgê Co** *var.* Elsen Nur. ⊚ C China
162 F7 **Dörgön Nuur** ⊚ NW Mongolia
77 Q12 **Dori** N Burkina
83 E24 **Doring** ≈ S South Africa
101 E16 **Dormagen** Nordrhein-Westfalen, W Germany
103 P4 **Dormans** Marne, N France
108 E6 **Dornach** Solothurn, NW Switzerland
Dorna Watra *see* Vatra Dornei
108 J7 **Dornbirn** Vorarlberg, W Austria
96 I7 **Dornoch** N Scotland, UK
96 J7 **Dornoch Firth** *inlet* N Scotland, UK
163 P7 **Dornod** ◈ *province* E Mongolia
163 N10 **Dornogovĭ** ◈ *province* SE Mongolia
77 P10 **Doro** Tombouctou, S Mali
116 L14 **Dorobanțu** Călărași, S Romania
111 J22 **Dorog** Komárom-Esztergom, N Hungary
126 I4 **Dorogobuzh** Smolenskaya Oblast', W Russian Federation
116 K8 **Dorohoi** Botoșani, NE Romania
93 H15 **Dorotea** Västerbotten, N Sweden
Dorpat *see* Tartu
180 G10 **Dorre Island** *island* Western Australia
183 U5 **Dorrigo** New South Wales, SE Australia
35 N1 **Dorris** California, W USA
14 H13 **Dorset** Ontario, SE Canada
97 K23 **Dorset** *cultural region* S England, UK
101 E14 **Dorsten** Nordrhein-Westfalen, W Germany
Dort *see* Dordrecht
101 F15 **Dortmund** Nordrhein-Westfalen, W Germany
100 F12 **Dortmund-Ems-Kanal** *canal* W Germany
136 L17 **Dörtyol** Hatay, S Turkey
142 L7 **Do Rūd** *var.* Dow Rūd, Durud. Lorestān, W Iran
79 O15 **Doruma** Orientale, N Dem. Rep. Congo
15 O12 **Dorval** ✕ (Montréal) Québec, SE Canada
45 T5 **Dos Bocas, Lago** ⊚ C Puerto Rico
104 K14 **Dos Hermanas** Andalucía, S Spain

◆ Country
● Country Capital
◇ Dependent Territory
○ Dependent Territory Capital
◈ Administrative Region
✕ International Airport
▲ Mountain
▲ Mountain Range
✱ Volcano
≈ River
⊚ Lake
⊞ Reservoir

Dospad Dagh *see* Rhodope Mountains
35 P10 **Dos Palos** California, W USA
114 I11 **Dospat** Smolyan, S Bulgaria
114 H11 **Dospat, Yazovir** ▣ SW Bulgaria
100 M11 **Dosse** ≈ NE Germany
77 S12 **Dosso** Dosso, SW Niger
77 S12 **Dosso** ◈ *department* SW Niger
144 G12 **Dossor** Atyrau, SW Kazakhstan
147 O10 **Do'stlik** Jizzax Viloyati, C Uzbekistan
147 V9 **Dostuk** Narynskaya Oblast', C Kyrgyzstan
145 X13 **Dostyk** *prev.* Druzhba. Almaty, SE Kazakhstan
23 R7 **Dothan** Alabama, S USA
39 T9 **Dot Lake** Alaska, USA
118 F12 **Dotnuva** Kaunas, C Lithuania
99 D19 **Dottignies** Hainaut, W Belgium
103 P2 **Douai** *prev.* Douay, *anc.* Duacum. Nord, N France
14 L9 **Douaire, Lac** ◎ Québec, SE Canada
79 D16 **Douala** *var.* Duala. Littoral, W Cameroon
79 D16 **Douala** ✕ Littoral, W Cameroon
102 F6 **Douarnenez** Finistère, NW France
102 E6 **Douarnenez, Baie de** *bay* NW France
Douay *see* Douai
25 O6 **Double Mountain Fork Brazos River** ≈ Texas, SW USA
23 O3 **Double Springs** Alabama, S USA
103 T8 **Doubs** ◈ *department* E France
108 C8 **Doubs** ≈ France/Switzerland
185 A22 **Doubtful Sound** *sound* South Island, NZ
184 J2 **Doubtless Bay** *bay* North Island, NZ
25 X9 **Doucette** Texas, SW USA
102 K8 **Doué-la-Fontaine** Maine-et-Loire, NW France
77 O11 **Douentza** Mopti, S Mali
65 D24 **Douglas** East Falkland, Falkland Islands
97 I16 **Douglas** ○ (Isle of Man) E Isle of Man
83 H23 **Douglas** Northern Cape, C South Africa
39 X13 **Douglas** Alexander Archipelago, Alaska, USA
37 O17 **Douglas** Arizona, SW USA
23 U7 **Douglas** Georgia, SE USA
33 Y15 **Douglas** Wyoming, C USA
38 L9 **Douglas, Cape** *headland* Alaska USA
10 J14 **Douglas Channel** *channel* British Columbia, W Canada
182 G3 **Douglas Creek** *seasonal river* South Australia
31 P5 **Douglas Lake** ◎ Michigan, N USA
21 O9 **Douglas Lake** ▣ Tennessee, S USA
39 Q13 **Douglas, Mount** ▲ Alaska, USA
194 I6 **Douglas Range** ⛰ Alexander Island, Antarctica
121 P9 **Doukáto, Akrotírio** *headland* Lefkáda, W Greece
103 O2 **Doullens** Somme, N France
Douma *see* Dūmā
79 F15 **Doumé** Est, E Cameroon
99 E21 **Dour** Hainaut, S Belgium
59 K18 **Dourada, Serra** ⛰ S Brazil
59 I21 **Dourados** Mato Grosso do Sul, S Brazil
103 N5 **Dourdan** Essonne, N France
104 I6 **Douro** *Sp.* Duero. ≈ Portugal/Spain *see also* Duero
104 G6 **Douro Litoral** *former province* N Portugal
Douvres *see* Dover
102 K15 **Douze** ≈ SW France
183 P17 **Dover** Tasmania, SE Australia
97 Q22 **Dover** *Fr.* Douvres; *Lat.* Dubris Portus. SE England, UK
21 Y3 **Dover** *state capital* Delaware, NE USA
19 P9 **Dover** New Hampshire, NE USA
18 J14 **Dover** New Jersey, NE USA
31 U12 **Dover** Ohio, N USA
20 H8 **Dover** Tennessee, S USA
97 Q23 **Dover, Strait of** *var.* Straits of Dover, *Fr.* Pas de Calais. *strait* England, UK/France
Dover, Straits of *see* Dover, Strait of
Dovlen *see* Devin
94 G11 **Dovre** Oppland, S Norway
94 G10 **Dovrefjell** *plateau* S Norway
Dovsk *see* Dowsk
83 M14 **Dowa** Central, C Malawi
31 O10 **Dowagiac** Michigan, N USA
143 N10 **Dow Gonbadān** *var.* Do Gonbadān, Gonbadān. Kohgīlūyeh va Būyer Aḩmad, SW Iran
148 M2 **Dowlatābād** Fāryāb, N Afghanistan
97 G16 **Down** *cultural region* SE Northern Ireland, UK
33 R16 **Downey** Idaho, NW USA
35 P5 **Downieville** California, W USA
97 G16 **Downpatrick** *Ir.* Dún Pádraig. SE Northern Ireland, UK
25 M3 **Downs** Kansas, C USA
18 J12 **Downsville** New York, NE USA
Dow Rūd *see* Do Rūd
29 V12 **Dows** Iowa, C USA
119 O17 **Dowsk** *Rus.* Dovsk. Homyel'skaya Voblasts', SE Belarus
35 Q4 **Doyle** California, W USA
18 I15 **Doylestown** Pennsylvania, NE USA
Doyransko, Ezero *see* Doïranis, Límnis
114 I8 **Doyrentsi** Lovech, N Bulgaria
164 G11 **Dōzen** *island* Oki-shotō, SW Japan
14 K9 **Dozois, Réservoir** ▣ Québec, SE Canada
74 D9 **Drâa** *seasonal river* S Morocco
Drâa, Hammada du *see* Dra, Hamada du
Drabble *see* José Enrique Rodó
117 Q5 **Drabiv** Cherkas'ka Oblast', C Ukraine
Drable *see* José Enrique Rodó
103 S13 **Drac** ≈ E France
Drač/Drac *see* Durrës
60 I8 **Dracena** São Paulo, S Brazil
98 M6 **Drachten** Friesland, N Netherlands
92 H11 **Drag** *Lapp.* Ájluokta. Nordland, C Norway
116 L14 **Dragalina** Călăraşi, SE Romania
116 I14 **Drăgăneşti-Olt** Olt, S Romania
116 J14 **Drăgăneşti-Vlaşca** Teleorman, S Romania
116 I13 **Drăgăşani** Vâlcea, SW Romania
114 G9 **Dragoman** Sofiya, W Bulgaria
115 L25 **Dragonáda** *island* SE Greece
Dragonera, Isla *see* Sa Dragonera
45 T14 **Dragon's Mouths, The** *strait* Trinidad and Tobago/Venezuela
95 J23 **Dragør** København, E Denmark
114 F10 **Dragovishtitsa** Kyustendil, W Bulgaria
103 U15 **Draguignan** Var, SE France
74 E9 **Dra, Hamada du** *var.* Hammada du Drâa, Haut Plateau du Dra. *plateau* W Algeria
Dra, Haut Plateau du *see* Dra, Hamada du
119 H19 **Drahichyn** *Pol.* Drohiczyn Poleski, *Rus.* Drogichin. Brestskaya Voblasts', SW Belarus
29 N4 **Drake** North Dakota, N USA
83 K23 **Drakensberg** ⛰ Lesotho/South Africa
194 F3 **Drake Passage** *passage* Atlantic Ocean/Pacific Ocean
114 L8 **Dralfa** Tŭrgovishte, N Bulgaria
114 I12 **Dráma** *var.* Dhráma. Anatolikí Makedonía kai Thráki, NE Greece
Dramburg *see* Drawsko Pomorskie
95 H15 **Drammen** Buskerud, S Norway
95 H15 **Drammensfjorden** *fjord* S Norway
92 H1 **Drangajökull** ▲ NW Iceland
95 F16 **Drangedal** Telemark, S Norway
92 I2 **Drangsnes** Vestfirdhir, NW Iceland
Drann *see* Dravinja
109 T10 **Drau** *var.* Drava, *Eng.* Drave, *Hung.* Dráva. ≈ C Europe *see also* Drava
112 F7 **Drava** *var.* Drau, *Eng.* Drave, *Hung.* Dráva. ≈ C Europe *see also* Drau
Dráva *see* Drau/Drava
Drave *see* Drau/Drava
109 W10 **Dravinja** *Ger.* Drann. ≈ NE Slovenia
109 V9 **Dravograd** *Ger.* Unterdrauburg; *prev.* Spodnji Dravograd. N Slovenia
110 F10 **Drawa** ≈ NW Poland
110 F9 **Drawno** Zachodnio-pomorskie, NW Poland
110 F9 **Drawsko Pomorskie** *Ger.* Dramburg. Zachodnio-pomorskie, NW Poland
29 R3 **Drayton** North Dakota, N USA
11 P14 **Drayton Valley** Alberta, SW Canada
186 B6 **Dreikikir** East Sepik, NW PNG
Dreikirchen *see* Teiuş
98 N7 **Drenthe** ◈ *province* NE Netherlands
115 H15 **Drépano, Akrotírio** *var.* Akra Dhrepanon. *headland* N Greece
Drepanum *see* Trapani
14 D17 **Dresden** Ontario, S Canada
101 O16 **Dresden** Sachsen, E Germany
20 G8 **Dresden** Tennessee, S USA
118 M11 **Dretun'** *Rus.* Dretun'. Vitsyebskaya Voblasts', N Belarus
102 M5 **Dreux** *anc.* Drocae, Durocasses. Eure-et-Loir, C France
94 I11 **Drevsjø** Hedmark, S Norway
22 K3 **Drew** Mississippi, S USA
110 F10 **Drezdenko** *Ger.* Driesen. Lubuskie, W Poland
98 J12 **Driebergen** *var.* Driebergen-Rijsenburg. Utrecht, C Netherlands
Driebergen-Rijsenburg *see* Driebergen
Driesen *see* Drezdenko
97 N16 **Driffield** E England, UK
65 D25 **Driftwood Point** *headland* East Falkland, Falkland Islands
33 S14 **Driggs** Idaho, NW USA
Drin *see* Drinit, Lumi i
112 K12 **Drina** ≈ Bosnia and Herzegovina/Serbia and Montenegro (Yugo.)
Drin, Gulf of *see* Drinit, Gjiri i
113 K18 **Drinit, Gjiri i** *var.* Pellg i Drinit, *Eng.* Gulf of Drin. *gulf* NW Albania
113 L17 **Drinit, Lumi i** *var.* Drin. ≈ NW Albania
Drinit, Pellg i *see* Drinit, Gjiri i
Drinit të Zi, Lumi i *see* Black Drin
113 L22 **Drino** *var.* Drino, Drínos Pótamos, *Alb.* Lumi i Drinos. ≈ Albania/Greece
Drinos, Lumi i/Drínos Pótamos *see* Drino
25 S11 **Dripping Springs** Texas, SW USA
25 S15 **Driscoll** Texas, SW USA
22 H5 **Driskill Mountain** ▲ Louisiana, S USA
Drissa *see* Drysa
94 G10 **Driva** ≈ S Norway
112 E13 **Drniš** *It.* Šibenik-Knin, S Croatia
95 H15 **Drøbak** Akershus, S Norway
116 G13 **Drobeta-Turnu Severin** *prev.* Turnu Severin. Mehedinţi, SW Romania
Drocae *see* Dreux
116 M8 **Drochia** *Rus.* Drokiya. N Moldova
97 F17 **Drogheda** *Ir.* Droichead Átha. NE Ireland
Drogichin *see* Drahichyn
Drogobych *see* Drohobych
Drohiczyn Poleski *see* Drahichyn
116 H6 **Drohobych** *Pol.* Drohobycz, *Rus.* Drogobych. L'vivs'ka Oblast', NW Ukraine
Drohobycz *see* Drohobych
Droichead Átha *see* Drogheda
Droicheadna Bandan *see* Bandon
Droichead na Banna *see* Banbridge
Droim Mór *see* Dromore
Drokiya *see* Drochia
103 R13 **Drôme** ◈ *department* E France
103 S13 **Drôme** ≈ E France
97 G15 **Dromore** *Ir.* Droim Mór. SE Northern Ireland, UK
106 A9 **Dronero** Piemonte, NE Italy
102 L12 **Dronne** ≈ SW France
195 Q3 **Dronning Maud Land** *physical region* Antarctica
98 K6 **Dronrijp** *Fris.* Dronryp. Friesland, N Netherlands
Dronryp *see* Dronrijp
98 L9 **Dronten** Flevoland, C Netherlands
Drontheim *see* Trondheim
102 L13 **Dropt** ≈ SW France
149 T4 **Drosh** North-West Frontier Province, NW Pakistan
Drossen *see* Ośno Lubuskie
Drug *see* Durg
118 I12 **Drūkšiai** ◎ NE Lithuania
Druk-yul *see* Bhutan
11 Q16 **Drumheller** Alberta, SW Canada
33 Q10 **Drummond** Montana, NW USA
31 R4 **Drummond Island** *island* Michigan, N USA
Drummond Island *see* Tabiteuea
21 X7 **Drummond, Lake** ◎ Virginia, NE USA
15 P12 **Drummondville** Québec, SE Canada
39 T11 **Drum, Mount** ▲ Alaska, USA
27 O9 **Drumright** Oklahoma, C USA
99 J14 **Drunen** Noord-Brabant, S Netherlands
Druskienniki *see* Druskininkai
119 F15 **Druskininkai** *Pol.* Druskienniki. Alytus, S Lithuania
98 K13 **Druten** Gelderland, SE Netherlands
118 K11 **Druya** Vitsyebskaya Voblasts', NW Belarus
117 S2 **Druzhba** Sums'ka Oblast', NE Ukraine
Druzhba *see* Dostyk, Kazakhstan
Druzhba *see* Pitnak, Uzbekistan
123 R7 **Druzhina** Respublika Sakha (Yakutiya), NE Russian Federation
117 X7 **Druzhkivka** Donets'ka Oblast', E Ukraine
112 E12 **Drvar** Federacija Bosna I Hercegovina, Bosnia and Herzegovina
113 G15 **Drvenik** Split-Dalmacija, SE Croatia
114 K9 **Dryanovo** Gabrovo, N Bulgaria
26 G7 **Dry Cimarron River** ≈ Kansas/Oklahoma, C USA
12 B11 **Dryden** Ontario, C Canada
24 M11 **Dryden** Texas, SW USA
195 Q14 **Drygalski Ice Tongue** *ice feature* Antarctica
118 L11 **Drysa** *Rus.* Drissa. ≈ N Belarus
23 V17 **Dry Tortugas** *island* Florida, SE USA
79 D15 **Dschang** Ouest, W Cameroon
54 J5 **Duaca** Lara, N Venezuela
Duacum *see* Douai
Duala *see* Douala
45 N9 **Duarte, Pico** ▲ C Dominican Republic
140 J5 **Ḑubā** Tabūk, NW Saudi Arabia
Dubai *see* Dubayy
117 N9 **Dubăsari** *Rus.* Dubossary. NE Moldova
117 N9 **Dubăsari Reservoir** ▣ NE Moldova
8 M10 **Dubawnt** ≈ Nunavut, NW Canada
8 L9 **Dubawnt Lake** ◎ Northwest Territories/Nunavut, N Canada
30 L6 **Du Bay, Lake** ▣ Wisconsin, N USA
141 U7 **Dubayy** *Eng.* Dubai. Dubayy, NE UAE
141 W7 **Dubayy** *Eng.* Dubai. ✕ Dubayy, NE UAE
183 R7 **Dubbo** New South Wales, SE Australia
108 G7 **Dübendorf** Zürich, NW Switzerland
97 F18 **Dublin** *Ir.* Baile Átha Cliath; *anc.* Eblana. ● (Ireland), E Ireland
23 U5 **Dublin** Georgia, SE USA
25 R7 **Dublin** Texas, SW USA
97 G18 **Dublin** *Ir.* Baile Átha Cliath; *anc.* Eblana. *cultural region* E Ireland
97 G18 **Dublin Airport** ✕ E Ireland
189 V12 **Dublon** *var.* Tonoas. *island* Chuuk Islands, C Micronesia
126 K2 **Dubna** Moskovskaya Oblast', W Russian Federation
111 G19 **Dubňany** *Ger.* Dubnian. Jihomoravský Kraj, SE Czech Republic
Dubnian *see* Dubňany
111 I19 **Dubnica nad Váhom** *Hung.* Máriatölgyes; *prev.* Dubnicz. Trenčiansky Kraj, W Slovakia
Dubnicz *see* Dubnica nad Váhom
116 K4 **Dubno** Rivnens'ka Oblast', NW Ukraine
18 D13 **Du Bois** Pennsylvania, NE USA
33 R13 **Dubois** Idaho, NW USA
33 T14 **Dubois** Wyoming, C USA
Dubossary *see* Dubăsari
127 O10 **Dubovka** Volgogradskaya Oblast', SW Russian Federation
76 H14 **Dubréka** Guinée-Maritime, SW Guinea
14 B7 **Dubreuilville** Ontario, S Canada
Dubris Portus *see* Dover
119 L20 **Dubrova** *Rus.* Dubrova. Homyel'skaya Voblasts', SE Belarus
126 I5 **Dubrovka** Bryanskaya Oblast', W Russian Federation
113 H16 **Dubrovnik** *It.* Ragusa. Dubrovnik-Neretva, SE Croatia
113 I16 **Dubrovnik** ✕ Dubrovnik-Neretva, SE Croatia
113 F16 **Dubrovnik-Neretva** *off.* Dubrovačko-Neretvanska Županija. ◈ *province* SE Croatia
Dubrovno *see* Dubrowna
116 L2 **Dubrovytsya** Rivnens'ka Oblast', NW Ukraine
119 O14 **Dubrowna** *Rus.* Dubrovno. Vitsyebskaya Voblasts', N Belarus
29 Z13 **Dubuque** Iowa, C USA
118 E12 **Dubysa** ≈ C Lithuania
167 U11 **Đức Cơ** Gia Lai, C Vietnam
191 V12 **Duc de Gloucester, Îles du** *Eng.* Duke of Gloucester Islands. *island group* C French Polynesia
111 C15 **Duchcov** *Ger.* Dux. Ústecký Kraj, NW Czech Republic
37 N3 **Duchesne** Utah, W USA
191 P17 **Ducie Island** *atoll* E Pitcairn Islands
11 W15 **Duck Bay** Manitoba, S Canada
23 X17 **Duck Key** *island* Florida Keys, Florida, SE USA
11 T14 **Duck Lake** Saskatchewan, S Canada
11 V15 **Duck Mountain** ⛰ Manitoba, S Canada
20 I9 **Duck River** ≈ Tennessee, S USA
20 M10 **Ducktown** Tennessee, S USA
167 U10 **Đức Phô** Quang Ngai, C Vietnam
Đức Tho *see* Lin Camh
167 U13 **Đức Trong** *var.* Liên Nghia. Lâm Đông, S Vietnam
D-U-D *see* Dalap-Uliga-Djarrit
99 M25 **Dudelange** *var.* Forge du Sud, *Ger.* Dudelingen. Luxembourg, S Luxembourg
Dudelingen *see* Dudelange
101 J15 **Duderstadt** Niedersachsen, C Germany
153 N15 **Dūdhi** Uttar Pradesh, N India
122 K8 **Dudinka** Taymyrskiy (Dolgano-Nenetskiy) Avtonomnyy Okrug, N Russian Federation
97 L20 **Dudley** C England, UK
154 G13 **Dudna** ≈ C India
76 L16 **Duékoué** W Ivory Coast
104 M5 **Dueñas** Castilla-León, N Spain
104 K4 **Duerna** ≈ NW Spain
105 O6 **Duero** *Port.* Douro. ≈ Portugal/Spain *see also* Douro
Duesseldorf *see* Düsseldorf
21 P12 **Due West** South Carolina, SE USA
195 P11 **Dufek Coast** *physical region* Antarctica
99 H17 **Duffel** Antwerpen, C Belgium
35 S2 **Duffer Peak** ▲ Nevada, W USA
187 Q9 **Duff Islands** *island group* E Solomon Islands
Dufour, Pizzo/Dufour, Punta *see* Dufour Spitze
108 E12 **Dufour Spitze** *It.* Pizzo Dufour, Punta Dufour. ▲ Italy/Switzerland
112 D9 **Duga Resa** Karlovac, C Croatia
22 H5 **Dugdemona River** ≈ Louisiana, S USA
154 J12 **Duggīpar** Mahārāshtra, C India
112 B13 **Dugi Otok** *var.* Isola Grossa, *It.* Isola Lunga. *island* W Croatia
113 F14 **Dugopolje** Split-Dalmacija, S Croatia
160 L8 **Du He** ≈ C China
54 M11 **Duida, Cerro** ▲ S Venezuela
Duinekerke *see* Dunkerque
101 E15 **Duisburg** *prev.* Duisburg-Hamborn. Nordrhein-Westfalen, W Germany
Duisburg-Hamborn *see* Duisburg
99 F14 **Duiveland** *island* SW Netherlands
98 M12 **Duiven** Gelderland, E Netherlands
139 W10 **Dujaylah, Hawr ad** ◎ S Iraq
160 H9 **Dujiangyan** *var.* Guanxian, Guan Xian. Sichuan, C China
81 L18 **Dujuuma** Shabeellaha Hoose, S Somalia
Dūkān *see* Dokan
39 Z14 **Duke Island** *island* Alexander Archipelago, Alaska, USA
Dukelský Priesmy/Dukelský Průsmyk *see* Dukla Pass
Duke of Gloucester Islands *see* Duc de Gloucester, Îles du
81 F14 **Duk Faiwil** Jonglei, SE Sudan
141 T7 **Dukhān** C Qatar
Dukhan Heights *see* Dukhān, Jabal
143 N16 **Dukhān, Jabal** *var.* Dukhan Heights. *hill range* S Qatar
127 Q7 **Dukhovnitskoye** Saratovskaya Oblast', W Russian Federation
126 H4 **Dukhovshchina** Smolenskaya Oblast', W Russian Federation
Dukielska, Przełęcz *see* Dukla Pass
111 N17 **Dukla** Podkarpackie, SE Poland
Duklai Hág *see* Dukla Pass
111 N18 **Dukla Pass** *Cz.* Dukelský Průsmyk, *Ger.* Dukla-Pass, *Hung.* Duklai Hág, *Pol.* Przełęcz Dukielska, *Slvk.* Dukelský Priesmy. *pass* Poland/Slovakia
Dukou *see* Panzhihua
118 I12 **Dūkštas** Utena, E Lithuania
162 M8 **Dulaan** Hentiy, C Mongolia
159 R10 **Dulan** *var.* Qagan Us. Qinghai, C China
37 R8 **Dulce** New Mexico, SW USA
43 N16 **Dulce, Golfo** *gulf* S Costa Rica
Dulce, Golfo *see* Izabal, Lago de
42 K6 **Dulce Nombre de Culmí** Olancho, C Honduras
62 L9 **Dulce, Río** ≈ C Argentina
123 Q9 **Dulgalakh** ≈ NE Russian Federation
114 M8 **Dŭlgopol** Varna, E Bulgaria
153 V14 **Dullabchara** Assam, NE India
20 D3 **Dulles** ✕ (Washington DC) Virginia, NE USA
101 E14 **Dülmen** Nordrhein-Westfalen, W Germany
114 M7 **Dulovo** Silistra, NE Bulgaria
29 W5 **Duluth** Minnesota, N USA
138 H7 **Dūmā** *Fr.* Douma. Dimashq, SW Syria
171 O8 **Dumagasa Point** *headland* Mindanao, S Philippines
171 P6 **Dumaguete** *var.* Dumaguete City. Negros, C Philippines
168 J10 **Dumai** Sumatera, W Indonesia
183 T4 **Dumaresq River** ≈ New South Wales/Queensland, SE Australia
27 W13 **Dumas** Arkansas, C USA
25 N1 **Dumas** Texas, SW USA
138 I7 **Ḑumayr** Dimashq, W Syria
96 I12 **Dumbarton** W Scotland, UK
96 I12 **Dumbarton** *cultural region* C Scotland, UK
187 Q17 **Dumbéa** Province Sud, S New Caledonia
111 K19 **Ďumbier** *Ger.* Djumbir, *Hung.* Gyömbér. ▲ C Slovakia
116 I11 **Dumbrăveni** *Ger.* Elisabethstedt, *Hung.* Erzsébetváros; *prev.* Ebesfalva, Eppeschdorf, Ibaşfalău. Sibiu, C Romania
116 L12 **Dumbrăveni** Vrancea, E Romania
97 J14 **Dumfries** S Scotland, UK
97 J14 **Dumfries** *cultural region* SW Scotland, UK
153 R15 **Dumka** Jhārkhand, NE India
Dümmer *see* Dümmersee
100 G12 **Dümmersee** *var.* Dümmer. ◎ NW Germany
14 J11 **Dumoine** ≈ Québec, SE Canada
14 J10 **Dumoine, Lac** ◎ Québec, SE Canada
195 V16 **Dumont d'Urville** *French research station* Antarctica
195 W15 **Dumont d'Urville Sea** S Pacific Ocean
14 K11 **Dumont, Lac** ◎ Québec, SE Canada
75 W7 **Dumyāt** *Eng.* Damietta. N Egypt
Duna *see* Don, Russian Federation
Duna *see* Danube, C Europe
Düna *see* Western Dvina
Dünaburg *see* Daugavpils
111 J24 **Dunaföldvár** Tolna, C Hungary
Dunaj *see* Wien, Austria
Dunaj *see* Danube, C Europe
111 L18 **Dunajec** ≈ S Poland
111 H21 **Dunajská Streda** *Hung.* Dunaszerdahely. Trnavský Kraj, W Slovakia
Dunapentele *see* Dunaújváros
Dunărea *see* Danube
116 M13 **Dunărea Veche, Braţul** ≈ SE Romania
117 N13 **Dunării, Delta** *delta* SE Romania
Dunaszerdahely *see* Dunajská Streda
111 J23 **Dunaújváros** *prev.* Dunapentele, Sztálinváros. Fejér, C Hungary
Dunav *see* Danube
114 J8 **Dunavska Ravnina** *Eng.* Danubian Plain. *plain* N Bulgaria
114 G7 **Dunavtsi** Vidin, NW Bulgaria
123 S15 **Dunay** Primorskiy Kray, SE Russian Federation
Dunayevtsy *see* Dunayivtsi
116 L7 **Dunayivtsi** *Rus.* Dunayevtsy. Khmel'nyts'ka Oblast', NW Ukraine
185 F22 **Dunback** Otago, South Island, NZ
10 L17 **Duncan** Vancouver Island, British Columbia, SW Canada
37 O15 **Duncan** Arizona, SW USA
26 M12 **Duncan** Oklahoma, C USA
Duncan Island *see* Pinzón, Isla
151 Q20 **Duncan Passage** *strait* Andaman Sea/Bay of Bengal
96 K6 **Duncansby Head** *headland* N Scotland, UK
14 G12 **Dunchurch** Ontario, S Canada
118 D7 **Dundaga** Talsi, NW Latvia
14 G14 **Dundalk** Ontario, S Canada
97 F16 **Dundalk** *Ir.* Dún Dealgan. NE Ireland
21 X3 **Dundalk** Maryland, NE USA
97 F16 **Dundalk Bay** *Ir.* Cuan Dhún Dealgan. *bay* NE Ireland
14 G16 **Dundas** Ontario, S Canada
180 L12 **Dundas, Lake** *salt lake* Western Australia
163 O7 **Dundbürd** Hentiy, E Mongolia
Dún Dealgan *see* Dundalk
15 N13 **Dundee** Québec, SE Canada
83 K22 **Dundee** KwaZulu/Natal, E South Africa
96 K11 **Dundee** E Scotland, UK
31 R10 **Dundee** Michigan, N USA
25 R5 **Dundee** Texas, SW USA
194 H3 **Dundee Island** *island* Antarctica
162 L9 **Dundgovĭ** ◈ *province* C Mongolia
97 G16 **Dundrum Bay** *Ir.* Cuan Dhún Droma. *inlet* NW Irish Sea
11 T15 **Dundurn** Saskatchewan, S Canada
162 E6 **Dund-Us** Hovd, W Mongolia
185 F23 **Dunedin** Otago, South Island, NZ
183 R7 **Dunedoo** New South Wales, SE Australia
97 D14 **Dunfanaghy** *Ir.* Dún Fionnachaidh. NW Ireland
96 J12 **Dunfermline** C Scotland, UK
Dún Fionnachaidh *see* Dunfanaghy
149 V10 **Dunga Bunga** Punjab, E Pakistan
97 F15 **Dungannon** *Ir.* Dún Geanainn. C Northern Ireland, UK
Dun Garbháin *see* Dungarvan
152 F15 **Dūngarpur** Rājasthān, N India
97 E21 **Dungarvan** *Ir.* Dun Garbháin. S Ireland
101 N21 **Dungau** *cultural region* SE Germany
Dún Geanainn *see* Dungannon
97 P23 **Dungeness** *headland* SE England, UK
63 I23 **Dungeness, Punta** *headland* S Argentina
Dungloe *see* Dunglow
97 D14 **Dunglow** *var.* Dungloe, *Ir.* An Clochán Liath. NW Ireland
183 T7 **Dungog** New South Wales, SE Australia
79 O16 **Dungu** Orientale, NE Dem. Rep. Congo
168 L8 **Dungun** *var.* Kuala Dungun. Terengganu, Peninsular Malaysia
80 I6 **Dungûnab** Red Sea, NE Sudan
15 P13 **Dunham** Québec, SE Canada
Dunheved *see* Launceston
Dunholme *see* Durham
163 X10 **Dunhua** Jilin, NE China
159 P8 **Dunhuang** Gansu, N China
182 L12 **Dunkeld** Victoria, SE Australia
103 O1 **Dunkerque** *Eng.* Dunkirk, *Flem.* Duinekerke; *prev.* Dunquerque. Nord, N France
97 K23 **Dunkery Beacon** ▲ SW England, UK
18 C11 **Dunkirk** New York, NE USA
Dunkirk *see* Dunkerque
77 P17 **Dunkwa** SW Ghana
97 G18 **Dún Laoghaire** *Eng.* Dunleary; *prev.* Kingstown. E Ireland
29 S14 **Dunlap** Iowa, C USA
20 L10 **Dunlap** Tennessee, S USA
Dunleary *see* Dún Laoghaire
Dún Mánmhaí *see* Dunmanway
97 B21 **Dunmanway** *Ir.* Dún Mánmhaí. SW Ireland
18 I13 **Dunmore** Pennsylvania, NE USA
21 U10 **Dunn** North Carolina, SE USA
Dún na nGall *see* Donegal
23 V11 **Dunnellon** Florida, SE USA
96 J6 **Dunnet Head** *headland* N Scotland, UK
29 N14 **Dunning** Nebraska, C USA
65 B24 **Dunnose Head Settlement** West Falkland, Falkland Islands
14 G17 **Dunnville** Ontario, S Canada
Dún Pádraig *see* Downpatrick
Dunquerque *see* Dunkerque
Dunqulah *see* Dongola
96 L12 **Duns** SE Scotland, UK
29 N2 **Dunseith** North Dakota, N USA
35 N2 **Dunsmuir** California, W USA
97 N21 **Dunstable** *Lat.* Durocobrivae. E England, UK
185 D21 **Dunstan Mountains** ⛰ South Island, NZ
103 O9 **Dun-sur-Auron** Cher, C France
185 F21 **Duntroon** Canterbury, South Island, NZ
149 T10 **Dunyāpur** Punjab, E Pakistan
163 U5 **Duobukur He** ≈ NE China
163 R12 **Duolun** *var.* Dolonnur. Nei Mongol Zizhiqu, N China
167 Q14 **Dương Đông** Kiên Giang, S Vietnam
114 G10 **Dupnitsa** *prev.* Marek, Stanke Dimitrov. Kyustendil, W Bulgaria
28 L8 **Dupree** South Dakota, N USA
33 Q7 **Dupuyer** Montana, NW USA
141 Y11 **Duqm** *var.* Daqm. E Oman
63 F23 **Duque de York, Isla** *island* S Chile

◆ Country ● Country Capital ◇ Dependent Territory ○ Dependent Territory Capital ◈ Administrative Region ✕ International Airport ▲ Mountain ⛰ Mountain Range ⩚ Volcano ≈ River ◎ Lake ▣ Reservoir

181 N4 **Durack Range** ▲ Western Australia
136 K10 **Durağan** Sinop, N Turkey
103 S15 **Durance** ≈ SE France
31 R9 **Durand** Michigan, N USA
30 I6 **Durand** Wisconsin, N USA
40 K10 **Durango** *var.* Victoria de Durango. Durango, W Mexico
105 P3 **Durango** País Vasco, N Spain
37 Q8 **Durango** Colorado, C USA
40 J9 **Durango** ◈ *state* C Mexico
114 O7 **Durankulak** *Rom.* Răcari; *prev.* Blatnitsa, Duranulac. Dobrich, NE Bulgaria
22 L4 **Durant** Mississippi, S USA
27 P13 **Durant** Oklahoma, C USA
Duranulac *see* Durankulak
105 N6 **Duratón** ≈ N Spain
61 E19 **Durazno** *var.* San Pedro de Durazno. Durazno, C Uruguay
61 E19 **Durazno** ◈ *department* C Uruguay
Durazzo *see* Durrës
83 K23 **Durban** *var.* Port Natal. KwaZulu/Natal, E South Africa
83 K23 **Durban** × KwaZulu/Natal, E South Africa
118 C9 **Durbe** *Ger.* Durben. Liepāja, W Latvia
Durben *see* Durbe
99 K21 **Durbuy** Luxembourg, SE Belgium
105 N15 **Dúrcal** Andalucía, S Spain
112 F8 **Đurđevac** *Ger.* Sankt Georgen, *Hung.* Szentgyörgy; *prev.* Djurdjevac, Gjurgjevac. Koprivnica-Križevci, N Croatia
113 K15 **Đurđevica Tara** Montenegro, SW Serbia and Montenegro (Yugo.)
97 L24 **Durdle Door** *natural arch* S England, UK
158 L3 **Düre** Xinjiang Uygur Zizhiqu, W China
101 D16 **Düren** *anc.* Marcodurum. Nordrhein-Westfalen, W Germany
154 K12 **Durg** *prev.* Drug. Chhattīsgarh, C India
153 U13 **Durgapur** Dhaka, N Bangladesh
153 R15 **Durgāpur** West Bengal, NE India
14 F14 **Durham** Ontario, S Canada
97 M14 **Durham** *hist.* Dunholme. N England, UK
21 U9 **Durham** North Carolina, SE USA
97 L15 **Durham** *cultural region* N England, UK
168 J10 **Duri** Sumatera, W Indonesia
Duria Major *see* Dora Baltea
Duria Minor *see* Dora Riparia
Durlas *see* Thurles
141 P8 **Ḑurmā** Ar Riyāḑ, C Saudi Arabia
113 J15 **Durmitor** ▲ N Serbia and Montenegro (Yugo.)
96 H6 **Durness** N Scotland, UK
109 Y3 **Dürnkrut** Niederösterreich, E Austria
Durnovaria *see* Dorchester
Durobrivae *see* Rochester
Durocasses *see* Dreux
Durocobrivae *see* Dunstable
Durocortorum *see* Reims
Durostorum *see* Silistra
Durovernum *see* Canterbury
113 K20 **Durrës** *var.* Durrësi, Dursi, *It.* Durazzo, *SCr.* Drač, *Turk.* Draç. Durrës, W Albania
113 K19 **Durrës** ◈ *district* W Albania
Durrësi *see* Durrës
97 A21 **Dursey Island** *Ir.* Oileán Baoi. *island* SW Ireland
Dursi *see* Durrës
Duru *see* Wuchuan
Durud *see* Dō Rūd
14 P12 **Durusu** İstanbul, NW Turkey
14 O12 **Durusu Gölü** ◎ NW Turkey
138 I9 **Durūz, Jabal ad** ▲ SW Syria
184 K13 **D'Urville Island** *island* C NZ
171 X12 **D'Urville, Tanjung** *headland* Papua, E Indonesia
146 H14 **Duşak** *Rus.* Dushak. Ahal Welaýaty, S Turkmenistan
Dusa Mareb/Dusa Marreb *see* Dhuusa Marreeb
118 I11 **Dusetos** Utena, NE Lithuania
Dushak *see* Duşak
160 K12 **Dushan** Guizhou, S China
147 P13 **Dushanbe** *var.* Dyushambe; *prev.* Stalinabad, *Taj.* Stalinobod. ● (Tajikistan) W Tajikistan
147 P13 **Dushanbe** × W Tajikistan
137 T9 **Dushet'i** E Georgia
18 H13 **Dushore** Pennsylvania, NE USA
185 A23 **Dusky Sound** *sound* South Island, NZ
101 E15 **Düsseldorf** *var.* Duesseldorf. Nordrhein-Westfalen, W Germany
147 P14 **Dŭsti** *Rus.* Dusti. SW Tajikistan
194 **Dustin Island** *island* Antarctica
Dutch East Indies *see* Indonesia
Dutch Guiana *see* Surinam
38 L17 **Dutch Harbor** Unalaska Island, Alaska, USA
36 J3 **Dutch Mount** ▲ Utah, W USA
Dutch New Guinea *see* Papua
Dutch West Indies *see* Netherlands Antilles
83 H20 **Dutlwe** Kweneng, S Botswana
125 U8 **Dutovo** Respublika Komi, NW Russian Federation
77 V13 **Dutsan Wai** *var.* Dutsen Wai. Kaduna, C Nigeria
77 W13 **Dutse** Jigawa, N Nigeria
Dutsen Wai *see* Dutsan Wai
Duttia *see* Datia
14 E17 **Dutton** Ontario, S Canada
36 L7 **Dutton, Mount** ▲ Utah, W USA
162 E7 **Duut** Hovd, W Mongolia
14 K11 **Duval, Lac** ◎ Québec, SE Canada
127 W3 **Duvan** Respublika Bashkortostan, W Russian Federation
138 L9 **Duwaykhilat Satīḩ ar Ruwayshid** *seasonal river* SE Jordan
Dux *see* Duchcov
160 J13 **Duyang Shan** ▲ S China
167 T14 **Duyên Hai** Tra Vinh, S Vietnam
160 K12 **Duyun** Guizhou, S China
136 G11 **Düzce** Bolu, NW Turkey
Duzdab *see* Zāhedān
Duzenkyr, Khrebet *see* Duzkyr, Khrebet
146 I16 **Duzkyr, Khrebet** *prev.* Khrebet Duzenkyr. ▲ S Turkmenistan
Dvina Bay *see* Chëshskaya Guba
Dvinsk *see* Daugavpils
126 L7 **Dvinskaya Guba** *bay* NW Russian Federation
112 E10 **Dvor** Sisak-Moslavina, C Croatia
117 W5 **Dvorichna** Kharkivs'ka Oblast', E Ukraine
111 F16 **Dvůr Králové nad Labem** *Ger.* Königinhof an der Elbe. Královéhradecký Kraj, NE Czech Republic
154 A10 **Dwārka** Gujarāt, W India
30 M12 **Dwight** Illinois, N USA
98 N8 **Dwingeloo** Drenthe, NE Netherlands
33 N10 **Dworshak Reservoir** ⊡ Idaho, NW USA
Dyal *see* Dyaul Island
Dyanev *see* Galkynyş
Dyatlovo *see* Dzyatlava
186 G5 **Dyaul Island** *var.* Djaul, Dyal. *island* NE PNG
20 G8 **Dyer** Tennessee, S USA
9 S5 **Dyer, Cape** *headland* Baffin Island, Nunavut, NE Canada
20 F8 **Dyersburg** Tennessee, S USA
29 Y13 **Dyersville** Iowa, C USA
97 I21 **Dyfed** *cultural region* SW Wales, UK
Dyfrdwy, Afon *see* Dee
Dyhernfurth *see* Brzeg Dolny
111 E19 **Dyje** *var.* Thaya. ≈ Austria/Czech Republic *see also* Thaya
117 T5 **Dykanska** Poltavs'ka Oblast', C Ukraine
127 N16 **Dykhtau** ▲ SW Russian Federation
111 A16 **Dyleń** *Ger.* Tillenberg. ▲ NW Czech Republic
110 K9 **Dylewska Góra** ▲ N Poland
117 O4 **Dymer** Kyyivs'ka Oblast', N Ukraine
117 W7 **Dymytrov** *Rus.* Dimitrov. Donets'ka Oblast', SE Ukraine
111 O17 **Dynów** Podkarpackie, SE Poland
29 X13 **Dysart** Iowa, C USA
Dysna *see* Dzisna
115 D18 **Dytikí Ellás** *Eng.* Greece West. ◈ *region* C Greece
115 C14 **Dytikí Makedonía** *Eng.* Macedonia West. ◈ *region* N Greece
Dyurmen'tyube *see* Dermentobe
127 U4 **Dyurtyuli** Respublika Bashkortostan, W Russian Federation
Dyushambe *see* Dushanbe
162 I7 **Dzaanhushuu** Arhangay, C Mongolia
Dza Chu *see* Mekong
162 I8 **Dzadgay** Bayanhongor, C Mongolia
162 H8 **Dzag** Bayanhongor, C Mongolia
162 H10 **Dzalaa** Bayanhongor, C Mongolia
172 J14 **Dzaoudzi** E Mayotte
Dzaudzhikau *see* Vladikavkaz
162 G7 **Dzavhan** ◈ *province* NW Mongolia
162 G7 **Dzavhan Gol** ≈ NW Mongolia
162 J7 **Dzegstey** Arhangay, C Mongolia
127 O3 **Dzerzhinsk** Nizhegorodskaya Oblast', W Russian Federation
Dzerzhinsk *see* Dzyarzhynsk, Belarus
Dzerzhinsk *see* Dzerzhyns'k, Ukraine
Dzerzhinskiy *see* Nar'yan-Mar
Dzerzhinskoye *see* Tokzhaylau
117 X7 **Dzerzhyns'k** *Rus.* Dzerzhinsk. Donets'ka Oblast', SE Ukraine
116 M5 **Dzerzhyns'k** Zhytomyrs'ka Oblast', N Ukraine
Dzhailgan *see* Jayilgan
145 N14 **Dzhalagash** *Kaz.* Zhalashash. Kzylorda, S Kazakhstan
147 T10 **Dzhalal-Abad** *Kir.* Jalal-Abad. Dzhalal-Abadskaya Oblast', W Kyrgyzstan
147 S9 **Dzhalal-Abadskaya Oblast'** *Kir.* Jalal-Abad Oblasty. ◈ *province* W Kyrgyzstan
Dzhalilabad *see* Cälilabad
Dzhambeyty *see* Zhympity
Dzhambulskaya Oblast' *see* Zhambyl
144 D9 **Dzhanibek** *var.* Dzhanybek, *Kaz.* Zhanibek, Zhänibek. Zapadnyy Kazakhstan, W Kazakhstan
Dzhankel'dy *see* Jongeldi
117 T12 **Dzhankoy** Respublika Krym, S Ukraine
145 V14 **Dzhansugurov** *Kaz.* Zhansügirov. Almaty, SE Kazakhstan
147 R9 **Dzhany-Bazar** *var.* Yangibazar. Dzhalal-Abadskaya Oblast', W Kyrgyzstan
Dzhanybek *see* Dzhanibek
123 P8 **Dzhardzhan** Respublika Sakha (Yakutiya), NE Russian Federation
Dzharkurgan *see* Jarqo'rg'on
117 S11 **Dzharylhats'ka Zatoka** *gulf* S Ukraine
Dzhayilgan *see* Jayilgan
Dzhebel *see* Jebel
147 T14 **Dzhelandy** SE Tajikistan
147 Y7 **Dzhergalan** *Kir.* Jyrgalan. Issyk-Kul'skaya Oblast', NE Kyrgyzstan
Dzherzinskoye *see* Tokzhaylau
Dzhetygara *see* Zhitikara
Dzhetysay *see* Zhetysay.
Dzhezkazgan *see* Zhezkazgan
Dzhigirbent *see* Jigerbent
Dzhirgatal' *see* Jirgatol
Dzhizak *see* Jizzakh
Dzhizakskaya Oblast' *see* Jizzax Viloyati
123 P8 **Dzhugdzhur, Khrebet** ▲ E Russian Federation
Dzhul'fa *see* Culfa
Dzhuma *see* Juma
145 W14 **Dzhungarskiy Alatau** ▲ China/Kazakhstan
144 M14 **Dzhusaly** *Kaz.* Zholsaly. Kzylorda, SW Kazakhstan
146 J12 **Dzhynlykum, Peski** *desert* E Turkmenistan
110 L9 **Działdowo** Warmińsko-Mazurskie, C Poland
111 L16 **Działoszyce** Świętokrzyskie, C Poland
41 X11 **Dzidzantún** Yucatán, E Mexico
111 G15 **Dzierżoniów** *Ger.* Reichenbach. Dolnośląskie, SW Poland
41 X11 **Dzilam de Bravo** Yucatán, E Mexico
118 L12 **Dzisna** *Rus.* Disna. Vitsyebskaya Voblasts', N Belarus
118 K12 **Dzisna** *Lith.* Dysna, *Rus.* Disna. ≈ Belarus/Lithuania
119 G20 **Dzivin** *Rus.* Divin. Brestskaya Voblasts', SW Belarus
119 M15 **Dzmitravichy** *Rus.* Dmitrovichi. Minskaya Voblasts', C Belarus
162 M8 **Dzogsool** Töv, C Mongolia
Dzungarian Basin *see* Junggar Pendi
162 G5 **Dzür** Dzavhan, W Mongolia
163 Q8 **Dzüünbulag** Dornod, E Mongolia
163 O8 **Dzüünbulag** Sühbaatar, E Mongolia
162 H7 **Dzuunmod** Dzavhan, C Mongolia
162 L8 **Dzuunmod** Töv, C Mongolia
Dzüün Soyonï Nuruu *see* Eastern Sayans
162 F8 **Dzüyl** Govĭ-Altay, SW Mongolia
Dzvina *see* Western Dvina
119 J16 **Dzyarzhynsk** *Rus.* Dzerzhinsk; *prev.* Kaydanovo. Minskaya Voblasts', C Belarus
119 H17 **Dzyatlava** *Pol.* Zdzięcioł, *Rus.* Dyatlovo. Hrodzyenskaya Voblasts', W Belarus

E

E *see* Hubei
Éadan Doire *see* Edenderry
37 W6 **Eads** Colorado, C USA
37 O13 **Eagar** Arizona, SW USA
39 T8 **Eagle** Alaska, USA
13 S8 **Eagle** ≈ Newfoundland and Labrador, E Canada
10 I3 **Eagle** ≈ Yukon Territory, NW Canada
29 T7 **Eagle Bend** Minnesota, N USA
28 M8 **Eagle Butte** South Dakota, N USA
29 V12 **Eagle Grove** Iowa, C USA
19 R2 **Eagle Lake** Maine, NE USA
25 U11 **Eagle Lake** Texas, SW USA
12 A11 **Eagle Lake** ◎ Ontario, S Canada
35 P3 **Eagle Lake** ◎ California, W USA
19 R3 **Eagle Lake** ◎ Maine, NE USA
29 Y3 **Eagle Mountain** ▲ Minnesota, N USA
25 T6 **Eagle Mountain Lake** ⊡ Texas, SW USA
37 S9 **Eagle Nest Lake** ⊡ New Mexico, SW USA
25 P13 **Eagle Pass** Texas, SW USA
65 C25 **Eagle Passage** *passage* SW Atlantic Ocean
35 R8 **Eagle Peak** ▲ California, W USA
35 Q2 **Eagle Peak** ▲ California, W USA
37 P13 **Eagle Peak** ▲ New Mexico, SW USA
10 I4 **Eagle Plain** Yukon Territory, NW Canada
32 G15 **Eagle Point** Oregon, NW USA
186 P10 **Eagle Point** *headland* SE PNG
39 R11 **Eagle River** Alaska, USA
30 M2 **Eagle River** Michigan, N USA
30 L4 **Eagle River** Wisconsin, N USA
21 S6 **Eagle Rock** Virginia, NE USA
36 J13 **Eagletail Mountains** ▲ Arizona, SW USA
167 U12 **Ea Hleo** Đăc Lăc, S Vietnam
167 U12 **Ea Kar** Đăc Lăc, S Vietnam
Eanjum *see* Anjum
Eanodat *see* Enontekiö
12 B10 **Ear Falls** Ontario, C Canada
27 X10 **Earle** Arkansas, C USA
35 R12 **Earlimart** California, W USA
20 I6 **Earlington** Kentucky, S USA
14 H8 **Earlton** Ontario, S Canada
29 T13 **Early** Iowa, C USA
96 J11 **Earn** ≈ N Scotland, UK
185 C21 **Earnslaw, Mount** ▲ South Island, NZ
24 M4 **Earth** Texas, SW USA
21 P11 **Easley** South Carolina, SE USA
East *see* Est
East Açores Fracture Zone *see* East Azores Fracture Zone
97 P19 **East Anglia** *physical region* E England, UK
15 Q12 **East Angus** Québec, SE Canada
East Antarctica *see* Greater Antarctica
18 E10 **East Aurora** New York, NE USA
East Australian Basin *see* Tasman Basin
East Azerbaijan *see* Āzarbāyjān-e Sharqī
64 L9 **East Azores Fracture Zone** *var.* East Açores Fracture Zone. *tectonic feature* E Atlantic Ocean
22 M11 **East Bay** *bay* Louisiana, S USA
25 V11 **East Bernard** Texas, SW USA
29 V8 **East Bethel** Minnesota, N USA
East Borneo *see* Kalimantan Timur
97 P23 **Eastbourne** SE England, UK
15 R11 **East-Broughton** Québec, SE Canada
44 M5 **East Caicos** *island* E Turks and Caicos Islands
184 R7 **East Cape** *headland* North Island, NZ
192 P4 **East China Sea** *Chin.* Dong Hai. *sea* W Pacific Ocean
97 P19 **East Dereham** E England, UK
30 J9 **East Dubuque** Illinois, N USA
11 S17 **Eastend** Saskatchewan, S Canada
193 S10 **Easter Fracture Zone** *tectonic feature* E Pacific Ocean
Easter Island *see* Pascua, Isla de
81 J18 **Eastern** ◈ *province* Kenya
153 Q12 **Eastern** ◈ *zone* E Nepal
82 L13 **Eastern** ◈ *province* E Zambia
83 H24 **Eastern Cape** *off.* Eastern Cape Province, *Afr.* Oos-Kaap. ◈ *province* SE South Africa
Eastern Desert *see* Sahara el Sharqîya
81 F15 **Eastern Equatoria** ◈ *state* SE Sudan
Eastern Euphrates *see* Murat Nehri
155 J17 **Eastern Ghats** ▲ SE India
186 E7 **Eastern Highlands** ◈ *province* C PNG
155 K25 **Eastern Province** ◈ *province* E Sri Lanka
Eastern Region *see* Ash Sharqīyah
122 L13 **Eastern Sayans** *Mong.* Dzüün Soyonï Nuruu, *Rus.* Vostochnyy Sayan. ▲ Mongolia/Russian Federation
Eastern Scheldt *see* Oosterschelde
Eastern Sierra Madre *see* Madre Oriental, Sierra
Eastern Transvaal *see* Mpumalanga
11 W14 **Easterville** Manitoba, C Canada
Easterwâlde *see* Oosterwolde
63 M23 **East Falkland** *var.* Isla Soledad. *island* E Falkland Islands
19 P12 **East Falmouth** Massachusetts, NE USA
East Fayu *see* Fayu
East Flanders *see* Oost Vlaanderen
39 S6 **East Fork Chandalar River** ≈ Alaska, USA
29 U12 **East Fork Des Moines River** ≈ Iowa/Minnesota, C USA
East Frisian Islands *see* Ostfriesische Inseln
18 K10 **East Glenville** New York, NE USA
29 R4 **East Grand Forks** Minnesota, N USA
97 O23 **East Grinstead** SE England, UK
18 M12 **East Hartford** Connecticut, NE USA
18 M13 **East Haven** Connecticut, NE USA
173 T9 **East Indiaman Ridge** *undersea feature* E Indian Ocean
East Java *see* Jawa Timur
31 Q6 **East Jordan** Michigan, N USA
East Kalimantan *see* Kalimantan Timur
East Kazakhstan *see* Vostochnyy Kazakhstan
96 I12 **East Kilbride** S Scotland, UK
25 R7 **Eastland** Texas, SW USA
31 Q9 **East Lansing** Michigan, N USA
35 X11 **East Las Vegas** Nevada, W USA
97 M23 **Eastleigh** S England, UK
31 V12 **East Liverpool** Ohio, N USA
83 J25 **East London** *Afr.* Oos-Londen; *prev.* Emonti, Port Rex. Eastern Cape, S South Africa
96 K12 **East Lothian** *cultural region* SE Scotland, UK
12 I10 **Eastmain** Québec, E Canada
12 J10 **Eastmain** ≈ Québec, C Canada
15 P13 **Eastman** Québec, SE Canada
23 U6 **Eastman** Georgia, SE USA
192 I7 **East Mariana Basin** *undersea feature* W Pacific Ocean
30 K11 **East Moline** Illinois, N USA
186 H7 **East New Britain** ◈ *province* E PNG
29 T15 **East Nishnabotna River** ≈ Iowa, C USA
197 V12 **East Novaya Zemlya Trough** *var.* Novaya Zemlya Trough. *undersea feature* W Kara Sea
East Nusa Tenggara *see* Nusa Tenggara Timur
21 X4 **Easton** Maryland, NE USA
18 I14 **Easton** Pennsylvania, NE USA
193 R16 **East Pacific Rise** *undersea feature* E Pacific Ocean
East Pakistan *see* Bangladesh
31 V12 **East Palestine** Ohio, N USA
30 L12 **East Peoria** Illinois, N USA
23 S3 **East Point** Georgia, SE USA
19 U6 **Eastport** Maine, NE USA
27 Z8 **East Prairie** Missouri, C USA
19 O12 **East Providence** Rhode Island, NE USA
20 L11 **East Ridge** Tennessee, S USA
97 N16 **East Riding** *cultural region* N England, UK
18 F9 **East Rochester** New York, NE USA
30 K15 **East Saint Louis** Illinois, N USA
65 K21 **East Scotia Basin** *undersea feature* SE Scotia Sea
157 Y7 **East Sea** *var.* Sea of Japan, *Rus.* Yapanskoye More. *sea* NW Pacific Ocean *see also* Japan, Sea of
186 B6 **East Sepik** ◈ *province* NW PNG
173 N4 **East Sheba Ridge** *undersea feature* W Arabian Sea
East Siberian Sea *see* Vostochno-Sibirskoye More
18 I14 **East Stroudsburg** Pennsylvania, NE USA
East Tasmanian Rise/East Tasmania Plateau/East Tasmania Rise *see* East Tasman Plateau
192 I12 **East Tasman Plateau** *var.* East Tasmanian Rise, East Tasmania Plateau, East Tasmania Rise. *undersea feature* SW Tasman Sea
64 L7 **East Thulean Rise** *undersea feature* N Atlantic Ocean
171 R16 **East Timor** *var* Loro Sae *prev.* Portuguese Timor, Timor Timur ◆ *country* SE Asia
21 Y6 **Eastville** Virginia, NE USA
35 R7 **East Walker River** ≈ California/Nevada, W USA
182 D1 **Eateringinna Creek** ≈ South Australia
37 T3 **Eaton** Colorado, C USA
15 Q12 **Eaton** ≈ Québec, SE Canada
11 S16 **Eatonia** Saskatchewan, S Canada
31 Q10 **Eaton Rapids** Michigan, N USA
23 U4 **Eatonton** Georgia, SE USA
32 H9 **Eatonville** Washington, NW USA
30 J6 **Eau Claire** Wisconsin, N USA
Eau Claire, Lac à L' *see* St.Clair, Lake
12 J7 **Eau Claire, Lac à l'** ◎ Québec, SE Canada
30 I6 **Eau Claire River** ≈ Wisconsin, N USA
188 J16 **Eauripik Atoll** *atoll* Caroline Islands, C Micronesia
192 H7 **Eauripik Rise** *undersea feature* W Pacific Ocean
102 K15 **Eauze** Gers, S France
41 P11 **Ébano** San Luis Potosí, C Mexico
97 K21 **Ebbw Vale** SE Wales, UK
79 E17 **Ebebiyin** NE Equatorial Guinea
95 H22 **Ebeltoft** Århus, C Denmark
109 X5 **Ebenfurth** Niederösterreich, E Austria
18 D14 **Ebensburg** Pennsylvania, NE USA
109 S5 **Ebensee** Oberösterreich, N Austria
101 H20 **Eberbach** Baden-Württemberg, SW Germany
121 U8 **Eber Gölü** *salt lake* C Turkey
109 U9 **Eberndorf** *Slvn.* Dobrla Vas. Kärnten, S Austria
109 R4 **Eberschwang** Oberösterreich, N Austria
100 O11 **Eberswalde-Finow** Brandenburg, E Germany
Ebesfalva *see* Dumbrăveni
165 T4 **Ebetsu** *var.* Ebetu. Hokkaidō, NE Japan
Ebetu *see* Ebetsu
Ebinayon *see* Evinayong
158 I4 **Ebinur Hu** ◎ NW China
138 I3 **Ebla** *Ar.* Tell Mardīkh. *site of ancient city* Idlib, NW Syria
Eblana *see* Dublin
108 H7 **Ebnat** Sankt Gallen, NE Switzerland
107 L18 **Eboli** Campania, S Italy
79 E16 **Ebolowa** Sud, S Cameroon
79 N21 **Ebombo** Kasai Oriental, C Dem. Rep. Congo
189 T9 **Ebon Atoll** *var.* Epoon. *atoll* Ralik Chain, S Marshall Islands
Ebora *see* Évora
Eboracum *see* York
Eborodunum *see* Yverdon
101 J19 **Ebrach** Bayern, C Germany
109 X5 **Ebreichsdorf** Niederösterreich, E Austria
105 S6 **Ebro** ≈ NE Spain
105 N3 **Ebro, Embalse del** ⊡ N Spain
120 G7 **Ebro Fan** *undersea feature* W Mediterranean Sea
Eburacum *see* York
Ebusus *see* Eivissa
99 F20 **Écaussinnes-d'Enghien** Hainaut, SW Belgium
Ecbatana *see* Hamadān
21 Q6 **Eccles** West Virginia, NE USA
115 L14 **Eceabat** Çanakkale, NW Turkey
171 O2 **Echague** Luzon, N Philippines
Ech Cheliff/Ech Chleff *see* Chlef
Echeng *see* Ezhou
115 C18 **Echinádes** *island group* W Greece
114 J12 **Echínos** *var.* Ehinos, Ekhínos. Anatolikí Makedonía kai Thráki, NE Greece
164 J12 **Echizen-misaki** *headland* Honshū, SW Japan
Echmiadzin *see* Ejmiatsin
8 J8 **Echo Bay** Northwest Territories, NW Canada
35 Y11 **Echo Bay** Nevada, W USA
36 L9 **Echo Cliffs** *cliff* Arizona, SW USA
14 C10 **Echo Lake** ◎ Ontario, S Canada
35 Q7 **Echo Summit** ▲ California, W USA
14 L8 **Échouani, Lac** ◎ Québec, SE Canada
99 L17 **Echt** Limburg, SE Netherlands
101 H22 **Echterdingen** × (Stuttgart) Baden-Württemberg, SW Germany
99 N24 **Echternach** Grevenmacher, E Luxembourg
183 N11 **Echuca** Victoria, SE Australia
104 L14 **Ecija** *anc.* Astigi. Andalucía, SW Spain
Eckengraf *see* Viesīte
100 I7 **Eckernförde** Schleswig-Holstein, N Germany
100 J7 **Eckernförder Bucht** *inlet* N Germany
102 L7 **Écommoy** Sarthe, NW France
14 L10 **Écorce, Lac de l'** ◎ Québec, SE Canada
15 Q8 **Écorces, Rivière aux** ≈ Québec, SE Canada
56 C7 **Ecuador** *off.* Republic of Ecuador. ◆ *republic* NW South America
80 L10 **Ed** *var.* Edd. SE Eritrea
95 I17 **Ed** Västra Götaland, S Sweden
98 I9 **Edam** Noord-Holland, C Netherlands
96 K4 **Eday** *island* NE Scotland, UK
25 S17 **Edcouch** Texas, SW USA
Edd *see* Ed
80 C11 **Ed Da'ein** Southern Darfur, W Sudan
80 G11 **Ed Damazin** *var.* Ad Damazīn. Blue Nile, E Sudan
80 G8 **Ed Damer** *var.* Ad Damar, Ad Dāmir. River Nile, NE Sudan
80 E8 **Ed Debba** Northern, N Sudan
80 F10 **Ed Dueim** *var.* Ad Duwaym, Ad Duwēm. White Nile, C Sudan
183 Q16 **Eddystone Point** *headland* Tasmania, SE Australia
97 I25 **Eddystone Rocks** *rocks* SW England, UK
29 W15 **Eddyville** Iowa, C USA
20 H7 **Eddyville** Kentucky, S USA
98 L12 **Ede** Gelderland, C Netherlands
77 T16 **Ede** Osun, SW Nigeria
79 D16 **Edéa** Littoral, SW Cameroon
111 M20 **Edelény** Borsod-Abaúj-Zemplén, NE Hungary
183 R12 **Eden** New South Wales, SE Australia
21 T8 **Eden** North Carolina, SE USA
25 P9 **Eden** Texas, SW USA
97 K14 **Eden** ≈ NW England, UK
83 I23 **Edenburg** Free State, C South Africa
185 D24 **Edendale** Southland, South Island, NZ
97 E18 **Edenderry** *Ir.* Éadan Doire. C Ireland
182 L11 **Edenhope** Victoria, SE Australia
21 X8 **Edenton** North Carolina, SE USA
101 G16 **Eder** ≈ NW Germany
101 H15 **Edersee** ◎ W Germany
Edessa *see* Şanlıurfa
114 E13 **Édessa** *var.* Édhessa. Kentrikí Makedonía, N Greece
Edfu *see* Idfu
29 P16 **Edgar** Nebraska, C USA
19 P13 **Edgartown** Martha's Vineyard, Massachusetts, NE USA
39 X13 **Edgecumbe, Mount** ▲ Baranof Island, Alaska, USA
21 Q13 **Edgefield** South Carolina, SE USA
29 P6 **Edgeley** North Dakota, N USA
28 I11 **Edgemont** South Dakota, N USA
92 O3 **Edgeøya** *island* S Svalbard
27 Q4 **Edgerton** Kansas, C USA
29 S10 **Edgerton** Minnesota, N USA
21 X3 **Edgewood** Maryland, NE USA
25 V6 **Edgewood** Texas, SW USA
Édhessa *see* Édessa
29 V9 **Edina** Minnesota, N USA
27 U2 **Edina** Missouri, C USA
25 S17 **Edinburg** Texas, SW USA
65 M24 **Edinburgh** *var.* Settlement of Edinburgh. ○ (Tristan da Cunha) NW Tristan da Cunha
96 J12 **Edinburgh** ● S Scotland, UK
31 P14 **Edinburgh** Indiana, N USA
96 J12 **Edinburgh** × S Scotland, UK
116 L8 **Edineţ** *var.* Edineţi, *Rus.* Yedintsy. NW Moldova
Edineţi *see* Edineţ
Edingen *see* Enghien
136 B9 **Edirne** *Eng.* Adrianople; *anc.* Adrianopolis, Hadrianopolis. Edirne, NW Turkey
136 B11 **Edirne** ◈ *province* NW Turkey
18 K15 **Edison** New Jersey, NE USA
21 S15 **Edisto Island** South Carolina, SE USA
21 R14 **Edisto River** ≈ South Carolina, SE USA
33 S10 **Edith, Mount** ▲ Montana, NW USA
27 N10 **Edmond** Oklahoma, C USA
32 H8 **Edmonds** Washington, NW USA
11 Q14 **Edmonton** Alberta, SW Canada

◆ Country ● Country Capital ◇ Dependent Territory ○ Dependent Territory Capital ◈ Administrative Region × International Airport ▲ Mountain ▲ Mountain Range Volcano ≈ River ◎ Lake ⊡ Reservoir

20 K7 **Edmonton** Kentucky, S USA
11 Q14 **Edmonton** × Alberta, SW Canada
29 P3 **Edmore** North Dakota, N USA
13 N13 **Edmundston** New Brunswick, SE Canada
25 U12 **Edna** Texas, SW USA
39 X14 **Edna Bay** Kosciusko Island, Alaska, USA
77 U16 **Edo** ◈ *state* S Nigeria
106 F6 **Edolo** Lombardia, N Italy
64 L6 **Edoras Bank** *undersea feature* C Atlantic Ocean
96 G7 **Edrachillis Bay** *bay* NW Scotland, UK
136 B12 **Edremit** Balıkesir, NW Turkey
136 B12 **Edremit Körfezi** *gulf* NW Turkey
95 P14 **Edsbro** Stockholm, C Sweden
95 N18 **Edsbruk** Kalmar, S Sweden
94 M12 **Edsbyn** Gävleborg, C Sweden
11 O14 **Edson** Alberta, SW Canada
62 K13 **Eduardo Castex** La Pampa, C Argentina
58 F12 **Eduardo Gomes** × (Manaus) Amazonas, NW Brazil
Edwardesabad *see* Bannu
81 E19 **Edward, Lake** *var.* Albert Edward Nyanza, Edward Nyanza, Lac Idi Amin, Lake Rutanzige. ⊚ Uganda/Dem. Rep. Congo
Edward Nyanza *see* Edward, Lake
22 K5 **Edwards** Mississippi, S USA
25 O10 **Edwards Plateau** *plain* Texas, SW USA
30 J11 **Edwards River** ≈ Illinois, N USA
30 K15 **Edwardsville** Illinois, N USA
195 O13 **Edward VII Peninsula** *peninsula* Antarctica
195 X4 **Edward VIII Gulf** *bay* Antarctica
10 J11 **Edziza, Mount** ▲ British Columbia, W Canada
8 K10 **Edzo** *prev.* Rae-Edzo. Northwest Territories, NW Canada
39 N12 **Eek** Alaska, USA
99 D16 **Eeklo** *var.* Eekloo. Oost-Vlaanderen, NW Belgium
Eekloo *see* Eeklo
39 N12 **Eek River** ≈ Alaska, USA
98 N6 **Eelde** Drenthe, NE Netherlands
34 L5 **Eel River** ≈ California, W USA
31 P12 **Eel River** ≈ Indiana, N USA
Eems *see* Ems
98 O4 **Eemshaven** Groningen, NE Netherlands
98 O5 **Eems Kanaal** *canal* NE Netherlands
98 M11 **Eerbeek** Gelderland, E Netherlands
99 C17 **Eernegem** West-Vlaanderen, W Belgium
99 J15 **Eersel** Noord-Brabant, S Netherlands
Eesti Vabariik *see* Estonia
187 R14 **Efate** *var.* Éfaté, Fr. Vaté *prev.* Sandwich Island. *island* C Vanuatu
109 S4 **Eferding** Oberösterreich, N Austria
30 M15 **Effingham** Illinois, N USA
117 N15 **Eforie-Nord** Constanţa, SE Romania
117 N15 **Eforie Sud** Constanţa, E Romania
Efyrnwy, Afon *see* Vyrnwy
163 N7 **Eg** Hentiy, N Mongolia
107 G23 **Egadi, Isole** *island group* S Italy
35 X6 **Egan Range** ▲ Nevada, W USA
14 K12 **Eganville** Ontario, SE Canada
Ege Denizi *see* Aegean Sea
39 O14 **Egegik** Alaska, USA
111 L21 **Eger** *Ger.* Erlau. Heves, NE Hungary
Eger *see* Cheb, Czech Republic
Eger *see* Ohre, Czech Republic/Germany
173 P8 **Egeria Fracture Zone** *tectonic feature* W Indian Ocean
95 C17 **Egersund** Rogaland, S Norway
108 J7 **Egg** Vorarlberg, NW Austria
101 H14 **Egge-gebirge** ▲ C Germany
109 Q4 **Eggelsberg** Oberösterreich, N Austria
109 W2 **Eggenburg** Niederösterreich, NE Austria
101 N22 **Eggenfelden** Bayern, SE Germany
18 J17 **Egg Harbor City** New Jersey, NE USA
65 G25 **Egg Island** *island* W Saint Helena
183 N14 **Egg Lagoon** Tasmania, SE Australia
99 I20 **Éghezèe** Namur, C Belgium
92 L2 **Egilsstadhir** Austurland, E Iceland
Egina *see* Aígina
Egindibulaq *see* Yegindybulak
Egio *see* Aígio
103 N12 **Égletons** Corrèze, C France
98 H9 **Egmond aan Zee** Noord-Holland, NW Netherlands
Egmont *see* Taranaki, Mount
134 J10 **Egmont, Cape** *headland* North Island, NZ
Egoli *see* Johannesburg
Eğri Palanka *see* Kriva Palanka
55 G23 **Egtved** Vejle, C Denmark
123 U5 **Egvekinot** Chukotskiy Avtonomnyy Okrug, NE Russian Federation
75 V9 **Egypt** *off.* Arab Republic of Egypt, *Ar.* Jumhūrīyah Miṣr al 'Arabīyah; *prev.* United Arab Republic, *anc.* Aegyptus. ◆ *republic* NE Africa
30 L17 **Egypt, Lake Of** ⊟ Illinois, N USA
162 I14 **Ehen Hudag** *var.* Alx Youqi. Nei Mongol Zizhiqu, N China
164 F14 **Ehime** *off.* Ehime-ken. ◈ *prefecture* Shikoku, SW Japan
101 I23 **Ehingen** Baden-Württemberg, S Germany
Ehinos *see* Echínos
21 R14 **Ehrhardt** South Carolina, SE USA
108 L7 **Ehrwald** Tirol, W Austria
191 W6 **Eiao** *island* Îles Marquises, NE French Polynesia
105 P2 **Eibar** País Vasco, N Spain
98 O11 **Eibergen** Gelderland, E Netherlands
109 V9 **Eibiswald** Steiermark, SE Austria
109 P8 **Eichham** ▲ SW Austria
101 J15 **Eichsfeld** *hill range* C Germany
101 K21 **Eichstätt** Bayern, SE Germany
100 H8 **Eider** ≈ N Germany
94 E13 **Eidfjord** Hordaland, S Norway
94 D13 **Eidfjorden** *fjord* S Norway
94 F9 **Eidsvåg** Møre og Romsdal, S Norway
95 I14 **Eidsvoll** Akershus, S Norway
92 N2 **Eidsvollfjellet** ▲ NW Svalbard
Eier-Berg *see* Suur Munamägi
101 D18 **Eifel** *plateau* W Germany
108 E9 **Eiger** ▲ C Switzerland
96 G10 **Eigg** *island* W Scotland, UK
155 D24 **Eight Degree Channel** *channel* India/Maldives
44 G1 **Eight Mile Rock** Grand Bahama Island, N Bahamas
194 J9 **Eights Coast** *physical region* Antarctica
180 K6 **Eighty Mile Beach** *beach* Western Australia
99 L18 **Eijsden** Limburg, SE Netherlands
95 G15 **Eikeren** ⊚ S Norway
Eil *see* Eyl
Eilat *see* Elat
183 O12 **Eildon** Victoria, SE Australia
183 O12 **Eildon, Lake** ⊚ Victoria, SE Australia
80 E8 **Eilei** Northern Kordofan, C Sudan
101 N15 **Eilenburg** Sachsen, E Germany
94 H13 **Eina** Oppland, S Norway
Ein 'Avedat *see* En 'Avedat
101 I14 **Einbeck** Niedersachsen, C Germany
99 K15 **Eindhoven** Noord-Brabant, S Netherlands
108 G8 **Einsiedeln** Schwyz, NE Switzerland
Eipel *see* Ipel'
Éire *see* Ireland, Republic of
Éireann, Muir *see* Irish Sea
Eirik Outer Ridge *see* Eirik Ridge
64 I6 **Eirik Ridge** *var.* Eirik Outer Ridge. *undersea feature* E Labrador Sea
92 I3 **Eiríksjökull** ▲ C Iceland
59 B14 **Eirunepé** Amazonas, N Brazil
99 L17 **Eisden** Limburg, NE Belgium
83 F18 **Eiseb** ≈ Botswana/Namibia
Eisen *see* Yŏngch'ŏn
101 J16 **Eisenach** Thüringen, C Germany
Eisenburg *see* Vasvár
109 U6 **Eisenerz** Steiermark, SE Austria
100 Q13 **Eisenhüttenstadt** Brandenburg, E Germany
109 U10 **Eisenkappel** *Slvn.* Železna Kapela. Kärnten, S Austria
Eisenmarkt *see* Hunedoara
109 Y5 **Eisenstadt** Burgenland, E Austria
Eishū *see* Yŏngju
119 H15 **Eišiškės** Vilnius, SE Lithuania
101 L15 **Eisleben** Sachsen-Anhalt, C Germany
190 I3 **Eita** Tarawa, W Kiribati
Eitape *see* Aitape
105 V11 **Eivissa** *var.* Iviza, *Cast.* Ibiza; *anc.* Ebusus. Eivissa, Spain, W Mediterranean Sea
105 V10 **Eivissa** *var.* Iviza, *Cast.* Ibiza; *anc.* Ebusus. *island* Islas Baleares, Spain, W Mediterranean Sea
105 R4 **Ejea de los Caballeros** Aragón, NE Spain
40 E8 **Ejido Insurgentes** Baja California Sur, W Mexico
Ejin Qi *see* Dalain Hob
Ejmiadzın *see* Ejmiatsin
137 T12 **Ejmiatsin** *var.* Ejmiadzın, Etchmiadzin, *Rus.* Echmiadzin. W Armenia
77 P16 **Ejura** C Ghana
41 R16 **Ejutla** *var.* Ejutla de Crespo. Oaxaca, SE Mexico
Ejutla de Crespo *see* Ejutla
33 Y10 **Ekalaka** Montana, NW USA
Ekapa *see* Cape Town
Ekaterinodar *see* Krasnodar
93 L20 **Ekenäs** *Fin.* Tammisaari. Etelä-Suomi, SW Finland
146 B13 **Ekerem** *Rus.* Okarem. Balkan Welaýaty, W Turkmenistan
184 M13 **Eketahuna** Manawatu-Wanganui, North Island, NZ
Ekhínos *see* Echínos
123 U5 **Ekiatapskiy Khrebet** ▲ NE Russian Federation
145 T8 **Ekibastuz** Pavlodar, NE Kazakhstan
123 R13 **Ekimchan** Amurskaya Oblast', SE Russian Federation
95 O15 **Ekoln** ⊚ C Sweden
80 I7 **Ekowit** Red Sea, NE Sudan
95 L19 **Eksjö** Jönköping, S Sweden
93 I15 **Ekträsk** Västerbotten, N Sweden
39 O13 **Ekuk** Alaska, USA
12 F9 **Ekwan** ≈ Ontario, C Canada
39 O13 **Ekwok** Alaska, USA
166 M6 **Ela** Mandalay, C Burma
El Aaiun *see* El Ayoun
81 N15 **Ēl Ābrēd** Somali, E Ethiopia
115 F22 **Elafónisos** *island* S Greece
115 F22 **Elafonísou, Porthmós** *strait* S Greece
El-Aïoun *see* El Ayoun
75 U8 **El 'Alamein** *var.* Al 'Alamayn. N Egypt
41 Q12 **El Alazán** Veracruz-Llave, C Mexico
57 J18 **El Alto** *var.* La Paz. × (La Paz) La Paz, W Bolivia
Elam *see* Īlām
El Amparo *see* El Amparo de Apure
54 I8 **El Amparo de Apure** *var.* El Amparo. Apure, C Venezuela
171 R13 **Elara** Pulau Ambelau, E Indonesia
El Araïch/El Araïche *see* Larache
40 D6 **El Arco** Baja California, NW Mexico
75 X7 **El 'Arîsh** *var.* Al 'Arīsh. NE Egypt
115 L25 **Elása** *island* SE Greece
El Asnam *see* Chlef
Elassón *see* Elassóna
115 E15 **Elassóna** *prev.* Elassón. Thessalía, C Greece
105 N2 **El Astillero** Cantabria, N Spain
138 F14 **Elat** *var.* Eilat, Elath. Southern, S Israel
Elat, Gulf of *see* Aqaba, Gulf of
Elath *see* Elat, Israel
Elath *see* Al 'Aqabah, Jordan
115 C17 **Eláti** ▲ Lefkáda, Iónioi Nísoi, Greece, C Mediterranean Sea
183 L16 **Elato Atoll** *atoll* Caroline Islands, C Micronesia
80 C7 **El'Atrun** Northern Darfur, NW Sudan
74 H6 **El Ayoun** *var.* El Aaiun, El-Aïoun, La Youne. NE Morocco
137 N14 **Elazığ** *var.* Elâziğ, Elâziz. Elazığ, E Turkey
137 O14 **Elazığ** *var.* Elâziğ, Elâziz. ◈ *province* C Turkey
Elâziz *see* Elazığ
Azraq, Bahr el *see* Blue Nile
23 Q7 **Elba** Alabama, S USA
106 E13 **Elba, Isola d'** *island* Archipelago Toscano, C Italy
123 S13 **El'ban** Khabarovskiy Kray, E Russian Federation
54 F6 **El Banco** Magdalena, N Colombia
El Barco *see* O Barco
104 L8 **El Barco de Ávila** Castilla-León, N Spain
El Barco de Valdeorras *see* O Barco
138 H7 **El Barouk, Jabal** ▲ C Lebanon
113 L20 **Elbasan** *var.* Elbasani. Elbasan, C Albania
113 L20 **Elbasan** ◈ *district* C Albania
Elbasani *see* Elbasan
54 K6 **El Baúl** Cojedes, C Venezuela
100 K10 **Elbe** *Cz.* Labe. ≈ Czech Republic/Germany
100 L13 **Elbe-Havel-Kanal** *canal* E Germany
100 K9 **Elbe-Lübeck-Kanal** *canal* N Germany
El Beni *see* Beni
138 H7 **El Beqaa** *var.* Al Biqā', Bekaa Valley. *valley* E Lebanon
25 R6 **Elbert** Texas, SW USA
37 R5 **Elbert, Mount** ▲ Colorado, C USA
23 U3 **Elberton** Georgia, SE USA
100 K11 **Elbe-Seiten-Kanal** *canal* N Germany
102 M4 **Elbeuf** Seine-Maritime, N France
Elbing *see* Elbląg
136 M15 **Elbistan** Kahramanmaraş, S Turkey
110 K7 **Elbląg** *var.* Elblag, *Ger.* Elbing. Warmińsko-Mazurskie, NE Poland
43 N10 **El Bluff** Región Autónoma Atlántico Sur, SE Nicaragua
63 H17 **El Bolsón** Río Negro, W Argentina
105 P11 **El Bonillo** Castilla-La Mancha, C Spain
El Bordo *see* Patía
El Boulaida/El Boulaïda *see* Blida
11 T16 **Elbow** Saskatchewan, S Canada
29 S7 **Elbow Lake** Minnesota, N USA
127 N16 **El'brus** *var.* Gora El'brus. ▲ SW Russian Federation
El'brus, Gora *see* El'brus
126 M15 **El'brusskiy** Karachayevo-Cherkesskaya Respublika, SW Russian Federation
81 D14 **El Buhayrat** *var.* Lakes State. ◈ *state* S Sudan
El Bur *see* Ceel Buur
98 L10 **Elburg** Gelderland, E Netherlands
105 O6 **El Burgo de Osma** Castilla-León, C Spain
Elburz Mountains *see* Alborz, Reshteh-ye Kūhhā-ye
35 V17 **El Cajon** California, W USA
63 H22 **El Calafate** *var.* Calafate. Santa Cruz, S Argentina
55 Q8 **El Callao** Bolívar, E Venezuela
25 U12 **El Campo** Texas, SW USA
54 I7 **El Cantón** Barinas, W Venezuela
35 Q8 **El Capitan** ▲ California, W USA
54 H5 **El Carmelo** Zulia, NW Venezuela
62 J5 **El Carmen** Jujuy, NW Argentina
54 E5 **El Carmen de Bolívar** Bolívar, NW Colombia
55 O8 **El Casabe** Bolívar, SE Venezuela
42 M12 **El Castillo de La Concepción** Río San Juan, SE Nicaragua
El Cayo *see* San Ignacio
35 X17 **El Centro** California, W USA
55 N6 **El Chaparro** Anzoátegui, NE Venezuela
105 S12 **Elche** *Cat.* Elx; *anc.* Ilici, *Lat.* Illicis. País Valenciano, E Spain
105 Q12 **Elche de la Sierra** Castilla-La Mancha, C Spain
41 U15 **El Chichonal, Volcán** ☗ SE Mexico
40 C2 **El Chinero** Baja California, NW Mexico
181 R1 **Elcho Island** *island* Wessel Islands, Northern Territory, N Australia
63 H18 **El Corcovado** Chubut, SW Argentina
105 R12 **Elda** País Valenciano, E Spain
100 M10 **Elde** ≈ NE Germany
98 L12 **Elden** Gelderland, E Netherlands
81 J16 **El Der** *spring/well* S Ethiopia
El Dere *see* Ceel Dheere
40 E3 **El Desemboque** Sonora, NW Mexico
54 F5 **El Difícil** *var.* Ariguaní. Magdalena, N Colombia
123 R10 **El'dikan** Respublika Sakha (Yakutiya), NE Russian Federation
El Djazaïr *see* Alger
El Djelfa *see* Djelfa
29 X15 **Eldon** Iowa, C USA
27 U5 **Eldon** Missouri, C USA
54 E13 **El Doncello** Caquetá, S Colombia
29 W13 **Eldora** Iowa, C USA
60 G12 **Eldorado** Misiones, NE Argentina
40 I9 **El Dorado** Sinaloa, C Mexico
27 U14 **El Dorado** Arkansas, C USA
30 M17 **Eldorado** Illinois, N USA
27 O6 **El Dorado** Kansas, C USA
26 K12 **Eldorado** Oklahoma, C USA
25 O9 **Eldorado** Texas, SW USA
55 Q8 **El Dorado** Bolívar, E Venezuela
54 F10 **El Dorado** × (Bogotá) Cundinamarca, C Colombia
El Dorado *see* California
27 O6 **El Dorado Lake** ⊟ Kansas, C USA
27 S6 **El Dorado Springs** Missouri, C USA
81 H18 **Eldoret** Rift Valley, W Kenya
29 Z14 **Eldridge** Iowa, C USA
95 J21 **Eldsberga** Halland, S Sweden
25 R4 **Electra** Texas, SW USA
37 Q7 **Electra Lake** ⊟ Colorado, C USA
38 B8 **'Ele'ele** *var.* Eleele. Kaua'i, Hawai'i, USA, C Pacific Ocean
Elefantes *see* Olifants
115 H19 **Elefsína** *prev.* Elevsís. Attikí, C Greece
115 G19 **Eléftheres** *anc.* Eleutherae. *site of ancient city* Attikí/Stereá Ellás, C Greece
114 I13 **Eleftheroúpoli** *prev.* Elevtheroúpolis. Anatolikí Makedonía kai Thráki, NE Greece
74 F10 **El Eglab** ▲ SW Algeria
118 F10 **Eleja** Jelgava, C Latvia
Elek *see* Ilek
119 G14 **Elektrėnai** Vilnius, SE Lithuania
126 L3 **Elektrostal'** Moskovskaya Oblast', W Russian Federation
81 H15 **Elemi Triangle** *disputed region* Kenya/Sudan
54 G16 **El Encanto** Amazonas, S Colombia
37 R14 **Elephant Butte Reservoir** ⊟ New Mexico, SW USA
Éléphant, Chaîne de l' *see* Dâmrei, Chuŏr Phmun
194 G2 **Elephant Island** *island* South Shetland Islands, Antarctica
Elephant River *see* Olifants
El Escorial *see* San Lorenzo de El Escorial
Élesd *see* Aleşd
114 F11 **Eleshnitsa** ≈ W Bulgaria
137 S13 **Eleşkirt** Ağrı, E Turkey
42 F5 **El Estor** Izabal, E Guatemala
Eleutherae *see* Eléftheres
44 I2 **Eleuthera Island** *island* N Bahamas
37 S5 **Elevenmile Canyon Reservoir** ⊟ Colorado, C USA
27 W8 **Eleven Point River** ≈ Arkansas/Missouri, C USA
Elevsís *see* Elefsína
Elevtheroúpolis *see* Eleftheroúpoli
75 W8 **El Faiyûm** *var.* Al Fayyūm. N Egypt
80 B10 **El Fasher** *var.* Al Fāshir. Northern Darfur, W Sudan
75 W8 **El Fashn** *var.* Al Fashn. C Egypt
El Ferrol/El Ferrol del Caudillo *see* Ferrol
39 W13 **Elfin Cove** Chichagof Island, Alaska, USA
105 W4 **El Fluvià** ≈ NE Spain
40 H7 **El Fuerte** Sinaloa, W Mexico
80 D11 **El Fula** Western Kordofan, C Sudan
El Gedaref *see* Gedaref
80 A10 **El Geneina** *var.* Ajjinena, Al-Genain, Al Junaynah. Western Darfur, W Sudan
96 J8 **Elgin** NE Scotland, UK
30 M10 **Elgin** Illinois, N USA
29 P14 **Elgin** Nebraska, C USA
35 Y9 **Elgin** Nevada, W USA
28 L6 **Elgin** North Dakota, N USA
26 M12 **Elgin** Oklahoma, C USA
25 T10 **Elgin** Texas, SW USA
123 R9 **El'ginskiy** Respublika Sakha (Yakutiya), NE Russian Federation
75 W8 **El Gîza** *var.* Al Jīzah, Gîza, Gizeh. N Egypt
74 J8 **El Goléa** *var.* Al Golea. C Algeria
40 D2 **El Golfo de Santa Clara** Sonora, NW Mexico
81 G18 **Elgon, Mount** ▲ E Uganda
105 T4 **El Grado** Aragón, NE Spain
94 I10 **Elgspiggen** ▲ S Norway
40 L6 **El Guaje, Laguna** ⊟ NE Mexico
54 H6 **El Guayabo** Zulia, W Venezuela
77 O6 **El Guettâra** *oasis* N Mali
76 J6 **El Hammâmi** *desert* N Mauritania
76 M5 **El Hank** *cliff* N Mauritania
El Haseke *see* Al Ḥasakah
80 H10 **El Hawata** Gedaref, E Sudan
El Higo *see* Higos
171 T16 **Eliase** Pulau Selaru, E Indonesia
Elías Piña *see* Comendador
25 R6 **Eliasville** Texas, SW USA
Elichpur *see* Achalpur
37 V13 **Elida** New Mexico, SW USA
115 F18 **Elikónas** ▲ C Greece
39 N9 **Elim** Alaska, USA
Elimberrum *see* Auch
Eliocroca *see* Lorca
61 B16 **Elisa** Santa Fe, C Argentina
Elisabethstedt *see* Dumbrăveni
Élisabethville *see* Lubumbashi
127 O13 **Elista** Respublika Kalmykiya, SW Russian Federation
182 I9 **Elizabeth** South Australia
21 Q3 **Elizabeth** West Virginia, NE USA
19 Q9 **Elizabeth, Cape** *headland* Maine, NE USA
21 Y8 **Elizabeth City** North Carolina, SE USA
21 P8 **Elizabethton** Tennessee, S USA
30 M17 **Elizabethtown** Illinois, N USA
20 K6 **Elizabethtown** Kentucky, S USA
18 L7 **Elizabethtown** New York, NE USA
21 U11 **Elizabethtown** North Carolina, SE USA
18 G15 **Elizabethtown** Pennsylvania, NE USA
74 E6 **El-Jadida** *prev.* Mazagan. W Morocco
El Jafr *see* Jafr, Qā' al
80 F11 **El Jebelein** White Nile, E Sudan
110 N8 **Ełk** *Ger.* Lyck. Warmińsko-Mazurskie, NE Poland
110 O8 **Ełk** ≈ NE Poland
29 Y12 **Elkader** Iowa, C USA
80 G9 **El Kamlin** Gezira, C Sudan
33 N11 **Elk City** Idaho, NW USA
26 K10 **Elk City** Oklahoma, C USA
27 P7 **Elk City Lake** ⊟ Kansas, C USA
34 M5 **Elk Creek** California, W USA
28 J10 **Elk Creek** ≈ South Dakota, N USA
74 M5 **El Kef** *var.* Al Kāf, Le Kef. NW Tunisia
74 F7 **El Kelâa Srarhna** *var.* Kal al Sraghna. C Morocco
El Kerak *see* Al Karak
11 P17 **Elkford** British Columbia, SW Canada
El Khalil *see* Hebron
80 E7 **El Khandaq** Northern, N Sudan
75 W10 **El Khârga** *var.* Al Khārijah. C Egypt
31 P11 **Elkhart** Indiana, N USA
26 H7 **Elkhart** Kansas, C USA
25 V8 **Elkhart** Texas, SW USA
30 M7 **Elkhart Lake** ⊚ Wisconsin, N USA
El Khartûm *see* Khartoum
37 Q3 **Elkhead Mountains** ▲ Colorado, C USA
18 I12 **Elk Hill** ▲ Pennsylvania, NE USA
138 G8 **El Khiyam** *var.* Al Khiyām, Khiam. S Lebanon
29 S15 **Elkhorn** Nebraska, C USA
30 M9 **Elkhorn** Wisconsin, N USA
29 R14 **Elkhorn River** ≈ Nebraska, C USA
127 O16 **El'khotovo** Respublika Severnaya Osetiya, SW Russian Federation
114 L10 **Elkhovo** *prev.* Kizilagach. Yambol, E Bulgaria
21 R8 **Elkin** North Carolina, SE USA
21 S4 **Elkins** West Virginia, NE USA
195 X3 **Elkins, Mount** ▲ Antarctica
14 G8 **Elk Lake** Ontario, S Canada
31 P6 **Elk Lake** ⊚ Michigan, N USA
18 F12 **Elkland** Pennsylvania, NE USA
35 W3 **Elko** Nevada, W USA
11 R14 **Elk Point** Alberta, SW Canada
29 R12 **Elk Point** South Dakota, N USA
29 V8 **Elk River** Minnesota, N USA
20 J10 **Elk River** ≈ Alabama/Tennessee, S USA
21 R4 **Elk River** ≈ West Virginia, NE USA
20 I7 **Elkton** Kentucky, S USA
21 Y2 **Elkton** Maryland, NE USA
29 R10 **Elkton** South Dakota, N USA
20 I10 **Elkton** Tennessee, S USA
21 U5 **Elkton** Virginia, NE USA
El Kuneitra *see* Al Qunayṭirah
81 L15 **El Kure** Somali, E Ethiopia
80 D12 **El Lagowa** Western Kordofan, C Sudan
39 S12 **Ellamar** Alaska, USA
Ellás *see* Greece
23 S6 **Ellaville** Georgia, SE USA
8 I3 **Ellef Ringnes Island** *island* Nunavut, N Canada
29 V10 **Ellendale** Minnesota, N USA
29 P7 **Ellendale** North Dakota, N USA
36 M6 **Ellen, Mount** ▲ Utah, W USA
32 I9 **Ellensburg** Washington, NW USA
18 K12 **Ellenville** New York, NE USA
Ellep *see* Lib
21 T10 **Ellerbe** North Carolina, SE USA
9 N2 **Ellesmere Island** *island* Queen Elizabeth Islands, Nunavut, N Canada
185 H19 **Ellesmere, Lake** ⊚ South Island, NZ
97 K18 **Ellesmere Port** C England, UK
31 O14 **Ellettsville** Indiana, N USA
99 E19 **Ellezelles** Hainaut, SW Belgium
8 L7 **Ellice** ≈ Nunavut, NE Canada
Ellice Islands *see* Tuvalu
Ellichpur *see* Achalpur
21 W3 **Ellicott City** Maryland, NE USA
23 S2 **Ellijay** Georgia, SE USA
27 W7 **Ellington** Missouri, C USA
26 L5 **Ellinwood** Kansas, C USA
83 J24 **Elliot** Eastern Cape, SE South Africa
14 D10 **Elliot Lake** Ontario, S Canada
181 X6 **Elliot, Mount** ▲ Queensland, E Australia
21 T5 **Elliott Knob** ▲ Virginia, NE USA
26 K4 **Ellis** Kansas, C USA
182 F8 **Elliston** South Australia
22 M7 **Ellisville** Mississippi, S USA
105 V5 **El Llobregat** ≈ NE Spain
96 L9 **Ellon** NE Scotland, UK
Ellore *see* Elūru
21 S13 **Elloree** South Carolina, SE USA
26 M4 **Ellsworth** Kansas, C USA
19 S7 **Ellsworth** Maine, NE USA
30 I6 **Ellsworth** Wisconsin, N USA
26 M11 **Ellsworth, Lake** ⊟ Oklahoma, C USA
194 K9 **Ellsworth Land** *physical region* Antarctica
194 L9 **Ellsworth Mountains** ▲ Antarctica
101 J21 **Ellwangen** Baden-Württemberg, S Germany
18 B14 **Ellwood City** Pennsylvania, NE USA
108 H8 **Elm** Glarus, NE Switzerland
32 G9 **Elma** Washington, NW USA
121 V13 **El Maḥalla el Kubra** *var.* Al Maḥallah al Kubrā, Mahalla el Kubra. N Egypt
74 E9 **El Mahbas** *var.* Mahbés. SW Western Sahara
63 H17 **El Maitén** Chubut, W Argentina
136 E16 **Elmalı** Antalya, SW Turkey
80 G10 **El Manaqil** Gezira, C Sudan
54 M12 **El Mango** Amazonas, S Venezuela
75 W7 **El Manşûra** *var.* Al Manşūrah, Manşûra. N Egypt
55 P8 **El Manteco** Bolívar, E Venezuela
29 O16 **Elm Creek** Nebraska, C USA
El Mediyya *see* Médéa
77 V9 **Elméki** Agadez, C Niger
108 K7 **Elmen** Tirol, W Austria
18 I16 **Elmer** New Jersey, NE USA
138 G6 **El Mina** *var.* Al Mīnā'. N Lebanon
75 W9 **El Minya** *var.* Al Minyā, Minya. C Egypt
14 F15 **Elmira** Ontario, S Canada
18 G11 **Elmira** New York, NE USA
36 K13 **El Mirage** Arizona, SW USA
29 O7 **Elm Lake** ⊟ South Dakota, N USA
El Moján *see* San Rafael
105 N7 **El Molar** Madrid, C Spain
76 L7 **El Mrâyer** *well* C Mauritania
76 L5 **El Mreiti** *well* N Mauritania
76 L8 **El Mreyyé** *desert* E Mauritania
29 P8 **Elm River** ≈ North Dakota/South Dakota, N USA
100 I9 **Elmshorn** Schleswig-Holstein, N Germany
80 D12 **El Muglad** Western Kordofan, C Sudan
El Muwaqqar *see* Al Muwaqqar
14 G14 **Elmvale** Ontario, S Canada
30 K12 **Elmwood** Illinois, N USA
26 J8 **Elmwood** Oklahoma, C USA
103 P17 **Elne** *anc.* Illiberis. Pyrénées-Orientales, S France
54 F11 **El Nevado, Cerro** *elevation* C Colombia
171 N5 **El Nido** Palawan, W Philippines
62 I12 **El Nihuil** Mendoza, W Argentina
75 W7 **El Nouzha** × (Alexandria) N Egypt
80 E10 **El Obeid** *var.* Al Obayyid, Al Ubayyiḍ. Northern Kordofan, C Sudan
41 O13 **El Oro** México, S Mexico
56 B8 **El Oro** ◈ *province* SW Ecuador
61 B19 **Elortondo** Santa Fe, C Argentina
54 J8 **Elorza** Apure, C Venezuela
El Ouâdi *see* El Oued
74 L7 **El Oued** *var.* Al Oued, El Ouâdi, El Wad. NE Algeria
36 L15 **Eloy** Arizona, SW USA
55 Q7 **El Palmar** Bolívar, E Venezuela
40 K8 **El Palmito** Durango, W Mexico
55 P7 **El Pao** Bolívar, E Venezuela
54 K5 **El Pao** Cojedes, N Venezuela
42 J7 **El Paraíso** El Paraíso, S Honduras
42 I7 **El Paraíso** ◈ *department* SE Honduras
30 L12 **El Paso** Illinois, N USA
24 G8 **El Paso** Texas, SW USA
24 G8 **El Paso** × Texas, SW USA
105 U7 **El Perello** Cataluña, NE Spain
55 P5 **El Pilar** Sucre, NE Venezuela
42 F7 **El Pital, Cerro** ▲ El Salvador/Honduras
35 Q9 **El Portal** California, W USA
40 J3 **El Porvenir** Chihuahua, N Mexico
43 U14 **El Porvenir** San Blas, N Panama
105 W6 **El Prat de Llobregat** Cataluña, NE Spain
42 H5 **El Progreso** Yoro, NW Honduras
42 A2 **El Progreso** *off.* Departamento de El Progreso. ◈ *department* C Guatemala
El Progreso *see* Guastatoya
104 L9 **El Puente del Arzobispo** Castilla-La Mancha, C Spain

◆ COUNTRY
● COUNTRY CAPITAL
◇ DEPENDENT TERRITORY
○ DEPENDENT TERRITORY CAPITAL
◈ ADMINISTRATIVE REGION
× INTERNATIONAL AIRPORT
▲ MOUNTAIN
▲ MOUNTAIN RANGE
☗ VOLCANO
≈ RIVER
⊚ LAKE
⊟ RESERVOIR

104 J15 **El Puerto de Santa María** Andalucía, S Spain
62 I8 **El Puesto** Catamarca, NW Argentina
El Qâhira see Cairo
75 V10 **El Qaşr** var. Al Qaşr. C Egypt
El Qatrani see Al Qaţrānah
40 I10 **El Quelite** Sinaloa, C Mexico
62 G9 **Elqui, Río** ≈ N Chile
El Quneitra see Al Qunayţirah
El Quseir see Al Quşayr
El Quweira see Al Quwayrah
141 O15 **El-Rahaba** ✕ (Şan'ā') W Yemen
42 M10 **El Rama** Región Autónoma Atlántico Sur, SE Nicaragua
43 W16 **El Real** var. El Real de Santa María. Darién, SE Panama
El Real de Santa María see El Real
26 M10 **El Reno** Oklahoma, C USA
40 K9 **El Rodeo** Durango, C Mexico
104 J13 **El Ronquillo** Andalucía, S Spain
11 S16 **Elrose** Saskatchewan, S Canada
30 K8 **Elroy** Wisconsin, N USA
25 S17 **Elsa** Texas, SW USA
75 W8 **El Şaff** var. Aş Şaff. N Egypt
40 J10 **El Salto** Durango, C Mexico
42 D8 **El Salvador** off. Republica de El Salvador. ◆ republic Central America
54 K7 **El Samán de Apure** Apure, C Venezuela
14 D7 **Elsas** Ontario, S Canada
40 F3 **El Sásabe** var. Aduana del Sásabe. Sonora, NW Mexico
Elsass see Alsace
40 J5 **El Sáuz** Chihuahua, N Mexico
27 W4 **Elsberry** Missouri, C USA
45 P9 **El Seibo** var. Santa Cruz de El Seibo, Santa Cruz del Seibo. E Dominican Republic
42 B7 **El Semillero Barra Nahualate** Escuintla, SW Guatemala
Elsene see Ixelles
Elsen Nur see Dorgê Co
36 L6 **Elsinore** Utah, W USA
Elsinore see Helsingør
99 L18 **Elsloo** Limburg, SE Netherlands
60 G13 **El Soberbio** Misiones, NE Argentina
55 N6 **El Socorro** Guárico, C Venezuela
54 L6 **El Sombrero** Guárico, N Venezuela
98 L10 **Elspeet** Gelderland, E Netherlands
98 L12 **Elst** Gelderland, E Netherlands
101 O15 **Elsterwerda** Brandenburg, E Germany
40 J4 **El Sueco** Chihuahua, N Mexico
El Suweida see As Suwaydā'
El Suweis see Suez
54 D12 **El Tambo** Cauca, SW Colombia
193 P13 **Eltanin Fracture Zone** tectonic feature SE Pacific Ocean
105 X5 **El Ter** ≈ NE Spain
184 K11 **Eltham** Taranaki, North Island, NZ
55 O6 **El Tigre** Anzoátegui, NE Venezuela
El Tigrito see San José de Guanipa
54 J5 **El Tocuyo** Lara, N Venezuela
127 Q10 **El'ton** Volgogradskaya Oblast', SW Russian Federation
32 K10 **Eltopia** Washington, NW USA
105 Z8 **El Toro** var. Mare de Déu del Toro. ▲ Menorca, Spain, W Mediterranean Sea
61 A18 **El Trébol** Santa Fe, C Argentina
40 J13 **El Tuito** Jalisco, SW Mexico
75 X8 **El Ţûr** var. Aţ Ţūr. NE Egypt
155 K16 **Elūru** prev. Ellore. Andhra Pradesh, E India
118 H13 **Elva** Ger. Elwa. Tartumaa, SE Estonia
37 R9 **El Vado Reservoir** ⊞ New Mexico, SW USA
43 S15 **El Valle** Coclé, C Panama
104 I11 **Elvas** Portalegre, C Portugal
54 K7 **El Venado** Apure, C Venezuela
105 V6 **El Vendrell** Cataluña, NE Spain
94 I13 **Elverum** Hedmark, S Norway
42 I9 **El Viejo** Chinandega, NW Nicaragua
54 G7 **El Viejo, Cerro** ▲ C Colombia
54 H6 **El Vigía** Mérida, NW Venezuela
105 Q4 **El Villar de Arnedo** La Rioja, N Spain
59 A14 **Elvira** Amazonas, W Brazil
Elwa see Elva
El Wad see El Oued
81 K17 **El Wak** North Eastern, NE Kenya
33 R7 **Elwell, Lake** ⊞ Montana, NW USA
31 P13 **Elwood** Indiana, N USA
27 R3 **Elwood** Kansas, C USA
29 N16 **Elwood** Nebraska, C USA
Elx see Elche
97 O20 **Ely** E England, UK
29 X4 **Ely** Minnesota, N USA
35 X6 **Ely** Nevada, W USA
El Yopal see Yopal
31 T11 **Elyria** Ohio, N USA
45 S9 **El Yunque** ▲ E Puerto Rico
101 F23 **Elz** ≈ SW Germany
187 R14 **Emae** island Shepherd Islands, C Vanuatu
118 I5 **Emajõgi** Ger. Embach. ≈ SE Estonia
Emāmrūd see Shāhrūd
149 Q2 **Emām Şāḩeb** var. Emam Saheb, Hazarat Imam. Kunduz, NE Afghanistan
Emāmshahr see Shāhrūd
95 M20 **Emån** ≈ S Sweden
144 J11 **Emba** Kaz. Embi. Aktyubinsk, W Kazakhstan
144 H12 **Emba** Kaz. Zhem. ≈ W Kazakhstan
Embach see Emajõgi
62 K5 **Embarcación** Salta, N Argentina
30 M15 **Embarras River** ≈ Illinois, N USA
Embi see Emba
81 I19 **Embu** Eastern, C Kenya
100 E10 **Emden** Niedersachsen, NW Germany
160 H9 **Emei Shan** ▲ Sichuan, C China
29 Q4 **Emerado** North Dakota, N USA
181 X8 **Emerald** Queensland, E Australia
Emerald Isle see Montserrat
57 J15 **Emero, Río** ≈ W Bolivia
11 Y17 **Emerson** Manitoba, S Canada
29 T15 **Emerson** Iowa, C USA
29 R13 **Emerson** Nebraska, C USA
36 M5 **Emery** Utah, W USA
Emesa see Ḩimş
136 E13 **Emet** Kütahya, W Turkey
186 B8 **Emeti** Western, SW PNG
35 V3 **Emigrant Pass** pass Nevada, W USA
78 I6 **Emi Koussi** ▲ N Chad
Emilia see Emilia-Romagna
41 V15 **Emiliano Zapata** Chiapas, SE Mexico
106 E9 **Emilia-Romagna** prev. Emilia, anc. Æmilia. ◈ region N Italy
158 J3 **Emin** var. Dorbiljin. Xinjiang Uygur Zizhiqu, NW China
149 W8 **Emīnābād** Punjab, E Pakistan
21 L5 **Eminence** Kentucky, S USA
27 W7 **Eminence** Missouri, C USA
114 N9 **Emine, Nos** headland E Bulgaria
158 I3 **Emin He** ≈ NW China
186 G4 **Emirau Island** island N PNG
136 F13 **Emirdağ** Afyon, W Turkey
95 M21 **Emmaboda** Kalmar, S Sweden
118 E5 **Emmaste** Hiiumaa, W Estonia
18 I15 **Emmaus** Pennsylvania, NE USA
183 U4 **Emmaville** New South Wales, SE Australia
108 E9 **Emme** ≈ W Switzerland
98 L8 **Emmeloord** Flevoland, N Netherlands
98 O8 **Emmen** Drenthe, NE Netherlands
108 F8 **Emmen** Luzern, C Switzerland
101 F23 **Emmendingen** Baden-Württemberg, SW Germany
98 P8 **Emmer-Compascuum** Drenthe, NE Netherlands
101 D14 **Emmerich** Nordrhein-Westfalen, W Germany
29 U12 **Emmetsburg** Iowa, C USA
32 M14 **Emmett** Idaho, NW USA
38 M10 **Emmonak** Alaska, USA
Emona see Ljubljana
Emonti see East London
24 L12 **Emory Peak** ▲ Texas, SW USA
40 F6 **Empalme** Sonora, NW Mexico
83 L23 **Empangeni** KwaZulu/Natal, E South Africa
61 C14 **Empedrado** Corrientes, NE Argentina
192 K3 **Emperor Seamounts** undersea feature NW Pacific Ocean
192 L3 **Emperor Trough** undersea feature N Pacific Ocean
35 R4 **Empire** Nevada, W USA
Empire State of the South see Georgia
Emplawas see Amplawas
106 F11 **Empoli** Toscana, C Italy
27 P5 **Emporia** Kansas, C USA
21 W7 **Emporia** Virginia, NE USA
18 E13 **Emporium** Pennsylvania, NE USA
Empty Quarter see Ar Rub' al Khālī
100 E10 **Ems** Dut. Eems. ≈ NW Germany
100 F13 **Emsdetten** Nordrhein-Westfalen, NW Germany
Ems-Hunte Canal see Küstenkanal
100 F10 **Ems-Jade-Kanal** canal NW Germany
100 F11 **Emsland** cultural region NW Germany
182 D3 **Emu Junction** South Australia
163 T3 **Emur He** ≈ NE China
55 R8 **Enachu Landing** NW Guyana
93 F16 **Enafors** Jämtland, C Sweden
94 N11 **Enånger** Gävleborg, C Sweden
96 G7 **Enard Bay** bay NW Scotland, UK
Enaretrāsk see Inarijärvi
171 X14 **Enarotali** Papua, E Indonesia
138 E12 **En 'Avedat** var. Ein 'Avedat. well S Israel
165 T2 **Enbetsu** Hokkaidō, NE Japan
61 H16 **Encantadas, Serra das** ▲▲ S Brazil
40 E7 **Encantado, Cerro** ▲ NW Mexico
62 P7 **Encarnación** Itapúa, S Paraguay
40 M12 **Encarnación de Díaz** Jalisco, SW Mexico
77 O17 **Enchi** SW Ghana
25 Q14 **Encinal** Texas, SW USA
35 U17 **Encinitas** California, W USA
25 S16 **Encino** Texas, SW USA
54 H6 **Encontrados** Zulia, NW Venezuela
182 I10 **Encounter Bay** inlet South Australia
61 F15 **Encruzilhada** Rio Grande do Sul, S Brazil
61 H16 **Encruzilhada do Sul** Rio Grande do Sul, S Brazil
111 M20 **Encs** Borsod-Abaúj-Zemplén, NE Hungary
193 P3 **Endeavour Seamount** undersea feature N Pacific Ocean
181 V1 **Endeavour Strait** strait Queensland, NE Australia
171 O16 **Endeh** Flores, S Indonesia
95 G23 **Endelave** island C Denmark
191 T4 **Enderbury Island** atoll Phoenix Islands, C Kiribati
11 N16 **Enderby** British Columbia, SW Canada
195 W4 **Enderby Land** physical region Antarctica
173 N14 **Enderby Plain** undersea feature S Indian Ocean
29 Q6 **Enderlin** North Dakota, N USA
Endersdorf see Jędrzejów
28 K16 **Enders Reservoir** ⊞ Nebraska, C USA
18 H11 **Endicott** New York, NE USA
39 P7 **Endicott Mountains** ▲▲ Alaska, USA
118 I5 **Endla Raba** wetland C Estonia
117 T9 **Enerhodar** Zaporiz'ka Oblast', SE Ukraine
57 F14 **Ene, Río** ≈ C Peru
189 N4 **Enewetak Atoll** var. Ānewetak, Eniwetok. atoll Ralik Chain, W Marshall Islands
114 L13 **Enez** Edirne, NW Turkey
21 W8 **Enfield** North Carolina, SE USA
186 B7 **Enga** ◈ province W PNG
45 Q9 **Engaño, Cabo** headland E Dominican Republic
164 U3 **Engaru** Hokkaidō, NE Japan
138 F11 **'En Gedi** Southern, E Israel
108 F9 **Engelberg** Unterwalden, C Switzerland
21 Y9 **Engelhard** North Carolina, SE USA
127 P8 **Engel's** Saratovskaya Oblast', W Russian Federation
101 G24 **Engen** Baden-Württemberg, SW Germany
Engeten see Aiud
168 K15 **Enggano, Pulau** island W Indonesia
80 J8 **Enghershatu** ▲ N Eritrea
99 F19 **Enghien** Dut. Edingen. Hainaut, SW Belgium
27 V12 **England** Arkansas, C USA
97 M20 **England** Lat. Anglia. national region UK
14 H8 **Englehart** Ontario, S Canada
37 T4 **Englewood** Colorado, C USA
31 O16 **English** Indiana, N USA
39 Q13 **English Bay** Alaska, USA
English Bazar see Ingrāj Bāzār
97 N25 **English Channel** var. The Channel, Fr. la Manche. channel NW Europe
194 J7 **English Coast** physical region Antarctica
105 S11 **Enguera** País Valenciano, E Spain
118 E8 **Engure** Tukums, W Latvia
118 E8 **Engures Ezers** ◎ NW Latvia
137 R9 **Enguri** Rus. Inguri. ≈ NW Georgia
Engyum see Gangi
26 M9 **Enid** Oklahoma, C USA
22 L3 **Enid Lake** ⊞ Mississippi, S USA
189 Y2 **Enigu** island Ratak Chain, SE Marshall Islands
Enikale Strait see Kerch Strait
147 Z8 **Enil'chek** Issyk-Kul'skaya Oblast', E Kyrgyzstan
115 F17 **Enipéfs** ≈ C Greece
165 S4 **Eniwa** Hokkaidō, NE Japan
Eniwetok see Enewetak Atoll
Enjiang see Yongfeng
123 S11 **Enkan, Mys** headland NE Russian Federation
Enkeldoorn see Chivhu
98 J8 **Enkhuizen** Noord-Holland, NW Netherlands
109 Q4 **Enknach** ≈ N Austria
95 N15 **Enköping** Uppsala, C Sweden
107 K24 **Enna** var. Castrogiovanni, Henna. Sicilia, Italy, C Mediterranean Sea
80 D11 **En Nahud** Western Kordofan, C Sudan
138 F8 **En Nâqoûra** var. An Nāqūrah. SW Lebanon
En Nazira see Nazerat
78 K8 **Ennedi** plateau E Chad
101 E15 **Ennepetal** Nordrhein-Westfalen, W Germany
183 P4 **Enngonia** New South Wales, SE Australia
97 C19 **Ennis** Ir. Inis. W Ireland
33 R11 **Ennis** Montana, NW USA
25 U7 **Ennis** Texas, SW USA
97 F20 **Enniscorthy** Ir. Inis Córthaidh. SE Ireland
97 E15 **Enniskillen** var. Inniskilling, Ir. Inis Ceithleann. SW Northern Ireland, UK
97 B19 **Ennistimon** Ir. Inis Díomáin. W Ireland
109 T4 **Enns** Oberösterreich, N Austria
109 T4 **Enns** ≈ C Austria
93 O16 **Eno** Itä-Suomi, E Finland
24 M5 **Enochs** Texas, SW USA
93 N17 **Enonkoski** Isä-Suomi, E Finland
92 K10 **Enontekiö** Lapp. Eanodat. Lappi, N Finland
21 Q11 **Enoree** South Carolina, SE USA
21 P11 **Enoree River** ≈ South Carolina, SE USA
18 M6 **Enosburg Falls** Vermont, NE USA
171 N13 **Enrekang** Sulawesi, C Indonesia
45 N10 **Enriquillo** SW Dominican Republic
45 N9 **Enriquillo, Lago** ◎ SW Dominican Republic
98 L9 **Ens** Flevoland, N Netherlands
98 P11 **Enschede** Overijssel, E Netherlands
40 B2 **Ensenada** Baja California, NW Mexico
101 E20 **Ensheim** ✕ (Saarbrücken) Saarland, W Germany
160 L9 **Enshi** Hubei, C China
164 L14 **Enshū-nada** gulf SW Japan
23 O8 **Ensley** Florida, SE USA
Enso see Svetogorsk
81 F18 **Entebbe** S Uganda
81 F18 **Entebbe** ✕ C Uganda
101 M18 **Entenbühl** ▲ Czech Republic/Germany
98 N10 **Enter** Overijssel, E Netherlands
23 Q7 **Enterprise** Alabama, S USA
32 L11 **Enterprise** Oregon, NW USA
36 J7 **Enterprise** Utah, W USA
32 J8 **Entiat** Washington, NW USA
105 P15 **Entinas, Punta de las** headland S Spain
108 F8 **Entlebuch** Luzern, W Switzerland
108 F8 **Entlebuch** valley C Switzerland
63 I22 **Entrada, Punta** headland S Argentina
103 O13 **Entraygues-sur-Truyère** Aveyron, S France
187 O14 **Entrecasteaux, Récifs d'** reef N New Caledonia
61 C17 **Entre Ríos** off. Provincia de Entre Ríos. ◈ province NE Argentina
42 K7 **Entre Ríos, Cordillera** ▲▲ Honduras/Nicaragua
104 G9 **Entroncamento** Santarém, C Portugal
77 V16 **Enugu** Enugu, S Nigeria
77 U16 **Enugu** ◈ state SE Nigeria
123 V5 **Enurmino** Chukotskiy Avtonomnyy Okrug, NE Russian Federation
54 E9 **Envigado** Antioquia, W Colombia
59 B15 **Envira** Amazonas, W Brazil
Enyélé see Enyellé
79 I16 **Enyellé** var. Enyélé. La Likouala, NE Congo
101 H21 **Enz** ≈ SW Germany
165 N13 **Enzan** Yamanashi, Honshū, S Japan
104 I2 **Eo** ≈ NW Spain
Eochaill see Youghal
Eochaille, Cuan see Youghal Bay
107 K22 **Eolie, Isole** var. Isole Lipari, Eng. Aeolian Islands, Lipari Islands. island group S Italy
189 U12 **Eot** island Chuuk, C Micronesia
115 J25 **Epáno Archánes** var. Áno Arkhánai; prev. Epáno Arkhánai. Kríti, Greece, E Mediterranean Sea
Epáno Arkhánai see Epáno Archánes
115 G14 **Epanomí** Kentrikí Makedonía, N Greece
98 M10 **Epe** Gelderland, E Netherlands
77 S16 **Epe** Lagos, S Nigeria
79 I17 **Epéna** La Likouala, NE Congo
Eperies/Eperjes see Prešov
103 Q4 **Épernay** anc. Sparnacum. Marne, N France
36 L5 **Ephraim** Utah, W USA
18 H15 **Ephrata** Pennsylvania, NE USA
32 J8 **Ephrata** Washington, NW USA
187 R14 **Epi** var. Épi. island C Vanuatu
105 R6 **Épila** Aragón, NE Spain
103 T6 **Épinal** Vosges, NE France
Epiphania see Ḩamāh
Epirus see Ípeiros
121 P3 **Episkopí** SW Cyprus
Episkopi Bay see Episkopí, Kólpos
121 P3 **Episkopí, Kólpos** var. Episkopi Bay. bay SE Cyprus
Epitoli see Pretoria
Epoon see Ebon Atoll
Eporedia see Ivrea
Eppeschdorf see Dumbrăveni
101 H21 **Eppingen** Baden-Württemberg, SW Germany
83 E18 **Epukiro** Omaheke, E Namibia
29 Y13 **Epworth** Iowa, C USA
143 O10 **Eqlīd** var. Iqlid. Fārs, C Iran
Equality State see Wyoming
79 J18 **Equateur** off. Région de l' Equateur. ◈ region N Dem. Rep. Congo
151 K22 **Equatorial Channel** channel S Maldives
79 B17 **Equatorial Guinea** off. Republic of Equatorial Guinea. ◆ republic C Africa
121 V11 **Eratosthenes Tablemount** undersea feature E Mediterranean Sea
Erautini see Johannesburg
136 L12 **Erbaa** Tokat, N Turkey
101 E19 **Erbeskopf** ▲ W Germany
Erbil see Arbīl
121 P2 **Ercan** ✕ (Nicosia) N Cyprus
Ercegnovi see Herceg-Novi
137 T14 **Erçek Gölü** ◎ E Turkey
137 S14 **Erciş** Van, E Turkey
136 K14 **Erciyes Dağı** anc. Argaeus. ▲ C Turkey
111 J22 **Érd** Ger. Hanselbeck. Pest, C Hungary
Erdaobaihe see Baihe
159 O12 **Erdaogou** Qinghai, W China
163 X11 **Erdao Jiang** ≈ NE China
Erdăt-Sângeorz see Sângeorgiu de Pădure
136 C11 **Erdek** Balıkesir, NW Turkey
Erdély see Transylvania
Erdélyi-Havasok see Carpaţii Meridionali
136 J17 **Erdemli** İçel, S Turkey
162 K6 **Erdenet** Orhon, N Mongolia
162 I8 **Erdenetsogt** Bayanhongor, C Mongolia
78 K7 **Erdi** plateau NE Chad
78 L7 **Erdi Ma** desert NE Chad
101 M23 **Erding** Bayern, SE Germany
Erdőszáda see Ardusat
Erdőszentgyörgy see Sângeorgiu de Pădure
102 I7 **Erdre** ≈ NW France
195 R13 **Erebus, Mount** ▲ Ross Island, Antarctica
61 H14 **Erechim** Rio Grande do Sul, S Brazil
163 O7 **Ereen Davaanī Nuruu** ▲▲ NE Mongolia
163 Q6 **Ereentsav** Dornod, NE Mongolia
136 I16 **Ereğli** Konya, S Turkey
136 I15 **Ereğli Gölü** ◎ W Turkey
115 A15 **Ereíkoussa** island Iónioi Nísoi, Greece, C Mediterranean Sea
163 O11 **Erenhot** var. Erlian. Nei Mongol Zizhiqu, NE China
104 M6 **Eresma** ≈ N Spain
115 K17 **Eresós** var. Eressós. Lésvos, E Greece
Eressós see Eresós
Erevan see Yerevan
Ereymentaū see Yereymentau
99 K21 **Érezée** Luxembourg, SE Belgium
74 G7 **Erfoud** SE Morocco
101 D16 **Erft** ≈ W Germany
101 K16 **Erfurt** Thüringen, C Germany
137 P15 **Ergani** Diyarbakır, SE Turkey
163 N11 **Ergel** Dornogovĭ, SE Mongolia
Ergene Irmaği see Ergene Çayı
162 L11 **Ergenetsogt** Ömnögovĭ, S Mongolia
136 C10 **Ergene Çayı** var. Ergene Irmağı. ≈ NW Turkey
118 I9 **Ērgļi** Madona, C Latvia
78 H11 **Erguig, Bahr** ≈ SW Chad
163 S5 **Ergun** var. Labudalin, prev. Ergun Youqi. Nei Mongol Zizhiqu, N China
Ergun He see Argun
Ergun Youqi see Ergun
Ergun Zuoqi see Genhe
160 F12 **Er Hai** ◎ SW China
102 G4 **Er, Îles d'** island group NW France
106 K4 **Ería** ≈ NW Spain
80 H8 **Eriba** Kassala, NE Sudan
96 I6 **Eriboll, Loch** inlet NW Scotland, UK
65 Q18 **Erica Seamount** undersea feature SW Indian Ocean
107 H23 **Erice** Sicilia, Italy, C Mediterranean Sea
104 E10 **Ericeira** Lisboa, C Portugal
96 H10 **Ericht, Loch** ◎ C Scotland, UK
26 J11 **Erick** Oklahoma, C USA
18 B11 **Erie** Pennsylvania, NE USA
18 E9 **Erie Canal** canal New York, NE USA
Érié, Lac see Erie, Lake
31 T10 **Erie, Lake** Fr. Lac Érié. ◎ Canada/USA
Erigabo see Ceerigaabo
77 N8 **'Erigât** desert N Mali
Erigavo see Ceerigaabo
92 P2 **Erik Eriksenstretet** strait E Svalbard
11 X15 **Eriksdale** Manitoba, S Canada
189 V6 **Erikub Atoll** var. Ādkup. atoll Ratak Chain, C Marshall Islands
Erimanthos see Erýmanthos
165 T6 **Erimo** Hokkaidō, NE Japan
165 T6 **Erimo-misaki** headland Hokkaidō, NE Japan
20 H8 **Erin** Tennessee, S USA
96 E9 **Eriskay** island NW Scotland, UK
Erithraí see Erythrés
80 I9 **Eritrea** off. State of Eritrea, Tig. Ērtra. ◆ transitional government E Africa
Erivan see Yerevan
101 D16 **Erkelenz** Nordrhein-Westfalen, W Germany
95 P15 **Erken** ◎ C Sweden
101 K19 **Erlangen** Bayern, S Germany
160 G9 **Erlang Shan** ▲ C China
Erlau see Eger
109 V5 **Erlauf** ≈ NE Austria
181 Q8 **Erldunda Roadhouse** Northern Territory, N Australia
Erlian see Erenhot
27 T15 **Erling, Lake** ⊞ Arkansas, USA
109 O8 **Erlsbach** Tirol, W Austria
Ermak see Aksu
98 K10 **Ermelo** Gelderland, C Netherlands
83 K21 **Ermelo** Mpumalanga, NE South Africa
136 H17 **Ermenek** Karaman, S Turkey
Érmihályfalva see Valea lui Mihai
115 G20 **Ermióni** Pelopónnisos, S Greece
115 J20 **Ermoúpoli** var. Hermoupolis; prev. Ermoúpolis. Sýros, Kykládes, Greece, Aegean Sea
Ermoúpolis see Ermoúpoli
Ernabella see Pukatja
155 G22 **Ernākulam** Kerala, SW India
102 J6 **Ernée** Mayenne, NW France
61 H14 **Ernestina, Barragem** ⊞ S Brazil
54 E4 **Ernesto Cortissoz** ✕ (Barranquilla) Atlántico, N Colombia
155 H21 **Erode** Tamil Nādu, SE India
Eroj see Iroj
83 C19 **Erongo** ◈ district W Namibia
99 F21 **Erquelinnes** Hainaut, S Belgium
74 G7 **Er-Rachidia** var. Ksar al Soule. E Morocco
80 E11 **Er Rahad** var. Ar Rahad. Northern Kordofan, C Sudan
Er Ramle see Ramla
83 O15 **Errego** Zambézia, NE Mozambique
Errenteria see Rentería
Er Rif/Er Riff see Rif
97 D14 **Errigal Mountain** Ir. An Earagail. ▲ N Ireland
97 A15 **Erris Head** Ir. Ceann Iorrais. headland W Ireland
187 S15 **Erromango** island S Vanuatu
Error Guyot see Error Tablemount
173 O4 **Error Tablemount** var. Error Guyot. undersea feature W Indian Ocean
80 G11 **Er Roseires** Blue Nile, E Sudan
Erseka see Ersekë
113 M22 **Ersekë** var. Erseka, Kolonjë. Korçë, SE Albania
Érsekújvár see Nové Zámky
29 S4 **Erskine** Minnesota, N USA
103 V6 **Erstein** Bas-Rhin, NE France
108 G9 **Erstfeld** Uri, C Switzerland
158 M3 **Ertai** Xinjiang Uygur Zizhiqu, NW China
126 M7 **Ertil'** Voronezhskaya Oblast', W Russian Federation
Ertis see Irtysh, C Asia
Ertis see Irtyshsk, Kazakhstan
158 K2 **Ertix He** Rus. Chërnyy Irtysh. ≈ China/Kazakhstan
Ērtra see Eritrea
21 P9 **Erwin** North Carolina, SE USA
114 L12 **Erydropótamos** Bul. Byala Reka. ≈ Bulgaria/Greece
115 E19 **Erýmanthos** var. Erimanthos. ▲ S Greece
115 G19 **Erythrés** prev. Erithraí. Stereá Ellás, C Greece
160 F12 **Eryuan** var. Yuhu. Yunnan, SW China
109 U6 **Erzbach** ≈ W Austria
Erzerum see Erzurum
101 N17 **Erzgebirge** Cz. Krušné Hory, Eng. Ore Mountains. ▲▲ Czech Republic/Germany see also Krušné Hory
122 L14 **Erzin** Respublika Tyva, S Russian Federation
137 O13 **Erzincan** var. Erzinjan. Erzincan, E Turkey
137 N13 **Erzincan** var. Erzinjan. ◈ province NE Turkey
Erzinjan see Erzincan
Erzsébetváros see Dumbrăveni
137 Q13 **Erzurum** prev. Erzerum. Erzurum, NE Turkey
137 Q12 **Erzurum** prev. Erzerum. ◈ province NE Turkey
186 G9 **Esa'ala** Normanby Island, SE PNG
165 T2 **Esashi** Hokkaidō, NE Japan
165 Q9 **Esashi** var. Esasi. Iwate, Honshū, C Japan
165 Q5 **Esasho** Hokkaidō, N Japan
Esasi see Esashi
95 F23 **Esbjerg** Ribe, W Denmark
Esbo see Espoo
36 L7 **Escalante** Utah, W USA
36 M7 **Escalante River** ≈ Utah, W USA
14 L12 **Escalier, Réservoir l'** ⊞ Québec, SE Canada
40 K7 **Escalón** Chihuahua, N Mexico
104 M8 **Escalona** Castilla-La Mancha, C Spain
23 O8 **Escambia River** ≈ Florida, SE USA
31 N5 **Escanaba** Michigan, N USA
31 N4 **Escanaba River** ≈ Michigan, N USA
105 R8 **Escandón, Puerto de** pass E Spain
41 W14 **Escárcega** Campeche, SE Mexico
171 O1 **Escarpada Point** headland Luzon, N Philippines
23 N8 **Escatawpa River** ≈ Alabama/Mississippi, S USA
103 P2 **Escaut** ≈ N France
Escaut see Scheldt
99 M25 **Esch-sur-Alzette** Luxembourg, S Luxembourg
101 J15 **Eschwege** Hessen, C Germany
101 D16 **Eschweiler** Nordrhein-Westfalen, W Germany
Esclaves, Grand Lac des see Great Slave Lake
45 O8 **Escocesa, Bahía** bay N Dominican Republic
43 W15 **Escocés, Punta** headland NE Panama
35 U17 **Escondido** California, W USA
42 M10 **Escondido, Río** ≈ SE Nicaragua
15 S7 **Escoumins, Rivière des** ≈ Québec, SE Canada
37 O13 **Escudilla Mountain** ▲ Arizona, SW USA
40 J11 **Escuinapa** var. Escuinapa de Hidalgo. Sinaloa, C Mexico
Escuinapa de Hidalgo see Escuinapa
42 C6 **Escuintla** Escuintla, S Guatemala
41 V17 **Escuintla** Chiapas, SE Mexico
42 A2 **Escuintla** off. Departamento de Escuintla. ◈ department S Guatemala
15 W7 **Escuminac** ≈ Québec, SE Canada
79 D16 **Eséka** Centre, SW Cameroon
136 I12 **Esenboğa** ✕ (Ankara) Ankara, C Turkey
146 B13 **Esenguly** Rus. Gasan-Kuli. Balkan Welaýaty, W Turkmenistan
136 D17 **Eşen Çayı** ≈ SW Turkey
105 T4 **Ésera** ≈ NE Spain
143 N8 **Eşfahān** Eng. Isfahan; anc. Aspadana. Eşfahān, C Iran
143 O7 **Eşfahān** off. Ostān-e Eşfahān. ◈ province C Iran
105 N5 **Esgueva** ≈ N Spain
149 Q3 **Eshkamesh** Takhār, NE Afghanistan
149 T2 **Eshkāshem** Badakhshān, NE Afghanistan
83 L23 **Eshowe** KwaZulu/Natal, E South Africa
143 T5 **'Eshqābād** Khorāsān, NE Iran
Esh Sham see Dimashq
Esh Sharā see Ash Sharāh
Esik see Yesik
Esil see Ishim, Kazakhstan/Russian Federation
Esil see Yesil', Kazakhstan
183 V2 **Esk** Queensland, E Australia
184 O11 **Eskdale** Hawke's Bay, North Island, NZ
Eski Dzhumaya see Türgovishte
92 L2 **Eskifjördhur** Austurland, E Iceland
139 S3 **Eski Kaļak** var. Askī Kalak, Kalak. N Iraq
95 N16 **Eskilstuna** Södermanland, C Sweden
8 H6 **Eskimo Lakes** lakes Northwest Territories, NW Canada
9 O10 **Eskimo Point** headland Nunavut, E Canada
Eskimo Point see Arviat
139 Q2 **Eski Mosul** N Iraq
147 T10 **Eski-Nookat** var. Iski-Nauket. Oshskaya Oblast', SW Kyrgyzstan
136 F12 **Eskişehir** var. Eskishehr. Eskişehir, W Turkey

136 F13 **Eskişehir** *var.* Eski shehr. ◈ *province* NW Turkey
Eskishehr *see* Eskişehir
104 K5 **Esla** ≈ NW Spain
142 J6 **Eslāmābād** *var.* Eslāmābād-e Gharb; *prev.* Harunabad, Shāhābād. Kermānshāhān, W Iran
Eslāmābād-e Gharb *see* Eslāmābād
148 J4 **Eslām Qal'eh** *Pash.* Islam Qala. Herāt, W Afghanistan
95 K23 **Eslöv** Skåne, S Sweden
143 S12 **Esmā'īlābād** Kermān, S Iran
143 U8 **Esmā'īlābād** Khorāsān, E Iran
136 D14 **Eşme** Uşak, W Turkey
44 G6 **Esmeralda** Camagüey, E Cuba
63 F21 **Esmeralda, Isla** *island* S Chile
56 B5 **Esmeraldas** Esmeraldas, N Ecuador
56 B5 **Esmeraldas** ◈ *province* NW Ecuador
Esna *see* Isna
14 B6 **Esnagi Lake** ◎ Ontario, S Canada
143 V14 **Espakeh** Sīstān va Balūchestān, SE Iran
103 O13 **Espalion** Aveyron, S France
España *see* Spain
14 E11 **Espanola** Ontario, S Canada
37 S10 **Espanola** New Mexico, SW USA
57 C18 **Española, Isla** *var.* Hood Island. *island* Galapagos Islands, Ecuador, E Pacific Ocean
104 M13 **Espejo** Andalucía, S Spain
94 C13 **Espeland** Hordaland, S Norway
100 G12 **Espelkamp** Nordrhein-Westfalen, NW Germany
38 M8 **Espenberg, Cape** *headland* Alaska, USA
180 L13 **Esperance** Western Australia
186 L9 **Esperance, Cape** *headland* Guadacanal, C Solomon Islands
57 P18 **Esperancita** Santa Cruz, E Bolivia
61 B17 **Esperanza** Santa Fe, C Argentina
40 G6 **Esperanza** Sonora, NW Mexico
24 H9 **Esperanza** Texas, SW USA
194 H3 **Esperanza** *Argentinian research station* Antarctica
104 E12 **Espichel, Cabo** *headland* S Portugal
54 E10 **Espinal** Tolima, C Colombia
104 G6 **Espinho** Aveiro, N Portugal
59 N18 **Espinosa** Minas Gerais, SE Brazil
103 O15 **Espinouse** ▲ S France
60 Q8 **Espírito Santo** *off.* Estado do Espírito Santo. ◈ *state* E Brazil
187 P13 **Espiritu Santo** *var.* Santo. *island* W Vanuatu
41 Z13 **Espíritu Santo, Bahía del** *bay* SE Mexico
40 F9 **Espíritu Santo, Isla del** *island* W Mexico
41 Y12 **Espita** Yucatán, SE Mexico
15 Y7 **Espoir, Cap d'** *headland* Québec, SE Canada
Esponsede/Esponsende *see* Esposende
93 L20 **Espoo** *Swe.* Esbo. Etelä-Suomi, S Finland
104 G5 **Esposende** *var.* Esponsede, Esponsende. Braga, N Portugal
83 M18 **Espungabera** Manica, SW Mozambique
63 H17 **Esquel** Chubut, SW Argentina
10 L17 **Esquimalt** Vancouver Island, British Columbia, SW Canada
61 C16 **Esquina** Corrientes, NE Argentina
42 E6 **Esquipulas** Chiquimula, SE Guatemala
42 K9 **Esquipulas** Matagalpa, C Nicaragua
94 I8 **Essandjøen** ◎ S Norway
74 E7 **Essaouira** *prev.* Mogador. W Morocco
Esseg *see* Osijek
Es Semara *see* Smara
99 G15 **Essen** Antwerpen, N Belgium
101 E15 **Essen** *var.* Essen an der Ruhr. Nordrhein-Westfalen, W Germany
Essen an der Ruhr *see* Essen
74 I5 **Es Senia** ✕ (Oran) NW Algeria
55 T8 **Essequibo Islands** *island group* N Guyana
55 T11 **Essequibo River** ≈ C Guyana
14 C18 **Essex** Ontario, S Canada
29 T16 **Essex** Iowa, C USA
97 P21 **Essex** *cultural region* E England, UK
31 R8 **Essexville** Michigan, N USA
101 H22 **Esslingen** *var.* Esslingen am Neckar. Baden-Württemberg, SW Germany
Esslingen am Neckar *see* Esslingen
103 N6 **Essonne** ◈ *department* N France
Es Suweida *see* As Suwaydā'
79 F16 **Est** *Eng.* East. ◈ *province* SE Cameroon
104 I1 **Estaca de Bares, Punta da** *point* NW Spain
24 M5 **Estacado, Llano** *plain* New Mexico/Texas, SW USA
63 K25 **Estados, Isla de los** *prev. Eng.* Staten Island. *island* S Argentina
143 P12 **Eşţahbān** Fārs, S Iran
14 F11 **Estaire** Ontario, S Canada
37 S12 **Estancia** New Mexico, SW USA
59 P16 **Estância** Sergipe, E Brazil
104 G7 **Estarreja** Aveiro, N Portugal
102 M17 **Estats, Pic d'** *Sp.* Pico d'Estats. ▲ France/Spain
Estats, Pico d' *see* Estats, Pic d'
83 K23 **Estcourt** KwaZulu/Natal, E South Africa
106 H8 **Este** *anc.* Ateste. Veneto, NE Italy
42 J9 **Estelí** Estelí, NW Nicaragua
42 J9 **Estelí** ◈ *department* NW Nicaragua
105 Q4 **Estella** *Bas.* Lizarra. Navarra, N Spain
29 R9 **Estelline** South Dakota, N USA
25 P4 **Estelline** Texas, SW USA
104 L14 **Estepa** Andalucía, S Spain
104 L16 **Estepona** Andalucía, S Spain
39 R9 **Ester** Alaska, USA
11 V16 **Esterhazy** Saskatchewan, S Canada
37 S3 **Estes Park** Colorado, C USA
11 V17 **Estevan** Saskatchewan, S Canada
29 T11 **Estherville** Iowa, C USA
21 R15 **Estill** South Carolina, SE USA
103 Q6 **Estissac** Aube, N France
15 T9 **Est, Lac de l'** ◎ Québec, SE Canada
Estland *see* Estonia
11 S16 **Eston** Saskatchewan, S Canada
118 G5 **Estonia** *off.* Republic of Estonia, *Est.* Eesti Vabariik, *Ger.* Estland, *Latv.* Igaunija; *prev.* Estonian SSR, *Rus.* Estonskaya SSR. ◆ *republic* NE Europe
Estonskaya SSR *see* Estonia
104 E11 **Estoril** Lisboa, W Portugal
59 L14 **Estreito** Maranhão, E Brazil
104 I8 **Estrela, Serra da** ▲ C Portugal
40 D3 **Estrella, Punta** *headland* NW Mexico
Estremadura *see* Extremadura
104 F10 **Estremadura** *cultural and historical region* W Portugal
104 H11 **Estremoz** Évora, S Portugal
79 D18 **Estuaire** *off.* Province de l'Estuaire, *var.* L'Estuaire. ◈ *province* NW Gabon
Eszék *see* Osijek
111 I22 **Esztergom** *Ger.* Gran; *anc.* Strigonium. Komárom-Esztergom, N Hungary
152 K11 **Etah** Uttar Pradesh, N India
189 R17 **Etal Atoll** *atoll* Mortlock Islands, C Micronesia
99 K24 **Étalle** Luxembourg, SE Belgium
103 N6 **Étampes** Essonne, N France
182 J1 **Etamunbanie, Lake** *salt lake* South Australia
103 N1 **Étaples** Pas-de-Calais, N France
152 K12 **Etāwah** Uttar Pradesh, N India
15 R10 **Etchemin** ≈ Québec, SE Canada
Etchmiadzin *see* Ejmiatsin
40 G7 **Etchojoa** Sonora, NW Mexico
93 L19 **Etelä-Suomi** ◈ *province* S Finland
83 B16 **Etengua** Kunene, NW Namibia
99 K25 **Éthe** Luxembourg, SE Belgium
11 W15 **Ethelbert** Manitoba, S Canada
80 H12 **Ethiopia** *off.* Federal Democratic Republic of Ethiopia; *prev.* Abyssinia, People's Democratic Republic of Ethiopia. ◆ *republic* E Africa
80 I13 **Ethiopian Highlands** *var.* Ethiopian Plateau. *plateau* N Ethiopia
Ethiopian Plateau *see* Ethiopian Highlands
34 M2 **Etna** California, W USA
18 B14 **Etna** Pennsylvania, NE USA
94 G12 **Etna** ≈ S Norway
107 L24 **Etna, Monte** *Eng.* Mount Etna. ⛰ Sicilia, Italy, C Mediterranean Sea
Etna, Mount *see* Etna, Monte
95 C15 **Etne** Hordaland, S Norway
Etoliko *see* Aitolikó
39 Y14 **Etolin Island** *island* Alexander Archipelago, Alaska, USA
38 L12 **Etolin Strait** *strait* Alaska, USA
83 C17 **Etosha Pan** *salt lake* N Namibia
79 G18 **Etoumbi** Cuvette, NW Congo
20 M10 **Etowah** Tennessee, S USA
23 S2 **Etowah River** ≈ Georgia, SE USA
146 B13 **Etrek** *var.* Gyzyletrek, *Rus.* Kizyl-Atrek. Balkan Welaýaty, W Turkmenistan
146 C13 **Etrek** *Per.* Rūd-e Atrak, *Rus.* Atrak, Atrek. ≈ Iran/Turkmenistan
102 L3 **Étretat** Seine-Maritime, N France
114 H9 **Etropole** Sofiya, W Bulgaria
Etsch *see* Adige
Et Tafila *see* Aţ Ţafīlah
99 M23 **Ettelbrück** Diekirch, C Luxembourg
189 V12 **Etten** *atoll* Chuuk Islands, C Micronesia
99 H14 **Etten-Leur** Noord-Brabant, S Netherlands
76 G7 **Et Tîdra** *var.* Ile Tîdra. *island* Dakhlet Nouâdhibou, NW Mauritania
101 G21 **Ettlingen** Baden-Württemberg, SW Germany
102 M2 **Eu** Seine-Maritime, N France
193 W16 **'Eua** *prev.* Middleburg Island. *island* Tongatapu Group, SE Tonga
193 W15 **Eua Iki** *island* Tongatapu Group, S Tonga
Euboea *see* Évvoia
181 O12 **Eucla** Western Australia
31 U11 **Euclid** Ohio, N USA
27 W14 **Eudora** Arkansas, C USA
27 Q4 **Eudora** Kansas, C USA
182 J9 **Eudunda** South Australia
23 R6 **Eufaula** Alabama, S USA
27 Q11 **Eufaula** Oklahoma, C USA
27 Q11 **Eufaula Lake** *var.* Eufaula Reservoir. ⊞ Oklahoma, C USA
Eufaula Reservoir *see* Eufaula Lake
32 F13 **Eugene** Oregon, NW USA
40 B6 **Eugenia, Punta** *headland* W Mexico
183 Q8 **Eugowra** New South Wales, SE Australia
104 I2 **Eume** ≈ NW Spain
104 H2 **Eume, Embalse do** ⊞ NW Spain
Eumolpias *see* Plovdiv
59 O18 **Eunápolis** Bahia, SE Brazil
22 H8 **Eunice** Louisiana, S USA
37 W15 **Eunice** New Mexico, SW USA
99 M19 **Eupen** Liège, E Belgium
138 J9 **Euphrates** *Ar.* Al Furāt, *Turk.* Firat Nehri. ≈ SW Asia
138 L3 **Euphrates Dam** *dam* N Syria
22 M4 **Eupora** Mississippi, S USA
93 K19 **Eura** Länsi-Suomi, W Finland
93 K19 **Eurajoki** Länsi-Suomi, W Finland
102 L4 **Eure** ◈ *department* N France
102 M4 **Eure** ≈ N France
102 M6 **Eure-et-Loir** ◈ *department* C France
34 K3 **Eureka** California, W USA
27 P6 **Eureka** Kansas, C USA
33 O6 **Eureka** Montana, NW USA
35 V5 **Eureka** Nevada, W USA
29 O7 **Eureka** South Dakota, N USA
36 L4 **Eureka** Utah, W USA
32 K10 **Eureka** Washington, NW USA
27 S9 **Eureka Springs** Arkansas, C USA
182 K6 **Eurinilla Creek** *seasonal river* South Australia
183 O11 **Euroa** Victoria, SE Australia
172 M9 **Europa** *island* W Madagascar
104 L3 **Europa, Picos de** ▲ N Spain
104 L16 **Europa Point** *headland* S Gibraltar
86-91 **Europe** *continent*
98 F12 **Europoort** Zuid-Holland, W Netherlands
Euskadi *see* País Vasco
101 D17 **Euskirchen** Nordrhein-Westfalen, W Germany
23 W11 **Eustis** Florida, SE USA
182 M9 **Euston** New South Wales, SE Australia
23 N5 **Eutaw** Alabama, S USA
100 K8 **Eutin** Schleswig-Holstein, N Germany
10 K14 **Eutsuk Lake** ⊞ British Columbia, SW Canada
Euxine Sea *see* Black Sea
83 C16 **Evale** Cunene, SW Angola
37 T3 **Evans** Colorado, C USA
11 P14 **Evansburg** Alberta, SW Canada
29 X13 **Evansdale** Iowa, C USA
183 V4 **Evans Head** New South Wales, SE Australia
12 J11 **Evans, Lac** ◎ Québec, SE Canada
37 S5 **Evans, Mount** ▲ Colorado, C USA
9 Q8 Nunavut, N Canada
31 N10 **Evanston** Illinois, N USA
33 S17 **Evanston** Wyoming, C USA
14 D11 **Evansville** Manitoulin Island, Ontario, S Canada
31 N16 **Evansville** Indiana, N USA
30 L9 **Evansville** Wisconsin, N USA
25 S8 **Evant** Texas, SW USA
143 P13 **Evaz** Fārs, S Iran
29 W4 **Eveleth** Minnesota, N USA
182 E3 **Evelyn Creek** *seasonal river* South Australia
181 Q2 **Evelyn, Mount** ▲ Northern Territory, N Australia
122 K10 **Evenkiyskiy Avtonomnyy Okrug** ◈ *autonomous district* N Russian Federation
183 R13 **Everard, Cape** *headland* Victoria, SE Australia
182 F6 **Everard, Lake** *salt lake* South Australia
182 C2 **Everard Ranges** ▲ South Australia
153 R11 **Everest, Mount** *Chin.* Qomolangma Feng, *Nep.* Sagarmatha. ▲ China/Nepal
18 E15 **Everett** Pennsylvania, NE USA
32 H7 **Everett** Washington, NW USA
99 E17 **Evergem** Oost-Vlaanderen, NW Belgium
23 X16 **Everglades City** Florida, SE USA
23 Y16 **Everglades, The** *wetland* Florida, SE USA
23 P7 **Evergreen** Alabama, S USA
37 T4 **Evergreen** Colorado, C USA
Evergreen State *see* Washington
97 L21 **Evesham** C England, UK
103 T10 **Évian-les-Bains** Haute-Savoie, E France
93 K16 **Evijärvi** Länsi-Suomi, W Finland
79 D17 **Evinayong** *var.* Ebinayon, Evinayoung. C Equatorial Guinea
Evinayoung *see* Evinayong
115 E18 **Évinos** ≈ C Greece
95 E17 **Evje** Aust-Agder, S Norway
Evmolpia *see* Plovdiv
104 H11 **Évora** *anc.* Ebora, *Lat.* Liberalitas Julia. Évora, C Portugal
104 G11 **Évora** ◈ *district* S Portugal
102 M4 **Évreux** *anc.* Civitas Eburovicum. Eure, N France
102 K6 **Évron** Mayenne, NW France
114 L13 **Évros** *Bul.* Maritsa, *Turk.* Meriç; *anc.* Hebrus. ≈ SE Europe *see also* Maritsa/Meriç
115 F21 **Evrótas** ≈ S Greece
103 O5 **Évry** Essonne, N France
25 O8 **E.V.Spence Reservoir** ⊞ Texas, SW USA
115 I18 **Évvoia** *Lat.* Euboea. *island* C Greece
38 D9 **'Ewa Beach** *var.* Ewa Beach. O'ahu, Hawai'i, USA, C Pacific Ocean
32 L9 **Ewan** Washington, NW USA
44 K12 **Ewarton** C Jamaica
81 J18 **Ewaso Ng'iro** *var.* Nyiro. ≈ C Kenya
29 P13 **Ewing** Nebraska, C USA
194 J5 **Ewing Island** *island* Antarctica
65 P17 **Ewing Seamount** *undersea feature* E Atlantic Ocean
158 L6 **Ewirgol** Xinjiang Uygur Zizhiqu, W China
79 G19 **Ewo** Cuvette, W Congo
27 T4 **Excelsior Springs** Missouri, C USA
97 J23 **Exe** ≈ SW England, UK
194 L12 **Executive Committee Range** ▲ Antarctica
14 E16 **Exeter** Ontario, S Canada
97 J24 **Exeter** *anc.* Isca Damnoniorum. SW England, UK
35 R11 **Exeter** California, W USA
19 P10 **Exeter** New Hampshire, NE USA
Exin *see* Kcynia
29 T14 **Exira** Iowa, C USA
97 J23 **Exmoor** *moorland* SW England, UK
21 Y6 **Exmore** Virginia, NE USA
180 G8 **Exmouth** Western Australia
97 J24 **Exmouth** SW England, UK
180 G8 **Exmouth Gulf** *gulf* Western Australia
173 V8 **Exmouth Plateau** *undersea feature* E Indian Ocean
115 J20 **Exompourgo** *ancient monument* Tínos, Kykládes, Greece, Aegean Sea
104 I10 **Extremadura** *var.* Estremadura. ◈ *autonomous community* W Spain
78 F12 **Extrême-Nord** *Eng.* Extreme North. ◈ *province* N Cameroon
Extreme North *see* Extrême-Nord
44 I3 **Exuma Cays** *islets* C Bahamas
44 I3 **Exuma Sound** *sound* C Bahamas
81 H20 **Eyasi, Lake** ◎ N Tanzania
95 F17 **Eydehavn** Aust-Agder, S Norway
96 L12 **Eyemouth** SE Scotland, UK
96 G7 **Eye Peninsula** *peninsula* NW Scotland, UK
80 Q13 **Eyl** *It.* Eil. Nugaal, E Somalia
103 N11 **Eymoutiers** Haute-Vienne, C France
Eyo (lower course) *see* Uolo, Río
29 X10 **Eyota** Minnesota, N USA
182 H2 **Eyre Basin, Lake** *salt lake* South Australia
182 I1 **Eyre Creek** *seasonal river* Northern Territory/South Australia
185 C22 **Eyre Mountains** ▲ South Island, NZ
182 H3 **Eyre North, Lake** *salt lake* South Australia
182 G7 **Eyre Peninsula** *peninsula* South Australia
182 H4 **Eyre South, Lake** *salt lake* South Australia
95 B18 **Eysturoy** *Dan.* Østerø *Island* Faeroe Islands
61 D20 **Ezeiza** ✕ (Buenos Aires) Buenos Aires, E Argentina
Ezeres *see* Ezeriş
116 F12 **Ezeriş** *Hung.* Ezeres. Caraş-Severin, W Romania
161 O9 **Ezhou** *prev.* Echeng. Hubei, C China
125 R11 **Ezhva** Respublika Komi, NW Russian Federation
136 B12 **Ezine** Çanakkale, NW Turkey
Ezo *see* Hokkaidō
Ezra/Ezraa *see* Izra'

F

191 P7 **Faaa** Tahiti, W French Polynesia
191 P7 **Faaa** ✕ (Papeete) Tahiti, W French Polynesia
95 H24 **Faaborg** *var.* Fåborg. Fyn, C Denmark
151 K19 **Faadhippolhu Atoll** *var.* Fadiffolu, Lhaviyani Atoll. *atoll* N Maldives
191 U10 **Faaite** *atoll* Îles Tuamotu, C French Polynesia
191 Q8 **Faaone** Tahiti, W French Polynesia
24 H8 **Fabens** Texas, SW USA
94 H12 **Fåberg** Oppland, S Norway
Fåborg *see* Faaborg
106 I12 **Fabriano** Marche, C Italy
145 U16 **Fabrichnyy** Almaty, SE Kazakhstan
54 F10 **Facatativá** Cundinamarca, C Colombia
77 X9 **Fachi** Agadez, C Niger
188 B16 **Facpi Point** *headland* W Guam
18 I13 **Factoryville** Pennsylvania, NE USA
78 K8 **Fada** Borkou-Ennedi-Tibesti, E Chad
77 Q13 **Fada-Ngourma** E Burkina
123 N6 **Faddeya, Zaliv** *bay* N Russian Federation
123 Q5 **Faddeyevskiy, Ostrov** *island* Novosibirskiye Ostrova, NE Russian Federation
141 W12 **Fadhī** S Oman
106 H10 **Faenza** *anc.* Faventia. Emilia-Romagna, N Italy
64 M5 **Faeroe-Iceland Ridge** *undersea feature* NW Norwegian Sea
64 M5 **Faeroe Islands** *Dan.* Færøerne, *Faer.* Føroyar. ◇ *Danish external territory* N Atlantic Ocean
Færøerne *see* Faeroe Islands
64 N6 **Faeroe-Shetland Trough** *undersea feature* NE Atlantic Ocean
104 H6 **Fafe** Braga, N Portugal
80 K13 **Fafen Shet'** ≈ E Ethiopia
193 V15 **Fafo** *island* Tongatapu Group, S Tonga
192 I16 **Fagaloa Bay** *bay* Upolu, E Samoa
192 H15 **Fagamālo** Savai'i, N Samoa
116 I12 **Făgăraş** *Ger.* Fogarasch, *Hung.* Fogaras. Braşov, C Romania
95 M20 **Fagerhult** Kalmar, S Sweden
94 G13 **Fagernes** Oppland, S Norway
92 I9 **Fagernes** Troms, N Norway
95 M14 **Fagersta** Västmanland, C Sweden
77 W13 **Faggo** *var.* Foggo. Bauchi, N Nigeria
Faghman *see* Fughmah
Fagibina, Lake *see* Faguibine, Lac
63 J25 **Fagnano, Lago** ◎ S Argentina
99 G22 **Fagne** *hill range* S Belgium
77 N10 **Faguibine, Lac** *var.* Lake Fagibina. ◎ NW Mali
Fahaheel *see* Al Fuḩayḩīl
Fahlun *see* Falun
143 U12 **Fahraj** Kermān, SE Iran
64 P5 **Faial** Madeira, Portugal, NE Atlantic Ocean
64 N2 **Faial** *var.* Ilha do Faial. *island* Azores, Portugal, NE Atlantic Ocean
Faial, Ilha do *see* Faial
108 G10 **Faido** Ticino, S Switzerland
Faifo *see* Hôi An
Failaka Island *see* Faylakah
190 G12 **Faioa, Île** *island* N Wallis and Futuna
181 W8 **Fairbairn Reservoir** ⊞ Queensland, E Australia
39 R9 **Fairbanks** Alaska, USA
21 U12 **Fair Bluff** North Carolina, SE USA
31 R14 **Fairborn** Ohio, N USA
23 S3 **Fairburn** Georgia, SE USA
30 M12 **Fairbury** Illinois, N USA
29 Q17 **Fairbury** Nebraska, C USA
29 T9 **Fairfax** Minnesota, N USA
27 O8 **Fairfax** Oklahoma, C USA
21 R14 **Fairfax** South Carolina, SE USA
35 N8 **Fairfield** California, W USA
33 O14 **Fairfield** Idaho, NW USA
30 M16 **Fairfield** Illinois, N USA
29 X15 **Fairfield** Iowa, C USA
33 R8 **Fairfield** Montana, NW USA
31 Q14 **Fairfield** Ohio, N USA
25 U8 **Fairfield** Texas, SW USA
27 T7 **Fair Grove** Missouri, C USA
19 P12 **Fairhaven** Massachusetts, NE USA
23 N8 **Fairhope** Alabama, S USA
96 L4 **Fair Isle** *island* NE Scotland, UK
185 F20 **Fairlie** Canterbury, South Island, NZ
29 U11 **Fairmont** Minnesota, N USA
29 Q16 **Fairmont** Nebraska, C USA
21 S3 **Fairmont** West Virginia, NE USA
31 P13 **Fairmount** Indiana, N USA
18 H10 **Fairmount** New York, NE USA
29 R7 **Fairmount** North Dakota, N USA
37 S5 **Fairplay** Colorado, C USA
18 F9 **Fairport** New York, NE USA
11 O12 **Fairview** Alberta, W Canada
26 L9 **Fairview** Oklahoma, C USA
36 L4 **Fairview** Utah, W USA
35 T6 **Fairview Peak** ▲ Nevada, W USA
188 H14 **Fais** *atoll* Caroline Islands, W Micronesia
149 U8 **Faisalābād** *prev.* Lyallpur. Punjab, NE Pakistan
Faisaliya *see* Fayṣalīyah
28 L8 **Faith** South Dakota, N USA
153 N12 **Faizābād** Uttar Pradesh, N India
Faizabad/Faizābād *see* Feyẕābād
45 S9 **Fajardo** E Puerto Rico
139 R9 **Fajj, Wādī al** *dry watercourse* S Iraq
140 K4 **Fajr, Bi'r** *well* NW Saudi Arabia
191 W10 **Fakahina** *atoll* Îles Tuamotu, C French Polynesia
190 L10 **Fakaofo Atoll** *island* SE Tokelau
191 U10 **Fakarava** *atoll* Îles Tuamotu, C French Polynesia
127 T2 **Fakel** Udmurtskaya Respublika, NW Russian Federation
97 P19 **Fakenham** E England, UK
171 U13 **Fakfak** Papua, E Indonesia
153 T12 **Fakīragrām** Assam, NE India
114 M10 **Fakiyska Reka** ≈ SE Bulgaria
95 J24 **Fakse** Storstrøm, SE Denmark
95 J24 **Fakse Bugt** *bay* SE Denmark
95 J24 **Fakse Ladeplads** Storstrøm, SE Denmark
163 V11 **Faku** Liaoning, NE China
76 J14 **Falaba** N Sierra Leone
102 K5 **Falaise** Calvados, N France
114 H12 **Falakró** ▲ NE Greece
189 T12 **Falalu** *island* Chuuk, C Micronesia
166 L4 **Falam** Chin State, W Burma
143 N8 **Falāvarjān** Eşfahān, C Iran
116 M11 **Fălciu** Vaslui, E Romania
54 I4 **Falcón** *off.* Estado Falcón. ◈ *state* NW Venezuela
106 J12 **Falconara Marittima** Marche, C Italy
Falcone, Capo del *see* Falcone, Punta del
107 A16 **Falcone, Punta del** *var.* Capo del Falcone. *headland* Sardegna, Italy, C Mediterranean Sea
11 Y16 **Falcon Lake** Manitoba, S Canada
Falcon Lake *see* Falcón, Presa/Falcon Reservoir
41 O7 **Falcón, Presa** *var.* Falcon Lake, Falcon Reservoir. ⊞ Mexico/USA *see also* Falcon Reservoir
25 Q16 **Falcon Reservoir** *var.* Falcon Lake, Presa Falcón. ⊞ Mexico/USA *see also* Falcón, Presa
190 L10 **Fale** *island* Fakaofo Atoll, SE Tokelau
192 F15 **Faleālupo** Savai'i, NW Samoa
190 B10 **Falefatu** *island* Funafuti Atoll, C Tuvalu
192 G15 **Fālelima** Savai'i, NW Samoa
95 N18 **Falerum** Östergötland, S Sweden
Faleshty *see* Făleşti
116 M9 **Făleşti** *Rus.* Faleshty. NW Moldova
25 S15 **Falfurrias** Texas, SW USA
11 O13 **Falher** Alberta, W Canada
Falkenau an der Eger *see* Sokolov
95 J21 **Falkenberg** Halland, S Sweden
Falkenberg *see* Niemodlin
Falkenburg in Pommern *see* Złocieniec
100 N12 **Falkensee** Brandenburg, NE Germany
96 J12 **Falkirk** C Scotland, UK
65 I20 **Falkland Escarpment** *undersea feature* SW Atlantic Ocean
63 K24 **Falkland Islands** *var.* Falklands, Islas Malvinas. ◇ *UK dependent territory* SW Atlantic Ocean
65 I20 **Falkland Plateau** *var.* Argentine Rise. *undersea feature* SW Atlantic Ocean
Falklands *see* Falkland Islands
63 M23 **Falkland Sound** *var.* Estrecho de San Carlos. *strait* C Falkland Islands
Falknov nad Ohří *see* Sokolov
115 H21 **Falkonéra** *island* S Greece
95 K18 **Falköping** Västra Götaland, S Sweden
139 U8 **Fallāḩ** E Iraq
35 U16 **Fallbrook** California, W USA
189 U12 **Falleallej Pass** *passage* Chuuk Islands, C Micronesia
93 J14 **Fällfors** Västerbotten, N Sweden
194 I6 **Fallières Coast** *physical region* Antarctica
100 I11 **Fallingbostel** Niedersachsen, NW Germany
33 X9 **Fallon** Montana, NW USA
35 S5 **Fallon** Nevada, W USA
19 O12 **Fall River** Massachusetts, NE USA
27 P6 **Fall River Lake** ⊞ Kansas, C USA
35 O3 **Fall River Mills** California, W USA
21 W4 **Falls Church** Virginia, NE USA
29 S17 **Falls City** Nebraska, C USA
25 S12 **Falls City** Texas, SW USA
Falluja *see* Al Fallūjah
77 S12 **Falmey** Dosso, SW Niger
45 W10 **Falmouth** Antigua, Antigua and Barbuda
44 J11 **Falmouth** W Jamaica
97 H25 **Falmouth** SW England, UK
20 M4 **Falmouth** Kentucky, S USA
19 P13 **Falmouth** Massachusetts, NE USA
21 W5 **Falmouth** Virginia, NE USA
189 U12 **Falos** *island* Chuuk, C Micronesia
83 E26 **False Bay** *Afr.* Valsbaai. *bay* SW South Africa
155 K17 **False Divi Point** *headland* E India
38 M16 **False Pass** Unimak Island, Alaska, USA
154 P12 **False Point** *headland* E India
105 U6 **Falset** Cataluña, NE Spain
95 I25 **Falster** *island* SE Denmark
116 K9 **Fălticeni** *Hung.* Falticsén. Suceava, NE Romania
Falticsén *see* Fălticeni
94 M13 **Falun** *var.* Fahlun. Dalarna, C Sweden
Famagusta *see* Gazimağusa
Famagusta Bay *see* Gazimağusa Körfezi
62 I8 **Famatina** La Rioja, NW Argentina
99 J21 **Famenne** *physical region* SE Belgium
113 D22 **Fan** *var.* Fani. ≈ N Albania
77 X15 **Fan** ≈ E Nigeria
76 M12 **Fana** Koulikoro, SW Mali
115 K19 **Fána** *ancient harbour* Chíos, SE Greece
189 V13 **Fanan** *island* Chuuk, C Micronesia
189 U12 **Fanapanges** *island* Chuuk, C Micronesia
115 L20 **Fanári, Akrotírio** *headland* Ikaría, Dodekánisos, Greece, Aegean Sea
45 Q13 **Fancy** Saint Vincent, Saint Vincent and the Grenadines
172 I5 **Fandriana** Fianarantsoa, SE Madagascar
167 O6 **Fang** Chiang Mai, NW Thailand
80 E13 **Fangak** Jonglei, SE Sudan
191 W10 **Fangatau** *atoll* Îles Tuamotu, C French Polynesia
191 X12 **Fangataufa** *island* Îles Tuamotu, SE French Polynesia
193 V15 **Fanga Uta** *bay* S Tonga
161 N7 **Fangcheng** Henan, C China
160 K15 **Fangchenggang** *var.* Fangcheng Gezu Zizhixian; *prev.* Fangcheng. Guangxi Zhuangzu Zizhiqu, S China
161 S15 **Fangshan** S Taiwan
163 X8 **Fangzheng** Heilongjiang, NE China
Fani *see* Fan
119 K16 **Fanipal'** *Rus.* Fanipol'. Minskaya Voblasts', C Belarus
Fanipol' *see* Fanipal'
25 T13 **Fannin** Texas, SW USA
Fanning Island *see* Tabuaeran
94 G8 **Fannrem** Sør-Trøndelag, S Norway
106 I11 **Fano** *anc.* Colonia Julia Fanestris, Fanum Fortunae. Marche, C Italy
95 E23 **Fanø** *island* W Denmark
167 R5 **Fan Si Pan** ▲ N Vietnam
Fanum Fortunae *see* Fano
Fao *see* Al Fāw
141 W7 **Faq'** *var.* Al Faqa. Dubayy, E UAE
Farab *see* Farap
194 H5 **Faraday** *UK research station* Antarctica

◆ Country
● Country Capital
◇ Dependent Territory
○ Dependent Territory Capital
◈ Administrative Region
✕ International Airport
▲ Mountain
▲ Mountain Range
⛰ Volcano
≈ River
◎ Lake
⊞ Reservoir

185 G16 **Faraday, Mount** ▲ South Island, NZ
79 P16 **Faradje** Orientale, NE Dem. Rep. Congo
Faradofay *see* Tôlañaro
172 I7 **Farafangana** Fianarantsoa, SE Madagascar
148 J7 **Farāh** *var.* Farah, Fararud. Farāh, W Afghanistan
148 K7 **Farāh** ◆ *province* W Afghanistan
148 J7 **Farāh Rūd** ≈ W Afghanistan
188 K7 **Farallon de Medinilla** *island* C Northern Mariana Islands
188 J2 **Farallon de Pajaros** *var.* Uracas. *island* N Northern Mariana Islands
76 J14 **Faranah** Haute-Guinée, S Guinea
146 K12 **Farap** *Rus.* Farab. Lebap Welaýaty, NE Turkmenistan
Fararud *see* Farāh
140 M13 **Farasān, Jazā'ir** *island group* SW Saudi Arabia
172 I5 **Faratsiho** Antananarivo, C Madagascar
188 K15 **Faraulep Atoll** *atoll* Caroline Islands, C Micronesia
99 H20 **Farciennes** Hainaut, S Belgium
105 O14 **Fardes** ≈ S Spain
191 S10 **Fare** Huahine, W French Polynesia
97 M23 **Fareham** S England, UK
39 P11 **Farewell** Alaska, USA
184 H13 **Farewell, Cape** *headland* South Island, NZ
Farewell, Cape *see* Nunap Isua
184 I13 **Farewell Spit** *spit* South Island, NZ
95 I17 **Färgelanda** Västra Götaland, S Sweden
Farghona Valley *see* Fergana Valley
147 R10 **Farg'ona Viloyati** *Rus.* Ferganskaya Oblast'. ◆ *province* E Uzbekistan
Farghona, Wodii/Farghona Wodiysi *see* Fergana Valley
23 V8 **Fargo** Georgia, SE USA
29 R5 **Fargo** North Dakota, N USA
147 S10 **Farg'ona** *Rus.* Fergana; *prev.* Novyy Margilan. Farg'ona Viloyati, E Uzbekistan
29 V10 **Faribault** Minnesota, N USA
152 J11 **Farīdābād** Haryāna, N India
152 H8 **Farīdkot** Punjab, NW India
153 T15 **Faridpur** Dhaka, C Bangladesh
121 P14 **Fārigh, Wādī al** ≈ N Libya
172 I4 **Farihy Alaotra** ⊚ C Madagascar
94 M11 **Färila** Gävleborg, C Sweden
104 E9 **Farilhões** *island* C Portugal
76 G12 **Farim** NW Guinea-Bissau
Farish *see* Forish
141 T11 **Fāris, Qalamat** *well* SE Saudi Arabia
95 N21 **Färjestaden** Kalmar, S Sweden
149 R2 **Farkhār** Takhār, NE Afghanistan
147 Q14 **Farkhor** *Rus.* Parkhar. SW Tajikistan
116 F12 **Fârliug** *prev.* Fîrliug, *Hung.* Furluk. Caraş-Severin, SW Romania
115 M21 **Farmakonísi** *island* Dodekánisos, Greece, Aegean Sea
30 M13 **Farmer City** Illinois, N USA
31 N14 **Farmersburg** Indiana, N USA
25 U6 **Farmersville** Texas, SW USA
22 H5 **Farmerville** Louisiana, S USA
29 X16 **Farmington** Iowa, C USA
19 Q6 **Farmington** Maine, NE USA
29 V9 **Farmington** Minnesota, N USA
27 X6 **Farmington** Missouri, C USA
19 O9 **Farmington** New Hampshire, NE USA
37 P9 **Farmington** New Mexico, SW USA
36 L2 **Farmington** Utah, W USA
21 W9 **Farmville** North Carolina, SE USA
21 U6 **Farmville** Virginia, NE USA
97 N22 **Farnborough** S England, UK
97 N22 **Farnham** S England, UK
10 J7 **Faro** Yukon Territory, W Canada
104 G14 **Faro** Faro, S Portugal
104 G14 **Faro** ◆ *district* S Portugal
104 G14 **Faro** ✕ Faro, S Portugal
78 F13 **Faro** ≈ Cameroon/Nigeria
95 Q18 **Fårö** Gotland, SE Sweden
Faro, Punta del *see* Peloro, Capo
95 Q18 **Fårösund** Gotland, SE Sweden
173 N7 **Farquhar Group** *island group* S Seychelles
18 B13 **Farrell** Pennsylvania, NE USA
152 K11 **Farrukhābād** Uttar Pradesh, N India
143 P11 **Fārs** *off.* Ostān-e Fārs; *anc.* Persis. ◆ *province* S Iran
115 F16 **Fársala** Thessalía, C Greece
143 R4 **Fārsīān** Golestān, N Iran
Fars, Khalīj-e *see* Gulf, The
95 G21 **Farsø** Nordjylland, N Denmark
95 D18 **Farsund** Vest-Agder, S Norway
141 U14 **Fartak, Ra's** *headland* E Yemen
60 H13 **Fartura, Serra da** ▲ S Brazil
Farvel, Kap *see* Nunap Isua
24 L4 **Farwell** Texas, SW USA
194 I9 **Farwell Island** *island* Antarctica
152 L9 **Far Western** ◆ *zone* W Nepal
148 M3 **Fāryāb** ◆ *province* N Afghanistan
143 P12 **Fasā** Fārs, S Iran
141 U12 **Fasad, Ramlat** *desert* SW Oman
107 P17 **Fasano** Puglia, SE Italy
92 L3 **Fáskrúdhsfjördhur** Austurland, E Iceland
117 O5 **Fastiv** *Rus.* Fastov. Kyyivs'ka Oblast', NW Ukraine
97 B22 **Fastnet Rock** *Ir.* Carraig Aonair. *island* SW Ireland
Fastov *see* Fastiv
190 C9 **Fatato** *island* Funafuti Atoll, C Tuvalu
152 K12 **Fatehgarh** Uttar Pradesh, N India
149 U6 **Fatehjang** Punjab, E Pakistan
152 G11 **Fatehpur** Rājasthān, N India
152 L13 **Fatehpur** Uttar Pradesh, N India
126 J7 **Fatezh** Kurskaya Oblast', W Russian Federation
76 G11 **Fatick** W Senegal
104 G9 **Fátima** Santarém, W Portugal
136 M11 **Fatsa** Ordu, N Turkey
Fatshan *see* Foshan
190 D12 **Fatua, Pointe** *var.* Pointe Nord. *headland* Île Futuna, S Wallis and Futuna
191 X7 **Fatu Hiva** *island* Îles Marquises, NE French Polynesia
Fatunda *see* Fatundu
79 H21 **Fatundu** *var.* Fatunda. Bandundu, W Dem. Rep. Congo
187 S11 **Fatutaka** *island*, E Soloman Islands
29 O8 **Faulkton** South Dakota, N USA
116 L13 **Făurei** *prev.* Filimon Sîrbu. Brăila, SE Romania
92 G12 **Fauske** Nordland, C Norway
11 P13 **Faust** Alberta, W Canada
99 L23 **Fauvillers** Luxembourg, SE Belgium
107 J24 **Favara** Sicilia, Italy, C Mediterranean Sea
Faventia *see* Faenza
107 G23 **Favignana, Isola** *island* Isole Egadi, S Italy
12 D8 **Fawn** ≈ Ontario, SE Canada
Faxa Bay *see* Faxaflói
92 H3 **Faxaflói** *Eng.* Faxa Bay. *bay* W Iceland
78 I7 **Faya** *prev.* Faya-Largeau, Largeau. Borkou-Ennedi-Tibesti, N Chad
Faya-Largeau *see* Faya
187 Q16 **Fayaoué** Province des Îles Loyauté, C New Caledonia
138 M5 **Faydāt** *hill range* E Syria
23 O3 **Fayette** Alabama, S USA
29 X12 **Fayette** Iowa, C USA
22 J6 **Fayette** Mississippi, S USA
27 U4 **Fayette** Missouri, C USA
27 S9 **Fayetteville** Arkansas, C USA
21 U10 **Fayetteville** North Carolina, SE USA
20 J10 **Fayetteville** Tennessee, S USA
25 U11 **Fayetteville** Texas, SW USA
21 R5 **Fayetteville** West Virginia, NE USA
141 R4 **Faylakah** *var.* Failaka Island. *island* E Kuwait
139 T10 **Fayṣalīyah** *var.* Faisaliya. S Iraq
189 P15 **Fayu** *var.* East Fayu. *island* Hall Islands, C Micronesia
152 G8 **Fāzilka** Punjab, NW India
Fdérick *see* Fdérik
76 J6 **Fdérik** *var.* Fdérick, *Fr.* Fort Gouraud. Tiris Zemmour, NW Mauritania
Feabhail, Loch *see* Foyle, Lough
97 B20 **Feale** ≈ SW Ireland
21 V12 **Fear, Cape** *headland* Bald Head Island, North Carolina, SE USA
35 O6 **Feather River** ≈ California, W USA
185 M14 **Featherston** Wellington, North Island, NZ
102 L3 **Fécamp** Seine-Maritime, N France
Fédala *see* Mohammedia
61 D17 **Federación** Entre Ríos, E Argentina
61 D17 **Federal** Entre Ríos, E Argentina
77 T15 **Federal Capital District** ◆ *capital territory* C Nigeria
Federal Capital Territory *see* Australian Capital Territory
Federal District *see* Distrito Federal
21 Y4 **Federalsburg** Maryland, NE USA
74 M6 **Fedjaj, Chott el** *var.* Chott el Fejaj, Shaṭṭ al Fijāj. *salt lake* C Tunisia
94 B13 **Fedje** *island* S Norway
144 M7 **Fedorovka** Kostanay, N Kazakhstan
127 U6 **Fedorovka** Respublika Bashkortostan, W Russian Federation
Fëdory *see* Fyadory
117 U11 **Fedotova Kosa** *spit* SE Ukraine
189 V13 **Fefan** *atoll* Chuuk Islands, C Micronesia
111 O21 **Fehérgyarmat** Szabolcs-Szatmár-Bereg, E Hungary
Fehér-Körös *see* Crişul Alb
Fehértemplom *see* Bela Crkva
Fehérvölgy *see* Albac
100 L7 **Fehmarn** *island* N Germany
95 H25 **Fehmarn Belt** *Dan.* Femern Bælt, *Ger.* Fehmarnbelt. *strait* Denmark/Germany *see also* Femern Bælt
Fehmarnbelt *see* Fehmarn Belt/Femern Bælt
109 X8 **Fehring** Steiermark, SE Austria
59 B15 **Feijó** Acre, W Brazil
184 M12 **Feilding** Manawatu-Wanganui, North Island, NZ
Feira *see* Feira de Santana
59 O17 **Feira de Santana** *var.* Feira. Bahia, E Brazil
109 X7 **Feistritz** ≈ SE Austria
Feistritz *see* Ilirska Bistrica
161 P8 **Feixi** *var.* Shangpai. Anhui, E China
Fejaj, Chott el *see* Fedjaj, Chott el
111 I23 **Fejér** *off.* Fejér Megye. ◆ *county* W Hungary
95 I24 **Fejø** *island* SE Denmark
136 K15 **Feke** Adana, S Turkey
Feketehalom *see* Codlea
Fekete-Körös *see* Crişul Negru
109 T3 **Feldaist** ≈ N Austria
109 W8 **Feldbach** Steiermark, SE Austria
101 F24 **Feldberg** ▲ SW Germany
116 J12 **Feldioara** *Ger.* Marienburg, *Hung.* Földvár. Braşov, C Romania
108 I7 **Feldkirch** *anc.* Clunia. Vorarlberg, W Austria
109 S9 **Feldkirchen in Kärnten** *Slvn.* Trg. Kärnten, S Austria
Félegyháza *see* Kiskunfélegyháza
192 H16 **Feleolo** ✕ (Āpia) Upolu, C Samoa
104 H6 **Felgueiras** Porto, N Portugal
Felicitas Julia *see* Lisboa
172 J16 **Félicité** *island* Inner Islands, NE Seychelles
151 K20 **Felidhu Atoll** *atoll* C Maldives
41 Y13 **Felipe Carrillo Puerto** Quintana Roo, SE Mexico
97 Q21 **Felixstowe** E England, UK
103 N11 **Felletin** Creuse, C France
Fellin *see* Viljandi
Felsőbánya *see* Baia Sprie
Felsőmuzslya *see* Mužlja
Felsővisó *see* Vişeu de Sus
35 N10 **Felton** California, W USA
106 H7 **Feltre** Veneto, NE Italy
95 H25 **Femern Bælt** *Ger.* Fehmarnbelt. Fehmarn Belt. *strait* Denmark/Germany *see also* Fehmarn Belt
95 I24 **Femø** *island* SE Denmark
94 I10 **Femunden** ⊚ S Norway
104 H2 **Fene** Galicia, NW Spain
14 I14 **Fenelon Falls** Ontario, SE Canada
189 U13 **Feneppi** *atoll* Chuuk Islands, C Micronesia
137 O11 **Fener Burnu** *headland* N Turkey
115 J14 **Fengári** ▲ Samothráki, E Greece
163 V13 **Fengcheng** *var.* Feng-cheng, Fenghwangcheng. Liaoning, NE China
160 K11 **Fenggang** *var.* Longquan. Guizhou, S China
161 S9 **Fenghua** Zhejiang, SE China
Fenghwangcheng *see* Fengcheng
Fengjiaba *see* Wangcang
160 L9 **Fengjie** *var.* Yong'an. Chongqing Shi, C China
160 M14 **Fengkai** *var.* Jiangkou. Guangdong, S China
161 T13 **Fenglin** *Jap.* Hōrin. C Taiwan
161 P1 **Fengning** *prev.* Dagezhen. Hebei, E China
160 E13 **Fengqing** *var.* Fengshan. Yunnan, SW China
161 O6 **Fengqiu** Henan, C China
161 Q2 **Fengrun** Hebei, E China
Fengshan *see* Fengqing, Yunnan, China
Fengshan *see* Luoyuan, Fujian, China
163 T4 **Fengshui Shan** ▲ NE China
161 P14 **Fengshun** Guangdong, S China
Fengtien *see* Liaoning, China
Fengtien *see* Shenyang, China
160 J7 **Fengxian** *var.* Feng Xian; *prev.* Shuangshipu. Shaanxi, C China
Fengxiang *see* Luobei
163 P13 **Fengzhen** Nei Mongol Zizhiqu, N China
160 M6 **Fen He** ≈ C China
153 V15 **Feni** Chittagong, E Bangladesh
186 I6 **Feni Islands** *island group* NE PNG
38 H17 **Fenimore Pass** *strait* Aleutian Islands, Alaska, USA
Fennern *see* Vändra
30 J9 **Fennimore** Wisconsin, N USA
172 J4 **Fenoarivo** Toamasina, E Madagascar
95 I24 **Fensmark** Storstrøm, SE Denmark
97 O19 **Fens, The** *wetland* E England, UK
31 R9 **Fenton** Michigan, N USA
190 K10 **Fenua Fala** *island* SE Tokelau
190 F12 **Fenuafo'ou, Île** *island* E Wallis and Futuna
190 L10 **Fenua Loa** *island* Fakaofo Atoll, E Tokelau
160 M4 **Fenyang** Shanxi, C China
117 U13 **Feodosiya** *var.* Kefe, *It.* Kaffa; *anc.* Theodosia. Respublika Krym, S Ukraine
94 I10 **Feragen** ⊚ S Norway
74 L5 **Fer, Cap de** *headland* NE Algeria
31 O16 **Ferdinand** Indiana, N USA
Ferdinand *see* Montana, Bulgaria
Ferdinand *see* Mihail Kogălniceanu, Romania
Ferdinandsberg *see* Oţelu Roşu
143 T7 **Ferdows** *var.* Firdaus; *prev.* Tūn. Khorāsān, E Iran
103 Q5 **Fère-Champenoise** Marne, N France
Ferencz-József Csúcs *see* Gerlachovský štít
107 J16 **Ferentino** Lazio, C Italy
114 L13 **Féres** Anatolikí Makedonía kai Thráki, NE Greece
Fergana *see* Farg'ona
147 S10 **Fergana Valley** *var.* Farghona Valley, *Rus.* Ferganskaya Dolina, *Taj.* Wodii Farghona, *Uzb.* Farghona Wodiysi. *basin* Tajikistan/Uzbekistan
Ferganskaya Dolina *see* Fergana Valley
Ferganskaya Oblast' *see* Farg'ona Viloyati
147 U9 **Ferganskiy Khrebet** ▲ C Kyrgyzstan
14 F15 **Fergus** Ontario, S Canada
29 S6 **Fergus Falls** Minnesota, N USA
186 G9 **Fergusson Island** *var.* Kaluwawa. *island* SE PNG
111 K22 **Ferihegy** ✕ (Budapest) Budapest, C Hungary
Ferizaj *see* Uroševac
77 N14 **Ferkessédougou** N Ivory Coast
109 T10 **Ferlach** *Slvn.* Borovlje. Kärnten, S Austria
97 E16 **Fermanagh** *cultural region* SW Northern Ireland, UK
106 J13 **Fermo** *anc.* Firmum Picenum. Marche, C Italy
104 J6 **Fermoselle** Castilla-León, N Spain
97 D20 **Fermoy** *Ir.* Mainistir Fhear Maí. SW Ireland
23 W8 **Fernandina Beach** Amelia Island, Florida, SE USA
57 A17 **Fernandina, Isla** *var.* Narborough Island. *island* Galapagos Islands, Ecuador, E Pacific Ocean
65 K14 **Fernando de Noronha** *island* E Brazil
Fernando Po/Fernando Póo *see* Bioco, Isla de
60 J7 **Fernandópolis** São Paulo, S Brazil
104 M13 **Fernán Núñez** Andalucía, S Spain
83 Q14 **Fernão Veloso, Baia de** *bay* NE Mozambique
34 K3 **Ferndale** California, W USA
32 H6 **Ferndale** Washington, NW USA
11 P17 **Fernie** British Columbia, SW Canada
35 R5 **Fernley** Nevada, W USA
Ferozepore *see* Firozpur
107 N18 **Ferrandina** Basilicata, S Italy
106 G9 **Ferrara** *anc.* Forum Alieni. Emilia-Romagna, N Italy
120 F9 **Ferrat, Cap** *headland* NW Algeria
107 D20 **Ferrato, Capo** *headland* Sardegna, Italy, C Mediterranean Sea
104 G12 **Ferreira do Alentejo** Beja, S Portugal
56 B11 **Ferreñafe** Lambayeque, W Peru
108 C12 **Ferret** Valais, SW Switzerland
102 I13 **Ferret, Cap** *headland* W France
22 I6 **Ferriday** Louisiana, S USA
Ferro *see* Hierro
107 D16 **Ferro, Capo** *headland* Sardegna, Italy, C Mediterranean Sea
104 H2 **Ferrol** *var.* El Ferrol; *prev.* El Ferrol del Caudillo. Galicia, NW Spain
56 B12 **Ferrol, Península de** *peninsula* W Peru
36 M5 **Ferron** Utah, W USA
21 S7 **Ferrum** Virginia, NE USA
23 O8 **Ferry Pass** Florida, SE USA
Ferryville *see* Menzel Bourguiba
29 S4 **Fertile** Minnesota, N USA
Fertő *see* Neusiedler See
98 L5 **Ferwerd** *Fris.* Ferwert. Friesland, N Netherlands
Ferwert *see* Ferwerd
74 G6 **Fès** *Eng.* Fez. N Morocco
79 I22 **Feshi** Bandundu, SW Dem. Rep. Congo
29 O4 **Fessenden** North Dakota, N USA
Festenberg *see* Twardogóra
27 X5 **Festus** Missouri, C USA
116 M14 **Feteşti** Ialomiţa, SE Romania
136 D17 **Fethiye** Muğla, SW Turkey
96 M1 **Fetlar** *island* NE Scotland, UK
95 I15 **Fetsund** Akershus, S Norway
12 L5 **Feuilles, Lac aux** ⊚ Québec, E Canada
12 L5 **Feuilles, Rivière aux** ≈ Québec, E Canada
99 M23 **Feulen** Diekirch, C Luxembourg
103 Q11 **Feurs** Loire, E France
95 F18 **Fevik** Aust-Agder, S Norway
123 R13 **Fevral'sk** Amurskaya Oblast', SE Russian Federation
149 S2 **Feyẕābād** *var.* Faizabad, Faizābād, Feyzābād, Fyzabad. Badakhshān, NE Afghanistan
Fez *see* Fès
97 J19 **Ffestiniog** NW Wales, UK
Fhóid Duibh, Cuan an *see* Blacksod Bay
62 I8 **Fiambalá** Catamarca, NW Argentina
172 I6 **Fianarantsoa** Fianarantsoa, C Madagascar
172 H6 **Fianarantsoa** ◆ *province* SE Madagascar
78 G12 **Fianga** Mayo-Kébbi, SW Chad
Ficce *see* Fichē
80 J12 **Fichē** *It.* Ficce. Oromo, C Ethiopia
101 N17 **Fichtelberg** ▲ Czech Republic/Germany
101 M18 **Fichtelgebirge** ▲ SE Germany
101 M19 **Fichtelnaab** ≈ SE Germany
106 E9 **Fidenza** Emilia-Romagna, N Italy
113 K21 **Fier** *var.* Fieri. Fier, SW Albania
113 K21 **Fier** ◆ *district* W Albania
Fieri *see* Fier
Fierza *see* Fierzë
113 L17 **Fierzë** *var.* Fierza. Shkodër, N Albania
113 L17 **Fierzës, Liqeni i** ⊚ N Albania
108 F10 **Fiesch** Valais, SW Switzerland
106 G11 **Fiesole** Toscana, C Italy
138 G12 **Fifah** Aṭ Ṭafilah, W Jordan
96 K11 **Fife** *var.* Kingdom of Fife. *cultural region* E Scotland, UK
96 K11 **Fife Ness** *headland* E Scotland, UK
Fifteen Twenty Fracture Zone *see* Barracuda Fracture Zone
103 N13 **Figeac** Lot, S France
95 N19 **Figeholm** Kalmar, SE Sweden
Figig *see* Figuig
83 J18 **Figtree** Matabeleland South, SW Zimbabwe
104 F8 **Figueira da Foz** Coimbra, W Portugal
105 X4 **Figueres** Cataluña, E Spain
74 H7 **Figuig** *var.* Figig. E Morocco
Fijāj, Shaṭṭ al *see* Fedjaj, Chott el
187 Y15 **Fiji** *off.* Sovereign Democratic Republic of Fiji, *Fij.* Viti. ◆ *republic* SW Pacific Ocean
192 K9 **Fiji** *island group* SW Pacific Ocean
105 P14 **Filabres, Sierra de los** ▲ SE Spain
83 K18 **Filabusi** Matabeleland South, S Zimbabwe
42 K13 **Filadelfia** Guanacaste, W Costa Rica
111 K20 **Fil'akovo** *Hung.* Fülek. Banskobystrický Kraj, C Slovakia
195 N5 **Filchner Ice Shelf** *ice shelf* Antarctica
14 J11 **Fildegrand** ≈ Québec, SE Canada
33 O15 **Filer** Idaho, NW USA
116 H14 **Filiaşi** Dolj, SW Romania
115 B16 **Filiátes** Ípeiros, W Greece
115 D21 **Filiatrá** Pelopónnisos, S Greece
107 K22 **Filicudi, Isola** *island* Isole Eolie, S Italy
141 Y10 **Filim** E Oman
Filimon Sîrbu *see* Făurei
77 S11 **Filingué** Tillabéri, W Niger
114 K13 **Filiouri** ≈ NE Greece
114 I13 **Fílippoi** *anc.* Philippi. *site of ancient city* Anatolikí Makedonía kai Thráki, NE Greece
95 L15 **Filipstad** Värmland, C Sweden
108 I9 **Filisur** Graubünden, S Switzerland
94 E12 **Filefjell** ▲ S Norway
35 R14 **Fillmore** California, W USA
36 K5 **Fillmore** Utah, W USA
14 J10 **Fils, Lac du** ⊚ Québec, SE Canada
136 H11 **Filyos Çayı** ≈ N Turkey
195 Q2 **Fimbulheimen** *physical region* Antarctica
195 Q1 **Fimbul Ice Shelf** *ice shelf* Antarctica
106 G9 **Finale Emilia** Emilia-Romagna, C Italy
106 C10 **Finale Ligure** Liguria, NW Italy
105 P14 **Fiñana** Andalucía, S Spain
172 I6 **Finandrahana** Fianarantsoa, SE Madagascar
21 S6 **Fincastle** Virginia, NE USA
99 M25 **Findel** ✕ (Luxembourg) Luxembourg, C Luxembourg
96 J9 **Findhorn** ≈ N Scotland, UK
31 R12 **Findlay** Ohio, N USA
18 G11 **Finger Lakes** *lakes* New York, NE USA
83 L14 **Fingoè** Tete, NW Mozambique
136 E17 **Finike** Antalya, SW Turkey
102 F6 **Finistère** ◆ *department* NW France
186 D7 **Finisterre Range** ▲ N PNG
181 Q8 **Finke** Northern Territory, N Australia
109 S10 **Finkenstein** Kärnten, S Austria
189 Y15 **Finkol, Mount** *var.* Mount Crozer. ▲ Kosrae, E Micronesia
93 L17 **Finland** *off.* Republic of Finland, *Fin.* Suomen Tasavalta, Suomi. ◆ *republic* N Europe
126 F12 **Finland, Gulf of** *Est.* Soome Laht, *Fin.* Suomenlahti, *Ger.* Finnischer Meerbusen, *Rus.* Finskiy Zaliv, *Swe.* Finska Viken. *gulf* E Baltic Sea
10 L11 **Finlay** ≈ British Columbia, W Canada
183 O10 **Finley** New South Wales, SE Australia
29 Q4 **Finley** North Dakota, N USA
Finnischer Meerbusen *see* Finland, Gulf of
92 K9 **Finnmark** ◆ *county* N Norway
92 K9 **Finnmarksvidda** *physical region* N Norway
92 I9 **Finnsnes** Troms, N Norway
186 E7 **Finschhafen** Morobe, C PNG
94 E13 **Finse** Hordaland, S Norway
Finska Viken/Finskiy Zaliv *see* Finland, Gulf of
95 M17 **Finspång** Östergötland, S Sweden
108 F10 **Finsteraarhorn** ▲ Switzerland
101 O14 **Finsterwalde** Brandenburg, E Germany
185 A23 **Fiordland** *physical region* South Island, NZ
106 E9 **Fiorenzuola d'Arda** Emilia-Romagna, C Italy
Firat Nehri *see* Euphrates
Firdaus *see* Ferdows
18 M14 **Fire Island** *island* New York, NE USA
106 G11 **Firenze** *Eng.* Florence; *anc.* Florentia. Toscana, C Italy
106 G10 **Firenzuola** Toscana, C Italy
14 C6 **Fire River** Ontario, S Canada
Firliug *see* Fârliug
61 B19 **Firmat** Santa Fe, C Argentina
103 Q12 **Firminy** Loire, E France
Firmum Picenum *see* Fermo
152 J12 **Fīrozābād** Uttar Pradesh, N India
152 G8 **Fīrozpur** *var.* Ferozepore. Punjab, NW India
First State *see* Delaware
143 O12 **Fīrūzābād** Fārs, S Iran
Fischamend *see* Fischamend Markt
109 Y4 **Fischamend Markt** *var.* Fischamend. Niederösterreich, NE Austria
109 W6 **Fischbacher Alpen** ▲ E Austria
Fischhausen *see* Primorsk
83 D21 **Fish** *var.* Vis. ≈ S Namibia
83 E24 **Fish** *Afr.* Vis. ≈ SW South Africa
11 X15 **Fisher Branch** Manitoba, S Canada
11 X15 **Fisher River** Manitoba, S Canada
19 N13 **Fishers Island** *island* New York, NE USA
37 U8 **Fishers Peak** ▲ Colorado, C USA
9 P9 **Fisher Strait** *strait* Nunavut, N Canada
97 H21 **Fishguard** *Wel.* Abergwaun. SW Wales, UK
19 R2 **Fish River Lake** ⊚ Maine, NE USA
194 K6 **Fiske, Cape** *headland* Antarctica
103 P4 **Fismes** Marne, N France
104 F3 **Fisterra, Cabo** *headland* NW Spain
19 N11 **Fitchburg** Massachusetts, NE USA
96 L3 **Fitful Head** *headland* NE Scotland, UK
95 C14 **Fitjar** Hordaland, S Norway
192 H16 **Fito** ▲ Upolu, C Samoa
23 U6 **Fitzgerald** Georgia, SE USA
180 M5 **Fitzroy Crossing** Western Australia
63 G21 **Fitzroy, Monte** *var.* Cerro Chaltel. ▲ S Argentina
181 Y8 **Fitzroy River** ≈ Queensland, E Australia
180 L5 **Fitzroy River** ≈ Western Australia
14 E12 **Fitzwilliam Island** *island* Ontario, S Canada
107 J15 **Fiuggi** Lazio, C Italy
Fiume *see* Rijeka
107 H15 **Fiumicino** Lazio, C Italy
Fiumicino *see* Leonardo da Vinci
106 E10 **Fivizzano** Toscana, C Italy
79 O21 **Fizi** Sud Kivu, E Dem. Rep. Congo
Fizuli *see* Füzuli
92 I11 **Fjällåsen** Norrbotten, N Sweden
95 G20 **Fjerritslev** Nordjylland, N Denmark
F.J.S. *see* Franz Josef Strauss
95 L16 **Fjugesta** Örebro, C Sweden
Fladstrand *see* Frederikshavn
37 V5 **Flagler** Colorado, C USA
23 X10 **Flagler Beach** Florida, SE USA
36 L11 **Flagstaff** Arizona, SW USA
65 H24 **Flagstaff Bay** *bay* Saint Helena, C Atlantic Ocean
19 P5 **Flagstaff Lake** ⊚ Maine, NE USA
94 E13 **Flåm** Sogn og Fjordane, S Norway
15 O8 **Flamand** ≈ Québec, SE Canada
30 J5 **Flambeau River** ≈ Wisconsin, N USA
97 O16 **Flamborough Head** *headland* E England, UK
100 N13 **Fläming** *hill range* NE Germany
16 H8 **Flaming Gorge Reservoir** ⊞ Utah/Wyoming, NW USA
99 B18 **Flanders** *Dut.* Vlaanderen, *Fr.* Flandre. *cultural region* Belgium/France
Flandre *see* Flanders
29 R10 **Flandreau** South Dakota, N USA
96 D6 **Flannan Isles** *island group* NW Scotland, UK
28 M6 **Flasher** North Dakota, N USA
93 G15 **Flåsjön** ⊚ N Sweden
39 O11 **Flat** Alaska, USA
92 H1 **Flateyri** Vestfirdhir, NW Iceland
33 P8 **Flathead Lake** ⊚ Montana, NW USA
173 Y15 **Flat Island** *Fr.* Île Plate. *island* N Mauritius
25 T11 **Flatonia** Texas, SW USA
185 M14 **Flat Point** *headland* North Island, NZ
27 X6 **Flat River** Missouri, C USA
31 P8 **Flat River** ≈ Michigan, N USA
31 P14 **Flatrock River** ≈ Indiana, N USA
32 E6 **Flattery, Cape** *headland* Washington, NW USA
64 B12 **Flatts Village** *var.* The Flatts Village. C Bermuda
108 H7 **Flawil** Sankt Gallen, NE Switzerland
97 N22 **Fleet** S England, UK
97 K16 **Fleetwood** NW England, UK
18 H15 **Fleetwood** Pennsylvania, NE USA
95 D18 **Flekkefjord** Vest-Agder, S Norway
21 N5 **Flemingsburg** Kentucky, S USA
18 J15 **Flemington** New Jersey, NE USA
64 I7 **Flemish Cap** *undersea feature* NW Atlantic Ocean
95 N16 **Flen** Södermanland, C Sweden
100 I6 **Flensburg** Schleswig-Holstein, N Germany
100 J6 **Flensburger Förde** *inlet* Denmark/Germany
102 K5 **Flers** Orne, N France
95 C14 **Flesland** ✕ (Bergen) Hordaland, S Norway
Flessingue *see* Vlissingen
21 P10 **Fletcher** North Carolina, SE USA
31 R6 **Fletcher Pond** ⊚ Michigan, N USA
102 L15 **Fleurance** Gers, S France
108 B8 **Fleurier** Neuchâtel, W Switzerland
99 H20 **Fleurus** Hainaut, S Belgium
103 N7 **Fleury-les-Aubrais** Loiret, C France
98 K10 **Flevoland** ◆ *province* C Netherlands
Flickertail State *see* North Dakota
108 H9 **Flims** Glarus, NE Switzerland
182 F8 **Flinders Island** *island* Investigator Group, South Australia
183 P14 **Flinders Island** *island* Furneaux Group, Tasmania, SE Australia

182 I6 **Flinders Ranges** ▲ South Australia
181 U5 **Flinders River** ∿ Queensland, NE Australia
11 V13 **Flin Flon** Manitoba, C Canada
97 K18 **Flint** NE Wales, UK
31 R9 **Flint** Michigan, N USA
97 J18 **Flint** cultural region NE Wales, UK
27 O7 **Flint Hills** hill range Kansas, C USA
191 Y6 **Flint Island** island Line Islands, E Kiribati
23 S4 **Flint River** ∿ Georgia, SE USA
31 R9 **Flint River** ∿ Michigan, N USA
189 X12 **Flipper Point** headland C Wake Island
94 I13 **Flisa** Hedmark, S Norway
94 J13 **Flisa** ∿ S Norway
122 J5 **Flissingskiy, Mys** headland Novaya Zemlya, NW Russian Federation
Flitsch see Bovec
105 U6 **Flix** Cataluña, NE Spain
95 J19 **Floda** Västra Götaland, S Sweden
101 O16 **Flöha** ∿ E Germany
25 O4 **Flomot** Texas, SW USA
29 V5 **Floodwood** Minnesota, N USA
30 M15 **Flora** Illinois, N USA
103 P14 **Florac** Lozère, S France
23 Q8 **Florala** Alabama, S USA
103 S4 **Florange** Moselle, NE France
Floreana, Isla see Santa María, Isla
23 O2 **Florence** Alabama, S USA
36 L14 **Florence** Arizona, SW USA
37 T6 **Florence** Colorado, C USA
27 O5 **Florence** Kansas, C USA
20 M4 **Florence** Kentucky, S USA
32 E13 **Florence** Oregon, NW USA
21 T12 **Florence** South Carolina, SE USA
25 S9 **Florence** Texas, SW USA
Florence see Firenze
54 E13 **Florencia** Caquetá, S Colombia
99 H21 **Florennes** Namur, S Belgium
Florentia see Firenze
63 J18 **Florentino Ameghino, Embalse** ◎ S Argentina
99 J24 **Florenville** Luxembourg, SE Belgium
42 E3 **Flores** Petén, N Guatemala
61 E19 **Flores** ◈ department S Uruguay
171 O16 **Flores** island Nusa Tenggara, C Indonesia
64 M1 **Flores** island Azores, Portugal, NE Atlantic Ocean
Floreshty see Florești
Flores, Lago de see Petén Itzá, Lago
Flores, Laut see Flores Sea
171 N15 **Flores Sea** Ind. Laut Flores. sea C Indonesia
116 M8 **Florești** Rus. Floreshty. N Moldova
25 S12 **Floresville** Texas, SW USA
59 N14 **Floriano** Piauí, E Brazil
61 K14 **Florianópolis** prev. Destêrro. state capital Santa Catarina, S Brazil
44 G6 **Florida** Camagüey, C Cuba
61 F19 **Florida** Florida, S Uruguay
61 F19 **Florida** ◈ department S Uruguay
23 U9 **Florida** off. State of Florida; also known as Peninsular State, Sunshine State. ◈ state SE USA
23 Y17 **Florida Bay** bay Florida, SE USA
54 G8 **Floridablanca** Santander, N Colombia
23 Y17 **Florida Keys** island group Florida, SE USA
37 Q16 **Florida Mountains** ▲ New Mexico, SW USA
64 D10 **Florida, Straits of** strait Atlantic Ocean/Gulf of Mexico
114 D13 **Flórina** var. Phlórina. Dytikí Makedonía, N Greece
27 X4 **Florissant** Missouri, C USA
94 C11 **Florø** Sogn og Fjordane, S Norway
115 L22 **Floúda, Akrotírio** headland Astypálaia, Kykládes, Greece, Aegean Sea
21 S7 **Floyd** Virginia, NE USA
25 N4 **Floydada** Texas, SW USA
Flüela Wisshorn see Weisshorn
98 K7 **Fluessen** ◎ N Netherlands
105 S5 **Flúmen** ∿ NE Spain
107 C20 **Flumendosa** ∿ Sardegna, Italy, C Mediterranean Sea
31 R9 **Flushing** Michigan, N USA
Flushing see Vlissingen
25 O6 **Fluvanna** Texas, SW USA
186 B8 **Fly** ∿ Indonesia/PNG
194 I10 **Flying Fish, Cape** headland Thurston Island, Antarctica
Flylân see Vlieland
193 Y15 **Foa** island Ha'apai Group, C Tonga
11 U15 **Foam Lake** Saskatchewan, S Canada
113 J14 **Foča** var Srbinje, Republika Srpska, Bosnia and Herzegovina
116 L12 **Focșani** Vrancea, E Romania
Fogaras/Fogarasch see Făgăraș
107 M16 **Foggia** Puglia, SE Italy
Foggo see Faggo
76 D10 **Fogo** island Ilhas de Sotavento, SW Cape Verde
13 U11 **Fogo Island** island Newfoundland and Labrador, E Canada
109 U7 **Fohnsdorf** Steiermark, SE Austria
100 G7 **Föhr** island NW Germany
104 F14 **Fóia** ▲ S Portugal
14 I10 **Foins, Lac aux** ◎ Québec, SE Canada
103 N17 **Foix** Ariège, S France
126 I5 **Fokino** Bryanskaya Oblast', W Russian Federation
123 S15 **Fokino** Primorskiy Oblast', SE Russian Federation
Fola, Cnoc see Bloody Foreland
94 E13 **Folarskardnuten** ▲ S Norway
92 G11 **Folda** fjord C Norway
93 E14 **Folda** fjord C Norway
Földvár see Feldioara
93 F14 **Foldereid** Nord-Trøndelag, C Norway
115 J22 **Folégandros** island Kykládes, Greece, Aegean Sea
23 O9 **Foley** Alabama, S USA
29 U7 **Foley** Minnesota, N USA
14 E7 **Foleyet** Ontario, S Canada
95 D14 **Folgefonni** glacier S Norway
106 I13 **Foligno** Umbria, C Italy
97 Q23 **Folkestone** SE England, UK
23 W8 **Folkston** Georgia, SE USA
94 H10 **Folldal** Hedmark, S Norway
25 P1 **Follett** Texas, SW USA
106 F13 **Follonica** Toscana, C Italy
21 T15 **Folly Beach** South Carolina, SE USA
35 O7 **Folsom** California, W USA
116 M12 **Foltești** Galați, E Romania
172 H14 **Fomboni** Mohéli, S Comoros
18 K10 **Fonda** New York, NE USA
11 S10 **Fond-du-Lac** Saskatchewan, C Canada
30 M8 **Fond du Lac** Wisconsin, N USA
11 T10 **Fond-du-Lac** ∿ Saskatchewan, C Canada
190 C9 **Fongafale** var. Funafuti. ● (Tuvalu) Funafuti Atoll, SE Tuvalu
190 G8 **Fongafale** atoll C Tuvalu
107 C18 **Fonni** Sardegna, Italy, C Mediterranean Sea
189 V12 **Fono** island Chuuk, C Micronesia
54 G4 **Fonseca** La Guajira, N Colombia
Fonseca, Golfo de see Fonseca, Gulf of
42 H8 **Fonseca, Gulf of** Sp. Golfo de Fonseca. gulf Central America
103 O6 **Fontainebleau** Seine-et-Marne, N France
63 G19 **Fontana, Lago** ◎ W Argentina
21 N10 **Fontana Lake** ⊟ North Carolina, SE USA
107 L24 **Fontanarossa** × (Catania) Sicilia, Italy, C Mediterranean Sea
11 N11 **Fontas** ∿ British Columbia, W Canada
58 D12 **Fonte Boa** Amazonas, N Brazil
102 J10 **Fontenay-le-Comte** Vendée, NW France
33 T16 **Fontenelle Reservoir** ⊟ Wyoming, C USA
193 Y14 **Fonualei** island Vava'u Group, N Tonga
111 H24 **Fonyód** Somogy, W Hungary
Foochow see Fuzhou
39 Q10 **Foraker, Mount** ▲ Alaska, USA
187 R14 **Forari** Éfaté, C Vanuatu
103 U4 **Forbach** Moselle, NE France
183 Q8 **Forbes** New South Wales, SE Australia
77 T17 **Forcados** Delta, S Nigeria
103 S14 **Forcalquier** Alpes-de-Haute-Provence, SE France
101 K19 **Forchheim** Bayern, SE Germany
35 R13 **Ford City** California, W USA
94 D11 **Førde** Sogn og Fjordane, S Norway
31 N4 **Ford River** ∿ Michigan, N USA
183 O4 **Fords Bridge** New South Wales, SE Australia
20 J6 **Fordsville** Kentucky, S USA
27 U13 **Fordyce** Arkansas, C USA
76 I14 **Forécariah** Guinée-Maritime, SW Guinea
197 O14 **Forel, Mont** ▲ SE Greenland
11 R17 **Foremost** Alberta, SW Canada
14 D16 **Forest** Ontario, S Canada
22 L5 **Forest** Mississippi, S USA
31 S12 **Forest** Ohio, N USA
29 V11 **Forest City** Iowa, C USA
21 Q10 **Forest City** North Carolina, SE USA
32 G11 **Forest Grove** Oregon, NW USA
183 P17 **Forestier Peninsula** peninsula Tasmania, SE Australia
29 V8 **Forest Lake** Minnesota, N USA
23 S3 **Forest Park** Georgia, SE USA
29 Q3 **Forest River** ∿ North Dakota, N USA
15 T6 **Forestville** Québec, SE Canada
103 Q11 **Forez, Monts du** ▲ C France
96 K10 **Forfar** E Scotland, UK
26 J8 **Forgan** Oklahoma, C USA
Forge du Sud see Dudelange
101 J24 **Forggensee** ◎ S Germany
147 N10 **Forish** Rus. Farish. Jizzax Viloyati, C Uzbekistan
20 F9 **Forked Deer River** ∿ Tennessee, S USA
32 F7 **Forks** Washington, NW USA
92 N2 **Forlandsundet** sound W Svalbard
106 H10 **Forlì** anc. Forum Livii. Emilia-Romagna, N Italy
29 Q7 **Forman** North Dakota, N USA
97 K17 **Formby** NW England, UK
105 V11 **Formentera** anc. Ophiusa, Lat. Frumentum. island Islas Baleares, Spain, W Mediterranean Sea
Formentor, Cabo de see Formentor, Cap de
105 Y9 **Formentor, Cap de** var. Cabo de Formentor, Cape Formentor. headland Mallorca, Spain, W Mediterranean Sea
Formentor, Cape see Formentor, Cap de
107 J16 **Formia** Lazio, C Italy
62 O7 **Formosa** Formosa, NE Argentina
62 M6 **Formosa** off. Provincia de Formosa. ◈ province NE Argentina
Formosa/Formo'sa see Taiwan
59 L17 **Formosa, Serra** ▲ C Brazil
Formosa Strait see Taiwan Strait
95 H15 **Fornebu** × (Oslo) Akershus, S Norway
25 U6 **Forney** Texas, SW USA
95 H21 **Fornæs** headland C Denmark
106 E9 **Fornovo di Taro** Emilia-Romagna, C Italy
117 T14 **Foros** Respublika Krym, S Ukraine
Føroyar see Faeroe Islands
96 J8 **Forres** NE Scotland, UK
27 X11 **Forrest City** Arkansas, C USA
39 Y15 **Forrester Island** island Alexander Archipelago, Alaska, USA
25 N7 **Forsan** Texas, SW USA
181 V5 **Forsayth** Queensland, NE Australia
95 L19 **Forserum** Jönköping, S Sweden
95 K15 **Forshaga** Värmland, C Sweden
93 L19 **Forssa** Etelä-Suomi, S Finland
101 Q14 **Forst** Lus. Baršć Łužyca. Brandenburg, E Germany
183 U7 **Forster-Tuncurry** New South Wales, SE Australia
23 T4 **Forsyth** Georgia, SE USA
27 T8 **Forsyth** Missouri, C USA
33 W10 **Forsyth** Montana, NW USA
149 U11 **Fort Abbās** Punjab, E Pakistan
12 G10 **Fort Albany** Ontario, C Canada
55 L13 **Fortaleza** Pando, N Bolivia
58 P13 **Fortaleza** prev. Ceará. state capital Ceará, NE Brazil
59 D16 **Fortaleza** Rondônia, W Brazil
56 C13 **Fortaleza, Río** ∿ W Peru
Fort-Archambault see Sarh
21 U3 **Fort Ashby** West Virginia, NE USA
96 I9 **Fort Augustus** N Scotland, UK
Fort-Bayard see Zhanjiang
33 S8 **Fort Benton** Montana, NW USA
35 Q1 **Fort Bidwell** California, W USA
34 L5 **Fort Bragg** California, W USA
31 N16 **Fort Branch** Indiana, N USA
Fort-Bretonnet see Bousso
33 T17 **Fort Bridger** Wyoming, C USA
Fort-Cappolani see Tidjikja
Fort Charlet see Djanet
Fort-Chimo see Kuujjuaq
11 R10 **Fort Chipewyan** Alberta, C Canada
Fort Cobb Lake see Fort Cobb Reservoir
26 L11 **Fort Cobb Reservoir** var. Fort Cobb Lake. ⊟ Oklahoma, C USA
37 T3 **Fort Collins** Colorado, C USA
14 K12 **Fort-Coulonge** Québec, SE Canada
Fort-Crampel see Kaga Bandoro
Fort-Dauphin see Tôlañaro
24 K10 **Fort Davis** Texas, SW USA
37 O10 **Fort Defiance** Arizona, SW USA
45 Q12 **Fort-de-France** prev. Fort-Royal. ○ (Martinique) W Martinique
45 P12 **Fort-de-France, Baie de** bay W Martinique
Fort de Kock see Bukittinggi
23 P6 **Fort Deposit** Alabama, S USA
29 U13 **Fort Dodge** Iowa, C USA
13 S10 **Forteau** Quebec, E Canada
106 E11 **Forte dei Marmi** Toscana, C Italy
14 H17 **Fort Erie** Ontario, S Canada
180 H7 **Fortescue River** ∿ Western Australia
19 S2 **Fort Fairfield** Maine, NE USA
Fort-Foureau see Kousséri
12 A11 **Fort Frances** Ontario, S Canada
Fort Franklin see Déljne
23 R7 **Fort Gaines** Georgia, SE USA
37 T8 **Fort Garland** Colorado, C USA
21 P5 **Fort Gay** West Virginia, NE USA
Fort George see La Grande Rivière
27 Q10 **Fort Gibson** Oklahoma, C USA
27 Q9 **Fort Gibson Lake** ⊟ Oklahoma, C USA
8 H7 **Fort Good Hope** var. Good Hope. Northwest Territories, NW Canada
23 V4 **Fort Gordon** Georgia, SE USA
Fort Gouraud see Fdérik
96 I11 **Forth** ∿ C Scotland, UK
Fort Hall see Murang'a
24 H8 **Fort Hancock** Texas, SW USA
Fort Hertz see Putao
96 K12 **Forth, Firth of** estuary E Scotland, UK
14 L14 **Forthton** Ontario, SE Canada
14 M8 **Fortier** ∿ Québec, SE Canada
Fortín General Eugenio Garay see General Eugenio A. Garay
Fort Jameson see Chipata
Fort Johnston see Mangochi
19 R1 **Fort Kent** Maine, NE USA
Fort-Lamy see Ndjamena
23 Z15 **Fort Lauderdale** Florida, SE USA
21 R11 **Fort Lawn** South Carolina, SE USA
8 H10 **Fort Liard** var. Liard. Northwest Territories, W Canada
44 M8 **Fort-Liberté** NE Haiti
21 N9 **Fort Loudoun Lake** ⊟ Tennessee, S USA
37 T3 **Fort Lupton** Colorado, C USA
11 R12 **Fort MacKay** Alberta, C Canada
11 Q17 **Fort Macleod** var. MacLeod. Alberta, SW Canada
29 Y16 **Fort Madison** Iowa, C USA
Fort Manning see Mchinji
25 P9 **Fort McKavett** Texas, SW USA
11 R12 **Fort McMurray** Alberta, C Canada
8 G7 **Fort McPherson** var. McPherson. Northwest Territories, NW Canada
21 R11 **Fort Mill** South Carolina, SE USA
Fort-Millot see Ngouri
37 U3 **Fort Morgan** Colorado, C USA
23 W14 **Fort Myers** Florida, SE USA
23 W15 **Fort Myers Beach** Florida, SE USA
10 M10 **Fort Nelson** British Columbia, W Canada
10 M10 **Fort Nelson** ∿ British Columbia, W Canada
Fort Norman see Tulita
23 Q2 **Fort Payne** Alabama, S USA
33 W7 **Fort Peck** Montana, NW USA
33 V8 **Fort Peck Lake** ⊟ Montana, NW USA
23 Y13 **Fort Pierce** Florida, SE USA
29 N10 **Fort Pierre** South Dakota, N USA
81 E18 **Fort Portal** SW Uganda
8 J10 **Fort Providence** var. Providence. Northwest Territories, W Canada
11 U16 **Fort Qu'Appelle** Saskatchewan, S Canada
Fort-Repoux see Akjoujt
8 K10 **Fort Resolution** var. Resolution. Northwest Territories, W Canada
33 T13 **Fortress Mountain** ▲ Wyoming, C USA
Fort Rosebery see Mansa
Fort-Rousset see Owando
Fort-Royal see Fort-de-France
12 I10 **Fort Rupert** prev. Rupert House. Québec, SE Canada
8 H13 **Fort St.James** British Columbia, SW Canada
11 N12 **Fort St.John** British Columbia, W Canada
Fort Sandeman see Zhob
11 Q14 **Fort Saskatchewan** Alberta, SW Canada
27 R6 **Fort Scott** Kansas, C USA
12 E6 **Fort Severn** Ontario, C Canada
31 R12 **Fort Shawnee** Ohio, N USA
144 E14 **Fort-Shevchenko** Mangistau, W Kazakhstan
Fort-Sibut see Sibut
8 I10 **Fort Simpson** var. Simpson. Northwest Territories, W Canada
8 K11 **Fort Smith** district capital Northwest Territories, W Canada
27 R10 **Fort Smith** Arkansas, C USA
37 T13 **Fort Stanton** New Mexico, SW USA
24 L9 **Fort Stockton** Texas, SW USA
37 U12 **Fort Sumner** New Mexico, SW USA
26 K8 **Fort Supply** Oklahoma, C USA
26 K8 **Fort Supply Lake** ⊟ Oklahoma, C USA
29 O10 **Fort Thompson** South Dakota, N USA
Fort-Trinquet see Bîr Mogreïn
105 R12 **Fortuna** Murcia, SE Spain
34 K3 **Fortuna** California, W USA
28 J2 **Fortuna** North Dakota, N USA
23 T5 **Fort Valley** Georgia, SE USA
11 P11 **Fort Vermilion** Alberta, W Canada
Fort Victoria see Masvingo
31 P13 **Fortville** Indiana, N USA
23 P9 **Fort Walton Beach** Florida, SE USA
31 P12 **Fort Wayne** Indiana, N USA
96 H10 **Fort William** N Scotland, UK
25 T6 **Fort Worth** Texas, SW USA
28 M7 **Fort Yates** North Dakota, N USA
39 S7 **Fort Yukon** Alaska, USA
Forum Alieni see Ferrara
Forum Julii see Fréjus
Forum Livii see Forlì
143 Q15 **Forūr, Jazīreh-ye** island S Iran
94 H7 **Fosen** physical region S Norway
161 N14 **Foshan** var. Fatshan, Fo-shan, Namhoi. Guangdong, S China
Fossa Claudia see Chioggia
106 B9 **Fossano** Piemonte, NW Italy
99 H21 **Fosses-la-Ville** Namur, S Belgium
32 J12 **Fossil** Oregon, NW USA
Foss Lake see Foss Reservoir
106 I11 **Fossombrone** Marche, C Italy
26 K10 **Foss Reservoir** var. Foss Lake. ⊟ Oklahoma, C USA
29 S4 **Fosston** Minnesota, N USA
183 O13 **Foster** Victoria, SE Australia
11 T12 **Foster Lakes** ◎ Saskatchewan, C Canada
31 S12 **Fostoria** Ohio, N USA
79 D19 **Fougamou** Ngounié, C Gabon
102 J6 **Fougères** Ille-et-Vilaine, NW France
Fou-hsin see Fuxin
27 S14 **Fouke** Arkansas, C USA
96 K2 **Foula** island NE Scotland, UK
65 D24 **Foul Bay** bay East Falkland, Falkland Islands
97 P21 **Foulness Island** island SE England, UK
185 F15 **Foulwind, Cape** headland South Island, NZ
79 E15 **Foumban** Ouest, NW Cameroon
172 H13 **Foumbouni** Grande Comore, NW Comoros
195 N8 **Foundation Ice Stream** glacier Antarctica
37 T6 **Fountain** Colorado, C USA
36 L4 **Fountain Green** Utah, W USA
21 P11 **Fountain Inn** South Carolina, SE USA
27 S11 **Fourche LaFave River** ∿ Arkansas, C USA
33 Z13 **Four Corners** Wyoming, C USA
103 Q2 **Fourmies** Nord, N France
38 J17 **Four Mountains, Islands of** island group Aleutian Islands, Alaska, USA
173 P17 **Fournaise, Piton de la** ▲ SE Réunion
14 J8 **Fournière, Lac** ◎ Québec, SE Canada
115 L20 **Foúrnoi** island Dodekánisos, Greece, Aegean Sea
64 K13 **Four North Fracture Zone** tectonic feature W Atlantic Ocean
Fouron-Saint-Martin see Sint-Martens-Voeren
30 L3 **Fourteen Mile Point** headland Michigan, N USA
76 I13 **Fouta Djallon** var. Futa Jallon. ▲ W Guinea
185 C25 **Foveaux Strait** strait S NZ
35 Q11 **Fowler** California, W USA
37 U6 **Fowler** Colorado, C USA
31 N12 **Fowler** Indiana, N USA
182 D7 **Fowlers Bay** bay South Australia
25 R13 **Fowlerton** Texas, SW USA
142 M3 **Fowman** var. Fuman, Fumen. Gīlān, NW Iran
65 C25 **Fox Bay East** West Falkland, Falkland Islands
65 C25 **Fox Bay West** West Falkland, Falkland Islands
14 J14 **Foxboro** Ontario, SE Canada
11 O14 **Fox Creek** Alberta, W Canada
64 G5 **Foxe Basin** sea Nunavut, N Canada
64 G5 **Foxe Channel** channel Nunavut, N Canada
95 I16 **Foxen** ◎ C Sweden
9 Q7 **Foxe Peninsula** peninsula Baffin Island, Nunavut, NE Canada
185 E19 **Fox Glacier** West Coast, South Island, NZ
38 L17 **Fox Islands** island Aleutian Islands, Alaska, USA
30 M10 **Fox Lake** Illinois, N USA
11 V12 **Fox Mine** Manitoba, C Canada
35 R3 **Fox Mountain** ▲ Nevada, W USA
65 E25 **Fox Point** headland East Falkland, Falkland Islands
30 M11 **Fox River** ∿ Illinois/Wisconsin, N USA
30 L7 **Fox River** ∿ Wisconsin, N USA
184 L13 **Foxton** Manawatu-Wanganui, North Island, NZ
11 S16 **Fox Valley** Saskatchewan, S Canada
11 W16 **Foxwarren** Manitoba, S Canada
97 E14 **Foyle, Lough** Ir. Loch Feabhail. inlet N Ireland
194 H5 **Foyn Coast** physical region Antarctica
104 I2 **Foz** Galicia, NW Spain
60 I12 **Foz do Areia, Represa de** ⊟ S Brazil
59 A16 **Foz do Breu** Acre, W Brazil
83 A16 **Foz do Cunene** Namibe, SW Angola
60 G12 **Foz do Iguaçu** Paraná, S Brazil
58 C12 **Foz do Mamoriá** Amazonas, NW Brazil
105 T6 **Fraga** Aragón, NE Spain
44 F5 **Fragoso, Cayo** island C Cuba
61 G18 **Fraile Muerto** Cerro Largo, NE Uruguay
99 H21 **Fraire** Namur, S Belgium
99 L21 **Fraiture, Baraque de** hill SE Belgium
Frakštát see Hlohovec
197 S10 **Fram Basin** var. Amundsen Basin. undersea feature Arctic Ocean
99 F20 **Frameries** Hainaut, S Belgium
19 O11 **Framingham** Massachusetts, NE USA
60 L7 **Franca** São Paulo, S Brazil
187 O15 **Français, Récif des** reef W New Caledonia
107 K14 **Francavilla al Mare** Abruzzo, C Italy
107 P18 **Francavilla Fontana** Puglia, SE Italy
102 M8 **France** off. French Republic, It./Sp. Francia; prev. Gaul, Gaule, Lat. Gallia. ◆ republic W Europe
45 O8 **Francés Viejo, Cabo** headland NE Dominican Republic
79 F19 **Franceville** var. Massoukou, Masuku. Haut-Ogooué, E Gabon
79 F19 **Franceville** × Haut-Ogooué, E Gabon
Francfort see Frankfurt am Main
103 T8 **Franche-Comté** ◈ region E France
Francia see France
29 O11 **Francis Case, Lake** ⊟ South Dakota, N USA
60 H12 **Francisco Beltrão** Paraná, S Brazil
Francisco I. Madero see Villa Madero
61 A21 **Francisco Madero** Buenos Aires, E Argentina
42 H6 **Francisco Morazán** prev. Tegucigalpa. ◈ department C Honduras
83 J18 **Francistown** North East, NE Botswana
Franconian Forest see Frankenwald
Franconian Jura see Fränkische Alb
98 K6 **Franeker** Fris. Frjentsjer. Friesland, N Netherlands
Frankenalb see Fränkische Alb
101 H16 **Frankenberg** Hessen, C Germany
101 J20 **Frankenhöhe** hill range C Germany
31 R8 **Frankenmuth** Michigan, N USA
101 F20 **Frankenstein** hill W Germany
Frankenstein/Frankenstein in Schlesien see Ząbkowice Śląskie
101 G20 **Frankenthal** Rheinland-Pfalz, W Germany
101 L18 **Frankenwald** Eng. Franconian Forest. ▲ C Germany
44 J12 **Frankfield** C Jamaica
14 J14 **Frankford** Ontario, SE Canada
31 O13 **Frankfort** Indiana, N USA
27 O3 **Frankfort** Kansas, C USA
20 L5 **Frankfort** state capital Kentucky, S USA
Frankfort on the Main see Frankfurt am Main
Frankfurt see Słubice, Poland
Frankfurt see Frankfurt am Main, Germany
101 G18 **Frankfurt am Main** var. Frankfurt, Fr. Francfort; prev. Eng. Frankfort on the Main. Hessen, SW Germany
100 Q12 **Frankfurt an der Oder** Brandenburg, E Germany
101 L21 **Fränkische Alb** var. Frankenalb, Eng. Franconian Jura. ▲ S Germany
101 I18 **Fränkische Saale** ∿ C Germany
101 L19 **Fränkische Schweiz** hill range C Germany
23 R4 **Franklin** Georgia, SE USA
31 P14 **Franklin** Indiana, N USA
20 J7 **Franklin** Kentucky, S USA
22 I9 **Franklin** Louisiana, S USA
29 O17 **Franklin** Nebraska, C USA
21 N10 **Franklin** North Carolina, SE USA
18 C13 **Franklin** Pennsylvania, NE USA
20 J9 **Franklin** Tennessee, S USA
25 U9 **Franklin** Texas, SW USA
21 X7 **Franklin** Virginia, NE USA
21 T4 **Franklin** West Virginia, NE USA
30 M9 **Franklin** Wisconsin, N USA
8 I6 **Franklin Bay** inlet Northwest Territories, N Canada
32 K7 **Franklin D.Roosevelt Lake** ⊟ Washington, NW USA
35 W4 **Franklin Lake** ◎ Nevada, W USA
185 B22 **Franklin Mountains** ▲ South Island, NZ
39 R5 **Franklin Mountains** ▲ Alaska, USA
39 N4 **Franklin, Point** headland Alaska, USA
183 O17 **Franklin River** ∿ Tasmania, SE Australia
22 K8 **Franklinton** Louisiana, S USA
21 U9 **Franklinton** North Carolina, SE USA
Frankstadt see Frenštát pod Radhoštěm
25 V7 **Frankston** Texas, SW USA
33 U12 **Frannie** Wyoming, C USA
15 U5 **Franquelin** Québec, SE Canada
15 U5 **Franquelin** ∿ Québec, SE Canada
83 C18 **Fransfontein** Kunene, NW Namibia
93 H17 **Fränsta** Västernorrland, C Sweden
122 J3 **Frantsa-Iosifa, Zemlya** Eng. Franz Josef Land. island group N Russian Federation
185 E18 **Franz Josef Glacier** West Coast, South Island, NZ
Franz Josef Land see Frantsa-Iosifa, Zemlya
Franz-Josef Spitze see Gerlachovský štít
101 L23 **Franz Josef Strauss** abbrev. F.J.S. × (München) Bayern, SE Germany
107 A19 **Frasca, Capo della** headland Sardegna, Italy, C Mediterranean Sea
107 I15 **Frascati** Lazio, C Italy
11 N14 **Fraser** ∿ British Columbia, SW Canada
83 G24 **Fraserburg** Western Cape, SW South Africa
96 L8 **Fraserburgh** NE Scotland, UK
181 Z9 **Fraser Island** var. Great Sandy Island. island Queensland, E Australia
10 L14 **Fraser Lake** British Columbia, SW Canada
10 L15 **Fraser Plateau** plateau British Columbia, SW Canada
184 P10 **Frasertown** Hawke's Bay, North Island, NZ
99 E19 **Frasnes-lez-Buissenal** Hainaut, SW Belgium
108 I7 **Frastanz** Vorarlberg, NW Austria
14 B8 **Frater** Ontario, S Canada
Fraubach see Baia Mare
Frauenburg see Saldus, Latvia
Frauenburg see Frombork, Poland
108 H6 **Frauenfeld** Thurgau, NE Switzerland
109 Z5 **Frauenkirchen** Burgenland, E Austria
61 D19 **Fray Bentos** Río Negro, W Uruguay
61 F19 **Fray Marcos** Florida, S Uruguay
29 S6 **Frazee** Minnesota, N USA
104 M5 **Frechilla** Castilla-León, N Spain
30 I4 **Frederic** Wisconsin, N USA
95 G23 **Fredericia** Vejle, C Denmark
21 W3 **Frederick** Maryland, NE USA
26 L12 **Frederick** Oklahoma, C USA
29 P7 **Frederick** South Dakota, N USA
29 X12 **Fredericksburg** Iowa, C USA
25 R10 **Fredericksburg** Texas, SW USA
21 W5 **Fredericksburg** Virginia, NE USA
39 X13 **Frederick Sound** sound Alaska, USA

◆ Country ● Country Capital ◇ Dependent Territory ○ Dependent Territory Capital ◈ Administrative Region × International Airport ▲ Mountain ▲ Mountain Range Volcano ∿ River ◎ Lake ⊟ Reservoir

27 X6 **Fredericktown** Missouri, C USA
60 H13 **Frederico Westphalen** Rio Grande do Sul, S Brazil
13 O15 **Fredericton** New Brunswick, SE Canada
95 I22 **Frederiksborg** *off.* Frederiksborgs Amt. ◈ *county* E Denmark
Frederikshåb *see* Paamiut
95 H19 **Frederikshavn** *prev.* Fladstrand. Nordjylland, N Denmark
95 J22 **Frederikssund** Frederiksborg, E Denmark
45 T9 **Frederiksted** Saint Croix, S Virgin Islands (US)
95 I22 **Frederiksværk** *var.* Frederiksværk og Hanehoved. Frederiksborg, E Denmark
Frederiksværk og Hanehoved *see* Frederiksværk
54 E9 **Fredonia** Antioquia, W Colombia
36 K8 **Fredonia** Arizona, SW USA
27 P7 **Fredonia** Kansas, C USA
18 C11 **Fredonia** New York, NE USA
35 P4 **Fredonyer Pass** *pass* California, W USA
93 I15 **Fredrika** Västerbotten, N Sweden
95 L14 **Fredriksberg** Dalarna, C Sweden
Fredrikshald *see* Halden
Fredrikshamn *see* Hamina
95 H16 **Fredrikstad** Østfold, S Norway
30 K16 **Freeburg** Illinois, N USA
18 K15 **Freehold** New Jersey, NE USA
18 H14 **Freeland** Pennsylvania, NE USA
182 J5 **Freeling Heights** ▲ South Australia
35 Q7 **Freel Peak** ▲ California, W USA
9 Z9 **Freels, Cape** *headland* Newfoundland and Labrador, E Canada
29 Q11 **Freeman** South Dakota, N USA
44 G1 **Freeport** Grand Bahama Island, N Bahamas
30 L10 **Freeport** Illinois, N USA
25 W12 **Freeport** Texas, SW USA
44 G1 **Freeport** ✕ Grand Bahama Island, N Bahamas
25 R14 **Freer** Texas, SW USA
83 I22 **Free State** *off.* Free State Province; *prev.* Orange Free State, *Afr.* Oranje Vrystaat. ◈ *province* C South Africa
Free State *see* Maryland
76 G15 **Freetown** ● (Sierra Leone) W Sierra Leone
172 J16 **Frégate** *island* Inner Islands, NE Seychelles
104 J12 **Fregenal de la Sierra** Extremadura, W Spain
182 C2 **Fregon** South Australia
102 H5 **Fréhel, Cap** *headland* NW France
94 F8 **Frei** Møre og Romsdal, S Norway
101 O16 **Freiberg** Sachsen, E Germany
101 O16 **Freiberger Mulde** ≈ E Germany
Freiburg *see* Fribourg, Switzerland
Freiburg *see* Freiburg im Breisgau, Germany
101 F23 **Freiburg im Breisgau** *var.* Freiburg, *Fr.* Fribourg-en-Brisgau. Baden-Württemberg, SW Germany
Freiburg in Schlesien *see* Świebodzice
Freie Hansestadt Bremen *see* Bremen
Freie und Hansestadt Hamburg *see* Brandenburg
101 L22 **Freising** Bayern, SE Germany
109 T3 **Freistadt** Oberösterreich, N Austria
Freistadtl *see* Hlohovec
101 O16 **Freital** Sachsen, E Germany
Freiwaldau *see* Jeseník
104 J6 **Freixo de Espada à Cinta** Bragança, N Portugal
103 U15 **Fréjus** *anc.* Forum Julii. Var, SE France
180 I13 **Fremantle** Western Australia
35 N9 **Fremont** California, W USA
31 Q11 **Fremont** Indiana, N USA
29 W15 **Fremont** Iowa, C USA
31 P8 **Fremont** Michigan, N USA
29 R15 **Fremont** Nebraska, C USA
31 S11 **Fremont** Ohio, N USA
33 T14 **Fremont Peak** ▲ Wyoming, C USA
36 M6 **Fremont River** ≈ Utah, W USA
21 O9 **French Broad River** ≈ Tennessee, S USA
21 N5 **Frenchburg** Kentucky, S USA
18 C12 **French Creek** ≈ Pennsylvania, NE USA
32 K15 **Frenchglen** Oregon, NW USA
55 Y10 **French Guiana** *var.* Guiana, Guyane. ◇ *French overseas department* N South America
French Guinea *see* Guinea
31 O15 **French Lick** Indiana, N USA
185 J14 **French Pass** Marlborough, South Island, NZ
191 T11 **French Polynesia** ◇ *French overseas territory* C Polynesia
French Republic *see* France
14 F11 **French River** ≈ Ontario, S Canada
French Somaliland *see* Djibouti
173 P12 **French Southern and Antarctic Territories** *Fr.* Terres Australes et Antarctiques Françaises. ◇ *French overseas territory* S Indian Ocean
French Sudan *see* Mali
French Territory of the Afars and Issas *see* Djibouti
French Togoland *see* Togo
74 J6 **Frenda** NW Algeria
111 I18 **Frenštát pod Radhoštěm** *Ger.* Frankstadt. Moravskoslezský Kraj, E Czech Republic
76 M17 **Fresco** S Ivory Coast
195 U16 **Freshfield, Cape** *headland* Antarctica
40 L10 **Fresnillo** *var.* Fresnillo de González Echeverría. Zacatecas, C Mexico
Fresnillo de González Echeverría *see* Fresnillo
35 Q10 **Fresno** California, W USA
Freu, Cabo del *see* Freu, Cap des
105 Y9 **Freu, Cap des** *var.* Cabo del Freu. *headland* Mallorca, Spain, W Mediterranean Sea
101 G22 **Freudenstadt** Baden-Württemberg, SW Germany
Freudenthal *see* Bruntál
183 Q17 **Freycinet Peninsula** *peninsula* Tasmania, SE Australia
76 H14 **Fria** Guinée-Maritime, W Guinea
83 A17 **Fria, Cape** *headland* NW Namibia
35 Q10 **Friant** California, W USA
62 K8 **Frías** Catamarca , N Argentina
108 D9 **Fribourg** *Ger.* Freiburg. Fribourg, W Switzerland
108 C9 **Fribourg** *Ger.* Freiburg. ◈ *canton* W Switzerland
Fribourg-en-Brisgau *see* Freiburg im Breisgau
32 G7 **Friday Harbor** San Juan Islands, Washington, NW USA
Friedau *see* Ormož
101 K23 **Friedberg** Bayern, S Germany
101 H18 **Friedberg** Hessen, W Germany
Friedeberg Neumark *see* Strzelce Krajeńskie
Friedek-Mistek *see* Frýdek-Místek
Friedland *see* Pravdinsk
101 I24 **Friedrichshafen** Baden-Württemberg, S Germany
Friedrichstadt *see* Jaunjelgava
29 Q16 **Friend** Nebraska, C USA
Friendly Islands *see* Tonga
55 V9 **Friendship** Coronie, N Surinam
30 L7 **Friendship** Wisconsin, N USA
109 T8 **Friesach** Kärnten, S Austria
101 F22 **Friesenheim** Baden-Württemberg, SW Germany
98 K6 **Friesland** ◈ *province* N Netherlands
60 Q10 **Frio, Cabo** *headland* SE Brazil
24 M3 **Friona** Texas, SW USA
42 L12 **Frío, Río** ≈ N Costa Rica
25 R13 **Frio River** ≈ Texas, SW USA
99 M25 **Frisange** Luxembourg, S Luxembourg
Frisches Haff *see* Vistula Lagoon
36 J6 **Frisco Peak** ▲ Utah, W USA
18 L12 **Frissell, Mount** ▲ Connecticut, NE USA
95 J19 **Fristad** Västra Götaland, S Sweden
25 N2 **Fritch** Texas, SW USA
95 J19 **Fritsla** Västra Götaland, S Sweden
101 H16 **Fritzlar** Hessen, C Germany
106 H6 **Friuli-Venezia Giulia** ◈ *region* NE Italy
Frjentsjer *see* Franeker
196 L13 **Frobisher Bay** *inlet* Baffin Island, Nunavut, NE Canada
Frobisher Bay *see* Iqaluit
11 S12 **Frobisher Lake** ◎ Saskatchewan, C Canada
94 G7 **Frohavet** *sound* C Norway
Frohenbruck *see* Veselí nad Lužnicí
109 V7 **Frohnleiten** Steiermark, SE Austria
99 G22 **Froidchapelle** Hainaut, S Belgium
127 O9 **Frolovo** Volgogradskaya Oblast', SW Russian Federation
110 K7 **Frombork** *Ger.* Frauenburg. Warmińsko-Mazurskie, NE Poland
97 L22 **Frome** SW England, UK
182 I4 **Frome Creek** *seasonal river* South Australia
182 J6 **Frome Downs** South Australia
182 J5 **Frome, Lake** *salt lake* South Australia
Fronicken *see* Wronki
104 H10 **Fronteira** Portalegre, C Portugal
40 M7 **Frontera** Coahuila de Zaragoza, NE Mexico
41 U14 **Frontera** Tabasco, SE Mexico
40 G3 **Fronteras** Sonora, NW Mexico
103 Q16 **Frontignan** Hérault, S France
54 D8 **Frontino** Antioquia, NW Colombia
21 V4 **Front Royal** Virginia, NE USA
107 J16 **Frosinone** *anc.* Frusino. Lazio, C Italy
107 K16 **Frosolone** Molise, C Italy
25 U7 **Frost** Texas, SW USA
21 U2 **Frostburg** Maryland, NE USA
23 X13 **Frostproof** Florida, SE USA
Frostviken *see* Kvarnbergsvattnet
95 M15 **Frövi** Örebro, C Sweden
94 F7 **Frøya** *island* W Norway
37 P5 **Fruita** Colorado, C USA
28 J9 **Fruitdale** South Dakota, N USA
23 W11 **Fruitland Park** Florida, SE USA
Frumentum *see* Formentera
147 S11 **Frunze** Batkenskaya Oblast', SW Kyrgyzstan
Frunze *see* Bishkek
117 O9 **Frunzivka** Odes'ka Oblast', SW Ukraine
Frusino *see* Frosinone
108 E9 **Frutigen** Bern, W Switzerland
111 I17 **Frýdek-Místek** *Ger.* Friedek-Mistek. Moravskoslezský Kraj, E Czech Republic
193 V16 **Fua'amotu** Tongatapu, S Tonga
190 A9 **Fuafatu** *island* Funafuti Atoll, C Tuvalu
190 A9 **Fuagea** *island* Funafuti Atoll, C Tuvalu
190 B8 **Fualifeke** *atoll* C Tuvalu
190 A8 **Fualopa** *island* Funafuti Atoll, C Tuvalu
151 K22 **Fuammulah** *var.* Gnaviyani Atoll. *atoll* S Maldives
161 R11 **Fu'an** Fujian, SE China
Fu-chien *see* Fujian
Fu-chou *see* Fuzhou
164 G13 **Fuchū** *var.* Hutyû. Hiroshima, Honshū, SW Japan
160 M13 **Fuchuan** Guangxi Zhuangzu Zizhiqu, S China
165 R8 **Fudai** Iwate, Honshū, C Japan
161 S11 **Fuding** Fujian, SE China
81 J20 **Fudua** *spring/well* S Kenya
104 M16 **Fuengirola** Andalucía, S Spain
104 J12 **Fuente de Cantos** Extremadura, W Spain
104 J11 **Fuente del Maestre** Extremadura, W Spain
104 L12 **Fuente Obejuna** Andalucía, S Spain
104 L6 **Fuentesaúco** Castilla-León, N Spain
62 O3 **Fuerte Olimpo** *var.* Olimpo. Alto Paraguay, NE Paraguay
40 H8 **Fuerte, Río** ≈ C Mexico
64 Q11 **Fuerteventura** *island* Islas Canarias, Spain, NE Atlantic Ocean
141 S14 **Fughmah** *var.* Faghman, Fugma. C Yemen
92 M2 **Fuglehuken** *headland* W Svalbard
95 B18 **Fugloy** *Dan.* Fuglø *Island* Faeroe Islands
197 T15 **Fugløya Bank** *undersea feature* E Norwegian Sea
166 E11 **Fugong** Yunnang, SW China
Fugma *see* Fughmah
81 K16 **Fugugo** *spring/well* NE Kenya
158 L2 **Fuhai** *var.* Burultokay. Xinjiang Uygur Zizhiqu, NW China
161 P10 **Fu He** ≈ S China
Fuhkien *see* Fujian
100 J9 **Fuhlsbüttel** ✕ (Hamburg) Hamburg, N Germany
101 L14 **Fuhne** ≈ C Germany
Fu-hsin *see* Fuxin
Fujairah *see* Al Fujayrah
164 M14 **Fuji** *var.* Huzi. Shizuoka, Honshū, S Japan
161 Q12 **Fujian** *var.* Fu-chien, Fuhkien, Fujian Sheng, Fukien, Min. ◈ *province* SE China
160 I9 **Fu Jiang** ≈ C China
Fujian Sheng *see* Fujian
164 M14 **Fujieda** *var.* Hujieda. Shizuoka, Honshū, S Japan
Fuji, Mount/Fujiyama *see* Fuji-san
163 Y7 **Fujin** Heilongjiang, NE China
164 M13 **Fujinomiya** *var.* Huzinomiya. Shizuoka, Honshū, S Japan
164 N13 **Fuji-san** *var.* Fujiyama, *Eng.* Mount Fuji. ▲ Honshū, SE Japan
165 N14 **Fujisawa** *var.* Huzisawa. Kanagawa, Honshū, S Japan
165 T3 **Fukagawa** *var.* Hukagawa. Hokkaidō, NE Japan
158 L5 **Fukang** Xinjiang Uygur Zizhiqu, W China
165 P7 **Fukaura** Aomori, Honshū, C Japan
193 W15 **Fukave** *island* Tongatapu Group, S Tonga
Fukien *see* Fujian
164 J13 **Fukuchiyama** *var.* Hukutiyama. Kyōto, Honshū, SW Japan
164 A14 **Fukue** *var.* Hukue. Nagasaki, Fukue-jima, SW Japan
164 A13 **Fukue-jima** *island* Gotō-rettō, SW Japan
164 K12 **Fukui** *var.* Hukui. Fukui, Honshū, SW Japan
164 K12 **Fukui** *off.* Fukui-ken, *var.* Hukui. ◈ *prefecture* Honshū, SW Japan
164 D13 **Fukuoka** *var.* Hukuoka; *hist.* Najima. Fukuoka, Kyūshū, SW Japan
164 D13 **Fukuoka** *off.* Fukuoka-ken, *var.* Hukuoka. ◈ *prefecture* Kyūshū, SW Japan
165 P11 **Fukushima** *var.* Hukusima. Fukushima, Honshū, C Japan
165 Q6 **Fukushima** Hokkaidō, NE Japan
165 Q12 **Fukushima** *off.* Fukushima-ken, *var.* Hukusima. ◈ *prefecture* Honshū, C Japan
164 G13 **Fukuyama** *var.* Hukuyama. Hiroshima, Honshū, SW Japan
76 G13 **Fulacunda** C Guinea-Bissau
187 Z15 **Fulaga** *island* Lau Group, E Fiji
101 I17 **Fulda** Hessen, C Germany
29 S10 **Fulda** Minnesota, N USA
101 I16 **Fulda** ≈ C Germany
Fülek *see* Fil'akovo
Fulin *see* Hanyuan
160 K10 **Fuling** Chongqing Shi, C China
35 T15 **Fullerton** California, SE USA
29 P15 **Fullerton** Nebraska, C USA
108 M8 **Fulpmes** Tirol, W Austria
20 G8 **Fulton** Kentucky, S USA
23 N2 **Fulton** Mississippi, S USA
27 V4 **Fulton** Missouri, C USA
18 H9 **Fulton** New York, NE USA
Fuman/Fumen *see* Fowman
103 R3 **Fumay** Ardennes, N France
102 M13 **Fumel** Lot-et-Garonne, SW France
190 B10 **Funafara** *atoll* C Tuvalu
190 C9 **Funafuti** ✕ Funafuti Atoll, C Tuvalu
Funafuti *see* Fongafale
190 F8 **Funafuti Atoll** *atoll* C Tuvalu
190 B9 **Funangongo** *atoll* C Tuvalu
93 F17 **Funäsdalen** Jämtland, C Sweden
64 O6 **Funchal** Madeira, Portugal, NE Atlantic Ocean
64 P5 **Funchal** ✕ Madeira, Portugal, NE Atlantic Ocean
54 F5 **Fundación** Magdalena, N Colombia
104 I8 **Fundão** *var.* Fundão. Castelo Branco, C Portugal
13 O16 **Fundy, Bay of** *bay* Canada/USA
Fünen *see* Fyn
54 C13 **Fúnes** Nariño, SW Colombia
Fünfkirchen *see* Pécs
83 M19 **Funhalouro** Inhambane, S Mozambique
161 R6 **Funing** Jiangsu, E China
160 I14 **Funing** *var.* Xinhua. Yunnan, SW China
160 M7 **Funiu Shan** ⛰ C China
77 U13 **Funtua** Katsina, N Nigeria
161 R12 **Fuqing** Fujian, SE China
83 M14 **Furancungo** Tete, NW Mozambique
116 I15 **Furculeşti** Teleorman, S Romania
Füred *see* Balatonfüred
165 W4 **Füren-ko** ◎ Hokkaidō, NE Japan
143 R12 **Fürg** Fārs, S Iran
Furluk *see* Fârliug
Fürmanov/Furmanovka *see* Moyynkum
Furmanovo *see* Zhalpaktal
59 L20 **Furnas, Represa de** ▣ SE Brazil
183 Q14 **Furneaux Group** *island group* Tasmania, SE Australia
Furnes *see* Veurne
160 J10 **Furong Jiang** ≈ S China
138 I5 **Furqlus** Ḩimş, W Syria
100 F12 **Fürstenau** Niedersachsen, NW Germany
109 X8 **Fürstenfeld** Steiermark, SE Austria
101 L23 **Fürstenfeldbruck** Bayern, S Germany
100 P12 **Fürstenwalde** Brandenburg, NE Germany
101 K20 **Fürth** Bayern, S Germany
109 W3 **Furth bei Göttweig** Niederösterreich, NW Austria
165 R3 **Furubira** Hokkaidō, NE Japan
94 L12 **Furudal** Dalarna, C Sweden
164 L12 **Furukawa** Gifu, Honshū, SW Japan
165 Q10 **Furukawa** *var.* Hurukawa. Miyagi, Honshū, C Japan
54 F10 **Fusagasugá** Cundinamarca, C Colombia
Fusan *see* Pusan
Fushë-Arëzi/Fushë-Arrësi *see* Fushë-Arrëz
113 L18 **Fushë-Arrëz** *var.* Fushë-Arëzi, Fushë-Arrësi. Shkodër, N Albania
Fushë-Kruja *see* Fushë-Krujë
113 K19 **Fushë-Krujë** *var.* Fushë-Kruja. Durrës, C Albania
163 V12 **Fushun** *var.* Fou-shan, Fu-shun. Liaoning, NE China
Fusin *see* Fuxin
108 G10 **Fusio** Ticino, S Switzerland
163 X11 **Fusong** Jilin, NE China
101 K24 **Füssen** Bayern, S Germany
160 K15 **Fusui** *prev.* Funan. Guangxi Zhuangzu Zizhiqu, S China
Futa Jallon *see* Fouta Djallon
63 G18 **Futaleufú** Los Lagos, S Chile
112 K10 **Futog** Serbia, NW Serbia and Montenegro (Yugo.)
165 O14 **Futtsu** *var.* Huttu. Chiba, Honshū, S Japan
187 S15 **Futuna** *island* S Vanuatu
190 D12 **Futuna, Île** *island* S Wallis and Futuna
161 Q11 **Futun Xi** ≈ SE China
160 L5 **Fuxian** *var.* Fu Xian. Shaanxi, C China
Fuxian *see* Wafangdian
160 G13 **Fuxian Hu** ◎ SW China
163 U12 **Fuxin** *var.* Fou-hsin, Fu-hsin, Fusin. Liaoning, NE China
Fuxing *see* Wangmo
161 P7 **Fuyang** Anhui, E China
161 O4 **Fuyang He** ≈ E China
163 U7 **Fuyu** Heilongjiang, NE China
Fuyu/Fu-yü *see* Songyuan
163 Z6 **Fuyuan** Heilongjiang, NE China
158 M3 **Fuyun** *var.* Koktokay. Xinjiang Uygur Zizhiqu, NW China
111 L22 **Füzesabony** Heves, E Hungary
161 R12 **Fuzhou** *var.* Foochow, Fu-chou. Fujian, SE China
161 P11 **Fuzhou** *prev.* Linchuan. Jiangxi, S China
137 W13 **Füzuli** *Rus.* Fizuli. SW Azerbaijan
119 I20 **Fyadory** *Rus.* Fëdory. Brestskaya Voblasts', SW Belarus
95 G24 **Fyn** *off.* Fyns Amt, *var.* Fünen. ◈ *county* C Denmark
95 G23 **Fyn** *Ger.* Fünen. *island* C Denmark
96 H12 **Fyne, Loch** *inlet* W Scotland, UK
95 E16 **Fyresvatn** ◎ S Norway
FYR Macedonia/FYROM *see* Macedonia, FYR
Fyzabad *see* Feyzābād

G

81 O14 **Gaalkacyo** *var.* Galka'yo, *It.* Galcaio. Mudug, C Somalia
146 J11 **Gabakly** *Rus.* Kabakly. Lebap Welaýaty, NE Turkmenistan
114 H8 **Gabare** Vratsa, NW Bulgaria
102 K15 **Gabas** ≈ SW France
Gabasumdo *see* Tongde
35 T7 **Gabbs** Nevada, W USA
82 B12 **Gabela** Cuanza Sul, W Angola
Gaberones *see* Gaborone
189 X14 **Gabert** *island* Caroline Islands, E Micronesia
74 M7 **Gabès** *var.* Qābis. E Tunisia
74 M6 **Gabès, Golfe de** *Ar.* Khalīj Qābis. *gulf* E Tunisia
Gablonz an der Neisse *see* Jablonec nad Nisou
Gablös *see* Cavalese
79 E18 **Gabon** *off.* Gabonese Republic. ◆ *republic* C Africa
83 I20 **Gaborone** *prev.* Gaberones. ● (Botswana) South East, SE Botswana
83 I20 **Gaborone** ✕ South East, SE Botswana
104 K8 **Gabriel y Galán, Embalse de** ▣ W Spain
143 U15 **Gābrīk, Rūd-e** ≈ SE Iran
114 J9 **Gabrovo** Gabrovo, N Bulgaria
114 J9 **Gabrovo** ◈ *province* N Bulgaria
76 H12 **Gabú** *prev.* Nova Lamego. E Guinea-Bissau
29 O6 **Gackle** North Dakota, N USA
113 I15 **Gacko** Republika Srpska, Bosnia and Herzegovina
155 F17 **Gadag** Karnātaka, W India
93 G15 **Gäddede** Jämtland, C Sweden
159 S12 **Gadê** Qinghai, C China
Gades/Gadier/Gadir/Gadire *see* Cádiz
105 P15 **Gádor, Sierra de** ⛰ S Spain
149 S15 **Gadra** Sind, SE Pakistan
23 Q3 **Gadsden** Alabama, S USA
36 H15 **Gadsden** Arizona, SW USA
Gadyach *see* Hadyach
79 H15 **Gadzi** Mambéré-Kadéï, SW Central African Republic
116 J13 **Găeşti** Dâmboviţa, S Romania
107 J17 **Gaeta** Lazio, C Italy
107 J17 **Gaeta, Golfo di** *var.* Gulf of Gaeta. *gulf* C Italy
188 L14 **Gaferut** *atoll* Caroline Islands, W Micronesia
21 Q10 **Gaffney** South Carolina, SE USA
Gäfle *see* Gävle
Gäfleborg *see* Gävleborg
74 M6 **Gafsa** *var.* Qafşah. W Tunisia
Gafurov *see* Ghafurov
147 O10 **Gagarin** Jizzax Viloyati, C Uzbekistan
101 G21 **Gaggenau** Baden-Württemberg, SW Germany
188 F16 **Gagil Tamil** *var.* Gagil-Tomil. *island* Caroline Islands, W Micronesia
Gagil-Tomil *see* Gagil Tamil
127 O4 **Gagino** Nizhegorodskaya Oblast', W Russian Federation
107 Q19 **Gagliano del Capo** Puglia, SE Italy
94 L13 **Gagnef** Dalarna, C Sweden
76 M17 **Gagnoa** C Ivory Coast
13 N10 **Gagnon** Québec, E Canada
Gago Coutinho *see* Lumbala N'Guimbo
137 P8 **Gagra** NW Georgia
31 S13 **Gahanna** Ohio, N USA
143 R13 **Gahkom** Hormozgān, S Iran
Gahnpa *see* Ganta
57 Q19 **Gaíba, Laguna** ◎ E Bolivia
153 T13 **Gaibanda** *var.* Gaibandah. Rajshahi, NW Bangladesh
Gaibandah *see* Gaibanda
Gaibhlte, Cnoc Mór na n *see* Galtymore Mountain
109 R9 **Gail** ≈ S Austria
101 I21 **Gaildorf** Baden-Württemberg, S Germany
103 N15 **Gaillac** *var.* Gaillac-sur-Tarn. Tarn, S France
Gaillac-sur-Tarn *see* Gaillac
Gaillimh *see* Galway
Gaillimhe, Cuan na *see* Galway Bay
109 Q9 **Gailtaler Alpen** ⛰ S Austria
63 J17 **Gaimán** Chaco, S Argentina
20 K8 **Gainesboro** Tennessee, S USA
23 V10 **Gainesville** Florida, SE USA
23 T2 **Gainesville** Georgia, SE USA
27 U8 **Gainesville** Missouri, C USA
25 T5 **Gainesville** Texas, SW USA
109 X5 **Gainfarn** Niederösterreich, NE Austria
97 N18 **Gainsborough** E England, UK
182 G6 **Gairdner, Lake** *salt lake* South Australia
Gaissane *see* Gáissát
92 L8 **Gáissát** *var.* Gaissane. ⛰ N Norway
43 T15 **Gaital, Cerro** ▲ C Panama
21 W3 **Gaithersburg** Maryland, NE USA
163 U13 **Gaizhou** Liaoning, NE China
Gaizina Kalns *see* Gaiziņkalns
118 H7 **Gaiziņkalns** *var.* Gaizina Kalns. ▲ E Latvia
Gajac *see* Villeneuve-sur-Lot
39 S10 **Gakona** Alaska, USA
Galaassiya *see* Galaosiyo
Galāğil *see* Jalājil
Galam, Pulau *see* Gelam, Pulau
62 J6 **Galán, Cerro** ▲ NW Argentina
111 H21 **Galanta** *Hung.* Galánta. Trnavský Kraj, W Slovakia
146 L11 **Galaosiyo** *Rus.* Galaassiya. Buxoro Viloyati, C Uzbekistan
57 B17 **Galápagos** *off.* Provincia de Galápagos. ◈ *province* Ecuador, E Pacific Ocean
193 P8 **Galapagos Fracture Zone** *tectonic feature* E Pacific Ocean
193 S9 **Galapagos Rise** *undersea feature* E Pacific Ocean
96 K13 **Galashiels** SE Scotland, UK
116 M12 **Galaţi** *Ger.* Galatz. Galaţi, E Romania
116 L12 **Galaţi** ◈ *county* E Romania
107 Q19 **Galatina** Puglia, SE Italy
107 Q19 **Galatone** Puglia, SE Italy
Galatz *see* Galaţi
21 R8 **Galax** Virginia, NE USA
146 J16 **Galaýmor** *Rus.* Kala-i-Mor. Mary Welaýaty, S Turkmenistan
Galcaio *see* Gaalkacyo
64 P11 **Gáldar** Gran Canaria, Islas Canarias, NE Atlantic Ocean
94 F11 **Galdhøpiggen** ▲ S Norway
40 I4 **Galeana** Chihuahua, N Mexico
41 O9 **Galeana** Nuevo León, NE Mexico
60 P9 **Galeão** ✕ (Rio de Janeiro) Rio de Janeiro, SE Brazil
171 R10 **Galela** Pulau Halmahera, E Indonesia
39 O9 **Galena** Alaska, USA
30 K10 **Galena** Illinois, N USA
27 R7 **Galena** Kansas, C USA
27 T8 **Galena** Missouri, C USA
45 V15 **Galeota Point** *headland* Trinidad, Trinidad and Tobago
105 P13 **Galera** Andalucía, S Spain
45 Y16 **Galera Point** *headland* Trinidad, Trinidad and Tobago
56 A5 **Galera, Punta** *headland* NW Ecuador
30 K12 **Galesburg** Illinois, N USA
30 J7 **Galesville** Wisconsin, N USA
18 F12 **Galeton** Pennsylvania, NE USA
116 H9 **Gâlgău** *Hung.* Galgó; *prev.* Gîlgău. Sălaj, NW Romania
Galgó *see* Gâlgău
Galgóc *see* Hlohovec
81 N15 **Galguduud** *off.* Gobolka Galguduud. ◈ *region* E Somalia
137 Q9 **Gali** W Georgia
125 N14 **Galich** Kostromskaya Oblast', NW Russian Federation
114 H7 **Galiche** Vratsa, NW Bulgaria
104 H3 **Galicia** *anc.* Gallaecia. ◈ *autonomous community* NW Spain
64 M8 **Galicia Bank** *undersea feature* E Atlantic Ocean
Galilee *see* HaGalil
181 W7 **Galilee, Lake** ◎ Queensland, NE Australia
Galilee, Sea of *see* Tiberias, Lake
106 E11 **Galileo Galilei** ✕ (Pisa) Toscana, C Italy
31 S12 **Galion** Ohio, N USA
Galka'yo *see* Gaalkacyo
146 K12 **Galkynyş** *prev. Rus.* Deynau, Dyanev, *Turkm.* Dänew. Lebap Welaýaty, NE Turkmenistan
80 H11 **Gallabat** Gedaref, E Sudan
Gallaecia *see* Galicia
106 C7 **Gallarate** Lombardia, NW Italy
27 S2 **Gallatin** Missouri, C USA
20 J8 **Gallatin** Tennessee, S USA
33 R11 **Gallatin Peak** ▲ Montana, NW USA
33 R12 **Gallatin River** ≈ Montana/Wyoming, NW USA
155 J26 **Galle** *prev.* Point de Galle. Southern Province, SW Sri Lanka
105 S5 **Gállego** ≈ NE Spain
193 Q8 **Gallego Rise** *undersea feature* E Pacific Ocean
Gallegos *see* Río Gallegos
63 H23 **Gallegos, Río** ≈ Argentina/Chile
Gallia *see* France
22 K10 **Galliano** Louisiana, S USA
114 G13 **Gallikós** ≈ N Greece
37 S12 **Gallinas Peak** ▲ New Mexico, SW USA
54 H3 **Gallinas, Punta** *headland* NE Colombia
37 T11 **Gallinas River** ≈ New Mexico, SW USA
107 Q19 **Gallipoli** Puglia, SE Italy
Gallipoli *see* Gelibolu
Gallipoli Peninsula *see* Gelibolu Yarımadası
31 T15 **Gallipolis** Ohio, N USA
92 J12 **Gällivare** *Lapp.* Váhtjer. Norrbotten, N Sweden
109 T4 **Gallneukirchen** Oberösterreich, N Austria
105 Q7 **Gallo** ≈ C Spain
93 G17 **Gällö** Jämtland, C Sweden
107 I23 **Gallo, Capo** *headland* Sicilia, Italy, C Mediterranean Sea
37 P13 **Gallo Mountains** ⛰ New Mexico, SW USA
18 G8 **Galloo Island** *island* New York, NE USA
97 H15 **Galloway, Mull of** *headland* S Scotland, UK
37 P10 **Gallup** New Mexico, SW USA
105 R5 **Gallur** Aragón, NE Spain
Galma *see* Guelma
35 O8 **Galt** California, W USA
74 C10 **Galtat-Zemmour** C Western Sahara
95 G22 **Galten** Århus, C Denmark
97 D20 **Galtymore Mountain** *Ir.* Cnoc Mór na nGaibhlte. ▲ S Ireland
97 D20 **Galty Mountains** *Ir.* Na Gaibhlte. ⛰ S Ireland
30 K11 **Galva** Illinois, N USA
25 X12 **Galveston** Texas, SW USA
25 W11 **Galveston Bay** *inlet* Texas, SW USA
25 W12 **Galveston Island** *island* Texas, SW USA
61 B18 **Gálvez** Santa Fe, C Argentina
97 C18 **Galway** *Ir.* Gaillimh. W Ireland
97 B18 **Galway** *Ir.* Gaillimh. *cultural region* W Ireland
97 B18 **Galway Bay** *Ir.* Cuan na Gaillimhe. *bay* W Ireland
83 F18 **Gam** Otjozondjupa, NE Namibia
164 L14 **Gamagōri** Aichi, Honshū, SW Japan
54 F7 **Gamarra** Cesar, N Colombia
Gámas *see* Kaamanen
158 L17 **Gamba** Xizang Zizhiqu, W China
Gamba *see* Zamtang

◆ Country ● Country Capital ◇ Dependent Territory ○ Dependent Territory Capital ◈ Administrative Region ✕ International Airport ▲ Mountain ⛰ Mountain Range Ѫ Volcano ≈ River ◎ Lake ▣ Reservoir

77 P14 **Gambaga** NE Ghana
80 G13 **Gambēla** Gambēla, W Ethiopia
83 H14 **Gambēla** ◈ *region*, W Ethiopia
38 K10 **Gambell** Saint Lawrence Island, Alaska, USA
76 E12 **Gambia** *off.* Republic of The Gambia, The Gambia. ◆ *republic* W Africa
76 I12 **Gambia** *Fr.* Gambie. ≈ W Africa
64 K12 **Gambia Plain** *undersea feature* E Atlantic Ocean
Gambie *see* Gambia
31 T13 **Gambier** Ohio, N USA
191 Y13 **Gambier, Îles** *island group* E French Polynesia
182 G10 **Gambier Islands** *island group* South Australia
79 H19 **Gamboma** Plateaux, E Congo
79 G16 **Gamboula** Mambéré-Kadéï, SW Central African Republic
37 P10 **Gamerco** New Mexico, SW USA
137 V12 **Gamış Dağı** ▲ W Azerbaijan
Gamlakarleby *see* Kokkola
95 N18 **Gamleby** Kalmar, S Sweden
Gammelstad *see* Gammelstaden
93 J14 **Gammelstaden** *var.* Gammelstad. Norrbotten, N Sweden
Gammouda *see* Sidi Bouzid
155 J25 **Gampaha** Western Province, W Sri Lanka
155 K25 **Gampola** Central Province, C Sri Lanka
167 S5 **Gâm, Sông** ≈ N Vietnam
92 L7 **Gamvik** Finnmark, N Norway
150 H13 **Gan** Addu Atoll, C Maldives
Gan *see* Gansu, China
Gan *see* Jiangxi, China
Ganaane *see* Juba
37 O10 **Ganado** Arizona, SW USA
25 U12 **Ganado** Texas, SW USA
14 L14 **Gananoque** Ontario, SE Canada
Ganāveh *see* Bandar-e Gonāveh
137 V11 **Gäncä** *Rus.* Gyandzha; *prev.* Kirovabad, Yelisavetpol. W Azerbaijan
Ganchi *see* Ghonchí
Gand *see* Gent
82 B13 **Ganda** *var.* Mariano Machado, *Port.* Vila Mariano Machado. Benguela, W Angola
79 L22 **Gandajika** Kasai Oriental, S Dem. Rep. Congo
153 O12 **Gandak** *Nep.* Nārāyāni. ≈ India/Nepal
13 U11 **Gander** Newfoundland and Labrador, SE Canada
13 U11 **Gander** ✕ Newfoundland and Labrador, E Canada
100 G11 **Ganderkesee** Niedersachsen, NW Germany
105 T7 **Gandesa** Cataluña, NE Spain
154 B10 **Gāndhīdhām** Gujarāt, W India
154 D10 **Gāndhīnagar** Gujarāt, W India
154 F9 **Gāndhi Sāgar** ◎ C India
105 T11 **Gandía** País Valenciano, E Spain
159 O10 **Gang** Qinghai, W China
152 G9 **Gangānagar** Rājasthān, NW India
152 I12 **Gangāpur** Rājasthān, N India
153 S17 **Ganga Sāgar** West Bengal, NE India
Gangavathi *see* Gangāwati
155 G17 **Gangāwati** *var.* Gangavathi. Karnātaka, C India
159 S9 **Gangca** *var.* Shaliuhe. Qinghai, C China
158 H14 **Gangdisê Shan** *Eng.* Kailas Range. ⛰ W China
103 Q15 **Ganges** Hérault, S France
153 P13 **Ganges** *Ben.* Padma. ≈ Bangladesh/India *see also* Padma
Ganges Cone *see* Ganges Fan
173 S3 **Ganges Fan** *var.* Ganges Cone. *undersea feature* N Bay of Bengal
153 U17 **Ganges, Mouths of the** *delta* Bangladesh/India
107 K23 **Gangi** *anc.* Engyum. Sicilia, Italy, C Mediterranean Sea
152 K8 **Gangotri** Uttaranchal, N India
Gangra *see* Çankırı
153 S11 **Gangtok** Sikkim, N India
159 W11 **Gangu** Gansu, C China
163 U5 **Gan He** ≈ NE China
171 S12 **Gani** Pulau Halmahera, E Indonesia
161 O12 **Gan Jiang** ≈ S China
163 U11 **Ganjig** *var.* Horqin Zuoyi Houqi. Nei Mongol Zizhiqu, N China
146 H15 **Gannaly** Ahal Welaýaty, S Turkmenistan
163 U7 **Gannan** Heilongjiang, NE China
103 P10 **Gannat** Allier, C France
33 T14 **Gannett Peak** ▲ Wyoming, C USA
29 O10 **Gannvalley** South Dakota, N USA
Ganqu *see* Lhünzhub
109 Y3 **Gänserndorf** Niederösterreich, NE Austria
Gansos, Lago dos *see* Goose Lake
159 T9 **Gansu** *var.* Gan, Gansu Sheng, Kansu. ◈ *province* N China
Gansu Sheng *see* Gansu
76 K16 **Ganta** *var.* Gahnpa. NE Liberia
182 H11 **Gantheaume, Cape** *headland* South Australia
Gantsevichi *see* Hantsavichy
151 Q6 **Ganyu** *var.* Qingkou. Jiangsu, E China
144 D12 **Ganyushkino** Atyrau, SW Kazakhstan
161 O12 **Ganzhou** Jiangxi, S China
Ganzhou *see* Zhangye
77 Q10 **Gao** Gao, E Mali
77 R10 **Gao** ◈ *region* SE Mali
161 O10 **Gao'an** Jiangxi, S China
Gaocheng *see* Litang
Gaoleshan *see* Xianfeng
161 R5 **Gaomi** Shandong, E China
161 N5 **Gaoping** Shanxi, C China
159 S8 **Gaotai** Gansu, N China
Gaoth Dobhair *see* Gweedore
77 O14 **Gaoua** SW Burkina
76 I13 **Gaoual** Moyenne-Guinée, N Guinea
Gaoxiong *see* Kaohsiung
161 R7 **Gaoyou** *var.* Dayishan. Jiangsu, E China
161 R7 **Gaoyou Hu** ◎ E China
160 M15 **Gaozhou** Guangdong, S China
103 T13 **Gap** *anc.* Vapincum. Hautes-Alpes, SE France
146 E9 **Gaplaňgyr Platosy** *Rus.* Plato Kaplangky. *ridge* Turkmenistan/Uzbekistan
158 G13 **Gar** *var.* Gar Xincun. Xizang Zizhiqu, W China
Garabekevyul *see* Garabekewül
146 L13 **Garabekewül** *Rus.* Garabekevyul, Karabekaul. Lebap Welaýaty, E Turkmenistan
146 K15 **Garabil Belentligi** *Rus.* Vozvyshennost' Karabil'. ⛰ S Turkmenistan
146 B9 **Garabogaz Aylagy** *Rus.* Zaliv Kara-Bogaz-Gol. *bay* NW Turkmenistan
146 A9 **Garabogazköl** *Rus.* Kara-Bogaz-Kol. Balkan Welaýaty, NW Turkmenistan
43 V16 **Garachiné** Darién, SE Panama
43 V16 **Garachiné, Punta** *headland* SE Panama
146 K12 **Garagan** *Rus.* Karagan. Ahal Welaýaty, C Turkmenistan
54 G10 **Garagoa** Boyacá, C Colombia
146 A11 **Garagöl** *Rus.* Karagel'. Balkan Welaýaty, W Turkmenistan
146 F12 **Garagum** *var.* Garagumy, Qara Qum, *Eng.* Black Sand Desert, Kara Kum; *prev.* Peski Karakumy. *desert* C Turkmenistan
146 E12 **Garagum Kanaly** *var.* Kara Kum Canal, *Rus.* Garagumskiy Kanal, Karakumskiy Kanal. *canal* C Turkmenistan
Garagumskiy Kanal *see* Garagum Kanaly
Garagumy *see* Garagum
183 S4 **Garah** New South Wales, SE Australia
64 O11 **Garajonay** ▲ Gomera, Islas Canarias, NE Atlantic Ocean
114 M8 **Gara Khitrino** Shumen, NE Bulgaria
76 L13 **Garalo** Sikasso, SW Mali
Garam *see* Hron
146 L14 **Garamätnyýaz** *Rus.* Karamet-Niyaz. Lebap Welaýaty, E Turkmenistan
Garamszentkereszt *see* Žiar nad Hronom
77 Q13 **Garango** S Burkina
59 Q15 **Garanhuns** Pernambuco, E Brazil
188 H5 **Garapan** Saipan, S Northern Mariana Islands
Gárasavvon *see* Karesuando
Gárassavon *see* Kaaresuvanto
78 J13 **Garba** Bamingui-Bangoran, N Central African Republic
Garba *see* Jiulong
81 L16 **Garbahaarrey** *It.* Garba Harre. Gedo, SW Somalia
Garba Harre *see* Garbahaarrey
81 J18 **Garba Tula** Eastern, C Kenya
27 N9 **Garber** Oklahoma, C USA
34 L4 **Garberville** California, W USA
100 I12 **Garbsen** Niedersachsen, N Germany
Garbo *see* Lhozhag
60 K9 **Garça** São Paulo, S Brazil
104 L10 **García de Solá, Embalse de** ⊡ C Spain
103 Q14 **Gard** ◈ *department* S France
103 Q14 **Gard** ≈ S France
106 F7 **Garda, Lago di** *var.* Benaco, *Eng.* Lake Garda, *Ger.* Gardasee. ◎ NE Italy
Garda, Lake *see* Garda, Lago di
Gardan Divāl *see* Gardan Dīwāl
149 Q5 **Gardan Dīwāl** *var.* Gardan Divāl. Wardag, C Afghanistan
103 S15 **Gardanne** Bouches-du-Rhône, SE France
Gardasee *see* Garda, Lago di
100 L12 **Gardelegen** Sachsen-Anhalt, C Germany
14 B10 **Garden** ≈ Ontario, S Canada
23 X6 **Garden City** Georgia, SE USA
26 I6 **Garden City** Kansas, C USA
27 S5 **Garden City** Missouri, C USA
25 N8 **Garden City** Texas, SW USA
23 P3 **Gardendale** Alabama, S USA
31 P5 **Garden Island** *island* Michigan, N USA
22 M11 **Garden Island Bay** *bay* Louisiana, S USA
31 O5 **Garden Peninsula** *peninsula* Michigan, N USA
Garden State *see* New Jersey
95 I14 **Gardermoen** Akershus, S Norway
Gardeyz *see* Gardēz
149 Q6 **Gardēz** *prev.* Gardeyz, Gordiaz. Paktīā, E Afghanistan
93 G14 **Gardiken** ◎ N Sweden
19 Q7 **Gardiner** Maine, NE USA
33 S12 **Gardiner** Montana, NW USA
19 N13 **Gardiners Island** *island* New York, NE USA
Gardner Island *see* Nikumaroro
19 T6 **Gardner Lake** ◎ Maine, NE USA
35 Q6 **Gardnerville** Nevada, W USA
Gardo *see* Qardho
106 F7 **Gardone Val Trompia** Lombardia, N Italy
Garegegasnjárga *see* Karigasniemi
38 F17 **Gareloi Island** *island* Aleutian Islands, Alaska, USA
Gares *see* Puente la Reina
106 B10 **Garessio** Piemonte, NE Italy
32 M9 **Garfield** Washington, NW USA
31 U11 **Garfield Heights** Ohio, N USA
Gargaliani *see* Gargaliánoi
115 D21 **Gargaliánoi** *var.* Gargaliani. Pelopónnisos, S Greece
107 N15 **Gargano, Promontorio del** *headland* SE Italy
108 J8 **Gargellen** Graubünden, W Switzerland
93 I14 **Gargnäs** Västerbotten, N Sweden
118 C11 **Gargždai** Klaipėda, W Lithuania
154 J13 **Garhchiroli** Mahārāshtra, C India
153 O15 **Garhwa** Jhārkhand, N India
171 V13 **Gariau** Papua, E Indonesia
83 E24 **Garies** Northern Cape, W South Africa
109 K17 **Garigliano** ≈ C Italy
81 K19 **Garissa** Coast, E Kenya
21 V11 **Garland** North Carolina, SE USA
25 T6 **Garland** Texas, SW USA
36 L1 **Garland** Utah, W USA
106 D8 **Garlasco** Lombardia, N Italy
119 F14 **Garliava** Kaunas, S Lithuania
Garm *see* Gharm
142 M9 **Garm, Āb-e** *var.* Rūd-e Khersān. ≈ SW Iran
101 K25 **Garmisch-Partenkirchen** Bayern, S Germany
143 O5 **Garmsār** *prev.* Qishlaq. Semnān, N Iran
Garmser *see* Darvīshān
29 V12 **Garner** Iowa, C USA
21 U9 **Garner** North Carolina, SE USA
27 Q5 **Garnett** Kansas, C USA
99 M25 **Garnich** Luxembourg, SW Luxembourg
182 M8 **Garnpung, Lake** *salt lake* New South Wales, SE Australia
Garoe *see* Garoowe
Garoet *see* Garut
153 U13 **Gāro Hills** *hill range* NE India
102 K13 **Garonne** *anc.* Garumna. ≈ S France
80 P13 **Garoowe** *var.* Garoe. Nugaal, N Somalia
78 F12 **Garoua** *var.* Garua. Nord, N Cameroon
79 G14 **Garoua Boulaï** Est, E Cameroon
77 O10 **Garou, Lac** ◎ C Mali
95 L16 **Garphyttan** Örebro, C Sweden
29 R11 **Garretson** South Dakota, N USA
31 Q11 **Garrett** Indiana, N USA
33 Q10 **Garrison** Montana, NW USA
28 M4 **Garrison** North Dakota, N USA
25 X8 **Garrison** Texas, SW USA
28 L4 **Garrison Dam** *dam* North Dakota, N USA
104 J9 **Garrovillas** Extremadura, W Spain
146 D12 **Garrygala** *Rus.* Kara-Kala. Balkan Welaýaty, W Turkmenistan
8 L8 **Garry Lake** ◎ Nunavut, N Canada
Gars *see* Gars am Kamp
109 W3 **Gars am Kamp** *var.* Gars. Niederösterreich, NE Austria
81 K20 **Garsen** Coast, S Kenya
Garshy *see* Garşy
14 F10 **Garson** Ontario, S Canada
109 T5 **Garsten** Oberösterreich, N Austria
146 A9 **Garşy** *var.* Garshy, *Rus.* Karshi. Balkan Welaýaty, NW Turkmenistan
Gartar *see* Qianning
102 M10 **Gartempe** ≈ C France
Gartog *see* Markam
Garua *see* Garoua
83 D21 **Garub** Karas, SW Namibia
Garumna *see* Garonne
169 P16 **Garut** *prev.* Garoet. Jawa, C Indonesia
185 C20 **Garvie Mountains** ⛰ South Island, NZ
110 N12 **Garwolin** Mazowieckie, E Poland
25 U12 **Garwood** Texas, SW USA
Gar Xincun *see* Gar
31 N11 **Gary** Indiana, N USA
25 X7 **Gary** Texas, SW USA
158 G13 **Gar Zangbo** ≈ W China
160 F8 **Garzê** Sichuan, C China
54 E12 **Garzón** Huila, S Colombia
Gasan-Kuli *see* Esenguly
31 P13 **Gas City** Indiana, N USA
102 K15 **Gascogne** *Eng.* Gascony. *cultural region* S France
Gascogne, Golfe de *see* Gascony, Gulf of
26 V5 **Gasconade River** ≈ Missouri, C USA
Gascony *see* Gascogne
180 H9 **Gascoyne Junction** Western Australia
173 V8 **Gascoyne Plain** *undersea feature* E Indian Ocean
180 H9 **Gascoyne River** ≈ Western Australia
192 J11 **Gascoyne Tablemount** *undersea feature* N Tasman Sea
149 X3 **Gasherbrum** ▲ NE Pakistan
Gas Hu *see* Gas Hure Hu
77 X12 **Gashua** Yobe, NE Nigeria
159 N9 **Gas Hure Hu** *var.* Gas Hu. ◎ C China
186 G7 **Gasmata** New Britain, E PNG
23 V14 **Gasparilla Island** *island* Florida, SE USA
169 O13 **Gaspar, Selat** *strait* W Indonesia
15 Y6 **Gaspé** Québec, SE Canada
15 Z6 **Gaspé, Cap de** *headland* Québec, SE Canada
15 X6 **Gaspé, Péninsule de** *var.* Péninsule de la Gaspésie. *peninsula* Québec, SE Canada
Gaspésie, Péninsule de la *see* Gaspé, Péninsule de
77 W15 **Gassol** Taraba, E Nigeria
Gastein *see* Badgastein
21 R10 **Gastonia** North Carolina, SE USA
21 V8 **Gaston, Lake** ⊡ North Carolina/Virginia, SE USA
115 D19 **Gastoúni** Dytikí Elláda, S Greece
63 I17 **Gastre** Chubut, S Argentina
Gat *see* Ghāt
105 P15 **Gata, Cabo de** *headland* S Spain
Gata, Cape *see* Gátas, Akrotíri
105 T11 **Gata de Gorgos** País Valenciano, E Spain
116 E12 **Gătaia** *Ger.* Gataja, *Hung.* Gátalja; *prev.* Gáttája. Timiş, W Romania
Gataja/Gátalja *see* Gătaia
121 P3 **Gátas, Akrotíri** *var.* Cape Gata. *headland* S Cyprus
104 J8 **Gata, Sierra de** ⛰ W Spain
124 G13 **Gatchina** Leningradskaya Oblast', NW Russian Federation
21 P8 **Gate City** Virginia, NE USA
97 M14 **Gateshead** NE England, UK
21 X8 **Gatesville** North Carolina, SE USA
25 S8 **Gatesville** Texas, SW USA
14 L12 **Gatineau** Québec, SE Canada
14 L11 **Gatineau** ≈ Ontario/Québec, SE Canada
21 N9 **Gatlinburg** Tennessee, S USA
Gatooma *see* Kadoma
Gáttája *see* Gătaia
43 T14 **Gatún, Lago** ⊡ C Panama
59 N14 **Gaturiano** Piauí, NE Brazil
97 O22 **Gatwick** ✕ (London) SE England, UK
187 Y14 **Gau** *prev.* Ngau. *island* C Fiji
187 R12 **Gaua** *var.* Santa Maria. *island* Banks Island, N Vanuatu
104 L16 **Gaucín** Andalucía, S Spain
Gauhāti *see* Guwāhāti
118 I8 **Gauja** *Ger.* Aa. ≈ Estonia/Latvia
118 I7 **Gaujiena** Alūksne, NE Latvia
Gaul/Gaule *see* France
94 H9 **Gauldalen** *valley* S Norway
21 R5 **Gauley River** ≈ West Virginia, NE USA
99 D19 **Gaurain-Ramecroix** Hainaut, SW Belgium
95 F15 **Gaustatoppen** ▲ S Norway
83 J21 **Gauteng** *off.* Gauteng Province; *prev.* Pretoria-Witwatersrand-Vereeniging. ◈ *province* NE South Africa
Gauteng *see* Germiston, South Africa
Gauteng *see* Johannesburg, South Africa
143 P14 **Gāvbandī** Hormozgān, S Iran
115 H25 **Gavdopoúla** *island* SE Greece
115 H26 **Gávdos** *island* SE Greece
102 K16 **Gave de Pau** *var.* Gave-de-Pay. ≈ SW France
Gave-de-Pay *see* Gave de Pau
102 J16 **Gave d'Oloron** ≈ SW France
99 E18 **Gavere** Oost-Vlaanderen, NW Belgium
94 N13 **Gävle** *var.* Gäfle; *prev.* Gefle. Gävleborg, C Sweden
94 M11 **Gävleborg** *var.* Gäfleborg, Gefleborg. ◈ *county* C Sweden
94 O13 **Gävlebukten** *bay* C Sweden
124 L16 **Gavrilov-Yam** Yaroslavskaya Oblast', W Russian Federation
182 I9 **Gawler** South Australia
182 G7 **Gawler Ranges** *hill range* South Australia
Gawso *see* Goaso
162 H11 **Gaxun Nur** ◎ N China
153 P14 **Gaya** Bihār, N India
77 S13 **Gaya** Dosso, SW Niger
Gaya *see* Kyjov
31 Q6 **Gaylord** Michigan, N USA
29 U9 **Gaylord** Minnesota, N USA
181 Y9 **Gayndah** Queensland, E Australia
125 T12 **Gayny** Komi-Permyatskiy Avtonomnyy Okrug, NW Russian Federation
Gaysin *see* Haysyn
Gayvorno *see* Hayvoron
138 E11 **Gaza** *Ar.* Ghazzah, *Heb.* 'Azza. NE Gaza Strip
83 L20 **Gaza** *off.* Província de Gaza. ◈ *province* SW Mozambique
Gaz-Achak *see* Gazojak
Gazalkent *see* G'azalkent
147 Q9 **G'azalkent** *Rus.* Gazalkent. Toshkent Viloyati, E Uzbekistan
Gazandzhyk/Gazanjyk *see* Bereket
77 V12 **Gazaoua** Maradi, S Niger
138 E11 **Gaza Strip** *Ar.* Qiṭā' Ghazzah. *disputed region* SW Asia
Gazgan *see* G'ozg'on
Gazi Antep *see* Gaziantep
136 M16 **Gaziantep** *var.* Gazi Antep; *prev.* Aintab, Antep. Gaziantep, S Turkey
136 M17 **Gaziantep** *var.* Gazi Antep. ◈ *province* S Turkey
114 M13 **Gaziköy** Tekirdağ, NW Turkey
121 Q2 **Gazimağusa** *var.* Famagusta, *Gk.* Ammóchostos. E Cyprus
121 Q2 **Gazimağusa Körfezi** *var.* Famagusta Bay, *Gk.* Kólpos Ammóchostos. *bay* E Cyprus
146 K11 **Gazli** Buxoro Viloyati, C Uzbekistan
146 I9 **Gazojak** *Rus.* Gaz-Achak. Lebap Welaýaty, NE Turkmenistan
79 K15 **Gbadolite** Equateur, NW Dem. Rep. Congo
76 K16 **Gbanga** *var.* Gbarnga. N Liberia
Gbarnga *see* Gbanga
77 S14 **Gbéroubouè** *var.* Béroubouay. N Benin
77 W16 **Gboko** Benue, S Nigeria
Gcuwa *see* Butterworth
110 J7 **Gdańsk** *Fr.* Dantzig, *Ger.* Danzig. Pomorskie, N Poland
Gdan'skaya Bukhta/Gdańsk, Gulf of *see* Danzig, Gulf of
Gdańska, Zakota *see* Danzig, Gulf of
Gdingen *see* Gdynia
124 F13 **Gdov** Pskovskaya Oblast', W Russian Federation
110 I6 **Gdynia** *Ger.* Gdingen. Pomorskie, N Poland
26 M10 **Geary** Oklahoma, C USA
Geavvú *see* Kevo
76 H12 **Gêba, Rio** ≈ C Guinea-Bissau
136 E11 **Gebze** Kocaeli, NW Turkey
80 H10 **Gedaref** *var.* Al Qaḍārif, El Gedaref. Gedaref, E Sudan
80 H10 **Gedaref** ◈ *state* E Sudan
80 B11 **Gedid Ras el Fil** Southern Darfur, W Sudan
101 I23 **Gedinne** Namur, SE Belgium
136 E13 **Gediz** Kütahya, W Turkey
136 C14 **Gediz Nehri** ≈ W Turkey
81 N14 **Gedlegubē** Somali, E Ethiopia
81 L17 **Gedo** *off.* Gobolka Gedo. ◈ *region* SW Somalia
95 I25 **Gedser** Storstrøm, SE Denmark
99 I16 **Geel** *var.* Gheel. Antwerpen, N Belgium
183 N13 **Geelong** Victoria, SE Australia
Ge'e'mu *see* Golmud
99 I14 **Geertruidenberg** Noord-Brabant, S Netherlands
100 H10 **Geeste** ≈ NW Germany
100 J10 **Geesthacht** Schleswig-Holstein, N Germany
183 P17 **Geeveston** Tasmania, SE Australia
Gefle *see* Gävle
Gefleborg *see* Gävleborg
158 G13 **Gê'gyai** Xizang Zizhiqu, W China
77 X12 **Geidam** Yobe, NE Nigeria
11 T11 **Geikie** ≈ Saskatchewan, C Canada
94 F13 **Geilo** Buskerud, S Norway
94 E10 **Geiranger** Møre og Romsdal, S Norway
101 I22 **Geislingen** *var.* Geislingen an der Steige. Baden-Württemberg, SW Germany
Geislingen an der Steige *see* Geislingen
81 F20 **Geita** Mwanza, NW Tanzania
95 G15 **Geithus** Buskerud, S Norway
160 H14 **Gejiu** *var.* Kochiu. Yunnan, S China
Gëkdepe *see* Gökdepe
146 E9 **Geklengkui, Solonchak** *var.* Solonchak Goklenkuy. *salt marsh* NW Turkmenistan
81 D14 **Gel** ≈ W Sudan
107 K25 **Gela** *prev.* Terranova di Sicilia. Sicilia, Italy, C Mediterranean Sea
159 N13 **Geladaindong** ▲ C China
81 N14 **Geladī** Somali, E Ethiopia
169 P13 **Gelam, Pulau** *var.* Pulau Galam. *island* N Indonesia
Gelaozu Miaozu Zizhixian *see* Wuchuan
98 L11 **Gelderland** *prev. Eng.* Guelders. ◈ *province* E Netherlands
98 J13 **Geldermalsen** Gelderland, C Netherlands
101 D14 **Geldern** Nordrhein-Westfalen, W Germany
99 K15 **Geldrop** Noord-Brabant, SE Netherlands
99 L17 **Geleen** Limburg, SE Netherlands
126 K14 **Gelendzhik** Krasnodarskiy Kray, SW Russian Federation
Gelib *see* Jilib
136 B11 **Gelibolu** *Eng.* Gallipoli. Çanakkale, NW Turkey
115 L14 **Gelibolu Yarımadası** *Eng.* Gallipoli Peninsula. *peninsula* NW Turkey
81 O14 **Gellinsor** Mudug, C Somalia
101 H18 **Gelnhausen** Hessen, C Germany
101 E14 **Gelsenkirchen** Nordrhein-Westfalen, W Germany
83 C20 **Geluk** Hardap, SW Namibia
99 H20 **Gembloux** Namur, Belgium
79 J16 **Gemena** Equateur, NW Dem. Rep. Congo
99 L14 **Gemert** Noord-Brabant, SE Netherlands
136 E11 **Gemlik** Bursa, NW Turkey
Gem of the Mountains *see* Idaho
106 J6 **Gemona del Friuli** Friuli-Venezia Giulia, NE Italy
Gem State *see* Idaho
Genalē Wenz *see* Juba
169 R10 **Genali, Danau** ◎ Borneo, N Indonesia
99 G19 **Genappe** Wallon Brabant, C Belgium
137 P14 **Genç** Bingöl, E Turkey
Genck *see* Genk
98 M9 **Genemuiden** Overijssel, E Netherlands
63 K14 **General Acha** La Pampa, C Argentina
61 C21 **General Alvear** Buenos Aires, E Argentina
62 I12 **General Alvear** Mendoza, W Argentina
61 B20 **General Arenales** Buenos Aires, E Argentina
61 D21 **General Belgrano** Buenos Aires, E Argentina
194 H3 **General Bernardo O'Higgins** *Chilean research station* Antarctica
41 O8 **General Bravo** Nuevo León, NE Mexico
62 M7 **General Capdevila** Chaco, N Argentina
General Carrera, Lago *see* Buenos Aires, Lago
41 N9 **General Cepeda** Coahuila de Zaragoza, NE Mexico
63 K15 **General Conesa** Río Negro, E Argentina
61 G18 **General Enrique Martínez** Treinta y Tres, E Uruguay
62 L3 **General Eugenio A. Garay** *var.* Fortín General Eugenio Garay; *prev.* Yrendagüé. Nueva Asunción, NW Paraguay
61 C18 **General Galarza** Entre Ríos, E Argentina
61 E22 **General Guido** Buenos Aires, E Argentina
General José F.Uriburu *see* Zárate
61 E22 **General Juan Madariaga** Buenos Aires, E Argentina
41 O16 **General Juan N Alvarez** ✕ (Acapulco) Guerrero, S Mexico
61 B22 **General La Madrid** Buenos Aires, E Argentina
61 E21 **General Lavalle** Buenos Aires, E Argentina
General Machado *see* Camacupa
62 I8 **General Manuel Belgrano, Cerro** ▲ W Argentina
41 O8 **General Mariano Escobero** ✕ (Monterrey) Nuevo León, NE Mexico
61 B20 **General O'Brien** Buenos Aires, E Argentina
62 K13 **General Pico** La Pampa, C Argentina
62 M7 **General Pinedo** Chaco, N Argentina
61 B20 **General Pinto** Buenos Aires, E Argentina
61 E22 **General Pirán** Buenos Aires, E Argentina
43 N15 **General, Río** ≈ S Costa Rica
63 I15 **General Roca** Río Negro, C Argentina
171 Q8 **General Santos** *off.* General Santos City. Mindanao, S Philippines
41 O9 **General Terán** Nuevo León, NE Mexico
114 N7 **General Toshevo** *Rom.* I.G.Duca, *prev.* Casim, Kasimköj. Dobrich, NE Bulgaria
61 B20 **General Viamonte** Buenos Aires, E Argentina
61 A20 **General Villegas** Buenos Aires, E Argentina
Gênes *see* Genova
18 E11 **Genesee River** ≈ New York/Pennsylvania, NE USA
30 K11 **Geneseo** Illinois, N USA
18 F10 **Geneseo** New York, NE USA
57 L14 **Geneshuaya, Río** ≈ N Bolivia
23 Q8 **Geneva** Alabama, S USA
30 M10 **Geneva** Illinois, N USA
29 Q16 **Geneva** Nebraska, C USA
18 G10 **Geneva** New York, NE USA
31 U10 **Geneva** Ohio, NE USA
Geneva *see* Genève
108 B10 **Geneva, Lake** *Fr.* Lac de Genève, Lac Léman, le Léman, *Ger.* Genfer See. ◎ France/Switzerland
108 A10 **Genève** *Eng.* Geneva, *Ger.* Genf, *It.* Ginevra. Genève, SW Switzerland
108 A11 **Genève** *Eng.* Geneva, *Ger.* Genf, *It.* Ginevra. ◈ *canton* SW Switzerland
108 A10 **Genève** *var.* Geneva. ✕ Vaud, SW Switzerland
Genève, Lac de *see* Geneva, Lake
Genf *see* Genève
Genfer See *see* Geneva, Lake
163 T5 **Genhe** *prev.* Ergun Zuoqi. Nei Mongol Zizhiqu, N China
163 S5 **Gen He** ≈ NE China
Genichesk *see* Heniches'k
104 L14 **Genil** ≈ S Spain
99 K18 **Genk** *var.* Genck. Limburg, NE Belgium
164 C13 **Genkai-nada** *gulf* Kyūshū, SW Japan
107 C19 **Gennargentu, Monti del** ▲ Sardegna, Italy, C Mediterranean Sea
99 M14 **Gennep** Limburg, SE Netherlands
30 M10 **Genoa** Illinois, N USA
29 Q15 **Genoa** Nebraska, C USA
Genoa *see* Genova
Genoa, Gulf of *see* Genova, Golfo di
106 D10 **Genova** *Eng.* Genoa, *Fr.* Gênes; *anc.* Genua. Liguria, NW Italy
106 D10 **Genova, Golfo di** *Eng.* Gulf of Genoa. *gulf* NW Italy
57 C17 **Genovesa, Isla** *var.* Tower Island. *island* Galapagos Islands, Ecuador, E Pacific Ocean
Genshū *see* Wŏnju
99 E17 **Gent** *Eng.* Ghent, *Fr.* Gand. Oost-Vlaanderen, NW Belgium
169 N16 **Genteng** Jawa, C Indonesia
100 M12 **Genthin** Sachsen-Anhalt, E Germany
27 R9 **Gentry** Arkansas, C USA
Genua *see* Genova
107 I15 **Genzano di Roma** Lazio, C Italy
Geokchay *see* Göyçay
Geok-Tepe *see* Gökdepe
122 I3 **Georga, Zemlya** *Eng.* George Land. *island* Zemlya Frantsa-Iosifa, N Russian Federation
83 G26 **George** Western Cape, S South Africa
29 S11 **George** Iowa, C USA
13 O5 **George** ≈ Newfoundland and Labrador/Québec, E Canada
45 T11 **George FL Charles** ✕ (Castries) *prev.* Vigie NE Saint Lucia
65 C25 **George Island** *island* S Falkland Islands
183 R10 **George, Lake** ◎ New South Wales, SE Australia
81 E18 **George, Lake** ◎ SW Uganda
23 W10 **George, Lake** ◎ Florida, SE USA
18 L8 **George, Lake** ⊡ New York, NE USA
George Land *see* Georga, Zemlya
Georgenburg *see* Jurbarkas
George River *see* Kangiqsualujjuaq
64 G8 **Georges Bank** *undersea feature* W Atlantic Ocean

◆ Country ● Country Capital ◇ Dependent Territory ○ Dependent Territory Capital ◈ Administrative Region ✕ International Airport ▲ Mountain ⛰ Mountain Range ⟁ Volcano ≈ River ◎ Lake ⊡ Reservoir

185 *A21* **George Sound** *sound* South Island, NZ
65 *F15* **Georgetown** ○ (Ascension Island) NW Ascension Island
181 *V5* **Georgetown** Queensland, NE Australia
183 *P15* **George Town** Tasmania, SE Australia
44 *I4* **George Town** Great Exuma Island, C Bahamas
44 *D8* **George Town** *var.* Georgetown. ○ (Cayman Islands) Grand Cayman, SW Cayman Islands
76 *H12* **Georgetown** E Gambia
55 *T8* **Georgetown** ● (Guyana) N Guyana
168 *I7* **George Town** *var.* Penang, Pinang. Pinang, Peninsular Malaysia
45 *Y14* **Georgetown** Saint Vincent, Saint Vincent and the Grenadines
21 *Y4* **Georgetown** Delaware, NE USA
23 *R6* **Georgetown** Georgia, SE USA
20 *M5* **Georgetown** Kentucky, S USA
21 *T13* **Georgetown** South Carolina, SE USA
25 *S10* **Georgetown** Texas, SW USA
55 *T8* **Georgetown** ✕ N Guyana
195 *U16* **George V Coast** *physical region* Antarctica
195 *T15* **George V Land** *physical region* Antarctica
194 *J7* **George VI Ice Shelf** *ice shelf* Antarctica
194 *J6* **George VI Sound** *sound* Antarctica
25 *S14* **George West** Texas, SW USA
137 *R9* **Georgia** *off.* Republic of Georgia, *Geor.* Sak'art'velo, *Rus.* Gruzinskaya SSR, Gruziya; *prev.* Georgian SSR. ◆ *republic* SW Asia
23 *S5* **Georgia** *off.* State of Georgia; also known as Empire State of the South, Peach State. ◈ *state* SE USA
14 *F12* **Georgian Bay** *lake bay* Ontario, S Canada
10 *L17* **Georgia, Strait of** *strait* British Columbia, W Canada
Georgi Dimitrov *see* Kostenets
Georgi Dimitrov, Yazovir *see* Koprinka, Yazovir
114 *M9* **Georgi Traykov, Yazovir** ⊟ NE Bulgaria
Georgiu-Dezh *see* Liski
145 *W10* **Georgiyevka** Vostochnyy Kazakhstan, E Kazakhstan
Georgiyevka *see* Korday
127 *N15* **Georgiyevsk** Stavropol'skiy Kray, SW Russian Federation
100 *G13* **Georgsmarienhütte** Niedersachsen, NW Germany
195 *O1* **Georg von Neumayer** *German research station* Antarctica
101 *M16* **Gera** Thüringen, E Germany
101 *K16* **Gera** ~ C Germany
99 *E19* **Geraardsbergen** Oost-Vlaanderen, SW Belgium
115 *F21* **Geráki** Pelopónnisos, S Greece
27 *W5* **Gerald** Missouri, C USA
185 *G20* **Geraldine** Canterbury, South Island, NZ
180 *H11* **Geraldton** Western Australia
12 *E11* **Geraldton** Ontario, S Canada
60 *J12* **Geral, Serra** ▲ S Brazil
103 *U6* **Gérardmer** Vosges, NE France
Gerasa *see* Jarash
Gerdauen *see* Zheleznodorozhnyy
39 *Q11* **Gerdine, Mount** ▲ Alaska, USA
136 *H11* **Gerede** Bolu, N Turkey
136 *H11* **Gerede Çayı** ~ N Turkey
148 *M8* **Gereshk** Helmand, SW Afghanistan
101 *L24* **Geretsried** Bayern, S Germany
105 *P14* **Gérgal** Andalucía, S Spain
28 *I14* **Gering** Nebraska, C USA
35 *R3* **Gerlach** Nevada, W USA
Gerlachfalvi Csúcs/Gerlachovka *see* Gerlachovský štít
111 *L18* **Gerlachovský štít** *var.* Gerlachovka, *Ger.* Gerlsdorfer Spitze, *Hung.* Gerlachfalvi Csúcs; *prev.* Stalinov Štít, *Ger.* Franz-Josef Spitze, *Hung.* Ferencz-József Csúcs. ▲ N Slovakia
108 *E8* **Gerlafingen** Solothurn, NW Switzerland
Gerlsdorfer Spitze *see* Gerlachovský štít
139 *V3* **Germak** E Iraq
German East Africa *see* Tanzania
Germanicopolis *see* Çankırı
Germanicum, Mare/German Ocean *see* North Sea
Germanovichi *see* Hyermanavichy
German Southwest Africa *see* Namibia
20 *E10* **Germantown** Tennessee, S USA
101 *I15* **Germany** *off.* Federal Republic of Germany, *Ger.* Bundesrepublik Deutschland, Deutschland. ◆ *federal republic* N Europe
101 *L23* **Germering** Bayern, SE Germany
83 *J21* **Germiston** *var.* Gauteng. Gauteng, NE South Africa
Gernika *see* Gernika-Lumo
105 *P2* **Gernika-Lumo** *var.* Gernika, Guernica, Guernica y Lumo. País Vasco, N Spain
164 *L12* **Gero** Gifu, Honshū, SW Japan
115 *F22* **Geroliménas** Pelopónnisos, S Greece
Gerona *see* Girona
99 *H21* **Gerpinnes** Hainaut, S Belgium
102 *L15* **Gers** ◈ *department* S France
102 *L14* **Gers** ~ S France
Gerunda *see* Girona
136 *K10* **Gerze** Sinop, N Turkey
158 *I13* **Gêrzê** *var.* Luring. Xizang Zizhiqu, W China
Gesoriacum/Gessoriacum *see* Boulogne-sur-Mer
99 *J21* **Gesves** Namur, SE Belgium
93 *J20* **Geta** Åland, SW Finland
105 *N8* **Getafe** Madrid, C Spain
95 *J21* **Getinge** Halland, S Sweden
18 *F16* **Gettysburg** Pennsylvania, NE USA
29 *N8* **Gettysburg** South Dakota, N USA
194 *K12* **Getz Ice Shelf** *ice shelf* Antarctica
137 *S15* **Gevaş** Van, SE Turkey
Gevgeli *see* Gevgelija
113 *Q20* **Gevgelija** *var.* Đevđelija, Djevdjelija, *Turk.* Gevgeli. SE FYR Macedonia
103 *T10* **Gex** Ain, E France
92 *I3* **Geysir** *physical region* SW Iceland
136 *F11* **Geyve** Sakarya, NW Turkey
80 *G10* **Gezira** ◈ *state* E Sudan
109 *V3* **Gföhl** Niederösterreich, N Austria
83 *H22* **Ghaap Plateau** *Afr.* Ghaapplato. *plateau* C South Africa
Ghaapplato *see* Ghaap Plateau
Ghaba *see* Al Ghābah
138 *J8* **Ghāb, Tall** ▲ SE Syria
139 *Q9* **Ghadaf, Wādī al** *dry watercourse* C Iraq
Ghadamès *see* Ghadāmis
74 *M9* **Ghadāmis** *var.* Ghadamès, Rhadames. W Libya
141 *Y10* **Ghadan** E Oman
75 *O10* **Ghaddūwah** C Libya
147 *Q11* **Ghafurov** *Rus.* Gafurov; *prev.* Sovetabad. NW Tajikistan
153 *N12* **Ghāghara** ~ S Asia
149 *P13* **Ghaibi Dero** Sind, SE Pakistan
141 *Y10* **Ghalat** E Oman
147 *O11* **G'allaorol** Jizzax Viloyati, C Uzbekistan
139 *W11* **Ghamūkah, Hawr** ◎ S Iraq
77 *P15* **Ghana** *off.* Republic of Ghana. ◆ *republic* W Africa
141 *X12* **Ghānah** *spring/well* S Oman
Ghanongga *see* Ranongga
Ghansi/Ghansiland *see* Ghanzi
83 *F18* **Ghanzi** *var.* Khanzi. Ghanzi, W Botswana
83 *G19* **Ghanzi** *var.* Ghansi, Ghansiland, Khanzi. ◈ *district* C Botswana
Ghap'an *see* Kapan
138 *F13* **Gharandal** Ma'ān, SW Jordan
Gharbt, Jabal al *see* Liban, Jebel
74 *K7* **Ghardaïa** N Algeria
139 *U14* **Gharibiyah, Sha'īb al** ~ S Iraq
147 *R12* **Gharm** *Rus.* Garm. C Tajikistan
149 *P17* **Gharo** Sind, SE Pakistan
139 *W10* **Gharrāf, Shaṭṭ al** ~ S Iraq
Gharvān *see* Gharyān
75 *O7* **Gharyān** *var.* Gharvān. NW Libya
74 *M11* **Ghāt** *var.* Gat. SW Libya
Ghawdex *see* Gozo
141 *U8* **Ghayathi** Abū Ẓaby, W UAE
Ghazāl, Baḥr al *see* Ghazal, Bahr el
78 *H9* **Ghazal, Bahr el** *var.* Soro. *seasonal river* C Chad
80 *E13* **Ghazal, Bahr el** *var.* Baḥr al Ghazāl. ~ S Sudan
74 *H6* **Ghazaouet** NW Algeria
152 *J10* **Ghāziābād** Uttar Pradesh, N India
153 *O13* **Ghāzīpur** Uttar Pradesh, N India
149 *Q6* **Ghaznī** *var.* Ghazni. Ghaznī, E Afghanistan
149 *P7* **Ghaznī** ◈ *province* SE Afghanistan
Ghazzah *see* Gaza
Gheel *see* Geel
Ghelīzāne *see* Relizane
Ghent *see* Gent
Gheorghe Brațul *see* Sfântu Gheorghe, Brațul
Gheorghe Gheorghiu-Dej *see* Onești
116 *J10* **Gheorgheni** *prev.* Gheorghieni, Sînt-Miclăuș, *Ger.* Niklasmarkt, *Hung.* Gyergyószentmiklós. Harghita, C Romania
Gheorghieni *see* Gheorgheni
116 *H10* **Gherla** *Ger.* Neuschliss, *Hung.* Szamosújvár; *prev.* Armenierstadt. Cluj, NW Romania
Gheweifat *see* Ghuwayfāt
Ghilan *see* Gīlān
107 *C18* **Ghilarza** Sardegna, Italy, C Mediterranean Sea
Ghilizane *see* Relizane
Ghimbi *see* Gīmbī
Ghiriș *see* Câmpia Turzii
103 *Y15* **Ghisonaccia** Corse, France, C Mediterranean Sea
147 *Q11* **Ghonchí** *Rus.* Ganchi. NW Tajikistan
Ghor *see* Ghowr
153 *T13* **Ghoraghat** Rajshahi, NW Bangladesh
149 *R13* **Ghotki** Sind, SE Pakistan
148 *M5* **Ghowr** *var.* Ghor. ◈ *province* C Afghanistan
147 *T13* **Ghŭdara** *var.* Gudara, *Rus.* Kudara. SE Tajikistan
153 *R13* **Ghugri** ~ N India
147 *S14* **Ghund** *Rus.* Gunt. ~ SE Tajikistan
Ghurdaqah *see* Hurghada
148 *J5* **Ghūrīān** Herāt, W Afghanistan
141 *T8* **Ghuwayfāt** *var.* Gheweifat. Abū Ẓaby, W UAE
121 *O14* **Ghuzayyil, Sabkhat** *salt lake* N Libya
115 *G17* **Giáltra** Évvoia, C Greece
Giamame *see* Jamaame
167 *U13* **Gia Nghia** *var.* Åak Nông. Đăc Lăc, S Vietnam
114 *F13* **Giannitsá** *var.* Yiannitsá. Kentrikí Makedonía, N Greece
107 *F14* **Giannutri, Isola di** *island* Archipelago Toscano, C Italy
96 *F13* **Giant's Causeway** *Ir.* Clochán an Aifir. *lava flow* N Northern Ireland, UK
167 *S15* **Gia Rai** Minh Hai, S Vietnam
107 *L24* **Giarre** Sicilia, Italy, C Mediterranean Sea
44 *I7* **Gibara** Holguín, E Cuba
29 *O16* **Gibbon** Nebraska, C USA
32 *K11* **Gibbon** Oregon, NW USA
33 *P11* **Gibbonsville** Idaho, NW USA
64 *A13* **Gibb's Hill** *hill* S Bermuda
92 *I9* **Gibostad** Troms, N Norway
104 *I14* **Gibraleón** Andalucía, S Spain
104 *L16* **Gibraltar** ○ (Gibraltar) S Gibraltar
104 *L16* **Gibraltar** ◇ *UK dependent territory* SW Europe
Gibraltar, Détroit de/Gibraltar, Estrecho de *see* Gibraltar, Strait of
104 *J17* **Gibraltar, Strait of** *Fr.* Détroit de Gibraltar, *Sp.* Estrecho de Gibraltar. *strait* Atlantic Ocean/ Mediterranean Sea
31 *S11* **Gibsonburg** Ohio, N USA
30 *M13* **Gibson City** Illinois, N USA
180 *L8* **Gibson Desert** *desert* Western Australia
10 *L17* **Gibsons** British Columbia, SW Canada
149 *N12* **Gīdār** Baluchistān, SW Pakistan
155 *I17* **Giddalūr** Andhra Pradesh, E India
24 *U10* **Giddings** Texas, SW USA
27 *Y8* **Gideon** Missouri, C USA
81 *I15* **Gīdolē** Southern, S Ethiopia
118 *H13* **Giedraičiai** Utena, E Lithuania
103 *O7* **Gien** Loiret, C France
101 *G17* **Giessen** Hessen, W Germany
98 *O6* **Gieten** Drenthe, NE Netherlands
23 *Y13* **Gifford** Florida, SE USA
9 *O5* **Gifford** ~ Baffin Island, Nunavut, NE Canada
100 *J12* **Gifhorn** Niedersachsen, N Germany
11 *P13* **Gift Lake** Alberta, W Canada
164 *K13* **Gifu** *var.* Gihu. Gifu, Honshū, SW Japan
164 *L13* **Gifu** *off.* Gifu-ken, *var.* Gihu. ◈ *prefecture* Honshū, SW Japan
126 *M13* **Gigant** Rostovskaya Oblast', SW Russian Federation
40 *E8* **Giganta, Sierra de la** ▲ W Mexico
54 *E12* **Gigante** Huila, S Colombia
114 *I7* **Gigen** Pleven, N Bulgaria
Giggiga *see* Jijiga
96 *G12* **Gigha Island** *island* SW Scotland, UK
107 *E14* **Giglio, Isola del** *island* Archipelago Toscano, C Italy
Gihu *see* Gifu
146 *L11* **G'ijduvon** *Rus.* Gizhduvan. Buxoro Viloyati, C Uzbekistan
104 *L2* **Gijón** *var.* Xixón. Asturias, NW Spain
81 *D20* **Gikongoro** SW Rwanda
36 *K14* **Gila Bend** Arizona, SW USA
36 *J14* **Gila Bend Mountains** ▲ Arizona, SW USA
37 *N14* **Gila Mountains** ▲ Arizona, SW USA
36 *I15* **Gila Mountains** ▲ Arizona, SW USA
142 *M4* **Gīlān** *off.* Ostān-e Gīlān; *var.* Ghilan, Guilan. ◈ *province* NW Iran
Gilani *see* Gnjilane
36 *L14* **Gila River** ~ Arizona, SW USA
29 *W4* **Gilbert** Minnesota, N USA
Gilbert Islands *see* Tungaru
10 *L16* **Gilbert, Mount** ▲ British Columbia, SW Canada
181 *U4* **Gilbert River** ~ Queensland, NE Australia
193 *N3* **Gilbert Seamounts** *undersea feature* NE Pacific Ocean
33 *S7* **Gildford** Montana, NW USA
83 *P15* **Gilé** Zambézia, NE Mozambique
30 *K4* **Gile Flowage** ◎ Wisconsin, N USA
182 *G7* **Giles, Lake** *salt lake* South Australia
75 *U12* **Gilf Kebir Plateau** *Ar.* Haḍabat al Jilf al Kabīr. *plateau* SW Egypt
183 *R6* **Gilgandra** New South Wales, SE Australia
Gilgâu *see* Gâlgău
81 *I19* **Gilgil** Rift Valley, SW Kenya
183 *S4* **Gil Gil Creek** ~ New South Wales, SE Australia
149 *V3* **Gilgit** Jammu and Kashmir, NE Pakistan
149 *V3* **Gilgit** ~ N Pakistan
11 *X11* **Gillam** Manitoba, C Canada
95 *J22* **Gilleleje** Frederiksborg, E Denmark
30 *K14* **Gillespie** Illinois, N USA
27 *W13* **Gillett** Arkansas, C USA
33 *X12* **Gillette** Wyoming, C USA
97 *P22* **Gillingham** SE England, UK
195 *X6* **Gillock Island** *island* Antarctica
173 *O16* **Gillot** ✕ (St-Denis) N Réunion
65 *H25* **Gill Point** *headland* E Saint Helena
30 *M12* **Gilman** Illinois, N USA
25 *W6* **Gilmer** Texas, SW USA
Gilolo *see* Halmahera, Pulau
81 *G14* **Gīlo Wenz** ~ SW Ethiopia
35 *O10* **Gilroy** California, W USA
123 *Q12* **Gilyuy** ~ SE Russian Federation
99 *I14* **Gilze** Noord-Brabant, S Netherlands
165 *R16* **Gima** Okinawa, Kume-jima, SW Japan
80 *H13* **Gīmbī** *It.* Ghimbi. Oromo, C Ethiopia
45 *T12* **Gimie, Mount** ▲ C Saint Lucia
11 *X16* **Gimli** Manitoba, S Canada
Gimma *see* Jīma
95 *O14* **Gimo** Uppsala, C Sweden
102 *L15* **Gimone** ~ S France
Gimpoe *see* Gimpu
171 *N12* **Gimpu** *prev.* Gimpoe. Sulawesi, C Indonesia
182 *F5* **Gina** South Australia
Ginevra *see* Genève
99 *J19* **Gingelom** Limburg, NE Belgium
180 *I12* **Gingin** Western Australia
171 *Q7* **Gingoog** Mindanao, S Philippines
81 *K14* **Gīnīr** Oromo, C Ethiopia
Giohar *see* Jawhar
107 *O17* **Gioia del Colle** Puglia, SE Italy
107 *M22* **Gioia, Golfo di** *gulf* S Italy
Giona *see* Gkióna
115 *I16* **Gioúra** *island* Vóreioi Sporádes, Greece, Aegean Sea
107 *O17* **Giovinazzo** Puglia, SE Italy
Gipeswic *see* Ipswich
Gipuzkoa *see* Guipúzcoa
Giran *see* Ilan
30 *K14* **Girard** Illinois, N USA
27 *R7* **Girard** Kansas, C USA
25 *O6* **Girard** Texas, SW USA
54 *E10* **Girardot** Cundinamarca, C Colombia
172 *M7* **Giraud Seamount** *undersea feature* SW Indian Ocean
83 *A15* **Girault** ~ SW Angola
96 *L9* **Girdle Ness** *headland* NE Scotland, UK
137 *N11* **Giresun** *var.* Kerasunt; *anc.* Cerasus, Pharnacia. Giresun, NE Turkey
137 *N12* **Giresun** *var.* Kerasunt. ◈ *province* NE Turkey
137 *N12* **Giresun Dağları** ▲ N Turkey
75 *X10* **Girga** *var.* Girgeh, Jirjā. C Egypt
Girgeh *see* Girga
Girgenti *see* Agrigento
153 *Q15* **Girīdīh** Jhārkhand, NE India
183 *P6* **Girilambone** New South Wales, SE Australia
Girin *see* Jilin
121 *W10* **Girne** *Gk.* Kerýneia, Kyrenia. N Cyprus
Giron *see* Kiruna
105 *X5* **Girona** *var.* Gerona; *anc.* Gerunda. Cataluña, NE Spain
105 *W5* **Girona** *var.* Gerona ◈ *province* Cataluña, NE Spain
102 *J12* **Gironde** ◈ *department* SW France
102 *J11* **Gironde** *estuary* SW France
105 *V5* **Gironella** Cataluña, NE Spain
103 *N15* **Girou** ~ S France
97 *H14* **Girvan** W Scotland, UK
24 *M9* **Girvin** Texas, SW USA
184 *Q9* **Gisborne** Gisborne, North Island, NZ
184 *P9* **Gisborne** *off.* Gisborne District. ◈ *unitary authority* North Island, NZ
Giseifu *see* Üijŏngbu
Gisenye *see* Gisenyi
81 *D19* **Gisenyi** *var.* Gisenye. NW Rwanda
95 *K20* **Gislaved** Jönköping, S Sweden
103 *N4* **Gisors** Eure, N France
Gissar *see* Hisor
147 *P12* **Gissar Range** *Rus.* Gissarskiy Khrebet. ▲ Tajikistan/Uzbekistan
Gissarskiy Khrebet *see* Gissar Range
99 *B16* **Gistel** West-Vlaanderen, W Belgium
108 *F9* **Giswil** Unterwalden, C Switzerland
115 *B16* **Gitánes** *ancient monument* Ípeiros, W Greece
81 *E20* **Gitarama** C Rwanda
81 *E20* **Gitega** C Burundi
Githio *see* Gýtheio
108 *H11* **Giubiasco** Ticino, S Switzerland
106 *K13* **Giulianova** Abruzzo, C Italy
Giulie, Alpi *see* Julian Alps
Giumri *see* Gyumri
116 *M13* **Giurgeni** Ialomița, SE Romania
116 *J15* **Giurgiu** Giurgiu, S Romania
116 *J14* **Giurgiu** ◈ *county* SE Romania
95 *F22* **Give** Vejle, C Denmark
103 *R2* **Givet** Ardennes, N France
103 *R11* **Givors** Rhône, E France
83 *K19* **Giyani** Limpopos, NE South Africa
80 *I13* **Giyon** Oromo, C Ethiopia
Giza/Gizeh *see* El Gîza
75 *V8* **Giza, Pyramids of** *ancient monument* N Egypt
Gizhduvan *see* G'ijduvon
123 *U8* **Gizhiga** Magadanskaya Oblast', E Russian Federation
123 *T9* **Gizhiginskaya Guba** *bay* E Russian Federation
186 *K8* **Gizo** Gizo, NW Solomon Islands
110 *N7* **Giżycko** *Ger.* Warmińsko-Mazurskie, NE Poland
Gízymałów *see* Hrymayliv
Gjakovë *see* Đakovica
94 *F12* **Gjende** ◎ S Norway
95 *F17* **Gjerstad** Aust-Agder, S Norway
Gjilan *see* Gnjilane
Gjinokastër *see* Gjirokastër
113 *L23* **Gjirokastër** *var.* Gjirokastra; *prev.* Gjinokastër, *Gk.* Argyrokastron, *It.* Argirocastro. Gjirokastër, S Albania
113 *L22* **Gjirokastër** ◈ *district* S Albania
8 *M7* **Gjoa Haven** King William Island, Nunavut, NW Canada
94 *H13* **Gjøvik** Oppland, S Norway
113 *J22* **Gjuhëzës, Kepi i** *headland* SW Albania
Gjurgjevac *see* Đurđevac
115 *E18* **Gkióna** *var.* Giona. ▲ C Greece
121 *R3* **Gkréko, Akrotíri** *var.* Cape Greco, Pidálion. *headland* E Cyprus
99 *I18* **Glabbeek-Zuurbemde** Vlaams Brabant, C Belgium
13 *R14* **Glace Bay** Cape Breton Island, Nova Scotia, SE Canada
11 *O16* **Glacier** British Columbia, SW Canada
39 *W12* **Glacier Bay** *inlet* Alaska, USA
32 *I7* **Glacier Peak** ▲ Washington, NW USA
21 *Q7* **Glade Spring** Virginia, NE USA
25 *W7* **Gladewater** Texas, SW USA
181 *Y8* **Gladstone** Queensland, E Australia
182 *I8* **Gladstone** South Australia
11 *X16* **Gladstone** Manitoba, S Canada
31 *O5* **Gladstone** Michigan, N USA
27 *R4* **Gladstone** Missouri, C USA
31 *Q7* **Gladwin** Michigan, N USA
95 *J15* **Glafsfjorden** ◎ C Sweden
92 *H2* **Gláma** *physical region* NW Iceland
94 *I12* **Glåma** *var.* Glommen. Glomma. ~ S Norway
112 *F13* **Glamoč** Federacija Bosna I Hercegovina, NE Bosnia and Herzegovina
97 *J22* **Glamorgan** *cultural region* S Wales, UK
95 *G24* **Glamsbjerg** Fyn, C Denmark
171 *Q8* **Glan** Mindanao, S Philippines
95 *M17* **Glan** ◎ S Sweden
109 *T9* **Glan** ~ SE Austria
101 *F19* **Glan** ~ W Germany
Glaris *see* Glarus
108 *H9* **Glarner Alpen** *Eng.* Glarus Alps. ▲ E Switzerland
108 *H8* **Glarus** Glarus, E Switzerland
108 *H9* **Glarus** *Fr.* Glaris. ◈ *canton* C Switzerland
Glarus Alps *see* Glarner Alpen
27 *N3* **Glasco** Kansas, C USA
96 *I12* **Glasgow** S Scotland, UK
20 *K7* **Glasgow** Kentucky, S USA
27 *T4* **Glasgow** Missouri, C USA
33 *W7* **Glasgow** Montana, NW USA
21 *T6* **Glasgow** Virginia, NE USA
96 *I12* **Glasgow** ✕ W Scotland, UK
11 *S14* **Glaslyn** Saskatchewan, S Canada
18 *I16* **Glassboro** New Jersey, NE USA
24 *L10* **Glass Mountains** ▲ Texas, SW USA
97 *K23* **Glastonbury** SW England, UK
Glatz *see* Kłodzko
101 *N16* **Glauchau** Sachsen, E Germany
Glavn'a Morava *see* Velika Morava
113 *N16* **Glavnik** Serbia, S Serbia and Montenegro (Yugo.)
127 *T1* **Glazov** Udmurtskaya Respublika, NW Russian Federation
Głda *see* Gwda
109 *U8* **Gleinalpe** ▲ SE Austria
109 *W8* **Gleisdorf** Steiermark, SE Austria
Gleiwitz *see* Gliwice
39 *S11* **Glenallen** Alaska, USA
102 *F7* **Glénan, Îles** *island group* NW France
185 *G21* **Glenavy** Canterbury, South Island, NZ
10 *H5* **Glenboyle** Yukon Territory, NW Canada
21 *X3* **Glen Burnie** Maryland, NE USA
36 *L8* **Glen Canyon** *canyon* Utah, W USA
36 *L8* **Glen Canyon Dam** *dam* Arizona, SW USA
30 *K15* **Glen Carbon** Illinois, N USA
14 *E17* **Glencoe** Ontario, S Canada
83 *K22* **Glencoe** KwaZulu/Natal, E South Africa
29 *U9* **Glencoe** Minnesota, N USA
96 *H10* **Glen Coe** *valley* N Scotland, UK
36 *K13* **Glendale** Arizona, SW USA
35 *S15* **Glendale** California, W USA
182 *G5* **Glendambo** South Australia
33 *Y8* **Glendive** Montana, NW USA
33 *Y15* **Glendo** Wyoming, C USA
55 *S10* **Glendor Mountains** ▲ C Guyana
182 *K12* **Glenelg River** ~ South Australia/Victoria, SE Australia
29 *P4* **Glenfield** North Dakota, N USA
25 *V12* **Glen Flora** Texas, SW USA
181 *P7* **Glen Helen** Northern Territory, N Australia
183 *U5* **Glen Innes** New South Wales, SE Australia
31 *P6* **Glen Lake** ◎ Michigan, N USA
10 *I7* **Glenlyon Peak** ▲ Yukon Territory, W Canada
37 *N16* **Glenn, Mount** ▲ Arizona, SW USA
33 *N15* **Glenns Ferry** Idaho, NW USA
23 *W6* **Glennville** Georgia, SE USA
10 *J10* **Glenora** British Columbia, W Canada
182 *M11* **Glenorchy** Victoria, SE Australia
183 *V5* **Glenreagh** New South Wales, SE Australia
33 *X15* **Glenrock** Wyoming, C USA
96 *K11* **Glenrothes** E Scotland, UK
18 *L9* **Glens Falls** New York, NE USA
97 *D14* **Glenties** *Ir.* Na Gleannta. NW Ireland
28 *L5* **Glen Ullin** North Dakota, N USA
21 *R4* **Glenville** West Virginia, NE USA
27 *T12* **Glenwood** Arkansas, C USA
29 *S15* **Glenwood** Iowa, C USA
29 *T7* **Glenwood** Minnesota, N USA
36 *L5* **Glenwood** Utah, W USA
30 *I5* **Glenwood City** Wisconsin, N USA
37 *Q4* **Glenwood Springs** Colorado, C USA
108 *F10* **Gletsch** Valais, S Switzerland
Glevum *see* Gloucester
29 *U14* **Glidden** Iowa, C USA
112 *E9* **Glina** Sisak-Moslavina, NE Croatia
94 *F11* **Glittertind** ▲ S Norway
111 *J16* **Gliwice** *Ger.* Gleiwitz. Śląskie, S Poland
36 *M14* **Globe** Arizona, SW USA
Globino *see* Hlobyne
108 *L9* **Glockturm** ▲ SW Austria
116 *L9* **Glodeni** *Rus.* Glodyany. N Moldova
109 *S9* **Glödnitz** Kärnten, S Austria
Glodyany *see* Glodeni
Glogau *see* Głogów
109 *W6* **Gloggnitz** Niederösterreich, E Austria
110 *F13* **Głogów** *Ger.* Glogau, Glogow. Dolnośląskie, SW Poland
111 *I16* **Głogówek** *Ger.* Oberglogau. Opolskie, S Poland
92 *G12* **Glomfjord** Nordland, C Norway
Glommen *see* Glåma
93 *I14* **Glommersträsk** Norrbotten, N Sweden
172 *I1* **Glorieuses, Nosy** *island group* N Madagascar
65 *C25* **Glorious Hill** *hill* East Falkland, Falkland Islands
38 *J12* **Glory of Russia Cape** *headland* Saint Matthew Island, Alaska, USA
22 *J7* **Gloster** Mississippi, S USA
183 *U7* **Gloucester** New South Wales, SE Australia
186 *F7* **Gloucester** New Britain, E PNG
97 *L21* **Gloucester** *hist.* Caer Glou, *Lat.* Glevum. C England, UK
19 *P10* **Gloucester** Massachusetts, NE USA
21 *X6* **Gloucester** Virginia, NE USA
97 *K21* **Gloucestershire** *cultural region* C England, UK
31 *T14* **Glouster** Ohio, N USA
42 *H3* **Glovers Reef** *reef* E Belize
18 *K10* **Gloversville** New York, NE USA
110 *K12* **Głowno** Łódź, C Poland
111 *H16* **Głubczyce** *Ger.* Leobschütz. Opolskie, S Poland
126 *L11* **Glubokiy** Rostovskaya Oblast', SW Russian Federation
145 *W9* **Glubokoye** Vostochnyy Kazakhstan, E Kazakhstan
Glubokoye *see* Hlybokaye
111 *H16* **Głuchołazy** *Ger.* Ziegenhais. Opolskie, S Poland
100 *I9* **Glückstadt** Schleswig-Holstein, N Germany
Glukhov *see* Hlukhiv
Glushkevichi *see* Hlushkavichy
Glusk/Glussk *see* Hlusk
Glybokaya *see* Hlyboka
95 *F21* **Glyngøre** Viborg, NW Denmark
127 *Q9* **Gmelinka** Volgogradskaya Oblast', SW Russian Federation
109 *R8* **Gmünd** Kärnten, S Austria
109 *U2* **Gmünd** Niederösterreich, N Austria
Gmünd *see* Schwäbisch Gmünd
109 *S5* **Gmunden** Oberösterreich, N Austria
Gmundner See *see* Traunsee
94 *N10* **Gnarp** Gävleborg, C Sweden
109 *W8* **Gnas** Steiermark, SE Austria
Gnesen *see* Gniezno
95 *O16* **Gnesta** Södermanland, C Sweden
110 *H11* **Gniezno** *Ger.* Gnesen. Wielkopolskie, C Poland
113 *O17* **Gnjilane** *var.* Gilani, *Alb.* Gjilan. Serbia, S Serbia and Montenegro (Yugo.)
95 *K20* **Gnosjö** Jönköping, S Sweden
155 *E17* **Goa** *prev.* Old Goa, Vela Goa, Velha Goa. Goa, W India
155 *E17* **Goa** *var.* Old Goa. ◈ *state* W India
Goabddális *see* Kåbdalis
42 *H7* **Goascorán, Río** ~ El Salvador/Honduras
77 *O16* **Goaso** *var.* Gawso. W Ghana
81 *K14* **Goba** *It.* Oromo, S Ethiopia
83 *C20* **Gobabed** Erongo, W Namibia
83 *E19* **Gobabis** Omaheke, E Namibia
Gobannium *see* Abergavenny
64 *M7* **Goban Spur** *undersea feature* NW Atlantic Ocean
Gobbà *see* Goba
63 *H21* **Gobernador Gregores** Santa Cruz, S Argentina
61 *F14* **Gobernador Ingeniero Virasoro** Corrientes, NE Argentina
162 *L12* **Gobi** *desert* China/Mongolia
164 *I14* **Gobō** Wakayama, Honshū, SW Japan
101 *D14* **Goch** Nordrhein-Westfalen, W Germany
83 *E20* **Gochas** Hardap, S Namibia
155 *I14* **Godāvari** *var.* Godavari. ~ C India
155 *L16* **Godāvari, Mouths of the** *delta* E India
15 *V5* **Godbout** Québec, SE Canada
15 *U5* **Godbout** ~ Québec, SE Canada
15 *U5* **Godbout Est** ~ Québec, SE Canada
27 *N6* **Goddard** Kansas, C USA
14 *E15* **Goderich** Ontario, S Canada
Godhavn *see* Qeqertarsuaq
154 *E10* **Godhra** Gujarāt, W India
Göding *see* Hodonín
111 *K22* **Gödöllő** Pest, N Hungary
62 *H11* **Godoy Cruz** Mendoza, W Argentina
11 *Y11* **Gods** ~ Manitoba, C Canada
11 *Y13* **Gods Lake** Manitoba, C Canada
11 *X13* **Gods Lake** ◎ Manitoba, C Canada

◆ Country ● Country Capital ◇ Dependent Territory ○ Dependent Territory Capital ◈ Administrative Region ✕ International Airport ▲ Mountain ▲ Mountain Range ⊼ Volcano ~ River ◎ Lake ⊟ Reservoir

Godthaab/Godthåb see Nuuk
Godwin Austen, Mount see K2
Goede Hoop, Kaap de see Good Hope, Cape of
Goedgegun see Nhlangano
Goeie Hoop, Kaap die see Good Hope, Cape of
13 O7 **Goélands, Lac aux** ◎ Québec, SE Canada
98 E13 **Goeree** island SW Netherlands
99 F15 **Goes** Zeeland, SW Netherlands
Goettingen see Göttingen
19 O10 **Goffstown** New Hampshire, NE USA
14 E8 **Gogama** Ontario, S Canada
30 L3 **Gogebic, Lake** ◎ Michigan, N USA
30 K3 **Gogebic Range** hill range Michigan/Wisconsin, N USA
137 V13 **Gogi, Mount** Arm. Gogi Lerr, Az. Küküdağ. ▲ Armenia/Azerbaijan
126 F12 **Gogland, Ostrov** island NW Russian Federation
111 I15 **Gogolin** Opolskie, S Poland
Gogonou see Gogounou
77 S14 **Gogounou** var. Gogonou. N Benin
152 I10 **Gohāna** Haryāna, N India
59 K18 **Goianésia** Goiás, C Brazil
59 K18 **Goiânia** prev. Goyania. state capital Goiás, C Brazil
59 K18 **Goiás** Goiás, C Brazil
59 J18 **Goiás** off. Estado de Goiás; prev. Goiaz, Goyaz. ◆ state C Brazil
Goiaz see Goiás
159 R14 **Goinsargoin** Xizang Zizhiqu, W China
60 H10 **Goio-Erê** Paraná, SW Brazil
99 I15 **Goirle** Noord-Brabant, S Netherlands
104 H8 **Góis** Coimbra, N Portugal
165 Q8 **Gojōme** Akita, Honshū, NW Japan
149 U9 **Gojra** Punjab, E Pakistan
136 A11 **Gökçeada** var. Imroz Adası, Gk. Imbros. island NW Turkey
Gökçeada see İmroz
146 F13 **Gökdepe** Rus. Gëkdepe, Geok-Tepe. Ahal Welaýaty, C Turkmenistan
136 I10 **Gökırmak** ≈ N Turkey
Goklenkuy, Solonchak see Geklengkui, Solonchak
136 C16 **Gökova Körfezi** gulf SW Turkey
136 K15 **Göksu** ≈ S Turkey
136 L15 **Göksun** Kahramanmaraş, C Turkey
136 I17 **Göksu Nehri** ≈ S Turkey
83 J16 **Gokwe** Midlands, NW Zimbabwe
94 F13 **Gol** Buskerud, S Norway
153 X12 **Golāghāt** Assam, NE India
110 H10 **Gołańcz** Wielkopolskie, C Poland
138 G8 **Golan Heights** Ar. Al Jawlān, Heb. HaGolan. ▲ SW Syria
Golārā see Ārān
Golaya Pristan see Hola Prystan'
143 T11 **Golbāf** Kermān, C Iran
136 M15 **Gölbaşı** Adıyaman, S Turkey
109 P9 **Gölbner** ▲ SW Austria
30 M17 **Golconda** Illinois, N USA
35 T3 **Golconda** Nevada, W USA
136 E11 **Gölcük** Kocaeli, NW Turkey
108 I7 **Goldach** Sankt Gallen, NE Switzerland
110 N7 **Gołdap** Ger. Goldap. Warmińsko-Mazurskie, NE Poland
32 E15 **Gold Beach** Oregon, NW USA
Goldberg see Złotoryja
183 V3 **Gold Coast** cultural region Queensland, E Australia
39 R10 **Gold Creek** Alaska, USA
11 O16 **Golden** British Columbia, SW Canada
37 T4 **Golden** Colorado, C USA
184 I13 **Golden Bay** bay South Island, NZ
27 R7 **Golden City** Missouri, C USA
32 I11 **Goldendale** Washington, NW USA
Goldener Tisch see Zlatý Stôl
44 L13 **Golden Grove** E Jamaica
14 J12 **Golden Lake** ◎ Ontario, SE Canada
22 K10 **Golden Meadow** Louisiana, S USA
45 V10 **Golden Rock** ✕ (Basseterre) Saint Kitts, Saint Kitts and Nevis
Golden State, The see California
83 K16 **Golden Valley** Mashonaland West, N Zimbabwe
35 U9 **Goldfield** Nevada, W USA
Goldingen see Kuldīga
Goldmarkt see Zlatna
10 K17 **Gold River** Vancouver Island, British Columbia, SW Canada
21 V10 **Goldsboro** North Carolina, SE USA
24 M8 **Goldsmith** Texas, SW USA
25 R8 **Goldthwaite** Texas, SW USA
137 R11 **Göle** Ardahan, NE Turkey
Golema Ada see Ostrovo
114 H9 **Golema Planina** ▲ W Bulgaria
114 F9 **Golemi Vrŭkh** ▲ W Bulgaria
110 D8 **Goleniów** Ger. Gollnow. Zachodnio-pomorskie, NW Poland
149 R3 **Golestān** ◆ province N Iran
35 Q14 **Goleta** California, W USA
43 O16 **Golfito** Puntarenas, SE Costa Rica
25 T13 **Goliad** Texas, SW USA
113 L14 **Golija** ▲ SW Serbia and Montenegro (Yugo.)
Golinka see Gongbo'gyamda
113 O16 **Goljak** ▲ SE Serbia and Montenegro (Yugo.)
136 M12 **Gölköy** Ordu, N Turkey
Gollel see Lavumisa
109 X3 **Göllersbach** ≈ NE Austria
Gollnow see Goleniów
Golmo see Golmud
159 P10 **Golmud** var. Ge'e'mu, Golmo, Chin. Ko-erh-mu. Qinghai, C China
103 Y14 **Golo** ≈ Corse, France, C Mediterranean Sea
Golovanevsk see Holovanivs'k
Golovchin see Halowchyn
39 N9 **Golovin** Alaska, USA
142 M7 **Golpāyegān** var. Gulpaigan. Eşfahān, W Iran
Golshan see Ṭabas
Gol'shany see Hal'shany
96 J7 **Golspie** N Scotland, UK
112 O11 **Golubac** Serbia, NE Serbia and Montenegro (Yugo.)
110 J9 **Golub-Dobrzyń** Kujawski-pomorskie, C Poland
145 S7 **Golubovka** Pavlodar, N Kazakhstan
82 B11 **Golungo Alto** Cuanza Norte, NW Angola
114 M8 **Golyama Kamchiya** ≈ E Bulgaria
114 L8 **Golyama Reka** ≈ N Bulgaria
114 H11 **Golyama Syutkya** ▲ SW Bulgaria
114 I12 **Golyam Perelik** ▲ S Bulgaria
114 I11 **Golyam Persenk** ▲ S Bulgaria
79 P19 **Goma** Nord Kivu, NE Dem. Rep. Congo
Gomati see Gumti
77 X14 **Gombe** Gombe, E Nigeria
77 Y14 **Gombi** Adamawa, E Nigeria
Gombroon see Bandar-e 'Abbās
Gomel' see Homyel'
Gomel'skaya Oblast' see Homyel'skaya Voblasts'
64 N11 **Gomera** island Islas Canarias, Spain, NE Atlantic Ocean
40 I5 **Gómez Farias** Chihuahua, N Mexico
40 L8 **Gómez Palacio** Durango, C Mexico
158 J13 **Gomo** Xizang Zizhiqu, W China
143 T6 **Gonābād** var. Gunabad. Khorāsān, NE Iran
44 L8 **Gonaïves** var. Les Gonaïves. N Haiti
123 Q12 **Gonam** ≈ NE Russian Federation
44 L9 **Gonâve, Canal de la** var. Canal de Sud. channel N Caribbean Sea
44 K9 **Gonâve, Golfe de la** gulf N Caribbean Sea
Gonāveh see Bandar-e Gonāveh
44 K9 **Gonâve, Île de la** island C Haiti
Gonbadān see Dow Gonbadān
143 Q3 **Gonbad-e Kāvūs** var. Gunbad-i-Qawus. Golestān, N Iran
152 M12 **Gonda** Uttar Pradesh, N India
Gondar see Gonder
80 I11 **Gonder** var. Gondar. Amhara, N Ethiopia
78 J13 **Gondey** Moyen-Chari, S Chad
154 J12 **Gondia** Mahārāshtra, C India
104 G6 **Gondomar** Porto, NW Portugal
136 C12 **Gönen** Balıkesir, W Turkey
136 C12 **Gönen Çayı** ≈ NW Turkey
159 O15 **Gongbo'gyamda** var. Golinka. Xizang Zizhiqu, W China
159 N16 **Gonggar** var. Gyixong. Xizang Zizhiqu, W China
160 G9 **Gongga Shan** ▲ C China
159 T10 **Gonghe** var. Qabqa. Qinghai, C China
Gongjiang see Yudu
158 I5 **Gongliu** var. Tokkuztara. Xinjiang Uygur Zizhiqu, NW China
77 W14 **Gongola** ≈ E Nigeria
Gongoleh State see Jonglei
183 P5 **Gongolgon** New South Wales, SE Australia
159 Q6 **Gongpoquan** Gansu, N China
Gongquan see Gongxian
Gongtang see Damxung
160 I10 **Gongxian** var. Gongquan, Gong Xian. Sichuan, C China
157 V10 **Gongzhuling** prev. Huaide. Jilin, NE China
159 S14 **Gonjo** Xizang Zizhiqu, W China
107 B20 **Gonnesa** Sardegna, Italy, C Mediterranean Sea
Gonni/Gónnos see Gónnoi
115 F15 **Gónnoi** var. Gonni, Gónnos; prev. Dereli. Thessalía, C Greece
164 C13 **Gōnoura** Nagasaki, Iki, SW Japan
35 O11 **Gonzales** California, W USA
22 J9 **Gonzales** Louisiana, S USA
25 T12 **Gonzales** Texas, SW USA
41 P11 **González** Tamaulipas, C Mexico
21 V6 **Goochland** Virginia, NE USA
195 X14 **Goodenough, Cape** headland Antarctica
186 F9 **Goodenough Island** var. Morata. island SE PNG
Good Hope see Fort Good Hope
39 N8 **Goodhope Bay** bay Alaska, USA
83 D26 **Good Hope, Cape of** Afr. Kaap de Goede Hoop, Kaap die Goeie Hoop. headland SW South Africa
10 K10 **Good Hope Lake** British Columbia, W Canada
83 E23 **Goodhouse** Northern Cape, W South Africa
33 O15 **Gooding** Idaho, NW USA
26 H3 **Goodland** Kansas, C USA
173 Y15 **Goodlands** NW Mauritius
20 J8 **Goodlettsville** Tennessee, S USA
39 N13 **Goodnews** Alaska, USA
25 O3 **Goodnight** Texas, SW USA
183 Q4 **Goodooga** New South Wales, SE Australia
29 N4 **Goodrich** North Dakota, N USA
25 W10 **Goodrich** Texas, SW USA
29 X10 **Goodview** Minnesota, N USA
26 H8 **Goodwell** Oklahoma, C USA
97 N17 **Goole** E England, UK
183 O8 **Goolgowi** New South Wales, SE Australia
182 I10 **Goolwa** South Australia
181 Y11 **Goondiwindi** Queensland, E Australia
98 O11 **Goor** Overijssel, E Netherlands
Goose Bay see Happy Valley-Goose Bay
33 V13 **Gooseberry Creek** ≈ Wyoming, C USA
21 S14 **Goose Creek** South Carolina, SE USA
63 M23 **Goose Green** var. Prado del Ganso. East Falkland, Falkland Islands
16 D8 **Goose Lake** var. Lago dos Gansos. ◎ California/Oregon, W USA
29 Q4 **Goose River** ≈ North Dakota, N USA
153 T16 **Gopalganj** Dhaka, S Bangladesh
153 O12 **Gopālganj** Bihār, N India
Gopher State see Minnesota
101 I22 **Göppingen** Baden-Württemberg, SW Germany
110 G13 **Góra** Ger. Guhrau. Dolnośląskie, SW Poland
110 M12 **Góra Kalwaria** Mazowieckie, C Poland
153 O12 **Gorakhpur** Uttar Pradesh, N India
Gorany see Harany
113 J14 **Goražde** Federacija Bosna I Hercegovina, Bosnia and Herzegovina
Gorbovichi see Harbavichy
Gorče Petrov see Đorče Petrov
193 P4 **Gorda Ridges** undersea feature NE Pacific Ocean
Gordiaz see Gardēz
78 K12 **Gordil** Vakaga, N Central African Republic
23 U5 **Gordon** Georgia, SE USA
28 K12 **Gordon** Nebraska, C USA
25 R7 **Gordon** Texas, SW USA
28 L13 **Gordon Creek** ≈ Nebraska, C USA
63 I25 **Gordon, Isla** island S Chile
183 O17 **Gordon, Lake** ◎ Tasmania, SE Australia
183 O17 **Gordon River** ≈ Tasmania, SE Australia
21 V5 **Gordonsville** Virginia, NE USA
80 H13 **Gorē** Oromo, C Ethiopia
185 D24 **Gore** Southland, South Island, NZ
78 H13 **Goré** Logone-Oriental, S Chad
14 D11 **Gore Bay** Manitoulin Island, Ontario, S Canada
25 Q5 **Goree** Texas, SW USA
137 O11 **Görele** Giresun, NE Turkey
19 N6 **Gore Mountain** ▲ Vermont, NE USA
39 R13 **Gore Point** headland Alaska, USA
37 R4 **Gore Range** ▲ Colorado, C USA
97 F19 **Gorey** Ir. Guaire. SE Ireland
143 R12 **Gorgāb** Kermān, S Iran
143 Q4 **Gorgān** var. Astarabad, Astrabad, Gurgan; prev. Asterābād, anc. Hyrcania. Golestān, N Iran
143 Q4 **Gorgān, Rūd-e** ≈ N Iran
76 I10 **Gorgol** ◆ region S Mauritania
106 D12 **Gorgona, Isola di** island Archipelago Toscano, C Italy
19 P8 **Gorham** Maine, NE USA
137 T10 **Gori** C Georgia
98 I13 **Gorinchem** var. Gorkum. Zuid-Holland, C Netherlands
137 V13 **Goris** SE Armenia
124 K16 **Goritsy** Tverskaya Oblast', W Russian Federation
106 J7 **Gorizia** Ger. Görz. Friuli-Venezia Giulia, NE Italy
116 G13 **Gorj** ◆ county SW Romania
109 W12 **Gorjanci** var. Uskočke Planine, Žumberak, Žumberačko Gorje, Ger. Uskokengebirge; prev. Sichelburger Gerbirge. ▲ Croatia/Slovenia see also Žumberačko Gorje
Görkau see Jirkov
Gorki see Horki
Gor'kiy see Nizhniy Novgorod
Gor'kiy Reservoir see Gor'kovskoye Vodokhranilishche
Gorkum see Gorinchem
95 I23 **Gørlev** Vestsjælland, E Denmark
111 M17 **Gorlice** Małopolskie, S Poland
101 Q15 **Görlitz** Sachsen, E Germany
Görlitz see Zgorzelec
Gorlovka see Horlivka
25 R7 **Gorman** Texas, SW USA
21 T3 **Gormania** West Virginia, NE USA
Gorna Dzhumaya see Blagoevgrad
114 K8 **Gorna Oryakhovitsa** Veliko Tŭrnovo, N Bulgaria
114 J8 **Gorna Studena** Veliko Tŭrnovo, N Bulgaria
Gornja Mužlja see Mužlja
109 X9 **Gornja Radgona** Ger. Oberradkersburg. NE Slovenia
112 M13 **Gornji Milanovac** Serbia, C Serbia and Montenegro (Yugo.)
112 G13 **Gornji Vakuf** var. Uskoplje. Federacija Bosna I Hercegovina, W Bosnia and Herzegovina
122 J13 **Gorno-Altaysk** Respublika Altay, S Russian Federation
Gorno-Altayskaya Respublika see Altay, Respublika
123 N12 **Gorno-Chuyskiy** Irkutskaya Oblast', C Russian Federation
125 V14 **Gornozavodsk** Permskaya Oblast', NW Russian Federation
122 I13 **Gornyak** Altayskiy Kray, S Russian Federation
123 O14 **Gornyy** Chitinskaya Oblast', S Russian Federation
127 R8 **Gornyy** Saratovskaya Oblast', W Russian Federation
Gornyy Altay see Altay, Respublika
127 O10 **Gornyy Balykley** Volgogradskaya Oblast', SW Russian Federation
80 I13 **Goroch'an** ▲ W Ethiopia
Gorodenka see Horodenka
127 O3 **Gorodets** Nizhegorodskaya Oblast', W Russian Federation
Gorodets see Haradzyets
Gorodeya see Haradzyeya
127 P6 **Gorodishche** Penzenskaya Oblast', W Russian Federation
Gorodishche see Horodyshche
Gorodnya see Horodnya
Gorodok see Haradok
Gorodok/Gorodok Yagellonski see Horodok
126 M13 **Gorodovikovsk** Respublika Kalmykiya, SW Russian Federation
186 D7 **Goroka** Eastern Highlands, C PNG
Gorokhov see Horokhiv
127 N3 **Gorokhovets** Vladimirskaya Oblast', W Russian Federation
77 Q11 **Gorom-Gorom** NE Burkina
171 U13 **Gorong, Kepulauan** island group E Indonesia
83 M17 **Gorongosa** Sofala, C Mozambique
171 P11 **Gorontalo** Sulawesi, C Indonesia
171 P11 **Gorontalo** off. Propinsi Gorontalo. ◆ province N Indonesia
Gorontalo, Teluk see Tomini, Gulf of
110 L7 **Górowo Iławeckie** Ger. Landsberg. Warmińsko-Mazurskie, NE Poland
98 M7 **Gorredijk** Fris. De Gordyk. Friesland, N Netherlands
98 M11 **Gorssel** Gelderland, E Netherlands
109 T8 **Görtschitz** ≈ S Austria
Goryn see Horyn'
Görz see Gorizia
110 E10 **Gorzów Wielkopolski** Ger. Landsberg, Landsberg an der Warthe. Lubuskie, W Poland
108 G9 **Göschenen** Uri, C Switzerland
165 O11 **Gosen** Niigata, Honshū, C Japan
183 T8 **Gosford** New South Wales, SE Australia
31 P11 **Goshen** Indiana, N USA
18 K13 **Goshen** New York, NE USA
Goshoba see Goşoba
165 Q7 **Goshogawara** var. Gosyogawara. Aomori, Honshū, C Japan
101 J14 **Goslar** Niedersachsen, C Germany
27 Y9 **Gosnell** Arkansas, C USA
146 B10 **Goşoba** var. Goshoba, Rus. Koshoba. Balkanskiy Velayat, NW Turkmenistan
112 C11 **Gospić** Lika-Senj, C Croatia
97 N23 **Gosport** S England, UK
94 D9 **Gossa** island S Norway
108 H7 **Gossau** Sankt Gallen, NE Switzerland
99 G20 **Gosselies** var. Goss'lies. Hainaut, S Belgium
77 P10 **Gossi** Tombouctou, C Mali
Goss'lies see Gosselies
113 N18 **Gostivar** W FYR Macedonia
Gostomel' see Hostomel'
110 G12 **Gostyń** var. Gostyn. Wielkopolskie, C Poland
110 K11 **Gostynin** Mazowieckie, C Poland
Gosyogawara see Goshogawara
95 J18 **Göta Älv** ≈ S Sweden
95 N17 **Göta kanal** canal S Sweden
95 K18 **Götaland** cultural region S Sweden
95 H17 **Göteborg** Eng. Gothenburg. Västra Götaland, S Sweden
77 X16 **Gotel Mountains** ▲ E Nigeria
95 K17 **Götene** Västra Götaland, S Sweden
Gotera see San Francisco
101 K16 **Gotha** Thüringen, C Germany
29 N15 **Gothenburg** Nebraska, C USA
Gothenburg see Göteborg
77 R12 **Gothèye** Tillabéri, SW Niger
Gothland see Gotland
95 P19 **Gotland** var. Gothland, Gottland. ◆ county SE Sweden
95 O18 **Gotland** island SE Sweden
164 B13 **Gotō-rettō** island group SW Japan
114 H12 **Gotse Delchev** prev. Nevrokop. Blagoevgrad, SW Bulgaria
95 P17 **Gotska Sandön** island SE Sweden
101 I15 **Göttingen** var. Goettingen. Niedersachsen, C Germany
Gottland see Gotland
93 I16 **Gottne** Västernorrland, C Sweden
Gottschee see Kočevje
Gottwaldov see Zlín
Gôtu see Gōtsu
146 B11 **Goturdepe** Rus. Koturdepe. Balkan Welaýaty, W Turkmenistan
108 I7 **Götzis** Vorarlberg, NW Austria
98 H12 **Gouda** Zuid-Holland, C Netherlands
76 I11 **Goudiri** var. Goudiry. E Senegal
Goudiry see Goudiri
77 X12 **Goudoumaria** Diffa, S Niger
15 R9 **Gouffre, Rivière du** ≈ Québec, SE Canada
65 M19 **Gough Fracture Zone** tectonic feature S Atlantic Ocean
65 M19 **Gough Island** island Tristan da Cunha, S Atlantic Ocean
15 N8 **Gouin, Réservoir** ▣ Québec, SE Canada
14 B10 **Goulais River** Ontario, S Canada
183 R9 **Goulburn** New South Wales, SE Australia
183 O11 **Goulburn River** ≈ Victoria, SE Australia
195 O10 **Gould Coast** physical region Antarctica
Goulimime see Guelmime
114 F13 **Gouménissa** Kentrikí Makedonía, N Greece
77 O10 **Goundam** Tombouctou, NW Mali
78 H12 **Goundi** Moyen-Chari, S Chad
78 G12 **Gounou-Gaya** Mayo-Kébbi, SW Chad
77 O12 **Gourci** var. Gourcy. NW Burkina
Gourcy see Gourci
102 M13 **Gourdon** Lot, S France
77 W11 **Gouré** Zinder, SE Niger
102 G6 **Gourin** Morbihan, NW France
77 P10 **Gourma-Rharous** Tombouctou, C Mali
103 N4 **Gournay-en-Bray** Seine-Maritime, N France
78 J6 **Gouro** Borkou-Ennedi-Tibesti, N Chad
104 H8 **Gouveia** Guarda, N Portugal
18 I7 **Gouverneur** New York, NE USA
99 L21 **Gouvy** Luxembourg, E Belgium
45 R14 **Gouyave** var. Charlotte Town. NW Grenada
Goverla, Gora see Hoverla, Hora
59 N20 **Governador Valadares** Minas Gerais, SE Brazil
171 R8 **Governor Generoso** Mindanao, S Philippines
44 I2 **Governor's Harbour** Eleuthera Island, C Bahamas
162 F9 **Govĭ-Altay** ◆ province SW Mongolia
162 I10 **Govĭ Altayn Nuruu** ▲ S Mongolia
154 L9 **Govind Ballabh Pant Sāgar** ▣ C India
152 I7 **Govind Sāgar** ▣ NE India
162 M8 **Govĭ-Sumber** ◆ province C Mongolia
Govurdak see Gowurdak
18 D11 **Gowanda** New York, NE USA
148 J10 **Gowd-e Zereh, Dasht-e** var. Guad-i-Zirreh. marsh SW Afghanistan
14 F8 **Gowganda** Ontario, S Canada
14 G8 **Gowganda Lake** ◎ Ontario, S Canada
29 U13 **Gowrie** Iowa, C USA
147 N14 **Gowurdak** Rus. Govurdak; prev. Guardak. Lebap Welaýaty, E Turkmenistan
61 C15 **Goya** Corrientes, NE Argentina
Goyania see Goiânia
137 X11 **Göyçay** Rus. Geokchay. C Azerbaijan
146 D10 **Goymat** Rus. Koymat. Balkan Welaýaty, NW Turkmenistan
146 D10 **Goymatdag** Rus. Gory Koymatdag. hill range NW Turkmenistan
136 F12 **Göynük** Bolu, NW Turkey
165 R9 **Goyō-san** ▲ Honshū, C Japan
78 K11 **Goz Beïda** Ouaddaï, SE Chad
146 M10 **G'ozg'on** Rus. Gazgan. Navoiy Viloyati, C Uzbekistan
158 H11 **Gozha Co** ◎ W China
121 O15 **Gozo** Malt. Ghawdex. island N Malta
80 H9 **Göz Regeb** Kassala, NE Sudan
Gozyô see Gojō
83 H25 **Graaff-Reinet** Eastern Cape, S South Africa
Graasten see Gråsten
76 L17 **Grabo** SW Ivory Coast
112 P11 **Grabovica** Serbia, E Serbia and Montenegro (Yugo.)
110 I13 **Grabów nad Prosną** Wielkopolskie, C Poland
108 I8 **Grabs** Sankt Gallen, NE Switzerland
112 D12 **Gračac** Zadar, C Croatia
112 I11 **Gračanica** Federacija Bosna I Hercegovina, NE Bosnia and Herzegovina
14 L11 **Gracefield** Québec, SE Canada
99 K19 **Grâce-Hollogne** Liège, E Belgium
23 R8 **Graceville** Florida, SE USA
29 R8 **Graceville** Minnesota, N USA
42 G6 **Gracias** Lempira, W Honduras
Gracias see Lempira
42 L5 **Gracias a Dios** ◆ department E Honduras
43 O6 **Gracias a Dios, Cabo de** headland Honduras/Nicaragua
64 O2 **Graciosa** var. Ilha Graciosa. island Azores, Portugal, NE Atlantic Ocean
64 Q11 **Graciosa** island Islas Canarias, Spain, NE Atlantic Ocean
Graciosa, Ilha see Graciosa
112 I11 **Gradačac** Federacija Bosna I Hercegovina, N Bosnia and Herzegovina
59 J15 **Gradaús, Serra dos** ▲ C Brazil
104 L3 **Gradefes** Castilla-León, N Spain
Gradiška see Bosanska Gradiška
Gradizhsk see Hradyz'k
106 J7 **Grado** Friuli-Venezia Giulia, NE Italy
104 K2 **Grado** Asturias, N Spain
113 P19 **Gradsko** C FYR Macedonia
37 V11 **Grady** New Mexico, SW USA
29 T12 **Graettinger** Iowa, C USA
101 M23 **Grafing** Bayern, SE Germany
25 S6 **Graford** Texas, SW USA
183 V5 **Grafton** New South Wales, SE Australia
29 Q3 **Grafton** North Dakota, N USA
21 S3 **Grafton** West Virginia, NE USA
21 T9 **Graham** North Carolina, SE USA
25 R6 **Graham** Texas, SW USA
Graham Bell Island see Greem-Bell, Ostrov
10 I13 **Graham Island** island Queen Charlotte Islands, British Columbia, SW Canada
19 S6 **Graham Lake** ◎ Maine, NE USA
194 H4 **Graham Land** physical region Antarctica
37 N15 **Graham, Mount** ▲ Arizona, SW USA
Grahamstad see Grahamstown
83 I25 **Grahamstown** Afr. Grahamstad. Eastern Cape, S South Africa
Grahovo see Bosansko Grahovo
169 S17 **Grajagan, Teluk** bay Jawa, S Indonesia
59 L14 **Grajaú** Maranhão, E Brazil
58 M13 **Grajaú, Rio** ≈ NE Brazil
110 O8 **Grajewo** Podlaskie, NE Poland
95 F24 **Gram** Sønderjylland, SW Denmark
103 N13 **Gramat** Lot, S France
22 H5 **Grambling** Louisiana, S USA
115 C14 **Grámmos** ▲ Albania/Greece
96 I9 **Grampian Mountains** ▲ C Scotland, UK
182 L12 **Grampians, The** ▲ Victoria, SE Australia
98 O9 **Gramsbergen** Overijssel, E Netherlands
113 L21 **Gramsh** var. Gramshi. Elbasan, C Albania
Gramshi see Gramsh
Gran see Hron, Slovakia
Gran see Esztergom, Hungary
54 F11 **Granada** Meta, C Colombia
42 J10 **Granada** Granada, SW Nicaragua
105 N14 **Granada** Andalucía, S Spain
37 W6 **Granada** Colorado, C USA
42 J11 **Granada** ◆ department SW Nicaragua
105 N14 **Granada** ◆ province Andalucía, S Spain
63 I21 **Gran Altiplanicie Central** plain S Argentina
97 E17 **Granard** Ir. Gránard. C Ireland
63 J20 **Gran Bajo** basin S Argentina
63 J15 **Gran Bajo del Gualicho** basin E Argentina
63 I21 **Gran Bajo de San Julián** basin SE Argentina
25 S7 **Granbury** Texas, SW USA
15 P12 **Granby** Québec, SE Canada
27 S8 **Granby** Missouri, C USA
37 S3 **Granby, Lake** ▣ Colorado, C USA
64 O12 **Gran Canaria** var. Grand Canary. island Islas Canarias, Spain, NE Atlantic Ocean
62 M5 **Gran Chaco** var. Chaco. lowland plain South America
45 R14 **Grand Anse** SW Grenada
Grand-Anse see Portsmouth
44 G1 **Grand Bahama Island** island N Bahamas
Grand Balé see Tui
103 U7 **Grand Ballon** Ger. Ballon de Guebwiller. ▲ NE France
13 T13 **Grand Bank** Newfoundland and Labrador, SE Canada
64 I7 **Grand Banks of Newfoundland and Labrador** undersea feature NW Atlantic Ocean
Grand Bassa see Buchanan
77 N17 **Grand-Bassam** var. Bassam. SE Ivory Coast
14 E16 **Grand Bend** Ontario, S Canada
76 L17 **Grand-Bérébi** var. Grand-Béréby. SW Ivory Coast
Grand-Béréby see Grand-Bérébi
45 X11 **Grand-Bourg** Marie-Galante, SE Guadeloupe
44 M6 **Grand Caicos** var. Middle Caicos. island C Turks and Caicos Islands
14 K12 **Grand Calumet, Île du** island Québec, SE Canada
97 E18 **Grand Canal** Ir. An Chanáil Mhór. canal C Ireland
Grand Canary see Gran Canaria
36 K10 **Grand Canyon** Arizona, SW USA
36 J9 **Grand Canyon** canyon Arizona, SW USA
Grand Canyon State see Arizona
44 D8 **Grand Cayman** island SW Cayman Islands
11 R14 **Grand Centre** Alberta, SW Canada
76 L17 **Grand Cess** SE Liberia
108 D12 **Grand Combin** ▲ S Switzerland
32 K8 **Grand Coulee** Washington, NW USA
32 J8 **Grand Coulee** valley Washington, NW USA
45 X5 **Grand Cul-de-Sac Marin** bay N Guadeloupe
Grand Duchy of Luxembourg see Luxembourg
63 I22 **Grande, Bahía** bay S Argentina
11 N14 **Grande Cache** Alberta, W Canada
103 U12 **Grande Casse** ▲ E France
172 G12 **Grande Comore** var. Njazidja, Great Comoro. island NW Comoros
61 G18 **Grande, Cuchilla** hill range E Uruguay
45 S5 **Grande de Añasco, Río** ≈ W Puerto Rico
Grande de Chiloé, Isla see Chiloé, Isla de

◆ Country ● Country Capital ◇ Dependent Territory ○ Dependent Territory Capital ◆ Administrative Region ✕ International Airport ▲ Mountain ▲ Mountain Range ⅄ Volcano ≈ River ◎ Lake ▣ Reservoir

58 J12 **Grande de Gurupá, Ilha** *river island* NE Brazil
57 K21 **Grande de Lipez, Río** ≈ SW Bolivia
45 U6 **Grande de Loíza, Río** ≈ E Puerto Rico
45 T5 **Grande de Manatí, Río** ≈ C Puerto Rico
42 L9 **Grande de Matagalpa, Río** ≈ C Nicaragua
40 K12 **Grande de Santiago, Río** *var.* Santiago. ≈ C Mexico
43 O15 **Grande de Térraba, Río** *var.* Río Térraba. ≈ SE Costa Rica
12 J9 **Grande Deux, Réservoir la** ▣ Québec, E Canada
60 O10 **Grande, Ilha** *island* SE Brazil
11 O13 **Grande Prairie** Alberta, W Canada
74 I8 **Grand Erg Occidental** *desert* W Algeria
74 L9 **Grand Erg Oriental** *desert* Algeria/Tunisia
59 J20 **Grande, Rio** ≈ S Brazil
16 K16 **Grande, Rio** *var.* Río Bravo, *Sp.* Río Bravo del Norte, Bravo del Norte. ≈ Mexico/USA
57 M18 **Grande, Río** ≈ C Bolivia
15 Y7 **Grande-Rivière** Québec, SE Canada
15 Y6 **Grande Rivière** ≈ Québec, SE Canada
44 M8 **Grande-Rivière-du-Nord** N Haiti
62 K9 **Grande, Salina** *var.* Gran Salitral. *salt lake* C Argentina
15 S7 **Grandes-Bergeronnes** Québec, SE Canada
40 K4 **Grande, Sierra** ▲▲ N Mexico
103 S12 **Grandes Rousses** ▲▲ E France
63 K17 **Grandes, Salinas** *salt lake* E Argentina
45 Y5 **Grande Terre** *island* E West Indies
15 X5 **Grande-Vallée** Québec, SE Canada
45 Y5 **Grande Vigie, Pointe de la** *headland* Grande Terre, N Guadeloupe
13 N14 **Grand Falls** New Brunswick, SE Canada
13 T11 **Grand Falls** Newfoundland and Labrador, SE Canada
24 L9 **Grandfalls** Texas, SW USA
21 P9 **Grandfather Mountain** ▲ North Carolina, SE USA
26 L13 **Grandfield** Oklahoma, C USA
11 N17 **Grand Forks** British Columbia, SW Canada
29 R4 **Grand Forks** North Dakota, N USA
31 O9 **Grand Haven** Michigan, N USA
Grandichi *see* Hrandzichy
29 P15 **Grand Island** Nebraska, C USA
31 O3 **Grand Island** *island* Michigan, N USA
22 K10 **Grand Isle** Louisiana, S USA
65 A23 **Grand Jason** *island* Jason Islands, NW Falkland Islands
37 P5 **Grand Junction** Colorado, C USA
20 F10 **Grand Junction** Tennessee, S USA
14 J9 **Grand-Lac-Victoria** Québec, SE Canada
14 J9 **Grand lac Victoria** ◎ Québec, SE Canada
77 N17 **Grand-Lahou** *var.* Grand Lahu. S Ivory Coast
Grand Lahu *see* Grand-Lahou
37 S3 **Grand Lake** Colorado, C USA
13 S11 **Grand Lake** ◎ Newfoundland and Labrador, E Canada
22 G9 **Grand Lake** ◎ Louisiana, S USA
31 R5 **Grand Lake** ◎ Michigan, N USA
31 Q13 **Grand Lake** ▣ Ohio, N USA
27 R9 **Grand Lake O' The Cherokees** *var.* Lake O' The Cherokees. ▣ Oklahoma, C USA
31 Q9 **Grand Ledge** Michigan, N USA
102 I8 **Grand-Lieu, Lac de** ◎ NW France
19 U6 **Grand Manan Channel** *channel* Canada/USA
13 O15 **Grand Manan Island** *island* New Brunswick, SE Canada
29 Y4 **Grand Marais** Minnesota, N USA
15 P10 **Grand-Mère** Quebec, SE Canada
37 P5 **Grand Mesa** ▲▲ Colorado, C USA
108 C10 **Grand Muveran** ▲ W Switzerland
104 G12 **Grândola** Setúbal, S Portugal
Grand Paradis *see* Gran Paradiso
187 O15 **Grand Passage** *passage* N New Caledonia
77 R16 **Grand-Popo** S Benin
29 Z3 **Grand Portage** Minnesota, N USA
25 T6 **Grand Prairie** Texas, SW USA
11 W14 **Grand Rapids** Manitoba, C Canada
31 P9 **Grand Rapids** Michigan, N USA
29 V5 **Grand Rapids** Minnesota, N USA
14 L10 **Grand-Remous** Québec, SE Canada
14 F15 **Grand River** ≈ Ontario, S Canada
31 P9 **Grand River** ≈ Michigan, N USA
27 T3 **Grand River** ≈ Missouri, C USA
28 M7 **Grand River** ≈ South Dakota, N USA
45 Q11 **Grand' Rivière** N Martinique
32 F11 **Grand Ronde** Oregon, NW USA
32 L11 **Grand Ronde River** ≈ Oregon/Washington, NW USA
Grand-Saint-Bernard, Col du *see* Great Saint Bernard Pass
25 V6 **Grand Saline** Texas, SW USA
55 X10 **Grand-Santi** W French Guiana
Grandsee *see* Grandson
108 B9 **Grandson** *prev.* Grandsee. Vaud, W Switzerland
172 J16 **Grand Sœur** *island* Les Sœurs, NE Seychelles
33 S14 **Grand Teton** ▲ Wyoming, C USA
31 P5 **Grand Traverse Bay** *lake bay* Michigan, N USA
45 N6 **Grand Turk** ○ (Turks and Caicos Islands) Grand Turk Island, S Turks and Caicos Islands
45 N6 **Grand Turk Island** *island* SE Turks and Caicos Islands
103 S13 **Grand Veymont** ▲ E France
11 W15 **Grandview** Manitoba, S Canada
27 R4 **Grandview** Missouri, C USA
36 I10 **Grand Wash Cliffs** *cliff* Arizona, SW USA
14 J8 **Granet, Lac** ◎ Québec, SE Canada
95 L14 **Grangärde** Dalarna, C Sweden
44 H12 **Grange Hill** W Jamaica
96 J12 **Grangemouth** C Scotland, UK
25 T10 **Granger** Texas, SW USA
32 J10 **Granger** Washington, NW USA
33 T17 **Granger** Wyoming, C USA
Granges *see* Grenchen
95 L14 **Grängesberg** Dalarna, C Sweden
33 N11 **Grangeville** Idaho, NW USA
10 K13 **Granisle** British Columbia, SW Canada
30 K15 **Granite City** Illinois, N USA
29 S9 **Granite Falls** Minnesota, N USA
21 Q9 **Granite Falls** North Carolina, SE USA
36 K12 **Granite Mountain** ▲ Arizona, SW USA
33 T12 **Granite Peak** ▲ Montana, NW USA
35 T2 **Granite Peak** ▲ Nevada, W USA
36 J3 **Granite Peak** ▲ Utah, W USA
Granite State *see* New Hampshire
107 H24 **Granitola, Capo** *headland* Sicilia, Italy, C Mediterranean Sea
185 H15 **Granity** West Coast, South Island, NZ
Gran Lago *see* Nicaragua, Lago de
63 J18 **Gran Laguna Salada** ◎ S Argentina
Gran Malvina, Isla *see* West Falkland
95 L18 **Gränna** Jönköping, S Sweden
105 W5 **Granollers** *var.* Granollérs. Cataluña, NE Spain
106 A7 **Gran Paradiso** *Fr.* Grand Paradis. ▲ NW Italy
Gran Pilastro *see* Hochfeiler
Gran Salitral *see* Grande, Salina
Gran San Bernardo, Passo di *see* Great Saint Bernard Pass
Gran Santiago *see* Santiago
107 J14 **Gran Sasso d'Italia** ▲▲ C Italy
100 N11 **Gransee** Brandenburg, NE Germany
28 L15 **Grant** Nebraska, C USA
27 R1 **Grant City** Missouri, C USA
97 N19 **Grantham** E England, UK
65 D24 **Grantham Sound** *sound* East Falkland, Falkland Islands
194 K13 **Grant Island** *island* Antarctica
45 Z14 **Grantley Adams** ✕ (Bridgetown) SE Barbados
35 S7 **Grant, Mount** ▲ Nevada, W USA
96 J9 **Grantown-on-Spey** N Scotland, UK
35 W8 **Grant Range** ▲▲ Nevada, W USA
37 Q11 **Grants** New Mexico, SW USA
30 I4 **Grantsburg** Wisconsin, N USA
32 F15 **Grants Pass** Oregon, NW USA
36 K3 **Grantsville** Utah, W USA
21 R4 **Grantsville** West Virginia, NE USA
102 I5 **Granville** Manche, N France
11 V12 **Granville Lake** ◎ Manitoba, C Canada
25 V8 **Grapeland** Texas, SW USA
25 T6 **Grapevine** Texas, SW USA
83 K20 **Graskop** Mpumalanga, NE South Africa
95 P14 **Gräsö** Uppsala, C Sweden
93 I19 **Gräsö** *island* C Sweden
103 U15 **Grasse** Alpes-Maritimes, SE France
18 E14 **Grassflat** Pennsylvania, NE USA
33 U9 **Grassrange** Montana, NW USA
18 J6 **Grass River** ≈ New York, NE USA
35 P6 **Grass Valley** California, W USA
183 N14 **Grassy** Tasmania, SE Australia
28 K4 **Grassy Butte** North Dakota, N USA
21 R5 **Grassy Knob** ▲ West Virginia, NE USA
95 G24 **Gråsten** *var.* Graasten. Sønderjylland, SW Denmark
95 J18 **Grästorp** Västra Götaland, S Sweden
Gratianopolis *see* Grenoble
109 V8 **Gratwein** Steiermark, SE Austria
Gratz *see* Graz
108 I9 **Graubünden** *Fr.* Grisons, *It.* Grigioni. ◈ *canton* SE Switzerland
Graudenz *see* Grudziądz
103 N15 **Graulhet** Tarn, S France
105 T4 **Graus** Aragón, NE Spain
61 I16 **Gravataí** Rio Grande do Sul, S Brazil
98 L13 **Grave** Noord-Brabant, SE Netherlands
11 T17 **Gravelbourg** Saskatchewan, S Canada
103 N1 **Gravelines** Nord, N France
Graven *see* Grez-Doiceau
14 H13 **Gravenhurst** Ontario, S Canada
33 O10 **Grave Peak** ▲ Idaho, NW USA
102 I11 **Grave, Pointe de** *headland* W France
183 S4 **Gravesend** New South Wales, SE Australia
97 P22 **Gravesend** SE England, UK
107 N17 **Gravina in Puglia** Puglia, SE Italy
103 S8 **Gray** Haute-Saône, E France
23 T4 **Gray** Georgia, SE USA
195 V16 **Gray, Cape** *headland* Antarctica
32 F9 **Grayland** Washington, NW USA
39 N10 **Grayling** Alaska, USA
31 Q6 **Grayling** Michigan, N USA
32 F8 **Grays Harbor** *inlet* Washington, NW USA
21 O5 **Grayson** Kentucky, S USA
37 S4 **Grays Peak** ▲ Colorado, C USA
30 M16 **Grayville** Illinois, N USA
109 V8 **Graz** *prev.* Gratz. Steiermark, SE Austria
104 L15 **Grazalema** Andalucía, S Spain
113 P15 **Grdelica** Serbia, SE Serbia and Montenegro (Yugo.)
44 H1 **Great Abaco** *var.* Abaco Island. *island* N Bahamas
Great Admiralty Island *see* Manus Island
Great Alfold *see* Great Hungarian Plain
Great Ararat *see* Büyükağrı Dağı
181 U8 **Great Artesian Basin** *lowlands* Queensland, C Australia
181 O12 **Great Australian Bight** *bight* S Australia
64 E11 **Great Bahama Bank** *undersea feature* E Gulf of Mexico
184 M4 **Great Barrier Island** *island* N NZ
181 X4 **Great Barrier Reef** *reef* Queensland, NE Australia
18 L11 **Great Barrington** Massachusetts, NE USA
16 E9 **Great Basin** *basin* W USA
8 I8 **Great Bear Lake** *Fr.* Grand Lac de l'Ours. ◎ Northwest Territories, NW Canada
Great Belt *see* Storebælt
26 L5 **Great Bend** Kansas, C USA
97 A20 **Great Blasket Island** *Ir.* An Blascaod Mór. *island* SW Ireland
Great Britain *see* Britain
151 Q23 **Great Channel** *channel* Andaman Sea/Indian Ocean
166 J10 **Great Coco Island** *island* SW Burma
Great Crosby *see* Crosby
21 X7 **Great Dismal Swamp** *wetland* North Carolina/Virginia, SE USA
33 V16 **Great Divide Basin** *basin* Wyoming, C USA
181 W7 **Great Dividing Range** ▲▲ NE Australia
14 D12 **Great Duck Island** *island* Ontario, S Canada
Great Elder Reservoir *see* Waconda Lake
195 V8 **Greater Antarctica** *var.* East Antarctica. *physical region* Antarctica
44 G8 **Greater Antilles** *island group* West Indies
184 I1 **Great Exhibition Bay** *inlet* North Island, NZ
44 H4 **Great Exuma Island** *island* C Bahamas
33 R8 **Great Falls** Montana, NW USA
21 R11 **Great Falls** South Carolina, SE USA
Great Glen *see* Mor, Glen
Great Grimsby *see* Grimsby
44 I4 **Great Guana Cay** *island* C Bahamas
64 I5 **Great Hellefiske Bank** *undersea feature* N Atlantic Ocean
111 L24 **Great Hungarian Plain** *var.* Great Alfold, Plain of Hungary, *Hung.* Alföld. *plain* SE Europe
44 L7 **Great Inagua** *var.* Inagua Islands. *island* S Bahamas
Great Indian Desert *see* Thar Desert
83 G25 **Great Karoo** *var.* Great Karroo, High Veld, *Afr.* Groot Karoo, Hoë Karoo. *plateau region* S South Africa
Great Karroo *see* Great Karoo
Great Kei *see* Groot-Kei
Great Khingan Range *see* Da Hinggan Ling
14 E11 **Great La Cloche Island** *island* Ontario, S Canada
183 P16 **Great Lake** ◎ Tasmania, SE Australia
Great Lake *see* Tônlé Sap
9 R15 **Great Lakes** *lakes* Ontario, Canada/USA
Great Lakes State *see* Michigan
97 L20 **Great Malvern** W England, UK
184 M5 **Great Mercury Island** *island* N NZ
Great Meteor Seamount *see* Great Meteor Tablemount
64 K10 **Great Meteor Tablemount** *var.* Great Meteor Seamount. *undersea feature* E Atlantic Ocean
31 Q14 **Great Miami River** ≈ Ohio, N USA
151 Q24 **Great Nicobar** *island* Nicobar Islands, India, NE Indian Ocean
97 O19 **Great Ouse** *var.* Ouse. ≈ E England, UK
183 Q17 **Great Oyster Bay** *bay* Tasmania, SE Australia
44 I13 **Great Pedro Bluff** *headland* W Jamaica
21 T12 **Great Pee Dee River** ≈ North Carolina/South Carolina, SE USA
16 J9 **Great Plains** *var.* High Plains. *plains* Canada/USA
37 W6 **Great Plains Reservoirs** ▣ Colorado, C USA
19 Q13 **Great Point** *headland* Nantucket Island, Massachusetts, NE USA
81 J14 **Great Rift Valley** *var.* Rift Valley. *depression* Asia/Africa
81 I23 **Great Ruaha** ≈ S Tanzania
18 K10 **Great Sacandaga Lake** ▣ New York, NE USA
108 C12 **Great Saint Bernard Pass** *Fr.* Col du Grand-Saint-Bernard, *It.* Passo di Gran San Bernardo. *pass* Italy/Switzerland
44 F1 **Great Sale Cay** *island* N Bahamas
Great Salt Desert *see* Kavīr, Dasht-e
36 K1 **Great Salt Lake** *salt lake* Utah, W USA
36 J3 **Great Salt Lake Desert** *plain* Utah, W USA
26 M8 **Great Salt Plains Lake** ▣ Oklahoma, C USA
75 T9 **Great Sand Sea** *desert* Egypt/Libya
180 L6 **Great Sandy Desert** *desert* Western Australia
Great Sandy Desert *see* Ar Rub' al Khālī
Great Sandy Island *see* Fraser Island
187 Y13 **Great Sea Reef** *reef* Vanua Levu, N Fiji
38 H17 **Great Sitkin Island** *island* Aleutian Islands, Alaska, USA
8 J10 **Great Slave Lake** *Fr.* Grand Lac des Esclaves. ◎ Northwest Territories, NW Canada
21 O10 **Great Smoky Mountains** ▲▲ North Carolina/Tennessee, SE USA
10 L11 **Great Snow Mountain** ▲ British Columbia, W Canada
64 A12 **Great Sound** *bay* Bermuda, NW Atlantic Ocean
180 M10 **Great Victoria Desert** *desert* South Australia/Western Australia
194 H2 **Great Wall** *Chinese research station* South Shetland Islands, Antarctica
19 T7 **Great Wass Island** *island* Maine, NE USA
97 Q19 **Great Yarmouth** *var.* Yarmouth. E England, UK
139 S1 **Great Zab** *Ar.* Az Zāb al Kabīr, *Kurd.* Zē-i Bādīnān, *Turk.* Büyükzap Suyu. ≈ Iraq/Turkey
95 I17 **Grebbestad** Västra Götaland, S Sweden
Grebenka *see* Hrebinka
42 M13 **Grecia** Alajuela, C Costa Rica
61 E18 **Greco** Río Negro, W Uruguay
Greco, Cape *see* Gkréko, Akrotíri
104 L8 **Gredos, Sierra de** ▲▲ W Spain
18 F9 **Greece** New York, NE USA
115 E17 **Greece** *off.* Hellenic Republic, *Gk.* Ellás; *anc.* Hellas. ◆ *republic* SE Europe
Greece Central *see* Stereá Ellás
Greece West *see* Dytikí Ellás
37 T3 **Greeley** Colorado, C USA
29 P14 **Greeley** Nebraska, C USA
122 K3 **Greem-Bell, Ostrov** *Eng.* Graham Bell Island. *island* Zemlya Frantsa-Iosifa, N Russian Federation
30 M6 **Green Bay** Wisconsin, N USA
31 N6 **Green Bay** *lake bay* Michigan/Wisconsin, N USA
21 S5 **Greenbrier River** ≈ West Virginia, NE USA
29 S2 **Greenbush** Minnesota, N USA
183 R12 **Green Cape** *headland* New South Wales, SE Australia
31 O14 **Greencastle** Indiana, N USA
18 F16 **Greencastle** Pennsylvania, NE USA
27 T2 **Green City** Missouri, C USA
21 O9 **Greeneville** Tennessee, S USA
35 O11 **Greenfield** California, W USA
31 P14 **Greenfield** Indiana, N USA
29 U15 **Greenfield** Iowa, C USA
18 M11 **Greenfield** Massachusetts, NE USA
27 S7 **Greenfield** Missouri, C USA
31 S14 **Greenfield** Ohio, N USA
20 G8 **Greenfield** Tennessee, S USA
30 M9 **Greenfield** Wisconsin, N USA
27 T9 **Green Forest** Arkansas, C USA
37 T7 **Greenhorn Mountain** ▲ Colorado, C USA
Green Island *see* Lü Tao
186 I6 **Green Islands** *var.* Nissan Islands. *island group* NE PNG
11 S14 **Green Lake** Saskatchewan, C Canada
30 L8 **Green Lake** ◎ Wisconsin, N USA
197 O14 **Greenland** *Dan.* Grønland, *Inuit* Kalaallit Nunaat. ◇ *Danish external territory* NE North America
197 R13 **Greenland Plain** *undersea feature* N Greenland Sea
197 R14 **Greenland Sea** *sea* Arctic Ocean
37 R4 **Green Mountain Reservoir** ▣ Colorado, C USA
18 M8 **Green Mountains** ▲▲ Vermont, NE USA
Green Mountain State *see* Vermont
96 H12 **Greenock** W Scotland, UK
39 T5 **Greenough, Mount** ▲ Alaska, USA
186 A6 **Green River** Sandaun, NW PNG
37 N5 **Green River** Utah, W USA
33 U17 **Green River** Wyoming, C USA
16 H9 **Green River** ≈ W USA
30 K11 **Green River** ≈ Illinois, N USA
20 J7 **Green River** ≈ Kentucky, S USA
28 K5 **Green River** ≈ North Dakota, N USA
37 N6 **Green River** ≈ Utah, W USA
33 T16 **Green River** ≈ Wyoming, C USA
20 L7 **Green River Lake** ▣ Kentucky, S USA
23 O5 **Greensboro** Alabama, S USA
23 U3 **Greensboro** Georgia, SE USA
21 T9 **Greensboro** North Carolina, SE USA
31 P14 **Greensburg** Indiana, N USA
26 K6 **Greensburg** Kansas, C USA
20 L7 **Greensburg** Kentucky, S USA
18 C15 **Greensburg** Pennsylvania, NE USA
37 O13 **Greens Peak** ▲ Arizona, SW USA
21 V12 **Green Swamp** *wetland* North Carolina, SE USA
21 O4 **Greenup** Kentucky, S USA
36 M16 **Green Valley** Arizona, SW USA
76 K17 **Greenville** *var.* Sino, Sinoe. SE Liberia
23 P6 **Greenville** Alabama, S USA
23 T8 **Greenville** Florida, SE USA
23 S4 **Greenville** Georgia, SE USA
30 L15 **Greenville** Illinois, N USA
20 I7 **Greenville** Kentucky, S USA
19 Q5 **Greenville** Maine, NE USA
31 P9 **Greenville** Michigan, N USA
22 J4 **Greenville** Mississippi, S USA
21 W9 **Greenville** North Carolina, SE USA
31 Q13 **Greenville** Ohio, N USA
19 O12 **Greenville** Rhode Island, NE USA
21 P11 **Greenville** South Carolina, SE USA
25 U6 **Greenville** Texas, SW USA
31 T12 **Greenwich** Ohio, N USA
27 S11 **Greenwood** Arkansas, C USA
31 O14 **Greenwood** Indiana, N USA
22 K4 **Greenwood** Mississippi, S USA
21 P12 **Greenwood** South Carolina, SE USA
21 Q12 **Greenwood, Lake** ▣ South Carolina, SE USA
21 P11 **Greer** South Carolina, SE USA
27 V10 **Greers Ferry Lake** ▣ Arkansas, C USA
27 S13 **Greeson, Lake** ▣ Arkansas, C USA
29 O12 **Gregory** South Dakota, N USA
182 J3 **Gregory, Lake** *salt lake* South Australia
180 J9 **Gregory Lake** ◎ Western Australia
181 V5 **Gregory Range** ▲▲ Queensland, E Australia
Greifenberg/Greifenberg in Pommern *see* Gryfice
Greifenhagen *see* Gryfino
100 O8 **Greifswald** Mecklenburg-Vorpommern, NE Germany
100 O8 **Greifswalder Bodden** *bay* NE Germany
109 U4 **Grein** Oberösterreich, N Austria
101 M17 **Greiz** Thüringen, C Germany
Gremicha/Gremiha *see* Gremikha
124 M4 **Gremikha** *var.* Gremicha, Gremiha. Murmanskaya Oblast', NW Russian Federation
125 V14 **Gremyachinsk** Permskaya Oblast', NW Russian Federation
Grenå *see* Grenaa
95 H21 **Grenaa** *var.* Grenå. Århus, C Denmark
22 L3 **Grenada** Mississippi, S USA
45 W15 **Grenada** ◆ *commonwealth republic* SE West Indies
22 L3 **Grenada Lake** ▣ Mississippi, S USA
45 Y14 **Grenadines, The** *island group* Grenada/St Vincent and the Grenadines
108 D7 **Grenchen** *Fr.* Granges. Solothurn, NW Switzerland
183 Q9 **Grenfell** New South Wales, SE Australia
11 V16 **Grenfell** Saskatchewan, S Canada
92 J1 **Grenivík** Nordhurland Eystra, N Iceland
103 S12 **Grenoble** *anc.* Cularo, Gratianopolis. Isère, E France
28 J2 **Grenora** North Dakota, N USA
92 N8 **Grense-Jakobselv** Finnmark, N Norway
45 S14 **Grenville** E Grenada
32 G11 **Gresham** Oregon, NW USA
Gresk *see* Hresk
106 B7 **Gressoney-St-Jean** Valle d'Aosta, NW Italy
22 K9 **Gretna** Louisiana, S USA
21 T7 **Gretna** Virginia, NE USA
98 F13 **Grevelingen** *inlet* S North Sea
100 F13 **Greven** Nordrhein-Westfalen, NW Germany
115 D15 **Grevená** Dytikí Makedonía, N Greece
101 D16 **Grevenbroich** Nordrhein-Westfalen, W Germany
99 N24 **Grevenmacher** Grevenmacher, E Luxembourg
99 M24 **Grevenmacher** ◈ *district* E Luxembourg
100 K9 **Grevesmühlen** Mecklenburg-Vorpommern, N Germany
185 H16 **Grey** ≈ South Island, NZ
33 V12 **Greybull** Wyoming, C USA
33 U13 **Greybull River** ≈ Wyoming, C USA
65 A24 **Grey Channel** *sound* Falkland Islands
Greyerzer See *see* Gruyère, Lac de la
13 T10 **Grey Islands** *island group* Newfoundland and Labrador, E Canada
18 L10 **Greylock, Mount** ▲ Massachusetts, NE USA
185 G17 **Greymouth** West Coast, South Island, NZ
181 U10 **Grey Range** ▲▲ New South Wales/Queensland, E Australia
97 G18 **Greystones** *Ir.* Na Clocha Liatha. E Ireland
185 M14 **Greytown** Wellington, North Island, NZ
83 K23 **Greytown** KwaZulu/Natal, E South Africa
Greytown *see* San Juan del Norte
99 H19 **Grez-Doiceau** *Dut.* Graven. Wallon Brabant, C Belgium
115 J19 **Griá, Akrotírio** *headland* Ándros, Kykládes, Greece, Aegean Sea
127 N8 **Gribanovskiy** Voronezhskaya Oblast', W Russian Federation
78 I13 **Gribingui** ≈ N Central African Republic
35 O6 **Gridley** California, W USA
83 G23 **Griekwastad** Northern Cape, C South Africa
23 S4 **Griffin** Georgia, SE USA
183 O9 **Griffith** New South Wales, SE Australia
14 F13 **Griffith Island** *island* Ontario, S Canada
21 W10 **Grifton** North Carolina, SE USA
Grigioni *see* Graubünden
119 H14 **Grigiškes** Vilnius, SE Lithuania
117 N10 **Grigoriopol** C Moldova
147 X7 **Grigor'yevka** Issyk-Kul'skaya Oblast', E Kyrgyzstan
193 U8 **Grijalva Ridge** *undersea feature* E Pacific Ocean
41 U15 **Grijalva, Río** *var.* Tabasco. ≈ Guatemala/Mexico
98 N5 **Grijpskerk** Groningen, NE Netherlands
83 C22 **Grillenthal** Karas, SW Namibia
79 J15 **Grimari** Ouaka, C Central African Republic
Grimaylov *see* Hrymayliv
99 G18 **Grimbergen** Vlaams Brabant, C Belgium
183 N15 **Grim, Cape** *headland* Tasmania, SE Australia
100 N8 **Grimmen** Mecklenburg-Vorpommern, NE Germany
14 G16 **Grimsby** Ontario, S Canada
97 O17 **Grimsby** *prev.* Great Grimsby. E England, UK
92 J1 **Grímsey** *var.* Grimsey. *island* N Iceland
11 O12 **Grimshaw** Alberta, W Canada
95 F18 **Grimstad** Aust-Agder, S Norway
92 H4 **Grindavík** Reykjanes, W Iceland
108 F9 **Grindelwald** Bern, S Switzerland
95 F23 **Grindsted** Ribe, W Denmark
29 W14 **Grinnell** Iowa, C USA
8 K4 **Grinnell Peninsula** *peninsula* Nunavut, N Canada
109 U10 **Grintovec** ▲ N Slovenia
9 N3 **Grise Fiord** *var.* Ausuituq. Nunavut, N Canada
182 H1 **Griselda, Lake** *salt lake* South Australia
Grisons *see* Graubünden
95 P14 **Grisslehamn** Stockholm, C Sweden
29 T15 **Griswold** Iowa, C USA
102 M1 **Griz Nez, Cap** *headland* N France
112 P13 **Grljan** Serbia, E Serbia and Montenegro (Yugo.)
112 E11 **Grmeč** ▲▲ NW Bosnia and Herzegovina
99 H16 **Grobbendonk** Antwerpen, N Belgium
Grobin *see* Grobiņa
118 C10 **Grobiņa** *Ger.* Grobin. Liepāja, W Latvia
83 K20 **Groblersdal** Mpumalanga, NE South Africa
83 G23 **Groblershoop** Northern Cape, W South Africa
Gródek Jagielloński *see* Horodok
109 Q6 **Grödig** Salzburg, W Austria
111 H15 **Grodków** Opolskie, S Poland
Grodnenskaya Oblast' *see* Hrodzyenskaya Voblasts'
Grodno *see* Hrodna
110 L12 **Grodzisk Mazowiecki** Mazowieckie, C Poland
110 F12 **Grodzisk Wielkopolski** Wielkolpolskie, C Poland
Grodzyanka *see* Hradzyanka
98 O12 **Groenlo** Gelderland, E Netherlands
83 E22 **Groenrivier** Karas, SE Namibia
25 U8 **Groesbeck** Texas, SW USA
98 L13 **Groesbeek** Gelderland, SE Netherlands
102 G7 **Groix, Îles de** *island group* NW France
110 M12 **Grójec** Mazowieckie, C Poland
65 K15 **Gröll Seamount** *undersea feature* C Atlantic Ocean
100 E13 **Gronau** *var.* Gronau in Westfalen. Nordrhein-Westfalen, NW Germany
Gronau in Westfalen *see* Gronau
93 F15 **Grong** Nord-Trøndelag, C Norway

◆ Country ● Country Capital ◇ Dependent Territory ○ Dependent Territory Capital ◈ Administrative Region ✕ International Airport ▲ Mountain ▲▲ Mountain Range Volcano ≈ River ◎ Lake ▣ Reservoir

95 N22 **Grönhögen** Kalmar, S Sweden
98 N5 **Groningen** Groningen, NE Netherlands
55 W9 **Groningen** Saramacca, N Surinam
98 N5 **Groningen** ◈ province NE Netherlands
Grønland see Greenland
108 H11 **Grono** Graubünden, S Switzerland
95 M20 **Grönskåra** Kalmar, S Sweden
25 O2 **Groom** Texas, SW USA
35 W9 **Groom Lake** ◎ Nevada, W USA
83 H25 **Groot** ∽ S South Africa
181 S2 **Groote Eylandt** island Northern Territory, N Australia
98 M6 **Grootegast** Groningen, NE Netherlands
83 D17 **Grootfontein** Otjozondjupa, N Namibia
83 E22 **Groot Karasberge** ⛰ S Namibia
Groot Karoo see Great Karoo
83 J25 **Groot-Kei** Eng. Great Kei. ∽ S South Africa
45 T10 **Gros Islet** N Saint Lucia
44 L8 **Gros-Morne** NW Haiti
13 S11 **Gros Morne** ▲ Newfoundland and Labrador, E Canada
103 R9 **Grosne** ∽ C France
45 S12 **Gros Piton** ▲ SW Saint Lucia
Grossa, Isola see Dugi Otok
Grossbetschkerek see Zrenjanin
Grosse Isper see Grosse Ysper
Grosse Kokel see Târnava Mare
101 M21 **Grosse Laaber** var. Grosse Laber. ∽ SE Germany
Grosse Laber see Grosse Laaber
Grosse Morava see Velika Morava
101 O15 **Grossenhain** Sachsen, E Germany
109 Y4 **Grossenzersdorf** Niederösterreich, NE Austria
101 O21 **Grosser Arber** ▲ SE Germany
101 K17 **Grosser Beerberg** ▲ C Germany
101 G18 **Grosser Feldberg** ▲ W Germany
109 O8 **Grosser Löffler** It. Monte Lovello. ▲ Austria/Italy
109 N8 **Grosser Möseler** var. Mesule. ▲ Austria/Italy
100 J8 **Grosser Plöner See** ◎ N Germany
101 O21 **Grosser Rachel** ▲ SE Germany
Grosser Sund see Suur Väin
15 V6 **Grosses-Roches** Québec, SE Canada
109 P8 **Grosses Weiesbachhorn** var. Wiesbachhorn. ▲ W Austria
106 F13 **Grosseto** Toscana, C Italy
101 M22 **Grosse Vils** ∽ SE Germany
109 U4 **Grosse Ysper** var. Grosse Isper. ∽ N Austria
101 G19 **Gross-Gerau** Hessen, W Germany
109 U3 **Gross Gerungs** Niederösterreich, N Austria
109 P8 **Grossglockner** ▲ W Austria
Grosskanizsa see Nagykanizsa
Gross-Karol see Carei
Grosskikinda see Kikinda
109 W9 **Grossklein** Steiermark, SE Austria
Grosskoppe see Velká Deštná
Grossmeseritsch see Velké Meziříčí
Grossmichel see Michalovce
101 H19 **Grossostheim** Bayern, C Germany
109 X7 **Grosspetersdorf** Burgenland, SE Austria
109 T5 **Grossraming** Oberösterreich, C Austria
101 P14 **Grossräschen** Brandenburg, E Germany
Grossrauschenbach see Revúca
Gross-Sankt-Johannis see Suure-Jaani
Gross-Schlatten see Abrud
109 V2 **Gross-Siegharts** Niederösterreich, N Austria
Gross-Skaisgirren see Bol'shakovo
Gross-Steffelsdorf see Rimavská Sobota
Gross Strehlitz see Strzelce Opolskie
109 O8 **Grossvenediger** ▲ W Austria
Grosswardein see Oradea
Gross Wartenberg see Syców
109 U11 **Grosuplje** C Slovenia
99 H17 **Grote Nete** ∽ N Belgium
94 E10 **Grotli** Oppland, S Norway
19 N13 **Groton** Connecticut, NE USA
29 P8 **Groton** South Dakota, N USA
107 P18 **Grottaglie** Puglia, SE Italy
107 L17 **Grottaminarda** Campania, S Italy
106 K13 **Grottammare** Marche, C Italy
21 U5 **Grottoes** Virginia, NE USA
Grou see Grouw
13 N10 **Groulx, Monts** ⛰ Québec, E Canada
14 E7 **Groundhog** ∽ Ontario, S Canada
36 J1 **Grouse Creek** Utah, W USA
36 J1 **Grouse Creek Mountains** ⛰ Utah, W USA
98 L6 **Grouw** Fris. Grou. Friesland, N Netherlands
27 R8 **Grove** Oklahoma, C USA
31 S13 **Grove City** Ohio, N USA
18 B13 **Grove City** Pennsylvania, NE USA
23 O6 **Grove Hill** Alabama, S USA
33 S15 **Grover** Wyoming, C USA
35 P13 **Grover City** California, W USA
25 Y11 **Groves** Texas, SW USA
19 O7 **Groveton** New Hampshire, NE USA
25 W9 **Groveton** Texas, SW USA
35 J15 **Growler Mountains** ⛰ Arizona, SW USA
Grozdovo see Bratya Daskalovi
127 P16 **Groznyy** Chechenskaya Respublika, SW Russian Federation
Grubeshov see Hrubieszów
112 G9 **Grubišno Polje** Bjelovar-Bilogora, NE Croatia
Grudovo see Sredets
110 J9 **Grudziądz** Ger. Graudenz. Kujawsko-pomorskie, C Poland
25 R17 **Grulla** var. La Grulla. Texas, SW USA
40 K14 **Grullo** Jalisco, SW Mexico
95 K16 **Grums** Värmland, C Sweden
109 S5 **Grünau im Almtal** Oberösterreich, N Austria
101 H17 **Grünberg** Hessen, W Germany
Grünberg/Grünberg in Schlesien see Zielona Góra
Grünberg in Schlesien see Zielona Góra
92 H3 **Grundarfjördhur** Vestfirdhir, W Iceland
21 P7 **Grundy** Virginia, NE USA
29 W13 **Grundy Center** Iowa, C USA
Grüneberg see Zielona Góra
25 N1 **Gruver** Texas, SW USA
108 C9 **Gruyère, Lac de la** Ger. Greyerzer See. ◎ SW Switzerland
108 C9 **Gruyères** Fribourg, W Switzerland
118 E11 **Gruzdžiai** Šiauliai, N Lithuania
Gruzinskaya SSR/Gruziya see Georgia
Gryada Akkyr see Akgyr Erezi
126 L7 **Gryazi** Lipetskaya Oblast', W Russian Federation
124 M14 **Gryazovets** Vologodskaya Oblast', NW Russian Federation
111 M17 **Grybów** Małopolskie, SE Poland
94 M13 **Grycksbo** Dalarna, C Sweden
110 E8 **Gryfice** Ger. Greifenberg, Greifenberg in Pommern. Zachodnio-pomorskie, NW Poland
110 D9 **Gryfino** Ger. Greifenhagen. Zachodnio-pomorskie, NW Poland
92 H9 **Gryllefjord** Troms, N Norway
95 L15 **Grythyttan** Örebro, C Sweden
108 D10 **Gstaad** Bern, W Switzerland
43 P14 **Guabito** Bocas del Toro, NW Panama
44 G7 **Guacanayabo, Golfo de** gulf S Cuba
40 I7 **Guachochi** Chihuahua, N Mexico
104 J11 **Guadajira** ∽ SW Spain
104 M13 **Guadajoz** ∽ S Spain
40 L13 **Guadalajara** Jalisco, C Mexico
105 O8 **Guadalajara** Ar. Wad Al-Hajarah; anc. Arriaca. Castilla-La Mancha, C Spain
105 O7 **Guadalajara** ◈ province Castilla-La Mancha, C Spain
104 K12 **Guadalcanal** Andalucía, S Spain
186 L10 **Guadalcanal** off. Guadalcanal Province. ◈ province C Solomon Islands
186 M9 **Guadalcanal** island C Solomon Islands
105 O12 **Guadalén** ∽ S Spain
105 R13 **Guadalentín** ∽ SE Spain
104 K15 **Guadalete** ∽ SW Spain
105 O13 **Guadalimar** ∽ S Spain
105 P12 **Guadalmena** ∽ S Spain
104 L11 **Guadalmez** ∽ W Spain
105 S7 **Guadalope** ∽ E Spain
104 K13 **Guadalquivir** ∽ W Spain
104 J14 **Guadalquivir, Marismas del** var. Las Marismas. wetland SW Spain
40 M11 **Guadalupe** Zacatecas, C Mexico
57 E16 **Guadalupe** Ica, W Peru
104 L10 **Guadalupe** Extremadura, W Spain
36 L14 **Guadalupe** Arizona, SW USA
35 P13 **Guadalupe** California, W USA
Guadalupe see Canelones
40 J3 **Guadalupe Bravos** Chihuahua, N Mexico
40 A4 **Guadalupe, Isla** island NW Mexico
37 U15 **Guadalupe Mountains** ⛰ New Mexico/Texas, SW USA
24 J8 **Guadalupe Peak** ▲ Texas, SW USA
25 R11 **Guadalupe River** ∽ SW USA
104 K10 **Guadalupe, Sierra de** ⛰ W Spain
40 K9 **Guadalupe Victoria** Durango, C Mexico
40 I8 **Guadalupe y Calvo** Chihuahua, N Mexico
105 N7 **Guadarrama** Madrid, C Spain
105 N7 **Guadarrama** ∽ C Spain
104 M7 **Guadarrama, Puerto de** pass C Spain
105 N9 **Guadarrama, Sierra de** ⛰ C Spain
105 Q9 **Guadazaón** ∽ C Spain
45 X10 **Guadeloupe** ◇ French overseas department E West Indies
45 W10 **Guadeloupe Passage** passage E Caribbean Sea
104 H13 **Guadiana** ∽ Portugal/Spain
105 O13 **Guadiana Menor** ∽ S Spain
105 Q8 **Guadiela** ∽ C Spain
105 O14 **Guadix** Andalucía, S Spain
Guad-i-Zirreh see Gowd-e Zereh, Dasht-e
193 T12 **Guafo Fracture Zone** tectonic feature SE Pacific Ocean
63 F18 **Guafo, Isla** island S Chile
42 I6 **Guaimaca** Francisco Morazán, C Honduras
54 J12 **Guainía** off. Comisaría del Guainía. ◈ province E Colombia
54 K12 **Guainía, Río** ∽ Colombia/Venezuela
55 O9 **Guaiquinima, Cerro** elevation SE Venezuela
62 O7 **Guairá** off. Departamento del Guairá. ◈ department S Paraguay
60 G10 **Guaíra** Paraná, S Brazil
60 L7 **Guaíra** São Paulo, S Brazil
Guaire see Gorey
63 F18 **Guaiteca, Isla** island S Chile
44 G6 **Guajaba, Cayo** headland C Cuba
59 D16 **Guajará-Mirim** Rondônia, W Brazil
Guajira see La Guajira
54 H3 **Guajira, Península de la** peninsula N Colombia
42 I6 **Gualaco** Olancho, C Honduras
34 L7 **Gualala** California, W USA
42 E5 **Gualán** Zacapa, C Guatemala
61 C19 **Gualeguay** Entre Ríos, E Argentina
61 D18 **Gualeguaychú** Entre Ríos, E Argentina
61 C18 **Gualeguay, Río** ∽ E Argentina
63 K16 **Gualicho, Salina del** salt lake E Argentina
188 B15 **Guam** ◇ US unincorporated territory W Pacific Ocean
63 F19 **Guamblin, Isla** island Archipiélago de los Chonos, S Chile
61 A22 **Guaminí** Buenos Aires, E Argentina
40 H8 **Guamúchil** Sinaloa, C Mexico
54 H4 **Guana** var. Misión de Guana. Zulia, NW Venezuela
44 C4 **Guanabacoa** La Habana, W Cuba
42 K13 **Guanacaste** off. Provincia de Guanacaste. ◈ province NW Costa Rica
42 K12 **Guanacaste, Cordillera de** ⛰ NW Costa Rica
40 J8 **Guanaceví** Durango, C Mexico
44 A5 **Guanahacabibes, Golfo de** gulf W Cuba
42 K4 **Guanaja, Isla de** island Islas de la Bahía, N Honduras
44 C4 **Guanajay** La Habana, W Cuba
41 N12 **Guanajuato** Guanajuato, C Mexico
40 M12 **Guanajuato** ◈ state C Mexico
54 J6 **Guanare** Portuguesa, N Venezuela
54 K7 **Guanare, Río** ∽ W Venezuela
54 J6 **Guanarito** Portuguesa, NW Venezuela
160 M3 **Guancen Shan** ⛰ C China
62 I9 **Guandacol** La Rioja, W Argentina
44 A5 **Guane** Pinar del Río, W Cuba
161 N14 **Guangdong** var. Guangdong Sheng, Kuang-tung, Kwangtung, Yue. ◈ province S China
Guangdong Sheng see Guangdong
Guanghua see Laohekou
Guangju see Kwangju
160 I13 **Guangnan** var. Liancheng. Yunnan, SW China
161 N8 **Guangshui** prev. Yingshan. Hubei, C China
Guangxi see Guangxi Zhuangzu Zizhiqu
160 K14 **Guangxi Zhuangzu Zizhiqu** var. Guangxi, Gui, Kuang-hsi, Kwangsi, Eng. Kwangsi Chuang Autonomous Region. ◈ autonomous region S China
160 J8 **Guangyuan** var. Kuang-yuan, Kwangyuan. Sichuan, C China
161 N14 **Guangzhou** var. Kuang-chou, Kwangchow, Eng. Canton. Guangdong, S China
59 N19 **Guanhães** Minas Gerais, SE Brazil
160 I12 **Guanling** var. Guanling Buyeizu Miaozu Zizhixian. Guizhou, S China
Guanling Buyeizu Miaozu Zizhixian see Guanling
55 N5 **Guanta** Anzoátegui, NE Venezuela
44 J8 **Guantánamo** Guantánamo, SE Cuba
44 J8 **Guantánamo, Bahía de** Eng. Guantanamo Bay. US military installation SE Cuba
Guantánamo Bay see Guantánamo, Bahía de
Guanxian see Dujiangyan
161 Q6 **Guanyun** Jiangsu, E China
54 C12 **Guapí** Cauca, SW Colombia
43 N13 **Guápiles** Limón, NE Costa Rica
61 I15 **Guaporé** Rio Grande do Sul, S Brazil
59 E17 **Guaporé, Rio** var. Río Iténez. ∽ Bolivia/Brazil see also Iténez, Río
56 B7 **Guaranda** Bolívar, C Ecuador
60 H11 **Guaraniaçu** Paraná, S Brazil
59 O20 **Guarapari** Espírito Santo, SE Brazil
60 I12 **Guarapuava** Paraná, S Brazil
60 J8 **Guararapes** São Paulo, S Brazil
105 S4 **Guara, Sierra de** ⛰ NE Spain
60 N10 **Guaratinguetá** São Paulo, S Brazil
104 I7 **Guarda** Guarda, N Portugal
104 I7 **Guarda** ◈ district N Portugal
Guardak see Gowurdak
104 M3 **Guardo** Castilla-León, N Spain
104 K11 **Guareña** Extremadura, W Spain
60 J11 **Guaricana, Pico** ▲ S Brazil
54 L6 **Guárico** off. Estado Guárico. ◈ state N Venezuela
44 J7 **Guarico, Punta** headland E Cuba
54 L7 **Guárico, Río** ∽ C Venezuela
60 M10 **Guarujá** São Paulo, SE Brazil
61 L22 **Guarulhos** ✕ (São Paulo) São Paulo, S Brazil
43 R17 **Guarumal** Veraguas, S Panama
Guasapa see Guasopa
40 H8 **Guasave** Sinaloa, C Mexico
54 I8 **Guasdualito** Apure, C Venezuela
55 Q7 **Guasipati** Bolívar, E Venezuela
186 I9 **Guasopa** var. Guasapa. Woodlark Island, SE PNG
106 F9 **Guastalla** Emilia-Romagna, C Italy
42 D6 **Guastatoya** var. El Progreso. El Progreso, C Guatemala
42 D5 **Guatemala** off. Republic of Guatemala. ◆ republic Central America
42 A2 **Guatemala** off. Departamento de Guatemala. ◈ department S Guatemala
193 S7 **Guatemala Basin** undersea feature E Pacific Ocean
Guatemala City see Ciudad de Guatemala
45 V14 **Guatuaro Point** headland Trinidad, Trinidad and Tobago
186 B8 **Guavi** ∽ SW PNG
54 G13 **Guaviare** off. Comisaría Guaviare. ◈ province S Colombia
54 J11 **Guaviare, Río** ∽ E Colombia
61 E15 **Guaviravi** Corrientes, NE Argentina
54 G12 **Guayabero, Río** ∽ SW Colombia
45 U6 **Guayama** E Puerto Rico
42 J7 **Guayambre, Río** ∽ S Honduras
Guayanas, Macizo de las see Guiana Highlands
45 V6 **Guayanés, Punta** headland E Puerto Rico
42 J6 **Guayape, Río** ∽ C Honduras
56 B7 **Guayaquil** var. Santiago de Guayaquil. Guayas, SW Ecuador
Guayaquil see Simon Bolivar
56 A8 **Guayaquil, Golfo de** var. Gulf of Guayaquil. gulf SW Ecuador
Guayaquil, Gulf of see Guayaquil, Golfo de
56 A7 **Guayas** ◈ province W Ecuador
62 N7 **Guaycurú, Río** ∽ NE Argentina
40 F6 **Guaymas** Sonora, NW Mexico
45 U5 **Guaynabo** E Puerto Rico
80 H12 **Guba** Benishangul, W Ethiopia
146 H8 **Gubadag** Turkm. Tel'man; prev. Tel'mansk. Daşoguz Welaýaty, N Turkmenistan
125 T1 **Guba Dolgaya** Nenetskiy Avtonomnyy Okrug, NW Russian Federation
125 V13 **Gubakha** Permskaya Oblast', NW Russian Federation
106 I12 **Gubbio** Umbria, C Italy
100 Q13 **Guben** var. Wilhelm-Pieck-Stadt. Brandenburg, E Germany
Guben see Gubin
110 D12 **Gubin** Ger. Guben. Lubuskie, W Poland
126 K8 **Gubkin** Belgorodskaya Oblast', W Russian Federation
Gudara see Ghŭdara
105 S8 **Gúdar, Sierra de** ⛰ E Spain
137 P8 **Gudaut'a** NW Georgia
94 G12 **Gudbrandsdalen** valley S Norway
95 G21 **Gudenå** var. Gudenaa. ∽ C Denmark
Gudenaa see Gudenå
127 P16 **Gudermes** Chechenskaya Respublika, SW Russian Federation
155 J18 **Gūdūr** Andhra Pradesh, E India
146 B13 **Gudurolum** Balkan Welaýaty, W Turkmenistan
94 D13 **Gudvangen** Sogn og Fjordane, S Norway
103 U7 **Guebwiller** Haut-Rhin, NE France
Guéckédou see Guékédou
14 K8 **Guéguen, Lac** ◎ Québec, SE Canada
76 J15 **Guékédou** var. Guéckédou. Guinée-Forestière, S Guinea
41 R16 **Guelatao** Oaxaca, SE Mexico
Guelders see Gelderland
78 G11 **Guélengdeng** Mayo-Kébbi, W Chad
74 L5 **Guelma** var. Gâlma. NE Algeria
74 D8 **Guelmime** var. Goulimime. SW Morocco
14 G15 **Guelph** Ontario, S Canada
102 I7 **Guémené-Penfao** Loire-Atlantique, NW France
102 I7 **Guer** Morbihan, NW France
78 I11 **Guéra** off. Préfecture du Guéra. ◈ prefecture S Chad
102 H8 **Guérande** Loire-Atlantique, NW France
78 K9 **Guéréda** Biltine, E Chad
103 N10 **Guéret** Creuse, C France
Guernica/Guernica y Lumo see Gernika-Lumo
33 Z15 **Guernsey** Wyoming, C USA
97 K25 **Guernsey** island Channel Islands, NW Europe
76 J10 **Guérou** Assaba, S Mauritania
25 R16 **Guerra** Texas, SW USA
41 O15 **Guerrero** ◈ state S Mexico
40 D6 **Guerrero Negro** Baja California Sur, NW Mexico
103 P9 **Gueugnon** Saône-et-Loire, C France
76 M17 **Guéyo** S Ivory Coast
107 L15 **Guglionesi** Molise, C Italy
188 K5 **Guguan** island C Northern Mariana Islands
Guhrau see Góra
Gui see Guangxi Zhuangzu Zizhiqu
Guiana see French Guiana
55 P10 **Guiana Highlands** var. Macizo de las Guayanas. ⛰ N South America
Guiba see Juba
102 I7 **Guichen** Ille-et-Vilaine, NW France
Guichi see Chizhou
61 E18 **Guichón** Paysandú, W Uruguay
77 U12 **Guidan-Roumji** Maradi, S Niger
Guidder see Guider
159 T10 **Guide** var. Heyin. Qinghai, C China
78 F12 **Guider** var. Guidder. Nord, N Cameroon
76 I11 **Guidimaka** ◈ region S Mauritania
77 W12 **Guidimouni** Zinder, S Niger
76 G10 **Guier, Lac de** var. Lac de Guiers. ◎ N Senegal
160 L14 **Guigang** prev. Guixian, Gui Xian. Guangxi Zhuangzu Zizhiqu, S China
76 L16 **Guiglo** W Ivory Coast
54 L5 **Güigüe** Carabobo, N Venezuela
83 M20 **Guijá** Gaza, S Mozambique
42 E7 **Güija, Lago de** ◎ El Salvador/Guatemala
160 L14 **Gui Jiang** var. Gui Shui. ∽ S China
104 K8 **Guijuelo** Castilla-León, N Spain
Guilan see Gīlān
97 N22 **Guildford** SE England, UK
19 R5 **Guildford** Maine, NE USA
19 O7 **Guildhall** Vermont, NE USA
103 R13 **Guilherand** Ardèche, E France
160 L13 **Guilin** var. Kuei-lin, Kweilin. Guangxi Zhuangzu Zizhiqu, S China
12 J6 **Guillaume-Delisle, Lac** ◎ Québec, NE Canada
103 U13 **Guillestre** Hautes-Alpes, SE France
104 H6 **Guimarães** var. Guimaráes. Braga, N Portugal
58 D11 **Guimarães Rosas, Pico** ▲ NW Brazil
23 N3 **Guin** Alabama, S USA
Güina see Wina
76 I14 **Guinea** off. Republic of Guinea, var. Guinée; prev. French Guinea, People's Revolutionary Republic of Guinea. ◆ republic W Africa
64 N13 **Guinea Basin** undersea feature E Atlantic Ocean
76 E12 **Guinea-Bissau** off. Republic of Guinea-Bissau, Fr. Guinée-Bissau, Port. Guiné-Bissau; prev. Portuguese Guinea. ◆ republic W Africa
64 O13 **Guinea, Gulf of** Fr. Golfe de Guinée. gulf E Atlantic Ocean
Guiné-Bissau see Guinea-Bissau
Guinée see Guinea
Guinée-Bissau see Guinea-Bissau
76 K15 **Guinée-Forestière** ◈ state SE Guinea
Guinée, Golfe de see Guinea, Gulf of
76 H13 **Guinée-Maritime** ◈ state W Guinea
44 C4 **Güines** La Habana, W Cuba
102 G5 **Guingamp** Côtes d'Armor, NW France
105 P3 **Guipúzcoa** Basq. Gipuzkoa. ◈ province País Vasco, N Spain
44 C5 **Güira de Melena** La Habana, W Cuba
74 G8 **Guir, Hamada du** desert Algeria/Morocco
55 P5 **Güiria** Sucre, NE Venezuela
Gui Shui see Gui Jiang
104 H2 **Guitiriz** Galicia, NW Spain
77 N17 **Guitri** S Ivory Coast
171 Q5 **Guiuan** Samar, C Philippines
Gui Xian/Guixian see Guigang
160 J12 **Guiyang** var. Kuei-Yang, Kuei-yang, Kueyang, Kweiyang; prev. Kweichu. Guizhou, S China
160 J12 **Guizhou** var. Guizhou Sheng, Kuei-chou, Kweichow, Qian. ◈ province S China
Guizhou Sheng see Guizhou
102 J13 **Gujan-Mestras** Gironde, SW France
154 B10 **Gujarāt** var. Gujerat. ◈ state W India
149 V6 **Gūjar Khān** Punjab, E Pakistan
Gujerat see Gujarāt
149 V7 **Gujrānwāla** Punjab, NE Pakistan
149 V7 **Gujrāt** Punjab, E Pakistan
146 B8 **Gulandag** Rus. Gory Kulandag. ⛰ W Turkmenistan
159 U9 **Gulang** Gansu, C China
183 R6 **Gulargambone** New South Wales, SE Australia
155 G15 **Gulbarga** Karnātaka, C India
118 J8 **Gulbene** Ger. Alt-Schwanenburg. Gulbene, NE Latvia
147 U10 **Gul'cha** Kir. Gülchö. Oshskaya Oblast', SW Kyrgyzstan
Gülchö see Gul'cha
173 T10 **Gulden Draak Seamount** undersea feature E Indian Ocean
136 J16 **Gülek Boğazı** var. Cilician Gates. pass S Turkey
186 D8 **Gulf** ◈ province S PNG
23 O9 **Gulf Breeze** Florida, SE USA
23 V13 **Gulfport** Florida, SE USA
22 M9 **Gulfport** Mississippi, S USA
23 O9 **Gulf Shores** Alabama, S USA
141 T5 **Gulf, The** var. Persian Gulf Ar. Khalīj al 'Arabī, Per. Khalīj-e Fars. gulf SW Asia
183 R7 **Gulgong** New South Wales, SE Australia
160 I11 **Gulin** Sichuan, C China
171 U14 **Gulir** Pulau Kasiui, E Indonesia
Gulistan see Guliston
147 P10 **Guliston** Rus. Gulistan. Sirdaryo Viloyati, E Uzbekistan
163 T6 **Guliya Shan** ▲ NE China
Gulja see Yining
39 S11 **Gulkana** Alaska, USA
11 S17 **Gull Lake** Saskatchewan, S Canada
31 P10 **Gull Lake** ◎ Michigan, N USA
29 T6 **Gull Lake** ◎ Minnesota, N USA
95 L16 **Gullspång** Västra Götaland, S Sweden
136 B15 **Güllük Körfezi** prev. Akbük Limanı. bay W Turkey
152 H5 **Gulmarg** Jammu and Kashmir, NW India
Gulpaigan see Golpāyegān
99 L18 **Gulpen** Limburg, SE Netherlands
Gul'shad see Gul'shat
145 S13 **Gul'shat** var. Gul'shad. Karaganda, E Kazakhstan
81 F17 **Gulu** N Uganda
114 K10 **Gŭlŭbovo** Stara Zagora, C Bulgaria
114 I7 **Gulyantsi** Pleven, N Bulgaria
Gulyaypole see Hulyaypole
Guma see Pishan
Gümai see Darlag
79 K16 **Gumba** Equateur, NW Dem. Rep. Congo
Gumbinnen see Gusev
81 H24 **Gumbiro** Ruvuma, S Tanzania
146 B11 **Gumdag** prev. Kum-Dag. Balkan Welaýaty, W Turkmenistan
77 W12 **Gumel** Jigawa, N Nigeria
105 N5 **Gumiel de Hizán** Castilla-León, N Spain
Gumire see Gumine
153 P16 **Gumla** Jhārkhand, N India
Gumma see Gunma
101 F16 **Gummersbach** Nordrhein-Westfalen, W Germany
77 T13 **Gummi** Zamfara, NW Nigeria
Gumpolds see Humpolec
153 N13 **Gumti** var. Gomati. ∽ N India
Gümülcine/Gümüljina see Komotiní
Gümüşane see Gümüşhane
137 O12 **Gümüşhane** var. Gümüşane, Gumushkhane. Gümüşhane, NE Turkey
137 O12 **Gümüşhane** var. Gümüşane, Gumushkhane. ◈ province NE Turkey
Gumushkhane see Gümüşhane
171 V14 **Gumzai** Pulau Kola, E Indonesia
154 H9 **Guna** Madhya Pradesh, C India
Gunabad see Gonābād
Gunan see Qijiang
Gunbad-i-Qawus see Gonbad-e Kāvūs
183 O9 **Gunbar** New South Wales, SE Australia
183 O9 **Gun Creek** seasonal river New South Wales, SE Australia
183 Q10 **Gundagai** New South Wales, SE Australia
79 K17 **Gundji** Equateur, N Dem. Rep. Congo
155 G20 **Gundlupet** Karnātaka, W India
136 G16 **Gündoğmuş** Antalya, S Turkey
137 O14 **Güney Doğu Toroslar** ⛰ SE Turkey
79 J21 **Gungu** Bandundu, SW Dem. Rep. Congo
127 P17 **Gunib** Respublika Dagestan, SW Russian Federation
112 J11 **Gunja** Vukovar-Srijem, E Croatia
31 P9 **Gun Lake** ◎ Michigan, N USA
165 N12 **Gunma** off. Gunma-ken, var. Gumma. ◈ prefecture Honshū, S Japan
197 P15 **Gunnbjørn Fjeld** var. Gunnbjörns Bjerge. ▲ C Greenland
183 S6 **Gunnedah** New South Wales, SE Australia
173 Y15 **Gunner's Quoin** var. Coin de Mire. island N Mauritius
37 R6 **Gunnison** Colorado, C USA
36 L5 **Gunnison** Utah, W USA
37 P5 **Gunnison River** ∽ Colorado, C USA
21 X2 **Gunpowder River** ∽ Maryland, NE USA
Güns see Kőszeg
Gunsan see Kunsan
109 S4 **Gunskirchen** Oberösterreich, N Austria
Gunt see Ghund
155 H17 **Guntakal** Andhra Pradesh, C India
23 Q2 **Guntersville** Alabama, S USA
23 Q2 **Guntersville Lake** ⊡ Alabama, S USA
109 X4 **Guntramsdorf** Niederösterreich, E Austria
155 J16 **Guntūr** var. Guntur. Andhra Pradesh, SE India
168 H10 **Gunungsitoli** Pulau Nias, W Indonesia
155 M14 **Gunupur** Orissa, E India
101 J23 **Günz** ∽ S Germany
Gunzan see Kunsan
101 J22 **Günzburg** Bayern, S Germany
101 K21 **Gunzenhausen** Bayern, S Germany
Guovdageaidu see Kautokeino
161 P7 **Guoyang** Anhui, E China
116 G11 **Gurahonţ** Hung. Honctő. Arad, W Romania
Gurahumora see Gura Humorului

116 K9 **Gura Humorului** *Ger.* Gurahumora. Suceava, NE Romania
158 K4 **Gurbantünggüt Shamo** *desert* W China
152 H7 **Gurdāspur** Punjab, N India
27 T13 **Gurdon** Arkansas, C USA
Gurdzhaani *see* Gurjaani
Gurgan *see* Gorgān
152 I10 **Gurgaon** Haryāna, N India
59 M15 **Gurguéia, Rio** ≈ NE Brazil
55 Q7 **Guri, Embalse de** ⊞ E Venezuela
137 V10 **Gurjaani** *Rus.* Gurdzhaani. E Georgia
109 T8 **Gurk** Kärnten, S Austria
109 T9 **Gurk** *Slvn.* Krka. ≈ S Austria
Gurkfeld *see* Krško
114 K9 **Gurkovo** *prev.* Kolupchii. Stara Zagora, C Bulgaria
109 S9 **Gurktaler Alpen** ▲ S Austria
146 H8 **Gurlan** *Rus.* Gurlen. Xorazm Viloyati, W Uzbekistan
Gurlen *see* Gurlan
83 M16 **Guro** Manica, C Mozambique
136 M14 **Gürün** Sivas, C Turkey
59 K16 **Gurupi** Tocantins, C Brazil
58 L12 **Gurupi, Rio** ≈ NE Brazil
152 E14 **Guru Sikhar** ▲ NW India
Gur'yev/Gur'yevskaya Oblast' *see* Atyrau
77 U13 **Gusau** Zamfara, NW Nigeria
126 C3 **Gusev** *Ger.* Gumbinnen. Kaliningradskaya Oblast', W Russian Federation
146 J17 **Gushgy** *Rus.* Kushka. ≈ S Turkmenistan
Gushgy *see* Serhetabat
Gushiago *see* Gushiegu
77 Q14 **Gushiegu** *var.* Gushiago. NE Ghana
165 S17 **Gushikawa** Okinawa, Okinawa, SW Japan
113 L16 **Gusinje** Montenegro, SW Serbia and Montenegro (Yugo.)
126 M4 **Gus'-Khrustal'nyy** Vladimirskaya Oblast', W Russian Federation
107 B19 **Guspini** Sardegna, Italy, C Mediterranean Sea
109 X8 **Güssing** Burgenland, SE Austria
109 V6 **Gusswerk** Steiermark, E Austria
92 O2 **Gustav Adolf Land** *physical region* NE Svalbard
195 X5 **Gustav Bull Mountains** ▲ Antarctica
39 W13 **Gustavus** Alaska, USA
92 O1 **Gustav V Land** *physical region* NE Svalbard
35 P9 **Gustine** California,W USA
25 R8 **Gustine** Texas, SW USA
100 M9 **Güstrow** Mecklenburg-Vorpommern, NE Germany
95 N18 **Gusum** Östergötland, S Sweden
Guta/Gúta *see* Kolárovo
Gutenstein *see* Ravne na Koroškem
101 G14 **Gütersloh** Nordrhein-Westfalen, W Germany
27 N10 **Guthrie** Oklahoma, C USA
25 P5 **Guthrie** Texas, SW USA
29 U14 **Guthrie Center** Iowa, C USA
41 Q13 **Gutiérrez Zamora** Veracruz-Llave, E Mexico
Gutta *see* Kolárovo
29 Y12 **Guttenberg** Iowa, C USA
Guttentag *see* Dobrodzień
Guttstadt *see* Dobre Miasto
162 G8 **Guulin** Govĭ-Altay, C Mongolia
153 V12 **Guwāhāti** *prev.* Gauhāti. Assam, NE India
139 R3 **Guwēr** *var.* Al Kuwayr, Al Quwayr, Quwair. N Iraq
146 A10 **Guwlumaýak** *Rus.* Kuuli-Mayak. Balkan Welaýaty, NW Turkmenistan
55 R9 **Guyana** *off.* Cooperative Republic of Guyana; *prev.* British Guiana. ◆ *republic* N South America
21 P5 **Guyandotte River** ≈ West Virginia, NE USA
Guyane *see* French Guiana
Guyi *see* Sanjiang
26 H8 **Guymon** Oklahoma, C USA
146 K12 **Guynuk** Lebap Welaýaty, NE Turkmenistan
Guyong *see* Jiangle
21 O9 **Guyot, Mount** ▲ North Carolina/Tennessee, SE USA
183 U5 **Guyra** New South Wales, SE Australia
159 W10 **Guyuan** Ningxia, N China
Guzar *see* G'uzor
147 N13 **G'uzor** *Rus.* Guzar. Qashqadaryo Viloyati, S Uzbekistan
121 P2 **Güzelyurt** *Gk.* Mórfou, Morphou. W Cyprus
121 N2 **Güzelyurt Körfezi** *var.* Morfou Bay, Morphou Bay, *Gk.* Kólpos Mórfou. *bay* W Cyprus
Guzhou *see* Rongjiang
40 I3 **Guzmán** Chihuahua, N Mexico
119 B14 **Gvardeysk** *Ger.* Tapaiu. Kaliningradskaya Oblast', W Russian Federation
Gvardeyskoye *see* Hvardiys'ke
183 R5 **Gwabegar** New South Wales, SE Australia
148 J16 **Gwādar** *var.* Gwadur. Baluchistān, SW Pakistan
148 J16 **Gwādar East Bay** *bay* SW Pakistan
148 J16 **Gwādar West Bay** *bay* SW Pakistan
Gwadur *see* Gwādar
83 J17 **Gwai** Matabeleland North, W Zimbabwe
154 I7 **Gwalior** Madhya Pradesh, C India
83 J18 **Gwanda** Matabeleland South, SW Zimbabwe
79 N15 **Gwane** Orientale, N Dem. Rep. Congo
83 I17 **Gwayi** ≈ W Zimbabwe
110 G8 **Gwda** *var.* Głda, *Ger.* Küddow. ≈ NW Poland
97 C14 **Gweebarra Bay** *Ir.* Béal an Bheara. *inlet* W Ireland
97 D14 **Gweedore** *Ir.* Gaoth Dobhair. NW Ireland
Gwelo *see* Gweru
97 K21 **Gwent** *cultural region* S Wales, UK
83 K17 **Gweru** *prev.* Gwelo. Midlands, C Zimbabwe
29 Q7 **Gwinner** North Dakota, N USA
77 Y13 **Gwoza** Borno, NE Nigeria
Gwy *see* Wye
183 R4 **Gwydir River** ≈ New South Wales, SE Australia
97 I19 **Gwynedd** *var.* Gwyneth. *cultural region* NW Wales, UK
Gwyneth *see* Gwynedd
159 O16 **Gyaca** *var.* Ngarrab. Xizang Zizhiqu, W China
Gya'gya *see* Saga
Gyaijêpozhanggê *see* Zhidoi
Gyaisi *see* Jiulong
115 M22 **Gyalí** *var.* Yialí. *island* Dodekánisos, Greece, Aegean Sea
Gyamotang *see* Dêngqên
Gyandzha *see* Gäncä
Gyangkar *see* Dinggyê
158 M16 **Gyangzê** Xizang Zizhiqu, W China
158 L14 **Gyaring Co** ◎ W China
159 Q12 **Gyaring Hu** ◎ C China
115 I20 **Gyáros** *var.* Yioúra. *island* Kykládes, Greece, Aegean Sea
122 J7 **Gyda** Yamalo-Nenetskiy Avtonomnyy Okrug, N Russian Federation
122 J7 **Gydanskiy Poluostrov** *Eng.* Gyda Peninsula. *peninsula* N Russian Federation
Gyda Peninsula *see* Gydanskiy Poluostrov
Gyêgu *see* Yushu
Gyéres *see* Câmpia Turzii
Gyergyószentmiklós *see* Gheorgheni
Gyergyótölgyes *see* Tulgheş
Gyertyámos *see* Cărpiniş
Gyeva *see* Detva
Gyigang *see* Zayü
Gyixong *see* Gonggar
95 I23 **Gyldenløveshøj** *hill range* C Denmark
181 Z10 **Gympie** Queensland, E Australia
166 L7 **Gyobingauk** Pegu, SW Burma
111 M23 **Gyomaendrőd** Békés, SE Hungary
Gyömbér *see* Ďumbier
111 L22 **Gyöngyös** Heves, NE Hungary
111 H22 **Győr** *Ger.* Raab; *Lat.* Arrabona. Győr-Moson-Sopron, NW Hungary
111 G22 **Győr-Moson-Sopron** *off.* Győr-Moson-Sopron Megye. ◆ *county* NW Hungary
11 X15 **Gypsumville** Manitoba, S Canada
12 M4 **Gyrfalcon Islands** *island group* Nunavut, NE Canada
95 N14 **Gysinge** Gävleborg, C Sweden
115 F22 **Gýtheio** *var.* Githio; *prev.* Yíthion. Pelopónnisos, S Greece
146 L13 **Gyuichbirleshik** Lebap Welaýaty, E Turkmenistan
111 N24 **Gyula** *Rom.* Jula. Békés, SE Hungary
Gyulafehérvár *see* Alba Iulia
Gyulovo *see* Roza
137 T11 **Gyumri** *var.* Giumri, *Rus.* Kumayri; *prev.* Aleksandropol', Leninakan. W Armenia
146 D13 **Gyunuzyndag, Gora** ▲ W Turkmenistan
Gyzylarbat *see* Serdar
146 J15 **Gyzylbaýdak** *Rus.* Krasnoye Znamya. Mary Welaýaty, S Turkmenistan
Gyzyletrek *see* Etrek
146 D10 **Gyzylgaýa** *Rus.* Kizyl-Kaya. Balkan Welaýaty, NW Turkmenistan
146 K12 **Gyzylsuw** *Rus.* Kizyl-Su. Balkan Welaýaty, W Turkmenistan
126 J3 **Gzhatsk** Smolenskaya Oblast', W Russian Federation

H

159 T12 **Ha** W Bhutan
Haabai *see* Ha'apai Group
99 H17 **Haacht** Vlaams Brabant, C Belgium
109 T4 **Haag** Niederösterreich, NE Austria
194 L8 **Haag Nunataks** ▲ Antarctica
92 N2 **Haakon VII Land** *physical region* NW Svalbard
98 O11 **Haaksbergen** Overijssel, E Netherlands
99 E14 **Haamstede** Zeeland, SW Netherlands
193 Y15 **Ha'ano** *island* Ha'apai Group, C Tonga
193 Y15 **Ha'apai Group** *var.* Haabai. *island group* C Tonga
93 L15 **Haapajärvi** Oulu, C Finland
93 L17 **Haapamäki** Länsi-Suomi, W Finland
93 L15 **Haapavesi** Oulu, C Finland
191 N7 **Haapiti** Moorea, W French Polynesia
118 F4 **Haapsalu** *Ger.* Hapsal. Läänemaa, W Estonia
Ha'Arava *see* 'Arabah, Wādī al
95 G24 **Haarby** *var.* Hårby. Fyn, C Denmark
98 H10 **Haarlem** *prev.* Harlem. Noord-Holland, W Netherlands
185 D19 **Haast** West Coast, South Island, NZ
185 C20 **Haast** ≈ South Island, NZ
185 D20 **Haast Pass** *pass* South Island, NZ
193 W16 **Ha'atua** 'Eau, E Tonga
149 P15 **Hab** ≈ SW Pakistan
141 W7 **Haba** *var.* Al Haba. Dubayy, NE UAE
158 K2 **Habahe** *var.* Kaba. Xinjiang Uygur Zizhiqu, NW China
141 U13 **Ḩabarūt** *var.* Habrut. SW Oman
81 J18 **Habaswein** North Eastern, NE Kenya
99 L24 **Habay-la-Neuve** Luxembourg, SE Belgium
139 S8 **Ḩabbānīyah, Buḩayrat** ◎ C Iraq
Habelschwerdt *see* Bystrzyca Kłodzka
153 V14 **Habiganj** Chittagong, NE Bangladesh
163 Q12 **Habirag** Nei Mongol Zizhiqu, N China
95 L19 **Habo** Västra Götaland, S Sweden
123 V14 **Habomai Islands** *island group* Kuril'skiye Ostrova, SE Russian Federation
165 S2 **Haboro** Hokkaidō, NE Japan
153 S16 **Habra** West Bengal, NE India
Habrut *see* Ḩabarūt
143 P17 **Ḩabshān** Abū Ẓaby, C UAE
54 E14 **Hacha** Putumayo, S Colombia
165 X13 **Hachijō** Tōkyō, Hachijō-jima, SE Japan
165 X13 **Hachijō-jima** *var.* Hatizyô Zima. *island* Izu-shotō, SE Japan
164 L12 **Hachiman** Gifu, Honshū, SW Japan
165 P7 **Hachimori** Akita, Honshū, C Japan
165 R7 **Hachinohe** Aomori, Honshū, C Japan
93 G17 **Hackås** Jämtland, C Sweden
18 K14 **Hackensack** New Jersey, NE USA
Hadama *see* Nazrēt
141 W13 **Ḩadbaram** S Oman
139 U13 **Ḩaddānīyah** *well* S Iraq
96 K12 **Haddington** SE Scotland, UK
141 Z8 **Ḩadd, Ra's al** *headland* NE Oman
Haded *see* Xadeed
77 W12 **Hadejia** Jigawa, N Nigeria
77 W12 **Hadejia** ≈ N Nigeria
138 F9 **Ḩadera** *var.* Khadera. Haifa, C Israel
Hadersleben *see* Haderslev
95 G24 **Haderslev** *Ger.* Hadersleben. Sønderjylland, SW Denmark
151 J21 **Hadhdhunmathi Atoll** *var.* Haddummati Atoll, Laamu Atoll. *atoll* S Maldives
Hadhramaut *see* Ḩaḑramawt
141 W17 **Hadīboh** Suquṭrā, SE Yemen
158 K9 **Hadilik** Xinjiang Uygur Zizhiqu, W China
136 H16 **Hadım** Konya, S Turkey
140 K7 **Hadīyah** Al Madīnah, W Saudi Arabia
8 L5 **Hadley Bay** *bay* Victoria Island, Nunavut, N Canada
167 S6 **Ha Đông** *var.* Hadong. Ha Tây, N Vietnam
141 R15 **Ḩaḑramawt** *Eng.* Hadhramaut. ▲ S Yemen
Hadria *see* Adria
Hadrianopolis *see* Edirne
Hadria Picena *see* Apricena
95 G22 **Hadsten** Århus, C Denmark
95 G21 **Hadsund** Nordjylland, N Denmark
117 S4 **Hadyach** *Rus.* Gadyach. Poltavs'ka Oblast', NE Ukraine
112 I13 **Hadžići** Federacija Bosna I Hercegovina, SE Bosnia and Herzegovina
163 W14 **Haeju** S North Korea
Haerbin/Haerhpin/ Ha-erh-pin *see* Harbin
141 P5 **Ḩafar al Bāṭin** Ash Sharqīyah, N Saudi Arabia
11 T15 **Hafford** Saskatchewan, S Canada
136 M13 **Hafik** Sivas, N Turkey
149 V8 **Hāfizābād** Punjab, E Pakistan
92 H4 **Hafnarfjördhur** Reykjanes, W Iceland
Hafnia *see* København, Denmark
Hafnia *see* Denmark
Hafren *see* Severn
Hafun *see* Xaafuun
Hafun, Ras *see* Xaafuun, Raas
80 G10 **Hag 'Abdullah** Sinnar, E Sudan
81 K18 **Hagadera** North Eastern, E Kenya
138 G8 **HaGalil** *Eng.* Galilee. ▲ N Israel
14 G10 **Hagar** Ontario, S Canada
155 G18 **Hagari** *var.* Vedāvati. ≈ W India
188 B16 **Hagåtña** *var.* Agana, Agaña. ○ (Guam) NW Guam
100 M13 **Hagelberg** *hill* NE Germany
39 N14 **Hagemeister Island** *island* Alaska, USA
101 F15 **Hagen** Nordrhein-Westfalen, W Germany
100 K10 **Hagenow** Mecklenburg-Vorpommern, N Germany
10 K15 **Hagensborg** British Columbia, SW Canada
80 I13 **Hägere Hiywet** *var.* Agere Hiywet, Ambo. Oromo, C Ethiopia
33 O15 **Hagerman** Idaho, NW USA
37 U14 **Hagerman** New Mexico, SW USA
21 V2 **Hagerstown** Maryland, NE USA
14 G16 **Hagersville** Ontario, S Canada
102 J15 **Hagetmau** Landes, SW France
95 K14 **Hagfors** Värmland, C Sweden
93 G16 **Häggenås** Jämtland, C Sweden
164 E12 **Hagi** Yamaguchi, Honshū, SW Japan
167 S5 **Ha Giang** Ha Giang, N Vietnam
Hagios Evstrátios *see* Ágios Efstrátios
HaGolan *see* Golan Heights
103 T4 **Hagondange** Moselle, NE France
97 B18 **Hag's Head** *Ir.* Ceann Caillí. *headland* W Ireland
102 I3 **Hague, Cap de la** *headland* N France
103 V5 **Haguenau** Bas-Rhin, NE France
165 X16 **Hahajima-rettō** *island group* SE Japan
15 R8 **Ha! Ha!, Lac** ◎ Québec, SE Canada
172 H13 **Hahaya** ✕ (Moroni) Grande Comore, NW Comoros
22 K9 **Hahnville** Louisiana, S USA
83 E22 **Haib** Karas, S Namibia
Haibak *see* Āybak
149 N15 **Haibo** ≈ SW Pakistan
Haibowan *see* Wuhai
163 U12 **Haicheng** Liaoning, NE China
Haida *see* Nový Bor
Haidarabad *see* Hyderābād
Haidenschaft *see* Ajdovščina
167 T6 **Hai Dương** Hai Hưng, N Vietnam
138 F9 **Haifa** ◆ *district* NW Israel
Haifa *see* Ḩefa
Haifa, Bay of *see* Ḩefa, Mifraẓ
161 P14 **Haifeng** Guangdong, S China
Haifong *see* Hai Phong
161 P3 **Hai He** ≈ E China
Haikang *see* Leizhou
160 L17 **Haikou** *var.* Hai-k'ou, Hoihow, *Fr.* Hoï-Hao. Hainan, S China
140 M6 **Ḩā'il** Ḩā'il, NW Saudi Arabia
141 N5 **Ḩā'il** *off.* Minṭaqah Ḩā'il. ◆ *province* N Saudi Arabia
Hai-la-erh *see* Hailar
163 S6 **Hailar** *var.* Hai-la-erh; *prev.* Hulun. Nei Mongol Zizhiqu, N China
163 S6 **Hailar He** ≈ NE China
33 P14 **Hailey** Idaho, NW USA
14 H9 **Haileybury** Ontario, S Canada
163 X9 **Hailin** Heilongjiang, NE China
Ḩā'il, Minṭaqah *see* Ḩā'il
Hailong *see* Meihekou
93 K14 **Hailuoto** *Swe.* Karlö. *island* W Finland
Haima *see* Haymā'
Haimen *see* Taizhou
160 M17 **Hainan** *var.* Hainan Sheng, Qiong. ◆ *province* S China
160 K17 **Hainan Dao** *island* S China
Hainan Sheng *see* Hainan
Hainan Strait *see* Qiongzhou Haixia
Hainasch *see* Ainaži
Hainau *see* Chojnów
99 E20 **Hainaut** ◆ *province* SW Belgium
Hainburg *see* Hainburg an der Donau
109 Z4 **Hainburg an der Donau** *var.* Hainburg. Niederösterreich, NE Austria
39 W12 **Haines** Alaska, USA
32 L12 **Haines** Oregon, NW USA
23 W12 **Haines City** Florida, SE USA
10 H8 **Haines Junction** Yukon Territory, W Canada
109 W4 **Hainfeld** Niederösterreich, NE Austria
101 N16 **Hainichen** Sachsen, E Germany
167 T6 **Hai Phong** *var.* Haifong, Haiphong. N Vietnam
161 S12 **Haitan Dao** *island* SE China
44 K8 **Haiti** *off.* Republic of Haiti. ◆ *republic* C West Indies
35 T11 **Haiwee Reservoir** ⊞ California, W USA
80 I7 **Haiya** Red Sea, NE Sudan
159 T10 **Haiyan** *var.* Sanjiaocheng. Qinghai, W China
160 M13 **Haiyang Shan** ▲ S China
159 V10 **Haiyuan** Ningxia, N China
Hajda *see* Nový Bor
111 M22 **Hajdú-Bihar** *off.* Hajdú-Bihar Megye. ◆ *county* E Hungary
111 N22 **Hajdúböszörmény** Hajdú-Bihar, E Hungary
111 N22 **Hajdúhadház** Hajdú-Bihar, E Hungary
111 N21 **Hajdúnánás** Hajdú-Bihar, E Hungary
111 N22 **Hajdúszoboszló** Hajdú-Bihar, E Hungary
142 I3 **Ḩājī Ebrāhīm, Kūh-e** ▲ Iran/Iraq
165 O9 **Hajiki-zaki** *headland* Sado, C Japan
Hajîne *see* Abū Ḩardān
153 P13 **Hājīpur** Bihār, N India
141 N14 **Ḩajjah** W Yemen
139 U11 **Ḩajjama** S Iraq
143 R12 **Ḩājjīābād** Hormozgān, C Iran
139 U14 **Ḩājj, Thaqb al** *well* S Iraq
113 L16 **Hajla** ▲ SW Serbia and Montenegro (Yugo.)
110 P10 **Hajnówka** *Ger.* Hermhausen. Podlaskie, NE Poland
166 K4 **Haka** Chin State, W Burma
Hakapehi *see* Punaauia
Hakâri *see* Hakkâri
137 T16 **Hakkâri** *var.* Çölemerik, Hakâri. Hakkâri, SE Turkey
137 T16 **Hakkâri** *var.* Hakkari. ◆ *province* SE Turkey
92 J12 **Hakkas** Norrbotten, N Sweden
164 J14 **Hakken-zan** ▲ Honshū, SW Japan
165 R7 **Hakkōda-san** ▲ Honshū, C Japan
165 T2 **Hako-dake** ▲ Hokkaidō, NE Japan
165 R5 **Hakodate** Hokkaidō, NE Japan
164 L11 **Hakui** Ishikawa, Honshū, SW Japan
190 B16 **Hakupu** SE Niue
164 L12 **Haku-san** ▲ Honshū, SW Japan
Hal *see* Halle
149 Q15 **Hāla** Sind, SE Pakistan
138 I3 **Ḩalab** *Eng.* Aleppo, *Fr.* Alep; *anc.* Beroea. Ḩalab, NW Syria
138 I3 **Ḩalab** *off.* Muḩāfaẓat Ḩalab, *var.* Aleppo, Halab. ◆ *governorate* NW Syria
138 I3 **Ḩalab** ✕ Ḩalab, NW Syria
141 O8 **Halabān** *var.* Halībān. Ar Riyāḑ, C Saudi Arabia
139 V4 **Ḩalabja** NE Iraq
146 L13 **Halaç** *Rus.* Khalach. Lebap Welaýaty, E Turkmenistan
190 A16 **Halagigie Point** *headland* W Niue
75 Z11 **Halaib** SE Egypt
190 G12 **Halalo** Île Uvea, N Wallis and Futuna
Halandri *see* Chalándri
141 X13 **Ḩalāniyāt, Juzur al** *var.* Jazā'ir Bin Ghalfān, *Eng.* Kuria Muria Islands. *island group* S Oman
141 W13 **Ḩalāniyāt, Khalīj al** *Eng.* Kuria Muria Bay. *bay* S Oman
Halas *see* Kiskunhalas
38 G11 **Hālawa** *var.* Halawa. Hawai'i, USA, C Pacific Ocean
38 F9 **Hālawa, Cape** *var.* Cape Halawa *headland* Moloka'i, Hawai'i, USA, C Pacific Ocean
162 H6 **Halban** Hövsgöl, N Mongolia
101 K14 **Halberstadt** Sachsen-Anhalt, C Germany
184 M12 **Halcombe** Manawatu-Wanganui, North Island, NZ
95 I16 **Halden** *prev.* Fredrikshald. Østfold, S Norway
100 L13 **Haldensleben** Sachsen-Anhalt, C Germany
Háldi *see* Halti
153 S17 **Haldia** West Bengal, NE India
152 K10 **Haldwāni** Uttaranchal, N India
38 F10 **Haleakalā** *var.* Haleakala *crater* Maui, Hawai'i, USA, C Pacific Ocean
25 N4 **Hale Center** Texas, SW USA
99 J18 **Halen** Limburg, NE Belgium
23 O2 **Haleyville** Alabama, S USA
77 O17 **Half Assini** SW Ghana
35 R8 **Half Dome** ▲ California, W USA
185 C25 **Halfmoon Bay** *var.* Oban. Stewart Island, Southland, NZ
182 E5 **Half Moon Lake** *salt lake* South Australia
163 R7 **Halhgol** Dornod, E Mongolia
Haliacmon *see* Aliákmonas
Halibān *see* Ḩalabān
14 I13 **Haliburton** Ontario, SE Canada
14 I12 **Haliburton Highlands** *var.* Madawaska Highlands. *hill range* Ontario, SE Canada
13 Q15 **Halifax** Nova Scotia, SE Canada
97 L17 **Halifax** N England, UK
21 W8 **Halifax** North Carolina, SE USA
21 U7 **Halifax** Virginia, NE USA
13 Q15 **Halifax** ✕ Nova Scotia, SE Canada
143 T13 **Halīl Rūd** *seasonal river* SE Iran
138 I6 **Ḩalīmah** ▲ Lebanon/Syria
162 G8 **Haliun** Govĭ-Altay, W Mongolia
118 I3 **Haljala** *Ger.* Halljal. Lääne-Virumaa, N Estonia
39 Q4 **Halkett, Cape** *headland* Alaska, USA
Halkida *see* Chalkída
96 J6 **Halkirk** N Scotland, UK
15 X7 **Hall** ≈ Québec, SE Canada
Hall *see* Schwäbisch Hall
93 H15 **Hälla** Västerbotten, N Sweden
96 J6 **Halladale** ≈ N Scotland, UK
95 J21 **Halland** ◆ *county* S Sweden
23 Z15 **Hallandale** Florida, SE USA
95 K22 **Hallandsås** *physical region* S Sweden
9 P6 **Hall Beach** Nunavut, N Canada
99 G19 **Halle** *Fr.* Hal. Vlaams Brabant, C Belgium
101 M15 **Halle** *var.* Halle an der Saale. Sachsen-Anhalt, C Germany
Halle an der Saale *see* Halle
35 W3 **Halleck** Nevada, W USA
95 L15 **Hällefors** Örebro, C Sweden
95 N16 **Hälleforsnäs** Södermanland, C Sweden
109 Q6 **Hallein** Salzburg, N Austria
101 L15 **Halle-Neustadt** Sachsen-Anhalt, C Germany
25 U12 **Hallettsville** Texas, SW USA
195 N4 **Halley** *UK research station* Antarctica
28 L4 **Halliday** North Dakota, N USA
37 S2 **Halligan Reservoir** ⊞ Colorado, C USA
100 G7 **Halligen** *island group* N Germany
94 G13 **Hallingdal** *valley* S Norway
38 J12 **Hall Island** *island* Alaska, USA
Hall Island *see* Maiana
189 P15 **Hall Islands** *island group* C Micronesia
118 H6 **Halliste** ≈ S Estonia
Halljal *see* Haljala
93 I15 **Hällnäs** Västerbotten, N Sweden
29 R2 **Hallock** Minnesota, N USA
9 S6 **Hall Peninsula** *peninsula* Baffin Island, Nunavut, NE Canada
20 F9 **Halls** Tennessee, S USA
95 M16 **Hallsberg** Örebro, C Sweden
181 N5 **Halls Creek** Western Australia
182 L12 **Halls Gap** Victoria, SE Australia
95 N15 **Hallstahammar** Västmanland, C Sweden
109 R6 **Hallstatt** Salzburg, W Austria
109 R6 **Hallstatter See** ◎ C Austria
95 P14 **Hallstavik** Stockholm, C Sweden
24 X7 **Hallsville** Texas, SW USA
103 P1 **Halluin** Nord, N France
Halmahera, Laut *see* Halmahera Sea
171 R11 **Halmahera, Pulau** *prev.* Djailolo, Gilolo, Jailolo. *island* E Indonesia
171 S12 **Halmahera Sea** *Ind.* Laut Halmahera. *sea* E Indonesia
95 J21 **Halmstad** Halland, S Sweden
119 N15 **Halowchyn** *Rus.* Golovchin. Mahilyowskaya Voblasts', E Belarus
95 H20 **Hals** Nordjylland, N Denmark
94 F8 **Halsa** Møre og Romsdal, S Norway
119 I15 **Hal'shany** *Rus.* Gol'shany. Hrodzyenskaya Voblasts', W Belarus
Hälsingborg *see* Helsingborg
29 R5 **Halstad** Minnesota, N USA
27 N6 **Halstead** Kansas, C USA
99 G15 **Halsteren** Noord-Brabant, S Netherlands
93 L16 **Halsua** Länsi-Suomi, W Finland
101 E14 **Haltern** Nordrhein-Westfalen, W Germany
92 J9 **Halti** *var.* Haltiatunturi, *Lapp.* Háldi. ▲ Finland/Norway
Haltiatunturi *see* Halti
116 J6 **Halych** Ivano-Frankivs'ka Oblast', W Ukraine
Halycus *see* Platani
103 P3 **Ham** Somme, N France
Hama *see* Ḩamāh
164 F12 **Hamada** Shimane, Honshū, SW Japan
142 L6 **Hamadān** *anc.* Ecbatana. Hamadān, W Iran
142 L6 **Hamadān** *off.* Ostān-e Hamadān. ◆ *province* W Iran
138 I5 **Ḩamāh** *var.* Hama; *anc.* Epiphania, *Bibl.* Hamath. Ḩamāh, W Syria
138 I5 **Ḩamāh** *off.* Muḩāfaẓat Ḩamāh, *var.* Hama. ◆ *governorate* C Syria
165 S3 **Hamamasu** Hokkaidō, NE Japan
164 L14 **Hamamatsu** *var.* Hamamatu. Shizuoka, Honshū, S Japan
Hamamatu *see* Hamamatsu
165 W14 **Hamanaka** Hokkaidō, NE Japan
164 L14 **Hamana-ko** ◎ Honshū, S Japan
94 I13 **Hamar** *prev.* Storhammer. Hedmark, S Norway
141 U10 **Ḩamārir al Kidan, Qalamat** *well* E Saudi Arabia
164 I12 **Hamasaka** Hyōgo, Honshū, SW Japan
Hamath *see* Ḩamāh
165 T1 **Hamatonbetsu** Hokkaidō, NE Japan
155 K26 **Hambantota** Southern Province, SE Sri Lanka
Hambourg *see* Hamburg
100 J9 **Hamburg** Hamburg, N Germany
27 V14 **Hamburg** Arkansas, C USA
29 S16 **Hamburg** Iowa, C USA
18 D10 **Hamburg** New York, NE USA
100 I10 **Hamburg** *Fr.* Hambourg. ◆ *state* N Germany
148 K5 **Hamdam Āb, Dasht-e** *Pash.* Dasht-i Hamdamab. ▲ W Afghanistan
Hamdamab, Dasht-i *see* Hamdam Āb, Dasht-e
18 M13 **Hamden** Connecticut, NE USA
140 K6 **Ḩamḑ, Wādī al** *dry watercourse* W Saudi Arabia
93 K18 **Hämeenkyrö** Länsi-Suomi, W Finland
93 L19 **Hämeenlinna** *Swe.* Tavastehus. Etelä-Suomi, S Finland
HaMelaḩ, Yam *see* Dead Sea
Hamelin *see* Hameln
100 I13 **Hameln** *Eng.* Hamelin. Niedersachsen, N Germany
180 I8 **Hamersley Range** ▲ Western Australia
163 Y12 **Hamgyŏng-sanmaek** ▲ N North Korea
163 X13 **Hamhŭng** C North Korea
159 O6 **Hami** *var.* Ha-mi, *Uigh.* Kumul, Qomul. Xinjiang Uygur Zizhiqu, NW China
139 X10 **Ḩāmid Amīn** E Iraq
141 W11 **Hamīdān, Khawr** *oasis* SE Saudi Arabia
138 H5 **Ḩamīdīyah** *var.* Hamīdīyé. Ṭarṭūs, W Syria
114 L12 **Hamidiye** Edirne, NW Turkey
Hamīdīyé *see* Ḩamīdīyah
182 L12 **Hamilton** Victoria, SE Australia
64 B12 **Hamilton** ○ (Bermuda) C Bermuda
14 G16 **Hamilton** Ontario, S Canada
184 M7 **Hamilton** Waikato, North Island, NZ
96 I12 **Hamilton** S Scotland, UK
23 N3 **Hamilton** Alabama, S USA
38 M10 **Hamilton** Alaska, USA
30 J13 **Hamilton** Illinois, N USA
27 S3 **Hamilton** Missouri, C USA
33 P10 **Hamilton** Montana, NW USA
25 S8 **Hamilton** Texas, SW USA
14 G16 **Hamilton** ✕ Ontario, SE Canada
64 I6 **Hamilton Bank** *undersea feature* SE Labrador Sea
182 E1 **Hamilton Creek** *seasonal river* South Australia
13 R8 **Hamilton Inlet** *inlet* Newfoundland and Labrador, E Canada
27 T12 **Hamilton, Lake** ⊞ Arkansas, C USA
35 W6 **Hamilton, Mount** ▲ Nevada, W USA
75 S8 **Ḩamīm, Wādī al** ≈ NE Libya
93 N19 **Hamina** *Swe.* Fredrikshamn. Etelä-Suomi, S Finland
11 W16 **Hamiota** Manitoba, S Canada
152 L13 **Hamīrpur** Uttar Pradesh, N India
Hamis Musait *see* Khamīs Mushayt
21 T11 **Hamlet** North Carolina, SE USA
25 P6 **Hamlin** Texas, SW USA
21 P5 **Hamlin** West Virginia, NE USA
31 O7 **Hamlin Lake** ◎ Michigan, N USA

◆ Country • Country Capital ◇ Dependent Territory ○ Dependent Territory Capital ◆ Administrative Region ✕ International Airport ▲ Mountain ▲ Mountain Range ⊼ Volcano ≈ River ◎ Lake ⊞ Reservoir

101 F14 **Hamm** *var.* Hamm in Westfalen. Nordrhein-Westfalen, W Germany
Ḩammāmāt, Khalīj al *see* Hammamet, Golfe de
75 N5 **Hammamet, Golfe de** *Ar.* Khalīj al Ḩammāmāt. *gulf* NE Tunisia
139 R3 **Ḩammān al 'Alīl** N Iraq
139 X12 **Ḩammār, Hawr al** ◎ SE Iraq
93 J20 **Hammarland** Åland, SW Finland
93 H16 **Hammarstrand** Jämtland, C Sweden
93 O17 **Hammaslahti** Itä-Suomi, E Finland
99 F17 **Hamme** Oost-Vlaanderen, NW Belgium
100 H10 **Hamme** ≈ NW Germany
95 G22 **Hammel** Århus, C Denmark
101 I18 **Hammelburg** Bayern, C Germany
99 H18 **Hamme-Mille** Wallon Brabant, C Belgium
100 H10 **Hamme-Oste-Kanal** *canal* NW Germany
93 G16 **Hammerdal** Jämtland, C Sweden
92 K8 **Hammerfest** Finnmark, N Norway
101 D14 **Hamminkeln** Nordrhein-Westfalen, W Germany
Hamm in Westfalen *see* Hamm
26 K10 **Hammon** Oklahoma, C USA
31 N11 **Hammond** Indiana, N USA
22 K8 **Hammond** Louisiana, S USA
99 K20 **Hamoir** Liège, E Belgium
99 J21 **Hamois** Namur, SE Belgium
99 K16 **Hamont** Limburg, NE Belgium
185 F22 **Hampden** Otago, South Island, NZ
19 R6 **Hampden** Maine, NE USA
97 M23 **Hampshire** *cultural region* S England, UK
13 O15 **Hampton** New Brunswick, SE Canada
27 U14 **Hampton** Arkansas, C USA
29 V12 **Hampton** Iowa, C USA
19 P10 **Hampton** New Hampshire, NE USA
21 R14 **Hampton** South Carolina, SE USA
21 P8 **Hampton** Tennessee, S USA
21 X7 **Hampton** Virginia, NE USA
94 L11 **Hamra** Gävleborg, C Sweden
80 D10 **Hamrat esh Sheikh** Northern Kordofan, C Sudan
139 S5 **Ḩamrīn, Jabal** ⛰ N Iraq
121 P16 **Hamrun** C Malta
167 U14 **Ham Thuân Nam** Bình Thuận, S Vietnam
Hāmūn, Daryācheh-ye *see* Şāberī, Hāmūn-e/Sīstān, Daryācheh-ye
Hamwih *see* Southampton
38 G10 **Hāna** *var.* Hana. Maui, Hawai'i, USA, C Pacific Ocean
21 S14 **Hanahan** South Carolina, SE USA
38 B8 **Hanalei** Kaua'i, Hawai'i, USA, C Pacific Ocean
167 U10 **Ha Nam** Quang Nam-Đa Năng, C Vietnam
165 Q9 **Hanamaki** Iwate, Honshū, C Japan
38 F10 **Hanamanioa, Cape** *headland* Maui, Hawai'i, USA, C Pacific Ocean
190 B16 **Hanan** ✕ (Alofi) SW Niue
101 H18 **Hanau** Hessen, W Germany
8 L9 **Hanbury** ≈ Northwest Territories, NW Canada
Hâncești *see* Hîncești
10 M15 **Hanceville** British Columbia, SW Canada
23 P3 **Hanceville** Alabama, S USA
Hancewicze *see* Hantsavichy
160 L6 **Hancheng** Shaanxi, C China
21 V2 **Hancock** Maryland, NE USA
30 M3 **Hancock** Michigan, N USA
29 S8 **Hancock** Minnesota, N USA
18 I12 **Hancock** New York, NE USA
80 Q12 **Handa** Bari, NE Somalia
161 O5 **Handan** *var.* Han-tan. Hebei, E China
95 P16 **Handen** Stockholm, C Sweden
81 J22 **Handeni** Tanga, E Tanzania
37 Q7 **Handies Peak** ▲ Colorado, C USA
111 J19 **Handlová** *Ger.* Krickerhäu, *Hung.* Nyitrabánya; *prev.* *Ger.* Kriegerhaj. Trenčiansky Kraj, W Slovakia
165 O13 **Haneda** ✕ (Tōkyō) Tōkyō, Honshū, S Japan
138 F13 **HaNegev** *Eng.* Negev. *desert* S Israel
35 Q11 **Hanford** California, W USA
191 V16 **Hanga Roa** Easter Island, Chile, E Pacific Ocean
162 H7 **Hangayn Nuruu** ⛰ C Mongolia
Hang-chou/Hangchow *see* Hangzhou
95 K20 **Hånger** Jönköping, S Sweden
Hangö *see* Hanko
161 R9 **Hangzhou** *var.* Hang-chou, Hangchow. Zhejiang, SE China
162 F5 **Hanhöhiy Uul** ⛰ NW Mongolia
146 I14 **Hanhowuz** *Rus.* Khauz-Khan. Ahal Welaýaty, S Turkmenistan
146 I14 **Hanhowuz Suw Howdany** *Rus.* Khauzkhanskoye Vodokhranilishche. ▣ S Turkmenistan
137 P15 **Hani** Diyarbakır, SE Turkey
Hania *see* Chaniá
141 R11 **Ḩanīsh al Kabīr, Jazīrat al** *island* SW Yemen
Hanka, Lake *see* Khanka, Lake
93 M17 **Hankasalmi** Länsi-Suomi, W Finland
29 R7 **Hankinson** North Dakota, N USA
93 K20 **Hanko** *Swe.* Hangö. Etelä-Suomi, SW Finland
Han-kou/Han-k'ou/Hankow *see* Wuhan
36 M6 **Hanksville** Utah, W USA
152 K6 **Hanle** Jammu and Kashmir, NW India
185 I17 **Hanmer Springs** Canterbury, South Island, NZ
11 R16 **Hanna** Alberta, SW Canada
27 V3 **Hannibal** Missouri, C USA
180 M3 **Hann, Mount** ▲ Western Australia
100 I12 **Hannover** *Eng.* Hanover. Niedersachsen, NW Germany
99 J19 **Hannut** Liège, C Belgium
95 L22 **Hanöbukten** *bay* S Sweden
167 T6 **Ha Nôi** *Eng.* Hanoi, *Fr.* Hanoï. ● (Vietnam) N Vietnam
14 F14 **Hanover** Ontario, S Canada
31 P15 **Hanover** Indiana, N USA
18 G16 **Hanover** Pennsylvania, NE USA
21 W6 **Hanover** Virginia, NE USA
Hanover *see* Hannover
63 G23 **Hanover, Isla** *island* S Chile
Hanselbeck *see* Érd
195 X5 **Hansen Mountains** ⛰ Antarctica
160 M8 **Han Shui** ≈ C China
152 H10 **Hānsi** Haryāna, NW India
95 F20 **Hanstholm** Viborg, NW Denmark
Han-tan *see* Handan
158 H6 **Hantengri Feng** *var.* Pik Khan-Tengri. ▲ China/Kazakhstan *see also* Khan-Tengri, Pik
119 I18 **Hantsavichy** *Pol.* Hancewicze, *Rus.* Gantsevichi. Brestskaya Voblasts', SW Belarus
Hanyang *see* Caidian
Hanyang *see* Wuhan
160 H10 **Hanyuan** *var.* Fulin. Sichuan, C China
Hanyuan *see* Xihe
160 J7 **Hanzhong** Shaanxi, C China
191 W11 **Hao** *atoll* Îles Tuamotu, C French Polynesia
153 S16 **Hāora** *prev.* Howrah. West Bengal, NE India
78 K8 **Haouach, Ouadi** *dry watercourse* E Chad
92 K13 **Haparanda** Norrbotten, N Sweden
25 N3 **Happy** Texas, SW USA
34 M1 **Happy Camp** California, W USA
13 Q9 **Happy Valley-Goose Bay** *prev.* Goose Bay. Newfoundland and Labrador, E Canada
Hapsal *see* Haapsalu
152 J10 **Hāpur** Uttar Pradesh, N India
138 F12 **HaQatan, HaMakhtesh** ◈ S Israel
140 I4 **Ḩaql** Tabūk, NW Saudi Arabia
171 U14 **Har** Pulau Kai Besar, E Indonesia
162 M8 **Haraat** Dundgovĭ, C Mongolia
141 R8 **Ḩaraḑ** *var.* Haradh. Ash Sharqīyah, E Saudi Arabia
Haradh *see* Ḩaraḑ
118 N12 **Haradok** *Rus.* Gorodok. Vitsyebskaya Voblasts', N Belarus
92 J13 **Harads** Norrbotten, N Sweden
119 G19 **Haradzyets** *Rus.* Gorodets. Brestskaya Voblasts', SW Belarus
119 J17 **Haradzyeya** *Rus.* Gorodeya. Minskaya Voblasts', C Belarus
191 V10 **Haraiki** *atoll* Îles Tuamotu, C French Polynesia
165 Q11 **Haramachi** Fukushima, Honshū, E Japan
118 M12 **Harany** *Rus.* Gorany. Vitsyebskaya Voblasts', N Belarus
83 L16 **Harare** *prev.* Salisbury. ● (Zimbabwe) Mashonaland East, NE Zimbabwe
83 L16 **Harare** ✕ Mashonaland East, NE Zimbabwe
78 J10 **Haraz-Djombo** Batha, C Chad
119 O16 **Harbavichy** *Rus.* Gorbovichi. Mahilyowskaya Voblasts', E Belarus
76 J16 **Harbel** W Liberia
163 W8 **Harbin** *var.* Haerbin, Ha-erh-pin, Kharbin; *prev.* Haerhpin, Pingkiang, Pinkiang. Heilongjiang, NE China
31 S7 **Harbor Beach** Michigan, N USA
13 T13 **Harbour Breton** Newfoundland and Labrador, E Canada
65 D25 **Harbours, Bay of** *bay* East Falkland, Falkland Islands
Hârby *see* Haarby
36 I13 **Harcuvar Mountains** ⛰ Arizona, SW USA
108 I7 **Hard** Vorarlberg, NW Austria
154 H11 **Harda Khās** Madhya Pradesh, C India
95 D14 **Hardanger** *physical region* S Norway
95 D14 **Hardangerfjorden** *fjord* S Norway
94 E13 **Hardangerjøkulen** *glacier* S Norway
95 E14 **Hardangervidda** *plateau* S Norway
83 D20 **Hardap** ◈ *district* S Namibia
21 R15 **Hardeeville** South Carolina, SE USA
98 L5 **Hardegarijp** *Fris.* Hurdegaryp. Friesland, N Netherlands
98 O9 **Hardenberg** Overijssel, E Netherlands
183 Q5 **Harden-Murrumburrah** New South Wales, SE Australia
98 K10 **Harderwijk** Gelderland, C Netherlands
30 J14 **Hardin** Illinois, N USA
33 V11 **Hardin** Montana, NW USA
23 R5 **Harding, Lake** ▣ Alabama/Georgia, SE USA
20 J6 **Hardinsburg** Kentucky, S USA
98 I13 **Hardinxveld-Giessendam** Zuid-Holland, C Netherlands
11 R15 **Hardisty** Alberta, SW Canada
152 L12 **Hardoi** Uttar Pradesh, N India
23 U4 **Hardwick** Georgia, SE USA
27 W9 **Hardy** Arkansas, C USA
94 D10 **Hareid** Møre og Romsdal, S Norway
8 H7 **Hare Indian** ≈ Northwest Territories, NW Canada
99 D18 **Harelbeke** *var.* Harlebeke. West-Vlaanderen, W Belgium
Harem *see* Ḩārim
100 E11 **Haren** Niedersachsen, NW Germany
98 N6 **Haren** Groningen, NE Netherlands
80 L13 **Hārer** Hārer, E Ethiopia
95 P14 **Harg** Uppsala, C Sweden
Hargeisa *see* Hargeysa
80 M13 **Hargeysa** *var.* Hargeisa. Woqooyi Galbeed, NW Somalia
116 J10 **Harghita** ◈ *county* NE Romania
25 S17 **Hargill** Texas, SW USA
162 J8 **Harhorin** Övörhangay, C Mongolia
159 Q9 **Har Hu** ◎ C China
Hariana *see* Haryāna
141 P15 **Ḩarīb** W Yemen
168 M12 **Hari, Batang** *prev.* Djambi. ≈ Sumatera, W Indonesia
152 J9 **Haridwār** *prev.* Hardwar. Uttaranchal, N India
155 F18 **Harihar** Karnātaka, W India
185 F18 **Harihari** West Coast, South Island, NZ
138 I3 **Ḩārim** *var.* Harem. Idlib, W Syria
98 F13 **Haringvliet** *channel* SW Netherlands
98 F13 **Haringvlietdam** *dam* SW Netherlands
149 U5 **Harīpur** North-West Frontier Province, NW Pakistan
148 J4 **Harīrūd** *var.* Tedzhen, *Turkm.* Tejen. ≈ Afghanistan/Iran *see also* Tejen
93 K18 **Harjavalta** Länsi-Suomi, W Finland
Härjehågna *see* Østrehogna
118 G4 **Harjumaa** *off.* Harju Maakond. ◈ *province* NW Estonia
21 X11 **Harkers Island** North Carolina, SE USA
139 S1 **Harki** N Iraq
29 T14 **Harlan** Iowa, C USA
21 O7 **Harlan** Kentucky, S USA
29 N17 **Harlan County Lake** ▣ Nebraska, C USA
116 L9 **Hârlău** *var.* Hîrlău. Iași, NE Romania
Harlebeke *see* Harelbeke
33 U7 **Harlem** Montana, NW USA
Harlem *see* Haarlem
95 G22 **Harlev** Århus, C Denmark
98 K6 **Harlingen** *Fris.* Harns. Friesland, N Netherlands
25 T17 **Harlingen** Texas, SW USA
97 O21 **Harlow** E England, UK
33 T10 **Harlowton** Montana, NW USA
94 N11 **Harmånger** Gävleborg, C Sweden
98 I11 **Harmelen** Utrecht, C Netherlands
29 X11 **Harmony** Minnesota, N USA
32 J14 **Harney Basin** *basin* Oregon, NW USA
16 D7 **Harney Basin** ⛰ Oregon, NW USA
32 J14 **Harney Lake** ◎ Oregon, NW USA
28 J10 **Harney Peak** ▲ South Dakota, N USA
93 H17 **Härnösand** *var.* Hernösand. Västernorrland, C Sweden
Harns *see* Harlingen
162 F6 **Har Nuur** ◎ NW Mongolia
105 P4 **Haro** La Rioja, N Spain
40 F6 **Haro, Cabo** *headland* NW Mexico
94 D9 **Harøy** *island* S Norway
97 N21 **Harpenden** E England, UK
76 L18 **Harper** *var.* Cape Palmas. NE Liberia
26 M7 **Harper** Kansas, C USA
32 L13 **Harper** Oregon, NW USA
25 Q10 **Harper** Texas, SW USA
35 U13 **Harper Lake** *salt flat* California, W USA
39 T9 **Harper, Mount** ▲ Alaska, USA
95 J21 **Harplinge** Halland, S Sweden
36 J13 **Harquahala Mountains** ⛰ Arizona, SW USA
141 T15 **Ḩarrah** SE Yemen
12 H11 **Harricana** ≈ Québec, SE Canada
20 M9 **Harriman** Tennessee, S USA
13 R11 **Harrington Harbour** Québec, E Canada
64 B12 **Harrington Sound** *bay* Bermuda, NW Atlantic Ocean
96 F8 **Harris** *physical region* NW Scotland, UK
27 X10 **Harrisburg** Arkansas, C USA
30 M17 **Harrisburg** Illinois, N USA
28 I14 **Harrisburg** Nebraska, C USA
32 F12 **Harrisburg** Oregon, NW USA
18 G15 **Harrisburg** *state capital* Pennsylvania, NE USA
182 F6 **Harris, Lake** ◎ South Australia
23 W11 **Harris, Lake** ◎ Florida, SE USA
83 J22 **Harrismith** Free State, E South Africa
27 T9 **Harrison** Arkansas, C USA
31 Q7 **Harrison** Michigan, N USA
28 I12 **Harrison** Nebraska, C USA
39 Q5 **Harrison Bay** *inlet* Alaska, USA
22 I6 **Harrisonburg** Louisiana, S USA
21 U4 **Harrisonburg** Virginia, NE USA
13 R7 **Harrison, Cape** *headland* Newfoundland and Labrador, E Canada
27 R5 **Harrisonville** Missouri, C USA
Harris Ridge *see* Lomonosov Ridge
192 M3 **Harris Seamount** *undersea feature* N Pacific Ocean
96 F8 **Harris, Sound of** *strait* NW Scotland, UK
31 R6 **Harrisville** Michigan, N USA
21 R3 **Harrisville** West Virginia, NE USA
20 M6 **Harrodsburg** Kentucky, S USA
97 M16 **Harrogate** N England, UK
25 Q4 **Harrold** Texas, SW USA
27 S5 **Harry S.Truman Reservoir** ▣ Missouri, C USA
100 G13 **Harsewinkel** Nordrhein-Westfalen, W Germany
116 M14 **Hârşova** *prev.* Hîrşova. Constanța, SE Romania
92 H10 **Harstad** Troms, N Norway
31 O8 **Hart** Michigan, N USA
24 M4 **Hart** Texas, SW USA
10 I5 **Hart** ≈ Yukon Territory, NW Canada
83 F23 **Hartbees** ≈ C South Africa
109 X7 **Hartberg** Steiermark, SE Austria
182 I10 **Hart, Cape** *headland* South Australia
95 E14 **Hårteigen** ▲ S Norway
23 Q7 **Hartford** Alabama, S USA
27 R11 **Hartford** Arkansas, C USA
18 M12 **Hartford** *state capital* Connecticut, NE USA
20 J6 **Hartford** Kentucky, S USA
31 P10 **Hartford** Michigan, N USA
29 R11 **Hartford** South Dakota, N USA
30 M8 **Hartford** Wisconsin, N USA
31 P13 **Hartford City** Indiana, N USA
29 Q13 **Hartington** Nebraska, C USA
13 N14 **Hartland** New Brunswick, SE Canada
97 H23 **Hartland Point** *headland* SW England, UK
97 M15 **Hartlepool** N England, UK
29 T12 **Hartley** Iowa, C USA
24 M1 **Hartley** Texas, SW USA
32 J15 **Hart Mountain** ▲ Oregon, NW USA
173 U10 **Hartog Ridge** *undersea feature* W Indian Ocean
93 M18 **Hartola** Etelä-Suomi, S Finland
23 P2 **Hartselle** Alabama, S USA
23 S3 **Hartsfield Atlanta** ✕ Georgia, SE USA
27 Q11 **Hartshorne** Oklahoma, C USA
21 S12 **Hartsville** South Carolina, SE USA
20 K8 **Hartsville** Tennessee, S USA
27 U7 **Hartville** Missouri, C USA
23 U2 **Hartwell** Georgia, SE USA
21 O11 **Hartwell Lake** ▣ Georgia/South Carolina, SE USA
Hartz *see* Harts
Harunabad *see* Eslāmābād
162 E6 **Har-Us** Hovd, W Mongolia
162 E6 **Har Us Nuur** ◎ NW Mongolia
30 M10 **Harvard** Illinois, N USA
29 P16 **Harvard** Nebraska, C USA
37 R5 **Harvard, Mount** ▲ Colorado, C USA
31 N11 **Harvey** Illinois, N USA
29 N4 **Harvey** North Dakota, N USA
97 Q21 **Harwich** E England, UK
152 H10 **Haryāna** *var.* Hariana. ◈ *state* N India
141 Y9 **Ḩaryān, Ṭawī al** *spring/well* NE Oman
101 J14 **Harz** ⛰ C Germany
Hasakah *see* Al Ḩasakah
165 Q9 **Hasama** Miyagi, Honshū, C Japan
136 J15 **Hasan Dağı** ▲ C Turkey
139 T9 **Ḩasan Ibn Ḩassūn** C Iraq
149 R6 **Ḩasan Khēl** *var.* Ahmad Khel. Paktīā, SE Afghanistan
100 F12 **Hase** ≈ NW Germany
Haselberg *see* Krasnoznamensk
100 F12 **Haselünne** Niedersachsen, NW Germany
162 K9 **Hashaat** Dundgovĭ, C Mongolia
Hashemite Kingdom of Jordan *see* Jordan
139 V8 **Hāshimah** E Iraq
141 W13 **Ḩāsik** S Oman
149 U10 **Hāsilpur** Punjab, E Pakistan
Hasimoto *see* Hashimoto
27 Q10 **Haskell** Oklahoma, C USA
25 Q6 **Haskell** Texas, SW USA
114 M11 **Hasköy** Edirne, NW Turkey
95 L24 **Hasle** Bornholm, E Denmark
97 N23 **Haslemere** SE England, UK
102 I16 **Hasparren** Pyrénées-Atlantiques, SW France
Hassakeh *see* Al Ḩasakah
155 G19 **Hassan** Karnātaka, W India
36 J13 **Hassayampa River** ≈ Arizona, SW USA
101 J18 **Hassberge** *hill range* C Germany
94 N10 **Hassela** Gävleborg, C Sweden
99 J18 **Hasselt** Limburg, NE Belgium
98 M9 **Hasselt** Overijssel, E Netherlands
Hassetché *see* Al Ḩasakah
101 J18 **Hassfurt** Bayern, C Germany
74 L9 **Hassi Bel Guebbour** E Algeria
74 L8 **Hassi Messaoud** E Algeria
95 K22 **Hässleholm** Skåne, S Sweden
Hasta Colonia/Hasta Pompeia *see* Asti
183 O13 **Hastings** Victoria, SE Australia
184 O11 **Hastings** Hawke's Bay, North Island, NZ
97 P23 **Hastings** SE England, UK
31 P9 **Hastings** Michigan, N USA
29 W9 **Hastings** Minnesota, N USA
29 P16 **Hastings** Nebraska, C USA
95 K22 **Hästveda** Skåne, S Sweden
92 J8 **Hasvik** Finnmark, N Norway
37 V6 **Haswell** Colorado, C USA
162 I10 **Hatansuudal** Bayanhongor, C Mongolia
163 P9 **Hatavch** Sühbaatar, E Mongolia
136 K17 **Hatay** ◈ *province* S Turkey
37 R15 **Hatch** New Mexico, SW USA
36 K7 **Hatch** Utah, W USA
20 F9 **Hatchie River** ≈ Tennessee, S USA
116 G12 **Haţeg** *Ger.* Wallenthal, *Hung.* Hátszeg; *prev.* Hatzeg, Hötzing. Hunedoara, SW Romania
165 O17 **Hateruma-jima** *island* Yaeyama-shotō, SW Japan
183 N8 **Hatfield** New South Wales, SE Australia
162 I5 **Hatgal** Hövsgöl, N Mongolia
153 V16 **Hathazari** Chittagong, SE Bangladesh
141 T13 **Hathūt, Hişā'** *oasis* NE Yemen
167 R14 **Ha Tiên** Kiên Giang, S Vietnam
167 T8 **Ha Tinh** Ha Tinh, N Vietnam
Hatiôzi *see* Hachiōji
138 F12 **Ḩaṭira, Haré** *hill range* S Israel
167 R6 **Hat Lot** Sơn La, N Vietnam
45 P16 **Hato Airport** ✕ (Willemstad) Curaçao, SW Netherlands Antilles
54 H9 **Hato Corozal** Casanare, C Colombia
Hato del Volcán *see* Volcán
45 P9 **Hato Mayor** E Dominican Republic
Hatra *see* Al Ḩaḑr
Hatria *see* Adria
Hátszeg *see* Haţeg
143 R16 **Hattā** Dubayy, NE UAE
182 L9 **Hattah** Victoria, SE Australia
98 M9 **Hattem** Gelderland, E Netherlands
21 Z10 **Hatteras** Hatteras Island, North Carolina, SE USA
21 Z10 **Hatteras, Cape** *headland* North Carolina, SE USA
21 Z9 **Hatteras Island** *island* North Carolina, SE USA
64 F10 **Hatteras Plain** *undersea feature* W Atlantic Ocean
93 G14 **Hattfjelldal** Troms, N Norway
22 M7 **Hattiesburg** Mississippi, S USA
29 Q4 **Hatton** North Dakota, N USA
Hatton Bank *see* Hatton Ridge
64 L6 **Hatton Ridge** *var.* Hatton Bank. *undersea feature* N Atlantic Ocean
191 W6 **Hatutu** *island* Îles Marquises, NE French Polynesia
111 K22 **Hatvan** Heves, NE Hungary
167 O16 **Hat Yai** *var.* Ban Hat Yai. Songkhla, SW Thailand
Hatzeg *see* Haţeg
Hatzfeld *see* Jimbolia
80 N13 **Haud** *plateau* Ethiopia/Somalia
95 D18 **Hauge** Rogaland, S Norway
95 C15 **Haugesund** Rogaland, S Norway
109 X2 **Haugsdorf** Niederösterreich, NE Austria
184 M9 **Hauhungaroa Range** ⛰ North Island, NZ
95 E15 **Haukeligrend** Telemark, S Norway
93 L14 **Haukipudas** Oulu, C Finland
93 M17 **Haukivesi** ◎ SE Finland
93 M17 **Haukivuori** Isä-Suomi, E Finland
Hauptkanal *see* Havelländ Grosse
187 N10 **Hauraha** San Cristobal, SE Solomon Islands
184 L5 **Hauraki Gulf** *gulf* North Island, NZ
185 B24 **Hauroko, Lake** ◎ South Island, NZ
167 S14 **Hâu, Sông** ≈ S Vietnam
92 N12 **Hautajärvi** Lappi, NE Finland
74 F7 **Haut Atlas** *Eng.* High Atlas. ⛰ C Morocco
79 M17 **Haut-Congo** *off.* Région du Haut-Congo; *prev.* Haut-Zaïre. ◈ *region* NE Dem. Rep. Congo
103 Y14 **Haute-Corse** ◈ *department* Corse, France, C Mediterranean Sea
102 L16 **Haute-Garonne** ◈ *department* S France
76 J13 **Haute-Guinée** ◈ *state* NE Guinea
79 K14 **Haute-Kotto** ◈ *prefecture* E Central African Republic
103 P12 **Haute-Loire** ◈ *department* C France
103 R6 **Haute-Marne** ◈ *department* N France
102 M3 **Haute-Normandie** ◈ *region* N France
15 U6 **Hauterive** Québec, SE Canada
103 T13 **Hautes-Alpes** ◈ *department* SE France
103 S7 **Haute-Saône** ◈ *department* E France
103 T10 **Haute-Savoie** ◈ *department* E France
99 M20 **Hautes Fagnes** *Ger.* Hohes Venn. ⛰ E Belgium
102 K16 **Hautes-Pyrénées** ◈ *department* S France
99 L23 **Haute Sûre, Lac de la** ▣ NW Luxembourg
102 M11 **Haute-Vienne** ◈ *department* C France
19 S8 **Haut, Isle au** *island* Maine, NE USA
79 M14 **Haut-Mbomou** ◈ *préfecture* SE Central African Republic
103 Q2 **Hautmont** Nord, N France
79 F19 **Haut-Ogooué** *off.* Province du Haut-Ogooué, *var.* Le Haut-Ogooué. ◈ *province* SE Gabon
Haut-Ogooué, Le *see* Haut-Ogooué
103 U7 **Haut-Rhin** ◈ *department* NE France
74 I6 **Hauts Plateaux** *plateau* Algeria/Morocco
38 D9 **Hau'ula** *var.* Hauula. O'ahu, Hawai'i, USA, C Pacific Ocean
101 O22 **Hauzenberg** Bayern, SE Germany
30 K13 **Havana** Illinois, N USA
Havana *see* La Habana
97 N23 **Havant** S England, UK
35 Y14 **Havasu, Lake** ▣ Arizona/California, W USA
95 J23 **Havdrup** Roskilde, E Denmark
100 N10 **Havel** ≈ NE Germany
99 J21 **Havelange** Namur, SE Belgium
100 M11 **Havelberg** Sachsen-Anhalt, NE Germany
149 U5 **Haveliān** North-West Frontier Province, NW Pakistan
100 N12 **Havelländ Grosse** *var.* Hauptkanal. *canal* NE Germany
14 J14 **Havelock** Ontario, SE Canada
185 J14 **Havelock** Marlborough, South Island, NZ
21 X11 **Havelock** North Carolina, SE USA
184 O11 **Havelock North** Hawke's Bay, North Island, NZ
98 M8 **Havelte** Drenthe, NE Netherlands
27 N6 **Haven** Kansas, C USA
97 H21 **Haverfordwest** SW Wales, UK
97 P20 **Haverhill** E England, UK
19 O10 **Haverhill** Massachusetts, NE USA
93 G17 **Haverö** Västernorrland, C Sweden
111 I17 **Havířov** Moravskoslezský Kraj, E Czech Republic
111 E17 **Havlíčkův Brod** *Ger.* Deutsch-Brod; *prev.* Německý Brod. Vysočina, C Czech Republic
92 K7 **Havøysund** Finnmark, N Norway
33 T7 **Havre** Montana, NW USA
Havre *see* le Havre
99 F20 **Havré** Hainaut, S Belgium
13 P11 **Havre-St-Pierre** Québec, E Canada
136 B10 **Havsa** Edirne, NW Turkey
38 D8 **Hawai'i** *off.* State of Hawai'i; also known as Aloha State, Paradise of the Pacific *var.* Hawaii. ◈ *state* USA, C Pacific Ocean
38 G12 **Hawai'i** *var.* Hawaii. *island* Hawaiian Islands, USA, C Pacific Ocean
192 M5 **Hawaiian Islands** *prev.* Sandwich Islands. *island group* Hawaii, USA, C Pacific Ocean
192 L5 **Hawaiian Ridge** *undersea feature* N Pacific Ocean
193 N6 **Hawaiian Trough** *undersea feature* N Pacific Ocean
29 R12 **Hawarden** Iowa, C USA
Hawash *see* Āwash
139 P6 **Ḩawbayn al Gharbīyah** C Iraq
185 D21 **Hawea, Lake** ◎ South Island, NZ
184 K11 **Hawera** Taranaki, North Island, NZ
20 J5 **Hawesville** Kentucky, S USA
38 G11 **Hāwī** *var.* Hawi. Hawai'i, USA, C Pacific Ocean
96 K13 **Hawick** SE Scotland, UK
139 S4 **Ḩawījah** C Iraq
139 Y10 **Ḩawīzah, Hawr al** ◎ S Iraq
185 E21 **Hawkdun Range** ⛰ South Island, NZ
184 P10 **Hawke Bay** *bay* North Island, NZ
182 I6 **Hawker** South Australia
184 N11 **Hawke's Bay** *off.* Hawkes Bay Region. ◈ *region* North Island, NZ
149 O16 **Hawkes Bay** *bay* SE Pakistan
15 N12 **Hawkesbury** Ontario, SE Canada
Hawkeye State *see* Iowa
23 T5 **Hawkinsville** Georgia, SE USA
14 B7 **Hawk Junction** Ontario, S Canada
21 N10 **Haw Knob** ▲ North Carolina/Tennessee, SE USA
21 Q9 **Hawksbill Mountain** ▲ North Carolina, SE USA
33 Z16 **Hawk Springs** Wyoming, C USA
Hawlēr *see* Arbīl
29 S5 **Hawley** Minnesota, N USA
25 P7 **Hawley** Texas, SW USA
141 R14 **Ḩawrā'** C Yemen
139 P7 **Ḩawrān, Wadi** *dry watercourse* W Iraq
21 T9 **Haw River** ≈ North Carolina, SE USA
139 U5 **Hawshqūrah** E Iraq
35 S7 **Hawthorne** Nevada, W USA
37 W3 **Haxtun** Colorado, C USA
183 N9 **Hay** New South Wales, SE Australia
11 O10 **Hay** ≈ W Canada
171 S13 **Haya** Pulau Seram, E Indonesia
165 R9 **Hayachine-san** ▲ Honshū, C Japan
103 S4 **Hayange** Moselle, NE France
HaYarden *see* Jordan
Hayastani Hanrapetut'yun *see* Armenia
Hayasui-seto *see* Hōyo-kaikyō
39 N9 **Haycock** Alaska, USA
36 M14 **Hayden** Arizona, SW USA
37 Q3 **Hayden** Colorado, C USA
28 M10 **Hayes** South Dakota, N USA
11 X13 **Hayes** ≈ Manitoba, C Canada
9 P12 **Hayes** ≈ Nunavut, NE Canada

◆ COUNTRY ● COUNTRY CAPITAL ◇ DEPENDENT TERRITORY ○ DEPENDENT TERRITORY CAPITAL ◈ ADMINISTRATIVE REGION ✕ INTERNATIONAL AIRPORT ▲ MOUNTAIN ⛰ MOUNTAIN RANGE 🌋 VOLCANO ≈ RIVER ◎ LAKE ▣ RESERVOIR

28 M16 **Hayes Center** Nebraska, C USA
39 S10 **Hayes, Mount** ▲ Alaska, USA
21 N11 **Hayesville** North Carolina, SE USA
35 X10 **Hayford Peak** ▲ Nevada, W USA
34 M3 **Hayfork** California, W USA
Hayir, Qasr al *see* Ḩayr al Gharbī, Qaşr al
163 P8 **Haylaastay** Sühbaatar, E Mongolia
14 I12 **Hay Lake** ◎ Ontario, SE Canada
141 X11 **Haymā'** *var.* Haima. C Oman
136 H13 **Haymana** Ankara, C Turkey
138 J7 **Ḩaymūr, Jabal** ▲ W Syria
Haynau *see* Chojnów
22 G4 **Haynesville** Louisiana, S USA
23 P6 **Hayneville** Alabama, S USA
114 M12 **Hayrabolu** Tekirdağ, NW Turkey
136 C10 **Hayrabolu Deresi** ~ NW Turkey
138 J6 **Ḩayr al Gharbī, Qaşr al** *var.* Qasr al Hayir, Qasr al Hir al Gharbi. *ruins* Ḩimş, C Syria
138 L5 **Ḩayr ash Sharqī, Qaşr al** *var.* Qasr al Hir Ash Sharqī. *ruins* Ḩimş, C Syria
8 J10 **Hay River** Northwest Territories, W Canada
26 K4 **Hays** Kansas, C USA
28 K12 **Hay Springs** Nebraska, C USA
65 H25 **Haystack, The** ▲ NE Saint Helena
27 N7 **Haysville** Kansas, C USA
117 O7 **Haysyn** *Rus.* Gaysin. Vinnyts'ka Oblast', C Ukraine
27 Y9 **Hayti** Missouri, C USA
29 Q9 **Hayti** South Dakota, N USA
117 O8 **Hayvoron** *Rus.* Gayvorno. Kirovohrads'ka Oblast', C Ukraine
35 N9 **Hayward** California, W USA
30 J4 **Hayward** Wisconsin, N USA
97 O23 **Haywards Heath** SE England, UK
146 A11 **Hazar** *prev. Rus.* Cheleken. Balkan Welaýaty, W Turkmenistan
143 S11 **Hazārān, Kūh-e** *var.* Kūh-e ā Hazr. ▲ SE Iran
Hazarat Imam *see* Emām Şāḩeb
21 O7 **Hazard** Kentucky, S USA
137 O15 **Hazar Gölü** ◎ C Turkey
153 P15 **Hazārībāg** *var.* Hazāribāgh. Jhārkhand, N India
Hazāribāgh *see* Hazārībāg
103 O1 **Hazebrouck** Nord, N France
30 K9 **Hazel Green** Wisconsin, N USA
192 K9 **Hazel Holme Bank** *undersea feature* S Pacific Ocean
10 K13 **Hazelton** British Columbia, SW Canada
29 N6 **Hazelton** North Dakota, N USA
35 R5 **Hazen** Nevada, W USA
28 L5 **Hazen** North Dakota, N USA
38 L12 **Hazen Bay** *bay* E Bering Sea
9 N1 **Hazen, Lake** ◎ Nunavut, N Canada
139 S5 **Hazīm, Bi'r** *well* C Iraq
23 V6 **Hazlehurst** Georgia, SE USA
22 K6 **Hazlehurst** Mississippi, S USA
18 K15 **Hazlet** New Jersey, NE USA
146 I9 **Hazorasp** *Rus.* Khazarosp. Xorazm Viloyati, W Uzbekistan
147 R13 **Hazratishoh, Qatorkŭhi** *var.* Khrebet Khazretishi, *Rus.* Khrebet Khozretishi. ▲ S Tajikistan
Hazr, Kūh-e ā *see* Hazārān, Kūh-e
149 U6 **Hazro** Punjab, E Pakistan
23 R7 **Headland** Alabama, S USA
182 C6 **Head of Bight** *headland* South Australia
33 N10 **Headquarters** Idaho, NW USA
34 M7 **Healdsburg** California, W USA
27 N13 **Healdton** Oklahoma, C USA
183 O12 **Healesville** Victoria, SE Australia
39 R10 **Healy** Alaska, USA
173 R13 **Heard and McDonald Islands** ◇ *Australian external territory* S Indian Ocean
173 R13 **Heard Island** *island* Heard and McDonald Islands, S Indian Ocean
25 U9 **Hearne** Texas, SW USA
12 F12 **Hearst** Ontario, S Canada
194 J5 **Hearst Island** *island* Antarctica
Heart of Dixie *see* Alabama
28 L5 **Heart River** ~ North Dakota, N USA
31 T13 **Heath** Ohio, N USA
183 N11 **Heathcote** Victoria, SE Australia
97 N22 **Heathrow** ✕ (London) SE England, UK
21 X5 **Heathsville** Virginia, NE USA
27 R11 **Heavener** Oklahoma, C USA
25 R15 **Hebbronville** Texas, SW USA
163 Q13 **Hebei** *var.* Hebei Sheng, Hopeh, Hopei, Ji; *prev.* Chihli. ◈ *province* E China
Hebei Sheng *see* Hebei
36 M3 **Heber City** Utah, W USA
27 V10 **Heber Springs** Arkansas, C USA
161 N5 **Hebi** Henan, C China
32 F11 **Hebo** Oregon, NW USA
96 F9 **Hebrides, Sea of the** *sea* NW Scotland, UK
13 P5 **Hebron** Newfoundland and Labrador, E Canada
31 N11 **Hebron** Indiana, N USA
29 Q17 **Hebron** Nebraska, C USA
28 L5 **Hebron** North Dakota, N USA
138 F11 **Hebron** *var.* Al Khalīl, El Khalil, *Heb.* Hevron; *anc.* Kiriath-Arba. S West Bank
Hebrus *see* Évros/Maritsa/Meriç
95 N14 **Heby** Västmanland, C Sweden
10 I14 **Hecate Strait** *strait* British Columbia, W Canada
41 W12 **Hecelchakán** Campeche, SE Mexico
160 K13 **Hechi** *var.* Jinchengjiang. Guangxi Zhuangzu Zizhiqu, S China
101 H23 **Hechingen** Baden-Württemberg, S Germany
99 K17 **Hechtel** Limburg, NE Belgium
160 J9 **Hechuan** Chongqing Shi, C China
29 P7 **Hecla** South Dakota, N USA
9 N1 **Hecla, Cape** *headland* Nunavut, N Canada
29 T9 **Hector** Minnesota, N USA
95 F17 **Hede** Jämtland, C Sweden
95 M14 **Hedemora** Dalarna, C Sweden
92 K13 **Hedenäset** Norrbotten, N Sweden
95 G23 **Hedensted** Vejle, C Denmark
95 N14 **Hedesunda** Gävleborg, C Sweden
95 N14 **Hedesundafjord** ◎ C Sweden
25 O3 **Hedley** Texas, SW USA
94 I12 **Hedmark** ◈ *county* S Norway
165 T16 **Hedo-misaki** *headland* Okinawa, SW Japan
29 X15 **Hedrick** Iowa, C USA
99 L16 **Heel** Limburg, SE Netherlands
189 Y12 **Heel Point** *point* Wake Island
98 H9 **Heemskerk** Noord-Holland, W Netherlands
98 M10 **Heerde** Gelderland, E Netherlands
98 L7 **Heerenveen** *Fris.* It Hearrenfean. Friesland, N Netherlands
98 I8 **Heerhugowaard** Noord-Holland, NW Netherlands
92 O3 **Heer Land** *physical region* C Svalbard
99 M18 **Heerlen** Limburg, SE Netherlands
99 J19 **Heers** Limburg, NE Belgium
Heerwegen *see* Polkowice
98 K13 **Heesch** Noord-Brabant, S Netherlands
99 K15 **Heeze** Noord-Brabant, SE Netherlands
138 F8 **Ḩefa** *var.* Haifa; *hist.* Caiffa, Caiphas, *anc.* Sycaminum. Haifa, N Israel
138 F8 **Ḩefa, Mifraz** *Eng.* Bay of Haifa. *bay* N Israel
161 Q8 **Hefei** *var.* Hofei; *hist.* Luchow. Anhui, E China
23 R3 **Heflin** Alabama, S USA
163 X7 **Hegang** Heilongjiang, NE China
164 L10 **Hegura-jima** *island* SW Japan
Heguri-jima *see* Heigun-tō
Hei *see* Heilongjiang
100 H8 **Heide** Schleswig-Holstein, N Germany
101 G20 **Heidelberg** Baden-Württemberg, SW Germany
83 J21 **Heidelberg** Gauteng, NE South Africa
22 M6 **Heidelberg** Mississippi, S USA
Heidenheim *see* Heidenheim an der Brenz
101 J22 **Heidenheim an der Brenz** *var.* Heidenheim. Baden-Württemberg, S Germany
109 U2 **Heidenreichstein** Niederösterreich, N Austria
164 F14 **Heigun-tō** *var.* Heguri-jima. *island* SW Japan
163 W5 **Heihe** *prev.* Ai-hun. Heilongjiang, NE China
159 S8 **Hei He** ~ C China
Hei-ho *see* Nagqu
83 J22 **Heilbron** Free State, N South Africa
101 H21 **Heilbronn** Baden-Württemberg, SW Germany
Heiligenbeil *see* Mamonovo
109 Q8 **Heiligenblut** Tirol, W Austria
100 K7 **Heiligenhafen** Schleswig-Holstein, N Germany
Heiligenkreuz *see* Žiar nad Hronom
101 J15 **Heiligenstadt** Thüringen, C Germany
Heilong Jiang *see* Amur
163 W8 **Heilongjiang** *var.* Hei, Heilongjiang Sheng, Hei-lung-chiang, Heilungkiang. ◈ *province* NE China
Heilongjiang Sheng *see* Heilongjiang
98 H9 **Heiloo** Noord-Holland, NW Netherlands
Heilsberg *see* Lidzbark Warmiński
Hei-lung-chiang/Heilungkiang *see* Heilongjiang
92 I4 **Heimaey** *var.* Heimaæy. *island* S Iceland
94 H8 **Heimdal** Sør-Trøndelag, S Norway
Heinaste *see* Ainaži
93 N17 **Heinävesi** Itä-Suomi, E Finland
99 M22 **Heinerscheid** Diekirch, N Luxembourg
98 M10 **Heino** Overijssel, E Netherlands
93 M18 **Heinola** Etelä-Suomi, S Finland
101 C16 **Heinsberg** Nordrhein-Westfalen, W Germany
163 U12 **Heishan** Liaoning, NE China
160 H8 **Heishui** *var.* Luhua. Sichuan, C China
99 H17 **Heist-op-den-Berg** Antwerpen, C Belgium
Heitō *see* P'ingtung
171 X15 **Heitske** Papua, E Indonesia
Hejanah *see* Al Hījānah
Hejaz *see* Al Ḩijāz
160 M14 **He Jiang** ~ S China
Hejiayan *see* Lüeyang
158 K6 **Hejing** Xinjiang Uygur Zizhiqu, NW China
Héjjasfalva *see* Vânători
Heka *see* Hoika
137 N14 **Hekimhan** Malatya, C Turkey
92 J4 **Hekla** ▲ S Iceland
Hekou *see* Yajiang, Sichuan, China
Hekou *see* Yanshan, Jiangxi, China
110 J6 **Hel** *Ger.* Hela. Pomorskie, N Poland
Hela *see* Hel
93 F17 **Helagsfjället** ▲ C Sweden
159 W8 **Helan** *var.* Xigang. Ningxia, N China
162 K14 **Helan Shan** ▲ N China
99 M16 **Helden** Limburg, SE Netherlands
27 X12 **Helena** Arkansas, C USA
33 R10 **Helena** *state capital* Montana, NW USA
96 H12 **Helensburgh** W Scotland, UK
184 K5 **Helensville** Auckland, North Island, NZ
95 L20 **Helgasjön** ◎ S Sweden
100 G8 **Helgoland** *Eng.* Heligoland. *island* NW Germany
Helgoland Bay *see* Helgoländer Bucht
100 G8 **Helgoländer Bucht** *var.* Helgoland Bay, Heligoland Bight. *bay* NW Germany
Heligoland *see* Helgoland
Heligoland Bight *see* Helgoländer Bucht
Heliopolis *see* Baalbek
92 I4 **Hella** Sudhurland, SW Iceland
Hellas *see* Greece
143 N11 **Ḩelleh, Rūd-e** ~ S Iran
98 N10 **Hellendoorn** Overijssel, E Netherlands
Hellenic Republic *see* Greece
121 Q10 **Hellenic Trough** *undersea feature* Aegean Sea, C Mediterranean Sea
94 E10 **Hellesylt** Møre og Romsdal, S Norway
98 F13 **Hellevoetsluis** Zuid-Holland, SW Netherlands
105 Q12 **Hellín** Castilla-La Mancha, C Spain
115 H19 **Hellinikon** ✕ (Athína) Attikí, C Greece
32 M12 **Hells Canyon** *valley* Idaho/Oregon, NW USA
148 L9 **Helmand** ◈ *province* S Afghanistan
148 K10 **Helmand, Daryā-ye** *var.* Rūd-e Hīrmand. ~ Afghanistan/Iran *see also* Hīrmand, Rūd-e
Helmantica *see* Salamanca
101 K15 **Helme** ~ C Germany
99 L15 **Helmond** Noord-Brabant, S Netherlands
96 J7 **Helmsdale** N Scotland, UK
100 K13 **Helmstedt** Niedersachsen, N Germany
163 Y10 **Helong** Jilin, NE China
36 M4 **Helper** Utah, W USA
100 O10 **Helpter Berge** *hill* NE Germany
95 J22 **Helsingborg** *prev.* Hälsingborg. Skåne, S Sweden
Helsingfors *see* Helsinki
95 J22 **Helsingør** *Eng.* Elsinore. Frederiksborg, E Denmark
93 M20 **Helsinki** *Swe.* Helsingfors. ● (Finland) Etelä-Suomi, S Finland
97 H25 **Helston** SW England, UK
Heltau *see* Cisnădie
61 C17 **Helvecia** Santa Fe, C Argentina
97 K15 **Helvellyn** ▲ NW England, UK
Helvetia *see* Switzerland
75 W8 **Helwân** *var.* Hilwân, Hulwan, Hulwân. N Egypt
97 N21 **Hemel Hempstead** E England, UK
35 U16 **Hemet** California, W USA
28 J13 **Hemingford** Nebraska, C USA
21 T13 **Hemingway** South Carolina, SE USA
92 G13 **Hemnesberget** Nordland, C Norway
25 Y8 **Hemphill** Texas, SW USA
25 V11 **Hempstead** Texas, SW USA
95 P20 **Hemse** Gotland, SE Sweden
94 F13 **Hemsedal** *valley* S Norway
159 T11 **Henan** *var.* Henan Mongolzu Zizhixian, Yêgainnyin. Qinghai, C China
161 N6 **Henan** *var.* Henan Sheng, Honan, Yu. ◈ *province* C China
184 L4 **Hen and Chickens** *island group* N NZ
Henan Mongolzu Zizhixian/Henan Sheng *see* Henan
105 O7 **Henares** ~ C Spain
165 P7 **Henashi-zaki** *headland* Honshū, C Japan
102 I16 **Hendaye** Pyrénées-Atlantiques, SW France
136 F11 **Hendek** Sakarya, NW Turkey
61 B21 **Henderson** Buenos Aires, E Argentina
20 I5 **Henderson** Kentucky, S USA
35 X11 **Henderson** Nevada, W USA
21 V8 **Henderson** North Carolina, SE USA
20 G10 **Henderson** Tennessee, S USA
25 W7 **Henderson** Texas, SW USA
30 J12 **Henderson Creek** ~ Illinois, N USA
186 M9 **Henderson Field** ✕ (Honiara) Guadalcanal, C Solomon Islands
191 O17 **Henderson Island** *atoll* N Pitcairn Islands
21 O10 **Hendersonville** North Carolina, SE USA
20 J8 **Hendersonville** Tennessee, S USA
143 O14 **Hendorābī, Jazīreh-ye** *island* S Iran
55 V10 **Hendrik Top** *var.* Hendriktop. *elevation* C Surinam
Hendū Kosh *see* Hindu Kush
14 L12 **Heney, Lac** ◎ Québec, SE Canada
Hengchow *see* Hengyang
161 S15 **Hengchun** S Taiwan
159 R16 **Hengduan Shan** ▲ SW China
98 N12 **Hengelo** Gelderland, E Netherlands
98 O10 **Hengelo** Overijssel, E Netherlands
Hengnan *see* Hengyang
161 N11 **Hengshan** Hunan, S China
160 L4 **Hengshan** Shaanxi, C China
161 O4 **Hengshui** Hebei, E China
161 N12 **Hengyang** *var.* Hengnan, Heng-yang; *prev.* Hengchow. Hunan, S China
117 U11 **Heniches'k** *Rus.* Genichesk. Khersons'ka Oblast', S Ukraine
21 Z4 **Henlopen, Cape** *headland* Delaware, NE USA
Henna *see* Enna
94 M10 **Hennan** Gävleborg, C Sweden
102 G7 **Hennebont** Morbihan, NW France
30 L11 **Hennepin** Illinois, N USA
26 M9 **Hennessey** Oklahoma, C USA
100 N12 **Hennigsdorf** *var.* Hennigsdorf bei Berlin. Brandenburg, NE Germany
Hennigsdorf bei Berlin *see* Hennigsdorf
19 N9 **Henniker** New Hampshire, NE USA
25 S5 **Henrietta** Texas, SW USA
Henrique de Carvalho *see* Saurimo
30 L12 **Henry** Illinois, N USA
21 Y7 **Henry, Cape** *headland* Virginia, NE USA
27 P10 **Henryetta** Oklahoma, C USA
194 M7 **Henry Ice Rise** *ice cap* Antarctica
9 Q5 **Henry Kater, Cape** *headland* Baffin Island, Nunavut, NE Canada
33 R13 **Henrys Fork** ~ Idaho, NW USA
14 E15 **Hensall** Ontario, S Canada
100 J9 **Henstedt-Ulzburg** Schleswig-Holstein, N Germany
163 N7 **Hentiy** ◈ *province* N Mongolia
162 M7 **Hentiyn Nuruu** ▲ N Mongolia
183 P10 **Henty** New South Wales, SE Australia
166 L8 **Henzada** Irrawaddy, SW Burma
Heping *see* Huishui
101 G19 **Heppenheim** Hessen, W Germany
32 J11 **Heppner** Oregon, NW USA
160 L15 **Hepu** *var.* Lianzhou. Guangxi Zhuangzu Zizhiqu, S China
92 J2 **Heradhsvötn** ~ C Iceland
Herakleion *see* Irákleio
148 K5 **Herāt** *var.* Herat; *anc.* Aria. Herāt, W Afghanistan
148 J5 **Herāt** ◈ *province* W Afghanistan
103 P14 **Hérault** ◈ *department* S France
103 P15 **Hérault** ~ S France
11 T16 **Herbert** Saskatchewan, S Canada
185 F22 **Herbert** Otago, South Island, NZ
38 J17 **Herbert Island** *island* Aleutian Islands, Alaska, USA
Herbertshöhe *see* Kokopo
15 Q7 **Herbertville** Québec, SE Canada
101 G17 **Herborn** Hessen, W Germany
113 I17 **Herceg-Novi** *It.* Castelnuovo; *prev.* Ercegnovi. Montenegro, SW Serbia and Montenegro (Yugo.)
11 X10 **Herchmer** Manitoba, C Canada
186 E8 **Hercules Bay** *bay* E PNG
92 K2 **Herdhubreidh** ▲ C Iceland
42 M13 **Heredia** Heredia, C Costa Rica
42 M12 **Heredia** *off.* Provincia de Heredia. ◈ *province* N Costa Rica
97 K21 **Hereford** W England, UK
24 M3 **Hereford** Texas, SW USA
15 Q13 **Hereford, Mont** ▲ Québec, SE Canada
97 K21 **Herefordshire** *cultural region* W England, UK
191 U11 **Hereheretue** *atoll* Îles Tuamotu, C French Polynesia
105 N10 **Herencia** Castilla-La Mancha, C Spain
99 H18 **Herent** Vlaams Brabant, C Belgium
99 I16 **Herentals** *var.* Herenthals. Antwerpen, N Belgium
Herenthals *see* Herentals
99 H17 **Herenthout** Antwerpen, N Belgium
95 J23 **Herfølge** Roskilde, E Denmark
100 G13 **Herford** Nordrhein-Westfalen, NW Germany
27 O5 **Herington** Kansas, C USA
108 H7 **Herisau** *Fr.* Hérisau. Appenzell Ausser Rhoden, NE Switzerland
Héristal *see* Herstal
99 J18 **Herk-de-Stad** Limburg, NE Belgium
Herkulesbad/Herkulesfürdő *see* Băile Herculane
Herlen Gol/Herlen He *see* Kerulen
35 Q4 **Herlong** California, W USA
97 L26 **Herm** *island* Channel Islands
109 R9 **Hermagor** *Slvn.* Šmohor. Kärnten, S Austria
29 S7 **Herman** Minnesota, N USA
96 L1 **Herma Ness** *headland* NE Scotland, UK
27 V4 **Hermann** Missouri, C USA
181 Q8 **Hermannsburg** Northern Territory, N Australia
Hermannstadt *see* Sibiu
94 E12 **Hermansverk** Sogn og Fjordane, S Norway
138 H6 **Hermel** *var.* Hirmil. NE Lebanon
Hermhausen *see* Hajnówka
183 P6 **Hermidale** New South Wales, SE Australia
55 X9 **Herminadorp** Sipaliwini, NE Surinam
32 K11 **Hermiston** Oregon, NW USA
27 T6 **Hermitage** Missouri, C USA
186 D4 **Hermit Islands** *island group* N PNG
25 O7 **Hermleigh** Texas, SW USA
138 G7 **Hermon, Mount** *Ar.* Jabal ash Shaykh. ▲ S Syria
Hermopolis Parva *see* Damanhûr
28 J10 **Hermosa** South Dakota, N USA
40 F5 **Hermosillo** Sonora, NW Mexico
Hermoupolis *see* Ermoúpoli
111 N20 **Hernád** *var.* Hornád, *Ger.* Kundert. ~ Hungary/Slovakia
61 C18 **Hernández** Entre Ríos, E Argentina
23 V11 **Hernando** Florida, SE USA
22 L1 **Hernando** Mississippi, S USA
105 Q2 **Hernani** País Vasco, N Spain
99 F19 **Herne** Vlaams Brabant, C Belgium
101 E14 **Herne** Nordrhein-Westfalen, W Germany
95 F22 **Herning** Ringkøbing, W Denmark
Hernösand *see* Härnösand
121 U11 **Herodotus Basin** *undersea feature* E Mediterranean Sea
121 Q12 **Herodotus Trough** *undersea feature* C Mediterranean Sea
29 T11 **Heron Lake** Minnesota, N USA
Herowābād *see* Khalkhāl
95 G16 **Herre** Telemark, S Norway
29 N7 **Herreid** South Dakota, N USA
101 H22 **Herrenberg** Baden-Württemberg, S Germany
104 L14 **Herrera** Andalucía, S Spain
43 R17 **Herrera** *off.* Provincia de Herrera. ◈ *province* S Panama
104 L10 **Herrera del Duque** Extremadura, W Spain
104 M4 **Herrera de Pisuerga** Castilla-León, N Spain
41 Z13 **Herrero, Punta** *headland* SE Mexico
183 P16 **Herrick** Tasmania, SE Australia
30 L17 **Herrin** Illinois, N USA
20 M6 **Herrington Lake** ▣ Kentucky, S USA
95 K18 **Herrljunga** Västra Götaland, S Sweden
103 N16 **Hers** ~ S France
10 I1 **Herschel Island** *island* Yukon Territory, NW Canada
99 I17 **Herselt** Antwerpen, C Belgium
18 G15 **Hershey** Pennsylvania, NE USA
99 K19 **Herstal** *Fr.* Héristal. Liège, E Belgium
97 O21 **Hertford** E England, UK
21 X8 **Hertford** North Carolina, SE USA
97 O21 **Hertfordshire** *cultural region* E England, UK
181 Z9 **Hervey Bay** Queensland, E Australia
101 O14 **Herzberg** Brandenburg, E Germany
99 E18 **Herzele** Oost-Vlaanderen, NW Belgium
101 K20 **Herzogenaurach** Bayern, SE Germany
109 W4 **Herzogenburg** Niederösterreich, NE Austria
Herzogenbusch *see* 's-Hertogenbosch
103 N2 **Hesdin** Pas-de-Calais, N France
160 K14 **Heshan** Guangxi Zhuangzu Zizhiqu, S China
159 X10 **Heshui** *var.* Xihuachi. Gansu, C China
99 M25 **Hespérange** Luxembourg, SE Luxembourg
35 U14 **Hesperia** California, W USA
37 P7 **Hesperus Mountain** ▲ Colorado, C USA
10 J6 **Hess** ~ Yukon Territory, NW Canada
Hesse *see* Hessen
101 J21 **Hesselberg** ▲ S Germany
95 I22 **Hesselo** *island* E Denmark
101 H17 **Hessen** *Eng./Fr.* Hesse. ◈ *state* C Germany
192 L6 **Hess Tablemount** *undersea feature* C Pacific Ocean
27 N6 **Hesston** Kansas, C USA
93 G15 **Hestskjøltoppen** ▲ C Norway
97 K18 **Heswall** NW England, UK
153 P12 **Hetauda** Central, C Nepal
Hétfalu *see* Săcele
28 K7 **Hettinger** North Dakota, N USA
101 L14 **Hettstedt** Sachsen-Anhalt, C Germany
92 P3 **Heuglin, Kapp** *headland* SE Svalbard
187 N10 **Heuru** San Cristobal, SE Solomon Islands
99 J17 **Heusden** Limburg, NE Belgium
98 J13 **Heusden** Noord-Brabant, S Netherlands
102 K3 **Hève, Cap de la** *headland* N France
99 H18 **Heverlee** Vlaams Brabant, C Belgium
111 L22 **Heves** Heves, NE Hungary
111 L22 **Heves** *off.* Heves Megye. ◈ *county* NE Hungary
Hevron *see* Hebron
45 Y13 **Hewanorra** ✕ (Saint Lucia) S Saint Lucia
Hexian *see* Hezhou
160 L6 **Heyang** Shaanxi, C China
Heydebrech *see* Kędzierzyn-Kozle
Heydekrug *see* Šilutė
Heyin *see* Guide
97 K16 **Heysham** NW England, UK
161 O14 **Heyuan** Guangdong, S China
182 L12 **Heywood** Victoria, SE Australia
180 K3 **Heywood Islands** *island group* Western Australia
161 O6 **Heze** *var.* Caozhou. Shandong, E China
159 U11 **Hezheng** Gansu, C China
160 M13 **Hezhou** *var.* Babu; *prev.* Hexian. Guangxi Zhuangzu Zizhiqu, S China
159 U11 **Hezuo** Gansu, C China
23 Z16 **Hialeah** Florida, SE USA
27 Q3 **Hiawatha** Kansas, C USA
36 M4 **Hiawatha** Utah, W USA
29 V4 **Hibbing** Minnesota, N USA
183 N17 **Hibbs, Point** *headland* Tasmania, SE Australia
20 F8 **Hickman** Kentucky, S USA
21 Q9 **Hickory** North Carolina, SE USA
21 Q9 **Hickory, Lake** ▣ North Carolina, SE USA
184 Q7 **Hicks Bay** Gisborne, North Island, NZ
25 S8 **Hico** Texas, SW USA
165 T4 **Hidaka** Hokkaidō, NE Japan
164 I12 **Hidaka** Hyōgo, Honshū, SW Japan
165 T5 **Hidaka-sanmyaku** ▲ Hokkaidō, NE Japan
41 O6 **Hidalgo** *var.* Villa Hidalgo. Coahuila de Zaragoza, NE Mexico
41 N8 **Hidalgo** Nuevo León, NE Mexico
41 O10 **Hidalgo** Tamaulipas, C Mexico
41 O13 **Hidalgo** ◈ *state* C Mexico
40 J7 **Hidalgo del Parral** *var.* Parral. Chihuahua, N Mexico
100 N7 **Hiddensee** *island* NE Germany
80 G6 **Hidiglib, Wadi** ~ NE Sudan
109 U6 **Hieflau** Salzburg, E Austria
187 P16 **Hienghène** Province Nord, C New Caledonia
Hierosolyma *see* Jerusalem
64 N12 **Hierro** *var.* Ferro. *island* Islas Canarias, Spain, NE Atlantic Ocean
164 G13 **Higashi-Hiroshima** *var.* Higasihirosima. Hiroshima, Honshū, SW Japan
164 C12 **Higashi-suidō** *strait* SW Japan
Higasihirosima *see* Higashi-Hiroshima
Higasine *see* Higashine
25 P1 **Higgins** Texas, SW USA
31 P7 **Higgins Lake** ◎ Michigan, N USA
27 S4 **Higginsville** Missouri, C USA
High Atlas *see* Haut Atlas
30 M5 **High Falls Reservoir** ▣ Wisconsin, N USA
44 K12 **Highgate** C Jamaica
25 X11 **High Island** Texas, SW USA
31 O5 **High Island** *island* Michigan, N USA
30 K15 **Highland** Illinois, N USA
31 N10 **Highland Park** Illinois, N USA
21 O10 **Highlands** North Carolina, SE USA
11 O11 **High Level** Alberta, W Canada
29 O9 **Highmore** South Dakota, N USA
171 N3 **High Peak** ▲ Luzon, N Philippines
High Plains *see* Great Plains
21 S9 **High Point** North Carolina, SE USA
18 J13 **High Point** *hill* New Jersey, NE USA
11 P13 **High Prairie** Alberta, W Canada
11 Q16 **High River** Alberta, SW Canada
21 S9 **High Rock Lake** ▣ North Carolina, SE USA
23 V9 **High Springs** Florida, SE USA
High Veld *see* Great Karoo
97 J24 **High Willhays** ▲ SW England, UK
97 N22 **High Wycombe** *prev.* Chepping Wycombe, Chipping Wycombe. SE England, UK
41 P12 **Higos** *var.* El Higo. Veracruz-Llave, E Mexico
102 I16 **Higuer, Cap** *headland* NE Spain
45 R5 **Higüero, Punta** *headland* W Puerto Rico
45 P9 **Higüey** *var.* Salvaleón de Higüey. E Dominican Republic
190 G11 **Hihifo** ✕ (Matā'utu) Île Uvea, N Wallis and Futuna
81 N16 **Hiiraan** *off.* Gobolka Hiiraan. ◈ *region* C Somalia
118 E4 **Hiiumaa** *off.* Hiiumaa Maakond. ◈ *province* W Estonia
118 D4 **Hiiumaa** *Ger.* Dagden, *Swe.* Dagö. *island* W Estonia
Hijanah *see* Al Hījānah
105 S6 **Híjar** Aragón, NE Spain
191 V10 **Hikueru** *atoll* Îles Tuamotu, C French Polynesia
184 K3 **Hikurangi** Northland, North Island, NZ
184 Q8 **Hikurangi** ▲ North Island, NZ
192 L11 **Hikurangi Trench** *var.* Hikurangi Trough. *undersea feature* SW Pacific Ocean
Hikurangi Trough *see* Hikurangi Trench
190 B15 **Hikutavake** NW Niue
121 Q12 **Hilāl, Ra's al** *headland* N Libya
61 A24 **Hilario Ascasubi** Buenos Aires, E Argentina
101 K17 **Hildburghausen** Thüringen, C Germany
101 E15 **Hilden** Nordrhein-Westfalen, W Germany
100 I13 **Hildesheim** Niedersachsen, N Germany
33 T9 **Hilger** Montana, NW USA
Hili *see* Hilli
Hilla *see* Al Ḩillah
45 O14 **Hillaby, Mount** ▲ N Barbados
95 K19 **Hillared** Västra Götaland, S Sweden
195 R12 **Hillary Coast** *physical region* Antarctica
42 G2 **Hill Bank** Orange Walk, N Belize
33 O14 **Hill City** Idaho, NW USA
26 K3 **Hill City** Kansas, C USA
29 V5 **Hill City** Minnesota, N USA

◆ Country ● Country Capital ◇ Dependent Territory ○ Dependent Territory Capital ◈ Administrative Region ✕ International Airport ▲ Mountain ▲ Mountain Range ✱ Volcano ~ River ◎ Lake ▣ Reservoir

28 J10 **Hill City** South Dakota, N USA
65 C24 **Hill Cove Settlement** West Falkland, Falkland Islands
98 H10 **Hillegom** Zuid-Holland, W Netherlands
95 J22 **Hillerød** Frederiksborg, E Denmark
36 M7 **Hillers, Mount** ▲ Utah, W USA
153 S13 **Hilli** var. Hili. Rajshahi, NW Bangladesh
29 R11 **Hills** Minnesota, N USA
30 L14 **Hillsboro** Illinois, N USA
27 N5 **Hillsboro** Kansas, C USA
27 X5 **Hillsboro** Missouri, C USA
19 N10 **Hillsboro** New Hampshire, NE USA
37 Q14 **Hillsboro** New Mexico, SW USA
29 R4 **Hillsboro** North Dakota, N USA
31 R14 **Hillsboro** Ohio, N USA
32 G11 **Hillsboro** Oregon, NW USA
25 T8 **Hillsboro** Texas, SW USA
30 K8 **Hillsboro** Wisconsin, N USA
23 Y14 **Hillsboro Canal** *canal* Florida, SE USA
45 Y15 **Hillsborough** Carriacou, N Grenada
97 G15 **Hillsborough** E Northern Ireland, UK
21 U9 **Hillsborough** North Carolina, SE USA
31 Q10 **Hillsdale** Michigan, N USA
183 O8 **Hillston** New South Wales, SE Australia
21 R7 **Hillsville** Virginia, NE USA
96 L2 **Hillswick** NE Scotland, UK
Hill Tippera see Tripura
38 H11 **Hilo** Hawai'i, USA, C Pacific Ocean
18 F9 **Hilton** New York, NE USA
14 C10 **Hilton Beach** Ontario, S Canada
21 R16 **Hilton Head Island** South Carolina, SE USA
21 R16 **Hilton Head Island** *island* South Carolina, SE USA
99 J15 **Hilvarenbeek** Noord-Brabant, S Netherlands
98 J11 **Hilversum** Noord-Holland, C Netherlands
Hilwân see Helwân
152 J7 **Himāchal Pradesh** ◈ *state* NW India
Himalaya/Himalaya Shan see Himalayas
152 M9 **Himalayas** var. Himalaya, Chin. Himalaya Shan. ▲ S Asia
171 P6 **Himamaylan** Negros, C Philippines
93 K15 **Himanka** Länsi-Suomi, W Finland
Himara see Himarë
113 L23 **Himarë** var. Himara. Vlorë, S Albania
138 M2 **Ḩimār, Wādī al** *dry watercourse* N Syria
154 D9 **Himatnagar** Gujarāt, W India
109 Y4 **Himberg** Niederösterreich, E Austria
164 I13 **Himeji** var. Himezi. Hyōgo, Honshū, SW Japan
164 E14 **Hime-jima** *island* SW Japan
Himezi see Himeji
164 L13 **Himi** Toyama, Honshū, SW Japan
109 S9 **Himmelberg** Kärnten, S Austria
138 I5 **Ḩimş** var. Homs; anc. Emesa. Ḩimş, C Syria
138 K6 **Ḩimş** off. Muḩāfaẓat Ḩimş, var. Homs. ◈ *governorate* C Syria
138 I5 **Ḩimş, Buḩayrat** var. Buḩayrat Qaţţīnah. ◎ W Syria
171 R7 **Hinatuan** Mindanao, S Philippines
117 N10 **Hînceşti** var. Hânceşti; prev. Kotovsk. C Moldova
44 M9 **Hinche** C Haiti
181 X5 **Hinchinbrook Island** *island* Queensland, NE Australia
39 S12 **Hinchinbrook Island** *island* Alaska, USA
97 M19 **Hinckley** C England, UK
29 V7 **Hinckley** Minnesota, N USA
36 K5 **Hinckley** Utah, W USA
18 J9 **Hinckley Reservoir** ▣ New York, NE USA
152 I12 **Hindaun** Rājasthān, N India
Hindenburg/Hindenburg in Oberschlesien see Zabrze
Hindiya see Al Hindīyah
21 O6 **Hindman** Kentucky, S USA
182 L10 **Hindmarsh, Lake** ◎ Victoria, SE Australia
185 G19 **Hinds** Canterbury, South Island, NZ
185 G19 **Hinds** ∽ South Island, NZ
95 H23 **Hindsholm** *island* C Denmark
149 S4 **Hindu Kush** Per. Hendū Kosh. ▲ Afghanistan/Pakistan
155 H19 **Hindupur** Andhra Pradesh, E India
11 O12 **Hines Creek** Alberta, W Canada
23 W6 **Hinesville** Georgia, SE USA
154 I12 **Hinganghāt** Mahārāshtra, C India
149 N15 **Hingol** ∽ SW Pakistan
154 H13 **Hingoli** Mahārāshtra, C India
137 R13 **Hınıs** Erzurum, E Turkey
92 O2 **Hinlopenstretet** *strait* N Svalbard
92 G10 **Hinnøya** Lapp. Iinnasuolu. *island* C Norway
108 H10 **Hinterrhein** ∽ SW Switzerland
11 O14 **Hinton** Alberta, SW Canada
26 M10 **Hinton** Oklahoma, C USA
21 R6 **Hinton** West Virginia, NE USA
Hios see Chíos
41 N8 **Hipolito** Coahuila de Zaragoza, NE Mexico
Hipponium see Vibo Valentia
164 B13 **Hirado** Nagasaki, Hirado-shima, SW Japan
164 B13 **Hirado-shima** *island* SW Japan
165 P16 **Hirakubo-saki** *headland* Ishigaki-jima, SW Japan
154 M11 **Hīrākud Reservoir** ▣ E India
Hir al Gharbi, Qasr al see Ḩayr al Gharbī, Qaşr al
165 Q16 **Hirara** Okinawa, Miyako-jima, SW Japan
Qasr al Hir Ash Sharqī see Ḩayr ash Sharqī, Qaşr al
164 G12 **Hirata** Shimane, Honshū, SW Japan
Hiratuka see Hiratsuka
136 I13 **Hirfanlı Barajı** ▣ C Turkey
155 G18 **Hiriyūr** Karnātaka, W India
Hirlău see Hârlău
148 K10 **Hīrmand, Rūd-e** var. Daryā-ye Helmand. ∽ Afghanistan/Iran **see also** Helmand, Daryā-ye
Hirmil see Hermel
165 T5 **Hiroo** Hokkaidō, NE Japan
165 Q7 **Hirosaki** Aomori, Honshū, C Japan
164 F13 **Hiroshima** var. Hirosima. Hiroshima, Honshū, SW Japan
164 G13 **Hiroshima** off. Hiroshima-ken, var. Hirosima. ◈ *prefecture* Honshū, SW Japan
Hirosima see Hiroshima
Hirschberg/Hirschberg im Riesengebirge/Hirschberg in Schlesien see Jelenia Góra
103 Q3 **Hirson** Aisne, N France
Hirşova see Hârşova
95 G19 **Hirtshals** Nordjylland, N Denmark
152 H10 **Hisār** Haryāna, NW India
186 E9 **Hisiu** Central, SW PNG
147 P13 **Hisor** Rus. Gissar. W Tajikistan
Hispalis see Sevilla
Hispana/Hispania see Spain
44 M7 **Hispaniola** *island* Dominion Republic/Haiti
64 F11 **Hispaniola Basin** var. Hispaniola Trough. *undersea feature* SW Atlantic Ocean
Hispaniola Trough see Hispaniola Basin
Histonium see Vasto
139 R7 **Hit** SW Iraq
165 P14 **Hita** Ōita, Kyūshū, SW Japan
165 P12 **Hitachi** var. Hitati. Ibaraki, Honshū, S Japan
165 P12 **Hitachi-Ōta** var. Hitatiôta. Ibaraki, Honshū, S Japan
Hitati see Hitachi
Hitatiôta see Hitachi-Ōta
97 O21 **Hitchin** E England, UK
191 Q7 **Hitiaa** Tahiti, W French Polynesia
164 D15 **Hitoyoshi** var. Hitoyosi. Kumamoto, Kyūshū, SW Japan
Hitoyosi see Hitoyoshi
94 F7 **Hitra** prev. Hitteren. *island* S Norway
Hitteren see Hitra
187 Q11 **Hiu** *island* Torres Islands, N Vanuatu
165 O11 **Hiuchiga-take** ▲ Honshū, C Japan
191 X7 **Hiva Oa** *island* Îles Marquises, N French Polynesia
20 M10 **Hiwassee Lake** ▣ North Carolina, SE USA
20 M10 **Hiwassee River** ∽ SE USA
95 H20 **Hjallerup** Nordjylland, N Denmark
95 M16 **Hjälmaren** Eng. Lake Hjalmar. ◎ C Sweden
Hjalmar, Lake see Hjälmaren
95 C14 **Hjellestad** Hordaland, S Norway
95 D16 **Hjelmeland** Rogaland, S Norway
94 G10 **Hjerkinn** Oppland, S Norway
95 L18 **Hjo** Västra Götaland, S Sweden
95 G19 **Hjørring** Nordjylland, N Denmark
167 O1 **Hkakabo Razi** ▲ Burma/China
167 N1 **Hkring Bum** ▲ N Burma
83 L21 **Hlathikulu** var. Hlatikulu. S Swaziland
Hlatikulu see Hlathikulu
Hliboka see Hlyboka
111 F17 **Hlinsko** var. Hlinsko v Čechách. Pardubický Kraj, C Czech Republic
Hlinsko v Čechách see Hlinsko
117 S6 **Hlobyne** Rus. Globino. Poltavs'ka Oblast', NE Ukraine
111 H20 **Hlohovec** Ger. Freistadtl, Hung. Galgóc; prev. Frakštát. Trnavský Kraj, W Slovakia
83 J23 **Hlotse** var. Leribe. NW Lesotho
111 I17 **Hlučín** Ger. Hultschin, Pol. Hulczyn. Moravskoslezský Kraj, E Czech Republic
117 S2 **Hlukhiv** Rus. Glukhov. Sums'ka Oblast', NE Ukraine
119 K21 **Hlushkavichy** Rus. Glushkevichi. Homyel'skaya Voblasts', SE Belarus
119 L18 **Hlusk** Rus. Glusk, Glussk. Mahilyowskaya Voblasts', E Belarus
116 K8 **Hlyboka** Ger. Hliboka, Rus. Glybokaya. Chernivets'ka Oblast', W Ukraine
118 K13 **Hlybokaye** Rus. Glubokoye. Vitsyebskaya Voblasts', N Belarus
77 Q16 **Ho** SE Ghana
167 S6 **Hoa Binh** Hoa Binh, N Vietnam
83 E20 **Hoachanas** Hardap, C Namibia
Hoai Nhơn see Bông Sơn
167 T8 **Hoa Lac** Quang Binh, C Vietnam
167 S5 **Hoang Liên Sơn** ▲ N Vietnam
83 B17 **Hoanib** ∽ NW Namibia
33 S15 **Hoback Peak** ▲ Wyoming, C USA
183 P17 **Hobart** prev. Hobarton, Hobart Town. *state capital* Tasmania, SE Australia
26 L11 **Hobart** Oklahoma, C USA
183 P17 **Hobart** ✕ Tasmania, SE Australia
Hobarton/Hobart Town see Hobart
37 W14 **Hobbs** New Mexico, SW USA
194 L12 **Hobbs Coast** *physical region* Antarctica
23 Z14 **Hobe Sound** Florida, SE USA
Hobicaurikány see Uricani
54 E12 **Hobo** Huila, S Colombia
99 G16 **Hoboken** Antwerpen, N Belgium
158 K3 **Hoboksar** var. Hoboksar Mongol Zizhixian. Xinjiang Uygur Zizhiqu, NW China
Hoboksar Mongol Zizhixian see Hoboksar
95 G21 **Hobro** Nordjylland, N Denmark
21 X10 **Hobucken** North Carolina, SE USA
95 O20 **Hoburgen** *headland* SE Sweden
81 P15 **Hobyo** It. Obbia. Mudug, E Somalia
109 R8 **Hochalmspitze** ▲ SW Austria
109 Q4 **Hochburg** Oberösterreich, N Austria
103 F8 **Hochdorf** Luzern, N Switzerland
109 N8 **Hochfeiler** It. Gran Pilastro. ▲ Austria/Italy
167 T14 **Hô Chi Minh** var. Ho Chi Minh City; prev. Saigon. S Vietnam
Ho Chi Minh City see Hô Chi Minh
108 I7 **Höchst** Vorarlberg, NW Austria
Höchstadt see Höchstadt an der Aisch
101 K19 **Höchstadt an der Aisch** var. Höchstadt. Bayern, C Germany
108 L9 **Hochwilde** It. L'Altissima. ▲ Austria/Italy
109 S7 **Hochwildstelle** ▲ C Austria
31 T14 **Hocking River** ∽ Ohio, N USA
Hoctúm see Hoctún
41 X12 **Hoctún** var. Hoctúm. Yucatán, E Mexico
Hodeida see Al Ḩudaydah
20 K6 **Hodgenville** Kentucky, S USA
11 T17 **Hodgeville** Saskatchewan, S Canada
76 L9 **Hodh ech Chargui** ◈ *region* E Mauritania
Hodh el Garbi see Hodh el Gharbi
76 J10 **Hodh el Gharbi** var. Hodh el Garbi. ◈ *region* S Mauritania
111 L25 **Hódmezővásárhely** Csongrád, SE Hungary
74 J6 **Hodna, Chott El** var. Chott el-Hodna, Ar. Shatt al-Hodna. *salt lake* N Algeria
Hodna, Shatt al- see Hodna, Chott El
111 G19 **Hodonín** Ger. Göding. Jihomoravský Kraj, SE Czech Republic
162 G6 **Hödrögö** Dzavhan, N Mongolia
Hodság/Hodschag see Odžaci
39 R7 **Hodzana River** ∽ Alaska, USA
Hoei see Huy
99 H19 **Hoeilaart** Vlaams Brabant, C Belgium
Hoë Karoo see Great Karoo
98 F12 **Hoek van Holland** Eng. Hook of Holland. Zuid-Holland, W Netherlands
98 L11 **Hoenderloo** Gelderland, E Netherlands
99 L18 **Hoensbroek** Limburg, SE Netherlands
163 Y11 **Hoeryŏng** NE North Korea
99 K18 **Hoeselt** Limburg, NE Belgium
98 K11 **Hoevelaken** Gelderland, C Netherlands
Hoey see Huy
101 M18 **Hof** Bayern, SE Germany
Höfdhakaupstadhur see Skagaströnd
Hofei see Hefei
101 G18 **Hofheim am Taunus** Hessen, W Germany
Hofmarkt see Odorheiu Secuiesc
92 L3 **Höfn** Austurland, SE Iceland
94 N13 **Hofors** Gävleborg, C Sweden
92 J6 **Hofsjökull** *glacier* C Iceland
92 J1 **Hofsós** Nordhurland Vestra, N Iceland
164 E13 **Hōfu** Yamaguchi, Honshū, SW Japan
Hofuf see Al Hufūf
95 J22 **Höganäs** Skåne, S Sweden
183 P14 **Hogan Group** *island group* Tasmania, SE Australia
23 R4 **Hogansville** Georgia, SE USA
39 P8 **Hogatza River** ∽ Alaska, USA
28 I14 **Hogback Mountain** ▲ Nebraska, C USA
95 G14 **Høgevarde** ▲ S Norway
Högfors see Karkkila
31 P5 **Hog Island** *island* Michigan, N USA
21 Y6 **Hog Island** *island* Virginia, NE USA
Hogoley Islands see Chuuk Islands
95 N20 **Högsby** Kalmar, S Sweden
36 K1 **Hogup Mountains** ▲ Utah, W USA
101 E17 **Hohe Acht** ▲ W Germany
Hohenelbe see Vrchlabí
108 I7 **Hohenems** Vorarlberg, W Austria
Hohenmauth see Vysoké Mýto
Hohensalza see Inowrocław
Hohenstadt see Zábřeh
Hohenstein in Ostpreussen see Olsztynek
20 I9 **Hohenwald** Tennessee, S USA
101 L17 **Hohenwarte-Stausee** ▣ C Germany
Hohes Venn see Hautes Fagnes
109 Q8 **Hohe Tauern** ▲ W Austria
163 O13 **Hohhot** var. Huhehot, Huhuohaote, Mong. Kukukhoto; prev. Kweisui, Kwesui. Nei Mongol Zizhiqu, N China
103 U6 **Hohneck** ▲ NE France
77 Q16 **Hohoe** E Ghana
164 E12 **Hōhoku** Yamaguchi, Honshū, SW Japan
159 O11 **Hoh Sai Hu** ◎ C China
159 N11 **Hoh Xil Hu** ◎ C China
158 L11 **Hoh Xil Shan** ▲ W China
167 U10 **Hôi An** prev. Faifo. Quang Nam-Đa Nãng, C Vietnam
Hoï-Hao/Hoihow see Haikou
159 S11 **Hoika** prev. Heka. Qinghai, W China
81 F17 **Hoima** W Uganda
26 L5 **Hoisington** Kansas, C USA
146 D12 **Hojagala** Rus. Khodzhakala. Balkan Welaýaty, W Turkmenistan
146 M13 **Hojambaz** Rus. Khodzhambas. Lebap Welaýaty, E Turkmenistan
95 H23 **Højby** Fyn, C Denmark
95 F24 **Højer** Sønderjylland, SW Denmark
164 E14 **Hōjō** var. Hôzyô. Ehime, Shikoku, SW Japan
184 J3 **Hokianga Harbour** *inlet* SE Tasman Sea
185 F17 **Hokitika** West Coast, South Island, NZ
165 U4 **Hokkai-dō** ◈ *territory* Hokkaidō, NE Japan
165 T3 **Hokkaidō** prev. Ezo, Yeso, Yezo. *island* NE Japan
95 G15 **Hokksund** Buskerud, S Norway
143 S4 **Hokmābād** Khorāsān, N Iran
Hokō see P'ohang
Hoko-guntō/Hoko-shotō see P'enghu Liehtao
Hoktemberyan see Armavir
94 F13 **Hol** Buskerud, S Norway
117 R11 **Hola Prystan'** Rus. Golaya Pristan. Khersons'ka Oblast', S Ukraine
95 I23 **Holbæk** Vestsjælland, E Denmark
162 G6 **Holboo** Dzavhan, W Mongolia
183 P10 **Holbrook** New South Wales, SE Australia
37 N11 **Holbrook** Arizona, SW USA
27 S5 **Holden** Missouri, C USA
36 K5 **Holden** Utah, W USA
27 O11 **Holdenville** Oklahoma, C USA
29 O16 **Holdrege** Nebraska, C USA
35 X3 **Hole in the Mountain Peak** ▲ Nevada, W USA
155 G20 **Hole Narsipur** Karnātaka, W India
111 H18 **Holešov** Ger. Holleschau. Zlínský Kraj, E Czech Republic
45 N14 **Holetown** prev. Jamestown. W Barbados
31 Q12 **Holgate** Ohio, N USA
44 I7 **Holguín** Holguín, SE Cuba
23 V12 **Holiday** Florida, SE USA
39 O12 **Holitna River** ∽ Alaska, USA
94 J13 **Höljes** Värmland, C Sweden
109 X3 **Hollabrunn** Niederösterreich, NE Austria
36 L3 **Holladay** Utah, W USA
11 X16 **Holland** Manitoba, S Canada
31 O9 **Holland** Michigan, N USA
25 T9 **Holland** Texas, SW USA
Holland see Netherlands
22 K4 **Hollandale** Mississippi, S USA
Hollandia see Jayapura
Hollandsch Diep see Hollands Diep
99 H14 **Hollands Diep** var. Hollandsch Diep. *channel* SW Netherlands
Holleschau see Holešov
25 R5 **Holliday** Texas, SW USA
18 E15 **Hollidaysburg** Pennsylvania, NE USA
21 S6 **Hollins** Virginia, NE USA
26 J12 **Hollis** Oklahoma, C USA
35 O10 **Hollister** California, W USA
27 T8 **Hollister** Missouri, C USA
93 M19 **Hollola** Etelä-Suomi, S Finland
98 K4 **Hollum** Friesland, N Netherlands
95 J23 **Höllviksnäs** Skåne, S Sweden
37 W6 **Holly** Colorado, C USA
31 R9 **Holly** Michigan, N USA
21 S14 **Holly Hill** South Carolina, SE USA
21 W11 **Holly Ridge** North Carolina, SE USA
22 L1 **Holly Springs** Mississippi, S USA
23 Z15 **Hollywood** Florida, SE USA
8 J6 **Holman** Victoria Island, Northwest Territories, N Canada
92 I2 **Hólmavík** Vestfirdhir, NW Iceland
30 J7 **Holmen** Wisconsin, N USA
23 R8 **Holmes Creek** ∽ Alabama/Florida, SE USA
95 H16 **Holmestrand** Vestfold, S Norway
93 J16 **Holmön** *island* N Sweden
95 E22 **Holmsland Klit** *beach* W Denmark
93 J16 **Holmsund** Västerbotten, N Sweden
95 Q18 **Holmudden** *headland* SE Sweden
138 F10 **Ḩolon** var. Kholon. Tel Aviv, C Israel
117 P8 **Holovanivs'k** Rus. Golovanevsk. Kirovohrads'ka Oblast', C Ukraine
95 F21 **Holstebro** Ringkøbing, W Denmark
95 F23 **Holsted** Ribe, W Denmark
29 T13 **Holstein** Iowa, C USA
Holsteinborg/Holsteinsborg/Holstenborg/Holstensborg see Sisimiut
21 O8 **Holston River** ∽ Tennessee, S USA
31 Q9 **Holt** Michigan, N USA
98 N10 **Holten** Overijssel, E Netherlands
27 P3 **Holton** Kansas, C USA
27 U5 **Holts Summit** Missouri, C USA
35 X17 **Holtville** California, W USA
98 L5 **Holwerd** Fris. Holwert. Friesland, N Netherlands
Holwert see Holwerd
39 O11 **Holy Cross** Alaska, USA
37 R4 **Holy Cross, Mount Of The** ▲ Colorado, C USA
97 I18 **Holyhead** Wel. Caer Gybi. NW Wales, UK
97 H18 **Holy Island** *island* NW Wales, UK
96 L12 **Holy Island** *island* NE England, UK
37 W3 **Holyoke** Colorado, C USA
18 M11 **Holyoke** Massachusetts, NE USA
101 I14 **Holzminden** Niedersachsen, C Germany
81 G19 **Homa Bay** Nyanza, W Kenya
Homāyūnshahr see Khomeynīshahr
77 P11 **Hombori** Mopti, S Mali
101 E20 **Homburg** Saarland, SW GermanyQ5
9 R5 **Home Bay** *bay* Baffin Bay, Nunavut, NE Canada
Homenau see Humenné
39 Q13 **Homer** Alaska, USA
22 H4 **Homer** Louisiana, S USA
18 H10 **Homer** New York, NE USA
23 V7 **Homerville** Georgia, SE USA
23 Y16 **Homestead** Florida, SE USA
27 O9 **Hominy** Oklahoma, C USA
94 H8 **Hommelvik** Sør-Trøndelag, S Norway
95 C16 **Hommersåk** Rogaland, S Norway
155 H15 **Homnābād** Karnātaka, C India
22 J7 **Homochitto River** ∽ Mississippi, S USA
83 N20 **Homoine** Inhambane, SE Mozambique
112 O12 **Homoljske Planine** ▲ E Serbia and Montenegro (Yugo.)
Homonna see Humenné
Homs see Al Khums, Libya
Homs see Ḩimş, Syria
119 P19 **Homyel'** Rus. Gomel'. Homyel'skaya Voblasts', SE Belarus
118 L12 **Homyel'** Vitsyebskaya Voblasts', N Belarus
119 L19 **Homyel'skaya Voblasts'** prev. Rus. Gomel'skaya Oblast'. ◈ *province* SE Belarus
Honan see Henan, China
Honan see Luoyang, China
165 U4 **Honbetsu** Hokkaidō, NE Japan
Honctő see Gurahonţ
54 E9 **Honda** Tolima, C Colombia
83 D24 **Hondeklip** Afr. Hondeklipbaai. Northern Cape, W South Africa
Hondeklipbaai see Hondeklip
11 Q13 **Hondo** Alberta, W Canada
164 C15 **Hondo** Kumamoto, Shimo-jima, SW Japan
25 Q12 **Hondo** Texas, SW USA
42 G1 **Hondo** ∽ Central America
Hondo see Honshū
42 G6 **Honduras** off. Republic of Honduras. ◆ *republic* Central America
Honduras, Golfo de see Honduras, Gulf of
42 H4 **Honduras, Gulf of** Sp. Golfo de Honduras. *gulf* W Caribbean Sea
11 V12 **Hone** Manitoba, C Canada
21 P12 **Honea Path** South Carolina, SE USA
95 H14 **Hønefoss** Buskerud, S Norway
31 S12 **Honey Creek** ∽ Ohio, N USA
25 V5 **Honey Grove** Texas, SW USA
35 Q4 **Honey Lake** ◎ California, W USA
102 L4 **Honfleur** Calvados, N France
Hon Gai see Hông Gai
161 O8 **Hong'an** prev. Huang'an. Hubei, C China
Hongay see Hông Gai
167 T6 **Hông Gai** var. Hon Gai, Hongay. Quang Ninh, N Vietnam
161 O15 **Honghai Wan** *bay* N South China Sea
Hông Hà, Sông see Red River
161 O7 **Hong He** ∽ C China
161 N9 **Hong Hu** ◎ C China
160 L11 **Hongjiang** Hunan, S China
Hongjiang see Wangcang
161 O15 **Hong Kong** Chin. Xianggang. S China
160 L4 **Hongliu He** ∽ C China
159 P8 **Hongliuwan** var. Aksay, Aksay Kazakzu Zizhixian. Gansu, N China
159 P7 **Hongliuyuan** Gansu, N China
163 O9 **Hongor** Dornogovĭ, SE Mongolia
161 S8 **Hongqiao** ✕ (Shanghai) Shanghai Shi, E China
160 K14 **Hongshui He** ∽ S China
160 M5 **Hongtong** Shanxi, C China
164 J15 **Hongū** Wakayama, Honshū, SW Japan
Honguedo, Détroit d' see Honguedo Passage
15 Y5 **Honguedo Passage** var. Honguedo Strait, Fr. Détroit d'Honguedo. *strait* Québec, E Canada
Honguedo Strait see Honguedo Passage
Hongwan see Hongwansi
159 S8 **Hongwansi** var. Sunan, Sunan Yugurzu Zizhixian; prev. Hongwan. Gansu, N China
163 X13 **Hongwŏn** E North Korea
160 H7 **Hongyuan** var. Qiongxi; prev. Hurama. Sichuan, C China
161 Q7 **Hongze Hu** var. Hung-tse Hu. ◎ E China
186 L9 **Honiara** ● (Solomon Islands) Guadalcanal, C Solomon Islands
165 P8 **Honjō** var. Honzyô. Akita, Honshū, C Japan
93 K18 **Honkajoki** Länsi-Suomi, W Finland
92 K7 **Honningsvåg** Finnmark, N Norway
95 I19 **Hönö** Västra Götaland, S Sweden
38 G11 **Honoka'a** var. Honokaa. Hawai'i, USA, C Pacific Ocean
38 D9 **Honolulu** ◎ O'ahu, Hawai'i, USA, C Pacific Ocean
38 H11 **Honomū** var. Honomu. Hawai'i, USA, C Pacific Ocean
105 P10 **Honrubia** Castilla-La Mancha, C Spain
164 M12 **Honshū** var. Hondo, Honsyû. *island* SW Japan
Honsyû see Honshū
Honte see Westerschelde
Honzyô see Honjō
8 K8 **Hood** ∽ Nunavut, NW Canada
Hood Island see Española, Isla
32 H11 **Hood, Mount** ▲ Oregon, NW USA
32 H11 **Hood River** Oregon, NW USA
98 H10 **Hoofddorp** Noord-Holland, W Netherlands
99 G15 **Hoogerheide** Noord-Brabant, S Netherlands
98 N8 **Hoogeveen** Drenthe, NE Netherlands
98 O6 **Hoogezand-Sappemeer** Groningen, NE Netherlands
98 J8 **Hoogkarspel** Noord-Holland, NW Netherlands
98 N5 **Hoogkerk** Groningen, NE Netherlands
98 G13 **Hoogvliet** Zuid-Holland, SW Netherlands
26 I8 **Hooker** Oklahoma, C USA
97 E21 **Hook Head** Ir. Rinn Duáin. *headland* SE Ireland
Hook of Holland see Hoek van Holland
162 J9 **Hoolt** Övörhangay, C Mongolia
39 W13 **Hoonah** Chichagof Island, Alaska, USA
38 L11 **Hooper Bay** Alaska, USA
31 N13 **Hoopeston** Illinois, N USA
95 K22 **Höör** Skåne, S Sweden
98 I9 **Hoorn** Noord-Holland, NW Netherlands
18 L10 **Hoosic River** ∽ New York, NE USA
Hoosier State see Indiana
35 Y11 **Hoover Dam** *dam* Arizona/Nevada, W USA
162 I9 **Höövör** Övörhangay, C Mongolia
137 Q11 **Hopa** Artvin, NE Turkey
18 J14 **Hopatcong** New Jersey, NE USA
10 M17 **Hope** British Columbia, SW Canada
39 R12 **Hope** Alaska, USA
27 T14 **Hope** Arkansas, C USA
31 P14 **Hope** Indiana, N USA
29 Q5 **Hope** North Dakota, N USA
13 Q7 **Hopedale** Newfoundland and Labrador, NE Canada
Hopeh/Hopei see Hebei
180 K13 **Hope, Lake** *salt lake* Western Australia
41 X13 **Hopelchén** Campeche, SE Mexico
21 U11 **Hope Mills** North Carolina, SE USA
183 O7 **Hope, Mount** New South Wales, SE Australia
92 P4 **Hopen** *island* SE Svalbard
197 Q4 **Hope, Point** *headland* Alaska, USA
12 M3 **Hopes Advance, Cap** *headland* Québec, NE Canada
182 L10 **Hopetoun** Victoria, SE Australia
83 H23 **Hopetown** Northern Cape, W South Africa
21 W6 **Hopewell** Virginia, NE USA
109 O7 **Hopfgarten-im-Brixental** Tirol, W Austria
181 N8 **Hopkins Lake** *salt lake* Western Australia
182 M12 **Hopkins River** ∽ Victoria, SE Australia
20 I7 **Hopkinsville** Kentucky, S USA
34 M6 **Hopland** California, W USA
95 G24 **Hoptrup** Sønderjylland, SW Denmark
Hoqin Zuoyi Zhongji see Baokang
32 F9 **Hoquiam** Washington, NW USA
29 R6 **Horace** North Dakota, N USA
137 R12 **Horasan** Erzurum, NE Turkey
101 G22 **Horb am Neckar** Baden-Württemberg, S Germany
95 K23 **Hörby** Skåne, S Sweden
43 P16 **Horconcitos** Chiriquí, W Panama
95 C14 **Hordaland** ◈ *county* S Norway
116 H13 **Horezu** Vâlcea, SW Romania
108 G7 **Horgen** Zürich, N Switzerland
162 I7 **Horgo** Arhangay, C Mongolia
Hörin see Fenglin
163 O13 **Horinger** Nei Mongol Zizhiqu, N China
162 I9 **Horiult** Bayanhongor, C Mongolia
11 U17 **Horizon** Saskatchewan, S Canada
192 K9 **Horizon Bank** *undersea feature* S Pacific Ocean
192 L10 **Horizon Deep** *undersea feature* W Pacific Ocean
95 L14 **Hörken** Örebro, S Sweden
119 O15 **Horki** Rus. Gorki. Mahilyowskaya Voblasts', E Belarus
195 O10 **Horlick Mountains** ▲ Antarctica
117 X7 **Horlivka** Rom. Adâncata, Rus. Gorlovka. Donets'ka Oblast', E Ukraine
143 V11 **Ḩormak** Sīstān va Balūchestān, SE Iran
143 R13 **Hormozgān** off. Ostān-e Hormozgān. ◈ *province* S Iran
Hormoz, Tangeh-ye see Hormuz, Strait of

◆ Country ● Country Capital ◇ Dependent Territory ○ Dependent Territory Capital ◈ Administrative Region ✕ International Airport ▲ Mountain ▲ Mountain Range ✗ Volcano ∽ River ◎ Lake ▣ Reservoir

141 W6 **Hormuz, Strait of** *var.* Strait of Ormuz, *Per.* Tangeh-ye Hormoz. *strait* Iran/Oman
109 W2 **Horn** Niederösterreich, NE Austria
95 M18 **Horn** Östergötland, S Sweden
8 J9 **Horn** ≈ Northwest Territories, NW Canada
Hornád *see* Hernád
8 I6 **Hornaday** ≈ Northwest Territories, NW Canada
92 H13 **Hornavan** ◎ N Sweden
65 C24 **Hornby Mountains** *hill range* West Falkland, Falkland Islands
Horn, Cape *see* Hornos, Cabo de
97 O18 **Horncastle** E England, UK
95 N14 **Horndal** Dalarna, C Sweden
93 I16 **Hörnefors** Västerbotten, N Sweden
18 F11 **Hornell** New York, NE USA
Horné Nové Mesto *see* Kysucké Nové Mesto
12 F12 **Hornepayne** Ontario, S Canada
94 D10 **Hornindalsvatnet** ◎ S Norway
101 G22 **Hornisgrinde** ▲ SW Germany
22 M9 **Horn Island** *island* Mississippi, S USA
Hornja Łužica *see* Oberlausitz
63 J26 **Hornos, Cabo de** *Eng.* Cape Horn. *headland* S Chile
117 S10 **Hornostayivka** Khersons'ka Oblast', S Ukraine
183 T9 **Hornsby** New South Wales, SE Australia
97 O16 **Hornsea** E England, UK
94 O11 **Hornslandet** *peninsula* C Sweden
95 H22 **Hornslet** Århus, C Denmark
92 O4 **Hornsundtind** ▲ S Svalbard
Horochów *see* Horokhiv
116 J7 **Horodenka** *Rus.* Gorodenka. Ivano-Frankivs'ka Oblast', W Ukraine
117 Q2 **Horodnya** *Rus.* Gorodnya. Chernihivs'ka Oblast', NE Ukraine
116 K6 **Horodok** Khmel'nyts'ka Oblast', W Ukraine
116 H5 **Horodok** *Pol.* Gródek Jagielloński, *Rus.* Gorodok, Gorodok Yagellonski. L'vivs'ka Oblast', NW Ukraine
117 Q6 **Horodyshche** *Rus.* Gorodishche. Cherkas'ka Oblast', C Ukraine
165 T3 **Horokanai** Hokkaidō, NE Japan
116 J4 **Horokhiv** *Pol.* Horochów, *Rus.* Gorokhov. Volyns'ka Oblast', NW Ukraine
165 T4 **Horoshiri-dake** *var.* Horosiri Dake. ▲ Hokkaidō, N Japan
Horosiri Dake *see* Horoshiri-dake
111 C17 **Hořovice** *Ger.* Horowitz. Středočeský Kraj, W Czech Republic
Horowitz *see* Hořovice
Horqin Zuoyi Houqi *see* Ganjig
Horqin Zuoyi Zhongji *see* Bayan Huxu
62 O5 **Horqueta** Concepción, C Paraguay
55 O12 **Horqueta Minas** Amazonas, S Venezuela
95 J20 **Horred** Västra Götaland, S Sweden
151 J19 **Horsburgh Atoll** *atoll* N Maldives
20 K7 **Horse Cave** Kentucky, S USA
37 V6 **Horse Creek** ≈ Colorado, C USA
27 S6 **Horse Creek** ≈ Missouri, C USA
18 G11 **Horseheads** New York, NE USA
37 P13 **Horse Mount** ▲ New Mexico, SW USA
95 G22 **Horsens** Vejle, C Denmark
65 F25 **Horse Pasture Point** *headland* W Saint Helena
33 N13 **Horseshoe Bend** Idaho, NW USA
36 L13 **Horseshoe Reservoir** ⊟ Arizona, SW USA
64 M9 **Horseshoe Seamounts** *undersea feature* E Atlantic Ocean
182 L11 **Horsham** Victoria, SE Australia
97 O23 **Horsham** SE England, UK
99 M15 **Horst** Limburg, SE Netherlands
64 N2 **Horta** Faial, Azores, Portugal, NE Atlantic Ocean
95 H16 **Horten** Vestfold, S Norway
111 M23 **Hortobágy-Berettyó** ≈ E Hungary
27 Q3 **Horton** Kansas, C USA
8 I7 **Horton** ≈ Northwest Territories, NW Canada
95 I23 **Hørve** Vestsjælland, E Denmark
95 L22 **Hörvik** Blekinge, S Sweden
138 E11 **Horvot Haluza** *var.* Khorvot Khalutsa. *ruins* Southern, S Israel
14 E7 **Horwood Lake** ◎ Ontario, S Canada
116 K4 **Horyn'** *Rus.* Goryn. ≈ NW Ukraine
81 I14 **Hosa'ina** *var.* Hosseina, *It.* Hosanna. Southern, S Ethiopia
Hosanna *see* Hosa'ina
101 H18 **Hösbach** Bayern, C Germany
Hose Mountains *see* Hose, Pegunungan
169 T9 **Hose, Pegunungan** *var.* Hose Mountains. ▲ East Malaysia
148 L15 **Hoshāb** Baluchistān, SW Pakistan
154 H10 **Hoshangābād** Madhya Pradesh, C India
116 L4 **Hoshcha** Rivnens'ka Oblast', NW Ukraine
152 I7 **Hoshiārpur** Punjab, NW India
162 J7 **Höshööt** Arhangay, C Mongolia
99 M23 **Hosingen** Diekirch, NE Luxembourg
186 G7 **Hoskins** New Britain, E PNG
155 G17 **Hospet** Karnātaka, C India
104 K4 **Hospital de Orbigo** Castilla-León, N Spain
Hospitalet *see* L'Hospitalet de Llobregat
92 N13 **Hossa** Oulu, E Finland
Hosseina *see* Hosa'ina
Hosszúmezjő *see* Câmpulung Moldovenesc
63 I25 **Hoste, Isla** *island* S Chile
117 O4 **Hostomel'** *Rus.* Gostomel'. Kyyivs'ka Oblast', N Ukraine
155 H20 **Hosūr** Tamil Nādu, SE India
167 N8 **Hot** Chiang Mai, NW Thailand
158 G10 **Hotan** *var.* Khotan, *Chin.* Ho-t'ien. Xinjiang Uygur Zizhiqu, NW China
158 H9 **Hotan He** ≈ NW China
83 G22 **Hotazel** Northern Cape, N South Africa
37 Q5 **Hotchkiss** Colorado, C USA
35 V7 **Hot Creek Range** ▲ Nevada, W USA
Hote *see* Hoti
171 T13 **Hoti** *var.* Hote. Pulau Seram, E Indonesia
Ho-t'ien *see* Hotan
Hotin *see* Khotyn
93 H15 **Hoting** Jämtland, C Sweden
162 L14 **Hotong Qagan Nur** ◎ N China
162 J8 **Hotont** Arhangay, C Mongolia
27 T12 **Hot Springs** Arkansas, C USA
28 J11 **Hot Springs** South Dakota, N USA
21 S5 **Hot Springs** Virginia, NE USA
35 Q4 **Hot Springs Peak** ▲ California, W USA
27 T12 **Hot Springs Village** Arkansas, C USA
Hotspur Bank *see* Hotspur Seamount
65 J16 **Hotspur Seamount** *var.* Hotspur Bank. *undersea feature* C Atlantic Ocean
8 J8 **Hottah Lake** ◎ Northwest Territories, NW Canada
44 K9 **Hotte, Massif de la** ▲ SW Haiti
99 K21 **Hotton** Luxembourg, SE Belgium
Hötzing *see* Haţeg
187 P17 **Houaïlou** Province Nord, C New Caledonia
74 K5 **Houari Boumediène** ✕ (Alger) N Algeria
167 P6 **Houayxay** *var.* Ban Houayxay, Ban Houei Sai. Bokèo, N Laos
103 N5 **Houdan** Yvelines, N France
99 F20 **Houdeng-Goegnies** *var.* Houdeng-Gœgnies. Hainaut, S Belgium
102 K14 **Houeillès** Lot-et-Garonne, SW France
99 L22 **Houffalize** Luxembourg, SE Belgium
30 M3 **Houghton** Michigan, N USA
31 Q7 **Houghton Lake** Michigan, N USA
31 Q7 **Houghton Lake** ◎ Michigan, N USA
19 T3 **Houlton** Maine, NE USA
160 M5 **Houma** Shanxi, C China
193 U15 **Houma** 'Eua, C Tonga
193 U16 **Houma** Tongatapu, S Tonga
22 J10 **Houma** Louisiana, S USA
196 V16 **Houma Taloa** *headland* Tongatapu, S Tonga
77 O13 **Houndé** SW Burkina
102 J12 **Hourtin-Carcans, Lac d'** ◎ SW France
36 J5 **House Range** ▲ Utah, W USA
10 K13 **Houston** British Columbia, SW Canada
39 R11 **Houston** Alaska, USA
29 X10 **Houston** Minnesota, N USA
22 M3 **Houston** Mississippi, S USA
27 V7 **Houston** Missouri, C USA
25 W11 **Houston** Texas, SW USA
25 W11 **Houston** ✕ Texas, SW USA
98 J12 **Houten** Utrecht, C Netherlands
99 K17 **Houthalen** Limburg, NE Belgium
99 I22 **Houyet** Namur, SE Belgium
95 H22 **Hov** Århus, C Denmark
95 L17 **Hova** Västra Götaland, S Sweden
162 E6 **Hovd** *var.* Khovd, Kobdo; *prev.* Jirgalanta. Hovd, W Mongolia
162 J10 **Hovd** Övörhangay, C Mongolia
162 E7 **Hovd** ◈ *province* W Mongolia
162 C5 **Hovd Gol** ≈ NW Mongolia
97 O23 **Hove** SE England, UK
29 N8 **Hoven** South Dakota, N USA
116 I8 **Hoverla, Hora** *Rus.* Gora Goverla. ▲ W Ukraine
162 H8 **Höviyn Am** Bayanhongor, C Mongolia
95 M21 **Hovmantorp** Kronoberg, S Sweden
163 N11 **Hövsgöl** Dornogovĭ, SE Mongolia
162 I5 **Hөvsgөl** Hөvsgөl ◈ *province* N Mongolia
Hovsgol, Lake *see* Hövsgöl Nuur
162 J5 **Hövsgöl Nuur** *var.* Lake Hovsgol. ◎ N Mongolia
78 L9 **Howa, Ouadi** *var.* Wādi Howar. ≈ Chad/Sudan ***see also*** Howar, Wādi
27 P7 **Howard** Kansas, C USA
29 Q10 **Howard** South Dakota, N USA
25 N10 **Howard Draw** *valley* Texas, SW USA
29 U8 **Howard Lake** Minnesota, N USA
80 B8 **Howar, Wādi** *var.* Ouadi Howa. ≈ Chad/Sudan ***see also*** Howa, Ouadi
25 U5 **Howe** Texas, SW USA
183 R12 **Howe, Cape** *headland* New South Wales/Victoria, SE Australia
31 R9 **Howell** Michigan, N USA
28 L9 **Howes** South Dakota, N USA
83 K23 **Howick** KwaZulu/Natal, E South Africa
Howrah *see* Hāora
27 W9 **Hoxie** Arkansas, C USA
26 J3 **Hoxie** Kansas, C USA
101 I14 **Höxter** Nordrhein-Westfalen, W Germany
158 K6 **Hoxud** Xinjiang Uygur Zizhiqu, NW China
96 J5 **Hoy** *island* N Scotland, UK
43 S17 **Hoya, Cerro** ▲ S Panama
94 D12 **Høyanger** Sogn og Fjordane, S Norway
101 P15 **Hoyerswerda** *Lus.* Wojerecy. Sachsen, E Germany
164 E14 **Hōyo-kaikyō** *var.* Hayasui-seto. *strait* SW Japan
104 J8 **Hoyos** Extremadura, W Spain
29 W4 **Hoyt Lakes** Minnesota, N USA
137 O14 **Hozat** Tunceli, E Turkey
Hôzyô *see* Hōjō
111 F16 **Hradec Králové** *Ger.* Königgrätz. Královéhradecký Kraj, N Czech Republic
Hradecký Kraj *see* Královéhradecký Kraj
111 B16 **Hradiště** *Ger.* Burgstadlberg. ▲ NW Czech Republic
117 R6 **Hradyz'k** *Rus.* Gradizhsk. Poltavs'ka Oblast', NE Ukraine
119 M16 **Hradzyanka** *Rus.* Grodzyanka. Mahilyowskaya Voblasts', E Belarus
119 F16 **Hrandzichy** *Rus.* Grandichi. Hrodzyenskaya Voblasts', W Belarus
111 H18 **Hranice** *Ger.* Mährisch-Weisskirchen. Olomoucký Kraj, E Czech Republic
112 I13 **Hrasnica** Federacija Bosna I Hercegovina, SE Bosnia and Herzegovina
109 V11 **Hrastnik** C Slovenia
137 U12 **Hrazdan** *Rus.* Razdan. C Armenia
137 T12 **Hrazdan** *var.* Zanga, *Rus.* Razdan. ≈ C Armenia
117 R5 **Hrebinka** *Rus.* Grebenka. Poltavs'ka Oblast', NE Ukraine
119 K17 **Hresk** *Rus.* Gresk. Minskaya Voblasts', C Belarus
Hrisoupoli *see* Chrysoúpoli
119 F16 **Hrodna** *Pol.* Grodno. Hrodzyenskaya Voblasts', W Belarus
119 F16 **Hrodzyenskaya Voblasts'** *prev. Rus.* Grodnenskaya Oblast'. ◈ *province* W Belarus
111 J21 **Hron** *Ger.* Gran, *Hung.* Garam. ≈ C Slovakia
111 Q14 **Hrubieszów** *Rus.* Grubeshov. Lubelskie, E Poland
112 F13 **Hrvace** Split-Dalmacija, SE Croatia
Hrvatska *see* Croatia
112 F10 **Hrvatska Kostajnica** *var.* Kostajnica. Sisak-Moslavina, C Croatia
Hrvatsko Grahovo *see* Bosansko Grahovo
116 K6 **Hrymayliv** *Pol.* Gizymałów, *Rus.* Grimaylov. Ternopil's'ka Oblast', W Ukraine
167 N4 **Hsenwi** Shan State, E Burma
Hsia-men *see* Xiamen
Hsiang-t'an *see* Xiangtan
Hsi Chiang *see* Xi Jiang
167 N6 **Hsihseng** Shan State, C Burma
161 S13 **Hsinchu** *municipality* N Taiwan
Hsing-k'ai Hu *see* Khanka, Lake
Hsi-ning/Hsining *see* Xining
Hsinking *see* Changchun
Hsin-yang *see* Xinyang
161 S14 **Hsinying** *var.* Sinying, *Jap.* Shinei. C Taiwan
167 N4 **Hsipaw** Shan State, C Burma
Hsu-chou *see* Xuzhou
161 S13 **Hsüeh Shan** ▲ N Taiwan
Hu *see* Shanghai Shi
83 B18 **Huab** ≈ W Namibia
57 M21 **Huacaya** Chuquisaca, S Bolivia
57 J19 **Huachacalla** Oruro, SW Bolivia
159 X9 **Huachi** *var.* Rouyuanchengzi. Gansu, C China
57 N16 **Huachi, Laguna** ◎ N Bolivia
57 D14 **Huacho** Lima, W Peru
163 Y8 **Huachuan** Heilongjiang, NE China
163 P12 **Huade** Nei Mongol Zizhiqu, N China
163 W10 **Huadian** Jilin, NE China
56 E13 **Huagaruncho, Cordillera** ▲ C Peru
Hua Hin *see* Ban Hua Hin
191 S10 **Huahine** *island* Îles Sous le Vent, W French Polynesia
Huahua, Rio *see* Wawa, Río
167 R8 **Huai** ≈ E Thailand
161 Q7 **Huai'an** *var.* Qingjiang; *prev.* Huaiyin. Jiangsu, E China
161 P6 **Huaibei** Anhui, E China
Huaide *see* Gongzhuling
157 T10 **Huai He** ≈ C China
160 L11 **Huaihua** Hunan, S China
161 N14 **Huaiji** Guangdong, S China
161 O2 **Huailai** *var.* Shacheng. Hebei, E China
161 P7 **Huainan** *var.* Huai-nan, Hwainan. Anhui, E China
161 N2 **Huairen** Shanxi, C China
161 O7 **Huaiyang** Henan, C China
Huaiyin *see* Huai'an
167 N16 **Huai Yot** Trang, SW Thailand
41 Q15 **Huajuapan** *var.* Huajuapan de León. Oaxaca, SE Mexico
Huajuapan de León *see* Huajuapan
41 O9 **Hualahuises** Nuevo León, NE Mexico
36 I11 **Hualapai Mountains** ▲ Arizona, SW USA
36 I11 **Hualapai Peak** ▲ Arizona, SW USA
62 J7 **Hualfín** Catamarca, N Argentina
161 T13 **Hualien** *var.* Hwalien, *Jap.* Karen. C Taiwan
56 E10 **Huallaga, Río** ≈ N Peru
56 C11 **Huamachuco** La Libertad, C Peru
41 Q14 **Huamantla** Tlaxcala, S Mexico
82 C13 **Huambo** *Port.* Nova Lisboa. Huambo, C Angola
82 B13 **Huambo** ◈ *province* C Angola
41 P15 **Huamuxtitlán** Guerrero, S Mexico
163 Y8 **Huanan** Heilongjiang, NE China
63 H17 **Huancache, Sierra** ▲ SW Argentina
57 I17 **Huancané** Puno, SE Peru
57 F16 **Huancapi** Ayacucho, C Peru
57 E15 **Huancavelica** Huancavelica, SW Peru
57 E15 **Huancavelica** *off.* Departamento de Huancavelica. ◈ *department* W Peru
57 E14 **Huancayo** Junín, C Peru
57 K20 **Huanchaca, Cerro** ▲ S Bolivia
56 C12 **Huandoy, Nevado** ▲ W Peru
161 O8 **Huangchuan** Henan, C China
161 O9 **Huanggang** Hubei, C China
Huang Hai *see* Yellow Sea
157 Q8 **Huang He** *var.* Yellow River. ≈ C China
161 Q4 **Huanghe Kou** *delta* E China
160 L5 **Huangling** Shaanxi, C China
163 P13 **Huangqi Hai** ◎ N China
161 Q9 **Huang Shan** ▲ Anhui, E China
161 Q9 **Huangshan** *var.* Tunxi. Anhui, E China
161 O9 **Huangshi** *var.* Huang-shih, Hwangshih. Hubei, C China
Huang-shih *see* Huangshi
160 L5 **Huangtu Gaoyuan** *plateau* C China
61 B22 **Huanguelén** Buenos Aires, E Argentina
161 S10 **Huangyan** Zhejiang, SE China
159 T10 **Huangyuan** Qinghai, C China
159 T10 **Huangzhong** *var.* Lushar. Qinghai, C China
163 W12 **Huanren** *var.* Huanren Manzu Zizhixian. Liaoning, NE China
Huanren Manzu Zizhixian *see* Huanren
57 F15 **Huanta** Ayacucho, C Peru
56 E13 **Huánuco** Huánuco, C Peru
56 D13 **Huánuco** *off.* Departamento de Huánuco. ◈ *department* C Peru
57 K19 **Huanuni** Oruro, W Bolivia
159 X9 **Huanxian** Gansu, C China
161 S12 **Huap'ing Yu** *island* N Taiwan
62 H3 **Huara** Tarapacá, N Chile
57 D14 **Huaral** Lima, W Peru
Huarás *see* Huaraz
56 D13 **Huaraz** *var.* Huarás. Ancash, W Peru
57 I16 **Huari Huari, Río** ≈ S Peru
56 C13 **Huarmey** Ancash, W Peru
40 H4 **Huásabas** Sonora, NW Mexico
56 D8 **Huasaga, Río** ≈ Ecuador/Peru
167 O15 **Hua Sai** Nakhon Si Thammarat, SW Thailand
56 D12 **Huascarán, Nevado** ▲ W Peru
62 G8 **Huasco** Atacama, N Chile
62 G8 **Huasco, Río** ≈ C Chile
159 S11 **Huashikia** Qinghai, W China
40 G7 **Huatabampo** Sonora, NW Mexico
159 W10 **Huating** Gansu, C China
167 S7 **Huatt, Phou** ▲ N Vietnam
41 Q14 **Huatusco** *var.* Huatusco de Chicuellar. Veracruz-Llave, C Mexico
Huatusco de Chicuellar *see* Huatusco
41 P13 **Huauchinango** Puebla, S Mexico
Huaunta *see* Wounta
41 R15 **Huautla** *var.* Huautla de Jiménez. Oaxaca, SE Mexico
Huautla de Jiménez *see* Huautla
161 O5 **Huaxian** *var.* Daokou, Hua Xian. Henan, C China
Huazangsi *see* Tianzhu
29 V13 **Hubbard** Iowa, C USA
25 U8 **Hubbard** Texas, SW USA
25 Q6 **Hubbard Creek Lake** ◎ Texas, SW USA
31 R6 **Hubbard Lake** ◎ Michigan, N USA
160 M9 **Hubei** *var.* E, Hubei Sheng, Hupeh, Hupei. ◈ *province* C China
Hubei Sheng *see* Hubei
109 P8 **Huben** Tirol, W Austria
31 R13 **Huber Heights** Ohio, N USA
155 F17 **Hubli** Karnātaka, SW India
163 X12 **Huch'ang** N North Korea
97 M18 **Hucknall** C England, UK
97 L17 **Huddersfield** N England, UK
95 O16 **Huddinge** Stockholm, C Sweden
94 N11 **Hudiksvall** Gävleborg, C Sweden
29 W13 **Hudson** Iowa, C USA
19 O11 **Hudson** Massachusetts, NE USA
31 Q11 **Hudson** Michigan, N USA
30 H6 **Hudson** Wisconsin, N USA
11 V14 **Hudson Bay** Saskatchewan, S Canada
12 G6 **Hudson Bay** *bay* NE Canada
195 T16 **Hudson, Cape** *headland* Antarctica
Hudson, Détroit d' *see* Hudson Strait
27 Q9 **Hudson, Lake** ⊟ Oklahoma, C USA
18 K9 **Hudson River** ≈ New Jersey/New York, NE USA
10 M12 **Hudson's Hope** British Columbia, W Canada
12 L2 **Hudson Strait** *Fr.* Détroit d'Hudson. *strait* Nunavut/Québec, NE Canada
Hudūd ash Shamālīyah, Minṭaqat al *see* Al Ḥudūd ash Shamālīyah
Hudur *see* Xuddur
167 U9 **Huê** Thưa Thiên-Huê, C Vietnam
104 J7 **Huebra** ≈ W Spain
24 H8 **Hueco Mountains** ▲ Texas, SW USA
116 G10 **Huedin** *Hung.* Bánffyhunyad. Cluj, NW Romania
40 J10 **Huehuento, Cerro** ▲ C Mexico
42 B5 **Huehuetenango** Huehuetenango, W Guatemala
42 B4 **Huehuetenango** *off.* Departamento de Huehuetenango. ◈ *department* W Guatemala
40 L11 **Huejuquilla** Jalisco, SW Mexico
41 P12 **Huejutla** *var.* Huejutla de Reyes. Hidalgo, C Mexico
Huejutla de Reyes *see* Huejutla
102 G6 **Huelgoat** Finistère, NW France
105 O13 **Huelma** Andalucía, S Spain
104 I14 **Huelva** *anc.* Onuba. Andalucía, SW Spain
104 I13 **Huelva** ◈ *province* Andalucía, SW Spain
104 J13 **Huelva** ≈ SW Spain
105 Q14 **Huercal-Overa** Andalucía, S Spain
37 Q9 **Huerfano Mountain** ▲ New Mexico, SW USA
37 T7 **Huerfano River** ≈ Colorado, C USA
105 S12 **Huertas, Cabo** *headland* SE Spain
105 R6 **Huerva** ≈ N Spain
105 S4 **Huesca** *anc.* Osca. Aragón, NE Spain
105 T4 **Huesca** ◈ *province* Aragón, NE Spain
105 P13 **Huéscar** Andalucía, S Spain
41 N15 **Huetamo** *var.* Huetamo de Núñez. Michoacán de Ocampo, SW Mexico
Huetamo de Núñez *see* Huetamo
105 P8 **Huete** Castilla-La Mancha, C Spain
23 P4 **Hueytown** Alabama, S USA
28 L16 **Hugh Butler Lake** ⊟ Nebraska, C USA
181 V6 **Hughenden** Queensland, NE Australia
182 A6 **Hughes** South Australia
39 P8 **Hughes** Alaska, USA
27 X11 **Hughes** Arkansas, C USA
25 W6 **Hughes Springs** Texas, SW USA
37 V5 **Hugo** Colorado, C USA
27 Q13 **Hugo** Oklahoma, C USA
27 Q13 **Hugo Lake** ⊟ Oklahoma, C USA
26 H7 **Hugoton** Kansas, C USA
Huhehot/Huhohaote *see* Hohhot
Huhttán *see* Kvikkjokk
161 R13 **Hui'an** *var.* Luocheng. Fujian, SE China
184 O9 **Huiarau Range** ▲ North Island, NZ
83 D22 **Huib-Hoch Plateau** *plateau* S Namibia
41 O13 **Huichapán** Hidalgo, C Mexico
Huicheng *see* Shexian
163 W13 **Hŭich'ŏn** C North Korea
54 E12 **Huila** *off.* Departamento del Huila. ◈ *province* S Colombia
83 B15 **Huíla** ◈ *province* SW Angola
54 D11 **Huila, Nevado del** *elevation* C Colombia
83 B15 **Huíla Plateau** *plateau* S Angola
160 G12 **Huili** Sichuan, C China
161 P4 **Huimin** Shandong, E China
163 W11 **Huinan** *var.* Chaoyang. Jilin, NE China
62 K12 **Huinca Renancó** Córdoba, C Argentina
159 V10 **Huining** *var.* Huishi. Gansu, C China
Huishi *see* Huining
160 J12 **Huishui** *var.* Heping. Guizhou, S China
102 L6 **Huisne** ≈ NW France
98 L12 **Huissen** Gelderland, SE Netherlands
159 N11 **Huiten Nur** ◎ C China
93 K19 **Huittinen** Länsi-Suomi, W Finland
41 O15 **Huitzuco** *var.* Huitzuco de los Figueroa. Guerrero, S Mexico
Huitzuco de los Figueroa *see* Huitzuco
159 W11 **Huixian** *var.* Hui Xian. Gansu, C China
41 V17 **Huixtla** Chiapas, SE Mexico
160 H12 **Huize** *var.* Zhongping. Yunnan, SW China
98 J10 **Huizen** Noord-Holland, C Netherlands
161 O14 **Huizhou** Guangdong, S China
162 J6 **Hujirt** Arhangay, C Mongolia
162 J8 **Hujirt** Övörhangay, C Mongolia
162 K8 **Hujirt** Töv, C Mongolia
Hukagawa *see* Fukagawa
Hŭksan-chedo *see* Hŭksan-gundo
163 W17 **Hŭksan-gundo** *var.* Hŭksan-chedo. *island group* SW South Korea
Hukue *see* Fukue
Hukui *see* Fukui
83 G20 **Hukuntsi** Kgalagadi, SW Botswana
Hukuoka *see* Fukuoka
Hukusima *see* Fukushima
Hukutiyama *see* Fukuchiyama
Hukuyama *see* Fukuyama
163 W8 **Hulan** Heilongjiang, NE China
163 W8 **Hulan He** ≈ NE China
31 Q4 **Hulbert Lake** ◎ Michigan, N USA
Hulczyn *see* Hlučín
Huliao *see* Dabu
163 Z8 **Hulin** Heilongjiang, NE China
163 S9 **Hulingol** *prev.* Huolin Gol. Nei Mongol Zizhiqu, N China
14 L12 **Hull** Québec, SE Canada
29 S12 **Hull** Iowa, C USA
Hull *see* Kingston upon Hull
Hull Island *see* Orona
99 F16 **Hulst** Zeeland, SW Netherlands
163 Q7 **Hulstay** Dornod, NE Mongolia
Hultschin *see* Hlučín
95 M19 **Hultsfred** Kalmar, S Sweden
163 T13 **Huludao** *prev.* Jinxi, Lianshan. Liaoning, NE China
Hulun *see* Hailar
Hu-lun Ch'ih *see* Hulun Nur
163 Q6 **Hulun Nur** *var.* Hu-lun Ch'ih; *prev.* Dalai Nor. ◎ NE China
Hulwan/Hulwân *see* Helwân
117 V8 **Hulyaypole** *Rus.* Gulyaypole. Zaporiz'ka Oblast', SE Ukraine
163 V4 **Huma** Heilongjiang, NE China
45 V6 **Humacao** E Puerto Rico
163 U4 **Huma He** ≈ NE China
62 J5 **Humahuaca** Jujuy, N Argentina
59 E14 **Humaitá** Amazonas, N Brazil
62 N7 **Humaitá** Ñeembucú, S Paraguay
83 H26 **Humansdorp** Eastern Cape, S South Africa
27 S6 **Humansville** Missouri, C USA
40 I8 **Humaya, Río** ≈ C Mexico
83 C16 **Humbe** Cunene, SW Angola
97 N17 **Humber** *estuary* E England, UK
97 N17 **Humberside** *cultural region* E England, UK
Humberto *see* Umberto
25 W11 **Humble** Texas, SW USA
11 U15 **Humboldt** Saskatchewan, S Canada
29 U12 **Humboldt** Iowa, C USA
27 Q6 **Humboldt** Kansas, C USA
29 S17 **Humboldt** Nebraska, C USA
35 S3 **Humboldt** Nevada, W USA
20 G9 **Humboldt** Tennessee, S USA
34 K3 **Humboldt Bay** *bay* California, W USA
35 S4 **Humboldt Lake** ◎ Nevada, W USA
35 S4 **Humboldt River** ≈ Nevada, W USA
35 T5 **Humboldt Salt Marsh** *wetland* Nevada, W USA
183 P11 **Hume, Lake** ◎ New South Wales/Victoria, SE Australia
111 N19 **Humenné** *Ger.* Homenau, *Hung.* Homonna. Prešovský Kraj, E Slovakia
29 V15 **Humeston** Iowa, C USA
54 J5 **Humocaro Bajo** Lara, N Venezuela
29 Q14 **Humphrey** Nebraska, C USA
35 S9 **Humphreys, Mount** ▲ California, W USA
36 L11 **Humphreys Peak** ▲ Arizona, SW USA
111 E17 **Humpolec** *Ger.* Gumpolds, Humpoletz. Vysočina, C Czech Republic
Humpoletz *see* Humpolec
93 K19 **Humppila** Etelä-Suomi, S Finland
32 F8 **Humptulips** Washington, NW USA
42 H7 **Humuya, Río** ≈ W Honduras
75 P9 **Hūn** N Libya
Hunabasi *see* Funabashi
92 I1 **Húnaflói** *bay* NW Iceland
160 M11 **Hunan** *var.* Hunan Sheng, Xiang. ◈ *province* S China
Hunan Sheng *see* Hunan
163 Y10 **Hunchun** Jilin, NE China
95 I22 **Hundested** Frederiksborg, E Denmark
Hundred Mile House *see* 100 Mile House
116 G12 **Hunedoara** *Ger.* Eisenmarkt, *Hung.* Vajdahunyad. Hunedoara, SW Romania
116 G12 **Hunedoara** ◈ *county* W Romania
101 I17 **Hünfeld** Hessen, C Germany
111 H23 **Hungary** *off.* Republic of Hungary, *Ger.* Ungarn, *Hung.* Magyarország, *Rom.* Ungaria, *SCr.* Madarska, *Ukr.* Uhorshchyna; *prev.* Hungarian People's Republic. ◆ *republic* C Europe
Hungary, Plain of *see* Great Hungarian Plain
162 F6 **Hungiy** Dzavhan, W Mongolia
163 X13 **Hŭngnam** E North Korea
33 P8 **Hungry Horse Reservoir** ⊟ Montana, NW USA
Hungt'ou *see* Lan Yü
Hung-tse Hu *see* Hongze Hu
167 T6 **Hưng Yên** Hai Hưng, N Vietnam
Hunjiang *see* Baishan
95 I18 **Hunnebostrand** Västra Götaland, S Sweden
101 E19 **Hunsrück** ▲ W Germany
97 P18 **Hunstanton** E England, UK
155 G20 **Hunsūr** Karnātaka, E India
162 I7 **Hunt** Arhangay, C Mongolia
101 G12 **Hunte** ≈ NW Germany
29 Q5 **Hunter** North Dakota, N USA
25 S11 **Hunter** Texas, SW USA
185 D20 **Hunter** ≈ South Island, NZ
183 N15 **Hunter Island** *island* Tasmania, SE Australia
18 K11 **Hunter Mountain** ▲ New York, NE USA
185 B23 **Hunter Mountains** ▲ South Island, NZ
183 S7 **Hunter River** ≈ New South Wales, SE Australia
32 L7 **Hunters** Washington, NW USA

◆ Country ● Country Capital ◇ Dependent Territory ○ Dependent Territory Capital ◈ Administrative Region ✕ International Airport ▲ Mountain ▲ Mountain Range Ⅹ Volcano ≈ River ◎ Lake ⊟ Reservoir

185 F20 **Hunters Hills, The** *hill range* South Island, NZ
184 M12 **Hunterville** Manawatu-Wanganui, North Island, NZ
31 N16 **Huntingburg** Indiana, N USA
97 O20 **Huntingdon** E England, UK
18 E15 **Huntingdon** Pennsylvania, NE USA
20 G9 **Huntingdon** Tennessee, S USA
97 O20 **Huntingdonshire** *cultural region* C England, UK
31 P12 **Huntington** Indiana, N USA
32 L13 **Huntington** Oregon, NW USA
25 X9 **Huntington** Texas, SW USA
36 M5 **Huntington** Utah, W USA
21 P5 **Huntington** West Virginia, NE USA
35 T16 **Huntington Beach** California, W USA
35 W4 **Huntington Creek** ≈ Nevada, W USA
184 L7 **Huntly** Waikato, North Island, NZ
96 K8 **Huntly** NE Scotland, UK
10 K8 **Hunt, Mount** ▲ Yukon Territory, NW Canada
14 H12 **Huntsville** Ontario, S Canada
23 P2 **Huntsville** Alabama, S USA
27 S9 **Huntsville** Arkansas, C USA
27 U3 **Huntsville** Missouri, C USA
20 M8 **Huntsville** Tennessee, S USA
25 V10 **Huntsville** Texas, SW USA
36 L2 **Huntsville** Utah, W USA
41 W12 **Hunucmá** Yucatán, SE Mexico
149 W3 **Hunza** *var.* Karīmābād. Jammu and Kashmir, NE Pakistan
149 W3 **Hunza** ≈ NE Pakistan
Hunze *see* Oostermoers Vaart
158 H4 **Huocheng** *var.* Shuiding. Xinjiang Uygur Zizhiqu, NW China
161 N6 **Huojia** Henan, C China
Huolin Gol *see* Hulingol
186 N14 **Huon** *reef* N New Caledonia
186 E7 **Huon Peninsula** *headland* C PNG
Huoshao Dao *see* Lü Tao
Huoshao Tao *see* Lan Yü
Hupeh/Hupei *see* Hubei
Hurama *see* Hongyuan
Hurano *see* Furano
95 H14 **Hurdalsjøen** ⊚ S Norway
14 E13 **Hurd, Cape** *headland* Ontario, S Canada
Hurdegaryp *see* Hardegarijp
29 N4 **Hurdsfield** North Dakota, N USA
162 J7 **Hüremt** Bulgan, C Mongolia
162 J8 **Hüremt** Övörhangay, C Mongolia
75 X9 **Hurghada** *var.* Al Ghurdaqah, Ghurdaqah. E Egypt
37 P15 **Hurley** New Mexico, SW USA
30 K4 **Hurley** Wisconsin, N USA
21 Y4 **Hurlock** Maryland, NE USA
29 P10 **Huron** South Dakota, N USA
31 S6 **Huron, Lake** ⊚ Canada/USA
31 N3 **Huron Mountains** *hill range* Michigan, N USA
36 J8 **Hurricane** Utah, W USA
21 P5 **Hurricane** West Virginia, NE USA
36 J8 **Hurricane Cliffs** *cliff* Arizona, SW USA
23 V6 **Hurricane Creek** ≈ Georgia, SE USA
94 E12 **Hurrungane** ▲ S Norway
101 E16 **Hürth** Nordrhein-Westfalen, W Germany
Hurukawa *see* Furukawa
185 I17 **Hurunui** ≈ South Island, NZ
95 F21 **Hurup** Viborg, NW Denmark
117 T14 **Hurzuf** Respublika Krym, S Ukraine
Huş *see* Huşi
95 B19 **Húsavík** *Dan.* Husevig Faeroe Islands
92 K1 **Húsavík** Nordhurland Eystra, NE Iceland
116 M10 **Huşi** *var.* Huş. Vaslui, E Romania
95 L19 **Huskvarna** Jönköping, S Sweden
39 P8 **Huslia** Alaska, USA
Husn *see* Al Ḥuṣn
95 C15 **Husnes** Hordaland, S Norway
94 D8 **Hustadvika** *sea area* S Norway
Husté *see* Khust
100 H7 **Husum** Schleswig-Holstein, N Germany
93 I16 **Husum** Västernorrland, C Sweden
116 K6 **Husyatyn** Ternopil's'ka Oblast', W Ukraine
Huszt *see* Khust
162 K6 **Hutag** Bulgan, N Mongolia
26 M6 **Hutchinson** Kansas, C USA
29 U9 **Hutchinson** Minnesota, N USA
23 Y13 **Hutchinson Island** *island* Florida, SE USA
36 L11 **Hutch Mountain** ▲ Arizona, SW USA
141 O14 **Ḥūth** NW Yemen
186 I7 **Hutjena** Buka Island, NE PNG
109 T8 **Hüttenberg** Kärnten, S Austria
25 T10 **Hutto** Texas, SW USA
Huttu *see* Futtsu
108 E8 **Huttwil** Bern, W Switzerland
158 K5 **Hutubi** Xinjiang Uygur Zizhiqu, NW China
161 N4 **Hutuo He** ≈ C China
Hutyû *see* Fuchū
185 E20 **Huxley, Mount** ▲ South Island, NZ
99 J20 **Huy** *Dut.* Hoei, Hoey. Liège, E Belgium
161 R8 **Huzhou** *var.* Wuxing. Zhejiang, SE China
Huzi *see* Fuji
Huzieda *see* Fujieda
Huzinomiya *see* Fujinomiya
Huzisawa *see* Fujisawa
Huziyosida *see* Fuji-Yoshida
92 I2 **Hvammstangi** Nordhurland Vestra, N Iceland
92 K4 **Hvannadalshnúkur** ▲ S Iceland
113 E15 **Hvar** *It.* Lesina. Split-Dalmacija, S Croatia
113 F15 **Hvar** *It.* Lesina; *anc.* Pharus. *island* S Croatia
117 T13 **Hvardiys'ke** *Rus.* Gvardeyskoye. Respublika Krym, S Ukraine
92 I4 **Hveragerdhi** Sudhurland, SW Iceland
95 E22 **Hvide Sande** Ringkøbing, W Denmark
92 I3 **Hvítá** ≈ C Iceland
95 G15 **Hvittingfoss** Buskerud, S Norway
92 I4 **Hvolsvöllur** Sudhurland, SW Iceland
Hwach'ŏn-chŏsuji *see* P'aro-ho
Hwainan *see* Huainan
Hwalien *see* Hualien
83 I16 **Hwange** *prev.* Wankie. Matabeleland North, W Zimbabwe
Hwang-Hae *see* Yellow Sea
Hwangshih *see* Huangshi
83 L17 **Hwedza** Mashonaland East, E Zimbabwe
63 G20 **Hyades, Cerro** ▲ S Chile
19 Q12 **Hyannis** Massachusetts, NE USA
28 L13 **Hyannis** Nebraska, C USA
162 F6 **Hyargas Nuur** ⊚ NW Mongolia
Hybla/Hybla Major *see* Paternò
39 Y14 **Hydaburg** Prince of Wales Island, Alaska, USA
185 F22 **Hyde** Otago, South Island, NZ
21 O7 **Hyden** Kentucky, S USA
18 K12 **Hyde Park** New York, NE USA
39 Z14 **Hyder** Alaska, USA
155 I15 **Hyderābād** *var.* Haidarabad. Andhra Pradesh, C India
149 Q16 **Hyderābād** *var.* Haidarabad. Sind, SE Pakistan
103 T16 **Hyères** Var, SE France
103 T16 **Hyères, Îles d'** *island group* S France
118 K12 **Hyermanavichy** *Rus.* Germanovichi. Vitsyebskaya Voblasts', N Belarus
163 X12 **Hyesan** NE North Korea
10 K8 **Hyland** ≈ Yukon Territory, NW Canada
95 K20 **Hyltebruk** Halland, S Sweden
18 D16 **Hyndman** Pennsylvania, NE USA
33 P14 **Hyndman Peak** ▲ Idaho, NW USA
164 I13 **Hyōgo** *off.* Hyōgo-ken. ◈ *prefecture* Honshū, SW Japan
Hypanis *see* Kuban'
Hypsas *see* Belice
Hyrcania *see* Gorgān
36 L1 **Hyrum** Utah, W USA
93 N14 **Hyrynsalmi** Oulu, C Finland
33 V10 **Hysham** Montana, NW USA
11 N13 **Hythe** Alberta, W Canada
97 Q23 **Hythe** SE England, UK
164 D15 **Hyūga** Miyazaki, Kyūshū, SW Japan
Hyvinge *see* Hyvinkää
93 L19 **Hyvinkää** *Swe.* Hyvinge. Etelä-Suomi, S Finland

I

118 J9 **Iacobeni** *Ger.* Jakobeny. Suceava, NE Romania
Iader *see* Zadar
172 I7 **Iakora** Fianarantsoa, SE Madagascar
116 K14 **Ialomiţa** *var.* Jalomitsa. ◈ *county* SE Romania
116 K14 **Ialomiţa** ≈ SE Romania
117 N10 **Ialoveni** *Rus.* Yaloveny. C Moldova
117 N11 **Ialpug** *var.* Ialpugul Mare, *Rus.* Yalpug. ≈ Moldova/Ukraine
Ialpugul Mare *see* Ialpug
23 T8 **Iamonia, Lake** ⊚ Florida, SE USA
116 L13 **Ianca** Brăila, SE Romania
116 M10 **Iaşi** *Ger.* Jassy. Iaşi, NE Romania
116 L9 **Iaşi** *Ger.* Jassy, Yassy. ◈ *county* NE Romania
114 J13 **Íasmos** Anatolikí Makedonía kai Thráki, NE Greece
22 H6 **Iatt, Lake** ⊡ Louisiana, S USA
58 B11 **Iauaretê** Amazonas, NW Brazil
171 N3 **Iba** Luzon, N Philippines
77 S16 **Ibadan** Oyo, SW Nigeria
54 E10 **Ibagué** Tolima, C Colombia
60 J10 **Ibaiti** Paraná, S Brazil
36 J4 **Ibapah Peak** ▲ Utah, W USA
113 M15 **Ibar** *Alb.* Ibër. ≈ C Serbia and Montenegro (Yugo.)
165 P13 **Ibaraki** *off.* Ibaraki-ken. ◈ *prefecture* Honshū, S Japan
56 C5 **Ibarra** *var.* San Miguel de Ibarra. Imbabura, N Ecuador
Ibaşfalău *see* Dumbrăveni
141 O16 **Ibb** W Yemen
100 F13 **Ibbenbüren** Nordrhein-Westfalen, NW Germany
79 H16 **Ibenga** ≈ N Congo
Iber *see* Ibar
57 I14 **Iberia** Madre de Dios, E Peru
Iberia *see* Spain
Iberian Mountains *see* Ibérico, Sistema
64 M8 **Iberian Plain** *undersea feature* E Atlantic Ocean
Ibérica, Cordillera *see* Ibérico, Sistema
105 P6 **Ibérico, Sistema** *var.* Cordillera Ibérica, *Eng.* Iberian Mountains. ⛰ NE Spain
12 K7 **Iberville, Lac d'** ⊚ Québec, NE Canada
77 T14 **Ibeto** Niger, W Nigeria
77 W15 **Ibi** Taraba, C Nigeria
105 S11 **Ibi** País Valenciano, E Spain
59 L20 **Ibiá** Minas Gerais, SE Brazil
61 F15 **Ibicuí, Rio** ≈ S Brazil
61 C19 **Ibicuy** Entre Ríos, E Argentina
61 F16 **Ibirapuitã** ≈ S Brazil
Ibiza *see* Eivissa
133 J4 **Ibn Wardān, Qaşr** *ruins* Ḥamāh, C Syria
Ibo *see* Sassandra
188 E9 **Ibobang** Babeldaob, N Palau
171 V13 **Ibonma** Papua, E Indonesia
59 N17 **Ibotirama** Bahia, E Brazil
141 Y8 **Ibrā** NE Oman
127 Q4 **Ibresi** Chuvashskaya Respublika, W Russian Federation
141 X8 **'Ibrī** NW Oman
164 C16 **Ibusuki** Kagoshima, Kyūshū, SW Japan
57 E16 **Ica** Ica, SW Peru
57 E16 **Ica** *off.* Departamento de Ica. ◈ *department* SW Peru
58 C11 **Içana** Amazonas, NW Brazil
Icaria *see* Ikaría
58 B13 **Içá, Rio** *var.* Río Putumayo. ≈ NW South America *see also* Putumayo, Río
136 I17 **İçel** *var.* Ichili. ◈ *province* S Turkey
92 I3 **Iceland** *off.* Republic of Iceland, *Dan.* Island, *Icel.* Ísland. ◆ *republic* N Atlantic Ocean
64 L5 **Iceland Basin** *undersea feature* N Atlantic Ocean
Icelandic Plateau *see* Iceland Plateau
197 Q15 **Iceland Plateau** *var.* Icelandic Plateau. *undersea feature* S Greenland Sea
155 E16 **Ichalkaranji** Mahārāshtra, W India
164 D15 **Ichifusa-yama** ▲ Kyūshū, SW Japan
Ichili *see* İçel
164 K13 **Ichinomiya** *var.* Itinomiya. Aichi, Honshū, SW Japan
165 Q9 **Ichinoseki** *var.* Itinoseki. Iwate, Honshū, C Japan
117 R3 **Ichnya** Chernihivs'ka Oblast', NE Ukraine
57 L17 **Ichoa, Río** ≈ C Bolivia
I-ch'un *see* Yichun
Iconium *see* Konya
Iculisma *see* Angoulême
39 U12 **Icy Bay** *inlet* Alaska, USA
39 N5 **Icy Cape** *headland* Alaska, USA
39 W13 **Icy Strait** *strait* Alaska, USA
27 R13 **Idabel** Oklahoma, C USA
29 T13 **Ida Grove** Iowa, C USA
77 U16 **Idah** Kogi, S Nigeria
33 N13 **Idaho** *off.* State of Idaho; *also known as* Gem of the Mountains, Gem State. ◈ *state* NW USA
33 N14 **Idaho City** Idaho, NW USA
33 R14 **Idaho Falls** Idaho, NW USA
121 P2 **Idálion** *var.* Dhali. C Cyprus
25 N5 **Idalou** Texas, SW USA
104 I9 **Idanha-a-Nova** Castelo Branco, C Portugal
101 E19 **Idar-Oberstein** Rheinland-Pfalz, SW Germany
118 J3 **Ida-Virumaa** *off.* Ida-Viru Maakond. ◈ *province* NE Estonia
124 J8 **Idel'** Respublika Kareliya, NW Russian Federation
79 C15 **Idenao** Sud-Ouest, SW Cameroon
Idenburg-rivier *see* Taritatu, Sungai
Idensalmi *see* Iisalmi
162 I6 **Ider** Hövsgöl, C Mongolia
75 X10 **Idfu** *var.* Edfu. SE Egypt
Ídhi Óros *see* Ídi
Ídhra *see* Ýdra
168 H7 **Idi** Sumatera, W Indonesia
115 I25 **Ídi** *var.* Ídhi Óros. ⛰ Kríti, Greece, E Mediterranean Sea
Idi Amin, Lac *see* Edward, Lake
106 G10 **Idice** ≈ N Italy
76 G9 **Idini** Trarza, W Mauritania
79 J21 **Idiofa** Bandundu, SW Dem. Rep. Congo
39 O10 **Iditarod River** ≈ Alaska, USA
95 M14 **Idkerberget** Dalarna, C Sweden
138 I3 **Idlib** Idlib, NW Syria
138 I4 **Idlib** *off.* Muḥāfaẓat Idlib. ◈ *governorate* NW Syria
Idra *see* Ýdra
94 J11 **Idre** Dalarna, C Sweden
Idria *see* Idrija
109 S11 **Idrija** *It.* Idria. W Slovenia
101 G18 **Idstein** Hessen, W Germany
83 J25 **Idutywa** Eastern Cape, SE South Africa
Idzhevan *see* Ijevan
118 G9 **Iecava** Bauska, S Latvia
165 T16 **Ie-jima** *var.* Ii-shima. *island* Nansei-shotō, SW Japan
99 B18 **Ieper** *Fr.* Ypres. West-Vlaanderen, W Belgium
115 K25 **Ierápetra** Kríti, Greece, E Mediterranean Sea
115 G22 **Iérax, Akrotírio** *headland* S Greece
Ierisós *see* Ierissós
115 H14 **Ierissós** *var.* Ierisós. Kentrikí Makedonía, N Greece
116 I11 **Iernut** *Hung.* Radnót. Mureş, C Romania
106 J12 **Iesi** *var.* Jesi. Marche, C Italy
92 K9 **Iešjávri** *var.* Jiesjavrre. ⊚ N Norway
Iesolo *see* Jesolo
188 K16 **Ifalik Atoll** *atoll* Caroline Islands, C Micronesia
172 I6 **Ifanadiana** Fianarantsoa, SE Madagascar
77 T16 **Ife** Osun, SW Nigeria
77 V8 **Iferouâne** Agadez, N Niger
Iferten *see* Yverdon
92 L8 **Ifjord** Finnmark, N Norway
77 R8 **Ifôghas, Adrar des** *var.* Adrar des Iforas. ⛰ NE Mali
Iforas, Adrar des *see* Ifôghas, Adrar des
182 D6 **Ifould lake** *salt lake* South Australia
74 G6 **Ifrane** C Morocco
171 S11 **Iga** Pulau Halmahera, E Indonesia
81 G18 **Iganga** SE Uganda
60 L7 **Igarapava** São Paulo, S Brazil
122 K9 **Igarka** Krasnoyarskiy Kray, N Russian Federation
Igaunija *see* Estonia
I.G.Duca *see* General Toshevo
Igel *see* Jihlava
137 T12 **Iğdır** ◈ *province* E Turkey
94 N11 **Iggesund** Gävleborg, C Sweden
39 P7 **Igikpak, Mount** ▲ Alaska, USA
39 P13 **Igiugig** Alaska, USA
Iglau/Iglawa/Igława *see* Jihlava
107 B20 **Iglesias** Sardegna, Italy, C Mediterranean Sea
127 V4 **Iglino** Respublika Bashkortostan, W Russian Federation
Igló *see* Spišská Nová Ves
9 O6 **Igloolik** Nunavut, N Canada
12 B11 **Ignace** Ontario, S Canada
118 I12 **Ignalina** Utena, E Lithuania
127 Q5 **Ignatovka** Ul'yanovskaya Oblast', W Russian Federation
124 K12 **Ignatovo** Vologodskaya Oblast', NW Russian Federation
114 N11 **İğneada** Kırklareli, NW Turkey
121 S7 **İğneada Burnu** *headland* NW Turkey
115 B16 **Igoumenítsa** Ípeiros, W Greece
127 T2 **Igra** Udmurtskaya Respublika, NW Russian Federation
122 H9 **Igrim** Khanty-Mansiyskiy Avtonomnyy Okrug, N Russian Federation
60 G12 **Iguaçu, Rio** *Sp.* Río Iguazú. ≈ Argentina/Brazil *see also* Iguazú, Río
59 I22 **Iguaçu, Salto do** *Sp.* Cataratas del Iguazú; *prev.* Victoria Falls. *waterfall* Argentina/Brazil *see also* Iguazú, Cataratas del
41 O15 **Iguala** *var.* Iguala de la Independencia. Guerrero, S Mexico
105 V5 **Igualada** Cataluña, NE Spain
Iguala de la Independencia *see* Iguala
60 G12 **Iguazú, Cataratas del** *Port.* Salto do Iguaçu, *prev.* Victoria Falls. *waterfall* Argentina/Brazil *see also* Iguaçu, Salto do
62 Q6 **Iguazú, Río** *Port.* Rio Iguaçu. ≈ Argentina/Brazil *see also* Iguaçu, Rio
79 D19 **Iguéla** Ogooué-Maritime, SW Gabon
Iguid, Erg *see* Iguîdi, 'Erg
74 F9 **Iguîdi, 'Erg** *var.* Erg Iguid. *desert* Algeria/Mauritania
172 K2 **Iharaña** *prev.* Vohémar. Antsiraňana, NE Madagascar
151 K18 **Ihavandippolhu Atoll** *var.* Ihavandiffulu Atoll. *atoll* N Maldives
162 M11 **Ih Bulag** Ömnögovĭ, S Mongolia
165 T16 **Iheya-jima** *island* Nansei-shotō, SW Japan
162 L8 **Ihhayrhan** Töv, C Mongolia
172 I6 **Ihosy** Fianarantsoa, S Madagascar
162 L7 **Ihsüüj** Töv, C Mongolia
93 L14 **Ii** Oulu, C Finland
164 M13 **Iida** Nagano, Honshū, S Japan
93 M14 **Iijoki** ≈ C Finland
Iinnasuolu *see* Hinnøya
118 J4 **Iisaku** *Ger.* Isaak. Ida-Virumaa, NE Estonia
93 M16 **Iisalmi** *var.* Idensalmi. Itä-Suomi, C Finland
165 N11 **Iiyama** Nagano, Honshū, S Japan
77 S16 **Ijebu-Ode** Ogun, SW Nigeria
137 U11 **Ijevan** *Rus.* Idzhevan. N Armenia
98 H9 **IJmuiden** Noord-Holland, W Netherlands
98 M12 **IJssel** *var.* Yssel. ≈ Netherlands/Germany
98 J8 **IJsselmeer** *prev.* Zuider Zee. ⊚ N Netherlands
98 L9 **IJsselmuiden** Overijssel, E Netherlands
98 I12 **IJsselstein** Utrecht, C Netherlands
61 G14 **Ijuí** Rio Grande do Sul, S Brazil
61 G14 **Ijuí, Rio** ≈ S Brazil
189 R8 **Ijuw** NE Nauru
99 E16 **IJzendijke** Zeeland, SW Netherlands
99 A18 **Ijzer** ≈ W Belgium
93 K18 **Ikaalinen** Länsi-Suomi, W Finland
172 I6 **Ikalamavony** Fianarantsoa, SE Madagascar
185 G16 **Ikamatua** West Coast, South Island, NZ
77 U16 **Ikare** Ondo, SW Nigeria
115 L20 **Ikaría** *var.* Kariot, Nicaria, Nikaria; *anc.* Icaria. *island* Dodekánisos, Greece, Aegean Sea
95 F22 **Ikast** Ringkøbing, W Denmark
184 O9 **Ikawhenua Range** ⛰ North Island, NZ
165 U4 **Ikeda** Hokkaidō, NE Japan
164 H14 **Ikeda** Tokushima, Shikoku, SW Japan
77 S16 **Ikeja** Lagos, SW Nigeria
79 L19 **Ikela** Equateur, C Dem. Rep. Congo
114 H10 **Ikhtiman** Sofiya, W Bulgaria
164 C13 **Iki** *island* SW Japan
127 O13 **Iki Burul** Respublika Kalmykiya, SW Russian Federation
137 P11 **İkizdere** Rize, NE Turkey
39 P14 **Ikolik, Cape** *headland* Kodiak Island, Alaska, USA
77 V17 **Ikom** Cross River, SE Nigeria
172 I6 **Ikongo** *prev.* Fort-Carnot. Fianarantsoa, SE Madagascar
39 P5 **Ikpikpuk River** ≈ Alaska, USA
190 H1 **Iku** *prev.* Lone Tree Islet. *atoll* Tungaru, W Kiribati
164 I12 **Ikuno** Hyōgo, Honshū, SW Japan
190 H16 **Ikurangi** ▲ Rarotonga, S Cook Islands
171 X14 **Ilaga** Papua, E Indonesia
171 O2 **Ilagan** Luzon, N Philippines
153 R12 **Ilam** Eastern, E Nepal
142 J7 **Īlām** *var.* Elam. Īlām, W Iran
142 J8 **Īlām** *off.* Ostān-e Īlām. ◈ *province* W Iran
161 T13 **Ilan** *Jap.* Giran. N Taiwan
146 G9 **Ilanly Obvodnitel'nyy Kanal** *canal* N Turkmenistan
122 L12 **Ilanskiy** Krasnoyarskiy Kray, S Russian Federation
108 H9 **Ilanz** Graubünden, S Switzerland
77 S16 **Ilaro** Ogun, SW Nigeria
57 I17 **Ilave** Puno, S Peru
110 K8 **Iława** *Ger.* Deutsch-Eylau. Warmińsko-Mazurskie, NE Poland
123 P10 **Il'benge** Respublika Sakha (Yakutiya), NE Russian Federation
145 U14 **Ile** *var.* Ili, *Chin.* Ili He, *Rus.* Reka Ili. ≈ China/Kazakhstan *see also* Ili He
11 S13 **Île-à-la-Crosse** Saskatchewan, C Canada
79 J21 **Ilebo** *prev.* Port-Francqui. Kasai Occidental, W Dem. Rep. Congo
103 N5 **Île-de-France** ◈ *region* N France
144 I9 **Ilek** *Kaz.* Elek. ≈ Kazakhstan/Russian Federation
Ilerda *see* Lleida
77 T16 **Ilesha** Osun, SW Nigeria
187 Q16 **Îles Loyauté, Province des** ◈ *province* E New Caledonia
11 X12 **Ilford** Manitoba, C Canada
97 I23 **Ilfracombe** SW England, UK
136 I11 **Ilgaz Dağları** ⛰ N Turkey
136 G15 **Ilgın** Konya, W Turkey
60 I7 **Ilha Solteira** São Paulo, S Brazil
104 G7 **Ílhavo** Aveiro, N Portugal
59 O18 **Ilhéus** Bahia, E Brazil
Ili *see* Ile/Ili He
116 G11 **Ilia** *Hung.* Marosillye. Hunedoara, SW Romania
39 P13 **Iliamna** Alaska, USA
39 P13 **Iliamna Lake** ⊚ Alaska, USA
137 N13 **Iliç** Erzincan, C Turkey
Il'ichevsk *see* Şärur, Azerbaijan
Il'ichevsk *see* Illichivs'k, Ukraine
Ilici *see* Elche
37 V2 **Iliff** Colorado, C USA
171 Q7 **Iligan** *off.* Iligan City. Mindanao, S Philippines
171 Q7 **Iligan Bay** *bay* S Philippines
158 I5 **Ili He** *var.* Ili, *Kaz.* Ile, *Rus.* Reka Ili. ≈ China/Kazakhstan *see also* Ile
56 C6 **Iliniza** ▲ N Ecuador
Ilinski *see* Il'inskiy
125 U14 **Il'inskiy** *var.* Ilinski. Permskaya Oblast', NW Russian Federation
123 T13 **Il'inskiy** Ostrov Sakhalin, Sakhalinskaya Oblast', SE Russian Federation
18 I10 **Ilion** New York, NE USA
38 E9 **'Ilio Point** *var.* Ilio Point *headland* Moloka'i, Hawai'i, USA, C Pacific Ocean
109 T13 **Ilirska Bistrica** *prev.* Bistrica, *Ger.* Feistritz, Illyrisch-Feistritz, *It.* Villa del Nevoso. SW Slovenia
137 Q16 **Ilisu Barajı** ⊡ SE Turkey
155 G17 **Ilkal** Karnātaka, C India
97 M19 **Ilkeston** C England, UK
121 O16 **Il-Kullana** *headland* SW Malta
108 J8 **Ill** ≈ W Austria
103 U6 **Ill** ≈ NE France
62 G10 **Illapel** Coquimbo, C Chile
Illaue Fartak Trench *see* Alula-Fartak Trench
182 C2 **Illbillee, Mount** ▲ South Australia
102 I6 **Ille-et-Vilaine** ◈ *department* NW France
77 T11 **Illéla** Tahoua, SW Niger
101 J24 **Iller** ≈ S Germany
101 J23 **Illertissen** Bayern, S Germany
105 N8 **Illescas** Castilla-La Mancha, C Spain
Ille-sur-la-Têt *see* Ille-sur-Têt
103 O17 **Ille-sur-Têt** *var.* Ille-sur-la-Têt. Pyrénées-Orientales, S France
Illiberis *see* Elne
117 P11 **Illichivs'k** *Rus.* Il'ichevsk. Odes'ka Oblast', SW Ukraine
Illicis *see* Elche
102 M6 **Illiers-Combray** Eure-et-Loir, C France
30 K12 **Illinois** *off.* State of Illinois; *also known as* Prairie State, Sucker State. ◈ *state* C USA
30 J13 **Illinois River** ≈ Illinois, N USA
117 N6 **Illintsi** Vinnyts'ka Oblast', C Ukraine
Illiturgis *see* Andújar
74 M10 **Illizi** SE Algeria
27 Y7 **Illmo** Missouri, C USA
Illur co *see* Lorca
Illuro *see* Mataró
Illyrisch-Feistritz *see* Ilirska Bistrica
101 K16 **Ilm** ≈ C Germany
101 K17 **Ilmenau** Thüringen, C Germany
126 H14 **Il'men', Ozero** ⊚ NW Russian Federation
57 H18 **Ilo** Moquegua, SW Peru
171 O6 **Iloilo** *off.* Iloilo City. Panay Island, C Philippines
112 K10 **Ilok** *Hung.* Újlak. Serbia, NW Serbia and Montenegro (Yugo.)
93 O16 **Ilomantsi** Itä-Suomi, E Finland
42 F8 **Ilopango, Lago de** *volcanic lake* C El Salvador
77 T15 **Ilorin** Kwara, W Nigeria
117 X8 **Ilovays'k** *Rus.* Ilovaysk. Donets'ka Oblast', SE Ukraine
127 O10 **Ilovlya** Volgogradskaya Oblast', SW Russian Federation
127 O10 **Ilovlya** ≈ SW Russian Federation
123 V8 **Il'pyrskoy** Koryakskiy Avtonomnyy Okrug, E Russian Federation
126 K14 **Il'skiy** Krasnodarskiy Kray, SW Russian Federation
182 B2 **Iltur** South Australia
171 Y13 **Ilugwa** Papua, E Indonesia
Iluh *see* Batman
118 I11 **Ilūkste** Daugvapils, SE Latvia
171 U14 **Ilur** Pulau Gorong, E Indonesia
32 F10 **Ilwaco** Washington, NW USA
Il'yaly *see* Ýylanly
Ilyasbaba Burnu *see* Tekke Burnu
127 U9 **Ilych** ≈ NW Russian Federation
101 O21 **Ilz** ≈ SE Germany
111 M14 **Iłża** Radom, SE Poland
164 G13 **Imabari** *var.* Imaharu. Ehime, Shikoku, SW Japan
Imaharu *see* Imabari
165 O12 **Imaichi** *var.* Imaiti. Tochigi, Honshū, S Japan
Imaiti *see* Imaichi
164 K12 **Imajō** Fukui, Honshū, SW Japan
139 R9 **Imām Ibn Hāshim** C Iraq
139 T11 **Imān 'Abd Allāh** S Iraq
126 J4 **Imandra, Ozero** ⊚ NW Russian Federation
164 F15 **Imano-yama** ▲ Shikoku, SW Japan
164 C13 **Imari** Saga, Kyūshū, SW Japan
Imarssuak Mid-Ocean Seachannel *see* Imarssuak Seachannel
64 J6 **Imarssuak Seachannel** *var.* Imarssuak Mid-Ocean Seachannel. *channel* N Atlantic Ocean
93 N18 **Imatra** Etelä-Suomi, S Finland
164 K13 **Imazu** Shiga, Honshū, SW Japan
56 C6 **Imbabura** ◈ *province* N Ecuador
55 R9 **Imbaimadai** W Guyana
61 K14 **Imbituba** Santa Catarina, S Brazil
27 W9 **Imboden** Arkansas, C USA
Imbros *see* Gökçeada
Imeni 26 Bakinskikh Komissarov *see* 26 Bakı Komissarı/Uzboý
125 N13 **Imeni Babushkina** Vologodskaya Oblast', NW Russian Federation
126 J7 **Imeni Karla Libknekhta** Kurskaya Oblast', W Russian Federation
Imeni Mollanepesa *see* Mollanepes Adyndaky
Imeni S.A.Niyazova *see* S.A.Nyýazow Adyndaky
Imeni Sverdlova Rudnik *see* Sverdlovs'k
188 E9 **Imeong** Babeldaob, N Palau
81 L14 **Imī** Somali, E Ethiopia
115 M21 **Imia** *Turk.* Kardak. *island* Dodekánisos, Greece, Aegean Sea
Imishli *see* İmişli
137 X12 **İmişli** *Rus.* Imishli. C Azerbaijan
163 X14 **Imjin-gang** ≈ North Korea/South Korea
35 S3 **Imlay** Nevada, W USA
31 S9 **Imlay City** Michigan, N USA
23 X15 **Immokalee** Florida, SE USA
77 U17 **Imo** ◈ *state* SE Nigeria
106 G10 **Imola** Emilia-Romagna, N Italy
186 A5 **Imonda** Sandaun, NW PNG
Imoschi *see* Imotski
113 G14 **Imotski** *It.* Imoschi. Split-Dalmacija, SE Croatia
59 L14 **Imperatriz** Maranhão, NE Brazil
106 B10 **Imperia** Liguria, NW Italy
57 E15 **Imperial** Lima, W Peru
35 X17 **Imperial** California, W USA
28 L16 **Imperial** Nebraska, C USA
24 M9 **Imperial** Texas, SW USA
35 Y17 **Imperial Dam** *dam* California, W USA
79 I17 **Impfondo** La Likouala, NE Congo
153 X14 **Imphāl** Manipur, NE India
103 P9 **Imphy** Nièvre, C France
106 G11 **Impruneta** Toscana, C Italy
115 K15 **İmroz** *var.* Gökçeada. Çanakkale, NW Turkey
Imroz Adası *see* Gökçeada
108 L7 **Imst** Tirol, W Austria
40 F3 **Imuris** Sonora, NW Mexico
164 M13 **Ina** Nagano, Honshū, S Japan
65 M18 **Inaccessible Island** *island* W Tristan da Cunha
115 F20 **Inachos** ≈ S Greece
188 H6 **I Naftan, Puntan** *headland* Saipan, S Northern Mariana Islands
Inagua Islands *see* Great Inagua/Little Inagua
185 H15 **Inangahua** West Coast, South Island, NZ
57 I14 **Iñapari** Madre de Dios, E Peru
188 B17 **Inarajan** SE Guam
92 L10 **Inari** *Lapp.* Anár, Aanaar. Lappi, N Finland
92 L10 **Inarijärvi** *Lapp.* Aanaarjävri, *Swe.* Enareträsk. ⊚ N Finland
92 L9 **Inarijoki** *Lapp.* Anárjohka. ≈ Finland/Norway
Ināu *see* Ineu
165 P11 **Inawashiro-ko** *var.* Inawasiro Ko. ⊚ Honshū, C Japan
Inawasiro Ko *see* Inawashiro-ko
62 H7 **Inca de Oro** Atacama, N Chile

115 J15 **İnce Burnu** headland NW Turkey
136 K9 **İnce Burnu** headland N Turkey
136 I17 **İncekum Burnu** headland S Turkey
76 G7 **Inchiri** ◈ region NW Mauritania
163 X15 **Inch'ŏn** off. Inch'ŏn-gwangyŏksi, Jap. Jinsen; prev. Chemulpo. NW South Korea
163 X15 **Inch'on** × (Sŏul) NW South Korea
83 M17 **Inchope** Manica, C Mozambique
Incoronata see Kornat
103 Y15 **Incudine, Monte** ▲ Corse, France, C Mediterranean Sea
60 M10 **Indaiatuba** São Paulo, S Brazil
93 H17 **Indal** Västernorrland, C Sweden
93 H17 **Indalsälven** ≈ C Sweden
40 K8 **Inde** Durango, C Mexico
Indefatigable Island see Santa Cruz, Isla
35 S10 **Independence** California, W USA
29 X13 **Independence** Iowa, C USA
27 P7 **Independence** Kansas, C USA
20 M4 **Independence** Kentucky, S USA
27 R4 **Independence** Missouri, C USA
21 R8 **Independence** Virginia, NE USA
30 J7 **Independence** Wisconsin, N USA
197 R12 **Independence Fjord** fjord N Greenland
Independence Island see Malden Island
35 W2 **Independence Mountains** ⛰ Nevada, W USA
57 K18 **Independencia** Cochabamba, C Bolivia
57 E16 **Independencia, Bahía de la** bay W Peru
Independencia, Monte see Adam, Mount
116 M12 **Independenţa** Galaţi, SE Romania
Inderagiri see Indragiri, Sungai
Inderbor see Inderborskiy
144 F11 **Inderborskiy** Kaz. Inderbor. Atyrau, W Kazakhstan
151 I14 **India** off. Republic of India, var. Indian Union, Union of India, Hind. Bhārat. ◆ republic S Asia
India see Inđija
18 D14 **Indiana** Pennsylvania, NE USA
31 N13 **Indiana** off. State of Indiana; also known as The Hoosier State. ◈ state N USA
31 O14 **Indianapolis** state capital Indiana, N USA
11 O10 **Indian Cabins** Alberta, W Canada
42 G1 **Indian Church** Orange Walk, N Belize
Indian Desert see Thar Desert
11 U16 **Indian Head** Saskatchewan, S Canada
31 O4 **Indian Lake** ◎ Michigan, N USA
18 K9 **Indian Lake** ◎ New York, NE USA
31 R13 **Indian Lake** ▣ Ohio, N USA
180-181 **Indian Ocean** ocean
29 V15 **Indianola** Iowa, C USA
22 K4 **Indianola** Mississippi, S USA
36 J6 **Indian Peak** ▲ Utah, W USA
23 Y13 **Indian River** lagoon Florida, SE USA
35 W10 **Indian Springs** Nevada, W USA
23 Y14 **Indiantown** Florida, SE USA
59 K19 **Indiara** Goiás, S Brazil
125 Q4 **Indiga** Nenetskiy Avtonomnyy Okrug, NW Russian Federation
123 R9 **Indigirka** ≈ NE Russian Federation
112 L10 **Inđija** Hung. India; prev. Indjija. Serbia, N Serbia and Montenegro (Yugo.)
35 V16 **Indio** California, W USA
42 M12 **Indio, Río** ≈ SE Nicaragua
152 I10 **Indira Gandhi International** × (Delhi) Delhi, N India
151 Q23 **Indira Point** headland Andaman and Nicobar Islands, India, NE Indian Ocean
Indjija see Inđija
173 N11 **Indomed Fracture Zone** tectonic feature SW Indian Ocean
170 L12 **Indonesia** off. Republic of Indonesia, Ind. Republik Indonesia; prev. Dutch East Indies, Netherlands East Indies, United States of Indonesia. ◆ republic SE Asia
Indonesian Borneo see Kalimantan
154 G10 **Indore** Madhya Pradesh, C India
168 L11 **Indragiri, Sungai** var. Batang Kuantan, Inderagiri. ≈ Sumatera, W Indonesia
Indramajoe/Indramaju see Indramayu
169 P15 **Indramayu** prev. Indramajoe, Indramaju. Jawa, C Indonesia
155 K14 **Indrāvati** ≈ S India
103 N9 **Indre** ◈ department C France
102 M8 **Indre** ≈ C France
94 D13 **Indre Ålvik** Hordaland, S Norway
102 L8 **Indre-et-Loire** ◈ department C France
Indreville see Châteauroux
152 G3 **Indus** Chin. Yindu He; prev. Yin-tu Ho. ≈ S Asia
Indus Cone see Indus Fan
173 P3 **Indus Fan** var. Indus Cone. undersea feature N Arabian Sea
149 P17 **Indus, Mouths of the** delta S Pakistan
83 I24 **Indwe** Eastern Cape, SE South Africa
136 I10 **İnebolu** Kastamonu, N Turkey
77 P8 **I-n-Échaï** oasis C Mali
114 M13 **İnecik** Tekirdağ, NW Turkey
136 E12 **İnegöl** Bursa, NW Turkey
Inessa see Biancavilla
116 F10 **Ineu** Hung. Borosjenő; prev. Inău. Arad, W Romania
Ineul/Ineu, Vîrful see Ineu, Vârful
116 J9 **Ineu, Vârful** var. Ineul; prev. Vîrful Ineu. ▲ N Romania
21 P6 **Inez** Kentucky, S USA
74 E8 **Inezgane** × (Agadir) W Morocco
41 T17 **Inferior, Laguna** lagoon S Mexico
40 M15 **Infiernillo, Presa del** ▣ S Mexico
104 L2 **Infiesto** Asturias, N Spain
93 L20 **Ingå** Fin. Inkoo. Etelä-Suomi, S Finland
77 U10 **Ingal** var. I-n-Gall. Agadez, C Niger
I-n-Gall see Ingal
99 C18 **Ingelmunster** West-Vlaanderen, W Belgium
79 I18 **Ingende** Equateur, W Dem. Rep. Congo
62 L5 **Ingeniero Guillermo Nueva Juárez** Formosa, N Argentina
63 H16 **Ingeniero Jacobacci** Río Negro, C Argentina
14 F16 **Ingersoll** Ontario, S Canada
162 K6 **Ingettolgoy** Bulgan, N Mongolia
181 W5 **Ingham** Queensland, NE Australia
146 M11 **Ingichka** Samarqand Viloyati, C Uzbekistan
97 L16 **Ingleborough** ▲ N England, UK
25 T14 **Ingleside** Texas, SW USA
184 K10 **Inglewood** Taranaki, North Island, NZ
35 S15 **Inglewood** California, W USA
101 L21 **Ingolstadt** Bayern, S Germany
33 V9 **Ingomar** Montana, NW USA
13 R14 **Ingonish Beach** Cape Breton Island, Nova Scotia, SE Canada
153 S14 **Ingrāj Bāzār** prev. English Bazar. West Bengal, NE India
25 Q11 **Ingram** Texas, SW USA
195 X7 **Ingrid Christensen Coast** physical region Antarctica
74 K14 **I-n-Guezzam** S Algeria
Ingulets see Inhulets'
Inguri see Enguri
Ingushetia/Ingushetiya, Respublika see Ingushskaya Respublika
127 O15 **Ingushskaya Respublika** var. Respublika Ingushetiya, Eng. Ingushetia. ◈ autonomous republic SW Russian Federation
83 N20 **Inhambane** Inhambane, SE Mozambique
83 M20 **Inhambane** off. Província de Inhambane. ◈ province S Mozambique
83 N17 **Inhaminga** Sofala, C Mozambique
83 N20 **Inharrime** Inhambane, SE Mozambique
83 M18 **Inhassoro** Inhambane, E Mozambique
117 S9 **Inhulets'** Rus. Ingulets. Dnipropetrovs'ka Oblast', E Ukraine
117 R10 **Inhulets'** Rus. Ingulets. ≈ S Ukraine
105 Q10 **Iniesta** Castilla-La Mancha, C Spain
I-ning see Yining
54 K11 **Inírida, Río** ≈ E Colombia
Inis see Ennis
Inis Ceithleann see Enniskillen
Inis Córthaidh see Enniscorthy
Inis Díomáin see Ennistimon
97 A17 **Inishbofin** Ir. Inis Bó Finne. island W Ireland
97 B18 **Inisheer** var. Inishere, Ir. Inis Oírr. island W Ireland
Inishere see Inisheer
97 B18 **Inishmaan** Ir. Inis Meáin. island W Ireland
97 A18 **Inishmore** Ir. Árainn. island W Ireland
96 E13 **Inishtrahull** Ir. Inis Trá Tholl. island NW Ireland
97 A17 **Inishturk** Ir. Inis Toirc. island W Ireland
Inkoo see Ingå
185 J16 **Inland Kaikoura Range** ⛰ South Island, NZ
Inland Sea see Seto-naikai
21 P11 **Inman** South Carolina, SE USA
108 L7 **Inn** ≈ C Europe
197 O11 **Innaanganeq** var. Kap York. headland NW Greenland
182 K2 **Innamincka** South Australia
92 G12 **Inndyr** Nordland, C Norway
42 G3 **Inner Channel** inlet SE Belize
96 F11 **Inner Hebrides** island group W Scotland, UK
172 H15 **Inner Islands** var. Central Group. island group NE Seychelles
Inner Mongolia/Inner Mongolian Autonomous Region see Nei Mongol Zizhiqu
96 G8 **Inner Sound** strait NW Scotland, UK
100 J13 **Innerste** ≈ C Germany
181 W5 **Innisfail** Queensland, NE Australia
11 Q15 **Innisfail** Alberta, SW Canada
Inniskilling see Enniskillen
39 O11 **Innoko River** ≈ Alaska, USA
Innosima see Innoshima
Innsbruch see Innsbruck
108 M7 **Innsbruck** var. Innsbruch. Tirol, W Austria
79 I19 **Inongo** Bandundu, W Dem. Rep. Congo
Inoucdjouac see Inukjuak
Inowrazlaw see Inowrocław
110 I10 **Inowrocław** Ger. Hohensalza; prev. Inowrazlaw. Kujawski-pomorskie, C Poland
57 K18 **Inquisivi** La Paz, W Bolivia
Inrin see Yüanlin
77 O8 **I-n-Sâkâne, 'Erg** desert N Mali
74 J10 **I-n-Salah** var. In Salah. C Algeria
127 O5 **Insar** Respublika Mordoviya, W Russian Federation
189 X15 **Insiaf** Kosrae, E Micronesia
94 L13 **Insjön** Dalarna, C Sweden
Insterburg see Chernyakhovsk
Insula see Lille
116 L13 **Însurăţei** Brăila, SE Romania
125 V6 **Inta** Respublika Komi, NW Russian Federation
77 R9 **I-n-Tebezas** Kidal, E Mali
Interamna see Teramo
Interamna Nahars see Terni
28 L11 **Interior** South Dakota, N USA
108 E9 **Interlaken** Bern, SW Switzerland
29 V2 **International Falls** Minnesota, N USA
167 O7 **Inthanon, Doi** ▲ NW Thailand
42 G7 **Intibucá** ◈ department SW Honduras
42 G8 **Intipucá** La Unión, SE El Salvador
61 B15 **Intiyaco** Santa Fe, C Argentina
116 K12 **Întorsura Buzăului** Ger. Bozau, Hung. Bodzafordulő. Covasna, E Romania
22 H9 **Intracoastal Waterway** inland waterway system Louisiana, S USA
25 V13 **Intracoastal Waterway** inland waterway system Texas, SW USA
108 G11 **Intragna** Ticino, S Switzerland
165 P14 **Inubō-zaki** headland Honshū, S Japan
164 E14 **Inukai** Ōita, Kyūshū, SW Japan
12 I5 **Inukjuak** var. Inoucdjouac; prev. Port Harrison. Québec, NE Canada
63 I24 **Inútil, Bahía** bay S Chile
Inuuvik see Inuvik
9 R8 **Inuvik** var. Inuuvik. Northwest Territories, NW Canada
164 L13 **Inuyama** Aichi, Honshū, SW Japan
56 G13 **Inuya, Río** ≈ E Peru
127 U13 **In'va** ≈ NW Russian Federation
96 H11 **Inveraray** W Scotland, UK
185 C24 **Invercargill** Southland, South Island, NZ
183 T5 **Inverell** New South Wales, SE Australia
96 I8 **Invergordon** N Scotland, UK
11 P16 **Invermere** British Columbia, SW Canada
13 R14 **Inverness** Cape Breton Island, Nova Scotia, SE Canada
96 I8 **Inverness** N Scotland, UK
23 V11 **Inverness** Florida, SE USA
96 I9 **Inverness** cultural region NW Scotland, UK
96 K9 **Inverurie** NE Scotland, UK
182 F8 **Investigator Group** island group South Australia
173 T7 **Investigator Ridge** undersea feature E Indian Ocean
182 H10 **Investigator Strait** strait South Australia
29 R11 **Inwood** Iowa, C USA
123 S10 **Inya** ≈ E Russian Federation
Inyanga see Nyanga
83 M16 **Inyangani** ▲ NE Zimbabwe
83 J17 **Inyathi** Matabeleland North, SW Zimbabwe
35 T12 **Inyokern** California, W USA
35 T10 **Inyo Mountains** ⛰ California, W USA
127 P6 **Inza** Ul'yanovskaya Oblast', W Russian Federation
127 W5 **Inzer** Respublika Bashkortostan, W Russian Federation
127 N7 **Inzhavino** Tambovskaya Oblast', W Russian Federation
115 C16 **Ioánnina** var. Janina, Yannina. Ípeiros, W Greece
164 B17 **Iō-jima** var. Iwojima. island Nansei-shotō, SW Japan
126 L4 **Iokan'ga** ≈ NW Russian Federation
27 Q6 **Iola** Kansas, C USA
Iolcus see Iolkós
115 G16 **Iolkós** anc. Iolcus. site of ancient city Thessalía, C Greece
Iolotan' see Ýolöten
83 A16 **Iona** Namibe, SW Angola
96 F11 **Iona** island W Scotland, UK
116 M15 **Ion Corvin** Constanţa, SE Romania
35 P7 **Ione** California, W USA
116 I13 **Ioneşti** Vâlcea, SW Romania
31 Q9 **Ionia** Michigan, N USA
Ionia Basin see Ionian Basin
121 O10 **Ionian Basin** var. Ionia Basin. undersea feature Ionian Sea, C Mediterranean Sea
Ionian Islands see Iónioi Nísoi
121 O10 **Ionian Sea** Gk. Iónio Pélagos, It. Mar Ionio. sea C Mediterranean Sea
115 B17 **Iónioi Nísoi** Eng. Ionian Islands. ◈ region W Greece
115 B17 **Iónioi Nísoi** Eng. Ionian Islands. island group W Greece
Ionio, Mar/Iónio Pélagos see Ionian Sea
Iordan see Yordon
137 U10 **Iori** var. Qabırrı. ≈ Azerbaijan/Georgia
Iorrais, Ceann see Erris Head
115 J22 **Íos** Íos, Kykládes, Greece, Aegean Sea
115 J22 **Íos** var. Nio. island Kykládes, Greece, Aegean Sea
22 G9 **Iowa** Louisiana, S USA
29 V13 **Iowa** off. State of Iowa; also known as The Hawkeye State. ◈ state C USA
29 Y14 **Iowa City** Iowa, C USA
29 V13 **Iowa Falls** Iowa, C USA
25 R4 **Iowa Park** Texas, SW USA
29 Y14 **Iowa River** ≈ Iowa, C USA
119 M19 **Ipa** Rus. Ipa. ≈ SE Belarus
59 N20 **Ipatinga** Minas Gerais, SE Brazil
127 N13 **Ipatovo** Stavropol'skiy Kray, SW Russian Federation
115 C16 **Ípeiros** Eng. Epirus. ◈ region W Greece
Ipek see Peć
111 J21 **Ipel'** var. Ipoly, Ger. Eipel. ≈ Hungary/Slovakia
54 C13 **Ipiales** Nariño, SW Colombia
189 V14 **Ipis** atoll Chuuk Islands, C Micronesia
59 A14 **Ipixuna** Amazonas, W Brazil
168 J8 **Ipoh** Perak, Peninsular Malaysia
Ipoly see Ipel'
187 S15 **Ipota** Erromango, S Vanuatu
79 K14 **Ippy** Ouaka, C Central African Republic
114 L13 **Ipsala** Edirne, NW Turkey
Ipsario see Ypsário
183 V3 **Ipswich** Queensland, E Australia
97 Q20 **Ipswich** hist. Gipeswic. E England, UK
29 O8 **Ipswich** South Dakota, N USA
Iput' see Iputs'
119 P18 **Iputs'** Rus. Iput'. ≈ Belarus/Russian Federation
9 R7 **Iqaluit** prev. Frobisher Bay. Baffin Island, Nunavut, NE Canada
159 P9 **Iqe** Qinghai, W China
159 P9 **Iqe He** ≈ C China
Iqlid see Eqlīd
62 G3 **Iquique** Tarapacá, N Chile
56 G8 **Iquitos** Loreto, N Peru
25 N9 **Iraan** Texas, SW USA
79 K14 **Ira Banda** Haute-Kotto, E Central African Republic
165 P16 **Irabu-jima** island Miyako-shotō, SW Japan
55 Y9 **Iracoubo** N French Guiana
60 H13 **Iraí** Rio Grande do Sul, S Brazil
114 G12 **Irákleia** Kentrikí Makedonía, N Greece
115 J21 **Irákleia** island Kykládes, Greece, Aegean Sea
115 J25 **Irákleio** var. Herakleion, Eng. Candia; prev. Iráklion. Kríti, Greece, E Mediterranean Sea
115 J25 **Irákleio** × Kríti, Greece, E Mediterranean Sea
115 F15 **Irákleio** anc. Heracleum. castle Kentrikí Makedonía, N Greece
Iráklion see Irákleio
143 O7 **Iran** off. Islamic Republic of Iran; prev. Persia. ◆ republic SW Asia
58 F13 **Iranduba** Amazonas, NW Brazil
143 Q9 **Iranian Plateau** var. Plateau of Iran. plateau N Iran
169 U9 **Iran, Pegunungan** var. Iran Mountains. ⛰ Indonesia/Malaysia
Iran, Plateau of see Iranian Plateau
143 W13 **Īrānshahr** Sīstān va Balūchestān, SE Iran
55 P5 **Irapa** Sucre, NE Venezuela
41 N13 **Irapuato** Guanajuato, C Mexico
139 R7 **Iraq** off. Republic of Iraq, Ar. 'Irāq. ◆ republic SW Asia
60 J12 **Irati** Paraná, S Brazil
105 R3 **Irati** ≈ N Spain
125 T8 **Irayël'** Respublika Komi, NW Russian Federation
43 N13 **Irazú, Volcán** ✳ C Costa Rica
Irbenskiy Zaliv/Irbes Šaurums see Irbe Strait
118 D7 **Irbe Strait** Est. Kura Kurk, Latv. Irbes Šaurums, Rus. Irbenskiy Zaliv; prev. Est. Irbe Väin. strait Estonia/Latvia
Irbe Väin see Irbe Strait
138 G9 **Irbid** Irbid, N Jordan
138 G9 **Irbid** off. Muḥāfaẓat Irbid. ◈ governorate N Jordan
Irbil see Arbil
109 S6 **Irdning** Steiermark, SE Austria
79 I18 **Irebu** Equateur, W Dem. Rep. Congo
97 D17 **Ireland** var. Republic of Ireland, Ir. Éire. ◆ republic NW Europe
64 A12 **Ireland Island North** island W Bermuda
64 A12 **Ireland Island South** island W Bermuda
Ireland, Republic of see Ireland
127 V15 **Iren'** ≈ NW Russian Federation
185 A22 **Irene, Mount** ▲ South Island, NZ
Irgalem see Yirga 'Alem
144 L11 **Irgiz** Aktyubinsk, C Kazakhstan
Irian see New Guinea
Irian Barat see Papua
Irian Jaya see Papua
Irian, Teluk see Cenderawasih, Teluk
78 K9 **Iriba** Biltine, NE Chad
127 X7 **Iriklinskoye Vodokhranilishche** ▣ W Russian Federation
81 H23 **Iringa** Iringa, C Tanzania
81 H23 **Iringa** ◈ region S Tanzania
165 O16 **Iriomote-jima** island Sakishima-shotō, SW Japan
42 L4 **Iriona** Colón, NE Honduras
58 I13 **Iriri, Rio** ≈ C Brazil
Iris see Yeşilırmak
35 W9 **Irish, Mount** ▲ Nevada, W USA
97 H17 **Irish Sea** Ir. Muir Éireann. sea C British Isles
139 U12 **Irjal ash Shaykhīyah** S Iraq
147 U11 **Irkeshtam** Oshskaya Oblast', SW Kyrgyzstan
122 M13 **Irkutsk** Irkutskaya Oblast', S Russian Federation
122 M12 **Irkutskaya Oblast'** ◈ province S Russian Federation
Irlir, Gora see Irlir Tog'i
146 K8 **Irlir Tog'i** var. Gora Irlir. ▲ N Uzbekistan
Irminger Basin see Reykjanes Basin
21 R12 **Irmo** South Carolina, SE USA
102 E6 **Iroise** sea NW France
189 X2 **Iroj** var. Eroj. island Ratak Chain, SE Marshall Islands
182 H7 **Iron Baron** South Australia
14 C10 **Iron Bridge** Ontario, S Canada
20 H10 **Iron City** Tennessee, S USA
14 I13 **Irondale** ≈ Ontario, SE Canada
182 H7 **Iron Knob** South Australia
30 M5 **Iron Mountain** Michigan, N USA
30 M4 **Iron River** Michigan, N USA
30 J3 **Iron River** Wisconsin, N USA
27 X6 **Ironton** Missouri, C USA
31 S15 **Ironton** Ohio, N USA
30 K4 **Ironwood** Michigan, N USA
12 H12 **Iroquois Falls** Ontario, S Canada
31 N12 **Iroquois River** ≈ Illinois/Indiana, N USA
164 M15 **Irō-zaki** headland Honshū, S Japan
Irpen' see Irpin'
117 O4 **Irpin'** Rus. Irpen'. Kyyivs'ka Oblast', N Ukraine
117 O4 **Irpin'** Rus. Irpen'. ≈ N Ukraine
141 Q16 **'Irqah** SW Yemen
166 K8 **Irrawaddy** var. Ayeyarwady. ◈ division SW Burma
166 L6 **Irrawaddy** var. Ayeyarwady. ≈ W Burma
166 K8 **Irrawaddy, Mouths of the** delta SW Burma
117 N4 **Irsha** ≈ N Ukraine
116 H7 **Irshava** Zakarpats'ka Oblast', W Ukraine
107 N18 **Irsina** Basilicata, S Italy
Irtish see Irtysh
122 H11 **Irtysh** var. Irtish, Kaz. Ertis. ≈ C Asia
145 S7 **Irtyshsk** Kaz. Ertis. Pavlodar, NE Kazakhstan
79 P17 **Irumu** Orientale, E Dem. Rep. Congo
105 Q2 **Irún** País Vasco, N Spain
Iruña see Pamplona
105 Q3 **Irurtzun** Navarra, N Spain
96 I13 **Irvine** W Scotland, UK
21 N6 **Irvine** Kentucky, S USA
25 T6 **Irving** Texas, SW USA
20 K5 **Irvington** Kentucky, S USA
Isaak see Iisaku
28 L8 **Isabel** South Dakota, N USA
186 L8 **Isabel** off. Isabel Province. ◈ province N Solomon Islands
171 O8 **Isabela** Basilan Island, SW Philippines
45 S5 **Isabela** W Puerto Rico
45 N8 **Isabela, Cabo** headland NW Dominican Republic
57 A18 **Isabela, Isla** var. Albemarle Island. island Galapagos Islands, Ecuador, E Pacific Ocean
40 I12 **Isabela, Isla** island C Mexico
42 K9 **Isabella, Cordillera** ⛰ NW Nicaragua
35 S12 **Isabella Lake** ▣ California, W USA
31 N2 **Isabelle, Point** headland Michigan, N USA
Isabel Segunda see Vieques
116 M13 **Isaccea** Tulcea, E Romania
92 H1 **Ísafjarðardjúp** inlet NW Iceland
92 H1 **Ísafjördhur** Vestfirdhir, NW Iceland
164 C14 **Isahaya** Nagasaki, Kyūshū, SW Japan
149 S7 **Īsa Khel** Punjab, E Pakistan
172 H7 **Isalo** var. Massif de L'Isalo. ⛰ SW Madagascar
Isalo, Massif de L' see Isalo
79 K20 **Isandja** Kasai Occidental, C Dem. Rep. Congo
187 R15 **Isangel** Tanna, S Vanuatu
79 M18 **Isangi** Orientale, C Dem. Rep. Congo
101 L24 **Isar** ≈ Austria/Germany
101 M23 **Isar-Kanal** canal SE Germany
Isbarta see Isparta
Isca Damnoniorum see Exeter
107 K18 **Ischia** var. Isola d'Ischia; anc. Aenaria. Campania, S Italy
107 J18 **Ischia, Isola d'** island S Italy
54 B12 **Iscuandé** var. Santa Bárbara. Nariño, SW Colombia
164 K14 **Ise** Mie, Honshū, SW Japan
100 J12 **Ise** ≈ N Germany
95 I23 **Isefjord** fjord E Denmark
Iseghem see Izegem
192 M14 **Iselin Seamount** undersea feature S Pacific Ocean
Isenhof see Püssi
106 E7 **Iseo** Lombardia, N Italy
103 U12 **Iseran, Col de l'** pass E France
103 S11 **Isère** ◈ department E France
103 S12 **Isère** ≈ E France
101 F15 **Iserlohn** Nordrhein-Westfalen, W Germany
107 K16 **Isernia** var. Æsernia. Molise, C Italy
165 N12 **Isesaki** Gunma, Honshū, S Japan
77 S15 **Iseyin** Oyo, W Nigeria
Isfahan see Eşfahān
147 Q11 **Isfana** Batkenskaya Oblast', SW Kyrgyzstan
147 R11 **Isfara** N Tajikistan
149 O4 **Isfi Maidān** Ghowr, N Afghanistan
92 O3 **Isfjorden** fjord W Svalbard
Isha Baydhabo see Baydhabo
127 V11 **Isherim, Gora** ▲ NW Russian Federation
127 Q5 **Isheyevka** Ul'yanovskaya Oblast', W Russian Federation
165 P16 **Ishigaki** Okinawa, Ishigaki-jima, SW Japan
165 P16 **Ishigaki-jima** var. Isigaki Zima. island Sakishima-shotō, SW Japan
165 R3 **Ishikari-wan** bay Hokkaidō, NE Japan
165 S16 **Ishikawa** var. Isikawa. Okinawa, Okinawa, SW Japan
164 K11 **Ishikawa** off. Ishikawa-ken, var. Isikawa. ◈ prefecture Honshū, SW Japan
122 H11 **Ishim** Tyumenskaya Oblast', C Russian Federation
122 H11 **Ishim** Kaz. Esil. ≈ Kazakhstan/Russian Federation
127 V6 **Ishimbay** Respublika Bashkortostan, W Russian Federation
145 O9 **Ishimskoye** Akmola, C Kazakhstan
165 Q10 **Ishinomaki** var. Isinomaki. Miyagi, Honshū, C Japan
165 P13 **Ishioka** var. Isioka. Ibaraki, Honshū, S Japan
Ishkashim see Ishkoshim
Ishkashimskiy Khrebet see Ishkoshim, Qatorkŭhi
147 S15 **Ishkoshim** Rus. Ishkashim. S Tajikistan
147 S15 **Ishkoshim, Qatorkŭhi** Rus. Ishkashimskiy Khrebet. ⛰ SE Tajikistan
31 N4 **Ishpeming** Michigan, N USA
147 N11 **Ishtixon** Rus. Ishtykhan. Samarqand Viloyati, C Uzbekistan
Ishtykhan see Ishtixon
153 T15 **Ishurdi** var. Iswardi. Rajshahi, W Bangladesh
61 G17 **Isidoro Noblia** Cerro Largo, NE Uruguay
102 J4 **Isigny-sur-Mer** Calvados, N France
Isikari Gawa see Ishikari-gawa
Isikawa see Ishikawa
136 C11 **Işıklar Dağı** ⛰ NW Turkey
107 C19 **Isili** Sardegna, Italy, C Mediterranean Sea
122 H12 **Isil'kul'** Omskaya Oblast', C Russian Federation
Isinomaki see Ishinomaki
Isioka see Ishioka
81 I18 **Isiolo** Eastern, C Kenya
79 O16 **Isiro** Orientale, NE Dem. Rep. Congo
92 P2 **Isispynten** headland NE Svalbard
123 P11 **Isit** Respublika Sakha (Yakutiya), NE Russian Federation
149 O2 **Iskabad Canal** canal N Afghanistan
147 Q9 **Iskandar** Rus. Iskander. Toshkent Viloyati, E Uzbekistan
Iskander see Iskandar
Iskăr see Iskŭr
121 Q2 **Iskele** var. Trikomo, Gk. Tríkomon. E Cyprus
136 K17 **İskenderun** Eng. Alexandretta. Hatay, S Turkey
138 H2 **İskenderun Körfezi** Eng. Gulf of Alexandretta. gulf S Turkey
136 J11 **İskilip** Çorum, N Turkey
Iski-Nauket see Eski-Nookat
114 J11 **Iskra** prev. Popovo. Kŭrdzhali, S Bulgaria
114 G10 **Iskŭr** var. Iskăr. ≈ NW Bulgaria
114 H10 **Iskŭr, Yazovir** prev. Yazovir Stalin. ▣ W Bulgaria
41 S15 **Isla** Veracruz-Llave, SE Mexico
119 J15 **Islach** Rus. Isloch'. ≈ C Belarus
104 H14 **Isla Cristina** Andalucía, S Spain
Isla de León see San Fernando
149 U6 **Islāmābād** ● (Pakistan) Federal Capital Territory Islāmābād, NE Pakistan
149 V6 **Islāmābād** × Federal Capital Territory Islāmābād, NE Pakistan
Islamabad see Anantnāg
149 R17 **Islāmkot** Sind, SE Pakistan
23 Y17 **Islamorada** Florida Keys, Florida, SE USA
153 P14 **Islāmpur** Bihār, N India
Islam Qala see Eslām Qal'eh
Island/Ísland see Iceland
18 K16 **Island Beach** spit New Jersey, NE USA
19 S4 **Island Falls** Maine, NE USA
182 H6 **Island Lagoon** ◎ South Australia
11 Y13 **Island Lake** ◎ Manitoba, C Canada
29 W5 **Island Lake Reservoir** ▣ Minnesota, N USA
33 R13 **Island Park** Idaho, NW USA
19 N6 **Island Pond** Vermont, NE USA
184 K2 **Islands, Bay of** inlet North Island, NZ
103 R7 **Is-sur-Tille** Côte d'Or, C France
42 J3 **Islas de la Bahía** ◈ department N Honduras
65 L20 **Islas Orcadas Rise** undersea feature S Atlantic Ocean
96 F12 **Islay** island SW Scotland, UK
116 I15 **Islaz** Teleorman, S Romania
29 V7 **Isle** Minnesota, N USA
102 M12 **Isle** ≈ W France
97 I16 **Isle of Man** ◇ UK crown dependency NW Europe
21 X7 **Isle of Wight** Virginia, NE USA
97 M24 **Isle of Wight** cultural region S England, UK
191 Y3 **Isles Lagoon** ◎ Kiritimati, E Kiribati
37 R11 **Isleta Pueblo** New Mexico, SW USA
Isloch' see Islach

◆ Country ● Country Capital ◇ Dependent Territory ○ Dependent Territory Capital ◈ Administrative Region × International Airport ▲ Mountain ⛰ Mountain Range ✳ Volcano ≈ River ◎ Lake ▣ Reservoir

61 E19 **Ismael Cortinas** Flores, S Uruguay
Ismailia *see* Ismâ'ilîya
75 W7 **Ismâ'ilîya** *var.* Ismailia. N Egypt
Ismailly *see* İsmayıllı
137 X11 **İsmayıllı** *Rus.* Ismailly. C Azerbaijan
Ismid *see* İzmit
75 X10 **Isna** *var.* Esna. SE Egypt
93 K18 **Isojoki** Länsi-Suomi, W Finland
82 M12 **Isoka** Northern, NE Zambia
Isola d'Ischia *see* Ischia
Isola d'Istria *see* Izola
Isonzo *see* Soča
15 U4 **Isoukustouc** ≈ Québec, SE Canada
136 F15 **İsparta** *var.* Isbarta. İsparta, SW Turkey
136 F15 **İsparta** *var.* Isbarta. ◆ *province* SW Turkey
114 M7 **Isperikh** *prev.* Kemanlar. Razgrad, N Bulgaria
107 L26 **Ispica** Sicilia, Italy, C Mediterranean Sea
148 J14 **Ispikān** Baluchistān, SW Pakistan
137 Q12 **İspir** Erzurum, NE Turkey
138 E12 **Israel** *off.* State of Israel, *var.* Medinat Israel, *Heb.* Yisrael, Yisra'el. ◆ *republic* SW Asia
Issa *see* Vis
55 S9 **Issano** C Guyana
76 M16 **Issia** SW Ivory Coast
Issiq Köl *see* Issyk-Kul', Ozero
103 P11 **Issoire** Puy-de-Dôme, C France
103 N9 **Issoudun** *anc.* Uxellodunum. Indre, C France
81 H22 **Issuna** Singida, C Tanzania
Issyk *see* Yesik
Issyk-Kul' *see* Balykchy
147 X7 **Issyk-Kul', Ozero** *var.* Issiq Köl, *Kir.* Ysyk-Köl. ◎ E Kyrgyzstan
147 X7 **Issyk-Kul'skaya Oblast'** *Kir.* Ysyk-Köl Oblasty. ◆ *province* E Kyrgyzstan
149 Q7 **Īstādeh-ye Moqor, Āb-e-** *var.* Āb-i-Istāda. ◎ SE Afghanistan
136 D11 **İstanbul** *Bul.* Tsarigrad, *Eng.* Istanbul; *prev.* Constantinople, *anc.* Byzantium. İstanbul, NW Turkey
114 P12 **İstanbul** ◆ *province* NW Turkey
114 P12 **İstanbul Boğazı** *var.* Bosporus Thracius, *Eng.* Bosphorus, Bosporus, *Turk.* Karadeniz Boğazı. *strait* NW Turkey
Istarska Županija *see* Istra
115 G19 **Isthmía** Pelopónnisos, S Greece
115 G17 **Istiaía** Évvoia, C Greece
54 D9 **Istmina** Chocó, W Colombia
23 W13 **Istokpoga, Lake** ◎ Florida, SE USA
112 A9 **Istra** *off.* Istarska županija. ◆ *province* NW Croatia
112 I10 **Istra** *Eng.* Istria, *Ger.* Istrien. *cultural region* NW Croatia
103 R15 **Istres** Bouches-du-Rhône, SE France
Istria/Istrien *see* Istra
Iswardi *see* Ishurdi
127 V7 **Isyangulovo** Respublika Bashkortostan, W Russian Federation
62 O6 **Itá** Central, S Paraguay
59 O17 **Itaberaba** Bahia, E Brazil
59 M20 **Itabira** *prev.* Presidente Vargas. Minas Gerais, SE Brazil
59 O18 **Itabuna** Bahia, E Brazil
59 J18 **Itacaiu** Mato Grosso, S Brazil
58 G12 **Itacoatiara** Amazonas, N Brazil
54 D9 **Itagüí** Antioquia, W Colombia
60 D13 **Itá Ibaté** Corrientes, NE Argentina
60 G11 **Itaipú, Represa de** ⊞ Brazil/Paraguay
58 H13 **Itaituba** Pará, NE Brazil
60 K13 **Itajaí** Santa Catarina, S Brazil
Italia/Italiana, Republica/Italian Republic, The *see* Italy
Italian Somaliland *see* Somalia
25 T7 **Italy** Texas, SW USA
106 G12 **Italy** *off.* The Italian Republic, *It.* Italia, Repubblica Italiana. ◆ *republic* S Europe
59 O19 **Itamaraju** Bahia, E Brazil
59 C14 **Itamarati** Amazonas, W Brazil
59 M19 **Itambé, Pico de** ▲ SE Brazil
164 J13 **Itami** ✕ (Ōsaka) Ōsaka, Honshū, SW Japan
115 H15 **Ítamos** ▲ N Greece
153 W11 **Itānagar** Arunāchal Pradesh, NE India
Itany *see* Litani
59 N19 **Itaobim** Minas Gerais, SE Brazil
59 P15 **Itaparica, Represa de** ⊞ E Brazil
58 M13 **Itapecuru-Mirim** Maranhão, E Brazil
60 Q8 **Itaperuna** Rio de Janeiro, SE Brazil
59 O18 **Itapetinga** Bahia, E Brazil
60 L10 **Itapetininga** São Paulo, S Brazil
60 K10 **Itapeva** São Paulo, S Brazil
53 O13 **Itapipoca** Ceará, E Brazil
60 M9 **Itapira** São Paulo, S Brazil
60 K8 **Itápolis** São Paulo, S Brazil
60 K10 **Itaporanga** São Paulo, S Brazil
62 P7 **Itapúa** *off.* Departamento de Itapúa. ◆ *department* SE Paraguay
59 E15 **Itapuã do Oeste** Rondônia, W Brazil
61 E15 **Itaqui** Rio Grande do Sul, S Brazil
60 K10 **Itararé** São Paulo, S Brazil
60 K10 **Itararé, Rio** ≈ S Brazil
154 H11 **Itārsi** Madhya Pradesh, C India
25 T7 **Itasca** Texas, SW USA
Itassi *see* Vieille Case
93 N17 **Itä-Suomi** ◆ *province* E Finland
60 D13 **Itatí** Corrientes, NE Argentina
60 K10 **Itatinga** São Paulo, S Brazil
115 F18 **Itéas, Kólpos** *gulf* C Greece
57 N15 **Iténez, Río** *var.* Rio Guaporé. ≈ Bolivia/Brazil *see also* Guaporé, Rio
54 H11 **Iteviate, Río** ≈ C Colombia
100 I13 **Ith** *hill range* C Germany
31 Q8 **Ithaca** Michigan, N USA
18 H11 **Ithaca** New York, NE USA
115 C18 **Itháki** Itháki, Iónioi Nísoi, Greece, C Mediterranean Sea
115 C18 **Itháki** *island* Iónioi Nísoi, Greece, C Mediterranean Sea
It Hearrenfean *see* Heerenveen
79 L17 **Itimbiri** ≈ N Dem. Rep. Congo
Itinomiya *see* Ichinomiya
Itinoseki *see* Ichinoseki
39 Q5 **Itkilik River** ≈ Alaska, USA
164 M11 **Itoigawa** Niigata, Honshū, C Japan
15 R6 **Itomamo, Lac** ◎ Québec, SE Canada
165 S17 **Itoman** Okinawa, SW Japan
102 M5 **Iton** ≈ N France
57 M16 **Itonamas Río** ≈ NE Bolivia
Itoupé, Mont *see* Sommet Tabulaire
Itseqqortoormiit *see* Ittoqqortoormiit
22 K4 **Itta Bena** Mississippi, S USA
107 B17 **Ittiri** Sardegna, Italy, C Mediterranean Sea
197 Q14 **Ittoqqortoormiit** *var.* Itseqqortoormiit, *Dan.* Scoresbysund, *Eng.* Scoresby Sound. Tunu, C Greenland
60 M10 **Itu** São Paulo, S Brazil
54 D8 **Ituango** Antioquia, NW Colombia
59 A14 **Ituí, Rio** ≈ NW Brazil
79 O20 **Itula** Sud Kivu, E Dem. Rep. Congo
59 K19 **Itumbiara** Goiás, C Brazil
55 T9 **Ituni** E Guyana
41 X13 **Iturbide** Campeche, SE Mexico
Ituri *see* Aruwimi
123 V13 **Iturup, Ostrov** *island* Kuril'skiye Ostrova, SE Russian Federation
60 L7 **Ituverava** São Paulo, S Brazil
59 C15 **Ituxi, Rio** ≈ W Brazil
61 E14 **Ituzaingó** Corrientes, NE Argentina
101 K18 **Itz** ≈ C Germany
100 I9 **Itzehoe** Schleswig-Holstein, N Germany
23 N2 **Iuka** Mississippi, S USA
60 I11 **Ivaiporã** Paraná, S Brazil
60 I11 **Ivaí, Rio** ≈ S Brazil
92 L10 **Ivalo** *Lapp.* Avveel, Avvil. Lappi, N Finland
92 L10 **Ivalojoki** *Lapp.* Avreel. ≈ N Finland
119 H20 **Ivanava** *Pol.* Janów, Janów Poleski, *Rus.* Ivanovo. Brestskaya Voblasts', SW Belarus
Ivangorod *see* Dęblin
Ivangrad *see* Berane
183 N7 **Ivanhoe** New South Wales, SE Australia
29 S9 **Ivanhoe** Minnesota, N USA
14 D8 **Ivanhoe** ≈ Ontario, S Canada
112 E8 **Ivanić-Grad** Sisak-Moslavina, N Croatia
117 T10 **Ivanivka** Khersons'ka Oblast', S Ukraine
117 P10 **Ivanivka** Odes'ka Oblast', SW Ukraine
113 L14 **Ivanjica** Serbia, C Serbia and Montenegro (Yugo.)
112 G11 **Ivanjska** *var.* Potkozarje. Republika Srpska, NW Bosnia & Herzegovina
111 H21 **Ivanka** ✕ (Bratislava) Bratislavský Kraj, W Slovakia
117 O3 **Ivankiv** *Rus.* Ivankov. Kyyivs'ka Oblast', N Ukraine
Ivankov *see* Ivankiv
39 O15 **Ivanof Bay** Alaska, USA
116 J7 **Ivano-Frankivs'k** *Ger.* Stanislau, *Pol.* Stanisławów, *Rus.* Ivano-Frankovsk; *prev.* Stanislav. Ivano-Frankivs'ka Oblast', W Ukraine
Ivano-Frankivs'k *see* Ivano-Frankivs'ka Oblast'
116 I7 **Ivano-Frankivs'ka Oblast'** *var.* Ivano-Frankivs'k, *Rus.* Ivano-Frankovskaya Oblast'; *prev.* Stanislavskaya Oblast'. ◆ *province* W Ukraine
Ivano-Frankovsk *see* Ivano-Frankivs'k
Ivano-Frankovskaya Oblast' *see* Ivano-Frankivs'ka Oblast'
124 M16 **Ivanovo** Ivanovskaya Oblast', W Russian Federation
Ivanovo *see* Ivanava
124 M16 **Ivanovskaya Oblast'** ◆ *province* W Russian Federation
35 X12 **Ivanpah Lake** ◎ California, W USA
112 E7 **Ivanščica** ▲ NE Croatia
114 M8 **Ivanski** Shumen, NE Bulgaria
127 R7 **Ivanteyevka** Saratovskaya Oblast', W Russian Federation
Ivantsevichi/Ivatsevichi *see* Ivatsevichy
116 I4 **Ivanychi** Volyns'ka Oblast', NW Ukraine
119 H18 **Ivatsevichy** *Pol.* Iwacewicze, *Rus.* Ivantsevichi, Ivatsevichi. Brestskaya Voblasts', SW Belarus
114 L12 **Ivaylovgrad** Khaskovo, S Bulgaria
114 K11 **Ivaylovgrad, Yazovir** ⊞ S Bulgaria
122 G9 **Ivdel'** Sverdlovskaya Oblast', C Russian Federation
Ivenets *see* Ivyanyets
116 L12 **Iveşti** Galaţi, E Romania
Ivgovuotna *see* Lyngen
Ivigtut *see* Ivittuut
79 F18 **Ivindo** ≈ Congo/Gabon
59 I21 **Ivinheima** Mato Grosso do Sul, SW Brazil
196 M15 **Ivittuut** *var.* Ivigtut. Kitaa, S Greenland
Iviza *see* Eivissa
172 I6 **Ivohibe** Fianarantsoa, SE Madagascar
Ivoire, Côte d' *see* Ivory Coast
76 L15 **Ivory Coast** *off.* Republic of the Ivory Coast, *Fr.* Côte d'Ivoire, République de la Côte d'Ivoire. ◆ *republic* W Africa
95 L22 **Ivösjön** ◎ S Sweden
106 B7 **Ivrea** *anc.* Eporedia. Piemonte, NW Italy
12 J2 **Ivujivik** Québec, NE Canada
119 J16 **Ivyanyets** *Rus.* Ivenets. Minskaya Voblasts', C Belarus
Iv'ye *see* Iwye
Iwacewicze *see* Ivatsevichy
165 R8 **Iwaizumi** Iwate, Honshū, NE Japan
165 P12 **Iwaki** Fukushima, Honshū, N Japan
164 F13 **Iwakuni** Yamaguchi, Honshū, SW Japan
165 S4 **Iwamizawa** Hokkaidō, NE Japan
165 R4 **Iwanai** Hokkaidō, NE Japan
165 Q10 **Iwanuma** Miyagi, Honshū, C Japan
164 L14 **Iwata** Shizuoka, Honshū, S Japan
165 R8 **Iwate** Iwate, Honshū, N Japan
165 R8 **Iwate** *off.* Iwate-ken. ◆ *prefecture* Honshū, C Japan
Iwje *see* Iwye
77 S16 **Iwo** Oyo, SW Nigeria
Iwojima *see* Iō-jima
119 I16 **Iwye** *Pol.* Iwje, *Rus.* Iv'ye. Hrodzyenskaya Voblasts', W Belarus
42 C4 **Ixcán, Río** ≈ Guatemala/Mexico
99 G18 **Ixelles** *Dut.* Elsene. Brussels, C Belgium
57 J16 **Ixiamas** La Paz, NW Bolivia
41 O13 **Ixmiquilpan** *var.* Ixmiquilpán. Hidalgo, C Mexico
83 K23 **Ixopo** KwaZulu/Natal, E South Africa
Ixtacchuatl, Volcán *see* Iztaccíhuatl, Volcán
40 M16 **Ixtapa** Guerrero, S Mexico
41 S16 **Ixtepec** Oaxaca, SE Mexico
40 K12 **Ixtlán** *var.* Ixtlán del Río. Nayarit, C Mexico
Ixtlán del Río *see* Ixtlán
122 H11 **Iyevlevo** Tyumenskaya Oblast', C Russian Federation
164 F14 **Iyo** Ehime, Shikoku, SW Japan
Iyomisima *see* Iyomishima
164 E14 **Iyo-nada** *sea* S Japan
42 E4 **Izabal** *off.* Departamento de Izabal. ◆ *department* E Guatemala
42 F5 **Izabal, Lago de** *prev.* Golfo Dulce. ◎ E Guatemala
143 O9 **Īzad Khvāst** Fārs, C Iran
41 X12 **Izamal** Yucatán, SE Mexico
127 Q16 **Izberbash** Respublika Dagestan, SW Russian Federation
99 C18 **Izegem** *prev.* Iseghem. West-Vlaanderen, W Belgium
142 M9 **Īzeh** Khūzestān, SW Iran
165 T16 **Izena-jima** *island* Nansei-shotō, SW Japan
114 N10 **Izgrev** Burgas, E Bulgaria
127 T2 **Izhevsk** *prev.* Ustinov. Udmurtskaya Respublika, NW Russian Federation
125 S7 **Izhma** Respublika Komi, NW Russian Federation
127 S7 **Izhma** ≈ NW Russian Federation
141 X8 **Izkī** NE Oman
Izmail *see* Izmayil
117 N13 **Izmayil** *Rus.* Izmail. Odes'ka Oblast', SW Ukraine
136 B14 **İzmir** *prev.* Smyrna. İzmir, W Turkey
136 C14 **İzmir** *prev.* Smyrna. ◆ *province* W Turkey
136 E11 **İzmit** *var.* Ismid; *anc.* Astacus. Kocaeli, NW Turkey
104 M14 **Iznájar** Andalucía, S Spain
104 M14 **Iznajar, Embalse de** ⊞ S Spain
105 N14 **Iznalloz** Andalucía, S Spain
136 E11 **İznik** Bursa, NW Turkey
136 E12 **İznik Gölü** ◎ NW Turkey
126 M14 **Izobil'nyy** Stavropol'skiy Kray, SW Russian Federation
109 S13 **Izola** *It.* Isola d'Istria. SW Slovenia
138 H9 **Izra'** *var.* Ezra, Ezraa. Dar'ā, S Syria
41 P14 **Iztaccíhuati, Volcán** *var.* Volcán Ixtaccíhuatal. ※ S Mexico
42 C7 **Iztapa** Escuintla, SE Guatemala
Izúcar de Matamoros *see* Matamoros
165 N14 **Izu-hantō** *peninsula* Honshū, S Japan
164 C12 **Izuhara** Nagasaki, Tsushima, SW Japan
164 J14 **Izumiōtsu** Ōsaka, Honshū, SW Japan
164 I14 **Izumi-Sano** Ōsaka, Honshū, SW Japan
164 G12 **Izumo** Shimane, Honshū, SW Japan
Izu Shichito *see* Izu-shotō
192 H5 **Izu Trench** *undersea feature* NW Pacific Ocean
122 K6 **Izvestiy TsIK, Ostrova** *island* N Russian Federation
114 G10 **Izvor** Pernik, W Bulgaria
116 L5 **Izyaslav** Khmel'nyts'ka Oblast', W Ukraine
117 W6 **Izyum** Kharkivs'ka Oblast', E Ukraine

J

95 M18 **Jaala** Etelä-Suomi, S Finland
140 J5 **Jabal ash Shifā** *desert* NW Saudi Arabia
141 U8 **Jabal az Ẓannah** *var.* Jebel Dhanna. Abū Ẓaby, W UAE
138 E11 **Jabalīya** *var.* Jabāliyah. NE Gaza Strip
Jabāliyah *see* Jabalīya
105 N11 **Jabalón** ≈ C Spain
154 J10 **Jabalpur** *prev.* Jubbulpore. Madhya Pradesh, C India
141 N15 **Jabal Zuqar, Jazīrat** *var.* Az Zuqur. *island* SW Yemen
Jabat *see* Jabwot
138 J3 **Jabbūl, Sabkhat al** *salt flat* NW Syria
181 P1 **Jabiru** Northern Territory, N Australia
138 H4 **Jablah** *var.* Jeble, *Fr.* Djéblé. Al Lādhiqīyah, W Syria
112 C11 **Jablanac** Lika-Senj, W Croatia
113 H14 **Jablanica** Federacija Bosna I Hercegovina, SW Bosnia and Herzegovina
113 M20 **Jablanica** *Alb.* Mali i Jabllanicës, *var.* Malet e Jabllanicës. ▲ Albania/FYR Macedonia *see also* Jabllanicës, Mali i
Jabllanicës, Malet e *see* Jablanica/Jabllanicës, Mali i
113 M20 **Jabllanicës, Mali i** *var.* Malet e Jabllanicës, *Mac.* Jablanica. ▲ Albania/FYR Macedonia *see also* Jablanica
111 E15 **Jablonec nad Nisou** *Ger.* Gablonz an der Neisse. Liberecký Kraj, N Czech Republic
Jabłonków/Jablunkau *see* Jablunkov
110 J9 **Jabłonowo Pomorskie** Kujawski-pomorskie, C Poland
111 J17 **Jablunkov** *Ger.* Jablunkau, *Pol.* Jabłonków. Moravskoslezský Kraj, E Czech Republic
59 Q15 **Jaboatão** Pernambuco, E Brazil
60 L8 **Jaboticabal** São Paulo, S Brazil
189 U7 **Jabwot** *var.* Jabat, Jebat, Jōwat. *island* Ralik Chain, S Marshall Islands
105 S4 **Jaca** Aragón, NE Spain
42 B4 **Jacaltenango** Huehuetenango, W Guatemala
59 G14 **Jacaré-a-Canga** Pará, NE Brazil
60 N10 **Jacareí** São Paulo, S Brazil
59 I18 **Jaciara** Mato Grosso, W Brazil
59 E15 **Jaciparaná** Rondônia, W Brazil
19 P5 **Jackman** Maine, NE USA
35 X1 **Jackpot** Nevada, W USA
20 M8 **Jacksboro** Tennessee, S USA
25 S6 **Jacksboro** Texas, SW USA
23 N7 **Jackson** Alabama, S USA
35 P7 **Jackson** California, W USA
23 T4 **Jackson** Georgia, SE USA
21 O6 **Jackson** Kentucky, S USA
22 J8 **Jackson** Louisiana, S USA
31 Q10 **Jackson** Michigan, N USA
29 T11 **Jackson** Minnesota, N USA
22 K5 **Jackson** *state capital* Mississippi, S USA
27 Y7 **Jackson** Missouri, C USA
21 W8 **Jackson** North Carolina, SE USA
31 T15 **Jackson** Ohio, NE USA
20 G9 **Jackson** Tennessee, S USA
33 S14 **Jackson** Wyoming, C USA
185 C19 **Jackson Bay** *bay* South Island, NZ
186 E9 **Jackson Field** ✕ (Port Moresby) Central/National Capital District, S PNG
185 C20 **Jackson Head** *headland* South Island, NZ
23 S8 **Jackson, Lake** ◎ Florida, SE USA
33 S13 **Jackson Lake** ◎ Wyoming, C USA
194 J6 **Jackson, Mount** ▲ Antarctica
37 U3 **Jackson Reservoir** ◎ Colorado, C USA
23 Q3 **Jacksonville** Alabama, S USA
27 V11 **Jacksonville** Arkansas, C USA
23 W8 **Jacksonville** Florida, SE USA
30 K14 **Jacksonville** Illinois, N USA
21 W11 **Jacksonville** North Carolina, SE USA
25 W7 **Jacksonville** Texas, SW USA
23 X9 **Jacksonville Beach** Florida, SE USA
44 L9 **Jacmel** *var.* Jaquemel. S Haiti
Jacob *see* Nkayi
149 Q12 **Jacobābād** Sind, SE Pakistan
55 T11 **Jacobs Ladder Falls** *waterfall* S Guyana
45 O11 **Jaco, Pointe** *headland* N Dominica
15 Q9 **Jacques-Cartier** ≈ Québec, SE Canada
13 P11 **Jacques-Cartier, Détroit de** *var.* Jacques-Cartier Passage. *strait* Gulf of St. Lawrence/St. Lawrence River
15 W6 **Jacques-Cartier, Mont** ▲ Québec, SE Canada
Jacques-Cartier Passage *see* Jacques-Cartier, Détroit de
61 H16 **Jacuí, Rio** ≈ S Brazil
60 L11 **Jacupiranga** São Paulo, S Brazil
100 G10 **Jade** ≈ NW Germany
100 G10 **Jadebusen** *bay* NW Germany
Jadotville *see* Likasi
Jadransko More/Jadransko Morje *see* Adriatic Sea
105 O7 **Jadraque** Castilla-La Mancha, C Spain
56 C10 **Jaén** Cajamarca, N Peru
105 N13 **Jaén** Andalucía, SW Spain
105 N13 **Jaén** ◆ *province* Andalucía, S Spain
155 J23 **Jaffna** Northern Province, N Sri Lanka
155 K23 **Jaffna Lagoon** *lagoon* N Sri Lanka
19 N10 **Jaffrey** New Hampshire, NE USA
138 H13 **Jafr, Qā' al** *var.* El Jafr. *salt pan* S Jordan
152 J9 **Jagādhri** Haryāna, N India
118 H4 **Jägala** *var.* Jägala Jõgi, *Ger.* Jaggowal. ≈ NW Estonia
Jägala Jõgi *see* Jägala
Jagannath *see* Puri
155 L14 **Jagdalpur** Chhattīsgarh, C India
163 U5 **Jagdaqi** Nei Mongol Zizhiqu, N China
Jägerndorf *see* Krnov
Jaggowal *see* Jägala
139 O2 **Jaghjaghah, Nahr** ≈ N Syria
112 N13 **Jagodina** *prev.* Svetozarevo. Serbia, C Serbia and Montenegro (Yugo.)
112 K12 **Jagodnja** ▲ W Serbia and Montenegro (Yugo.)
101 I20 **Jagst** ≈ SW Germany
155 I14 **Jagtiāl** Andhra Pradesh, C India
61 H18 **Jaguarão** Rio Grande do Sul, S Brazil
61 H18 **Jaguarão, Rio** *var.* Río Yaguarón. ≈ Brazil/Uruguay
60 K11 **Jaguariaíva** Paraná, S Brazil
44 D5 **Jagüey Grande** Matanzas, W Cuba
153 P14 **Jahānābād** Bihār, N India
Jahra *see* Al Jahrā'
143 P12 **Jahrom** *var.* Jahrum. Fārs, S Iran
Jahrum *see* Jahrom
Jailolo *see* Halmahera, Pulau
Jainat *see* Chai Nat
Jainti *see* Jayanti
152 H12 **Jaipur** *prev.* Jeypore. Rājasthān, N India
153 T14 **Jaipur Hat** Rajshahi, NW Bangladesh
152 D11 **Jaisalmer** Rājasthān, NW India
154 O12 **Jājapur** Orissa, E India
143 R4 **Jājarm** Khorāsān, NE Iran
112 G12 **Jajce** Federacija Bosna I Hercegovina, W Bosnia and Herzegovina
Jajı *see* 'Alī Kheyl
83 D17 **Jakalsberg** Otjozondjupa, N Namibia
169 O15 **Jakarta** *prev.* Djakarta, *Dut.* Batavia. ● (Indonesia) Jawa, C Indonesia
10 I8 **Jakes Corner** Yukon Territory, W Canada
152 H9 **Jākhal** Haryāna, NW India
Jakobeny *see* Iacobeni
93 K16 **Jakobstad** *Fin.* Pietarsaari. Länsi-Suomi, W Finland
Jakobstadt *see* Jēkabpils
113 O18 **Jakupica** ▲ C FYR Macedonia
37 W15 **Jal** New Mexico, SW USA
141 P7 **Jalājil** *var.* Ğalāğıl. Ar Riyāḍ, C Saudi Arabia
Jalal-Abad *see* Dzhalal-Abad, Dzhalal-Abadskaya Oblast', W Kyrgyzstan
149 S5 **Jalālābād** *var.* Jalalabad, Jelalabad. Nangarhār, E Afghanistan
Jalal-Abad Oblasty *see* Dzhalal-Abadskaya Oblast'
149 V7 **Jalālpur** Punjab, E Pakistan
149 T11 **Jalālpur Pīrwāla** Punjab, E Pakistan
152 H8 **Jalandhar** *prev.* Jullundur. Punjab, N India
42 J7 **Jalán, Río** ≈ S Honduras
42 E6 **Jalapa** Jalapa, C Guatemala
42 J7 **Jalapa** Nueva Segovia, NW Nicaragua
42 A3 **Jalapa** *off.* Departamento de Jalapa. ◆ *department* SE Guatemala
42 E6 **Jalapa, Río** ≈ SE Guatemala
143 X13 **Jālaq** Sīstān va Balūchestān, SE Iran
93 K17 **Jalasjärvi** Länsi-Suomi, W Finland
149 O8 **Jaldak** Zābul, SE Afghanistan
60 J7 **Jales** São Paulo, S Brazil
154 P11 **Jaleshwar** *var.* Jaleswar. Orissa, NE India
Jaleswar *see* Jaleshwar
154 F12 **Jalgaon** Mahārāshtra, C India
139 W12 **Jalībah** S Iraq
139 W13 **Jalīb Shahāb** S Iraq
77 X15 **Jalingo** Taraba, E Nigeria
40 K13 **Jalisco** ◆ *state* SW Mexico
154 G13 **Jālna** Mahārāshtra, W India
Jalomitsa *see* Ialomiţa
105 R5 **Jalón** ≈ N Spain
152 E13 **Jālor** Rājasthān, N India
112 K11 **Jalovik** Serbia, W Serbia and Montenegro (Yugo.)
40 L12 **Jalpa** Zacatecas, C Mexico
153 S12 **Jalpāiguri** West Bengal, NE India
41 O12 **Jalpán** *var.* Jalpan. Querétaro de Arteaga, C Mexico
75 S9 **Jālū** *var.* Jūlā. NE Libya
189 U8 **Jaluit Atoll** *var.* Jālwōj. *atoll* Ralik Chain, S Marshall Islands
Jālwōj *see* Jaluit Atoll
81 L18 **Jamaame** *It.* Giamame; *prev.* Margherita. Jubbada Hoose, S Somalia
77 W13 **Jamaare** ≈ NE Nigeria
44 G9 **Jamaica** ◆ *commonwealth republic* W West Indies
44 I9 **Jamaica Channel** *channel* Haiti/Jamaica
153 T14 **Jamalpur** Dhaka, N Bangladesh
153 Q14 **Jamālpur** Bihār, NE India
168 L9 **Jamaluang** *var.* Jemaluang. Johor, Peninsular Malaysia
59 I14 **Jamanxim, Rio** ≈ C Brazil
56 B8 **Jambeli, Canal de** *channel* S Ecuador
99 I20 **Jambes** Namur, SE Belgium
168 L12 **Jambi** *var.* Telanaipura; *prev.* Djambi. Sumatera, W Indonesia
168 K12 **Jambi** *off.* Propinsi Jambi, *var.* Djambi. ◆ *province* W Indonesia
Jamdena *see* Yamdena, Pulau
12 H8 **James Bay** *bay* Ontario/Québec, E Canada
63 F19 **James, Isla** *island* Archipiélago de los Chonos, S Chile
181 Q8 **James Ranges** ▲ Northern Territory, C Australia
29 P8 **James River** ≈ North Dakota/South Dakota, N USA
21 X7 **James River** ≈ Virginia, NE USA
194 H4 **James Ross Island** *island* Antarctica
182 I8 **Jamestown** South Australia
65 G25 **Jamestown** ○ (Saint Helena) NW Saint Helena
35 P8 **Jamestown** California, W USA
20 L7 **Jamestown** Kentucky, S USA
18 D11 **Jamestown** New York, NE USA
29 P5 **Jamestown** North Dakota, N USA
20 L8 **Jamestown** Tennessee, S USA
Jamestown *see* Holetown
15 N10 **Jamet** ≈ Québec, SE Canada
41 Q17 **Jamiltepec** *var.* Santiago Jamiltepec. Oaxaca, SE Mexico
95 F20 **Jammerbugten** *bay* Skagerrak, E North Sea
152 H6 **Jammu** *prev.* Jummoo. Jammu and Kashmir, NW India
152 I5 **Jammu and Kashmir** *var.* Jammu-Kashmir, Kashmir. ◆ *state* NW India
149 V4 **Jammu and Kashmir** *disputed region* India/Pakistan
154 B10 **Jāmnagar** *prev.* Navanagar. Gujarāt, W India
149 S11 **Jāmpur** Punjab, E Pakistan
93 L18 **Jämsä** Länsi-Suomi, W Finland
93 L18 **Jämsänkoski** Länsi-Suomi, W Finland
153 Q16 **Jamshedpur** Jhārkhand, NE India
94 K9 **Jämtland** ◆ *county* C Sweden
153 Q14 **Jamūi** Bihār, NE India
153 T14 **Jamuna** ≈ N Bangladesh
Jamuna *see* Brahmaputra
Jamundá *see* Nhamundá, Rio
54 D11 **Jamundí** Valle del Cauca, SW Colombia
153 Q12 **Janakpur** Central, C Nepal
59 N18 **Janaúba** Minas Gerais, SE Brazil
58 K11 **Janaucu, Ilha** *island* NE Brazil
143 Q7 **Jandaq** Eşfahān, C Iran
64 Q11 **Jandia, Punta de** *headland* Fuerteventura, Islas Canarias, Spain, NE Atlantic Ocean
59 B14 **Jandiatuba, Rio** ≈ NW Brazil
105 N12 **Jándula** ≈ S Spain
29 V10 **Janesville** Minnesota, N USA
30 L9 **Janesville** Wisconsin, N USA
149 N13 **Jangal** Baluchistān, SW Pakistan
83 N20 **Jangamo** Inhambane, SE Mozambique
155 J14 **Jangaon** Andhra Pradesh, C India
153 S14 **Jangipur** West Bengal, NE India
Janina *see* Ioánnina
Janischken *see* Joniškis
112 J11 **Janja** Republika Srpska, NE Bosnia and Herzegovina
Jankovac *see* Jánoshalma
197 Q15 **Jan Mayen** ◇ *Norwegian dependency* N Atlantic Ocean
197 R15 **Jan Mayen Fracture Zone** *tectonic feature* Greenland Sea/Norwegian Sea
197 R15 **Jan Mayen Ridge** *undersea feature* Greenland Sea/Norwegian Sea
40 H3 **Janos** Chihuahua, N Mexico
111 K25 **Jánoshalma** *SCr.* Jankovac. Bács-Kiskun, S Hungary
Janow/Janów *see* Jonava, Lithuania
Janów *see* Ivanava, Belarus
110 H10 **Janowiec Wielkopolski** *Ger.* Janowitz. Kujawski-pomorskie, C Poland
Janowitz *see* Janowiec Wielkopolski
111 O15 **Janów Lubelski** Lubelskie, E Poland
Janów Poleski *see* Ivanava
83 H25 **Jansenville** Eastern Cape, S South Africa
59 M18 **Januária** Minas Gerais, SE Brazil
Janūbīyah, Al Bādiyah al *see* Ash Shāmīyah
102 I7 **Janzé** Ille-et-Vilaine, NW France
154 F10 **Jaora** Madhya Pradesh, C India
164 K11 **Japan** *var.* Nippon, *Jap.* Nihon. ◆ *monarchy* E Asia
192 H4 **Japan Basin** *undersea feature* N Sea of Japan
192 H4 **Japan, Sea of** *var.* East Sea, *Rus.* Yapanskoye More. *sea* NW Pacific Ocean *see also* East Sea
192 H4 **Japan Trench** *undersea feature* NW Pacific Ocean
Japen *see* Yapen, Pulau
59 A15 **Japiim** *var.* Máncio Lima. Acre, W Brazil
58 D12 **Japurá** Amazonas, N Brazil
58 C12 **Japurá, Rio** *var.* Río Caquetá, Yapurá. ≈ Brazil/Colombia *see also* Caquetá, Río
43 W17 **Jaqué** Darién, SE Panama
Jaquemel *see* Jacmel
Jarablos *see* Jarābulus
138 K2 **Jarābulus** *var.* Jarablos, Jerablus, *Fr.* Djérablous. Ḩalab, N Syria
60 K13 **Jaraguá do Sul** Santa Catarina, S Brazil
104 K9 **Jaraicejo** Extremadura, W Spain
104 K9 **Jaráiz de la Vera** Extremadura, W Spain
105 O7 **Jarama** ≈ C Spain
63 J20 **Jaramillo** Santa Cruz, SE Argentina

◆ Country
● Country Capital
◇ Dependent Territory
○ Dependent Territory Capital
◆ Administrative Region
✕ International Airport
▲ Mountain
▲ Mountain Range
※ Volcano
≈ River
◎ Lake
⊞ Reservoir

Jarandilla de la Vega *see* Jarandilla de la Vera
104 *K8* **Jarandilla de la Vera** ***var.*** Jarandilla de la Vega. Extremadura, W Spain
149 *V9* **Jarānwāla** Punjab, E Pakistan
138 *G9* **Jarash** ***var.*** Jerash; ***anc.*** Gerasa. Irbid, NW Jordan
Jarbah, Jazīrat *see* Jerba, Île de
94 *N13* **Järbo** Gävleborg, C Sweden
Jardan *see* Yordon
44 *F7* **Jardines de la Reina, Archipiélago de los** *island group* C Cuba
162 *J7* **Jargalant** Arhangay, C Mongolia
162 *I8* **Jargalant** Bayanhongor, C Mongolia
162 *D7* **Jargalant** Bayan-Ölgiy, W Mongolia
162 *K6* **Jargalant** Bulgan, N Mongolia
162 *G9* **Jargalant** Govĭ-Altay, W Mongolia
Jarīd, Shaṭṭ al *see* Jerid, Chott el
58 *I11* **Jari, Rio** ***var.*** Jary. ≈ N Brazil
141 *N7* **Jarīr, Wādī al** *dry watercourse* C Saudi Arabia
Jarja *see* Yur'ya
94 *L13* **Järna** ***var.*** Dala-Jarna. Dalarna, C Sweden
95 *O16* **Järna** Stockholm, C Sweden
102 *K11* **Jarnac** Charente, W France
110 *H12* **Jarocin** Wielkopolskie, C Poland
111 *F16* **Jaroměř** ***Ger.*** Jermer. Královéhradecký Kraj, N Czech Republic
Jaroslau *see* Jarosław
111 *O16* **Jarosław** ***Ger.*** Jaroslau, ***Rus.*** Yaroslav. Podkarpackie, SE Poland
93 *F16* **Järpen** Jämtland, C Sweden
147 *O14* **Jarqo'rg'on** ***Rus.*** Dzharkurgan. Surxondaryo Viloyati, S Uzbekistan
139 *P2* **Jarrāh, Wadi** *dry watercourse* NE Syria
Jars, Plain of *see* Xiangkhoang, Plateau de
162 *K14* **Jartai Yanchi** ◎ N China
59 *E16* **Jaru** Rondônia, W Brazil
Jarud Qi *see* Lubei
118 *I4* **Järva-Jaani** ***Ger.*** Sankt-Johannis. Järvamaa, N Estonia
118 *G5* **Järvakandi** ***Ger.*** Jerwakant. Raplamaa, NW Estonia
118 *H4* **Järvamaa** ***off.*** Järva Maakond. ◈ *province* N Estonia
93 *L19* **Järvenpää** Etelä-Suomi, S Finland
14 *G17* **Jarvis** Ontario, S Canada
192 *M8* **Jarvis Island** ◇ *US unincorporated territory* C Pacific Ocean
94 *M11* **Järvsö** Gävleborg, C Sweden
Jary *see* Jari, Rio
112 *M9* **Jaša Tomić** Serbia, NE Serbia and Montenegro (Yugo.)
112 *D12* **Jasenice** Zadar, SW Croatia
138 *I11* **Jashshat al 'Adlah, Wādī al** *dry watercourse* C Jordan
77 *Q16* **Jasikan** E Ghana
143 *T15* **Jāsk** Hormozgān, SE Iran
146 *F6* **Jasliq** ***Rus.*** Zhaslyk. Qoraqalpog'iston Respublikasi, NW Uzbekistan
111 *N17* **Jasło** Podkarpackie, SE Poland
11 *U16* **Jasmin** Saskatchewan, S Canada
65 *A23* **Jason Islands** *island group* NW Falkland Islands
194 *I4* **Jason Peninsula** *peninsula* Antarctica
31 *N15* **Jasonville** Indiana, N USA
11 *O15* **Jasper** Alberta, SW Canada
14 *L13* **Jasper** Ontario, SE Canada
23 *O3* **Jasper** Alabama, S USA
27 *T9* **Jasper** Arkansas, C USA
23 *U8* **Jasper** Florida, SE USA
31 *N16* **Jasper** Indiana, N USA
29 *R11* **Jasper** Minnesota, N USA
27 *S7* **Jasper** Missouri, C USA
20 *K10* **Jasper** Tennessee, S USA
25 *Y9* **Jasper** Texas, SW USA
11 *O15* **Jasper National Park** *national park* Alberta/British Columbia, SW Canada
Jassy *see* Iaşi
113 *N14* **Jastrebac** ⛰ SE Serbia and Montenegro (Yugo.)
112 *D9* **Jastrebarsko** Zagreb, N Croatia
Jastrow *see* Jastrowie
110 *G9* **Jastrowie** ***Ger.*** Jastrow. Wielkopolskie, C Poland
111 *J17* **Jastrzębie-Zdrój** Śląskie, S Poland
111 *L22* **Jászapáti** Jász-Nagykun-Szolnok, E Hungary
111 *L22* **Jászberény** Jász-Nagykun-Szolnok, E Hungary
111 *L23* **Jász-Nagykun-Szolnok** ***off.*** Jász-Nagykun-Szolnok Megye. ◈ *county* E Hungary
59 *J19* **Jataí** Goiás, C Brazil
58 *G12* **Jatapu, Serra do** ⛰ N Brazil
41 *W16* **Jatate, Río** ≈ SE Mexico
149 *P17* **Jāti** Sind, SE Pakistan
44 *F6* **Jatibonico** Sancti Spíritus, C Cuba
169 *O16* **Jatiluhur, Danau** ◎ Jawa, S Indonesia
Jativa *see* Xátiva
149 *S11* **Jattoi** Punjab, E Pakistan
60 *L9* **Jaú** São Paulo, S Brazil
58 *F11* **Jauaperi, Rio** ≈ N Brazil
99 *I19* **Jauche** Wallon Brabant, C Belgium
Jauer *see* Jawor
Jauf *see* Al Jawf
149 *U7* **Jauharābād** Punjab, E Pakistan
57 *E14* **Jauja** Junín, C Peru
41 *O10* **Jaumave** Tamaulipas, C Mexico
118 *H10* **Jaunjelgava** ***Ger.*** Friedrichstadt. Aizkraukle, S Latvia
Jaunlatgale *see* Pytalovo
118 *I8* **Jaunpiebalga** Gulbene, NE Latvia
118 *E9* **Jaunpils** Tukums, C Latvia
153 *N13* **Jaunpur** Uttar Pradesh, N India
29 *N8* **Java** South Dakota, N USA
Java *see* Jawa
105 *R9* **Javalambre** ▲ E Spain
173 *V7* **Java Ridge** *undersea feature* E Indian Ocean
59 *A14* **Javari, Rio** ***var.*** Yavarí. ≈ Brazil/Peru
163 *O7* **Javarthushuu** Dornod, NE Mongolia
169 *Q15* **Java Sea** ***Ind.*** Laut Jawa. *sea* W Indonesia
173 *U7* **Java Trench** ***var.*** Sunda Trench. *undersea feature* E Indian Ocean
105 *T11* **Jávea** ***Cat.*** Xàbia. País Valenciano, E Spain
163 *O7* **Javhlant** Hentiy, E Mongolia
63 *G20* **Javier, Isla** *island* S Chile
113 *L14* **Javor** ⛰ Bosnia and Herzegovina/Serbia and Montenegro (Yugo.)
111 *K20* **Javorie** ***Hung.*** Jávoros. ▲ S Slovakia
Jávoros *see* Javorie
93 *J14* **Jävre** Norrbotten, N Sweden
192 *E8* **Jawa** ***Eng.*** Java; ***prev.*** Djawa. *island* C Indonesia
169 *O16* **Jawa Barat** ***off.*** Propinsi Jawa Barat, ***Eng.*** West Java. ◈ *province* S Indonesia
Jawa, Laut *see* Java Sea
139 *R3* **Jawān** NW Iraq
169 *P16* **Jawa Tengah** ***off.*** Propinsi Jawa Tengah, ***Eng.*** Central Java. ◈ *province* S Indonesia
169 *R16* **Jawa Timur** ***off.*** Propinsi Jawa Timur, ***Eng.*** East Java. ◈ *province* S Indonesia
81 *N17* **Jawhar** ***var.*** Jowhar, ***It.*** Giohar. Shabeellaha Dhexe, S Somalia
111 *F14* **Jawor** ***Ger.*** Jauer. Dolnośląskie, SW Poland
Jaworów *see* Yavoriv
111 *J16* **Jaworzno** Śląskie, S Poland
Jaxartes *see* Syr Darya
27 *R9* **Jay** Oklahoma, C USA
Jayabum *see* Chaiyaphum
Jayanath *see* Chai Nat
153 *T12* **Jayanti** ***prev.*** Jainti. West Bengal, NE India
171 *X14* **Jaya, Puncak** ***prev.*** Puntjak Carstensz, Puntjak Sukarno. ▲ Papua, E Indonesia
171 *Z13* **Jayapura** ***var.*** Djajapura, ***Dut.*** Hollandia; ***prev.*** Kotabaru, Sukarnapura. Papua, E Indonesia
Jay Dairen *see* Dalian
Jayhawker State *see* Kansas
147 *S12* **Jayilgan** ***Rus.*** Dzhailgan, Dzhayilgan. C Tajikistan
155 *L14* **Jaypur** ***var.*** Jeypore, Jeypur. Orissa, E India
25 *O6* **Jayton** Texas, SW USA
143 *U13* **Jaz Murian, Hāmūn-e** ◎ SE Iran
138 *M4* **Jazrah** Ar Raqqah, C Syria
138 *G6* **Jbaïl** ***var.*** Jebeil, Jubayl, Jubeil; ***anc.*** Biblical Gebal, Bybles. W Lebanon
25 *O7* **J.B.Thomas, Lake** ⊞ Texas, SW USA
Jdaïdé *see* Judaydah
35 *X12* **Jean** Nevada, W USA
22 *I9* **Jeanerette** Louisiana, S USA
44 *L8* **Jean-Rabel** NW Haiti
143 *T12* **Jebāl Bārez, Kūh-e** ⛰ SE Iran
Jebat *see* Jabwot
77 *T15* **Jebba** Kwara, W Nigeria
Jebeil *see* Jbaïl
116 *E12* **Jebel** ***Hung.*** Széphely; ***prev. Hung.*** Zsebely. Timiş, W Romania
146 *B11* **Jebel** ***Rus.*** Dzhebel. Balkan Welaýaty, W Turkmenistan
Jebel, Bahr el *see* White Nile
Jebel Dhanna *see* Jabal aẓ Ẓannah
Jeble *see* Jablah
96 *K13* **Jedburgh** SE Scotland, UK
Jedda *see* Jiddah
111 *L15* **Jędrzejów** ***Ger.*** Endersdorf. Świętokrzyskie, C Poland
100 *K12* **Jeetze** ***var.*** Jeetzel. ≈ C Germany
Jeetzel *see* Jeetze
29 *U14* **Jefferson** Iowa, C USA
21 *Q8* **Jefferson** North Carolina, SE USA
25 *X6* **Jefferson** Texas, SW USA
30 *M9* **Jefferson** Wisconsin, N USA
27 *U5* **Jefferson City** *state capital* Missouri, C USA
33 *R10* **Jefferson City** Montana, NW USA
21 *N9* **Jefferson City** Tennessee, S USA
35 *U7* **Jefferson, Mount** ▲ Nevada, W USA
32 *H12* **Jefferson, Mount** ▲ Oregon, NW USA
20 *L5* **Jeffersontown** Kentucky, S USA
31 *P16* **Jeffersonville** Indiana, N USA
33 *V15* **Jeffrey City** Wyoming, C USA
77 *T13* **Jega** Kebbi, NW Nigeria
Jehol *see* Chengde
62 *P5* **Jejui-Guazú, Río** ≈ E Paraguay
118 *I10* **Jēkabpils** ***Ger.*** Jakobstadt. Jēkabpils, S Latvia
23 *W7* **Jekyll Island** *island* Georgia, SE USA
169 *R13* **Jelai, Sungai** ≈ Borneo, N Indonesia
Jelalabad *see* Jalālābād
111 *H14* **Jelcz-Laskowice** Dolnośląskie, SW Poland
111 *E14* **Jelenia Góra** ***Ger.*** Hirschberg, Hirschberg im Riesengebirge, Hirschberg in Riesengebirge, Hirschberg in Schlesien. Dolnośląskie, SW Poland
153 *S11* **Jelep La** *pass* N India
118 *F9* **Jelgava** ***Ger.*** Mitau. Jelgava, C Latvia
112 *L13* **Jelica** ⛰ C Serbia and Montenegro (Yugo.)
20 *M8* **Jellico** Tennessee, S USA
95 *G23* **Jelling** Vejle, C Denmark
169 *N9* **Jemaja, Pulau** *island* W Indonesia
Jemaluang *see* Jamaluang
99 *E20* **Jemappes** Hainaut, S Belgium
169 *S17* **Jember** ***prev.*** Djember. Jawa, C Indonesia
99 *I20* **Jemeppe-sur-Sambre** Namur, S Belgium
37 *R10* **Jemez Pueblo** New Mexico, SW USA
158 *K2* **Jeminay** Xinjiang Uygur Zizhiqu, NW China
189 *U5* **Jemo Island** *atoll* Ratak Chain, C Marshall Islands
169 *U11* **Jempang, Danau** ◎ Borneo, N Indonesia
101 *L16* **Jena** Thüringen, C Germany
22 *I6* **Jena** Louisiana, S USA
108 *I8* **Jenaz** Graubünden, SE Switzerland
109 *N7* **Jenbach** Tirol, W Austria
171 *N15* **Jeneponto** ***prev.*** Djeneponto. Sulawesi, C Indonesia
138 *F9* **Jenīn** N West Bank
21 *P7* **Jenkins** Kentucky, S USA
27 *P9* **Jenks** Oklahoma, C USA
Jenné *see* Djenné
109 *X8* **Jennersdorf** Burgenland, SE Austria
22 *H9* **Jennings** Louisiana, S USA
9 *N7* **Jenny Lind Island** *island* Nunavut, N Canada
23 *Y13* **Jensen Beach** Florida, SE USA
9 *P6* **Jens Munk Island** *island* Nunavut, NE Canada
59 *O17* **Jequié** Bahia, E Brazil
59 *O18* **Jequitinhonha, Rio** ≈ E Brazil
Jerablus *see* Jarābulus
74 *H6* **Jerada** NE Morocco
Jerash *see* Jarash
75 *N7* **Jerba, Île de** ***var.*** Djerba, Jazīrat Jarbah. *island* E Tunisia
44 *K9* **Jérémie** SW Haiti
Jerez *see* Jeréz de la Frontera, Spain
Jeréz *see* Jerez de García Salinas, Mexico
40 *L11* **Jerez de García Salinas** ***var.*** Jeréz. Zacatecas, C Mexico
104 *J15* **Jeréz de la Frontera** ***var.*** Jerez; ***prev.*** Xeres. Andalucía, SW Spain
104 *I12* **Jeréz de los Caballeros** Extremadura, W Spain
Jergucati *see* Jorgucat
138 *G10* **Jericho** ***Ar.*** Arīḩā, ***Heb.*** Yeriḩo. E West Bank
74 *M7* **Jerid, Chott el** ***var.*** Shaṭṭ al Jarīd. *salt lake* SW Tunisia
183 *O10* **Jerilderie** New South Wales, SE Australia
Jerischmarkt *see* Câmpia Turzii
92 *K11* **Jerisjärvi** ◎ NW Finland
Jermentau *see* Yereymentau
Jermer *see* Jaroměř
36 *K11* **Jerome** Arizona, SW USA
33 *O15* **Jerome** Idaho, NW USA
97 *L26* **Jersey** *island* Channel Islands, NW Europe
18 *K14* **Jersey City** New Jersey, NE USA
18 *F13* **Jersey Shore** Pennsylvania, NE USA
30 *K14* **Jerseyville** Illinois, N USA
104 *K8* **Jerte** ≈ W Spain
138 *F10* **Jerusalem** ***Ar.*** Al Quds, Al Quds ash Sharīf, ***Heb.*** Yerushalayim; ***anc.*** Hierosolyma. ● (Israel) Jerusalem, NE Israel
138 *G10* **Jerusalem** ◈ *district* E Israel
183 *S10* **Jervis Bay** New South Wales, SE Australia
183 *S10* **Jervis Bay Territory** ◈ *territory* SE Australia
Jerwakant *see* Järvakandi
109 *S10* **Jesenice** ***Ger.*** Assling. NW Slovenia
111 *H16* **Jeseník** ***Ger.*** Freiwaldau. Olomoucký Kraj, E Czech Republic
Jesi *see* Iesi
106 *I8* **Jesolo** ***var.*** Iesolo. Veneto, NE Italy
Jesselton *see* Kota Kinabalu
95 *I14* **Jessheim** Akershus, S Norway
153 *T15* **Jessore** Khulna, W Bangladesh
23 *W6* **Jesup** Georgia, SE USA
41 *S15* **Jesús Carranza** Veracruz-Llave, SE Mexico
62 *K10* **Jesús María** Córdoba, C Argentina
26 *K6* **Jetmore** Kansas, C USA
103 *Q2* **Jeumont** Nord, N France
95 *H14* **Jevnaker** Oppland, S Norway
Jewe *see* Jõhvi
25 *V9* **Jewett** Texas, SW USA
19 *N12* **Jewett City** Connecticut, NE USA
Jewish Autonomous Oblast *see* Yevreyskaya Avtonomnaya Oblast'
Jeypore/Jeypur *see* Jaypur, Orissa, India
Jeypore *see* Jaipur, Rājasthān, India
113 *L17* **Jezercës, Maja e** ▲ N Albania
111 *B18* **Jezerní Hora** ▲ SW Czech Republic
154 *F10* **Jhābua** Madhya Pradesh, C India
152 *H14* **Jhālāwār** Rājasthān, N India
Jhang/Jhang Sadar *see* Jhang Sadr
149 *U9* **Jhang Sadr** ***var.*** Jhang, Jhang Sadar. Punjab, NE Pakistan
152 *J13* **Jhānsi** Uttar Pradesh, N India
153 *O16* **Jhārkhand** ◈ *state* NE India
154 *M11* **Jhārsuguda** Orissa, E India
149 *V7* **Jhelum** Punjab, NE Pakistan
Jhenaidaha *see* Jhenida
153 *T15* **Jhenida** ***var.*** Jhenaidaha. Dhaka, W Bangladesh
149 *P16* **Jhimpīr** Sind, SE Pakistan
Jhind *see* Jīnd
149 *R16* **Jhudo** Sind, SE Pakistan
Jhumra *see* Chak Jhumra
152 *H11* **Jhunjhunūn** Rājasthān, N India
Ji *see* Hebei, China
Ji *see* Jilin, China
Jiading *see* Xinfeng
153 *S14* **Jiāganj** West Bengal, NE India
160 *J7* **Jialing Jiang** ≈ C China
163 *Y7* **Jiamusi** ***var.*** Chia-mu-ssu, Kiamusze. Heilongjiang, NE China
161 *O11* **Ji'an** Jiangxi, S China
163 *W12* **Ji'an** Jilin, NE China
163 *T13* **Jianchang** Liaoning, NE China
Jianchang *see* Nancheng
160 *F11* **Jianchuan** ***var.*** Jinhuan. Yunnan, SW China
158 *M4* **Jiangjunmiao** Xinjiang Uygur Zizhiqu, W China
160 *K11* **Jiangkou** ***var.*** Shuangjiang. Guizhou, S China
Jiangkou *see* Fengkai
161 *Q12* **Jiangle** ***var.*** Guyong. Fujian, SE China
161 *N15* **Jiangmen** Guangdong, S China
Jiangna *see* Yanshan
161 *Q10* **Jiangshan** Zhejiang, SE China
161 *Q7* **Jiangsu** ***var.*** Chiang-su, Jiangsu Sheng, Kiangsu, Su. ◈ *province* E China
Jiangsu Sheng *see* Jiangsu
161 *O11* **Jiangxi** ***var.*** Chiang-hsi, Gan, Jiangxi Sheng, Kiangsi. ◈ *province* S China
Jiangxi Sheng *see* Jiangxi
160 *I8* **Jiangyou** ***prev.*** Zhongba. Sichuan, C China
161 *N9* **Jianli** ***var.*** Rongcheng. Hubei, C China
161 *Q11* **Jian'ou** Fujian, SE China
163 *S12* **Jianping** ***var.*** Yebaishou. Liaoning, NE China
Jianshe *see* Baiyü
160 *L9* **Jianshi** ***var.*** Yezhou. Hubei, C China
161 *Q11* **Jianyang** Fujian, SE China
160 *I9* **Jianyang** Sichuan, C China
163 *X10* **Jiaohe** Jilin, NE China
Jiaojiang *see* Taizhou
Jiaoxian *see* Jiaozhou
161 *R5* **Jiaozhou** ***prev.*** Jiaoxian. Shandong, E China
161 *N6* **Jiaozuo** Henan, C China
Jiashan *see* Mingguang
158 *F8* **Jiashi** ***var.*** Payzawat. Xinjiang Uygur Zizhiqu, NW China
154 *L9* **Jiāwān** Madhya Pradesh, C India
161 *S9* **Jiaxing** Zhejiang, SE China
Jiayi *see* Chiai
163 *X6* **Jiayin** ***var.*** Chaoyang. Heilongjiang, NE China
159 *R8* **Jiayuguan** Gansu, N China
Jibhalanta *see* Uliastay
138 *M4* **Jibli** Ar Raqqah, C Syria
116 *H9* **Jibou** ***Hung.*** Zsibó. Sălaj, NW Romania
141 *Z9* **Jibsh, Ra's al** *headland* E Oman
Jibuti *see* Djibouti
111 *E15* **Jičín** ***Ger.*** Jitschin. Královéhradecký Kraj, N Czech Republic
140 *K10* **Jiddah** ***Eng.*** Jedda. ● (Saudi Arabia) Makkah, W Saudi Arabia
141 *W11* **Jiddat al Ḩarāsīs** *desert* C Oman
Jiesjavrre *see* Iešjávri
160 *M4* **Jiexiu** Shanxi, C China
161 *P14* **Jieyang** Guangdong, S China
119 *F14* **Jieznas** Kaunas, S Lithuania
Jīfa', Bi'r *see* Jif'īyah, Bi'r
141 *P15* **Jif'īyah, Bi'r** ***var.*** Bi'r Jīfa'. *well* C Yemen
77 *W13* **Jigawa** ◈ *state* N Nigeria
146 *J10* **Jigerbent** ***Rus.*** Dzhigirbent. Lebap Welaýaty, NE Turkmenistan
44 *I7* **Jiguaní** Granma, E Cuba
159 *T12* **Jigzhi** ***var.*** Chugqênsumdo. Qinghai, C China
Jih-k'a-tse *see* Xigazê
111 *E18* **Jihlava** ***Ger.*** Iglau, ***Pol.*** Igława. Vysočina, C Czech Republic
111 *E18* **Jihlava** ***var.*** Igel, ***Ger.*** Iglawa. ≈ S Czech Republic
Jihlavský Kraj *see* Vysočina
111 *C18* **Jihočeský Kraj** ***prev.*** Budějovický Kraj. ◈ *region* S Czech Republic
111 *G19* **Jihomoravský Kraj** ***prev.*** Brněnský Kraj. ◈ *region* SE Czech Republic
74 *L5* **Jijel** ***var.*** Djidjel; ***prev.*** Djidjelli. NE Algeria
116 *L9* **Jijia** ≈ N Romania
80 *L13* **Jijiga** ***It.*** Giggiga. Somali, E Ethiopia
105 *S12* **Jijona** ***var.*** Xixona. País Valenciano, E Spain
Jilf al Kabīr, Haḑabat al *see* Gilf Kebir Plateau
81 *L18* **Jilib** ***It.*** Gelib. Jubbada Dhexe, S Somalia
163 *W10* **Jilin** ***var.*** Chi-lin, Girin, Kirin; ***prev.*** Yungki, Yunki. Jilin, NE China
163 *W10* **Jilin** ***var.*** Chi-lin, Girin, Ji, Jilin Sheng, Kirin. ◈ *province* NE China
163 *W11* **Jilin Hada Ling** ⛰ NE China
Jilin Sheng *see* Jilin
163 *S4* **Jiliu He** ≈ NE China
105 *Q6* **Jiloca** ≈ N Spain
81 *I14* **Jīma** ***var.*** Jimma, ***It.*** Gimma. Oromo, C Ethiopia
44 *M9* **Jimaní** W Dominican Republic
116 *E11* **Jimbolia** ***Ger.*** Hatzfeld, ***Hung.*** Zsombolya. Timiş, W Romania
104 *K16* **Jimena de la Frontera** Andalucía, S Spain
40 *K7* **Jiménez** Chihuahua, N Mexico
41 *N5* **Jiménez** Coahuila de Zaragoza, NE Mexico
41 *P9* **Jiménez** ***var.*** Santander Jiménez. Tamaulipas, C Mexico
40 *L10* **Jiménez del Teul** Zacatecas, C Mexico
77 *Y14* **Jimeta** Adamawa, E Nigeria
Jimma *see* Jīma
158 *M5* **Jimsar** Xinjiang Uygur Zizhiqu, NW China
18 *I14* **Jim Thorpe** Pennsylvania, NE USA
Jin *see* Shanxi, China
Jin *see* Tianjin Shi, China
161 *P5* **Jinan** ***var.*** Chinan, Chi-nan, Tsinan. Shandong, E China
Jin'an *see* Songpan
Jinbi *see* Dayao
159 *T8* **Jinchang** Gansu, N China
161 *N5* **Jincheng** Shanxi, C China
Jincheng *see* Wuding
Jinchengjiang *see* Hechi
152 *I9* **Jīnd** ***prev.*** Jhind. Haryāna, NW India
183 *Q11* **Jindabyne** New South Wales, SE Australia
111 *O18* **Jindřichův Hradec** ***Ger.*** Neuhaus. Jihočeský Kraj, S Czech Republic
Jing *see* Beijing Shi, China
Jing *see* Jinghe, China
159 *X10* **Jingchuan** Gansu, C China
161 *Q10* **Jingdezhen** Jiangxi, S China
161 *O12* **Jinggangshan** Jiangxi, S China
161 *P3* **Jinghai** Tianjin Shi, E China
160 *K6* **Jing He** ≈ C China
158 *I4* **Jinghe** ***var.*** Jing. Xinjiang Uygur Zizhiqu, NW China
160 *F15* **Jinghong** ***var.*** Yunjinghong. Yunnan, SW China
160 *M9* **Jingmen** Hubei, C China
163 *X10* **Jingpo Hu** ◎ NE China
160 *M8* **Jing Shan** ⛰ C China
159 *V9* **Jingtai** ***var.*** Yitiaoshan. Gansu, C China
160 *J14* **Jingxi** ***var.*** Xinjing. Guangxi Zhuangzu Zizhiqu, S China
Jing Xian *see* Jingzhou, Hunan
163 *W11* **Jingyu** Jilin, NE China
159 *V10* **Jingyuan** Gansu, C China
160 *M9* **Jingzhou** ***prev.*** Shashi, Sha-shih, Shasi. Hubei, C China
160 *L12* **Jingzhou** ***var.*** Jing Xian, Jingzhou Miaozu Dongzu Zizhixian, Quyang. Hunan, S China
Jingzhou Miaozu Dongzu Zizhixian *see* Jingzhou, Hunan
161 *R10* **Jinhua** Zhejiang, SE China
Jinhuan *see* Jianchuan
163 *P13* **Jining** Nei Mongol Zizhiqu, N China
161 *P5* **Jining** Shandong, E China
81 *G18* **Jinja** S Uganda
161 *R13* **Jinjiang** ***var.*** Qingyang. Fujian, SE China
161 *O11* **Jin Jiang** ≈ S China
Jinjiang *see* Chengmai
171 *V15* **Jin, Kepulauan** *island group* E Indonesia
Jinmen Dao *see* Chinmen Tao
42 *J9* **Jinotega** Jinotega, NW Nicaragua
42 *K7* **Jinotega** ◈ *department* N Nicaragua
42 *J11* **Jinotepe** Carazo, SW Nicaragua
160 *L13* **Jinping** ***var.*** Sanjiang. Guizhou, S China
160 *H14* **Jinping** Yunnan, SW China
Jinsen *see* Inch'ŏn
160 *J11* **Jinsha** Guizhou, S China
157 *N12* **Jinsha Jiang** ***Eng.*** Yangtze. ≈ SW China
160 *M10* **Jinshi** Hunan, S China
Jinshi *see* Xinning
159 *R7* **Jinta** Gansu, N China
161 *Q12* **Jin Xi** ≈ SE China
Jinxi *see* Huludao
Jinxian *see* Jinzhou
161 *P6* **Jinxiang** Shandong, E China
161 *P8* **Jinzhai** ***var.*** Meishan. Anhui, E China
161 *N4* **Jinzhong** ***var.*** Yuci. Shanxi, C China
163 *U14* **Jinzhou** ***prev.*** Jinxian. Liaoning, NE China
163 *T12* **Jinzhou** ***var.*** Chin-chou, Chinchow; ***prev.*** Chinhsien. Liaoning, NE China
Jinzhu *see* Daocheng
138 *H12* **Jinz, Qā' al** ◎ C Jordan
56 *A7* **Jipijapa** Manabí, W Ecuador
42 *F8* **Jiquilisco** Usulután, S El Salvador
Jirgalanta *see* Hovd
147 *S12* **Jirgatol** ***Rus.*** Dzhirgatal'. C Tajikistan
Jirjā *see* Girga
111 *B15* **Jirkov** ***Ger.*** Görkau. Ústecký Kraj, NW Czech Republic
Jiroft *see* Sabzvārān
160 *L11* **Jishou** Hunan, S China
Jisr ash Shadadi *see* Ash Shadādah
116 *I14* **Jitaru** Olt, S Romania
Jitschin *see* Jičín
116 *H14* **Jiu** ***Ger.*** Schil, Schyl, ***Hung.*** Zsil, Zsily. ≈ S Romania
161 *R11* **Jiufeng Shan** ⛰ SE China
161 *P9* **Jiujiang** Jiangxi, S China
161 *O10* **Jiuling Shan** ⛰ S China
160 *G10* **Jiulong** ***var.*** Garba, ***Tib.*** Gyaisi. Sichuan, C China
161 *Q13* **Jiulong Jiang** ≈ SE China
161 *Q12* **Jiulong Xi** ≈ SE China
159 *R8* **Jiuquan** ***var.*** Suzhou. Gansu, N China
160 *K17* **Jiusuo** Hainan, S China
163 *W10* **Jiutai** Jilin, NE China
160 *K13* **Jiuwan Dashan** ⛰ S China
160 *I7* **Jiuzhaigou** ***prev.*** Nanping. Sichuan, C China
148 *I16* **Jīwani** Baluchistān, SW Pakistan
163 *Y8* **Jixi** Heilongjiang, NE China
163 *Y7* **Jixian** Heilongjiang, NE China
160 *M5* **Jixian** ***var.*** Ji Xian. Shanxi, C China
Jiza *see* Al Jīzah
141 *N13* **Jīzān** ***var.*** Qīzān. Jīzān, SW Saudi Arabia
141 *N13* **Jīzān** ***var.*** Minṭaqat Jīzān. ◈ *province* SW Saudi Arabia
140 *K6* **Jizl, Wādī al** *dry watercourse* W Saudi Arabia
164 *H12* **Jizō-zaki** *headland* Honshū, SW Japan
141 *U14* **Jiz', Wādī al** *dry watercourse* E Yemen
147 *O11* **Jizzakh** ***Rus.*** Dzhizak. Jizzax Viloyati, C Uzbekistan
147 *N10* **Jizzax Viloyati** ***Rus.*** Dzhizakskaya Oblast'. ◈ *province* C Uzbekistan
60 *I13* **Joaçaba** Santa Catarina, S Brazil
Joal *see* Joal-Fadiout
76 *F11* **Joal-Fadiout** ***prev.*** Joal. W Senegal
76 *E10* **João Barrosa** Boa Vista, E Cape Verde
João Belo *see* Xai-Xai
João de Almeida *see* Chibia
59 *Q15* **João Pessoa** ***prev.*** Paraíba. *state capital* Paraíba, E Brazil
25 *X7* **Joaquin** Texas, SW USA
62 *K6* **Joaquín V.González** Salta, N Argentina
Joazeiro *see* Juazeiro
Jo'burg *see* Johannesburg
109 *O7* **Jochberger Ache** ≈ W Austria
Jo-ch'iang *see* Ruoqiang
92 *K12* **Jock** Norrbotten, N Sweden
42 *I5* **Jocón** Yoro, N Honduras
105 *O13* **Jódar** Andalucía, S Spain
152 *F12* **Jodhpur** Rājasthān, NW India
99 *I19* **Jodoigne** Wallon Brabant, C Belgium
95 *I22* **Jægerspris** Frederiksborg, E Denmark
93 *O16* **Joensuu** Itä-Suomi, E Finland
95 *C17* **Jæren** *physical region* S Norway
37 *W4* **Joes** Colorado, C USA
191 *Z3* **Joe's Hill** *hill* Kiritimati, NE Kiribati
165 *N11* **Jōetsu** ***var.*** Zyôetu. Niigata, Honshū, C Japan
83 *M18* **Jofane** Inhambane, S Mozambique
153 *R12* **Jogbani** Bihār, NE India
118 *I5* **Jõgeva** ***Ger.*** Laisholm. Jõgevamaa, E Estonia
118 *I4* **Jõgevamaa** ***off.*** Jõgeva Maakond. ◈ *province* E Estonia
155 *E18* **Jog Falls** *waterfall* Karnātaka, W India
143 *S4* **Joghatāy** Khorāsān, NE Iran
153 *U12* **Jogīghopa** Assam, NE India
152 *I7* **Jogindarnagar** Himāchal Pradesh, N India
Jogjakarta *see* Yogyakarta
164 *L11* **Jōhana** Toyama, Honshū, SW Japan
83 *J21* **Johannesburg** ***var.*** Egoli, Erautini, Gauteng, ***abbrev.*** Jo'burg. Gauteng, NE South Africa
35 *T13* **Johannesburg** California, W USA
83 *I21* **Johannesburg** ✕ Gauteng, NE South Africa
Johannisburg *see* Pisz
149 *P14* **Johi** Sind, SE Pakistan
55 *T13* **Johi Village** S Guyana
32 *K13* **John Day** Oregon, NW USA
32 *I11* **John Day River** ≈ Oregon, NW USA
18 *L14* **John F Kennedy** ✕ (New York) Long Island, New York, NE USA
21 *V8* **John H.Kerr Reservoir** ***var.*** Buggs Island Lake, Kerr Lake. ⊞ North Carolina/Virginia, SE USA
37 *V6* **John Martin Reservoir** ⊞ Colorado, C USA
96 *K6* **John o'Groats** N Scotland, UK
27 *P5* **John Redmond Reservoir** ⊞ Kansas, C USA
39 *Q7* **John River** ≈ Alaska, USA
26 *H6* **Johnson** Kansas, C USA
18 *M7* **Johnson** Vermont, NE USA
18 *D13* **Johnsonburg** Pennsylvania, NE USA
18 *H11* **Johnson City** New York, NE USA
21 *P8* **Johnson City** Tennessee, S USA
25 *R10* **Johnson City** Texas, SW USA
35 *S12* **Johnsondale** California, W USA
10 *I8* **Johnsons Crossing** Yukon Territory, W Canada
21 *T13* **Johnsonville** South Carolina, SE USA
21 *Q13* **Johnston** South Carolina, SE USA
192 *M6* **Johnston Atoll** ◇ *US unincorporated territory* C Pacific Ocean
30 *L17* **Johnston City** Illinois, N USA
180 *K12* **Johnston, Lake** *salt lake* Western Australia
31 *S13* **Johnstown** Ohio, N USA
18 *D15* **Johnstown** Pennsylvania, NE USA
168 *L10* **Johor** ***var.*** Johore. ◈ *state* Peninsular Malaysia
Johor Baharu *see* Johor Bahru
168 *K10* **Johor Bahru** ***var.*** Johor Baharu, Johore Bahru. Johor, Peninsular Malaysia
Johore *see* Johor
Johore Bahru *see* Johor Bahru
118 *K3* **Jõhvi** ***Ger.*** Jewe. Ida-Virumaa, NE Estonia
103 *P7* **Joigny** Yonne, C France
Joinvile *see* Joinville
60 *K12* **Joinville** ***var.*** Joinvile. Santa Catarina, S Brazil
103 *R6* **Joinville** Haute-Marne, N France
194 *H3* **Joinville Island** *island* Antarctica
41 *O15* **Jojutla** ***var.*** Jojutla de Juárez. Morelos, S Mexico
Jojutla de Juárez *see* Jojutla
92 *I12* **Jokkmokk** ***Lapp.*** Dálvvadis. Norrbotten, N Sweden
92 *L2* **Jökulsá á Dal** ≈ E Iceland
92 *K2* **Jökulsá á Fjöllum** ≈ NE Iceland
Jokyakarta *see* Yogyakarta
30 *M11* **Joliet** Illinois, N USA
15 *O11* **Joliette** Québec, SE Canada
171 *O8* **Jolo** Jolo Island, SW Philippines
94 *D11* **Jølstravatnet** ◎ S Norway
169 *S16* **Jombang** ***prev.*** Djombang. Jawa, S Indonesia
159 *R14* **Jomda** Xizang Zizhiqu, W China
118 *G13* **Jonava** ***Ger.*** Janow, ***Pol.*** Janów. Kaunas, C Lithuania
146 *L11* **Jondor** ***Rus.*** Zhondor. Buxoro Viloyati, C Uzbekistan
159 *V11* **Jonê** Gansu, C China
27 *X9* **Jonesboro** Arkansas, C USA
23 *S4* **Jonesboro** Georgia, SE USA
30 *L17* **Jonesboro** Illinois, N USA
22 *H5* **Jonesboro** Louisiana, S USA

21 P8 **Jonesboro** Tennessee, S USA
19 T6 **Jonesport** Maine, NE USA
9 N4 **Jones Sound** *channel* Nunavut, N Canada
22 I6 **Jonesville** Louisiana, S USA
31 Q10 **Jonesville** Michigan, N USA
21 Q11 **Jonesville** South Carolina, SE USA
146 K10 **Jongeldi** *Rus.* Dzhankel'dy. Buxoro Viloyati, C Uzbekistan
81 F14 **Jonglei** Jonglei, SE Sudan
81 F14 **Jonglei** *var.* Gongoleh State. ◈ *state* SE Sudan
81 F14 **Jonglei Canal** *canal* S Sudan
118 F11 **Joniškėlis** Panevėžys, N Lithuania
118 F10 **Joniškis** *Ger.* Janischken. Šiauliai, N Lithuania
95 L19 **Jönköping** Jönköping, S Sweden
95 K20 **Jönköping** ◈ *county* S Sweden
15 Q7 **Jonquière** Québec, SE Canada
41 V15 **Jonuta** Tabasco, SE Mexico
102 K12 **Jonzac** Charente-Maritime, W France
27 R7 **Joplin** Missouri, C USA
33 W8 **Jordan** Montana, NW USA
138 H12 **Jordan** *off.* Hashemite Kingdom of Jordan, *Ar.* Al Mamlakah al Urdunīyah al Hāshimīyah, Al Urdunn; *prev.* Transjordan. ◆ *monarchy* SW Asia
138 G9 **Jordan** *Ar.* Urdunn, *Heb.* HaYarden. ≈ SW Asia
Jordan Lake *see* B.Everett Jordan Reservoir
111 K17 **Jordanów** Małopolskie, S Poland
32 M15 **Jordan Valley** Oregon, NW USA
138 G9 **Jordan Valley** *valley* N Israel
57 D15 **Jorge Chávez International** *var.* Lima. ✖ (Lima) Lima, W Peru
113 L23 **Jorgucat** *var.* Jergucati, Jorgucati. Gjirokastër, S Albania
Jorgucati *see* Jorgucat
153 X12 **Jorhāt** Assam, NE India
93 J14 **Jörn** Västerbotten, N Sweden
37 R14 **Jornada Del Muerto** *valley* New Mexico, SW USA
93 N17 **Joroinen** Isä-Suomi, E Finland
95 C16 **Jørpeland** Rogaland, S Norway
77 W14 **Jos** Plateau, C Nigeria
171 Q8 **Jose Abad Santos** *var.* Trinidad. Mindanao, S Philippines
61 F19 **José Batlle y Ordóñez** *var.* Batlle y Ordóñez. Florida, C Uruguay
63 H18 **José de San Martín** Chubut, S Argentina
61 E19 **José Enrique Rodó** *var.* Rodó, José E.Rodo; *prev.* Drabble, Drable. Soriano, SW Uruguay
José E.Rodo *see* José Enrique Rodó
Josefsdorf *see* Žabalj
44 C4 **José Martí** ✖ (La Habana) Cuidad de La Habana, N Cuba
61 F19 **José Pedro Varela** *var.* José P.Varela. Lavalleja, S Uruguay
181 N2 **Joseph Bonaparte Gulf** *gulf* N Australia
37 N11 **Joseph City** Arizona, SW USA
13 O9 **Joseph, Lake** ◎ Newfoundland and Labrador, E Canada
14 G13 **Joseph, Lake** ◎ Ontario, S Canada
186 C6 **Josephstaal** Madang, N PNG
José P.Varela *see* José Pedro Varela
59 J14 **José Rodrigues** Pará, N Brazil
152 K9 **Joshīmath** Uttaranchal, N India
25 T7 **Joshua** Texas, SW USA
35 V15 **Joshua Tree** California, W USA
77 V14 **Jos Plateau** *plateau* C Nigeria
102 H6 **Josselin** Morbihan, NW France
Jos Sudarso *see* Yos Sudarso, Pulau
94 E11 **Jostedalsbreen** *glacier* S Norway
94 F12 **Jotunheimen** ▲ S Norway
138 G7 **Joûnié** *var.* Junīyah. W Lebanon
25 R13 **Jourdanton** Texas, SW USA
98 L7 **Joure** *Fris.* De Jouwer. Friesland, N Netherlands
93 M18 **Joutsa** Länsi-Suomi, W Finland
93 N18 **Joutseno** Etelä-Suomi, S Finland
92 M12 **Joutsijärvi** Lappi, NE Finland
108 A9 **Joux, Lac de** ◎ W Switzerland
44 D5 **Jovellanos** Matanzas, W Cuba
153 V13 **Jowai** Meghālaya, NE India
Jöwat *see* Jabwot
Jowhar *see* Jawhar
143 O12 **Jowkān** Fārs, S Iran
143 Q10 **Jowzam** Kermān, C Iran
149 N2 **Jowzjān** ◈ *province* N Afghanistan
Józseffalva *see* Žabalj
J.Storm Thurmond Reservoir *see* Clark Hill Lake
45 T6 **Juana Díaz** C Puerto Rico
40 L9 **Juan Aldama** Zacatecas, C Mexico
32 F7 **Juan de Fuca, Strait of** *strait* Canada/USA
Juan Fernandez Islands *see* Juan Fernández, Islas
193 S11 **Juan Fernández, Islas** *Eng.* Juan Fernandez Islands. *island group* W Chile
55 O4 **Juangriego** Nueva Esparta, NE Venezuela
56 D11 **Juanjuí** *var.* Juanjuy. San Martín, N Peru
Juanjuy *see* Juanjuí
93 N16 **Juankoski** Itä-Suomi, C Finland
Juan Lacaze *see* Juan L.Lacaze
61 E20 **Juan L.Lacaze** *var.* Juan Lacaze, Puerto Sauce; *prev.* Sauce. Colonia, SW Uruguay
62 L5 **Juan Solá** Salta, N Argentina
63 F21 **Juan Stuven, Isla** *island* S Chile
59 H16 **Juará** Mato Grosso, W Brazil
41 N7 **Juárez** *var.* Villa Juárez. Coahuila de Zaragoza, NE Mexico
40 C2 **Juárez, Sierra de** ▲ NW Mexico
59 O15 **Juazeiro** *prev.* Joazeiro. Bahia, E Brazil
59 P14 **Juazeiro do Norte** Ceará, E Brazil
81 F15 **Juba** *var.* Jūbā. Bahr el Gabel, S Sudan
81 L17 **Juba** *Amh.* Genalē Wenz, *It.* Guiba, *Som.* Ganaane, Webi Jubba. ≈ Ethiopia/Somalia
194 H2 **Jubany** *Argentinian research station* Antarctica
Jubayl *see* Jbaïl
81 L18 **Jubbada Dhexe** *off.* Gobolka Jubbada Dhexe. ◈ *region* SW Somalia
81 K18 **Jubbada Hoose** ◈ *region* SW Somalia
Jubba, Webi *see* Juba
Jubbulpore *see* Jabalpur
Jubeil *see* Jbaïl
74 B9 **Juby, Cap** *headland* SW Morocco
105 R10 **Júcar** *var.* Jucar. ≈ C Spain
40 L12 **Juchipila** Zacatecas, C Mexico
41 S16 **Juchitán** *var.* Juchitán de Zaragosa. Oaxaca, SE Mexico
Juchitán de Zaragosa *see* Juchitán
138 G11 **Judaea** *cultural region* Israel/West Bank
138 F11 **Judaean Hills** *Heb.* Haré Yehuda. *hill range* E Israel
138 H8 **Judaydah** *Fr.* Jdaïdé. Dimashq, W Syria
139 P11 **Judayyidat Hāmir** S Iraq
109 U8 **Judenburg** Steiermark, C Austria
33 T8 **Judith River** ≈ Montana, NW USA
27 V11 **Judsonia** Arkansas, C USA
141 P14 **Jufrah, Wādī al** *dry watercourse* NW Yemen
Jugar *see* Sêrxü
Jugoslavija/Jugoslavija, Savezna Republika *see* Serbia and Montenegro (Yugo.)
42 K10 **Juigalpa** Chontales, S Nicaragua
161 T13 **Juishui** C Taiwan
100 E9 **Juist** *island* NW Germany
59 M21 **Juiz de Fora** Minas Gerais, SE Brazil
62 J5 **Jujuy** *off.* Provincia de Jujuy. ◈ *province* N Argentina
Jujuy *see* San Salvador de Jujuy
92 J11 **Jukkasjärvi** *Lapp.* Čohkkiras. Norrbotten, N Sweden
Jula *see* Gyula, Hungary
Jūlā *see* Jālū, Libya
37 W2 **Julesburg** Colorado, C USA
Julia Beterrae *see* Béziers
57 I17 **Juliaca** Puno, SE Peru
181 U6 **Julia Creek** Queensland, C Australia
35 V17 **Julian** California, W USA
98 H7 **Julianadorp** Noord-Holland, NW Netherlands
109 S11 **Julian Alps** *Ger.* Julische Alpen, *It.* Alpi Giulie, *Slvn.* Julijske Alpe. ▲ Italy/Slovenia
55 V11 **Juliana Top** ▲ C Surinam
Julianehåb *see* Qaqortoq
Julijske Alpe *see* Julian Alps
40 J6 **Julimes** Chihuahua, N Mexico
Julio Briga *see* Bragança, Portugal
Juliobriga *see* Logroño, Spain
61 G15 **Júlio de Castilhos** Rio Grande do Sul, S Brazil
Juliomagus *see* Angers
Julische Alpen *see* Julian Alps
Jullundur *see* Jalandhar
147 N11 **Juma** *Rus.* Dzhuma. Samarqand Viloyati, C Uzbekistan
161 O3 **Juma He** ≈ E China
81 L18 **Jumboo** Jubbada Hoose, S Somalia
35 Y11 **Jumbo Peak** ▲ Nevada, W USA
105 R12 **Jumilla** Murcia, SE Spain
153 N10 **Jumla** Mid Western, NW Nepal
Jummoo *see* Jammu
Jumna *see* Yamuna
Jumporn *see* Chumphon
30 K5 **Jump River** ≈ Wisconsin, N USA
154 B11 **Jūnāgadh** *var.* Junagarh. Gujarāt, W India
Junagarh *see* Jūnāgadh
161 Q6 **Junan** *var.* Shizilu. Shandong, E China
62 G11 **Juncal, Cerro** ▲ C Chile
25 Q10 **Junction** Texas, SW USA
36 K6 **Junction** Utah, W USA
27 O4 **Junction City** Kansas, C USA
32 F13 **Junction City** Oregon, NW USA
60 M10 **Jundiaí** São Paulo, S Brazil
39 X12 **Juneau** *state capital* Alaska, USA
30 M8 **Juneau** Wisconsin, N USA
105 U6 **Juneda** Cataluña, NE Spain
183 Q9 **Junee** New South Wales, SE Australia
35 R8 **June Lake** California, W USA
Jungbunzlau *see* Mladá Boleslav
158 L4 **Junggar Pendi** *Eng.* Dzungarian Basin. *basin* NW China
99 N24 **Junglinster** Grevenmacher, C Luxembourg
18 F14 **Juniata River** ≈ Pennsylvania, NE USA
61 B20 **Junín** Buenos Aires, E Argentina
57 E14 **Junín** Junín, C Peru
57 F14 **Junín** *off.* Departamento de Junín. ◈ *department* C Peru
63 H15 **Junín de los Andes** Neuquén, W Argentina
57 D14 **Junín, Lago de** ◎ C Peru
Junīyah *see* Joûnié
Junkseylon *see* Phuket
160 I11 **Junlian** Sichuan, C China
25 O11 **Juno** Texas, SW USA
92 J11 **Junosuando** *Lapp.* Čunusavvon. Norrbotten, N Sweden
93 H16 **Junsele** Västernorrland, C Sweden
Junten *see* Sunch'ŏn
32 L14 **Juntura** Oregon, NW USA
93 N14 **Juntusranta** Oulu, E Finland
118 H11 **Juodupė** Panevėžys, NE Lithuania
119 H14 **Juozapinės Kalnas** ▲ SE Lithuania
99 K19 **Juprelle** Liège, E Belgium
80 D13 **Jur** ≈ C Sudan
103 S9 **Jura** ◈ *department* E France
108 C7 **Jura** ◈ *canton* NW Switzerland
108 B8 **Jura** *var.* Jura Mountains. ▲ France/Switzerland
96 G12 **Jura** *island* SW Scotland, UK
Juraciszki *see* Yuratsishki
54 C8 **Juradó** Chocó, NW Colombia
Jura Mountains *see* Jura
96 G12 **Jura, Sound of** *strait* W Scotland, UK
139 V15 **Juraybīyāt, Bi'r** *well* S Iraq
118 E13 **Jurbarkas** *Ger.* Georgenburg, Jurburg. Tauragė, W Lithuania
99 F20 **Jurbise** Hainaut, SW Belgium
Jurburg *see* Jurbarkas
118 F9 **Jūrmala** Riga, C Latvia
58 D13 **Juruá** Amazonas, NW Brazil
58 C13 **Juruá, Río** *var.* Río Yuruá. ≈ Brazil/Peru
59 G16 **Juruena** Mato Grosso, W Brazil
59 G16 **Juruena** ≈ W Brazil
165 Q6 **Jūsan-ko** ◎ Honshū, C Japan
25 O6 **Justiceburg** Texas, SW USA
Justinianopolis *see* Kirşehir
62 K11 **Justo Daract** San Luis, C Argentina
59 C14 **Jutaí** Amazonas, W Brazil
58 C13 **Jutaí, Rio** ≈ NW Brazil
100 N13 **Jüterbog** Brandenburg, E Germany
42 E6 **Jutiapa** Jutiapa, S Guatemala
42 A3 **Jutiapa** *off.* Departamento de Jutiapa. ◈ *department* SE Guatemala
42 J6 **Juticalpa** Olancho, C Honduras
82 I13 **Jutila** North Western, NW Zambia
Jutland *see* Jylland
93 N16 **Juuka** Itä-Suomi, E Finland
93 N17 **Juva** Isä-Suomi, SE Finland
Juvavum *see* Salzburg
44 A6 **Juventud, Isla de la** *var.* Isla de Pinos, *Eng.* Isle of Youth; *prev.* The Isle of the Pines. *island* W Cuba
161 Q5 **Juxian** *var.* Chengyang, Ju Xian. Shandong, E China
161 P6 **Juye** Shandong, E China
113 O15 **Južna Morava** *Ger.* Südliche Morava. ≈ SE Serbia and Montenegro (Yugo.)
83 H20 **Jwaneng** Southern, S Botswana
95 I23 **Jyderup** Vestsjælland, E Denmark
95 F22 **Jylland** *Eng.* Jutland. *peninsula* W Denmark
Jyrgalan *see* Dzhergalan
93 M17 **Jyväskylä** Länsi-Suomi, W Finland

K

155 X3 **K2** *Chin.* Qogir Feng, *Eng.* Mount Godwin Austen. ▲ China/Pakistan
38 D9 **Ka'a'awa** *var.* Kaaawa. O'ahu, Hawai'i, USA, C Pacific Ocean
81 G16 **Kaabong** NE Uganda
Kaaden *see* Kadaň
55 V9 **Kaaimanston** Sipaliwini, N Surinam
Kaakhka *see* Kaka
Kaala *see* Caála
187 O16 **Kaala-Gomen** Province Nord, W New Caledonia
92 L9 **Kaamanen** *Lapp.* Gámas. Lappi, N Finland
Kaapstad *see* Cape Town
Kaarasjoki *see* Karasjok
Kaaresuanto *see* Karesuando
92 J10 **Kaaresuvanto** *Lapp.* Gárassavon. Lappi, N Finland
93 K19 **Kaarina** Länsi-Suomi, W Finland
99 I14 **Kaatsheuvel** Noord-Brabant, S Netherlands
93 N16 **Kaavi** Itä-Suomi, C Finland
Ka'a'wa *see* Kaaawa
Kaba *see* Habahe
171 O14 **Kabaena, Pulau** *island* C Indonesia
Kabakly *see* Gabakly
76 J14 **Kabala** N Sierra Leone
81 E19 **Kabale** SW Uganda
55 U10 **Kabalebo Rivier** ≈ W Surinam
79 N22 **Kabalo** Katanga, SE Dem. Rep. Congo
145 W13 **Kabanbay** *Kaz.* Qabanbay *prev.* Andreyevka, *Kaz.* Andreevka. Almaty, SE Kazakhstan
79 O21 **Kabambare** Maniema, E Dem. Rep. Congo
187 Y15 **Kabara** *prev.* Kambara. *island* Lau Group, E Fiji
Kabardino-Balkaria *see* Kabardino-Balkarskaya Respublika
126 M15 **Kabardino-Balkarskaya Respublika** *Eng.* Kabardino-Balkaria. ◈ *autonomous republic* SW Russian Federation
79 O19 **Kabare** Sud Kivu, E Dem. Rep. Congo
171 T11 **Kabarei** Papua, E Indonesia
171 P7 **Kabasalan** Mindanao, S Philippines
77 U15 **Kabba** Kogi, S Nigeria
92 I13 **Kåbdalis** *Lapp.* Goabddális. Norrbotten, N Sweden
138 M6 **Kabd aş Şārim** *hill range* E Syria
14 B7 **Kabenung Lake** ◎ Ontario, S Canada
29 W3 **Kabetogama Lake** ◎ Minnesota, N USA
Kabia, Pulau *see* Kabin, Pulau
79 M22 **Kabinda** Kasai Oriental, SE Dem. Rep. Congo
Kabinda *see* Cabinda
171 O15 **Kabin, Pulau** *var.* Pulau Kabia. *island* W Indonesia
171 P16 **Kabir** Pulau Pantar, S Indonesia
149 T10 **Kabīrwāla** Punjab, E Pakistan
78 I13 **Kabo** Ouham, NW Central African Republic
Kābol *see* Kābul
83 H14 **Kabompo** North Western, W Zambia
83 H14 **Kabompo** ≈ W Zambia
79 M22 **Kabongo** Katanga, SE Dem. Rep. Congo
120 K11 **Kaboudia, Rass** *headland* E Tunisia
143 U4 **Kabūd Gonbad** Khorāsān, NE Iran
142 L5 **Kabūd Rāhang** Hamadān, W Iran
82 L12 **Kabuko** Northern, NE Zambia
149 Q5 **Kābul** *var.* Kabul, *Per.* Kābol. ● (Afghanistan) Kābul, E Afghanistan
149 Q5 **Kābul** *Eng.* Kabul, *Per.* Kābol. ◈ *province* E Afghanistan
149 Q5 **Kābul** ✖ Kābul, E Afghanistan
149 R5 **Kabul** *var.* Daryā-ye Kābul. ≈ Afghanistan/Pakistan *see also* Kābul, Daryā-ye
149 S5 **Kābul, Daryā-ye** *var.* Kabul. ≈ Afghanistan/Pakistan *see also* Kabul
79 O25 **Kabunda** Katanga, SE Dem. Rep. Congo
171 R9 **Kaburuang, Pulau** *island* Kepulauan Talaud, N Indonesia
80 G8 **Kabushiya** River Nile, NE Sudan
83 J14 **Kabwe** Central, C Zambia
186 E7 **Kabwum** Morobe, C PNG
113 N17 **Kačanik** Serbia, S Serbia and Montenegro (Yugo.)
118 F13 **Kačerginė** Kaunas, C Lithuania
117 S13 **Kacha** Respublika Krym, S Ukraine
154 A10 **Kachchh, Gulf of** *var.* Gulf of Cutch, Gulf of Kutch. *gulf* W India
154 I11 **Kachchhidhāna** Madhya Pradesh, C India
149 Q11 **Kachchh, Rann of** *var.* Rann of Kachh, Rann of Kutch. *salt marsh* India/Pakistan
39 Q13 **Kachemak Bay** *bay* Alaska, USA
Kachh, Rann of *see* Kachchh, Rann of
77 V14 **Kachia** Kaduna, C Nigeria
167 N2 **Kachin State** ◈ *state* N Burma
145 T7 **Kachiry** Pavlodar, NE Kazakhstan
137 Q11 **Kaçkar Dağları** ▲ NE Turkey
155 C21 **Kadamatt Island** *island* Lakshadweep, India, N Indian Ocean
111 B15 **Kadaň** *Ger.* Kaaden.Ústecký Kraj, NW Czech Republic
167 N11 **Kadan Kyun** *prev.* King Island. *island* Mergui Archipelago, S Burma
187 X15 **Kadavu** *prev.* Kandavu. *island* S Fiji
187 X15 **Kadavu Passage** *channel* S Fiji
79 G16 **Kadéï** ≈ Cameroon/Central African Republic
Kadhimain *see* Al Kāẓimīyah
Kadijica *see* Kadiytsa
114 M13 **Kadıköy Barajı** ⊞ NW Turkey
182 I8 **Kadina** South Australia
136 H15 **Kadınhanı** Konya, C Turkey
76 M14 **Kadiolo** Sikasso, S Mali
136 L16 **Kadirli** Osmaniye, S Turkey
114 G11 **Kadiytsa** *Mac.* Kadijica. ▲ Bulgaria/FYR Macedonia
28 L10 **Kadoka** South Dakota, N USA
127 N5 **Kadom** Ryazanskaya Oblast', W Russian Federation
83 K16 **Kadoma** *prev.* Gatooma. Mashonaland West, C Zimbabwe
80 E12 **Kadugli** Southern Kordofan, S Sudan
77 V14 **Kaduna** Kaduna, C Nigeria
77 V14 **Kaduna** ◈ *state* C Nigeria
77 V15 **Kaduna** ≈ N Nigeria
124 K14 **Kaduy** Vologodskaya Oblast', NW Russian Federation
154 E13 **Kadwa** ≈ W India
123 S9 **Kadykchan** Magadanskaya Oblast', E Russian Federation
Kadzharan *see* K'ajaran
125 T7 **Kadzherom** Respublika Komi, NW Russian Federation
147 X8 **Kadzhi-Say** *Kir.* Kajisay. Issyk-Kul'skaya Oblast', NE Kyrgyzstan
76 I10 **Kaédi** Gorgol, S Mauritania
78 G12 **Kaélé** Extrême-Nord, N Cameroon
38 C9 **Ka'ena Point** *var.* Kaena Point *headland* O'ahu, Hawai'i, USA, C Pacific Ocean
184 J2 **Kaeo** Northland, North Island, NZ
163 X14 **Kaesŏng** *var.* Kaesŏng-si. S North Korea
Kaesŏng-si *see* Kaesŏng
Kaewieng *see* Kavieng
79 L24 **Kafakumba** Katanga, S Dem. Rep. Congo
Kafan *see* Kapan
77 V14 **Kafanchan** Kaduna, C Nigeria
Kaffa *see* Feodosiya
76 G11 **Kaffrine** C Senegal
Kafiau *see* Kofiau, Pulau
115 I19 **Kafiréas, Akrotírio** *headland* Évvoia, C Greece
115 I19 **Kafiréos, Stenó** *strait* Évvoia/Kykládes, Greece, Aegean Sea
Kafirnigan *see* Kofarnihon
Kafo *see* Kafu
Kafr ash Shaykh/Kafrel Sheik *see* Kafr el Sheikh
75 W7 **Kafr el Sheikh** *var.* Kafr ash Shaykh, Kafrel Sheik. N Egypt
81 F17 **Kafu** *var.* Kafo. ≈ W Uganda
83 J15 **Kafue** Lusaka, SE Zambia
83 I14 **Kafue** ≈ C Zambia
164 K12 **Kaga** Ishikawa, Honshū, SW Japan
79 J14 **Kaga Bandoro** *prev.* Fort-Crampel. Nana-Grébizi, C Central African Republic
81 E18 **Kagadi** W Uganda
38 H17 **Kagalaska Island** *island* Aleutian Islands, Alaska, USA
Kagan *see* Kogon
Kaganovichabad *see* Kolkhozobod
Kagarlyk *see* Kaharlyk
164 H14 **Kagawa** *off.* Kagawa-ken. ◈ *prefecture* Shikoku, SW Japan
154 J13 **Kagaznagar** Andhra Pradesh, C India
93 J14 **Kåge** Västerbotten, N Sweden
81 E19 **Kagera** *var.* Ziwa Magharibi, *Eng.* West Lake. ◈ *region* NW Tanzania
81 E19 **Kagera** *var.* Akagera. ≈ Rwanda/Tanzania *see also* Akagera
76 L5 **Kâgheţ** *var.* Karet. *physical region* N Mauritania
Kagi *see* Chiai
137 S12 **Kağızman** Kars, NE Turkey
188 I6 **Kagman Point** *headland* Saipan, S Northern Mariana Islands
164 C16 **Kagoshima** *var.* Kagosima. Kagoshima, Kyūshū, SW Japan
164 C16 **Kagoshima** *off.* Kagoshima-ken, *var.* Kagosima. ◈ *prefecture* Kyūshū, SW Japan
Kagosima *see* Kagoshima
Kagul *see* Cahul
Kagul, Ozero *see* Kahul, Ozero
38 B8 **Kahala Point** *headland* Kaua'i, Hawai'i, USA, C Pacific Ocean
81 F21 **Kahama** Shinyanga, NW Tanzania
117 P5 **Kaharlyk** *Rus.* Kagarlyk. Kyyivs'ka Oblast', N Ukraine
169 T13 **Kahayan, Sungai** ≈ Borneo, C Indonesia
79 I22 **Kahemba** Bandundu, SW Dem. Rep. Congo
185 A23 **Kaherekoau Mountains** ▲ South Island, NZ
143 W14 **Kahīrī** *var.* Kūhīrī. Sīstān va Balūchestān, SE Iran
101 L16 **Kahla** Thüringen, C Germany
101 G15 **Kahler Asten** ▲ W Germany
149 Q4 **Kahmard, Daryā-ye** *prev.* Darya-i-Surkhab. ≈ NE Afghanistan
143 T13 **Kahnūj** Kermān, SE Iran
27 V1 **Kahoka** Missouri, C USA
38 E10 **Kaho'olawe** *var.* Kahoolawe *island* Hawai'i, USA, C Pacific Ocean
136 M16 **Kahramanmaraş** *var.* Kahraman Maraş, Maraş, Marash. Kahramanmaraş, S Turkey
136 L15 **Kahramanmaraş** *var.* Kahraman Maraş, Maraş, Marash. ◈ *province* C Turkey
Kahror/Kahror Pakka *see* Karor Pacca
137 N15 **Kâhta** Adıyaman, S Turkey
38 D8 **Kahuku** O'ahu, Hawai'i, USA, C Pacific Ocean
38 D8 **Kahuku Point** *headland* O'ahu, Hawai'i, USA, C Pacific Ocean
116 M12 **Kahul, Ozero** *var.* Lacul Cahul, *Rus.* Ozero Kagul. ◎ Moldova/Ukraine
143 V11 **Kahūrak** Sīstān va Balūchestān, SE Iran
184 G13 **Kahurangi Point** *headland* South Island, NZ
149 V6 **Kahūta** Punjab, E Pakistan
77 S14 **Kaiama** Kwara, W Nigeria
186 D7 **Kaiapit** Morobe, C PNG
185 I18 **Kaiapoi** Canterbury, South Island, NZ
36 K9 **Kaibab Plateau** *plain* Arizona, SW USA
171 U14 **Kai Besar, Pulau** *island* Kepulauan Kai, E Indonesia
36 L9 **Kaibito Plateau** *plain* Arizona, SW USA
158 K6 **Kaidu He** *var.* Karaxahar. ≈ NW China
55 S10 **Kaieteur Falls** *waterfall* C Guyana
161 O6 **Kaifeng** Henan, C China
184 J3 **Kaihu** Northland, North Island, NZ
Kaihua *see* Wenshan
171 U14 **Kai Kecil, Pulau** *island* Kepulauan Kai, E Indonesia
169 U16 **Kai, Kepulauan** *prev.* Kei Islands. *island group* Maluku, SE Indonesia
184 J3 **Kaikohe** Northland, North Island, NZ
185 J16 **Kaikoura** Canterbury, South Island, NZ
185 J16 **Kaikoura Peninsula** *peninsula* South Island, NZ
Kailas Range *see* Gangdisê Shan
160 K12 **Kaili** Guizhou, S China
38 F10 **Kailua** Maui, Hawai'i, USA, C Pacific Ocean
Kailua *see* Kalaoa
38 G11 **Kalaoa** *var.* Kailua. Hawai'i, USA, C Pacific Ocean
38 G11 **Kailua-Kona** *var.* Kona. Hawai'i, USA, C Pacific Ocean
186 B7 **Kaim** ≈ W PNG
171 X14 **Kaima** Papua, E Indonesia
184 M7 **Kaimai Range** ▲ North Island, NZ
114 E13 **Kaïmaktsalán** ▲ Greece/FYR Macedonia
185 C20 **Kaimanawa Mountains** ▲ North Island, NZ
118 E4 **Käina** *Ger.* Keinis; *prev.* Keina. Hiiumaa, W Estonia
109 V7 **Kainach** ≈ SE Austria
164 I14 **Kainan** Tokushima, Shikoku, SW Japan
164 H15 **Kainan** Wakayama, Honshū, SW Japan
147 U7 **Kaindy** *Kir.* Kayyngdy. Chuyskaya Oblast', N Kyrgyzstan
77 T14 **Kainji Dam** *dam* W Nigeria
Kainji Lake *see* Kainji Reservoir
77 T14 **Kainji Reservoir** *var.* Kainji Lake. ⊞ W Nigeria
186 D8 **Kaintiba** *var.* Kamina. Gulf, S PNG
92 K12 **Kainulaisjärvi** Norrbotten, N Sweden
184 K5 **Kaipara Harbour** *harbour* North Island, NZ
152 I10 **Kairāna** Uttar Pradesh, N India
74 M6 **Kairouan** *var.* Al Qayrawān. E Tunisia
Kaisaria *see* Kayseri
101 F20 **Kaiserslautern** Rheinland-Pfalz, SW Germany
118 G13 **Kaišiadorys** Kaunas, S Lithuania
184 I2 **Kaitaia** Northland, North Island, NZ
185 E24 **Kaitangata** Otago, South Island, NZ
152 I9 **Kaithal** Haryāna, NW India
Kaitong *see* Tongyu
169 N13 **Kait, Tanjung** *headland* Sumatera, W Indonesia
38 E9 **Kaiwi Channel** *channel* Hawai'i, USA, C Pacific Ocean
160 K9 **Kaixian** *var.* Kai Xian. Sichuan, C China
163 V11 **Kaiyuan** *var.* K'ai-yüan. Liaoning, NE China
160 H14 **Kaiyuan** Yunnan, SW China
39 O9 **Kaiyuh Mountains** ▲ Alaska, USA
93 M15 **Kajaani** *Swe.* Kajana. Oulu, C Finland
149 N7 **Kajakī, Band-e** ◎ C Afghanistan
Kajan *see* Kayan, Sungai
Kajana *see* Kajaani
137 V13 **K'ajaran** *Rus.* Kadzharan. SE Armenia
Kajisay *see* Kadzhi-Say
113 O20 **Kajmakčalan** ▲ S FYR Macedonia
Kajnar *see* Kaynar
149 N6 **Kajrān** Urūzgān, C Afghanistan
149 N5 **Kaj Rūd** ≈ C Afghanistan
146 G14 **Kaka** *Rus.* Kaakhka. Ahal Welaýaty, S Turkmenistan
12 C12 **Kakabeka Falls** Ontario, S Canada
83 F23 **Kakamas** Northern Cape, W South Africa
81 H18 **Kakamega** Western, W Kenya
112 H13 **Kakanj** Federacija Bosna I Hercegovina, Bosnia and Herzegovina
185 F22 **Kakanui Mountains** ▲ South Island, NZ
184 K11 **Kakaramea** Taranaki, North Island, NZ
76 J16 **Kakata** C Liberia
184 M11 **Kakatahi** Manawatu-Wanganui, North Island, NZ
113 M23 **Kakavi** Gjirokastër, S Albania
147 O14 **Kakaydi** Surxondaryo Viloyati, S Uzbekistan
164 F13 **Kake** Hiroshima, Honshū, SW Japan
39 X13 **Kake** Kupreanof Island, Alaska, USA
171 P14 **Kakea** Pulau Wowoni, C Indonesia
164 M14 **Kakegawa** Shizuoka, Honshū, S Japan
165 V16 **Kakeromajima** Kagoshima, SW Japan
143 T6 **Kākhak** *var.* Kākhk. Khorāsān, E Iran
118 L11 **Kakhanavichy** *Rus.* Kokhanovichi. Vitsyebskaya Voblasts', N Belarus
39 P13 **Kakhonak** Alaska, USA
117 S10 **Kakhovka** Khersons'ka Oblast', S Ukraine
117 U9 **Kakhovs'ka Vodoskhovyshche** *Rus.* Kakhovskoye Vodokhranilishche. ⊞ SE Ukraine
Kakhovskoye Vodokhranilishche *see* Kakhovs'ka Vodoskhovyshche
117 T11 **Kakhovs'kyy Kanal** *canal* S Ukraine
Kakia *see* Khakhea
155 L16 **Kākināda** *prev.* Cocanada. Andhra Pradesh, E India
Kākisalmi *see* Priozersk
164 I13 **Kakogawa** Hyōgo, Honshū, SW Japan
81 F18 **Kakoge** C Uganda
145 O7 **Kak, Ozero** ◎ N Kazakhstan
Ka-Krem *see* Malyy Yenisey
Kakshaal-Too, Khrebet *see* Kokshaal-Tau
39 S5 **Kaktovik** Alaska, USA
165 Q11 **Kakuda** Miyagi, Honshū, C Japan
165 Q8 **Kakunodate** Akita, Honshū, C Japan
Kalaallit Nunaat *see* Greenland
149 T7 **Kālābāgh** Punjab, E Pakistan
171 Q16 **Kalabahi** Pulau Alor, S Indonesia
188 I5 **Kalabera** Saipan, S Northern Mariana Islands
83 G14 **Kalabo** Western, W Zambia
126 M9 **Kalach** Voronezhskaya Oblast', W Russian Federation

◆ Country ● Country Capital ◇ Dependent Territory ○ Dependent Territory Capital ◈ Administrative Region ✖ International Airport ▲ Mountain ▲ Mountain Range ⛰ Volcano ≈ River ◎ Lake ⊞ Reservoir

127 N10 **Kalach-na-Donu** Volgogradskaya Oblast', SW Russian Federation
166 K5 **Kaladan** ≈ W Burma
14 K14 **Kaladar** Ontario, SE Canada
38 G13 **Ka Lae** *var.* South Cape, South Point. *headland* Hawai'i, USA, C Pacific Ocean
83 G19 **Kalahari Desert** *desert* Southern Africa
38 B8 **Kalāheo** *var.* Kalaheo. Kaua'i, Hawai'i, USA, C Pacific Ocean
Kalaikhum *see* Qal'aikhum
Kala-i-Mor *see* Galaýmor
93 K15 **Kalajoki** Oulu, W Finland
Kalak *see* Eski Kaļak
Kal al Sraghna *see* El Kelâa Srarhna
32 G10 **Kalama** Washington, NW USA
Kalámai *see* Kalámata
115 G14 **Kalamariá** Kentrikí Makedonía, N Greece
115 E21 **Kalámata** *prev.* Kalámai. Pelopónnisos, S Greece
31 P10 **Kalamazoo** Michigan, N USA
31 P9 **Kalamazoo River** ≈ Michigan, N USA
Kalambaka *see* Kalampáka
117 S13 **Kalamits'ka Zatoka** *Rus.* Kalamitskiy Zaliv. *gulf* S Ukraine
Kalamitskiy Zaliv *see* Kalamits'ka Zatoka
115 H18 **Kálamos** Attikí, C Greece
115 C18 **Kálamos** *island* Iónioi Nísoi, Greece, C Mediterranean Sea
115 D15 **Kalampáka** *var.* Kalambaka. Thessalía, C Greece
Kalan *see* Călan, Romania
Kalan *see* Tunceli, Turkey
117 S11 **Kalanchak** Khersons'ka Oblast', S Ukraine
38 G11 **Kalaoa** *var.* Kailua. Hawai'i, USA, C Pacific Ocean
171 O15 **Kalaotoa, Pulau** *island* W Indonesia
155 J24 **Kala Oya** ≈ NW Sri Lanka
Kalarash *see* Călărași
93 H17 **Kälarne** Jämtland, C Sweden
143 V15 **Kalar Rūd** ≈ SE Iran
167 R9 **Kalasin** *var.* Muang Kalasin. Kalasin, E Thailand
149 O8 **Kālat** *Per.* Qalāt. Zābul, S Afghanistan
149 O11 **Kālat** *var.* Kelat, Khelat. Baluchistān, SW Pakistan
115 J14 **Kalathriá, Akrotírio** *headland* Samothráki, NE Greece
193 W17 **Kalau** *island* Tongatapu Group, SE Tonga
38 E9 **Kalaupapa** Moloka'i, Hawai'i, USA, C Pacific Ocean
127 N13 **Kalaus** ≈ SW Russian Federation
Kalávrita *see* Kalávryta
115 E19 **Kalávryta** *var.* Kalávrita. Dytikí Ellás, S Greece
141 Y10 **Kalbān** W Oman
180 H11 **Kalbarri** Western Australia
145 X10 **Kalbinskiy Khrebet** *Kaz.* Qalba Zhotasy. ▲ E Kazakhstan
144 G10 **Kaldygayty** ≈ W Kazakhstan
136 I12 **Kalecik** Ankara, N Turkey
79 O19 **Kalehe** Sud Kivu, E Dem. Rep. Congo
79 P22 **Kalemie** *prev.* Albertville. Katanga, SE Dem. Rep. Congo
166 L4 **Kalemyo** Sagaing, W Burma
82 H12 **Kalene Hill** North Western, NW Zambia
Kale Sultanie *see* Çanakkale
124 I7 **Kalevala** Respublika Kareliya, NW Russian Federation
166 L4 **Kalewa** Sagaing, C Burma
Kalgan *see* Zhangjiakou
39 Q12 **Kalgin Island** *island* Alaska, USA
180 L12 **Kalgoorlie** Western Australia
Kali *see* Sārda
115 E17 **Kaliakoúda** ▲ C Greece
114 O8 **Kaliakra, Nos** *headland* NE Bulgaria
115 F19 **Kaliánoi** Pelopónnisos, S Greece
115 N24 **Kalí Límni** ▲ Kárpathos, SE Greece
79 N20 **Kalima** Maniema, E Dem. Rep. Congo
169 S11 **Kalimantan** *Eng.* Indonesian Borneo. *geopolitical region* Borneo, C Indonesia
169 Q11 **Kalimantan Barat** *off.* Propinsi Kalimantan Barat, *Eng.* West Borneo, West Kalimantan. ◆ *province* N Indonesia
169 T13 **Kalimantan Selatan** *off.* Propinsi Kalimantan Selatan, *Eng.* South Borneo, South Kalimantan. ◆ *province* N Indonesia
169 R12 **Kalimantan Tengah** *off.* Propinsi Kalimantan Tengah, *Eng.* Central Borneo, Central Kalimantan. ◆ *province* N Indonesia
169 U10 **Kalimantan Timur** *off.* Propinsi Kalimantan Timur, *Eng.* East Borneo, East Kalimantan. ◆ *province* N Indonesia
Kálimnos *see* Kálymnos
153 S12 **Kālimpang** West Bengal, NE India
Kalinin *see* Tver', Russian Federation
Kalinin *see* Boldumsaz, Turkmenistan
Kalininabad *see* Kalininobod
126 B3 **Kaliningrad** Kaliningradskaya Oblast', W Russian Federation
Kaliningrad *see* Kaliningradskaya Oblast'
126 A3 **Kaliningradskaya Oblast'** *var.* Kaliningrad. ◆ *province and enclave* W Russian Federation
Kalinino *see* Tashir
147 P14 **Kalininobod** *Rus.* Kalininabad. SW Tajikistan
127 O8 **Kalininsk** Saratovskaya Oblast', W Russian Federation
Kalininsk *see* Boldumsaz
Kalinisk *see* Cupcina
119 M19 **Kalinkavichy** *Rus.* Kalinkovichi. Homyel'skaya Voblasts', SE Belarus
Kalinkovichi *see* Kalinkavichy
81 G18 **Kaliro** SE Uganda
Kalisch/Kalish *see* Kalisz
33 O7 **Kalispell** Montana, NW USA
110 I13 **Kalisz** *Ger.* Kalisch, *Rus.* Kalish; *anc.* Calisia. Wielkopolskie, C Poland
110 F9 **Kalisz Pomorski** *Ger.* Kallies. Zachodnio-pomorskie, NW Poland
126 M10 **Kalitva** ≈ SW Russian Federation
81 F21 **Kaliua** Tabora, C Tanzania
92 K13 **Kalix** Norrbotten, N Sweden
92 J11 **Kalixfors** Norrbotten, N Sweden
145 T8 **Kalkaman** Pavlodar, NE Kazakhstan
Kalkandelen *see* Tetovo
181 O4 **Kalkarindji** Northern Territory, N Australia
31 P6 **Kalkaska** Michigan, N USA
95 F16 **Kall** Jämtland, C Sweden
189 X2 **Kallalen** *var.* Calalen. *island* Ratak Chain, SE Marshall Islands
118 J5 **Kallaste** *Ger.* Krasnogor. Tartumaa, SE Estonia
93 N16 **Kallavesi** ◎ SE Finland
115 F17 **Kallídromo** ▲ C Greece
Kallies *see* Kalisz Pomorski
95 M22 **Kallinge** Blekinge, S Sweden
115 L16 **Kalloní** Lésvos, E Greece
93 F16 **Kallsjön** ◎ C Sweden
95 N21 **Kalmar** *var.* Calmar. Kalmar, S Sweden
95 M19 **Kalmar** *var.* Calmar. ◆ *county* S Sweden
95 N20 **Kalmarsund** *strait* S Sweden
148 L16 **Kalmat, Khor** *Eng.* Kalmat Lagoon. *lagoon* SW Pakistan
Kalmat Lagoon *see* Kalmat, Khor
117 X9 **Kal'mius** ≈ E Ukraine
99 H15 **Kalmthout** Antwerpen, N Belgium
Kalmykia/Kalmykiya-Khal'mg Tangch, Respublika *see* Kalmykiya, Respublika
127 O12 **Kalmykiya, Respublika** *var.* Respublika Kalmykiya-Khal'mg Tangch, *Eng.* Kalmykia; *prev.* Kalmytskaya ASSR. ◆ *autonomous republic* SW Russian Federation
Kalmytskaya ASSR *see* Kalmykiya, Respublika
118 F9 **Kalnciems** Jelgava, C Latvia
114 L10 **Kalnitsa** ≈ SE Bulgaria
111 J24 **Kalocsa** Bács-Kiskun, S Hungary
114 J9 **Kalofer** Plovdiv, C Bulgaria
38 E10 **Kalohi Channel** *channel* Hawai'i, USA, C Pacific Ocean
83 I16 **Kalomo** Southern, S Zambia
29 X14 **Kalona** Iowa, C USA
115 K22 **Kalotási, Akrotírio** *headland* Amorgós, Kykládes, Greece, Aegean Sea
152 J8 **Kalpa** Himāchal Pradesh, N India
115 C15 **Kalpáki** Ípeiros, W Greece
155 C22 **Kalpeni Island** *island* Lakshadweep, India, N Indian Ocean
152 K13 **Kālpi** Uttar Pradesh, N India
158 G7 **Kalpin** Xinjiang Uygur Zizhiqu, NW China
149 P16 **Kalri Lake** ◎ SE Pakistan
143 R5 **Kāl Shūr** ≈ N Iran
39 N11 **Kalskag** Alaska, USA
95 B18 **Kalsoy** *Dan.* Kalsø *Island* Faeroe Islands
39 O9 **Kaltag** Alaska, USA
108 H7 **Kaltbrunn** Sankt Gallen, NE Switzerland
Kaltdorf *see* Pruszków
77 X14 **Kaltungo** Gombe, E Nigeria
126 K4 **Kaluga** Kaluzhskaya Oblast', W Russian Federation
155 J26 **Kalu Ganga** ≈ S Sri Lanka
82 J13 **Kalulushi** Copperbelt, C Zambia
180 M2 **Kalumburu** Western Australia
95 H23 **Kalundborg** Vestsjælland, E Denmark
82 K11 **Kalungwishi** ≈ N Zambia
149 T8 **Kalūr Kot** Punjab, E Pakistan
116 I6 **Kalush** *Pol.* Kałusz. Ivano-Frankivs'ka Oblast', W Ukraine
Kałusz *see* Kalush
110 N11 **Kałuszyn** Mazowieckie, C Poland
155 J26 **Kalutara** Western Province, SW Sri Lanka
Kaluwawa *see* Fergusson Island
126 I5 **Kaluzhskaya Oblast'** ◆ *province* W Russian Federation
119 E14 **Kalvarija** *Pol.* Kalwaria. Marijampolė, S Lithuania
93 K15 **Kalvià** Länsi-Suomi, W Finland
109 U6 **Kalwang** Steiermark, E Austria
Kalwaria *see* Kalvarija
154 D13 **Kalyān** Mahārāshtra, W India
124 K16 **Kalyazin** Tverskaya Oblast', W Russian Federation
115 D18 **Kalydón** *anc.* Calydon. *site of ancient city* Dytikí Ellás, C Greece
115 M21 **Kálymnos** *var.* Kálimnos. Kálymnos, Dodekánisos, Greece, Aegean Sea
115 M21 **Kálymnos** *var.* Kálimnos. *island* Dodekánisos, Greece, Aegean Sea
117 O5 **Kalynivka** Kyyivs'ka Oblast', N Ukraine
117 N6 **Kalynivka** Vinnyts'ka Oblast', C Ukraine
42 M10 **Kama** *var.* Cama. Región Autónoma Atlántico Sur, SE Nicaragua
165 R9 **Kamaishi** *var.* Kamaisi. Iwate, Honshū, C Japan
Kamaisi *see* Kamaishi
118 H11 **Kamajai** Panevėžys, NE Lithuania
118 H13 **Kamajai** Utena, E Lithuania
149 U9 **Kamālia** Punjab, NE Pakistan
83 I14 **Kamalondo** North Western, NW Zambia
136 I13 **Kaman** Kırşehir, C Turkey
79 O20 **Kamanyola** Sud Kivu, E Dem. Rep. Congo
141 N14 **Kamarān** *island* W Yemen
55 R9 **Kamarang** W Guyana
Kāmāreddi/Kamareddy *see* Rāmāreddi
Kama Reservoir *see* Kamskoye Vodokhranilishche
148 K13 **Kamarod** Baluchistān, SW Pakistan
171 P14 **Kamaru** Pulau Buton, C Indonesia
77 S13 **Kamba** Kebbi, NW Nigeria
Kambaeng Petch *see* Kamphaeng Phet
180 L12 **Kambalda** Western Australia
149 P13 **Kambar** *var.* Qambar. Sind, SE Pakistan
Kambara *see* Kabara
76 I14 **Kambia** W Sierra Leone
Kambos *see* Kámpos
79 N25 **Kambove** Katanga, SE Dem. Rep. Congo
Kambryk *see* Cambrai
123 V10 **Kamchatka** ≈ E Russian Federation
Kamchatka *see* Kamchatka, Poluostrov
Kamchatka Basin *see* Komandorskaya Basin
123 U10 **Kamchatka, Poluostrov** *Eng.* Kamchatka. *peninsula* E Russian Federation
123 V10 **Kamchatskaya Oblast'** ◆ *province* E Russian Federation
123 V10 **Kamchatskiy Zaliv** *gulf* E Russian Federation
114 N9 **Kamchiya** ≈ E Bulgaria
114 L9 **Kamchiya, Yazovir** ⊞ E Bulgaria
Kamdesh *see* Kāmdeysh
149 T4 **Kāmdeysh** *var.* Kamdesh. Kunar, E Afghanistan
118 M13 **Kamen'** *Rus.* Kamen'. Vitsyebskaya Voblasts', N Belarus
Kamenets *see* Kamyanyets
Kamenets-Podol'skaya Oblast' *see* Khmel'nyts'ka Oblast'
Kamenets-Podol'skiy *see* Kam''yanets'-Podil's'kyy
113 Q18 **Kamenica** NE FYR Macedonia
112 A11 **Kamenjak, Rt** *headland* NW Croatia
144 F8 **Kamenka** Zapadnyy Kazakhstan, NW Kazakhstan
125 O6 **Kamenka** Arkhangel'skaya Oblast', NW Russian Federation
126 O6 **Kamenka** Penzenskaya Oblast', W Russian Federation
127 L8 **Kamenka** Voronezhskaya Oblast', W Russian Federation
Kamenka *see* Camenca, Moldova
Kamenka *see* Kam''yanka, Ukraine
Kamenka-Bugskaya *see* Kam''yanka-Buz'ka
Kamenka Dneprovskaya *see* Kam''yanka-Dniprovs'ka
Kamen Kashirskiy *see* Kamin'-Kashyrs'kyy
1028 L15 **Kamennomostskiy** Respublika Adygeya, SW Russian Federation
126 L11 **Kamenolomni** Rostovskaya Oblast', SW Russian Federation
127 P8 **Kamenskiy** Saratovskaya Oblast', W Russian Federation
Kamenskoye *see* Dniprodzerzhyns'k
126 L11 **Kamensk-Shakhtinskiy** Rostovskaya Oblast', SW Russian Federation
101 P15 **Kamenz** Sachsen, E Germany
164 J13 **Kameoka** Kyōto, Honshū, SW Japan
126 M3 **Kameshkovo** Vladimirskaya Oblast', W Russian Federation
164 C11 **Kami-Agata** Nagasaki, Tsushima, SW Japan
33 N10 **Kamiah** Idaho, NW USA
Kamień Koszyrski *see* Kamin'-Kashyrs'kyy
110 H9 **Kamień Krajeński** *Ger.* Kamin in Westpreussen. Kujawsko-pomorskie, C Poland
111 F15 **Kamienna Góra** *Ger.* Landeshut, Landeshut in Schlesien. Dolnośląskie, SW Poland
110 D8 **Kamień Pomorski** *Ger.* Cammin in Pommern. Zachodnio-pomorskie, NW Poland
165 R5 **Kamiiso** Hokkaidō, NE Japan
79 L22 **Kamiji** Kasai Oriental, S Dem. Rep. Congo
165 T3 **Kamikawa** Hokkaidō, NE Japan
164 B15 **Kami-Koshiki-jima** *island* SW Japan
79 M23 **Kamina** Katanga, S Dem. Rep. Congo
Kamina *see* Kaintiba
42 C6 **Kaminaljuyú** *ruins* Guatemala, C Guatemala
Kamin in Westpreussen *see* Kamień Krajeński
116 J2 **Kamin'-Kashyrs'kyy** *Pol.* Kamień Koszyrski, *Rus.* Kamen Kashirskiy. Volyns'ka Oblast', NW Ukraine
165 Q5 **Kaminokuni** Hokkaidō, NE Japan
165 P10 **Kaminoyama** Yamagata, Honshū, C Japan
39 Q13 **Kamishak Bay** *bay* Alaska, USA
165 U4 **Kami-Shihoro** Hokkaidō, NE Japan
Kamishli *see* Al Qāmishlī
Kamissar *see* Kamsar
164 C11 **Kami-Tsushima** Nagasaki, Tsushima, SW Japan
79 O20 **Kamituga** Sud Kivu, E Dem. Rep. Congo
164 B17 **Kamiyaku** Kagoshima, Yaku-shima, SW Japan
11 N16 **Kamloops** British Columbia, SW Canada
107 G25 **Kamma** Sicilia, Italy, C Mediterranean Sea
192 K4 **Kammu Seamount** *undersea feature* N Pacific Ocean
109 U11 **Kamnik** *Ger.* Stein. C Slovenia
Kamniške Alpe *see* Kamniško-Savinjske Alpe
109 T10 **Kamniško-Savinjske Alpe** *var.* Kamniške Alpe, Sanntaler Alpen, *Ger.* Steiner Alpen. ▲ N Slovenia
165 O14 **Kamogawa** Chiba, Honshū, S Japan
149 W8 **Kāmoke** Punjab, E Pakistan
82 L13 **Kamoto** Eastern, E Zambia
109 V3 **Kamp** ≈ N Austria
81 F18 **Kampala** ● (Uganda) S Uganda
168 K11 **Kampar, Sungai** ≈ Sumatera, W Indonesia
98 L9 **Kampen** Overijssel, E Netherlands
79 N20 **Kampene** Maniema, E Dem. Rep. Congo
29 Q9 **Kampeska, Lake** ◎ South Dakota, N USA
167 O9 **Kamphaeng Phet** *var.* Kambaeng Petch. Kamphaeng Phet, W Thailand
Kampo *see* Campo, Cameroon
Kampo *see* Ntem, Cameroon/Equatorial Guinea
167 S12 **Kâmpóng Cham** *prev.* Kompong Cham. Kâmpóng Cham, C Cambodia
167 R12 **Kâmpóng Chhnăng** *prev.* Kompong. Kâmpóng Chhnăng, C Cambodia
167 R12 **Kâmpóng Khleăng** *prev.* Kompong Kleang. Siĕmréab, NW Cambodia
167 Q14 **Kâmpóng Saôm** *prev.* Kompong Som, Sihanoukville. Kâmpóng Saôm, SW Cambodia
167 R13 **Kâmpóng Spoe** *prev.* Kompong Speu. Kâmpóng Spœ, S Cambodia
121 O2 **Kámpos** *var.* Kambos. NW Cyprus
167 R14 **Kâmpôt** Kâmpôt, SW Cambodia
Kamptee *see* Kāmthi
77 O14 **Kampti** SW Burkina
Kampuchea *see* Cambodia
169 Q9 **Kampung Sirik** Sarawak, East Malaysia
11 V15 **Kamsack** Saskatchewan, S Canada
76 H13 **Kamsar** *var.* Kamissar. Guinée-Maritime, W Guinea
127 R4 **Kamskoye Ust'ye** Respublika Tatarstan, W Russian Federation
127 U14 **Kamskoye Vodokhranilishche** *var.* Kama Reservoir. ⊞ NW Russian Federation
154 I12 **Kāmthi** *prev.* Kamptee. Mahārāshtra, C India
Kamuela *see* Waimea
165 R3 **Kamuenai** Hokkaidō, NE Japan
165 T5 **Kamui-dake** ▲ Hokkaidō, NE Japan
165 R3 **Kamui-misaki** *headland* Hokkaidō, NE Japan
43 O15 **Kámuk, Cerro** ▲ SE Costa Rica
116 K7 **Kam''yanets'-Podil's'kyy** *Rus.* Kamenets-Podol'skiy. Khmel'nyts'ka Oblast', W Ukraine
117 Q6 **Kam''yanka** *Rus.* Kamenka. Cherkas'ka Oblast', C Ukraine
116 I5 **Kam''yanka-Buz'ka** *Rus.* Kamenka-Bugskaya. L'vivs'ka Oblast', NW Ukraine
117 T9 **Kam''yanka-Dniprovs'ka** *Rus.* Kamenka Dneprovskaya. Zaporiz'ka Oblast', SE Ukraine
119 F19 **Kamyanyets** *Rus.* Kamenets. Brestskaya Voblasts', SW Belarus
127 P9 **Kamyshin** Volgogradskaya Oblast', SW Russian Federation
127 Q13 **Kamyzyak** Astrakhanskaya Oblast', SW Russian Federation
12 K8 **Kanaaupscow** ≈ Québec, C Canada
36 K8 **Kanab** Utah, W USA
36 K9 **Kanab Creek** ≈ Arizona/Utah, SW USA
187 Y14 **Kanacea** *prev.* Kanathea. Taveuni, N Fiji
38 G17 **Kanaga Island** *island* Aleutian Islands, Alaska, USA
38 G17 **Kanaga Volcano** ▲ Kanaga Island, Alaska, USA
165 N14 **Kanagawa** *off.* Kanagawa-ken. ◆ *prefecture* Honshū, S Japan
13 Q8 **Kanairiktok** ≈ Newfoundland and Labrador, E Canada
Kanaky *see* New Caledonia
79 K22 **Kananga** *prev.* Luluabourg. Kasai Occidental, S Dem. Rep. Congo
Kananur *see* Cannanore
Kanara *see* Karnātaka
36 J7 **Kanarraville** Utah, W USA
127 Q4 **Kanash** Chuvashskaya Respublika, W Russian Federation
Kanathea *see* Kanacea
21 Q4 **Kanawha River** ≈ West Virginia, NE USA
164 L13 **Kanayama** Gifu, Honshū, SW Japan
164 L11 **Kanazawa** Ishikawa, Honshū, SW Japan
166 M4 **Kanbalu** Sagaing, C Burma
166 L8 **Kanbe** Yangon, SW Burma
167 O11 **Kanchanaburi** Kanchanaburi, W Thailand
Kānchenjunga *see* Kangchenjunga
145 V11 **Kanchingiz, Khrebet** ▲ E Kazakhstan
155 J19 **Kānchīpuram** *prev.* Conjeeveram. Tamil Nādu, SE India
149 N8 **Kandahār** *Per.* Qandahār. Kandahār, S Afghanistan
149 N9 **Kandahār** *Per.* Qandahār. ◆ *province* SE Afghanistan
Kandalakša *see* Kandalaksha
124 I5 **Kandalaksha** *var.* Kandalakša, *Fin.* Kantalahti. Murmanskaya Oblast', NW Russian Federation
Kandalaksha Gulf / Kandalakshskaya Guba *see* Kandalakshskiy Zaliv
126 K6 **Kandalakshskiy Zaliv** *var.* Kandalakshskaya Guba, *Eng.* Kandalaksha Gulf. *bay* NW Russian Federation
Kandalangodi *see* Kandalangoti
83 G17 **Kandalangoti** *var.* Kandalangodi. Ngamiland, NW Botswana
169 U13 **Kandangan** Borneo, C Indonesia
Kandau *see* Kandava
118 E8 **Kandava** *Ger.* Kandau. Tukums, W Latvia
Kandavu *see* Kadavu
77 R14 **Kandé** *var.* Kanté. NE Togo
101 F23 **Kandel** ▲ SW Germany
186 C7 **Kandep** Enga, W PNG
149 R12 **Kandh Kot** Sind, SE Pakistan
77 S13 **Kandi** N Benin
149 P14 **Kandiāro** Sind, SE Pakistan
136 F11 **Kandıra** Kocaeli, NW Turkey
183 S8 **Kandos** New South Wales, SE Australia
148 M16 **Kandrāch** *var.* Kanrach. Baluchistān, SW Pakistan
172 I4 **Kandreho** Mahajanga, C Madagascar
186 F7 **Kandrian** New Britain, E PNG
Kandukur *see* Kondukūr
155 K25 **Kandy** Central Province, C Sri Lanka
144 I10 **Kandyagash** *Kaz.* Qandyaghash; *prev.* Oktyabr'sk. Aktyubinsk, W Kazakhstan
18 D12 **Kane** Pennsylvania, NE USA
64 I11 **Kane Fracture Zone** *tectonic feature* NW Atlantic Ocean
Kaněka *see* Kanëvka
78 G9 **Kanem** *off.* Préfecture du Kanem. ◆ *prefecture* W Chad
38 D9 **Kāne'ohe** *var.* Kaneohe. O'ahu, Hawai'i, USA, C Pacific Ocean
Kanestron, Akrotírio *see* Palioúri, Akrotírio
Kanëv *see* Kaniv
124 M5 **Kanëvka** *var.* Kaněka. Murmanskaya Oblast', NW Russian Federation
126 K13 **Kanevskaya** Krasnodarskiy Kray, SW Russian Federation
Kanevskoye Vodokhranilishche *see* Kanivs'ke Vodoskhovyshche
165 P9 **Kaneyama** Yamagata, Honshū, C Japan
83 G20 **Kang** Kgalagadi, C Botswana
76 L13 **Kangaba** Koulikoro, SW Mali
136 M13 **Kangal** Sivas, C Turkey
143 O13 **Kangān** Būshehr, S Iran
143 S15 **Kangān** Hormozgān, SE Iran
168 J6 **Kangar** Perlis, Peninsular Malaysia
76 L13 **Kangaré** Sikasso, S Mali
182 F10 **Kangaroo Island** *island* South Australia
93 M17 **Kangasniemi** Itä-Suomi, E Finland
142 K6 **Kangāvar** *var.* Kangāwar. Kermānshāh, W Iran
Kangāwar *see* Kangāvar
153 S11 **Kangchenjunga** *var.* Kānchenjunga. ▲ NE India
160 G9 **Kangding** *var.* Lucheng, *Tib.* Dardo. Sichuan, C China
169 U16 **Kangean, Kepulauan** *island group* S Indonesia
169 T16 **Kangean, Pulau** *island* Kepulauan Kangean, S Indonesia
197 N14 **Kangerlussuaq** *Dan.* Sondre Strømfjord ✕ Kitaa, W Greenland
197 Q15 **Kangertittivaq** *Dan.* Scoresby Sund. *fjord* E Greenland
167 O2 **Kangfang** Kachin State, N Burma
163 X12 **Kanggye** N North Korea
197 P15 **Kangikajik** *var.* Kap Brewster. *headland* E Greenland
13 N5 **Kangiqsualujjuaq** *prev.* George River, Port-Nouveau-Quebec. Québec, E Canada
12 L2 **Kangiqsujuaq** *prev.* Maricourt, Wakeham Bay. Québec, NE Canada
12 M4 **Kangirsuk** *prev.* Bellin, Payne. Québec, E Canada
Kangle *see* Wanzai
158 J15 **Kangmar** Xizang Zizhiqu, W China
158 M16 **Kangmar** Xizang Zizhiqu, W China
163 Y14 **Kangnŭng** *Jap.* Kōryō. NE South Korea
79 D18 **Kango** Estuaire, NW Gabon
152 I7 **Kāngra** Himāchal Pradesh, NW India
153 Q16 **Kangsabati Reservoir** ⊞ N India
159 O17 **Kangto** ▲ China/India
159 W12 **Kangxian** *var.* Kang Xian, Zuitai, Zuitaizi. Gansu, C China
166 L4 **Kani** Sagaing, C Burma
76 M15 **Kani** NW Ivory Coast
79 M23 **Kaniama** Katanga, S Dem. Rep. Congo
Kanibadam *see* Konibodom
169 V6 **Kanibongan** Sabah, East Malaysia
185 F17 **Kaniere** West Coast, South Island, NZ
185 G17 **Kaniere, Lake** ◎ South Island, NZ
188 E17 **Kanifaay** Yap, W Micronesia
127 O4 **Kanin Kamen'** ▲ NW Russian Federation
125 N3 **Kanin Nos** Nenetskiy Avtonomnyy Okrug, NW Russian Federation
127 N3 **Kanin Nos, Mys** *headland* NW Russian Federation
127 O5 **Kanin, Poluostrov** *peninsula* NW Russian Federation
139 V8 **Kāni Sakht** E Iraq
139 T3 **Kāni Sulaymān** N Iraq
165 Q6 **Kanita** Aomori, Honshū, C Japan
117 Q5 **Kaniv** *Rus.* Kanëv. Cherkas'ka Oblast', C Ukraine
182 K11 **Kaniva** Victoria, SE Australia
117 Q5 **Kanivs'ke Vodoskhovyshche** *Rus.* Kanevskoye Vodokhranilishche. ⊞ C Ukraine
112 L8 **Kanjiža** *Ger.* Altkanischa, *Hung.* Magyarkanizsa, Ókanizsa; *prev.* Stara Kanjiža. Serbia, N Serbia and Montenegro (Yugo.)
93 K18 **Kankaanpää** Länsi-Suomi, W Finland
30 M12 **Kankakee** Illinois, N USA
31 O11 **Kankakee River** ≈ Illinois/Indiana, N USA
76 K14 **Kankan** Haute-Guinée, E Guinea
154 K13 **Kānker** Chhattīsgarh, C India
76 J10 **Kankossa** Assaba, S Mauritania
167 N12 **Kanmaw Kyun** *var.* Kisseraing, Kithareng. *island* Mergui Archipelago, S Burma
164 F12 **Kanmuri-yama** ▲ Kyūshū, SW Japan
21 R10 **Kannapolis** North Carolina, SE USA
93 L16 **Kannonkoski** Länsi-Suomi, W Finland
Kannur *see* Cannanore
93 K15 **Kannus** Länsi-Suomi, W Finland
77 V13 **Kano** Kano, N Nigeria
77 V13 **Kano** ◆ *state* N Nigeria
77 V13 **Kano** ✕ Kano, N Nigeria
164 G14 **Kan'onji** *var.* Kanonzi. Kagawa, Shikoku, SW Japan
Kanonzi *see* Kan'onji
26 M5 **Kanopolis Lake** ⊞ Kansas, C USA
36 K5 **Kanosh** Utah, W USA
169 R9 **Kanowit** Sarawak, East Malaysia
164 C16 **Kanoya** Kagoshima, Kyūshū, SW Japan
152 L13 **Kānpur** *Eng.* Cawnpore. Uttar Pradesh, N India
Kanrach *see* Kandrāch
164 I14 **Kansai** ✕ (Ōsaka) Ōsaka, Honshū, SW Japan
27 R9 **Kansas** Oklahoma, C USA
26 L5 **Kansas** *off.* State of Kansas; also known as Jayhawker State, Sunflower State. ◆ *state* C USA
27 R4 **Kansas City** Kansas, C USA
27 R4 **Kansas City** Missouri, C USA
27 R3 **Kansas City** ✕ Missouri, C USA
27 P4 **Kansas River** ≈ Kansas, C USA
122 L14 **Kansk** Krasnoyarskiy Kray, S Russian Federation
Kansu *see* Gansu
147 V7 **Kant** Chuyskaya Oblast', N Kyrgyzstan
Kantalahti *see* Kandalaksha
167 N16 **Kantang** *var.* Ban Kantang. Trang, SW Thailand
115 H25 **Kántanos** Kríti, Greece, E Mediterranean Sea
77 R12 **Kantchari** E Burkina
Kanté *see* Kandé
Kantemir *see* Cantemir
126 L9 **Kantemirovka** Voronezhskaya Oblast', W Russian Federation
167 R11 **Kantharalak** Si Sa Ket, E Thailand
Kantipur *see* Kathmandu
39 Q9 **Kantishna River** ≈ Alaska, USA
191 S3 **Kanton** *var.* Abariringa, Canton Island; *prev.* Mary Island. *atoll* Phoenix Islands, C Kiribati
97 C20 **Kanturk** *Ir.* Ceann Toirc. SW Ireland
55 T11 **Kanuku Mountains** ▲ S Guyana
165 O12 **Kanuma** Tochigi, Honshū, S Japan
83 H20 **Kanye** Southern, SE Botswana
83 H17 **Kanyu** Ngamiland, C Botswana
166 M7 **Kanyutkwin** Pegu, C Burma
79 M24 **Kanzenze** Katanga, SE Dem. Rep. Congo
193 Y15 **Kao** *island* Kotu Group, W Tonga
161 S14 **Kaohsiung** *var.* Gaoxiong, *Jap.* Takao, Takow. S Taiwan
161 S14 **Kaohsiung** ✕ S Taiwan
Kaokaona *see* Kirakira
83 B17 **Kaoko Veld** ▲ N Namibia
76 G11 **Kaolack** *var.* Kaolak. W Senegal
Kaolak *see* Kaolack
Kaolan *see* Lanzhou
186 M8 **Kaolo** San Jorge, N Solomon Islands
83 H14 **Kaoma** Western, W Zambia
38 B8 **Kapa'a** *var.* Kapaa. Kaua'i, Hawai'i, USA, C Pacific Ocean
113 J16 **Kapa Moračka** ▲ SW Serbia and Montenegro (Yugo.)
137 V13 **Kapan** *Rus.* Kafan; *prev.* Ghap'an. SE Armenia

82 L13 **Kapandashila** Northern, NE Zambia
79 L23 **Kapanga** Katanga, S Dem. Rep. Congo
145 U15 **Kapchagay** *Kaz.* Kapshaghay. Almaty, SE Kazakhstan
145 V15 **Kapchagayskoye Vodokhranilishche** *Kaz.* Qapshagay Böyeni. ⊡ SE Kazakhstan
99 F15 **Kapelle** Zeeland, SW Netherlands
99 G16 **Kapellen** Antwerpen, N Belgium
95 P15 **Kapellskär** Stockholm, C Sweden
81 H18 **Kapenguria** Rift Valley, W Kenya
109 V6 **Kapfenberg** Steiermark, C Austria
83 J14 **Kapiri Mposhi** Central, C Zambia
149 R4 **Kāpīsā** ◈ *province* E Afghanistan
12 G10 **Kapiskau** ~ Ontario, C Canada
184 K13 **Kapiti Island** *island* C NZ
78 K9 **Kapka, Massif du** ⛰ E Chad
Kaplamada *see* Kaubalatmada, Gunung
22 H9 **Kaplan** Louisiana, S USA
Kaplangky, Plato *see* Gaplañgyr Platosy
111 D19 **Kaplice** *Ger.* Kaplitz. Jihočeský Kraj, S Czech Republic
Kaplitz *see* Kaplice
Kapoche *see* Capoche
171 T12 **Kapocol** Papua, E Indonesia
167 N14 **Kapoe** Ranong, SW Thailand
Kapoeas *see* Kapuas, Sungai
81 G15 **Kapoeta** Eastern Equatoria, SE Sudan
111 I25 **Kapos** ~ S Hungary
111 H25 **Kaposvár** Somogy, SW Hungary
94 H13 **Kapp** Oppland, S Norway
100 I7 **Kappeln** Schleswig-Holstein, N Germany
Kaproncza *see* Koprivnica
109 P7 **Kaprun** Salzburg, C Austria
Kapshaghay *see* Kapchagay
Kapstad *see* Cape Town
Kapsukas *see* Marijampolė
171 Y13 **Kaptiau** Papua, E Indonesia
119 L19 **Kaptsevichy** *Rus.* Koptsevichi. Homyel'skaya Voblasts', SE Belarus
Kapuas Hulu, Banjaran/Kapuas Hulu, Pegunungan *see* Kapuas Mountains
169 S10 **Kapuas Mountains** *Ind.* Banjaran Kapuas Hulu, Pegunungan Kapuas Hulu. ⛰ Indonesia/Malaysia
169 P11 **Kapuas, Sungai** ~ Borneo, N Indonesia
169 T13 **Kapuas, Sungai** *prev.* Kapoeas. ~ Borneo, C Indonesia
182 J9 **Kapunda** South Australia
152 H8 **Kapūrthala** Punjab, N India
12 G12 **Kapuskasing** Ontario, S Canada
14 D6 **Kapuskasing** ~ Ontario, S Canada
127 P11 **Kapustin Yar** Astrakhanskaya Oblast', SW Russian Federation
82 K11 **Kaputa** Northern, NE Zambia
111 G22 **Kapuvár** Győr-Moson-Sopron, NW Hungary
Kapydzhik, Gora *see* Qazangödağ
119 J17 **Kapyl'** *Rus.* Kopyl'. Minskaya Voblasts', C Belarus
43 N9 **Kara** *var.* Cara. Región Autónoma Atlántico Sur, E Nicaragua
77 R14 **Kara** *var.* Lama-Kara. NE Togo
77 Q14 **Kara** ~ N Togo
144 L7 **Karabalyk** *Kaz.* Komsomol, Komsomolets. Kostanay, N Kazakhstan
147 U7 **Kara-Balta** Chuyskaya Oblast', N Kyrgyzstan
144 G11 **Karabau** Atyrau, W Kazakhstan
146 E7 **Karabaur', Uval** *Kaz.* Korabavur Pastligi, *Uzb.* Qorabowur Kirlari. *physical region* Kazakhstan/Uzbekistan
Karabekaul *see* Garabekewül
Karabil', Vozvyshennost' *see* Garabil Belentligi
Kara-Bogaz-Gol *see* Garabogazköl
Kara-Bogaz-Gol, Zaliv *see* Garabogaz Aylagy
145 R15 **Karaboget** *Kaz.* Qaraböget. Zhambyl, S Kazakhstan
136 H11 **Karabük** Karabük, NW Turkey
136 H11 **Karabük** ◈ *province* NW Turkey
122 L12 **Karabula** Krasnoyarskiy Kray, C Russian Federation
145 V14 **Karabulak** *Kaz.* Qarabulaq. Almaty, SE Kazakhstan
145 Y11 **Karabulak** *Kaz.* Qarabulaq. Vostochnyy Kazakhstan, E Kazakhstan
145 Q17 **Karabulak** *Kaz.* Qarabulaq. Yuzhnyy Kazakhstan, S Kazakhstan
136 C17 **Kara Burnu** *headland* SW Turkey
144 K10 **Karabutak** *Kaz.* Qarabutaq. Aktyubinsk, W Kazakhstan
136 D12 **Karacabey** Bursa, NW Turkey
114 O12 **Karacaköy** İstanbul, NW Turkey
114 M12 **Karacaoğlan** Kırklareli, NW Turkey
Karachay-Cherkessia *see* Karachayevo-Cherkesskaya Respublika
126 L15 **Karachayevo-Cherkesskaya Respublika** *Eng.* Karachay-Cherkessia. ◈ *autonomous republic* SW Russian Federation
126 M15 **Karachayevsk** Karachayevo-Cherkesskaya Respublika, SW Russian Federation
126 J6 **Karachev** Bryanskaya Oblast', W Russian Federation
149 O16 **Karāchi** Sind, SE Pakistan
149 O16 **Karāchi** ✕ Sind, S Pakistan
Karácsonkő *see* Piatra-Neamț
155 E15 **Karād** Mahārāshtra, W India
136 H16 **Karadağ** ▲ S Turkey
147 T10 **Karadar'ya** *Uzb.* Qoradaryo. ~ Kyrgyzstan/Uzbekistan
Karadeniz *see* Black Sea
Karadeniz Boğazı *see* İstanbul Boğazı
146 B13 **Karadepe** Balkan Welaýaty, W Turkmenistan
Karadzhar *see* Qorajar
Karaferiye *see* Véroia
Karagan *see* Garagan
145 R10 **Karaganda** *Kaz.* Qaraghandy. Karaganda, C Kazakhstan
145 R10 **Karaganda** *off.* Karagandinskaya Oblast', *Kaz.* Qaraghandy Oblysy. ◈ *province* C Kazakhstan
Karagandinskaya Oblast' *see* Karaganda
145 T10 **Karagayly** *Kaz.* Qaraghayly. Karaganda, C Kazakhstan
Karagel' *see* Garagöl
123 U9 **Karaginskiy, Ostrov** *island* E Russian Federation
197 T1 **Karaginskiy Zaliv** *bay* E Russian Federation
137 P13 **Karagöl Dağları** ⛰ NE Turkey
114 L13 **Karahisar** Edirne, NW Turkey
127 V3 **Karaidel'** Respublika Bashkortostan, W Russian Federation
127 V3 **Karaidel'skiy** Respublika Bashkortostan, W Russian Federation
114 L13 **Karaidemir Barajı** ⊡ NW Turkey
155 J21 **Kāraikāl** Pondicherry, SE India
155 I22 **Kāraikkudi** Tamil Nādu, SE India
145 Y11 **Kara Irtysh** *Rus.* Chërnyy Irtysh. ~ NE Kazakhstan
143 N5 **Karaj** Tehrān, N Iran
168 K8 **Karak** Pahang, Peninsular Malaysia
Karak *see* Al Karak
147 T11 **Kara-Kabak** Oshskaya Oblast', SW Kyrgyzstan
Kara-Kala *see* Garrygala
Karakala *see* Oqqal'a
Karakalpakstan, Respublika *see* Qoraqalpog'iston Respublikasi
Karakalpakya *see* Qoraqalpog'iston
Karakax *see* Moyu
158 G10 **Karakax He** ~ NW China
121 X8 **Karakaya Barajı** ⊡ C Turkey
171 Q9 **Karakelang, Pulau** *island* N Indonesia
Karakılısse *see* Ağrı
Karak, Muḩāfaẓat al *see* Al Karak
Kara-Köl *see* Kara-Kul'
147 Y7 **Karakol** *prev.* Przheval'sk. Issyk-Kul'skaya Oblast', NE Kyrgyzstan
147 X8 **Karakol** *var.* Karakolka. Issyk-Kul'skaya Oblast', NE Kyrgyzstan
Karakolka *see* Karakol
149 W2 **Karakoram Highway** *road* China/Pakistan
149 Z3 **Karakoram Pass** *Chin.* Karakoram Shankou. *pass* C Asia
152 I3 **Karakoram Range** ⛰ C Asia
Karakoram Shankou *see* Karakoram Pass
Karaköse *see* Ağrı
145 P14 **Karakoyyn, Ozero** *Kaz.* Qaraqoyyn. ◎ C Kazakhstan
83 F19 **Karakubis** Ghanzi, W Botswana
147 T9 **Kara-Kul'** *Kir.* Kara-Köl. Dzhalal-Abadskaya Oblast', W Kyrgyzstan
Karakul' *see* Qarokŭl, Tajikistan
Karakul' *see* Qorako'l, Uzbekistan
147 U10 **Kara-Kul'dzha** Oshskaya Oblast', SW Kyrgyzstan
127 T3 **Karakulino** Udmurtskaya Respublika, NW Russian Federation
Karakul', Ozero *see* Qarokŭl
Kara Kum *see* Garagum
Kara Kum Canal/Karakumskiy Kanal *see* Garagum Kanaly
Karakumy, Peski *see* Garagum
83 E17 **Karakuwisa** Okavango, NE Namibia
122 M13 **Karam** Irkutskaya Oblast', S Russian Federation
Karamai *see* Karamay
169 T14 **Karamain, Pulau** *island* N Indonesia
136 I16 **Karaman** Karaman, S Turkey
136 H16 **Karaman** ◈ *province* S Turkey
114 M8 **Karamandere** ~ NE Bulgaria
158 J4 **Karamay** *var.* Karamai, Kelamayi, *prev. Chin.* K'o-la-ma-i. Xinjiang Uygur Zizhiqu, NW China
169 U14 **Karambu** Borneo, N Indonesia
185 H14 **Karamea** West Coast, South Island, NZ
185 H14 **Karamea** ~ South Island, NZ
185 G15 **Karamea Bight** *gulf* South Island, NZ
Karamet-Niyaz *see* Garamätnyýaz
158 K10 **Karamiran He** ~ NW China
147 S11 **Karamyk** Oshskaya Oblast', SW Kyrgyzstan
169 U17 **Karangasem** Bali, S Indonesia
154 H12 **Kāranja** Mahārāshtra, C India
Karanpur *see* Karanpura
152 F9 **Karanpura** *var.* Karanpur. Rājasthān, NW India
Karánsebes/Karansebesch *see* Caransebeș
145 T14 **Karaoy** *Kaz.* Qaraoy. Almaty, SE Kazakhstan
114 N7 **Karapelit** *Rom.* Stejarul. Dobrich, NE Bulgaria
136 I15 **Karapınar** Konya, C Turkey
83 D22 **Karas** ◈ *district* S Namibia
147 Y8 **Kara-Say** Issyk-Kul'skaya Oblast', NE Kyrgyzstan
83 E22 **Karasburg** Karas, S Namibia
Kara Sea *see* Karskoye More
92 K9 **Kárášjohka** *var.* Karašjoka. ~ N Norway
92 L9 **Karasjok** *Fin.* Kaarasjoki, *Lap.* Kárášjohka. Finnmark, N Norway
Karašjokka *see* Kárášjohka
Kara Strait *see* Karskiye Vorota, Proliv
Kara Su *see* Mesta/Néstos
145 N8 **Karasu** *Kaz.* Qarasū. Kostanay, N Kazakhstan
136 F11 **Karasu** Sakarya, NW Turkey
Karasubazar *see* Bilohirs'k
122 I12 **Karasuk** Novosibirskaya Oblast', C Russian Federation
145 U13 **Karatal** *Kaz.* Qaratal. ~ SE Kazakhstan
136 K17 **Karataş** Adana, S Turkey
145 Q16 **Karatau** *Kaz.* Qaratau. Zhambyl, S Kazakhstan
Karatau *see* Karatau, Khrebet
145 P16 **Karatau, Khrebet** *var.* Karatau, *Kaz.* Qaratau. ⛰ S Kazakhstan
144 G13 **Karaton** *Kaz.* Qaraton. Atyrau, W Kazakhstan
164 C13 **Karatsu** *var.* Karatu. Saga, Kyūshū, SW Japan
Karatu *see* Karatsu
122 K8 **Karaul** Taymyrskiy (Dolgano-Nenetskiy) Avtonomnyy Okrug, N Russian Federation
Karaulbazar *see* Qorovulbozor
Karauzyak *see* Qorao'zak
115 D16 **Karáva** ▲ C Greece
Karavanke *see* Karawanken
115 F22 **Karavás** Kýthira, S Greece
113 J20 **Karavastasë, Laguna e** *var.* Kënet' e Karavastas, Kravasta Lagoon. *lagoon* W Albania
Karavastas, Kënet' e *see* Karavastasë, Laguna e
118 I5 **Karavere** Tartumaa, E Estonia
115 L23 **Karavonísia** *island* Kykládes, Greece, Aegean Sea
169 O15 **Karawang** *prev.* Krawang. Jawa, C Indonesia
109 T10 **Karawanken** *Slvn.* Karavanke. ⛰ Austria/Serbia and Montenegro (Yugo.)
Karaxahar *see* Kaidu He
137 R13 **Karayazı** Erzurum, NE Turkey
145 Q12 **Karazhal** Karaganda, C Kazakhstan
139 S9 **Karbalā'** *var.* Kerbala, Kerbela. S Iraq
94 L11 **Kårböle** Gävleborg, C Sweden
111 M23 **Karcag** Jász-Nagykun-Szolnok, E Hungary
Kardak *see* Imia
114 N7 **Kardam** Dobrich, NE Bulgaria
115 M22 **Kardámaina** Kos, Dodekánisos, Greece, Aegean Sea
Kardamila *see* Kardámyla
115 L18 **Kardámyla** *var.* Kardamila, Kardhámila. Chíos, E Greece
Kardeljevo *see* Ploče
Kardh *see* Qardho
Kardhámila *see* Kardámyla
Kardhítsa *see* Kardítsa
115 E16 **Kardítsa** *var.* Kardhítsa. Thessalía, C Greece
118 E4 **Kärdla** *Ger.* Kertel. Hiiumaa, W Estonia
Karelia *see* Kareliya, Respublika
119 I16 **Karelichy** *Pol.* Korelicze, *Rus.* Korelichi. Hrodzyenskaya Voblasts', W Belarus
126 I10 **Kareliya, Respublika** *prev.* Karel'skaya ASSR, *Eng.* Karelia. ◈ *autonomous republic* NW Russian Federation
Karel'skaya ASSR *see* Kareliya, Respublika
81 E22 **Karema** Rukwa, W Tanzania
Karen *see* Hualien
83 I14 **Karenda** Central, C Zambia
167 N8 **Karen State** *var.* Kawthule State, Kayin State. ◈ *state* S Burma
92 J10 **Karesuando** *Fin.* Kaaresuanto, *Lapp.* Gárasavvon. Norrbotten, N Sweden
Karet *see* Kâgheț
Kareyz-e-Elyās/Kārez Iliās *see* Kārīz-e Elyās
122 J11 **Kargasok** Tomskaya Oblast', C Russian Federation
122 I12 **Kargat** Novosibirskaya Oblast', C Russian Federation
136 J11 **Kargı** Çorum, N Turkey
152 I5 **Kargil** Jammu and Kashmir, NW India
Kargilik *see* Yecheng
124 L11 **Kargopol'** Arkhangel'skaya Oblast', NW Russian Federation
110 F12 **Kargowa** *Ger.* Unruhstadt. Lubuskie, W Poland
77 X13 **Kari** Bauchi, E Nigeria
83 J15 **Kariba** Mashonaland West, N Zimbabwe
83 J16 **Kariba, Lake** ⊡ Zambia/Zimbabwe
165 Q4 **Kariba-yama** ▲ Hokkaidō, NE Japan
83 C19 **Karibib** Erongo, C Namibia
92 L9 **Karigasniemi** *Lapp.* Garegegasnjárga. Lappi, N Finland
184 J2 **Karikari, Cape** *headland* North Island, NZ
Karīmābād *see* Hunza
169 P12 **Karimata, Kepulauan** *island group* N Indonesia
169 P12 **Karimata, Pulau** *island* Kepulauan Karimata, N Indonesia
169 O11 **Karimata, Selat** *strait* W Indonesia
155 I14 **Karīmnagar** Andhra Pradesh, C India
186 C7 **Karimui** Chimbu, C PNG
169 Q15 **Karimunjawa, Pulau** *island* S Indonesia
80 N12 **Karin** Woqooyi Galbeed, N Somalia
Kariot *see* Ikaría
93 L20 **Karis** *Fin.* Karjaa. Etelä-Suomi, SW Finland
Káristos *see* Kárystos
148 J4 **Kārīz-e Elyās** *var.* Kareyz-e-Elyās, Kārez Iliās. Herāt, NW Afghanistan
Karjaa *see* Karis
145 T10 **Karkaralinsk** *Kaz.* Qarqaraly. Karaganda, E Kazakhstan
186 D6 **Karkar Island** *island* N PNG
143 N7 **Karkas, Kūh-e** ▲ C Iran
142 K8 **Karkheh, Rūd-e** ~ SW Iran
115 L20 **Karkinágrio** Ikaría, Dodekánisos, Greece, Aegean Sea
117 R12 **Karkinits'ka Zatoka** *Rus.* Karkinitskiy Zaliv. *gulf* S Ukraine
Karkinitskiy Zaliv *see* Karkinits'ka Zatoka
93 L19 **Karkkila** *Swe.* Högfors. Etelä-Suomi, S Finland
93 M19 **Kärkölä** Etelä-Suomi, S Finland
182 G9 **Karkoo** South Australia
Karkūk *see* Kirkūk
118 D5 **Kärla** *Ger.* Kergel. Saaremaa, W Estonia
Karleby *see* Kokkola
110 F7 **Karlino** *Ger.* Körlin an der Persante. Zachodnio-pomorskie, NW Poland
137 Q13 **Karlıova** Bingöl, E Turkey
117 U6 **Karlivka** Poltavs'ka Oblast', C Ukraine
Karl-Marx-Stadt *see* Chemnitz
Karlö *see* Hailuoto
112 C11 **Karlobag** *It.* Carlopago. Lika-Senj, W Croatia
112 D9 **Karlovac** *Ger.* Karlstadt, *Hung.* Károlyváros. Karlovac, C Croatia
112 C10 **Karlovac** *off.* Karlovačka Županija. ◈ *province* C Croatia
Karlovačka Županija *see* Karlovac
111 A16 **Karlovarský Kraj** ◈ W Czech Republic
114 J9 **Karlovo** *prev.* Levskigrad. Plovdiv, C Bulgaria
111 A16 **Karlovy Vary** *Ger.* Karlsbad; *prev. Eng.* Carlsbad. Karlovarský Kraj, W Czech Republic
Karlsbad *see* Karlovy Vary
95 L17 **Karlsborg** Västra Götaland, S Sweden
Karlsburg *see* Alba Iulia
95 L22 **Karlshamn** Blekinge, S Sweden
95 L16 **Karlskoga** Örebro, C Sweden
95 M22 **Karlskrona** Blekinge, S Sweden
101 G21 **Karlsruhe** *var.* Carlsruhe. Baden-Württemberg, SW Germany
95 K16 **Karlstad** Värmland, C Sweden
29 R3 **Karlstad** Minnesota, N USA
101 I18 **Karlstadt** Bayern, C Germany
Karlstadt *see* Karlovac
39 Q14 **Karluk** Kodiak Island, Alaska, USA
Karluk *see* Qarluq
119 O17 **Karma** *Rus.* Korma. Homyel'skaya Voblasts', SE Belarus
155 F14 **Karmāla** Mahārāshtra, W India
146 M11 **Karmana** Navoiy Viloyati, C Uzbekistan
138 G8 **Karmi'él** *var.* Carmiel. Northern, N Israel
95 B16 **Karmøy** *island* S Norway
152 I9 **Karnāl** Haryāna, N India
153 W15 **Karnaphuli Reservoir** ⊡ NE India
155 F17 **Karnātaka** *var.* Kanara; *prev.* Maisur, Mysore. ◈ *state* W India
25 S13 **Karnes City** Texas, SW USA
109 P9 **Karnische Alpen** *It.* Alpi Carniche. ⛰ Austria/Italy
114 M9 **Karnobat** Burgas, E Bulgaria
109 Q9 **Kärnten** *off.* Land Kärnten, *Eng.* Carinthia, *Slvn.* Koroška. ◈ *state* S Austria
Karnul *see* Kurnool
83 K16 **Karoi** Mashonaland West, N Zimbabwe
Karol *see* Carei
Károly-Fehérvár *see* Alba Iulia
Károlyváros *see* Karlovac
82 M12 **Karonga** Northern, N Malawi
147 W10 **Karool-Tëbë** Narynskaya Oblast', C Kyrgyzstan
182 J9 **Karoonda** South Australia
149 S9 **Karor Lāl Esan** Punjab, E Pakistan
149 T11 **Karor Pacca** *var.* Kahror, Kahror Pakka. Punjab, E Pakistan
171 N12 **Karosa** Sulawesi, C Indonesia
Karpaten *see* Carpathian Mountains
115 L22 **Karpáthio Pélagos** *sea* Dodekánisos, Greece, Aegean Sea
115 N24 **Kárpathos** Kárpathos, SE Greece
115 N24 **Kárpathos** *It.* Scarpanto; *anc.* Carpathos, Carpathus. *island* SE Greece
Karpathos Strait *see* Karpathou, Stenó
115 N24 **Karpathou, Stenó** *var.* Karpathos Strait, Scarpanto Strait. *strait* Dodekánisos, Greece, Aegean Sea
Karpaty *see* Carpathian Mountains
115 E17 **Karpenísi** *prev.* Karpenísion. Stereá Ellás, C Greece
Karpenísion *see* Karpenísi
Karpilovka *see* Aktsyabrski
125 O8 **Karpogory** Arkhangel'skaya Oblast', NW Russian Federation
180 I7 **Karratha** Western Australia
137 S12 **Kars** *var.* Qars. Kars, NE Turkey
137 S12 **Kars** *var.* Qars. ◈ *province* NE Turkey
145 O12 **Karsakpay** *Kaz.* Qarsaqbay. Karaganda, C Kazakhstan
93 L15 **Kärsämäki** Oulu, C Finland
Karsau *see* Kārsava
118 K9 **Kārsava** *Ger.* Karsau; *prev. Rus.* Korsovka. Ludza, E Latvia
Karshi Turkmenistan *see* Garşy
Karshi Uzbekistan *see* Qarshi
Karshinskaya Step *see* Qarshi Cho'li
Karshinskiy Kanal *see* Qarshi Kanali
122 H7 **Karskiye Vorota, Proliv** *Eng.* Kara Strait. *strait* N Russian Federation
122 J6 **Karskoye More** *Eng.* Kara Sea. *sea* Arctic Ocean
93 L17 **Karstula** Länsi-Suomi, W Finland
127 Q5 **Karsun** Ul'yanovskaya Oblast', W Russian Federation
122 F11 **Kartaly** Chelyabinskaya Oblast', C Russian Federation
18 E13 **Karthaus** Pennsylvania, NE USA
110 I7 **Kartuzy** Pomorskie, NW Poland
165 R8 **Karumai** Iwate, Honshū, C Japan
181 U4 **Karumba** Queensland, NE Australia
142 L10 **Kārūn** *var.* Rūd-e Kārūn. ~ SW Iran
92 K13 **Karungi** Norrbotten, N Sweden
92 K13 **Karunki** Lappi, N Finland
Kārūn, Rūd-e *see* Kārūn
155 H21 **Karūr** Tamil Nādu, SE India
93 K17 **Karvia** Länsi-Suomi, W Finland
111 J17 **Karviná** *Ger.* Karwin, *Pol.* Karwina; *prev.* Nová Karvinná. Moravskoslezský Kraj, E Czech Republic
155 E17 **Kārwār** Karnātaka, W India
108 M7 **Karwendelgebirge** ⛰ Austria/Germany
Karwin/Karwina *see* Karviná
115 I14 **Karyés** *var.* Karies. Ágion Óros, N Greece
115 I19 **Kárystos** *var.* Káristos. Évvoia, C Greece
136 E17 **Kaş** Antalya, SW Turkey
39 Y14 **Kasaan** Prince of Wales Island, Alaska, USA
164 I13 **Kasai** Hyōgo, Honshū, SW Japan
79 K21 **Kasai** *var.* Cassai, Kassai. ~ Angola/Dem. Rep. Congo
79 K22 **Kasai Occidental** *off.* Région Kasai Occidental. ◈ *region* S Dem. Rep. Congo
79 L21 **Kasai Oriental** *off.* Région Kasai Oriental. ◈ *region* C Dem. Rep. Congo
79 L24 **Kasaji** Katanga, S Dem. Rep. Congo
82 L12 **Kasama** Northern, N Zambia
Kasan *see* Koson
83 H16 **Kasane** Chobe, NE Botswana
81 E23 **Kasanga** Rukwa, W Tanzania
79 G21 **Kasangulu** Bas-Congo, W Dem. Rep. Congo
Kasansay *see* Kosonsoy
Kasargen *see* Kasari
155 E20 **Kāsaragod** Kerala, SW India
118 P13 **Kasari** *var.* Kasari Jõgi, *Ger.* Kasargen. ~ W Estonia
Kasari Jõgi *see* Kasari
8 L11 **Kasba Lake** ◎ Northwest Territories/Nunavut, N Canada
Kaschau *see* Košice
164 B16 **Kaseda** Kagoshima, Kyūshū, SW Japan
83 I14 **Kasempa** North Western, NW Zambia
79 O24 **Kasenga** Katanga, SE Dem. Rep. Congo
79 P17 **Kasenye** *var.* Kasenyi. Orientale, NE Dem. Rep. Congo
Kasenyi *see* Kasenye
81 E18 **Kasese** SW Uganda
79 O19 **Kasese** Maniema, E Dem. Rep. Congo
152 J11 **Kāsganj** Uttar Pradesh, N India
143 U4 **Kashaf Rūd** ~ NE Iran
143 N7 **Kāshān** Eşfahān, C Iran
126 M10 **Kashary** Rostovskaya Oblast', SW Russian Federation
39 O12 **Kashegelok** Alaska, USA
Kashgar *see* Kashi
158 E7 **Kashi** *Chin.* Kaxgar, K'o-shih, *Uigh.* Kashgar. Xinjiang Uygur Zizhiqu, NW China
164 J14 **Kashihara** *var.* Kasihara. Nara, Honshū, SW Japan
165 P13 **Kashima-nada** *gulf* S Japan
124 K15 **Kashin** Tverskaya Oblast', W Russian Federation
152 K10 **Kāshīpur** Uttaranchal, N India
126 L4 **Kashira** Moskovskaya Oblast', W Russian Federation
165 N11 **Kashiwazaki** *var.* Kasiwazaki. Niigata, Honshū, C Japan
Kashkadar'inskaya Oblast' *see* Qashqadaryo Viloyati
143 T5 **Kāshmar** *var.* Turshiz; *prev.* Solṭānābād, Torshiz. Khorāsān, NE Iran
Kashmir *see* Jammu and Kashmir
149 R12 **Kashmor** Sind, SE Pakistan
149 S5 **Kashmūnḍ Ghar** *Eng.* Kashmund Range. ⛰ E Afghanistan
Kashmund Range *see* Kashmūnḍ Ghar
Kasi *see* Vārānasi
153 O12 **Kasia** Uttar Pradesh, N India
39 N12 **Kasigluk** Alaska, USA
Kasihara *see* Kashihara
39 R12 **Kasilof** Alaska, USA
Kasima *see* Kashima
Kasimköj *see* General Toshevo
126 M4 **Kasimov** Ryazanskaya Oblast', W Russian Federation
79 P18 **Kasindi** Nord Kivu, E Dem. Rep. Congo
82 M12 **Kasitu** ~ N Malawi
Kasiwa *see* Kashiwa
Kasiwazaki *see* Kashiwazaki
30 L14 **Kaskaskia River** ~ Illinois, N USA
93 J17 **Kaskinen** *Swe.* Kaskö. Länsi-Suomi, W Finland
Kaskö *see* Kaskinen
Kas Kong *see* Kŏng, Kaôh
11 O17 **Kaslo** British Columbia, SW Canada
Käsmark *see* Kežmarok
169 T12 **Kasongan** Borneo, C Indonesia
79 N21 **Kasongo** Maniema, E Dem. Rep. Congo
79 H22 **Kasongo-Lunda** Bandundu, SW Dem. Rep. Congo
115 M24 **Kásos** *island* S Greece
Kasos Strait *see* Kasou, Stenó
115 M25 **Kasou, Stenó** *var.* Kasos Strait. *strait* Dodekánisos /Kríti, Greece, Aegean Sea
137 T10 **Kaspi** C Georgia
114 M8 **Kaspichan** Shumen, NE Bulgaria
Kaspiy Mangy Oypaty *see* Caspian Depression
127 Q16 **Kaspiysk** Respublika Dagestan, SW Russian Federation
Kaspiyskiy *see* Lagan'
Kaspiyskoye More/Kaspiy Tengizi *see* Caspian Sea
Kassa *see* Košice
Kassai *see* Kasai
80 I9 **Kassala** Kassala, E Sudan
80 H9 **Kassala** ◈ *state* NE Sudan
115 G15 **Kassándra** *prev.* Pallíni; *anc.* Pallene. *peninsula* NE Greece
115 G15 **Kassándras, Akrotírio** *headland* N Greece
115 H15 **Kassándras, Kólpos** *var.* Kólpos Toronaíos. *gulf* N Greece
139 Y11 **Kassārah** E Iraq
101 I15 **Kassel** *prev.* Cassel. Hessen, C Germany
74 M6 **Kasserine** *var.* Al Qaşrayn. W Tunisia
14 J14 **Kasshabog Lake** ◎ Ontario, SE Canada
139 O5 **Kassīr, Sabkhat al** ◎ E Syria
29 W10 **Kasson** Minnesota, N USA
115 C17 **Kassópi** *site of ancient city* Ípeiros, W Greece
115 N24 **Kastállou, Akrotírio** *headland* Kárpathos, SE Greece
136 I11 **Kastamonu** *var.* Castamoni, Kastamuni. Kastamonu, N Turkey
136 I10 **Kastamonu** *var.* Kastamuni. ◈ *province* N Turkey
Kastamuni *see* Kastamonu
115 E14 **Kastaneá** Kentrikí Makedonía, N Greece
115 H24 **Kastélli** Kríti, Greece, E Mediterranean Sea
Kastellórizon *see* Megísti
95 N21 **Kastlösa** Kalmar, S Sweden
115 D14 **Kastoría** Dytikí Makedonía, N Greece
126 K7 **Kastornoye** Kurskaya Oblast', W Russian Federation
115 I21 **Kástro** Sífnos, Kykládes, Greece, Aegean Sea
95 J23 **Kastrup** ✕ (København) København, E Denmark
119 Q17 **Kastsyukovichy** *Rus.* Kostyukovichi. Mahilyowskaya Voblasts', E Belarus
119 O18 **Kastsyukowka** *Rus.* Kostyukovka. Homyel'skaya Voblasts', SE Belarus
164 D13 **Kasuga** Fukuoka, Kyūshū, SW Japan
164 L13 **Kasugai** Aichi, Honshū, SW Japan
81 E21 **Kasulu** Kigoma, W Tanzania
164 I12 **Kasumi** Hyōgo, Honshū, SW Japan
127 R17 **Kasumkent** Respublika Dagestan, SW Russian Federation
82 M13 **Kasungu** Central, C Malawi
149 W9 **Kasūr** Punjab, E Pakistan
83 G15 **Kataba** Western, W Zambia
19 R4 **Katahdin, Mount** ▲ Maine, NE USA
79 M20 **Katako-Kombe** Kasai Oriental, C Dem. Rep. Congo
39 T12 **Katalla** Alaska, USA
Katana *see* Qaṭanā
79 L24 **Katanga** *off.* Région du Katanga; *prev.* Shaba. ◈ *region* SE Dem. Rep. Congo
122 M11 **Katanga** ~ C Russian Federation
154 J11 **Katangi** Madhya Pradesh, C India
180 J13 **Katanning** Western Australia
189 P8 **Kata Tjuta** *var.* Mount Olga ▲ Northern Territory, C Australia
Katawaz *see* Zarghūn Shahr
151 Q22 **Katchall Island** *island* Nicobar Islands, India, NE Indian Ocean
115 F14 **Kateríni** Kentrikí Makedonía, N Greece
117 P7 **Kateryno pil'** Cherkas'ka Oblast', C Ukraine

◆ Country ● Country Capital ◇ Dependent Territory ○ Dependent Territory Capital ◈ Administrative Region ✕ International Airport ▲ Mountain ⛰ Mountain Range Volcano ~ River ◎ Lake ⊡ Reservoir

166 M3 **Katha** Sagaing, N Burma
181 P2 **Katherine** Northern Territory, N Australia
154 B11 **Kāthiāwār Peninsula** peninsula W India
153 P11 **Kathmandu** prev. Kantipur. ● (Nepal) Central, C Nepal
152 H7 **Kathua** Jammu and Kashmir, NW India
76 L12 **Kati** Koulikoro, SW Mali
153 R13 **Katihār** Bihār, NE India
184 N7 **Katikati** Bay of Plenty, North Island, NZ
83 H16 **Katima Mulilo** Caprivi, NE Namibia
77 N15 **Katiola** C Ivory Coast
191 V10 **Katiu** atoll Îles Tuamotu, C French Polynesia
117 N12 **Katlabukh, Ozero** ◎ SW Ukraine
39 P14 **Katmai, Mount** ▲ Alaska, USA
154 J9 **Katni** Madhya Pradesh, C India
115 D19 **Káto Achaïa** var. Kato Ahaia, Káto Akhaïa. Dytikí Ellás, S Greece
Kato Ahaia/Káto Akhaïa see Káto Achaïa
121 P2 **Kato Lakatámeia** var. Kato Lakatamia. C Cyprus
Kato Lakatamia see Kato Lakatámeia
79 N22 **Katompi** Katanga, SE Dem. Rep. Congo
83 K14 **Katondwe** Lusaka, C Zambia
114 H12 **Káto Nevrokópi** prev. Káto Nevrokópion. Anatolikí Makedonía kai Thráki, NE Greece
Káto Nevrokópion see Káto Nevrokópi
81 E18 **Katonga** ≈ S Uganda
115 F15 **Káto Ólympos** ▲▲ C Greece
115 D17 **Katoúna** Dytikí Ellás, C Greece
115 E19 **Káto Vlasiá** Dytikí Makedonía, S Greece
111 J16 **Katowice** Ger. Kattowitz. Śląskie, S Poland
153 S15 **Kātoya** West Bengal, NE India
136 E16 **Katrançık Dağı** ▲▲ SW Turkey
95 N16 **Katrineholm** Södermanland, C Sweden
96 I11 **Katrine, Loch** ◎ C Scotland, UK
77 V12 **Katsina** Katsina, N Nigeria
77 U12 **Katsina** ◈ state N Nigeria
164 C13 **Katsumoto** Nagasaki, Iki, SW Japan
165 P13 **Katsuta** var. Katuta. Ibaraki, Honshū, S Japan
165 O14 **Katsuura** var. Katuura. Chiba, Honshū, S Japan
164 K12 **Katsuyama** var. Katuyama. Fukui, Honshū, SW Japan
164 H12 **Katsuyama** Okayama, Honshū, SW Japan
Kattakurgan see Kattaqo'rg'on
147 N11 **Kattaqo'rg'on** Rus. Kattakurgan. Samarqand Viloyati, C Uzbekistan
115 O23 **Kattavía** Ródos, Dodekánisos, Greece, Aegean Sea
95 I21 **Kattegat** Dan. Kattegatt. strait N Europe
Kattegatt see Kattegat
95 P19 **Katthammarsvik** Gotland, SE Sweden
Kattowitz see Katowice
122 J13 **Katun'** ≈ S Russian Federation
Katuta see Katsuta
Katuura see Katsuura
Katuyama see Katsuyama
Katwijk see Katwijk aan Zee
98 G11 **Katwijk aan Zee** var. Katwijk. Zuid-Holland, W Netherlands
38 B8 **Kaua‘i** var. Kauai. island Hawaiian Islands, Hawai‘i, USA, C Pacific Ocean
38 C8 **Kaua‘i Channel** var. Kauai Channel. channel Hawai‘i, USA, C Pacific Ocean
171 R13 **Kaubalatmada, Gunung** var. Kaplamada. ▲ Pulau Buru, E Indonesia
191 U10 **Kauehi** atoll Îles Tuamotu, C French Polynesia
Kauen see Kaunas
101 K24 **Kaufbeuren** Bayern, S Germany
25 U7 **Kaufman** Texas, SW USA
101 I15 **Kaufungen** Hessen, C Germany
93 K17 **Kauhajoki** Länsi-Suomi, W Finland
93 K16 **Kauhava** Länsi-Suomi, W Finland
30 M7 **Kaukauna** Wisconsin, N USA
92 L11 **Kaukonen** Lappi, N Finland
38 A8 **Kaulakahi Channel** channel Hawai‘i, USA, C Pacific Ocean
38 E9 **Kaunakakai** Moloka‘i, Hawai‘i, USA, C Pacific Ocean
38 F12 **Kaunā Point** var. Kauna Point. headland Hawai‘i, USA, C Pacific Ocean
118 F13 **Kaunas** Ger. Kauen, Pol. Kowno; prev. Rus. Kovno. Kaunas, C Lithuania
118 F13 **Kaunas** ◈ province C Lithuania
186 C6 **Kaup** East Sepik, NW PNG
77 U12 **Kaura Namoda** Zamfara, NW Nigeria
Kaushany see Căuşeni
93 K16 **Kaustinen** Länsi-Suomi, W Finland
99 M23 **Kautenbach** Diekirch, NE Luxembourg
92 K10 **Kautokeino** Lap. Guovdageaidnu. Finnmark, N Norway
Kavadar see Kavadarci
113 P19 **Kavadarci** Turk. Kavadar. C FYR Macedonia
Kavaja see Kavajë
113 K20 **Kavajë** It. Cavaia, Kavaja. Tiranë, W Albania
114 M13 **Kavak Çayı** ≈ NW Turkey
Kavakli see Topolovgrad
114 I13 **Kavála** prev. Kaválla. Anatolikí Makedonía kai Thráki, NE Greece
114 I13 **Kaválas, Kólpos** gulf Aegean Sea, NE Mediterranean Sea
155 J17 **Kāvali** Andhra Pradesh, E India
Kaválla see Kavála
Kavango see Cubango/Okavango
155 C21 **Kavaratti** Lakshadweep, SW India
114 O8 **Kavarna** Dobrich, NE Bulgaria
118 G12 **Kavarskas** Utena, E Lithuania
76 I13 **Kavendou** ▲ C Guinea
Kavengo see Cubango/Okavango
155 F20 **Kāveri** var. Cauvery. ≈ S India
186 G5 **Kavieng** var. Kaewieng. NE PNG
83 H16 **Kavimba** Chobe, NE Botswana
83 I15 **Kavingu** Southern, S Zambia
143 Q6 **Kavīr, Dasht-e** var. Great Salt Desert. salt pan N Iran
Kavirondo Gulf see Winam Gulf
Kavkaz see Caucasus
95 K23 **Kävlinge** Skåne, S Sweden
82 G12 **Kavungo** Moxico, E Angola
165 Q8 **Kawabe** Akita, Honshū, C Japan
165 R9 **Kawai** Iwate, Honshū, C Japan
38 A8 **Kawaihoa Point** headland Ni‘ihau, Hawai‘i, USA, C Pacific Ocean
184 K3 **Kawakawa** Northland, North Island, NZ
82 I13 **Kawama** North Western, NW Zambia
82 K11 **Kawambwa** Luapula, N Zambia
154 K11 **Kawardha** Chhattīsgarh, C India
14 I14 **Kawartha Lakes** ◎ Ontario, SE Canada
165 O13 **Kawasaki** Kanagawa, Honshū, S Japan
171 R12 **Kawassi** Pulau Obi, E Indonesia
165 R6 **Kawauchi** Aomori, Honshū, C Japan
184 L5 **Kawau Island** island N NZ
184 N10 **Kaweka Range** ▲▲ North Island, NZ
Kawelecht see Puhja
184 O8 **Kawerau** Bay of Plenty, North Island, NZ
184 L8 **Kawhia** Waikato, North Island, NZ
184 K8 **Kawhia Harbour** inlet North Island, NZ
35 V8 **Kawich Peak** ▲ Nevada, W USA
35 V9 **Kawich Range** ▲▲ Nevada, W USA
14 G12 **Kawigamog Lake** ◎ Ontario, S Canada
171 P9 **Kawio, Kepulauan** island group N Indonesia
167 N9 **Kawkareik** Karen State, S Burma
27 O8 **Kaw Lake** ⊟ Oklahoma, C USA
166 M3 **Kawlin** Sagaing, N Burma
Kawm Umbū see Kôm Ombo
Kawthule State see Karen State
Kaxgar see Kashi
158 D7 **Kaxgar He** ≈ NW China
158 J5 **Kax He** ≈ NW China
77 P12 **Kaya** C Burkina
167 N6 **Kayah State** ◈ state C Burma
39 T12 **Kayak Island** island Alaska, USA
114 M11 **Kayalıköy Barajı** ⊟ NW Turkey
155 G23 **Kāyamkulam** Kerala, SW India
166 M8 **Kayan** Yangon, SW Burma
169 V9 **Kayan, Sungai** prev. Kajan. ≈ Borneo, C Indonesia
144 F14 **Kaydak, Sor** salt flat SW Kazakhstan
Kaydanovo see Dzyarzhynsk
37 N9 **Kayenta** Arizona, SW USA
76 J11 **Kayes** Kayes, W Mali
76 J11 **Kayes** ◈ region SW Mali
Kayin State see Karen State
145 U10 **Kaynar** var. Kajnar. Vostochnyy Kazakhstan, E Kazakhstan
Kaynary see Căinari
83 H15 **Kayoya** Western, W Zambia
Kayrakkum see Qayroqqum
Kayrakkumskoye Vodokhranilishche see Qayroqqum, Obanbori
136 K14 **Kayseri** var. Kaisaria; anc. Caesarea Mazaca, Mazaca. Kayseri, C Turkey
136 K14 **Kayseri** var. Kaisaria. ◈ province C Turkey
36 L2 **Kaysville** Utah, W USA
Kayyngdy see Kaindy
14 L11 **Kazabazua** Québec, SE Canada
14 L12 **Kazabazua** ≈ Québec, SE Canada
123 Q7 **Kazach'ye** Respublika Sakha (Yakutiya), NE Russian Federation
Kazakdar'ya see Qozoqdaryo
146 E9 **Kazakhlyshor, Solonchak** var. Solonchak Shorkazakhly. salt marsh NW Turkmenistan
Kazakhskaya SSR/Kazakh Soviet Socialist Republic see Kazakhstan
145 R9 **Kazakhskiy Melkosopochnik** Eng. Kazakh Uplands, Kirghiz Steppe, Kaz. Saryarqa. uplands C Kazakhstan
144 L12 **Kazakhstan** off. Republic of Kazakhstan, var. Kazakstan, Kaz. Qazaqstan, Qazaqstan Respublikasy; prev. Kazakh Soviet Socialist Republic, Rus. Kazakhskaya SSR. ◆ republic C Asia
Kazakh Uplands see Kazakhskiy Melkosopochnik
Kazakstan see Kazakhstan
144 L14 **Kazalinsk** Kzylorda, S Kazakhstan
127 R4 **Kazan'** Respublika Tatarstan, W Russian Federation
127 R4 **Kazan'** ✕ Respublika Tatarstan, W Russian Federation
8 M10 **Kazan** ≈ Nunavut, NW Canada
Kazandzhik see Bereket
117 R8 **Kazanka** Mykolayivs'ka Oblast', S Ukraine
Kazanketken see Qozonketkan
Kazanlik see Kazanlŭk
114 J9 **Kazanlŭk** prev. Kazanlik. Stara Zagora, C Bulgaria
165 Y16 **Kazan-rettō** Eng. Volcano Islands. island group SE Japan
117 V12 **Kazantip, Mys** headland S Ukraine
147 U9 **Kazarman** Narynskaya Oblast', C Kyrgyzstan
Kazatin see Kozyatyn
Kazbegi see Kazbek
Kazbegi see Qazbegi
137 T9 **Kazbek** var. Kazbegi, Geor. Mqinvartsveri. ▲ N Georgia
82 M13 **Kazembe** Eastern, NE Zambia
143 N11 **Kāzerūn** Fārs, S Iran
125 R12 **Kazhym** Respublika Komi, NW Russian Federation
Kazi Ahmad see Qāzi Ahmad
Kazi Magomed see Qazimämmäd
136 H16 **Kâzımkarabekir** Karaman, S Turkey
111 M20 **Kazincbarcika** Borsod-Abaúj-Zemplén, NE Hungary
119 H17 **Kazlowshchyna** Pol. Kozlowszczyzna, Rus. Kozlovshchina. Hrodzyenskaya Voblasts', W Belarus
119 E14 **Kazlų Rūda** Marijampolė, S Lithuania
144 E9 **Kaztalovka** Zapadnyy Kazakhstan, W Kazakhstan
79 K22 **Kazumba** Kasai Occidental, S Dem. Rep. Congo
165 Q8 **Kazuno** Akita, Honshū, C Japan
Kazvin see Qazvīn
118 J12 **Kaz'yany** Rus. Koz'yany. Vitsyebskaya Voblasts', NW Belarus
122 H9 **Kazym** ≈ N Russian Federation
110 H10 **Kcynia** Ger. Exin. Kujawsko-pomorskie, C Poland
115 I20 **Kéa** Kéa, Kykládes, Greece, Aegean Sea
115 I20 **Kéa** prev. Kéos, anc. Ceos. island Kykládes, Greece, Aegean Sea
38 H11 **Kea‘au** var. Keaau. Hawai‘i, USA, C Pacific Ocean
38 F11 **Keāhole Point** var. Keahole Point. headland Hawai‘i, USA, C Pacific Ocean
38 G12 **Kealakekua** Hawai‘i, USA, C Pacific Ocean
38 H11 **Kea, Mauna** ▲ Hawai‘i, USA, C Pacific Ocean
37 N10 **Keams** Arizona, SW USA
Kéamu see Aneityum
29 O16 **Kearney** Nebraska, C USA
36 L3 **Kearns** Utah, W USA
115 H20 **Kéas, Stenó** strait SE Greece
137 O14 **Keban Barajı** dam C Turkey
137 O14 **Keban Barajı** ⊟ C Turkey
77 S13 **Kebbi** ◈ state NW Nigeria
76 G10 **Kébémèr** NW Senegal
74 M7 **Kebili** var. Qibilī. C Tunisia
138 H4 **Kebīr, Nahr el** ≈ NW Syria
80 A10 **Kebkabiya** Northern Darfur, W Sudan
92 I11 **Kebnekaise** ▲ N Sweden
81 M14 **K'ebrī Dehar** Somali, E Ethiopia
148 K15 **Kech** ≈ SW Pakistan
10 K10 **Kechika** ≈ British Columbia, W Canada
111 K23 **Kecskemét** Bács-Kiskun, C Hungary
168 J6 **Kedah** ◈ state Peninsular Malaysia
118 F12 **Kėdainiai** Kaunas, C Lithuania
Kedder see Kehra
13 N13 **Kedgwick** New Brunswick, SE Canada
169 R16 **Kediri** Jawa, C Indonesia
171 Y13 **Kedir Sarmi** Papua, E Indonesia
163 V7 **Kedong** Heilongjiang, NE China
76 I12 **Kédougou** SE Senegal
122 I11 **Kedrovyy** Tomskaya Oblast', C Russian Federation
111 H16 **Kędzierzyn-Koźle** Ger. Heydebrech. Opolskie, S Poland
8 H8 **Keele** ≈ Northwest Territories, NW Canada
10 K6 **Keele Peak** ▲ Yukon Territory, NW Canada
Keelung see Chilung
19 N10 **Keene** New Hampshire, NE USA
99 H17 **Keerbergen** Vlaams Brabant, C Belgium
83 E21 **Keetmanshoop** Karas, S Namibia
12 A11 **Keewatin** Ontario, S Canada
29 V4 **Keewatin** Minnesota, N USA
115 B18 **Kefallinía** var. Kefallonía. island Iónioi Nísoi, Greece, C Mediterranean Sea
Kefallonía see Kefallinía
115 M22 **Kéfalos** Kos, Dodekánisos, Greece, Aegean Sea
171 Q17 **Kefamenanu** Timor, C Indonesia
138 F10 **Kefar Sava** var. Kfar Saba. Central, C Israel
Kefe see Feodosiya
77 V15 **Keffi** Nassarawa, C Nigeria
92 H4 **Keflavík** ✕ (Reykjavík) Reykjanes, W Iceland
92 H4 **Keflavík** Reykjanes, W Iceland
Kegalee see Kegalla
155 J25 **Kegalla** var. Kegalee, Kegalle. Sabaragamuwa Province, C Sri Lanka
Kegalle see Kegalla
Kegayli see Kegeyli
Kegel see Keila
145 W16 **Kegen** Almaty, SE Kazakhstan
146 H7 **Kegeyli** var. Kegayli. Qoraqalpog'iston Respublikasi, W Uzbekistan
101 F22 **Kehl** Baden-Württemberg, SW Germany
118 H3 **Kehra** Ger. Kedder. Harjumaa, NW Estonia
117 U6 **Kehychivka** Kharkivs'ka Oblast', E Ukraine
97 L17 **Keighley** N England, UK
Kei Islands see Kai, Kepulauan
Keijō see Sŏul
118 G3 **Keila** Ger. Kegel. Harjumaa, NW Estonia
Keilberg see Klínovec
83 F23 **Keimoes** Northern Cape, W South Africa
Keina/Keinis see Kāina
Keishū see Kyŏngju
77 T11 **Keïta** Tahoua, C Niger
78 J12 **Kéïta, Bahr** var. Doka. ≈ S Chad
182 K10 **Keith** South Australia
96 K8 **Keith** NE Scotland, UK
26 K3 **Keith Sebelius Lake** ⊟ Kansas, C USA
32 G11 **Keizer** Oregon, NW USA
38 A8 **Kekaha** Kaua‘i, Hawai‘i, USA, C Pacific Ocean
147 U10 **Këk-Art** prev. Alaykel', Alay-Kuu. Oshskaya Oblast', SW Kyrgyzstan
147 W10 **Këk-Aygyr** var. Keyaygyr. Narynskaya Oblast', C Kyrgyzstan
147 V9 **Këk-Dzhar** Narynskaya Oblast', C Kyrgyzstan
14 L8 **Kekek** ≈ Québec, SE Canada
185 K15 **Kekerengu** Canterbury, South Island, NZ
111 L21 **Kékes** ▲ N Hungary
171 P17 **Kekneno, Gunung** ▲ Timor, S Indonesia
147 S9 **Këk-Tash** Kir. Kök-Tash. Dzhalal-Abadskaya Oblast', W Kyrgyzstan
81 M15 **K'elafo** Somali, E Ethiopia
169 U10 **Kelai, Sungai** ≈ Borneo, N Indonesia
Kelamayi see Karamay
Kelang see Klang
168 K7 **Kelantan** ◈ state Peninsular Malaysia
Kelantan see Kelantan, Sungai
168 K7 **Kelantan, Sungai** var. Kelantan. ≈ Peninsular Malaysia
Kelat see Kālat
Kelcyra see Këlcyrë
113 L22 **Këlcyrë** var. Kelcyra. Gjirokastër, S Albania
Kelifskiy Uzboy see Kelif Uzboýy
146 L14 **Kelif Uzboýy** Rus. Kelifskiy Uzboy. salt marsh E Turkmenistan
137 O12 **Kelkit** Gümüşhane, NE Turkey
136 M12 **Kelkit Çayı** ≈ N Turkey
77 W11 **Kellé** Zinder, S Niger
79 G18 **Kéllé** Cuvette, W Congo
145 P7 **Kellerovka** Severnyy Kazakhstan, N Kazakhstan
8 I5 **Kellett, Cape** headland Banks Island, Northwest Territories, NW Canada
31 S11 **Kelleys Island** island Ohio, N USA
33 N8 **Kellogg** Idaho, NW USA
92 M12 **Kelloselkä** Lappi, N Finland
97 F17 **Kells** Ir. Ceanannas. E Ireland
118 E12 **Kelmė** Šiauliai, C Lithuania
99 M19 **Kelmis** var. La Calamine. Liège, E Belgium
78 H12 **Kélo** Tandjilé, SW Chad
83 I14 **Kelongwa** North Western, NW Zambia
11 N17 **Kelowna** British Columbia, SW Canada
11 X12 **Kelsey** Manitoba, C Canada
34 M6 **Kelseyville** California, W USA
96 K13 **Kelso** SE Scotland, UK
32 G10 **Kelso** Washington, NW USA
195 W15 **Keltie, Cape** headland Antarctica
Keltsy see Kielce
168 L9 **Keluang** var. Kluang. Johor, Peninsular Malaysia
168 M11 **Kelume** Pulau Lingga, W Indonesia
11 U15 **Kelvington** Saskatchewan, S Canada
124 J7 **Kem'** Respublika Kareliya, NW Russian Federation
126 I7 **Kem'** ≈ NW Russian Federation
137 O13 **Kemah** Erzincan, E Turkey
137 N13 **Kemaliye** Erzincan, C Turkey
Kemaman see Cukai
Kemanlar see Isperikh
10 K14 **Kemano** British Columbia, SW Canada
Kemarat see Khemmarat
171 P12 **Kembani** Pulau Peleng, N Indonesia
136 F17 **Kemer** Antalya, SW Turkey
122 J12 **Kemerovo** prev. Shcheglovsk. Kemerovskaya Oblast', C Russian Federation
122 K12 **Kemerovskaya Oblast'** ◈ province S Russian Federation
92 L13 **Kemi** Lappi, NW Finland
92 M12 **Kemijärvi** Swe. Kemiträsk. Lappi, N Finland
92 M12 **Kemijärvi** ◎ N Finland
92 L13 **Kemijoki** ≈ NW Finland
147 V7 **Kemin** prev. Bystrovka. Chuyskaya Oblast', N Kyrgyzstan
92 L13 **Keminmaa** Lappi, NW Finland
Kemins Island see Nikumaroro
Kemiö see Kimito
Kemiträsk see Kemijärvi
127 P5 **Kemlya** Respublika Mordoviya, W Russian Federation
99 B18 **Kemmel** West-Vlaanderen, W Belgium
33 S16 **Kemmerer** Wyoming, C USA
Kemmuna see Comino
79 I14 **Kémo** ◈ prefecture S Central African Republic
25 U7 **Kemp** Texas, SW USA
93 L14 **Kempele** Oulu, C Finland
101 D15 **Kempen** Nordrhein-Westfalen, W Germany
25 Q5 **Kemp, Lake** ◎ Texas, SW USA
195 W5 **Kemp Land** physical region Antarctica
25 S9 **Kempner** Texas, SW USA
44 H3 **Kemp's Bay** Andros Island, W Bahamas
183 U6 **Kempsey** New South Wales, SE Australia
101 J24 **Kempten** Bayern, S Germany
15 N9 **Kempt, Lac** ◎ Québec, SE Canada
183 P17 **Kempton** Tasmania, SE Australia
154 J9 **Ken** ≈ C India
39 R12 **Kenai** Alaska, USA
39 R12 **Kenai Peninsula** peninsula Alaska, USA
21 V11 **Kenansville** North Carolina, SE USA
146 A10 **Kenar** prev. Rus. Ufra. Balkan Welaýaty, NW Turkmenistan
121 U13 **Kenâyis, Râs el** headland N Egypt
97 K16 **Kendal** NW England, UK
23 Y16 **Kendall** Florida, SE USA
9 O8 **Kendall, Cape** headland Nunavut, E Canada
18 J15 **Kendall Park** New Jersey, NE USA
31 Q11 **Kendallville** Indiana, N USA
171 P14 **Kendari** Sulawesi, C Indonesia
169 Q13 **Kendawangan** Borneo, C Indonesia
154 O12 **Kendrāpāra** var. Kendrāparha. Orissa, E India
Kendrāparha see Kendrāpāra
154 O11 **Kendujhargarh** prev. Keonjihargarh. Orissa, E India
25 S13 **Kenedy** Texas, SW USA
Kënekesir see Könekesir
76 J15 **Kenema** SE Sierra Leone
29 P16 **Kenesaw** Nebraska, C USA
Këneurgench see Köneürgenç
79 H21 **Kenge** Bandundu, SW Dem. Rep. Congo
Kengen see Kangen
167 O5 **Keng Tung** var. Kentung. Shan State, E Burma
83 F23 **Kenhardt** Northern Cape, W South Africa
76 J12 **Kéniéba** Kayes, W Mali
Kenimekh see Konimex
169 U7 **Keningau** Sabah, East Malaysia
74 F6 **Kénitra** prev. Port-Lyautey. NW Morocco
21 V9 **Kenly** North Carolina, SE USA
97 B21 **Kenmare** Ir. Neidín. S Ireland
28 L2 **Kenmare** North Dakota, N USA
97 A21 **Kenmare River** Ir. An Ribhéar. inlet NE Atlantic Ocean
18 D10 **Kenmore** New York, NE USA
25 W8 **Kennard** Texas, SW USA
29 N10 **Kennebec** South Dakota, N USA
19 Q7 **Kennebec River** ≈ Maine, NE USA
19 P9 **Kennebunk** Maine, NE USA
39 R13 **Kennedy Entrance** strait Alaska, USA
166 L3 **Kennedy Peak** ▲ W Burma
22 K9 **Kenner** Louisiana, S USA
180 I8 **Kenneth Range** ▲▲ Western Australia
27 Y9 **Kennett** Missouri, C USA
18 I16 **Kennett Square** Pennsylvania, NE USA
32 K10 **Kennewick** Washington, NW USA
12 E11 **Kenogami** ≈ Ontario, S Canada
15 Q7 **Kénogami, Lac** ◎ Québec, SE Canada
14 G8 **Kenogami Lake** Ontario, S Canada
14 F7 **Kenogamissi Lake** ◎ Ontario, S Canada
10 I6 **Keno Hill** Yukon Territory, NW Canada
12 A11 **Kenora** Ontario, S Canada
31 N9 **Kenosha** Wisconsin, N USA
13 P14 **Kensington** Prince Edward Island, SE Canada
26 L3 **Kensington** Kansas, C USA
32 I11 **Kent** Oregon, NW USA
24 J9 **Kent** Texas, SW USA
32 H8 **Kent** Washington, NW USA
97 P22 **Kent** cultural region SE England, UK
145 P16 **Kentau** Yuzhnyy Kazakhstan, S Kazakhstan
183 P14 **Kent Group** island group Tasmania, SE Australia
31 N12 **Kentland** Indiana, N USA
31 R12 **Kenton** Ohio, N USA
8 K7 **Kent Peninsula** peninsula Nunavut, N Canada
115 F14 **Kentrikí Makedonía** Eng. Macedonia Central. ◈ region N Greece
20 J6 **Kentucky** off. Commonwealth of Kentucky; also known as The Bluegrass State. ◈ state C USA
20 H8 **Kentucky Lake** ⊟ Kentucky/Tennessee, S USA
Kentung see Keng Tung
13 P15 **Kentville** Nova Scotia, SE Canada
22 K8 **Kentwood** Louisiana, S USA
31 P9 **Kentwood** Michigan, N USA
81 H17 **Kenya** off. Republic of Kenya. ◆ republic E Africa
Kenya, Mount see Kirinyaga
168 L7 **Kenyir, Tasik** var. Tasek Kenyir. ◎ Peninsular Malaysia
29 W10 **Kenyon** Minnesota, N USA
29 Y16 **Keokuk** Iowa, C USA
Keonjihargarh see Kendujhargarh
Kéos see Kéa
29 X16 **Keosauqua** Iowa, C USA
29 X15 **Keota** Iowa, C USA
21 O11 **Keowee, Lake** ⊟ South Carolina, SE USA
124 I7 **Kepa** var. Kepe. Respublika Kareliya, NW Russian Federation
Kepe see Kepa
189 O13 **Kepirohi Falls** waterfall Pohnpei, E Micronesia
185 B22 **Kepler Mountains** ▲▲ South Island, NZ
111 I14 **Kępno** Wielkopolskie, C Poland
65 C24 **Keppel Island** island N Falkland Islands
Keppel Island see Niuatoputapu
65 C23 **Keppel Sound** sound N Falkland Islands
136 D12 **Kepsut** Balıkesir, NW Turkey
168 M11 **Kepulauan Riau** off. Propinsi Kepulauan Riau. ◈ province NW Indonesia
171 V13 **Kerai** Papua, E Indonesia
Kerak see Al Karak
155 F22 **Kerala** ◈ state S India
165 R16 **Kerama-rettō** island group SW Japan
183 N10 **Kerang** Victoria, SE Australia
Kerasunt see Giresun
115 H19 **Keratéa** var. Keratea. Attikí, C Greece
93 M19 **Kerava** Swe. Kervo. Etelä-Suomi, S Finland
Kerbala/Kerbela see Karbalā'
32 F15 **Kerby** Oregon, NW USA
117 W12 **Kerch** Rus. Kerch'. Respublika Krym, SE Ukraine
Kerchens'ka Protska/Kerchenskiy Proliv see Kerch Strait
117 V13 **Kerchens'kyy Pivostriv** peninsula S Ukraine
121 V4 **Kerch Strait** var. Bosporus Cimmerius, Enikale Strait, Rus. Kerchenskiy Proliv, Ukr. Kerchens'ka Protska. strait Black Sea/Sea of Azov
152 K8 **Kerdārnāth** Uttaranchal, N India
Kerdilio see Kerdýlio
114 H13 **Kerdýlio** var. Kerdilio. ▲ N Greece
186 D8 **Kerema** Gulf, S PNG
Keremitlik see Lyulyakovo
136 I9 **Kerempe Burnu** headland N Turkey
80 J9 **Keren** var. Cheren. C Eritrea
25 U7 **Kerens** Texas, SW USA
184 M6 **Kerepehi** Waikato, North Island, NZ
145 P10 **Kerey, Ozero** ◎ C Kazakhstan
Kergel see Kärla
173 Q12 **Kerguelen** island C French Southern and Antarctic Territories
173 Q13 **Kerguelen Plateau** undersea feature S Indian Ocean
115 C20 **Kerí** Zákynthos, Iónioi Nísoi, Greece, C Mediterranean Sea
81 H19 **Kericho** Rift Valley, W Kenya
184 K2 **Kerikeri** Northland, North Island, NZ
93 O17 **Kerimäki** Isä-Suomi, E Finland
168 K12 **Kerinci, Gunung** ▲ Sumatera, W Indonesia
Keriya see Yutian
158 H9 **Keriya He** ≈ NW China
98 J9 **Kerkbuurt** Noord-Holland, C Netherlands
98 J13 **Kerkdriel** Gelderland, C Netherlands
75 N6 **Kerkenah, Îles de** var. Kerkenna Islands, Ar. Juzur Qarqannah. island group E Tunisia
Kerkenna Islands see Kerkenah, Îles de
115 M20 **Kerketévs** ▲ Sámos, Dodekánisos, Greece, Aegean Sea
29 T8 **Kerkhoven** Minnesota, N USA
Kerki see Atamyrat
Kerkichi see Kerkiçi
146 M14 **Kerkiçi** Rus. Kerkichi. Lebap Welaýaty, E Turkmenistan
115 F16 **Kerkíneo** prehistoric site Thessalía, C Greece
114 G12 **Kerkinitis, Límni** ◎ N Greece
Kérkira see Kérkyra
99 M18 **Kerkrade** Limburg, SE Netherlands
Kerkuk see Kirkūk
115 B16 **Kérkyra** ✕ Kérkyra, Iónioi Nísoi, Greece, C Mediterranean Sea
115 B16 **Kérkyra** var. Kérkira, Eng. Corfu. Kérkyra, Iónioi Nísoi, Greece, C Mediterranean Sea
115 A16 **Kérkyra** var. Kérkira, Eng. Corfu. island Iónioi Nísoi, Greece, C Mediterranean Sea
192 K10 **Kermadec Islands** island group NZ, SW Pacific Ocean
192 L11 **Kermadec Trench** undersea feature SW Pacific Ocean
143 S10 **Kermān** var. Kirman; anc. Carmana. Kermān, C Iran
143 R11 **Kermān** off. Ostān-e Kermān, var. Kirman; anc. Carmania. ◈ province SE Iran
143 U12 **Kermān, Bīābān-e** var. Kerman Desert. desert SE Iran
142 K6 **Kermānshāh** var. Qahremānshahr, prev. Bākhtarān. Kermānshāh, W Iran
143 Q9 **Kermānshāh** Yazd, C Iran
142 J6 **Kermānshāh** off. Ostān-e Kermānshāh; prev. Bākhtarān, Kermānshāhān. ◈ province W Iran
Kermānshāhān see Kermānshāh
114 L10 **Kermen** Sliven, C Bulgaria
24 L8 **Kermit** Texas, SW USA
21 P6 **Kermit** West Virginia, NE USA
21 S9 **Kernersville** North Carolina, SE USA

◆ Country
● Country Capital
◇ Dependent Territory
○ Dependent Territory Capital
◈ Administrative Region
✕ International Airport
▲ Mountain
▲▲ Mountain Range
Volcano
≈ River
◎ Lake
⊟ Reservoir

35 S12 **Kern River** ≈ California, W USA
35 S12 **Kernville** California, W USA
115 K21 **Kéros** *island* Kykládes, Greece, Aegean Sea
76 K14 **Kérouané** Haute-Guinée, SE Guinea
101 D16 **Kerpen** Nordrhein-Westfalen, W Germany
146 I11 **Kerpichli** Lebap Welaýaty, NE Turkmenistan
24 M1 **Kerrick** Texas, SW USA
Kerr Lake *see* John H.Kerr Reservoir
11 S15 **Kerrobert** Saskatchewan, S Canada
25 Q11 **Kerrville** Texas, SW USA
97 B20 **Kerry** *Ir.* Ciarraí. *cultural region* SW Ireland
21 S11 **Kershaw** South Carolina, SE USA
Kertel *see* Kärdla
95 H23 **Kerteminde** Fyn, C Denmark
163 Q7 **Kerulen** *Chin.* Herlen He, *Mong.* Herlen Gol. ≈ China/Mongolia
Kervo *see* Kerava
Kerýneia *see* Girne
12 H11 **Kesagami Lake** ◎ Ontario, SE Canada
93 O17 **Kesälahti** Itä-Suomi, E Finland
136 B11 **Keşan** Edirne, NW Turkey
165 R9 **Kesennuma** Miyagi, Honshū, C Japan
163 V7 **Keshan** Heilongjiang, NE China
30 M6 **Keshena** Wisconsin, N USA
136 I13 **Keskin** Kırıkkale, C Turkey
Késmárk *see* Kežmarok
124 I6 **Kesten'ga** *var.* Kest Enga. Respublika Kareliya, NW Russian Federation
98 K12 **Kesteren** Gelderland, C Netherlands
14 H14 **Keswick** Ontario, S Canada
97 K15 **Keswick** NW England, UK
111 H24 **Keszthely** Zala, SW Hungary
122 K11 **Ket'** ≈ C Russian Federation
77 R17 **Keta** SE Ghana
169 Q12 **Ketapang** Borneo, C Indonesia
127 O12 **Ketchenery** *prev.* Sovetskoye. Respublika Kalmykiya, SW Russian Federation
39 Y14 **Ketchikan** Revillagigedo Island, Alaska, USA
33 O14 **Ketchum** Idaho, NW USA
Kete/Kete Krakye *see* Kete-Krachi
77 Q15 **Kete-Krachi** *var.* Kete, Kete Krakye. E Ghana
98 L9 **Ketelmeer** *channel* E Netherlands
149 P17 **Keti Bandar** Sind, SE Pakistan
145 W16 **Ketmen', Khrebet** ⛰ SE Kazakhstan
77 S16 **Kétou** SE Benin
110 M7 **Kętrzyn** *Ger.* Rastenburg. Warmińsko-Mazurskie, NE Poland,
97 N20 **Kettering** C England, UK
31 R14 **Kettering** Ohio, N USA
18 F13 **Kettle Creek** ≈ Pennsylvania, NE USA
32 L7 **Kettle Falls** Washington, NW USA
14 D16 **Kettle Point** *headland* Ontario, S Canada
29 V6 **Kettle River** ≈ Minnesota, N USA
186 B7 **Ketu** ≈ W PNG
18 G10 **Keuka Lake** ◎ New York, NE USA
Keupriya *see* Primorsko
93 L17 **Keuruu** Länsi-Suomi, W Finland
Kevevára *see* Kovin
92 L9 **Kevo** *Lapp.* Geavvú. Lappi, N Finland
44 M6 **Kew** North Caicos, N Turks and Caicos Islands
30 K11 **Kewanee** Illinois, N USA
31 N7 **Kewaunee** Wisconsin, N USA
30 M3 **Keweenaw Bay** ◎ Michigan, N USA
31 N2 **Keweenaw Peninsula** *peninsula* Michigan, N USA
31 N2 **Keweenaw Point** *headland* Michigan, N USA
29 N12 **Keya Paha River** ≈ Nebraska/South Dakota, N USA
Keyaygyr *see* Këk-Aygyr
23 Z16 **Key Biscayne** Florida, SE USA
26 G8 **Keyes** Oklahoma, C USA
23 Y17 **Key Largo** Key Largo, Florida, SE USA
21 U3 **Keyser** West Virginia, NE USA
27 O9 **Keystone Lake** ▣ Oklahoma, C USA
36 L16 **Keystone Peak** ▲ Arizona, SW USA
Keystone State *see* Pennsylvania
21 U7 **Keysville** Virginia, NE USA
27 T3 **Keytesville** Missouri, C USA
23 W17 **Key West** Florida Keys, Florida, SE USA
127 T1 **Kez** Udmurtskaya Respublika, NW Russian Federation
Kezdivásárhely *see* Târgu Secuiesc
122 M12 **Kezhma** Krasnoyarskiy Kray, C Russian Federation
111 L18 **Kežmarok** *Ger.* Käsmark, *Hung.* Késmárk. Prešovský Kraj, E Slovakia
Kfar Saba *see* Kefar Sava
83 F20 **Kgalagadi** ◈ *district* SW Botswana
83 I20 **Kgatleng** ◈ *district* SE Botswana
188 F8 **Kgkeklau** Babeldaob, N Palau
125 R6 **Khabarikha** *var.* Chabaricha. Respublika Komi, NW Russian Federation
123 S14 **Khabarovsk** Khabarovskiy Kray, SE Russian Federation
123 R11 **Khabarovskiy Kray** ◈ *territory* E Russian Federation
141 W7 **Khabb** Abū Ẓaby, E UAE
Khabour, Nahr al *see* Khābūr, Nahr al
Khabura *see* Al Khābūrah
139 N2 **Khābūr, Nahr al** *var.* Nahr al Khabour. ≈ Syria/Turkey
Khachmas *see* Xaçmaz
80 B12 **Khadari** ≈ W Sudan
Khadera *see* Hadera
141 X12 **Khādhil** *var.* Khudal. SE Oman
155 E14 **Khadki** *prev.* Kirkee. Mahārāshtra, W India
126 L14 **Khadyzhensk** Krasnodarskiy Kray, SW Russian Federation
114 N9 **Khadzhiyska Reka** ≈ E Bulgaria
117 P10 **Khadzhybeys'kyy Lyman** ◎ SW Ukraine
138 K3 **Khafsah** Ḩalab, N Syria
152 M13 **Khāga** Uttar Pradesh, N India
153 Q13 **Khagaria** Bihār, NE India
149 Q13 **Khairpur** Sind, SE Pakistan
122 K13 **Khakasiya, Respublika** *prev.* Khakasskaya Avtonomnaya Oblast', *Eng.* Khakassia. ◈ *autonomous republic* C Russian Federation
Khakassia/Khakasskaya Avtonomnaya Oblast' *see* Khakasiya, Respublika
167 N9 **Kha Khaeng, Khao** ▲ W Thailand
83 G20 **Khakhea** *var.* Kakia. Southern, S Botswana
Khalach *see* Halaç
Khalándrion *see* Chalándri
127 W7 **Khalilovo** Orenburgskaya Oblast', W Russian Federation
Khalkabad *see* Xalqobod
142 L3 **Khalkhāl** *prev.* Herowābād. Ardabīl, NW Iran
Khalkidhikí *see* Chalkidikí
Khalkís *see* Chalkída
125 W3 **Khal'mer-Yu** Respublika Komi, NW Russian Federation
119 M14 **Khalopyenichy** *Rus.* Kholopenichi. Minskaya Voblasts', NE Belarus
Khalturin *see* Orlov
141 Y10 **Khalūf** *var.* Al Khaluf. E Oman
154 K10 **Khamaria** Madhya Pradesh, C India
154 D11 **Khambhāt** Gujarāt, W India
154 C12 **Khambhāt, Gulf of** *Eng.* Gulf of Cambay. *gulf* W India
167 U10 **Khâm Đu'c** Quang Nam-Đa Năng, C Vietnam
154 G12 **Khāmgaon** Mahārāshtra, C India
141 O14 **Khamir** *var.* Khamr. W Yemen
141 N12 **Khamīs Mushayṭ** *var.* Hamīs Musait. 'Asīr, SW Saudi Arabia
123 P10 **Khampa** Respublika Sakha (Yakutiya), NE Russian Federation
Khamr *see* Khamir
83 C19 **Khan** ≈ W Namibia
149 Q2 **Khānābād** Kunduz, NE Afghanistan
Khân Abou Châmâte/Khan Abou Ech Cham *see* Khān Abū Shāmāt
138 I7 **Khān Abū Shāmāt** *var.* Khân Abou Châmâte, Khan Abou Ech Cham. Dimashq, W Syria
Khān al Baghdādī *see* Al Baghdādī
Khān al Maḩāwīl *see* Al Maḩāwīl
139 T7 **Khān al Mashāhidah** C Iraq
139 T10 **Khān al Muşallá** S Iraq
139 U6 **Khānaqīn** E Iraq
139 T11 **Khān ar Ruḩbah** S Iraq
139 P2 **Khān as Sūr** N Iraq
139 T8 **Khān Āzād** C Iraq
154 N13 **Khandaparha** *prev.* Khandpara. Orissa, E India
Khandpara *see* Khandaparha
149 T2 **Khandūd** *var.* Khandud, Wakhan. Badakhshān, NE Afghanistan
154 G11 **Khandwa** Madhya Pradesh, C India
123 R10 **Khandyga** Respublika Sakha (Yakutiya), NE Russian Federation
149 T10 **Khānewāl** Punjab, NE Pakistan
149 S10 **Khāngarh** Punjab, E Pakistan
Khanh Hung *see* Soc Trăng
Khaniá *see* Chaniá
Khanka *see* Xonqa
163 Z8 **Khanka, Lake** *var.* Hsing-k'ai Hu, Lake Hanka, *Chin.* Xingkai Hu, *Rus.* Ozero Khanka. ◎ China/Russian Federation
Khanka, Ozero *see* Khanka, Lake
Khankendi *see* Xankändi
Khanlar *see* Xanlar
123 O9 **Khannya** ≈ NE Russian Federation
149 S12 **Khānpur** Punjab, SE Pakistan
149 S12 **Khānpur** Punjab, E Pakistan
138 I4 **Khān Shaykhūn** *var.* Khan Sheikhun. Idlib, NW Syria
Khan Sheikhun *see* Khān Shaykhūn
145 S15 **Khantau** Zhambyl, S Kazakhstan
145 W16 **Khan Tengri, Pik** ▲ SE Kazakhstan
167 S9 **Khanthabouli** *prev.* Savannakhét. Savannakhét, S Laos
127 V8 **Khanty-Mansiyskiy Avtonomnyy Okrug** ◈ *autonomous district* C Russian Federation
139 R4 **Khānūqah** C Iraq
138 E11 **Khān Yūnis** *var.* Khān Yūnus. S Gaza Strip
Khān Yūnus *see* Khān Yūnis
Khanzi *see* Ghanzi
139 U5 **Khān Zūr** E Iraq
167 N10 **Khao Laem Reservoir** ▣ W Thailand
123 O14 **Khapcheranga** Chitinskaya Oblast', S Russian Federation
127 Q12 **Kharabali** Astrakhanskaya Oblast', SW Russian Federation
153 R16 **Kharagpur** West Bengal, NE India
139 V11 **Kharā'ib 'Abd al Karīm** S Iraq
143 Q8 **Kharānaq** Yazd, C Iran
Kharbin *see* Harbin
146 H13 **Khardzhagaz** Ahal Welaýaty, C Turkmenistan
Khārga Oasis *see* Great Oasis, The
154 F11 **Khargon** Madhya Pradesh, C India
149 V7 **Khāriān** Punjab, NE Pakistan
117 X8 **Kharisyz'k** Donets'ka Oblast', E Ukraine
117 V5 **Kharkiv** *Rus.* Khar'kov. Kharkivs'ka Oblast', NE Ukraine
117 V5 **Kharkiv** ✈ Kharkivs'ka Oblast', E Ukraine
Kharkiv *see* Kharkivs'ka Oblast'
117 U5 **Kharkivs'ka Oblast'** *var.* Kharkiv, *Rus.* Khar'kovskaya Oblast'. ◈ *province* E Ukraine
Khar'kov *see* Kharkiv
Khar'kovskaya Oblast' *see* Kharkivs'ka Oblast'
124 L3 **Kharlovka** Murmanskaya Oblast', NW Russian Federation
114 K11 **Kharmanli** Khaskovo, S Bulgaria
114 K11 **Kharmanliyska Reka** ≈ S Bulgaria
124 M13 **Kharovsk** Vologodskaya Oblast', NW Russian Federation
80 F9 **Khartoum** *var.* El Khartûm, Khartum. ● (Sudan) Khartoum, C Sudan
80 F9 **Khartoum** ◈ *state* NE Sudan
80 F9 **Khartoum** ✈ Khartoum, C Sudan
80 F9 **Khartoum North** Khartoum, C Sudan
117 X8 **Khartsyz'k** *Rus.* Khartsyzsk. Donets'ka Oblast', SE Ukraine
Khartsyzsk *see* Khartsyz'k
Khartum *see* Khartoum
Khasab *see* Al Khaşab
123 S15 **Khasan** Primorskiy Kray, SE Russian Federation
127 P16 **Khasavyurt** Respublika Dagestan, SW Russian Federation
143 W12 **Khāsh** *prev.* Vāsht. Sīstān va Balūchestān, SE Iran
148 K8 **Khāsh, Dasht-e** *Eng.* Khash Desert. *desert* SW Afghanistan
Khash Desert *see* Khāsh, Dasht-e
Khashim Al Qirba/Khashm al Qirbah *see* Khashm el Girba
80 H9 **Khashm el Girba** *var.* Khashim Al Qirba, Khashm al Qirbah. Kassala, E Sudan
138 G14 **Khashsh, Jabal al** ▲ S Jordan
137 S10 **Khashuri** C Georgia
153 V13 **Khāsi Hills** *hill range* NE India
114 K11 **Khaskovo** Khaskovo, S Bulgaria
114 K11 **Khaskovo** ◈ *province* S Bulgaria
122 M7 **Khatanga** ≈ N Russian Federation
Khatanga, Gulf of *see* Khatangskiy Zaliv
123 N7 **Khatangskiy Zaliv** *var.* Gulf of Khatanga. *bay* N Russian Federation
141 W7 **Khatmat al Malāḩah** N Oman
143 S16 **Khaṭmat al Malāḩah** Ash Shāriqah, E UAE
123 V7 **Khatyrka** Chukotskiy Avtonomnyy Okrug, NE Russian Federation
Khauz-Khan *see* Hanhowuz
Khauzkhanskoye Vodokhranilishche *see* Hanhowuz Suw Howdany
Khavaling *see* Khovaling
Khavast *see* Xovos
139 W10 **Khawrah, Nahr al** ≈ S Iraq
Khawr Barakah *see* Baraka
141 W7 **Khawr Fakkān** *var.* Khor Fakkan. Ash Shāriqah, NE UAE
140 L6 **Khaybar** Al Madīnah, NW Saudi Arabia
Khaybar, Kowtal-e *see* Khyber Pass
147 S11 **Khaydarkan** *var.* Khaydarken. Batkenskaya Oblast', SW Kyrgyzstan
Khaydarken *see* Khaydarkan
127 U2 **Khaypudyrskaya Guba** *bay* NW Russian Federation
139 S1 **Khayrūzuk** E Iraq
Khazar, Baḩr-e/Khazar, Daryā-ye *see* Caspian Sea
Khazarosp *see* Hazorasp
Khazretishi, Khrebet *see* Hazratishoh, Qatorkŭhi
Khelat *see* Kālat
74 F6 **Khemisset** NW Morocco
167 R10 **Khemmarat** *var.* Kemarat. Ubon Ratchathani, E Thailand
74 L6 **Khenchela** *var.* Khenchla. NE Algeria
Khenchla *see* Khenchela
74 G7 **Khénifra** C Morocco
Khersān, Rūd-e *see* Garm, Āb-e
117 R10 **Kherson** Khersons'ka Oblast', S Ukraine
Kherson *see* Khersons'ka Oblast'
117 S14 **Khersones, Mys** *Rus.* Mys Khersonesskiy. *headland* S Ukraine
Khersonesskiy, Mys *see* Khersones, Mys
117 R10 **Khersons'ka Oblast'** *var.* Kherson, *Rus.* Khersonskaya Oblast'. ◈ *province* S Ukraine
Khersonskaya Oblast' *see* Khersons'ka Oblast'
122 L8 **Kheta** ≈ N Russian Federation
167 S8 **Khe Ve** Quang Binh, C Vietnam
149 U7 **Khewra** Punjab, E Pakistan
Khiam *see* El Khiyam
126 J4 **Khibiny** ⛰ NW Russian Federation
126 K3 **Khimki** Moskovskaya Oblast', W Russian Federation
147 S12 **Khingov** *Rus.* Obi-Khingou. ≈ C Tajikistan
Khíos *see* Chíos
149 R15 **Khipro** Sind, SE Pakistan
139 S10 **Khirr, Wādī al** *dry watercourse* S Iraq
114 I10 **Khisarya** Plovdiv, C Bulgaria
Khiva *see* Xiva
167 N9 **Khlong Khlung** Kamphaeng Phet, W Thailand
167 N15 **Khlong Thom** Krabi, SW Thailand
167 P12 **Khlung** Chantaburi, S Thailand
Khmel'nik *see* Khmil'nyk
Khmel'nitskaya Oblast' *see* Khmel'nyts'ka Oblast'
Khmel'nitskiy *see* Khmel 'nyts'kyy
116 K5 **Khmel'nyts'ka Oblast'** *var.* Khmel'nyts'kyy, *Rus.* Khmel'nitskaya Oblast'; *prev.* Kamenets-Podol'skaya Oblast'. ◈ *province* NW Ukraine
116 L6 **Khmel 'nyts'kyy** *Rus.* Khmel'nitskiy; *prev.* Proskurov. Khmel'nyts'ka Oblast', W Ukraine
Khmel'nyts'kyy *see* Khmel'nyts'ka Oblast'
116 M6 **Khmil'nyk** *Rus.* Khmel'nik. Vinnyts'ka Oblast', C Ukraine
144 I10 **Khobda** *prev.* Novoalekseyevka. Aktyubinsk, W Kazakhstan
137 R9 **Khobi** W Georgia
119 P15 **Khodasy** *Rus.* Khodosy. Mahilyowskaya Voblasts', E Belarus
116 I6 **Khodoriv** *Pol.* Chodorów, *Rus.* Khodorov. L'vivs'ka Oblast', NW Ukraine
Khodorov *see* Khodoriv
Khodosy *see* Khodasy
Khodzhakala *see* Hojagala
Khodzhambas *see* Hojambaz
Khodzhent *see* Khŭjand
Khodzheyli *see* Xo'jayli
Khoi *see* Khvoy
Khojend *see* Khŭjand
Khokand *see* Qo'qon
126 L8 **Khokhol'skiy** Voronezhskaya Oblast', W Russian Federation
167 P10 **Khok Samrong** Lop Buri, C Thailand
149 P2 **Kholm** *var.* Tashqurghan, *Pash.* Khulm. Balkh, N Afghanistan
124 H15 **Kholm** Novgorodskaya Oblast', W Russian Federation
Kholm *see* Chełm
Kholmech' *see* Kholmyech
123 T13 **Kholmsk** Ostrov Sakhalin, Sakhalinskaya Oblast', SE Russian Federation
119 O19 **Kholmyech** *Rus.* Kholmech'. Homyel'skaya Voblasts', SE Belarus
Kholon *see* Holon
Kholopenichi *see* Khalopyenichy
83 D19 **Khomas** ◈ *district* C Namibia
83 D19 **Khomas Hochland** *var.* Khomasplato. *plateau* C Namibia
Khomasplato *see* Khomas Hochland
Khomein *see* Khomeyn
142 M7 **Khomeyn** *var.* Khomein, Khumain. Markazī, W Iran
143 N8 **Khomeynīshahr** *prev.* Homāyūnshahr. Eşfahān, C Iran
Khoms *see* Al Khums
Khong Sedone *see* Muang Khôngxédôn
167 Q9 **Khon Kaen** *var.* Muang Khon Kaen. Khon Kaen, E Thailand
167 Q9 **Khon San** Khon Kaen, E Thailand
123 R8 **Khonuu** Respublika Sakha (Yakutiya), NE Russian Federation
127 N8 **Khopër** *var.* Khoper. ≈ SW Russian Federation
123 S14 **Khor** Khabarovskiy Kray, SE Russian Federation
143 S6 **Khorāsān** *off.* Ostān-e Khorāsān, *var.* Khorassan, Khurasan. ◈ *province* NE Iran
Khorassan *see* Khorāsān
Khorat *see* Nakhon Ratchasima
154 O13 **Khordha** *prev.* Khurda. Orissa, E India
125 U4 **Khorey-Ver** Nenetskiy Avtonomnyy Okrug, NW Russian Federation
Khorezmskaya Oblast' *see* Xorazm Viloyati
Khor Fakkan *see* Khawr Fakkān
145 W15 **Khorgos** Almaty, SE Kazakhstan
123 N13 **Khorinsk** Respublika Buryatiya, S Russian Federation
83 C18 **Khorixas** Kunene, NW Namibia
141 O17 **Khormaksar** *var.* Aden. ✈ ('Adan) SW Yemen
Khormal *see* Khurmāl
Khormuj *see* Khvormūj
Khorog *see* Khorugh
117 S5 **Khorol** Poltavs'ka Oblast', NE Ukraine
142 L7 **Khorramābād** *var.* Khurramabad. Lorestān, W Iran
142 K10 **Khorramshahr** *var.* Khurramshahr, Muhammerah; *prev.* Mohammerah. Khūzestān, SW Iran
147 S14 **Khorugh** *Rus.* Khorog. S Tajikistan
127 Q12 **Khosheutovo** Astrakhanskaya Oblast', SW Russian Federation
Khotan *see* Hotan
Khorvot Khalutsa *see* Horvot Haluza
Khotimsk *see* Khotsimsk
Khotin *see* Khotyn
119 R16 **Khotsimsk** *Rus.* Khotimsk. Mahilyowskaya Voblasts', E Belarus
116 K7 **Khotyn** *Rom.* Hotin, *Rus.* Khotin. Chernivets'ka Oblast', W Ukraine
74 F7 **Khouribga** C Morocco
147 Q13 **Khovaling** *Rus.* Khavaling. SW Tajikistan
Khovd *see* Hovd
149 R6 **Khowst** Paktīā, E Afghanistan
Khoy *see* Khvoy
119 N20 **Khoyniki** *Rus.* Khoyniki. Homyel'skaya Voblasts', SE Belarus
Khozretishi, Khrebet *see* Hazratishoh, Qatorkŭhi
Khrisoúpolis *see* Chrysoúpoli
144 J10 **Khromtau** *Kaz.* Khromtaū. Aktyubinsk, W Kazakhstan
Khrysokhou Bay *see* Chrysochoú, Kólpos
117 O7 **Khrystynivka** Cherkas'ka Oblast', C Ukraine
167 R10 **Khuang Nai** Ubon Ratchathani, E Thailand
Khudal *see* Khādhil
Khudat *see* Xudat
149 W9 **Khudiān** Punjab, E Pakistan
Khudzhand *see* Khŭjand
147 O13 **Khufar** Surxondaryo Viloyati, S Uzbekistan
83 G21 **Khuis** Kgalagadi, SW Botswana
147 Q11 **Khŭjand** *var.* Khodzhent, Khojend, *Rus.* Khudzhand; *prev.* Leninabad, *Taj.* Leninobod. N Tajikistan
167 R11 **Khukhan** Si Sa Ket, E Thailand
Khulm *see* Kholm
153 T16 **Khulna** Khulna, SW Bangladesh
153 T16 **Khulna** ◈ *division* SW Bangladesh
Khumain *see* Khomeyn
Khums *see* Al Khums
149 W2 **Khunjerāb Pass** *Chin.* Kunjirap Daban. *pass* China/Pakistan *see also* Kunjirap Daban
153 P16 **Khunti** Jhārkhand, N India
167 N7 **Khun Yuam** Mae Hong Son, NW Thailand
Khurais *see* Khurayş
Khurasan *see* Khorāsān
141 R7 **Khurayş** *var.* Khurais. Ash Sharqīyah, C Saudi Arabia
Khurda *see* Khordha
152 J11 **Khurja** Uttar Pradesh, N India
139 V4 **Khurmāl** *var.* Khormal. NE Iraq
Khurramabad *see* Khorramābād
Khurramshahr *see* Khorramshahr
149 U7 **Khushāb** Punjab, NE Pakistan
116 H8 **Khust** *Cz.* Chust, Husté, *Hung.* Huszt. Zakarpats'ka Oblast', W Ukraine
80 D11 **Khuwei** Western Kordofan, C Sudan
149 O13 **Khuzdār** Baluchistān, SW Pakistan
142 L9 **Khūzestān** *off.* Ostān-e Khūzestān, *var.* Khuzistan; *prev.* Arabistan, *anc.* Susiana. ◈ *province* SW Iran
Khuzistan *see* Khūzestān
149 R2 **Khvājeh Ghār** *var.* Khwajaghar, Khwaja-i-Ghar. Takhār, NE Afghanistan
127 Q7 **Khvalynsk** Saratovskaya Oblast', W Russian Federation
143 N12 **Khvormūj** *var.* Khormuj. Būshehr, S Iran
142 I2 **Khvoy** *var.* Khoi, Khoy. Āžarbāyjān-e Bākhtarī, NW Iran
Khwajaghar/Khwaja-i-Ghar *see* Khvājeh Ghār
149 S5 **Khyber Pass** *var.* Kowtal-e Khaybar. *pass* Afghanistan/Pakistan
186 L8 **Kia** Santa Isabel, N Solomon Islands
183 S10 **Kiama** New South Wales, SE Australia
79 O22 **Kiambi** Katanga, SE Dem. Rep. Congo
27 Q12 **Kiamichi Mountains** ⛰ Oklahoma, C USA
27 Q12 **Kiamichi River** ≈ Oklahoma, C USA
14 M10 **Kiamika, Réservoir** ▣ Québec, SE Canada
Kiamusze *see* Jiamusi
39 N7 **Kiana** Alaska, USA
Kiangmai *see* Chiang Mai
Kiang-ning *see* Nanjing
Kiangsi *see* Jiangxi
Kiangsu *see* Jiangsu
93 M14 **Kiantajärvi** ◎ E Finland
115 F19 **Kiáto** *prev.* Kiáton. Pelopónnisos, S Greece
Kiáton *see* Kiáto
Kiayi *see* Chiai
79 E21 **Kibangou** Le Niari, SW Congo
Kibarty *see* Kybartai
92 M8 **Kiberg** Finnmark, N Norway
95 F22 **Kibæk** Ringkøbing, W Denmark
79 N20 **Kibombo** Maniema, E Dem. Rep. Congo
81 E20 **Kibondo** Kigoma, NW Tanzania
81 J15 **Kibre Mengist** *var.* Adola. Oromo, C Ethiopia
Kıbrıs/Kıbrıs Cumhuriyeti *see* Cyprus
81 E20 **Kibungo** *var.* Kibungu. SE Rwanda
Kibungu *see* Kibungo
113 N19 **Kičevo** SW FYR Macedonia
125 P13 **Kichmengskiy Gorodok** Vologodskaya Oblast', NW Russian Federation
30 J8 **Kickapoo River** ≈ Wisconsin, N USA
11 P16 **Kicking Horse Pass** *pass* Alberta/British Columbia, SW Canada
77 R9 **Kidal** Kidal, C Mali
77 Q8 **Kidal** ◈ *region* NE Mali
171 Q8 **Kidapawan** Mindanao, S Philippines
97 L20 **Kidderminster** C England, UK
76 I11 **Kidira** E Senegal
184 O11 **Kidnappers, Cape** *headland* North Island, NZ
100 J8 **Kiel** Schleswig-Holstein, N Germany
111 L15 **Kielce** *Rus.* Keltsy. Świętokrzyskie, C Poland
100 K7 **Kieler Bucht** *bay* N Germany
100 J7 **Kieler Förde** *inlet* N Germany
167 U13 **Kiên Đu'c** *var.* Đak Lap. Đăc Lăc, S Vietnam
79 N24 **Kienge** Katanga, SE Dem. Rep. Congo
100 Q12 **Kietz** Brandenburg, NE Germany
Kiev *see* Kyyiv
Kiev Reservoir *see* Kyyivs'ke Vodoskhovyshche
76 J10 **Kiffa** Assaba, S Mauritania
115 H19 **Kifisiá** Attikí, C Greece
115 F18 **Kifisós** ≈ C Greece
139 U5 **Kifrī** N Iraq
81 D20 **Kigali** ● (Rwanda) C Rwanda
81 E20 **Kigali** ✈ C Rwanda
137 P13 **Kiği** Bingöl, E Turkey
81 E21 **Kigoma** Kigoma, W Tanzania
81 E21 **Kigoma** ◈ *region* W Tanzania
38 F10 **Kīhei** *var.* Kihei. Maui, Hawai'i, USA, C Pacific Ocean
93 K17 **Kihniö** Länsi-Suomi, W Finland
118 F6 **Kihnu** *var.* Kihnu Saar, *Ger.* Kühnö. *island* SW Estonia
Kihnu Saar *see* Kihnu
38 A8 **Kii Landing** Ni'ihau, Hawai'i, USA, C Pacific Ocean
93 L14 **Kiiminki** Oulu, C Finland
164 J14 **Kii-Nagashima** *var.* Nagashima. Mie, Honshū, SW Japan
164 J14 **Kii-sanchi** ⛰ Honshū, SW Japan
92 L11 **Kiistala** Lappi, N Finland
164 I15 **Kii-suidō** *strait* S Japan
165 V16 **Kikai-shima** *var.* Kikaiga-shima. *island* Nansei-shotō, SW Japan
112 M8 **Kikinda** *Ger.* Grosskikinda, *Hung.* Nagykikinda; *prev.* Velika Kikinda. Serbia, N Serbia and Montenegro (Yugo.)
Kikládhes *see* Kykládes
165 Q5 **Kikonai** Hokkaidō, NE Japan
186 C8 **Kikori** Gulf, S PNG
186 C8 **Kikori** ≈ W PNG
165 O14 **Kikuchi** *var.* Kikuti. Kumamoto, Kyūshū, SW Japan
Kikuti *see* Kikuchi
127 N8 **Kikvidze** Volgogradskaya Oblast', SW Russian Federation
14 I10 **Kikwissi, Lac** ◎ Québec, SE Canada
79 I21 **Kikwit** Bandundu, W Dem. Rep. Congo
95 K15 **Kil** Värmland, C Sweden
94 N12 **Kilafors** Gävleborg, C Sweden
38 B8 **Kīlauea** *var.* Kilauea. Kaua'i, Hawai'i, USA, C Pacific Ocean
38 H12 **Kīlauea Caldera** *var.* Kilauea Caldera *crater* Hawai'i, USA, C Pacific Ocean
109 V4 **Kilb** Niederösterreich, C Austria
39 O12 **Kilbuck Mountains** ⛰ Alaska, USA
163 Y12 **Kilchu** NE North Korea
97 F18 **Kilcock** *Ir.* Cill Choca. E Ireland
183 V2 **Kilcoy** Queensland, E Australia
97 F18 **Kildare** *Ir.* Cill Dara. E Ireland
97 F18 **Kildare** *Ir.* Cill Dara. *cultural region* E Ireland
126 K2 **Kil'din, Ostrov** *island* NW Russian Federation
25 W7 **Kilgore** Texas, SW USA
Kilien Mountains *see* Qilian Shan
114 K9 **Kilifarevo** Veliko Tŭrnovo, N Bulgaria
81 K20 **Kilifi** Coast, SE Kenya
189 U9 **Kili Island** *var.* Kōle. *island* Ralik Chain, S Marshall Islands
149 V2 **Kilik Pass** *pass* Afghanistan/China
Kilimane *see* Quelimane
81 I21 **Kilimanjaro** ◈ *region* E Tanzania
81 I20 **Kilimanjaro** *var.* Uhuru Peak. ▲ NE Tanzania
Kilimbangara *see* Kolombangara
Kilinailau Islands *see* Tulun Islands
81 K23 **Kilindoni** Pwani, E Tanzania
118 H6 **Kilingi-Nõmme** *Ger.* Kurkund. Pärnumaa, SW Estonia
136 M17 **Kilis** Kilis, S Turkey
136 M16 **Kilis** ◈ *province* S Turkey
117 N12 **Kiliya** *Rom.* Chilia-Nouă. Odes'ka Oblast', SW Ukraine
97 B19 **Kilkee** *Ir.* Cill Chaoi. W Ireland
97 E19 **Kilkenny** *Ir.* Cill Chainnigh. S Ireland
97 E19 **Kilkenny** *Ir.* Cill Chainnigh. *cultural region* S Ireland
97 B18 **Kilkieran Bay** *Ir.* Cuan Chill Chiaráin. *bay* W Ireland
114 G13 **Kilkís** Kentrikí Makedonía, N Greece
97 C15 **Killala Bay** *Ir.* Cuan Chill Ala. *inlet* NW Ireland
11 R15 **Killam** Alberta, SW Canada
183 U3 **Killarney** Queensland, E Australia
11 W17 **Killarney** Manitoba, S Canada

◆ Country ● Country Capital ◇ Dependent Territory ○ Dependent Territory Capital ◈ Administrative Region ✈ International Airport ▲ Mountain ⛰ Mountain Range ※ Volcano ≈ River ◎ Lake ▣ Reservoir

14 E11 **Killarney** Ontario, S Canada
97 B20 **Killarney** *Ir.* Cill Airne. SW Ireland
28 K4 **Killdeer** North Dakota, N USA
28 J4 **Killdeer Mountains** ▲ North Dakota, N USA
45 V15 **Killdeer River** ≈ Trinidad, Trinidad and Tobago
25 S9 **Killeen** Texas, SW USA
39 P6 **Killik River** ≈ Alaska, USA
9 T7 **Killinek Island** *island* Nunavut, NE Canada
Killini *see* Kyllíni
115 C19 **Killínis, Akrotírio** *headland* S Greece
97 D15 **Killybegs** *Ir.* Na Cealla Beaga. NW Ireland
Kilmain *see* Quelimane
96 I13 **Kilmarnock** W Scotland, UK
21 X6 **Kilmarnock** Virginia, NE USA
125 S16 **Kil'mez'** Kirovskaya Oblast', NW Russian Federation
127 S2 **Kil'mez'** Udmurtskaya Respublika, NW Russian Federation
127 R16 **Kil'mez'** ≈ NW Russian Federation
92 J10 **Kilpisjarvi** Lappi, N Finland
97 B19 **Kilrush** *Ir.* Cill Rois. W Ireland
79 O24 **Kilwa** Katanga, SE Dem. Rep. Congo
Kilwa *see* Kilwa Kivinje
81 J24 **Kilwa Kivinje** *var.* Kilwa. Lindi, SE Tanzania
81 J24 **Kilwa Masoko** Lindi, SE Tanzania
171 T13 **Kilwo** Pulau Seram, E Indonesia
114 P12 **Kilyos** İstanbul, NW Turkey
37 V8 **Kim** Colorado, C USA
169 U7 **Kimanis, Teluk** *bay* Sabah, East Malaysia
182 H8 **Kimba** South Australia
28 I15 **Kimball** Nebraska, C USA
29 O11 **Kimball** South Dakota, N USA
79 I21 **Kimbao** Bandundu, SW Dem. Rep. Congo
186 F7 **Kimbe** New Britain, E PNG
186 G7 **Kimbe Bay** *inlet* New Britain, E PNG
11 P17 **Kimberley** British Columbia, SW Canada
83 H23 **Kimberley** Northern Cape, C South Africa
180 M4 **Kimberley Plateau** *plateau* Western Australia
33 P15 **Kimberly** Idaho, NW USA
163 Y12 **Kimch'aek** *prev.* Sŏngjin. E North Korea
163 Y15 **Kimch'ŏn** C South Korea
163 Z16 **Kim Hae** *var.* Pusan. × (Pusan) SE South Korea
Kími *see* Kými
93 K20 **Kimito** *Swe.* Kemiö. Länsi-Suomi, W Finland
165 R4 **Kimobetsu** Hokkaidō, NE Japan
115 I21 **Kímolos** *island* Kykládes, Greece, Aegean Sea
115 I21 **Kímolou Sífnou, Stenó** *strait* Kykládes, Greece, Aegean Sea
126 L5 **Kimovsk** Tul'skaya Oblast', W Russian Federation
Kimpolung *see* Câmpulung Moldovenesc
124 K16 **Kimry** Tverskaya Oblast', W Russian Federation
79 H21 **Kimvula** Bas-Congo, SW Dem. Rep. Congo
169 U6 **Kinabalu, Gunung** ▲ East Malaysia
Kinabatangan *see* Kinabatangan, Sungai
169 V7 **Kinabatangan, Sungai** *var.* Kinabatangan. ≈ East Malaysia
115 L21 **Kínaros** *island* Kykládes, Greece, Aegean Sea
11 O15 **Kinbasket Lake** ⊞ British Columbia, SW Canada
96 I7 **Kinbrace** N Scotland, UK
14 E14 **Kincardine** Ontario, S Canada
96 K10 **Kincardine** *cultural region* E Scotland, UK
79 K21 **Kinda** Kasai Occidental, SE Dem. Rep. Congo
79 M24 **Kinda** Katanga, SE Dem. Rep. Congo
166 L3 **Kindat** Sagaing, N Burma
109 V6 **Kindberg** Steiermark, C Austria
22 H8 **Kinder** Louisiana, S USA
98 H13 **Kinderdijk** Zuid-Holland, SW Netherlands
7 M17 **Kinder Scout** ▲ C England, UK
1 S16 **Kindersley** Saskatchewan, S Canada
I14 **Kindia** Guinée-Maritime, SW Guinea
B11 **Kindley Field** *air base* E Bermuda
R6 **Kindred** North Dakota, N USA
7 N20 **Kindu** *prev.* Kindu-Port-Empain. Maniema, C Dem. Rep. Congo
Kindu-Port-Empain *see* Kindu
12 S6 **Kinel'** Samarskaya Oblast', W Russian Federation
125 N15 **Kineshma** Ivanovskaya Oblast', W Russian Federation
King *see* King William's Town
140 K10 **King Abdul Aziz** × (Makkah) Makkah, W Saudi Arabia
21 X6 **King and Queen Court House** Virginia, NE USA
King Charles Islands *see* Kong Karls Land
King Christian IX Land *see* Kong Christian IX Land
King Christian X Land *see* Kong Christian X Land
35 O11 **King City** California, W USA
27 R2 **King City** Missouri, C USA
38 M16 **King Cove** Alaska, USA
26 M10 **Kingfisher** Oklahoma, C USA
King Frederik VI Coast *see* Kong Frederik VI Kyst
King Frederik VIII Land *see* Kong Frederik VIII Land
65 B24 **King George Bay** *bay* West Falkland, Falkland Islands
194 G3 **King George Island** *var.* King George Land. *island* South Shetland Islands, Antarctica
12 I6 **King George Islands** *island group* Nunavut, C Canada
King George Land *see* King George Island
124 G13 **Kingisepp** Leningradskaya Oblast', NW Russian Federation
183 N14 **King Island** *island* Tasmania, SE Australia
10 J15 **King Island** *island* British Columbia, SW Canada
King Island *see* Kadan Kyun
Kingissepp *see* Kuressaare
141 Q7 **King Khalid** × (Ar Riyāḍ) Ar Riyāḍ, C Saudi Arabia
35 S2 **King Lear Peak** ▲ Nevada, W USA
195 Y8 **King Leopold and Queen Astrid Land** *physical region* Antarctica
180 M4 **King Leopold Ranges** ▲ Western Australia
36 I11 **Kingman** Arizona, SW USA
26 M6 **Kingman** Kansas, C USA
192 L7 **Kingman Reef** ◇ *US territory* C Pacific Ocean
79 N20 **Kingombe** Maniema, E Dem. Rep. Congo
182 F5 **Kingoonya** South Australia
194 J10 **King Peninsula** *peninsula* Antarctica
39 P13 **King Salmon** Alaska, USA
35 Q6 **Kings Beach** California, W USA
35 R11 **Kingsburg** California, W USA
182 I10 **Kingscote** South Australia
King's County *see* Offaly
194 H2 **King Sejong** *South Korean research station* Antarctica
183 T9 **Kingsford Smith** × (Sydney) New South Wales, SE Australia
11 P17 **Kingsgate** British Columbia, SW Canada
23 W8 **Kingsland** Georgia, SE USA
29 S13 **Kingsley** Iowa, C USA
97 O19 **King's Lynn** *var.* Bishop's Lynn, Kings Lynn, Lynn, Lynn Regis. E England, UK
21 Q10 **Kings Mountain** North Carolina, SE USA
180 K4 **King Sound** *sound* Western Australia
37 N2 **Kings Peak** ▲ Utah, W USA
21 O8 **Kingsport** Tennessee, S USA
35 R11 **Kings River** ≈ California, W USA
183 P17 **Kingston** Tasmania, SE Australia
14 K14 **Kingston** Ontario, SE Canada
44 K13 **Kingston** ● (Jamaica) E Jamaica
185 C22 **Kingston** Otago, South Island, NZ
19 P12 **Kingston** Massachusetts, NE USA
27 S3 **Kingston** Missouri, C USA
18 K12 **Kingston** New York, NE USA
31 S14 **Kingston** Ohio, N USA
19 O13 **Kingston** Rhode Island, NE USA
20 M9 **Kingston** Tennessee, S USA
35 W12 **Kingston Peak** ▲ California, W USA
182 J11 **Kingston Southeast** South Australia
97 N17 **Kingston upon Hull** *var.* Hull. E England, UK
97 N22 **Kingston upon Thames** SE England, UK
45 P14 **Kingstown** ● (Saint Vincent and the Grenadines) Saint Vincent, Saint Vincent and the Grenadines
Kingstown *see* Dún Laoghaire
21 T13 **Kingstree** South Carolina, SE USA
64 L8 **Kings Trough** *undersea feature* E Atlantic Ocean
14 C18 **Kingsville** Ontario, S Canada
25 S15 **Kingsville** Texas, SW USA
21 W6 **King William** Virginia, NE USA
8 M7 **King William Island** *island* Nunavut, N Canada Arctic Ocean
83 I25 **King William's Town** *var.* King, Kingwilliamstown. Eastern Cape, S South Africa
21 T3 **Kingwood** West Virginia, NE USA
136 C13 **Kınık** İzmir, W Turkey
79 G21 **Kinkala** Le Pool, S Congo
165 R10 **Kinka-san** *headland* Honshū, C Japan
184 M8 **Kinleith** Waikato, North Island, NZ
95 J19 **Kinna** Västra Götaland, S Sweden
96 L8 **Kinnaird Head** *var.* Kinnairds Head. *headland* NE Scotland, UK
95 K20 **Kinnared** Halland, S Sweden
Kinneret, Yam *see* Tiberias, Lake
155 K24 **Kinniyai** Eastern Province, NE Sri Lanka
93 L16 **Kinnula** Länsi-Suomi, W Finland
14 I8 **Kinojévis** ≈ Québec, SE Canada
164 I14 **Kino-kawa** ≈ Honshū, SW Japan
11 U11 **Kinoosao** Saskatchewan, C Canada
99 L17 **Kinrooi** Limburg, NE Belgium
96 J11 **Kinross** C Scotland, UK
96 J11 **Kinross** *cultural region* C Scotland, UK
97 C21 **Kinsale** *Ir.* Cionn tSáile. SW Ireland
95 D14 **Kinsarvik** Hordaland, S Norway
79 G21 **Kinshasa** *prev.* Léopoldville. ● (Dem. Rep. Congo) Kinshasa, W Dem. Rep. Congo
79 G21 **Kinshasa** *off.* Ville de Kinshasa, *var.* Kinshasa City. ◈ *region* SW Dem. Rep. Congo
79 G21 **Kinshasa** × Kinshasa, SW Dem. Rep. Congo
Kinshasa City *see* Kinshasa
117 U9 **Kins'ka** ≈ SE Ukraine
26 K6 **Kinsley** Kansas, C USA
21 W10 **Kinston** North Carolina, SE USA
77 P15 **Kintampo** W Ghana
182 B1 **Kintore, Mount** ▲ South Australia
96 G13 **Kintyre** *peninsula* W Scotland, UK
96 G13 **Kintyre, Mull of** *headland* W Scotland, UK
166 M4 **Kin-u** Sagaing, C Burma
12 G8 **Kinushseo** ≈ Ontario, C Canada
11 P13 **Kinuso** Alberta, W Canada
154 I13 **Kinwat** Mahārāshtra, C India
81 F16 **Kinyeti** ▲ S Sudan
101 I17 **Kinzig** ≈ SW Germany
Kioga, Lake *see* Kyoga, Lake
26 M8 **Kiowa** Kansas, C USA
27 P12 **Kiowa** Oklahoma, C USA
Kiparissía *see* Kyparissía
14 H10 **Kipawa, Lac** ◎ Québec, SE Canada
81 G24 **Kipengere Range** ▲ SW Tanzania
81 E23 **Kipili** Rukwa, W Tanzania
81 K20 **Kipini** Coast, SE Kenya
11 V16 **Kipling** Saskatchewan, S Canada
38 M13 **Kipnuk** Alaska, USA
97 F18 **Kippure** *Ir.* Cipiúr. ▲ E Ireland
79 N25 **Kipushi** Katanga, SE Dem. Rep. Congo
187 N10 **Kirakira** *var.* Kaokaona. San Cristobal, SE Solomon Islands
155 K14 **Kirandul** *var.* Bailādila. Chhattīsgarh, C India
155 I21 **Kīranūr** Tamil Nādu, SE India
119 N21 **Kiraw** *Rus.* Kirovo. Homyel'skaya Voblasts', SE Belarus
119 M17 **Kirawsk** *Rus.* Kirovsk; *prev.* Startsy. Mahilyowskaya Voblasts', E Belarus
118 F5 **Kirbla** Läänemaa, W Estonia
25 Y9 **Kirbyville** Texas, SW USA
114 M12 **Kırcasalih** Edirne, NW Turkey
109 W8 **Kirchbach** *var.* Kirchbach in Steiermark. Steiermark, SE Austria
Kirchbach in Steiermark *see* Kirchbach
108 H7 **Kirchberg** Sankt Gallen, NE Switzerland
109 S5 **Kirchdorf an der Krems** Oberösterreich, N Austria
Kirchheim *see* Kirchheim unter Teck
101 I22 **Kirchheim unter Teck** *var.* Kirchheim. Baden-Württemberg, SW Germany
Kirdzhali *see* Kŭrdzhali
123 N13 **Kirenga** ≈ S Russian Federation
123 N12 **Kirensk** Irkutskaya Oblast', C Russian Federation
Kirghizia *see* Kyrgyzstan
145 S16 **Kirghiz Range** *Rus.* Kirgizskiy Khrebet; *prev.* Alexander Range. ▲ Kazakhstan/Kyrgyzstan
Kirghiz SSR *see* Kyrgyzstan
Kirghiz Steppe *see* Kazakhskiy Melkosopochnik
Kirgizskaya SSR *see* Kyrgyzstan
Kirgizskiy Khrebet *see* Kirghiz Range
79 I19 **Kiri** Bandundu, W Dem. Rep. Congo
Kiriath-Arba *see* Hebron
191 R3 **Kiribati** *off.* Republic of Kiribati. ◆ *republic* C Pacific Ocean
136 L17 **Kırıkhan** Hatay, S Turkey
136 I13 **Kırıkkale** Kırıkkale, C Turkey
136 C10 **Kırıkkale** ◈ *province* C Turkey
124 L13 **Kirillov** Vologodskaya Oblast', NW Russian Federation
Kirin *see* Jilin
81 I18 **Kirinyaga** *prev.* Mount Kenya. ▲ C Kenya
124 H13 **Kirishi** *var.* Kirisi. Leningradskaya Oblast', NW Russian Federation
164 C16 **Kirishima-yama** ▲ Kyūshū, SW Japan
Kirisi *see* Kirishi
191 Y2 **Kiritimati** × Kiritimati, E Kiribati
191 Y2 **Kiritimati** *prev.* Christmas Island. *atoll* Line Islands, E Kiribati
186 G9 **Kiriwina Island** *Eng.* Trobriand Island. *island* SE PNG
186 G9 **Kiriwina Islands** *var.* Trobriand Islands. *island group* S PNG
96 K12 **Kirkcaldy** E Scotland, UK
97 I14 **Kirkcudbright** S Scotland, UK
97 I14 **Kirkcudbright** *cultural region* S Scotland, UK
Kirkee *see* Khadki
92 M8 **Kirkenes** *Fin.* Kirkkoniemi. Finnmark, N Norway
95 I14 **Kirkenær** Hedmark, S Norway
92 J4 **Kirkjubæjarklaustur** Sudhurland, S Iceland
Kirk-Kilissa *see* Kırklareli
Kirkkoniemi *see* Kirkenes
93 L20 **Kirkkonummi** *Swe.* Kyrkslätt. Etelä-Suomi, S Finland
14 G7 **Kirkland Lake** Ontario, S Canada
136 C9 **Kırklareli** *prev.* Kirk-Kilissa. Kırklareli, NW Turkey
136 I13 **Kırklareli** ◈ *province* NW Turkey
185 F20 **Kirkliston Range** ▲ South Island, NZ
14 D10 **Kirkpatrick Lake** ◎ Ontario, S Canada
195 Q11 **Kirkpatrick, Mount** ▲ Antarctica
27 U2 **Kirksville** Missouri, C USA
139 T4 **Kirkūk** *var.* Karkūk, Kerkuk. N Iraq
139 U7 **Kir Kush** E Iraq
96 K5 **Kirkwall** NE Scotland, UK
83 H25 **Kirkwood** Eastern Cape, S South Africa
27 X5 **Kirkwood** Missouri, C USA
Kirman *see* Kermān
Kir Moab/Kir of Moab *see* Al Karak
126 I5 **Kirov** Kaluzhskaya Oblast', W Russian Federation
125 R14 **Kirov** *prev.* Vyatka. Kirovskaya Oblast', NW Russian Federation
Kirov *see* Balpyk Bi, Kazakhstan
Kirov/Kirova *see* Kopbirlik, Kazakhstan
Kirovabad *see* Gäncä, Azerbaijan
Kirovabad *see* Panj, Tajikistan
Kirovakan *see* Vanadzor
Kirovo *see* Kiraw, Belarus
Kirovo/Kirovograd *see* Kirovohrad, Ukraine
Kirovo *see* Beshariq, Uzbekistan
125 R14 **Kirovo-Chepetsk** Kirovskaya Oblast', NW Russian Federation
Kirovogradskaya Oblast'/Kirovohrad *see* Kirovohrads'ka Oblast'
117 R7 **Kirovohrad** *Rus.* Kirovograd; *prev.* Kirovo, Yelizavetgrad, Zinov'yevsk. Kirovohrads'ka Oblast', C Ukraine
117 P7 **Kirovohrads'ka Oblast'** *var.* Kirovohrad, *Rus.* Kirovogradskaya Oblast'. ◈ *province* C Ukraine
124 J4 **Kirovsk** Murmanskaya Oblast', NW Russian Federation
Kirovsk *see* Babadaýhan, Turkmenistan
Kirovsk *see* Kirawsk, Belarus
117 X7 **Kirovs'k** Luhans'ka Oblast', E Ukraine
122 E9 **Kirovskaya Oblast'** ◈ *province* NW Russian Federation
117 X8 **Kirov'ske** Donets'ka Oblast', E Ukraine
117 U13 **Kirovs'ke** *Rus.* Kirovskoye. Respublika Krym, S Ukraine
Kirovskiy *see* Balpyk Bi/Ust'yevoye
Kirovskoye *see* Kyzyl-Adyr
Kirovskoye *see* Kirovs'ke
146 E11 **Kirpili** Ahal Welaýaty, C Turkmenistan
96 K10 **Kirriemuir** E Scotland, UK
125 S13 **Kirs** Kirovskaya Oblast', NW Russian Federation
127 N7 **Kirsanov** Tambovskaya Oblast', W Russian Federation
136 J14 **Kırşehir** *anc.* Justinianopolis. Kırşehir, C Turkey
136 I13 **Kırşehir** ◈ *province* C Turkey
149 P4 **Kirthar Range** ▲ S Pakistan
37 P9 **Kirtland** New Mexico, SW USA
Kirun/Kirun' *see* Chilung
92 J11 **Kiruna** *Lapp.* Giron. Norrbotten, N Sweden
79 M18 **Kirundu** Orientale, NE Dem. Rep. Congo
26 L3 **Kirwin Reservoir** ⊞ Kansas, C USA
127 Q4 **Kirya** Chuvashskaya Respublika, W Russian Federation
Kiryat Gat *see* Qiryat Gat
95 M18 **Kisa** Östergötland, S Sweden
165 P9 **Kisakata** Akita, Honshū, C Japan
Kisalföld *see* Little Alföld
79 L18 **Kisangani** *prev.* Stanleyville. Orientale, NE Dem. Rep. Congo
39 N12 **Kisaralik River** ≈ Alaska, USA
165 O14 **Kisarazu** Chiba, Honshū, S Japan
111 I22 **Kisbér** Komárom-Esztergom, NW Hungary
11 V17 **Kisbey** Saskatchewan, S Canada
122 J13 **Kiselevsk** Kemerovskaya Oblast', S Russian Federation
153 R13 **Kishanganj** Bihār, NE India
152 G12 **Kishangarh** Rājasthān, N India
Kishegyes *see* Mali Idoš
77 S15 **Kishi** Oyo, W Nigeria
Kishinev *see* Chişinău
Kishiözen *see* Malyy Uzen'
164 I14 **Kishiwada** *var.* Kisiwada. Ōsaka, Honshū, SW Japan
143 P14 **Kīsh, Jazīreh-ye** *var.* Qeys. *island* S Iran
145 R7 **Kishkenekol'** *prev.* Kzyltu. *Kaz.* Qyzyltu; Severnyy Kazakhstan, N Kazakhstan
152 I6 **Kishtwār** Jammu and Kashmir, NW India
81 H19 **Kisii** Nyanza, SW Kenya
81 J23 **Kisiju** Pwani, E Tanzania
Kisiwada *see* Kishiwada
Kisjenő *see* Chişineu-Criş
38 E17 **Kiska Island** *island* Aleutian Islands, Alaska, USA
Kiskapus *see* Copşa Mică
111 M22 **Kiskőrei-víztároló** ⊞ E Hungary
Kis-Küküllo *see* Târnava Mică
111 L24 **Kiskunfélegyháza** *var.* Félegyháza. Bács-Kiskun, C Hungary
111 K25 **Kiskunhalas** *var.* Halas. Bács-Kiskun, S Hungary
111 K24 **Kiskunmajsa** Bács-Kiskun, S Hungary
127 N15 **Kislovodsk** Stavropol'skiy Kray, SW Russian Federation
81 L18 **Kismaayo** *var.* Chisimayu, Kismayu, *It.* Chisimaio. Jubbada Hoose, S Somalia
Kismayu *see* Kismaayo
164 M13 **Kiso-sanmyaku** ▲ Honshū, S Japan
Kisseraing *see* Kanmaw Kyun
76 K14 **Kissidougou** Guinée-Forestière, S Guinea
23 X12 **Kissimmee** Florida, SE USA
23 X12 **Kissimmee, Lake** ◎ Florida, SE USA
23 X13 **Kissimmee River** ≈ Florida, SE USA
11 V13 **Kississing Lake** ◎ Manitoba, C Canada
111 L24 **Kistelek** Csongrád, SE Hungary
Kistna *see* Krishna
111 M23 **Kisújszállás** Jász-Nagykun-Szolnok, E Hungary
164 G12 **Kisuki** Shimane, Honshū, SW Japan
81 H18 **Kisumu** *prev.* Port Florence. Nyanza, W Kenya
Kisutzaneustadtl *see* Kysucké Nové Mesto
111 O20 **Kisvárda** *Ger.* Kleinwardein. Szabolcs-Szatmár-Bereg, E Hungary
81 J24 **Kiswere** Lindi, SE Tanzania
Kiszucaújhely *see* Kysucké Nové Mesto
76 K12 **Kita** Kayes, W Mali
207 N14 **Kitaa** ◈ *province* W Greenland
Kitab *see* Kitob
165 Q4 **Kitahiyama** Hokkaidō, NE Japan
165 P12 **Kita-Ibaraki** Ibaraki, Honshū, S Japan
165 X16 **Kita-Iō-jima** *Eng.* San Alessandro. *island* SE Japan
165 Q9 **Kitakami** Iwate, Honshū, C Japan
165 P11 **Kitakata** Fukushima, Honshū, C Japan
164 D13 **Kitakyūshū** *var.* Kitakyûsyû. Fukuoka, Kyūshū, SW Japan
Kitakyûsyû *see* Kitakyūshū
81 H18 **Kitale** Rift Valley, W Kenya
165 U3 **Kitami** Hokkaidō, NE Japan
165 T2 **Kitami-sanchi** ▲ Hokkaidō, NE Japan
37 W5 **Kit Carson** Colorado, C USA
180 M12 **Kitchener** Western Australia
14 F16 **Kitchener** Ontario, S Canada
93 O17 **Kitee** Itä-Suomi, E Finland
81 G16 **Kitgum** N Uganda
Kithareng *see* Kanmaw Kyun
Kíthira *see* Kýthira
Kíthnos *see* Kýthnos
10 J13 **Kitimat** British Columbia, SW Canada
92 L11 **Kitinen** ≈ N Finland
147 N12 **Kitob** *Rus.* Kitab. Qashqadaryo Viloyati, S Uzbekistan
116 K7 **Kitsman'** *Ger.* Kotzman, *Rom.* Cozmeni, *Rus.* Kitsman. Chernivets'ka Oblast', W Ukraine
164 E14 **Kitsuki** *var.* Kituki. Ōita, Kyūshū, SW Japan
18 C14 **Kittanning** Pennsylvania, NE USA
19 P10 **Kittery** Maine, NE USA
92 L11 **Kittilä** Lappi, N Finland
109 Z4 **Kittsee** Burgenland, E Austria
81 J19 **Kitui** Eastern, S Kenya
Kituki *see* Kitsuki
81 G22 **Kitunda** Tabora, C Tanzania
10 K13 **Kitwanga** British Columbia, SW Canada
82 J13 **Kitwe** *var.* Kitwe-Nkana. Copperbelt, C Zambia
Kitwe-Nkana *see* Kitwe
109 O7 **Kitzbühel** Tirol, W Austria
109 O7 **Kitzbüheler Alpen** ▲ W Austria
101 J19 **Kitzingen** Bayern, SE Germany
153 Q14 **Kiul** Bihār, NE India
186 A7 **Kiunga** Western, SW PNG
93 M16 **Kiuruvesi** Itä-Suomi, C Finland
38 M7 **Kivalina** Alaska, USA
92 L13 **Kivalo** *ridge* C Finland
116 J3 **Kivertsi** *Pol.* Kiwerce, *Rus.* Kivertsy. Volyns'ka Oblast', NW Ukraine
Kivertsy *see* Kivertsi
93 L16 **Kivijärvi** Länsi-Suomi, W Finland
95 L23 **Kivik** Skåne, S Sweden
118 J3 **Kiviõli** Ida-Virumaa, NE Estonia
Kivu, Lac *see* Kivu, Lake
79 P20 **Kivu, Lake** *Fr.* Lac Kivu. ◎ Rwanda/Dem. Rep. Congo
186 C9 **Kiwai Island** *island* SW PNG
39 N8 **Kiwalik** Alaska, USA
Kiwerce *see* Kivertsi
Kiyev *see* Kyyiv
145 R10 **Kiyevka** Karaganda, C Kazakhstan
Kiyevskaya Oblast' *see* Kyyivs'ka Oblast'
Kiyevskoye Vodokhranilishche *see* Kyyivs'ke Vodoskhovyshche
136 D10 **Kıyıköy** Kırklareli, NW Turkey
145 O9 **Kiyma** Akmola, C Kazakhstan
125 V13 **Kizel** Permskaya Oblast', NW Russian Federation
125 O12 **Kizema** *var.* Kizëma. Arkhangel'skaya Oblast', NW Russian Federation
Kizilagach *see* Elkhovo
136 H12 **Kızılcahamam** Ankara, N Turkey
136 J10 **Kızıl Irmak** ≈ C Turkey
Kızılkoca *see* Şefaatli
Kizil Kum *see* Kyzyl Kum
137 P16 **Kızıltepe** Mardin, SE Turkey
Ki Zil Uzen *see* Qezel Owzan, Rūd-e
127 Q16 **Kizilyurt** Respublika Dagestan, SW Russian Federation
127 Q15 **Kizlyar** Respublika Dagestan, SW Russian Federation
127 S3 **Kizner** Udmurtskaya Respublika, NW Russian Federation
Kizyl-Arvat *see* Serdar
Kizyl-Atrek *see* Etrek
Kizyl-Kaya *see* Gyzylgaya
Kizyl-Su *see* Gyzylsuw
95 H16 **Kjerkøy** *island* S Norway
Kjølen *see* Kölen
92 L7 **Kjøllefjord** Finnmark, N Norway
92 H11 **Kjøpsvik** Nordland, C Norway
169 N12 **Klabat, Teluk** *bay* Pulau Bangka, W Indonesia
112 I12 **Kladanj** Federacija Bosan I Hercegovina, C Bosnia and Herzegovina
171 X16 **Kladar** Papua, E Indonesia
111 C16 **Kladno** Středočeský Kraj, NW Czech Republic
112 P11 **Kladovo** Serbia, E Serbia and Montenegro (Yugo.)
167 P12 **Klaeng** Rayong, S Thailand
109 T9 **Klagenfurt** *Slvn.* Celovec. Kärnten, S Austria
118 B11 **Klaipėda** *Ger.* Memel. Klaipėda, NW Lithuania
118 C11 **Klaipėda** ◈ *province* W Lithuania
95 B18 **Klaksvík** *Dan.* Klaksvig Faeroe Islands
34 L2 **Klamath** California, W USA
32 H16 **Klamath Falls** Oregon, NW USA
34 M1 **Klamath Mountains** ▲ California/Oregon, W USA
34 L2 **Klamath River** ≈ California/Oregon, W USA
168 K9 **Klang** *var.* Kelang; *prev.* Port Swettenham. Selangor, Peninsular Malaysia
94 J13 **Klarälven** ≈ Norway/Sweden
111 B15 **Klášterec nad Ohří** *Ger.* Klösterle an der Eger. Ústecký Kraj, NW Czech Republic
111 B18 **Klatovy** *Ger.* Klattau. Plzeňský Kraj, W Czech Republic
Klattau *see* Klatovy
Klausenburg *see* Cluj-Napoca
39 Y14 **Klawock** Prince of Wales Island, Alaska, USA
98 P8 **Klazienaveen** Drenthe, NE Netherlands
Kleck *see* Klyetsk
110 H11 **Kłecko** Wielkolpolskie, C Poland
110 I11 **Kleczew** Wielkopolskie, C Poland
10 L15 **Kleena Kleene** British Columbia, SW Canada
83 D20 **Klein Aub** Hardap, C Namibia
Kleine Donau *see* Mosoni-Duna
101 O14 **Kleine Elster** ≈ E Germany
Kleine Kokel *see* Târnava Mică
99 I16 **Kleine Nete** ≈ N Belgium
Kleines Ungarisches Tiefland *see* Little Alföld
83 E22 **Klein Karas** Karas, S Namibia
Kleinkopisch *see* Copşa Mică
Klein-Marien *see* Väike-Maarja
Kleinschlatten *see* Zlatna
83 D23 **Kleinsee** Northern Cape, W South Africa
Kleinwardein *see* Kisvárda
115 C16 **Kleisoúra** Ípeiros, W Greece
95 C17 **Klepp** Rogaland, S Norway
83 I22 **Klerksdorp** North-West, N South Africa
126 I5 **Kletnya** Bryanskaya Oblast', W Russian Federation
Kletsk *see* Klyetsk
101 D14 **Kleve** *Eng.* Cleves, *Fr.* Clèves; *prev.* Cleve. Nordrhein-Westfalen, W Germany
113 J16 **Kličevo** Montenegro, SW Serbia and Montenegro (Yugo.)
119 M16 **Klichaw** *Rus.* Klichev. Mahilyowskaya Voblasts', E Belarus
Klichev *see* Klichaw
119 Q16 **Klimavichy** *Rus.* Klimovichi. Mahilyowskaya Voblasts', E Belarus
114 M7 **Kliment** Shumen, NE Bulgaria
Klimovichi *see* Klimavichy
93 G14 **Klimpfjäll** Västerbotten, N Sweden
126 K3 **Klin** Moskovskaya Oblast', W Russian Federation
113 M16 **Klina** Serbia, S Serbia and Montenegro (Yugo.)
111 B15 **Klínovec** *Ger.* Keilberg. ▲ NW Czech Republic
95 P19 **Klintehamn** Gotland, SE Sweden
127 R8 **Klintsovka** Saratovskaya Oblast', W Russian Federation
126 H6 **Klintsy** Bryanskaya Oblast', W Russian Federation
95 K22 **Klippan** Skåne, S Sweden
92 G13 **Klippen** Västerbotten, N Sweden
121 P2 **Klirou** W Cyprus
114 I9 **Klisura** Plovdiv, C Bulgaria
95 F20 **Klitmøller** Viborg, NW Denmark
112 F11 **Ključ** Federacija Bosna I Hercegovina, NW Bosnia and Herzegovina
111 J14 **Kłobuck** Śląskie, S Poland
110 J11 **Kłodawa** Wielkopolskie, C Poland
111 G16 **Kłodzko** *Ger.* Glatz. Dolnośląskie, SW Poland
95 I14 **Kløfta** Akershus, S Norway
112 P12 **Kločočevac** Serbia, E Serbia and Montenegro (Yugo.)
118 G3 **Klooga** *Ger.* Lodensee. Harjumaa, NW Estonia
99 F15 **Kloosterzande** Zeeland, SW Netherlands
113 L19 **Klos** *var.* Klosi. Dibër, C Albania
Klosi *see* Klos
Klösterle an der Eger *see* Klášterec nad Ohří

109 *X3* **Klosterneuburg** Niederösterreich, NE Austria
108 *J9* **Klosters** Graubünden, SE Switzerland
108 *G7* **Kloten** Zürich, N Switzerland
108 *G7* **Kloten** ✈ (Zürich) Zürich, N Switzerland
100 *K12* **Klötze** Sachsen-Anhalt, C Germany
12 *K3* **Klotz, Lac** ⊚ Québec, NE Canada
101 *O15* **Klotzsche** ✈ (Dresden) Sachsen, E Germany
10 *H7* **Kluane Lake** ⊚ Yukon Territory, W Canada
Kluang see Keluang
111 *I14* **Kluczbork** Ger. Kreuzburg, Kreuzburg in Oberschlesien. Opolskie, S Poland
39 *W12* **Klukwan** Alaska, USA
Klyastitsy see Klyastsitsy
118 *L11* **Klyastsitsy** Rus. Klyastitsy. Vitsyebskaya Voblasts', N Belarus
127 *T5* **Klyavlino** Samarskaya Oblast', W Russian Federation
127 *N3* **Klyaz'ma** ≈ W Russian Federation
119 *J17* **Klyetsk** Pol. Kleck, Rus. Kletsk. Minskaya Voblasts', SW Belarus
147 *S8* **Klyuchevka** Talasskaya Oblast', NW Kyrgyzstan
123 *V10* **Klyuchevskaya Sopka, Vulkan** ✱ E Russian Federation
95 *D17* **Knaben** Vest-Agder, S Norway
Knanzi see Ghanzi
95 *K21* **Knäred** Halland, S Sweden
97 *M16* **Knaresborough** N England, UK
114 *H8* **Knezha** Vratsa, NW Bulgaria
25 *O9* **Knickerbocker** Texas, SW USA
28 *K5* **Knife River** ≈ North Dakota, N USA
10 *K16* **Knight Inlet** inlet British Columbia, W Canada
39 *S12* **Knight Island** island Alaska, USA
97 *K20* **Knighton** E Wales, UK
35 *O7* **Knights Landing** California, W USA
112 *E13* **Knin** Šibenik-Knin, S Croatia
25 *Q12* **Knippal** Texas, SW USA
109 *U7* **Knittelfeld** Steiermark, C Austria
95 *O15* **Knivsta** Uppsala, C Sweden
113 *P14* **Knjaževac** Serbia, E Serbia and Montenegro (Yugo.)
27 *S4* **Knob Noster** Missouri, C USA
99 *D15* **Knokke-Heist** West-Vlaanderen, NW Belgium
95 *H20* **Knøsen** hill N Denmark
Knosós see Knossos
115 *J25* **Knossos** Gk. Knosós. prehistoric site Kríti, Greece, E Mediterranean Sea
25 *N7* **Knott** Texas, SW USA
194 *K5* **Knowles, Cape** headland Antarctica
31 *O11* **Knox** Indiana, N USA
29 *O3* **Knox** North Dakota, N USA
18 *C13* **Knox** Pennsylvania, NE USA
189 *X8* **Knox Atoll** var. Nadikdik, Narikrik. atoll Ratak Chain, SE Marshall Islands
10 *H13* **Knox, Cape** headland Graham Island, British Columbia, SW Canada
25 *P5* **Knox City** Texas, SW USA
195 *Y11* **Knox Coast** physical region Antarctica
31 *T12* **Knox Lake** ⊠ Ohio, N USA
23 *T5* **Knoxville** Georgia, SE USA
30 *K12* **Knoxville** Illinois, N USA
29 *W15* **Knoxville** Iowa, C USA
21 *N9* **Knoxville** Tennessee, S USA
197 *P11* **Knud Rasmussen Land** physical region N Greenland
Knüll see Knüllgebirge
101 *I16* **Knüllgebirge** var. Knüll. ▲▲ C Germany
Knyazhevo see Sredishte
Knyazhitsy see Knyazhytsy
119 *O15* **Knyazhytsy** Rus. Knyazhitsy. Mahilyowskaya Voblasts', E Belarus
83 *G26* **Knysna** Western Cape, SW South Africa
Koartac see Quaqtaq
169 *N13* **Koba** Pulau Bangka, W Indonesia
164 *D16* **Kobayashi** var. Kobayasi. Miyazaki, Kyūshū, SW Japan
Kobayasi see Kobayashi
Kobdo see Hovd
164 *I13* **Kōbe** Hyōgo, Honshū, SW Japan
Kobelyaki see Kobelyaky
117 *T6* **Kobelyaky** Rus. Kobelyaki. Poltavs'ka Oblast', NE Ukraine
95 *J22* **København** Eng. Copenhagen; anc. Hafnia. ● (Denmark) Sjælland, København, E Denmark
95 *J23* **København** off. Københavns Amt. ◈ county E Denmark
76 *K10* **Kobenni** Hodh el Gharbi, S Mauritania
171 *T13* **Kobi** Pulau Seram, E Indonesia
101 *F17* **Koblenz** prev. Coblenz, Fr. Coblence, anc. Confluentes. Rheinland-Pfalz, W Germany
108 *F6* **Koblenz** Aargau, N Switzerland
124 *J14* **Kobozha** Novgorodskaya Oblast', W Russian Federation
Kobrin see Kobryn
171 *V15* **Kobroor, Pulau** island Kepulauan Aru, E Indonesia
119 *G19* **Kobryn** Pol. Kobryn, Rus. Kobrin. Brestskaya Voblasts', SW Belarus
39 *O7* **Kobuk** Alaska, USA
39 *O7* **Kobuk River** ≈ Alaska, USA
137 *Q10* **K'obulet'i** W Georgia
123 *P10* **Kobyay** Respublika Sakha (Yakutiya), NE Russian Federation
136 *E11* **Kocaeli** ◈ province NW Turkey
113 *P18* **Kočani** NE FYR Macedonia
112 *K12* **Koceljevo** Serbia, W Serbia and Montenegro (Yugo.)
109 *U12* **Kočevje** Ger. Gottschee. S Slovenia
153 *T12* **Koch Bihār** West Bengal, NE India
122 *M9* **Kochechum** ≈ N Russian Federation
101 *I20* **Kocher** ≈ SW Germany
125 *T13* **Kochevo** Komi-Permyatskiy Avtonomnyy Okrug, NW Russian Federation
164 *G14* **Kōchi** var. Kôti. Kōchi, Shikoku, SW Japan
164 *G14* **Kōchi** off. Kōchi-ken, var. Kôti. ◈ prefecture Shikoku, SW Japan
Kochi see Cochin
Kochiu see Gejiu
Kochkor see Kochkorka
147 *V8* **Kochkorka** Kir. Kochkor. Narynskaya Oblast', C Kyrgyzstan
125 *V5* **Kochmes** Respublika Komi, NW Russian Federation
127 *P15* **Kochubey** Respublika Dagestan, SW Russian Federation
115 *I17* **Kochýlas** ▲ Skýros, Vóreioi Sporádes, Greece, Aegean Sea
110 *O13* **Kock** Lubelskie, E Poland
81 *J19* **Kodacho** spring/well S Kenya
155 *K24* **Koddiyar Bay** bay NE Sri Lanka
39 *Q14* **Kodiak** Kodiak Island, Alaska, USA
39 *Q14* **Kodiak Island** island Alaska, USA
154 *B12* **Kodīnār** Gujarāt, W India
124 *M9* **Kodino** Arkhangel'skaya Oblast', NW Russian Federation
122 *M12* **Kodinsk** Krasnoyarskiy Kray, C Russian Federation
80 *F12* **Kodok** Upper Nile, SE Sudan
117 *N8* **Kodyma** Odes'ka Oblast', SW Ukraine
99 *B17* **Koekelare** West-Vlaanderen, W Belgium
Koeln see Köln
Koepang see Kupang
Ko-erh-mu see Golmud
99 *J17* **Koersel** Limburg, NE Belgium
83 *E21* **Koës** Karas, SE Namibia
Koetai see Mahakam, Sungai
Koetaradja see Bandaaceh
36 *I14* **Kofa Mountains** ▲▲ Arizona, SW USA
171 *Y15* **Kofarau** Papua, E Indonesia
147 *P13* **Kofarnihon** Rus. Kofarnikhon; prev. Ordzhonikidzeabad, Taj. Orjonikidzeobod, Yangi-Bazar. W Tajikistan
147 *P14* **Kofarnihon** Rus. Kafirnigan. ≈ SW Tajikistan
Kofarnikhon see Kofarnihon
114 *M11* **Kofçaz** Kırklareli, NW Turkey
115 *J25* **Kófinas** ▲ Kríti, Greece, E Mediterranean Sea
121 *P3* **Kofínou** var. Kophinou. S Cyprus
109 *V8* **Köflach** Steiermark, SE Austria
77 *Q17* **Koforidua** SE Ghana
164 *H12* **Kōfu** Tottori, Honshū, SW Japan
164 *M13* **Kōfu** var. Kôhu. Yamanashi, Honshū, S Japan
81 *F22* **Koga** Tabora, C Tanzania
Kogălniceanu see Mihail Kogălniceanu
13 *P6* **Kogaluk** ≈ Newfoundland and Labrador, E Canada
12 *J4* **Kogaluk** ≈ Québec, NE Canada
122 *I10* **Kogalym** Khanty-Mansiyskiy Avtonomnyy Okrug, C Russian Federation
95 *J23* **Køge** Roskilde, E Denmark
95 *J23* **Køge Bugt** bay E Denmark
77 *U16* **Kogi** ◈ state C Nigeria
146 *L11* **Kogon** Rus. Kagan. Buxoro Viloyati, C Uzbekistan
163 *Y17* **Kōgŭm-do** island S South Korea
Kőhalom see Rupea
149 *T6* **Kohāt** North-West Frontier Province, NW Pakistan
118 *G4* **Kohila** Ger. Koil. Raplamaa, NW Estonia
153 *X13* **Kohīma** Nāgāland, E India
Koh I Noh see Büyükağrı Dağı
142 *L10* **Kohgīlūyeh va Būyer Aḥmad** off. Ostān-e Kohgīlūyeh va Būyer Aḥmad, var. Boyer Ahmadī va Kohkīlūyeh. ◈ province SW Iran
Kohsān see Kūhestān
118 *J3* **Kohtla-Järve** Ida-Virumaa, NE Estonia
Kôhu see Kōfu
117 *N10* **Kohyl'nyk** Rom. Cogîlnic. ≈ Moldova/Ukraine
165 *N11* **Koide** Niigata, Honshū, C Japan
10 *G7* **Koidern** Yukon Territory, W Canada
76 *J15* **Koidu** E Sierra Leone
118 *I4* **Koigi** Järvamaa, C Estonia
Koil see Kohila
172 *H13* **Koimbani** Grande Comore, NW Comoros
139 *T3* **Koi Sanjaq** var. Koysanjaq, Küysanjaq. N Iraq
93 *O16* **Koitere** ⊚ E Finland
Koivisto see Primorsk
163 *Z16* **Kōje-do** Jap. Kyōsai-tō. island S South Korea
80 *J13* **K'ok'a Hāyk'** ⊚ C Ethiopia
Kokand see Qo'qon
182 *F6* **Kokatha** South Australia
Kokcha see Ko'kcha
Kokchetav see Kokshetau
93 *K18* **Kokemäenjoki** ≈ SW Finland
171 *W14* **Kokenau** var. Kokonau. Papua, E Indonesia
83 *E22* **Kokerboom** Karas, SE Namibia
119 *N14* **Kokhanava** Rus. Kokhanovo. Vitsyebskaya Voblasts', NE Belarus
Kokhanovichi see Kakhanavichy
Kokhanovo see Kokhanava
Kök-Janggak see Kok-Yangak
93 *K16* **Kokkola** Swe. Karleby; prev. Swe. Gamlakarleby. Länsi-Suomi, W Finland
158 *L3* **Kok Kuduk** well N China
118 *H9* **Koknese** Aizkraukle, C Latvia
77 *T13* **Koko** Kebbi, W Nigeria
186 *E9* **Kokoda** Northern, S PNG
76 *K12* **Kokofata** Kayes, W Mali
39 *N6* **Kokolik River** ≈ Alaska, USA
31 *O13* **Kokomo** Indiana, N USA
Kokonau see Kokenau
Koko Nor see Qinghai Hu, China
Koko Nor see Qinghai, China
186 *H6* **Kokopo** var. Kopopo; prev. Herbertshöhe. New Britain, E PNG
145 *X10* **Kokpekti** Kaz. Kökpekti. Vostochnyy Kazakhstan, E Kazakhstan
145 *X11* **Kokpekti** ≈ E Kazakhstan
39 *P9* **Kokrines** Alaska, USA
39 *P9* **Kokrines Hills** ▲▲ Alaska, USA
145 *P17* **Koksaray** Yuzhnyy Kazakhstan, S Kazakhstan
147 *X9* **Kokshaal-Tau** Rus. Khrebet Kakshaal-Too. ▲▲ China/Kyrgyzstan
145 *P7* **Kokshetau** Kaz. Kökshetaū; prev. Kokchetav. Akmola, N Kazakhstan
99 *A17* **Koksijde** West-Vlaanderen, W Belgium
12 *M5* **Koksoak** ≈ Québec, E Canada
83 *K24* **Kokstad** KwaZulu/Natal, E South Africa
145 *W15* **Koktal** Kaz. Köktal. Almaty, SE Kazakhstan
145 *Q12* **Koktas** ≈ C Kazakhstan
Kök-Tash see Kĕk-Tash
Koktokay see Fuyun
147 *T9* **Kok-Yangak** Kir. Kök-Janggak. Dzhalal-Abadskaya Oblast', W Kyrgyzstan
158 *F9* **Kokyar** Xinjiang Uygur Zizhiqu, W China
149 *O13* **Kolāchi** var. Kulachi. ≈ SW Pakistan
76 *J15* **Kolahun** N Liberia
171 *O14* **Kolaka** Sulawesi, C Indonesia
Kolam see Quilon
K'o-la-ma-i see Karamay
Kola Peninsula see Kol'skiy Poluostrov
155 *H19* **Kolār** Karnātaka, E India
155 *H19* **Kolār Gold Fields** Karnātaka, E India
92 *K11* **Kolari** Lappi, NW Finland
111 *I21* **Kolárovo** Ger. Gutta; prev. Guta, Hung. Gúta. Nitriansky Kraj, SW Slovakia
113 *K16* **Kolašin** Montenegro, SW Serbia and Montenegro (Yugo.)
152 *F11* **Kolāyat** Rājasthān, NW India
95 *N15* **Kolbäck** Västmanland, C Sweden
Kolbcha see Kowbcha
197 *Q15* **Kolbeinsey Ridge** undersea feature Denmark Strait/Norwegian Sea
Kolberg see Kołobrzeg
95 *H15* **Kolbotn** Akershus, S Norway
111 *N16* **Kolbuszowa** Podkarpackie, SE Poland
126 *L3* **Kol'chugino** Vladimirskaya Oblast', W Russian Federation
76 *H12* **Kolda** S Senegal
95 *G23* **Kolding** Vejle, C Denmark
79 *M17* **Kole** Orientale, N Dem. Rep. Congo
79 *K20* **Kole** Kasai Oriental, SW Dem. Rep. Congo
Kōle see Kili Island
Kolepom, Pulau see Yos Sudarso, Pulau
118 *H3* **Kolga Laht** Ger. Kolko-Wiek. bay N Estonia
127 *Q3* **Kolguyev, Ostrov** island NW Russian Federation
155 *E16* **Kolhāpur** Mahārāshtra, SW India
151 *K21* **Kolhumadulu Atoll** var. Kolumadulu Atoll, Thaa Atoll. atoll S Maldives
93 *O16* **Koli** var. Kolinkylä. Itä-Suomi, E Finland
39 *O13* **Koliganek** Alaska, USA
111 *E16* **Kolín** Ger. Kolin. Středočeský Kraj, C Czech Republic
Kolinkylä see Koli
190 *E12* **Koliu** Île Futuna, W Wallis and Futuna
118 *E7* **Kolka** Talsi, NW Latvia
118 *E7* **Kolkasrags** prev. Eng. Cape Domesnes. headland NW Latvia
Kolkhozabad see Kolkhozobod
147 *P14* **Kolkhozobod** Rus. Kolkhozabad; prev. Kaganovichabad, Tugalan. SW Tajikistan
Kolki/Kołki see Kolky
Kolko-Wiek see Kolga Laht
116 *K3* **Kolky** Pol. Kołki, Rus. Kolki. Volyns'ka Oblast', NW Ukraine
Kollam see Quilon
155 *G20* **Kollegāl** Karnātaka, W India
98 *M5* **Kollum** Friesland, N Netherlands
Kolmar see Colmar
101 *E16* **Köln** var. Koeln, Eng./Fr. Cologne; prev. Cöln, anc. Colonia Agrippina, Oppidum Ubiorum. Nordrhein-Westfalen, W Germany
110 *N9* **Kolno** Podlaskie, NE Poland
110 *J12* **Koło** Wielkopolskie, C Poland
38 *B8* **Kōloa** var. Koloa. Kaua'i, Hawai'i, USA, C Pacific Ocean
110 *E7* **Kołobrzeg** Ger. Kolberg. Zachodnio-pomorskie, NW Poland
126 *H4* **Kolodnya** Smolenskaya Oblast', W Russian Federation
190 *E13* **Kolofau, Mont** ✱ Île Alofi, S Wallis and Futuna
125 *O14* **Kologriv** Kostromskaya Oblast', NW Russian Federation
76 *L12* **Kolokani** Koulikoro, W Mali
77 *N13* **Koloko** W Burkina
186 *K8* **Kolombangara** var. Kilimbangara, Nduke. island New Georgia Islands, NW Solomon Islands
Kolomea see Kolomyya
126 *L4* **Kolomna** Moskovskaya Oblast', W Russian Federation
116 *J7* **Kolomyya** Ger. Kolomea. Ivano-Frankivs'ka Oblast', W Ukraine
76 *M13* **Kolondiéba** Sikasso, SW Mali
193 *V15* **Kolonga** Tongatapu, S Tonga
189 *U16* **Kolonia** var. Colonia. Pohnpei, E Micronesia
Kolonja see Kolonjë
113 *K21* **Kolonjë** var. Kolonja. Fier, C Albania
Kolonjë see Ersekë
Kolotambu see Avuavu
193 *U15* **Kolovai** Tongatapu, S Tonga
Kolozsvár see Cluj-Napoca
112 *C9* **Kolpa** Ger. Kulpa, SCr. Kupa. ≈ Croatia/Slovenia
122 *J11* **Kolpashevo** Tomskaya Oblast', C Russian Federation
124 *H13* **Kolpino** Leningradskaya Oblast', NW Russian Federation
100 *M10* **Kölpinsee** ⊚ NE Germany
146 *K8* **Ko'lquduq** Rus. Kulkuduk. Navoiy Viloyati, N Uzbekistan
126 *K5* **Kol'skiy Poluostrov** Eng. Kola Peninsula. peninsula NW Russian Federation
127 *T6* **Koltubanovskiy** Orenburgskaya Oblast', W Russian Federation
112 *L11* **Kolubara** ≈ C Serbia and Montenegro (Yugo.)
Kolupchii see Gurkovo
110 *K13* **Koluszki** Łodzkie, C Poland
127 *T6* **Kolva** ≈ NW Russian Federation
93 *E14* **Kolvereid** Nord-Trøndelag, W Norway
148 *L15* **Kolwa** Baluchistān, SW Pakistan
79 *M24* **Kolwezi** Katanga, S Dem. Rep. Congo
123 *S7* **Kolyma** ≈ NE Russian Federation
Kolyma Lowland see Kolymskaya Nizmennost'
Kolyma Range/Kolymskiy, Khrebet see Kolymskoye Nagor'ye
123 *S7* **Kolymskaya Nizmennost'** Eng. Kolyma Lowland. lowlands NE Russian Federation
123 *S7* **Kolymskoye** Respublika Sakha (Yakutiya), NE Russian Federation
123 *U8* **Kolymskoye Nagor'ye** var. Khrebet Kolymskiy, Eng. Kolyma Range. ▲▲ E Russian Federation
123 *V5* **Kolyuchinskaya Guba** bay NE Russian Federation
145 *W15* **Kol'zhat** Almaty, SE Kazakhstan
114 *G8* **Kom** ▲ NW Bulgaria
80 *I13* **Koma** Oromo, C Ethiopia
77 *X12* **Komadugu Gana** ≈ NE Nigeria
164 *M13* **Komagane** Nagano, Honshū, S Japan
79 *P17* **Komanda** Orientale, NE Dem. Rep. Congo
197 *U1* **Komandorskaya Basin** var. Kamchatka Basin. undersea feature SW Bering Sea
123 *W9* **Komandorskiye Ostrova** Eng. Commander Islands. island group E Russian Federation
Kománfalva see Comănești
111 *I22* **Komárno** Ger. Komorn, Hung. Komárom. Nitriansky Kraj, SW Slovakia
111 *I22* **Komárom** Komárom-Esztergom, NW Hungary
Komárom see Komárno
111 *I22* **Komárom-Esztergom** off. Komárom-Esztergom Megye. ◈ county N Hungary
164 *K11* **Komatsu** var. Komatu. Ishikawa, Honshū, SW Japan
Komatu see Komatsu
83 *D17* **Kombat** Otjozondjupa, N Namibia
Kombissiguiri see Kombissiri
77 *P13* **Kombissiri** var. Kombissiguiri. C Burkina
188 *E10* **Komebail Lagoon** lagoon N Palau
81 *F20* **Kome Island** island N Tanzania
Komeyo see Wandai
117 *P10* **Kominternivs'ke** Odes'ka Oblast', SW Ukraine
125 *R12* **Komi-Permyatskiy Avtonomnyy Okrug** ◈ autonomous district W Russian Federation
127 *R8* **Komi, Respublika** ◈ autonomous republic NW Russian Federation
111 *I25* **Komló** Baranya, SW Hungary
Kommunarsk see Alchevs'k
147 *S12* **Kommunizm, Qullai** ▲ E Tajikistan
186 *B7* **Komo** Southern Highlands, W PNG
170 *M16* **Komodo, Pulau** island Nusa Tenggara, S Indonesia
77 *N15* **Komoé** var. Komoé Fleuve. ≈ E Ivory Coast
Komoé Fleuve see Komoé
75 *X11* **Kôm Ombo** var. Kawm Umbū. SE Egypt
79 *F20* **Komono** La Lékoumou, SW Congo
171 *Y16* **Komoran** Papua, E Indonesia
171 *Y16* **Komoran, Pulau** island E Indonesia
Komorn see Komárno
Komornok see Comorâște
Komosolabad see Komsomolobod
Komotau see Chomutov
114 *K13* **Komotiní** var. Gümüljina, Turk. Gümülcine. Anatolikí Makedonía kai Thráki, NE Greece
113 *K16* **Komovi** ▲▲ SW Serbia and Montenegro (Yugo.)
117 *R8* **Kompaniyivka** Kirovohrads'ka Oblast', C Ukraine
Kompong see Kâmpóng Chhnăng
Kompong Cham see Kâmpóng Cham
Kompong Kleang see Kâmpóng Khleăng
Kompong Som see Kâmpóng Saôm
Kompong Speu see Kâmpóng Spoe
Komrat see Comrat
Komsomol see Komsomol'skiy, Atyrau, Kazakhstan
Komsomol/Komsomolets see Karabalyk, Kostanay, Kazakhstan
122 *K14* **Komsomolets, Ostrov** island Severnaya Zemlya, N Russian Federation
144 *F13* **Komsomolets, Zaliv** lake gulf SW Kazakhstan
147 *Q12* **Komsomolobod** Rus. Komosolabad. C Tajikistan
124 *M16* **Komsomol'sk** Ivanovskaya Oblast', W Russian Federation
117 *S6* **Komsomol's'k** Poltavs'ka Oblast', C Ukraine
146 *M11* **Komsomol'sk** Navoiy Viloyati, N Uzbekistan
144 *G12* **Komsomol'skiy** Kaz. Komsomol. Atyrau, W Kazakhstan
125 *W4* **Komsomol'skiy** Respublika Komi, NW Russian Federation
123 *S13* **Komsomol'sk-na-Amure** Khabarovskiy Kray, SE Russian Federation
Komsomol'sk-na-Ustyurte see Kubla-Ustyurt
144 *K10* **Komsomol'skoye** Aktyubinsk, NW Kazakhstan
127 *Q8* **Komsomol'skoye** Saratovskaya Oblast', W Russian Federation
145 *P10* **Kon** ≈ C Kazakhstan
Kona see Kailua-Kona
124 *K16* **Konakovo** Tverskaya Oblast', W Russian Federation
143 *V15* **Konārak** Sīstān va Balūchestān, SE Iran
Konarhā see Kunar
27 *O11* **Konawa** Oklahoma, C USA
122 *H10* **Konda** ≈ C Russian Federation
154 *L13* **Kondagaon** Chhattīsgarh, C India
14 *K10* **Kondiaronk, Lac** ⊚ Québec, SE Canada
180 *J13* **Kondinin** Western Australia
81 *H21* **Kondoa** Dodoma, C Tanzania
127 *P6* **Kondol'** Penzenskaya Oblast', W Russian Federation
114 *N10* **Kondolovo** Burgas, E Bulgaria
171 *Z16* **Kondomirat** Papua, E Indonesia
124 *J10* **Kondopoga** Respublika Kareliya, NW Russian Federation
Kondoz see Kunduz
155 *J17* **Kondukūr** var. Kandukur. Andhra Pradesh, E India
Kondūz see Kunduz
187 *P16* **Koné** Province Nord, W New Caledonia
146 *E13* **Könekesir** Rus. Kënekesir. Balkan Welaýaty, W Turkmenistan
146 *G8* **Köneürgenç** var. Köneürgench, Rus. Këneurgench; prev. Kunya-Urgench. Daşoguz Welaýaty, N Turkmenistan
Köneürgench see Köneürgenç
77 *N15* **Kong** N Ivory Coast
39 *S5* **Kongakut River** ≈ Alaska, USA
197 *O14* **Kong Christian IX Land** Eng. King Christian IX Land. physical region SE Greenland
197 *P13* **Kong Christian X Land** Eng. King Christian X Land. physical region E Greenland
197 *N13* **Kong Frederik IX Land** Eng. King Frederik IX Land. physical region SW Greenland
197 *Q12* **Kong Frederik VIII Land** Eng. King Frederik VIII Land. physical region NE Greenland
197 *N15* **Kong Frederik VI Kyst** Eng. King Frederik VI Coast. physical region SE Greenland
167 *P13* **Kông, Kaôh** prev. Kas Kong. island SW Cambodia
92 *P2* **Kong Karls Land** Eng. King Charles Islands. island group SE Svalbard
81 *G14* **Kong Kong** ≈ SE Sudan
Kongo see Congo (river)
83 *G16* **Kongola** Caprivi, NE Namibia
79 *N21* **Kongolo** Katanga, E Dem. Rep. Congo
81 *F14* **Kongor** Jonglei, SE Sudan
197 *Q14* **Kong Oscar Fjord** fjord E Greenland
77 *P12* **Kongoussi** N Burkina
95 *G15* **Kongsberg** Buskerud, S Norway
92 *Q2* **Kongsøya** island Kong Karls Land, E Svalbard
95 *I14* **Kongsvinger** Hedmark, S Norway
Kongtong see Pingliang
167 *T11* **Kông, Tônle** Lao. Xê Kong. ≈ Cambodia/Laos
158 *E8* **Kongur Shan** ▲ NW China
81 *I22* **Kongwa** Dodoma, C Tanzania
Kong, Xê see Kông, Tônle
Konia see Konya
147 *R11* **Konibodom** Rus. Kanibadam. N Tajikistan
111 *K15* **Koniecpol** Śląskie, S Poland
Konieh see Konya
Königgrätz see Hradec Králové
Königinhof an der Elbe see Dvůr Králové nad Labem
101 *K23* **Königsbrunn** Bayern, S Germany
Königshütte see Chorzów
101 *O24* **Königssee** ⊚ SE Germany
109 *S8* **Königstuhl** ▲ S Austria
109 *U3* **Königswiesen** Oberösterreich, N Austria
101 *E17* **Königswinter** Nordrhein-Westfalen, W Germany
146 *M11* **Konimex** Rus. Kenimekh. Navoiy Viloyati, N Uzbekistan
110 *I12* **Konin** Ger. Kuhnau. Wielkopolskie, C Poland
Koninkrijk der Nederlanden see Netherlands
113 *L24* **Konispol** var. Konispoli. Vlorë, S Albania
Konispoli see Konispol
115 *C15* **Kónitsa** Ípeiros, W Greece
Konitz see Chojnice
108 *D8* **Köniz** Bern, W Switzerland
113 *H14* **Konjic** Federacija Bosna I Hercegovina, C Bosnia and Herzegovina
92 *J10* **Könkämäälven** ≈ Finland/Sweden
155 *D14* **Konkan** W India
83 *D22* **Konkiep** ≈ S Namibia
76 *I14* **Konkouré** ≈ W Guinea
77 *O11* **Konna** Mopti, S Mali
186 *H6* **Konogaiang, Mount** ▲ New Ireland, NE PNG
186 *H5* **Konogogo** New Ireland, NE PNG
108 *E9* **Konolfingen** Bern, W Switzerland
77 *P16* **Konongo** C Ghana
186 *H5* **Konos** New Ireland, NE PNG
124 *M12* **Konosha** Arkhangel'skaya Oblast', NW Russian Federation
117 *R3* **Konotop** Sums'ka Oblast', NE Ukraine
158 *L7* **Konqi He** ≈ NW China
111 *L14* **Końskie** Świętokrzyskie, C Poland
Konstantinovka see Kostyantynivka
126 *M11* **Konstantinovsk** Rostovskaya Oblast', SW Russian Federation
101 *H24* **Konstanz** var. Constanz, Eng. Constance; hist. Kostnitz, anc. Constantia. Baden-Württemberg, S Germany
Konstanza see Constanța
77 *T14* **Kontagora** Niger, W Nigeria
78 *E13* **Kontcha** Nord, N Cameroon
99 *G17* **Kontich** Antwerpen, N Belgium
93 *O16* **Kontiolahti** Itä-Suomi, E Finland
93 *M15* **Kontiomäki** Oulu, C Finland
167 *U11* **Kon Tum** var. Kontum. Kon Tum, C Vietnam
Konur see Sulakyurt
136 *H15* **Konya** var. Konieh; prev. Konia, anc. Iconium. Konya, C Turkey
136 *H15* **Konya** var. Konia, Konieh. ◈ province C Turkey
145 *T13* **Konyrat** var. Kounradskiy, Kaz. Qongyrat. Karaganda, C Kazakhstan
145 *W15* **Konyrolen** Almaty, SE Kazakhstan
81 *I19* **Konza** Eastern, S Kenya
98 *I9* **Koog aan den Zaan** Noord-Holland, C Netherlands
182 *E7* **Koonibba** South Australia
31 *O11* **Koontz Lake** Indiana, N USA
171 *U12* **Koor** Papua, E Indonesia
183 *R9* **Koorawatha** New South Wales, SE Australia
118 *J5* **Koosa** Tartumaa, E Estonia
33 *N7* **Kootenai** var. Kootenay. ≈ Canada/USA see also Kootenay
11 *P17* **Kootenay** var. Kootenai. ≈ Canada/USA see also Kootenai
83 *F24* **Kootjieskolk** Northern Cape, W South Africa
113 *M15* **Kopaonik** ▲▲ S Serbia and Montenegro (Yugo.)
Kopar see Koper
92 *K1* **Kópasker** Nordhurland Eystra, N Iceland
92 *H4* **Kópavogur** Reykjanes, W Iceland
145 *U13* **Kopbirlik** prev. Kīrov, Kirova. Almaty, SE Kazakhstan
109 *S13* **Koper** It. Capodistria; prev. Kopar. SW Slovenia
95 *C16* **Kopervik** Rogaland, S Norway
Köpetdag Gershi/Kopetdag, Khrebet see Koppeh Dāgh
Kophinou see Kofínou
182 *G8* **Kopi** South Australia
Kopiago see Lake Copiago
153 *W12* **Kopili** ≈ NE India
95 *M15* **Köping** Västmanland, C Sweden
113 *K17* **Koplik** var. Kopliku. Shkodër, NW Albania
Kopliku see Koplik
Kopopo see Kokopo
94 *I11* **Koppang** Hedmark, S Norway
Kopparberg see Dalarna
143 *S3* **Koppeh Dāgh** Rus. Khrebet Kopetdag, Turkm. Köpetdag Gershi. ▲▲ Iran/Turkmenistan
Koppename see Coppename Rivier
95 *J15* **Koppom** Värmland, C Sweden
Kopreinitz see Koprivnica
114 *K9* **Koprinka, Yazovir** prev. Yazovir Georgi Dimitrov. ⊠ C Bulgaria
112 *F7* **Koprivnica** Ger. Kopreinitz, Hung. Kaproncza. Koprivnica-Križevci, N Croatia

◆ COUNTRY ● COUNTRY CAPITAL ◇ DEPENDENT TERRITORY ○ DEPENDENT TERRITORY CAPITAL ◈ ADMINISTRATIVE REGION ✈ INTERNATIONAL AIRPORT ▲ MOUNTAIN ▲▲ MOUNTAIN RANGE ✱ VOLCANO ≈ RIVER ⊚ LAKE ⊠ RESERVOIR

112 F8 **Koprivnica-Križevci** *off.* Koprivničko-Križevačka Županija. ◈ *province* N Croatia
111 I17 **Kopřivnice** *Ger.* Nesselsdorf. Moravskoslezský Kraj, E Czech Republic
Köprülü *see* Veles
Koptsevichi *see* Kaptsevichy
Kopyl' *see* Kapyl'
119 O14 **Kopys'** *Rus.* Kopys'. Vitsyebskaya Voblasts', NE Belarus
113 M18 **Korab** ▲ Albania/FYR Macedonia
Korabavur Pastligi *see* Karabaur', Uval
81 M14 **K'orahē** Somali, E Ethiopia
115 L16 **Kórakas, Akrotírio** *headland* Lésvos, E Greece
112 D9 **Korana** ⩫ C Croatia
155 L14 **Korāput** Orissa, E India
Korat *see* Nakhon Ratchasima
167 Q9 **Korat Plateau** *plateau* E Thailand
139 T1 **Kōrāwa, Sar-i** ▲ NE Iraq
154 L11 **Korba** Chhattīsgarh, C India
101 H15 **Korbach** Hessen, C Germany
Korça *see* Korçë
113 M21 **Korçë** *var.* Korça, *Gk.* Korytsa, *It.* Corriza; *prev.* Koritsa. Korçë, SE Albania
113 M21 **Korçë** ◈ *district* SE Albania
113 G15 **Korčula** *It.* Curzola. Dubrovnik-Neretva, S Croatia
113 F15 **Korčula** *It.* Curzola; *anc.* Corcyra Nigra. *island* S Croatia
113 F15 **Korčulanski Kanal** *channel* S Croatia
145 T6 **Korday** *prev.* Georgiyevka. Zhambyl, SE Kazakhstan
142 J5 **Kordestān** *off.* Ostān-e Kordestān, *var.* Kurdestan. ◈ *province* W Iran
143 P4 **Kord Kūy** *var.* Kurd Kui. Golestān, N Iran
163 V13 **Korea Bay** *bay* China/North Korea
Korea, Democratic People's Republic of *see* North Korea
171 T15 **Koreare** Pulau Yamdena, E Indonesia
Korea, Republic of *see* South Korea
163 Z17 **Korea Strait** *Jap.* Chōsen-kaikyō, *Kor.* Taehan-haehyŏp. *channel* Japan/South Korea
Korelichi/Korelicze *see* Karelichy
80 J11 **Korem** Tigray, N Ethiopia
77 U11 **Korén Adoua** ⩫ C Niger
126 I7 **Korenevo** Kurskaya Oblast', W Russian Federation
126 L13 **Korenovsk** Krasnodarskiy Kray, SW Russian Federation
116 L4 **Korets'** *Pol.* Korzec, *Rus.* Korets. Rivnens'ka Oblast', NW Ukraine
194 L7 **Korff Ice Rise** *ice cap* Antarctica
145 Q10 **Korgalzhyn** *var.* Kurgal'dzhino, Kurgal'dzhinsky, *Kaz.* Qorgazhyn. Akmola, C Kazakhstan
92 G13 **Korgen** Troms, N Norway
147 R9 **Korgon-Dĕbĕ** Dzhalal-Abadskaya Oblast', W Kyrgyzstan
76 M14 **Korhogo** N Ivory Coast
115 F19 **Korinthiakós Kólpos** *Eng.* Gulf of Corinth; *anc.* Corinthiacus Sinus. *gulf* C Greece
115 F19 **Kórinthos** *Eng.* Corinth; *anc.* Corinthus. Pelopónnisos, S Greece
113 M18 **Koritnik** ▲ S Serbia and Montenegro (Yugo.)
Koritsa *see* Korçë
165 P11 **Kōriyama** Fukushima, Honshū, C Japan
136 E16 **Korkuteli** Antalya, SW Turkey
158 K6 **Korla** *Chin.* K'u-erh-lo. Xinjiang Uygur Zizhiqu, NW China
122 J10 **Korliki** Khanty-Mansiyskiy Avtonomnyy Okrug, C Russian Federation
Körlin an der Persante *see* Karlino
Korma *see* Karma
14 D8 **Kormak** Ontario, S Canada
Kormakíti, Akrotíri/Kormakiti, Cape/Kormakítis *see* Koruçam Burnu
111 G23 **Körmend** Vas, W Hungary
139 T5 **Kōrmōr** E Iraq
112 C13 **Kornat** *It.* Incoronata. *island* W Croatia
Korneshty *see* Corneşti
109 X3 **Korneuburg** Niederösterreich, NE Austria
145 P7 **Korneyevka** Severnyy Kazakhstan, N Kazakhstan
95 I17 **Kornsjø** Østfold, S Norway
77 O11 **Koro** Mopti, S Mali
187 Y14 **Koro** *island* C Fiji
186 B7 **Koroba** Southern Highlands, W PNG
126 K8 **Korocha** Belgorodskaya Oblast', W Russian Federation
136 H12 **Köroğlu Dağları** ⛰ C Turkey
183 V6 **Korogoro Point** *headland* New South Wales, SE Australia
81 J21 **Korogwe** Tanga, E Tanzania
182 L13 **Koroit** Victoria, SE Australia
187 X15 **Korolevu** Viti Levu, W Fiji
190 I17 **Koromiri** *island* S Cook Islands
171 Q8 **Koronadal** Mindanao, S Philippines
115 E22 **Koróni** Pelopónnisos, S Greece
114 G13 **Korónia, Límni** ⊚ N Greece
110 I9 **Koronowo** *Ger.* Krone an der Brahe. Kujawski-pomorskie, C Poland
117 R2 **Korop** Chernihivs'ka Oblast', N Ukraine
115 H19 **Koropí** Attikí, C Greece
188 C8 **Koror** *var.* Oreor. ● (Palau) Oreor, N Palau
Koror *see* Oreor
Kőrös *see* Križevci
111 L23 **Körös** ⩫ E Hungary
Körösbánya *see* Baia de Criş
187 Y14 **Koro Sea** *sea* C Fiji
Koroška *see* Kärnten
117 N3 **Korosten'** Zhytomyrs'ka Oblast', NW Ukraine
Korostyshev *see* Korostyshiv
117 N4 **Korostyshiv** *Rus.* Korostyshev. Zhytomyrs'ka Oblast', N Ukraine
127 V3 **Korotaikha** ⩫ NW Russian Federation
122 J9 **Korotchayevo** Yamalo-Nenetskiy Avtonomnyy Okrug, N Russian Federation
78 I8 **Koro Toro** Borkou-Ennedi-Tibesti, N Chad
39 N16 **Korovin Island** *island* Shumagin Islands, Alaska, USA
187 X14 **Korovou** Viti Levu, W Fiji
93 M17 **Korpilahti** Länsi-Suomi, W Finland
92 K12 **Korpilombolo** *Lapp.* Dállogilli. Norrbotten, N Sweden
123 T13 **Korsakov** Ostrov Sakhalin, Sakhalinskaya Oblast', SE Russian Federation
93 J16 **Korsholm** *Fin.* Mustasaari. Länsi-Suomi, W Finland
95 I23 **Korsør** Vestsjælland, E Denmark
Korsovka *see* Kārsava
117 P6 **Korsun'-Shevchenkivs'kyy** *Rus.* Korsun'-Shevchenkovskiy. Cherkas'ka Oblast', C Ukraine
Korsun'-Shevchenkovskiy *see* Korsun'-Shevchenkivs'kyy
99 C17 **Kortemark** West-Vlaanderen, W Belgium
99 H18 **Kortenberg** Vlaams Brabant, C Belgium
99 K18 **Kortessem** Limburg, NE Belgium
99 E14 **Kortgene** Zeeland, SW Netherlands
80 F8 **Korti** Northern, N Sudan
99 C18 **Kortrijk** *Fr.* Courtrai. West-Vlaanderen, W Belgium
121 O2 **Kornuçam Burnu** *var.* Cape Kormakiti, Kormakítis, *Gk.* Akrotíri Kormakíti. *headland* N Cyprus
183 O13 **Korumburra** Victoria, SE Australia
Koryak Range *see* Koryakskoye Nagor'ye
123 V8 **Koryakskiy Avtonomnyy Okrug** ◈ *autonomous district* E Russian Federation
Koryakskiy Khrebet *see* Koryakskoye Nagor'ye
123 V7 **Koryakskoye Nagor'ye** *var.* Koryakskiy Khrebet, *Eng.* Koryak Range. ⛰ NE Russian Federation
125 P11 **Koryazhma** Arkhangel'skaya Oblast', NW Russian Federation
Köryō *see* Kangnŭng
Korytsa *see* Korçë
117 Q2 **Koryukivka** Chernihivs'ka Oblast', N Ukraine
Korzec *see* Korets'
115 N21 **Kos** Kos, Dodekánisos, Greece, Aegean Sea
115 M21 **Kos** *It.* Coo; *anc.* Cos. *island* Dodekánisos, Greece, Aegean Sea
125 T12 **Kosa** Komi-Permyatskiy Avtonomnyy Okrug, NW Russian Federation
127 T13 **Kosa** ⩫ NW Russian Federation
164 B12 **Kō-saki** *headland* Nagasaki, Tsushima, SW Japan
163 X13 **Kosan** SE North Korea
119 H18 **Kosava** *Rus.* Kosovo. Brestskaya Voblasts', SW Belarus
Kosch *see* Kose
144 G12 **Koschagyl** *Kaz.* Qosshaghyl. Atyrau, W Kazakhstan
110 G12 **Kościan** *Ger.* Kosten. Wielkopolskie, C Poland
110 I7 **Kościerzyna** Pomorskie, NW Poland
22 L4 **Kosciusko** Mississippi, S USA
Kosciusko, Mount *see* Kosciuszko, Mount
183 R11 **Kosciuszko, Mount** *prev.* Mount Kosciusko ▲ New South Wales, SE Australia
118 H4 **Kose** *Ger.* Kosch. Harjumaa, NW Estonia
114 G6 **Koshava** Vidin, NW Bulgaria
147 U9 **Kosh-Dëbë** *var.* Koshtebë. Narynskaya Oblast', C Kyrgyzstan
K'o-shih *see* Kashi
164 B16 **Koshikijima-rettō** *var.* Kosikizima Rettô. *island group* SW Japan
145 W13 **Koshkarkol', Ozero** ⊚ SE Kazakhstan
30 L9 **Koshkonong, Lake** ⊚ Wisconsin, N USA
Koshoba *see* Goşoba
164 M12 **Kōshoku** *var.* Kôsyoku. Nagano, Honshū, S Japan
Koshtebë *see* Kosh-Dëbë
Kōshū *see* Kwangju
111 N19 **Košice** *Ger.* Kaschau, *Hung.* Kassa. Košický Kraj, E Slovakia
111 M20 **Košický Kraj** ◈ *region* E Slovakia
Kosigaya *see* Koshigaya
Kosikizima Rettô *see* Koshikijima-rettō
153 R12 **Kosi Reservoir** ⊠ E Nepal
116 J8 **Kosiv** Ivano-Frankivs'ka Oblast', W Ukraine
145 O11 **Koskol'** Karaganda, C Kazakhstan
125 Q9 **Koslan** Respublika Komi, NW Russian Federation
Köslin *see* Koszalin
146 M12 **Koson** *Rus.* Kasan. Qashqadaryo Viloyati, S Uzbekistan
163 Y13 **Kosŏng** SE North Korea
147 S9 **Kosonsoy** *Rus.* Kasansay. Namangan Viloyati, E Uzbekistan
113 M16 **Kosovo** *prev.* Autonomous Province of Kosovo and Metohija. *region* S Serbia and Montenegro (Yugo.)
Kosovo *see* Kosava
Kosovo and Metohija, Autonomous Province of *see* Kosovo
113 N16 **Kosovo Polje** Serbia, S Serbia and Montenegro (Yugo.)
113 O16 **Kosovska Kamenica** Serbia, SE Serbia and Montenegro (Yugo.)
113 M16 **Kosovska Mitrovica** *Alb.* Mitrovicë; *prev.* Mitrovica, Titova Mitrovica. Serbia, S Serbia and Montenegro (Yugo.)
189 X17 **Kosrae** ◈ *state* E Micronesia
189 Y14 **Kosrae** *prev.* Kusaie. *island* Caroline Islands, E Micronesia
25 U9 **Kosse** Texas, SW USA
109 P6 **Kössen** Tirol, W Austria
76 M16 **Kossou, Lac de** ⊚ C Ivory Coast
Kossukavak *see* Krumovgrad
Kostajnica *see* Hrvatska Kostajnica
150 M7 **Kostanay** *var.* Kustanay, *Kaz.* Qostanay. N Kazakhstan
150 L8 **Kostanay** *var.* Kostanayskaya Oblast, *Kaz.* Qostanay Oblysy. ◈ *province* N Kazakhstan
Kostanayskaya Oblast *see* Kostanay
Kostamus *see* Kostomuksha
Kosten *see* Kościan
114 H10 **Kostenets** *prev.* Georgi Dimitrov. Sofiya, W Bulgaria
80 F10 **Kosti** White Nile, C Sudan
Kostnitz *see* Konstanz
124 H7 **Kostomuksha** *Fin.* Kostamus. Respublika Kareliya, NW Russian Federation
116 K3 **Kostopil'** *Rus.* Kostopol'. Rivnens'ka Oblast', NW Ukraine
Kostopol' *see* Kostopil'
124 M15 **Kostroma** Kostromskaya Oblast', NW Russian Federation
127 N14 **Kostroma** ⩫ NW Russian Federation
125 N14 **Kostromskaya Oblast'** ◈ *province* NW Russian Federation
110 D11 **Kostrzyn** *Ger.* Cüstrin, Küstrin. Lubuskie, W Poland
110 H11 **Kostrzyn** Wielkolpolskie, C Poland
117 X7 **Kostyantynivka** *Rus.* Konstantinovka. Donets'ka Oblast', SE Ukraine
Kostyukovichi *see* Kastsyukovichy
Kostyukovka *see* Kastsyukowka
Kōsyoku *see* Kōshoku
125 U6 **Kos'yu** Respublika Komi, NW Russian Federation
127 U6 **Kos'yu** ⩫ NW Russian Federation
110 F7 **Koszalin** *Ger.* Köslin. Zachodnio-pomorskie, NW Poland
111 F22 **Kőszeg** *Ger.* Güns. Vas, W Hungary
152 H13 **Kota** *prev.* Kotah. Rājasthān, N India
168 K12 **Kota Baru** Sumatera, W Indonesia
169 U13 **Kotabaru** Pulau Laut, C Indonesia
Kotabaru *see* Jayapura
168 K6 **Kota Bharu** *var.* Kota Baharu, Kota Bahru. Kelantan, Peninsular Malaysia
Kotaboemi *see* Kotabumi
168 M14 **Kotabumi** *prev.* Kotaboemi. Sumatera, W Indonesia
149 S10 **Kot Addu** Punjab, E Pakistan
Kotah *see* Kota
169 U7 **Kota Kinabalu** *prev.* Jesselton. Sabah, East Malaysia
169 U7 **Kota Kinabalu** × Sabah, East Malaysia
92 M12 **Kotala** Lappi, N Finland
Kotamobagoe *see* Kotamobagu
171 Q11 **Kotamobagu** *prev.* Kotamobagoe. Sulawesi, C Indonesia
155 L14 **Kotapad** *var.* Kotapārh. Orissa, E India
Kotapārh *see* Kotapad
166 N17 **Ko Ta Ru Tao** *island* SW Thailand
169 R13 **Kotawaringin, Teluk** *bay* Borneo, C Indonesia
149 Q13 **Kot Diji** Sind, SE Pakistan
152 K9 **Kotdwāra** Uttaranchal, N India
125 Q14 **Kotel'nich** Kirovskaya Oblast', NW Russian Federation
127 N12 **Kotel'nikovo** Volgogradskaya Oblast', SW Russian Federation
123 Q6 **Kotel'nyy, Ostrov** *island* Novosibirskiye Ostrova, N Russian Federation
117 T5 **Kotel'va** Poltavs'ka Oblast', C Ukraine
101 M14 **Köthen** *var.* Cöthen. Sachsen-Anhalt, C Germany
Kôti *see* Kōchi
81 G17 **Kotido** NE Uganda
93 N19 **Kotka** Etelä-Suomi, S Finland
125 P11 **Kotlas** Arkhangel'skaya Oblast', NW Russian Federation
38 M10 **Kotlik** Alaska, USA
77 Q17 **Kotoka** × (Accra) S Ghana
Kotonu *see* Cotonou
113 J17 **Kotor** *It.* Cattaro. Montenegro, SW Serbia and Montenegro (Yugo.)
Kotor *see* Kotoriba
112 F7 **Kotoriba** *Hung.* Kotor. Medimurje, N Croatia
113 I17 **Kotorska, Boka** *It.* Bocche di Cattaro. *bay* Montenegro, SW Serbia and Montenegro (Yugo.)
112 H11 **Kotorsko** Republika Srpska, N Bosnia and Herzegovina
112 G11 **Kotor Varoš** Republika Srpska, N Bosnia and Herzegovina
Koto Sho/Kotosho *see* Lan Yü
126 M7 **Kotovsk** Tambovskaya Oblast', W Russian Federation
117 O9 **Kotovs'k** *Rus.* Kotovsk. Odes'ka Oblast', SW Ukraine
Kotovsk *see* Hînceşti
119 G16 **Kotra** *Rus.* Kotra. ⩫ W Belarus
149 P16 **Kotri** Sind, SE Pakistan
109 Q9 **Kötschach** Kärnten, S Austria
155 K15 **Kottagūdem** Andhra Pradesh, E India
155 F21 **Kottappadi** Kerala, SW India
155 G23 **Kottayam** Kerala, SW India
Kottbus *see* Cottbus
Kotte *see* Sri Jayawardanapura
79 K15 **Kotto** ⩫ Central African Republic/Dem. Rep. Congo
193 X15 **Kotu Group** *island group* W Tonga
Koturdepe *see* Goturdepe
122 M9 **Kotuy** ⩫ N Russian Federation
83 M16 **Kotwa** Mashonaland East, NE Zimbabwe
39 N7 **Kotzebue** Alaska, USA
38 M7 **Kotzebue Sound** *inlet* Alaska, USA
Kotzenan *see* Chocianów
Kotzman *see* Kitsman'
77 R14 **Kouandé** NW Benin
79 J15 **Kouango** Ouaka, S Central African Republic
77 O13 **Koudougou** C Burkina
98 K7 **Koudum** Friesland, N Netherlands
115 L25 **Koufonísi** *island* SE Greece
115 K21 **Koufonísi** *island* Kykládes, Greece, Aegean Sea
38 M8 **Kougarok Mountain** ▲ Alaska, USA
79 E20 **Kouilou** ⩫ S Congo
121 O3 **Koúklia** SW Cyprus
79 E19 **Koulamoutou** Ogooué-Lolo, C Gabon
76 L12 **Koulikoro** Koulikoro, SW Mali
76 L11 **Koulikoro** ◈ *region* SW Mali
187 P16 **Koumac** Province Nord, W New Caledonia
165 N12 **Koumi** Nagano, Honshū, S Japan
78 I13 **Koumra** Moyen-Chari, S Chad
Kounadougou *see* Koundougou
76 M15 **Kounahiri** C Ivory Coast
76 I12 **Koundâra** Moyenne-Guinée, NW Guinea
77 N13 **Koundougou** *var.* Kounadougou. C Burkina
76 H11 **Koungheul** C Senegal
Kounradskiy *see* Konyrat
25 X10 **Kountze** Texas, SW USA
77 Q13 **Koupéla** C Burkina
77 N13 **Kouri** Sikasso, SW Mali
55 Y9 **Kourou** N French Guiana
114 J12 **Kouroú** ⩫ NE Greece
76 K14 **Kouroussa** Haute-Guinée, C Guinea
Kousseir *see* Al Quşayr
78 G11 **Kousséri** *prev.* Fort-Foureau. Extrême-Nord, NE Cameroon
Kouteifé *see* Al Quṭayfah
76 M13 **Koutiala** Sikasso, S Mali
76 M13 **Kouto** NW Ivory Coast
93 M19 **Kouvola** Etelä-Suomi, S Finland
79 G18 **Kouyou** ⩫ C Congo
112 M10 **Kovačica** *Hung.* Antafalva; *prev.* Kovacsicza. Serbia, N Serbia and Montenegro (Yugo.)
Kovacsicza *see* Kovačica
Kővárhosszúfalu *see* Satulung
Kovászna *see* Covasna
124 I4 **Kovdor** Murmanskaya Oblast', NW Russian Federation
126 I5 **Kovdozero, Ozero** ⊚ NW Russian Federation
116 J3 **Kovel'** *Pol.* Kowel. Volyns'ka Oblast', NW Ukraine
112 M11 **Kovin** *Hung.* Kevevára; *prev.* Temes-Kubin. Serbia, NE Serbia and Montenegro (Yugo.)
Kovno *see* Kaunas
127 N3 **Kovrov** Vladimirskaya Oblast', W Russian Federation
127 O5 **Kovylkino** Respublika Mordoviya, W Russian Federation
110 J11 **Kowal** Kujawsko-pomorskie, C Poland
110 J9 **Kowalewo Pomorskie** *Ger.* Schönsee. Kujawsko-pomorskie, C Poland
Kowasna *see* Covasna
119 M16 **Kowbcha** *Rus.* Kolbcha. Mahilyowskaya Voblasts', E Belarus
Koweit *see* Kuwait
Kowel *see* Kovel'
185 F17 **Kowhitirangi** West Coast, South Island, NZ
161 O15 **Kowloon** *Chin.* Jiulong. Hong Kong, S China
Kowno *see* Kaunas
159 N7 **Kox Kuduk** *well* NW China
136 D16 **Köyceğiz** Muğla, SW Turkey
125 N6 **Koyda** Arkhangel'skaya Oblast', NW Russian Federation
Koymat *see* Goymat
Koymatdag, Gory *see* Goymatdag
Koyna Reservoir *see* Shivāji Sāgar
165 P9 **Koyoshi-gawa** ⩫ Honshū, C Japan
Koysanjaq *see* Koi Sanjaq
Koytash *see* Qo'ytosh
146 M14 **Köytendag** *prev. Rus.* Charshanga, Charshangy, *Turkm.* Charshangngy. Lebap Welaýaty, E Turkmenistan
39 N9 **Koyuk** Alaska, USA
39 N9 **Koyuk River** ⩫ Alaska, USA
39 O9 **Koyukuk** Alaska, USA
39 O9 **Koyukuk River** ⩫ Alaska, USA
136 J13 **Kozaklı** Nevşehir, C Turkey
136 K16 **Kozan** Adana, S Turkey
115 E14 **Kozáni** Dytikí Makedonía, N Greece
112 F10 **Kozara** ⛰ NW Bosnia and Herzegovina
Kozarska Dubica *see* Bosanska Dubica
117 P3 **Kozelets'** *Rus.* Kozelets. Chernihivs'ka Oblast', NE Ukraine
117 S6 **Kozel'shchyna** Poltavs'ka Oblast', C Ukraine
126 J5 **Kozel'sk** Kaluzhskaya Oblast', W Russian Federation
Kozhikode *see* Calicut
127 V9 **Kozhimiz, Gora** ▲ NW Russian Federation
126 L9 **Kozhozero, Ozero** ⊚ NW Russian Federation
125 T7 **Kozhva** *var.* Kozya. Respublika Komi, NW Russian Federation
127 T7 **Kozhva** ⩫ NW Russian Federation
110 N13 **Kozienice** Mazowieckie, C Poland
125 U6 **Kozhim** Respublika Komi, NW Russian Federation
109 S13 **Kozina** SW Slovenia
114 H7 **Kozloduy** Vratsa, NW Bulgaria
127 Q3 **Kozlovka** Chuvashskaya Respublika, W Russian Federation
Kozlowshchina/Kozlowszczyzna *see* Kazlowshchyna
127 P3 **Koz'modem'yansk** Respublika Mariy El, W Russian Federation
116 J6 **Kozova** Ternopil's'ka Oblast', W Ukraine
113 P20 **Kožuf** ▲ S FYR Macedonia
165 N15 **Kōzu-shima** *island* E Japan
Kozya *see* Kozhva
Koz'yany *see* Kaz'yany
117 N5 **Kozyatyn** *Rus.* Kazatin. Vinnyts'ka Oblast', C Ukraine
77 Q16 **Kpalimé** *var.* Palimé. SW Togo
77 Q16 **Kpandu** E Ghana
99 F15 **Krabbendijke** Zeeland, SW Netherlands
167 N15 **Krabi** *var.* Muang Krabi. Krabi, SW Thailand
167 N13 **Kra Buri** Ranong, SW Thailand
167 S12 **Krâchéh** *prev.* Kratie. Krâchéh, E Cambodia
95 G17 **Kragerø** Telemark, S Norway
112 M13 **Kragujevac** Serbia, C Serbia and Montenegro (Yugo.)
Krainburg *see* Kranj
166 N13 **Kra, Isthmus of** *isthmus* Malaysia/Thailand
112 D12 **Krajina** *cultural region* SW Croatia
Krakatau, Pulau *see* Rakata, Pulau
Krakau *see* Małopolskie
111 L16 **Kraków** *Eng.* Cracow, *Ger.* Krakau; *anc.* Cracovia. Małopolskie, S Poland
100 L9 **Krakower See** ⊚ NE Germany
167 Q11 **Krâlănh** Siĕmréab, NW Cambodia
45 Q16 **Kralendijk** Bonaire, E Netherlands Antilles
112 B10 **Kraljevica** *It.* Porto Re. Primorje-Gorski Kotar, NW Croatia
112 M13 **Kraljevo** *prev.* Rankovićevo. Serbia, C Serbia and Montenegro (Yugo.)
111 E16 **Královéhradecký Kraj** *prev.* Hradecký Kraj. ◈ *region* N Czech Republic
Kralup an der Moldau *see* Kralupy nad Vltavou
111 C16 **Kralupy nad Vltavou** *Ger.* Kralup an der Moldau. Středočeský Kraj, NW Czech Republic
117 W7 **Kramators'k** *Rus.* Kramatorsk. Donets'ka Oblast', SE Ukraine
93 H17 **Kramfors** Västernorrland, C Sweden
115 D15 **Kranéa** Dytikí Makedonía, N Greece
108 M7 **Kranebitten** × (Innsbruck) Tirol, W Austria
115 G20 **Kranídi** Pelopónnisos, S Greece
109 T11 **Kranj** *Ger.* Krainburg. NW Slovenia
115 F16 **Krannón** *battleground* Thessalía, C Greece
Kranz *see* Zelenogradsk
112 D7 **Krapina** Krapina-Zagorje, N Croatia
112 E8 **Krapina** ⩫ N Croatia
112 D8 **Krapina-Zagorje** *off.* Krapinsko-Zagorska Županija. ◈ *province* N Croatia
114 L7 **Krapinets** ⩫ NE Bulgaria
111 I15 **Krapkowice** *Ger.* Krappitz. Opolskie, S Poland
Krappitz *see* Krapkowice
125 O12 **Krasavino** Vologodskaya Oblast', NW Russian Federation
122 H6 **Krasino** Novaya Zemlya, Arkhangel'skaya Oblast', N Russian Federation
123 S15 **Kraskino** Primorskiy Kray, SE Russian Federation
118 J11 **Krāslava** Krāslava, SE Latvia
119 M14 **Krasnaluki** *Rus.* Krasnoluki. Vitsyebskaya Voblasts', N Belarus
119 P17 **Krasnapollye** *Rus.* Krasnopol'ye. Mahilyowskaya Voblasts', E Belarus
126 L15 **Krasnaya Polyana** Krasnodarskiy Kray, SW Russian Federation
119 J18 **Krasnaya Slabada** *var.* Chyrvonaya Slabada, *Rus.* Krasnaya Sloboda. Minskaya Voblasts', S Belarus
Krasnaya Sloboda *see* Krasnaya Slabada
119 J15 **Krasnaye** *Rus.* Krasnoye. Minskaya Voblasts', C Belarus
111 O14 **Kraśnik** *Ger.* Kratznick. Lubelskie, E Poland
117 O9 **Krasni Okny** Odes'ka Oblast', SW Ukraine
145 P7 **Krasnoarmeysk** Severnyy Kazakhstan, N Kazakhstan
127 P8 **Krasnoarmeysk** Saratovskaya Oblast', W Russian Federation
Krasnoarmeysk *see* Krasnoarmiys'k/Tayynsha
123 T6 **Krasnoarmeyskiy** Chukotskiy Avtonomnyy Okrug, NE Russian Federation
117 W7 **Krasnoarmiys'k** *Rus.* Krasnoarmeysk. Donets'ka Oblast', SE Ukraine
125 P11 **Krasnoborsk** Arkhangel'skaya Oblast', NW Russian Federation
126 K14 **Krasnodar** *prev.* Ekaterinodar, Yekaterinodar. Krasnodarskiy Kray, SW Russian Federation
126 K13 **Krasnodarskiy Kray** ◈ *territory* SW Russian Federation
117 Z7 **Krasnodon** Luhans'ka Oblast', E Ukraine
Krasnogor *see* Kallaste
127 T2 **Krasnogorskoye** *Latv.* Sarkaņi. Udmurtskaya Respublika, NW Russian Federation
Krasnograd *see* Krasnohrad
Krasnogvardeysk *see* Bulung'ur
126 M13 **Krasnogvardeyskoye** Stavropol'skiy Kray, SW Russian Federation
Krasnogvardeyskoye *see* Krasnohvardiys'ke
117 U6 **Krasnohrad** *Rus.* Krasnograd. Kharkivs'ka Oblast', E Ukraine
117 S12 **Krasnohvardiys'ke** *Rus.* Krasnogvardeyskoye. Respublika Krym, S Ukraine
123 P14 **Krasnokamensk** Chitinskaya Oblast', S Russian Federation
125 U14 **Krasnokamsk** Permskaya Oblast', W Russian Federation
127 U8 **Krasnokholm** Orenburgskaya Oblast', W Russian Federation
117 U5 **Krasnokuts'k** *Rus.* Krasnokutsk. Kharkivs'ka Oblast', E Ukraine
126 L7 **Krasnolesnyy** Voronezhskaya Oblast', W Russian Federation
Krasnoluki *see* Krasnaluki
Krasnoosol'skoye Vodokhranilishche *see* Chervonooskil's'ke Vodoskhovyshche
117 S11 **Krasnoperekops'k** *Rus.* Krasnoperekopsk. Respublika Krym, S Ukraine
117 U4 **Krasnopillya** Sums'ka Oblast', NE Ukraine
Krasnopol'ye *see* Krasnapollye
124 L5 **Krasnoshchel'ye** Murmanskaya Oblast', NW Russian Federation
127 O5 **Krasnoslobodsk** Respublika Mordoviya, W Russian Federation
127 T2 **Krasnoslobodsk** Volgogradskaya Oblast', SW Russian Federation
Krasnostav *see* Krasnystaw
127 V5 **Krasnousol'skiy** Respublika Bashkortostan, W Russian Federation
125 U12 **Krasnovishersk** Permskaya Oblast', NW Russian Federation
Krasnovodsk *see* Türkmenbaşy
Krasnovodskiy Zaliv *see* Türkmenbaşy Aylagy
146 B10 **Krasnovodskoye Plato** *Turkm.* Krasnowodsk Platosy. *plateau* NW Turkmenistan
Krasnowodsk Aylagy *see* Türkmenbaşy Aylagy
Krasnowodsk Platosy *see* Krasnovodskoye Plato
122 K12 **Krasnoyarsk** Krasnoyarskiy Kray, S Russian Federation
127 X7 **Krasnoyarskiy** Orenburgskaya Oblast', W Russian Federation
122 K11 **Krasnoyarskiy Kray** ◈ *territory* C Russian Federation
Krasnoye *see* Krasnaye
Krasnoye Znamya *see* Gyzylbaýdak
125 R11 **Krasnozatonskiy** Respublika Komi, NW Russian Federation
118 D13 **Krasnoznamensk** *prev.* Lasdehnen, *Ger.* Haselberg. Kaliningradskaya Oblast', W Russian Federation
126 K4 **Krasnoznamensk** Moskovskaya Oblast', W Russian Federation
117 R11 **Krasnoznam"yans'kyy Kanal** *canal* S Ukraine
111 P14 **Krasnystaw** *Rus.* Krasnostav. Lubelskie, SE Poland
126 H4 **Krasnyy** Smolenskaya Oblast', W Russian Federation
127 P2 **Krasnyye Baki** Nizhegorodskaya Oblast', W Russian Federation
127 Q13 **Krasnyye Barrikady** Astrakhanskaya Oblast', SW Russian Federation
124 K15 **Krasnyy Kholm** Tverskaya Oblast', W Russian Federation
127 Q8 **Krasnyy Kut** Saratovskaya Oblast', W Russian Federation
Krasnyy Liman *see* Krasnyy Lyman
117 Y7 **Krasnyy Luch** *prev.* Krindachevka. Luhans'ka Oblast', E Ukraine
117 X6 **Krasnyy Lyman** *Rus.* Krasnyy Liman. Donets'ka Oblast', SE Ukraine

◆ COUNTRY ◇ DEPENDENT TERRITORY ◈ ADMINISTRATIVE REGION ▲ MOUNTAIN ⛰ VOLCANO ⊚ LAKE
● COUNTRY CAPITAL ○ DEPENDENT TERRITORY CAPITAL × INTERNATIONAL AIRPORT ⛰ MOUNTAIN RANGE ⩫ RIVER ⊠ RESERVOIR

127 R3 **Krasnyy Steklovar** Respublika Mariy El, W Russian Federation
127 P8 **Krasnyy Tekstil'shchik** Saratovskaya Oblast', W Russian Federation
127 R13 **Krasnyy Yar** Astrakhanskaya Oblast', SW Russian Federation
Krassóvár *see* Caraşova
116 L5 **Krasyliv** Khmel'nyts'ka Oblast', W Ukraine
111 O21 **Kraszna** ***Rom.*** Crasna. ≈ Hungary/Romania
Kratie *see* Krâchéh
113 P17 **Kratovo** NE FYR Macedonia
Kratznick *see* Kraśnik
171 Y13 **Krau** Papua, E Indonesia
167 Q13 **Krâvanh, Chuŏr Phnum** ***Eng.*** Cardamom Mountains, ***Fr.*** Chaîne des Cardamomes. ▲ W Cambodia
Kravasta Lagoon *see* Karavastasë, Laguna e
Krawang *see* Karawang
Kraxatau *see* Rakata, Pulau
127 Q15 **Kraynovka** Respublika Dagestan, SW Russian Federation
118 D12 **Kražiai** Šiauliai, C Lithuania
27 P11 **Krebs** Oklahoma, C USA
101 D15 **Krefeld** Nordrhein-Westfalen, W Germany
Kreisstadt *see* Krosno Odrzańskie
115 D17 **Kremastón, Technití Límni** ◻ C Greece
Kremenchug *see* Kremenchuk
Kremenchugskoye Vodokhranilishche/ Kremenchuk Reservoir *see* Kremenchuts'ke Vodoskhovyshche
117 S6 **Kremenchuk** ***Rus.*** Kremenchug. Poltavs'ka Oblast', NE Ukraine
117 R6 **Kremenchuts'ke Vodoskhovyshche** ***Eng.*** Kremenchuk Reservoir, ***Rus.*** Kremenchugskoye Vodokhranilishche. ◻ C Ukraine
116 K5 **Kremenets'** ***Pol.*** Krzemieniec, ***Rus.*** Kremenets. Ternopil's'ka Oblast', W Ukraine
Kremennaya *see* Kreminna
117 X6 **Kreminna** ***Rus.*** Kremennaya. Luhans'ka Oblast', E Ukraine
37 R4 **Kremmling** Colorado, C USA
109 V3 **Krems** ≈ NE Austria
Krems *see* Krems an der Donau
109 W3 **Krems an der Donau** ***var.*** Krems. Niederösterreich, N Austria
Kremsier *see* Kroměříž
109 S4 **Kremsmünster** Oberösterreich, N Austria
38 M17 **Krenitzin Islands** *island* Aleutian Islands, Alaska, USA
Kresena *see* Kresna
114 G11 **Kresna** ***var.*** Kresena. Blagoevgrad, SW Bulgaria
112 O12 **Krespoljin** Serbia, E Serbia and Montenegro (Yugo.)
25 N4 **Kress** Texas, SW USA
123 V6 **Kresta, Zaliv** *bay* E Russian Federation
115 D20 **Kréstena** ***prev.*** Selinoús. Dytikí Ellás, S Greece
124 H14 **Kresttsy** Novgorodskaya Oblast', W Russian Federation
Kretikon Delagos *see* Kritikó Pélagos
118 C11 **Kretinga** ***Ger.*** Krottingen. Klaipėda, NW Lithuania
Kreutz *see* Cristuru Secuiesc
Kreuz *see* Križevci, Croatia
Kreuz *see* Risti, Estonia
Kreuzburg/Kreuzburg in Oberschlesien *see* Kluczbork
Kreuzingen *see* Bol'shakovo
108 H6 **Kreuzlingen** Thurgau, NE Switzerland
101 K25 **Kreuzspitze** ▲ S Germany
101 F16 **Kreuztal** Nordrhein-Westfalen, W Germany
119 I15 **Kreva** ***Rus.*** Krevo. Hrodzyenskaya Voblasts', W Belarus
Krevo *see* Kreva
Kría Vrísi *see* Krýa Vrýsi
79 D16 **Kribi** Sud, SW Cameroon
Krichëv *see* Krychaw
Krickerhäu/Kriegerhaj *see* Handlová
109 W6 **Krieglach** Steiermark, E Austria
108 F8 **Kriens** Luzern, W Switzerland
Krimmitschau *see* Crimmitschau
98 H12 **Krimpen aan den IJssel** Zuid-Holland, SW Netherlands
Krindachevka *see* Krasnyy Luch
115 G25 **Kríos, Akrotírio** *headland* Kríti, Greece, E Mediterranean Sea
155 J16 **Krishna** ***prev.*** Kistna. ≈ C India
155 H20 **Krishnagiri** Tamil Nādu, SE India
155 K17 **Krishna, Mouths of the** *delta* SE India
153 S15 **Krishnanagar** West Bengal, N India
155 G20 **Krishnarājāsāgara Reservoir** ◻ W India
95 N19 **Kristdala** Kalmar, S Sweden
Kristiania *see* Oslo
95 E18 **Kristiansand** ***var.*** Christiansand. Vest-Agder, S Norway
95 L22 **Kristianstad** Skåne, S Sweden
94 F8 **Kristiansund** ***var.*** Christiansund. Møre og Romsdal, S Norway
Kristiinankaupunki *see* Kristinestad
93 I14 **Kristineberg** Västerbotten, N Sweden
95 L16 **Kristinehamn** Värmland, C Sweden
93 J17 **Kristinestad** ***Fin.*** Kristiinankaupunki. Länsi-Suomi, W Finland
Kristyor *see* Crişcior
115 J25 **Kríti** ***Eng.*** Crete. ◆ *region* Greece, Aegean Sea
115 J24 **Kríti** ***Eng.*** Crete. *island* Greece, Aegean Sea
115 J23 **Kritikó Pélagos** ***var.*** Kretikon Delagos, ***Eng.*** Sea of Crete; ***anc.*** Mare Creticum. *sea* Greece, Aegean Sea
Kriulyany *see* Criuleni
112 I12 **Krivaja** ≈ NE Bosnia and Herzegovina
Krivaja *see* Mali Idoš
113 P17 **Kriva Palanka** ***Turk.*** Eğri Palanka. NE FYR Macedonia
Krivichi *see* Kryvychy
114 H8 **Krivodol** Vratsa, NW Bulgaria
126 M10 **Krivorozh'ye** Rostovskaya Oblast', SW Russian Federation
Krivoshin *see* Kryvoshyn
Krivoy Rog *see* Kryvyy Rih
112 F7 **Križevci** ***Ger.*** Kreuz, ***Hung.*** Kőrös. Varaždin, NE Croatia
112 B10 **Krk** ***It.*** Veglia. Primorje-Gorski Kotar, NW Croatia
112 B10 **Krk** ***It.*** Veglia; ***anc.*** Curieta. *island* NW Croatia
109 V12 **Krka** ≈ SE Slovenia
Krka *see* Gurk
109 R11 **Krn** ▲ NW Slovenia
111 H16 **Krnov** ***Ger.*** Jägerndorf. Moravskoslezský Kraj, E Czech Republic
Kroatien *see* Croatia
95 G14 **Krøderen** Buskerud, S Norway
95 G14 **Krøderen** ◎ S Norway
Kroi *see* Krui
95 N17 **Krokek** Östergötland, S Sweden
93 G16 **Krokom** Jämtland, C Sweden
117 S2 **Krolevets'** ***Rus.*** Krolevets. Sums'ka Oblast', NE Ukraine
Królewska Huta *see* Chorzów
111 H18 **Kroměříž** ***Ger.*** Kremsier. Zlínský Kraj, E Czech Republic
98 I9 **Krommenie** Noord-Holland, C Netherlands
126 J6 **Kromy** Orlovskaya Oblast', W Russian Federation
101 L18 **Kronach** Bayern, E Germany
Krone an der Brahe *see* Koronowo
167 Q13 **Krŏng Kaôh Kŏng** Kaôh Kŏng, SW Cambodia
95 K21 **Kronoberg** ◆ *county* S Sweden
123 V10 **Kronotskiy Zaliv** *bay* E Russian Federation
195 O2 **Kronprinsesse Märtha Kyst** *physical region* Antarctica
195 V3 **Kronprins Olav Kyst** *physical region* Antarctica
124 G12 **Kronshtadt** Leningradskaya Oblast', NW Russian Federation
Kronstadt *see* Braşov
83 I22 **Kroonstad** Free State, C South Africa
123 O12 **Kropotkin** Irkutskaya Oblast', C Russian Federation
126 L14 **Kropotkin** Krasnodarskiy Kray, SW Russian Federation
110 J11 **Krośniewice** Łódzkie, C Poland
111 N17 **Krosno** ***Ger.*** Krossen. Podkarpackie, SE Poland
110 E12 **Krosno Odrzańskie** ***Ger.*** Crossen, Kreisstadt. Lubuskie, W Poland
Krossen *see* Krosno
Krotoschin *see* Krotoszyn
110 H13 **Krotoszyn** ***Ger.*** Krotoschin. Wielkopolskie, C Poland
Krottingen *see* Kretinga
Krousón *see* Krousónas
115 J25 **Krousónas** ***prev.*** Krousón, Kroussón. Kríti, Greece, E Mediterranean Sea
Kroussón *see* Krousónas
Krraba *see* Krrabë
113 L20 **Krrabë** ***var.*** Krraba. Tiranë, C Albania
113 L17 **Krrabit, Mali i** ▲ N Albania
109 W12 **Krško** ***Ger.*** Gurkfeld; ***prev.*** Videm-Krško. E Slovenia
83 K19 **Kruger National Park** *national park* Limpopo, N South Africa
83 J21 **Krugersdorp** Gauteng, NE South Africa
38 D16 **Krugloi Point** *headland* Agattu Island, Alaska, USA
Krugloye *see* Kruhlaye
119 N15 **Kruhlaye** ***Rus.*** Krugloye. Mahilyowskaya Voblasts', E Belarus
168 L15 **Krui** ***var.*** Kroi. Sumatera, SW Indonesia
99 G16 **Kruibeke** Oost-Vlaanderen, N Belgium
83 G25 **Kruidfontein** Western Cape, SW South Africa
99 F15 **Kruiningen** Zeeland, SW Netherlands
Kruja *see* Krujë
113 L19 **Krujë** ***var.*** Kruja, ***It.*** Croia. Durrës, C Albania
Krulevshchina *see* Krulewshchyna
118 K13 **Krulewshchyna** ***Rus.*** Krulevshchina. Vitsyebskaya Voblasts', N Belarus
25 T6 **Krum** Texas, SW USA
101 J23 **Krumbach** Bayern, S Germany
113 M17 **Krumë** Kukës, NE Albania
Krummau *see* Český Krumlov
114 K12 **Krumovgrad** ***prev.*** Kossukavak. Kŭrdzhali, S Bulgaria
114 K12 **Krumovitsa** ≈ S Bulgaria
114 L10 **Krumovo** Yambol, E Bulgaria
167 O11 **Krung Thep** ***var.*** Krung Thep Mahanakhon, ***Eng.*** Bangkok. ● (Thailand) Bangkok, C Thailand
167 O11 **Krung Thep, Ao** ***var.*** Bight of Bangkok. *bay* S Thailand
Krung Thep Mahanakhon *see* Krung Thep
Krupa/Krupa na Uni *see* Bosanska Krupa
119 M15 **Krupki** ***Rus.*** Krupki. Minskaya Voblasts', C Belarus
95 G24 **Kruså** ***var.*** Krusaa. Sønderjylland, SW Denmark
Krusaa *see* Kruså
113 N14 **Kruševac** Serbia, C Serbia and Montenegro (Yugo.)
113 N19 **Kruševo** SW FYR Macedonia
111 A15 **Krušné Hory** ***Eng.*** Ore Mountains, ***Ger.*** Erzgebirge. ▲ Czech Republic/Germany *see also* Erzgebirge
39 W13 **Kruzof Island** *island* Alexander Archipelago, Alaska, USA
114 F13 **Krýa Vrýsi** ***var.*** Kría Vrísi. Kentrikí Makedonía, N Greece
119 P16 **Krychaw** ***Rus.*** Krichëv. Mahilyowskaya Voblasts', E Belarus
64 K11 **Krylov Seamount** *undersea feature* E Atlantic Ocean
Krym *see* Krym, Respublika
117 S13 **Krym, Respublika** ***var.*** Krym, ***Eng.*** Crimea, Crimean Oblast; ***prev. Rus.*** Krymskaya ASSR, Krymskaya Oblast'. ◆ *province* SE Ukraine
126 K14 **Krymsk** Krasnodarskiy Kray, SW Russian Federation
Krymskaya ASSR/ Krymskaya Oblast' *see* Krym, Respublika
117 T13 **Kryms'ki Hory** ▲ S Ukraine
117 T13 **Kryms'kyy Pivostriv** *peninsula* S Ukraine
111 M18 **Krynica** ***Ger.*** Tannenhof. Małopolskie, S Poland
117 P8 **Kryve Ozero** Odes'ka Oblast', SW Ukraine
119 I18 **Kryvoshyn** ***Rus.*** Krivoshin. Brestskaya Voblasts', SW Belarus
119 K14 **Kryvychy** ***Rus.*** Krivichi. Minskaya Voblasts', C Belarus
117 S8 **Kryvyy Rih** ***Rus.*** Krivoy Rog. Dnipropetrovs'ka Oblast', SE Ukraine
117 N8 **Kryzhopil'** Vinnyts'ka Oblast', C Ukraine
Krzemieniec *see* Kremenets'
111 J14 **Krzepice** Śląskie, S Poland
110 F10 **Krzyż Wielkopolski** Wielkopolskie, C Poland
Ksar al Kabir *see* Ksar-el-Kebir
Ksar al Soule *see* Er-Rachidia
74 J5 **Ksar El Boukhari** N Algeria
74 G5 **Ksar-el-Kebir** ***var.*** Alcázar, Ksar al Kabir, Ksar-el-Kébir, ***Ar.*** Al-Kasr al-Kebir, Al-Qsar al-Kbir, ***Sp.*** Alcazarquivir. NW Morocco
Ksar-el-Kébir *see* Ksar-el-Kebir
110 H12 **Książ Wielkopolski** ***Ger.*** Xions. Wielkopolskie, C Poland
127 O3 **Kstovo** Nizhegorodskaya Oblast', W Russian Federation
169 T8 **Kuala Belait** W Brunei
Kuala Dungun *see* Dungun
169 S10 **Kualakerian** Borneo, C Indonesia
169 S12 **Kualakuayan** Borneo, C Indonesia
168 K8 **Kuala Lipis** Pahang, Peninsular Malaysia
168 K9 **Kuala Lumpur** ● (Malaysia) Kuala Lumpur, Peninsular Malaysia
168 K9 **Kuala Lumpur International** ✕ Selangor, Peninsular Malaysia
Kuala Pelabohan Kelang *see* Pelabuhan Klang
169 U7 **Kuala Penyu** Sabah, East Malaysia
38 E9 **Kualapu'u** ***var.*** Kualapuu. Moloka'i, Hawai'i, USA, C Pacific Ocean
168 L7 **Kuala Terengganu** ***var.*** Kuala Trengganu. Terengganu, Peninsular Malaysia
168 L11 **Kualatungkal** Sumatera, W Indonesia
171 P11 **Kuandang** Sulawesi, N Indonesia
163 V12 **Kuandian** ***var.*** Kuandian Manzu Zizhixian. Liaoning, NE China
Kuandian Manzu Zizhixian *see* Kuandian
Kuando-Kubango *see* Cuando Cubango
Kuang-chou *see* Guangzhou
Kuang-hsi *see* Guangxi Zhuangzu Zizhiqu
Kuang-tung *see* Guangdong
Kuang-yuan *see* Guangyuan
Kuantan, Batang *see* Indragiri, Sungai
Kuanza Norte *see* Cuanza Norte
Kuanza Sul *see* Cuanza Sul
Kuba *see* Quba
Kubango *see* Cubango/Okavango
141 X8 **Kubārah** NW Oman
93 H16 **Kubbe** Västernorrland, C Sweden
80 A11 **Kubbum** Southern Darfur, W Sudan
126 L13 **Kubenskoye, Ozero** ◎ NW Russian Federation
146 G6 **Kubla-Ustyurt** ***Rus.*** Komsomol'sk-na-Ustyurte. Qoraqalpog'iston Respublikasi, NW Uzbekistan
164 G15 **Kubokawa** Kōchi, Shikoku, SW Japan
114 L7 **Kubrat** ***prev.*** Balbunar. Razgrad, N Bulgaria
112 O13 **Kučajske Planine** ▲ E Serbia and Montenegro (Yugo.)
165 T1 **Kuccharo-ko** ◎ Hokkaidō, N Japan
112 O11 **Kučevo** Serbia, NE Serbia and Montenegro (Yugo.)
Kuchan *see* Qūchān
169 Q10 **Kuching** ***prev.*** Sarawak. Sarawak, East Malaysia
169 Q10 **Kuching** ✕ Sarawak, East Malaysia
164 B17 **Kuchinoerabu-jima** *island* Nansei-shotō, SW Japan
164 C14 **Kuchinotsu** Nagasaki, Kyūshū, SW Japan
109 Q6 **Kuchl** Salzburg, NW Austria
148 L9 **Kūchnay Darweyshān** Helmand, S Afghanistan
Kuchurgan *see* Kuchurhan
117 O9 **Kuchurhan** ***Rus.*** Kuchurgan. ≈ NE Ukraine
Kuçova *see* Kuçovë
113 L21 **Kuçovë** ***var.*** Kuçova; ***prev.*** Qyteti Stalin. Berat, C Albania
136 D11 **Küçük Çekmece** İstanbul, NW Turkey
164 F14 **Kudamatsu** ***var.*** Kudamatu. Yamaguchi, Honshū, SW Japan
Kudamatu *see* Kudamatsu
Kudara *see* Ghŭdara
169 V6 **Kudat** Sabah, East Malaysia
Küddow *see* Gwda
155 G17 **Kūdligi** Karnātaka, W India
Kudowa *see* Kudowa-Zdrój
111 F16 **Kudowa-Zdrój** ***Ger.*** Kudowa. Wałbrzych, SW Poland
117 P9 **Kudryavtsivka** Mykolayivs'ka Oblast', S Ukraine
169 R16 **Kudus** ***prev.*** Koedoes. Jawa, C Indonesia
125 T13 **Kudymkar** Komi-Permyatskiy Avtonomnyy Okrug, NW Russian Federation
Kudzsir *see* Cugir
Kuei-chou *see* Guizhou
Kuei-lin *see* Guilin
Kuei-yang *see* Guiyang
K'u-erh-lo *see* Korla
Kueyang *see* Guiyang
Kufa *see* Al Kūfah
136 E14 **Küfiçayı** ≈ C Turkey
109 O6 **Kufstein** Tirol, W Austria
145 V14 **Kugaly** ***Kaz.*** Qoghaly. Almaty, SE Kazakhstan
8 K8 **Kugluktuk** ***var.*** Qurlurtuuq ***prev.*** Coppermine. Nunavut, NW Canada
143 Y13 **Kūhak** Sīstān va Balūchestān, SE Iran
143 R9 **Kūhbonān** Kermān, C Iran
148 J5 **Kūhestān** ***var.*** Kohsān. Herāt, W Afghanistan
93 N15 **Kuhmo** Oulu, E Finland
93 L18 **Kuhmoinen** Länsi-Suomi, W Finland
Kuhnau *see* Konin
Kühnö *see* Kihnu
143 O8 **Kūhpāyeh** Eşfahān, C Iran
167 O12 **Kui Buri** ***var.*** Ban Kui Nua. Prachuap Khiri Khan, SW Thailand
Kuibyshev *see* Kuybyshevskoye Vodokhranilishche
82 D13 **Kuito** ***Port.*** Silva Porto. Bié, C Angola
39 X14 **Kuiu Island** *island* Alexander Archipelago, Alaska, USA
92 L13 **Kuivaniemi** Oulu, C Finland
77 V14 **Kujama** Kaduna, C Nigeria
110 I10 **Kujawsko-pomorskie** ◆ *province*, C Poland
165 R8 **Kuji** ***var.*** Kuzi. Iwate, Honshū, C Japan
Kujto, Ozero *see* Kuyto, Ozero
Kujū-renzan *see* Kujū-san
164 D14 **Kujū-san** ***var.*** Kujū-renzan. ▲ Kyūshū, SW Japan
43 N7 **Kukalaya, Rio** ***var.*** Rio Cuculaya, Rio Kukulaya. ≈ NE Nicaragua
113 O16 **Kukavica** ***var.*** Vlajna. ▲ SE Serbia and Montenegro (Yugo.)
146 M10 **Ko'k'cha** ***Rus.*** Kokcha. Buxoro Viloyati, C Uzbekistan
113 M18 **Kukës** ***var.*** Kukësi. Kukës, NE Albania
113 L18 **Kukës** ◆ *district* NE Albania
Kukësi *see* Kukës
186 D8 **Kukipi** Gulf, S PNG
127 S3 **Kukmor** Respublika Tatarstan, W Russian Federation
Kukong *see* Shaoguan
39 N6 **Kukpowruk River** ≈ Alaska, USA
38 M6 **Kukpuk River** ≈ Alaska, USA
Kukukhoto *see* Hohhot
Kukulaya, Rio *see* Kukalaya, Rio
189 W12 **Kuk Point** *headland* NW Wake Island
146 G11 **Kukurtli** Ahal Welaýaty, C Turkmenistan
Kül *see* Kūl, Rūd-e
114 F7 **Kula** Vidin, NW Bulgaria
136 D14 **Kula** Manisa, W Turkey
112 K9 **Kula** Serbia, NW Serbia and Montenegro (Yugo.)
149 S8 **Kulāchi** North-West Frontier Province, NW Pakistan
Kulachi *see* Kolāchi
144 F11 **Kulagino** ***Kaz.*** Kūlagino. Atyrau, W Kazakhstan
168 L10 **Kulai** Johor, Peninsular Malaysia
114 M7 **Kulak** ≈ NE Bulgaria
153 T11 **Kula Kangri** ***var.*** Kulhakangri. ▲ Bhutan/China
144 E13 **Kulaly, Ostrov** *island* SW Kazakhstan
145 S16 **Kulan** ***Kaz.*** Qulan; ***prev.*** Lugovoy, Lugovoye. Zhambyl, S Kazakhstan
147 V9 **Kulanak** Narynskaya Oblast', C Kyrgyzstan
Kulandag, Gory *see* Gulandag
153 V14 **Kulaura** Chittagong, NE Bangladesh
118 D9 **Kuldīga** ***Ger.*** Goldingen. Kuldīga, W Latvia
Kuldja *see* Yining
Kul'dzhuktau, Gory *see* Quljuqtov-Toghi
127 N4 **Kulebaki** Nizhegorodskaya Oblast', W Russian Federation
112 E11 **Kulen Vakuf** ***var.*** Spasovo, Federacija Bosna I Hercegovina, NW Bosnia and Herzegovina
181 Q9 **Kulgera Roadhouse** Northern Territory, N Australia
Kulhakangri *see* Kula Kangri
127 T1 **Kuliga** Udmurtskaya Respublika, NW Russian Federation
Kulkuduk *see* Ko'lquduq
118 G4 **Kullamaa** Läänemaa, W Estonia
197 O12 **Kullorsuaq** ***var.*** Kuvdlorssuak. Kitaa, C Greenland
29 O6 **Kulm** North Dakota, N USA
Kulm *see* Chełmno
146 D12 **Kul'mach** ***prev. Turkm.*** Isgender. Balkan Welaýaty, W Turkmenistan
101 L18 **Kulmbach** Bayern, SE Germany
Kulmsee *see* Chełmża
147 Q14 **Kŭlob** ***Rus.*** Kulyab. SW Tajikistan
92 M13 **Kuloharju** Lappi, N Finland
125 N7 **Kuloy** Arkhangel'skaya Oblast', NW Russian Federation
127 N7 **Kuloy** ≈ NW Russian Federation
137 Q14 **Kulp** Diyarbakır, SE Turkey
Kulpa *see* Kolpa
77 P14 **Kulpawn** ≈ N Ghana
143 R13 **Kūl, Rūd-e** ***var.*** Kül. ≈ S Iran
144 G12 **Kul'sary** ***Kaz.*** Qulsary. Atyrau, W Kazakhstan
153 R15 **Kulti** West Bengal, NE India
93 G14 **Kultsjön** ◎ N Sweden
136 I14 **Kulu** Konya, W Turkey
123 S9 **Kulu** ≈ E Russian Federation
122 I13 **Kulunda** Altayskiy Kray, S Russian Federation
145 T7 **Kulunda Steppe** ***Kaz.*** Qulyndy Zhazyghy, ***Rus.*** Kulundinskaya Ravnina. *grassland* Kazakhstan/Russian Federation
Kulundinskaya Ravnina *see* Kulunda Steppe
182 M9 **Kulwin** Victoria, SE Australia
Kulyab *see* Kŭlob
117 Q3 **Kulykivka** Chernihivs'ka Oblast', N Ukraine
Kum *see* Qom
164 F14 **Kuma** Ehime, Shikoku, SW Japan
127 P14 **Kuma** ≈ SW Russian Federation
165 O12 **Kumagaya** Saitama, Honshū, S Japan
165 Q5 **Kumaishi** Hokkaidō, NE Japan
169 R13 **Kumai, Teluk** *bay* Borneo, C Indonesia
127 Y7 **Kumak** Orenburgskaya Oblast', W Russian Federation
164 C14 **Kumamoto** Kumamoto, Kyūshū, SW Japan
164 D15 **Kumamoto** ***off.*** Kumamoto-ken. ◆ *prefecture* Kyūshū, SW Japan
164 J15 **Kumano** Mie, Honshū, SW Japan
Kumanova *see* Kumanovo
113 O17 **Kumanovo** ***Turk.*** Kumanova. N FYR Macedonia
185 G17 **Kumara** West Coast, South Island, NZ
180 J8 **Kumarina Roadhouse** Western Australia
153 T15 **Kumarkhali** Khulna, W Bangladesh
77 P16 **Kumasi** ***prev.*** Coomassie. C Ghana
Kumayri *see* Gyumri
79 D15 **Kumba** Sud-Ouest, W Cameroon
114 N13 **Kumbağ** Tekirdağ, NW Turkey
155 J21 **Kumbakonam** Tamil Nādu, SE India
Kum-Dag *see* Gumdag
165 R16 **Kume-jima** *island* Nansei-shotō, SW Japan
127 V6 **Kumertau** Respublika Bashkortostan, W Russian Federation
35 R4 **Kumiva Peak** ▲ Nevada, W USA
159 N8 **Kum Kuduk** *well* NW China
159 N7 **Kumkuduk** Xinjiang Uygur Zizhiqu, W China
Kumkurgan *see* Qumqo'rg'on
95 M16 **Kumla** Örebro, C Sweden
136 E17 **Kumluca** Antalya, SW Turkey
100 N9 **Kummerower See** ◎ NE Germany
77 X14 **Kumo** Gombe, E Nigeria
145 O13 **Kumola** ≈ C Kazakhstan
167 N1 **Kumon Range** ▲ N Burma
83 F22 **Kums** Karas, SE Namibia
155 E18 **Kumta** Karnātaka, W India
158 L6 **Kümük** Xinjiang Uygur Zizhiqu, W China
38 H12 **Kumukahi, Cape** *headland* Hawai'i, USA, C Pacific Ocean
127 Q17 **Kumukh** Respublika Dagestan, SW Russian Federation
Kumul *see* Hami
127 N9 **Kumylzhenskaya** Volgogradskaya Oblast', SW Russian Federation
141 W6 **Kumzār** N Oman
149 S4 **Kunar** ***Per.*** Konarhā. ◆ *province* E Afghanistan
Kunashiri *see* Kunashir, Ostrov
123 U14 **Kunashir, Ostrov** ***var.*** Kunashiri. *island* Kuril'skiye Ostrova, SE Russian Federation
118 J3 **Kunda** Lääne-Virumaa, NE Estonia
152 M13 **Kunda** Uttar Pradesh, N India
155 E19 **Kundāpura** ***var.*** Coondapoor. Karnātaka, W India
79 O24 **Kundelungu, Monts** ▲ S Dem. Rep. Congo
Kundert *see* Hernád
186 D7 **Kundiawa** Chimbu, W PNG
Kundla *see* Sāvarkundla
168 L10 **Kundur, Pulau** *island* W Indonesia
149 Q2 **Kunduz** ***var.*** Kondoz, Kunduz, Qondūz, ***Per.*** Konduz. Kunduz, NE Afghanistan
149 Q2 **Kunduz** ***Per.*** Kondūz. ◆ *province* NE Afghanistan
Kuneitra *see* Al Qunayţirah
83 B18 **Kunene** ◆ *district* NE Namibia
83 A16 **Kunene** ***var.*** Cunene. ≈ Angola/Namibia *see also* Cunene
Kūnes *see* Xinyuan
158 J5 **Künes He** ≈ NW China
95 I19 **Kungälv** Västra Götaland, S Sweden
147 W7 **Kungei Ala-Tau** ***Rus.*** Khrebet Kyungëy Ala-Too, ***Kir.*** Küngöy Ala-Too. ▲ Kazakhstan/Kyrgyzstan
Küngöy Ala-Too *see* Kungei Ala-Tau
Kungrad *see* Qo'ng'irot
95 J19 **Kungsbacka** Halland, S Sweden
95 I18 **Kungshamn** Västra Götaland, S Sweden
95 M16 **Kungsör** Västmanland, C Sweden
79 J16 **Kungu** Equateur, NW Dem. Rep. Congo
125 V15 **Kungur** Permskaya Oblast', NW Russian Federation
166 L9 **Kungyangon** Yangon, SW Burma
111 M22 **Kunhegyes** Jász-Nagykun-Szolnok, E Hungary
167 O5 **Kunhing** Shan State, E Burma
158 D9 **Kunjirap Daban** ***var.*** Khūnjerāb Pass. *pass* China/Pakistan *see also* Khūnjerāb Pass
Kunlun Mountains *see* Kunlun Shan
158 H10 **Kunlun Shan** ***Eng.*** Kunlun Mountains. ▲ NW China
159 P11 **Kunlun Shankou** *pass* C China
160 G13 **Kunming** ***var.*** K'un-ming; ***prev.*** Yunnan. Yunnan, SW China
165 R4 **Kunnui** Hokkaidō, NE Japan
95 B18 **Kunoy** ***Dan.*** Kunø *Island* Faeroe Islands
163 X16 **Kunsan** ***var.*** Gunsan, ***Jap.*** Gunzan. W South Korea
111 L24 **Kunszentmárton** Jász-Nagykun-Szolnok, E Hungary
111 J23 **Kunszentmiklós** Bács-Kiskun, C Hungary
181 N3 **Kununurra** Western Australia
Kunyang *see* Pingyang
Kunya-Urgench *see* Köneürgenç
Kunyé *see* Pins, Île des
169 T11 **Kunyi** Borneo, C Indonesia
101 I20 **Künzelsau** Baden-Württemberg, S Germany
161 S10 **Kuocang Shan** ▲ SE China
124 H5 **Kuoloyarvi** ***var.*** Luolajarvi. Murmanskaya Oblast', NW Russian Federation
93 N16 **Kuopio** Itä-Suomi, C Finland
93 K17 **Kuortane** Länsi-Suomi, W Finland
93 M18 **Kuortti** Itä-Suomi, E Finland
Kupa *see* Kolpa
171 P17 **Kupang** ***prev.*** Koepang. Timor, C Indonesia
39 Q5 **Kuparuk River** ≈ Alaska, USA
Kupchino *see* Cupcina
186 E9 **Kupiano** Central, S PNG
180 M4 **Kupingarri** Western Australia
122 I12 **Kupino** Novosibirskaya Oblast', C Russian Federation
118 H11 **Kupiškis** Panevėžys, NE Lithuania
114 L13 **Küplü** Edirne, NW Turkey
39 X13 **Kupreanof Island** *island* Alexander Archipelago, Alaska, USA
39 O16 **Kupreanof Point** *headland* Alaska, USA
112 G13 **Kupres** Federacija Bosna I Hercegovina, SW Bosnia and Herzegovina
117 W5 **Kup"yans'k** ***Rus.*** Kupyansk. Kharkivs'ka Oblast', E Ukraine
117 W5 **Kup"yans'k-Vuzlovyy** Kharkivs'ka Oblast', E Ukraine
158 I6 **Kuqa** Xinjiang Uygur Zizhiqu, NW China
Kür *see* Kura
137 W11 **Kura** ***Az.*** Kür, ***Geor.*** Mtkvari, ***Turk.*** Kura Nehri. ≈ SW Asia
55 R8 **Kuracki** NW Guyana
Kura Kurk *see* Irbe Strait
147 Q10 **Kurama Range** ***Rus.*** Kuraminskiy Khrebet. ▲ Tajikistan/Uzbekistan
Kuraminskiy Khrebet *see* Kurama Range
Kura Nehri *see* Kura
119 J14 **Kuranyets** ***Rus.*** Kurenets. Minskaya Voblasts', C Belarus
164 H13 **Kurashiki** ***var.*** Kurasiki. Okayama, Honshū, SW Japan
154 L10 **Kurasia** Chhattīsgarh, C India
Kurasiki *see* Kurashiki
164 H12 **Kurayoshi** ***var.*** Kurayosi. Tottori, Honshū, SW Japan
Kurayosi *see* Kurayoshi
163 X6 **Kurbin He** ≈ NE China
145 X10 **Kurchum** ***Kaz.*** Kürshim. Vostochnyy Kazakhstan, E Kazakhstan
145 Y10 **Kurchum** ≈ E Kazakhstan
137 X11 **Kürdämir** ***Rus.*** Kyurdamir. C Azerbaijan
Kurdestan *see* Kordestān
139 S1 **Kurdistan** *cultural region* SW Asia
Kurd Kui *see* Kord Kūy
155 F15 **Kurduvādi** Mahārāshtra, W India
114 J11 **Kŭrdzhali** ***var.*** Kirdzhali. Kŭrdzhali, S Bulgaria
114 K11 **Kŭrdzhali** ◆ *province* S Bulgaria
114 J11 **Kŭrdzhali, Yazovir** ◻ S Bulgaria

◆ Country ● Country Capital ◇ Dependent Territory ○ Dependent Territory Capital ◆ Administrative Region ✕ International Airport ▲ Mountain ▲ Mountain Range ☀ Volcano ≈ River ◎ Lake ◻ Reservoir

164 F13 **Kure** Hiroshima, Honshū, SW Japan
192 K5 **Kure Atoll** *var.* Ocean Island. *atoll* Hawaiian Islands, Hawaii, USA, C Pacific Ocean
136 J10 **Küre Dağları** ⛰ N Turkey
Kurenets *see* Kuranyets
118 E6 **Kuressaare** *Ger.* Arensburg; *prev.* Kingissepp. Saaremaa, W Estonia
122 K9 **Kureyka** Krasnoyarskiy Kray, N Russian Federation
122 K9 **Kureyka** ≈ N Russian Federation
Kurgal'dzhino/Kurgal'dzhinskiy *see* Korgalzhyn
122 G11 **Kurgan** Kurganskaya Oblast', C Russian Federation
126 L14 **Kurganinsk** Krasnodarskiy Kray, SW Russian Federation
122 G11 **Kurganskaya Oblast'** ◈ *province* C Russian Federation
Kurgan-Tyube *see* Qŭrghonteppa
191 O2 **Kuria** *prev.* Woodle Island. *island* Tungaru, W Kiribati
Kuria Muria Bay *see* Ḥalānīyāt, Khalīj al
Kuria Muria Islands *see* Ḥalānīyāt, Juzur al
153 T13 **Kurigram** Rajshahi, N Bangladesh
93 K17 **Kurikka** Länsi-Suomi, W Finland
192 I3 **Kurile Basin** *undersea feature* NW Pacific Ocean
Kurile Islands *see* Kuril'skiye Ostrova
Kurile-Kamchatka Depression *see* Kurile Trench
192 J3 **Kurile Trench** *var.* Kurile-Kamchatka Depression. *undersea feature* NW Pacific Ocean
127 Q9 **Kurilovka** Saratovskaya Oblast', W Russian Federation
123 U13 **Kuril'sk** Kuril'skiye Ostrova, Sakhalinskaya Oblats', SE Russian Federation
122 G11 **Kuril'skiye Ostrova** *Eng.* Kurile Islands. *island group* SE Russian Federation
42 M9 **Kurinwas, Río** ≈ E Nicaragua
Kurisches Haff *see* Courland Lagoon
Kurkund *see* Kilingi-Nõmme
126 M4 **Kurlovskiy** Vladimirskaya Oblast', W Russian Federation
80 G12 **Kurmuk** Blue Nile, SE Sudan
Kurna *see* Al Qurnah
155 H17 **Kurnool** *var.* Karnul. Andhra Pradesh, S India
164 M11 **Kurobe** Toyama, Honshū, SW Japan
165 Q7 **Kuroishi** *var.* Kuroisi. Aomori, Honshū, C Japan
Kuroisi *see* Kuroishi
165 O12 **Kuroiso** Tochigi, Honshū, S Japan
165 Q4 **Kuromatsunai** Hokkaidō, NE Japan
164 B17 **Kuro-shima** *island* SW Japan
185 F21 **Kurow** Canterbury, South Island, NZ
127 N15 **Kursavka** Stavropol'skiy Kray, SW Russian Federation
118 E11 **Kuršėnai** Šiauliai, N Lithuania
Kürshim *see* Kurchum
Kurshskaya Kosa/Kuršių Nerija *see* Courland Spit
126 J7 **Kursk** Kurskaya Oblast', W Russian Federation
126 I7 **Kurskaya Oblast'** ◈ *province* W Russian Federation
Kurskiy Zaliv *see* Courland Lagoon
113 N15 **Kuršumlija** Serbia, S Serbia and Montenegro (Yugo.)
137 R15 **Kurtalan** Siirt, SE Turkey
Kurtbunar *see* Tervel
Kurt-Dere *see* Vŭlchidol
Kurtitsch/Kürtös *see* Curtici
Kurtty *see* Kurty
145 U15 **Kurty** *var.* Kurtty. ≈ SE Kazakhstan
93 L18 **Kuru** Länsi-Suomi, W Finland
80 C13 **Kuru** ≈ W Sudan
114 M13 **Kuru Dağı** ⛰ NW Turkey
158 L7 **Kuruktag** ⛰ NW China
83 G22 **Kuruman** Northern Cape, N South Africa
164 D14 **Kurume** Fukuoka, Kyūshū, SW Japan
123 N13 **Kurumkan** Respublika Buryatiya, S Russian Federation
155 J25 **Kurunegala** North Western Province, C Sri Lanka
55 T10 **Kurupukari** C Guyana
125 U10 **Kur"ya** Respublika Komi, NW Russian Federation
144 E15 **Kuryk** *prev.* Yeraliyev. Mangistau, SW Kazakhstan
136 B15 **Kuşadası** Aydın, SW Turkey
115 M19 **Kuşadası Körfezi** *gulf* SW Turkey
164 A17 **Kusagaki-guntō** *island* SW Japan
Kusaie *see* Kosrae
145 T12 **Kusak** ≈ C Kazakhstan
Kusary *see* Qusar
167 P7 **Ku Sathan, Doi** ▲ NW Thailand
164 J13 **Kusatsu** *var.* Kusatu. Shiga, Honshū, SW Japan
Kusatu *see* Kusatsu
138 F11 **Kuseifa** Southern, C Israel
136 C12 **Kuş Gölü** ◎ NW Turkey
126 L12 **Kushchevskaya** Krasnodarskiy Kray, SW Russian Federation
164 D16 **Kushima** *var.* Kusima. Miyazaki, Kyūshū, SW Japan
164 I15 **Kushimoto** Wakayama, Honshū, SW Japan
165 V4 **Kushiro** *var.* Kusiro. Hokkaidō, NE Japan
148 K4 **Kūshk** Herāt, W Afghanistan
Kushka *see* Gushgy/Serhetabat
145 N8 **Kushmurun** *Kaz.* Qusmuryn. Kostanay, N Kazakhstan
145 N8 **Kushmurun, Ozero** *Kaz.* Qusmuryn. ◎ N Kazakhstan
127 U4 **Kushnarenkovo** Respublika Bashkortostan, W Russian Federation
Kushrabat *see* Qo'shrabot
153 T15 **Kushtia** *var.* Kustia. Khulna, W Bangladesh
Kusikino *see* Kushikino
Kusima *see* Kushima
Kusiro *see* Kushiro
38 M13 **Kuskokwim Bay** *bay* Alaska, USA
39 P11 **Kuskokwim Mountains** ⛰ Alaska, USA
39 N12 **Kuskokwim River** ≈ Alaska, USA
108 G7 **Küsnacht** Zürich, N Switzerland
165 V4 **Kussharo-ko** *var.* Kussyaro. ◎ Hokkaidō, NE Japan
Küssnacht *see* Küssnacht am Rigi
108 F8 **Küssnacht am Rigi** *var.* Küssnacht. Schwyz, C Switzerland
Kussyaro *see* Kussharo-ko
Kustanay *see* Kostanay
Küstence/Küstendje *see* Constanța
100 F11 **Küstenkanal** *var.* Ems-Hunte Canal. *canal* NW Germany
Küstrin *see* Kostrzyn
Kustia *see* Kushtia
171 R11 **Kusu** Pulau Halmahera, E Indonesia
170 L16 **Kuta** Pulau Lombok, S Indonesia
139 T4 **Kutabān** N Iraq
136 E13 **Kütahya** *prev.* Kutaia. Kütahya, W Turkey
136 E13 **Kütahya** *var.* Kutaia. ◈ *province* W Turkey
Kutai *see* Mahakam, Sungai
Kutaia *see* Kütahya
137 R9 **K'ut'aisi** W Georgia
Kūt al 'Amārah *see* Al Kūt
Kut al Hai/Kūt al Ḩayy *see* Al Ḩayy
Kut al Imara *see* Al Kūt
123 Q11 **Kutana** Respublika Sakha (Yakutiya), NE Russian Federation
Kutaradja/Kutaraja *see* Bandaaceh
165 R4 **Kutchan** Hokkaidō, NE Japan
Kutch, Gulf of *see* Kachchh, Gulf of
Kutch, Rann of *see* Kachchh, Rann of
112 F9 **Kutina** Sisak-Moslavina, NE Croatia
112 H9 **Kutjevo** Požega-Slavonija, NE Croatia
111 E17 **Kutná Hora** *Ger.* Kuttenberg. Středočeský Kraj, C Czech Republic
110 K12 **Kutno** Łódzkie, C Poland
Kuttenberg *see* Kutná Hora
79 I20 **Kutu** Bandundu, W Dem. Rep. Congo
153 V17 **Kutubdia Island** *island* SE Bangladesh
80 B10 **Kutum** Northern Darfur, W Sudan
147 Y7 **Kuturgu** Issyk-Kul'skaya Oblast', E Kyrgyzstan
12 M5 **Kuujjuaq** *prev.* Fort-Chimo. Québec, E Canada
12 I7 **Kuujjuarapik** Québec, C Canada
Kuuli-Mayak *see* Guwlumaýak
118 I6 **Kuulse magi** ▲ S Estonia
92 N13 **Kuusamo** Oulu, E Finland
93 M19 **Kuusankoski** Etelä-Suomi, S Finland
127 W7 **Kuvandyk** Orenburgskaya Oblast', W Russian Federation
Kuvango *see* Cubango
Kuvasay *see* Quvasoy
Kuvdlorssuak *see* Kullorsuaq
124 I16 **Kuvshinovo** Tverskaya Oblast', W Russian Federation
141 Q4 **Kuwait** *off.* State of Kuwait, *var.* Dawlat al Kuwait, Koweit, Kuweit. ◆ *monarchy* SW Asia
Kuwait *see* Al Kuwayt
Kuwait Bay *see* Kuwayt, Jūn al
Kuwait City *see* Al Kuwayt
Kuwait, Dawlat al *see* Kuwait
Kuwajleen *see* Kwajalein Atoll
164 K13 **Kuwana** Mie, Honshū, SW Japan
139 X9 **Kuwayt** E Iraq
142 K11 **Kuwayt, Jūn al** *var.* Kuwait Bay. *bay* E Kuwait
Kuweit *see* Kuwait
117 P10 **Kuyal'nyts'kyy Lyman** ◎ SW Ukraine
122 I12 **Kuybyshev** Novosibirskaya Oblast', C Russian Federation
Kuybyshev *see* Bolgar, Respublika Tatarstan, Russian Federation
Kuybyshev *see* Samara
117 W9 **Kuybysheve** *Rus.* Kuybyshevo. Zaporiz'ka Oblast', SE Ukraine
Kuybyshevo *see* Kuybysheve
Kuybyshev Reservoir *see* Kuybyshevskoye Vodokhranilishche
Kuybyshevskaya Oblast' *see* Samarskaya Oblast'
Kuybyshevskiy *see* Novoishimskiy
127 R4 **Kuybyshevskoye Vodokhranilishche** *var.* Kuibyshev, *Eng.* Kuybyshev Reservoir. ▣ W Russian Federation
123 S9 **Kuydusun** Respublika Sakha (Yakutiya), NE Russian Federation
125 U16 **Kuyeda** Permskaya Oblast', NW Russian Federation
Küysanjaq *see* Koi Sanjaq
126 I7 **Kuyto, Ozero** *var.* Ozero Kujto. ◎ NW Russian Federation
158 J4 **Kuytun** Xinjiang Uygur Zizhiqu, NW China
122 M13 **Kuytun** Irkutskaya Oblast', S Russian Federation
55 S12 **Kuyuwini Landing** S Guyana
Kuzi *see* Kuji
38 M9 **Kuzitrin River** ≈ Alaska, USA
127 P6 **Kuznetsk** Penzenskaya Oblast', W Russian Federation
116 K3 **Kuznetsovs'k** Rivnens'ka Oblast', NW Ukraine
124 K6 **Kuzomen'** Murmanskaya Oblast', NW Russian Federation
165 R8 **Kuzumaki** Iwate, Honshū, C Japan
92 H9 **Kvaløya** *island* N Norway
92 K8 **Kvalsund** Finnmark, N Norway
94 G11 **Kvam** Oppland, S Norway
127 X7 **Kvarkeno** Orenburgskaya Oblast', W Russian Federation
93 G15 **Kvarnbergsvattnet** *var.* Frostviken. ◎ N Sweden
112 A11 **Kvarner** *var.* Carnaro, *It.* Quarnero. *gulf* W Croatia
112 B11 **Kvarnerić** *channel* W Croatia
39 O14 **Kvichak Bay** *bay* Alaska, USA
92 H12 **Kvikkjokk** *Lapp.* Huhttán. Norrbotten, N Sweden
95 D17 **Kvina** ≈ S Norway
92 Q1 **Kvitøya** *island* NE Svalbard
95 F16 **Kviteseid** Telemark, S Norway
95 H24 **Kværndrup** Fyn, C Denmark
79 H20 **Kwa** ≈ W Dem. Rep. Congo
77 Q15 **Kwadwokurom** C Ghana
186 M8 **Kwailibesi** Malaita, N Solomon Islands
189 S6 **Kwajalein Atoll** *var.* Kuwajleen. *atoll* Ralik Chain, C Marshall Islands
55 W9 **Kwakoegron** Brokopondo, N Surinam
81 J21 **Kwale** Coast, S Kenya
77 U17 **Kwale** Delta, S Nigeria
79 H20 **Kwamouth** Bandundu, W Dem. Rep. Congo
Kwando *see* Cuando
Kwangchow *see* Guangzhou
Kwangchu *see* Kwangju
163 X16 **Kwangju** *off.* Kwangju-gwangyŏksi, *var.* Guangju, Kwangchu, *Jap.* Kōshū. SW South Korea
79 H20 **Kwango** *Port.* Cuango. ≈ Angola/Dem. Rep. Congo *see also* Cuango
Kwangsi/Kwangsi Chuang Autonomous Region *see* Guangxi Zhuangzu Zizhiqu
Kwangtung *see* Guangdong
Kwangyuan *see* Guangyuan
81 F17 **Kwania, Lake** ◎ C Uganda
Kwanza *see* Cuanza
77 S15 **Kwara** ◈ *state* SW Nigeria
83 K22 **KwaZulu/Natal** *off.* KwaZulu/Natal Province; *prev.* Natal. ◈ *province* E South Africa
Kweichow *see* Guizhou
Kweichu *see* Guiyang
Kweilin *see* Guilin
Kweisui *see* Hohhot
Kweiyang *see* Guiyang
83 K17 **Kwekwe** *prev.* Que Que. Midlands, C Zimbabwe
83 G20 **Kweneng** ◈ *district* S Botswana
Kwesui *see* Hohhot
39 N12 **Kwethluk** Alaska, USA
39 N12 **Kwethluk River** ≈ Alaska, USA
110 J8 **Kwidzyń** *Ger.* Marienwerder. Pomorskie, N Poland
38 M13 **Kwigillingok** Alaska, USA
186 E9 **Kwikila** Central, S PNG
79 I20 **Kwilu** ≈ W Dem. Rep. Congo
Kwito *see* Cuito
171 U12 **Kwoka, Gunung** ▲ Papua, E Indonesia
78 I12 **Kyabé** Moyen-Chari, S Chad
183 O11 **Kyabram** Victoria, SE Australia
166 M9 **Kyaikkami** *prev.* Amherst. Mon State, S Burma
166 L9 **Kyaiklat** Irrawaddy, SW Burma
166 M8 **Kyaikto** Mon State, S Burma
123 N14 **Kyakhta** Respublika Buryatiya, S Russian Federation
182 G8 **Kyancutta** South Australia
167 T8 **Ky Anh** Ha Tinh, N Vietnam
166 L5 **Kyaukpadaung** Mandalay, C Burma
166 J6 **Kyaukpyu** Arakan State, W Burma
166 M5 **Kyaukse** Mandalay, C Burma
166 L8 **Kyaunggon** Irrawaddy, SW Burma
119 E14 **Kybartai** *Pol.* Kibarty. Marijampolė, S Lithuania
152 I7 **Kyelang** Himāchal Pradesh, NW India
111 G19 **Kyjov** *Ger.* Gaya. Jihomoravský Kraj, SE Czech Republic
115 J21 **Kykládes** *var.* Kikládhes, *Eng.* Cyclades. *island group* SE Greece
25 S11 **Kyle** Texas, SW USA
96 G9 **Kyle of Lochalsh** N Scotland, UK
101 D18 **Kyll** ≈ W Germany
115 F19 **Kyllíni** *var.* Killini. ▲ S Greece
93 M19 **Kymijoki** ≈ S Finland
115 H18 **Kými, Akrotírio** *headland* Évvoia, C Greece
125 W14 **Kyn** Permskaya Oblast', NW Russian Federation
183 N12 **Kyneton** Victoria, SE Australia
81 G17 **Kyoga, Lake** *var.* Lake Kioga. ◎ C Uganda
164 J12 **Kyōga-misaki** *headland* Honshū, SW Japan
183 V4 **Kyogle** New South Wales, SE Australia
163 W15 **Kyŏnggi-man** *bay* NW South Korea
163 Z16 **Kyŏngju** *Jap.* Keishū. SE South Korea
Kyŏngsŏng *see* Sŏul
Kyōsai-tō *see* Kŏje-do
81 F19 **Kyotera** S Uganda
164 J13 **Kyōto** Kyōto, Honshū, SW Japan
164 J13 **Kyōto** *off.* Kyōto-fu, *var.* Kyōto Hu. ◈ *urban prefecture* Honshū, SW Japan
Kyōto-fu/Kyōto Hu *see* Kyōto
115 D21 **Kyparissía** *var.* Kiparissía. Pelopónnisos, S Greece
115 D20 **Kyparissiakós Kólpos** *gulf* S Greece
Kyperounda *see* Kyperoúnta
121 P3 **Kyperoúnta** *var.* Kyperounda. C Cyprus
Kypros *see* Cyprus
115 H16 **Kyrá Panagía** *island* Vóreioi Sporádes, Greece, Aegean Sea
Kyrenia *see* Girne
Kyrenia Mountains *see* Beşparmak Dağları
Kyrgyz Republic *see* Kyrgyzstan
147 U9 **Kyrgyzstan** *off.* Kyrgyz Republic, *var.* Kirghizia; *prev.* Kirgizskaya SSR, Kirghiz SSR, Republic of Kyrgyzstan. ◆ *republic* C Asia
100 M11 **Kyritz** Brandenburg, NE Germany
Kyrkslätt *see* Kirkkonummi
94 G8 **Kyrksæterøra** Sør-Trøndelag, S Norway
125 U8 **Kyrta** Respublika Komi, NW Russian Federation
111 J18 **Kysucké Nové Mesto** *prev.* Horné Nové Mesto, *Ger.* Kisutzaneustadtl, Oberneustadtl, *Hung.* Kiszucaújhely. Žilinský Kraj, N Slovakia
117 N12 **Kytay, Ozero** ◎ SW Ukraine
115 F23 **Kýthira** *var.* Kíthira, *It.* Cerigo; *Lat.* Cythera. Kýthira, S Greece
115 F23 **Kýthira** *var.* Kíthira, *It.* Cerigo; *Lat.* Cythera. *island* S Greece
115 I20 **Kýthnos** Kýthnos, Kykládes, Greece, Aegean Sea
115 I20 **Kýthnos** *var.* Kíthnos, Thermiá, *It.* Termia; *anc.* Cythnos. *island* Kykládes, Greece, Aegean Sea
115 I20 **Kýthnou, Stenó** *strait* Kykládes, Greece, Aegean Sea
Kyungëy Ala-Too, Khrebet *see* Kungei Ala-Tau
Kyurdamir *see* Kürdämir
146 C11 **Kürendag** *Rus.* Gora Kyuren. ▲ W Turkmenistan
Kyuren, Gora *see* Kürendag
164 D15 **Kyūshū** *var.* Kyûsyû. *island* SW Japan
192 H6 **Kyushu-Palau Ridge** *var.* Kyusyu-Palau Ridge. *undersea feature* W Pacific Ocean
114 F10 **Kyustendil** *anc.* Pautalia. Kyustendil, W Bulgaria
114 G11 **Kyustendil** ◈ *province* W Bulgaria
Kyûsyû *see* Kyūshū
Kyusyu-Palau Ridge *see* Kyushu-Palau Ridge
123 P8 **Kyusyur** Respublika Sakha (Yakutiya), NE Russian Federation
183 P10 **Kywong** New South Wales, SE Australia
117 P4 **Kyyiv** *Eng.* Kiev, *Rus.* Kiyev. ● (Ukraine) Kyyivs'ka Oblast', N Ukraine
Kyyiv *see* Kyyivs'ka Oblast'
117 O4 **Kyyivs'ka Oblast'** *var.* Kyyiv, *Rus.* Kiyevskaya Oblast'. ◈ *province* N Ukraine
117 P3 **Kyyivs'ke Vodoskhovyshche** *Eng.* Kiev Reservoir, *Rus.* Kiyevskoye Vodokhranilishche. ▣ N Ukraine
93 L16 **Kyyjärvi** Länsi-Suomi, W Finland
122 K14 **Kyzyl** Respublika Tyva, C Russian Federation
147 S8 **Kyzyl-Adyr** *prev.* Kirovskoye. Talasskaya Oblast', NW Kyrgyzstan
145 V14 **Kyzylagash** Almaty, SE Kazakhstan
146 C13 **Kyzylbair** Balkan Welaýaty, W Turkmenistan
Kyzyl-Dzhiik, Pereval *see* Uzbel Shankou
145 S7 **Kyzylkak, Ozero** ◎ NE Kazakhstan
145 X11 **Kyzylkesek** Vostochnyy Kazakhstan, E Kazakhstan
147 S10 **Kyzyl-Kiya** *Kir.* Kyzyl-Kyya. Batkenskaya Oblast', SW Kyrgyzstan
144 L11 **Kyzylkol', Ozero** ◎ C Kazakhstan
151 N15 **Kyzylorda** *var.* Kzyl-Orda, Qizil Orda *Kaz.* Qyzylorda; *prev.* Perovsk. Kyzylorda, S Kazakhstan
150 L14 **Kyzylorda** *off.* Kyzylordinskaya Oblast' *Kaz.* Qyzylorda Oblysy. ◈ *province* S Kazakhstan
122 K14 **Kyzyl Kum** *var.* Kizil Kum, Qizil Qum, *Uzb.* Qizilqum. *desert* Kazakhstan/Uzbekistan
Kyzyl-Kyya *see* Kyzyl-Kiya
Kyzylrabat *see* Qizilravot
Kyzylrabot *see* Qizilrabot
Kyzylsu *see* Kyzyl-Suu
147 X7 **Kyzyl-Suu** *prev.* Pokrovka. Issyk-Kul'skaya Oblast', NE Kyrgyzstan
147 S12 **Kyzyl-Suu** *var.* Kyzylsu. ≈ Kyrgyzstan/Tajikistan
147 X8 **Kyzyl-Tuu** Issyk-Kul'skaya Oblast', E Kyrgyzstan
145 Q12 **Kyzylzhar** *Kaz.* Qyzylzhar. Karaganda, C Kazakhstan
Kzyl-Orda *see* Kyzylorda
Kyzylordinskaya Oblast' *see* Kyzylorda
Kzyltu *see* Kishkenekol'

L

109 X2 **Laa an der Thaya** Niederösterreich, NE Austria
63 K15 **La Adela** La Pampa, SE Argentina
Laagen *see* Numedalslågen
109 S5 **Laakirchen** Oberösterreich, N Austria
Laaland *see* Lolland
104 I11 **La Albuera** Extremadura, W Spain
105 O7 **La Alcarria** *physical region* C Spain
104 K14 **La Algaba** Andalucía, S Spain
105 P9 **La Almarcha** Castilla-La Mancha, C Spain
105 R6 **La Almunia de Doña Godina** Aragón, NE Spain
41 N5 **La Amistad, Presa** ▣ NW Mexico
118 F4 **Läänemaa** *off.* Lääne Maakond. ◈ *province* NW Estonia
118 I3 **Lääne-Virumaa** *off.* Lääne-Viru Maakond. ◈ *province* NE Estonia
62 J9 **La Antigua, Salina** *salt lake* W Argentina
99 E17 **Laarne** Oost-Vlaanderen, NW Belgium
80 O13 **Laas Caanood** Nugaal, N Somalia
41 O9 **La Ascensión** Nuevo León, NE Mexico
80 N12 **Laas Dhaareed** Woqooyi Galbeed, N Somalia
55 O4 **La Asunción** Nueva Esparta, NE Venezuela
Laatokka *see* Ladozhskoye Ozero
100 I13 **Laatzen** Niedersachsen, NW Germany
38 E9 **Lā'au Point** *var.* Laau Point. *headland* Moloka'i, Hawai'i, USA, C Pacific Ocean
42 D6 **La Aurora** ✈ (Ciudad de Guatemala) Guatemala, C Guatemala
74 C9 **Laâyoune** *var.* Aaiún. ○ (Western Sahara) NW Western Sahara
126 L14 **Laba** ≈ SW Russian Federation
40 M6 **La Babia** Coahuila de Zaragoza, NE Mexico
15 R7 **La Baie** Québec, SE Canada
171 P16 **Labala** Pulau Lomblen, S Indonesia
62 K8 **La Banda** Santiago del Estero, N Argentina
La Banda Oriental *see* Uruguay
104 K4 **La Bañeza** Castilla-León, N Spain
40 M13 **La Barca** Jalisco, SW Mexico
40 K14 **La Barra de Navidad** Jalisco, C Mexico
187 Y13 **Labasa** *prev.* Lambasa. Vanua Levu, N Fiji
102 H8 **la Baule-Escoublac** Loire-Atlantique, NW France
Labe *see* Elbe
76 I13 **Labé** Moyenne-Guinée, NW Guinea
23 X14 **La Belle** Florida, SE USA
15 N11 **Labelle** Québec, SE Canada
10 H7 **Laberge, Lake** ◎ Yukon Territory, W Canada
Labes *see* Łobez
Labiau *see* Polessk
112 A10 **Labin** *It.* Albona. Istra, NW Croatia
126 L14 **Labinsk** Krasnodarskiy Kray, SW Russian Federation
105 X5 **La Bisbal d'Empordà** Cataluña, NE Spain
119 P16 **Labkovichy** *Rus.* Lobkovichi. Mahilyowskaya Voblasts', E Belarus
15 S4 **La Blache, Lac de** ◎ Québec, SE Canada
171 P4 **Labo** Luzon, N Philippines
Laboehanbadjo *see* Labuhanbajo
Laborca *see* Laborec
111 N18 **Laborec** *Hung.* Laborca. ≈ E Slovakia
108 D11 **La Borgne** ≈ S Switzerland
45 T12 **Laborie** SW Saint Lucia
79 F21 **La Bouenza** ◈ *province* S Congo
102 J14 **Labouheyre** Landes, SW France
62 L12 **Laboulaye** Córdoba, C Argentina
13 Q7 **Labrador** *cultural region* Newfoundland and Labrador, SW Canada
64 I6 **Labrador Basin** *var.* Labrador Sea Basin. *undersea feature* Labrador Sea
13 N9 **Labrador City** Newfoundland and Labrador, E Canada
13 Q5 **Labrador Sea** *sea* NW Atlantic Ocean
Labrador Sea Basin *see* Labrador Basin
Labrang *see* Xiahe
54 G9 **Labranzagrande** Boyacá, C Colombia
45 U15 **La Brea** Trinidad, Trinidad and Tobago
59 D14 **Lábrea** Amazonas, N Brazil
15 S6 **Labrieville** Québec, SE Canada
102 K14 **Labrit** Landes, SW France
108 C9 **La Broye** ≈ SW Switzerland
103 N15 **Labruguière** Tarn, S France
168 M11 **Labu** Pulau Singkep, W Indonesia
169 T7 **Labuan** *var.* Victoria. Labuan, East Malaysia
169 T7 **Labuan** ◈ *federal territory* East Malaysia
Labuan *see* Labuan, Pulau
169 T7 **Labuan, Pulau** *var.* Labuan. *island* East Malaysia
Labudalin *see* Ergun
171 N16 **Labuhanbajo** *prev.* Laboehanbadjo. Flores, S Indonesia
168 J9 **Labuhanbilik** Sumatera, N Indonesia
168 G8 **Labuhanhaji** Sumatera, W Indonesia
Labuk *see* Labuk, Sungai
Labuk Bay *see* Labuk, Teluk
169 V7 **Labuk, Sungai** *var.* Labuk. ≈ East Malaysia
169 W6 **Labuk, Teluk** *var.* Labuk Bay, Telukan Labuk. *bay* S Sulu Sea
Labuk, Telukan *see* Labuk, Teluk
166 K9 **Labutta** Irrawaddy, SW Burma
122 I8 **Labytnangi** Yamalo-Nenetskiy Avtonomnyy Okrug, N Russian Federation
78 F10 **Lac** *off.* Préfecture du Lac. ◈ *prefecture* W Chad
113 K19 **Laç** *var.* Laci. Lezhë, C Albania
57 K19 **Lacajahuira, Rio** ≈ W Bolivia
La Calamine *see* Kelmis
62 G11 **La Calera** Valparaíso, C Chile
13 P11 **Lac-Allard** Québec, E Canada
104 L13 **La Campana** Andalucía, S Spain
102 J12 **Lacanau** Gironde, SW France
42 C2 **Lacandón, Sierra del** ⛰ Guatemala/Mexico
La Cañiza *see* A Cañiza
41 W16 **Lacantún, Río** ≈ SE Mexico
103 Q3 **la Capelle** Aisne, N France
112 K10 **Laćarak** Serbia, NW Serbia and Montenegro (Yugo.)
62 L11 **La Carlota** Córdoba, C Argentina
104 L13 **La Carlota** Andalucía, S Spain
105 N12 **La Carolina** Andalucía, S Spain
103 O15 **Lacaune** Tarn, S France
15 P7 **Lac-Bouchette** Québec, SE Canada
Laccadive Islands/Laccadive Minicoy and Amindivi Islands, the *see* Lakshadweep
11 Y16 **Lac du Bonnet** Manitoba, S Canada
30 L4 **Lac du Flambeau** Wisconsin, N USA
15 P8 **Lac-Édouard** Québec, SE Canada
42 I4 **La Ceiba** Atlántida, N Honduras
54 E9 **La Ceja** Antioquia, W Colombia
182 J11 **Lacepede Bay** *bay* South Australia
32 G9 **Lacey** Washington, NW USA
103 P12 **la Chaise-Dieu** Haute-Loire, C France
114 G13 **Lachanás** Kentrikí Makedonía, N Greece
126 L11 **Lacha, Ozero** ◎ NW Russian Federation
103 O8 **la Charité-sur-Loire** Nièvre, C France
103 N9 **la Châtre** Indre, C France
108 C8 **La Chaux-de-Fonds** Neuchâtel, W Switzerland
Lach Dera *see* Dheere Laaq
108 G8 **Lachen** Schwyz, C Switzerland
183 Q8 **Lachlan River** ≈ New South Wales, SE Australia
43 T15 **La Chorrera** Panamá, C Panama
15 V7 **Lac-Humqui** Québec, SE Canada
15 N12 **Lachute** Québec, SE Canada
Lachyn *see* Laçın
Laci *see* Laç
137 W13 **Laçın** *Rus.* Lachyn. SW Azerbaijan
103 S16 **la Ciotat** *anc.* Citharista. Bouches-du-Rhône, SE France
18 D10 **Lackawanna** New York, NE USA
11 Q13 **Lac La Biche** Alberta, SW Canada
Lac La Martre *see* Wha Ti
15 R12 **Lac-Mégantic** *var.* Mégantic. Québec, SE Canada
Lacobriga *see* Lagos
40 G5 **La Colorada** Sonora, NW Mexico
11 Q15 **Lacombe** Alberta, SW Canada
30 L12 **Lacon** Illinois, N USA
43 P16 **La Concepción** *var.* Concepción. Chiriquí, W Panama
54 H5 **La Concepción** Zulia, NW Venezuela
54 H5 **La Concepción** Zulia, NW Venezuela
107 C19 **Laconi** Sardegna, Italy, C Mediterranean Sea
19 O9 **Laconia** New Hampshire, NE USA
61 H19 **La Coronilla** Rocha, E Uruguay
La Coruña *see* A Coruña
103 O11 **la Courtine** Creuse, C France
102 J16 **Lacq** Pyrénées-Atlantiques, SW France
15 P9 **La Croche** Québec, SE Canada
29 X3 **la Croix, Lac** ◎ Canada/USA
26 K5 **La Crosse** Kansas, C USA
21 V7 **La Crosse** Virginia, NE USA
32 L9 **La Crosse** Washington, NW USA
30 J7 **La Crosse** Wisconsin, N USA
54 C13 **La Cruz** Nariño, SW Colombia
42 K12 **La Cruz** Guanacaste, NW Costa Rica
40 I10 **La Cruz** Sinaloa, W Mexico
61 F19 **La Cruz** Florida, S Uruguay
42 M9 **La Cruz de Río Grande** Región Autónoma Atlántico Sur, E Nicaragua
54 J4 **La Cruz de Taratara** Falcón, N Venezuela
15 Q10 **Lac-St-Charles** Québec, SE Canada
40 M6 **La Cuesta** Coahuila de Zaragoza, NE Mexico
57 A17 **La Cumbra, Volcán** ✶ Galapagos Islands, Ecuador, E Pacific Ocean
152 J5 **Ladākh Range** ⛰ NE India
26 I5 **Ladder Creek** ≈ Kansas, C USA
45 X10 **la Désirade** *atoll* E Guadeloupe
Lādhiqīyah, Muḩāfaẓat al *see* Al Lādhiqīyah
83 F25 **Ladismith** Western Cape, SW South Africa
152 G11 **Lādnūn** Rājasthān, NW India

◆ Country ● Country Capital ◇ Dependent Territory ○ Dependent Territory Capital ◈ Administrative Region ✈ International Airport ▲ Mountain ⛰ Mountain Range ✶ Volcano ≈ River ◎ Lake ▣ Reservoir

Ladoga, Lake *see* Ladozhskoye Ozero
115 E19 **Ládon** ≈ S Greece
54 E9 **La Dorada** Caldas, C Colombia
126 H11 **Ladozhskoye Ozero** *Eng.* Lake Ladoga, *Fin.* Laatokka. ◎ NW Russian Federation
37 R12 **Ladron Peak** ▲ New Mexico, SW USA
124 J11 **Ladva-Vetka** Respublika Kareliya, NW Russian Federation
183 Q15 **Lady Barron** Tasmania, SE Australia
14 G9 **Lady Evelyn Lake** ◎ Ontario, S Canada
23 W11 **Lady Lake** Florida, SE USA
10 L17 **Ladysmith** Vancouver Island, British Columbia, SW Canada
83 J22 **Ladysmith** KwaZulu/Natal, E South Africa
30 J5 **Ladysmith** Wisconsin, N USA
145 P9 **Ladyzhenka** Akmola, C Kazakhstan
186 E7 **Lae** Morobe, W PNG
189 R6 **Lae Atoll** *atoll* Ralik Chain, W Marshall Islands
40 C3 **La Encantada, Cerro de** ▲ NW Mexico
94 E12 **Lærdalsøyri** Sogn og Fjordane, S Norway
55 N11 **La Esmeralda** Amazonas, S Venezuela
42 G7 **La Esperanza** Intibucá, SW Honduras
30 K8 **La Farge** Wisconsin, N USA
23 R5 **Lafayette** Alabama, S USA
37 T4 **Lafayette** Colorado, C USA
23 R2 **La Fayette** Georgia, SE USA
31 O13 **Lafayette** Indiana, N USA
22 I9 **Lafayette** Louisiana, S USA
20 K8 **Lafayette** Tennessee, S USA
19 N7 **Lafayette, Mount** ▲ New Hampshire, NE USA
La Fe *see* Santa Fé
103 P3 **la Fère** Aisne, N France
102 L6 **la Ferté-Bernard** Sarthe, NW France
102 K5 **la Ferté-Macé** Orne, N France
103 N7 **la Ferté-St-Aubin** Loiret, C France
103 P5 **la Ferté-sous-Jouarre** Seine-et-Marne, N France
77 V15 **Lafia** Nassarawa, C Nigeria
77 T15 **Lafiagi** Kwara, W Nigeria
11 T17 **Lafleche** Saskatchewan, S Canada
102 K7 **la Flèche** Sarthe, NW France
109 X7 **Lafnitz** *Hung.* Lapines. ≈ Austria/Hungary
187 P17 **La Foa** Province Sud, S New Caledonia
20 M8 **La Follette** Tennessee, S USA
15 N12 **Lafontaine** Québec, SE Canada
22 K10 **Lafourche, Bayou** ≈ Louisiana, S USA
62 K6 **La Fragua** Santiago del Estero, N Argentina
54 H7 **La Fría** Táchira, NW Venezuela
104 J7 **La Fuente de San Esteban** Castilla-León, N Spain
186 C7 **Lagaip** ≈ W PNG
61 B15 **La Gallareta** Santa Fe, C Argentina
127 Q14 **Lagan'** *prev.* Kaspiyskiy. Respublika Kalmykiya, SW Russian Federation
95 L20 **Lagan** Kronoberg, S Sweden
95 K21 **Lågan** ≈ S Sweden
92 L2 **Lagarfljót** *var.* Lögurinn. ◎ E Iceland
37 R7 **La Garita Mountains** ▲ Colorado, C USA
171 O2 **Lagawe** Luzon, N Philippines
78 F13 **Lagdo** Nord, N Cameroon
78 F13 **Lagdo, Lac de** ◎ N Cameroon
100 H13 **Lage** Nordrhein-Westfalen, W Germany
94 H12 **Lågen** ≈ S Norway
61 J14 **Lages** Santa Catarina, S Brazil
Lágesvuotna *see* Laksefjorden
149 R4 **Laghmān** ◈ *province* E Afghanistan
74 J6 **Laghouat** N Algeria
105 Q10 **La Gineta** Castilla-La Mancha, C Spain
115 E21 **Lagkáda** *var.* Langada. Pelopónnisos, S Greece
114 G13 **Lagkadás** *var.* Langades, Langadhás. Kentrikí Makedonía, N Greece
115 E20 **Lagkádia** *var.* Langádhia, Langadia. Pelopónnisos, S Greece
54 F6 **La Gloria** Cesar, N Colombia
41 O7 **La Gloria** Nuevo León, NE Mexico
92 N3 **Lågneset** *headland* W Svalbard
104 G14 **Lagoa** Faro, S Portugal
La Goagira *see* La Guajira
Lago Agrio *see* Nueva Loja
61 I14 **Lagoa Vermelha** Rio Grande do Sul, S Brazil
137 V10 **Lagodekhi** SE Georgia
42 C7 **La Gomera** Escuintla, S Guatemala
Lagone *see* Logone
107 M19 **Lagonegro** Basilicata, S Italy
63 G16 **Lago Ranco** Los Lagos, S Chile
77 S16 **Lagos** Lagos, SW Nigeria
104 F14 **Lagos** *anc.* Lacobriga. Faro, S Portugal
77 S16 **Lagos** ◈ *state* SW Nigeria
40 M12 **Lagos de Moreno** Jalisco, SW Mexico
Lagosta *see* Lastovo
74 A12 **Lagouira** SW Western Sahara
92 O1 **Lågøya** *island* N Svalbard
32 L11 **La Grande** Oregon, NW USA
103 Q14 **la Grande-Combe** Gard, S France
12 K9 **La Grande Rivière** *var.* Fort George. ≈ Québec, SE Canada
23 R4 **La Grange** Georgia, SE USA
31 P11 **Lagrange** Indiana, N USA
20 L5 **La Grange** Kentucky, S USA
27 V2 **La Grange** Missouri, C USA
21 V10 **La Grange** North Carolina, SE USA
25 U11 **La Grange** Texas, SW USA
105 N7 **La Granja** Castilla-León, N Spain
55 Q9 **La Gran Sabana** *grassland* E Venezuela
54 H7 **La Grita** Táchira, NW Venezuela
La Grulla *see* Grulla
15 R11 **La Guadeloupe** Québec, SE Canada
54 F12 **La Guaira** Distrito Federal, N Venezuela
54 G4 **La Guajira** *off.* Departamento de La Guajira, *var.* Guajira, La Goagira. ◈ *province* NE Colombia
188 I4 **Lagua Lichan, Punta** *headland* Saipan, S Northern Mariana Islands
18 K14 **La Guardia** ✕ (New York) Long Island, New York, NE USA
La Guardia/Laguardia *see* A Guarda
105 P4 **Laguardia** País Vasco, N Spain
La Gudiña *see* A Gudiña
103 O9 **la Guerche-sur-l'Aubois** Cher, C France
103 O13 **Laguiole** Aveyron, S France
83 F26 **L'Agulhas** *var.* Agulhas. W Cape, SW South Africa
61 K14 **Laguna** Santa Catarina, S Brazil
37 Q11 **Laguna** New Mexico, SW USA
35 T16 **Laguna Beach** California, W USA
35 Y17 **Laguna Dam** *dam* Arizona/California, W USA
40 L7 **Laguna El Rey** Coahuila de Zaragoza, N Mexico
35 V17 **Laguna Mountains** ▲ California, W USA
61 B17 **Laguna Paiva** Santa Fe, C Argentina
62 H3 **Lagunas** Tarapacá, N Chile
56 E9 **Lagunas** Loreto, N Peru
57 M20 **Lagunillas** Santa Cruz, SE Bolivia
54 H6 **Lagunillas** Mérida, NW Venezuela
44 C4 **La Habana** *var.* Havana. ● (Cuba) Ciudad de La Habana, W Cuba
169 W7 **Lahad Datu** Sabah, East Malaysia
169 W7 **Lahad Datu, Teluk** *var.* Telukan Lahad Datu, Teluk Darvel, Teluk Datu; *prev.* Darvel Bay. *bay* Sabah, East Malaysia
38 F10 **Lahaina** Maui, Hawai'i, USA, C Pacific Ocean
168 L14 **Lahat** Sumatera, W Indonesia
La Haye *see* 's-Gravenhage
Lahej *see* Laḩij
62 G9 **La Higuera** Coquimbo, N Chile
141 S13 **Lahī, Ḩisā' al** *spring/well* NE Yemen
141 O16 **Laḩij** *var.* Laḩj, *Eng.* Lahej. SW Yemen
142 M3 **Lāhījān** Gīlān, NW Iran
119 I19 **Lahishyn** *Pol.* Lohiszyn, *Rus.* Logishin. Brestskaya Voblasts', SW Belarus
Laḩj *see* Laḩij
101 F18 **Lahn** ≈ W Germany
Lähn *see* Wleń
95 J21 **Laholm** Halland, S Sweden
95 J21 **Laholmsbukten** *bay* S Sweden
35 R6 **Lahontan Reservoir** ▣ Nevada, W USA
149 W8 **Lahore** Punjab, NE Pakistan
149 W8 **Lahore** ✕ Punjab, E Pakistan
55 Q6 **La Horqueta** Delta Amacuro, NE Venezuela
119 K15 **Lahoysk** *Rus.* Logoysk. Minskaya Voblasts', C Belarus
101 F22 **Lahr** Baden-Württemberg, S Germany
93 M19 **Lahti** *Swe.* Lahtis. Etelä-Suomi, S Finland
Lahtis *see* Lahti
40 M14 **La Huacana** Michoacán de Ocampo, SW Mexico
40 K14 **La Huerta** Jalisco, SW Mexico
78 H12 **Laï** *prev.* Behagle, De Behagle. Tandjilé, S Chad
Laibach *see* Ljubljana
167 Q5 **Lai Châu** Lai Châu, N Vietnam
38 D9 **Lā'ie** *var.* Laie. O'ahu, Hawai'i, USA, C Pacific Ocean
102 L5 **l'Aigle** Orne, N France
103 Q7 **Laignes** Côte d'Or, C France
93 K17 **Laihia** Länsi-Suomi, W Finland
Laila *see* Laylā
83 F25 **Laingsburg** Western Cape, SW South Africa
109 U2 **Lainsitz** *Cz.* Lužnice. ≈ Austria/Czech Republic
96 I7 **Lairg** N Scotland, UK
81 I17 **Laisamis** Eastern, N Kenya
Laisberg *see* Leisi
127 R4 **Laishevo** Respublika Tatarstan, W Russian Federation
Laisholm *see* Jõgeva
92 H13 **Laisvall** Norrbotten, N Sweden
93 K19 **Laitila** Länsi-Suomi, W Finland
161 P5 **Laiwu** Shandong, E China
161 R4 **Laixi** *var.* Shuiji. Shandong, E China
161 R4 **Laiyang** Shandong, E China
161 O3 **Laiyuan** Hebei, E China
161 R4 **Laizhou** *var.* Ye Xian. Shandong, E China
161 Q4 **Laizhou Wan** *var.* Laichow Bay. *bay* E China
37 S8 **La Jara** Colorado, C USA
61 I15 **Lajeado** Rio Grande do Sul, S Brazil
112 L12 **Lajkovac** Serbia, C Serbia and Montenegro (Yugo.)
111 K25 **Lajosmizse** Bács-Kiskun, C Hungary
Lajta *see* Leitha
40 I6 **La Junta** Chihuahua, N Mexico
37 V7 **La Junta** Colorado, C USA
92 J13 **Lakaträsk** Norrbotten, N Sweden
Lak Dera *see* Dheere Laaq
Lakeamu *see* Lakekamu
29 P12 **Lake Andes** South Dakota, N USA
22 H9 **Lake Arthur** Louisiana, S USA
187 Z15 **Lakeba** *prev.* Lakemba. *island* Lau Group, E Fiji
187 Z14 **Lakeba Passage** *channel* E Fiji
29 S10 **Lake Benton** Minnesota, N USA
23 V9 **Lake Butler** Florida, SE USA
183 P8 **Lake Cargelligo** New South Wales, SE Australia
22 G9 **Lake Charles** Louisiana, S USA
27 X9 **Lake City** Arkansas, C USA
37 Q7 **Lake City** Colorado, C USA
23 V9 **Lake City** Florida, SE USA
29 U13 **Lake City** Iowa, C USA
31 P7 **Lake City** Michigan, N USA
29 W9 **Lake City** Minnesota, N USA
21 T13 **Lake City** South Carolina, SE USA
29 Q7 **Lake City** South Dakota, N USA
20 M8 **Lake City** Tennessee, S USA
10 L17 **Lake Cowichan** Vancouver Island, British Columbia, SW Canada
29 U10 **Lake Crystal** Minnesota, N USA
25 T6 **Lake Dallas** Texas, SW USA
97 K15 **Lake District** *physical region* NW England, UK
18 D10 **Lake Erie Beach** New York, NE USA
29 T11 **Lakefield** Minnesota, N USA
25 V6 **Lake Fork Reservoir** ▣ Texas, SW USA
30 M9 **Lake Geneva** Wisconsin, N USA
18 L9 **Lake George** New York, NE USA
9 R7 **Lake Harbour** Baffin Island, Nunavut, NE Canada
36 I12 **Lake Havasu City** Arizona, SW USA
25 W12 **Lake Jackson** Texas, SW USA
186 D8 **Lakekamu** *var.* Lakeamu. ≈ S PNG
180 K13 **Lake King** Western Australia
23 V12 **Lakeland** Florida, SE USA
23 U7 **Lakeland** Georgia, SE USA
181 W4 **Lakeland Downs** Queensland, NE Australia
11 P16 **Lake Louise** Alberta, SW Canada
Lakemba *see* Lakeba
29 V11 **Lake Mills** Iowa, C USA
39 Q10 **Lake Minchumina** Alaska, USA
Lakemti *see* Nek'emtē
186 A7 **Lake Murray** Western, SW PNG
80 F5 **Lake Nasser** *var.* Buhayrat Nasir, Buḩayrat Nāşir, Buheiret Nâsir. ◎ Egypt/Sudan
31 R9 **Lake Orion** Michigan, N USA
190 B16 **Lakepa** NE Niue
29 T11 **Lake Park** Iowa, C USA
18 K7 **Lake Placid** New York, NE USA
18 K9 **Lake Pleasant** New York, NE USA
34 M6 **Lakeport** California, W USA
29 Q10 **Lake Preston** South Dakota, N USA
22 J5 **Lake Providence** Louisiana, S USA
185 E20 **Lake Pukaki** Canterbury, South Island, NZ
183 Q12 **Lakes Entrance** Victoria, SE Australia
37 N12 **Lakeside** Arizona, SW USA
35 V17 **Lakeside** California, W USA
23 S9 **Lakeside** Florida, SE USA
28 K13 **Lakeside** Nebraska, C USA
32 E13 **Lakeside** Oregon, NW USA
21 W6 **Lakeside** Virginia, NE USA
Lakes State *see* El Buhayrat
Lake State *see* Michigan
185 F20 **Lake Tekapo** Canterbury, South Island, NZ
21 O10 **Lake Toxaway** North Carolina, SE USA
29 T13 **Lake View** Iowa, C USA
32 I16 **Lakeview** Oregon, NW USA
25 O3 **Lakeview** Texas, SW USA
27 W14 **Lake Village** Arkansas, C USA
23 W12 **Lake Wales** Florida, SE USA
37 T4 **Lakewood** Colorado, C USA
18 K15 **Lakewood** New Jersey, NE USA
18 C11 **Lakewood** New York, NE USA
31 T11 **Lakewood** Ohio, N USA
23 Y13 **Lakewood Park** Florida, SE USA
23 Z14 **Lake Worth** Florida, SE USA
152 H4 **Lake Wular** ◎ NE India
124 H11 **Lakhdenpokh'ya** Respublika Kareliya, NW Russian Federation
152 L11 **Lakhīmpur** Uttar Pradesh, N India
154 J11 **Lakhnādon** Madhya Pradesh, C India
Lakhnau *see* Lucknow
154 A9 **Lakhpat** Gujarāt, W India
119 K19 **Lakhva** *Rus.* Lakhva. Brestskaya Voblasts', SW Belarus
26 I6 **Lakin** Kansas, C USA
149 S7 **Lakki Marwat** North-West Frontier Province, NW Pakistan
115 F21 **Lakonía** *historical region* S Greece
115 F22 **Lakonikós Kólpos** *gulf* S Greece
76 M17 **Lakota** S Ivory Coast
29 U11 **Lakota** Iowa, C USA
29 P3 **Lakota** North Dakota, N USA
Lak Sao *see* Ban Lakxao
92 L8 **Laksefjorden** *Lapp.* Lágesvuotna. *fjord* N Norway
92 K8 **Lakselv** *Lapp.* Leavdnja. Finnmark, N Norway
155 B21 **Lakshadweep** *prev.* the Laccadive, Minicoy and Amindivi Islands. ◈ *union territory* India, N Indian Ocean
155 C22 **Lakshadweep** *Eng.* Laccadive Islands. *island group* India, N Indian Ocean
153 S17 **Lakshmikāntapur** West Bengal, NE India
112 G11 **Laktaši** Republika Srpska, N Bosnia and Herzegovina
149 V7 **Lāla Mūsa** Punjab, NE Pakistan
la Laon *see* Laon
114 M11 **Lalapaşa** Edirne, NW Turkey
83 P14 **Lalaua** Nampula, N Mozambique
105 S10 **L'Alcúdia** *var.* L'Alcudia. País Valenciano, E Spain
80 J11 **Lalibela** Amhara, N Ethiopia,
153 T12 **Lalmanirhat** Rajshahi, N Bangladesh
79 F20 **La Lékoumou** ◈ *province* SW Congo
42 E8 **La Libertad** La Libertad, SW El Salvador
42 E3 **La Libertad** Petén, N Guatemala
42 H6 **La Libertad** Comayagua, SW Honduras
40 E4 **La Libertad** *var.* Puerto Libertad. Sonora, NW Mexico
42 K10 **La Libertad** Chontales, S Nicaragua
42 A9 **La Libertad** ◈ *department* SW El Salvador
56 B11 **La Libertad** *off.* Departamento de La Libertad. ◈ *department* W Peru
62 G11 **La Ligua** Valparaíso, C Chile
139 U5 **La'li Khān** E Iraq
79 F19 **La Likouala** ◈ *province* NE Congo
104 H3 **Lalín** Galicia, NW Spain
102 L13 **Lalinde** Dordogne, SW France
104 K16 **La Línea** *var.* La Línea de la Concepción. Andalucía, S Spain
La Línea de la Concepción *see* La Línea
152 J14 **Lalitpur** Uttar Pradesh, N India
153 P11 **Lalitpur** Central, C Nepal
152 K10 **Lālkua** Uttaranchal, N India
11 R12 **La Loche** Saskatchewan, C Canada
102 M6 **la Loupe** Eure-et-Loir, C France
99 G20 **La Louvière** Hainaut, S Belgium
L'Altissima *see* Hochwilde
104 L14 **La Luisiana** Andalucía, S Spain
37 S14 **La Luz** New Mexico, SW USA
107 D16 **La Maddalena** Sardegna, Italy, C Mediterranean Sea
62 J7 **La Madrid** Tucumán, N Argentina
Lama-Kara *see* Kara
15 S8 **La Malbaie** Québec, SE Canada
167 T10 **Lamam** Xékong, S Laos
105 P10 **La Mancha** *physical region* C Spain
la Manche *see* English Channel
187 R13 **Lamap** Malekula, C Vanuatu
37 W6 **Lamar** Colorado, C USA
27 S7 **Lamar** Missouri, C USA
21 S12 **Lamar** South Carolina, SE USA
107 C19 **La Marmora, Punta** ▲ Sardegna, Italy, C Mediterranean Sea
8 I9 **La Martre, Lac** ◎ Northwest Territories, NW Canada
56 D10 **Lamas** San Martín, N Peru
42 I5 **La Masica** Atlántida, NW Honduras
103 R12 **Lamastre** Ardèche, E France
La Matepec *see* Santa Ana, Volcán de
44 I7 **La Maya** Santiago de Cuba, E Cuba
109 S5 **Lambach** Oberösterreich, N Austria
168 I11 **Lambak** Pulau Pini, W Indonesia
102 H5 **Lamballe** Côtes d'Armor, NW France
79 D18 **Lambaréné** Moyen-Ogooué, W Gabon
Lambasa *see* Labasa
56 B11 **Lambayeque** Lambayeque, W Peru
56 A10 **Lambayeque** *off.* Departamento de Lambayeque. ◈ *department* NW Peru
97 G17 **Lambay Island** *Ir.* Reachrainn. *island* E Ireland
186 G6 **Lambert, Cape** *headland* New Britain, E PNG
195 W6 **Lambert Glacier** *glacier* Antarctica
29 T10 **Lamberton** Minnesota, N USA
27 X4 **Lambert-Saint Louis** ✕ Missouri, C USA
31 R11 **Lambertville** Michigan, N USA
18 J15 **Lambertville** New Jersey, NE USA
171 N12 **Lambogo** Sulawesi, N Indonesia
106 D8 **Lambro** ≈ N Italy
33 W11 **Lame Deer** Montana, NW USA
104 H6 **Lamego** Viseu, N Portugal
187 Q14 **Lamen Bay** Épi, C Vanuatu
45 X6 **Lamentin** Basse Terre, N Guadeloupe
Lamentin *see* le Lamentin
182 K10 **Lameroo** South Australia
54 F10 **La Mesa** Cundinamarca, C Colombia
35 U17 **La Mesa** California, W USA
37 R16 **La Mesa** New Mexico, SW USA
25 N6 **Lamesa** Texas, SW USA
107 N21 **Lamezia Terme** Calabria, SE Italy
115 F17 **Lamía** Stereá Ellás, C Greece
171 O8 **Lamitan** Basilan Island, SW Philippines
187 Y14 **Lamiti** Gau, C Fiji
171 T11 **Lamlam** Papua, E Indonesia
188 B16 **Lamlam, Mount** ▲ SW Guam
109 Q6 **Lammer** ≈ E Austria
185 E23 **Lammerlaw Range** ▲ South Island, NZ
95 L20 **Lammhult** Kronoberg, S Sweden
93 L18 **Lammi** Etelä-Suomi, S Finland
189 U11 **Lamoil** *island* Chuuk, C Micronesia
35 W3 **Lamoille** Nevada, W USA
18 M7 **Lamoille River** ≈ Vermont, NE USA
30 J13 **La Moine River** ≈ Illinois, N USA
171 P4 **Lamon Bay** *bay* Luzon, N Philippines
29 V16 **Lamoni** Iowa, C USA
35 R13 **Lamont** California, W USA
27 N8 **Lamont** Oklahoma, C USA
54 E13 **La Montañita** *var.* Montañita. Caquetá, S Colombia
43 N8 **La Mosquitia** *var.* Miskito Coast, *Eng.* Mosquito Coast. *coastal region* E Nicaragua
102 I9 **la Mothe-Achard** Vendée, NW France
188 L15 **Lamotrek Atoll** *atoll* Caroline Islands, C Micronesia
29 P6 **La Moure** North Dakota, N USA
167 O8 **Lampang** *var.* Muang Lampang. Lampang, NW Thailand
167 R9 **Lam Pao Reservoir** ▣ E Thailand
25 S9 **Lampasas** Texas, SW USA
25 S9 **Lampasas River** ≈ Texas, SW USA
41 N7 **Lampazos** *var.* Lampazos de Naranjo. Nuevo León, NE Mexico
Lampazos de Naranjo *see* Lampazos
115 E19 **Lámpeia** Dytikí Ellás, S Greece
101 G19 **Lampertheim** Hessen, W Germany
97 I20 **Lampeter** SW Wales, UK
167 O7 **Lamphun** *var.* Lampun, Muang Lamphun. Lamphun, NW Thailand
11 X10 **Lamprey** Manitoba, C Canada
Lampun *see* Lamphun
168 M15 **Lampung** *off.* Propinsi Lampung. ◈ *province* SW Indonesia
126 K6 **Lamskoye** Lipetskaya Oblast', W Russian Federation
81 K20 **Lamu** Coast, SE Kenya
43 N14 **La Muerte, Cerro** ▲ C Costa Rica
103 S13 **la Mure** Isère, E France
37 S10 **Lamy** New Mexico, SW USA
119 J18 **Lan'** *Rus.* Lan'. ≈ C Belarus
38 E10 **Lāna'i** *var.* Lanai. *island* Hawai'i, USA, C Pacific Ocean
38 E10 **Lāna'i City** *var.* Lanai City. Lāna'i, Hawai'i, USA, C Pacific Ocean
99 L18 **Lanaken** Limburg, NE Belgium
171 Q7 **Lanao, Lake** *var.* Lake Sultan Alonto. ◎ Mindanao, S Philippines
96 J12 **Lanark** S Scotland, UK
96 I13 **Lanark** *cultural region* C Scotland, UK
104 L9 **La Nava de Ricomalillo** Castilla-La Mancha, C Spain
166 M13 **Lanbi Kyun** *prev.* Sullivan Island. *island* Mergui Archipelago, S Burma
Lancang Jiang *see* Mekong
97 K17 **Lancashire** *cultural region* NW England, UK
15 N13 **Lancaster** Ontario, SE Canada
97 K16 **Lancaster** NW England, UK
35 T14 **Lancaster** California, W USA
20 M6 **Lancaster** Kentucky, S USA
27 U1 **Lancaster** Missouri, C USA
19 O7 **Lancaster** New Hampshire, NE USA
18 D10 **Lancaster** New York, NE USA
31 T14 **Lancaster** Ohio, N USA
18 H16 **Lancaster** Pennsylvania, NE USA
21 R11 **Lancaster** South Carolina, SE USA
25 U7 **Lancaster** Texas, SW USA
21 X5 **Lancaster** Virginia, NE USA
30 J9 **Lancaster** Wisconsin, N USA
9 O4 **Lancaster Sound** *sound* Nunavut, N Canada
Lan-chou/Lan-chow/ Lanchow *see* Lanzhou
107 K14 **Lanciano** Abruzzo, C Italy
111 O16 **Łańcut** Podkarpackie, SE Poland
169 Q11 **Landak, Sungai** ≈ Borneo, N Indonesia
Landao *see* Lantau Island
Landau *see* Landau an der Isar, Bayern, Germany
Landau *see* Landau in der Pfalz, Rheinland-Pfalz, Germany
101 N22 **Landau an der Isar** *var.* Landau. Bayern, SE Germany
101 F20 **Landau in der Pfalz** *var.* Landau. Rheinland-Pfalz, SW Germany
Land Burgenland *see* Burgenland
108 K8 **Landeck** Tirol, W Austria
99 J19 **Landen** Vlaams Brabant, C Belgium
33 U15 **Lander** Wyoming, C USA
102 F5 **Landerneau** Finistère, NW France
95 K20 **Landeryd** Halland, S Sweden
102 J15 **Landes** ◈ *department* SW France
Landeshut/Landeshut in Schlesien *see* Kamienna Góra
105 R9 **Landete** Castilla-La Mancha, C Spain
99 M18 **Landgraaf** Limburg, SE Netherlands
102 F5 **Landivisiau** Finistère, NW France
Land of Enchantment *see* New Mexico
Land of Opportunity *see* Arkansas
Land of Steady Habits *see* Connecticut
Land of the Midnight Sun *see* Alaska
108 I8 **Landquart** Graubünden, SE Switzerland
108 J9 **Landquart** ≈ Austria/Switzerland
21 P10 **Landrum** South Carolina, SE USA
Landsberg *see* Górowo Iławeckie, Warmińsko-Mazurskie, NE Poland
Landsberg *see* Gorzów Wielkopolski, Gorzów, Poland
101 K23 **Landsberg am Lech** Bayern, S Germany
Landsberg an der Warthe *see* Gorzów Wielkopolski
8 J4 **Lands End** *headland* Northwest Territories, NW Canada
97 G25 **Land's End** *headland* SW England, UK
101 M22 **Landshut** Bayern, SE Germany
Landskron *see* Lanškroun
95 J22 **Landskrona** Skåne, S Sweden
98 I10 **Landsmeer** Noord-Holland, C Netherlands
95 J19 **Landvetter** ✕ (Göteborg) Västra Götaland, S Sweden
Landwarów *see* Lentvaris
23 R5 **Lanett** Alabama, S USA
108 C8 **La Neuveville** *var.* Neuveville, *Ger.* Neuenstadt. Neuchâtel, W Switzerland
95 G21 **Langå** *var.* Langaa. Århus, C Denmark
Langaa *see* Langå
158 G14 **La'nga Co** ◎ W China
Langada *see* Lagkáda
Langades/Langadhás *see* Lagkadás
Langádhia/Langadia *see* Lagkádia
147 T14 **Langar** *Rus.* Lyangar. SE Tajikistan
146 M10 **Langar** *Rus.* Lyangar. Navoiy Viloyati, C Uzbekistan
142 M3 **Langarūd** Gīlān, NW Iran
11 V16 **Langbank** Saskatchewan, S Canada
29 P2 **Langdon** North Dakota, N USA
103 P12 **Langeac** Haute-Loire, C France
102 L8 **Langeais** Indre-et-Loire, C France
80 I8 **Langeb, Wadi** ≈ NE Sudan
Långed *see* Dals Långed
95 G25 **Langeland** *island* S Denmark
99 B18 **Langemark** West-Vlaanderen, W Belgium
101 G18 **Langen** Hessen, W Germany
101 J22 **Langenau** Baden-Württemberg, S Germany
11 V16 **Langenburg** Saskatchewan, S Canada
101 E16 **Langenfeld** Nordrhein-Westfalen, W Germany
108 L8 **Längenfeld** Tirol, W Austria
100 I12 **Langenhagen** Niedersachsen, N Germany
100 I12 **Langenhagen** ✕ (Hannover) Niedersachsen, NW Germany
109 W3 **Langenlois** Niederösterreich, NE Austria
108 E7 **Langenthal** Bern, NW Switzerland
109 W6 **Langenwang** Steiermark, E Austria
109 X3 **Langenzersdorf** Niederösterreich, E Austria
100 F9 **Langeoog** *island* NW Germany
95 H23 **Langeskov** Fyn, C Denmark
95 G16 **Langesund** Telemark, S Norway
95 G17 **Langesundsfjorden** *fjord* S Norway
94 D10 **Langevåg** Møre og Romsdal, S Norway
161 P3 **Langfang** Hebei, E China
94 E9 **Langfjorden** *fjord* S Norway
29 Q8 **Langford** South Dakota, N USA
169 I10 **Langgapayung** Sumatera, W Indonesia
106 E9 **Langhirano** Emilia-Romagna, C Italy
97 K14 **Langholm** S Scotland, UK
92 I3 **Langjökull** *glacier* C Iceland
168 I6 **Langkawi, Pulau** *island* Peninsular Malaysia
166 M14 **Langkha Tuk, Khao** ▲ SW Thailand
14 L8 **Langlade** Québec, SE Canada
10 M17 **Langley** British Columbia, SW Canada
167 S7 **Lang Mô** Thanh Hoa, N Vietnam
Langnau *see* Langnau im Emmental
108 E8 **Langnau im Emmental** *var.* Langnau. Bern, W Switzerland
103 Q13 **Langogne** Lozère, S France
102 K13 **Langon** Gironde, SW France
La Ngounié *see* Ngounié
92 G10 **Langøya** *island* C Norway
158 G14 **Langqên Zangbo** ≈ China/India
104 K2 **Langreo** *var.* Sama de Langreo. Asturias, N Spain
103 S7 **Langres** Haute-Marne, N France
103 R8 **Langres, Plateau de** *plateau* C France

◆ COUNTRY ● COUNTRY CAPITAL ◇ DEPENDENT TERRITORY ○ DEPENDENT TERRITORY CAPITAL ◈ ADMINISTRATIVE REGION ✕ INTERNATIONAL AIRPORT ▲ MOUNTAIN ▲ MOUNTAIN RANGE ※ VOLCANO ≈ RIVER ◎ LAKE ▣ RESERVOIR

168 H8 **Langsa** Sumatera, W Indonesia
93 H16 **Långsele** Västernorrland, C Sweden
162 L12 **Lang Shan** ▲ N China
95 M14 **Långshyttan** Dalarna, C Sweden
167 T5 **Lang Sơn** *var.* Langson. Lang Sơn, N Vietnam
167 N14 **Lang Suan** Chumphon, SW Thailand
93 J14 **Långträsk** Norrbotten, N Sweden
25 N11 **Langtry** Texas, SW USA
103 P16 **Languedoc** *cultural region* S France
103 P15 **Languedoc-Roussillon** ◈ *region* S France
27 X10 **L'Anguille River** ~ Arkansas, C USA
93 I16 **Långviksmon** Västernorrland, N Sweden
101 K22 **Langweid** Bayern, S Germany
160 J8 **Langzhong** Sichuan, C China
Lan Hsü *see* Lan Yü
11 U15 **Lanigan** Saskatchewan, S Canada
116 K5 **Lanivtsi** Ternopil's'ka Oblast', W Ukraine
137 Y13 **Länkäran** *Rus.* Lenkoran'. S Azerbaijan
102 L16 **Lannemezan** Hautes-Pyrénées, S France
102 G5 **Lannion** Côtes d'Armor, NW France
14 M11 **L'Annonciation** Québec, SE Canada
105 V5 **L'Anoia** ~ NE Spain
18 I15 **Lansdale** Pennsylvania, NE USA
14 L14 **Lansdowne** Ontario, SE Canada
152 K9 **Lansdowne** Uttaranchal, N India
30 M3 **L'Anse** Michigan, N USA
15 S7 **L'Anse-St-Jean** Québec, SE Canada
93 K18 **Länsi-Suomi** ◈ *province* W Finland
29 Y11 **Lansing** Iowa, C USA
27 R4 **Lansing** Kansas, C USA
31 Q9 **Lansing** *state capital* Michigan, N USA
92 J12 **Lansjärv** Norrbotten, N Sweden
111 G17 **Lanškroun** *Ger.* Landskron. Pardubický Kraj, C Czech Republic
167 N16 **Lanta, Ko** *island* S Thailand
161 O15 **Lantau Island** *Cant.* Tai Yue Shan, *Chin.* Landao. *island* Hong Kong, S China
Lan-ts'ang Chiang *see* Mekong
171 O11 **Lanu** Sulawesi, N Indonesia
107 D19 **Lanusei** Sardegna, Italy, C Mediterranean Sea
102 H7 **Lanvaux, Landes de** *physical region* NW France
163 W8 **Lanxi** Heilongjiang, NE China
161 R10 **Lanxi** Zhejiang, SE China
La Nyanga *see* Nyanga
161 T15 **Lan Yü** *var.* Huoshao Tao, *var.* Hungt'ou, Lan Hsü, Lanyü, *Eng.* Orchid Island; *prev.* Kotosho, Koto Sho. *island* SE Taiwan
64 P11 **Lanzarote** *island* Islas Canarias, Spain, NE Atlantic Ocean
159 V10 **Lanzhou** *var.* Lan-chou, Lanchow, Lan-chow; *prev.* Kaolan. Gansu, C China
106 B8 **Lanzo Torinese** Piemonte, NE Italy
171 O1 **Laoag** Luzon, N Philippines
171 Q5 **Laoang** Samar, C Philippines
167 R5 **Lao Cai** Lao Cai, N Vietnam
Laodicea/Laodicea ad Mare *see* Al Lādhiqīyah
Laoet *see* Laut, Pulau
163 T11 **Laoha He** ~ NE China
160 M8 **Laohekou** *prev.* Guanghua. Hubei, C China
Laoi, An *see* Lee
97 E19 **Laois** *prev.* Leix, Queen's County. *cultural region* C Ireland
Laojunmiao *see* Yumen
163 W12 **Lao Ling** ▲ NE China
64 Q11 **La Oliva** *var.* Oliva. Fuerteventura, Islas Canarias, Spain, NE Atlantic Ocean
Lao, Loch *see* Belfast Lough
Laolong *see* Longchuan
Lao Mangnai *see* Mangnai
103 P3 **Laon** *var.* la Laon; *anc.* Laudunum. Aisne, N France
Lao People's Democratic Republic *see* Laos
54 M3 **La Orchila, Isla** *island* N Venezuela
64 O11 **La Orotava** Tenerife, Islas Canarias, Spain, NE Atlantic Ocean
57 E14 **La Oroya** Junín, C Peru
167 Q7 **Laos** *off.* Lao People's Democratic Republic. ◆ *republic* SE Asia
161 R5 **Laoshan Wan** *bay* E China
163 Y10 **Laoye Ling** ▲ NE China
60 J12 **Lapa** Paraná, S Brazil
103 P10 **Lapalisse** Allier, C France
54 F9 **La Palma** Cundinamarca, C Colombia
42 F7 **La Palma** Chalatenango, N El Salvador
43 W16 **La Palma** Darién, SE Panama
64 N11 **La Palma** *island* Islas Canarias, Spain, NE Atlantic Ocean
104 J14 **La Palma del Condado** Andalucía, S Spain
61 F18 **La Paloma** Durazno, C Uruguay
61 G20 **La Paloma** Rocha, E Uruguay
61 A21 **La Pampa** *off.* Provincia de La Pampa. ◈ *province* C Argentina
55 P8 **La Paragua** Bolívar, E Venezuela
119 O16 **Lapatsichy** *Rus.* Lopatichi. Mahilyowskaya Voblasts', E Belarus
61 C16 **La Paz** Entre Ríos, E Argentina
62 I11 **La Paz** Mendoza, C Argentina
57 J18 **La Paz** *var.* La Paz de Ayacucho. ● (Bolivia-legislative and administrative capital) La Paz, W Bolivia
42 H6 **La Paz** La Paz, SW Honduras
40 F9 **La Paz** Baja California Sur, NW Mexico
61 F20 **La Paz** Canelones, S Uruguay
57 J16 **La Paz** ◈ *department* W Bolivia
42 B9 **La Paz** ◈ *department* S El Salvador
42 G7 **La Paz** ◈ *department* SW Honduras
La Paz *see* El Alto, Bolivia
La Paz *see* Robles, Colombia
La Paz *see* La Paz Centro, Nicaragua
40 F9 **La Paz, Bahía de** *bay* W Mexico
42 I10 **La Paz Centro** *var.* La Paz. León, W Nicaragua
La Paz de Ayacucho *see* La Paz
54 J15 **La Pedrera** Amazonas, SE Colombia
31 S9 **Lapeer** Michigan, N USA
40 K6 **La Perla** Chihuahua, N Mexico
165 T1 **La Perouse Strait** *Jap.* Sōya-kaikyō, *Rus.* Proliv Laperuza. *strait* Japan/Russian Federation
63 I14 **La Perra, Salitral de** *salt lake* C Argentina
Laperuza, Proliv *see* La Perouse Strait
41 Q10 **La Pesca** Tamaulipas, C Mexico
40 M13 **La Piedad Cavadas** Michoacán de Ocampo, C Mexico
Lapines *see* Lafnitz
93 M16 **Lapinlahti** Itä-Suomi, C Finland
Lápithos *see* Lapta
22 K9 **Laplace** Louisiana, S USA
45 X12 **La Plaine** SE Dominica
173 P16 **la Plaine-des-Palmistes** C Réunion
92 K11 **Lapland** *Fin.* Lappi, *Swe.* Lappland. *cultural region* N Europe
28 M8 **La Plant** South Dakota, N USA
61 D20 **La Plata** Buenos Aires, E Argentina
54 D12 **La Plata** Huila, SW Colombia
21 W4 **La Plata** Maryland, NE USA
La Plata *see* Sucre
45 U6 **la Plata, Río de** ~ C Puerto Rico
105 W4 **La Pobla de Lillet** Cataluña, NE Spain
105 U4 **La Pobla de Segur** Cataluña, NE Spain
15 S9 **La Pocatière** Québec, SE Canada
104 L3 **La Pola de Gordón** Castilla-León, N Spain
31 O11 **La Porte** Indiana, N USA
18 H13 **Laporte** Pennsylvania, NE USA
29 X13 **La Porte City** Iowa, C USA
62 J8 **La Posta** Catamarca, C Argentina
40 E8 **La Poza Grande** Baja California Sur, W Mexico
93 K16 **Lappajärvi** Länsi-Suomi, W Finland
93 L16 **Lappajärvi** ◎ W Finland
93 N18 **Lappeenranta** *Swe.* Villmanstrand. Etelä-Suomi, S Finland
93 J17 **Lappfjärd** *Fin.* Lapväärtti. Länsi-Suomi, W Finland
92 L12 **Lappi** *Swe.* Lappland. ◈ *province* N Finland
Lappi *see* Lapland
Lappland *see* Lappi
Lappland *see* Lapland, N Europe
Lappo *see* Lapua
61 C23 **Laprida** Buenos Aires, E Argentina
25 P13 **La Pryor** Texas, SW USA
136 B11 **Lâpseki** Çanakkale, NW Turkey
121 P2 **Lapta** *Gk.* Lápithos. NW Cyprus
Laptev Sea *see* Laptevykh, More
122 N6 **Laptevykh, More** *Eng.* Laptev Sea. *sea* Arctic Ocean
93 K16 **Lapua** *Swe.* Lappo. Länsi-Suomi, W Finland
105 P3 **La Puebla de Arganzón** País Vasco, N Spain
104 L14 **La Puebla de Cazalla** Andalucía, S Spain
104 M9 **La Puebla de Montalbán** Castilla-La Mancha, C Spain
54 I6 **La Puerta** Trujillo, NW Venezuela
Lapurdum *see* Bayonne
40 E7 **La Purísima** Baja California Sur, W Mexico
Lapväärtti *see* Lappfjärd
110 O10 **Łapy** Podlaskie, NE Poland
80 D6 **Laqiya Arba'in** Northern, NW Sudan
62 J4 **La Quiaca** Jujuy, N Argentina
107 J14 **L'Aquila** *var.* Aquila, Aquila degli Abruzzo. Abruzzo, C Italy
143 Q13 **Lār** Fārs, S Iran
54 J5 **Lara** *off.* Estado Lara. ◈ *state* NW Venezuela
104 G2 **Laracha** Galicia, NW Spain
74 G5 **Larache** *var.* al Araïch, El Araïch, El Araîche, *anc.* Lixus. NW Morocco
103 T14 **Laragne-Montéglin** Hautes-Alpes, SE France
104 M13 **La Rambla** Andalucía, S Spain
33 Y17 **Laramie** Wyoming, C USA
33 X15 **Laramie Mountains** ▲ Wyoming, C USA
33 Y16 **Laramie River** ~ Wyoming, C USA
60 H12 **Laranjeiras do Sul** Paraná, S Brazil
Larantoeka *see* Larantuka
171 P16 **Larantuka** *prev.* Larantoeka. Flores, C Indonesia
171 U15 **Larat** Pulau Larat, E Indonesia
171 U15 **Larat, Pulau** *island* Kepulauan Tanimbar, E Indonesia
95 P19 **Lärbro** Gotland, SE Sweden
106 A9 **Larche, Col de** *pass* France/Italy
14 H8 **Larder Lake** Ontario, S Canada
105 O2 **Laredo** Cantabria, N Spain
25 Q15 **Laredo** Texas, SW USA
40 H9 **La Reforma** Sinaloa, W Mexico
98 N11 **Laren** Gelderland, E Netherlands
98 J11 **Laren** Noord-Holland, C Netherlands
102 K13 **la Réole** Gironde, SW France
La Réunion *see* Réunion
Largeau *see* Faya
103 U13 **l'Argentière-la-Bessée** Hautes-Alpes, SE France
149 O4 **Lar Gerd** *var.* Largird. Balkh, N Afghanistan
Largird *see* Lar Gerd
23 V12 **Largo** Florida, SE USA
37 Q9 **Largo, Canon** *valley* New Mexico, SW USA
44 D6 **Largo, Cayo** *island* W Cuba
23 Z17 **Largo, Key** *island* Florida Keys, Florida, SE USA
96 H12 **Largs** W Scotland, UK
102 I16 **la Rhune** *var.* Larrún. ▲ France/Spain *see also* Larrún
la Riege *see* Ariège
29 Q4 **Larimore** North Dakota, N USA
107 L15 **Larino** Molise, C Italy
Lario *see* Como, Lago di
62 J9 **La Rioja** La Rioja, NW Argentina
62 I9 **La Rioja** *off.* Provincia de La Rioja. ◈ *province* NW Argentina
105 O4 **La Rioja** ◈ *autonomous community* N Spain
115 F16 **Lárisa** *var.* Larissa. Thessalía, C Greece
Larissa *see* Lárisa
149 Q13 **Lārkāna** *var.* Larkhana. Sind, SE Pakistan
Larkhana *see* Lārkāna
Larnaca *see* Lárnaka
121 Q3 **Lárnaka** *var.* Larnaca, Larnax. SE Cyprus
121 Q3 **Lárnaka** ✕ SE Cyprus
Larnax *see* Lárnaka
97 G14 **Larne** *Ir.* Latharna. E Northern Ireland, UK
26 L5 **Larned** Kansas, C USA
104 L3 **La Robla** Castilla-León, N Spain
104 I10 **La Roca de la Sierra** Extremadura, W Spain
99 K22 **La Roche-en-Ardenne** Luxembourg, SE Belgium
102 L11 **la Rochefoucauld** Charente, W France
102 J10 **la Rochelle** *anc.* Rupella. Charente-Maritime, W France
102 I9 **la Roche-sur-Yon** *prev.* Bourbon Vendée, Napoléon-Vendée. Vendée, NW France
105 Q10 **La Roda** Castilla-La Mancha, C Spain
104 L14 **La Roda de Andalucía** Andalucía, S Spain
45 P9 **La Romana** E Dominican Republic
11 T13 **La Ronge** Saskatchewan, C Canada
11 U13 **La Ronge, Lac** ◎ Saskatchewan, C Canada
22 K10 **Larose** Louisiana, S USA
42 M7 **La Rosita** Región Autónoma Atlántico Norte, NE Nicaragua
181 Q3 **Larrimah** Northern Territory, N Australia
62 N11 **Larroque** Entre Ríos, E Argentina
105 Q2 **Larrún** *Fr.* la Rhune. ▲ France/Spain *see also* la Rhune
195 X6 **Lars Christensen Coast** *physical region* Antarctica
39 Q14 **Larsen Bay** Kodiak Island, Alaska, USA
194 I5 **Larsen Ice Shelf** *ice shelf* Antarctica
8 M6 **Larsen Sound** *sound* Nunavut, N Canada
La Rúa *see* A Rúa de Valdeorras
102 K16 **Laruns** Pyrénées-Atlantiques, SW France
95 G16 **Larvik** Vestfold, S Norway
La-sa *see* Lhasa
171 S13 **Lasahata** Pulau Seram, E Indonesia
Lasahau *see* Lasihao
37 O6 **La Sal** Utah, W USA
14 C17 **La Salle** Ontario, S Canada
30 L11 **La Salle** Illinois, N USA
45 O9 **Las Americas** ✕ (Santo Domingo) S Dominican Republic
79 G17 **La Sangha** ◈ *province* N Congo
37 V6 **Las Animas** Colorado, C USA
108 D10 **La Sarine** *var.* Sarine. ~ SW Switzerland
108 B9 **La Sarraz** Vaud, W Switzerland
12 H12 **La Sarre** Québec, SE Canada
54 L3 **Las Aves, Islas** *var.* Islas de Aves. *island group* N Venezuela
55 N7 **Las Bonitas** Bolívar, C Venezuela
104 K15 **Las Cabezas de San Juan** Andalucía, S Spain
61 G19 **Lascano** Rocha, E Uruguay
62 I5 **Lascar, Volcán** ▲ N Chile
41 T15 **Las Choapas** *var.* Choapas. Veracruz-Llave, SE Mexico
37 R15 **Las Cruces** New Mexico, SW USA
Lasdehnen *see* Krasnoznamensk
105 V4 **La See d'Urgel** *var.* La Seu d'Urgell, Seo de Urgel. Cataluña, NE Spain
La Selle *see* Selle, Pic de la
62 G9 **La Serena** Coquimbo, C Chile
104 K11 **La Serena** *physical region* W Spain
La Seu d'Urgell *see* La See d'Urgel
103 T16 **la Seyne-sur-Mer** Var, SE France
61 D21 **Las Flores** Buenos Aires, E Argentina
62 H9 **Las Flores** San Juan, W Argentina
11 S14 **Lashburn** Saskatchewan, S Canada
62 I11 **Las Heras** Mendoza, W Argentina
167 N4 **Lashio** Shan State, E Burma
148 M8 **Lashkar Gāh** *var.* Lash-Kar-Gar'. Helmand, S Afghanistan
Lash-Kar-Gar' *see* Lashkar Gāh
171 P14 **Lasihao** *var.* Lasahau. Pulau Muna, C Indonesia
107 N21 **La Sila** ▲ SW Italy
63 H23 **La Silueta, Cerro** ▲ S Chile
42 L9 **La Sirena** Región Autónoma Atlántico Sur, E Nicaragua
110 J13 **Łask** Łódzkie, C Poland
109 V11 **Laško** *Ger.* Tüffer. C Slovenia
63 H14 **Las Lajas** Neuquén, W Argentina
63 H15 **Las Lajas, Cerro** ▲ W Argentina
62 M6 **Las Lomitas** Formosa, N Argentina
41 V16 **Las Margaritas** Chiapas, SE Mexico
Las Marismas *see* Guadalquivir, Marismas del
54 M6 **Las Mercedes** Guárico, N Venezuela
42 F6 **Las Minas, Cerro** ▲ W Honduras
105 O11 **La Solana** Castilla-La Mancha, C Spain
45 Q14 **La Soufrière** ▲ Saint Vincent, Saint Vincent and the Grenadines
102 M10 **la Souterraine** Creuse, C France
62 N7 **Las Palmas** Chaco, N Argentina
43 Q16 **Las Palmas** Veraguas, W Panama
64 P12 **Las Palmas** *var.* Las Palmas de Gran Canaria. Gran Canaria, Islas Canarias, Spain, NE Atlantic Ocean
64 P12 **Las Palmas** ◈ *province* Islas Canarias, Spain, NE Atlantic Ocean
64 Q12 **Las Palmas** ✕ Gran Canaria, Islas Canarias, Spain, NE Atlantic Ocean
Las Palmas de Gran Canaria *see* Las Palmas
40 D6 **Las Palomas** Baja California Sur, W Mexico
105 P10 **Las Pedroñeras** Castilla-La Mancha, C Spain
106 E10 **La Spezia** Liguria, NW Italy
61 F20 **Las Piedras** Canelones, S Uruguay
63 J18 **Las Plumas** Chubut, S Argentina
61 B18 **Las Rosas** Santa Fe, C Argentina
Lassa *see* Lhasa
35 O4 **Lassen Peak** ▲ California, W USA
194 K6 **Lassiter Coast** *physical region* Antarctica
109 V9 **Lassnitz** ~ SE Austria
15 O12 **L'Assomption** Québec, SE Canada
15 N11 **L'Assomption** ~ Québec, SE Canada
43 S17 **Las Tablas** Los Santos, S Panama
Lastarria, Volcán *see* Azufre, Volcán
37 V4 **Last Chance** Colorado, C USA
Last Frontier, The *see* Alaska
11 U16 **Last Mountain Lake** ◎ Saskatchewan, S Canada
62 H9 **Las Tórtolas, Cerro** ▲ W Argentina
61 C14 **Las Toscas** Santa Fe, C Argentina
79 F19 **Lastoursville** Ogooué-Lolo, E Gabon
113 F16 **Lastovo** *It.* Lagosta. *island* SW Croatia
113 F16 **Lastovski Kanal** *channel* SW Croatia
40 E6 **Las Tres Vírgenes, Volcán** ▲ W Mexico
40 F4 **Las Trincheras** Sonora, NW Mexico
55 N8 **Las Trincheras** Bolívar, E Venezuela
44 H7 **Las Tunas** *var.* Victoria de las Tunas. Las Tunas, E Cuba
La Suisse *see* Switzerland
40 I5 **Las Varas** Chihuahua, N Mexico
40 J12 **Las Varas** Nayarit, C Mexico
62 L10 **Las Varillas** Córdoba, E Argentina
35 X11 **Las Vegas** Nevada, W USA
37 T10 **Las Vegas** New Mexico, SW USA
187 P10 **Lata** Nendö, Solomon Islands
13 R10 **La Tabatière** Québec, E Canada
56 C6 **Latacunga** Cotopaxi, C Ecuador
194 I7 **Latady Island** *island* Antarctica
54 E14 **La Tagua** Putumayo, S Colombia
Latakia *see* Al Lādhiqīyah
92 J10 **Lätäseno** ~ NW Finland
14 H9 **Latchford** Ontario, S Canada
14 J13 **Latchford Bridge** Ontario, SE Canada
193 Y14 **Late** *island* Vava'u Group, N Tonga
153 P15 **Lātehār** Jhārkhand, N India
15 R7 **Laterrière** Québec, SE Canada
102 J13 **la Teste** Gironde, SW France
25 V8 **Latexo** Texas, SW USA
18 L10 **Latham** New York, NE USA
Latharna *see* Larne
108 B9 **La Thielle** *var.* Thièle. ~ W Switzerland
27 R3 **Lathrop** Missouri, C USA
107 I16 **Latina** *prev.* Littoria. Lazio, C Italy
41 R14 **La Tinaja** Veracruz-Llave, S Mexico
106 J7 **Latisana** Friuli-Venezia Giulia, NE Italy
Latium *see* Lazio
115 K25 **Lató** *site of ancient city* Kríti, Greece, E Mediterranean Sea
187 Q17 **La Tontouta** ✕ (Noumea) Province Sud, S New Caledonia
55 N4 **La Tortuga, Isla** *var.* Isla Tortuga. *island* N Venezuela
108 C10 **La Tour-de-Peilz** *var.* La Tour de Peilz. Vaud, SW Switzerland
103 S11 **la Tour-du-Pin** Isère, E France
102 J11 **la Tremblade** Charente-Maritime, W France
102 L10 **la Trimouille** Vienne, W France
42 J9 **La Trinidad** Estelí, NW Nicaragua
41 V16 **La Trinitaria** Chiapas, SE Mexico
45 Q11 **la Trinité** E Martinique
15 U7 **La Trinité-des-Monts** Québec, SE Canada
18 C15 **Latrobe** Pennsylvania, NE USA
183 P13 **La Trobe River** ~ Victoria, SE Australia
Lattakia/Lattaquié *see* Al Lādhiqīyah
171 S13 **Latu** Pulau Seram, E Indonesia
15 P9 **La Tuque** Québec, SE Canada
155 G14 **Lātūr** Mahārāshtra, C India
118 G8 **Latvia** *off.* Republic of Latvia, *Ger.* Lettland, *Latv.* Latvija, Latvijas Republika; *prev.* Latvian SSR, *Rus.* Latviyskaya SSR. ◆ *republic* NE Europe
Latvian SSR/ Latvija/Latvijas Republika/Latviyskaya SSR *see* Latvia
186 H7 **Lau** New Britain, E PNG
101 O15 **Lauchhammer** Brandenburg, E Germany
Laudunum *see* Laon
Laudus *see* St-Lô
Lauenburg/Lauenburg in Pommern *see* Lębork
101 L20 **Lauf an der Pegnitz** Bayern, SE Germany
108 D7 **Laufen** Basel, NW Switzerland
109 P5 **Lauffen** Salzburg, NW Austria
92 I2 **Laugarbakki** Nordhurland Vestra, N Iceland
92 I4 **Laugarvatn** Sudhurland, SW Iceland
31 O3 **Laughing Fish Point** *headland* Michigan, N USA
187 Z14 **Lau Group** *island group* E Fiji
Lauis *see* Lugano
93 M17 **Laukaa** Länsi-Suomi, W Finland
118 D12 **Laukuva** Tauragė, W Lithuania
Laun *see* Louny
183 P16 **Launceston** Tasmania, SE Australia
97 I24 **Launceston** *anc.* Dunheved. SW England, UK
54 C13 **La Unión** Nariño, SW Colombia
42 H8 **La Unión** La Unión, SE El Salvador
42 I6 **La Unión** Olancho, C Honduras
40 M15 **La Unión** Guerrero, S Mexico
41 Y14 **La Unión** Quintana Roo, E Mexico
105 S13 **La Unión** Murcia, SE Spain
54 L7 **La Unión** Barinas, C Venezuela
42 B10 **La Unión** ◈ *department* E El Salvador
38 H11 **Laupāhoehoe** *var.* Laupahoehoe. Hawai'i, USA, C Pacific Ocean
101 I23 **Laupheim** Baden-Württemberg, S Germany
181 W3 **Laura** Queensland, NE Australia
189 X2 **Laura** *atoll* Majuro Atoll, SE Marshall Islands
Laurana *see* Lovran
54 L8 **La Urbana** Bolívar, C Venezuela
21 Y4 **Laurel** Delaware, NE USA
23 V14 **Laurel** Florida, SE USA
21 W3 **Laurel** Maryland, NE USA
22 M6 **Laurel** Mississippi, S USA
33 U11 **Laurel** Montana, NW USA
29 R13 **Laurel** Nebraska, C USA
18 H15 **Laureldale** Pennsylvania, NE USA
18 C16 **Laurel Hill** *ridge* Pennsylvania, NE USA
29 T12 **Laurens** Iowa, C USA
21 P11 **Laurens** South Carolina, SE USA
Laurentian Highlands *see* Laurentian Mountains
15 P10 **Laurentian Mountains** *var.* Laurentian Highlands, *Fr.* Les Laurentides. *plateau* Newfoundland and Labrador/Québec, Canada
15 O12 **Laurentides** Québec, SE Canada
Laurentides, Les *see* Laurentian Mountains
107 M19 **Lauria** Basilicata, S Italy
194 I1 **Laurie Island** *island* Antarctica
21 T11 **Laurinburg** North Carolina, SE USA
30 M2 **Laurium** Michigan, N USA
Lauru *see* Choiseul
108 B9 **Lausanne** *It.* Losanna. Vaud, SW Switzerland
101 Q16 **Lausche** *Cz.* Luže. ▲ Czech Republic/Germany *see also* Luže
101 Q16 **Lausitzer Bergland** *var.* Lausitzer Gebirge, *Cz.* Gory Lużyckie, Lužické Hory, *Eng.* Lusatian Mountains. ▲ E Germany
Lausitzer Gebirge *see* Lausitzer Bergland
Lausitzer Neisse *see* Neisse
103 T12 **Lautaret, Col du** *pass* SE France
63 G15 **Lautaro** Araucanía, C Chile
101 F21 **Lauter** ~ W Germany
108 I7 **Lauterach** Vorarlberg, NW Austria
101 I17 **Lauterbach** Hessen, C Germany
108 E9 **Lauterbrunnen** Bern, C Switzerland
169 U14 **Laut Kecil, Kepulauan** *island group* N Indonesia
187 X14 **Lautoka** Viti Levu, W Fiji
169 O8 **Laut, Pulau** *prev.* Laoet. *island* Borneo, C Indonesia
169 V14 **Laut, Pulau** *island* Kepulauan Natuna, W Indonesia
169 U13 **Laut, Selat** *strait* Borneo, C Indonesia
168 H8 **Laut Tawar, Danau** ◎ Sumatera, NW Indonesia
189 V14 **Lauvergne Island** *island* Chuuk, C Micronesia
98 M5 **Lauwers Meer** ◎ N Netherlands
98 M4 **Lauwersoog** Groningen, NE Netherlands
102 M14 **Lauzerte** Tarn-et-Garonne, S France
25 U13 **Lavaca Bay** *bay* Texas, SW USA
25 U12 **Lavaca River** ~ Texas, SW USA
15 O12 **Laval** Québec, SE Canada
102 J6 **Laval** Mayenne, NW France
15 T6 **Laval** ~ Québec, SE Canada
61 F19 **Lavalleja** ◈ *department* S Uruguay
15 O12 **Lavaltrie** Québec, SE Canada
186 M10 **Lavanggu** Rennell, S Solomon Islands
143 O14 **Lāvān, Jazīreh-ye** *island* S Iran
109 U8 **Lavant** ~ S Austria
118 G5 **Lavassaare** *Ger.* Lawassaar. Pärnumaa, SW Estonia
104 L3 **La Vecilla de Curueño** Castilla-León, N Spain
45 N8 **La Vega** *var.* Concepción de la Vega. C Dominican Republic
La Vela *see* La Vela de Coro
54 J4 **La Vela de Coro** *var.* La Vela. Falcón, N Venezuela
103 N17 **Lavelanet** Ariège, S France
107 M17 **Lavello** Basilicata, S Italy
36 J8 **La Verkin** Utah, W USA
26 J8 **Laverne** Oklahoma, C USA
25 S12 **La Vernia** Texas, SW USA
93 K18 **Lavia** Länsi-Suomi, W Finland
14 I12 **Lavieille, Lake** ◎ Ontario, SE Canada
94 C12 **Lavik** Sogn og Fjordane, S Norway
La Vila Joíosa *see* Villajoyosa
33 U10 **Lavina** Montana, NW USA
194 H5 **Lavoisier Island** *island* Antarctica
23 U2 **Lavonia** Georgia, SE USA
103 R13 **la Voulte-sur-Rhône** Ardèche, E France
123 W5 **Lavrentiya** Chukotskiy Avtonomnyy Okrug, NE Russian Federation
115 H20 **Lávrio** *prev.* Lávrion. Attikí, C Greece
Lávrion *see* Lávrio
83 L22 **Lavumisa** *prev.* Gollel. SE Swaziland
149 T4 **Lawarai Pass** *pass* N Pakistan
Lawassaar *see* Lavassaare
141 P16 **Lawdar** SW Yemen
25 Q7 **Lawn** Texas, SW USA
195 Y4 **Law Promontory** *headland* Antarctica
77 O14 **Lawra** NW Ghana
185 E23 **Lawrence** Otago, South Island, NZ
31 P14 **Lawrence** Indiana, N USA
27 Q4 **Lawrence** Kansas, C USA
19 O10 **Lawrence** Massachusetts, NE USA
20 L5 **Lawrenceburg** Kentucky, S USA
20 I10 **Lawrenceburg** Tennessee, S USA
23 T3 **Lawrenceville** Georgia, SE USA
31 N15 **Lawrenceville** Illinois, N USA
21 V7 **Lawrenceville** Virginia, NE USA
27 S3 **Lawson** Missouri, C USA
26 L12 **Lawton** Oklahoma, C USA
140 I4 **Lawz, Jabal al** ▲ NW Saudi Arabia
95 L16 **Laxå** Örebro, C Sweden
127 T5 **Laya** ~ NW Russian Federation
57 I19 **La Yarada** Tacna, SW Peru
141 S15 **Layjūn** C Yemen
141 Q9 **Laylā** *var.* Laila. Ar Riyāḑ, C Saudi Arabia
23 P4 **Lay Lake** ◎ Alabama, S USA
45 P14 **Layou** Saint Vincent, Saint Vincent and the Grenadines
La Youne *see* El Ayoun
192 L5 **Laysan Island** *island* Hawaiian Islands, Hawaii, USA, C Pacific Ocean
36 L2 **Layton** Utah, W USA
34 L5 **Laytonville** California, N USA
172 H17 **Lazare, Pointe** *headland* Mahé, NE Seychelles
123 T12 **Lazarev** Khabarovskiy Kray, SE Russian Federation
112 L12 **Lazarevac** Serbia, C Serbia and Montenegro (Yugo.)
65 N22 **Lazarev Sea** *sea* Antarctica
40 M15 **Lázaro Cárdenas** Michoacán de Ocampo, SW Mexico
119 F15 **Lazdijai** Alytus, S Lithuania
107 H15 **Lazio** *anc.* Latium. ◈ *region* C Italy
111 A16 **Lázně Kynžvart** *Ger.* Bad Königswart. Karlovarský Kraj, W Czech Republic
Lazovsk *see* Sîngerei
167 R12 **Leach** Poŭthĭsăt, W Cambodia
27 X9 **Leachville** Arkansas, C USA
28 I9 **Lead** South Dakota, N USA
11 S16 **Leader** Saskatchewan, S Canada
19 S6 **Lead Mountain** ▲ Maine, NE USA
37 R5 **Leadville** Colorado, C USA
11 V12 **Leaf Rapids** Manitoba, C Canada
22 M7 **Leaf River** ~ Mississippi, S USA
25 W11 **League City** Texas, SW USA

◆ Country ● Country Capital ◇ Dependent Territory ○ Dependent Territory Capital ◈ Administrative Region ✕ International Airport ▲ Mountain ▲ Mountain Range ▲ Volcano ~ River ◎ Lake ▣ Reservoir

92 K8 **Leaibevuotna** *Nor.* Olderfjord. Finnmark, N Norway
23 N7 **Leakesville** Mississippi, S USA
25 Q11 **Leakey** Texas, SW USA
Leal *see* Lihula
83 G15 **Lealui** Western, W Zambia
Leamhcán *see* Lucan
14 C18 **Leamington** Ontario, S Canada
Leamington/Leamington Spa *see* Royal Leamington Spa
Leammi *see* Lemmenjoki
25 S10 **Leander** Texas, SW USA
60 F13 **Leandro N.Alem** Misiones, NE Argentina
97 A20 **Leane, Lough** *Ir.* Loch Léin. ◎ SW Ireland
180 G8 **Learmouth** Western Australia
Leau *see* Zoutleeuw
L'Eau d'Heure *see* Plate Taille, Lac de la
190 D12 **Leava** Île Futuna, S Wallis and Futuna
Leavdnja *see* Lakselv
27 R3 **Leavenworth** Kansas, C USA
32 I8 **Leavenworth** Washington, NW USA
92 L8 **Leavvajohka** *var.* Levajok, Lævvajok. Finnmark, N Norway
27 R4 **Leawood** Kansas, C USA
110 H6 **Łeba** *Ger.* Leba. Pomorskie, N Poland
110 I6 **Łeba** *Ger.* Leba. ≈ N Poland
101 D20 **Lebach** Saarland, SW Germany
Łeba, Jezioro *see* Łebsko, Jezioro
171 P8 **Lebak** Mindanao, S Philippines
31 O13 **Lebanon** Indiana, N USA
20 L6 **Lebanon** Kentucky, S USA
27 U6 **Lebanon** Missouri, C USA
19 N9 **Lebanon** New Hampshire, NE USA
32 G12 **Lebanon** Oregon, NW USA
18 H15 **Lebanon** Pennsylvania, NE USA
20 J8 **Lebanon** Tennessee, S USA
21 P7 **Lebanon** Virginia, NE USA
138 G6 **Lebanon** *off.* Republic of Lebanon, *Ar.* Al Lubnān, *Fr.* Liban. ◆ *republic* SW Asia
20 K6 **Lebanon Junction** Kentucky, S USA
Lebanon, Mount *see* Liban, Jebel
146 J10 **Lebap** Lebapskiy Velayat, NE Turkmenistan
Lebapskiy Velayat *see* Lebap Welaýaty
146 H11 **Lebap Welaýaty** *Rus.* Lebapskiy Velayat; *prev. Rus.* Chardzhevskaya Oblast', *Turkm.* Chärjew Oblasty. ◈ *province* E Turkmenistan
Lebasee *see* Łebsko, Jezioro
99 F17 **Lebbeke** Oost-Vlaanderen, NW Belgium
35 S14 **Lebec** California, W USA
Lebedin *see* Lebedyn
123 Q11 **Lebedinyy** Respublika Sakha (Yakutiya), NE Russian Federation
126 L6 **Lebedyan'** Lipetskaya Oblast', W Russian Federation
117 T4 **Lebedyn** *Rus.* Lebedin. Sums'ka Oblast', NE Ukraine
12 I12 **Lebel-sur-Quévillon** Québec, SE Canada
92 L8 **Lebesby** Finnmark, N Norway
102 M9 **le Blanc** Indre, C France
27 P5 **Lebo** Kansas, C USA
79 L15 **Lebo** Orientale, N Dem. Rep. Congo
110 H6 **Lębork** *var.* Lębórk, *Ger.* Lauenburg, Lauenburg in Pommern. Pomorskie, N Poland
103 O17 **le Boulou** Pyrénées-Orientales, S France
108 A9 **Le Brassus** Vaud, W Switzerland
104 J15 **Lebrija** Andalucía, S Spain
110 G6 **Łebsko, Jezioro** *Ger.* Lebasee; *prev.* Jezioro Łeba. ◎ N Poland
63 F14 **Lebu** Bío Bío, C Chile
Lebyazh'ye *see* Akku
104 F6 **Leça da Palmeira** Porto, N Portugal
103 U15 **le Cannet** Alpes-Maritimes, SE France
Le Cap *see* Cap-Haïtien
103 P2 **le Cateau-Cambrésis** Nord, N France
107 Q18 **Lecce** Puglia, SE Italy
106 D7 **Lecco** Lombardia, N Italy
29 V10 **Le Center** Minnesota, N USA
108 J7 **Lech** Vorarlberg, W Austria
101 K22 **Lech** ≈ Austria/Germany
115 D19 **Lechainá** *var.* Lehena, Lekhainá. Dytikí Ellás, S Greece
102 J11 **le Château d'Oléron** Charente-Maritime, W France
103 R3 **le Chesne** Ardennes, N France
103 R13 **le Cheylard** Ardèche, E France
108 K7 **Lechtaler Alpen** ⛰ W Austria
100 H6 **Leck** Schleswig-Holstein, N Germany
14 L9 **Lecointre, Lac** ◎ Québec, SE Canada
22 H7 **Lecompte** Louisiana, S USA
103 Q9 **le Creusot** Saône-et-Loire, C France
Lecumberri *see* Lekunberri
110 P13 **Łęczna** Lubelskie, E Poland
110 J12 **Łęczyca** *Ger.* Lentschiza, *Rus.* Lenchitsa. Łódzkie, C Poland
100 F10 **Leda** ≈ NW Germany
109 Y9 **Ledava** ≈ NE Slovenia
99 F17 **Lede** Oost-Vlaanderen, NW Belgium
104 K6 **Ledesma** Castilla-León, N Spain
45 Q12 **le Diamant** SW Martinique
172 J16 **Le Digue** *island* Inner Islands, NE Seychelles
103 Q10 **le Donjon** Allier, C France
102 M10 **le Dorat** Haute-Vienne, C France
Ledo Salinarius *see* Lons-le-Saunier
11 Q14 **Leduc** Alberta, SW Canada
123 V7 **Ledyanaya, Gora** ▲ E Russian Federation
97 C21 **Lee** *Ir.* An Laoi. ≈ SW Ireland
29 U5 **Leech Lake** ◎ Minnesota, N USA
26 K10 **Leedey** Oklahoma, C USA
97 M17 **Leeds** N England, UK
23 P4 **Leeds** Alabama, S USA
29 O3 **Leeds** North Dakota, N USA
98 N6 **Leek** Groningen, NE Netherlands
99 K15 **Leende** Noord-Brabant, SE Netherlands
100 F10 **Leer** Niedersachsen, NW Germany
98 J13 **Leerdam** Zuid-Holland, C Netherlands
98 K12 **Leersum** Utrecht, C Netherlands
23 W11 **Leesburg** Florida, SE USA
21 V3 **Leesburg** Virginia, NE USA
27 R4 **Lees Summit** Missouri, C USA
22 G7 **Leesville** Louisiana, S USA
25 S12 **Leesville** Texas, SW USA
31 U13 **Leesville Lake** ⊟ Ohio, N USA
Leesville Lake *see* Smith Mountain Lake
183 P9 **Leeton** New South Wales, SE Australia
98 L6 **Leeuwarden** *Fris.* Ljouwert. Friesland, N Netherlands
180 I14 **Leeuwin, Cape** *headland* Western Australia
35 R8 **Lee Vining** California, W USA
45 V8 **Leeward Islands** *island group* E West Indies
Leeward Islands *see* Vent, Îles Sous le, W French Polynesia
Leeward Islands *see* Sotavento, Ilhas de, Cape Verde
79 G20 **Léfini** ≈ SE Congo
Lefka *see* Lefke
115 C17 **Lefkáda** *prev.* Levkás. Lefkáda, Iónioi Nísoi, Greece, C Mediterranean Sea
115 B17 **Lefkáda** *It.* Santa Maura; *prev.* Levkás, *anc.* Leucas. *island* Iónioi Nísoi, Greece, C Mediterranean Sea
115 H25 **Lefká Óri** ⛰ Kríti, Greece, E Mediterranean Sea
115 B16 **Lefkímmi** *var.* Levkímmi. Kérkyra, Iónioi Nísoi, Greece, C Mediterranean Sea
Lefkoşa/Lefkosía *see* Nicosia
25 O2 **Lefors** Texas, SW USA
45 R12 **le François** E Martinique
180 L12 **Lefroy, Lake** *salt lake* Western Australia
Legaceaster *see* Chester
105 N8 **Leganés** Madrid, C Spain
171 P4 **Legaspi** *off.* Legaspi City. Luzon, N Philippines
Leghorn *see* Livorno
110 M11 **Legionowo** Mazowieckie, C Poland
99 K24 **Léglise** Luxembourg, SE Belgium
106 G8 **Legnago** Lombardia, NE Italy
106 D7 **Legnano** Veneto, NE Italy
111 F14 **Legnica** *Ger.* Liegnitz. Dolnośląskie, SW Poland
35 Q9 **Le Grand** California, W USA
103 Q15 **le Grau-du-Roi** Gard, S France
183 U3 **Legume** New South Wales, SE Australia
102 L4 **le Havre** *Eng.* Havre; *prev.* le Havre-de-Grâce. Seine-Maritime, N France
le Havre-de-Grâce *see* le Havre
Lehena *see* Lechainá
36 L3 **Lehi** Utah, W USA
18 I14 **Lehighton** Pennsylvania, NE USA
29 O6 **Lehr** North Dakota, N USA
38 A8 **Lehua Island** *island* Hawaiian Islands, Hawai'i, USA, C Pacific Ocean
149 S9 **Leiah** Punjab, NE Pakistan
109 W9 **Leibnitz** Steiermark, SE Austria
97 M19 **Leicester** *Lat.* Batae Coritanorum. C England, UK
97 M19 **Leicestershire** *cultural region* C England, UK
98 H11 **Leiden** *prev.* Leyden, *anc.* Lugdunum Batavorum. Zuid-Holland, W Netherlands
98 H11 **Leiderdorp** Zuid-Holland, W Netherlands
98 G11 **Leidschendam** Zuid-Holland, W Netherlands
99 D18 **Leie** *Fr.* Lys. ≈ Belgium/France
Leifear *see* Lifford
184 L4 **Leigh** Auckland, North Island, NZ
97 K17 **Leigh** NW England, UK
182 I5 **Leigh Creek** South Australia
23 O2 **Leighton** Alabama, S USA
97 M21 **Leighton Buzzard** E England, UK
Léim an Bhradáin *see* Leixlip
Léim an Mhadaidh *see* Limavady
Léime, Ceann *see* Loop Head, Ireland
Léime, Ceann *see* Slyne Head, Ireland
101 G20 **Leimen** Baden-Württemberg, SW Germany
100 I13 **Leine** ≈ NW Germany
101 J15 **Leinefelde** Thüringen, C Germany
Léin, Loch *see* Leane, Lough
97 D19 **Leinster** *Ir.* Cúige Laighean. *cultural region* E Ireland
97 F19 **Leinster, Mount** *Ir.* Stua Laighean. ▲ SE Ireland
119 F15 **Leipalingis** Alytus, S Lithuania
92 J12 **Leipojärvi** Norrbotten, N Sweden
31 R12 **Leipsic** Ohio, N USA
Leipsic *see* Leipzig
115 M20 **Leipsoí** *island* Dodekánisos, Greece, Aegean Sea
101 M15 **Leipzig** *Pol.* Lipsk; *hist.* Leipsic, *anc.* Lipsia. Sachsen, E Germany
101 M15 **Leipzig Halle** × Sachsen, E Germany
104 G9 **Leiria** *anc.* Collipo. Leiria, C Portugal
104 F9 **Leiria** ◈ *district* C Portugal
95 C15 **Leirvik** Hordaland, S Norway
118 E5 **Leisi** *Ger.* Laisberg. Saaremaa, W Estonia
104 J3 **Leitariegos, Puerto de** *pass* NW Spain
20 J6 **Leitchfield** Kentucky, S USA
109 Y5 **Leitha** *Hung.* Lajta. ≈ Austria/Hungary
Leitir Ceanainn *see* Letterkenny
Leitmeritz *see* Litoměřice
Leitomischl *see* Litomyšl
97 D16 **Leitrim** *Ir.* Liatroim. *cultural region* NW Ireland
115 F18 **Leivádia** *prev.* Levádhia. Stereá Ellás, C Greece
Leix *see* Laois
97 F18 **Leixlip** *Eng.* Salmon Leap, *Ir.* Léim an Bhradáin. E Ireland
64 N8 **Leixões** Porto, N Portugal
161 N12 **Leiyang** Hunan, S China
160 L16 **Leizhou** *var.* Haikang. Guangdong, S China
160 L16 **Leizhou Bandao** *var.* Luichow Peninsula. *peninsula* S China
98 H13 **Lek** ≈ SW Netherlands
114 I13 **Lekánis** ⛰ NE Greece
172 H13 **Le Kartala** ▲ Grande Comore, NW Comoros
Le Kef *see* El Kef
79 G20 **Lékéti, Monts de la** ⛰ S Congo
Lekhainá *see* Lechainá
114 H8 **Lekhchevo** Montana, NW Bulgaria
92 G11 **Leknes** Nordland, C Norway
79 E21 **Le Kouilou** ◈ *province* SW Congo
94 L13 **Leksand** Dalarna, C Sweden
126 H8 **Leksozero, Ozero** ◎ NW Russian Federation
105 Q3 **Lekunberri** *var.* Lecumberri. Navarra, N Spain
171 S11 **Lelai, Tanjung** *headland* Pulau Halmahera, N Indonesia
45 Q12 **le Lamentin** *var.* Lamentin. C Martinique
45 Q12 **le Lamentin** × (Fort-de-France) C Martinique
31 P6 **Leland** Michigan, N USA
22 J4 **Leland** Mississippi, S USA
95 J16 **Lelång** *var.* Lelången. ◎ S Sweden
Lelången *see* Lelång
Lel'chitsy *see* Lyel'chytsy
le Léman *see* Geneva, Lake
Leli *see* Tianlin
25 O3 **Lelia Lake** Texas, SW USA
113 I14 **Lelija** ▲ SE Bosnia and Herzegovina
108 C8 **Le Locle** Neuchâtel, W Switzerland
189 Y14 **Lelu** Kosrae, E Micronesia
Lelu *see* Lelu Island
189 Y14 **Lelu Island** *var.* Lelu. *island* Kosrae, E Micronesia
55 W9 **Lelydorp** Wanica, N Surinam
98 K9 **Lelystad** Flevoland, C Netherlands
63 K25 **Le Maire, Estrecho de** *strait* S Argentina
168 L10 **Lemang** Pulau Rangsang, W Indonesia
186 I7 **Lemankoa** Buka Island, NE PNG
Léman, Lac *see* Geneva, Lake
102 L6 **le Mans** Sarthe, NW France
29 S12 **Le Mars** Iowa, C USA
109 S3 **Lembach im Mühlkreis** Oberösterreich, N Austria
101 G23 **Lemberg** ▲ SW Germany
Lemberg *see* L'viv
Lemdiyya *see* Médéa
121 P3 **Lemesós** *var.* Limassol. SW Cyprus
100 H13 **Lemgo** Nordrhein-Westfalen, W Germany
33 P13 **Lemhi Range** ⛰ Idaho, NW USA
9 S6 **Lemieux Islands** *island group* Nunavut, NE Canada
171 O11 **Lemito** Sulawesi, N Indonesia
92 L10 **Lemmenjoki** *Lapp.* Leammi. ≈ NE Finland
98 L7 **Lemmer** *Fris.* De Lemmer. Friesland, N Netherlands
28 L7 **Lemmon** South Dakota, N USA
36 M15 **Lemmon, Mount** ▲ Arizona, SW USA
Lemnos *see* Límnos
31 O14 **Lemon, Lake** ◎ Indiana, N USA
102 J5 **le Mont St-Michel** *castle* Manche, N France
35 Q11 **Lemoore** California, W USA
189 T13 **Lemotol Bay** *bay* Chuuk Islands, C Micronesia
45 Y5 **le Moule** *var.* Moule. Grande Terre, NE Guadeloupe
Lemovices *see* Limoges
Le Moyen-Ogooué *see* Moyen-Ogooué
12 M6 **le Moyne, Lac** ◎ Québec, E Canada
93 L18 **Lempäälä** Länsi-Suomi, W Finland
42 E7 **Lempa, Río** ≈ Central America
42 F7 **Lempira** *prev.* Gracias. ◈ *department* SW Honduras
Lemsalu *see* Limbaži
107 N17 **Le Murge** ⛰ SE Italy
127 V6 **Lemva** ≈ NW Russian Federation
95 F21 **Lemvig** Ringkøbing, W Denmark
166 K8 **Lemyethna** Irrawaddy, SW Burma
30 K10 **Lena** Illinois, N USA
123 P9 **Lena** ≈ NE Russian Federation
173 N13 **Lena Tablemount** *undersea feature* S Indian Ocean
Lenchitsa *see* Łęczyca
59 N17 **Lençóis** Bahia, E Brazil
60 K9 **Lençóis Paulista** São Paulo, S Brazil
109 Y9 **Lendava** *Hung.* Lendva, *Ger.* Unterlimbach; *prev.* Dolnja Lendava. NE Slovenia
83 F20 **Lendepas** Hardap, SE Namibia
124 H9 **Lendery** Respublika Kareliya, NW Russian Federation
Lendum *see* Lens
Lendva *see* Lendava
27 R4 **Lenexa** Kansas, C USA
109 Q5 **Lengau** Oberösterreich, N Austria
145 Q17 **Lenger** Yuzhnyy Kazakhstan, S Kazakhstan
Lenghu *see* Lenghuzhen
159 O9 **Lenghuzhen** *var.* Lenghu. Qinghai, C China
159 T9 **Lenglong Ling** ▲ N China
108 D7 **Lengnau** Bern, W Switzerland
160 M12 **Lengshuitan** Hunan, S China
95 M20 **Lenhovda** Kronoberg, S Sweden
79 E20 **Le Niari** ◈ *province* SW Congo
Lenin *see* Akdepe, Turkmenistan
Lenin *see* Uzynkol', Kazakhstan
Leninabad *see* Khŭjand
Leninakan *see* Gyumri
Lenina, Pik *see* Lenin Peak
117 V12 **Lenine** *Rus.* Lenino. Respublika Krym, S Ukraine
Leningor *see* Leninogorsk
147 Q13 **Leningrad** *Rus.* Leningradskiy; *prev.* Mŭ'minobod, *Rus.* Muminabad. SW Tajikistan
Leningrad *see* Sankt-Peterburg
126 L13 **Leningradskaya** Krasnodarskiy Kray, SW Russian Federation
195 S16 **Leningradskaya** *Russian research station* Antarctica
124 H12 **Leningradskaya Oblast'** ◈ *province* NW Russian Federation
Leningradskiy *see* Leningrad
Lenino *see* Lenine, Ukraine
Lenino *see* Lyenina, Belarus
Leninobod *see* Khŭjand
145 X9 **Leninogorsk** *Kaz.* Leningor. Vostochnyy Kazakhstan, E Kazakhstan
127 T5 **Leninogorsk** Respublika Tatarstan, W Russian Federation
147 T12 **Lenin Peak** *Rus.* Pik Lenina, *Taj.* Qullai Lenin. ▲ Kyrgyzstan/Tajikistan
147 S8 **Leninpol'** Talasskaya Oblast', NW Kyrgyzstan
Lenin, Qullai *see* Lenin Peak
127 P11 **Leninsk** Volgogradskaya Oblast', SW Russian Federation
Leninsk *see* Akdepe, Turkmenistan
Leninsk *see* Asaka, Uzbekistan
Leninsk *see* Baykonyr, Kazakhstan
145 T8 **Leninskiy** Pavlodar, E Kazakhstan
122 I13 **Leninsk-Kuznetskiy** Kemerovskaya Oblast', S Russian Federation
125 P15 **Leninskoye** Kirovskaya Oblast', NW Russian Federation
Leninskoye *see* Uzynkol'
Leninsk-Turkmenski *see* Türkmenabat
Leninváros *see* Tiszaújváros
Lenkoran' *see* Länkäran
101 F15 **Lenne** ≈ W Germany
101 G16 **Lennestadt** Nordrhein-Westfalen, W Germany
29 R11 **Lennox** South Dakota, N USA
63 J25 **Lennox, Isla** *Eng.* Lennox Island. *island* S Chile
Lennox Island *see* Lennox, Isla
21 Q9 **Lenoir** North Carolina, SE USA
20 M9 **Lenoir City** Tennessee, S USA
108 C7 **Le Noirmont** Jura, NW Switzerland
14 L9 **Lenôtre, Lac** ◎ Québec, SE Canada
29 U15 **Lenox** Iowa, C USA
103 O2 **Lens** *anc.* Lendum, Lentium. Pas-de-Calais, N France
123 O11 **Lensk** Respublika Sakha (Yakutiya), NE Russian Federation
111 F24 **Lenti** Zala, SW Hungary
Lentia *see* Linz
93 N14 **Lentiira** Oulu, E Finland
107 L25 **Lentini** *anc.* Leontini. Sicilia, Italy, C Mediterranean Sea
Lentium *see* Lens
Lentschiza *see* Łęczyca
93 N15 **Lentua** ◎ E Finland
119 H14 **Lentvaris** *Pol.* Landwarów. Vilnius, SE Lithuania
108 F7 **Lenzburg** Aargau, N Switzerland
109 R5 **Lenzing** Oberösterreich, N Austria
77 P13 **Léo** SW Burkina
109 V7 **Leoben** Steiermark, C Austria
Leobschütz *see* Głubczyce
44 L9 **Léogâne** S Haiti
171 O11 **Leok** Sulawesi, N Indonesia
29 O7 **Leola** South Dakota, N USA
97 K20 **Leominster** W England, UK
19 N11 **Leominster** Massachusetts, NE USA
29 V16 **Leon** Iowa, C USA
40 M12 **León** *var.* León de los Aldamas. Guanajuato, C Mexico
42 I10 **León** León, NW Nicaragua
104 L4 **León** Castilla-León, NW Spain
42 I9 **León** ◈ *department* W Nicaragua
104 K4 **León** ◈ *province* Castilla-León, NW Spain
León *see* Cotopaxi
102 I15 **Léon** Landes, SW France
25 V9 **Leona** Texas, SW USA
180 K11 **Leonara** Western Australia
25 U5 **Leonard** Texas, SW USA
107 H15 **Leonardo da Vinci** *prev.* Fiumicino. × (Roma) Lazio, C Italy
21 X5 **Leonardtown** Maryland, NE USA
25 Q13 **Leona River** ≈ Texas, SW USA
41 Z11 **Leona Vicario** Quintana Roo, SE Mexico
101 H21 **Leonberg** Baden-Württemberg, SW Germany
62 M3 **León, Cerro** ▲ NW Paraguay
León de los Aldamas *see* León
109 T4 **Leonding** Oberösterreich, N Austria
107 I14 **Leonessa** Lazio, C Italy
107 K24 **Leonforte** Sicilia, Italy, C Mediterranean Sea
183 O13 **Leongatha** Victoria, SE Australia
115 F21 **Leonídi** Pelopónnisos, S Greece
104 J4 **León, Montes de** ⛰ NW Spain
25 S8 **Leon River** ≈ Texas, SW USA
Leontini *see* Lentini
Léopold II, Lac *see* Mai-Ndombe, Lac
99 J17 **Leopoldsburg** Limburg, NE Belgium
Léopoldville *see* Kinshasa
26 I5 **Leoti** Kansas, C USA
116 M11 **Leova** *Rus.* Leovo. SW Moldova
Leovo *see* Leova
102 G8 **le Palais** Morbihan, NW France
27 X10 **Lepanto** Arkansas, C USA
169 N13 **Lepar, Pulau** *island* W Indonesia
104 I14 **Lepe** Andalucía, S Spain
Lepel' *see* Lyepyel'
83 I19 **Lephephe** Kweneng, SE Botswana
161 Q10 **Leping** Jiangxi, S China
Lépontiennes, Alpes/Lepontine, Alpi *see* Lepontine Alps
108 G10 **Lepontine Alps** *Fr.* Alpes Lépontiennes, *It.* Alpi Lepontine. ⛰ Italy/Switzerland
79 G20 **Le Pool** ◈ *province* S Congo
173 O16 **le Port** NW Réunion
103 N1 **le Portel** Pas-de-Calais, N France
93 N17 **Leppävirta** Itä-Suomi, C Finland
45 Q11 **le Prêcheur** NW Martinique
Lepsi *see* Lepsy
145 V13 **Lepsy** *Kaz.* Lepsi. Almaty, SE Kazakhstan
145 V13 **Lepsy** *Kaz.* Lepsi. ≈ SE Kazakhstan
Le Puglie *see* Puglia
103 Q12 **le Puy** *prev.* le Puy-en-Velay, *hist.* Anicium, Podium Anicensis. Haute-Loire, C France
le Puy-en-Velay *see* le Puy
Le Raizet *see* le Raizet
45 X11 **le Raizet** *var.* Le Raizet. × (Pointe-à-Pitre) Grande Terre, C Guadeloupe
107 J24 **Lercara Friddi** Sicilia, Italy, C Mediterranean Sea
78 G12 **Léré** Mayo-Kébbi, SW Chad
Leribe *see* Hlotse
106 E10 **Lerici** Liguria, NW Italy
54 I14 **Lérida** Vaupés, SE Colombia
Lérida *see* Lleida
105 N5 **Lerma** Castilla-León, N Spain
40 M13 **Lerma, Río** ≈ C Mexico
115 F20 **Lérna** *prehistoric site* Pelopónnisos, S Greece
45 R11 **le Robert** E Martinique
115 M21 **Léros** *island* Dodekánisos, Greece, Aegean Sea
30 L13 **Le Roy** Illinois, N USA
27 Q6 **Le Roy** Kansas, C USA
29 W11 **Le Roy** Minnesota, N USA
18 E10 **Le Roy** New York, NE USA
Lerrnayin Gharabakh *see* Nagorno-Karabakh
95 J19 **Lerum** Västra Götaland, S Sweden
96 M2 **Lerwick** NE Scotland, UK
45 Y6 **les Abymes** *var.* Abymes. Grande Terre, C Guadeloupe
les Albères *see* Albères, Chaîne des
102 M4 **les Andelys** Eure, N France
45 Q12 **les Anses-d'Arlets** SW Martinique
105 U6 **Les Borges Blanques** *var.* Borjas Blancas. Cataluña, NE Spain
Lesbos *see* Lésvos
Les Cayes *see* Cayes
31 Q4 **Les Cheneaux Islands** *island* Michigan, N USA
103 T12 **les Écrins** ▲ E France
108 C10 **Le Sépey** Vaud, W Switzerland
15 T7 **Les Escoumins** Québec, SE Canada
Les Gonaïves *see* Gonaïves
Lesh/Leshi *see* Lezhë
160 H9 **Leshan** Sichuan, C China
108 D11 **Les Haudères** Valais, SW Switzerland
102 J9 **les Herbiers** Vendée, NW France
125 O8 **Leshukonskoye** Arkhangel'skaya Oblast', NW Russian Federation
Lesina *see* Hvar
107 M15 **Lesina, Lago di** ◎ SE Italy
114 K13 **Lesítse** ⛰ NE Greece
94 G10 **Lesja** Oppland, S Norway
95 L15 **Lesjöfors** Värmland, C Sweden
111 O18 **Lesko** Podkarpackie, SE Poland
113 O15 **Leskovac** Serbia, SE Serbia and Montenegro (Yugo.)
113 M22 **Leskovik** *var.* Leskoviku. Korçë, S Albania
Leskoviku *see* Leskovik
33 P14 **Leslie** Idaho, NW USA
31 Q10 **Leslie** Michigan, N USA
Leśna/Lesnaya *see* Lyasnaya
102 F5 **Lesneven** Finistère, NW France
112 J11 **Lešnica** Serbia, W Serbia and Montenegro (Yugo.)
125 S13 **Lesnoy** Kirovskaya Oblast', NW Russian Federation
122 G10 **Lesnoy** Sverdlovskaya Oblast', C Russian Federation
122 K12 **Lesosibirsk** Krasnoyarskiy Kray, C Russian Federation
83 J23 **Lesotho** *off.* Kingdom of Lesotho; *prev.* Basutoland. ◆ *monarchy* S Africa
102 J12 **Lesparre-Médoc** Gironde, SW France
108 C8 **Les Ponts-de-Martel** Neuchâtel, W Switzerland
102 I9 **les Sables-d'Olonne** Vendée, NW France
103 P1 **Lesquin** × Nord, N France
109 S7 **Lessach** *var.* Lessachbach. ≈ E Austria
Lessachbach *see* Lessach
45 W11 **les Saintes** *var.* Îles des Saintes. *island group* S Guadeloupe
74 L5 **Les Salines** × (Annaba) NE Algeria
99 J22 **Lesse** ≈ SE Belgium
95 M21 **Lessebo** Kronoberg, S Sweden
194 M10 **Lesser Antarctica** *var.* West Antarctica. *physical region* Antarctica
45 P15 **Lesser Antilles** *island group* E West Indies
137 T10 **Lesser Caucasus** *Rus.* Malyy Kavkaz. ⛰ SW Asia
Lesser Khingan Range *see* Xiao Hinggan Ling
11 P13 **Lesser Slave Lake** ◎ Alberta, W Canada
Lesser Sunda Islands *see* Nusa Tenggara
99 E19 **Lessines** Hainaut, SW Belgium
103 R16 **les Stes-Maries-de-la-Mer** Bouches-du-Rhône, SE France
14 G15 **Lester B.Pearson** *var.* Toronto. × (Toronto) Ontario, S Canada
29 U9 **Lester Prairie** Minnesota, N USA
93 L16 **Lestijärvi** Länsi-Suomi, W Finland
L'Estuaire *see* Estuaire
29 U9 **Le Sueur** Minnesota, N USA
108 B8 **Les Verrières** Neuchâtel, W Switzerland
115 L17 **Lésvos** *anc.* Lesbos. *island* E Greece
110 G12 **Leszno** *Ger.* Lissa. Wielkopolskie, C Poland
83 L20 **Letaba** Limpopo, NE South Africa
173 P17 **le Tampon** SW Réunion
97 O21 **Letchworth** E England, UK
111 G25 **Letenye** Zala, SW Hungary
11 Q17 **Lethbridge** Alberta, SW Canada
55 S11 **Lethem** S Guyana
83 H18 **Letiahau** ≈ W Botswana
54 J18 **Leticia** Amazonas, S Colombia
171 S16 **Leti, Kepulauan** *island group* E Indonesia
83 I18 **Letlhakane** Central, C Botswana
83 H20 **Letlhakeng** Kweneng, SE Botswana
114 J8 **Letnitsa** Lovech, N Bulgaria
103 N1 **le Touquet-Paris-Plage** Pas-de-Calais, N France
166 L8 **Letpadan** Pegu, SW Burma
166 K6 **Letpan** Arakan State, W Burma
102 M2 **le Tréport** Seine-Maritime, N France
166 M12 **Letsôk-aw Kyun** *var.* Letsutan Island; *prev.* Domel Island. *island* Mergui Archipelago, S Burma
Letsutan Island *see* Letsôk-aw Kyun
97 E14 **Letterkenny** *Ir.* Leitir Ceanainn. NW Ireland
Lettland *see* Latvia
116 M6 **Letychiv** Khmel'nyts'ka Oblast', W Ukraine
Lëtzebuerg *see* Luxembourg
116 H14 **Leu** Dolj, SW Romania
Leucas *see* Lefkáda
103 P17 **Leucate** Aude, S France
103 P17 **Leucate, Étang de** ◎ S France
108 E10 **Leuk** Valais, SW Switzerland
108 E10 **Leukerbad** Valais, SW Switzerland
Leusden *see* Leusden-Centrum
98 K11 **Leusden-Centrum** *var.* Leusden. Utrecht, C Netherlands
Leutensdorf *see* Litvínov
Leutschau *see* Levoča
99 H18 **Leuven** *Fr.* Louvain, *Ger.* Löwen. Vlaams Brabant, C Belgium
99 I20 **Leuze** Namur, C Belgium
Leuze *see* Leuze-en-Hainaut
99 E19 **Leuze-en-Hainaut** *var.* Leuze. Hainaut, SW Belgium
Léva *see* Levice
Levádhia *see* Leivádia
Levajok *see* Leavvajohka
36 L4 **Levan** Utah, W USA
93 E16 **Levanger** Nord-Trøndelag, C Norway
121 S12 **Levantine Basin** *undersea feature* E Mediterranean Sea
106 D10 **Levanto** Liguria, W Italy
107 H23 **Levanzo, Isola di** *island* Isole Egadi, S Italy
127 Q17 **Levashi** Respublika Dagestan, SW Russian Federation
24 M5 **Levelland** Texas, SW USA
39 P13 **Levelock** Alaska, USA
101 E16 **Leverkusen** Nordrhein-Westfalen, W Germany
111 J21 **Levice** *Ger.* Lewentz, Lewenz, *Hung.* Léva. Nitriansky Kraj, SW Slovakia
106 G6 **Levico Terme** Trentino-Alto Adige, N Italy
115 E20 **Levídi** Pelopónnisos, S Greece
103 P14 **le Vigan** Gard, S France
184 L13 **Levin** Manawatu-Wanganui, North Island, NZ
15 R10 **Lévis** *var.* Levis. Québec, SE Canada
21 P6 **Levisa Fork** ≈ Kentucky/Virginia, S USA
115 L21 **Levítha** *island* Kykládes, Greece, Aegean Sea

◆ Country
● Country Capital
◇ Dependent Territory
○ Dependent Territory Capital
◈ Administrative Region
× International Airport
▲ Mountain
⛰ Mountain Range
Volcano
≈ River
◎ Lake
⊟ Reservoir

18 L14 **Levittown** Long Island, New York, NE USA
18 J15 **Levittown** Pennsylvania, NE USA
Levkás *see* Lefkáda
Levkímmi *see* Lefkímmi
111 L19 **Levoča** *Ger.* Leutschau, *Hung.* Locse. Prešovský Kraj, E Slovakia
Lévrier, Baie du *see* Nouâdhibou, Dakhlet
103 N9 **Levroux** Indre, C France
114 J8 **Levski** Pleven, N Bulgaria
Levskigrad *see* Karlovo
126 L6 **Lev Tolstoy** Lipetskaya Oblast', W Russian Federation
187 X14 **Levuka** Ovalau, C Fiji
166 L6 **Lewe** Mandalay, C Burma
Lewentz/Lewenz *see* Levice
97 O23 **Lewes** SE England, UK
21 Z4 **Lewes** Delaware, NE USA
29 Q12 **Lewis and Clark Lake** ⊡ Nebraska/South Dakota, N USA
18 G14 **Lewisburg** Pennsylvania, NE USA
20 J10 **Lewisburg** Tennessee, S USA
21 S6 **Lewisburg** West Virginia, NE USA
96 F6 **Lewis, Butt of** *headland* NW Scotland, UK
96 F7 **Lewis, Isle of** *island* NW Scotland, UK
35 U4 **Lewis, Mount** ▲ Nevada, W USA
185 H16 **Lewis Pass** *pass* South Island, NZ
33 P7 **Lewis Range** ▲ Montana, NW USA
23 O3 **Lewis Smith Lake** ⊡ Alabama, S USA
32 M10 **Lewiston** Idaho, NW USA
19 P7 **Lewiston** Maine, NE USA
29 X10 **Lewiston** Minnesota, N USA
18 D9 **Lewiston** New York, NE USA
36 L1 **Lewiston** Utah, W USA
30 K13 **Lewistown** Illinois, N USA
33 T9 **Lewistown** Montana, NW USA
27 T14 **Lewisville** Arkansas, C USA
25 T6 **Lewisville** Texas, SW USA
25 T6 **Lewisville, Lake** ⊡ Texas, SW USA
Le Woleu-Ntem *see* Woleu-Ntem
23 U3 **Lexington** Georgia, SE USA
20 M5 **Lexington** Kentucky, S USA
22 L4 **Lexington** Mississippi, S USA
27 S4 **Lexington** Missouri, C USA
29 N16 **Lexington** Nebraska, C USA
21 S9 **Lexington** North Carolina, SE USA
27 N11 **Lexington** Oklahoma, C USA
21 R12 **Lexington** South Carolina, SE USA
20 G9 **Lexington** Tennessee, S USA
25 T10 **Lexington** Texas, SW USA
21 T6 **Lexington** Virginia, NE USA
21 X5 **Lexington Park** Maryland, NE USA
Leyden *see* Leiden
102 J14 **Leyre** ≈ SW France
171 Q5 **Leyte** *island* C Philippines
171 Q6 **Leyte Gulf** *gulf* E Philippines
111 O16 **Leżajsk** Podkarpackie, SE Poland
Lezha *see* Lezhë
113 K18 **Lezhë** *var.* Lezha; *prev.* Lesh, Leshi. Lezhë, NW Albania
113 K18 **Lezhë** ◆ *district* NW Albania
103 O16 **Lézignan-Corbières** Aude, S France
126 J7 **L'gov** Kurskaya Oblast', W Russian Federation
159 P15 **Lhari** Xizang Zizhiqu, W China
159 N16 **Lhasa** *var.* La-sa, Lassa. Xizang Zizhiqu, W China
159 O15 **Lhasa He** ≈ W China
158 K16 **Lhazê** *var.* Quxar. Xizang Zizhiqu, W China
158 K14 **Lhazhong** Xizang Zizhiqu, W China
168 H7 **Lhoksukon** Sumatera, W Indonesia
159 Q15 **Lhorong** *var.* Zito. Xizang Zizhiqu, W China
105 W6 **L'Hospitalet de Llobregat** *var.* Hospitalet. Cataluña, NE Spain
153 R11 **Lhotse** ▲ China/Nepal
159 N17 **Lhozhag** *var.* Garbo. Xizang Zizhiqu, W China
159 O16 **Lhünzê** *var.* Xingba. Xizang Zizhiqu, W China
159 N15 **Lhünzhub** *var.* Ganqu. Xizang Zizhiqu, W China
167 N8 **Li** Lamphun, NW Thailand
161 P12 **Liancheng** *var.* Lianfeng. Fujian, SE China
Liancheng *see* Guangnan, Yunnan, China
Liancheng *see* Qinglong, Guizhou, China
Lianfeng *see* Liancheng
160 K9 **Liangping** *var.* Liangshan. Chongqing Shi, C China
Liangshan *see* Liangping
Liangzhou *see* Wuwei
161 O9 **Liangzi Hu** ◎ C China
161 R12 **Lianjiang** Fujian, SE China
160 L15 **Lianjiang** Guangdong, S China
Lianjiang *see* Xingguo
161 O13 **Lianping** *var.* Yuanshan. Guangdong, S China
Lianshan *see* Huludao
Lian Xian *see* Lianzhou
160 M11 **Lianyuan** *prev.* Lantian. Hunan, S China
161 Q6 **Lianyungang** *var.* Xinpu. Jiangsu, E China
161 N13 **Lianzhou** *var.* Linxian; *prev.* Lian Xian. Guangdong, S China
Lianzhou *see* Hepu
Liao *see* Liaoning
161 P5 **Liaocheng** Shandong, E China
163 U13 **Liaodong Bandao** *var.* Liaotung Peninsula. *peninsula* NE China
163 T13 **Liaodong Wan** *Eng.* Gulf of Lantung, Gulf of Liaotung. *gulf* NE China
163 U11 **Liao He** ≈ NE China
163 U12 **Liaoning** *var.* Liao, Liaoning Sheng, Shengking; *hist.* Fengtien, Shenking. ◆ *province* NE China
Liaoning Sheng *see* Liaoning
Liaotung, Gulf of *see* Liaodong Wan
Liaotung Peninsula *see* Liaodong Bandao
163 V12 **Liaoyang** *var.* Liao-yang. Liaoning, NE China
163 V11 **Liaoyuan** *var.* Dongliao, Shuang-liao, *Jap.* Chengchiatun. Jilin, NE China
163 U12 **Liaozhong** Liaoning, NE China
Liaqatabad *see* Piplān
10 M10 **Liard** ≈ W Canada
Liard *see* Fort Liard
10 L10 **Liard River** British Columbia, W Canada
149 O15 **Liāri** Baluchistān, SW Pakistan
Liatroim *see* Leitrim
189 S6 **Lib** *var.* Ellep. *island* Ralik Chain, C Marshall Islands
Liban *see* Lebanon
138 H6 **Liban, Jebel** *Ar.* Jabal al Gharbt, Jabal Lubnān, *Eng.* Mount Lebanon. ▲ C Lebanon
Libau *see* Liepāja
33 N7 **Libby** Montana, NW USA
79 I16 **Libenge** Equateur, NW Dem. Rep. Congo
26 I7 **Liberal** Kansas, C USA
27 R7 **Liberal** Missouri, C USA
Liberalitas Julia *see* Évora
111 D15 **Liberec** *Ger.* Reichenberg. Liberecký Kraj, N Czech Republic
111 D15 **Liberecký Kraj** ◆ *region* N Czech Republic
42 K12 **Liberia** Guanacaste, NW Costa Rica
76 K17 **Liberia** *off.* Republic of Liberia. ◆ *republic* W Africa
61 D16 **Libertad** Corrientes, NE Argentina
61 E20 **Libertad** San José, S Uruguay
54 I7 **Libertad** Barinas, NW Venezuela
54 K6 **Libertad** Cojedes, N Venezuela
62 G12 **Libertador** *off.* Región del Libertador General Bernardo O'Higgins. ◆ *region* C Chile
Libertador General San Martín *see* Ciudad de Libertador General San Martín
20 L6 **Liberty** Kentucky, S USA
22 J7 **Liberty** Mississippi, S USA
27 R4 **Liberty** Missouri, C USA
18 J12 **Liberty** New York, NE USA
21 T9 **Liberty** North Carolina, SE USA
Libian Desert *see* Libyan Desert
99 J23 **Libin** Luxembourg, SE Belgium
160 K13 **Libo** *var.* Yuping. Guizhou, S China
Libohova *see* Libohovë
113 L23 **Libohovë** *var.* Libohova. Gjirokastër, S Albania
81 K18 **Liboi** North Eastern, E Kenya
102 K13 **Libourne** Gironde, SW France
99 K23 **Libramont** Luxembourg, SE Belgium
113 M20 **Librazhd** *var.* Librazhdi. Elbasan, E Albania
Librazhdi *see* Librazhd
79 C18 **Libreville** ● (Gabon) Estuaire, NW Gabon
75 P10 **Libya** *off.* Socialist People's Libyan Arab Jamahiriya, *Ar.* Al Jamāhīrīyah al 'Arabīyah al Lībīyah ash Sha'bīyah al Ishtirākīyah; *prev.* Libyan Arab Republic. ◆ *Islamic state* N Africa
75 T11 **Libyan Desert** *var.* Libian Desert, *Ar.* Aş Şahrā' al Lībīyah. *desert* N Africa
75 T8 **Libyan Plateau** *var.* Aḍ Diffah. *plateau* Egypt/Libya
Lībīyah, Aş Şahrā' al *see* Libyan Desert
62 G12 **Licantén** Maule, C Chile
107 J25 **Licata** *anc.* Phintias. Sicilia, Italy, C Mediterranean Sea
137 P14 **Lice** Diyarbakır, SE Turkey
97 L19 **Lichfield** C England, UK
83 N14 **Lichinga** Niassa, N Mozambique
109 V3 **Lichtenau** Niederösterreich, N Austria
83 I21 **Lichtenburg** North-West, N South Africa
101 K18 **Lichtenfels** Bayern, SE Germany
98 O12 **Lichtenvoorde** Gelderland, E Netherlands
Lichtenwald *see* Sevnica
99 C17 **Lichtervelde** West-Vlaanderen, W Belgium
160 L9 **Lichuan** Hubei, C China
27 V7 **Licking** Missouri, C USA
20 M4 **Licking River** ≈ Kentucky, S USA
112 C11 **Lički Osik** Lika-Senj, C Croatia
Ličko-Senjska Županija *see* Lika-Senj
107 K19 **Licosa, Punta** *headland* S Italy
119 H16 **Lida** *Rus.* Lida. Hrodzyenskaya Voblasts', W Belarus
93 H17 **Liden** Västernorrland, C Sweden
29 R7 **Lidgerwood** North Dakota, N USA
Lidhorikíon *see* Lidoríki
95 K21 **Lidhult** Kronoberg, S Sweden
95 P16 **Lidingö** Stockholm, C Sweden
95 K17 **Lidköping** Västra Götaland, S Sweden
Lido di Iesolo *see* Lido di Jesolo
106 I8 **Lido di Jesolo** *var.* Lido di Iesolo. Veneto, NE Italy
107 H15 **Lido di Ostia** Lazio, C Italy
Lidokhorikion *see* Lidoríki
115 E18 **Lidoríki** *prev.* Lidhorikíon, Lidokhorikion. Stereá Ellás, C Greece
110 K9 **Lidzbark** Warmińsko-Mazurskie, NE Poland
110 L7 **Lidzbark Warmiński** *Ger.* Heilsberg. Warmińsko-Mazurskie, NE Poland
109 U3 **Liebenau** Oberösterreich, N Austria
181 P7 **Liebig, Mount** ▲ Northern Territory, C Australia
109 V8 **Lieboch** Steiermark, SE Austria
108 I8 **Liechtenstein** *off.* Principality of Liechtenstein. ◆ *principality* C Europe
99 F18 **Liedekerke** Vlaams Brabant, C Belgium
99 K19 **Liège** *Dut.* Luik, *Ger.* Lüttich. Liège, E Belgium
99 K20 **Liège** *Dut.* Luik. ◆ *province* E Belgium
Liegnitz *see* Legnica
93 O16 **Lieksa** Itä-Suomi, E Finland
118 F10 **Lielupe** ≈ Latvia/Lithuania
118 G9 **Lielvārde** Ogre, C Latvia
167 U13 **Liên Hương** *var.* Tuy Phong. Binh Thuận, S Vietnam
Liên Nghia *see* Đưc Trong
109 P9 **Lienz** Tirol, W Austria
118 B10 **Liepāja** *Ger.* Libau. Liepāja, W Latvia
99 H17 **Lier** *Fr.* Lierre. Antwerpen, N Belgium
95 H15 **Lierbyen** Buskerud, S Norway
99 L21 **Lierneux** Liège, E Belgium
Lierre *see* Lier
101 D18 **Lieser** ≈ W Germany
109 U7 **Liesing** ≈ E Austria
108 E6 **Liestal** Basel-Land, N Switzerland
Lietuva *see* Lithuania
Lievenhof *see* Līvāni
103 O2 **Liévin** Pas-de-Calais, N France
14 M9 **Lièvre, Rivière du** ≈ Québec, SE Canada
109 T6 **Liezen** Steiermark, C Austria
97 E14 **Lifford** *Ir.* Leifear. NW Ireland
187 Q16 **Lifou** *island* Îles Loyauté, E New Caledonia
193 Y15 **Lifuka** *island* Ha'apai Group, C Tonga
171 P4 **Ligao** Luzon, N Philippines
Liger *see* Loire
42 H1 **Lighthouse Reef** *reef* E Belize
183 Q4 **Lightning Ridge** New South Wales, SE Australia
103 N9 **Lignières** Cher, C France
103 S5 **Ligny-en-Barrois** Meuse, NE France
83 P15 **Ligonha** ≈ NE Mozambique
31 P11 **Ligonier** Indiana, N USA
81 I25 **Ligunga** Ruvuma, S Tanzania
106 D9 **Ligure, Appennino** *Eng.* Ligurian Mountains. ▲ NW Italy
Ligure, Mar *see* Ligurian Sea
106 C9 **Liguria** ◆ *region* NW Italy
Ligurian Mountains *see* Ligure, Appennino
120 K6 **Ligurian Sea** *Fr.* Mer Ligurienne, *It.* Mar Ligure. *sea* N Mediterranean Sea
Ligurienne, Mer *see* Ligurian Sea
186 H5 **Lihir Group** *island group* NE PNG
38 B8 **Līhu'e** *var.* Lihue. Kaua'i, Hawai'i, USA, C Pacific Ocean
118 F5 **Lihula** *Ger.* Leal. Läänemaa, W Estonia
124 I2 **Liinakhamari** *var.* Linacmamari. Murmanskaya Oblast', NW Russian Federation
Liivi Laht *see* Riga, Gulf of
160 F11 **Lijiang** *var.* Dayan, Lijiang Naxizu Zizhixian. Yunnan, SW China
Lijiang Naxizu Zizhixian *see* Lijiang
112 C11 **Lika-Senj** *off.* Ličko-Senjska Županija. ◆ *province* W Croatia
79 N25 **Likasi** *prev.* Jadotville. Katanga, SE Dem. Rep. Congo
79 L16 **Likati** Orientale, N Dem. Rep. Congo
10 M15 **Likely** British Columbia, SW Canada
153 Y11 **Likhapāni** Assam, NE India
124 J16 **Likhoslavl'** Tverskaya Oblast', W Russian Federation
189 U5 **Likiep Atoll** *atoll* Ratak Chain, C Marshall Islands
95 D18 **Liknes** Vest-Agder, S Norway
79 H18 **Likouala** ≈ N Congo
79 H18 **Likouala aux Herbes** ≈ E Congo
190 B16 **Liku** E Niue
Likupang, Selat *see* Bangka, Selat
27 Y8 **Lilbourn** Missouri, C USA
103 X14 **l'Île-Rousse** Corse, France, C Mediterranean Sea
109 W5 **Lilienfeld** Niederösterreich, NE Austria
161 N11 **Liling** Hunan, S China
95 J18 **Lilla Edet** Västra Götaland, S Sweden
103 P1 **Lille** *var.* l'Isle, *Dut.* Rijssel, *Flem.* Ryssel; *prev.* Lisle, *anc.* Insula. Nord, N France
95 G24 **Lillebælt** *var.* Lille Bælt, *Eng.* Little Belt. *strait* S Denmark
102 L3 **Lillebonne** Seine-Maritime, N France
94 H12 **Lillehammer** Oppland, S Norway
103 O1 **Lillers** Pas-de-Calais, N France
95 F18 **Lillesand** Aust-Agder, S Norway
95 I15 **Lillestrøm** Akershus, S Norway
93 F18 **Lillhärdal** Jämtland, C Sweden
21 U10 **Lillington** North Carolina, SE USA
105 O9 **Lillo** Castilla-La Mancha, C Spain
10 M16 **Lillooet** British Columbia, SW Canada
83 M14 **Lilongwe** ● (Malawi) Central, W Malawi
83 M14 **Lilongwe** × Central, W Malawi
83 M14 **Lilongwe** ≈ W Malawi
171 P7 **Liloy** Mindanao, S Philippines
Lilybaeum *see* Marsala
182 J7 **Lilydale** South Australia
183 P16 **Lilydale** Tasmania, SE Australia
113 J14 **Lim** ≈ Bosnia and Herzegovina/Serbia and Montenegro (Yugo.)
57 D15 **Lima** ● (Peru) Lima, W Peru
94 K13 **Lima** Dalarna, C Sweden
31 R12 **Lima** Ohio, NE USA
57 D14 **Lima** ◆ *department* W Peru
Lima *see* Jorge Chávez International
104 G5 **Lima, Rio** *Sp.* Limia ≈ Portugal/Spain *see also* Limia
111 L17 **Limanowa** Małopolskie, S Poland
168 M11 **Limas** Pulau Sebangka, W Indonesia
Limassol *see* Lemesós
97 F14 **Limavady** *Ir.* Léim an Mhadaidh. NW Northern Ireland, UK
63 J14 **Limay Mahuida** La Pampa, C Argentina
63 H15 **Limay, Río** ≈ W Argentina
101 N16 **Limbach-Oberfrohna** Sachsen, E Germany
81 F22 **Limba Limba** ≈ C Tanzania
107 C17 **Limbara, Monte** ▲ Sardegna, Italy, C Mediterranean Sea
118 G7 **Limbaži** *Est.* Lemsalu. Limbaži, N Latvia
44 M8 **Limbé** N Haiti
99 L19 **Limbourg** Liège, E Belgium
99 K17 **Limburg** ◆ *province* NE Belgium
99 L16 **Limburg** ◆ *province* SE Netherlands
101 F17 **Limburg an der Lahn** Hessen, W Germany
94 K13 **Limedsforsen** Dalarna, C Sweden
60 L9 **Limeira** São Paulo, S Brazil
97 C19 **Limerick** *Ir.* Luimneach. SW Ireland
97 C20 **Limerick** *Ir.* Luimneach. *cultural region* SW Ireland
19 S2 **Limestone** Maine, NE USA
25 U9 **Limestone, Lake** ◎ Texas, SW USA
39 P12 **Lime Village** Alaska, USA
95 F20 **Limfjorden** *fjord* N Denmark
95 J23 **Limhamn** Skåne, S Sweden
104 H5 **Limia** *Port.* Rio Lima ≈ Portugal/Spain *see also* Lima, Rio
93 L14 **Liminka** Oulu, C Finland
Limín Vathéos *see* Sámos
115 G17 **Límni** Évvoia, C Greece
115 J15 **Límnos** *anc.* Lemnos. *island* E Greece
102 M11 **Limoges** *anc.* Augustoritum Lemovicensium, Lemovices. Haute-Vienne, C France
37 U5 **Limon** Colorado, C USA
43 O13 **Limón** *var.* Puerto Limón. Limón, E Costa Rica
42 K4 **Limón** Colón, NE Honduras
43 N13 **Limón** *off.* Provincia de Limón. ◆ *province* E Costa Rica
106 A10 **Limone Piemonte** Piemonte, NE Italy
Limones *see* Valdéz
Limonum *see* Poitiers
103 N11 **Limousin** ◆ *region* C France
103 N16 **Limoux** Aude, S France
83 L19 **Limpopo** *var.* Crocodile. ≈ S Africa
83 J20 **Limpopo** *prev.* Northern Province, Northern Transvaal. ◆ *province* NE South Africa
160 K17 **Limu Ling** ▲ S China
113 M20 **Lin** *var.* Lini. Elbasan, E Albania
Linacmamari *see* Liinakhamari
62 G13 **Linares** Maule, C Chile
54 C13 **Linares** Nariño, SW Colombia
41 O9 **Linares** Nuevo León, NE Mexico
105 N12 **Linares** Andalucía, S Spain
107 G15 **Linaro, Capo** *headland* C Italy
106 D8 **Linate** × (Milano) Lombardia, N Italy
167 T8 **Lin Camh** *prev.* Đưc Tho. Ha Tinh, N Vietnam
160 F13 **Lincang** Yunnan, SW China
Lincheng *see* Lingao
Linchuan *see* Fuzhou
61 B20 **Lincoln** Buenos Aires, E Argentina
185 H19 **Lincoln** Canterbury, South Island, NZ
97 N18 **Lincoln** *anc.* Lindum, Lindum Colonia. E England, UK
35 O6 **Lincoln** California, W USA
30 L13 **Lincoln** Illinois, N USA
26 M4 **Lincoln** Kansas, C USA
19 S5 **Lincoln** Maine, NE USA
27 T5 **Lincoln** Missouri, C USA
29 R16 **Lincoln** *state capital* Nebraska, C USA
32 F11 **Lincoln City** Oregon, NW USA
167 X10 **Lincoln Island** *island* E Paracel Islands
197 Q11 **Lincoln Sea** *sea* Arctic Ocean
97 N18 **Lincolnshire** *cultural region* E England, UK
21 R10 **Lincolnton** North Carolina, SE USA
25 V7 **Lindale** Texas, SW USA
101 I25 **Lindau** *var.* Lindau am Bodensee. Bayern, S Germany
Lindau am Bodensee *see* Lindau
123 P9 **Linde** ≈ NE Russian Federation
55 T9 **Linden** E Guyana
23 O6 **Linden** Alabama, S USA
20 H9 **Linden** Tennessee, S USA
25 X6 **Linden** Texas, SW USA
18 J16 **Lindenwold** New Jersey, NE USA
95 M15 **Lindesberg** Örebro, C Sweden
95 D18 **Lindesnes** *headland* S Norway
Líndhos *see* Líndos
81 K24 **Lindi** Lindi, SE Tanzania
81 J24 **Lindi** ◆ *region* SE Tanzania
79 N17 **Lindi** ≈ NE Dem. Rep. Congo
163 V7 **Lindian** Heilongjiang, NE China
185 E21 **Lindis Pass** *pass* South Island, NZ
83 J22 **Lindley** Free State, C South Africa
95 J19 **Lindome** Västra Götaland, S Sweden
163 S10 **Lindong** *var.* Bairin Zuoqi. Nei Mongol Zizhiqu, N China
115 O23 **Líndos** *var.* Líndhos. Ródos, Dodekánisos, Greece, Aegean Sea
14 I14 **Lindsay** Ontario, SE Canada
35 R11 **Lindsay** California, W USA
33 X8 **Lindsay** Montana, NW USA
27 N11 **Lindsay** Oklahoma, C USA
27 N5 **Lindsborg** Kansas, C USA
95 N21 **Lindsdal** Kalmar, S Sweden
Lindum/Lindum Colonia *see* Lincoln
191 W3 **Line Islands** *island group* E Kiribati
Linëvo *see* Linova
160 M5 **Linfen** *var.* Lin-fen. Shanxi, C China
155 F18 **Linganamakki Reservoir** ⊡ SW India
160 L17 **Lingao** *var.* Lincheng. Hainan, S China
171 N3 **Lingayen** Luzon, N Philippines
160 M6 **Lingbao** *var.* Guolüezhen. Henan, C China
94 N12 **Lingbo** Gävleborg, C Sweden
Lingeh *see* Bandar-e Langeh
100 E12 **Lingen** *var.* Lingen an der Ems. Niedersachsen, NW Germany
Lingen an der Ems *see* Lingen
168 M11 **Lingga, Kepulauan** *island group* W Indonesia
168 L11 **Lingga, Pulau** *island* Kepulauan Lingga, W Indonesia
14 J14 **Lingham Lake** ◎ Ontario, SE Canada
94 M13 **Linghed** Dalarna, C Sweden
33 Z15 **Lingle** Wyoming, C USA
18 G15 **Linglestown** Pennsylvania, NE USA
79 K18 **Lingomo II** Equateur, NW Dem. Rep. Congo
160 L15 **Lingshan** Guangxi Zhuangzu Zizhiqu, S China
160 L17 **Lingshui** *var.* Lingshui Lizu Zizhixian. Hainan, S China
Lingshui Lizu Zizhixian *see* Lingshui
155 G16 **Lingsugūr** Karnātaka, C India
107 L23 **Linguaglossa** Sicilia, Italy, C Mediterranean Sea
76 H10 **Linguère** N Senegal
159 W8 **Lingwu** Ningxia, N China
Lingxi Hunan, China *see* Yongshun
Lingxi Zhejiang, China *see* Cangnan
Lingxian/Ling Xian *see* Yanling
163 S12 **Lingyuan** Liaoning, NE China
163 U4 **Linhai** Heilongjiang, NE China
161 S10 **Linhai** *var.* Taizhou. Zhejiang, SE China
59 O20 **Linhares** Espírito Santo, SE Brazil
162 M13 **Linhe** Nei Mongol Zizhiqu, N China
Lini *see* Lin
139 S1 **Linik, Chiyā-ē** ▲ N Iraq
95 M18 **Linköping** Östergötland, S Sweden
163 Y8 **Linkou** Heilongjiang, NE China
118 F11 **Linkuva** Šiauliai, N Lithuania
27 V5 **Linn** Missouri, C USA
25 S16 **Linn** Texas, SW USA
27 T2 **Linneus** Missouri, C USA
96 H10 **Linnhe, Loch** *inlet* W Scotland, UK
119 G19 **Linova** *Rus.* Linëvo. Brestskaya Voblasts', SW Belarus
161 O5 **Linqing** Shandong, E China
60 K8 **Lins** São Paulo, S Brazil
93 F17 **Linsell** Jämtland, C Sweden
160 J9 **Linshui** Sichuan, C China
44 K12 **Linstead** C Jamaica
159 U11 **Lintan** Gansu, N China
159 V11 **Lintao** Gansu, C China
15 S12 **Lintère** ≈ Québec, SE Canada
108 H8 **Linth** ≈ NW Switzerland
108 H8 **Linthal** Glarus, NE Switzerland
31 N15 **Linton** Indiana, N USA
29 N6 **Linton** North Dakota, N USA
163 R11 **Linxi** Nei Mongol Zizhiqu, N China
159 U11 **Linxia** *var.* Linxia Huizu Zizhizhou. Gansu, C China
Linxia Huizu Zizhizhou *see* Linxia
Linxian *see* Lianzhou
161 Q6 **Linyi** Shandong, S China
161 P4 **Linyi** Shandong, E China
160 M6 **Linyi** Shanxi, C China
109 T4 **Linz** *anc.* Lentia. Oberösterreich, N Austria
159 S8 **Linze** *var.* Shahepu. Gansu, N China
44 J13 **Lionel Town** C Jamaica
103 Q16 **Lion, Golfe du** *Eng.* Gulf of Lion, Gulf of Lions; *anc.* Sinus Gallicus. *gulf* S France
Lion, Gulf of/Lions, Gulf of *see* Lion, Golfe du
83 K16 **Lions Den** Mashonaland West, N Zimbabwe
14 F13 **Lion's Head** Ontario, S Canada
Lios Ceannúir, Bá *see* Liscannor Bay
Lios Mór *see* Lismore
Lios na gCearrbhach *see* Lisburn
Lios Tuathail *see* Listowel
79 G17 **Liouesso** La Sangha, N Congo
Liozno *see* Lyozna
171 O4 **Lipa** *off.* Lipa City. Luzon, N Philippines
25 S7 **Lipan** Texas, SW USA
Lipari Islands/Lipari, Isole *see* Eolie, Isole
107 L22 **Lipari, Isola** *island* Isole Eolie, S Italy
116 L8 **Lipcani** *Rus.* Lipkany. N Moldova
93 N17 **Liperi** Itä-Suomi, E Finland
126 L7 **Lipetsk** Lipetskaya Oblast', W Russian Federation
126 K6 **Lipetskaya Oblast'** ◆ *province* W Russian Federation
57 K22 **Lipez, Cordillera de** ▲ SW Bolivia
110 E10 **Lipiany** *Ger.* Lippehne. Zachodnio-pomorskie, W Poland
112 G9 **Lipik** Požega-Slavonija, NE Croatia
124 L12 **Lipin Bor** Vologodskaya Oblast', NW Russian Federation
160 L12 **Liping** *var.* Defeng. Guizhou, S China
Lipkany *see* Lipcani
119 H15 **Lipnishki** *Rus.* Lipnishki. Hrodzyenskaya Voblasts', W Belarus
110 J10 **Lipno** Kujawsko-pomorskie, C Poland
116 F11 **Lipova** *Hung.* Lippa. Arad, W Romania
Lipovets *see* Lypovets'
Lippa *see* Lipova
101 E14 **Lippe** ≈ W Germany
Lippehne *see* Lipiany
101 G14 **Lippstadt** Nordrhein-Westfalen, W Germany
25 P1 **Lipscomb** Texas, SW USA
Lipsia/Lipsk *see* Leipzig
Liptau-Sankt-Nikolaus/Liptószentmiklós *see* Liptovský Mikuláš
111 K19 **Liptovský Mikuláš** *Ger.* Liptau-Sankt-Nikolaus, *Hung.* Liptószentmiklós. Žilinský Kraj, N Slovakia
183 O13 **Liptrap, Cape** *headland* Victoria, SE Australia
160 L13 **Lipu** Guangxi Zhuangzu Zizhiqu, S China
141 X12 **Liqbi** S Oman
81 G17 **Lira** N Uganda
57 F15 **Lircay** Huancavelica, C Peru
107 J15 **Liri** ≈ C Italy
144 M8 **Lisakovsk** Kostanay, NW Kazakhstan
79 K17 **Lisala** Equateur, N Dem. Rep. Congo
104 F11 **Lisboa** *Eng.* Lisbon; *anc.* Felicitas Julia, Olisipo. ● (Portugal) Lisboa, W Portugal
104 F10 **Lisboa** ◆ *Eng.* Lisbon. *district* C Portugal
19 N7 **Lisbon** New Hampshire, NE USA
29 Q6 **Lisbon** North Dakota, N USA
Lisbon *see* Lisboa
19 Q8 **Lisbon Falls** Maine, NE USA
97 G15 **Lisburn** *Ir.* Lios na gCearrbhach. E Northern Ireland, UK
38 L6 **Lisburne, Cape** *headland* Alaska, USA
97 B19 **Liscannor Bay** *Ir.* Bá Lios Ceannúir. *inlet* W Ireland
113 Q18 **Lisec** ▲ E FYR Macedonia
160 F13 **Lishe Jiang** ≈ SW China
160 M4 **Lishi** Shanxi, C China
163 V10 **Lishu** Jilin, NE China
161 R10 **Lishui** Zhejiang, SE China
192 L5 **Lisianski Island** *island* Hawaiian Islands, Hawaii, USA, C Pacific Ocean
Lisichansk *see* Lysychans'k
102 L4 **Lisieux** *anc.* Noviomagus. Calvados, N France
126 L8 **Liski** *prev.* Georgiu-Dezh. Voronezhskaya Oblast', W Russian Federation
Lisle/l'Isle *see* Lille
103 N4 **l'Isle-Adam** Val-d'Oise, N France
103 R15 **l'Isle-sur-la-Sorgue** Vaucluse, SE France
15 S9 **L'Islet** Québec, SE Canada
182 M12 **Lismore** Victoria, SE Australia
97 D20 **Lismore** *Ir.* Lios Mór. S Ireland
Lissa *see* Vis, Croatia
Lissa *see* Leszno, Poland
98 H11 **Lisse** Zuid-Holland, W Netherlands
95 D18 **Lista** *peninsula* S Norway
95 D18 **Listafjorden** *fjord* S Norway
195 R13 **Lister, Mount** ▲ Antarctica
126 M8 **Listopadovka** Voronezhskaya Oblast', W Russian Federation
14 F15 **Listowel** Ontario, S Canada
97 B20 **Listowel** *Ir.* Lios Tuathail. SW Ireland
160 L14 **Litang** Guangxi Zhuangzu Zizhiqu, S China
160 F9 **Litang** *var.* Gaocheng. Sichuan, C China
160 F10 **Litang Qu** ≈ C China
55 X12 **Litani** *var.* Itany. ≈ French Guiana/Surinam
138 G8 **Lītani, Nahr el** *var.* Nahr al Litant. ≈ C Lebanon
Litant, Nahr al *see* Lītani, Nahr el
Litauen *see* Lithuania
30 K14 **Litchfield** Illinois, N USA
29 U8 **Litchfield** Minnesota, N USA
36 K13 **Litchfield Park** Arizona, SW USA
183 S8 **Lithgow** New South Wales, SE Australia
115 I26 **Líthino, Akrotírio** *headland* Kríti, Greece, E Mediterranean Sea
118 D12 **Lithuania** *off.* Republic of Lithuania, *Ger.* Litauen, *Lith.* Lietuva, *Pol.* Litwa, *Rus.* Litva; *prev.* Lithuanian SSR, *Rus.* Litovskaya SSR. ◆ *republic* NE Europe
Lithuanian SSR *see* Lithuania
109 U11 **Litija** *Ger.* Littai. C Slovenia
18 H15 **Lititz** Pennsylvania, NE USA
115 F15 **Litóchoro** *var.* Litohoro, Litókhoron. Kentrikí Makedonía, N Greece
Litohoro/Litókhoron *see* Litóchoro

◆ Country ● Country Capital ◇ Dependent Territory ○ Dependent Territory Capital ◆ Administrative Region × International Airport ▲ Mountain ▲ Mountain Range ⩕ Volcano ≈ River ◎ Lake ⊡ Reservoir

111 C15 Litoměřice Ger. Ústecký Kraj, NW Czech Republic
111 F17 Litomyšl Ger. Pardubický Kraj, C Czech Republic
111 G17 Litovel Ger. Littau. Olomoucký Kraj, E Czech Republic
123 S13 Litovko Khabarovskiy Kray, SE Russian Federation
Litovskaya SSR see Lithuania
Littai see Litija
Littau see Litovel
44 G1 Little Abaco var. Abaco Island. island N Bahamas
111 I21 Little Alföld Ger. Kleines Ungarisches Tiefland, Hung. Kisalföld, Slvk. Podunajská Rovina. plain Hungary/Slovakia
151 Q20 Little Andaman island Andaman Islands, India, NE Indian Ocean
26 M5 Little Arkansas River ≈ Kansas, C USA
184 L4 Little Barrier Island island N NZ
Little Belt see Lillebælt
38 M11 Little Black River ≈ Alaska, USA
27 O2 Little Blue River ≈ Kansas/Nebraska, C USA
44 D8 Little Cayman island E Cayman Islands
11 X11 Little Churchill ≈ Manitoba, C Canada
166 J10 Little Coco Island island SW Burma
36 L10 Little Colorado River ≈ Arizona, SW USA
14 E11 Little Current Manitoulin Island, Ontario, S Canada
12 E11 Little Current ≈ Ontario, S Canada
38 L8 Little Diomede Island island Alaska, USA
44 I4 Little Exuma island C Bahamas
29 U7 Little Falls Minnesota, N USA
18 J10 Little Falls New York, NE USA
24 M5 Littlefield Texas, SW USA
29 V3 Littlefork Minnesota, N USA
29 V3 Little Fork River ≈ Minnesota, N USA
11 N16 Little Fort British Columbia, SW Canada
11 Y14 Little Grand Rapids Manitoba, C Canada
97 N23 Littlehampton SE England, UK
35 T2 Little Humboldt River ≈ Nevada, W USA
44 K6 Little Inagua var. Inagua Islands. island S Bahamas
21 Q4 Little Kanawha River ≈ West Virginia, NE USA
83 F25 Little Karoo plateau S South Africa
39 O16 Little Koniuji Island island Shumagin Islands, Alaska, USA
44 H12 Little London W Jamaica
13 R10 Little Mecatina Fr. Rivière du Petit Mécatina. ≈ Newfoundland and Labrador/Québec, E Canada
96 F8 Little Minch, The strait NW Scotland, UK
27 T13 Little Missouri River ≈ Arkansas, USA
28 J7 Little Missouri River ≈ NW USA
28 J3 Little Muddy River ≈ North Dakota, N USA
151 Q22 Little Nicobar island Nicobar Islands, India, NE Indian Ocean
27 R6 Little Osage River ≈ Missouri, C USA
97 P20 Little Ouse ≈ E England, UK
149 V2 Little Pamir Pash. Pāmīr-e Khord, Rus. Malyy Pamir. ▲▲ Afghanistan/Tajikistan
21 U12 Little Pee Dee River ≈ North Carolina/South Carolina, SE USA
27 V10 Little Red River ≈ Arkansas, C USA
Little Rhody see Rhode Island
185 I19 Little River Canterbury, South Island, NZ
21 U12 Little River South Carolina, SE USA
27 Y9 Little River ≈ Arkansas/Missouri, C USA
27 R13 Little River ≈ Arkansas/Oklahoma, USA
23 T7 Little River ≈ Georgia, SE USA
22 H6 Little River ≈ Louisiana, S USA
25 T10 Little River ≈ Texas, SW USA
27 V12 Little Rock state capital Arkansas, C USA
31 N8 Little Sable Point headland Michigan, N USA
103 U11 Little Saint Bernard Pass Fr. Col du Petit St-Bernard, It. Colle di Piccolo San Bernardo. pass France/Italy
36 K7 Little Salt Lake ◎ Utah, W USA
180 K8 Little Sandy Desert desert Western Australia
29 S13 Little Sioux River ≈ Iowa, C USA
38 E17 Little Sitkin Island island Aleutian Islands, Alaska, USA
11 O13 Little Smoky Alberta, W Canada
11 O14 Little Smoky ≈ Alberta, W Canada
37 P3 Little Snake River ≈ Colorado, C USA
64 A12 Little Sound bay Bermuda, NW Atlantic Ocean
37 T4 Littleton Colorado, C USA
19 N7 Littleton New Hampshire, NE USA
18 D11 Little Valley New York, NE USA
30 M15 Little Wabash River ≈ Illinois, N USA
14 D10 Little White River ≈ Ontario, S Canada
28 M12 Little White River ≈ South Dakota, N USA
25 R5 Little Wichita River ≈ Texas, SW USA
142 I4 Little Zab Ar. Nahraz Zāb aş Şaghīr, Kurd. Zē-i Kōya, Per. Rūdkhāneh-ye Zāb-e Kūchek. ≈ Iran/Iraq
79 D15 Littoral ◈ province W Cameroon
Littoria see Latina
Litva/Litwa see Lithuania
111 B15 Litvínov Ger. Ústecký Kraj, NW Czech Republic
116 M6 Lityn Vinnyts'ka Oblast', C Ukraine
Liu-chou/Liuchow see Liuzhou
163 W11 Liuhe Jilin, NE China
83 Q15 Liúpo Nampula, NE Mozambique
83 G14 Liuwa Plain plain W Zambia
160 L13 Liuzhou var. Liu-chou, Liuchow. Guangxi Zhuangzu Zizhiqu, S China
116 H8 Livada Hung. Sárköz. Satu Mare, NW Romania
115 J20 Liváda, Akrotírio headland Tínos, Kykládes, Greece, Aegean Sea
115 L21 Livádi island Kykládes, Greece, Aegean Sea
Livanátai see Livanátes
115 G18 Livanátes prev. Livanátai. Stereá Ellás, C Greece
118 I10 Līvāni Ger. Lievenhof. Preiļi, SE Latvia
65 E25 Lively Island island SE Falkland Islands
65 D25 Lively Sound sound SE Falkland Islands
39 R8 Livengood Alaska, USA
106 I7 Livenza ≈ NE Italy
35 O6 Live Oak California, W USA
23 U9 Live Oak Florida, SE USA
35 O9 Livermore California, W USA
20 I6 Livermore Kentucky, S USA
19 Q7 Livermore Falls Maine, NE USA
24 J10 Livermore, Mount ▲ Texas, SW USA
97 K17 Liverpool NW England, UK
183 S7 Liverpool Range ▲▲ New South Wales, SE Australia
96 J12 Livingston C Scotland, UK
23 N5 Livingston Alabama, S USA
35 P9 Livingston California, W USA
22 J8 Livingston Louisiana, S USA
33 S11 Livingston Montana, NW USA
20 L8 Livingston Tennessee, S USA
25 W9 Livingston Texas, SW USA
42 F4 Livingston Izabal, E Guatemala
83 I16 Livingstone var. Maramba. Southern, S Zambia
185 B22 Livingstone Mountains ▲▲ South Island, NZ
80 K13 Livingstone Mountains ▲▲ S Tanzania
82 N12 Livingstonia Northern, N Malawi
194 G4 Livingston Island island Antarctica
25 W9 Livingston, Lake ▣ Texas, SW USA
112 F13 Livno Federacija Bosna I Hercegovina, SW Bosnia and Herzegovina
126 K7 Livny Orlovskaya Oblast', W Russian Federation
93 M14 Livojoki ≈ C Finland
31 R10 Livonia Michigan, N USA
106 E11 Livorno Eng. Leghorn. Toscana, C Italy
Livramento see Santana do Livramento
141 U8 Liwā var. Al Liwā'. oasis region S UAE
81 I24 Liwale Lindi, SE Tanzania
159 W9 Liwangbu Ningxia, N China
83 N15 Liwonde Southern, S Malawi
159 V11 Lixian var. Li Xian. Gansu, C China
160 H8 Lixian var. Li Xian, Zagunao. Sichuan, C China
Lixian Jiang see Black River
115 B18 Lixoúri prev. Lixoúrion. Kefallinía, Iónioi Nísoi, Greece, C Mediterranean Sea
Lixoúrion see Lixoúri
Lixus see Larache
Lizarra see Estella
33 U15 Lizard Head Peak ▲ Wyoming, C USA
97 H25 Lizard Point headland SW England, UK
112 L12 Ljig Serbia, C Serbia and Montenegro (Yugo.)
Ljouwert see Leeuwarden
Ljubelj see Loibl Pass
109 U11 Ljubljana Ger. Laibach, It. Lubiana; anc. Aemona, Emona. ● (Slovenia) C Slovenia
109 T11 Ljubljana × C Slovenia
113 N17 Ljuboten ▲ S Serbia and Montenegro (Yugo.)
95 P19 Ljugarn Gotland, SE Sweden
84 G7 Ljungan ≈ N Sweden
93 F17 Ljungan ≈ C Sweden
95 K21 Ljungby Kronoberg, S Sweden
95 M17 Ljungsbro Östergötland, S Sweden
95 I18 Ljungskile Västra Götaland, S Sweden
94 M11 Ljusdal Gävleborg, C Sweden
94 M11 Ljusnan ≈ C Sweden
94 N12 Ljusne Gävleborg, C Sweden
95 P15 Ljusterö Stockholm, C Sweden
109 X9 Ljutomer Ger. Luttenberg. NE Slovenia
63 G15 Llaima, Volcán ▲ S Chile
105 X4 Llançà var. Llansá. Cataluña, NE Spain
97 J21 Llandovery C Wales, UK
97 J20 Llandrindod Wells E Wales, UK
97 J18 Llandudno N Wales, UK
97 I21 Llanelli prev. Llanelly. SW Wales, UK
Llanelly see Llanelli
104 M2 Llanes Asturias, N Spain
97 K19 Llangollen NE Wales, UK
25 R10 Llano Texas, SW USA
25 Q10 Llano River ≈ Texas, SW USA
54 I9 Llanos physical region Colombia/Venezuela
63 G16 Llanquihue, Lago ◎ S Chile
Llansá see Llançà
105 U5 Lleida Cast. Lérida; anc. Ilerda. Cataluña, NE Spain
105 U5 Lleida Cast. Lérida ◈ province Cataluña, NE Spain
104 K12 Llerena Extremadura, W Spain
105 S9 Llíria País Valenciano, E Spain
105 W4 Llivia Cataluña, NE Spain
105 O3 Llodio País Vasco, N Spain
105 X5 Lloret de Mar Cataluña, NE Spain
Llorri see Tossal de l'Orri
11 L11 Lloyd George, Mount ▲ British Columbia, W Canada
11 R14 Lloydminster Alberta/Saskatchewan, SW Canada
36 L6 Loa Utah, W USA
169 S8 Loagan Bunut ◎ East Malaysia
38 G12 Loa, Mauna ▲ Hawai'i, USA, C Pacific Ocean
Loanda see Luanda
79 J22 Loange ≈ S Dem. Rep. Congo
79 E21 Loango Le Kouilou, S Congo
106 B10 Loano Liguria, NW Italy
62 H4 Loa, Río ≈ N Chile
83 I20 Lobatse var. Lobatsi. Kgatleng, SE Botswana
Lobatsi see Lobatse
101 Q15 Löbau Sachsen, E Germany
79 H16 Lobaye ◈ prefecture SW Central African Republic
79 I16 Lobaye ≈ SW Central African Republic
99 G21 Lobbes Hainaut, S Belgium
61 D23 Lobería Buenos Aires, E Argentina
110 F8 Łobez Ger. Labes. Zachodnio-pomorskie, NW Poland
82 A13 Lobito Benguela, W Angola
Lobkovichi see Labkovichy
Lob Nor see Lop Nur
171 V13 Lobo Papua, E Indonesia
104 J11 Lobón Extremadura, W Spain
61 D20 Lobos Buenos Aires, E Argentina
40 E4 Lobos, Cabo headland NW Mexico
40 F6 Lobos, Isla island NW Mexico
Lobositz see Lovosice
Lobsens see Łobżenica
Loburi see Lop Buri
110 H9 Łobżenica Ger. Lobsens. Wielkopolskie, C Poland
108 G11 Locarno Ger. Luggarus. Ticino, S Switzerland
96 E9 Lochboisdale NW Scotland, UK
98 N11 Lochem Gelderland, E Netherlands
102 M8 Loches Indre-et-Loire, C France
Loch Garman see Wexford
96 H12 Lochgilphead W Scotland, UK
96 H7 Lochinver N Scotland, UK
96 F8 Lochmaddy NW Scotland, UK
96 J10 Lochnagar ▲ C Scotland, UK
99 E17 Lochristi Oost-Vlaanderen, NW Belgium
96 H9 Lochy, Loch ◎ N Scotland, UK
182 G8 Lock South Australia
97 J14 Lockerbie S Scotland, UK
27 S13 Lockesburg Arkansas, C USA
183 P10 Lockhart New South Wales, SE Australia
25 S11 Lockhart Texas, SW USA
18 F13 Lock Haven Pennsylvania, NE USA
25 N4 Lockney Texas, SW USA
100 O12 Löcknitz ≈ NE Germany
18 E9 Lockport New York, NE USA
167 T13 Lôc Ninh Sông Be, S Vietnam
107 N23 Locri Calabria, SW Italy
Locse see Levoča
27 T2 Locust Creek ≈ Missouri, C USA
23 P3 Locust Fork ≈ Alabama, S USA
27 Q9 Locust Grove Oklahoma, C USA
94 E11 Lodalskåpa ▲ S Norway
183 N10 Loddon River ≈ Victoria, SE Australia
Lodensee see Klooga
103 P15 Lodève anc. Luteva. Hérault, S France
124 I12 Lodeynoye Pole Leningradskaya Oblast', NW Russian Federation
33 V11 Lodge Grass Montana, NW USA
28 J15 Lodgepole Creek ≈ Nebraska/Wyoming, C USA
149 T11 Lodhrān Punjab, E Pakistan
106 D8 Lodi Lombardia, NW Italy
35 O8 Lodi California, W USA
31 T12 Lodi Ohio, N USA
92 H10 Lødingen Nordland, C Norway
79 L20 Lodja Kasai Oriental, C Dem. Rep. Congo
37 O3 Lodore, Canyon of canyon Colorado, C USA
105 Q4 Lodosa Navarra, N Spain
81 H16 Lodwar Rift Valley, NW Kenya
110 K13 Łódź Rus. Lodz. Łódź, C Poland
110 J13 Łódzkie ◈ province C Poland
167 P8 Loei var. Loey, Muang Loei. Loei, C Thailand
98 I11 Loenen Utrecht, C Netherlands
167 R9 Loeng Nok Tha Yasothon, E Thailand
83 F24 Loeriesfontein Northern Cape, W South Africa
95 H20 Læsø island N Denmark
Loewoek see Luwuk
Loey see Loei
76 J16 Lofa ≈ N Liberia
109 P6 Lofer Salzburg, C Austria
92 F11 Lofoten var. Lofoten Islands. island group C Norway
Lofoten Islands see Lofoten
95 N18 Loftahammar Kalmar, S Sweden
127 O10 Log Volgogradskaya Oblast', SW Russian Federation
77 S12 Loga Dosso, SW Niger
29 S14 Logan Iowa, C USA
26 K3 Logan Kansas, C USA
31 T14 Logan Ohio, N USA
36 L1 Logan Utah, W USA
21 P6 Logan West Virginia, NE USA
35 Y10 Logandale Nevada, W USA
19 O11 Logan International × (Boston) Massachusetts, NE USA
11 N16 Logan Lake British Columbia, SW Canada
23 Q4 Logan Martin Lake ▣ Alabama, S USA
10 G8 Logan, Mount ▲ Yukon Territory, W Canada
32 I7 Logan, Mount ▲ Washington, NW USA
33 P7 Logan Pass pass Montana, NW USA
31 O12 Logansport Indiana, N USA
22 F6 Logansport Louisiana, S USA
Logar see Lowgar
Logishin see Lahishyn
Log na Coille see Lugnaquillia Mountain
78 G11 Logone var. Lagone. ≈ Cameroon/Chad
78 G13 Logone-Occidental off. Préfecture du Logone-Occidental. ◈ prefecture SW Chad
78 H13 Logone Occidental ≈ SW Chad
78 G13 Logone-Oriental off. Préfecture du Logone-Oriental. ◈ prefecture SW Chad
78 H13 Logone Oriental ≈ SW Chad
Logone Oriental see Pendé
L'Ogooué-Ivindo see Ogooué-Ivindo
L'Ogooué-Lolo see Ogooué-Lolo
L'Ogooué-Maritime see Ogooué-Maritime
Logoysk see Lahoysk
105 P4 Logroño anc. Vareia, Lat. Juliobriga. La Rioja, N Spain
104 L10 Logrosán Extremadura, W Spain
95 G20 Løgstør Nordjylland, N Denmark
95 H22 Løgten Århus, C Denmark
95 F24 Løgumkloster Sønderjylland, SW Denmark
Lögurinn see Lagarfljót
153 P15 Lohārdaga Jhārkhand, N India
152 H10 Lohāru Haryāna, N India
101 D15 Lohausen × (Düsseldorf) Nordrhein-Westfalen, W Germany
189 O14 Lohd Pohnpei, E Micronesia
92 L12 Lohiniva Lappi, N Finland
Lohiszyn see Lahishyn
93 L20 Lohja var. Lojo. Etelä-Suomi, S Finland
169 V11 Lohjanan Borneo, C Indonesia
25 Q9 Lohn Texas, SW USA
100 G12 Lohne Niedersachsen, NW Germany
Lohr see Lohr am Main
101 I18 Lohr am Main var. Lohr. Bayern, C Germany
109 T10 Loibl Pass Ger. Loiblpass, Slvn. Ljubelj. pass Austria/Slovenia
167 N6 Loi-Kaw Kayah State, C Burma
93 K19 Loimaa Länsi-Suomi, W Finland
103 O6 Loing ≈ C France
167 R6 Loi, Phou ▲ N Laos
102 L7 Loir ≈ C France
103 Q11 Loire ◈ department E France
102 M7 Loire var. Liger. ≈ C France
102 I7 Loire-Atlantique ◈ department NW France
103 O7 Loiret ◈ department C France
102 M8 Loir-et-Cher ◈ department C France
101 L24 Loisach ≈ SE Germany
56 B9 Loja Loja, S Ecuador
104 M14 Loja Andalucía, S Spain
56 B9 Loja ◈ province S Ecuador
Lojo see Lohja
116 J4 Lokachi Volyns'ka Oblast', NW Ukraine
79 M20 Lokandu Maniema, C Dem. Rep. Congo
92 M11 Lokan Tekojärvi ◎ NE Finland
137 Z11 Lökbatan Rus. Lokbatan. E Azerbaijan
99 F17 Lokeren Oost-Vlaanderen, NW Belgium
Lokhvitsa see Lokhvytsya
117 S4 Lokhvytsya Rus. Lokhvitsa. Poltavs'ka Oblast', NE Ukraine
81 H17 Lokichar Rift Valley, NW Kenya
81 G16 Lokichokio Rift Valley, NW Kenya
81 H16 Lokitaung Rift Valley, NW Kenya
92 M11 Lokka Lappi, N Finland
94 G8 Løkken Verk Sør-Trøndelag, S Norway
124 G16 Loknya Pskovskaya Oblast', W Russian Federation
77 V15 Loko Nassarawa, C Nigeria
77 U15 Lokoja Kogi, C Nigeria
81 H17 Lokori Rift Valley, W Kenya
77 R16 Lokossa S Benin
118 I3 Loksa Ger. Loxa. Harjumaa, NW Estonia
9 T7 Loks Land island Nunavut, NE Canada
80 C13 Lol ≈ S Sudan
76 K15 Lola Guinée-Forestière, SE Guinea
35 Q5 Lola, Mount ▲ California, W USA
81 H20 Loliondo Arusha, NE Tanzania
95 H25 Lolland prev. Laaland. island S Denmark
186 G6 Lolobau Island island E PNG
79 E16 Lolodorf Sud, SW Cameroon
114 G7 Lom prev. Lom-Palanka. Oblast Montana, NW Bulgaria
114 G7 Lom ≈ Montana, NW Bulgaria
79 M19 Lomami ≈ C Dem. Rep. Congo
57 F17 Lomas Arequipa, SW Peru
63 I23 Lomas, Bahía bay S Chile
61 D20 Lomas de Zamora Buenos Aires, E Argentina
61 D20 Loma Verde Buenos Aires, E Argentina
180 K4 Lombadina Western Australia
106 E6 Lombardia Eng. Lombardy. ◈ region N Italy
Lombardy see Lombardia
102 M15 Lombez Gers, S France
171 Q16 Lomblen, Pulau island Nusa Tenggara, S Indonesia
173 W7 Lombok Basin undersea feature E Indian Ocean
170 L16 Lombok, Pulau island Nusa Tenggara, C Indonesia
77 Q16 Lomé ● (Togo) S Togo
77 Q16 Lomé × S Togo
79 L19 Lomela Kasai Oriental, C Dem. Rep. Congo
25 R9 Lometa Texas, SW USA
79 F16 Lomié Est, SE Cameroon
30 M8 Lomira Wisconsin, N USA
95 K23 Lomma Skåne, S Sweden
99 J16 Lommel Limburg, N Belgium
96 I11 Lomond, Loch ◎ C Scotland, UK
197 R9 Lomonosov Ridge var. Harris Ridge, Rus. Khrebet Lomonsova. undersea feature Arctic Ocean
Lomonsova, Khrebet see Lomonosov Ridge
Lom-Palanka see Lom
Lomphat see Lumphăt
35 P14 Lompoc California, W USA
167 P9 Lom Sak var. Muang Lom Sak. Phetchabun, C Thailand
110 N9 Łomża Rus. Lomzha. Podlaskie, NE Poland
Lomzha see Łomża
155 D14 Lonāvale prev. Lonaula. Mahārāshtra, W India
63 G15 Loncoche Araucanía, C Chile
63 H14 Loncopue Neuquén, W Argentina
99 G17 Londerzeel Vlaams Brabant, C Belgium
Londinium see London
14 E16 London Ontario, S Canada
191 Y2 London Kiritimati, E Kiribati
97 O22 London anc. Augusta, Lat. Londinium. ● (UK) SE England, UK
21 N7 London Kentucky, S USA
31 S13 London Ohio, NE USA
25 Q10 London Texas, SW USA
97 O22 London City × SE England, UK
97 E14 Londonderry var. Derry, Ir. Doire. NW Northern Ireland, UK
97 F14 Londonderry cultural region NW Northern Ireland, UK
180 M2 Londonderry, Cape headland Western Australia
63 H25 Londonderry, Isla island S Chile
43 O7 Londres, Cayos reef NE Nicaragua
60 I10 Londrina Paraná, S Brazil
27 N13 Lone Grove Oklahoma, C USA
14 E12 Lonely Island island Ontario, S Canada
35 T8 Lone Mountain ▲ Nevada, W USA
25 V6 Lone Oak Texas, SW USA
35 T11 Lone Pine California, W USA
Lone Star State see Texas
83 D14 Longa Cuando Cubango, C Angola
82 B12 Longa ≈ W Angola
83 E15 Longa ≈ SE Angola
Long'an see Pingwu
197 S4 Longa, Proliv Eng. Long Strait. strait NE Russian Federation
44 J13 Long Bay bay W Jamaica
21 V13 Long Bay bay North Carolina/South Carolina, E USA
35 T16 Long Beach California, W USA
22 M9 Long Beach Mississippi, S USA
18 L14 Long Beach Long Island, New York, NE USA
32 F9 Long Beach Washington, NW USA
18 K16 Long Beach Island island New Jersey, NE USA
65 M25 Longbluff headland SW Tristan da Cunha
23 U13 Longboat Key island Florida, SE USA
18 K15 Long Branch New Jersey, NE USA
44 J5 Long Cay island SE Bahamas
Longcheng see Xiaoxian
161 P14 Longchuan var. Laolong. Guangdong, S China
Longchuan see Nanhua
Longchuan Jiang see Shweli
32 K12 Long Creek Oregon, NW USA
159 W10 Longde Ningxia, N China
183 P16 Longford Tasmania, SE Australia
97 D17 Longford Ir. An Longfort. C Ireland
97 E17 Longford Ir. An Longfort. cultural region C Ireland
Longgang see Dazu
163 W11 Longgang Shan ▲▲ NE China
161 P1 Longhua Hebei, E China
169 U11 Longiram Borneo, C Indonesia
44 J4 Long Island island C Bahamas
12 H8 Long Island island Nunavut, C Canada
186 D7 Long Island var. Arop Island. island N PNG
18 L14 Long Island island New York, NE USA
18 M14 Long Island Sound sound NE USA
160 K13 Long Jiang ≈ S China
163 U7 Longjiang Heilongjiang, NE China
163 Y10 Longjing var. Yanji. Jilin, NE China
161 R4 Longkou Shandong, E China
12 E11 Longlac Ontario, S Canada
19 S1 Long Lake ◎ Maine, NE USA
31 O6 Long Lake ◎ Michigan, N USA
31 R5 Long Lake ◎ Michigan, N USA
29 N6 Long Lake ◎ North Dakota, N USA
30 J4 Long Lake ▣ Wisconsin, N USA
99 K23 Longlier Luxembourg, SE Belgium
160 I13 Longlin var. Longlin Gezu Zizhixian, Xinzhou. Guangxi Zhuangzu Zizhiqu, S China
37 T3 Longmont Colorado, C USA
29 N13 Long Pine Nebraska, C USA
Longping see Luodian
14 F17 Long Point headland Ontario, S Canada
14 K15 Long Point headland Ontario, SE Canada
184 P10 Long Point headland North Island, NZ
30 L2 Long Point headland Michigan, N USA
14 G17 Long Point Bay lake bay Ontario, S Canada
29 T7 Long Prairie Minnesota, N USA
Longquan see Fenggang
13 S11 Long Range Mountains hill range Newfoundland and Labrador, E Canada
65 H25 Long Range Point headland SE Saint Helena
181 V8 Longreach Queensland, E Australia
160 H7 Longriba Sichuan, C China
160 L10 Longshan var. Min'an. Hunan, S China
37 S3 Longs Peak ▲ Colorado, C USA
Long Strait see Longa, Proliv
102 K8 Longué Maine-et-Loire, NW France
13 P11 Longue-Pointe Québec, E Canada
103 S4 Longuyon Meurthe-et-Moselle, NE France
25 W7 Longview Texas, SW USA
32 G10 Longview Washington, NW USA
65 H25 Longwood C Saint Helena
25 P7 Longworth Texas, SW USA
103 S3 Longwy Meurthe-et-Moselle, NE France
159 V11 Longxi Gansu, C China
Longxian see Wengyuan
167 S14 Long Xuyên var. Longxuyen. An Giang, S Vietnam
161 Q13 Longyan Fujian, SE China
92 O3 Longyearbyen ○ (Svalbard) Spitsbergen, W Svalbard
160 J15 Longzhou Guangxi Zhuangzu Zizhiqu, S China
Longzhouping see Changyang
100 F12 Löningen Niedersachsen, NW Germany
27 V11 Lonoke Arkansas, C USA
95 L21 Lönsboda Skåne, S Sweden
103 S9 Lons-le-Saunier anc. Ledo Salinarius. Jura, E France
31 O15 Loogootee Indiana, N USA
31 Q9 Looking Glass River ≈ Michigan, N USA
21 X11 Lookout, Cape headland North Carolina, SE USA
39 O6 Lookout Ridge ridge Alaska, USA
181 N11 Loongana Western Australia
99 I14 Loon op Zand Noord-Brabant, S Netherlands
97 A19 Loop Head Ir. Ceann Léime. headland W Ireland
109 V4 Loosdorf Niederösterreich, NE Austria
158 G10 Lop Xinjiang Uygur Zizhiqu, NW China
112 J11 Lopare Republika Srpska, NE Bosnia and Herzegovina
Lopatichi see Lapatsichy
127 Q15 Lopatin Respublika Dagestan, SW Russian Federation
127 P7 Lopatino Penzenskaya Oblast', W Russian Federation
167 P10 Lop Buri var. Loburi. Lop Buri, C Thailand
25 R16 Lopeno Texas, SW USA
79 C18 Lopez, Cap headland W Gabon
98 I12 Lopik Utrecht, C Netherlands
Lop Nor see Lop Nur
158 M7 Lop Nur var. Lob Nor, Lop Nor, Lo-pu Po. seasonal lake NW China
Lopnur see Yuli
79 K17 Lopori ≈ NW Dem. Rep. Congo
98 O5 Loppersum Groningen, NE Netherlands
92 I8 Lopphavet sound N Norway
Lo-pu Po see Lop Nur
Lora see Lowrah
182 F3 Lora Creek seasonal river South Australia
104 K13 Lora del Río Andalucía, S Spain
148 M11 Lora, Hāmūn-i wetland SW Pakistan
31 T11 Lorain Ohio, N USA
25 O7 Loraine Texas, SW USA
31 R13 Loramie, Lake ▣ Ohio, N USA
105 Q13 Lorca Ar. Lurka; anc. Eliocroca, Lat. Illur co. Murcia, S Spain
192 I10 Lord Howe Island island E Australia
Lord Howe Island see Ontong Java Atoll
192 J11 Lord Howe Rise undersea feature SW Pacific Ocean
192 J10 Lord Howe Seamounts undersea feature W Pacific Ocean
37 P15 Lordsburg New Mexico, SW USA
186 E5 Lorengau var. Lorungau. Manus Island, N PNG

25 N5 **Lorenzo** Texas, SW USA
142 K7 **Lorestān** off. Ostān-e Lorestān, var. Luristan. ◆ province W Iran
57 M17 **Loreto** Beni, N Bolivia
106 J12 **Loreto** Marche, C Italy
40 F8 **Loreto** Baja California Sur, W Mexico
40 M11 **Loreto** Zacatecas, C Mexico
56 E9 **Loreto** off. Departamento de Loreto. ◆ department NE Peru
81 K18 **Lorian Swamp** swamp E Kenya
54 E6 **Lorica** Córdoba, NW Colombia
102 G7 **Lorient** prev. l'Orient. Morbihan, NW France
111 K22 **Lőrinci** Heves, NE Hungary
14 G11 **Loring** Ontario, S Canada
33 V6 **Loring** Montana, NW USA
103 R13 **Loriol-sur-Drôme** Drôme, E France
21 U12 **Loris** South Carolina, SE USA
57 I18 **Loriscota, Laguna** ⊚ S Peru
183 N13 **Lorne** Victoria, SE Australia
96 G11 **Lorn, Firth of** inlet W Scotland, UK
Loro Sae see East Timor
101 F24 **Lörrach** Baden-Württemberg, S Germany
103 T5 **Lorraine** ◆ region NE France
Lorungau see Lorengau
94 L11 **Los** Gävleborg, C Sweden
35 P14 **Los Alamos** California, W USA
37 S10 **Los Alamos** New Mexico, SW USA
42 F5 **Los Amates** Izabal, E Guatemala
35 S15 **Los Angeles** California, W USA
35 S15 **Los Angeles** ✕ California, W USA
63 G14 **Los Ángeles** Bío Bío, C Chile
35 T13 **Los Angeles Aqueduct** aqueduct California, W USA
Losanna see Lausanne
63 H20 **Los Antiguos** Santa Cruz, SW Argentina
189 Q16 **Losap Atoll** atoll C Micronesia
35 P10 **Los Banos** California, W USA
104 K16 **Los Barrios** Andalucía, S Spain
62 L5 **Los Blancos** Salta, N Argentina
42 L12 **Los Chiles** Alajuela, NW Costa Rica
105 O2 **Los Corrales de Buelna** Cantabria, N Spain
25 T17 **Los Fresnos** Texas, SW USA
35 N9 **Los Gatos** California, W USA
110 O11 **Łosice** Mazowieckie, E Poland
112 B11 **Lošinj** Ger. Lussin, It. Lussino. island W Croatia
Los Jardines see Ngetik Atoll
63 G15 **Los Lagos** Los Lagos, C Chile
63 F17 **Los Lagos** off. Región de los Lagos. ◆ region C Chile
Loslau see Wodzisław Śląski
64 N11 **Los Llanos** var. Los Llanos de Aridane. La Palma, Islas Canarias, Spain, NE Atlantic Ocean
Los Llanos de Aridane see Los Llanos
37 R11 **Los Lunas** New Mexico, SW USA
63 I16 **Los Menucos** Río Negro, C Argentina
40 H8 **Los Mochis** Sinaloa, C Mexico
35 N4 **Los Molinos** California, W USA
104 M9 **Los Navalmorales** Castilla-La Mancha, C Spain
25 S15 **Los Olmos Creek** ~ Texas, SW USA
Losonc/Losontz see Lučenec
167 S5 **Lô, Sông** Chin. Panlong Jiang. ~ China/Vietnam
44 B5 **Los Palacios** Pinar del Río, W Cuba
104 K14 **Los Palacios y Villafranca** Andalucía, S Spain
171 R16 **Lospalos** E East Timor
37 R12 **Los Pinos Mountains** ▲ New Mexico, SW USA
37 R11 **Los Ranchos De Albuquerque** New Mexico, SW USA
40 M14 **Los Reyes** Michoacán de Ocampo, SW Mexico
56 B7 **Los Ríos** ◆ province C Ecuador
64 O11 **Los Rodeos** ✕ (Santa Cruz de Tenerife) Tenerife, Islas Canarias, Spain, NE Atlantic Ocean
54 L4 **Los Roques, Islas** island group N Venezuela
43 S17 **Los Santos** Los Santos, S Panama
43 S17 **Los Santos** off. Provincia de Los Santos. ◆ province S Panama
Los Santos see Los Santos de Maimona
104 J12 **Los Santos de Maimona** var. Los Santos. Extremadura, W Spain
98 P10 **Losser** Overijssel, E Netherlands
96 J8 **Lossiemouth** NE Scotland, UK
61 B14 **Los Tábanos** Santa Fe, C Argentina
54 J4 **Los Taques** Falcón, N Venezuela
14 G11 **Lost Channel** Ontario, S Canada
54 L5 **Los Teques** Miranda, N Venezuela
35 Q12 **Lost Hills** California, W USA
36 I7 **Lost Peak** ▲ Utah, W USA
33 P11 **Lost Trail Pass** pass Montana, NW USA
186 G9 **Losuia** Kiriwina Island, SE PNG
62 G10 **Los Vilos** Coquimbo, C Chile
105 N10 **Los Yébenes** Castilla-La Mancha, C Spain
103 N13 **Lot** ◆ department S France
103 N13 **Lot** ~ S France
63 F14 **Lota** Bío Bío, C Chile
81 G15 **Lotagipi Swamp** wetland Kenya/Sudan
102 K14 **Lot-et-Garonne** ◆ department SW France
83 K21 **Lothair** Mpumalanga, NE South Africa
33 R7 **Lothair** Montana, NW USA
79 L20 **Loto** Kasai Oriental, C Dem. Rep. Congo
192 H16 **Lotofagā** Upolu, SE Samoa
108 E10 **Lötschbergtunnel** tunnel Valais, SW Switzerland
25 T9 **Lott** Texas, SW USA
126 H3 **Lotta** var. Lutto. ~ Finland/Russian Federation
184 Q7 **Lottin Point** headland North Island, NZ
Lötzen see Giżycko
Loualaba see Lualaba
167 P6 **Louangnamtha** var. Luong Nam Tha. Louang Namtha, N Laos
167 Q7 **Louangphabang** var. Louangphrabang, Luang Prabang. Louangphabang, N Laos
Louangphrabang see Louangphabang
194 H5 **Loubet Coast** physical region Antarctica
Loubomo see Dolisie
Louch see Loukhi
102 H6 **Loudéac** Côtes d'Armor, NW France
160 M11 **Loudi** Hunan, S China
79 F21 **Loudima** La Bouenza, S Congo
20 M9 **Loudon** Tennessee, S USA
31 T12 **Loudonville** Ohio, N USA
102 L8 **Loudun** Vienne, W France
102 K7 **Loué** Sarthe, NW France
76 G10 **Louga** NW Senegal
97 M19 **Loughborough** C England, UK
8 L4 **Lougheed Island** island Nunavut, N Canada
97 C18 **Loughrea** Ir. Baile Locha Riach. W Ireland
103 S9 **Louhans** Saône-et-Loire, C France
21 P5 **Louisa** Kentucky, S USA
21 V5 **Louisa** Virginia, NE USA
21 V9 **Louisburg** North Carolina, SE USA
37 U2 **Louise** Texas, SW USA
15 P11 **Louiseville** Québec, SE Canada
27 W3 **Louisiana** Missouri, C USA
22 G8 **Louisiana** off. State of Louisiana; also known as Creole State, Pelican State. ◆ state S USA
186 E5 **Lou Island** island N PNG
83 K19 **Louis Trichardt** Limpopo, NE South Africa
23 V4 **Louisville** Georgia, SE USA
30 M15 **Louisville** Illinois, N USA
20 K5 **Louisville** Kentucky, S USA
22 M4 **Louisville** Mississippi, S USA
29 S15 **Louisville** Nebraska, C USA
192 L11 **Louisville Ridge** undersea feature S Pacific Ocean
124 J6 **Loukhi** var. Louch. Respublika Kareliya, NW Russian Federation
79 H19 **Loukoléla** Cuvette, E Congo
104 G14 **Loulé** Faro, S Portugal
111 C16 **Louny** Ger. Laun. Ústecký kraj NW Czech Republic
29 O15 **Loup City** Nebraska, C USA
29 P15 **Loup River** ~ Nebraska, C USA
15 S9 **Loup, Rivière du** ~ Québec, SE Canada
12 K7 **Loups Marins, Lacs des** lakes Québec, NE Canada
102 K16 **Lourdes** Hautes-Pyrénées, S France
Lourenço Marques see Maputo
104 F11 **Loures** Lisboa, C Portugal
104 F10 **Lourinhã** Lisboa, C Portugal
115 C16 **Loúros** ~ W Greece
104 G8 **Lousã** Coimbra, N Portugal
160 M10 **Lou Shui** ~ C China
183 O5 **Louth** New South Wales, SE Australia
97 O18 **Louth** E England, UK
97 F17 **Louth** Ir. Lú. cultural region NE Ireland
115 H15 **Loutrá** Kentrikí Makedonía, N Greece
115 G19 **Loutráki** Pelopónnisos, S Greece
Louvain see Leuven
99 H19 **Louvain-la Neuve** Wallon Brabant, C Belgium
14 J8 **Louvicourt** Québec, SE Canada
102 M4 **Louviers** Eure, N France
30 K14 **Lou Yaeger, Lake** ⊠ Illinois, N USA
93 J15 **Lövånger** Västerbotten, N Sweden
126 J14 **Lovat'** ~ NW Russian Federation
113 J17 **Lovćen** ▲ S Serbia and Montenegro (Yugo.)
114 I8 **Lovech** Lovech, N Bulgaria
114 I9 **Lovech** ◆ province N Bulgaria
25 V9 **Lovelady** Texas, SW USA
37 T3 **Loveland** Colorado, C USA
33 U12 **Lovell** Wyoming, C USA
Lovello, Monte see Grosser Löffler
35 S4 **Lovelock** Nevada, W USA
106 E7 **Lovere** Lombardia, N Italy
30 L10 **Loves Park** Illinois, N USA
26 M2 **Lovewell Reservoir** ⊠ Kansas, C USA
93 M19 **Loviisa** Swe. Lovisa. Etelä-Suomi, S Finland
37 V15 **Loving** New Mexico, SW USA
21 U6 **Lovingston** Virginia, NE USA
37 V14 **Lovington** New Mexico, SW USA
Lovisa see Loviisa
111 C15 **Lovosice** Ger. Lobositz. Ústecký Kraj, NW Czech Republic
124 K4 **Lovozero** Murmanskaya Oblast', NW Russian Federation
126 K4 **Lovozero, Ozero** ⊚ NW Russian Federation
112 B9 **Lovran** It. Laurana. Primorje-Gorski Kotar, NW Croatia
116 E11 **Lovrin** Ger. Lowrin. Timiș, W Romania
82 E10 **Lóvua** Lunda Norte, NE Angola
82 G12 **Lóvua** Moxico, E Angola
65 D25 **Low Bay** bay East Falkland, Falkland Islands
9 P9 **Low, Cape** headland Nunavut, E Canada
33 N10 **Lowell** Idaho, NW USA
19 O10 **Lowell** Massachusetts, NE USA
Löwen see Leuven
Löwenberg in Schlesien see Lwówek Śląski
Lower Austria see Niederösterreich
Lower Bann see Bann
Lower California see Baja California
Lower Danube see Niederösterreich
185 L14 **Lower Hutt** Wellington, North Island, NZ
39 N11 **Lower Kalskag** Alaska, USA
35 O1 **Lower Klamath Lake** ⊚ California, W USA
35 Q2 **Lower Lake** ⊚ California/Nevada, W USA
97 E15 **Lower Lough Erne** ⊚ SW Northern Ireland, UK
Lower Lusatia see Niederlausitz
Lower Normandy see Basse-Normandie, France
10 K9 **Lower Post** British Columbia, W Canada
29 T4 **Lower Red Lake** ⊚ Minnesota, N USA
Lower Rhine see Neder Rijn
Lower Saxony see Niedersachsen
Lower Tunguska see Nizhnyaya Tunguska
97 Q19 **Lowestoft** E England, UK
149 Q5 **Lowgar** var. Logar. ◆ province E Afghanistan
182 H7 **Low Hill** South Australia
110 K12 **Łowicz** Łódzkie, C Poland
33 N13 **Lowman** Idaho, NW USA
149 P8 **Lowrah** var. Lora. ~ SE Afghanistan
Lowrin see Lovrin
183 N17 **Low Rocky Point** headland Tasmania, SE Australia
18 I8 **Lowville** New York, NE USA
Loxa see Loksa
182 K9 **Loxton** South Australia
81 G21 **Loya** Tabora, C Tanzania
30 K6 **Loyal** Wisconsin, N USA
18 G13 **Loyalsock Creek** ~ Pennsylvania, NE USA
35 Q5 **Loyalton** California, W USA
Lo-yang see Luoyang
187 Q16 **Loyauté, Îles** island group S New Caledonia
Loyev see Loyew
119 O20 **Loyew** Rus. Loyev. Homyel'skaya Voblasts', SE Belarus
125 S13 **Loyno** Kirovskaya Oblast', NW Russian Federation
103 P13 **Lozère** ◆ department S France
103 Q14 **Lozère, Mont** ▲ S France
112 J11 **Loznica** Serbia, W Serbia and Montenegro (Yugo.)
117 V7 **Lozova** Rus. Lozovaya. Kharkivs'ka Oblast', E Ukraine
Lozovaya see Lozova
105 N7 **Lozoyuela** Madrid, C Spain
Lœvvajok see Leavvajohka
Lu see Shandong, China
Lú see Louth, Ireland
82 F12 **Luacano** Moxico, E Angola
79 N21 **Lualaba** Fr. Loualaba. ~ SE Dem. Rep. Congo
83 H14 **Luampa** Western, NW Zambia
83 H15 **Luampa Kuta** Western, W Zambia
161 P8 **Lu'an** Anhui, E China
104 K2 **Luanco** Asturias, N Spain
82 A11 **Luanda** var. Loanda, Port. São Paulo de Loanda. ● (Angola) Luanda, NW Angola
82 A11 **Luanda** ◆ province NW Angola
82 A11 **Luanda** ✕ Luanda, NW Angola
82 D12 **Luando** ~ C Angola
Luang see Tapi, Mae Nam
83 G14 **Luanginga** var. Luanguinga. ~ Angola/Zambia
167 N15 **Luang, Khao** ▲ SW Thailand
Luang Prabang see Louangphabang
167 P8 **Luang Prabang Range** Th. Thiukhaoluang Phrahang. ▲ Laos/Thailand
167 N16 **Luang, Thale** lagoon S Thailand
Luangua, Rio see Luangwa
82 E11 **Luangue** ~ NE Angola
Luanguinga see Luanginga
83 K15 **Luangwa** var. Aruângua. Lusaka, C Zambia
83 K14 **Luangwa** var. Aruângua, Rio Luangua. ~ Mozambique/Zambia
161 Q2 **Luan He** ~ E China
190 G11 **Luaniva, Île** island E Wallis and Futuna
161 P2 **Luanping** var. Anjiangying. Hebei, E China
82 J13 **Luanshya** Copperbelt, C Zambia
62 K13 **Luan Toro** La Pampa, C Argentina
161 Q2 **Luanxian** var. Luan Xian. Hebei, E China
82 J12 **Luapula** ◆ province N Zambia
79 O25 **Luapula** ~ Dem. Rep. Congo/Zambia
104 J2 **Luarca** Asturias, N Spain
169 R10 **Luar, Danau** ⊚ Borneo, N Indonesia
79 L25 **Luashi** Katanga, S Dem. Rep. Congo
82 G12 **Luau** Port. Vila Teixeira de Sousa. Moxico, NE Angola
79 C16 **Luba** prev. San Carlos. Isla de Bioco, NW Equatorial Guinea
42 F4 **Lubaantun** ruins Toledo, S Belize
111 P16 **Lubaczów** var. Lúbaczów. Podkarpackie, SE Poland
Lubale see Lubalo
82 E11 **Lubalo** Lunda Norte, NE Angola
82 E11 **Lubalo** var. Lubale. ~ Angola/Zaire
118 J9 **Lubāna** Madona, E Latvia
Lubānas Ezers see Lubāns
171 N4 **Lubang Island** island N Philippines
83 B15 **Lubango** Port. Sá da Bandeira. Huíla, SW Angola
118 J9 **Lubāns** var. Lubānas Ezers. ⊚ E Latvia
79 M21 **Lubao** Kasai Oriental, C Dem. Rep. Congo
110 O13 **Lubartów** Ger. Qumälisch. Lubelskie, E Poland
100 G13 **Lübbecke** Nordrhein-Westfalen, NW Germany
100 O13 **Lübben** Brandenburg, E Germany
101 P14 **Lübbenau** Brandenburg, E Germany
25 N5 **Lubbock** Texas, SW USA
Lubcz see Lyubcha
19 U6 **Lubec** Maine, NE USA
100 K9 **Lübeck** Schleswig-Holstein, N Germany
100 K8 **Lübecker Bucht** bay N Germany
79 M21 **Lubefu** Kasai Oriental, C Dem. Rep. Congo
163 T10 **Lubei** var. Jarud Qi. Nei Mongol Zizhiqu, N China
111 O14 **Lubelska, Wyżyna** plateau SE Poland
111 O14 **Lubelskie** ◆ province E Poland
Lubembe see Luembe
Lüben see Lubin
144 H9 **Lubenka** Zapadnyy Kazakhstan, W Kazakhstan
79 P18 **Lubero** Nord Kivu, E Dem. Rep. Congo
79 L22 **Lubi** ~ S Dem. Rep. Congo
Lubiana see Ljubljana
110 J11 **Lubień Kujawski** Kujawsko-pomorskie, C Poland
110 F13 **Lubin** Ger. Lüben. Dolnośląskie, SW Poland
111 O14 **Lublin** Rus. Lyublin. Lubelskie, E Poland
111 J15 **Lubliniec** Śląskie, S Poland
Lubnān, Jabal see Liban, Jebel
117 R5 **Lubny** Poltavs'ka Oblast', NE Ukraine
Luboml see Lyuboml'
110 G11 **Luboń** Ger. Peterhof. Wielkolpolskie, C Poland
110 D12 **Lubsko** Ger. Sommerfeld. Lubuskie, W Poland
79 N24 **Lubudi** Katanga, SE Dem. Rep. Congo
168 L13 **Lubuklinggau** Sumatera, W Indonesia
79 N25 **Lubumbashi** prev. Élisabethville. Katanga, SE Dem. Rep. Congo
83 I14 **Lubungu** Central, C Zambia
110 E12 **Lubuskie** ◆ province W Poland
79 N18 **Lubutu** Maniema, E Dem. Rep. Congo
Luca see Lucca
82 C11 **Lucala** ~ W Angola
14 E16 **Lucan** Ontario, S Canada
97 F18 **Lucan** Ir. Leamhcán. E Ireland
Lucanian Mountains see Lucano, Appennino
107 M18 **Lucano, Appennino** Eng. Lucanian Mountains. ▲ S Italy
82 F11 **Lucapa** var. Lukapa. Lunda Norte, NE Angola
29 V15 **Lucas** Iowa, C USA
61 C18 **Lucas González** Entre Ríos, E Argentina
65 C25 **Lucas Point** headland West Falkland, Falkland Islands
31 S15 **Lucasville** Ohio, N USA
106 F11 **Lucca** anc. Luca. Toscana, C Italy
44 H12 **Lucea** W Jamaica
97 H15 **Luce Bay** inlet SW Scotland, UK
22 M8 **Lucedale** Mississippi, S USA
171 O4 **Lucena** off. Lucena City. Luzon, N Philippines
104 M14 **Lucena** Andalucía, S Spain
105 S8 **Lucena del Cid** País Valenciano, E Spain
111 D15 **Lučenec** Ger. Losontz, Hung. Losonc. Banskobystrický Kraj, C Slovakia
Lucentum see Alicante
107 M16 **Lucera** Puglia, SE Italy
Lucerna/Lucerne see Luzern
Lucerne, Lake of see Vierwaldstätter See
40 J4 **Lucero** Chihuahua, N Mexico
123 S14 **Luchegorsk** Primorskiy Kray, SE Russian Federation
105 Q13 **Luchena** ~ SE Spain
Lucheng see Kangding
82 N13 **Lucheringo** var. Luchulingo. ~ N Mozambique
Luchesa see Luchosa
Luchin see Luchyn
118 N13 **Luchosa** Rus. Luchesa. ~ N Belarus
Luchow see Hefei
100 K11 **Lüchow** Mecklenburg-Vorpommern, N Germany
Luchulingo see Lucheringo
119 N17 **Luchyn** Rus. Luchin. Homyel'skaya Voblasts', SE Belarus
55 U11 **Lucie Rivier** ~ W Surinam
182 K11 **Lucindale** South Australia
83 A14 **Lucira** Namibe, SW Angola
Łuck see Luts'k
101 O14 **Luckau** Brandenburg, E Germany
100 N13 **Luckenwalde** Brandenburg, E Germany
14 E15 **Lucknow** Ontario, S Canada
152 L12 **Lucknow** var. Lakhnau. Uttar Pradesh, N India
102 J10 **Luçon** Vendée, NW France
44 I7 **Lucrecia, Cabo** headland E Cuba
82 F13 **Lucusse** Moxico, E Angola
Lüda see Dalian
114 M9 **Luda Kamchiya** ~ E Bulgaria
Ludasch see Luduș
114 I10 **Luda Yana** ~ C Bulgaria
112 F7 **Ludbreg** Varaždin, N Croatia
29 P7 **Ludden** North Dakota, N USA
101 F15 **Lüdenscheid** Nordrhein-Westfalen, W Germany
83 C21 **Lüderitz** prev. Angra Pequena. Karas, SW Namibia
152 H8 **Ludhiāna** Punjab, N India
31 O7 **Ludington** Michigan, N USA
97 K20 **Ludlow** W England, UK
35 W14 **Ludlow** California, W USA
28 J7 **Ludlow** South Dakota, N USA
18 M9 **Ludlow** Vermont, NE USA
114 L7 **Ludogorie** physical region NE Bulgaria
23 W6 **Ludowici** Georgia, SE USA
Ludsan see Ludza
116 I10 **Luduș** Ger. Ludasch, Hung. Marosludas. Mureș, C Romania
95 M14 **Ludvika** Dalarna, C Sweden
101 H21 **Ludwigsburg** Baden-Württemberg, SW Germany
100 O13 **Ludwigsfelde** Brandenburg, NE Germany
101 G20 **Ludwigshafen** var. Ludwigshafen am Rhein. Rheinland-Pfalz, W Germany
Ludwigshafen am Rhein see Ludwigshafen
101 L20 **Ludwigskanal** canal SE Germany
100 L10 **Ludwigslust** Mecklenburg-Vorpommern, N Germany
118 K10 **Ludza** Ger. Ludsan. Ludza, E Latvia
79 K21 **Luebo** Kasai Occidental, SW Dem. Rep. Congo
25 Q6 **Lueders** Texas, SW USA
79 N20 **Lueki** Maniema, C Dem. Rep. Congo
82 F10 **Luembe** var. Lubembe. ~ Angola/Dem. Rep. Congo
82 E13 **Luena** var. Lwena, Port. Luso. Moxico, E Angola
79 M24 **Luena** Katanga, SE Dem. Rep. Congo
82 K12 **Luena** Northern, NE Zambia
82 F13 **Luena** ~ E Angola
83 F16 **Luengue** ~ SE Angola
83 G15 **Lueti** ~ Angola/Zambia
160 J7 **Lüeyang** var. Hejiayan. Shaanxi, C China
161 P14 **Lufeng** Guangdong, S China
79 N24 **Lufira** ~ SE Dem. Rep. Congo
79 N25 **Lufira, Lac de Retenue de la** var. Lac Tshangalele. ⊠ SE Dem. Rep. Congo
25 W8 **Lufkin** Texas, SW USA
82 L11 **Lufubu** ~ N Zambia
124 G14 **Luga** Leningradskaya Oblast', NW Russian Federation
126 G13 **Luga** ~ NW Russian Federation
Luganer See see Lugano, Lago di
108 H11 **Lugano** Ger. Lauis. Ticino, S Switzerland
108 H12 **Lugano, Lago di** var. Ceresio, Ger. Luganer See. ⊚ S Switzerland
Lugansk see Luhans'k
187 Q13 **Luganville** Espiritu Santo, C Vanuatu
Lugdunum see Lyon
Lugdunum Batavorum see Leiden
83 O15 **Lugela** Zambézia, NE Mozambique
83 O16 **Lugela** ~ C Mozambique
82 P13 **Lugenda, Rio** ~ N Mozambique
Luggarus see Locarno
Lugh Ganana see Luuq
97 G19 **Lugnaquillia Mountain** Ir. Log na Coille. ▲ E Ireland
106 H10 **Lugo** Emilia-Romagna, N Italy
104 I3 **Lugo** anc. Lugus Augusti. Galicia, NW Spain
104 I3 **Lugo** ◆ province Galicia, NW Spain
21 R12 **Lugoff** South Carolina, SE USA
116 F12 **Lugoj** Ger. Lugosch, Hung. Lugos. Timiș, W Romania
Lugos/Lugosch see Lugoj
Lugovoy/Lugovoye see Kulan
158 I13 **Lugu** Xizang Zizhiqu, W China
Lugus Augusti see Lugo
Luguvallium/Luguvallum see Carlisle
117 Y7 **Luhans'k** Rus. Lugansk; prev. Voroshilovgrad. Luhans'ka Oblast', E Ukraine
117 Y7 **Luhans'k** ✕ Luhans'ka Oblast', E Ukraine
117 X6 **Luhans'ka Oblast'** var. Luhans'k; prev. Voroshilovgrad, Rus. Voroshilovgradskaya Oblast'. ◆ province E Ukraine
161 Q7 **Luhe** Jiangsu, E China
171 S13 **Luhu** Pulau Seram, E Indonesia
Luhua see Heishui
160 G8 **Luhuo** var. Xindu, Tib. Zhaggo. Sichuan, C China
116 M3 **Luhyny** Zhytomyrs'ka Oblast', N Ukraine
83 G15 **Lui** ~ W Zambia
83 G16 **Luiana** ~ SE Angola
83 L15 **Luia, Rio** var. Ruya. ~ Mozambique/Zimbabwe
Luichow Peninsula see Leizhou Bandao
Luik see Liège
82 C13 **Luimbale** Huambo, C Angola
Luimneach see Limerick
106 D6 **Luino** Lombardia, N Italy
82 E13 **Luio** ~ E Angola
92 L11 **Luiro** ~ NE Finland
79 N25 **Luishia** Katanga, SE Dem. Rep. Congo
59 M19 **Luislândia do Oeste** Minas Gerais, SE Brazil
40 K5 **Luis L.León, Presa** ⊠ N Mexico
Luis Muñoz Marin see San Juan
195 N5 **Luitpold Coast** physical region Antarctica
79 K22 **Luiza** Kasai Occidental, S Dem. Rep. Congo
61 D20 **Luján** Buenos Aires, E Argentina
79 N24 **Lukafu** Katanga, SE Dem. Rep. Congo
Lukapa see Lucapa
112 I11 **Lukavac** Federacija Bosna I Hercegovina, NE Bosnia and Herzegovina
79 I20 **Lukenie** ~ C Dem. Rep. Congo
79 H19 **Lukolela** Equateur, W Dem. Rep. Congo
119 M14 **Lukoml'skaye, Vozyera** Rus. Ozero Lukoml'skoye. ⊚ N Belarus
Lukoml'skoye, Ozero see Lukoml'skaye, Vozyera
114 I8 **Lukovit** Lovech, N Bulgaria
110 O12 **Łuków** Ger. Bogendorf. Lubelskie, E Poland
127 O4 **Lukoyanov** Nizhegorodskaya Oblast', W Russian Federation
79 N22 **Lukuga** ~ SE Dem. Rep. Congo
79 F21 **Lukula** Bas-Congo, SW Dem. Rep. Congo
83 G14 **Lukulu** Western, NW Zambia
189 R17 **Lukunor Atoll** atoll Mortlock Islands, C Micronesia
82 J12 **Lukwesa** Luapula, NE Zambia
93 K14 **Luleå** Norrbotten, N Sweden
92 J13 **Luleälven** ~ N Sweden
136 C10 **Lüleburgaz** Kırklareli, NW Turkey
160 M4 **Lüliang Shan** ▲ C China
79 O21 **Lulimba** Maniema, E Dem. Rep. Congo
22 K9 **Luling** Louisiana, S USA
25 T11 **Luling** Texas, SW USA
79 I18 **Lulonga** ~ NW Dem. Rep. Congo
79 K22 **Lulua** ~ S Dem. Rep. Congo
Luluabourg see Kananga
192 L17 **Luma** Ta'ū, E American Samoa
169 S17 **Lumajang** Jawa, C Indonesia
158 G12 **Lumajangdong Co** ⊚ W China
82 G13 **Lumbala Kaquengue** Moxico, E Angola
83 F14 **Lumbala N'Guimbo** var. Nguimbo, Port. Gago Coutinho, Vila Gago Coutinho. Moxico, E Angola
21 T11 **Lumber River** ~ North Carolina/South Carolina, SE USA
Lumber State see Maine
22 L8 **Lumberton** Mississippi, S USA
21 U11 **Lumberton** North Carolina, SE USA
105 R4 **Lumbier** Navarra, N Spain
83 Q15 **Lumbo** Nampula, NE Mozambique
124 M4 **Lumbovka** Murmanskaya Oblast', NW Russian Federation
104 J7 **Lumbrales** Castilla-León, N Spain
153 W13 **Lumding** Assam, NE India
82 F12 **Lumege** var. Lumeje. Moxico, E Angola
Lumeje see Lumege
99 J17 **Lummen** Limburg, NE Belgium
93 J20 **Lumparland** Åland, SW Finland
167 T11 **Lumphăt** prev. Lomphat. Rôtânôkiri, NE Cambodia
11 U16 **Lumsden** Saskatchewan, S Canada
185 C23 **Lumsden** Southland, South Island, NZ
169 N14 **Lumut, Tanjung** headland Sumatera, W Indonesia
157 P4 **Lün** Töv, C Mongolia
116 I13 **Luna Corbului** Argeș, S Romania
95 K23 **Lund** Skåne, S Sweden
35 X6 **Lund** Nevada, W USA
82 D11 **Lunda Norte** ◆ province NE Angola
82 E12 **Lunda Sul** ◆ province NE Angola
82 M13 **Lundazi** Eastern, NE Zambia
95 G16 **Lunde** Telemark, S Norway
Lundenburg see Břeclav
95 C17 **Lundevatnet** ⊚ S Norway
Lundi see Runde
97 I23 **Lundy** island SW England, UK
100 J10 **Lüneburg** Niedersachsen, N Germany
100 J11 **Lüneburger Heide** heathland NW Germany
103 Q15 **Lunel** Hérault, S France
101 F14 **Lünen** Nordrhein-Westfalen, W Germany
13 P16 **Lunenburg** Nova Scotia, SE Canada
21 V7 **Lunenburg** Virginia, NE USA
103 T5 **Lunéville** Meurthe-et-Moselle, NE France
83 I14 **Lunga** ~ C Zambia
Lunga, Isola see Dugi Otok
158 H12 **Lungdo** Xizang Zizhiqu, W China
158 I14 **Lunggar** Xizang Zizhiqu, W China
76 I15 **Lungi** ✕ (Freetown) W Sierra Leone
Lungkiang see Qiqihar
Lungleh see Lunglei
153 W15 **Lunglei** prev. Lungleh. Mizoram, NE India
158 L15 **Lungsang** Xizang Zizhiqu, W China
82 E13 **Lungué-Bungo** var. Lungwebungu. ~ Angola/Zambia **see also** Lungwebungu
83 G14 **Lungwebungu** var. Lungué-Bungo. ~ Angola/Zambia **see also** Lungué-Bungo
152 F12 **Lūni** Rājasthān, N India
152 F12 **Lūni** ~ N India
Luninets see Luninyets
35 S7 **Luning** Nevada, W USA
Łuniniec see Luninyets
127 P6 **Lunino** Penzenskaya Oblast', W Russian Federation
119 J19 **Luninyets** Pol. Łuniniec, Rus. Luninets. Brestskaya Voblasts', SW Belarus

◆ Country ● Country Capital ◇ Dependent Territory ○ Dependent Territory Capital ◆ Administrative Region ✕ International Airport ▲ Mountain ▲ Mountain Range ⊼ Volcano ~ River ⊚ Lake ⊠ Reservoir

152 F10 **Lūnkaransar** Rājasthān, NW India
119 G17 **Lunna** Pol. Łunna, Rus. Lunna. Hrodzyenskaya Voblasts', W Belarus
76 I15 **Lunsar** W Sierra Leone
83 K14 **Lunsemfwa** ≈ C Zambia
158 J6 **Luntai** var. Bügür. Xinjiang Uygur Zizhiqu, NW China
98 K11 **Lunteren** Gelderland, C Netherlands
109 U5 **Lunz am See** Niederösterreich, C Austria
163 Y7 **Luobei** var. Fengxiang. Heilongjiang, NE China
Luocheng see Hui'an
160 J13 **Luodian** var. Longping. Guizhou, S China
160 M15 **Luoding** Guangdong, S China
160 M6 **Luo He** ≈ C China
160 L5 **Luo He** ≈ C China
161 N7 **Luohe** Henan, C China
Luolajarvi see Kuoloyarvi
Luong Nam Tha see Louangnamtha
160 L13 **Luoqing Jiang** ≈ S China
161 O8 **Luoshan** Henan, C China
161 O12 **Luoxiao Shan** ⛰ S China
161 N6 **Luoyang** var. Honan, Lo-yang. Henan, C China
161 R12 **Luoyuan** var. Fengshan. Fujian, SE China
79 F21 **Luozi** Bas-Congo, W Dem. Rep. Congo
83 J17 **Lupane** Matabeleland North, W Zimbabwe
160 I12 **Lupanshui** prev. Shuicheng. Guizhou, S China
169 R10 **Lupar, Batang** ≈ East Malaysia
Lupatia see Altamura
116 G12 **Lupeni** Hung. Lupény. Hunedoara, SW Romania
Lupény see Lupeni
82 N13 **Lupiliche** Niassa, N Mozambique
83 E14 **Lupire** Cuando Cubango, E Angola
79 L22 **Luputa** Kasai Oriental, S Dem. Rep. Congo
121 P16 **Luqa** ✕ (Valletta) S Malta
159 U11 **Luqu** var. Ma'ai. Gansu, C China
45 U5 **Luquillo, Sierra de** ⛰ E Puerto Rico
26 L4 **Luray** Kansas, C USA
21 U4 **Luray** Virginia, NE USA
103 T7 **Lure** Haute-Saône, E France
82 D11 **Luremo** Lunda Norte, NE Angola
97 F15 **Lurgan** Ir. An Lorgain. S Northern Ireland, UK
57 K18 **Luribay** La Paz, W Bolivia
Luring see Gêrzê
83 Q14 **Lúrio** Nampula, NE Mozambique
83 P14 **Lúrio, Rio** ≈ NE Mozambique
Luristan see Lorestān
Lurka see Lorca
83 J15 **Lusaka** ● (Zambia) Lusaka, SE Zambia
83 J15 **Lusaka** ◈ province C Zambia
83 J15 **Lusaka** ✕ Lusaka, C Zambia
79 L21 **Lusambo** Kasai Oriental, C Dem. Rep. Congo
186 F8 **Lusancay Islands and Reefs** island group SE PNG
79 I21 **Lusanga** Bandundu, SW Dem. Rep. Congo
79 N21 **Lusangi** Maniema, E Dem. Rep. Congo
Lusatian Mountains see Lausitzer Bergland
Lushar see Huangzhong
Lushnja see Lushnjë
113 K21 **Lushnjë** var. Lushnja. Fier, C Albania
81 J21 **Lushoto** Tanga, E Tanzania
102 L10 **Lusignan** Vienne, W France
33 Z15 **Lusk** Wyoming, C USA
Luso see Luena
102 L10 **Lussac-les-Châteaux** Vienne, W France
Lussin/Lussino see Lošinj
Lussinpiccolo see Mali Lošinj
108 I7 **Lustenau** Vorarlberg, W Austria
161 T14 **Lü Tao** var. Huoshao Dao, Lütao, Eng. Green Island. island SE Taiwan
Lūt, Baḩrat/Lut, Bahret see Dead Sea
22 K9 **Lutcher** Louisiana, S USA
143 T9 **Lūt, Dasht-e** var. Kavīr-e Lūt. desert E Iran
83 F14 **Lutembo** Moxico, E Angola
Lutetia/Lutetia Parisiorum see Paris
Luteva see Lodève
14 G15 **Luther Lake** ◎ Ontario, S Canada
186 K8 **Luti** Choiseul Island, NW Solomon Islands
Lūt, Kavīr-e see Lūt, Dasht-e
97 N21 **Luton** SE England, UK
97 N21 **Luton** ✕ (London) SE England, UK
108 B10 **Lutry** Vaud, SW Switzerland
8 K10 **Lutsel'k'e** prev. Snowdrift. Northwest Territories, W Canada
29 Y4 **Lutsen** Minnesota, N USA
116 J4 **Luts'k** Pol. Łuck, Rus. Lutsk. Volyns'ka Oblast', NW Ukraine
Luttenberg see Ljutomer
Lüttich see Liège
83 G25 **Luttig** Western Cape, SW South Africa
Lutto see Lotta
82 E13 **Lutuai** Moxico, E Angola
117 Y7 **Lutuhyne** Luhans'ka Oblast', E Ukraine
171 V14 **Lutur, Pulau** island Kepulauan Aru, E Indonesia
23 V12 **Lutz** Florida, SE USA
Lutzow-Holm Bay see Lützow Holmbukta
195 V2 **Lützow Holmbukta** var. Lutzow-Holm Bay. bay Antarctica
81 L16 **Luuq** It. Lugh Ganana. Gedo, SW Somalia
92 M12 **Luusua** Lappi, NE Finland
23 Q6 **Luverne** Alabama, S USA
29 S11 **Luverne** Minnesota, N USA
79 O22 **Luvua** ≈ SE Dem. Rep. Congo
82 F13 **Luvuei** Moxico, E Angola
81 H24 **Luwego** ≈ S Tanzania
82 K12 **Luwingu** Northern, NE Zambia
171 P12 **Luwuk** prev. Loewoek. Sulawesi, C Indonesia
23 N3 **Luxapallila Creek** ≈ Alabama/Mississippi, S USA
99 M25 **Luxembourg** ● (Luxembourg) Luxembourg, S Luxembourg
99 M25 **Luxembourg** off. Grand Duchy of Luxembourg, var. Lëtzebuerg, Luxemburg. ◆ monarchy NW Europe
99 J23 **Luxembourg** ◈ province SE Belgium
99 L24 **Luxembourg** ◈ district S Luxembourg
31 N6 **Luxemburg** Wisconsin, N USA
Luxemburg see Luxembourg
103 U7 **Luxeuil-les-Bains** Haute-Saône, E France
160 E13 **Luxi** prev. Mangshi. Yunnan, SW China
82 E10 **Luxico** ≈ Angola/Dem. Rep. Congo
75 X10 **Luxor** Ar. Al Uqşur. E Egypt
75 X10 **Luxor** ✕ C Egypt
160 M4 **Luya Shan** ⛰ C China
102 J15 **Luy de Béarn** ≈ SW France
102 J15 **Luy de France** ≈ SW France
125 P12 **Luza** Kirovskaya Oblast', NW Russian Federation
127 Q12 **Luza** ≈ NW Russian Federation
104 I16 **Luz, Costa de la** coastal region SW Spain
111 K20 **Luže** var. Lausche. ▲ Czech Republic/Germany **see also** Lausche
108 F8 **Luzern** Fr. Lucerne, It. Lucerna. Luzern, C Switzerland
108 E8 **Luzern** Fr. Lucerne. ◈ canton C Switzerland
160 L13 **Luzhai** Guangxi Zhuangzu Zizhiqu, S China
118 K12 **Luzhki** Rus. Luzhki. Vitsyebskaya Voblasts', N Belarus
160 I10 **Luzhou** Sichuan, C China
Lužická Nisa see Neisse
Lužické Hory see Lausitzer Bergland
Lužnice see Lainsitz
171 O2 **Luzon** island N Philippines
171 N1 **Luzon Strait** strait Philippines/Taiwan
116 I5 **L'viv** Ger. Lemberg, Pol. Lwów, Rus. L'vov. L'vivs'ka Oblast', W Ukraine
L'viv see L'vivs'ka Oblast'
116 I4 **L'vivs'ka Oblast'** var. L'viv, Rus. L'vovskaya Oblast'. ◈ province NW Ukraine
L'vov see L'viv
L'vovskaya Oblast' see L'vivs'ka Oblast'
Lwena see Luena
Lwów see L'viv
110 F11 **Lwówek** Ger. Neustadt bei Pinne. Wielkolpolskie, C Poland
111 E14 **Lwówek Śląski** Ger. Löwenberg in Schlesien. Dolnośląskie, SW Poland
119 I18 **Lyakhavichy** Rus. Lyakhovichi. Brestskaya Voblasts', SW Belarus
Lyakhovichi see Lyakhavichy
185 B22 **Lyall, Mount** ▲ South Island, NZ
Lyallpur see Faisalābād
Lyangar see Langar
124 H11 **Lyaskelya** Respublika Kareliya, NW Russian Federation
119 I18 **Lyasnaya** Rus. Lesnaya. Brestskaya Voblasts', SW Belarus
119 F19 **Lyasnaya** Pol. Leśna, Rus. Lesnaya. ≈ SW Belarus
124 H15 **Lychkovo** Novgorodskaya Oblast', W Russian Federation
Lyck see Ełk
93 I15 **Lycksele** Västerbotten, N Sweden
18 G13 **Lycoming Creek** ≈ Pennsylvania, NE USA
Lycopolis see Asyūt
195 N3 **Lyddan Island** island Antarctica
83 K20 **Lydenburg** Mpumalanga, NE South Africa
119 L20 **Lyel'chytsy** Rus. Lel'chitsy. Homyel'skaya Voblasts', SE Belarus
119 P14 **Lyenina** Rus. Lenino. Mahilyowskaya Voblasts', E Belarus
118 L13 **Lyepyel'** Rus. Lepel'. Vitsyebskaya Voblasts', N Belarus
25 S17 **Lyford** Texas, SW USA
95 E17 **Lygna** ≈ S Norway
18 G14 **Lykens** Pennsylvania, NE USA
115 E21 **Lykódimo** ▲ S Greece
97 K24 **Lyme Bay** bay S England, UK
97 K24 **Lyme Regis** S England, UK
110 L7 **Łyna** Ger. Alle. ≈ N Poland
29 P12 **Lynch** Nebraska, C USA
20 J10 **Lynchburg** Tennessee, S USA
21 T6 **Lynchburg** Virginia, NE USA
21 T12 **Lynches River** ≈ South Carolina, SE USA
32 H6 **Lynden** Washington, NW USA
182 I5 **Lyndhurst** South Australia
27 Q5 **Lyndon** Kansas, C USA
19 N7 **Lyndonville** Vermont, NE USA
95 D18 **Lyngdal** Vest-Agder, S Norway
92 I9 **Lyngen** Lapp. Ivgovuotna. inlet Arctic Ocean
95 G17 **Lyngør** Aust-Agder, S Norway
92 I9 **Lyngseidet** Troms, N Norway
19 P11 **Lynn** Massachusetts, NE USA
Lynn see King's Lynn
23 R9 **Lynn Haven** Florida, SE USA
11 V11 **Lynn Lake** Manitoba, C Canada
Lynn Regis see King's Lynn
118 I13 **Lyntupy** Rus. Lyntupy. Vitsyebskaya Voblasts', NW Belarus
103 R11 **Lyon** Eng. Lyons; anc. Lugdunum. Rhône, E France
8 I6 **Lyon, Cape** headland Northwest Territories, NW Canada
18 K6 **Lyon Mountain** ▲ New York, NE USA
103 Q11 **Lyonnais, Monts du** ⛰ C France
65 N25 **Lyon Point** headland SE Tristan da Cunha
182 E5 **Lyons** South Australia
37 T3 **Lyons** Colorado, C USA
23 V6 **Lyons** Georgia, SE USA
26 M5 **Lyons** Kansas, C USA
29 R14 **Lyons** Nebraska, C USA
18 G10 **Lyons** New York, NE USA
Lyons see Lyon
118 O13 **Lyozna** Rus. Liozno. Vitsyebskaya Voblasts', NE Belarus
117 S4 **Lypova Dolyna** Sums'ka Oblast', NE Ukraine
117 N6 **Lypovets'** Rus. Lipovets. Vinnyts'ka Oblast', C Ukraine
Lys see Leie
111 I18 **Lysá Hora** ▲ E Czech Republic
95 D16 **Lysefjorden** fjord S Norway
95 I18 **Lysekil** Västra Götaland, S Sweden
Lýsi see Akdoğan
33 V14 **Lysite** Wyoming, C USA
127 P3 **Lyskovo** Nizhegorodskaya Oblast', W Russian Federation
108 D8 **Lyss** Bern, W Switzerland
95 H22 **Lystrup** Århus, C Denmark
125 V14 **Lys'va** Permskaya Oblast', NW Russian Federation
117 P6 **Lysyanka** Cherkas'ka Oblast', C Ukraine
117 X6 **Lysychans'k** Rus. Lisichansk. Luhans'ka Oblast', E Ukraine
97 K17 **Lytham St Anne's** NW England, UK
185 I19 **Lyttelton** Canterbury, South Island, NZ
10 M17 **Lytton** British Columbia, SW Canada
119 L18 **Lyuban'** Rus. Lyuban'. Minskaya Voblasts', S Belarus
119 L18 **Lyubanskaye Vodaskhovishcha** ▣ C Belarus
116 M5 **Lyubar** Zhytomyrs'ka Oblast', N Ukraine
Lyubashëvka see Lyubashivka
117 O8 **Lyubashivka** Rus. Lyubashëvka. Odes'ka Oblast', SW Ukraine
119 I16 **Lyubcha** Pol. Lubcz, Rus. Lyubcha. Hrodzyenskaya Voblasts', W Belarus
126 L4 **Lyubertsy** Moskovskaya Oblast', W Russian Federation
116 K2 **Lyubeshiv** Volyns'ka Oblast', NW Ukraine
124 M14 **Lyubim** Yaroslavskaya Oblast', NW Russian Federation
114 K11 **Lyubimets** Khaskovo, S Bulgaria
Lyublin see Lublin
116 I3 **Lyuboml'** Pol. Luboml. Volyns'ka Oblast', NW Ukraine
Lyubotin see Lyubotyn
117 U5 **Lyubotyn** Rus. Lyubotin. Kharkivs'ka Oblast', E Ukraine
126 I5 **Lyudinovo** Kaluzhskaya Oblast', W Russian Federation
127 T2 **Lyuk** Udmurtskaya Respublika, NW Russian Federation
114 M9 **Lyulyakovo** prev. Keremitlik. Burgas, E Bulgaria
119 I18 **Lyusina** Rus. Lyusino. Brestskaya Voblasts', SW Belarus
Lyusino see Lyusina

M

138 G9 **Ma'ād** Irbid, N Jordan
Ma'ai see Luqu
Maalahti see Malax
Maale see Male'
138 G13 **Ma'ān** Ma'ān, SW Jordan
138 H13 **Ma'ān** off. Muḩāfaẓat Ma'ān, var. Ma'an, Ma'ān. ◈ governorate S Jordan
93 M16 **Maaninka** Itä-Suomi, C Finland
162 K7 **Maanĭt** Bulgan, C Mongolia
162 M8 **Maanĭt** Töv, C Mongolia
93 N15 **Maanselkä** Oulu, C Finland
161 Q8 **Ma'anshan** Anhui, E China
188 F16 **Maap** island Caroline Islands, W Micronesia
118 H3 **Maardu** Ger. Maart. Harjumaa, NW Estonia
Ma'aret-en-Nu'man see Ma'arrat an Nu'mān
99 K16 **Maarheeze** Noord-Brabant, SE Netherlands
Maarianhamina see Mariehamn
138 I4 **Ma'arrat an Nu'mān** var. Ma'aret-en-Nu'man, Fr. Maarret enn Naamâne. Idlib, NW Syria
Maarret enn Naamâne see Ma'arrat an Nu'mān
98 I11 **Maarssen** Utrecht, C Netherlands
Maart see Maardu
99 L17 **Maas** Fr. Meuse. ≈ W Europe **see also** Meuse
99 M15 **Maasbree** Limburg, SE Netherlands
99 L17 **Maaseik** prev. Maeseyck. Limburg, NE Belgium
171 Q6 **Maasin** Leyte, C Philippines
99 L17 **Maasmechelen** Limburg, NE Belgium
98 G12 **Maassluis** Zuid-Holland, SW Netherlands
99 L18 **Maastricht** var. Maestricht; anc. Traietum ad Mosam, Traiectum Tungorum. Limburg, SE Netherlands
183 N18 **Maatsuyker Group** island group Tasmania, SE Australia
Maba see Qujiang
83 L20 **Mabalane** Gaza, S Mozambique
25 V7 **Mabank** Texas, SW USA
97 O18 **Mablethorpe** E England, UK
171 V12 **Maboi** Papua, E Indonesia
83 M19 **Mabote** Inhambane, S Mozambique
32 J10 **Mabton** Washington, NW USA
Mabuchi-gawa see Mabechi-gawa
83 H20 **Mabutsane** Southern, S Botswana
63 G19 **Macá, Cerro** ▲ S Chile
60 Q9 **Macaé** Rio de Janeiro, SE Brazil
82 N13 **Macaloge** Niassa, N Mozambique
Macan see Bonerate, Kepulauan
161 N15 **Macao** Chin. Aomen, Port. Macau. S China
104 H9 **Mação** Santarém, C Portugal
58 J11 **Macapá** state capital Amapá, N Brazil
43 S17 **Macaracas** Los Santos, S Panama
55 P6 **Macare, Caño** ≈ NE Venezuela
55 Q6 **Macareo, Caño** ≈ NE Venezuela
Macarsca see Makarska
MacArthur see Ormoc
182 L12 **Macarthur** Victoria, SE Australia
56 C7 **Macas** Morona Santiago, SE Ecuador
Macassar see Makassar
59 Q14 **Macau** Rio Grande do Norte, E Brazil
Macau see Macao
Macău see Makó, Hungary
65 E24 **Macbride Head** headland East Falkland, Falkland Islands
23 V9 **Macclenny** Florida, SE USA
97 L18 **Macclesfield** C England, UK
192 F6 **Macclesfield Bank** undersea feature N South China Sea
MacCluer Gulf see Berau, Teluk
181 N7 **Macdonald, Lake** salt lake Western Australia
181 Q7 **Macdonnell Ranges** ⛰ Northern Territory, C Australia
96 K8 **Macduff** NE Scotland, UK
104 I6 **Macedo de Cavaleiros** Bragança, N Portugal
Macedonia Central see Kentrikí Makedonía
Macedonia East and Thrace see Anatolikí Makedonía kai Thráki
113 O19 **Macedonia, FYR** off. the Former Yugoslav Republic of Macedonia, var. Macedonia, Mac. Makedonija, abbrev. FYR Macedonia, FYROM. ◆ republic SE Europe
Macedonia West see Dytikí Makedonía
59 Q16 **Maceió** state capital Alagoas, E Brazil
76 K15 **Macenta** Guinée-Forestière, SE Guinea
106 J12 **Macerata** Marche, C Italy
11 S11 **MacFarlane** ≈ Saskatchewan, C Canada
182 H7 **Macfarlane, Lake** var. Lake Mcfarlane. ◎ South Australia
Macgillicuddy's Reeks Mountains see Macgillycuddy's Reeks
97 B21 **Macgillycuddy's Reeks** var. Macgillicuddy's Reeks Mountains, Ir. Na Cruacha Dubha. ⛰ SW Ireland
11 X16 **MacGregor** Manitoba, S Canada
149 O10 **Mach** Baluchistān, SW Pakistan
56 C6 **Machachi** Pichincha, C Ecuador
83 M19 **Machaila** Gaza, S Mozambique
Machaire Fíolta see Magherafelt
Machaire Rátha see Maghera
81 I19 **Machakos** Eastern, S Kenya
56 B8 **Machala** El Oro, SW Ecuador
Machali see Madoi
83 J19 **Machaneng** Central, SE Botswana
83 M18 **Machanga** Sofala, E Mozambique
80 G13 **Machar Marshes** wetland SE Sudan
102 I8 **Machecoul** Loire-Atlantique, NW France
161 O8 **Macheng** Hubei, C China
155 J16 **Mācherla** Andhra Pradesh, C India
153 O11 **Machhapuchhre** ▲ C Nepal
19 T6 **Machias** Maine, NE USA
19 R3 **Machias River** ≈ Maine, NE USA
19 T6 **Machias River** ≈ Maine, NE USA
64 P5 **Machico** Madeira, Portugal, NE Atlantic Ocean
155 K16 **Machilīpatnam** var. Bandar Masulipatnam. Andhra Pradesh, E India
54 G5 **Machiques** Zulia, NW Venezuela
57 G15 **Machupicchu** Cusco, C Peru
83 M20 **Macia** var. Vila de Macia. Gaza, S Mozambique
Macías Nguema Biyogo see Bioco, Isla de
116 M13 **Măcin** Tulcea, SE Romania
183 T4 **Macintyre River** ≈ New South Wales/Queensland, SE Australia
181 Y7 **Mackay** Queensland, NE Australia
181 O7 **Mackay, Lake** salt lake Northern Territory/Western Australia
10 M13 **Mackenzie** British Columbia, W Canada
8 I9 **Mackenzie** ≈ Northwest Territories, NW Canada
195 Y6 **Mackenzie Bay** bay Antarctica
10 J1 **Mackenzie Bay** bay NW Canada
8 K3 **Mackenzie King Island** island Queen Elizabeth Islands, Northwest Territories, N Canada
8 H8 **Mackenzie Mountains** ⛰ Northwest Territories, NW Canada
31 Q5 **Mackinac, Straits of** ◎ Michigan, N USA
194 K5 **Mackintosh, Cape** headland Antarctica
11 R15 **Macklin** Saskatchewan, S Canada
183 V6 **Macksville** New South Wales, SE Australia
183 V5 **Maclean** New South Wales, SE Australia
83 J24 **Maclear** Eastern Cape, SE South Africa
183 U6 **Macleay River** ≈ New South Wales, SE Australia
MacLeod see Fort Macleod
180 G9 **Macleod, Lake** ◎ Western Australia
10 I6 **Macmillan** ≈ Yukon Territory, NW Canada
30 J12 **Macomb** Illinois, N USA
107 B18 **Macomer** Sardegna, Italy, C Mediterranean Sea
82 Q13 **Macomia** Cabo Delgado, NE Mozambique
23 T5 **Macon** Georgia, SE USA
23 N4 **Macon** Mississippi, S USA
27 U3 **Macon** Missouri, C USA
103 R10 **Mâcon** anc. Matisco, Matisco Ædourum. Saône-et-Loire, C France
22 J6 **Macon, Bayou** ≈ Arkansas/Louisiana, S USA
82 G13 **Macondo** Moxico, E Angola
83 M16 **Macossa** Manica, C Mozambique
11 T12 **Macoun Lake** ◎ Saskatchewan, C Canada
30 K14 **Macoupin Creek** ≈ Illinois, N USA
Macouria see Tonate
83 N18 **Macovane** Inhambane, SE Mozambique
183 N17 **Macquarie Harbour** inlet Tasmania, SE Australia
192 J13 **Macquarie Island** island NZ, SW Pacific Ocean
183 T8 **Macquarie, Lake** lagoon New South Wales, SE Australia
183 Q6 **Macquarie Marshes** wetland New South Wales, SE Australia
192 K13 **Macquarie Ridge** undersea feature SW Pacific Ocean
183 Q6 **Macquarie River** ≈ New South Wales, SE Australia
183 P17 **Macquarie River** ≈ Tasmania, SE Australia
195 V5 **Mac. Robertson Land** physical region Antarctica
97 C21 **Macroom** Ir. Maigh Chromtha. SW Ireland
42 G5 **Macuelizo** Santa Bárbara, NW Honduras
182 G2 **Macumba River** ≈ South Australia
57 I16 **Macusani** Puno, S Peru
56 E8 **Macusari, Río** ≈ N Peru
41 U15 **Macuspana** Tabasco, SE Mexico
138 G10 **Ma'dabā** var. Mādabā, Madeba; anc. Medeba. 'Al Āşimah, NW Jordan
172 G2 **Madagascar** off. Democratic Republic of Madagascar, Malg. Madagasikara; prev. Malagasy Republic. ◆ republic W Indian Ocean
172 I5 **Madagascar** island W Indian Ocean
173 O9 **Madagascar Basin** undersea feature W Indian Ocean
172 M10 **Madagascar Plateau** var. Madagascar Ridge, Madagascar Rise, Rus. Madagaskarskiy Khrebet. undersea feature W Indian Ocean
Madagascar Ridge/Madagascar Rise see Madagascar Plateau
Madagasikara see Madagascar
Madagaskarskiy Khrebet see Madagascar Plateau
64 N2 **Madalena** Pico, Azores, Portugal, NE Atlantic Ocean
77 Y6 **Madama** Agadez, NE Niger
114 J12 **Madan** Smolyan, S Bulgaria
155 I19 **Madanapalle** Andhra Pradesh, E India
186 D7 **Madang** Madang, N PNG
186 C6 **Madang** ◈ province N PNG
146 G7 **Madaniyat** Rus. Madeniyet. Qoraqalpog'iston Respublikasi, W Uzbekistan
Madanīyīn see Médenine
77 U11 **Madaoua** Tahoua, SW Niger
Madaras see Vtáčnik
153 U15 **Madaripur** Dhaka, C Bangladesh
77 U12 **Madarounfa** Maradi, S Niger
Madarska see Hungary
Madau see Madaw
186 H9 **Madau Island** island SE PNG
146 B13 **Madaw** Rus. Madau. Balkan Welaýaty, W Turkmenistan
19 S1 **Madawaska** Maine, NE USA
14 J13 **Madawaska** ≈ Ontario, SE Canada
Madawaska Highlands see Haliburton Highlands
166 M4 **Madaya** Mandalay, C Burma
107 K17 **Maddaloni** Campania, S Italy
29 O3 **Maddock** North Dakota, N USA
99 I14 **Made** Noord-Brabant, S Netherlands
Madeba see Ma'dabā
64 L9 **Madeira** var. Ilha de Madeira. island Madeira, Portugal, NE Atlantic Ocean
Madeira, Ilha de see Madeira
64 O5 **Madeira Islands** Port. Região Autoónoma da Madeira. ◈ autonomous region Madeira, Portugal, NE Atlantic Ocean
64 L9 **Madeira Plain** undersea feature E Atlantic Ocean
64 L9 **Madeira Ridge** undersea feature E Atlantic Ocean
59 F14 **Madeira, Rio** Sp. Río Madera. ≈ Bolivia/Brazil **see also** Madera, Río
101 J25 **Mädelegabel** ▲ Austria/Germany
15 X6 **Madeleine** ≈ Québec, SE Canada
15 X5 **Madeleine, Cap de la** headland Québec, SE Canada
13 Q13 **Madeleine, Îles de la** Eng. Magdalen Islands. island group Québec, E Canada
29 U10 **Madelia** Minnesota, N USA
35 P3 **Madeline** California, W USA
30 K3 **Madeline Island** island Apostle Islands, Wisconsin, N USA
137 O15 **Maden** Elazığ, SE Turkey
145 V12 **Madeniyet** Vostochnyy Kazakhstan, E Kazakhstan
Madeniyet see Madaniyat
40 H5 **Madera** Chihuahua, N Mexico
35 Q10 **Madera** California, W USA
56 L13 **Madera, Río** Port. Rio Madeira. ≈ Bolivia/Brazil **see also** Madeira, Rio
106 D6 **Madesimo** Lombardia, N Italy
141 O14 **Madhāb, Wādī** dry watercourse NW Yemen
153 R13 **Madhepura** prev. Madhipure. Bihār, NE India
Madhipure see Madhepura
153 Q13 **Madhubani** Bihār, N India
153 Q15 **Madhupur** Jhārkhand, NE India
154 I10 **Madhya Pradesh** prev. Central Provinces and Berar. ◈ state C India
57 K15 **Madidi, Río** ≈ W Bolivia
155 F20 **Madikeri** prev. Mercara. Karnātaka, W India
27 O13 **Madill** Oklahoma, C USA
79 G21 **Madimba** Bas-Congo, SW Dem. Rep. Congo
138 M4 **Ma'dīn** Ar Raqqah, C Syria
Madīnah, Minţaqat al see Al Madīnah
76 M14 **Madinani** NW Ivory Coast
141 O17 **Madīnat ash Sha'b** prev. Al Ittiḩād. SW Yemen
138 K3 **Madīnat ath Thawrah** var. Ath Thawrah. Ar Raqqah, N Syria Asia
173 O6 **Madingley Rise** undersea feature W Indian Ocean
79 E21 **Madingo-Kayes** Le Kouilou, S Congo
79 F21 **Madingou** La Bouenza, S Congo
Madioen see Madiun
23 U8 **Madison** Florida, SE USA
23 T3 **Madison** Georgia, SE USA
31 P15 **Madison** Indiana, N USA
27 P6 **Madison** Kansas, C USA
19 Q6 **Madison** Maine, NE USA
29 S9 **Madison** Minnesota, N USA
22 K5 **Madison** Mississippi, S USA
29 Q14 **Madison** Nebraska, C USA
29 R10 **Madison** South Dakota, N USA
21 V5 **Madison** Virginia, NE USA
21 Q5 **Madison** West Virginia, NE USA
30 L9 **Madison** state capital Wisconsin, N USA
21 T6 **Madison Heights** Virginia, NE USA
20 I6 **Madisonville** Kentucky, S USA
20 M10 **Madisonville** Tennessee, S USA
25 V9 **Madisonville** Texas, SW USA
169 R16 **Madiun** prev. Madioen. Jawa, C Indonesia
Madjene see Majene
14 J14 **Madoc** Ontario, SE Canada
Madoera see Madura, Pulau
81 J18 **Mado Gashi** North Eastern, E Kenya
159 R11 **Madoi** var. Machali. Qinghai, C China
189 O13 **Madolenihmw** Pohnpei, E Micronesia
118 I9 **Madona** Ger. Modohn. Madona, E Latvia
107 J23 **Madonie** ⛰ Sicilia, Italy, C Mediterranean Sea
141 Y11 **Madrakah, Ra's** headland E Oman
32 I12 **Madras** Oregon, NW USA
Madras see Chennai
57 H14 **Madre de Dios** off. Departamento de Madre de Dios. ◈ department E Peru
63 F22 **Madre de Dios, Isla** island S Chile
57 J14 **Madre de Dios, Río** ≈ Bolivia/Peru
25 T16 **Madre, Laguna** ◎ Texas, SW USA
41 Q9 **Madre, Laguna** lagoon NE Mexico
37 Q12 **Madre Mount** ▲ New Mexico, SW USA
105 N8 **Madrid** ● (Spain) Madrid, C Spain
29 V14 **Madrid** Iowa, C USA
105 N7 **Madrid** ◈ autonomous community C Spain
105 N10 **Madridejos** Castilla-La Mancha, C Spain
104 L7 **Madrigal de las Altas Torres** Castilla-León, N Spain
104 K10 **Madrigalejo** Extremadura, W Spain
34 L3 **Mad River** ≈ California, W USA
42 J8 **Madriz** ◈ department NW Nicaragua
104 K10 **Madroñera** Extremadura, W Spain
181 N12 **Madura** Western Australia
Madura see Madurai
155 H22 **Madurai** prev. Madura, Mathurai. Tamil Nādu, S India
169 S16 **Madura, Pulau** prev. Madoera. island C Indonesia
169 S16 **Madura, Selat** strait C Indonesia

◆ Country ● Country Capital ◇ Dependent Territory ○ Dependent Territory Capital ◈ Administrative Region ✕ International Airport ▲ Mountain ⛰ Mountain Range Volcano ≈ River ◎ Lake ▣ Reservoir

127 Q17 **Madzhalis** Respublika Dagestan, SW Russian Federation
114 K12 **Madzharovo** Khaskovo, S Bulgaria
83 M14 **Madzimoyo** Eastern, E Zambia
165 O12 **Maebashi** var. Maebasi, Mayebashi. Gunma, Honshū, S Japan
Maebasi see Maebashi
167 O6 **Mae Chan** Chiang Rai, NW Thailand
167 N7 **Mae Hong Son** var. Maehongson, Muai To. Mae Hong Son, NW Thailand
Mae Nam Khong see Mekong
167 Q7 **Mae Nam Nan** ≈ NW Thailand
167 O10 **Mae Nam Tha Chin** ≈ W Thailand
167 P7 **Mae Nam Yom** ≈ W Thailand
37 O3 **Maeser** Utah, W USA
Maeseyck see Maaseik
167 N9 **Mae Sot** var. Ban Mae Sot. Tak, W Thailand
Maestricht see Maastricht
167 O7 **Mae Suai** var. Ban Mae Suai. Chiang Rai, NW Thailand
167 O7 **Mae Tho, Doi** ▲ NW Thailand
172 I4 **Maevatanana** Mahajanga, C Madagascar
187 R13 **Maéwo** prev. Aurora. island C Vanuatu
171 S11 **Mafa** Pulau Halmahera, E Indonesia
83 I23 **Mafeteng** W Lesotho
99 J21 **Maffe** Namur, SE Belgium
183 P12 **Maffra** Victoria, SE Australia
81 K23 **Mafia** island E Tanzania
81 J23 **Mafia Channel** sea waterway E Tanzania
83 I21 **Mafikeng** North-West, N South Africa
60 J12 **Mafra** Santa Catarina, S Brazil
104 F10 **Mafra** Lisboa, C Portugal
143 Q17 **Mafraq** Abū Ẓaby, C UAE
Mafraq/Mafraq, Muḥāfaẓat al see Al Mafraq
123 T10 **Magadan** Magadanskaya Oblast', E Russian Federation
123 T9 **Magadanskaya Oblast'** ◈ province E Russian Federation
108 G11 **Magadino** Ticino, S Switzerland
63 G23 **Magallanes** off. Región de Magallanes y de la Antártica Chilena. ◈ region S Chile
Magallanes see Punta Arenas
Magallanes, Estrecho de see Magellan, Strait of
14 I10 **Maganasipi, Lac** ◎ Québec, SE Canada
54 F6 **Magangué** Bolívar, N Colombia
Magareva see Mangareva
77 V12 **Magaria** Zinder, S Niger
186 F10 **Magarida** Central, SW PNG
171 O2 **Magat** ≈ Luzon, N Philippines
27 T11 **Magazine Mountain** ▲ Arkansas, C USA
76 I15 **Magburaka** C Sierra Leone
123 Q13 **Magdagachi** Amurskaya Oblast', SE Russian Federation
62 O12 **Magdalena** Buenos Aires, E Argentina
57 M15 **Magdalena** Beni, N Bolivia
40 F4 **Magdalena** Sonora, NW Mexico
37 Q13 **Magdalena** New Mexico, SW USA
54 F5 **Magdalena** off. Departamento del Magdalena. ◈ province N Colombia
40 E9 **Magdalena, Bahía** bay W Mexico
63 G19 **Magdalena, Isla** island Archipiélago de los Chonos, S Chile
40 D8 **Magdalena, Isla** island W Mexico
54 F7 **Magdalena, Río** ≈ C Colombia
40 F4 **Magdalena, Río** ≈ NW Mexico
Magdalen Islands see Madeleine, Îles de la
100 L13 **Magdeburg** Sachsen-Anhalt, C Germany
22 L6 **Magee** Mississippi, S USA
169 Q16 **Magelang** Jawa, C Indonesia
192 K7 **Magellan Rise** undersea feature C Pacific Ocean
63 H24 **Magellan, Strait of** Sp. Estrecho de Magallanes. strait Argentina/Chile
106 D7 **Magenta** Lombardia, NW Italy
Magerøy see Magerøya
92 K7 **Magerøya** var. Magerøy, Lapp. Máhkarávju. island N Norway
164 C17 **Mage-shima** island Nansei-shotō, SW Japan
108 G11 **Maggia** Ticino, S Switzerland
108 G10 **Maggia** ≈ SW Switzerland
Maggiore, Lago see Maggiore, Lake
106 C6 **Maggiore, Lake** It. Lago Maggiore. ◎ Italy/Switzerland
44 I12 **Maggotty** W Jamaica
76 I10 **Maghama** Gorgol, S Mauritania
97 F14 **Maghera** Ir. Machaire Rátha. C Northern Ireland, UK
97 F15 **Magherafelt** Ir. Machaire Fíolta. C Northern Ireland, UK
188 H6 **Magicienne Bay** bay Saipan, S Northern Mariana Islands
105 O13 **Magina** ▲ S Spain
81 H24 **Magingo** Ruvuma, S Tanzania
112 H11 **Maglaj** Federacija Bosna I Hercegovina, N Bosnia and Herzegovina
107 Q19 **Maglie** Puglia, SE Italy
36 L2 **Magna** Utah, W USA
Magnesia see Manisa
14 G12 **Magnetawan** ≈ Ontario, S Canada
27 T14 **Magnolia** Arkansas, C USA
22 K7 **Magnolia** Mississippi, S USA
25 V10 **Magnolia** Texas, SW USA
Magnolia State see Mississippi
95 J15 **Magnor** Hedmark, S Norway
187 Y14 **Mago** prev. Mango. island Lau Group, E Fiji
83 L15 **Màgoé** Tete, NW Mozambique
15 Q13 **Magog** Québec, SE Canada
83 J15 **Magoye** Southern, S Zambia
41 Q12 **Magozal** Veracruz-Llave, C Mexico
14 B7 **Magpie** ≈ Ontario, S Canada
11 Q17 **Magrath** Alberta, SW Canada
105 R10 **Magro** ≈ E Spain
76 I9 **Magta' Lahjar** var. Magta Lahjar, Magta' Lahjar, Magtá Lahjar. Brakna, SW Mauritania
83 L20 **Magude** Maputo, S Mozambique
77 Y12 **Magumeri** Borno, NE Nigeria
189 O14 **Magur Islands** island group Caroline Islands, C Micronesia
Magway see Magwe
166 L6 **Magwe** var. Magway. Magwe, W Burma
166 L6 **Magwe** var. Magway. ◈ division C Burma
Magyar-Becse see Bečej
Magyarkanizsa see Kanjiža
Magyarország see Hungary
Magyarzsombor see Zimbor
142 J4 **Mahābād** var. Mehabad; prev. Sāūjbulāgh. Āžarbāyjān-e Bākhtarī, NW Iran
172 H5 **Mahabo** Toliara, W Madagascar
Maha Chai see Samut Sakhon
155 D14 **Mahād** Mahārāshtra, W India
81 N17 **Mahadday Weyne** Shabeellaha Dhexe, C Somalia
79 Q17 **Mahagi** Orientale, NE Dem. Rep. Congo
Mahāil see Muhāyil
172 I4 **Mahajamba** seasonal river NW Madagascar
152 G10 **Mahājan** Rājasthān, NW India
172 I3 **Mahajanga** var. Majunga. Mahajanga, NW Madagascar
172 I3 **Mahajanga** ◈ province W Madagascar
172 I3 **Mahajanga** ✕ Mahajanga, NW Madagascar
169 U10 **Mahakam, Sungai** var. Koetai, Kutai. ≈ Borneo, C Indonesia
83 I19 **Mahalapye** var. Mahalatswe. Central, SE Botswana
Mahalatswe see Mahalapye
Mahalla el Kubra see El Maḥalla el Kubra
171 O13 **Mahalona** Sulawesi, C Indonesia
Mahameru see Semeru, Gunung
143 S11 **Mahān** Kermān, E Iran
154 N12 **Mahānadi** ≈ E India
172 J5 **Mahanoro** Toamasina, E Madagascar
153 P13 **Mahārājganj** Bihār, N India
154 G13 **Mahārāshtra** ◈ state W India
172 I4 **Mahavavy** seasonal river N Madagascar
155 K24 **Mahaweli Ganga** ≈ C Sri Lanka
Mahbés see El Mahbas
155 J15 **Mahbūbābād** Andhra Pradesh, E India
155 H16 **Mahbūbnagar** Andhra Pradesh, C India
140 M8 **Mahd adh Dhahab** Al Madīnah, W Saudi Arabia
55 S9 **Mahdia** C Guyana
75 N6 **Mahdia** var. Al Mahdīyah, Mehdia. NE Tunisia
155 F20 **Mahe** Fr. Mahé; prev. Mayyali. Pondicherry, SW India
172 I16 **Mahé** ✕ Mahé, NE Seychelles
172 H16 **Mahé** island Inner Islands, NE Seychelles
173 Y17 **Mahebourg** SE Mauritius
152 L10 **Mahendranagar** Far Western, W Nepal
81 I23 **Mahenge** Morogoro, SE Tanzania
185 F22 **Maheno** Otago, South Island, NZ
154 D9 **Mahesāna** Gujarāt, W India
154 F11 **Maheshwar** Madhya Pradesh, C India
151 F14 **Mahi** ≈ N India
184 Q10 **Mahia Peninsula** peninsula North Island, NZ
119 O16 **Mahilyow** Rus. Mogilëv. Mahilyowskaya Voblasts', E Belarus
119 M16 **Mahilyowskaya Voblasts'** prev. Rus. Mogilëvskaya Oblast'. ◈ province E Belarus
191 P7 **Mahina** Tahiti, W French Polynesia
185 E23 **Mahinerangi, Lake** ◎ South Island, NZ
Máhkarávju see Magerøya
83 L22 **Mahlabatini** KwaZulu/Natal, E South Africa
166 L5 **Mahlaing** Mandalay, C Burma
109 X8 **Mahldorf** Steiermark, SE Austria
Maḥmūd-e 'Erāqī see Maḥmūd-e Rāqī
149 R4 **Maḥmūd-e Rāqī** var. Mahmūd-e 'Erāqī. Kāpīsā, NE Afghanistan
Mahmudiya see Al Maḥmūdīyah
29 S5 **Mahnomen** Minnesota, N USA
152 K14 **Mahoba** Uttar Pradesh, N India
105 Z9 **Mahón** Cat. Maó, Eng. Port Mahon; anc. Portus Magonis. Menorca, Spain, W Mediterranean Sea
18 D14 **Mahoning Creek Lake** ▦ Pennsylvania, NE USA
105 Q10 **Mahora** Castilla-La Mancha, C Spain
Mähren see Moravia
Mährisch-Budwitz see Moravské Budějovice
Mährisch-Kromau see Moravský Krumlov
Mährisch-Neustadt see Uničov
Mährisch-Schönberg see Šumperk
Mährisch-Trübau see Moravská Třebová
Mährisch-Weisskirchen see Hranice
Māh-Shahr see Bandar-e Māhshahr
79 N19 **Mahulu** Maniema, E Dem. Rep. Congo
154 C12 **Mahuva** Gujarāt, W India
114 N11 **Mahya Dağı** ▲ NW Turkey
105 T6 **Maials** var. Mayals. Cataluña, NE Spain
191 O2 **Maiana** prev. Hall Island. atoll Tungaru, W Kiribati
191 S11 **Maiao** var. Tapuaemanu, Tubuai-Manu. island Îles du Vent, W French Polynesia
54 H4 **Maicao** La Guajira, N Colombia
Mai Ceu/Mai Chio see Maych'ew
103 U8 **Maîche** Doubs, E France
97 N22 **Maidenhead** S England, UK
11 S15 **Maidstone** Saskatchewan, S Canada
97 P22 **Maidstone** SE England, UK
77 Y13 **Maiduguri** Borno, NE Nigeria
108 I8 **Maienfeld** Sankt Gallen, NE Switzerland
116 J12 **Măieruş** Hung. Szászmagyarós. Braşov, C Romania
Maigh Chromtha see Macroom
Maigh Eo see Mayo
55 N9 **Maigualida, Sierra** ⛰ S Venezuela
154 K9 **Maihar** Madhya Pradesh, C India
154 K11 **Maikala Range** ⛰ C India
Mailand see Milano
152 L11 **Mailāni** Uttar Pradesh, N India
149 U10 **Māilsi** Punjab, E Pakistan
147 R8 **Maimak** Talasskaya Oblast', NW Kyrgyzstan
Maimāna see Meymaneh
Maimansingh see Mymensingh
171 V13 **Maimawa** Papua, E Indonesia
Maimuna see Al Maymūnah
101 G18 **Main** ≈ C Germany
115 F22 **Maïna** ancient monument Pelopónnisos, S Greece
115 E20 **Maínalo** ⛰ S Greece
101 L22 **Mainburg** Bayern, SE Germany
Main Camp see Banana
14 E12 **Main Channel** lake channel Ontario, S Canada
79 I20 **Mai-Ndombe, Lac** prev. Lac Léopold II. ◎ W Dem. Rep. Congo
101 K20 **Main-Donau-Kanal** canal SE Germany
19 R6 **Maine** off. State of Maine; also known as Lumber State, Pine Tree State. ◈ state NE USA
102 K6 **Maine** cultural region NW France
102 J7 **Maine-et-Loire** ◈ department NW France
19 Q9 **Maine, Gulf of** gulf NE USA
77 X12 **Maïné-Soroa** Diffa, SE Niger
167 N2 **Maingkwan** var. Mungkawn. Kachin State, N Burma
Mainistir Fhear Maí see Fermoy
Mainistirna Búille see Boyle
Mainistir na Corann see Midleton
Mainistir na Féile see Abbeyfeale
96 J5 **Mainland** island Orkney, N Scotland, UK
96 L2 **Mainland** island Shetland, NE Scotland, UK
159 P16 **Mainling** var. Tungdor. Xizang Zizhiqu, W China
152 K12 **Mainpuri** Uttar Pradesh, N India
103 N5 **Maintenon** Eure-et-Loir, C France
172 H4 **Maintirano** Mahajanga, W Madagascar
93 M15 **Mainua** Oulu, C Finland
101 G18 **Mainz** Fr. Mayence. Rheinland-Pfalz, SW Germany
76 I9 **Maio** var. Vila do Maio. Maio, S Cape Verde
76 E10 **Maio** var. Mayo. island Ilhas de Sotavento, SE Cape Verde
62 G12 **Maipo, Río** ≈ C Chile
62 H12 **Maipo, Volcán** ▲ W Argentina
61 E22 **Maipú** Buenos Aires, E Argentina
62 I11 **Maipú** Mendoza, E Argentina
62 H11 **Maipú** Santiago, C Chile
54 L5 **Maiquetía** Distrito Federal, N Venezuela
108 I10 **Maira** It. Mera. ≈ Italy/Switzerland
106 A9 **Maira** ≈ NW Italy
153 V12 **Mairābari** Assam, NE India
44 K7 **Maisí** Guantánamo, E Cuba
118 H13 **Maišiagala** Vilnius, SE Lithuania
153 V17 **Maiskhal Island** island SE Bangladesh
167 N13 **Mai Sombun** Chumphon, SW Thailand
Maisur see Karnātaka, India
Maisur see Mysore, India
183 T8 **Maitland** New South Wales, SE Australia
182 I9 **Maitland** South Australia
14 F15 **Maitland** ≈ Ontario, S Canada
195 R1 **Maitri** Indian research station Antarctica
159 N15 **Maizhokunggar** Xizang Zizhiqu, W China
43 O10 **Maíz, Islas del** var. Corn Islands. island group SE Nicaragua
164 J12 **Maizuru** Kyōto, Honshū, SW Japan
54 F6 **Majagual** Sucre, N Colombia
41 Z13 **Majahual** Quintana Roo, E Mexico
Mājeej see Mejit Island
171 N13 **Majene** prev. Madjene. Sulawesi, C Indonesia
43 V15 **Majé, Serranía de** ⛰ E Panama
112 I11 **Majevica** ⛰ NE Bosnia and Herzegovina
81 H15 **Majī** Southern, S Ethiopia
141 X7 **Majīs** NW Oman
Majorca see Mallorca
Mājro see Majuro Atoll
Majunga see Mahajanga
189 Y3 **Majuro** ✕ Majuro Atoll, SE Marshall Islands
189 Y2 **Majuro Atoll** var. Mājro. atoll Ratak Chain, SE Marshall Islands
189 X2 **Majuro Lagoon** lagoon Majuro Atoll, SE Marshall Islands
76 H11 **Maka** C Senegal
79 F20 **Makabana** Le Niari, SW Congo
38 D9 **Mākaha** var. Makaha. O'ahu, Hawai'i, USA, C Pacific Ocean
38 B8 **Makahū'ena Point** var. Makahuena Point. headland Kaua'i, Hawai'i, USA, C Pacific Ocean
38 D9 **Makakilo City** O'ahu, Hawai'i, USA, C Pacific Ocean
83 H18 **Makalamabedi** Central, C Botswana
Makale see Mek'elē
158 K17 **Makalu** Chin. Makaru Shan. ▲ China/Nepal
81 G23 **Makampi** Mbeya, S Tanzania
145 X12 **Makanchi** Kaz. Maqanshy. Vostochnyy Kazakhstan, E Kazakhstan
42 M8 **Makantaka** Región Autónoma Atlántico Norte, NE Nicaragua
190 B16 **Makapu Point** headland W Niue
185 C24 **Makarewa** Southland, South Island, NZ
117 O4 **Makariv** Kyyivs'ka Oblast', N Ukraine
185 D20 **Makarora** ≈ South Island, NZ
123 T13 **Makarov** Ostrov Sakhalin, Sakhalinskaya Oblast', SE Russian Federation
197 R9 **Makarov Basin** undersea feature Arctic Ocean
192 I5 **Makarov Seamount** undersea feature W Pacific Ocean
113 F15 **Makarska** It. Macarsca. Split-Dalmacija, SE Croatia
Makaru Shan see Makalu
125 O15 **Makar'yev** Kostromskaya Oblast', NW Russian Federation
82 L11 **Makasa** Northern, NE Zambia
Makasar, Selat see Makassar Straits
170 M14 **Makassar** var. Macassar, Makasar; prev. Ujungpandang. Sulawesi, C Indonesia
192 F7 **Makassar Straits** Ind. Selat Makasar. strait C Indonesia
144 G12 **Makat** Kaz. Maqat. Atyrau, SW Kazakhstan
191 T10 **Makatea** island Îles Tuamotu, C French Polynesia
139 U7 **Makātū** E Iraq
172 H6 **Makay** var. Massif du Makay. ⛰ SW Madagascar
114 J12 **Makaza** pass Bulgaria/Greece
Makedonija see Macedonia, FYR
190 B16 **Makefu** W Niue
191 V10 **Makemo** atoll Îles Tuamotu, C French Polynesia
76 I15 **Makeni** C Sierra Leone
Makenzen see Orlyak
Makeyevka see Makiyivka
127 Q16 **Makhachkala** prev. Petrovsk-Port. Respublika Dagestan, SW Russian Federation
144 F11 **Makhambet** Atyrau, W Kazakhstan
Makharadze see Ozurget'i
139 W13 **Makhfar Al Buşayyah** S Iraq
139 R4 **Makhmūr** N Iraq
138 I11 **Makhrūq, Wadi al** dry watercourse E Jordan
139 R4 **Makḥūl, Jabal** ⛰ C Iraq
141 R13 **Makhyah, Wādī** dry watercourse N Yemen
171 V13 **Maki** Papua, E Indonesia
185 G21 **Makikihi** Canterbury, South Island, NZ
191 O2 **Makin** prev. Pitt Island. atoll Tungaru, W Kiribati
81 I20 **Makindu** Eastern, S Kenya
145 Q8 **Makinsk** Akmola, N Kazakhstan
187 N10 **Makira** off. Makira Province. ◈ province SE Solomon Islands
Makira see San Cristobal
117 X8 **Makiyivka** Rus. Makeyevka; prev. Dmitriyevsk. Donets'ka Oblast', E Ukraine
140 L10 **Makkah** Eng. Mecca. Makkah, W Saudi Arabia
140 M10 **Makkah** var. Minṭaqat Makkah. ◈ province W Saudi Arabia
13 R7 **Makkovik** Newfoundland and Labrador, NE Canada
98 K6 **Makkum** Friesland, N Netherlands
Mako see Makung
111 M25 **Makó** Rom. Macău. Csongrád, SE Hungary
14 G9 **Makobe Lake** ◎ Ontario, S Canada
79 F18 **Makokou** Ogooué-Ivindo, NE Gabon
81 G23 **Makongolosi** Mbeya, S Tanzania
81 E19 **Makota** SW Uganda
79 G18 **Makoua** Cuvette, C Congo
110 M10 **Maków Mazowiecki** Mazowieckie, C Poland
111 K17 **Maków Podhalański** Małopolskie, S Poland
143 V14 **Makran** cultural region Iran/Pakistan
152 G12 **Makrāna** Rājasthān, N India
143 U15 **Makran Coast** coastal region SE Iran
119 F20 **Makrany** Rus. Mokrany. Brestskaya Voblasts', SW Belarus
Makrinoros see Makrynóros
115 H20 **Makrónisosi** island Kykládes, Greece, Aegean Sea
115 D17 **Makrynóros** var. Makrinoros. ⛰ C Greece
115 G19 **Makryplági** ▲ C Greece
Maksamaa see Maxmo
124 J15 **Maksatikha** var. Maksatha, Maksaticha. Tverskaya Oblast', W Russian Federation
154 G10 **Maksi** Madhya Pradesh, C India
142 I1 **Mākū** Āžarbāyjān-e Bākhtarī, NW Iran
153 Y11 **Mākum** Assam, NE India
Makun see Makung
161 R14 **Makung** prev. Mako, Makun. W Taiwan
164 B16 **Makurazaki** Kagoshima, Kyūshū, SW Japan
77 V15 **Makurdi** Benue, C Nigeria
38 L17 **Makushin Volcano** ♨ Unalaska Island, Alaska, USA
83 K16 **Makwiro** Mashonaland West, N Zimbabwe
57 D15 **Mala** Lima, W Peru
Mala see Mallow, Ireland
Mala see Malaita, Solomon Islands
93 I14 **Malå** Västerbotten, N Sweden
190 G12 **Mala'atoli** Île Uvea, E Wallis and Futuna
171 P8 **Malabang** E Mindanao, S Philippines
155 E21 **Malabār Coast** coast SW India
79 C16 **Malabo** prev. Santa Isabel. ● (Equatorial Guinea) Isla de Bioco, NW Equatorial Guinea
79 C16 **Malabo** ✕ Isla de Bioco, N Equatorial Guinea
Malaca see Málaga
Malacca see Melaka
168 I7 **Malacca, Strait of** Ind. Selat Malaka. strait Indonesia/Malaysia
Malacka see Malacky
111 G20 **Malacky** Hung. Malacka. Bratislavský Kraj, W Slovakia
33 R16 **Malad City** Idaho, NW USA
117 Q4 **Mala Divytsya** Chernihivs'ka Oblast', N Ukraine
119 J15 **Maladzyechna** Pol. Molodeczno, Rus. Molodechno. Minskaya Voblasts', C Belarus
190 D12 **Malaee** Île Futuna, N Wallis and Futuna
37 V15 **Malaga** New Mexico, SW USA
54 G8 **Málaga** Santander, C Colombia
104 M15 **Málaga** anc. Malaca. Andalucía, S Spain
104 L15 **Málaga** ◈ province Andalucía, S Spain
104 M15 **Málaga** ✕ Andalucía, S Spain
Malagasy Republic see Madagascar
105 N10 **Malagón** Castilla-La Mancha, C Spain
97 G18 **Malahide** Ir. Mullach Íde. E Ireland
187 N9 **Malaita** off. Malaita Province. ◈ province N Solomon Islands
187 N8 **Malaita** var. Mala. island N Solomon Islands
80 F13 **Malakal** Upper Nile, S Sudan
112 C10 **Mala Kapela** ⛰ NW Croatia
25 V7 **Malakoff** Texas, SW USA
Malakula see Malekula
149 V7 **Malakwāl** var. Mālikwāla. Punjab, E Pakistan
186 E7 **Malalamai** Madang, W PNG
GG Q11 **Malamala** Sulawesi, C Indonesia
169 S17 **Malang** Jawa, C Indonesia
83 O14 **Malanga** Niassa, N Mozambique
Malange see Malanje
92 I9 **Malangen** sound N Norway
82 C11 **Malanje** var. Malange. Malanje, NW Angola
82 C11 **Malanje** var. Malange. ◈ province N Angola
148 M16 **Malān, Rās** headland SW Pakistan
77 S13 **Malanville** NE Benin
Malapane see Ozimek
155 F21 **Malappuram** Kerala, SW India
43 T17 **Mala, Punta** headland S Panama
95 N16 **Mälaren** ◎ C Sweden
62 H13 **Malargüe** Mendoza, W Argentina
14 J8 **Malartic** Québec, SE Canada
119 F20 **Malaryta** Pol. Maloryta, Rus. Malorita. Brestskaya Voblasts', SW Belarus
63 J19 **Malaspina** Chubut, SE Argentina
39 U12 **Malaspina Glacier** glacier Alaska, USA
137 N15 **Malatya** anc. Melitene. Malatya, SE Turkey
136 M14 **Malatya** ◈ province C Turkey
117 Q7 **Mala Vyska** Rus. Malaya Viska. Kirovohrads'ka Oblast', S Ukraine
83 M14 **Malawi** off. Republic of Malawi; prev. Nyasaland, Nyasaland Protectorate. ◆ republic S Africa
Malawi, Lake see Nyasa, Lake
93 J17 **Malax** Fin. Maalahti. Länsi-Suomi, W Finland
124 H14 **Malaya Vishera** Novgorodskaya Oblast', W Russian Federation
Malaya Viska see Mala Vyska
171 Q7 **Malaybalay** Mindanao, S Philippines
142 L6 **Malāyer** prev. Daulatabad. Hamadān, W Iran
168 J7 **Malay Peninsula** peninsula Malaysia/Thailand
168 L7 **Malaysia** var. Federation of Malaysia; prev. the separate territories of Federation of Malaya, Sarawak and Sabah (North Borneo) and Singapore. ◆ monarchy SE Asia
137 R14 **Malazgirt** Muş, E Turkey
15 R8 **Malbaie** ≈ Québec, SE Canada
77 T12 **Malbaza** Tahoua, S Niger
110 J7 **Malbork** Ger. Marienburg, Marienburg in Westpreussen. Pomorskie, N Poland
100 N9 **Malchin** Mecklenburg-Vorpommern, N Germany
100 M9 **Malchiner See** ◎ NE Germany
99 D16 **Maldegem** Oost-Vlaanderen, NW Belgium
98 L13 **Malden** Gelderland, SE Netherlands
19 O11 **Malden** Massachusetts, NE USA
27 Y8 **Malden** Missouri, C USA
191 X4 **Malden Island** prev. Independence Island. atoll E Kiribati
173 Q6 **Maldives** off. Maldivian Divehi, Republic of Maldives. ◆ republic N Indian Ocean
Maldivian Divehi see Maldives
97 P21 **Maldon** E England, UK
61 G20 **Maldonado** Maldonado, S Uruguay
61 G20 **Maldonado** ◈ department S Uruguay
41 P17 **Maldonado, Punta** headland S Mexico
151 K19 **Male'** Div. Maale ● (Maldives) Male' Atoll, C Maldives
106 G6 **Malè** Trentino-Alto Adige, N Italy
76 K13 **Maléa** var. Maléya. Haute-Guinée, NE Guinea
115 G22 **Maléas, Akrotírio** headland S Greece
115 L17 **Maléas, Akrotírio** headland Lésvos, E Greece
151 K19 **Male' Atoll** var. Kaafu Atoll. atoll C Maldives
Malebo, Pool see Stanley Pool
154 E12 **Mālegaon** Mahārāshtra, W India
81 F15 **Malek** Jonglei, S Sudan
187 Q13 **Malekula** var. Malakula; prev. Mallicolo. island W Vanuatu
189 Y15 **Malem** Kosrae, E Micronesia
83 O15 **Malema** Nampula, N Mozambique
79 N23 **Malemba-Nkulu** Katanga, SE Dem. Rep. Congo
124 K9 **Malen'ga** Respublika Kareliya, NW Russian Federation
95 M20 **Målerås** Kalmar, S Sweden
103 O6 **Malesherbes** Loiret, C France
115 G18 **Malesína** Stereá Ellás, E Greece
Maléya see Maléa
127 O15 **Malgobek** Chechenskaya Respublika, SW Russian Federation
105 X5 **Malgrat de Mar** Cataluña, NE Spain
80 C9 **Malha** Northern Darfur, W Sudan
139 Q5 **Malḥāt** C Iraq
32 K14 **Malheur Lake** ◎ Oregon, NW USA
32 L14 **Malheur River** ≈ Oregon, NW USA
76 I13 **Mali** Moyenne-Guinée, NW Guinea
77 O9 **Mali** off. Republic of Mali, Fr. République du Mali; prev. French Sudan, Sudanese Republic. ◆ republic W Africa
171 Q16 **Maliana** W East Timor
167 O2 **Mali Hka** ≈ N Burma
Mali Idjoš see Mali Iđoš
112 K8 **Mali Iđoš** var. Mali Idjoš, Hung. Kishegyes; prev. Krivaja. Serbia, N Serbia and Montenegro (Yugo.)
112 K9 **Mali Kanal** canal N Serbia and Montenegro (Yugo.)
171 P12 **Maliku** Sulawesi, N Indonesia
Malik, Wadi al see Milk, Wadi el
Mālikwāla see Malakwāl
167 N11 **Mali Kyun** var. Tavoy Island. island Mergui Archipelago, S Burma
95 M19 **Målilla** Kalmar, S Sweden
112 B11 **Mali Lošinj** It. Lussinpiccolo. Primorje-Gorski Kotar, W Croatia
Malin see Malyn
171 P7 **Malindang, Mount** ▲ Mindanao, S Philippines
81 K20 **Malindi** Coast, SE Kenya
Malines see Mechelen
96 E13 **Malin Head** Ir. Cionn Mhálanna. headland NW Ireland
171 O11 **Malino, Gunung** ▲ Sulawesi, N Indonesia
113 M21 **Maliq** var. Maliqi. Korçë, SE Albania
Maliqi see Maliq
171 Q8 **Malita** Mindanao, S Philippines
154 G12 **Malkāpur** Mahārāshtra, C India
136 B10 **Malkara** Tekirdağ, NW Turkey
119 J19 **Mal'kavichy** Rus. Mal'kovichi. Brestskaya Voblasts', SW Belarus
Malkiye see Al Mālikīyah
114 L11 **Malko Sharkovo, Yazovir** ▦ SE Bulgaria
114 N11 **Malko Tŭrnovo** Burgas, E Bulgaria
Mal'kovichi see Mal'kavichy

183 R12 **Mallacoota** Victoria, SE Australia
96 G10 **Mallaig** N Scotland, UK
182 I9 **Mallala** South Australia
75 W9 **Mallawi** C Egypt
105 R5 **Mallén** Aragón, NE Spain
106 F5 **Malles Venosta** Ger. Mals im Vinschgau. Trentino-Alto Adige, N Italy
Mallicolo see Malekula
109 Q8 **Mallnitz** Salzburg, S Austria
105 W9 **Mallorca** Eng. Majorca; anc. Baleares Major. island Islas Baleares, Spain, W Mediterranean Sea
97 C20 **Mallow** Ir. Mala. SW Ireland
93 E15 **Malm** Nord-Trøndelag, C Norway
95 L19 **Malmbäck** Jönköping, S Sweden
92 J12 **Malmberget** Lapp. Malmivaara. Norrbotten, N Sweden
99 M20 **Malmédy** Liège, E Belgium
83 E25 **Malmesbury** Western Cape, SW South Africa
Malmivaara see Malmberget
95 N16 **Malmköping** Södermanland, C Sweden
95 K23 **Malmö** Skåne, S Sweden
95 K23 **Malmo** × Skåne, S Sweden
45 Q16 **Malmok** headland Bonaire, S Netherlands Antilles
95 M18 **Malmslätt** Östergötland, S Sweden
125 R16 **Malmyzh** Kirovskaya Oblast', NW Russian Federation
187 Q13 **Malo** island W Vanuatu
126 J7 **Maloarkhangel'sk** Orlovskaya Oblast', W Russian Federation
Maļoeļap see Maloelap Atoll
189 V6 **Maloelap Atoll** var. Maļoeļap. atoll E Marshall Islands
Maloenda see Malunda
108 I10 **Maloja** Graubünden, S Switzerland
82 L12 **Malole** Northern, NE Zambia
171 O3 **Malolos** Luzon, N Philippines
18 K6 **Malone** New York, NE USA
79 K25 **Malonga** Katanga, S Dem. Rep. Congo
111 L15 **Małopolska** plateau S Poland
111 K17 **Małopolskie** ◆ province S Poland
Malorita/Maloryta see Malaryta
124 K9 **Maloshuyka** Arkhangel'skaya Oblast', NW Russian Federation
114 G10 **Mal'ovitsa** ▲ W Bulgaria
145 V15 **Malovodnoye** Almaty, SE Kazakhstan
94 C10 **Måløy** Sogn og Fjordane, S Norway
126 K4 **Maloyaroslavets** Kaluzhskaya Oblast', W Russian Federation
122 G7 **Malozemel'skaya Tundra** physical region NW Russian Federation
104 J10 **Malpartida de Cáceres** Extremadura, W Spain
104 K9 **Malpartida de Plasencia** Extremadura, W Spain
106 C7 **Malpensa** × (Milano) Lombardia, N Italy
76 J6 **Malqteïr** desert N Mauritania
Mals im Vinschgau see Malles Venosta
118 J10 **Malta** Rēzekne, SE Latvia
33 V7 **Malta** Montana, NW USA
120 M11 **Malta** off. Republic of Malta. ◆ republic C Mediterranean Sea
109 R8 **Malta** var. Maltabach. ≈ S Austria
120 M11 **Malta** island Malta, C Mediterranean Sea
Maltabach see Malta
Malta, Canale di see Malta Channel
120 M11 **Malta Channel** It. Canale di Malta. strait Italy/Malta
83 D20 **Maltahöhe** Hardap, SW Namibia
97 N16 **Malton** N England, UK
171 R13 **Maluku** off. Propinsi Maluku, Dut. Molukken, Eng. Moluccas. ◆ province E Indonesia
171 R13 **Maluku** Dut. Molukken, Eng. Moluccas; prev. Spice Islands. island group E Indonesia
Maluku, Laut see Molucca Sea
171 R11 **Maluku Utara** off. Propinsi Maluku Utara. ◆ province E Indonesia
77 V13 **Malumfashi** Katsina, N Nigeria
171 N13 **Malunda** prev. Maloenda. Sulawesi, C Indonesia
94 K13 **Malung** Dalarna, C Sweden
94 K13 **Malungsfors** Dalarna, C Sweden
186 M8 **Maluu** var. Malu'u. Malaita, N Solomon Islands
155 D16 **Mālvan** Mahārāshtra, W India
Malventum see Benevento
27 U12 **Malvern** Arkansas, C USA
29 S15 **Malvern** Iowa, C USA
44 I13 **Malvern** ▲ W Jamaica
Malvinas, Islas see Falkland Islands
117 N4 **Malyn** Rus. Malin. Zhytomyrs'ka Oblast', N Ukraine
127 O11 **Malyye Derbety** Respublika Kalmykiya, SW Russian Federation
Malyy Kavkaz see Lesser Caucasus
123 Q6 **Malyy Lyakhovskiy, Ostrov** island NE Russian Federation
Malyy Pamir see Little Pamir
122 N5 **Malyy Taymyr, Ostrov** island Severnaya Zemlya, N Russian Federation
144 E10 **Malyy Uzen'** Kaz. Kishiözen. ≈ Kazakhstan/Russian Federation
122 L14 **Malyy Yenisey** var. Ka-Krem. ≈ S Russian Federation
127 S3 **Mamadysh** Respublika Tatarstan, W Russian Federation
117 N14 **Mamaia** Constanța, E Romania
187 W14 **Mamanuca Group** island group Yasawa Group, W Fiji
146 L13 **Mamash** Lebap Welaýaty, E Turkmenistan
79 O17 **Mambasa** Orientale, NE Dem. Rep. Congo
171 X13 **Mamberamo, Sungai** ≈ Papua, E Indonesia
79 G15 **Mambéré** ≈ SW Central African Republic
79 G15 **Mambéré-Kadéï** ◆ prefecture SW Central African Republic
Mambij see Manbij
79 H18 **Mambili** ≈ W Congo
83 N18 **Mambone** var. Nova Mambone. Inhambane, E Mozambique
171 O4 **Mamburao** Mindoro, N Philippines
172 I16 **Mamelles** island Inner Islands, NE Seychelles
99 M25 **Mamer** Luxembourg, SW Luxembourg
102 L6 **Mamers** Sarthe, NW France
79 D15 **Mamfe** Sud-Ouest, W Cameroon
145 P6 **Mamlyutka** Severnyy Kazakhstan, N Kazakhstan
36 M15 **Mammoth** Arizona, SW USA
33 S12 **Mammoth Hot Springs** Wyoming, C USA
Mamoedjoe see Mamuju
119 A14 **Mamonovo** Ger. Heiligenbeil. Kaliningradskaya Oblast', W Russian Federation
57 L14 **Mamoré, Rio** ≈ Bolivia/Brazil
76 I14 **Mamou** Moyenne-Guinée, W Guinea
22 H8 **Mamou** Louisiana, S USA
172 I14 **Mamoudzou** ○ (Mayotte) C Mayotte
172 I3 **Mampikony** Mahajanga, N Madagascar
77 P16 **Mampong** C Ghana
110 M7 **Mamry, Jezioro** Ger. Mauersee. ◎ NE Poland
171 N13 **Mamuju** prev. Mamoedjoe. Sulawesi, S Indonesia
83 F19 **Mamuno** Ghanzi, W Botswana
113 K19 **Mamuras** var. Mamurasi, Mamurras. Lezhë, C Albania
Mamurasi/Mamurras see Mamuras
76 L16 **Man** W Ivory Coast
55 X9 **Mana** NW French Guiana
56 A6 **Manabí** ◆ province W Ecuador
42 G4 **Manabique, Punta** var. Cabo Tres Puntas. headland E Guatemala
54 G11 **Manacacías, Río** ≈ C Colombia
58 F13 **Manacapuru** Amazonas, N Brazil
171 Q11 **Manado** prev. Menado. Sulawesi, C Indonesia
188 H5 **Managaha** island S Northern Mariana Islands
99 G20 **Manage** Hainaut, S Belgium
42 J10 **Managua** ● (Nicaragua) Managua, W Nicaragua
42 J10 **Managua** ◆ department W Nicaragua
42 J10 **Managua** × Managua, W Nicaragua
42 J10 **Managua, Lago de** var. Xolotlán. ◎ W Nicaragua
Manah see Bilād Manah
18 K16 **Manahawkin** New Jersey, NE USA
184 K11 **Manaia** Taranaki, North Island, NZ
172 J6 **Manakara** Fianarantsoa, SE Madagascar
152 J7 **Manāli** Himāchal Pradesh, NW India
Ma, Nam see Mā, Sông
Manama see Al Manāmah
186 D6 **Manam Island** island N PNG
172 I7 **Mananara** ≈ SE Madagascar
182 M9 **Manangatang** Victoria, SE Australia
172 J6 **Mananjary** Fianarantsoa, SE Madagascar
76 L14 **Manankoro** Sikasso, SW Mali
76 J12 **Manantali, Lac de** ◎ W Mali
Manáos see Manaus
185 B23 **Manapouri** Southland, South Island, NZ
185 B23 **Manapouri, Lake** ◎ South Island, NZ
58 F13 **Manaquiri** Amazonas, NW Brazil
Manar see Mannar
158 K5 **Manas** Xinjiang Uygur Zizhiqu, NW China
153 U12 **Manas** var. Dangme Chu. ≈ Bhutan/India
147 R8 **Manas, Gora** ▲ Kyrgyzstan/Uzbekistan
158 K3 **Manas Hu** ◎ NW China
153 P10 **Manaslu** ▲ C Nepal
37 S8 **Manassa** Colorado, C USA
21 W4 **Manassas** Virginia, NE USA
45 T5 **Manatí** C Puerto Rico
171 R16 **Manatuto** N East Timor
186 E8 **Manau** Northern, S PNG
54 H4 **Manaure** La Guajira, N Colombia
58 F12 **Manaus** prev. Manáos. state capital Amazonas, NW Brazil
136 G17 **Manavgat** Antalya, SW Turkey
184 M13 **Manawatu** ≈ North Island, NZ
184 L11 **Manawatu-Wanganui** off. Manawatu-Wanganui Region. ◆ region North Island, NZ
171 R7 **Manay** Mindanao, S Philippines
138 K2 **Manbij** var. Mambij, Fr. Membidj. Ḥalab, N Syria
105 N13 **Mancha Real** Andalucía, S Spain
102 I4 **Manche** ◆ department N France
97 L17 **Manchester** Lat. Mancunium. NW England, UK
23 S5 **Manchester** Georgia, SE USA
29 Y13 **Manchester** Iowa, C USA
21 N7 **Manchester** Kentucky, S USA
19 O10 **Manchester** New Hampshire, NE USA
20 K10 **Manchester** Tennessee, S USA
18 M9 **Manchester** Vermont, NE USA
97 L18 **Manchester** × NW England, UK
149 P15 **Manchhar Lake** ◎ SE Pakistan
Man-chou-li see Manzhouli
163 U11 **Manchuria** cultural region NE China
Máncio Lima see Japiim
Mancunium see Manchester
148 J15 **Mand** Baluchistān, SW Pakistan
Mand see Mand, Rūd-e
81 H25 **Manda** Iringa, SW Tanzania
172 H6 **Mandabe** Toliara, W Madagascar
162 I5 **Mandal** Hövsgöl, N Mongolia
162 L7 **Mandal** Töv, C Mongolia
95 E18 **Mandal** Vest-Agder, S Norway
166 L5 **Mandalay** Mandalay, C Burma
166 M6 **Mandalay** ◆ division C Burma
152 L9 **Mandalgovĭ** Dundgovĭ, C Mongolia
139 V7 **Mandalī** E Iraq
95 E18 **Mandalselva** ≈ S Norway
163 P11 **Mandalt** var. Sonid Zuoqi. Nei Mongol Zizhiqu, N China
28 M5 **Mandan** North Dakota, N USA
Mandargiri Hill see Mandār Hill
153 R14 **Mandār Hill** prev. Mandargiri Hill. Bihār, NE India
170 M13 **Mandar, Teluk** bay Sulawesi, C Indonesia
107 C19 **Mandas** Sardegna, Italy, C Mediterranean Sea
Mandasor see Mandsaur
81 L16 **Mandera** North Eastern, NE Kenya
33 V13 **Manderson** Wyoming, C USA
44 J12 **Mandeville** C Jamaica
22 K9 **Mandeville** Louisiana, S USA
152 I7 **Mandi** Himāchal Pradesh, NW India
76 K14 **Mandiana** Haute-Guinée, E Guinea
149 U10 **Mandi Būrewāla** var. Būrewāla. Punjab, E Pakistan
152 G9 **Mandi Dabwāli** Haryāna, NW India
Mandidzudzure see Chimanimani
83 M15 **Mandié** Manica, NW Mozambique
83 N14 **Mandimba** Niassa, N Mozambique
57 Q19 **Mandioré, Laguna** ◎ E Bolivia
154 J10 **Mandla** Madhya Pradesh, C India
83 M20 **Mandlakazi** var. Manjacaze. Gaza, S Mozambique
95 E24 **Mandø** var. Manø. island W Denmark
Mandoúdhion/Mandoudi see Mantoúdi
115 G19 **Mándra** Attikí, C Greece
172 I7 **Mandrare** ≈ S Madagascar
114 M10 **Mandra, Yazovir** salt lake SE Bulgaria
107 L23 **Mandrazzi, Portella** pass Sicilia, Italy, C Mediterranean Sea
172 J3 **Mandritsara** Mahajanga, N Madagascar
143 O13 **Mand, Rūd-e** var. Mand. ≈ S Iran
154 F9 **Mandsaur** prev. Mandasor. Madhya Pradesh, C India
154 F11 **Māndu** Madhya Pradesh, C India
169 W8 **Mandul, Pulau** island N Indonesia
83 G15 **Mandundu** Western, W Zambia
180 I13 **Mandurah** Western Australia
107 P18 **Manduria** Puglia, SE Italy
155 G20 **Mandya** Karnātaka, C India
77 P12 **Mané** C Burkina
106 E8 **Manerbio** Lombardia, NW Italy
Manevichi see Manevychi
116 K3 **Manevychi** Pol. Maniewicze, Rus. Manevichi. Volyns'ka Oblast', NW Ukraine
107 N16 **Manfredonia** Puglia, SE Italy
107 N16 **Manfredonia, Golfo di** gulf Adriatic Sea, N Mediterranean Sea
77 P13 **Manga** C Burkina
59 L16 **Mangabeiras, Chapada das** ▲ E Brazil
79 J20 **Mangai** Bandundu, W Dem. Rep. Congo
190 L17 **Mangaia** island group S Cook Islands
184 M9 **Mangakino** Waikato, North Island, NZ
116 M15 **Mangalia** anc. Callatis. Constanța, SE Romania
78 J11 **Mangalmé** Guéra, SE Chad
155 E19 **Mangalore** Karnātaka, W India
191 Y13 **Mangareva** var. Magareva. island Îles Tuamotu, SE French Polynesia
83 I23 **Mangaung** Free State, C South Africa
Mangaung see Bloemfontein
154 K9 **Mangawān** Madhya Pradesh, C India
184 M11 **Mangaweka** Manawatu-Wanganui, North Island, NZ
184 N11 **Mangaweka** ▲ North Island, NZ
79 P17 **Mangbwalu** Orientale, NE Dem. Rep. Congo
101 L24 **Mangfall** ≈ SE Germany
169 P13 **Manggar** Pulau Belitung, W Indonesia
166 M2 **Mangin Range** ▲ N Burma
139 R1 **Mangish** N Iraq
144 F15 **Mangistau** Kaz. Mangqystaū Oblysy; prev. Mangyshlakskaya. ◆ province SW Kazakhstan
Mangit see Mang'it
146 H8 **Mang'it** Rus. Mangit. Qoraqalpog'iston Respublikasi, W Uzbekistan
54 A13 **Manglares, Cabo** headland SW Colombia
149 V6 **Mangla Reservoir** ⊞ NE Pakistan
159 N9 **Mangnai** var. Lao Mangnai. Qinghai, C China
Mango see Mago, Fiji
Mango see Sansanné-Mango, Togo
Mangoche see Mangochi
83 N14 **Mangochi** var. Mangoche; prev. Fort Johnston. Southern, SE Malawi
77 N14 **Mangodara** SW Burkina
172 H6 **Mangoky** ≈ W Madagascar
171 Q12 **Mangole, Pulau** island Kepulauan Sula, E Indonesia
184 J2 **Mangonui** Northland, North Island, NZ
Mangqystaū Oblysy see Mangistau
Mangqystaū Shyghanaghy see Mangyshlakskiy Zaliv
104 H7 **Mangualde** Viseu, N Portugal
61 H18 **Mangueira, Lagoa** ◎ S Brazil
77 X6 **Manguéni, Plateau du** ▲ NE Niger
163 T4 **Mangui** Nei Mongol Zizhiqu, N China
26 K11 **Mangum** Oklahoma, C USA
79 O18 **Manguredjipa** Nord Kivu, E Dem. Rep. Congo
83 L16 **Mangwendi** Mashonaland East, E Zimbabwe
144 F15 **Mangyshlak, Plato** plateau SW Kazakhstan
144 E14 **Mangyshlakskiy Zaliv** Kaz. Mangqystaū Shyghanaghy. gulf SW Kazakhstan
Mangyshlaskaya see Mangistau
162 I5 **Manhan** Hövsgöl, N Mongolia
27 O4 **Manhattan** Kansas, C USA
99 L21 **Manhay** Luxembourg, SE Belgium
83 L21 **Manhiça** prev. Vila de Manhiça. Maputo, S Mozambique
83 L21 **Manhoca** Maputo, S Mozambique
59 N20 **Manhuaçu** Minas Gerais, SE Brazil
143 R11 **Mānī** Kermān, C Iran
54 H10 **Maní** Casanare, C Colombia
83 M17 **Manica** var. Vila de Manica. Manica, W Mozambique
83 M17 **Manica** off. Província de Manica. ◆ province W Mozambique
83 L17 **Manicaland** ◆ province E Zimbabwe
15 U5 **Manic Deux, Réservoir** ⊞ Québec, SE Canada
Manich see Manych
59 F14 **Manicoré** Amazonas, N Brazil
13 N11 **Manicouagan** Québec, SE Canada
13 N11 **Manicouagan** ≈ Québec, SE Canada
15 U6 **Manicouagan, Péninsule de** peninsula Québec, SE Canada
13 N11 **Manicouagan, Réservoir** ◎ Québec, E Canada
15 T4 **Manic Trois, Réservoir** ⊞ Québec, SE Canada
79 M20 **Maniema** off. Région du Maniema. ◆ region E Dem. Rep. Congo
Maniewicze see Manevychi
160 F8 **Maniganggo** Sichuan, C China
11 Y15 **Manigotagan** Manitoba, S Canada
153 R13 **Manihāri** Bihār, N India
191 U9 **Manihi** island Îles Tuamotu, C French Polynesia
190 L13 **Manihiki** atoll N Cook Islands
192 M8 **Manihiki Plateau** undersea feature C Pacific Ocean
196 M14 **Maniitsoq** var. Manîtsoq, Dan. Sukkertoppen. Kita, S Greenland
153 T15 **Manikganj** Dhaka, C Bangladesh
152 M14 **Mānikpur** Uttar Pradesh, N India
171 N4 **Manila** off. City of Manila. ● (Philippines) Luzon, N Philippines
27 Y9 **Manila** Arkansas, C USA
189 N16 **Manila Reef** reef W Micronesia
183 T6 **Manilla** New South Wales, SE Australia
192 P6 **Maniloa** island Tongatapu Group, S Tonga
123 U8 **Manily** Koryakskiy Avtonomnyy Okrug, E Russian Federation
171 V12 **Manim, Pulau** island E Indonesia
168 I11 **Maninjau, Danau** ◎ Sumatera, W Indonesia
153 W13 **Manipur** ◆ state NE India
153 X14 **Manipur Hills** hill range E India
136 C14 **Manisa** var. Manissa; prev. Saruhan, anc. Magnesia. Manisa, W Turkey
136 C13 **Manisa** var. Manissa. ◆ province W Turkey
Manissa see Manisa
31 O7 **Manistee** Michigan, N USA
31 P7 **Manistee River** ≈ Michigan, N USA
31 O4 **Manistique** Michigan, N USA
31 P4 **Manistique Lake** ◎ Michigan, N USA
11 W13 **Manitoba** ◆ province S Canada
11 X16 **Manitoba, Lake** ◎ Manitoba, S Canada
11 X17 **Manitou** Manitoba, S Canada
31 N2 **Manitou Island** island Michigan, N USA
14 H11 **Manitou Lake** ◎ Ontario, SE Canada
12 G15 **Manitoulin Island** island Ontario, S Canada
37 T5 **Manitou Springs** Colorado, C USA
14 G12 **Manitouwabing Lake** ◎ Ontario, S Canada
12 E12 **Manitouwadge** Ontario, S Canada
12 G15 **Manitowaning** Manitoulin Island, Ontario, S Canada
14 B7 **Manitowik Lake** ◎ Ontario, S Canada
31 N7 **Manitowoc** Wisconsin, N USA
Manîtsoq see Maniitsoq
139 O7 **Mānī', Wādī al** dry watercourse W Iraq
12 J14 **Maniwaki** Québec, SE Canada
171 W13 **Maniwori** Papua, E Indonesia
54 E10 **Manizales** Caldas, W Colombia
112 F11 **Manjača** ▲ NW Bosnia and Herzegovina
Manjacaze see Mandlakazi
180 J14 **Manjimup** Western Australia
109 V4 **Mank** Niederösterreich, C Austria
79 I17 **Mankanza** Equateur, NW Dem. Rep. Congo
153 N12 **Mankāpur** Uttar Pradesh, N India
26 M3 **Mankato** Kansas, C USA
29 U10 **Mankato** Minnesota, N USA
117 O7 **Man'kivka** Cherkas'ka Oblast', C Ukraine
76 M15 **Mankono** C Ivory Coast
11 T17 **Mankota** Saskatchewan, S Canada
155 K23 **Mankulam** Northern Province, N Sri Lanka
39 Q9 **Manley Hot Springs** Alaska, USA
18 H10 **Manlius** New York, NE USA
105 W5 **Manlleu** Cataluña, NE Spain
29 V11 **Manly** Iowa, C USA
154 E13 **Manmād** Mahārāshtra, W India
182 J7 **Mannahill** South Australia
155 J23 **Mannar** var. Manar. Northern Province, NW Sri Lanka
155 I24 **Mannar, Gulf of** gulf India/Sri Lanka
155 J23 **Mannar Island** island N Sri Lanka
Mannersdorf see Mannersdorf am Leithagebirge
109 Y5 **Mannersdorf am Leithagebirge** var. Mannersdorf. Niederösterreich, E Austria
109 Y6 **Mannersdorf an der Rabnitz** Burgenland, E Austria
101 G20 **Mannheim** Baden-Württemberg, SW Germany
11 O12 **Manning** Alberta, W Canada
29 T14 **Manning** Iowa, C USA
28 K5 **Manning** North Dakota, N USA
21 S13 **Manning** South Carolina, SE USA
191 Y2 **Manning, Cape** headland Kiritimati, NE Kiribati
21 S3 **Mannington** West Virginia, NE USA
182 A1 **Mann Ranges** ▲ South Australia
107 C19 **Mannu** ≈ Sardegna, Italy, C Mediterranean Sea
11 R14 **Mannville** Alberta, SW Canada
76 J15 **Mano** ≈ Liberia/Sierra Leone
Manø see Mandø
39 O13 **Manokotak** Alaska, USA
171 V12 **Manokwari** Papua, E Indonesia
79 N22 **Manono** Shaba, SE Dem. Rep. Congo
25 T10 **Manor** Texas, SW USA
97 D16 **Manorhamilton** Ir. Cluainín. NW Ireland
103 S15 **Manosque** Alpes-de-Haute-Provence, SE France
12 L11 **Manouane, Lac** ◎ Québec, SE Canada
163 W12 **Manp'o** var. Manp'ojin. NW North Korea
Manp'ojin see Manp'o
191 T4 **Manra** prev. Sydney Island. atoll Phoenix Islands, C Kiribati
105 V5 **Manresa** Cataluña, NE Spain
152 H9 **Mānsa** Punjab, NW India
82 J12 **Mansa** prev. Fort Rosebery. Luapula, N Zambia
76 G12 **Mansa Konko** C Gambia
15 Q11 **Manseau** Québec, SE Canada
149 U5 **Mānsehra** North-West Frontier Province, NW Pakistan
9 Q9 **Mansel Island** island Nunavut, NE Canada
183 O12 **Mansfield** Victoria, SE Australia
97 M18 **Mansfield** C England, UK
27 S11 **Mansfield** Arkansas, C USA
22 G6 **Mansfield** Louisiana, S USA
19 O12 **Mansfield** Massachusetts, NE USA
31 T12 **Mansfield** Ohio, N USA
18 G12 **Mansfield** Pennsylvania, NE USA
18 M7 **Mansfield, Mount** ▲ Vermont, NE USA
59 M16 **Mansidão** Bahia, E Brazil
102 L11 **Mansle** Charente, W France
76 G12 **Mansôa** C Guinea-Bissau
Manşûra see El Manşûra
Mansurabad see Mehrān, Rūd-e
56 A6 **Manta** Manabí, W Ecuador
56 A6 **Manta, Bahía de** bay W Ecuador
57 F14 **Mantaro, Río** ≈ C Peru
35 O8 **Manteca** California, W USA
54 J7 **Mantecal** Apure, C Venezuela
31 N11 **Manteno** Illinois, N USA
21 Y9 **Manteo** Roanoke Island, North Carolina, SE USA
Mantes-Gassicourt see Mantes-la-Jolie
103 N5 **Mantes-la-Jolie** prev. Mantes-Gassicourt, Mantes-sur-Seine, anc. Medunta. Yvelines, N France
Mantes-sur-Seine see Mantes-la-Jolie
36 L5 **Manti** Utah, W USA
Mantinea see Mantíneia
115 F20 **Mantíneia** anc. Mantinea. site of ancient city Pelopónnisos, S Greece
59 M21 **Mantiqueira, Serra da** ▲ S Brazil
29 W10 **Mantorville** Minnesota, N USA
115 G17 **Mantoúdi** var. Mandoudi; prev. Mandoúdhion. Évvoia, C Greece
Mantoue see Mantova
106 F8 **Mantova** Eng. Mantua, Fr. Mantoue. Lombardia, NW Italy
93 M19 **Mäntsälä** Etelä-Suomi, S Finland
93 L17 **Mänttä** Länsi-Suomi, W Finland
Mantua see Mantova
125 O14 **Manturovo** Kostromskaya Oblast', NW Russian Federation
93 M18 **Mäntyharju** Ita-Suomi, SE Finland
92 M13 **Mäntyjärvi** Lappi, N Finland
190 L16 **Manuae** island S Cook Islands
191 Q10 **Manuae** atoll Îles Sous le Vent, W French Polynesia
192 L16 **Manua Islands** island group E American Samoa
40 L5 **Manuel Benavides** Chihuahua, N Mexico
61 D21 **Manuel J.Cobo** Buenos Aires, E Argentina
58 M12 **Manuel Luís, Recife** reef E Brazil
61 F15 **Manuel Viana** Rio Grande do Sul, S Brazil
59 I14 **Manuel Zinho** Pará, N Brazil
191 V11 **Manuhangi** atoll Îles Tuamotu, C French Polynesia
185 E22 **Manuherikia** ≈ South Island, NZ
171 P13 **Manui, Pulau** island N Indonesia
Manukau see Manurewa
184 L6 **Manukau Harbour** harbour North Island, NZ
191 Z2 **Manulu Lagoon** ◎ Kiritimati, E Kiribati
182 J7 **Manunda Creek** seasonal river South Australia
57 K15 **Manupari, Río** ≈ N Bolivia
184 L6 **Manurewa** var. Manukau. Auckland, North Island, NZ
57 K15 **Manurimi, Río** ≈ NW Bolivia
186 D5 **Manus** ◆ province N PNG
186 D5 **Manus Island** var. Great Admiralty Island. island N PNG
171 T16 **Manuwui** Pulau Babar, E Indonesia
29 Q3 **Manvel** North Dakota, N USA
33 Z14 **Manville** Wyoming, C USA
22 G6 **Many** Louisiana, S USA
81 H21 **Manyara, Lake** ◎ NE Tanzania
126 L12 **Manych** var. Manich. ≈ SW Russian Federation
127 N13 **Manych-Gudilo, Ozero** salt lake SW Russian Federation
83 H14 **Manyinga** North Western, NW Zambia
105 O11 **Manzanares** Castilla-La Mancha, C Spain
44 H7 **Manzanillo** Granma, E Cuba
40 K14 **Manzanillo** Colima, SW Mexico
40 K14 **Manzanillo, Bahía** bay SW Mexico
37 S11 **Manzano Mountains** ▲ New Mexico, SW USA
37 R12 **Manzano Peak** ▲ New Mexico, SW USA
163 R6 **Manzhouli** var. Man-chou-li. Nei Mongol Zizhiqu, N China
Manzil Bū Ruqaybah see Menzel Bourguiba
139 X9 **Manzilīyah** E Iraq
83 L21 **Manzini** prev. Bremersdorp. C Swaziland
83 L21 **Manzini** × (Mbabane) C Swaziland
78 G10 **Mao** Kanem, W Chad
45 N8 **Mao** NW Dominican Republic
Maó see Mahón
Maoemere see Maumere
159 W9 **Maojing** Gansu, N China
171 Y14 **Maoke, Pegunungan** Dut. Sneeuw-gebergte, Eng. Snow Mountains. ▲ Papua, E Indonesia
Maol Réidh, Caoc see Mweelrea
160 M15 **Maoming** Guangdong, S China
160 H8 **Maoxian** var. Mao Xian; prev. Fengyizhen. Sichuan, C China
83 L19 **Mapai** Gaza, SW Mozambique
158 H15 **Mapam Yumco** ◎ W China
83 I15 **Mapanza** Southern, S Zambia
54 J4 **Maparari** Falcón, N Venezuela
41 U17 **Mapastepec** Chiapas, SE Mexico
169 V9 **Mapat, Pulau** island N Indonesia
171 Y15 **Mapi** Papua, E Indonesia
171 V11 **Mapia, Kepulauan** island group E Indonesia
40 L8 **Mapimí** Durango, C Mexico
83 N19 **Mapinhane** Inhambane, SE Mozambique
55 N7 **Mapire** Monagas, NE Venezuela
11 S17 **Maple Creek** Saskatchewan, S Canada
31 Q9 **Maple River** ≈ Michigan, N USA
29 P7 **Maple River** ≈ North Dakota/South Dakota, N USA
29 S13 **Mapleton** Iowa, C USA
29 U10 **Mapleton** Minnesota, N USA

29 R5 **Mapleton** North Dakota, N USA
32 F13 **Mapleton** Oregon, NW USA
36 L3 **Mapleton** Utah, W USA
192 K5 **Mapmaker Seamounts** *undersea feature* N Pacific Ocean
186 B6 **Maprik** East Sepik, NW PNG
83 L21 **Maputo** *prev.* Lourenço Marques. ● (Mozambique) Maputo, S Mozambique
83 L21 **Maputo** ◈ *province* S Mozambique
83 L21 **Maputo** × Maputo, S Mozambique
Maqanshy *see* Makanchi
Maqat *see* Makat
113 K19 **Maqë** ≈ NW Albania
113 M19 **Maqellarë** Dibër, C Albania
159 S12 **Maqên** *var.* Dawo; *prev.* Dawu. Qinghai, C China
159 S11 **Maqên Kangri** ▲ C China
159 U12 **Maqu** *var.* Nyinma. Gansu, C China
104 M9 **Maqueda** Castilla-La Mancha, C Spain
82 B9 **Maquela do Zombo** Uíge, NW Angola
63 I16 **Maquinchao** Río Negro, C Argentina
29 Z13 **Maquoketa** Iowa, C USA
29 Y13 **Maquoketa River** ≈ Iowa, C USA
14 F13 **Mar** Ontario, S Canada
95 F13 **Mår** ◎ S Norway
81 G19 **Mara** ◈ *region* N Tanzania
191 P8 **Maraa** Tahiti, W French Polynesia
58 D12 **Maraã** Amazonas, NW Brazil
191 O8 **Maraa, Pointe** *headland* Tahiti, W French Polynesia
59 K14 **Marabá** Pará, NE Brazil
54 H5 **Maracaibo** Zulia, NW Venezuela
Maracaibo, Gulf of *see* Venezuela, Golfo de
54 H5 **Maracaibo, Lago de** *var.* Lake Maracaibo. *inlet* NW Venezuela
Maracaibo, Lake *see* Maracaibo, Lago de
58 K10 **Maracá, Ilha de** *island* NE Brazil
59 H20 **Maracaju, Serra de** ▲ S Brazil
58 I11 **Maracanaquará, Planalto** ▲ NE Brazil
54 L5 **Maracay** Aragua, N Venezuela
Marada *see* Marādah
75 R9 **Marādah** *var.* Marada. N Libya
77 U12 **Maradi** Maradi, S Niger
77 U11 **Maradi** ◈ *department* S Niger
81 E21 **Maragarazi** *var.* Muragarazi. ≈ Burundi/Tanzania
Maragha *see* Marāgheh
142 J3 **Marāgheh** *var.* Maragha. Āžarbāyjān-e Khāvarī, NW Iran
141 P7 **Marāh** *var.* Marrāt. Ar Riyāḍ, C Saudi Arabia
55 N11 **Marahuaca, Cerro** ▲ S Venezuela
27 R5 **Marais des Cygnes River** ≈ Kansas/Missouri, C USA
58 L11 **Marajó, Baía de** *bay* N Brazil
59 K12 **Marajó, Ilha de** *island* N Brazil
191 O2 **Marakei** *atoll* Tungaru, W Kiribati
Marakesh *see* Marrakech
81 I18 **Maralal** Rift Valley, C Kenya
83 G21 **Maralaleng** Kgalagadi, S Botswana
145 U8 **Maraldy, Ozero** ◎ NE Kazakhstan
182 C5 **Maralinga** South Australia
Máramarossziget *see* Sighetu Marmației
187 N9 **Maramasike** *var.* Small Malaita. *island* N Solomon Islands
Maramba *see* Livingstone
194 H3 **Marambio** *Argentinian research station* Antarctica
116 H9 **Maramureș** ◈ *county* NW Romania
36 L15 **Marana** Arizona, SW USA
105 P7 **Maranchón** Castilla-La Mancha, C Spain
142 J2 **Marand** *var.* Merend. Āžarbāyjān-e Khāvarī, NW Iran
Marandellas *see* Marondera
58 L13 **Maranhão** *off.* Estado do Maranhão. ◈ *state* E Brazil
104 H10 **Maranhão, Barragem do** ⊞ C Portugal
149 O11 **Mārān, Koh-i** ▲ SW Pakistan
106 J7 **Marano, Laguna di** *lagoon* NE Italy
56 E9 **Marañón, Río** ≈ N Peru
102 J10 **Marans** Charente-Maritime, W France
83 M20 **Marão** Inhambane, S Mozambique
185 B23 **Mararoa** ≈ South Island, NZ
Maraş/Marash *see* Kahramanmaraş
07 M19 **Maratea** Basilicata, S Italy
04 G11 **Marateca** Setúbal, S Portugal
15 B20 **Marathiá, Akrotírio** *headland* Zákynthos, Iónioi Nísoi, Greece, C Mediterranean Sea
12 E12 **Marathon** Ontario, S Canada
23 Y17 **Marathon** Florida Keys, Florida, SE USA
24 L10 **Marathon** Texas, SW USA
Marathón *see* Marathónas
115 H19 **Marathónas** *prev.* Marathón. Attikí, C Greece
169 W9 **Maratua, Pulau** *island* N Indonesia
59 O18 **Maraú** Bahia, SE Brazil
143 R3 **Marāveh Tappeh** Golestān, N Iran
24 L11 **Maravillas Creek** ≈ Texas, SW USA
186 D8 **Marawaka** Eastern Highlands, C PNG
171 Q7 **Marawi** Mindanao, S Philippines
137 Y11 **Märäzä** *Rus.* Maraza. E Azerbaijan
Marbat *see* Mirbāṭ
104 L16 **Marbella** Andalucía, S Spain
180 J7 **Marble Bar** Western Australia
36 L9 **Marble Canyon** *canyon* Arizona, SW USA
25 S10 **Marble Falls** Texas, SW USA
27 Y7 **Marble Hill** Missouri, C USA
33 T15 **Marbleton** Wyoming, C USA
Marburg *see* Maribor
Marburg *see* Marburg an der Lahn, Germany
101 H16 **Marburg an der Lahn** *hist.* Marburg. Hessen, W Germany
111 H23 **Marcal** ≈ W Hungary
42 G7 **Marcala** La Paz, SW Honduras
111 H24 **Marcali** Somogy, SW Hungary
83 A16 **Marca, Ponta da** *headland* SW Angola
59 I16 **Marcelândia** Mato Grosso, W Brazil
27 T3 **Marceline** Missouri, C USA
60 I13 **Marcelino Ramos** Rio Grande do Sul, S Brazil
55 Y12 **Marcel, Mont** ▲ S French Guiana
97 O19 **March** E England, UK
109 Z3 **March** *var.* Morava. ≈ C Europe *see also* Morava
106 I12 **Marche** *Eng.* Marches. ◈ *region* C Italy
103 N11 **Marche** *cultural region* C France
99 J21 **Marche-en-Famenne** Luxembourg, SE Belgium
104 K14 **Marchena** Andalucía, S Spain
57 B17 **Marchena, Isla** *var.* Bindloe Island. *island* Galapagos Islands, Ecuador, E Pacific Ocean
Marches *see* Marche
99 J20 **Marchin** Liège, E Belgium
181 S1 **Marchinbar Island** *island* Wessel Islands, Northern Territory, N Australia
62 L9 **Mar Chiquita, Laguna** ◎ C Argentina
103 Q10 **Marcigny** Saône-et-Loire, C France
23 W16 **Marco** Florida, SE USA
Marcodurum *see* Düren
59 O15 **Marcolândia** Pernambuco, E Brazil
106 I8 **Marco Polo** × (Venezia) Veneto, NE Italy
Marcq *see* Mark
116 M8 **Mărculești** *Rus.* Markuleshty. N Moldova
29 S12 **Marcus** Iowa, C USA
39 S11 **Marcus Baker, Mount** ▲ Alaska, USA
192 I5 **Marcus Island** *var.* Minami Tori Shima. *island* E Japan
18 K8 **Marcy, Mount** ▲ New York, NE USA
149 T5 **Mardān** North-West Frontier Province, N Pakistan
63 N14 **Mar del Plata** Buenos Aires, E Argentina
137 Q16 **Mardin** Mardin, SE Turkey
137 Q16 **Mardin** ◈ *province* SE Turkey
137 Q16 **Mardin Dağları** ▲ SE Turkey
162 J9 **Mardzad** Övörhangay, C Mongolia
187 R17 **Maré** *island* Îles Loyauté, E New Caledonia
Marea Neagră *see* Black Sea
Mare de Déu del Toro *see* El Toro
181 W4 **Mareeba** Queensland, NE Australia
96 G8 **Maree, Loch** ◎ N Scotland, UK
Mareeq *see* Mereeg
Marek *see* Dupnitsa
76 J11 **Maréna** Kayes, W Mali
190 I2 **Marenanuka** *atoll* Tungaru, W Kiribati
29 X14 **Marengo** Iowa, C USA
102 J11 **Marennes** Charente-Maritime, W France
107 G23 **Marettimo, Isola** *island* Isole Egadi, S Italy
24 K10 **Marfa** Texas, SW USA
57 P17 **Marfil, Laguna** ◎ E Bolivia
Marganets *see* Marhanets'
25 Q4 **Margaret** Texas, SW USA
180 I14 **Margaret River** Western Australia
186 C7 **Margarima** Southern Highlands, W PNG
55 N4 **Margarita, Isla de** *island* N Venezuela
115 I25 **Margarites** Kríti, Greece, E Mediterranean Sea
97 Q22 **Margate** *prev.* Mergate. SE England, UK
23 Z15 **Margate** Florida, SE USA
Margelan *see* Marg'ilon
103 P13 **Margeride, Montagnes de la** ▲ C France
Margherita *see* Jamaame
107 N16 **Margherita di Savoia** Puglia, SE Italy
Margherita, Lake *see* Ābaya Hāyk'
81 E18 **Margherita Peak** *Fr.* Pic Marguerite. ▲ Uganda/Dem. Rep. Congo
149 O4 **Marghī** Bāmīān, N Afghanistan
116 G9 **Marghita** *Hung.* Margitta. Bihor, NW Romania
Margilan *see* Marg'ilon
147 S10 **Marg'ilon** *var.* Margelan, *Rus.* Margilan. Farg'ona Viloyati, E Uzbekistan
116 K8 **Marginea** Suceava, NE Romania
Margitta *see* Marghita
148 K9 **Mārgow, Dasht-e** *desert* SW Afghanistan
99 L18 **Margraten** Limburg, SE Netherlands
10 M15 **Marguerite** British Columbia, SW Canada
15 V3 **Marguerite** ≈ Québec, SE Canada
194 I6 **Marguerite Bay** *bay* Antarctica
Marguerite, Pic *see* Margherita Peak
117 T9 **Marhanets'** *Rus.* Marganets. Dnipropetrovs'ka Oblast', E Ukraine
186 B9 **Mari** Western, SW PNG
191 R12 **Maria** *island* Îles Australes, SW French Polynesia
191 Y12 **Maria** *atoll* Groupe Actéon, SE French Polynesia
40 I12 **María Cleofas, Isla** *island* C Mexico
62 H4 **María Elena** *var.* Oficina María Elena. Antofagasta, N Chile
95 G21 **Mariager** Århus, C Denmark
61 C22 **María Ignacia** Buenos Aires, E Argentina
183 P17 **Maria Island** *island* Tasmania, SE Australia
40 H12 **María Madre, Isla** *island* C Mexico
40 I12 **María Magdalena, Isla** *island* C Mexico
192 H6 **Mariana Islands** *island group* Guam/Northern Mariana Islands
192 H6 **Mariana Trench** *var.* Challenger Deep. *undersea feature* W Pacific Ocean
153 X12 **Mariāni** Assam, NE India
27 X11 **Marianna** Arkansas, C USA
23 R8 **Marianna** Florida, SE USA
172 J16 **Marianne** *island* Inner Islands, NE Seychelles
95 M19 **Mariannelund** Jönköping, S Sweden
61 D15 **Mariano I.Loza** Corrientes, NE Argentina
Mariano Machado *see* Ganda
111 A16 **Mariánské Lázně** *Ger.* Marienbad. Karlovarský Kraj, W Czech Republic
Máriaradna *see* Radna
33 S7 **Marias River** ≈ Montana, NW USA
Maria-Theresiopel *see* Subotica
Máriatölgyes *see* Dubnica nad Váhom
184 H1 **Maria van Diemen, Cape** *headland* North Island, NZ
109 V5 **Mariazell** Steiermark, E Austria
141 P15 **Mar'ib** W Yemen
95 I25 **Maribo** Storstrøm, S Denmark
109 W9 **Maribor** *Ger.* Marburg. NE Slovenia
Marica *see* Maritsa
35 R13 **Maricopa** California, W USA
Maricourt *see* Kangiqsujuaq
81 D15 **Maridi** Western Equatoria, SW Sudan
194 M11 **Marie Byrd Land** *physical region* Antarctica
193 P14 **Marie Byrd Seamount** *undersea feature* N Amundsen Sea
45 X11 **Marie-Galante** *var.* Ceyre to the Caribs. *island* SE Guadeloupe
45 Y6 **Marie-Galante, Canal de** *channel* S Guadeloupe
93 J20 **Mariehamn** *Fin.* Maarianhamina. Åland, SW Finland
44 C4 **Mariel** La Habana, W Cuba
99 H22 **Mariembourg** Namur, S Belgium
Marienbad *see* Mariánské Lázně
Marienburg *see* Alūksne, Latvia
Marienburg *see* Malbork, Poland
Marienburg *see* Feldioara, Romania
Marienburg in Westpreussen *see* Malbork
Marienhausen *see* Viļaka
83 D20 **Mariental** Hardap, SW Namibia
18 D13 **Marienville** Pennsylvania, NE USA
Marienwerder *see* Kwidzyń
58 C12 **Marié, Rio** ≈ NW Brazil
95 K17 **Mariestad** Västra Götaland, S Sweden
23 S3 **Marietta** Georgia, SE USA
31 U14 **Marietta** Ohio, N USA
27 N13 **Marietta** Oklahoma, C USA
81 H18 **Marigat** Rift Valley, W Kenya
103 S16 **Marignane** Bouches-du-Rhône, SE France
Marignano *see* Melegnano
45 O11 **Marigot** NE Dominica
122 K12 **Mariinsk** Kemerovskaya Oblast', S Russian Federation
127 Q3 **Mariinskiy Posad** Respublika Mariy El, W Russian Federation
119 E14 **Marijampolė** *prev.* Kapsukas. Marijampolė, S Lithuania
Marijampolė ◈ *province* SW Lithuania
114 G12 **Marikostenovo** Blagoevgrad, SW Bulgaria
60 J9 **Marília** São Paulo, S Brazil
82 D11 **Marimba** Malanje, NW Angola
139 T1 **Marī Mīlā** E Iraq
104 G4 **Marín** Galicia, NW Spain
35 N10 **Marina** California, W USA
Marina di Catanzaro *see* Catanzaro Marina
Mar'ina Gorka *see* Mar"ina Horka
119 L17 **Mar"ina Horka** *Rus.* Mar'ina Gorka. Minskaya Voblasts', C Belarus
171 O4 **Marinduque** *island* C Philippines
31 S9 **Marine City** Michigan, N USA
31 N6 **Marinette** Wisconsin, N USA
60 I10 **Maringá** Paraná, S Brazil
83 N16 **Maringuè** Sofala, C Mozambique
104 F9 **Marinha Grande** Leiria, C Portugal
107 I15 **Marino** Lazio, C Italy
59 A15 **Mário Lobão** Acre, W Brazil
23 O5 **Marion** Alabama, S USA
27 Y11 **Marion** Arkansas, C USA
30 L17 **Marion** Illinois, N USA
31 P13 **Marion** Indiana, N USA
29 X13 **Marion** Iowa, C USA
27 O5 **Marion** Kansas, C USA
20 H6 **Marion** Kentucky, S USA
21 P9 **Marion** North Carolina, SE USA
31 S12 **Marion** Ohio, N USA
21 T12 **Marion** South Carolina, SE USA
21 Q7 **Marion** Virginia, NE USA
27 O5 **Marion Lake** ⊞ Kansas, C USA
21 S13 **Marion, Lake** ⊞ South Carolina, SE USA
27 S8 **Marionville** Missouri, C USA
55 N7 **Maripa** Bolívar, E Venezuela
55 X11 **Maripasoula** W French Guiana
35 Q9 **Mariposa** California, W USA
61 G19 **Mariscala** Lavalleja, S Uruguay
62 M4 **Mariscal Estigarribia** Boquerón, NW Paraguay
56 C6 **Mariscal Sucre** *var.* Quito. × (Quito) Pichincha, C Ecuador
30 K16 **Marissa** Illinois, N USA
103 U14 **Maritime Alps** *Fr.* Alpes Maritimes, *It.* Alpi Marittime. ▲ France/Italy
Maritimes, Alpes *see* Maritime Alps
Maritime Territory *see* Primorskiy Kray
114 K11 **Maritsa** *var.* Marica, *Gk.* Évros, *Turk.* Meriç; *anc.* Hebrus. ≈ SW Europe *see also* Évros/Meriç
Maritsa *see* Simeonovgrad
Marittime, Alpi *see* Maritime Alps
Maritzburg *see* Pietermaritzburg
117 X9 **Mariupol'** *prev.* Zhdanov. Donets'ka Oblast', SE Ukraine
55 Q6 **Mariusa, Caño** ≈ NE Venezuela
142 J5 **Marīvān** *prev.* Dezh Shāhpūr. Kordestān, W Iran
127 R3 **Mariyets** Respublika Mariy El, W Russian Federation
Mariyskaya ASSR *see* Mariy El, Respublika
118 G4 **Märjamaa** *Ger.* Merjama. Raplamaa, NW Estonia
99 I15 **Mark** *Fr.* Marcq. ≈ Belgium/Netherlands
81 N17 **Marka** *var.* Merca. Shabeellaha Hoose, S Somalia
145 Z10 **Markakol', Ozero** *Kaz.* Marqaköl. ◎ E Kazakhstan
76 M12 **Markala** Ségou, W Mali
159 S15 **Markam** *var.* Gartog. Xizang Zizhiqu, W China
95 K21 **Markaryd** Kronoberg, S Sweden
142 L7 **Markazī** *off.* Ostān-e Markazī. ◈ *province* W Iran
14 F14 **Markdale** Ontario, S Canada
27 X10 **Marked Tree** Arkansas, C USA
98 N11 **Markelo** Overijssel, E Netherlands
98 J9 **Markermeer** ◎ C Netherlands
97 N20 **Market Harborough** C England, UK
97 N18 **Market Rasen** E England, UK
123 O10 **Markha** ≈ NE Russian Federation
12 H16 **Markham** Ontario, S Canada
25 V12 **Markham** Texas, SW USA
186 E7 **Markham** ≈ C PNG
195 Q11 **Markham, Mount** ▲ Antarctica
110 M11 **Marki** Mazowieckie, C Poland
158 F8 **Markit** Xinjiang Uygur Zizhiqu, NW China
117 Y5 **Markivka** *Rus.* Markovka. Luhans'ka Oblast', E Ukraine
35 Q7 **Markleeville** California, W USA
98 L8 **Marknesse** Flevoland, N Netherlands
79 H14 **Markounda** *var.* Marcounda. Ouham, NW Central African Republic
Markovka *see* Markivka
123 U7 **Markovo** Chukotskiy Avtonomnyy Okrug, NE Russian Federation
127 P8 **Marks** Saratovskaya Oblast', W Russian Federation
22 K2 **Marks** Mississippi, S USA
22 I7 **Marksville** Louisiana, S USA
101 I19 **Marktheidenfeld** Bayern, C Germany
101 J24 **Marktoberdorf** Bayern, S Germany
101 M18 **Marktredwitz** Bayern, E Germany
Markt-Übelbach *see* Übelbach
27 V3 **Mark Twain Lake** ⊞ Missouri, C USA
Markuleshty *see* Mărculești
101 E14 **Marl** Nordrhein-Westfalen, W Germany
182 E2 **Marla** South Australia
181 Y8 **Marlborough** Queensland, E Australia
97 M22 **Marlborough** S England, UK
185 I15 **Marlborough** *off.* Marlborough District. ◈ *unitary authority* South Island, NZ
103 P3 **Marle** Aisne, N France
31 S8 **Marlette** Michigan, N USA
25 T9 **Marlin** Texas, SW USA
21 S5 **Marlinton** West Virginia, NE USA
26 M12 **Marlow** Oklahoma, C USA
155 E17 **Marmagao** Goa, W India
Marmanda *see* Marmande
102 L13 **Marmande** *anc.* Marmanda. Lot-et-Garonne, SW France
136 C11 **Marmara** Balıkesir, NW Turkey
136 D11 **Marmara Denizi** *Eng.* Sea of Marmara. *sea* NW Turkey
114 N13 **Marmaraereğlisi** Tekirdağ, NW Turkey
Marmara, Sea of *see* Marmara Denizi
136 C16 **Marmaris** Muğla, SW Turkey
28 J6 **Marmarth** North Dakota, N USA
21 Q5 **Marmet** West Virginia, NE USA
106 H5 **Marmolada, Monte** ▲ N Italy
104 M13 **Marmolejo** Andalucía, S Spain
14 J14 **Marmora** Ontario, SE Canada
39 Q14 **Marmot Bay** *bay* Alaska, USA
103 Q4 **Marne** ◈ *department* N France
103 Q4 **Marne** ≈ N France
137 U10 **Marneuli** *prev.* Borchalo, Sarvani. S Georgia
78 I13 **Maro** Moyen-Chari, S Chad
54 L12 **Maroa** Amazonas, S Venezuela
172 J3 **Maroantsetra** Toamasina, NE Madagascar
191 W11 **Marokau** *atoll* Îles Tuamotu, C French Polynesia
172 J5 **Marolambo** Toamasina, E Madagascar
172 J2 **Maromokotro** ▲ N Madagascar
83 L16 **Marondera** *prev.* Marandellas. Mashonaland East, NE Zimbabwe
55 X9 **Maroni** *Dut.* Marowijne. ≈ French Guiana/Surinam
183 V2 **Maroochydore-Mooloolaba** Queensland, E Australia
171 N14 **Maros** Sulawesi, C Indonesia
116 H11 **Maros** *var.* Mureş, Mureşul, *Ger.* Marosch, Mieresch. ≈ Hungary/Romania *see also* Mureş
Marosch *see* Maros/Mureş
Maroshévíz *see* Toplița
Marosillye *see* Ilia
Marosludas *see* Luduș
Marosújvár/Marosújvárakna *see* Ocna Mureș
Marosvásárhely *see* Târgu Mureș
191 V14 **Marotiri** *var.* Îlots de Bass, Morotiri. *island group* Îles Australes, SW French Polynesia
78 G12 **Maroua** Extrême-Nord, N Cameroon
55 X12 **Marouini Rivier** ≈ SE Surinam
172 I3 **Marovoay** Mahajanga, NW Madagascar
55 W9 **Marowijne** ◈ *district* NE Surinam
Marowijne *see* Maroni
Marqaköl *see* Markakol', Ozero
193 P8 **Marquesas Fracture Zone** *tectonic feature* E Pacific Ocean
Marquesas Islands *see* Marquises, Îles
23 W17 **Marquesas Keys** *island group* Florida, SE USA
29 Y12 **Marquette** Iowa, C USA
31 N3 **Marquette** Michigan, N USA
103 N1 **Marquise** Pas-de-Calais, N France
191 X7 **Marquises, Îles** *Eng.* Marquesas Islands. *island group* N French Polynesia
183 Q6 **Marra Creek** ≈ New South Wales, SE Australia
80 B10 **Marra Hills** *plateau* W Sudan
80 B11 **Marra, Jebel** ▲ W Sudan
74 E7 **Marrakech** *var.* Marakesh, *Eng.* Marrakesh; *prev.* Morocco. W Morocco
Marrakesh *see* Marrakech
Marrāt *see* Marāh
183 N15 **Marrawah** Tasmania, SE Australia
182 I4 **Marree** South Australia
81 L17 **Marrehan** ▲ SW Somalia
83 N17 **Marromeu** Sofala, C Mozambique
104 J17 **Marroquí, Punta** *headland* SW Spain
183 N8 **Marrowie Creek** *seasonal river* New South Wales, SE Australia
83 O14 **Marrupa** Niassa, N Mozambique
182 D1 **Marryat** South Australia
75 Y10 **Marsa 'Alam** SE Egypt
75 R8 **Marsá al Burayqah** *var.* Al Burayqah. N Libya
81 J17 **Marsabit** Eastern, N Kenya
107 H23 **Marsala** *anc.* Lilybaeum. Sicilia, Italy, C Mediterranean Sea
121 P16 **Marsaxlokk Bay** *bay* SE Malta
65 G15 **Mars Bay** *bay* Ascension Island, C Atlantic Ocean
101 H15 **Marsberg** Nordrhein-Westfalen, W Germany
11 R15 **Marsden** Saskatchewan, S Canada
98 H7 **Marsdiep** *strait* NW Netherlands
103 R16 **Marseille** *Eng.* Marseilles; *anc.* Massilia. Bouches-du-Rhône, SE France
Marseille-Marignane *see* Provence
30 M11 **Marseilles** Illinois, N USA
Marseilles *see* Marseille
76 J16 **Marshall** W Liberia
39 N11 **Marshall** Alaska, USA
27 U9 **Marshall** Arkansas, C USA
31 N14 **Marshall** Illinois, N USA
31 Q10 **Marshall** Michigan, N USA
29 S9 **Marshall** Minnesota, N USA
27 T4 **Marshall** Missouri, C USA
21 O9 **Marshall** North Carolina, SE USA
25 X6 **Marshall** Texas, SW USA
189 S4 **Marshall Islands** *off.* Republic of the Marshall Islands. ◆ *republic* W Pacific Ocean
192 K6 **Marshall Seamounts** *undersea feature* SW Pacific Ocean
29 W13 **Marshalltown** Iowa, C USA
19 P12 **Marshfield** Massachusetts, NE USA
27 T7 **Marshfield** Missouri, C USA
30 K6 **Marshfield** Wisconsin, N USA
44 H1 **Marsh Harbour** Great Abaco, W Bahamas
19 S3 **Mars Hill** Maine, NE USA
21 P9 **Mars Hill** North Carolina, SE USA
22 H10 **Marsh Island** *island* Louisiana, S USA
21 S11 **Marshville** North Carolina, SE USA
15 W5 **Marsoui** Québec, SE Canada
15 R8 **Mars, Rivière à** ≈ Québec, SE Canada
95 O15 **Märsta** Stockholm, C Sweden
95 H24 **Marstal** Fyn, C Denmark
95 I19 **Marstrand** Västra Götaland, S Sweden
25 U8 **Mart** Texas, SW USA
166 M9 **Martaban** *var.* Moktama. Mon State, S Burma
166 L9 **Martaban, Gulf of** *gulf* S Burma
107 Q19 **Martano** Puglia, SE Italy
Martapoera *see* Martapura
169 T13 **Martapura** *prev.* Martapoera. Borneo, C Indonesia
99 L23 **Martelange** Luxembourg, SE Belgium
114 L7 **Marten** Ruse, N Bulgaria
14 H10 **Marten River** Ontario, S Canada
11 T15 **Martensville** Saskatchewan, S Canada
Marteskirch *see* Târnăveni
Martes Tolosane *see* Martres-Tolosane
115 K25 **Mártha** Kríti, Greece, E Mediterranean Sea
183 Q6 **Marthaguy Creek** ≈ New South Wales, SE Australia
19 P13 **Martha's Vineyard** *island* Massachusetts, NE USA
108 C11 **Martigny** Valais, SW Switzerland
103 R16 **Martigues** Bouches-du-Rhône, SE France
111 J19 **Martin** *Ger.* Sankt Martin, *Hung.* Turócszentmárton; *prev.* Turčianský Svätý Martin. Žilinský Kraj, N Slovakia
28 L11 **Martin** South Dakota, N USA
20 G8 **Martin** Tennessee, S USA
105 S7 **Martín** ≈ E Spain
107 P18 **Martina Franca** Puglia, SE Italy
185 M14 **Martinborough** Wellington, North Island, NZ
25 S11 **Martindale** Texas, SW USA
35 N8 **Martinez** California, W USA
23 V3 **Martinez** Georgia, SE USA
41 Q13 **Martínez de La Torre** Veracruz-Llave, E Mexico
45 Y12 **Martinique** ◇ *French overseas department* E West Indies
Martinique Channel *see* Martinique Passage
45 X12 **Martinique Passage** *var.* Dominica Channel, Martinique Channel. *channel* Dominica/Martinique
23 Q5 **Martin Lake** ⊞ Alabama, S USA
115 G18 **Martíno** *prev.* Martínon. Stereá Ellás, C Greece
Martínon *see* Martíno
194 J11 **Martin Peninsula** *peninsula* Antarctica
39 S5 **Martin Point** *headland* Alaska, USA
109 V3 **Martinsberg** Niederösterreich, NE Austria
21 V3 **Martinsburg** West Virginia, NE USA
31 V13 **Martins Ferry** Ohio, N USA
Martinskirch *see* Târnăveni
31 O14 **Martinsville** Indiana, N USA
21 S8 **Martinsville** Virginia, NE USA
65 K16 **Martin Vaz, Ilhas** *island group* E Brazil
Martök *see* Martuk
184 M12 **Marton** Manawatu-Wanganui, North Island, NZ
105 N13 **Martos** Andalucía, S Spain
102 M16 **Martres-Tolosane** *var.* Martes Tolosane. Haute-Garonne, S France
92 M11 **Martti** Lappi, NE Finland
144 I9 **Martuk** *Kaz.* Martök. Aktyubinsk, NW Kazakhstan
137 U12 **Martuni** E Armenia
58 L11 **Marudá** Pará, E Brazil
169 V6 **Marudu, Teluk** *bay* East Malaysia
149 O8 **Ma'rūf** Kandahār, SE Afghanistan
164 H13 **Marugame** Kagawa, Shikoku, SW Japan
185 H16 **Maruia** ≈ South Island, NZ
98 M6 **Marum** Groningen, NE Netherlands
187 R13 **Marum, Mount** ▲ Ambrym, C Vanuatu
79 P23 **Marungu** ▲ SE Dem. Rep. Congo
191 Y12 **Marutea** *atoll* Groupe Actéon, C French Polynesia
143 O11 **Marv Dasht** *var.* Mervdasht. Fārs, S Iran
103 P13 **Marvejols** Lozère, S France
27 X12 **Marvell** Arkansas, C USA
36 L6 **Marvine, Mount** ▲ Utah, W USA
139 Q7 **Marwānīyah** C Iraq
152 F13 **Mārwār** *var.* Marwar Junction. Rājasthān, N India
Marwar Junction *see* Mārwār
11 R14 **Marwayne** Alberta, SW Canada
146 I14 **Mary** *prev.* Merv. Mary Welaýaty, S Turkmenistan
Mary *see* Mary Welaýaty
181 Z9 **Maryborough** Queensland, E Australia
182 M11 **Maryborough** Victoria, SE Australia
Maryborough *see* Port Laoise
83 G23 **Marydale** Northern Cape, W South Africa
117 W8 **Mar"yinka** Donets'ka Oblast', E Ukraine
Mary Island *see* Kanton
21 W4 **Maryland** *off.* State of Maryland; *also known as* America in Miniature, Cockade State, Free State, Old Line State. ◈ *state* NE USA
25 P7 **Maryneal** Texas, SW USA
97 J15 **Maryport** NW England, UK
13 U13 **Marystown** Newfoundland and Labrador, SE Canada
36 K6 **Marysvale** Utah, W USA
35 O6 **Marysville** California, W USA
27 O3 **Marysville** Kansas, C USA
31 S13 **Marysville** Michigan, N USA
31 S9 **Marysville** Ohio, N USA

◆ COUNTRY ● COUNTRY CAPITAL ◇ DEPENDENT TERRITORY ○ DEPENDENT TERRITORY CAPITAL ◈ ADMINISTRATIVE REGION × INTERNATIONAL AIRPORT ▲ MOUNTAIN ▲ MOUNTAIN RANGE Ꞩ VOLCANO ≈ RIVER ◎ LAKE ⊞ RESERVOIR

32 H7 **Marysville** Washington, NW USA
27 R2 **Maryville** Missouri, C USA
21 N9 **Maryville** Tennessee, S USA
146 I15 **Mary Welayaty** var. Mary, Rus. Maryyskiy Velayat. ◈ province S Turkmenistan
Maryyskiy Velayat see Mary Welaýaty
Marzūq see Murzuq
42 J11 **Masachapa** var. Puerto Masachapa. Managua, W Nicaragua
81 G19 **Masai Mara National Reserve** reserve C Kenya
81 I21 **Masai Steppe** grassland NW Tanzania
81 F19 **Masaka** SW Uganda
169 T15 **Masalembo Besar, Pulau** island S Indonesia
137 Y13 **Masallı** Rus. Masally. S Azerbaijan
Masally see Masallı
171 N13 **Masamba** Sulawesi, C Indonesia
Masampo see Masan
163 Y16 **Masan** prev. Masampo. S South Korea
Masandam Peninsula see Musandam Peninsula
81 J25 **Masasi** Mtwara, SE Tanzania
Masawa see Massawa
42 J10 **Masaya** Masaya, W Nicaragua
42 J10 **Masaya** ◈ department W Nicaragua
171 P5 **Masbate** Masbate, N Philippines
171 P5 **Masbate** island C Philippines
74 I6 **Mascara** var. Mouaskar. NW Algeria
173 O7 **Mascarene Basin** undersea feature W Indian Ocean
173 O9 **Mascarene Islands** island group W Indian Ocean
173 N9 **Mascarene Plain** undersea feature W Indian Ocean
173 O7 **Mascarene Plateau** undersea feature W Indian Ocean
194 H5 **Mascart, Cape** headland Adelaide Island, Antarctica
62 J10 **Mascasín, Salinas de** salt lake C Argentina
40 K13 **Mascota** Jalisco, C Mexico
15 O12 **Mascouche** Québec, SE Canada
124 J9 **Masel'gskaya** Respublika Kareliya, NW Russian Federation
83 J23 **Maseru** ● (Lesotho) W Lesotho
83 J23 **Maseru** ✕ W Lesotho
Mashaba see Mashava
160 K14 **Mashan** var. Baishan. Guangxi Zhuangzu Zizhiqu, S China
83 K17 **Mashava** prev. Mashaba. Masvingo, SE Zimbabwe
143 U4 **Mashhad** var. Meshed. Khorāsān, NE Iran
165 S3 **Mashike** Hokkaidō, NE Japan
Mashīz see Bardsīr
149 N14 **Mashkai** ≈ SW Pakistan
143 X13 **Māshkel** var. Rūd-i Māshkel, Rūd-e Māshkīd. ≈ Iran/Pakistan
148 K12 **Māshkel, Hāmūn-i** salt marsh SW Pakistan
Māshkel, Rūd-i/Māshkīd, Rūd-e see Māshkel
83 K15 **Mashonaland Central** ◈ province N Zimbabwe
83 K16 **Mashonaland East** ◈ province NE Zimbabwe
83 J16 **Mashonaland West** ◈ province NW Zimbabwe
Mashtagi see Maştağa
141 S14 **Masīlah, Wādī al** dry watercourse SE Yemen
79 I21 **Masi-Manimba** Bandundu, SW Dem. Rep. Congo
81 F17 **Masindi** W Uganda
81 I19 **Masinga Reservoir** ⊡ S Kenya
Maṣīra see Maṣīrah, Jazīrat
Masira, Gulf of see Maṣīrah, Khalīj
141 Y10 **Maṣīrah, Jazīrat** var. Masīra. island E Oman
141 Y10 **Maṣīrah, Khalīj** var. Gulf of Masira. bay E Oman
Masis see Büyükağrı Dağı
79 O19 **Masisi** Nord Kivu, E Dem. Rep. Congo
Masjed-e Soleymān see Masjed Soleymān
142 L9 **Masjed Soleymān** var. Masjed-e Soleymān, Masjid-i Sulaiman. Khūzestān, SW Iran
Masjid-i Sulaiman see Masjed Soleymān
Maskat see Masqaţ
139 Q7 **Maskhān** C Iraq
141 X8 **Maskin** var. Miskin. NW Oman
97 B17 **Mask, Lough** Ir. Loch Measca. ◎ W Ireland
114 N10 **Maslen Nos** headland E Bulgaria
172 K3 **Masoala, Tanjona** headland NE Madagascar
Masohi see Amahai
31 Q9 **Mason** Michigan, N USA
31 R14 **Mason** Ohio, N USA
25 Q10 **Mason** Texas, SW USA
21 P4 **Mason** West Virginia, NE USA
185 B25 **Mason Bay** bay Stewart Island, NZ
30 K13 **Mason City** Illinois, N USA
29 V12 **Mason City** Iowa, C USA
167 S7 **Mā, Sông** var. Nam Ma. ≈ Laos/Vietnam
18 B16 **Masontown** Pennsylvania, NE USA
141 Y8 **Masqaţ** var. Maskat, Eng. Muscat. ● (Oman) NE Oman
106 E10 **Massa** Toscana, C Italy
18 M11 **Massachusetts** off. Commonwealth of Massachusetts; also known as Bay State, Old Bay State, Old Colony State. ◈ state NE USA
19 P11 **Massachusetts Bay** bay Massachusetts, NE USA
35 R2 **Massacre Lake** ◎ Nevada, W USA
107 O18 **Massafra** Puglia, SE Italy
108 G11 **Massagno** Ticino, S Switzerland
78 G11 **Massaguet** Chari-Baguirmi, W Chad
Massakori see Massakory
78 G10 **Massakory** var. Massakori; prev. Dagana. Chari-Baguirmi, W Chad
78 H11 **Massalassef** Chari-Baguirmi, SW Chad
106 F13 **Massa Marittima** Toscana, C Italy
82 B11 **Massangano** Cuanza Norte, NW Angola
83 M18 **Massangena** Gaza, S Mozambique
80 J9 **Massawa** var. Masawa, Amh. Mits'iwa. E Eritrea
80 K9 **Massawa Channel** channel E Eritrea
18 J6 **Massena** New York, NE USA
78 H11 **Massenya** Chari-Baguirmi, SW Chad
10 I13 **Masset** Graham Island, British Columbia, SW Canada
102 L16 **Masseube** Gers, S France
14 E11 **Massey** Ontario, S Canada
103 P12 **Massiac** Cantal, C France
103 P12 **Massif Central** plateau C France
Massilia see Marseille
31 U12 **Massillon** Ohio, N USA
77 N12 **Massina** Ségou, W Mali
83 N19 **Massinga** Inhambane, SE Mozambique
83 L20 **Massingir** Gaza, SW Mozambique
195 Z10 **Masson Island** island Antarctica
Massoukou see Franceville
137 Z11 **Maştağa** Rus. Mashtagi, Mastaga. E Azerbaijan
Mastanli see Momchilgrad
184 M13 **Masterton** Wellington, North Island, NZ
18 M14 **Mastic** Long Island, New York, NE USA
149 O10 **Mastung** Baluchistān, SW Pakistan
119 J20 **Mastva** Rus. Mostva. ≈ SW Belarus
119 G17 **Masty** Rus. Mosty. Hrodzyenskaya Voblasts', W Belarus
164 F12 **Masuda** Shimane, Honshū, SW Japan
92 J11 **Masugnsbyn** Norrbotten, N Sweden
Masuku see Franceville
83 K17 **Masvingo** prev. Fort Victoria, Nyanda, Victoria. Masvingo, SE Zimbabwe
83 K18 **Masvingo** prev. Victoria. ◈ province SE Zimbabwe
138 H5 **Maşyāf** Fr. Misiaf. Ḩamāh, C Syria
Masyû Ko see Mashū-ko
110 E9 **Maszewo** Zachodniopomorskie, NW Poland
83 I17 **Matabeleland North** ◈ province W Zimbabwe
83 J18 **Matabeleland South** ◈ province S Zimbabwe
82 O13 **Mataca** Niassa, N Mozambique
14 G8 **Matachewan** Ontario, S Canada
79 F22 **Matadi** Bas-Congo, W Dem. Rep. Congo
25 O4 **Matador** Texas, SW USA
42 J9 **Matagalpa** Matagalpa, C Nicaragua
42 K9 **Matagalpa** ◈ department W Nicaragua
12 I12 **Matagami** Québec, S Canada
25 U13 **Matagorda** Texas, SW USA
25 U13 **Matagorda Bay** inlet Texas, SW USA
25 U14 **Matagorda Island** island Texas, SW USA
25 V13 **Matagorda Peninsula** headland Texas, SW USA
191 Q8 **Mataiea** Tahiti, W French Polynesia
191 T9 **Mataiva** atoll Îles Tuamotu, C French Polynesia
183 O7 **Matakana** New South Wales, SE Australia
184 N7 **Matakana Island** island NE NZ
83 C15 **Matala** Huíla, SW Angola
190 G12 **Matala'a Pointe** headland Île Uvea, N Wallis and Futuna
155 K25 **Matale** Central Province, C Sri Lanka
190 E12 **Matalesina, Pointe** headland Île Alofi, W Wallis and Futuna
76 I10 **Matam** NE Senegal
184 M8 **Matamata** Waikato, North Island, NZ
77 V12 **Matameye** Zinder, S Niger
40 L8 **Matamoros** Coahuila de Zaragoza, NE Mexico
41 P15 **Matamoros** var. Izúcar de Matamoros. Puebla, S Mexico
41 Q8 **Matamoros** Tamaulipas, C Mexico
75 S13 **Ma'ṭan as Sārah** SE Libya
82 J12 **Matanda** Luapula, N Zambia
81 J24 **Matandu** ≈ S Tanzania
15 V6 **Matane** Québec, SE Canada
15 V6 **Matane** ≈ Québec, SE Canada
77 S12 **Matankari** Dosso, SW Niger
39 R11 **Matanuska River** ≈ Alaska, USA
54 G7 **Matanza** Santander, N Colombia
44 D4 **Matanzas** Matanzas, NW Cuba
15 V7 **Matapédia** ≈ Québec, SE Canada
15 V6 **Matapédia, Lac** ◎ Québec, SE Canada
190 B17 **Mata Point** headland SE Niue
190 D12 **Matapu, Pointe** headland Île Futuna, W Wallis and Futuna
62 G12 **Mataquito, Río** ≈ C Chile
155 K26 **Matara** Southern Province, S Sri Lanka
115 D18 **Matarágka** var. Mataránga. Dytikí Elláda, C Greece
170 K16 **Mataram** Pulau Lombok, C Indonesia
Mataránga see Matarágka
181 Q3 **Mataranka** Northern Territory, N Australia
105 W6 **Mataró** anc. Illuro. Cataluña, E Spain
184 O8 **Matata** Bay of Plenty, North Island, NZ
192 K16 **Matātula, Cape** headland Tutuila, W American Samoa
185 D24 **Mataura** Southland, South Island, NZ
185 D24 **Mataura** ≈ South Island, NZ
Mata Uta see Matā'utu
190 G11 **Matā'utu** var. Mata Uta. ○ (Wallis and Futuna) Île Uvea, Wallis and Futuna
192 H16 **Matāutu** Upolu, C Samoa
190 G12 **Matā'utu, Baie de** bay Île Uvea, Wallis and Futuna
191 P7 **Mataval, Baie de** bay Tahiti, W French Polynesia
190 I16 **Matavera** Rarotonga, S Cook Islands
191 V16 **Mataveri** Easter Island, Chile, E Pacific Ocean
191 V17 **Mataveri** ✕ (Easter Island) Easter Island, Chile, E Pacific Ocean
184 P9 **Matawai** Gisborne, North Island, NZ
15 O10 **Matawin** ≈ Québec, SE Canada
145 V13 **Matay** Almaty, SE Kazakhstan
14 K8 **Matchi-Manitou, Lac** ◎ Québec, SE Canada
41 O10 **Matehuala** San Luis Potosí, C Mexico
45 V13 **Matelot** Trinidad, Trinidad and Tobago
83 M15 **Matenge** Tete, NW Mozambique
107 O18 **Matera** Basilicata, S Italy
111 O21 **Mátészalka** Szabolcs-Szatmár-Bereg, E Hungary
93 H17 **Matfors** Västernorrland, C Sweden
102 K11 **Matha** Charente-Maritime, W France
21 X6 **Mathews** Virginia, NE USA
25 S14 **Mathis** Texas, SW USA
152 J11 **Mathura** prev. Muttra. Uttar Pradesh, N India
Mathurai see Madurai
171 R7 **Mati** Mindanao, S Philippines
Matianus see Orūmīyeh, Daryācheh-ye
Matiara see Matiāri
149 Q15 **Matiāri** var. Matiara. Sind, SE Pakistan
41 S16 **Matías Romero** Oaxaca, SE Mexico
43 O13 **Matina** Limón, E Costa Rica
14 D10 **Matinenda Lake** ◎ Ontario, S Canada
19 R8 **Matinicus Island** island Maine, NE USA
Matisco/Matisco Ædourum see Mâcon
149 Q16 **Mātli** Sind, SE Pakistan
97 M18 **Matlock** C England, UK
59 F18 **Mato Grosso** prev. Vila Bela da Santíssima Trindade. Mato Grosso, W Brazil
59 G17 **Mato Grosso** off. Estado de Mato Grosso; prev. Matto Grosso. ◈ state W Brazil
60 H8 **Mato Grosso do Sul** off. Estado de Mato Grosso do Sul. ◈ state S Brazil
59 I18 **Mato Grosso, Planalto de** plateau C Brazil
104 G6 **Matosinhos** prev. Matozinhos. Porto, NW Portugal
Matou see Pingguo
55 Z10 **Matoury** NE French Guiana
Matozinhos see Matosinhos
111 L21 **Mátra** ▲▲ N Hungary
141 Y8 **Maṭraḥ** var. Mutrah. NE Oman
116 L12 **Mătrăşeşti** Vrancea, E Romania
108 M8 **Matrei Am Brenner** Tirol, W Austria
109 P8 **Matrei in Osttirol** Tirol, W Austria
76 I15 **Matru** SW Sierra Leone
75 U7 **Maṭrūḥ** var. Mersa Maṭrūḥ; anc. Paraetonium. NW Egypt
165 U16 **Matsubara** var. Matubara. Kagoshima, Tokuno-shima, SW Japan
164 G12 **Matsue** var. Matsuye, Matue. Shimane, Honshū, SW Japan
165 Q6 **Matsumae** Hokkaidō, NE Japan
164 M12 **Matsumoto** var. Matumoto. Nagano, Honshū, S Japan
164 K14 **Matsusaka** var. Matsuzaka, Matusaka. Mie, Honshū, SW Japan
161 S12 **Matsu Tao** Chin. Mazu Dao. island NW Taiwan
Matsutō see Mattō
164 F14 **Matsuyama** var. Matuyama. Ehime, Shikoku, SW Japan
Matsuye see Matsue
Matsuzaka see Matsusaka
164 M14 **Matsuzaki** Shizuoka, Honshū, S Japan
14 F8 **Mattagami** ≈ Ontario, S Canada
14 F8 **Mattagami Lake** ◎ Ontario, S Canada
62 K12 **Mattaldi** Córdoba, C Argentina
21 Y9 **Mattamuskeet, Lake** ◎ North Carolina, SE USA
21 W6 **Mattaponi River** ≈ Virginia, NE USA
14 I11 **Mattawa** Ontario, SE Canada
14 I11 **Mattawa** ≈ Ontario, SE Canada
19 S5 **Mattawamkeag** Maine, NE USA
19 S4 **Mattawamkeag Lake** ◎ Maine, NE USA
108 D11 **Matterhorn** It. Monte Cervino. ▲ Italy/Switzerland see also Cervino, Monte
35 W1 **Matterhorn** ▲ Nevada, W USA
32 L12 **Matterhorn** var. Sacajawea Peak. ▲ Oregon, NW USA
35 R8 **Matterhorn Peak** ▲ California, W USA
109 Y5 **Mattersburg** Burgenland, E Austria
108 E11 **Matter Vispa** ≈ S Switzerland
55 R7 **Matthews Ridge** N Guyana
44 K7 **Matthew Town** Great Inagua, S Bahamas
109 Q4 **Mattighofen** Oberösterreich, NW Austria
107 N16 **Mattinata** Puglia, SE Italy
141 T9 **Maṭṭī, Sabkhat** salt flat Saudi Arabia/UAE
18 M14 **Mattituck** Long Island, New York, NE USA
164 L11 **Mattō** var. Matsutō. Ishikawa, Honshū, SW Japan
Matto Grosso see Mato Grosso
30 M14 **Mattoon** Illinois, N USA
57 L16 **Mattos, Río** ≈ C Bolivia
Mattu see Metu
169 R9 **Matu** Sarawak, East Malaysia
57 E14 **Matucana** Lima, W Peru
Matudo see Matsudo
Matue see Matsue
187 Y15 **Matuku** island S Fiji
112 B9 **Matulji** Primorje-Gorski Kotar, NW Croatia
Matumoto see Matsumoto
55 P5 **Maturín** Monagas, NE Venezuela
Matusaka see Matsusaka
Matuura see Matsuura
Matuyama see Matsuyama
126 K11 **Matveyev Kurgan** Rostovskaya Oblast', SW Russian Federation
127 O8 **Matyshevo** Volgogradskaya Oblast', SW Russian Federation
153 O13 **Mau** var. Maunāth Bhanjan. Uttar Pradesh, N India
83 O14 **Maúa** Niassa, N Mozambique
102 M17 **Maubermé, Pic de** var. Tuc de Moubermé, Sp. Pico Mauberme; prev. Tuc de Maubermé. ▲ France/Spain see also Moubermé, Tuc de
Mauberme, Pico see Maubermé, Pic de/Moubermé, Tuc de
Maubermé, Tuc de see Maubermé, Pic de/Moubermé, Tuc de
103 Q2 **Maubeuge** Nord, N France
166 L8 **Maubin** Irrawaddy, SW Burma
152 L13 **Maudaha** Uttar Pradesh, N India
183 N9 **Maude** New South Wales, SE Australia
195 P3 **Maudheimvidda** physical region Antarctica
65 N22 **Maud Rise** undersea feature S Atlantic Ocean
109 Q4 **Mauerkirchen** Oberösterreich, NW Austria
Mauersee see Mamry, Jezioro
188 K2 **Maug Islands** island group N Northern Mariana Islands
103 Q15 **Mauguio** Hérault, S France
193 N5 **Maui** island Hawai'i, USA, C Pacific Ocean
190 M16 **Mauke** atoll S Cook Islands
62 G13 **Maule** off. Región del Maule. ◈ region C Chile
102 J9 **Mauléon** Deux-Sèvres, W France
102 J16 **Mauléon-Licharre** Pyrénées-Atlantiques, SW France
62 G13 **Maule, Río** ≈ C Chile
63 G17 **Maullín** Los Lagos, S Chile
Maulmain see Moulmein
31 R11 **Maumee** Ohio, N USA
31 Q12 **Maumee River** ≈ Indiana/Ohio, N USA
27 U11 **Maumelle** Arkansas, C USA
27 T11 **Maumelle, Lake** ⊡ Arkansas, C USA
171 O16 **Maumere** prev. Maoemere. Flores, S Indonesia
83 G17 **Maun** Ngamiland, C Botswana
Maunāth Bhanjan see Mau
Maunawai see Waimea
190 H16 **Maungaroa** ▲ Rarotonga, S Cook Islands
184 K3 **Maungatapere** Northland, North Island, NZ
184 K4 **Maungaturoto** Northland, North Island, NZ
191 R10 **Maupiti** var. Maurua. island Îles Sous le Vent, W French Polynesia
152 K14 **Mau Rānīpur** Uttar Pradesh, N India
22 K9 **Maurepas, Lake** ◎ Louisiana, S USA
103 T16 **Maures** ▲▲ SE France
103 O12 **Mauriac** Cantal, C France
Maurice see Mauritius
65 J20 **Maurice Ewing Bank** undersea feature SW Atlantic Ocean
182 C4 **Maurice, Lake** salt lake South Australia
18 I17 **Maurice River** ≈ New Jersey, NE USA
25 Y10 **Mauriceville** Texas, SW USA
98 K12 **Maurik** Gelderland, C Netherlands
76 H8 **Mauritania** off. Islamic Republic of Mauritania, Ar. Mūrītānīyah. ◆ republic W Africa
173 W15 **Mauritius** off. Republic of Mauritius, Fr. Maurice. ◆ republic W Indian Ocean
173 N9 **Mauritius Trench** undersea feature W Indian Ocean
102 H6 **Mauron** Morbihan, NW France
103 N13 **Maurs** Cantal, C France
Maurua see Maupiti
Maury Mid-Ocean Channel see Maury Seachannel
64 L6 **Maury Seachannel** var. Maury Mid-Ocean Channel. undersea feature N Atlantic Ocean
30 K8 **Mauston** Wisconsin, N USA
109 R8 **Mauterndorf** Salzburg, NW Austria
109 T4 **Mauthausen** Oberösterreich, N Austria
109 Q9 **Mauthen** Kärnten, S Austria
83 F15 **Mavinga** Cuando Cubango, SE Angola
83 M17 **Mavita** Manica, W Mozambique
115 K22 **Mavrópetra, Akrotírio** headland Thíra, Kykládes, Greece, Aegean Sea
115 F16 **Mavrovoúni** ▲ C Greece
184 Q8 **Mawhai Point** headland North Island, NZ
166 L3 **Mawlaik** Sagaing, C Burma
Mawlamyine see Moulmein
141 N14 **Mawr, Wādī** dry watercourse NW Yemen
195 X5 **Mawson** Australian research station Antarctica
195 X5 **Mawson Coast** physical region Antarctica
28 M4 **Max** North Dakota, N USA
41 W12 **Maxcanú** Yucatán, SE Mexico
Maxesibebi see Mount Ayliff
109 Q5 **Maxglan** ✕ (Salzburg) Salzburg, W Austria
93 K16 **Maxmo** Fin. Maksamaa. Länsi-Suomi, W Finland
21 T11 **Maxton** North Carolina, SE USA
25 R8 **May** Texas, SW USA
186 B6 **May** ≈ NW PNG
123 R10 **Maya** ≈ E Russian Federation
151 Q19 **Māyābandar** Andaman and Nicobar Islands, India, E Indian Ocean
Mayadin see Al Mayādīn
44 L5 **Mayaguana** island SE Bahamas
44 L5 **Mayaguana Passage** passage SE Bahamas
45 S6 **Mayagüez** W Puerto Rico
45 R6 **Mayagüez, Bahía de** bay W Puerto Rico
Mayals see Maials
79 G20 **Mayama** Le Pool, SE Congo
37 V8 **Maya, Mesa De** ▲ Colorado, C USA
143 R4 **Mayamey** Semnān, N Iran
42 F3 **Maya Mountains** Sp. Montañas Mayas. ▲▲ Belize/Guatemala
44 I7 **Mayarí** Holguín, E Cuba
Mayas, Montañas see Maya Mountains
18 I17 **May, Cape** headland New Jersey, NE USA
80 J11 **Maych'ew** var. Mai Chio, It. Mai Ceu. Tigray, N Ethiopia
138 I2 **Maydān Ikbiz** Ḩalab, N Syria
149 Q5 **Maydān Shahr** Wardag, E Afghanistan
80 O12 **Maydh** Sanaag, N Somalia
Maydī see Mīdī
Mayebashi see Maebashi
Mayence see Mainz
102 K6 **Mayenne** Mayenne, NW France
102 J6 **Mayenne** ◈ department NW France
102 J7 **Mayenne** ≈ N France
36 K12 **Mayer** Arizona, SW USA
22 J4 **Mayersville** Mississippi, S USA
11 P14 **Mayerthorpe** Alberta, SW Canada
21 S12 **Mayesville** South Carolina, SE USA
185 G19 **Mayfield** Canterbury, South Island, NZ
33 N14 **Mayfield** Idaho, NW USA
20 G7 **Mayfield** Kentucky, S USA
36 L5 **Mayfield** Utah, W USA
162 K9 **Mayhan** Övörhangay, C Mongolia
37 T14 **Mayhill** New Mexico, SW USA
145 T9 **Maykain** Kaz. Mayqayyng. Pavlodar, NE Kazakhstan
126 L14 **Maykop** Respublika Adygeya, SW Russian Federation
Maylibash see Maylybas
Mayli-Say see Mayluu-Suu
147 T9 **Mayluu-Suu** prev. Mayli-Say, Kir. Mayly-Say. Dzhalal-Abadskaya Oblast', W Kyrgyzstan
144 L14 **Maylybas** prev. Maylibash. Kyzylorda, S Kazakhstan
Mayly-Say see Mayluu-Suu
Maymana see Meymaneh
166 M5 **Maymyo** Mandalay, C Burma
123 V7 **Mayn** ≈ NE Russian Federation
127 Q5 **Mayna** Ul'yanovskaya Oblast', W Russian Federation
21 N8 **Maynardville** Tennessee, S USA
14 J13 **Maynooth** Ontario, SE Canada
10 I6 **Mayo** Yukon Territory, NW Canada
23 U9 **Mayo** Florida, SE USA
97 B16 **Mayo** Ir. Maigh Eo. cultural region W Ireland
Mayo see Maio
78 G12 **Mayo-Kébbi** off. Préfecture du Mayo-Kébbi, var. Mayo-Kébi. ◈ prefecture SW Chad
Mayo-Kébi see Mayo-Kébbi
79 F19 **Mayoko** Le Niari, SW Congo
171 P4 **Mayon Volcano** ✷ Luzon, N Philippines
61 A24 **Mayor Buratovich** Buenos Aires, E Argentina
104 L4 **Mayorga** Castilla-León, N Spain
184 N6 **Mayor Island** island NE NZ
Mayor Pablo Lagerenza see Capitán Pablo Lagerenza
173 I14 **Mayotte** ◇ French territorial collectivity E Africa
Mayoumba see Mayumba
Mayqayyng see Maykain
44 J13 **May Pen** C Jamaica
171 O1 **Mayraira Point** headland Luzon, N Philippines
109 N8 **Mayrhofen** Tirol, W Austria
186 A6 **May River** East Sepik, NW PNG
123 R13 **Mayskiy** Amurskaya Oblast', SE Russian Federation
127 O15 **Mayskiy** Kabardino-Balkarskaya Respublika, SW Russian Federation
145 U9 **Mayskoye** Pavlodar, NE Kazakhstan
18 J17 **Mays Landing** New Jersey, NE USA
21 N4 **Maysville** Kentucky, S USA
27 R2 **Maysville** Missouri, C USA
79 D20 **Mayumba** var. Mayoumba. Nyanga, S Gabon
31 S8 **Mayville** Michigan, N USA
18 C11 **Mayville** New York, NE USA
29 Q4 **Mayville** North Dakota, N USA
Mayyali see Mahe
Mayyit, Al Baḩr al see Dead Sea
83 J15 **Mazabuka** Southern, S Zambia
Mazaca see Kayseri
Mazagan see El-Jadida
32 J7 **Mazama** Washington, NW USA
103 O15 **Mazamet** Tarn, S France
143 O4 **Māzandarān** off. Ostān-e Māzandarān. ◈ province N Iran
156 F7 **Mazar** Xinjiang Uygur Zizhiqu, NW China
107 H24 **Mazara del Vallo** Sicilia, Italy, C Mediterranean Sea
149 O2 **Mazār-e Sharīf** var. Mazār-i Sharif. Balkh, N Afghanistan
Mazār-i Sharif see Mazār-e Sharīf
105 R13 **Mazarrón** Murcia, SE Spain
105 R14 **Mazarrón, Golfo de** gulf SE Spain
55 S9 **Mazaruni River** ≈ N Guyana
42 B6 **Mazatenango** Suchitepéquez, SW Guatemala
40 I10 **Mazatlán** Sinaloa, C Mexico
36 L12 **Mazatzal Mountains** ▲▲ Arizona, SW USA
118 D10 **Mažeikiai** Telšiai, NW Lithuania
118 D7 **Mazirbe** Talsi, NW Latvia
40 G5 **Mazocahui** Sonora, NW Mexico
57 I18 **Mazocruz** Puno, S Peru
Mazoe, Rio see Mazowe
79 N21 **Mazomeno** Maniema, E Dem. Rep. Congo
159 Q6 **Mazong Shan** ▲ N China
83 L16 **Mazowe** var. Rio Mazoe. ≈ Mozambique/Zimbabwe
110 L11 **Mazowieckie** ◈ province C Poland
Mazra'a see Al Mazra'ah
138 G6 **Mazraat Kfar Debiâne** C Lebanon
118 H7 **Mazsalaca** Est. Väike-Salatsi, Ger. Salisburg. Valmiera, N Latvia
110 L9 **Mazury** physical region NE Poland
119 M20 **Mazyr** Rus. Mozyr'. Homyel'skaya Voblasts', SE Belarus
107 K25 **Mazzarino** Sicilia, Italy, C Mediterranean Sea
Mba see Ba
83 L21 **Mbabane** ● (Swaziland) NW Swaziland
Mbacké see Mbaké
77 N16 **Mbahiakro** E Ivory Coast
79 I16 **Mbaïki** var. M'Baiki. Lobaye, SW Central African Republic
79 F14 **Mbakaou, Lac de** ◎ C Cameroon
76 G11 **Mbaké** var. Mbacké. W Senegal
82 L11 **Mbala** prev. Abercorn. Northern, NE Zambia
83 J18 **Mbalabala** prev. Balla Balla. Matabeleland South, SW Zimbabwe
81 G18 **Mbale** E Uganda
79 E16 **Mbalmayo** var. M'Balmayo. Centre, S Cameroon
81 H25 **Mbamba Bay** Ruvuma, S Tanzania
79 I18 **Mbandaka** prev. Coquilhatville. Equateur, NW Dem. Rep. Congo
82 B9 **M'Banza Congo** var. Mbanza Congo; prev. São Salvador, São Salvador do Congo. Zaire, NW Angola
79 G21 **Mbanza-Ngungu** Bas-Congo, W Dem. Rep. Congo
81 E19 **Mbarara** SW Uganda
79 L15 **Mbari** ≈ SE Central African Republic
81 I24 **Mbarika Mountains** ▲▲ S Tanzania
83 J24 **Mbashe** ≈ S South Africa
Mbatiki see Batiki
78 F13 **Mbé** Nord, N Cameroon
81 J24 **Mbemkuru** var. Mbwemkuru. ≈ S Tanzania
Mbengga see Beqa
172 H13 **Mbéni** Grande Comore, NW Comoros
83 K18 **Mberengwa** Midlands, S Zimbabwe
81 G24 **Mbeya** Mbeya, SW Tanzania
81 G23 **Mbeya** ◈ region S Tanzania
79 E19 **Mbigou** Ngounié, C Gabon
Mbilua see Vella Lavella
79 F19 **Mbinda** Le Niari, SW Congo
79 D17 **Mbini** W Equatorial Guinea
Mbini see Uolo, Río
83 L18 **Mbizi** Masvingo, SE Zimbabwe
81 G23 **Mbogo** Mbeya, W Tanzania
79 N15 **Mboki** Haut-Mbomou, SE Central African Republic
79 G18 **Mbomo** Cuvette, NW Congo
79 L15 **Mbomou** ◈ prefecture SE Central African Republic
Mbomou/M'Bomu/Mbomu see Bomu
76 F11 **Mbour** W Senegal
76 I10 **Mbout** Gorgol, S Mauritania
79 J14 **Mbrès** var. Mbrés. Nana-Grébizi, C Central African Republic
79 L22 **Mbuji-Mayi** prev. Bakwanga. Kasai Oriental, S Dem. Rep. Congo
81 H21 **Mbulu** Arusha, N Tanzania
186 E5 **M'bunai** var. Bunai. Manus Island, N PNG
62 N8 **Mburucuyá** Corrientes, NE Argentina
Mbutha see Buca
Mbwemkuru see Mbemkuru
81 G21 **Mbwikwe** Singida, C Tanzania
13 O15 **McAdam** New Brunswick, SE Canada
25 O5 **McAdoo** Texas, SW USA
35 V2 **McAfee Peak** ▲ Nevada, W USA
27 P11 **McAlester** Oklahoma, C USA
25 S17 **McAllen** Texas, SW USA
21 S11 **McBee** South Carolina, SE USA
11 N14 **McBride** British Columbia, SW Canada
24 M9 **McCamey** Texas, SW USA
33 R15 **McCammon** Idaho, NW USA
35 X11 **McCarran** ✕ (Las Vegas) Nevada, W USA
39 T11 **McCarthy** Alaska, USA
30 M5 **McCaslin Mountain** hill Wisconsin, N USA
25 O2 **McClellan Creek** ≈ Texas, SW USA
21 T14 **McClellanville** South Carolina, SE USA
8 L6 **McClintock Channel** channel Nunavut, N Canada
195 R12 **McClintock, Mount** ▲ Antarctica

◆ Country ● Country Capital ◇ Dependent Territory ○ Dependent Territory Capital ◈ Administrative Region ✕ International Airport ▲ Mountain ▲▲ Mountain Range ✷ Volcano ≈ River ◎ Lake ⊡ Reservoir

35 N2 **McCloud** California, W USA
35 N3 **McCloud River** ≈ California, W USA
35 Q9 **McClure, Lake** ▣ California, W USA
197 O8 **McClure Strait** strait Northwest Territories, N Canada
29 N4 **McClusky** North Dakota, N USA
21 T11 **McColl** South Carolina, SE USA
22 K7 **McComb** Mississippi, S USA
18 E16 **McConnellsburg** Pennsylvania, NE USA
31 T14 **McConnelsville** Ohio, N USA
28 M17 **McCook** Nebraska, C USA
21 P13 **McCormick** South Carolina, SE USA
11 W16 **McCreary** Manitoba, S Canada
27 W11 **McCrory** Arkansas, C USA
25 T10 **McDade** Texas, SW USA
23 O8 **McDavid** Florida, SE USA
35 T1 **McDermitt** Nevada, W USA
23 S4 **McDonough** Georgia, SE USA
36 L12 **McDowell Mountains** ⛰ Arizona, SW USA
20 H8 **McEwen** Tennessee, S USA
35 R12 **McFarland** California, W USA
Mcfarlane, Lake see Macfarlane, Lake
27 P12 **McGee Creek Lake** ▣ Oklahoma, C USA
27 W13 **McGehee** Arkansas, C USA
35 X5 **Mcgill** Nevada, W USA
14 K11 **McGillivray, Lac** ⊚ Québec, SE Canada
39 P10 **Mcgrath** Alaska, USA
25 T8 **McGregor** Texas, SW USA
33 O12 **McGuire, Mount** ▲ Idaho, NW USA
83 M14 **Mchinji** prev. Fort Manning. Central, W Malawi
28 M7 **McIntosh** South Dakota, N USA
9 S7 **McKeand** ≈ Baffin Island, Nunavut, NE Canada
191 R4 **McKean Island** island Phoenix Islands, C Kiribati
30 J13 **McKee Creek** ≈ Illinois, N USA
18 C15 **Mckeesport** Pennsylvania, NE USA
21 V7 **McKenney** Virginia, NE USA
20 G8 **McKenzie** Tennessee, S USA
185 B20 **McKerrow, Lake** ⊚ South Island, NZ
39 Q10 **McKinley, Mount** var. Denali. ▲ Alaska, USA
39 R10 **McKinley Park** Alaska, USA
34 K3 **McKinleyville** California, W USA
25 U6 **McKinney** Texas, SW USA
26 J5 **McKinney, Lake** ⊚ Kansas, C USA
28 M7 **McLaughlin** South Dakota, N USA
25 O2 **McLean** Texas, SW USA
30 M16 **Mcleansboro** Illinois, N USA
11 O13 **McLennan** Alberta, W Canada
14 L9 **McLennan, Lac** ⊚ Québec, SE Canada
10 M13 **McLeod Lake** British Columbia, W Canada
27 N10 **McLoud** Oklahoma, C USA
32 G15 **McLoughlin, Mount** ▲ Oregon, NW USA
8 J4 **M'Clure Strait** strait NW Canada
37 U15 **McMillan, Lake** ▣ New Mexico, SW USA
32 G11 **McMinnville** Oregon, NW USA
20 K9 **McMinnville** Tennessee, S USA
195 R13 **McMurdo** US research station Antarctica
24 H9 **McNary** Texas, SW USA
37 N13 **Mcnary** Arizona, SW USA
27 N5 **McPherson** Kansas, C USA
McPherson see Fort McPherson
23 U6 **McRae** Georgia, SE USA
29 P4 **McVille** North Dakota, N USA
83 J25 **Mdantsane** Eastern Cape, SE South Africa
167 T6 **Me** Ninh Binh, N Vietnam
26 J7 **Meade** Kansas, C USA
39 O5 **Meade River** ≈ Alaska, USA
35 Y11 **Mead, Lake** ▣ Arizona/Nevada, W USA
24 M5 **Meadow** Texas, SW USA
11 S14 **Meadow Lake** Saskatchewan, C Canada
35 Y10 **Meadow Valley Wash** ≈ Nevada, W USA
22 J7 **Meadville** Mississippi, S USA
18 B12 **Meadville** Pennsylvania, NE USA
14 F14 **Meaford** Ontario, S Canada
Meáin, Inis see Inishmaan
104 G8 **Mealhada** Aveiro, N Portugal
13 R8 **Mealy Mountains** ⛰ Newfoundland and Labrador, E Canada
11 O10 **Meander River** Alberta, W Canada
32 E11 **Meares, Cape** headland Oregon, NW USA
Measca, Loch see Mask, Lough
97 F17 **Meath** Ir. An Mhí. cultural region E Ireland
11 T14 **Meath Park** Saskatchewan, S Canada
103 O5 **Meaux** Seine-et-Marne, N France
21 T9 **Mebane** North Carolina, SE USA
171 U12 **Mebo, Gunung** ▲ Papua, E Indonesia
94 I8 **Mebonden** Sør-Trøndelag, S Norway
82 A10 **Mebridege** ≈ NW Angola
35 W16 **Mecca** California, W USA
Mecca see Makkah
29 Y14 **Mechanicsville** Iowa, C USA
18 L10 **Mechanicville** New York, NE USA
99 H17 **Mechelen** Eng. Mechlin, Fr. Malines. Antwerpen, C Belgium
188 C8 **Mecherchar** var. Eil Malk. island Palau Islands, Palau
101 D17 **Mechernich** Nordrhein-Westfalen, W Germany
126 L12 **Mechetinskaya** Rostovskaya Oblast', SW Russian Federation
114 J11 **Mechka** ≈ S Bulgaria
Mechlin see Mechelen
61 D23 **Mechongué** Buenos Aires, E Argentina
115 L14 **Mecidiye** Edirne, NW Turkey
101 I24 **Meckenbeuren** Baden-Württemberg, S Germany
100 L8 **Mecklenburger Bucht** bay N Germany
100 M10 **Mecklenburgische Seenplatte** wetland NE Germany
100 L9 **Mecklenburg-Vorpommern** ◆ state NE Germany
83 Q15 **Meconta** Nampula, NE Mozambique
111 I25 **Mecsek** ⛰ SW Hungary
83 P14 **Mecubúri** ≈ N Mozambique
83 Q14 **Mecúfi** Cabo Delgado, NE Mozambique
82 O13 **Mecula** Niassa, N Mozambique
168 I8 **Medan** Sumatera, E Indonesia
61 A24 **Médanos** var. Medanos. Buenos Aires, E Argentina
61 C19 **Médanos** Entre Ríos, E Argentina
155 K24 **Medawachchiya** North Central Province, N Sri Lanka
106 C8 **Mede** Lombardia, N Italy
74 J5 **Médéa** var. El Mediyya, Lemdiyya. N Algeria
Medeba see Ma'dabā
54 E8 **Medellín** Antioquia, NW Colombia
100 H9 **Medem** ≈ NW Germany
98 J8 **Medemblik** Noord-Holland, NW Netherlands
75 N7 **Médenine** var. Madanīyīn. SE Tunisia
76 G9 **Mederdra** Trarza, SW Mauritania
Medeshamstede see Peterborough
42 F4 **Medesto Mendez** Izabal, NE Guatemala
19 O11 **Medford** Massachusetts, NE USA
27 N8 **Medford** Oklahoma, C USA
32 G15 **Medford** Oregon, NW USA
30 K6 **Medford** Wisconsin, N USA
39 P10 **Medfra** Alaska, USA
116 M14 **Medgidia** Constanța, SE Romania
Medgyes see Mediaș
43 O5 **Media Luna, Arrecifes de la** reef E Honduras
60 G11 **Medianeira** Paraná, S Brazil
29 Y15 **Mediapolis** Iowa, C USA
116 I11 **Mediaș** Ger. Mediasch, Hung. Medgyes. Sibiu, C Romania
41 S15 **Medias Aguas** Veracruz-Llave, SE Mexico
Mediasch see Mediaș
106 G10 **Medicina** Emilia-Romagna, C Italy
33 X16 **Medicine Bow** Wyoming, C USA
37 S2 **Medicine Bow Mountains** ⛰ Colorado/Wyoming, C USA
33 X16 **Medicine Bow River** ≈ Wyoming, C USA
11 R17 **Medicine Hat** Alberta, SW Canada
26 L7 **Medicine Lodge** Kansas, C USA
26 L7 **Medicine Lodge River** ≈ Kansas/Oklahoma, C USA
112 E7 **Međimurje** off. Međimurska Županija. ◆ province N Croatia
Međimurska Županija see Međimurje
54 G10 **Medina** Cundinamarca, C Colombia
18 E9 **Medina** New York, NE USA
29 O5 **Medina** North Dakota, N USA
31 T11 **Medina** Ohio, N USA
25 Q11 **Medina** Texas, SW USA
Medina see Al Madīnah
105 P6 **Medinaceli** Castilla-León, N Spain
104 L6 **Medina del Campo** Castilla-León, N Spain
104 L5 **Medina de Ríoseco** Castilla-León, N Spain
Médina Gonassé see Médina Gounas
76 H12 **Médina Gounas** var. Médina Gonassé. S Senegal
25 S12 **Medina River** ≈ Texas, SW USA
104 K16 **Medina Sidonia** Andalucía, S Spain
Medinat Israel see Israel
119 H14 **Medininkai** Vilnius, SE Lithuania
153 R16 **Medinīpur** West Bengal, NE India
Mediolanum see Saintes, France
Mediolanum see Milano, Italy
Mediomatrica see Metz
121 Q11 **Mediterranean Ridge** undersea feature C Mediterranean Sea
121 O16 **Mediterranean Sea** Fr. Mer Méditerranée. sea Africa/Asia/Europe
Méditerranée, Mer see Mediterranean Sea
79 N17 **Medje** Orientale, NE Dem. Rep. Congo
114 G7 **Medkovets** Montana, NW Bulgaria
93 J15 **Medle** Västerbotten, N Sweden
127 W7 **Mednogorsk** Orenburgskaya Oblast', W Russian Federation
123 W9 **Mednyy, Ostrov** island E Russian Federation
102 J12 **Médoc** cultural region SW France
159 Q16 **Mêdog** Xizang Zizhiqu, W China
28 J5 **Medora** North Dakota, N USA
79 E17 **Médouneu** Woleu-Ntem, N Gabon
106 I7 **Meduna** ≈ NE Italy
Medunta see Mantes-la-Jolie
Medvedica see Medveditsa
126 J16 **Medveditsa** var. Medvedica. ≈ W Russian Federation
127 O9 **Medveditsa** ≈ SW Russian Federation
112 E8 **Medvednica** ⛰ NE Croatia
125 R15 **Medvedok** Kirovskaya Oblast', NW Russian Federation
123 S6 **Medvezh'i, Ostrova** island group NE Russian Federation
124 J9 **Medvezh'yegorsk** Respublika Kareliya, NW Russian Federation
109 T11 **Medvode** Ger. Zwischenwässern. NW Slovenia
126 J4 **Medyn'** Kaluzhskaya Oblast', W Russian Federation
180 J10 **Meekatharra** Western Australia
37 Q4 **Meeker** Colorado, C USA
13 T12 **Meelpaeg Lake** ⊚ Newfoundland and Labrador, E Canada
Meenen see Menen
101 M16 **Meerane** Sachsen, E Germany
101 D15 **Meerbusch** Nordrhein-Westfalen, W Germany
98 I12 **Meerkerk** Zuid-Holland, C Netherlands
99 L18 **Meerssen** var. Mersen. Limburg, SE Netherlands
152 J10 **Meerut** Uttar Pradesh, N India
33 U13 **Meeteetse** Wyoming, C USA
99 K17 **Meeuwen** Limburg, NE Belgium
81 J16 **Mēga** Oromo, C Ethiopia
81 J16 **Mēga Escarpment** escarpment S Ethiopia
Megála Kalívia see Megála Kalývia
115 E16 **Megála Kalývia** var. Megála Kalívia. Thessalía, C Greece
115 H14 **Megáli Panagiá** var. Megáli Panayía. Kentrikí Makedonía, N Greece
Megáli Panayía see Megáli Panagiá
Megáli Préspa, Límni see Prespa, Lake
114 K12 **Megálo Livádi** ▲ Bulgaria/Greece
115 E20 **Megalópoli** prev. Megalópolis. Pelopónnisos, S Greece
Megalópolis see Megalópoli
171 U12 **Megamo** Papua, E Indonesia
115 C18 **Meganísi** island Iónioi Nísoi, Greece, C Mediterranean Sea
Meganom, Mys see Mehanom, Mys
Mégantic see Lac-Mégantic
15 R12 **Mégantic, Mont** ▲ Québec, SE Canada
115 G19 **Mégara** Attikí, C Greece
25 R5 **Megargel** Texas, SW USA
98 K13 **Megen** Noord-Brabant, S Netherlands
153 U13 **Meghālaya** ◆ state NE India
153 U16 **Meghna** ≈ S Bangladesh
137 V13 **Meghri** Rus. Megri. SE Armenia
115 Q23 **Megísti** var. Kastellórizon. island SE Greece
Megri see Meghri
Mehabad see Mahābād
116 F13 **Mehadia** Hung. Mehádia. Caraș-Severin, SW Romania
92 L7 **Mehamn** Finnmark, N Norway
117 U13 **Mehanom, Mys** Rus. Mys Meganom. headland S Ukraine
149 P14 **Mehar** Sind, SE Pakistan
180 J8 **Meharry, Mount** ▲ Western Australia
Mehdia see Mahdia
116 G14 **Mehedinți** ◆ county SW Romania
153 S15 **Meherpur** Khulna, W Bangladesh
21 W8 **Meherrin River** ≈ North Carolina/Virginia, SE USA
Meheso see Mī'ēso
191 T11 **Mehetia** island Îles du Vent, W French Polynesia
118 K6 **Mehikoorma** Tartumaa, E Estonia
Me Hka see Nmai Hka
143 N5 **Mehrabad** × (Tehrān) Tehrān, N Iran
142 J7 **Mehrān** Īlām, W Iran
143 Q14 **Mehrān, Rūd-e** prev. Mansurabad. ≈ W Iran
143 Q9 **Mehrīz** Yazd, C Iran
149 R5 **Mehtarlām** var. Mehtar Lām, Meterlam, Methariam, Metharlam. Laghmān, E Afghanistan
103 N8 **Mehun-sur-Yèvre** Cher, C France
79 G14 **Meiganga** Adamaoua, NE Cameroon
160 H10 **Meigu** var. Bapu. Sichuan, C China
163 W11 **Meihekou** var. Hailong. Jilin, NE China
99 L15 **Meijel** Limburg, SE Netherlands
Meijiang see Ningdu
166 M5 **Meiktila** Mandalay, C Burma
Meilbhe, Loch see Melvin, Lough
108 G7 **Meilen** Zürich, N Switzerland
Meilu see Wuchuan
161 T12 **Meinhua Yu** island N Taiwan
101 J17 **Meiningen** Thüringen, C Germany
108 F9 **Meiringen** Bern, S Switzerland
Meishan see Jinzhai
101 O15 **Meissen** var. Meißen. Sachsen, E Germany
101 I15 **Meissner** ▲ C Germany
99 K25 **Meix-devant-Virton** Luxembourg, SE Belgium
Mei Xian see Meizhou
Meixing see Xinjin
161 P13 **Meizhou** var. Meixian, Mei Xian. Guangdong, S China
42 F7 **Mejicanos** San Salvador, C El Salvador
Méjico see Mexico
62 G5 **Mejillones** Antofagasta, N Chile
189 V5 **Mejit Island** var. Mājeej. island Ratak Chain, NE Marshall Islands
79 F17 **Mékambo** Ogooué-Ivindo, NE Gabon
80 J10 **Mek'elē** var. Makale. Tigray, N Ethiopia
74 I10 **Mekerrhane, Sebkha** var. Sebkha Meqerghane, Sebkra Mekerrhane. salt flat C Algeria
Mekerrhane, Sebkra see Mekerrhane, Sebkha
76 G10 **Mékhé** NW Senegal
146 G14 **Mekhinli** Ahal Welaýaty, C Turkmenistan
15 P9 **Mékinac, Lac** ⊚ Québec, SE Canada
Meklong see Samut Songhram
74 G6 **Meknès** N Morocco
167 S10 **Mekong** var. Lan-ts'ang Chiang, Cam. Mékôngk, Chin. Lancang Jiang, Lao. Mènam Khong, Th. Mae Nam Khong, Tib. Dza Chu, Vtn. Sông Tiên Giang. ≈ SE Asia
Mékôngk see Mekong
167 T15 **Mekong, Mouths of the** delta S Vietnam
38 L12 **Mekoryuk** Nunivak Island, Alaska, USA
77 R14 **Mékrou** ≈ N Benin
168 K9 **Melaka** var. Malacca. Melaka, Peninsular Malaysia
168 L9 **Melaka** var. Malacca. ◆ state Peninsular Malaysia
Melaka, Selat see Malacca, Strait of
192 I7 **Melanesia** island group W Pacific Ocean
192 J7 **Melanesian Basin** undersea feature W Pacific Ocean
171 R9 **Melanguane** Pulau Karakelang, N Indonesia
169 R11 **Melawi, Sungai** ≈ Borneo, N Indonesia
183 N12 **Melbourne** state capital Victoria, SE Australia
27 V9 **Melbourne** Arkansas, C USA
23 Y12 **Melbourne** Florida, SE USA
29 W14 **Melbourne** Iowa, C USA
92 G10 **Melbu** Nordland, C Norway
Melchor de Mencos see Ciudad Melchor de Mencos
63 F19 **Melchor, Isla** island Archipiélago de los Chonos, S Chile
40 M9 **Melchor Ocampo** Zacatecas, C Mexico
14 C11 **Meldrum Bay** Manitoulin Island, Ontario, S Canada
Meleda see Mljet
106 D8 **Melegnano** prev. Marignano. Lombardia, N Italy
188 F9 **Melekeok** var. Melekeiok. Babeldaob, N Palau
112 L9 **Melenci** Hung. Melencze. Serbia, N Serbia and Montenegro (Yugo.)
Melencze see Melenci
127 N4 **Melenki** Vladimirskaya Oblast', W Russian Federation
127 V6 **Meleuz** Respublika Bashkortostan, W Russian Federation
12 L6 **Mélèzes, Rivière aux** ≈ Québec, C Canada
78 I11 **Melfi** Guéra, S Chad
107 M17 **Melfi** Basilicata, S Italy
11 U14 **Melfort** Saskatchewan, S Canada
104 H4 **Melgaço** Viana do Castelo, N Portugal
105 N4 **Melgar de Fernamental** Castilla-León, N Spain
74 L6 **Melghir, Chott** var. Chott Melrhir. salt lake E Algeria
94 H8 **Melhus** Sør-Trøndelag, S Norway
104 H3 **Melide** Galicia, NW Spain
Meligalá see Meligalás
115 E21 **Meligalás** prev. Meligalá. Pelopónnisos, S Greece
60 L12 **Mel, Ilha do** island S Brazil
120 E10 **Melilla** anc. Rusaddir, Russadir. Melilla, Spain, N Africa
63 G18 **Melimoyu, Monte** ▲ S Chile
169 V11 **Melintang, Danau** ⊚ Borneo, N Indonesia
117 U7 **Melioratyvne** Dnipropetrovs'ka Oblast', E Ukraine
62 G11 **Melipilla** Santiago, C Chile
115 I25 **Mélissa, Akrotírio** headland Kríti, Greece, E Mediterranean Sea
11 W17 **Melita** Manitoba, S Canada
Melita see Mljet
Melitene see Malatya
107 M23 **Melito di Porto Salvo** Calabria, SW Italy
117 U10 **Melitopol'** Zaporiz'ka Oblast', S Ukraine
109 V4 **Melk** Niederösterreich, NE Austria
95 K15 **Mellan-Fryken** ⊚ C Sweden
99 E17 **Melle** Oost-Vlaanderen, NW Belgium
100 G13 **Melle** Niedersachsen, NW Germany
95 J17 **Mellerud** Västra Götaland, S Sweden
102 K10 **Melle-sur-Bretonne** Deux-Sèvres, W France
29 P8 **Mellette** South Dakota, N USA
121 O15 **Mellieha** E Malta
80 B10 **Mellit** Northern Darfur, W Sudan
75 N7 **Mellita** × SE Tunisia
63 G21 **Mellizo Sur, Cerro** ▲ S Chile
100 G9 **Mellum** island NW Germany
83 L22 **Melmoth** KwaZulu/Natal, E South Africa
111 D16 **Mělník** Ger. Melnik. Středočeský Kraj, NW Czech Republic
122 J12 **Mel'nikovo** Tomskaya Oblast', C Russian Federation
61 G18 **Melo** Cerro Largo, NE Uruguay
Melodunum see Melun
Melrhir, Chott see Melghir, Chott
183 P7 **Melrose** New South Wales, SE Australia
182 I7 **Melrose** South Australia
29 T7 **Melrose** Minnesota, N USA
33 Q11 **Melrose** Montana, NW USA
37 V12 **Melrose** New Mexico, SW USA
108 I8 **Mels** Sankt Gallen, NE Switzerland
Melsetter see Chimanimani
33 V9 **Melstone** Montana, NW USA
101 I16 **Melsungen** Hessen, C Germany
92 L12 **Meltaus** Lappi, NW Finland
97 N19 **Melton Mowbray** C England, UK
82 Q13 **Meluco** Cabo Delgado, NE Mozambique
103 O5 **Melun** anc. Melodunum. Seine-et-Marne, N France
80 F12 **Melut** Upper Nile, SE Sudan
27 P5 **Melvern Lake** ▣ Kansas, C USA
11 V16 **Melville** Saskatchewan, S Canada
Melville Bay/Melville Bugt see Qimusseriarsuaq
45 O11 **Melville Hall** × (Dominica) NE Dominica
181 O1 **Melville Island** island Northern Territory, N Australia
8 K5 **Melville Island** island Parry Islands, Northwest Territories, NW Canada
9 W9 **Melville, Lake** ⊚ Newfoundland and Labrador, E Canada
9 O7 **Melville Peninsula** peninsula Nunavut, NE Canada
Melville Sound see Viscount Melville Sound
25 Q9 **Melvin** Texas, SW USA
97 D15 **Melvin, Lough** Ir. Loch Meilbhe. ⊚ S Northern Ireland, UK/Ireland
169 S12 **Memala** Borneo, C Indonesia
113 L22 **Memaliaj** Gjirokastër, S Albania
83 Q14 **Memba** Nampula, NE Mozambique
83 Q14 **Memba, Baia de** inlet NE Mozambique
Membidj see Manbij
Memel see Neman, NE Europe
Memel see Klaipėda, Lithuania
101 J23 **Memmingen** Bayern, S Germany
27 U1 **Memphis** Missouri, C USA
20 E10 **Memphis** Tennessee, S USA
25 P3 **Memphis** Texas, SW USA
20 E10 **Memphis** × Tennessee, S USA
15 Q13 **Memphrémagog, Lac** var. Lake Memphremagog. ⊚ Canada/USA see also Memphremagog, Lake
19 N6 **Memphremagog, Lake** var. Lac Memphrémagog. ⊚ Canada/USA see also Memphrémagog, Lac
117 Q2 **Mena** Chernihivs'ka Oblast', NE Ukraine
27 S12 **Mena** Arkansas, C USA
Menaam see Menaldum
Menado see Manado
106 D6 **Menaggio** Lombardia, N Italy
29 T6 **Menahga** Minnesota, N USA
77 R10 **Ménaka** Goa, E Mali
98 K5 **Menaldum** Fris. Menaam. Friesland, N Netherlands
Mènam Khong see Mekong
74 E7 **Menara** × (Marrakech) C Morocco
25 Q9 **Menard** Texas, SW USA
193 Q12 **Menard Fracture Zone** tectonic feature E Pacific Ocean
30 M7 **Menasha** Wisconsin, N USA
Mencezi Garagum see Merkezi Garagumy
193 U9 **Mendaña Fracture Zone** tectonic feature E Pacific Ocean
169 S13 **Mendawai, Sungai** ≈ Borneo, C Indonesia
103 P13 **Mende** anc. Mimatum. Lozère, S France
81 J14 **Mendebo** ⛰ C Ethiopia
80 J9 **Mendefera** prev. Adi Ugri. S Eritrea
197 S7 **Mendeleyev Ridge** undersea feature Arctic Ocean
127 T3 **Mendeleyevsk** Respublika Tatarstan, W Russian Federation
101 F15 **Menden** Nordrhein-Westfalen, W Germany
22 L6 **Mendenhall** Mississippi, S USA
38 L13 **Mendenhall, Cape** headland Nunivak Island, Alaska, USA
41 P9 **Méndez** var. Villa de Méndez. Tamaulipas, C Mexico
80 H13 **Mendī** Oromo, C Ethiopia
186 C7 **Mendi** Southern Highlands, W PNG
97 K22 **Mendip Hills** var. Mendips. hill range S England, UK
Mendips see Mendip Hills
34 L6 **Mendocino** California, W USA
34 J3 **Mendocino, Cape** headland California, W USA
193 N4 **Mendocino Fracture Zone** tectonic feature NE Pacific Ocean
35 P10 **Mendota** California, W USA
30 L11 **Mendota** Illinois, N USA
30 K8 **Mendota, Lake** ⊚ Wisconsin, N USA
62 I11 **Mendoza** Mendoza, W Argentina
62 I12 **Mendoza** off. Provincia de Mendoza. ◆ province W Argentina
108 H12 **Mendrisio** Ticino, S Switzerland
168 L10 **Mendung** Pulau Mendol, W Indonesia
54 I5 **Mene de Mauroa** Falcón, NW Venezuela
54 I5 **Mene Grande** Zulia, NW Venezuela
136 B14 **Menemen** İzmir, W Turkey
99 C18 **Menen** var. Meenen, Fr. Menin. West-Vlaanderen, W Belgium
163 Q8 **Menengiyn Tal** plain E Mongolia
189 R9 **Meneng Point** headland SW Nauru
92 L10 **Menesjärvi** Lapp. Menešjávri. Lappi, N Finland
Menešjávri see Menesjärvi
107 I24 **Menfi** Sicilia, Italy, C Mediterranean Sea
161 P7 **Mengcheng** Anhui, E China
160 F15 **Menghai** Yunnan, SW China
160 F15 **Mengla** Yunnan, SW China
65 F24 **Menguera Point** headland East Falkland, Falkland Islands
160 M13 **Mengzhu Ling** ⛰ S China
160 H14 **Mengzi** Yunnan, SW China
Menin see Menen
182 L7 **Menindee** New South Wales, SE Australia
182 L7 **Menindee Lake** ⊚ New South Wales, SE Australia
182 J10 **Meningie** South Australia
103 O5 **Mennecy** Essonne, N France
29 Q12 **Menno** South Dakota, N USA
114 H13 **Menoíkio** ⛰ NE Greece
31 N5 **Menominee** Michigan, N USA
30 M5 **Menominee River** ≈ Michigan/Wisconsin, N USA
30 M8 **Menomonee Falls** Wisconsin, N USA
30 I6 **Menomonie** Wisconsin, N USA
83 D14 **Menongue** var. Vila Serpa Pinto, Port. Serpa Pinto. Cuando Cubango, C Angola
120 H8 **Menorca** Eng. Minorca; anc. Balearis Minor. island Islas Baleares, Spain, W Mediterranean Sea
105 S13 **Menor, Mar** lagoon SE Spain
39 S10 **Mentasta Lake** ⊚ Alaska, USA
39 S10 **Mentasta Mountains** ⛰ Alaska, USA
168 I13 **Mentawai, Kepulauan** island group W Indonesia
168 I12 **Mentawai, Selat** strait W Indonesia
168 M12 **Mentok** Pulau Bangka, W Indonesia
103 V15 **Menton** It. Mentone. Alpes-Maritimes, SE France
24 K8 **Mentone** Texas, SW USA
Mentone see Menton
31 U11 **Mentor** Ohio, N USA
169 U10 **Menyapa, Gunung** ▲ Borneo, N Indonesia
159 T9 **Menyuan** var. Menyuan Huizu Zizhixian. Qinghai, C China
Menyuan Huizu Zizhixian see Menyuan
74 M5 **Menzel Bourguiba** var. Manzil Bū Ruqaybah; prev. Ferryville. N Tunisia
136 M15 **Menzelet Barajı** ▣ C Turkey
127 T4 **Menzelinsk** Respublika Tatarstan, W Russian Federation
180 K11 **Menzies** Western Australia
195 V6 **Menzies, Mount** ▲ Antarctica
40 J6 **Meoqui** Chihuahua, N Mexico
83 N14 **Meponda** Niassa, NE Mozambique
98 M8 **Meppel** Drenthe, NE Netherlands
100 E12 **Meppen** Niedersachsen, NW Germany
Meqerghane, Sebkha see Mekerrhane, Sebkha
105 T6 **Mequinenza, Embalse de** ▣ NE Spain
30 M8 **Mequon** Wisconsin, N USA
Mera see Maira
182 D3 **Meramangye, Lake** salt lake South Australia
27 W5 **Meramec River** ≈ Missouri, C USA
Meran see Merano
168 K13 **Merangin** ≈ Sumatera, W Indonesia
106 G5 **Merano** Ger. Meran. Trentino-Alto Adige, N Italy
168 K8 **Merapuh Lama** Pahang, Peninsular Malaysia
106 D7 **Merate** Lombardia, N Italy
169 U13 **Meratus, Pegunungan** ⛰ Borneo, N Indonesia
171 Y16 **Merauke, Sungai** ≈ Papua, E Indonesia
182 L9 **Merbein** Victoria, SE Australia
99 F21 **Merbes-le-Château** Hainaut, S Belgium
Merca see Marka
54 C13 **Mercaderes** Cauca, SW Colombia
Mercara see Madikeri
35 P9 **Merced** California, W USA
61 C20 **Mercedes** Buenos Aires, E Argentina
61 D15 **Mercedes** Corrientes, NE Argentina
62 J11 **Mercedes** prev. Villa Mercedes. San Luis, C Argentina
61 D19 **Mercedes** Soriano, SW Uruguay
25 S17 **Mercedes** Texas, SW USA
35 R9 **Merced Peak** ▲ California, W USA
35 P9 **Merced River** ≈ California, W USA
18 B13 **Mercer** Pennsylvania, NE USA
99 G18 **Merchtem** Vlaams Brabant, C Belgium
15 O13 **Mercier** Québec, SE Canada
25 Q9 **Mercury** Texas, SW USA
184 M5 **Mercury Islands** island group N NZ
19 O9 **Meredith** New Hampshire, NE USA
65 B25 **Meredith, Cape** var. Cabo Belgrano. headland West Falkland, Falkland Islands
37 V6 **Meredith, Lake** ⊚ Colorado, C USA
25 N2 **Meredith, Lake** ▣ Texas, SW USA
81 O16 **Mereeg** var. Mareeq, It. Meregh. Galguduud, E Somalia
117 V5 **Merefa** Kharkivs'ka Oblast', E Ukraine
Meregh see Mereeg
99 E17 **Merelbeke** Oost-Vlaanderen, NW Belgium
Merend see Marand

◆ Country ● Country Capital ◇ Dependent Territory ○ Dependent Territory Capital ◈ Administrative Region × International Airport ▲ Mountain ⛰ Mountain Range Volcano ≈ River ⊚ Lake ▣ Reservoir

167 T12 **Mereuch** Môndól Kiri, E Cambodia
Mergate *see* Margate
167 N12 **Mergui** Tenasserim, S Burma
166 M12 **Mergui Archipelago** *island group* S Burma
114 L12 **Meriç** Edirne, NW Turkey
114 L12 **Meriç** *Bul.* Maritsa, *Gk.* Évros; *anc.* Hebrus. ≈ SE Europe *see also* Évros/Maritsa
41 X12 **Mérida** Yucatán, SW Mexico
104 J11 **Mérida** *anc.* Augusta Emerita. Extremadura, W Spain
54 I6 **Mérida** Mérida, W Venezuela
54 H7 **Mérida** *off.* Estado Mérida. ❖ *state* W Venezuela
18 M13 **Meriden** Connecticut, NE USA
22 M5 **Meridian** Mississippi, S USA
25 S8 **Meridian** Texas, SW USA
102 J13 **Mérignac** Gironde, SW France
102 J13 **Mérignac** × (Bordeaux) Gironde, SW France
93 J18 **Merikarvia** Länsi-Suomi, W Finland
183 R12 **Merimbula** New South Wales, SE Australia
182 L9 **Meringur** Victoria, SE Australia
Merín, Laguna *see* Mirim Lagoon
97 I19 **Merioneth** *cultural region* W Wales, UK
188 A11 **Merir** *island* Palau Islands, N Palau
188 B17 **Merizo** SW Guam
Merjama *see* Märjamaa
145 S16 **Merke** Zhambyl, S Kazakhstan
25 P7 **Merkel** Texas, SW USA
146 E12 **Merkezi Garagumy** *var.* Mencezi Garagum, *Rus.* Tsentral'nyye Nizmennyye Garagumy. *desert* C Turkmenistan
119 F15 **Merkinė** Alytus, S Lithuania
99 G16 **Merksem** Antwerpen, N Belgium
99 I15 **Merksplas** Antwerpen, N Belgium
Merkulovichi *see* Myerkulavichy
119 G15 **Merkys** ≈ S Lithuania
32 F15 **Merlin** Oregon, NW USA
61 C20 **Merlo** Buenos Aires, E Argentina
138 G8 **Meron, Haré** ▲ N Israel
74 K6 **Merouane, Chott** *salt lake* NE Algeria
80 F7 **Merowe** Northern, N Sudan
180 J12 **Merredin** Western Australia
97 I14 **Merrick** ▲ S Scotland, UK
32 H16 **Merrill** Oregon, NW USA
30 L5 **Merrill** Wisconsin, N USA
31 N11 **Merrillville** Indiana, N USA
19 O10 **Merrimack River** ≈ Massachusetts/New Hampshire, NE USA
28 L12 **Merriman** Nebraska, C USA
11 N17 **Merritt** British Columbia, SW Canada
23 Y12 **Merritt Island** Florida, SE USA
23 Y11 **Merritt Island** *island* Florida, SE USA
28 M12 **Merritt Reservoir** ⊞ Nebraska, C USA
183 S7 **Merriwa** New South Wales, SE Australia
183 O8 **Merriwagga** New South Wales, SE Australia
22 G8 **Merryville** Louisiana, S USA
80 K9 **Mersa Fatma** E Eritrea
102 M7 **Mer St-Aubin** Loir-et-Cher, C France
Mersa Maṭrûḥ *see* Maṭrûḥ
99 M24 **Mersch** Luxembourg, C Luxembourg
101 M15 **Merseburg** Sachsen-Anhalt, C Germany
Mersen *see* Meerssen
97 K18 **Mersey** ≈ NW England, UK
136 J17 **Mersin** İçel, S Turkey
168 L9 **Mersing** Johor, Peninsular Malaysia
118 E8 **Mērsrags** Talsi, NW Latvia
152 G12 **Merta** *var.* Merta City. Rājasthān, N India
Merta City *see* Merta
152 F12 **Merta Road** Rājasthān, N India
97 J21 **Merthyr Tydfil** S Wales, UK
104 H13 **Mértola** Beja, S Portugal
144 G14 **Mertvyy Kultuk, Sor** *salt flat* SW Kazakhstan
195 V16 **Mertz Glacier** *glacier* Antarctica
99 M24 **Mertzig** Diekirch, C Luxembourg
25 O9 **Mertzon** Texas, SW USA
81 I18 **Meru** Eastern, C Kenya
103 N4 **Méru** Oise, N France
81 I20 **Meru, Mount** ▲ NE Tanzania
Merv *see* Mary
Mervdasht *see* Marv Dasht
136 K11 **Merzifon** Amasya, N Turkey
101 D20 **Merzig** Saarland, SW Germany
36 L14 **Mesa** Arizona, SW USA
29 V4 **Mesabi Range** ▲ Minnesota, N USA
54 H6 **Mesa Bolívar** Mérida, NW Venezuela
107 Q18 **Mesagne** Puglia, SE Italy
39 P12 **Mesa Mountain** ▲ Alaska, USA
115 J25 **Mesará** *lowland* Kríti, Greece, E Mediterranean Sea
37 S14 **Mescalero** New Mexico, SW USA
101 G15 **Meschede** Nordrhein-Westfalen, W Germany
137 Q12 **Mescit Dağları** ▲ NE Turkey
189 V13 **Mesegon** *island* Chuuk, C Micronesia
Meseritz *see* Międzyrzecz
54 F11 **Mesetas** Meta, C Colombia
Meshchera Lowland *see* Meshcherskaya Nizina
126 M4 **Meshcherskaya Nizina** *Eng.* Meshchera Lowland. *basin* W Russian Federation
126 J5 **Meshchovsk** Kaluzhskaya Oblast', W Russian Federation
125 R9 **Meshchura** Respublika Komi, NW Russian Federation
Meshed *see* Mashhad
Meshed-i-Sar *see* Bābolsar
80 E13 **Meshra'er Req** Warab, S Sudan
37 R15 **Mesilla** New Mexico, SW USA
108 H10 **Mesocco** *Ger.* Misox. Ticino, S Switzerland
115 D18 **Mesolóngi** *prev.* Mesolóngion. Dytikí Ellás, W Greece
Mesolóngion *see* Mesolóngi
14 E8 **Mesomikenda Lake** ◎ Ontario, S Canada
61 D15 **Mesopotamia** *var.* Mesopotamia Argentina. *physical region* NE Argentina
Mesopotamia Argentina *see* Mesopotamia
35 Y10 **Mesquite** Nevada, W USA
82 Q13 **Messalo, Rio** *var.* Mualo. ≈ NE Mozambique
Messana/Messene *see* Messina
99 L25 **Messancy** Luxembourg, SE Belgium
107 M23 **Messina** *var.* Messana, Messene; *anc.* Zancle. Sicilia, Italy, C Mediterranean Sea
Messina *see* Musina
Messina, Strait of *see* Messina, Stretto di
107 M23 **Messina, Stretto di** *Eng.* Strait of Messina. *strait* SW Italy
115 E21 **Messíni** Pelopónnisos, S Greece
115 E21 **Messinía** *peninsula* S Greece
115 E22 **Messiniakós Kólpos** *gulf* S Greece
122 J8 **Messoyakha** ≈ N Russian Federation
114 H11 **Mesta** *Gk.* Néstos, *Turk.* Kara Su. ≈ Bulgaria/Greece *see also* Néstos
Mestghanem *see* Mostaganem
137 R8 **Mestia** *var.* Mestiya. N Georgia
Mestiya *see* Mestia
115 K18 **Mestón, Akrotírio** *headland* Chíos, E Greece
106 H8 **Mestre** Veneto, NE Italy
59 M16 **Mestre, Espigão** ▲ E Brazil
169 N14 **Mesuji** ≈ Sumatera, W Indonesia
Mesule *see* Grosser Möseler
10 J10 **Meszah Peak** ▲ British Columbia, W Canada
54 G11 **Meta** *off.* Departamento del Meta. ❖ *province* C Colombia
15 Q8 **Metabetchouane** ≈ Québec, SE Canada
9 S7 **Meta Incognita Peninsula** *peninsula* Baffin Island, Nunavut, NE Canada
22 K9 **Metairie** Louisiana, S USA
32 M6 **Metaline Falls** Washington, NW USA
62 K6 **Metán** Salta, N Argentina
82 N13 **Metangula** Niassa, N Mozambique
42 E7 **Metapán** Santa Ana, NW El Salvador
54 K9 **Meta, Río** ≈ Colombia/Venezuela
106 I11 **Metauro** ≈ C Italy
80 H11 **Metema** Amhara, N Ethiopia
115 D15 **Metéora** *religious building* Thessalía, C Greece
65 O20 **Meteor Rise** *undersea feature* SW Indian Ocean
186 G5 **Meteran** New Hanover, NE PNG
Meterlam/Methariam/Metharlam *see* Mehtarlām
115 G20 **Methanon** *peninsula* S Greece
32 J6 **Methow River** ≈ Washington, NW USA
19 O10 **Methuen** Massachusetts, NE USA
185 G19 **Methven** Canterbury, South Island, NZ
Metis *see* Metz
113 G15 **Metković** Dubrovnik-Neretva, SE Croatia
39 Y14 **Metlakatla** Annette Island, Alaska, USA
109 V13 **Metlika** *Ger.* Möttling. SE Slovenia
109 T8 **Metnitz** Kärnten, S Austria
27 W12 **Meto, Bayou** ≈ Arkansas, C USA
168 M15 **Metro** Sumatera, W Indonesia
30 M17 **Metropolis** Illinois, N USA
Metropolitan *see* Santiago
35 N8 **Metropolitan Oakland** × California, W USA
115 D15 **Métsovo** *prev.* Métsovon. Ípeiros, C Greece
Métsovon *see* Métsovo
23 V5 **Metter** Georgia, SE USA
99 H21 **Mettet** Namur, S Belgium
101 D20 **Mettlach** Saarland, SW Germany
Mettu *see* Metu
80 H13 **Metu** *var.* Mattu, Mettu. Oromo, C Ethiopia
169 T10 **Metulang** Borneo, N Indonesia
138 G8 **Metulla** Northern, N Israel
103 T4 **Metz** *anc.* Divodurum Mediomatricum, Mediomatrica, Metis. Moselle, NE France
101 H22 **Metzingen** Baden-Württemberg, S Germany
168 G8 **Meulaboh** Sumatera, W Indonesia
99 D18 **Meulebeke** West-Vlaanderen, W Belgium
103 U6 **Meurthe** ≈ NE France
103 S5 **Meurthe-et-Moselle** ❖ *department* NE France
103 S4 **Meuse** ❖ *department* NE France
84 F10 **Meuse** *Dut.* Maas. ≈ W Europe *see also* Maas
Mexcala, Río *see* Balsas, Río
25 U8 **Mexia** Texas, SW USA
58 K11 **Mexiana, Ilha** *island* NE Brazil
40 C1 **Mexicali** Baja California, NW Mexico
27 V4 **Mexico** Missouri, C USA
18 H9 **Mexico** New York, NE USA
40 L7 **Mexico** *off.* United Mexican States, *var.* Méjico, México, *Sp.* Estados Unidos Mexicanos. ◆ *federal republic* N Central America
41 O14 **México** *var.* Ciudad de México, *Eng.* Mexico City. ● (Mexico) México, C Mexico
41 O13 **México** ❖ *state* S Mexico
Mexico City *see* México
México, Golfo de *see* Mexico, Gulf of
44 B4 **Mexico, Gulf of** *Sp.* Golfo de México. *gulf* W Atlantic Ocean
Meyadine *see* Al Mayādīn
39 Y14 **Meyers Chuck** Etolin Island, Alaska, USA
148 M3 **Meymaneh** *var.* Maimāna, Maymana. Fāryāb, NW Afghanistan
143 N7 **Meymeh** Eşfahān, C Iran
123 V7 **Meynypil'gyno** Chukotskiy Avtonomnyy Okrug, NE Russian Federation
108 A10 **Meyrin** Genève, SW Switzerland
166 L7 **Mezaligon** Irrawaddy, SW Burma
41 O15 **Mezcala** Guerrero, S Mexico
114 H8 **Mezdra** Vratsa, NW Bulgaria
103 P16 **Mèze** Hérault, S France
125 O6 **Mezen'** Arkhangel'skaya Oblast', NW Russian Federation
127 P8 **Mezen'** ≈ NW Russian Federation
Mezen, Bay of *see* Mezenskaya Guba
103 Q13 **Mézenc, Mont** ▲ C France
127 O8 **Mezenskaya Guba** *var.* Bay of Mezen. *bay* NW Russian Federation
Mezha *see* Myazha
122 H6 **Mezhdusharskiy, Ostrov** *island* Novaya Zemlya, N Russian Federation
Mezhëvo *see* Myezhava
127 W4 **Mezhgor'ye** Respublika Bashkortostan, W Russian Federation
Mezhgor'ye *see* Mizhhir"ya
117 V8 **Mezhova** Dnipropetrovs'ka Oblast', E Ukraine
10 J12 **Meziadin Junction** British Columbia, W Canada
111 G16 **Mezileské Sedlo** *var.* Przełęcz Międzyleska. *pass* Czech Republic/Poland
102 L14 **Mézin** Lot-et-Garonne, SW France
111 M24 **Mezőberény** Békés, SE Hungary
111 M25 **Mezőhegyes** Békés, SE Hungary
111 M25 **Mezőkovácsháza** Békés, SE Hungary
111 M21 **Mezőkövesd** Borsod-Abaúj-Zemplén, NE Hungary
Mezőtelegd *see* Tileagd
111 M23 **Mezőtúr** Jász-Nagykun-Szolnok, E Hungary
40 K10 **Mezquital** Durango, C Mexico
106 G6 **Mezzolombardo** Trentino-Alto Adige, N Italy
82 L13 **Mfuwe** Northern, N Zambia
121 O15 **Mġarr** Gozo, N Malta
126 H6 **Mglin** Bryanskaya Oblast', W Russian Federation
Mhálanna, Cionn *see* Malin Head
154 G10 **Mhow** Madhya Pradesh, C India
Miadzioł Nowy *see* Myadzyel
171 O6 **Miagao** Panay Island, C Philippines
41 R17 **Miahuatlán** *var.* Miahuatlán de Porfirio Díaz. Oaxaca, SE Mexico
Miahuatlán de Porfirio Díaz *see* Miahuatlán
104 K10 **Miajadas** Extremadura, W Spain
Miajlar *see* Myājlār
36 M14 **Miami** Arizona, SW USA
23 Z16 **Miami** Florida, SE USA
27 R8 **Miami** Oklahoma, C USA
25 O2 **Miami** Texas, SW USA
23 Z16 **Miami** × Florida, SE USA
23 Z16 **Miami Beach** Florida, SE USA
23 Y15 **Miami Canal** *canal* Florida, SE USA
31 R14 **Miamisburg** Ohio, N USA
149 U10 **Miān Channūn** Punjab, E Pakistan
142 J4 **Miāndowāb** *var.* Miandub, Miyāndoāb. Āžarbāyjān-e Bākhtarī, NW Iran
172 H5 **Miandrivazo** Toliara, C Madagascar
Miandub *see* Miāndowāb
142 K3 **Miāneh** *var.* Miyāneh. Āžarbāyjān-e Khāvarī, NW Iran
149 O16 **Miāni Hōr** *lagoon* S Pakistan
160 G10 **Mianning** Sichuan, C China
149 T7 **Miānwāli** Punjab, NE Pakistan
160 J7 **Mianxian** *var.* Mian Xian. Shaanxi, C China
160 I8 **Mianyang** Sichuan, C China
Mianyang *see* Xiantao
161 R3 **Miaodao Qundao** *island group* E China
161 S13 **Miaoli** N Taiwan
122 F11 **Miass** Chelyabinskaya Oblast', C Russian Federation
110 G8 **Miastko** *Ger.* Rummelsburg in Pommern. Pomorskie, N Poland
Miava *see* Myjava
11 O15 **Mica Creek** British Columbia, SW Canada
160 J7 **Micang Shan** ▲ C China
Mi Chai *see* Nong Khai
111 O19 **Michalovce** *Ger.* Grossmichel, *Hung.* Nagymihály. Košický Kraj, E Slovakia
99 M20 **Michel, Baraque** *hill* E Belgium
39 S5 **Michelson, Mount** ▲ Alaska, USA
45 P9 **Miches** E Dominican Republic
30 M4 **Michigamme, Lake** ◎ Michigan, N USA
30 M4 **Michigamme Reservoir** ⊞ Michigan, N USA
31 N4 **Michigamme River** ≈ Michigan, N USA
31 O7 **Michigan** *off.* State of Michigan; also known as Great Lakes State, Lake State, Wolverine State. ❖ *state* N USA
31 O11 **Michigan City** Indiana, N USA
31 O8 **Michigan, Lake** ◎ N USA
31 P2 **Michipicoten Bay** *lake bay* Ontario, N Canada
14 A8 **Michipicoten Island** *island* Ontario, S Canada
14 B7 **Michipicoten River** Ontario, S Canada
Michurin *see* Tsarevo
126 M6 **Michurinsk** Tambovskaya Oblast', W Russian Federation
Mico, Punta/Mico, Punto *see* Monkey Point
42 L10 **Mico, Río** ≈ SE Nicaragua
45 T12 **Micoud** SE Saint Lucia
189 N16 **Micronesia** *off.* Federated States of Micronesia. ◆ *federation* W Pacific Ocean
192 J7 **Micronesia** *island group* W Pacific Ocean
169 O9 **Midai, Pulau** *island* Kepulauan Natuna, W Indonesia
Mid-Atlantic Cordillera *see* Mid-Atlantic Ridge
65 M17 **Mid-Atlantic Ridge** *var.* Mid-Atlantic Cordillera, Mid-Atlantic Rise, Mid-Atlantic Swell. *undersea feature* Atlantic Ocean
Mid-Atlantic Rise/Mid-Atlantic Swell *see* Mid-Atlantic Ridge
99 E15 **Middelburg** Zeeland, SW Netherlands
83 H24 **Middelburg** Eastern Cape, S South Africa
83 K21 **Middelburg** Mpumalanga, NE South Africa
95 G23 **Middelfart** Fyn, C Denmark
98 G13 **Middelharnis** Zuid-Holland, SW Netherlands
99 B16 **Middelkerke** West-Vlaanderen, W Belgium
98 I9 **Middenbeemster** Noord-Holland, C Netherlands
98 I8 **Middenmeer** Noord-Holland, NW Netherlands
35 Q2 **Middle Alkali Lake** ◎ California, W USA
193 S6 **Middle America Trench** *undersea feature* E Pacific Ocean
151 P19 **Middle Andaman** *island* Andaman Islands, India, NE Indian Ocean
Middle Atlas *see* Moyen Atlas
21 R3 **Middlebourne** West Virginia, NE USA
23 W9 **Middleburg** Florida, SE USA
Middleburg Island *see* 'Eua
Middle Caicos *see* Grand Caicos
25 N8 **Middle Concho River** ≈ Texas, SW USA
Middle Congo *see* Congo (Republic of)
39 R6 **Middle Fork Chandalar River** ≈ Alaska, USA
39 Q7 **Middle Fork Koyukuk River** ≈ Alaska, USA
33 O12 **Middle Fork Salmon River** ≈ Idaho, NW USA
11 T15 **Middle Lake** Saskatchewan, S Canada
28 L13 **Middle Loup River** ≈ Nebraska, C USA
185 E22 **Middlemarch** Otago, South Island, NZ
31 T15 **Middleport** Ohio, N USA
29 U14 **Middle Raccoon River** ≈ Iowa, C USA
29 R3 **Middle River** ≈ Minnesota, N USA
21 N8 **Middlesboro** Kentucky, S USA
97 M15 **Middlesbrough** N England, UK
42 G3 **Middlesex** Stann Creek, C Belize
97 N22 **Middlesex** *cultural region* SE England, UK
13 P15 **Middleton** Nova Scotia, SE Canada
20 F10 **Middleton** Tennessee, S USA
30 L9 **Middleton** Wisconsin, N USA
39 S13 **Middleton Island** *island* Alaska, USA
34 M7 **Middletown** California, W USA
21 Y2 **Middletown** Delaware, NE USA
18 K15 **Middletown** New Jersey, NE USA
18 K13 **Middletown** New York, NE USA
31 R14 **Middletown** Ohio, N USA
18 G15 **Middletown** Pennsylvania, NE USA
141 N14 **Midī** *var.* Maydī. NW Yemen
103 O16 **Midi, Canal du** *canal* S France
102 K17 **Midi de Bigorre, Pic du** ▲ S France
102 K17 **Midi d'Ossau, Pic du** ▲ SW France
173 R7 **Mid-Indian Basin** *undersea feature* N Indian Ocean
173 P7 **Mid-Indian Ridge** *var.* Central Indian Ridge. *undersea feature* C Indian Ocean
103 N14 **Midi-Pyrénées** ❖ *region* S France
25 N8 **Midkiff** Texas, SW USA
14 G13 **Midland** Ontario, S Canada
31 R8 **Midland** Michigan, N USA
28 M10 **Midland** South Dakota, N USA
24 M8 **Midland** Texas, SW USA
83 K17 **Midlands** ❖ *province* C Zimbabwe
97 D21 **Midleton** *Ir.* Mainistir na Corann. SW Ireland
25 T7 **Midlothian** Texas, SW USA
96 K12 **Midlothian** *cultural region* S Scotland, UK
172 I7 **Midongy** Fianarantsoa, S Madagascar
102 K15 **Midou** ≈ SW France
192 J6 **Mid-Pacific Mountains** *var.* Mid-Pacific Seamounts. *undersea feature* NW Pacific Ocean
Mid-Pacific Seamounts *see* Mid-Pacific Mountains
171 Q7 **Midsayap** Mindanao, S Philippines
36 L3 **Midway** Utah, W USA
192 L5 **Midway Islands** ◇ US *territory* C Pacific Ocean
33 X14 **Midwest** Wyoming, C USA
27 N10 **Midwest City** Oklahoma, C USA
152 M10 **Mid Western** ❖ *zone* W Nepal
98 P5 **Midwolda** Groningen, NE Netherlands
137 Q16 **Midyat** Mardin, SE Turkey
114 F8 **Midzhur** *SCr.* Midžor. ▲ Bulgaria/Serbia and Montenegro (Yugo.) *see also* Midžor
113 Q14 **Midžor** *Bul.* Midzhur. ▲ Bulgaria/Serbia and Montenegro (Yugo.) *see also* Midzhur
164 K14 **Mie** *off.* Mie-ken. ❖ *prefecture* Honshū, SW Japan
111 L16 **Miechów** Małopolskie, S Poland
110 F11 **Międzychód** *Ger.* Mitteldorf. Wielkopolskie, C Poland
Międzyleska, Przełęcz *see* Mezileské Sedlo
110 O12 **Międzyrzec Podlaski** Lubelskie, E Poland
110 E11 **Międzyrzecz** *Ger.* Meseritz. Lubelskie, W Poland
Mie-ken *see* Mie
102 L16 **Miélan** Gers, S France
111 N16 **Mielec** Podkarpackie, SE Poland
95 L21 **Mien** ◎ S Sweden
41 O8 **Mier** Tamaulipas, C Mexico
116 J11 **Miercurea-Ciuc** *Ger.* Szeklerburg, *Hung.* Csíkszereda. Harghita, C Romania
Mieresch *see* Maros/Mureş
Mieres del Camín *see* Mieres del Camino
104 K2 **Mieres del Camino** *var.* Mieres del Camín. Asturias, NW Spain
99 K15 **Mierlo** Noord-Brabant, SE Netherlands
41 O10 **Mier y Noriega** Nuevo León, NE Mexico
Mies *see* Stříbro
80 K13 **Mī'ēso** *var.* Meheso, Oromo. C Ethiopia
Miesso *see* Mī'ēso
110 D10 **Mieszkowice** *Ger.* Bärwalde Neumark. Zachodnio-pomorskie, W Poland
18 G14 **Mifflinburg** Pennsylvania, NE USA
18 F14 **Mifflintown** Pennsylvania, NE USA
41 R15 **Miguel Alemán, Presa** ⊞ SE Mexico
40 L9 **Miguel Asua** *var.* Miguel Auza. Zacatecas, C Mexico
Miguel Auza *see* Miguel Asua
43 S15 **Miguel de la Borda** *var.* Donoso. Colón, C Panama
41 N13 **Miguel Hidalgo** × (Guadalajara) Jalisco, SW Mexico
40 H7 **Miguel Hidalgo, Presa** ⊞ W Mexico
116 J14 **Mihăileşti** Giurgiu, S Romania
116 M14 **Mihail Kogălniceanu** *var.* Kogălniceanu; *prev.* Caramurat, Ferdinand. Constanţa, SE Romania
117 N14 **Mihai Viteazu** Constanţa, SE Romania
136 G12 **Mihalıççık** Eskişehir, NW Turkey
164 G13 **Mihara** Hiroshima, Honshū, SW Japan
165 N14 **Mihara-yama** ✻ Miyako-jima, SE Japan
105 S8 **Mijares** ≈ E Spain
98 I11 **Mijdrecht** Utrecht, C Netherlands
165 S4 **Mikasa** Hokkaidō, NE Japan
Mikashevichi *see* Mikashevichy
119 K19 **Mikashevichy** *Pol.* Mikaszewicze, *Rus.* Mikashevichi. Brestskaya Voblasts', SW Belarus
Mikaszewicze *see* Mikashevichy
126 L5 **Mikhaylov** Ryazanskaya Oblast', W Russian Federation
Mikhaylovgrad *see* Montana
195 Z8 **Mikhaylov Island** *island* Antarctica
145 T6 **Mikhaylovka** Pavlodar, N Kazakhstan
127 N9 **Mikhaylovka** Volgogradskaya Oblast', SW Russian Federation
Mikhaylovka *see* Mykhaylivka
81 K24 **Mikindani** Mtwara, SE Tanzania
93 N18 **Mikkeli** *Swe.* Sankt Michel. Itä-Suomi, E Finland
110 M8 **Mikołajki** *Ger.* Nikolaiken. Warmińsko-Mazurskie, NE Poland
Míkonos *see* Mýkonos
114 I9 **Mikre** Lovech, N Bulgaria
114 C13 **Mikrí Préspa, Límni** ◎ N Greece
127 P4 **Mikulkin, Mys** *headland* NW Russian Federation
81 I23 **Mikumi** Morogoro, SE Tanzania
125 R10 **Mikun'** Respublika Komi, NW Russian Federation
164 K13 **Mikuni** Fukui, Honshū, SW Japan
165 X13 **Mikura-jima** *island* E Japan
29 V7 **Milaca** Minnesota, N USA
62 J10 **Milagro** La Rioja, C Argentina
56 B7 **Milagro** Guayas, SW Ecuador
31 P4 **Milakokia Lake** ◎ Michigan, N USA
30 J1 **Milan** Illinois, N USA
31 R10 **Milan** Michigan, N USA
27 T2 **Milan** Missouri, C USA
37 Q11 **Milan** New Mexico, SW USA
20 G9 **Milan** Tennessee, S USA
Milan *see* Milano
95 F15 **Miland** Telemark, S Norway
83 N15 **Milange** Zambézia, NE Mozambique
106 D8 **Milano** *Eng.* Milan, *Ger.* Mailand; *anc.* Mediolanum. Lombardia, N Italy
25 U10 **Milano** Texas, SW USA
136 C15 **Milas** Muğla, SW Turkey
119 K21 **Milashavichy** *Rus.* Milashevichi. Homyel'skaya Voblasts', SE Belarus
Milashevichi *see* Milashavichy
119 I18 **Milavidy** *Rus.* Milovidy. Brestskaya Voblasts', SW Belarus
107 L23 **Milazzo** *anc.* Mylae. Sicilia, Italy, C Mediterranean Sea
29 R8 **Milbank** South Dakota, N USA
19 T7 **Milbridge** Maine, NE USA
100 L11 **Milde** ≈ C Germany
14 F14 **Mildmay** Ontario, S Canada
182 L9 **Mildura** Victoria, SE Australia
137 X12 **Mil Düzü** *Rus.* Mil'skaya Ravnina, Mil'skaya Step'. *physical region* C Azerbaijan
160 H13 **Mile** *var.* Miyang. Yunnan, SW China
Mile *see* Mili Atoll
181 Y10 **Miles** Queensland, E Australia
25 P8 **Miles** Texas, SW USA
33 X9 **Miles City** Montana, NW USA
11 U17 **Milestone** Saskatchewan, S Canada
107 N22 **Mileto** Calabria, SW Italy
107 K16 **Miletto, Monte** ▲ C Italy
18 M13 **Milford** Connecticut, NE USA
21 Y3 **Milford** *var.* Milford City. Delaware, NE USA
29 T11 **Milford** Iowa, C USA
19 S6 **Milford** Maine, NE USA
29 R16 **Milford** Nebraska, C USA
19 O10 **Milford** New Hampshire, NE USA
18 J13 **Milford** Pennsylvania, NE USA
25 T7 **Milford** Texas, SW USA
36 K6 **Milford** Utah, W USA
Milford *see* Milford Haven
Milford City *see* Milford
97 H21 **Milford Haven** *prev.* Milford. SW Wales, UK
27 O4 **Milford Lake** ⊞ Kansas, C USA
185 B21 **Milford Sound** Southland, South Island, NZ
185 B21 **Milford Sound** *inlet* South Island, NZ
Milhau *see* Millau
Milh, Bahr al *see* Razāzah, Buḥayrat ar
139 T10 **Milh, Wādī al** *dry watercourse* S Iraq
189 W8 **Mili Atoll** *var.* Mile. *atoll* Ratak Chain, SE Marshall Islands
110 H13 **Milicz** Dolnośląskie, SW Poland
107 L25 **Militello in Val di Catania** Sicilia, Italy, C Mediterranean Sea
123 V10 **Mil'kovo** Kamchatskaya Oblast', E Russian Federation
11 R17 **Milk River** Alberta, SW Canada
44 J13 **Milk River** ≈ C Jamaica
33 W7 **Milk River** ≈ Montana, NW USA
80 D9 **Milk, Wadi el** *var.* Wadi al Malik. ≈ C Sudan
99 L14 **Mill** Noord-Brabant, SE Netherlands
103 P14 **Millau** *var.* Milhau; *anc.* Æmilianum. Aveyron, S France
14 I14 **Millbrook** Ontario, SE Canada
23 U4 **Milledgeville** Georgia, SE USA
12 C12 **Mille Lacs, Lac des** ◎ Ontario, S Canada
29 V6 **Mille Lacs Lake** ◎ Minnesota, N USA
23 V4 **Millen** Georgia, SE USA
191 Y5 **Millennium Island** *prev.* Caroline Island, Thornton Island. *atoll* Line Islands, E Kiribati
29 O9 **Miller** South Dakota, N USA
30 K5 **Miller Dam Flowage** ◎ Wisconsin, N USA
39 U12 **Miller, Mount** ▲ Alaska, USA
126 L10 **Millerovo** Rostovskaya Oblast', SW Russian Federation
37 N17 **Miller Peak** ▲ Arizona, SW USA
31 T12 **Millersburg** Ohio, N USA
18 G15 **Millersburg** Pennsylvania, NE USA
185 D23 **Millers Flat** Otago, South Island, NZ
25 Q8 **Millersview** Texas, SW USA
106 B10 **Millesimo** Piemonte, NE Italy
12 C12 **Milles Lacs, Lac des** ◎ Ontario, SW Canada
25 Q13 **Millett** Texas, SW USA
103 N11 **Millevaches, Plateau de** *plateau* C France
182 K12 **Millicent** South Australia
98 M13 **Millingen aan den Rijn** Gelderland, SE Netherlands
20 E10 **Millington** Tennessee, S USA
19 R4 **Millinocket** Maine, NE USA
19 R4 **Millinocket Lake** ◎ Maine, NE USA
195 Z11 **Mill Island** *island* Antarctica
183 T3 **Millmerran** Queensland, E Australia
109 R9 **Millstatt** Kärnten, S Austria
97 B19 **Milltown Malbay** *Ir.* Sráid na Cathrach. W Ireland
18 J17 **Millville** New Jersey, NE USA
27 S13 **Millwood Lake** ⊞ Arkansas, C USA
Milne Bank *see* Milne Seamounts
186 G10 **Milne Bay** ❖ *province* SE PNG
64 J8 **Milne Seamounts** *var.* Milne Bank. *undersea feature* N Atlantic Ocean
29 Q6 **Milnor** North Dakota, N USA
19 R5 **Milo** Maine, NE USA
115 I22 **Mílos** Mílos, Kykládes, Greece, Aegean Sea
115 I22 **Mílos** *island* Kykládes, Greece, Aegean Sea

◆ Country ● Country Capital ◇ Dependent Territory ○ Dependent Territory Capital ❖ Administrative Region × International Airport ▲ Mountain ▲ Mountain Range ✻ Volcano ≈ River ◎ Lake ⊞ Reservoir

110 H11 Miłosław Wielkopolskie, C Poland
113 K19 Milot var. Miloti. Lezhë, C Albania
Miloti see Milot
117 Z5 Milove Luhans'ka Oblast', E Ukraine
Milovidy see Milavidy
182 L4 Milparinka New South Wales, SE Australia
35 N9 Milpitas California, W USA
Mil'skaya Ravnina/Mil'skaya Step' see Mil Düzü
14 G15 Milton Ontario, S Canada
185 E24 Milton Otago, South Island, NZ
21 Y4 Milton Delaware, NE USA
23 P8 Milton Florida, SE USA
18 G14 Milton Pennsylvania, NE USA
18 L7 Milton Vermont, NE USA
32 K11 Milton-Freewater Oregon, NW USA
97 N21 Milton Keynes SE England, UK
27 N3 Miltonvale Kansas, C USA
161 N10 Miluo Hunan, S China
30 M9 Milwaukee Wisconsin, N USA
Milyang see Miryang
Mimatum see Mende
37 Q15 Mimbres Mountains ▲ New Mexico, SW USA
182 D2 Mimili South Australia
102 J14 Mimizan Landes, SW France
Mimmaya see Minmaya
79 E19 Mimongo Ngounié, C Gabon
Min see Fujian
35 T7 Mina Nevada, W USA
143 S14 Mīnāb Hormozgān, SE Iran
Mīnā Baranīs see Berenice
149 R9 Mīna Bāzār Baluchistān, SW Pakistan
165 X17 Minami-Iō-jima Eng. San Augustine. island SE Japan
Min'an see Longshan
165 R5 Minami-Kayabe Hokkaidō, NE Japan
164 C17 Minamitane Kagoshima, Tanega-shima, SW Japan
Minami Tori Shima see Marcus Island
62 J4 Mina Pirquitas Jujuy, NW Argentina
173 O3 Mīnā' Qābūs NE Oman
61 F19 Minas Lavalleja, S Uruguay
13 P15 Minas Basin bay Nova Scotia, SE Canada
61 F17 Minas de Corrales Rivera, NE Uruguay
44 A5 Minas de Matahambre Pinar del Río, W Cuba
104 J13 Minas de Ríotinto Andalucía, S Spain
60 K7 Minas Gerais off. Estado de Minas Gerais. ◆ state E Brazil
42 E5 Minas, Sierra de las ▲ E Guatemala
41 T15 Minatitlán Veracruz-Llave, E Mexico
166 L6 Minbu Magwe, W Burma
149 V10 Minchinābād Punjab, E Pakistan
63 G17 Minchinmávida, Volcán ▲ S Chile
96 G7 Minch, The var. North Minch. strait NW Scotland, UK
106 F8 Mincio anc. Mincius. ~ N Italy
Mincius see Mincio
26 M11 Minco Oklahoma, C USA
171 Q7 Mindanao island S Philippines
Mindanao Sea see Bohol Sea
101 J23 Mindel ~ S Germany
101 J23 Mindelheim Bayern, S Germany
Mindello see Mindelo
76 C9 Mindelo var. Mindello; prev. Porto Grande. São Vicente, N Cape Verde
14 I13 Minden Ontario, SE Canada
100 H13 Minden anc. Minthun. Nordrhein-Westfalen, NW Germany
22 G5 Minden Louisiana, S USA
29 O16 Minden Nebraska, C USA
35 Q6 Minden Nevada, W USA
182 L8 Mindona Lake seasonal lake New South Wales, SE Australia
171 O4 Mindoro island N Philippines
171 N5 Mindoro Strait strait W Philippines
159 S9 Mine Gansu, N China
97 E21 Mine Head Ir. Mionn Ard. headland S Ireland
97 J23 Minehead SW England, UK
59 J19 Mineiros Goiás, C Brazil
25 V6 Mineola Texas, SW USA
25 S13 Mineral Texas, SW USA
127 N15 Mineral'nyye Vody Stavropol'skiy Kray, SW Russian Federation
30 K9 Mineral Point Wisconsin, N USA
25 S6 Mineral Wells Texas, SW USA
36 K6 Minersville Utah, W USA
31 U12 Minerva Ohio, N USA
107 N17 Minervino Murge Puglia, SE Italy
103 O16 Minervois physical region S France
158 I10 Minfeng var. Niya. Xinjiang Uygur Zizhiqu, NW China
79 O25 Minga Katanga, SE Dem. Rep. Congo
137 W11 Mingäçevir Rus. Mingechaur, Mingechevir. C Azerbaijan
137 W11 Mingäçevir Su Anbarı Rus. Mingechaurskoye Vodokhranilishche, Mingechevirskoye Vodokhranilishche. ⊞ NW Azerbaijan
166 L8 Mingaladon ✕ (Yangon) Yangon, SW Burma
13 P11 Mingan Québec, E Canada
149 U5 Mingāora var. Mingora, Mongora. North-West Frontier Province, N Pakistan
146 K8 Mingbuloq Rus. Mynbulak. Navoiy Viloyati, N Uzbekistan
146 K9 Mingbuloq Botig'I Rus. Vpadina Mynbulak. depression N Uzbekistan
Mingechaur/Mingechevir see Mingäçevir
Mingechaurskoye Vodokhranilishche/Mingechevirskoye Vodokhranilishche see Mingäçevir Su Anbarı
161 Q7 Mingguang prev. Jiashan. Anhui, S China
166 L4 Mingin Sagaing, C Burma
105 Q10 Minglanilla Castilla-La Mancha, C Spain
31 V13 Mingo Junction Ohio, N USA
Mingora see Mingāora
163 V7 Mingshui Heilongjiang, NE China
Mingteke Daban see Mintaka Pass
83 Q14 Minguri Nampula, NE Mozambique
159 U10 Minhe var. Shangchuankou. Qinghai, C China
166 L6 Minhla Magwe, W Burma
167 S14 Minh Lương Kiên Giang, S Vietnam
104 G5 Minho, Rio Sp. Miño. ~ Portugal/Spain see also Miño
104 G5 Minho former province N Portugal
155 C24 Minicoy Island island SW India
33 P15 Minidoka Idaho, NW USA
118 C11 Minija ~ W Lithuania
180 G9 Minilya Western Australia
14 E8 Minisinakwa Lake ◎ Ontario, S Canada
45 T12 Ministre Point headland S Saint Lucia
11 V15 Minitonas Manitoba, S Canada
Minius see Miño
161 R12 Min Jiang ~ SE China
160 H10 Min Jiang ~ C China
182 H9 Minlaton South Australia
165 Q6 Minmaya var. Mimmaya. Aomori, Honshū, C Japan
77 U14 Minna Niger, C Nigeria
165 P16 Minna-jima island Sakishima-shotō, SW Japan
27 N4 Minneapolis Kansas, C USA
29 U9 Minneapolis Minnesota, N USA
29 V8 Minneapolis-Saint Paul ✕ Minnesota, N USA
11 W16 Minnedosa Manitoba, S Canada
26 J7 Minneola Kansas, C USA
29 S7 Minnesota off. State of Minnesota; also known as Gopher State, New England of the West, North Star State. ◆ state N USA
29 S9 Minnesota River ~ Minnesota/South Dakota, N USA
29 V9 Minnetonka Minnesota, N USA
29 O3 Minnewaukan North Dakota, N USA
182 F7 Minnipa South Australia
104 H2 Miño Galicia, NW Spain
104 G5 Miño var. Mino, Minius, Port. Rio Minho. ~ Portugal/Spain see also Minho, Rio
30 L4 Minocqua Wisconsin, N USA
30 L12 Minonk Illinois, N USA
Minorca see Menorca
28 M3 Minot North Dakota, N USA
159 U8 Minqin Gansu, N China
119 J16 Minsk ● (Belarus) Minskaya Voblasts', C Belarus
119 L16 Minsk ✕ Minskaya Voblasts', C Belarus
Minskaya Oblast' see Minskaya Voblasts'
119 K16 Minskaya Voblasts' prev. Rus. Minskaya Oblast'. ◆ province C Belarus
119 J16 Minskaya Wzvyshsha ▲ C Belarus
110 N12 Mińsk Mazowiecki var. Nowo-Minsk. Mazowieckie, C Poland
31 Q13 Minster Ohio, N USA
79 F15 Minta Centre, C Cameroon
149 W2 Mintaka Pass Chin. Mingteke Daban. pass China/Pakistan
115 D20 Mínthi ▲ S Greece
Minthun see Minden
13 O14 Minto New Brunswick, SE Canada
10 H6 Minto Yukon Territory, W Canada
39 R9 Minto Alaska, USA
29 Q3 Minto North Dakota, N USA
12 K6 Minto, Lac ◎ Québec, C Canada
195 R16 Minto, Mount ▲ Antarctica
11 U17 Minton Saskatchewan, S Canada
189 R15 Minto Reef atoll Caroline Islands, C Micronesia
37 R4 Minturn Colorado, C USA
107 J16 Minturno Lazio, C Italy
122 K13 Minusinsk Krasnoyarskiy Kray, S Russian Federation
108 G11 Minusio Ticino, S Switzerland
79 E17 Minvoul Woleu-Ntem, N Gabon
141 R13 Minwakh N Yemen
159 V11 Minxian var. Min Xian. Gansu, C China
Minya see El Minya
31 R6 Mio Michigan, N USA
Mionn Ard see Mine Head
158 L5 Miquan Xinjiang Uygur Zizhiqu, NW China
119 I17 Mir Hrodzyenskaya Voblasts', W Belarus
106 H8 Mira Veneto, NE Italy
104 G13 Mira, Rio ~ S Portugal
12 K15 Mirabel var. Montreal. ✕ (Montréal) Québec, SE Canada
60 Q8 Miracema Rio de Janeiro, SE Brazil
54 G9 Miraflores Boyacá, C Colombia
40 G10 Miraflores Baja California Sur, W Mexico
44 L9 Miragoâne S Haiti
155 E16 Miraj Mahārāshtra, W India
61 E23 Miramar Buenos Aires, E Argentina
103 R15 Miramas Bouches-du-Rhône, SE France
102 K12 Mirambeau Charente-Maritime, W France
102 L13 Miramont-de-Guyenne Lot-et-Garonne, SW France
115 L25 Mirampéllou Kólpos gulf Kriti, Greece, E Mediterranean Sea
158 L8 Miran Xinjiang Uygur Zizhiqu, NW China
54 M5 Miranda off. Estado Miranda. ◆ state N Venezuela
Miranda de Corvo see Miranda do Corvo
105 O3 Miranda de Ebro La Rioja, N Spain
104 G8 Miranda do Corvo var. Miranda de Corvo. Coimbra, N Portugal
104 J6 Miranda do Douro Bragança, N Portugal
102 L15 Mirande Gers, S France
104 I6 Mirandela Bragança, N Portugal
25 R15 Mirando City Texas, SW USA
106 G9 Mirandola Emilia-Romagna, N Italy
60 I8 Mirandópolis São Paulo, S Brazil
60 K8 Mirassol São Paulo, S Brazil
104 J3 Miravalles ▲ NW Spain
42 L12 Miravalles, Volcán ⚹ NW Costa Rica
141 W13 Mirbāṭ var. Marbat. S Oman
44 M9 Mirebalais C Haiti
103 T6 Mirecourt Vosges, NE France
103 N16 Mirepoix Ariège, S France
Mirgorod see Myrhorod
139 W10 Mīr Ḩājī Khalīl E Iraq
169 T8 Miri Sarawak, East Malaysia
77 W12 Miria Zinder, S Niger
182 F5 Mirikata South Australia
54 K4 Mirimire Falcón, N Venezuela
61 H18 Mirim Lagoon var. Lake Mirim, Sp. Laguna Merín. lagoon Brazil/Uruguay
Mirim, Lake see Mirim Lagoon
Mírina see Mýrina
172 H14 Miringoni Mohéli, S Comoros
143 W11 Mīrjāveh Sīstān va Balūchestān, SE Iran
195 Z9 Mirny Russian research station Antarctica
124 M10 Mirnyy Arkhangel'skaya Oblast', NW Russian Federation
123 O10 Mirnyy Respublika Sakha (Yakutiya), NE Russian Federation
Mironovka see Myronivka
110 F9 Mirosławiec Zachodnio-pomorskie, NW Poland
Mirovo see Vrattsa
100 N10 Mirow Mecklenburg-Vorpommern, N Germany
152 G6 Mīrpur Jammu and Kashmir, NW India
Mīrpur see New Mīrpur
149 P17 Mīrpur Batoro Sind, SE Pakistan
149 Q16 Mīrpur Khās Sind, SE Pakistan
149 P17 Mīrpur Sakro Sind, SE Pakistan
143 T14 Mīr Shahdād Hormozgān, S Iran
Mirtoan Sea see Mirtóo Pélagos
115 G21 Mirtóo Pélagos Eng. Mirtoan Sea; anc. Myrtoum Mare. sea S Greece
163 Z16 Miryang var. Milyang, Jap. Mitsuō. SE South Korea
Mirzachirla see Murzechirla
164 E14 Misaki Ehime, Shikoku, SW Japan
41 Q13 Misantla Veracruz-Llave, E Mexico
165 R7 Misawa Aomori, Honshū, C Japan
57 G14 Mishagua, Río ~ C Peru
163 Z8 Mishan Heilongjiang, NE China
31 O11 Mishawaka Indiana, N USA
39 N6 Misheguk Mountain ▲ Alaska, USA
165 N14 Mishima var. Misima. Shizuoka, Honshū, S Japan
164 E12 Mi-shima island SW Japan
127 V4 Mishkino Respublika Bashkortostan, W Russian Federation
153 Y10 Mishmi Hills hill range NE India
161 N11 Mi Shui ~ S China
Misiaf see Maşyāf
107 J23 Misilmeri Sicilia, Italy, C Mediterranean Sea
Misima see Mishima
Misión de Guana see Guana
60 F13 Misiones off. Provincia de Misiones. ◆ province NE Argentina
62 P8 Misiones off. Departamento de las Misiones. ◆ department S Paraguay
Misión San Fernando see San Fernando
Miskin see Maskin
Miskito Coast see La Mosquitia
43 O7 Miskitos, Cayos island group NE Nicaragua
111 M21 Miskolc Borsod-Abaúj-Zemplén, NE Hungary
171 T12 Misool, Pulau island Maluku, E Indonesia
Misox see Mesocco
29 Y3 Misquah Hills hill range Minnesota, N USA
75 P7 Mişrātah var. Misurata. NW Libya
14 C7 Missanabie Ontario, S Canada
58 E10 Missão Catrimani Roraima, N Brazil
14 D6 Missinaibi ~ Ontario, S Canada
14 C7 Missinaibi Lake ◎ Ontario, S Canada
11 T13 Missinipe Saskatchewan, C Canada
28 M11 Mission South Dakota, N USA
25 S17 Mission Texas, SW USA
12 F10 Missisa Lake ◎ Ontario, C Canada
18 M6 Missisquoi Bay lake bay Canada/USA
14 C10 Mississagi ~ Ontario, S Canada
14 G15 Mississauga Ontario, S Canada
31 P12 Mississinewa Lake ⊞ Indiana, N USA
31 P12 Mississinewa River ~ Indiana/Ohio, N USA
22 K4 Mississippi off. State of Mississippi; also known as Bayou State, Magnolia State. ◆ state SE USA
14 K13 Mississippi ~ Ontario, SE Canada
22 M10 Mississippi Delta delta Louisiana, S USA
64 D10 Mississippi Fan undersea feature N Gulf of Mexico
14 L13 Mississippi Lake ◎ Ontario, SE Canada
17 O11 Mississippi River ~ C USA
22 M9 Mississippi Sound sound Alabama/Mississippi, S USA
33 P9 Missoula Montana, NW USA
27 T5 Missouri off. State of Missouri; also known as Bullion State, Show Me State. ◆ state C USA
25 V11 Missouri City Texas, SW USA
16 L9 Missouri River ~ C USA
15 Q6 Mistassibi ~ Québec, SE Canada
15 P6 Mistassini Québec, SE Canada
15 P6 Mistassini ~ Québec, SE Canada
12 J11 Mistassini, Lac ◎ Québec, SE Canada
109 Y3 Mistelbach an der Zaya Niederösterreich, NE Austria
107 L24 Misterbianco Sicilia, Italy, C Mediterranean Sea
95 N19 Misterhult Kalmar, S Sweden
57 H17 Misti, Volcán ▲ S Peru
Mistras see Mystrás
107 K23 Mistretta anc. Amestratus. Sicilia, Italy, C Mediterranean Sea
164 F12 Misumi Shimane, Honshū, SW Japan
Misurata see Mişrātah
83 O14 Mitande Niassa, N Mozambique
40 J13 Mita, Punta de headland C Mexico
55 W12 Mitaraka, Massif du ▲ NE South America
Mitau see Jelgava
181 X9 Mitchell Queensland, E Australia
14 E15 Mitchell Ontario, S Canada
28 I13 Mitchell Nebraska, C USA
32 J12 Mitchell Oregon, NW USA
29 P11 Mitchell South Dakota, N USA
23 P5 Mitchell Lake ⊞ Alabama, S USA
31 P7 Mitchell, Lake ◎ Michigan, N USA
21 P9 Mitchell, Mount ▲ North Carolina, SE USA
181 V3 Mitchell River ~ Queensland, NE Australia
97 D20 Mitchelstown Ir. Baile Mhistéala. SW Ireland
14 M9 Mitchinamécus, Lac ◎ Québec, SE Canada
Mitèmboni see Mitemele, Río
79 D17 Mitemele, Río var. Mitèmboni, Temboni, Utamboni. ~ S Equatorial Guinea
149 S12 Mithānkot Punjab, E Pakistan
149 T7 Mitha Tiwāna Punjab, E Pakistan
149 R17 Mithi Sind, SE Pakistan
Míthimna see Míthymna
Mi Tho see My Tho
115 L16 Míthymna var. Míthimna. Lésvos, E Greece
190 L16 Mitiaro island S Cook Islands
Mitilíni see Mytilíni
15 U7 Mitis ~ Québec, SE Canada
41 R16 Mitla Oaxaca, SE Mexico
165 P13 Mito Ibaraki, Honshū, S Japan
92 N2 Mitra, Kapp headland W Svalbard
184 M13 Mitre ▲ North Island, NZ
185 B21 Mitre Peak ▲ South Island, NZ
39 O15 Mitrofania Island island Alaska, USA
Mitrovica/Mitrowitz see Sremska Mitrovica, Serbia, Serbia and Montenegro (Yugo.)
Mitrovica/Mitrovicë see Kosovska Mitrovica, Serbia, Serbia and Montenegro (Yugo.)
172 H12 Mitsamiouli Grande Comore, NW Comoros
172 I3 Mitsinjo Mahajanga, NW Madagascar
Mits'iwa see Massawa
172 H13 Mitsoudjé Grande Comore, NW Comoros
Mitspe Ramon see Mizpé Ramon
165 T5 Mitsuishi Hokkaidō, NE Japan
165 O11 Mitsuke var. Mituke. Niigata, Honshū, C Japan
Mitsuō see Miryang
164 C12 Mitsushima Nagasaki, Tsushima, SW Japan
100 G12 Mittelandkanal canal NW Germany
108 J7 Mittelberg Vorarlberg, NW Austria
Mitteldorf see Międzychód
Mittelstadt see Baia Sprie
Mitterburg see Pazin
109 P7 Mittersill Salzburg, NW Austria
101 N16 Mittweida Sachsen, E Germany
54 J13 Mitú Vaupés, SE Colombia
Mituke see Mitsuke
Mitumba, Chaîne des/Mitumba Range see Mitumba, Monts
79 O22 Mitumba, Monts var. Chaîne des Mitumba, Mitumba Range. ▲ E Dem. Rep. Congo
79 N23 Mitwaba Katanga, SE Dem. Rep. Congo
79 E18 Mitzic Woleu-Ntem, N Gabon
82 K11 Miueru Wantipa, Lake ◎ N Zambia
165 N14 Miura Kanagawa, Honshū, S Japan
165 Q10 Miyagi off. Miyagi-ken. ◆ prefecture Honshū, C Japan
138 M7 Miyāh, Wādī al dry watercourse E Syria
165 X13 Miyake Tōkyō, Miyako-jima, SE Japan
165 R8 Miyako Iwate, Honshū, C Japan
165 Q16 Miyako-jima island Sakishima-shotō, SW Japan
164 D16 Miyakonojō var. Miyakonzyô. Miyazaki, Kyūshū, SW Japan
Miyakonzyô see Miyakonojō
165 Q16 Miyako-shotō island group SW Japan
144 G11 Miyaly Atyrau, W Kazakhstan
Miyāndoāb see Miāndowāb
Miyāneh see Mīāneh
Miyang see Mile
164 D16 Miyazaki Miyazaki, Kyūshū, SW Japan
164 D16 Miyazaki off. Miyazaki-ken. ◆ prefecture Kyūshū, SW Japan
164 J12 Miyazu Kyōto, Honshū, SW Japan
Miyory see Myory
164 G12 Miyoshi var. Miyosi. Hiroshima, Honshū, SW Japan
Miyosi see Miyoshi
Miza see Mizë
81 H14 Mīzan Teferī Southern, S Ethiopia
Mizda see Mizdah
75 O8 Mizdah var. Mizda. NW Libya
113 K20 Mizë var. Miza. Fier, W Albania
97 A22 Mizen Head Ir. Carn Uí Néid. headland SW Ireland
116 H7 Mizhhir"ya Rus. Mezhgor'ye. Zakarpats'ka Oblast', W Ukraine
160 L4 Mizhi Shaanxi, C China
116 K13 Mizil Prahova, SE Romania
114 H7 Miziya Vratsa, NW Bulgaria
153 W15 Mizo Hills hill range E India
153 W15 Mizoram ◆ state NE India
138 F12 Mizpé Ramon var. Mitspe Ramon. Southern, S Israel
57 L19 Mizque Cochabamba, C Bolivia
57 M19 Mizque, Río ~ C Bolivia
165 Q9 Mizusawa Iwate, Honshū, C Japan
95 M18 Mjölby Östergötland, S Sweden
95 G15 Mjøndalen Buskerud, S Norway
95 J19 Mjörn ◎ S Sweden
94 I13 Mjøsa var. Mjøsen. ◎ S Norway
Mjøsen see Mjøsa
81 G21 Mkalama Singida, C Tanzania
80 K13 Mkata ~ C Tanzania
83 K14 Mkushi Central, C Zambia
83 L22 Mkuze KwaZulu/Natal, E South Africa
81 J22 Mkwaja Tanga, E Tanzania
111 D16 Mladá Boleslav Ger. Jungbunzlau. Středočeský Kraj, N Czech Republic
112 M12 Mladenovac Serbia, C Serbia and Montenegro (Yugo.)
114 L11 Mladinovo Khaskovo, S Bulgaria
113 O17 Mlado Nagoričane N FYR Macedonia
Mlanje see Mulanje
112 N12 Mlava ~ E Serbia and Montenegro (Yugo.)
110 L9 Mława Mazowieckie, C Poland
113 G16 Mljet It. Meleda; anc. Melita. island S Croatia
116 K4 Mlyniv Rivnens'ka Oblast', NW Ukraine
83 I21 Mmabatho North-West, N South Africa
83 I19 Mmashoro Central, E Botswana
44 J7 Moa Holguín, E Cuba
76 J15 Moa ~ Guinea/Sierra Leone
37 O6 Moab Utah, W USA
181 V1 Moa Island island Queensland, NE Australia
187 Y15 Moala island S Fiji
83 L21 Moamba Maputo, SW Mozambique
79 F19 Moanda var. Mouanda. Haut-Ogooué, SE Gabon
83 M15 Moatize Tete, NW Mozambique
79 P22 Moba Katanga, E Dem. Rep. Congo
Mobay see Montego Bay
79 K15 Mobaye Basse-Kotto, S Central African Republic
79 K15 Mobayi-Mbongo Equateur, NW Dem. Rep. Congo
25 P2 Mobeetie Texas, SW USA
27 U3 Moberly Missouri, C USA
23 N8 Mobile Alabama, S USA
23 N9 Mobile Bay bay Alabama, S USA
23 N8 Mobile River ~ Alabama, S USA
29 N8 Mobridge South Dakota, N USA
Mobutu Sese Seko, Lac see Albert, Lake
45 N8 Moca N Dominican Republic
Moçâmedes see Namibe
167 S6 Môc Châu Sơn La, N Vietnam
187 Z15 Moce island Lau Group, E Fiji
83 Q15 Moçambique Nampula, NE Mozambique
Mocha see Al Mukhā
193 T11 Mocha Fracture Zone tectonic feature SE Pacific Ocean
63 F14 Mocha, Isla island C Chile
56 C12 Moche, Río ~ W Peru
167 S14 Môc Hoa Long An, S Vietnam
83 I20 Mochudi Kgatleng, SE Botswana
82 Q13 Mocímboa da Praia var. Vila de Mocímboa da Praia. Cabo Delgado, N Mozambique
94 L13 Mockfjärd Dalarna, C Sweden
21 R9 Mocksville North Carolina, SE USA
32 F8 Moclips Washington, NW USA
82 C13 Môco var. Morro de Môco. ▲ W Angola
54 D13 Mocoa Putumayo, SW Colombia
60 M8 Mococa São Paulo, S Brazil
Môco, Morro de see Môco
40 H8 Mocorito Sinaloa, C Mexico
40 J4 Moctezuma Chihuahua, N Mexico
41 N11 Moctezuma San Luis Potosí, C Mexico
40 G4 Moctezuma Sonora, NW Mexico
41 P12 Moctezuma, Río ~ C Mexico
Mó, Cuan see Clew Bay
83 O16 Mocuba Zambézia, NE Mozambique
103 U12 Modane Savoie, E France
106 F9 Modena anc. Mutina. Emilia-Romagna, N Italy
36 I7 Modena Utah, W USA
35 O9 Modesto California, W USA
107 L25 Modica anc. Motyca. Sicilia, Italy, C Mediterranean Sea
83 J20 Modimolle prev. Nylstroom. Limpopo, NE South Africa
79 K17 Modjamboli Equateur, N Dem. Rep. Congo
109 X4 Mödling Niederösterreich, NE Austria
Modohn see Madona
163 N8 Modot Hentiy, C Mongolia
171 V14 Modowi Papua, E Indonesia
112 I12 Modračko Jezero ⊞ NE Bosnia and Herzegovina
112 I10 Modriča Republika Srpska, N Bosnia and Herzegovina
183 O13 Moe Victoria, SE Australia
Moearatewe see Muaratewe
Moei, Mae Nam see Thaungyin
94 H13 Moelv Hedmark, S Norway
92 I10 Moen Troms, N Norway
Moen see Weno, Micronesia
Möen see Møn, Denmark
Moena see Muna, Pulau
36 M10 Moenkopi Wash ~ Arizona, SW USA
185 F22 Moeraki Point headland South Island, NZ
99 F16 Moerbeke Oost-Vlaanderen, NW Belgium
99 H14 Moerdijk Noord-Brabant, S Netherlands
Moero, Lac see Mweru, Lake
101 D15 Moers var. Mörs. Nordrhein-Westfalen, W Germany
Moesi see Musi, Air
Moeskroen see Mouscron
96 J13 Moffat S Scotland, UK
185 C22 Moffat Peak ▲ South Island, NZ
152 H8 Moga Punjab, N India
79 N19 Moga Sud Kivu, E Dem. Rep. Congo
Mogadiscio/Mogadishu see Muqdisho
Mogador see Essaouira
104 J6 Mogadouro Bragança, N Portugal
167 N2 Mogaung Kachin State, N Burma
110 L13 Mogielnica Mazowieckie, C Poland
Mogilëv see Mahilyow
Mogilev-Podol'skiy see Mohyliv-Podil's'kyy
Mogilëvskaya Oblast' see Mahilyowskaya Voblasts'
110 I11 Mogilno Kujawsko-pomorskie, C Poland
60 L9 Mogi-Mirim var. Moji-Mirim. São Paulo, S Brazil
83 Q15 Mogincual Nampula, NE Mozambique
114 E13 Moglenítsas ~ N Greece
106 H8 Mogliano Veneto Veneto, NE Italy
113 M21 Moglicë Korçë, SE Albania
123 O13 Mogocha Chitinskaya Oblast', S Russian Federation
122 J11 Mogochin Tomskaya Oblast', C Russian Federation
80 F13 Mogogh Jonglei, SE Sudan
171 U12 Mogoi Papua, E Indonesia
166 M4 Mogok Mandalay, C Burma
37 P14 Mogollon Mountains ▲ New Mexico, SW USA
36 M12 Mogollon Rim cliff Arizona, SW USA
61 E23 Mogotes, Punta headland E Argentina
42 J8 Mogotón ▲ NW Nicaragua
104 I14 Moguer Andalucía, S Spain
111 I26 Mohács Baranya, SW Hungary
185 C20 Mohaka ~ North Island, NZ
28 M2 Mohall North Dakota, N USA
Moḩammadābād see Dargaz
74 F6 Mohammedia prev. Fédala. NW Morocco
74 F6 Mohammed V ✕ (Casablanca) W Morocco
Mohammerah see Khorramshahr
36 H10 Mohave, Lake ⊞ Arizona/Nevada, W USA
36 I12 Mohave Mountains ▲ Arizona, SW USA
36 I15 Mohawk Mountains ▲ Arizona, SW USA
18 J10 Mohawk River ~ New York, NE USA
163 T3 Mohe var. Xilinji. Heilongjiang, NE China
95 L20 Moheda Kronoberg, S Sweden
172 H13 Mohéli var. Mwali, Mohilla, Mohila, Fr. Moili. island S Comoros
152 I11 Mohendergarh Haryāna, N India
38 K12 Mohican, Cape headland Nunivak Island, Alaska, USA
Mohn see Muhu
101 G15 Möhne ~ W Germany
101 G15 Möhne-Stausee ⊞ W Germany
92 P2 Mohn, Kapp headland NW Svalbard
197 S14 Mohns Ridge undersea feature Greenland Sea/Norwegian Sea
57 I17 Moho Puno, SE Peru
Mohokare see Caledon
95 L17 Moholm Västra Götaland, S Sweden

◆ Country ● Country Capital ◇ Dependent Territory ○ Dependent Territory Capital ◆ Administrative Region ✕ International Airport ▲ Mountain ▲ Mountain Range ⚹ Volcano ~ River ◎ Lake ⊞ Reservoir

36 J11 **Mohon Peak** ▲ Arizona, SW USA
81 J23 **Mohoro** Pwani, E Tanzania
Mohra see Moravice
Mohrungen see Morąg
116 M7 **Mohyliv-Podil's'kyy** Rus. Mogilev-Podol'skiy. Vinnyts'ka Oblast', C Ukraine
95 D17 **Moi** Rogaland, S Norway
116 K11 **Moinești** Hung. Mojnest. Bacău, E Romania
Móinteach Mílic see Mountmellick
14 J14 **Moira** ≈ Ontario, SE Canada
92 G13 **Mo i Rana** Nordland, C Norway
153 X14 **Moirāng** Manipur, NE India
115 J25 **Moíres** Kríti, Greece, E Mediterranean Sea
118 H6 **Mõisaküla** Ger. Moiseküll. Viljandimaa, S Estonia
Moiseküll see Mõisaküla
15 W4 **Moisie** Québec, E Canada
15 W3 **Moisie** ≈ Québec, SE Canada
102 M14 **Moissac** Tarn-et-Garonne, S France
78 I13 **Moïssala** Moyen-Chari, S Chad
55 O7 **Moitaco** Bolívar, E Venezuela
95 P15 **Möja** Stockholm, C Sweden
105 Q14 **Mojácar** Andalucía, S Spain
35 T13 **Mojave** California, W USA
35 V13 **Mojave Desert** plain California, W USA
35 V13 **Mojave River** ≈ California, W USA
Moji-Mirim see Mogi-Mirim
113 K15 **Mojkovac** Montenegro, SW Serbia and Montenegro (Yugo.)
Mojnest see Moinești
Mōka see Mooka
153 Q13 **Mokāma** prev. Mokameh, Mukama. Bihār, N India
79 O25 **Mokambo** Katanga, SE Dem. Rep. Congo
Mokameh see Mokāma
38 D9 **Mōkapu Point** var. Mokapu Point headland O'ahu, Hawai'i, USA, C Pacific Ocean
184 L9 **Mokau** Waikato, North Island, NZ
184 L9 **Mokau** ≈ North Island, NZ
35 P7 **Mokelumne River** ≈ California, W USA
83 J23 **Mokhotlong** NE Lesotho
Mokil Atoll see Mwokil Atoll
95 N14 **Möklinta** Västmanland, C Sweden
184 L4 **Mokohinau Islands** island group N NZ
153 X12 **Mokokchūng** Nāgāland, NE India
78 F12 **Mokolo** Extrême-Nord, N Cameroon
83 J20 **Mokopane** prev. Potgietersrus. Limpopo, NE South Africa
185 D24 **Mokoreta** ≈ South Island, NZ
163 X17 **Mokp'o** Jap. Moppo. SW South Korea
113 L16 **Mokra Gora** ▲▲ S Serbia and Montenegro (Yugo.)
Mokrany see Makrany
127 O5 **Moksha** ≈ W Russian Federation
Moktama see Martaban
77 T14 **Mokwa** Niger, W Nigeria
99 J16 **Mol** prev. Moll. Antwerpen, N Belgium
107 O17 **Mola di Bari** Puglia, SE Italy
Molai see Moláoi
41 P13 **Molango** Hidalgo, C Mexico
115 F22 **Moláoi** var. Molai. Pelopónnisos, S Greece
41 Z12 **Molas del Norte, Punta** var. Punta Molas. headland SE Mexico
Molas, Punta see Molas del Norte, Punta
105 R11 **Molatón** ▲ C Spain
97 K18 **Mold** NE Wales, UK
Moldau see Moldova
Moldau see Vltava, Czech Republic
Moldavia see Moldova
Moldavian SSR/Moldavskaya SSR see Moldova
94 E9 **Molde** Møre og Romsdal, S Norway
Moldotau, Khrebet see Moldo-Too, Khrebet
147 V9 **Moldo-Too, Khrebet** prev. Khrebet Moldotau. ▲▲ C Kyrgyzstan
116 K9 **Moldova** ≈ N Romania
116 K9 **Moldova** Eng. Moldavia, Ger. Moldau. former province NE Romania
116 L9 **Moldova** off. Republic of Moldova, var. Moldavia; prev. Moldavian SSR, Rus. Moldavskaya SSR. ◆ republic SE Europe
116 F13 **Moldova Nouă** Ger. Neumoldowa, Hung. Újmoldova. Caraș-Severin, SW Romania
116 F13 **Moldova Veche** Ger. Altmoldowa, Hung. Ómoldova. Caraș-Severin, SW Romania
Moldoveanul see Vârful Moldoveanu
83 I20 **Molepolole** Kweneng, SE Botswana
44 L8 **Môle-St-Nicolas** NW Haiti
118 H13 **Molėtai** Utena, E Lithuania
107 O17 **Molfetta** Puglia, SE Italy
171 P11 **Molibagu** Sulawesi, N Indonesia
62 G12 **Molina** Maule, C Chile
105 Q7 **Molina de Aragón** Castilla-La Mancha, C Spain
105 R13 **Molina de Segura** Murcia, SE Spain
30 J11 **Moline** Illinois, N USA
27 P7 **Moline** Kansas, C USA
79 P23 **Moliro** Katanga, SE Dem. Rep. Congo
107 K16 **Molise** ◈ region S Italy
95 K15 **Molkom** Värmland, C Sweden
Moll see Mol
109 Q9 **Möll** ≈ S Austria
146 I14 **Mollanepes Adyndaky** Rus. Imeni Mollanepesa. Mary Welaýaty, S Turkmenistan
95 J22 **Mölle** Skåne, S Sweden
57 H18 **Mollendo** Arequipa, SW Peru
105 U5 **Mollerussa** Cataluña, NE Spain
108 H8 **Mollis** Glarus, NE Switzerland
95 J19 **Mölndal** Västra Götaland, S Sweden
95 J19 **Mölnlycke** Västra Götaland, S Sweden
117 U9 **Molochans'k** Rus. Molochansk. Zaporiz'ka Oblast', SE Ukraine
117 U10 **Molochna** Rus. Molochnaya. ≈ S Ukraine
Molochnaya see Molochna
117 U10 **Molochnyy Lyman** bay N Black Sea
Molodechno/Molodeczno see Maladzyechna
195 V3 **Molodezhnaya** Russian research station Antarctica
126 J14 **Mologa** ≈ NW Russian Federation
38 E9 **Moloka'i** var. Molokai. island Hawai'i, USA, C Pacific Ocean
193 O5 **Molokai Fracture Zone** tectonic feature NE Pacific Ocean
124 K15 **Molokovo** Tverskaya Oblast', W Russian Federation
127 Q14 **Moloma** ≈ NW Russian Federation
183 R8 **Molong** New South Wales, SE Australia
83 H21 **Molopo** seasonal river Botswana/South Africa
115 F17 **Mólos** Stereá Ellás, C Greece
171 O11 **Molosipat** Sulawesi, N Indonesia
Molotov see Severodvinsk,
Molotov see Perm'
79 G17 **Moloundou** Est, SE Cameroon
103 U5 **Molsheim** Bas-Rhin, NE France
11 X13 **Molson Lake** ◎ Manitoba, C Canada
Moluccas see Maluku
171 Q12 **Molucca Sea** Ind. Laut Maluku. sea E Indonesia
Molukken see Maluku
83 O15 **Molumbo** Zambézia, N Mozambique
171 T15 **Molu, Pulau** island Maluku, E Indonesia
83 P16 **Moma** Nampula, NE Mozambique
171 X14 **Momats** ≈ Papua, E Indonesia
42 J11 **Mombacho, Volcán** ⛰ SW Nicaragua
81 K21 **Mombasa** Coast, SE Kenya
81 J21 **Mombasa** ✕ Coast, SE Kenya
Mombetsu see Monbetsu
114 J12 **Momchilgrad** prev. Mastanli. Kŭrdzhali, S Bulgaria
99 F23 **Momignies** Hainaut, S Belgium
54 E6 **Momil** Córdoba, NW Colombia
42 I10 **Momotombo, Volcán** ⛰ W Nicaragua
56 B5 **Mompiche, Ensenada de** bay NW Ecuador
79 K18 **Mompono** Equateur, NW Dem. Rep. Congo
54 F6 **Mompós** Bolívar, NW Colombia
95 J24 **Møn** prev. Möen. island SE Denmark
36 L4 **Mona** Utah, W USA
Mona, Canal de la see Mona Passage
96 E8 **Monach Islands** island group NW Scotland, UK
103 V14 **Monaco** var. Monaco-Ville; anc. Monoecus. ● (Monaco) S Monaco
103 V14 **Monaco** off. Principality of Monaco. ◆ monarchy W Europe
Monaco see München
Monaco-Ville see Monaco
96 I9 **Monadhliath Mountains** ▲▲ N Scotland, UK
55 O6 **Monagas** off. Estado Monagas. ◈ state NE Venezuela
97 F16 **Monaghan** Ir. Muineachán. N Ireland
97 E16 **Monaghan** Ir. Muineachán. cultural region N Ireland
43 S16 **Monagrillo** Herrera, S Panama
24 L8 **Monahans** Texas, SW USA
45 Q9 **Mona, Isla** island W Puerto Rico
45 Q9 **Mona Passage** Sp. Canal de la Mona. channel Dominican Republic/Puerto Rico
43 O14 **Mona, Punta** headland E Costa Rica
155 K25 **Monaragala** Uva Province, SE Sri Lanka
33 S9 **Monarch** Montana, NW USA
10 H14 **Monarch Mountain** ▲ British Columbia, SW Canada
Monasterio see Monesterio
Monasterzyska see Monastyrys'ka
Monastir see Bitola
Monastyriska see Monastyrys'ka
117 O7 **Monastyryshche** Cherkas'ka Oblast', C Ukraine
116 J6 **Monastyrys'ka** Pol. Monasterzyska, Rus. Monastyriska. Ternopil's'ka Oblast', W Ukraine
79 E15 **Monatélé** Centre, SW Cameroon
165 U2 **Monbetsu** var. Mombetsu, Monbetu. Hokkaidō, NE Japan
Monbetu see Monbetsu
106 B8 **Moncalieri** Piemonte, NW Italy
104 G4 **Monção** Viana do Castelo, N Portugal
105 Q5 **Moncayo** ▲ N Spain
105 Q5 **Moncayo, Sierra del** ▲▲ N Spain
124 I4 **Monchegorsk** Murmanskaya Oblast', NW Russian Federation
101 D15 **Mönchengladbach** prev. München-Gladbach. Nordrhein-Westfalen, W Germany
104 F14 **Monchique** Faro, S Portugal
104 G14 **Monchique, Serra de** ▲▲ S Portugal
21 S14 **Moncks Corner** South Carolina, SE USA
41 N7 **Monclova** Coahuila de Zaragoza, NE Mexico
Moncorvo see Torre de Moncorvo
13 P14 **Moncton** New Brunswick, SE Canada
104 F8 **Mondego, Cabo** headland N Portugal
104 G8 **Mondego, Rio** ≈ N Portugal
104 I2 **Mondoñedo** Galicia, NW Spain
99 N25 **Mondorf-les-Bains** Grevenmacher, SE Luxembourg
102 M7 **Mondoubleau** Loir-et-Cher, C France
30 J6 **Mondovi** Wisconsin, N USA
106 B9 **Mondovì** Piemonte, NW Italy
105 P3 **Mondragón** var. Arrasate. País Vasco, N Spain
107 J17 **Mondragone** Campania, S Italy
109 R5 **Mondsee** ◎ N Austria
115 G22 **Monemvasía** Pelopónnisos, S Greece
18 B15 **Monessen** Pennsylvania, NE USA
104 J12 **Monesterio** var. Monasterio. Extremadura, W Spain
14 L8 **Monet** Québec, SE Canada
27 S8 **Monett** Missouri, C USA
27 X9 **Monette** Arkansas, C USA
14 G11 **Monetville** Ontario, S Canada
106 J7 **Monfalcone** Friuli-Venezia Giulia, NE Italy
104 H10 **Monforte** Portalegre, C Portugal
104 I4 **Monforte de Lemos** Galicia, NW Spain
81 I24 **Monga** Lindi, SE Tanzania
79 L16 **Monga** Orientale, N Dem. Rep. Congo
81 F15 **Mongalla** Bahr el Gabel, S Sudan
153 U11 **Mongar** E Bhutan
167 U6 **Mong Cai** Quang Ninh, N Vietnam
180 I11 **Mongers Lake** salt lake Western Australia
186 K8 **Mongga** Kolombangara, NW Solomon Islands
167 O6 **Möng Hpayak** Shan State, E Burma
Monghyr see Munger
106 B10 **Mongioie** ▲ NW Italy
167 N5 **Möng Küng** Shan State, E Burma
Mongla see Mungla
188 C15 **Mongmong** C Guam
167 N6 **Möng Nai** Shan State, E Burma
78 I11 **Mongo** Guéra, C Chad
76 I14 **Mongo** ≈ N Sierra Leone
163 I8 **Mongolia** Mong. Mongol Uls. ◆ republic E Asia
Mongolküre see Zhaosu
Mongol Uls see Mongolia
79 E17 **Mongomo** E Equatorial Guinea
77 Y12 **Mongonu** var. Monguno. Borno, NE Nigeria
Mongora see Mingāora
78 K11 **Mongororo** Ouaddaï, SE Chad
Mongos, Chaîne des see Bongo, Massif des
79 I16 **Mongoumba** Lobaye, SW Central African Republic
Mongrove, Punta see Cayacal, Punta
83 G15 **Mongu** Western, W Zambia
76 I10 **Mônguel** Gorgol, SW Mauritania
Monguno see Mongonu
167 N4 **Möng Yai** Shan State, E Burma
167 O5 **Möng Yang** Shan State, E Burma
167 N3 **Möng Yu** Shan State, E Burma
162 K8 **Mönhbulag** Övörhangay, C Mongolia
Mönh Sarĭdag see Munku-Sardyk, Gora
186 P9 **Moni** ≈ S Papau New Guinea
115 I15 **Moní Megístis Lávras** monastery Kentrikí Makedonía, N Greece
115 F18 **Moní Osíou Loúkas** monastery Stereá Ellás, C Greece
54 F9 **Moniquirá** Boyacá, C Colombia
103 Q12 **Monistrol-sur-Loire** Haute-Loire, C France
35 V7 **Monitor Range** ▲▲ Nevada, W USA
115 I14 **Moní Vatopedíou** monastery Kentrikí Makedonía, N Greece
Monkchester see Newcastle upon Tyne
83 N14 **Monkey Bay** Southern, SE Malawi
43 N11 **Monkey Point** var. Punta Mico, Punte Mono, Punto Mico. headland SE Nicaragua
Monkey River see Monkey River Town
42 G3 **Monkey River Town** var. Monkey River. Toledo, SE Belize
14 M13 **Monkland** Ontario, SE Canada
79 J19 **Monkoto** Equateur, NW Dem. Rep. Congo
97 K21 **Monmouth** Wel. Trefynwy. SE Wales, UK
30 J12 **Monmouth** Illinois, N USA
32 F12 **Monmouth** Oregon, NW USA
97 K21 **Monmouth** cultural region SE Wales, UK
98 I10 **Monnickendam** Noord-Holland, C Netherlands
77 R15 **Mono** ≈ C Togo
Monoecus see Monaco
35 R8 **Mono Lake** ◎ California, W USA
115 O23 **Monólithos** Ródos, Dodekánisos, Greece, Aegean Sea
19 Q12 **Monomoy Island** island Massachusetts, NE USA
31 O12 **Monon** Indiana, N USA
29 Y12 **Monona** Iowa, C USA
30 L9 **Monona** Wisconsin, N USA
18 B15 **Monongahela** Pennsylvania, NE USA
18 B16 **Monongahela River** ≈ NE USA
107 P17 **Monopoli** Puglia, SE Italy
Mono, Punte see Monkey Point
111 K23 **Monor** Pest, C Hungary
Monostor see Beli Manastir
78 K8 **Monou** Borkou-Ennedi-Tibesti, NE Chad
105 S12 **Monovar** Cat. Monover País Valenciano, E Spain
Monover see Monovar
105 R7 **Monreal del Campo** Aragón, NE Spain
107 I23 **Monreale** Sicilia, Italy, C Mediterranean Sea
23 T3 **Monroe** Georgia, SE USA
29 W14 **Monroe** Iowa, C USA
22 I5 **Monroe** Louisiana, S USA
31 S10 **Monroe** Michigan, N USA
18 K13 **Monroe** New York, NE USA
21 S11 **Monroe** North Carolina, SE USA
36 L6 **Monroe** Utah, W USA
32 H7 **Monroe** Washington, NW USA
30 L9 **Monroe** Wisconsin, N USA
27 V3 **Monroe City** Missouri, C USA
31 O15 **Monroe Lake** ▣ Indiana, N USA
23 O7 **Monroeville** Alabama, S USA
18 C15 **Monroeville** Pennsylvania, NE USA
76 J16 **Monrovia** ● (Liberia) W Liberia
76 J16 **Monrovia** ✕ W Liberia
105 T7 **Monroyo** Aragón, NE Spain
99 F20 **Mons** Dut. Bergen. Hainaut, S Belgium
104 I8 **Monsanto** Castelo Branco, C Portugal
106 H8 **Monselice** Veneto, NE Italy
166 M9 **Mon State** ◈ state S Burma
98 G12 **Monster** Zuid-Holland, W Netherlands
95 N20 **Mönsterås** Kalmar, S Sweden
101 F17 **Montabaur** Rheinland-Pfalz, W Germany
106 G8 **Montagnana** Veneto, NE Italy
35 N1 **Montague** California, W USA
25 S5 **Montague** Texas, SW USA
183 S11 **Montague Island** island New South Wales, SE Australia
39 S12 **Montague Island** island Alaska, USA
39 S13 **Montague Strait** strait N Gulf of Alaska
102 J8 **Montaigu** Vendée, NW France
Montaigu see Scherpenheuvel
105 S7 **Montalbán** Aragón, NE Spain
106 G13 **Montalcino** Toscana, C Italy
104 H5 **Montalegre** Vila Real, N Portugal
114 G8 **Montana** prev. Ferdinand, Mikhaylovgrad. Montana, NW Bulgaria
108 D10 **Montana** Valais, SW Switzerland
39 R11 **Montana** Alaska, USA
114 G8 **Montana** ◈ province NW Bulgaria
33 T9 **Montana** off. State of Montana; also known as Mountain State, Treasure State. ◈ state NW USA
104 J10 **Montánchez** Extremadura, W Spain
Montañita see La Montañita
15 Q8 **Mont-Apica** Québec, SE Canada
104 G10 **Montargil** Portalegre, C Portugal
104 G10 **Montargil, Barragem de** ▣ C Portugal
103 O7 **Montargis** Loiret, C France
103 O4 **Montataire** Oise, N France
102 M14 **Montauban** Tarn-et-Garonne, S France
19 N14 **Montauk** Long Island, New York, NE USA
19 N14 **Montauk Point** headland Long Island, New York, NE USA
103 Q7 **Montbard** Côte d'Or, C France
103 U7 **Montbéliard** Doubs, E France
25 W11 **Mont Belvieu** Texas, SW USA
105 U6 **Montblanc** var. Montblanch. Cataluña, NE Spain
Montblanch see Montblanc
103 Q11 **Montbrison** Loire, E France
Montcalm, Lake see Dogai Coring
103 Q9 **Montceau-les-Mines** Saône-et-Loire, C France
103 U12 **Mont Cenis, Col du** pass E France
102 K15 **Mont-de-Marsan** Landes, SW France
103 O3 **Montdidier** Somme, N France
187 Q17 **Mont-Dore** Province Sud, S New Caledonia
20 K10 **Monteagle** Tennessee, S USA
57 M20 **Monteagudo** Chuquisaca, S Bolivia
41 R16 **Monte Albán** ruins Oaxaca, S Mexico
105 R11 **Montealegre del Castillo** Castilla-La Mancha, C Spain
59 N18 **Monte Azul** Minas Gerais, SE Brazil
14 M12 **Montebello** Québec, SE Canada
106 H7 **Montebelluna** Veneto, NE Italy
60 G13 **Montecarlo** Misiones, NE Argentina
61 D16 **Monte Caseros** Corrientes, NE Argentina
60 J13 **Monte Castelo** Santa Catarina, S Brazil
106 F11 **Montecatini Terme** Toscana, C Italy
42 H7 **Montecillos, Cordillera de** ▲▲ W Honduras
62 I12 **Monte Comén** Mendoza, W Argentina
44 M8 **Monte Cristi** var. San Fernando de Monte Cristi. NW Dominican Republic
58 C13 **Monte Cristo** Amazonas, W Brazil
107 E14 **Montecristo, Isola di** island Archipelago Toscano, C Italy
Monte Croce Carnico, Passo di see Plöcken Pass
58 J12 **Monte Dourado** Pará, NE Brazil
40 L11 **Monte Escobedo** Zacatecas, C Mexico
106 I13 **Montefalco** Umbria, C Italy
107 H14 **Montefiascone** Lazio, C Italy
105 N14 **Montefrío** Andalucía, S Spain
44 I11 **Montego Bay** var. Mobay. W Jamaica
Montego Bay see Sangster
104 J8 **Montehermoso** Extremadura, W Spain
104 F10 **Montejunto, Serra de** ▲ C Portugal
Monteleone di Calabria see Vibo Valentia
54 E7 **Montelíbano** Córdoba, NW Colombia
103 R13 **Montélimar** anc. Acunum Acusio, Montilium Adhemari. Drôme, E France
104 K15 **Montellano** Andalucía, S Spain
35 Y2 **Montello** Nevada, W USA
30 L8 **Montello** Wisconsin, N USA
63 J18 **Montemayor, Meseta de** plain SE Argentina
41 O9 **Montemorelos** Nuevo León, NE Mexico
104 G11 **Montemor-o-Novo** Évora, S Portugal
104 G8 **Montemor-o-Velho** var. Montemor-o-Vélho. Coimbra, N Portugal
104 H7 **Montemuro, Serra de** ▲ N Portugal
102 K12 **Montendre** Charente-Maritime, W France
61 I15 **Montenegro** Rio Grande do Sul, S Brazil
113 J16 **Montenegro** Serb. Crna Gora. ◈ republic SW Serbia and Montenegro (Yugo.)
62 G10 **Monte Patria** Coquimbo, N Chile
45 O9 **Monte Plata** E Dominican Republic
83 P14 **Montepuez** Cabo Delgado, N Mozambique
83 P14 **Montepuez** ≈ N Mozambique
106 G13 **Montepulciano** Toscana, C Italy
62 L6 **Monte Quemado** Santiago del Estero, N Argentina
103 O6 **Montereau-Faut-Yonne** anc. Condate. Seine-St-Denis, N France
35 N11 **Monterey** California, W USA
20 L9 **Monterey** Tennessee, S USA
21 T5 **Monterey** Virginia, NE USA
Monterey see Monterrey
35 N10 **Monterey Bay** bay California, W USA
54 D6 **Montería** Córdoba, NW Colombia
57 N18 **Montero** Santa Cruz, C Bolivia
62 J7 **Monteros** Tucumán, C Argentina
104 I5 **Monterrei** Galicia, NW Spain
41 O8 **Monterrey** var. Monterey. Nuevo León, NE Mexico
32 F9 **Montesano** Washington, NW USA
107 M19 **Montesano sulla Marcellana** Campania, S Italy
107 N16 **Monte Sant' Angelo** Puglia, SE Italy
59 O16 **Monte Santo** Bahia, E Brazil
107 D18 **Monte Santu, Capo di** headland Sardegna, Italy, C Mediterranean Sea
59 M19 **Montes Claros** Minas Gerais, SE Brazil
107 K14 **Montesilvano Marina** Abruzzo, C Italy
23 P4 **Montevallo** Alabama, S USA
106 G12 **Montevarchi** Toscana, C Italy
29 S9 **Montevideo** Minnesota, N USA
61 F20 **Montevideo** ● (Uruguay) Montevideo, S Uruguay
37 S7 **Monte Vista** Colorado, C USA
23 T5 **Montezuma** Georgia, SE USA
29 W14 **Montezuma** Iowa, C USA
26 J6 **Montezuma** Kansas, C USA
103 U12 **Montgenèvre, Col de** pass France/Italy
97 K20 **Montgomery** E Wales, UK
23 Q5 **Montgomery** state capital Alabama, S USA
29 V9 **Montgomery** Minnesota, N USA
18 G13 **Montgomery** Pennsylvania, NE USA
21 Q5 **Montgomery** West Virginia, NE USA
97 K19 **Montgomery** cultural region E Wales, UK
Montgomery see Sāhīwāl
27 V4 **Montgomery City** Missouri, C USA
35 S8 **Montgomery Pass** pass Nevada, W USA
102 K12 **Montguyon** Charente-Maritime, W France
108 C10 **Monthey** Valais, SW Switzerland
27 V13 **Monticello** Arkansas, C USA
23 T4 **Monticello** Florida, SE USA
23 T8 **Monticello** Georgia, SE USA
30 M13 **Monticello** Illinois, N USA
31 O12 **Monticello** Indiana, N USA
29 Y13 **Monticello** Iowa, C USA
20 L7 **Monticello** Kentucky, S USA
29 V8 **Monticello** Minnesota, N USA
22 K7 **Monticello** Mississippi, S USA
27 V2 **Monticello** Missouri, C USA
18 J12 **Monticello** New York, NE USA
37 O7 **Monticello** Utah, W USA
106 F8 **Montichiari** Lombardia, N Italy
102 M12 **Montignac** Dordogne, SW France
99 G21 **Montignies-le-Tilleul** var. Montigny-le-Tilleul. Hainaut, S Belgium
14 J8 **Montigny, Lac de** ◎ Québec, SE Canada
103 S6 **Montigny-le-Roi** Haute-Marne, N France
Montigny-le-Tilleul see Montignies-le-Tilleul
43 R16 **Montijo** Veraguas, S Panama
104 F11 **Montijo** Setúbal, W Portugal
104 J11 **Montijo** Extremadura, W Spain
Montilium Adhemari see Montélimar
104 M13 **Montilla** Andalucía, S Spain
102 L3 **Montivilliers** Seine-Maritime, N France
15 U7 **Mont-Joli** Québec, SE Canada
14 M10 **Mont-Laurier** Québec, SE Canada
15 X5 **Mont-Louis** Québec, SE Canada
103 N17 **Mont-Louis** var. Mont Louis. Pyrénées-Orientales, S France
103 O10 **Montluçon** Allier, C France
15 R10 **Montmagny** Québec, SE Canada
103 S3 **Montmédy** Meuse, NE France
103 P5 **Montmirail** Marne, N France
15 R9 **Montmorency** ≈ Québec, SE Canada
102 M10 **Montmorillon** Vienne, W France
107 J14 **Montorio al Vomano** Abruzzo, C Italy
104 M13 **Montoro** Andalucía, S Spain
33 S16 **Montpelier** Idaho, NW USA
29 P6 **Montpelier** North Dakota, N USA
18 M7 **Montpelier** state capital Vermont, NE USA
103 Q15 **Montpellier** Hérault, S France
102 L12 **Montpon-Ménestérol** Dordogne, SW France
12 K15 **Montréal** Eng. Montreal. Québec, SE Canada
14 G8 **Montreal** ≈ Ontario, S Canada
14 C8 **Montreal** ≈ Ontario, S Canada
Montreal see Mirabel
11 T14 **Montreal Lake** ◎ Saskatchewan, C Canada
14 B9 **Montreal River** Ontario, S Canada
103 N2 **Montreuil** Pas-de-Calais, N France
102 K8 **Montreuil-Bellay** Maine-et-Loire, NW France
108 C10 **Montreux** Vaud, SW Switzerland
108 B9 **Montricher** Vaud, W Switzerland
96 K10 **Montrose** E Scotland, UK
27 W14 **Montrose** Arkansas, C USA
37 Q6 **Montrose** Colorado, C USA
29 Y16 **Montrose** Iowa, C USA
18 H12 **Montrose** Pennsylvania, NE USA
21 X5 **Montross** Virginia, NE USA
15 O12 **Mont-St-Hilaire** Québec, SE Canada
103 S3 **Mont-St-Martin** Meurthe-et-Moselle, NE France
45 V10 **Montserrat** var. Emerald Isle. ◇ UK dependent territory E West Indies
105 V5 **Montserrat** ▲ NE Spain
104 M7 **Montuenga** Castilla-León, N Spain
99 M19 **Montzen** Liège, E Belgium
37 N8 **Monument Valley** valley Arizona/Utah, SW USA
166 L4 **Monywa** Sagaing, C Burma
106 D7 **Monza** Lombardia, N Italy
83 J15 **Monze** Southern, S Zambia
105 T5 **Monzón** Aragón, NE Spain
25 T9 **Moody** Texas, SW USA
98 L13 **Mook** Limburg, SE Netherlands
165 O12 **Mooka** var. Mōka. Tochigi, Honshū, S Japan
182 K3 **Moomba** South Australia
14 G13 **Moon** ≈ Ontario, S Canada
Moon see Muhu
181 Y10 **Moonie** Queensland, E Australia
193 O5 **Moonless Mountains** undersea feature E Pacific Ocean
182 L13 **Moonlight Head** headland Victoria, SE Australia
Moon-Sund see Väinameri
182 H8 **Moonta** South Australia
Moor see Mór
180 I12 **Moora** Western Australia
98 H12 **Moordrecht** Zuid-Holland, C Netherlands
33 T9 **Moore** Montana, NW USA
27 N11 **Moore** Oklahoma, C USA
25 R12 **Moore** Texas, SW USA
191 S10 **Moorea** island Îles du Vent, W French Polynesia
21 U3 **Moorefield** West Virginia, NE USA
23 X14 **Moore Haven** Florida, SE USA
180 J11 **Moore, Lake** ◎ Western Australia
19 N7 **Moore Reservoir** ▣ New Hampshire/Vermont, NE USA
44 G1 **Moores Island** island N Bahamas
21 R10 **Mooresville** North Carolina, SE USA
29 R5 **Moorhead** Minnesota, N USA
22 K4 **Moorhead** Mississippi, S USA
99 F18 **Moorsel** Oost-Vlaanderen, C Belgium
99 C18 **Moorslede** West-Vlaanderen, W Belgium
18 L8 **Moosalamoo, Mount** ▲ Vermont, NE USA
101 M22 **Moosburg an der Isar** Bayern, SE Germany
33 S14 **Moose** Wyoming, C USA
12 H11 **Moose** ≈ Ontario, S Canada

◆ Country ● Country Capital ◇ Dependent Territory ○ Dependent Territory Capital ◈ Administrative Region ✕ International Airport ▲ Mountain ▲▲ Mountain Range ⛰ Volcano ≈ River ◎ Lake ▣ Reservoir

12 H10 **Moose Factory** Ontario, S Canada
19 Q4 **Moosehead Lake** ◎ Maine, NE USA
11 U16 **Moose Jaw** Saskatchewan, S Canada
11 V14 **Moose Lake** Manitoba, C Canada
29 W6 **Moose Lake** Minnesota, N USA
19 P6 **Mooselookmeguntic Lake** ◎ Maine, NE USA
39 R12 **Moose Pass** Alaska, USA
19 P5 **Moose River** ≈ Maine, NE USA
18 J9 **Moose River** ≈ New York, NE USA
11 V16 **Moosomin** Saskatchewan, S Canada
12 H10 **Moosonee** Ontario, SE Canada
19 N12 **Moosup** Connecticut, NE USA
83 N16 **Mopeia** Zambézia, NE Mozambique
83 H18 **Mopipi** Central, C Botswana
Moppo *see* Mokp'o
77 N11 **Mopti** Mopti, C Mali
77 O11 **Mopti** ◆ *region* S Mali
57 H18 **Moquegua** Moquegua, SE Peru
57 H18 **Moquegua** *off.* Departamento de Moquegua. ◆ *department* S Peru
111 I23 **Mór** *Ger.* Moor. Fejér, C Hungary
78 G11 **Mora** Extrême-Nord, N Cameroon
104 G11 **Mora** Évora, S Portugal
105 N9 **Mora** Castilla-La Mancha, C Spain
94 L12 **Mora** Dalarna, C Sweden
29 V7 **Mora** Minnesota, N USA
37 T10 **Mora** New Mexico, SW USA
113 J17 **Morača** ≈ SW Serbia and Montenegro (Yugo.)
152 K10 **Morādābād** Uttar Pradesh, N India
105 U6 **Móra d'Ebre** *var.* Mora de Ebro. Cataluña, NE Spain
Mora de Ebro *see* Móra d'Ebre
105 S8 **Mora de Rubielos** Aragón, NE Spain
172 H4 **Morafenobe** Mahajanga, W Madagascar
110 K8 **Morąg** *Ger.* Mohrungen. Warmińsko-Mazurskie, NE Poland,
111 L25 **Mórahalom** Csongrád, S Hungary
105 N11 **Moral de Calatrava** Castilla-La Mancha, C Spain
63 G19 **Moraleda, Canal** *strait* SE Pacific Ocean
54 J3 **Morales** Bolívar, N Colombia
54 D12 **Morales** Cauca, SW Colombia
42 F5 **Morales** Izabal, E Guatemala
172 J5 **Moramanga** Toamasina, E Madagascar
27 Q6 **Moran** Kansas, C USA
25 Q7 **Moran** Texas, SW USA
181 X7 **Moranbah** Queensland, NE Australia
44 L13 **Morant Bay** E Jamaica
96 G10 **Morar, Loch** ◎ N Scotland, UK
Morata *see* Goodenough Island
105 Q12 **Moratalla** Murcia, SE Spain
108 C8 **Morat, Lac de** *Ger.* Murtensee. ◎ W Switzerland
84 I11 **Morava** *var.* March. ≈ C Europe *see also* March
Morava *see* Moravia, Czech Republic
Morava *see* Velika Morava, Serbia and Montenegro (Yugo.)
29 W15 **Moravia** Iowa, C USA
111 F18 **Moravia** *Cz.* Morava, *Ger.* Mähren. *cultural region* E Czech Republic
111 H17 **Moravice** *Ger.* Mohra. ≈ NE Czech Republic
118 E12 **Moravița** Timiș, SW Romania
111 G17 **Moravská Třebová** *Ger.* Mährisch-Trübau. Pardubický Kraj, C Czech Republic
111 E19 **Moravské Budějovice** *Ger.* Mährisch-Budwitz. Vysočina, C Czech Republic
111 H17 **Moravskoslezský Kraj** *prev.* Ostravský Kraj. ◆ *region* E Czech Republic
111 F19 **Moravský Krumlov** *Ger.* Mährisch-Kromau. Jihomoravský Kraj, SE Czech Republic
96 J8 **Moray** *cultural region* N Scotland, UK
96 J8 **Moray Firth** *inlet* N Scotland, UK
42 B10 **Morazán** ◆ *department* NE El Salvador
154 C10 **Morbi** Gujarāt, W India
102 G7 **Morbihan** ◆ *department* NW France
Mörbisch *see* Mörbisch am See
109 Y5 **Mörbisch am See** *var.* Mörbisch. Burgenland, E Austria
95 N21 **Mörbylånga** Kalmar, S Sweden
102 J14 **Morcenx** Landes, SW France
Morcheh Khort *see* Mürcheh Khvort
163 T5 **Mordaga** Nei Mongol Zizhiqu, N China
11 X17 **Morden** Manitoba, S Canada
Mordovskaya ASSR/Mordvinia *see* Mordoviya, Respublika
127 N5 **Mordoviya, Respublika** *prev.* Mordovskaya ASSR, *Eng.* Mordovia, Mordvinia. ◆ *autonomous republic* W Russian Federation
126 M7 **Mordovo** Tambovskaya Oblast', W Russian Federation
Morea *see* Pelopónnisos
28 K8 **Moreau River** ≈ South Dakota, N USA
97 K16 **Morecambe** NW England, UK
97 K16 **Morecambe Bay** *inlet* NW England, UK
183 S4 **Moree** New South Wales, SE Australia
21 N5 **Morehead** Kentucky, S USA
21 X11 **Morehead City** North Carolina, SE USA
27 Y8 **Morehouse** Missouri, C USA
108 E10 **Mörel** Valais, SW Switzerland
54 D13 **Morelia** Caquetá, S Colombia
41 N14 **Morelia** Michoacán de Ocampo, S Mexico
105 T7 **Morella** País Valenciano, E Spain
40 I7 **Morelos** Chihuahua, N Mexico
41 O15 **Morelos** ◆ *state* S Mexico
154 H7 **Morena** Madhya Pradesh, C India
104 L12 **Morena, Sierra** ▲ S Spain
37 O14 **Morenci** Arizona, SW USA
31 R11 **Morenci** Michigan, N USA
116 J13 **Moreni** Dâmbovița, S Romania
94 D9 **Møre og Romsdal** ◆ *county* S Norway
10 I14 **Moresby Island** *island* Queen Charlotte Islands, British Columbia, SW Canada
183 W2 **Moreton Island** *island* Queensland, E Australia
103 O3 **Moreuil** Somme, N France
35 V7 **Morey Peak** ▲ Nevada, W USA
127 U4 **More-Yu** ≈ NW Russian Federation
103 T9 **Morez** Jura, E France
Mórfou *see* Güzelyurt
Morfou Bay/Mórfou, Kólpos *see* Güzelyurt Körfezi
182 I8 **Morgan** South Australia
23 S7 **Morgan** Georgia, SE USA
25 S8 **Morgan** Texas, SW USA
22 J10 **Morgan City** Louisiana, S USA
20 H6 **Morganfield** Kentucky, S USA
35 O10 **Morgan Hill** California, W USA
21 Q9 **Morganton** North Carolina, SE USA
20 J7 **Morgantown** Kentucky, S USA
21 S2 **Morgantown** West Virginia, NE USA
108 B10 **Morges** Vaud, SW Switzerland
148 M4 **Morghāb, Daryā-ye** *Rus.* Murgab, Murghab, *Turkm.* Murgap, Murgap Deryasy. ≈ Afghanistan/Turkmenistan *see also* Murgap
96 I9 **Mor, Glen** *var.* Glen Albyn, Great Glen. *valley* N Scotland, UK
103 T5 **Morhange** Moselle, NE France
158 M5 **Mori** *var.* Mori Kazak Zizhixian. Xinjiang Uygur Zizhiqu, NW China
165 R5 **Mori** Hokkaidō, NE Japan
35 Y6 **Moriah, Mount** ▲ Nevada, W USA
37 S11 **Moriarty** New Mexico, SW USA
54 J12 **Morichal** Guaviare, E Colombia
Mori Kazak Zizhixian *see* Mori
Morin Dawa Daurzu Zizhiqi *see* Nirji
11 Q14 **Morinville** Alberta, SW Canada
165 R8 **Morioka** Iwate, Honshū, C Japan
183 T8 **Morisset** New South Wales, SE Australia
165 Q8 **Moriyoshi-yama** ▲ Honshū, C Japan
92 K13 **Morjärv** Norrbotten, N Sweden
127 R3 **Morki** Respublika Mariy El, W Russian Federation
123 N10 **Morkoka** ≈ NE Russian Federation
102 F5 **Morlaix** Finistère, NW France
95 M20 **Mörlunda** Kalmar, S Sweden
107 N19 **Mormanno** Calabria, SW Italy
36 L11 **Mormon Lake** ◎ Arizona, SW USA
35 Y10 **Mormon Peak** ▲ Nevada, W USA
Mormon State *see* Utah
45 Y5 **Morne-à-l'Eau** Grande Terre, N Guadeloupe
29 Y15 **Morning Sun** Iowa, C USA
193 S12 **Mornington Abyssal Plain** *undersea feature* SE Pacific Ocean
63 F22 **Mornington, Isla** *island* S Chile
181 T4 **Mornington Island** *island* Wellesley Islands, Queensland, N Australia
115 E18 **Mórnos** ≈ C Greece
149 P14 **Moro** Sind, SE Pakistan
32 I11 **Moro** Oregon, NW USA
186 E8 **Morobe** Morobe, C PNG
186 E8 **Morobe** ◆ *province* C PNG
31 N12 **Morocco** Indiana, N USA
74 E8 **Morocco** *off.* Kingdom of Morocco, *Ar.* Al Mamlakah. ◆ *monarchy* N Africa
Morocco *see* Marrakech
81 I22 **Morogoro** Morogoro, E Tanzania
81 H24 **Morogoro** ◆ *region* SE Tanzania
171 Q7 **Moro Gulf** *gulf* S Philippines
41 N13 **Moroleón** Guanajuato, C Mexico
172 H6 **Morombe** Toliara, W Madagascar
44 G5 **Morón** Ciego de Ávila, C Cuba
54 K5 **Morón** Carabobo, N Venezuela
Morón *see* Morón de la Frontera
163 N8 **Mörön** Hentiy, C Mongolia
162 I6 **Mörön** Hövsgöl, N Mongolia
56 D8 **Morona, Río** ≈ N Peru
56 C8 **Morona Santiago** ◆ *province* E Ecuador
172 H5 **Morondava** Toliara, W Madagascar
104 K14 **Morón de la Frontera** *var.* Morón. Andalucía, S Spain
172 G13 **Moroni** ● (Comoros) Grande Comore, NW Comoros
171 S10 **Morotai, Pulau** *island* Maluku, E Indonesia
Morotiri *see* Marotiri
81 H17 **Moroto** NE Uganda
Morozov *see* Bratan
126 M11 **Morozovsk** Rostovskaya Oblast', SW Russian Federation
97 L14 **Morpeth** N England, UK
Morphou *see* Güzelyurt
Morphou Bay *see* Güzelyurt Körfezi
28 I13 **Morrill** Nebraska, C USA
27 U11 **Morrilton** Arkansas, C USA
11 Q16 **Morrin** Alberta, SW Canada
184 M7 **Morrinsville** Waikato, North Island, NZ
11 X16 **Morris** Manitoba, S Canada
30 M11 **Morris** Illinois, N USA
29 S8 **Morris** Minnesota, N USA
14 M13 **Morrisburg** Ontario, SE Canada
197 R11 **Morris Jesup, Kap** *headland* N Greenland
182 B1 **Morris, Mount** ▲ South Australia
30 K10 **Morrison** Illinois, N USA
36 K13 **Morristown** Arizona, SW USA
18 J14 **Morristown** New Jersey, NE USA
21 O8 **Morristown** Tennessee, S USA
42 L11 **Morrito** Río San Juan, SW Nicaragua
35 P13 **Morro Bay** California, W USA
95 L22 **Mörrum** Blekinge, S Sweden
83 N16 **Morrumbala** Zambézia, NE Mozambique
83 N20 **Morrumbene** Inhambane, SE Mozambique
95 F21 **Mors** *island* NW Denmark
Mörs *see* Moers
25 N1 **Morse** Texas, SW USA
127 N6 **Morshansk** Tambovskaya Oblast', W Russian Federation
102 L5 **Mortagne-au-Perche** Orne, N France
102 J8 **Mortagne-sur-Sèvre** Vendée, NW France
104 G8 **Mortágua** Viseu, N Portugal
102 J5 **Mortain** Manche, N France
106 C8 **Mortara** Lombardia, N Italy
59 J17 **Mortes, Rio das** ≈ C Brazil
182 M12 **Mortlake** Victoria, SE Australia
Mortlock Group *see* Takuu Islands
189 Q17 **Mortlock Islands** *prev.* Nomoi Islands. *island group* C Micronesia
29 T9 **Morton** Minnesota, N USA
22 L5 **Morton** Mississippi, S USA
24 M5 **Morton** Texas, SW USA
32 H9 **Morton** Washington, NW USA
45 U15 **Moruga** Trinidad, Trinidad and Tobago
183 P9 **Morundah** New South Wales, SE Australia
Moruroa *see* Mururoa
183 S11 **Moruya** New South Wales, SE Australia
103 Q8 **Morvan** *physical region* C France
185 G21 **Morven** Canterbury, South Island, NZ
183 O13 **Morwell** Victoria, SE Australia
127 N6 **Morzhovets, Ostrov** *island* NW Russian Federation
126 J4 **Mosal'sk** Kaluzhskaya Oblast', W Russian Federation
101 H20 **Mosbach** Baden-Württemberg, SW Germany
95 E18 **Mosby** Vest-Agder, S Norway
33 V9 **Mosby** Montana, NW USA
32 M9 **Moscow** Idaho, NW USA
20 F10 **Moscow** Tennessee, S USA
Moscow *see* Moskva
101 D19 **Mosel** *Fr.* Moselle. ≈ W Europe *see also* Moselle
103 T4 **Moselle** ◆ *department* NE France
103 T6 **Moselle** *Ger.* Mosel. ≈ W Europe *see also* Mosel
32 K9 **Moses Lake** ◎ Washington, NW USA
83 I18 **Mosetse** Central, E Botswana
92 H4 **Mosfellsbær** Sudhurland, SW Iceland
185 F23 **Mosgiel** Otago, South Island, NZ
126 M11 **Mosha** ≈ NW Russian Federation
81 I20 **Moshi** Kilimanjaro, NE Tanzania
110 G12 **Mosina** Wielkolpolskie, C Poland
30 L6 **Mosinee** Wisconsin, N USA
92 F13 **Mosjøen** Nordland, C Norway
123 S12 **Moskal'vo** Ostrov Sakhalin, Sakhalinskaya Oblast', SE Russian Federation
92 I13 **Moskosel** Norrbotten, N Sweden
126 K4 **Moskovskaya Oblast'** ◆ *province* W Russian Federation
Moskovskiy *see* Moskva
126 J3 **Moskva** *Eng.* Moscow. ● (Russian Federation) Gorod Moskva, W Russian Federation
147 Q14 **Moskva** *Rus.* Moskovskiy; *prev.* Chubek. SW Tajikistan
126 L4 **Moskva** ≈ W Russian Federation
83 I20 **Mosomane** Kgatleng, SE Botswana
Moson and Magyaróvár *see* Mosonmagyaróvár
111 H21 **Mosoni-Duna** *Ger.* Kleine Donau. ≈ NW Hungary
111 H21 **Mosonmagyaróvár** *Ger.* Wieselburg-Ungarisch-Altenburg; *prev.* Moson and Magyaróvár, *Ger.* Wieselburg and Ungarisch-Altenburg. Győr-Moson-Sopron, NW Hungary
Mospino *see* Mospyne
117 X8 **Mospyne** *Rus.* Mospino. Donets'ka Oblast', E Ukraine
54 B12 **Mosquera** Nariño, SW Colombia
37 U10 **Mosquero** New Mexico, SW USA
Mosquito Coast *see* La Mosquitia
31 U11 **Mosquito Creek Lake** ▣ Ohio, N USA
Mosquito Gulf *see* Mosquitos, Golfo de los
23 X11 **Mosquito Lagoon** *wetland* Florida, SE USA
43 N10 **Mosquito, Punta** *headland* E Nicaragua
43 W14 **Mosquito, Punta** *headland* NE Panama
43 Q15 **Mosquitos, Golfo de los** *Eng.* Mosquito Gulf. *gulf* N Panama
95 H16 **Moss** Østfold, S Norway
Mossâmedes *see* Namibe
22 G8 **Moss Bluff** Louisiana, S USA
185 C23 **Mossburn** Southland, South Island, NZ
83 G26 **Mosselbaai** *var.* Mosselbai, *Eng.* Mossel Bay. Western Cape, SW South Africa
Mosselbai/Mossel Bay *see* Mosselbaai
79 F20 **Mossendjo** Le Niari, SW Congo
183 N8 **Mossgiel** New South Wales, SE Australia
101 H22 **Mössingen** Baden-Württemberg, S Germany
181 W4 **Mossman** Queensland, NE Australia
59 P14 **Mossoró** Rio Grande do Norte, NE Brazil
23 N9 **Moss Point** Mississippi, S USA
183 S9 **Moss Vale** New South Wales, SE Australia
32 G9 **Mossyrock** Washington, NW USA
111 B15 **Most** *Ger.* Brüx. Ústecký Kraj, NW Czech Republic
121 P16 **Mosta** *var.* Musta. C Malta
74 I5 **Mostaganem** *var.* Mestghanem. NW Algeria
113 H14 **Mostar** Federacija Bosna I Hercegovina, S Bosnia and Herzegovina
61 J17 **Mostardas** Rio Grande do Sul, S Brazil
116 K14 **Mostiștea** ≈ S Romania
Mostva *see* Mastva
Mosty *see* Masty
116 H5 **Mostys'ka** L'vivs'ka Oblast', W Ukraine
Mosul *see* Al Mawṣil
95 F15 **Møsvatnet** ◎ S Norway
80 J12 **Mot'a** Amhara, N Ethiopia
79 H16 **Motaba** ≈ N Congo
105 O10 **Mota del Cuervo** Castilla-La Mancha, C Spain
104 L5 **Mota del Marqués** Castilla-León, N Spain
42 F5 **Motagua, Río** ≈ Guatemala/Honduras
119 H19 **Motal'** Brestskaya Voblasts', SW Belarus
95 L17 **Motala** Östergötland, S Sweden
191 X7 **Motane** *var.* Mohotani. *island* Îles Marquises, NE French Polynesia
152 K13 **Moth** Uttar Pradesh, N India
Mother of Presidents/Mother of States *see* Virginia
96 I12 **Motherwell** C Scotland, UK
153 P12 **Motīhāri** Bihār, N India
105 Q10 **Motilla del Palancar** Castilla-La Mancha, C Spain
184 N7 **Motiti Island** *island* NE NZ
65 E25 **Motley Island** *island* SE Falkland Islands
83 J19 **Motloutse** ≈ E Botswana
41 V17 **Motozintla de Mendoza** Chiapas, SE Mexico
105 N15 **Motril** Andalucía, S Spain
116 G13 **Motru** Gorj, SW Romania
165 Q4 **Motsuta-misaki** *headland* Hokkaidō, NE Japan
28 L6 **Mott** North Dakota, N USA
Möttling *see* Metlika
107 O18 **Mottola** Puglia, SE Italy
184 P8 **Motu** ≈ North Island, NZ
185 I14 **Motueka** Tasman, South Island, NZ
185 I14 **Motueka** ≈ South Island, NZ
Motu Iti *see* Tupai
41 X12 **Motul** *var.* Motul de Felipe Carrillo Puerto. Yucatán, SE Mexico
Motul de Felipe Carrillo Puerto *see* Motul
191 U17 **Motu Nui** *island* Easter Island, Chile, E Pacific Ocean
191 Q10 **Motu One** *var.* Bellingshausen. *atoll* Îles Sous le Vent, W French Polynesia
190 I16 **Motutapu** *island* E Cook Islands
193 V15 **Motu Tapu** *island* Tongatapu Group, S Tonga
184 L5 **Motutapu Island** *island* N NZ
Motyca *see* Modica
Mouanda *see* Moanda
Mouaskar *see* Mascara
105 U3 **Moubermé, Tuc de** *Fr.* Pic de Maubermé, *Sp.* Pico Mauberme; *prev.* Tuc de Maubermé. ▲ France/Spain *see also* Maubermé, Pic de
45 N7 **Mouchoir Passage** *passage* SE Turks and Caicos Islands
76 I9 **Moudjéria** Tagant, SW Mauritania
108 C9 **Moudon** Vaud, W Switzerland
Mouhoun *see* Black Volta
79 E19 **Mouila** Ngounié, C Gabon
79 K14 **Mouka** Haute-Kotto, C Central African Republic
Moukden *see* Shenyang
183 N10 **Moulamein** New South Wales, SE Australia
Moulamein Creek *see* Billabong Creek
74 F6 **Moulay-Bousselham** NW Morocco
Moule *see* le Moule
80 M11 **Moulhoulé** N Djibouti
103 P9 **Moulins** Allier, C France
166 M9 **Moulmein** *var.* Maulmain, Mawlamyine. Mon State, S Burma
166 L8 **Moulmeingyun** Irrawaddy, SW Burma
74 G6 **Moulouya** *var.* Mulucha, Muluya, Mulwiya. *seasonal river* NE Morocco
23 O2 **Moulton** Alabama, S USA
29 W16 **Moulton** Iowa, C USA
25 T11 **Moulton** Texas, SW USA
23 T7 **Moultrie** Georgia, SE USA
21 S14 **Moultrie, Lake** ▣ South Carolina, SE USA
22 K3 **Mound Bayou** Mississippi, S USA
30 L17 **Mound City** Illinois, N USA
27 R6 **Mound City** Kansas, C USA
27 Q2 **Mound City** Missouri, C USA
29 N7 **Mound City** South Dakota, N USA
78 H13 **Moundou** Logone-Occidental, SW Chad
27 P10 **Mounds** Oklahoma, C USA
21 R2 **Moundsville** West Virginia, NE USA
167 Q12 **Moŭng Roessei** Bătdâmbâng, W Cambodia
Moun Hou *see* Black Volta
8 H8 **Mountain** ≈ Northwest Territories, NW Canada
37 S12 **Mountainair** New Mexico, SW USA
35 V1 **Mountain City** Nevada, W USA
21 Q8 **Mountain City** Tennessee, S USA
27 U7 **Mountain Grove** Missouri, C USA
27 U9 **Mountain Home** Arkansas, C USA
33 N15 **Mountain Home** Idaho, NW USA
25 Q11 **Mountain Home** Texas, SW USA
29 W4 **Mountain Iron** Minnesota, N USA
29 T10 **Mountain Lake** Minnesota, N USA
23 S3 **Mountain Park** Georgia, SE USA
35 W12 **Mountain Pass** *pass* California, W USA
27 T12 **Mountain Pine** Arkansas, C USA
39 Y14 **Mountain Point** Annette Island, Alaska, USA
Mountain State *see* Montana, USA
Mountain State *see* West Virginia, USA
27 V7 **Mountain View** Arkansas, C USA
38 H12 **Mountain View** Hawai'i, USA, C Pacific Ocean
27 V10 **Mountain View** Missouri, C USA
38 M11 **Mountain Village** Alaska, USA
21 R8 **Mount Airy** North Carolina, SE USA
83 K24 **Mount Ayliff** *Xh.* Maxesibebi. Eastern Cape, SE South Africa
29 U16 **Mount Ayr** Iowa, C USA
182 J9 **Mount Barker** South Australia
180 J14 **Mount Barker** Western Australia
183 P11 **Mount Beauty** Victoria, SE Australia
14 E16 **Mount Brydges** Ontario, S Canada
31 N16 **Mount Carmel** Illinois, N USA
30 K10 **Mount Carroll** Illinois, N USA
31 S9 **Mount Clemens** Michigan, N USA
185 E19 **Mount Cook** Canterbury, South Island, NZ
83 L16 **Mount Darwin** Mashonaland Central, NE Zimbabwe
19 S7 **Mount Desert Island** *island* Maine, NE USA
23 W11 **Mount Dora** Florida, SE USA
182 G5 **Mount Eba** South Australia
25 W8 **Mount Enterprise** Texas, SW USA
182 J4 **Mount Fitton** South Australia
83 J24 **Mount Fletcher** Eastern Cape, SE South Africa
14 F15 **Mount Forest** Ontario, S Canada
182 K12 **Mount Gambier** South Australia
181 W5 **Mount Garnet** Queensland, NE Australia
21 P6 **Mount Gay** West Virginia, NE USA
31 S12 **Mount Gilead** Ohio, N USA
186 C7 **Mount Hagen** Western Highlands, C PNG
18 J16 **Mount Holly** New Jersey, NE USA
21 R10 **Mount Holly** North Carolina, SE USA
27 T12 **Mount Ida** Arkansas, C USA
181 T6 **Mount Isa** Queensland, C Australia
21 U4 **Mount Jackson** Virginia, NE USA
18 D12 **Mount Jewett** Pennsylvania, NE USA
18 L13 **Mount Kisco** New York, NE USA
18 B15 **Mount Lebanon** Pennsylvania, NE USA
182 J8 **Mount Lofty Ranges** ▲ South Australia
180 J10 **Mount Magnet** Western Australia
184 N7 **Mount Maunganui** Bay of Plenty, North Island, NZ
97 E18 **Mountmellick** *Ir.* Móinteach Mílic. C Ireland
30 L10 **Mount Morris** Illinois, N USA
31 R9 **Mount Morris** Michigan, N USA
18 F10 **Mount Morris** New York, NE USA
18 B16 **Mount Morris** Pennsylvania, NE USA
30 K15 **Mount Olive** Illinois, N USA
21 V10 **Mount Olive** North Carolina, SE USA
21 N4 **Mount Olivet** Kentucky, S USA
29 Y15 **Mount Pleasant** Iowa, C USA
31 Q8 **Mount Pleasant** Michigan, N USA
18 C15 **Mount Pleasant** Pennsylvania, NE USA
21 T14 **Mount Pleasant** South Carolina, SE USA
20 I9 **Mount Pleasant** Tennessee, S USA
25 W6 **Mount Pleasant** Texas, SW USA
36 L4 **Mount Pleasant** Utah, W USA
63 N23 **Mount Pleasant** ✕ (Stanley) East Falkland, Falkland Islands
97 G25 **Mount's Bay** *inlet* SW England, UK
35 N2 **Mount Shasta** California, W USA
30 J13 **Mount Sterling** Illinois, N USA
21 N5 **Mount Sterling** Kentucky, S USA
18 E15 **Mount Union** Pennsylvania, NE USA
23 V6 **Mount Vernon** Georgia, SE USA
30 L16 **Mount Vernon** Illinois, N USA
20 M6 **Mount Vernon** Kentucky, S USA
27 S7 **Mount Vernon** Missouri, C USA
31 T13 **Mount Vernon** Ohio, N USA
32 K13 **Mount Vernon** Oregon, NW USA
25 W6 **Mount Vernon** Texas, SW USA
32 H7 **Mount Vernon** Washington, NW USA
20 L5 **Mount Washington** Kentucky, S USA
182 F8 **Mount Wedge** South Australia
30 L14 **Mount Zion** Illinois, N USA
181 Y9 **Moura** Queensland, NE Australia
58 F12 **Moura** Amazonas, NW Brazil
104 H12 **Moura** Beja, S Portugal
104 I12 **Mourão** Évora, S Portugal
76 L11 **Mourdiah** Koulikoro, W Mali
78 K7 **Mourdi, Dépression du** *desert lowland* Chad/Sudan
102 J16 **Mourenx** Pyrénées-Atlantiques, SW France
Mourgana *see* Mourgkána
115 C15 **Mourgkána** *var.* Mourgana. ▲ Albania/Greece
97 G16 **Mourne Mountains** *Ir.* Beanna Boirche. ▲ SE Northern Ireland, UK
115 I15 **Moúrtzeflos, Akrotírio** *headland* Límnos, E Greece
99 C19 **Mouscron** *Dut.* Moeskroen. Hainaut, W Belgium
Mouse River *see* Souris River
78 H10 **Moussoro** Kanem, W Chad
103 T11 **Moûtiers** Savoie, E France
172 J14 **Moutsamoudou** *var.* Mutsamudu. Anjouan, SE Comoros
74 K11 **Mouydir, Monts de** ▲ S Algeria
79 F20 **Mouyondzi** La Bouenza, S Congo
115 E16 **Mouzáki** *prev.* Mouzákion. Thessalía, C Greece
Mouzákion *see* Mouzáki
29 S13 **Moville** Iowa, C USA
82 E13 **Moxico** ◆ *province* E Angola
172 I14 **Moya** Anjouan, SE Comoros
40 L12 **Moyahua** Zacatecas, C Mexico
81 J16 **Moyalē** Oromo, C Ethiopia
76 I15 **Moyamba** W Sierra Leone
74 G7 **Moyen Atlas** *Eng.* Middle Atlas. ▲ N Morocco
78 H13 **Moyen-Chari** *off.* Préfecture du Moyen-Chari. ◆ *prefecture* S Chad
Moyen-Congo *see* Congo (Republic of)
83 J24 **Moyeni** *var.* Quthing. SW Lesotho
76 H13 **Moyenne-Guinée** ◆ *state* NW Guinea
79 D18 **Moyen-Ogooué** *off.* Province du Moyen-Ogooué, *var.* Le Moyen-Ogooué. ◆ *province* C Gabon
103 S4 **Moyeuvre-Grande** Moselle, NE France
33 N7 **Moyie Springs** Idaho, NW USA
146 G6 **Mo'ynoq** *Rus.* Muynak. Qoraqalpog'iston Respublikasi, NW Uzbekistan
81 F16 **Moyo** NW Uganda
56 D10 **Moyobamba** San Martín, NW Peru
78 H10 **Moyto** Chari-Baguirmi, W Chad
158 G9 **Moyu** *var.* Karakax. Xinjiang Uygur Zizhiqu, NW China
122 M9 **Moyyero** ≈ N Russian Federation
145 S15 **Moyynkum** *var.* Furmanovka, *Kaz.* Fürmanov. Zhambyl, S Kazakhstan
145 Q15 **Moyynkum, Peski** *Kaz.* Moyynqum. *desert* S Kazakhstan
Moyynqum *see* Moyynkum, Peski
145 S12 **Moyynty** Karaganda, C Kazakhstan
145 S12 **Moyynty** ≈ C Kazakhstan
Mozambika, Lakandranon' i *see* Mozambique Channel
83 M18 **Mozambique** *off.* Republic of Mozambique; *prev.* People's Republic of Mozambique, Portuguese East Africa. ◆ *republic* S Africa
Mozambique Basin *see* Natal Basin
Mozambique, Canal de *see* Mozambique Channel
83 P17 **Mozambique Channel** *Fr.* Canal de Mozambique, *Mal.* Lakandranon' i Mozambika. *strait* W Indian Ocean
172 L11 **Mozambique Escarpment** *var.* Mozambique Scarp. *undersea feature* SW Indian Ocean
172 L10 **Mozambique Plateau** *var.* Mozambique Rise. *undersea feature* SW Indian Ocean
Mozambique Rise *see* Mozambique Plateau
Mozambique Scarp *see* Mozambique Escarpment
127 O15 **Mozdok** Respublika Severnaya Osetiya, SW Russian Federation

◆ Country ● Country Capital ◇ Dependent Territory ○ Dependent Territory Capital ◆ Administrative Region ✕ International Airport ▲ Mountain ▲ Mountain Range ☗ Volcano ≈ River ◎ Lake ▣ Reservoir

57 K17 **Mozetenes, Serranías de** ▲ C Bolivia
126 J4 **Mozhaysk** Moskovskaya Oblast', W Russian Federation
127 T3 **Mozhga** Udmurtskaya Respublika, NW Russian Federation
Mozyr' see Mazyr
79 P22 **Mpala** Katanga, E Dem. Rep. Congo
79 G19 **Mpama** ~ C Congo
81 E22 **Mpanda** Rukwa, W Tanzania
82 L11 **Mpande** Northern, NE Zambia
83 J18 **Mphoengs** Matabeleland South, SW Zimbabwe
81 F18 **Mpigi** S Uganda
82 L13 **Mpika** Northern, NE Zambia
83 J14 **Mpima** Central, C Zambia
82 J13 **Mpongwe** Copperbelt, C Zambia
82 K11 **Mporokoso** Northern, N Zambia
79 H20 **Mpouya** Plateaux, SE Congo
77 P16 **Mpraeso** C Ghana
82 L11 **Mpulungu** Northern, N Zambia
83 K21 **Mpumalanga** *prev.* Eastern Transvaal, *Afr.* Oos-Transvaal. ◆ *province* NE South Africa
83 D16 **Mpungu** Okavango, N Namibia
81 I22 **Mpwapwa** Dodoma, C Tanzania
Mqinvartsveri see Kazbek
110 M8 **Mrągowo** *Ger.* Sensburg. Warmińsko-Mazurskie, NE Poland,
127 V6 **Mrakovo** Respublika Bashkortostan, W Russian Federation
172 I13 **Mramani** Anjouan, E Comoros
112 F12 **Mrkonjić Grad** Republika Srpska, W Bosnia and Herzegovina
110 H9 **Mrocza** Kujawsko-pomorskie, NW Poland
126 I14 **Msta** ~ NW Russian Federation
Mtkvari see Kura
Mtoko see Mutoko
126 K6 **Mtsensk** Orlovskaya Oblast', W Russian Federation
81 K24 **Mtwara** Mtwara, SE Tanzania
81 J25 **Mtwara** ◆ *region* SE Tanzania
104 G14 **Mu** ▲ S Portugal
193 V15 **Mu'a** Tongatapu, S Tonga
Muai To see Mae Hong Son
83 P16 **Mualama** Zambézia, NE Mozambique
Mualo see Messalo, Rio
79 E22 **Muanda** Bas-Congo, SW Dem. Rep. Congo
Muang Chiang Rai see Chiang Rai
167 R6 **Muang Ham** Houaphan, N Laos
167 S8 **Muang Hinboun** Khammouan, C Laos
Muang Kalasin see Kalasin
Muang Khammouan see Thakhèk
167 S11 **Muang Không** Champasak, S Laos
167 S10 **Muang Khôngxédôn** *var.* Khong Sedone. Salavan, S Laos
Muang Khon Kaen see Khon Kaen
167 Q6 **Muang Khoua** Phôngsali, N Laos
Muang Krabi see Krabi
Muang Lampang see Lampang
Muang Lamphun see Lamphun
Muang Loei see Loei
Muang Lom Sak see Lom Sak
Muang Nakhon Sawan see Nakhon Sawan
167 Q6 **Muang Namo** Oudômxai, N Laos
Muang Nan see Nan
167 Q6 **Muang Ngoy** Louangphabang, N Laos
167 Q5 **Muang Ou Tai** Phôngsali, N Laos
Muang Pak Lay see Pak Lay
Muang Pakxan see Pakxan
167 T10 **Muang Pakxong** Champasak, S Laos
167 S9 **Muang Phalan** *var.* Muang Phalane. Savannakhét, S Laos
Muang Phalane see Muang Phalan
Muang Phan see Phan
Muang Phayao see Phayao
Muang Phichit see Phichit
167 T9 **Muang Phin** Savannakhét, S Laos
Muang Phitsanulok see Phitsanulok
Muang Phrae see Phrae
Muang Roi Et see Roi Et
Muang Sakon Nakhon see Sakon Nakhon
Muang Samut Prakan see Samut Prakan
167 P6 **Muang Sing** Louang Namtha, N Laos
Muang Ubon see Ubon Ratchathani
Muang Uthai Thani see Uthai Thani
167 P7 **Muang Vangviang** Viangchan, C Laos
Muang Xaignabouri see Xaignabouli
Muang Xay see Xai
167 S9 **Muang Xépôn** *var.* Sepone. Savannakhét, S Laos
168 K10 **Muar** *var.* Bandar Maharani. Johor, Peninsular Malaysia
168 I9 **Muara** Sumatera, W Indonesia
168 L13 **Muarabeliti** Sumatera, W Indonesia
168 K12 **Muarabungo** Sumatera, W Indonesia
168 L13 **Muaraenim** Sumatera, W Indonesia
169 T11 **Muarajuloi** Borneo, C Indonesia
169 U12 **Muarakaman** Borneo, C Indonesia
168 H12 **Muarasigep** Pulau Siberut, W Indonesia
168 L12 **Muaratembesi** Sumatera, W Indonesia
169 T12 **Muaratewe** *var.* Muarateweh; *prev.* Moearatewe. Borneo, C Indonesia
Muarateweh see Muaratewe
169 U10 **Muarawahau** Borneo, N Indonesia
138 G13 **Mubārak, Jabal** ▲ S Jordan
153 N13 **Mubārakpur** Uttar Pradesh, N India
Mubarek see Muborak
81 F18 **Mubende** SW Uganda
77 Y14 **Mubi** Adamawa, NE Nigeria
146 M12 **Muborak** *Rus.* Mubarek. Qashqadaryo Viloyati, S Uzbekistan
171 U12 **Mubrani** Papua, E Indonesia
127 N7 **Muchkapskiy** Tambovskaya Oblast', W Russian Federation
96 G10 **Muck** *island* W Scotland, UK
82 Q13 **Mucojo** Cabo Delgado, N Mozambique
82 F12 **Muconda** Lunda Sul, NE Angola
54 I10 **Muco, Río** ~ E Colombia
83 O16 **Mucubela** Zambézia, NE Mozambique
42 J5 **Mucupina, Monte** ▲ N Honduras
136 J14 **Mucur** Kirşehir, C Turkey
143 U8 **Mūd** Khorāsān, E Iran
163 Y9 **Mudanjiang** *var.* Mu-tan-chiang. Heilongjiang, NE China
163 Y9 **Mudan Jiang** ~ NE China
136 D11 **Mudanya** Bursa, NW Turkey
28 K8 **Mud Butte** South Dakota, N USA
155 G16 **Muddebihāl** Karnātaka, C India
27 P12 **Muddy Boggy Creek** ~ Oklahoma, C USA
36 M6 **Muddy Creek** ~ Utah, W USA
37 V7 **Muddy Creek Reservoir** ⊞ Colorado, C USA
33 W15 **Muddy Gap** Wyoming, C USA
35 Y11 **Muddy Peak** ▲ Nevada, W USA
183 R7 **Mudgee** New South Wales, SE Australia
29 S3 **Mud Lake** ◎ Minnesota, N USA
29 P7 **Mud Lake Reservoir** ⊞ South Dakota, N USA
167 N9 **Mudon** Mon State, S Burma
81 O14 **Mudug** *off.* Gobolka Mudug. ◆ *region* NE Somalia
81 O14 **Mudug** *var.* Mudugh. *plain* N Somalia
Mudugh see Mudug
83 Q15 **Muecate** Nampula, NE Mozambique
82 Q13 **Mueda** Cabo Delgado, NE Mozambique
42 L10 **Muelle de los Bueyes** Región Autónoma Atlántico Sur, SE Nicaragua
Muenchen see München
83 M14 **Muende** Tete, NW Mozambique
25 T5 **Muenster** Texas, SW USA
Muenster see Münster
43 O6 **Muerto, Cayo** *reef* NE Nicaragua
41 T17 **Muerto, Mar** *lagoon* SE Mexico
64 F11 **Muertos Trough** *undersea feature* N Caribbean Sea
83 H14 **Mufaya Kuta** Western, NW Zambia
82 J13 **Mufulira** Copperbelt, C Zambia
161 O10 **Mufu Shan** ▲ C China
Mugalzhar Taūlary see Mugodzhary, Gory
137 Y12 **Muğan Düzü** *Rus.* Muganskaya Ravnina, Muganskaya Step'. *physical region* S Azerbaijan
Muganskaya Ravnina/Muganskaya Step' see Muğan Düzü
106 K8 **Muggia** Friuli-Venezia Giulia, NE Italy
153 N14 **Mughal Sarāi** Uttar Pradesh, N India
Mughla see Muğla
141 W11 **Mughshin** *var.* Muqshin. S Oman
147 S12 **Mughsu** *Rus.* Muksu. ~ C Tajikistan
164 H14 **Mugi** Tokushima, Shikoku, SW Japan
136 C16 **Muğla** *var.* Mughla. Muğla, SW Turkey
136 C16 **Muğla** *var.* Mughla. ◆ *province* SW Turkey
144 J11 **Mugodzhary, Gory** *Kaz.* Mugalzhar Taūlary. ▲ W Kazakhstan
83 O15 **Mugulama** Zambézia, NE Mozambique
139 U9 **Muḩammad** E Iraq
139 R8 **Muḩammadīyah** C Iraq
80 I6 **Muhammad Qol** Red Sea, NE Sudan
75 Y9 **Muhammad, Râs** *headland* E Egypt
Muhammerah see Khorramshahr
140 M12 **Muhāyil** *var.* Mahāil. 'Asīr, SW Saudi Arabia
139 O7 **Muḩaywīr** W Iraq
101 H21 **Mühlacker** Baden-Württemberg, SW Germany
Mühlbach see Sebeş
Mühldorf see Mühldorf am Inn
101 N23 **Mühldorf am Inn** *var.* Mühldorf. Bayern, SE Germany
101 J15 **Mühlhausen** *var.* Mühlhausen in Thüringen. Thüringen, C Germany
Mühlhausen in Thüringen see Mühlhausen
195 Q2 **Mühlig-Hofmann Mountains** ▲ Antarctica
93 L14 **Muhos** Oulu, C Finland
138 K6 **Mūḩ, Sabkhat al** ◎ C Syria
118 E5 **Muhu** *Ger.* Mohn, Moon. *island* W Estonia
81 F19 **Muhutwe** Kagera, NW Tanzania
Muhu Väin see Väinameri
98 J10 **Muiden** Noord-Holland, C Netherlands
193 W15 **Mui Hopohoponga** *headland* Tongatapu, S Tonga
Muikamachi see Muika
Muinchille see Cootehill
Muineachán see Monaghan
97 F19 **Muine Bheag** *Eng.* Bagenalstown. SE Ireland
56 B5 **Muisne** Esmeraldas, NW Ecuador
83 P14 **Muite** Nampula, NE Mozambique
41 Z11 **Mujeres, Isla** *island* E Mexico
116 G7 **Mukacheve** *Hung.* Munkács, *Rus.* Mukachevo. Zakarpats'ka Oblast', W Ukraine
Mukachevo see Mukacheve
169 R9 **Mukah** Sarawak, East Malaysia
Mukalla see Al Mukallā
Mukama see Mokāma
Mukāshafa/Mukashshafah see Mukayshīfah
139 S6 **Mukayshīfah** *var.* Mukāshafa, Mukashshafah. N Iraq
167 R9 **Mukdahan** Mukdahan, E Thailand
Mukden see Shenyang
155 Y15 **Mukojima-rettō** *Eng.* Parry group. *island group* SE Japan
146 M14 **Mukry** Lebap Welaýaty, E Turkmenistan
Muksu see Mughsu
153 U14 **Muktagacha** *var.* Muktagachha Dhaka, N Bangladesh
Muktagachha see Muktagacha
82 K13 **Mukuku** Central, C Zambia
82 K11 **Mukupa Kaoma** Northern, NE Zambia
81 I18 **Mukutan** Rift Valley, W Kenya
83 F16 **Mukwe** Caprivi, NE Namibia
105 R13 **Mula** Murcia, SE Spain
151 K20 **Mulaku Atoll** *var.* Meemu Atoll. *atoll* C Maldives
83 J15 **Mulalika** Lusaka, C Zambia
163 X8 **Mulan** Heilongjiang, NE China
83 N15 **Mulanje** *var.* Mlanje. Southern, S Malawi
40 H5 **Mulatos** Sonora, NW Mexico
23 P3 **Mulberry Fork** ~ Alabama, S USA
39 P12 **Mulchatna River** ~ Alaska, USA
125 W4 **Mul'da** Respublika Komi, NW Russian Federation
101 M14 **Mulde** ~ E Germany
27 R10 **Muldrow** Oklahoma, C USA
40 E7 **Mulegé** Baja California Sur, W Mexico
108 I10 **Mulegns** Graubünden, S Switzerland
79 M21 **Mulenda** Kasai Oriental, C Dem. Rep. Congo
24 M4 **Muleshoe** Texas, SW USA
83 O15 **Mulevala** Zambézia, NE Mozambique
183 P5 **Mulgoa Creek** *seasonal river* New South Wales, SE Australia
105 O15 **Mulhacén** *var.* Cerro de Mulhacén. ▲ S Spain
Mulhacén, Cerro de see Mulhacén
Mülhausen see Mulhouse
101 E24 **Mülheim** Baden-Württemberg, SW Germany
101 E15 **Mülheim** *var.* Mulheim an der Ruhr. Nordrhein-Westfalen, W Germany
Mulheim an der Ruhr see Mülheim
103 U7 **Mulhouse** *Ger.* Mülhausen. Haut-Rhin, NE France
160 G11 **Muli** *var.* Qiaowa, Muli Zangzu Zizhixian. Sichuan, C China
171 X15 **Muli** *channel* Papua, E Indonesia
163 Y9 **Muling** Heilongjiang, NE China
Mullach Íde see Malahide
Mullaitivu see Mullaittivu
155 K23 **Mullaittivu** *var.* Mullaitivu. Northern Province, N Sri Lanka
33 N8 **Mullan** Idaho, NW USA
28 M13 **Mullen** Nebraska, C USA
183 Q6 **Mullengudgery** New South Wales, SE Australia
21 Q6 **Mullens** West Virginia, NE USA
Müller-gerbergte see Muller, Pegunungan
169 T10 **Muller, Pegunungan** *Dut.* Müller-gerbergte. ▲ Borneo, C Indonesia
31 Q5 **Mullett Lake** ◎ Michigan, N USA
18 J16 **Mullica River** ~ New Jersey, NE USA
25 R8 **Mullin** Texas, SW USA
97 E17 **Mullingar** *Ir.* An Muileann gCearr. C Ireland
21 T12 **Mullins** South Carolina, SE USA
96 G11 **Mull, Isle of** *island* W Scotland, UK
127 R5 **Mullovka** Ul'yanovskaya Oblast', W Russian Federation
95 K19 **Mullsjö** Västra Götaland, S Sweden
183 V4 **Mullumbimby** New South Wales, SE Australia
83 H15 **Mulobezi** Western, SW Zambia
83 C15 **Mulondo** Huíla, SW Angola
83 G15 **Mulonga Plain** *plain* W Zambia
79 N23 **Mulongo** Katanga, SE Dem. Rep. Congo
149 T10 **Multān** Punjab, E Pakistan
93 L17 **Multia** Länsi-Suomi, W Finland
Mulucha see Moulouya
83 J14 **Mulungushi** Central, C Zambia
83 K14 **Mulungwe** Central, C Zambia
Muluya see Moulouya
27 N7 **Mulvane** Kansas, C USA
183 O10 **Mulwala** New South Wales, SE Australia
Mulwiya see Moulouya
182 K6 **Mulyungarie** South Australia
154 D13 **Mumbai** *prev.* Bombay. Mahārāshtra, W India
154 D13 **Mumbai** × Mahārāshtra, W India
83 D14 **Mumbué** Bié, C Angola
186 E8 **Mumeng** Morobe, C PNG
171 V12 **Mumi** Papua, E Indonesia
Muminabad/Mū'minobod see Leningrad
127 Q13 **Mumra** Astrakhanskaya Oblast', SW Russian Federation
41 X12 **Muna** Yucatán, SE Mexico
123 O9 **Muna** ~ NE Russian Federation
152 C12 **Munābāo** Rājasthān, NW India
Munamägi see Suur Munamägi
171 O14 **Muna, Pulau** *prev.* Moena. *island* C Indonesia
101 L18 **Münchberg** Bayern, E Germany
101 L23 **München** *var.* Muenchen, *Eng.* Munich, *It.* Monaco. Bayern, SE Germany
München-Gladbach see Mönchengladbach
108 E6 **Münchenstein** Basel-Land, NW Switzerland
10 L10 **Muncho Lake** British Columbia, W Canada
31 P13 **Muncie** Indiana, N USA
18 G13 **Muncy** Pennsylvania, NE USA
11 Q14 **Mundare** Alberta, SW Canada
25 Q5 **Munday** Texas, SW USA
31 N10 **Mundelein** Illinois, N USA
101 I15 **Münden** Niedersachsen, C Germany
105 Q12 **Mundo** ~ S Spain
82 B12 **Munenga** Cuanza Sul, NW Angola
105 P11 **Munera** Castilla-La Mancha, C Spain
20 E9 **Munford** Tennessee, S USA
20 K7 **Munfordville** Kentucky, S USA
182 D5 **Mungala** South Australia
83 M16 **Mungári** Manica, C Mozambique
79 O16 **Mungbere** Orientale, NE Dem. Rep. Congo
153 Q13 **Munger** *prev.* Monghyr. Bihār, NE India
182 I2 **Mungeranie** South Australia
Mu Nggava see Rennell
169 O10 **Mungguresak, Tanjung** *headland* Borneo, N Indonesia
Mungiki see Bellona
183 R4 **Mungindi** New South Wales, SE Australia
Mungkawn see Maingkwan
153 T16 **Mungla** *var.* Mongla. Khulna, S Bangladesh
82 C13 **Mungo** Huambo, W Angola
188 F16 **Munguuy Bay** *bay* Yap, W Micronesia
82 E13 **Munhango** Bié, C Angola
Munich see München
105 S7 **Muniesa** Aragón, NE Spain
31 O4 **Munising** Michigan, N USA
Munkács see Mukacheve
95 I17 **Munkedal** Västra Götaland, S Sweden
95 K15 **Munkfors** Värmland, C Sweden
122 M14 **Munku-Sardyk, Gora** *var.* Mönh Sarĭdag. ▲ Mongolia/Russian Federation
99 E18 **Munkzwalm** Oost-Vlaanderen, NW Belgium
167 R10 **Mun, Mae Nam** ~ E Thailand
153 U15 **Munshiganj** Dhaka, C Bangladesh
108 D8 **Münsingen** Bern, W Switzerland
103 U6 **Munster** Haut-Rhin, NE France
100 J11 **Munster** Niedersachsen, NW Germany
97 B20 **Munster** *Ir.* Cúige Mumhan. *cultural region* S Ireland
100 F13 **Münster** *var.* Muenster, Münster in Westfalen. Nordrhein-Westfalen, W Germany
108 F10 **Münster** Valais, S Switzerland
Münsterberg in Schlesien see Ziębice
Münster in Westfalen see Münster
100 E13 **Münsterland** *cultural region* NW Germany
100 F13 **Münster-Osnabruck** × Nordrhein-Westfalen, NW Germany
31 R4 **Munuscong Lake** ◎ Michigan, N USA
83 K17 **Munyati** ~ C Zimbabwe
109 R3 **Münzkirchen** Oberösterreich, N Austria
92 K11 **Muodoslompolo** Norrbotten, N Sweden
92 M13 **Muojärvi** ◎ NE Finland
167 S6 **Mương Khên** Hoa Binh, N Vietnam
Muong Sai see Xai
167 Q7 **Muong Xiang Ngeun** *var.* Xieng Ngeun. Louangphabang, N Laos
92 K11 **Muonio** Lappi, N Finland
Muonioälv/Muoniojoki see Muonionjoki
92 K11 **Muonionjoki** *var.* Muoniojoki, *Swe.* Muonioälv. ~ Finland/Sweden
83 N17 **Mupa** ~ C Mozambique
83 E16 **Mupini** Okavango, NE Namibia
80 F8 **Muqaddam, Wadi** ~ N Sudan
138 K9 **Muqāṭ** Al Mafraq, E Jordan
141 X7 **Muqaz** N Oman
81 N17 **Muqdisho** *Eng.* Mogadishu, *It.* Mogadiscio. ● (Somalia) Banaadir, S Somalia
81 N17 **Muqdisho** × Banaadir, E Somalia
Muqshin see Mughshin
109 T8 **Mur** *SCr.* Mura. ~ C Europe
Mura see Mur
137 T14 **Muradiye** Van, E Turkey
Muragarazi see Maragarazi
165 O10 **Murakami** Niigata, Honshū, C Japan
63 G22 **Murallón, Cerro** ▲ S Argentina
81 E20 **Muramvya** C Burundi
81 I19 **Murang'a** *prev.* Fort Hall. Central, SW Kenya
81 H16 **Murangering** Rift Valley, NW Kenya
Murapara see Murupara
140 M5 **Murār, Bi'r al** *well* NW Saudi Arabia
125 Q13 **Murashi** Kirovskaya Oblast', NW Russian Federation
103 O12 **Murat** Cantal, C France
114 N12 **Muratlı** Tekirdağ, NW Turkey
137 R14 **Murat Nehri** *var.* Eastern Euphrates; *anc.* Arsanias. ~ NE Turkey
107 D20 **Muravera** Sardegna, Italy, C Mediterranean Sea
165 P10 **Murayama** Yamagata, Honshū, C Japan
121 R13 **Muraysah, Ra's al** *headland* N Libya
104 I6 **Murça** Vila Real, N Portugal
80 Q11 **Murcanyo** Bari, NE Somalia
143 N8 **Mürcheh Khvort** *var.* Morcheh Khort. Eşfahān, C Iran
185 H15 **Murchison** Tasman, South Island, NZ
185 B22 **Murchison Mountains** ▲ South Island, NZ
180 I10 **Murchison River** ~ Western Australia
105 R13 **Murcia** Murcia, SE Spain
105 Q13 **Murcia** ◆ *autonomous community* SE Spain
103 O13 **Mur-de-Barrez** Aveyron, S France
182 G8 **Murdinga** South Australia
28 M10 **Murdo** South Dakota, N USA
15 X6 **Murdochville** Québec, SE Canada
109 W9 **Mureck** Steiermark, SE Austria
114 M13 **Mürefte** Tekirdağ, NW Turkey
116 I10 **Mureş** ◆ *county* N Romania
84 J11 **Mureş** *var.* Maros, Mureşul, *Ger.* Marosch, Mieresch. ~ Hungary/Romania *see also* Maros
Mureşul see Maros/Mureş
102 M16 **Muret** Haute-Garonne, S France
27 T13 **Murfreesboro** Arkansas, C USA
21 W8 **Murfreesboro** North Carolina, SE USA
20 J9 **Murfreesboro** Tennessee, S USA
Murgab see Morghāb, Daryā-ye/Murgap/Murghob
146 I14 **Murgap** *Rus.* Murgap. Mary Welaýaty, S Turkmenistan
146 J16 **Murgap** *var.* Murgap Deryasy, Murghab, *Pash.* Daryā-ye Morghāb, *Rus.* Murgab. ~ Afghanistan/Turkmenistan *see also* Morghāb, Daryā-ye
Murgap Deryasy see Morghāb, Daryā-ye/Murgap
114 H9 **Murgash** ▲ W Bulgaria
Murghab see Morghāb, Daryā-ye/Murgap
147 U13 **Murghob** *Rus.* Murgab. SE Tajikistan
147 U13 **Murghob** *Rus.* Murgab. ~ SE Tajikistan
181 Z10 **Murgon** Queensland, E Australia
190 I16 **Muri** Rarotonga, S Cook Islands
108 F7 **Muri** Aargau, W Switzerland
108 D8 **Muri** *var.* Muri bei Bern. Bern, W Switzerland
104 K3 **Murias de Paredes** Castilla-León, N Spain
Muri bei Bern see Muri
82 F11 **Muriege** Lunda Sul, NE Angola
189 P14 **Murilo Atoll** *atoll* Hall Islands, C Micronesia
Mūrītānīyah see Mauritania
100 N10 **Müritz** *var.* Müritzee. ◎ NE Germany
Müritzee see Müritz
100 L10 **Müritz-Elde-Kanal** *canal* N Germany
184 K6 **Muriwai Beach** Auckland, North Island, NZ
92 J13 **Murjek** Norrbotten, N Sweden
124 J3 **Murmansk** Murmanskaya Oblast', NW Russian Federation
124 I4 **Murmanskaya Oblast'** ◆ *province* NW Russian Federation
197 V14 **Murmansk Rise** *undersea feature* SW Barents Sea
124 J3 **Murmashi** Murmanskaya Oblast', NW Russian Federation
126 M5 **Murmino** Ryazanskaya Oblast', W Russian Federation
101 K24 **Murnau** Bayern, SE Germany
103 X16 **Muro, Capo di** *headland* Corse, France, C Mediterranean Sea
107 M18 **Muro Lucano** Basilicata, S Italy
127 N4 **Murom** Vladimirskaya Oblast', W Russian Federation
122 I11 **Muromtsevo** Omskaya Oblast', C Russian Federation
165 R5 **Muroran** Hokkaidō, NE Japan
104 G3 **Muros** Galicia, NW Spain
104 F3 **Muros e Noia, Ría de** *estuary* NW Spain
164 H15 **Muroto** Kōchi, Shikoku, SW Japan
164 H15 **Muroto-zaki** *headland* Shikoku, SW Japan
116 L7 **Murovani Kurylivtsi** Vinnyts'ka Oblast', C Ukraine
110 G11 **Murowana Goślina** Wielkolpolskie, C Poland
32 M14 **Murphy** Idaho, NW USA
21 N10 **Murphy** North Carolina, SE USA
35 P8 **Murphys** California, W USA
30 L17 **Murphysboro** Illinois, N USA
29 V15 **Murray** Iowa, C USA
20 H8 **Murray** Kentucky, S USA
182 J10 **Murray Bridge** South Australia
193 N4 **Murray Fracture Zone** *tectonic feature* NE Pacific Ocean
192 H11 **Murray, Lake** ◎ SW PNG
21 P12 **Murray, Lake** ⊞ South Carolina, SE USA
10 K8 **Murray, Mount** ▲ Yukon Territory, NW Canada
Murray Range see Murray Ridge
173 O3 **Murray Ridge** *var.* Murray Range. *undersea feature* N Arabian Sea
183 N10 **Murray River** ~ SE Australia
182 K10 **Murrayville** Victoria, SE Australia
149 U5 **Murree** Punjab, E Pakistan
101 I21 **Murrhardt** Baden-Württemberg, S Germany
183 O9 **Murrumbidgee River** ~ New South Wales, SE Australia
83 P15 **Murrupula** Nampula, NE Mozambique
183 T7 **Murrurundi** New South Wales, SE Australia
109 X9 **Murska Sobota** *Ger.* Olsnitz. NE Slovenia
154 G12 **Murtajāpur** *prev.* Murtazapur. Mahārāshtra, C India
77 S16 **Murtala Muhammed** × (Lagos) Ogun, SW Nigeria
Murtazapur see Murtajāpur
108 C8 **Murten** Neuchâtel, W Switzerland
Murtensee see Morat, Lac de
182 L11 **Murtoa** Victoria, SE Australia
92 N13 **Murtovaara** Oulu, E Finland
Murua Island see Woodlark Island
155 D14 **Murud** Mahārāshtra, W India
184 O9 **Murupara** *var.* Murapara. Bay of Plenty, North Island, NZ
191 X12 **Mururoa** *var.* Moruroa. *atoll* Îles Tuamotu, SE French Polynesia
Murviedro see Sagunto
154 J9 **Murwāra** Madhya Pradesh, N India
183 V4 **Murwillumbah** New South Wales, SE Australia
146 H11 **Murzechirla** *prev.* Mirzachirla. Ahal Welaýaty, C Turkmenistan
Murzuk see Murzuq
75 O11 **Murzuq** *var.* Marzūq, Murzuk. SW Libya
Murzuq, Edeyin see Murzuq, Idhān
75 N11 **Murzuq, Ḩamādat** *plateau* W Libya
75 O11 **Murzuq, Idhān** *var.* Edeyin Murzuq. *desert* SW Libya
109 W6 **Mürzzuschlag** Steiermark, E Austria
137 Q14 **Muş** *var.* Mush. Muş, E Turkey
137 Q14 **Muş** *var.* Mush. ◆ *province* E Turkey
186 F9 **Musa** ~ S PNG
118 G11 **Mūša** ~ Latvia/Lithuania
75 X8 **Mûsa, Gebel** ▲ NE Egypt
Musaiyib see Al Musayyib
Musa Khel see Mūsā Khel Bazār
149 R9 **Mūsā Khel Bazār** *var.* Musa Khel. Baluchistān, SW Pakistan
114 H10 **Musala** ▲ W Bulgaria
168 H10 **Musala, Pulau** *island* W Indonesia
83 I15 **Musale** Southern, S Zambia
141 Y9 **Muşalla** NE Oman
141 W6 **Musandam Peninsula** *Ar.* Masandam Peninsula. *peninsula* N Oman
Musay'id see Umm Sa'īd
Muscat see Masqaţ
Muscat and Oman see Oman
29 Y14 **Muscatine** Iowa, C USA
Muscat Sīb Airport see Seeb
31 O15 **Muscatuck River** ~ Indiana, N USA
30 K8 **Muscoda** Wisconsin, N USA
185 F19 **Musgrave, Mount** ▲ South Island, NZ
181 P9 **Musgrave Ranges** ▲ South Australia
Mush see Muş
138 H12 **Mushayyish, Qaşr al** *castle* Ma'ān, C Jordan
79 H20 **Mushie** Bandundu, W Dem. Rep. Congo
168 M13 **Musi, Air** *prev.* Moesi. ~ Sumatera, W Indonesia
192 M4 **Musicians Seamounts** *undersea feature* N Pacific Ocean
54 D8 **Musinga, Alto** ▲ NW Colombia
29 T2 **Muskeg Bay** *lake bay* Minnesota, N USA
31 O8 **Muskegon** Michigan, N USA
31 O8 **Muskegon Heights** Michigan, N USA
31 P8 **Muskegon River** ~ Michigan, N USA
31 T14 **Muskingum River** ~ Ohio, N USA
95 P16 **Muskö** Stockholm, C Sweden
Muskogean see Tallahassee
27 Q10 **Muskogee** Oklahoma, C USA
14 H13 **Muskoka, Lake** ◎ Ontario, S Canada
80 H8 **Musmar** Red Sea, NE Sudan
83 K14 **Musofu** Central, C Zambia
81 G19 **Musoma** Mara, N Tanzania
82 L13 **Musoro** Central, C Zambia
186 F4 **Mussau Island** *island* NE PNG
98 P7 **Musselkanaal** Groningen, NE Netherlands
33 V9 **Musselshell River** ~ Montana, NW USA
82 C12 **Mussende** Cuanza Sul, NW Angola
102 L12 **Mussidan** Dordogne, SW France
83 K19 **Musina** *prev.* Messina. Limpopo, NE South Africa
99 L25 **Musson** Luxembourg, SE Belgium
152 J9 **Mussoorie** Uttaranchal, N India
Musta see Mosta
152 M13 **Mustafābād** Uttar Pradesh, N India
136 D12 **Mustafakemalpaşa** Bursa, NW Turkey
Mustafa-Pasha see Svilengrad
81 M15 **Mustahīl** Somali, E Ethiopia

◆ COUNTRY ● COUNTRY CAPITAL ◇ DEPENDENT TERRITORY ○ DEPENDENT TERRITORY CAPITAL ◆ ADMINISTRATIVE REGION × INTERNATIONAL AIRPORT ▲ MOUNTAIN ▲ MOUNTAIN RANGE ⚠ VOLCANO ~ RIVER ◎ LAKE ⊞ RESERVOIR

24 M7 **Mustang Draw** *valley* Texas, SW USA
25 T14 **Mustang Island** *island* Texas, SW USA
Mustasaari *see* Korsholm
Mustér *see* Disentis
63 I19 **Musters, Lago** ◎ S Argentina
45 Y14 **Mustique** *island* C Saint Vincent and the Grenadines
118 I6 **Mustla** Viljandimaa, S Estonia
118 J4 **Mustvee** *Ger.* Tschorna. Jõgevamaa, E Estonia
42 L9 **Musún, Cerro** ▲ NE Nicaragua
183 T7 **Muswellbrook** New South Wales, SE Australia
111 M18 **Muszyna** Małopolskie, SE Poland
136 I17 **Mut** İçel, S Turkey
75 V10 **Mût** *var.* Mut. C Egypt
109 V9 **Muta** N Slovenia
190 B15 **Mutalau** N Niue
Mu-tan-chiang *see* Mudanjiang
82 I13 **Mutanda** North Western, NW Zambia
59 O17 **Mutá, Ponta do** *headland* E Brazil
83 L17 **Mutare** *var.* Mutari; *prev.* Umtali. Manicaland, E Zimbabwe
Mutari *see* Mutare
54 D8 **Mutatá** Antioquia, NW Colombia
Mutina *see* Modena
83 L16 **Mutoko** *prev.* Mtoko. Mashonaland East, NE Zimbabwe
81 J20 **Mutomo** Eastern, S Kenya
Mutrah *see* Maṭraḥ
79 M24 **Mutshatsha** Katanga, S Dem. Rep. Congo
165 R6 **Mutsu** *var.* Mutu. Aomori, Honshū, N Japan
165 R6 **Mutsu-wan** *bay* N Japan
108 E6 **Muttenz** Basel-Land, NW Switzerland
185 A26 **Muttonbird Islands** *island group* SW NZ
Mutu *see* Mutsu
83 O15 **Mutuáli** Nampula, N Mozambique
82 D13 **Mutumbo** Bié, C Angola
189 Y14 **Mutunte, Mount** *var.* Mount Buache. ▲ Kosrae, E Micronesia
155 K24 **Mutur** Eastern Province, E Sri Lanka
92 L13 **Muurola** Lappi, NW Finland
162 M14 **Mu Us Shadi** *var.* Ordos Desert, *prev.* Mu Us Shamo. *desert* N China
Mu Us Shamo *see* Mu Us Shadi
82 B11 **Muxima** Bengo, NW Angola
124 I8 **Muyezerskiy** Respublika Kareliya, NW Russian Federation
81 E20 **Muyinga** NE Burundi
42 K9 **Muy Muy** Matagalpa, C Nicaragua
Muynak *see* Mo'ynoq
79 N22 **Muyumba** Katanga, SE Dem. Rep. Congo
149 V5 **Muzaffarābād** Jammu and Kashmir, NE Pakistan
149 S10 **Muzaffargarh** Punjab, E Pakistan
152 J9 **Muzaffarnagar** Uttar Pradesh, N India
153 P13 **Muzaffarpur** Bihār, N India
158 H6 **Muzat He** ≈ W China
83 L15 **Muze** Tete, NW Mozambique
122 H8 **Muzhi** Yamalo-Nenetskiy Avtonomnyy Okrug, N Russian Federation
102 H7 **Muzillac** Morbihan, NW France
Muzkol, Khrebet *see* Muzqūl, Qatorkŭhi
112 L9 **Mužlja** *Hung.* Felsőmuzslya; *prev.* Gornja Mužlja. Serbia, N Serbia and Montenegro (Yugo.)
54 F9 **Muzo** Boyacá, C Colombia
83 J15 **Muzoka** Southern, S Zambia
39 Y15 **Muzon, Cape** *headland* Dall Island, Alaska, USA
40 M6 **Múzquiz** Coahuila de Zaragoza, NE Mexico
147 U13 **Muzqŭl, Qatorkŭhi** *Rus.* Khrebet Muzkol. ▲ SE Tajikistan
158 G10 **Muztag** ▲ NW China
158 K10 **Muz Tag** ▲ W China
158 D8 **Muztagata** ▲ NW China
83 K17 **Mvuma** *prev.* Umvuma. Midlands, C Zimbabwe
82 L13 **Mwanya** Eastern, E Zambia
81 G20 **Mwanza** Mwanza, NW Tanzania
79 N23 **Mwanza** Katanga, SE Dem. Rep. Congo
81 F20 **Mwanza** ◐ *region* N Tanzania
82 M13 **Mwase Lundazi** Eastern, E Zambia
97 B17 **Mweelrea** *Ir.* Caoc Maol Réidh. ▲ W Ireland
79 K21 **Mweka** Kasai Occidental, C Dem. Rep. Congo
82 K12 **Mwenda** Luapula, N Zambia
79 L22 **Mwene-Ditu** Kasai Oriental, S Dem. Rep. Congo
83 L18 **Mwenezi** ≈ S Zimbabwe
79 O20 **Mwenga** Sud Kivu, E Dem. Rep. Congo
82 K11 **Mweru, Lake** *var.* Lac Moero. ◎ Dem. Rep. Congo/Zambia
82 H13 **Mwinilunga** North Western, NW Zambia
189 V16 **Mwokil Atoll** *var.* Mokil Atoll. *atoll* Caroline Islands, E Micronesia
Myadel' *see* Myadzyel
118 J13 **Myadzyel** *Pol.* Miadzioł Nowy, *Rus.* Myadel'. Minskaya Voblasts', N Belarus
152 C12 **Myājlār** *var.* Miajlar. Rājasthān, NW India
123 T9 **Myakit** Magadanskaya Oblast', E Russian Federation
23 W13 **Myakka River** ≈ Florida, SE USA
124 L14 **Myaksa** Vologodskaya Oblast', NW Russian Federation
183 U8 **Myall Lake** ◎ New South Wales, SE Australia
166 L7 **Myanaung** Irrawaddy, SW Burma
Myanmar *see* Burma
166 K8 **Myaungmya** Irrawaddy, SW Burma
118 N11 **Myazha** *Rus.* Mezha. Vitsyebskaya Voblasts', NE Belarus
119 O18 **Myerkulavichy** *Rus.* Merkulovichi. Homyel'skaya Voblasts', SE Belarus
119 N14 **Myezhava** *Rus.* Mezhëvo. Vitsyebskaya Voblasts', NE Belarus
166 L5 **Myingyan** Mandalay, C Burma
167 N2 **Myitkyina** Kachin State, N Burma
166 M5 **Myittha** Mandalay, C Burma
111 H19 **Myjava** *Hung.* Miava. Trenčiansky Kraj, W Slovakia
Myjeldino *see* Myyëldino
117 U9 **Mykhaylivka** *Rus.* Mikhaylovka. Zaporiz'ka Oblast', SE Ukraine
95 A18 **Mykines** *Dan.* Myggenaes *Island* Faeroe Islands
116 I5 **Mykolayiv** L'vivs'ka Oblast', W Ukraine
117 Q10 **Mykolayiv** *Rus.* Nikolayev. Mykolayivs'ka Oblast', S Ukraine
117 Q10 **Mykolayiv** ✕ Mykolayivs'ka Oblast', S Ukraine
Mykolayiv *see* Mykolayivs'ka Oblast'
117 P9 **Mykolayivka** Odes'ka Oblast', SW Ukraine
117 S13 **Mykolayivka** Respublika Krym, S Ukraine
117 P9 **Mykolayivs'ka Oblast'** *var.* Mykolayiv, *Rus.* Nikolayevskaya Oblast'. ◐ *province* S Ukraine
115 J20 **Mýkonos** Mýkonos, Kykládes, Greece, Aegean Sea
115 K20 **Mýkonos** *var.* Míkonos. *island* Kykládes, Greece, Aegean Sea
125 R7 **Myla** Respublika Komi, NW Russian Federation
Mylae *see* Milazzo
93 M19 **Myllykoski** Etelä-Suomi, S Finland
Mymensing *see* Mymensingh
153 U14 **Mymensingh** *var.* Maimansingh, Mymensing; *prev.* Nasirābād. Dhaka, N Bangladesh
93 K19 **Mynämäki** Länsi-Suomi, W Finland
145 S14 **Mynaral** *Kaz.* Myngaral. Zhambyl, S Kazakhstan
Mynbulak *see* Mingbuloq
Mynbulak, Vpadina *see* Mingbuloq Botighi
Myngaral *see* Mynaral
166 K5 **Myohaung** Arakan State, W Burma
163 W13 **Myohyang-sanmaek** ▲ C North Korea
164 M11 **Myōkō-san** ▲ Honshū, S Japan
83 J15 **Myooye** Central, C Zambia
118 K12 **Myory** *prev.* Miyory. Vitsyebskaya Voblasts', N Belarus
92 J4 **Mýrdalsjökull** *glacier* S Iceland
92 G10 **Myre** Nordland, C Norway
117 S5 **Myrhorod** *Rus.* Mirgorod. Poltavs'ka Oblast', NE Ukraine
115 J15 **Mýrina** *var.* Mírina. Límnos, SE Greece
117 P5 **Myronivka** *Rus.* Mironovka. Kyyivs'ka Oblast', N Ukraine
21 U13 **Myrtle Beach** South Carolina, SE USA
32 F14 **Myrtle Creek** Oregon, NW USA
183 P11 **Myrtleford** Victoria, SE Australia
32 E14 **Myrtle Point** Oregon, NW USA
115 K25 **Mýrtos** Kríti, Greece, E Mediterranean Sea
Myrtoum Mare *see* Mirtóo Pélagos
93 G17 **Myrviken** Jämtland, C Sweden
95 I15 **Mysen** Østfold, S Norway
124 L15 **Myshkin** Yaroslavskaya Oblast', NW Russian Federation
111 K17 **Myślenice** Małopolskie, S Poland
110 D10 **Myślibórz** Zachodnio-pomorskie, NW Poland
155 G20 **Mysore** *var.* Maisur. Karnātaka, W India
Mysore *see* Karnātaka
115 F21 **Mystrás** *var.* Mistras. Pelopónnisos, S Greece
125 T12 **Mysy** Komi-Permyatskiy Avtonomnyy Okrug, NW Russian Federation
111 K15 **Myszków** Śląskie, S Poland
167 T14 **My Tho** *var.* Mi Tho. Tiên Giang, S Vietnam
Mytilene *see* Mytilíni
115 L17 **Mytilíni** *var.* Mitilíni; *anc.* Mytilene. Lésvos, E Greece
126 K3 **Mytishchi** Moskovskaya Oblast', W Russian Federation
37 N3 **Myton** Utah, W USA
92 K2 **Mývatn** ◎ C Iceland
125 T11 **Myyëldino** *var.* Myjeldino. Respublika Komi, NW Russian Federation
82 M13 **Mzimba** Northern, NW Malawi
82 M12 **Mzuzu** Northern, N Malawi

N

101 M19 **Naab** ≈ SE Germany
98 G12 **Naaldwijk** Zuid-Holland, W Netherlands
38 G12 **Nā'ālehu** *var.* Naalehu. Hawai'i, USA, C Pacific Ocean
93 K19 **Naantali** *Swe.* Nådendal. Länsi-Suomi, W Finland
98 J10 **Naarden** Noord-Holland, C Netherlands
109 U4 **Naarn** ≈ N Austria
97 F18 **Naas** *Ir.* An Nás, Nás na Ríogh. C Ireland
92 M9 **Näätämöjoki** *Lapp.* Njávdám. ≈ NE Finland
83 E23 **Nababeep** *var.* Nababiep. Northern Cape, W South Africa
Nababiep *see* Nababeep
Nabadwip *see* Navadwīp
164 J14 **Nabari** Mie, Honshū, SW Japan
Nabatié *see* Nabatîyé
138 G8 **Nabatîyé** *var.* An Nabatīyah at Taḥtā, Nabatié, Nabatiyet et Tahta. SW Lebanon
Nabatiyet et Tahta *see* Nabatîyé
187 X14 **Nabavatu** Vanua Levu, N Fiji
190 I2 **Nabeina** *island* Tungaru, W Kiribati
127 T4 **Naberezhnyye Chelny** *prev.* Brezhnev. Respublika Tatarstan, W Russian Federation
39 T10 **Nabesna** Alaska, USA
39 T10 **Nabesna River** ≈ Alaska, USA
75 N5 **Nabeul** *var.* Nābul. NE Tunisia
152 I9 **Nābha** Punjab, NW India
171 W13 **Nabire** Papua, E Indonesia
141 O15 **Nabī Shu'ayb, Jabal an** ▲ W Yemen
138 F10 **Nablus** *var.* Nābulus, *Heb.* Shekhem; *anc.* Neapolis, *Bibl.* Shechem. N West Bank
187 X14 **Nabouwalu** Vanua Levu, N Fiji
Nābul *see* Nabeul
Nābulus *see* Nablus
187 Y13 **Nabuna** Vanua Levu, N Fiji
83 Q14 **Nacala** Nampula, NE Mozambique
42 H8 **Nacaome** Valle, S Honduras
Na Cealla Beaga *see* Killybegs
Na-ch'ii *see* Nagqu
164 J15 **Nachikatsuura** *var.* Nachi-Katsuura. Wakayama, Honshū, SE Japan
81 J24 **Nachingwea** Lindi, SE Tanzania
111 F16 **Náchod** Královéhradecký Kraj, N Czech Republic
Na Clocha Liatha *see* Greystones
40 G3 **Naco** Sonora, NW Mexico
25 X8 **Nacogdoches** Texas, SW USA
40 G4 **Nacozari de García** Sonora, NW Mexico
Nada *see* Danzhou
77 O14 **Nadawli** NW Ghana
104 I3 **Nadela** Galicia, NW Spain
Nådendal *see* Naantali
144 M7 **Nadezhdinka** *prev.* Nadezhdinskiy. Kostanay, N Kazakhstan
Nadezhdinskiy *see* Nadezhdinka
Nadgan *see* Nadqān, Qalamat
187 W14 **Nadi** *prev.* Nandi. Viti Levu, W Fiji
187 X14 **Nadi** *prev.* Nandi. ✕ Viti Levu, W Fiji
154 D10 **Nadiād** Gujarāt, W India
Nadikdik *see* Knox Atoll
116 E11 **Nădlac** *Ger.* Nadlak, *Hung.* Nagylak. Arad, W Romania
Nadlak *see* Nădlac
74 H6 **Nador** *prev.* Villa Nador. NE Morocco
141 S9 **Nadqān, Qalamat** *var.* Nadgan. *well* E Saudi Arabia
111 N22 **Nádudvar** Hajdú-Bihar, E Hungary
121 O15 **Nadur** Gozo, N Malta
187 X13 **Naduri** *prev.* Nanduri. Vanua Levu, N Fiji
116 I7 **Nadvirna** *Pol.* Nadwórna, *Rus.* Nadvornaya. Ivano-Frankivs'ka Oblast', W Ukraine
124 J8 **Nadvoitsy** Respublika Kareliya, NW Russian Federation
Nadvornaya/Nadwórna *see* Nadvirna
122 I9 **Nadym** Yamalo-Nenetskiy Avtonomnyy Okrug, N Russian Federation
122 I9 **Nadym** ≈ C Russian Federation
186 E7 **Nadzab** Morobe, C PNG
77 X13 **Nafada** Gombe, E Nigeria
108 H8 **Näfels** Glarus, NE Switzerland
115 E18 **Náfpaktos** *var.* Návpaktos. Dytikí Ellás, C Greece
115 F20 **Náfplio** *prev.* Návplion. Pelopónnisos, S Greece
139 U6 **Naft Khāneh** E Iraq
149 N13 **Nag** Baluchistān, SW Pakistan
171 P4 **Naga** *off.* Naga City; *prev.* Nueva Caceres. Luzon, N Philippines
Nagaarzê *see* Nagarzê
12 F11 **Nagagami** ≈ Ontario, S Canada
164 F14 **Nagahama** Ehime, Shikoku, SW Japan
153 X12 **Nāga Hills** ▲ NE India
165 P10 **Nagai** Yamagata, Honshū, C Japan
Na Gaibhlte *see* Galty Mountains
39 N16 **Nagai Island** *island* Shumagin Islands, Alaska, USA
153 X12 **Nāgāland** ◐ *state* NE India
164 M11 **Nagano** Nagano, Honshū, S Japan
164 M12 **Nagano** *off.* Nagano-ken. ◐ *prefecture* Honshū, S Japan
165 N11 **Nagaoka** Niigata, Honshū, C Japan
153 W12 **Nagaon** *prev.* Nowgong. Assam, NE India
155 J21 **Nāgappattinam** *var.* Negapatam, Negapattinam. Tamil Nādu, SE India
Nagara Nayok *see* Nakhon Nayok
Nagara Panom *see* Nakhon Phanom
Nagara Pathom *see* Nakhon Pathom
Nagara Sridharmaraj *see* Nakhon Si Thammarat
Nagara Svarga *see* Nakhon Sawan
155 H16 **Nāgārjuna Sāgar** ⊞ E India
42 I10 **Nagarote** León, SW Nicaragua
158 M16 **Nagarzê** *var.* Nagaarzê. Xizang Zizhiqu, W China
164 C14 **Nagasaki** Nagasaki, Kyūshū, SW Japan
164 C14 **Nagasaki** *off.* Nagasaki-ken. ◐ *prefecture* Kyūshū, SW Japan
Nagashima *see* Kii-Nagashima
164 E12 **Nagato** Yamaguchi, Honshū, SW Japan
152 F11 **Nāgaur** Rājasthān, NW India
154 F10 **Nāgda** Madhya Pradesh, C India
98 L8 **Nagele** Flevoland, N Netherlands
155 H24 **Nāgercoil** Tamil Nādu, SE India
153 X12 **Nāginimāra** Nāgāland, NE India
Na Gleannta *see* Glenties
165 T16 **Nago** Okinawa, Okinawa, SW Japan
154 K9 **Nāgod** Madhya Pradesh, C India
155 J26 **Nagoda** Southern Province, S Sri Lanka
101 G22 **Nagold** Baden-Württemberg, SW Germany
Nagorno-Karabakhskaya Avtonomnaya Oblast *see* Nagorno-Karabakh
123 Q12 **Nagornyy** Respublika Sakha (Yakutiya), NE Russian Federation
137 V12 **Nagorno-Karabakh** *var.* Nagorno-Karabakhskaya Avtonomnaya Oblast , *Arm.* Lerrnayin Gharabakh, *Az.* Dağliq Qarabağ, *Rus.* Nagornyy Karabakh. *former autonomous region* SW Azerbaijan
Nagornyy Karabakh *see* Nagorno-Karabakh
125 R13 **Nagorsk** Kirovskaya Oblast', NW Russian Federation
164 K13 **Nagoya** Aichi, Honshū, SW Japan
154 I12 **Nāgpur** Mahārāshtra, C India
156 K10 **Nagqu** *Chin.* Na-ch'ii; *prev.* Hei-ho. Xizang Zizhiqu, W China
152 J8 **Nag Tibba Range** ▲ N India
45 O8 **Nagua** NE Dominican Republic
111 H25 **Nagyatád** Somogy, SW Hungary
Nagybánya *see* Baia Mare
Nagybecskerek *see* Zrenjanin
Nagydisznód *see* Cisnădie
Nagyenyed *see* Aiud
111 N21 **Nagykálló** Szabolcs-Szatmár-Bereg, E Hungary
111 G25 **Nagykanizsa** *Ger.* Grosskanizsa. Zala, SW Hungary
Nagykároly *see* Carei
111 K22 **Nagykáta** Pest, C Hungary
Nagykikinda *see* Kikinda
111 K23 **Nagykőrös** Pest, C Hungary
Nagy-Küküllő *see* Târnava Mare
Nagylak *see* Nădlac
Nagymihály *see* Michalovce
Nagyrőce *see* Revúca
Nagysomkút *see* Şomcuta Mare
Nagysurány *see* Šurany
Nagyszalonta *see* Salonta
Nagyszeben *see* Sibiu
Nagyszentmiklós *see* Sânnicolau Mare
Nagyszöllös *see* Vynohradiv
Nagyszombat *see* Trnava
Nagytapolcsány *see* Topoľčany
Nagyvárad *see* Oradea
165 S17 **Naha** Okinawa, Okinawa, SW Japan
152 J8 **Nāhan** Himāchal Pradesh, NW India
Nahang, Rūd-e *see* Nihing
Nahariya *see* Nahariyya
138 F8 **Nahariyya** *var.* Nahariya. Northern, N Israel
142 L6 **Nahāvand** *var.* Nehavend. Hamadān, W Iran
101 F19 **Nahe** ≈ SW Germany
Na h-Iarmhidhe *see* Westmeath
189 O13 **Nahnalaud** ▲ Pohnpei, E Micronesia
Nahoi, Cape *see* Cumberland, Cape
Nahtavárr *see* Nattavaara
63 H16 **Nahuel Huapi, Lago** ◎ W Argentina
23 W7 **Nahunta** Georgia, SE USA
40 J6 **Naica** Chihuahua, N Mexico
11 U15 **Naicam** Saskatchewan, S Canada
Naiman Qi *see* Daqin Tal
158 M4 **Naimin Bulak** *spring* NW China
13 P6 **Nain** Newfoundland and Labrador, NE Canada
143 P8 **Nā'īn** Eşfahān, C Iran
152 K10 **Naini Tāl** Uttaranchal, N India
154 J11 **Nainpur** Madhya Pradesh, C India
96 J8 **Nairn** N Scotland, UK
96 I8 **Nairn** *cultural region* NE Scotland, UK
81 I19 **Nairobi** ● (Kenya) Nairobi Area, S Kenya
81 I19 **Nairobi** ✕ Nairobi Area, S Kenya
82 P13 **Nairoto** Cabo Delgado, NE Mozambique
118 G3 **Naissaar** *island* N Estonia
Naissus *see* Niš
187 Z14 **Naitaba** *var.* Naitauba; *prev.* Naitamba. *island* Lau Group, E Fiji
Naitamba/Naitauba *see* Naitaba
81 I19 **Naivasha** Rift Valley, SW Kenya
81 H19 **Naivasha, Lake** ◎ SW Kenya
Najaf *see* An Najaf
143 N8 **Najafābād** *var.* Nejafabad. Eşfahān, C Iran
141 N7 **Najd** *var.* Nejd. *cultural region* C Saudi Arabia
105 O4 **Nájera** La Rioja, N Spain
105 P4 **Najerilla** ≈ N Spain
163 U7 **Naji** *var.* Arun Qi. Nei Mongol Zizhiqu, N China
152 J9 **Najībābād** Uttar Pradesh, N India
Najima *see* Fukuoka
163 Y11 **Najin** NE North Korea
139 T9 **Najm al Ḥassūn** C Iraq
141 O13 **Najrān** *var.* Abā as Su'ūd. Najrān, S Saudi Arabia
141 P12 **Najrān** *off.* Minṭaqat al Najrān. ◐ *province* S Saudi Arabia
165 T2 **Nakagawa** Hokkaidō, NE Japan
38 F9 **Nākālele Point** *var.* Nakalele Point *headland* Maui, Hawai'i, USA, C Pacific Ocean
164 D13 **Nakama** Fukuoka, Kyūshū, SW Japan
Nakambé *see* White Volta
Nakamti *see* Nek'emtē
164 F15 **Nakamura** Kōchi, Shikoku, SW Japan
186 H7 **Nakanai Mountains** ▲ New Britain, E PNG
164 H11 **Nakano-shima** *island* Oki-shotō, SW Japan
165 Q6 **Nakasato** Aomori, Honshū, C Japan
165 T5 **Nakasatsunai** Hokkaidō, NE Japan
165 W4 **Nakashibetsu** Hokkaidō, NE Japan
81 F18 **Nakasongola** C Uganda
165 T1 **Nakatonbetsu** Hokkaidō, NE Japan
164 L13 **Nakatsugawa** *var.* Nakatugawa. Gifu, Honshū, SW Japan
Nakatu *see* Nakatsu
Nakatugawa *see* Nakatsugawa
Naka-umi *see* Nakano-umi
Nakdong *see* Naktong-gang
Nakel *see* Nakło nad Notecią
80 J8 **Nakfa** N Eritrea
Nakhichevan' *see* Naxçıvan
123 S15 **Nakhodka** Primorskiy Kray, SE Russian Federation
122 J8 **Nakhodka** Yamalo-Nenetskiy Avtonomnyy Okrug, N Russian Federation
Nakhon Navok *see* Nakhon Nayok
167 P11 **Nakhon Nayok** *var.* Nagara Nayok, Nakhon Navok. Nakhon Nayok, C Thailand
167 O11 **Nakhon Pathom** *var.* Nagara Pathom, Nakorn Pathom. Nakhon Pathom, W Thailand
167 R8 **Nakhon Phanom** *var.* Nagara Panom. Nakhon Phanom, E Thailand
167 Q10 **Nakhon Ratchasima** *var.* Khorat, Korat. Nakhon Ratchasima, E Thailand
167 O9 **Nakhon Sawan** *var.* Muang Nakhon Sawan, Nagara Svarga. Nakhon Sawan, W Thailand
167 N15 **Nakhon Si Thammarat** *var.* Nagara Sridharmaraj, Nakhon Sithammaraj. Nakhon Si Thammarat, SW Thailand
Nakhon Sithammaraj *see* Nakhon Si Thammarat
139 Y11 **Nakhrash** SE Iraq
10 I9 **Nakina** British Columbia, W Canada
110 H9 **Nakło nad Notecią** *Ger.* Nakel. Kujawsko-pomorskie, C Poland
39 P13 **Naknek** Alaska, USA
152 H8 **Nakodar** Punjab, NW India
82 M11 **Nakonde** Northern, NE Zambia
Nakorn Pathom *see* Nakhon Pathom
95 H24 **Nakskov** Storstrøm, SE Denmark
163 Y15 **Naktong-gang** *var.* Nakdong, *Jap.* Rakutō-kō. ≈ C South Korea
83 H18 **Nakuru** Rift Valley, SW Kenya
81 H19 **Nakuru, Lake** ◎ Rift Valley, C Kenya
11 O17 **Nakusp** British Columbia, SW Canada
149 N15 **Nāl** ≈ W Pakistan
162 M7 **Nalayh** Töv, C Mongolia
153 V12 **Nalbāri** Assam, NE India
63 G19 **Nalcayec, Isla** *island* Archipiélago de los Chonos, S Chile
127 N15 **Nal'chik** Kabardino-Balkarskaya Respublika, SW Russian Federation
155 I16 **Nalgonda** Andhra Pradesh, C India
153 S14 **Nalhāti** West Bengal, NE India
153 U14 **Nalitabari** Dhaka, N Bangladesh
155 I17 **Nallamala Hills** ▲ E India
136 G12 **Nallıhan** Ankara, NW Turkey
104 K2 **Nalón** ≈ NW Spain
167 N3 **Nalong** Kachin State, N Burma
75 N8 **Nālūt** NW Libya
171 T14 **Nama** Pulau Manawoka, E Indonesia
189 Q16 **Nama** *island* C Micronesia
83 O16 **Namacurra** Zambézia, NE Mozambique
188 F9 **Namai Bay** *bay* Babeldaob, N Palau
29 W2 **Namakan Lake** ◎ Canada/USA
143 O6 **Namak, Daryācheh-ye** *marsh* N Iran
143 T6 **Namak, Kavīr-e** *salt pan* NE Iran
167 O6 **Namaklwe** Shan State, E Burma
Namaksār, Kowl-e/Namakzār, Daryācheh-ye *see* Namakzar
148 I5 **Namakzar** *Pash.* Daryācheh-ye Namakzār, Kowl-e Namaksār. *marsh* Afghanistan/Iran
171 V15 **Namalau** Pulau Jursian, E Indonesia
81 I20 **Namanga** Rift Valley, S Kenya
147 S10 **Namangan** Namangan Viloyati, E Uzbekistan
Namanganskaya Oblast' *see* Namangan Viloyati
147 R10 **Namangan Viloyati** *Rus.* Namanganskaya Oblast'. ◐ *province* E Uzbekistan
83 Q14 **Namapa** Nampula, NE Mozambique
83 C21 **Namaqualand** *physical region* S Namibia
81 G18 **Namasagali** C Uganda
186 H6 **Namatanai** New Ireland, NE PNG
83 I14 **Nambala** Central, C Zambia
81 J23 **Nambanje** Lindi, SE Tanzania
83 G16 **Nambiya** Ngamiland, N Botswana
183 V2 **Nambour** Queensland, E Australia
183 V6 **Nambucca Heads** New South Wales, SE Australia
159 N15 **Nam Co** ◎ W China
167 R5 **Nam Cum** Lai Châu, N Vietnam
Namdik *see* Namorik Atoll
167 T6 **Nam Định** Nam Ha, N Vietnam
99 I20 **Namêche** Namur, SE Belgium
30 J4 **Namekagon Lake** ◎ Wisconsin, N USA
188 F10 **Namekakl Passage** *passage* Babeldaob, N Palau
Namen *see* Namur
83 P15 **Nametil** Nampula, NE Mozambique
163 X14 **Nam-gang** ≈ C North Korea
163 Y16 **Nam-gang** ≈ S South Korea
163 Y17 **Namhae-do** *Jap.* Nankai-tō. *island* S South Korea
Namhoi *see* Foshan
83 C19 **Namib Desert** *desert* W Namibia
83 A15 **Namibe** *Port.* Moçâmedes, Mossâmedes. Namibe, SW Angola
83 A15 **Namibe** ◐ *province* SE Angola
83 C18 **Namibia** *off.* Republic of Namibia, *var.* South West Africa, *Afr.* Suidwes-Afrika, *Ger.* Deutsch-Südwestafrika; *prev.* German Southwest Africa, South-West Africa. ◆ *republic* S Africa
65 O17 **Namibia Plain** *undersea feature* S Atlantic Ocean
165 Q11 **Namie** Fukushima, Honshū, C Japan
165 Q7 **Namioka** Aomori, Honshū, C Japan
40 I5 **Namiquipa** Chihuahua, N Mexico
159 P15 **Namjagbarwa Feng** ▲ W China
Namka *see* Doilungdêqên
171 R13 **Namlea** Pulau Buru, E Indonesia
158 L16 **Namling** Xizang Zizhiqu, W China
Namnetes *see* Nantes
167 R8 **Nam Ngum** ≈ C Laos
Namo *see* Namu Atoll
183 R5 **Namoi River** ≈ New South Wales, SE Australia
189 Q17 **Namoluk Atoll** *atoll* Mortlock Islands, C Micronesia
189 O15 **Namonuito Atoll** *atoll* Caroline Islands, C Micronesia
189 T9 **Namorik Atoll** *var.* Namdik. *atoll* Ralik Chain, S Marshall Islands
167 Q6 **Nam Ou** ≈ N Laos
32 M14 **Nampa** Idaho, NW USA
76 M11 **Nampala** Ségou, W Mali
163 W14 **Namp'o** SW North Korea
83 P15 **Nampula** Nampula, NE Mozambique
83 P15 **Nampula** *off.* Província de Nampula. ◐ *province* NE Mozambique
163 W13 **Namsan-ni** NW North Korea
Namslau *see* Namysłów
93 E15 **Namsos** Nord-Trøndelag, C Norway
93 F14 **Namsskogan** Nord-Trøndelag, C Norway
123 Q10 **Namsty** Respublika Sakha (Yakutiya), NE Russian Federation
167 O6 **Nam Teng** ≈ E Burma
167 P6 **Nam Tha** ≈ N Laos
167 N4 **Namtu** Shan State, E Burma
10 J15 **Namu** British Columbia, SW Canada
189 T7 **Namu Atoll** *var.* Namo. *atoll* Ralik Chain, C Marshall Islands
187 Y15 **Namuka-i-lau** *island* Lau Group, E Fiji
83 O15 **Namuli, Mont** ▲ NE Mozambique
83 P14 **Namuno** Cabo Delgado, N Mozambique
99 I20 **Namur** *Dut.* Namen. Namur, SE Belgium
99 H21 **Namur** *Dut.* Namen. ◐ *province* S Belgium
83 D17 **Namutoni** Kunene, N Namibia
163 Y16 **Namwŏn** *Jap.* Nangen. S South Korea
111 H14 **Namysłów** *Ger.* Namslau. Opolskie, S Poland
167 P7 **Nan** *var.* Muang Nan. Nan, NW Thailand
79 G15 **Nana** ≈ W Central African Republic
165 R5 **Nanae** Hokkaidō, NE Japan
79 I14 **Nana-Grébizi** ◐ *prefecture* N Central African Republic
10 L17 **Nanaimo** Vancouver Island, British Columbia, SW Canada
38 C9 **Nānākuli** *var.* Nanakuli. O'ahu, Hawai'i, USA, C Pacific Ocean
79 G15 **Nana-Mambéré** ◐ *prefecture* W Central African Republic
161 R13 **Nan'an** Fujian, SE China
183 U2 **Nanango** Queensland, E Australia
164 L11 **Nanao** Ishikawa, Honshū, SW Japan
161 Q14 **Nan'ao Dao** *island* S China
164 L10 **Nanatsu-shima** *island* SW Japan
56 F8 **Nanay, Río** ≈ NE Peru
160 J8 **Nanbu** Sichuan, C China
163 X7 **Nancha** Heilongjiang, NE China
161 P10 **Nanchang** *var.* Nan-ch'ang, Nanch'ang-hsien. Jiangxi, S China
Nanch'ang-hsien *see* Nanchang
161 P11 **Nancheng** *var.* Jianchang. Jiangxi, S China
Nan-ching *see* Nanjing
160 J9 **Nanchong** Sichuan, C China
160 J10 **Nanchuan** Chongqing Shi, C China
103 T5 **Nancy** Meurthe-et-Moselle, NE France

185 A22 **Nancy Sound** *sound* South Island, NZ
152 L9 **Nanda Devi** ▲ NW India
42 J11 **Nandaime** Granada, SW Nicaragua
160 K13 **Nandan** Guangxi Zhuangzu Zizhiqu, S China
155 H14 **Nānded** Mahārāshtra, C India
183 S5 **Nandewar Range** ▲ New South Wales, SE Australia
Nandi *see* Nadi
160 E13 **Nanding He** ≈ China/Vietnam
Nándorhgy *see* Oţelu Roşu
154 E11 **Nandurbār** Mahārāshtra, W India
Nanduri *see* Naduri
155 I17 **Nandyāl** Andhra Pradesh, E India
161 P11 **Nanfeng** *var.* Qincheng. Jiangxi, S China
Nang *see* Nangxian
79 E15 **Nanga Eboko** Centre, C Cameroon
149 W4 **Nanga Parbat** ▲ India/Pakistan
169 R11 **Nangapinoh** Borneo, C Indonesia
149 R5 **Nangarhār** ◆ *province* E Afghanistan
169 S11 **Nangaserawai** *var.* Nangah Serawai. Borneo, C Indonesia
169 Q12 **Nangatayap** Borneo, C Indonesia
Nangen *see* Namwŏn
103 P5 **Nangis** Seine-et-Marne, N France
163 X13 **Nangnim-sanmaek** ▲ C North Korea
161 O4 **Nangong** Hebei, E China
159 Q14 **Nangqên** *var.* Xangda. Qinghai, C China
167 Q10 **Nang Rong** Buri Ram, E Thailand
159 O16 **Nangxian** *var.* Nang. Xizang Zizhiqu, W China
Nan Hai *see* South China Sea
160 L8 **Nan He** ≈ C China
160 F12 **Nanhua** *var.* Longchuan. Yunnan, SW China
Naniwa *see* Ōsaka
155 G20 **Nanjangūd** Karnātaka, W India
161 Q8 **Nanjing** *var.* Nan-ching, Nanking; *prev.* Chianning, Chian-ning, Kiang-ning. Jiangsu, E China
Nankai-tō *see* Namhae-do
161 O12 **Nankang** *var.* Rongjiang. Jiangxi, S China
Nanking *see* Nanjing
161 N13 **Nan Ling** ▲ S China
160 L15 **Nanliu Jiang** ≈ S China
189 P13 **Nan Madol** *ruins* Temwen Island, E Micronesia
160 K15 **Nanning** *var.* Nan-ning; *prev.* Yung-ning. Guangxi Zhuangzu Zizhiqu, S China
196 M15 **Nanortalik** Kitaa, S Greenland
Nanouki *see* Aranuka
160 H13 **Nanpan Jiang** ≈ S China
152 M11 **Nānpāra** Uttar Pradesh, N India
161 Q12 **Nanping** *var.* Nan-p'ing; *prev.* Yenping. Fujian, SE China
Nanping *see* Jiuzhaigou
Nanpu *see* Pucheng
161 R12 **Nanri Dao** *island* SE China
165 S16 **Nansei-shotō** *Eng.* Ryukyu Islands. *island group* SW Japan
Nansei Syotō Trench *see* Ryukyu Trench
197 T10 **Nansen Basin** *undersea feature* Arctic Ocean
197 T10 **Nansen Cordillera** *var.* Arctic-Mid Oceanic Ridge, Nansen Ridge. *undersea feature* Arctic Ocean
Nansen Ridge *see* Nansen Cordillera
Nansha Qundao *see* Spratly Islands
12 K3 **Nantais, Lac** ◎ Québec, NE Canada
103 N5 **Nanterre** Hauts-de-Seine, N France
102 I8 **Nantes** *Bret.* Naoned; *anc.* Condivincum, Namnetes. Loire-Atlantique, NW France
14 G17 **Nanticoke** Ontario, S Canada
18 H13 **Nanticoke** Pennsylvania, NE USA
21 Y4 **Nanticoke River** ≈ Delaware/Maryland, NE USA
11 Q17 **Nanton** Alberta, SW Canada
161 S8 **Nantong** Jiangsu, E China
161 S13 **Nant'ou** W Taiwan
103 S10 **Nantua** Ain, E France
19 Q13 **Nantucket** Nantucket Island, Massachusetts, NE USA
19 Q13 **Nantucket Island** *island* Massachusetts, NE USA
19 Q13 **Nantucket Sound** *sound* Massachusetts, NE USA
82 P13 **Nantulo** Cabo Delgado, N Mozambique
189 O12 **Nanuh** Pohnpei, E Micronesia
190 D6 **Nanumaga** *var.* Nanumanga. *atoll* NW Tuvalu
Nanumanga *see* Nanumaga
190 D5 **Nanumea Atoll** *atoll* NW Tuvalu
59 O19 **Nanuque** Minas Gerais, SE Brazil
171 R10 **Nanusa, Kepulauan** *island group* N Indonesia
163 U4 **Nanweng He** ≈ NE China
160 I10 **Nanxi** Sichuan, C China
161 N10 **Nanxian** *var.* Nan Xian, Nanzhou. Hunan, S China
161 N7 **Nanyang** *var.* Nan-yang. Henan, C China
161 P6 **Nanyang Hu** ◎ E China
165 P10 **Nan'yō** Yamagata, Honshū, C Japan
81 I18 **Nanyuki** Central, C Kenya
160 M8 **Nanzhang** Hubei, C China
Nanzhou *see* Nanxian
105 T11 **Nao, Cabo de La** *headland* E Spain
12 M9 **Naococane, Lac** ◎ Québec, E Canada
153 S14 **Naogaon** Rajshahi, NW Bangladesh
Naokot *see* Naukot
187 R13 **Naone** Maewo, C Vanuatu
Naoned *see* Nantes
115 E14 **Náousa** Kentrikí Makedonía, N Greece
35 N8 **Napa** California, W USA
39 O11 **Napaimiut** Alaska, USA
39 N12 **Napakiak** Alaska, USA
122 J7 **Napalkovo** Yamalo-Nenetskiy Avtonomnyy Okrug, N Russian Federation
12 I16 **Napanee** Ontario, SE Canada
39 N12 **Napaskiak** Alaska, USA
167 S5 **Na Phac** Cao Băng, N Vietnam
184 O11 **Napier** Hawke's Bay, North Island, NZ
195 X3 **Napier Mountains** ▲ Antarctica
15 O13 **Napierville** Québec, SE Canada
23 W15 **Naples** Florida, SE USA
25 W5 **Naples** Texas, SW USA
Naples *see* Napoli
160 I14 **Napo** Guangxi Zhuangzu Zizhiqu, S China
56 C6 **Napo** ◆ *province* NE Ecuador
29 O6 **Napoleon** North Dakota, N USA
31 R11 **Napoleon** Ohio, N USA
Napoléon-Vendée *see* la Roche-sur-Yon
22 J9 **Napoleonville** Louisiana, S USA
107 K17 **Napoli** *Eng.* Naples, *Ger.* Neapel; *anc.* Neapolis. Campania, S Italy
107 J18 **Napoli, Golfo di** *gulf* S Italy
57 F7 **Napo, Río** ≈ Ecuador/Peru
191 W9 **Napuka** *island* Îles Tuamotu, C French Polynesia
142 J3 **Naqadeh** Āžarbāyjān-e Bākhtarī, NW Iran
139 U6 **Naqnah** E Iraq
Nar *see* Nera
164 J14 **Nara** Nara, Honshū, SW Japan
76 L11 **Nara** Koulikoro, W Mali
164 J14 **Nara** *off.* Nara-ken. ◆ *prefecture* Honshū, SW Japan
149 R14 **Nāra Canal** *irrigation canal* S Pakistan
182 K11 **Naracoorte** South Australia
183 P8 **Naradhan** New South Wales, SE Australia
Naradhivas *see* Narathiwat
56 B8 **Naranjal** Guayas, W Ecuador
57 Q19 **Naranjos** Santa Cruz, E Bolivia
41 Q12 **Naranjos** Veracruz-Llave, E Mexico
159 Q6 **Naran Sebstein Bulag** *spring* NW China
143 X12 **Narānū** Sīstān va Balūchestān, SE Iran
164 B14 **Narao** Nagasaki, Nakadōri-jima, SW Japan
155 J16 **Narasaraopet** Andhra Pradesh, E India
158 J5 **Narat** Xinjiang Uygur Zizhiqu, W China
167 P17 **Narathiwat** *var.* Naradhivas. Narathiwat, SW Thailand
37 V10 **Nara Visa** New Mexico, SW USA
Nārāyāni *see* Gandak
Narbada *see* Narmada
Narbo Martius *see* Narbonne
103 P16 **Narbonne** *anc.* Narbo Martius. Aude, S France
Narborough Island *see* Fernandina, Isla
104 J2 **Narcea** ≈ NW Spain
152 J9 **Narendranagar** Uttaranchal, N India
Nares Abyssal Plain *see* Nares Plain
64 G11 **Nares Plain** *var.* Nares Abyssal Plain. *undersea feature* NW Atlantic Ocean
197 P10 **Nares Strait** *Dan.* Nares Stræde. *strait* Canada/Greenland
Nares Stræde *see* Nares Strait
110 O9 **Narew** ≈ E Poland
155 F17 **Nargund** Karnātaka, W India
83 D20 **Narib** Hardap, S Namibia
Narikrik *see* Knox Atoll
Narin Gol *see* Dong He
54 B13 **Nariño** *off.* Departamento de Nariño. ◆ *province* SW Colombia
165 P13 **Narita** Chiba, Honshū, S Japan
165 P13 **Narita** ✕ (Tōkyō) Chiba, Honshū, S Japan
Nariya *see* An Nu'ayrīyah
162 F5 **Nariyn Gol** ≈ Mongolia/Russian Federation
152 J8 **Narkanda** Himāchal Pradesh, NW India
92 L13 **Narkaus** Lappi, NW Finland
154 E11 **Narmada** *var.* Narbada. ≈ C India
152 H11 **Narnaul** *var.* Nārnaul. Haryāna, N India
107 I14 **Narni** Umbria, C Italy
107 J24 **Naro** Sicilia, Italy, C Mediterranean Sea
Narodichi *see* Narodychi
127 V7 **Narodnaya, Gora** ▲ NW Russian Federation
117 N3 **Narodychi** *Rus.* Narodichi. Zhytomyrs'ka Oblast', N Ukraine
126 J4 **Naro-Fominsk** Moskovskaya Oblast', W Russian Federation
81 H19 **Narok** Rift Valley, SW Kenya
104 H2 **Narón** Galicia, NW Spain
183 S11 **Narooma** New South Wales, SE Australia
Narova *see* Narva
Narovlya *see* Narowlya
149 W8 **Nārowāl** Punjab, E Pakistan
119 N20 **Narowlya** *Rus.* Narovlya. Homyel'skaya Voblasts', SE Belarus
93 J17 **Närpes** *Fin.* Närpiö. Länsi-Suomi, W Finland
Närpiö *see* Närpes
183 S5 **Narrabri** New South Wales, SE Australia
183 P9 **Narrandera** New South Wales, SE Australia
183 Q4 **Narran Lake** ◎ New South Wales, SE Australia
183 Q4 **Narran River** ≈ New South Wales/Queensland, SE Australia
180 J13 **Narrogin** Western Australia
183 Q7 **Narromine** New South Wales, SE Australia
21 R6 **Narrows** Virginia, NE USA
196 M15 **Narsarsuaq** ✕ Kitaa, S Greenland
154 I10 **Narsimhapur** Madhya Pradesh, C India
Narsingdi *see* Narsinghdi
153 U15 **Narsinghdi** *var.* Narsingdi. Dhaka, C Bangladesh
154 H9 **Narsinghgarh** Madhya Pradesh, C India
163 Q11 **Nart** Nei Mongol Zizhiqu, N China
Nartës, Gjol i/Nartës, Laguna e *see* Nartës, Liqeni i
113 J22 **Nartës, Liqeni i** *var.* Gjol i Nartës, Laguna e Nartës. ◎ SW Albania
115 F17 **Nartháki** ▲ C Greece
127 O15 **Nartkala** Kabardino-Balkarskaya Respublika, SW Russian Federation
118 K3 **Narva** Ida-Virumaa, NE Estonia
118 K4 **Narva** *prev.* Narova. ≈ Estonia/Russian Federation
118 J3 **Narva Bay** *Est.* Narva Laht, *Ger.* Narwa-Bucht, *Rus.* Narvskiy Zaliv. *bay* Estonia/Russian Federation
Narva Laht *see* Narva Bay
126 F13 **Narva Reservoir** *Est.* Narva Veehoidla, *Rus.* Narvskoye Vodokhranilishche. ⊟ Estonia/Russian Federation
Narva Veehoidla *see* Narva Reservoir
92 H10 **Narvik** Nordland, C Norway
Narvskiy Zaliv *see* Narva Bay
Narvskoye Vodokhranilishche *see* Narva Reservoir
Narwa-Bucht *see* Narva Bay
152 I9 **Narwāna** Haryāna, NW India
125 R4 **Nar'yan-Mar** *prev.* Beloshchel'ye, Dzerzhinskiy. Nenetskiy Avtonomnyy Okrug, NW Russian Federation
122 J12 **Narym** Tomskaya Oblast', C Russian Federation
145 Y10 **Narymskiy Khrebet** *Kaz.* Naryn Zhotasy. ▲ E Kazakhstan
147 W9 **Naryn** Narynskaya Oblast', C Kyrgyzstan
147 U8 **Naryn** ≈ Kyrgyzstan/Uzbekistan
145 W16 **Narynkol** *Kaz.* Narynqol. Almaty, SE Kazakhstan
Naryn Oblasty *see* Narynskaya Oblast'
Narynqol *see* Narynkol
147 V9 **Narynskaya Oblast'** *Kir.* Naryn Oblasty. ◆ *province* C Kyrgyzstan
Naryn Zhotasy *see* Narymskiy Khrebet
126 J6 **Naryshkino** Orlovskaya Oblast', W Russian Federation
95 L14 **Nås** Dalarna, C Sweden
92 G13 **Nasafjellet** *Lapp.* Násávárre. ▲ C Norway
93 H16 **Näsåker** Västernorrland, C Sweden
187 Y14 **Nasau** Koro, C Fiji
116 I9 **Năsăud** *Ger.* Nussdorf, *Hung.* Naszód. Bistriţa-Năsăud, N Romania
Násávárre *see* Nasafjellet
103 P13 **Nasbinals** Lozère, S France
Na Sceirí *see* Skerries
Nase *see* Naze
185 E22 **Naseby** Otago, South Island, NZ
143 R10 **Nāşerīyeh** Kermān, C Iran
25 X5 **Nash** Texas, SW USA
154 E13 **Nāshik** *prev.* Nāsik. Mahārāshtra, W India
56 E7 **Nashiño, Río** ≈ Ecuador/Peru
29 W12 **Nashua** Iowa, C USA
33 W7 **Nashua** Montana, NW USA
19 O10 **Nashua** New Hampshire, NE USA
27 S13 **Nashville** Arkansas, C USA
23 U7 **Nashville** Georgia, SE USA
30 L16 **Nashville** Illinois, N USA
31 O14 **Nashville** Indiana, N USA
21 V9 **Nashville** North Carolina, SE USA
20 J8 **Nashville** *state capital* Tennessee, S USA
20 J9 **Nashville** ✕ Tennessee, S USA
64 H10 **Nashville Seamount** *undersea feature* NW Atlantic Ocean
112 H9 **Našice** Osijek-Baranja, E Croatia
110 M11 **Nasielsk** Mazowieckie, C Poland
93 K18 **Näsijärvi** ◎ SW Finland
Nāsik *see* Nāshik
80 G13 **Nasir** Upper Nile, SE Sudan
149 Q12 **Nasīrābād** Baluchistān, SW Pakistan
148 K15 **Nasīrābād** Baluchistān, SW Pakistan
Nasīrābād *see* Mymensingh
Nasir, Buhayrat/Nâşir, Buḥeiret *see* Nasser, Lake
Nāsiri *see* Ahvāz
Nasiriya *see* An Nāşirīyah
Nás na Ríogh *see* Naas
107 L23 **Naso** Sicilia, Italy, C Mediterranean Sea
Nasratabad *see* Zābol
10 J11 **Nass** ≈ British Columbia, SW Canada
77 V15 **Nassarawa** Nassarawa, C Nigeria
44 H2 **Nassau** ● (Bahamas) New Providence, N Bahamas
44 H2 **Nassau** ✕ New Providence, C Bahamas
190 J13 **Nassau** *island* N Cook Islands
23 W8 **Nassau Sound** *sound* Florida, SE USA
108 L7 **Nassereith** Tirol, W Austria
95 L19 **Nässjö** Jönköping, S Sweden
99 K22 **Nassogne** Luxembourg, SE Belgium
12 J6 **Nastapoka Islands** *island group* Nunavut, C Canada
93 M19 **Nastola** Etelä-Suomi, S Finland
171 O4 **Nasugbu** Luzon, N Philippines
94 N11 **Näsviken** Gävleborg, C Sweden
Naszód *see* Năsăud
83 I17 **Nata** Central, NE Botswana
54 E11 **Natagaima** Tolima, C Colombia
59 Q14 **Natal** Rio Grande do Norte, E Brazil
168 I11 **Natal** Sumatera, N Indonesia
Natal *see* KwaZulu/Natal
173 L10 **Natal Basin** *var.* Mozambique Basin. *undersea feature* W Indian Ocean
25 R12 **Natalia** Texas, SW USA
172 L10 **Natal Valley** *undersea feature* SW Indian Ocean
Natanya *see* Netanya
143 O7 **Naţanz** Eşfahān, C Iran
13 Q11 **Natashquan** Québec, E Canada
13 Q10 **Natashquan** ≈ Newfoundland and Labrador/Québec, E Canada
22 J7 **Natchez** Mississippi, S USA
22 G6 **Natchitoches** Louisiana, S USA
108 E10 **Naters** Valais, S Switzerland
Nathanya *see* Netanya
92 O3 **Nathorst Land** *physical region* W Svalbard
Nathula *see* Nacula
186 E9 **National Capital District** ◆ *province* S PNG
35 U17 **National City** California, W USA
184 M10 **National Park** Manawatu-Wanganui, North Island, NZ
77 R14 **Natitingou** NW Benin
40 B5 **Natividad, Isla** *island* W Mexico
165 Q10 **Natori** Miyagi, Honshū, C Japan
18 C14 **Natrona Heights** Pennsylvania, NE USA
81 H20 **Natron, Lake** ◎ Kenya/Tanzania
Natsrat *see* Nazerat
166 L7 **Nattalin** Pegu, C Burma
92 J12 **Nattavaara** *Lapp.* Nahtavárr. Norrbotten, N Sweden
109 S3 **Natternbach** Oberösterreich, N Austria
95 M22 **Nättraby** Blekinge, S Sweden
169 P10 **Natuna Besar, Pulau** *island* Kepulauan Natuna, W Indonesia
169 O9 **Natuna Islands** *see* Natuna, Kepulauan
169 O9 **Natuna, Kepulauan** *var.* Natuna Islands. *island group* W Indonesia
169 N9 **Natuna, Laut** *sea* W Indonesia
21 N6 **Natural Bridge** *tourist site* Kentucky, C USA
173 V11 **Naturaliste Fracture Zone** *tectonic feature* E Indian Ocean
173 V10 **Naturaliste Plateau** *undersea feature* E Indian Ocean
Nau *see* Nov
103 O14 **Naucelle** Aveyron, S France
83 D20 **Nauchas** Hardap, C Namibia
108 K9 **Nauders** Tirol, W Austria
Naugard *see* Nowogard
118 F12 **Naujamiestis** Panevėžys, C Lithuania
118 E10 **Naujoji Akmenė** Šiauliai, NW Lithuania
149 R16 **Naukot** *var.* Naokot. Sind, SE Pakistan
101 L16 **Naumburg** *var.* Naumburg an der Saale. Sachsen-Anhalt, C Germany
Naumburg am Queis *see* Nowogrodziec
Naumburg an der Saale *see* Naumburg
191 W15 **Naunau** *ancient monument* Easter Island, Chile, E Pacific Ocean
138 G10 **Nā'ūr** 'Al Āşimah, W Jordan
189 Q8 **Nauru** *off.* Republic of Nauru; *prev.* Pleasant Island. ◆ *republic* W Pacific Ocean
189 Q9 **Nauru International** ✕ S Nauru
Nausari *see* Navsāri
19 Q12 **Nauset Beach** *beach* Massachusetts, NE USA
Naushahra *see* Nowshera
149 P14 **Naushahro Fīroz** Sind, SE Pakistan
Naushara *see* Nowshera
187 X14 **Nausori** Viti Levu, W Fiji
56 F9 **Nauta** Loreto, N Peru
153 O12 **Nautanwa** Uttar Pradesh, N India
41 R13 **Nautla** Veracruz-Llave, E Mexico
Nauzad *see* Now Zād
41 N6 **Nava** Coahuila de Zaragoza, NE Mexico
Navabad *see* Navobod
104 L6 **Nava del Rey** Castilla-León, N Spain
153 S15 **Navadwīp** *prev.* Nabadwip. West Bengal, NE India
104 M9 **Navahermosa** Castilla-La Mancha, C Spain
119 I16 **Navahrudak** *Pol.* Nowogródek, *Rus.* Novogrudok. Hrodzyenskaya Voblasts', W Belarus
119 I16 **Navahrudskaye Wzvyshsha** ▲ W Belarus
36 M8 **Navajo Mount** ▲ Utah, W USA
37 Q9 **Navajo Reservoir** ⊟ New Mexico, SW USA
104 K9 **Navalmoral de la Mata** Extremadura, W Spain
104 K10 **Navalvillar de Pelea** Extremadura, W Spain
97 F17 **Navan** *Ir.* An Uaimh. E Ireland
Navanagar *see* Jāmnagar
118 L12 **Navapolatsk** *Rus.* Novopolotsk. Vitsyebskaya Voblasts', N Belarus
149 P6 **Nāvar, Dasht-e** *Pash.* Dasht-i-Nawar. *desert* C Afghanistan
123 W6 **Navarin, Mys** *headland* NE Russian Federation
63 J25 **Navarino, Isla** *island* S Chile
105 Q4 **Navarra** *Eng./Fr.* Navarre. ◆ *autonomous community* N Spain
Navarre *see* Navarra
105 P4 **Navarrete** La Rioja, N Spain
61 C20 **Navarro** Buenos Aires, E Argentina
105 O12 **Navas de San Juan** Andalucía, S Spain
25 V10 **Navasota** Texas, SW USA
25 U9 **Navasota River** ≈ Texas, SW USA
44 I9 **Navassa Island** ◇ *US unincorporated territory* C West Indies
119 L19 **Navasyolki** *Rus.* Novosëlki. Homyel'skaya Voblasts', SE Belarus
119 H17 **Navayel'nya** *Pol.* Nowojelnia, *Rus.* Novoyel'nya. Hrodzyenskaya Voblasts', W Belarus
171 Y13 **Naver** Papua, E Indonesia
118 H5 **Navesti** ≈ C Estonia
104 J2 **Navia** Asturias, N Spain
104 J2 **Navia** ≈ NW Spain
59 I21 **Naviraí** Mato Grosso do Sul, SW Brazil
126 I6 **Navlya** Bryanskaya Oblast', W Russian Federation
187 X13 **Navoalevu** Vanua Levu, N Fiji
147 R12 **Navobod** *Rus.* Navabad, Novabad. C Tajikistan
147 P13 **Navobod** *Rus.* Navabad. W Tajikistan
Navoi *see* Navoiy
146 M11 **Navoiy** *Rus.* Navoi. Navoiy Viloyati, C Uzbekistan
Navoiyskaya Oblast' *see* Navoiy Viloyati
40 G7 **Navojoa** Sonora, NW Mexico
Navolat *see* Navolato
42 H9 **Navolato** *var.* Navolat. Sinaloa, C Mexico
187 Q13 **Navonda** Ambae, C Vanuatu
Návpaktos *see* Náfpaktos
Návplion *see* Náfplio
77 P14 **Navrongo** N Ghana
154 D12 **Navsāri** *var.* Nausari. Gujarāt, W India
187 X15 **Navua** Viti Levu, W Fiji
138 H8 **Nawá** Dar'ā, S Syria
Nawabashah *see* Nawābshāh
153 S14 **Nawabganj** Rajshahi, NW Bangladesh
153 S14 **Nawābganj** Uttar Pradesh, N India
149 Q15 **Nawābshāh** *var.* Nawabashah. Sind, S Pakistan
153 P14 **Nawāda** Bihār, N India
152 H11 **Nawalgarh** Rājasthān, N India
Nawāl, Sabkhat an *see* Noual, Sebkhet en
Nawar, Dasht-i- *see* Nāvar, Dasht-e
167 N4 **Nawnghkio** *var.* Nawngkio. Shan State, C Burma
Nawngkio *see* Nawnghkio
146 K8 **Navoiy Viloyati** *Rus.* Navoiyskaya Oblast'. ◆ *province* N Uzbekistan
137 U13 **Naxçıvan** *Rus.* Nakhichevan'. SW Azerbaijan
160 I10 **Naxi** Sichuan, C China
115 K21 **Náxos** *var.* Naxos. Náxos, Kykládes, Greece, Aegean Sea
115 K21 **Náxos** *island* Kykládes, Greece, Aegean Sea
40 J11 **Nayarit** ◆ *state* C Mexico
187 Y14 **Nayau** *island* Lau Group, E Fiji
143 S8 **Nāy Band** Yazd, E Iran
165 T2 **Nayoro** Hokkaidō, NE Japan
104 F9 **Nazaré** *var.* Nazare. Leiria, C Portugal
24 M4 **Nazareth** Texas, SW USA
Nazareth *see* Nazerat
173 O8 **Nazareth Bank** *undersea feature* W Indian Ocean
40 K9 **Nazas** Durango, C Mexico
57 F16 **Nazca** Ica, S Peru
193 U9 **Nazca Ridge** *undersea feature* E Pacific Ocean
165 V15 **Naze** *var.* Nase. Kagoshima, Amami-ōshima, SW Japan
138 G9 **Nazerat** *var.* Natsrat, *Ar.* En Nazira, *Eng.* Nazareth. Northern, N Israel
137 R14 **Nazik Gölü** ◎ E Turkey
136 C15 **Nazilli** Aydın, SW Turkey
137 P14 **Nazimiye** Tunceli, E Turkey
Nazinon *see* Red Volta
10 L15 **Nazko** British Columbia, SW Canada
127 O16 **Nazran'** Ingushskaya Respublika, SW Russian Federation
80 J13 **Nazrēt** *var.* Adama, Hadama. Oromo, C Ethiopia
Nazwāh *see* Nizwá
82 J13 **Nchanga** Copperbelt, C Zambia
82 J11 **Nchelenge** Luapula, N Zambia
Ncheu *see* Ntcheu
Ndaghamcha, Sebkra de *see* Te-n-Dghâmcha, Sebkhet
81 G21 **Ndala** Tabora, C Tanzania
82 B11 **N'Dalatando** *Port.* Salazar, Vila Salazar. Cuanza Norte, NW Angola
77 S14 **Ndali** C Benin
81 E18 **Ndeke** SW Uganda
78 J13 **Ndélé** Bamingui-Bangoran, N Central African Republic
79 E19 **Ndendé** Ngounié, S Gabon
79 E20 **Ndindi** Nyanga, S Gabon
78 G11 **Ndjamena** *var.* N'Djamena; *prev.* Fort-Lamy. ● (Chad) Chari-Baguirmi, W Chad
78 G11 **Ndjamena** ✕ Chari-Baguirmi, W Chad
79 D18 **Ndjolé** Moyen-Ogooué, W Gabon
82 J13 **Ndola** Copperbelt, C Zambia
Ndrhamcha, Sebkha de *see* Te-n-Dghâmcha, Sebkhet
79 L15 **Ndu** Orientale, N Dem. Rep. Congo
81 H21 **Nduguti** Singida, C Tanzania
186 M9 **Nduindui** Guadalcanal, C Solomon Islands
Nduke *see* Kolombangara
115 F16 **Néa Anchiálos** *var.* Nea Anhialos, Néa Ankhíalos. Thessalía, C Greece
Nea Anhialos/Néa Ankhíalos *see* Néa Anchiálos
115 H18 **Néa Artáki** Évvoia, C Greece
97 F15 **Neagh, Lough** ◎ E Northern Ireland, UK
32 F7 **Neah Bay** Washington, NW USA
115 J22 **Nea Kaméni** *island* Kykládes, Greece, Aegean Sea
181 O8 **Neale, Lake** ◎ Northern Territory, C Australia
182 G2 **Neales River** *seasonal river* South Australia
115 G14 **Néa Moudanía** *var.* Néa Moudhaniá. Kentrikí Makedonía, N Greece
Néa Moudhaniá *see* Néa Moudanía
116 K10 **Neamţ** ◆ *county* NE Romania
Neapel *see* Napoli
115 D14 **Neápoli** *prev.* Neápolis. Dytikí Makedonía, N Greece
115 K25 **Neápoli** Kríti, Greece, E Mediterranean Sea
115 G22 **Neápoli** Pelopónnisos, S Greece
Neapolis *see* Napoli, Italy
Neapolis *see* Nablus, West Bank
Neápolis *see* Neápoli, Greece
38 D16 **Near Islands** *island group* Aleutian Islands, Alaska, USA
97 J21 **Neath** S Wales, UK
114 H13 **Néa Zíchni** *var.* Néa Zíkhni; *prev.* Néa Zíkhna. Kentrikí Makedonía, NE Greece
Néa Zíkhna/Néa Zíkhni *see* Néa Zíchni
42 C5 **Nebaj** Quiché, W Guatemala
77 P13 **Nebbou** S Burkina
Nebitdag *see* Balkanabat
54 M13 **Neblina, Pico da** ▲ NW Brazil
124 I13 **Nebolchi** Novgorodskaya Oblast', W Russian Federation
36 L4 **Nebo, Mount** ▲ Utah, W USA
28 L14 **Nebraska** *off.* State of Nebraska; also known as Blackwater State, Cornhusker State, Tree Planters State. ◆ *state* C USA
29 S16 **Nebraska City** Nebraska, C USA
107 K23 **Nebrodi, Monti** *var.* Monti Caronie. ▲ Sicilia, Italy, C Mediterranean Sea
10 L14 **Nechako** ≈ British Columbia, SW Canada
29 Q2 **Neche** North Dakota, N USA
25 V8 **Neches** Texas, SW USA
25 W8 **Neches River** ≈ Texas, SW USA
101 H20 **Neckar** ≈ SW Germany
101 H20 **Neckarsulm** Baden-Württemberg, SW Germany
192 L5 **Necker Island** *island* C British Virgin Islands
61 D23 **Necochea** Buenos Aires, E Argentina
104 H2 **Neda** Galicia, NW Spain
115 E20 **Nédas** ≈ S Greece
25 Y11 **Nederland** Texas, SW USA
Nederland *see* Netherlands
98 K12 **Neder Rijn** *Eng.* Lower Rhine. ≈ C Netherlands
99 L16 **Nederweert** Limburg, SE Netherlands
95 G16 **Nedre Tokke** ◎ S Norway
Nedrigaylov *see* Nedryhayliv
117 S3 **Nedryhayliv** *Rus.* Nedrigaylov. Sums'ka Oblast', NE Ukraine
98 O11 **Neede** Gelderland, E Netherlands
33 T13 **Needle Mountain** ▲ Wyoming, C USA
35 Y14 **Needles** California, W USA
97 M24 **Needles, The** *rocks* Isle of Wight, S England, UK
62 O7 **Ñeembucú** *off.* Departamento de Ñeembucú. ◆ *department* SW Paraguay
30 M7 **Neenah** Wisconsin, N USA
11 W16 **Neepawa** Manitoba, S Canada
99 K16 **Neerpelt** Limburg, NE Belgium
74 M6 **Nefta** ✕ W Tunisia
126 L15 **Neftegorsk** Krasnodarskiy Kray, SW Russian Federation
127 U3 **Neftekamsk** Respublika Bashkortostan, W Russian Federation
127 O14 **Neftekumsk** Stavropol'skiy Kray, SW Russian Federation
Neftezavodsk *see* Seýdi
82 C10 **Negage** *var.* N'Gage. Uíge, NW Angola
Negapatam/Negapattinam *see* Nāgappattinam
169 T17 **Negara** Bali, Indonesia
169 T13 **Negara** Borneo, C Indonesia
Negara Brunei Darussalam *see* Brunei
31 N4 **Negaunee** Michigan, N USA
81 J15 **Negēlē** *var.* Negelli, *It.* Neghelli. Oromo, C Ethiopia
Negelli *see* Negēlē
Negeri Pahang Darul Makmur *see* Pahang
Negeri Selangor Darul Ehsan *see* Selangor
168 K9 **Negeri Sembilan** *var.* Negri Sembilan. ◆ *state* Peninsular Malaysia
92 P3 **Negerpynten** *headland* S Svalbard
Negev *see* HaNegev
Neghelli *see* Negēlē
116 I12 **Negoiu** *var.* Negoiul. ▲ S Romania
Negoiul *see* Negoiu
82 P13 **Negomane** *var.* Negomano. Cabo Delgado, N Mozambique
Negomano *see* Negomane
155 J25 **Negombo** Western Province, SW Sri Lanka
Negoreloye *see* Nyeharelaye
112 P12 **Negotin** Serbia, E Serbia and Montenegro (Yugo.)
113 P19 **Negotino** C FYR Macedonia
56 A10 **Negra, Punta** *headland* NW Peru
104 G3 **Negreira** Galicia, NW Spain
116 L10 **Negreşti** Vaslui, E Romania
Negreşti *see* Negreşti-Oaş
116 H8 **Negreşti-Oaş** *Hung.* Avasfelsőfalu; *prev.* Negreşti. Satu Mare, NE Romania
44 H12 **Negril** W Jamaica
Negri Sembilan *see* Negeri Sembilan
63 K15 **Negro, Río** ≈ E Argentina
62 N7 **Negro, Río** ≈ NE Argentina
57 N17 **Negro, Río** ≈ E Bolivia
62 O5 **Negro, Río** ≈ C Paraguay
58 D12 **Negro, Río** ≈ N South America

◆ Country ● Country Capital ◇ Dependent Territory ○ Dependent Territory Capital ◆ Administrative Region ✕ International Airport ▲ Mountain ▲ Mountain Range ⚠ Volcano ◎ Lake ≈ River ⊟ Reservoir

61 E18 **Negro, Río** ≈ Brazil/Uruguay
Negro, Río see Sico Tinto, Río, Honduras
Negro, Río see Chixoy, Río, Guatemala/Mexico
171 P6 **Negros** island C Philippines
116 M15 **Negru Vodă** Constanţa, SE Romania
13 P13 **Neguac** New Brunswick, SE Canada
14 B7 **Negwazu, Lake** ◎ Ontario, S Canada
Négyfalu see Săcele
32 F10 **Nehalem** Oregon, NW USA
32 F10 **Nehalem River** ≈ Oregon, NW USA
Nehavend see Nahāvand
143 V9 **Nehbandān** Khorāsān, E Iran
163 V6 **Nehe** Heilongjiang, NE China
193 Y14 **Neiafu** 'Uta Vava'u, N Tonga
45 N9 **Neiba** var. Neyba. SW Dominican Republic
Néid, Carn Uí see Mizen Head
92 M9 **Neiden** Finnmark, N Norway
Neidín see Kenmare
Néifinn see Nephin
103 S10 **Neige, Crêt de la** ▲ E France
173 O16 **Neiges, Piton des** ▲ C Réunion
15 R9 **Neiges, Rivière des** ≈ Québec, SE Canada
160 I10 **Neijiang** Sichuan, C China
30 K6 **Neillsville** Wisconsin, N USA
Nei Monggol Zizhiqu/ Nei Mongol see Nei Mongol Zizhiqu
163 Q10 **Nei Mongol Gaoyuan** plateau NE China
163 O12 **Nei Mongol Zizhiqu** var. Nei Mongol, Eng. Inner Mongolia, Inner Mongolian Autonomous Region; prev. Nei Monggol Zizhiqu. ◈ autonomous region N China
161 O4 **Neiqiu** Hebei, E China
Neiriz see Neyrīz
101 Q16 **Neisse** Cz. Lužická Nisa, Ger. Lausitzer Neisse, Pol. Nisa, Nysa Łużycka. ≈ C Europe
Neisse see Nysa
54 E11 **Neiva** Huila, S Colombia
160 M7 **Neixiang** Henan, C China
Nejafabad see Najafābād
11 V9 **Nejanilini Lake** ◎ Manitoba, C Canada
Nejd see Najd
80 I13 **Nek'emtē** var. Lakemti, Nakamti. Oromo, C Ethiopia
126 M9 **Nekhayevskiy** Volgogradskaya Oblast', SW Russian Federation
30 K7 **Nekoosa** Wisconsin, N USA
Neksø see Nexø
115 C16 **Nekyomanteío** ancient monument Ípeiros, W Greece
104 H7 **Nelas** Viseu, N Portugal
124 H16 **Nelidovo** Tverskaya Oblast', W Russian Federation
29 P13 **Neligh** Nebraska, C USA
123 R11 **Nel'kan** Khabarovskiy Kray, E Russian Federation
92 M10 **Nellim** var. Nellimö, Lapp. Njellim. Lappi, N Finland
Nellimö see Nellim
155 J18 **Nellore** Andhra Pradesh, E India
123 T14 **Nel'ma** Khabarovskiy Kray, SE Russian Federation
61 B17 **Nelson** Santa Fe, C Argentina
11 O17 **Nelson** British Columbia, SW Canada
185 I14 **Nelson** Nelson, South Island, NZ
97 L17 **Nelson** NW England, UK
29 P17 **Nelson** Nebraska, C USA
185 J14 **Nelson** ◈ unitary authority South Island, NZ
11 X12 **Nelson** ≈ Manitoba, C Canada
183 U8 **Nelson Bay** New South Wales, SE Australia
182 K13 **Nelson, Cape** headland Victoria, SE Australia
63 G23 **Nelson, Estrecho** strait SE Pacific Ocean
11 W12 **Nelson House** Manitoba, C Canada
30 J4 **Nelson Lake** ◎ Wisconsin, N USA
31 T14 **Nelsonville** Ohio, N USA
27 S2 **Nelsoon River** ≈ Iowa/Missouri, C USA
83 K21 **Nelspruit** Mpumalanga, NE South Africa
76 L10 **Néma** Hodh ech Chargui, SE Mauritania
118 D13 **Neman** Ger. Ragnit. Kaliningradskaya Oblast', W Russian Federation
84 I9 **Neman** Bel. Nyoman, Ger. Memel, Lith. Nemunas, Pol. Niemen, Rus. Neman. ≈ NE Europe
Nemausus see Nîmes
115 F19 **Neméa** Pelopónnisos, S Greece
Německý Brod see Havlíčkův Brod
14 D7 **Nemegosenda** ≈ Ontario, S Canada
14 D8 **Nemegosenda Lake** ◎ Ontario, S Canada
119 H14 **Nemencinė** Vilnius, SE Lithuania
Nemetocenna see Arras
Nemirov see Nemyriv
103 O6 **Nemours** Seine-et-Marne, N France
Nemunas see Neman
165 W4 **Nemuro** Hokkaidō, NE Japan
165 W4 **Nemuro-hantō** peninsula Hokkaidō, NE Japan
165 W3 **Nemuro-kaikyō** strait Japan/Russian Federation
165 W4 **Nemuro-wan** bay N Japan
116 H5 **Nemyriv** Rus. Nemirov. L'vivs'ka Oblast', NW Ukraine
117 N7 **Nemyriv** Rus. Nemirov. Vinnyts'ka Oblast', C Ukraine
97 D19 **Nenagh** Ir. An tAonach. C Ireland
39 R9 **Nenana** Alaska, USA
39 R9 **Nenana River** ≈ Alaska, USA
187 P10 **Nendö** var. Swallow Island. island Santa Cruz Islands, E Solomon Islands
97 O19 **Nene** ≈ E England, UK
125 R4 **Nenetskiy Avtonomnyy Okrug** ◈ autonomous district NW Russian Federation
191 W11 **Nengonengo** atoll Îles Tuamotu, C French Polynesia
163 U6 **Nen Jiang** var. Nonni. ≈ NE China
163 V6 **Nenjiang** Heilongjiang, NE China
189 P16 **Neoch** atoll Caroline Islands, C Micronesia
115 D18 **Neochóri** Dytikí Ellás, C Greece
27 Q7 **Neodesha** Kansas, C USA
29 S14 **Neola** Iowa, C USA
115 M19 **Néon Karlovási** var. Néon Karlovásion. Sámos, Dodekánisos, Greece, Aegean Sea
Néon Karlovásion see Néon Karlovási
115 E16 **Néon Monastíri** Thessalía, C Greece
27 R8 **Neosho** Missouri, C USA
27 Q7 **Neosho River** ≈ Kansas/Oklahoma, C USA
123 N12 **Nepa** ≈ C Russian Federation
153 N10 **Nepal** off. Kingdom of Nepal. ◆ monarchy S Asia
152 M11 **Nepalganj** Mid Western, SW Nepal
14 L13 **Nepean** Ontario, SE Canada
36 L4 **Nephi** Utah, W USA
97 B16 **Nephin** Ir. Néifinn. ▲ W Ireland
18 K15 **Neptune** New Jersey, NE USA
182 G10 **Neptune Islands** island group South Australia
107 I14 **Nera** anc. Nar. ≈ C Italy
102 L14 **Nérac** Lot-et-Garonne, SW France
111 D16 **Neratovice** Ger. Neratowitz. Středočeský Kraj, C Czech Republic
Neratowitz see Neratovice
123 O13 **Nercha** ≈ S Russian Federation
123 O13 **Nerchinsk** Chitinskaya Oblast', S Russian Federation
123 P14 **Nerchinskiy Zavod** Chitinskaya Oblast', S Russian Federation
124 M15 **Nerekhta** Kostromskaya Oblast', NW Russian Federation
118 H10 **Nereta** Aizkraukle, S Latvia
106 K13 **Nereto** Abruzzo, C Italy
113 H15 **Neretva** ≈ Bosnia and Herzegovina/Croatia
115 C17 **Nerikós** ruins Lefkáda, Iónioi Nísoi, Greece, C Mediterranean Sea
83 F15 **Neriquinha** Cuando Cubango, SE Angola
118 I13 **Neris** Bel. Viliya, Pol. Wilia; prev. Pol. Wilja. ≈ Belarus/Lithuania
Neris see Viliya
105 N15 **Nerja** Andalucía, S Spain
126 L16 **Nerl'** ≈ W Russian Federation
105 P12 **Nerpio** Castilla-La Mancha, C Spain
104 J13 **Nerva** Andalucía, S Spain
98 L4 **Nes** Friesland, N Netherlands
94 G13 **Nesbyen** Buskerud, S Norway
92 L2 **Neskaupstadhur** Austurland, E Iceland
92 F13 **Nesna** Nordland, C Norway
26 K5 **Ness City** Kansas, C USA
Nesselsdorf see Kopřivnice
108 H7 **Nesslau** Sankt Gallen, NE Switzerland
96 I9 **Ness, Loch** ◎ N Scotland, UK
Nesterov see Zhovkva
114 I12 **Néstos** Bul. Mesta, Turk. Kara Su. ≈ Bulgaria/Greece see also Mesta
95 C14 **Nesttun** Hordaland, S Norway
Nesvizh see Nyasvizh
138 F9 **Netanya** var. Natanya, Nathanya. Central, C Israel
98 I9 **Netherlands** off. Kingdom of the Netherlands, var. Holland, Dut. Koninkrijk der Nederlanden, Nederland. ◆ monarchy NW Europe
45 S9 **Netherlands Antilles** prev. Dutch West Indies. ◇ Dutch autonomous region S Caribbean Sea
Netherlands East Indies see Indonesia
Netherlands Guiana see Surinam
Netherlands New Guinea see Papua
116 L4 **Netishyn** Khmel'nyts'ka Oblast', W Ukraine
138 E11 **Netivot** Southern, S Israel
107 O21 **Neto** ≈ S Italy
9 Q6 **Nettilling Lake** ◎ Baffin Island, Nunavut, N Canada
29 V3 **Nett Lake** ◎ Minnesota, N USA
107 I16 **Nettuno** Lazio, C Italy
Netum see Noto
41 U16 **Netzahualcóyotl, Presa** ▣ SE Mexico
Netze see Noteć
Neu Amerika see Puławy
Neubetsche see Novi Bečej
Neubidschow see Nový Bydžov
Neubistritz see Nová Bystřice
100 N9 **Neubrandenburg** Mecklenburg-Vorpommern, NE Germany
101 K22 **Neuburg an der Donau** Bayern, S Germany
108 C8 **Neuchâtel** Ger. Neuenburg. Neuchâtel, W Switzerland
108 C8 **Neuchâtel** Ger. Neuenburg. ◈ canton W Switzerland
108 C8 **Neuchâtel, Lac de** Ger. Neuenburger See. ◎ W Switzerland
Neudorf see Spišská Nová Ves
100 L10 **Neue Elde** canal N Germany
Neuenburg see Neuchâtel
Neuenburg an der Elbe see Nymburk
Neuenburger See see Neuchâtel, Lac de
108 F7 **Neuenhof** Aargau, N Switzerland
100 H11 **Neuenland** × (Bremen) Bremen, NW Germany
Neuenstadt see La Neuveville
101 C18 **Neuerburg** Rheinland-Pfalz, W Germany
99 K24 **Neufchâteau** Luxembourg, SE Belgium
103 S6 **Neufchâteau** Vosges, NE France
102 M3 **Neufchâtel-en-Bray** Seine-Maritime, N France
109 S3 **Neufelden** Oberösterreich, N Austria
Neugradisk see Nova Gradiška
Neuhaus see Jindřichův Hradec
Neuhäusel see Nové Zámky
108 G6 **Neuhausen** var. Neuhausen am Rheinfall. Schaffhausen, N Switzerland
Neuhausen am Rheinfall see Neuhausen
101 I17 **Neuhof** Hessen, C Germany
Neuhof see Zgierz
Neukuhren see Pionerskiy
Neu-Langenburg see Tukuyu
109 W4 **Neulengbach** Niederösterreich, NE Austria
113 G15 **Neum** Federacija Bosna I Hercegovina, S Bosnia and Herzegovina
Neumark see Nowy Targ, Nowy Sącz, Poland
Neumark see Nowe Miasto Lubawskie, Toruń, Poland
Neumarkt see Neumarkt im Hausruckkreis, Oberösterreich, Austria
Neumarkt see Neumarkt am Wallersee, Salzburg, Austria
Neumarkt see Środa Śląska, Wrocław, Poland
Neumarkt see Târgu Secuiesc, Covasna, Romania
Neumarkt see Târgu Mureş, Mureş, Romania
109 Q5 **Neumarkt am Wallersee** var. Neumarkt. Salzburg, NW Austria
109 R4 **Neumarkt im Hausruckkreis** var. Neumarkt. Oberösterreich, N Austria
101 L20 **Neumarkt in der Oberpfalz** Bayern, SE Germany
Neumarktl see Tržič
Neumoldowa see Moldova Nouă
100 J8 **Neumünster** Schleswig-Holstein, N Germany
109 X5 **Neunkirchen** var. Neunkirchen am Steinfeld. Niederösterreich, E Austria
101 E20 **Neunkirchen** Saarland, SW Germany
Neunkirchen am Steinfeld see Neunkirchen
Neuoderberg see Bohumín
63 I15 **Neuquén** Neuquén, SE Argentina
63 H14 **Neuquén** off. Provincia de Neuquén. ◈ province W Argentina
63 H14 **Neuquén, Río** ≈ W Argentina
Neurode see Nowa Ruda
100 N11 **Neuruppin** Brandenburg, NE Germany
Neusalz an der Oder see Nowa Sól
Neu Sandec/Neusandez see Małopolskie
101 K22 **Neusäss** Bayern, S Germany
Neusatz see Novi Sad
Neuschliss see Gherla
21 N8 **Neuse River** ≈ North Carolina, SE USA
109 Z5 **Neusiedl am See** Burgenland, E Austria
111 G22 **Neusiedler See** Hung. Fertő. ◎ Austria/Hungary
Neusohl see Banská Bystrica
101 D15 **Neuss** anc. Novaesium, Novesium. Nordrhein-Westfalen, W Germany
Neuss see Nyon
Neustadt see Neustadt an der Aisch, Bayern, Germany
Neustadt see Neustadt bei Coburg, Bayern, Germany
Neustadt see Prudnik, Opole, Poland
Neustadt see Baia Mare, Maramureş, Romania
100 I12 **Neustadt am Rübenberge** Niedersachsen, N Germany
101 J19 **Neustadt an der Aisch** var. Neustadt. Bayern, C Germany
Neustadt an der Haardt see Neustadt an der Weinstrasse
101 F20 **Neustadt an der Weinstrasse** prev. Neustadt an der Haardt, hist. Niewenstat, anc. Nova Civitas. Rheinland-Pfalz, SW Germany
101 K18 **Neustadt bei Coburg** var. Neustadt. Bayern, C Germany
Neustadt bei Pinne see Lwówek
Neustadt in Oberschlesien see Prudnik
Neustadtl see Novo mesto
Neustadtl in Mähren see Nové Město na Moravě
Neustettin see Szczecinek
108 M8 **Neustift im Stubaital** var. Stubaital. Tirol, W Austria
100 N10 **Neustrelitz** Mecklenburg-Vorpommern, NE Germany
Neutitschein see Nový Jičín
Neutra see Nitra
101 J22 **Neu-Ulm** Bayern, S Germany
Neuveville see La Neuveville
103 N12 **Neuvic** Corrèze, C France
Neuwarp see Nowe Warpno
100 G9 **Neuwerk** island NW Germany
101 E17 **Neuwied** Rheinland-Pfalz, W Germany
Neuzen see Terneuzen
126 H12 **Neva** ≈ NW Russian Federation
29 V14 **Nevada** Iowa, C USA
27 R6 **Nevada** Missouri, C USA
35 R5 **Nevada** off. State of Nevada; also known as Battle Born State, Sagebrush State, Silver State. ◈ state W USA
35 P6 **Nevada City** California, W USA
124 G16 **Nevel'** Pskovskaya Oblast', W Russian Federation
123 T14 **Nevel'sk** Ostrov Sakhalin, Sakhalinskaya Oblast', SE Russian Federation
123 Q13 **Never** Amurskaya Oblast', SE Russian Federation
127 Q6 **Neverkino** Penzenskaya Oblast', W Russian Federation
103 P9 **Nevers** anc. Noviodunum. Nièvre, C France
18 J12 **Neversink River** ≈ New York, NE USA
183 Q6 **Nevertire** New South Wales, SE Australia
113 H15 **Nevesinje** Republika Srpska, S Bosnia and Herzegovina
118 G12 **Nevėžis** ≈ C Lithuania
126 M14 **Nevinnomyssk** Stavropol'skiy Kray, SW Russian Federation
45 W10 **Nevis** island Saint Kitts and Nevis
Nevoso, Monte see Veliki Snežnik
Nevrokop see Gotse Delchev
136 J14 **Nevşehir** var. Nevshehr. Nevşehir, C Turkey
136 J14 **Nevşehir** var. Nevshehr. ◈ province C Turkey
Nevshehr see Nevşehir
122 G10 **Nev'yansk** Sverdlovskaya Oblast', C Russian Federation
81 J25 **Newala** Mtwara, SE Tanzania
31 P16 **New Albany** Indiana, N USA
22 M2 **New Albany** Mississippi, S USA
29 Y11 **New Albin** Iowa, C USA
55 U8 **New Amsterdam** E Guyana
183 Q4 **New Angledool** New South Wales, SE Australia
21 Y2 **Newark** Delaware, NE USA
18 K14 **Newark** New Jersey, NE USA
18 G10 **Newark** New York, NE USA
31 T13 **Newark** Ohio, N USA
Newark see Newark-on-Trent
35 W5 **Newark Lake** ◎ Nevada, W USA
97 N18 **Newark-on-Trent** var. Newark. C England, UK
22 M7 **New Augusta** Mississippi, S USA
19 P12 **New Bedford** Massachusetts, NE USA
32 G11 **Newberg** Oregon, NW USA
21 X10 **New Bern** North Carolina, SE USA
20 F8 **Newbern** Tennessee, S USA
31 P4 **Newberry** Michigan, N USA
21 Q12 **Newberry** South Carolina, SE USA
18 F15 **New Bloomfield** Pennsylvania, NE USA
25 X5 **New Boston** Texas, SW USA
25 S11 **New Braunfels** Texas, SW USA
31 Q13 **New Bremen** Ohio, N USA
97 F18 **Newbridge** Ir. An Droichead Nua. C Ireland
18 B14 **New Brighton** Pennsylvania, NE USA
18 M12 **New Britain** Connecticut, NE USA
186 G7 **New Britain** island E PNG
192 I8 **New Britain Trench** undersea feature W Pacific Ocean
18 J15 **New Brunswick** New Jersey, NE USA
15 V8 **New Brunswick** Fr. Nouveau-Brunswick. ◈ province SE Canada
18 K13 **Newburgh** New York, NE USA
97 M22 **Newbury** S England, UK
19 P10 **Newburyport** Massachusetts, NE USA
77 T14 **New Bussa** Niger, W Nigeria
187 O17 **New Caledonia** var. Kanaky, Fr. Nouvelle-Calédonie. ◇ French overseas territory SW Pacific Ocean
187 O15 **New Caledonia** island SW Pacific Ocean
192 K10 **New Caledonia Basin** undersea feature W Pacific Ocean
183 T8 **Newcastle** New South Wales, SE Australia
13 O14 **Newcastle** New Brunswick, SE Canada
14 I15 **Newcastle** Ontario, SE Canada
97 C20 **Newcastle** Ir. An Caisleán Nua. SW Ireland
83 K22 **Newcastle** KwaZulu/Natal, E South Africa
97 G16 **Newcastle** Ir. An Caisleán Nua. SE Northern Ireland, UK
31 P13 **New Castle** Indiana, N USA
20 L5 **New Castle** Kentucky, S USA
27 N11 **Newcastle** Oklahoma, C USA
18 B13 **New Castle** Pennsylvania, NE USA
25 R6 **Newcastle** Texas, SW USA
36 J7 **Newcastle** Utah, W USA
21 S6 **New Castle** Virginia, NE USA
33 Z13 **Newcastle** Wyoming, C USA
45 W10 **Newcastle** × Nevis, Saint Kitts and Nevis
97 L14 **Newcastle** × NE England, UK
Newcastle see Newcastle upon Tyne
97 L18 **Newcastle-under-Lyme** C England, UK
97 M14 **Newcastle upon Tyne** var. Newcastle; hist. Monkchester, Lat. Pons Aelii. NE England, UK
181 Q4 **Newcastle Waters** Northern Territory, N Australia
Newchwang see Yingkou
18 K13 **New City** New York, NE USA
31 U13 **Newcomerstown** Ohio, N USA
18 G15 **New Cumberland** Pennsylvania, NE USA
21 R1 **New Cumberland** West Virginia, NE USA
152 I10 **New Delhi** ● (India) Delhi, N India
11 O17 **New Denver** British Columbia, SW Canada
28 J9 **Newell** South Dakota, N USA
21 Q13 **New Ellenton** South Carolina, SE USA
22 J6 **Newellton** Louisiana, S USA
28 K6 **New England** North Dakota, N USA
19 P8 **New England** cultural region NE USA
New England of the West see Minnesota
183 U5 **New England Range** ⛰ New South Wales, SE Australia
64 G9 **New England Seamounts** var. Bermuda-New England Seamount Arc. undersea feature W Atlantic Ocean
38 M14 **Newenham, Cape** headland Alaska, USA
138 F11 **Newé Zohar** Southern, E Israel
18 D9 **Newfane** New York, NE USA
97 M23 **New Forest** physical region S England, UK
13 T12 **Newfoundland** Fr. Terre-Neuve. island Newfoundland and Labrador, SE Canada
13 R9 **Newfoundland and Labrador** Fr. Terre Neuve. ◈ province E Canada
65 J8 **Newfoundland Basin** undersea feature NW Atlantic Ocean
64 I8 **Newfoundland Ridge** undersea feature NW Atlantic Ocean
64 J8 **Newfoundland Seamounts** undersea feature N Sargasso Sea
18 G16 **New Freedom** Pennsylvania, NE USA
186 K9 **New Georgia** island New Georgia Islands, NW Solomon Islands
186 K8 **New Georgia Islands** island group NW Solomon Islands
186 L8 **New Georgia Sound** var. The Slot. sound E Solomon Sea
30 L9 **New Glarus** Wisconsin, N USA
13 Q15 **New Glasgow** Nova Scotia, SE Canada
New Goa see Panaji
186 A6 **New Guinea** Dut. Nieuw Guinea, Ind. Irian. island Indonesia/PNG
192 H8 **New Guinea Trench** undersea feature SW Pacific Ocean
32 I6 **Newhalem** Washington, NW USA
39 P13 **Newhalen** Alaska, USA
29 X13 **Newhall** Iowa, C USA
14 F16 **New Hamburg** Ontario, S Canada
19 N9 **New Hampshire** off. State of New Hampshire; also known as The Granite State. ◈ state NE USA
29 W12 **New Hampton** Iowa, C USA
186 G5 **New Hanover** island NE PNG
18 M13 **New Haven** Connecticut, NE USA
31 Q12 **New Haven** Indiana, N USA
27 W5 **New Haven** Missouri, C USA
97 P23 **Newhaven** SE England, UK
10 K13 **New Hazelton** British Columbia, SW Canada
New Hebrides see Vanuatu
192 K9 **New Hebrides Trench** undersea feature N Coral Sea
18 H15 **New Holland** Pennsylvania, NE USA
22 I9 **New Iberia** Louisiana, S USA
186 G5 **New Ireland** ◈ province NE PNG
186 G5 **New Ireland** island NE PNG
65 A24 **New Island** island W Falkland Islands
18 J15 **New Jersey** off. State of New Jersey; also known as The Garden State. ◈ state NE USA
18 C14 **New Kensington** Pennsylvania, NE USA
21 W6 **New Kent** Virginia, NE USA
27 O8 **Newkirk** Oklahoma, C USA
21 Q9 **Newland** North Carolina, SE USA
28 L6 **New Leipzig** North Dakota, N USA
14 H9 **New Liskeard** Ontario, S Canada
22 G7 **Newllano** Louisiana, S USA
19 N13 **New London** Connecticut, NE USA
29 Y15 **New London** Iowa, C USA
29 T8 **New London** Minnesota, N USA
27 V3 **New London** Missouri, C USA
30 M7 **New London** Wisconsin, N USA
27 Y8 **New Madrid** Missouri, C USA
180 J8 **Newman** Western Australia
194 M13 **Newman Island** island Antarctica
14 H15 **Newmarket** Ontario, S Canada
97 P20 **Newmarket** E England, UK
19 P10 **Newmarket** New Hampshire, NE USA
21 U4 **New Market** Virginia, NE USA
21 R2 **New Martinsville** West Virginia, NE USA
31 U14 **New Matamoras** Ohio, N USA
32 M12 **New Meadows** Idaho, NW USA
26 R12 **New Mexico** off. State of New Mexico; also known as Land of Enchantment, Sunshine State. ◈ state SW USA
149 V6 **New Mirpur** var. Mirpur. Sind, SE Pakistan
151 T17 **New Moore Island** island E India
23 S4 **Newnan** Georgia, SE USA
183 P17 **New Norfolk** Tasmania, SE Australia
22 K9 **New Orleans** Louisiana, S USA
22 K9 **New Orleans** × Louisiana, S USA
18 K12 **New Paltz** New York, NE USA
31 U12 **New Philadelphia** Ohio, N USA
184 K10 **New Plymouth** Taranaki, North Island, NZ
97 M24 **Newport** S England, UK
97 K22 **Newport** SE Wales, UK
27 W10 **Newport** Arkansas, C USA
31 N13 **Newport** Indiana, N USA
22 M3 **Newport** Kentucky, S USA
31 W9 **Newport** Minnesota, N USA
34 F12 **Newport** Oregon, NW USA
21 O13 **Newport** Rhode Island, NE USA
23 O9 **Newport** Tennessee, S USA
21 N6 **Newport** Vermont, NE USA
34 M7 **Newport** Washington, NW USA
23 X7 **Newport News** Virginia, NE USA
99 N20 **Newport Pagnell** SE England, UK
25 U12 **New Port Richey** Florida, SE USA
31 V9 **New Prague** Minnesota, N USA
44 H3 **New Providence** island N Bahamas
99 H24 **Newquay** SW England, UK
99 I20 **New Quay** SW Wales, UK
31 V10 **New Richland** Minnesota, N USA
13 X7 **New-Richmond** Québec, SE Canada
31 R15 **New Richmond** Ohio, N USA
32 I5 **New Richmond** Wisconsin, N USA
44 G1 **New River** ≈ N Belize
57 T12 **New River** ≈ SE Guyana
23 R6 **New River** ≈ West Virginia, NE USA
44 G1 **New River Lagoon** ◎ N Belize
24 J8 **New Roads** Louisiana, S USA
20 L14 **New Rochelle** New York, NE USA
31 O4 **New Rockford** North Dakota, N USA
97 P23 **New Romney** SE England, UK
97 F20 **New Ross** Ir. Ros Mhic Thriúin. SE Ireland
97 F16 **Newry** Ir. An tIúr. SE Northern Ireland, UK
28 M5 **New Salem** North Dakota, N USA
New Sarum see Salisbury
29 W14 **New Sharon** Iowa, C USA
New Siberian Islands see Novosibirskiye Ostrova
23 X11 **New Smyrna Beach** Florida, SE USA
183 O7 **New South Wales** ◈ state SE Australia
39 O13 **New Stuyahok** Alaska, USA
21 N8 **New Tazewell** Tennessee, S USA
38 M12 **Newtok** Alaska, USA
23 S7 **Newton** Georgia, SE USA
29 W14 **Newton** Iowa, C USA
27 N6 **Newton** Kansas, C USA
19 O11 **Newton** Massachusetts, NE USA
22 M5 **Newton** Mississippi, S USA
18 J14 **Newton** New Jersey, NE USA
21 R9 **Newton** North Carolina, SE USA
25 Y9 **Newton** Texas, SW USA
97 J24 **Newton Abbot** SW England, UK
96 K13 **Newton St Boswells** SE Scotland, UK
97 I14 **Newton Stewart** S Scotland, UK
92 O2 **Newtontoppen** ▲ C Svalbard
28 K3 **New Town** North Dakota, N USA
97 J20 **Newtown** E Wales, UK
97 G15 **Newtownabbey** Ir. Baile na Mainistreach. E Northern Ireland, UK
97 G15 **Newtownards** Ir. Baile Nua na hArda. SE Northern Ireland, UK
29 U10 **New Ulm** Minnesota, N USA
28 K10 **New Underwood** South Dakota, N USA
25 V10 **New Waverly** Texas, SW USA
18 K14 **New York** New York, NE USA
18 G10 **New York** ◈ state NE USA
35 X13 **New York Mountains** ⛰ California, W USA
184 K12 **New Zealand** abbrev. NZ. ◆ commonwealth republic SW Pacific Ocean
95 M24 **Nexø** var. Neksø. Bornholm, E Denmark
125 O15 **Neya** Kostromskaya Oblast', NW Russian Federation
Neyba see Neiba
143 Q12 **Neyrīz** var. Neiriz, Niriz. Fārs, S Iran
143 T4 **Neyshābūr** var. Nishapur. Khorāsān, NE Iran
155 J21 **Neyveli** Tamil Nādu, SE India
Nezhin see Nizhyn
33 N10 **Nezperce** Idaho, NW USA
22 H8 **Nezpique, Bayou** ≈ Louisiana, S USA
77 Y13 **Ngadda** ≈ NE Nigeria
N'Gage see Negage
185 G16 **Ngahere** West Coast, South Island, NZ
77 Z12 **Ngala** Borno, NE Nigeria
83 G17 **Ngamiland** ◈ district N Botswana
158 K16 **Ngamring** Xizang Zizhiqu, W China
81 K19 **Ngangerabeli Plain** plain SE Kenya
158 I14 **Ngangla Ringco** ◎ W China
158 G13 **Nganglong Kangri** ▲ W China
158 K15 **Ngangzê Co** ◎ W China
79 F14 **Ngaoundéré** var. N'Gaoundéré. Adamaoua, N Cameroon
81 E20 **Ngara** Kagera, NW Tanzania
188 F8 **Ngardmau Bay** bay Babeldaob, N Palau

◆ Country
● Country Capital
◇ Dependent Territory
○ Dependent Territory Capital
◈ Administrative Region
× International Airport
▲ Mountain
⛰ Mountain Range
Volcano
≈ River
◎ Lake
▣ Reservoir

188 F7 **Ngaregur** *island* Palau Islands, N Palau
Ngarrab *see* Gyaca
184 L7 **Ngaruawahia** Waikato, North Island, NZ
184 N11 **Ngaruroro** ≈ North Island, NZ
190 I16 **Ngatangiia** Rarotonga, S Cook Islands
184 M6 **Ngatea** Waikato, North Island, NZ
166 L8 **Ngathainggyaung** Irrawaddy, SW Burma
Ngatik *see* Ngetik Atoll
Ngau *see* Gau
188 C7 **Ngcheangel** *var.* Kayangel Islands. *island* Palau Islands, N Palau
188 E10 **Ngchemiangel** Babeldaob, N Palau
188 C8 **Ngeaur** *var.* Angaur. *island* Palau Islands, S Palau
188 E10 **Ngerkeai** Babeldaob, N Palau
188 F9 **Ngermechau** Babeldaob, N Palau
188 C8 **Ngeruktabel** *prev.* Urukthapel. *island* Palau Islands, S Palau
188 F8 **Ngetbong** Babeldaob, N Palau
189 T17 **Ngetik Atoll** *var.* Ngatik; *prev.* Los Jardines. *atoll* Caroline Islands, E Micronesia
188 E10 **Ngetkip** Babeldaob, N Palau
Nggamea *see* Qamea
83 C16 **N'Giva** *var.* Ondjiva, *Port.* Vila Pereira de Eça. Cunene, S Angola
79 G20 **Ngo** Plateaux, SE Congo
167 S7 **Ngoc Lac** Thanh Hoa, N Vietnam
79 G17 **Ngoko** ≈ Cameroon/Congo
81 H19 **Ngorengore** Rift Valley, SW Kenya
159 Q11 **Ngoring Hu** ◎ C China
Ngorolaka *see* Banifing
81 H20 **Ngorongoro Crater** *crater* N Tanzania
79 D19 **Ngounié** *off.* Province de la Ngounié, *var.* La Ngounié. ◐ *province* S Gabon
79 D19 **Ngounié** ≈ Congo/Gabon
78 H10 **Ngoura** *var.* NGoura. Chari-Baguirmi, W Chad
78 G10 **Ngouri** *var.* NGouri; *prev.* Fort-Millot. Lac, W Chad
77 Y10 **Ngourti** Diffa, E Niger
77 Y11 **Nguigmi** *var.* N'Guigmi. Diffa, SE Niger
Nguimbo *see* Lumbala N'Guimbo
188 F15 **Ngulu Atoll** *atoll* Caroline Islands, W Micronesia
187 R14 **Nguna** *island* C Vanuatu
N'Gunza *see* Sumbe
169 U17 **Ngurah Rai** ✕ (Bali) Bali, S Indonesia
77 W12 **Nguru** Yobe, NE Nigeria
Ngwaketze *see* Southern
83 I16 **Ngweze** ≈ S Zambia
83 M17 **Nhamatanda** Sofala, C Mozambique
58 G12 **Nhamundá, Rio** *var.* Jamundá, Yamundá. ≈ N Brazil
60 J7 **Nhandeara** São Paulo, S Brazil
N'Harea *see* Nharêa
82 D12 **Nharêa** *var.* N'Harea, Nhareia. Bié, W Angola
Nhareia *see* Nharêa
167 V12 **Nha Trang** Khanh Hoa, S Vietnam
182 L11 **Nhill** Victoria, SE Australia
83 L22 **Nhlangano** *prev.* Goedgegun. SW Swaziland
181 S1 **Nhulunbuy** Northern Territory, N Australia
77 N10 **Niafounké** Tombouctou, W Mali
31 N5 **Niagara** Wisconsin, N USA
14 H16 **Niagara** ≈ Ontario, S Canada
14 G15 **Niagara Escarpment** *hill range* Ontario, S Canada
14 H16 **Niagara Falls** Ontario, S Canada
18 D9 **Niagara Falls** New York, NE USA
17 S7 **Niagara Falls** *waterfall* Canada/USA
76 K12 **Niagassola** *var.* Nyagassola. Haute-Guinée, NE Guinea
77 R12 **Niamey** ● (Niger) Niamey, SW Niger
77 R12 **Niamey** ✕ Niamey, SW Niger
77 R14 **Niamtougou** N Togo
79 O16 **Niangara** Orientale, NE Dem. Rep. Congo
77 O10 **Niangay, Lac** ◎ E Mali
77 N14 **Niangoloko** SW Burkina
27 U6 **Niangua River** ≈ Missouri, C USA
79 O17 **Nia-Nia** Orientale, NE Dem. Rep. Congo
19 N13 **Niantic** Connecticut, NE USA
163 U7 **Nianzishan** Heilongjiang, NE China
168 H10 **Nias, Pulau** *island* W Indonesia
82 O13 **Niassa** *off.* Província do Niassa. ◐ *province* N Mozambique
191 U10 **Niau** *island* Îles Tuamotu, C French Polynesia
95 G20 **Nibe** Nordjylland, N Denmark
189 Q8 **Nibok** N Nauru
118 C10 **Nīca** Liepāja, W Latvia
Nicaea *see* Nice
42 J9 **Nicaragua** *off.* Republic of Nicaragua. ◆ *republic* Central America
42 K11 **Nicaragua, Lago de** *var.* Cocibolca, Gran Lago, *Eng.* Lake Nicaragua. ◎ S Nicaragua
Nicaragua, Lake *see* Nicaragua, Lago de
64 D11 **Nicaraguan Rise** *undersea feature* NW Caribbean Sea
Nicaria *see* Ikaría
107 N21 **Nicastro** Calabria, SW Italy
103 V15 **Nice** *It.* Nizza; *anc.* Nicaea. Alpes-Maritimes, SE France
Nice *see* Côte d'Azur
Nicephorium *see* Ar Raqqah
12 M9 **Nichicun, Lac** ◎ Québec, E Canada
164 D16 **Nichinan** *var.* Nitinan. Miyazaki, Kyūshū, SW Japan
44 E4 **Nicholas Channel** *channel* N Cuba
Nicholas II Land *see* Severnaya Zemlya
149 U2 **Nicholas Range** *Pash.* Selseleh-ye Kūh-e Vākhān, *Taj.* Qatorkŭhi Vakhon. ▲▲ Afghanistan/Tajikistan
20 M6 **Nicholasville** Kentucky, S USA
44 G2 **Nicholls Town** Andros Island, NW Bahamas
21 U12 **Nichols** South Carolina, SE USA
55 U9 **Nickerie** ◐ *district* NW Surinam
55 V9 **Nickerie Rivier** ≈ NW Surinam
151 P22 **Nicobar Islands** *island group* India, E Indian Ocean
116 L9 **Nicolae Bălcescu** Botoşani, NE Romania
15 P11 **Nicolet** Québec, SE Canada
15 Q12 **Nicolet** ≈ Québec, SE Canada
31 Q4 **Nicolet, Lake** ◎ Michigan, N USA
29 U10 **Nicollet** Minnesota, N USA
61 F19 **Nico Pérez** Florida, S Uruguay
Nicopolis *see* Nikopol, Bulgaria
Nicopolis *see* Nikópoli, Greece
121 P2 **Nicosia** *Gk.* Lefkosía, *Turk.* Lefkoşa. ● (Cyprus) C Cyprus
107 K24 **Nicosia** Sicilia, Italy, C Mediterranean Sea
107 N22 **Nicotera** Calabria, SW Italy
42 K13 **Nicoya** Guanacaste, W Costa Rica
42 L14 **Nicoya, Golfo de** *gulf* W Costa Rica
42 L14 **Nicoya, Península de** *peninsula* NW Costa Rica
Nictheroy *see* Niterói
118 B12 **Nida** *Ger.* Nidden. Klaipėda, SW Lithuania
111 L15 **Nida** ≈ S Poland
Nidaros *see* Trondheim
108 D8 **Nidau** Bern, W Switzerland
101 H17 **Nidda** ≈ W Germany
Nidden *see* Nida
95 F17 **Nidelva** ≈ S Norway
110 L9 **Nidzica** *Ger.* Niedenburg. Warmińsko-Mazurskie, NE Poland,
100 H6 **Niebüll** Schleswig-Holstein, N Germany
Niedenburg *see* Nidzica
99 N25 **Niederanven** Luxembourg, C Luxembourg
103 V4 **Niederbronn-les-Bains** Bas-Rhin, NE France
Niederdonau *see* Niederösterreich
109 S7 **Niedere Tauern** ▲▲ C Austria
101 P14 **Niederlausitz** *Eng.* Lower Lusatia, *Lus.* Donja Łužyca. *physical region* E Germany
109 U5 **Niederösterreich** *off.* Land Niederösterreich, *Eng.* Lower Austria, *Ger.* Niederdonau; *prev.* Lower Danube. ◐ *state* NE Austria
100 G12 **Niedersachsen** *Eng.* Lower Saxony, *Fr.* Basse-Saxe. ◐ *state* NW Germany
79 D17 **Niefang** *var.* Sevilla de Niefang. NW Equatorial Guinea
83 G23 **Niekerkshoop** Northern Cape, W South Africa
99 G17 **Niel** Antwerpen, N Belgium
Niélé *see* Niellé
76 M14 **Niellé** *var.* Niélé. N Ivory Coast
79 O22 **Niemba** Katanga, E Dem. Rep. Congo
111 G15 **Niemcza** *Ger.* Nimptsch. Dolnośląskie, SW Poland
Niemen *see* Neman
92 J13 **Niemisel** Norrbotten, N Sweden
111 H15 **Niemodlin** *Ger.* Falkenberg. Opolskie, S Poland
76 M13 **Niéna** Sikasso, SW Mali
100 H12 **Nienburg** Niedersachsen, N Germany
100 N13 **Nieplitz** ≈ NE Germany
111 L16 **Niepołomice** Małopolskie, S Poland
101 D14 **Niers** ≈ Germany/Netherlands
101 Q15 **Niesky** *Lus.* Niska. Sachsen, E Germany
Nieświeź *see* Nyasvizh
Nieuport *see* Nieuwpoort
98 O8 **Nieuw-Amsterdam** Drenthe, NE Netherlands
55 W9 **Nieuw Amsterdam** Commewijne, NE Surinam
99 M14 **Nieuw-Bergen** Limburg, SE Netherlands
98 O7 **Nieuw-Buinen** Drenthe, NE Netherlands
98 J12 **Nieuwegein** Utrecht, C Netherlands
98 P6 **Nieuwe Pekela** Groningen, NE Netherlands
98 P5 **Nieuweschans** Groningen, NE Netherlands
Nieuw Guinea *see* New Guinea
98 I11 **Nieuwkoop** Zuid-Holland, C Netherlands
98 M9 **Nieuwleusen** Overijssel, S Netherlands
98 J11 **Nieuw-Loosdrecht** Utrecht, C Netherlands
55 U9 **Nieuw Nickerie** Nickerie, NW Surinam
98 P5 **Nieuwolda** Groningen, NE Netherlands
99 B17 **Nieuwpoort** *var.* Nieuport. West-Vlaanderen, W Belgium
99 G14 **Nieuw-Vossemeer** Noord-Brabant, S Netherlands
98 F7 **Nieuw-Weerdinge** Drenthe, NE Netherlands
40 L10 **Nieves** Zacatecas, C Mexico
64 O11 **Nieves, Pico de las** ▲ Gran Canaria, Islas Canarias, Spain, NE Atlantic Ocean
103 P8 **Nièvre** ◐ *department* C France
Niewenstat *see* Neustadt an der Weinstrasse
136 I15 **Niğde** Niğde, C Turkey
136 I15 **Niğde** ◐ *province* C Turkey
83 I21 **Nigel** Gauteng, NE South Africa
77 V10 **Niger** *off.* Republic of Niger. ◆ *republic* W Africa
77 T14 **Niger** ◐ *state* C Nigeria
77 T13 **Niger** ≈ W Africa
Niger Cone *see* Niger Fan
64 P13 **Niger Fan** *var.* Niger Cone. *undersea feature* E Atlantic Ocean
77 T13 **Nigeria** *off.* Federal Republic of Nigeria. ◆ *federal republic* W Africa
77 T17 **Niger, Mouths of the** *delta* S Nigeria
185 C24 **Nightcaps** Southland, South Island, NZ
14 F7 **Night Hawk Lake** ◎ Ontario, S Canada
65 M19 **Nightingale Island** *island* S Tristan da Cunha, S Atlantic Ocean
38 M12 **Nightmute** Alaska, USA
114 G13 **Nigríta** Kentrikí Makedonía, NE Greece
143 J15 **Nihing** *Per.* Rūd-e Nahang. ≈ Iran/Pakistan
191 V10 **Nihiru** *atoll* Îles Tuamotu, C French Polynesia
Nihommatsu *see* Nihonmatsu
Nihon *see* Japan
165 P11 **Nihonmatsu** *var.* Nihommatsu, Nihonmatu. Fukushima, Honshū, C Japan
Nihonmatu *see* Nihonmatsu
62 I12 **Nihuil, Embalse del** ⊠ W Argentina
165 O10 **Niigata** Niigata, Honshū, C Japan
155 O11 **Niigata** *off.* Niigata-ken. ◐ *prefecture* Honshū, C Japan
165 G14 **Niihama** Ehime, Shikoku, SW Japan
38 A8 **Ni'ihau** *var.* Niihau. *island* Hawai'i, USA, C Pacific Ocean
165 X12 **Nii-jima** *island* E Japan
165 H12 **Niimi** Okayama, Honshū, SW Japan
165 O10 **Niitsu** *var.* Niitu. Niigata, Honshū, C Japan
Niitu *see* Niitsu
105 P15 **Níjar** Andalucía, S Spain
98 K11 **Nijkerk** Gelderland, C Netherlands
99 H16 **Nijlen** Antwerpen, N Belgium
98 L13 **Nijmegen** *Ger.* Nimwegen; *anc.* Noviomagus. Gelderland, SE Netherlands
98 N10 **Nijverdal** Overijssel, E Netherlands
190 G16 **Nikao** Rarotonga, S Cook Islands
Nikaria *see* Ikaría
124 I2 **Nikel'** Murmanskaya Oblast', NW Russian Federation
171 Q17 **Nikiniki** Timor, S Indonesia
77 S14 **Nikki** E Benin
Niklasmarkt *see* Gheorgheni
39 P10 **Nikolai** Alaska, USA
Nikolaiken *see* Mikołajki
Nikolainkaupunki *see* Länsi-Suomi
Nikolayev *see* Mykolayiv
Nikolayevka *see* Zhetigen
127 P9 **Nikolayevsk** Volgogradskaya Oblast', SW Russian Federation
Nikolayevskaya Oblast' *see* Mykolayivs'ka Oblast'
123 S12 **Nikolayevsk-na-Amure** Khabarovskiy Kray, SE Russian Federation
127 P6 **Nikol'sk** Penzenskaya Oblast', W Russian Federation
125 O13 **Nikol'sk** Vologodskaya Oblast', NW Russian Federation
Nikol'sk *see* Ussuriysk
38 K17 **Nikolski** Umnak Island, Alaska, USA
Nikol'skiy *see* Satpayev
127 V7 **Nikol'skoye** Orenburgskaya Oblast', W Russian Federation
Nikol'sk-Ussuriyskiy *see* Ussuriysk
114 J7 **Nikopol** *anc.* Nicopolis. Pleven, N Bulgaria
117 S9 **Nikopol'** Dnipropetrovs'ka Oblast', SE Ukraine
115 C17 **Nikópoli** *anc.* Nicopolis. *site of ancient city* Ípeiros, W Greece
136 M12 **Niksar** Tokat, N Turkey
143 V14 **Nīkshahr** Sīstān va Balūchestān, SE Iran
113 J16 **Nikšić** Montenegro, SW Serbia and Montenegro (Yugo.)
191 R4 **Nikumaroro** *prev.* Gardner Island, Kemins Island. *atoll* Phoenix Islands, C Kiribati
191 P3 **Nikunau** *var.* Nukunau; *prev.* Byron Island. *atoll* Tungaru, W Kiribati
155 G21 **Nilambūr** Kerala, SW India
35 X16 **Niland** California, W USA
75 X9 **Nile** *Ar.* Nahr an Nīl. ≈ N Africa
80 G8 **Nile** *former province* NW Uganda
75 W7 **Nile Delta** *delta* N Egypt
121 U13 **Nile Fan** *undersea feature* E Mediterranean Sea
31 O11 **Niles** Michigan, N USA
31 V11 **Niles** Ohio, N USA
155 F20 **Nīleswaram** Kerala, SW India
14 K10 **Nilgaut, Lac** ◎ Québec, SE Canada
158 I5 **Nilka** Xinjiang Uygur Zizhiqu, NW China
Nīl, Nahr an *see* Nile
93 N16 **Nilsiä** Itä-Suomi, C Finland
154 F9 **Nīmach** Madhya Pradesh, C India
152 G14 **Nimbāhera** Rājasthān, N India
76 L15 **Nimba, Monts** *var.* Nimba Mountains. ▲▲ W Africa
Nimba Mountains *see* Nimba, Monts
Nimburg *see* Nymburk
103 Q15 **Nîmes** *anc.* Nemausus, Nismes. Gard, S France
152 H11 **Nīm ka Thāna** Rājasthān, N India
183 R11 **Nimmitabel** New South Wales, SE Australia
Nimptsch *see* Niemcza
195 R11 **Nimrod Glacier** *glacier* Antarctica
Nimroze *see* Nīmrūz
148 K8 **Nīmrūz** *var.* Nimroze; *prev.* Chakhānsūr. ◐ *province* SW Afghanistan
81 F16 **Nimule** Eastern Equatoria, S Sudan
Nimwegen *see* Nijmegen
155 C23 **Nine Degree Channel** *channel* India/Maldives
18 G9 **Ninemile Point** *headland* New York, NE USA
173 S8 **Ninetyeast Ridge** *undersea feature* E Indian Ocean
183 P13 **Ninety Mile Beach** *beach* Victoria, SE Australia
184 I2 **Ninety Mile Beach** *beach* North Island, NZ
21 P12 **Ninety Six** South Carolina, SE USA
163 Y9 **Ning'an** Heilongjiang, NE China
161 S9 **Ningbo** *var.* Ning-po, Yin-hsien; *prev.* Ninghsien. Zhejiang, SE China
161 U12 **Ningde** Fujian, SE China
161 P12 **Ningdu** *var.* Meijiang. Jiangxi, S China
Ning'er *see* Pu'er
186 A7 **Ningerum** Western, SW PNG
161 R9 **Ningguo** Anhui, E China
161 S9 **Ninghai** Zhejiang, SE China
Ning-hsia *see* Ningxia
Ninghsien *see* Ningbo
160 J15 **Ningming** *var.* Chengzhong. Guangxi Zhuangzu Zizhiqu, S China
160 H11 **Ningnan** *var.* Pisha. Sichuan, C China
Ning-po *see* Ningbo
Ningsia/Ningsia Hui/Ningsia Hui Autonomous Region *see* Ningxia
160 J5 **Ningxia** *off.* Ningxia Huizu Zizhiqu, *var.* Ning-hsia, Ningsia, *Eng.* Ningsia Hui, Ningsia Hui Autonomous Region. ◐ *autonomous region* N China
159 X10 **Ningxian** Gansu, N China
167 T7 **Ninh Binh** Ninh Binh, N Vietnam
167 V12 **Ninh Hoa** Khanh Hoa, S Vietnam
186 C4 **Ninigo Group** *island group* N PNG
39 Q12 **Ninilchik** Alaska, USA
27 N7 **Ninnescah River** ≈ Kansas, C USA
195 U16 **Ninnis Glacier** *glacier* Antarctica
165 R8 **Ninohe** Iwate, Honshū, C Japan
99 F18 **Ninove** Oost-Vlaanderen, C Belgium
171 O4 **Ninoy Aquino** ✕ (Manila) Luzon, N Philippines
Nio *see* Íos
29 P12 **Niobrara** Nebraska, C USA
28 M12 **Niobrara River** ≈ Nebraska/Wyoming, C USA
79 I20 **Nioki** Bandundu, W Dem. Rep. Congo
76 M11 **Niono** Ségou, C Mali
76 K11 **Nioro** *var.* Nioro du Sahel. Kayes, W Mali
76 G11 **Nioro du Rip** SW Senegal
Nioro du Sahel *see* Nioro
102 K10 **Niort** Deux-Sèvres, W France
172 H14 **Nioumachoua** Mohéli, S Comoros
186 C7 **Nipa** Southern Highlands, W PNG
11 U14 **Nipawin** Saskatchewan, S Canada
12 D12 **Nipigon** Ontario, S Canada
12 D11 **Nipigon, Lake** ◎ Ontario, S Canada
11 S13 **Nipin** ≈ Saskatchewan, C Canada
14 G11 **Nipissing, Lake** ◎ Ontario, S Canada
35 P13 **Nipomo** California, W USA
Nippon *see* Japan
138 K6 **Niqniqiyah, Jabal an** ▲ C Syria
62 I9 **Niquivil** San Juan, W Argentina
171 Y13 **Nirabotong** Papua, E Indonesia
Niriz *see* Neyrīz
163 U7 **Nirji** *var.* Morin Dawa Daurzu Zizhiqu. Nei Mongol Zizhiqu, N China
155 I14 **Nirmal** Andhra Pradesh, C India
153 Q13 **Nirmāli** Bihār, NE India
113 O14 **Niš** *Eng.* Nish, *Ger.* Nisch; *anc.* Naissus. Serbia, SE Serbia and Montenegro (Yugo.)
104 H9 **Nisa** Portalegre, C Portugal
Nisa *see* Neisse
141 P4 **Niṣab** Al Ḥudūd ash Shamālīyah, N Saudi Arabia
141 Q15 **Niṣāb** *var.* Anṣāb. SW Yemen
113 P14 **Nišava** *Bul.* Nishava. ≈ Bulgaria/Serbia and Montenegro (Yugo.) *see also* Nishava
107 K25 **Niscemi** Sicilia, Italy, C Mediterranean Sea
Nisch/Nish *see* Niš
165 R4 **Niseko** Hokkaidō, NE Japan
Nishapur *see* Neyshābūr
114 G9 **Nishava** *var.* Nišava. ≈ Bulgaria/Serbia and Montenegro (Yugo.) *see also* Nišava
118 L11 **Nishcha** *Rus.* Nishcha. ≈ N Belarus
165 C17 **Nishinoomote** Kagoshima, Tanega-shima, SW Japan
165 X15 **Nishino-shima** *Eng.* Rosario. *island* Ogasawara-shotō, SE Japan
165 I13 **Nishiwaki** *var.* Nisiwaki. Hyōgo, Honshū, SW Japan
141 U14 **Nishtūn** SE Yemen
Nisiros *see* Nísyros
Nisiwaki *see* Nishiwaki
Niska *see* Niesky
113 O14 **Niška Banja** Serbia, SE Serbia and Montenegro (Yugo.)
12 D6 **Niskibi** ≈ Ontario, C Canada
111 O15 **Nisko** Podkarpackie, SE Poland
10 H7 **Nisling** ≈ Yukon Territory, W Canada
99 H22 **Nismes** Namur, S Belgium
Nismes *see* Nîmes
116 M10 **Nisporeni** *Rus.* Nisporeny. W Moldova
Nisporeny *see* Nisporeni
95 K20 **Nissan** ≈ S Sweden
Nissan Islands *see* Green Islands
95 F16 **Nisser** ◎ S Norway
95 E21 **Nissum Bredning** *inlet* NW Denmark
29 U6 **Nisswa** Minnesota, N USA
Nistru *see* Dniester
115 M22 **Nísyros** *var.* Nisiros. *island* Dodekánisos, Greece, Aegean Sea
118 H8 **Nītaure** Cēsis, C Latvia
60 P10 **Niterói** *prev.* Nictheroy. Rio de Janeiro, SE Brazil
14 F16 **Nith** ≈ Ontario, S Canada
96 J13 **Nith** ≈ S Scotland, UK
Nitinan *see* Nichinan
111 I21 **Nitra** *Ger.* Neutra, *Hung.* Nyitra. Nitriansky Kraj, SW Slovakia
111 I20 **Nitra** *Ger.* Neutra, *Hung.* Nyitra. ≈ W Slovakia
111 I21 **Nitriansky Kraj** ◐ *region* SW Slovakia
21 Q5 **Nitro** West Virginia, NE USA
95 H14 **Nittedal** Akershus, S Norway
Niuatobutabu *see* Niuatoputapu
193 X13 **Niuatoputapu** *var.* Niuatobutabu; *prev.* Keppel Island. *island* N Tonga
193 U15 **Niu'Aunofa** *headland* Tongatapu, S Tonga
Niuchwang *see* Yingkou
190 B16 **Niue** ◇ *self-governing territory in free association with NZ* S Pacific Ocean
190 F10 **Niulakita** *var.* Nurakita. *atoll* S Tuvalu
190 E6 **Niutao** *atoll* NW Tuvalu
93 L15 **Nivala** Oulu, C Finland
102 I15 **Nive** ≈ SW France
99 G19 **Nivelles** Wallon Brabant, C Belgium
103 P8 **Nivernais** *cultural region* C France
15 N8 **Niverville, Lac** ◎ Québec, SE Canada
27 T7 **Nixa** Missouri, C USA
35 R5 **Nixon** Nevada, W USA
25 S12 **Nixon** Texas, SW USA
Niya *see* Minfeng
Niyazov *see* Nyýazow
155 H14 **Nizāmābād** Andhra Pradesh, C India
155 H15 **Nizām Sāgar** ◎ C India
127 N16 **Nizhegorodskaya Oblast'** ◐ *province* W Russian Federation
Nizhnegorskiy *see* Nyzhn'ohirs'kyy
127 S4 **Nizhnekamsk** Respublika Tatarstan, W Russian Federation
127 U3 **Nizhnekamskoye Vodokhranilishche** ⊠ W Russian Federation
123 S14 **Nizhneleninskoye** Yevreyskaya Avtonomnaya Oblast', SE Russian Federation
122 L13 **Nizhneudinsk** Irkutskaya Oblast', S Russian Federation
122 I10 **Nizhnevartovsk** Khanty-Mansiyskiy Avtonomnyy Okrug, C Russian Federation
123 Q7 **Nizhneyansk** Respublika Sakha (Yakutiya), NE Russian Federation
127 Q11 **Nizhniy Baskunchak** Astrakhanskaya Oblast', SW Russian Federation
127 O6 **Nizhniy Lomov** Penzenskaya Oblast', W Russian Federation
127 P3 **Nizhniy Novgorod** *prev.* Gor'kiy. Nizhegorodskaya Oblast', W Russian Federation
125 T8 **Nizhniy Odes** Respublika Komi, NW Russian Federation
Nizhniy Pyandzh *see* Panji Poyon
122 G10 **Nizhniy Tagil** Sverdlovskaya Oblast', C Russian Federation
125 T9 **Nizhnyaya-Omra** Respublika Komi, NW Russian Federation
125 P5 **Nizhnyaya Pesha** Nenetskiy Avtonomnyy Okrug, NW Russian Federation
117 Q3 **Nizhyn** *Rus.* Nezhin. Chernihivs'ka Oblast', NE Ukraine
136 M17 **Nizip** Gaziantep, S Turkey
141 X8 **Nizwá** *var.* Nazwāh. NE Oman
Nizza *see* Nice
106 C9 **Nizza Monferrato** Piemonte, NE Italy
Njávdám *see* Näätämöjoki
Njellim *see* Nellim
81 H24 **Njombe** Iringa, S Tanzania
81 G23 **Njombe** ≈ C Tanzania
92 I10 **Njunis** ▲ N Norway
93 H17 **Njurunda** Västernorrland, C Sweden
94 N11 **Njutånger** Gävleborg, C Sweden
79 D14 **Nkambe** Nord-Ouest, NW Cameroon
Nkata Bay *see* Nkhata Bay
79 F21 **Nkayi** *prev.* Jacob. La Bouenza, S Congo
83 J17 **Nkayi** Matabeleland North, W Zimbabwe
82 N13 **Nkhata Bay** *var.* Nkata Bay. Northern, N Malawi
81 E22 **Nkonde** Kigoma, N Tanzania
79 D15 **Nkongsamba** *var.* N'Kongsamba. Littoral, W Cameroon
83 E16 **Nkurenkuru** Okavango, N Namibia
77 Q15 **Nkwanta** E Ghana
167 O2 **Nmai Hka** *var.* Me Hka. ≈ N Burma
Noardwâlde *see* Noordwolde
39 N7 **Noatak** Alaska, USA
39 N7 **Noatak River** ≈ Alaska, USA
Nobeji *see* Noheji
164 E15 **Nobeoka** Miyazaki, Kyūshū, SW Japan
27 N11 **Noble** Oklahoma, C USA
31 P13 **Noblesville** Indiana, N USA
165 R5 **Noboribetsu** *var.* Noboribetu. Hokkaidō, NE Japan
Noboribetu *see* Noboribetsu
59 H18 **Nobres** Mato Grosso, W Brazil
107 N21 **Nocera Terinese** Calabria, S Italy
41 Q16 **Nochixtlán** *var.* Asunción Nochixtlán. Oaxaca, SE Mexico
25 S5 **Nocona** Texas, SW USA
63 K21 **Nodales, Bahía de los** *bay* S Argentina
27 Q2 **Nodaway River** ≈ Iowa/Missouri, C USA
27 R8 **Noel** Missouri, C USA
95 C17 **Nærbø** Rogaland, S Norway
95 I24 **Næstved** Storstrøm, SE Denmark
40 H3 **Nogales** Chihuahua, NW Mexico
40 F3 **Nogales** Sonora, NW Mexico
36 M17 **Nogales** Arizona, SW USA
Nogal Valley *see* Dooxo Nugaaleed
102 K15 **Nogaro** Gers, S France
110 J7 **Nogat** ≈ N Poland
164 D12 **Nōgata** Fukuoka, Kyūshū, SW Japan
127 P15 **Nogayskaya Step'** *steppe* SW Russian Federation
102 M6 **Nogent-le-Rotrou** Eure-et-Loir, C France
103 O4 **Nogent-sur-Oise** Oise, N France
103 P6 **Nogent-sur-Seine** Aube, N France
122 L10 **Noginsk** Evenkiyskiy Avtonomnyy Okrug, N Russian Federation
126 L3 **Noginsk** Moskovskaya Oblast', W Russian Federation
123 T12 **Nogliki** Ostrov Sakhalin, Sakhalinskaya Oblast', SE Russian Federation
164 K12 **Nōgōhaku-san** ▲ Honshū, SW Japan
162 D5 **Nogoonnuur** Bayan-Ölgiy, NW Mongolia
61 C18 **Nogoyá** Entre Ríos, E Argentina
111 K21 **Nógrád** *off.* Nógrád Megye. ◐ *county* N Hungary
105 U5 **Noguera Pallaresa** ≈ NE Spain
105 U4 **Noguera Ribagorçana** ≈ NE Spain
101 E19 **Nohfelden** Saarland, SW Germany
38 A8 **Nohili Point** *headland* Kaua'i, Hawai'i, USA, C Pacific Ocean
104 G3 **Noia** Galicia, NW Spain
103 N16 **Noire, Montagne** ▲▲ S France
15 P12 **Noire, Rivière** ≈ Québec, SE Canada
14 J10 **Noire, Rivière** ≈ Québec, SE Canada
Noire, Rivière *see* Black River
102 G6 **Noires, Montagnes** ▲▲ NW France
102 H8 **Noirmoutier-en-l'Île** Vendée, NW France
102 H8 **Noirmoutier, Île de** *island* NW France
187 Q10 **Noka** Nendö, E Solomon Islands
83 G17 **Nokaneng** Ngamiland, NW Botswana
93 L18 **Nokia** Länsi-Suomi, W Finland
148 K11 **Nok Kundi** Baluchistān, SW Pakistan
30 L14 **Nokomis** Illinois, N USA
30 K5 **Nokomis, Lake** ⊠ Wisconsin, N USA
78 G9 **Nokou** Kanem, W Chad
187 Q12 **Nokuku** Espiritu Santo, W Vanuatu
95 J18 **Nol** Västra Götaland, S Sweden
79 H16 **Nola** Sangha-Mbaéré, SW Central African Republic
25 P7 **Nolan** Texas, SW USA
125 R15 **Nolinsk** Kirovskaya Oblast', NW Russian Federation
95 B19 **Nólsoy** *Dan.* Nolsø *Island* Faeroe Islands
186 B7 **Nomad** Western, SW Papau New Guinea
164 B16 **Noma-zaki** *headland* Kyūshū, SW Japan
40 K10 **Nombre de Dios** Durango, C Mexico
42 I5 **Nombre de Dios, Cordillera** ▲▲ N Honduras
38 M9 **Nome** Alaska, USA
29 Q6 **Nome** North Dakota, N USA
38 M9 **Nome, Cape** *headland* Alaska, USA
Nōmi-jima *see* Nishi-Nōmi-jima
14 M11 **Nominingue, Lac** ◎ Québec, SE Canada
Nomoi Islands *see* Mortlock Islands
164 B16 **Nomo-zaki** *headland* Kyūshū, SW Japan
193 X15 **Nomuka** *island* Nomuka Group, C Tonga
193 X15 **Nomuka Group** *island group* W Tonga
189 Q15 **Nomwin Atoll** *atoll* Hall Islands, C Micronesia
8 L10 **Nonacho Lake** ◎ Northwest Territories, NW Canada
Nondaburi *see* Nonthaburi
39 P12 **Nondalton** Alaska, USA
163 V10 **Nong'an** Jilin, NE China
167 P10 **Nong Bua Khok** Nakhon Ratchasima, C Thailand
167 Q9 **Nong Bua Lamphu** Udon Thani, E Thailand
167 R7 **Nông Hèt** Xiangkhoang, N Laos
Nongkaya *see* Nong Khai
167 Q8 **Nong Khai** *var.* Mi Chai, Nongkaya. Nong Khai, E Thailand
167 N14 **Nong Met** Surat Thani, SW Thailand
83 L22 **Nongoma** KwaZulu/Natal, E South Africa
167 P9 **Nong Phai** Phetchabun, C Thailand
153 U13 **Nongstoin** Meghālaya, NE India
83 C19 **Nonidas** Erongo, N Namibia
Nonni *see* Nen Jiang
40 I7 **Nonoava** Chihuahua, N Mexico

◆ Country
● Country Capital
◇ Dependent Territory
○ Dependent Territory Capital
◐ Administrative Region
✕ International Airport
▲ Mountain
▲▲ Mountain Range
Volcano
≈ River
◎ Lake
⊠ Reservoir

191 O3 **Nonouti** *prev.* Sydenham Island. *atoll* Tungaru, W Kiribati
167 O11 **Nonthaburi** *var.* Nondaburi, Nontha Buri. Nonthaburi, C Thailand
102 L11 **Nontron** Dordogne, SW France
181 P1 **Noonamah** Northern Territory, N Australia
28 K2 **Noonan** North Dakota, N USA
99 E14 **Noord-Beveland** *var.* North Beveland. *island* SW Netherlands
99 J14 **Noord-Brabant** *Eng.* North Brabant. ◈ *province* S Netherlands
98 H7 **Noorder Haaks** *spit* NW Netherlands
98 H9 **Noord-Holland** *Eng.* North Holland. ◈ *province* NW Netherlands
Noordhollandsch Kanaal *see* Noordhollands Kanaal
98 H8 **Noordhollands Kanaal** *var.* Noordhollandsch Kanaal. *canal* NW Netherlands
Noord-Kaap *see* Northern Cape
98 L8 **Noordoostpolder** *island* N Netherlands
45 P16 **Noordpunt** *headland* Curaçao, C Netherlands Antilles
98 I8 **Noord-Scharwoude** Noord-Holland, NW Netherlands
Noordwes *see* North-West
98 G11 **Noordwijk aan Zee** Zuid-Holland, W Netherlands
98 H11 **Noordwijkerhout** Zuid-Holland, W Netherlands
98 M7 **Noordwolde** *Fris.* Noardwâlde. Friesland, N Netherlands
Noordzee *see* North Sea
98 H10 **Noordzee-Kanaal** *canal* NW Netherlands
93 K18 **Noormarkku** *Swe.* Norrmark. Länsi-Suomi, W Finland
39 N8 **Noorvik** Alaska, USA
10 J17 **Nootka Sound** *inlet* British Columbia, W Canada
82 A9 **Nóqui** Zaire, NW Angola
95 L15 **Nora** Örebro, C Sweden
147 Q13 **Norak** *Rus.* Nurek. W Tajikistan
13 I13 **Noranda** Quebec, SE Canada
29 W12 **Nora Springs** Iowa, C USA
95 M14 **Norberg** Västmanland, C Sweden
14 K13 **Norcan Lake** ⊚ Ontario, SE Canada
197 R12 **Nord** Avannaarsua, N Greenland
78 F13 **Nord** *Eng.* North. ◈ *province* N Cameroon
103 P2 **Nord** ◈ *department* N France
92 P1 **Nordaustlandet** *island* NE Svalbard
95 G24 **Nordborg** *Ger.* Nordburg. Sønderjylland, SW Denmark
Nordburg *see* Nordborg
95 F23 **Nordby** Ribe, W Denmark
11 P15 **Nordegg** Alberta, SW Canada
100 E9 **Norden** Niedersachsen, NW Germany
100 G10 **Nordenham** Niedersachsen, NW Germany
122 M6 **Nordenshel'da, Arkhipelag** *island group* N Russian Federation
92 O3 **Nordenskiold Land** *physical region* W Svalbard
100 E9 **Norderney** *island* NW Germany
100 J9 **Norderstedt** Schleswig-Holstein, N Germany
94 C11 **Nordfjord** *physical region* S Norway
94 D11 **Nordfjord** *fjord* S Norway
94 D11 **Nordfjordeid** Sogn og Fjordane, S Norway
92 G11 **Nordfold** Nordland, C Norway
Nordfriesische Inseln *see* North Frisian Islands
100 H7 **Nordfriesland** *cultural region* N Germany
101 K15 **Nordhausen** Thüringen, C Germany
25 T13 **Nordheim** Texas, SW USA
94 C13 **Nordhordland** *physical region* S Norway
100 E12 **Nordhorn** Niedersachsen, NW Germany
92 I1 **Nordhurfjördhur** Vestfirdhir, NW Iceland
92 J1 **Nordhurland Eystra** ◈ *region* N Iceland
92 I2 **Nordhurland Vestra** ◈ *region* N Iceland
172 H16 **Nord, Île du** *island* Inner Islands, NE Seychelles
95 F20 **Nordjylland** *off.* Nordjyllands Amt. ◈ *county* N Denmark
92 K7 **Nordkapp** *Eng.* North Cape. *headland* N Norway
92 O1 **Nordkapp** *headland* N Svalbard
92 L7 **Nordkinn** *headland* N Norway
79 N19 **Nord Kivu** *off.* Région du Nord Kivu. ◈ *region* E Dem. Rep. Congo
92 G12 **Nordland** ◈ *county* C Norway
101 J21 **Nördlingen** Bayern, S Germany
93 I16 **Nordmaling** Västerbotten, N Sweden
95 K15 **Nordmark** Värmland, C Sweden
Nord, Mer du *see* North Sea
94 F8 **Nordmøre** *physical region* S Norway
100 I8 **Nord-Ostee-Kanal** *canal* N Germany
79 D14 **Nord-Ouest** *Eng.* North-West. ◈ *province* NW Cameroon
Nord-Ouest, Territoires du *see* Northwest Territories
103 N2 **Nord-Pas-de-Calais** ◈ *region* N France
101 F19 **Nordpfälzer Bergland** ▲ W Germany
Nord, Pointe *see* Fatua, Pointe
187 P16 **Nord, Province** ◈ *province* C New Caledonia
101 D14 **Nordrhein-Westfalen** *Eng.* North Rhine-Westphalia, *Fr.* Rhénanie du Nord-Westphalie. ◈ *state* W Germany
Nordsee/Nordsjøen/Nordsøen *see* North Sea
100 H7 **Nordstrand** *island* N Germany
93 E15 **Nord-Trøndelag** ◈ *county* C Norway
97 E19 **Nore** *Ir.* An Fheoir. ≈ S Ireland
29 Q14 **Norfolk** Nebraska, C USA
21 X7 **Norfolk** Virginia, NE USA
97 P19 **Norfolk** *cultural region* E England, UK
192 K10 **Norfolk Island** ◇ *Australian external territory* SW Pacific Ocean
192 K10 **Norfolk Ridge** *undersea feature* W Pacific Ocean
27 U8 **Norfork Lake** ⊟ Arkansas/Missouri, C USA
98 N6 **Norg** Drenthe, NE Netherlands
Norge *see* Norway
95 D14 **Norheimsund** Hordaland, S Norway
25 S16 **Norias** Texas, SW USA
164 L12 **Norikura-dake** ▲ Honshū, S Japan
122 K8 **Noril'sk** Taymyrskiy (Dolgano-Nenetskiy) Avtonomnyy Okrug, N Russian Federation
14 I13 **Norland** Ontario, SE Canada
21 V8 **Norlina** North Carolina, SE USA
30 L13 **Normal** Illinois, N USA
27 N11 **Norman** Oklahoma, C USA
Norman *see* Tulita
186 G9 **Normanby Island** *island* SE PNG
Normandes, Îles *see* Channel Islands
58 G9 **Normandia** Roraima, N Brazil
102 L5 **Normandie** *Eng.* Normandy. *cultural region* N France
102 J5 **Normandie, Collines de** *hill range* NW France
Normandy *see* Normandie
25 V9 **Normangee** Texas, SW USA
21 Q10 **Norman, Lake** ⊟ North Carolina, SE USA
44 K13 **Norman Manley** × (Kingston) E Jamaica
181 U5 **Norman River** ≈ Queensland, NE Australia
181 U4 **Normanton** Queensland, NE Australia
8 I8 **Norman Wells** Northwest Territories, NW Canada
12 H12 **Normétal** Québec, S Canada
11 V15 **Norquay** Saskatchewan, S Canada
94 N11 **Norra Dellen** ⊚ C Sweden
93 G15 **Norråker** Jämtland, C Sweden
94 N12 **Norrala** Gävleborg, C Sweden
Norra Ny *see* Stöllet
92 G13 **Norra Storjfjället** ▲ N Sweden
92 I13 **Norrbotten** ◈ *county* N Sweden
95 G23 **Nørre Aaby** *var.* Nørre Åby. Fyn, C Denmark
Nørre Åby *see* Nørre Aaby
95 I24 **Nørre Alslev** Storstrøm, SE Denmark
95 E23 **Nørre Nebel** Ribe, W Denmark
95 G20 **Nørresundby** Nordjylland, N Denmark
21 N8 **Norris Lake** ⊟ Tennessee, S USA
18 I15 **Norristown** Pennsylvania, NE USA
95 N17 **Norrköping** Östergötland, S Sweden
Norrmark *see* Noormarkku
94 N13 **Norrsundet** Gävleborg, C Sweden
95 P15 **Norrtälje** Stockholm, C Sweden
180 L12 **Norseman** Western Australia
93 I14 **Norsjö** Västerbotten, N Sweden
95 G16 **Norsjø** ⊚ S Norway
123 R13 **Norsk** Amurskaya Oblast', SE Russian Federation
Norske Havet *see* Norwegian Sea
187 Q13 **Norsup** Malekula, C Vanuatu
191 V15 **Norte, Cabo** *headland* Easter Island, Chile, E Pacific Ocean
54 F7 **Norte de Santander** *off.* Departamento de Norte de Santander. ◈ *province* N Colombia
61 E21 **Norte, Punta** *headland* E Argentina
21 R13 **North** South Carolina, SE USA
North *see* Nord
18 L10 **North Adams** Massachusetts, NE USA
113 L17 **North Albanian Alps** *Alb.* Bjeshkët e Namuna, *SCr.* Prokletije. ▲ Albania/Serbia and Montenegro (Yugo.)
97 M15 **Northallerton** N England, UK
180 J12 **Northam** Western Australia
83 J20 **Northam** Northern, N South Africa
2-7 **North America** *continent*
18 M11 **North Amherst** Massachusetts, NE USA
97 N20 **Northampton** C England, UK
97 M20 **Northamptonshire** *cultural region* C England, UK
151 P18 **North Andaman** *island* Andaman Islands, India, NE Indian Ocean
65 D25 **North Arm** East Falkland, Falkland Islands
21 Q13 **North Augusta** South Carolina, SE USA
173 W8 **North Australian Basin** *Fr.* Bassin Nord de l' Australie. *undersea feature* E Indian Ocean
31 R11 **North Baltimore** Ohio, N USA
11 T15 **North Battleford** Saskatchewan, S Canada
14 H11 **North Bay** Ontario, S Canada
12 H6 **North Belcher Islands** *island group* Belcher Islands, Nunavut, C Canada
29 R15 **North Bend** Nebraska, C USA
32 E14 **North Bend** Oregon, NW USA
96 K12 **North Berwick** SE Scotland, UK
North Beveland *see* Noord-Beveland
North Borneo *see* Sabah
183 P5 **North Bourke** New South Wales, SE Australia
North Brabant *see* Noord-Brabant
182 F2 **North Branch Neales** *seasonal river* South Australia
44 M6 **North Caicos** *island* NW Turks and Caicos Islands
26 L10 **North Canadian River** ≈ Oklahoma, C USA
31 U12 **North Canton** Ohio, N USA
13 R13 **North, Cape** *headland* Cape Breton Island, Nova Scotia, SE Canada
184 I1 **North Cape** *headland* North Island, NZ
186 G5 **North Cape** *headland* New Ireland, NE PNG
North Cape *see* Nordkapp
18 J17 **North Cape May** New Jersey, NE USA
12 C9 **North Caribou Lake** ⊚ Ontario, C Canada
21 U10 **North Carolina** *off.* State of North Carolina; *also known as* Old North State, Tar Heel State, Turpentine State. ◈ *state* SE USA
North Celebes *see* Sulawesi Utara
155 J24 **North Central Province** ◈ *province* N Sri Lanka
31 S4 **North Channel** *lake channel* Canada/USA
97 G14 **North Channel** *strait* Northern Ireland/Scotland, UK
21 S14 **North Charleston** South Carolina, SE USA
31 N10 **North Chicago** Illinois, N USA
195 Y10 **Northcliffe Glacier** *glacier* Antarctica
31 Q14 **North College Hill** Ohio, N USA
25 O8 **North Concho River** ≈ Texas, SW USA
19 O8 **North Conway** New Hampshire, NE USA
27 V14 **North Crossett** Arkansas, C USA
28 L4 **North Dakota** *off.* State of North Dakota; *also known as* Flickertail State, Peace Garden State, Sioux State. ◈ *state* N USA
North Devon Island *see* Devon Island
97 O22 **North Downs** *hill range* SE England, UK
18 C11 **North East** Pennsylvania, NE USA
83 I18 **North East** ◈ *district* NE Botswana
65 G15 **North East Bay** *bay* Ascension Island, C Atlantic Ocean
38 L10 **Northeast Cape** *headland* Saint Lawrence Island, Alaska, USA
81 J17 **North Eastern** ◈ *province* Kenya
North East Frontier Agency/North East Frontier Agency of Assam *see* Arunāchal Pradesh
65 E25 **North East Island** *island* E Falkland Islands
189 V11 **Northeast Island** *island* Chuuk, C Micronesia
44 L12 **North East Point** *headland* E Jamaica
44 L6 **Northeast Point** *headland* Great Inagua, S Bahamas
44 K5 **Northeast Point** *headland* Acklins Island, SE Bahamas
191 Z2 **Northeast Point** *headland* Kiritimati, E Kiribati
44 H2 **Northeast Providence Channel** *channel* N Bahamas
101 J14 **Northeim** Niedersachsen, C Germany
29 X14 **North English** Iowa, C USA
138 G8 **Northern** ◈ *district* N Israel
82 M12 **Northern** ◈ *region* N Malawi
186 F8 **Northern** ◈ *province* S PNG
80 D7 **Northern** ◈ *state* N Sudan
82 K12 **Northern** ◈ *province* NE Zambia
80 B13 **Northern Bahr el Ghazal** ◈ *state* SW Sudan
Northern Border Region *see* Al Ḥudūd ash Shamālīyah
83 F24 **Northern Cape** *off.* Northern Cape Province, *Afr.* Noord-Kaap. ◈ *province* W South Africa
190 K14 **Northern Cook Islands** *island group* N Cook Islands
80 B8 **Northern Darfur** ◈ *state* NW Sudan
Northern Dvina *see* Severnaya Dvina
97 F14 **Northern Ireland** *var.* The Six Counties. *political division* UK
80 D9 **Northern Kordofan** ◈ *state* C Sudan
187 Z14 **Northern Lau Group** *island group* Lau Group, NE Fiji
188 K3 **Northern Mariana Islands** ◇ *US commonwealth territory* W Pacific Ocean
155 J23 **Northern Province** ◈ *province* N Sri Lanka
Northern Province *see* Limpopo
Northern Rhodesia *see* Zambia
Northern Sporades *see* Vóreioi Sporádes
182 D1 **Northern Territory** ◈ *territory* N Australia
Northern Transvaal *see* Limpopo
Northern Ural Hills *see* Severnyye Uvaly
84 I9 **North European Plain** *plain* N Europe
27 V2 **North Fabius River** ≈ Missouri, C USA
65 D24 **North Falkland Sound** *sound* N Falkland Islands
29 V9 **Northfield** Minnesota, N USA
19 O9 **Northfield** New Hampshire, NE USA
192 K9 **North Fiji Basin** *undersea feature* N Coral Sea
97 Q22 **North Foreland** *headland* SE England, UK
35 P6 **North Fork American River** ≈ California, W USA
39 R7 **North Fork Chandalar River** ≈ Alaska, USA
28 K7 **North Fork Grand River** ≈ North Dakota/South Dakota, N USA
21 O6 **North Fork Kentucky River** ≈ Kentucky, S USA
39 Q7 **North Fork Koyukuk River** ≈ Alaska, USA
39 Q10 **North Fork Kuskokwim River** ≈ Alaska, USA
26 K11 **North Fork Red River** ≈ Oklahoma/Texas, SW USA
26 K3 **North Fork Solomon River** ≈ Kansas, C USA
23 W14 **North Fort Myers** Florida, SE USA
31 P5 **North Fox Island** *island* Michigan, N USA
100 G6 **North Frisian Islands** *var.* Nordfriesische Inseln. *island group* N Germany
197 N9 **North Geomagnetic Pole** *pole* Arctic Ocean
18 M13 **North Haven** Connecticut, NE USA
184 J5 **North Head** *headland* North Island, NZ
18 L6 **North Hero** Vermont, NE USA
35 O7 **North Highlands** California, W USA
North Holland *see* Noord-Holland
81 I16 **North Horr** Eastern, N Kenya
151 K21 **North Huvadhu Atoll** *var.* Gaafu Alifu Atoll. *atoll* S Maldives
65 A24 **North Island** *island* W Falkland Islands
184 N9 **North Island** *island* N NZ
21 U14 **North Island** *island* South Carolina, SE USA
31 O11 **North Judson** Indiana, N USA
North Kazakhstan *see* Severnyy Kazakhstan
31 V10 **North Kingsville** Ohio, N USA
163 Y13 **North Korea** *off.* Democratic People's Republic of Korea, *Kor.* Chosŏn-minjujuŭi-inmin-kanghwaguk. ◆ *republic* E Asia
153 X11 **North Lakhimpur** Assam, NE India
184 J3 **Northland** *off.* Northland Region. ◈ *region* North Island, NZ
192 K11 **Northland Plateau** *undersea feature* S Pacific Ocean
35 X11 **North Las Vegas** Nevada, W USA
31 O11 **North Liberty** Indiana, N USA
29 X14 **North Liberty** Iowa, C USA
27 V12 **North Little Rock** Arkansas, C USA
28 M13 **North Loup River** ≈ Nebraska, C USA
151 K18 **North Maalhosmadulu Atoll** *var.* North Malosmadulu Atoll, Raa Atoll. *atoll* N Maldives
31 U10 **North Madison** Ohio, N USA
31 P12 **North Manchester** Indiana, N USA
31 P6 **North Manitou Island** *island* Michigan, N USA
29 U10 **North Mankato** Minnesota, N USA
23 Z15 **North Miami** Florida, SE USA
151 K18 **North Miladummadulu Atoll** *atoll* N Maldives
North Minch *see* Minch, The
23 W15 **North Naples** Florida, SE USA
192 J9 **North New Hebrides Trench** *undersea feature* N Coral Sea
23 Y15 **North New River Canal** ≈ Florida, SE USA
151 K20 **North Nilandhe Atoll** *var.* Faafu Atoll. *atoll* C Maldives
36 L2 **North Ogden** Utah, W USA
North Ossetia *see* Severnaya Osetiya-Alaniya, Respublika
35 S10 **North Palisade** ▲ California, W USA
189 U11 **North Pass** *passage* Chuuk Islands, C Micronesia
28 M15 **North Platte** Nebraska, C USA
33 X17 **North Platte River** ≈ C USA
65 G14 **North Point** *headland* Ascension Island, C Atlantic Ocean
172 I16 **North Point** *headland* Mahé, NE Seychelles
31 S6 **North Point** *headland* Michigan, N USA
31 R5 **North Point** *headland* Michigan, N USA
39 S9 **North Pole** Alaska, USA
197 R9 **North Pole** *pole* Arctic Ocean
23 O4 **Northport** Alabama, S USA
23 W14 **North Port** Florida, SE USA
32 L6 **Northport** Washington, NW USA
32 L12 **North Powder** Oregon, NW USA
29 U13 **North Raccoon River** ≈ Iowa, C USA
North Rhine-Westphalia *see* Nordrhein-Westfalen
97 M16 **North Riding** *cultural region* N England, UK
96 G5 **North Rona** *island* NW Scotland, UK
96 K4 **North Ronaldsay** *island* NE Scotland, UK
36 L2 **North Salt Lake** Utah, W USA
11 P15 **North Saskatchewan** ≈ Alberta/Saskatchewan, S Canada
35 X5 **North Schell Peak** ▲ Nevada, W USA
North Scotia Ridge *see* South Georgia Ridge
96 M12 **North Sea** *Dan.* Nordsøen, *Dut.* Noordzee, *Fr.* Mer du Nord, *Ger.* Nordsee, *Nor.* Nordsjøen; *prev.* German Ocean, *Lat.* Mare Germanicum. *sea* NW Europe
35 T6 **North Shoshone Peak** ▲ Nevada, W USA
North Siberian Lowland/North Siberian Plain *see* Severo-Sibirskaya Nizmennost'
29 R13 **North Sioux City** South Dakota, N USA
96 K4 **North Sound, The** *sound* N Scotland, UK
183 T4 **North Star** New South Wales, SE Australia
North Star State *see* Minnesota
183 V3 **North Stradbroke Island** *island* Queensland, E Australia
North Sulawesi *see* Sulawesi Utara
North Sumatra *see* Sumatera Utara
14 D17 **North Sydenham** ≈ Ontario, S Canada
18 H9 **North Syracuse** New York, NE USA
184 K9 **North Taranaki Bight** *gulf* North Island, NZ
12 H9 **North Twin Island** *island* Nunavut, C Canada
96 E8 **North Uist** *island* NW Scotland, UK
97 L14 **Northumberland** *cultural region* N England, UK
181 Y7 **Northumberland Isles** *island group* Queensland, NE Australia
13 Q14 **Northumberland Strait** *strait* SE Canada
32 G14 **North Umpqua River** ≈ Oregon, NW USA
45 Q13 **North Union** Saint Vincent, Saint Vincent and the Grenadines
10 L17 **North Vancouver** British Columbia, SW Canada
18 K9 **Northville** New York, NE USA
97 Q19 **North Walsham** E England, UK
39 T10 **Northway** Alaska, USA
83 G21 **North-West** *off.* North-West Province, *Afr.* Noordwes. ◈ *province* N South Africa
North-West *see* Nord-Ouest
64 I6 **Northwest Atlantic Mid-Ocean Canyon** *undersea feature* N Atlantic Ocean
180 G8 **North West Cape** *headland* Western Australia
38 J9 **Northwest Cape** *headland* Saint Lawrence Island, Alaska, USA
82 H13 **North Western** ◈ *province* W Zambia
155 J24 **North Western Province** ◈ *province* W Sri Lanka
149 U4 **North-West Frontier Province** ◈ *province* NW Pakistan
96 H8 **North West Highlands** ▲ N Scotland, UK
192 J4 **Northwest Pacific Basin** *undersea feature* NW Pacific Ocean
191 Y2 **Northwest Point** *headland* Kiritimati, E Kiribati
44 G1 **Northwest Providence Channel** *channel* N Bahamas
13 Q8 **North West River** Newfoundland and Labrador, E Canada
8 J9 **Northwest Territories** *Fr.* Territoires du Nord-Ouest. ◈ *territory* NW Canada
97 K18 **Northwich** C England, UK
25 Q5 **North Wichita River** ≈ Texas, SW USA
18 J17 **North Wildwood** New Jersey, NE USA
21 R9 **North Wilkesboro** North Carolina, SE USA
19 P8 **North Windham** Maine, NE USA
197 Q6 **Northwind Plain** *undersea feature* Arctic Ocean
29 V11 **Northwood** Iowa, C USA
29 Q4 **Northwood** North Dakota, N USA
97 M15 **North York Moors** *moorland* N England, UK
25 V9 **North Zulch** Texas, SW USA
26 K2 **Norton** Kansas, C USA
31 S13 **Norton** Ohio, N USA
21 P7 **Norton** Virginia, NE USA
39 N9 **Norton Bay** *bay* Alaska, USA
Norton de Matos *see* Balombo
31 O9 **Norton Shores** Michigan, N USA
38 M10 **Norton Sound** *inlet* Alaska, USA
27 Q3 **Nortonville** Kansas, C USA
102 I8 **Nort-sur-Erdre** Loire-Atlantique, NW France
195 N2 **Norvegia, Cape** *headland* Antarctica
18 L13 **Norwalk** Connecticut, NE USA
29 V14 **Norwalk** Iowa, C USA
31 S11 **Norwalk** Ohio, N USA
19 P7 **Norway** Maine, NE USA
31 N5 **Norway** Michigan, N USA
93 E17 **Norway** *off.* Kingdom of Norway, *Nor.* Norge. ◆ *monarchy* N Europe
11 X13 **Norway House** Manitoba, C Canada
197 R16 **Norwegian Basin** *undersea feature* NW Norwegian Sea
84 D6 **Norwegian Sea** *Nor.* Norske Havet. *sea* NE Atlantic Ocean
197 S17 **Norwegian Trench** *undersea feature* NE North Sea
14 F16 **Norwich** Ontario, S Canada
97 Q19 **Norwich** E England, UK
19 N13 **Norwich** Connecticut, NE USA
18 I11 **Norwich** New York, NE USA
29 U9 **Norwood** Minnesota, N USA
31 Q15 **Norwood** Ohio, N USA
14 H11 **Nosbonsing, Lake** ⊚ Ontario, S Canada
Nösen *see* Bistriţa
165 T1 **Noshappu-misaki** *headland* Hokkaidō, NE Japan
165 P7 **Noshiro** *var.* Nosiro; *prev.* Noshirominato. Akita, Honshū, C Japan
Noshirominato/Nosiro *see* Noshiro
117 Q3 **Nosivka** *Rus.* Nosovka. Chernihivs'ka Oblast', NE Ukraine
Nosop *see* Nossob
125 S4 **Nosovaya** Nenetskiy Avtonomnyy Okrug, NW Russian Federation
Nosovka *see* Nosivka
143 V11 **Noşratābād** Sīstān va Balūchestān, E Iran
95 J18 **Nossebro** Västra Götaland, S Sweden
96 K6 **Noss Head** *headland* N Scotland, UK
Nossi-Bé *see* Be, Nosy
83 E20 **Nossob** *var.* Nosop, Nossop. ≈ Botswana/Namibia
172 J2 **Nosy Be** × Antsirañana, N Madagascar
172 J6 **Nosy Varika** Fianarantsoa, SE Madagascar
14 L10 **Notawassi** ≈ Québec, SE Canada
14 M9 **Notawassi, Lac** ⊚ Québec, SE Canada
36 J5 **Notch Peak** ▲ Utah, W USA
110 G10 **Noteć** *Ger.* Netze. ≈ NW Poland
Nóties Sporádes *see* Dodekánisos
115 J22 **Nótion Aigaíon** *Eng.* Aegean South. ◈ *region* E Greece
115 H18 **Nótios Evvoïkós Kólpos** *gulf* E Greece
115 B16 **Nótio Stenó Kérkyras** *strait* W Greece
107 L25 **Noto** *anc.* Netum. Sicilia, Italy, C Mediterranean Sea
164 M10 **Noto** Ishikawa, Honshū, SW Japan
95 G15 **Notodden** Telemark, S Norway
107 L25 **Noto, Golfo di** *gulf* Sicilia, Italy, C Mediterranean Sea
164 L10 **Noto-hantō** *peninsula* Honshū, SW Japan
164 L11 **Noto-jima** *island* SW Japan
13 T11 **Notre Dame Bay** *bay* Newfoundland and Labrador, E Canada
15 P6 **Notre-Dame-de-Lorette** Québec, SE Canada
14 L11 **Notre-Dame-de-Pontmain** Québec, SE Canada
15 T8 **Notre-Dame-du-Lac** Québec, SE Canada
15 Q6 **Notre-Dame-du-Rosaire** Québec, SE Canada
15 U8 **Notre-Dame, Monts** ▲ Québec, S Canada
77 R16 **Notsé** S Togo
14 G14 **Nottawasaga** ≈ Ontario, S Canada
14 G14 **Nottawasaga Bay** *lake bay* Ontario, S Canada
12 I11 **Nottaway** ≈ Québec, SE Canada
23 S1 **Nottely Lake** ⊟ Georgia, SE USA
95 H16 **Nøtterøy** *island* S Norway
97 M19 **Nottingham** C England, UK
9 E14 **Nottingham Island** *island* Nunavut, NE Canada
97 P8 **Nottinghamshire** *cultural region* C England, UK
21 V7 **Nottoway** Virginia, NE USA
21 V7 **Nottoway River** ≈ Virginia, NE USA
76 G7 **Nouâdhibou** *prev.* Port-Étienne. Dakhlet Nouâdhibou, W Mauritania
76 G7 **Nouâdhibou** × Dakhlet Nouâdhibou, W Mauritania
76 F7 **Nouâdhibou, Dakhlet** *prev.* Baie du Lévrier. *bay* W Mauritania
76 F7 **Nouâdhibou, Râs** *prev.* Cap Blanc. *headland* NW Mauritania
76 G9 **Nouakchott** ● (Mauritania) Nouakchott District, SW Mauritania
76 G9 **Nouakchott** × Trarza, SW Mauritania
120 J11 **Noual, Sebkhet en** *var.* Sabkhat an Nawāl. *salt flat* C Tunisia
76 G8 **Nouâmghâr** *var.* Nouamrhar. Dakhlet Nouâdhibou, W Mauritania
Nouamrhar *see* Nouâmghâr
Nouă Sulița *see* Novoselytsya
187 Q17 **Nouméa** ○ (New Caledonia) Province Sud, S New Caledonia
79 E15 **Noun** ≈ C Cameroon
77 N12 **Nouna** W Burkina
83 H24 **Noupoort** Northern Cape, C South Africa
Nouveau-Brunswick *see* New Brunswick
Nouveau-Comptoir *see* Wemindji
15 T4 **Nouvel, Lacs** ⊚ Québec, SE Canada
15 W7 **Nouvelle** Québec, SE Canada
15 W7 **Nouvelle** ≈ Québec, SE Canada
Nouvelle-Calédonie *see* New Caledonia
Nouvelle Écosse *see* Nova Scotia
103 R3 **Nouzonville** Ardennes, N France
147 Q11 **Nov** *Rus.* Nau. NW Tajikistan
59 I21 **Nova Alvorada** Mato Grosso do Sul, SW Brazil
Novabad *see* Navobod
111 D19 **Nová Bystřice** *Ger.* Neubistritz. Jihočeský Kraj, S Czech Republic
116 H13 **Novaci** Gorj, SW Romania
Nova Civitas *see* Neustadt an der Weinstrasse

◆ Country ● Country Capital ◇ Dependent Territory ○ Dependent Territory Capital ◈ Administrative Region × International Airport ▲ Mountain ▲ Mountain Range Volcano ≈ River ⊚ Lake ⊟ Reservoir

Novaesium see Neuss
60 H10 **Nova Esperança** Paraná, S Brazil
106 H11 **Novafeltria** Marche, C Italy
60 Q9 **Nova Friburgo** Rio de Janeiro, SE Brazil
82 D12 **Nova Gaia** *var.* Cambundi-Catembo. Malanje, NE Angola
109 S12 **Nova Gorica** W Slovenia
112 G10 **Nova Gradiška** *Ger.* Neugradisk, *Hung.* Újgradiska. Brod-Posavina, NE Croatia
60 K7 **Nova Granada** São Paulo, S Brazil
60 O10 **Nova Iguaçu** Rio de Janeiro, SE Brazil
117 S10 **Nova Kakhovka** *Rus.* Novaya Kakhovka. Khersons'ka Oblast', SE Ukraine
Nová Karvinná see Karviná
Nova Lamego see Gabú
Nova Lisboa see Huambo
112 C11 **Novalja** Lika-Senj, W Croatia
119 M14 **Novalukoml'** *Rus.* Novolukoml'. Vitsyebskaya Voblasts', N Belarus
Nova Mambone see Mambone
83 P16 **Nova Nabúri** Zambézia, NE Mozambique
117 Q9 **Nova Odesa** *var.* Novaya Odessa. Mykolayivs'ka Oblast', S Ukraine
60 H10 **Nova Olímpia** Paraná, S Brazil
61 I15 **Nova Prata** Rio Grande do Sul, S Brazil
14 H12 **Novar** Ontario, S Canada
106 C7 **Novara** *anc.* Novaria. Piemonte, NW Italy
Novaria see Novara
117 P7 **Novarkanels'k** Kirovohrads'ka Oblast', C Ukraine
13 P15 **Nova Scotia** *Fr.* Nouvelle Écosse. ◈ *province* SE Canada
64 G8 **Nova Scotia** *physical region* SE Canada
34 M8 **Novato** California, W USA
192 M7 **Nova Trough** *undersea feature* W Pacific Ocean
116 L7 **Nova Ushtsya** Khmel'nyts'ka Oblast', W Ukraine
83 M17 **Nova Vanduzi** Manica, C Mozambique
117 U5 **Nova Vodolaha** *Rus.* Novaya Vodolaga. Kharkivs'ka Oblast', E Ukraine
123 O12 **Novaya Chara** Chitinskaya Oblast', S Russian Federation
122 M12 **Novaya Igirma** Irkutskaya Oblast', C Russian Federation
Novaya Kakhovka see Nova Kakhovka
144 E10 **Novaya Kazanka** Zapadnyy Kazakhstan, W Kazakhstan
124 I12 **Novaya Ladoga** Leningradskaya Oblast', NW Russian Federation
127 R5 **Novaya Malykla** Ul'yanovskaya Oblast', W Russian Federation
Novaya Odessa see Nova Odesa
123 Q5 **Novaya Sibir', Ostrov** *island* Novosibirskiye Ostrova, NE Russian Federation
Novaya Vodolaga see Nova Vodolaha
119 P17 **Novaya Yel'nya** *Rus.* Novaya Yel'nya. Mahilyowskaya Voblasts', E Belarus
122 I6 **Novaya Zemlya** *island group* N Russian Federation
Novaya Zemlya Trough see East Novaya Zemlya Trough
114 K10 **Nova Zagora** Sliven, C Bulgaria
105 S12 **Novelda** País Valenciano, E Spain
111 H19 **Nové Mesto nad Váhom** *Ger.* Waagneustadtl, *Hung.* Vágújhely. Trenčiansky Kraj, W Slovakia
111 F17 **Nové Město na Moravě** *Ger.* Neustadtl in Mähren. Vysočina, C Czech Republic
Novesium see Neuss
111 I21 **Nové Zámky** *Ger.* Neuhäusel, *Hung.* Érsekújvár. Nitriansky Kraj, SW Slovakia
Novgorod see Velikiy Novgorod
Novgorod-Severskiy see Novhorod-Sivers'kyy
122 C7 **Novgorodskaya Oblast'** ◈ *province* W Russian Federation
117 R8 **Novhorodka** Kirovohrads'ka Oblast', C Ukraine
117 R2 **Novhorod-Sivers'kyy** *Rus.* Novgorod-Severskiy. Chernihivs'ka Oblast', NE Ukraine
31 R10 **Novi** Michigan, N USA
Novi see Novi Vinodolski
112 L9 **Novi Bečej** *prev.* Új-Becse, Vološinovo, *Ger.* Neubetsche, *Hung.* Törökbecse. Serbia, N Serbia and Montenegro (Yugo.)
25 Q8 **Novice** Texas, SW USA
112 A9 **Novigrad** Istra, NW Croatia
Novi Grad see Bosanski Novi
114 G9 **Novi Iskŭr** Sofiya-Grad, W Bulgaria
106 C9 **Novi Ligure** Piemonte, NW Italy
99 L22 **Noville** Luxembourg, SE Belgium
194 I10 **Noville Peninsula** *peninsula* Thurston Island, Antarctica
Noviodunum see Soissons, Aisne, France
Noviodunum see Nevers, Nièvre, France
Noviodunum see Nyon, Vaud, Switzerland
Noviomagus see Lisieux, France
Noviomagus see Nijmegen, Netherlands
114 M8 **Novi Pazar** Shumen, NE Bulgaria
113 M15 **Novi Pazar** *Turk.* Yenipazar. Serbia, S Serbia and Montenegro (Yugo.)
112 K10 **Novi Sad** *Ger.* Neusatz, *Hung.* Újvidék. Serbia, N Serbia and Montenegro (Yugo.)
117 T6 **Novi Sanzhary** Poltavs'ka Oblast', C Ukraine
112 H12 **Novi Travnik** *prev.* Pučarevo. Federacija Bosna I Hercegovina, C Bosnia and Herzegovina
112 B10 **Novi Vinodolski** *var.* Novi. Primorje-Gorski Kotar, NW Croatia
58 F12 **Novo Airão** Amazonas, N Brazil
127 N14 **Novoaleksandrovsk** Stavropol'skiy Kray, SW Russian Federation
Novoalekseyevka see Khobda
127 N9 **Novoanninskiy** Volgogradskaya Oblast', SW Russian Federation
58 F13 **Novo Aripuanã** Amazonas, N Brazil
117 Y6 **Novoaydar** Luhans'ka Oblast', E Ukraine
117 X9 **Novoazovs'k** *Rus.* Novoazovsk. Donets'ka Oblast', E Ukraine
123 R14 **Novobureyskiy** Amurskaya Oblast', SE Russian Federation
127 Q3 **Novocheboksarsk** Chuvashskaya Respublika, W Russian Federation
127 R5 **Novocheremshansk** Ul'yanovskaya Oblast', W Russian Federation
126 L12 **Novocherkassk** Rostovskaya Oblast', SW Russian Federation
127 R6 **Novodevich'ye** Samarskaya Oblast', W Russian Federation
124 M8 **Novodvinsk** Arkhangel'skaya Oblast', NW Russian Federation
Novograd-Volynskiy see Novohrad-Volyns'kyy
Novogrudok see Navahrudak
61 I15 **Novo Hamburgo** Rio Grande do Sul, S Brazil
59 H16 **Novo Horizonte** Mato Grosso, W Brazil
60 K8 **Novo Horizonte** São Paulo, S Brazil
116 M4 **Novohrad-Volyns'kyy** *Rus.* Novograd-Volynskiy. Zhytomyrs'ka Oblast', N Ukraine
145 O7 **Novoishimskiy** *prev.* Kuybyshevskiy. Severnyy Kazakhstan, N Kazakhstan
144 L14 **Novokazalinsk** see Ayteke Bi
126 M8 **Novokhopersk** Voronezhskaya Oblast', W Russian Federation
127 R6 **Novokuybyshevsk** Samarskaya Oblast', W Russian Federation
122 J13 **Novokuznetsk** *prev.* Stalinsk. Kemerovskaya Oblast', S Russian Federation
195 R1 **Novolazarevskaya** *Russian research station* Antarctica
Novolukoml' see Novalukoml'
109 V12 **Novo mesto** *Ger.* Rudolfswert; *prev. Ger.* Neustadtl. SE Slovenia
126 K15 **Novomikhaylovskiy** Krasnodarskiy Kray, SW Russian Federation
112 L8 **Novo Miloševo** Serbia, N Serbia and Montenegro (Yugo.)
Novomirgorod see Novomyrhorod
126 L5 **Novomoskovsk** Tul'skaya Oblast', W Russian Federation
117 U7 **Novomoskovs'k** *Rus.* Novomoskovsk. Dnipropetrovs'ka Oblast', E Ukraine
117 V8 **Novomykolayivka** Zaporiz'ka Oblast', SE Ukraine
117 Q7 **Novomyrhorod** *Rus.* Novomirgorod. Kirovohrads'ka Oblast', S Ukraine
127 N8 **Novonikolayevskiy** Volgogradskaya Oblast', SW Russian Federation
127 P10 **Novonikol'skoye** Volgogradskaya Oblast', SW Russian Federation
127 X7 **Novoorsk** Orenburgskaya Oblast', W Russian Federation
126 M13 **Novopokrovskaya** Krasnodarskiy Kray, SW Russian Federation
Novopolotsk see Navapolatsk
117 Y5 **Novopskov** Luhans'ka Oblast', E Ukraine
Novoradomsk see Radomsko
Novo Redondo see Sumbe
127 R8 **Novorepnoye** Saratovskaya Oblast', W Russian Federation
126 K14 **Novorossiysk** Krasnodarskiy Kray, SW Russian Federation
Novorossiyskiy/Novorossiyskoye see Akzhar
124 F15 **Novorzhev** Pskovskaya Oblast', W Russian Federation
Novoselitsa see Novoselytsya
117 S12 **Novoselivs'ke** Respublika Krym, S Ukraine
Novosëlki see Navasyolki
114 G6 **Novo Selo** Vidin, NW Bulgaria
113 M14 **Novo Selo** Serbia, C Serbia and Montenegro (Yugo.)
116 K8 **Novoselytsya** *Rom.* Nouă Suliţa, *Rus.* Novoselitsa. Chernivets'ka Oblast', W Ukraine
127 U7 **Novosergiyevka** Orenburgskaya Oblast', W Russian Federation
126 L11 **Novoshakhtinsk** Rostovskaya Oblast', SW Russian Federation
122 J12 **Novosibirsk** Novosibirskaya Oblast', C Russian Federation
122 J12 **Novosibirskaya Oblast'** ◈ *province* C Russian Federation
122 M4 **Novosibirskiye Ostrova** *Eng.* New Siberian Islands. *island group* N Russian Federation
126 K6 **Novosil'** Orlovskaya Oblast', W Russian Federation
124 G16 **Novosokol'niki** Pskovskaya Oblast', W Russian Federation
127 Q6 **Novospasskoye** Ul'yanovskaya Oblast', W Russian Federation
127 X8 **Novotroitsk** Orenburgskaya Oblast', W Russian Federation
Novotroitskoye see Brlik, Kazakhstan
Novotroitskoye see Novotroyits'ke, Ukraine
117 T11 **Novotroyits'ke** *Rus.* Novotroitskoye. Khersons'ka Oblast', S Ukraine
Novoukrainka see Novoukrayinka
117 Q8 **Novoukrayinka** *Rus.* Novoukrainka. Kirovohrads'ka Oblast', C Ukraine
127 Q5 **Novoul'yanovsk** Ul'yanovskaya Oblast', W Russian Federation
127 W8 **Novouralets** Orenburgskaya Oblast', W Russian Federation
122 G10 **Novoural'ske** Chelyabinskaya Oblast', S Russian Federation
Novo-Urgench see Urganch
116 I4 **Novovolyns'k** *Rus.* Novovolynsk. Volyns'ka Oblast', NW Ukraine
117 S9 **Novovorontsovka** Khersons'ka Oblast', S Ukraine
147 Y7 **Novovoznesenovka** Issyk-Kul'skaya Oblast', E Kyrgyzstan
125 R14 **Novovyatsk** Kirovskaya Oblast', NW Russian Federation
Novoyel'nya see Navayel'nya
124 I7 **Novoye Yushozero** Respublika Kareliya, NW Russian Federation
117 O6 **Novozhyvotiv** Vinnyts'ka Oblast', C Ukraine
126 H6 **Novozybkov** Bryanskaya Oblast', W Russian Federation
112 F9 **Novska** Sisak-Moslavina, NE Croatia
Nový Bohumín see Bohumín
111 D15 **Nový Bor** *Ger.* Haida; *prev.* Bor u České Lípy, Hajda. Liberecký Kraj, N Czech Republic
111 E16 **Nový Bydžov** *Ger.* Neubidschow. Královéhradecký Kraj, N Czech Republic
119 G18 **Novy Dvor** *Rus.* Novyy Dvor. Hrodzyenskaya Voblasts', W Belarus
111 I17 **Nový Jičín** *Ger.* Neutitschein. Moravskoslezský Kraj, E Czech Republic
118 K12 **Novy Pahost** *Rus.* Novyy Pogost. Vitsyebskaya Voblasts', NW Belarus
Novyy Bug see Novyy Buh
117 R9 **Novyy Buh** *Rus.* Novyy Bug. Mykolayivs'ka Oblast', S Ukraine
117 Q4 **Novyy Bykiv** Chernihivs'ka Oblast', N Ukraine
Novyy Dvor see Novy Dvor
Novyye Aneny see Anenii Noi
127 P7 **Novyye Burasy** Saratovskaya Oblast', W Russian Federation
Novyy Margilan see Farg'ona
126 K8 **Novyy Oskol** Belgorodskaya Oblast', W Russian Federation
Novyy Pogost see Novy Pahost
127 R2 **Novyy Tor"yal** Respublika Mariy El, W Russian Federation
123 N12 **Novyy Uoyan** Respublika Buryatiya, S Russian Federation
122 J9 **Novyy Urengoy** Yamalo-Nenetskiy Avtonomnyy Okrug, N Russian Federation
Novyy Uzen' see Zhanaozen
111 N16 **Nowa Dęba** Podkarpackie, SE Poland
111 G15 **Nowa Ruda** *Ger.* Neurode. Dolnośląskie, SW Poland
110 F12 **Nowa Sól** *var.* Nowasól, *Ger.* Neusalz an der Oder. Lubuskie, W Poland
27 Q8 **Nowata** Oklahoma, C USA
142 M6 **Nowbarān** Markazī, W Iran
110 J8 **Nowe** Kujawski-pomorskie, C Poland
110 K9 **Nowe Miasto Lubawskie** *Ger.* Neumark. Warmińsko-Mazurskie, NE Poland
110 L13 **Nowe Miasto nad Pilicą** Mazowieckie, C Poland
110 D8 **Nowe Warpno** *Ger.* Neuwarp. Zachodnio-pomorskie, NW Poland
Nowgong see Nagaon
110 E8 **Nowogard** *var.* Nowógard, *Ger.* Naugard. Zachodnio-pomorskie, NW Poland
110 N9 **Nowogród** Podlaskie, NE Poland
Nowogródek see Navahrudak
111 E14 **Nowogrodziec** *Ger.* Naumburg am Queis. Dolnośląskie, SW Poland
Nowojelnia see Navayel'nya
Nowo-Minsk see Mińsk Mazowiecki
33 V13 **Nowood River** ⟿ Wyoming, C USA
Nowo-Święciany see Švenčionėliai
183 S10 **Nowra-Bomaderry** New South Wales, SE Australia
149 T5 **Nowshera** *var.* Naushahra, Naushara. North-West Frontier Province, NE Pakistan
110 J7 **Nowy Dwór Gdański** *Ger.* Tiegenhof. Pomorskie, N Poland
110 L11 **Nowy Dwór Mazowiecki** Mazowieckie, C Poland
111 M17 **Nowy Sącz** *Ger.* Neu Sandec. Małopolskie, S Poland
111 L18 **Nowy Targ** *Ger.* Neumark. Małopolskie, S Poland
110 F11 **Nowy Tomyśl** *var.* Nowy Tomysl. Wielkolpolskie, C Poland
148 M7 **Now Zād** *var.* Nauzad. Helmand, S Afghanistan
23 N4 **Noxubee River** ⟿ Alabama/Mississippi, S USA
122 I10 **Noyabr'sk** Yamalo-Nenetskiy Avtonomnyy Okrug, N Russian Federation
102 L8 **Noyant** Maine-et-Loire, NW France
39 X14 **Noyes Island** *island* Alexander Archipelago, Alaska, USA
103 O3 **Noyon** Oise, N France
102 I7 **Nozay** Loire-Atlantique, NW France
82 L12 **Nsando** Northern, NE Zambia
83 N16 **Nsanje** Southern, S Malawi
77 Q17 **Nsawam** SE Ghana
79 E16 **Nsimalen** ✕ Centre, C Cameroon
82 K12 **Nsombo** Northern, NE Zambia
82 H13 **Ntambu** North Western, NW Zambia
83 N14 **Ntcheu** *var.* Ncheu. Central, S Malawi
79 D17 **Ntem** *prev.* Campo, Kampo. ⟿ Cameroon/Equatorial Guinea
83 I14 **Ntemwa** North Western, NW Zambia
Ntlenyana, Mount see Thabana Ntlenyana
79 I19 **Ntomba, Lac** *var.* Lac Tumba. ◎ NW Dem. Rep. Congo
81 E19 **Ntungamo** SW Uganda
81 E18 **Ntusi** SW Uganda
83 H18 **Ntwetwe Pan** *salt lake* NE Botswana
93 M15 **Nuasjärvi** ◎ C Finland
80 F11 **Nuba Mountains** ▲ C Sudan
80 G6 **Nubian Desert** *desert* NE Sudan
116 G10 **Nucet** *Hung.* Diófás. Bihor, W Romania
Nu Chiang see Salween
145 U9 **Nuclear Testing Ground** *nuclear site* Pavlodar, E Kazakhstan
56 E9 **Nucuray, Río** ⟿ N Peru
25 R14 **Nueces River** ⟿ Texas, SW USA
11 V9 **Nueltin Lake** ◎ Manitoba/Nunavut, C Canada
99 K15 **Nuenen** Noord-Brabant, S Netherlands
62 G6 **Nuestra Señora, Bahía** *bay* N Chile
61 D14 **Nuestra Señora Rosario de Caa Catí** Corrientes, NE Argentina
54 J9 **Nueva Antioquia** Vichada, E Colombia
Nueva Caceres see Naga
41 O7 **Nueva Ciudad Guerrera** Tamaulipas, C Mexico
55 N4 **Nueva Esparta** *off.* Estado Nueva Esparta. ◈ *state* NE Venezuela
44 C5 **Nueva Gerona** Isla de la Juventud, S Cuba
42 H8 **Nueva Guadalupe** San Miguel, E El Salvador
42 M11 **Nueva Guinea** Región Autónoma Atlántico Sur, SE Nicaragua
61 D19 **Nueva Helvecia** Colonia, SW Uruguay
63 J25 **Nueva, Isla** *island* S Chile
40 M14 **Nueva Italia** Michoacán de Ocampo, SW Mexico
56 D6 **Nueva Loja** *var.* Lago Agrio. Sucumbíos, NE Ecuador
42 F6 **Nueva Ocotepeque** *prev.* Ocotepeque. Ocotepeque, W Honduras
61 D19 **Nueva Palmira** Colonia, SW Uruguay
41 N6 **Nueva Rosita** Coahuila de Zaragoza, NE Mexico
42 E7 **Nueva San Salvador** *prev.* Santa Tecla. La Libertad, SW El Salvador
42 J8 **Nueva Segovia** ◈ *department* NW Nicaragua
Nueva Tabarca see Plana, Isla
Nueva Villa de Padilla see Nuevo Padilla
61 B21 **Nueve de Julio** Buenos Aires, E Argentina
44 H6 **Nuevitas** Camagüey, E Cuba
61 D18 **Nuevo Berlín** Río Negro, W Uruguay
40 I4 **Nuevo Casas Grandes** Chihuahua, N Mexico
43 T14 **Nuevo Chagres** Colón, C Panama
41 W15 **Nuevo Coahuila** Campeche, E Mexico
63 K17 **Nuevo, Golfo** *gulf* S Argentina
41 O7 **Nuevo Laredo** Tamaulipas, NE Mexico
41 N8 **Nuevo León** ◈ *state* NE Mexico
41 P10 **Nuevo Padilla** *var.* Nueva Villa de Padilla. Tamaulipas, C Mexico
56 E6 **Nuevo Rocafuerte** Orellana, E Ecuador
162 G6 **Nuga** Dzavhan, W Mongolia
80 O13 **Nugaal** *off.* Gobolka Nugaal. ◈ *region* N Somalia
185 E24 **Nugget Point** *headland* South Island, NZ
186 J5 **Nuguria Islands** *island group* E PNG
184 P10 **Nuhaka** Hawke's Bay, North Island, NZ
138 M10 **Nuhaydayn, Wādī an** *dry watercourse* W Iraq
190 E7 **Nui Atoll** *atoll* W Tuvalu
Nu Jiang see Salween
Nûk see Nuuk
182 G7 **Nukey Bluff** *hill* South Australia
Nukha see Şäki
123 T9 **Nukh Yablonevyy, Gora** ▲ E Russian Federation
186 K7 **Nukiki** Choiseul Island, NW Solomon Islands
186 B6 **Nuku** Sandaun, NW PNG
193 W15 **Nuku** *island* Tongatapu Group, NE Tonga
193 U15 **Nuku'alofa** Tongatapu, S Tonga
193 Y16 **Nuku'alofa** ● (Tonga) Tongatapu, S Tonga
190 G12 **Nukuatea** *island* N Wallis and Futuna
190 F7 **Nukufetau Atoll** *atoll* C Tuvalu
190 G12 **Nukuhifala** *island* E Wallis and Futuna
191 W7 **Nuku Hiva** *island* Îles Marquises, NE French Polynesia
193 O8 **Nuku Hiva Island** *island* Îles Marquises, N French Polynesia
190 F9 **Nukulaelae Atoll** *var.* Nukulailai. *atoll* E Tuvalu
Nukulailai see Nukulaelae Atoll
190 G11 **Nukuloa** *island* N Wallis and Futuna
186 L6 **Nukumanu Islands** *prev.* Tasman Group. *island group* NE PNG
Nukunau see Nikunau
190 J9 **Nukunonu Atoll** *island* C Tokelau
190 J9 **Nukunonu Village** Nukunonu Atoll, C Tokelau
189 S18 **Nukuoro Atoll** *atoll* Caroline Islands, S Micronesia
146 H8 **Nukus** Qoraqalpog'iston Respublikasi, W Uzbekistan
190 G11 **Nukutapu** *island* N Wallis and Futuna
39 O9 **Nulato** Alaska, USA
39 O10 **Nulato Hills** ▲ Alaska, USA
105 T9 **Nules** País Valenciano, E Spain
Nuling see Sultan Kudarat
182 C6 **Nullarbor** South Australia
180 M11 **Nullarbor Plain** *plateau* South Australia/Western Australia
163 S12 **Nulu'erhu Shan** ▲ N China
77 X14 **Numan** Adamawa, E Nigeria
165 S3 **Numata** Hokkaidō, NE Japan
81 C15 **Numatinna** ⟿ W Sudan
95 F14 **Numedalen** *valley* S Norway
95 G14 **Numedalslågen** *var.* Laagen. ⟿ S Norway
93 L19 **Nummela** Etelä-Suomi, S Finland
183 O11 **Numurkah** Victoria, SE Australia
196 L16 **Nunap Isua** *var.* Uummannarsuaq, *Dan.* Kap Farvel, *Eng.* Cape Farewell. *headland* S Greenland
9 N8 **Nunavut** ◈ *Territory* N Canada
54 H9 **Nunchia** Casanare, C Colombia
97 M20 **Nuneaton** C England, UK
153 W14 **Nungba** Manipur, NE India
38 L12 **Nunivak Island** *island* Alaska, USA
152 I5 **Nun Kun** ▲ NW India
98 L10 **Nunspeet** Gelderland, E Netherlands
107 C18 **Nuoro** Sardegna, Italy, C Mediterranean Sea
75 R12 **Nuqayy, Jabal** *hill range* S Libya
54 C9 **Nuquí** Chocó, W Colombia
143 O4 **Nūr** Māzandarān, N Iran
145 Q9 **Nura** ⟿ N Kazakhstan
143 N11 **Nūrābād** Fārs, C Iran
Nurakita see Niulakita
Nurata see Nurota
Nuratau, Khrebet see Nurota Tizmasi
136 L17 **Nur Dağları** ▲ S Turkey
Nurek see Norak
Nuremberg see Nürnberg
136 M15 **Nurhak** Kahramanmaraş, S Turkey
182 J9 **Nuriootpa** South Australia
127 S5 **Nurlat** Respublika Tatarstan, W Russian Federation
93 N15 **Nurmes** Itä-Suomi, E Finland
101 K20 **Nürnberg** *Eng.* Nuremberg. Bayern, S Germany
101 K20 **Nürnberg** ✕ Bayern, SE Germany
146 M10 **Nurota** *Rus.* Nurata. Navoiy Viloyati, C Uzbekistan
147 N10 **Nurota Tizmasi** *Rus.* Khrebet Nuratau. ▲ C Uzbekistan
149 T8 **Nūrpur** Punjab, E Pakistan
183 P6 **Nurri, Mount** *hill* New South Wales, SE Australia
25 T13 **Nursery** Texas, SW USA
171 O16 **Nusa Tenggara** *Eng.* Lesser Sunda Islands. *island group* East Timor/ Indonesia
169 V17 **Nusa Tenggara Barat** *off.* Propinsi Nusa Tenggara Barat, *Eng.* West Nusa Tenggara. ◈ *province* S Indonesia
171 O16 **Nusa Tenggara Timur** *off.* Propinsi Nusa Tenggara Timur, *Eng.* East Nusa Tenggara. ◈ *province* S Indonesia
171 U14 **Nusawulan** Papua, E Indonesia
137 Q16 **Nusaybin** *var.* Nisibin. Manisa, SE Turkey
39 O14 **Nushagak Bay** *bay* Alaska, USA
39 O13 **Nushagak Peninsula** *headland* Alaska, USA
39 O13 **Nushagak River** ⟿ Alaska, USA
160 E11 **Nu Shan** ▲ SW China
149 N11 **Nushki** Baluchistān, SW Pakistan
Nussdorf see Năsăud
112 J9 **Nuštar** Vukovar-Srijem, E Croatia
99 L18 **Nuth** Limburg, SE Netherlands
100 N13 **Nuthe** ⟿ NE Germany
Nutmeg State see Connecticut
39 T10 **Nutzotin Mountains** ▲ Alaska, USA
64 I5 **Nuuk** *var.* Nûk, *Dan.* Godthaab, Godthåb. ○ (Greenland). Kitaa, SW Greenland
92 L13 **Nuupas** Lappi, NW Finland
191 O7 **Nuupere, Pointe** *headland* Moorea, W French Polynesia
191 O7 **Nuuroa, Pointe** *headland* Tahiti, W French Polynesia
Nüürst see Baga Nuur
Nuwara see Nuwara Eliya
155 K25 **Nuwara Eliya** *var.* Nuwara. Central Province, S Sri Lanka
182 E7 **Nuyts Archipelago** *island group* South Australia
83 F17 **Nxaunxau** Ngamiland, NW Botswana
39 N12 **Nyac** Alaska, USA
122 H9 **Nyagan'** Khanty-Mansiyskiy Avtonomnyy Okrug, N Russian Federation
Nyagassola see Niagassola
Nyagquka see Yajiang
81 I18 **Nyahururu** Central, W Kenya
182 M10 **Nyah West** Victoria, SE Australia
158 M15 **Nyainqêntanglha Feng** ▲ W China
159 N15 **Nyainqêntanglha Shan** ▲ W China
80 B11 **Nyala** Southern Darfur, W Sudan
83 M16 **Nyamapanda** Mashonaland East, NE Zimbabwe
81 H25 **Nyamtumbo** Ruvuma, S Tanzania
Nyanda see Masvingo
124 M11 **Nyandoma** Arkhangel'skaya Oblast', NW Russian Federation
83 M16 **Nyanga** *prev.* Inyanga. Manicaland, E Zimbabwe
79 D20 **Nyanga** *off.* Province de la Nyanga, *var.* La Nyanga. ◈ *province* SW Gabon
79 E20 **Nyanga** ⟿ Congo/Gabon
81 F20 **Nyantakara** Kagera, NW Tanzania
81 G19 **Nyanza** ◈ *province* W Kenya
81 E21 **Nyanza-Lac** S Burundi
82 N13 **Nyasa, Lake** *var.* Lake Malawi; *prev.* Lago Nyassa. ◎ E Africa
Nyasaland/Nyasaland Protectorate see Malawi
Nyassa, Lago see Nyasa, Lake
119 J17 **Nyasvizh** *Pol.* Nieśwież, *Rus.* Nesvizh. Minskaya Voblasts', C Belarus
166 M8 **Nyaunglebin** Pegu, SW Burma
166 M5 **Nyaung-u** Magwe, C Burma
95 H24 **Nyborg** Fyn, C Denmark
95 N21 **Nybro** Kalmar, S Sweden
119 J16 **Nyeharelaye** *Rus.* Negoreloye. Minskaya Voblasts', C Belarus
195 W3 **Nye Mountains** ▲ Antarctica
81 I19 **Nyeri** Central, C Kenya
118 M11 **Nyeshcharda, Vozyera** ◎ N Belarus
92 O2 **Ny-Friesland** *physical region* N Svalbard
95 L14 **Nyhammar** Dalarna, C Sweden
160 F7 **Nyikog Qu** ⟿ C China
158 L14 **Nyima** Xizang Zizhiqu, W China
83 L14 **Nyimba** Eastern, E Zambia
159 P16 **Nyingchi** *var.* Pula. Xizang Zizhiqu, W China
Nyinma see Maqu
111 O21 **Nyírbátor** Szabolcs-Szatmár-Bereg, E Hungary
111 N21 **Nyíregyháza** Szabolcs-Szatmár-Bereg, NE Hungary
Nyiro see Ewaso Ng'iro
Nyitra see Nitra
Nyitrabánya see Handlová
93 K16 **Nykarleby** *Fin.* Uusikaarlepyy. Länsi-Suomi, W Finland
95 I25 **Nykøbing** Storstrøm, SE Denmark
95 I22 **Nykøbing** Vestsjælland, C Denmark
95 F21 **Nykøbing** Viborg, NW Denmark
95 N17 **Nyköping** Södermanland, S Sweden
95 L15 **Nykroppa** Värmland, C Sweden
Nylstroom see Modimolle
183 P7 **Nymagee** New South Wales, SE Australia
183 V5 **Nymboida** New South Wales, SE Australia
183 U5 **Nymboida River** ⟿ New South Wales, SE Australia
111 D16 **Nymburk** *var.* Neuenburg an der Elbe, *Ger.* Nimburg. Středočeský Kraj, C Czech Republic
95 O16 **Nynäshamn** Stockholm, C Sweden
183 Q6 **Nyngan** New South Wales, SE Australia
Nyoman see Neman
108 A10 **Nyon** *Ger.* Neuss; *anc.* Noviodunum. Vaud, SW Switzerland
79 D16 **Nyong** ⟿ SW Cameroon
103 S14 **Nyons** Drôme, E France
79 D14 **Nyos, Lac** *Eng.* Lake Nyos. ◎ NW Cameroon
Nyos, Lake see Nyos, Lac
125 U11 **Nyrob** *var.* Nyrov. Permskaya Oblast', NW Russian Federation
Nyrov see Nyrob
111 H15 **Nysa** *Ger.* Neisse. Opolskie, S Poland
Nysa Łużycka see Neisse
Nyslott see Savonlinna
32 M13 **Nyssa** Oregon, NW USA
Nystad see Uusikaupunki
95 I25 **Nysted** Storstrøm, SE Denmark
125 U14 **Nytva** Permskaya Oblast', NW Russian Federation
165 P8 **Nyūdō-zaki** *headland* Honshū, C Japan
125 P9 **Nyukhcha** Arkhangel'skaya Oblast', NW Russian Federation
126 H8 **Nyuk, Ozero** *var.* Ozero Njuk. ◎ NW Russian Federation
125 O12 **Nyuksenitsa** *var.* Njuksenica. Vologodskaya Oblast', NW Russian Federation
79 O22 **Nyunzu** Katanga, SE Dem. Rep. Congo
123 O10 **Nyurba** Respublika Sakha (Yakutiya), NE Russian Federation
123 O11 **Nyuya** Respublika Sakha (Yakutiya), NE Russian Federation

146 K12 **Nyýazow** Rus. Niyazov. Lebap Welaýaty, NE Turkmenistan
117 T10 **Nyzhni Sirohozy** Khersons'ka Oblast', S Ukraine
117 U12 **Nyzhn'ohirs'kyy** Rus. Nizhnegorskiy. Respublika Krym, S Ukraine
81 G21 **Nzega** Tabora, C Tanzania
76 K15 **Nzérékoré** Guinée-Forestière, SE Guinea
82 A10 **N'Zeto** prev. Ambrizete. Zaire, NW Angola
79 M24 **Nzilo, Lac** prev. Lac Delcommune. ⊚ SE Dem. Rep. Congo

O

29 O11 **Oacoma** South Dakota, N USA
29 N9 **Oahe Dam** dam South Dakota, N USA
28 M9 **Oahe, Lake** ⊠ North Dakota/South Dakota, N USA
38 C9 **O'ahu** var. Oahu island Hawai'i, USA, C Pacific Ocean
165 V4 **O-Akan-dake** ▲ Hokkaidō, NE Japan
182 K8 **Oakbank** South Australia
19 P13 **Oak Bluffs** Martha's Vineyard, New York, NE USA
36 K4 **Oak City** Utah, W USA
37 R3 **Oak Creek** Colorado, C USA
35 P8 **Oakdale** California, W USA
22 H8 **Oakdale** Louisiana, S USA
29 P7 **Oakes** North Dakota, N USA
22 J4 **Oak Grove** Louisiana, S USA
97 N19 **Oakham** C England, UK
32 H7 **Oak Harbor** Washington, NW USA
21 R5 **Oak Hill** West Virginia, NE USA
35 N8 **Oakland** California, W USA
29 T15 **Oakland** Iowa, C USA
19 Q7 **Oakland** Maine, NE USA
21 T3 **Oakland** Maryland, NE USA
29 R14 **Oakland** Nebraska, C USA
31 N11 **Oak Lawn** Illinois, N USA
33 P16 **Oakley** Idaho, NW USA
26 I4 **Oakley** Kansas, C USA
31 N10 **Oak Park** Illinois, N USA
11 X16 **Oak Point** Manitoba, S Canada
32 G13 **Oakridge** Oregon, NW USA
20 M9 **Oak Ridge** Tennessee, S USA
184 K10 **Oakura** Taranaki, North Island, NZ
22 L7 **Oak Vale** Mississippi, S USA
14 G16 **Oakville** Ontario, S Canada
25 V8 **Oakwood** Texas, SW USA
185 F22 **Oamaru** Otago, South Island, NZ
96 F13 **Oa, Mull of** headland W Scotland, UK
171 O11 **Oan** Sulawesi, N Indonesia
185 J17 **Oaro** Canterbury, South Island, NZ
35 X2 **Oasis** Nevada, W USA
195 S15 **Oates Land** physical region Antarctica
183 P17 **Oatlands** Tasmania, SE Australia
36 I11 **Oatman** Arizona, SW USA
41 R16 **Oaxaca** var. Oaxaca de Juárez; prev. Antequera. Oaxaca, SE Mexico
41 Q16 **Oaxaca** ◆ state SE Mexico
Oaxaca de Juárez see Oaxaca
122 I19 **Ob'** ~ C Russian Federation
14 G9 **Obabika Lake** ⊚ Ontario, S Canada
Obagan see Ubagan
118 M12 **Obal'** Rus. Obol'. Vitsyebskaya Voblasts', N Belarus
79 E16 **Obala** Centre, SW Cameroon
14 C6 **Oba Lake** ⊚ Ontario, S Canada
164 J12 **Obama** Fukui, Honshū, SW Japan
96 H11 **Oban** W Scotland, UK
Oban see Halfmoon Bay
Obando see Puerto Inírida
104 I4 **O Barco** var. El Barco, El Barco de Valdeorras, O Barco de Valdeorras. Galicia, NW Spain
O Barco de Valdeorras see O Barco
Obbia see Hobyo
93 J16 **Obbola** Västerbotten, N Sweden
Obbrovazzo see Obrovac
Obchuga see Abchuha
Obdorsk see Salekhard
Óbecse see Bečej
118 I11 **Obeliai** Panevėžys, NE Lithuania
60 F13 **Oberá** Misiones, NE Argentina
108 E8 **Oberburg** Bern, W Switzerland
109 Q9 **Oberdrauburg** Salzburg, S Austria
Oberglogau see Głogówek
109 W4 **Ober Grafendorf** Niederösterreich, NE Austria
101 E15 **Oberhausen** Nordrhein-Westfalen, W Germany
Oberhollabrunn see Tulln
Oberlaibach see Vrhnika
101 Q15 **Oberlausitz** Lus. Hornja Łužica. physical region E Germany
26 J2 **Oberlin** Kansas, C USA
22 H8 **Oberlin** Louisiana, S USA
31 T11 **Oberlin** Ohio, N USA
103 U5 **Obernai** Bas-Rhin, NE France
109 R4 **Obernberg-am-Inn** Oberösterreich, N Austria
Oberndorf see Oberndorf am Neckar
101 G23 **Oberndorf am Neckar** var. Oberndorf. Baden-Württemberg, SW Germany
109 Q5 **Oberndorf bei Salzburg** Salzburg, W Austria
Oberneustadtl see Kysucké Nové Mesto
183 S8 **Oberon** New South Wales, SE Australia
109 Q4 **Oberösterreich** off. Land Oberösterreich, Eng. Upper Austria. ◆ state NW Austria
Oberpahlen see Põltsamaa
101 M19 **Oberpfälzer Wald** ▲ SE Germany
109 Y6 **Oberpullendorf** Burgenland, E Austria
Oberradkersburg see Gornja Radgona
101 G18 **Oberursel** Hessen, W Germany
109 Q8 **Obervellach** Salzburg, S Austria
109 X7 **Oberwart** Burgenland, SE Austria
Oberwischau see Vişeu de Sus
109 T7 **Oberwölz** var. Oberwölz-Stadt. Steiermark, SE Austria
Oberwölz-Stadt see Oberwölz
31 S13 **Obetz** Ohio, N USA
Ob', Gulf of see Obskaya Guba
54 G8 **Obia** Santander, C Colombia
58 H12 **Óbidos** Pará, NE Brazil
104 F10 **Óbidos** Leiria, C Portugal
Obidovichi see Abidavichy
147 Q13 **Obigarm** W Tajikistan
165 T2 **Obihiro** Hokkaidō, NE Japan
Obi-Khingou see Khingov
147 P13 **Obikiik** SW Tajikistan
113 N16 **Obilić** Serbia, S Serbia and Montenegro (Yugo.)
127 O12 **Obil'noye** Respublika Kalmykiya, SW Russian Federation
20 F8 **Obion** Tennessee, S USA
20 F8 **Obion River** ~ Tennessee, S USA
171 S12 **Obi, Pulau** island Maluku, E Indonesia
165 S2 **Obira** Hokkaidō, NE Japan
127 N11 **Oblivskaya** Rostovskaya Oblast', SW Russian Federation
123 R14 **Obluch'ye** Yevreyskaya Avtonomnaya Oblast', SE Russian Federation
126 K4 **Obninsk** Kaluzhskaya Oblast', W Russian Federation
114 J8 **Obnova** Pleven, N Bulgaria
79 N15 **Obo** Haut-Mbomou, E Central African Republic
159 T9 **Obo** Qinghai, C China
80 M11 **Obock** E Djibouti
Obol' see Obal'
Obolyanka see Abalyanka
171 V13 **Obome** Papua, E Indonesia
110 G11 **Oborniki** Wielkolpolskie, C Poland
79 G19 **Obouya** Cuvette, C Congo
126 J8 **Oboyan'** Kurskaya Oblast', W Russian Federation
124 M9 **Obozerskiy** Arkhangel'skaya Oblast', NW Russian Federation
112 L11 **Obrenovac** Serbia, N Serbia and Montenegro (Yugo.)
112 D12 **Obrovac** It. Obbrovazzo. Zadar, SW Croatia
Obrovo see Abrova
35 Q3 **Observation Peak** ▲ California, W USA
122 J8 **Obskaya Guba** Eng. Gulf of Ob'. gulf N Russian Federation
173 N13 **Ob' Tablemount** undersea feature S Indian Ocean
173 T10 **Ob' Trench** undersea feature E Indian Ocean
77 P16 **Obuasi** S Ghana
117 P5 **Obukhiv** Rus. Obukhov. Kyyivs'ka Oblast', N Ukraine
Obukhov see Obukhiv
127 U14 **Obva** ~ NW Russian Federation
117 V10 **Obytichna Kosa** spit SE Ukraine
117 V10 **Obytichna Zatoka** gulf SE Ukraine
105 O3 **Oca** ~ N Spain
23 W10 **Ocala** Florida, SE USA
40 M7 **Ocampo** Coahuila de Zaragoza, NE Mexico
54 G7 **Ocaña** Norte de Santander, N Colombia
105 N9 **Ocaña** Castilla-La Mancha, C Spain
106 N4 **O Carballiño** Cast. Carballiño Galicia, NW Spain
37 T9 **Ocate** New Mexico, SW USA
Ocavango see Okavango
54 D14 **Occidental, Cordillera** ▲ W Colombia
57 D14 **Occidental, Cordillera** ▲ W S America
21 Q6 **Oceana** West Virginia, NE USA
21 Z4 **Ocean City** Maryland, NE USA
18 J17 **Ocean City** New Jersey, NE USA
10 K15 **Ocean Falls** British Columbia, SW Canada
Ocean Island see Kure Atoll
Ocean Island see Banaba
64 J9 **Oceanographer Fracture Zone** tectonic feature NW Atlantic Ocean
35 U17 **Oceanside** California, W USA
22 M9 **Ocean Springs** Mississippi, S USA
Ocean State see Rhode Island
25 O9 **O C Fisher Lake** ⊠ Texas, SW USA
117 Q10 **Ochakiv** Rus. Ochakov. Mykolayivs'ka Oblast', S Ukraine
Ochakov see Ochakiv
Ochamchira see Och'amch'ire
137 Q9 **Och'amch'ire** Rus. Ochamchira. W Georgia
Ochansk see Okhansk
125 T15 **Ocher** Permskaya Oblast', NW Russian Federation
115 I19 **Óchi** ▲ Évvoia, C Greece
165 W4 **Ochiishi-misaki** headland Hokkaidō, NE Japan
23 S9 **Ochlockonee River** ~ Florida/Georgia, SE USA
44 K12 **Ocho Rios** C Jamaica
Ochrida see Ohrid
Ochrida, Lake see Ohrid, Lake
101 J19 **Ochsenfurt** Bayern, C Germany
23 U7 **Ocilla** Georgia, SE USA
94 N13 **Ockelbo** Gävleborg, C Sweden
Ocker see Oker
95 I19 **Öckerö** Västra Götaland, S Sweden
23 U6 **Ocmulgee River** ~ Georgia, SE USA
116 H11 **Ocna Mureş** Hung. Marosújvár; prev. Ocna Mureşului; prev. Hung. Marosújvárakna. Alba, C Romania
Ocna Mureşului see Ocna Mureş
116 H11 **Ocna Sibiului** Ger. Salzburg, Hung. Vizakna. Sibiu, C Romania
116 H13 **Ocnele Mari** prev. Vioara. Vâlcea, S Romania
116 L7 **Ocniţa** Rus. Oknitsa. N Moldova
23 U4 **Oconee, Lake** ⊠ Georgia, SE USA
23 U5 **Oconee River** ~ Georgia, SE USA
30 M9 **Oconomowoc** Wisconsin, N USA
30 M6 **Oconto** Wisconsin, N USA
30 M6 **Oconto Falls** Wisconsin, N USA
30 M6 **Oconto River** ~ Wisconsin, N USA
104 I3 **O Corgo** Galicia, NW Spain
41 V16 **Ocosingo** Chiapas, SE Mexico
42 J8 **Ocotal** Nueva Segovia, NW Nicaragua
42 F6 **Ocotepeque** ◆ department W Honduras
Ocotepeque see Nueva Ocotepeque
40 L13 **Ocotlán** Jalisco, SW Mexico
41 R16 **Ocotlán** var. Ocotlán de Morelos. Oaxaca, SE Mexico
Ocotlán de Morelos see Ocotlán
41 U16 **Ocozocuautla** Chiapas, SE Mexico
21 Y10 **Ocracoke Island** island North Carolina, SE USA
102 I3 **Octeville** Manche, N France
October Revolution Island see Oktyabr'skoy Revolyutsii, Ostrov
43 R17 **Ocú** Herrera, S Panama
83 Q14 **Ocua** Cabo Delgado, NE Mozambique
Ocumare see Ocumare del Tuy
54 M5 **Ocumare del Tuy** var. Ocumare. Miranda, N Venezuela
77 P17 **Oda** SE Ghana
165 G12 **Ōda** var. Oda. Shimane, Honshū, SW Japan
92 K3 **Ódáðahraun** lava flow C Iceland
165 Q7 **Ōdate** Akita, Honshū, C Japan
165 N14 **Odawara** Kanagawa, Honshū, S Japan
95 D14 **Odda** Hordaland, S Norway
95 G22 **Odder** Århus, C Denmark
Oddur see Xuddur
29 T13 **Odebolt** Iowa, C USA
104 H14 **Odeleite** Faro, S Portugal
25 Q4 **Odell** Texas, SW USA
25 T14 **Odem** Texas, SW USA
104 F13 **Odemira** Beja, S Portugal
136 C14 **Ödemiş** İzmir, SW Turkey
Ödenburg see Sopron
83 I22 **Odendaalsrus** Free State, C South Africa
Odenpäh see Otepää
95 H23 **Odense** Fyn, C Denmark
101 H19 **Odenwald** ▲ W Germany
84 H10 **Oder** Cz./Pol. Odra. ~ C Europe
Oderberg see Bohumín
100 P11 **Oderbruch** wetland Germany/Poland
Oderhaff see Szczeciński, Zalew
100 O11 **Oder-Havel-Kanal** canal NE Germany
Oderhellen see Odorheiu Secuiesc
100 P13 **Oder-Spree-Kanal** canal NE Germany
Odertal see Zdzieszowice
106 I7 **Oderzo** Veneto, NE Italy
117 P10 **Odesa** Rus. Odessa. Odes'ka Oblast', SW Ukraine
Odesa see Odes'ka Oblast'
95 L18 **Ödeshög** Östergötland, S Sweden
117 O9 **Odes'ka Oblast'** var. Odesa, Rus. Odesskaya Oblast'. ◆ province SW Ukraine
24 M8 **Odessa** Texas, SW USA
32 K8 **Odessa** Washington, NW USA
Odessa see Odesa
Odesskaya Oblast' see Odes'ka Oblast'
122 H12 **Odesskoye** Omskaya Oblast', C Russian Federation
Odessus see Varna
102 F6 **Odet** ~ NW France
104 J14 **Odiel** ~ SW Spain
76 L14 **Odienné** NW Ivory Coast
171 O4 **Odiongan** Tablas Island, C Philippines
116 L12 **Odobeşti** Vrancea, E Romania
110 H13 **Odolanów** Ger. Adelnau. Wielkopolskie, C Poland
167 R13 **Ŏdôngk** Kâmpóng Spoe, S Cambodia
25 N6 **O'donnell** Texas, SW USA
98 O7 **Odoorn** Drenthe, NE Netherlands
Odorhei see Odorheiu Secuiesc
116 J11 **Odorheiu Secuiesc** Ger. Oderhellen, Hung. Vámosudvarhely; prev. Odorhei; Ger. Hofmarkt. Harghita, C Romania
Odra see Oder
112 J9 **Odžaci** Ger. Hodschag, Hung. Hodság. Serbia, NW Serbia and Montenegro (Yugo.)
59 N14 **Oeiras** Piauí, E Brazil
104 F11 **Oeiras** Lisboa, C Portugal
101 G14 **Oelde** Nordrhein-Westfalen, W Germany
28 J11 **Oelrichs** South Dakota, N USA
Oels/Oels in Schlesien see Oleśnica
101 M17 **Oelsnitz** Sachsen, E Germany
29 X12 **Oelwein** Iowa, C USA
Oeniadae see Oiniádes
191 N17 **Oeno Island** atoll Pitcairn Islands, C Pacific Ocean
Oesel see Saaremaa
108 L7 **Oetz** var. Ötz. Tirol, W Austria
137 P11 **Of** Trabzon, NE Turkey
30 K15 **O'Fallon** Illinois, N USA
27 W4 **O'Fallon** Missouri, C USA
107 N16 **Ofanto** ~ S Italy
97 D18 **Offaly** Ir. Ua Uíbh Fhailí; prev. King's County. cultural region C Ireland
101 H18 **Offenbach** var. Offenbach am Main. Hessen, W Germany
Offenbach am Main see Offenbach
101 F22 **Offenburg** Baden-Württemberg, SW Germany
182 C2 **Officer Creek** seasonal river South Australia
Oficina María Elena see María Elena
Oficina Pedro de Valdivia see Pedro de Valdivia
115 K22 **Ofidoússa** island Kykládes, Greece, Aegean Sea
Ofiral see Sharm el Sheikh
92 H10 **Ofotfjorden** fjord N Norway
192 L16 **Ofu** island Manua Islands, E American Samoa
165 R9 **Ōfunato** Iwate, Honshū, C Japan
165 P8 **Oga** Akita, Honshū, C Japan
Ogaadeen see Ogadēn
165 Q9 **Ogachi** Akita, Honshū, C Japan
165 P9 **Ogachi-tōge** pass Honshū, C Japan
81 N14 **Ogadēn** Som. Ogaadeen. plateau Ethiopia/Somalia
165 P8 **Oga-hantō** peninsula Honshū, C Japan
165 K13 **Ōgaki** Gifu, Honshū, SW Japan
28 L15 **Ogallala** Nebraska, C USA
168 M14 **Ogan, Air** ~ Sumatera, W Indonesia
165 Y15 **Ogasawara-shotō** Eng. Bonin Islands. island group SE Japan
14 I9 **Ogascanane, Lac** ⊚ Québec, SE Canada
165 R7 **Ogawara-ko** ⊚ Honshū, C Japan
77 T15 **Ogbomosho** var. Ogmoboso. Oyo, W Nigeria
Ogbomoso see Ogbomosho
29 U13 **Ogden** Iowa, C USA
36 L2 **Ogden** Utah, W USA
18 I6 **Ogdensburg** New York, NE USA
23 W5 **Ogeechee River** ~ Georgia, SE USA
Oger see Ogre
146 F6 **Og'iyon Sho'rxogi** wetland NW Uzbekistan
165 N10 **Ogi** Niigata, Sado, C Japan
10 H5 **Ogilvie** Yukon Territory, NW Canada
10 H4 **Ogilvie** ~ Yukon Territory, NW Canada
10 H5 **Ogilvie Mountains** ▲ Yukon Territory, NW Canada
Oginskiy Kanal see Ahinski Kanal
146 B10 **Oglanly** Balkan Welaýaty, W Turkmenistan
23 T5 **Oglethorpe** Georgia, SE USA
23 T2 **Oglethorpe, Mount** ▲ Georgia, SE USA
106 F7 **Oglio** anc. Ollius. ~ N Italy
103 T8 **Ognon** ~ E France
123 R13 **Ogodzha** Amurskaya Oblast', S Russian Federation
77 W16 **Ogoja** Cross River, S Nigeria
12 C10 **Ogoki** ~ Ontario, S Canada
12 D11 **Ogoki Lake** ⊚ Ontario, C Canada
162 K10 **Ögöömör** Ömnögovĭ, S Mongolia
79 F19 **Ogooué** ~ Congo/Gabon
79 E18 **Ogooué-Ivindo** off. Province de l'Ogooué-Ivindo, var. L'Ogooué-Ivindo. ◆ province N Gabon
79 E19 **Ogooué-Lolo** off. Province de l'Ogooué-Lolo, var. L'Ogooué-Lolo. ◆ province C Gabon
79 C19 **Ogooué-Maritime** off. Province de l'Ogooué-Maritime, var. L'Ogooué-Maritime. ◆ province W Gabon
165 D14 **Ogōri** Fukuoka, Kyūshū, SW Japan
114 H7 **Ogosta** ~ NW Bulgaria
112 Q9 **Ogražden** Bul. Ograzhden. ▲ Bulgaria/FYR Macedonia see also Ograzhden
114 G12 **Ograzhden** Mac. Orgražden. ▲ Bulgaria/FYR Macedonia see also Ogražden
118 G9 **Ogre** Ger. Oger. Ogre, C Latvia
118 H9 **Ogre** ~ C Latvia
112 C10 **Ogulin** Karlovac, NW Croatia
77 S16 **Ogun** ◆ state SW Nigeria
Ogurdzhaly, Ostrov see Ogurjaly Adasy
146 A12 **Ogurjaly Adasy** Rus. Ogurdzhaly, Ostrov. island W Turkmenistan
77 U16 **Ogwashi-Uku** Delta, S Nigeria
185 B23 **Ohai** Southland, South Island, NZ
147 Q10 **Ohangaron** Rus. Akhangaran. Toshkent Viloyati, E Uzbekistan
147 Q10 **Ohangaron** Rus. Akhangaran. ~ E Uzbekistan
83 C16 **Ohangwena** ◆ district N Namibia
30 M10 **O'Hare** ✕ (Chicago) Illinois, N USA
165 R6 **Ōhata** Aomori, Honshū, C Japan
184 L13 **Ohau** Manawatu-Wanganui, North Island, NZ
185 E20 **Ohau, Lake** ⊚ South Island, NZ
Ohcejohka see Utsjoki
99 J20 **Ohey** Namur, SE Belgium
191 X15 **O'Higgins, Cabo** headland Easter Island, Chile, E Pacific Ocean
O'Higgins, Lago see San Martín, Lago
31 S12 **Ohio** off. State of Ohio; also known as The Buckeye State. ◆ state N USA
17 P11 **Ohio River** ~ N USA
Ohlau see Oława
101 H16 **Ohm** ~ C Germany
193 W16 **Ohonua** 'Eua, E Tonga
23 V5 **Ohoopee River** ~ Georgia, SE USA
100 L12 **Ohre** Ger. Eger. ~ Czech Republic/Germany
Ohri see Ohrid
113 M20 **Ohrid** Turk. Ochrida, Ohri. SW FYR Macedonia
113 M20 **Ohrid, Lake** var. Lake Ochrida, Alb. Liqeni i Ohrit, Mac. Ohridsko Ezero. ⊚ Albania/FYR Macedonia
Ohridsko Ezero/Ohrit, Liqeni i see Ohrid, Lake
184 L9 **Ohura** Manawatu-Wanganui, North Island, NZ
58 J9 **Oiapoque** Amapá, E Brazil
58 J10 **Oiapoque, Rio** var. Fleuve l'Oyapok, Oyapock. ~ Brazil/French Guiana see also Oyapok, Fleuve l'
15 O9 **Oies, Île aux** island Québec, SE Canada
92 L13 **Oijärvi** Oulu, C Finland
92 L12 **Oikarainen** Lappi, N Finland
188 F10 **Oikuul** Babeldaob, N Palau
18 C13 **Oil City** Pennsylvania, NE USA
18 C12 **Oil Creek** ~ Pennsylvania, NE USA
35 R13 **Oildale** California, W USA
Oileán Ciarral see Castleisland
Oil Islands see Chagos Archipelago
115 D18 **Oiniádes** anc. Oeniadae. site of ancient city Dytikí Ellás, W Greece
115 L18 **Oinoússes** island E Greece
Oírr, Inis see Inisheer
99 J15 **Oirschot** Noord-Brabant, S Netherlands
103 N4 **Oise** ◆ department N France
103 P3 **Oise** ~ N France
99 J14 **Oisterwijk** Noord-Brabant, S Netherlands
45 O14 **Oistins** S Barbados
165 E4 **Ōita** Ōita, Kyūshū, SW Japan
165 D14 **Ōita** off. Ōita-ken. ◆ prefecture Kyūshū, SW Japan
115 E17 **Oíti** ▲ C Greece
165 S4 **Oiwake** Hokkaidō, NE Japan
35 R14 **Ojai** California, W USA
94 K13 **Öje** Dalarna, C Sweden
93 J14 **Öjebyn** Norrbotten, N Sweden
165 B13 **Ojika-jima** island SW Japan
40 K5 **Ojinaga** Chihuahua, N Mexico
40 M11 **Ojo Caliente** var. Ojocaliente. Zacatecas, C Mexico
40 D6 **Ojo de Liebre, Laguna** var. Laguna Scammon, Scammon Lagoon. lagoon W Mexico
62 I7 **Ojos del Salado, Cerro** ▲ W Argentina
105 R7 **Ojos Negros** Aragón, NE Spain
40 M12 **Ojuelos de Jalisco** Aguascalientes, C Mexico
127 N4 **Oka** ~ W Russian Federation
83 D19 **Okahandja** Otjozondjupa, C Namibia
184 L9 **Okahukura** Manawatu-Wanganui, North Island, NZ
184 J3 **Okaihau** Northland, North Island, NZ
83 D18 **Okakarara** Otjozondjupa, N Namibia
13 P5 **Okak Islands** island group Newfoundland and Labrador, E Canada
10 M17 **Okanagan** ~ British Columbia, SW Canada
11 N17 **Okanagan Lake** ⊚ British Columbia, SW Canada
Ókanizsa see Kanjiža
83 C16 **Okankolo** Otjikoto, N Namibia
32 K6 **Okanogan River** ~ Washington, NW USA
83 D18 **Okaputa** Otjozondjupa, N Namibia
149 V9 **Okāra** Punjab, E Pakistan
26 M10 **Okarche** Oklahoma, C USA
Okarem see Ekerem
189 X14 **Okat Harbor** harbour Kosrae, E Micronesia
22 M5 **Okatibbee Creek** ~ Mississippi, S USA
83 C17 **Okaukuejo** Kunene, N Namibia
Okavanggo see Cubango/Okavango
83 E17 **Okavango** ◆ district NW Namibia
83 G17 **Okavango** var. Cubango, Kavango, Kavengo, Kubango, Okavanggo, Port. Ocavango. ~ S Africa see also Cubango
83 G17 **Okavango Delta** wetland N Botswana
164 M12 **Okaya** Nagano, Honshū, S Japan
164 H13 **Okayama** Okayama, Honshū, SW Japan
164 H13 **Okayama** off. Okayama-ken. ◆ prefecture Honshū, SW Japan
164 L14 **Okazaki** Aichi, Honshū, C Japan
110 M12 **Okęcie** ✕ (Warszawa) Mazowieckie, C Poland
23 Y13 **Okeechobee** Florida, SE USA
23 Y14 **Okeechobee, Lake** ⊚ Florida, SE USA
26 M9 **Okeene** Oklahoma, C USA
23 V8 **Okefenokee Swamp** wetland Georgia, SE USA
97 J24 **Okehampton** SW England, UK
27 P10 **Okemah** Oklahoma, C USA
77 U16 **Okene** Kogi, S Nigeria
100 K13 **Oker** var. Ocker. ~ NW Germany
101 J14 **Oker-Stausee** ⊚ C Germany
123 T12 **Okha** Ostrov Sakhalin, Sakhalinskaya Oblast', SE Russian Federation
125 U15 **Okhansk** var. Ochansk. Permskaya Oblast', NW Russian Federation
123 S10 **Okhotsk** Khabarovskiy Kray, E Russian Federation
192 J2 **Okhotsk, Sea of** sea NW Pacific Ocean
117 T4 **Okhtyrka** Rus. Akhtyrka. Sums'ka Oblast', NE Ukraine
83 E23 **Okiep** Northern Cape, W South Africa
Oki-guntō see Oki-shotō
164 H11 **Oki-kaikyō** strait SW Japan
165 P16 **Okinawa** Okinawa, SW Japan
165 S16 **Okinawa** off. Okinawa-ken. ◆ prefecture Okinawa, SW Japan
165 S16 **Okinawa** island SW Japan
165 U16 **Okinoerabu-jima** island Nansei-shotō, SW Japan
164 F15 **Okino-shima** island SW Japan
164 H11 **Oki-shotō** var. Oki-guntō. island group SW Japan
77 T16 **Okitipupa** Ondo, SW Nigeria
166 L8 **Okkan** Pegu, SW Burma
27 N10 **Oklahoma** off. State of Oklahoma; also known as The Sooner State. ◆ state C USA
27 N11 **Oklahoma City** state capital Oklahoma, C USA
25 Q4 **Oklaunion** Texas, SW USA
23 W10 **Oklawaha River** ~ Florida, SE USA
27 P10 **Okmulgee** Oklahoma, C USA
Oknitsa see Ocniţa
22 M3 **Okolona** Mississippi, S USA
165 U2 **Okoppe** Hokkaidō, NE Japan
11 Q16 **Okotoks** Alberta, SW Canada
80 H6 **Oko, Wadi** ~ NE Sudan
79 G19 **Okoyo** Cuvette, W Congo
77 S15 **Okpara** ~ Benin/Nigeria
92 J8 **Øksfjord** Finnmark, N Norway
125 R4 **Oksino** Nenetskiy Avtonomnyy Okrug, NW Russian Federation
92 G13 **Oksskolten** ▲ C Norway
Oksu see Oqsu
144 M8 **Oktyabr'skiy** Kostanay, N Kazakhstan
186 B7 **Ok Tedi** Western, W PNG
Oktemberyan see Armavir
166 M7 **Oktwin** Pegu, C Burma
127 R6 **Oktyabr'sk** Samarskaya Oblast', W Russian Federation
Oktyabr'sk see Kandyagash
125 N12 **Oktyabr'skiy** Arkhangel'skaya Oblast', NW Russian Federation
122 E10 **Oktyabr'skiy** Kamchatskaya Oblast', E Russian Federation
127 T5 **Oktyabr'skiy** Respublika Bashkortostan, W Russian Federation
127 O11 **Oktyabr'skiy** Volgogradskaya Oblast', SW Russian Federation
Oktyabr'skiy see Aktsyabrski
127 V7 **Oktyabr'skoye** Orenburgskaya Oblast', W Russian Federation
122 M5 **Oktyabr'skoy Revolyutsii, Ostrov** Eng. October Revolution Island. island Severnaya Zemlya, N Russian Federation
164 C15 **Ōkuchi** var. Ōkuti. Kagoshima, Kyūshū, SW Japan
Okulovka see Uglovka
165 Q4 **Okushiri-tō** var. Okusiri Tô. island NE Japan
Okusiri Tô see Okushiri-tō
77 S15 **Okuta** Kwara, W Nigeria
Ōkuti see Ōkuchi
83 F19 **Okwa** var. Chapman's. ~ Botswana/Namibia
123 T10 **Ola** Magadanskaya Oblast', E Russian Federation
27 T11 **Ola** Arkansas, C USA
Ola see Ala
35 T11 **Olacha Peak** ▲ California, W USA
92 J1 **Ólafsfjördhur** Nordhurland Eystra, N Iceland
92 H3 **Ólafsvík** Vesturland, W Iceland
Oláhbrettye see Bretea-Română
Oláhszentgyörgy see Sângeorz-Băi
Oláh-Toplicza see Toplița
35 T11 **Olancha** California, W USA
42 J5 **Olanchito** Yoro, C Honduras
42 J6 **Olancho** ◆ department E Honduras
95 O20 **Öland** island S Sweden
95 O19 **Ölands norra udde** headland S Sweden
95 N22 **Ölands södra udde** headland S Sweden
182 K7 **Olary** South Australia
27 R4 **Olathe** Kansas, C USA
61 C22 **Olavarría** Buenos Aires, E Argentina
92 O2 **Olav V Land** physical region C Svalbard
111 H14 **Oława** Ger. Ohlau. Dolnośląskie, SW Poland
107 D17 **Olbia** prev. Terranova Pausania. Sardegna, Italy, C Mediterranean Sea
44 G5 **Old Bahama Channel** channel Bahamas/Cuba
Old Bay State/Old Colony State see Massachusetts
10 H2 **Old Crow** Yukon Territory, NW Canada
Old Dominion see Virginia
Oldeberkeap see Oldeberkoop
98 M7 **Oldeberkoop** Fris. Oldeberkeap. Friesland, N Netherlands
98 L10 **Oldebroek** Gelderland, E Netherlands
98 L8 **Oldemarkt** Overijssel, N Netherlands
94 E11 **Olden** Sogn og Fjordane, C Norway
100 G10 **Oldenburg** Niedersachsen, NW Germany
100 K8 **Oldenburg** var. Oldenburg in Holstein. Schleswig-Holstein, N Germany
Oldenburg in Holstein see Oldenburg
98 P10 **Oldenzaal** Overijssel, E Netherlands
Olderfjord see Leaibevuotna
18 J8 **Old Forge** New York, NE USA
Old Goa see Goa
97 L17 **Oldham** NW England, UK
39 Q14 **Old Harbor** Kodiak Island, Alaska, USA
44 J13 **Old Harbour** C Jamaica

◆ Country ● Country Capital ◇ Dependent Territory ○ Dependent Territory Capital ◆ Administrative Region ✕ International Airport ▲ Mountain ▲ Mountain Range Volcano ~ River ⊚ Lake ⊠ Reservoir

97 C22 **Old Head of Kinsale** *Ir.* An Seancheann. *headland* SW Ireland
20 J8 **Old Hickory Lake** ⊠ Tennessee, S USA
Old Line State *see* Maryland
Old North State *see* North Carolina
81 I17 **Ol Doinyo Lengeyo** ⛰ C Kenya
11 Q16 **Olds** Alberta, SW Canada
19 O7 **Old Speck Mountain** ▲ Maine, NE USA
19 S6 **Old Town** Maine, NE USA
11 T17 **Old Wives Lake** ◎ Saskatchewan, S Canada
162 J7 **Öldziyt** Arhangay, C Mongolia
163 N10 **Öldziyt** Dornogovĭ, SE Mongolia
188 H6 **Oleai** *var.* San Jose. Saipan, S Northern Mariana Islands
18 E11 **Olean** New York, NE USA
110 O7 **Olecko** *Ger.* Treuburg. Warmińsko-Mazurskie, NE Poland
106 C7 **Oleggio** Piemonte, NE Italy
123 P11 **Olëkma** Amurskaya Oblast', SE Russian Federation
123 P12 **Olëkma** ≈ C Russian Federation
123 P11 **Olëkminsk** Respublika Sakha (Yakutiya), NE Russian Federation
117 W7 **Oleksandrivka** Donets'ka Oblast', E Ukraine
117 R7 **Oleksandrivka** *Rus.* Aleksandrovka. Kirovohrads'ka Oblast', C Ukraine
117 Q9 **Oleksandrivka** Mykolayivs'ka Oblast', S Ukraine
117 S7 **Oleksandriya** *Rus.* Aleksandriya. Kirovohrads'ka Oblast', C Ukraine
93 B20 **Ølen** Hordaland, S Norway
124 J4 **Olenegorsk** Murmanskaya Oblast', NW Russian Federation
123 N9 **Olenëk** Respublika Sakha (Yakutiya), NE Russian Federation
123 N9 **Olenëk** ≈ NE Russian Federation
123 O7 **Olenëkskiy Zaliv** *bay* N Russian Federation
124 K6 **Olenitsa** Murmanskaya Oblast', NW Russian Federation
102 I11 **Oléron, Île d'** *island* W France
111 H14 **Oleśnica** *Ger.* Oels, Oels in Schlesien. Dolnośląskie, SW Poland
111 I15 **Olesno** *Ger.* Rosenberg. Opolskie, S Poland
116 M3 **Olevs'k** *Rus.* Olevsk. Zhytomyrs'ka Oblast', N Ukraine
123 S15 **Ol'ga** Primorskiy Kray, SE Russian Federation
Olga, Mount *see* Kata Tjuta
92 P2 **Olgastretet** *strait* E Svalbard
162 D5 **Ölgiy** Bayan-Ölgiy, W Mongolia
95 F23 **Ølgod** Ribe, W Denmark
104 H14 **Olhão** Faro, S Portugal
93 L14 **Olhava** Oulu, C Finland
112 B12 **Olib** *It.* Ulbo. *island* W Croatia
83 B16 **Olifa** Kunene, NW Namibia
83 E20 **Olifants** *var.* Elephant River. ≈ E Namibia
83 E25 **Olifants** *var.* Elefantes. ≈ SW South Africa
83 G22 **Olifantshoek** Northern Cape, N South Africa
188 L15 **Olimarao Atoll** *atoll* Caroline Islands, C Micronesia
Ólimbos *see* Ólympos
Olimpo *see* Fuerte Olimpo
59 Q15 **Olinda** Pernambuco, E Brazil
Olinthos *see* Ólynthos
83 I20 **Oliphants Drift** Kgatleng, SE Botswana
Olisipo *see* Lisboa
Olita *see* Alytus
105 Q4 **Olite** Navarra, N Spain
62 K10 **Oliva** Córdoba, C Argentina
105 T11 **Oliva** País Valenciano, E Spain
104 I12 **Oliva de la Frontera** Extremadura, W Spain
Olivares *see* Olivares de Júcar
62 H9 **Olivares, Cerro de** ▲ N Chile
105 P9 **Olivares de Júcar** *var.* Olivares. Castilla-La Mancha, C Spain
22 L1 **Olive Branch** Mississippi, S USA
21 O5 **Olive Hill** Kentucky, S USA
35 O6 **Olivehurst** California, W USA
104 G7 **Oliveira de Azeméis** Aveiro, N Portugal
104 I11 **Olivenza** Extremadura, W Spain
11 N17 **Oliver** British Columbia, SW Canada
103 N7 **Olivet** Loiret, C France
29 Q12 **Olivet** South Dakota, N USA
29 T9 **Olivia** Minnesota, N USA
185 C20 **Olivine Range** ⛰ South Island, NZ
108 H10 **Olivone** Ticino, S Switzerland
Ölkeyek *see* Ul'kayak
127 O9 **Ol'khovka** Volgogradskaya Oblast', SW Russian Federation
111 K16 **Olkusz** Małopolskie, S Poland
22 I6 **Olla** Louisiana, S USA
62 I4 **Ollagüe, Volcán** *var.* Oyahue, Volcán Oyahue. ▲ N Chile
189 U13 **Ollan** *island* Chuuk, C Micronesia
188 F7 **Ollei** Babeldaob, N Palau
Ollius *see* Oglio
108 C10 **Ollon** Vaud, W Switzerland
147 Q10 **Olmaliq** *Rus.* Almalyk. Toshkent Viloyati, E Uzbekistan
104 M6 **Olmedo** Castilla-León, N Spain
56 B10 **Olmos** Lambayeque, W Peru
Olmütz *see* Olomouc
30 M15 **Olney** Illinois, N USA
25 R5 **Olney** Texas, SW USA
95 L22 **Olofström** Blekinge, S Sweden
187 N9 **Olomburi** Malaita, N Solomon Islands
111 H17 **Olomouc** *Ger.* Olmütz, *Pol.* Ołomuniec. Olomoucký Kraj, E Czech Republic
111 H18 **Olomoucký Kraj** ◈ region E Czech Republic
Ołomuniec *see* Olomouc
122 D7 **Olonets** Respublika Kareliya, NW Russian Federation
171 N3 **Olongapo** *off.* Olongapo City. Luzon, N Philippines
102 J16 **Oloron-Ste-Marie** Pyrénées-Atlantiques, SW France
192 L16 **Olosega** *island* Manua Islands, E American Samoa
105 W4 **Olot** Cataluña, NE Spain
146 K12 **Olot** *Rus.* Alat. Buxoro Viloyati, C Uzbekistan
112 I12 **Olovo** Federacija Bosna I Hercegovina, E Bosnia and Herzegovina
123 O14 **Olovyannaya** Chitinskaya Oblast', S Russian Federation
123 T7 **Oloy** ≈ NE Russian Federation
101 F16 **Olpe** Nordrhein-Westfalen, W Germany
109 N8 **Olperer** ▲ SW Austria
Olshanka *see* Vil'shanka
Ol'shany *see* Al'shany
Olsnitz *see* Murska Sobota
98 M10 **Olst** Overijssel, E Netherlands
110 L8 **Olsztyn** *Ger.* Allenstein. Warmińsko-Mazurskie, NE Poland,
110 L8 **Olsztynek** *Ger.* Hohenstein in Ostpreussen. Warmińsko-Mazurskie, NE Poland,
116 I14 **Olt** ◈ *county* SW Romania
116 I14 **Olt** *var.* Oltul, *Ger.* Alt. ≈ S Romania
108 E7 **Olten** Solothurn, NW Switzerland
116 K14 **Oltenița** *prev. Eng.* Oltenitsa, *anc.* Constantiola. Călărași, SE Romania
Oltenitsa *see* Oltenița
116 H14 **Olteț** ≈ S Romania
24 M4 **Olton** Texas, SW USA
137 R12 **Oltu** Erzurum, NE Turkey
Oltul *see* Olt
146 G7 **Oltynko'l** Qoraqalpog'iston Respublikasi, NW Uzbekistan
161 S15 **Oluan Pi** *Eng.* Cape Olwanpi. *headland* S Taiwan
Ólubló *see* Stará L'ubovňa
137 R11 **Olur** Erzurum, NE Turkey
104 L15 **Olvera** Andalucía, S Spain
Ol'viopol' *see* Pervomays'k
Olwanpi, Cape *see* Oluan Pi
32 G9 **Olympia** *state capital* Washington, NW USA
115 D20 **Olympía** Dytikí Ellás, S Greece
182 H5 **Olympic Dam** South Australia
32 F7 **Olympic Mountains** ⛰ Washington, NW USA
121 O3 **Ólympos** *var.* Troodos, *Eng.* Mount Olympus. ▲ C Cyprus
115 F15 **Ólympos** *var.* Ólimbos, *Eng.* Mount Olympus. ▲ N Greece
115 L17 **Ólympos** ▲ Lésvos, E Greece
16 C5 **Olympus, Mount** ▲ Washington, NW USA
Olympus, Mount *see* Ólympos
115 G14 **Ólynthos** *var.* Olinthos; *anc.* Olynthus. *site of ancient city* Kentrikí Makedonía, N Greece
Olynthus *see* Ólynthos
117 Q3 **Olyshivka** Chernihivs'ka Oblast', N Ukraine
123 W8 **Olyutorskiy, Mys** *headland* E Russian Federation
123 V8 **Olyutorskiy Zaliv** *bay* E Russian Federation
186 M10 **Om** ≈ W PNG
158 I13 **Oma** Xizang Zizhiqu, W China
165 R6 **Ōma** Aomori, Honshū, C Japan
127 P6 **Oma** ≈ NW Russian Federation
164 M12 **Ōmachi** *var.* Ōmati. Nagano,Honshū, S Japan
165 Q8 **Ōmagari** Akita, Honshū, C Japan
97 E15 **Omagh** *Ir.* An Ómaigh. W Northern Ireland, UK
29 S15 **Omaha** Nebraska, C USA
83 E19 **Omaheke** ◈ *district* W Namibia
141 W10 **Oman** *off.* Sultanate of Oman, *Ar.* Salṭanat 'Umān; *prev.* Muscat and Oman. ◆ *monarchy* SW Asia
141 Y7 **Oman, Gulf of** *Ar.* Khalīj 'Umān. *gulf* N Arabian Sea
184 J3 **Omapere** Northland, North Island, NZ
185 E20 **Omarama** Canterbury, South Island, NZ
112 F11 **Omarska** Republika Srpska, NW Bosnia and Herzegovina
83 C18 **Omaruru** Erongo, NW Namibia
83 C19 **Omaruru** ≈ W Namibia
83 E17 **Omatako** ≈ NE Namibia
Ōmati *see* Ōmachi
83 E18 **Omawewozonyanda** Omaheke, E Namibia
165 R6 **Oma-zaki** *headland* Honshū, C Japan
Ombai *see* Alor, Pulau
83 C16 **Ombalantu** Omusati, N Namibia
79 H15 **Ombella-Mpoko** ◈ *prefecture* S Central African Republic
Ombetsu *see* Onbetsu
83 B17 **Ombombo** Kunene, NW Namibia
79 D19 **Omboué** Ogooué-Maritime, W Gabon
106 G13 **Ombrone** ≈ C Italy
80 F9 **Omdurman** *var.* Umm Durmān. Khartoum, C Sudan
165 N13 **Ōme** Tōkyō, Honshū, S Japan
106 C6 **Omegna** Piemonte, NE Italy
183 P12 **Omeo** Victoria, SE Australia
138 F11 **'Omer** Southern, C Israel
41 P16 **Ometepec** Guerrero, S Mexico
42 K11 **Ometepe, Isla de** *island* S Nicaragua
Om Hager *see* Om Hajer
80 I10 **Om Hajer** *var.* Om Hager. SW Eritrea
165 I13 **Ōmi-Hachiman** *var.* Ōmihachiman. Shiga, Honshū, SW Japan
10 L12 **Omineca Mountains** ⛰ British Columbia, W Canada
113 F14 **Omiš** *It.* Almissa. Split-Dalmacija, S Croatia
112 B10 **Omišalj** Primorje-Gorski Kotar, NW Croatia
83 D19 **Omitara** Khomas, C Namibia
41 O16 **Omitlán, Río** ≈ S Mexico
39 X14 **Ommaney, Cape** *headland* Baranof Island, Alaska, USA
98 N9 **Ommen** Overijssel, E Netherlands
162 K11 **Ömnögovĭ** ◈ *province* S Mongolia
191 X7 **Omoa** Fatu Hira, NE French Polynesia
Omo Botego *see* Omo Wenz
Ómoldova *see* Moldova Veche
123 T7 **Omolon** Chukotskiy Avtonomnyy Okrug, NE Russian Federation
123 T7 **Omolon** ≈ NE Russian Federation
123 Q8 **Omoloy** ≈ NE Russian Federation
165 P8 **Omono-gawa** ≈ Honshū, C Japan
81 I14 **Omo Wenz** *var.* Omo Botego. ≈ Ethiopia/Kenya
122 H12 **Omsk** Omskaya Oblast', C Russian Federation
122 H11 **Omskaya Oblast'** ◈ *province* C Russian Federation
165 U2 **Ōmu** Hokkaidō, NE Japan
110 M9 **Omulew** ≈ NE Poland
116 J12 **Omul, Vârful** *prev.* Vîrful Omu. ▲ C Romania
83 D16 **Omundaungilo** Ohangwena, N Namibia
164 C14 **Ōmura** Nagasaki, Kyūshū, SW Japan
83 B17 **Omusati** ◈ *district* N Namibia
164 C14 **Ōmuta** Fukuoka, Kyūshū, SW Japan
125 S14 **Omutninsk** Kirovskaya Oblast', NW Russian Federation
Omu, Vîrful *see* Omul, Vârful
29 V7 **Onamia** Minnesota, N USA
21 Y5 **Onancock** Virginia, NE USA
14 E10 **Onaping Lake** ◎ Ontario, S Canada
30 M12 **Onarga** Illinois, N USA
15 R6 **Onatchiway, Lac** ◎ Québec, SE Canada
29 S14 **Onawa** Iowa, C USA
165 U5 **Onbetsu** *var.* Ombetsu. Hokkaidō, NE Japan
83 B16 **Oncócua** Cunene, SW Angola
105 S9 **Onda** País Valenciano, E Spain
111 N18 **Ondava** ≈ NE Slovakia
Ondjiva *see* N'Giva
77 T16 **Ondo** Ondo, SW Nigeria
77 T16 **Ondo** ◈ *state* SW Nigeria
163 N8 **Öndörhaan** *var.* Undur Khan; *prev.* Tsetsen Khan. Hentiy, E Mongolia
83 D18 **Ondundazongonda** Otjozondjupa, N Namibia
151 K21 **One and Half Degree Channel** *channel* S Maldives
187 Z15 **Oneata** *island* Lau Group, E Fiji
124 L9 **Onega** Arkhangel'skaya Oblast', NW Russian Federation
122 E7 **Onega** ≈ NW Russian Federation
Onega Bay *see* Onezhskaya Guba
Onega, Lake *see* Onezhskoye Ozero
18 I10 **Oneida** New York, NE USA
20 M8 **Oneida** Tennessee, S USA
18 H9 **Oneida Lake** ◎ New York, NE USA
29 P13 **O'Neill** Nebraska, C USA
123 V12 **Onekotan, Ostrov** *island* Kuril'skiye Ostrova, SE Russian Federation
23 P3 **Oneonta** Alabama, S USA
18 J11 **Oneonta** New York, NE USA
190 I16 **Oneroa** *island* S Cook Islands
116 K11 **Onești** *Hung.* Onyest; *prev.* Gheorghe Gheorghiu-Dej. Bacău, E Romania
193 V15 **Onevai** *island* Tongatapu Group, S Tonga
108 A11 **Onex** Genève, SW Switzerland
126 K8 **Onezhskaya Guba** *Eng.* Onega Bay. *bay* NW Russian Federation
122 D7 **Onezhskoye Ozero** *Eng.* Lake Onega. ◎ NW Russian Federation
83 C16 **Ongandjera** Omusati, N Namibia
184 N12 **Ongaonga** Hawke's Bay, North Island, NZ
162 K9 **Ongi** Dundgovĭ, C Mongolia
162 J8 **Ongi** Övörhangay, C Mongolia
163 W14 **Ongjin** SW North Korea
155 J17 **Ongole** Andhra Pradesh, E India
162 K8 **Ongon** Övörhangay, C Mongolia
Ongtüstik Qazaqstan Oblysy *see* Yuzhnyy Kazakhstan
99 I21 **Onhaye** Namur, S Belgium
166 M8 **Onhne** Pegu, SW Burma
137 S9 **Oni** N Georgia
29 N9 **Onida** South Dakota, N USA
164 F15 **Onigajō-yama** ▲ Shikoku, SW Japan
172 H7 **Onilahy** ≈ S Madagascar
77 U16 **Onitsha** Anambra, S Nigeria
164 I13 **Ono** Hyōgo, Honshū, SW Japan
187 K15 **Ono** *island* SW Fiji
164 K12 **Ōno** Fukui, Honshū, SW Japan
164 E13 **Onoda** Yamaguchi, Honshū, SW Japan
187 Z16 **Ono-i-lau** *island* SE Fiji
164 D13 **Onojō** *var.* Ōnozyô. Fukuoka, Kyūshū, SW Japan
Onomiti *see* Onomichi
163 O7 **Onon Gol** ≈ N Mongolia
Ononte *see* Orontes
55 N6 **Onoto** Anzoátegui, NE Venezuela
191 O3 **Onotoa** *prev.* Clerk Island. *atoll* Tungaru, W Kiribati
Ōnozyô *see* Ōnojō
95 I19 **Onsala** Halland, S Sweden
83 E23 **Onseepkans** Northern Cape, W South Africa
104 F4 **Ons, Illa de** *island* NW Spain
180 H7 **Onslow** Western Australia
21 W11 **Onslow Bay** *bay* North Carolina, E USA
98 P6 **Onstwedde** Groningen, NE Netherlands
164 C16 **On-take** ▲ Kyūshū, SW Japan
35 T15 **Ontario** California, W USA
32 M13 **Ontario** Oregon, NW USA
12 D10 **Ontario** ◈ *province* S Canada
9 P14 **Ontario, Lake** ◎ Canada/USA
Onteniente *see* Ontinyent
105 S11 **Ontinyent** *var.* Onteniente. País Valenciano, E Spain
93 N15 **Ontojärvi** ◎ E Finland
30 L3 **Ontonagon** Michigan, N USA
30 L3 **Ontonagon River** ≈ Michigan, N USA
186 M7 **Ontong Java Atoll** *prev.* Lord Howe Island. *atoll* N Solomon Islands
192 I7 **Ontong Java Rise** *undersea feature* W Pacific Ocean
Onuba *see* Huelva
55 W9 **Onverwacht** Para, N Surinam
Onyest *see* Onești
182 J7 **Oodla Wirra** South Australia
182 F2 **Oodnadatta** South Australia
182 C5 **Ooldea** South Australia
27 Q8 **Oologah Lake** ⊠ Oklahoma, C USA
Oos-Kaap *see* Eastern Cape
Oos-Londen *see* East London
99 E17 **Oostakker** Oost-Vlaanderen, NW Belgium
99 D15 **Oostburg** Zeeland, SW Netherlands
98 K9 **Oostelijk-Flevoland** *polder* C Netherlands
99 B16 **Oostende** *Eng.* Ostend, *Fr.* Ostende. West-Vlaanderen, NW Belgium
99 B16 **Oostende** ✕ West-Vlaanderen, NW Belgium
98 L12 **Oosterbeek** Gelderland, SE Netherlands
99 I14 **Oosterhout** Noord-Brabant, S Netherlands
98 O6 **Oostermoers Vaart** *var.* Hunze. ≈ NE Netherlands
99 F14 **Oosterschelde** *Eng.* Eastern Scheldt. *inlet* SW Netherlands
99 E14 **Oosterscheldedam** *dam* SW Netherlands
98 M7 **Oosterwolde** *Fris.* Easterwâlde. Friesland, N Netherlands
98 I9 **Oosthuizen** Noord-Holland, NW Netherlands
99 H16 **Oostmalle** Antwerpen, N Belgium
Oos-Transvaal *see* Mpumalanga
99 E15 **Oost-Souburg** Zeeland, SW Netherlands
99 E17 **Oost-Vlaanderen** *Eng.* East Flanders. ◈ *province* NW Belgium
98 J5 **Oost-Vlieland** Friesland, N Netherlands
98 F12 **Oostvoorne** Zuid-Holland, SW Netherlands
Ootacamund *see* Udagamandalam
98 O10 **Ootmarsum** Overijssel, E Netherlands
10 K14 **Ootsa Lake** ⊠ British Columbia, SW Canada
114 L8 **Opaka** Tŭrgovishte, N Bulgaria
79 M18 **Opala** Orientale, C Dem. Rep. Congo
125 Q13 **Oparino** Kirovskaya Oblast', NW Russian Federation
14 H8 **Opasatica, Lac** ◎ Québec, SE Canada
112 B9 **Opatija** *It.* Abbazia. Primorje-Gorski Kotar, NW Croatia
111 N15 **Opatów** Świętokrzyskie, C Poland
111 I17 **Opava** *Ger.* Troppau. Moravskoslezský Kraj, E Czech Republic
111 H16 **Opava** *Ger.* Oppa. ≈ NE Czech Republic
Ópazova *see* Stara Pazova
Ópécska *see* Pecica
14 E8 **Opeepeesway Lake** ◎ Ontario, S Canada
23 R5 **Opelika** Alabama, S USA
22 I8 **Opelousas** Louisiana, S USA
186 G6 **Open Bay** *bay* New Britain, E PNG
14 I12 **Opeongo Lake** ◎ Ontario, SE Canada
99 K17 **Opglabbeek** Limburg, NE Belgium
33 W6 **Opheim** Montana, NW USA
39 P10 **Ophir** Alaska, USA
Ophiusa *see* Formentera
79 N18 **Opienge** Orientale, E Dem. Rep. Congo
185 G20 **Opihi** ≈ South Island, NZ
12 J9 **Opinaca** ≈ Québec, C Canada
12 J10 **Opinaca, Réservoir** ⊠ Québec, E Canada
117 T5 **Opishnya** *Rus.* Oposhnya. Poltavs'ka Oblast', NE Ukraine
98 I8 **Opmeer** Noord-Holland, NW Netherlands
77 V17 **Opobo** Akwa Ibom, S Nigeria
124 F16 **Opochka** Pskovskaya Oblast', W Russian Federation
110 L13 **Opoczno** Łodzkie, C Poland
111 I15 **Opole** *Ger.* Oppeln. Opolskie, S Poland
111 H15 **Opolskie** ◈ *province* S Poland
Opornyy *see* Borankul
104 G4 **O Porriño** *var.* Porriño. Galicia, NW Spain
Oporto *see* Porto
Oposhnya *see* Opishnya
184 P8 **Opotiki** Bay of Plenty, North Island, NZ
23 Q7 **Opp** Alabama, S USA
Oppa *see* Opava
94 G9 **Oppdal** Sør-Trøndelag, S Norway
Oppeln *see* Opole
107 N23 **Oppido Mamertina** Calabria, SW Italy
Oppidum Ubiorum *see* Köln
94 F12 **Oppland** ◈ *county* S Norway
118 J12 **Opsa** *Rus.* Opsa. Vitsyebskaya Voblasts', NW Belarus
26 I8 **Optima Lake** ⊠ Oklahoma, C USA
184 J11 **Opunake** Taranaki, North Island, NZ
191 N6 **Opunohu, Baie d'** *bay* Moorea, W French Polynesia
83 B17 **Opuwo** Kunene, NW Namibia
146 H6 **Oqqal'a** *var.* Akkala, *Rus.* Karakala. Qoraqalpog'iston Respublikasi, NW Uzbekistan
147 V13 **Oqsu** *Rus.* Oksu. ≈ SE Tajikistan
147 P14 **Oqtogh, Qatorkŭhi** *Rus.* Khrebet Aktau. ⛰ SW Tajikistan
146 M11 **Oqtosh** *Rus.* Aktash. Samarqand Viloyati, C Uzbekistan
147 N11 **Oqtov Tizmasi** *Rus.* Khrebet Aktau. ⛰ C Uzbekistan
30 J12 **Oquawka** Illinois, N USA
144 J10 **Or'** *Kaz.* Or. ≈ Kazakhstan/Russian Federation
36 M15 **Oracle** Arizona, SW USA
147 N13 **O'radaryo** *Rus.* Uradar'ya. ≈ S Uzbekistan
116 F9 **Oradea** *prev.* Oradea Mare, *Ger.* Grosswardein, *Hung.* Nagyvárad. Bihor, NW Romania
Oradea Mare *see* Oradea
113 M17 **Orahovac** *Alb.* Rahovec. Serbia, S Serbia and Montenegro (Yugo.)
112 H9 **Orahovica** Virovitica-Podravina, NE Croatia
152 K13 **Orai** Uttar Pradesh, N India
92 K12 **Orajärvi** Lappi, NW Finland
Or Akiva *see* Or 'Aqiva
Oral *see* Ural'sk
74 I5 **Oran** *var.* Ouahran, Wahran. NW Algeria
183 R8 **Orange** New South Wales, SE Australia
103 R14 **Orange** *anc.* Arausio. Vaucluse, SE France
25 Y10 **Orange** Texas, SW USA
21 V5 **Orange** Virginia, NE USA
21 R13 **Orangeburg** South Carolina, SE USA
58 J9 **Orange, Cabo** *headland* NE Brazil
29 S12 **Orange City** Iowa, C USA
Orange Cone *see* Orange Fan
172 J10 **Orange Fan** *var.* Orange Cone. *undersea feature* SW Indian Ocean
Orange Free State *see* Free State
25 S14 **Orange Grove** Texas, SW USA
18 K13 **Orange Lake** New York, NE USA
23 V10 **Orange Lake** ◎ Florida, SE USA
Orange Mouth/Orangemund *see* Oranjemund
23 W9 **Orange Park** Florida, SE USA
83 E23 **Orange River** *Afr.* Oranjerivier. ≈ S Africa
14 G15 **Orangeville** Ontario, S Canada
36 M5 **Orangeville** Utah, W USA
42 G1 **Orange Walk** Orange Walk, N Belize
42 F1 **Orange Walk** ◈ *district* NW Belize
100 N11 **Oranienburg** Brandenburg, NE Germany
98 O7 **Oranjekanaal** *canal* NE Netherlands
83 D23 **Oranjemund** *var.* Orangemund; *prev.* Orange Mouth. Karas, SW Namibia
Oranjerivier *see* Orange River
45 N16 **Oranjestad** ○ (Aruba) W Aruba
Oranje Vrystaat *see* Free State
Orany *see* Varėna
83 H18 **Orapa** Central, C Botswana
138 F9 **Or 'Aqiva** *var.* Or Akiva. Haifa, N Israel
112 I10 **Orašje** Federacija Bosna I Hercegovina, N Bosnia and Herzegovina
116 G11 **Orăștie** *Ger.* Broos, *Hung.* Szászváros. Hunedoara, W Romania
Orașul Stalin *see* Brașov
111 K18 **Orava** *Hung.* Árva, *Pol.* Orawa. ≈ N Slovakia
Oravainen *see* Oravais
93 K16 **Oravais** *Fin.* Oravainen. Länsi-Suomi, W Finland
Oravicabánya *see* Oravița
116 F13 **Oravița** *Ger.* Orawitza, *Hung.* Oravicabánya. Caraș-Severin, SW Romania
Orawa *see* Orava
185 B24 **Orawia** Southland, South Island, NZ
Orawitza *see* Oravița
103 P16 **Orb** ≈ S France
106 C9 **Orba** ≈ NW Italy
158 H12 **Orba Co** ◎ W China
108 B9 **Orbe** Vaud, W Switzerland
107 G14 **Orbetello** Toscana, C Italy
104 K3 **Orbigo** ≈ NW Spain
183 Q12 **Orbost** Victoria, SE Australia
95 O14 **Örbyhus** Uppsala, C Sweden
194 I1 **Orcadas** *Argentinian research station* South Orkney Islands, Antarctica
105 P12 **Orcera** Andalucía, S Spain
33 P9 **Orchard Homes** Montana, NW USA
37 P5 **Orchard Mesa** Colorado, C USA
18 D10 **Orchard Park** New York, NE USA
Orchid Island *see* Lan Yü
115 G18 **Orchómenos** *var.* Orhomenos, Orkhómenos; *prev.* Skripón, *anc.* Orchomenus. Stereá Ellás, C Greece
Orchomenus *see* Orchómenos
106 B7 **Orco** ≈ NW Italy
103 R8 **Or, Côte d'** *physical region* C France
29 O14 **Ord** Nebraska, C USA
Ordat' *see* Ordats'
119 O15 **Ordats'** *Rus.* Ordat'. Mahilyowskaya Voblasts', E Belarus
36 K8 **Orderville** Utah, W USA
104 H2 **Ordes** Galicia, NW Spain
35 V14 **Ord Mountain** ▲ California, W USA
163 N14 **Ordos** *prev.* Dongsheng. Nei Mongol Zizhiqu, N China
Ordos Desert *see* Mu Us Shadi
188 B16 **Ordot** C Guam
137 N11 **Ordu** *anc.* Cotyora. Ordu, N Turkey
136 M11 **Ordu** ◈ *province* N Turkey
137 V14 **Ordubad** SW Azerbaijan
105 O3 **Orduña** País Vasco, N Spain
37 U6 **Ordway** Colorado, C USA
117 T9 **Ordzhonikidze** Dnipropetrovs'ka Oblast', E Ukraine
Ordzhonikidze *see* Denisovka, Kazakhstan
Ordzhonikidze *see* Vladikavkaz, Russian Federation
Ordzhonikidze *see* Yenakiyeve, Ukraine
Ordzhonikidzeabad *see* Kofarnihon
55 U9 **Orealla** E Guyana
113 G15 **Orebić** *It.* Sabbioncello. Dubrovnik-Neretva, S Croatia
95 M16 **Örebro** Örebro, C Sweden
95 L16 **Örebro** ◈ *county* C Sweden
25 W6 **Ore City** Texas, SW USA
30 L10 **Oregon** Illinois, N USA
27 Q2 **Oregon** Missouri, C USA
31 R11 **Oregon** Ohio, N USA
32 H13 **Oregon** *off.* State of Oregon; also known as Beaver State, Sunset State, Valentine State, Webfoot State. ◈ *state* NW USA
32 G11 **Oregon City** Oregon, NW USA
95 P14 **Öregrund** Uppsala, C Sweden
Orekhov *see* Orikhiv
126 L3 **Orekhovo-Zuyevo** Moskovskaya Oblast', W Russian Federation
Orekhovsk *see* Arekhawsk
Orel *see* Oril'
126 J6 **Orël** Orlovskaya Oblast', W Russian Federation
56 E11 **Orellana** Loreto, N Peru
56 E6 **Orellana** ◈ *province* NE Ecuador
104 L11 **Orellana, Embalse de** ⊠ W Spain
36 L3 **Orem** Utah, W USA
Ore Mountains *see* Erzgebirge/Krušné Hory
127 V7 **Orenburg** *prev.* Chkalov. Orenburgskaya Oblast', W Russian Federation
127 V7 **Orenburg** ✕ Orenburgskaya Oblast', W Russian Federation
127 T7 **Orenburgskaya Oblast'** ◈ *province* W Russian Federation
Orense *see* Ourense
188 C8 **Oreor** *var.* Koror. *island* N Palau
Oreor *see* Koror
185 B24 **Orepuki** Southland, South Island, NZ
114 L12 **Orestiáda** *prev.* Orestiás. Anatolikí Makedonía kai Thráki, NE Greece
Orestiás *see* Orestiáda
Öresund/Øresund *see* Sound, The
185 C23 **Oreti** ≈ South Island, NZ
184 L5 **Orewa** Auckland, North Island, NZ
65 A25 **Orford, Cape** *headland* West Falkland, Falkland Islands
44 B5 **Órganos, Sierra de los** ⛰ W Cuba
37 R15 **Organ Peak** ▲ New Mexico, SW USA
105 N9 **Orgaz** Castilla-La Mancha, C Spain
Orgeyev *see* Orhei
162 I6 **Orgil** Hövsgöl, C Mongolia
105 O15 **Orgiva** *var.* Órjiva. Andalucía, S Spain
162 I9 **Örgön** Bayanhongor, C Mongolia
117 N9 **Orhei** *var.* Orheiu, *Rus.* Orgeyev. N Moldova
Orheiu *see* Orhei
105 R3 **Orhi** *var.* Orhy, Pico de Orhy, Pic d'Orhy. ▲ France/Spain **see also** Orhy
Orhomenos *see* Orchómenos
162 K6 **Orhon** ◈ *province* N Mongolia
162 L6 **Orhon Gol** ≈ N Mongolia
102 J16 **Orhy** *var.* Orhi, Pico de Orhy, Pic d'Orhy. ▲ France/Spain **see also** Orhi
Orhy, Pic d'/Orhy, Pico de *see* Orhi/Orhy
34 L2 **Orick** California, W USA
32 L6 **Orient** Washington, NW USA
57 I17 **Oriental, Cordillera** ⛰ Bolivia/Peru
54 F10 **Oriental, Cordillera** ⛰ C Colombia
63 M15 **Oriente** Buenos Aires, E Argentina

◆ Country ● Country Capital ◇ Dependent Territory ○ Dependent Territory Capital ◈ Administrative Region ✕ International Airport ▲ Mountain ⛰ Mountain Range 🌋 Volcano ≈ River ◎ Lake ⊠ Reservoir

105 R12 **Orihuela** País Valenciano, E Spain
117 V9 **Orikhiv** *Rus.* Orekhov. Zaporiz'ka Oblast', SE Ukraine
113 K22 **Orikum** *var.* Orikumi. Vlorë, SW Albania
Orikumi *see* Orikum
117 V6 **Oril'** *Rus.* Orel. ≈ E Ukraine
14 H14 **Orillia** Ontario, S Canada
93 M19 **Orimattila** Etelä-Suomi, S Finland
33 Y15 **Orin** Wyoming, C USA
54 M7 **Orinoco, Río** ≈ Colombia/Venezuela
186 C9 **Oriomo** Western, SW PNG
30 K11 **Orion** Illinois, N USA
29 Q5 **Oriska** North Dakota, N USA
153 P17 **Orissa** ◈ *state* NE India
Orissaar *see* Orissaare
118 E5 **Orissaare** *Ger.* Orissaar. Saaremaa, W Estonia
107 B19 **Oristano** Sardegna, Italy, C Mediterranean Sea
107 A19 **Oristano, Golfo di** *gulf* Sardegna, Italy, C Mediterranean Sea
54 D13 **Orito** Putumayo, SW Colombia
93 L18 **Orivesi** Häme, SW Finland
93 N17 **Orivesi** ◎ Länsi-Suomi, SE Finland
58 H12 **Oriximiná** Pará, NE Brazil
41 Q14 **Orizaba** Veracruz-Llave, E Mexico
41 Q14 **Orizaba, Volcán Pico de** *var.* Citlaltépetl. ▲ S Mexico
95 I16 **Ørje** Østfold, S Norway
113 I16 **Orjen** ▲ Bosnia and Herzegovina/Serbia and Montenegro (Yugo.)
Orjiva *see* Orgiva
94 G8 **Orkanger** Sør-Trøndelag, S Norway
94 G8 **Orkdalen** *valley* S Norway
95 K22 **Örkelljunga** Skåne, S Sweden
Orkhaniye *see* Botevgrad
Orkhómenos *see* Orchómenos
94 H9 **Orkla** ≈ S Norway
Orkney *see* Orkney Islands
65 J22 **Orkney Deep** *undersea feature* Scotia Sea/Weddell Sea
96 J4 **Orkney Islands** *var.* Orkney, Orkneys. *island group* N Scotland, UK
Orkneys *see* Orkney Islands
24 K8 **Orla** Texas, SW USA
35 N5 **Orland** California, W USA
23 X11 **Orlando** Florida, SE USA
23 X12 **Orlando** × Florida, SE USA
107 K23 **Orlando, Capo d'** *headland* Sicilia, Italy, C Mediterranean Sea
Orlau *see* Orlová
103 N6 **Orléanais** *cultural region* C France
34 L2 **Orleans** California, W USA
19 Q12 **Orleans** Massachusetts, NE USA
103 N7 **Orléans** *anc.* Aurelianum. Loiret, C France
15 R10 **Orléans, Île d'** *island* Québec, SE Canada
Orléansville *see* Chlef
111 F16 **Orlice** *Ger.* Adler. ≈ NE Czech Republic
122 L13 **Orlik** Respublika Buryatiya, S Russian Federation
125 Q14 **Orlov** *prev.* Khalturin. Kirovskaya Oblast', NW Russian Federation
111 I17 **Orlová** *Ger.* Orlau, *Pol.* Orłowa. Moravskoslezský Kraj, E Czech Republic
Orlov, Mys *see* Orlovskiy, Mys
126 I6 **Orlovskaya Oblast'** ◈ *province* W Russian Federation
126 M5 **Orlovskiy, Mys** *var.* Mys Orlov. *headland* NW Russian Federation
Orłowa *see* Orlová
103 O5 **Orly** × (Paris) Essonne, N France
119 G16 **Orlya** *Rus.* Orlya. Hrodzyenskaya Voblasts', W Belarus
114 M7 **Orlyak** *prev.* Makenzen, Trubchular, *Rom.* Trupcilar. Dobrich, NE Bulgaria
148 L16 **Ormāra** Baluchistān, SW Pakistan
171 P5 **Ormoc** *off.* Ormoc City, *var.* MacArthur. Leyte, C Philippines
23 X10 **Ormond Beach** Florida, SE USA
109 X10 **Ormož** *Ger.* Friedau. NE Slovenia
14 J13 **Ormsby** Ontario, SE Canada
97 K17 **Ormskirk** NW England, UK
Ormsö *see* Vormsi
15 N13 **Ormstown** Québec, SE Canada
Ormuz, Strait of *see* Hormuz, Strait of
103 T8 **Ornans** Doubs, E France
102 K5 **Orne** ◈ *department* N France
102 K5 **Orne** ≈ N France
92 G12 **Ørnes** Nordland, C Norway
110 L7 **Orneta** Warmińsko-Mazurskie, NE Poland
95 P16 **Ornö** Stockholm, C Sweden
37 Q3 **Orno Peak** ▲ Colorado, C USA
93 I16 **Örnsköldsvik** Västernorrland, C Sweden
163 X13 **Oro** E North Korea
45 T6 **Orocovis** C Puerto Rico
54 H10 **Orocué** Casanare, E Colombia
77 N13 **Orodara** SW Burkina
105 S4 **Oroel, Peña de** ▲ N Spain
33 N10 **Orofino** Idaho, NW USA
162 I9 **Orog Nuur** ◎ S Mongolia
35 U14 **Oro Grande** California, W USA
37 S15 **Orogrande** New Mexico, SW USA
191 Q7 **Orohena, Mont** 🌋 Tahiti, W French Polynesia
Orolaunum *see* Arlon
Orol Dengizi *see* Aral Sea
189 S15 **Oroluk Atoll** *atoll* Caroline Islands, C Micronesia
80 J13 **Oromo** ◈ *region* C Ethiopia
13 O15 **Oromocto** New Brunswick, SE Canada
191 S4 **Orona** *prev.* Hull Island. *atoll* Phoenix Islands, C Kiribati
191 V17 **Orongo** *ancient monument* Easter Island, Chile, E Pacific Ocean
138 I3 **Orontes** *var.* Ononte, *Ar.* Nahr el Aassi, Nahr al 'Āṣī. ≈ SW Asia
104 L9 **Oropesa** Castilla-La Mancha, C Spain
105 T8 **Oropesa** País Valenciano, E Spain
Oropeza *see* Cochabamba
Oroqen Zizhiqi *see* Alihe
171 P7 **Oroquieta** *var.* Oroquieta City. Mindanao, S Philippines
40 J8 **Oro, Río del** ≈ C Mexico
59 O14 **Orós, Açude** ⊞ E Brazil
107 D18 **Orosei, Golfo di** *gulf* Tyrrhenian Sea, C Mediterranean Sea
111 M24 **Orosháza** Békés, SE Hungary
Orosirá Rodhópis *see* Rhodope Mountains
111 I22 **Oroszlány** Komárom-Esztergom, W Hungary
188 B16 **Orote Peninsula** *peninsula* W Guam
123 T9 **Orotukan** Magadanskaya Oblast', E Russian Federation
35 O5 **Oroville** California, W USA
32 K6 **Oroville** Washington, NW USA
35 O5 **Oroville, Lake** ⊞ California, W USA
64 I7 **Orphan Knoll** *undersea feature* NW Atlantic Ocean
29 V3 **Orr** Minnesota, N USA
95 M21 **Orrefors** Kalmar, S Sweden
182 I7 **Orroroo** South Australia
31 T12 **Orrville** Ohio, N USA
94 L12 **Orsa** Dalarna, C Sweden
Orschowa *see* Orşova
Orschütz *see* Orzyc
119 O14 **Orsha** *Rus.* Orsha. Vitsyebskaya Voblasts', NE Belarus
127 Q2 **Orshanka** Respublika Mariy El, W Russian Federation
108 C11 **Orsières** Valais, SW Switzerland
127 X8 **Orsk** Orenburgskaya Oblast', W Russian Federation
116 F13 **Orşova** *Ger.* Orschowa, *Hung.* Orsova. Mehedinți, SW Romania
94 D10 **Ørsta** Møre og Romsdal, S Norway
95 O15 **Örsundsbro** Uppsala, C Sweden
136 D16 **Ortaca** Muğla, SW Turkey
107 M16 **Orta Nova** Puglia, SE Italy
136 I17 **Orta Toroslar** ▲ S Turkey
54 E11 **Ortega** Tolima, W Colombia
104 H1 **Ortegal, Cabo** *headland* NW Spain
Ortelsburg *see* Szczytno
102 J15 **Orthez** Pyrénées-Atlantiques, SW France
57 K14 **Orthon, Río** ≈ N Bolivia
60 J10 **Ortigueira** Paraná, S Brazil
104 H1 **Ortigueira** Galicia, NW Spain
106 H5 **Ortisei** *Ger.* Sankt-Ulrich. Trentino-Alto Adige, N Italy
40 F6 **Ortiz** Sonora, NW Mexico
54 L5 **Ortiz** Guárico, N Venezuela
Ortler *see* Ortles
106 F5 **Ortles** *Ger.* Ortler. ▲ N Italy
107 K14 **Ortona** Abruzzo, C Italy
29 R8 **Ortonville** Minnesota, N USA
147 W8 **Orto-Tokoy** Issyk-Kul'skaya Oblast', NE Kyrgyzstan
93 I15 **Örträsk** Västerbotten, N Sweden
100 J12 **Örtze** ≈ NW Germany
Oruba *see* Aruba
142 I3 **Orūmīyeh** *var.* Rizaiyeh, Urmia, Urmiyeh; *prev.* Reẓā'īyeh. Āzarbāyjān-e Bākhtarī, NW Iran
142 J3 **Orūmīyeh, Daryācheh-ye** *var.* Matianus, Sha Hi, Urumi Yeh, *Eng.* Lake Urmia; *prev.* Daryācheh-ye Reẓā'īyeh. ◎ NW Iran
57 K19 **Oruro** Oruro, W Bolivia
57 J19 **Oruro** ◈ *department* W Bolivia
95 I18 **Orust** *island* S Sweden
Orūzgān/Orūzgān *see* Ūrūzgān
106 H13 **Orvieto** *anc.* Velsuna. Umbria, C Italy
194 K7 **Orville Coast** *physical region* Antarctica
114 H7 **Oryakhovo** Vratsa, NW Bulgaria
Oryokko *see* Yalu
117 R5 **Orzhytsya** Poltavs'ka Oblast', C Ukraine
110 M9 **Orzyc** *Ger.* Orschütz. ≈ NE Poland
110 N8 **Orzysz** *Ger.* Arys. Warmińsko-Mazurskie, NE Poland
94 I10 **Os** Hedmark, S Norway
125 U15 **Osa** Permskaya Oblast', NW Russian Federation
29 W11 **Osage** Iowa, C USA
27 U5 **Osage Beach** Missouri, C USA
27 P5 **Osage City** Kansas, C USA
27 U7 **Osage Fork River** ≈ Missouri, C USA
27 U5 **Osage River** ≈ Missouri, C USA
164 J13 **Ōsaka** *hist.* Naniwa. Ōsaka, Honshū, SW Japan
164 I13 **Ōsaka** *off.* Ōsaka-fu, *var.* Ōsaka Hu. ◈ *urban prefecture* Honshū, SW Japan
Ōsaka-fu/Ōsaka Hu *see* Ōsaka
145 R10 **Osakarovka** Karaganda, C Kazakhstan
29 T7 **Osakis** Minnesota, N USA
43 N16 **Osa, Península de** *peninsula* S Costa Rica
60 M10 **Osasco** São Paulo, S Brazil
27 R5 **Osawatomie** Kansas, C USA
26 L3 **Osborne** Kansas, C USA
173 S8 **Osborn Plateau** *undersea feature* E Indian Ocean
95 L21 **Osby** Skåne, S Sweden
Osca *see* Huesca
92 N2 **Oscar II Land** *physical region* W Svalbard
27 Y10 **Osceola** Arkansas, C USA
29 V15 **Osceola** Iowa, C USA
27 S6 **Osceola** Missouri, C USA
29 Q15 **Osceola** Nebraska, C USA
101 N15 **Oschatz** Sachsen, E Germany
100 K13 **Oschersleben** Sachsen-Anhalt, C Germany
31 R7 **Oscoda** Michigan, N USA
Ösel *see* Saaremaa
94 H6 **Osen** Sør-Trøndelag, S Norway
94 J12 **Osensjøen** ◎ S Norway
164 A14 **Ōse-zaki** *headland* Fukue-jima, SW Japan
147 T10 **Osh** Oshskaya Oblast', SW Kyrgyzstan
83 C16 **Oshakati** Oshana, N Namibia
83 C16 **Oshana** ◈ *district* N Namibia
14 H15 **Oshawa** Ontario, SE Canada
165 R10 **Oshika-hantō** *peninsula* Honshū, C Japan
83 C16 **Oshikango** Ohangwena, N Namibia
Oshikoto *see* Otjikoto
165 P5 **Ō-shima** *island* NE Japan
165 N14 **Ō-shima** *island* S Japan
165 Q5 **Oshima-hantō** ▲ Hokkaidō, NE Japan
83 D17 **Oshivelo** Otjikoto, N Namibia
28 K14 **Oshkosh** Nebraska, C USA
30 M7 **Oshkosh** Wisconsin, N USA
Oshmyany *see* Ashmyany
Osh Oblasty *see* Oshskaya Oblast'
77 T16 **Oshogbo** *var.* Osogbo. Osun, W Nigeria
147 T11 **Oshskaya Oblast'** *Kir.* Osh Oblasty. ◈ *province* SW Kyrgyzstan
Oshun *see* Osun
79 J20 **Oshwe** Bandundu, C Dem. Rep. Congo
Osiek *see* Osijek
112 I9 **Osijek** *prev.* Osiek, Osjek, *Ger.* Esseg, *Hung.* Eszék. Osijek-Baranja, E Croatia
112 I9 **Osijek-Baranja** *off.* Osječko-Baranjska Županija. ◈ *province* E Croatia
106 J12 **Osimo** Marche, C Italy
122 M12 **Osinovka** Irkutskaya Oblast', C Russian Federation
Osintorf *see* Asintorf
112 N11 **Osipaonica** Serbia, NE Serbia and Montenegro (Yugo.)
Osipenko *see* Berdyans'k
Osipovichi *see* Asipovichy
Osječko-Baranjska Županija *see* Osijek-Baranja
Osjek *see* Osijek
29 W15 **Oskaloosa** Iowa, C USA
27 Q4 **Oskaloosa** Kansas, C USA
95 N20 **Oskarshamn** Kalmar, S Sweden
95 J21 **Oskarström** Halland, S Sweden
14 M8 **Oskélanéo** Québec, SE Canada
Öskemen *see* Ust'-Kamenogorsk
Oskil *see* Oskol
117 W5 **Oskol** *Ukr.* Oskil. ≈ Russian Federation/Ukraine
93 D20 **Oslo** *prev.* Christiania, Kristiania. • (Norway) Oslo, S Norway
93 D20 **Oslo** ◈ *county* S Norway
93 D21 **Oslofjorden** *fjord* S Norway
155 G15 **Osmānābād** Mahārāshtra, C India
136 J11 **Osmancık** Çorum, N Turkey
136 L16 **Osmaniye** Osmaniye, S Turkey
136 L16 **Osmaniye** ◈ *province* S Turkey
95 O16 **Ösmo** Stockholm, C Sweden
118 E3 **Osmussaar** *island* W Estonia
100 G13 **Osnabrück** Niedersachsen, NW Germany
110 D11 **Ośno Lubuskie** *Ger.* Drossen. Lubuskie, W Poland
Osogbo *see* Oshogbo
113 P19 **Osogov Mountains** *var.* Osogovske Planine, Osogovski Planina, *Mac.* Osogovski Planini. ▲ Bulgaria/FYR Macedonia
Osogovske Planine/ Osogovski Planina/ Osogovski Planini *see* Osogov Mountains
165 R6 **Osore-yama** ▲ Honshū, C Japan
Oşorhei *see* Târgu Mureş
61 J16 **Osório** Rio Grande do Sul, S Brazil
63 G16 **Osorno** Los Lagos, C Chile
104 M4 **Osorno** Castilla-León, N Spain
11 N17 **Osoyoos** British Columbia, SW Canada
95 C14 **Osøyro** Hordaland, S Norway
54 J6 **Ospino** Portuguesa, N Venezuela
98 K13 **Oss** Noord-Brabant, S Netherlands
104 H11 **Ossa** ▲ S Portugal
115 F15 **Óssa** ▲ C Greece
23 X6 **Ossabaw Island** *island* Georgia, SE USA
23 X6 **Ossabaw Sound** *sound* Georgia, SE USA
183 O16 **Ossa, Mount** ▲ Tasmania, SE Australia
104 H11 **Ossa, Serra d'** ▲ SE Portugal
77 U16 **Osse** ≈ S Nigeria
30 J6 **Osseo** Wisconsin, N USA
109 S9 **Ossiacher See** ◎ S Austria
18 K13 **Ossining** New York, NE USA
123 V9 **Ossora** Koryakskiy Avtonomnyy Okrug, E Russian Federation
124 I15 **Ostashkov** Tverskaya Oblast', W Russian Federation
100 H9 **Oste** ≈ NW Germany
Ostee *see* Baltic Sea
Ostend/Ostende *see* Oostende
117 P3 **Oster** Chernihivs'ka Oblast', N Ukraine
95 O14 **Österbybruk** Uppsala, C Sweden
95 M19 **Österbymo** Östergotland, S Sweden
94 K12 **Österdalälven** ≈ C Sweden
94 I12 **Østerdalen** *valley* S Norway
95 L18 **Östergötland** ◈ *county* S Sweden
100 H10 **Osterholz-Scharmbeck** Niedersachsen, NW Germany
Östermark *see* Teuva
Östermyra *see* Seinäjoki
Osterode/Osterode in Ostpreussen *see* Ostróda
94 J11 **Østrehogna** *prev.* Härjåhågnen *Swe.* Härjahågnen, Härjehågna. ▲ Norway/Sweden
101 J14 **Osterode am Harz** Niedersachsen, C Germany
94 C13 **Osterøy** *island* S Norway
Österreich *see* Austria
93 G16 **Östersund** Jämtland, C Sweden
95 N14 **Östervåla** Västmanland, C Sweden
101 H22 **Ostfildern** Baden-Württemberg, SW Germany
95 H16 **Østfold** ◈ *county* S Norway
100 E9 **Ostfriesische Inseln** *Eng.* East Frisian Islands. *island group* NW Germany
100 F10 **Ostfriesland** *historical region* NW Germany
95 P14 **Östhammar** Uppsala, C Sweden
Ostia Aterni *see* Pescara
106 G8 **Ostiglia** Lombardia, N Italy
95 J14 **Östmark** Värmland, C Sweden
95 K22 **Östra Ringsjön** ◎ S Sweden
111 I17 **Ostrava** Moravskoslezský Kraj, E Czech Republic
Ostravský Kraj *see* Moravskoslezský Kraj
110 K8 **Ostróda** *Ger.* Osterode, Osterode in Ostpreussen. Warmińsko-Mazurskie, NE Poland
Ostrog/Ostróg *see* Ostroh
126 L8 **Ostrogozhsk** Voronezhskaya Oblast', W Russian Federation
116 L4 **Ostroh** *Pol.* Ostróg, *Rus.* Ostrog. Rivnens'ka Oblast', NW Ukraine
110 N9 **Ostrołęka** *Ger.* Wiesenhof, *Rus.* Ostrolenka. Mazowieckie, C Poland
111 A16 **Ostrov** *Ger.* Schlackenwerth. Karlovarský Kraj, W Czech Republic
124 F15 **Ostrov** *Latv.* Austrava. Pskovskaya Oblast', W Russian Federation
Ostrovets *see* Ostrowiec Świętokrzyski
113 M21 **Ostrovicës, Mali i** ▲ SE Albania
165 Z2 **Ostrov Iturup** *island* NE Russian Federation
124 M4 **Ostrovnoy** Murmanskaya Oblast', NW Russian Federation
114 L7 **Ostrovo** *prev.* Golema Ada. Razgrad, N Bulgaria
125 N15 **Ostrovskoye** Kostromskaya Oblast', NW Russian Federation
Ostrów *see* Ostrów Wielkopolski
Ostrowiec *see* Ostrowiec Świętokrzyski
111 M14 **Ostrowiec Świętokrzyski** *var.* Ostrowiec, *Rus.* Ostrovets. Świętokrzyskie, C Poland
110 P13 **Ostrów Lubelski** Lubelskie, E Poland
110 N10 **Ostrów Mazowiecka** *var.* Ostrów Mazowiecki. Mazowieckie, C Poland
Ostrów Mazowiecki *see* Ostrów Mazowiecka
Ostrowo *see* Ostrów Wielkopolski
110 H13 **Ostrów Wielkopolski** *var.* Ostrów, *Ger.* Ostrowo. Wielkopolskie, C Poland
Ostryna *see* Astryna
110 I13 **Ostrzeszów** Wielkopolskie, C Poland
107 P18 **Ostuni** Puglia, SE Italy
Ostyako-Voguls'k *see* Khanty-Mansiysk
Osum *see* Osumit, Lumi i
114 I9 **Osŭm** ≈ N Bulgaria
164 C17 **Ōsumi-hantō** ▲ Kyūshū, SW Japan
164 C17 **Ōsumi-kaikyō** *strait* SW Japan
113 L22 **Osumit, Lumi i** *var.* Osum. ≈ SE Albania
77 T16 **Osun** *var.* Oshun. ◈ *state* SW Nigeria
104 L14 **Osuna** Andalucía, S Spain
60 J8 **Osvaldo Cruz** São Paulo, S Brazil
Osveya *see* Asvyeya
18 J7 **Oswegatchie River** ≈ New York, NE USA
27 Q7 **Oswego** Kansas, C USA
18 H9 **Oswego** New York, NE USA
97 K19 **Oswestry** W England, UK
111 J16 **Oświęcim** *Ger.* Auschwitz. Małopolskie, S Poland
185 E22 **Otago** *off.* Otago Region. ◈ *region* South Island, NZ
185 F23 **Otago Peninsula** *peninsula* South Island, NZ
165 F13 **Ōtake** Hiroshima, Honshū, SW Japan
184 L13 **Otaki** Wellington, North Island, NZ
93 M15 **Otanmäki** Oulu, C Finland
145 T15 **Otar** Zhambyl, SE Kazakhstan
165 R4 **Otaru** Hokkaidō, NE Japan
185 C24 **Otatara** Southland, South Island, NZ
185 C24 **Otautau** Southland, South Island, NZ
93 M18 **Otava** Isä-Suomi, E Finland
111 B18 **Otava** *Ger.* Wottawa. ≈ SW Czech Republic
56 C6 **Otavalo** Imbabura, N Ecuador
83 D17 **Otavi** Otjozondjupa, N Namibia
165 P12 **Ōtawara** Tochigi, Honshū, S Japan
83 B16 **Otchinjau** Cunene, SW Angola
116 F12 **Oțelu Roşu** *Ger.* Ferdinandsberg, *Hung.* Nándorhgy. Caras-Severin, SW Romania
185 E21 **Otematata** Canterbury, South Island, NZ
118 I6 **Otepää** *Ger.* Odenpäh. Valgamaa, SE Estonia
32 K9 **Othello** Washington, NW USA
115 A15 **Othonoí** *island* Iónioi Nísoi, Greece, C Mediterranean Sea
Othris *see* Óthrys
115 F17 **Óthrys** *var.* Othris. ▲ C Greece
77 Q14 **Oti** ≈ N Togo
40 K10 **Otinapa** Durango, C Mexico
185 G17 **Otira** West Coast, South Island, NZ
37 V3 **Otis** Colorado, C USA
12 L10 **Otish, Monts** ▲ Québec, E Canada
83 C17 **Otjikondo** Kunene, N Namibia
83 C17 **Otjikoto** *var.* Oshikoto. ◈ *district* N Namibia
83 E18 **Otjinene** Omaheke, NE Namibia
83 D18 **Otjiwarongo** Otjozondjupa, N Namibia
83 D18 **Otjosondu** *var.* Otjosundu. Otjozondjupa, C Namibia
Otjosundu *see* Otjosondu
83 D18 **Otjozondjupa** ◈ *district* C Namibia
112 C11 **Otočac** Lika-Senj, W Croatia
Otog Qi *see* Ulan
112 J10 **Otok** Vukovar-Srijem, E Croatia
116 K14 **Otopeni** × (București) București, S Romania
184 L8 **Otorohanga** Waikato, North Island, NZ
12 D9 **Otoskwin** ≈ Ontario, C Canada
165 G14 **Ōtoyo** Kōchi, Shikoku, SW Japan
95 E16 **Otra** ≈ S Norway
107 R19 **Otranto** Puglia, SE Italy
Otranto, Canale d' *see* Otranto, Strait of
107 Q18 **Otranto, Strait of** *It.* Canale d'Otranto. *strait* Albania/Italy
111 H18 **Otrokovice** *Ger.* Otrokowitz. Zlínský Kraj, E Czech Republic
Otrokowitz *see* Otrokovice
31 P10 **Otsego** Michigan, N USA
31 Q6 **Otsego Lake** ◎ Michigan, N USA
18 I11 **Otselic River** ≈ New York, NE USA
164 J14 **Ōtsu** *var.* Ōtu. Shiga, Honshū, SW Japan
94 G11 **Otta** Oppland, S Norway
189 U13 **Otta** *island* Chuuk, C Micronesia
94 F11 **Otta** ≈ S Norway
189 U13 **Otta Pass** *passage* Chuuk Islands, C Micronesia
95 J22 **Ottarp** Skåne, S Sweden
14 L12 **Ottawa** • (Canada) Ontario, SE Canada
30 L11 **Ottawa** Illinois, N USA
27 Q5 **Ottawa** Kansas, C USA
31 R12 **Ottawa** Ohio, N USA
14 L12 **Ottawa** *var.* Uplands. × Ontario, SE Canada
14 M12 **Ottawa** *Fr.* Outaouais. ≈ Ontario/Québec, SE Canada
12 I4 **Ottawa Islands** *island group* Nunavut, C Canada
18 L8 **Otter Creek** ≈ Vermont, NE USA
36 L6 **Otter Creek Reservoir** ⊞ Utah, W USA
98 L11 **Otterlo** Gelderland, E Netherlands
94 D9 **Otterøya** *island* S Norway
29 S6 **Otter Tail Lake** ◎ Minnesota, N USA
29 R7 **Otter Tail River** ≈ Minnesota, C USA
95 H23 **Otterup** Fyn, C Denmark
99 H19 **Ottignies** Wallon Brabant, C Belgium
101 L23 **Ottobrunn** Bayern, SE Germany
29 X15 **Ottumwa** Iowa, C USA
Ōtu *see* Ōtsu
83 B16 **Otuazuma** Kunene, NW Namibia
Otuki *see* Ōtsuki
77 V16 **Oturkpo** Benue, S Nigeria
193 Y15 **Otu Tolu Group** *island group* SE Tonga
182 M13 **Otway, Cape** *headland* Victoria, SE Australia
63 H24 **Otway, Seno** *inlet* S Chile
Ötz *see* Oetz
108 L8 **Ötztaler Ache** ≈ W Austria
108 L9 **Ötztaler Alpen** *It.* Alpi Venoste. ▲ SW Austria
27 T12 **Ouachita, Lake** ⊞ Arkansas, C USA
27 R11 **Ouachita Mountains** ▲ Arkansas/Oklahoma, C USA
27 U13 **Ouachita River** ≈ Arkansas/Louisiana, C USA
Ouadaï *see* Ouaddaï
76 J7 **Ouadâne** *var.* Ouadane. Adrar, C Mauritania
78 K13 **Ouadda** Haute-Kotto, N Central African Republic
78 J10 **Ouaddaï** *off.* Préfecture du Ouaddaï, *var.* Ouadaï, Wadai. ◈ *prefecture* SE Chad
77 P13 **Ouagadougou** *var.* Wagadugu. • (Burkina) C Burkina
77 P13 **Ouagadougou** × C Burkina
77 O12 **Ouahigouya** NW Burkina
Ouahran *see* Oran
79 J14 **Ouaka** ◈ *prefecture* C Central African Republic
79 J15 **Ouaka** ≈ S Central African Republic
Oualam *see* Ouallam
76 M9 **Oualâta** *var.* Oualata. Hodh ech Chargui, SE Mauritania
77 R11 **Ouallam** *var.* Oualam. Tillabéri, W Niger
172 H14 **Ouanani** Mohéli, S Comoros
55 Z10 **Ouanary** E French Guiana
78 L13 **Ouanda Djallé** Vakaga, NE Central African Republic
79 N14 **Ouando** Haut-Mbomou, SE Central African Republic
79 L15 **Ouango** Mbomou, S Central African Republic
77 N14 **Ouangolodougou** *var.* Wangolodougou. N Ivory Coast
172 I13 **Ouani** Anjouan, SE Comoros
79 M15 **Ouara** ≈ E Central African Republic
76 K7 **Ouarâne** *desert* C Mauritania
15 O11 **Ouareau** ≈ Québec, SE Canada
74 K7 **Ouargla** *var.* Wargla. NE Algeria
74 F8 **Ouarzazate** S Morocco
77 Q11 **Ouatagouna** Gao, E Mali
74 G6 **Ouazzane** *var.* Ouezzane, *Ar.* Wazan, Wazzan. N Morocco
Oubangui *see* Ubangi
Oubangui-Chari *see* Central African Republic
Oubari, Edeyen d' *see* Awbāri, Idhān
98 G13 **Oud-Beijerland** Zuid-Holland, SW Netherlands
98 F13 **Ouddorp** Zuid-Holland, SW Netherlands
77 P9 **Oudeïka** *oasis* C Mali
98 G13 **Oude Maas** ≈ SW Netherlands
99 E18 **Oudenaarde** *Fr.* Audenarde. Oost-Vlaanderen, SW Belgium
99 H14 **Oudenbosch** Noord-Brabant, S Netherlands
98 P6 **Oude Pekela** Groningen, NE Netherlands
Ouderkerk *see* Ouderkerk aan den Amstel
98 I10 **Ouderkerk aan den Amstel** *var.* Ouderkerk. Noord-Holland, C Netherlands
98 I6 **Oudeschild** Noord-Holland, NW Netherlands
99 G14 **Oude-Tonge** Zuid-Holland, SW Netherlands
98 I12 **Oudewater** Utrecht, C Netherlands
Oudjda *see* Oujda
98 L5 **Oudkerk** Friesland, N Netherlands
102 J7 **Oudon** ≈ NW France
98 I9 **Oudorp** Noord-Holland, NW Netherlands
83 G25 **Oudtshoorn** Western Cape, SW South Africa
99 I16 **Oud-Turnhout** Antwerpen, N Belgium
74 F7 **Oued-Zem** C Morocco
187 P16 **Ouégoa** Province Nord, C New Caledonia
76 L13 **Ouéléssébougou** *var.* Ouolossébougou. Koulikoro, SW Mali
77 N16 **Ouellé** E Ivory Coast
77 R16 **Ouémé** ≈ C Benin
77 O13 **Ouessa** S Burkina
102 D5 **Ouessant, Île d'** *Eng.* Ushant. *island* NW France
79 H17 **Ouésso** La Sangha, NW Congo
79 D15 **Ouest** *Eng.* West. ◈ *province* W Cameroon
190 G11 **Ouest, Baie de l'** *bay* Îles Wallis, Wallis and Futuna
15 Y7 **Ouest, Pointe de l'** *headland* Québec, SE Canada
Ouezzane *see* Ouazzane
99 K20 **Ouffet** Liège, E Belgium
79 H14 **Ouham** ◈ *prefecture* NW Central African Republic
78 I13 **Ouham** ≈ Central African Republic/Chad
79 G14 **Ouham-Pendé** ◈ *prefecture* W Central African Republic
77 R16 **Ouidah** *Eng.* Whydah, Wida. S Benin
74 H6 **Oujda** *Ar.* Oudjda, Ujda. NE Morocco
76 I7 **Oujeft** Adrar, C Mauritania
93 L15 **Oulainen** Oulu, C Finland
Ould Yanja *see* Ould Yenjé
76 J10 **Ould Yenjé** *var.* Ould Yanja. Guidimaka, S Mauritania
93 L14 **Oulu** *Swe.* Uleåborg. Oulu, C Finland
93 M14 **Oulu** *Swe.* Uleåborg. ◈ *province* N Finland
93 L15 **Oulujärvi** *Swe.* Uleträsk. ◎ C Finland
93 M14 **Oulujoki** *Swe.* Uleälv. ≈ C Finland
93 L14 **Oulunsalo** Oulu, C Finland
106 A8 **Oulx** Piemonte, NE Italy
78 J9 **Oum-Chalouba** Borkou-Ennedi-Tibesti, NE Chad
76 M16 **Oumé** C Ivory Coast
74 F7 **Oum er Rbia** ≈ C Morocco
78 J10 **Oum-Hadjer** Batha, E Chad
92 K10 **Ounasjoki** ≈ N Finland
78 J7 **Ounianga Kébir** Borkou-Ennedi-Tibesti, N Chad
Ouolossébougou *see* Ouéléssébougou
Oup *see* Auob
99 K19 **Oupeye** Liège, E Belgium
99 N21 **Our** ≈ NW Europe
37 Q7 **Ouray** Colorado, C USA
103 R7 **Ource** ≈ C France
104 G9 **Ourém** Santarém, C Portugal
104 H4 **Ourense** *Cast.* Orense; *Lat.* Aurium. Galicia, NW Spain
104 I4 **Ourense** *Cast.* Orense ◈ *province* Galicia, NW Spain
59 O15 **Ouricuri** Pernambuco, E Brazil
60 J9 **Ourinhos** São Paulo, S Brazil
104 G13 **Ourique** Beja, S Portugal
59 M20 **Ouro Preto** Minas Gerais, NE Brazil
Ours, Grand Lac de l' *see* Great Bear Lake
99 K20 **Ourthe** ≈ E Belgium
165 Q9 **Ōu-sanmyaku** ▲ Honshū, C Japan
97 M17 **Ouse** ≈ N England, UK
Ouse *see* Great Ouse
102 H7 **Oust** ≈ NW France
Outaouais *see* Ottawa
15 T4 **Outardes Quatre, Réservoir** ⊞ Québec, SE Canada
15 T5 **Outardes, Rivière aux** ≈ Québec, SE Canada
96 E8 **Outer Hebrides** *var.* Western Isles. *island group* NW Scotland, UK
30 K3 **Outer Island** *island* Apostle Islands, Wisconsin, N USA
35 S16 **Outer Santa Barbara Passage** *passage* California, SW USA
104 G3 **Outes** Galicia, NW Spain
83 C18 **Outjo** Kunene, N Namibia
11 T16 **Outlook** Saskatchewan, S Canada
93 N16 **Outokumpu** Itä-Suomi, E Finland
96 M2 **Out Skerries** *island group* NE Scotland, UK
187 Q16 **Ouvéa** *island* Îles Loyauté, NE New Caledonia
103 S14 **Ouvèze** ≈ SE France
182 L9 **Ouyen** Victoria, SE Australia
39 Q14 **Ouzinkie** Kodiak Island, Alaska, USA
137 O13 **Ovacık** Tunceli, E Turkey
106 C9 **Ovada** Piemonte, NE Italy

◆ Country • Country Capital ◇ Dependent Territory ○ Dependent Territory Capital ◈ Administrative Region × International Airport ▲ Mountain ▲ Mountain Range 🌋 Volcano ≈ River ◎ Lake ⊞ Reservoir

187 X14 **Ovalau** island C Fiji
62 G9 **Ovalle** Coquimbo, N Chile
83 C17 **Ovamboland** physical region N Namibia
54 L10 **Ovana, Cerro** ▲ S Venezuela
104 G7 **Ovar** Aveiro, N Portugal
114 L10 **Ovcharitsa, Yazovir** ▣ SE Bulgaria
54 E6 **Ovejas** Sucre, NW Colombia
101 E16 **Overath** Nordrhein-Westfalen, W Germany
98 F13 **Overflakkee** island SW Netherlands
99 H19 **Overijse** Vlaams Brabant, C Belgium
98 N10 **Overijssel** ◈ province E Netherlands
98 M9 **Overijssels Kanaal** canal E Netherlands
92 K13 **Överkalix** Norrbotten, N Sweden
27 R4 **Overland Park** Kansas, C USA
99 L14 **Overloon** Noord-Brabant, SE Netherlands
99 K16 **Overpelt** Limburg, NE Belgium
35 Y10 **Overton** Nevada, W USA
25 W7 **Overton** Texas, SW USA
92 K13 **Övertorneå** Norrbotten, N Sweden
95 N18 **Överum** Kalmar, S Sweden
92 G13 **Överuman** ◎ N Sweden
117 P11 **Ovidiopol'** Odes'ka Oblast', SW Ukraine
116 M14 **Ovidiu** Constanța, SE Romania
45 N10 **Oviedo** SW Dominican Republic
104 K2 **Oviedo** anc. Asturias. Asturias, NW Spain
104 K2 **Oviedo** ✕ Asturias, N Spain
Ovilava see Wels
118 D7 **Oviši** Ventspils, W Latvia
146 K10 **Ovminzatov-Tog'lari** Rus. Gory Auminzatau. ▲ N Uzbekistan
162 H6 **Övögdiy** Dzavhan, C Mongolia
163 P10 **Ovoot** Sühbaatar, SE Mongolia
157 O4 **Övörhangay** ◈ province C Mongolia
94 E12 **Øvre Årdal** Sogn og Fjordane, S Norway
95 J14 **Övre Fryken** ◎ C Sweden
92 J11 **Övre Soppero** Lapp. Badje-Sohppar. Norrbotten, N Sweden
117 N3 **Ovruch** Zhytomyrs'ka Oblast', N Ukraine
162 J8 **Övt** Övörhangay, C Mongolia
185 E24 **Owaka** Otago, South Island, NZ
79 H18 **Owando** prev. Fort-Rousset. Cuvette, C Congo
164 J14 **Owase** Mie, Honshū, SW Japan
27 P9 **Owasso** Oklahoma, C USA
29 V10 **Owatonna** Minnesota, N USA
173 O4 **Owen Fracture Zone** tectonic feature W Arabian Sea
185 H15 **Owen, Mount** ▲ South Island, NZ
185 H15 **Owen River** Tasman, South Island, NZ
44 D8 **Owen Roberts** ✕ Grand Cayman, Cayman Islands
20 I6 **Owensboro** Kentucky, S USA
35 T11 **Owens Lake** salt flat California, W USA
14 F14 **Owen Sound** Ontario, S Canada
14 F13 **Owen Sound** ◎ Ontario, S Canada
35 T10 **Owens River** ≈ California, W USA
186 F9 **Owen Stanley Range** ▲ S PNG
27 V5 **Owensville** Missouri, C USA
20 M4 **Owenton** Kentucky, S USA
77 U17 **Owerri** Imo, S Nigeria
184 M10 **Owhango** Manawatu-Wanganui, North Island, NZ
21 N5 **Owingsville** Kentucky, S USA
77 T16 **Owo** Ondo, SW Nigeria
31 R9 **Owosso** Michigan, N USA
35 V1 **Owyhee** Nevada, W USA
32 L14 **Owyhee, Lake** ◎ Oregon, NW USA
32 L15 **Owyhee River** ≈ Idaho/Oregon, NW USA
92 K1 **Öxarfjördhur** var. Axarfjördhur. fjord N Iceland
94 K12 **Oxberg** Dalarna, C Sweden
11 V17 **Oxbow** Saskatchewan, S Canada
95 O17 **Oxelösund** Södermanland, S Sweden
185 H18 **Oxford** Canterbury, South Island, NZ
97 M21 **Oxford** Lat. Oxonia. S England, UK
23 Q3 **Oxford** Alabama, S USA
22 L2 **Oxford** Mississippi, S USA
29 N16 **Oxford** Nebraska, C USA
18 I11 **Oxford** New York, NE USA
21 U8 **Oxford** North Carolina, SE USA
31 Q14 **Oxford** Ohio, N USA
18 H16 **Oxford** Pennsylvania, NE USA
11 X12 **Oxford House** Manitoba, C Canada
29 Y13 **Oxford Junction** Iowa, C USA
11 X12 **Oxford Lake** ◎ Manitoba, C Canada
97 M21 **Oxfordshire** cultural region S England, UK
Oxia see Oxyá
41 X12 **Oxkutzcab** Yucatán, SE Mexico
35 R15 **Oxnard** California, W USA
Oxonia see Oxford
14 I12 **Oxtongue** ≈ Ontario, SE Canada
Oxus see Amu Darya
115 E15 **Oxyá** var. Oxia. ▲ C Greece
164 L11 **Oyabe** Toyama, Honshū, SW Japan
Oyahue/Oyahue, Volcán see Ollagüe, Volcán
165 O12 **Oyama** Tochigi, Honshū, S Japan
Oyapock see Oiapoque, Rio
55 Z10 **Oyapok, Baie de L'** bay Brazil/French Guiana
55 Z11 **Oyapok, Fleuve l'** var. Oyapock, Rio Oiapoque. ≈ Brazil/French Guiana **see also** Oiapoque, Rio
79 E17 **Oyem** Woleu-Ntem, N Gabon
11 R16 **Oyen** Alberta, SW Canada
95 I15 **Øyeren** ◎ S Norway
162 G6 **Oygon** Dzavhan, N Mongolia
96 I7 **Oykel** ≈ N Scotland, UK
123 R9 **Oymyakon** Respublika Sakha (Yakutiya), NE Russian Federation
79 H19 **Oyo** Cuvette, C Congo
77 S15 **Oyo** Oyo, W Nigeria
77 S15 **Oyo** ◈ state SW Nigeria
56 D13 **Oyón** Lima, C Peru
103 S10 **Oyonnax** Ain, E France
146 L10 **Oyoqig'itma** Rus. Ayakagytma. Buxoro Viloyati, C Uzbekistan
146 M9 **Oyoqquduq** Rus. Ayakkuduk. Navoiy Viloyati, N Uzbekistan
32 F9 **Oysterville** Washington, NW USA
95 D14 **Øystese** Hordaland, S Norway
147 U10 **Oy-Tal** Oshskaya Oblast', SW Kyrgyzstan
147 T10 **Oy-Tal** ≈ SW Kyrgyzstan
145 S16 **Oytal** Zhambyl, S Kazakhstan
Oyyl see Uil
Ozarichi see Azarychy
23 R7 **Ozark** Alabama, S USA
27 S10 **Ozark** Arkansas, C USA
27 T8 **Ozark** Missouri, C USA
27 T8 **Ozark Plateau** plain Arkansas/Missouri, C USA
27 T6 **Ozarks, Lake of the** ▣ Missouri, C USA
192 L10 **Ozbourn Seamount** undersea feature W Pacific Ocean
111 L20 **Ózd** Borsod-Abaúj-Zemplén, NE Hungary
112 D11 **Ozeblin** ▲ C Croatia
123 V11 **Ozernovskiy** Kamchatskaya Oblast', E Russian Federation
144 M7 **Ozërnoye** var. Ozërnyy. Kostanay, N Kazakhstan
124 I15 **Ozërnyy** Tverskaya Oblast', W Russian Federation
Ozërnyy see Ozërnoye
115 D18 **Ozerós, Límni** ◎ W Greece
122 F11 **Ozërsk** Chelyabinskaya Oblast', C Russian Federation
119 D14 **Ozersk** prev. Darkehnen, Ger. Angerapp. Kaliningradskaya Oblast', W Russian Federation
126 L4 **Ozery** Moskovskaya Oblast', W Russian Federation
Özgön see Uzgen
107 C17 **Ozieri** Sardegna, Italy, C Mediterranean Sea
111 I15 **Ozimek** Ger. Malapane. Opolskie, S Poland
127 R8 **Ozinki** Saratovskaya Oblast', W Russian Federation
Oziya see Ojiya
25 O10 **Ozona** Texas, SW USA
Ozorkov see Ozorków
110 J12 **Ozorków** Rus. Ozorkov. Łódź, C Poland
164 F14 **Ōzu** Ehime, Shikoku, SW Japan
137 R10 **Ozurget'i** prev. Makharadze. W Georgia

P

99 J17 **Paal** Limburg, NE Belgium
196 M14 **Paamiut** var. Pâmiut, Dan. Frederikshåb. Kitaa, S Greenland
167 N8 **Pa-an** Karen State, S Burma
101 L22 **Paar** ≈ SE Germany
83 E26 **Paarl** Western Cape, SW South Africa
93 L15 **Paavola** Oulu, C Finland
96 E8 **Pabbay** island NW Scotland, UK
153 T15 **Pabna** Rajshahi, W Bangladesh
109 U4 **Pabneukirchen** Oberösterreich, N Austria
118 H13 **Pabradė** Pol. Podbrodzie. Vilnius, SE Lithuania
56 L13 **Pacahuaras, Río** ≈ N Bolivia
Pacaraima, Sierra/Pacaraim, Serra see Pakaraima Mountains
56 B11 **Pacasmayo** La Libertad, W Peru
42 D6 **Pacaya, Volcán de** ▲ S Guatemala
115 K23 **Pachía** island Kykládes, Greece, Aegean Sea
107 L26 **Pachino** Sicilia, Italy, C Mediterranean Sea
56 F12 **Pachitea, Río** ≈ C Peru
154 I11 **Pachmarhi** Madhya Pradesh, C India
121 P3 **Páchna** var. Pakhna. SW Cyprus
115 H25 **Páchnes** ▲ Kríti, Greece, E Mediterranean Sea
54 F9 **Pacho** Cundinamarca, C Colombia
154 F12 **Pāchora** Mahārāshtra, C India
41 P13 **Pachuca** var. Pachuca de Soto. Hidalgo, C Mexico
Pachuca de Soto see Pachuca
27 W5 **Pacific** Missouri, C USA
192 L14 **Pacific-Antarctic Ridge** undersea feature S Pacific Ocean
32 F8 **Pacific Beach** Washington, NW USA
35 N10 **Pacific Grove** California, W USA
29 S15 **Pacific Junction** Iowa, C USA
198-199 **Pacific Ocean** ocean
113 J15 **Pačir** ▲ SW Serbia and Montenegro (Yugo.)
182 L5 **Packsaddle** New South Wales, SE Australia
32 H9 **Packwood** Washington, NW USA
Padalung see Phatthalung
168 J12 **Padang** Sumatera, W Indonesia
168 L9 **Padang Endau** Pahang, Peninsular Malaysia
Padangpandjang see Padangpanjang
168 I11 **Padangpanjang** prev. Padangpandjang. Sumatera, W Indonesia
168 I10 **Padangsidempuan** prev. Padangsidimpoean. Sumatera, W Indonesia
Padangsidimpoean see Padangsidempuan
124 I9 **Padany** Respublika Kareliya, NW Russian Federation
93 M18 **Padasjoki** Etelä-Suomi, S Finland
57 M22 **Padcaya** Tarija, S Bolivia
101 H14 **Paderborn** Nordrhein-Westfalen, NW Germany
Padeşul/Padeş, Vîrful see Padeş, Vârful
116 F12 **Padeş, Vârful** var. Padeşul; prev. Vîrful Padeş. ▲ W Romania
112 L10 **Padinska Skela** Serbia, N Serbia and Montenegro (Yugo.)
Padma see Brahmaputra
153 S14 **Padma** var. Ganges. ≈ Bangladesh/India **see also** Ganges
106 H8 **Padova** Eng. Padua; anc. Patavium. Veneto, NE Italy
82 A10 **Padrão, Ponta do** headland NW Angola
25 T16 **Padre Island** island Texas, SW USA
104 G3 **Padrón** Galicia, NW Spain
118 K13 **Padsvillye** Rus. Podsvil'ye. Vitsyebskaya Voblasts', N Belarus
182 K11 **Padthaway** South Australia
Padua see Padova
20 G7 **Paducah** Kentucky, S USA
25 P4 **Paducah** Texas, SW USA
105 N15 **Padul** Andalucía, S Spain
191 P8 **Paea** Tahiti, W French Polynesia
185 L14 **Paekakariki** Wellington, North Island, NZ
163 X11 **Paektu-san** var. Baitou Shan. ▲ China/North Korea
163 V15 **Paengnyŏng-do** island NW South Korea
184 M7 **Paeroa** Waikato, North Island, NZ
54 D12 **Páez** Cauca, SW Colombia
121 O3 **Páfos** var. Paphos. W Cyprus
121 O3 **Páfos** ✕ SW Cyprus
83 L19 **Pafúri** Gaza, SW Mozambique
112 C12 **Pag** It. Pago. Lika-Senj, W Croatia
112 B11 **Pag** It. Pago. island Zadar, SW Croatia
171 P7 **Pagadian** Mindanao, S Philippines
168 J13 **Pagai Selatan, Pulau** island Kepulauan Mentawai, W Indonesia
168 J13 **Pagai Utara, Pulau** island Kepulauan Mentawai, W Indonesia
188 K4 **Pagan** island C Northern Mariana Islands
115 G16 **Pagasitikós Kólpos** gulf E Greece
36 L8 **Page** Arizona, SW USA
29 Q5 **Page** North Dakota, N USA
118 D13 **Pagėgiai** Ger. Pogegen. Tauragė, SW Lithuania
21 S11 **Pageland** South Carolina, SE USA
81 G16 **Pager** ≈ NE Uganda
149 Q5 **Paghmān** Kābul, E Afghanistan
Pago see Pag
188 C16 **Pago Bay** bay E Guam, W Pacific Ocean
115 M20 **Pagóndas** var. Pagóndhas. Sámos, Dodekánisos, Greece, Aegean Sea
Pagóndhas see Pagóndas
192 J16 **Pago Pago** ○ (American Samoa) Tutuila, W American Samoa
37 R8 **Pagosa Springs** Colorado, C USA
38 H12 **Pāhala** var. Pahala. Hawai'i, USA, C Pacific Ocean
168 K8 **Pahang** off. Negeri Pahang Darul Makmur. ◈ state Peninsular Malaysia
Pahang see Pahang, Sungai
168 L8 **Pahang, Sungai** var. Pahang, Sungei Pahang. ≈ Peninsular Malaysia
149 S8 **Pahārpur** North-West Frontier Province, NW Pakistan
185 B24 **Pahia Point** headland South Island, NZ
184 M13 **Pahiatua** Manawatu-Wanganui, North Island, NZ
38 H12 **Pāhoa** var. Pahoa. Hawai'i, USA, C Pacific Ocean
23 Y14 **Pahokee** Florida, SE USA
35 X9 **Pahranagat Range** ▲ Nevada, W USA
35 W11 **Pahrump** Nevada, W USA
Pahsien see Chongqing
35 V9 **Pahute Mesa** ▲ Nevada, W USA
167 N7 **Pai** Mae Hong Son, NW Thailand
38 F10 **Pā'ia** var. Paia. Maui, Hawai'i, USA, C Pacific Ocean
Pai-ch'eng see Baicheng
118 H4 **Paide** Ger. Weissenstein. Järvamaa, N Estonia
97 J24 **Paignton** SW England, UK
184 K3 **Paihia** Northland, North Island, NZ
93 M18 **Päijänne** ◎ S Finland
114 F13 **Páïko** ▲ N Greece
57 M17 **Paila, Río** ≈ C Bolivia
167 Q12 **Pailin** Bātdâmbâng, W Cambodia
54 F6 **Pailitas** Cesar, N Colombia
38 F9 **Pailolo Channel** channel Hawai'i, USA, C Pacific Ocean
93 K19 **Paimio** Swe. Pemar. Länsi-Suomi, W Finland
165 O16 **Paimi-saki** var. Yaeme-saki. headland Iriomote-jima, SW Japan
102 G5 **Paimpol** Côtes d'Armor, NW France
168 J12 **Painan** Sumatera, W Indonesia
63 G23 **Paine, Cerro** ▲ S Chile
31 U11 **Painesville** Ohio, N USA
31 S14 **Paint Creek** ≈ Ohio, N USA
36 L10 **Painted Desert** desert Arizona, SW USA
Paint Hills see Wemindji
30 M4 **Paint River** ≈ Michigan, N USA
25 P8 **Paint Rock** Texas, SW USA
21 O6 **Paintsville** Kentucky, S USA
Paisance see Piacenza
96 I12 **Paisley** W Scotland, UK
32 I15 **Paisley** Oregon, NW USA
105 R10 **País Valenciano** var. Valencia, Cat. València; anc. Valentia. ◈ autonomous community NE Spain
105 O3 **País Vasco** Basq. Euskadi, Eng. The Basque Country, Sp. Provincias Vascongadas. ◈ autonomous community N Spain
56 A9 **Paita** Piura, NW Peru
169 V6 **Paitan, Teluk** bay Sabah, East Malaysia
104 H7 **Paiva, Rio** ≈ N Portugal
92 K12 **Pajala** Norrbotten, N Sweden
104 K3 **Pajares, Puerto de** pass NW Spain
54 G9 **Pajárito** Boyacá, C Colombia
54 G4 **Pajaro** La Guajira, S Colombia
Pakanbaru see Pekanbaru
55 Q10 **Pakaraima Mountains** var. Serra Pacaraim, Sierra Pacaraima. ▲ N South America
167 P10 **Pak Chong** Nakhon Ratchasima, C Thailand
123 V8 **Pakhachi** Koryakskiy Avtonomnyy Okrug, E Russian Federation
Pakhna see Páchna
189 U16 **Pakin Atoll** atoll Caroline Islands, E Micronesia
149 Q12 **Pakistan** off. Islamic Republic of Pakistan, var. Islami Jamhuriya e Pakistan. ◆ republic S Asia
Pakistan, Islami Jamhuriya e see Pakistan
167 P8 **Pak Lay** var. Muang Pak Lay. Xaignabouli, C Laos
Paknam see Samut Prakan
166 L5 **Pakokku** Magwe, C Burma
110 I10 **Pakość** Ger. Pakosch. Kujawski-pomorskie, C Poland
Pakosch see Pakość
149 V10 **Pākpattan** Punjab, E Pakistan
167 O15 **Pak Phanang** var. Ban Pak Phanang. Nakhon Si Thammarat, SW Thailand
112 G9 **Pakrac** Hung. Pakrácz. Požega-Slavonija, NE Croatia
Pakrácz see Pakrac
118 F11 **Pakruojis** Šiauliai, N Lithuania
111 J24 **Paks** Tolna, S Hungary
Pak Sane see Pakxan
Paksé see Pakxé
167 Q10 **Pak Thong Chai** Nakhon Ratchasima, C Thailand
149 R6 **Paktiā** ◈ province SE Afghanistan
149 Q7 **Paktīkā** ◈ province SE Afghanistan
171 N12 **Pakuli** Sulawesi, C Indonesia
81 F17 **Pakwach** NW Uganda
167 R8 **Pakxan** var. Muang Pakxan, Pak Sane. Bolikhamxai, C Laos
167 S10 **Pakxé** var. Paksé. Champasak, S Laos
78 G12 **Pala** Mayo-Kébbi, SW Chad
61 A17 **Palacios** Santa Fe, C Argentina
25 V13 **Palacios** Texas, SW USA
105 X5 **Palafrugell** Cataluña, NE Spain
107 L24 **Palagonia** Sicilia, Italy, C Mediterranean Sea
113 E17 **Palagruža** It. Pelagosa. island SW Croatia
115 G20 **Palaiá Epídavros** Pelopónnisos, S Greece
121 P3 **Palaichóri** var. Palekhori. C Cyprus
115 H25 **Palaiochóra** Kríti, Greece, E Mediterranean Sea
115 A15 **Palaiolastrítsa** religious building Kérkyra, Iónioi Nísoi, Greece, C Mediterranean Sea
115 J19 **Palaiópoli** Ándros, Kykládes, Greece, Aegean Sea
103 N5 **Palaiseau** Essonne, N France
Palakkad see Pālghāt
154 N11 **Pāla Laharha** Orissa, E India
83 G19 **Palamakoloi** Ghanzi, C Botswana
115 E16 **Palamás** Thessalía, C Greece
105 X5 **Palamós** Cataluña, NE Spain
118 J5 **Palamuse** Ger. Sankt-Bartholomäi. Jõgevamaa, E Estonia
183 Q14 **Palana** Tasmania, SE Australia
123 U9 **Palana** Koryakskiy Avtonomnyy Okrug, E Russian Federation
118 C11 **Palanga** Ger. Polangen. Klaipėda, NW Lithuania
143 V10 **Palangān, Kūh-e** ▲ E Iran
Palangkaraja see Palangkaraya
169 T12 **Palangkaraya** prev. Palangkaraja. Borneo, C Indonesia
155 H22 **Palani** Tamil Nādu, SE India
Palanka see Bačka Palanka
154 D9 **Pālanpur** Gujarāt, W India
Palantia see Palencia
83 I19 **Palapye** Central, SE Botswana
155 J19 **Palār** ≈ SE India
104 H3 **Palas de Rei** Galicia, NW Spain
123 T9 **Palatka** Magadanskaya Oblast', E Russian Federation
23 W10 **Palatka** Florida, SE USA
188 B9 **Palau** var. Belau. ◆ republic W Pacific Ocean
192 G16 **Palauli Bay** bay Savai'i, Samoa, C Pacific Ocean
167 N11 **Palaw** Tenasserim, S Burma
170 M6 **Palawan** island W Philippines
171 N6 **Palawan Passage** passage W Philippines
192 E7 **Palawan Trough** undersea feature S South China Sea
155 H23 **Pālayankottai** Tamil Nādu, SE India
107 L25 **Palazzolo Acreide** anc. Acrae. Sicilia, Italy, C Mediterranean Sea
118 G3 **Paldiski** prev. Baltiski, Eng. Baltic Port, Ger. Baltischport. Harjumaa, NW Estonia
112 I13 **Pale** Republika Srpska, E Bosnia and Herzegovina
Palekhori see Palaichóri
168 L13 **Palembang** Sumatera, W Indonesia
63 G18 **Palena** Los Lagos, S Chile
63 G18 **Palena, Río** ≈ S Chile
104 M5 **Palencia** anc. Palantia, Pallantia. Castilla-León, NW Spain
104 M3 **Palencia** ◈ province Castilla-León, N Spain
35 X15 **Palen Dry Lake** ◎ California, W USA
41 V15 **Palenque** Chiapas, SE Mexico
41 V15 **Palenque** var. Ruinas de Palenque. ruins Chiapas, SE Mexico
45 O9 **Palenque, Punta** headland S Dominican Republic
Palenque, Ruinas de see Palenque
Palerme see Palermo
107 I23 **Palermo** Fr. Palerme; anc. Panhormus, Panormus. Sicilia, Italy, C Mediterranean Sea
25 V8 **Palestine** Texas, SW USA
25 V7 **Palestine, Lake** ▣ Texas, SW USA
107 I15 **Palestrina** Lazio, C Italy
166 K5 **Paletwa** Chin State, W Burma
155 G21 **Pālghāt** var. Palakkad; prev. Pulicat. Kerala, SW India
152 F13 **Pāli** Rājasthān, N India
167 N16 **Palian** Trang, SW Thailand
189 O12 **Palikir** ● (Micronesia) Pohnpei, E Micronesia
Palimé see Kpalimé
107 L19 **Palinuro, Capo** headland S Italy
115 H15 **Palioúri, Akrotírio** var. Akra Kanestron. headland N Greece
33 R14 **Palisades Reservoir** ▣ Idaho, NW USA
99 J23 **Paliseul** Luxembourg, SE Belgium
154 C11 **Pālitāna** Gujarāt, W India
118 F4 **Palivere** Läänemaa, W Estonia
41 V14 **Palizada** Campeche, SE Mexico
93 L18 **Pälkäne** Länsi-Suomi, W Finland
155 J22 **Palk Strait** strait India/Sri Lanka
155 J23 **Pallai** Northern Province, NW Sri Lanka
Pallantia see Palencia
106 C6 **Pallanza** Piemonte, NE Italy
127 Q9 **Pallasovka** Volgogradskaya Oblast', SW Russian Federation
Pallene/Pallíni see Kassándra
185 L15 **Palliser Bay** bay North Island, NZ
185 L15 **Palliser, Cape** headland North Island, NZ
191 U9 **Palliser, Îles** island group Îles Tuamotu, C French Polynesia
105 X9 **Palma** var. Palma de Mallorca. Mallorca, Spain, W Mediterranean Sea
105 X9 **Palma** ✕ Mallorca, Spain, W Mediterranean Sea
82 Q12 **Palma** Cabo Delgado, N Mozambique
105 X10 **Palma, Badia de** bay Mallorca, Spain, W Mediterranean Sea
104 L13 **Palma del Río** Andalucía, S Spain
Palma de Mallorca see Palma
107 J25 **Palma di Montechiaro** Sicilia, Italy, C Mediterranean Sea
106 J7 **Palmanova** Friuli-Venezia Giulia, NE Italy
54 J7 **Palmarito** Apure, C Venezuela
43 N15 **Palmar Sur** Puntarenas, SE Costa Rica
60 I12 **Palmas** Paraná, S Brazil
59 K16 **Palmas** var. Palmas do Tocantins. Tocantins, C Brazil
76 L18 **Palmas, Cape** Fr. Cap des Palmès. headland SW Ivory Coast
Palmas do Tocantins see Palmas
54 D11 **Palmaseca** ✕ (Cali) Valle del Cauca, SW Colombia
107 B21 **Palmas, Golfo di** gulf Sardegna, Italy, C Mediterranean Sea
44 I7 **Palma Soriano** Santiago de Cuba, E Cuba
23 Y12 **Palm Bay** Florida, SE USA
35 T14 **Palmdale** California, W USA
61 H14 **Palmeira das Missões** Rio Grande do Sul, S Brazil
82 A11 **Palmeirinhas, Ponta das** headland NW Angola
39 R11 **Palmer** Alaska, USA
19 N11 **Palmer** Massachusetts, NE USA
25 U7 **Palmer** Texas, SW USA
194 H4 **Palmer** US research station Antarctica
15 R11 **Palmer** ≈ Québec, SE Canada
37 T5 **Palmer Lake** Colorado, C USA
194 J6 **Palmer Land** physical region Antarctica
14 F15 **Palmerston** Ontario, SE Canada
185 F22 **Palmerston** Otago, South Island, NZ
190 K15 **Palmerston** island S Cook Islands
Palmerston see Darwin
184 M12 **Palmerston North** Manawatu-Wanganui, North Island, NZ
Palmés, Cap des see Palmas, Cape
23 V13 **Palmetto** Florida, SE USA
Palmetto State see South Carolina
107 M22 **Palmi** Calabria, SW Italy
54 D11 **Palmira** Valle del Cauca, W Colombia
56 F8 **Palmira, Río** ≈ N Peru
61 D19 **Palmitas** Soriano, SW Uruguay
Palmnicken see Yantarnyy
35 V15 **Palm Springs** California, W USA
27 V2 **Palmyra** Missouri, C USA
18 G10 **Palmyra** New York, NE USA
18 G15 **Palmyra** Pennsylvania, NE USA
21 V5 **Palmyra** Virginia, NE USA
Palmyra see Tudmur
192 L7 **Palmyra Atoll** ◇ US privately owned unincorporated territory C Pacific Ocean
154 P12 **Palmyras Point** headland E India
35 N9 **Palo Alto** California, W USA
25 O1 **Palo Duro Creek** ≈ Texas, SW USA
Paloe see Palu
Paloe see Denpasar, Bali, C Indonesia
168 L9 **Paloh** Johor, Peninsular Malaysia
80 F12 **Paloich** Upper Nile, SE Sudan
40 I3 **Palomas** Chihuahua, N Mexico
107 I15 **Palombara Sabina** Lazio, C Italy
105 S13 **Palos, Cabo de** headland SE Spain
104 I14 **Palos de la Frontera** Andalucía, S Spain
60 G11 **Palotina** Paraná, S Brazil
32 M9 **Palouse** Washington, NW USA
32 L9 **Palouse River** ≈ Washington, NW USA
35 Y16 **Palo Verde** California, W USA
57 E16 **Palpa** Ica, W Peru
95 M16 **Pålsboda** Örebro, C Sweden
93 M15 **Paltamo** Oulu, C Finland
171 N12 **Palu** prev. Paloe. Sulawesi, C Indonesia
137 P14 **Palu** Elazığ, E Turkey
152 I11 **Palwal** Haryāna, N India
123 U6 **Palyavaam** ≈ NE Russian Federation
77 Q13 **Pama** SE Burkina
172 J14 **Pamandzi** ✕ (Mamoudzou) Petite-Terre, E Mayotte
Pamangkat see Pemangkat
143 R11 **Pā Mazār** Kermān, C Iran
83 N19 **Pambarra** Inhambane, SE Mozambique
171 X12 **Pamdai** Papua, E Indonesia
103 N16 **Pamiers** Ariège, S France
147 T14 **Pamir** var. Daryā-ye Pāmīr, Taj. Dar"yoi Pomir. ≈ Afghanistan/Tajikistan **see also** Pāmīr, Daryā-ye
Pamir/Pāmīr, Daryā-ye see Pamirs
149 U1 **Pāmīr, Daryā-ye** var. Pamir, Taj. Dar"yoi Pomir. ≈ Afghanistan/Tajikistan **see also** Pamir
Pāmīr-e Khord see Little Pamir
147 U13 **Pamirs** Pash. Daryā-ye Pāmīr, Rus. Pamir. ▲ C Asia
Pâmiut see Paamiut
21 X10 **Pamlico River** ≈ North Carolina, SE USA
21 Y10 **Pamlico Sound** sound North Carolina, SE USA
25 O2 **Pampa** Texas, SW USA
Pampa Aullagas, Lago see Poopó, Lago
61 B21 **Pampa Húmeda** grassland E Argentina
56 A10 **Pampa las Salinas** salt lake NW Peru
57 F15 **Pampas** Huancavelica, C Peru
62 K13 **Pampas** plain C Argentina
55 O4 **Pampatar** Nueva Esparta, NE Venezuela
Pampeluna see Pamplona
104 H8 **Pampilhosa da Serra** var. Pampilhosa de Serra. Coimbra, N Portugal
173 Y15 **Pamplemousses** N Mauritius
54 G7 **Pamplona** Norte de Santander, N Colombia
105 Q3 **Pamplona** Basq. Iruña; prev. Pampeluna, anc. Pompaelo. Navarra, N Spain
114 I11 **Pamporovo** prev. Vasil Kolarov. Smolyan, S Bulgaria
136 D15 **Pamukkale** Denizli, W Turkey
21 W5 **Pamunkey River** ≈ Virginia, NE USA
152 K5 **Pamzal** Jammu and Kashmir, NW India
30 L14 **Pana** Illinois, N USA
41 Y11 **Panabá** Yucatán, SE Mexico
35 Y8 **Panaca** Nevada, W USA
115 E19 **Panachaikó** ▲ S Greece
14 F11 **Panache Lake** ◎ Ontario, S Canada
114 I10 **Panagyurishte** Pazardzhik, C Bulgaria
168 M16 **Panaitan, Pulau** island S Indonesia
115 D18 **Panaitolikó** ▲ C Greece
155 E17 **Panaji** var. Pangim, Panjim, New Goa. Goa, W India
43 T14 **Panama** off. Republic of Panama. ◆ republic Central America
43 T15 **Panamá** var. Ciudad de Panamá, Eng. Panama City. ● (Panama) Panamá, C Panama
43 U14 **Panamá** off. Provincia de Panamá. ◈ province E Panama
43 U15 **Panamá, Bahía de** bay N Gulf of Panama
193 T7 **Panama Basin** undersea feature E Pacific Ocean
43 T15 **Panama Canal** canal E Panama
23 R9 **Panama City** Florida, SE USA
43 T14 **Panama City** ✕ Panamá, C Panama
Panama City see Panamá
23 Q9 **Panama City Beach** Florida, SE USA
43 T17 **Panamá, Golfo de** var. Gulf of Panama. gulf S Panama
Panama, Gulf of see Panamá, Golfo de
Panama, Isthmus of see Panamá, Istmo de
43 T15 **Panamá, Istmo de** Eng. Isthmus of Panama; prev. Isthmus of Darien. isthmus E Panama
35 U11 **Panamint Range** ▲ California, W USA
107 L22 **Panarea, Isola** island Isole Eolie, S Italy

◆ Country ● Country Capital ◇ Dependent Territory ○ Dependent Territory Capital ◈ Administrative Region ✕ International Airport ▲ Mountain ▲ Mountain Range ▲ Volcano ≈ River ◎ Lake ▣ Reservoir

106 G9 **Panaro** ≈ N Italy
171 P6 **Panay Gulf** *gulf* C Philippines
171 P5 **Panay Island** *island* C Philippines
35 W7 **Pancake Range** ⛰ Nevada, W USA
112 M11 **Pančevo** *Ger.* Pantschowa, *Hung.* Pancsova. Serbia, N Serbia and Montenegro (Yugo.)
113 M15 **Pančićev Vrh** ▲ SW Serbia and Montenegro (Yugo.)
116 L12 **Panciu** Vrancea, E Romania
116 F10 **Pâncota** *Hung.* Pankota; *prev.* Pîncota. Arad, W Romania
Pancsova *see* Pančevo
83 N20 **Panda** Inhambane, SE Mozambique
171 X12 **Pandaidori, Kepulauan** *island group* E Indonesia
25 N11 **Pandale** Texas, SW USA
169 P12 **Pandang Tikar, Pulau** *island* N Indonesia
61 F20 **Pan de Azúcar** Maldonado, S Uruguay
118 H11 **Pandėlys** Panevėžys, NE Lithuania
155 F15 **Pandharpur** Mahārāshtra, W India
182 J1 **Pandie Pandie** South Australia
171 O12 **Pandiri** Sulawesi, C Indonesia
61 F20 **Pando** Canelones, S Uruguay
57 J14 **Pando** ◐ *department* N Bolivia
192 K9 **Pandora Bank** *undersea feature* W Pacific Ocean
95 G20 **Pandrup** Nordjylland, N Denmark
153 V12 **Pandu** Assam, NE India
79 J15 **Pandu** Equateur, NW Dem. Rep. Congo
Paneas *see* Bāniyās
59 F15 **Panelas** Mato Grosso, W Brazil
118 G12 **Panevėžys** Panevėžys, C Lithuania
118 G11 **Panevėžys** ◐ *province* NE Lithuania
Panfilov *see* Zharkent
127 N9 **Panfilovo** Volgogradskaya Oblast', SW Russian Federation
79 N17 **Panga** Orientale, N Dem. Rep. Congo
193 Y15 **Pangai** Lifuka, C Tonga
114 H13 **Pangaío** ⛰ N Greece
79 G20 **Pangala** Le Pool, S Congo
81 J22 **Pangani** Tanga, E Tanzania
81 I21 **Pangani** ≈ NE Tanzania
186 K8 **Panggoe** Choiseul Island, NW Solomon Islands
79 N20 **Pangi** Maniema, E Dem. Rep. Congo
Pangim *see* Panaji
168 H8 **Pangkalanbrandan** Sumatera, W Indonesia
Pangkalanbun *see* Pangkalanbuun
169 R13 **Pangkalanbuun** *var.* Pangkalanbun. Borneo, C Indonesia
169 N12 **Pangkalpinang** Pulau Bangka, W Indonesia
11 U17 **Pangman** Saskatchewan, S Canada
Pang-Nga *see* Phang-Nga
9 S6 **Pangnirtung** Baffin Island, Nunavut, NE Canada
152 K6 **Pangong Tso** *var.* Bangong Co. ◎ China/India *see also* Bangong Co
36 K7 **Panguitch** Utah, W USA
186 J7 **Panguna** Bougainville Island, NE PNG
171 N8 **Pangutaran Group** *island group* Sulu Archipelago, SW Philippines
25 N2 **Panhandle** Texas, SW USA
Panhormus *see* Palermo
171 W14 **Paniai, Danau** ◎ Papua, E Indonesia
79 L21 **Pania-Mutombo** Kasai Oriental, C Dem. Rep. Congo
Panicherevo *see* Dolno Panicherevo
187 P16 **Panié, Mont** ▲ C New Caledonia
152 I10 **Pānīpat** Haryāna, N India
147 Q14 **Panj** *Rus.* Pyandzh; *prev.* Kirovabad. SW Tajikistan
147 P15 **Panj** *Rus.* Pyandzh. ≈ Afghanistan/Tajikistan
149 O5 **Panjāb** Bāmīān, C Afghanistan
147 O12 **Panjakent** *Rus.* Pendzhikent. W Tajikistan
148 L14 **Panjgūr** Baluchistān, SW Pakistan
Panjim *see* Panaji
163 U12 **Panjin** Liaoning, NE China
147 P14 **Panji Poyon** *Rus.* Nizhniy Pyandzh. SW Tajikistan
149 Q4 **Panjshīr** ≈ E Afghanistan
Pankota *see* Pâncota
77 W14 **Pankshin** Plateau, C Nigeria
163 Y10 **Pan Ling** ⛰ N China
Panlong Jiang *see* Lô, Sông
154 J9 **Panna** Madhya Pradesh, C India
99 M16 **Panningen** Limburg, SE Netherlands
149 R13 **Pāno Āqil** Sind, SE Pakistan
121 P3 **Páno Léfkara** S Cyprus
121 O3 **Páno Panagiá** *var.* Pano Panaya. W Cyprus
Pano Panaya *see* Páno Panagiá
Panopolis *see* Akhmīm
29 U14 **Panora** Iowa, C USA
60 I8 **Panorama** São Paulo, S Brazil
115 I24 **Pánormos** Kríti, Greece, E Mediterranean Sea
Panormus *see* Palermo
163 W11 **Panshi** Jilin, NE China
59 H19 **Pantanal** *var.* Pantanalmato-Grossense. *swamp* SW Brazil
Pantanalmato-Grossense *see* Pantanal
61 H16 **Pântano Grande** Rio Grande do Sul, S Brazil
171 Q16 **Pantar, Pulau** *island* Kepulauan Alor, S Indonesia
21 X9 **Pantego** North Carolina, SE USA
107 G25 **Pantelleria** *anc.* Cossyra, Cosyra. Sicilia, Italy, C Mediterranean Sea
107 G25 **Pantelleria, Isola di** *island* SW Italy
Pante Macassar/Pante Makassar *see* Pante Makasar
171 Q16 **Pante Makasar** *var.* Pante Macassar, Pante Makassar. W East Timor
152 K10 **Pantnagar** Uttaranchal, N India
115 A15 **Pantokrátoras** ▲ Kérkyra, Iónioi Nísoi, Greece, C Mediterranean Sea
Pantschowa *see* Pančevo
41 P11 **Pánuco** Veracruz-Llave, E Mexico
41 P11 **Pánuco, Río** ≈ C Mexico
160 I12 **Panxian** Guizhou, S China
168 I10 **Panyabungan** Sumatera, N Indonesia
77 W14 **Panyam** Plateau, C Nigeria
157 N13 **Panzhihua** *prev.* Dukou, Tu-k'ou. Sichuan, C China
79 I22 **Panzi** Bandundu, SW Dem. Rep. Congo
42 E5 **Panzós** Alta Verapaz, E Guatemala
Pao-chi/Paoki *see* Baoji
Pao-king *see* Shaoyang
107 N20 **Paola** Calabria, SW Italy
121 P16 **Paola** E Malta
27 R5 **Paola** Kansas, C USA
31 O15 **Paoli** Indiana, N USA
187 R14 **Paonangisu** Éfaté, C Vanuatu
171 S13 **Paoni** *var.* Pauni. Pulau Seram, E Indonesia
37 Q5 **Paonia** Colorado, C USA
191 O7 **Paopao** Moorea, W French Polynesia
Pao-shan *see* Baoshan
Pao-ting *see* Baoding
Pao-t'ou/Paotow *see* Baotou
79 H14 **Paoua** Ouham-Pendé, W Central African Republic
Pap *see* Pop
111 H23 **Pápa** Veszprém, W Hungary
42 J12 **Papagayo, Golfo de** *gulf* NW Costa Rica
38 H11 **Pāpa'ikou** *var.* Papaikou. Hawai'i, USA, C Pacific Ocean
41 R15 **Papaloapan, Río** ≈ S Mexico
184 L6 **Papakura** Auckland, North Island, NZ
41 Q13 **Papantla** *var.* Papantla de Olarte. Veracruz-Llave, E Mexico
Papantla de Olarte *see* Papantla
191 P8 **Papara** Tahiti, W French Polynesia
184 K4 **Paparoa** Northland, North Island, NZ
185 G16 **Paparoa Range** ⛰ South Island, NZ
115 K20 **Pápas, Akrotírio** *headland* Ikaría, Dodekánisos, Greece, Aegean Sea
96 L2 **Papa Stour** *island* NE Scotland, UK
184 L6 **Papatoetoe** Auckland, North Island, NZ
185 E25 **Papatowai** Otago, South Island, NZ
96 K4 **Papa Westray** *island* NE Scotland, UK
191 T10 **Papeete** ○ (French Polynesia) Tahiti, W French Polynesia
100 F11 **Papenburg** Niedersachsen, NW Germany
98 H13 **Papendrecht** Zuid-Holland, SW Netherlands
191 Q7 **Papenoo** Tahiti, W French Polynesia
191 Q7 **Papenoo Rivière** ≈ Tahiti, W French Polynesia
191 N7 **Papetoai** Moorea, W French Polynesia
92 L3 **Papey** *island* E Iceland
Paphos *see* Páfos
40 H5 **Papigochic, Río** ≈ NW Mexico
118 E10 **Papilė** Šiauliai, NW Lithuania
29 S15 **Papillion** Nebraska, C USA
15 T5 **Papinachois** ≈ Québec, SE Canada
171 X13 **Papua** *var.* Irian Barat, West Irian, West New Guinea, West Papua ; *prev.* Dutch New Guinea, Irian Jaya, Netherlands New Guinea. ◐ *province* E Indonesia
186 C9 **Papua, Gulf of** *gulf* S PNG
186 C8 **Papua New Guinea** *off.* Independent State of Papua New Guinea; *prev.* Territory of Papua and New Guinea, *abbrev.* PNG. ◆ *commonwealth republic* NW Melanesia
192 H8 **Papua Plateau** *undersea feature* N Coral Sea
112 G9 **Papuk** ⛰ NE Croatia
167 N8 **Papun** Karen State, S Burma
42 L14 **Paquera** Puntarenas, W Costa Rica
55 V9 **Para** ◐ *district* N Surinam
58 I13 **Pará** *off.* Estado do Pará. ◐ *state* NE Brazil
Pará *see* Belém
180 I8 **Paraburdoo** Western Australia
57 E16 **Paracas, Península de** *peninsula* W Peru
59 L19 **Paracatu** Minas Gerais, NE Brazil
192 E6 **Paracel Islands** ◇ *disputed territory* SE Asia
182 I6 **Parachilna** South Australia
149 R6 **Pārachinār** North-West Frontier Province, NW Pakistan
112 N13 **Paraćin** Serbia, C Serbia and Montenegro (Yugo.)
14 K8 **Paradis** Québec, SE Canada
39 N11 **Paradise** *var.* Paradise Hill. Alaska, USA
35 O5 **Paradise** California, W USA
35 X11 **Paradise** Nevada, W USA
Paradise Hill *see* Paradise
37 R11 **Paradise Hills** New Mexico, SW USA
Paradise of the Pacific *see* Hawaii
36 L13 **Paradise Valley** Arizona, SW USA
35 T2 **Paradise Valley** Nevada, W USA
115 O22 **Paradisi** ✈ (Ródos) Ródos, Dodekánisos, Greece, Aegean Sea
154 P12 **Pārādwīp** Orissa, E India
Paraetonium *see* Maṭrūḥ
117 R4 **Parafiyivka** Chernihivs'ka Oblast', N Ukraine
36 K7 **Paragonah** Utah, W USA
27 X9 **Paragould** Arkansas, C USA
47 X8 **Paraguaçu** *var.* Paraguassú. ≈ E Brazil
60 J9 **Paraguaçu Paulista** São Paulo, S Brazil
54 H4 **Paraguaipoa** Zulia, NW Venezuela
62 O6 **Paraguarí** Paraguarí, S Paraguay
62 O7 **Paraguarí** *off.* Departamento de Paraguarí. ◐ *department* S Paraguay
55 O8 **Paragua, Río** ≈ SE Venezuela
57 O16 **Paraguá, Río** ≈ NE Bolivia
Paraguassú *see* Paraguaçu
62 N5 **Paraguay** ◆ *republic* C South America
47 U10 **Paraguay** *var.* Río Paraguay. ≈ C South America
Parahiba/Parahyba *see* Paraíba
59 P15 **Paraíba** *off.* Estado da Paraíba; *prev.* Parahiba, Parahyba. ◐ *state* E Brazil
Paraíba *see* João Pessoa
60 P9 **Paraíba do Sul, Rio** ≈ SE Brazil
Parainen *see* Pargas
43 N14 **Paraíso** Cartago, C Costa Rica
41 U14 **Paraíso** Tabasco, SE Mexico
57 O17 **Paraíso, Río** ≈ E Bolivia
Parajd *see* Praid
77 S14 **Parakou** C Benin
121 Q12 **Paralimni** E Cyprus
115 G18 **Paralímni, Límni** ◎ C Greece
55 W8 **Paramaribo** ● (Surinam) Paramaribo, N Surinam
55 W9 **Paramaribo** ◐ *district* N Surinam
55 W9 **Paramaribo** ✈ Paramaribo, N Surinam
Paramithiá *see* Paramythiá
56 C13 **Paramonga** Lima, W Peru
123 V12 **Paramushir, Ostrov** *island* SE Russian Federation
115 C16 **Paramythiá** *var.* Paramithiá. Ípeiros, W Greece
42 M10 **Paraná** Entre Ríos, E Argentina
60 H11 **Paraná** *off.* Estado do Paraná. ◐ *state* S Brazil
47 U11 **Paraná** *var.* Alto Paraná. ≈ C South America
60 K12 **Paranaguá** Paraná, S Brazil
59 J20 **Paranaíba, Rio** ≈ E Brazil
61 C19 **Paraná Ibicuy, Río** ≈ E Argentina
59 H15 **Paranaíta** Mato Grosso, W Brazil
60 H9 **Paranapanema, Rio** ≈ S Brazil
60 K11 **Paranapiacaba, Serra do** ⛰ S Brazil
60 H10 **Paranavaí** Paraná, S Brazil
143 N5 **Parandak** Markazī, W Iran
114 I12 **Paranéstio** Anatolikí Makedonía kai Thráki, NE Greece
191 W11 **Paraoa** *atoll* Îles Tuamotu, C French Polynesia
184 L13 **Paraparaumu** Wellington, North Island, NZ
57 N20 **Parapeti, Río** ≈ SE Bolivia
54 L10 **Paraque, Cerro** ▲ W Venezuela
154 I11 **Parasiya** Madhya Pradesh, C India
115 M23 **Paraspóri, Akrotírio** *headland* Kárpathos, SE Greece
60 O10 **Parati** Rio de Janeiro, SE Brazil
59 K14 **Parauapebas** Pará, N Brazil
103 Q10 **Paray-le-Monial** Saône-et-Loire, C France
Parbatsar *see* Parvatsar
154 G13 **Parbhani** Mahārāshtra, C India
100 L10 **Parchim** Mecklenburg-Vorpommern, N Germany
Parchwitz *see* Prochowice
110 P13 **Parczew** Lubelskie, E Poland
60 L8 **Pardo, Rio** ≈ S Brazil
111 E16 **Pardubice** *Ger.* Pardubitz. Pardubický Kraj, C Czech Republic
111 E17 **Pardubický Kraj** ◐ region C Czech Republic
Pardubitz *see* Pardubice
119 F16 **Parechcha** *Pol.* Porzecze, *Rus.* Porech'ye. Hrodzyenskaya Voblasts', W Belarus
59 F17 **Parecis, Chapada dos** *var.* Serra dos Parecis. ⛰ W Brazil
Parecis, Serra dos *see* Parecis, Chapada dos
104 M4 **Paredes de Nava** Castilla-León, N Spain
189 U12 **Parem** *island* Chuuk, C Micronesia
189 O12 **Parem Island** *island* E Micronesia
184 I1 **Parengarenga Harbour** *inlet* North Island, NZ
15 N8 **Parent** Québec, SE Canada
102 J14 **Parentis-en-Born** Landes, SW France
Parenzo *see* Poreč
185 G20 **Pareora** Canterbury, South Island, NZ
171 N14 **Parepare** Sulawesi, C Indonesia
115 B16 **Párga** Ípeiros, W Greece
93 K20 **Pargas** *Swe.* Parainen. Länsi-Suomi, W Finland
64 O5 **Pargo, Ponta do** *headland* Madeira, Portugal, NE Atlantic Ocean
Paria, Golfo de *see* Paria, Gulf of
55 N6 **Pariaguán** Anzoátegui, NE Venezuela
45 X17 **Paria, Gulf of** *var.* Golfo de Paria. *gulf* Trinidad and Tobago/Venezuela
57 I15 **Pariamanu, Río** ≈ E Peru
36 L8 **Paria River** ≈ Utah, W USA
Parichi *see* Parychy
40 M14 **Paricutín, Volcán** ✱ C Mexico
43 P16 **Parida, Isla** *island* SW Panama
55 T8 **Parika** NE Guyana
93 O18 **Parikkala** Etelä-Suomi, S Finland
58 E10 **Parima, Serra** *var.* Sierra Parima. ⛰ Brazil/Venezuela *see also* Parima, Sierra
55 N11 **Parima, Sierra** *var.* Serra Parima. ⛰ Brazil/Venezuela *see also* Parima, Serra
57 F17 **Parinacochas, Laguna** ◎ SW Peru
56 A9 **Pariñas, Punta** *headland* NW Peru
58 H12 **Parintins** Amazonas, N Brazil
103 O5 **Paris** *anc.* Lutetia, Lutetia Parisiorum, Parisii. ● (France) Paris, N France
191 Y2 **Paris** Kiritimati, E Kiribati
27 S11 **Paris** Arkansas, C USA
33 S16 **Paris** Idaho, NW USA
31 N14 **Paris** Illinois, N USA
20 M5 **Paris** Kentucky, S USA
27 V3 **Paris** Missouri, C USA
20 H8 **Paris** Tennessee, S USA
25 V5 **Paris** Texas, SW USA
Parisii *see* Paris
43 S16 **Parita** Herrera, S Panama
43 S16 **Parita, Bahía de** *bay* S Panama
Parkan/Párkány *see* Štúrovo
93 K18 **Parkano** Länsi-Suomi, W Finland
27 N6 **Park City** Kansas, C USA
36 L3 **Park City** Utah, W USA
36 I12 **Parker** Arizona, SW USA
23 R9 **Parker** Florida, SE USA
29 R11 **Parker** South Dakota, N USA
35 Z14 **Parker Dam** California, W USA
29 W13 **Parkersburg** Iowa, C USA
21 Q3 **Parkersburg** West Virginia, NE USA
29 T7 **Parkers Prairie** Minnesota, N USA
171 P8 **Parker Volcano** ✱ Mindanao, S Philippines
181 W13 **Parkes** New South Wales, SE Australia
30 K4 **Park Falls** Wisconsin, N USA
Parkhar *see* Farkhor
14 E16 **Parkhill** Ontario, S Canada
29 T5 **Park Rapids** Minnesota, N USA
29 Q3 **Park River** North Dakota, N USA
29 Q11 **Parkston** South Dakota, N USA
10 L17 **Parksville** Vancouver Island, British Columbia, SW Canada
37 S3 **Parkview Mountain** ▲ Colorado, C USA
105 N8 **Parla** Madrid, C Spain
29 S8 **Parle, Lac qui** ◎ Minnesota, N USA
115 F20 **Parlía Tyroú** Pelopónnisos, S Greece
155 G14 **Parli Vaijnāth** Mahārāshtra, C India
106 F9 **Parma** Emilia-Romagna, N Italy
31 T11 **Parma** Ohio, N USA
Parnahyba *see* Parnaíba
58 N13 **Parnaíba** *var.* Parnahyba. Piauí, E Brazil
65 J14 **Parnaíba Ridge** *undersea feature* C Atlantic Ocean
58 N13 **Parnaíba, Rio** ≈ NE Brazil
115 F18 **Parnassós** ⛰ C Greece
185 J17 **Parnassus** Canterbury, South Island, NZ
182 H10 **Parndana** South Australia
115 H19 **Párnitha** ⛰ C Greece
115 F21 **Párnon** ⛰ S Greece
118 G5 **Pärnu** *Ger.* Pernau, *Latv.* Pērnava; *prev. Rus.* Pernov. Pärnumaa, SW Estonia
118 G6 **Pärnu** *var.* Parnu Jõgi, *Ger.* Pernau. ≈ SW Estonia
118 G5 **Pärnu-Jaagupi** *Ger.* Sankt-Jakobi. Pärnumaa, SW Estonia
Parnu Jõgi *see* Pärnu
118 G5 **Pärnu Laht** *Ger.* Pernauer Bucht. *bay* SW Estonia
118 F5 **Pärnumaa** *off.* Pärnu Maakond. ◐ *province* SW Estonia
153 T11 **Paro** W Bhutan
153 T11 **Paro** ✈ (Thimphu) W Bhutan
185 G17 **Paroa** West Coast, South Island, NZ
163 X14 **P'aro-ho** *var.* Hwach'ŏn-chŏsuji. ▣ N South Korea
183 N6 **Paroo River** *seasonal river* New South Wales/ Queensland, SE Australia
Paropamisus Range *see* Sefīdkūh, Selseleh-ye
115 J21 **Páros** Páros, Kykládes, Greece, Aegean Sea
115 J21 **Páros** *island* Kykládes, Greece, Aegean Sea
36 K7 **Parowan** Utah, W USA
103 U13 **Parpaillon** ⛰ SE France
108 I9 **Parpan** Graubünden, S Switzerland
62 G13 **Parral** Maule, C Chile
Parral *see* Hidalgo del Parral
183 T9 **Parramatta** New South Wales, SE Australia
21 Y6 **Parramore Island** *island* Virginia, NE USA
40 M8 **Parras** *var.* Parras de la Fuente. Coahuila de Zaragoza, NE Mexico
Parras de la Fuente *see* Parras
42 M14 **Parrita** Puntarenas, S Costa Rica
8 L5 **Parry Channel** *channel* N Canada
14 G13 **Parry Island** *island* Ontario, S Canada
8 M4 **Parry Islands** *island group* Nunavut, NW Canada
14 G12 **Parry Sound** Ontario, S Canada
110 F7 **Parsęta** *Ger.* Persante. ≈ NW Poland
28 L3 **Parshall** North Dakota, N USA
27 Q7 **Parsons** Kansas, C USA
20 H9 **Parsons** Tennessee, S USA
21 T3 **Parsons** West Virginia, NE USA
Parsonstown *see* Birr
100 P11 **Parsteiner See** ◎ NE Germany
107 I24 **Partanna** Sicilia, Italy, C Mediterranean Sea
108 J8 **Partenen** Graubünden, E Switzerland
102 K9 **Parthenay** Deux-Sèvres, W France
95 J19 **Partille** Västra Götaland, S Sweden
107 I23 **Partinico** Sicilia, Italy, C Mediterranean Sea
111 I20 **Partizánske** *prev.* Šimonovany; *Hung.* Simony. Trenčiansky Kraj, W Slovakia
58 H11 **Paru de Oeste, Rio** ≈ N Brazil
182 K9 **Paruna** South Australia
58 I11 **Paru, Rio** ≈ N Brazil
Parvān *see* Parwān
155 M14 **Pārvatipuram** Andhra Pradesh, E India
152 G12 **Parvatsar** *prev.* Parbatsar. Rājasthān, N India
149 Q5 **Parwān** *Per.* Parvān. ◐ *province* E Afghanistan
158 I15 **Paryang** Xizang Zizhiqu, W China
119 M18 **Parychy** *Rus.* Parichi. Homyel'skaya Voblasts', SE Belarus
83 J21 **Parys** Free State, C South Africa
35 T15 **Pasadena** California, W USA
25 W11 **Pasadena** Texas, SW USA
56 B8 **Pasaje** El Oro, SW Ecuador
137 T9 **P'asanauri** N Georgia
168 I13 **Pasapuat** Pulau Pagai Utara, W Indonesia
167 N7 **Pasawng** Kayah State, C Burma
114 L13 **Paşayiğit** Edirne, NW Turkey
23 N9 **Pascagoula** Mississippi, S USA
22 M8 **Pascagoula River** ≈ Mississippi, S USA
116 F12 **Paşcani** *Hung.* Páskán. Iaşi, NE Romania
109 T4 **Pasching** Oberösterreich, N Austria
32 K10 **Pasco** Washington, NW USA
56 E13 **Pasco** *off.* Departamento de Pasco. ◐ *department* C Peru
191 N11 **Pascua, Isla de** *var.* Rapa Nui, *Eng.* Easter Island. *island* E Pacific Ocean
63 G21 **Pascua, Río** ≈ S Chile
103 N1 **Pas-de-Calais** ◐ *department* N France
100 P10 **Pasewalk** Mecklenburg-Vorpommern, NE Germany
11 T10 **Pasfield Lake** ◎ Saskatchewan, C Canada
Pa-shih Hai-hsia *see* Bashi Channel
Pashkeni *see* Bolyarovo
Pashmakli *see* Smolyan
153 X10 **Pāsighāt** Arunāchel Pradesh, NE India
137 Q12 **Pasinler** Erzurum, NE Turkey
Pasi Oloy, Qatorkŭhi *see* Zaalayskiy Khrebet
42 E3 **Pasión, Río de la** ≈ N Guatemala
168 J12 **Pasirganting** Sumatera, W Indonesia
Pasirpangarayan *see* Bagansiapiapi
168 K6 **Pasir Puteh** *var.* Pasir Putih. Kelantan, Peninsular Malaysia
169 R9 **Pasir, Tanjung** *headland* East Malaysia
95 N20 **Påskallavik** Kalmar, S Sweden
Páskán *see* Paşcani
Paskevicha, Zaliv *see* Tushchybas, Zaliv
110 K7 **Pasłęk** *Ger.* Preußisch Holland. Warmińsko-Mazurskie, NE Poland
110 K7 **Pasłęka** *Ger.* Passarge. ≈ N Poland
148 K16 **Pasni** Baluchistān, SW Pakistan
63 I18 **Paso de Indios** Chubut, S Argentina
54 L7 **Paso del Caballo** Guárico, N Venezuela
61 E15 **Paso de los Libres** Corrientes, NE Argentina
61 E18 **Paso de los Toros** Tacuarembó, C Uruguay
35 P12 **Paso Robles** California, W USA
15 Y7 **Paspébiac** Québec, SE Canada
11 U14 **Pasquia Hills** ⛰ Saskatchewan, S Canada
149 W7 **Pasrūr** Punjab, E Pakistan
30 M1 **Passage Island** *island* Michigan, N USA
65 B24 **Passage Islands** *island group* W Falkland Islands
8 K5 **Passage Point** *headland* Banks Island, Northwest Territories, NW Canada
Passarge *see* Pasłęka
115 C15 **Passarón** *ancient monument* Ípeiros, W Greece
Passarowitz *see* Požarevac
101 O22 **Passau** Bayern, SE Germany
22 M9 **Pass Christian** Mississippi, S USA
107 L26 **Passero, Capo** *headland* Sicilia, Italy, C Mediterranean Sea
171 P5 **Passi** Panay Island, C Philippines
61 H14 **Passo Fundo** Rio Grande do Sul, S Brazil
60 H13 **Passo Fundo, Barragem de** ▣ S Brazil
61 H15 **Passo Real, Barragem de** ▣ S Brazil
59 L20 **Passos** Minas Gerais, NE Brazil
167 X10 **Passu Keah** *island* S Paracel Islands
118 J13 **Pastavy** *Pol.* Postawy, *Rus.* Postavy. Vitsyebskaya Voblasts', NW Belarus
56 D7 **Pastaza** ◐ *province* E Ecuador
56 D9 **Pastaza, Río** ≈ Ecuador/Peru
61 A21 **Pasteur** Buenos Aires, E Argentina
15 V3 **Pasteur** ≈ Québec, SE Canada
147 Q12 **Pastigav** *Rus.* Pastigov. W Tajikistan
Pastigov *see* Pastigav
54 C13 **Pasto** Nariño, SW Colombia
38 M10 **Pastol Bay** *bay* Alaska, USA
37 O8 **Pastora Peak** ▲ Arizona, SW USA
105 O8 **Pastrana** Castilla-La Mancha, C Spain
169 S16 **Pasuruan** *prev.* Pasoeroean. Jawa, C Indonesia
118 F11 **Pasvalys** Panevėžys, N Lithuania
111 K21 **Pásztó** Nógrád, N Hungary
189 U12 **Pata** *var.* Patta. *atoll* Chuuk Islands, C Micronesia
36 M16 **Patagonia** Arizona, SW USA
63 H20 **Patagonia** *physical region* Argentina/Chile
Patalung *see* Phatthalung
154 D9 **Pātan** Gujarāt, W India
154 J10 **Pātan** Madhya Pradesh, C India
171 S11 **Patani** Pulau Halmahera, E Indonesia
Patani *see* Pattani
15 V7 **Patapédia Est** ≈ Québec, SE Canada
116 K13 **Pătârlagele** *prev.* Pătîriagele. Buzău, SE Romania
Patavium *see* Padova
182 I5 **Patawarta Hill** ▲ South Australia
182 L10 **Patchewollock** Victoria, SE Australia
184 K11 **Patea** Taranaki, North Island, NZ
184 K11 **Patea** ≈ North Island, NZ
77 U15 **Pategi** Kwara, C Nigeria
81 K20 **Pate Island** *var.* Patta Island. *island* SE Kenya
105 S10 **Paterna** País Valenciano, E Spain
109 R9 **Paternion** *Slvn.* Špatrjan. Kärnten, S Austria
107 L24 **Paternò** *anc.* Hybla, Hybla Major. Sicilia, Italy, C Mediterranean Sea
32 J7 **Pateros** Washington, NW USA
18 J14 **Paterson** New Jersey, NE USA
32 J10 **Paterson** Washington, NW USA
185 C25 **Paterson Inlet** *inlet* Stewart Island, NZ
98 N6 **Paterswolde** Drenthe, NE Netherlands
152 H7 **Pathānkot** Himāchal Pradesh, N India
Pathein *see* Bassein
33 W15 **Pathfinder Reservoir** ▣ Wyoming, C USA
167 O11 **Pathum Thani** *var.* Patumdhani, Prathum Thani. Pathum Thani, C Thailand
54 C12 **Patía** *var.* El Bordo. Cauca, SW Colombia
152 I9 **Patiāla** *var.* Puttiala. Punjab, NW India
54 B12 **Patía, Río** ≈ SW Colombia
188 D15 **Pati Point** *headland* NE Guam
Pătîriagele *see* Pătârlagele
56 C13 **Pativilca** Lima, W Peru
166 M1 **Pātkai Bum** *var.* Patkai Range. ⛰ Burma/India
Patkai Range *see* Pātkai Bum
115 L20 **Pátmos** Pátmos, Dodekánisos, Greece, Aegean Sea
115 L20 **Pátmos** *island* Dodekánisos, Greece, Aegean Sea
153 P13 **Patna** *var.* Azimabad. Bihār, N India
154 M12 **Patnāgarh** Orissa, E India
171 O5 **Patnongon** Panay Island, C Philippines
137 S13 **Patnos** Ağrı, E Turkey
60 H12 **Pato Branco** Paraná, S Brazil
31 O16 **Patoka Lake** ◎ Indiana, N USA
92 L9 **Patoniva** *Lapp.* Buoddobohki. Lappi, N Finland
113 K21 **Patos** *var.* Patosi. Fier, SW Albania
Patos *see* Patos de Minas
59 K19 **Patos de Minas** *var.* Patos. Minas Gerais, NE Brazil
Patosi *see* Patos
61 I17 **Patos, Lagoa dos** *lagoon* S Brazil
62 J9 **Patquía** La Rioja, C Argentina
115 E19 **Pátra** *Eng.* Patras; *prev.* Pátrai. Dytikí Ellás, S Greece
Pátrai/Patras *see* Pátra
115 D18 **Patraïkós Kólpos** *gulf* S Greece
92 G2 **Patreksfjördhur** Vestfirdhir, W Iceland
24 M7 **Patricia** Texas, SW USA
63 F21 **Patricio Lynch, Isla** *island* S Chile
Patta *see* Pata
Patta Island *see* Pate Island
167 O16 **Pattani** *var.* Patani. Pattani, SW Thailand
167 P12 **Pattaya** Chon Buri, S Thailand
19 S4 **Patten** Maine, NE USA
35 O9 **Patterson** California, W USA
22 J10 **Patterson** Louisiana, S USA
35 R7 **Patterson, Mount** ▲ California, W USA
31 P4 **Patterson, Point** *headland* Michigan, N USA
107 L23 **Patti** Sicilia, Italy, C Mediterranean Sea
107 L23 **Patti, Golfo di** *gulf* Sicilia, Italy, C Mediterranean Sea
93 L14 **Pattijoki** Oulu, W Finland
193 Q4 **Patton Escarpment** *undersea feature* E Pacific Ocean
27 S2 **Pattonsburg** Missouri, C USA
193 N2 **Patton Seamount** *undersea feature* NE Pacific Ocean
10 J12 **Pattullo, Mount** ▲ British Columbia, W Canada
Patuakhali *see* Patukhali
42 M5 **Patuca, Río** ≈ E Honduras
153 U16 **Patukhali** *var.* Patuakhali. Khulna, S Bangladesh
Patumdhani *see* Pathum Thani
40 M14 **Pátzcuaro** Michoacán de Ocampo, SW Mexico
42 C6 **Patzicía** Chimaltenango, S Guatemala
102 K16 **Pau** Pyrénées-Atlantiques, SW France
102 J12 **Pauillac** Gironde, SW France
166 L5 **Pauk** Magwe, W Burma
8 I6 **Paulatuk** Northwest Territories, NW Canada
42 K5 **Paulayá, Río** ≈ NE Honduras

◆ Country ● Country Capital ◇ Dependent Territory ○ Dependent Territory Capital ◐ Administrative Region ✈ International Airport ▲ Mountain ⛰ Mountain Range ✱ Volcano ≈ River ◎ Lake ▣ Reservoir

22 M6 **Paulding** Mississippi, S USA
31 Q12 **Paulding** Ohio, N USA
29 S12 **Paullina** Iowa, C USA
59 P15 **Paulo Afonso** Bahia, E Brazil
38 M16 **Pauloff Harbor** *var.* Pavlor Harbour. Sanak Island, Alaska, USA
27 N12 **Pauls Valley** Oklahoma, C USA
166 L7 **Paungde** Pegu, C Burma
Pauni *see* Paoni
152 K9 **Pauri** Uttaranchal, N India
Pautalia *see* Kyustendil
142 J5 **Pāveh** Kermānshāh, NW Iran
126 L5 **Pavelets** Ryazanskaya Oblast', W Russian Federation
106 D8 **Pavia** *anc.* Ticinum. Lombardia, N Italy
118 C9 **Pāvilosta** Liepāja, W Latvia
125 P14 **Pavino** Kostromskaya Oblast', NW Russian Federation
114 J8 **Pavlikeni** Veliko Tŭrnovo, N Bulgaria
145 T8 **Pavlodar** Pavlodar, NE Kazakhstan
145 S9 **Pavlodar** *off.* Pavlodarskaya Oblast', *Kaz.* Pavlodar Oblysy. ◈ *province* NE Kazakhstan
Pavlodar Oblysy/Pavlodarskaya Oblast' *see* Pavlodar
Pavlograd *see* Pavlohrad
117 U7 **Pavlohrad** *Rus.* Pavlograd. Dnipropetrovs'ka Oblast', E Ukraine
Pavlor Harbour *see* Pauloff Harbour
145 R9 **Pavlovka** Akmola, C Kazakhstan
127 V4 **Pavlovka** Respublika Bashkortostan, W Russian Federation
127 Q7 **Pavlovka** Ul'yanovskaya Oblast', W Russian Federation
127 N3 **Pavlovo** Nizhegorodskaya Oblast', W Russian Federation
126 L9 **Pavlovsk** Voronezhskaya Oblast', W Russian Federation
126 L13 **Pavlovskaya** Krasnodarskiy Kray, SW Russian Federation
117 S7 **Pavlysh** Kirovohrads'ka Oblast', C Ukraine
106 F10 **Pavullo nel Frignano** Emilia-Romagna, C Italy
27 P8 **Pawhuska** Oklahoma, C USA
21 U13 **Pawleys Island** South Carolina, SE USA
167 N6 **Pawn** ≈ C Burma
30 K14 **Pawnee** Illinois, N USA
27 O9 **Pawnee** Oklahoma, C USA
37 U2 **Pawnee Buttes** ▲ Colorado, C USA
29 S17 **Pawnee City** Nebraska, C USA
26 K5 **Pawnee River** ≈ Kansas, C USA
31 O10 **Paw Paw** Michigan, N USA
31 O10 **Paw Paw Lake** Michigan, N USA
19 O12 **Pawtucket** Rhode Island, NE USA
Pax Augusta *see* Badajoz
115 I25 **Paximádia** *island* SE Greece
Pax Julia *see* Beja
115 B16 **Paxoí** *island* Iónioi Nísoi, Greece, C Mediterranean Sea
39 S10 **Paxson** Alaska, USA
147 O11 **Paxtakor** Jizzax Viloyati, C Uzbekistan
30 M13 **Paxton** Illinois, N USA
124 J11 **Pay** Respublika Kareliya, NW Russian Federation
166 M8 **Payagyi** Pegu, SW Burma
108 C9 **Payerne** *Ger.* Peterlingen. Vaud, W Switzerland
32 M13 **Payette** Idaho, NW USA
32 M13 **Payette River** ≈ Idaho, NW USA
127 V2 **Pay-Khoy, Khrebet** ▲▲ NW Russian Federation
Payne *see* Kangirsuk
12 K4 **Payne, Lac** ◎ Québec, NE Canada
29 T8 **Paynesville** Minnesota, N USA
169 S8 **Payong, Tanjung** *headland* East Malaysia
Payo Obispo *see* Chetumal
61 D18 **Paysandú** Paysandú, W Uruguay
61 D17 **Paysandú** ◈ *department* W Uruguay
102 I7 **Pays de la Loire** ◈ *region* NW France
36 L12 **Payson** Arizona, SW USA
36 L4 **Payson** Utah, W USA
127 W4 **Payyer, Gora** ▲ NW Russian Federation
Payzawat *see* Jiashi
137 Q11 **Pazar** Rize, NE Turkey
136 F10 **Pazarbaşı Burnu** *headland* NW Turkey
136 M16 **Pazarcık** Kahramanmaraş, S Turkey
114 I10 **Pazardzhik** *prev.* Tatar Pazardzhik. Pazardzhik, C Bulgaria
114 H11 **Pazardzhik** ◈ *province* C Bulgaria
54 H9 **Paz de Ariporo** Casanare, E Colombia
112 A10 **Pazin** *Ger.* Mitterburg, *It.* Pisino. Istra, NW Croatia
42 D7 **Paz, Río** ≈ El Salvador/Guatemala
113 O18 **Pčinja** ≈ N FYR Macedonia
193 V15 **Pea** Tongatapu, S Tonga
27 O6 **Peabody** Kansas, C USA
11 O12 **Peace** ≈ Alberta/British Columbia, W Canada
Peace Garden State *see* North Dakota
11 Q10 **Peace Point** Alberta, C Canada
11 O12 **Peace River** Alberta, W Canada
23 W13 **Peace River** ≈ Florida, SE USA
11 N17 **Peachland** British Columbia, SW Canada
36 J10 **Peach Springs** Arizona, SW USA
Peach State *see* Georgia
23 S4 **Peachtree City** Georgia, SE USA
189 Y13 **Peacock Point** *point* SE Wake Island
97 M18 **Peak District** *physical region* C England, UK
183 Q7 **Peak Hill** New South Wales, SE Australia
65 G15 **Peak, The** ▲ C Ascension Island
105 O13 **Peal de Becerro** Andalucía, S Spain
189 X11 **Peale Island** *island* N Wake Island
37 O6 **Peale, Mount** ▲ Utah, W USA
39 O4 **Peard Bay** *bay* Alaska, USA
23 Q7 **Pea River** ≈ Alabama/Florida, S USA
25 W11 **Pearland** Texas, SW USA
38 D9 **Pearl City** O'ahu, Hawai'i, USA, C Pacific Ocean
38 D9 **Pearl Harbor** *inlet* O'ahu, Hawai'i, USA, C Pacific Ocean
Pearl Islands *see* Perlas, Archipiélago de las
Pearl Lagoon *see* Perlas, Laguna de
22 M5 **Pearl River** ≈ Louisiana/Mississippi, S USA
25 Q13 **Pearsall** Texas, SW USA
23 U7 **Pearson** Georgia, SE USA
25 P4 **Pease River** ≈ Texas, SW USA
12 F7 **Peawanuk** Ontario, C Canada
83 P16 **Pebane** Zambézia, NE Mozambique
65 C23 **Pebble Island** *island* N Falkland Islands
65 C23 **Pebble Island Settlement** Pebble Island, N Falkland Islands
113 L16 **Peć** *Alb.* Pejë, *Turk.* Ipek. Serbia, S Serbia and Montenegro (Yugo.)
25 R8 **Pecan Bayou** ≈ Texas, SW USA
22 H10 **Pecan Island** Louisiana, S USA
60 L12 **Peças, Ilha das** *island* S Brazil
30 L10 **Pecatonica River** ≈ Illinois/Wisconsin, N USA
108 G10 **Peccia** Ticino, S Switzerland
Pechenegi *see* Pechenihy
Pechenezhskoye Vodokhranilishche *see* Pecheniz'ke Vodoskhovyshche
124 I2 **Pechenga** *Fin.* Petsamo. Murmanskaya Oblast', NW Russian Federation
117 V5 **Pechenihy** *Rus.* Pechenegi. Kharkivs'ka Oblast', E Ukraine
117 V5 **Pecheniz'ke Vodoskhovyshche** *Rus.* Pechenezhskoye Vodokhranilishche. ▣ E Ukraine
125 U7 **Pechora** Respublika Komi, NW Russian Federation
127 R6 **Pechora** ≈ NW Russian Federation
Pechora Bay *see* Pechorskaya Guba
Pechora Sea *see* Pechorskoye More
127 S3 **Pechorskaya Guba** *Eng.* Pechora Bay. *bay* NW Russian Federation
122 H7 **Pechorskoye More** *Eng.* Pechora Sea. *sea* NW Russian Federation
116 E11 **Pecica** *Ger.* Petschka, *Hung.* Ópécska. Arad, W Romania
24 K8 **Pecos** Texas, SW USA
25 N11 **Pecos River** ≈ New Mexico/Texas, SW USA
111 I25 **Pécs** *Ger.* Fünfkirchen; *Lat.* Sopianae. Baranya, SW Hungary
43 T17 **Pedasí** Los Santos, S Panama
Pedde *see* Pedja
183 O17 **Pedder, Lake** ◎ Tasmania, SE Australia
44 M10 **Pedernales** SW Dominican Republic
55 Q5 **Pedernales** Delta Amacuro, NE Venezuela
25 R10 **Pedernales River** ≈ Texas, SW USA
62 H6 **Pedernales, Salar de** *salt lake* N Chile
Pedhoulas *see* Pedoulás
55 X11 **Pédima** *var.* Malavate. SW French Guiana
182 F1 **Pedirka** South Australia
171 S11 **Pediwang** Pulau Halmahera, E Indonesia
118 I5 **Pedja** *var.* Pedja Jõgi, *Ger.* Pedde. ≈ E Estonia
Pedja Jõgi *see* Pedja
121 O3 **Pedoulás** *var.* Pedhoulas. W Cyprus
59 N18 **Pedra Azul** Minas Gerais, NE Brazil
104 I3 **Pedrafita, Porto de** *var.* Puerto de Piedrafita. *pass* NW Spain
76 E9 **Pedra Lume** Sal, NE Cape Verde
43 P16 **Pedregal** Chiriquí, W Panama
54 J4 **Pedregal** Falcón, N Venezuela
40 L9 **Pedriceña** Durango, C Mexico
60 L11 **Pedro Barros** São Paulo, S Brazil
39 Q13 **Pedro Bay** Alaska, USA
62 H4 **Pedro de Valdivia** *var.* Oficina Pedro de Valdivia. Antofagasta, N Chile
62 P4 **Pedro Juan Caballero** Amambay, E Paraguay
63 L15 **Pedro Luro** Buenos Aires, E Argentina
105 O10 **Pedro Muñoz** Castilla-La Mancha, C Spain
155 J22 **Pedro, Point** *headland* NW Sri Lanka
182 K9 **Peebinga** South Australia
96 J13 **Peebles** SE Scotland, UK
31 S15 **Peebles** Ohio, N USA
96 I12 **Peebles** *cultural region* SE Scotland, UK
18 K13 **Peekskill** New York, NE USA
97 I16 **Peel** W Isle of Man
8 G7 **Peel** ≈ Northwest Territories/Yukon Territory, NW Canada
8 K5 **Peel Point** *headland* Victoria Island, Northwest Territories, NW Canada
8 M5 **Peel Sound** *passage* Nunavut, N Canada
100 N9 **Peene** ≈ NE Germany
99 K17 **Peer** Limburg, NE Belgium
14 H14 **Pefferlaw** Ontario, S Canada
185 I18 **Pegasus Bay** *bay* South Island, NZ
121 O3 **Pégeia** *var.* Peyia. SW Cyprus
109 V7 **Peggau** Steiermark, SE Austria
101 L19 **Pegnitz** Bayern, SE Germany
101 L19 **Pegnitz** ≈ SE Germany
105 T11 **Pego** País Valenciano, E Spain
166 L8 **Pegu** *var.* Bago. Pegu, SW Burma
166 L7 **Pegu** ◈ *division* S Burma
189 N13 **Pehleng** Pohnpei, E Micronesia
114 M12 **Pehlivanköy** Kırklareli, NW Turkey
77 R14 **Péhonko** C Benin
61 B21 **Pehuajó** Buenos Aires, E Argentina
Pei-ching *see* Beijing/Beijing Shi
100 J13 **Peine** Niedersachsen, C Germany
Pei-p'ing *see* Beijing/Beijing Shi
Peipsi Järv/Peipus-See *see* Peipus, Lake
118 J5 **Peipus, Lake** *Est.* Peipsi Järv, *Ger.* Peipus-See, *Rus.* Chudskoye Ozero. ◎ Estonia/Russian Federation
115 H19 **Peiraías** *prev.* Piraiévs, *Eng.* Piraeus. Attikí, C Greece
Peisern *see* Pyzdry
60 I8 **Peixe, Rio do** ≈ S Brazil
59 I16 **Peixoto de Azevedo** Mato Grosso, W Brazil
168 O11 **Pejantan, Pulau** *island* W Indonesia
Pejë *see* Peć
112 N11 **Pek** ≈ E Serbia and Montenegro (Yugo.)
167 R7 **Pèk** *var.* Xieng Khouang; *prev.* Xiangkhoang. Xiangkhoang, N Laos
169 Q16 **Pekalongan** Jawa, C Indonesia
168 K11 **Pekanbaru** *var.* Pakanbaru. Sumatera, W Indonesia
30 L12 **Pekin** Illinois, N USA
Peking *see* Beijing/Beijing Shi
Pelabohan Kelang/Pelabuhan Kelang *see* Pelabuhan Klang
168 J9 **Pelabuhan Klang** *var.* Kuala Pelabohan Kelang, Pelabohan Kelang, Pelabuhan Kelang, Port Klang, Port Swettenham. Selangor, Peninsular Malaysia
120 L11 **Pelagie, Isole** *island group* SW Italy
Pelagosa *see* Palagruža
22 L5 **Pelahatchie** Mississippi, S USA
169 T14 **Pelaihari** *var.* Pleihari. Borneo, C Indonesia
103 U14 **Pelat, Mont** ▲ SE France
116 F12 **Peleaga, Vârful** *prev.* Vîrful Peleaga. ▲ W Romania
Peleaga, Vîrful *see* Peleaga, Vârful
123 O11 **Peleduy** Respublika Sakha (Yakutiya), NE Russian Federation
14 C18 **Pelee Island** *island* Ontario, S Canada
45 Q11 **Pelée, Montagne** ⚶ N Martinique
14 D18 **Pelee, Point** *headland* Ontario, S Canada
171 P12 **Pelei** Pulau Peleng, N Indonesia
Peleliu *see* Beliliou
171 P12 **Peleng, Pulau** *island* Kepulauan Banggai, N Indonesia
23 T7 **Pelham** Georgia, SE USA
111 E18 **Pelhřimov** *Ger.* Pilgram. Vysočina, C Czech Republic
39 W13 **Pelican** Chichagof Island, Alaska, USA
191 Z3 **Pelican Lagoon** ◎ Kiritimati, E Kiribati
29 U6 **Pelican Lake** ◎ Minnesota, N USA
29 V3 **Pelican Lake** ◎ Minnesota, N USA
30 L5 **Pelican Lake** ◎ Wisconsin, N USA
44 G1 **Pelican Point** Grand Bahama Island, N Bahamas
83 B19 **Pelican Point** *headland* W Namibia
29 S6 **Pelican Rapids** Minnesota, N USA
Pelican State *see* Louisiana
11 U13 **Pelikan Narrows** Saskatchewan, C Canada
115 L18 **Pelinaío** ▲ Chíos, E Greece
Pelinnaeum *see* Pelinnaío
115 E16 **Pelinnaío** *anc.* Pelinnaeum. *ruins* Thessalía, C Greece
113 N20 **Pelister** ▲ SW FYR Macedonia
113 G15 **Pelješac** *peninsula* S Croatia
92 M12 **Pelkosenniemi** Lappi, NE Finland
29 W15 **Pella** Iowa, C USA
114 F13 **Pélla** *site of ancient city* Kentrikí Makedonía, N Greece
23 Q3 **Pell City** Alabama, S USA
61 A22 **Pellegrini** Buenos Aires, E Argentina
92 K12 **Pello** Lappi, NW Finland
100 G7 **Pellworm** *island* N Germany
10 H6 **Pelly** ≈ Yukon Territory, NW Canada
9 N7 **Pelly Bay** Nunavut, N Canada
10 I8 **Pelly Mountains** ▲▲ Yukon Territory, W Canada
Pélmonostor *see* Beli Manastir
37 P13 **Pelona Mountain** ▲ New Mexico, SW USA
Peloponnese/Peloponnesus *see* Pelopónnisos
115 E20 **Pelopónnisos** *Eng.* Peloponnese. ◈ *region* S Greece
115 E20 **Pelopónnisos** *var.* Morea, *Eng.* Peloponnese; *anc.* Peloponnesus. *peninsula* S Greece
107 L23 **Peloritani, Monti** *anc.* Pelorus and Neptunius. ▲▲ Sicilia, Italy, C Mediterranean Sea
107 M22 **Peloro, Capo** *var.* Punta del Faro. *headland* S Italy
Pelorus and Neptunius *see* Peloritani, Monti
61 H17 **Pelotas** Rio Grande do Sul, S Brazil
61 I14 **Pelotas, Rio** ≈ S Brazil
92 K10 **Peltovuoma** *Lapp.* Bealdovuopmi. Lappi, N Finland
19 R4 **Pemadumcook Lake** ◎ Maine, NE USA
169 Q16 **Pemalang** Jawa, C Indonesia
169 P10 **Pemangkat** *var.* Pamangkat. Borneo, C Indonesia
Pemar *see* Paimio
168 I9 **Pematangsiantar** Sumatera, W Indonesia
83 Q14 **Pemba** *prev.* Port Amelia, Porto Amélia. Cabo Delgado, NE Mozambique
81 J22 **Pemba** ◈ *region* E Tanzania
81 K21 **Pemba** *island* E Tanzania
83 Q14 **Pemba, Baia de** *inlet* NE Mozambique
81 J21 **Pemba Channel** *channel* E Tanzania
180 J14 **Pemberton** Western Australia
10 M16 **Pemberton** British Columbia, SW Canada
29 Q2 **Pembina** North Dakota, N USA
29 Q2 **Pembina** ≈ Canada/USA
11 P15 **Pembina** ≈ Alberta, SW Canada
171 X16 **Pembre** Papua, E Indonesia
14 K12 **Pembroke** Ontario, SE Canada
97 H21 **Pembroke** SW Wales, UK
23 W6 **Pembroke** Georgia, SE USA
21 U11 **Pembroke** North Carolina, SE USA
21 R7 **Pembroke** Virginia, NE USA
97 H21 **Pembroke** *cultural region* SW Wales, UK
Pembuang, Sungai *see* Seruyan, Sungai
43 S15 **Peña Blanca, Cerro** ▲ C Panama
104 K8 **Peña de Francia, Sierra de la** ▲▲ W Spain
104 G6 **Penafiel** *var.* Peñafiel. Porto, N Portugal
105 N6 **Peñafiel** Castilla-León, N Spain
105 S8 **Peñagolosa** ▲ E Spain
105 N7 **Peñalara, Pico de** ▲ C Spain
171 X16 **Penambo, Banjaran** *var.* Banjaran Tama Abu, Penambo Range. ▲▲ Indonesia/Malaysia
Penambo Range *see* Penambo, Banjaran
41 O10 **Peña Nevada, Cerro** ▲ C Mexico
Penang *see* Pinang, Pulau, Peninsular Malaysia
Penang *see* Pinang
Penang *see* George Town
60 J8 **Penápolis** São Paulo, S Brazil
104 L7 **Peñaranda de Bracamonte** Castilla-León, N Spain
105 S8 **Peñarroya** ▲ E Spain
104 L12 **Peñarroya-Pueblonuevo** Andalucía, S Spain
97 K22 **Penarth** S Wales, UK
104 K1 **Peñas, Cabo de** *headland* N Spain
63 F20 **Penas, Golfo de** *gulf* S Chile
Pen-ch'i *see* Benxi
79 H14 **Pendé** *var.* Logone Oriental. ≈ Central African Republic/Chad
76 I14 **Pendembu** E Sierra Leone
29 R13 **Pender** Nebraska, C USA
Penderma *see* Bandırma
32 K11 **Pendleton** Oregon, NW USA
32 M7 **Pend Oreille, Lake** ◎ Idaho, NW USA
32 M7 **Pend Oreille River** ≈ Idaho/Washington, NW USA
Pendzhikent *see* Panjakent
Peneius *see* Pineiós
104 G8 **Penela** Coimbra, N Portugal
14 G13 **Penetanguishene** Ontario, S Canada
151 H15 **Penganga** ≈ C India
161 T12 **P'engchia Yu** *island* N Taiwan
79 M21 **Penge** Kasai Oriental, C Dem. Rep. Congo
Penghu Archipelago/P'enghu Ch'üntao/Penghu Islands *see* P'enghu Liehtao
161 R14 **P'enghu Liehtao** *var.* P'enghu Ch'üntao, Penghu Islands, *Eng.* Penghu Archipelago, Pescadores, *Jap.* Hoko-guntō, Hoko-shotō. *island group* W Taiwan
Penghu Shuidao/P'enghu Shuitao *see* Pescadores Channel
161 R4 **Penglai** *var.* Dengzhou. Shandong, E China
Peng-pu *see* Bengbu
Penhsihu *see* Benxi
Penibético, Sistema *see* Béticos, Sistemas
104 F10 **Peniche** Leiria, W Portugal
169 U17 **Penida, Nusa** *island* S Indonesia
Peninsular State *see* Florida
105 T8 **Peñíscola** País Valenciano, E Spain
40 M13 **Pénjamo** Guanajuato, C Mexico
Penki *see* Benxi
102 F7 **Penmarch, Pointe de** *headland* NW France
107 L15 **Penna, Punta della** *headland* C Italy
107 K14 **Penne** Abruzzo, C Italy
Penner *see* Penneru
155 J18 **Penneru** *var.* Penner. ≈ C India
182 I10 **Penneshaw** South Australia
18 C14 **Penn Hills** Pennsylvania, NE USA
Penninae, Alpes/Pennine, Alpi *see* Pennine Alps
108 D11 **Pennine Alps** *Fr.* Alpes Pennines, *It.* Alpi Pennine; *Lat.* Alpes Penninae. ▲▲ Italy/Switzerland
Pennine Chain *see* Pennines
97 L15 **Pennines** *var.* Pennine Chain. ▲▲ N England, UK
Pennines, Alpes *see* Pennine Alps
21 O8 **Pennington Gap** Virginia, NE USA
18 I16 **Penns Grove** New Jersey, NE USA
18 I16 **Pennsville** New Jersey, NE USA
18 E14 **Pennsylvania** *off.* Commonwealth of Pennsylvania; also known as The Keystone State. ◈ *state* NE USA
18 G10 **Penn Yan** New York, NE USA
124 H16 **Peno** Tverskaya Oblast', W Russian Federation
19 R7 **Penobscot Bay** *bay* Maine, NE USA
19 S5 **Penobscot River** ≈ Maine, NE USA
182 K12 **Penola** South Australia
40 K9 **Peñón Blanco** Durango, C Mexico
182 E7 **Penong** South Australia
43 S16 **Penonomé** Coclé, C Panama
190 L13 **Penrhyn** *atoll* N Cook Islands
192 M9 **Penrhyn Basin** *undersea feature* C Pacific Ocean
183 S9 **Penrith** New South Wales, SE Australia
97 K15 **Penrith** NW England, UK
23 O9 **Pensacola** Florida, SE USA
23 O9 **Pensacola Bay** *bay* Florida, SE USA
195 N7 **Pensacola Mountains** ▲▲ Antarctica
182 L12 **Penshurst** Victoria, SE Australia
187 R13 **Pentecost** *Fr.* Pentecôte. *island* C Vanuatu
15 V4 **Pentecôte** ≈ Québec, SE Canada
Pentecôte *see* Pentecost
15 V4 **Pentecôte, Lac** ◎ Québec, SE Canada
8 H15 **Penticton** British Columbia, SW Canada
96 J6 **Pentland Firth** *strait* N Scotland, UK
96 J12 **Pentland Hills** *hill range* S Scotland, UK
171 Q12 **Penu** Pulau Taliabu, E Indonesia
155 H18 **Penukonda** Andhra Pradesh, E India
166 L7 **Penwegon** Pegu, C Burma
24 M8 **Penwell** Texas, SW USA
97 J21 **Pen y Fan** ▲ SE Wales, UK
97 L16 **Pen-y-ghent** ▲ N England, UK
127 O6 **Penza** Penzenskaya Oblast', W Russian Federation
97 G25 **Penzance** SW England, UK
127 N6 **Penzenskaya Oblast'** ◈ *province* W Russian Federation
123 U7 **Penzhina** ≈ E Russian Federation
123 U9 **Penzhinskaya Guba** *bay* E Russian Federation
Penzig *see* Pieńsk
36 K13 **Peoria** Arizona, SW USA
30 L12 **Peoria** Illinois, N USA
30 L12 **Peoria Heights** Illinois, N USA
31 N11 **Peotone** Illinois, N USA
18 J11 **Pepacton Reservoir** ▣ New York, NE USA
76 I15 **Pepel** W Sierra Leone
30 I6 **Pepin, Lake** ▣ Minnesota/Wisconsin, N USA
99 L20 **Pepinster** Liège, E Belgium
113 L20 **Peqin** *var.* Peqini. Elbasan, C Albania
Peqini *see* Peqin
40 D7 **Pequeña, Punta** *headland* W Mexico
168 J8 **Perak** ◈ *state* Peninsular Malaysia
105 R7 **Perales del Alfambra** Aragón, NE Spain
115 C15 **Pérama** *var.* Perama. Ípeiros, W Greece
92 M13 **Perä-Posio** Lappi, NE Finland
15 Z6 **Percé** Québec, SE Canada
15 Z6 **Percé, Rocher** *island* Québec, S Canada
102 L5 **Perche, Collines de** ▲ N France
109 X4 **Perchtoldsdorf** Niederösterreich, NE Austria
180 L6 **Percival Lakes** *lakes* Western Australia
105 T3 **Perdido, Monte** ▲ NE Spain
23 O8 **Perdido River** ≈ Alabama/Florida, S USA
Perece Vela Basin *see* West Mariana Basin
116 G7 **Perechyn** Zakarpats'ka Oblast', W Ukraine
54 E10 **Pereira** Risaralda, W Colombia
60 I7 **Pereira Barreto** São Paulo, S Brazil
59 G15 **Pereirinha** Pará, N Brazil
127 N10 **Perelazovskiy** Volgogradskaya Oblast', SW Russian Federation
127 S7 **Perelyub** Saratovskaya Oblast', W Russian Federation
31 P7 **Pere Marquette River** ≈ Michigan, N USA
Peremyshl *see* Podkarpackie
116 I5 **Peremyshlyany** L'vivs'ka Oblast', W Ukraine
Pereshchepino *see* Pereshchepyne
116 L9 **Pereshchepyne** *Rus.* Pereshchepino. Dnipropetrovs'ka Oblast', E Ukraine
126 L16 **Pereslavl'-Zalesskiy** Yaroslavskaya Oblast', W Russian Federation
117 Y7 **Pereval's'k** Luhans'ka Oblast', E Ukraine
127 U7 **Perevolotskiy** Orenburgskaya Oblast', W Russian Federation
Pereyaslav-Khmel'nitskiy *see* Pereyaslav-Khmel'nyts'kyy
117 Q5 **Pereyaslav-Khmel'nyts'kyy** *Rus.* Pereyaslav-Khmel'nitskiy. Kyyivs'ka Oblast', N Ukraine
109 U4 **Perg** Oberösterreich, N Austria
61 B19 **Pergamino** Buenos Aires, E Argentina
106 G6 **Pergine Valsugana** *Ger.* Persen. Trentino-Alto Adige, N Italy
29 S6 **Perham** Minnesota, N USA
93 L16 **Perho** Länsi-Suomi, W Finland
116 E11 **Periam** *Ger.* Perjamosch, *Hung.* Perjámos. Timiş, W Romania
15 Q6 **Péribonca** ≈ Québec, SE Canada
12 L11 **Péribonca, Lac** ◎ Québec, SE Canada
15 Q6 **Péribonca, Petite Rivière** ≈ Québec, SE Canada
15 Q7 **Péribonka** Québec, SE Canada
40 I9 **Pericos** Sinaloa, C Mexico
169 Q10 **Perigi** Borneo, C Indonesia
102 L12 **Périgueux** *anc.* Vesuna. Dordogne, SW France
54 G5 **Perijá, Serranía de** ▲▲ Columbia/Venezuela
115 H17 **Peristéra** *island* Vóreioi Sporádes, Greece, Aegean Sea
63 H20 **Perito Moreno** Santa Cruz, S Argentina
155 G22 **Periyāl** *var.* Periyār. ≈ SW India
Periyār *see* Periyāl
155 G23 **Periyār Lake** ◎ S India
Perjámos/Perjamosch *see* Periam
27 O9 **Perkins** Oklahoma, C USA
116 L7 **Perkivtsi** Chernivets'ka Oblast', W Ukraine
43 U15 **Perlas, Archipiélago de las** *Eng.* Pearl Islands. *island group* SE Panama
43 O10 **Perlas, Cayos de** *reef* SE Nicaragua
43 N9 **Perlas, Laguna de** *Eng.* Pearl Lagoon. *lagoon* E Nicaragua
43 N10 **Perlas, Punta de** *headland* E Nicaragua
100 L11 **Perleberg** Brandenburg, N Germany
Perlepe *see* Prilep
168 I6 **Perlis** ◈ *state* Peninsular Malaysia
125 U14 **Perm'** *prev.* Molotov. Permskaya Oblast', NW Russian Federation
113 M22 **Përmet** *var.* Përmeti, Prëmet. Gjirokastër, S Albania
Përmeti *see* Përmet
125 U15 **Permskaya Oblast'** ◈ *province* NW Russian Federation
59 P15 **Pernambuco** *off.* Estado de Pernambuco. ◈ *state* E Brazil
Pernambuco *see* Recife
Pernambuco Abyssal Plain *see* Pernambuco Plain
47 Y6 **Pernambuco Plain** *var.* Pernambuco Abyssal Plain. *undersea feature* E Atlantic Ocean
65 K15 **Pernambuco Seamounts** *undersea feature* C Atlantic Ocean
182 H6 **Pernatty Lagoon** *salt lake* South Australia
Pernau *see* Pärnu
Pernauer Bucht *see* Pärnu Laht
Pērnava *see* Pärnu
114 G9 **Pernik** *prev.* Dimitrovo. Pernik, W Bulgaria
114 G10 **Pernik** ◈ *province* W Bulgaria
93 K20 **Perniö** *Swe.* Bjärnå. Länsi-Suomi, W Finland
109 X5 **Pernitz** Niederösterreich, E Austria
Pernov *see* Pärnu
103 O3 **Péronne** Somme, N France
14 L8 **Péronne, Lac** ◎ Québec, SE Canada
106 A8 **Perosa Argentina** Piemonte, NE Italy
41 Q14 **Perote** Veracruz-Llave, E Mexico
Pérouse *see* Perugia
191 W15 **Pérouse, Bahía de la** *bay* Easter Island, Chile, E Pacific Ocean
Perovsk *see* Kyzylorda
103 O17 **Perpignan** Pyrénées-Orientales, S France
113 M20 **Përrenjas** *var.* Përrenjasi, Prenjas, Prenjasi. Elbasan, E Albania
Përrenjasi *see* Përrenjas
92 O2 **Perriertoppen** ▲ C Svalbard
25 S6 **Perrin** Texas, SW USA
23 Y16 **Perrine** Florida, SE USA
37 S12 **Perro, Laguna del** ◎ New Mexico, SW USA
102 G5 **Perros-Guirec** Côtes d'Armor, NW France
23 T9 **Perry** Florida, SE USA
23 T5 **Perry** Georgia, SE USA
29 U14 **Perry** Iowa, C USA
18 E10 **Perry** New York, NE USA
27 N9 **Perry** Oklahoma, C USA
27 Q3 **Perry Lake** ▣ Kansas, C USA
31 R11 **Perrysburg** Ohio, N USA
25 O1 **Perryton** Texas, SW USA
39 O15 **Perryville** Alaska, USA
27 U11 **Perryville** Arkansas, C USA
27 Y6 **Perryville** Missouri, C USA
Persante *see* Parsęta
Persen *see* Pergine Valsugana
Pershay *see* Pyarshai
117 V7 **Pershotravens'k** Dnipropetrovs'ka Oblast', E Ukraine
117 W9 **Pershotravneve** Donets'ka Oblast', E Ukraine
Persia *see* Iran
Persian Gulf *see* Gulf, The
Persis *see* Fārs
95 K22 **Perstorp** Skåne, S Sweden
137 O14 **Pertek** Tunceli, C Turkey
183 P16 **Perth** Tasmania, SE Australia

◆ Country ● Country Capital ◇ Dependent Territory ○ Dependent Territory Capital ◈ Administrative Region ✕ International Airport ▲ Mountain ▲▲ Mountain Range ⚶ Volcano ≈ River ◎ Lake ▣ Reservoir

180 I13 **Perth** *state capital* Western Australia
14 L13 **Perth** Ontario, SE Canada
96 J11 **Perth** C Scotland, UK
180 I12 **Perth** ✕ Western Australia
96 J10 **Perth** *cultural region* C Scotland, UK
173 V10 **Perth Basin** *undersea feature* SE Indian Ocean
103 S15 **Pertuis** Vaucluse, SE France
103 Y16 **Pertusato, Capo** *headland* Corse, France, C Mediterranean Sea
30 L11 **Peru** Illinois, N USA
31 P12 **Peru** Indiana, N USA
57 E13 **Peru** *off.* Republic of Peru. ◆ *republic* W South America
Peru *see* Beru
193 T9 **Peru Basin** *undersea feature* E Pacific Ocean
193 U8 **Peru-Chile Trench** *undersea feature* E Pacific Ocean
112 F13 **Perućko Jezero** ◎ S Croatia
106 H13 **Perugia** *Fr.* Pérouse; *anc.* Perusia. Umbria, C Italy
Perugia, Lake of *see* Trasimeno, Lago
61 D15 **Perugorría** Corrientes, NE Argentina
60 M11 **Peruíbe** São Paulo, S Brazil
155 B21 **Perumalpār** *reef* India, N Indian Ocean
Perusia *see* Perugia
99 D20 **Péruwelz** Hainaut, SW Belgium
137 R15 **Pervari** Siirt, SE Turkey
127 O4 **Pervomaysk** Nizhegorodskaya Oblast', W Russian Federation
117 X7 **Pervomays'k** Luhans'ka Oblast', E Ukraine
117 P8 **Pervomays'k** *prev.* Ol'viopol'. Mykolayivs'ka Oblast', S Ukraine
117 S12 **Pervomays'ke** Respublika Krym, S Ukraine
125 R14 **Pervomayskiy** Kirovskaya Oblast', NW Russian Federation
127 V7 **Pervomayskiy** Orenburgskaya Oblast', W Russian Federation
126 M6 **Pervomayskiy** Tambovskaya Oblast', W Russian Federation
117 V6 **Pervomays'kyy** Kharkivs'ka Oblast', E Ukraine
122 F10 **Pervoural'sk** Sverdlovskaya Oblast', C Russian Federation
123 V11 **Pervyy Kuril'skiy Proliv** *strait* E Russian Federation
99 I19 **Perwez** Walloon Brabant, C Belgium
106 I11 **Pesaro** *anc.* Pisaurum. Marche, C Italy
35 N9 **Pescadero** California, W USA
Pescadores *see* P'enghu Liehtao
161 S14 **Pescadores Channel** *var.* Penghu Shuidao, P'enghu Shuitao. *channel* W Taiwan
107 K14 **Pescara** *anc.* Aternum, Ostia Aterni. Abruzzo, C Italy
107 K15 **Pescara** ≈ C Italy
106 F11 **Pescia** Toscana, C Italy
108 C8 **Peseux** Neuchâtel, W Switzerland
127 P6 **Pesha** ≈ NW Russian Federation
149 T5 **Peshāwar** North-West Frontier Province, N Pakistan
149 T6 **Peshāwar** ✕ North-West Frontier Province, N Pakistan
113 M19 **Peshkopi** *var.* Peshkopia, Peshkopija. Dibër, NE Albania
Peshkopia/Peshkopija *see* Peshkopi
114 I11 **Peshtera** Pazardzhik, C Bulgaria
31 N6 **Peshtigo** Wisconsin, N USA
31 N6 **Peshtigo River** ≈ Wisconsin, N USA
Peski *see* Pyeski
Peski Taskuduk *see* Tosquduq Qumlari
125 S13 **Peskovka** Kirovskaya Oblast', NW Russian Federation
103 S8 **Pesmes** Haute-Saône, E France
104 H6 **Peso da Régua** *var.* Pêso da Regua. Vila Real, N Portugal
40 F5 **Pesqueira** Sonora, NW Mexico
102 J13 **Pessac** Gironde, SW France
111 J23 **Pest** *off.* Pest Megye. ◈ *county* C Hungary
124 J14 **Pestovo** Novgorodskaya Oblast', W Russian Federation
40 M15 **Petacalco, Bahía** *bay* W Mexico
Petach-Tikva/Petah Tiqva *see* Petaḥ Tiqwa
138 F10 **Petaḥ Tiqwa** *var.* Petach-Tikva, Petah Tiqva, Petakh Tikva.Tel Aviv, C Israel
Petakh Tikva *see* Petaḥ Tiqwa
93 L17 **Petäjävesi** Länsi-Suomi, W Finland
22 M7 **Petal** Mississippi, S USA
115 I19 **Petalioí** *island* C Greece
115 H19 **Petalión, Kólpos** *gulf* E Greece
115 J19 **Pétalo** ▲ Ándros, Kykládes, Greece, Aegean Sea
34 M8 **Petaluma** California, W USA
99 L25 **Pétange** Luxembourg, SW Luxembourg
54 M5 **Petare** Miranda, N Venezuela
41 N16 **Petatlán** Guerrero, S Mexico
83 L14 **Petauke** Eastern, E Zambia
14 J12 **Petawawa** Ontario, SE Canada
14 J11 **Petawawa** ≈ Ontario, SE Canada
Petchaburi *see* Phetchaburi
42 D2 **Petén** *off.* Departamento del Petén. ◈ *department* N Guatemala
42 D2 **Petén Itzá, Lago** *var.* Lago de Flores. ◎ N Guatemala
30 K7 **Petenwell Lake** ▣ Wisconsin, N USA
14 D6 **Peterbell** Ontario, S Canada
182 I7 **Peterborough** South Australia
14 I14 **Peterborough** Ontario, SE Canada
97 N20 **Peterborough** *prev.* Medeshamstede. E England, UK
19 N10 **Peterborough** New Hampshire, NE USA
96 L8 **Peterhead** NE Scotland, UK
Peterhof *see* Luboń
193 Q14 **Peter I Island** ◇ *Norwegian dependency* Antarctica
194 H9 **Peter I Island** *var.* Peter I øy. *island* Antarctica
Peter I øy *see* Peter I Island
97 M14 **Peterlee** N England, UK
Peterlingen *see* Payerne
197 P14 **Petermann Bjerg** ▲ C Greenland
11 S12 **Peter Pond Lake** ◎ Saskatchewan, C Canada
39 X13 **Petersburg** Mytkof Island, Alaska, USA
30 K13 **Petersburg** Illinois, N USA
31 N16 **Petersburg** Indiana, N USA
29 Q3 **Petersburg** North Dakota, N USA
25 N5 **Petersburg** Texas, SW USA
21 V7 **Petersburg** Virginia, NE USA
21 T4 **Petersburg** West Virginia, NE USA
100 H12 **Petershagen** Nordrhein-Westfalen, NW Germany
55 S9 **Peters Mine** *var.* Peter's Mine. N Guyana
107 O21 **Petilia Policastro** Calabria, SW Italy
44 M9 **Pétionville** S Haiti
45 X6 **Petit-Bourg** Basse Terre, C Guadeloupe
15 Y5 **Petit-Cap** Québec, SE Canada
45 Y6 **Petit Cul-de-Sac Marin** *bay* C Guadeloupe
44 M9 **Petite-Rivière-de-l'Artibonite** C Haiti
173 X16 **Petite Rivière Noire, Piton de la** ▲ C Mauritius
15 R9 **Petite-Rivière-St-François** Québec, SE Canada
44 L9 **Petit-Goâve** S Haiti
Petitjean *see* Sidi-Kacem
13 N10 **Petit Lac Manicouagan** ◎ Québec, E Canada
19 T7 **Petit Manan Point** *headland* Maine, NE USA
Petit Mécatina, Rivière du *see* Little Mecatina
11 N10 **Petitot** ≈ Alberta/British Columbia, W Canada
45 S12 **Petit Piton** ▲ SW Saint Lucia
Petit-Popo *see* Aného
Petit St-Bernard, Col du *see* Little Saint Bernard Pass
13 O8 **Petitsikapau Lake** ◎ Newfoundland and Labrador, E Canada
92 L11 **Petkula** Lappi, N Finland
41 X12 **Peto** Yucatán, SE Mexico
62 G10 **Petorca** Valparaíso, C Chile
31 Q5 **Petoskey** Michigan, N USA
138 G14 **Petra** *archaeological site* Ma'ān, W Jordan
Petra *see* Wādī Mūsā
115 F14 **Pétras, Sténa** *pass* N Greece
123 S16 **Petra Velikogo, Zaliv** *bay* SE Russian Federation
Petrel *see* Petrer
14 K15 **Petre, Point** *headland* Ontario, SE Canada
105 S12 **Petrer** *var.* Petrel. País Valenciano, E Spain
125 U11 **Petretsovo** Permskaya Oblast', NW Russian Federation
114 G12 **Petrich** Blagoevgrad, SW Bulgaria
187 P15 **Petrie, Récif** *reef* N New Caledonia
37 N11 **Petrified Forest** *prehistoric site* Arizona, SW USA
Petrikau *see* Piotrków Trybunalski
Petrikov *see* Pyetrykaw
116 H12 **Petrila** *Hung.* Petrilla. Hunedoara, W Romania
Petrilla *see* Petrila
112 E9 **Petrinja** Sisak-Moslavina, C Croatia
Petroaleksandrovsk *see* Türtkül
Petrőcz *see* Bački Petrovac
124 G12 **Petrodvorets** *Fin.* Pietarhovi. Leningradskaya Oblast', NW Russian Federation
Petrograd *see* Sankt-Peterburg
Petrokov *see* Piotrków Trybunalski
54 G6 **Petrólea** Norte de Santander, NE Colombia
14 D16 **Petrolia** Ontario, S Canada
25 S4 **Petrolia** Texas, SW USA
59 O15 **Petrolina** Pernambuco, E Brazil
45 T6 **Petrona, Punta** *headland* C Puerto Rico
Petropavl *see* Petropavlovsk
117 V7 **Petropavlivka** Dnipropetrovs'ka Oblast', E Ukraine
145 P6 **Petropavlovsk** *Kaz.* Petropavl. Severnyy Kazakhstan, N Kazakhstan
123 V11 **Petropavlovsk-Kamchatskiy** Kamchatskaya Oblast', E Russian Federation
60 P9 **Petrópolis** Rio de Janeiro, SE Brazil
116 H12 **Petroşani** *var.* Petroşeni, *Ger.* Petroschen, *Hung.* Petrozsény. Hunedoara, W Romania
Petroschen/Petroşeni *see* Petroşani
Petroskoi *see* Petrozavodsk
Petrovac/Petrovácz *see* Bački Petrovac
113 J17 **Petrovac na Moru** Montenegro, SW Serbia and Montenegro (Yugo.)
117 S8 **Petrove** Kirovohrads'ka Oblast', C Ukraine
113 O18 **Petrovec** C FYR Macedonia
Petrovgrad *see* Zrenjanin
127 P7 **Petrovsk** Saratovskaya Oblast', W Russian Federation
124 J9 **Petrovskiy Yam** Respublika Kareliya, NW Russian Federation
Petrovsk-Port *see* Makhachkala
127 P9 **Petrov Val** Volgogradskaya Oblast', SW Russian Federation
124 J11 **Petrozavodsk** *Fin.* Petroskoi. Respublika Kareliya, NW Russian Federation
Petrozsény *see* Petroşani
83 D20 **Petrusdal** Hardap, C Namibia
117 T7 **Petrykivka** Dnipropetrovs'ka Oblast', E Ukraine
Petsamo *see* Pechenga
Petschka *see* Pecica
Pettau *see* Ptuj
109 S5 **Pettenbach** Oberösterreich, C Austria
25 S13 **Pettus** Texas, SW USA
122 G12 **Petukhovo** Kurganskaya Oblast', C Russian Federation
Petuna *see* Songyuan
109 R4 **Peuerbach** Oberösterreich, N Austria
62 G12 **Peumo** Libertador, C Chile
123 T6 **Pevek** Chukotskiy Avtonomnyy Okrug, NE Russian Federation
27 X5 **Pevely** Missouri, C USA
Peyia *see* Pégeia
102 J15 **Peyrehorade** Landes, SW France
126 J14 **Peza** ≈ NW Russian Federation
103 P16 **Pézenas** Hérault, S France
111 H20 **Pezinok** *Ger.* Bösing, *Hung.* Bazin. Bratislavský Kraj, W Slovakia
101 L22 **Pfaffenhofen an der Ilm** Bayern, SE Germany
108 G7 **Pfäffikon** Schwyz, C Switzerland
101 F20 **Pfälzer Wald** *hill range* W Germany
101 N22 **Pfarrkirchen** Bayern, SE Germany
101 G21 **Pforzheim** Baden-Württemberg, SW Germany
101 H24 **Pfullendorf** Baden-Württemberg, S Germany
108 K8 **Pfunds** Tirol, W Austria
101 G19 **Pfungstadt** Hessen, W Germany
83 L20 **Phalaborwa** Limpopo, NE South Africa
152 E11 **Phalodi** Rājasthān, NW India
152 E12 **Phalsund** Rājasthān, NW India
155 E15 **Phaltan** Mahārāshtra, W India
167 O7 **Phan** *var.* Muang Phan. Chiang Rai, NW Thailand
167 O14 **Phangan, Ko** *island* SW Thailand
166 M15 **Phang-Nga** *var.* Pang-Nga, Phangnga. Phangnga, SW Thailand
Phan Rang/Phanrang *see* Phan Rang-Thap Cham
167 V13 **Phan Rang-Thap Cham** *var.* Phanrang, Phan Rang, Phan Rang Thap Cham. Ninh Thuân, S Vietnam
167 U13 **Phan Ri** Bình Thuân, S Vietnam
167 u13 **Phan Thiêt** Bình Thuân, S Vietnam
Pharnacia *see* Giresun
25 S17 **Pharr** Texas, SW USA
Pharus *see* Hvar
167 N16 **Phatthalung** *var.* Padalung, Patalung. Phatthalung, SW Thailand
167 O7 **Phayao** *var.* Muang Phayao. Phayao, NW Thailand
11 U10 **Phelps Lake** ◎ Saskatchewan, C Canada
21 X9 **Phelps Lake** ◎ North Carolina, SE USA
23 R5 **Phenix City** Alabama, S USA
167 T8 **Pheo** Quang Binh, C Vietnam
Phet Buri *see* Phetchaburi
167 O11 **Phetchaburi** *var.* Bejraburi, Petchaburi, Phet Buri. Phetchaburi, SW Thailand
167 O9 **Phichit** *var.* Bichitra, Muang Phichit, Pichit. Phichit, C Thailand
22 M5 **Philadelphia** Mississippi, S USA
18 I7 **Philadelphia** New York, NE USA
18 I16 **Philadelphia** Pennsylvania, NE USA
18 I16 **Philadelphia** ✕ Pennsylvania, NE USA
Philadelphia *see* 'Ammān
28 L10 **Philip** South Dakota, N USA
99 H22 **Philippeville** Namur, S Belgium
Philippeville *see* Skikda
21 S3 **Philippi** West Virginia, NE USA
Philippi *see* Fílippoi
195 Y9 **Philippi Glacier** *glacier* Antarctica
192 G6 **Philippine Basin** *undersea feature* W Pacific Ocean
171 O5 **Philippines** *off.* Republic of the Philippines. ◆ *republic* SE Asia
171 P3 **Philippine Sea** *sea* W Pacific Ocean
192 F6 **Philippine Trench** *undersea feature* W Philippine Sea
83 H23 **Philippolis** Free State, C South Africa
Philippopolis *see* Plovdiv, Bulgaria
Philippopolis *see* Shahbā', Syria
45 V9 **Philipsburg** Sint Maarten, N Netherlands Antilles
33 P10 **Philipsburg** Montana, NW USA
39 R6 **Philip Smith Mountains** ▲▲ Alaska, USA
152 H8 **Phillaur** Punjab, N India
183 N13 **Phillip Island** *island* Victoria, SE Australia
25 N2 **Phillips** Texas, SW USA
30 K5 **Phillips** Wisconsin, N USA
26 K3 **Phillipsburg** Kansas, C USA
18 I14 **Phillipsburg** New Jersey, NE USA
21 S7 **Philpott Lake** ▣ Virginia, NE USA
Phintias *see* Licata
167 P9 **Phitsanulok** *var.* Bisnulok, Muang Phitsanulok, Pitsanulok. Phitsanulok, C Thailand
Phlórina *see* Flórina
Phnom Penh *see* Phnum Penh
167 S13 **Phnum Penh** *var.* Phnom Penh. ● (Cambodia) Phnum Penh, S Cambodia
167 S11 **Phnum Tbêng Meanchey** Preăh Vihéar, N Cambodia
36 K13 **Phoenix** *state capital* Arizona, SW USA
Phoenix Island *see* Rawaki
191 R3 **Phoenix Islands** *island group* C Kiribati
18 I15 **Phoenixville** Pennsylvania, NE USA
83 K22 **Phofung** *var.* Mont-aux-Sources. ▲ N Lesotho
167 Q10 **Phon** Khon Kaen, E Thailand
167 Q5 **Phôngsali** *var.* Phong Saly. Phôngsali, N Laos
Phong Saly *see* Phôngsali
167 Q8 **Phônhông** C Laos
167 R5 **Phô Rang** Lao Cai, N Vietnam
Phort Láirge, Cuan *see* Waterford Harbour
167 N10 **Phra Chedi Sam Ong** Kanchanaburi, W Thailand
167 O8 **Phrae** *var.* Muang Phrae, Prae. Phrae, NW Thailand
Phra Nakhon Si Ayutthaya *see* Ayutthaya
167 M14 **Phra Thong, Ko** *island* SW Thailand
Phu Cương *see* Thu Dâu Môt
166 M15 **Phuket** *var.* Bhuket, Puket, *Mal.* Ujung Salang; *prev.* Junkseylon, Salang. Phuket, SW Thailand
166 M15 **Phuket** ✕ Phuket, SW Thailand
166 M15 **Phuket, Ko** *island* SW Thailand
154 N12 **Phulabāni** *prev.* Phulbani. Orissa, E India
Phulbani *see* Phulabāni
167 U9 **Phu Lôc** Th,a Thiên-Huê, C Vietnam
167 S13 **Phumĭ Banam** Prey Vêng, S Cambodia
167 R13 **Phumĭ Chŏâm** Kâmpóng Spœ, SW Cambodia
167 T11 **Phumĭ Kalêng** Stœng Trêng, NE Cambodia
167 S12 **Phumĭ Kâmpóng Trâbêk** *prev.* Phum Kompong Trabek. Kâmpóng Thum, C Cambodia
167 Q11 **Phumĭ Koŭk Kduŏch** Bătdâmbâng, NW Cambodia
167 T11 **Phumĭ Labăng** Rôtânôkiri, NE Cambodia
167 S11 **Phumĭ Mlu Prey** Preăh Vihéar, N Cambodia
167 R11 **Phumĭ Moŭng** Siĕmréab, NW Cambodia
167 Q12 **Phumĭ Prâmaôy** Poŭthĭsăt, W Cambodia
167 Q13 **Phumĭ Samĭt** Kaôh Kŏng, SW Cambodia
167 R11 **Phumĭ Sâmraông** *prev.* Phum Samrong. Siĕmréab, NW Cambodia
167 S12 **Phumĭ Siĕmbok** Stœng Trêng, N Cambodia
167 S11 **Phumĭ Thalabârĭvăt** Stœng Trêng, N Cambodia
167 R13 **Phumĭ Veal Renh** Kâmpôt, SW Cambodia
167 P13 **Phumĭ Yeay Sên** Kaôh Kông, SW Cambodia
Phum Kompong Trabek *see* Phumĭ Kâmpóng Trâbêk
Phum Samrong *see* Phumĭ Sâmraông
167 V11 **Phu My** Bình Định, C Vietnam
167 S14 **Phung Hiêp** Cân Thơ, S Vietnam
153 T12 **Phuntsholing** SW Bhutan
167 R15 **Phươc Long** Minh Hai, S Vietnam
167 R14 **Phu Quôc, Đao** *var.* Phu Quoc Island. *island* S Vietnam
Phu Quoc Island *see* Phu Quôc, Đao
167 S6 **Phu Tho** Vinh Phu, N Vietnam
Phu Vinh *see* Tra Vinh
189 T13 **Piaanu Pass** *passage* Chuuk Islands, C Micronesia
106 E8 **Piacenza** *Fr.* Paisance; *anc.* Placentia. Emilia-Romagna, N Italy
107 K14 **Pianella** Abruzzo, C Italy
107 M15 **Pianosa, Isola** *island* Archipelago Toscano, C Italy
171 U13 **Piar** Papua, E Indonesia
45 U14 **Piarco** *var.* Port of Spain. ✕ (Port-of-Spain) Trinidad, Trinidad and Tobago
110 M12 **Piaseczno** Mazowieckie, C Poland
116 I15 **Piatra** Teleorman, S Romania
116 L10 **Piatra-Neamţ** *Hung.* Karácsonkő. Neamţ, NE Romania
Piauhy *see* Piauí
59 N15 **Piauí** *off.* Estado do Piauí; *prev.* Piauhy. ◈ *state* E Brazil
106 I7 **Piave** ≈ NE Italy
107 K24 **Piazza Armerina** *var.* Chiazza. Sicilia, Italy, C Mediterranean Sea
81 G14 **Pibor** *Amh.* Pībor Wenz. ≈ Ethiopia/Sudan
81 G14 **Pibor Post** Jonglei, SE Sudan
Pībor Wenz *see* Pibor
Pibrans *see* Příbram
36 K11 **Picacho Butte** ▲ Arizona, SW USA
40 D4 **Picachos, Cerro** ▲ NW Mexico
103 O4 **Picardie** *Eng.* Picardy. ◈ *region* N France
Picardy *see* Picardie
22 L8 **Picayune** Mississippi, S USA
Piccolo San Bernardo, Colle di *see* Little Saint Bernard Pass
62 K5 **Pichanal** Salta, N Argentina
147 P12 **Pichandar** W Tajikistan
27 R8 **Picher** Oklahoma, C USA
62 G12 **Pichilemu** Libertador, C Chile
40 F9 **Pichilingue** Baja California Sur, W Mexico
56 B6 **Pichincha** ◈ *province* N Ecuador
56 C6 **Pichincha** ▲ N Ecuador
Pichit *see* Phichit
41 U15 **Pichucalco** Chiapas, SE Mexico
22 L5 **Pickens** Mississippi, S USA
21 O11 **Pickens** South Carolina, SE USA
14 G11 **Pickerel** ≈ Ontario, S Canada
14 H15 **Pickering** Ontario, S Canada
97 N16 **Pickering** N England, UK
31 S13 **Pickerington** Ohio, N USA
12 C10 **Pickle Lake** Ontario, C Canada
29 P12 **Pickstown** South Dakota, N USA
25 V6 **Pickton** Texas, SW USA
23 N1 **Pickwick Lake** ▣ S USA
64 N2 **Pico** *var.* Ilha do Pico. *island* Azores, Portugal, NE Atlantic Ocean
63 J19 **Pico de Salamanca** Chubut, SE Argentina
Pico, Ilha do *see* Pico
59 O14 **Picos** Piauí, E Brazil
63 I20 **Pico Truncado** Santa Cruz, SE Argentina
183 S9 **Picton** New South Wales, SE Australia
14 K15 **Picton** Ontario, SE Canada
185 K14 **Picton** Marlborough, South Island, NZ
63 H15 **Piĉun Leufú, Arroyo** ≈ SW Argentina
Pidálion *see* Gkréko, Akrotíri
155 K25 **Pidurutalagala** ▲ S Sri Lanka
116 K6 **Pidvolochys'k** Ternopil's'ka Oblast', W Ukraine
107 K16 **Piedimonte Matese** Campania, S Italy
27 X7 **Piedmont** Missouri, C USA
21 P11 **Piedmont** South Carolina, SE USA
17 S12 **Piedmont** *escarpment* E USA
Piedmont *see* Piemonte
31 U13 **Piedmont Lake** ◎ Ohio, N USA
104 M11 **Piedrabuena** Castilla-La Mancha, C Spain
Piedrafita, Puerto de *see* Pedrafita, Porto de
104 L8 **Piedrahita** Castilla-León, N Spain
41 N6 **Piedras Negras** *var.* Ciudad Porfirio Díaz. Coahuila de Zaragoza, NE Mexico
61 E21 **Piedras, Punta** *headland* E Argentina
57 I14 **Piedras, Río de las** ≈ E Peru
111 J16 **Piekary Śląskie** Śląskie, S Poland
93 M17 **Pieksämäki** Isä-Suomi, E Finland
109 V5 **Pielach** ≈ NE Austria
93 M16 **Pielavesi** Itä-Suomi, C Finland
93 M16 **Pielavesi** ◎ C Finland
93 N16 **Pielinen** *var.* Pielisjärvi. ◎ E Finland
Pielisjärvi *see* Pielinen
106 A8 **Piemonte** *Eng.* Piedmont. ◈ *region* NW Italy
111 L18 **Pieniny** ▲▲ Poland/Slovakia
111 E14 **Pieńsk** *Ger.* Penzig. Dolnośląskie, SW Poland
29 Q13 **Pierce** Nebraska, C USA
11 R14 **Pierceland** Saskatchewan, C Canada
115 E14 **Piéria** ▲▲ N Greece
29 N10 **Pierre** *state capital* South Dakota, N USA
102 K16 **Pierrefitte-Nestalas** Hautes-Pyrénées, S France
103 R14 **Pierrelatte** Drôme, E France
15 P11 **Pierreville** Québec, SE Canada
15 O7 **Pierriche** ≈ Québec, SE Canada
111 H20 **Piešt'any** *Ger.* Pistyan, *Hung.* Pöstyén. Trnavský, W Slovakia
109 X5 **Piesting** ≈ E Austria
Pietarhovi *see* Petrodvorets
Pietari *see* Sankt-Peterburg
Pietarsaari *see* Jakobstad
83 K23 **Pietermaritzburg** *var.* Maritzburg. KwaZulu/Natal, E South Africa
Pietersburg *see* Polokwane
107 K24 **Pietraperzia** Sicilia, Italy, C Mediterranean Sea
107 N22 **Pietra Spada, Passo della** *pass* SW Italy
83 K22 **Piet Retief** Mpumalanga, E South Africa
116 I9 **Pietrosul, Vârful** *prev.* Vîrful Pietrosu. ▲ N Romania
116 J10 **Pietrosul, Vârful** *prev.* Vîrful Pietrosu. ▲ N Romania
Pietrosu, Vîrful *see* Pietrosul, Vârful
106 I6 **Pieve di Cadore** Veneto, NE Italy
14 C18 **Pigeon Bay** *lake bay* Ontario, S Canada
27 X8 **Piggott** Arkansas, C USA
83 L21 **Piggs Peak** NW Swaziland
Pigs, Bay of *see* Cochinos, Bahía de
61 A23 **Pigüé** Buenos Aires, E Argentina
41 O12 **Piguícas** ▲ C Mexico
193 W15 **Piha Passage** *passage* S Tonga
Pihkva Järv *see* Pskov, Lake
93 N18 **Pihlajavesi** ◎ SE Finland
93 J18 **Pihlava** Länsi-Suomi, W Finland
93 L16 **Pihtipudas** Länsi-Suomi, W Finland
40 L14 **Pihuamo** Jalisco, SW Mexico
189 U11 **Piis Moen** *var.* Pis. *atoll* Chuuk Islands, C Micronesia
41 U17 **Pijijiapán** Chiapas, SE Mexico
98 G12 **Pijnacker** Zuid-Holland, W Netherlands
42 H5 **Pijol, Pico** ▲ NW Honduras
Pikaar *see* Bikar Atoll
124 I13 **Pikalevo** Leningradskaya Oblast', NW Russian Federation
188 M15 **Pikelot** *island* Caroline Islands, C Micronesia
30 M5 **Pike River** ≈ Wisconsin, N USA
37 T5 **Pikes Peak** ▲ Colorado, C USA
21 P6 **Pikeville** Kentucky, S USA
20 L9 **Pikeville** Tennessee, S USA
Pikinni *see* Bikini Atoll
79 H18 **Pikounda** La Sangha, C Congo
110 G9 **Piła** *Ger.* Schneidemühl. Wielkopolskie, C Poland
62 N6 **Pilagá, Riacho** ≈ NE Argentina
61 D20 **Pilar** Buenos Aires, E Argentina
62 N7 **Pilar** *var.* Villa del Pilar. Ñeembucú, S Paraguay
62 N6 **Pilcomayo, Río** ≈ C South America
147 R12 **Pildon** *Rus.* Pil'don. C Tajikistan
Piles *see* Pylés
Pilgram *see* Pelhřimov
152 L10 **Pīlībhīt** Uttar Pradesh, N India
110 M13 **Pilica** ≈ C Poland
115 G16 **Pílio** ▲▲ C Greece
111 J22 **Pilisvörösvár** Pest, N Hungary
65 G15 **Pillar Bay** *bay* Ascension Island, C Atlantic Ocean
183 P17 **Pillar, Cape** *headland* Tasmania, SE Australia
Pillau *see* Baltiysk
183 R5 **Pilliga** New South Wales, SE Australia
44 H8 **Pilón** Granma, E Cuba
Pilos *see* Pýlos
11 W17 **Pilot Mound** Manitoba, S Canada
21 S8 **Pilot Mountain** North Carolina, SE USA
39 O14 **Pilot Point** Alaska, USA
25 T5 **Pilot Point** Texas, SW USA
32 K11 **Pilot Rock** Oregon, NW USA
38 M11 **Pilot Station** Alaska, USA
Pilsen *see* Plzeň
111 K18 **Pilsko** ▲ N Slovakia
Pilten *see* Piltene
118 D8 **Piltene** *Ger.* Pilten. Ventspils, W Latvia
111 M16 **Pilzno** Podkarpackie, SE Poland
Pilzno *see* Plzeň
37 N14 **Pima** Arizona, SW USA
58 H13 **Pimenta** Pará, N Brazil
59 F16 **Pimenta Bueno** Rondônia, W Brazil
56 B11 **Pimentel** Lambayeque, W Peru
105 S6 **Pina** Aragón, NE Spain
119 I20 **Pina** *Rus.* Pina. ≈ SW Belarus
40 E2 **Pinacate, Sierra del** ▲ NW Mexico
63 H22 **Pináculo, Cerro** ▲ S Argentina
191 X11 **Pinaki** *atoll* Îles Tuamotu, E French Polynesia
37 N15 **Pinaleno Mountains** ▲▲ Arizona, SW USA
171 P4 **Pinamalayan** Mindoro, N Philippines
169 Q10 **Pinang** Borneo, C Indonesia
168 J7 **Pinang** *var.* Penang. ◈ *state* Peninsular Malaysia
Pinang *see* Pinang, Pulau, Peninsular Malaysia
Pinang *see* George Town
168 J7 **Pinang, Pulau** *var.* Penang, Pinang; *prev.* Prince of Wales Island. *island* Peninsular Malaysia
44 B5 **Pinar del Río** Pinar del Río, W Cuba
114 N11 **Pınarhisar** Kırklareli, NW Turkey
171 O3 **Pinatubo, Mount** ※ Luzon, N Philippines
11 Y16 **Pinawa** Manitoba, S Canada
11 Q17 **Pincher Creek** Alberta, SW Canada
30 L16 **Pinckneyville** Illinois, N USA
Pincota *see* Pâncota
111 L15 **Pińczów** Świętokrzyskie, C Poland
149 U7 **Pind Dādan Khān** Punjab, E Pakistan
Píndhos/Píndhos Óros *see* Píndos
149 V8 **Pindi Bhattiān** Punjab, E Pakistan
149 U6 **Pindi Gheb** Punjab, E Pakistan
115 D15 **Píndos** *var.* Píndhos Óros, *Eng.* Pindus Mountains; *prev.* Píndhos. ▲▲ C Greece
Pindus Mountains *see* Píndos
18 J16 **Pine Barrens** *physical region* New Jersey, NE USA
27 V12 **Pine Bluff** Arkansas, C USA
23 X11 **Pine Castle** Florida, SE USA
29 V7 **Pine City** Minnesota, N USA
181 P2 **Pine Creek** Northern Territory, N Australia
35 V4 **Pine Creek** ≈ Nevada, W USA
18 F13 **Pine Creek** ≈ Pennsylvania, NE USA
27 Q13 **Pine Creek Lake** ▣ Oklahoma, C USA
33 T15 **Pinedale** Wyoming, C USA
11 X15 **Pine Dock** Manitoba, S Canada
11 Y16 **Pine Falls** Manitoba, S Canada
35 R10 **Pine Flat Lake** ▣ California, W USA
125 N8 **Pinega** Arkhangel'skaya Oblast', NW Russian Federation
127 N8 **Pinega** ≈ NW Russian Federation
15 N12 **Pine Hill** Québec, SE Canada

11 T12 **Pinehouse Lake** ◎ Saskatchewan, C Canada
21 T10 **Pinehurst** North Carolina, SE USA
115 D19 **Pineiós** ≈ S Greece
115 E16 **Pineiós** *var.* Piniós; *anc.* Peneius. ≈ C Greece
29 W10 **Pine Island** Minnesota, N USA
23 V15 **Pine Island** *island* Florida, SE USA
194 K10 **Pine Island Glacier** *glacier* Antarctica
25 X9 **Pineland** Texas, SW USA
23 V13 **Pinellas Park** Florida, SE USA
10 M13 **Pine Pass** *pass* British Columbia, W Canada
8 J10 **Pine Point** Northwest Territories, W Canada
28 K12 **Pine Ridge** South Dakota, N USA
29 U6 **Pine River** Minnesota, N USA
31 Q8 **Pine River** ≈ Michigan, N USA
30 M4 **Pine River** ≈ Wisconsin, N USA
106 A8 **Pinerolo** Piemonte, NE Italy
25 W6 **Pines, Lake O' the** ⊞ Texas, SW USA
Pines, The Isle of the *see* Juventud, Isla de la
Pine Tree State *see* Maine
21 N7 **Pineville** Kentucky, S USA
22 H7 **Pineville** Louisiana, S USA
27 R8 **Pineville** Missouri, C USA
21 R10 **Pineville** North Carolina, SE USA
21 Q6 **Pineville** West Virginia, NE USA
33 V8 **Piney Buttes** *physical region* Montana, NW USA
160 H14 **Pingbian** *var.* Pingbian Miaozu Zizhixian, Yuping. Yunnan, SW China
Pingbian Miaozu Zizhixian *see* Pingbian
157 S9 **Pingdingshan** Henan, C China
161 R4 **Pingdu** Shandong, E China
189 W16 **Pingelap Atoll** *atoll* Caroline Islands, E Micronesia
160 K14 **Pingguo** *var.* Matou. Guangxi Zhuangzu Zizhiqu, S China
161 Q13 **Pinghe** *var.* Xiaoxi. Fujian, SE China
P'ing-hsiang *see* Pingxiang
161 N10 **Pingjiang** Hunan, S China
Pingkiang *see* Harbin
160 L8 **Pingli** Shaanxi, C China
159 W10 **Pingliang** *var.* Kongtong, P'ing-liang. Gansu, C China
159 W8 **Pingluo** Ningxia, N China
Pingma *see* Tiandong
167 O7 **Ping, Mae Nam** ≈ W Thailand
161 Q1 **Pingquan** Hebei, E China
29 P5 **Pingree** North Dakota, N USA
163 W9 **Pingshan** Jilin, NE China
Pingsiang *see* Pingxiang
161 S14 **P'ingtung** *Jap.* Heitō. S Taiwan
160 I8 **Pingwu** *var.* Long'an. Sichuan, C China
160 J15 **Pingxiang** Guangxi Zhuangzu Zizhiqu, S China
161 O11 **Pingxiang** *var.* P'ing-hsiang; *prev.* Pingsiang. Jiangxi, S China
161 S11 **Pingyang** *var.* Kunyang. Zhejiang, SE China
161 P5 **Pingyi** Shandong, E China
161 P5 **Pingyin** Shandong, E China
60 H13 **Pinhalzinho** Santa Catarina, S Brazil
60 I12 **Pinhão** Paraná, S Brazil
61 H17 **Pinheiro Machado** Rio Grande do Sul, S Brazil
104 I7 **Pinhel** Guarda, N Portugal
Piniós *see* Pineiós
168 I11 **Pini, Pulau** *island* Kepulauan Batu, W Indonesia
109 Y7 **Pinka** ≈ SE Austria
109 X7 **Pinkafeld** Burgenland, SE Austria
Pinkiang *see* Harbin
10 M12 **Pink Mountain** British Columbia, W Canada
166 M3 **Pinlebu** Sagaing, N Burma
38 J12 **Pinnacle Island** *island* Alaska, USA
180 I12 **Pinnacles, The** *tourist site* Western Australia
182 K10 **Pinnaroo** South Australia
Pinne *see* Pniewy
100 I9 **Pinneberg** Schleswig-Holstein, N Germany
115 I15 **Pínnes, Akrotírio** *headland* N Greece
Pinos, Isla de *see* Juventud, Isla de la
35 R14 **Pinos, Mount** ▲ California, W USA
105 R12 **Pinoso** País Valenciano, E Spain
105 N14 **Pinos-Puente** Andalucía, S Spain
41 Q17 **Pinotepa Nacional** *var.* Santiago Pinotepa Nacional. Oaxaca, SE Mexico
114 F13 **Pínovo** ▲ N Greece
187 R17 **Pins, Île des** *var.* Kunyé. *island* E New Caledonia
119 I20 **Pinsk** *Pol.* Pińsk. Brestskaya Voblasts', SW Belarus
14 D18 **Pins, Pointe aux** *headland* Ontario, S Canada
57 B16 **Pinta, Isla** *var.* Abingdon. *island* Galapagos Islands, Ecuador, E Pacific Ocean
125 Q12 **Pinyug** Kirovskaya Oblast', NW Russian Federation
57 B17 **Pinzón, Isla** *var.* Duncan Island. *island* Galapagos Islands, Ecuador, E Pacific Ocean
35 Y8 **Pioche** Nevada, W USA
106 F13 **Piombino** Toscana, C Italy
122 L5 **Pioner, Ostrov** *island* Severnaya Zemlya, N Russian Federation
118 A13 **Pionerskiy** *Ger.* Neukuhren. Kaliningradskaya Oblast', W Russian Federation
110 N13 **Pionki** Mazowieckie, C Poland
184 L9 **Piopio** Waikato, North Island, NZ
110 K13 **Piotrków Trybunalski** *Ger.* Petrikau, *Rus.* Petrokov. Łodzkie, C Poland
152 F12 **Pīpār Road** Rājasthān, N India
115 I16 **Pipéri** *island* Vóreioi Sporádes, Greece, Aegean Sea
29 S10 **Pipestone** Minnesota, N USA
12 C9 **Pipestone** ≈ Ontario, C Canada
61 E21 **Pipinas** Buenos Aires, E Argentina
149 T7 **Piplān** *prev.* Liaqatabad. Punjab, E Pakistan
15 R5 **Pipmuacan, Réservoir** ⊞ Québec, SE Canada
Piqan *see* Shanshan
31 R13 **Piqua** Ohio, N USA
105 P5 **Piqueras, Puerto de** *pass* N Spain
60 H11 **Piquiri, Rio** ≈ S Brazil
60 L9 **Piracicaba** São Paulo, S Brazil
Piraeus/Piraiévs *see* Peiraías
60 K10 **Piraju** São Paulo, S Brazil
60 K9 **Pirajuí** São Paulo, S Brazil
63 G21 **Pirámide, Cerro** ▲ S Chile
Piramiva *see* Pyramíva
109 R13 **Piran** *It.* Pirano. SW Slovenia
62 N6 **Pirané** Formosa, N Argentina
59 J18 **Piranhas** Goiás, S Brazil
Pirano *see* Piran
142 I4 **Pīrānshahr** Āžarbāyjān-e Bākhtarī, NW Iran
59 M19 **Pirapora** Minas Gerais, NE Brazil
60 I9 **Pirapòzinho** São Paulo, S Brazil
61 G19 **Piraraja** Lavalleja, S Uruguay
60 L9 **Pirassununga** São Paulo, S Brazil
45 V6 **Pirata, Monte** ▲ E Puerto Rico
60 I13 **Piratuba** Santa Catarina, S Brazil
114 I9 **Pirdop** *prev.* Srednogorie. Sofiya, W Bulgaria
191 P7 **Pirea** Tahiti, W French Polynesia
59 K18 **Pirenópolis** Goiás, S Brazil
153 S13 **Pirganj** Rajshahi, NW Bangladesh
Pirgi *see* Pyrgí
Pírgos *see* Pýrgos
61 F20 **Piriápolis** Maldonado, S Uruguay
114 G11 **Pirin** ▲ SW Bulgaria
Pirineos *see* Pyrenees
58 N13 **Piripiri** Piauí, E Brazil
118 H4 **Pirita** *var.* Pirita Jõgi. ≈ NW Estonia
Pirita Jõgi *see* Pirita
54 J6 **Píritu** Portuguesa, N Venezuela
93 L18 **Pirkkala** Länsi-Suomi, W Finland
101 F20 **Pirmasens** Rheinland-Pfalz, SW Germany
101 P16 **Pirna** Sachsen, E Germany
Piroe *see* Piru
113 Q15 **Pirot** Serbia, SE Serbia and Montenegro (Yugo.)
152 H6 **Pīr Panjāl Range** ▲ NE India
43 W16 **Pirre, Cerro** ▲ SE Panama
137 Y11 **Pirsaat** *Rus.* Pirsagat. ≈ E Azerbaijan
Pirsagat *see* Pirsaat
143 V11 **Pīr Shūrān, Selseleh-ye** ▲ SE Iran
92 M12 **Pirttikoski** Lappi, N Finland
Pirttikylä *see* Pörtom
171 R13 **Piru** *prev.* Piroe. Pulau Seram, E Indonesia
Piryatin *see* Pyryatyn
Pis *see* Piis Moen
106 F11 **Pisa** *var.* Pisae. Toscana, C Italy
Pisae *see* Pisa
189 V12 **Pisar** *atoll* Chuuk Islands, C Micronesia
Pisaurum *see* Pesaro
14 M10 **Piscatosine, Lac** ◎ Québec, SE Canada
109 W7 **Pischeldorf** Steiermark, SE Austria
Pischk *see* Simeria
107 L19 **Pisciotta** Campania, S Italy
57 E16 **Pisco** Ica, SW Peru
116 G9 **Pișcolt** *Hung.* Piskolt. Satu Mare, NW Romania
57 E16 **Pisco, Río** ≈ E Peru
111 C18 **Písek** Budějovický Kraj, S Czech Republic
31 R14 **Pisgah** Ohio, N USA
Pisha *see* Ningnan
158 F9 **Pishan** *var.* Guma. Xinjiang Uygur Zizhiqu, NW China
117 N8 **Pishchanka** Vinnyts'ka Oblast', C Ukraine
113 K21 **Pishë** Fier, SW Albania
143 X14 **Pīshīn** Sīstān va Balūchestān, SE Iran
149 O9 **Pishīn** North-West Frontier Province, NW Pakistan
149 N11 **Pishin Lora** *var.* Psein Lora, *Pash.* Pseyn Bowr. ≈ SW Pakistan
Pishma *see* Pizhma
Pishpek *see* Bishkek
171 O14 **Pising** Pulau Kabaena, C Indonesia
Pisino *see* Pazin
Piski *see* Simeria
Piskolt *see* Pișcolt
147 Q9 **Piskom** *Rus.* Pskem. ≈ E Uzbekistan
Piskom Tizmasi *see* Pskemskiy Khrebet
35 P13 **Pismo Beach** California, W USA
77 P12 **Pissila** C Burkina
62 H8 **Pissis, Monte** ▲ N Argentina
41 X12 **Piste** Yucatán, E Mexico
107 O18 **Pisticci** Basilicata, S Italy
106 F11 **Pistoia** *anc.* Pistoria, Pistoriæ. Toscana, C Italy
32 E15 **Pistol River** Oregon, NW USA
Pistoria/Pistoriæ *see* Pistoia
15 U5 **Pistuacanis** ≈ Québec, SE Canada
Pistyan *see* Piešt'any
104 M5 **Pisuerga** ≈ N Spain
110 N8 **Pisz** *Ger.* Johannisburg. Warmińsko-Mazurskie, NE Poland
76 I13 **Pita** Moyenne-Guinée, NW Guinea
54 D12 **Pitalito** Huila, S Colombia
60 I11 **Pitanga** Paraná, S Brazil
182 M9 **Pitarpunga Lake** *salt lake* New South Wales, SE Australia
193 P10 **Pitcairn Island** *island* S Pitcairn Islands
193 P10 **Pitcairn Islands** ◇ *UK dependent territory* C Pacific Ocean
93 J14 **Piteå** Norrbotten, N Sweden
92 I13 **Piteälven** ≈ N Sweden
116 I13 **Pitești** Argeș, S Romania
Pithagorio *see* Pythagóreio
180 I12 **Pithara** Western Australia
103 N6 **Pithiviers** Loiret, C France
152 L9 **Pithorāgarh** Uttaranchal, N India
188 B16 **Piti** W Guam
106 G13 **Pitigliano** Toscana, C Italy
40 F3 **Pitiquito** Sonora, NW Mexico
Pitkäranta *see* Pitkyaranta
38 M11 **Pitkas Point** Alaska, USA
124 H11 **Pitkyaranta** *Fin.* Pitkäranta. Respublika Kareliya, NW Russian Federation
96 J10 **Pitlochry** C Scotland, UK
18 I16 **Pitman** New Jersey, NE USA
146 I9 **Pitnak** *Rus.* Druzhba. Xorazm Viloyati, W Uzbekistan
112 G8 **Pitomača** Virovitica-Podravina, NE Croatia
35 O2 **Pit River** ≈ California, W USA
63 G15 **Pitrufquén** Araucanía, S Chile
Pitsanulok *see* Phitsanulok
Pitschen *see* Byczyna
Pitsunda *see* Bichvint'a
109 X6 **Pitten** ≈ E Austria
10 J14 **Pitt Island** *island* British Columbia, W Canada
Pitt Island *see* Makin
22 M3 **Pittsboro** Mississippi, S USA
21 T9 **Pittsboro** North Carolina, SE USA
27 R7 **Pittsburg** Kansas, C USA
25 W6 **Pittsburg** Texas, SW USA
18 B14 **Pittsburgh** Pennsylvania, NE USA
30 J14 **Pittsfield** Illinois, N USA
19 R6 **Pittsfield** Maine, NE USA
18 L11 **Pittsfield** Massachusetts, NE USA
183 U3 **Pittsworth** Queensland, E Australia
62 I8 **Pituil** La Rioja, NW Argentina
56 A10 **Piura** Piura, NW Peru
56 A9 **Piura** *off.* Departamento de Piura. ◈ *department* NW Peru
35 S13 **Piute Peak** ▲ California, W USA
113 J15 **Piva** ≈ SW Serbia and Montenegro (Yugo.)
117 V5 **Pivdenne** Kharkivs'ka Oblast', E Ukraine
117 P8 **Pivdennyy Buh** *Rus.* Yuzhnyy Bug. ≈ S Ukraine
54 F5 **Pivijay** Magdalena, N Colombia
109 T13 **Pivka** *prev.* Šent Peter, *Ger.* Sankt Peter, *It.* San Pietro del Carso. SW Slovenia
117 U13 **Pivnichno-Kryms'kyy Kanal** *canal* S Ukraine
113 J15 **Pivsko Jezero** ◎ SW Serbia and Montenegro (Yugo.)
111 M18 **Piwniczna** Małopolskie, S Poland
35 R12 **Pixley** California, W USA
127 Q15 **Pizhma** *var.* Pishma. ≈ NW Russian Federation
13 U13 **Placentia** Newfoundland and Labrador, SE Canada
Placentia *see* Piacenza
13 U13 **Placentia Bay** *inlet* Newfoundland and Labrador, SE Canada
171 P5 **Placer** Masbate, N Philippines
35 P7 **Placerville** California, W USA
44 F5 **Placetas** Villa Clara, C Cuba
113 Q18 **Plačkovica** ▲ E FYR Macedonia
36 L2 **Plain City** Utah, W USA
22 G4 **Plain Dealing** Louisiana, S USA
31 O14 **Plainfield** Indiana, N USA
18 K14 **Plainfield** New Jersey, NE USA
33 O8 **Plains** Montana, NW USA
24 L6 **Plains** Texas, SW USA
29 X10 **Plainview** Minnesota, N USA
29 Q13 **Plainview** Nebraska, C USA
25 N4 **Plainview** Texas, SW USA
26 K4 **Plainville** Kansas, C USA
115 L25 **Pláka, Akrotírio** *headland* Kríti, Greece, E Mediterranean Sea
115 J15 **Pláka, Akrotírio** *headland* Límnos, E Greece
113 N19 **Plakenska Planina** ▲ SW FYR Macedonia
44 K5 **Plana Cays** *islets* SE Bahamas
105 S12 **Plana, Isla** *var.* Nueva Tabarca. *island* E Spain
59 L18 **Planaltina** Goiás, S Brazil
83 O14 **Planalto Moçambicano** *plateau* N Mozambique
112 N10 **Plandište** Serbia, NE Serbia and Montenegro (Yugo.)
100 N13 **Plane** ≈ NE Germany
54 E6 **Planeta Rica** Córdoba, NW Colombia
29 P11 **Plankinton** South Dakota, N USA
30 M11 **Plano** Illinois, N USA
25 U6 **Plano** Texas, SW USA
23 W12 **Plant City** Florida, SE USA
22 J9 **Plaquemine** Louisiana, S USA
104 K9 **Plasencia** Extremadura, W Spain
112 P7 **Plaska** Podlaskie, NE Poland
114 C10 **Plaški** Karlovac, C Croatia
113 N19 **Plasnica** SW FYR Macedonia
13 N14 **Plaster Rock** New Brunswick, SE Canada
107 J24 **Platani** *anc.* Halycus. ≈ Sicilia, Italy, C Mediterranean Sea
115 G17 **Plataniá** Thessalía, C Greece
115 G24 **Plátanos** Kríti, Greece, E Mediterranean Sea
65 H18 **Plata, Río de la** *var.* River Plate. *estuary* Argentina/Uruguay
77 V15 **Plateau** ◈ *state* C Nigeria
79 G19 **Plateaux** *var.* Région des Plateaux. ◈ *province* C Congo
92 P1 **Platen, Kapp** *headland* NE Svalbard
Plate, River *see* Plata, Río de la
99 G22 **Plate Taille, Lac de la** *var.* L'Eau d'Heure. ◎ SE Belgium
Plathe *see* Płoty
39 N13 **Platinum** Alaska, USA
54 F5 **Plato** Magdalena, N Colombia
29 O11 **Platte** South Dakota, N USA
27 R3 **Platte City** Missouri, C USA
Plattensee *see* Balaton
27 R3 **Platte River** ≈ Iowa/Missouri, USA
29 Q15 **Platte River** ≈ Nebraska, C USA
37 T3 **Platteville** Colorado, C USA
30 K9 **Platteville** Wisconsin, N USA
101 N21 **Plattling** Bayern, SE Germany
27 R3 **Plattsburg** Missouri, C USA
18 L6 **Plattsburgh** New York, NE USA
29 S15 **Plattsmouth** Nebraska, C USA
101 M17 **Plauen** *var.* Plauen im Vogtland. Sachsen, E Germany
Plauen im Vogtland *see* Plauen
100 M10 **Plauer See** ◎ NE Germany
113 L16 **Plav** Montenegro, SW Serbia and Montenegro (Yugo.)
118 I10 **Pļaviņas** *Ger.* Stockmannshof. Aizkraukle, S Latvia
126 K5 **Plavsk** Tul'skaya Oblast', W Russian Federation
41 Z12 **Playa del Carmen** Quintana Roo, E Mexico
40 J12 **Playa Los Corchos** Nayarit, SW Mexico
37 P16 **Playas Lake** ◎ New Mexico, SW USA
41 S15 **Playa Vicenté** Veracruz-Llave, SE Mexico
167 U11 **Plây Cu** *var.* Pleiku. Gia Lai, C Vietnam
28 L3 **Plaza** North Dakota, N USA
63 I15 **Plaza Huincul** Neuquén, C Argentina
36 L3 **Pleasant Grove** Utah, W USA
29 V14 **Pleasant Hill** Iowa, C USA
27 R4 **Pleasant Hill** Missouri, C USA
Pleasant Island *see* Nauru
36 K13 **Pleasant, Lake** ⊞ Arizona, SW USA
19 P8 **Pleasant Mountain** ▲ Maine, NE USA
27 R5 **Pleasanton** Kansas, C USA
25 R12 **Pleasanton** Texas, SW USA
185 G20 **Pleasant Point** Canterbury, South Island, NZ
19 R5 **Pleasant River** ≈ Maine, NE USA
18 J17 **Pleasantville** New Jersey, NE USA
103 N12 **Pléaux** Cantal, C France
111 B19 **Plechý** *Ger.* Plöckenstein. ▲ Austria/Czech Republic
Pleebo *see* Plibo
Pleihari *see* Pelaihari
Pleiku *see* Plây Cu
101 M16 **Pleisse** ≈ E Germany
Plencia *see* Plentzia
184 O7 **Plenty, Bay of** *bay* North Island, NZ
33 Y6 **Plentywood** Montana, NW USA
105 O2 **Plentzia** *var.* Plencia. País Vasco, N Spain
102 H5 **Plérin** Côtes d'Armor, NW France
124 M10 **Plesetsk** Arkhangel'skaya Oblast', NW Russian Federation
Pleshchenitsy *see* Plyeshchanitsy
Pleskau *see* Pskov
Pleskauer See *see* Pskov, Lake
Pleskava *see* Pskov
112 E8 **Pleso International** ✕ (Zagreb) Zagreb, NW Croatia
Pless *see* Pszczyna
15 Q11 **Plessisville** Québec, SE Canada
110 H12 **Pleszew** Wielkopolskie, C Poland
12 L10 **Plétipi, Lac** ◎ Québec, SE Canada
101 F15 **Plettenberg** Nordrhein-Westfalen, W Germany
114 I8 **Pleven** *prev.* Plevna. Pleven, N Bulgaria
114 I8 **Pleven** ◈ *province* N Bulgaria
Plevlja/Plevlje *see* Pljevlja
Plevna *see* Pleven
Plezzo *see* Bovec
Pliberk *see* Bleiburg
76 L17 **Plibo** *var.* Pleebo. SE Liberia
121 R11 **Pliny Trench** *undersea feature* C Mediterranean Sea
118 K13 **Plisa** *Rus.* Plissa. Vitsyebskaya Voblasts', N Belarus
Plissa *see* Plisa
112 D11 **Plitvica Selo** Lika-Senj, W Croatia
112 D11 **Plješevica** ▲ C Croatia
113 K14 **Pljevlja** *prev.* Plevlja, Plevlje. Montenegro, N Serbia and Montenegro (Yugo.)
Ploça *see* Ploçë
Plocce *see* Ploče
113 G15 **Ploče** *It.* Plocce; *prev.* Kardeljevo. Dubrovnik-Neretva, SE Croatia
113 K22 **Ploçë** *var.* Ploça. Vlorë, SW Albania
110 K11 **Płock** *Ger.* Plozk. Mazowieckie, C Poland
109 Q10 **Plöcken Pass** *Ger.* Plöckenpass, *It.* Passo di Monte Croce Carnico. *pass* SW Austria
Plöckenstein *see* Plechý
99 B19 **Ploegsteert** Hainaut, W Belgium
102 H6 **Ploërmel** Morbihan, NW France
Ploești *see* Ploiești
116 K13 **Ploiești** *prev.* Ploești. Prahova, SE Romania
115 L17 **Plomári** *prev.* Plomárion. Lésvos, E Greece
Plomárion *see* Plomári
103 O12 **Plomb du Cantal** ▲ C France
183 V6 **Plomer, Point** *headland* New South Wales, SE Australia
100 J8 **Plön** Schleswig-Holstein, N Germany
110 L11 **Płońsk** Mazowieckie, C Poland
119 J20 **Plotnitsa** *Rus.* Plotnitsa. Brestskaya Voblasts', SW Belarus
110 E8 **Płoty** *Ger.* Plathe. Zachodnio-pomorskie, NW Poland
102 G7 **Plouay** Morbihan, NW France
111 D15 **Ploučnice** *Ger.* Polzen. ≈ NE Czech Republic
114 I10 **Plovdiv** *prev.* Eumolpias, *anc.* Evmolpia, Philippopolis, *Lat.* Trimontium. Plovdiv, C Bulgaria 24.47
116 J11 **Plovdiv** ◈ *province* C Bulgaria
30 L6 **Plover** Wisconsin, N USA
Plozk *see* Płock
27 U11 **Plumerville** Arkansas, C USA
19 P10 **Plum Island** *island* Massachusetts, NE USA
32 M9 **Plummer** Idaho, NW USA
83 J18 **Plumtree** Matabeleland South, SW Zimbabwe
118 D11 **Plungė** Telšiai, W Lithuania
113 J15 **Plužine** Montenegro, SW Serbia and Montenegro (Yugo.)
119 K14 **Plyeshchanitsy** *Rus.* Pleshchenitsy. Minskaya Voblasts', N Belarus
45 V10 **Plymouth** ○ (Montserrat) SW Montserrat
97 I24 **Plymouth** SW England, UK
31 O11 **Plymouth** Indiana, N USA
19 P12 **Plymouth** Massachusetts, NE USA
19 N8 **Plymouth** New Hampshire, NE USA
21 X9 **Plymouth** North Carolina, SE USA
30 M8 **Plymouth** Wisconsin, N USA
97 J20 **Plynlimon** ▲ C Wales, UK
124 G14 **Plyussa** Pskovskaya Oblast', W Russian Federation
111 B17 **Plzeň** *Ger.* Pilsen, *Pol.* Pilzno. Plzeňský Kraj, W Czech Republic
111 B17 **Plzeňský Kraj** ◈ *region* W Czech Republic
110 F11 **Pniewy** *Ger.* Pinne. Wielkolpolskie, C Poland
106 D8 **Po** ≈ N Italy
77 P13 **Pô** S Burkina
42 M13 **Poás, Volcán** ▲ NW Costa Rica
77 S16 **Pobè** S Benin
123 S8 **Pobeda, Gora** ▲ NE Russian Federation
Pobeda Peak *see* Pobedy, Pik/Tomür Feng
147 Z7 **Pobedy, Pik** *var.* Pobeda Peak, *Chin.* Tomür Feng. ▲ China/Kyrgyzstan *see also* Tomür Feng
110 H11 **Pobiedziska** *Ger.* Pudewitz. Wielkolpolskie, C Poland
Po, Bocche del *see* Po, Foci del
27 W9 **Pocahontas** Arkansas, C USA
29 U12 **Pocahontas** Iowa, C USA
33 Q15 **Pocatello** Idaho, NW USA
167 S13 **Pochentong** ✕ (Phnum Penh) Phnum Penh, S Cambodia
126 I6 **Pochep** Bryanskaya Oblast', W Russian Federation
126 H4 **Pochinok** Smolenskaya Oblast', W Russian Federation
41 R17 **Pochutla** *var.* San Pedro Pochutla. Oaxaca, SE Mexico
62 I6 **Pocitos, Salar** *var.* Salar Quiróm. *salt lake* NW Argentina
101 O22 **Pocking** Bayern, SE Germany
186 I10 **Pocklington Reef** *reef* SE PNG
59 P15 **Poço da Cruz, Açude** ⊞ E Brazil
27 R11 **Pocola** Oklahoma, C USA
21 Y5 **Pocomoke City** Maryland, NE USA
59 L21 **Poços de Caldas** Minas Gerais, NE Brazil
124 H14 **Podberez'ye** Novgorodskaya Oblast', NW Russian Federation
Podbrodzie *see* Pabradė
125 U8 **Podcher'ye** Respublika Komi, NW Russian Federation
111 E16 **Poděbrady** *Ger.* Podiebrad. Středočeský Kraj, C Czech Republic
126 L9 **Podgorenskiy** Voronezhskaya Oblast', W Russian Federation
113 J17 **Podgorica** *prev.* Titograd. Montenegro, SW Serbia and Montenegro (Yugo.)
113 K17 **Podgorica** ✕ Montenegro, SW Serbia and Montenegro (Yugo.)
122 L12 **Podgornyy** Krasnoyarskiy Kray, C Russian Federation
109 T13 **Podgrad** SW Slovenia
Podiebrad *see* Poděbrady
116 M5 **Podil's'ka Vysochina** *plateau* W Ukraine
Podium Anicensis *see* le Puy
122 L11 **Podkamennaya Tunguska** *Eng.* Stony Tunguska. ≈ C Russian Federation
113 N17 **Podkarpackie** ◈ *province* SE Poland
Pod Klošter *see* Arnoldstein
110 O9 **Podlaskie** ◈ *province* NE Poland
127 Q8 **Podlesnoye** Saratovskaya Oblast', W Russian Federation
126 K4 **Podol'sk** Moskovskaya Oblast', W Russian Federation
76 H10 **Podor** N Senegal
125 P12 **Podosinovets** Kirovskaya Oblast', NW Russian Federation
124 I12 **Podporozh'ye** Leningradskaya Oblast', NW Russian Federation
Podravska Slatina *see* Slatina, Croatia
112 J13 **Podromanlja** Republika Srpska, SE Bosnia & Herzegovina
Podsvil'ye *see* Padsvillye
116 L9 **Podu Iloaiei** *prev.* Podul Iloaiei. Iași, NE Romania
113 N15 **Podujevo** Serbia, S Serbia and Montenegro (Yugo.)
Podul Iloaiei *see* Podu Iloaiei
Podunajská Rovina *see* Little Alföld
124 M12 **Podyuga** Arkhangel'skaya Oblast', NW Russian Federation
56 A9 **Poechos, Embalse** ◎ NW Peru
55 W10 **Poeketi** Sipaliwini, E Surinam
100 L8 **Poel** *island* N Germany
83 M20 **Poelela, Lagoa** ◎ S Mozambique
Poerwodadi *see* Purwodadi
Poetovio *see* Ptuj
83 E23 **Pofadder** Northern Cape, W South Africa
106 I9 **Po, Foci del** *var.* Bocche del Po. ≈ NE Italy
116 E12 **Pogănis** ≈ W Romania
Pogegen *see* Pagėgiai
106 G12 **Poggibonsi** Toscana, C Italy
107 I14 **Poggio Mirteto** Lazio, C Italy
109 V4 **Pöggstall** Niederösterreich, N Austria
116 L13 **Pogoanele** Buzău, SE Romania
Pogónion *see* Delvináki
113 M21 **Pogradec** *var.* Pogradeci. Korçë, SE Albania
Pogradeci *see* Pogradec
123 S15 **Pogranichnyy** Primorskiy Kray, SE Russian Federation
38 M16 **Pogromni Volcano** ▲ Unimak Island, Alaska, USA
163 Z15 **P'ohang** *Jap.* Hokō. E South Korea
15 T9 **Pohénégamook, Lac** ◎ Québec, SE Canada
93 L20 **Pohja** *Swe.* Pojo. Etelä-Suomi, SW Finland
Pohjanlahti *see* Bothnia, Gulf of
189 U16 **Pohnpei** ◈ *state* E Micronesia
189 O12 **Pohnpei** ✕ Pohnpei, E Micronesia
189 O12 **Pohnpei** *prev.* Ponape Ascension Island. *island* E Micronesia
111 F19 **Pohořelice** *Ger.* Pohrlitz. Jihomoravský Kraj, SE Czech Republic
109 V10 **Pohorje** *Ger.* Bacher. ▲ N Slovenia
117 N6 **Pohrebyshche** Vinnyts'ka Oblast', C Ukraine
Pohrlitz *see* Pohořelice
161 P9 **Po Hu** ◎ E China
116 G15 **Poiana Mare** Dolj, S Romania
Poictiers *see* Poitiers
127 N6 **Poim** Penzenskaya Oblast', W Russian Federation
159 N15 **Poindo** Xizang Zizhiqu, W China
195 Y13 **Poinsett, Cape** *headland* Antarctica
29 R9 **Poinsett, Lake** ◎ South Dakota, N USA
22 I10 **Point Au Fer Island** *island* Louisiana, S USA
39 X14 **Point Baker** Prince of Wales Island, Alaska, USA
25 U13 **Point Comfort** Texas, SW USA
Point de Galle *see* Galle
44 K10 **Pointe à Gravois** *headland* SW Haiti
22 L10 **Pointe a la Hache** Louisiana, S USA
45 Y6 **Pointe-à-Pitre** Grande Terre, C Guadeloupe
15 U7 **Pointe-au-Père** Québec, SE Canada
15 V5 **Pointe-aux-Anglais** Québec, SE Canada
45 T10 **Pointe du Cap** *headland* N Saint Lucia
79 E21 **Pointe-Noire** Le Kouilou, S Congo
45 X6 **Pointe Noire** Basse Terre, W Guadeloupe
79 E21 **Pointe-Noire** ✕ Le Kouilou, S Congo
45 U15 **Point Fortin** Trinidad, Trinidad and Tobago
38 M6 **Point Hope** Alaska, USA
39 N5 **Point Lay** Alaska, USA
18 B16 **Point Marion** Pennsylvania, NE USA
18 K16 **Point Pleasant** New Jersey, NE USA
21 P4 **Point Pleasant** West Virginia, NE USA
45 R14 **Point Salines** ✕ (St.George's) SW Grenada
102 L9 **Poitiers** *prev.* Poictiers, *anc.* Limonum. Vienne, W France
102 K9 **Poitou** *cultural region* W France
102 K10 **Poitou-Charentes** ◈ *region* W France
103 N3 **Poix-de-Picardie** Somme, N France
Pojo *see* Pohja
37 S10 **Pojoaque** New Mexico, SW USA
152 E11 **Pokaran** Rājasthān, NW India
183 R4 **Pokataroo** New South Wales, SE Australia
119 P18 **Pokats'** *Rus.* Pokot'. ≈ SE Belarus
29 V5 **Pokegama Lake** ◎ Minnesota, N USA
184 L6 **Pokeno** Waikato, North Island, NZ
153 O11 **Pokhara** Western, C Nepal

127 *T6* **Pokhvistnevo** Samarskaya Oblast', W Russian Federation
55 *W10* **Pokigron** Sipaliwini, C Surinam
92 *L10* **Pokka** *Lapp.* Bohkká. Lappi, N Finland
79 *N16* **Poko** Orientale, NE Dem. Rep. Congo
Pokot' *see* Pokats'
Po-ko-to Shan *see* Bogda Shan
147 *S7* **Pokrovka** Talasskaya Oblast', NW Kyrgyzstan
Pokrovka *see* Kyzyl-Suu
117 *V8* **Pokrovs'ke** *Rus.* Pokrovskoye. Dnipropetrovs'ka Oblast', E Ukraine
Pokrovskoye *see* Pokrovs'ke
Pola *see* Pula
37 *N10* **Polacca** Arizona, SW USA
104 *L2* **Pola de Laviana** Asturias, N Spain
104 *K2* **Pola de Lena** Asturias, N Spain
104 *L2* **Pola de Siero** Asturias, N Spain
191 *Y3* **Poland** Kiritimati, E Kiribati
110 *H12* **Poland** *off.* Republic of Poland, *var.* Polish Republic, *Pol.* Polska, Rzeczpospolita Polska; *prev. Pol.* Polska Rzeczpospolita Ludowa, Polish People's Republic. ◆ *republic* C Europe
Polangen *see* Palanga
110 *G7* **Polanów** *Ger.* Pollnow. Zachodnio-pomorskie, NW Poland
136 *H13* **Polatlı** Ankara, C Turkey
118 *L12* **Polatsk** *Rus.* Polotsk. Vitsyebskaya Voblasts', N Belarus
110 *F8* **Połczyn-Zdrój** *Ger.* Bad Polzin. Zachodnio-pomorskie, NW Poland
Polekhatum *see* Pulhatyn
149 *Q3* **Pol-e Khomrī** *var.* Pul-i-Khumri. Baghlān, NE Afghanistan
197 *S10* **Pole Plain** *undersea feature* Arctic Ocean
143 *P5* **Pol-e Safīd** *var.* Pol-e-Sefid, Pul-i-Sefid. Māzandarān, N Iran
Pol-e-Sefid *see* Pol-e Safīd
118 *B13* **Polessk** *Ger.* Labiau. Kaliningradskaya Oblast', W Russian Federation
Polesskoye *see* Polis'ke
171 *N13* **Polewali** Sulawesi, C Indonesia
114 *G11* **Polezhan** ▲ SW Bulgaria
78 *F13* **Poli** Nord, N Cameroon
Poli *see* Pólis
107 *M19* **Policastro, Golfo di** *gulf* S Italy
110 *D8* **Police** *Ger.* Politz. Zachodniopomorskie, NW Poland
172 *I17* **Police, Pointe** *headland* Mahé, NE Seychelles
115 *L17* **Polichnítos** *var.* Polihnitos, Políkhnitos. Lésvos, E Greece
Poligiros *see* Polýgyros
107 *P17* **Polignano a Mare** Puglia, SE Italy
103 *S9* **Poligny** Jura, E France
Polihnitos *see* Polichnítos
Polikastro/Políkastron *see* Polýkastro
Políkhnitos *see* Polichnítos
114 *K8* **Polikrayshte** Veliko Tŭrnovo, N Bulgaria
171 *O3* **Polillo Islands** *island group* N Philippines
109 *Q9* **Polinik** ▲ SW Austria
121 *O2* **Pólis** *var.* Poli. W Cyprus
Polish People's Republic *see* Poland
Polish Republic *see* Poland
117 *O3* **Polis'ke** *Rus.* Polesskoye. Kyyivs'ka Oblast', N Ukraine
107 *N22* **Polistena** Calabria, SW Italy
Politz *see* Police
Políyiros *see* Polýgyros
29 *V14* **Polk City** Iowa, C USA
110 *F13* **Polkowice** *Ger.* Heerwegen. Dolnośląskie, SW Poland
155 *G22* **Pollāchi** Tamil Nādu, SE India
109 *W7* **Pöllau** Steiermark, SE Austria
189 *T13* **Polle** *atoll* Chuuk Islands, C Micronesia
Pollnow *see* Polanów
29 *N7* **Pollock** South Dakota, N USA
92 *L8* **Polmak** Finnmark, N Norway
30 *L10* **Polo** Illinois, N USA
193 *V15* **Poloa** *island* Tongatapu Group, N Tonga
42 *E5* **Polochic, Río** ≈ C Guatemala
Pologi *see* Polohy
117 *V9* **Polohy** *Rus.* Pologi. Zaporiz'ka Oblast', SE Ukraine
83 *K20* **Polokwane** *prev.* Pietersburg. Limpopo, NE South Africa
14 *M10* **Polonais, Lac des** ⊚ Québec, SE Canada
61 *G20* **Polonio, Cabo** *headland* E Uruguay
155 *K24* **Polonnaruwa** North Central Province, C Sri Lanka
116 *L5* **Polonne** *Rus.* Polonnoye. Khmel'nyts'ka Oblast', NW Ukraine
Polonnoye *see* Polonne
Polotsk *see* Polatsk
109 *T7* **Pöls** *var.* Pölsbach. ≈ E Austria
Pölsbach *see* Pöls
Polska/Polska, Rzeczpospolita/Polska Rzeczpospolita Ludowa *see* Poland
114 *L10* **Polski Gradets** Stara Zagora, C Bulgaria
114 *K8* **Polsko Kosovo** Ruse, N Bulgaria
33 *P8* **Polson** Montana, NW USA
117 *T6* **Poltava** Poltavs'ka Oblast', NE Ukraine
Poltava *see* Poltavs'ka Oblast'
117 *R5* **Poltavs'ka Oblast'** *var.* Poltava, *Rus.* Poltavskaya Oblast'. ◈ *province* NE Ukraine
Poltavskaya Oblast' *see* Poltavs'ka Oblast'
Poltoratsk *see* Aşgabat
118 *I5* **Põltsamaa** *Ger.* Oberpahlen. Jõgevamaa, E Estonia
118 *I4* **Põltsamaa** *var.* Põltsamaa Jõgi. ≈ C Estonia
Põltsamaa Jõgi *see* Põltsamaa
122 *I8* **Poluy** ≈ N Russian Federation
118 *J6* **Põlva** *Ger.* Pölwe. Põlvamaa, SE Estonia
93 *N16* **Polvijärvi** Itä-Suomi, E Finland
Pölwe *see* Põlva
115 *I22* **Polýaigos** *island* Kykládes, Greece, Aegean Sea
115 *I22* **Polyaígou Folégandrou, Stenó** *strait* Kykládes, Greece, Aegean Sea
124 *J3* **Polyarnyy** Murmanskaya Oblast', NW Russian Federation
127 *W5* **Polyarnyy Ural** ⛰ NW Russian Federation
115 *G14* **Polýgyros** *var.* Poligiros, Políyiros. Kentrikí Makedonía, N Greece
114 *F13* **Polýkastro** *var.* Polikastro; *prev.* Políkastron. Kentrikí Makedonía, N Greece
193 *O9* **Polynesia** *island group* C Pacific Ocean
115 *J15* **Polýochni** *site of ancient city* Límnos, E Greece
41 *Y13* **Polyuc** Quintana Roo, E Mexico
109 *V10* **Polzela** C Slovenia
Polzen *see* Ploučnice
56 *D12* **Pomabamba** Ancash, C Peru
185 *D23* **Pomahaka** ≈ South Island, NZ
106 *F12* **Pomarance** Toscana, C Italy
104 *G9* **Pombal** Leiria, C Portugal
76 *D9* **Pombas** Santo Antão, NW Cape Verde
83 *N19* **Pomene** Inhambane, SE Mozambique
110 *G8* **Pomerania** *cultural region* Germany/Poland
110 *D7* **Pomeranian Bay** *Ger.* Pommersche Bucht, *Pol.* Zatoka Pomorska. *bay* Germany/Poland
31 *T15* **Pomeroy** Ohio, N USA
32 *L10* **Pomeroy** Washington, NW USA
117 *Q8* **Pomichna** Kirovohrads'ka Oblast', C Ukraine
186 *H7* **Pomio** New Britain, E PNG
Pomir, Dar"yoi *see* Pamir/Pāmīr, Daryā-ye
27 *T6* **Pomme de Terre Lake** ⊞ Missouri, C USA
29 *S8* **Pomme de Terre River** ≈ Minnesota, N USA
Pommersche Bucht *see* Pomeranian Bay
35 *T15* **Pomona** California, W USA
114 *N9* **Pomorie** Burgas, E Bulgaria
Pomorska, Zatoka *see* Pomeranian Bay
110 *H8* **Pomorskie** ◈ *province* N Poland
127 *Q4* **Pomorskiy Proliv** *strait* NW Russian Federation
125 *T10* **Pomozdino** Respublika Komi, NW Russian Federation
Pompaelo *see* Pamplona
23 *Z15* **Pompano Beach** Florida, SE USA
107 *K18* **Pompei** Campania, S Italy
33 *V10* **Pompeys Pillar** Montana, NW USA
Ponape Ascension Island *see* Pohnpei
29 *R13* **Ponca** Nebraska, C USA
27 *O8* **Ponca City** Oklahoma, C USA
45 *T6* **Ponce** C Puerto Rico
23 *X10* **Ponce de Leon Inlet** *inlet* Florida, SE USA
22 *K8* **Ponchatoula** Louisiana, S USA
26 *M8* **Pond Creek** Oklahoma, C USA
155 *J20* **Pondicherry** *var.* Puduchcheri, *Fr.* Pondichéry. Pondicherry, SE India
151 *I20* **Pondicherry** *var.* Puduchcheri, *Fr.* Pondichéry. ◈ *union territory* India
Pondichéry *see* Pondicherry
197 *N11* **Pond Inlet** Baffin Island, Nunavut, NE Canada
187 *P16* **Ponérihouen** Province Nord, C New Caledonia
104 *J4* **Ponferrada** Castilla-León, NW Spain
184 *N13* **Pongaroa** Manawatu-Wanganui, North Island, NZ
167 *Q12* **Pong Nam Ron** Chantaburi, S Thailand
81 *C14* **Pongo** ≈ S Sudan
152 *I7* **Pong Reservoir** ⊞ N India
111 *N14* **Poniatowa** Lubelskie, E Poland
167 *R12* **Pônley** Kâmpóng Chhnăng, C Cambodia
155 *I20* **Ponnaiyār** ≈ SE India
11 *Q15* **Ponoka** Alberta, SW Canada
127 *U6* **Ponomarevka** Orenburgskaya Oblast', W Russian Federation
169 *Q17* **Ponorogo** Jawa, C Indonesia
124 *M5* **Ponoy** Murmanskaya Oblast', NW Russian Federation
122 *F6* **Ponoy** ≈ NW Russian Federation
102 *K11* **Pons** Charente-Maritime, W France
Pons *see* Ponts
Pons Aelii *see* Newcastle upon Tyne
Pons Vetus *see* Pontevedra
99 *G20* **Pont-à-Celles** Hainaut, S Belgium
102 *K16* **Pontacq** Pyrénées-Atlantiques, SW France
64 *P3* **Ponta Delgada** São Miguel, Azores, Portugal, NE Atlantic Ocean
64 *P3* **Ponta Delgado** × São Miguel, Azores, Portugal, NE Atlantic Ocean
64 *N2* **Ponta do Pico** ▲ Pico, Azores, Portugal, NE Atlantic Ocean
60 *J11* **Ponta Grossa** Paraná, S Brazil
103 *S5* **Pont-à-Mousson** Meurthe-et-Moselle, NE France
103 *T9* **Pontarlier** Doubs, E France
106 *G11* **Pontassieve** Toscana, C Italy
102 *L4* **Pont-Audemer** Eure, N France
22 *K9* **Pontchartrain, Lake** ⊚ Louisiana, S USA
102 *I8* **Pontchâteau** Loire-Atlantique, NW France
103 *R10* **Pont-de-Vaux** Ain, E France
104 *G4* **Ponteareas** Galicia, NW Spain
106 *J6* **Pontebba** Friuli-Venezia Giulia, NE Italy
104 *G4* **Ponte Caldelas** Galicia, NW Spain
107 *J16* **Pontecorvo** Lazio, C Italy
104 *G5* **Ponte da Barca** Viana do Castelo, N Portugal
104 *G5* **Ponte de Lima** Viana do Castelo, N Portugal
106 *F11* **Pontedera** Toscana, C Italy
104 *H10* **Ponte de Sor** Portalegre, C Portugal
104 *H2* **Pontedeume** Galicia, NW Spain
106 *F6* **Ponte di Legno** Lombardia, N Italy
11 *T17* **Ponteix** Saskatchewan, S Canada
59 *N20* **Ponte Nova** Minas Gerais, NE Brazil
59 *G18* **Pontes e Lacerda** Mato Grosso, W Brazil
104 *G4* **Pontevedra** *anc.* Pons Vetus. Galicia, NW Spain
104 *G3* **Pontevedra** ◈ *province* Galicia, NW Spain
104 *G4* **Pontevedra, Ría de** *estuary* NW Spain
30 *M12* **Pontiac** Illinois, N USA
31 *R9* **Pontiac** Michigan, N USA
169 *P11* **Pontianak** Borneo, C Indonesia
107 *I16* **Pontino, Agro** *plain* C Italy
Pontisarae *see* Pontoise
102 *H6* **Pontivy** Morbihan, NW France
102 *F6* **Pont-l'Abbé** Finistère, NW France
103 *N4* **Pontoise** *anc.* Briva Isarae, Cergy-Pontoise, Pontisarae. Val-d'Oise, N France
11 *W13* **Ponton** Manitoba, C Canada
102 *J5* **Pontorson** Manche, N France
22 *M2* **Pontotoc** Mississippi, S USA
25 *R9* **Pontotoc** Texas, SW USA
106 *E10* **Pontremoli** Toscana, C Italy
108 *J10* **Pontresina** Graubünden, S Switzerland
105 *U5* **Ponts** *var.* Pons. Cataluña, NE Spain
103 *R14* **Pont-St-Esprit** Gard, S France
97 *K21* **Pontypool** *Wel.* Pontypŵl. SE Wales, UK
97 *J22* **Pontypridd** S Wales, UK
Pontypŵl *see* Pontypool
43 *R17* **Ponuga** Veraguas, SE Panama
184 *L6* **Ponui Island** *island* N NZ
119 *K14* **Ponya** *Rus.* Ponya. ≈ N Belarus
107 *I17* **Ponziane, Isole** *island* C Italy
182 *F7* **Poochera** South Australia
97 *L24* **Poole** S England, UK
25 *S6* **Poolville** Texas, SW USA
Poona *see* Pune
182 *M8* **Pooncarie** New South Wales, SE Australia
183 *N6* **Poopelloe Lake** *seasonal lake* New South Wales, SE Australia
57 *K19* **Poopó** Oruro, C Bolivia
57 *K19* **Poopó, Lago** *var.* Lago Pampa Aullagas. ⊚ W Bolivia
184 *L3* **Poor Knights Islands** *island* N NZ
39 *P10* **Poorman** Alaska, USA
182 *E3* **Pootnoura** South Australia
147 *R10* **Pop** *Rus.* Pap. Namangan Viloyati, E Uzbekistan
117 *X7* **Popasna** *Rus.* Popasnaya. Luhans'ka Oblast', E Ukraine
Popasnaya *see* Popasna
54 *D12* **Popayán** Cauca, SW Colombia
99 *B18* **Poperinge** West-Vlaanderen, W Belgium
123 *N7* **Popigay** Taymyrskiy (Dolgano-Nenetskiy) Avtonomnyy Okrug, N Russian Federation
123 *N7* **Popigay** ≈ N Russian Federation
117 *O5* **Popil'nya** Zhytomyrs'ka Oblast', N Ukraine
182 *K8* **Popiltah Lake** *seasonal lake* New South Wales, SE Australia
33 *X7* **Poplar** Montana, NW USA
11 *Y14* **Poplar** ≈ Manitoba, C Canada
27 *X8* **Poplar Bluff** Missouri, C USA
33 *X6* **Poplar River** ≈ Montana, NW USA
41 *P14* **Popocatépetl** ⚲ S Mexico
79 *H21* **Popokabaka** Bandundu, SW Dem. Rep. Congo
107 *J15* **Popoli** Abruzzo, C Italy
186 *F9* **Popondetta** Northern, S PNG
112 *F9* **Popovača** Sisak-Moslavina, NE Croatia
114 *J10* **Popovitsa** Tŭrgovishte, C Bulgaria
114 *L8* **Popovo** Tŭrgovishte, N Bulgaria
Popovo *see* Iskra
Popper *see* Poprad
30 *M5* **Popple River** ≈ Wisconsin, N USA
111 *L19* **Poprad** *Ger.* Deutschendorf, *Hung.* Poprád. Prešovský Kraj, E Slovakia
111 *L18* **Poprad** *Ger.* Popper, *Hung.* Poprád. ≈ Poland/Slovakia
111 *L19* **Poprad-Tatry** × (Poprad) Prešovský Kraj, E Slovakia
21 *X7* **Poquoson** Virginia, NE USA
149 *O15* **Porāli** ≈ SW Pakistan
184 *N12* **Porangahau** Hawke's Bay, North Island, NZ
59 *K17* **Porangatu** Goiás, C Brazil
119 *G18* **Porazava** *Pol.* Porozow, *Rus.* Porozovo. Hrodzyenskaya Voblasts', W Belarus
154 *A11* **Porbandar** Gujarāt, W India
10 *I13* **Porcher Island** *island* British Columbia, SW Canada
104 *M13* **Porcuna** Andalucía, S Spain
14 *F7* **Porcupine** Ontario, S Canada
64 *M6* **Porcupine Bank** *undersea feature* N Atlantic Ocean
11 *V15* **Porcupine Hills** ⛰ Manitoba/Saskatchewan, S Canada
30 *L3* **Porcupine Mountains** *hill range* Michigan, N USA
64 *M7* **Porcupine Plain** *undersea feature* E Atlantic Ocean
8 *G7* **Porcupine River** ≈ Canada/USA
106 *I7* **Pordenone** *anc.* Portenau. Friuli-Venezia Giulia, NE Italy
54 *H9* **Pore** Casanare, E Colombia
112 *A9* **Poreč** *It.* Parenzo. Istra, NW Croatia
60 *I9* **Porecatu** Paraná, *M15*S Brazil
Porech'ye *see* Parechcha
127 *P4* **Poretskoye** Chuvashskaya Respublika, W Russian Federation
77 *Q13* **Porga** N Benin
186 *B7* **Porgera** Enga, W PNG
93 *K18* **Pori** *Swe.* Björneborg. Länsi-Suomi, W Finland
185 *L14* **Porirua** Wellington, North Island, NZ
92 *I12* **Porjus** *Lapp.* Bårjås. Norrbotten, N Sweden
124 *G14* **Porkhov** Pskovskaya Oblast', W Russian Federation
55 *O4* **Porlamar** Nueva Esparta, NE Venezuela
102 *I8* **Pornic** Loire-Atlantique, NW France
186 *B7* **Poroma** Southern Highlands, W PNG
123 *T13* **Poronaysk** Ostrov Sakhalin, Sakhalinskaya Oblast', SE Russian Federation
115 *G20* **Póros** Póros, S Greece
115 *C19* **Póros** Kefallinía, Iónioi Nísoi, Greece, C Mediterranean Sea
115 *G20* **Póros** *island* S Greece
81 *G24* **Poroto Mountains** ⛰ SW Tanzania
112 *B10* **Porozina** Primorje-Gorski Kotar, NW Croatia
Porozovo/Porozow *see* Porazava
195 *X15* **Porpoise Bay** *bay* Antarctica
65 *G15* **Porpoise Point** *headland* NE Ascension Island
65 *C25* **Porpoise Point** *headland* East Falkland, Falkland Islands
108 *C6* **Porrentruy** Jura, NW Switzerland
106 *F10* **Porretta Terme** Emilia-Romagna, C Italy
Porriño *see* O Porriño
92 *L7* **Porsangerfjorden** *Lapp.* Porsángguvuotna. *fjord* N Norway
92 *K8* **Porsangerhalvøya** *peninsula* N Norway
Porsángguvuotna *see* Porsangerfjorden
95 *G16* **Porsgrunn** Telemark, S Norway
136 *E13* **Porsuk Çayı** ≈ C Turkey
Porsy *see* Boldumsaz
57 *N18* **Portachuelo** Santa Cruz, C Bolivia
182 *I9* **Port Adelaide** South Australia
97 *F15* **Portadown** *Ir.* Port An Dúnáin. S Northern Ireland, UK
31 *P10* **Portage** Michigan, N USA
18 *D15* **Portage** Pennsylvania, NE USA
30 *K8* **Portage** Wisconsin, N USA
30 *M3* **Portage Lake** ⊚ Michigan, N USA
11 *X16* **Portage la Prairie** Manitoba, S Canada
31 *R11* **Portage River** ≈ Ohio, N USA
27 *Y8* **Portageville** Missouri, C USA
28 *L2* **Portal** North Dakota, N USA
10 *L17* **Port Alberni** Vancouver Island, British Columbia, SW Canada
14 *E15* **Port Albert** Ontario, S Canada
104 *I10* **Portalegre** *anc.* Ammaia, Amoea. Portalegre, E Portugal
104 *H10* **Portalegre** ◈ *district* C Portugal
37 *V12* **Portales** New Mexico, SW USA
39 *X14* **Port Alexander** Baranof Island, Alaska, USA
83 *I25* **Port Alfred** Eastern Cape, S South Africa
10 *J16* **Port Alice** Vancouver Island, British Columbia, SW Canada
22 *J8* **Port Allen** Louisiana, S USA
Port Amelia *see* Pemba
Port An Dúnáin *see* Portadown
32 *G7* **Port Angeles** Washington, NW USA
44 *L12* **Port Antonio** NE Jamaica
115 *D16* **Pórta Panagiá** *religious building* Thessalía, C Greece
25 *T14* **Port Aransas** Texas, SW USA
97 *E18* **Portarlington** *Ir.* Cúil an tSúdaire. C Ireland
183 *P17* **Port Arthur** Tasmania, SE Australia
25 *Y11* **Port Arthur** Texas, SW USA
96 *G12* **Port Askaig** W Scotland, UK
182 *I7* **Port Augusta** South Australia
44 *M9* **Port-au-Prince** ● (Haiti) C Haiti
44 *M9* **Port-au-Prince** × E Haiti
22 *I8* **Port Barre** Louisiana, S USA
151 *Q19* **Port Blair** Andaman and Nicobar Islands, SE India
25 *X12* **Port Bolivar** Texas, SW USA
105 *X4* **Portbou** Cataluña, NE Spain
77 *N17* **Port Bouet** × (Abidjan) SE Ivory Coast
182 *I8* **Port Broughton** South Australia
14 *F17* **Port Burwell** Ontario, S Canada
12 *G17* **Port Burwell** Québec, NE Canada
182 *M13* **Port Campbell** Victoria, SE Australia
15 *V4* **Port-Cartier** Québec, SE Canada
185 *F23* **Port Chalmers** Otago, South Island, NZ
23 *W14* **Port Charlotte** Florida, SE USA
38 *L9* **Port Clarence** Alaska, USA
10 *I13* **Port Clements** Graham Island, British Columbia, SW Canada
31 *S11* **Port Clinton** Ohio, N USA
14 *H17* **Port Colborne** Ontario, S Canada
15 *Y7* **Port-Daniel** Québec, SE Canada
Port Darwin *see* Darwin
183 *O17* **Port Davey** *headland* Tasmania, SE Australia
44 *K8* **Port-de-Paix** NW Haiti
181 *W4* **Port Douglas** Queensland, NE Australia
10 *J13* **Port Edward** British Columbia, SW Canada
83 *K24* **Port Edward** KwaZulu/Natal, SE South Africa
58 *J12* **Portel** Pará, NE Brazil
104 *H12* **Portel** Évora, S Portugal
14 *E14* **Port Elgin** Ontario, S Canada
45 *Y14* **Port Elizabeth** Bequia, Saint Vincent and the Grenadines
83 *I26* **Port Elizabeth** Eastern Cape, S South Africa
96 *G13* **Port Ellen** W Scotland, UK
Portenau *see* Pordenone
97 *H16* **Port Erin** SW Isle of Man
45 *Q13* **Porter Point** *headland* Saint Vincent, Saint Vincent and the Grenadines
185 *G18* **Porters Pass** *pass* South Island, NZ
83 *E25* **Porterville** Western Cape, SW South Africa
35 *R12* **Porterville** California, W USA
Port-Étienne *see* Nouâdhibou
182 *L13* **Port Fairy** Victoria, SE Australia
184 *M4* **Port Fitzroy** Great Barrier Island, Auckland, NE NZ
Port Florence *see* Kisumu
Port-Francqui *see* Ilebo
79 *C18* **Port-Gentil** Ogooué-Maritime, W Gabon
182 *I7* **Port Germein** South Australia
22 *J6* **Port Gibson** Mississippi, S USA
39 *Q13* **Port Graham** Alaska, USA
77 *U17* **Port Harcourt** Rivers, S Nigeria
10 *J16* **Port Hardy** Vancouver Island, British Columbia, SW Canada
Port Harrison *see* Inukjuak
13 *R14* **Port Hawkesbury** Cape Breton Island, Nova Scotia, SE Canada
180 *I6* **Port Hedland** Western Australia
39 *O15* **Port Heiden** Alaska, USA
97 *I19* **Porthmadog** *var.* Portmadoc. NW Wales, UK
14 *I15* **Port Hope** Ontario, SE Canada
13 *S9* **Port Hope Simpson** Newfoundland and Labrador, E Canada
65 *C24* **Port Howard Settlement** West Falkland, Falkland Islands
31 *T9* **Port Huron** Michigan, N USA
107 *K17* **Portici** Campania, S Italy
137 *Y13* **Port-Iliç** *Rus.* Port Il'ich. SE Azerbaijan
Port Il'ich *see* Port-Iliç
104 *G14* **Portimão** *var.* Vila Nova de Portimão. Faro, S Portugal
25 *T17* **Port Isabel** Texas, SW USA
18 *J13* **Port Jervis** New York, NE USA
55 *S7* **Port Kaituma** NW Guyana
126 *K12* **Port-Katon** Rostovskaya Oblast', SW Russian Federation
183 *S9* **Port Kembla** New South Wales, SE Australia
182 *F8* **Port Kenny** South Australia
Port Klang *see* Pelabuhan Klang
Port Láirge *see* Waterford
183 *S8* **Portland** New South Wales, SE Australia
182 *L13* **Portland** Victoria, SE Australia
184 *K4* **Portland** Northland, North Island, NZ
31 *Q13* **Portland** Indiana, N USA
19 *P8* **Portland** Maine, NE USA
31 *Q9* **Portland** Michigan, N USA
29 *Q4* **Portland** North Dakota, N USA
32 *G11* **Portland** Oregon, NW USA
20 *J8* **Portland** Tennessee, S USA
25 *T14* **Portland** Texas, SW USA
32 *G11* **Portland** × Oregon, NW USA
182 *L13* **Portland Bay** *bay* Victoria, SE Australia
44 *K13* **Portland Bight** *bay* S Jamaica
97 *L24* **Portland Bill** *var.* Bill of Portland. *headland* S England, UK
Portland, Bill of *see* Portland Bill
183 *P15* **Portland, Cape** *headland* Tasmania, SE Australia
10 *J12* **Portland Inlet** *inlet* British Columbia, W Canada
184 *P11* **Portland Island** *island* E NZ
65 *F15* **Portland Point** *headland* SW Ascension Island
44 *J13* **Portland Point** *headland* C Jamaica
103 *P16* **Port-la-Nouvelle** Aude, S France
Portlaoighise *see* Port Laoise
97 *E18* **Port Laoise** *var.* Portlaoise, *Ir.* Portlaoighise; *prev.* Maryborough. C Ireland
25 *U13* **Port Lavaca** Texas, SW USA
182 *G9* **Port Lincoln** South Australia
39 *Q14* **Port Lions** Kodiak Island, Alaska, USA
76 *I15* **Port Loko** W Sierra Leone
65 *E24* **Port Louis** East Falkland, Falkland Islands
45 *Y5* **Port-Louis** Grande Terre, N Guadeloupe
173 *X16* **Port Louis** ● (Mauritius) NW Mauritius
Port Louis *see* Scarborough
Port-Lyautey *see* Kénitra
182 *K12* **Port MacDonnell** South Australia
183 *U7* **Port Macquarie** New South Wales, SE Australia
Portmadoc *see* Porthmadog
Port Mahon *see* Mahón
44 *K12* **Port Maria** C Jamaica
10 *K16* **Port McNeill** Vancouver Island, British Columbia, SW Canada
13 *P11* **Port-Menier** Île d'Anticosti, Québec, E Canada
39 *N15* **Port Moller** Alaska, USA
44 *L13* **Port Morant** E Jamaica
44 *K13* **Portmore** C Jamaica
186 *D9* **Port Moresby** ● (PNG) Central/National Capital District, SW PNG
Port Natal *see* Durban
25 *Y11* **Port Neches** Texas, SW USA
182 *G9* **Port Neill** South Australia
15 *S6* **Portneuf** ≈ Québec, SE Canada
15 *R6* **Portneuf, Lac** ⊚ Québec, SE Canada
83 *D23* **Port Nolloth** Northern Cape, W South Africa
18 *J17* **Port Norris** New Jersey, NE USA
Port-Nouveau-Québec *see* Kangiqsualujjuaq
104 *G6* **Porto** *Eng.* Oporto; *anc.* Portus Cale. Porto, NW Portugal
104 *G6* **Porto** *var.* Pôrto. ◈ *district* N Portugal
104 *G6* **Porto** × Porto, W Portugal
61 *I16* **Porto Alegre** *var.* Pôrto Alegre. *state capital* Rio Grande do Sul, S Brazil
Porto Alexandre *see* Tombua
82 *B12* **Porto Amboim** Cuanza Sul, NW Angola
Porto Amélia *see* Pemba
Porto Bello *see* Portobelo
43 *T14* **Portobelo** *var.* Porto Bello, Puerto Bello. Colón, N Panama
60 *G10* **Pôrto Camargo** Paraná, S Brazil
25 *U13* **Port O'Connor** Texas, SW USA
Pôrto de Mós *see* Porto de Moz
58 *J12* **Porto de Moz** *var.* Pôrto de Mós. Pará, NE Brazil
64 *O5* **Porto do Moniz** Madeira, Portugal, NE Atlantic Ocean
59 *H16* **Porto dos Gaúchos** Mato Grosso, W Brazil
Porto Edda *see* Sarandë
107 *J24* **Porto Empedocle** Sicilia, Italy, C Mediterranean Sea
59 *H20* **Porto Esperança** Mato Grosso do Sul, SW Brazil
106 *E13* **Portoferraio** Toscana, C Italy
96 *G6* **Port of Ness** NW Scotland, UK
45 *U14* **Port-of-Spain** ● (Trinidad and Tobago) Trinidad, Trinidad and Tobago
Port of Spain *see* Piarco
103 *X15* **Porto, Golfe de** *gulf* Corse, France, C Mediterranean Sea
Porto Grande *see* Mindelo
106 *I7* **Portogruaro** Veneto, NE Italy
35 *P5* **Portola** California, W USA
187 *Q13* **Port-Olry** Espiritu Santo, C Vanuatu
93 *J17* **Pörtom** *Fin.* Pirttikylä. Länsi-Suomi, W Finland
Port Omna *see* Portumna
59 *G21* **Porto Murtinho** Mato Grosso do Sul, SW Brazil
59 *K16* **Porto Nacional** Tocantins, C Brazil
77 *S16* **Porto-Novo** ● (Benin) S Benin
23 *X10* **Port Orange** Florida, SE USA
32 *G8* **Port Orchard** Washington, NW USA
Porto Re *see* Kraljevica
32 *E15* **Port Orford** Oregon, NW USA
Porto Rico *see* Puerto Rico
106 *J13* **Porto San Giorgio** Marche, C Italy
107 *F14* **Porto San Stefano** Toscana, C Italy
64 *P5* **Porto Santo** *var.* Vila Baleira. Porto Santo, Madeira, Portugal, NE Atlantic Ocean
64 *Q5* **Porto Santo** × Porto Santo, Madeira, Portugal, NE Atlantic Ocean
64 *P5* **Porto Santo** *var.* Ilha do Porto Santo. *island* Madeira, Portugal, NE Atlantic Ocean
60 *H9* **Porto São José** Paraná, S Brazil
59 *O19* **Porto Seguro** Bahia, E Brazil
107 *B17* **Porto Torres** Sardegna, Italy, C Mediterranean Sea
59 *J23* **Porto União** Santa Catarina, S Brazil
103 *Y16* **Porto-Vecchio** Corse, France, C Mediterranean Sea
59 *E15* **Porto Velho** *var.* Velho. *state capital* Rondônia, W Brazil
56 *A6* **Portoviejo** *var.* Puertoviejo. Manabí, W Ecuador
185 *B26* **Port Pegasus** *bay* Stewart Island, NZ

◆ Country ◇ Dependent Territory ◈ Administrative Region ▲ Mountain ⚲ Volcano ⊚ Lake
● Country Capital ○ Dependent Territory Capital × International Airport ⛰ Mountain Range ≈ River ⊞ Reservoir

14 *H15* **Port Perry** Ontario, SE Canada
183 *N12* **Port Phillip Bay** *harbour* Victoria, SE Australia
182 *I8* **Port Pirie** South Australia
96 *G9* **Portree** N Scotland, UK
Port Rex *see* East London
Port Rois *see* Portrush
44 *K13* **Port Royal** E Jamaica
21 *R15* **Port Royal** South Carolina, SE USA
21 *R15* **Port Royal Sound** *inlet* South Carolina, SE USA
97 *F14* **Portrush** *Ir.* Port Rois. N Northern Ireland, UK
75 *W7* **Port Said** *Ar.* Būr Sa'īd. N Egypt
23 *R9* **Port Saint Joe** Florida, SE USA
23 *Y11* **Port Saint John** Florida, SE USA
83 *K24* **Port St.Johns** Eastern Cape, SE South Africa
103 *R16* **Port-Saint-Louis-du-Rhône** Bouches-du-Rhône, SE France
44 *K10* **Port Salut** SW Haiti
65 *E24* **Port Salvador** *inlet* East Falkland, Falkland Islands
65 *D24* **Port San Carlos** East Falkland, Falkland Islands
13 *S10* **Port Saunders** Newfoundland and Labrador, SE Canada
83 *K24* **Port Shepstone** KwaZulu/Natal, E South Africa
45 *O11* **Portsmouth** *var.* Grand-Anse. NW Dominica
97 *N24* **Portsmouth** S England, UK
19 *P10* **Portsmouth** New Hampshire, NE USA
31 *S15* **Portsmouth** Ohio, N USA
21 *X7* **Portsmouth** Virginia, NE USA
14 *E17* **Port Stanley** Ontario, S Canada
65 *B25* **Port Stephens** *inlet* West Falkland, Falkland Islands
65 *B25* **Port Stephens Settlement** West Falkland, Falkland Islands
97 *F14* **Portstewart** *Ir.* Port Stíobhaird. N Northern Ireland, UK
Port Stíobhaird *see* Portstewart
80 *I7* **Port Sudan** Red Sea, NE Sudan
22 *L10* **Port Sulphur** Louisiana, S USA
Port Swettenham *see* Klang/Pelabuhan Klang
97 *J22* **Port Talbot** S Wales, UK
92 *L11* **Porttipahdan Tekojärvi** ◎ N Finland
32 *G7* **Port Townsend** Washington, NW USA
104 *H9* **Portugal** *off.* Republic of Portugal. ◆ *republic* SW Europe
105 *O2* **Portugalete** País Vasco, N Spain
54 *J6* **Portuguesa** *off.* Estado Portuguesa. ◐ *state* N Venezuela
Portuguese East Africa *see* Mozambique
Portuguese Guinea *see* Guinea-Bissau
Portuguese Timor *see* East Timor
Portuguese West Africa *see* Angola
97 *D18* **Portumna** *Ir.* Port Omna. W Ireland
Portus Cale *see* Porto
Portus Magnus *see* Almería
Portus Magonis *see* Mahón
103 *P17* **Port-Vendres** *var.* Port Vendres. Pyrénées-Orientales, S France
182 *H9* **Port Victoria** South Australia
187 *Q14* **Port-Vila** *var.* Vila. ● (Vanuatu) Éfaté, C Vanuatu
182 *I9* **Port Wakefield** South Australia
31 *N8* **Port Washington** Wisconsin, N USA
57 *J14* **Porvenir** Pando, NW Bolivia
63 *I24* **Porvenir** Magallanes, S Chile
61 *D18* **Porvenir** Paysandú, W Uruguay
93 *M19* **Porvoo** *Swe.* Borgå. Etelä-Suomi, S Finland
Porzecze *see* Parechcha
104 *M10* **Porzuna** Castilla-La Mancha, C Spain
61 *E14* **Posadas** Misiones, NE Argentina
104 *L13* **Posadas** Andalucía, S Spain
Poschega *see* Požega
108 *J11* **Poschiavino** ≈ Italy/Switzerland
108 *J10* **Poschiavo** *Ger.* Puschlav. Graubünden, S Switzerland
112 *D12* **Posedarje** Zadar, SW Croatia
Posen *see* Poznań
126 *L14* **Poshekhon'ye** Yaroslavskaya Oblast', W Russian Federation
92 *M13* **Posio** Lappi, NE Finland
Poskam *see* Zepu
Posnania *see* Poznań
171 *O12* **Poso** Sulawesi, C Indonesia
171 *O12* **Poso, Danau** ◎ Sulawesi, C Indonesia
137 *R10* **Posof** Ardahan, NE Turkey
25 *R6* **Possum Kingdom Lake** ⊞ Texas, SW USA
25 *N6* **Post** Texas, SW USA
Postavy/Postawy *see* Pastavy
12 *I7* **Poste-de-la-Baleine** Québec, NE Canada
99 *M17* **Posterholt** Limburg, SE Netherlands
83 *G22* **Postmasburg** Northern Cape, N South Africa
Pôsto Diuarum *see* Campo de Diauarum
59 *I16* **Pôsto Jacaré** Mato Grosso, W Brazil
109 *T12* **Postojna** *Ger.* Adelsberg, *It.* Postumia. SW Slovenia
Postumia *see* Postojna
29 *X12* **Postville** Iowa, C USA
Pöstyén *see* Piešťany
113 *G14* **Posušje** Federacija Bosna I Herzegovina, SE Bosnia & Herzegovina
171 *O16* **Pota** Flores, C Indonesia
115 *G23* **Potamós** Antikýthira, S Greece
55 *S9* **Potaru River** ≈ C Guyana
83 *I21* **Potchefstroom** North-West, N South Africa
27 *R11* **Poteau** Oklahoma, C USA
25 *R12* **Poteet** Texas, SW USA
115 *G14* **Poteídaia** *site of ancient city* Kentrikí Makedonía, N Greece
Potentia *see* Potenza
107 *M18* **Potenza** *anc.* Potentia. Basilicata, S Italy
185 *A24* **Poteriteri, Lake** ◎ South Island, NZ
104 *M2* **Potes** Cantabria, N Spain
Potgietersrus *see* Mokopane
25 *S12* **Poth** Texas, SW USA
32 *J9* **Potholes Reservoir** ⊞ Washington, NW USA
137 *Q9* **P'ot'i** W Georgia
77 *X13* **Potiskum** Yobe, NE Nigeria
Potkozarje *see* Ivanjska
32 *M9* **Potlatch** Idaho, NW USA
33 *N9* **Pot Mountain** ▲ Idaho, NW USA
113 *H14* **Potoci** Federacija Bosna I Hercegovina, SE Bosnia & Herzegovina
21 *V3* **Potomac River** ≈ NE USA
27 *W6* **Potosi** Missouri, C USA
57 *L20* **Potosí** Potosí, S Bolivia
42 *H9* **Potosí** Chinandega, NW Nicaragua
57 *K21* **Potosí** ◐ *department* SW Bolivia
62 *H7* **Potrerillos** Atacama, N Chile
42 *H5* **Potrerillos** Cortés, NW Honduras
62 *H8* **Potro, Cerro del** ▲ N Chile
100 *N12* **Potsdam** Brandenburg, NE Germany
18 *J7* **Potsdam** New York, NE USA
109 *X5* **Pottendorf** Niederösterreich, E Austria
109 *X5* **Pottenstein** Niederösterreich, E Austria
18 *I15* **Pottstown** Pennsylvania, NE USA
18 *H14* **Pottsville** Pennsylvania, NE USA
155 *L25* **Pottuvil** Eastern Province, SE Sri Lanka
149 *U6* **Potwar Plateau** *plateau* NE Pakistan
102 *J7* **Pouancé** Maine-et-Loire, W France
15 *R6* **Poulin de Courval, Lac** ◎ Québec, SE Canada
18 *L9* **Poultney** Vermont, NE USA
187 *O16* **Poum** Province Nord, W New Caledonia
59 *L21* **Pouso Alegre** Minas Gerais, NE Brazil
192 *I16* **Poutasi** Upolu, SE Samoa
167 *R12* **Poŭthĭsăt** *prev.* Pursat. Poŭthĭsăt, W Cambodia
167 *R12* **Poŭthĭsăt, Stœng** *prev.* Pursat. ≈ W Cambodia
102 *J9* **Pouzauges** Vendée, NW France
Po, Valle del *see* Po Valley
106 *F8* **Po Valley** *It.* Valle del Po. *valley* N Italy
111 *I19* **Považská Bystrica** *Ger.* Waagbistritz, *Hung.* Vágbeszterce. Trenčiansky Kraj, W Slovakia
124 *J10* **Povenets** Respublika Kareliya, NW Russian Federation
184 *Q9* **Poverty Bay** *inlet* North Island, NZ
112 *K12* **Povlen** ▲ W Serbia and Montenegro (Yugo.)
104 *G6* **Póvoa de Varzim** Porto, NW Portugal
127 *N8* **Povorino** Voronezhskaya Oblast', W Russian Federation
Povungnituk *see* Puvirnituq
12 *J3* **Povungnituk, Rivière de** ≈ Québec, NE Canada
14 *H11* **Powassan** Ontario, S Canada
35 *U17* **Poway** California, W USA
33 *W14* **Powder River** Wyoming, C USA
33 *Y10* **Powder River** ≈ Montana/Wyoming, NW USA
32 *L12* **Powder River** ≈ Oregon, NW USA
33 *W13* **Powder River Pass** *pass* Wyoming, C USA
33 *U12* **Powell** Wyoming, C USA
65 *I22* **Powell Basin** *undersea feature* NW Weddell Sea
36 *M8* **Powell, Lake** ◎ Utah, W USA
37 *R4* **Powell, Mount** ▲ Colorado, C USA
10 *L17* **Powell River** British Columbia, SW Canada
31 *N5* **Powers** Michigan, N USA
28 *K2* **Powers Lake** North Dakota, N USA
21 *V6* **Powhatan** Virginia, NE USA
31 *V13* **Powhatan Point** Ohio, N USA
97 *J20* **Powys** *cultural region* E Wales, UK
187 *P17* **Poya** Province Nord, C New Caledonia
161 *P10* **Poyang Hu** ◎ S China
30 *L7* **Poygan, Lake** ◎ Wisconsin, N USA
109 *Y2* **Poysdorf** Niederösterreich, NE Austria
112 *N11* **Požarevac** *Ger.* Passarowitz. Serbia, NE Serbia and Montenegro (Yugo.)
41 *Q13* **Poza Rica** *var.* Poza Rica de Hidalgo. Veracruz-Llave, E Mexico
Poza Rica de Hidalgo *see* Poza Rica
112 *L13* **Požega** *Prev.* Slavonska Požega; *Ger.* Poschega, *Hung.* Pozsega. Požega-Slavonija, NE Croatia
112 *H9* **Požega-Slavonija** *off.* Požeško-Slavonska Županija. ◐ *province* NE Croatia
125 *U13* **Pozhva** Komi-Permyatskiy Avtonomnyy Okrug, NW Russian Federation
110 *G11* **Poznań** *Ger.* Posen, Posnania. Wielkolpolskie, C Poland
105 *O13* **Pozo Alcón** Andalucía, S Spain
62 *H3* **Pozo Almonte** Tarapacá, N Chile
104 *L12* **Pozoblanco** Andalucía, S Spain
105 *Q11* **Pozo Cañada** Castilla-La Mancha, C Spain
62 *N5* **Pozo Colorado** Presidente Hayes, C Paraguay
63 *J20* **Pozos, Punta** *headland* S Argentina
Pozsega *see* Požega
Pozsony *see* Bratislava
55 *N5* **Pozuelos** Anzoátegui, NE Venezuela
107 *L26* **Pozzallo** Sicilia, Italy, C Mediterranean Sea
107 *K17* **Pozzuoli** *anc.* Puteoli. Campania, S Italy
77 *P17* **Pra** ≈ S Ghana
111 *C19* **Prachatice** *Ger.* Prachatitz. Jihočeský Kraj, S Czech Republic
Prachatitz *see* Prachatice
167 *P11* **Prachin Buri** *var.* Prachinburi. Prachin Buri, C Thailand
Prachuab Girikhand *see* Prachuap Khiri Khan
167 *O12* **Prachuap Khiri Khan** *var.* Prachuab Girikhand. Prachuap Khiri Khan, SW Thailand
111 *H16* **Praděd** *Ger.* Altvater. ▲ NE Czech Republic
54 *D11* **Pradera** Valle del Cauca, SW Colombia
103 *O17* **Prades** Pyrénées-Orientales, S France
59 *O19* **Prado** Bahia, SE Brazil
54 *E11* **Prado** Tolima, C Colombia
Prado del Ganso *see* Goose Green
Prae *see* Phrae
Prag/Praga/Prague *see* Praha
27 *O10* **Prague** Oklahoma, C USA
111 *D16* **Praha** *Eng.* Prague, *Ger.* Prag, *Pol.* Praga. ● (Czech Republic) Středočeský Kraj, NW Czech Republic
116 *J13* **Prahova** ◐ *county* SE Romania
116 *J13* **Prahova** ≈ S Romania
76 *E10* **Praia** ● (Cape Verde) Santiago, S Cape Verde
83 *M21* **Praia do Bilene** Gaza, S Mozambique
83 *M20* **Praia do Xai-Xai** Gaza, S Mozambique
116 *J10* **Praid** *Hung.* Parajd. Harghita, C Romania
26 *J3* **Prairie Dog Creek** ≈ Kansas/Nebraska, C USA
30 *J9* **Prairie du Chien** Wisconsin, N USA
27 *S9* **Prairie Grove** Arkansas, C USA
31 *P10* **Prairie River** ≈ Michigan, N USA
Prairie State *see* Illinois
25 *V11* **Prairie View** Texas, SW USA
167 *Q10* **Prakhon Chai** Buri Ram, E Thailand
109 *R4* **Pram** ≈ N Austria
109 *S4* **Prambachkirchen** Oberösterreich, N Austria
118 *H2* **Prangli** *island* N Estonia
154 *J13* **Prānhita** ≈ C India
172 *I15* **Praslin** *island* Inner Islands, NE Seychelles
115 *O23* **Prasonísi, Akrotírio** *headland* Ródos, Dodekánisos, Greece, Aegean Sea
111 *I14* **Praszka** Opolskie, S Poland
119 *M18* **Pratasy** *Rus.* Protasy. Homyel'skaya Voblasts', SE Belarus
167 *Q10* **Prathai** Nakhon Ratchasima, E Thailand
Prathet Thai *see* Thailand
Prathum Thani *see* Pathum Thani
63 *F21* **Prat, Isla** *island* S Chile
106 *G11* **Prato** Toscana, C Italy
103 *O17* **Prats-de-Mollo-la-Preste** Pyrénées-Orientales, S France
26 *L6* **Pratt** Kansas, C USA
108 *E6* **Pratteln** Basel-Land, NW Switzerland
193 *O2* **Pratt Seamount** *undersea feature* N Pacific Ocean
23 *P5* **Prattville** Alabama, S USA
Praust *see* Pruszcz Gdański
114 *M7* **Pravda** *prev.* Dogrular. Silistra, NE Bulgaria
119 *B14* **Pravdinsk** *Ger.* Friedland. Kaliningradskaya Oblast', W Russian Federation
104 *K2* **Pravia** Asturias, N Spain
118 *L12* **Prazaroki** *Rus.* Prozoroki. Vitsyebskaya Voblasts', N Belarus
Prázsmár *see* Prejmer
167 *S11* **Preăh Vihéar** Preăh Vihéar, N Cambodia
116 *J12* **Predeal** *Hung.* Predeál. Braşov, C Romania
109 *S8* **Predlitz** Steiermark, SE Austria
11 *V15* **Preeceville** Saskatchewan, S Canada
Preenkuln *see* Priekule
102 *K6* **Pré-en-Pail** Mayenne, NW France
109 *T4* **Pregarten** Oberösterreich, N Austria
54 *H7* **Pregonero** Táchira, NW Venezuela
118 *J10* **Preiļi** *Ger.* Preli. Preiļi, SE Latvia
116 *J12* **Prejmer** *Ger.* Tartlau, *Hung.* Prázsmár. Braşov, S Romania
113 *J16* **Prekornica** ▲ SW Serbia and Montenegro (Yugo.)
Preli *see* Preiļi
Prëmet *see* Përmet
100 *M12* **Premnitz** Brandenburg, NE Germany
25 *S15* **Premont** Texas, SW USA
113 *H14* **Prenj** ▲ S Bosnia and Herzegovina
Prenjas/Prenjasi *see* Përrenjas
22 *L7* **Prentiss** Mississippi, S USA
Preny *see* Prienai
100 *O10* **Prenzlau** Brandenburg, NE Germany
123 *N11* **Preobrazhenka** Irkutskaya Oblast', C Russian Federation
166 *J9* **Preparis Island** *island* SW Burma
Prerau *see* Přerov
111 *H18* **Přerov** *Ger.* Prerau. Olomoucký Kraj, E Czech Republic
Preschau *see* Prešov
14 *M14* **Prescott** Ontario, SE Canada
36 *K12* **Prescott** Arizona, SW USA
27 *T13* **Prescott** Arkansas, C USA
32 *L10* **Prescott** Washington, NW USA
30 *H6* **Prescott** Wisconsin, N USA
185 *A24* **Preservation Inlet** *inlet* South Island, NZ
112 *O7* **Preševo** Serbia, SE Serbia and Montenegro (Yugo.)
29 *N10* **Presho** South Dakota, N USA
58 *M13* **Presidente Dutra** Maranhão, E Brazil
60 *I8* **Presidente Epitácio** São Paulo, S Brazil
62 *N5* **Presidente Hayes** *off.* Departamento de Presidente Hayes. ◐ *department* C Paraguay
60 *I9* **Presidente Prudente** São Paulo, S Brazil
Presidente Stroessner *see* Ciudad del Este
Presidente Vargas *see* Itabira
60 *I8* **Presidente Venceslau** São Paulo, S Brazil
193 *O10* **President Thiers Seamount** *undersea feature* C Pacific Ocean
24 *J11* **Presidio** Texas, SW USA
Preslav *see* Veliki Preslav
111 *M19* **Prešov** *var.* Preschau, *Ger.* Eperies, *Hung.* Eperjes. Prešovský Kraj, E Slovakia
111 *M19* **Prešovský Kraj** ◐ *region* E Slovakia
113 *N20* **Prespa, Lake** *Alb.* Liqen i Prespës, *Gk.* Límni Megáli Préspa, Limni Prespa, *Mac.* Prespansko Ezero, *Serb.* Prespansko Jezero. ◎ SE Europe
Prespa, Limni/Prespansko Ezero/Prespansko Jezero/Prespës, Liqen i *see* Prespa, Lake
19 *S2* **Presque Isle** Maine, NE USA
18 *B11* **Presque Isle** *headland* Pennsylvania, NE USA
Pressburg *see* Bratislava
77 *P17* **Prestea** SW Ghana
111 *B17* **Přeštice** *Ger.* Pschestitz. Plzeňský Kraj, W Czech Republic
97 *K17* **Preston** NW England, UK
23 *S6* **Preston** Georgia, SE USA
33 *R16* **Preston** Idaho, NW USA
29 *Z13* **Preston** Iowa, C USA
29 *X11* **Preston** Minnesota, N USA
21 *O6* **Prestonsburg** Kentucky, S USA
96 *I13* **Prestwick** W Scotland, UK
83 *J21* **Pretoria** *var.* Epitoli, Tshwane. ● (South Africa-administrative capital) Gauteng, NE South Africa
Pretoria-Witwatersrand-Vereeniging *see* Gauteng
Pretusha *see* Pretushë
113 *M21* **Pretushë** *var.* Pretusha. Korçë, SE Albania
Preussisch Eylau *see* Bagrationovsk
Preussisch-Stargard *see* Starogard Gdański
Preußisch Holland *see* Pasłęk
115 *C17* **Préveza** Ípeiros, W Greece
37 *V3* **Prewitt Reservoir** ⊞ Colorado, C USA
167 *S13* **Prey Vêng** Prey Vêng, S Cambodia
144 *M12* **Priaral'skiye Karakumy, Peski** *desert* SW Kazakhstan
123 *P14* **Priargunsk** Chitinskaya Oblast', S Russian Federation
38 *K14* **Pribilof Islands** *island group* Alaska, USA
113 *K14* **Priboj** Serbia, W Serbia and Montenegro (Yugo.)
111 *C17* **Příbram** *Ger.* Pibrans. Středočeský Kraj, W Czech Republic
36 *M4* **Price** Utah, W USA
37 *N5* **Price River** ≈ Utah, W USA
23 *N8* **Prichard** Alabama, S USA
25 *R8* **Priddy** Texas, SW USA
105 *P8* **Priego** Castilla-La Mancha, C Spain
104 *M14* **Priego de Córdoba** Andalucía, S Spain
118 *C10* **Priekule** *Ger.* Preenkuln. Liepāja, SW Latvia
118 *C12* **Priekulė** *Ger.* Prökuls. Klaipėda, W Lithuania
119 *F14* **Prienai** *Pol.* Preny. Kaunas, S Lithuania
83 *G23* **Prieska** Northern Cape, C South Africa
32 *M7* **Priest Lake** ⊞ Idaho, NW USA
32 *M7* **Priest River** Idaho, NW USA
104 *M3* **Prieta, Peña** ▲ N Spain
40 *J10* **Prieto, Cerro** ▲ C Mexico
111 *J19* **Prievidza** *var.* Priewitz, *Ger.* Priwitz, *Hung.* Privigye. Trenčiansky Kraj, C Slovakia
Priewitz *see* Prievidza
112 *F10* **Prijedor** Republika Srpska, NW Bosnia & Herzegovina
113 *K14* **Prijepolje** Serbia, W Serbia and Montenegro (Yugo.)
Prikaspiyskaya Nizmennost' *see* Caspian Depression
113 *O19* **Prilep** *Turk.* Perlepe. S FYR Macedonia
108 *B9* **Prilly** Vaud, SW Switzerland
Priluki *see* Pryluky
62 *L10* **Primero, Río** ≈ C Argentina
29 *S12* **Primghar** Iowa, C USA
112 *B9* **Primorje-Gorski Kotar** *off.* Primorsko-Goranska Županija. ◐ *province* NW Croatia
118 *A13* **Primorsk** *Ger.* Fischhausen. Kaliningradskaya Oblast', W Russian Federation
124 *G12* **Primorsk** *Fin.* Koivisto. Leningradskaya Oblast', NW Russian Federation
Primorsk/Primorskoye *see* Prymors'k
123 *S14* **Primorskiy Kray** *prev. Eng.* Maritime Territory. ◐ *territory* SE Russian Federation
114 *N10* **Primorsko** *prev.* Keupriya. Burgas, E Bulgaria
126 *K13* **Primorsko-Akhtarsk** Krasnodarskiy Kray, SW Russian Federation
117 *U13* **Primors'kyy** Respublika Krym, S Ukraine
113 *D14* **Primošten** Šibenik-Knin, S Croatia
11 *R13* **Primrose Lake** ◎ Saskatchewan, C Canada
11 *T14* **Prince Albert** Saskatchewan, S Canada
83 *G25* **Prince Albert** Western Cape, SW South Africa
8 *J5* **Prince Albert Peninsula** *peninsula* Victoria Island, Northwest Territories, NW Canada
8 *J6* **Prince Albert Sound** *inlet* Northwest Territories, N Canada
8 *J5* **Prince Alfred, Cape** *headland* Northwest Territories, NW Canada
9 *P6* **Prince Charles Island** *island* Nunavut, NE Canada
195 *W6* **Prince Charles Mountains** ▲ Antarctica
Prince-Édouard, Île-du *see* Prince Edward Island
172 *M13* **Prince Edward Fracture Zone** *tectonic feature* SW Indian Ocean
13 *P14* **Prince Edward Island** *Fr.* Île-du Prince-Édouard. ◐ *province* SE Canada
13 *Q14* **Prince Edward Island** *Fr.* Île-du Prince-Édouard. *island* SE Canada
173 *M12* **Prince Edward Islands** *island group* S South Africa
21 *X4* **Prince Frederick** Maryland, NE USA
10 *M14* **Prince George** British Columbia, SW Canada
21 *W6* **Prince George** Virginia, NE USA
8 *L3* **Prince Gustaf Adolf Sea** *sea* Nunavut, N Canada
197 *Q3* **Prince of Wales, Cape** *headland* Alaska, USA
9 *N3* **Prince of Wales Icefield** *ice feature* Nunavut, N Canada
181 *V1* **Prince of Wales Island** *island* Queensland, E Australia
8 *L5* **Prince of Wales Island** *island* Queen Elizabeth Islands, Nunavut, NW Canada
39 *Y14* **Prince of Wales Island** *island* Alexander Archipelago, Alaska, USA
Prince of Wales Island *see* Pinang, Pulau
8 *J5* **Prince of Wales Strait** *strait* Northwest Territories, N Canada
8 *K4* **Prince Patrick Island** *island* Parry Islands, Northwest Territories, NW Canada
9 *N5* **Prince Regent Inlet** *channel* Nunavut, N Canada
10 *J13* **Prince Rupert** British Columbia, SW Canada
Prince's Island *see* Príncipe
21 *Y5* **Princess Anne** Maryland, NE USA
195 *R1* **Princess Astrid Kyst** *physical region* Antarctica
181 *W2* **Princess Charlotte Bay** *bay* Queensland, NE Australia
195 *W7* **Princess Elizabeth Land** *physical region* Antarctica
10 *J14* **Princess Royal Island** *island* British Columbia, SW Canada
45 *U15* **Princes Town** Trinidad, Trinidad and Tobago
11 *N17* **Princeton** British Columbia, SW Canada
30 *L11* **Princeton** Illinois, N USA
31 *N16* **Princeton** Indiana, N USA
29 *Z14* **Princeton** Iowa, C USA
20 *H7* **Princeton** Kentucky, S USA
29 *V8* **Princeton** Minnesota, N USA
27 *S1* **Princeton** Missouri, C USA
18 *J15* **Princeton** New Jersey, NE USA
21 *R6* **Princeton** West Virginia, NE USA
39 *S12* **Prince William Sound** *inlet* Alaska, USA
79 *C17* **Príncipe** *var.* Príncipe Island, *Eng.* Prince's Island. *island* N Sao Tome and Principe
Príncipe Island *see* Príncipe
32 *I13* **Prineville** Oregon, NW USA
28 *J11* **Pringle** South Dakota, N USA
25 *N1* **Pringle** Texas, SW USA
99 *H14* **Prinsenbeek** Noord-Brabant, S Netherlands
98 *L6* **Prinses Margriet Kanaal** *canal* N Netherlands
195 *T2* **Prinsesse Ragnhild Kyst** *physical region* Antarctica
195 *U2* **Prins Harald Kyst** *physical region* Antarctica
92 *N2* **Prins Karls Forland** *island* W Svalbard
43 *N8* **Prinzapolka** Región Autónoma Atlántico Norte, NE Nicaragua
42 *L8* **Prinzapolka, Río** ≈ NE Nicaragua
122 *H9* **Priob'ye** Khanty-Mansiyskiy Avtonomnyy Okrug, N Russian Federation
104 *H1* **Prior, Cabo** *headland* NW Spain
29 *V9* **Prior Lake** Minnesota, N USA
124 *H11* **Priozersk** *Fin.* Käkisalmi. Leningradskaya Oblast', NW Russian Federation
119 *J20* **Pripet** *Bel.* Prypyats', *Ukr.* Pryp"yat'. ≈ Belarus/Ukraine
119 *J20* **Pripet Marshes** *wetland* Belarus/Ukraine
Prishtinë *see* Priština
126 *J8* **Pristen'** Kurskaya Oblast', W Russian Federation
113 *N16* **Priština** *Alb.* Prishtinë. Serbia, S Serbia and Montenegro (Yugo.)
100 *M10* **Pritzwalk** Brandenburg, NE Germany
103 *R13* **Privas** Ardèche, E France
107 *I16* **Priverno** Lazio, C Italy
Privigye *see* Prievidza
112 *C12* **Privlaka** Zadar, SW Croatia
124 *M15* **Privolzhsk** Ivanovskaya Oblast', NW Russian Federation
127 *P7* **Privolzhskaya Vozvyshennost'** *var.* Volga Uplands. ▲ W Russian Federation
127 *P8* **Privolzhskoye** Saratovskaya Oblast', W Russian Federation
Priwitz *see* Prievidza
127 *N13* **Priyutnoye** Respublika Kalmykiya, SW Russian Federation
113 *M17* **Prizren** *Alb.* Prizreni. Serbia, S Serbia and Montenegro (Yugo.)
Prizreni *see* Prizren
107 *I24* **Prizzi** Sicilia, Italy, C Mediterranean Sea
113 *P18* **Probištip** NE FYR Macedonia
169 *S16* **Probolinggo** Jawa, C Indonesia
Probstberg *see* Wyszków
111 *F14* **Prochowice** *Ger.* Parchwitz. Dolnośląskie, SW Poland
29 *W5* **Proctor** Minnesota, N USA
25 *R8* **Proctor** Texas, SW USA
25 *R8* **Proctor Lake** ⊞ Texas, SW USA
155 *I18* **Proddatūr** Andhra Pradesh, E India
104 *H9* **Proença-a-Nova** Castelo Branco, C Portugal
95 *I24* **Præstø** Storstrøm, SE Denmark
99 *I21* **Profondeville** Namur, SE Belgium
41 *W11* **Progreso** Yucatán, SE Mexico
123 *R14* **Progress** Amurskaya Oblast', SE Russian Federation
127 *O15* **Prokhladnyy** Kabardino-Balkarskaya Respublika, SW Russian Federation
Prokletije *see* North Albanian Alps
Prökuls *see* Priekulė
113 *O15* **Prokuplje** Serbia, SE Serbia and Montenegro (Yugo.)
124 *H14* **Proletariy** Novgorodskaya Oblast', W Russian Federation
126 *M12* **Proletarsk** Rostovskaya Oblast', SW Russian Federation
126 *J8* **Proletarskiy** Belgorodskaya Oblast', W Russian Federation
166 *L7* **Prome** *var.* Pyè. Pegu, C Burma
60 *J8* **Promissão** São Paulo, S Brazil
60 *J8* **Promissão, Represa de** ⊞ S Brazil
125 *V4* **Promyshlennyy** Respublika Komi, NW Russian Federation
119 *O16* **Pronya** *Rus.* Pronya. ≈ E Belarus
10 *M11* **Prophet River** British Columbia, W Canada
30 *K11* **Prophetstown** Illinois, N USA
59 *P16* **Propriá** Sergipe, E Brazil
103 *X16* **Propriano** Corse, France, C Mediterranean Sea
Prościejów *see* Prostějov
Proskurov *see* Khmel 'nyts'kyy
114 *H12* **Prosotsáni** Anatolikí Makedonía kai Thráki, NE Greece
171 *Q7* **Prosperidad** Mindanao, S Philippines
32 *J10* **Prosser** Washington, NW USA
Prossnitz *see* Prostějov
111 *G18* **Prostějov** *Ger.* Prossnitz, *Pol.* Prościejów. Olomoucký Kraj, E Czech Republic
117 *V8* **Prosyana** Dnipropetrovs'ka Oblast', E Ukraine
111 *L16* **Proszowice** Małopolskie, S Poland
Protasy *see* Pratasy
172 *J11* **Protea Seamount** *undersea feature* SW Indian Ocean
115 *D21* **Próti** *island* S Greece
114 *N8* **Provadiya** Varna, E Bulgaria
103 *S15* **Provence** *prev.* Marseille-Marignane. ✕ (Marseille) Bouches-du-Rhône, SE France
103 *T14* **Provence** *cultural region* SE France
103 *T14* **Provence-Alpes-Côte d'Azur** ◐ *region* SE France
20 *H6* **Providence** Kentucky, S USA
19 *N12* **Providence** *state capital* Rhode Island, NE USA
36 *L1* **Providence** Utah, W USA
Providence *see* Fort Providence
14 *D12* **Providence Bay** Manitoulin Island, Ontario, S Canada
23 *R6* **Providence Canyon** *valley* Alabama/Georgia, S USA
22 *I5* **Providence, Lake** ◎ Louisiana, S USA
35 *X13* **Providence Mountains** ▲ California, W USA
44 *L6* **Providenciales** *island* W Turks and Caicos Islands
19 *Q12* **Provincetown** Massachusetts, NE USA
103 *P5* **Provins** Seine-et-Marne, N France
36 *L3* **Provo** Utah, W USA
11 *R15* **Provost** Alberta, SW Canada
112 *G13* **Prozor** Federacija Bosna I Hercegovina, SE Bosnia & Herzegovina
Prozoroki *see* Prazaroki
60 *I11* **Prudentópolis** Paraná, S Brazil
39 *R5* **Prudhoe Bay** Alaska, USA
39 *R4* **Prudhoe Bay** *bay* Alaska, USA
111 *H16* **Prudnik** *Ger.* Neustadt, Neustadt in Oberschlesien. Opolskie, S Poland

◆ Country ◇ Dependent Territory ◐ Administrative Region ▲ Mountain ⩕ Volcano ◎ Lake
● Country Capital ○ Dependent Territory Capital ✕ International Airport ▲ Mountain Range ≈ River ⊞ Reservoir

119 J16 **Prudy** Rus. Prudy. Minskaya Voblasts', C Belarus
101 D18 **Prüm** Rheinland-Pfalz, W Germany
101 D18 **Prüm** ≈ W Germany
Prusa see Bursa
110 J7 **Pruszcz Gdański** Ger. Praust. Pomorskie, N Poland
110 M12 **Pruszków** Ger. Kaltdorf. Mazowieckie, C Poland
116 K8 **Prut** Ger. Pruth. ≈ E Europe
Pruth see Prut
108 L8 **Prutz** Tirol, W Austria
Pružana see Pruzhany
119 G19 **Pruzhany** Pol. Prużana. Brestskaya Voblasts', SW Belarus
124 I11 **Pryazha** Respublika Kareliya, NW Russian Federation
117 U10 **Pryazovs'ke** Zaporiz'ka Oblast', SE Ukraine
Prychornomors'ka Nyzovyna see Black Sea Lowland
Prydniprovs'ka Nyzovyna/Prydnyaprowskaya Nizina see Dnieper Lowland
195 Y7 **Prydz Bay** bay Antarctica
117 R4 **Pryluky** Rus. Priluki. Chernihivs'ka Oblast', NE Ukraine
117 V10 **Prymors'k** Rus. Primorsk; prev. Primorskoye. Zaporiz'ka Oblast', SE Ukraine
27 Q9 **Pryor** Oklahoma, C USA
33 U11 **Pryor Creek** ≈ Montana, NW USA
Pryp"yat'/Prypyats' see Pripet
110 M10 **Przasnysz** Mazowieckie, C Poland
111 K14 **Przedbórz** Łodzkie, S Poland
111 P17 **Przemyśl** Rus. Peremyshl. Podkarpackie, SE Poland
111 O16 **Przeworsk** Podkarpackie, SE Poland
Przheval'sk see Karakol
110 L13 **Przysucha** Mazowieckie, SE Poland
115 H18 **Psachná** var. Psahna, Psakhná. Évvoia, C Greece
Psahna/Psakhná see Psachná
115 K18 **Psará** island E Greece
115 I16 **Psathoúra** island Vóreioi Sporádes, Greece, Aegean Sea
Pschestitz see Přeštice
Psein Lora see Pishin Lora
117 S5 **Psël** ≈ Russian Federation/Ukraine
115 M21 **Psérimos** island Dodekánisos, Greece, Aegean Sea
Pseyn Bowr see Pishin Lora
Pskem see Piskom
147 R8 **Pskemskiy Khrebet** Uzb. Piskom Tizmasi. ⛰ Kyrgyzstan/Uzbekistan
124 F14 **Pskov** Ger. Pleskau, Latv. Pleskava. Pskovskaya Oblast', W Russian Federation
118 K6 **Pskov, Lake** Est. Pihkva Järv, Ger. Pleskauer See, Rus. Pskovskoye Ozero. ◎ Estonia/Russian Federation
124 F15 **Pskovskaya Oblast'** ◈ province W Russian Federation
Pskovskoye Ozero see Pskov, Lake
112 G9 **Psunj** ⛰ NE Croatia
111 J17 **Pszczyna** Ger. Pless. Śląskie, S Poland
Ptačnik/Ptacsnik see Vtáčnik
115 D17 **Ptéri** ▲ C Greece
Ptich' see Ptsich
115 E14 **Ptolemaïda** prev. Ptolemaïs. Dytikí Makedonía, N Greece
Ptolemaïs see Ptolemaïda, Greece
Ptolemaïs see 'Akko, Israel
119 M19 **Ptsich** Rus. Ptich'. Homyel'skaya Voblasts', SE Belarus
119 M18 **Ptsich** Rus. Ptich'. ≈ SE Belarus
109 X10 **Ptuj** Ger. Pettau; anc. Poetovio. NE Slovenia
61 A23 **Puán** Buenos Aires, E Argentina
192 H15 **Pu'apu'a** Savai'i, C Samoa
192 G15 **Puava, Cape** headland Savai'i, NW Samoa
56 F12 **Pucallpa** Ucayali, C Peru
57 J17 **Pucarani** La Paz, NW Bolivia
Pučarevo see Novi Travnik
157 U12 **Pucheng** var. Nanpu. Fujian, SE China
160 L6 **Pucheng** Shaanxi, C China
125 N16 **Puchezh** Ivanovskaya Oblast', W Russian Federation
111 I19 **Púchov** Hung. Puhó. Trenčiansky Kraj, W Slovakia
116 J13 **Pucioasa** Dâmbovița, S Romania
110 I6 **Puck** Pomorskie, N Poland
30 L8 **Puckaway Lake** ◎ Wisconsin, N USA
63 G15 **Pucón** Araucanía, S Chile
93 M14 **Pudasjärvi** Oulu, C Finland
148 L8 **Püdeh Tal, Shelleh-ye** ≈ SW Afghanistan
127 S1 **Pudem** Udmurtskaya Respublika, NW Russian Federation
Pudewitz see Pobiedziska
124 K11 **Pudozh** Respublika Kareliya, NW Russian Federation
97 M17 **Pudsey** N England, UK
Puduchcheri see Pondicherry
151 H21 **Pudukkottai** Tamil Nādu, SE India
171 Z13 **Pue** Papua, E Indonesia
41 P14 **Puebla** var. Puebla de Zaragoza. Puebla, S Mexico
41 P15 **Puebla** ◈ state S Mexico
104 L11 **Puebla de Alcocer** Extremadura, W Spain
Puebla de Don Fabrique see Puebla de Don Fadrique
105 P13 **Puebla de Don Fadrique** var. Puebla de Don Fabrique. Andalucía, S Spain
104 J11 **Puebla de la Calzada** Extremadura, W Spain
104 J5 **Puebla de Sanabria** Castilla-León, N Spain
104 I4 **Puebla de Trives** see A Pobla de Trives
Puebla de Zaragoza see Puebla
37 T6 **Pueblo** Colorado, C USA
37 N10 **Pueblo Colorado Wash** valley Arizona, SW USA
61 C16 **Pueblo Libertador** Corrientes, NE Argentina
40 J10 **Pueblo Nuevo** Durango, C Mexico
42 J8 **Pueblo Nuevo** Estelí, NW Nicaragua
54 J3 **Pueblo Nuevo** Falcón, N Venezuela
42 B6 **Pueblo Nuevo Tiquisate** var. Tiquisate. Escuintla, SW Guatemala
41 Q11 **Pueblo Viejo, Laguna de** lagoon E Mexico
63 J14 **Puelches** La Pampa, C Argentina
104 L14 **Puente-Genil** Andalucía, S Spain
105 Q3 **Puente la Reina** Bas. Gares. Navarra, N Spain
104 L12 **Puente Nuevo, Embalse de** ⊡ S Spain
57 D14 **Puente Piedra** Lima, W Peru
160 F14 **Pu'er** var. Ning'er. Yunnan, SW China
45 V6 **Puerca, Punta** headland E Puerto Rico
37 R12 **Puerco, Rio** ≈ New Mexico, SW USA
57 J17 **Puerto Acosta** La Paz, W Bolivia
63 G19 **Puerto Aisén** Aisén, S Chile
41 R17 **Puerto Ángel** Oaxaca, SE Mexico
Puerto Argentino see Stanley
41 T17 **Puerto Arista** Chiapas, SE Mexico
43 O16 **Puerto Armuelles** Chiriquí, SW Panama
Puerto Arrecife see Arrecife
54 D14 **Puerto Asís** Putumayo, SW Colombia
54 L9 **Puerto Ayacucho** Amazonas, SW Venezuela
57 C18 **Puerto Ayora** Galapagos Islands, Ecuador, E Pacific Ocean
57 C18 **Puerto Baquerizo Moreno** var. Baquerizo Moreno. Galapagos Islands, Ecuador, E Pacific Ocean
42 G4 **Puerto Barrios** Izabal, E Guatemala
Puerto Bello see Portobelo
54 F8 **Puerto Berrío** Antioquia, C Colombia
54 F9 **Puerto Boyaca** Boyacá, C Colombia
54 K4 **Puerto Cabello** Carabobo, N Venezuela
43 N7 **Puerto Cabezas** var. Bilwi. Región Autónoma Atlántico Norte, NE Nicaragua
54 L9 **Puerto Carreño** Vichada, E Colombia
54 E4 **Puerto Colombia** Atlántico, N Colombia
42 H4 **Puerto Cortés** Cortés, NW Honduras
54 J4 **Puerto Cumarebo** Falcón, N Venezuela
Puerto de Cabras see Puerto del Rosario
55 Q5 **Puerto de Hierro** Sucre, NE Venezuela
64 O11 **Puerto de la Cruz** Tenerife, Islas Canarias, Spain, NE Atlantic Ocean
64 Q11 **Puerto del Rosario** var. Puerto de Cabras. Fuerteventura, Islas Canarias, Spain, NE Atlantic Ocean
63 J20 **Puerto Deseado** Santa Cruz, SE Argentina
40 F8 **Puerto Escondido** Baja California Sur, W Mexico
41 R17 **Puerto Escondido** Oaxaca, SE Mexico
60 G12 **Puerto Esperanza** Misiones, NE Argentina
56 D6 **Puerto Francisco de Orellana** var. Coca. Orellana, N Ecuador
54 H10 **Puerto Gaitán** Meta, C Colombia
Puerto Gallegos see Río Gallegos
60 G12 **Puerto Iguazú** Misiones, NE Argentina
56 F12 **Puerto Inca** Huánuco, N Peru
54 L11 **Puerto Inírida** var. Obando. Guainía, E Colombia
42 K13 **Puerto Jesús** Guanacaste, NW Costa Rica
41 Z11 **Puerto Juárez** Quintana Roo, SE Mexico
55 N5 **Puerto La Cruz** Anzoátegui, NE Venezuela
54 E14 **Puerto Leguízamo** Putumayo, S Colombia
43 N5 **Puerto Lempira** Gracias a Dios, E Honduras
Puerto Libertad see La Libertad
54 I11 **Puerto Limón** Meta, E Colombia
54 D13 **Puerto Limón** Putumayo, SW Colombia
Puerto Limón see Limón
105 N11 **Puertollano** Castilla-La Mancha, C Spain
63 K17 **Puerto Lobos** Chubut, SE Argentina
54 I3 **Puerto López** La Guajira, N Colombia
105 Q14 **Puerto Lumbreras** Murcia, SE Spain
41 V17 **Puerto Madero** Chiapas, SE Mexico
63 K17 **Puerto Madryn** Chubut, S Argentina
Puerto Magdalena see Bahía Magdalena
57 J15 **Puerto Maldonado** Madre de Dios, E Peru
Puerto Masachapa see Masachapa
Puerto México see Coatzacoalcos
63 G17 **Puerto Montt** Los Lagos, C Chile
41 Z12 **Puerto Morelos** Quintana Roo, SE Mexico
54 L10 **Puerto Nariño** Vichada, E Colombia
63 H23 **Puerto Natales** Magallanes, S Chile
43 X15 **Puerto Obaldía** San Blas, NE Panama
44 H6 **Puerto Padre** Las Tunas, E Cuba
54 L9 **Puerto Páez** Apure, C Venezuela
40 E3 **Puerto Peñasco** Sonora, NW Mexico
55 N5 **Puerto Píritu** Anzoátegui, NE Venezuela
45 N8 **Puerto Plata** var. San Felipe de Puerto Plata. N Dominican Republic
45 N8 **Puerto Plata** ✕ N Dominican Republic
Puerto Presidente Stroessner see Ciudad del Este
171 N6 **Puerto Princesa** off. Puerto Princesa City. Palawan, W Philippines
Puerto Princesa City see Puerto Princesa
Puerto Príncipe see Camagüey
Puerto Quellón see Quellón
60 F13 **Puerto Rico** Misiones, NE Argentina
57 K14 **Puerto Rico** Pando, N Bolivia
54 E12 **Puerto Rico** Caquetá, S Colombia
45 U5 **Puerto Rico** off. Commonwealth of Puerto Rico; prev. Porto Rico. ◇ US commonwealth territory C West Indies
64 F11 **Puerto Rico** island C West Indies
64 G11 **Puerto Rico Trench** undersea feature NE Caribbean Sea
54 I8 **Puerto Rondón** Arauca, E Colombia
Puerto San José see San José
63 J21 **Puerto San Julián** var. San Julián. Santa Cruz, SE Argentina
63 I22 **Puerto Santa Cruz** var. Santa Cruz. Santa Cruz, SE Argentina
Puerto Sauce see Juan L.Lacaze
57 Q20 **Puerto Suárez** Santa Cruz, E Bolivia
54 D13 **Puerto Umbría** Putumayo, SW Colombia
40 J13 **Puerto Vallarta** Jalisco, SW Mexico
63 G16 **Puerto Varas** Los Lagos, C Chile
42 M13 **Puerto Viejo** Heredia, NE Costa Rica
Puertoviejo see Portoviejo
57 B18 **Puerto Villamil** var. Villamil. Galapagos Islands, Ecuador, E Pacific Ocean
54 F8 **Puerto Wilches** Santander, N Colombia
63 H20 **Pueyrredón, Lago** var. Lago Cochrane. ◎ S Argentina
127 R7 **Pugachëv** Saratovskaya Oblast', W Russian Federation
127 T3 **Pugachëvo** Udmurtskaya Respublika, NW Russian Federation
32 H8 **Puget Sound** sound Washington, NW USA
107 O17 **Puglia** var. Le Puglie, Eng. Apulia. ◈ region SE Italy
107 N17 **Puglia, Canosa di** anc. Canusium. Puglia, SE Italy
118 I6 **Puhja** Ger. Kawelecht. Tartumaa, SE Estonia
Puhó see Púchov
105 V4 **Puigcerdà** Cataluña, NE Spain
Puigmal see Puigmal d'Err
103 N17 **Puigmal d'Err** var. Puigmal. ▲ S France
76 I16 **Pujehun** S Sierra Leone
Puka see Pukë
185 E20 **Pukaki, Lake** ◎ South Island, NZ
38 F10 **Pukalani** Maui, Hawai'i, USA, C Pacific Ocean
190 J13 **Pukapuka** atoll N Cook Islands
191 X9 **Pukapuka** atoll Îles Tuamotu, E French Polynesia
Pukari Neem see Purekkari Neem
191 X11 **Pukarua** var. Pukaruha. atoll Îles Tuamotu, E French Polynesia
Pukaruha see Pukarua
14 A7 **Pukaskwa** ≈ Ontario, S Canada
11 V12 **Pukatawagan** Manitoba, C Canada
191 X16 **Pukatikei, Maunga** ☒ Easter Island, Chile, E Pacific Ocean
182 C1 **Pukatja** var. Ernabella. South Australia
163 Y12 **Pukch'ŏng** E North Korea
113 L18 **Pukë** var. Puka. Shkodër, N Albania
184 L6 **Pukekohe** Auckland, North Island, NZ
184 L7 **Pukemiro** Waikato, North Island, NZ
190 D12 **Puke, Mont** ▲ Île Futuna, W Wallis and Futuna
Puket see Phuket
185 C20 **Puketeraki Range** ⛰ South Island, NZ
184 N13 **Puketoi Range** ⛰ North Island, NZ
185 F21 **Pukeuri Junction** Otago, South Island, NZ
119 L16 **Pukhavichy** Rus. Pukhovichi. Minskaya Voblasts', C Belarus
Pukhovichi see Pukhavichy
124 M10 **Puksoozero** Arkhangel'skaya Oblast', NW Russian Federation
112 A10 **Pula** It. Pola; prev. Pulj. Istra, NW Croatia
Pula see Nyingchi
163 U14 **Pulandian** var. Xinjin. Liaoning, NE China
163 T14 **Pulandian Wan** bay NE China
189 O15 **Pulap Atoll** atoll Caroline Islands, C Micronesia
18 H9 **Pulaski** New York, NE USA
20 I10 **Pulaski** Tennessee, S USA
21 R7 **Pulaski** Virginia, NE USA
171 Y14 **Pulau, Sungai** ≈ Papua, E Indonesia
110 N13 **Puławy** Ger. Neu Amerika. Lubelskie, E Poland
146 I16 **Pulhatyn** Rus. Polekhatum; prev. Pul'-I-Khatum. Ahal Welaýaty, S Turkmenistan
101 E16 **Pulheim** Nordrhein-Westfalen, W Germany
Pulicat see Pālghāt
155 J19 **Pulicat Lake** lagoon SE India
Pul'-I-Khatum see Pulhatyn
Pul-i-Khumri see Pol-e Khomrī
Pul-i-Sefid see Pol-e Safid
Pulj see Pula
109 W2 **Pulkau** ≈ NE Austria
93 L15 **Pulkkila** Oulu, C Finland
122 C7 **Pul'kovo** ✕ (Sankt-Peterburg) Leningradskaya Oblast', NW Russian Federation
32 M9 **Pullman** Washington, NW USA
108 B10 **Pully** Vaud, SW Switzerland
40 F7 **Púlpita, Punta** headland W Mexico
110 M10 **Pułtusk** Mazowieckie, C Poland
158 H10 **Pulu** Xinjiang Uygur Zizhiqu, W China
137 P13 **Pülümür** Tunceli, E Turkey
189 N16 **Pulusuk** island Caroline Islands, C Micronesia
189 N16 **Puluwat Atoll** atoll Caroline Islands, C Micronesia
25 N11 **Pumpville** Texas, SW USA
191 P7 **Punaauia** var. Hakapehi. Tahiti, W French Polynesia
56 B8 **Puná, Isla** island SW Ecuador
185 G16 **Punakaiki** West Coast, South Island, NZ
153 T11 **Punakha** C Bhutan
57 L18 **Punata** Cochabamba, C Bolivia
155 E14 **Pune** prev. Poona. Mahārāshtra, W India
83 M17 **Pungoè, Rio** var. Púnguè, Pungwe. ≈ C Mozambique
21 X10 **Pungo River** ≈ North Carolina, SE USA
Púnguè/Pungwe see Pungoè, Rio
79 N19 **Punia** Maniema, E Dem. Rep. Congo
62 H8 **Punilla, Sierra de la** ⛰ W Argentina
161 P14 **Puning** Guangdong, S China
62 G10 **Punitaqui** Coquimbo, C Chile
152 H8 **Punjab** ◈ state NW India
149 T9 **Punjab** prev. West Punjab, Western Punjab. ◈ province E Pakistan
93 O17 **Punkaharju** var. Punkasalmi. Isä-Suomi, E Finland
Punkasalmi see Punkaharju
57 I17 **Puno** Puno, SE Peru
57 H17 **Puno** off. Departamento de Puno. ◈ department S Peru
61 B24 **Punta Alta** Buenos Aires, E Argentina
63 H24 **Punta Arenas** prev. Magallanes. Magallanes, S Chile
45 T6 **Punta, Cerro de** ▲ C Puerto Rico
43 T15 **Punta Chame** Panamá, C Panama
57 G17 **Punta Colorada** Arequipa, SW Peru
40 F9 **Punta Coyote** Baja California Sur, W Mexico
62 G8 **Punta de Díaz** Atacama, N Chile
61 G20 **Punta del Este** Maldonado, S Uruguay
63 K17 **Punta Delgada** Chubut, SE Argentina
55 O5 **Punta de Mata** Monagas, NE Venezuela
55 O4 **Punta de Piedras** Nueva Esparta, NE Venezuela
42 F4 **Punta Gorda** Toledo, SE Belize
43 N11 **Punta Gorda** Región Autónoma Atlántico Sur, SE Nicaragua
23 W14 **Punta Gorda** Florida, SE USA
42 M11 **Punta Gorda, Río** ≈ SE Nicaragua
62 H6 **Punta Negra, Salar de** salt lake N Chile
40 D5 **Punta Prieta** Baja California, NW Mexico
42 L13 **Puntarenas** Puntarenas, W Costa Rica
42 L13 **Puntarenas** off. Provincia de Puntarenas. ◈ province W Costa Rica
54 J4 **Punto Fijo** Falcón, N Venezuela
105 S4 **Puntón de Guara** ▲ N Spain
18 D14 **Punxsutawney** Pennsylvania, NE USA
93 M14 **Puolanka** Oulu, C Finland
57 J17 **Pupuya, Nevado** ▲ W Bolivia
Puqi see Chibi
57 F16 **Puquio** Ayacucho, S Peru
122 J9 **Pur** ≈ N Russian Federation
186 D7 **Purari** ≈ S PNG
27 N11 **Purcell** Oklahoma, C USA
11 O16 **Purcell Mountains** ⛰ British Columbia, SW Canada
105 P14 **Purchena** Andalucía, S Spain
27 S8 **Purdy** Missouri, C USA
118 I2 **Purekkari Neem** prev. Pukari Neem. headland N Estonia
37 U7 **Purgatoire River** ≈ Colorado, C USA
Purgstall see Purgstall an der Erlauf
109 V5 **Purgstall an der Erlauf** var. Purgstall. Niederösterreich, NE Austria
154 O13 **Puri** var. Jagannath. Orissa, E India
Puriramya see Buriram
109 X4 **Purkersdorf** Niederösterreich, NE Austria
98 I9 **Purmerend** Noord-Holland, C Netherlands
151 G16 **Pūrna** ≈ C India
Purnea see Pūrnia
153 R13 **Pūrnia** prev. Purnea. Bihār, NE India
Pursat see Poŭthĭsăt, Poŭthĭsăt, W Cambodia
Pursat see Poŭthĭsăt, Stœng, W Cambodia
Purulia see Puruliya
150 L13 **Puruliya** prev. Purulia. West Bengal, NE India
47 G7 **Purus, Rio** Sp. Río Purús. ≈ Brazil/Peru
186 C9 **Purutu Island** island SW PNG
93 N17 **Puruvesi** ◎ SE Finland
22 L7 **Purvis** Mississippi, S USA
114 J11 **Pŭrvomay** prev. Borisovgrad. Plovdiv, C Bulgaria
169 R16 **Purwodadi** prev. Poerwodadi. Jawa, C Indonesia
169 P16 **Purwokerto** prev. Poerwokerto. Jawa, C Indonesia
169 P16 **Purworejo** prev. Poerworedjo. Jawa, C Indonesia
20 H8 **Puryear** Tennessee, S USA
154 H13 **Pusad** Mahārāshtra, C India
163 Z16 **Pusan** off. Pusan-gwangyŏksi, var. Busan, Jap. Fusan. SE South Korea
168 H7 **Pusatgajo, Pegunungan** ⛰ Sumatera, NW Indonesia
Puschlav see Poschiavo
Pushkin see Tsarskoye Selo
127 Q8 **Pushkino** Saratovskaya Oblast', W Russian Federation
Pushkino see Biläsuvar
111 M22 **Püspökladány** Hajdú-Bihar, E Hungary
118 J3 **Püssi** Ger. Isenhof. Ida-Virumaa, NE Estonia
116 I5 **Pustomyty** L'vivs'ka Oblast', W Ukraine
124 F16 **Pustoshka** Pskovskaya Oblast', W Russian Federation
Pusztakalán see Călan
167 N1 **Putao** prev. Fort Hertz. Kachin State, N Burma
184 M8 **Putaruru** Waikato, North Island, NZ
Puteoli see Pozzuoli
161 R12 **Putian** Fujian, SE China
107 O17 **Putignano** Puglia, SE Italy
Puting see De'an
Putivl' see Putyvl'
41 Q16 **Putla** var. Putla de Guerrero. Oaxaca, SE Mexico
Putla de Guerrero see Putla
19 N12 **Putnam** Connecticut, NE USA
25 Q7 **Putnam** Texas, SW USA
18 M10 **Putney** Vermont, NE USA
111 L20 **Putnok** Borsod-Abaúj-Zemplén, NE Hungary
Putorana, Gory/Putorana Mountains see Putorana, Plato
122 L8 **Putorana, Plato** var. Gory Putorana, Eng. Putorana Mountains. ⛰ N Russian Federation
168 K9 **Putrajaya** ● (Malaysia), Kuala Lumpur, Peninsular Malaysia
62 H2 **Putre** Tarapacá, N Chile
155 J24 **Puttalam** North Western Province, W Sri Lanka
155 J24 **Puttalam Lagoon** lagoon W Sri Lanka
99 H17 **Putte** Antwerpen, C Belgium
94 E10 **Puttegga** ▲ S Norway
98 K11 **Putten** Gelderland, C Netherlands
100 K7 **Puttgarden** Schleswig-Holstein, N Germany
Puttiala see Patiāla
101 D20 **Püttlingen** Saarland, SW Germany
54 D14 **Putumayo** off. Intendencia del Putumayo. ◈ province S Colombia
56 H8 **Putumayo, Río** var. Rio Içá. ≈ NW South America see also Içá, Rio
169 P11 **Putus, Tanjung** headland Borneo, N Indonesia
116 J8 **Putyla** Chernivets'ka Oblast', W Ukraine
117 S3 **Putyvl'** Rus. Putivl'. Sums'ka Oblast', NE Ukraine
93 M18 **Puula** ◎ SE Finland
93 N18 **Puumala** Isä-Suomi, E Finland
118 I5 **Puurmani** Ger. Talkhof. Jõgevamaa, E Estonia
99 G17 **Puurs** Antwerpen, N Belgium
38 P10 **Pu'u 'Ula'ula** var. Red Hill. ▲ Maui, Hawai'i, USA, C Pacific Ocean
38 A8 **Pu'uwai** var. Puuwai. Ni'ihau, Hawai'i, USA, C Pacific Ocean
12 J4 **Puvirnituq** prev. Povungnituk. Québec, NE Canada
32 H8 **Puyallup** Washington, NW USA
161 O5 **Puyang** Henan, C China
161 R9 **Puyang Jiang** var. Tsien Tang. ≈ SE China
103 O11 **Puy-de-Dôme** ◈ department C France
103 N15 **Puylaurens** Tarn, S France
102 M13 **Puy-l'Evêque** Lot, S France
103 N17 **Puymorens, Col de** pass S France
56 C7 **Puyo** Pastaza, C Ecuador
185 A24 **Puysegur Point** headland South Island, NZ
148 J8 **Pūzak, Hāmūn-e** Pash. Hāmūn-i-Puzak. ◎ SW Afghanistan
Puzak, Hāmūn-i- see Pūzak, Hāmūn-e
81 J23 **Pwani** Eng. Coast. ◈ region E Tanzania
79 O23 **Pweto** Katanga, SE Dem. Rep. Congo
97 I19 **Pwllheli** NW Wales, UK
189 O14 **Pwok** Pohnpei, E Micronesia
122 I9 **Pyakupur** ≈ N Russian Federation
124 M6 **Pyalitsa** Murmanskaya Oblast', NW Russian Federation
124 K10 **Pyal'ma** Respublika Kareliya, NW Russian Federation
Pyandzh see Panj
126 I6 **Pyaozero, Ozero** ◎ NW Russian Federation
166 L9 **Pyapon** Irrawaddy, SW Burma
119 J15 **Pyarshai** Rus. Pershay. Minskaya Voblasts', C Belarus
122 K8 **Pyasina** ≈ N Russian Federation
114 I10 **Pyasŭchnik, Yazovir** ⊡ C Bulgaria
Pyatikhatki see P"yatykhatky
117 S7 **P"yatykhatky** Rus. Pyatikhatki. Dnipropetrovs'ka Oblast', E Ukraine
166 M6 **Pyawbwe** Mandalay, C Burma
127 T3 **Pychas** Udmurtskaya Respublika, NW Russian Federation
Pyè see Prome
166 K6 **Pyechin** Chin State, W Burma
119 G17 **Pyeski** Rus. Peski. Hrodzyenskaya Voblasts', W Belarus
119 L19 **Pyetrykaw** Rus. Petrikov. Homyel'skaya Voblasts', SE Belarus
93 M16 **Pyhajärvi** ◎ C Finland
93 O17 **Pyhäjärvi** ◎ SE Finland
93 L15 **Pyhäjoki** Oulu, W Finland
93 L15 **Pyhäjoki** ≈ W Finland
93 M15 **Pyhäntä** Oulu, C Finland
93 M16 **Pyhäsalmi** Oulu, C Finland
93 O17 **Pyhäselkä** ◎ SE Finland
93 M19 **Pyhtää** Swe. Pyttis. Etelä-Suomi, S Finland
166 M6 **Pyinmana** Mandalay, C Burma
115 N24 **Pylés** var. Piles. Kárpathos, SE Greece
115 D21 **Pýlos** var. Pilos. Pelopónnisos, S Greece
18 B12 **Pymatuning Reservoir** ⊡ Ohio/Pennsylvania, NE USA
163 X15 **P'yŏngt'aek** NW South Korea
163 V14 **P'yŏngyang** var. P'yŏngyang-si, Eng. Pyongyang. ● (North Korea) SW North Korea
P'yŏngyang-si see P'yŏngyang
35 Q4 **Pyramid Lake** ◎ Nevada, W USA
37 P15 **Pyramid Mountains** ⛰ New Mexico, SW USA
37 R5 **Pyramid Peak** ▲ Colorado, C USA
115 D17 **Pyramíva** var. Piramiva. ▲ C Greece
Pyrenaei Montes see Pyrenees
102 L17 **Pyrenees** Fr. Pyrénées, Sp. Pirineos; anc. Pyrenaei Montes. ⛰ SW Europe
102 J16 **Pyrénées-Atlantiques** ◈ department SW France
103 N17 **Pyrénées-Orientales** ◈ department S France
115 L19 **Pyrgí** var. Pirgi. Chíos, E Greece
115 D20 **Pýrgos** var. Pírgos. Dytikí Ellás, S Greece
Pyritz see Pyrzyce
115 E19 **Pýrros** ≈ S Greece
117 R4 **Pyryatyn** Rus. Piryatin. Poltavs'ka Oblast', NE Ukraine
110 D9 **Pyrzyce** Ger. Pyritz. Zachodnio-pomorskie, NW Poland
124 F15 **Pytalovo** Latv. Abrene; prev. Jaunlatgale. Pskovskaya Oblast', W Russian Federation
115 M20 **Pythagóreio** var. Pithagorio. Sámos, Dodekánisos, Greece, Aegean Sea
14 L11 **Pythonga, Lac** ◎ Québec, SE Canada
Pyttis see Pyhtää
166 M7 **Pyu** Pegu, C Burma
166 M8 **Pyuntaza** Pegu, SW Burma
153 N11 **Pyuthan** Mid Western, W Nepal
110 H12 **Pyzdry** Ger. Peisern. Wielkopolskie, C Poland

Q

138 H13 **Qā' al Jafr** ◎ S Jordan
197 O11 **Qaanaaq** var. Qânâq, Dan. Thule. Avannaarsua, N Greenland
138 G7 **Qabb Eliâs** E Lebanon
Qabil see Al Qābil
Qabırrı see Iori
Qābis see Gabès
Qābis, Khalīj see Gabès, Golfe de
Qabqa see Gonghe
141 S14 **Qabr Hūd** C Yemen
Qacentina see Constantine
148 L4 **Qādes** Bādghīs, NW Afghanistan
139 T11 **Qādisīyah** S Iraq
143 O4 **Qa'emshahr** prev. 'Alīābad, Shāhī. Māzandarān, N Iran
143 U7 **Qā'en** var. Qain, Qāyen. Khorāsān, E Iran
141 U13 **Qafa** spring/well SW Oman
Qafşah see Gafsa
163 Q12 **Qagan Nur** var. Xulun Hobot Qagan, Zhengxiangbai Qi. Nei Mongol Zizhiqu, N China
163 V9 **Qagan Nur** ◎ NE China
163 Q11 **Qagan Nur** ◎ N China
Qagan Us see Dulan

◆ Country ◇ Dependent Territory ◈ Administrative Region ▲ Mountain ☒ Volcano ◎ Lake
● Country Capital ○ Dependent Territory Capital ✕ International Airport ⛰ Mountain Range ≈ River ⊡ Reservoir

158 H13 **Qagcaka** Xizang Zizhiqu, W China
Qagcheng see Xiangcheng
Qahremānshahr see Kermānshāh
159 Q10 **Qaidam He** ≈ C China
156 L8 **Qaidam Pendi** basin C China
Qain see Qā'en
Qala Āhangarān see Chaghcharān
139 U3 **Qalā Diza** var. Qal 'at Dīzah. NE Iraq
Qal'ah Sālih see Qal'at Şāliḥ
147 R13 **Qal'aikhum** Rus. Kalaikhum. S Tajikistan
Qala Nau see Qal'eh-ye Now
141 V17 **Qalansīyah** Suquṭrā, W Yemen
Qala Panja see Qal'eh-ye Panjeh
Qala Shāhar see Qal'eh Shahr
Qalāt see Kalāt
139 W9 **Qal'at Aḥmad** E Iraq
141 N11 **Qal'at Bīshah** 'Asīr, SW Saudi Arabia
138 H4 **Qal'at Burzay** Ḥamāh, W Syria
Qal 'at Dīzah see Qalā Diza
139 W9 **Qal'at Ḥusayh** E Iraq
139 V10 **Qal'at Majnūnah** S Iraq
139 X11 **Qal'at Şāliḥ** var. Qal'ah Sālih. E Iraq
139 V10 **Qal'at Sukkar** SE Iraq
Qalba Zhotasy see Kalbinskiy Khrebet
143 Q12 **Qal'eh Biābān** Fārs, S Iran
149 N4 **Qal'eh Shahr** Pash. Qala Shāhar. Sar-e Pol, N Afghanistan
148 L4 **Qal'eh-ye Now** var. Qala Nau. Bādghīs, NW Afghanistan
149 T2 **Qal'eh-ye Panjeh** var. Qala Panja. Badakhshān, NE Afghanistan
Qamar Bay see Qamar, Ghubbat al
141 U14 **Qamar, Ghubbat al** Eng. Qamar Bay. bay Oman/Yemen
141 V13 **Qamar, Jabal al** ⛰ SW Oman
147 N12 **Qamashi** Qashqadaryo Viloyati, S Uzbekistan
Qambar see Kambar
159 R14 **Qamdo** Xizang Zizhiqu, W China
75 R7 **Qamīnis** NE Libya
Qamishly see Al Qāmishlī
Qânâq see Qaanaaq
Qandahār see Kandahār
80 Q11 **Qandala** Bari, NE Somalia
Qandyaghash see Kandyagash
138 L2 **Qanṭarī** Ar Raqqah, N Syria
Qapiciğ Dağı see Qazangödağ
158 H5 **Qapqal** var. Qapqal Xibe Zizhixian. Xinjiang Uygur Zizhiqu, NW China
Qapqal Xibe Zizhixian see Qapqal
Qapshagay Böyeni see Kapchagayskoye Vodokhranilishche
Qaptugang see Zadoi
196 M15 **Qaqortoq** Dan. Julianehåb. Kitaa, S Greenland
75 U8 **Qâra** var. Qārah. NW Egypt
139 T4 **Qara Anjīr** N Iraq
Qarabāgh see Qarah Bāgh
Qaraböget see Karaboget
Qarabulaq see Karabulak
Qarabutaq see Karabutak
Qaraghandy/Qaraghandy Oblysy see Karaganda
Qaraghayly see Karagayly
139 U4 **Qara Gol** NE Iraq
Qārah see Qâra
148 J4 **Qarah Bāgh** var. Qarabāgh. Herāt, NW Afghanistan
138 G7 **Qaraoun, Lac de** var. Buḥayrat al Qir'awn. ◎ S Lebanon
Qaraoy see Karaoy
Qaraqoyyn see Karakoyyn, Ozero
Qara Qum see Garagum
Qarasū see Karasu
Qaratal see Karatal
Qarataū see Karatau, Khrebet, Kazakhstan
Qarataū see Karatau, Zhambyl, Kazakhstan
Qaraton see Karaton
80 P13 **Qardho** var. Kardh, It. Gardo. Bari, N Somalia
142 M6 **Qareh Chāy** ≈ N Iran
142 K2 **Qareh Sū** ≈ NW Iran
Qariateïne see Al Qaryatayn
Qarkilik see Ruoqiang
147 O13 **Qarluq** Rus. Karluk. Surxondaryo Viloyati, S Uzbekistan
147 U12 **Qarokŭl** Rus. Karakul'. E Tajikistan
147 T12 **Qarokŭl** Rus. Ozero Karakul'. ◎ E Tajikistan
Qarqan see Qiemo
158 K9 **Qarqan He** ≈ NW China
Qarqannah, Juzur see Kerkenah, Îles de
Qarqaraly see Karkaralinsk
149 O1 **Qarqīn** Jowzjān, N Afghanistan
Qars see Kars
Qarsaqbay see Karsakpay
146 M12 **Qarshi** Rus. Karshi; prev. Bek-Budi. Qashqadaryo Viloyati, S Uzbekistan
146 L12 **Qarshi Cho'li** Rus. Karshinskaya Step. grassland S Uzbekistan
146 M13 **Qarshi Kanali** Rus. Karshinskiy Kanal. canal Turkmenistan/Uzbekistan
Qaryatayn see Al Qaryatayn
146 M12 **Qashqadaryo Viloyati** Rus. Kashkadar'inskaya Oblast'. ⬖ province S Uzbekistan
Qasigianguit see Qasigiannguit
197 N13 **Qasigiannguit** var. Qasigianguit, Dan. Christianshåb. Kitaa, C Greenland
Qaşim, Minṭaqat see Al Qaşīm
139 P8 **Qaşr 'Amij** C Iraq
139 R9 **Qaşr Darwīshāh** C Iraq
142 J6 **Qaşr-e Shīrīn** Kermānshāh, W Iran
75 V10 **Qasr Farâfra** W Egypt
Qassim see Al Qaşīm
141 O16 **Qa'ṭabah** SW Yemen
138 H7 **Qaṭanā** var. Katana. Dimashq, S Syria
143 N15 **Qatar** off. State of Qatar, Ar. Dawlat Qaṭar. ◆ monarchy SW Asia
Qatrana see Al Qaṭrānah
143 Q12 **Qaṭrūyeh** Fārs, S Iran
Qattara Depression/Qaṭṭārah, Munkhafaḍ al see Qaṭṭâra, Monkhafad el
75 U8 **Qaṭṭâra, Monkhafad el** var. Munkhafaḍ al Qaṭṭārah, Eng. Qattara Depression. desert NW Egypt
Qaṭṭīnah, Buḥayrat see Ḥimṣ, Buḥayrat
Qaydār see Qeydār
Qāyen see Qā'en
147 Q11 **Qayroqqum** Rus. Kayrakkum. NW Tajikistan
147 Q10 **Qayroqqum, Obanbori** Rus. Kayrakkumskoye Vodokhranilishche. ▣ NW Tajikistan
137 V13 **Qazangödağ** Rus. Gora Kapydzhik, Turk. Qapiciğ Dağı. ▲ SW Azerbaijan
139 U7 **Qazānīyah** var. Dhū Shaykh. E Iraq
Qazaqstan/Qazaqstan Respublikasy see Kazakhstan
137 T9 **Qazbegi** Rus. Kazbegi. NE Georgia
149 P15 **Qāzi Ahmad** var. Kazi Ahmad. Sind, SE Pakistan
137 Y12 **Qazimämmäd** Rus. Kazi Magomed. SE Azerbaijan
Qazris see Cáceres
142 M4 **Qazvīn** var. Kazvin. Qazvīn, N Iran
142 M5 **Qazvīn** ⬖ province N Iran
187 Z13 **Qelelevu Lagoon** lagoon NE Fiji
75 X10 **Qena** var. Qinā; anc. Caene, Caenepolis. E Egypt
113 L23 **Qeparo** Vlorë, S Albania
Qeqertarssuaq see Qeqertarsuaq
197 N13 **Qeqertarsuaq** var. Qeqertarssuaq, Dan. Godhavn. Kitaa, Greenland
196 M13 **Qeqertarsuaq** island W Greenland
197 N13 **Qeqertarsuup Tunua** Dan. Disko Bugt. inlet W Greenland
Qerveh see Qorveh
143 S14 **Qeshm** Hormozgān, S Iran
143 R14 **Qeshm** var. Jazīreh-ye Qeshm, Qeshm Island. island S Iran
Qeshm Island/Qeshm, Jazīreh-ye see Qeshm
142 L4 **Qeydār** var. Qaydār. Zanjān, NW Iran
142 K5 **Qezel Owzan, Rūd-e** var. Ki Zil Uzen, Qi Zil Uzun. ≈ NW Iran
Qian see Guizhou
161 Q2 **Qian'an** Hebei, E China
Qian Gorlo/Qian Gorlos/Qian Gorlos Mongolzu Zizhixian/Qianguozhen see Qianguo
163 V9 **Qianguo** var. Qian Gorlo, Qian Gorlos, Qian Gorlos Mongolzu Zizhixian, Qianguozhen. Jilin, NE China
161 N9 **Qianjiang** Hubei, C China
160 K10 **Qianjiang** Sichuan, C China
160 L14 **Qian Jiang** ≈ S China
160 G9 **Qianning** var. Gartar. Sichuan, C China
163 U13 **Qian Shan** ⛰ NE China
160 H10 **Qianwei** var. Yujin. Sichuan, C China
160 J11 **Qianxi** Guizhou, S China
Qiaotou see Datong
Qiaowa see Muli
159 Q7 **Qiaowan** Gansu, N China
Qibilī see Kebili
158 K9 **Qiemo** var. Qarqan. Xinjiang Uygur Zizhiqu, NW China
160 J10 **Qijiang** var. Gunan. Chongqing Shi, C China
159 N5 **Qijiaojing** Xinjiang Uygur Zizhiqu, NW China
Qike see Xunke
149 P9 **Qila Saifullāh** Baluchistān, SW Pakistan
159 S9 **Qilian** var. Babao. Qinghai, C China
159 N8 **Qilian Shan** var. Kilien Mountains. ⛰ N China
197 O11 **Qimusseriarsuaq** Dan. Melville Bugt, Eng. Melville Bay. bay NW Greenland
Qinā see Qena
159 W11 **Qin'an** Gansu, C China
Qincheng see Nanfeng
Qing see Qinghai
163 W7 **Qing'an** Heilongjiang, NE China
161 R5 **Qingdao** var. Ching-Tao, Ch'ing-tao, Tsingtao, Tsintao, Ger. Tsingtau. Shandong, E China
163 V8 **Qinggang** Heilongjiang, NE China
Qinggil see Qinghe
159 P11 **Qinghai** var. Chinghai, Koko Nor, Qing, Qinghai Sheng, Tsinghai. ⬖ province C China
159 S10 **Qinghai Hu** var. Ch'ing Hai, Tsing Hai, Mong. Koko Nor. ◎ C China
Qinghai Sheng see Qinghai
158 M3 **Qinghe** var. Qinggil. Xinjiang Uygur Zizhiqu, NW China
160 L4 **Qingjian** Shaanxi, C China
160 L9 **Qing Jiang** ≈ C China
Qingjiang see Huai'an
Qingkou see Ganyu
160 L12 **Qinglong** var. Liancheng. Guizhou, S China
161 Q2 **Qinglong** Hebei, E China
Qingshan see Wudalianchi
159 R12 **Qingshuihe** Qinghai, C China
159 X10 **Qingyang** var. Xifeng. Gansu, C China
Qingyang see Jinjiang
161 N14 **Qingyuan** Guangdong, S China
163 V11 **Qingyuan** var. Qingyuan Manzu Zizhixian. Liaoning, NE China
Qingyuan Manzu Zizhixian see Qingyuan
158 L13 **Qingzang Gaoyuan** var. Xizang Gaoyuan, Eng. Plateau of Tibet. plateau W China
161 Q4 **Qingzhou** prev. Yidu. Shandong, E China
157 R9 **Qin He** ≈ C China
161 Q2 **Qinhuangdao** Hebei, E China
160 K7 **Qin Ling** ⛰ C China
Qin Xian see Qinxian
161 N5 **Qinxian** var. Qin Xian. Shanxi, C China
161 N6 **Qinyang** Henan, C China
160 K15 **Qinzhou** Guangxi Zhuangzu Zizhiqu, S China
Qiong see Hainan
160 L17 **Qionghai** prev. Jiaji. Hainan, S China
160 H9 **Qionglai** Sichuan, C China
160 H8 **Qionglai Shan** ⛰ C China
Qiongxi see Hongyuan
160 L17 **Qiongzhou Haixia** var. Hainan Strait. strait S China
163 U7 **Qiqihar** var. Ch'i-ch'i-ha-erh, Tsitsihar; prev. Lungkiang. Heilongjiang, NE China
143 P12 **Qīr** Fārs, S Iran
158 H10 **Qira** Xinjiang Uygur Zizhiqu, NW China
Qir'awn, Buḥayrat al see Qaraoun, Lac de
138 F11 **Qiryat Gat** var. Kiryat Gat. Southern, C Israel
138 G8 **Qiryat Shemona** Northern, N Israel
Qishlaq see Garmsār
141 U14 **Qishn** SE Yemen
138 G9 **Qishon, Naḥal** ≈ N Israel
Qita Ghazzah see Gaza Strip
156 K5 **Qitai** Xinjiang Uygur Zizhiqu, NW China
163 Y8 **Qitaihe** Heilongjiang, NE China
141 W12 **Qitbīt, Wādī** dry watercourse S Oman
161 O5 **Qixian** var. Qi Xian, Zhaoge. Henan, C China
Qizān see Jīzān
Qizil Orda see Kyzylorda
Qizil Qum/Qizilqum see Kyzyl Kum
147 V14 **Qizilrabot** Rus. Kyzylrabot. SE Tajikistan
146 J10 **Qizilravot** Rus. Kyzylrabat. Buxoro Viloyati, C Uzbekistan
Qi Zil Uzun see Qezel Owzan, Rūd-e
139 S4 **Qizil Yār** N Iraq
Qoghaly see Kugaly
Qogir Feng see K2
143 N6 **Qom** var. Kum, Qum. Qom, N Iran
143 N6 **Qom** ⬖ province N Iran
Qomisheh see Shahreẓā
Qomolangma Feng see Everest, Mount
142 M7 **Qom, Rūd-e** ≈ C Iran
Qomsheh see Shahreẓā
Qomul see Hami
Qondūz see Kunduz
146 G7 **Qo'ng'irot** Rus. Kungrad. Qoraqalpog'iston Respublikasi, NW Uzbekistan
Qongyrat see Konyrat
Qoqek see Tacheng
147 R10 **Qo'qon** var. Khokand, Rus. Kokand. Farg'ona Viloyati, E Uzbekistan
Qorabowur Kirlari see Karabaur', Uval
Qoradaryo see Karadar'ya
146 G6 **Qorajar** Rus. Karadzhar. Qoraqalpog'iston Respublikasi, NW Uzbekistan
146 K12 **Qorako'l** Rus. Karakul'. Buxoro Viloyati, C Uzbekistan
146 H7 **Qorao'zak** Rus. Karauzyak. Qoraqalpog'iston Respublikasi, NW Uzbekistan
146 E5 **Qoraqalpog'iston** Rus. Karakalpakya. Qoraqalpog'iston Respublikasi, NW Uzbekistan
146 G7 **Qoraqalpog'iston Respublikasi** Rus. Respublika Karakalpakstan. ⬖ autonomous republic NW Uzbekistan
Qorgazhyn see Kurgal'dzhino
138 H6 **Qornet es Saouda** ▲ NE Lebanon
146 L12 **Qorovulbozor** Rus. Karaulbazar. Buxoro Viloyati, C Uzbekistan
142 K5 **Qorveh** var. Qerveh, Qurveh. Kordestān, W Iran
147 N11 **Qo'shrabot** Rus. Kushrabat. Samarqand Viloyati, C Uzbekistan
Qosshaghyl see Koschagyl
Qostanay/Qostanay Oblysy see Kostanay
143 P12 **Qoṭbābād** Fārs, S Iran
143 R13 **Qoṭbābād** Hormozgān, S Iran
138 H6 **Qoubaïyât** var. Al Qubayyāt. N Lebanon
Qoussantîna see Constantine
158 K16 **Qowowuyag** see Cho Oyu
147 O11 **Qo'ytosh** Rus. Koytash. Jizzax Viloyati, C Uzbekistan
146 G7 **Qozonketkan** Rus. Kazanketken. Qoraqalpog'iston Respublikasi, W Uzbekistan
146 H6 **Qozoqdaryo** Rus. Kazakdar'ya. Qoraqalpog'iston Respublikasi, NW Uzbekistan
19 N11 **Quabbin Reservoir** ▣ Massachusetts, NE USA
100 F12 **Quakenbrück** Niedersachsen, NW Germany
18 I15 **Quakertown** Pennsylvania, NE USA
182 M10 **Quambatook** Victoria, SE Australia
25 Q4 **Quanah** Texas, SW USA
167 V10 **Quang Ngai** var. Quangngai, Quang Nghia. Quang Ngai, C Vietnam
Quang Nghia see Quang Ngai
167 T9 **Quang Tri** Quang Tri, C Vietnam
Quanjiang see Suichuan
Quan Long see Ca Mau
152 L4 **Quanshuigou** China/India
161 R13 **Quanzhou** var. Ch'uan-chou, Tsinkiang; prev. Chin-chiang. Fujian, SE China
160 M12 **Quanzhou** Guangxi Zhuangzu Zizhiqu, S China
11 V16 **Qu'Appelle** ≈ Saskatchewan, S Canada
12 M3 **Quaqtaq** prev. Koartac. Québec, NE Canada
61 E16 **Quaraí** Rio Grande do Sul, S Brazil
59 H24 **Quaraí, Rio** Sp. Río Cuareim. ≈ Brazil/Uruguay **see also** Cuareim, Río
171 N13 **Quarles, Pegunungan** ⛰ Sulawesi, C Indonesia
Quarnero see Kvarner
107 C20 **Quartu Sant' Elena** Sardegna, Italy, C Mediterranean Sea
29 X13 **Quasqueton** Iowa, C USA
173 X16 **Quatre Bornes** W Mauritius
172 I17 **Quatre Bornes** Mahé, NE Seychelles
137 X10 **Quba** Rus. Kuba. N Azerbaijan
Qubba see Ba'qūbah
143 T3 **Qūchān** var. Kuchan. Khorāsān, NE Iran
183 R10 **Queanbeyan** New South Wales, SE Australia
15 Q10 **Québec** var. Quebec. Québec, SE Canada
14 K10 **Québec** var. Quebec. ⬖ province SE Canada
61 D17 **Quebracho** Paysandú, W Uruguay
101 K14 **Quedlinburg** Sachsen-Anhalt, C Germany
138 H10 **Queen Alia** ✕ ('Ammān) 'Al 'Ammān, C Jordan
10 L16 **Queen Bess, Mount** ▲ British Columbia, SW Canada
10 I14 **Queen Charlotte** British Columbia, SW Canada
65 B24 **Queen Charlotte Bay** bay West Falkland, Falkland Islands
10 H14 **Queen Charlotte Islands** Fr. Îles de la Reine-Charlotte. island group British Columbia, SW Canada
10 I15 **Queen Charlotte Sound** sea area British Columbia, W Canada
10 J16 **Queen Charlotte Strait** strait British Columbia, W Canada
27 U1 **Queen City** Missouri, C USA
25 X5 **Queen City** Texas, SW USA
8 L3 **Queen Elizabeth Islands** Fr. Îles de la Reine-Élisabeth. island group Nunavut, N Canada
195 Y10 **Queen Mary Coast** physical region Antarctica
65 N24 **Queen Mary's Peak** ▲ C Tristan da Cunha
196 M8 **Queen Maud Gulf** gulf Arctic Ocean
195 P11 **Queen Maud Mountains** ⛰ Antarctica
Queen's County see Laois
181 U7 **Queensland** ⬖ state N Australia
192 I9 **Queensland Plateau** undersea feature N Coral Sea
183 O16 **Queenstown** Tasmania, SE Australia
185 C22 **Queenstown** Otago, South Island, NZ
83 I24 **Queenstown** Eastern Cape, S South Africa
Queenstown see Cobh
32 F8 **Queets** Washington, NW USA
61 D18 **Queguay Grande, Río** ≈ W Uruguay
59 O16 **Queimadas** Bahia, E Brazil
82 D11 **Quela** Malanje, NW Angola
83 O16 **Quelimane** var. Kilimane, Kilmain, Quilimane. Zambézia, NE Mozambique
63 G18 **Quellón** var. Puerto Quellón. Los Lagos, S Chile
Quelpart see Cheju-do
37 P12 **Quemado** New Mexico, SW USA
25 O12 **Quemado** Texas, SW USA
44 K7 **Quemado, Punta de** headland E Cuba
Quemoy see Chinmen Tao
62 K13 **Quemú Quemú** La Pampa, E Argentina
155 E17 **Quepem** Goa, W India
42 M14 **Quepos** Puntarenas, S Costa Rica
Que Que see Kwekwe
61 D23 **Quequén** Buenos Aires, E Argentina
61 D23 **Quequén Grande, Río** ≈ E Argentina
61 C23 **Quequén Salado, Río** ≈ E Argentina
Quera see Chur
41 N13 **Querétaro** Querétaro de Arteaga, C Mexico
40 F4 **Querobabi** Sonora, NW Mexico
42 M13 **Quesada** var. Ciudad Quesada, San Carlos. Alajuela, N Costa Rica
105 O13 **Quesada** Andalucía, S Spain
161 O7 **Queshan** Henan, C China
10 M15 **Quesnel** British Columbia, SW Canada
37 S9 **Questa** New Mexico, SW USA
102 H7 **Questembert** Morbihan, NW France
57 K22 **Quetena, Río** ≈ SW Bolivia
149 O10 **Quetta** Baluchistān, SW Pakistan
Quetzalcoalco see Coatzacoalcos
Quetzaltenango see Quezaltenango
56 B6 **Quevedo** Los Ríos, C Ecuador
42 B6 **Quezaltenango** var. Quetzaltenango. Quezaltenango, W Guatemala
42 A2 **Quezaltenango** off. Departamento de Quezaltenango, var. Quetzaltenango. ⬖ department SW Guatemala
42 E6 **Quezaltepeque** Chiquimula, SE Guatemala
170 M6 **Quezon** Palawan, W Philippines
161 P5 **Qufu** Shandong, E China
82 B12 **Quibala** Cuanza Sul, NW Angola
82 B11 **Quibaxe** var. Quibaxi. Cuanza Norte, NW Angola
Quibaxi see Quibaxe
54 D9 **Quibdó** Chocó, W Colombia
102 G7 **Quiberon** Morbihan, NW France
102 G7 **Quiberon, Baie de** bay NW France
54 J5 **Quíbor** Lara, N Venezuela
42 C4 **Quiché** off. Departamento del Quiché. ⬖ department W Guatemala
99 E21 **Quiévrain** Hainaut, S Belgium
40 I9 **Quila** Sinaloa, C Mexico
83 B14 **Quilengues** Huíla, SW Angola
Quilimane see Quelimane
57 G15 **Quillabamba** Cusco, C Peru
57 L18 **Quillacollo** Cochabamba, C Bolivia
62 H4 **Quillagua** Antofagasta, N Chile
103 N17 **Quillan** Aude, S France
11 U15 **Quill Lakes** ◎ Saskatchewan, S Canada
62 G11 **Quillota** Valparaíso, C Chile
155 G23 **Quilon** var. Kolam, Kollam. Kerala, SW India
181 V9 **Quilpie** Queensland, C Australia
149 O4 **Quil-Qala** Bāmīān, N Afghanistan
62 L7 **Quimilí** Santiago del Estero, C Argentina
57 O19 **Quimome** Santa Cruz, E Bolivia
102 F6 **Quimper** anc. Quimper Corentin. Finistère, NW France
Quimper Corentin see Quimper
102 G7 **Quimperlé** Finistère, NW France
32 F8 **Quinault** Washington, NW USA
32 F8 **Quinault River** ≈ Washington, NW USA
35 P5 **Quincy** California, W USA
23 S8 **Quincy** Florida, SE USA
30 I13 **Quincy** Illinois, N USA
19 O11 **Quincy** Massachusetts, NE USA
32 J9 **Quincy** Washington, NW USA
54 E10 **Quindío** off. Departamento del Quindío. ⬖ province C Colombia
54 E10 **Quindío, Nevado del** ▲ C Colombia
62 J10 **Quines** San Luis, C Argentina
39 N13 **Quinhagak** Alaska, USA
76 G13 **Quinhámel** W Guinea-Bissau
Qui Nhon/Quinhon see Quy Nhơn
Quinindé see Rosa Zárate
25 U6 **Quinlan** Texas, SW USA
61 H17 **Quinta** Rio Grande do Sul, S Brazil
105 O10 **Quintanar de la Orden** Castilla-La Mancha, C Spain
41 X13 **Quintana Roo** ⬖ state SE Mexico
105 S6 **Quinto** Aragón, NE Spain
108 G10 **Quinto** Ticino, S Switzerland
27 Q11 **Quinton** Oklahoma, C USA
62 K12 **Quinto, Río** ≈ C Argentina
82 A10 **Quinzau** Zaire, NW Angola
14 H8 **Quinze, Lac des** ◎ Québec, SE Canada
83 B15 **Quipungo** Huíla, C Angola
62 G13 **Quirihue** Bío Bío, C Chile
82 D12 **Quirima** Malanje, NW Angola
183 T6 **Quirindi** New South Wales, SE Australia
55 P5 **Quiriquire** Monagas, NE Venezuela
14 D10 **Quirke Lake** ◎ Ontario, S Canada
61 B21 **Quiroga** Buenos Aires, E Argentina
104 I4 **Quiroga** Galicia, NW Spain
Quiróm, Salar see Pocitos, Salar
56 B9 **Quiroz, Río** ≈ NW Peru
82 Q13 **Quissanga** Cabo Delgado, NE Mozambique
83 M20 **Quissico** Inhambane, S Mozambique
25 O4 **Quitaque** Texas, SW USA
82 Q13 **Quiterajo** Cabo Delgado, NE Mozambique
23 T6 **Quitman** Georgia, SE USA
22 M6 **Quitman** Mississippi, S USA
25 V6 **Quitman** Texas, SW USA
56 C6 **Quito** ● (Ecuador) Pichincha, N Ecuador
Quito see Mariscal Sucre
58 P13 **Quixadá** Ceará, E Brazil
83 Q15 **Quixaxe** Nampula, NE Mozambique
160 J9 **Qu Jiang** ≈ C China
161 R10 **Qu Jiang** ≈ SE China
161 N13 **Qujiang** var. Maba. Guangdong, S China
160 H12 **Qujing** Yunnan, SW China
Qulan see Kulan
163 T8 **Qulin Gol** prev. Chaor He. ≈ N China
146 L10 **Quljuqtov-Tog'lari** Rus. Gory Kul'dzhuktau. ▲ C Uzbekistan
Qulsary see Kul'sary
Qulyndy Zhazyghy see Kulunda Steppe
Qum see Qom
Qumälisch see Lubartów
159 P11 **Qumar He** ≈ C China
159 Q12 **Qumarlêb** var. Yuegaitan. Qinghai, C China
Qumisheh see Shahreẓā
147 O14 **Qumqo'rg'on** Rus. Kumkurgan. Surxondaryo Viloyati, S Uzbekistan
Qunaytirah/Qunaytirah, Muḥāfaẓat al/Qunaytra see Al Qunayṭirah
189 V12 **Quoi** island Chuuk, C Micronesia
9 N8 **Quoich** ≈ Nunavut, NE Canada
83 E26 **Quoin Point** headland SW South Africa
182 I7 **Quorn** South Australia
Qurein see Al Kuwayt
147 P14 **Qŭrghonteppa** Rus. Kurgan-Tyube. SW Tajikistan
Qurlurtuuq see Kugluktuk
Qurveh see Qorveh
Qusair see Quseir
137 X10 **Qusar** Rus. Kusary. NE Azerbaijan
Quşayr see Al Quşayr
75 Y10 **Quseir** var. Al Quşayr, Qusair. E Egypt
142 I2 **Qūshchī** Āžarbāyjān-e Bākhtarī, N Iran
Qusmuryn see Kushmurun, Kostanay, Kazakhstan
Qusmuryn see Kushmurun, Ozero, Kazakhstan
Quṭayfah/Qutayfe/Quteife see Al Quṭayfah
Quthing see Moyeni
147 S10 **Quvasoy** Rus. Kuvasay. Farg'ona Viloyati, E Uzbekistan
Quwair see Guwēr
Quxar see Lhazê
Qu Xian see Quzhou
159 N16 **Qūxū** var. Xoi. Xizang Zizhiqu, W China
Quyang see Jingzhou, Hunan
167 V13 **Quy Chanh** Ninh Thuận, S Vietnam
167 V11 **Quy Nhơn** var. Quinhon, Qui Nhon. Binh Định, C Vietnam
161 R10 **Quzhou** var. Qu Xian. Zhejiang, SE China
Qyteti Stalin see Kuçovë
Qyzylorda/Qyzylorda Oblysy see Kyzylorda
Qyzyltū see Kishkenekol'
Qyzylzhar see Kyzylzhar

R

109 R4 **Raab** Oberösterreich, N Austria
109 X8 **Raab** Hung. Rába. ≈ Austria/Hungary **see also** Rába
Raab see Győr
109 V2 **Raabs an der Thaya** Niederösterreich, E Austria
93 L14 **Raahe** Swe. Brahestad. Oulu, W Finland
98 M10 **Raalte** Overijssel, E Netherlands
99 I14 **Raamsdonksveer** Noord-Brabant, S Netherlands
92 L12 **Raanujärvi** Lappi, NW Finland
96 G9 **Raasay** island NW Scotland, UK
118 H3 **Raasiku** Ger. Rasik. Harjumaa, NW Estonia
112 B11 **Rab** It. Arbe. Primorje-Gorski Kotar, NW Croatia
112 B11 **Rab** It. Arbe. island NW Croatia
171 N16 **Raba** Sumbawa, S Indonesia
111 G22 **Rába** Ger. Raab. ≈ Austria/Hungary **see also** Raab
112 A10 **Rabac** Istra, NW Croatia
104 I2 **Rábade** Galicia, NW Spain
80 F10 **Rabak** White Nile, C Sudan
186 G9 **Rabaraba** Milne Bay, SE PNG
102 K16 **Rabastens-de-Bigorre** Hautes-Pyrénées, S France
121 O16 **Rabat** W Malta
74 F6 **Rabat** var. al Dar al Baida. ● (Morocco) NW Morocco
Rabat see Victoria
186 H6 **Rabaul** New Britain, E PNG
Rabbah Ammon/Rabbath Ammon see 'Ammān
28 K8 **Rabbit Creek** ≈ South Dakota, N USA
14 H10 **Rabbit Lake** ◎ Ontario, S Canada
187 Y14 **Rabi** prev. Rambi. island N Fiji
140 K9 **Rābigh** Makkah, W Saudi Arabia
42 D5 **Rabinal** Baja Verapaz, C Guatemala
168 G9 **Rabi, Pulau** island NW Indonesia, East Indies
111 L17 **Rabka** Małopolskie, S Poland
155 F16 **Rabkavi** Karnātaka, W India
Râbniţa see Rîbniţa
109 Y6 **Rabnitz** ≈ E Austria
124 J7 **Rabocheostrovsk** Respublika Kareliya, NW Russian Federation
23 U1 **Rabun Bald** ▲ Georgia, SE USA
75 S11 **Rabyānah** SE Libya
75 S11 **Rabyānah, Ramlat** var. Rebiana Sand Sea, Şaḥrā' Rabyānah. desert SE Libya
Rabyānah, Şaḥrā' see Rabyānah, Ramlat
116 L11 **Răcăciuni** Bacău, E Romania
Racaka see Riwoqê
107 J24 **Racalmuto** Sicilia, Italy, C Mediterranean Sea
116 J14 **Răcari** Dâmboviţa, SE Romania
Răcari see Durankulak
116 F13 **Răcăşdia** Hung. Rakasd. Caraş-Severin, SW Romania
106 B9 **Racconigi** Piemonte, NE Italy
31 T15 **Raccoon Creek** ≈ Ohio, N USA
13 V13 **Race, Cape** headland Newfoundland and Labrador, E Canada
22 K10 **Raceland** Louisiana, S USA
19 Q12 **Race Point** headland Massachusetts, NE USA
167 S14 **Rach Gia** Kiên Giang, S Vietnam
167 S14 **Rach Gia, Vinh** bay S Vietnam
76 J8 **Rachid** Tagant, C Mauritania

110 L10 **Raciąż** Mazowieckie, C Poland
111 I16 **Racibórz** *Ger.* Ratibor. Śląskie, S Poland
31 N9 **Racine** Wisconsin, N USA
14 D7 **Racine Lake** ◎ Ontario, S Canada
111 J23 **Ráckeve** Pest, C Hungary
Rácz-Becse *see* Bečej
141 O15 **Radā'** *var.* Ridā'. W Yemen
113 O15 **Radan** ▲ SE Serbia and Montenegro (Yugo.)
63 J19 **Rada Tilly** Chubut, SE Argentina
116 K8 **Rădăuţi** *Ger.* Radautz, *Hung.* Rádóc. Suceava, N Romania
116 L8 **Rădăuţi-Prut** Botoşani, NE Romania
Radautz *see* Rădăuţi
Radbusa *see* Radbuza
111 A17 **Radbuza** *Ger.* Radbusa. ⇝ SE Czech Republic
20 K6 **Radcliff** Kentucky, S USA
139 O2 **Radd, Wādī ar** *dry watercourse* N Syria
95 H16 **Råde** Østfold, S Norway
109 V11 **Radeče** *Ger.* Ratschach. C Slovenia
Radein *see* Radenci
116 J4 **Radekhiv** *Pol.* Radziechów, *Rus.* Radekhov. L'vivs'ka Oblast', W Ukraine
Radekhov *see* Radekhiv
109 X9 **Radenci** *Ger.* Radein; *prev.* Radinci. NE Slovenia
109 S9 **Radenthein** Kärnten, S Austria
21 R7 **Radford** Virginia, NE USA
154 C9 **Rādhanpur** Gujarāt, W India
Radinci *see* Radenci
127 Q6 **Radishchevo** Ul'yanovskaya Oblast', W Russian Federation
12 I9 **Radisson** Québec, E Canada
11 P16 **Radium Hot Springs** British Columbia, SW Canada
116 F11 **Radna** *Hung.* Máriaradna. Arad, W Romania
114 K10 **Radnevo** Stara Zagora, C Bulgaria
97 J20 **Radnor** *cultural region* E Wales, UK
Radnót *see* Iernut
Rádóc *see* Rădăuţi
101 H24 **Radolfzell am Bodensee** Baden-Württemberg, S Germany
110 M13 **Radom** Mazowieckie, C Poland
116 I14 **Radomireşti** Olt, S Romania
111 K14 **Radomsko** *Rus.* Novoradomsk. Łodzkie, C Poland
117 N4 **Radomyshl'** Zhytomyrs'ka Oblast', N Ukraine
113 P19 **Radoviš** *prev.* Radovište. E FYR Macedonia
Radovište *see* Radoviš
95 B13 **Radøy** *island* S Norway
109 R7 **Radstadt** Salzburg, NW Austria
182 E8 **Radstock, Cape** *headland* South Australia
119 G15 **Radun'** *Rus.* Radun'. Hrodzyenskaya Voblasts', W Belarus
126 M3 **Raduzhnyy** Vladimirskaya Oblast', W Russian Federation
118 F11 **Radviliškis** Šiauliai, N Lithuania
11 U17 **Radville** Saskatchewan, S Canada
140 K7 **Raḍwá, Jabal** ▲ W Saudi Arabia
111 P16 **Radymno** Podkarpackie, SE Poland
116 J5 **Radyvyliv** Rivnens'ka Oblast', NW Ukraine
Radziechów *see* Radekhiv
110 I11 **Radziejów** Kujawsko-pomorskie, C Poland
110 O12 **Radzyń Podlaski** Lubelskie, E Poland
8 J7 **Rae** ⇝ Nunavut, NW Canada
152 M13 **Rāe Bareli** Uttar Pradesh, N India
Rae-Edzo *see* Edzo
21 T11 **Raeford** North Carolina, SE USA
99 M19 **Raeren** Liège, E Belgium
9 N7 **Rae Strait** *strait* Nunavut, N Canada
184 L11 **Raetihi** Manawatu-Wanganui, North Island, NZ
191 U13 **Raevavae** *var.* Raivavae. *island* Îles Australes, SW French Polynesia
Rafa *see* Rafah
62 M10 **Rafaela** Santa Fe, E Argentina
138 E11 **Rafah** *var.* Rafa, Rafaḥ, *Heb.* Rafiaḥ, Raphiah. SW Gaza Strip
79 L15 **Rafaï** Mbomou, SE Central African Republic
141 O4 **Rafḥah** Al Ḥudūd ash Shamālīyah, N Saudi Arabia
Rafiaḥ *see* Rafah
143 R10 **Rafsanjān** Kermān, C Iran
80 B13 **Raga** Western Bahr el Ghazal, SW Sudan
19 S8 **Ragged Island** *island* Maine, NE USA
44 I5 **Ragged Island Range** *island group* S Bahamas
184 L7 **Raglan** Waikato, North Island, NZ
22 G8 **Ragley** Louisiana, S USA
Ragnit *see* Neman
107 K25 **Ragusa** Sicilia, Italy, C Mediterranean Sea
Ragusa *see* Dubrovnik
Ragusavecchia *see* Cavtat
171 P14 **Raha** Pulau Muna, C Indonesia
119 N17 **Rahachow** *Rus.* Rogachëv. Homyel'skaya Voblasts', SE Belarus
Rahaeng *see* Tak
138 F11 **Rahat** Southern, C Israel
140 L8 **Rahaṭ, Ḥarrat** *lavaflow* W Saudi Arabia
149 S12 **Rahīmyār Khān** Punjab, SE Pakistan
95 I14 **Råholt** Akershus, S Norway
Rahovec *see* Orahovac
191 S10 **Raiatea** *island* Îles Sous le Vent, W French Polynesia
155 H16 **Rāichūr** Karnātaka, C India
Raidestos *see* Tekirdağ
153 S13 **Rāiganj** West Bengal, NE India
154 M11 **Raigarh** Chhattīsgarh, C India
183 O16 **Railton** Tasmania, SE Australia
36 L8 **Rainbow Bridge** *natural arch* Utah, W USA
23 Q3 **Rainbow City** Alabama, S USA
11 N11 **Rainbow Lake** Alberta, W Canada
21 R5 **Rainelle** West Virginia, NE USA
32 G10 **Rainier** Oregon, NW USA
32 H9 **Rainier, Mount** ⚘ Washington, NW USA
23 Q2 **Rainsville** Alabama, S USA
12 B11 **Rainy Lake** ◎ Canada/USA
12 A11 **Rainy River** Ontario, C Canada
Raippaluoto *see* Replot
154 K12 **Raipur** Chhattīsgarh, C India
154 H10 **Raisen** Madhya Pradesh, C India
15 N13 **Raisin** ⇝ Ontario, SE Canada
31 R11 **Raisin, River** ⇝ Michigan, N USA
Raivavae *see* Raevavae
149 W9 **Rāiwind** Punjab, E Pakistan
171 T12 **Raja Ampat, Kepulauan** *island group* E Indonesia
155 L16 **Rājahmundry** Andhra Pradesh, E India
155 I18 **Rājampet** Andhra Pradesh, E India
Rajang *see* Rajang, Batang
169 S9 **Rajang, Batang** *var.* Rajang. ⇝ East Malaysia
149 S11 **Rājanpur** Punjab, E Pakistan
155 H23 **Rājapālaiyam** Tamil Nādu, SE India
152 E12 **Rājasthān** ◈ *state* NW India
153 T15 **Rājbari** Dhaka, C Bangladesh
153 R12 **Rājbiraj** Eastern, E Nepal
154 G9 **Rājgarh** Madhya Pradesh, C India
152 H10 **Rājgarh** Rājasthān, NW India
153 P14 **Rājgīr** Bihār, N India
110 O8 **Rajgród** Podlaskie, NE Poland
154 L12 **Rājim** Chhattīsgarh, C India
112 C11 **Rajinac, Mali** ▲ W Croatia
154 B10 **Rājkot** Gujarāt, W India
153 R14 **Rājmahal** Jhārkhand, NE India
153 Q14 **Rājmahal Hills** *hill range* N India
154 K12 **Rāj Nāndgaon** Chhattīsgarh, C India
152 I8 **Rājpura** Punjab, NW India
153 S14 **Rājshahi** *prev.* Rampur Boalia. Rājshahi, W Bangladesh
153 S13 **Rajshahi** ◈ *division* NW Bangladesh
190 K13 **Rakahanga** *atoll* N Cook Islands
185 H19 **Rakaia** Canterbury, South Island, NZ
185 G19 **Rakaia** ⇝ South Island, NZ
152 H3 **Rakaposhi** ▲ N India
Rakasd *see* Răcăşdia
169 N15 **Rakata, Pulau** *var.* Pulau Krakatau. *island* S Indonesia
141 U10 **Rakbah, Qalamat ar** *well* SE Saudi Arabia
Rakhine State *see* Arakan State
116 I8 **Rakhiv** Zakarpats'ka Oblast', W Ukraine
141 V13 **Rakhyūt** SW Oman
192 K9 **Rakiraki** Viti Levu, W Fiji
Rakka *see* Ar Raqqah
118 I4 **Rakke** Lääne-Virumaa, NE Estonia
95 I16 **Rakkestad** Østfold, S Norway
110 F12 **Rakoniewice** *Ger.* Rakwitz. Wielkolpolskie, C Poland
Rakonitz *see* Rakovník
83 H18 **Rakops** Central, C Botswana
111 C16 **Rakovník** *Ger.* Rakonitz. Středočeský Kraj, W Czech Republic
114 J10 **Rakovski** Plovdiv, C Bulgaria
Rakutō-kō *see* Naktong-gang
118 I3 **Rakvere** *Ger.* Wesenberg. Lääne-Virumaa, N Estonia
Rakwitz *see* Rakoniewice
22 L6 **Raleigh** Mississippi, S USA
21 U9 **Raleigh** *state capital* North Carolina, SE USA
21 Y11 **Raleigh Bay** *bay* North Carolina, SE USA
21 U9 **Raleigh-Durham** ✕ North Carolina, SE USA
189 S6 **Ralik Chain** *island group* Ralik Chain, W Marshall Islands
25 N5 **Ralls** Texas, SW USA
18 G13 **Ralston** Pennsylvania, NE USA
141 O16 **Ramādah** W Yemen
Ramadi *see* Ar Ramādī
105 N2 **Ramales de la Victoria** Cantabria, N Spain
138 F10 **Ramallah** C West Bank
61 C19 **Ramallo** Buenos Aires, E Argentina
155 H20 **Rāmanagaram** Karnātaka, E India
155 I23 **Rāmanāthapuram** Tamil Nādu, SE India
154 N12 **Rāmapur** Orissa, E India
155 I14 **Rāmāreddi** *var.* Kāmāreddi, Kamareddy. Andhra Pradesh, C India
138 F10 **Ramat Gan** Tel Aviv, W Israel
103 T6 **Rambervillers** Vosges, NE France
Rambi *see* Rabi
103 N5 **Rambouillet** Yvelines, N France
186 E5 **Rambutyo Island** *island* N PNG
153 Q12 **Ramechhap** Central, C Nepal
183 R12 **Rame Head** *headland* Victoria, SE Australia
126 L4 **Ramenskoye** Moskovskaya Oblast', W Russian Federation
124 J15 **Rameshki** Tverskaya Oblast', W Russian Federation
153 P14 **Rāmgarh** Jhārkhand, N India
152 D11 **Rāmgarh** Rājasthān, NW India
142 M9 **Rāmhormoz** *var.* Ram Hormuz, Ramuz. Khūzestān, SW Iran
Ram Hormuz *see* Rāmhormoz
Ram, Jebel *see* Ramm, Jabal
138 F10 **Ramla** *var.* Ramle, Ramleh, *Ar.* Er Ramle. Central, C Israel
Ramle/Ramleh *see* Ramla
138 F14 **Ramm, Jabal** *var.* Jebel Ram. ▲ SW Jordan
152 K10 **Rāmnagar** Uttaranchal, N India
95 N15 **Ramnäs** Västmanland, C Sweden
Râmnicul-Sărat *see* Râmnicu Sărat
116 L12 **Râmnicu Sărat** *prev.* Râmnicul-Sărat, Rîmnicu-Sărat. Buzău, E Romania
116 I13 **Râmnicu Vâlcea** *prev.* Rîmnicu Vîlcea. Vâlcea, C Romania
Ramokgwebana *see* Ramokgwebane
83 J18 **Ramokgwebane** *var.* Ramokgwebana. Central, NE Botswana
126 L7 **Ramon'** Voronezhskaya Oblast', W Russian Federation
35 V17 **Ramona** California, W USA
56 A10 **Ramón, Laguna** ◎ NW Peru
14 G7 **Ramore** Ontario, S Canada
40 M11 **Ramos** San Luis Potosí, C Mexico
41 N8 **Ramos Arizpe** Coahuila de Zaragoza, NE Mexico
40 J9 **Ramos, Río de** ⇝ C Mexico
83 I21 **Ramotswa** South East, S Botswana
39 R8 **Rampart** Alaska, USA
8 H8 **Ramparts** ⇝ Northwest Territories, NW Canada
152 K10 **Rāmpur** Uttar Pradesh, N India
154 F9 **Rāmpura** Madhya Pradesh, C India
Rampur Boalia *see* Rajshahi
166 K6 **Ramree Island** *island* W Burma
141 W6 **Rams** *var.* Ar Rams. Ra's al Khaymah, NE UAE
143 N4 **Rāmsar** *prev.* Sakhtsar. Māzandarān, N Iran
93 H16 **Ramsele** Västernorrland, N Sweden
21 T9 **Ramseur** North Carolina, SE USA
97 I16 **Ramsey** NE Isle of Man
97 I16 **Ramsey Bay** *bay* NE Isle of Man
14 E9 **Ramsey Lake** ◎ Ontario, S Canada
97 Q22 **Ramsgate** SE England, UK
94 M10 **Ramsjö** Gävleborg, C Sweden
154 I12 **Rāmtek** Mahārāshtra, C India
Ramtha *see* Ar Ramthā
Ramuz *see* Rāmhormoz
118 G12 **Ramygala** Panevėžys, C Lithuania
152 H14 **Rāna Pratāp Sāgar** ◎ N India
169 V7 **Ranau** Sabah, East Malaysia
168 L14 **Ranau, Danau** ◎ Sumatera, W Indonesia
62 H12 **Rancagua** Libertador, C Chile
99 G22 **Rance** Hainaut, S Belgium
102 H6 **Rance** ⇝ NW France
60 J9 **Rancharia** São Paulo, S Brazil
153 P15 **Rānchi** Jhārkhand, N India
61 D21 **Ranchos** Buenos Aires, E Argentina
37 S9 **Ranchos De Taos** New Mexico, SW USA
63 G16 **Ranco, Lago** ◎ C Chile
95 C16 **Randaberg** Rogaland, S Norway
29 U7 **Randall** Minnesota, N USA
107 L23 **Randazzo** Sicilia, Italy, C Mediterranean Sea
95 G21 **Randers** Århus, C Denmark
92 I12 **Randijaure** ◎ N Sweden
21 T9 **Randleman** North Carolina, SE USA
19 O11 **Randolph** Massachusetts, NE USA
29 Q13 **Randolph** Nebraska, C USA
36 M1 **Randolph** Utah, W USA
100 P9 **Randow** ⇝ NE Germany
95 H14 **Randsfjorden** ◎ S Norway
92 K13 **Råneå** Norrbotten, N Sweden
92 G12 **Ranelva** ⇝ C Norway
93 F15 **Ranemsletta** Nord-Trøndelag, C Norway
76 H10 **Ranérou** C Senegal
Ráneš *see* Ringvassøya
185 E22 **Ranfurly** Otago, South Island, NZ
167 P17 **Rangae** Narathiwat, SW Thailand
153 V16 **Rangamati** Chittagong, SE Bangladesh
184 I2 **Rangaunu Bay** *bay* North Island, NZ
19 P6 **Rangeley** Maine, NE USA
37 O4 **Rangely** Colorado, C USA
25 R7 **Ranger** Texas, SW USA
14 C9 **Ranger Lake** Ontario, S Canada
14 C9 **Ranger Lake** ◎ Ontario, S Canada
153 V12 **Rangia** Assam, NE India
185 I18 **Rangiora** Canterbury, South Island, NZ
191 T9 **Rangiroa** *atoll* Îles Tuamotu, W French Polynesia
184 N9 **Rangitaiki** ⇝ North Island, NZ
185 F19 **Rangitata** ⇝ South Island, NZ
184 M12 **Rangitikei** ⇝ North Island, NZ
184 L6 **Rangitoto Island** *island* N NZ
Rangkasbitoeng *see* Rangkasbitung
169 N16 **Rangkasbitung** *prev.* Rangkasbitoeng. Jawa, SW Indonesia
167 P9 **Rang, Khao** ▲ C Thailand
147 V13 **Rangkŭl** *Rus.* Rangkul'. SE Tajikistan
Rangkul' *see* Rangkŭl
Rangoon *see* Yangon
153 T13 **Rangpur** Rajshahi, N Bangladesh
155 F18 **Rānibennur** Karnātaka, W India
153 R15 **Rāniganj** West Bengal, NE India
149 Q13 **Rānīpur** Sind, SE Pakistan
Rāniyah *see* Rānya
25 N9 **Rankin** Texas, SW USA
9 O9 **Rankin Inlet** Nunavut, C Canada
183 P8 **Rankins Springs** New South Wales, SE Australia
Rankovićevo *see* Kraljevo
108 I7 **Rankweil** Vorarlberg, W Austria
Rann *see* Brežice
127 T8 **Ranneye** Orenburgskaya Oblast', W Russian Federation
96 I10 **Rannoch, Loch** ◎ C Scotland, UK
191 U17 **Rano Kau** *var.* Rano Kao. *crater* Easter Island, Chile, E Pacific Ocean
167 N14 **Ranong** Ranong, SW Thailand
186 J8 **Ranongga** *var.* Ghanongga. *island* NW Solomon Islands
191 W16 **Rano Raraku** *ancient monument* Easter Island, Chile, E Pacific Ocean
171 V12 **Ransiki** Papua, E Indonesia
92 K12 **Rantajärvi** Norrbotten, N Sweden
93 N17 **Rantasalmi** Isä-Suomi, SE Finland
169 U13 **Rantau** Borneo, C Indonesia
168 L10 **Rantau, Pulau** *var.* Pulau Tebingtinggi. *island* W Indonesia
171 N13 **Rantepao** Sulawesi, C Indonesia
30 M13 **Rantoul** Illinois, N USA
93 L15 **Rantsila** Oulu, C Finland
92 L13 **Ranua** Lappi, NW Finland
139 T2 **Rānya** *var.* Rāniyah. NE Iraq
157 X3 **Raohe** Heilongjiang, NE China
74 H9 **Raoui, Erg er** *desert* W Algeria
193 O10 **Rapa** *island* Îles Australes, S French Polynesia
191 V14 **Rapa Iti** *island* Îles Australes, SW French Polynesia
106 D10 **Rapallo** Liguria, NW Italy
Rapa Nui *see* Pascua, Isla de
Raphiah *see* Rafah
21 V5 **Rapidan River** ⇝ Virginia, NE USA
28 J10 **Rapid City** South Dakota, N USA
15 P8 **Rapide-Blanc** Québec, SE Canada
14 I8 **Rapide-Deux** Québec, SE Canada
118 K6 **Räpina** *Ger.* Rappin. Põlvamaa, SE Estonia
118 G4 **Rapla** *Ger.* Rappel. Raplamaa, NW Estonia
118 G4 **Raplamaa** *off.* Rapla Maakond. ◈ *province* NW Estonia
21 X6 **Rappahonnock River** ⇝ Virginia, NE USA
Rappel *see* Rapla
108 G7 **Rapperswil** Sankt Gallen, NE Switzerland
Rappin *see* Räpina
153 N12 **Rāpti** ⇝ N India
57 K16 **Rapulo, Río** ⇝ E Bolivia
Raqqah/Raqqah, Muḥāfaẓat al *see* Ar Raqqah
18 J8 **Raquette Lake** ◎ New York, NE USA
18 J6 **Raquette River** ⇝ New York, NE USA
191 V10 **Raraka** *atoll* Îles Tuamotu, C French Polynesia
191 V10 **Raroia** *atoll* Îles Tuamotu, C French Polynesia
190 H15 **Rarotonga** ✕ Rarotonga, S Cook Islands, C Pacific Ocean
190 H16 **Rarotonga** *island* S Cook Islands, C Pacific Ocean
147 P12 **Rarz** W Tajikistan
Ras al 'Ain *see* Ra's al 'Ayn
139 N2 **Ra's al 'Ayn** *var.* Ras al 'Ain. Al Ḥasakah, N Syria
138 H3 **Ra's al Basīṭ** Al Lādhiqīyah, W Syria
Ra's al-Hafgī *see* Ra's al Khafjī
141 R5 **Ra's al Khafjī** *var.* Ra's al-Hafgī. Ash Sharqīyah, NE Saudi Arabia
Ras al-Khaimah/Ras al Khaimah *see* Ra's al Khaymah
143 R15 **Ra's al Khaymah** *var.* Ras al Khaimah. Ra's al Khaymah, NE UAE
143 R15 **Ra's al Khaymah** *var.* Ras al-Khaimah. ✕ Ra's al Khaymah, NE UAE
138 G13 **Ra's an Naqb** Ma'ān, S Jordan
61 B26 **Rasa, Punta** *headland* E Argentina
171 V12 **Rasawi** Papua, E Indonesia
Râşcani *see* Rişcani
80 J10 **Ras Dashen Terara** ▲ N Ethiopia
151 K19 **Rasdu Atoll** *atoll* C Maldives
118 E12 **Raseiniai** Kaunas, C Lithuania
75 X8 **Râs Ghârib** E Egypt
162 D6 **Rashaant** Bayan-Ölgiy, W Mongolia
162 L10 **Rashaant** Dundgovĭ, C Mongolia
162 J6 **Rashaant** Hövsgöl, N Mongolia
139 Y11 **Rashīd** E Iraq
75 V7 **Rashîd** *Eng.* Rosetta. N Egypt
142 M3 **Rasht** *var.* Resht. Gīlān, NW Iran
139 S2 **Rashwān** N Iraq
Rasik *see* Raasiku
113 M15 **Raška** Serbia, C Serbia and Montenegro (Yugo.)
119 P15 **Rasna** *Rus.* Ryasna. Mahilyowskaya Voblasts', E Belarus
116 J12 **Râşnov** *prev.* Rîşno, Rozsnyó, *Hung.* Barcarozsnyó. Braşov, C Romania
118 L11 **Rasony** *Rus.* Rossony. Vitsyebskaya Voblasts', N Belarus
Ra's Shamrah *see* Ugarit
127 N7 **Rasskazovo** Tambovskaya Oblast', W Russian Federation
119 O16 **Rasta** ⇝ E Belarus
Rastadt *see* Rastatt
Rastâne *see* Ar Rastān
141 S6 **Ra's Tannūrah** *Eng.* Ras Tanura. Ash Sharqīyah, NE Saudi Arabia
Ras Tanura *see* Ra's Tannūrah
101 G21 **Rastatt** *var.* Rastadt. Baden-Württemberg, SW Germany
Rastenburg *see* Kętrzyn
149 V7 **Rasūlnagar** Punjab, E Pakistan
189 U6 **Ratak Chain** *island group* Ratak Chain, E Marshall Islands
119 K15 **Ratamka** *Rus.* Ratomka. Minskaya Voblasts', C Belarus
93 G17 **Rätan** Jämtland, C Sweden
152 G11 **Ratangarh** Rājasthān, NW India
Rat Buri *see* Ratchaburi
167 O11 **Ratchaburi** *var.* Rat Buri. Ratchaburi, W Thailand
29 W15 **Rathbun Lake** ▣ Iowa, C USA
Ráth Caola *see* Rathkeale
166 K5 **Rathedaung** Arakan State, W Burma
100 M12 **Rathenow** Brandenburg, NE Germany
97 C19 **Rathkeale** *Ir.* Ráth Caola. SW Ireland
96 F13 **Rathlin Island** *Ir.* Reachlainn. *island* N Northern Ireland, UK
97 C20 **Ráthluirc** *Ir.* An Ráth. SW Ireland
Ratibor *see* Racibórz
Ratisbon/Ratisbona/Ratisbonne *see* Regensburg
Rätische Alpen *see* Rhaetian Alps
38 E17 **Rat Island** *island* Aleutian Islands, Alaska, USA
38 E17 **Rat Islands** *island group* Aleutian Islands, Alaska, USA
154 F10 **Ratlām** *prev.* Rutlam. Madhya Pradesh, C India
155 D15 **Ratnāgiri** Mahārāshtra, W India
155 K26 **Ratnapura** Sabaragamuwa Province, S Sri Lanka
116 J2 **Ratne** *Rus.* Ratno. Volyns'ka Oblast', NW Ukraine
Ratno *see* Ratne
Ratomka *see* Ratamka
37 U8 **Raton** New Mexico, SW USA
139 O7 **Ratqah, Wādī ar** *dry watercourse* W Iraq
Ratschach *see* Radeče
167 O16 **Rattaphum** Songkhla, SW Thailand
26 L6 **Rattlesnake Creek** ⇝ Kansas, C USA
94 L13 **Rättvik** Dalarna, C Sweden
100 K9 **Ratzeburg** Mecklenburg-Vorpommern, N Germany
100 K9 **Ratzeburger See** ◎ N Germany
10 J10 **Ratz, Mount** ▲ British Columbia, SW Canada
61 D22 **Rauch** Buenos Aires, E Argentina
41 U16 **Raudales** Chiapas, SE Mexico
Raudhatain *see* Ar Rawḍatayn
Raudnitz an der Elbe *see* Roudnice nad Labem
92 K1 **Raufarhöfn** Nordhurland Eystra, NE Iceland
94 H13 **Raufoss** Oppland, S Norway
Raukawa *see* Cook Strait
184 Q8 **Raukumara** ▲ North Island, NZ
192 K11 **Raukumara Plain** *undersea feature* N Coral Sea
184 P8 **Raukumara Range** ⛰ North Island, NZ
154 N11 **Rāulakela** *var.* Raurkela; *prev.* Rourkela. Orissa, E. India
95 F15 **Rauland** Telemark, S Norway
93 J19 **Rauma** *Swe.* Raumo. Länsi-Suomi, W Finland
94 F10 **Rauma** ⇝ S Norway
Raumo *see* Rauma
118 H8 **Rauna** Cēsis, C Latvia
169 T17 **Raung, Gunung** ▲ Jawa, S Indonesia
Raurkela *see* Rāulakela
95 J22 **Raus** Skåne, S Sweden
165 W3 **Rausu** Hokkaidō, NE Japan
165 W3 **Rausu-dake** ▲ Hokkaidō, NE Japan
93 M17 **Rautalampi** Itä-Suomi, C Finland
93 N16 **Rautavaara** Itä-Suomi, C Finland
116 M9 **Răutel** ⇝ C Moldova
93 O18 **Rautjärvi** Etelä-Suomi, S Finland
Rautu *see* Sosnovo
191 V11 **Ravahere** *atoll* Îles Tuamotu, C French Polynesia
107 J25 **Ravanusa** Sicilia, Italy, C Mediterranean Sea
143 S9 **Rāvar** Kermān, C Iran
147 Q11 **Ravat** Batkenskaya Oblast', SW Kyrgyzstan
18 K11 **Ravena** New York, NE USA
106 H10 **Ravenna** Emilia-Romagna, N Italy
29 O15 **Ravenna** Nebraska, C USA
31 U11 **Ravenna** Ohio, N USA
101 I24 **Ravensburg** Baden-Württemberg, S Germany
181 W4 **Ravenshoe** Queensland, NE Australia
180 K13 **Ravensthorpe** Western Australia
21 Q4 **Ravenswood** West Virginia, NE USA
149 U9 **Rāvi** ⇝ India/Pakistan
112 C9 **Ravna Gora** Primorje-Gorski Kotar, NW Croatia
109 U10 **Ravne na Koroškem** *Ger.* Gutenstein. N Slovenia
139 P6 **Rāwah** W Iraq
191 T4 **Rawaki** *prev.* Phoenix Island. *atoll* Phoenix Islands, C Kiribati
149 U6 **Rāwalpindi** Punjab, NE Pakistan
110 L13 **Rawa Mazowiecka** Łódzkie, C Poland
139 T2 **Rawāndiz** *var.* Rawandoz, Rawāndūz. N Iraq
Rawandoz/Rawāndūz *see* Rawāndiz
171 U12 **Rawas** Papua, E Indonesia
139 O4 **Rawḍah** ◎ E Syria
110 G13 **Rawicz** *Ger.* Rawitsch. Wielkopolskie, C Poland
Rawitsch *see* Rawicz
180 M11 **Rawlinna** Western Australia
33 W16 **Rawlins** Wyoming, C USA
63 K17 **Rawson** Chubut, SE Argentina
159 R16 **Rawu** Xizang Zizhiqu, W China
153 P12 **Raxaul** Bihār, N India
28 K3 **Ray** North Dakota, N USA
169 S11 **Raya, Bukit** ▲ Borneo, C Indonesia
155 I18 **Rāyachoti** Andhra Pradesh, E India
Rāyadrug *see* Rāyagarha
155 M14 **Rāyagarha** *prev.* Rāyadrug. Orissa, E India
138 H7 **Rayak** *var.* Rayaq, Riyāq. E Lebanon
Rayaq *see* Rayak
139 T2 **Rāyat** E Iraq
169 N12 **Raya, Tanjung** *headland* Pulau Bangka, W Indonesia
13 R13 **Ray, Cape** *headland* Newfoundland and Labrador, E Canada
123 Q13 **Raychikhinsk** Amurskaya Oblast', SE Russian Federation
127 U5 **Rayevskiy** Respublika Bashkortostan, W Russian Federation
11 Q17 **Raymond** Alberta, SW Canada
22 K6 **Raymond** Mississippi, S USA
32 F9 **Raymond** Washington, NW USA
183 T8 **Raymond Terrace** New South Wales, SE Australia
25 T17 **Raymondville** Texas, SW USA
11 U16 **Raymore** Saskatchewan, S Canada
39 Q8 **Ray Mountains** ⛰ Alaska, USA
22 H9 **Rayne** Louisiana, S USA
41 O12 **Rayón** San Luis Potosí, C Mexico
40 G4 **Rayón** Sonora, NW Mexico
167 P12 **Rayong** Rayong, S Thailand
25 T5 **Ray Roberts, Lake** ◎ Texas, SW USA
18 E15 **Raystown Lake** ▣ Pennsylvania, NE USA
141 V13 **Raysūt** SW Oman
27 R4 **Raytown** Missouri, C USA
22 I5 **Rayville** Louisiana, S USA
142 L5 **Razan** Hamadān, W Iran
139 S9 **Razāzah, Buḥayrat ar** *var.* Baḥr al Milḥ. ◎ C Iraq
114 L9 **Razboyna** ▲ E Bulgaria
Razdan *see* Hrazdan
Razdolnoye *see* Rozdol'ne
Razelm, Lacul *see* Razim, Lacul
139 U2 **Razga** E Iraq
114 L8 **Razgrad** Razgrad, N Bulgaria
114 L8 **Razgrad** ◈ *province* N Bulgaria
117 N13 **Razim, Lacul** *prev.* Lacul Razelm. *lagoon* NW Black Sea
114 G11 **Razlog** Blagoevgrad, SW Bulgaria
118 K10 **Rāznas Ezers** ◎ SE Latvia
102 E6 **Raz, Pointe du** *headland* NW France
Reachlainn *see* Rathlin Island
Reachrainn *see* Lambay Island
97 N22 **Reading** S England, UK
18 H15 **Reading** Pennsylvania, NE USA
62 K12 **Realicó** La Pampa, C Argentina
25 R15 **Realitos** Texas, SW USA
108 G9 **Realp** Uri, C Switzerland
167 Q12 **Reăng Kesei** Bătdâmbâng, W Cambodia
191 Y11 **Reao** *atoll* Îles Tuamotu, E French Polynesia
Reate *see* Rieti
180 L11 **Rebecca, Lake** ◎ Western Australia
Rebiana Sand Sea *see* Rabyānah, Ramlat
124 H8 **Reboly** Respublika Kareliya, NW Russian Federation
165 S1 **Rebun** Rebun-tō, NE Japan
165 S1 **Rebun-tō** *island* NE Japan
106 J12 **Recanati** Marche, C Italy
Rechitsa *see* Rechytsa
109 Y7 **Rechnitz** Burgenland, SE Austria
119 J20 **Rechytsa** *Rus.* Rechitsa. Brestskaya Voblasts', SW Belarus
119 O19 **Rechytsa** *Rus.* Rechitsa. Homyel'skaya Voblasts', SE Belarus
59 Q15 **Recife** *prev.* Pernambuco. *state capital* Pernambuco, E Brazil
83 I26 **Recife, Cape** *Afr.* Kaap Recife. *headland* S South Africa
Recife, Kaap *see* Recife, Cape
172 I16 **Récifs, Îles aux** *island* Inner Islands, NE Seychelles
101 E14 **Recklinghausen** Nordrhein-Westfalen, W Germany
100 M8 **Recknitz** ⇝ NE Germany
99 K23 **Recogne** Luxembourg, SE Belgium
61 C15 **Reconquista** Santa Fe, C Argentina
195 O6 **Recovery Glacier** *glacier* Antarctica
59 G15 **Recreio** Mato Grosso, W Brazil
27 X9 **Rector** Arkansas, C USA
110 E9 **Recz** *Ger.* Reetz Neumark. Zachodnio-pomorskie, NW Poland
99 L24 **Redange** *var.* Redange-sur-Attert. Diekirch, W Luxembourg

◆ Country
● Country Capital
◇ Dependent Territory
○ Dependent Territory Capital
◈ Administrative Region
✕ International Airport
▲ Mountain
⛰ Mountain Range
⚘ Volcano
⇝ River
◎ Lake
▣ Reservoir

Redange-sur-Attert see Redange
18 C13 Redbank Creek ≈ Pennsylvania, NE USA
13 S9 Red Bay Quebec, E Canada
23 N2 Red Bay Alabama, S USA
35 N4 Red Bluff California, W USA
24 J8 Red Bluff Reservoir ⊞ New Mexico/Texas, SW USA
30 K16 Red Bud Illinois, N USA
30 J5 Red Cedar River ≈ Wisconsin, N USA
11 R17 Redcliff Alberta, SW Canada
83 K17 Redcliff Midlands, C Zimbabwe
182 L9 Red Cliffs Victoria, SE Australia
29 P17 Red Cloud Nebraska, C USA
22 L8 Red Creek ≈ Mississippi, S USA
11 P15 Red Deer Alberta, SW Canada
11 Q16 Red Deer ≈ Alberta, SW Canada
39 O11 Red Devil Alaska, USA
35 N3 Redding California, W USA
97 L20 Redditch W England, UK
29 P9 Redfield South Dakota, N USA
24 J12 Redford Texas, SW USA
45 V13 Redhead Trinidad, Trinidad and Tobago
182 I8 Red Hill South Australia
Red Hill see Pu'u 'Ula'ula
26 K7 Red Hills hill range Kansas, C USA
13 T12 Red Indian Lake ◎ Newfoundland and Labrador, E Canada
124 J16 Redkino Tverskaya Oblast', W Russian Federation
12 A10 Red Lake Ontario, C Canada
36 I10 Red Lake salt flat Arizona, SW USA
29 S4 Red Lake Falls Minnesota, N USA
29 R4 Red Lake River ≈ Minnesota, N USA
35 U15 Redlands California, W USA
18 G16 Red Lion Pennsylvania, NE USA
33 U11 Red Lodge Montana, NW USA
32 H13 Redmond Oregon, NW USA
36 L5 Redmond Utah, W USA
32 H8 Redmond Washington, NW USA
Rednitz see Regnitz
29 T15 Red Oak Iowa, C USA
18 K12 Red Oaks Mill New York, NE USA
102 I7 Redon Ille-et-Vilaine, NW France
45 W10 Redonda island SW Antigua and Barbuda
104 G4 Redondela Galicia, NW Spain
104 H11 Redondo Évora, S Portugal
39 Q12 Redoubt Volcano ▲ Alaska, USA
11 Y16 Red River ≈ Canada/USA
167 S5 Red River var. Yuan, Chin. Yuan Jiang, Vtn. Sông Hông Hà. ≈ China/Vietnam
25 W4 Red River ≈ S USA
22 H7 Red River ≈ Louisiana, S USA
30 M6 Red River ≈ Wisconsin, N USA
Red Rock, Lake see Red Rock Reservoir
29 W14 Red Rock Reservoir var. Lake Red Rock. ⊞ Iowa, C USA
80 H7 Red Sea ◈ state NE Sudan
75 Y9 Red Sea anc. Sinus Arabicus. sea Africa/Asia
21 T11 Red Springs North Carolina, SE USA
8 I9 Redstone ≈ Northwest Territories, NW Canada
11 V17 Redvers Saskatchewan, S Canada
77 P13 Red Volta var. Nazinon, Fr. Volta Rouge. ≈ Burkina/Ghana
11 Q14 Redwater Alberta, SW Canada
28 M16 Red Willow Creek ≈ Nebraska, C USA
29 W9 Red Wing Minnesota, N USA
35 N9 Redwood City California, W USA
29 T9 Redwood Falls Minnesota, N USA
31 P7 Reed City Michigan, N USA
28 K6 Reeder North Dakota, N USA
35 R11 Reedley California, W USA
33 T11 Reedpoint Montana, NW USA
30 K8 Reedsburg Wisconsin, N USA
32 E13 Reedsport Oregon, NW USA
187 Q9 Reef Islands island group Santa Cruz Islands, E Solomon Islands
185 H16 Reefton West Coast, South Island, NZ
20 F8 Reelfoot Lake ◎ Tennessee, S USA
97 D17 Ree, Lough Ir. Loch Rí. ◎ C Ireland
Reengus see Ringas
35 U4 Reese River ≈ Nevada, W USA
98 M8 Reest ≈ E Netherlands
Reetz Neumark see Recz
Reevhtse see Rossvatnet
137 N13 Refahiye Erzincan, C Turkey
23 N4 Reform Alabama, S USA
95 K20 Reftele Jönköping, S Sweden
25 T14 Refugio Texas, SW USA
110 E8 Rega ≈ NW Poland
Regar see Tursunzoda
101 O21 Regen Bayern, SE Germany
101 M20 Regen ≈ SE Germany
101 M21 Regensburg Eng. Ratisbon, Fr. Ratisbonne; hist. Ratisbona, anc. Castra Regina, Reginum. Bayern, SE Germany
101 M21 Regenstauf Bayern, SE Germany
74 I10 Reggane C Algeria
98 N9 Regge ≈ E Netherlands
Reggio see Reggio nell' Emilia
Reggio Calabria see Reggio di Calabria
107 M23 Reggio di Calabria var. Reggio Calabria, Gk. Rhegion; anc. Regium, Rhegium. Calabria, SW Italy
Reggio Emilia see Reggio nell' Emilia
106 F9 Reggio nell' Emilia var. Reggio Emilia, abbrev. Reggio; anc. Regium Lepidum. Emilia-Romagna, N Italy
116 I10 Reghin Ger. Sächsisch-Reen, Hung. Szászrégen; prev. Reghinul Săsesc, Ger. Sächsisch-Regen. Mureș, C Romania
Reghinul Săsesc see Reghin
11 U16 Regina Saskatchewan, S Canada
11 U16 Regina × Saskatchewan, S Canada
55 Z10 Régina E French Guiana
11 U16 Regina Beach Saskatchewan, S Canada
Reginum see Regensburg
Registan see Rīgestān
60 L11 Registro São Paulo, S Brazil
Regium see Reggio di Calabria
Regium Lepidum see Reggio nell' Emilia
101 K19 Regnitz var. Rednitz. ≈ SE Germany
40 K10 Regocijo Durango, W Mexico
104 H12 Reguengos de Monsaraz Évora, S Portugal
101 M18 Rehau Bayern, E Germany
83 D19 Rehoboth Hardap, C Namibia
Rehoboth/Rehovoth see Reḥovot
21 Z4 Rehoboth Beach Delaware, NE USA
138 F10 Reḥovot var. Rehoboth, Rekhovot, Rehovoth. Central, C Israel
81 J20 Rei spring/well S Kenya
Reichenau see Rychnov nad Kněžnou, Czech Republic
Reichenau see Bogatynia, Poland
101 M17 Reichenbach var. Reichenbach im Vogtland. Sachsen, E Germany
Reichenbach see Dzierżoniów
Reichenbach im Vogtland see Reichenbach
Reichenberg see Liberec
181 O11 Reid Western Australia
23 V6 Reidsville Georgia, SE USA
21 T8 Reidsville North Carolina, SE USA
Reifnitz see Ribnica
97 O22 Reigate SE England, UK
Reikjavik see Reykjavík
102 I10 Ré, Île de island W France
37 N15 Reiley Peak ▲ Arizona, SW USA
103 Q4 Reims Eng. Rheims; anc. Durocortorum, Remi. Marne, N France
63 G23 Reina Adelaida, Archipiélago island group S Chile
45 O16 Reina Beatrix × (Oranjestad) C Aruba
108 F7 Reinach Aargau, W Switzerland
108 E6 Reinach Basel-Land, NW Switzerland
64 O11 Reina Sofía × (Tenerife) Tenerife, Islas Canarias, Spain, NE Atlantic Ocean
29 W13 Reinbeck Iowa, C USA
100 J10 Reinbek Schleswig-Holstein, N Germany
11 U12 Reindeer ≈ Saskatchewan, C Canada
11 U11 Reindeer Lake ◎ Manitoba/Saskatchewan, C Canada
Reine-Charlotte, Îles de la see Queen Charlotte Islands
Reine-Élisabeth, Îles de la see Queen Elizabeth Islands
94 F13 Reineskarvet ▲ S Norway
184 H1 Reinga, Cape headland North Island, NZ
105 N3 Reinosa Cantabria, N Spain
109 R8 Reisseck ▲ S Austria
21 W3 Reisterstown Maryland, NE USA
Reisui see Yŏsu
98 N5 Reitdiep ≈ NE Netherlands
191 V10 Reitoru atoll Îles Tuamotu, C French Polynesia
95 M17 Rejmyre Östergötland, S Sweden
Reka see Rijeka
Reka Ili see Ile/Ili He
95 N16 Rekarne Västmanland, C Sweden 16.04
Rekhovot see Reḥovot
8 K9 Reliance Northwest Territories, C Canada
33 U16 Reliance Wyoming, C USA
74 I5 Relizane var. Ghelîzâne, Ghilizane. NW Algeria
182 I7 Remarkable, Mount ▲ South Australia
54 E8 Remedios Antioquia, N Colombia
43 Q16 Remedios Veraguas, W Panama
42 D8 Remedios, Punta headland SW El Salvador
Remi see Reims
99 N25 Remich Grevenmacher, SE Luxembourg
99 J19 Remicourt Liège, E Belgium
14 H8 Rémigny, Lac ◎ Québec, SE Canada
55 Z10 Rémire NE French Guiana
127 N13 Remontnoye Rostovskaya Oblast', SW Russian Federation
171 U14 Remoon Pulau Kur, E Indonesia
99 L20 Remouchamps Liège, E Belgium
103 R15 Remoulins Gard, S France
173 X16 Rempart, Mont du var. Mount Rempart. hill W Mauritius
101 E15 Remscheid Nordrhein-Westfalen, W Germany
29 S12 Remsen Iowa, C USA
94 I12 Rena Hedmark, S Norway
94 I11 Renåa ≈ S Norway
Renaix see Ronse
113 H7 Rencēni Valmiera, N Latvia
118 D9 Renda Kuldīga, W Latvia
107 N20 Rende Calabria, SW Italy
99 K21 Rendeux Luxembourg, SE Belgium
Rendina see Rentína
30 L16 Rend Lake ⊞ Illinois, N USA
186 K9 Rendova island New Georgia Islands, NW Solomon Islands
100 I8 Rendsburg Schleswig-Holstein, N Germany
108 B9 Renens Vaud, SW Switzerland
14 K12 Renfrew Ontario, SE Canada
96 I12 Renfrew cultural region SW Scotland, UK
168 L11 Rengat Sumatera, W Indonesia
153 W12 Rengma Hills ▲▲ NE India
62 H12 Rengo Libertador, C Chile
116 M12 Reni Odes'ka Oblast', SW Ukraine
80 F11 Renk Upper Nile, E Sudan
93 L19 Renko Etelä-Suomi, S Finland
98 L12 Renkum Gelderland, SE Netherlands
182 K9 Renmark South Australia
186 L10 Rennell var. Mu Nggava. island S Solomon Islands
181 Q4 Renner Springs Roadhouse Northern Territory, N Australia
102 I6 Rennes Bret. Roazon; anc. Condate. Ille-et-Vilaine, NW France
195 S16 Rennick Glacier glacier Antarctica
11 Y16 Rennie Manitoba, S Canada
35 Q5 Reno Nevada, W USA
106 H10 Reno ≈ N Italy
35 Q5 Reno-Cannon × Nevada, W USA
83 F24 Renoster ≈ SW South Africa
15 T5 Renouard, Lac ◎ Québec, SE Canada
18 F13 Renovo Pennsylvania, NE USA
161 O3 Renqiu Hebei, E China
160 I9 Renshou Sichuan, C China
31 N12 Rensselaer Indiana, N USA
18 L11 Rensselaer New York, NE USA
105 Q2 Rentería Basq. Errenteria. País Vasco, N Spain
115 E17 Rentína var. Rendina. Thessalía, C Greece
29 T9 Renville Minnesota, N USA
77 O13 Réo W Burkina
15 O12 Repentigny Québec, SE Canada
146 K13 Repetek Lebap Welaýaty, E Turkmenistan
93 J16 Replot Fin. Raippaluoto. island W Finland
Reppen see Rzepin
Reps see Rupea
27 T7 Republic Missouri, C USA
32 K7 Republic Washington, NW USA
27 N3 Republican River ≈ Kansas/Nebraska, C USA
9 O7 Repulse Bay Northwest Territories, N Canada
56 F9 Requena Loreto, NE Peru
105 R10 Requena País Valenciano, E Spain
103 O14 Réquista Aveyron, S France
136 M12 Reşadiye Tokat, N Turkey
Reschenpass see Resia, Passo di
Reschitza see Reşiţa
113 N20 Resen Turk. Resne. SW FYR Macedonia
60 J11 Reserva Paraná, S Brazil
11 V15 Reserve Saskatchewan, S Canada
37 P13 Reserve New Mexico, SW USA
Reshetilovka see Reshetylivka
117 S6 Reshetylivka Rus. Reshetilovka. Poltavs'ka Oblast', NE Ukraine
Resht see Rasht
106 F5 Resia, Passo di Ger. Reschenpass. pass Austria/Italy
Resicabánya see Reşiţa
62 N7 Resistencia Chaco, NE Argentina
116 F12 Reşiţa Ger. Reschitza, Hung. Resicabánya. Caraş-Severin, W Romania
Resne see Resen
8 K4 Resolute var.. Qausuittuq. Nunavut, N Canada
Resolution see Fort Resolution
9 T7 Resolution Island island Nunavut, NE Canada
185 A23 Resolution Island island SW NZ
15 W7 Restigouche Québec, SE Canada
11 W17 Reston Manitoba, S Canada
14 H11 Restoule Lake ◎ Ontario, S Canada
54 F10 Restrepo Meta, C Colombia
42 B6 Retalhuleu Retalhuleu, SW Guatemala
42 A1 Retalhuleu off. Departamento de Retalhuleu. ◈ department SW Guatemala
97 N18 Retford C England, UK
103 Q3 Rethel Ardennes, N France
Rethimno/Réthimnon see Réthymno
115 I25 Réthymno var. Rethimno; prev. Réthimnon. Kríti, Greece, E Mediterranean Sea
Retiche, Alpi see Rhaetian Alps
99 J16 Retie Antwerpen, N Belgium
111 J21 Rétság Nógrád, N Hungary
109 W2 Retz Niederösterreich, NE Austria
173 N15 Réunion off. La Réunion. ◇ French overseas department W Indian Ocean
105 U6 Reus Cataluña, E Spain
99 J15 Reusel Noord-Brabant, S Netherlands
108 F7 Reuss ≈ NW Switzerland
Reuṭel see Ciuhuru
101 H22 Reutlingen Baden-Württemberg, S Germany
108 L7 Reutte Tirol, W Austria
99 M16 Reuver Limburg, SE Netherlands
28 K7 Reva South Dakota, N USA
Reval/Revel' see Tallinn
124 J4 Revda Murmanskaya Oblast', NW Russian Federation
122 F6 Revda Sverdlovskaya Oblast', C Russian Federation
103 N16 Revel Haute-Garonne, S France
11 O16 Revelstoke British Columbia, SW Canada
43 N13 Reventazón, Río ≈ E Costa Rica
106 G9 Revere Lombardia, N Italy
39 Y14 Revillagigedo Island island Alexander Archipelago, Alaska, USA
103 R3 Revin Ardennes, N France
92 O3 Revnosa headland C Svalbard
Revolyutsii, Pik see Revolyutsiya, Qullai
147 T13 Revolyutsiya, Qullai Rus. Pik Revolyutsii. ▲ SE Tajikistan
111 L19 Revúca Ger. Grossrauschenbach, Hung. Nagyrőce. Banskobystrický Kraj, C Slovakia
154 K9 Rewa Madhya Pradesh, C India
152 I11 Rewāri Haryāna, N India
33 R14 Rexburg Idaho, NW USA
78 G13 Rey Bouba Nord, NE Cameroon
92 L3 Reydharfjördhur Austurland, E Iceland
57 K16 Reyes Beni, NW Bolivia
34 L8 Reyes, Point headland California, W USA
54 B12 Reyes, Punta headland SW Colombia
136 L17 Reyhanlı Hatay, S Turkey
43 U16 Rey, Isla del island Archipiélago de las Perlas, SE Panama
92 H2 Reykhólar Vestfirdhir, W Iceland
92 K2 Reykjahlídh Nordhurland Eystra, NE Iceland
92 I4 Reykjanes ◈ region SW Iceland
197 O16 Reykjanes Basin var. Irminger Basin. undersea feature N Atlantic Ocean
197 N17 Reykjanes Ridge undersea feature N Atlantic Ocean
92 H4 Reykjavík var. Reikjavik. ● (Iceland) Höfudhborgarsvaedhi, W Iceland
18 D13 Reynoldsville Pennsylvania, NE USA
41 P8 Reynosa Tamaulipas, C Mexico
Reẕā'īyeh see Orūmīyeh
Reẕā'īyeh, Daryācheh-ye see Orūmīyeh, Daryācheh-ye
102 I8 Rezé Loire-Atlantique, NW France
118 K10 Rēzekne Ger. Rositten; prev. Rus. Rezhitsa. Rēzekne, SE Latvia
Rezhitsa see Rēzekne
117 N9 Rezina NE Moldova
114 N11 Rezovo Turk. Rezve. Burgas, E Bulgaria
114 N11 Rezovska Reka Turk. Rezve Deresi. ≈ Bulgaria/Turkey see also Rezve Deresi
Rezve see Rezovo
114 N11 Rezve Deresi Bul. Rezovska Reka. ≈ Bulgaria/Turkey see also Rezovska Reka
Rhadames see Ghadāmis
Rhaedestus see Tekirdağ
108 J10 Rhaetian Alps Fr. Alpes Rhétiques, Ger. Rätische Alpen, It. Alpi Retiche. ▲▲ C Europe
108 I8 Rhätikon ▲▲ C Europe
101 G14 Rheda-Wiedenbrück Nordrhein-Westfalen, W Germany
98 M12 Rheden Gelderland, E Netherlands
Rhegion/Rhegium see Reggio di Calabria
Rheims see Reims
Rhein see Rhine
101 E17 Rheinbach Nordrhein-Westfalen, W Germany
100 F13 Rheine var. Rheine in Westfalen. Nordrhein-Westfalen, NW Germany
Rheine in Westfalen see Rheine
Rheinfeld see Rheinfelden
101 F24 Rheinfelden Baden-Württemberg, S Germany
108 E6 Rheinfelden var. Rheinfeld. Aargau, N Switzerland
101 E17 Rheinisches Schiefergebirge var. Rhine State Uplands, Eng. Rhenish Slate Mountains. ▲▲ W Germany
101 D18 Rheinland-Pfalz Eng. Rhineland-Palatinate, Fr. Rhénanie-Palatinat. ◈ state W Germany
101 G18 Rhein/Main × (Frankfurt am Main) Hessen, W Germany
Rhénanie du Nord-Westphalie see Nordrhein-Westfalen
Rhénanie-Palatinat see Rheinland-Pfalz
98 K12 Rhenen Utrecht, C Netherlands
Rhenish Slate Mountains see Rheinisches Schiefergebirge
Rhétiques, Alpes see Rhaetian Alps
100 N10 Rhin ≈ NE Germany
Rhin see Rhine
101 E17 Rhine Dut. Rijn, Fr. Rhin, Ger. Rhein. ≈ W Europe
30 L5 Rhinelander Wisconsin, N USA
Rhineland-Palatinate see Rheinland-Pfalz
Rhine State Uplands see Rheinisches Schiefergebirge
100 N11 Rhinkanal canal NE Germany
81 F17 Rhino Camp NW Uganda
74 D7 Rhir, Cap headland W Morocco
106 D7 Rho Lombardia, N Italy
19 N12 Rhode Island off. State of Rhode Island and Providence Plantations; also known as Little Rhody, Ocean State. ◈ state NE USA
19 O13 Rhode Island island Rhode Island, NE USA
19 O13 Rhode Island Sound sound Maine/Rhode Island, NE USA
Rhodes see Ródos
Rhode-Saint-Genèse see Sint-Genesius-Rode
84 L14 Rhodes Basin undersea feature E Mediterranean Sea
Rhodesia see Zimbabwe
114 I12 Rhodope Mountains var. Rodhópi Óri, Bul. Rhodope Planina, Rodopi, Gk. Orosirá Rodhópis, Turk. Dospad Dagh. ▲▲ Bulgaria/Greece
Rhodope Planina see Rhodope Mountains
Rhodos see Ródos
101 I18 Rhön ▲▲ C Germany
103 Q10 Rhône ◈ department E France
103 R13 Rhône ≈ France/Switzerland
103 R12 Rhône-Alpes ◈ region E France
98 G13 Rhoon Zuid-Holland, SW Netherlands
96 G9 Rhum var. Rum. island W Scotland, UK
Rhuthun see Ruthin
97 J18 Rhyl NE Wales, UK
59 K18 Rialma Goiás, S Brazil
104 L3 Riaño Castilla-León, N Spain
105 O9 Riansáres ≈ C Spain
152 H6 Riāsi Jammu and Kashmir, NW India
168 K10 Riau off. Propinsi Riau. ◈ province W Indonesia
Riau Archipelago see Riau, Kepulauan
168 M11 Riau, Kepulauan var. Riau Archipelago, Dut. Riouw-Archipel. island group W Indonesia
105 O6 Riaza Castilla-León, N Spain
105 N6 Riaza ≈ N Spain
81 K17 Riba spring/well NE Kenya
104 H4 Ribadavia Galicia, NW Spain
104 J2 Ribadeo Galicia, NW Spain
104 L2 Ribadesella Asturias, N Spain
104 G10 Ribatejo former province C Portugal
83 P15 Ribáuè Nampula, N Mozambique
97 K17 Ribble ≈ NW England, UK
95 F23 Ribe Ribe, W Denmark
95 F23 Ribe off. Ribe Amt, var. Ripen. ◈ county W Denmark
104 G3 Ribeira Galicia, NW Spain
64 O5 Ribeira Brava Madeira, Portugal, NE Atlantic Ocean
64 P3 Ribeira Grande São Miguel, Azores, Portugal, NE Atlantic Ocean
60 L8 Ribeirão Preto São Paulo, S Brazil
60 L11 Ribeira, Rio ≈ S Brazil
107 I24 Ribera Sicilia, Italy, C Mediterranean Sea
57 L14 Riberalta Beni, N Bolivia
105 W4 Ribes de Freser Cataluña, NE Spain
30 L6 Rib Mountain ▲ Wisconsin, N USA
109 U12 Ribnica Ger. Reifnitz. S Slovenia
117 N9 Rîbniţa var. Râbniţa, Rus. Rybnitsa. NE Moldova
100 M8 Ribnitz-Damgarten Mecklenburg-Vorpommern, NE Germany
111 D16 Říčany Ger. Ritschan. Středočeský Kraj, W Czech Republic
29 U7 Rice Minnesota, N USA
30 J5 Rice Lake Wisconsin, N USA
14 I15 Rice Lake ◎ Ontario, S Canada
14 E8 Rice Lake ◎ Ontario, S Canada
23 V3 Richard B.Russell Lake ⊞ Georgia, SE USA
25 U6 Richardson Texas, SW USA
11 R11 Richardson ≈ Alberta, C Canada
10 I3 Richardson Mountains ▲▲ Yukon Territory, NW Canada
185 C21 Richardson Mountains ▲▲ South Island, NZ
42 F3 Richardson Peak ▲ SE Belize
76 G10 Richard Toll N Senegal
28 L5 Richardton North Dakota, N USA
14 F13 Rich, Cape headland Ontario, S Canada
102 L8 Richelieu Indre-et-Loire, C France
33 P15 Richfield Idaho, NW USA
36 K5 Richfield Utah, W USA
18 J10 Richfield Springs New York, NE USA
18 M6 Richford Vermont, NE USA
27 R6 Rich Hill Missouri, C USA
13 P14 Richibucto New Brunswick, SE Canada
108 G8 Richisau Glarus, NE Switzerland
23 S6 Richland Georgia, SE USA
27 U6 Richland Missouri, C USA
25 U8 Richland Texas, SW USA
32 K10 Richland Washington, NW USA
30 K8 Richland Center Wisconsin, N USA
21 W11 Richlands North Carolina, SE USA
21 Q7 Richlands Virginia, NE USA
25 R9 Richland Springs Texas, SW USA
183 S8 Richmond New South Wales, SE Australia
10 L17 Richmond British Columbia, SW Canada
14 L13 Richmond Ontario, SE Canada
15 Q12 Richmond Québec, SE Canada
185 I14 Richmond Tasman, South Island, NZ
35 N8 Richmond California, W USA
31 Q14 Richmond Indiana, N USA
20 M6 Richmond Kentucky, S USA
27 S4 Richmond Missouri, C USA
25 V11 Richmond Texas, SW USA
36 L1 Richmond Utah, W USA
21 W6 Richmond state capital Virginia, NE USA
14 H15 Richmond Hill Ontario, S Canada
185 J15 Richmond Range ▲▲ South Island, NZ
27 S12 Rich Mountain ▲ Arkansas, C USA
31 S13 Richwood Ohio, N USA
21 R5 Richwood West Virginia, NE USA
104 K5 Ricobayo, Embalse de ⊞ NW Spain
Ricomagus see Riom
Ridā' see Radā'
98 H13 Ridderkerk Zuid-Holland, SW Netherlands
33 N16 Riddle Idaho, NW USA
32 F14 Riddle Oregon, NW USA
14 L13 Rideau ≈ Ontario, SE Canada
35 T12 Ridgecrest California, W USA
18 L13 Ridgefield Connecticut, NE USA
22 K5 Ridgeland Mississippi, S USA
21 R15 Ridgeland South Carolina, SE USA
20 F8 Ridgely Tennessee, S USA
14 D17 Ridgetown Ontario, S Canada
Ridgeway see Ridgway
21 R12 Ridgeway South Carolina, SE USA
18 D13 Ridgway var. Ridgeway. Pennsylvania, NE USA
11 W16 Riding Mountain ▲▲ Manitoba, S Canada
Ried see Ried im Innkreis
109 R4 Ried im Innkreis var. Ried. Oberösterreich, NW Austria
109 X8 Riegersburg Steiermark, SE Austria
108 E6 Riehen Basel-Stadt, NW Switzerland
92 J9 Riehppegáisá var. Rieppe. ▲ N Norway
99 K18 Riemst Limburg, NE Belgium
Rieppe see Riehppegáisá
101 O15 Riesa Sachsen, E Germany
63 H24 Riesco, Isla island S Chile
107 K25 Riesi Sicilia, Italy, C Mediterranean Sea
83 F25 Riet ≈ SW South Africa
83 I23 Riet ≈ SW South Africa
118 D11 Rietavas Telšiai, W Lithuania
83 F19 Rietfontein Omaheke, E Namibia
107 I14 Rieti anc. Reate. Lazio, C Italy
84 D14 Rif var. Er Rif, Er Riff, Riff. ▲▲ N Morocco
Riff see Rif
37 Q4 Rifle Colorado, C USA
31 R7 Rifle River ≈ Michigan, N USA
81 H18 Rift Valley ◈ province Kenya
Rift Valley see Great Rift Valley
118 F9 Rīga Eng. Riga. ● (Latvia) Rīga, C Latvia
Rigaer Bucht see Riga, Gulf of
118 F6 Riga, Gulf of Est. Liivi Laht, Ger. Rigaer Bucht, Latv. Rīgas Jūras Līcis, Rus. Rizhskiy Zaliv; prev. Est. Riia Laht. gulf Estonia/Latvia
143 U12 Rīgān Kermān, SE Iran
Rīgas Jūras Līcis see Riga, Gulf of
15 N12 Rigaud ≈ Ontario/Québec, SE Canada
33 R14 Rigby Idaho, NW USA
148 M10 Rīgestān var. Registan. desert region S Afghanistan
32 M11 Riggins Idaho, NW USA
13 R8 Rigolet Newfoundland and Labrador, NE Canada
78 G9 Rig-Rig Kanem, W Chad
118 F4 Riguldi Läänemaa, W Estonia
Riia Laht see Riga, Gulf of
93 L19 Riihimäki Etelä-Suomi, S Finland
195 O2 Riiser-Larsen Ice Shelf ice shelf Antarctica
195 U2 Riiser-Larsen Peninsula peninsula Antarctica
65 P22 Riiser-Larsen Sea sea Antarctica
40 D2 Riíto Sonora, NW Mexico
112 B9 Rijeka Ger. Sankt Veit am Flaum, It. Fiume, Slvn. Reka; anc. Tarsatica. Primorje-Gorski Kotar, NW Croatia
99 I14 Rijen Noord-Brabant, S Netherlands
99 H15 Rijkevorsel Antwerpen, N Belgium
Rijn see Rhine
98 G11 Rijnsburg Zuid-Holland, W Netherlands
Rijssel see Lille
98 N10 Rijssen Overijssel, E Netherlands
98 G12 Rijswijk Eng. Ryswick. Zuid-Holland, W Netherlands
92 I10 Riksgränsen Norrbotten, N Sweden
165 U4 Rikubetsu Hokkaidō, NE Japan
165 R9 Rikuzen-Takata Iwate, Honshū, C Japan
27 O4 Riley Kansas, C USA
99 I17 Rillaar Vlaams Brabant, C Belgium
Rí, Loch see Ree, Lough
114 G11 Rilska Reka ≈ W Bulgaria
77 T12 Rima ≈ N Nigeria
141 N7 Rimah, Wādī ar var. Wādī ar Rummah. dry watercourse C Saudi Arabia
Rimaszombat see Rimavská Sobota

191 R12 **Rimatara** *island* Îles Australes, SW French Polynesia
111 L20 **Rimavská Sobota** *Ger.* Gross-Steffelsdorf, *Hung.* Rimaszombat. Banskobystrický Kraj, C Slovakia
11 Q15 **Rimbey** Alberta, SW Canada
95 P15 **Rimbo** Stockholm, C Sweden
95 M18 **Rimforsa** Östergötland, S Sweden
106 I11 **Rimini** *anc.* Ariminum. Emilia-Romagna, N Italy
Rîmnicu-Sărat *see* Râmnicu Sărat
Rîmnicu Vîlcea *see* Râmnicu Vâlcea
149 Y3 **Rimo Muztāgh** ▲ India/Pakistan
15 U7 **Rimouski** Québec, SE Canada
158 M16 **Rinbung** Xizang Zizhiqu, W China
162 I5 **Rinchinlhümbe** Hövsgöl, N Mongolia
62 I5 **Rincón, Cerro** ▲ N Chile
104 M15 **Rincón de la Victoria** Andalucía, S Spain
Rincón del Bonete, Lago Artificial de *see* Río Negro, Embalse del
105 Q4 **Rincón de Soto** La Rioja, N Spain
94 G8 **Rindal** Møre og Romsdal, S Norway
115 J20 **Ríneia** *island* Kykládes, Greece, Aegean Sea
152 H11 **Rīngas** *prev.* Reengus, Rīngus. Rājasthān, N India
95 H24 **Ringe** Fyn, C Denmark
94 H11 **Ringebu** Oppland, S Norway
Ringen *see* Rõngu
186 K8 **Ringgi** Kolombangara, NW Solomon Islands
23 R1 **Ringgold** Georgia, SE USA
22 G5 **Ringgold** Louisiana, S USA
25 S5 **Ringgold** Texas, SW USA
95 E22 **Ringkøbing** Ringkøbing, W Denmark
95 E21 **Ringkøbing** *off.* Ringkøbing Amt. ◆ *county* W Denmark
95 E22 **Ringkøbing Fjord** *fjord* W Denmark
33 S10 **Ringling** Montana, NW USA
27 N13 **Ringling** Oklahoma, C USA
94 H13 **Ringsaker** Hedmark, S Norway
95 I23 **Ringsted** Vestsjælland, E Denmark
Ringus *see* Rīngas
92 I9 **Ringvassøya** *Lapp.* Ráneš. *island* N Norway
18 K13 **Ringwood** New Jersey, NE USA
Rinn Duáin *see* Hook Head
100 H13 **Rinteln** Niedersachsen, NW Germany
Rio *see* Rio de Janeiro
115 E18 **Río** Dytikí Ellás, S Greece
56 C7 **Riobamba** Chimborazo, C Ecuador
60 P9 **Rio Bonito** Rio de Janeiro, SE Brazil
59 C16 **Rio Branco** *state capital* Acre, W Brazil
61 H18 **Río Branco** Cerro Largo, NE Uruguay
Rio Branco, Território de *see* Roraima
41 P8 **Río Bravo** Tamaulipas, C Mexico
63 G16 **Río Bueno** Los Lagos, C Chile
55 P5 **Río Caribe** Sucre, NE Venezuela
54 M5 **Río Chico** Miranda, N Venezuela
63 H18 **Río Cisnes** Aisén, S Chile
60 L9 **Rio Claro** São Paulo, S Brazil
45 V14 **Rio Claro** Trinidad, Trinidad and Tobago
54 J5 **Río Claro** Lara, N Venezuela
63 K15 **Río Colorado** Río Negro, E Argentina
62 K11 **Río Cuarto** Córdoba, C Argentina
60 P10 **Rio de Janeiro** *var.* Rio. *state capital* Rio de Janeiro, SE Brazil
60 P9 **Rio de Janeiro** *off.* Estado do Rio de Janeiro. ◆ *state* SE Brazil
43 R17 **Río de Jesús** Veraguas, S Panama
34 K3 **Rio Dell** California, W USA
60 K13 **Rio do Sul** Santa Catarina, S Brazil
63 I23 **Río Gallegos** *var.* Gallegos, Puerto Gallegos. Santa Cruz, S Argentina
61 I18 **Rio Grande** *var.* São Pedro do Rio Grande do Sul. Rio Grande do Sul, S Brazil
24 I9 **Rio Grande** ∽ Texas, SW USA
63 J24 **Río Grande** Tierra del Fuego, S Argentina
40 L10 **Río Grande** Zacatecas, C Mexico
42 J9 **Río Grande** León, NW Nicaragua
45 V5 **Río Grande** E Puerto Rico
25 R17 **Rio Grande City** Texas, SW USA
59 P14 **Rio Grande do Norte** *off.* Estado do Rio Grande do Norte. ◆ *state* E Brazil
61 G15 **Rio Grande do Sul** *off.* Estado do Rio Grande do Sul. ◆ *state* S Brazil
65 M17 **Rio Grande Fracture Zone** *tectonic feature* C Atlantic Ocean
65 J18 **Rio Grande Gap** *undersea feature* S Atlantic Ocean
Rio Grande Plateau *see* Rio Grande Rise
65 J18 **Rio Grande Rise** *var.* Rio Grande Plateau. *undersea feature* SW Atlantic Ocean
54 G4 **Ríohacha** La Guajira, N Colombia
43 S16 **Río Hato** Coclé, C Panama
25 T17 **Rio Hondo** Texas, SW USA
56 D10 **Rioja** San Martín, N Peru
41 Y11 **Río Lagartos** Yucatán, SE Mexico
103 P11 **Riom** *anc.* Ricomagus. Puy-de-Dôme, C France
104 F10 **Rio Maior** Santarém, C Portugal
103 O12 **Riom-ès-Montagnes** Cantal, C France
60 J12 **Rio Negro** Paraná, S Brazil
63 I15 **Río Negro** *off.* Provincia de Río Negro. ◆ *province* C Argentina
61 D18 **Río Negro** ◆ *department* W Uruguay
47 V12 **Río Negro, Embalse del** *var.* Lago Artificial de Rincón del Bonete. ⊠ C Uruguay
107 M17 **Rionero in Vulture** Basilicata, S Italy
137 S9 **Rioni** ∽ W Georgia
105 P12 **Riópar** Castilla-La Mancha, C Spain
61 H16 **Rio Pardo** Rio Grande do Sul, S Brazil
37 R11 **Rio Rancho Estates** New Mexico, SW USA
42 L11 **Río San Juan** ◆ *department* S Nicaragua
54 E9 **Ríosucio** Caldas, W Colombia
54 C7 **Ríosucio** Chocó, NW Colombia
62 K10 **Río Tercero** Córdoba, C Argentina
54 J5 **Río Tocuyo** Lara, N Venezuela
Riouw-Archipel *see* Riau, Kepulauan
59 J19 **Rio Verde** Goiás, C Brazil
41 O12 **Río Verde** *var.* Rioverde. San Luis Potosí, C Mexico
35 O8 **Rio Vista** California, W USA
112 M11 **Ripanj** Serbia, N Serbia and Montenegro (Yugo.)
106 J13 **Ripatransone** Marche, C Italy
Ripen *see* Ribe
22 M2 **Ripley** Mississippi, S USA
31 R15 **Ripley** Ohio, N USA
20 F9 **Ripley** Tennessee, S USA
21 Q4 **Ripley** West Virginia, NE USA
105 W4 **Ripoll** Cataluña, NE Spain
97 M16 **Ripon** N England, UK
30 M7 **Ripon** Wisconsin, N USA
107 L24 **Riposto** Sicilia, Italy, C Mediterranean Sea
99 L14 **Rips** Noord-Brabant, SE Netherlands
54 D9 **Risaralda** *off.* Departamento de Risaralda. ◆ *province* C Colombia
116 L8 **Rîşcani** *var.* Râşcani, *Rus.* Ryshkany. NW Moldova
152 J9 **Rishikesh** Uttaranchal, N India
165 S1 **Rishiri-tō** *var.* Risiri Tô. *island* NE Japan
165 S1 **Rishiri-yama** ▲ Rishiri-tō, NE Japan
25 R7 **Rising Star** Texas, SW USA
31 Q15 **Rising Sun** Indiana, N USA
Risiri Tô *see* Rishiri-tō
102 L4 **Risle** ∽ N France
Rişno *see* Râşnov
27 V13 **Rison** Arkansas, C USA
95 G17 **Risør** Aust-Agder, S Norway
92 H10 **Risøyhamn** Nordland, C Norway
101 I23 **Riss** ∽ S Germany
118 G4 **Risti** *Ger.* Kreuz. Läänemaa, W Estonia
15 V8 **Ristigouche** ∽ Québec, SE Canada
93 N18 **Ristiina** Isä-Suomi, E Finland
93 N14 **Ristijärvi** Oulu, C Finland
188 C14 **Ritidian Point** *headland* N Guam
Ritschan *see* Říčany
35 R9 **Ritter, Mount** ▲ California, W USA
31 T12 **Rittman** Ohio, N USA
32 L9 **Ritzville** Washington, NW USA
Riva *see* Riva del Garda
61 A21 **Rivadavia** Buenos Aires, E Argentina
108 F7 **Riva del Garda** var. Riva. Trentino-Alto Adige, N Italy
106 B8 **Rivarolo Canavese** Piemonte, W Italy
42 K11 **Rivas** Rivas, SW Nicaragua
42 J11 **Rivas** ◆ *department* SW Nicaragua
103 R11 **Rive-de-Gier** Loire, E France
61 A22 **Rivera** Buenos Aires, E Argentina
61 F16 **Rivera** Rivera, NE Uruguay
61 F17 **Rivera** ◆ *department* NE Uruguay
35 P9 **Riverbank** California, W USA
76 K17 **River Cess** SW Liberia
28 M4 **Riverdale** North Dakota, N USA
30 I6 **River Falls** Wisconsin, N USA
11 T16 **Riverhurst** Saskatchewan, S Canada
183 O10 **Riverina** *physical region* New South Wales, SE Australia
80 G8 **River Nile** ◆ *state* NE Sudan
63 F19 **Rivero, Isla** *island* Archipiélago de los Chonos, S Chile
11 W16 **Rivers** Manitoba, S Canada
77 U17 **Rivers** ◆ *state* S Nigeria
185 D23 **Riversdale** Southland, South Island, NZ
83 F26 **Riversdale** Western Cape, SW South Africa
35 U15 **Riverside** California, W USA
25 W9 **Riverside** Texas, SW USA
37 U3 **Riverside Reservoir** ⊠ Colorado, C USA
10 K15 **Rivers Inlet** British Columbia, SW Canada
10 K15 **Rivers Inlet** *inlet* British Columbia, SW Canada
11 X15 **Riverton** Manitoba, S Canada
185 C24 **Riverton** Southland, South Island, NZ
30 L13 **Riverton** Illinois, N USA
36 L3 **Riverton** Utah, W USA
33 V15 **Riverton** Wyoming, C USA
14 G10 **River Valley** Ontario, S Canada
13 P14 **Riverview** New Brunswick, SE Canada
103 O17 **Rivesaltes** Pyrénées-Orientales, S France
36 H11 **Riviera** Arizona, SW USA
25 S15 **Riviera** Texas, SW USA
23 Z14 **Riviera Beach** Florida, SE USA
15 Q10 **Rivière-à-Pierre** Québec, SE Canada
15 T9 **Rivière-Bleue** Québec, SE Canada
15 T8 **Rivière-du-Loup** Québec, SE Canada
173 Y15 **Rivière du Rempart** NE Mauritius
45 R12 **Rivière-Pilote** S Martinique
173 O17 **Rivière St-Etienne, Point de la** *headland* SW Réunion
13 S10 **Rivière-St-Paul** Québec, E Canada
Rivière Sèche *see* Bel Air
116 K4 **Rivne** *Pol.* Równe, *Rus.* Rovno. Rivnens'ka Oblast', NW Ukraine
Rivne *see* Rivnens'ka Oblast'
116 K3 **Rivnens'ka Oblast'** *var.* Rivne, *Rus.* Rovenskaya Oblast'. ◆ *province* NW Ukraine
106 B8 **Rivoli** Piemonte, NW Italy
159 Q14 **Riwoqê** *var.* Racaka. Xizang Zizhiqu, W China
99 H19 **Rixensart** Wallon Brabant, C Belgium
Riyadh/Riyāḍ, Minṭaqat ar *see* Ar Riyāḍ
Riyāq *see* Rayak
Rizaiyeh *see* Orūmīyeh
137 P11 **Rize** Rize, NE Turkey
137 P11 **Rize** *prev.* Çoruh. ◆ *province* NE Turkey
161 R5 **Rizhao** Shandong, E China
Rizhskiy Zaliv *see* Riga, Gulf of
Rizokarpaso/Rizokárpason *see* Dipkarpaz
107 O21 **Rizzuto, Capo** *headland* S Italy
95 F15 **Rjukan** Telemark, S Norway
95 D16 **Rjuven** ▲ S Norway
76 H9 **Rkiz** Trarza, W Mauritania
95 H14 **Roa** Oppland, S Norway
105 N5 **Roa** Castilla-León, N Spain
45 T9 **Road Town** ○ (British Virgin Islands) Tortola, C British Virgin Islands
96 F6 **Roag, Loch** *inlet* NW Scotland, UK
37 O5 **Roan Cliffs** *cliff* Colorado/Utah, W USA
21 P9 **Roan High Knob** *var.* Roan Mountain. ▲ North Carolina/Tennessee, SE USA
Roan Mountain *see* Roan High Knob
103 Q10 **Roanne** *anc.* Rodunma. Loire, E France
23 R4 **Roanoke** Alabama, S USA
21 S7 **Roanoke** Virginia, NE USA
21 Z9 **Roanoke Island** *island* North Carolina, SE USA
21 W8 **Roanoke Rapids** North Carolina, SE USA
21 X9 **Roanoke River** ∽ North Carolina/Virginia, SE USA
37 O4 **Roan Plateau** *plain* Utah, W USA
37 R5 **Roaring Fork River** ∽ Colorado, C USA
25 O5 **Roaring Springs** Texas, SW USA
42 J4 **Roatán** *var.* Coxen Hole, Coxin Hole. Islas de la Bahía, N Honduras
42 I4 **Roatán, Isla de** *island* Islas de la Bahía, N Honduras
Roat Kampuchea *see* Cambodia
Roazon *see* Rennes
143 T7 **Robāṭ-e Chāh Gonbad** Yazd, E Iran
143 R7 **Robāṭ-e Khān** Yazd, C Iran
143 T7 **Robāṭ-e Khvosh Āb** Yazd, E Iran
143 R8 **Robāṭ-e Posht-e Bādām** Yazd, NE Iran
143 Q8 **Robāṭ-e Rīzāb** Yazd, C Iran
192 L8 **Robbie Ridge** *undersea feature* W Pacific Ocean
21 T10 **Robbins** North Carolina, SE USA
183 N15 **Robbins Island** *island* Tasmania, SE Australia
21 N10 **Robbinsville** North Carolina, SE USA
182 J12 **Robe** South Australia
21 W9 **Robersonville** North Carolina, SE USA
25 P8 **Robert Lee** Texas, SW USA
35 V5 **Roberts Creek Mountain** ▲ Nevada, W USA
93 J15 **Robertsfors** Västerbotten, N Sweden
27 R11 **Robert S.Kerr Reservoir** ⊠ Oklahoma, C USA
38 L12 **Roberts Mountain** ▲ Nunivak Island, Alaska, USA
83 F26 **Robertson** Western Cape, SW South Africa
194 H4 **Robertson Island** *island* Antarctica
76 J16 **Robertsport** W Liberia
182 J8 **Robertstown** South Australia
Robert Williams *see* Caála
15 P7 **Roberval** Québec, SE Canada
31 N15 **Robinson** Illinois, N USA
193 U11 **Róbinson Crusoe, Isla** *island* Islas Juan Fernández, Chile, E Pacific Ocean
180 J9 **Robinson Range** ▲ Western Austral
182 M9 **Robinvale** Victoria, SE Australia
105 P11 **Robledo** Castilla-La Mancha, C Spain
54 G5 **Robles** *var.* La Paz, Robles La Paz. Cesar, N Colombia
Robles La Paz *see* Robles
11 V15 **Roblin** Manitoba, S Canada
11 S17 **Robsart** Saskatchewan, S Canada
11 N15 **Robson, Mount** ▲ British Columbia, SW Canada
25 T14 **Robstown** Texas, SW USA
25 P6 **Roby** Texas, SW USA
104 E11 **Roca, Cabo da** *headland* C Portugal
Rocadas *see* Xangongo
41 S14 **Roca Partida, Punta** *headland* C Mexico
47 X6 **Rocas, Atol das** *island* E Brazil
107 L18 **Roccadaspide** *var.* Rocca d'Aspide. Campania, S Italy
107 K15 **Roccaraso** Abruzzo, C Italy
106 H10 **Rocca San Casciano** Emilia-Romagna, C Italy
106 G13 **Roccastrada** Toscana, C Italy
61 G20 **Rocha** Rocha, E Uruguay
61 G19 **Rocha** ◆ *department* E Uruguay
97 L17 **Rochdale** NW England, UK
102 L11 **Rochechouart** Haute-Vienne, C France
99 J22 **Rochefort** Namur, SE Belgium
102 J11 **Rochefort** *var.* Rochefort sur Mer. Charente-Maritime, W France
Rochefort sur Mer *see* Rochefort
125 N10 **Rochegda** Arkhangel'skaya Oblast', NW Russian Federation
30 L10 **Rochelle** Illinois, N USA
25 Q9 **Rochelle** Texas, SW USA
15 V3 **Rochers Ouest, Rivière aux** ∽ Québec, SE Canada
97 O22 **Rochester** *anc.* Durobrivae. SE England, UK
31 O12 **Rochester** Indiana, N USA
29 W10 **Rochester** Minnesota, N USA
19 O9 **Rochester** New Hampshire, NE USA
18 F9 **Rochester** New York, NE USA
25 P5 **Rochester** Texas, SW USA
31 S9 **Rochester Hills** Michigan, N USA
Rocheuses, Montagnes/Rockies *see* Rocky Mountains
64 M6 **Rockall** *island* UK, N Atlantic Ocean
64 L6 **Rockall Bank** *undersea feature* N Atlantic Ocean
84 B8 **Rockall Rise** *undersea feature* N Atlantic Ocean
84 C9 **Rockall Trough** *undersea feature* N Atlantic Ocean
35 U2 **Rock Creek** ∽ Nevada, W USA
25 T10 **Rockdale** Texas, SW USA
195 N12 **Rockefeller Plateau** *plateau* Antarctica
30 K11 **Rock Falls** Illinois, N USA
23 Q5 **Rockford** Alabama, S USA
30 L10 **Rockford** Illinois, N USA
15 Q12 **Rock Forest** Québec, SE Canada
11 T17 **Rockglen** Saskatchewan, S Canada
181 Y8 **Rockhampton** Queensland, E Australia
21 R11 **Rock Hill** South Carolina, SE USA
180 I13 **Rockingham** Western Australia
21 T11 **Rockingham** North Carolina, SE USA
30 J11 **Rock Island** Illinois, N USA
25 U12 **Rock Island** Texas, SW USA
14 C10 **Rock Lake** Ontario, S Canada
29 O2 **Rock Lake** North Dakota, N USA
14 I12 **Rock Lake** ◎ Ontario, SE Canada
14 M12 **Rockland** Ontario, SE Canada
19 R7 **Rockland** Maine, NE USA
182 L11 **Rocklands Reservoir** ⊠ Victoria, SE Australia
35 O7 **Rocklin** California, W USA
23 R3 **Rockmart** Georgia, SE USA
31 N16 **Rockport** Indiana, N USA
27 Q1 **Rock Port** Missouri, C USA
25 T14 **Rockport** Texas, SW USA
32 I7 **Rockport** Washington, NW USA
29 S11 **Rock Rapids** Iowa, C USA
30 K11 **Rock River** ∽ Illinois/Wisconsin, N USA
44 I3 **Rock Sound** Eleuthera Island, C Bahamas
33 U17 **Rock Springs** Wyoming, C USA
25 P11 **Rocksprings** Texas, SW USA
55 T9 **Rockstone** C Guyana
29 S12 **Rock Valley** Iowa, C USA
31 N14 **Rockville** Indiana, N USA
21 W3 **Rockville** Maryland, NE USA
25 U6 **Rockwall** Texas, SW USA
29 U13 **Rockwell City** Iowa, C USA
31 S10 **Rockwood** Michigan, N USA
20 M9 **Rockwood** Tennessee, S USA
25 Q8 **Rockwood** Texas, SW USA
37 U6 **Rocky Ford** Colorado, C USA
14 D9 **Rocky Island Lake** ◎ Ontario, S Canada
21 V9 **Rocky Mount** North Carolina, SE USA
21 S7 **Rocky Mount** Virginia, NE USA
33 Q8 **Rocky Mountain** ▲ Montana, NW USA
11 P15 **Rocky Mountain House** Alberta, SW Canada
37 T3 **Rocky Mountain National Park** *national park* Colorado, C USA
16 I9 **Rocky Mountains** *var.* Rockies, *Fr.* Montagnes Rocheuses. ▲ Canada/USA
42 H1 **Rocky Point** *headland* NE Belize
83 A17 **Rocky Point** *headland* NW Namibia
95 F14 **Rødberg** Buskerud, S Norway
95 I25 **Rødby** Storstrøm, SE Denmark
95 I25 **Rødbyhavn** Storstrøm, SE Denmark
13 T10 **Roddickton** Newfoundland and Labrador, SE Canada
95 F23 **Rødding** Sønderjylland, SW Denmark
95 M22 **Rödeby** Blekinge, S Sweden
98 N6 **Roden** Drenthe, NE Netherlands
62 H9 **Rodeo** San Juan, W Argentina
103 O14 **Rodez** *anc.* Segodunum. Aveyron, S France
Rodholívos *see* Rodolívos
Rodhópi Óri *see* Rhodope Mountains
Ródhos/Rodi *see* Ródos
107 N15 **Rodi Garganico** Puglia, SE Italy
101 N20 **Roding** Bayern, SE Germany
113 J19 **Rodinit, Kepi i** *headland* W Albania
116 I9 **Rodnei, Munţii** ▲ N Romania
184 L4 **Rodney, Cape** *headland* North Island, NZ
38 L9 **Rodney, Cape** *headland* Alaska, USA
124 M16 **Rodniki** Ivanovskaya Oblast', W Russian Federation
119 Q16 **Rodnya** *Rus.* Rodnya. Mahilyowskaya Voblasts', E Belarus
Rodó *see* José Enrique Rodó
114 H13 **Rodolívos** *var.* Rodholívos. Kentrikí Makedonía, NE Greece
Rodopi *see* Rhodope Mountains
115 O22 **Ródos** *var.* Ródhos, *Eng.* Rhodes, *It.* Rodi. Ródos, Dodekánisos, Greece, Aegean Sea
115 O22 **Ródos** *var.* Ródhos, *Eng.* Rhodes, *It.* Rodi; *anc.* Rhodos. *island* Dodekánisos, Greece, Aegean Sea
Rodosto *see* Tekirdağ
59 A14 **Rodrigues** Amazonas, W Brazil
173 P8 **Rodrigues** *var.* Rodriquez. *island* E Mauritius
Rodriquez *see* Rodrigues
Rodunma *see* Roanne
180 I7 **Roebourne** Western Australia
83 J20 **Roedtan** Limpopo, NE South Africa
98 H11 **Roelofarendsveen** Zuid-Holland, W Netherlands
Roepat *see* Rupat, Pulau
Roer *see* Rur
99 M16 **Roermond** Limburg, SE Netherlands
99 C18 **Roeselare** *Fr.* Roulers; *prev.* Rousselaere. West-Vlaanderen, W Belgium
9 P8 **Roes Welcome Sound** *strait* Nunavut, N Canada
Roeteng *see* Ruteng
Rofreit *see* Rovereto
Rogachëv *see* Rahachow
57 L15 **Rogagua, Laguna** ◎ NW Bolivia
95 C16 **Rogaland** ◆ *county* S Norway
25 Y9 **Roganville** Texas, SW USA
109 W11 **Rogaška Slatina** *Ger.* Rohitsch-Sauerbrunn; *prev.* Rogatec-Slatina. E Slovenia
Rogatec-Slatina *see* Rogaška Slatina
112 J13 **Rogatica** Republika Srpska, SE Bosnia & Herzegovina
Rogatin *see* Rohatyn
93 F17 **Rogen** ◎ C Sweden
27 S9 **Rogers** Arkansas, C USA
29 P5 **Rogers** North Dakota, N USA
25 T9 **Rogers** Texas, SW USA
31 R5 **Rogers City** Michigan, N USA
Roger Simpson Island *see* Abemama
35 T14 **Rogers Lake** *salt flat* California, W USA
21 Q8 **Rogers, Mount** ▲ Virginia, NE USA
33 O16 **Rogerson** Idaho, NW USA
11 O16 **Rogers Pass** *pass* British Columbia, SW Canada
21 O8 **Rogersville** Tennessee, S USA
99 L16 **Roggel** Limburg, SE Netherlands
Roggeveen *see* Roggewein, Cabo
193 R10 **Roggeveen Basin** *undersea feature* E Pacific Ocean
191 X16 **Roggewein, Cabo** *var.* Roggeveen. *headland* Easter Island, Chile, E Pacific Ocean
103 Y13 **Rogliano** Corse, France, C Mediterranean Sea
107 N21 **Rogliano** Calabria, SW Italy
92 G12 **Rognan** Nordland, C Norway
100 K10 **Rögnitz** ∽ N Germany
Rogozhina/Rogozhinë *see* Rrogozhinë
110 G10 **Rogoźno** Wielkopolskie, C Poland
32 E15 **Rogue River** ∽ Oregon, NW USA
116 I6 **Rohatyn** *Rus.* Rogatin. Ivano-Frankivs'ka Oblast', W Ukraine
189 O14 **Rohi** Pohnpei, E Micronesia
Rohitsch-Sauerbrunn *see* Rogaška Slatina
149 Q13 **Rohri** Sind, SE Pakistan
152 I10 **Rohtak** Haryāna, N India
Roi Ed *see* Roi Et
167 R9 **Roi Et** *var.* Muang Roi Et, Roi Ed. Roi Et, E Thailand
191 U9 **Roi Georges, Îles du** *island group* Îles Tuamotu, C French Polynesia
153 Y10 **Roing** Arunāchal Pradesh, NE India
118 E7 **Roja** Talsi, NW Latvia
61 B20 **Rojas** Buenos Aires, E Argentina
149 R12 **Rojhān** Punjab, E Pakistan
41 Q12 **Rojo, Cabo** *headland* C Mexico
45 Q10 **Rojo, Cabo** *headland* W Puerto Rico
168 K10 **Rokan Kiri, Sungai** ∽ Sumatera, W Indonesia
Rokha *see* Rokhah
149 R4 **Rokhah** *var.* Rokha. Kāpīsā, E Afghanistan
118 I11 **Rokiškis** Panevėžys, NE Lithuania
165 R7 **Rokkasho** Aomori, Honshū, C Japan
111 B17 **Rokycany** *Ger.* Rokytzan. Plzeňský Kraj, NW Czech Republic
117 P6 **Rokytne** Kyyivs'ka Oblast', N Ukraine
116 L3 **Rokytne** Rivnens'ka Oblast', NW Ukraine
Rokytzan *see* Rokycany
158 L11 **Rola Co** ◎ W China
29 V13 **Roland** Iowa, C USA
95 D15 **Røldal** Hordaland, S Norway
98 O7 **Rolde** Drenthe, NE Netherlands
29 O2 **Rolette** North Dakota, N USA
27 V6 **Rolla** Missouri, C USA
29 O2 **Rolla** North Dakota, N USA
108 A10 **Rolle** Vaud, W Switzerland
181 X8 **Rolleston** Queensland, E Australia
185 H19 **Rolleston** Canterbury, South Island, NZ
185 G18 **Rolleston Range** ▲ South Island, NZ
14 H8 **Rollet** Québec, SE Canada
22 J4 **Rolling Fork** Mississippi, S USA
20 L6 **Rolling Fork** ∽ Kentucky, S USA
14 J11 **Rolphton** Ontario, SE Canada
Röm *see* Rømø
181 X10 **Roma** Queensland, E Australia
107 I15 **Roma** *Eng.* Rome. ● (Italy) Lazio, C Italy
95 P19 **Roma** Gotland, SE Sweden
21 T14 **Romain, Cape** *headland* South Carolina, SE USA
13 P11 **Romaine** ∽ Newfoundland and Labrador/Québec, E Canada
25 R17 **Roma Los Saenz** Texas, SW USA
114 H8 **Roman** Vratsa, NW Bulgaria
116 L10 **Roman** *Hung.* Románvásár. Neamţ, NE Romania
64 M13 **Romanche Fracture Zone** *tectonic feature* E Atlantic Ocean
61 C15 **Romang** Santa Fe, C Argentina
171 R15 **Romang, Pulau** *var.* Pulau Roma. *island* Kepulauan Damar, E Indonesia
171 R15 **Romang, Selat** *strait* Nusa Tenggara, S Indonesia
116 J11 **Romania** *Bul.* Rumŭniya, *Ger.* Rumänien, *Hung.* Románia, *Rom.* România, *SCr.* Rumunjska, *Ukr.* Rumuniya; *prev.* Republica Socialistă România, Roumania, Rumania, Socialist Republic of Romania, *Rom.* Romînia. ◆ *republic* SE Europe
117 T14 **Roman-Kash** ▲ S Ukraine
23 W16 **Romano, Cape** *headland* Florida, SE USA
44 G5 **Romano, Cayo** *island* C Cuba
123 O13 **Romanovka** Respublika Buryatiya, S Russian Federation
127 N8 **Romanovka** Saratovskaya Oblast', W Russian Federation
108 I6 **Romanshorn** Thurgau, NE Switzerland
103 R12 **Romans-sur-Isère** Drôme, E France
189 U12 **Romanum** *island* Chuuk, C Micronesia
Románvásár *see* Roman
39 S5 **Romanzof Mountains** ▲ Alaska, USA
Roma, Pulau *see* Romang, Pulau
103 S4 **Rombas** Moselle, NE France
23 R2 **Rome** Georgia, SE USA
18 I9 **Rome** New York, NE USA
Rome *see* Roma
31 S9 **Romeo** Michigan, N USA
Römerstadt *see* Rýmařov
Rometan *see* Romiton
103 P5 **Romilly-sur-Seine** Aube, N France
Romînia *see* Romania
146 L11 **Romiton** *Rus.* Rometan. Buxoro Viloyati, C Uzbekistan
21 U3 **Romney** West Virginia, NE USA
117 S4 **Romny** Sums'ka Oblast', NE Ukraine
95 E24 **Rømø** *Ger.* Röm. *island* SW Denmark
117 S5 **Romodan** Poltavs'ka Oblast', NE Ukraine
127 P5 **Romodanovo** Respublika Mordoviya, W Russian Federation
Romorantin *see* Romorantin-Lanthenay
103 N8 **Romorantin-Lanthenay** *var.* Romorantin. Loir-et-Cher, C France
94 F9 **Romsdal** *physical region* S Norway
94 F10 **Romsdalen** *valley* S Norway
94 E9 **Romsdalsfjorden** *fjord* S Norway
33 P8 **Ronan** Montana, NW USA
59 M14 **Roncador** Maranhão, E Brazil
186 M7 **Roncador Reef** *reef* N Solomon Islands
59 J17 **Roncador, Serra do** ▲ C Brazil
21 S6 **Ronceverte** West Virginia, NE USA
107 H14 **Ronciglione** Lazio, C Italy
104 L15 **Ronda** Andalucía, S Spain
94 G11 **Rondane** ▲ S Norway
104 L15 **Ronda, Serranía de** ▲ S Spain
95 H22 **Rønde** Århus, C Denmark
Röndik *see* Rongrik Atoll
59 E16 **Rondônia** *off.* Estado de Rondônia; *prev.* Território de Rondônia. ◆ *state* W Brazil
59 I18 **Rondonópolis** Mato Grosso, W Brazil
94 G11 **Rondslottet** ▲ S Norway
95 P20 **Ronehamn** Gotland, SE Sweden
160 L13 **Rong'an** *var.* Chang'an, Rongan. Guangxi Zhuangzu Zizhiqu, S China
Rongcheng *see* Jianli
189 R4 **Rongelap Atoll** *var.* Rōnļap. *atoll* Ralik Chain, NW Marshall Islands
Rongerik *see* Rongrik Atoll
160 K12 **Rongjiang** *var.* Guzhou. Guizhou, S China
160 L13 **Rong Jiang** ∽ S China
Rongjiang *see* Nankang
Rong, Kas *see* Rŭng, Kaôh
167 P8 **Rong Kwang** Phrae, NW Thailand
189 T4 **Rongrik Atoll** *var.* Röndik, Rongerik. *atoll* Ralik Chain, N Marshall Islands

189 X2 **Rongrong** *island* SE Marshall Islands
160 L13 **Rongshui** *var.* Rongshui Miaozu Zizhixian. Guangxi Zhuangzu Zizhiqu, S China
Rongshui Miaozu Zizhixian *see* Rongshui
118 I6 **Rõngu** *Ger.* Ringen. Tartumaa, SE Estonia
Rongwo *see* Tongren
160 L15 **Rongxian** *var.* Rong Xian. Guangxi Zhuangzu Zizhiqu, S China
Rongzhag *see* Danba
Roniu *see* Ronui, Mont
189 N13 **Ronkiti** Pohnpei, E Micronesia
Rōnlap *see* Rongelap Atoll
95 L24 **Rønne** Bornholm, E Denmark
95 M22 **Ronneby** Blekinge, S Sweden
194 J7 **Ronne Entrance** *inlet* Antarctica
194 L6 **Ronne Ice Shelf** *ice shelf* Antarctica
99 E19 **Ronse** *Fr.* Renaix. Oost-Vlaanderen, SW Belgium
191 R8 **Ronui, Mont** *var.* Roniu. Ж Tahiti, W French Polynesia
30 K14 **Roodhouse** Illinois, N USA
83 C19 **Rooibank** Erongo, W Namibia
65 N24 **Rookery Point** *headland* NE Tristan da Cunha
171 V13 **Roon, Pulau** *island* E Indonesia
173 V7 **Roo Rise** *undersea feature* E Indian Ocean
152 J9 **Roorkee** Uttaranchal, N India
99 H15 **Roosendaal** Noord-Brabant, S Netherlands
25 P10 **Roosevelt** Texas, SW USA
37 N3 **Roosevelt** Utah, W USA
47 T8 **Roosevelt** ≈ W Brazil
195 O13 **Roosevelt Island** *island* Antarctica
10 L10 **Roosevelt, Mount** ▲ British Columbia, W Canada
11 P17 **Roosville** British Columbia, SW Canada
29 X10 **Root River** ≈ Minnesota, N USA
111 N16 **Ropczyce** Podkarpackie, SE Poland
181 Q3 **Roper Bar** Northern Territory, N Australia
24 M5 **Ropesville** Texas, SW USA
102 K14 **Roquefort** Landes, SW France
61 C21 **Roque Pérez** Buenos Aires, E Argentina
58 E10 **Roraima** *off.* Estado de Roraima; *prev.* Território de Rio Branco, Território de Roraima. ◈ *state* N Brazil
58 F9 **Roraima, Mount** ▲ N South America
Ro Ro Reef *see* Malolo Barrier Reef
94 I9 **Røros** Sør-Trøndelag, S Norway
108 I7 **Rorschach** Sankt Gallen, NE Switzerland
93 E14 **Rørvik** Nord-Trøndelag, C Norway
119 G17 **Ros'** *Rus.* Ross'. Hrodzyenskaya Voblasts', W Belarus
119 G17 **Ros'** *Rus.* Ross'. ≈ W Belarus
117 O6 **Ros'** ≈ N Ukraine
44 K7 **Rosa, Lake** ◎ Great Inagua, S Bahamas
32 M9 **Rosalia** Washington, NW USA
191 W15 **Rosalia, Punta** *headland* Easter Island, Chile, E Pacific Ocean
45 P12 **Rosalie** E Dominica
35 T14 **Rosamond** California, W USA
35 S14 **Rosamond Lake** *salt flat* California, W USA
61 B18 **Rosario** Santa Fe, C Argentina
40 J11 **Rosario** Sinaloa, C Mexico
40 G6 **Rosario** Sonora, NW Mexico
62 O6 **Rosario** San Pedro, C Paraguay
61 E20 **Rosario** Colonia, SW Uruguay
54 H5 **Rosario** Zulia, NW Venezuela
Rosario *see* Rosarito
40 B4 **Rosario, Bahía del** *bay* NW Mexico
62 K6 **Rosario de la Frontera** Salta, N Argentina
61 C18 **Rosario del Tala** Entre Ríos, E Argentina
61 F16 **Rosário do Sul** Rio Grande do Sul, S Brazil
59 H18 **Rosário Oeste** Mato Grosso, W Brazil
40 E7 **Rosarito** Baja California, NW Mexico
40 B1 **Rosarito** *var.* Rosario. Baja California, NW Mexico
40 E7 **Rosarito** Baja California Sur, W Mexico
104 L9 **Rosarito, Embalse del** ▣ W Spain
107 N22 **Rosarno** Calabria, SW Italy
56 B5 **Rosa Zárate** *var.* Quinindé. Esmeraldas, SW Ecuador
Roscianum *see* Rossano
29 O8 **Roscoe** South Dakota, N USA
25 P7 **Roscoe** Texas, SW USA
102 F5 **Roscoff** Finistère, NW France
Ros Comáin *see* Roscommon
97 C17 **Roscommon** *Ir.* Ros Comáin. C Ireland
31 Q7 **Roscommon** Michigan, N USA
97 C17 **Roscommon** *Ir.* Ros Comáin. *cultural region* C Ireland
Ros. Cré *see* Roscrea
97 D19 **Roscrea** *Ir.* Ros. Cré. C Ireland
45 X12 **Roseau** *prev.* Charlotte Town. ● (Dominica) SW Dominica
29 S2 **Roseau** Minnesota, N USA
173 Y16 **Rose Belle** SE Mauritius
183 O16 **Rosebery** Tasmania, SE Australia
21 U11 **Roseboro** North Carolina, SE USA
25 T9 **Rosebud** Texas, SW USA
33 W10 **Rosebud Creek** ≈ Montana, NW USA
32 F14 **Roseburg** Oregon, NW USA
22 J3 **Rosedale** Mississippi, S USA
99 H21 **Rosée** Namur, S Belgium
55 U8 **Rose Hall** E Guyana
173 X16 **Rose Hill** W Mauritius
80 H12 **Roseires, Reservoir** *var.* Lake Rusayris. ▣ E Sudan
Rosenau *see* Rožnov pod Radhoštěm, Czech Republic
Rosenau *see* Rožňava, Slovakia
25 V11 **Rosenberg** Texas, SW USA
Rosenberg *see* Olesno, Poland
Rosenberg *see* Ružomberok, Slovakia
100 I10 **Rosengarten** Niedersachsen, N Germany
101 M24 **Rosenheim** Bayern, S Germany
Rosenhof *see* Zilupe
105 X4 **Roses** Cataluña, NE Spain
105 X4 **Roses, Golfe de** *gulf* NE Spain
107 K14 **Roseto degli Abruzzi** Abruzzo, C Italy
11 S16 **Rosetown** Saskatchewan, S Canada
Rosetta *see* Rashīd
35 O7 **Roseville** California, W USA
30 J12 **Roseville** Illinois, N USA
29 V8 **Roseville** Minnesota, N USA
29 R7 **Rosholt** South Dakota, N USA
106 F12 **Rosignano Marittimo** Toscana, C Italy
116 I14 **Roşiori de Vede** Teleorman, S Romania
114 K8 **Rositsa** ≈ N Bulgaria
Rositten *see* Rēzekne
95 J23 **Roskilde** Roskilde, E Denmark
95 I23 **Roskilde** *off.* Roskilde Amt. ◈ *county* E Denmark
Ros Láir *see* Rosslare
126 H5 **Roslavl'** Smolenskaya Oblast', W Russian Federation
32 I8 **Roslyn** Washington, NW USA
99 K14 **Rosmalen** Noord-Brabant, S Netherlands
Ros Mhic Thriúin *see* New Ross
113 P19 **Rosoman** C FYR Macedonia
102 F6 **Rosporden** Finistère, NW France
185 F17 **Ross** West Coast, South Island, NZ
10 J7 **Ross** ≈ Yukon Territory, W Canada
Ross' *see* Ros'
96 H8 **Ross and Cromarty** *cultural region* N Scotland, UK
107 O20 **Rossano** *anc.* Roscianum. Calabria, SW Italy
22 L5 **Ross Barnett Reservoir** ▣ Mississippi, S USA
11 W16 **Rossburn** Manitoba, S Canada
14 H13 **Rosseau** Ontario, S Canada
14 H13 **Rosseau, Lake** ◎ Ontario, S Canada
186 I10 **Rossel Island** *prev.* Yela Island. *island* SE PNG
195 P12 **Ross Ice Shelf** *ice shelf* Antarctica
13 P16 **Rossignol, Lake** ◎ Nova Scotia, SE Canada
83 C19 **Rössing** Erongo, W Namibia
195 Q14 **Ross Island** *island* Antarctica
Rossitten *see* Rybachiy
Rossiyskaya Federatsiya *see* Russian Federation
11 N17 **Rossland** British Columbia, SW Canada
97 F20 **Rosslare** *Ir.* Ros Láir. SE Ireland
97 F20 **Rosslare Harbour** Wexford, SE Ireland
101 M14 **Rosslau** Sachsen-Anhalt, E Germany
76 G10 **Rosso** Trarza, SW Mauritania
103 X14 **Rosso, Cap** *headland* Corse, France, C Mediterranean Sea
93 H16 **Rossön** Jämtland, C Sweden
97 K21 **Ross-on-Wye** W England, UK
Rossony *see* Rasony
126 L9 **Rossosh'** Voronezhskaya Oblast', W Russian Federation
181 Q7 **Ross River** Northern Territory, N Australia
10 J7 **Ross River** Yukon Territory, W Canada
205 O15 **Ross Sea** *sea* Antarctica
92 G13 **Røssvatnet** *Lapp.* Reevhtse. ◎ C Norway
23 R1 **Rossville** Georgia, SE USA
Rostak *see* Ar Rustāq
143 P14 **Rostāq** Hormozgān, S Iran
117 N5 **Rostavytsya** ≈ N Ukraine
11 T15 **Rosthern** Saskatchewan, S Canada
100 M8 **Rostock** Mecklenburg-Vorpommern, NE Germany
126 L16 **Rostov** Yaroslavskaya Oblast', W Russian Federation
Rostov *see* Rostov-na-Donu
126 L12 **Rostov-na-Donu** *var.* Rostov, *Eng.* Rostov-on-Don. Rostovskaya Oblast', SW Russian Federation
Rostov-on-Don *see* Rostov-na-Donu
126 L10 **Rostovskaya Oblast'** ◈ *province* SW Russian Federation
93 J14 **Rosvik** Norrbotten, N Sweden
23 S3 **Roswell** Georgia, SE USA
37 U14 **Roswell** New Mexico, SW USA
94 K12 **Rot** Dalarna, C Sweden
101 I23 **Rot** ≈ S Germany
104 J15 **Rota** Andalucía, S Spain
188 K9 **Rota** *island* S Northern Mariana Islands
25 P6 **Rotan** Texas, SW USA
Rotcher Island *see* Tamana
100 I11 **Rotenburg** Niedersachsen, NW Germany
Rotenburg *see* Rotenburg an der Fulda
101 I16 **Rotenburg an der Fulda** *var.* Rotenburg. Thüringen, C Germany
101 L18 **Roter Main** ≈ E Germany
101 K20 **Roth** Bayern, SE Germany
101 G16 **Rothaargebirge** ⛰ W Germany
Rothenburg *see* Rothenburg ob der Tauber
101 J20 **Rothenburg ob der Tauber** *var.* Rothenburg. Bayern, S Germany
194 H6 **Rothera** *UK research station* Antarctica
185 I17 **Rotherham** Canterbury, South Island, NZ
97 M17 **Rotherham** N England, UK
96 H12 **Rothesay** W Scotland, UK
108 E7 **Rothrist** Aargau, N Switzerland
194 H6 **Rothschild Island** *island* Antarctica
171 P17 **Roti, Pulau** *island* S Indonesia
183 O8 **Roto** New South Wales, SE Australia
184 N8 **Rotoiti, Lake** ◎ North Island, NZ
Rotomagus *see* Rouen
107 N19 **Rotondella** Basilicata, S Italy
103 X15 **Rotondo, Monte** ▲ Corse, France, C Mediterranean Sea
185 I15 **Rotoroa, Lake** ◎ South Island, NZ
184 N8 **Rotorua** Bay of Plenty, North Island, NZ
184 N8 **Rotorua, Lake** ◎ North Island, NZ
101 N22 **Rott** ≈ SE Germany
108 F10 **Rotten** ≈ S Switzerland
109 T6 **Rottenmann** Steiermark, E Austria
98 H12 **Rotterdam** Zuid-Holland, SW Netherlands
18 K10 **Rotterdam** New York, NE USA
95 M21 **Rottnen** ◎ S Sweden
98 N4 **Rottumeroog** *island* Waddeneilanden, NE Netherlands
98 N4 **Rottumerplaat** *island* Waddeneilanden, NE Netherlands
101 G23 **Rottweil** Baden-Württemberg, S Germany
191 O7 **Rotui, Mont** Ж Moorea, W French Polynesia
103 P1 **Roubaix** Nord, N France
111 C15 **Roudnice nad Labem** *Ger.* Raudnitz an der Elbe. Ústecký Kraj, NW Czech Republic
102 M4 **Rouen** *anc.* Rotomagus. Seine-Maritime, N France
171 X13 **Rouffaer Reserves** *reserve* Papua, E Indonesia
15 N10 **Rouge, Rivière** ≈ Québec, SE Canada
20 J6 **Rough River** ≈ Kentucky, S USA
20 J6 **Rough River Lake** ▣ Kentucky, S USA
Rouhaïbé *see* Ar Ruḩaybah
102 K11 **Rouillac** Charente, W France
Roulers *see* Roeselare
Roumania *see* Romania
173 Y15 **Round Island** *var.* Île Ronde. *island* NE Mauritius
14 J12 **Round Lake** ◎ Ontario, SE Canada
35 U7 **Round Mountain** Nevada, W USA
25 R10 **Round Mountain** Texas, SW USA
183 U5 **Round Mountain** ▲ New South Wales, SE Australia
25 S10 **Round Rock** Texas, SW USA
33 U10 **Roundup** Montana, NW USA
55 Y10 **Roura** NE French Guiana
Rourkela *see* Rāulakela
96 J4 **Rousay** *island* N Scotland, UK
Rousselaere *see* Roeselare
103 O17 **Roussillon** *cultural region* S France
15 V7 **Routhierville** Québec, SE Canada
99 K25 **Rouvroy** Luxembourg, SE Belgium
14 I7 **Rouyn-Noranda** Québec, SE Canada
Rouyuanchengzi *see* Huachi
92 L12 **Rovaniemi** Lappi, N Finland
106 E7 **Rovato** Lombardia, N Italy
125 N11 **Rovdino** Arkhangel'skaya Oblast', NW Russian Federation
Roven'ki *see* Roven'ky
117 Y8 **Roven'ky** *var.* Roven'ki. Luhans'ka Oblast', E Ukraine
Rovenskaya Oblast' *see* Rivnens'ka Oblast'
Rovenskaya Sloboda *see* Rovyenskaya Slabada
106 G7 **Rovereto** *Ger.* Rofreit. Trentino-Alto Adige, N Italy
167 S12 **Rôviĕng Tbong** Preăh Vihéar, N Cambodia
Rovigno *see* Rovinj
106 H8 **Rovigo** Veneto, NE Italy
112 A10 **Rovinj** *It.* Rovigno. Istra, NW Croatia
54 E10 **Rovira** Tolima, C Colombia
127 P9 **Rovnoye** Saratovskaya Oblast', W Russian Federation
82 Q12 **Rovuma, Rio** *var.* Ruvuma. ≈ Mozambique/Tanzania **see also** Ruvuma
119 O19 **Rovyenskaya Slabada** *Rus.* Rovenskaya Sloboda. Homyel'skaya Voblasts', SE Belarus
183 R5 **Rowena** New South Wales, SE Australia
21 T11 **Rowland** North Carolina, SE USA
9 P5 **Rowley** ≈ Baffin Island, Nunavut, NE Canada
9 P6 **Rowley Island** *island* Nunavut, NE Canada
173 W8 **Rowley Shoals** *reef* NW Australia
171 O4 **Roxas** Mindoro, N Philippines
171 P5 **Roxas City** Panay Island, C Philippines
21 U8 **Roxboro** North Carolina, SE USA
185 D23 **Roxburgh** Otago, South Island, NZ
96 K13 **Roxburgh** *cultural region* SE Scotland, UK
182 H5 **Roxby Downs** South Australia
95 M17 **Roxen** ◎ S Sweden
25 V5 **Roxton** Texas, SW USA
15 P12 **Roxton-Sud** Québec, SE Canada
33 U8 **Roy** Montana, NW USA
37 U10 **Roy** New Mexico, SW USA
97 E17 **Royal Canal** *Ir.* An Chanáil Ríoga. *canal* C Ireland
30 L1 **Royale, Isle** *island* Michigan, N USA
37 S6 **Royal Gorge** *valley* Colorado, C USA
97 M20 **Royal Leamington Spa** *var.* Leamington, Leamington Spa. C England, UK
97 O23 **Royal Tunbridge Wells** *var.* Tunbridge Wells. SE England, UK
24 L9 **Royalty** Texas, SW USA
102 J11 **Royan** Charente-Maritime, W France
65 B24 **Roy Cove Settlement** West Falkland, Falkland Islands
103 O3 **Roye** Somme, N France
95 H15 **Røyken** Buskerud, S Norway
93 F14 **Røyrvik** Nord-Trøndelag, C Norway
25 U6 **Royse City** Texas, SW USA
97 O21 **Royston** E England, UK
23 U2 **Royston** Georgia, SE USA
114 L10 **Roza** *prev.* Gyulovo. Yambol, E Bulgaria
113 L16 **Rožaje** Montenegro, SW Serbia and Montenegro (Yugo.)
110 M10 **Różan** Mazowieckie, C Poland
117 O10 **Rozdil'na** Odes'ka Oblast', SW Ukraine
117 S12 **Rozdol'ne** *Rus.* Razdolnoye. Respublika Krym, S Ukraine
145 Q9 **Rozhdestvenka** Akmola, C Kazakhstan
116 I6 **Rozhnyativ** Ivano-Frankivs'ka Oblast', W Ukraine
116 J3 **Rozhyshche** Volyns'ka Oblast', NW Ukraine
Roznau am Radhost *see* Rožnov pod Radhoštěm
111 L19 **Rožňava** *Ger.* Rosenau, *Hung.* Rozsnyó. Košický Kraj, E Slovakia
116 K10 **Roznov** Neamţ, NE Romania
111 I18 **Rožnov pod Radhoštěm** *Ger.* Rosenau, Roznau am Radhost. Zlínský Kraj, E Czech Republic
Rózsahegy *see* Ružomberok
Rozsnyó *see* Râşnov, Romania
Rozsnyó *see* Rožňava, Slovakia
113 K18 **Rranxë** Shkodër, NW Albania
113 L18 **Rrëshen** *var.* Rresheni, Rrshen. Lezhë, C Albania
Rresheni *see* Rrëshen
Rrogozhina *see* Rrogozhinë
113 K20 **Rrogozhinë** *var.* Rogozhina, Rogozhinë, Rrogozhina. Tiranë, W Albania
Rrshen *see* Rrëshen
112 O13 **Rtanj** ▲ E Serbia and Montenegro (Yugo.)
127 O7 **Rtishchevo** Saratovskaya Oblast', W Russian Federation
184 N12 **Ruahine Range** *var.* Ruarine. ⛰ North Island, NZ
185 L14 **Ruamahanga** ≈ North Island, NZ
Ruanda *see* Rwanda
184 M10 **Ruapehu, Mount** ▲ North Island, NZ
185 C25 **Ruapuke Island** *island* SW NZ
Ruarine *see* Ruahine Range
184 O9 **Ruatahuna** Bay of Plenty, North Island, NZ
184 Q8 **Ruatoria** Gisborne, North Island, NZ
184 K4 **Ruawai** Northland, North Island, NZ
15 N8 **Ruban** ≈ Québec, SE Canada
81 I22 **Rubeho Mountains** ⛰ C Tanzania
165 U3 **Rubeshibe** Hokkaidō, NE Japan
Rubezhnoye *see* Rubizhne
113 L18 **Rubik** Lezhë, C Albania
54 H7 **Rubio** Táchira, W Venezuela
117 X6 **Rubizhne** *Rus.* Rubezhnoye. Luhans'ka Oblast', E Ukraine
81 F20 **Rubondo Island** *island* N Tanzania
122 I13 **Rubtsovsk** Altayskiy Kray, S Russian Federation
39 P9 **Ruby** Alaska, USA
35 W3 **Ruby Dome** ▲ Nevada, W USA
35 W4 **Ruby Lake** ◎ Nevada, W USA
35 W4 **Ruby Mountains** ⛰ Nevada, W USA
33 Q12 **Ruby Range** ⛰ Montana, NW USA
118 C10 **Rucava** Liepāja, SW Latvia
Rūdān *see* Dehbārez
Rudelstadt *see* Ciechanowiec
Rudensk *see* Rudzyensk
119 G14 **Rūdiškės** Vilnius, S Lithuania
95 H24 **Rudkøbing** Fyn, C Denmark
145 V14 **Rudnichnyy** *Kaz.* Rūdnīchnyy. Almaty, SE Kazakhstan
125 S13 **Rudnichnyy** Kirovskaya Oblast', NW Russian Federation
114 N9 **Rudnik** Varna, E Bulgaria
Rudny *see* Rudnyy
126 H4 **Rudnya** Smolenskaya Oblast', W Russian Federation
127 O8 **Rudnya** Volgogradskaya Oblast', SW Russian Federation
144 M7 **Rudnyy** *var.* Rudny. Kostanay, N Kazakhstan
122 K3 **Rudol'fa, Ostrov** *island* Zemlya Frantsa-Iosifa, NW Russian Federation
Rudolf, Lake *see* Turkana, Lake
Rudolfswert *see* Novo mesto
101 L17 **Rudolstadt** Thüringen, C Germany
31 Q4 **Rudyard** Michigan, N USA
33 S7 **Rudyard** Montana, NW USA
119 K16 **Rudzyensk** *Rus.* Rudensk. Minskaya Voblasts', C Belarus
104 L6 **Rueda** Castilla-León, N Spain
114 F10 **Ruen** ▲ Bulgaria/FYR Macedonia
80 G10 **Rufa'a** Gezira, C Sudan
102 L10 **Ruffec** Charente, W France
21 R14 **Ruffin** South Carolina, SE USA
81 J23 **Rufiji** ≈ E Tanzania
61 A20 **Rufino** Santa Fe, C Argentina
76 F11 **Rufisque** W Senegal
83 K14 **Rufunsa** Lusaka, C Zambia
118 J9 **Rugāji** Balvi, E Latvia
161 R7 **Rugao** Jiangsu, E China
97 M20 **Rugby** C England, UK
29 N3 **Rugby** North Dakota, N USA
100 N7 **Rügen** *headland* NE Germany
Ruhaybeh *see* Ar Ruḩaybah
81 E19 **Ruhengeri** NW Rwanda
Ruhja *see* Rūjiena
100 M10 **Ruhner Berg** *hill* N Germany
118 F7 **Ruhnu** *var.* Ruhnu Saar, *Swe.* Runö. *island* SW Estonia
Ruhnu Saar *see* Ruhnu
101 G15 **Ruhr** ≈ W Germany
161 S11 **Rui'an** *var.* Rui an. Zhejiang, SE China
161 P10 **Ruichang** Jiangxi, S China
24 J11 **Ruidosa** Texas, SW USA
37 S14 **Ruidoso** New Mexico, SW USA
161 P12 **Ruijin** Jiangxi, S China
160 D13 **Ruili** Yunnan, SW China
98 N8 **Ruinen** Drenthe, NE Netherlands
99 D17 **Ruiselede** West-Vlaanderen, W Belgium
64 P5 **Ruivo de Santana, Pico** ▲ Madeira, Portugal, NE Atlantic Ocean
40 J12 **Ruiz** Nayarit, SW Mexico
54 E10 **Ruiz, Nevado del** Ж W Colombia
138 J9 **Rujaylah, Ḩarrat ar** *salt lake* N Jordan
Rujen *see* Rūjiena
118 H7 **Rūjiena** *Est.* Ruhja, *Ger.* Rujen. Valmiera, N Latvia
79 I18 **Ruki** ≈ W Dem. Rep. Congo
81 E22 **Rukwa** ◈ *region* SW Tanzania
81 F23 **Rukwa, Lake** ◎ SE Tanzania
25 P6 **Rule** Texas, SW USA
22 K3 **Ruleville** Mississippi, S USA
Rum *see* Rhum
112 K10 **Ruma** Serbia, N Serbia and Montenegro (Yugo.)
Rumadiya *see* Ar Ramādī
141 Q7 **Rumāḩ** Ar Riyāḑ, C Saudi Arabia
Rumaitha *see* Ar Rumaythah
Rumania/Rumänien *see* Romania
Rumänisch-Sankt-Georgen *see* Sângeorz-Băi
139 Y13 **Rumaylah** SE Iraq
139 P2 **Rumaylah, Wādī** *dry watercourse* NE Syria
171 U13 **Rumbati** Papua, E Indonesia
81 E14 **Rumbek** El Buhayrat, S Sudan
Rumburg *see* Rumburk
111 D14 **Rumburk** *Ger.* Rumburg. Ústecký Kraj, NW Czech Republic
44 J4 **Rum Cay** *island* C Bahamas
99 M26 **Rumelange** Luxembourg, S Luxembourg
99 D20 **Rumes** Hainaut, SW Belgium
19 P7 **Rumford** Maine, NE USA
110 I6 **Rumia** Pomorskie, N Poland
113 J17 **Rumija** ⛰ SW Serbia and Montenegro (Yugo.)
103 T11 **Rumilly** Haute-Savoie, E France
139 O6 **Rūmiyah** W Iraq
Rummah, Wādī ar *see* Rimah, Wādī ar
Rummelsburg in Pommern *see* Miastko
165 S3 **Rumoi** Hokkaidō, NE Japan
82 M12 **Rumphi** *var.* Rumpi. Northern, N Malawi
Rumpi *see* Rumphi
29 V7 **Rum River** ≈ Minnesota, N USA
188 F16 **Rumung** *island* Caroline Islands, W Micronesia
Rumuniya/Rumŭniya/Rumunjska *see* Romania
185 G16 **Runanga** West Coast, South Island, NZ
184 P7 **Runaway, Cape** *headland* North Island, NZ
97 K18 **Runcorn** C England, UK
118 K10 **Rundāni** Ludza, E Latvia
83 L18 **Runde** *var.* Lundi. ≈ SE Zimbabwe
83 E16 **Rundu** *var.* Runtu. Okavango, NE Namibia
93 I16 **Rundvik** Västerbotten, N Sweden
81 G20 **Runere** Mwanza, N Tanzania
25 S13 **Runge** Texas, SW USA
167 Q13 **Rŭng, Kaôh** *prev.* Kas Rong. *island* SW Cambodia
79 O16 **Rungu** Orientale, NE Dem. Rep. Congo
81 F23 **Rungwa** Rukwa, W Tanzania
81 G22 **Rungwa** Singida, C Tanzania
94 M13 **Runn** ◎ C Sweden
24 M4 **Running Water Draw** *valley* New Mexico/Texas, SW USA
Runö *see* Ruhnu
Runtu *see* Rundu
189 V12 **Ruo** *island* Caroline Islands, C Micronesia
158 L9 **Ruoqiang** *var.* Jo-ch'iang, *Uigh.* Charkhlik, Charkhliq, Qarkilik. Xinjiang Uygur Zizhiqu, NW China
159 S7 **Ruo Shui** ≈ N China
92 L8 **Ruostekfielbmá** *var.* Rustefjelbma Finnmark, N Norway
93 L18 **Ruovesi** Länsi-Suomi, W Finland
112 B9 **Rupa** Primorje-Gorski Kotar, NW Croatia
182 M11 **Rupanyup** Victoria, SE Australia
168 K9 **Rupat, Pulau** *prev.* Roepat. *island* W Indonesia
168 K10 **Rupat, Selat** *strait* Sumatera, W Indonesia
116 J11 **Rupea** *Ger.* Reps, *Hung.* Kőhalom; *prev.* Cohalm. Braşov, C Romania
99 G17 **Rupel** ≈ N Belgium
Rupella *see* la Rochelle
33 P15 **Rupert** Idaho, NW USA
21 R5 **Rupert** West Virginia, NE USA
Rupert House *see* Fort Rupert
12 J10 **Rupert, Rivière de** ≈ Québec, C Canada
194 M13 **Ruppert Coast** *physical region* Antarctica
100 N11 **Ruppiner Kanal** *canal* NE Germany
55 S11 **Rupununi River** ≈ S Guyana
101 D16 **Rur** *Dut.* Roer. ≈ Germany/Netherlands
58 H13 **Rurópolis Presidente Medici** Pará, N Brazil
191 S12 **Rurutu** *island* Îles Australes, SW French Polynesia
Rusaddir *see* Melilla
83 L17 **Rusape** Manicaland, E Zimbabwe
Rusayris, Lake *see* Roseires, Reservoir
Ruschuk/Rusçuk *see* Ruse
114 K7 **Ruse** *var.* Ruschuk, Rustchuk, *Turk.* Rusçuk. Ruse, N Bulgaria
114 L7 **Ruse** ◈ *province* N Bulgaria
109 W10 **Ruše** NE Slovenia
114 K7 **Rusenski Lom** ≈ N Bulgaria
97 G17 **Rush** *Ir.* An Ros. E Ireland
161 S4 **Rushan** *var.* Xiacun. Shandong, E China
Rushan *see* Rŭshon
Rushanskiy Khrebet *see* Rushon, Qatorkŭhi
29 V7 **Rush City** Minnesota, N USA
37 V5 **Rush Creek** ≈ Colorado, C USA
29 X10 **Rushford** Minnesota, N USA
154 N13 **Rushikulya** ≈ E India
14 D8 **Rush Lake** ◎ Ontario, S Canada
30 M7 **Rush Lake** ◎ Wisconsin, N USA
28 J10 **Rushmore, Mount** ▲ South Dakota, N USA
147 S13 **Rŭshon** *Rus.* Rushan. S Tajikistan
147 S14 **Rushon, Qatorkŭhi** *Rus.* Rushanskiy Khrebet. ⛰ SE Tajikistan
26 M12 **Rush Springs** Oklahoma, C USA
45 V15 **Rushville** Trinidad, Trinidad and Tobago
30 J13 **Rushville** Illinois, N USA
28 K12 **Rushville** Nebraska, C USA
183 O11 **Rushworth** Victoria, SE Australia
25 W8 **Rusk** Texas, SW USA
93 I14 **Rusksele** Västerbotten, N Sweden
118 C12 **Rusnė** Klaipėda, W Lithuania
114 M10 **Rusokastrenska Reka** ≈ E Bulgaria
Russadir *see* Melilla
109 X3 **Russbach** ≈ NE Austria
11 V16 **Russell** Manitoba, S Canada
184 K2 **Russell** Northland, North Island, NZ
26 L4 **Russell** Kansas, C USA
21 O4 **Russell** Kentucky, S USA
20 L7 **Russell Springs** Kentucky, S USA
23 O2 **Russellville** Alabama, S USA
27 T11 **Russellville** Arkansas, C USA
20 J7 **Russellville** Kentucky, S USA
101 G18 **Rüsselsheim** Hessen, W Germany
Russenes *see* Olderfjord
Russia *see* Russian Federation
Russian America *see* Alaska
122 J11 **Russian Federation** *off.* Russian Federation, *var.* Russia, *Latv.* Krievija, *Rus.* Rossiyskaya Federatsiya. ◆ *republic* Asia/Europe
39 N11 **Russian Mission** Alaska, USA
34 M7 **Russian River** ≈ California, W USA
194 L13 **Russkaya** *Russian research station* Antarctica
122 J5 **Russkaya Gavan'** Novaya Zemlya, Arkhangel'skaya Oblast', N Russian Federation
122 J5 **Russkiy, Ostrov** *island* N Russian Federation
109 Y5 **Rust** Burgenland, E Austria
Rustaq *see* Ar Rustāq
137 U10 **Rust'avi** SE Georgia
21 T7 **Rustburg** Virginia, NE USA
Rustchuk *see* Ruse
Rustefjelbma *see* Ruostekfielbmá
83 I21 **Rustenburg** North-West, N South Africa
22 H5 **Ruston** Louisiana, S USA
81 E21 **Rutana** SE Burundi
62 I4 **Rutana, Volcán** ▲ N Chile
Rutanzige, Lake *see* Edward, Lake
Rutba *see* Ar Ruṭbah
104 M14 **Rute** Andalucía, S Spain
171 N16 **Ruteng** *prev.* Roeteng. Flores, C Indonesia
194 L8 **Rutford Ice Stream** *ice feature* Antarctica
35 X6 **Ruth** Nevada, W USA
101 G15 **Rüthen** Nordrhein-Westfalen, W Germany
14 D17 **Rutherford** Ontario, S Canada
21 Q10 **Rutherfordton** North Carolina, SE USA
97 J18 **Ruthin** *Wel.* Rhuthun. NE Wales, UK
108 G7 **Rüti** Zürich, N Switzerland
Rutlam *see* Ratlām
18 M9 **Rutland** Vermont, NE USA

◆ Country ● Country Capital ◇ Dependent Territory ○ Dependent Territory Capital ◈ Administrative Region ✕ International Airport ▲ Mountain ⛰ Mountain Range Ж Volcano ≈ River ◎ Lake ▣ Reservoir

97 N19 **Rutland** *cultural region* C England, UK
21 N8 **Rutledge** Tennessee, S USA
158 G12 **Rutög** *var.* Rutog, Rutok. Xizang Zizhiqu, W China
Rutok *see* Rutög
79 P19 **Rutshuru** Nord Kivu, E Dem. Rep. Congo
98 L8 **Rutten** Flevoland, N Netherlands
127 Q17 **Rutul** Respublika Dagestan, SW Russian Federation
93 L14 **Ruukki** Oulu, C Finland
98 N11 **Ruurlo** Gelderland, E Netherlands
143 S15 **Ru'ūs al Jibāl** *headland* Oman/UAE
138 I7 **Ru'ūs aṭ Ṭiwāl, Jabal** ▲ W Syria
81 H23 **Ruvuma** ❖ *region* SE Tanzania
81 I25 **Ruvuma** *var.* Rio Rovuma. ≈ Mozambique/Tanzania *see also* Rovuma, Rio
Ruwais *see* Ar Ruways
138 L9 **Ruwayshid, Wadi ar** *dry watercourse* NE Jordan
141 Z10 **Ruways, Ra's ar** *headland* E Oman
79 P18 **Ruwenzori** ▲ Uganda/Dem. Rep. Congo
141 Y8 **Ruwī** NE Oman
114 F9 **Ruy** ▲ Bulgaria/Serbia and Montenegro (Yugo.)
Ruya *see* Luia, Rio
81 E20 **Ruyigi** E Burundi
127 P5 **Ruzayevka** Respublika Mordoviya, W Russian Federation
119 G18 **Ruzhany** *Rus.* Ruzhany. Brestskaya Voblasts', SW Belarus
114 I10 **Rŭzhevo Konare** *var.* Rŭzhevo Konare. Plovdiv, C Bulgaria
Ruzhin *see* Ruzhyn
114 G7 **Ruzhintsi** Vidin, NW Bulgaria
161 N6 **Ruzhou** Henan, C China
117 N5 **Ruzhyn** *Rus.* Ruzhin. Zhytomyrs'ka Oblast', N Ukraine
111 K19 **Ružomberok** *Ger.* Rosenberg, *Hung.* Rózsahegy. Žilinský Kraj, N Slovakia
111 C16 **Ruzyně** ✈ (Praha) Praha, C Czech Republic
81 D19 **Rwanda** *off.* Rwandese Republic; *prev.* Ruanda. ◆ *republic* C Africa
Rwandese Republic *see* Rwanda
95 G22 **Ry** Århus, C Denmark
Ryasna *see* Rasna
126 L5 **Ryazan'** Ryazanskaya Oblast', W Russian Federation
126 L5 **Ryazanskaya Oblast'** ❖ *province* W Russian Federation
126 M6 **Ryazhsk** Ryazanskaya Oblast', W Russian Federation
118 B13 **Rybachiy** *Ger.* Rossitten. Kaliningradskaya Oblast', W Russian Federation
126 J2 **Rybachiy, Poluostrov** *peninsula* NW Russian Federation
Rybach'ye *see* Balykchy
126 L15 **Rybinsk** *prev.* Andropov. Yaroslavskaya Oblast', W Russian Federation
126 K14 **Rybinskoye Vodokhranilishche** *Eng.* Rybinsk Reservoir, Rybinsk Sea. ⊠ W Russian Federation
Rybinsk Reservoir/Rybinsk Sea *see* Rybinskoye Vodokhranilishche
111 I16 **Rybnik** Śląskie, S Poland
Rybnitsa *see* Rîbniţa
111 F16 **Rychnov nad Kněžnou** *Ger.* Reichenau. Královéhradecký Kraj, N Czech Republic
110 I12 **Rychwał** Wielkolpolskie, C Poland
11 O13 **Rycroft** Alberta, W Canada
95 L21 **Ryd** Kronoberg, S Sweden
95 L20 **Rydaholm** Jönköping, S Sweden
194 I8 **Rydberg Peninsula** *peninsula* Antarctica
97 P23 **Rye** SE England, UK
33 T10 **Ryegate** Montana, NW USA
35 S3 **Rye Patch Reservoir** ⊠ Nevada, W USA
95 D15 **Ryfylke** *physical region* S Norway
95 H16 **Rygge** Østfold, S Norway
110 N13 **Ryki** Lubelskie, E Poland
Rykovo *see* Yenakiyeve
126 I7 **Ryl'sk** Kurskaya Oblast', W Russian Federation
183 S8 **Rylstone** New South Wales, SE Australia
111 H17 **Rýmařov** *Ger.* Römerstadt. Moravskoslezský Kraj, E Czech Republic
144 E11 **Ryn-Peski** *desert* W Kazakhstan
165 N10 **Ryōtsu** *var.* Ryôtu. Niigata, Sado, C Japan
Ryôtu *see* Ryōtsu
110 K10 **Rypin** Kujawsko-pomorskie, C Poland
Ryshkany *see* Rîşcani
Ryssel *see* Lille
Ryswick *see* Rijswijk
95 M24 **Rytterknægten** *hill* E Denmark
192 G5 **Ryukyu Trench** *var.* Nansei Syotō Trench. *undersea feature* S East China Sea
110 D11 **Rzepin** *Ger.* Reppen. Lubuskie, W Poland
111 N16 **Rzeszów** Podkarpackie, SE Poland
124 I16 **Rzhev** Tverskaya Oblast', W Russian Federation
Rzhishchev *see* Rzhyshchiv
117 P5 **Rzhyshchiv** *Rus.* Rzhishchev. Kyyivs'ka Oblast', N Ukraine

S

138 E11 **Sa'ad** Southern, W Israel
109 P7 **Saalach** ≈ W Austria
101 L14 **Saale** ≈ C Germany
101 L17 **Saalfeld** *var.* Saalfeld an der Saale. Thüringen, C Germany
Saalfeld *see* Zalewo
Saalfeld an der Saale *see* Saalfeld
108 C8 **Saane** ≈ W Switzerland
101 D19 **Saar** *Fr.* Sarre. ≈ France/Germany
101 E20 **Saarbrücken** *Fr.* Sarrebruck. Saarland, SW Germany
Saarburg *see* Sarrebourg
Saare *see* Saaremaa
118 D6 **Sääre** *var.* Sjar. Saaremaa, W Estonia
118 D5 **Saaremaa** *off.* Saare Maakond. ❖ *province* W Estonia
118 E6 **Saaremaa** *Ger.* Oesel, Ösel; *prev.* Saare. *island* W Estonia
92 L12 **Saarenkylä** Lappi, N Finland
Saargemund *see* Sarreguemines
93 L17 **Saarijärvi** Länsi-Suomi, W Finland
Saar in Mähren *see* Žďár nad Sázavou
92 M10 **Saariselkä** *Lapp.* Suoločielgi. Lappi, N Finland
92 L10 **Saariselkä** *hill range* NE Finland
101 D20 **Saarland** *Fr.* Sarre. ❖ *state* SW Germany
Saarlautern *see* Saarlouis
101 D20 **Saarlouis** *prev.* Saarlautern. Saarland, SW Germany
108 E11 **Saaser Vispa** ≈ S Switzerland
137 X12 **Saatlı** *Rus.* Saatly. C Azerbaijan
Saatly *see* Saatlı
Saaz *see* Žatec
45 V9 **Saba** *island* N Netherlands Antilles
138 J7 **Sab' Ābār** *var.* Sab'a Biyar, Sa'b Bi'ār. Ḥimṣ, C Syria
Sab'a Biyar *see* Sab' Ābār
112 K11 **Šabac** Serbia, W Serbia and Montenegro (Yugo.)
105 W5 **Sabadell** Cataluña, E Spain
164 K12 **Sabae** Fukui, Honshū, SW Japan
169 V7 **Sabah** *prev.* British North Borneo, North Borneo. ❖ *state* East Malaysia
168 J8 **Sabak** *var.* Sabak Bernam. Selangor, Peninsular Malaysia
Sabak Bernam *see* Sabak
38 D16 **Sabak, Cape** *headland* Agattu Island, Alaska, USA
81 J20 **Sabaki** ≈ S Kenya
142 L2 **Sabalān, Kuhhā-ye** ▲ NW Iran
154 H7 **Sabalgarh** Madhya Pradesh, C India
44 E4 **Sabana, Archipiélago de** *island group* C Cuba
42 H7 **Sabanagrande** *var.* Sabana Grande. Francisco Morazán, S Honduras
54 E5 **Sabanalarga** Atlántico, N Colombia
41 W14 **Sabancuy** Campeche, SE Mexico
45 N8 **Sabaneta** NW Dominican Republic
54 J4 **Sabaneta** Falcón, N Venezuela
188 H4 **Sabaneta, Puntan** *prev.* Ushi Point. *headland* Saipan, S Northern Mariana Islands
171 X14 **Sabang** Papua, E Indonesia
116 L10 **Săbăoani** Neamţ, NE Romania
155 J26 **Sabaragamuwa Province** ❖ *province* C Sri Lanka
Sabaria *see* Szombathely
154 D10 **Sābarmati** ≈ NW India
171 S10 **Sabatai** Pulau Morotai, E Indonesia
141 Q15 **Sab'atayn, Ramlat as** *desert* C Yemen
107 I16 **Sabaudia** Lazio, C Italy
57 J19 **Sabaya** Oruro, S Bolivia
Sa'b Bi'ār *see* Sab' Ābār
Sabbioncello *see* Orebić
148 I8 **Šāberī, Hāmūn-e** *var.* Daryācheh-ye Hāmūn, Daryācheh-ye Sīstān. ◎ Afghanistan/Iran *see also* Sīstān, Daryācheh-ye
27 P2 **Sabetha** Kansas, C USA
75 P10 **Sabhā** C Libya
Sabi *see* Save, Rio
118 E8 **Sabile** *Ger.* Zabeln. Talsi, NW Latvia
31 R14 **Sabina** Ohio, N USA
40 I3 **Sabinal** Chihuahua, N Mexico
25 Q12 **Sabinal** Texas, SW USA
25 Q11 **Sabinal River** ≈ Texas, SW USA
105 S4 **Sabiñánigo** Aragón, NE Spain
41 N6 **Sabinas** Coahuila de Zaragoza, NE Mexico
41 O8 **Sabinas Hidalgo** Nuevo León, NE Mexico
41 N6 **Sabinas, Río** ≈ NE Mexico
22 F9 **Sabine Lake** ◎ Louisiana/Texas, S USA
92 O3 **Sabine Land** *physical region* C Svalbard
25 W7 **Sabine River** ≈ Louisiana/Texas, SW USA
137 X12 **Sabirabad** C Azerbaijan
Sabkha *see* As Sabkhah
171 O4 **Sablayan** Mindoro, N Philippines
13 P16 **Sable, Cape** *headland* Newfoundland and Labrador, SE Canada
23 X17 **Sable, Cape** *headland* Florida, SE USA
13 R16 **Sable Island** *island* Nova Scotia, SE Canada
14 L11 **Sables, Lac des** ◎ Québec, SE Canada
14 E10 **Sables, Rivière aux** ≈ Ontario, S Canada
102 K7 **Sable-sur-Sarthe** Sarthe, NW France
127 U7 **Sablya, Gora** ▲ NW Russian Federation
77 U14 **Sabon Birnin Gwari** Kaduna, C Nigeria
77 V11 **Sabon Kafi** Zinder, C Niger
104 I6 **Sabor, Rio** ≈ N Portugal
14 J8 **Sabourin, Lac** ◎ Québec, SE Canada
102 J14 **Sabres** Landes, SW France
195 X13 **Sabrina Coast** *physical region* Antarctica
140 M11 **Sabt al Ulayā** 'Asīr, SW Saudi Arabia
104 I8 **Sabugal** Guarda, N Portugal
29 Z13 **Sabula** Iowa, C USA
141 N13 **Ṣabyā** Jīzān, SW Saudi Arabia
Sabzawar *see* Sabzevār
Sabzawaran *see* Sabzvārān
143 S4 **Sabzevār** *var.* Sabzawar. Khorāsān, NE Iran
143 T12 **Sabzvārān** *var.* Sabzawaran; *prev.* Jiroft. Kermān, SE Iran
Sacajawea Peak *see* Matterhorn
82 C9 **Sacandica** Uíge, NW Angola
42 A2 **Sacatepéquez** *off.* Departamento de Sacatepéquez. ❖ *department* S Guatemala
104 F11 **Sacavém** Lisboa, W Portugal
29 T13 **Sac City** Iowa, C USA
105 P8 **Sacedón** Castilla-La Mancha, C Spain
116 J12 **Săcele** *Ger.* Vierdörfer, *Hung.* Négyfalu; *prev. Ger.* Sieben Dörfer, *Hung.* Hétfalu. Braşov, C Romania
12 C8 **Sachigo** Ontario, C Canada
12 C7 **Sachigo** ≈ Ontario, C Canada
12 C8 **Sachigo Lake** ◎ Ontario, C Canada
163 Y16 **Sach'ŏn** *Jap.* Sansenhō; *prev.* Samch'ŏnpŏ. S South Korea
101 O15 **Sachsen** *Eng.* Saxony, *Fr.* Saxe. ❖ *state* E Germany
101 K14 **Sachsen-Anhalt** *Eng.* Saxony-Anhalt. ❖ *state* C Germany
109 R9 **Sachsenburg** Salzburg, S Austria
Sachsenfeld *see* Žalec
8 I5 **Sachs Harbour** Banks Island, Northwest Territories, N Canada
Sächsisch-Reen/Sächsisch-Regen *see* Reghin
18 H8 **Sackets Harbor** New York, NE USA
13 P14 **Sackville** New Brunswick, SE Canada
19 P9 **Saco** Maine, NE USA
19 P8 **Saco River** ≈ Maine/New Hampshire, NE USA
35 O7 **Sacramento** *state capital* California, W USA
37 T14 **Sacramento Mountains** ▲ New Mexico, SW USA
35 N6 **Sacramento River** ≈ California, W USA
35 N5 **Sacramento Valley** *valley* California, W USA
36 I10 **Sacramento Wash** *valley* Arizona, SW USA
105 N15 **Sacratif, Cabo** *headland* S Spain
116 F9 **Săcueni** *prev.* Săcuieni, *Hung.* Székelyhid. Bihor, W Romania
Săcuieni *see* Săcueni
105 R4 **Sádaba** Aragón, NE Spain
Sá da Bandeira *see* Lubango
138 I6 **Şadad** Ḥimṣ, W Syria
141 O13 **Ṣa'dah** NW Yemen
167 O16 **Sadao** Songkhla, SW Thailand
142 L8 **Sadd-e Dez, Daryācheh-ye** ◎ W Iran
19 S3 **Saddleback Mountain** *hill* Maine, NE USA
19 P6 **Saddleback Mountain** ▲ Maine, NE USA
167 S14 **Sa Đec** Đông Thap, S Vietnam
141 W13 **Sadḥ** S Oman
76 J11 **Sadiola** Kayes, W Mali
149 R12 **Sādiqābād** Punjab, E Pakistan
153 Y10 **Sadiya** Assam, NE India
139 W9 **Sa'dīyah, Hawr as** ◎ E Iraq
165 N9 **Sado** *var.* Sadoga-shima. *island* C Japan
Sadoga-shima *see* Sado
104 F12 **Sado, Rio** ≈ S Portugal
114 I8 **Sadovets** Pleven, N Bulgaria
127 O11 **Sadovoye** Respublika Kalmykiya, SW Russian Federation
105 W9 **Sa Dragonera** *var.* Isla Dragonera. *island* Islas Baleares, Spain, W Mediterranean Sea
95 H20 **Sæby** Nordjylland, N Denmark
105 P9 **Saelices** Castilla-La Mancha, C Spain
Saena Julia *see* Siena
Saetabicula *see* Alzira
114 O12 **Safaalan** Tekirdağ, NW Turkey
Safad *see* Ẕefat
Safāqis *see* Sfax
192 I16 **Safata Bay** *bay* Upolu, Samoa, C Pacific Ocean
Safed *see* Ẕefat
Safed, Āb-i- *see* Sefīd, Darya-ye
139 X11 **Şaffāf, Ḥawr aş** *wetland* S Iraq
95 J16 **Säffle** Värmland, C Sweden
37 N15 **Safford** Arizona, SW USA
74 E7 **Safi** W Morocco
143 V9 **Safīdābeh** Khorāsān, E Iran
142 M4 **Safīd, Rūd-e** ≈ NW Iran
126 I4 **Safonovo** Smolenskaya Oblast', W Russian Federation
136 H11 **Safranbolu** Karabük, N Turkey
139 Y13 **Safwān** SE Iraq
158 J16 **Saga** *var.* Gya'gya. Xizang Zizhiqu, W China
164 C14 **Saga** Saga, Kyūshū, SW Japan
164 C13 **Saga** *off.* Saga-ken. ❖ *prefecture* Kyūshū, SW Japan
165 P10 **Sagae** Yamagata, Honshū, C Japan
166 L3 **Sagaing** Sagaing, C Burma
166 L5 **Sagaing** ❖ *division* N Burma
165 N13 **Sagamihara** Kanagawa, Honshū, S Japan
165 N14 **Sagami-nada** *inlet* SW Japan
Sagan *see* Żagań
29 Y3 **Saganaga Lake** ◎ Minnesota, N USA
155 F18 **Sāgar** Karnātaka, W India
154 I9 **Sāgar** *prev.* Saugor. Madhya Pradesh, C India
15 S8 **Sagard** Québec, SE Canada
Sagarmatha *see* Everest, Mount
Sagebrush State *see* Nevada
143 V11 **Sāghand** Yazd, C Iran
19 N14 **Sag Harbor** Long Island, New York, NE USA
Saghez *see* Saqqez
31 R8 **Saginaw** Michigan, N USA
31 R8 **Saginaw Bay** *lake bay* Michigan, N USA
144 H11 **Sagiz** Atyrau, W Kazakhstan
64 H6 **Saglek Bank** *undersea feature* W Labrador Sea
13 P5 **Saglek Bay** *bay* SW Labrador Sea
Saglouc/Sagluk *see* Salluit
103 X15 **Sagonne, Golfe de** *gulf* Corse, France, C Mediterranean Sea
105 P13 **Sagra** ▲ S Spain
104 F14 **Sagres** Faro, S Portugal
37 S7 **Saguache** Colorado, C USA
44 J7 **Sagua de Tánamo** Holguín, E Cuba
44 E5 **Sagua la Grande** Villa Clara, C Cuba
15 R7 **Saguenay** ≈ Québec, SE Canada
74 C9 **Saguia al Hamra** *var.* Saqia al Hamra. ≈ N Western Sahara
Sagunt/Saguntum *see* Sagunto
105 S9 **Sagunto** *Cat.* Sagunt, *Ar.* Murviedro; *anc.* Saguntum. País Valenciano, E Spain
138 H10 **Saḥāb** 'Al 'Ammān, NW Jordan
54 E6 **Sahagún** Córdoba, NW Colombia
104 L4 **Sahagún** Castilla-León, N Spain
141 X8 **Saḥam** N Oman
74 M11 **Sahara** *desert* Libya/Algeria
75 U9 **Sahara el Gharbîya** *var.* Aş Şaḥrā' al Gharbīyah, *Eng.* Western Desert. *desert* C Egypt
75 X9 **Sahara el Sharqîya** *var.* Aş Şaḥrā' ash Sharqīyah, *Eng.* Arabian Desert, Eastern Desert. *desert* E Egypt
Saharan Atlas *see* Atlas Saharien
152 J9 **Sahāranpur** Uttar Pradesh, N India
64 L10 **Saharan Seamounts** *var.* Saharian Seamounts. *undersea feature* E Atlantic Ocean
153 Q13 **Saharsa** Bihār, NE India
77 P11 **Sahel** *physical region* C Africa
153 R14 **Sāhibganj** Jhārkhand, NE India
139 Q7 **Sahīlīyah** C Iraq
138 H4 **Sāḥilīyah, Jibāl as** ▲ NW Syria
114 M13 **Şahin** Tekirdağ, NW Turkey
149 U8 **Sāhīwāl** Punjab, E Pakistan
149 U9 **Sāhīwāl** *prev.* Montgomery. Punjab, E Pakistan
141 W11 **Saḥmah, Ramlat as** *desert* C Oman
139 T13 **Şaḥrā' al Ḥijārah** *desert* S Iraq
40 H5 **Sahuaripa** Sonora, NW Mexico
36 M16 **Sahuarita** Arizona, SW USA
40 L13 **Sahuayo** *var.* Sahuayo de José Mariá Morelos; *prev.* Sahuayo de Díaz, Sahuayo de Porfirio Díaz. Michoacán de Ocampo, SW Mexico
Sahuayo de Díaz/Sahuayo de José Mariá Morelos/Sahuayo de Porfirio Díaz *see* Sahuayo
173 W8 **Sahul Shelf** *undersea feature* N Timor Sea
167 P17 **Sai Buri** Pattani, SW Thailand
74 I6 **Saïda** NW Algeria
138 G7 **Saïda** *var.* Şaydā, Sayida; *anc.* Sidon. W Lebanon
Sa'īdābād *see* Sīrjān
80 B13 **Sa'id Bundas** Western Bahr el Ghazal, SW Sudan
186 E7 **Saidor** Madang, N PNG
153 S13 **Saidpur** *var.* Syedpur. Rajshahi, NW Bangladesh
108 C7 **Saignelégier** Jura, NW Switzerland
164 H11 **Saigō** Shimane, Dōgo, SW Japan
Saigon *see* Hô Chi Minh
163 P11 **Saihan Tal** *var.* Sonid Youqi. Nei Mongol Zizhiqu, N China
162 I12 **Saihan Toroi** Nei Mongol Zizhiqu, N China
Sai Hun *see* Syr Darya
92 M11 **Saija** Lappi, NE Finland
164 G14 **Saijō** Ehime, Shikoku, SW Japan
164 E15 **Saiki** Ōita, Kyūshū, SW Japan
93 N18 **Saimaa** ◎ SE Finland
93 N18 **Saimaa Canal** *Fin.* Saimaan Kanava, *Rus.* Saymenskiy Kanal. *canal* Finland/Russian Federation
Saimaan Kanava *see* Saimaa Canal
40 L10 **Saín Alto** Zacatecas, C Mexico
96 L12 **St Abb's Head** *headland* SE Scotland, UK
11 Y16 **St.Adolphe** Manitoba, S Canada
103 O15 **St-Affrique** Aveyron, S France
15 Q10 **St-Agapit** Québec, SE Canada
97 O21 **St Albans** *anc.* Verulamium. E England, UK
18 L6 **Saint Albans** Vermont, NE USA
21 Q5 **Saint Albans** West Virginia, NE USA
St Alban's Head *see* St.Aldhelm's Head
11 Q14 **St.Albert** Alberta, SW Canada
99 M24 **St. Aldhelm's Head** *var.* St.Alban's Head. *headland* S England, UK
15 S8 **St-Alexandre** Québec, SE Canada
15 O11 **St-Alexis-des-Monts** Québec, SE Canada
103 P2 **St-Amand-les-Eaux** Nord, N France
103 O9 **St-Amand-Montrond** *var.* St-Amand-Mont-Rond. Cher, C France
15 Q7 **St-Ambroise** Québec, SE Canada
173 P16 **St-André** NE Réunion
14 M12 **St-André-Avellin** Québec, SE Canada
102 K12 **St-André-de-Cubzac** Gironde, SW France
96 K11 **St Andrews** E Scotland, UK
23 Q9 **Saint Andrews Bay** *bay* Florida, SE USA
23 W7 **Saint Andrew Sound** *sound* Georgia, SE USA
Saint Anna Trough *see* Svyataya Anna Trough
44 J11 **St.Ann's Bay** C Jamaica
13 T10 **St.Anthony** Newfoundland and Labrador, SE Canada
33 R13 **Saint Anthony** Idaho, NW USA
182 M11 **Saint Arnaud** Victoria, SE Australia
185 I15 **St.Arnaud Range** ▲ South Island, NZ
15 T8 **St-Arsène** Québec, SE Canada
13 R10 **St-Augustin** Québec, E Canada
23 X9 **Saint Augustine** Florida, SE USA
97 H24 **St Austell** SW England, UK
103 T4 **St-Avold** Moselle, NE France
103 N17 **St-Barthélemy** ▲ S France
102 L17 **St-Béat** Haute-Garonne, S France
97 I15 **St Bees Head** *headland* NW England, UK
173 P16 **St-Benoit** E Réunion
103 T13 **St-Bonnet** Hautes-Alpes, SE France
St.Botolph's Town *see* Boston
97 G21 **St Brides Bay** *inlet* SW Wales, UK
102 H5 **St-Brieuc** Côtes d'Armor, NW France
102 H5 **St-Brieuc, Baie de** *bay* NW France
102 L7 **St-Calais** Sarthe, NW France
15 Q10 **St-Casimir** Québec, SE Canada
14 H16 **St.Catharines** Ontario, S Canada
45 S14 **St.Catherine, Mount** ▲ N Grenada
64 C11 **St Catherine Point** *headland* E Bermuda
23 X6 **Saint Catherines Island** *island* Georgia, SE USA
97 M24 **St Catherine's Point** *headland* S England, UK
103 N13 **St-Céré** Lot, S France
108 A10 **St.Cergue** Vaud, W Switzerland
103 R11 **St-Chamond** Loire, E France
33 S16 **Saint Charles** Idaho, NW USA
27 X4 **Saint Charles** Missouri, C USA
103 P13 **St-Chély-d'Apcher** Lozère, S France
Saint Christopher-Nevis *see* Saint Kitts and Nevis
31 S9 **Saint Clair** Michigan, N USA
14 D17 **St.Clair** ≈ Canada/USA
183 O17 **St.Clair, Lake** ◎ Tasmania, SE Australia
14 C17 **St.Clair, Lake** *var.* Lac à L'eau Claire. ◎ Canada/USA
31 S10 **Saint Clair Shores** Michigan, N USA
103 S10 **St-Claude** *anc.* Condate. Jura, E France
45 X6 **St-Claude** Basse Terre, SW Guadeloupe
23 X12 **Saint Cloud** Florida, SE USA
29 U8 **Saint Cloud** Minnesota, N USA
45 T9 **Saint Croix** *island* S Virgin Islands (US)
30 J4 **Saint Croix Flowage** ⊠ Wisconsin, N USA
19 T5 **Saint Croix River** ≈ Canada/USA
29 W7 **Saint Croix River** ≈ Minnesota/Wisconsin, N USA
45 S14 **St.David's** SE Grenada
97 H21 **St David's** SW Wales, UK
97 G21 **St David's Head** *headland* SW Wales, UK
64 C12 **St David's Island** *island* E Bermuda
173 O16 **St-Denis** ○ (Réunion) NW Réunion
103 U6 **St-Dié** Vosges, NE France
103 R5 **St-Dizier** *anc.* Desiderii Fanum. Haute-Marne, N France
15 N11 **St-Donat** Québec, SE Canada
15 N11 **Ste-Adèle** Québec, SE Canada
15 N11 **Ste-Agathe-des-Monts** Québec, SE Canada
172 I16 **Sainte Anne** *island* Inner Islands, NE Seychelles
11 Y16 **Ste.Anne** Manitoba, S Canada
45 R12 **Ste-Anne** Grande Terre, E Guadeloupe
45 Y6 **Ste-Anne** SE Martinique
15 Q10 **Ste-Anne** ≈ Québec, SE Canada
15 W6 **Ste-Anne-des-Monts** Québec, SE Canada
14 M10 **Ste-Anne-du-Lac** Québec, SE Canada
15 U4 **Ste-Anne, Lac** ◎ Québec, SE Canada
15 S10 **Ste-Apolline** Québec, SE Canada
15 U7 **Ste-Blandine** Québec, SE Canada
15 R10 **Ste-Claire** Québec, SE Canada
15 Q10 **Ste-Croix** Québec, SE Canada
108 B8 **Ste.Croix** Vaud, SW Switzerland
103 P14 **Ste-Énimie** Lozère, S France
27 Y6 **Sainte Genevieve** Missouri, C USA
103 S12 **St-Egrève** Isère, E France
39 T12 **Saint Elias, Cape** *headland* Kayak Island, Alaska, USA
39 U11 **Saint Elias, Mount** ▲ Alaska, USA
10 G8 **Saint Elias Mountains** ▲ Canada/USA
55 Y10 **St-Élie** N French Guiana
103 O10 **St-Eloy-les-Mines** Puy-de-Dôme, C France
15 R7 **Ste-Marguerite** ≈ Québec, SE Canada
15 S7 **Ste-Marguerite-Nord-Est** ≈ Québec, SE Canada
15 V4 **Ste-Marguerite, Pointe** *headland* Québec, SE Canada
15 R10 **Ste-Marie** Québec, SE Canada
45 Q11 **Ste-Marie** NE Martinique
173 P16 **Ste-Marie** NE Réunion
103 U6 **Ste-Marie-aux-Mines** Haut-Rhin, NE France
12 J14 **Ste-Marie, Lac** ⊠ Quebec, S Canada
172 K4 **Sainte Marie, Nosy** *island* E Madagascar
102 L8 **Ste-Maure-de-Touraine** Indre-et-Loire, C France
103 R4 **Ste-Menehould** Marne, NE France
Ste-Perpétue *see* Ste-Perpétue-de-l'Islet
15 S9 **Ste-Perpétue-de-l'Islet** *var.* Ste-Perpétue. Québec, SE Canada
45 X11 **Ste-Rose** Basse Terre, N Guadeloupe
173 P16 **Ste-Rose** E Réunion
11 W15 **Ste.Rose du Lac** Manitoba, S Canada
102 J11 **Saintes** *anc.* Mediolanum. Charente-Maritime, W France
45 X7 **Saintes, Canal des** *channel* SW Guadeloupe
Saintes, Îles des *see* les Saintes
173 P16 **Ste-Suzanne** N Réunion
15 P10 **Ste-Thècle** Québec, SE Canada
103 Q12 **St-Étienne** Loire, E France
102 M4 **St-Étienne-du-Rouvray** Seine-Maritime, N France
Saint Eustatius *see* Sint Eustatius
14 M11 **Ste-Véronique** Québec, SE Canada
15 T7 **St-Fabien** Québec, SE Canada
15 P7 **St-Félicien** Québec, SE Canada
15 O11 **St-Félix-de-Valois** Québec, SE Canada
103 Y14 **St-Florent** Corse, France, C Mediterranean Sea
103 Y14 **St-Florent, Golfe de** *gulf* Corse, France, C Mediterranean Sea
103 P6 **St-Florentin** Yonne, C France
103 N9 **St-Florent-sur-Cher** Cher, C France
103 P12 **St-Flour** Cantal, C France
26 H2 **Saint Francis** Kansas, C USA
83 H26 **St.Francis, Cape** *headland* S South Africa
27 X10 **Saint Francis River** ≈ Arkansas/Missouri, C USA
22 J8 **Saint Francisville** Louisiana, S USA
15 Q12 **St-François** ≈ Québec, SE Canada
45 Y6 **St-François** Grande Terre, E Guadeloupe
15 R11 **St-François, Lac** ◎ Québec, SE Canada
27 X7 **Saint Francois Mountains** ▲ Missouri, C USA
St-Gall/Saint Gall/St.Gallen *see* Sankt Gallen
102 L16 **St-Gaudens** Haute-Garonne, S France
15 R12 **St-Gédéon** Québec, SE Canada
181 X10 **Saint George** Queensland, E Australia
64 B12 **St George** N Bermuda
38 K15 **Saint George** Saint George Island, Alaska, USA
21 S14 **Saint George** South Carolina, SE USA
36 J8 **Saint George** Utah, W USA
13 R12 **St.George, Cape** *headland* Newfoundland and Labrador, E Canada
186 I6 **St.George, Cape** *headland* New Ireland, NE PNG
38 J15 **Saint George Island** *island* Pribilof Islands, Alaska, USA
23 S10 **Saint George Island** *island* Florida, SE USA
99 J19 **Saint-Georges** Liège, E Belgium
15 R11 **St-Georges** Québec, SE Canada
55 Z11 **St-Georges** E French Guiana
45 R14 **St.George's** ● (Grenada) SW Grenada
13 R12 **St.George's Bay** *inlet* Newfoundland and Labrador, E Canada
97 G21 **Saint George's Channel** *channel* Ireland/Wales, UK
186 H6 **St.George's Channel** *channel* NE PNG
64 B11 **St George's Island** *island* E Bermuda
99 I21 **Saint-Gérard** Namur, S Belgium
St-Germain *see* St-Germain-en-Laye
15 P12 **St-Germain-de-Grantham** Québec, SE Canada
103 N5 **St-Germain-en-Laye** *var.* St-Germain. Yvelines, N France
102 H8 **St-Gildas, Pointe du** *headland* NW France
103 R15 **St-Gilles** Gard, S France
102 I9 **St-Gilles-Croix-de-Vie** Vendée, NW France
173 O16 **St-Gilles-les-Bains** W Réunion
102 M16 **St-Girons** Ariège, S France
Saint Gotthard *see* Szentgotthárd
108 G9 **St.Gotthard Tunnel** *tunnel* Ticino, S Switzerland
97 H22 **St Govan's Head** *headland* SW Wales, UK
34 M7 **Saint Helena** California, W USA
65 F24 **Saint Helena** ◇ *UK dependent territory* C Atlantic Ocean
83 E25 **St.Helena Bay** *bay* SW South Africa
65 M16 **Saint Helena Fracture Zone** *tectonic feature* C Atlantic Ocean
34 M7 **Saint Helena, Mount** ▲ California, W USA
21 S15 **Saint Helena Sound** *inlet* South Carolina, SE USA

◆ Country ◇ Dependent Territory ❖ Administrative Region ▲ Mountain ☒ Volcano ◎ Lake
● Country Capital ○ Dependent Territory Capital ✈ International Airport ▲ Mountain Range ≈ River ⊠ Reservoir

31 Q7 **Saint Helen, Lake** ◎ Michigan, N USA
183 Q16 **Saint Helens** Tasmania, SE Australia
97 K18 **St Helens** NW England, UK
32 G10 **Saint Helens** Oregon, NW USA
32 H10 **Saint Helens, Mount** ☒ Washington, NW USA
97 L26 **St Helier** ○ (Jersey) S Jersey, Channel Islands
15 S9 **St-Hilarion** Québec, SE Canada
99 K22 **Saint-Hubert** Luxembourg, SE Belgium
15 T8 **St-Hubert** Québec, SE Canada
15 P12 **St-Hyacinthe** Québec, SE Canada
St.Iago de la Vega *see* Spanish Town
31 Q4 **Saint Ignace** Michigan, N USA
15 O10 **St-Ignace-du-Lac** Québec, SE Canada
12 D12 **St.Ignace Island** *island* Ontario, S Canada
108 C7 **St.Imier** Bern, W Switzerland
97 G25 **St Ives** SW England, UK
29 U10 **Saint James** Minnesota, N USA
10 I15 **St.James, Cape** *headland* Graham Island, British Columbia, SW Canada
15 O13 **St-Jean** *var.* St-Jean-sur-Richelieu. Québec, SE Canada
55 X9 **St-Jean** NW French Guiana
15 R8 **St-Jean** ≈ Québec, SE Canada
Saint-Jean-d'Acre *see* 'Akko
102 K11 **St-Jean-d'Angély** Charente-Maritime, W France
103 N7 **St-Jean-de-Braye** Loiret, C France
102 I16 **St-Jean-de-Luz** Pyrénées-Atlantiques, SW France
103 T12 **St-Jean-de-Maurienne** Savoie, E France
102 I9 **St-Jean-de-Monts** Vendée, NW France
103 Q14 **St-Jean-du-Gard** Gard, S France
15 Q7 **St-Jean, Lac** ◎ Québec, SE Canada
102 I16 **St-Jean-Pied-de-Port** Pyrénées-Atlantiques, SW France
15 S9 **St-Jean-Port-Joli** Québec, SE Canada
St-Jean-sur-Richelieu *see* St-Jean
15 N12 **St-Jérôme** Québec, SE Canada
25 T5 **Saint Jo** Texas, SW USA
13 O15 **St.John** New Brunswick, SE Canada
26 L6 **Saint John** Kansas, C USA
76 K16 **Saint John** ≈ C Liberia
45 T9 **Saint John** *island* C Virgin Islands (US)
22 I6 **Saint John, Lake** ◎ Louisiana, S USA
19 Q2 **Saint John** *Fr.* Saint-John. ≈ Canada/USA
45 W10 **St John's** ● (Antigua and Barbuda) Antigua, Antigua and Barbuda
13 V12 **St.John's** Newfoundland and Labrador, E Canada
37 O12 **Saint Johns** Arizona, SW USA
31 Q9 **Saint Johns** Michigan, N USA
13 V12 **St.John's** ✕ Newfoundland and Labrador, E Canada
23 X11 **Saint Johns River** ≈ Florida, SE USA
45 N12 **St.Joseph** W Dominica
173 P17 **St-Joseph** S Réunion
22 J6 **Saint Joseph** Louisiana, S USA
31 O10 **Saint Joseph** Michigan, N USA
27 R3 **Saint Joseph** Missouri, C USA
20 I10 **Saint Joseph** Tennessee, S USA
22 R9 **Saint Joseph Bay** *bay* Florida, SE USA
15 R11 **St-Joseph-de-Beauce** Québec, SE Canada
12 C10 **St.Joseph, Lake** ◎ Ontario, C Canada
31 Q11 **Saint Joseph River** ≈ N USA
14 C11 **Saint Joseph's Island** *island* Ontario, S Canada
15 N11 **St-Jovite** Québec, SE Canada
121 P16 **St Julian's** N Malta
St-Julien *see* St-Julien-en-Genevois
103 T10 **St-Julien-en-Genevois** *var.* St-Julien. Haute-Savoie, E France
102 M11 **St-Junien** Haute-Vienne, C France
103 Q11 **St-Just-St-Rambert** Loire, E France
96 D8 **St Kilda** *island* NW Scotland, UK
45 V10 **Saint Kitts** *island* Saint Kitts and Nevis
45 U10 **Saint Kitts and Nevis** *off.* Federation of Saint Christopher and Nevis, *var.* Saint Christopher-Nevis. ◆ *commonwealth republic* E West Indies
11 X16 **St.Laurent** Manitoba, S Canada
St-Laurent *see* St-Laurent-du-Maroni
55 X9 **St-Laurent-du-Maroni** *var.* St-Laurent. NW French Guiana
St-Laurent, Fleuve *see* St.Lawrence
102 J12 **St-Laurent-Médoc** Gironde, SW France
13 N12 **St.Lawrence** *Fr.* Fleuve St-Laurent. ≈ Canada/USA
13 Q12 **St.Lawrence, Gulf of** *gulf* NW Atlantic Ocean
38 K10 **Saint Lawrence Island** *island* Alaska, USA
14 M14 **Saint Lawrence River** ≈ Canada/USA
99 L25 **Saint-Léger** Luxembourg, SE Belgium
13 N14 **St.Léonard** New Brunswick, SE Canada
15 P11 **St-Léonard** Québec, SE Canada
173 O17 **St-Leu** W Réunion
102 J4 **St-Lô** *anc.* Briovera, Laudus. Manche, N France
11 T15 **St.Louis** Saskatchewan, S Canada
103 V7 **St-Louis** Haut-Rhin, NE France
173 O17 **St-Louis** S Réunion
76 G10 **Saint Louis** NW Senegal
27 X4 **Saint Louis** Missouri, C USA
29 W5 **Saint Louis River** ≈ Minnesota, N USA
103 T7 **St-Loup-sur-Semouse** Haute-Saône, E France
15 O12 **St-Luc** Québec, SE Canada
83 L22 **St.Lucia** KwaZulu/Natal, E South Africa
45 X13 **Saint Lucia** ◆ *commonwealth republic* SE West Indies
47 S3 **Saint Lucia** *island* SE West Indies
83 L22 **St.Lucia, Cape** *headland* E South Africa
45 Y13 **Saint Lucia Channel** *channel* Martinique/Saint Lucia
23 Y14 **Saint Lucie Canal** *canal* Florida, SE USA
23 Z13 **Saint Lucie Inlet** *inlet* Florida, SE USA
96 L2 **St Magnus Bay** *bay* N Scotland, UK
102 K10 **St-Maixent-l'École** Deux-Sèvres, W France
11 Y16 **St.Malo** Manitoba, S Canada
102 I5 **St-Malo** Ille-et-Vilaine, NW France
102 H4 **St-Malo, Golfe de** *gulf* NW France
44 L9 **St-Marc** C Haiti
44 L9 **St-Marc, Canal de** *channel* W Haiti
55 Y12 **Saint-Marcel, Mont** ▲ S French Guiana
103 S12 **St-Marcellin-le-Mollard** Isère, E France
96 K5 **St Margaret's Hope** NE Scotland, UK
32 M9 **Saint Maries** Idaho, NW USA
23 T9 **Saint Marks** Florida, SE USA
108 D11 **St.Martin** Valais, SW Switzerland
Saint Martin *see* Sint Maarten
31 O5 **Saint Martin Island** *island* Michigan, N USA
22 I9 **Saint Martinville** Louisiana, S USA
185 E20 **St.Mary, Mount** ▲ South Island, NZ
186 E8 **St.Mary, Mount** ▲ S PNG
182 I6 **Saint Mary Peak** ▲ South Australia
183 Q16 **Saint Marys** Tasmania, SE Australia
14 E16 **St.Marys** Ontario, S Canada
38 M11 **Saint Marys** Alaska, USA
23 W8 **Saint Marys** Georgia, SE USA
27 P4 **Saint Marys** Kansas, C USA
31 Q4 **Saint Marys** Ohio, N USA
21 R3 **Saint Marys** West Virginia, NE USA
23 W8 **Saint Marys River** ≈ Florida/Georgia, SE USA
31 Q4 **Saint Marys River** ≈ Michigan, N USA
102 D6 **St-Mathieu, Pointe** *headland* NW France
38 J12 **Saint Matthew Island** *island* Alaska, USA
21 R13 **Saint Matthews** South Carolina, SE USA
St.Matthew's Island *see* Zadetkyi Kyun
186 G4 **St.Matthias Group** *island group* NE PNG
108 C11 **St.Maurice** Valais, SW Switzerland
15 P9 **St-Maurice** ≈ Québec, SE Canada
102 J13 **St-Médard-en-Jalles** Gironde, SW France
39 N10 **Saint Michael** Alaska, USA
St.Michel *see* Mikkeli
15 N10 **St-Michel-des-Saints** Québec, SE Canada
103 S5 **St-Mihiel** Meuse, NE France
108 J10 **St.Moritz** *Ger.* Sankt Moritz, *Rmsch.* San Murezzan. Graubünden, SE Switzerland
102 H8 **St-Nazaire** Loire-Atlantique, NW France
Saint Nicholas *see* São Nicolau
Saint-Nicolas *see* Sint-Niklaas
103 N1 **St-Omer** Pas-de-Calais, N France
102 J11 **Saintonge** *cultural region* W France
15 S9 **St-Pacôme** Québec, SE Canada
15 S10 **St-Pamphile** Québec, SE Canada
15 S9 **St-Pascal** Québec, SE Canada
14 J11 **St-Patrice, Lac** ◎ Québec, SE Canada
11 R14 **St.Paul** Alberta, SW Canada
173 O16 **St-Paul** NW Réunion
38 K14 **Saint Paul** Saint Paul Island, Alaska, USA
29 V8 **Saint Paul** *state capital* Minnesota, N USA
29 P15 **Saint Paul** Nebraska, C USA
21 P7 **Saint Paul** Virginia, NE USA
77 Q17 **Saint Paul, Cape** *headland* S Ghana
103 O17 **St-Paul-de-Fenouillet** Pyrénées-Orientales, S France
65 K14 **Saint Paul Fracture Zone** *tectonic feature* E Atlantic Ocean
38 J14 **Saint Paul Island** *island* Pribilof Islands, Alaska, USA
102 J15 **St-Paul-les-Dax** Landes, SW France
21 U11 **Saint Pauls** North Carolina, SE USA
Saint Paul's Bay *see* San Pawl il-Bahar
191 R16 **St Paul's Point** *headland* Pitcairn Island, Pitcairn Islands
29 U10 **Saint Peter** Minnesota, N USA
97 L26 **St Peter Port** ○ (Guernsey) C Guernsey, Channel Islands
23 V13 **Saint Petersburg** Florida, SE USA
Saint Petersburg *see* Sankt-Peterburg
23 V13 **Saint Petersburg Beach** Florida, SE USA
173 P17 **St-Philippe** SE Réunion
45 Q11 **St-Pierre** NW Martinique
173 O17 **St-Pierre** SW Réunion
13 S13 **St-Pierre and Miquelon** *Fr.* Îles St-Pierre et Miquelon. ◇ *French territorial collectivity* NE North America
15 P11 **St-Pierre, Lac** ◎ Québec, SE Canada
102 F5 **St-Pol-de-Léon** Finistère, NW France
103 O2 **St-Pol-sur-Ternoise** Pas-de-Calais, N France
St. Pons *see* St-Pons-de-Thomières
103 O16 **St-Pons-de-Thomières** *var.* St.Pons. Hérault, S France
103 P10 **St-Pourçain-sur-Sioule** Allier, C France
15 S11 **St-Prosper** Québec, SE Canada
103 P3 **St-Quentin** Aisne, N France
15 R10 **St-Raphaël** Québec, SE Canada
103 U15 **St-Raphaël** Var, SE France
15 Q10 **St-Raymond** Québec, SE Canada
33 O9 **Saint Regis** Montana, NW USA
18 J7 **Saint Regis River** ≈ New York, NE USA
103 R15 **St-Rémy-de-Provence** Bouches-du-Rhône, SE France
15 V6 **St-René-de-Matane** Québec, SE Canada
102 M9 **St-Savin** Vienne, W France
15 S8 **St-Siméon** Québec, SE Canada
23 X7 **Saint Simons Island** *island* Georgia, SE USA
191 Y2 **Saint Stanislas Bay** *bay* Kiritimati, E Kiribati
13 O15 **St.Stephen** New Brunswick, SE Canada
39 X12 **Saint Terese** Alaska, USA
14 E17 **St.Thomas** Ontario, S Canada
29 Q2 **Saint Thomas** North Dakota, N USA
45 T9 **Saint Thomas** *island* W Virgin Islands (US)
Saint Thomas *see* São Tomé, Sao Tome and Principe
Saint Thomas *see* Charlotte Amalie, Virgin Islands (US)
15 P10 **St-Tite** Québec, SE Canada
Saint-Trond *see* Sint-Truiden
103 U16 **St-Tropez** Var, SE France
Saint Ubes *see* Setúbal
102 L3 **St-Valéry-en-Caux** Seine-Maritime, N France
103 Q9 **St-Vallier** Saône-et-Loire, C France
106 B7 **St-Vincent** Valle d'Aosta, NW Italy
45 Q14 **Saint Vincent** *island* N Saint Vincent and the Grenadines
Saint Vincent *see* São Vicente
45 W14 **Saint Vincent and the Grenadines** ◆ *commonwealth republic* SE West Indies
Saint Vincent, Cape *see* São Vicente, Cabo de
102 I15 **St-Vincent-de-Tyrosse** Landes, SW France
182 I9 **Saint Vincent, Gulf** *gulf* South Australia
23 R10 **Saint Vincent Island** *island* Florida, SE USA
45 T12 **Saint Vincent Passage** *passage* Saint Lucia/Saint Vincent and the Grenadines
183 N18 **Saint Vincent, Point** *headland* Tasmania, SE Australia
Saint-Vith *see* Sankt-Vith
11 S14 **St.Walburg** Saskatchewan, S Canada
St Wolfgangsee *see* Wolfgangsee
102 M11 **St-Yrieix-la-Perche** Haute-Vienne, C France
Saint Yves *see* Setúbal
15 Y5 **St-Yvon** Québec, SE Canada
188 H5 **Saipan** *island* ● (Northern Mariana Islands) S Northern Mariana Islands
188 H6 **Saipan Channel** *channel* S Northern Mariana Islands
188 H6 **Saipan International Airport** ✕ Saipan, S Northern Mariana Islands
74 G6 **Sais** ✕ (Fès) C Morocco
Saishū *see* Cheju
Saishū *see* Cheju-do
102 J16 **Saison** ≈ SW France
169 R10 **Sai, Sungai** ≈ Borneo, N Indonesia
165 N13 **Saitama** *off.* Saitama-ken. ◈ *prefecture* Honshū, S Japan
Saiyid Abid *see* Sayyid 'Abīd
57 J19 **Sajama, Nevado** ▲ W Bolivia
141 V13 **Sājir, Ras** *headland* S Oman
111 M20 **Sajószentpéter** Borsod-Abaúj-Zemplén, NE Hungary
83 F24 **Sak** ≈ SW South Africa
81 J18 **Saka** Coast, E Kenya
167 P11 **Sa Kaeo** Prachin Buri, C Thailand
164 J14 **Sakai** Ōsaka, Honshū, SW Japan
164 H14 **Sakaide** Kagawa, Shikoku, SW Japan
164 H12 **Sakaiminato** Tottori, Honshū, SW Japan
140 M3 **Sakākah** Al Jawf, NW Saudi Arabia
28 L4 **Sakakawea, Lake** ⊠ North Dakota, N USA
12 J9 **Sakami, Lac** ◎ Québec, C Canada
79 O26 **Sakania** Katanga, SE Dem. Rep. Congo
146 K12 **Sakar** Lebap Welaýaty, E Turkmenistan
172 H7 **Sakaraha** Toliara, SW Madagascar
146 I14 **Sakarçäge** *var.* Sakarchäge, *Rus.* Sakar-Chaga. Mary Welaýaty, C Turkmenistan
Sakar-Chaga/Sakarchäge *see* Sakarçäge
Sak'art'velo *see* Georgia
136 F11 **Sakarya** ◈ *province* NW Turkey
136 F12 **Sakarya Nehri** ≈ NW Turkey
150 K13 **Sakasaul'skiy** *var.* Saksaul'skoye *Kaz.* Sekseüil. Kyzylorda, S Kazakhstan
Saksaul'skoye *see* Sakasaul'skiy
165 P9 **Sakata** Yamagata, Honshū, C Japan
123 P9 **Sakha (Yakutiya), Respublika** *var.* Respublika Yakutiya, *Eng.* Yakutia. ◈ *autonomous republic* NE Russian Federation
Sakhalin *see* Sakhalin, Ostrov
192 I3 **Sakhalin, Ostrov** *var.* Sakhalin. *island* SE Russian Federation
123 U12 **Sakhalinskaya Oblast'** ◈ *province* SE Russian Federation
123 T12 **Sakhalinskiy Zaliv** *gulf* E Russian Federation
Sakhnovshchina *see* Sakhnovshchyna
117 U6 **Sakhnovshchyna** *Rus.* Sakhnovshchina. Kharkivs'ka Oblast', E Ukraine
Sakhon Nakhon *see* Sakon Nakhon
Sakhtsar *see* Rāmsar
Saki *see* Saky
137 W10 **Şäki** *Rus.* Sheki; *prev.* Nukha. NW Azerbaijan
118 E13 **Šakiai** *Ger.* Schaken. Marijampolė, S Lithuania
165 O16 **Sakishima-shotō** *var.* Sakisima Syotô. *island group* SW Japan
Sakiz *see* Saqqez
Sakiz-Adasi *see* Chíos
155 F19 **Sakleshpur** Karnātaka, E India
167 S9 **Sakon Nakhon** *var.* Muang Sakon Nakhon. Sakon Nakhon, E Thailand
149 P15 **Sakrand** Sind, SE Pakistan
83 F24 **Sak River** *Afr.* Sakrivier. Northern Cape, W South Africa
Sakrivier *see* Sak River
Saksaul'skiy *see* Saksaul'skoye
144 K13 **Saksaul'skoye** *prev.* Saksaul'skiy, *Kaz.* Sekseüil. Kzylorda, S Kazakhstan
95 I25 **Sakskøbing** Storstrøm, SE Denmark
165 N12 **Saku** Nagano, Honshū, S Japan
117 S13 **Saky** *Rus.* Saki. Respublika Krym, S Ukraine
76 E9 **Sal** *island* Ilhas de Barlavento, NE Cape Verde
127 N12 **Sal** ≈ SW Russian Federation
111 I21 **Sal'a** *Hung.* Sellye, Vágsellye. Nitriansky Kraj, SW Slovakia
95 N15 **Sala** Västmanland, C Sweden
15 N13 **Salaberry-de-Valleyfield** *var.* Valleyfield. Québec, SE Canada
118 G7 **Salacgrīva** *Est.* Salatsi. Limbaži, N Latvia
107 M18 **Sala Consilina** Campania, S Italy
40 C2 **Salada, Laguna** ◎ NW Mexico
61 D14 **Saladas** Corrientes, NE Argentina
61 C21 **Saladillo** Buenos Aires, E Argentina
61 B16 **Saladillo, Río** ≈ C Argentina
25 T9 **Salado** Texas, SW USA
63 J16 **Salado, Arroyo** ≈ SE Argentina
37 Q12 **Salado, Rio** ≈ New Mexico, SW USA
61 D21 **Salado, Río** ≈ E Argentina
62 J12 **Salado, Río** ≈ C Argentina
41 N7 **Salado, Río** ≈ NE Mexico
143 N6 **Salafchegān** *var.* Sarafjagān. Qom, N Iran
77 Q15 **Salaga** C Ghana
192 G5 **Sala'ilua** Savai'i, W Samoa
116 G9 **Sălaj** ◈ *county* NW Romania
83 H20 **Salajwe** Kweneng, SE Botswana
78 H9 **Salal** Kanem, W Chad
80 I6 **Salala** Red Sea, NE Sudan
141 V13 **Şalālah** SW Oman
42 D5 **Salamá** Baja Verapaz, C Guatemala
42 J6 **Salamá** Olancho, C Honduras
62 G10 **Salamanca** Coquimbo, C Chile
41 N13 **Salamanca** Guanajuato, C Mexico
104 K7 **Salamanca** *anc.* Helmantica, Salmantica. Castilla-León, NW Spain
18 D11 **Salamanca** New York, NE USA
104 J7 **Salamanca** ◈ *province* Castilla-León, W Spain
63 J19 **Salamanca, Pampa de** *plain* S Argentina
78 J12 **Salamat** *off.* Préfecture du Salamat. ◈ *prefecture* SE Chad
78 I12 **Salamat, Bahr** ≈ S Chad
54 F5 **Salamina** Magdalena, N Colombia
115 G19 **Salamína** *var.* Salamís. Salamína, C Greece
115 G19 **Salamína** *island* C Greece
Salamís *see* Salamína
138 I5 **Salamīyah** *var.* As Salamīyah. Ḩamāh, W Syria
31 P12 **Salamonie Lake** ⊠ Indiana, N USA
31 P12 **Salamonie River** ≈ Indiana, N USA
Salang *see* Phuket
192 I16 **Salani** Upolu, SE Samoa
118 C11 **Salantai** Klaipėda, NW Lithuania
104 K2 **Salas** Asturias, N Spain
105 O5 **Salas de los Infantes** Castilla-León, N Spain
102 M16 **Salat** ≈ S France
189 V13 **Salat** *island* Chuuk, C Micronesia
169 Q16 **Salatiga** Jawa, C Indonesia
189 V13 **Salat Pass** *passage* W Pacific Ocean
Salatsi *see* Salacgrīva
167 T10 **Salavan** *var.* Saravan, Saravane. Salavan, S Laos
127 V6 **Salavat** Respublika Bashkortostan, W Russian Federation
56 C12 **Salaverry** La Libertad, N Peru
171 T12 **Salawati, Pulau** *island* E Indonesia
193 R10 **Sala y Gomez** *island* Chile, E Pacific Ocean
Sala y Gomez Fracture Zone *see* Sala y Gomez Ridge
193 S10 **Sala y Gomez Ridge** *var.* Sala y Gomez Fracture Zone. *tectonic feature* SE Pacific Ocean
61 A22 **Salazar** Buenos Aires, E Argentina
54 G7 **Salazar** Norte de Santander, N Colombia
Salazar *see* N'Dalatando
173 P16 **Salazie** C Réunion
103 N8 **Salbris** Loir-et-Cher, C France
57 G15 **Salcantay, Nevado** ▲ C Peru
45 O8 **Salcedo** N Dominican Republic
39 S9 **Salcha River** ≈ Alaska, USA
119 H15 **Šalčininkai** Vilnius, SE Lithuania
Saldae *see* Béjaïa
54 E11 **Saldaña** Tolima, C Colombia
104 M4 **Saldaña** Castilla-León, N Spain
83 E25 **Saldanha** Western Cape, SW South Africa
Salduba *see* Zaragoza
61 B23 **Saldungaray** Buenos Aires, E Argentina
118 D9 **Saldus** *Ger.* Frauenburg. Saldus, W Latvia
183 P13 **Sale** Victoria, SE Australia
74 F6 **Salé** NW Morocco
74 F6 **Salé** ✕ (Rabat) W Morocco
Salehābād *see* Andīmeshk
170 M16 **Saleh, Teluk** *bay* Nusa Tenggara, S Indonesia
122 H8 **Salekhard** *prev.* Obdorsk. Yamalo-Nenetskiy Avtonomnyy Okrug, N Russian Federation
192 H16 **Sālelologa** Savai'i, C Samoa
155 H21 **Salem** Tamil Nādu, SE India
27 V9 **Salem** Arkansas, C USA
30 L15 **Salem** Illinois, N USA
31 P15 **Salem** Indiana, N USA
19 P11 **Salem** Massachusetts, NE USA
27 V6 **Salem** Missouri, C USA
18 I16 **Salem** New Jersey, NE USA
31 U12 **Salem** Ohio, N USA
32 G12 **Salem** *state capital* Oregon, NW USA
29 Q11 **Salem** South Dakota, N USA
36 L4 **Salem** Utah, W USA
21 S7 **Salem** Virginia, NE USA
21 R3 **Salem** West Virginia, NE USA
107 H23 **Salemi** Sicilia, Italy, C Mediterranean Sea
Salemy *see* As Sālimī
94 K12 **Sälen** Dalarna, C Sweden
107 Q18 **Salentina, Campi** Puglia, SE Italy
107 Q18 **Salentina, Penisola** *peninsula* SE Italy
107 L18 **Salerno** *anc.* Salernum. Campania, S Italy
107 L18 **Salerno, Golfo di** *Eng.* Gulf of Salerno. *gulf* S Italy
Salerno, Gulf of *see* Salerno, Golfo di
Salernum *see* Salerno
97 K17 **Salford** NW England, UK
Salgir *see* Salhyr
111 K21 **Salgótarján** Nógrád, N Hungary
59 O15 **Salgueiro** Pernambuco, E Brazil
94 C13 **Salhus** Hordaland, S Norway
117 T12 **Salhyr** *Rus.* Salgir. ≈ S Ukraine
171 Q9 **Salibabu, Pulau** *island* N Indonesia
37 S6 **Salida** Colorado, C USA
102 J15 **Salies-de-Béarn** Pyrénées-Atlantiques, SW France
136 C14 **Salihli** Manisa, W Turkey
119 K18 **Salihorsk** *Rus.* Soligorsk. Minskaya Voblasts', S Belarus
119 K18 **Salihorskaye Vodaskhovishcha** ⊠ C Belarus
83 N14 **Salima** Central, C Malawi
166 L5 **Salin** Magwe, W Burma
27 N4 **Salina** Kansas, C USA
36 L5 **Salina** Utah, W USA
41 S17 **Salina Cruz** Oaxaca, SE Mexico
107 L22 **Salina, Isola** *island* Isole Eolie, S Italy
44 J5 **Salina Point** *headland* Acklins Island, SE Bahamas
56 A7 **Salinas** Guayas, W Ecuador
40 M11 **Salinas** *var.* Salinas de Hidalgo. San Luis Potosí, C Mexico
45 T6 **Salinas** C Puerto Rico
35 O10 **Salinas** California, W USA
Salinas, Cabo de *see* Salines, Cap de ses
Salinas de Hidalgo *see* Salinas
82 A13 **Salinas, Ponta das** *headland* W Angola
45 O10 **Salinas, Punta** *headland* S Dominican Republic
Salinas, Río *see* Chixoy, Río
35 O11 **Salinas River** ≈ California, W USA
22 H6 **Saline Lake** ◎ Louisiana, S USA
25 R17 **Salineno** Texas, SW USA
27 V14 **Saline River** ≈ Arkansas, C USA
30 M17 **Saline River** ≈ Illinois, N USA
105 X10 **Salines, Cap de ses** *var.* Cabo de Salinas. *headland* Mallorca, Spain, W Mediterranean Sea
Salisburg *see* Mazsalaca
45 O12 **Salisbury** *var.* Baroui. W Dominica
97 M23 **Salisbury** *var.* New Sarum. S England, UK
21 Y4 **Salisbury** Maryland, NE USA
27 T3 **Salisbury** Missouri, C USA
21 S9 **Salisbury** North Carolina, SE USA
Salisbury *see* Harare
9 Q7 **Salisbury Island** *island* Nunavut, NE Canada
Salisbury, Lake *see* Bisina, Lake
97 L23 **Salisbury Plain** *plain* S England, UK
21 R14 **Salkehatchie River** ≈ South Carolina, SE USA
138 I9 **Şalkhad** As Suwaydā', SW Syria
92 M12 **Salla** Lappi, NE Finland
Sállan *see* Sørøya
103 U11 **Sallanches** Haute-Savoie, E France
105 V5 **Sallent** Cataluña, NE Spain
61 A22 **Salliqueló** Buenos Aires, E Argentina
27 R10 **Sallisaw** Oklahoma, C USA
80 I7 **Sallom** Red Sea, NE Sudan
12 J2 **Salluit** *prev.* Saglouc, Sagluk. Québec, NE Canada
Sallūm, Khalīj as *see* Salûm, Gulf of
13 S11 **Sally's Cove** Newfoundland and Labrador, E Canada
139 W9 **Salmān Bin 'Arāzah** E Iraq
Salmantica *see* Salamanca
142 I2 **Salmās** *prev.* Dilman, Shāpūr. Āžarbāyjān-e Bākhtarī, NW Iran
124 I11 **Salmi** Respublika Kareliya, NW Russian Federation
33 P12 **Salmon** Idaho, NW USA
11 N16 **Salmon Arm** British Columbia, SW Canada
192 L5 **Salmon Bank** *undersea feature* N Pacific Ocean
Salmon Leap *see* Leixlip
34 L2 **Salmon Mountains** ▲ California, W USA
14 J15 **Salmon Point** *headland* Ontario, SE Canada
33 N11 **Salmon River** ≈ Idaho, NW USA
18 K6 **Salmon River** ≈ New York, NE USA
33 N12 **Salmon River Mountains** ▲ Idaho, NW USA
18 I9 **Salmon River Reservoir** ⊠ New York, NE USA
93 K19 **Salo** Länsi-Suomi, W Finland
106 F7 **Salò** Lombardia, N Italy
Salona/Salonae *see* Solin
103 S15 **Salon-de-Provence** Bouches-du-Rhône, SE France
Salonica/Salonika *see* Thessaloníki
115 I14 **Salonikós, Akrotírio** *headland* Thásos, E Greece
116 F10 **Salonta** *Hung.* Nagyszalonta. Bihor, W Romania
104 I9 **Salor** ≈ W Spain
105 U6 **Salou** Cataluña, NE Spain
76 H11 **Saloum** ≈ C Senegal
42 H4 **Sal, Punta** *headland* NW Honduras
92 N3 **Salpynten** *headland* W Svalbard
138 I3 **Salqīn** Idlib, W Syria
93 F14 **Salsbruket** Nord-Trøndelag, C Norway
126 M13 **Sal'sk** Rostovskaya Oblast', SW Russian Federation
107 K25 **Salso** ≈ Sicilia, Italy, C Mediterranean Sea
107 J25 **Salso** ≈ Sicilia, Italy, C Mediterranean Sea
106 E9 **Salsomaggiore Terme** Emilia-Romagna, N Italy
Salt *see* As Salṭ
62 J6 **Salta** Salta, NW Argentina
62 K6 **Salta** *off.* Provincia de Salta. ◈ *province* N Argentina
97 I24 **Saltash** SW England, UK
24 I8 **Salt Basin** *basin* Texas, SW USA
11 V16 **Saltcoats** Saskatchewan, S Canada
30 L13 **Salt Creek** ≈ Illinois, N USA
24 J9 **Salt Draw** ≈ Texas, SW USA
97 F21 **Saltee Islands** *island group* SE Ireland
92 G12 **Saltfjorden** *inlet* C Norway
24 I8 **Salt Flat** Texas, SW USA
27 N8 **Salt Fork Arkansas River** ≈ Oklahoma, C USA
31 T13 **Salt Fork Lake** ⊠ Ohio, N USA
26 J11 **Salt Fork Red River** ≈ Oklahoma/Texas, C USA
95 J23 **Saltholm** *island* E Denmark
41 N8 **Saltillo** Coahuila de Zaragoza, NE Mexico
182 L5 **Salt Lake** *salt lake* New South Wales, SE Australia
37 V15 **Salt Lake** ◎ New Mexico, SW USA
36 K2 **Salt Lake City** *state capital* Utah, W USA
61 C20 **Salto** Buenos Aires, E Argentina
61 D17 **Salto** Salto, N Uruguay
61 E17 **Salto** ◈ *department* N Uruguay
107 I14 **Salto** ≈ C Italy
62 Q6 **Salto del Guairá** Canindeyú, E Paraguay
61 D17 **Salto Grande, Embalse de** *var.* Lago de Salto Grande. ⊠ Argentina/Uruguay
Salto Grande, Lago de *see* Salto Grande, Embalse de
35 W16 **Salton Sea** ◎ California, W USA
60 I12 **Salto Santiago, Represa de** ⊠ S Brazil
149 U7 **Salt Range** ▲ E Pakistan
36 M13 **Salt River** ≈ Arizona, SW USA
20 L5 **Salt River** ≈ Kentucky, S USA
27 V3 **Salt River** ≈ Missouri, C USA
95 F17 **Saltrød** Aust-Agder, S Norway
95 P16 **Saltsjöbaden** Stockholm, C Sweden
92 G12 **Saltstraumen** Nordland, C Norway
21 Q7 **Saltville** Virginia, NE USA
Saluces/Saluciae *see* Saluzzo
21 Q12 **Saluda** South Carolina, SE USA
21 X6 **Saluda** Virginia, NE USA
21 Q12 **Saluda River** ≈ South Carolina, SE USA
75 T7 **Salûm** *var.* As Sallūm. NW Egypt
152 F14 **Sālūmbar** Rājasthān, N India
75 T7 **Salûm, Gulf of** *Ar.* Khalīj as Sallūm. *gulf* Egypt/Libya
171 O11 **Salumpaga** Sulawesi, N Indonesia

◆ Country ● Country Capital ◇ Dependent Territory ○ Dependent Territory Capital ◈ Administrative Region ✕ International Airport ▲ Mountain ▲ Mountain Range ☒ Volcano ≈ River ◎ Lake ⊠ Reservoir

155 M14 Sālūr Andhra Pradesh, E India
55 Y9 Salut, Îles du island group N French Guiana
106 A9 Saluzzo Fr. Saluces; anc. Saluciae. Piemonte, NW Italy
63 F23 Salvación, Bahía bay S Chile
59 P17 Salvador prev. São Salvador. Bahia, E Brazil
65 E24 Salvador East Falkland, Falkland Islands
22 K10 Salvador, Lake ◎ Louisiana, S USA
Salvaleón de Higüey see Higüey
104 F10 Salvaterra de Magos Santarém, C Portugal
41 N13 Salvatierra Guanajuato, C Mexico
105 P3 Salvatierra Basq. Agurain. País Vasco, N Spain
Salwa/Salwah see As Salwā
166 M7 Salween Bur. Thanlwin, Chin. Nu Chiang, Nu Jiang. ⩪ SE Asia
137 Y12 Salyan Rus. Sal'yany. SE Azerbaijan
153 N11 Salyan var. Sallyana. Mid Western, W Nepal
Sal'yany see Salyan
21 O6 Salyersville Kentucky, S USA
109 V6 Salza ⩪ E Austria
109 Q7 Salzach ⩪ Austria/Germany
109 Q6 Salzburg anc. Juvavum. Salzburg, N Austria
109 O8 Salzburg off. Land Salzburg. ◆ state C Austria
Salzburg see Ocna Sibiului
Salzburg Alps see Salzburger Kalkalpen
109 Q7 Salzburger Kalkalpen Eng. Salzburg Alps. ▲ C Austria
100 J13 Salzgitter prev. Watenstedt-Salzgitter. Niedersachsen, C Germany
101 G14 Salzkotten Nordrhein-Westfalen, W Germany
100 K11 Salzwedel Sachsen-Anhalt, N Germany
152 D11 Sām Rājasthān, NW India
Šamac see Bosanski Šamac
54 G9 Samacá Boyacá, C Colombia
40 I7 Samachique Chihuahua, N Mexico
141 Y8 Şamad NE Oman
Sama de Langreo see Sama
Samaden see Samedan
57 M19 Samaipata Santa Cruz, C Bolivia
167 T10 Samakhixai var. Attapu, Attopeu. Attapu, S Laos
Samakov see Samokov
42 B6 Samalá, Río ⩪ SW Guatemala
40 J3 Samalayuca Chihuahua, N Mexico
155 L16 Sāmalkot Andhra Pradesh, E India
45 P8 Samaná var. Santa Bárbara de Samaná. E Dominican Republic
45 P8 Samaná, Bahía de bay E Dominican Republic
44 K4 Samana Cay island SE Bahamas
136 K17 Samandağı Hatay, S Turkey
149 P3 Samangān ◆ province N Afghanistan
Samangān see Āybak
165 T5 Samani Hokkaidō, NE Japan
54 C13 Samaniego Nariño, SW Colombia
171 Q5 Samar island C Philippines
127 S6 Samara prev. Kuybyshev. Samarskaya Oblast', W Russian Federation
127 S6 Samara ✕ Samarskaya Oblast', W Russian Federation
127 T7 Samara ⩪ W Russian Federation
117 V7 Samara ⩪ E Ukraine
186 G10 Samarai Milne Bay, SE PNG
Samarang see Semarang
138 G9 Samarian Hills hill range N Israel
54 L9 Samariapo Amazonas, C Venezuela
169 V11 Samarinda Borneo, C Indonesia
Samarkand see Samarqand
Samarkandskaya Oblast' see Samarqand Viloyati
Samarkandski/Samarkandskoye see Temirtau
Samarobriva see Amiens
147 N11 Samarqand Rus. Samarkand. Samarqand Viloyati, C Uzbekistan
146 M11 Samarqand Viloyati Rus. Samarkandskaya Oblast'. ◆ province C Uzbekistan
139 S6 Sāmarrā' C Iraq
127 R7 Samarskaya Oblast' prev. Kuybyshevskaya Oblast'. ◆ province W Russian Federation
153 Q13 Samastīpur Bihār, N India
76 L14 Samatiguila NW Ivory Coast
119 Q17 Samatsevichy Rus. Samotevichi. Mahilyowskaya Voblasts', E Belarus
Samawa see As Samāwah
137 Y11 Şamaxı Rus. Shemakha. E Azerbaijan
152 H6 Samba Jammu and Kashmir, NW India
79 K18 Samba Equateur, NW Dem. Rep. Congo
79 N21 Samba Maniema, E Dem. Rep. Congo
169 W10 Sambaliung, Pegunungan ▲ Borneo, N Indonesia
154 M11 Sambalpur Orissa, E India
169 Q10 Sambas, Sungai ⩪ Borneo, N Indonesia
172 K2 Sambava Antsirañana, NE Madagascar
152 J10 Sambhal Uttar Pradesh, N India
152 H12 Sāmbhar Salt Lake ◎ N India
107 N21 Sambiase Calabria, SW Italy
116 H5 Sambir Rus. Sambor. L'vivs'ka Oblast', NW Ukraine
82 C13 Sambo Huambo, C Angola
Sambor see Sambir
61 E21 Samborombón, Bahía bay NE Argentina
99 H20 Sambre ⩪ Belgium/France
43 V16 Sambú, Río ⩪ SE Panama
163 Z14 Samch'ŏk Jap. Sanchoku. NE South Korea
Samch'ŏnpŏ see Sach'ŏn
81 I21 Same Kilimanjaro, NE Tanzania
108 J10 Samedan Ger. Samaden. Graubünden, S Switzerland
82 K12 Samfya Luapula, N Zambia
141 W13 Samḩān, Jabal ▲ SW Oman
115 C18 Sámi Kefallinía, Iónioi Nísoi, Greece, C Mediterranean Sea
56 F10 Samiria, Río ⩪ N Peru
Samirum see Semīrom
137 V11 Şämkir Rus. Shamkhor. NW Azerbaijan
167 S7 Sam, Nam Vtn. Sông Chu. ⩪ Laos/Vietnam
Samnān see Semnān
Sam Neua see Xam Nua
75 P10 Samnū C Libya
192 H15 Samoa off. Independent State of Samoa, var. Sāmoa; prev. Western Samoa ◆ monarchy W Polynesia
192 L9 Sāmoa island group American /Samoa
192 M9 Samoa Basin undersea feature W Pacific Ocean
Sāmoa-i-Sisifo see Samoa
112 D8 Samobor Zagreb, N Croatia
114 H10 Samokov var. Samakov. Sofiya, W Bulgaria
111 H21 Šamorín Ger. Sommerein, Hung. Somorja. Trnavský Kraj, W Slovakia
115 M19 Sámos prev. Limín Vathéos. Sámos, Dodekánisos, Greece, Aegean Sea
115 M20 Sámos island Dodekánisos, Greece, Aegean Sea
Samosch see Szamos
168 I9 Samosir, Pulau island W Indonesia
Samotevichi see Samatsevichy
Samothrace see Samothráki
115 K14 Samothráki Samothráki, NE Greece
115 J14 Samothráki anc. Samothrace. island NE Greece
115 A15 Samothráki island Iónioi Nísoi, Greece, C Mediterranean Sea
Samotschin see Szamocin
Sampê see Xiangcheng
169 S13 Sampit Borneo, C Indonesia
169 S12 Sampit, Sungai ⩪ Borneo, N Indonesia
Sampoku see Sanpoku
186 H7 Sampun New Britain, E PNG
79 N24 Sampwe Katanga, SE Dem. Rep. Congo
25 X8 Sam Rayburn Reservoir ⊟ Texas, SW USA
167 Q6 Sam Sao, Phou ▲ Laos/Thailand
95 H22 Samsø island E Denmark
95 H23 Samsø Bælt channel E Denmark
167 T7 Sâm Sơn Thanh Hoa, N Vietnam
136 L11 Samsun anc. Amisus. Samsun, N Turkey
136 K11 Samsun ◆ province N Turkey
137 R9 Samtredia W Georgia
59 E15 Samuel, Represa de ⊟ W Brazil
167 O14 Samui, Ko island SW Thailand
Samundari see Samundri
149 U9 Samundri var. Samundari. Punjab, E Pakistan
137 X10 Samur ⩪ Azerbaijan/Russian Federation
137 Y11 Samur-Abşeron Kanalı Rus. Samur-Apsheronskiy Kanal. canal E Azerbaijan
Samur-Apsheronskiy Kanal see Samur-Abşeron Kanalı
167 O11 Samut Prakan var. Muang Samut Prakan, Paknam. Samut Prakan, C Thailand
167 O11 Samut Sakhon var. Maha Chai, Samut Sakorn, Tha Chin. Samut Sakhon, C Thailand
Samut Sakorn see Samut Sakhon
167 O11 Samut Songhram prev. Meklong. Samut Songkhram, SW Thailand
77 N12 San Ségou, C Mali
111 O15 San ⩪ SE Poland
141 O15 Şan'ā' Eng. Sana. ● (Yemen) W Yemen
112 F11 Sana ⩪ NW Bosnia and Herzegovina
80 O12 Sanaag off. Gobolka Sanaag. ◆ region N Somalia
114 J8 Sanadinovo Pleven, N Bulgaria
195 P1 Sanae South African research station Antarctica
139 Y10 Sanāf, Hawr as ◎ S Iraq
79 E15 Sanaga ⩪ C Cameroon
54 D12 San Agustín Huila, SW Colombia
171 R8 San Agustin, Cape headland Mindanao, S Philippines
37 Q13 San Agustin, Plains of plain New Mexico, SW USA
38 M16 Sanak Islands island group Aleutian Islands, Alaska, USA
193 U10 San Ambrosio, Isla Eng. San Ambrosio Island. island W Chile
San Ambrosio Island see San Ambrosio, Isla
171 Q12 Sanana Pulau Sanana, E Indonesia
171 Q12 Sanana, Pulau island Maluku, E Indonesia
142 K5 Sanandaj prev. Sinneh. Kordestān, W Iran
35 P8 San Andreas California, W USA
54 G8 San Andrés Santander, C Colombia
61 C20 San Andrés de Giles Buenos Aires, E Argentina
37 R14 San Andres Mountains ▲ New Mexico, SW USA
41 S15 San Andrés Tuxtla var. Tuxtla. Veracruz-Llave, E Mexico
25 P8 San Angelo Texas, SW USA
107 A20 San Antioco, Isola di island W Italy
42 F4 San Antonio Toledo, S Belize
62 G11 San Antonio Valparaíso, C Chile
188 H6 San Antonio Saipan, S Northern Mariana Islands
37 R13 San Antonio New Mexico, SW USA
25 R12 San Antonio Texas, SW USA
54 M11 San Antonio Amazonas, S Venezuela
54 I7 San Antonio Barinas, C Venezuela
55 O5 San Antonio Monagas, NE Venezuela
25 S12 San Antonio ✕ Texas, SW USA
San Antonio see San Antonio del Táchira
San Antonio Abad see Sant Antoni de Portmany
25 U13 San Antonio Bay inlet Texas, SW USA
61 E22 San Antonio, Cabo headland E Argentina
44 A5 San Antonio, Cabo de headland W Cuba
105 T11 San Antonio, Cabo de headland E Spain
54 H7 San Antonio de Caparo Táchira, W Venezuela
62 J5 San Antonio de los Cobres Salta, NE Argentina
54 H7 San Antonio del Táchira var. San Antonio. Táchira, W Venezuela
35 T15 San Antonio, Mount ▲ California, W USA
63 K16 San Antonio Oeste Río Negro, E Argentina
25 T13 San Antonio River ⩪ Texas, SW USA
54 J5 Sanare Lara, N Venezuela
103 T16 Sanary-sur-Mer Var, SE France
25 X8 San Augustine Texas, SW USA
141 T13 Sanāw var. Sanaw. NE Yemen
41 O11 San Bartolo San Luis Potosí, C Mexico
107 L16 San Bartolomeo in Galdo Campania, S Italy
106 K13 San Benedetto del Tronto Marche, C Italy
42 E3 San Benito Petén, N Guatemala
25 T17 San Benito Texas, SW USA
54 E6 San Benito Abad Sucre, N Colombia
35 P11 San Benito Mountain ▲ California, W USA
35 O10 San Benito River ⩪ California, W USA
108 H10 San Bernardino Graubünden, S Switzerland
35 U15 San Bernardino California, W USA
62 H11 San Bernardo Santiago, C Chile
40 J8 San Bernardo Durango, C Mexico
164 G12 Sanbe-san ▲ Kyūshū, SW Japan
40 J12 San Blas Nayarit, C Mexico
40 H8 San Blas Sinaloa, C Mexico
43 V14 San Blas off. Comarca de San Blas. ◆ special territory NE Panama
43 U14 San Blas, Archipiélago de island group NE Panama
23 Q10 San Blas, Cape headland Florida, SE USA
43 V14 San Blas, Cordillera de ▲ NE Panama
62 J8 San Blas de los Sauces Catamarca, NW Argentina
106 G8 San Bonifacio Veneto, NE Italy
29 S12 Sanborn Iowa, C USA
40 M7 San Buenaventura Coahuila de Zaragoza, NE Mexico
105 S5 San Caprasio ▲ N Spain
62 G13 San Carlos Bío Bío, C Chile
40 E9 San Carlos Baja California Sur, W Mexico
41 N5 San Carlos Coahuila de Zaragoza, NE Mexico
San Carlos, Estrecho de see Falkland Sound
41 P9 San Carlos Tamaulipas, C Mexico
42 L12 San Carlos Río San Juan, S Nicaragua
43 T16 San Carlos Panamá, C Panama
171 N3 San Carlos off. San Carlos City. Luzon, N Philippines
36 M14 San Carlos Arizona, SW USA
61 G20 San Carlos Maldonado, S Uruguay
54 K5 San Carlos Cojedes, N Venezuela
San Carlos see Quesada, Costa Rica
San Carlos see Luba, Equatorial Guinea
61 B17 San Carlos Centro Santa Fe, C Argentina
171 P6 San Carlos City Negros, C Philippines
San Carlos de Ancud see Ancud
63 H16 San Carlos de Bariloche Río Negro, SW Argentina
61 B21 San Carlos de Bolívar Buenos Aires, E Argentina
54 H6 San Carlos del Zulia Zulia, W Venezuela
54 L12 San Carlos de Río Negro Amazonas, S Venezuela
San Carlos, Estrecho de see Falkland Sound
36 M14 San Carlos Reservoir ⊟ Arizona, SW USA
42 M12 San Carlos, Río ⩪ N Costa Rica
65 D24 San Carlos Settlement East Falkland, Falkland Islands
61 C23 San Cayetano Buenos Aires, E Argentina
103 O8 Sancerre Cher, C France
158 G7 Sanchakou Xinjiang Uygur Zizhiqu, NW China
Sanchoku see Samch'ŏk
41 O12 San Ciro San Luis Potosí, C Mexico
105 P10 San Clemente Castilla-La Mancha, C Spain
35 T16 San Clemente California, W USA
61 E21 San Clemente del Tuyú Buenos Aires, E Argentina
35 S17 San Clemente Island island Channel Islands, California, W USA
103 O9 Sancoins Cher, C France
187 N10 San Cristobal var. Makira. island SE Solomon Islands
61 B16 San Cristóbal Santa Fe, C Argentina
44 B4 San Cristóbal Pinar del Río, W Cuba
45 O9 San Cristóbal var. Benemérita de San Cristóbal. S Dominican Republic
54 H7 San Cristóbal Táchira, W Venezuela
San Cristóbal see San Cristóbal de Las Casas
41 U16 San Cristóbal de Las Casas var. San Cristóbal. Chiapas, SE Mexico
187 N10 San Cristóbal, Isla var. Chatham Island. island Galapagos Islands, Ecuador, E Pacific Ocean
42 D5 San Cristóbal Verapaz Alta Verapaz, C Guatemala
44 F6 Sancti Spíritus Sancti Spíritus, C Cuba
103 O11 Sancy, Puy de ▲ C France
95 D15 Sand Rogaland, S Norway
169 W7 Sandakan Sabah, East Malaysia
182 K9 Sandalwood South Australia
Sandalwood Island see Sumba, Pulau
94 D11 Sandane Sogn og Fjordane, S Norway
114 G12 Sandanski prev. Sveti Vrach. Blagoevgrad, SW Bulgaria
76 J11 Sandaré Kayes, W Mali
95 J19 Sandared Västra Götaland, S Sweden
94 N12 Sandarne Gävleborg, C Sweden
186 B5 Sandaun prev. West Sepik. ◆ province NW PNG
96 K4 Sanday island NE Scotland, UK
31 P15 Sand Creek ⩪ Indiana, N USA
95 H15 Sande Vestfold, S Norway
95 H16 Sandefjord Vestfold, S Norway
77 O15 Sandégué E Ivory Coast
77 P14 Sandema N Ghana
37 O11 Sanders Arizona, SW USA
24 M11 Sanderson Texas, SW USA
23 U4 Sandersville Georgia, SE USA
92 H4 Sandgerdhi Sudhurland, SW Iceland
28 K14 Sand Hills ▲ Nebraska, C USA
25 S14 Sandia Texas, SW USA
35 T17 San Diego California, W USA
25 S14 San Diego Texas, SW USA
136 F14 Sandıklı Afyon, W Turkey
152 L12 Sandila Uttar Pradesh, N India
121 N15 San Dimitri, Ras var. San Dimitri Point. headland Gozo, NW Malta
168 J13 Sanding, Selat strait W Indonesia
30 J3 Sand Island island Apostle Islands, Wisconsin, N USA
95 C16 Sandnes Rogaland, S Norway
92 F13 Sandnessjøen Nordland, C Norway
79 L24 Sandoa Katanga, S Dem. Rep. Congo
111 N15 Sandomierz Rus. Sandomir. Świętokrzyskie, C Poland
Sandomir see Sandomierz
54 C13 Sandoná Nariño, SW Colombia
106 I7 San Donà di Piave Veneto, NE Italy
124 K14 Sandovo Tverskaya Oblast', W Russian Federation
166 K7 Sandoway Arakan State, W Burma
97 M24 Sandown S England, UK
95 B19 Sandoy Dan. Sandø Island Faeroe Islands
39 N16 Sand Point Popof Island, Alaska, USA
65 N24 Sand Point headland E Tristan da Cunha
31 R7 Sand Point headland Michigan, N USA
32 M7 Sandpoint Idaho, NW USA
93 H14 Sandsele Västerbotten, N Sweden
10 I14 Sandspit Moresby Island, British Columbia, SW Canada
27 P9 Sand Springs Oklahoma, C USA
29 W7 Sandstone Minnesota, N USA
36 K15 Sand Tank Mountains ▲ Arizona, SW USA
31 S8 Sandusky Michigan, N USA
31 S11 Sandusky Ohio, N USA
31 S12 Sandusky River ⩪ Ohio, N USA
83 D22 Sandverhaar Karas, S Namibia
95 L24 Sandvig Bornholm, E Denmark
95 H15 Sandvika Akershus, S Norway
94 N13 Sandviken Gävleborg, C Sweden
30 M11 Sandwich Illinois, N USA
Sandwich Island see Éfaté
Sandwich Islands see Hawaiian Islands
153 V16 Sandwip Island island SE Bangladesh
11 U12 Sandy Bay Saskatchewan, C Canada
183 N16 Sandy Cape headland Tasmania, SE Australia
36 L3 Sandy City Utah, W USA
31 U12 Sandy Creek ⩪ Ohio, N USA
21 O5 Sandy Hook Kentucky, S USA
18 K15 Sandy Hook headland New Jersey, NE USA
Sandykachi/Sandykgachy see Sandykgaçy
146 J15 Sandykgaçy var. Sandykgachy, Rus. Sandykachi. Mary Welaýaty, S Turkmenistan
146 L13 Sandykly Gumy Rus. Peski Sandykly. desert E Turkmenistan
Sandykly, Peski see Sandykly Gumy
11 Q13 Sandy Lake Alberta, W Canada
12 B8 Sandy Lake Ontario, C Canada
12 B8 Sandy Lake ◎ Ontario, C Canada
23 S3 Sandy Springs Georgia, SE USA
24 H8 San Elizario Texas, SW USA
99 L25 Sanem Luxembourg, SW Luxembourg
42 K5 San Esteban Olancho, C Honduras
105 O6 San Esteban de Gormaz Castilla-León, N Spain
40 E5 San Esteban, Isla island NW Mexico
San Eugenio/San Eugenio del Cuareim see Artigas
62 H11 San Felipe var. San Felipe de Aconcagua. Valparaíso, C Chile
40 D3 San Felipe Baja California, NW Mexico
40 N12 San Felipe Guanajuato, C Mexico
54 K5 San Felipe Yaracuy, NW Venezuela
44 B5 San Felipe, Cayos de island group W Cuba
San Felipe de Aconcagua see San Felipe
San Felipe de Puerto Plata see Puerto Plata
37 R11 San Felipe Pueblo New Mexico, SW USA
San Feliú de Guixols see Sant Feliu de Guíxols
193 T10 San Félix, Isla Eng. San Felix Island. island W Chile
San Felix Island see San Félix, Isla
54 L11 San Fernando de Atabapo Amazonas, S Venezuela
40 C4 San Fernando var. Misión San Fernando. Baja California, NW Mexico
41 P9 San Fernando Tamaulipas, C Mexico
171 N2 San Fernando Luzon, N Philippines
171 O3 San Fernando Luzon, N Philippines
104 J16 San Fernando prev. Isla de León. Andalucía, S Spain
45 U14 San Fernando Trinidad, Trinidad and Tobago
35 S15 San Fernando California, W USA
54 L7 San Fernando var. San Fernando de Apure. Apure, C Venezuela
San Fernando de Apure see San Fernando
62 L8 San Fernando del Valle de Catamarca var. Catamarca. Catamarca, NW Argentina
San Fernando de Monte Cristi see Monte Cristi
41 P9 San Fernando, Río ⩪ C Mexico
23 X11 Sanford Florida, SE USA
19 P9 Sanford Maine, NE USA
21 T10 Sanford North Carolina, SE USA
25 N2 Sanford Texas, SW USA
39 T10 Sanford, Mount ▲ Alaska, USA
42 G8 San Francisco var. Gotera, San Francisco Gotera. Morazán, E El Salvador
43 R16 San Francisco Veraguas, C Panama
171 N2 San Francisco var. Aurora. Luzon, N Philippines
35 L8 San Francisco California, W USA
54 H5 San Francisco Zulia, NW Venezuela
34 M8 San Francisco ✕ California, W USA
35 N9 San Francisco Bay bay California, W USA
61 C24 San Francisco de Bellocq Buenos Aires, E Argentina
40 I6 San Francisco de Borja Chihuahua, N Mexico
42 J6 San Francisco de la Paz Olancho, C Honduras
40 J7 San Francisco del Oro Chihuahua, N Mexico
40 M12 San Francisco del Rincón Jalisco, SW Mexico
45 O8 San Francisco de Macorís C Dominican Republic
San Francisco de Satipo see Satipo
San Francisco Gotera see San Francisco
San Francisco Telixtlahuaca see Telixtlahuaca
107 K23 San Fratello Sicilia, Italy, C Mediterranean Sea
San Fructuoso see Tacuarembó
82 C12 Sanga Cuanza Sul, NW Angola
56 C5 San Gabriel Carchi, N Ecuador
159 S15 Sa'ngain Xizang Zizhiqu, W China
154 E13 Sangamner Mahārāshtra, W India
152 H12 Sāngāner Rājasthān, N India
Sangān, Koh-i- see Sangān, Kūh-e
149 N6 Sangān, Kūh-e Pash. Koh-i-Sangān. ▲ C Afghanistan
123 P10 Sangar Respublika Sakha (Yakutiya), NE Russian Federation
169 V11 Sangasanga Borneo, C Indonesia
103 N1 Sangatte Pas-de-Calais, N France
107 B19 San Gavino Monreale Sardegna, Italy, C Mediterranean Sea
57 D16 Sangayan, Isla island W Peru
30 L14 Sangchris Lake ⊟ Illinois, N USA
171 N16 Sangeang, Pulau island S Indonesia
116 I10 Sângeorgiu de Pădure prev. Erdăt-Sângeorz, Sîngeorgiu de Pădure, Hung. Erdőszentgyörgy. Mureş, C Romania
116 I9 Sângeorz-Băi var. Singeroz Băi, Ger. Rumänisch-Sankt-Georgen, Hung. Oláhszentgyőrgy; prev. Sîngeorz-Băi. Bistriţa-Năsăud, N Romania
35 R10 Sanger California, W USA
25 T5 Sanger Texas, SW USA
Sângerei see Sîngerei
101 L15 Sangerhausen Sachsen-Anhalt, C Germany
45 S6 San Germán W Puerto Rico
San Germano see Cassino
161 N2 Sanggan He ⩪ E China
169 Q11 Sanggau Borneo, C Indonesia
79 H16 Sangha ⩪ Central African Republic/Congo
79 G16 Sangha-Mbaéré ◆ prefecture SW Central African Republic
149 Q15 Sānghar Sind, SE Pakistan
115 F22 Sangiás ▲ S Greece
Sangihe, Kepulauan see Sangir, Kepulauan
171 Q9 Sangihe, Pulau var. Sangir. island N Indonesia
54 G8 San Gil Santander, C Colombia
106 F12 San Gimignano Toscana, C Italy
148 M8 Sangīn var. Sangin. Helmand, S Afghanistan
107 O21 San Giovanni in Fiore Calabria, SW Italy
107 M16 San Giovanni Rotondo Puglia, SE Italy
106 G12 San Giovanni Valdarno Toscana, C Italy
Sangir see Sangihe, Pulau
171 Q10 Sangir, Kepulauan var. Kepulauan Sangihe. island group N Indonesia
162 K9 Sangiyn Dalay Dundgovĭ, C Mongolia
162 H9 Sangiyn Dalay Govĭ-Altay, C Mongolia
162 K11 Sangiyn Dalay Ömnögovĭ, S Mongolia
162 K8 Sangiyn Dalay Övörhangay, C Mongolia
163 Y15 Sangju Jap. Shōshū. C South Korea
167 R11 Sangkha Surin, E Thailand
169 W10 Sangkulirang Borneo, N Indonesia
169 W10 Sangkulirang, Teluk bay Borneo, N Indonesia
155 E16 Sāngli Mahārāshtra, W India
79 E16 Sangmélima Sud, S Cameroon
35 V15 San Gorgonio Mountain ▲ California, W USA
37 T8 Sangre de Cristo Mountains ▲ Colorado /New Mexico, C USA
61 A20 San Gregorio Santa Fe, C Argentina
61 F18 San Gregorio de Polanco Tacuarembó, C Uruguay
45 V14 Sangre Grande Trinidad, Trinidad and Tobago
159 N16 Sangri Xizang Zizhiqu, W China
152 H9 Sangrūr Punjab, NW India
44 I11 Sangster off. Sir Donald Sangster International Airport, var. Montego Bay. ✕ (Montego Bay) W Jamaica
59 G17 Sangue, Rio do ⩪ W Brazil
105 R4 Sangüesa Navarra, N Spain
61 C16 San Gustavo Entre Ríos, E Argentina
Sangyuan see Wuqiao
40 C6 San Hipólito, Punta headland W Mexico
23 W15 Sanibel Sanibel Island, Florida, SE USA
23 V15 Sanibel Island island Florida, SE USA
60 F13 San Ignacio Misiones, NE Argentina
42 F2 San Ignacio prev. Cayo, El Cayo. Cayo, W Belize
57 L16 San Ignacio Beni, N Bolivia
57 O18 San Ignacio Santa Cruz, E Bolivia
42 M14 San Ignacio var. San Ignacio de Acosta. San José, W Costa Rica
40 E6 San Ignacio Baja California Sur, W Mexico
40 J10 San Ignacio Sinaloa, W Mexico
56 B9 San Ignacio Cajamarca, N Peru
San Ignacio de Acosta see San Ignacio
40 D7 San Ignacio, Laguna lagoon W Mexico
12 I6 Sanikiluaq Belcher Islands, Nunavut, C Canada
171 O3 San Ildefonso Peninsula peninsula Luzon, N Philippines
Saniquillie see Sanniquellie
61 D20 San Isidro Buenos Aires, E Argentina
43 N14 San Isidro var. San Isidro de El General. San José, SE Costa Rica
San Isidro de El General see San Isidro
54 E5 San Jacinto Bolívar, N Colombia
35 U16 San Jacinto California, W USA
35 V15 San Jacinto Peak ▲ California, W USA
61 F14 San Javier Misiones, NE Argentina
61 C16 San Javier Santa Fe, C Argentina
105 S13 San Javier Murcia, SE Spain
61 D18 San Javier Río Negro, W Uruguay
61 C16 San Javier, Río ⩪ C Argentina
160 L12 Sanjiang var. Guyi, Sanjiang Dongzu Zizhixian. Guangxi Zhuangzu Zizhiqu, S China
Sanjiang see Jinping, Guizhou
Sanjiang Dongzu Zizhixian see Sanjiang
Sanjiaocheng see Haiyan
165 N11 Sanjō var. Sanzyô. Niigata, Honshū, C Japan
57 M15 San Joaquín Beni, N Bolivia
55 O5 San Joaquín Anzoátegui, NE Venezuela
35 O9 San Joaquin River ⩪ California, W USA
35 P10 San Joaquin Valley valley California, W USA
61 A18 San Jorge Santa Fe, C Argentina

◆ Country ● Country Capital ◇ Dependent Territory ○ Dependent Territory Capital ◆ Administrative Region ✕ International Airport ▲ Mountain ▲ Mountain Range ⚲ Volcano ⩪ River ◎ Lake ⊟ Reservoir

40 D3 **San Jorge, Bahía de** *bay* NW Mexico
San Jorge, Isla de *see* Weddell Island
63 J19 **San Jorge, Golfo** *var.* Gulf of San Jorge. *gulf* S Argentina
San Jorge, Gulf of *see* San Jorge, Golfo
188 K8 **San Jose** Tinian, S Northern Mariana Islands
35 N9 **San Jose** California, W USA
61 F14 **San José** Misiones, NE Argentina
57 P19 **San José** *var.* San José de Chiquitos. Santa Cruz, E Bolivia
42 M14 **San José** ● (Costa Rica) San José, C Costa Rica
42 C7 **San José** *var.* Puerto San José. Escuintla, S Guatemala
40 G6 **San José** Sonora, NW Mexico
105 U11 **San José** Eivissa, Spain, W Mediterranean Sea
54 H5 **San José** Zulia, NW Venezuela
42 M14 **San José** *off.* Provincia de San José. ◆ *province* W Costa Rica
61 E19 **San José** ◆ *department* S Uruguay
42 M13 **San José** ✈ Alajuela, C Costa Rica
San José *see* San José del Guaviare, Colombia
San José *see* San José de Mayo, S Uruguay
171 O3 **San Jose City** Luzon, N Philippines
San José de Cúcuta *see* Cúcuta
61 D16 **San José de Feliciano** Entre Ríos, E Argentina
55 O6 **San José de Guanipa** *var.* El Tigrito. Anzoátegui, NE Venezuela
62 I9 **San José de Jáchal** San Juan, W Argentina
40 G10 **San José del Cabo** Baja California Sur, W Mexico
54 G12 **San José del Guaviare** *var.* San José. Guaviare, S Colombia
61 E20 **San José de Mayo** *var.* San José. San José, S Uruguay
54 I10 **San José de Ocuné** Vichada, E Colombia
41 O9 **San José de Raíces** Nuevo León, NE Mexico
63 K17 **San José, Golfo** *gulf* E Argentina
40 F9 **San José, Isla** *island* W Mexico
43 U16 **San José, Isla** *island* SE Panama
25 U14 **San Jose Island** *island* Texas, SW USA
62 I10 **San Juan** San Juan, W Argentina
45 N9 **San Juan** *var.* San Juan de la Maguana. C Dominican Republic
57 E17 **San Juan** Ica, S Peru
45 U5 **San Juan** ○ (Puerto Rico) NE Puerto Rico
62 H10 **San Juan** *off.* Provincia de San Juan. ◆ *province* W Argentina
45 U5 **San Juan** *var.* Luis Muñoz Marin. ✈ NE Puerto Rico
San Juan *see* San Juan de los Morros
62 O7 **San Juan Bautista** Misiones, S Paraguay
35 O10 **San Juan Bautista** California, W USA
San Juan Bautista *see* Villahermosa
San Juan Bautista Cuicatlán *see* Cuicatlán
San Juan Bautista Tuxtepec *see* Tuxtepec
79 C17 **San Juan, Cabo** *headland* S Equatorial Guinea
105 S12 **San Juan de Alicante** País Valenciano, E Spain
54 H7 **San Juan de Colón** Táchira, NW Venezuela
40 L9 **San Juan de Guadalupe** Durango, C Mexico
San Juan de la Maguana *see* San Juan
54 G4 **San Juan del Cesar** La Guajira, N Colombia
40 L15 **San Juan de Lima, Punta** *headland* SW Mexico
42 I8 **San Juan de Limay** Estelí, NW Nicaragua
43 N12 **San Juan del Norte** *var.* Greytown. Río San Juan, SE Nicaragua
54 K4 **San Juan de los Cayos** Falcón, N Venezuela
40 M12 **San Juan de los Lagos** Jalisco, C Mexico
54 L5 **San Juan de los Morros** *var.* San Juan. Guárico, N Venezuela
40 K9 **San Juan del Río** Durango, C Mexico
41 O13 **San Juan del Río** Querétaro de Arteaga, C Mexico
42 J11 **San Juan del Sur** Rivas, SW Nicaragua
54 M9 **San Juan de Manapiare** Amazonas, S Venezuela
40 E7 **San Juanico** Baja California Sur, W Mexico
40 D7 **San Juanico, Punta** *headland* W Mexico
32 G6 **San Juan Islands** *island group* Washington, NW USA
40 I6 **San Juanito** Chihuahua, N Mexico
40 I12 **San Juanito, Isla** *island* C Mexico
37 R8 **San Juan Mountains** ▲ Colorado, C USA
54 E5 **San Juan Nepomuceno** Bolívar, NW Colombia
44 E5 **San Juan, Pico** ▲ C Cuba
191 W15 **San Juan, Punta** *headland* Easter Island, Chile, E Pacific Ocean
42 M12 **San Juan, Río** ≈ Costa Rica/Nicaragua
41 S15 **San Juan, Río** ≈ SE Mexico
37 O8 **San Juan River** ≈ Colorado/Utah, W USA
San Julián *see* Puerto San Julián
61 B17 **San Justo** Santa Fe, C Argentina
109 W5 **Sankt Aegyd-am-Neuwalde** Niederösterreich, E Austria
109 U9 **Sankt Andrä** *Slvn.* Šent Andraž. Kärnten, S Austria
Sankt Andrä *see* Szentendre
Sankt Anna *see* Sântana
108 K8 **Sankt Anton-am-Arlberg** Vorarlberg, W Austria
101 E16 **Sankt Augustin** Nordrhein-Westfalen, W Germany
Sankt-Bartholomäi *see* Palamuse
101 F24 **Sankt Blasien** Baden-Württemberg, SW Germany
109 R3 **Sankt Florian am Inn** Oberösterreich, N Austria
108 I7 **Sankt Gallen** *var.* St.Gallen, *Eng.* Saint Gall, *Fr.* St-Gall. Sankt Gallen, NE Switzerland
108 H8 **Sankt Gallen** *var.* St.Gallen, Eng. Saint Gall, *Fr.* St-Gall. ◆ *canton* NE Switzerland
108 J8 **Sankt Gallenkirch** Vorarlberg, W Austria
109 Q5 **Sankt Georgen** Salzburg, N Austria
Sankt Georgen *see* Đurđevac, Croatia
Sankt-Georgen *see* Sfântu Gheorghe, Romania
109 R6 **Sankt Gilgen** Salzburg, NW Austria
Sankt Gotthard *see* Szentgotthárd
101 E20 **Sankt Ingbert** Saarland, SW Germany
Sankt-Jakobi *see* Viru-Jaagupi, Lääne-Virumaa, Estonia
Sankt-Jakobi *see* Pärnu-Jaagupi, Pärnumaa, Estonia
Sankt Johann *see* Sankt Johann in Tirol
109 T7 **Sankt Johann am Tauern** Steiermark, E Austria
109 Q7 **Sankt Johann im Pongau** Salzburg, NW Austria
109 P6 **Sankt Johann in Tirol** *var.* Sankt Johann. Tirol, W Austria
Sankt-Johannis *see* Järva-Jaani
108 L8 **Sankt Leonhard** Tirol, W Austria
Sankt Margarethen *see* Sankt Margarethen im Burgenland
109 Y5 **Sankt Margarethen im Burgenland** *var.* Sankt Margarethen. Burgenland, E Austria
Sankt Martin *see* Martin
109 X8 **Sankt Martin an der Raab** Burgenland, SE Austria
109 U7 **Sankt Michael in Obersteiermark** Steiermark, SE Austria
Sankt Michel *see* Mikkeli
Sankt Moritz *see* St.Moritz
108 E11 **Sankt Niklaus** Valais, S Switzerland
109 S7 **Sankt Nikolai** *var.* Sankt Nikolai im Sölktal. Steiermark, SE Austria
Sankt Nikolai im Sölktal *see* Sankt Nikolai
109 U9 **Sankt Paul** *var.* Sankt Paul im Lavanttal. Kärnten, S Austria
Sankt Paul im Lavanttal *see* Sankt Paul
Sankt Peter *see* Pivka
109 W9 **Sankt Peter am Ottersbach** Steiermark, SE Austria
124 J13 **Sankt-Peterburg** *prev.* Leningrad, Petrograd, *Eng.* Saint Petersburg, *Fin.* Pietari. Leningradskaya Oblast', NW Russian Federation
100 H8 **Sankt Peter-Ording** Schleswig-Holstein, N Germany
109 V4 **Sankt Pölten** Niederösterreich, N Austria
109 W7 **Sankt Ruprecht** *var.* Sankt Ruprecht an der Raab. Steiermark, SE Austria
Sankt Ruprecht an der Raab *see* Sankt Ruprecht
Sankt-Ulrich *see* Ortisei
109 T4 **Sankt Valentin** Niederösterreich, C Austria
Sankt Veit am Flaum *see* Rijeka
109 T9 **Sankt Veit an der Glan** *Slvn.* Šent Vid. Kärnten, S Austria
99 M21 **Sankt-Vith** *var.* Saint-Vith. Liège, E Belgium
101 E20 **Sankt Wendel** Saarland, SW Germany
109 R6 **Sankt Wolfgang** Salzburg, NW Austria
79 K21 **Sankuru** ≈ C Dem. Rep. Congo
40 D8 **San Lázaro, Cabo** *headland* W Mexico
137 O16 **Şanlıurfa** *prev.* Sanli Urfa, Urfa, *anc.* Edessa. Şanlıurfa, S Turkey
137 O16 **Şanlıurfa** *prev.* Urfa. ◆ *province* SE Turkey
137 O16 **Şanlıurfa Yaylası** *plateau* SE Turkey
61 B18 **San Lorenzo** Santa Fe, C Argentina
57 M21 **San Lorenzo** Tarija, S Bolivia
56 C5 **San Lorenzo** Esmeraldas, N Ecuador
42 H8 **San Lorenzo** Valle, S Honduras
56 A6 **San Lorenzo, Cabo** *headland* W Ecuador
105 N8 **San Lorenzo de El Escorial** *var.* El Escorial. Madrid, C Spain
40 E5 **San Lorenzo, Isla** *island* NW Mexico
57 C14 **San Lorenzo, Isla** *island* W Peru
63 G20 **San Lorenzo, Monte** ▲ S Argentina
40 I9 **San Lorenzo, Río** ≈ C Mexico
104 J15 **Sanlúcar de Barrameda** Andalucía, S Spain
104 J14 **Sanlúcar la Mayor** Andalucía, S Spain
40 F11 **San Lucas** Baja California Sur, NW Mexico
40 E6 **San Lucas** *var.* Cabo San Lucas. Baja California Sur, W Mexico
40 G11 **San Lucas, Cabo** *var.* San Lucas Cape. *headland* W Mexico
San Lucas Cape *see* San Lucas, Cabo
62 J11 **San Luis** San Luis, C Argentina
42 E4 **San Luis** Petén, NE Guatemala
40 D2 **San Luis** *var.* San Luis Río Colorado. Sonora, NW Mexico
42 M7 **San Luis** Región Autónoma Atlántico Norte, NE Nicaragua
36 H15 **San Luis** Arizona, SW USA
37 T8 **San Luis** Colorado, C USA
54 J4 **San Luis** Falcón, N Venezuela
62 J11 **San Luis** *off.* Provincia de San Luis. ◆ *province* C Argentina
41 N12 **San Luis de la Paz** Guanajuato, C Mexico
40 K8 **San Luis del Cordero** Durango, C Mexico
40 D4 **San Luis, Isla** *island* NW Mexico
42 E6 **San Luis Jilotepeque** Jalapa, SE Guatemala
57 M16 **San Luis, Laguna de** ◎ NW Bolivia
35 P13 **San Luis Obispo** California, W USA
37 R7 **San Luis Peak** ▲ Colorado, C USA
41 N11 **San Luis Potosí** San Luis Potosí, C Mexico
41 N11 **San Luis Potosí** ◆ *state* C Mexico
35 O10 **San Luis Reservoir** ⊠ California, W USA
San Luis Río Colorado *see* San Luis
37 S8 **San Luis Valley** *basin* Colorado, C USA
107 C19 **Sanluri** Sardegna, Italy, C Mediterranean Sea
61 D23 **San Manuel** Buenos Aires, E Argentina
36 M15 **San Manuel** Arizona, SW USA
106 F11 **San Marcello Pistoiese** Toscana, C Italy
107 N20 **San Marco Argentano** Calabria, SW Italy
54 E6 **San Marcos** Sucre, N Colombia
42 M14 **San Marcos** San José, C Costa Rica
42 B5 **San Marcos** San Marcos, W Guatemala
42 F6 **San Marcos** Ocotepeque, SW Honduras
41 O16 **San Marcos** Guerrero, S Mexico
25 S11 **San Marcos** Texas, SW USA
42 A5 **San Marcos** *off.* Departamento de San Marcos. ◆ *department* W Guatemala
San Marcos de Arica *see* Arica
40 E6 **San Marcos, Isla** *island* W Mexico
106 H11 **San Marino** ● (San Marino) C San Marino
106 I11 **San Marino** *off.* Republic of San Marino. ◆ *republic* S Europe
62 I11 **San Martín** Mendoza, C Argentina
54 F11 **San Martín** Meta, C Colombia
56 D11 **San Martín** *off.* Departamento de San Martín. ◆ *department* C Peru
194 I5 **San Martín** *Argentinian research station* Antarctica
63 H16 **San Martín de los Andes** Neuquén, W Argentina
104 M8 **San Martín de Valdeiglesias** Madrid, C Spain
63 G21 **San Martín, Lago** *var.* Lago O'Higgins. ◎ S Argentina
106 H6 **San Martino di Castrozza** Trentino-Alto Adige, N Italy
57 N16 **San Martín, Río** ≈ N Bolivia
San Martín Texmelucan *see* Texmelucan
35 N9 **San Mateo** California, W USA
55 O6 **San Mateo** Anzoátegui, NE Venezuela
42 B4 **San Mateo Ixtatán** Huehuetenango, W Guatemala
57 Q18 **San Matías** Santa Cruz, E Bolivia
63 K16 **San Matías, Golfo** *var.* Gulf of San Matías. *gulf* E Argentina
San Matías, Gulf of *see* San Matías
15 O8 **Sanmaur** Québec, SE Canada
161 T10 **Sanmen Wan** *bay* E China
160 M6 **Sanmenxia** *var.* Shan Xian. Henan, C China
Sânmiclăuş Mare *see* Sânnicolau Mare
61 D14 **San Miguel** Corrientes, NE Argentina
57 L16 **San Miguel** Beni, N Bolivia
42 G8 **San Miguel** San Miguel, SE El Salvador
40 L6 **San Miguel** Coahuila de Zaragoza, N Mexico
40 J9 **San Miguel** *var.* San Miguel de Cruces. Durango, C Mexico
43 U16 **San Miguel** Panamá, SE Panama
35 P12 **San Miguel** California, W USA
42 B9 **San Miguel** ◆ *department* E El Salvador
41 N13 **San Miguel de Allende** Guanajuato, C Mexico
San Miguel de Cruces *see* San Miguel
San Miguel de Ibarra *see* Ibarra
61 D21 **San Miguel del Monte** Buenos Aires, E Argentina
62 J7 **San Miguel de Tucumán** *var.* Tucumán. Tucumán, N Argentina
43 V16 **San Miguel, Golfo de** *gulf* S Panama
35 P15 **San Miguel Island** *island* California, W USA
42 L11 **San Miguelito** Río San Juan, S Nicaragua
43 T15 **San Miguelito** Panamá, C Panama
57 N18 **San Miguel, Río** ≈ E Bolivia
56 D6 **San Miguel, Río** ≈ Colombia/Ecuador
40 I7 **San Miguel, Río** ≈ N Mexico
42 G8 **San Miguel, Volcán de** ⛰ SE El Salvador
161 Q12 **Sanming** Fujian, SE China
106 F11 **San Miniato** Toscana, C Italy
San Murezzan *see* St.Moritz
Sannār *see* Sennar
107 M15 **Sannicandro Garganico** Puglia, SE Italy
40 H6 **San Nicolás** Sonora, NW Mexico
61 C19 **San Nicolás de los Arroyos** Buenos Aires, E Argentina
35 R16 **San Nicolas Island** *island* Channel Islands, California, W USA
Sânnicolaul-Mare *see* Sânnicolau Mare
116 E11 **Sânnicolau Mare** *var.* Sânnicolaul-Mare, *Hung.* Nagyszentmiklós; *prev.* Sânmiclăuş Mare, Sînnicolau Mare. Timiş, W Romania
123 Q6 **Sannikova, Proliv** *strait* NE Russian Federation
76 K16 **Sanniquellie** *var.* Saniquillie. NE Liberia
165 R7 **Sannohe** Aomori, Honshū, C Japan
Sanntaler Alpen *see* Kamniško-Savinjske Alpe
111 O17 **Sanok** Podkarpackie, SE Poland
54 E5 **San Onofre** Sucre, NW Colombia
57 K21 **San Pablo** Potosí, S Bolivia
171 O4 **San Pablo** *off.* San Pablo City. Luzon, N Philippines
San Pablo Balleza *see* Balleza
35 N8 **San Pablo Bay** *bay* California, W USA
40 C6 **San Pablo, Punta** *headland* W Mexico
43 R16 **San Pablo, Río** ≈ C Panama
171 P4 **San Pascual** Burias Island, C Philippines
121 Q16 **San Pawl il-Bahar** *Eng.* Saint Paul's Bay. E Malta
61 C19 **San Pedro** Buenos Aires, E Argentina
62 K5 **San Pedro** Jujuy, N Argentina
60 G13 **San Pedro** Misiones, NE Argentina
42 H1 **San Pedro** Corozal, NE Belize
40 L8 **San Pedro** *var.* San Pedro de las Colonias. Coahuila de Zaragoza, NE Mexico
62 O5 **San Pedro** San Pedro, SE Paraguay
62 O6 **San Pedro** *off.* Departamento de San Pedro. ◆ *department* C Paraguay
77 N16 **San Pedro** ✈ (Yamoussoukro) C Ivory Coast
44 G6 **San Pedro** ≈ C Cuba
San Pedro *see* San Pedro del Pinatar
76 M17 **San-Pédro** S Ivory Coast
42 D5 **San Pedro Carchá** Alta Verapaz, C Guatemala
35 S16 **San Pedro Channel** *channel* California, W USA
62 I5 **San Pedro de Atacama** Antofagasta, N Chile
San Pedro de Durazno *see* Durazno
40 G5 **San Pedro de la Cueva** Sonora, NW Mexico
San Pedro de las Colonias *see* San Pedro
56 B11 **San Pedro de Lloc** La Libertad, NW Peru
105 S13 **San Pedro del Pinatar** *var.* San Pedro. Murcia, SE Spain
45 P9 **San Pedro de Macorís** SE Dominican Republic
40 C3 **San Pedro Mártir, Sierra** ▲ NW Mexico
San Pedro Pochutla *see* Pochutla
42 D2 **San Pedro, Río** ≈ Guatemala/Mexico
40 K10 **San Pedro, Río** ≈ C Mexico
104 J10 **San Pedro, Sierra de** ▲ W Spain
42 G5 **San Pedro Sula** Cortés, NW Honduras
San Pedro Tapanatepec *see* Tapanatepec
62 I4 **San Pedro, Volcán** ▲ N Chile
106 E7 **San Pellegrino Terme** Lombardia, N Italy
25 T16 **San Perlita** Texas, SW USA
San Pietro *see* Supetar
San Pietro del Carso *see* Pivka
107 A20 **San Pietro, Isola di** *island* W Italy
32 K7 **Sanpoil River** ≈ Washington, NW USA
165 O9 **Sanpoku** *var.* Sampoku. Niigata, Honshū, C Japan
40 C3 **San Quintín** Baja California, NW Mexico
40 B3 **San Quintín, Bahía de** *bay* NW Mexico
40 B3 **San Quintín, Cabo** *headland* NW Mexico
62 I12 **San Rafael** Mendoza, W Argentina
41 N9 **San Rafael** Nuevo León, NE Mexico
34 M8 **San Rafael** California, W USA
37 Q11 **San Rafael** New Mexico, SW USA
54 H4 **San Rafael** *var.* El Moján. Zulia, NW Venezuela
42 J8 **San Rafael del Norte** Jinotega, NW Nicaragua
42 J10 **San Rafael del Sur** Managua, SW Nicaragua
36 M5 **San Rafael Knob** ▲ Utah, W USA
35 Q14 **San Rafael Mountains** ▲ California, W USA
42 M13 **San Ramón** Alajuela, C Costa Rica
57 E14 **San Ramón** Junín, C Peru
61 F19 **San Ramón** Canelones, S Uruguay
62 K5 **San Ramón de la Nueva Orán** Salta, N Argentina
57 O16 **San Ramón, Río** ≈ E Bolivia
106 B11 **San Remo** Liguria, NW Italy
54 J3 **San Román, Cabo** *headland* NW Venezuela
61 C15 **San Roque** Corrientes, NE Argentina
188 I4 **San Roque** Saipan, S Northern Mariana Islands
104 K16 **San Roque** Andalucía, S Spain
25 R9 **San Saba** Texas, SW USA
25 Q9 **San Saba River** ≈ Texas, SW USA
61 D17 **San Salvador** Entre Ríos, E Argentina
42 F7 **San Salvador** ● (El Salvador) San Salvador, SW El Salvador
42 A10 **San Salvador** ◆ *department* C El Salvador
42 F8 **San Salvador** ✈ La Paz, S El Salvador
44 K4 **San Salvador** *prev.* Watlings Island. *island* E Bahamas
62 J5 **San Salvador de Jujuy** *var.* Jujuy. Jujuy, N Argentina
42 F7 **San Salvador, Volcán de** ⛰ C El Salvador
77 Q14 **Sansanné-Mango** *var.* Mango. N Togo
45 S5 **San Sebastián** W Puerto Rico
63 J24 **San Sebastián, Bahía** *bay* S Argentina
Sansenhō *see* Sach'ŏn
106 H12 **Sansepolcro** Toscana, C Italy
107 M16 **San Severo** Puglia, SE Italy
112 F11 **Sanski Most** Federacija Bosna I Hercegovina, NW Bosnia & Herzegovina
171 W12 **Sansundi** Papua, E Indonesia
104 K11 **Santa Amalia** Extremadura, W Spain
60 F13 **Santa Ana** Misiones, NE Argentina
57 L16 **Santa Ana** Beni, N Bolivia
42 E7 **Santa Ana** Santa Ana, NW El Salvador
40 F4 **Santa Ana** Sonora, NW Mexico
35 T16 **Santa Ana** California, W USA
55 N6 **Santa Ana** Nueva Esparta, NE Venezuela
42 A9 **Santa Ana** ◆ *department* NW El Salvador
Santa Ana de Coro *see* Coro
42 E7 **Santa Ana, Volcán de** *var.* La Matepec. ⛰ W El Salvador
40 J7 **Santa Barbara** Chihuahua, N Mexico
35 Q14 **Santa Barbara** California, W USA
42 G6 **Santa Bárbara** Santa Bárbara, W Honduras
54 L11 **Santa Bárbara** Amazonas, S Venezuela
54 I7 **Santa Bárbara** Barinas, W Venezuela
42 F5 **Santa Bárbara** ◆ *department* NW Honduras
Santa Bárbara *see* Iscuandé
35 Q15 **Santa Barbara Channel** *channel* California, W USA
Santa Bárbara de Samaná *see* Samaná
35 R16 **Santa Barbara Island** *island* Channel Islands, California, W USA
54 E5 **Santa Catalina** Bolívar, N Colombia
43 R15 **Santa Catalina** Bocas del Toro, W Panama
35 T17 **Santa Catalina, Gulf of** *gulf* California, W USA
40 F8 **Santa Catalina, Isla** *island* W Mexico
35 S16 **Santa Catalina Island** *island* Channel Islands, California, W USA
41 N8 **Santa Catarina** Nuevo León, NE Mexico
60 H13 **Santa Catarina** *off.* Estado de Santa Catarina. ◆ *state* S Brazil
Santa Catarina de Tepehuanes *see* Tepehuanes
60 L13 **Santa Catarina, Ilha de** *island* S Brazil
45 Q16 **Santa Catherina** Curaçao, C Netherlands Antilles
44 E5 **Santa Clara** Villa Clara, C Cuba
35 N9 **Santa Clara** California, W USA
36 J8 **Santa Clara** Utah, W USA
Santa Clara *see* Santa Clara de Olimar
61 F18 **Santa Clara de Olimar** *var.* Santa Clara. Cerro Largo, NE Uruguay
61 A17 **Santa Clara de Saguier** Santa Fe, C Argentina
Santa Coloma *see* Santa Coloma de Gramenet
105 X5 **Santa Coloma de Farners** *var.* Santa Coloma de Farnés. Cataluña, NE Spain
Santa Coloma de Farnés *see* Santa Coloma de Farners
105 W6 **Santa Coloma de Gramanet** *var.* Santa Coloma. Cataluña, NE Spain
104 G2 **Santa Comba** Galicia, NW Spain
Santa Comba *see* Uaco Cungo
104 H8 **Santa Comba Dão** Viseu, N Portugal
82 C10 **Santa Cruz** Uíge, NW Angola
57 N19 **Santa Cruz** *var.* Santa Cruz de la Sierra. Santa Cruz, C Bolivia
62 G12 **Santa Cruz** Libertador, C Chile
42 K13 **Santa Cruz** Guanacaste, W Costa Rica
44 I12 **Santa Cruz** W Jamaica
64 P6 **Santa Cruz** Madeira, Portugal, NE Atlantic Ocean
35 N10 **Santa Cruz** California, W USA
63 H20 **Santa Cruz** *off.* Provincia de Santa Cruz. ◆ *province* S Argentina
57 O18 **Santa Cruz** ◆ *department* E Bolivia
Santa Cruz *see* Viru-Viru
Santa Cruz *see* Puerto Santa Cruz
Santa Cruz Barillas *see* Barillas
59 O18 **Santa Cruz Cabrália** Bahia, E Brazil
Santa Cruz de El Seibo *see* El Seibo
64 N11 **Santa Cruz de la Palma** La Palma, Islas Canarias, Spain, NE Atlantic Ocean
Santa Cruz de la Sierra *see* Santa Cruz
105 O9 **Santa Cruz de la Zarza** Castilla-La Mancha, C Spain
42 C5 **Santa Cruz del Quiché** Quiché, W Guatemala
105 N8 **Santa Cruz del Retamar** Castilla-La Mancha, C Spain
Santa Cruz del Seibo *see* El Seibo
44 G7 **Santa Cruz del Sur** Camagüey, C Cuba
105 O11 **Santa Cruz de Mudela** Castilla-La Mancha, C Spain
64 Q11 **Santa Cruz de Tenerife** Tenerife, Islas Canarias, Spain, NE Atlantic Ocean
64 P11 **Santa Cruz de Tenerife** ◆ *province* Islas Canarias, Spain, NE Atlantic Ocean
60 K9 **Santa Cruz do Rio Pardo** São Paulo, S Brazil
61 H15 **Santa Cruz do Sul** Rio Grande do Sul, S Brazil
57 C17 **Santa Cruz, Isla** *var.* Indefatigable Island, Isla Chávez. *island* Galapagos Islands, Ecuador, E Pacific Ocean
40 F8 **Santa Cruz, Isla** *island* W Mexico
35 Q15 **Santa Cruz Island** *island* California, W USA
187 Q10 **Santa Cruz Islands** *island group* E Solomon Islands
63 I22 **Santa Cruz, Río** ≈ S Argentina
36 L15 **Santa Cruz River** ≈ Arizona, SW USA
61 C17 **Santa Elena** Entre Ríos, E Argentina
42 F2 **Santa Elena** Cayo, W Belize
25 R16 **Santa Elena** Texas, SW USA
56 A7 **Santa Elena, Bahía de** *bay* W Ecuador
55 R10 **Santa Elena de Uairén** Bolívar, E Venezuela
42 K12 **Santa Elena, Península** *peninsula* NW Costa Rica
56 A7 **Santa Elena, Punta** *headland* W Ecuador
104 L11 **Santa Eufemia** Andalucía, S Spain
107 N21 **Santa Eufemia, Golfo di** *gulf* S Italy
105 S4 **Santa Eulalia de Gállego** Aragón, NE Spain
105 V11 **Santa Eulalia del Río** Eivissa, Spain, W Mediterranean Sea
61 B17 **Santa Fe** Santa Fe, C Argentina
105 N14 **Santa Fe** Andalucía, S Spain
37 S10 **Santa Fe** *state capital* New Mexico, SW USA
61 B15 **Santa Fe** *off.* Provincia de Santa Fe. ◆ *province* C Argentina
Santa Fe *see* Bogotá
44 C6 **Santa Fé** *var.* La Fe. Isla de la Juventud, W Cuba
43 R16 **Santa Fé** Veraguas, C Panama
Santa Fe de Bogotá *see* Bogotá
60 J7 **Santa Fé do Sul** São Paulo, S Brazil
57 B18 **Santa Fe, Isla** *var.* Barrington Island. *island* Galapagos Islands, Ecuador, E Pacific Ocean
23 V9 **Santa Fe River** ≈ Florida, SE USA
59 M15 **Santa Filomena** Piauí, E Brazil
40 G10 **Santa Genoveva** ▲ W Mexico
153 S14 **Santahar** Rajshahi, NW Bangladesh
60 G11 **Santa Helena** Paraná, S Brazil
54 J5 **Santa Inés** Lara, N Venezuela
63 G24 **Santa Inés, Isla** *island* S Chile
62 J13 **Santa Isabel** La Pampa, C Argentina
43 U14 **Santa Isabel** Colón, N Panama
186 L8 **Santa Isabel** *var.* Bughotu. *island* N Solomon Islands
Santa Isabel *see* Malabo
58 D11 **Santa Isabel do Rio Negro** Amazonas, NW Brazil
61 C15 **Santa Lucia** Corrientes, NE Argentina
57 I17 **Santa Lucía** Puno, S Peru
61 F20 **Santa Lucía** *var.* Santa Lucia. Canelones, S Uruguay
42 B6 **Santa Lucía Cotzumalguapa** Escuintla, SW Guatemala
107 L23 **Santa Lucia del Mela** Sicilia, Italy, C Mediterranean Sea
35 O11 **Santa Lucia Range** ▲ California, W USA
40 D9 **Santa Margarita, Isla** *island* W Mexico
61 G15 **Santa Maria** Rio Grande do Sul, S Brazil
35 P13 **Santa Maria** California, W USA
64 Q4 **Santa Maria** ✈ Santa Maria, Azores, Portugal, NE Atlantic Ocean
64 P3 **Santa Maria** *island* Azores, Portugal, NE Atlantic Ocean
Santa Maria *see* Gaua.
62 J7 **Santa María** Catamarca, N Argentina
Santa María Asunción Tlaxiaco *see* Tlaxiaco
40 G9 **Santa María, Bahía** *bay* W Mexico
83 L21 **Santa Maria, Cabo de** *headland* S Mozambique
104 G15 **Santa Maria, Cabo de** *headland* S Portugal
44 J4 **Santa Maria, Cape** *headland* Long Island, C Bahamas
107 J17 **Santa Maria Capua Vetere** Campania, S Italy
59 M17 **Santa Maria da Vitória** Bahia, E Brazil

◆ Country ● Country Capital ◇ Dependent Territory ○ Dependent Territory Capital ◆ Administrative Region ✈ International Airport ▲ Mountain ▲ Mountain Range ⛰ Volcano ≈ River ◎ Lake ⊠ Reservoir

55 N9 **Santa Maria de Erebato** Bolívar, SE Venezuela
104 G7 **Santa Maria da Feira** Aveiro, N Portugal
55 N6 **Santa María de Ipire** Guárico, C Venezuela
Santa Maria del Buen Aire *see* Buenos Aires
40 J8 **Santa María del Oro** Durango, C Mexico
41 N12 **Santa María del Río** San Luis Potosí, C Mexico
Santa Maria di Castellabate *see* Castellabate
107 Q20 **Santa Maria di Leuca, Capo** *headland* SE Italy
108 K10 **Santa Maria-im-Münstertal** Graubünden, SE Switzerland
57 B18 **Santa María, Isla** *var.* Isla Floreana, Charles Island. *island* Galapagos Islands, Ecuador, E Pacific Ocean
40 J3 **Santa María, Laguna de** ⊚ N Mexico
61 G16 **Santa Maria, Rio** ≈ S Brazil
43 R16 **Santa María, Río** ≈ C Panama
36 J12 **Santa Maria River** ≈ Arizona, SW USA
107 G15 **Santa Marinella** Lazio, C Italy
54 F4 **Santa Marta** Magdalena, N Colombia
104 J11 **Santa Marta** Extremadura, W Spain
Santa Maura *see* Lefkáda
35 S15 **Santa Monica** California, W USA
116 F10 **Sântana** *Ger.* Sankt Anna, *Hung.* Újszentanna; *prev.* Sîntana. Arad, W Romania
61 F16 **Santana, Coxilha de** *hill range* S Brazil
61 H16 **Santana da Boa Vista** Rio Grande do Sul, S Brazil
61 F16 **Santana do Livramento** *prev.* Livramento. Rio Grande do Sul, S Brazil
105 N2 **Santander** Cantabria, N Spain
54 F8 **Santander** *off.* Departamento de Santander. ◆ *province* C Colombia
Santander Jiménez *see* Jiménez
Sant'Andrea *see* Svetac
107 B20 **Sant'Antioco** Sardegna, Italy, C Mediterranean Sea
105 V11 **Sant Antoni de Portmany** *Cas.* San Antonio Abad. Eivissa, Spain, W Mediterranean Sea
104 J13 **Santa Olalla del Cala** Andalucía, S Spain
35 R15 **Santa Paula** California, W USA
36 L4 **Santaquin** Utah, W USA
58 I12 **Santarém** Pará, N Brazil
104 G10 **Santarém** *anc.* Scalabis. Santarém, W Portugal
104 G10 **Santarém** ◆ *district* C Portugal
44 F4 **Santaren Channel** *channel* W Bahamas
54 K10 **Santa Rita** Vichada, E Colombia
188 B16 **Santa Rita** SW Guam
42 H5 **Santa Rita** Cortés, NW Honduras
40 E9 **Santa Rita** Baja California Sur, W Mexico
54 H5 **Santa Rita** Zulia, NW Venezuela
59 I19 **Santa Rita de Araguaia** Goiás, S Brazil
Santa Rita de Cassia *see* Cássia
61 D14 **Santa Rosa** Corrientes, NE Argentina
62 K13 **Santa Rosa** La Pampa, C Argentina
61 G14 **Santa Rosa** Rio Grande do Sul, S Brazil
58 E10 **Santa Rosa** Roraima, N Brazil
56 B8 **Santa Rosa** El Oro, SW Ecuador
57 I16 **Santa Rosa** Puno, S Peru
34 M7 **Santa Rosa** California, W USA
37 U11 **Santa Rosa** New Mexico, SW USA
55 O6 **Santa Rosa** Anzoátegui, NE Venezuela
42 A3 **Santa Rosa** *off.* Departamento de Santa Rosa. ◆ *department* SE Guatemala
Santa Rosa *see* Santa Rosa de Copán
63 J15 **Santa Rosa, Bajo de** *basin* E Argentina
42 F6 **Santa Rosa de Copán** *var.* Santa Rosa. Copán, W Honduras
54 E8 **Santa Rosa de Osos** Antioquia, C Colombia
35 Q15 **Santa Rosa Island** *island* California, W USA
23 O9 **Santa Rosa Island** *island* Florida, SE USA
40 E6 **Santa Rosalía** Baja California Sur, W Mexico
54 K6 **Santa Rosalía** Portuguesa, NW Venezuela
188 C15 **Santa Rosa, Mount** ▲ NE Guam
35 V16 **Santa Rosa Mountains** ▲ California, W USA
35 T2 **Santa Rosa Range** ▲ Nevada, W USA
62 M8 **Santa Sylvina** Chaco, N Argentina
Santa Tecla *see* Nueva San Salvador
61 B19 **Santa Teresa** Santa Fe, C Argentina
59 O20 **Santa Teresa** Espírito Santo, SE Brazil
107 M23 **Santa Teresa di Riva** Sicilia, Italy, C Mediterranean Sea
61 E21 **Santa Teresita** Buenos Aires, E Argentina
61 H19 **Santa Vitória do Palmar** Rio Grande do Sul, S Brazil
35 Q14 **Santa Ynez River** ≈ California, W USA
Sant Carles de la Rápida *see* Sant Carles de la Ràpita
105 U7 **Sant Carles de la Ràpita** *var.* Sant Carles de la Rápida. Cataluña, NE Spain
105 W5 **Sant Celoni** Cataluña, NE Spain
35 U17 **Santee** California, W USA
21 T13 **Santee River** ≈ South Carolina, SE USA
40 K15 **San Telmo, Punta** *headland* SW Mexico
107 O17 **Santeramo in Colle** Puglia, SE Italy
105 X5 **Sant Feliu de Guíxols** *var.* San Feliú de Guixols. Cataluña, NE Spain
105 W6 **Sant Feliu de Llobregat** Cataluña, NE Spain
106 C7 **Santhià** Piemonte, NE Italy
61 F15 **Santiago** Rio Grande do Sul, S Brazil
62 H11 **Santiago** *var.* Gran Santiago. ● (Chile) Santiago, C Chile
45 N8 **Santiago** *var.* Santiago de los Caballeros. N Dominican Republic
40 G10 **Santiago** Baja California Sur, W Mexico
41 O8 **Santiago** Nuevo León, NE Mexico
43 R16 **Santiago** Veraguas, S Panama
57 E16 **Santiago** Ica, SW Peru
104 G3 **Santiago** *var.* Santiago de Compostela, *Eng.* Compostella; *anc.* Campus Stellae. Galicia, NW Spain
62 H11 **Santiago** *off.* Región Metropolitana de Santiago, *var.* Metropolitan. ◆ *region* C Chile
62 H11 **Santiago** ✕ Santiago, C Chile
104 G3 **Santiago** ✕ Galicia, NW Spain
76 D10 **Santiago** *var.* São Tiago. *island* Ilhas de Sotavento, S Cape Verde
Santiago *see* Santiago de Cuba, Cuba
Santiago *see* Grande de Santiago, Río, Mexico
42 B6 **Santiago Atitlán** Sololá, SW Guatemala
43 Q16 **Santiago, Cerro** ▲ W Panama
Santiago de Compostela *see* Santiago
44 I8 **Santiago de Cuba** *var.* Santiago. Santiago de Cuba, E Cuba
Santiago de Guayaquil *see* Guayaquil
62 K8 **Santiago del Estero** Santiago del Estero, C Argentina
61 A15 **Santiago del Estero** *off.* Provincia de Santiago del Estero. ◆ *province* N Argentina
40 I8 **Santiago de los Caballeros** Sinaloa, W Mexico
Santiago de los Caballeros *see* Santiago, Dominican Republic
Santiago de los Caballeros *see* Guatemala, Guatemala
42 F8 **Santiago de María** Usulután, SE El Salvador
104 F12 **Santiago do Cacém** Setúbal, S Portugal
40 J12 **Santiago Ixcuintla** Nayarit, C Mexico
Santiago Jamiltepec *see* Jamiltepec
24 L11 **Santiago Mountains** ▲ Texas, SW USA
40 J9 **Santiago Papasquiaro** Durango, C Mexico
Santiago Pinotepa Nacional *see* Pinotepa Nacional
56 C8 **Santiago, Río** ≈ N Peru
40 M10 **San Tiburcio** Zacatecas, C Mexico
105 N2 **Santillana** Cantabria, N Spain
54 I5 **San Timoteo** Zulia, NW Venezuela
Santi Quaranta *see* Sarandë
Santissima Trinidad *see* Chilung
105 O12 **Santisteban del Puerto** Andalucía, S Spain
105 U7 **Sant Jordi, Golf de** *gulf* NE Spain
105 T8 **Sant Mateu** País Valenciano, E Spain
25 S7 **Santo** Texas, SW USA
Santo *see* Espiritu Santo
60 M10 **Santo Amaro, Ilha de** *island* SE Brazil
61 G14 **Santo Ângelo** Rio Grande do Sul, S Brazil
76 C9 **Santo Antão** *island* Ilhas de Barlavento, N Cape Verde
60 J10 **Santo Antônio da Platina** Paraná, S Brazil
58 C13 **Santo Antônio do Içá** Amazonas, N Brazil
57 Q18 **Santo Corazón, Río** ≈ E Bolivia
44 E5 **Santo Domingo** Villa Clara, C Cuba
45 O9 **Santo Domingo** *prev.* Ciudad Trujillo. ● (Dominican Republic) SE Dominican Republic
40 E8 **Santo Domingo** Baja California Sur, W Mexico
40 M10 **Santo Domingo** San Luis Potosí, C Mexico
42 L10 **Santo Domingo** Chontales, S Nicaragua
105 P4 **Santo Domingo de la Calzada** La Rioja, N Spain
56 B6 **Santo Domingo de los Colorados** Pichincha, NW Ecuador
Santo Domingo Tehuantepec *see* Tehuantepec
55 O6 **San Tomé** Anzoátegui, NE Venezuela
San Tomé de Guayana *see* Ciudad Guayana
105 R13 **Santomera** Murcia, SE Spain
105 O2 **Santoña** Cantabria, N Spain
Santorin/Santoríni *see* Thíra
60 M10 **Santos** São Paulo, S Brazil
65 J17 **Santos Plateau** *undersea feature* SW Atlantic Ocean
104 G6 **Santo Tirso** Porto, N Portugal
40 B2 **Santo Tomás** Baja California, NW Mexico
42 L10 **Santo Tomás** Chontales, S Nicaragua
42 G5 **Santo Tomás de Castilla** Izabal, E Guatemala
40 B2 **Santo Tomás, Punta** *headland* NW Mexico
57 H16 **Santo Tomás, Río** ≈ C Peru
57 B18 **Santo Tomás, Volcán** ※ Galapagos Islands, Ecuador, E Pacific Ocean
61 F14 **Santo Tomé** Corrientes, NE Argentina
Santo Tomé de Guayana *see* Ciudad Guayana
98 H10 **Santpoort** Noord-Holland, W Netherlands
Santurce *see* Santurtzi
105 O2 **Santurtzi** *var.* Santurce, Santurzi. País Vasco, N Spain
Santurzi *see* Santurtzi
63 G20 **San Valentín, Cerro** ▲ S Chile
42 F8 **San Vicente** San Vicente, C El Salvador
40 C2 **San Vicente** Baja California, NW Mexico
188 H6 **San Vicente** Saipan, S Northern Mariana Islands
42 B9 **San Vicente** ◆ *department* E El Salvador
104 I10 **San Vicente de Alcántara** Extremadura, W Spain
105 N2 **San Vicente de Barakaldo** *var.* Baracaldo. País Vasco, N Spain
57 E15 **San Vicente de Cañete** *var.* Cañete. Lima, W Peru
104 M2 **San Vicente de la Barquera** Cantabria, N Spain
54 E12 **San Vicente del Caguán** Caquetá, S Colombia
42 F8 **San Vicente, Volcán de** ※ C El Salvador
43 O15 **San Vito** Puntarenas, SE Costa Rica
106 I7 **San Vito al Tagliamento** Friuli-Venezia Giulia, NE Italy
107 H23 **San Vito, Capo** *headland* Sicilia, Italy, C Mediterranean Sea
107 P18 **San Vito dei Normanni** Puglia, SE Italy
160 L17 **Sanya** *var.* Ya Xian. Hainan, S China
83 J16 **Sanyati** ≈ N Zimbabwe
25 Q16 **San Ygnacio** Texas, SW USA
160 L6 **Sanyuan** Shaanxi, C China
123 P11 **Sanyyakhtakh** Respublika Sakha (Yakutiya), NE Russian Federation
146 J15 **S.A.Nyýazow Adyndaky** *Rus.* Imeni S.A.Niyazova. Mary Welaýaty, S Turkmenistan
82 C10 **Sanza Pombo** Uíge, NW Angola
Sanzyô *see* Sanjō
104 G14 **São Bartolomeu de Messines** Faro, S Portugal
60 M10 **São Bernardo do Campo** São Paulo, S Brazil
61 F15 **São Borja** Rio Grande do Sul, S Brazil
104 H14 **São Brás de Alportel** Faro, S Portugal
60 M10 **São Caetano do Sul** São Paulo, S Brazil
60 L9 **São Carlos** São Paulo, S Brazil
59 P16 **São Cristóvão** Sergipe, E Brazil
61 F15 **São Francisco de Assis** Rio Grande do Sul, S Brazil
58 K13 **São Félix** Pará, NE Brazil
São Félix *see* São Félix do Araguaia
59 J16 **São Félix do Araguaia** *var.* São Félix. Mato Grosso, W Brazil
59 J14 **São Félix do Xingu** Pará, NE Brazil
60 Q9 **São Fidélis** Rio de Janeiro, SE Brazil
76 D10 **São Filipe** Fogo, S Cape Verde
60 K12 **São Francisco do Sul** Santa Catarina, S Brazil
60 K12 **São Francisco, Ilha de** *island* S Brazil
59 P16 **São Francisco, Rio** ≈ E Brazil
61 G16 **São Gabriel** Rio Grande do Sul, S Brazil
60 P10 **São Gonçalo** Rio de Janeiro, SE Brazil
81 H23 **Sao Hill** Iringa, S Tanzania
60 R9 **São João da Barra** Rio de Janeiro, SE Brazil
104 G7 **São João da Madeira** Aveiro, N Portugal
58 M12 **São João de Cortes** Maranhão, E Brazil
59 M21 **São João del Rei** Minas Gerais, NE Brazil
59 N15 **São João do Piauí** Piauí, E Brazil
59 N14 **São João dos Patos** Maranhão, E Brazil
58 C11 **São Joaquim** Amazonas, NW Brazil
61 J14 **São Joaquim** Santa Catarina, S Brazil
60 L7 **São Joaquim da Barra** São Paulo, S Brazil
64 N2 **São Jorge** *island* Azores, Portugal, NE Atlantic Ocean
61 K14 **São José** Santa Catarina, S Brazil
60 M8 **São José do Rio Pardo** São Paulo, S Brazil
60 K8 **São José do Rio Preto** São Paulo, S Brazil
60 N10 **São Jose dos Campos** São Paulo, S Brazil
61 I17 **São Lourenço do Sul** Rio Grande do Sul, S Brazil
58 F11 **São Luís** Roraima, N Brazil
58 M12 **São Luís** *state capital* Maranhão, NE Brazil
58 M12 **São Luís, Ilha de** *island* NE Brazil
61 F14 **São Luiz Gonzaga** Rio Grande do Sul, S Brazil
104 I10 **São Mamede** ▲ C Portugal
São Mandol *see* São Manuel, Rio
47 U8 **São Manuel** ≈ C Brazil
59 H15 **São Manuel, Rio** *var.* São Mandol, Teles Pirés. ≈ C Brazil
58 C11 **São Marcelino** Amazonas, NW Brazil
58 N12 **São Marcos, Baía de** *bay* N Brazil
59 O20 **São Mateus** Espírito Santo, SE Brazil
60 J12 **São Mateus do Sul** Paraná, S Brazil
64 P3 **São Miguel** *island* Azores, Portugal, NE Atlantic Ocean
60 G13 **São Miguel d'Oeste** Santa Catarina, S Brazil
45 P9 **Saona, Isla** *island* SE Dominican Republic
172 H12 **Saondzou** ▲ Grande Comore, NW Comoros
103 R10 **Saône** ≈ E France
103 Q9 **Saône-et-Loire** ◆ *department* C France
76 D9 **São Nicolau** *Eng.* Saint Nicholas. *island* Ilhas de Barlavento, N Cape Verde
60 M10 **São Paulo** *state capital* São Paulo, S Brazil
60 K9 **São Paulo** *off.* Estado de São Paulo. ◆ *state* S Brazil
São Paulo de Loanda *see* Luanda
São Pedro do Rio Grande do Sul *see* Rio Grande
104 H7 **São Pedro do Sul** Viseu, N Portugal
64 K13 **São Pedro e São Paulo** *undersea feature* C Atlantic Ocean
59 M14 **São Raimundo das Mangabeiras** Maranhão, E Brazil
59 Q14 **São Roque, Cabo de** *headland* E Brazil
São Salvador/São Salvador do Congo *see* M'Banza Congo, Angola
São Salvador *see* Salvador, Brazil
60 N10 **São Sebastião, Ilha de** *island* S Brazil
83 N19 **São Sebastião, Ponta** *headland* C Mozambique
104 F13 **São Teotónio** Beja, S Portugal
São Tiago *see* Santiago
79 B18 **São Tomé** ● (Sao Tome and Principe) São Tomé, S Sao Tome and Principe
79 B18 **São Tomé** ✕ São Tomé, S Sao Tome and Principe
79 B18 **São Tomé** *Eng.* Saint Thomas. *island* S Sao Tome and Principe
79 B17 **Sao Tome and Principe** *off.* Democratic Republic of Sao Tome and Principe. ◆ *republic* E Atlantic Ocean
74 H9 **Saoura, Oued** ≈ NW Algeria
60 M10 **São Vicente** *Eng.* Saint Vincent. São Paulo, S Brazil
64 O5 **São Vicente** Madeira, Portugal, NE Atlantic Ocean
76 C9 **São Vicente** *Eng.* Saint Vincent. *island* Ilhas de Barlavento, N Cape Verde
São Vicente, Cabo de *see* São Vicente, Cabo de
104 F14 **São Vicente, Cabo de** *Eng.* Cape Saint Vincent, *Port.* Cabo de São Vicente. *headland* S Portugal
Sápai *see* Sápes
Sapaleri, Cerro *see* Zapaleri, Cerro
Saparoea *see* Saparua
171 S13 **Saparua** *prev.* Saparoea. C Indonesia
168 L11 **Sapat** Sumatera, W Indonesia
77 U17 **Sapele** Delta, S Nigeria
23 X7 **Sapelo Island** *island* Georgia, SE USA
23 X7 **Sapelo Sound** *sound* Georgia, SE USA
114 K13 **Sápes** *var.* Sápai. Anatolikí Makedonía kai Thráki, NE Greece
115 D22 **Sapiéntza** *island* S Greece
Sapir *see* Sappir
61 I15 **Sapiranga** Rio Grande do Sul, S Brazil
114 K13 **Sápka** ▲ NE Greece
56 D11 **Saposoa** San Martín, N Peru
119 F16 **Sapotskino** *Pol.* Sopockinie, *Rus.* Sopotskin. Hrodzyenskaya Voblasts', W Belarus
77 P13 **Sapoui** *var.* Sapouy. S Burkina
Sapouy *see* Sapoui
138 F12 **Sappir** *var.* Sapir. Southern, S Israel
165 S4 **Sapporo** Hokkaidō, NE Japan
107 M19 **Sapri** Campania, S Italy
169 T16 **Sapudi, Pulau** *island* S Indonesia
27 P9 **Sapulpa** Oklahoma, C USA
142 J4 **Saqqez** *var.* Saghez, Sakiz, Saqqiz. Kordestān, NW Iran
Saqqiz *see* Saqqez
139 U8 **Sarābādī** E Iraq
167 P10 **Sara Buri** *var.* Saraburi. Saraburi, C Thailand
24 K9 **Saragosa** Texas, SW USA
Saragossa *see* Zaragoza
Saragt *see* Sarahs
56 B8 **Saraguro** Loja, S Ecuador
146 I15 **Sarahs** *var.* Saragt, *Rus.* Serakhs. Ahal Welaýaty, S Turkmenistan
126 M6 **Sarai** Ryazanskaya Oblast', W Russian Federation
Sarāi *see* Saráy
154 M12 **Saraipāli** Chhattīsgarh, C India
149 T9 **Sarāi Sidhu** Punjab, E Pakistan
93 M15 **Säräisniemi** Oulu, C Finland
113 I14 **Sarajevo** ● (Bosnia and Herzegovina) Federacija Bosna I Hercegovina, SE Bosnia and Herzegovina
112 I13 **Sarajevo** ✕ Federacija Bosna I Hercegovina, C Bosnia and Herzegovina
143 V4 **Sarakhs** Khorāsān, NE Iran
115 H17 **Sarakíniko, Akrotírio** *headland* Évvoia, C Greece
115 I18 **Sarakinó** *island* Vóreioi Sporádes, Greece, Aegean Sea
127 V7 **Saraktash** Orenburgskaya Oblast', W Russian Federation
30 L15 **Sara, Lake** ⊞ Illinois, N USA
23 N8 **Saraland** Alabama, S USA
55 V9 **Saramacca** ◆ *district* N Surinam
55 V10 **Saramacca Rivier** ≈ C Surinam
166 M2 **Saramati** ▲ N Burma
145 R10 **Saran'** *Kaz.* Saran. Karagandy, C Kazakhstan
18 K7 **Saranac Lake** New York, NE USA
18 K7 **Saranac River** ≈ New York, NE USA
Saranda *see* Sarandë
113 L23 **Sarandë** *var.* Saranda, *It.* Porto Edda; *prev.* Santi Quaranta. Vlorë, S Albania
61 H14 **Sarandi** Rio Grande do Sul, S Brazil
61 F19 **Sarandí del Yí** Durazno, C Uruguay
61 F19 **Sarandí Grande** Florida, S Uruguay
171 Q8 **Sarangani Islands** *island group* S Philippines
127 P5 **Saransk** Respublika Mordoviya, W Russian Federation
115 C14 **Sarantáporos** ≈ N Greece
114 H9 **Sarantsi** Sofiya, W Bulgaria
127 T3 **Sarapul** Udmurtskaya Respublika, NW Russian Federation
Sarâqeb *see* Sarāqib
138 I3 **Sarāqib** *Fr.* Sarâqeb. Idlib, N Syria
54 J5 **Sarare** Lara, N Venezuela
55 O10 **Sarariña** Amazonas, S Venezuela
143 S10 **Sar Ashk** Kermān, C Iran
23 V13 **Sarasota** Florida, SE USA
117 O11 **Sarata** Odes'ka Oblast', SW Ukraine
116 I10 **Sărăţel** *Hung.* Szeretfalva. Bistriţa-Năsăud, N Romania
25 X10 **Saratoga** Texas, SW USA
18 K10 **Saratoga Springs** New York, NE USA
127 P8 **Saratov** Saratovskaya Oblast', W Russian Federation
127 P8 **Saratovskaya Oblast'** ◆ *province* W Russian Federation
127 Q7 **Saratovskoye Vodokhranilishche** ⊞ W Russian Federation
Saravan/Saravane *see* Salavan
169 S9 **Sarawak** ◆ *state* East Malaysia
Sarawak *see* Kuching
139 U6 **Saráy** *var.* Sarāi. E Iraq
136 D10 **Saray** Tekirdağ, NW Turkey
76 J12 **Saraya** SE Senegal
143 W14 **Sarbāz** Sīstān va Balūchestān, SE Iran
143 U8 **Sarbīsheh** Khorāsān, E Iran
111 J24 **Sárbogárd** Fejér, C Hungary
Şărcad *see* Sarkad
27 S7 **Sarcoxie** Missouri, C USA
152 L11 **Sārda** *Nep.* Kali. ≈ India/Nepal
152 G10 **Sardārshahr** Rājasthān, NW India
107 C18 **Sardegna** *Eng.* Sardinia. ◆ *region* Italy, C Mediterranean Sea
107 A18 **Sardegna** *Eng.* Sardinia. *island* Italy, C Mediterranean Sea
42 K13 **Sardinal** Guanacaste, NW Costa Rica
54 G7 **Sardinata** Norte de Santander, N Colombia
Sardinia *see* Sardegna
120 K8 **Sardinia-Corsica Trough** *undersea feature* Tyrrhenian Sea, C Mediterranean Sea
22 L2 **Sardis** Mississippi, S USA
22 L2 **Sardis Lake** ⊞ Mississippi, S USA
27 P12 **Sardis Lake** ⊞ Oklahoma, C USA
92 H12 **Sarek** ▲ N Sweden
149 N3 **Sar-e Pol** *var.* Sar-i-Pul. Sar-e Pol, N Afghanistan
149 O3 **Sar-e Pol** ◆ *province* N Afghanistan
Sar-e Pol *see* Sar-e Pol-e Žahāb
142 J6 **Sar-e Pol-e Žahāb** *var.* Sar-e Pol, Sar-i Pul. Kermānshāh, W Iran
147 T13 **Sarez, Kŭli** *Rus.* Sarezskoye Ozero. ⊚ SE Tajikistan
Sarezskoye Ozero *see* Sarez, Kŭli
64 G10 **Sargasso Sea** *sea* W Atlantic Ocean
149 U8 **Sargodha** Punjab, NE Pakistan
78 I13 **Sarh** *prev.* Fort-Archambault. Moyen-Chari, S Chad
143 P4 **Sārī** *var.* Sari, Sāri. Māzandarān, N Iran
115 N23 **Saría** *island* SE Greece
Sariasiya *see* Sariosiyo
40 F3 **Saric** Sonora, NW Mexico
188 K6 **Sarigan** *island* C Northern Mariana Islands
136 D14 **Sarıgöl** Manisa, SW Turkey
139 T6 **Sārihah** E Iraq
137 R12 **Sarıkamış** Kars, NE Turkey
169 R9 **Sarikei** Sarawak, East Malaysia
147 U12 **Sarikol Range** *Rus.* Sarykol'skiy Khrebet. ▲ China/Tajikistan
181 Y7 **Sarina** Queensland, NE Australia
Sarine *see* La Sarine
105 S5 **Sariñena** Aragón, NE Spain
147 O13 **Sariosiyo** *Rus.* Sariasiya. Surxondaryo Viloyati, S Uzbekistan
Sar-i-Pul *see* Sar-e Pol, Afghanistan
Sar-i Pul *see* Sar-e Pol-e Žahāb, Iran
Sariqamish Kŭli *see* Sarygamyş Köli
149 V1 **Sari Qŭl** *Rus.* Ozero Zurkul', *Taj.* Zŭrkŭl. ⊚ Afghanistan/Tajikistan *see also* Zŭrkŭl
75 Q12 **Sarīr Tībistī** *var.* Serir Tibesti. *desert* S Libya
25 S15 **Sarita** Texas, SW USA
163 W14 **Sariwŏn** SW North Korea
114 P12 **Sarıyer** İstanbul, NW Turkey
97 L26 **Sark** *Fr.* Sercq. *island* Channel Islands
111 N24 **Sarkad** *Rom.* Şărcad. Békés, SE Hungary
145 W14 **Sarkand** Almaty, SW Kazakhstan
Sarkaṇi *see* Krasnogorskoye
152 D11 **Sarkāri Tala** Rājasthān, NW India
136 G15 **Şarkîkaraağaç** *var.* Şarki Karaağaç. İsparta, SW Turkey
136 L13 **Şarkışla** Sivas, C Turkey
136 C11 **Şarköy** Tekirdağ, NW Turkey
Sárköz *see* Livada
Sarlat *see* Sarlat-la-Canéda
102 M13 **Sarlat-la-Canéda** *var.* Sarlat. Dordogne, SW France
109 S3 **Sarleinsbach** Oberösterreich, N Austria
171 Y12 **Sarmi** Papua, E Indonesia
63 I19 **Sarmiento** Chubut, S Argentina
63 H25 **Sarmiento, Monte** ▲ S Chile
94 J11 **Särna** Dalarna, C Sweden
108 F8 **Sarnen** Obwalden, C Switzerland
108 F9 **Sarner See** ⊚ C Switzerland
14 D16 **Sarnia** Ontario, S Canada
116 L3 **Sarny** Rivnens'ka Oblast', NW Ukraine
171 O13 **Saroako** Sulawesi, C Indonesia
118 L13 **Sarochyna** *Rus.* Sorochino. Vitsyebskaya Voblasts', N Belarus
168 L12 **Sarolangun** Sumatera, W Indonesia
165 U3 **Saroma** Hokkaidō, NE Japan
165 V3 **Saroma-ko** ⊚ Hokkaidō, NE Japan
Saronic Gulf *see* Saronikós Kólpos
115 H20 **Saronikós Kólpos** *Eng.* Saronic Gulf. *gulf* S Greece
106 D7 **Saronno** Lombardia, N Italy
136 B11 **Saros Körfezi** *gulf* NW Turkey
111 N20 **Sárospatak** Borsod-Abaúj-Zemplén, NE Hungary
127 O4 **Sarov** *prev.* Sarova. Respublika Mordoviya, SW Russian Federation
Sarova *see* Sarov
127 P12 **Sarpa** Respublika Kalmykiya, SW Russian Federation
127 P12 **Sarpa, Ozero** ⊚ SW Russian Federation
113 M18 **Šar Planina** ▲ FYR Macedonia/Serbia and Montenegro (Yugo.)
95 I16 **Sarpsborg** Østfold, S Norway
139 U5 **Sarqalā** N Iraq
103 U4 **Sarralbe** Moselle, NE France
Sarre *see* Saar, France/Germany
Sarre *see* Saarland, Germany
103 U5 **Sarrebourg** *Ger.* Saarburg. Moselle, NE France
Sarrebruck *see* Saarbrücken
103 U4 **Sarreguemines** *prev.* Saargemund. Moselle, NE France
104 I3 **Sarria** Galicia, NW Spain
105 S8 **Sarrión** Aragón, NE Spain
42 F4 **Sarstoon** *Sp.* Río Sarstún. ≈ Belize/Guatemala
Sarstún, Río *see* Sarstoon
123 Q9 **Sartang** ≈ NE Russian Federation
103 X16 **Sartène** Corse, France, C Mediterranean Sea
102 K7 **Sarthe** ◆ *department* NW France
102 K7 **Sarthe** ≈ N France
115 H15 **Sárti** Kentrikí Makedonía, N Greece
Sartu *see* Daqing
165 T1 **Sarufutsu** Hokkaidō, NE Japan
Saruhan *see* Manisa
152 G9 **Sarūpsar** Rājasthān, NW India
137 U13 **Şǝrur** *prev.* Il'ichevsk. SW Azerbaijan
Sarvani *see* Marneuli
111 G23 **Sárvár** Vas, W Hungary
143 P11 **Sarvestān** Fārs, S Iran
171 W12 **Sarwon** Papua, E Indonesia
Saryagach *see* Saryagash
145 P17 **Saryagash** *var.* Saryagach, *Kaz.* Saryaghash. Yuzhnyy Kazakhstan, S Kazakhstan
Saryaghash *see* Saryagash
Saryarqa *see* Kazakhskiy Melkosopochnik
147 W8 **Sary-Bulak** Narynskaya Oblast', C Kyrgyzstan
147 U10 **Sary-Bulak** Oshskaya Oblast', SW Kyrgyzstan
117 S14 **Sarych, Mys** *headland* S Ukraine
147 Z7 **Sary-Dzhaz** *var.* Aksu He. ≈ China/Kyrgyzstan *see also* Aksu He
146 F8 **Sarygamyş Köli** *Rus.* Sarykamyshkoye Ozero, *Uzb.* Sariqamish Kŭli. *salt lake* Kazakhstan/Uzbekistan
144 G13 **Sarykamys** *Kaz.* Saryqamys. Mangistau, SW Kazakhstan
Sarykamyshkoye Ozero *see* Sarygamyş Köli
145 N7 **Sarykol'** *prev.* Uritskiy. Kostanay, N Kazakhstan
Sarykol'skiy Khrebet *see* Sarikol Range
144 M10 **Sarykopa, Ozero** ⊚ C Kazakhstan
145 V15 **Saryozek** *Kaz.* Saryözek. Almaty, SE Kazakhstan
Saryqamys *see* Sarykamys
145 S13 **Saryshagan** *Kaz.* Saryshahan. Karaganda, SE Kazakhstan
Saryshahan *see* Saryshagan
145 O13 **Sarysu** ≈ S Kazakhstan
147 T11 **Sary-Tash** Oshskaya Oblast', SW Kyrgyzstan
145 T12 **Saryterek** Karaganda, C Kazakhstan
Saryyazynskoye Vodokhranilisshche *see* Saryýazy Suw Howdany
146 J15 **Saryýazy Suw Howdany** *Rus.* Saryyazynskoye Vodokhranilischche. ⊞ S Turkmenistan
145 T14 **Saryyesik-Atyrau, Peski** *desert* E Kazakhstan
106 E10 **Sarzana** Liguria, NW Italy
188 B17 **Sasalaguan, Mount** ▲ S Guam
153 O14 **Sasarām** Bihār, N India
186 M8 **Sasari, Mount** ▲ Santa Isabel, N Solomon Islands

◆ Country ● Country Capital ◇ Dependent Territory ○ Dependent Territory Capital ◆ Administrative Region ✕ International Airport ▲ Mountain ▲ Mountain Range ※ Volcano ≈ River ⊚ Lake ⊞ Reservoir

164 C13 **Sasebo** Nagasaki, Kyūshū, SW Japan
14 I9 **Saseginaga, Lac** ◎ Québec, SE Canada
Saseno *see* Sazan
11 R13 **Saskatchewan** ◈ *province* SW Canada
11 U14 **Saskatchewan** ≈ Manitoba/Saskatchewan, C Canada
11 T15 **Saskatoon** Saskatchewan, S Canada
11 T15 **Saskatoon** ✕ Saskatchewan, S Canada
123 N7 **Saskylakh** Respublika Sakha (Yakutiya), NE Russian Federation
42 L7 **Saslaya, Cerro** ▲ N Nicaragua
38 G17 **Sasmik, Cape** *headland* Tanaga Island, Alaska, USA
119 N19 **Sasnovy Bor** *Rus.* Sosnovyy Bor. Homyel'skaya Voblasts', SE Belarus
127 N5 **Sasovo** Ryazanskaya Oblast', W Russian Federation
25 S12 **Saspamco** Texas, SW USA
109 W9 **Sass** *var.* Sassbach. ≈ SE Austria
76 M17 **Sassandra** S Ivory Coast
76 M17 **Sassandra** *var.* Ibo, Sassandra Fleuve. ≈ S Ivory Coast
Sassandra Fleuve *see* Sassandra
107 B17 **Sassari** Sardegna, Italy, C Mediterranean Sea
Sassbach *see* Sass
98 H11 **Sassenheim** Zuid-Holland, W Netherlands
Sassmacken *see* Valdemārpils
100 O7 **Sassnitz** Mecklenburg-Vorpommern, NE Germany
99 E16 **Sas van Gent** Zeeland, SW Netherlands
145 W12 **Sasykkol', Ozero** ◎ E Kazakhstan
117 O12 **Sasyk Kunduk, Ozero** ◎ SW Ukraine
76 J12 **Satadougou** Kayes, SW Mali
105 V11 **Sa Talaiassa** ▲ Eivissa, Spain, W Mediterranean Sea
164 C17 **Sata-misaki** *headland* Kyūshū, SW Japan
26 I7 **Satanta** Kansas, C USA
155 E15 **Sātāra** Mahārāshtra, W India
192 G15 **Sātaua** Savai'i, NW Samoa
188 M16 **Satawal** *island* Caroline Islands, C Micronesia
189 R17 **Satawan Atoll** *atoll* Mortlock Islands, C Micronesia
23 Y12 **Satellite Beach** Florida, SE USA
95 M14 **Säter** Dalarna, C Sweden
Sathmar *see* Satu Mare
23 V7 **Satilla River** ≈ Georgia, SE USA
57 F14 **Satipo** *var.* San Francisco de Satipo. Junín, C Peru
122 F11 **Satka** Chelyabinskaya Oblast', C Russian Federation
153 T16 **Satkhira** Khulna, SW Bangladesh
146 J13 **Şatlyk** *Rus.* Shatlyk. Mary Welaýaty, C Turkmenistan
154 K9 **Satna** *prev.* Sutna. Madhya Pradesh, C India
103 R11 **Satolas** ✕ (Lyon) Rhône, E France
111 N20 **Sátoraljaújhely** Borsod-Abaúj-Zemplén, NE Hungary
145 O12 **Satpayev** *prev.* Nikol'skiy. Karaganda, C Kazakhstan
154 G11 **Sātpura Range** ⛰ C India
167 P12 **Sattahip** *var.* Ban Sattahip, Ban Sattahipp. Chon Buri, S Thailand
92 L11 **Sattanen** Lappi, NE Finland
Satul *see* Satun
116 H9 **Satulung** *Hung.* Kővárhosszúfalu. Maramureş, N Romania
Satul-Vechi *see* Staro Selo
116 G8 **Satu Mare** *Ger.* Sathmar, *Hung.* Szatmárnémeti. Satu Mare, NW Romania
116 G8 **Satu Mare** ◈ *county* NW Romania
167 N16 **Satun** *var.* Satul, Setul. Satun, SW Thailand
192 G16 **Satupaiteau** Savai'i, W Samoa
Sau *see* Sava
14 F14 **Sauble** ≈ Ontario, S Canada
14 F13 **Sauble Beach** Ontario, S Canada
61 C16 **Sauce** Corrientes, NE Argentina
Sauce *see* Juan L.Lacaze
36 K15 **Sauceda Mountains** ⛰ Arizona, SW USA
61 C17 **Sauce de Luna** Entre Ríos, E Argentina
63 L15 **Sauce Grande, Río** ≈ E Argentina
40 K6 **Saucillo** Chihuahua, N Mexico
95 D15 **Sauda** Rogaland, S Norway
145 Q16 **Saudakent** *Kaz.* Saūdakent; *prev.* Baykadam *Kaz.* Bayqadam. Zhambyl, S Kazakhstan
92 J2 **Saudhárkrókur** Nordhurland Vestra, N Iceland
141 P9 **Saudi Arabia** *off.* Kingdom of Saudi Arabia, *Ar.* Al 'Arabīyah as Su'ūdīyah, Al Mamlakah al 'Arabīyah as Su'ūdīyah. ◆ *monarchy* SW Asia
101 D19 **Sauer** *var.* Sûre. ≈ NW Europe *see also* Sûre
101 F15 **Sauerland** *forest* W Germany
14 F14 **Saugeen** ≈ Ontario, S Canada
18 K12 **Saugerties** New York, NE USA
Saugor *see* Sāgar
10 K15 **Saugstad, Mount** ▲ British Columbia, SW Canada
Sāūjbulāgh *see* Mahābād
102 J11 **Saujon** Charente-Maritime, W France
29 T7 **Sauk Centre** Minnesota, N USA
30 L8 **Sauk City** Wisconsin, N USA
29 U7 **Sauk Rapids** Minnesota, N USA
55 Y11 **Saül** C French Guiana
103 O7 **Sauldre** ≈ C France
101 I23 **Saulgau** Baden-Württemberg, SW Germany
103 Q8 **Saulieu** Côte d'Or, C France
118 G8 **Saulkrasti** Rīga, C Latvia
15 S6 **Sault-aux-Cochons, Rivière du** ≈ Québec, SE Canada
31 Q4 **Sault Sainte Marie** Michigan, N USA
12 F14 **Sault Ste.Marie** Ontario, S Canada
145 P7 **Saumalkol'** *prev.* Volodarskoye. Severnyy Kazakhstan, N Kazakhstan
190 E13 **Sauma, Pointe** *headland* Île Alofi, W Wallis and Futuna
171 T16 **Saumlaki** *var.* Saumlakki. Pulau Yamdena, E Indonesia
Saumlakki *see* Saumlaki
15 R12 **Saumon, Rivière au** ≈ Québec, SE Canada
102 K8 **Saumur** Maine-et-Loire, NW France
185 F23 **Saunders, Cape** *headland* South Island, NZ
195 N13 **Saunders Coast** *physical region* Antarctica
65 B23 **Saunders Island** *island* NW Falkland Islands
65 C24 **Saunders Island** Settlement Saunders Island, NW Falkland Islands
82 F11 **Saurimo** *Port.* Henrique de Carvalho, Vila Henrique de Carvalho. Lunda Sul, NE Angola
55 S11 **Sauriwaunawa** S Guyana
82 D12 **Sautar** Malanje, NW Angola
45 S13 **Sauteurs** N Grenada
102 K13 **Sauveterre-de-Guyenne** Gironde, SW France
119 O14 **Sava** *Rus.* Sava. Mahilyowskaya Voblasts', E Belarus
84 H11 **Sava** *Eng.* Save, *Ger.* Sau, *Hung.* Száva. ≈ SE Europe
42 J5 **Savá** Colón, N Honduras
33 Y8 **Savage** Montana, NW USA
183 N16 **Savage River** Tasmania, SE Australia
77 R15 **Savalou** S Benin
30 K10 **Savanna** Illinois, N USA
23 X6 **Savannah** Georgia, SE USA
27 R2 **Savannah** Missouri, C USA
20 H10 **Savannah** Tennessee, S USA
21 O12 **Savannah River** ≈ Georgia/South Carolina, SE USA
Savannakhét *see* Khanthabouli
44 H12 **Savanna-La-Mar** W Jamaica
12 B10 **Savant Lake** ◎ Ontario, S Canada
155 F17 **Savanūr** Karnātaka, W India
93 J16 **Sävar** Västerbotten, N Sweden
Savaria *see* Szombathely
154 C11 **Sāvarkundla** *var.* Kundla. Gujarāt, W India
116 F11 **Săvârşin** *Hung.* Soborsin; *prev.* Săvirşin. Arad, W Romania
136 C13 **Savaştepe** Balıkesir, W Turkey
147 P11 **Savat** *Rus.* Sawot. Sirdaryo Viloyati, E Uzbekistan
Sāvdijāri *see* Skaulo
83 N18 **Save** Inhambane, E Mozambique
102 L16 **Save** ≈ S France
83 L17 **Save** *var.* Sabi. ≈ Mozambique/Zimbabwe
Save *see* Sava
77 R15 **Savè** SE Benin
142 M6 **Sāveh** Markazī, W Iran
116 L8 **Săveni** Botoşani, NE Romania
103 N16 **Saverdun** Ariège, S France
103 U5 **Saverne** *var.* Zabern; *anc.* Tres Tabernae. Bas-Rhin, NE France
Savichi *see* Savichy
119 O21 **Savichy** *Rus.* Savichi. Homyel'skaya Voblasts', SE Belarus
106 B9 **Savigliano** Piemonte, NW Italy
Savigsivik *see* Savissivik
Savinichi *see* Savinichy
119 Q16 **Savinichy** *Rus.* Savinichi. Mahilyowskaya Voblasts', E Belarus
109 U10 **Savinja** ≈ C Slovenia
Savinski *see* Savinskiy
106 H11 **Savio** ≈ C Italy
Săvirşin *see* Săvârşin
197 C11 **Savissivik** *var.* Savigsivik. Avannaarsua, S Greenland
93 N18 **Savitaipale** Etelä-Suomi, S Finland
113 J15 **Šavnik** Montenegro, SW Serbia and Montenegro (Yugo.)
108 I9 **Savognin** Graubünden, S Switzerland
103 T12 **Savoie** ◈ *department* E France
106 C10 **Savona** Liguria, NW Italy
93 N17 **Savonlinna** *Swe.* Nyslott. Itä-Suomi, SE Finland
93 N17 **Savonranta** Itä-Suomi, SE Finland
38 K10 **Savoonga** Saint Lawrence Island, Alaska, USA
30 M13 **Savoy** Illinois, N USA
117 O8 **Savran'** Odes'ka Oblast', SW Ukraine
137 R11 **Şavşat** Artvin, NE Turkey
95 L19 **Sävsjö** Jönköping, S Sweden
Savu, Kepulauan *see* Sawu, Kepulauan
92 M11 **Savukoski** Lappi, NE Finland
Savu, Pulau *see* Sawu, Pulau
187 Y14 **Savusavu** Vanua Levu, N Fiji
171 O17 **Savu Sea** *Ind.* Laut Sawu. *sea* S Indonesia
83 H17 **Savute** Chobe, N Botswana
139 N7 **Şawāb 'Uqlat** *well* W Iraq
138 M7 **Şawāb, Wādī aş** *dry watercourse* W Iraq
152 H13 **Sawāi Mādhopur** Rājasthān, N India**Sawakin** *see* Suakin
167 F8 **Sawang Daen Din** Sakon Nakhon, E Thailand
167 O8 **Sawankhalok** *var.* Swankalok. Sukhothai, NW Thailand
165 P13 **Sawara** Chiba, Honshū, S Japan
37 R5 **Sawatch Range** ⛰ Colorado, C USA
141 N12 **Sawdā', Jabal** ▲ SW Saudi Arabia
75 P9 **Sawdā', Jabal as** ⛰ C Libya
Sawdirī *see* Sodiri
97 F14 **Sawel Mountain** ▲ C Northern Ireland, UK
Sawhāj *see* Sohāg
77 O15 **Sawla** N Ghana
Sawot *see* Savat
141 X12 **Şawqirah** *var.* Suqrah. S Oman
141 X12 **Şawqirah, Dawḩat** *var.* Ghubbat Sawqirah, Sukra Bay, Suqrah Bay. *bay* S Oman
Sawqirah, Ghubbat *see* Şawqirah, Dawḩat
183 V5 **Sawtell** New South Wales, SE Australia
138 K7 **Şawt, Wādī aş** *dry watercourse* S Syria
171 O17 **Sawu, Kepulauan** *var.* Kepulauan Savu. *island group* S Indonesia
Sawu, Laut *see* Savu Sea
171 O17 **Sawu, Pulau** *var.* Pulau Savu. *island* Kepulauan Sawu, S Indonesia
105 S12 **Sax** País Valenciano, E Spain
Saxe *see* Sachsen
108 C11 **Saxon** Valais, SW Switzerland
Saxony *see* Sachsen
Saxony-Anhalt *see* Sachsen-Anhalt
77 R12 **Say** Niamey, SW Niger
15 V7 **Sayabec** Québec, SE Canada
Sayaboury *see* Xaignabouli
145 U12 **Sayak** *Kaz.* Sayaq. Karaganda, E Kazakhstan
57 D14 **Sayán** Lima, W Peru
Sayaq *see* Sayak
146 K13 **Saýat** *Rus.* Sayat. Lebap Welaýaty, E Turkmenistan
42 D3 **Sayaxché** Petén, N Guatemala
Şaydā/Sayida *see* Saïda
141 T15 **Sayḩūt** E Yemen
29 U14 **Saylorville Lake** ⊠ Iowa, C USA
Saymenskiy Kanal *see* Saimaa Canal
163 N10 **Saynshand** Dornogovĭ, SE Mongolia
162 I11 **Saynshand** Ömnögovĭ, S Mongolia
162 F7 **Sayn-Ust** Govĭ-Altay, W Mongolia
Say-Ötesh *see* Say-Utës
138 I7 **Şayqal, Bahr** ◎ S Syria
Sayrab *see* Sayrob
158 H4 **Sayram Hu** ◎ NW China
26 K11 **Sayre** Oklahoma, C USA
18 H12 **Sayre** Pennsylvania, NE USA
18 K15 **Sayreville** New Jersey, NE USA
147 N13 **Sayrob** *Rus.* Sayrab. Surxondaryo Viloyati, S Uzbekistan
40 L13 **Sayula** Jalisco, SW Mexico
141 R14 **Say'ūn** *var.* Saywūn. C Yemen
144 G14 **Say-Utës** *Kaz.* Say-Ötesh. Mangistau, SW Kazakhstan
10 K16 **Sayward** Vancouver Island, British Columbia, SW Canada
Saywūn *see* Say'ūn
Sayyāl *see* As Sayyāl
139 U8 **Sayyid 'Abīd** *var.* Saiyid Abid. E Iraq
113 J22 **Sazan** *var.* Ishulli i Sazanit, *It.* Saseno. *island* SW Albania
Sazanit, Ishulli i *see* Sazan
Sazau/Sazawa *see* Sázava
111 E17 **Sázava** *var.* Sazau, *Ger.* Sazawa. ≈ C Czech Republic
124 J14 **Sazonovo** Vologodskaya Oblast', NW Russian Federation
102 G6 **Scaër** Finistère, NW France
97 J15 **Scafell Pike** ▲ NW England, UK
Scalabis *see* Santarém
96 M2 **Scalloway** N Scotland, UK
38 M11 **Scammon Bay** Alaska, USA
Scammon Lagoon/Scammon, Laguna *see* Ojo de Liebre, Laguna
84 F7 **Scandinavia** *geophysical region* NW Europe
Scania *see* Skåne
96 K5 **Scapa Flow** *sea basin* N Scotland, UK
107 K26 **Scaramia, Capo** *headland* Sicilia, Italy, C Mediterranean Sea
14 H15 **Scarborough** Ontario, SE Canada
45 Z16 **Scarborough** *prev.* Port Louis. Tobago, Trinidad and Tobago
97 N16 **Scarborough** N England, UK
185 I17 **Scargill** Canterbury, South Island, NZ
96 E7 **Scarp** *island* NW Scotland, UK
Scarpanto *see* Kárpathos
Scarpanto Strait *see* Karpathou, Stenó
107 G25 **Scauri** Sicilia, Italy, C Mediterranean Sea
Scealg, Bá na *see* Ballinskelligs Bay
Scebeli *see* Shebeli
100 K10 **Schaale** ≈ N Germany
100 K9 **Schaalsee** ◎ N Germany
99 G18 **Schaerbeek** Brussels, C Belgium
108 G6 **Schaffhausen** *Fr.* Schaffhouse. Schaffhausen, N Switzerland
108 G6 **Schaffhausen** *Fr.* Schaffhouse. ◈ *canton* N Switzerland
Schaffhouse *see* Schaffhausen
98 I8 **Schagen** Noord-Holland, NW Netherlands
Schaken *see* Šakiai
98 M10 **Schalkhaar** Overijssel, E Netherlands
109 R3 **Schärding** Oberösterreich, N Austria
100 G9 **Scharhörn** *island* NW Germany
Schässburg *see* Sighişoara
Schaulen *see* Šiauliai
30 M10 **Schaumburg** Illinois, N USA
Schebschi Mountains *see* Shebshi Mountains
98 P6 **Scheemda** Groningen, NE Netherlands
100 I10 **Scheessel** Niedersachsen, NW Germany
13 N8 **Schefferville** Québec, E Canada
Schelde *see* Scheldt
99 D18 **Scheldt** *Dut.* Schelde, *Fr.* Escaut. ≈ W Europe
35 X5 **Schell Creek Range** ⛰ Nevada, W USA
18 K10 **Schenectady** New York, NE USA
99 I17 **Scherpenheuvel** *Fr.* Montaigu. Vlaams Brabant, C Belgium
98 K11 **Scherpenzeel** Gelderland, C Netherlands
25 S12 **Schertz** Texas, SW USA
98 G11 **Scheveningen** Zuid-Holland, W Netherlands
98 G12 **Schiedam** Zuid-Holland, SW Netherlands
99 M24 **Schieren** Diekirch, NE Luxembourg
98 M4 **Schiermonnikoog** *Fris.* Skiermûntseach. Friesland, N Netherlands
98 M4 **Schiermonnikoog** *Fris.* Skiermûntseach. *island* Waddeneilanden, N Netherlands
99 K14 **Schijndel** Noord-Brabant, S Netherlands
Schil *see* Jiu
99 H16 **Schilde** Antwerpen, N Belgium
Schillen *see* Zhilino
103 V5 **Schiltigheim** Bas-Rhin, NE France
106 G7 **Schio** Veneto, NE Italy
98 H10 **Schiphol** ✕ (Amsterdam) Noord-Holland, C Netherlands
Schippenbeil *see* Sępopol
Schiria *see* Şiria
Schivelbein *see* Świdwin
115 D22 **Schíza** *island* S Greece
Schlackenwerth *see* Ostrov
109 R7 **Schladming** Steiermark, SE Austria
Schlan *see* Slaný
Schlanders *see* Silandro
100 I7 **Schlei** *inlet* N Germany
101 D17 **Schleiden** Nordrhein-Westfalen, W Germany
Schlelau *see* Szydłowiec
100 I7 **Schleswig** Schleswig-Holstein, N Germany
29 T13 **Schleswig** Iowa, C USA
100 H8 **Schleswig-Holstein** ◈ *state* N Germany
Schlettstadt *see* Sélestat
108 F7 **Schlieren** Zürich, N Switzerland
Schlochau *see* Człuchów
Schloppe *see* Człopa
101 I18 **Schlüchtern** Hessen, C Germany
101 J17 **Schmalkalden** Thüringen, C Germany
109 W2 **Schmida** ≈ NE Austria
65 P19 **Schmidt-Ott Seamount** *var.* Schmitt-Ott Seamount, Schmitt-Ott Tablemount. *undersea feature* SW Indian Ocean
Schmiegel *see* Śmigiel
Schmitt-Ott Seamount/ Schmitt-Ott Tablemount *see* Schmidt-Ott Seamount
15 V3 **Schmon** ≈ Québec, SE Canada
101 M18 **Schneeberg** ▲ W Germany
Schneeberg *see* Veliki Snežnik
Schnee-Eifel *see* Schneifel
Schneekoppe *see* Sněžka
Schneidemühl *see* Piła
101 D18 **Schneifel** *var.* Schnee-Eifel. *plateau* W Germany
Schnelle Körös/Schnelle Kreisch *see* Crişul Repede
100 I11 **Schneverdingen** *var.* Schneverdingen (Wümme). Niedersachsen, NW Germany
Schneverdingen (Wümme) *see* Schneverdingen
Schoden *see* Skuodas
18 K10 **Schoharie** New York, NE USA
18 K11 **Schoharie Creek** ≈ New York, NE USA
115 J21 **Schoinoússa** *island* Kykládes, Greece, Aegean Sea
100 L13 **Schönebeck** Sachsen-Anhalt, C Germany
Schöneck *see* Skarszewy
100 O12 **Schönefeld** ✕ (Berlin) Berlin, NE Germany
101 K24 **Schongau** Bayern, S Germany
100 K13 **Schöningen** Niedersachsen, C Germany
Schönlanke *see* Trzcianka
Schönsee *see* Kowalewo Pomorskie
31 P10 **Schoolcraft** Michigan, N USA
98 O8 **Schoonebeek** Drenthe, NE Netherlands
98 I12 **Schoonhoven** Zuid-Holland, C Netherlands
98 H8 **Schoorl** Noord-Holland, NW Netherlands
Schooten *see* Schoten
101 F24 **Schopfheim** Baden-Württemberg, SW Germany
101 I21 **Schorndorf** Baden-Württemberg, S Germany
100 F10 **Schortens** Niedersachsen, NW Germany
99 H16 **Schoten** *var.* Schooten. Antwerpen, N Belgium
183 Q17 **Schouten Island** *island* Tasmania, SE Australia
186 C5 **Schouten Islands** *island group* NW PNG
98 E13 **Schouwen** *island* SW Netherlands
45 Q12 **Schœlcher** W Martinique
Schreiberhau *see* Szklarska Poręba
109 U2 **Schrems** Niederösterreich, E Austria
101 L22 **Schrobenhausen** Bayern, SE Germany
18 L8 **Schroon Lake** ◎ New York, NE USA
108 J8 **Schruns** Vorarlberg, W Austria
Schubin *see* Szubin
25 U11 **Schulenburg** Texas, SW USA
Schuls *see* Scuol
108 E8 **Schüpfheim** Luzern, C Switzerland
35 S6 **Schurz** Nevada, W USA
101 I24 **Schussen** ≈ S Germany
Schüttenhofen *see* Sušice
29 R15 **Schuyler** Nebraska, C USA
18 L10 **Schuylerville** New York, NE USA
101 K20 **Schwabach** Bayern, SE Germany
Schwabenalb *see* Schwäbische Alb
101 I23 **Schwäbische Alb** *var.* Schwabenalb, *Eng.* Swabian Jura. ⛰ S Germany
101 I22 **Schwäbisch Gmünd** *var.* Gmünd. Baden-Württemberg, SW Germany
101 I21 **Schwäbisch Hall** *var.* Hall. Baden-Württemberg, SW Germany
101 H16 **Schwalm** ≈ C Germany
109 V9 **Schwanberg** Steiermark, SE Austria
108 H8 **Schwanden** Glarus, E Switzerland
101 M20 **Schwandorf** Bayern, SE Germany
109 S5 **Schwanenstadt** Oberösterreich, NW Austria
169 S11 **Schwaner, Pegunungan** ⛰ Borneo, N Indonesia
109 W5 **Schwarza** ≈ E Austria
109 P9 **Schwarzach** ≈ S Austria
101 M20 **Schwarzach** *Cz.* Černice. ≈ Czech Republic/Germany
Schwarzach *see* Schwarzach im Pongau, Austria
Schwarzach *see* Svratka, Czech Republic
109 Q7 **Schwarzach im Pongau** *var.* Schwarzach. Salzburg, NW Austria
Schwarzawa *see* Svratka
101 N14 **Schwarze Elster** ≈ E Germany
Schwarze Körös *see* Crişul Negru
108 D9 **Schwarzenburg** Bern, W Switzerland
83 D21 **Schwarzrand** ⛰ S Namibia
101 G23 **Schwarzwald** *Eng.* Black Forest. ⛰ SW Germany
Schwarzwasser *see* Wda
39 P7 **Schwatka Mountains** ⛰ Alaska, USA
109 N7 **Schwaz** Tirol, W Austria
109 Y4 **Schwechat** Niederösterreich, NE Austria
109 Y4 **Schwechat** ✕ (Wien) Wien, E Austria
100 P11 **Schwedt** Brandenburg, NE Germany
101 D19 **Schweich** Rheinland-Pfalz, SW Germany
Schweidnitz *see* Świdnica
101 J18 **Schweinfurt** Bayern, SE Germany
Schweiz *see* Switzerland
100 L9 **Schwerin** Mecklenburg-Vorpommern, N Germany
Schwerin *see* Skwierzyna
100 L9 **Schweriner See** ◎ N Germany
Schwertberg *see* Świecie
101 F15 **Schwerte** Nordrhein-Westfalen, W Germany
Schwiebus *see* Świebodzin
100 P13 **Schwielochsee** ◎ NE Germany
Schwihau *see* Švihov
Schwiz *see* Schwyz
108 G8 **Schwyz** *var.* Schwiz. Schwyz, C Switzerland
108 G8 **Schwyz** *var.* Schwiz. ◈ *canton* C Switzerland
14 J11 **Schyan** ≈ Québec, SE Canada
Schyl *see* Jiu
107 I24 **Sciacca** Sicilia, Italy, C Mediterranean Sea
Sciasciamana *see* Shashemenē
107 L26 **Scicli** Sicilia, Italy, C Mediterranean Sea
97 F25 **Scilly, Isles of** *island group* SW England, UK
111 H17 **Ščinawa** *Ger.* Steinau an der Elbe. Dolnośląskie, SW Poland
Scio *see* Chíos
31 S14 **Scioto River** ≈ Ohio, N USA
36 L5 **Scipio** Utah, W USA
33 X6 **Scobey** Montana, NW USA
183 T7 **Scone** New South Wales, SE Australia
Scoresby Sound/Scoresbysund *see* Ittoqqortoormiit
Scoresby Sund *see* Kangertittivaq
Scorno, Punta dello *see* Caprara, Punta
34 K3 **Scotia** California, W USA
47 Y14 **Scotia Plate** *tectonic feature*
47 V15 **Scotia Ridge** *undersea feature* S Atlantic Ocean
194 H2 **Scotia Sea** *sea* SW Atlantic Ocean
29 Q12 **Scotland** South Dakota, N USA
25 R5 **Scotland** Texas, SW USA
96 H11 **Scotland** *national region* UK
21 W8 **Scotland Neck** North Carolina, SE USA
195 R13 **Scott Base** *NZ research station* Antarctica
10 J16 **Scott, Cape** *headland* Vancouver Island, British Columbia, SW Canada
26 I5 **Scott City** Kansas, C USA
27 Y7 **Scott City** Missouri, C USA
195 R14 **Scott Coast** *physical region* Antarctica
18 C15 **Scottdale** Pennsylvania, NE USA
195 Y11 **Scott Glacier** *glacier* Antarctica
195 Q17 **Scott Island** *island* Antarctica
26 L11 **Scott, Mount** ▲ Oklahoma, USA
32 G15 **Scott, Mount** ▲ Oregon, NW USA
34 M1 **Scott River** ≈ California, W USA
28 I13 **Scottsbluff** Nebraska, C USA
23 Q2 **Scottsboro** Alabama, S USA
31 P15 **Scottsburg** Indiana, N USA
183 P16 **Scottsdale** Tasmania, SE Australia
36 L13 **Scottsdale** Arizona, SW USA
45 O12 **Scotts Head Village** *var.* Cachacrou. S Dominica
192 L14 **Scott Shoal** *undersea feature* S Pacific Ocean
20 K7 **Scottsville** Kentucky, S USA
29 U14 **Scranton** Iowa, C USA
18 I13 **Scranton** Pennsylvania, NE USA
186 B6 **Screw** ≈ NW PNG
29 R14 **Scribner** Nebraska, C USA
Scrobesbyrig' *see* Shrewsbury
14 I14 **Scugog** ≈ Ontario, SE Canada
14 I14 **Scugog, Lake** ◎ Ontario, SE Canada
97 N17 **Scunthorpe** E England, UK
108 K9 **Scuol** *Ger.* Schuls. Graubünden, E Switzerland
Scupi *see* Skopje
Scutari *see* Shkodër
113 K17 **Scutari, Lake** *Alb.* Liqeni i Shkodrës, *SCr.* Skadarsko Jezero. ◎ Albania/Serbia and Montenegro (Yugo.)
Scyros *see* Skýros
Scythopolis *see* Bet She'an
25 U13 **Seadrift** Texas, SW USA
21 Y4 **Seaford** *var.* Seaford City. Delaware, NE USA
Seaford City *see* Seaford
14 E15 **Seaforth** Ontario, S Canada
24 M6 **Seagraves** Texas, SW USA
11 X9 **Seal** ≈ Manitoba, C Canada
182 M10 **Sea Lake** Victoria, SE Australia
83 G26 **Seal, Cape** *headland* S South Africa
65 D26 **Sea Lion Islands** *island group* SE Falkland Islands
19 S8 **Seal Island** *island* Maine, NE USA
25 V11 **Sealy** Texas, SW USA
35 X12 **Searchlight** Nevada, W USA
27 V11 **Searcy** Arkansas, C USA
19 R7 **Searsport** Maine, NE USA
35 N10 **Seaside** California, W USA
32 F10 **Seaside** Oregon, NW USA
18 K16 **Seaside Heights** New Jersey, NE USA
32 H8 **Seattle** Washington, NW USA
32 H9 **Seattle-Tacoma** ✕ Washington, NW USA
185 J16 **Seaward Kaikoura Range** ⛰ South Island, NZ
42 J9 **Sébaco** Matagalpa, W Nicaragua
19 P8 **Sebago Lake** ◎ Maine, NE USA
169 S13 **Sebangan, Teluk** *bay* Borneo, C Indonesia
169 S13 **Sebanganu, Teluk** *bay* Borneo, C Indonesia
Sebaste/Sebastia *see* Sivas
23 Y12 **Sebastian** Florida, SE USA
40 C5 **Sebastían Vizcaíno, Bahía** *bay* NW Mexico
19 R6 **Sebasticook Lake** ◎ Maine, NE USA
34 M7 **Sebastopol** California, W USA
Sebastopol *see* Sevastopol'
169 W8 **Sebatik, Pulau** *island* N Indonesia
19 R5 **Sebec Lake** ◎ Maine, NE USA
76 K12 **Sébékoro** Kayes, W Mali
Sebenico *see* Šibenik
40 G6 **Seberi, Cerro** ▲ NW Mexico
116 H11 **Sebeş** *Ger.* Mühlbach, *Hung.* Szászsebes; *prev.* Sebeşu Săsesc. Alba, W Romania
Sebes-Körös *see* Crişul Repede
Sebeşu Săsesc *see* Sebeş
31 R8 **Sebewaing** Michigan, N USA
124 F16 **Sebezh** Pskovskaya Oblast', W Russian Federation
137 N12 **Şebinkarahisar** Giresun, N Turkey
116 F11 **Sebiş** *Hung.* Borossebes. Arad, W Romania
Sebkra Azz el Matti *see* Azzel Matti, Sebkha
19 Q4 **Seboomook Lake** ◎ Maine, NE USA
74 G6 **Sebou** *var.* Sebu. ≈ N Morocco
20 I6 **Sebree** Kentucky, S USA
23 X13 **Sebring** Florida, SE USA
Sebta *see* Ceuta
Sebu *see* Sebou
169 U13 **Sebuku, Pulau** *island* N Indonesia
169 W8 **Sebuku, Teluk** *bay* Borneo, N Indonesia
106 F10 **Secchia** ≈ N Italy
10 L17 **Sechelt** British Columbia, SW Canada
56 C12 **Sechín, Río** ≈ W Peru
56 A10 **Sechura, Bahía de** *bay* NW Peru
185 A22 **Secretary Island** *island* SW NZ
155 I15 **Secunderābād** *var.* Sikandarabad. Andhra Pradesh, C India
57 L17 **Sécure, Río** ≈ C Bolivia
118 D10 **Seda** Telšiai, NW Lithuania
27 T5 **Sedalia** Missouri, C USA
103 R3 **Sedan** Ardennes, N France
27 P7 **Sedan** Kansas, C USA
105 N3 **Sedano** Castilla-León, N Spain
104 H10 **Seda, Ribeira de** *stream* C Portugal
185 K15 **Seddon** Marlborough, South Island, NZ
185 H15 **Seddonville** West Coast, South Island, NZ
143 U7 **Sedeh** Khorāsān, E Iran
122 I11 **Sedel'nikovo** Omskaya Oblast', C Russian Federation0
138 E11 **Sederot** Southern, S Israel
65 B23 **Sedge Island** *island* NW Falkland Islands
76 G12 **Sédhiou** SW Senegal
11 U16 **Sedley** Saskatchewan, S Canada
Sedlez *see* Siedlce
117 Q2 **Sedniv** Chernihivs'ka Oblast', N Ukraine
36 L11 **Sedona** Arizona, SW USA
Sedunum *see* Sion
118 F12 **Šeduva** Šiauliai, N Lithuania
141 Y8 **Seeb** *var.* Muscat Sīb Airport. ✕ (Masqaţ) NE Oman
Seeb *see* As Sīb

◆ Country ● Country Capital ◇ Dependent Territory ○ Dependent Territory Capital ◈ Administrative Region ✕ International Airport ▲ Mountain ⛰ Mountain Range Ѫ Volcano ≈ River ◎ Lake ⊠ Reservoir

108 M7 **Seefeld-in-Tirol** Tirol, W Austria
83 E22 **Seeheim Noord** Karas, S Namibia
Seeland *see* Sjælland
195 N9 **Selig, Mount** ▲ Antarctica
Seeonee *see* Seoni
162 E6 **Seer** Hovd, W Mongolia
102 L5 **Sées** Orne, N France
101 J14 **Seesen** Niedersachsen, C Germany
Seesker Höhe *see* Szeska Góra
100 J10 **Seevetal** Niedersachsen, N Germany
109 V6 **Seewiesen** Steiermark, E Austria
136 J13 **Şefaatli** *var.* Kızılkoca. Yozgat, C Turkey
149 N3 **Sefid, Darya-ye** *Pash.* Āb-i-Safed. ≈ N Afghanistan
148 K5 **Sefid Kūh, Selseleh-ye** *Eng.* Paropamisus Range. ⛰ W Afghanistan
74 G6 **Sefrou** N Morocco
185 E19 **Sefton, Mount** ▲ South Island, NZ
171 S13 **Segaf, Kepulauan** *island group* E Indonesia
169 W7 **Segama, Sungai** ≈ East Malaysia
168 L9 **Segamat** Johor, Peninsular Malaysia
77 S13 **Ségbana** NE Benin
Segestica *see* Sisak
Segesvár *see* Sighişoara
171 T12 **Seget** Papua, E Indonesia
Segewold *see* Sigulda
124 J9 **Segezha** Respublika Kareliya, NW Russian Federation
Seghedin *see* Szeged
Segna *see* Senj
107 I16 **Segni** Lazio, C Italy
Segodunum *see* Rodez
105 S9 **Segorbe** País Valenciano, E Spain
76 M12 **Ségou** *var.* Segu. Ségou, C Mali
76 M12 **Ségou** ◈ *region* SW Mali
54 E8 **Segovia** Antioquia, N Colombia
105 N7 **Segovia** Castilla-León, C Spain
104 M6 **Segovia** ◈ *province* Castilla-León, N Spain
Segoviao Wangkí *see* Coco, Río
126 J9 **Segozero, Ozero** ◎ NW Russian Federation
105 U5 **Segre** ≈ NE Spain
102 J7 **Segré** Maine-et-Loire, NW France
Segu *see* Ségou
38 I17 **Seguam Island** *island* Aleutian Islands, Alaska, USA
38 I17 **Seguam Pass** *strait* Aleutian Islands, Alaska, USA
77 Y7 **Séguédine** Agadez, NE Niger
76 M15 **Séguéla** W Ivory Coast
25 S11 **Seguin** Texas, SW USA
38 E17 **Segula Island** *island* Aleutian Islands, Alaska, USA
62 K10 **Segundo, Río** ≈ C Argentina
105 Q12 **Segura** ≈ S Spain
105 P13 **Sierra de Segura** ⛰ S Spain
83 G18 **Sehithwa** Ngamiland, N Botswana
154 H10 **Sehore** Madhya Pradesh, C India
186 G9 **Sehulea** Normanby Island, S PNG
149 P15 **Sehwān** Sind, SE Pakistan
109 V8 **Seiersberg** Steiermark, SE Austria
26 L9 **Seiling** Oklahoma, C USA
103 S9 **Seille** ≈ E France
99 J20 **Seilles** Namur, SE Belgium
93 K17 **Seinäjoki** *Swe.* Östermyra. Länsi-Suomi, W Finland
12 B12 **Seine** ≈ Ontario, S Canada
102 M4 **Seine** ≈ N France
102 K4 **Seine, Baie de la** *bay* N France
Seine, Banc de la *see* Seine Seamount
103 O5 **Seine-et-Marne** ◈ *department* N France
102 L3 **Seine-Maritime** ◈ *department* N France
84 B14 **Seine Plain** *undersea feature* E Atlantic Ocean
84 B15 **Seine Seamount** *var.* Banc de la Seine. *undersea feature* E Atlantic Ocean
102 E6 **Sein, Île de** *island* NW France
171 Y14 **Seinma** Papua, E Indonesia
Seisbierrum *see* Sexbierum
109 U5 **Seitenstetten Markt** Niederösterreich, C Austria
Seiyu *see* Chŏnju
95 H22 **Sejerø** *island* E Denmark
110 P7 **Sejny** Podlaskie, NE Poland
81 G20 **Seke** Shinyanga, N Tanzania
164 L13 **Seki** Gifu, Honshū, SW Japan
161 U12 **Sekibi-sho** *island* China/Japan/Taiwan
165 U3 **Sekihoku-tōge** *pass* Hokkaidō, NE Japan
Sekondi *see* Sekondi-Takoradi
77 P17 **Sekondi-Takoradi** *var.* Sekondi. S Ghana
80 J11 **Sek'ot'a** Amhara, N Ethiopia
Sekseŭil *see* Saksaul'skiy
32 I9 **Selah** Washington, NW USA
168 J8 **Selangor** *var.* Negeri Selangor Darul Ehsan. ◈ *state* Peninsular Malaysia
Selânik *see* Thessaloníki
168 K10 **Selapanjang** Pulau Rantau, W Indonesia
167 R10 **Selaphum** Roi Et, E Thailand
171 T16 **Selaru, Pulau** *island* Kepulauan Tanimbar, E Indonesia
171 U13 **Selassi** Papua, E Indonesia
168 J7 **Selatan, Selat** *strait* Peninsular Malaysia
39 N8 **Selawik** Alaska, USA
39 N8 **Selawik Lake** ◎ Alaska, USA
171 N14 **Selayar, Selat** *strait* Sulawesi, C Indonesia
95 C14 **Selbjørnsfjorden** *fjord* S Norway
94 H8 **Selbusjøen** ◎ S Norway
97 M17 **Selby** N England, UK
29 N8 **Selby** South Dakota, N USA
21 Z4 **Selbyville** Delaware, NE USA
136 B15 **Selçuk** *var.* Akıncılar. İzmir, SW Turkey
39 Q13 **Seldovia** Alaska, USA
107 M18 **Sele** *anc.* Silarius. ≈ S Italy
83 J19 **Selebi-Phikwe** Central, E Botswana
42 B5 **Selegua, Río** ≈ W Guatemala
123 R13 **Selemdzha** ≈ SE Russian Federation
131 U7 **Selenga** *Mong.* Selenge Mörön. ≈ Mongolia/Russian Federation
162 K6 **Selenge** Bulgan, N Mongolia
162 J6 **Selenge** Hövsgöl, N Mongolia
79 I19 **Selenge** Bandundu, W Dem. Rep. Congo
162 L6 **Selenge** ◈ *province* N Mongolia
Selenge Mörön *see* Selenga
123 N14 **Selenginsk** Respublika Buryatiya, S Russian Federation
Selenica *see* Selenicë
113 K22 **Selenicë** *var.* Selenica. Vlorë, SW Albania
123 Q8 **Selennyakh** ≈ NE Russian Federation
100 J8 **Selenter See** ◎ N Germany
Sele Sound *see* Soela Väin
103 U6 **Sélestat** *Ger.* Schlettstadt. Bas-Rhin, NE France
Selety *see* Sileti
Seleucia *see* Silifke
92 I4 **Selfoss** Sudhurland, SW Iceland
28 M7 **Selfridge** North Dakota, N USA
76 I15 **Seli** ≈ N Sierra Leone
76 I11 **Sélibabi** *var.* Sélibaby. Guidimaka, S Mauritania
Sélibaby *see* Sélibabi
Selidovka/Selidovo *see* Selydove
126 I15 **Seliger, Ozero** ◎ W Russian Federation
36 J11 **Seligman** Arizona, SW USA
27 S8 **Seligman** Missouri, C USA
80 E6 **Selima Oasis** *oasis* N Sudan
76 L13 **Sélingué, Lac de** ◎ S Mali
Selinoús *see* Kréstena
18 G14 **Selinsgrove** Pennsylvania, NE USA
Selishche *see* Syelishcha
124 I16 **Selizharovo** Tverskaya Oblast', W Russian Federation
94 C10 **Selje** Sogn og Fjordane, S Norway
11 X16 **Selkirk** Manitoba, S Canada
96 K13 **Selkirk** SE Scotland, UK
96 K13 **Selkirk** *cultural region* SE Scotland, UK
11 O16 **Selkirk Mountains** ⛰ British Columbia, SW Canada
193 T11 **Selkirk Rise** *undersea feature* SE Pacific Ocean
115 F21 **Sellasía** Pelopónnisos, S Greece
44 M9 **Selle, Pic de la** *var.* La Selle. ▲ SE Haiti
102 M8 **Selles-sur-Cher** Loir-et-Cher, C France
36 K16 **Sells** Arizona, SW USA
Sellye *see* Sal'a
23 P5 **Selma** Alabama, S USA
35 Q11 **Selma** California, W USA
20 G10 **Selmer** Tennessee, S USA
173 N17 **Sel, Pointe au** *headland* W Réunion
Selseleh-ye Kūh-e Vākhān *see* Nicholas Range
127 S2 **Selty** Udmurtskaya Respublika, NW Russian Federation
Selukwe *see* Shurugwi
62 L9 **Selva** Santiago del Estero, N Argentina
11 T9 **Selwyn Lake** ◎ Northwest Territories/Saskatchewan, C Canada
10 K6 **Selwyn Mountains** ⛰ Yukon Territory, NW Canada
181 T6 **Selwyn Range** ⛰ Queensland, C Australia
117 W8 **Selydove** *var.* Selidovka, *Rus.* Selidovo. Donets'ka Oblast', SE Ukraine
Selzaete *see* Zelzate
Seman *see* Semanit, Lumi i
168 M15 **Semangka, Teluk** *bay* Sumatera, SW Indonesia
113 D22 **Semanit, Lumi i** *var.* Seman. ≈ W Albania
169 Q16 **Semarang** *var.* Samarang. Jawa, C Indonesia
169 Q10 **Sematan** Sarawak, East Malaysia
171 P17 **Semau, Pulau** *island* S Indonesia
169 V8 **Sembakung, Sungai** ≈ Borneo, N Indonesia
79 G17 **Sembé** La Sangha, NW Congo
169 S13 **Sembulu, Danau** ◎ Borneo, N Indonesia
Semendria *see* Smederevo
117 R1 **Semenivka** Chernihivs'ka Oblast', N Ukraine
117 S6 **Semenivka** *Rus.* Semenovka. Poltavs'ka Oblast', NE Ukraine
127 O3 **Semenov** Nizhegorodskaya Oblast', W Russian Federation
Semenovka *see* Semenivka
169 S17 **Semeru, Gunung** *var.* Mahameru. ▲ Jawa, S Indonesia
Semey *see* Semipalatinsk
Semezhevo *see* Syemyezhava
126 L7 **Semiluki** Voronezhskaya Oblast', W Russian Federation
33 W16 **Seminoe Reservoir** ⊞ Wyoming, C USA
27 O11 **Seminole** Oklahoma, C USA
24 M6 **Seminole** Texas, SW USA
23 S8 **Seminole, Lake** ⊞ Florida/Georgia, SE USA
Semiozernoye *see* Auliyekol'
145 V9 **Semipalatinsk** *Kaz.* Semey. Vostochnyy Kazakhstan, E Kazakhstan
143 O9 **Semīrom** *var.* Samirum. Eşfahān, C Iran
38 F17 **Semisopochnoi Island** *island* Aleutian Islands, Alaska, USA
169 R11 **Semitau** Borneo, C Indonesia
81 E18 **Semliki** ≈ Uganda/Dem. Rep. Congo
143 P5 **Semnān** *var.* Samnān. Semnān, N Iran
143 Q5 **Semnān** *off.* Ostān-e Semnān. ◈ *province* N Iran
99 K24 **Semois** ≈ SE Belgium
108 E8 **Sempacher See** ◎ C Switzerland
Sena *see* Vila de Sena
30 L12 **Senachwine Lake** ◎ Illinois, N USA
59 O14 **Senador Pompeu** Ceará, E Brazil
Sena Gallica *see* Senigallia
59 C15 **Sena Madureira** Acre, W Brazil
155 L25 **Senanayake Samudra** ◎ E Sri Lanka
83 G15 **Senanga** Western, SW Zambia
27 Y9 **Senath** Missouri, C USA
22 L2 **Senatobia** Mississippi, S USA
164 C16 **Sendai** Kagoshima, Kyūshū, SW Japan
165 Q10 **Sendai** Miyagi, Honshū, C Japan
165 Q11 **Sendai-wan** *bay* E Japan
101 J23 **Senden** Bayern, S Germany
154 F11 **Sendhwa** Madhya Pradesh, C India
111 H21 **Senec** *Ger.* Wartberg, *Hung.* Szenc; *prev.* Szempcz. Bratislavský Kraj, W Slovakia
27 P3 **Seneca** Kansas, C USA
27 R8 **Seneca** Missouri, C USA
32 K13 **Seneca** Oregon, NW USA
21 O11 **Seneca** South Carolina, SE USA
18 G11 **Seneca Lake** ◎ New York, NE USA
31 U13 **Senecaville Lake** ⊞ Ohio, N USA
76 G11 **Senegal** *off.* Republic of Senegal, *Fr.* Sénégal. ◆ *republic* W Africa
76 H9 **Senegal** *Fr.* Sénégal. ≈ W Africa
31 O4 **Seney Marsh** *wetland* Michigan, N USA
101 P14 **Senftenberg** Brandenburg, E Germany
82 L11 **Senga Hill** Northern, NE Zambia
158 G13 **Sênggê Zangbo** ≈ W China
171 Z13 **Senggi** Papua, E Indonesia
127 R5 **Sengiley** Ul'yanovskaya Oblast', W Russian Federation
63 I19 **Senguerr, Río** ≈ S Argentina
83 J16 **Sengwa** ≈ C Zimbabwe
Senia *see* Senj
111 H19 **Senica** *Ger.* Senitz, *Hung.* Szenice. Trnavský Kraj, W Slovakia
Seniça *see* Sjenica
106 J11 **Senigallia** *anc.* Sena Gallica. Marche, C Italy
136 F15 **Senirkent** Isparta, SW Turkey
Senitz *see* Senica
112 C10 **Senj** *Ger.* Zengg, *It.* Segna; *anc.* Senia. Lika-Senj, NW Croatia
163 O10 **Senj** Dornogovĭ, SE Mongolia
92 H9 **Senja** *prev.* Senjen. *island* N Norway
Senjen *see* Senja
161 U12 **Senkaku-shotō** *island group* SW Japan
137 R12 **Şenkaya** Erzurum, NE Turkey
83 I16 **Senkobo** Southern, S Zambia
103 O4 **Senlis** Oise, N France
167 T12 **Senmonorom** Môndól Kiri, E Cambodia
80 G10 **Sennar** *var.* Sannār. Sinnar, C Sudan
Senno *see* Syanno
Senones *see* Sens
109 W11 **Senovo** E Slovenia
103 P6 **Sens** *anc.* Agendicum, Senones. Yonne, C France
Sensburg *see* Mrągowo
167 S11 **Sên, Stœng** ≈ C Cambodia
42 F7 **Sensuntepeque** Cabañas, NE El Salvador
112 L8 **Senta** *Hung.* Zenta. Serbia, N Serbia and Montenegro (Yugo.)
Šent Andraž *see* Sankt Andrä
171 Y13 **Sentani, Danau** ◎ Papua, E Indonesia
28 J5 **Sentinel Butte** ▲ North Dakota, N USA
10 M13 **Sentinel Peak** ▲ British Columbia, W Canada
59 N16 **Sento Sé** Bahia, E Brazil
Šent Peter *see* Pivka
Šent Vid *see* Sankt Veit an der Glan
Seo de Urgel *see* La See d'Urgel
154 I7 **Seondha** Madhya Pradesh, C India
154 J11 **Seoni** *prev.* Seeonee. Madhya Pradesh, C India
Seoul *see* Sŏul
184 I13 **Separation Point** *headland* South Island, NZ
169 V10 **Sepasu** Borneo, N Indonesia
186 B6 **Sepik** ≈ Indonesia/PNG
Sepone *see* Muang Xépôn
110 M7 **Sępopol** *Ger.* Schippenbeil. Warmińsko-Mazurskie, NE Poland,
116 F10 **Şepreuş** *Hung.* Seprős. Arad, W Romania
Seprős *see* Şepreuş
Şepşi-Sângeorz/Sepsiszentgyörgy *see* Sfântu Gheorghe
15 W4 **Sept-Îles** Québec, SE Canada
105 N6 **Sepúlveda** Castilla-León, N Spain
104 K8 **Sequeros** Castilla-León, N Spain
104 L5 **Sequillo** ≈ NW Spain
32 G7 **Sequim** Washington, NW USA
35 S11 **Sequoia National Park** *national park* California, W USA
137 Q14 **Şerafettin Dağları** ⛰ E Turkey
127 N10 **Serafimovich** Volgogradskaya Oblast', SW Russian Federation
171 Q10 **Serai** Sulawesi, N Indonesia
99 K19 **Seraing** Liège, E Belgium
Sêraitang *see* Baima
Serajgonj *see* Shirajganj Ghat
Serakhs *see* Sarahs
171 W13 **Serami** Papua, E Indonesia
Seram, Laut *see* Ceram Sea
Serampore/Serampur *see* Shrīrāmpur
171 S13 **Seram, Pulau** *var.* Serang, *Eng.* Ceram. *island* Maluku, E Indonesia
169 N15 **Serang** Jawa, C Indonesia
Serang *see* Seram, Pulau
169 P9 **Serasan, Pulau** *island* Kepulauan Natuna, W Indonesia
169 P9 **Serasan, Selat** *strait* Indonesia/Malaysia
112 M12 **Serbia** *Ger.* Serbien, *Serb.* Srbija. ◈ *republic* Serbia and Montenegro (Yugo.)
112 M13 **Serbia and Montenegro (Yugo.)** *off.* Federal Republic of Serbia and Montenegro (Yugo.), *SCr.* Jugoslavija, Savezna Republika Jugoslavija. ◆ *federal republic* SE Europe
Serbien *see* Serbia
Sercq *see* Sark
146 D12 **Serdar** *prev. Rus.* Gyzylarbat, Kizyl-Arvat. Balkan Welaýaty, W Turkmenistan
Serdica *see* Sofiya
127 O7 **Serdobsk** Penzenskaya Oblast', W Russian Federation
145 X9 **Serebryansk** Vostochnyy Kazakhstan, E Kazakhstan
123 Q12 **Serebryanyy Bor** Respublika Sakha (Yakutiya), NE Russian Federation
111 H20 **Sered'** *Hung.* Szered. Trnavský Kraj, SW Slovakia
117 S1 **Seredyna-Buda** Sums'ka Oblast', NE Ukraine
118 E13 **Seredžius** Tauragė, C Lithuania
136 I14 **Şereflikoçhisar** Ankara, C Turkey
106 D7 **Seregno** Lombardia, N Italy
103 P7 **Serein** ≈ C France
168 K9 **Seremban** Negeri Sembilan, Peninsular Malaysia
81 H20 **Serengeti Plain** *plain* N Tanzania
82 K13 **Serenje** Central, E Zambia
Seres *see* Sérres
116 J5 **Seret** ≈ W Ukraine
Seret/Sereth *see* Siret
115 I21 **Serfopoúla** *island* Kykládes, Greece, Aegean Sea
127 P4 **Sergach** Nizhegorodskaya Oblast', W Russian Federation
29 S13 **Sergeant Bluff** Iowa, C USA
163 P7 **Sergelen** Dornod, NE Mongolia
163 O9 **Sergelen** Sühbaatar, E Mongolia
168 H8 **Sergeulangit, Pegunungan** ⛰ Sumatera, NW Indonesia
122 L5 **Sergeya Kirova, Ostrova** *island* N Russian Federation
Sergeyevichi *see* Syarhyeyevichy
145 O7 **Sergeyevka** Severnyy Kazakhstan, N Kazakhstan
Sergiopol *see* Ayagoz
59 P16 **Sergipe** *off.* Estado de Sergipe. ◈ *state* E Brazil
126 L3 **Sergiyev Posad** Moskovskaya Oblast', W Russian Federation
126 K5 **Sergozero, Ozero** ◎ NW Russian Federation
146 J17 **Serhetabat** *prev. Rus.* Gushgy, Kushka. Mary Welaýaty, S Turkmenistan
169 Q10 **Serian** Sarawak, East Malaysia
169 O15 **Seribu, Kepulauan** *island group* S Indonesia
115 I21 **Sérifos** *anc.* Seriphos. *island* Kykládes, Greece, Aegean Sea
115 I21 **Sérifou, Stenó** *strait* SE Greece
136 F16 **Serik** Antalya, SW Turkey
106 E7 **Serio** ≈ N Italy
Seriphos *see* Sérifos
Serir Tibesti *see* Sarīr Tibistī
Sêrkog *see* Sêrtar
127 S5 **Sernovodsk** Samarskaya Oblast', W Russian Federation
127 R2 **Sernur** Respublika Mariy El, W Russian Federation
110 M11 **Serock** Mazowieckie, C Poland
61 B18 **Serodino** Santa Fe, C Argentina
Seroei *see* Serui
105 P14 **Serón** Andalucía, S Spain
99 E14 **Serooskerke** Zeeland, SW Netherlands
105 T6 **Seròs** Cataluña, NE Spain
122 G10 **Serov** Sverdlovskaya Oblast', C Russian Federation
83 I19 **Serowe** Central, SE Botswana
104 H13 **Serpa** Beja, S Portugal
Serpa Pinto *see* Menongue
182 A4 **Serpentine Lakes** *salt lake* South Australia
45 T15 **Serpent's Mouth, The** *Sp.* Boca de la Serpiente. *strait* Trinidad and Tobago/Venezuela
Serpiente, Boca de la *see* Serpent's Mouth, The
126 K4 **Serpukhov** Moskovskaya Oblast', W Russian Federation
60 K13 **Serra do Mar** ⛰ S Brazil
Sérrai *see* Sérres
107 N22 **Serra San Bruno** Calabria, SW Italy
103 S14 **Serres** Hautes-Alpes, SE France
114 H13 **Sérres** *var.* Seres; *prev.* Sérrai. Kentrikí Makedonía, NE Greece
62 J9 **Serrezuela** Córdoba, C Argentina
59 O16 **Serrinha** Bahia, E Brazil
59 M19 **Serro** *var.* Sêrro. Minas Gerais, NE Brazil
Sêrro *see* Serro
Sert *see* Siirt
Sertá *see* Sertã
104 H9 **Sertã** *var.* Sertá. Castelo Branco, C Portugal
60 L8 **Sertãozinho** São Paulo, S Brazil
160 F7 **Sêrtar** *var.* Sêrkog. Sichuan, C China
171 W13 **Serui** *prev.* Seroei. Papua, E Indonesia
83 J19 **Serule** Central, E Botswana
169 S12 **Seruyan, Sungai** *var.* Sungai Pembuang. ≈ Borneo, N Indonesia
115 E14 **Sérvia** Dytikí Makedonía, N Greece
160 E7 **Sêrxü** *var.* Jugar. Sichuan, C China
123 R13 **Seryshevo** Amurskaya Oblast', SE Russian Federation
Sesana *see* Sežana
169 V8 **Sesayap, Sungai** ≈ Borneo, N Indonesia
Sesdlets *see* Siedlce
79 N17 **Sese** Orientale, N Dem. Rep. Congo
81 F18 **Sese Islands** *island group* S Uganda
83 H16 **Sesheke** *var.* Sesheko. Western, SE Zambia
Sesheko *see* Sesheke
106 C8 **Sesia** *anc.* Sessites. ≈ NW Italy
104 F11 **Sesimbra** Setúbal, S Portugal
115 N22 **Seskló** *island* Dodekánisos, Greece, Aegean Sea
30 L16 **Sesser** Illinois, N USA
Sessites *see* Sesia
106 G11 **Sesto Fiorentino** Toscana, C Italy
106 E7 **Sesto San Giovanni** Lombardia, N Italy
106 A8 **Sestriere** Piemonte, NE Italy
106 D10 **Sestri Levante** Liguria, NW Italy
107 C20 **Sestu** Sardegna, Italy, C Mediterranean Sea
112 E8 **Sesvete** Zagreb, N Croatia
118 G12 **Šeta** Kaunas, C Lithuania
Setabis *see* Xátiva
165 Q4 **Setana** Hokkaidō, NE Japan
103 Q16 **Sète** *prev.* Cette. Hérault, S France
58 J11 **Sete Ilhas** Amapá, NE Brazil
59 L20 **Sete Lagoas** Minas Gerais, NE Brazil
60 G10 **Sete Quedas, Ilha das** *island* S Brazil
92 I10 **Setermoen** Troms, N Norway
95 E17 **Setesdal** *valley* S Norway
43 W16 **Setetule, Cerro** ▲ SE Panama
21 Q5 **Seth** West Virginia, NE USA
Setia *see* Sezze
74 K5 **Sétif** *var.* Stif. N Algeria
164 L13 **Seto** Aichi, Honshū, SW Japan
164 G13 **Seto-naikai** *Eng.* Inland Sea. *sea* S Japan
165 V16 **Setouchi** *var.* Setoushi. Kagoshima, Amami-Ō-shima, SW Japan
74 F6 **Settat** W Morocco
79 D20 **Setté Cama** Ogooué-Maritime, SW Gabon
11 W13 **Setting Lake** ◎ Manitoba, C Canada
97 L16 **Settle** N England, UK
189 Y12 **Settlement** E Wake Island
104 F11 **Setúbal** *Eng.* Saint Ubes, Saint Yves. Setúbal, W Portugal
104 F11 **Setúbal** ◈ *district* S Portugal
104 F12 **Setúbal, Baía de** *bay* W Portugal
Setul *see* Satun
12 B10 **Seul, Lac** ◎ Ontario, S Canada
103 R8 **Seurre** Côte d'Or, C France
137 U11 **Sevan** C Armenia
137 V12 **Sevana Lich** *Eng.* Lake Sevan, *Rus.* Ozero Sevan. ◎ E Armenia
Sevan, Lake/Sevan, Ozero *see* Sevana Lich
77 N11 **Sévaré** Mopti, C Mali
117 S14 **Sevastopol'** *Eng.* Sebastopol. Respublika Krym, S Ukraine
25 R14 **Seven Sisters** Texas, SW USA
10 K13 **Seven Sisters Peaks** ▲ British Columbia, SW Canada
99 M15 **Sevenum** Limburg, SE Netherlands
103 P14 **Séverac-le-Château** Aveyron, S France
14 H13 **Severn** ≈ Ontario, S Canada
97 L21 **Severn** *Wel.* Hafren. ≈ England/Wales, UK
127 O11 **Severnaya Dvina** *var.* Northern Dvina. ≈ NW Russian Federation
127 N16 **Severnaya Osetiya-Alaniya, Respublika** *Eng.* North Ossetia; *prev.* Respublika Severnaya Osetiya, Severo-Osetinskaya SSR. ◈ *autonomous republic* SW Russian Federation
Severnaya Osetiya, Respublika *see* Severnaya Osetiya-Alaniya Respublika
122 M5 **Severnaya Zemlya** *var.* Nicholas II Land. *island group* N Russian Federation
127 T5 **Severnoye** Orenburgskaya Oblast', W Russian Federation
35 S3 **Severn Troughs Range** ⛰ Nevada, W USA
125 W3 **Severnyy** Respublika Komi, NW Russian Federation
144 I13 **Severnyy Chink Ustyurta** ⛰ W Kazakhstan
127 Q13 **Severnyye Uvaly** *var.* Northern Ural Hills. *hill range* NW Russian Federation
145 O6 **Severnyy Kazakhstan** *off.* Severo-Kazakhstanskaya Oblast', *var.* North Kazakhstan, *Kaz.* Soltüstik Qazaqstan Oblysy. ◈ *province* N Kazakhstan
127 V9 **Severnyy Ural** ⛰ NW Russian Federation
Severo-Alichurskiy Khrebet *see* Alichuri Shimolí, Qatorkŭhi
123 N12 **Severobaykal'sk** Respublika Buryatiya, S Russian Federation
Severodonetsk *see* Syeverodonets'k
124 M8 **Severodvinsk** *prev.* Molotov, Sudostroy. Arkhangel'skaya Oblast', NW Russian Federation
Severo-Kazakhstanskaya Oblast' *see* Severnyy Kazakhstan
123 U11 **Severo-Kuril'sk** Sakhalinskaya Oblast', SE Russian Federation
124 J3 **Severomorsk** Murmanskaya Oblast', NW Russian Federation
Severo-Osetinskaya SSR *see* Severnaya Osetiya-Alaniya, Respublika
122 M7 **Severo-Sibirskaya Nizmennost'** *var.* North Siberian Plain, *Eng.* North Siberian Lowland. *lowlands* N Russian Federation
122 G10 **Severoural'sk** Sverdlovskaya Oblast', C Russian Federation
122 L11 **Severo-Yeniseyskiy** Krasnoyarskiy Kray, C Russian Federation
122 J12 **Seversk** Tomskaya Oblast', C Russian Federation
126 M11 **Severskiy Donets** *Ukr.* Sivers'kyy Donets'. ≈ Russian Federation/Ukraine *see also* Sivers'kyy Donets'
92 M9 **Sevettijärvi** Lappi, N Finland
36 M5 **Sevier Bridge Reservoir** ⊞ Utah, W USA
36 J4 **Sevier Desert** *plain* Utah, W USA
36 J5 **Sevier Lake** ◎ Utah, W USA
21 N9 **Sevierville** Tennessee, S USA
104 J14 **Sevilla** *Eng.* Seville; *anc.* Hispalis. Andalucía, SW Spain
104 J13 **Sevilla** ◈ *province* Andalucía, SW Spain
Sevilla de Niefang *see* Niefang
43 O16 **Sevilla, Isla** *island* SW Panama
Seville *see* Sevilla
114 J9 **Sevlievo** Gabrovo, N Bulgaria
Sevluš/Sevlyush *see* Vynohradiv
109 V11 **Sevnica** *Ger.* Lichtenwald. E Slovenia
126 I7 **Sevsk** Bryanskaya Oblast', W Russian Federation
76 J15 **Sewa** ≈ E Sierra Leone
39 R12 **Seward** Alaska, USA
29 R15 **Seward** Nebraska, C USA
10 G8 **Seward Glacier** *glacier* Yukon Territory, W Canada
197 Q3 **Seward Peninsula** *peninsula* Alaska, USA
Seward's Folly *see* Alaska
62 H12 **Sewell** Libertador, C Chile
98 K5 **Sexbierum** *Fris.* Seisbierrum. Friesland, N Netherlands
11 O13 **Sexsmith** Alberta, W Canada
41 W13 **Seybaplaya** Campeche, SE Mexico
173 N6 **Seychelles** *off.* Republic of Seychelles. ◆ *republic* W Indian Ocean
173 N6 **Seychelles Bank** *var.* Le Banc des Seychelles. *undersea feature* W Indian Ocean
Seychelles, Le Banc des *see* Seychelles Bank
172 H17 **Seychellois, Morne** ▲ Mahé, NE Seychelles
92 L2 **Seydhisfjördhur** Austurland, E Iceland
146 J12 **Seýdi** *Rus.* Seydi; *prev.* Neftezavodsk. Lebap Welaýaty, E Turkmenistan
136 G16 **Seydişehir** Konya, SW Turkey
136 J13 **Seyfe Gölü** ◎ C Turkey
Seyhan *see* Adana
136 K16 **Seyhan Barajı** ⊞ S Turkey
136 K17 **Seyhan Nehri** ≈ S Turkey
136 F13 **Seyitgazi** Eskişehir, W Turkey
126 J7 **Seym** ≈ W Russian Federation
117 S3 **Seym** ≈ N Ukraine
123 T9 **Seymchan** Magadanskaya Oblast', E Russian Federation
114 N12 **Seymen** Tekirdağ, NW Turkey
183 O11 **Seymour** Victoria, SE Australia
83 I25 **Seymour** Eastern Cape, S South Africa
29 W16 **Seymour** Iowa, C USA
27 U7 **Seymour** Missouri, C USA
25 Q5 **Seymour** Texas, SW USA
114 M12 **Şeytan Deresi** ≈ NW Turkey
109 S12 **Sežana** *It.* Sesana. SW Slovenia
103 P5 **Sézanne** Marne, N France
107 I16 **Sezze** *anc.* Setia. Lazio, C Italy
115 H25 **Sfákia** Kríti, Greece, E Mediterranean Sea
115 D21 **Sfaktiría** *island* S Greece
116 J11 **Sfântu Gheorghe** *Ger.* Sankt-Georgen, *Hung.* Sepsiszentgyörgy; *prev.* Şepşi-Sângeorz, Sfîntu Gheorghe. Covasna, C Romania
117 N13 **Sfântu Gheorghe, Braţul** *var.* Gheorghe Braţul. ≈ E Romania
75 N6 **Sfax** *Ar.* Şafāqis. E Tunisia
75 N6 **Sfax** ✕ E Tunisia
Sfîntu Gheorghe *see* Sfântu Gheorghe
98 H13 **'s-Gravendeel** Zuid-Holland, SW Netherlands
98 F11 **'s-Gravenhage** *var.* Den Haag, *Eng.* The Hague, *Fr.* La Haye. ● (Netherlands-seat of government) Zuid-Holland, W Netherlands
98 G12 **'s-Gravenzande** Zuid-Holland, W Netherlands
Shaan/Shaanxi Sheng *see* Shaanxi

◆ Country
● Country Capital
◇ Dependent Territory
○ Dependent Territory Capital
◈ Administrative Region
✕ International Airport
▲ Mountain
⛰ Mountain Range
※ Volcano
≈ River
◎ Lake
⊞ Reservoir

159 X11 **Shaanxi** var. Shaan, Shaanxi Sheng, Shan-hsi, Shenshi, Shensi. ◆ province C China
Shaartuz see Shahrtuz
Shabani see Zvishavane
81 N17 **Shabeellaha Dhexe** off. Gobolka Shabeellaha Dhexe. ◆ region E Somalia
81 L17 **Shabeellaha Hoose** off. Gobolka Shabeellaha Hoose. ◆ region S Somalia
Shabeelle, Webi see Shebeli
114 O7 **Shabla** Dobrich, NE Bulgaria
114 O7 **Shabla, Nos** headland NE Bulgaria
13 N9 **Shabogama Lake** ◎ Newfoundland and Labrador, E Canada
79 N20 **Shabunda** Sud Kivu, E Dem. Rep. Congo
141 Q15 **Shabwah** C Yemen
158 F8 **Shache** var. Yarkant. Xinjiang Uygur Zizhiqu, NW China
Shacheng see Huailai
195 R12 **Shackleton Coast** physical region Antarctica
195 Z10 **Shackleton Ice Shelf** ice shelf Antarctica
Shaddādī see Ash Shadādah
28 K7 **Shadehill Reservoir** ▣ South Dakota, N USA
122 G11 **Shadrinsk** Kurganskaya Oblast', C Russian Federation
31 O12 **Shafer, Lake** ▣ Indiana, N USA
35 R13 **Shafter** California, W USA
24 J11 **Shafter** Texas, SW USA
97 L23 **Shaftesbury** S England, UK
185 F22 **Shag** ≈ South Island, NZ
145 V9 **Shagan** ≈ E Kazakhstan
39 O11 **Shageluk** Alaska, USA
122 K14 **Shagonar** Respublika Tyva, S Russian Federation
185 F22 **Shag Point** headland South Island, NZ
144 J12 **Shagyray, Plato** plain SW Kazakhstan
Shāhābād see Eslāmābād
168 K9 **Shah Alam** Selangor, Peninsular Malaysia
117 O12 **Shahany, Ozero** ◎ SW Ukraine
138 H9 **Shahbā'** anc. Philippopolis. As Suwaydā', S Syria
Shahbān see Ad Dayr
149 P17 **Shāhbandar** Sind, SE Pakistan
149 P13 **Shāhdād Kot** Sind, SW Pakistan
143 T10 **Shahdād, Namakzār-e** salt pan E Iran
149 Q15 **Shāhdādpur** Sind, SE Pakistan
154 K10 **Shahdol** Madhya Pradesh, C India
161 N7 **Sha He** ≈ C China
Shahepu see Linze
153 N13 **Shāhganj** Uttar Pradesh, N India
152 C11 **Shāhgarh** Rājasthān, NW India
Sha Hi see Orūmīyeh, Daryācheh-ye, Iran
Shāhī see Qā'emshahr, Māzandarān, Iran
139 Q6 **Shāhimah** var. Shahma. C Iraq
Shahjahanabad see Delhi
152 L11 **Shāhjahānpur** Uttar Pradesh, N India
Shahma see Shāhimah
149 U7 **Shāhpur** Punjab, E Pakistan
Shāhpur see Shāhpur Chākar
152 G13 **Shāhpura** Rājasthān, N India
149 Q15 **Shāhpur Chākar** var. Shāhpur. Sind, SE Pakistan
148 M5 **Shahrak** Ghowr, C Afghanistan
143 Q11 **Shahr-e Bābak** Kermān, C Iran
143 N8 **Shahr-e Kord** var. Shahr Kord. Chahār Maḩall va Bakhtīārī, C Iran
143 O9 **Shahreẕā** var. Qomisheh, Qumisheh, Shahriza; prev. Qomsheh. Eşfahān, C Iran
147 N12 **Shahrisabz** Rus. Shakhrisabz. Qashqadaryo Viloyati, S Uzbekistan
147 P11 **Shahriston** Rus. Shakhristan. NW Tajikistan
Shahriza see Shahreẕā
Shahr-i-Zabul see Zābol
Shahr Kord see Shahr-e Kord
147 P14 **Shahrtuz** Rus. Shaartuz. SW Tajikistan
143 Q4 **Shāhrūd** prev. Emāmrūd, Emāmshahr. Semnān, N Iran
Shahsavār/Shahsawar see Tonekābon
Shaidara see Step' Nardara
Shaikh Ābid see Shaykh 'Ābid
Shaikh Fāris see Shaykh Fāris
Shaikh Najm see Shaykh Najm
138 K5 **Sha'īr, Jabal** ▲ C Syria
154 G10 **Shājāpur** Madhya Pradesh, C India
80 J8 **Shakal, Ras** headland NE Sudan
83 G17 **Shakawe** Ngamiland, N Botswana
Shakhdarinskiy Khrebet see Shokhdara, Qatorkŭhi
Shakhrikhan see Sharixon
Shakhrisabz see Shahrisabz
Shakhristan see Shahriston
117 X8 **Shakhtars'k** Rus. Shakhtërsk. Donets'ka Oblast', SE Ukraine
Shakhtërsk see Shakhtars'k
145 R10 **Shakhtinsk** Karaganda, C Kazakhstan
126 L11 **Shakhty** Rostovskaya Oblast', SW Russian Federation
127 P2 **Shakhun'ya** Nizhegorodskaya Oblast', W Russian Federation
77 S15 **Shaki** Oyo, W Nigeria
81 J15 **Shakīso** Oromo, C Ethiopia
117 X8 **Shakmars'k** Donets'ka Oblast', E Ukraine
29 V9 **Shakopee** Minnesota, N USA
165 R3 **Shakotan-misaki** headland Hokkaidō, NE Japan
39 N9 **Shaktoolik** Alaska, USA
81 J14 **Shala Hāyk'** ◎ C Ethiopia
124 M10 **Shalakusha** Arkhangel'skaya Oblast', NW Russian Federation
145 U8 **Shalday** Pavlodar, NE Kazakhstan
127 P16 **Shali** Chechenskaya Respublika, SW Russian Federation
141 W12 **Shalim** var. Shelim. S Oman
Shaliuhe see Gangca
144 K12 **Shalkar** var. Chelkar. Aktyubinsk, W Kazakhstan
144 F9 **Shalkar, Ozero** prev. Chelkar, Ozero. ◎ W Kazakhstan
21 V12 **Shallotte** North Carolina, SE USA
25 N5 **Shallowater** Texas, SW USA
124 K11 **Shal'skiy** Respublika Kareliya, NW Russian Federation
160 F9 **Shaluli Shan** ▲ C China
81 F22 **Shama** ≈ C Tanzania
11 Z11 **Shamattawa** Manitoba, C Canada
12 F8 **Shamattawa** ≈ Ontario, C Canada
Shām, Bādiyat ash see Syrian Desert
Shamiya see Ash Shāmīyah
141 X8 **Shām, Jabal ash** var. Jebel Sham. ▲ NW Oman
Sham, Jebel see Shām, Jabal ash
Shamkhor see Şämkir
18 G14 **Shamokin** Pennsylvania, NE USA
25 P2 **Shamrock** Texas, SW USA
Sha'nabī, Jabal ash see Chambi, Jebel
139 Y12 **Shanāwah** E Iraq
Shancheng see Taining
159 T8 **Shandan** Gansu, N China
Shandī see Shendi
161 Q5 **Shandong** var. Lu, Shandong Sheng, Shantung. ◆ province E China
161 R4 **Shandong Bandao** var. Shantung Peninsula. peninsula E China
Shandong Peninsula see Shandong Bandao
Shandong Sheng see Shandong
139 U8 **Shandrūkh** E Iraq
83 J17 **Shangani** ≈ W Zimbabwe
161 O15 **Shangchuan Dao** island S China
Shangchuankou see Minhe
163 P12 **Shangdu** Nei Mongol Zizhiqu, N China
161 O11 **Shanggao** var. Aoyang. Jiangxi, S China
161 S8 **Shanghai** var. Shang-hai. Shanghai Shi, E China
Shanghai see Shanghai Shi
161 S8 **Shanghai Shi** var. Hu, Shanghai. ◆ municipality E China
161 P13 **Shanghang** Fujian, SE China
160 K14 **Shanglin** var. Dafeng. Guangxi Zhuangzu Zizhiqu, S China
83 G15 **Shangombo** Western, W Zambia
Shangpai see Feixi
161 O6 **Shangqiu** var. Zhuji. Henan, C China
161 Q10 **Shangrao** Jiangxi, S China
161 S9 **Shangyu** var. Baiguan. Zhejiang, SE China
163 X9 **Shangzhi** Heilongjiang, NE China
160 L7 **Shangzhou** var. Shang Xian. Shaanxi, C China
163 W9 **Shanhetun** Heilongjiang, NE China
Shan-hsi see Shaanxi, China
Shan-hsi see Shanxi, China
159 O6 **Shankou** Xinjiang Uygur Zizhiqu, W China
184 M13 **Shannon** Manawatu-Wanganui, North Island, NZ
97 B19 **Shannon** ✕ W Ireland
97 C17 **Shannon** Ir. An tSionainn. ≈ W Ireland
167 N6 **Shan Plateau** plateau E Burma
158 M6 **Shanshan** var. Piqan. Xinjiang Uygur Zizhiqu, NW China
Shansi see Shanxi
167 N5 **Shan State** ◆ state E Burma
Shantar Islands see Shantarskiye Ostrova
123 S12 **Shantarskiye Ostrova** Eng. Shantar Islands. island group E Russian Federation
161 Q14 **Shantou** var. Shan-t'ou, Swatow. Guangdong, S China
Shantung see Shandong
Shantung Peninsula see Shandong Bandao
163 O14 **Shanxi** var. Jin, Shan-hsi, Shansi, Shanxi Sheng. ◆ province C China
Shan Xian see Sanmenxia
161 P6 **Shanxian** var. Shan Xian. Shandong, E China
Shanxi Sheng see Shanxi
160 L7 **Shanyang** Shaanxi, C China
161 N13 **Shanyin** var. Daiyue. Shanxi, C China
161 O13 **Shaoguan** var. Shao-kuan, Cant. Kukong; prev. Ch'u-chiang. Guangdong, S China
Shao-kuan see Shaoguan
161 Q11 **Shaowu** Fujian, SE China
161 S9 **Shaoxing** Zhejiang, SE China
160 M12 **Shaoyang** var. Tangdukou. Hunan, S China
160 M11 **Shaoyang** var. Baoqing, Shao-yang; prev. Pao-king. Hunan, S China
96 K5 **Shapinsay** island NE Scotland, UK
127 S4 **Shapkina** ≈ NW Russian Federation
Shāpūr see Salmās
158 M4 **Shaqiuhe** Xinjiang Uygur Zizhiqu, W China
139 T2 **Shaqlāwa** var. Shaqlāwah. E Iraq
Shaqlāwah see Shaqlāwa
138 I8 **Shaqqā** As Suwaydā', S Syria
141 P7 **Shaqrā'** Ar Riyāḑ, C Saudi Arabia
Shaqrā see Shuqrah
145 W10 **Shar** var. Charsk. Vostochnyy Kazakhstan, E Kazakhstan
149 O6 **Sharan** Urūzgān, SE Afghanistan
Sharaqpur see Sharqpur
Sharbaqty see Shcherbakty
141 X12 **Sharbatāt** S Oman
141 X12 **Sharbithāt, Ras** var. Ra's Sharbatāt. headland S Oman
14 K14 **Sharbot Lake** Ontario, SE Canada
145 P17 **Shardara** var. Chardara. Yuzhnyy Kazakhstan, S Kazakhstan
Shardara Dalasy see Step' Nardara
162 F8 **Sharga** Govĭ-Altay, W Mongolia
162 H6 **Sharga** Hövsgöl, N Mongolia
116 M7 **Sharhorod** Vinnyts'ka Oblast', C Ukraine
162 K10 **Sharhulsan** Ömnögovĭ, S Mongolia
165 V3 **Shari** Hokkaidō, NE Japan
Shari see Chari
139 T6 **Shārī, Buḩayrat** ◎ C Iraq
147 S10 **Sharixon** Rus. Shakhrikhan. Andijon Viloyati, E Uzbekistan
Sharjah see Ash Shāriqah
118 K12 **Sharkawshchyna** var. Sharkowshchyna, Pol. Szarkowszczyzna, Rus. Sharkovshchina. Vitsyebskaya Voblasts', NW Belarus
180 G9 **Shark Bay** bay Western Australia
141 Y9 **Sharkh** E Oman
Sharkovshchina/Sharkowshchyna see Sharkawshchyna
127 U6 **Sharlyk** Orenburgskaya Oblast', W Russian Federation
Sharm ash Shaykh see Sharm el Sheikh
75 Y9 **Sharm el Sheikh** var. Ofiral, Sharm ash Shaykh. E Egypt
18 B13 **Sharon** Pennsylvania, NE USA
26 H4 **Sharon Springs** Kansas, C USA
31 Q14 **Sharonville** Ohio, N USA
Sharourah see Sharūrah
29 O10 **Sharpe, Lake** ▣ South Dakota, N USA
Sharqī, Al Jabal ash/Sharqi, Jebel esh see Anti-Lebanon
Sharqīyah, Al Minṭaqah ash see Ash Sharqīyah
133 I6 **Sharqīyat an Nabk, Jabal** ▲ W Syria
149 W8 **Sharqpur** var. Sharaqpur. Punjab, E Pakistan
141 Q13 **Sharūrah** var. Sharourah. Najrān, S Saudi Arabia
125 O14 **Shar'ya** Kostromskaya Oblast', NW Russian Federation
145 V15 **Sharyn** var. Charyn. ≈ SE Kazakhstan
Sharyn see Charyn
83 J18 **Shashe** Central, NE Botswana
83 J18 **Shashe** var. Shashi. ≈ Botswana/Zimbabwe
81 J14 **Shashemenē** var. Shashemene, Shashhamana, It. Sciasciamana. Oromo, C Ethiopia
Shashemenne/Shashhamana see Shashemenē
Shashi see Shashe
Shashi/Sha-shih/Shasi see Jingzhou, Hubei
35 N3 **Shasta Lake** ▣ California, W USA
35 N2 **Shasta, Mount** ▲ California, W USA
127 O4 **Shatki** Nizhegorodskaya Oblast', W Russian Federation
Shatlyk see Şatlyk
Shatra see Ash Shaṭrah
119 K17 **Shatsk** Rus. Shatsk. Minskaya Voblasts', C Belarus
127 N5 **Shatsk** Ryazanskaya Oblast', W Russian Federation
26 J9 **Shattuck** Oklahoma, C USA
145 P16 **Shaul'der** Yuzhnyy Kazakhstan, S Kazakhstan
11 S17 **Shaunavon** Saskatchewan, S Canada
Shavat see Shovot
158 K4 **Shawan** Xinjiang Uygur Zizhiqu, NW China
14 G12 **Shawanaga** Ontario, S Canada
30 M6 **Shawano** Wisconsin, N USA
30 M6 **Shawano Lake** ◎ Wisconsin, N USA
15 P10 **Shawinigan** prev. Shawinigan Falls. Québec, SE Canada
Shawinigan Falls see Shawinigan
15 P10 **Shawinigan-Sud** Québec, SE Canada
138 J5 **Shawmarīyah, Jabal ash** ▲ C Syria
27 O11 **Shawnee** Oklahoma, C USA
14 K12 **Shawville** Québec, SE Canada
145 Q16 **Shayan** var. Chayan. Yuzhnyy Kazakhstan, S Kazakhstan
Shaykh see Ash Shakk
139 W9 **Shaykh 'Ābid** var. Shaikh Ābid. E Iraq
139 Y10 **Shaykh Fāris** var. Shaikh Fāris. E Iraq
139 T7 **Shaykh Ḩātim** E Iraq
Shaykh, Jabal ash see Hermon, Mount
139 X10 **Shaykh Najm** var. Shaikh Najm. E Iraq
139 W9 **Shaykh Sa'd** E Iraq
147 T14 **Shazud** SE Tajikistan
119 N18 **Shchadryn** Rus. Shchedrin. Homyel'skaya Voblasts', SE Belarus
119 H18 **Shchara** ≈ SW Belarus
Shchedrin see Shchadryn
Shcheglovsk see Kemerovo
126 K5 **Shchëkino** Tul'skaya Oblast', W Russian Federation
125 S7 **Shchel'yayur** Respublika Komi, NW Russian Federation
145 U8 **Shcherbakty** Kaz. Sharbaqty. Pavlodar, E Kazakhstan
126 K7 **Shchigry** Kurskaya Oblast', W Russian Federation
Shchitkovichi see Shchytkavichy
117 Q2 **Shchors** Chernihivs'ka Oblast', N Ukraine
117 T8 **Shchors'k** Dnipropetrovs'ka Oblast', E Ukraine
Shchuchin see Shchuchyn
145 Q7 **Shchuchinsk** prev. Shchuchye. Akmola, N Kazakhstan
Shchuchye see Shchuchinsk
119 G16 **Shchuchyn** Pol. Szczuczyn Nowogródzki, Rus. Shchuchin. Hrodzyenskaya Voblasts', W Belarus
119 K17 **Shchytkavichy** Rus. Shchitkovichi. Minskaya Voblasts', C Belarus
122 J13 **Shebalino** Respublika Altay, S Russian Federation
126 J9 **Shebekino** Belgorodskaya Oblast', W Russian Federation
Shebelē Wenz, Wabē see Shebeli
81 L14 **Shebeli** Amh. Wabē Shebelē Wenz, It. Scebeli, Som. Webi Shabeelle. ≈ Ethiopia/Somalia
113 M20 **Shebenikut, Maja e** ▲ E Albania
149 N2 **Sheberghān** var. Shibarghān, Shiberghan, Shiberghān. Jowzjān, N Afghanistan
144 F14 **Shebir** Mangistau, SW Kazakhstan
31 N8 **Sheboygan** Wisconsin, N USA
77 X15 **Shebshi Mountains** var. Schebschi Mountains. ▲ E Nigeria
Shechem see Nablus
Shedadi see Ash Shadādah
13 P14 **Shediac** New Brunswick, SE Canada
126 L15 **Shedok** Krasnodarskiy Kray, SW Russian Federation
80 N12 **Sheekh** Woqooyi Galbeed, N Somalia
38 M11 **Sheenjek River** ≈ Alaska, USA
96 D13 **Sheep Haven** Ir. Cuan na gCaorach. inlet N Ireland
35 X10 **Sheep Range** ▲ Nevada, W USA
98 M13 **'s-Heerenberg** Gelderland, E Netherlands
97 P22 **Sheerness** SE England, UK
13 Q15 **Sheet Harbour** Nova Scotia, SE Canada
185 H18 **Sheffield** Canterbury, South Island, NZ
97 M18 **Sheffield** N England, UK
23 O2 **Sheffield** Alabama, S USA
29 V12 **Sheffield** Iowa, C USA
25 N10 **Sheffield** Texas, SW USA
63 H22 **Shehuen, Río** ≈ S Argentina
Shekhem see Nablus
149 V8 **Shekhūpura** Punjab, NE Pakistan
Sheki see Şäki
124 L14 **Sheksna** Vologodskaya Oblast', NW Russian Federation
123 T5 **Shelagskiy, Mys** headland NE Russian Federation
27 V3 **Shelbina** Missouri, C USA
13 P16 **Shelburne** Nova Scotia, SE Canada
14 G14 **Shelburne** Ontario, S Canada
33 R7 **Shelby** Montana, NW USA
21 Q10 **Shelby** North Carolina, SE USA
31 S12 **Shelby** Ohio, N USA
30 L14 **Shelbyville** Illinois, N USA
31 P14 **Shelbyville** Indiana, N USA
20 L5 **Shelbyville** Kentucky, S USA
27 V2 **Shelbyville** Missouri, C USA
20 J10 **Shelbyville** Tennessee, S USA
25 X8 **Shelbyville** Texas, SW USA
30 L14 **Shelbyville, Lake** ▣ Illinois, N USA
29 S12 **Sheldon** Iowa, C USA
38 M11 **Sheldons Point** Alaska, USA
Shelekhov Gulf see Shelikhova, Zaliv
123 U9 **Shelikhova, Zaliv** Eng. Shelekhov Gulf. gulf E Russian Federation
39 P14 **Shelikof Strait** strait Alaska, USA
Shelim see Shalīm
11 T14 **Shellbrook** Saskatchewan, S Canada
28 L3 **Shell Creek** ≈ North Dakota, N USA
Shellif see Chelif, Oued
22 I10 **Shell Keys** island group Louisiana, S USA
30 I4 **Shell Lake** Wisconsin, N USA
29 W12 **Shell Rock** Iowa, C USA
185 C26 **Shelter Point** headland Stewart Island, NZ
18 L13 **Shelton** Connecticut, NE USA
32 G8 **Shelton** Washington, NW USA
Shemakha see Şamaxı
145 W9 **Shemonaikha** Vostochnyy Kazakhstan, E Kazakhstan
127 Q4 **Shemursha** Chuvashskaya Respublika, W Russian Federation
38 D16 **Shemya Island** island Aleutian Islands, Alaska, USA
29 T16 **Shenandoah** Iowa, C USA
21 U4 **Shenandoah** Virginia, NE USA
21 U4 **Shenandoah Mountains** ridge West Virginia, NE USA
21 V3 **Shenandoah River** ≈ West Virginia, NE USA
77 W15 **Shendam** Plateau, C Nigeria
80 G8 **Shendi** var. Shandī. River Nile, NE Sudan
76 I15 **Shenge** SW Sierra Leone
146 L10 **Shengeldi** Rus. Chingildi. Navoiy Viloyati, N Uzbekistan
145 U15 **Shengel'dy** Almaty, SE Kazakhstan
113 K18 **Shëngjin** var. Shëngjini. Lezhë, NW Albania
Shëngjini see Shëngjin
Shengking see Liaoning
Sheng Xian/Shengxian see Shengzhou
161 S9 **Shengzhou** var. Shengxian, Sheng Xian. Zhejiang, SE China
Shenking see Liaoning
125 N11 **Shenkursk** Arkhangel'skaya Oblast', NW Russian Federation
160 L3 **Shenmu** Shaanxi, C China
113 L19 **Shën Noj i Madh** ▲ C Albania
160 L8 **Shennong Ding** var. Dashennongjia. ▲ C China
Shenshi/Shensi see Shaanxi
163 V12 **Shenyang** Chin. Shen-yang, Eng. Moukden, Mukden; prev. Fengtien. Liaoning, NE China
161 O15 **Shenzhen** Guangdong, S China
154 G8 **Sheopur** Madhya Pradesh, C India
116 L5 **Shepetivka** Rus. Shepetovka. Khmel'nyts'ka Oblast', NW Ukraine
Shepetovka see Shepetivka
25 W10 **Shepherd** Texas, SW USA
187 R14 **Shepherd Islands** island group C Vanuatu
20 K5 **Shepherdsville** Kentucky, S USA
183 O11 **Shepparton** Victoria, SE Australia
97 P22 **Sheppey, Isle of** island SE England, UK
Sherabad see Sherobod
9 O4 **Sherard, Cape** headland Nunavut, N Canada
97 L23 **Sherborne** S England, UK
76 H16 **Sherbro Island** island SW Sierra Leone
15 Q12 **Sherbrooke** Québec, SE Canada
29 T11 **Sherburn** Minnesota, N USA
78 H6 **Sherda** Borkou-Ennedi-Tibesti, N Chad
80 G7 **Shereik** River Nile, N Sudan
126 K3 **Sheremet'yevo** ✕ (Moskva) Moskovskaya Oblast', W Russian Federation
153 P14 **Shergāti** Bihār, N India
27 U12 **Sheridan** Arkansas, C USA
33 W12 **Sheridan** Wyoming, C USA
182 G8 **Sheringa** South Australia
25 U5 **Sherman** Texas, SW USA
194 J10 **Sherman Island** island Antarctica
19 S4 **Sherman Mills** Maine, NE USA
29 O15 **Sherman Reservoir** ▣ Nebraska, C USA
147 N14 **Sherobod** Rus. Sherabad. Surxondaryo Viloyati, S Uzbekistan
147 O13 **Sherobod** Rus. Sherabad. ≈ S Uzbekistan
153 T14 **Sherpur** Dhaka, N Bangladesh
37 T4 **Sherrelwood** Colorado, C USA
99 J14 **'s-Hertogenbosch** Fr. Bois-le-Duc, Ger. Herzogenbusch. Noord-Brabant, S Netherlands
28 M2 **Sherwood** North Dakota, N USA
11 Q14 **Sherwood Park** Alberta, SW Canada
56 F13 **Sheshea, Río** ≈ E Peru
143 T5 **Sheshtamad** Khorāsān, NE Iran
29 S10 **Shetek, Lake** ◎ Minnesota, N USA
96 M2 **Shetland Islands** island group NE Scotland, UK
144 F14 **Shetpe** Mangistau, SW Kazakhstan
154 C11 **Shetrunji** ≈ W India
Shevchenko see Aktau
117 W5 **Shevchenkove** Kharkivs'ka Oblast', E Ukraine
81 H14 **Shewa Gīmīra** Southern, S Ethiopia
161 Q9 **Shexian** var. Huicheng, She Xian. Anhui, E China
161 R6 **Sheyang** prev. Hede. Jiangsu, E China
29 O4 **Sheyenne** North Dakota, N USA
29 P4 **Sheyenne River** ≈ North Dakota, N USA
96 G7 **Shiant Islands** island group NW Scotland, UK
123 U12 **Shiashkotan, Ostrov** island Kuril'skiye Ostrova, SE Russian Federation
31 R9 **Shiawassee River** ≈ Michigan, N USA
141 R14 **Shibām** C Yemen
Shibarghān see Sheberghān
165 O10 **Shibata** var. Sibata. Niigata, Honshū, C Japan
Shiberghan/Shiberghān see Sheberghān
Shibh Jazīrat Sīnā' see Sinai
Shibīn al Kawm see Shibīn el Kôm
75 W8 **Shibîn el Kôm** var. Shibīn al Kawm. N Egypt
143 O13 **Shīb, Kūh-e** ▲ S Iran
12 D8 **Shibogama Lake** ◎ Ontario, C Canada
Shibotsu-jima see Zelënyy, Ostrov
164 B16 **Shibushi** Kagoshima, Kyūshū, SW Japan
189 U13 **Shichiyo Islands** island group Chuuk, C Micronesia
Shickshock Mountains see Chic-Chocs, Monts
145 S8 **Shiderti** var. Shiderty. Pavlodar, NE Kazakhstan
145 S9 **Shiderti** ≈ N Kazakhstan
Shiderty see Shiderti
96 G10 **Shiel, Loch** ◎ N Scotland, UK
164 J13 **Shiga** off. Shiga-ken, var. Siga. ◆ prefecture Honshū, SW Japan
Shigatse see Xigazê
141 U13 **Shiḩan** oasis NE Yemen
Shih-chia-chuang/Shihmen see Shijiazhuang
158 K4 **Shihezi** Xinjiang Uygur Zizhiqu, NW China
Shiichi see Shyichy
113 K19 **Shijak** var. Shijaku. Durrës, W Albania
Shijaku see Shijak
161 O4 **Shijiazhuang** var. Shih-chia-chuang; prev. Shihmen. Hebei, E China
165 R5 **Shikabe** Hokkaidō, NE Japan
149 Q13 **Shikārpur** Sind, S Pakistan
127 Q7 **Shikhany** Saratovskaya Oblast', W Russian Federation
189 V12 **Shiki Islands** island group Chuuk, C Micronesia
164 G14 **Shikoku** var. Sikoku. island SW Japan
192 H5 **Shikoku Basin** var. Sikoku Basin. undersea feature N Philippine Sea
164 G14 **Shikoku-sanchi** ▲ Shikoku, SW Japan
165 X4 **Shikotan, Ostrov** Jap. Shikotan-tō. island NE Russian Federation
Shikotan-tō see Shikotan, Ostrov
165 R4 **Shikotsu-ko** var. Sikotu Ko. ◎ Hokkaidō, NE Japan
81 N15 **Shilabo** Somali, E Ethiopia
127 X7 **Shil'da** Orenburgskaya Oblast', W Russian Federation
139 V3 **Shilēr, Āw-e** ≈ E Iraq
153 S12 **Shiliguri** prev. Siliguri. West Bengal, NE India
Shiliu see Changjiang
131 V7 **Shilka** ≈ S Russian Federation
18 H15 **Shillington** Pennsylvania, NE USA
153 V13 **Shillong** Meghālaya, NE India
126 M5 **Shilovo** Ryazanskaya Oblast', W Russian Federation
164 C14 **Shimabara** var. Simabara. Nagasaki, Kyūshū, SW Japan
164 C14 **Shimabara-wan** bay SW Japan
164 F12 **Shimane** off. Shimane-ken, var. Simane. ◆ prefecture Honshū, SW Japan
164 G11 **Shimane-hantō** peninsula Honshū, SW Japan
123 Q13 **Shimanovsk** Amurskaya Oblast', SE Russian Federation
Shimbir Berris see Shimbiris
80 O12 **Shimbiris** var. Shimbir Berris. ▲ N Somalia
165 T4 **Shimizu** Hokkaidō, NE Japan
164 M14 **Shimizu** var. Simizu. Shizuoka, Honshū, S Japan
152 I8 **Shimla** prev. Simla. Himāchal Pradesh, N India
Shimminato see Shinminato
165 N14 **Shimoda** var. Simoda. Shizuoka, Honshū, S Japan
165 O13 **Shimodate** var. Simodate. Ibaraki, Honshū, S Japan
155 F18 **Shimoga** Karnātaka, W India
164 C15 **Shimo-jima** island SW Japan
164 B15 **Shimo-Koshiki-jima** island SW Japan
81 J21 **Shimoni** Coast, S Kenya
164 D13 **Shimonoseki** var. Simonoseki; hist. Akamagaseki, Bakan. Yamaguchi, Honshū, SW Japan
124 G14 **Shimsk** Novgorodskaya Oblast', NW Russian Federation
141 W7 **Shināş** N Oman
148 J6 **Shīndand** Farāh, W Afghanistan
Shinei see Hsinying
25 T12 **Shiner** Texas, SW USA
167 N1 **Shingbwiyang** Kachin State, N Burma
145 W11 **Shingozha** Vostochnyy Kazakhstan, E Kazakhstan
164 J15 **Shingū** var. Singû. Wakayama, Honshū, SW Japan
14 F8 **Shining Tree** Ontario, S Canada
165 P9 **Shinjō** var. Sinzyô. Yamagata, Honshū, C Japan
96 I7 **Shin, Loch** ◎ N Scotland, UK
21 S3 **Shinnston** West Virginia, NE USA
138 I6 **Shinshār** Fr. Chinnchâr. Ḩimş, W Syria
Shinshū see Chinju
165 T4 **Shintoku** Hokkaidō, NE Japan
81 G20 **Shinyanga** Shinyanga, NW Tanzania
81 G20 **Shinyanga** ◆ region N Tanzania
165 Q10 **Shiogama** var. Siogama. Miyagi, Honshū, C Japan
164 M12 **Shiojiri** var. Sioziri. Nagano, Honshū, S Japan
164 I15 **Shiono-misaki** headland Honshū, SW Japan
165 Q12 **Shioya-zaki** headland Honshū, C Japan
114 J9 **Shipchenski Prokhod** pass C Bulgaria
160 G14 **Shiping** Yunnan, SW China
13 P13 **Shippagan** var. Shippegan. New Brunswick, SE Canada
Shippegan see Shippagan
18 F15 **Shippensburg** Pennsylvania, NE USA
37 O9 **Ship Rock** ▲ New Mexico, SW USA
37 P9 **Shiprock** New Mexico, SW USA
15 R6 **Shipshaw** ≈ Québec, SE Canada
123 V10 **Shipunskiy, Mys** headland E Russian Federation
160 K7 **Shiquan** Shaanxi, C China
122 K13 **Shira** Respublika Khakasiya, S Russian Federation
153 T14 **Shirajganj Ghat** var. Serajgonj, Sirajganj. Rajshahi, C Bangladesh
165 P12 **Shirakawa** var. Sirakawa. Fukushima, Honshū, C Japan
164 M13 **Shirane-san** ▲ Honshū, S Japan
165 U14 **Shiranuka** Hokkaidō, NE Japan
195 N12 **Shirase Coast** physical region Antarctica
165 U3 **Shirataki** Hokkaidō, NE Japan
143 O11 **Shirāz** var. Shīrāz. Fārs, S Iran
83 N15 **Shire** var. Chire. ≈ Malawi/Mozambique
162 G7 **Shiree** Dzavhan, W Mongolia

◆ Country ● Country Capital ◇ Dependent Territory ○ Dependent Territory Capital ◆ Administrative Region ✕ International Airport ▲ Mountain ▲ Mountain Range Volcano ≈ River ◎ Lake ▣ Reservoir

163 O9 **Shireet** Sühbaatar, SE Mongolia
165 W3 **Shiretoko-hantō** headland Hokkaidō, NE Japan
165 W3 **Shiretoko-misaki** headland Hokkaidō, NE Japan
127 N5 **Shiringushi** Respublika Mordoviya, W Russian Federation
148 M3 **Shīrīn Tagāb** Fāryāb, N Afghanistan
149 N2 **Shīrīn Tagāb** ≈ N Afghanistan
165 R6 **Shiriya-zaki** headland Honshū, C Japan
144 I12 **Shirkala, Gryada** plain W Kazakhstan
165 P10 **Shiroishi** var. Siroisi. Miyagi, Honshū, C Japan
Shirokoye see Shyroke
165 O10 **Shirone** var. Sirone. Niigata, Honshū, C Japan
164 L12 **Shirotori** Gifu, Honshū, SW Japan
197 T1 **Shirshov Ridge** undersea feature W Bering Sea
Shirshütür/Shirshyutyur, Peski see Şirşütür Gumy
143 T3 **Shīrvān** var. Shirwān. Khorāsān, NE Iran
Shirwa, Lake see Chilwa, Lake
Shirwān see Shīrvān
159 N5 **Shisanjianfang** Xinjiang Uygur Zizhiqu, W China
38 M16 **Shishaldin Volcano** ▲ Unimak Island, Alaska, USA
Shishchitsy see Shyshchytsy
38 M8 **Shishmaref** Alaska, USA
Shisur see Ash Shişar
164 L13 **Shitara** Aichi, Honshū, SW Japan
152 D12 **Shiv** Rājasthān, NW India
151 E15 **Shivāji Sāgar** prev. Konya Reservoir ⊠ W India
154 H8 **Shivpuri** Madhya Pradesh, C India
36 J9 **Shivwits Plateau** plain Arizona, SW USA
Shiwālik Range see Siwalik Range
160 M8 **Shiyan** Hubei, C China
Shizilu see Junan
160 H13 **Shizong** var. Danfeng. Yunnan, SW China
165 R10 **Shizugawa** Miyagi, Honshū, NE Japan
159 W8 **Shizuishan** var. Dawukou. Ningxia, N China
165 T5 **Shizunai** Hokkaidō, NE Japan
165 M14 **Shizuoka** var. Sizuoka. Shizuoka, Honshū, S Japan
164 M13 **Shizuoka** off. Shizuoka-ken, var. Sizuoka. ◇ prefecture Honshū, S Japan
Shklov see Shklow
119 N15 **Shklow** Rus. Shklov. Mahilyowskaya Voblasts', E Belarus
113 K18 **Shkodër** var. Shkodra, It. Scutari, SCr. Skadar. Shkodër, NW Albania
113 K17 **Shkodër** ◇ district NW Albania
Shkodra see Shkodër
Shkodrës, Liqeni i see Scutari, Lake
Shkumbî/Shkumbin see Shkumbinit, Lumi i
113 L20 **Shkumbinit, Lumi i** var. Shkumbî, Shkumbin. ≈ C Albania
Shligigh, Cuan see Sligo Bay
122 L4 **Shmidta, Ostrov** island Severnaya Zemlya, N Russian Federation
183 S10 **Shoalhaven River** ≈ New South Wales, SE Australia
11 W16 **Shoal Lake** Manitoba, S Canada
31 O15 **Shoals** Indiana, N USA
164 I13 **Shōdo-shima** island SW Japan
Shōka see Changhua
122 M5 **Shokal'skogo, Proliv** strait N Russian Federation
147 T14 **Shokhdara, Qatorkŭhi** Rus. Shakhdarinskiy Khrebet. ⛰ SE Tajikistan
145 P17 **Sholakkorgan** var. Chulakkurgan. Yuzhnyy Kazakhstan, S Kazakhstan
145 N9 **Sholaksay** Kostanay, N Kazakhstan
Sholāpur see Solāpur
Sholdaneshty see Şoldăneşti
Shoqpar see Chokpar
155 G21 **Shoranūr** Kerala, SW India
155 G16 **Shorāpur** Karnātaka, C India
30 M11 **Shorewood** Illinois, N USA
Shorkazakhly, Solonchak see Kazakhlyshor, Solonchak
145 Q9 **Shortandy** Akmola, C Kazakhstan
Shortepa/Shor Tepe see Shūr Tappeh
186 J7 **Shortland Island** var. Alu. island NW Solomon Islands
Shosambetsu see Shosanbetsu
165 S2 **Shosanbetsu** var. Shosambetsu. Hokkaidō, NE Japan
33 O15 **Shoshone** Idaho, NW USA
35 T6 **Shoshone Mountains** ⛰ Nevada, W USA
33 U12 **Shoshone River** ≈ Wyoming, C USA
83 I19 **Shoshong** Central, SE Botswana
33 V14 **Shoshoni** Wyoming, C USA
Shōshū see Sangju
117 S2 **Shostka** Sums'ka Oblast', NE Ukraine
185 C21 **Shotover** ≈ South Island, NZ
146 H9 **Shovot** Rus. Shavat. Xorazm Viloyati, W Uzbekistan
37 N12 **Show Low** Arizona, SW USA
Show Me State see Missouri
125 O4 **Shoyna** Nenetskiy Avtonomnyy Okrug, NW Russian Federation
124 M11 **Shozhma** Arkhangel'skaya Oblast', NW Russian Federation
117 Q7 **Shpola** Cherkas'ka Oblast', N Ukraine
Shqipëria/Shqipërisë, Republika e see Albania
22 G5 **Shreveport** Louisiana, S USA
97 K19 **Shrewsbury** hist. Scrobesbyrig'. W England, UK
152 D11 **Shri Mohangarh** prev. Sri Mohangorh. Rājasthān, NW India
153 S16 **Shrīrāmpur** prev. Serampore, Serampur. West Bengal, NE India
97 K19 **Shropshire** cultural region W England, UK
145 S16 **Shu** Kaz. Shū. Zhambyl, SE Kazakhstan
Shū see Chu
160 G13 **Shuangbai** var. Tuodian. Yunnan, SW China
163 W9 **Shuangcheng** Heilongjiang, NE China
Shuangcheng see Zherong
160 E14 **Shuangjiang** var. Weiyuan. Yunnan, SW China
Shuangjiang see Jiangkou
163 U10 **Shuangliao** var. Zhengjiatun. Jilin, NE China
Shuang-liao see Liaoyuan
163 Y7 **Shuangyashan** var. Shuang-ya-shan. Heilongjiang, NE China
Shu'aymiah see Shu'aymīyah
141 W12 **Shu'aymīyah** var. Shu'aymiah. S Oman
144 I10 **Shubarkuduk** Kaz. Shubarqudyq. Aktyubinsk, W Kazakhstan
Shubarqudyq see Shubarkuduk
145 N12 **Shubar-Tengiz, Ozero** ◎ C Kazakhstan
39 S5 **Shublik Mountains** ⛰ Alaska, USA
Shubrā al Khaymah see Shubrâ el Kheima
121 U13 **Shubrâ el Kheima** var. Shubrā al Khaymah. N Egypt
158 E8 **Shufu** Xinjiang Uygur Zizhiqu, NW China
147 S14 **Shughnon, Qatorkŭhi** Rus. Shugnanskiy Khrebet. ⛰ SE Tajikistan
Shugnanskiy Khrebet see Shughnon, Qatorkŭhi
161 Q6 **Shu He** ≈ E China
Shuiding see Huocheng
Shuidong see Dianbai
Shuiji see Laixi
Shū-Ile Taūlary see Chu-Iliyskiye Gory
Shuiluocheng see Zhuanglang
149 T10 **Shujāābād** Punjab, E Pakistan
159 W8 **Shulan** Jilin, NE China
158 E8 **Shule** Xinjiang Uygur Zizhiqu, NW China
Shuleh see Shule He
159 Q8 **Shule He** var. Shuleh, Sulo. ≈ C China
30 K9 **Shullsburg** Wisconsin, N USA
39 N16 **Shumagin Islands** island group Alaska, USA
146 G7 **Shumanay** Qoraqalpog'iston Respublikasi, W Uzbekistan
114 M8 **Shumen** Shumen, NE Bulgaria
114 M8 **Shumen** ◇ province NE Bulgaria
127 P4 **Shumerlya** Chuvashskaya Respublika, W Russian Federation
122 G11 **Shumikha** Kurganskaya Oblast', C Russian Federation
118 M12 **Shumilina** Rus. Shumilino. Vitsyebskaya Voblasts', NE Belarus
Shumilino see Shumilina
123 V11 **Shumshu, Ostrov** island SE Russian Federation
116 K5 **Shums'k** Ternopil's'ka Oblast', W Ukraine
39 O7 **Shungnak** Alaska, USA
Shunsen see Ch'unch'ŏn
Shuoxian see Shuozhou
161 N3 **Shuozhou** var. Shuoxian. Shanxi, C China
141 P16 **Shuqrah** var. Shaqrā. SW Yemen
Shurab see Shŭrob
147 O14 **Sho'rchi** Rus. Shurchi. Surxondaryo Viloyati, S Uzbekistan
147 R11 **Shŭrob** Rus. Shurab. NW Tajikistan
143 T10 **Shūr, Rūd-e** ≈ E Iran
149 O2 **Shūr Tappeh** var. Shortepa, Shor Tepe. Balkh, N Afghanistan
83 K17 **Shurugwi** prev. Selukwe. Midlands, C Zimbabwe
142 L8 **Shūsh** anc. Susa, Bibl. Shushan. Khūzestān, SW Iran
Shushan see Shūsh
142 L9 **Shūshtar** var. Shustar, Shushter. Khūzestān, SW Iran
Shushter/Shustar see Shūshtar
141 T9 **Shuṭfah, Qalamat** well E Saudi Arabia
139 V9 **Shuwayjah, Hawr ash** var. Hawr as Suwayqiyah. ◎ E Iraq
124 M16 **Shuya** Ivanovskaya Oblast', W Russian Federation
39 Q14 **Shuyak Island** island Alaska, USA
166 M4 **Shwebo** Sagaing, C Burma
166 L7 **Shwedaung** Pegu, W Burma
166 M7 **Shwegyin** Pegu, SW Burma
167 N4 **Shweli** Chin. Longchuan Jiang. ≈ Burma/China
166 M6 **Shwemyo** Mandalay, C Burma
Shyghys Qazagastan Oblysy see Vostochnyy Kazakhstan
Shyghys Qongyrat see Shygys Konyrat
145 T12 **Shygys Konyrat** var. Vostochno-Kounradskiy, Kaz. Shyghys Qongyrat. Karaganda, C Kazakhstan
119 M19 **Shyichy** Rus. Shiichi. Homyel'skaya Voblasts', SE Belarus
145 Q17 **Shymkent** prev. Chimkent. Yuzhnyy Kazakhstan, S Kazakhstan
Shyngghyrlaū see Chingirlau
152 J5 **Shyok** Jammu and Kashmir, NW India
117 S9 **Shyroke** Rus. Shirokoye. Dnipropetrovs'ka Oblast', E Ukraine
117 O9 **Shyryayeve** Odes'ka Oblast', SW Ukraine
117 S5 **Shyshaky** Poltavs'ka Oblast', C Ukraine
119 K17 **Shyshchytsy** Rus. Shishchitsy. Minskaya Voblasts', C Belarus
149 Y3 **Siachen Muztāgh** ⛰ NE Pakistan
Siadehan see Tākestān
148 M13 **Siāhān Range** ⛰ W Pakistan
142 I1 **Siāh Chashmeh** Āžarbāyjān-e Bākhtarī, N Iran
149 W7 **Siālkot** Punjab, NE Pakistan
186 E7 **Sialum** Morobe, C PNG
Siam see Thailand
Siam, Gulf of see Thailand, Gulf of
Sian see Xi'an
Siang see Brahmaputra
Siangtan see Xiangtan
169 N8 **Siantan, Pulau** island Kepulauan Anambas, W Indonesia
54 H11 **Siare, Río** ≈ C Colombia
171 R6 **Siargao Island** island S Philippines
186 F7 **Siassi** Umboi Island, C PNG
115 D14 **Siátista** Dytikí Makedonía, N Greece
166 K4 **Siatlai** Chin State, W Burma
171 P6 **Siaton** Negros, C Philippines
171 P6 **Siaton Point** headland Negros, C Philippines
118 F11 **Šiauliai** Ger. Schaulen. Šiauliai, N Lithuania
118 E11 **Šiauliai** ◇ province N Lithuania
171 Q10 **Siau, Pulau** island N Indonesia
83 J15 **Siavonga** Southern, SE Zambia
Siazan' see Siyäzän
Sibah see As Sibah
107 N20 **Sibari** Calabria, S Italy
Sibata see Shibata
127 X6 **Sibay** Respublika Bashkortostan, W Russian Federation
93 M19 **Sibbo** Fin. Sipoo. Etelä-Suomi, S Finland
112 D13 **Šibenik** It. Sebenico. Šibenik-Knin, S Croatia
Šibenik see Šibenik-Knin
112 E13 **Šibenik-Knin** off. Šibenska Županija. var. Šibenik. ◇ province S Croatia
Šibenska Županija see Šibenik-Knin
Siberia see Sibir'
Siberoet see Siberut, Pulau
168 H12 **Siberut, Pulau** prev. Siberoet. island Kepulauan Mentawai, W Indonesia
168 I12 **Siberut, Selat** strait W Indonesia
Sibetu see Shibetsu
149 P11 **Sibi** Baluchistān, SW Pakistan
186 B9 **Sibidiri** Western, SW PNG
123 N10 **Sibir'** var. Siberia. physical region NE Russian Federation
122 J13 **Sibirskiy** Altayskiy Kray, S Russian Federation
79 F20 **Sibiti** La Lékoumou, S Congo
81 G21 **Sibiti** ≈ C Tanzania
116 I12 **Sibiu** Ger. Hermannstadt, Hung. Nagyszeben. Sibiu, C Romania
116 I11 **Sibiu** ◇ county C Romania
29 S11 **Sibley** Iowa, C USA
169 R9 **Sibu** Sarawak, East Malaysia
Sibukawa see Shibukawa
42 G2 **Sibun** ≈ E Belize
79 I15 **Sibut** prev. Fort-Sibut. Kémo, S Central African Republic
171 P4 **Sibuyan Island** island C Philippines
171 P4 **Sibuyan Sea** sea C Philippines
189 U1 **Sibylla Island** island N Marshall Islands
11 N16 **Sicamous** British Columbia, SW Canada
Sichelburger Gebirge see Gorjanci/Žumberačko Gorje
167 N14 **Sichon** var. Ban Sichon, Si Chon. Nakhon Si Thammarat, SW Thailand
160 H9 **Sichuan** var. Chuan, Sichuan Sheng, Ssu-ch'uan, Szechuan, Szechwan. ◇ province C China
160 I9 **Sichuan Pendi** basin C China
Sichuan Sheng see Sichuan
103 S16 **Sicie, Cap** headland SE France
107 J24 **Sicilia** Eng. Sicily; anc. Trinacria. ◇ region Italy, C Mediterranean Sea
107 M24 **Sicilia** Eng. Sicily; anc. Trinacria. island Italy, C Mediterranean Sea
Sicilian Channel see Sicily, Strait of
Sicily see Sicilia
107 H24 **Sicily, Strait of** var. Sicilian Channel. strait C Mediterranean Sea
42 K5 **Sico Tinto, Río** var. Río Negro. ≈ NE Honduras
57 H16 **Sicuani** Cusco, S Peru
112 J10 **Šid** Serbia, NW Serbia and Montenegro (Yugo.)
115 A15 **Sidári** Kérkyra, Iónioi Nísoi, Greece, C Mediterranean Sea
169 Q11 **Sidas** Borneo, C Indonesia
98 O5 **Siddeburen** Groningen, NE Netherlands
154 D9 **Siddhapur** prev. Siddhpur, Sidhpur. Gujarāt, W India
Siddhpur see Siddhapur
155 I15 **Siddipet** Andhra Pradesh, C India
77 N14 **Sidéradougou** SW Burkina
107 N23 **Siderno** Calabria, SW Italy
Siders see Sierre
154 L9 **Sidhi** Madhya Pradesh, C India
Sidhirókastron see Sidirókastro
Sidhpur see Siddhapur
Sīdī al Hānī', Sabkhat see Sidi el Hani, Sebkhet de
75 U7 **Sidi Barrâni** NW Egypt
74 I6 **Sidi Bel Abbès** var. Sidi bel Abbès, Sidi-Bel-Abbès. NW Algeria
74 E7 **Sidi-Bennour** W Morocco
74 M6 **Sidi Bouzid** var. Gammouda, Sīdī Bu Zayd. C Tunisia
74 D8 **Sidi-Ifni** SW Morocco
74 G6 **Sidi-Kacem** prev. Petitjean. N Morocco
114 G12 **Sidirókastro** prev. Sidhirókastron. Kentrikí Makedonía, NE Greece
194 L12 **Sidley, Mount** ▲ Antarctica
29 S16 **Sidney** Iowa, C USA
33 Y7 **Sidney** Montana, NW USA
28 J15 **Sidney** Nebraska, C USA
18 I11 **Sidney** New York, NE USA
31 R13 **Sidney** Ohio, N USA
23 T2 **Sidney Lanier, Lake** ⊠ Georgia, SE USA
Sidon see Saïda
122 J9 **Sidorovsk** Yamalo-Nenetskiy Avtonomnyy Okrug, N Russian Federation
Sidra/Sidra, Gulf of see Surt, Khalīj, N Libya
Sidra see Surt, N Libya
Sīdī Bu Zayd see Sidi Bouzid
Siebenbürgen see Transylvania
Sieben Dörfer see Săcele
110 O12 **Siedlce** Ger. Sedlez, Rus. Sesdlets. Mazowieckie, C Poland
101 E16 **Sieg** ≈ W Germany
101 F16 **Siegen** Nordrhein-Westfalen, W Germany
109 X4 **Sieghartskirchen** Niederösterreich, E Austria
110 O11 **Siemiatycze** Podlaskie, NE Poland
167 T11 **Siĕmpang** Stœng Trêng, NE Cambodia
167 R11 **Siĕmréab** prev. Siemreap. Siĕmréab, NW Cambodia
Siemreap see Siĕmréab
106 G12 **Siena** Fr. Sienne; anc. Saena Julia. Toscana, C Italy
Sienne see Siena
92 K12 **Sieppijärvi** Lappi, NW Finland
110 J13 **Sieradz** Sieradz, C Poland
110 K10 **Sierpc** Mazowieckie, C Poland
24 I9 **Sierra Blanca** Texas, SW USA
37 S14 **Sierra Blanca Peak** ▲ New Mexico, SW USA
35 P5 **Sierra City** California, W USA
63 I16 **Sierra Colorada** Río Negro, S Argentina
62 I13 **Sierra del Nevado** ▲ W Argentina
63 J16 **Sierra Grande** Río Negro, E Argentina
76 G15 **Sierra Leone** off. Republic of Sierra Leone. ♦ republic W Africa
64 M13 **Sierra Leone Basin** undersea feature E Atlantic Ocean
Sierra Leone Ridge see Sierra Leone Rise
64 L13 **Sierra Leone Rise** var. Sierra Leone Ridge, Sierra Leone Schwelle. undersea feature E Atlantic Ocean
Sierra Leone Schwelle see Sierra Leone Rise
41 U17 **Sierra Madre** var. Sierra de Soconusco. ⛰ Guatemala/Mexico
37 R2 **Sierra Madre** ⛰ Colorado/Wyoming, C USA
41 P16 **Sierra Madre del Sur** ⛰ S Mexico
40 J8 **Sierra Madre Occidental** var. Western Sierra Madre. ⛰ C Mexico
41 O10 **Sierra Madre Oriental** var. Eastern Sierra Madre. ⛰ C Mexico
44 H8 **Sierra Maestra** ⛰ E Cuba
40 L7 **Sierra Mojada** Coahuila de Zaragoza, NE Mexico
105 O14 **Sierra Nevada** ⛰ S Spain
35 P6 **Sierra Nevada** ⛰ W USA
54 F4 **Sierra Nevada de Santa Marta** ⛰ NE Colombia
42 K5 **Sierra Río Tinto** ⛰ NE Honduras
24 J10 **Sierra Vieja** ⛰ Texas, SW USA
37 N16 **Sierra Vista** Arizona, SW USA
108 D10 **Sierre** Ger. Siders. Valais, SW Switzerland
36 L16 **Sierrita Mountains** ⛰ Arizona, SW USA
Siete Moai see Ahu Akivi
76 M15 **Sifié** W Ivory Coast
115 I21 **Sífnos** anc. Siphnos. island Kykládes, Greece, Aegean Sea
115 I21 **Sífnou, Stenó** strait SE Greece
Siga see Shiga
103 P16 **Sigean** Aude, S France
Sighet see Sighetu Marmației
Sighetul Marmației see Sighetu Marmației
116 I8 **Sighetu Marmației** var. Sighet, Sighetul Marmației, Hung. Máramarossziget. Maramureș, N Romania
116 I11 **Sighișoara** Ger. Schässburg, Hung. Segesvár. Mureș, C Romania
168 G7 **Sigli** Sumatera, W Indonesia
92 J1 **Siglufjördhur** Nordhurland Vestra, N Iceland
101 H23 **Sigmaringen** Baden-Württemberg, S Germany
101 N20 **Signalberg** ▲ SE Germany
36 I13 **Signal Peak** ▲ Arizona, SW USA
Signan see Xi'an
194 H1 **Signy** UK research station South Orkney Islands, Antarctica
29 X15 **Sigourney** Iowa, C USA
115 K17 **Sígri, Akrotírio** headland Lésvos, E Greece
47 N2 **Sigsbee Escarpment** undersea feature N Gulf of Mexico
56 C8 **Sigsig** Azuay, S Ecuador
95 O15 **Sigtuna** Stockholm, C Sweden
42 H6 **Siguatepeque** Comayagua, W Honduras
105 P7 **Sigüenza** Castilla-La Mancha, C Spain
105 R4 **Sigües** Aragón, NE Spain
76 K13 **Siguiri** Haute-Guinée, NE Guinea
118 G8 **Sigulda** Ger. Segewold. Rīga, C Latvia
Sihanoukville see Kâmpóng Saôm
108 G8 **Sihlsee** ◎ NW Switzerland
93 K18 **Siikainen** Länsi-Suomi, W Finland
93 M16 **Siilinjärvi** Itä-Suomi, C Finland
137 R15 **Siirt** var. Sert; anc. Tigranocerta. Siirt, SE Turkey
137 R15 **Siirt** var. Sert. ◇ province SE Turkey
187 N8 **Sikaiana** var. Stewart Islands. island group W Solomon Islands
Sikandarabad see Secunderābād
152 J11 **Sikandra Rao** Uttar Pradesh, N India
10 M11 **Sikanni Chief** British Columbia, W Canada
10 M11 **Sikanni Chief** ≈ British Columbia, W Canada
152 H11 **Sīkar** Rājasthān, N India
76 M13 **Sikasso** Sikasso, S Mali
76 L13 **Sikasso** ◇ region SW Mali
167 N3 **Sikaw** Kachin State, C Burma
83 H14 **Sikelenge** Western, W Zambia
27 Y7 **Sikeston** Missouri, C USA
93 J14 **Sikfors** Norrbotten, N Sweden
123 T14 **Sikhote-Alin', Khrebet** ⛰ SE Russian Federation
Siking see Xi'an
115 J22 **Síkinos** island Kykládes, Greece, Aegean Sea
153 S11 **Sikkim** Tib. Denjong. ◇ state N India
111 I26 **Siklós** Baranya, SW Hungary
Sikoku see Shikoku
Sikoku Basin see Shikoku Basin
83 G14 **Sikongo** Western, W Zambia
Sikotu Ko see Shikotsu-ko
Sikouri/Sikoúrion see Sykoúri
123 P8 **Siktyakh** Respublika Sakha (Yakutiya), NE Russian Federation
118 D12 **Šilalė** Tauragė, W Lithuania
106 G5 **Silandro** Ger. Schlanders. Trentino-Alto Adige, N Italy
41 N12 **Silao** Guanajuato, C Mexico
Silarius see Sele
153 W14 **Silchar** Assam, NE India
108 G9 **Silenen** Uri, C Switzerland
21 T9 **Siler City** North Carolina, SE USA
33 U11 **Silesia** Montana, NW USA
110 F13 **Silesia** physical region SW Poland
74 K12 **Silet** S Algeria
145 R8 **Sileti** var. Selety. ≈ N Kazakhstan
Siletitengiz see Siletiteniz, Ozero
145 R7 **Siletiteniz, Ozero** Kaz. Siletitengiz. ◎ N Kazakhstan
172 H16 **Silhouette** island Inner Islands, SE Seychelles
136 I17 **Silifke** anc. Seleucia. İçel, S Turkey
Siliguri see Shiliguri
156 J10 **Siling Co** ◎ W China
Silinhot see Xilinhot
192 G15 **Silisili** ▲ Savai'i, C Samoa
114 M6 **Silistra** var. Silistria; anc. Durostorum. Silistra, NE Bulgaria
116 M7 **Silistra** ◇ province NE Bulgaria
Silistria see Silistra
136 D10 **Silivri** İstanbul, NW Turkey
94 L13 **Siljan** ◎ C Sweden
95 G22 **Silkeborg** Århus, C Denmark
108 M8 **Sill** ≈ W Austria
105 S10 **Silla** País Valenciano, E Spain
62 H3 **Sillajguay, Cordillera** ▲ N Chile
118 K3 **Sillamäe** Ger. Sillamäggi. Ida-Virumaa, NE Estonia
Sillamäggi see Sillamäe
Sillein see Žilina
109 P9 **Sillian** Tirol, W Austria
112 B10 **Šilo** Primorje-Gorski Kotar, NW Croatia
27 R9 **Siloam Springs** Arkansas, C USA
25 X10 **Silsbee** Texas, SW USA
143 W15 **Sīlūp, Rūd-e** ≈ SE Iran
118 C12 **Šilutė** Ger. Heydekrug. Klaipėda, W Lithuania
137 Q15 **Silvan** Dıyarbakır, SE Turkey
108 J10 **Silvaplana** Graubünden, S Switzerland
Silva Porto see Kuito
58 M12 **Silva, Recife do** reef E Brazil
154 D12 **Silvassa** Dādra and Nagar Haveli, W India
29 X4 **Silver Bay** Minnesota, N USA
37 P15 **Silver City** New Mexico, SW USA
18 D10 **Silver Creek** New York, NE USA
37 N12 **Silver Creek** ≈ Arizona, SW USA
27 P4 **Silver Lake** Kansas, C USA
32 I14 **Silver Lake** Oregon, NW USA
35 T9 **Silver Peak Range** ⛰ Nevada, W USA
21 W3 **Silver Spring** Maryland, NE USA
Silver State see Nevada
Silver State see Colorado
37 Q7 **Silverton** Colorado, C USA
18 K16 **Silverton** New Jersey, NE USA
32 G11 **Silverton** Oregon, NW USA
25 N4 **Silverton** Texas, SW USA
104 G14 **Silves** Faro, S Portugal
54 D12 **Silvia** Cauca, SW Colombia
108 J9 **Silvrettagruppe** ⛰ Austria/Switzerland
Sily-Vajdej see Vulcan
108 L7 **Silz** Tirol, W Austria
172 I13 **Sima** Anjouan, SE Comoros
Simabara see Shimabara
Simada see Shimada
83 H15 **Simakando** Western, W Zambia
Simane see Shimane
119 L20 **Simanichy** Rus. Simonichi. Homyel'skaya Voblasts', SE Belarus
160 F14 **Simao** Yunnan, SW China
153 P12 **Simara** Central, C Nepal
14 I8 **Simard, Lac** ◎ Québec, SE Canada
136 D13 **Simav** Kütahya, W Turkey
136 D13 **Simav Çayı** ≈ NW Turkey
79 L18 **Simba** Orientale, N Dem. Rep. Congo
186 C7 **Simbai** Madang, N PNG
Simbirsk see Ul'yanovsk
14 F17 **Simcoe** Ontario, S Canada
14 H14 **Simcoe, Lake** ◎ Ontario, S Canada
80 J11 **Sīmēn** ⛰ N Ethiopia
114 K11 **Simeonovgrad** prev. Maritsa. Khaskovo, S Bulgaria
116 G11 **Simeria** Ger. Pischk, Hung. Piski. Hunedoara, W Romania
107 L24 **Simeto** ≈ Sicilia, Italy, C Mediterranean Sea
168 G9 **Simeulue, Pulau** island NW Indonesia
117 T13 **Simferopol'** Respublika Krym, S Ukraine
117 T13 **Simferopol'** ✕ Respublika Krym, S Ukraine
Simi see Sými
152 M9 **Simikot** Far Western, NW Nepal
54 F7 **Simití** Bolívar, N Colombia
114 G11 **Simitla** Blagoevgrad, SW Bulgaria
35 S15 **Simi Valley** California, W USA
Simizu see Shimizu
Simla see Shimla
Şimlăul Silvaniei/Şimleul Silvaniei see Şimleu Silvaniei
116 G9 **Şimleu Silvaniei** Hung. Szilágysomlyó; prev. Şimlăul Silvaniei, Şimleul Silvaniei. Sălaj, NW Romania
Simmer see Simmerbach
101 E19 **Simmerbach** var. Simmer. ≈ W Germany
101 F18 **Simmern** Rheinland-Pfalz, W Germany
22 I7 **Simmesport** Louisiana, S USA
119 F14 **Simnas** Alytus, S Lithuania
92 L13 **Simo** Lappi, NW Finland
Simoda see Shimoda
Simodate see Shimodate
92 M13 **Simojärvi** ◎ N Finland
92 L13 **Simojoki** ≈ NW Finland
41 U15 **Simojovel** var. Simojovel de Allende. Chiapas, SE Mexico
Simojovel de Allende see Simojovel
56 B7 **Simon Bolívar** var. Guayaquil. ✕ (Quayaquil) Guayas, W Ecuador
54 L5 **Simon Bolívar** ✕ (Caracas) Distrito Federal, N Venezuela
Simonichi see Simanichy
14 M12 **Simon, Lac** ◎ Québec, SE Canada
Simonoseki see Shimonoseki
Šimonovany see Partizánske
Simonstad see Simon's Town
83 E26 **Simon's Town** var. Simonstad. Western Cape, SW South Africa
Simony see Partizánske
Simotuma see Shimotsuma
Simpeln see Simplon
99 M18 **Simpelveld** Limburg, SE Netherlands
108 E11 **Simplon** var. Simpeln. Valais, SW Switzerland
108 E11 **Simplon Pass** pass S Switzerland
106 C6 **Simplon Tunnel** tunnel Italy/Switzerland
Simpson see Fort Simpson
182 G1 **Simpson Desert** desert Northern Territory/South Australia
10 J9 **Simpson Peak** ▲ British Columbia, W Canada
9 N7 **Simpson Peninsula** peninsula Nunavut, NE Canada
21 P11 **Simpsonville** South Carolina, SE USA
95 L23 **Simrishamn** Skåne, S Sweden
123 U13 **Simushir, Ostrov** island Kuril'skiye Ostrova, SE Russian Federation
Sinā'/Sinai Peninsula see Sinai
168 G9 **Sinabang** Sumatera, W Indonesia
81 N15 **Sina Dhaqa** Galguduud, C Somalia
75 X8 **Sinai** var. Sinai Peninsula, Ar. Shibh Jazīrat Sīnā', Sīnā'. physical region NE Egypt
116 J12 **Sinaia** Prahova, SE Romania
188 B16 **Sinajana** C Guam
40 H8 **Sinaloa** ◇ state C Mexico
54 H4 **Sinamaica** Zulia, NW Venezuela
163 X14 **Sinan-ni** SE North Korea
Sinano Gawa see Shinano-gawa
Sināwan see Sīnāwin
75 N8 **Sīnāwin** var. Sīnāwan. NW Libya
83 J16 **Sinazongwe** Southern, S Zambia
166 L6 **Sinbaungwe** Magwe, W Burma
166 L5 **Sinbyugyun** Magwe, W Burma
54 E6 **Since** Sucre, NW Colombia
54 E6 **Sincelejo** Sucre, NW Colombia
166 J5 **Sinchaingbyin** var. Zullapara. Arakan State, W Burma
23 U4 **Sinclair, Lake** ⊠ Georgia, SE USA
10 M14 **Sinclair Mills** British Columbia, SW Canada
149 Q14 **Sind** var. Sindh. ◇ province SE Pakistan
154 I8 **Sind** ≈ N India
95 H19 **Sindal** Nordjylland, N Denmark
171 P7 **Sindañgan** Mindanao, S Philippines
79 D19 **Sindara** Ngounié, W Gabon
152 E13 **Sindari** prev. Sindri. Rājasthān, N India
114 N8 **Sindel** Varna, E Bulgaria
101 H22 **Sindelfingen** Baden-Württemberg, SW Germany
155 G16 **Sindgi** Karnātaka, C India
Sindh see Sind
118 G5 **Sindi** Ger. Zintenhof. Pärnumaa, SW Estonia

136 C13 **Sındırgı** Balıkesir, W Turkey
77 N14 **Sindou** SW Burkina
Sindri see Sindari
149 T9 **Sind Sāgar Doāb** desert E Pakistan
126 M11 **Sinegorskiy** Rostovskaya Oblast', SW Russian Federation
123 S9 **Sinegor'ye** Magadanskaya Oblast', E Russian Federation
114 O12 **Sinekli** İstanbul, NW Turkey
104 F12 **Sines** Setúbal, S Portugal
104 F12 **Sines, Cabo de** headland S Portugal
92 L12 **Sinettä** Lappi, NW Finland
186 H6 **Sinewit, Mount** ▲ New Britain, C PNG
80 G11 **Singa** var. Sinja, Sinjah. Sinnar, E Sudan
78 J12 **Singako** Moyen-Chari, S Chad
Singan see Xi'an
168 K10 **Singapore** ● (Singapore) S Singapore
168 L10 **Singapore** off. Republic of Singapore. ◆ republic SE Asia
168 L10 **Singapore Strait** var. Strait of Singapore, Mal. Selat Singapura. strait Indonesia/Singapore
Singapore, Strait of/Singapura, Selat see Singapore Strait
169 U17 **Singaraja** Bali, C Indonesia
Singatoka see Sigatoka
167 O10 **Sing Buri** var. Singhaburi. Sing Buri, C Thailand
101 H24 **Singen** Baden-Württemberg, S Germany
Singeorgiu de Pădure see Sângeorgiu de Pădure
Singeorz-Băi/Singeroz Băi see Sângeorz-Băi
116 M9 **Sîngerei** var. Sângerei; prev. Lazovsk. N Moldova
Singhaburi see Sing Buri
81 H21 **Singida** Singida, C Tanzania
81 G22 **Singida** ◈ region C Tanzania
Singidunum see Beograd
166 M2 **Singkaling Hkamti** Sagaing, N Burma
171 N14 **Singkang** Sulawesi, C Indonesia
168 J11 **Singkarak, Danau** ◎ Sumatera, W Indonesia
169 N10 **Singkawang** Borneo, C Indonesia
168 M11 **Singkep, Pulau** island Kepulauan Lingga, W Indonesia
168 H9 **Singkilbaru** Sumatera, W Indonesia
183 T7 **Singleton** New South Wales, SE Australia
Singora see Songkhla
Singû see Shingū
Sining see Xining
107 D17 **Siniscola** Sardegna, Italy, C Mediterranean Sea
113 F14 **Sinj** Split-Dalmacija, SE Croatia
Sinja/Sinjah see Singa
Sinjajevina see Sinjavina
139 P3 **Sinjār** NW Iraq
139 P2 **Sinjār, Jabal** ▲ N Iraq
113 K15 **Sinjavina** var. Sinjajevina. ⛰ SW Serbia and Montenegro (Yugo.)
80 I7 **Sinkat** Red Sea, NE Sudan
Sinkiang/Sinkiang Uighur Autonomous Region see Xinjiang Uygur Zizhiqu
Sinmartin see Târnăveni
163 V13 **Sinmi-do** island NW North Korea
Sinminato see Shinminato
101 I18 **Sinn** ≈ C Germany
Sinnamarie see Sinnamary
55 Y9 **Sinnamary** var. Sinnamarie. N French Guiana
Sinn'anyô see Shinnanyō
80 G11 **Sinnar** ◈ state E Sudan
Sinneh see Sanandaj
18 E13 **Sinnemahoning Creek** ≈ Pennsylvania, NE USA
Sînnicolau Mare see Sânnicolau Mare
Sino/Sinoe see Greenville
Sinoe, Lacul see Sinoie, Lacul
Sinoia see Chinhoyi
117 N14 **Sinoie, Lacul** prev. Lacul Sinoe. lagoon SE Romania
59 H16 **Sinop** Mato Grosso, W Brazil
136 K10 **Sinop** anc. Sinope. Sinop, N Turkey
136 J10 **Sinop** ◈ province N Turkey
136 K10 **Sinop Burnu** headland N Turkey
Sinope see Sinop
163 Y12 **Sinp'o** E North Korea
101 H20 **Sinsheim** Baden-Württemberg, SW Germany
Sinsiro see Shinshiro
Sîntana see Sântana
169 R11 **Sintang** Borneo, C Indonesia
99 F14 **Sint Annaland** Zeeland, SW Netherlands
98 L5 **Sint Annaparochie** Friesland, N Netherlands
45 V9 **Sint Eustatius** Eng. Saint Eustatius. island N Netherlands Antilles
99 G19 **Sint-Genesius-Rode** Fr. Rhode-Saint-Genèse. Vlaams Brabant, C Belgium
99 F16 **Sint-Gillis-Waas** Oost-Vlaanderen, N Belgium
99 H17 **Sint-Katelijne-Waver** Antwerpen, C Belgium
99 E18 **Sint-Lievens-Houtem** Oost-Vlaanderen, NW Belgium
45 V9 **Sint Maarten** Eng. Saint Martin. island N Netherlands Antilles
99 F14 **Sint Maartensdijk** Zeeland, SW Netherlands
99 L19 **Sint-Martens-Voeren** Fr. Fouron-Saint-Martin. Limburg, NE Belgium
99 J14 **Sint-Michielsgestel** Noord-Brabant, S Netherlands
Sînt-Miclăuş see Gheorgheni
45 O16 **Sint Nicholaas** S Aruba
99 F16 **Sint-Niklaas** Fr. Saint-Nicolas. Oost-Vlaanderen, N Belgium
99 K14 **Sint-Oedenrode** Noord-Brabant, S Netherlands
25 T14 **Sinton** Texas, SW USA
99 G14 **Sint Philipsland** Zeeland, SW Netherlands
99 G19 **Sint-Pieters-Leeuw** Vlaams Brabant, C Belgium
104 E11 **Sintra** prev. Cintra. Lisboa, W Portugal
99 J18 **Sint-Truiden** Fr. Saint-Trond. Limburg, NE Belgium
99 H14 **Sint Willebrord** Noord-Brabant, S Netherlands
163 V13 **Sinŭiju** W North Korea
80 P13 **Sinujiif** Nugaal, NE Somalia
Sinus Aelaniticus see Aqaba, Gulf of
Sinus Gallicus see Lion, Golfe du
Sinyang see Xinyang
Sinyavka see Sinyawka
119 I18 **Sinyawka** Rus. Sinyavka. Minskaya Voblasts', SW Belarus
Sinying see Hsinying
Sinyukha see Synyukha
Sinzi-ko see Shinji-ko
Sinzyô see Shinjō
111 I24 **Sió** ≈ W Hungary
171 O7 **Siocon** Mindanao, S Philippines
111 I24 **Siófok** Somogy, C Hungary
Siogama see Shiogama
83 G15 **Sioma** Western, SW Zambia
108 D11 **Sion** Ger. Sitten; anc. Sedunum. Valais, SW Switzerland
103 O11 **Sioule** ≈ C France
29 S12 **Sioux Center** Iowa, C USA
29 R13 **Sioux City** Iowa, C USA
29 R11 **Sioux Falls** South Dakota, N USA
12 B11 **Sioux Lookout** Ontario, S Canada
29 T12 **Sioux Rapids** Iowa, C USA
Sioux State see North Dakota
Siozeri see Shiojiri
171 P6 **Sipalay** Negros, C Philippines
55 V11 **Sipaliwini** ◈ district S Surinam
45 U15 **Siparia** Trinidad, Trinidad and Tobago
Siphnos see Sífnos
163 V11 **Siping** var. Ssu-p'ing, Szeping; prev. Ssu-p'ing-chieh. Jilin, NE China
11 X12 **Sipiwesk** Manitoba, C Canada
11 W13 **Sipiwesk Lake** ◎ Manitoba, C Canada
195 O11 **Siple Coast** physical region Antarctica
194 K12 **Siple Island** island Antarctica
194 K13 **Siple, Mount** ▲ Siple Island, Antarctica
Sipoo see Sibbo
112 G12 **Šipovo** Republika Srpska, W Bosnia and Herzegovina
23 O4 **Sipsey River** ≈ Alabama, S USA
168 I13 **Sipura, Pulau** island W Indonesia
42 L10 **Siquia, Río** ≈ SE Nicaragua
43 N13 **Siquirres** Limón, E Costa Rica
54 J5 **Siquisique** Lara, N Venezuela
155 G19 **Sira** Karnātaka, W India
95 D16 **Sira** ≈ S Norway
167 P12 **Siracha** var. Ban Si Racha, Si Racha. Chon Buri, S Thailand
107 L25 **Siracusa** Eng. Syracuse. Sicilia, Italy, C Mediterranean Sea
Sirajganj see Shirajganj Ghat
Sirakawa see Shirakawa
11 N14 **Sir Alexander, Mount** ▲ British Columbia, W Canada
137 O12 **Şiran** Gümüşhane, NE Turkey
77 Q12 **Sirba** ≈ E Burkina
143 O17 **Şīr Banī Yās** island W UAE
95 D17 **Sirdalsvannet** ◎ S Norway
Sir Darya/Sirdaryo see Syr Darya
147 P10 **Sirdaryo** Sirdaryo Viloyati, E Uzbekistan
147 O11 **Sirdaryo Viloyati** Rus. Syrdar'inskaya Oblast'. ◈ province E Uzbekistan
Sir Donald Sangster International Airport see Sangster
181 S3 **Sir Edward Pellew Group** island group Northern Territory, NE Australia
116 K8 **Siret** Ger. Sereth, Hung. Szeret. Suceava, N Romania
116 K8 **Siret** var. Siretul, Ger. Sereth, Rus. Seret, Ukr. Siret. ≈ Romania/Ukraine
Siretul see Siret
140 K3 **Sirḥān, Wādī as** dry watercourse Jordan/Saudi Arabia
152 I8 **Sirhind** Punjab, N India
116 F11 **Şiria** Ger. Schiria. Arad, W Romania
Siria see Syria
143 S14 **Sīrīk** Hormozgān, SE Iran
167 P8 **Sirikit Reservoir** ⊡ N Thailand
58 K12 **Sirituba, Ilha** island NE Brazil
143 R11 **Sīrjān** prev. Sa'īdābād. Kermān, S Iran
182 H9 **Sir Joseph Banks Group** island group South Australia
92 K11 **Sirkka** Lappi, N Finland
Sirna see Sýrna
137 R16 **Şırnak** Şırnak, SE Turkey
137 S16 **Şırnak** ◈ province SE Turkey
Siroisi see Shiroishi
155 I14 **Sironcha** Mahārāshtra, C India
Sirone see Shirone
Síros see Sýros
Sirotino see Sirotsina
118 M12 **Sirotsina** Rus. Sirotino. Vitsyebskaya Voblasts', N Belarus
152 H9 **Sirsa** Haryāna, NW India
173 Y17 **Sir Seewoosagur Ramgoolam** ✕ (Port Louis) SE Mauritius
155 E18 **Sirsi** Karnātaka, W India
146 K12 **Şirşütür Gumy** var. Shirshütür, Rus. Peski Shirshyutyur. desert E Turkmenistan
Sirte see Surt
182 A2 **Sir Thomas, Mount** ▲ South Australia
Sirti, Gulf of see Surt, Khalīj
142 J5 **Sīrvān, Rūdkhāneh-ye** var. Nahr Diyālá, Sirwan. ≈ Iran/Iraq see also Diyālá, Nahr
118 H13 **Širvintos** Vilnius, SE Lithuania
Sirwan see Diyālá, Nahr/Sīrvān, Rūdkhāneh-ye
11 N15 **Sir Wilfrid Laurier, Mount** ▲ British Columbia, SW Canada
14 M10 **Sir-Wilfrid, Mont** ▲ Québec, SE Canada
Sisačko-Moslavačka Županija see Sisak-Moslavina
112 E9 **Sisak** var. Siscia, Ger. Sissek, Hung. Sziszek; anc. Segestica. Sisak-Moslavina, C Croatia
167 R10 **Si Sa Ket** var. Sisaket, Sri Saket. Si Sa Ket, E Thailand
112 E9 **Sisak-Moslavina** off. Sisačko-Moslavačka Županija. ◈ province C Croatia
167 O8 **Si Satchanalai** Sukhothai, NW Thailand
Siscia see Sisak
83 G22 **Sishen** Northern Cape, NW South Africa
137 U13 **Sisian** SE Armenia
197 N13 **Sisimiut** var. Holsteinborg, Holsteinsborg, Holstenborg, Holstensborg. Kitaa, S Greenland
30 M1 **Siskiwit Bay** lake bay Michigan, N USA
34 L1 **Siskiyou Mountains** ⛰ California/Oregon, W USA
167 Q11 **Sisŏphŏn** Bătdâmbâng, NW Cambodia
108 E7 **Sissach** Basel-Land, NW Switzerland
186 B5 **Sissano** Sandaun, NW PNG
Sissek see Sisak
29 R7 **Sisseton** South Dakota, N USA
143 W9 **Sīstān, Daryācheh-ye** var. Daryācheh-ye Hāmūn, Hāmūn-e Şāberī. ◎ Afghanistan/Iran see also Şāberī, Hāmūn-e
143 V12 **Sīstān va Balūchestān** off. Ostān-e Sīstān va Balūchestān, var. Balūchestān va Sīstān. ◈ province SE Iran
103 T14 **Sisteron** Alpes-de-Haute-Provence, SE France
32 H13 **Sisters** Oregon, NW USA
65 G15 **Sisters Peak** ▲ N Ascension Island
21 R3 **Sistersville** West Virginia, NE USA
Sistova see Svishtov
Sitakund see Sitakunda
153 V16 **Sitakunda** var. Sitakund. Chittagong, SE Bangladesh
153 P12 **Sītāmarhi** Bihār, N India
152 L11 **Sītāpur** Uttar Pradesh, N India
Sitaş Cristuru see Cristuru Secuiesc
115 L25 **Siteía** var. Sitía. Kríti, Greece, E Mediterranean Sea
105 V6 **Sitges** Cataluña, NE Spain
115 H15 **Sithoniá** peninsula NE Greece
Sitía see Siteía
54 F4 **Sitionuevo** Magdalena, N Colombia
39 X13 **Sitka** Baranof Island, Alaska, USA
39 Q15 **Sitkinak Island** island Trinity Islands, Alaska, USA
166 M7 **Sittang** var. Sittoung. ≈ S Burma
99 L17 **Sittard** Limburg, SE Netherlands
Sitten see Sion
108 H7 **Sitter** ≈ NW Switzerland
109 U10 **Sittersdorf** Kärnten, S Austria
Sittoung see Sittang
166 K6 **Sittwe** var. Akyab. Arakan State, W Burma
42 L8 **Siuna** Región Autónoma Atlántico Norte, NE Nicaragua
153 R15 **Siuri** West Bengal, NE India
Siut see Asyūt
123 Q13 **Sivaki** Amurskaya Oblast', SE Russian Federation
136 M13 **Sivas** anc. Sebastia, Sebaste. Sivas, C Turkey
136 M13 **Sivas** ◈ province C Turkey
137 O15 **Siverek** Şanlıurfa, S Turkey
117 X6 **Sivers'k** Donets'ka Oblast', E Ukraine
124 G13 **Siverskiy** Leningradskaya Oblast', NW Russian Federation
117 X6 **Sivers'kyy Donets'** Rus. Severskiy Donets. ≈ Russian Federation/Ukraine see also Severskiy Donets
125 W5 **Sivomaskinskiy** Respublika Komi, NW Russian Federation
136 G13 **Sivrihisar** Eskişehir, W Turkey
99 F22 **Sivry** Hainaut, S Belgium
123 V9 **Sivuchiy, Mys** headland E Russian Federation
75 U9 **Sīwa** var. Sīwah. NW Egypt
Sīwah see Sīwa
152 J9 **Siwalik Range** var. Shiwālik Range. ⛰ India/Nepal
153 O13 **Siwān** Bihār, N India
43 O14 **Sixaola, Río** ≈ Costa Rica/Panama
Six Counties, The see Northern Ireland
103 T16 **Six-Fours-les-Plages** Var, SE France
161 Q7 **Sixian** var. Si Xian. Anhui, E China
22 J9 **Six Mile Lake** ◎ Louisiana, S USA
139 V3 **Siyāh Gūz** E Iraq
155 L25 **Siyambalanduwa** Uva Province, SE Sri Lanka
137 Y10 **Siyäzän** Rus. Siazan'. NE Azerbaijan
Sizebolu see Sozopol
Sizuoka see Shizuoka
Sjar see Sääre
113 L15 **Sjenica** Turk. Seniça. Serbia, SW Serbia and Montenegro (Yugo.)
94 G11 **Sjoa** ≈ S Norway
95 K23 **Sjöbo** Skåne, S Sweden
95 I24 **Sjælland** Eng. Zealand, Ger. Seeland. island E Denmark
94 E9 **Sjøholt** Møre og Romsdal, S Norway
92 O1 **Sjuøyane** island group N Svalbard
Skadar see Shkodër
Skadarsko Jezero see Scutari, Lake
117 R11 **Skadovs'k** Khersons'ka Oblast', S Ukraine
92 I2 **Skagaströnd** prev. Höfdhakaupstadhur. Nordhurland Vestra, N Iceland
95 H19 **Skagen** Nordjylland, N Denmark
Skagerak see Skagerrak
95 L16 **Skagern** ◎ C Sweden
197 T17 **Skagerrak** var. Skagerak. channel N Europe
94 G12 **Skaget** ▲ S Norway
32 H7 **Skagit River** ≈ Washington, NW USA
39 W12 **Skagway** Alaska, USA
92 K8 **Skáidi** Finnmark, N Norway
115 F21 **Skála** Pelopónnisos, S Greece
116 K6 **Skalat** Pol. Skałat. Ternopil's'ka Oblast', W Ukraine
95 J22 **Skälderviken** inlet Denmark/Sweden
124 J3 **Skalistyy** Murmanskaya Oblast', NW Russian Federation
92 I12 **Skalka** ◎ N Sweden
114 I12 **Skalotí** Anatolikí Makedonía kai Thráki, NE Greece
95 G22 **Skanderborg** Århus, C Denmark
95 K22 **Skåne** Eng. Scania. ◈ county S Sweden
75 N6 **Skanès** ✕ (Sousse) E Tunisia
95 C15 **Skånevik** Hordaland, S Norway
95 M18 **Skänninge** Östergötland, S Sweden
95 J23 **Skanör med Falsterbo** Skåne, S Sweden
115 H17 **Skantzoúra** island Vóreioi Sporádes, Greece, Aegean Sea
95 K18 **Skara** Västra Götaland, S Sweden
95 M17 **Skärblacka** Östergötland, S Sweden
95 I18 **Skärhamn** Västra Götaland, S Sweden
95 I14 **Skarnes** Hedmark, S Norway
119 M21 **Skarodnaye** Rus. Skorodnoye. Homyel'skaya Voblasts', SE Belarus
110 I8 **Skarszewy** Ger. Schöneck. Pomorskie, NW Poland
111 M14 **Skarżysko-Kamienna** Świętokrzyskie, C Poland
95 K16 **Skattkärr** Värmland, C Sweden
118 D12 **Skaudvilė** Tauragė, SW Lithuania
92 J12 **Skaulo** Lapp. Sávdijári. Norrbotten, N Sweden
111 K17 **Skawina** Małopolskie, S Poland
10 K12 **Skeena** ≈ British Columbia, SW Canada
10 J11 **Skeena Mountains** ⛰ British Columbia, W Canada
97 O18 **Skegness** E England, UK
92 J4 **Skeidharársandur** coast S Iceland
93 J15 **Skellefteå** Västerbotten, N Sweden
93 I14 **Skellefteälven** ≈ N Sweden
93 J15 **Skelleftehamn** Västerbotten, N Sweden
25 O2 **Skellytown** Texas, SW USA
95 J19 **Skene** Västra Götaland, S Sweden
97 G17 **Skerries** Ir. Na Sceirí. E Ireland
95 H15 **Ski** Akershus, S Norway
115 G17 **Skíathos** Skíathos, Vóreioi Sporádes, Greece, Aegean Sea
115 G17 **Skíathos** island Vóreioi Sporádes, Greece, Aegean Sea
27 P9 **Skiatook** Oklahoma, C USA
27 P9 **Skiatook Lake** ⊡ Oklahoma, C USA
97 B22 **Skibbereen** Ir. An Sciobairín. SW Ireland
92 I9 **Skibotn** Troms, N Norway
119 F16 **Skidal'** Rus. Skidel'. Hrodzyenskaya Voblasts', W Belarus
97 K15 **Skiddaw** ▲ NW England, UK
Skidel' see Skidal'
25 T14 **Skidmore** Texas, SW USA
95 G16 **Skien** Telemark, S Norway
Skiermûntseach see Schiermonnikoog
110 L12 **Skierniewice** Łodzkie, C Poland
74 L5 **Skikda** prev. Philippeville. NE Algeria
30 M16 **Skillet Fork** ≈ Illinois, N USA
95 L19 **Skillingaryd** Jönköping, S Sweden
115 B19 **Skinári, Akrotírio** headland Zákynthos, Iónioi Nísoi, Greece, C Mediterranean Sea
95 M15 **Skinnskatteberg** Västmanland, C Sweden
182 M12 **Skipton** Victoria, SE Australia
97 L16 **Skipton** N England, UK
Skiropoula see Skyropoúla
Skíros see Skýros
95 F21 **Skive** Viborg, NW Denmark
94 F11 **Skjåk** Oppland, S Norway
92 K2 **Skjálfandafljót** ≈ C Iceland
95 F22 **Skjern** Ringkøbing, W Denmark
95 F22 **Skjern Å** var. Skjern Aa. ≈ W Denmark
Skjern Aa see Skjern Å
92 G12 **Skjerstad** Nordland, C Norway
92 J8 **Skjervøy** Troms, N Norway
92 I10 **Skjold** Troms, N Norway
111 I17 **Skoczów** Śląskie, S Poland
95 I24 **Skælskør** Vestsjælland, E Denmark
109 T11 **Škofja Loka** Ger. Bischoflack. NW Slovenia
94 N12 **Skog** Gävleborg, C Sweden
95 K16 **Skoghall** Värmland, C Sweden
31 N10 **Skokie** Illinois, N USA
116 H6 **Skole** L'vivs'ka Oblast', W Ukraine
115 D19 **Skóllis** ▲ S Greece
167 S13 **Skon** Kâmpóng Cham, C Cambodia
115 H17 **Skópelos** Skópelos, Vóreioi Sporádes, Greece, Aegean Sea
115 H17 **Skópelos** island Vóreioi Sporádes, Greece, Aegean Sea
126 L5 **Skopin** Ryazanskaya Oblast', W Russian Federation
113 N18 **Skopje** var. Üsküb, Turk. Üsküp; prev. Skoplje, anc. Scupi. ● (FYR Macedonia) N FYR Macedonia
113 O18 **Skopje** ✕ N FYR Macedonia
Skoplje see Skopje
110 I8 **Skórcz** Ger. Skurz. Pomorskie, N Poland
Skorodnoye see Skarodnaye
93 H16 **Skorped** Västernorrland, C Sweden
95 G21 **Skørping** Nordjylland, N Denmark
95 K18 **Skövde** Västra Götaland, S Sweden
123 Q13 **Skovorodino** Amurskaya Oblast', SE Russian Federation
19 Q6 **Skowhegan** Maine, NE USA
11 W15 **Skownan** Manitoba, S Canada
94 H13 **Skreia** Oppland, S Norway
Skripón see Orchómenos
118 H9 **Skriveri** Aizkraukle, S Latvia
118 J11 **Skrudaliena** Daugvapils, SE Latvia
118 D9 **Skrunda** Kuldīga, W Latvia
95 C16 **Skudeneshavn** Rogaland, S Norway
83 L20 **Skukuza** Mpumalanga, NE South Africa
97 B22 **Skull** Ir. An Scoil. SW Ireland
22 L3 **Skuna River** ≈ Mississippi, S USA
29 X15 **Skunk River** ≈ Iowa, C USA
118 C10 **Skuodas** Ger. Schoden, Pol. Szkudy. Klaipėda, NW Lithuania
95 K23 **Skurup** Skåne, S Sweden
Skurz see Skórcz
114 H8 **Skŭt** ≈ NW Bulgaria
94 O13 **Skutskär** Uppsala, C Sweden
95 B19 **Skúvoy** Dan. Skuø. Island Faeroe Islands
Skvira see Skvyra
117 O5 **Skvyra** Rus. Skvira. Kyyivs'ka Oblast', N Ukraine
39 Q11 **Skwentna** Alaska, USA
110 E11 **Skwierzyna** Ger. Schwerin. Lubuskie, W Poland
36 K13 **Sky Harbour** ✕ (Phoenix) Arizona, SW USA
96 G9 **Skye, Isle of** island NW Scotland, UK
32 I8 **Skykomish** Washington, NW USA
Skylge see Terschelling
63 F19 **Skyring, Peninsula** peninsula S Chile
63 H24 **Skyring, Seno** inlet S Chile
115 H17 **Skyropoúla** var. Skiropoula. island Vóreioi Sporádes, Greece, Aegean Sea
115 I17 **Skýros** var. Skíros. Skýros, Vóreioi Sporádes, Greece, Aegean Sea
115 I17 **Skýros** var. Skíros; anc. Scyros. island Vóreioi Sporádes, Greece, Aegean Sea
118 J12 **Slabodka** Rus. Slobodka. Vitsyebskaya Voblasts', NW Belarus
95 I23 **Slagelse** Vestsjælland, E Denmark
93 I14 **Slagnäs** Norrbotten, N Sweden
39 T10 **Slana** Alaska, USA
97 F20 **Slaney** Ir. An tSláine. ≈ SE Ireland
116 J13 **Slănic** Prahova, SE Romania
116 K11 **Slănic Moldova** Bacău, E Romania
113 H16 **Slano** Dubrovnik-Neretva, SE Croatia
124 F13 **Slantsy** Leningradskaya Oblast', NW Russian Federation
111 C16 **Slaný** Ger. Schlan. Střední Čechy, NW Czech Republic
111 I16 **Śląskie** ◈ province S Poland
12 C10 **Slate Falls** Ontario, S Canada
27 T4 **Slater** Missouri, C USA
112 H9 **Slatina** Hung. Szlatina; prev. Podravska Slatina. Virovitica-Podravina, NE Croatia
116 I14 **Slatina** Olt, S Romania
25 N5 **Slaton** Texas, SW USA
95 H14 **Slattum** Akershus, S Norway
11 R10 **Slave** ≈ Alberta/Northwest Territories, C Canada
11 P13 **Slave Lake** Alberta, SW Canada
122 I13 **Slavgorod** Altayskiy Kray, S Russian Federation
Slavgorod see Slawharad
Slavonia see Slavonija
112 G9 **Slavonija** Eng. Slavonia, Ger. Slawonien, Hung. Szlavonia, Szlavonország. cultural region NE Croatia
Slavonska Požega see Požega
112 H10 **Slavonski Brod** Ger. Brod, Hung. Bród; prev. Brod, Brod na Savi. Brod-Posavina, NE Croatia
116 L4 **Slavuta** Khmel'nyts'ka Oblast', NW Ukraine
117 P2 **Slavutych** Chernihivs'ka Oblast', N Ukraine
123 R15 **Slavyanka** Primorskiy Kray, SE Russian Federation
114 J8 **Slavyanovo** Pleven, N Bulgaria
Slavyansk see Slov"yans'k
126 K14 **Slavyansk-na-Kubani** Krasnodarskiy Kray, SW Russian Federation
119 N20 **Slavyechna** Rus. Slovechna. ≈ Belarus/Ukraine
119 O16 **Slawharad** Rus. Slavgorod. Mahilyowskaya Voblasts', E Belarus
110 G7 **Sławno** Zachodnio-pomorskie, NW Poland
Slawonien see Slavonija
29 S10 **Slayton** Minnesota, N USA
97 N18 **Sleaford** E England, UK
97 A20 **Slea Head** Ir. Ceann Sléibhe. headland SW Ireland
96 G9 **Sleat, Sound of** strait NW Scotland, UK
Sledyuki see Slyedzyuki
12 I5 **Sleeper Islands** island group Nunavut, C Canada
31 O6 **Sleeping Bear Point** headland Michigan, N USA
29 T10 **Sleepy Eye** Minnesota, N USA
39 O11 **Sleetmute** Alaska, USA
Sléibhe, Ceann see Slea Head
Slēmānī see As Sulaymānīyah
195 O5 **Slessor Glacier** glacier Antarctica
22 L9 **Slidell** Louisiana, S USA
18 K12 **Slide Mountain** ▲ New York, NE USA
98 I13 **Sliedrecht** Zuid-Holland, C Netherlands
121 P16 **Sliema** N Malta
97 G16 **Slieve Donard** ▲ SE Northern Ireland, UK
Sliezsko see Silesia
97 D16 **Sligo** Ir. Sligeach. NW Ireland
97 C16 **Sligo** Ir. Sligeach. cultural region NW Ireland
97 C15 **Sligo Bay** Ir. Cuan Shligigh. inlet NW Ireland
18 B13 **Slippery Rock** Pennsylvania, NE USA
95 P19 **Slite** Gotland, SE Sweden
114 L9 **Sliven** var. Slivno. Sliven, C Bulgaria
114 L10 **Sliven** ◈ province C Bulgaria
114 G9 **Slivnitsa** Sofiya, W Bulgaria
Slivno see Sliven
114 L7 **Slivo Pole** Ruse, N Bulgaria
29 S13 **Sloan** Iowa, C USA
35 X12 **Sloan** Nevada, W USA
Slobodka see Slabodka
125 R14 **Slobodskoy** Kirovskaya Oblast', NW Russian Federation
Slobodzeya see Slobozia
117 O10 **Slobozia** Rus. Slobodzeya. E Moldova
116 L14 **Slobozia** Ialomiţa, SE Romania
98 O5 **Slochteren** Groningen, NE Netherlands
119 H17 **Slonim** Pol. Słonim, Rus. Slonim. Hrodzyenskaya Voblasts', W Belarus
98 K7 **Sloter Meer** ◎ N Netherlands
Slot, The see New Georgia Sound
97 N22 **Slough** S England, UK
111 J20 **Slovakia** off. Slovenská Republika, Ger. Slowakei, Hung. Szlovákia, Slvk. Slovensko. ◆ republic C Europe
Slovak Ore Mountains see Slovenské rudohorie
Slovechna see Slavyechna
109 S12 **Slovenia** off. Republic of Slovenia, Ger. Slowenien, Slvn. Slovenija. ◆ republic SE Europe
Slovenija see Slovenia
109 V10 **Slovenj Gradec** Ger. Windischgraz. N Slovenia
109 W10 **Slovenska Bistrica** Ger. Windischfeistritz. NE Slovenia
Slovenská Republika see Slovakia
109 W10 **Slovenske Konjice** E Slovenia
111 K20 **Slovenské rudohorie** Eng. Slovak Ore Mountains, Ger. Slowakisches Erzgebirge, Ungarisches Erzgebirge. ⛰ C Slovakia
Slovensko see Slovakia
117 Y7 **Slov"yanoserbs'k** Luhans'ka Oblast', E Ukraine
117 W6 **Slov"yans'k** Rus. Slavyansk. Donets'ka Oblast', E Ukraine
Slowakei see Slovakia
Slowakisches Erzgebirge see Slovenské rudohorie
Slowenien see Slovenia
110 D11 **Słubice** Ger. Frankfurt. Lubuskie, W Poland
119 K19 **Sluch** Rus. Sluch'. ≈ C Belarus
116 L4 **Sluch** ≈ NW Ukraine
99 D16 **Sluis** Zeeland, SW Netherlands
112 D10 **Slunj** Hung. Szluin. Karlovac, C Croatia
110 I11 **Słupca** Wielkolpolskie, C Poland
110 G6 **Słupia** Ger. Stolpe. ≈ NW Poland
110 G6 **Słupsk** Ger. Stolp. Pomorskie, N Poland
119 K18 **Slutsk** Rus. Slutsk. Minskaya Voblasts', S Belarus
119 O16 **Slyedzyuki** Rus. Sledyuki. Mahilyowskaya Voblasts', E Belarus
97 A17 **Slyne Head** Ir. Ceann Léime. headland W Ireland
27 U14 **Smackover** Arkansas, C USA
95 L20 **Småland** cultural region S Sweden
95 K20 **Smålandsstenar** Jönköping, S Sweden
Small Malaita see Maramasike
13 O8 **Smallwood Reservoir** ⊡ Newfoundland and Labrador, S Canada
119 N14 **Smalyany** Rus. Smolyany. Vitsyebskaya Voblasts', N Belarus
119 L15 **Smalyavichy** Rus. Smolevichi. Minskaya Voblasts', C Belarus
74 C9 **Smara** var. Es Semara. N Western Sahara
119 I14 **Smarhon'** Pol. Smorgonie, Rus. Smorgon'. Hrodzyenskaya Voblasts', W Belarus
112 M11 **Smederevo** Ger. Semendria. Serbia, N Serbia and Montenegro (Yugo.)
112 M12 **Smederevska Palanka** Serbia, C Serbia and Montenegro (Yugo.)
95 M14 **Smedjebacken** Dalarna, C Sweden
116 L13 **Smeeni** Buzău, SE Romania
Smela see Smila
107 D16 **Smeralda, Costa** cultural region Sardegna, Italy, C Mediterranean Sea

111 J22 **Šmigiel** *Ger.* Schmiegel. Wielkolpolskie, C Poland
117 Q6 **Smila** *Rus.* Smela. Cherkas'ka Oblast', C Ukraine
98 N7 **Smilde** Drenthe, NE Netherlands
11 S16 **Smiley** Saskatchewan, S Canada
25 T12 **Smiley** Texas, SW USA
Smilten *see* Smiltene
118 I8 **Smiltene** *Ger.* Smilten. Valka, N Latvia
123 T13 **Smirnykh** Ostrov Sakhalin, Sakhalinskaya Oblast', SE Russian Federation
11 Q13 **Smith** Alberta, W Canada
39 P4 **Smith Bay** *bay* Alaska, USA
12 I3 **Smith, Cape** *headland* Québec, NE Canada
26 L3 **Smith Center** Kansas, C USA
10 K13 **Smithers** British Columbia, SW Canada
21 V10 **Smithfield** North Carolina, SE USA
36 L1 **Smithfield** Utah, W USA
21 X7 **Smithfield** Virginia, NE USA
12 I3 **Smith Island** *island* Nunavut, C Canada
Smith Island *see* Sumisu-jima
20 H7 **Smithland** Kentucky, S USA
21 T7 **Smith Mountain Lake** *var.* Leesville Lake. ⊠ Virginia, NE USA
34 L1 **Smith River** California, W USA
33 R9 **Smith River** ≈ Montana, NW USA
14 L13 **Smiths Falls** Ontario, SE Canada
33 N13 **Smiths Ferry** Idaho, NW USA
20 K7 **Smiths Grove** Kentucky, S USA
183 N15 **Smithton** Tasmania, SE Australia
18 L14 **Smithtown** Long Island, New York, NE USA
20 K9 **Smithville** Tennessee, S USA
25 T11 **Smithville** Texas, SW USA
Šmohor *see* Hermagor
35 Q4 **Smoke Creek Desert** *desert* Nevada, W USA
11 O14 **Smoky** ≈ Alberta, W Canada
182 E7 **Smoky Bay** South Australia
183 V6 **Smoky Cape** *headland* New South Wales, SE Australia
26 L4 **Smoky Hill River** ≈ Kansas, C USA
26 L4 **Smoky Hills** *hill range* Kansas, C USA
11 Q14 **Smoky Lake** Alberta, SW Canada
94 E8 **Smøla** *island* W Norway
126 H4 **Smolensk** Smolenskaya Oblast', W Russian Federation
126 H4 **Smolenskaya Oblast'** ◈ *province* W Russian Federation
Smolensk-Moscow Upland *see* Smolensko-Moskovskaya Vozvyshennost'
126 J3 **Smolensko-Moskovskaya Vozvyshennost'** *var.* Smolensk-Moscow Upland. ▲▲ W Russian Federation
Smolevichi *see* Smalyavichy
115 C15 **Smolikás** ▲ W Greece
114 I12 **Smolyan** *prev.* Pashmakli. Smolyan, S Bulgaria
114 I12 **Smolyan** ◈ *province* S Bulgaria
Smolyany *see* Smalyany
33 S15 **Smoot** Wyoming, C USA
12 G12 **Smooth Rock Falls** Ontario, S Canada
Smorgon'/Smorgonie *see* Smarhon'
95 K23 **Smygehamn** Skåne, S Sweden
194 I7 **Smyley Island** *island* Antarctica
21 Y3 **Smyrna** Delaware, NE USA
23 S3 **Smyrna** Georgia, SE USA
20 J9 **Smyrna** Tennessee, S USA
Smyrna *see* İzmir
97 I16 **Snaefell** ▲ C Isle of Man
92 H3 **Snaefellsjökull** ▲ W Iceland
10 J4 **Snake** ≈ Yukon Territory, NW Canada
29 O8 **Snake Creek** ≈ South Dakota, N USA
183 P13 **Snake Island** *island* Victoria, SE Australia
35 Y6 **Snake Range** ▲▲ Nevada, W USA
32 K10 **Snake River** ≈ NW USA
29 V6 **Snake River** ≈ Minnesota, N USA
28 L12 **Snake River** ≈ Nebraska, C USA
33 Q14 **Snake River Plain** *plain* Idaho, NW USA
93 E15 **Snåsa** Nord-Trøndelag, C Norway
21 O8 **Sneedville** Tennessee, S USA
98 K5 **Sneek** Friesland, N Netherlands
Sneeuw-gebergte *see* Maoke, Pegunungan
95 F22 **Snejbjerg** Ringkøbing, C Denmark
122 G11 **Snezhinsk** Chelyabinskaya Oblast', W Russian Federation
124 J3 **Snezhnogorsk** Murmanskaya Oblast', NW Russian Federation
122 K9 **Snezhnogorsk** Taymyrskiy (Dolgano-Nenetskiy) Avtonomnyy Okrug, N Russian Federation
Snezhnoye *see* Snizhne
111 G15 **Sněžka** *Ger.* Schneekoppe, *Pol.* Śnieżka. ▲ Czech Republic/Poland
110 N8 **Śniardwy, Jezioro** *Ger.* Spirdingsee. ◎ NE Poland
Sniečkus *see* Visaginas
Śnieżka *see* Sněžka
117 R10 **Snihurivka** Mykolayivs'ka Oblast', S Ukraine
116 I5 **Snilov** ✕ (L'viv) L'vivs'ka Oblast', W Ukraine
111 O19 **Snina** *Hung.* Szinna. Prešovský Kraj, E Slovakia
117 Y8 **Snizhne** *Rus.* Snezhnoye. Donets'ka Oblast', SE Ukraine
92 J3 **Snækollur** ▲ C Iceland
94 G10 **Snøhetta** *var.* Snohetta. ▲ S Norway
92 G12 **Snøtinden** ▲ C Norway
97 I18 **Snowdon** ▲ NW Wales, UK
97 I18 **Snowdonia** ▲▲ NW Wales, UK
8 K10 **Snowdrift** ≈ Northwest Territories, NW Canada
Snowdrift *see* Łutselk'e
37 N12 **Snowflake** Arizona, SW USA
21 Y5 **Snow Hill** Maryland, NE USA
21 W10 **Snow Hill** North Carolina, SE USA
194 H3 **Snowhill Island** *island* Antarctica
11 V13 **Snow Lake** Manitoba, C Canada
37 R5 **Snowmass Mountain** ▲ Colorado, C USA
18 M10 **Snow, Mount** ▲ Vermont, NE USA
34 M5 **Snow Mountain** ▲ California, W USA
Snow Mountains *see* Maoke, Pegunungan
33 N7 **Snowshoe Peak** ▲ Montana, NW USA
182 I8 **Snowtown** South Australia
36 K1 **Snowville** Utah, W USA
35 X3 **Snow Water Lake** ◎ Nevada, W USA
183 Q11 **Snowy Mountains** ▲▲ New South Wales/Victoria, SE Australia
183 Q12 **Snowy River** ≈ New South Wales/Victoria, SE Australia
44 K5 **Snug Corner** Acklins Island, SE Bahamas
167 T13 **Snuŏl** Krâchéh, E Cambodia
116 J7 **Snyatyn** *Rus.* Snyatyn. Ivano-Frankivs'ka Oblast', W Ukraine
26 L12 **Snyder** Oklahoma, C USA
25 O6 **Snyder** Texas, SW USA
172 H3 **Soalala** Mahajanga, W Madagascar
172 J4 **Soanierana-Ivongo** Toamasina, E Madagascar
171 R11 **Soasiu** *var.* Tidore. Pulau Tidore, E Indonesia
54 G8 **Soatá** Boyacá, C Colombia
172 I5 **Soavinandriana** Antananarivo, C Madagascar
77 V13 **Soba** Kaduna, C Nigeria
163 Y16 **Sobaek-sanmaek** ▲▲ S South Korea
80 F13 **Sobat** ≈ E Sudan
171 Z14 **Sobger, Sungai** ≈ Papua, E Indonesia
171 V13 **Sobiei** Papua, E Indonesia
126 M3 **Sobinka** Vladimirskaya Oblast', W Russian Federation
127 S7 **Sobolevo** Orenburgskaya Oblast', W Russian Federation
Soborsin *see* Săvârşin
164 D15 **Sobo-san** ▲ Kyūshū, SW Japan
111 G14 **Sobótka** Dolnośląskie, SW Poland
59 O15 **Sobradinho** Bahia, E Brazil
Sobradinho, Barragem de *see* Sobradinho, Represa de
59 O16 **Sobradinho, Represa de** *var.* Barragem de Sobradinho. ⊠ E Brazil
58 O13 **Sobral** Ceará, E Brazil
105 T4 **Sobrarbe** *physical region* NE Spain
109 R10 **Soča** *It.* Isonzo. ≈ Italy/Slovenia
110 L11 **Sochaczew** Mazowieckie, C Poland
126 L15 **Sochi** Krasnodarskiy Kray, SW Russian Federation
114 G13 **Sochós** *var.* Sohos, Sokhós. Kentrikí Makedonía, N Greece
191 R11 **Société, Archipel de la** *var.* Archipel de Tahiti, Îles de la Société, *Eng.* Society Islands. *island group* W French Polynesia
Société, Îles de la/Society Islands *see* Société, Archipel de la
21 T11 **Society Hill** South Carolina, SE USA
62 I5 **Socompa, Volcán** ▲ N Chile
Soconusco, Sierra de *see* Sierra Madre
54 G8 **Socorro** Santander, C Colombia
37 R13 **Socorro** New Mexico, SW USA
Socotra *see* Suquṭrā
167 S14 **Soc Trăng** *var.* Khanh *Hung.* Soc Trăng, S Vietnam
105 P10 **Socuéllamos** Castilla-La Mancha, C Spain
35 W13 **Soda Lake** *salt flat* California, W USA
92 L11 **Sodankylä** Lappi, N Finland
Sodari *see* Sodiri
33 R15 **Soda Springs** Idaho, NW USA
Soddo/Soddu *see* Sodo
20 L10 **Soddy Daisy** Tennessee, S USA
95 N14 **Söderfors** Uppsala, C Sweden
94 N12 **Söderhamn** Gävleborg, C Sweden
95 N17 **Söderköping** Östergötland, S Sweden
95 N17 **Södermanland** ◈ *county* C Sweden
95 O16 **Södertälje** Stockholm, C Sweden
80 D10 **Sodiri** *var.* Sawdirī, Sodari. Northern Kordofan, C Sudan
81 I14 **Sodo** *var.* Soddo, Soddu. Southern, S Ethiopia
94 N11 **Södra Dellen** ◎ C Sweden
95 M19 **Södra Vi** Kalmar, S Sweden
18 G9 **Sodus Point** *headland* New York, NE USA
171 Q17 **Soe** *prev.* Soë. Timor, C Indonesia
169 N15 **Soekarno-Hatta** ✕ (Jakarta) Jawa, S Indonesia
Soëla-Sund *see* Soela Väin
118 E5 **Soela Väin** *prev. Eng.* Sele Sound, *Ger.* Dagden-Sund, Soëla-Sund. *strait* W Estonia
Soemba *see* Sumba, Pulau
Soembawa *see* Sumbawa
Soemenep *see* Sumenep
Soengaipenoeh *see* Sungaipenuh
Soerabaja *see* Surabaya
101 G14 **Soest** Nordrhein-Westfalen, W Germany
98 J11 **Soest** Utrecht, C Netherlands
100 F11 **Soeste** ≈ NW Germany
98 J11 **Soesterberg** Utrecht, C Netherlands
115 E16 **Sofádes** *var.* Sofádhes. Thessalía, C Greece
Sofádhes *see* Sofádes
83 N18 **Sofala** Sofala, C Mozambique
83 N17 **Sofala** ◈ *province* C Mozambique
83 N18 **Sofala, Baia de** *bay* E Mozambique
172 J3 **Sofia** *seasonal river* NW Madagascar
Sofia *see* Sofiya
115 G19 **Sofikó** Pelopónnisos, S Greece
Sofi-Kurgan *see* Sopu-Korgon
114 G10 **Sofiya** *var.* Sophia, *Eng.* Sofia; *Lat.* Serdica. ● (Bulgaria) Sofiya-Grad, W Bulgaria
114 G9 **Sofiya** ✕ Sofiya-Grad, W Bulgaria
114 H9 **Sofiya** ◈ *province* W Bulgaria
114 G9 **Sofiya-Grad** ◈ *municipality* W Bulgaria
Sofiyevka *see* Sofiyivka
117 S8 **Sofiyivka** *Rus.* Sofiyevka. Dnipropetrovs'ka Oblast', E Ukraine
123 R13 **Sofiysk** Khabarovskiy Kray, SE Russian Federation
123 S12 **Sofiysk** Khabarovskiy Kray, SE Russian Federation
124 I6 **Sofporog** Respublika Kareliya, NW Russian Federation
165 Y14 **Sōfu-gan** *island* Izu-shotō, SE Japan
156 K10 **Sog** Xizang Zizhiqu, W China
54 G9 **Sogamoso** Boyacá, C Colombia
136 I11 **Soğanlı Çayı** ≈ N Turkey
94 E12 **Sogn** *physical region* S Norway
94 E12 **Sogndal** *see* Sogndalsfjøra.
94 E12 **Sogndalsfjøra** *var.* Sogndal. Sogn og Fjordane, S Norway
95 E18 **Søgne** Vest-Agder, S Norway
94 D12 **Sognefjorden** *fjord* NE North Sea
94 C12 **Sogn Og Fjordane** ◈ *county* S Norway
162 I11 **Sogo Nur** ◎ N China
159 T12 **Sogruma** Qinghai, W China
163 X17 **Sŏgwip'o** S South Korea
75 X10 **Sohâg** *var.* Sawhāj, Suliag. C Egypt
Sohar *see* Ṣuḥār
64 H9 **Sohm Plain** *undersea feature* NW Atlantic Ocean
100 H7 **Soholmer Au** ≈ N Germany
Sohos *see* Sochós
Sohrau *see* Żory
99 F20 **Soignies** Hainaut, SW Belgium
159 R15 **Soila** Xizang Zizhiqu, W China
103 P4 **Soissons** *anc.* Augusta Suessionum, Noviodunum. Aisne, N France
164 H13 **Sōja** Okayama, Honshū, SW Japan
152 F13 **Sojat** Rājasthān, N India
163 W13 **Sŏjosŏn-man** *inlet* W North Korea
116 I4 **Sokal'** *Rus.* Sokal. L'vivs'ka Oblast', NW Ukraine
163 Y14 **Sokch'o** N South Korea
136 B15 **Söke** Aydın, SW Turkey
189 N12 **Sokehs Island** *island* E Micronesia
79 M24 **Sokele** Katanga, SE Dem. Rep. Congo
147 R11 **Sokh** *Uzb.* Sŭkh. ≈ Kyrgyzstan/Uzbekistan
Sokh *see* So'x
Sokhós *see* Sochós
137 Q8 **Sokhumi** *Rus.* Sukhumi. NW Georgia
113 O14 **Sokobanja** Serbia, E Serbia and Montenegro (Yugo.)
77 R15 **Sokodé** C Togo
123 T10 **Sokol** Magadanskaya Oblast', E Russian Federation
124 M13 **Sokol** Vologodskaya Oblast', NW Russian Federation
110 P9 **Sokółka** Podlaskie, NE Poland
76 M11 **Sokolo** Ségou, W Mali
111 A16 **Sokolov** *Ger.* Falkenau an der Eger; *prev.* Falknov nad Ohří. Karlovarský Kraj, W Czech Republic
111 O16 **Sokołów Małopolski** Podkarpackie, SE Poland
110 O11 **Sokołów Podlaski** Mazowieckie, E Poland
76 G11 **Sokone** W Senegal
77 T12 **Sokoto** Sokoto, NW Nigeria
77 T12 **Sokoto** ◈ *state* NW Nigeria
77 S12 **Sokoto** ≈ NW Nigeria
Sokotra *see* Suquṭrā
147 U7 **Sokuluk** Chuyskaya Oblast', N Kyrgyzstan
116 L7 **Sokyryany** Chernivets'ka Oblast', W Ukraine
95 C16 **Sola** Rogaland, S Norway
187 R12 **Sola** Vanua Lava, N Vanuatu
95 C17 **Sola** ✕ (Stavanger) Rogaland, S Norway
81 H18 **Solai** Rift Valley, W Kenya
152 I8 **Solan** Himāchal Pradesh, N India
185 A25 **Solander Island** *island* SW NZ
Solano *see* Bahía Solano
155 F15 **Solāpur** *var.* Sholāpur. Mahārāshtra, W India
93 H16 **Solberg** Västernorrland, C Sweden
116 K9 **Solca** *Ger.* Solka. Suceava, N Romania
105 O16 **Sol, Costa del** *coastal region* S Spain
106 F5 **Solda** *Ger.* Sulden. Trentino-Alto Adige, N Italy
117 N9 **Şoldăneşti** *Rus.* Sholdaneshty. N Moldova
Soldau *see* Wkra
108 L8 **Sölden** Tirol, W Austria
27 P3 **Soldier Creek** ≈ Kansas, C USA
39 R12 **Soldotna** Alaska, USA
110 I10 **Solec Kujawski** Kujawsko-pomorskie, C Poland
61 B16 **Soledad** Santa Fe, C Argentina
55 E4 **Soledad** Atlántico, N Colombia
35 O11 **Soledad** California, W USA
55 O7 **Soledad** Anzoátegui, NE Venezuela
Soledad *see* East Falkland
Soledad, Isla *see* East Falkland
61 H15 **Soledade** Rio Grande do Sul, S Brazil
103 Y15 **Solenzara** Corse, France, C Mediterranean Sea
Soleure *see* Solothurn
94 C12 **Solheim** Hordaland, S Norway
127 N14 **Soligalich** Kostromskaya Oblast', NW Russian Federation
Soligorsk *see* Salihorsk
97 L20 **Solihull** C England, UK
125 U13 **Solikamsk** Permskaya Oblast', NW Russian Federation
127 V8 **Sol'-Iletsk** Orenburgskaya Oblast', W Russian Federation
57 G17 **Solimana, Nevado** ▲ S Peru
58 E13 **Solimões, Rio** ≈ C Brazil
113 E14 **Solin** *It.* Salona; *anc.* Salonae. Split-Dalmacija, S Croatia
101 E15 **Solingen** Nordrhein-Westfalen, W Germany
Solka *see* Solca
93 H16 **Sollefteå** Västernorrland, C Sweden
95 O15 **Sollentuna** Stockholm, C Sweden
94 L13 **Sollerön** Dalarna, C Sweden
101 I14 **Solling** *hill range* C Germany
95 O16 **Solna** Stockholm, C Sweden
126 K3 **Solnechnogorsk** Moskovskaya Oblast', W Russian Federation
123 R10 **Solnechnyy** Khabarovskiy Kray, SE Russian Federation
122 K13 **Solnechnyy** Krasnoyarskiy Kray, C Russian Federation
123 S13 **Solnechnyy** Respublika Sakha (Yakutiya), NE Russian Federation
107 L17 **Solofra** Campania, S Italy
168 J11 **Solok** Sumatera, W Indonesia
42 C6 **Sololá** Sololá, W Guatemala
42 A2 **Sololá** *off.* Departamento de Sololá. ◈ *department* SW Guatemala
81 J16 **Sololo** Eastern, N Kenya
42 C4 **Soloma** Huehuetenango, W Guatemala
38 M9 **Solomon** Alaska, USA
27 N4 **Solomon** Kansas, C USA
187 N9 **Solomon Islands** *prev.* British Solomon Islands Protectorate. ◆ *commonwealth republic* W Pacific Ocean
186 L7 **Solomon Islands** *island group* PNG/Solomon Islands
26 M3 **Solomon River** ≈ Kansas, C USA
186 H8 **Solomon Sea** *sea* W Pacific Ocean
31 U11 **Solon** Ohio, N USA
117 T8 **Solone** Dnipropetrovs'ka Oblast', E Ukraine
171 P16 **Solor, Kepulauan** *island group* S Indonesia
126 M4 **Solotcha** Ryazanskaya Oblast', W Russian Federation
108 D7 **Solothurn** *Fr.* Soleure. Solothurn, NW Switzerland
108 D7 **Solothurn** *Fr.* Soleure. ◈ *canton* NW Switzerland
126 J7 **Solovetskiye Ostrova** *island group* NW Russian Federation
105 V5 **Solsona** Cataluña, NE Spain
113 E14 **Šolta** *It.* Solta. *island* S Croatia
Solṭānābād *see* Kāshmar
142 L4 **Solṭānīyeh** Zanjān, NW Iran
100 I11 **Soltau** Niedersachsen, NW Germany
124 G14 **Sol'tsy** Novgorodskaya Oblast', W Russian Federation
Soltüstik Qazaqstan Oblysy *see* Severnyy Kazakhstan
Solun *see* Thessaloníki
113 O19 **Solunska Glava** ▲ C FYR Macedonia
95 L22 **Sölvesborg** Blekinge, S Sweden
97 J15 **Solway Firth** *inlet* England/Scotland, UK
82 I13 **Solwezi** North Western, NW Zambia
165 Q11 **Sōma** Fukushima, Honshū, C Japan
136 C13 **Soma** Manisa, W Turkey
81 M14 **Somali** ◈ *region* E Ethiopia
81 O15 **Somalia** *off.* Somali Democratic Republic, *Som.* Jamuuriyada Demuqraadiga Soomaaliyeed, Soomaaliya; *prev.* Italian Somaliland, Somaliland Protectorate. ◆ *republic* E Africa
173 N6 **Somali Basin** *undersea feature* W Indian Ocean
112 J8 **Sombor** *Hung.* Zombor. Serbia, NW Serbia and Montenegro (Yugo.)
99 H20 **Sombreffe** Namur, S Belgium
40 L10 **Sombrerete** Zacatecas, C Mexico
45 V8 **Sombrero** *island* N Anguilla
151 Q21 **Sombrero Channel** *channel* Nicobar Islands, India
116 H9 **Şomcuta Mare** *Hung.* Nagysomkút; *prev.* Somcuţa Mare. Maramureş, N Romania
167 R9 **Somdet** Kalasin, E Thailand
99 L15 **Someren** Noord-Brabant, SE Netherlands
93 L19 **Somero** Länsi-Suomi, W Finland
33 P7 **Somers** Montana, NW USA
64 A12 **Somerset** *var.* Somerset Village. W Bermuda
37 Q5 **Somerset** Colorado, C USA
20 M7 **Somerset** Kentucky, S USA
19 O12 **Somerset** Massachusetts, NE USA
97 K23 **Somerset** *cultural region* SW England, UK
Somerset East *see* Somerset-Oos
64 A12 **Somerset Island** *island* W Bermuda
197 N9 **Somerset Island** *island* Queen Elizabeth Islands, Nunavut, NW Canada
Somerset Nile *see* Victoria Nile
83 I25 **Somerset-Oos** *Eng.* Somerset East. Eastern Cape, S South Africa
83 E26 **Somerset-Wes** *Eng.* Somerset West. Western Cape, SW South Africa
Somerset West *see* Somerset-Wes
Somers Islands *see* Bermuda
18 J17 **Somers Point** New Jersey, NE USA
19 P9 **Somersworth** New Hampshire, NE USA
36 H15 **Somerton** Arizona, SW USA
18 J14 **Somerville** New Jersey, NE USA
20 F10 **Somerville** Tennessee, S USA
25 U10 **Somerville** Texas, SW USA
25 T10 **Somerville Lake** ⊠ Texas, SW USA
Someş/Somesch/Someşul *see* Szamos
103 N2 **Somme** ◈ *department* N France
103 N2 **Somme** ≈ N France
95 L18 **Sommen** Jönköping, S Sweden
95 M18 **Sommen** ◎ S Sweden
101 K16 **Sömmerda** Thüringen, C Germany
Sommerein *see* Šamorín
Sommerfeld *see* Lubsko
55 Y11 **Sommet Tabulaire** *var.* Mont Itoupé. ▲ S French Guiana
111 H25 **Somogy** *off.* Somogy Megye. ◈ *county* SW Hungary
Somorja *see* Šamorín
105 N7 **Somosierra, Puerto de** *pass* N Spain
187 Y14 **Somosomo** Taveuni, N Fiji
42 I9 **Somotillo** Chinandega, NW Nicaragua
42 I8 **Somoto** Madriz, NW Nicaragua
110 I11 **Sompolno** Wielkolpolskie, C Poland
105 S3 **Somport** *var.* Puerto de Somport, *Fr.* Col du Somport; *anc.* Summus Portus. *pass* France/Spain *see also* Somport, Col du
102 J17 **Somport, Col du** *var.* Puerto de Somport, *Sp.* Somport; *anc.* Summus Portus. *pass* France/Spain *see also* Somport
Somport, Puerto de *see* Somport/Somport, Col du
99 K15 **Son** Noord-Brabant, S Netherlands
95 H15 **Son** Akershus, S Norway
154 L9 **Son** *var.* Sone. ≈ C India
43 R16 **Soná** Veraguas, W Panama
Sonag *see* Zêkog
154 M12 **Sonapur** *prev.* Sonepur. Orissa, E India
95 G24 **Sønderborg** *Ger.* Sonderburg. Sønderjylland, SW Denmark
Sonderburg *see* Sønderborg
95 F24 **Sønderjylland** *off.* Sønderjyllands Amt. ◈ *county* SW Denmark
101 K15 **Sondershausen** Thüringen, C Germany
Søndre Strømfjord *see* Kangerlussuaq
106 E6 **Sondrio** Lombardia, N Italy
Sone *see* Son
Sonepur *see* Sonapur
57 K22 **Sonequera** ▲ S Bolivia
167 V12 **Sông Câu** Phu Yên, C Vietnam
167 R15 **Sông Đôc** Minh Hai, S Vietnam
81 H25 **Songea** Ruvuma, S Tanzania
163 X10 **Songhua Hu** ◎ NE China
163 Y7 **Songhua Jiang** *var.* Sungari. ≈ NE China
161 S8 **Songjiang** Shanghai Shi, E China
Sŏngjin *see* Kimch'aek
167 O16 **Songkhla** *var.* Songkla, *Mal.* Singora. Songkhla, SW Thailand
Songkla *see* Songkhla
163 T13 **Song Ling** ▲▲ NE China
163 W14 **Songnim** SW North Korea
82 B10 **Songo** Uíge, NW Angola
83 M15 **Songo** Tete, NW Mozambique
79 F21 **Songololo** Bas-Congo, SW Dem. Rep. Congo
160 H7 **Songpan** *var.* Jin'an, *Tib.* Sungpu. Sichuan, C China
163 Y17 **Sŏngsan** S South Korea
161 R11 **Songxi** Fujian, SE China
160 M6 **Songxian** *var.* Song Xian. Henan, C China
161 R10 **Songyang** *var.* Xiping. Zhejiang, SE China
163 V9 **Songyuan** *var.* Fu-yü, Petuna; *prev.* Fuyu. Jilin, NE China
Sonid Youqi *see* Saihan Tal
Sonid Zuoqi *see* Mandalt
152 I10 **Sonīpat** Haryāna, N India
93 M15 **Sonkajärvi** Itä-Suomi, C Finland
167 R6 **Sơn La** Sơn La, N Vietnam
149 O16 **Sonmiāni** Baluchistān, S Pakistan
149 O16 **Sonmiāni Bay** *bay* S Pakistan
101 K18 **Sonneberg** Thüringen, C Germany
101 N24 **Sonntagshorn** ▲ Austria/Germany
Sonoita *see* Sonoyta
40 E3 **Sonoita, Rio** *var.* Río Sonoyta. ≈ Mexico/USA
35 N7 **Sonoma** California, W USA
35 T3 **Sonoma Peak** ▲ Nevada, W USA
35 P8 **Sonora** California, W USA
25 O10 **Sonora** Texas, SW USA
40 F5 **Sonora** ◈ *state* NW Mexico
35 X17 **Sonoran Desert** *var.* Desierto de Altar. *desert* Mexico/USA *see also* Altar, Desierto de
40 G5 **Sonora, Río** ≈ NW Mexico
40 E2 **Sonoyta** *var.* Sonoita. Sonora, NW Mexico
Sonoyta, Río *see* Sonoita, Rio
142 K6 **Sonqor** *var.* Sunqur. Kermānshāh, W Iran
105 N9 **Sonseca** *var.* Sonseca con Casalgordo. Castilla-La Mancha, C Spain
Sonseca con Casalgordo *see* Sonseca
54 E9 **Sonsón** Antioquia, W Colombia
42 E7 **Sonsonate** Sonsonate, W El Salvador
42 A9 **Sonsonate** ◈ *department* SW El Salvador
188 A10 **Sonsorol Islands** *island group* S Palau
112 J9 **Sonta** *Hung.* Szond; *prev.* Szonta. Serbia, NW Serbia and Montenegro (Yugo.)
167 S6 **Sơn Tây** *var.* Sontay. Ha Tây, N Vietnam
101 J25 **Sonthofen** Bayern, S Germany
Soochow *see* Suzhou
Soomaaliya/Soomaaliyeed, Jamuuriyada Demuqraadiga *see* Somalia
Soome Laht *see* Finland, Gulf of
Sooner State *see* Oklahoma
23 V5 **Soperton** Georgia, SE USA
167 S6 **Sop Hao** Houaphan, N Laos
Sophia *see* Sofiya
171 S10 **Sopi** Pulau Morotai, E Indonesia
Sopianae *see* Pécs
171 U13 **Sopinusa** Papua, E Indonesia
81 B14 **Sopo** ≈ W Sudan
Sopockinie/Sopotskin *see* Sapotskino
114 I9 **Sopot** Plovdiv, C Bulgaria
110 I7 **Sopot** *Ger.* Zoppot. Pomorskie, N Poland
167 O8 **Sop Prap** *var.* Ban Sop Prap. Lampang, NW Thailand
111 G22 **Sopron** *Ger.* Ödenburg. Győr-Moson-Sopron, NW Hungary
147 U11 **Sopu-Korgon** *var.* Sofi-Kurgan. Oshskaya Oblast', SW Kyrgyzstan
152 H5 **Sopur** Jammu and Kashmir, NW India
107 J15 **Sora** Lazio, C Italy
154 N13 **Sorada** Orissa, E India
93 H17 **Söråker** Västernorrland, C Sweden
57 J17 **Sorata** La Paz, W Bolivia
Sorau/Sorau in der Niederlausitz *see* Żary
105 Q14 **Sorbas** Andalucía, S Spain
Sord/Sórd Choluim Chille *see* Swords
15 O11 **Sorel** Québec, SE Canada
183 P17 **Sorell** Tasmania, SE Australia
183 O17 **Sorell, Lake** ◎ Tasmania, SE Australia
106 E8 **Soresina** Lombardia, N Italy
95 D14 **Sørfjorden** *fjord* S Norway
94 N11 **Sörforsa** Gävleborg, C Sweden
103 R14 **Sorgues** Vaucluse, SE France
136 K13 **Sorgun** Yozgat, C Turkey
105 P5 **Soria** Castilla-León, N Spain
105 P6 **Soria** ◈ *province* Castilla-León, N Spain
61 D19 **Soriano** Soriano, SW Uruguay
61 D19 **Soriano** ◈ *department* SW Uruguay
92 O4 **Sørkapp** *headland* SW Svalbard
143 T5 **Sorkh, Kūh-e** ▲▲ NE Iran
Soro *see* Ghazal, Bahr el
95 I23 **Sorø** Vestsjælland, E Denmark
116 M8 **Soroca** *Rus.* Soroki. N Moldova
60 L10 **Sorocaba** São Paulo, S Brazil
Sorochino *see* Sarochyna
127 T7 **Sorochinsk** Orenburgskaya Oblast', W Russian Federation
Soroki *see* Soroca
188 H15 **Sorol** *atoll* Caroline Islands, W Micronesia
171 T12 **Sorong** Papua, E Indonesia
81 G17 **Soroti** C Uganda
Sørøy *see* Sørøya
92 J8 **Sørøya** *var.* Sørøy, *Lapp.* Sállan. *island* N Norway
104 G11 **Sorraia, Rio** ≈ C Portugal
92 I10 **Sørreisa** Troms, N Norway
107 K18 **Sorrento** *anc.* Surrentum. Campania, S Italy
104 H10 **Sor, Ribeira de** *stream* C Portugal
195 T3 **Sør Rondane Mountains** ▲▲ Antarctica
93 H14 **Sorsele** Västerbotten, N Sweden
107 B17 **Sorso** Sardegna, Italy, C Mediterranean Sea
171 P4 **Sorsogon** Luzon, N Philippines
105 U4 **Sort** Cataluña, NE Spain
124 H11 **Sortavala** Respublika Kareliya, NW Russian Federation
107 L25 **Sortino** Sicilia, Italy, C Mediterranean Sea
92 G10 **Sortland** Nordland, C Norway
94 G9 **Sør-Trøndelag** ◈ *county* S Norway
95 I15 **Sørumsand** Akershus, S Norway
118 D6 **Sõrve Säär** *headland* SW Estonia
95 K22 **Sösdala** Skåne, S Sweden
105 R4 **Sos del Rey Católico** Aragón, NE Spain
93 F15 **Sösjöfjällen** ▲ C Sweden
126 K7 **Sosna** ≈ W Russian Federation
62 H12 **Sosneado, Cerro** ▲ W Argentina
125 S9 **Sosnogorsk** Respublika Komi, NW Russian Federation
124 J8 **Sosnovets** Respublika Kareliya, NW Russian Federation
Sosnovets *see* Sosnowiec
127 Q3 **Sosnovka** Chuvashskaya Respublika, W Russian Federation
125 S16 **Sosnovka** Kirovskaya Oblast', NW Russian Federation
126 M6 **Sosnovka** Murmanskaya Oblast', NW Russian Federation
126 M6 **Sosnovka** Tambovskaya Oblast', W Russian Federation

◆ Country ● Country Capital ◇ Dependent Territory ○ Dependent Territory Capital ◈ Administrative Region ✕ International Airport ▲ Mountain ▲▲ Mountain Range Volcano ≈ River ◎ Lake ⊠ Reservoir

124 H12 **Sosnovo** *Fin.* Rautu. Leningradskaya Oblast', NW Russian Federation
Sosnovyy Bor *see* Sasnovy Bor
111 J16 **Sosnowiec** *Ger.* Sosnowitz, *Rus.* Sosnovets. Śląskie, S Poland
Sosnowitz *see* Sosnowiec
117 R2 **Sosnytsya** Chernihivs'ka Oblast', N Ukraine
109 V10 **Šoštanj** N Slovenia
122 G10 **Sos'va** Sverdlovskaya Oblast', C Russian Federation
54 D12 **Sotará, Volcán** ※ S Colombia
76 D10 **Sotavento, Ilhas de** *var.* Leeward Islands. *island group* S Cape Verde
93 N15 **Sotkamo** Oulu, C Finland
109 W11 **Sotla** ≈ E Slovenia
41 P10 **Soto la Marina** Tamaulipas, C Mexico
41 P10 **Soto la Marina, Río** ≈ C Mexico
95 B14 **Sotra** *island* S Norway
41 X12 **Sotuta** Yucatán, SE Mexico
79 F17 **Souanké** La Sangha, NW Congo
76 M17 **Soubré** S Ivory Coast
115 H24 **Soúda** *var.* Soúdha, *Eng.* Suda. Kríti, Greece, E Mediterranean Sea
Soúdha *see* Soúda
Soueida *see* As Suwaydā'
114 L12 **Souflí** *prev.* Souflíon. Anatolikí Makedonía kai Thráki, NE Greece
Souflíon *see* Souflí
45 S11 **Soufrière** W Saint Lucia
45 X6 **Soufrière** ※ Basse Terre, S Guadeloupe
102 M13 **Souillac** Lot, S France
173 Y17 **Souillac** S Mauritius
74 M5 **Souk Ahras** NE Algeria
74 E6 **Souk-el-Arba-Rharb** *var.* Souk el Arba du Rharb, Souk-el-Arba-du-Rharb, Souk-el-Arba-el-Rhab. NW Morocco
Soukhné *see* As Sukhnah
163 X14 **Sŏul** *off.* Sŏul-t'ŭkpyŏlsi, *Eng.* Seoul, *Jap.* Keijō; *prev.* Kyŏngsŏng. ● (South Korea) NW South Korea
102 J11 **Soulac-sur-Mer** Gironde, SW France
99 L19 **Soumagne** Liège, E Belgium
18 M14 **Sound Beach** Long Island, New York, NE USA
95 J22 **Sound, The** *Dan.* Øresund, *Swe.* Öresund. *strait* Denmark/Sweden
115 H20 **Soúnio, Akrotírio** *headland* C Greece
138 F8 **Soûr** *var.* Şūr; *anc.* Tyre. SW Lebanon
Sources, Mont-aux- *see* Phofung
104 G8 **Soure** Coimbra, N Portugal
11 W17 **Souris** Manitoba, S Canada
13 Q14 **Souris** Prince Edward Island, SE Canada
28 L2 **Souris River** *var.* Mouse River. ≈ Canada/USA
25 X10 **Sour Lake** Texas, SW USA
115 F17 **Sourpi** Thessalía, C Greece
104 H11 **Sousel** Portalegre, C Portugal
75 N6 **Sousse** *var.* Sūsah. NE Tunisia
14 H11 **South** ≈ Ontario, S Canada
South *see* Sud
83 G23 **South Africa** *off.* Republic of South Africa, *Afr.* Suid-Afrika. ◆ *republic* S Africa
48-53 **South America** *continent*
97 M23 **Southampton** *hist.* Hamwih, *Lat.* Clausentum. S England, UK
19 N14 **Southampton** Long Island, New York, NE USA
9 P8 **Southampton Island** *island* Nunavut, NE Canada
151 P20 **South Andaman** *island* Andaman Islands, India, NE Indian Ocean
13 Q6 **South Aulatsivik Island** *island* Newfoundland and Labrador, E Canada
182 E4 **South Australia** ◈ *state* S Australia
South Australian Abyssal Plain *see* South Australian Plain
192 G11 **South Australian Basin** *undersea feature* SW Indian Ocean
173 X12 **South Australian Plain** *var.* South Australian Abyssal Plain. *undersea feature* SE Indian Ocean
37 R13 **South Baldy** ▲ New Mexico, SW USA
23 Y14 **South Bay** Florida, SE USA
14 E12 **South Baymouth** Manitoulin Island, Ontario, S Canada
30 L10 **South Beloit** Illinois, N USA
31 O11 **South Bend** Indiana, N USA
25 R6 **South Bend** Texas, SW USA
32 F9 **South Bend** Washington, NW USA
South Beveland *see* Zuid-Beveland
South Borneo *see* Kalimantan Selatan
21 U7 **South Boston** Virginia, NE USA
182 F2 **South Branch Neales** *seasonal river* South Australia
21 U3 **South Branch Potomac River** ≈ West Virginia, NE USA
185 H19 **Southbridge** Canterbury, South Island, NZ
19 N12 **Southbridge** Massachusetts, NE USA
183 P17 **South Bruny Island** *island* Tasmania, SE Australia
18 L7 **South Burlington** Vermont, NE USA
44 M6 **South Caicos** *island* S Turks and Caicos Islands
South Cape *see* Ka Lae
23 V3 **South Carolina** *off.* State of South Carolina; also known as The Palmetto State. ◈ *state* SE USA
South Carpathians *see* Carpații Meridionali
South Celebes *see* Sulawesi Selatan
21 Q5 **South Charleston** West Virginia, NE USA
192 D7 **South China Basin** *undersea feature* SE South China Sea
169 R8 **South China Sea** *Chin.* Nan Hai, *Ind.* Laut Cina Selatan, *Vtn.* Biên Đông. *sea* SE Asia
33 Z10 **South Dakota** *off.* State of South Dakota; also known as The Coyote State, Sunshine State. ◈ *state* N USA
23 X10 **South Daytona** Florida, SE USA
37 R10 **South Domingo Pueblo** New Mexico, SW USA
97 N23 **South Downs** *hill range* SE England, UK
83 I21 **South East** ◈ *district* SE Botswana
65 H15 **South East Bay** *bay* Ascension Island, C Atlantic Ocean
183 O17 **South East Cape** *headland* Tasmania, SE Australia
38 K10 **Southeast Cape** *headland* Saint Lawrence Island, Alaska, USA
South-East Celebes *see* Sulawesi Tenggara
192 G12 **Southeast Indian Ridge** *undersea feature* Indian Ocean/Pacific Ocean
Southeast Island *see* Tagula Island
193 P13 **Southeast Pacific Basin** *var.* Belling Hausen Mulde. *undersea feature* SE Pacific Ocean
65 H15 **South East Point** *headland* SE Ascension Island
183 O14 **South East Point** *headland* Victoria, S Australia
191 Z3 **South East Point** *headland* Kiritimati, NE Kiribati
44 L5 **Southeast Point** *headland* Mayaguana, SE Bahamas
South-East Sulawesi *see* Sulawesi Tenggara
11 U12 **Southend** Saskatchewan, C Canada
97 P22 **Southend-on-Sea** E England, UK
83 H20 **Southern** *var.* Bangwaketse, Ngwaketze. ◈ *district* SE Botswana
81 I15 **Southern** ◈ *region* S Ethiopia
138 E13 **Southern** ◈ *district* S Israel
83 N15 **Southern** ◈ *region* S Malawi
83 I15 **Southern** ◈ *province* S Zambia
185 E19 **Southern Alps** ▲ South Island, NZ
190 K15 **Southern Cook Islands** *island group* S Cook Islands
180 K12 **Southern Cross** Western Australia
80 A12 **Southern Darfur** ◈ *state* W Sudan
186 B7 **Southern Highlands** ◈ *province* W PNG
11 V11 **Southern Indian Lake** ◎ Manitoba, C Canada
80 E11 **Southern Kordofan** ◈ *state* C Sudan
187 Z15 **Southern Lau Group** *island group* Lau Group, SE Fiji
173 S13 **Southern Ocean** *ocean*
21 T10 **Southern Pines** North Carolina, SE USA
155 J26 **Southern Province** ◈ *province* S Sri Lanka
96 I13 **Southern Uplands** ▲ S Scotland, UK
Southern Urals *see* Yuzhnyy Ural
183 P16 **South Esk River** ≈ Tasmania, SE Australia
11 U16 **Southey** Saskatchewan, S Canada
27 V2 **South Fabius River** ≈ Missouri, C USA
31 S10 **Southfield** Michigan, N USA
192 K10 **South Fiji Basin** *undersea feature* S Pacific Ocean
97 Q22 **South Foreland** *headland* SE England, UK
35 P7 **South Fork American River** ≈ California, W USA
28 K7 **South Fork Grand River** ≈ South Dakota, N USA
35 T12 **South Fork Kern River** ≈ California, W USA
39 Q7 **South Fork Koyukuk River** ≈ Alaska, USA
39 Q11 **South Fork Kuskokwim River** ≈ Alaska, USA
26 H2 **South Fork Republican River** ≈ C USA
26 L3 **South Fork Solomon River** ≈ Kansas, C USA
31 P5 **South Fox Island** *island* Michigan, N USA
20 G8 **South Fulton** Tennessee, S USA
195 U10 **South Geomagnetic Pole** *pole* Antarctica
65 J20 **South Georgia** *island* South Georgia and the South Sandwich Islands, SW Atlantic Ocean
65 K21 **South Georgia and the South Sandwich Islands** ◇ *UK dependent territory* SW Atlantic Ocean
181 Q1 **South Goulburn Island** *island* Northern Territory, N Australia
153 U16 **South Hatia Island** *island* SE Bangladesh
31 O10 **South Haven** Michigan, N USA
21 V7 **South Hill** Virginia, NE USA
South Holland *see* Zuid-Holland
21 P8 **South Holston Lake** ⊟ Tennessee/Virginia, S USA
26 M6 **South Hutchinson** Kansas, C USA
151 K21 **South Huvadhu Atoll** *var.* Gaafu Dhaalu Atoll. *atoll* S Maldives
173 U14 **South Indian Basin** *undersea feature* Indian Ocean/Pacific Ocean
11 W11 **South Indian Lake** Manitoba, C Canada
81 I17 **South Island** *island* NW Kenya
185 C20 **South Island** *island* S NZ
65 B23 **South Jason** *island* Jason Islands, NW Falkland Islands
South Kalimantan *see* Kalimantan Selatan
South Kazakhstan *see* Yuzhnyy Kazakhstan
163 X15 **South Korea** *off.* Republic of Korea, *Kor.* Taehan Min'guk. ◆ *republic* E Asia
35 Q6 **South Lake Tahoe** California, W USA
25 N6 **Southland** Texas, SW USA
185 B23 **Southland** *off.* Southland Region. ◈ *region* South Island, NZ
29 N15 **South Loup River** ≈ Nebraska, C USA
151 K19 **South Maalhosmadulu Atoll** *var.* Baa Atoll. *atoll* N Maldives
14 E15 **South Maitland** ≈ Ontario, S Canada
192 E8 **South Makassar Basin** *undersea feature* E Java Sea
31 O6 **South Manitou Island** *island* Michigan, N USA
151 K18 **South Miladummadulu Atoll** *atoll* N Maldives
21 X8 **South Mills** North Carolina, SE USA
8 H9 **South Nahanni** ≈ Northwest Territories, NW Canada
39 P13 **South Naknek** Alaska, USA
14 M13 **South Nation** ≈ Ontario, SE Canada
44 F9 **South Negril Point** *headland* W Jamaica
151 K20 **South Nilandhe Atoll** *var.* Dhaalu Atoll. *atoll* C Maldives
36 L2 **South Ogden** Utah, W USA
18 M14 **Southold** Long Island, New York, NE USA
194 H1 **South Orkney Islands** *island group* Antarctica
137 S9 **South Ossetia** *former autonomous region* SW Georgia
South Pacific Basin *see* Southwest Pacific Basin
19 P7 **South Paris** Maine, NE USA
33 U15 **South Pass** *pass* Wyoming, C USA
189 U13 **South Pass** *passage* Chuuk Islands, C Micronesia
20 K10 **South Pittsburg** Tennessee, S USA
28 K15 **South Platte River** ≈ Colorado/Nebraska, C USA
31 T16 **South Point** Ohio, N USA
65 G15 **South Point** *headland* S Ascension Island
31 R6 **South Point** *headland* Michigan, N USA
South Point *see* Ka Lae
195 P9 **South Pole** *pole* Antarctica
183 P17 **Southport** Tasmania, SE Australia
97 K17 **Southport** NW England, UK
21 V12 **Southport** North Carolina, SE USA
19 P8 **South Portland** Maine, NE USA
14 H12 **South River** Ontario, S Canada
21 U11 **South River** ≈ North Carolina, SE USA
96 K5 **South Ronaldsay** *island* NE Scotland, UK
36 L2 **South Salt Lake** Utah, W USA
65 L21 **South Sandwich Islands** *island group* SE South Georgia and South Sandwich Islands
65 K21 **South Sandwich Trench** *undersea feature* SW Atlantic Ocean
11 S16 **South Saskatchewan** ≈ Alberta/Saskatchewan, S Canada
65 I21 **South Scotia Ridge** *undersea feature* S Scotia Sea
11 V10 **South Seal** ≈ Manitoba, C Canada
194 G4 **South Shetland Islands** *island group* Antarctica
65 H22 **South Shetland Trough** *undersea feature* Atlantic Ocean/Pacific Ocean
97 M14 **South Shields** NE England, UK
29 R13 **South Sioux City** Nebraska, C USA
192 J9 **South Solomon Trench** *undersea feature* W Pacific Ocean
183 V3 **South Stradbroke Island** *island* Queensland, E Australia
South Sulawesi *see* Sulawesi Selatan
South Sumatra *see* Sumatera Selatan
184 K11 **South Taranaki Bight** *bight* SE Tasman Sea
South Tasmania Plateau *see* Tasman Plateau
36 M15 **South Tucson** Arizona, SW USA
12 H9 **South Twin Island** *island* Nunavut, C Canada
96 E9 **South Uist** *island* NW Scotland, UK
South-West *see* Sud-Ouest
South-West Africa/South West Africa *see* Namibia
65 F15 **South West Bay** *bay* Ascension Island, C Atlantic Ocean
183 N18 **South West Cape** *headland* Tasmania, SE Australia
185 B26 **South West Cape** *headland* Stewart Island, NZ
38 J10 **Southwest Cape** *headland* Saint Lawrence Island, Alaska, USA
Southwest Indian Ocean Ridge *see* Southwest Indian Ridge
173 N11 **Southwest Indian Ridge** *var.* Southwest Indian Ocean Ridge. *undersea feature* SW Indian Ocean
192 L10 **Southwest Pacific Basin** *var.* South Pacific Basin. *undersea feature* SE Pacific Ocean
44 H2 **South West Point** *headland* Great Abaco, N Bahamas
191 X3 **South West Point** *headland* Kiritimati, NE Kiribati
65 G25 **South West Point** *headland* SW Saint Helena
25 P5 **South Wichita River** ≈ Texas, SW USA
97 Q20 **Southwold** E England, UK
19 Q12 **South Yarmouth** Massachusetts, NE USA
116 J10 **Sovata** *Hung.* Szováta. Mureș, C Romania
107 N22 **Soverato** Calabria, SW Italy
Sovetabad *see* Ghafurov
126 C2 **Sovetsk** *Ger.* Tilsit. Kaliningradskaya Oblast', W Russian Federation
125 Q15 **Sovetsk** Kirovskaya Oblast', NW Russian Federation
127 N10 **Sovetskaya** Rostovskaya Oblast', SW Russian Federation
Sovetskoye *see* Ketchenery
146 I15 **Sovet"yab** *prev.* Sovet"yap. Ahal Welaýaty, S Turkmenistan
Sovet"yap *see* Sovet"yab
117 U12 **Sovyets'kyy** Respublika Krym, S Ukraine
83 I18 **Sowa** *var.* Sua. Central, NE Botswana
Sowa Pan *see* Sua Pan
83 J21 **Soweto** Gauteng, NE South Africa
147 R11 **So'x** *Rus.* Sokh. Farg'ona Viloyati, E Uzbekistan
Sōya-kaikyō *see* La Perouse Strait
165 T1 **Sōya-misaki** *headland* Hokkaidō, NE Japan
127 N7 **Soyana** ≈ NW Russian Federation
146 A8 **Soye, Mys** *var.* Mys Suz. *headland* NW Turkmenistan
82 A10 **Soyo** Zaire, NW Angola
80 J10 **Soyra** ▲ C Eritrea
Sozaq *see* Suzak
119 P16 **Sozh** *Rus.* Sozh. ≈ NE Europe
114 N10 **Sozopol** *prev.* Sizebolu *anc.* Apollonia. Burgas, E Bulgaria
172 J15 **Sœurs, Les** *island group* Inner Islands, W Seychelles
99 L20 **Spa** Liège, E Belgium
194 I7 **Spaatz Island** *island* Antarctica
144 M14 **Space Launching Centre** *space station* Kzylorda, S Kazakhstan
105 O7 **Spain** *off.* Kingdom of Spain, *Sp.* España; *anc.* Hispania, Iberia, *Lat.* Hispana. ◆ *monarchy* SW Europe
Spalato *see* Split
97 O19 **Spalding** E England, UK
14 D11 **Spanish** Ontario, S Canada
36 L3 **Spanish Fork** Utah, W USA
64 B12 **Spanish Point** *headland* C Bermuda
14 E9 **Spanish River** ≈ Ontario, S Canada
44 K13 **Spanish Town** *hist.* St.Iago de la Vega. C Jamaica
115 H24 **Spánta, Akrotírio** *headland* Kríti, Greece, E Mediterranean Sea
35 Q5 **Sparks** Nevada, W USA
Sparnacum *see* Épernay
95 N16 **Sparreholm** Södermanland, C Sweden
23 U4 **Sparta** Georgia, SE USA
30 K16 **Sparta** Illinois, N USA
31 P9 **Sparta** Michigan, N USA
21 R8 **Sparta** North Carolina, SE USA
20 L9 **Sparta** Tennessee, S USA
30 I7 **Sparta** Wisconsin, N USA
Sparta *see* Spárti
21 Q11 **Spartanburg** South Carolina, SE USA
115 F21 **Spárti** *Eng.* Sparta. Pelopónnisos, S Greece
107 B21 **Spartivento, Capo** *headland* Sardegna, Italy, C Mediterranean Sea
11 P17 **Sparwood** British Columbia, SW Canada
126 I4 **Spas-Demensk** Kaluzhskaya Oblast', W Russian Federation
126 M4 **Spas-Klepiki** Ryazanskaya Oblast', W Russian Federation
Spasovo *see* Kulen Vakuf
123 R15 **Spassk-Dal'niy** Primorskiy Kray, SE Russian Federation
126 M5 **Spassk-Ryazanskiy** Ryazanskaya Oblast', W Russian Federation
115 H19 **Spáta** Attikí, C Greece
121 Q11 **Spátha, Akrotírio** *headland* Kríti, Greece, E Mediterranean Sea
Špatrjan *see* Paternion
28 I9 **Spearfish** South Dakota, N USA
25 O1 **Spearman** Texas, SW USA
65 C25 **Speedwell Island** *island* S Falkland Islands
65 C25 **Speedwell Island Settlement** S Falkland Islands
65 G25 **Speery Island** *island* S Saint Helena
45 N14 **Speightstown** NW Barbados
106 I13 **Spello** Umbria, C Italy
39 R12 **Spenard** Alaska, USA
Spence Bay *see* Taloyoak
31 O14 **Spencer** Indiana, N USA
29 T12 **Spencer** Iowa, C USA
29 R12 **Spencer** Nebraska, C USA
21 S9 **Spencer** North Carolina, SE USA
20 L9 **Spencer** Tennessee, S USA
21 Q4 **Spencer** West Virginia, NE USA
30 K6 **Spencer** Wisconsin, N USA
182 G10 **Spencer, Cape** *headland* South Australia
39 V13 **Spencer, Cape** *headland* Alaska, USA
182 H9 **Spencer Gulf** *gulf* South Australia
18 F9 **Spencerport** New York, NE USA
31 Q12 **Spencerville** Ohio, N USA
115 E17 **Spercheiáda** *var.* Sperhiada, Sperkhiás. Stereá Ellás, C Greece
115 E17 **Spercheiós** ≈ C Greece
Sperhiada *see* Spercheiáda
95 G14 **Sperillen** ◎ S Norway
Sperkhiás *see* Spercheiáda
101 I18 **Spessart** *hill range* C Germany
Spétsai *see* Spétses
115 G21 **Spétses** *prev.* Spétsai. Spétses, S Greece
115 G21 **Spétses** *island* S Greece
96 J8 **Spey** ≈ NE Scotland, UK
101 G20 **Speyer** *Eng.* Spires; *anc.* Civitas Nemetum, Spira. Rheinland-Pfalz, SW Germany
101 G20 **Speyerbach** ≈ W Germany
107 N20 **Spezzano Albanese** Calabria, SW Italy
Spice Islands *see* Maluku
100 F9 **Spiekeroog** *island* NW Germany
109 W9 **Spielfeld** Steiermark, SE Austria
65 N21 **Spiess Seamount** *undersea feature* S Atlantic Ocean
108 E9 **Spiez** Bern, W Switzerland
98 G13 **Spijkenisse** Zuid-Holland, SW Netherlands
39 T6 **Spike Mountain** ▲ Alaska, USA
115 I25 **Spíli** Kríti, Greece, E Mediterranean Sea
108 D10 **Spillgerten** ▲ W Switzerland
118 F9 **Spilva** ✈ (Rīga) Riga, C Latvia
107 N17 **Spinazzola** Puglia, SE Italy
149 O9 **Spīn Būldak** Kandahār, S Afghanistan
Spira *see* Speyer
Spirdingsee *see* Śniardwy, Jezioro
Spires *see* Speyer
29 T11 **Spirit Lake** Iowa, C USA
29 T11 **Spirit Lake** ◎ Iowa, C USA
11 N13 **Spirit River** Alberta, W Canada
11 S14 **Spiritwood** Saskatchewan, S Canada
27 R11 **Spiro** Oklahoma, C USA
111 L19 **Spišská Nová Ves** *Ger.* Neudorf, Zipser Neudorf, *Hung.* Igló. Košický Kraj, E Slovakia
137 T11 **Spitak** NW Armenia
92 O2 **Spitsbergen** *island* NW Svalbard
Spittal *see* Spittal an der Drau
109 R9 **Spittal an der Drau** *var.* Spittal. Kärnten, S Austria
109 V3 **Spitz** Niederösterreich, NE Austria
94 D9 **Spjelkavik** Møre og Romsdal, S Norway
25 W10 **Splendora** Texas, SW USA
113 E14 **Split** *It.* Spalato. Split-Dalmacija, S Croatia
113 E14 **Split** ✈ Split-Dalmacija, S Croatia
113 E14 **Split-Dalmacija** *off.* Splitsko-Dalmatinska Županija. ◈ *province* S Croatia
11 X12 **Split Lake** ◎ Manitoba, C Canada
Splitsko-Dalmatinska Županija *see* Split-Dalmacija
108 H10 **Splügen** Graubünden, S Switzerland
Spodnji Dravograd *see* Dravograd
25 P12 **Spofford** Texas, SW USA
118 J11 **Špoģi** Daugvapils, SE Latvia
32 L8 **Spokane** Washington, NW USA
32 L8 **Spokane River** ≈ Washington, NW USA
106 I13 **Spoleto** Umbria, C Italy
30 I4 **Spooner** Wisconsin, N USA
30 K12 **Spoon River** ≈ Illinois, N USA
21 W5 **Spotsylvania** Virginia, NE USA
32 L8 **Sprague** Washington, NW USA
170 J5 **Spratly Island** *island* SW Spratly Islands
192 E6 **Spratly Islands** *Chin.* Nansha Qundao. ◇ *disputed territory* SE Asia
32 J12 **Spray** Oregon, NW USA
112 I11 **Spreča** ≈ N Bosnia and Herzegovina
100 P13 **Spree** ≈ E Germany
100 P13 **Spreewald** *wetland* NE Germany
101 P14 **Spremberg** Brandenburg, E Germany
25 W11 **Spring** Texas, SW USA
31 Q10 **Spring Arbor** Michigan, N USA
83 E23 **Springbok** Northern Cape, W South Africa
18 I15 **Spring City** Pennsylvania, NE USA
20 L9 **Spring City** Tennessee, S USA
36 L4 **Spring City** Utah, W USA
35 W3 **Spring Creek** Nevada, W USA
27 S9 **Springdale** Arkansas, C USA
31 Q14 **Springdale** Ohio, N USA
100 I13 **Springe** Niedersachsen, N Germany
37 U9 **Springer** New Mexico, SW USA
37 W7 **Springfield** Colorado, C USA
23 W5 **Springfield** Georgia, SE USA
30 K14 **Springfield** *state capital* Illinois, N USA
20 L6 **Springfield** Kentucky, S USA
18 M12 **Springfield** Massachusetts, NE USA
29 T10 **Springfield** Minnesota, N USA
27 T7 **Springfield** Missouri, C USA
31 R13 **Springfield** Ohio, N USA
32 G13 **Springfield** Oregon, NW USA
29 Q12 **Springfield** South Dakota, N USA
20 J8 **Springfield** Tennessee, S USA
18 M9 **Springfield** Vermont, NE USA
30 K14 **Springfield, Lake** ⊟ Illinois, N USA
55 T8 **Spring Garden** NE Guyana
30 K8 **Spring Green** Wisconsin, N USA
29 X11 **Spring Grove** Minnesota, N USA
22 G4 **Springhill** Louisiana, S USA
23 V12 **Spring Hill** Florida, SE USA
27 R4 **Spring Hill** Kansas, C USA
13 P15 **Springhill** Nova Scotia, SE Canada
20 I9 **Spring Hill** Tennessee, S USA
21 U10 **Spring Lake** North Carolina, SE USA
24 M4 **Springlake** Texas, SW USA
35 W11 **Spring Mountains** ▲ Nevada, W USA
65 B24 **Spring Point** West Falkland, Falkland Islands
27 W9 **Spring River** ≈ Arkansas/Missouri, C USA
27 S7 **Spring River** ≈ Missouri/Oklahoma, C USA
83 J21 **Springs** Gauteng, NE South Africa
185 H16 **Springs Junction** West Coast, South Island, NZ
181 X8 **Springsure** Queensland, E Australia
29 W11 **Spring Valley** Minnesota, N USA
18 K13 **Spring Valley** New York, NE USA
29 N12 **Springview** Nebraska, C USA
18 D11 **Springville** New York, NE USA
36 L3 **Springville** Utah, W USA
Sprottau *see* Szprotawa
15 V4 **Sproule, Pointe** *headland* Québec, SE Canada
11 Q14 **Spruce Grove** Alberta, SW Canada
21 T4 **Spruce Knob** ▲ West Virginia, NE USA
35 X3 **Spruce Mountain** ▲ Nevada, W USA
21 P9 **Spruce Pine** North Carolina, SE USA
98 G13 **Spui** ≈ SW Netherlands
107 O19 **Spulico, Capo** *headland* S Italy
25 O5 **Spur** Texas, SW USA
97 O17 **Spurn Head** *headland* E England, UK
99 H20 **Spy** Namur, S Belgium
95 I15 **Spydeberg** Østfold, S Norway
185 J17 **Spy Glass Point** *headland* South Island, NZ
10 L17 **Squamish** British Columbia, SW Canada
19 O8 **Squam Lake** ◎ New Hampshire, NE USA
19 S2 **Squa Pan Mountain** ▲ Maine, NE USA
39 N16 **Squaw Harbor** Unga Island, Alaska, USA
14 E11 **Squaw Island** *island* Ontario, S Canada
107 O22 **Squillace, Golfo di** *gulf* S Italy
107 Q18 **Squinzano** Puglia, SE Italy
Sráid na Cathrach *see* Milltown Malbay
167 S11 **Srâlau** Stœng Trêng, N Cambodia
Srath an Urláir *see* Stranorlar
112 G10 **Srbac** Republika Srpska, N Bosnia & Herzegovina
Srbinje *see* Foča
Srbija *see* Serbia
Srbobran *see* Donji Vakuf
112 K9 **Srbobran** *var.* Bácsszenttamás, *Hung.* Szenttamás. Serbia, N Serbia and Montenegro (Yugo.)
167 R13 **Srê Âmběl** Kaôh Kông, SW Cambodia
112 K13 **Srebrenica** Republika Srpska, E Bosnia & Herzegovina
112 I11 **Srebrenik** Federacija Bosna I Hercegovina, E Bosnia & Herzegovina
114 M10 **Sredets** *prev.* Grudovo. Burgas, E Bulgaria
114 K10 **Sredets** *prev.* Syulemeshlii. Stara Zagora, C Bulgaria
114 M10 **Sredetska Reka** ≈ SE Bulgaria
123 U9 **Sredinnyy Khrebet** ▲ E Russian Federation
114 N7 **Sredishte** *Rom.* Beibunar; *prev.* Knyazhevo. Dobrich, NE Bulgaria
114 I10 **Sredna Gora** ▲ C Bulgaria
123 R7 **Srednekolymsk** Respublika Sakha (Yakutiya), NE Russian Federation
126 K7 **Srednerusskaya Vozvyshennost'** *Eng.* Central Russian Upland. ▲ W Russian Federation
122 L9 **Srednesibirskoye Ploskogor'ye** *var.* Central Siberian Uplands, *Eng.* Central Siberian Plateau. ▲ N Russian Federation
127 V13 **Sredniy Ural** ▲ NW Russian Federation
167 T12 **Srê Khtŭm** Môndól Kiri, E Cambodia
111 G12 **Śrem** Wielkolpolskie, C Poland
112 K10 **Sremska Mitrovica** *prev.* Mitrovica, *Ger.* Mitrowitz. Serbia, NW Serbia and Montenegro (Yugo.)
167 R11 **Srêng, Stœng** ≈ NW Cambodia
167 R11 **Srê Noy** Siĕmréab, NW Cambodia
Srepok, Sông *see* Srêpôk, Tônle
167 T12 **Srêpôk, Tônle** *var.* Sông Srepok. ≈ Cambodia/Vietnam
123 P13 **Sretensk** Chitinskaya Oblast', S Russian Federation
169 R10 **Sri Aman** Sarawak, East Malaysia
117 R4 **Sribne** Chernihivs'ka Oblast', N Ukraine
155 I25 **Sri Jayawardanapura** *var* Sri Jayawardenepura; *prev.* Kotte. Western Province, W Sri Lanka
155 M14 **Srīkākulam** Andhra Pradesh, E India
155 I25 **Sri Lanka** *off.* Democratic Socialist Republic of Sri Lanka; *prev.* Ceylon. ◆ *republic* S Asia
173 R5 **Sri Lanka** *island* S Asia
153 V14 **Srimangal** Chittagong, E Bangladesh
Sri Mohangorh *see* Shri Mohangarh
152 H5 **Srīnagar** Jammu and Kashmir, N India
167 N10 **Srinagarind Reservoir** ⊟ W Thailand
155 F19 **Sringeri** Karnātaka, W India
155 K25 **Sri Pada** *Eng.* Adam's Peak. ▲ S Sri Lanka
Sri Saket *see* Si Sa Ket
111 G14 **Środa Śląska** *Ger.* Neumarkt. Dolnośląskie, SW Poland
110 H12 **Środa Wielkopolska** Wielkolpolskie, C Poland
Srpska Kostajnica *see* Bosanska Kostajnica
113 G14 **Srpska, Republika** ◈ *republic* Bosnia & Herzegovina
Srpski Brod *see* Bosanski Brod
Ssu-ch'uan *see* Sichuan
Ssu-p'ing/Ssu-p'ing-chieh *see* Siping
Stablo *see* Stavelot
99 G15 **Stabroek** Antwerpen, N Belgium
Stackeln *see* Strenči
96 I5 **Stack Skerry** *island* N Scotland, UK
100 I9 **Stade** Niedersachsen, NW Germany

◆ Country ◇ Dependent Territory ◈ Administrative Region ▲ Mountain ※ Volcano ◎ Lake
● Country Capital ○ Dependent Territory Capital ✈ International Airport ▲ Mountain Range ≈ River ⊟ Reservoir

94 C10 **Stadlandet** *peninsula* S Norway
109 R5 **Stadl-Paura** Oberösterreich, NW Austria
119 L20 **Stadolichy** ***Rus.*** Stodolichi. Homyel'skaya Voblasts', SE Belarus
98 P7 **Stadskanaal** Groningen, NE Netherlands
101 H16 **Stadtallendorf** Hessen, C Germany
101 K23 **Stadtbergen** Bayern, S Germany
108 G7 **Stäfa** Zürich, NE Switzerland
95 K23 **Staffanstorp** Skåne, S Sweden
101 K18 **Staffelstein** Bayern, C Germany
97 L19 **Stafford** C England, UK
26 L6 **Stafford** Kansas, C USA
21 W4 **Stafford** Virginia, NE USA
97 L19 **Staffordshire** *cultural region* C England, UK
19 N12 **Stafford Springs** Connecticut, NE USA
115 H14 **Stágira** Kentrikí Makedonía, N Greece
118 G7 **Staicele** Limbaži, N Latvia
Ştaierdorf-Anina *see* Anina
109 V8 **Stainz** Steiermark, SE Austria
Stájerlakanina *see* Anina
117 Y7 **Stakhanov** Luhans'ka Oblast', E Ukraine
108 E11 **Stalden** Valais, SW Switzerland
Stalin *see* Varna
Stalinabad *see* Dushanbe
Stalingrad *see* Volgograd
Staliniri *see* Ts'khinvali
Stalino *see* Donets'k
Stalinobod *see* Dushanbe
Stalinov Štít *see* Gerlachovský štít
Stalinsk *see* Novokuznetsk
Stalinskaya Oblast' *see* Donets'ka Oblast'
Stalinski Zaliv *see* Varnenski Zaliv
Stalin, Yazovir *see* Iskŭr, Yazovir
8 K2 **Stallworthy, Cape** *headland* Nunavut, N Canada
111 N15 **Stalowa Wola** Podkarpackie, SE Poland
114 I11 **Stamboliyski** Plovdiv, C Bulgaria
114 J8 **Stamboliyski, Yazovir** ▣ N Bulgaria
97 N19 **Stamford** E England, UK
18 L14 **Stamford** Connecticut, NE USA
25 P6 **Stamford** Texas, SW USA
25 Q6 **Stamford, Lake** ▣ Texas, SW USA
108 I10 **Stampa** Graubünden, SE Switzerland
Stampalia *see* Astypálaia
27 T14 **Stamps** Arkansas, C USA
92 G11 **Stamsund** Nordland, C Norway
27 R2 **Stanberry** Missouri, C USA
195 O3 **Stancomb-Wills Glacier** *glacier* Antarctica
83 K21 **Standerton** Mpumalanga, E South Africa
31 R7 **Standish** Michigan, N USA
20 M6 **Stanford** Kentucky, S USA
33 S9 **Stanford** Montana, NW USA
95 P19 **Stånga** Gotland, SE Sweden
94 I13 **Stange** Hedmark, S Norway
83 L23 **Stanger** KwaZulu/Natal, E South Africa
Stanimaka *see* Asenovgrad
Stanislau *see* Ivano-Frankivs'k
35 P8 **Stanislaus River** ≈ California, W USA
Stanislav *see* Ivano-Frankivs'k
Stanislavskaya Oblast' *see* Ivano-Frankivs'ka Oblast'
Stanisławów *see* Ivano-Frankivs'k
Stanke Dimitrov *see* Dupnitsa
183 O15 **Stanley** Tasmania, SE Australia
65 E24 **Stanley** ***var.*** Port Stanley, Puerto Argentino ○ (Falkland Islands) East Falkland, Falkland Islands
33 O13 **Stanley** Idaho, NW USA
28 L3 **Stanley** North Dakota, N USA
21 U4 **Stanley** Virginia, NE USA
30 J6 **Stanley** Wisconsin, N USA
79 G21 **Stanley Pool** ***var.*** Pool Malebo. ◎ Congo/Dem. Rep. Congo
155 H20 **Stanley Reservoir** ▣ S India
Stanleyville *see* Kisangani
42 G3 **Stann Creek** ◆ *district* SE Belize
Stann Creek *see* Dangriga
123 [illegible]12 **Stanovoy Khrebet** ▲ SE Russian Federation
108 [illegible] **Stans** Unterwalden, C Switzerland
97 O21 **Stansted** × (London) Essex, E England, UK
183 [illegible] **Stanthorpe** Queensland, E Australia
21 N[illegible] **Stanton** Kentucky, S USA
31 Q[illegible] **Stanton** Michigan, N USA
29 Q[illegible]4 **Stanton** Nebraska, C USA
28 L5 **Stanton** North Dakota, N USA
25 N7 **Stanton** Texas, SW USA
32 H7 **Stanwood** Washington, NW USA
117 Y7 **Stanychno-Luhans'ke** Luhans'ka Oblast', E Ukraine
108 K7 **Stanzach** Tirol, W Austria
98 M9 **Staphorst** Overijssel, E Netherlands
14 D18 **Staples** Ontario, S Canada
29 T6 **Staples** Minnesota, N USA
28 M14 **Stapleton** Nebraska, C USA
25 S8 **Star** Texas, SW USA
111 M14 **Starachowice** Świętokrzyskie, C Poland
Stara Kanjiža *see* Kanjiža
111 M18 **Stará L'ubovňa** ***Ger.*** Altlublau, ***Hung.*** Prešovský Kraj, E Slovakia
112 L10 **Stara Pazova** ***Ger.*** Altpasua, ***Hung.*** Ópazova. Serbia, N Serbia and Montenegro (Yugo.)
Stara Planina *see* Balkan Mountains
114 L9 **Stara Reka** ≈ C Bulgaria
116 M5 **Stara Synyava** Khmel'nyts'ka Oblast', W Ukraine
116 I2 **Stara Vyzhivka** Volyns'ka Oblast', NW Ukraine
Staraya Belitsa *see* Staraya Byelitsa
119 M14 **Staraya Byelitsa** ***Rus.*** Staraya Belitsa. Vitsyebskaya Voblasts', NE Belarus
127 R5 **Staraya Mayna** Ul'yanovskaya Oblast', W Russian Federation
119 O18 **Staraya Rudnya** ***Rus.*** Staraya Rudnya. Homyel'skaya Voblasts', SE Belarus
124 H14 **Staraya Russa** Novgorodskaya Oblast', W Russian Federation
114 K10 **Stara Zagora** ***Lat.*** Augusta Trajana. Stara Zagora, C Bulgaria
116 K10 **Stara Zagora** ◆ *province* C Bulgaria
29 S8 **Starbuck** Minnesota, N USA
191 W4 **Starbuck Island** ***prev.*** Volunteer Island. *island* E Kiribati
27 V13 **Star City** Arkansas, C USA
112 F13 **Staretina** ▲ W Bosnia and Herzegovina
Stargard in Pommern *see* Stargard Szczeciński
110 E9 **Stargard Szczeciński** ***Ger.*** Stargard in Pommern. Zachodnio-pomorskie, NW Poland
187 N10 **Star Harbour** *harbour* San Cristobal, SE Solomon Islands
Stari Bečej *see* Bečej
113 F15 **Stari Grad** ***It.*** Cittavecchia. Split-Dalmacija, S Croatia
124 J16 **Staritsa** Tverskaya Oblast', W Russian Federation
23 V9 **Starke** Florida, SE USA
22 M4 **Starkville** Mississippi, S USA
186 B7 **Star Mountains** ***Ind.*** Pegunungan Sterren. ▲ Indonesia/PNG
101 L23 **Starnberg** Bayern, SE Germany
101 L24 **Starnberger See** ◎ SE Germany
Starobel'sk *see* Starobil's'k
117 X8 **Starobesheve** Donets'ka Oblast', E Ukraine
117 Y6 **Starobil's'k** ***Rus.*** Starobel'sk. Luhans'ka Oblast', E Ukraine
Starobin *see* Starobyn
119 K18 **Starobyn** ***Rus.*** Starobin. Minskaya Voblasts', S Belarus
126 H6 **Starodub** Bryanskaya Oblast', W Russian Federation
110 I8 **Starogard Gdański** ***Ger.*** Preussisch-Stargard. Pomorskie, N Poland
145 P16 **Staroikan** Yuzhnyy Kazakhstan, S Kazakhstan
Starokonstantinov *see* Starokostyantyniv
116 L5 **Starokostyantyniv** ***Rus.*** Starokonstantinov. Khmel'nyts'ka Oblast', NW Ukraine
126 K12 **Starominskaya** Krasnodarskiy Kray, SW Russian Federation
114 L7 **Staro Selo** ***Rom.*** Satul-Vechi; ***prev.*** Star-Smil. Silistra, NE Bulgaria
126 K12 **Staroshcherbinovskaya** Krasnodarskiy Kray, SW Russian Federation
127 V6 **Starosubkhangulovo** Respublika Bashkortostan, W Russian Federation
35 S4 **Star Peak** ▲ Nevada, W USA
Star-Smil *see* Staro Selo
97 J25 **Start Point** *headland* SW England, UK
Startsy *see* Kirawsk
Starum *see* Stavoren
119 L18 **Staryya Darohi** ***Rus.*** Staryye Dorogi. Minskaya Voblasts', S Belarus
Staryye Dorogi *see* Staryya Darohi
127 T2 **Staryye Zyattsy** Udmurtskaya Respublika, NW Russian Federation
117 U13 **Staryy Krym** Respublika Krym, S Ukraine
126 K8 **Staryy Oskol** Belgorodskaya Oblast', W Russian Federation
116 H6 **Staryy Sambir** L'vivs'ka Oblast', W Ukraine
101 L14 **Stassfurt** ***var.*** Staßfurt. Sachsen-Anhalt, C Germany
111 M15 **Staszów** Świętokrzyskie, C Poland
29 W13 **State Center** Iowa, C USA
18 E14 **State College** Pennsylvania, NE USA
18 K15 **Staten Island** *island* New York, NE USA
Staten Island *see* Estados, Isla de los
23 U8 **Statenville** Georgia, SE USA
23 W5 **Statesboro** Georgia, SE USA
States, The *see* United States of America
21 R9 **Statesville** North Carolina, SE USA
95 G16 **Stathelle** Telemark, S Norway
30 K15 **Staunton** Illinois, N USA
21 T5 **Staunton** Virginia, NE USA
95 C16 **Stavanger** Rogaland, S Norway
99 L21 **Stavelot** ***Dut.*** Stablo. Liège, E Belgium
95 G16 **Stavern** Vestfold, S Norway
Stavers Island *see* Vostok Island
98 J7 **Stavoren** ***Fris.*** Starum. Friesland, N Netherlands
126 M14 **Stavropol'** ***prev.*** Voroshilovsk. Stavropol'skiy Kray, SW Russian Federation
Stavropol' *see* Tol'yatti
126 M14 **Stavropol'skaya Vozvyshennost'** ▲ SW Russian Federation
126 M14 **Stavropol'skiy Kray** ◆ *territory* SW Russian Federation
115 H14 **Stavrós** Kentrikí Makedonía, N Greece
115 J24 **Stavrós, Akrotírio** *headland* Kríti, Greece, E Mediterranean Sea
115 K21 **Stavrós, Akrotírio** *headland* Náxos, Kykládes, Greece, Aegean Sea
114 I12 **Stavroúpoli** ***prev.*** Stavroúpolis. Anatolikí Makedonía kai Thráki, NE Greece
Stavroúpolis *see* Stavroúpoli
117 O6 **Stavyshche** Kyyivs'ka Oblast', N Ukraine
182 M11 **Stawell** Victoria, SE Australia
110 N9 **Stawiski** Podlaskie, NE Poland
14 G14 **Stayner** Ontario, S Canada
37 R3 **Steamboat Springs** Colorado, C USA
20 M8 **Stearns** Kentucky, S USA
39 N10 **Stebbins** Alaska, USA
108 K7 **Steeg** Tirol, W Austria
27 Y9 **Steele** Missouri, C USA
29 N5 **Steele** North Dakota, N USA
194 J5 **Steele Island** *island* Antarctica
30 K16 **Steeleville** Illinois, N USA
27 W6 **Steelville** Missouri, C USA
99 G14 **Steenbergen** Noord-Brabant, S Netherlands
Steenkool *see* Bintuni
11 O10 **Steen River** Alberta, W Canada
98 M8 **Steenwijk** Overijssel, N Netherlands
65 A23 **Steeple Jason** *island* Jason Islands, NW Falkland Islands
116 L9 **Ştefăneşti** Botoşani, NE Romania
Stefanie, Lake *see* Ch'ew Bahir
8 L5 **Stefansson Island** *island* Nunavut, N Canada
117 O10 **Ştefan Vodă** ***Rus.*** Suvorovo. SE Moldova
63 H18 **Steffen, Cerro** ▲ S Chile
108 D9 **Steffisburg** Bern, C Switzerland
95 J24 **Stege** Storstrøm, SE Denmark
116 G10 **Ştei** ***Hung.*** Vaskohsziklás. Bihor, W Romania
Steier *see* Steyr
Steierdorf/Steierdorf-Anina *see* Anina
109 T7 **Steiermark** ***off.*** Land Steiermark, ***Eng.*** Styria. ◆ *state* C Austria
101 J19 **Steigerwald** *hill range* C Germany
99 L17 **Stein** Limburg, SE Netherlands
Stein *see* Stein an der Donau, Austria
Stein *see* Kamnik, Slovenia
108 M8 **Steinach** Tirol, W Austria
Steinamanger *see* Szombathely
109 W3 **Stein an der Donau** ***var.*** Stein. Niederösterreich, NE Austria
Steinau an der Elbe *see* Ścinawa
11 Y16 **Steinbach** Manitoba, S Canada
Steiner Alpen *see* Kamniško-Savinjske Alpe
99 L24 **Steinfort** Luxembourg, W Luxembourg
100 H12 **Steinhuder Meer** ◎ NW Germany
93 E15 **Steinkjer** Nord-Trøndelag, C Norway
Stejarul *see* Karapelit
99 F16 **Stekene** Oost-Vlaanderen, NW Belgium
83 E26 **Stellenbosch** Western Cape, SW South Africa
98 F13 **Stellendam** Zuid-Holland, SW Netherlands
39 T12 **Steller, Mount** ▲ Alaska, USA
103 Y14 **Stello, Monte** ▲ Corse, France, C Mediterranean Sea
106 F5 **Stelvio, Passo dello** *pass* Italy/Switzerland
103 R3 **Stenay** Meuse, NE France
100 L12 **Stendal** Sachsen-Anhalt, C Germany
118 E8 **Stende** Talsi, NW Latvia
182 H10 **Stenhouse Bay** South Australia
95 J23 **Stenløse** Frederiksborg, E Denmark
95 L19 **Stensjön** Jönköping, S Sweden
95 K18 **Stenstorp** Västra Götaland, S Sweden
95 I18 **Stenungsund** Västra Götaland, S Sweden
Stepanakert *see* Xankändi
137 T11 **Step'anavan** N Armenia
100 K9 **Stepenitz** ≈ N Germany
29 O10 **Stephan** South Dakota, N USA
29 R3 **Stephen** Minnesota, N USA
27 T14 **Stephens** Arkansas, C USA
184 J13 **Stephens, Cape** *headland* D'Urville Island, Marlborough, SW NZ
21 V3 **Stephens City** Virginia, NE USA
182 L6 **Stephens Creek** New South Wales, SE Australia
184 K13 **Stephens Island** *island* C NZ
31 N5 **Stephenson** Michigan, N USA
13 S12 **Stephenville** Newfoundland and Labrador, SE Canada
25 S7 **Stephenville** Texas, SW USA
145 P17 **Step' Nardara** ***Kaz.*** Shardara Dalasy; ***prev.*** Shaidara. *grassland* S Kazakhstan
145 R8 **Stepnogorsk** Akmola, C Kazakhstan
127 O15 **Stepnoye** Stavropol'skiy Kray, SW Russian Federation
145 Q8 **Stepnyak** Akmola, N Kazakhstan
192 J17 **Steps Point** *headland* Tutuila, W American Samoa
115 F17 **Stereá Ellás** ***Eng.*** Greece Central. ◆ *region* C Greece
83 J24 **Sterkspruit** Eastern Cape, SE South Africa
127 U6 **Sterlibashevo** Respublika Bashkortostan, W Russian Federation
39 R12 **Sterling** Alaska, USA
37 V3 **Sterling** Colorado, C USA
30 K11 **Sterling** Illinois, N USA
26 M5 **Sterling** Kansas, C USA
25 O8 **Sterling City** Texas, SW USA
31 S9 **Sterling Heights** Michigan, N USA
21 W3 **Sterling Park** Virginia, NE USA
37 V2 **Sterling Reservoir** ▣ Colorado, C USA
22 I5 **Sterlington** Louisiana, S USA
127 U6 **Sterlitamak** Respublika Bashkortostan, W Russian Federation
Sternberg *see* Šternberk
111 H17 **Šternberk** ***Ger.*** Sternberg. Olomoucký Kraj, E Czech Republic
141 V17 **Stēroh** Suquṭrā, S Yemen
110 G11 **Stęszew** Wielkolpolskie, C Poland
Stettin *see* Szczecin
Stettiner Haff *see* Szczeciński, Zalew
11 Q15 **Stettler** Alberta, SW Canada
31 V13 **Steubenville** Ohio, N USA
97 O21 **Stevenage** E England, UK
23 Q1 **Stevenson** Alabama, S USA
32 H11 **Stevenson** Washington, NW USA
182 E1 **Stevenson Creek** *seasonal river* South Australia
39 Q13 **Stevenson Entrance** *strait* Alaska, USA
30 L6 **Stevens Point** Wisconsin, N USA
39 R8 **Stevens Village** Alaska, USA
33 P10 **Stevensville** Montana, NW USA
93 E25 **Stevns Klint** *headland* E Denmark
10 J12 **Stewart** British Columbia, W Canada
10 J6 **Stewart** ≈ Yukon Territory, NW Canada
10 I6 **Stewart Crossing** Yukon Territory, NW Canada
63 H25 **Stewart, Isla** *island* S Chile
185 B25 **Stewart Island** *island* S NZ
181 W6 **Stewart, Mount** ▲ Queensland, E Australia
10 H6 **Stewart River** Yukon Territory, NW Canada
27 R3 **Stewartsville** Missouri, C USA
11 S16 **Stewart Valley** Saskatchewan, S Canada
29 W10 **Stewartville** Minnesota, N USA
Steyerlak-Anina *see* Anina
109 T5 **Steyr** ***var.*** Steier. Oberösterreich, N Austria
109 T5 **Steyr** ≈ NW Austria
29 P11 **Stickney** South Dakota, N USA
98 L5 **Stiens** Friesland, N Netherlands
Stif *see* Sétif
27 Q11 **Stigler** Oklahoma, C USA
107 N18 **Stigliano** Basilicata, S Italy
95 N17 **Stigtomta** Södermanland, C Sweden
10 I11 **Stikine** ≈ British Columbia, W Canada
Stilida/Stilís *see* Stylída
95 G22 **Stilling** Århus, C Denmark
29 W8 **Stillwater** Minnesota, N USA
27 O9 **Stillwater** Oklahoma, C USA
35 S5 **Stillwater Range** ▲ Nevada, W USA
18 I8 **Stillwater Reservoir** ▣ New York, NE USA
107 O22 **Stilo, Punta** *headland* S Italy
27 R10 **Stilwell** Oklahoma, C USA
113 N17 **Štimlje** Serbia, S Serbia and Montenegro (Yugo.)
25 N1 **Stinnett** Texas, SW USA
113 P18 **Štip** E FYR Macedonia
Stira *see* Stýra
96 J12 **Stirling** C Scotland, UK
96 I12 **Stirling** *cultural region* C Scotland, UK
180 J14 **Stirling Range** ▲ Western Australia
93 E16 **Stjørdalshalsen** Nord-Trøndelag, C Norway
Stochód *see* Stokhid
101 H24 **Stockach** Baden-Württemberg, S Germany
25 S12 **Stockdale** Texas, SW USA
109 X3 **Stockerau** Niederösterreich, NE Austria
93 H20 **Stockholm** ● (Sweden) Stockholm, C Sweden
95 O15 **Stockholm** ◆ *county* C Sweden
Stockmannshof *see* Pļaviņas
97 L18 **Stockport** NW England, UK
65 K15 **Stocks Seamount** *undersea feature* C Atlantic Ocean
35 O8 **Stockton** California, W USA
26 L3 **Stockton** Kansas, C USA
27 S6 **Stockton** Missouri, C USA
30 K3 **Stockton Island** *island* Apostle Islands, Wisconsin, N USA
27 S7 **Stockton Lake** ▣ Missouri, C USA
97 M15 **Stockton-on-Tees** ***var.*** Stockton on Tees. N England, UK
24 M10 **Stockton Plateau** *plain* Texas, SW USA
28 M16 **Stockville** Nebraska, C USA
93 H17 **Stöde** Västernorrland, C Sweden
Stodolichi *see* Stadolichy
167 S11 **Stœng Trêng** ***prev.*** Stung Treng. Stœng Trêng, NE Cambodia
113 M19 **Stogovo Karaorman** ▲ W FYR Macedonia
Stoke *see* Stoke-on-Trent
97 L19 **Stoke-on-Trent** ***var.*** Stoke. C England, UK
182 M15 **Stokes Point** *headland* Tasmania, SE Australia
116 J2 **Stokhid** ***Pol.*** Stochód, ***Rus.*** Stokhod. ≈ NW Ukraine
Stokhod *see* Stokhid
92 I4 **Stokkseyri** Sudhurland, SW Iceland
92 G10 **Stokmarknes** Nordland, C Norway
Stol *see* Veliki Krš
113 H15 **Stolac** Federacija Bosna I Hercegovina, S Bosnia and Herzegovina
Stolbce *see* Stowbtsy
101 D16 **Stolberg** ***var.*** Stolberg im Rheinland. Nordrhein-Westfalen, W Germany
Stolberg im Rheinland *see* Stolberg
123 P6 **Stolbovoy, Ostrov** *island* NE Russian Federation
Stolbtsy *see* Stowbtsy
119 J20 **Stolin** ***Rus.*** Stolin. Brestskaya Voblasts', SW Belarus
95 K14 **Stöllet** ***var.*** Norra Ny. Värmland, C Sweden
Stolp *see* Słupsk
Stolpe *see* Słupia
Stolpmünde *see* Ustka
115 F15 **Stómio** Thessalía, C Greece
14 J11 **Stonecliffe** Ontario, SE Canada
96 L10 **Stonehaven** NE Scotland, UK
97 M23 **Stonehenge** *ancient monument* Wiltshire, S England, UK
23 T3 **Stone Mountain** ▲ Georgia, SE USA
11 X16 **Stonewall** Manitoba, S Canada
21 S3 **Stonewood** West Virginia, NE USA
14 D17 **Stoney Point** Ontario, S Canada
92 H10 **Stonglandseidet** Troms, N Norway
65 N25 **Stonybeach Bay** *bay* Tristan da Cunha, SE Atlantic Ocean
35 N5 **Stony Creek** ≈ California, W USA
65 N25 **Stonyhill Point** *headland* S Tristan da Cunha
14 I14 **Stony Lake** ◎ Ontario, SE Canada
11 Q14 **Stony Plain** Alberta, SW Canada
21 R9 **Stony Point** North Carolina, SE USA
18 G8 **Stony Point** *headland* New York, NE USA
11 T10 **Stony Rapids** Saskatchewan, C Canada
39 P11 **Stony River** Alaska, USA
Stony Tunguska *see* Podkamennaya Tunguska
12 G10 **Stooping** ≈ Ontario, C Canada
100 I9 **Stör** ≈ N Germany
95 M15 **Storå** Örebro, S Sweden
95 J16 **Stora Gla** ◎ C Sweden
95 I16 **Stora Le** ***Nor.*** Store Le. ◎ Norway/Sweden
92 I12 **Stora Lulevatten** ◎ N Sweden
92 H13 **Storavan** ◎ N Sweden
93 I20 **Storby** Åland, SW Finland
94 E10 **Stordalen** Møre og Romsdal, S Norway
Storebelt *see* Storebælt
95 H23 **Storebælt** ***var.*** Store Bælt, ***Eng.*** Great Belt, Storebelt. *channel* Baltic Sea/Kattegat
95 M19 **Storebro** Kalmar, S Sweden
95 J24 **Store Heddinge** Storstrøm, SE Denmark
Store Le *see* Stora Le
93 E16 **Støren** Sør-Trøndelag, S Norway
92 O4 **Storfjorden** *fjord* S Norway
95 L15 **Storfors** Värmland, C Sweden
92 G13 **Storforshei** Nordland, C Norway
Storhammer *see* Hamar
100 L10 **Störkanal** *canal* N Germany
93 F16 **Storlien** Jämtland, C Sweden
183 P17 **Storm Bay** *inlet* Tasmania, SE Australia
29 T12 **Storm Lake** Iowa, C USA
29 S13 **Storm Lake** ◎ Iowa, C USA
96 G7 **Stornoway** NW Scotland, UK
Storojineţ *see* Storozhynets'
92 P1 **Storøya** *island* NE Svalbard
125 S10 **Storozhevsk** Respublika Komi, NW Russian Federation
Storozhinets *see* Storozhynets'
116 K8 **Storozhynets'** ***Ger.*** Storozynetz, ***Rom.*** Storojineţ, ***Rus.*** Storozhinets. Chernivets'ka Oblast', W Ukraine
Storozynetz *see* Storozhynets'
92 H11 **Storriten** ▲ C Norway
19 N12 **Storrs** Connecticut, NE USA
94 I11 **Storsjøen** ◎ S Norway
94 N13 **Storsjön** ◎ C Sweden
93 F16 **Storsjön** ◎ C Sweden
92 J9 **Storslett** Troms, N Norway
94 H11 **Storsølnkletten** ▲ S Norway
92 I9 **Storsteinnes** Troms, N Norway
95 I24 **Storstrøm** ***off.*** Storstrøms Amt. ◆ *county* SE Denmark
93 J14 **Storsund** Norrbotten, N Sweden
94 J9 **Storsylen** ***Swe.*** Sylarna. ▲ Norway/Sweden
92 H11 **Stortoppen** ▲ N Sweden
93 H14 **Storuman** Västerbotten, N Sweden
93 H14 **Storuman** ◎ N Sweden
94 N13 **Storvik** Gävleborg, C Sweden
95 O14 **Storvreta** Uppsala, C Sweden
29 V13 **Story City** Iowa, C USA
11 V17 **Stoughton** Saskatchewan, S Canada
19 O11 **Stoughton** Massachusetts, NE USA
30 L9 **Stoughton** Wisconsin, N USA
97 L23 **Stour** ≈ E England, UK
97 P21 **Stour** ≈ S England, UK
27 T5 **Stover** Missouri, C USA
95 G21 **Støvring** Nordjylland, N Denmark
119 J17 **Stowbtsy** ***Pol.*** Stolbce, ***Rus.*** Stolbtsy. Minskaya Voblasts', C Belarus
25 X11 **Stowell** Texas, SW USA
97 P20 **Stowmarket** E England, UK
114 N8 **Stozher** Dobrich, NE Bulgaria
97 E14 **Strabane** ***Ir.*** An Srath Bán. W Northern Ireland, UK
121 S11 **Strabo Trench** *undersea feature* C Mediterranean Sea
27 T7 **Strafford** Missouri, C USA
183 N17 **Strahan** Tasmania, SE Australia
111 C18 **Strakonice** ***Ger.*** Strakonitz. Jihočeský Kraj, S Czech Republic
Strakonitz *see* Strakonice
100 N8 **Stralsund** Mecklenburg-Vorpommern, NE Germany
99 L16 **Stramproy** Limburg, SE Netherlands
83 E26 **Strand** Western Cape, SW South Africa
94 E10 **Stranda** Møre og Romsdal, S Norway
97 G15 **Strangford Lough** ***Ir.*** Loch Cuan. *inlet* E Northern Ireland, UK
95 N16 **Strängnäs** Södermanland, C Sweden
97 E14 **Stranorlar** ***Ir.*** Srath an Urláir. NW Ireland
97 H14 **Stranraer** S Scotland, UK
11 U16 **Strasbourg** Saskatchewan, S Canada
103 V5 **Strasbourg** ***Ger.*** Strassburg; ***anc.*** Argentoratum. Bas-Rhin, NE France
37 U4 **Strasburg** Colorado, C USA
29 N7 **Strasburg** North Dakota, N USA
31 U12 **Strasburg** Ohio, N USA
21 U3 **Strasburg** Virginia, NE USA
117 N10 **Strășeni** ***var.*** Strasheny. C Moldova
Strasheny *see* Strășeni
109 T8 **Strassburg** Kärnten, S Austria
Strassburg *see* Strasbourg, France
Strassburg *see* Aiud, Romania
99 M25 **Strassen** Luxembourg, S Luxembourg
109 R5 **Strasswalchen** Salzburg, C Austria
14 F16 **Stratford** Ontario, S Canada
184 K10 **Stratford** Taranaki, North Island, NZ
35 Q11 **Stratford** California, W USA
29 V13 **Stratford** Iowa, C USA
27 O12 **Stratford** Oklahoma, C USA
25 N1 **Stratford** Texas, SW USA
30 K6 **Stratford** Wisconsin, N USA
Stratford *see* Stratford-upon-Avon
97 M20 **Stratford-upon-Avon** ***var.*** Stratford. C England, UK
183 O17 **Strathgordon** Tasmania, SE Australia
11 Q16 **Strathmore** Alberta, SW Canada
35 R11 **Strathmore** California, W USA
14 E16 **Strathroy** Ontario, S Canada
96 I6 **Strathy Point** *headland* N Scotland, UK
37 W4 **Stratton** Colorado, C USA
19 P6 **Stratton** Maine, NE USA
18 M10 **Stratton Mountain** ▲ Vermont, NE USA
101 N21 **Straubing** Bayern, SE Germany
100 O12 **Strausberg** Brandenburg, E Germany
32 K13 **Strawberry Mountain** ▲ Oregon, NW USA
29 X12 **Strawberry Point** Iowa, C USA
36 M3 **Strawberry Reservoir** ▣ Utah, W USA
36 M4 **Strawberry River** ≈ Utah, W USA
25 R7 **Strawn** Texas, SW USA
113 P17 **Straža** ▲ Bulgaria/FYR Macedonia
111 I19 **Strážov** ***Hung.*** Sztrazsó. ▲ NW Slovakia
182 F7 **Streaky Bay** South Australia
182 E7 **Streaky Bay** *bay* South Australia
30 L12 **Streator** Illinois, N USA
Streckenbach *see* Świdnik
111 C17 **Středočeský kraj** ◆ *region* C Czech Republic
Strednogorie *see* Pirdop
29 O6 **Streeter** North Dakota, N USA
25 U8 **Streetman** Texas, SW USA
116 G13 **Strehaia** Mehedinți, SW Romania
Strehlen *see* Strzelin
114 I10 **Strelcha** Pazardzhik, C Bulgaria
122 L12 **Strelka** Krasnoyarskiy Kray, C Russian Federation
126 L6 **Strel'na** ≈ NW Russian Federation
118 H7 **Strenči** ***Ger.*** Stackeln. Valka, N Latvia
108 K8 **Strengen** Tirol, W Austria
106 C6 **Stresa** Piemonte, NE Italy
Streshin *see* Streshyn
119 N18 **Streshyn** ***Rus.*** Streshin. Homyel'skaya Voblasts', SE Belarus
95 B18 **Streymoy** ***Dan.*** Strømø *Island* Faeroe Islands
95 G23 **Strib** Fyn, C Denmark
111 A17 **Stříbro** ***Ger.*** Mies. Plzeňský Kraj, W Czech Republic
186 B7 **Strickland** ≈ SW PNG
Striegau *see* Strzegom
Strigonium *see* Esztergom
98 H13 **Strijen** Zuid-Holland, SW Netherlands
63 H21 **Strobel, Lago** ◎ S Argentina
61 B25 **Stroeder** Buenos Aires, E Argentina
115 C20 **Strofádes** *island* Iónioi Nísoi, Greece, C Mediterranean Sea
Strofilia *see* Strofyliá
115 G17 **Strofyliá** ***var.*** Strofilia. Évvoia, C Greece
100 O10 **Strom** ≈ NE Germany
107 L22 **Stromboli** ※ Isola Stromboli, SW Italy
107 L22 **Stromboli, Isola** *island* Isole Eolie, S Italy
96 H9 **Stromeferry** N Scotland, UK
96 J5 **Stromness** N Scotland, UK
94 N11 **Strömsbruk** Gävleborg, C Sweden
29 Q15 **Stromsburg** Nebraska, C USA
95 K21 **Strömsnäsbruk** Kronoberg, S Sweden
95 I17 **Strömstad** Västra Götaland, S Sweden
93 G16 **Strömsund** Jämtland, C Sweden
93 G15 **Ströms Vattudal** *valley* N Sweden
27 V14 **Strong** Arkansas, C USA
Strongilí *see* Strongylí
107 O21 **Strongoli** Calabria, SW Italy
31 T11 **Strongsville** Ohio, N USA
115 Q23 **Strongylí** ***var.*** Strongilí. *island* SE Greece
96 K5 **Stronsay** *island* NE Scotland, UK
97 L21 **Stroud** C England, UK
27 O10 **Stroud** Oklahoma, C USA
18 I14 **Stroudsburg** Pennsylvania, NE USA
95 F21 **Struer** Ringkøbing, W Denmark
113 M20 **Struga** SW FYR Macedonia
Strugi-Kranyse *see* Strugi-Krasnyye
124 G14 **Strugi-Krasnyye** ***var.*** Strugi-Kranyse. Pskovskaya Oblast', W Russian Federation
114 G11 **Struma** ***Gk.*** Strymónas. ≈ Bulgaria/Greece ***see also*** Strymónas
97 G21 **Strumble Head** *headland* SW Wales, UK
113 Q19 **Strumeshnitsa** | Mac. Strumica. ≈ Bulgaria/FYR Macedonia
113 Q19 **Strumica** E FYR Macedonia
Strumica *see* Strumeshnitsa

◆ COUNTRY
● COUNTRY CAPITAL
◇ DEPENDENT TERRITORY
○ DEPENDENT TERRITORY CAPITAL
◆ ADMINISTRATIVE REGION
× INTERNATIONAL AIRPORT
▲ MOUNTAIN
▲ MOUNTAIN RANGE
※ VOLCANO
≈ RIVER
◎ LAKE
▣ RESERVOIR

114 G11 **Strumyani** Blagoevgrad, SW Bulgaria
31 V12 **Struthers** Ohio, N USA
114 I10 **Stryama** ≈ C Bulgaria
114 G13 **Strymónas** *Bul.* Struma. ≈ Bulgaria/Greece *see also* Struma
115 H14 **Strymonikós Kólpos** *gulf* N Greece
116 I6 **Stryy** L'vivs'ka Oblast', NW Ukraine
116 H6 **Stryy** ≈ W Ukraine
111 F14 **Strzegom** *Ger.* Striegau. Wałbrzych, SW Poland
110 E10 **Strzelce Krajeńskie** *Ger.* Friedeberg Neumark. Lubuskie, W Poland
111 I15 **Strzelce Opolskie** *Ger.* Gross Strehlitz. Opolskie, S Poland
182 K3 **Strzelecki Creek** *seasonal river* South Australia
182 J3 **Strzelecki Desert** *desert* South Australia
111 G15 **Strzelin** *Ger.* Strehlen. Dolnośląskie, SW Poland
110 I11 **Strzelno** Kujawsko-pomorskie, C Poland
111 N17 **Strzyżów** Podkarpackie, SE Poland
Stua Laighean *see* Leinster, Mount
23 Y13 **Stuart** Florida, SE USA
29 U14 **Stuart** Iowa, C USA
29 O13 **Stuart** Nebraska, C USA
21 S8 **Stuart** Virginia, NE USA
10 L13 **Stuart** ≈ British Columbia, SW Canada
39 N10 **Stuart Island** *island* Alaska, USA
10 L13 **Stuart Lake** ◎ British Columbia, SW Canada
185 B22 **Stuart Mountains** ▲ South Island, NZ
182 F3 **Stuart Range** *hill range* South Australia
Stubaital *see* Neustift im Stubaital
95 I24 **Stubbekøbing** Storstrøm, SE Denmark
45 P14 **Stubbs** Saint Vincent, Saint Vincent and the Grenadines
109 V6 **Stübming** ≈ E Austria
114 J11 **Studen Kladenets, Yazovir** ⊞ S Bulgaria
185 G21 **Studholme** Canterbury, South Island, NZ
Stuhlweissenberg *see* Székesfehérvár
Stuhm *see* Sztum
12 C7 **Stull Lake** ◎ Ontario, C Canada
Stung Treng *see* Stœng Trêng
126 L4 **Stupino** Moskovskaya Oblast', W Russian Federation
27 U4 **Sturgeon** Missouri, C USA
14 G10 **Sturgeon** ≈ Ontario, S Canada
31 N6 **Sturgeon Bay** Wisconsin, N USA
14 G11 **Sturgeon Falls** Ontario, S Canada
12 C11 **Sturgeon Lake** ◎ Ontario, S Canada
30 M3 **Sturgeon River** ≈ Michigan, N USA
20 H6 **Sturgis** Kentucky, S USA
31 P11 **Sturgis** Michigan, N USA
28 J9 **Sturgis** South Dakota, N USA
112 D10 **Šturlić** Federacija Bosna I Hercegovina, NW Bosnia and Herzegovina
111 J22 **Štúrovo** *Hung.* Párkány; *prev.* Parkan. Nitriansky Kraj, W Slovakia
182 L4 **Sturt, Mount** *hill* New South Wales, SE Australia
181 P4 **Sturt Plain** *plain* Northern Territory, N Australia
181 T9 **Sturt Stony Desert** *desert* South Australia
83 J25 **Stutterheim** Eastern Cape, S South Africa
101 H21 **Stuttgart** Baden-Württemberg, SW Germany
27 W12 **Stuttgart** Arkansas, C USA
92 H2 **Stykkishólmur** Vesturland, W Iceland
115 F17 **Stylída** *var.* Stilida, Stilís. Stereá Ellás, C Greece
116 K2 **Styr** *Rus.* Styr'. ≈ Belarus/Ukraine
115 I19 **Stýra** *var.* Stira. Évvoia, C Greece
Styria *see* Steiermark
Su *see* Jiangsu
Sua *see* Sowa
171 Q17 **Suai** W East Timor
54 G9 **Suaita** Santander, C Colombia
80 I7 **Suakin** *var.* Sawakin. Red Sea, NE Sudan
161 T13 **Suao** *Jap.* Suō. N Taiwan
Suao *see* Suau
83 I18 **Sua Pan** *var.* Sowa Pan. *salt lake* NE Botswana
40 G6 **Suaqui Grande** Sonora, NW Mexico
61 A16 **Suardi** Santa Fe, C Argentina
54 D11 **Suárez** Cauca, SW Colombia
186 G10 **Suau** *var.* Suao. Suaul Island, SE PNG
118 G12 **Subačius** Panevėžys, NE Lithuania
168 K9 **Subang** *prev.* Soebang. Jawa, C Indonesia
169 O16 **Subang** ✕ (Kuala Lumpur) Pahang, Peninsular Malaysia
118 I11 **Subate** Daugvapils, SE Latvia
139 N5 **Subaykhān** Dayr az Zawr, E Syria
Subei/Subei Mongolzu Zizhixian *see* Dangchengwan
169 P9 **Subi Besar, Pulau** *island* Kepulauan Natuna, W Indonesia
Subiyah *see* Aş Şubayhīyah
26 I7 **Sublette** Kansas, C USA
112 K8 **Subotica** *Ger.* Maria-Theresiopel, *Hung.* Szabadka. Serbia, N Serbia and Montenegro (Yugo.)
116 K9 **Suceava** *Ger.* Suczawa, *Hung.* Szucsava. Suceava, NE Romania
116 J9 **Suceava** ◈ *county* NE Romania
116 K9 **Suceava** *Ger.* Suczawa. ≈ N Romania
112 E12 **Sučevići** Zadar, SW Croatia
111 K17 **Sucha Beskidzka** Małopolskie, S Poland
111 M14 **Suchedniów** Świętokrzyskie, C Poland
42 A2 **Suchitepéquez** *off.* Departamento de Suchitepéquez. ◈ *department* SW Guatemala
Su-chou *see* Suzhou
Suchow *see* Suzhou, Jiangsu, China
Suchow *see* Xuzhou, Jiangsu, China
97 D17 **Suck** ≈ C Ireland
Sucker State *see* Illinois
186 F9 **Suckling, Mount** ▲ S PNG
57 L19 **Sucre** *hist.* Chuquisaca, La Plata. ● (Bolivia-legal capital) Chuquisaca, S Bolivia
54 E6 **Sucre** Santander, N Colombia
56 A7 **Sucre** Manabí, W Ecuador
54 E6 **Sucre** *off.* Departamento de Sucre. ◈ *province* N Colombia
55 O5 **Sucre** *off.* Estado Sucre. ◈ *state* NE Venezuela
56 D6 **Sucumbíos** ◈ *province* NE Ecuador
113 G15 **Sućuraj** Split-Dalmacija, S Croatia
58 K10 **Sucuriju** Amapá, NE Brazil
Suczawa *see* Suceava
79 E16 **Sud** *Eng.* South. ◈ *province* S Cameroon
126 K13 **Suda** ≈ NW Russian Federation
Suda *see* Soúda
117 U13 **Sudak** Respublika Krym, S Ukraine
24 M4 **Sudan** Texas, SW USA
80 C10 **Sudan** *off.* Republic of Sudan, *Ar.* Jumhuriyat as-Sudan; *prev.* Anglo-Egyptian Sudan. ◆ *republic* N Africa
Sudanese Republic *see* Mali
Sudan, Jumhuriyat as- *see* Sudan
14 F10 **Sudbury** Ontario, S Canada
97 P20 **Sudbury** E England, UK
Sud, Canal de *see* Gonâve, Canal de la
80 E13 **Sudd** *swamp region* S Sudan
100 K10 **Sude** ≈ N Germany
Sudest Island *see* Tagula Island
111 E15 **Sudeten** *var.* Sudetes, Sudetic Mountains, *Cz./Pol.* Sudety. ▲ Czech Republic/Poland
Sudetes/Sudetic Mountains/Sudety *see* Sudeten
92 G1 **Suðureyri** Vestfirdhir, NW Iceland
92 J4 **Suðurland** ◈ *region* S Iceland
95 B19 **Suðuroy** *Dan.* Suderø *Island* Faeroe Islands
124 M15 **Sudislavl'** Kostromskaya Oblast', NW Russian Federation
Südkarpaten *see* Carpaţii Meridionali
79 N20 **Sud Kivu** *off.* Région Sud Kivu. ◈ *region* E Dem. Rep. Congo
Südliche Morava *see* Južna Morava
100 E12 **Süd-Nord-Kanal** *canal* NW Germany
126 M3 **Sudogda** Vladimirskaya Oblast', W Russian Federation
Sudostroy *see* Severodvinsk
79 C15 **Sud-Ouest** *Eng.* South-West. ◈ *province* W Cameroon
173 X17 **Sud Ouest, Pointe** *headland* SW Mauritius
187 P17 **Sud, Province** ◈ *province* S New Caledonia
126 J8 **Sudzha** Kurskaya Oblast', W Russian Federation
81 D15 **Sue** ≈ S Sudan
105 S10 **Sueca** País Valenciano, E Spain
114 I10 **Săedinenie** Plovdiv, C Bulgaria
Suero *see* Alzira
75 X8 **Suez** *Ar.* As Suways, El Suweis. NE Egypt
75 W7 **Suez Canal** *Ar.* Qanāt as Suways. *canal* NE Egypt
75 X8 **Suez, Gulf of** *Ar.* Khalīj as Suways. *gulf* NE Egypt
11 R17 **Suffield** Alberta, SW Canada
21 X7 **Suffolk** Virginia, NE USA
97 P20 **Suffolk** *cultural region* E England, UK
142 J2 **Şūfīān** Āzarbāyjān-e Khāvarī, N Iran
31 N12 **Sugar Creek** ≈ Illinois, N USA
30 L13 **Sugar Creek** ≈ Illinois, N USA
31 R3 **Sugar Island** *island* Michigan, N USA
25 V11 **Sugar Land** Texas, SW USA
19 P6 **Sugarloaf Mountain** ▲ Maine, NE USA
65 G24 **Sugar Loaf Point** *headland* N Saint Helena
136 G16 **Suğla Gölü** ◎ SW Turkey
123 T8 **Sugoy** ≈ E Russian Federation
158 F7 **Sugun** Xinjiang Uygur Zizhiqu, W China
147 U1[illegible] **Sugut, Gora** ▲ SW Kyrgyzstan
169 V6 **Sugut, Sungai** ≈ East Malaysia
159 O9 **Suhai Hu** ◎ C China
162 K14 **Suhait** Nei Mongol Zizhiqu, N China
141 X7 **Şuḩār** *var.* Sohar. N Oman
162 L5 **Sühbaatar** Selenge, N Mongolia
163 P9 **Sühbaatar** ◈ *province* E Mongolia
101 K17 **Suhl** Thüringen, C Germany
108 F7 **Suhr** Aargau, N Switzerland
Sui'an *see* Zhangpu
161 O12 **Suichuan** *var.* Quanjiang. Jiangxi, S China
Suid-Afrika *see* South Africa
160 L4 **Suide** Shaanxi, C China
Suidwes-Afrika *see* Namibia
163 Y9 **Suifenhe** Heilongjiang, NE China
Suigen *see* Suwŏn
163 W8 **Suihua** Heilongjiang, NE China
Súilí, Loch *see* Swilly, Lough
161 Q6 **Suining** Jiangsu, E China
160 I9 **Suining** Sichuan, C China
103 Q4 **Suippes** Marne, N France
97 E20 **Suir** *Ir.* An tSiúir. ≈ S Ireland
165 J13 **Suita** Ōsaka, Honshū, SW Japan
160 L16 **Suixi** Guangdong, S China
Sui Xian *see* Suizhou
163 T13 **Suizhong** Liaoning, NE China
161 N8 **Suizhou** *prev.* Sui Xian. Hubei, C China
149 P17 **Sujāwal** Sind, SE Pakistan
169 O16 **Sukabumi** *prev.* Soekaboemi. Jawa, C Indonesia
169 Q12 **Sukadana, Teluk** *bay* Borneo, W Indonesia
165 P11 **Sukagawa** Fukushima, Honshū, C Japan
Sukarnapura *see* Jayapura
Sukarno, Puntjak *see* Jaya, Puncak
Sûkh *see* Sokh
114 N8 **Sukha Reka** ≈ NE Bulgaria
126 J5 **Sukhinichi** Kaluzhskaya Oblast', W Russian Federation
Sukhne *see* As Sukhnah
125 N12 **Sukhona** *var.* Tot'ma. ≈ NW Russian Federation
167 O8 **Sukhothai** *var.* Sukotai. Sukhothai, W Thailand
Sukhumi *see* Sokhumi
Sukkertoppen *see* Maniitsoq
149 Q13 **Sukkur** Sind, SE Pakistan
Sukotai *see* Sukhothai
Sukra Bay *see* Şawqirah, Dawḩat
125 V15 **Suksun** Permskaya Oblast', NW Russian Federation
165 F15 **Sukumo** Kōchi, Shikoku, SW Japan
94 B12 **Sula** *island* S Norway
127 Q5 **Sula** ≈ NW Russian Federation
117 R5 **Sula** ≈ N Ukraine
42 H6 **Sulaco, Río** ≈ NW Honduras
Sulaimaniya *see* As Sulaymānīyah
149 S10 **Sulaimān Range** ▲ C Pakistan
127 Q16 **Sulak** Respublika Dagestan, SW Russian Federation
127 Q16 **Sulak** ≈ SW Russian Federation
171 Q13 **Sula, Kepulauan** *island group* C Indonesia
136 I12 **Sulakyurt** *var.* Konur. Kırıkkale, N Turkey
171 P17 **Sulamu** Timor, S Indonesia
96 F5 **Sula Sgeir** *island* NW Scotland, UK
171 N13 **Sulawesi** *Eng.* Celebes. *island* C Indonesia
Sulawesi, Laut *see* Celebes Sea
171 N14 **Sulawesi Selatan** *off.* Propinsi Sulawesi Selatan, *Eng.* South Celebes, South Sulawesi. ◈ *province* C Indonesia
171 P12 **Sulawesi Tengah** *off.* Propinsi Sulawesi Tengah, *Eng.* Central Celebes, Central Sulawesi. ◈ *province* N Indonesia
171 O14 **Sulawesi Tenggara** *off.* Propinsi Sulawesi Tenggara, *Eng.* South-East Celebes, South-East Sulawesi. ◈ *province* C Indonesia
171 P11 **Sulawesi Utara** *off.* Propinsi Sulawesi Utara, *Eng.* North Celebes, North Sulawesi. ◈ *province* N Indonesia
139 T5 **Sulaymān Beg** N Iraq
95 D15 **Suldalsvatnet** ◎ S Norway
Sulden *see* Solda
110 E12 **Sulechów** *Ger.* Züllichau. Lubuskie, W Poland
110 E11 **Sulęcin** Lubuskie, W Poland
77 U14 **Suleja** Niger, C Nigeria
111 K14 **Sulejów** Łodzkie, S Poland
96 I5 **Sule Skerry** *island* N Scotland, UK
Suliag *see* Sohâg
76 J16 **Sulima** S Sierra Leone
117 O13 **Sulina** Tulcea, SE Romania
117 N13 **Sulina Braţul** ≈ SE Romania
100 H12 **Sulingen** Niedersachsen, NW Germany
Sulisjielmmá *see* Sulitjelma
92 H12 **Suliskongen** ▲ C Norway
92 H12 **Sulitjelma** *Lapp.* Sulisjielmmá. Nordland, C Norway
56 A9 **Sullana** Piura, NW Peru
23 N3 **Sulligent** Alabama, S USA
30 M14 **Sullivan** Illinois, N USA
31 N15 **Sullivan** Indiana, N USA
27 W5 **Sullivan** Missouri, C USA
Sullivan Island *see* Lanbi Kyun
96 M1 **Sullom Voe** NE Scotland, UK
103 O7 **Sully-sur-Loire** Loiret, C France
Sulmo *see* Sulmona
107 K15 **Sulmona** *anc.* Sulmo. Abruzzo, C Italy
Sulo *see* Shule He
114 M11 **Süloğlu** Edirne, NW Turkey
22 G9 **Sulphur** Louisiana, S USA
27 O12 **Sulphur** Oklahoma, C USA
28 K9 **Sulphur Creek** ≈ South Dakota, N USA
24 M5 **Sulphur Draw** ≈ Texas, SW USA
25 W5 **Sulphur River** ≈ Arkansas/Texas, SW USA
25 V6 **Sulphur Springs** Texas, SW USA
24 M6 **Sulphur Springs Draw** ≈ Texas, SW USA
14 D8 **Sultan** Ontario, S Canada
Sultānābād *see* Arāk
Sultan Alonto, Lake *see* Lanao, Lake
136 G15 **Sultan Dağları** ▲ C Turkey
114 N13 **Sultanköy** Tekirdağ, NW Turkey
171 Q7 **Sultan Kudarat** *var.* Nuling. Mindanao, S Philippines
152 M13 **Sultānpur** Uttar Pradesh, N India
171 O9 **Sulu Archipelago** *island group* SW Philippines
192 F7 **Sulu Basin** *undersea feature* SE South China Sea
Sülüktü *see* Sulyukta
Sulu, Laut *see* Sulu Sea
169 X6 **Sulu Sea** *Ind.* Laut Sulu. *sea* SW Philippines
145 O15 **Sulutobe** *Kaz.* Sulütöbe. Kyzylorda, S Kazakhstan
147 Q11 **Sulyukta** *Kir.* Sülüktü. Batkenskaya Oblast', SW Kyrgyzstan
Sulz *see* Sulz am Neckar
101 G22 **Sulz am Neckar** *var.* Sulz. Baden-Württemberg, SW Germany
101 L20 **Sulzbach-Rosenberg** Bayern, SE Germany
195 N13 **Sulzberger Bay** *bay* Antarctica
Sumail *see* Summēl
113 F15 **Sumartin** Split-Dalmacija, S Croatia
32 H6 **Sumas** Washington, NW USA
168 J10 **Sumatera** *Eng.* Sumatra. *island* W Indonesia
168 J12 **Sumatera Barat** *off.* Propinsi Sumatera Barat, *Eng.* West Sumatra. ◈ *province* W Indonesia
168 L13 **Sumatera Selatan** *off.* Propinsi Sumatera Selatan, *Eng.* South Sumatra. ◈ *province* W Indonesia
168 H10 **Sumatera Utara** *off.* Propinsi Sumatera Utara, *Eng.* North Sumatra. ◈ *province* W Indonesia
Sumatra *see* Sumatera
Šumava *see* Bohemian Forest
Sumayl *see* Summēl
139 U7 **Sumayr al Muḩammad** E Iraq
171 N17 **Sumba, Pulau** *Eng.* Sandalwood Island; *prev.* Soemba. *island* Nusa Tenggara, C Indonesia
146 D12 **Sumbar** ≈ W Turkmenistan
192 E9 **Sumbawa** *prev.* Soembawa. *island* Nusa Tenggara, C Indonesia
170 L16 **Sumbawabesar** Sumbawa, S Indonesia
81 F23 **Sumbawanga** Rukwa, W Tanzania
82 B12 **Sumbe** *prev.* N'Gunza, *Port.* Novo Redondo. Cuanza Sul, W Angola
96 M3 **Sumburgh Head** *headland* NE Scotland, UK
111 H23 **Sümeg** Veszprém, W Hungary
80 C12 **Sumeih** Southern Darfur, S Sudan
169 T16 **Sumenep** *prev.* Soemenep. Pulau Madura, C Indonesia
Sumgait *see* Sumqayıt, Azerbaijan
Sumgait *see* Sumqayıtçay, Azerbaijan
165 Y14 **Sumisu-jima** *Eng.* Smith Island. *island* SE Japan
139 Q2 **Summēl** *var.* Sumail, Sumayl. N Iraq
31 O5 **Summer Island** *island* Michigan, N USA
32 H15 **Summer Lake** ◎ Oregon, NW USA
11 N17 **Summerland** British Columbia, SW Canada
13 P14 **Summerside** Prince Edward Island, SE Canada
21 R5 **Summersville** West Virginia, NE USA
21 R5 **Summersville Lake** ⊞ West Virginia, NE USA
21 S13 **Summerton** South Carolina, SE USA
23 R2 **Summerville** Georgia, SE USA
21 S14 **Summerville** South Carolina, SE USA
39 R10 **Summit** Alaska, USA
35 V6 **Summit Mountain** ▲ Nevada, W USA
37 R8 **Summit Peak** ▲ Colorado, C USA
Summus Portus *see* Somport, Col du
29 X12 **Sumner** Iowa, C USA
22 K3 **Sumner** Mississippi, S USA
185 H17 **Sumner, Lake** ◎ South Island, NZ
37 U12 **Sumner, Lake** ⊞ New Mexico, SW USA
111 G17 **Šumperk** *Ger.* Mährisch-Schönberg. Olomoucký Kraj, E Czech Republic
42 F7 **Sumpul, Río** ≈ El Salvador/Honduras
137 Z11 **Sumqayıt** *Rus.* Sumgait. E Azerbaijan
137 Y11 **Sumqayıtçay** *Rus.* Sumgait. ≈ E Azerbaijan
147 R9 **Sumsar** Dzhalal-Abadskaya Oblast', W Kyrgyzstan
117 S3 **Sums'ka Oblast'** *var.* Sumy, *Rus.* Sumskaya Oblast'. ◈ *province* NE Ukraine
Sumskaya Oblast' *see* Sums'ka Oblast'
124 J8 **Sumskiy Posad** Respublika Kareliya, NW Russian Federation
21 S12 **Sumter** South Carolina, SE USA
117 T3 **Sumy** Sums'ka Oblast', NE Ukraine
Sumy *see* Sums'ka Oblast'
159 Q15 **Sumzom** Xizang Zizhiqu, W China
125 R15 **Suna** Kirovskaya Oblast', NW Russian Federation
126 I10 **Suna** ≈ NW Russian Federation
165 S3 **Sunagawa** Hokkaidō, NE Japan
153 V13 **Sunamganj** Chittagong, NE Bangladesh
163 W14 **Sunan** ✕ (P'yŏngyang) SW North Korea
Sunan/Sunan Yugurzu Zizhixian *see* Hongwansi
19 N9 **Sunapee Lake** ◎ New Hampshire, NE USA
139 P4 **Sunaysilah** *salt marsh* N Iraq
20 M8 **Sunbright** Tennessee, S USA
33 R6 **Sunburst** Montana, NW USA
183 N12 **Sunbury** Victoria, SE Australia
21 X8 **Sunbury** North Carolina, SE USA
18 G14 **Sunbury** Pennsylvania, NE USA
61 A17 **Sunchales** Santa Fe, C Argentina
163 W13 **Sunch'ŏn** SW North Korea
163 Y16 **Sunch'ŏn** *Jap.* Junten. S South Korea
36 K13 **Sun City** Arizona, SW USA
19 O9 **Suncook** New Hampshire, NE USA
161 P5 **Suncun** *prev.* Xinwen. Shandong, E China
Sunda Islands *see* Greater Sunda Islands
33 Z12 **Sundance** Wyoming, C USA
153 T17 **Sundarbans** *wetland* Bangladesh/India
154 M11 **Sundargarh** Orissa, E India
Sunda Trench *see* Java Trench
95 O16 **Sundbyberg** Stockholm, C Sweden
97 M14 **Sunderland** *var.* Wearmouth. NE England, UK
101 F15 **Sundern** Nordrhein-Westfalen, W Germany
136 F12 **Sündiken Dağları** ▲ C Turkey
24 M5 **Sundown** Texas, SW USA
11 P16 **Sundre** Alberta, SW Canada
14 H12 **Sundridge** Ontario, S Canada
93 H17 **Sundsvall** Västernorrland, C Sweden
26 H4 **Sunflower, Mount** ▲ Kansas, C USA
Sunflower State *see* Kansas
169 N14 **Sungaibuntu** Sumatera, SW Indonesia
168 K12 **Sungaidareh** Sumatera, W Indonesia
167 P17 **Sungai Kolok** *var.* Sungai Ko-Lok. Narathiwat, SW Thailand
168 K12 **Sungaipenuh** *prev.* Soengaipenoeh. Sumatera, W Indonesia
169 P11 **Sungaipinyuh** Borneo, C Indonesia
Sungari *see* Songhua Jiang
Sungei Pahang *see* Pahang, Sungai
167 O8 **Sung Men** Phrae, NW Thailand
83 M15 **Sungo** Tete, NW Mozambique
Sungpu *see* Songpan
168 M13 **Sungsang** Sumatera, W Indonesia
114 M9 **Sungurlare** Burgas, E Bulgaria
136 J12 **Sungurlu** Çorum, N Turkey
112 F9 **Sunja** Sisak-Moslavina, C Croatia
153 Q12 **Sun Koshi** ≈ E Nepal
94 F9 **Sunndalen** *valley* S Norway
94 F9 **Sunndalsøra** Møre og Romsdal, S Norway
95 K15 **Sunne** Värmland, C Sweden
95 O15 **Sunnersta** Uppsala, C Sweden
94 C11 **Sunnfjord** *physical region* S Norway
95 C15 **Sunnhordland** *physical region* S Norway
94 D10 **Sunnmøre** *physical region* S Norway
37 N4 **Sunnyside** Utah, W USA
32 J10 **Sunnyside** Washington, NW USA
35 N9 **Sunnyvale** California, W USA
30 L8 **Sun Prairie** Wisconsin, N USA
Sunqur *see* Sonqor
25 N1 **Sunray** Texas, SW USA
22 I8 **Sunset** Louisiana, S USA
25 S5 **Sunset** Texas, SW USA
Sunset State *see* Oregon
181 Z10 **Sunshine Coast** *cultural region* Queensland, E Australia
Sunshine State *see* Florida, USA
Sunshine State *see* New Mexico, USA
Sunshine State *see* South Dakota, USA
123 O10 **Suntar** Respublika Sakha (Yakutiya), NE Russian Federation
39 R10 **Suntrana** Alaska, USA
148 J15 **Suntsar** Baluchistān, SW Pakistan
163 W15 **Sunwi-do** *island* SW North Korea
163 W6 **Sunwu** Heilongjiang, NE China
77 O16 **Sunyani** W Ghana
Suō *see* Suao
93 M17 **Suolahti** Länsi-Suomi, W Finland
Suoločielgi *see* Saariselkä
Suomenlahti *see* Finland, Gulf of
Suomen Tasavalta/Suomi *see* Finland
93 N14 **Suomussalmi** Oulu, E Finland
165 E13 **Suō-nada** *sea* SW Japan
93 M17 **Suonenjoki** Itä-Suomi, C Finland
167 S13 **Suŏng** Kâmpóng Cham, C Cambodia
124 I10 **Suoyarvi** Respublika Kareliya, NW Russian Federation
Supanburi *see* Suphan Buri
57 D14 **Supe** Lima, W Peru
15 V7 **Supérieur, Lac** ◎ Québec, SE Canada
Supérieur, Lac *see* Superior, Lake
36 M14 **Superior** Arizona, SW USA
33 O9 **Superior** Montana, NW USA
29 P17 **Superior** Nebraska, C USA
30 I3 **Superior** Wisconsin, N USA
41 S17 **Superior, Laguna** *lagoon* S Mexico
31 N2 **Superior, Lake** *Fr.* Lac Supérieur. ◎ Canada/USA
36 L13 **Superstition Mountains** ▲ Arizona, SW USA
113 F14 **Supetar** *It.* San Pietro. Split-Dalmacija, S Croatia
167 O10 **Suphan Buri** *var.* Supanburi. Suphan Buri, W Thailand
171 V12 **Supiori, Pulau** *island* E Indonesia
188 K2 **Supply Reef** *reef* N Northern Mariana Islands
195 O7 **Support Force Glacier** *glacier* Antarctica
137 R10 **Sup'sa** *var.* Supsa. ≈ W Georgia
Sūq 'Abs *see* 'Abs
139 W12 **Sūq ash Shuyūkh** SE Iraq
138 H4 **Şuqaylibīyah** Ḩamāh, W Syria
161 Q6 **Suqian** Jiangsu, E China
Suqrah *see* Şawqirah
Suqrah Bay *see* Şawqirah, Dawḩat
141 V16 **Suquṭrā** *var.* Sokotra, *Eng.* Socotra. *island* SE Yemen
141 Z8 **Şūr** NE Oman
Şūr *see* Soûr
127 P5 **Sura** Penzenskaya Oblast', W Russian Federation
127 P4 **Sura** ≈ W Russian Federation
149 N12 **Sūrāb** Baluchistān, SW Pakistan
Surabaja *see* Surabaya
192 E8 **Surabaya** *prev.* Soerabaja, Surabaja. Jawa, C Indonesia
95 N15 **Surahammar** Västmanland, C Sweden
169 Q16 **Surakarta** *Eng.* Solo; *prev.* Soerakarta. Jawa, S Indonesia
Surakhany *see* Suraxanı
137 S10 **Surami** C Georgia
143 X13 **Sūrān** Sīstān va Balūchestān, SE Iran
111 I21 **Šurany** *Hung.* Nagysurány. Nitriansky Kraj, SW Slovakia
154 D12 **Sūrat** Gujarāt, W India
Suratdhani *see* Surat Thani
152 G9 **Sūratgarh** Rājasthān, NW India
167 N14 **Surat Thani** *var.* Suratdhani. Surat Thani, SW Thailand
119 Q16 **Suraw** *Rus.* Surov. ≈ E Belarus
137 Z11 **Suraxanı** *Rus.* Surakhany. E Azerbaijan
141 Y11 **Surayr** E Oman
138 K2 **Suraysāt** Ḩalab, N Syria
118 O12 **Surazh** *Rus.* Surazh. Vitsyebskaya Voblasts', NE Belarus
126 H6 **Surazh** Bryanskaya Oblast', W Russian Federation
191 V17 **Sur, Cabo** *headland* Easter Island, Chile, E Pacific Ocean
112 L11 **Surčin** Serbia, N Serbia and Montenegro (Yugo.)
116 H9 **Surduc** *Hung.* Szurduk. Sălaj, NW Romania
113 P16 **Surdulica** Serbia, SE Serbia and Montenegro (Yugo.)
99 L24 **Sûre** *var.* Sauer. ≈ W Europe *see also* Sauer
154 C10 **Surendranagar** Gujarāt, W India
18 K16 **Surf City** New Jersey, NE USA
183 V3 **Surfers Paradise** Queensland, E Australia
21 U13 **Surfside Beach** South Carolina, SE USA
102 J10 **Surgères** Charente-Maritime, W France
122 H10 **Surgut** Khanty-Mansiyskiy Avtonomnyy Okrug, C Russian Federation
122 K10 **Surgutikha** Krasnoyarskiy Kray, N Russian Federation
98 M6 **Surhuisterveen** Friesland, N Netherlands
105 V5 **Súria** Cataluña, NE Spain
143 P10 **Sūrīān** Fārs, S Iran
155 J15 **Suriāpet** Andhra Pradesh, C India
171 Q6 **Surigao** Mindanao, S Philippines
167 R10 **Surin** Surin, E Thailand
55 U11 **Surinam** *off.* Republic of Surinam, *var.* Suriname; *prev.* Dutch Guiana, Netherlands Guiana. ◆ *republic* N South America
Sūrīya/Sūrīyah, Al-Jumhūrīyah al-'Arabīyah as- *see* Syria
Surkhab, Darya-i- *see* Kahmard, Daryā-ye
Surkhandar'inskaya Oblast' *see* Surxondaryo Viloyati
Surkhandar'ya *see* Surxondaryo
Surkhet *see* Birendranagar
147 R12 **Surkhob** ≈ C Tajikistan
137 P11 **Sürmene** Trabzon, NE Turkey
Surov *see* Suraw
127 N11 **Surovikino** Volgogradskaya Oblast', SW Russian Federation
35 N11 **Sur, Point** *headland* California, W USA
187 N15 **Surprise, Île** *island* N New Caledonia
61 E22 **Sur, Punta** *headland* E Argentina
Surrentum *see* Sorrento
28 M3 **Surrey** North Dakota, N USA
97 O22 **Surrey** *cultural region* SE England, UK
21 X7 **Surry** Virginia, NE USA
108 F8 **Sursee** Luzern, W Switzerland
127 P6 **Sursk** Penzenskaya Oblast', W Russian Federation
127 P5 **Surskoye** Ul'yanovskaya Oblast', W Russian Federation
75 P8 **Surt** *var.* Sidra, Sirte. N Libya
95 I19 **Surte** Västra Götaland, S Sweden
75 Q8 **Surt, Khalīj** *Eng.* Gulf of Sidra, Gulf of Sirti, Sidra. *gulf* N Libya
92 I5 **Surtsey** *island* S Iceland
137 N17 **Suruç** Şanlıurfa, S Turkey
168 L13 **Surulangun** Sumatera, W Indonesia
147 P13 **Surxondaryo** *Rus.* Surkhandar'ya. ≈ Tajikistan/Uzbekistan
147 N13 **Surxondaryo Viloyati** *Rus.* Surkhandar'inskaya Oblast'. ◈ *province* S Uzbekistan
Süs *see* Susch
106 A8 **Susa** Piemonte, NE Italy
165 E12 **Susa** Yamaguchi, Honshū, SW Japan
Susa *see* Shūsh
113 E16 **Sušac** *It.* Cazza. *island* SW Croatia
Sūsah *see* Sousse
165 G14 **Susaki** Kōchi, Shikoku, SW Japan
165 I15 **Susami** Wakayama, Honshū, SW Japan
142 K9 **Süsangerd** *var.* Susangird. Khūzestān, SW Iran
Susangird *see* Süsangerd
35 P4 **Susanville** California, W USA
108 J9 **Susch** *var.* Süs. Graubünden, SE Switzerland
137 N12 **Suşehri** Sivas, N Turkey
Susiana *see* Khūzestān
111 B18 **Sušice** *Ger.* Schüttenhofen. Plzeňský Kraj, W Czech Republic
39 R11 **Susitna** Alaska, USA
39 R11 **Susitna River** ≈ Alaska, USA
127 Q3 **Suslonger** Respublika Mariy El, W Russian Federation
105 N14 **Suspiro del Moro, Puerto del** *pass* S Spain

18 H16 **Susquehanna River** ≈ New York/Pennsylvania, NE USA
13 O15 **Sussex** New Brunswick, SE Canada
18 J13 **Sussex** New Jersey, NE USA
21 W7 **Sussex** Virginia, NE USA
97 O23 **Sussex** *cultural region* S England, UK
183 S10 **Sussex Inlet** New South Wales, SE Australia
99 L17 **Susteren** Limburg, SE Netherlands
10 K12 **Sustut Peak** ▲ British Columbia, W Canada
123 S9 **Susuman** Magadanskaya Oblast', E Russian Federation
188 H6 **Susupe** Saipan, S Northern Mariana Islands
136 D12 **Susurluk** Balıkesir, NW Turkey
114 M13 **Susuzmüsellim** Tekirdağ, NW Turkey
136 F15 **Sütçüler** Isparta, SW Turkey
116 L13 **Şuţeşti** Brăila, SE Romania
83 F25 **Sutherland** Western Cape, SW South Africa
28 L15 **Sutherland** Nebraska, C USA
96 I7 **Sutherland** *cultural region* N Scotland, UK
185 B21 **Sutherland Falls** *waterfall* South Island, NZ
32 F14 **Sutherlin** Oregon, NW USA
149 V10 **Sutlej** ≈ India/Pakistan
Sutna *see* Satna
35 P7 **Sutter Creek** California, W USA
39 R11 **Sutton** Alaska, USA
29 Q16 **Sutton** Nebraska, C USA
21 R4 **Sutton** West Virginia, NE USA
12 F8 **Sutton** ≈ Ontario, C Canada
97 M19 **Sutton Coldfield** C England, UK
21 R4 **Sutton Lake** ⊞ West Virginia, NE USA
15 P13 **Sutton, Monts** *hill range* Québec, SE Canada
12 F8 **Sutton Ridges** ⛰ Ontario, C Canada
165 Q4 **Suttsu** Hokkaidō, NE Japan
39 P15 **Sutwik Island** *island* Alaska, USA
162 K7 **Süüj** Bulgan, C Mongolia
118 H5 **Suure-Jaani** *Ger.* Gross-Sankt-Johannis. Viljandimaa, S Estonia
118 J7 **Suur Munamägi** *var.* Munamägi, *Ger.* Eier-Berg. ▲ SE Estonia
118 F5 **Suur Väin** *Ger.* Grosser Sund. *strait* W Estonia
147 U8 **Suusamyr** Chuyskaya Oblast', C Kyrgyzstan
187 X14 **Suva** ● (Fiji) Viti Levu, W Fiji
187 X15 **Suva** ✕ Viti Levu, C Fiji
113 N18 **Suva Gora** ⛰ W FYR Macedonia
118 H11 **Suvainiškis** Panevėžys, NE Lithuania
Suvalkai/Suvalki *see* Suwałki
113 P15 **Suva Planina** ⛰ SE Serbia and Montenegro (Yugo.)
113 M17 **Suva Reka** Serbia, S Serbia and Montenegro (Yugo.)
126 K5 **Suvorov** Tul'skaya Oblast', W Russian Federation
117 N12 **Suvorove** Odes'ka Oblast', SW Ukraine
Suvorovo *see* Ştefan Vodă
Suwaik *see* As Suwayq
Suwaira *see* Aş Şuwayrah
110 O7 **Suwałki** *Lith.* Suvalkai, *Rus.* Suvalki. Podlaskie, NE Poland
167 R10 **Suwannaphum** Roi Et, E Thailand
23 V8 **Suwannee River** ≈ Florida/Georgia, SE USA
Şuwār *see* Aş Şuwār
190 K14 **Suwarrow** *atoll* N Cook Islands
Suwaydá/Suwaydā', **Muḩāfaẓat as** *see* As Suwaydā'
143 R16 **Suwaydān** *var.* Sweiham. Abū Ẓaby, E UAE
Suwayqiyah, Hawr as *see* Shuwayjah, Hawr ash
Suways, Khalīj as *see* Suez, Gulf of
Suways, Qanāt as *see* Suez Canal
Suweida *see* As Suwaydā'
Suweon *see* Suwŏn
163 X15 **Suwŏn** *var.* Suweon, *Jap.* Suigen. NW South Korea
Su Xian *see* Suzhou
143 R14 **Sūzā** Hormozgān, S Iran
145 P15 **Suzak** *Kaz.* Sozaq. Yuzhnyy Kazakhstan, S Kazakhstan
Suzaka *see* Suzuka
126 M3 **Suzdal'** Vladimirskaya Oblast', W Russian Federation
161 P7 **Suzhou** *var.* Su Xian. Anhui, E China
161 R8 **Suzhou** *var.* Soochow, Su-chou, Suchow; *prev.* Wuhsien. Jiangsu, E China
Suzhou *see* Jiuquan
163 V12 **Suzi He** ≈ NE China
Suz, Mys *see* Soye, Mys
165 M10 **Suzu** Ishikawa, Honshū, SW Japan
165 K14 **Suzuka** Mie, Honshū, SW Japan
165 N12 **Suzuka** *var.* Suzaka. Nagano, Honshū, S Japan
165 M10 **Suzu-misaki** *headland* Honshū, SW Japan
Svågälv *see* Svågan
94 M10 **Svågan** *var.* Svågälv. ≈ C Sweden
Svalava/Svaljava *see* Svalyava
92 O2 **Svalbard** ◇ *Norwegian dependency* Arctic Ocean
92 J2 **Svalbardhseyri** Nordhurland Eystra, N Iceland
95 K22 **Svalöv** Skåne, S Sweden
116 H7 **Svalyava** *Cz.* Svalava, Svaljava, *Hung.* Szolyva. Zakarpats'ka Oblast', W Ukraine
92 O2 **Svanbergfjellet** ▲ C Svalbard
95 M24 **Svaneke** Bornholm, E Denmark
95 L22 **Svängsta** Blekinge, S Sweden
95 J16 **Svanskog** Värmland, C Sweden
95 L16 **Svartå** Örebro, C Sweden
95 L15 **Svartälven** ≈ C Sweden
92 G12 **Svartisen** *glacier* C Norway
117 X6 **Svatove** *Rus.* Svatovo. Luhans'ka Oblast', E Ukraine
Svatovo *see* Svatove
Sväty Kríž nad Hronom *see* Žiar nad Hronom
167 Q11 **Svay Chék, Stœng** ≈ Cambodia/Thailand
167 S13 **Svay Riĕng** Svay Riĕng, S Cambodia
92 O3 **Sveagruva** Spitsbergen, W Svalbard
95 K23 **Svedala** Skåne, S Sweden
118 H12 **Svėdasai** Utena, NE Lithuania
93 G18 **Sveg** Jämtland, C Sweden
118 C12 **Švėkšna** Klaipėda, W Lithuania
94 C11 **Svelgen** Sogn og Fjordane, S Norway
95 H15 **Svelvik** Vestfold, S Norway
118 I13 **Švenčionėliai** *Pol.* Nowo-Święciany. Vilnius, SE Lithuania
118 I13 **Švenčionys** *Pol.* Swięciany. Vilnius, SE Lithuania
95 H24 **Svendborg** Fyn, C Denmark
95 K19 **Svenljunga** Västra Götaland, S Sweden
92 P2 **Svenskøya** *island* E Svalbard
93 G17 **Svenstavik** Jämtland, C Sweden
95 G20 **Svenstrup** Nordjylland, N Denmark
118 H12 **Šventoji** ≈ C Lithuania
117 Z8 **Sverdlovs'k** *Rus.* Sverdlovsk; *prev.* Imeni Sverdlova Rudnik. Luhans'ka Oblast', E Ukraine
Sverdlovsk *see* Yekaterinburg
127 W2 **Sverdlovskaya Oblast'** ◈ *province* C Russian Federation
8 M3 **Sverdrup Islands** *island group* Nunavut, N Canada
122 K6 **Sverdrup, Ostrov** *island* N Russian Federation
Sverige *see* Sweden
113 D15 **Svetac** *prev.* Sveti Andrea, *It.* Sant'Andrea. *island* SW Croatia
Sveti Andrea *see* Svetac
Sveti Nikola *see* Sveti Nikole
113 O18 **Sveti Nikole** *prev.* Sveti Nikola. C FYR Macedonia
Sveti Vrach *see* Sandanski
123 T14 **Svetlaya** Primorskiy Kray, SE Russian Federation
126 B2 **Svetlogorsk** Kaliningradskaya Oblast', W Russian Federation
122 K9 **Svetlogorsk** Krasnoyarskiy Kray, N Russian Federation
Svetlogorsk *see* Svyetlahorsk
127 N14 **Svetlograd** Stavropol'skiy Kray, SW Russian Federation
Svetlovodsk *see* Svitlovods'k
119 A14 **Svetlyy** *Ger.* Zimmerbude. Kaliningradskaya Oblast', W Russian Federation
127 Y8 **Svetlyy** Orenburgskaya Oblast', W Russian Federation
127 P8 **Svetlyy** Saratovskaya Oblast', SW Russian Federation
124 G11 **Svetogorsk** *Fin.* Enso. Leningradskaya Oblast', NW Russian Federation
Svetozarevo *see* Jagodina
111 B18 **Švihov** *Ger.* Schwihau. Plzeňský Kraj, W Czech Republic
112 E13 **Svilaja** ⛰ SE Croatia
112 N12 **Svilajnac** Serbia, C Serbia and Montenegro (Yugo.)
114 L11 **Svilengrad** *prev.* Mustafa-Pasha. Khaskovo, S Bulgaria
Svinecea Mare, Munte *see* Svinecea Mare, Vârful
116 F13 **Svinecea Mare, Vârful** *var.* Munte Svinecea Mare. ▲ SW Romania
95 B18 **Svínoy** *Dan.* Svinø *Island* Faeroe Islands
147 N14 **Svintsovyy Rudnik** *Turkm.* Swintsowy Rudnik. Lebap Welaýaty, E Turkmenistan
118 I13 **Svir** *Rus.* Svir'. Minskaya Voblasts', NW Belarus
126 I12 **Svir'** *canal* NW Russian Federation
Svir', Ozero *see* Svir, Vozyera
119 I14 **Svir, Vozyera** *Rus.* Ozero Svir'. ◎ C Belarus
114 J7 **Svishtov** *prev.* Sistova. Veliko Tŭrnovo, N Bulgaria
119 F18 **Svislach** *Pol.* Świsłocz, *Rus.* Svisloch'. Hrodzyenskaya Voblasts', W Belarus
119 M17 **Svislach** *Rus.* Svisloch'. Mahilyowskaya Voblasts', E Belarus
119 L17 **Svislach** *Rus.* Svisloch'. ≈ E Belarus
Svisloch' *see* Svislach
111 F17 **Svitavy** *Ger.* Zwittau. Pardubický Kraj, C Czech Republic
117 S6 **Svitlovods'k** *Rus.* Svetlovodsk. Kirovohrads'ka Oblast', C Ukraine
Svizzera *see* Switzerland
123 Q13 **Svobodnyy** Amurskaya Oblast', SE Russian Federation
114 G9 **Svoge** Sofiya, W Bulgaria
92 G11 **Svolvær** Nordland, C Norway
111 F18 **Svratka** *Ger.* Schwarzach, Schwarzawa. ≈ SE Czech Republic
113 P14 **Svrljig** Serbia, E Serbia and Montenegro (Yugo.)
197 U10 **Svyataya Anna Trough** *var.* Saint Anna Trough. *undersea feature* N Kara Sea
126 M4 **Svyatoy Nos, Mys** *headland* NW Russian Federation
119 N18 **Svyetlahorsk** *Rus.* Svetlogorsk. Homyel'skaya Voblasts', SE Belarus
Swabian Jura *see* Schwäbische Alb
97 P19 **Swaffham** E England, UK
23 V5 **Swainsboro** Georgia, SE USA
83 C19 **Swakop** ≈ W Namibia
83 C19 **Swakopmund** Erongo, W Namibia
97 M15 **Swale** ≈ N England, UK
Swallow Island *see* Nendö
99 M16 **Swalmen** Limburg, SE Netherlands
12 G8 **Swan** ≈ Ontario, C Canada
97 L24 **Swanage** S England, UK
182 M10 **Swan Hill** Victoria, SE Australia
11 P13 **Swan Hills** Alberta, W Canada
65 D24 **Swan Island** *island* C Falkland Islands
Swankalok *see* Sawankhalok
29 U10 **Swan Lake** ◎ Minnesota, N USA
21 Y10 **Swanquarter** North Carolina, SE USA
182 J9 **Swan Reach** South Australia
11 V15 **Swan River** Manitoba, S Canada
183 P17 **Swansea** Tasmania, SE Australia
97 J22 **Swansea** *Wel.* Abertawe. S Wales, UK
21 R13 **Swansea** South Carolina, SE USA
19 S7 **Swans Island** *island* Maine, NE USA
28 L17 **Swanson Lake** ⊞ Nebraska, C USA
31 R11 **Swanton** Ohio, N USA
110 G11 **Swarzędz** Poznań, C Poland
Swatow *see* Shantou
83 L22 **Swaziland** *off.* Kingdom of Swaziland. ◆ *monarchy* S Africa
93 G18 **Sweden** *off.* Kingdom of Sweden, *Swe.* Sverige. ◆ *monarchy* N Europe
Swedru *see* Agona Swedru
25 V12 **Sweeny** Texas, SW USA
33 R6 **Sweetgrass** Montana, NW USA
32 G12 **Sweet Home** Oregon, NW USA
25 T12 **Sweet Home** Texas, SW USA
27 T4 **Sweet Springs** Missouri, C USA
20 M10 **Sweetwater** Tennessee, S USA
25 P7 **Sweetwater** Texas, SW USA
33 V15 **Sweetwater River** ≈ Wyoming, C USA
Sweiham *see* Suwaydān
83 F26 **Swellendam** Western Cape, SW South Africa
111 G15 **Świdnica** *Ger.* Schweidnitz. Wałbrzych, SW Poland
111 O14 **Świdnik** *Ger.* Streckenbach. Lubelskie, E Poland
110 F8 **Świdwin** *Ger.* Schivelbein. Zachodnio-pomorskie, NW Poland
111 F15 **Świebodzice** *Ger.* Freiburg in Schlesien, Swiebodzice. Wałbrzych, SW Poland
110 E11 **Świebodzin** *Ger.* Schwiebus. Lubuskie, W Poland
Święciany *see* Švenčionys
110 I9 **Świecie** *Ger.* Schwertberg. Kujawsko-pomorskie, N Poland
111 L15 **Świętokrzyskie** ◈ *province* C Poland
11 T16 **Swift Current** Saskatchewan, S Canada
98 K9 **Swifterbant** Flevoland, C Netherlands
183 Q12 **Swifts Creek** Victoria, SE Australia
96 E13 **Swilly, Lough** *Ir.* Loch Súilí. *inlet* N Ireland
97 M22 **Swindon** S England, UK
Swinemünde *see* Świnoujście
110 D8 **Świnoujście** *Ger.* Swinemünde. Zachodnio-pomorskie, NW Poland
Swintsowyy Rudnik *see* Svintsovyy Rudnik
Świsłocz *see* Svislach
Swiss Confederation *see* Switzerland
108 E9 **Switzerland** *off.* Swiss Confederation, *Fr.* La Suisse, *Ger.* Schweiz, *It.* Svizzera; *anc.* Helvetia. ◆ *federal republic* C Europe
97 F17 **Swords** *Ir.* Sord, Sórd Choluim Chille. E Ireland
18 H13 **Swoyersville** Pennsylvania, NE USA
126 I10 **Syamozero, Ozero** ◎ NW Russian Federation
124 M13 **Syamzha** Vologodskaya Oblast', NW Russian Federation
118 N13 **Syanno** *Rus.* Senno. Vitsyebskaya Voblasts', NE Belarus
119 K16 **Syarhyeyevichy** *Rus.* Sergeyevichi. Minskaya Voblasts', C Belarus
124 I12 **Syas'stroy** Leningradskaya Oblast', NW Russian Federation
Sycaminum *see* Hefa
30 M10 **Sycamore** Illinois, N USA
126 J3 **Sychëvka** Smolenskaya Oblast', W Russian Federation
111 H14 **Syców** *Ger.* Gross Wartenberg. Dolnośląskie, SW Poland
14 E17 **Sydenham** ≈ Ontario, S Canada
Sydenham Island *see* Nonouti
183 T9 **Sydney** *state capital* New South Wales, SE Australia
13 R14 **Sydney** Cape Breton Island, Nova Scotia, SE Canada
Sydney Island *see* Manra
13 R14 **Sydney Mines** Cape Breton Island, Nova Scotia, SE Canada
Syedpur *see* Saidpur
119 K18 **Syelishcha** *Rus.* Selishche. Minskaya Voblasts', C Belarus
119 J18 **Syemyezhava** *Rus.* Semezhevo. Minskaya Voblasts', C Belarus
Syene *see* Aswān
117 X6 **Syeverodonets'k** *Rus.* Severodonetsk. Luhans'ka Oblast', E Ukraine
161 T6 **Syïao Shan** *island* SE China
100 H11 **Syke** Niedersachsen, NW Germany
94 D10 **Sykkylven** Møre og Romsdal, S Norway
115 F15 **Sykoúri** *var.* Sikouri; *prev.* Sikoúrion. Thessalía, C Greece
125 R11 **Syktyvkar** *prev.* Ust'-Sysol'sk. Respublika Komi, NW Russian Federation
23 Q4 **Sylacauga** Alabama, S USA
Sylarna *see* Storsylen
153 V14 **Sylhet** Chittagong, NE Bangladesh
100 G6 **Sylt** *island* NW Germany
21 O10 **Sylva** North Carolina, SE USA
127 V15 **Sylva** ≈ NW Russian Federation
23 W5 **Sylvania** Georgia, SE USA
31 R11 **Sylvania** Ohio, N USA
11 Q15 **Sylvan Lake** Alberta, SW Canada
33 T13 **Sylvan Pass** *pass* Wyoming, C USA
23 T7 **Sylvester** Georgia, SE USA
25 P6 **Sylvester** Texas, SW USA
10 L11 **Sylvia, Mount** ▲ British Columbia, W Canada
122 K11 **Sym** ≈ C Russian Federation
115 N22 **Sými** *var.* Simi. *island* Dodekánisos, Greece, Aegean Sea
117 U8 **Synel'nykove** Dnipropetrovs'ka Oblast', E Ukraine
125 U6 **Synya** Respublika Komi, NW Russian Federation
117 P7 **Synyukha** *Rus.* Sinyukha. ≈ S Ukraine
Syôbara *see* Shōbara
195 V2 **Syowa** *Japanese research station* Antarctica
26 H6 **Syracuse** Kansas, C USA
29 S16 **Syracuse** Nebraska, C USA
18 H10 **Syracuse** New York, NE USA
Syracuse *see* Siracusa
Syrdar'inskaya Oblast' *see* Sirdaryo Viloyati
Syrdarya *see* Syr Darya
144 L14 **Syr Darya** *var.* Sai Hun, Sir Darya, Syrdarya, *Kaz.* Syrdariya, *Rus.* Syrdar'ya, *Uzb.* Sirdaryo; *anc.* Jaxartes. ≈ C Asia
138 J6 **Syria** *off.* Syrian Arab Republic, *var.* Siria, Syrie, *Ar.* Al-Jumhūrīyah al-'Arabīyah as-Sūrīyah, Sūrīya. ◆ *republic* SW Asia
138 L9 **Syrian Desert** *Ar.* Al Hamad, Bādiyat ash Shām. *desert* SW Asia
Syrie *see* Syria
115 L22 **Sýrna** *var.* Sirna. *island* Kykládes, Greece, Aegean Sea
115 I20 **Sýros** *var.* Síros. *island* Kykládes, Greece, Aegean Sea
93 M18 **Sysmä** Etelä-Suomi, S Finland
127 R12 **Sysola** ≈ NW Russian Federation
Syulemeshlii *see* Sredets
127 S2 **Syumsi** Udmurtskaya Respublika, NW Russian Federation
114 K10 **Syuyutliyka** ≈ C Bulgaria
Syvash, Zaliv *see* Syvash, Zatoka
117 U12 **Syvash, Zatoka** *Rus.* Zaliv Syvash. *inlet* S Ukraine
127 Q6 **Syzran'** Samarskaya Oblast', W Russian Federation
Szabadka *see* Subotica
111 N21 **Szabolcs-Szatmár-Bereg** *off.* Szabolcs-Szatmár-Bereg Megye. ◈ *county* E Hungary
110 G10 **Szamocin** *Ger.* Samotschin. Wielkopolskie, C Poland
116 H8 **Szamos** *var.* Someş, Someşul, *Ger.* Samosch, Somesch. ≈ Hungary/Romania
Szamosújvár *see* Gherla
110 G11 **Szamotuły** Poznań, C Poland
Szarkowszczyzna *see* Sharkawshchyna
111 M24 **Szarvas** Békés, SE Hungary
Szászmagyarós *see* Măieruş
Szászrégen *see* Reghin
Szászsebes *see* Sebeş
Szászváros *see* Orăştie
Szatmárrnémeti *see* Satu Mare
Száva *see* Sava
111 P15 **Szczebrzeszyn** Lubelskie, E Poland
110 D9 **Szczecin** *Eng./Ger.* Stettin. Zachodnio-pomorskie, NW Poland
110 G8 **Szczecinek** *Ger.* Neustettin. Zachodnio-pomorskie, NW Poland
110 D8 **Szczeciński, Zalew** *var.* Stettiner Haff, *Ger.* Oderhaff. *bay* Germany/Poland
111 K15 **Szczekociny** Śląskie, S Poland
110 N8 **Szczuczyn** Podlaskie, NE Poland
Szczuczyn Nowogródzki *see* Shchuchyn
110 M8 **Szczytno** *Ger.* Ortelsburg. Warmińsko-Mazurskie, NE Poland,
Szechuan/Szechwan *see* Sichuan
111 K21 **Szécsény** Nógrád, N Hungary
111 L25 **Szeged** *Ger.* Szegedin, *Rom.* Seghedin. Csongrád, SE Hungary
Szegedin *see* Szeged
111 N23 **Szeghalom** Békés, SE Hungary
Székelyhid *see* Săcueni
Székelykeresztúr *see* Cristuru Secuiesc
111 I23 **Székesfehérvár** *Ger.* Stuhlweissenberg; *anc.* Alba Regia. Fejér, W Hungary
Szeklerburg *see* Miercurea-Ciuc
Szekler Neumarkt *see* Târgu Secuiesc
111 J25 **Szekszárd** Tolna, S Hungary
Szempcz/Szenc *see* Senec
Szenice *see* Senica
Szentágota *see* Agnita
111 J22 **Szentendre** *Ger.* Sankt Andrä. Pest, N Hungary
111 L24 **Szentes** Csongrád, SE Hungary
111 F23 **Szentgotthárd** *Eng.* Saint Gotthard, *Ger.* Sankt Gotthard. Vas, W Hungary
Szentgyörgy *see* Đurđevac
Szenttamás *see* Srbobran
Széphely *see* Jebel
Szeping *see* Siping
Szered *see* Sereď
111 N21 **Szerencs** Borsod-Abaúj-Zemplén, NE Hungary
Szeret *see* Siret
Szeretfalva *see* Sărăţel
110 N7 **Szeska Góra** *var.* Szeskie Wygórza, *Ger.* Seesker Höhe. *hill* NE Poland
Szeskie Wygórza *see* Szeska Góra
111 H25 **Szigetvár** Baranya, SW Hungary
Szilágysomlyó *see* Şimleu Silvaniei
Szinna *see* Snina
Sziszek *see* Sisak
Szitás-Keresztúr *see* Cristuru Secuiesc
111 E15 **Szklarska Poręba** *Ger.* Schreiberhau. Dolnośląskie, SW Poland
Szkudy *see* Skuodas
Szlatina *see* Slatina, Croatia
Szlavonia/Szlavonország *see* Slavonija
Szlovákia *see* Slovakia
Szluin *see* Slunj
111 L23 **Szolnok** Jász-Nagykun-Szolnok, C Hungary
Szolyva *see* Svalyava
111 G23 **Szombathely** *Ger.* Steinamanger; *anc.* Sabaria, Savaria. Vas, W Hungary
Szond/Szonta *see* Sonta
Szováta *see* Sovata
110 F13 **Szprotawa** *Ger.* Sprottau. Lubuskie, W Poland
Sztálinváros *see* Dunaújváros
Sztrazsó *see* Strážov
110 J8 **Sztum** *Ger.* Stuhm. Pomorskie, N Poland
110 H10 **Szubin** *Ger.* Schubin. Kujawsko-pomorskie, W Poland
Szucsava *see* Suceava
Szurduk *see* Surduc
111 M14 **Szydłowiec** *Ger.* Schlelau. Mazowieckie, C Poland

T

Taalintehdas *see* Dalsbruk
171 O4 **Taal, Lake** ◎ Luzon, NW Philippines
95 J23 **Taastrup** *var.* Tåstrup. København, E Denmark
111 I24 **Tab** Somogy, W Hungary
171 P4 **Tabaco** Luzon, N Philippines
186 G4 **Tabalo** Mussau Island, NE PNG
104 K5 **Tábara** Castilla-León, N Spain
186 H5 **Tabar Islands** *island group* NE PNG
Tabariya, Bahrat *see* Tiberias, Lake
143 S7 **Ţabas** *var.* Golshan. Yazd, C Iran
43 P15 **Tabasará, Serranía de** ⛰ W Panama
41 U15 **Tabasco** ◈ *state* SE Mexico
Tabasco *see* Grijalva, Río
127 Q2 **Tabashino** Respublika Mariy El, W Russian Federation
58 B13 **Tabatinga** Amazonas, N Brazil
74 G9 **Tabelbala** W Algeria
11 Q17 **Taber** Alberta, SW Canada
171 V15 **Taberfane** Pulau Trangan, E Indonesia
95 L19 **Taberg** Jönköping, S Sweden
191 O3 **Tabiteuea** *prev.* Drummond Island. *atoll* Tungaru, W Kiribati
171 O5 **Tablas Island** *island* C Philippines
184 Q10 **Table Cape** *headland* North Island, NZ
13 S13 **Table Mountain** ▲ Newfoundland and Labrador, E Canada
173 P17 **Table, Pointe de la** *headland* SE Réunion
27 S8 **Table Rock Lake** ⊞ Arkansas/Missouri, C USA
36 K14 **Table Top** ▲ Arizona, SW USA
186 D8 **Tabletop, Mount** ▲ C PNG
123 R7 **Tabor** Respublika Sakha (Yakutiya), NE Russian Federation
29 S15 **Tabor** Iowa, C USA
111 D18 **Tábor** Jihočeský Kraj, S Czech Republic
81 F21 **Tabora** Tabora, W Tanzania
81 F21 **Tabora** ◈ *region* C Tanzania
21 U12 **Tabor City** North Carolina, SE USA
147 Q10 **Taboshar** NW Tajikistan
76 L18 **Tabou** *var.* Tabu. S Ivory Coast
142 J2 **Tabrīz** *var.* Tebriz; *anc.* Tauris. Āżarbāyjān-e Khāvarī, NW Iran
Tabu *see* Tabou
191 W1 **Tabuaeran** *prev.* Fanning Island. *atoll* Line Islands, E Kiribati
171 O2 **Tabuk** Luzon, N Philippines
140 J4 **Tabūk** Tabūk, NW Saudi Arabia
140 J5 **Tabūk** *off.* Minṭaqat Tabūk. ◈ *province* NW Saudi Arabia
187 Q13 **Tabwemasana, Mount** ▲ Espiritu Santo, W Vanuatu
95 O15 **Täby** Stockholm, C Sweden
41 N14 **Tacámbaro** Michoacán de Ocampo, SW Mexico
42 A5 **Tacaná, Volcán** ℜ Guatemala/Mexico
43 X16 **Tacarcuna, Cerro** ▲ SE Panama
Tachau *see* Tachov
158 J3 **Tacheng** *var.* Qoqek. Xinjiang Uygur Zizhiqu, NW China
54 H7 **Táchira** *off.* Estado Táchira. ◈ *state* W Venezuela
161 T13 **Tachoshui** N Taiwan
111 A17 **Tachov** *Ger.* Tachau. Plzeňský Kraj, W Czech Republic
171 Q5 **Tacloban** *off.* Tacloban City. Leyte, C Philippines
57 I19 **Tacna** Tacna, SE Peru
57 H18 **Tacna** *off.* Departamento de Tacna. ◈ *department* S Peru
32 H8 **Tacoma** Washington, NW USA
18 L11 **Taconic Range** ⛰ NE USA
62 L6 **Taco Pozo** Formosa, N Argentina
57 M20 **Tacsara, Cordillera de** ⛰ S Bolivia
61 F17 **Tacuarembó** *prev.* San Fructuoso. Tacuarembó, C Uruguay
61 E18 **Tacuarembó** ◈ *department* C Uruguay
61 F17 **Tacuarembó, Río** ≈ C Uruguay
83 I14 **Taculi** North Western, NW Zambia
171 Q8 **Tacurong** Mindanao, S Philippines
77 V8 **Tadek** ≈ NW Niger
74 J9 **Tademaït, Plateau du** *plateau* C Algeria
187 R17 **Tadine** Province des Îles Loyauté, E New Caledonia
80 L11 **Tadjoura** E Djibouti
80 M11 **Tadjoura, Golfe de** *Eng.* Gulf of Tajura. *inlet* E Djibouti
Tadmor/Tadmur *see* Tudmur
11 W10 **Tadoule Lake** ◎ Manitoba, C Canada
15 S8 **Tadoussac** Québec, SE Canada
155 H18 **Tādpatri** Andhra Pradesh, E India
Tadzhikabad *see* Tojikobod
Tadzhikistan *see* Tajikistan
163 Y14 **T'aebaek-sanmaek** ⛰ E South Korea
163 V15 **Taechŏng-do** *island* NW South Korea
163 X13 **Taedong-gang** ≈ C North Korea
163 Y16 **Taegu** *off.* Taegu-gwangyŏksi, *var.* Daegu, *Jap.* Taikyū. SE South Korea
Taehan-haehyŏp *see* Korea Strait
Taehan Min'guk *see* South Korea
163 Y15 **Taejŏn** *off.* Taejŏn-gwangyŏksi, *Jap.* Taiden. C South Korea
193 Z13 **Tafahi** *island* N Tonga
105 Q4 **Tafalla** Navarra, N Spain
75 M12 **Tafassâsset, Oued** ≈ SE Algeria
77 W7 **Tafassâsset, Ténéré du** *desert* N Niger
55 U11 **Tafelberg** ▲ S Surinam
97 J21 **Taff** ≈ SE Wales, UK
Tafila/Ţafīlah, Muḩāfaẓat aţ *see* Aţ Ţafīlah
77 N15 **Tafiré** N Ivory Coast
142 M9 **Tafresh** Markazī, W Iran
143 Q9 **Taft** Yazd, C Iran
35 R13 **Taft** California, W USA
25 T14 **Taft** Texas, SW USA
143 W12 **Taftān, Kūh-e** ▲ SE Iran
35 R13 **Taft Heights** California, W USA
189 Y14 **Tafunsak** Kosrae, E Micronesia
192 G16 **Tāga** Savai'i, SW Samoa
149 O6 **Tagāb** Kāpīsā, E Afghanistan
39 O8 **Tagagawik River** ≈ Alaska, USA
165 Q10 **Tagajō** *var.* Tagazyô. Miyagi, Honshū, C Japan
126 K12 **Taganrog** Rostovskaya Oblast', SW Russian Federation
126 K12 **Taganrog, Gulf of** *Rus.* Taganrogskiy Zaliv, *Ukr.* Tahanroz'ka Zatoka. *gulf* Russian Federation/Ukraine
Taganrogskiy Zaliv *see* Taganrog, Gulf of
76 J8 **Tagant** ◈ *region* C Mauritania
148 M14 **Tagas** Baluchistān, SW Pakistan
171 O4 **Tagaytay** Luzon, N Philippines
Tagazyô *see* Tagajō
171 P6 **Tagbilaran** *var.* Tagbilaran City. Bohol, C Philippines
106 B10 **Taggia** Liguria, NW Italy
77 V9 **Taghouaji, Massif de** ▲ C Niger
107 J15 **Tagliacozzo** Lazio, C Italy
106 J7 **Tagliamento** ≈ NE Italy
149 N3 **Tagow Bāy** *var.* Bai. Sar-e Pol, N Afghanistan
146 H9 **Tagta** *var.* Tahta, *Rus.* Takhta. Daşoguz Welaýaty, N Turkmenistan
146 J16 **Tagtabazar** *Rus.* Takhtabazar. Mary Welaýaty, S Turkmenistan
59 L17 **Taguatinga** Tocantins, C Brazil
186 I10 **Tagula** Tagula Island, SE PNG
186 I11 **Tagula Island** *prev.* Southeast Island, Sudest Island. *island* SE PNG
171 Q7 **Tagum** Mindanao, S Philippines
54 C7 **Tagún, Cerro** *elevation* Colombia/Panama
105 P7 **Tagus** *Port.* Rio Tejo, *Sp.* Río Tajo. ≈ Portugal/Spain
64 M9 **Tagus Plain** *undersea feature* E Atlantic Ocean
191 S10 **Tahaa** *island* Îles Sous le Vent, W French Polynesia
191 U10 **Tahanea** *atoll* Îles Tuamotu, C French Polynesia
Tahanroz'ka Zatoka *see* Taganrog, Gulf of
74 K12 **Tahat** ▲ SE Algeria
163 U4 **Tahe** Heilongjiang, NE China
162 G9 **Tahilt** Govĭ-Altay, W Mongolia
191 T10 **Tahiti** *island* Îles du Vent, W French Polynesia
Tahiti, Archipel de *see* Société, Archipel de la
118 E4 **Tahkuna nina** *headland* W Estonia
148 K12 **Tāhlāb** ≈ W Pakistan
148 K12 **Tāhlāb, Dasht-i** *desert* SW Pakistan
27 R10 **Tahlequah** Oklahoma, C USA
35 Q6 **Tahoe City** California, W USA
35 P6 **Tahoe, Lake** ◎ California/Nevada, W USA
Tahoena *see* Tahuna
25 N6 **Tahoka** Texas, SW USA
32 F8 **Taholah** Washington, NW USA
77 T11 **Tahoua** Tahoua, W Niger
77 T11 **Tahoua** ◈ *department* W Niger
31 P3 **Tahquamenon Falls** *waterfall* Michigan, N USA
31 P4 **Tahquamenon River** ≈ Michigan, N USA
139 V10 **Taḩrīr** S Iraq
10 K17 **Tahsis** Vancouver Island, British Columbia, SW Canada
Tahta *see* Tagta
75 W9 **Ţahta** C Egypt
136 L15 **Tahtalı Dağları** ⛰ C Turkey
57 I14 **Tahuamanu, Río** ≈ Bolivia/Peru
56 F13 **Tahuanía, Río** ≈ E Peru
191 X7 **Tahuata** *island* Îles Marquises, NE French Polynesia
171 Q10 **Tahuna** *prev.* Tahoena. Pulau Sangihe, N Indonesia
76 L17 **Taï** SW Ivory Coast
161 P5 **Tai'an** Shandong, E China
191 R8 **Taiarapu, Presqu'île de** *peninsula* Tahiti, W French Polynesia
Taibad *see* Tāybād

◆ Country ◇ Dependent Territory ◈ Administrative Region ▲ Mountain ℜ Volcano ◎ Lake
● Country Capital ○ Dependent Territory Capital ✕ International Airport ⛰ Mountain Range ≈ River ⊞ Reservoir

160 K7 **Taibai Shan** ▲ C China
105 Q12 **Taibilla, Sierra de** ▲▲ S Spain
Taibus Qi *see* Baochang
Taichū *see* T'aichung
161 S13 **T'aichung** *Jap.* Taichū; *prev.* Taiwan. C Taiwan
Taiden *see* Taejŏn
185 E23 **Taieri** ≈ South Island, NZ
115 E21 **Taïgetos** ▲▲ S Greece
161 N4 **Taihang Shan** ▲▲ C China
184 M11 **Taihape** Manawatu-Wanganui, North Island, NZ
161 O7 **Taihe** Anhui, E China
161 O12 **Taihe** *var.* Chengjiang. Jiangxi, S China
Taihoku *see* T'aipei
161 R8 **Tai Hu** ◎ E China
161 P9 **Taihu** Anhui, E China
159 O9 **Taikang** *var.* Dorbod, Dorbod Mongolzu Zizhixian. Heilongjiang, NE China
161 O6 **Taikang** Henan, C China
165 T5 **Taiki** Hokkaidō, NE Japan
166 L8 **Taikkyi** Yangon, SW Burma
Taikyū *see* Taegu
163 U8 **Tailai** Heilongjiang, NE China
168 I12 **Taileleo** Pulau Siberut, W Indonesia
182 J10 **Tailem Bend** South Australia
96 I8 **Tain** N Scotland, UK
161 S14 **T'ainan** *Jap.* Tainan; *prev.* Dainan. S Taiwan
115 E22 **Taínaro, Akrotírio** *headland* S Greece
161 Q11 **Taining** *var.* Shancheng. Fujian, SE China
191 W7 **Taiohae** *prev.* Madisonville. Nuku Hiva, NE French Polynesia
161 T13 **T'aipei** *Jap.* Taihoku; *prev.* Daihoku. ● (Taiwan) N Taiwan
168 J7 **Taiping** Perak, Peninsular Malaysia
163 S8 **Taiping Ling** ▲ NE China
165 Q4 **Taisei** Hokkaidō, NE Japan
165 G12 **Taisha** Shimane, Honshū, SW Japan
109 R4 **Taiskirchen** Oberösterreich, NW Austria
63 F20 **Taitao, Peninsula de** *peninsula* S Chile
Taitō *see* T'aitung
161 T14 **T'aitung** *Jap.* Taitō. S Taiwan
92 M13 **Taivalkoski** Oulu, E Finland
93 K19 **Taivassalo** Länsi-Suomi, W Finland
161 T14 **Taiwan** *off.* Republic of China, *var.* Formosa, Formo'sa. ◆ *republic* E Asia
192 F5 **Taiwan** *var.* Formosa. *island* E Asia
Taiwan *see* T'aichung
T'aiwan Haihsia/Taiwan Haixia *see* Taiwan Strait
Taiwan Shan *see* Chungyang Shanmo
161 R13 **Taiwan Strait** *var.* Formosa Strait, *Chin.* T'aiwan Haihsia, Taiwan Haixia. *strait* China/Taiwan
161 N4 **Taiyuan** *prev.* T'ai-yuan, T'ai-yüan, Yangku. Shanxi, C China
161 R7 **Taizhou** Jiangsu, E China
161 S10 **Taizhou** *var.* Jiaojiang; *prev.* Haimen. Zhejiang, SE China
Taizhou *see* Linhai
141 O16 **Ta'izz** SW Yemen
141 O16 **Ta'izz** ✕ SW Yemen
75 P12 **Tajarhī** SW Libya
147 P13 **Tajikistan** *off.* Republic of Tajikistan, *Rus.* Tadzhikistan, *Taj.* Jumhurii Tojikiston; *prev.* Tajik S.S.R. ◆ *republic* C Asia
Tajik S.S.R *see* Tajikistan
165 O11 **Tajima** Fukushima, Honshū, C Japan
Tajoe *see* Tayu
Tajo, Río *see* Tagus
42 B5 **Tajumulco, Volcán** ⛰ W Guatemala
105 P7 **Tajuña** ≈ C Spain
Tajura, Gulf of *see* Tadjoura, Golfe de
167 O9 **Tak** *var.* Rahaeng. Tak, W Thailand
189 U4 **Taka Atoll** *var.* Tōke. *atoll* Ratak Chain, N Marshall Islands
165 P12 **Takahagi** Ibaraki, Honshū, S Japan
165 H13 **Takahashi** *var.* Takahasi. Okayama, Honshū, SW Japan
Takahasi *see* Takahashi
189 P12 **Takaieu Island** *island* E Micronesia
184 I13 **Takaka** Tasman, South Island, NZ
170 M14 **Takalar** Sulawesi, C Indonesia
165 H13 **Takamatsu** *var.* Takamatu. Kagawa, Shikoku, SW Japan
Takamatu *see* Takamatsu
165 D14 **Takamori** Kumamoto, Kyūshū, SW Japan
165 D16 **Takanabe** Miyazaki, Kyūshū, SW Japan
170 M16 **Takan, Gunung** ▲ Pulau Sumba, S Indonesia
165 Q7 **Takanosu** Akita, Honshū, C Japan
Takao *see* Kaohsiung
165 L11 **Takaoka** Toyama, Honshū, SW Japan
184 N12 **Takapau** Hawke's Bay, North Island, NZ
191 U9 **Takapoto** *atoll* Îles Tuamotu, C French Polynesia
184 L5 **Takapuna** Auckland, North Island, NZ
165 J3 **Takarazuka** Hyōgo, Honshū, SW Japan
191 U9 **Takaroa** *atoll* Îles Tuamotu, C French Polynesia
165 N12 **Takasaki** Gunma, Honshū, S Japan
164 L12 **Takayama** Gifu, Honshū, SW Japan
164 K12 **Takefu** *var.* Takehu. Fukui, Honshū, SW Japan
Takehu *see* Takefu
164 C14 **Takeo** Saga, Kyūshū, SW Japan
Takeo *see* Takêv
164 C17 **Take-shima** *island* Nansei-shotō, SW Japan
142 M5 **Tākestān** *var.* Takistan; *prev.* Siadehan. Qazvin, N Iran
164 D14 **Taketa** Ōita, Kyūshū, SW Japan
167 R13 **Takêv** *prev.* Takeo. Takêv, S Cambodia
167 O10 **Tak Fah** Nakhon Sawan, C Thailand
139 T13 **Takhādīd** *well* S Iraq
149 R3 **Takhār** ◈ *province* NE Afghanistan
Takhiatash *see* Taxiatosh
167 S13 **Ta Khmau** Kândal, S Cambodia
Takhta *see* Tagta
Takhtabazar *see* Tagtabazar
145 O8 **Takhtabrod** Severnyy Kazakhstan, N Kazakhstan
Takhtakupyr *see* Taxtako'pir
142 M8 **Takht-e Shāh, Kūh-e** ▲ C Iran
77 V12 **Takiéta** Zinder, S Niger
8 J8 **Takijuq Lake** ◎ Nunavut, NW Canada
165 S3 **Takikawa** Hokkaidō, NE Japan
165 U3 **Takinoue** Hokkaidō, NE Japan
Takistan *see* Tākestān
185 B23 **Takitimu Mountains** ▲▲ South Island, NZ
Takkaze *see* Tekezē
165 R7 **Takko** Aomori, Honshū, C Japan
10 L13 **Takla Lake** ◎ British Columbia, SW Canada
Takla Makan Desert *see* Taklimakan Shamo
158 H9 **Taklimakan Shamo** *Eng.* Takla Makan Desert. *desert* NW China
167 T12 **Takôk** Môndól Kiri, E Cambodia
39 P10 **Takotna** Alaska, USA
Takow *see* Kaohsiung
123 O12 **Taksimo** Respublika Buryatiya, S Russian Federation
164 C13 **Taku** Saga, Kyūshū, SW Japan
10 I10 **Taku** ≈ British Columbia, W Canada
166 M15 **Takua Pa** *var.* Ban Takua Pa. Phangnga, SW Thailand
77 W16 **Takum** Taraba, E Nigeria
191 V10 **Takume** *atoll* Îles Tuamotu, C French Polynesia
190 L16 **Takutea** *island* S Cook Islands
186 K6 **Takuu Islands** *prev.* Mortlock Group. *island group* NE PNG
119 L18 **Tal'** *Rus.* Tal'. Minskaya Voblasts', S Belarus
40 L13 **Tala** Jalisco, C Mexico
61 F19 **Tala** Canelones, S Uruguay
Talabriga *see* Aveiro, Portugal
Talabriga *see* Talavera de la Reina, Spain
119 N14 **Talachyn** *Rus.* Tolochin. Vitsyebskaya Voblasts', NE Belarus
149 U7 **Talagang** Punjab, E Pakistan
155 J23 **Talaimannar** Northern Province, NW Sri Lanka
117 R3 **Talalayivka** Chernihivs'ka Oblast', N Ukraine
43 O15 **Talamanca, Cordillera de** ▲▲ S Costa Rica
56 A9 **Talara** Piura, NW Peru
104 L11 **Talarrubias** Extremadura, W Spain
147 S8 **Talas** Talasskaya Oblast', NW Kyrgyzstan
147 S8 **Talas** ≈ NW Kyrgyzstan
186 G7 **Talasea** New Britain, E PNG
Talas Oblasty *see* Talasskaya Oblast'
147 S8 **Talasskaya Oblast'** *Kir.* Talas Oblasty. ◈ *province* NW Kyrgyzstan
147 S8 **Talasskiy Alatau, Khrebet** ▲▲ Kazakhstan/Kyrgyzstan
77 U12 **Talata Mafara** Zamfara, NW Nigeria
171 R9 **Talaud, Kepulauan** *island group* E Indonesia
104 M9 **Talavera de la Reina** *anc.* Caesarobriga, Talabriga. Castilla-La Mancha, C Spain
104 J11 **Talavera la Real** Extremadura, W Spain
186 F7 **Talawe, Mount** ▲ New Britain, C PNG
23 S5 **Talbotton** Georgia, SE USA
183 R7 **Talbragar River** ≈ New South Wales, SE Australia
62 G13 **Talca** Maule, C Chile
62 F13 **Talcahuano** Bío Bío, C Chile
154 N12 **Tālcher** Orissa, E India
25 W5 **Talco** Texas, SW USA
145 V14 **Taldykorgan** *Kaz.* Taldyqorghan; *prev.* Taldy-Kurgan. Almaty, SE Kazakhstan
Taldy-Kurgan/Taldyqorghan *see* Taldykorgan
147 Y7 **Taldy-Suu** Issyk-Kul'skaya Oblast', E Kyrgyzstan
147 U10 **Taldy-Suu** Oshskaya Oblast', SW Kyrgyzstan
Tal-e Khosravī *see* Yāsūj
193 Y15 **Taleki Tonga** *island* Otu Tolu Group, C Tonga
193 Y15 **Taleki Vavu'u** *island* Otu Tolu Group, C Tonga
102 J13 **Talence** Gironde, SW France
145 U16 **Talgar** *Kaz.* Talghar. Almaty, SE Kazakhstan
Talghar *see* Talgar
171 Q12 **Taliabu, Pulau** *island* Kepulauan Sula, C Indonesia
115 L22 **Taliarós, Akrotírio** *headland* Astypálaia, Kykládes, Greece, Aegean Sea
Ta-lien *see* Dalian
27 Q12 **Talihina** Oklahoma, C USA
Talimardzhan *see* Tollimarjon
Talin *see* T'alin
137 T12 **T'alin** *Rus.* Talin; *prev.* Verin Talin. W Armenia
81 E15 **Tali Post** Bahr el Gabel, S Sudan
Taliq-an *see* Tāloqān
Taliş Dağları *see* Talish Mountains
142 L2 **Talish Mountains** *Az.* Talış Dağları, *Per.* Kūhhā-ye Ţavālesh, *Rus.* Talyshskiye Gory. ▲▲ Azerbaijan/Iran
170 M16 **Taliwang** Sumbawa, C Indonesia
119 L17 **Tal'ka** *Rus.* Tal'ka. Minskaya Voblasts', C Belarus
39 R11 **Talkeetna** Alaska, USA
39 R11 **Talkeetna Mountains** ▲▲ Alaska, USA
Talkhof *see* Puurmani
92 H2 **Tálknafjördhur** Vestfirdhir, W Iceland
139 Q3 **Tall 'Abṭah** N Iraq
138 M2 **Tall Abyaḍ** *var.* Tell Abiad. Ar Raqqah, N Syria
23 Q4 **Talladega** Alabama, S USA
139 Q2 **Tall 'Afar** N Iraq
23 S8 **Tallahassee** *prev.* Muskogean. *state capital* Florida, SE USA
22 L2 **Tallahatchie River** ≈ Mississippi, S USA
Tall al Abyaḍ *see* At Tall al Abyaḍ
139 W12 **Tall al Laḥm** S Iraq
183 P11 **Tallangatta** Victoria, SE Australia
23 R4 **Tallapoosa River** ≈ Alabama/Georgia, S USA
103 T13 **Tallard** Hautes-Alpes, SE France
139 Q3 **Tall ash Sha'īr** N Iraq
23 O5 **Tallassee** Alabama, S USA
139 R4 **Tall 'Azbah** NW Iraq
138 I5 **Tall Bīsah** Ḥimṣ, W Syria
139 R3 **Tall Ḥassūnah** N Iraq
139 Q2 **Tall Ḥuqnah** *var.* Tell Huqnah. N Iraq
Tallin *see* Tallinn
118 G3 **Tallinn** *Ger.* Reval, *Rus.* Tallin; *prev.* Revel. ● (Estonia) Harjumaa, NW Estonia
118 H3 **Tallinn** ✕ Harjumaa, NW Estonia
138 H5 **Tall Kalakh** *var.* Tell Kalakh. Ḥimṣ, C Syria
139 R2 **Tall Kayf** NW Iraq
Tall Kūchak *see* Tall Kūshik
139 P2 **Tall Kūshik** *var.* Tall Kūchak. Al Ḥasakah, E Syria
31 U12 **Tallmadge** Ohio, N USA
22 J5 **Tallulah** Louisiana, S USA
139 Q2 **Tall 'Uwaynāt** NW Iraq
139 Q2 **Tall Ẓāhir** N Iraq
122 J13 **Tal'menka** Altayskiy Kray, S Russian Federation
122 K8 **Talnakh** Taymyrskiy (Dolgano-Nenetskiy) Avtonomnyy Okrug, N Russian Federation
117 P7 **Tal'ne** *Rus.* Tal'noye. Cherkas'ka Oblast', C Ukraine
Tal'noye *see* Tal'ne
80 E12 **Talodi** Southern Kordofan, C Sudan
188 B16 **Talofofo** SE Guam
188 B16 **Talofofo Bay** *bay* SE Guam
26 L9 **Taloga** Oklahoma, C USA
123 T10 **Talon** Magadanskaya Oblast', E Russian Federation
14 H11 **Talon, Lake** ◎ Ontario, S Canada
149 R2 **Tāloqān** *var.* Taliq-an. Takhār, NE Afghanistan
126 M8 **Talovaya** Voronezhskaya Oblast', W Russian Federation
9 N6 **Taloyoak** *prev.* Spence Bay. Nunavut, N Canada
25 Q8 **Talpa** Texas, SW USA
40 K13 **Talpa de Allende** Jalisco, C Mexico
23 S9 **Talquin, Lake** ⊠ Florida, SE USA
Talsen *see* Talsi
162 H9 **Talshand** Govĭ-Altay, C Mongolia
118 E8 **Talsi** *Ger.* Talsen. Talsi, NW Latvia
143 V11 **Tal Sīāh** Sīstān va Balūchestān, SE Iran
62 G6 **Taltal** Antofagasta, N Chile
8 K10 **Taltson** ≈ Northwest Territories, NW Canada
168 K11 **Taluk** Sumatera, W Indonesia
92 J8 **Talvik** Finnmark, N Norway
182 M7 **Talyawalka Creek** ≈ New South Wales, SE Australia
Talyshskiye Gory *see* Talish Mountains
29 W14 **Tama** Iowa, C USA
Tama Abu, Banjaran *see* Penambo, Banjaran
169 U9 **Tamabo, Banjaran** ▲▲ East Malaysia
190 B16 **Tamakautoga** SW Niue
127 N7 **Tamala** Penzenskaya Oblast', W Russian Federation
77 P15 **Tamale** C Ghana
191 P3 **Tamana** *prev.* Rotcher Island. *atoll* Tungaru, W Kiribati
74 K12 **Tamanrasset** *var.* Tamenghest. S Algeria
74 J13 **Tamanrasset** *wadi* Algeria/Mali
166 M2 **Tamanthi** Sagaing, N Burma
97 I24 **Tamar** ≈ SW England, UK
Tamar *see* Tudmur
54 H9 **Támara** Casanare, C Colombia
54 F7 **Tamar, Alto de** ▲ C Colombia
173 X16 **Tamarin** E Mauritius
105 T5 **Tamarite de Litera** *var.* Tararite de Llitera. Aragón, NE Spain
111 I24 **Tamási** Tolna, S Hungary
Tamatave *see* Toamasina
41 O9 **Tamaulipas** ◈ *state* C Mexico
41 P10 **Tamaulipas, Sierra de** ▲▲ C Mexico
56 F12 **Tamaya, Río** ≈ E Peru
40 I9 **Tamazula** Durango, C Mexico
40 L14 **Tamazula** Jalisco, C Mexico
Tamazulápam *see* Tamazulapán
41 Q15 **Tamazulapán** *var.* Tamazulápam. Oaxaca, SE Mexico
41 P12 **Tamazunchale** San Luis Potosí, C Mexico
76 H11 **Tambacounda** SE Senegal
83 M16 **Tambara** Manica, C Mozambique
77 T13 **Tambawel** Sokoto, NW Nigeria
186 M9 **Tambea** Guadalcanal, C Solomon Islands
169 N10 **Tambelan, Kepulauan** *island group* W Indonesia
57 E15 **Tambo de Mora** Ica, W Peru
170 L16 **Tambora, Gunung** ⛰ Sumbawa, S Indonesia
61 E17 **Tambores** Paysandú, W Uruguay
57 F14 **Tambo, Río** ≈ C Peru
56 F7 **Tamboryacu, Río** ≈ N Peru
126 M7 **Tambov** Tambovskaya Oblast', W Russian Federation
126 L6 **Tambovskaya Oblast'** ◈ *province* W Russian Federation
104 H3 **Tambre** ≈ NW Spain
169 V7 **Tambunan** Sabah, East Malaysia
81 C15 **Tambura** Western Equatoria, SW Sudan
Tamchaket *see* Tâmchekkeţ
76 J9 **Tâmchekkeţ** *var.* Tamchaket. Hodh el Gharbi, S Mauritania
167 T7 **Tam Điêp** Ninh Binh, N Vietnam
Tamdybulak *see* Tomdibuloq
54 H8 **Tame** Arauca, C Colombia
104 H6 **Tâmega, Rio** *Sp.* Río Támega. ≈ Portugal/Spain
115 H20 **Tamélos, Akrotírio** *headland* Kéa, Kykládes, Greece, Aegean Sea
Tamenghest *see* Tamanrasset
77 V8 **Tamgak, Adrar** ▲ C Niger
76 I13 **Tamgue** ▲ NW Guinea
41 Q12 **Tamiahua** Veracruz-Llave, E Mexico
41 Q12 **Tamiahua, Laguna de** *lagoon* E Mexico
23 Y16 **Tamiami Canal** *canal* Florida, SE USA
188 F17 **Tamil Harbor** *harbour* Yap, W Micronesia
155 H21 **Tamil Nādu** *prev.* Madras. ◈ *state* SE India
99 H20 **Tamines** Namur, S Belgium
116 E12 **Tamiš** *Ger.* Temesch, *Hung.* Temes, *SCr.* Tamiš. ≈ Romania/Serbia and Montenegro (Yugo.)
167 U10 **Tam Ky** Quang Nam-Đa Nâng, C Vietnam
Tammerfors *see* Tampere
Tammisaari *see* Ekenäs
95 N14 **Tämnaren** ◎ C Sweden
191 Q7 **Tamotoe, Passe** *passage* Tahiti, W French Polynesia
23 V12 **Tampa** Florida, SE USA
23 V12 **Tampa** ✕ Florida, SE USA
23 V13 **Tampa Bay** *bay* Florida, SE USA
93 L18 **Tampere** *Swe.* Tammerfors. Länsi-Suomi, W Finland
41 Q11 **Tampico** Tamaulipas, C Mexico
171 P14 **Tampo** Pulau Muna, C Indonesia
167 V11 **Tam Quan** Binh Đinh, C Vietnam
162 J13 **Tamsag Muchang** Nei Mongol Zizhiqu, N China
Tamsal *see* Tamsalu
118 I4 **Tamsalu** *Ger.* Tamsal. Lääne-Virumaa, NE Estonia
109 S8 **Tamsweg** Salzburg, SW Austria
166 L3 **Tamu** Sagaing, N Burma
41 P12 **Tamuín** San Luis Potosí, C Mexico
188 C15 **Tamuning** NW Guam
183 T6 **Tamworth** New South Wales, SE Australia
97 M19 **Tamworth** C England, UK
81 K19 **Tana** ≈ SE Kenya
Tana *see* Deatnu/Tenojoki
164 I15 **Tanabe** Wakayama, Honshū, SW Japan
92 L8 **Tana Bru** Finnmark, N Norway
39 T10 **Tanacross** Alaska, USA
92 L7 **Tanafjorden** *Lapp.* Deanuvuotna. *fjord* N Norway
38 G17 **Tanaga Island** *island* Aleutian Islands, Alaska, USA
38 G17 **Tanaga Volcano** ▲ Tanaga Island, Alaska, USA
107 M18 **Tanagro** ≈ S Italy
80 H11 **T'ana Hāyk'** *Eng.* Lake Tana. ◎ NW Ethiopia
168 H11 **Tanahbela, Pulau** *island* Kepulauan Batu, W Indonesia
171 H15 **Tanahjampea, Pulau** *island* W Indonesia
168 H11 **Tanahmasa, Pulau** *island* Kepulauan Batu, W Indonesia
Tanais *see* Don
152 L10 **Tanakpur** Uttaranchal, N India
Tana, Lake *see* T'ana Hāyk'
181 P5 **Tanami Desert** *desert* Northern Territory, N Australia
167 T14 **Tân An** Long An, S Vietnam
39 Q9 **Tanana** Alaska, USA
Tananarive *see* Antananarivo
39 Q9 **Tanana River** ≈ Alaska, USA
95 C16 **Tananger** Rogaland, S Norway
188 H5 **Tanapag** Saipan, S Northern Mariana Islands
188 H5 **Tanapag, Puetton** *bay* Saipan, S Northern Mariana Islands
106 C9 **Tanaro** ≈ N Italy
163 Y12 **Tanch'ŏn** E North Korea
40 M14 **Tancítaro, Cerro** ⛰ C Mexico
153 N12 **Tānda** Uttar Pradesh, N India
77 O15 **Tanda** E Ivory Coast
116 L14 **Ţăndărei** Ialomiţa, SE Romania
63 N14 **Tandil** Buenos Aires, E Argentina
78 H12 **Tandjilé** *off.* Préfecture du Tandjilé. ◈ *prefecture* SW Chad
Tandjoeng *see* Tanjung
Tandjoengpandan *see* Tanjungpandan
Tandjoengpinang *see* Tanjungpinang
Tandjoengredeb *see* Tanjungredeb
149 Q16 **Tando Allāhyār** Sind, SE Pakistan
149 Q17 **Tando Bāgo** Sind, SE Pakistan
149 Q16 **Tando Muhammad Khān** Sind, SE Pakistan
182 L7 **Tandou Lake** *seasonal lake* New South Wales, SE Australia
94 L11 **Tandsjöborg** Gävleborg, C Sweden
155 H15 **Tāndūr** Andhra Pradesh, C India
164 C17 **Tanega-shima** *island* Nansei-shotō, SW Japan
165 R7 **Taneichi** Iwate, Honshū, C Japan
Tanen Taunggyi *see* Tane Range
167 N8 **Tane Range** *Bur.* Tanen Taunggyi. ▲▲ W Thailand
111 P15 **Tanew** ≈ SE Poland
21 W2 **Taneytown** Maryland, NE USA
74 H12 **Tanezrouft** *desert* Algeria/Mali
138 L7 **Ţanf, Jabal aţ** ▲ SE Syria
81 J21 **Tanga** Tanga, E Tanzania
81 I22 **Tanga** ◈ *region* E Tanzania
153 T14 **Tangail** Dhaka, C Bangladesh
186 I5 **Tanga Islands** *island group* NE PNG
155 K26 **Tangalla** Southern Province, S Sri Lanka
Tanganyika and Zanzibar *see* Tanzania
81 D3 **Tanganyika, Lake** ◎ E Africa
56 E7 **Tangarana, Río** ≈ N Peru
Tangdukou *see* Shaoyang
191 V16 **Tangaroa, Maunga** ⛰ Easter Island, Chile, E Pacific Ocean
74 G5 **Tanger** *var.* Tangiers, Tangier, *Fr./Ger.* Tangerk, *Sp.* Tánger; *anc.* Tingis. NW Morocco
169 N15 **Tangerang** Jawa, C Indonesia
Tangerk *see* Tanger
100 M12 **Tangermünde** Sachsen-Anhalt, C Germany
159 O12 **Tanggulashan** *var.* Togton Heyan, *var.* Tuotuoheyan. Qinghai, C China
156 K10 **Tanggula Shan** *var.* Dangla, Tangla Range. ▲▲ W China
159 N13 **Tanggula Shan** ▲ W China
156 K10 **Tanggula Shankou** *Tib.* Dang La. *pass* W China
161 N7 **Tanghe** Henan, C China
149 T5 **Tāngi** North-West Frontier Province, NW Pakistan
Tangier *see* Tanger
21 Y5 **Tangier Island** *island* Virginia, NE USA
Tangiers *see* Tanger
22 K8 **Tangipahoa River** ≈ Louisiana, S USA
Tangla Range *see* Tanggula Shan
164 J12 **Tango-hantō** *peninsula* Honshū, SW Japan
156 I10 **Tangra Yumco** *var.* Tangro Tso. ◎ W China
Tangro Tso *see* Tangra Yumco
157 T7 **Tangshan** *var.* T'ang-shan. Hebei, E China
77 R14 **Tanguiéta** NW Benin
163 X7 **Tangwang He** ≈ NE China
163 X7 **Tangyuan** Heilongjiang, NE China
92 M11 **Tanhua** Lappi, N Finland
171 U16 **Tanimbar, Kepulauan** *island group* Maluku, E Indonesia
Tanintharyi *see* Tenasserim
139 U4 **Tānjarō** ≈ E Iraq
Tanjore *see* Thanjāvūr
169 U12 **Tanjung** *prev.* Tandjoeng. Borneo, C Indonesia
169 W9 **Tanjungbatu** Borneo, N Indonesia
Tanjungkarang *see* Bandarlampung
169 N13 **Tanjungpandan** *prev.* Tandjoengpandan. Pulau Belitung, W Indonesia
168 M10 **Tanjungpinang** *prev.* Tandjoengpinang. Pulau Bintan, W Indonesia
169 V9 **Tanjungredeb** *var.* Tanjungredep; *prev.* Tandjoengredeb. Borneo, C Indonesia
Tanjungredep *see* Tanjungredeb
149 S8 **Tānk** North-West Frontier Province, NW Pakistan
187 S15 **Tanna** *island* S Vanuatu
93 F17 **Tännäs** Jämtland, C Sweden
Tannenhof *see* Krynica
108 K7 **Tannheim** Tirol, W Austria
Tannu-Tuva *see* Tyva, Respublika
171 Q12 **Tano** Pulau Taliabu, E Indonesia
77 O17 **Tano** ≈ S Ghana
152 D10 **Tanot** Rājasthān, NW India
77 V11 **Tanout** Zinder, C Niger
41 P12 **Tanquián** San Luis Potosí, C Mexico
77 R13 **Tansarga** E Burkina
167 T13 **Tan Son Nhat** ✕ (Hô Chi Minh) Tây Ninh, S Vietnam
75 V8 **Tanta** *var.* Tantā, Tantâ. N Egypt
74 D9 **Tan-Tan** SW Morocco
41 P12 **Tantoyuca** Veracruz-Llave, E Mexico
152 J12 **Tāntpur** Uttar Pradesh, N India
Tan-tung *see* Dandong
38 M12 **Tanunak** Alaska, USA
166 L5 **Ta-nyaung** Magwe, W Burma
167 S5 **Tân Yên** Tuyên Quang, N Vietnam
81 F22 **Tanzania** *off.* United Republic of Tanzania, *Swa.* Jamhuri ya Muungano wa Tanzania; *prev.* German East Africa, Tanganyika and Zanzibar. ◆ *republic* E Africa
Tanzania, Jamhuri ya Muungano wa *see* Tanzania
Taoan/Tao'an *see* Taonan
163 T8 **Tao'er He** ≈ NE China
159 U11 **Tao He** ≈ C China
163 U9 **Taonan** *var.* Taoan, Tao'an. Jilin, NE China
T'aon-an *see* Baicheng
Taongi *see* Bokaak Atoll
107 M23 **Taormina** *anc.* Tauromenium. Sicilia, Italy, C Mediterranean Sea
37 S9 **Taos** New Mexico, SW USA
Taoudenit *see* Taoudenni
77 O6 **Taoudenni** *var.* Taoudenit. Tombouctou, N Mali
74 G6 **Taourirt** NE Morocco
161 S13 **T'aoyüan** *Jap.* Tōen. N Taiwan
118 I3 **Tapa** *Ger.* Taps. Lääne-Virumaa, NE Estonia
41 V17 **Tapachula** Chiapas, SE Mexico
Tapaiu *see* Gvardeysk
59 H14 **Tapajós, Rio** *var.* Tapajóz. ≈ NW Brazil
Tapajóz *see* Tapajós, Rio
61 C21 **Tapalqué** *var.* Tapalquén. Buenos Aires, E Argentina
Tapalquén *see* Tapalqué
Tapanahoni *see* Tapanahony Rivier
55 W11 **Tapanahony Rivier** *var.* Tapanahoni. ≈ E Surinam
41 T16 **Tapanatepec** *var.* San Pedro Tapanatepec. Oaxaca, SE Mexico
185 D23 **Tapanui** Otago, South Island, NZ
59 E14 **Tapauá** Amazonas, N Brazil
59 D15 **Tapauá, Rio** ≈ W Brazil
185 I14 **Tapawera** Tasman, South Island, NZ
61 I16 **Tapes** Rio Grande do Sul, S Brazil
76 K16 **Tapeta** C Liberia
154 H11 **Tāpi** *prev.* Tāpti. ≈ W India
104 J2 **Tapia de Casariego** Asturias, N Spain
56 F10 **Tapiche, Río** ≈ N Peru
167 N15 **Tapi, Mae Nam** *var.* Luang. ≈ SW Thailand
186 E8 **Tapini** Central, S PNG
Tapirapecó, Serra *see* Tapirapecó, Sierra
55 N13 **Tapirapecó, Sierra** *Port.* Serra Tapirapecó. ▲▲ Brazil/Venezuela
77 R13 **Tapoa** ≈ Benin/Niger
188 H5 **Tapochau, Mount** ▲ Saipan, S Northern Mariana Islands
111 H24 **Tapolca** Veszprém, W Hungary
21 X5 **Tappahannock** Virginia, NE USA
31 U13 **Tappan Lake** ⊠ Ohio, N USA
165 Q6 **Tappi-zaki** *headland* Honshū, C Japan
Taps *see* Tapa
Tāpti *see* Tāpi
185 J16 **Tapuaenuku** ▲ South Island, NZ
171 N8 **Tapul Group** *island group* Sulu Archipelago, SW Philippines
58 E11 **Tapurucuará** *var.* Tapuruquara. Amazonas, NW Brazil
Tapuruquara *see* Tapurucuará
192 J17 **Taputapu, Cape** *headland* Tutuila, W American Samoa
141 W13 **Ţāqah** S Oman
139 T3 **Taqtaq** N Iraq
61 J15 **Taquara** Rio Grande do Sul, S Brazil
59 H19 **Taquari, Rio** ≈ C Brazil
60 L8 **Taquaritinga** São Paulo, S Brazil
122 I11 **Tara** Omskaya Oblast', C Russian Federation
83 I16 **Tara** Southern, S Zambia
113 J15 **Tara** ≈ SW Serbia and Montenegro (Yugo.)
112 K13 **Tara** ▲▲ W Serbia and Montenegro (Yugo.)
77 W15 **Taraba** ◈ *state* E Nigeria
77 X15 **Taraba** ≈ E Nigeria
75 O7 **Tarābulus** *var.* Ţarābulus al Gharb, *Eng.* Tripoli. ● (Libya) NW Libya
75 O7 **Tarābulus** ✕ NW Libya
Tarābulus/Ţarābulus ash Shām *see* Tripoli
Ţarābulus al Gharb *see* Tarābulus
105 O7 **Taracena** Castilla-La Mancha, C Spain
117 N12 **Taraclia** *Rus.* Tarakilya. S Moldova
139 V10 **Tarād al Kahf** SE Iraq
183 R10 **Tarago** New South Wales, SE Australia
169 V8 **Tarakan** Borneo, C Indonesia
169 V9 **Tarakan, Pulau** *island* N Indonesia
Tarakilya *see* Taraclia
165 P16 **Tarama-jima** *island* Sakishima-shotō, SW Japan
184 K10 **Taranaki** *off.* Taranaki Region. ◈ *region* North Island, NZ
184 K10 **Taranaki, Mount** *var.* Egmont. ▲ North Island, NZ
105 O9 **Tarancón** Castilla-La Mancha, C Spain
188 M15 **Tarang Reef** *reef* C Micronesia
96 E7 **Taransay** *island* NW Scotland, UK
107 P18 **Taranto** *var.* Tarentum. Puglia, SE Italy
107 O19 **Taranto, Golfo di** *Eng.* Gulf of Taranto. *gulf* S Italy
Taranto, Gulf of *see* Taranto, Golfo di
62 G3 **Tarapacá** *off.* Región de Tarapacá. ◈ *region* N Chile
187 N9 **Tarapaina** Maramasike Island, N Solomon Islands
56 D10 **Tarapoto** San Martín, N Peru
138 M6 **Ţaraq an Na'jah** *hill range* E Syria
138 M6 **Ţaraq Sidāwī** *hill range* E Syria
103 Q11 **Tarare** Rhône, E France
Tararite de Llitera *see* Tamarite de Litera
184 M13 **Tararua Range** ▲▲ North Island, NZ
151 Q22 **Tarāsa Dwīp** *island* Nicobar Islands, India, NE Indian Ocean
103 Q15 **Tarascon** Bouches-du-Rhône, SE France
102 M17 **Tarascon-sur-Ariège** Ariège, S France
117 P6 **Tarashcha** Kyyivs'ka Oblast', N Ukraine
57 L18 **Tarata** Cochabamba, C Bolivia
57 I18 **Tarata** Tacna, SW Peru
190 H2 **Taratai** *atoll* Tungaru, W Kiribati
59 B15 **Tarauacá** Acre, W Brazil
59 B15 **Tarauacá, Rio** ≈ NW Brazil
191 Q8 **Taravao** Tahiti, W French Polynesia
191 R8 **Taravao, Baie de** *bay* Tahiti, W French Polynesia
191 Q8 **Taravao, Isthme de** *isthmus* Tahiti, W French Polynesia
103 X16 **Taravo** ≈ Corse, France, C Mediterranean Sea
190 I3 **Tarawa** ✕ Tarawa, W Kiribati
190 H2 **Tarawa** *atoll* Tungaru, W Kiribati
184 N10 **Tarawera** Hawke's Bay, North Island, NZ
184 N8 **Tarawera, Lake** ◎ North Island, NZ
184 N8 **Tarawera, Mount** ▲ North Island, NZ
105 S8 **Tarayuela** ▲ N Spain

◆ Country ● Country Capital ◇ Dependent Territory ○ Dependent Territory Capital ◈ Administrative Region ✕ International Airport ▲ Mountain ▲▲ Mountain Range ⛰ Volcano ≈ River ◎ Lake ⊠ Reservoir

151 R16 **Taraz** *prev.* Aulie Ata, Auliye-Ata, Dzhambul, Zhambyl, S Kazakhstan.
105 Q5 **Tarazona** Aragón, NE Spain
105 Q10 **Tarazona de la Mancha** Castilla-La Mancha, C Spain
145 X12 **Tarbagatay, Khrebet** ⛰ China/Kazakhstan
96 J8 **Tarbat Ness** *headland* N Scotland, UK
149 U5 **Tarbela Reservoir** ⊞ N Pakistan
96 H12 **Tarbert** W Scotland, UK
96 F7 **Tarbert** Western Isles, NW Scotland, UK
102 K16 **Tarbes** *anc.* Bigorra. Hautes-Pyrénées, S France
21 W9 **Tarboro** North Carolina, SE USA
Tarca *see* Torysa
106 J6 **Tarcento** Friuli-Venezia Giulia, NE Italy
182 F5 **Tarcoola** South Australia
105 S5 **Tardienta** Aragón, NE Spain
102 L11 **Tardoire** ≈ W France
183 U7 **Taree** New South Wales, SE Australia
92 K12 **Tärendö** *Lapp.* Deargget. Norrbotten, N Sweden
Tarentum *see* Taranto
74 C9 **Tarfaya** SW Morocco
116 J13 **Târgovişte** *prev.* Tîrgovişte. Dâmboviţa, S Romania
116 M12 **Târgu Bujor** *prev.* Tîrgu Bujor. Galaţi, E Romania
116 H13 **Târgu Cărbuneşti** *prev.* Tîrgu. Gorj, SW Romania
116 L9 **Târgu Frumos** *prev.* Tîrgu Frumos. Iaşi, NE Romania
116 H13 **Târgu Jiu** *prev.* Tîrgu Jiu. Gorj, W Romania
116 H9 **Târgu Lăpuş** *prev.* Tîrgu Lăpuş. Maramureş, N Romania
Târgul-Neamţ *see* Târgu-Neamţ
Târgul-Săcuiesc *see* Târgu Secuiesc
116 I10 **Târgu Mureş** *prev.* Oşorhei, Tîrgu Mures, *Ger.* Neumarkt, *Hung.* Marosvásárhely. Mureş, C Romania
116 K9 **Târgu-Neamţ** *var.* Târgul-Neamţ; *prev.* Tîrgu-Neamţ. Neamţ, NE Romania
116 K11 **Târgu Ocna** *Hung.* Aknavásár; *prev.* Tîrgu Ocna. Bacău, E Romania
116 K11 **Târgu Secuiesc** *Ger.* Neumarkt, Szekler Neumarkt, *Hung.* Kezdivásárhely; *prev.* Chezdi-Oşorheiu, Târgul-Săcuiesc, Tîrgu Secuiesc. Covasna, E Romania
145 X10 **Targyn** Vostochnyy Kazakhstan, E Kazakhstan
Tar Heel State *see* North Carolina
186 C7 **Tari** Southern Highlands, W PNG
143 P17 **Ţarif** Abū Ẓaby, C UAE
104 K16 **Tarifa** Andalucía, S Spain
57 M21 **Tarija** Tarija, S Bolivia
57 M21 **Tarija** ⬖ *department* S Bolivia
141 R14 **Tarīm** C Yemen
Tarim Basin *see* Tarim Pendi
81 G19 **Tarime** Mara, N Tanzania
158 J7 **Tarim He** ≈ NW China
159 H8 **Tarim Pendi** *Eng.* Tarim Basin. *basin* NW China
149 N7 **Tarīn Kowt** *var.* Terinkot. Urūzgān, C Afghanistan
171 O12 **Taripa** Sulawesi, C Indonesia
117 Q12 **Tarkhankut, Mys** *headland* S Ukraine
27 Q1 **Tarkio** Missouri, C USA
122 J9 **Tarko-Sale** Yamalo-Nenetskiy Avtonomnyy Okrug, N Russian Federation
77 P17 **Tarkwa** S Ghana
171 O3 **Tarlac** Luzon, N Philippines
95 F22 **Tarm** Ringkøbing, W Denmark
57 E14 **Tarma** Junín, C Peru
103 N15 **Tarn** ⬖ *department* S France
102 M15 **Tarn** ≈ S France
111 L22 **Tarna** ≈ C Hungary
92 G13 **Tärnaby** Västerbotten, N Sweden
149 P8 **Tarnak Rūd** ≈ SE Afghanistan
116 J11 **Târnava Mare** *Ger.* Grosse Kokel, *Hung.* Nagy-Küküllő; *prev.* Tîrnava Mare. ≈ S Romania
116 I11 **Târnava Mică** *Ger.* Kleine Kokel, *Hung.* Kis-Küküllő; *prev.* Tîrnava Mică. ≈ C Romania
116 I11 **Târnăveni** *Ger.* Marteskirch, Martinskirch, *Hung.* Dicsőszentmárton; *prev.* Sînmartin, Tîrnăveni. Mureş, C Romania
102 L14 **Tarn-et-Garonne** ⬖ *department* S France
111 P18 **Tarnica** ▲ SE Poland
111 N15 **Tarnobrzeg** Podkarpackie, SE Poland
125 N12 **Tarnogskiy Gorodok** Vologodskaya Oblast', NW Russian Federation
Tarnopol *see* Ternopil'
111 M16 **Tarnów** Małopolskie, SE Poland
Tarnowice/Tarnowitz *see* Tarnowskie Góry
111 J16 **Tarnowskie Góry** *var.* Tarnowice, Tarnowskie Gory, *Ger.* Tarnowitz. Śląskie, S Poland
95 N14 **Tärnsjö** Västmanland, C Sweden
106 E9 **Taro** ≈ NW Italy
186 I6 **Taron** New Ireland, NE PNG
74 E8 **Taroudannt** *var.* Taroudant. SW Morocco
Taroudant *see* Taroudannt
23 V12 **Tarpon, Lake** ◎ Florida, SE USA
23 V12 **Tarpon Springs** Florida, SE USA
107 G14 **Tarquinia** *anc.* Tarquinii; *hist.* Corneto. Lazio, C Italy
Tarquinii *see* Tarquinia
Tarraco *see* Tarragona
76 D10 **Tarrafal** Santiago, S Cape Verde
105 V6 **Tarragona** *anc.* Tarraco. Cataluña, E Spain
105 T7 **Tarragona** ⬖ *province* Cataluña, NE Spain
183 O17 **Tarraleah** Tasmania, SE Australia
23 P3 **Tarrant City** Alabama, S USA
185 D21 **Tarras** Otago, South Island, NZ
Tarrasa *see* Terrassa
105 U5 **Tàrrega** *var.* Tarrega. Cataluña, NE Spain
21 W9 **Tar River** ≈ North Carolina, SE USA
Tarsatica *see* Rijeka
136 J17 **Tarsus** İçel, S Turkey
62 K4 **Tartagal** Salta, N Argentina
137 V12 **Tärtär** *Rus.* Terter. ≈ SW Azerbaijan
102 J15 **Tartas** Landes, SW France
139 Q6 **Tārtasah** C Iraq
Tartlau *see* Prejmer
Tartous/Tartouss *see* Ṭarṭūs
118 J5 **Tartu** *Ger.* Dorpat; *prev. Rus.* Yurev, Yur'yev. Tartumaa, SE Estonia
118 I5 **Tartumaa** *off.* Tartu Maakond. ⬖ *province* E Estonia
138 H5 **Ṭarṭūs** *Fr.* Tartouss; *anc.* Tortosa. Ṭarṭūs, W Syria
138 H5 **Ṭarṭūs** *off.* Muḥāfaẓat Ṭarṭūs, *var.* Tartous, Tartus. ⬖ *governorate* W Syria
164 C16 **Tarumizu** Kagoshima, Kyūshū, SW Japan
126 K4 **Tarusa** Kaluzhskaya Oblast', W Russian Federation
117 N11 **Tarutyne** Odes'ka Oblast', SW Ukraine
162 I7 **Tarvagatyn Nuruu** ⛰ N Mongolia
106 J6 **Tarvisio** Friuli-Venezia Giulia, NE Italy
Tarvisium *see* Treviso
57 O16 **Tarvo, Río** ≈ E Bolivia
14 G8 **Tarzwell** Ontario, S Canada
40 K5 **Tasajera, Sierra de la** ⛰ N Mexico
145 S13 **Tasaral** Karaganda, C Kazakhstan
Tasböget *see* Tasbuget
145 N15 **Tasbuget** *Kaz.* Tasböget. Kzylorda, S Kazakhstan
108 E11 **Tasch** Valais, SW Switzerland
Tasek Kenyir *see* Kenyir, Tasik
122 J14 **Tashanta** Respublika Altay, S Russian Federation
Tashauz *see* Daşoguz
Tashi Chho Dzong *see* Thimphu
153 U11 **Tashigang** E Bhutan
137 T11 **Tashir** *prev.* Kalinino. N Armenia
143 Q11 **Tashk, Daryācheh-ye** ◎ C Iran
Tashkent *see* Toshkent
Tashkentskaya Oblast' *see* Toshkent Viloyati
Tashkepri *see* Daşköpri
Tash-Kömür *see* Tash-Kumyr
147 S9 **Tash-Kumyr** *Kir.* Tash-Kömür. Dzhalal-Abadskaya Oblast', W Kyrgyzstan
127 T7 **Tashla** Orenburgskaya Oblast', W Russian Federation
Tashqurghan *see* Kholm
122 J13 **Tashtagol** Kemerovskaya Oblast', S Russian Federation
95 H23 **Tåsinge** *island* C Denmark
12 M5 **Tasiujaq** Québec, E Canada
77 W11 **Tasker** Zinder, C Niger
145 W12 **Taskesken** Vostochnyy Kazakhstan, E Kazakhstan
136 J10 **Taşköprü** Kastamonu, N Turkey
Taskuduk, Peski *see* Goshquduq Qum
186 G5 **Taskul** New Ireland, NE PNG
137 S13 **Taşlıçay** Ağrı, E Turkey
185 H14 **Tasman** *off.* Tasman District. ⬖ *unitary authority* South Island, NZ
192 J12 **Tasman Basin** *var.* East Australian Basin. *undersea feature* S Tasman Sea
185 I14 **Tasman Bay** *inlet* South Island, NZ
192 I13 **Tasman Fracture Zone** *tectonic feature* S Indian Ocean
185 E19 **Tasman Glacier** *glacier* South Island, NZ
Tasman Group *see* Nukumanu Islands
183 N15 **Tasmania** *prev.* Van Diemen's Land. ⬖ *state* SE Australia
183 Q16 **Tasmania** *island* SE Australia
185 H14 **Tasman Mountains** ⛰ South Island, NZ
183 P17 **Tasman Peninsula** *peninsula* Tasmania, SE Australia
192 I11 **Tasman Plain** *undersea feature* W Tasman Sea
192 I12 **Tasman Plateau** *var.* South Tasmania Plateau. *undersea feature* SW Tasman Sea
192 I11 **Tasman Sea** *sea* SW Pacific Ocean
116 G9 **Tăşnad** *Ger.* Trestenberg, Trestendorf, *Hung.* Tasnád. Satu Mare, NW Romania
136 L11 **Taşova** Amasya, N Turkey
77 T10 **Tassara** Tahoua, W Niger
12 K4 **Tassialouc, Lac** ◎ Québec, C Canada
Tassili du Hoggar *see* Tassili ta-n-Ahaggar
74 L11 **Tassili-n-Ajjer** *plateau* E Algeria
74 K14 **Tassili ta-n-Ahaggar** *var.* Tassili du Hoggar. *plateau* S Algeria
59 M15 **Tasso Fragoso** Maranhão, E Brazil
Tåstrup *see* Taastrup
145 O9 **Tasty-Taldy** Akmola, C Kazakhstan
143 W10 **Tāsūkī** Sīstān va Balūchestān, SE Iran
111 I22 **Tata** *Ger.* Totis. Komárom-Esztergom, NW Hungary
74 E8 **Tata** SW Morocco
Tataaihoa, Pointe *see* Vénus, Pointe
111 I22 **Tatabánya** Komárom-Esztergom, NW Hungary
191 X10 **Tatakoto** *atoll* Îles Tuamotu, E French Polynesia
75 N7 **Tataouine** *var.* Taṭāwīn. SE Tunisia
55 O5 **Tataracual, Cerro** ▲ NE Venezuela
117 O12 **Tatarbunary** Odes'ka Oblast', SW Ukraine
119 M17 **Tatarka** *Rus.* Tatarka. Mahilyowskaya Voblasts', E Belarus
Tatar Pazardzhik *see* Pazardzhik
122 I12 **Tatarsk** Novosibirskaya Oblast', C Russian Federation
Tatarskaya ASSR *see* Tatarstan, Respublika
123 T13 **Tatarskiy Proliv** *Eng.* Tatar Strait. *strait* SE Russian Federation
127 R4 **Tatarstan, Respublika** *prev.* Tatarskaya ASSR. ⬖ *autonomous republic* W Russian Federation
Tatar Strait *see* Tatarskiy Proliv
Taṭāwīn *see* Tataouine
171 N12 **Tate** Sulawesi, N Indonesia
141 N11 **Tathlith** 'Asīr, S Saudi Arabia
141 O11 **Tathlīth, Wādī** *dry watercourse* S Saudi Arabia
183 R11 **Tathra** New South Wales, SE Australia
127 P8 **Tatishchevo** Saratovskaya Oblast', W Russian Federation
39 S12 **Tatitlek** Alaska, USA
10 L15 **Tatla Lake** British Columbia, SW Canada
121 Q2 **Tatlısu** *Gk.* Akanthoú. N Cyprus
11 Z10 **Tatnam, Cape** *headland* Manitoba, C Canada
Tatra/Tátra *see* Tatra Mountains
111 K18 **Tatra Mountains** *Ger.* Tatra, *Hung.* Tátra, *Pol./Slvk.* Tatry. ⛰ Poland/Slovakia
Tatry *see* Tatra Mountains
164 I13 **Tatsuno** *var.* Tatuno. Hyōgo, Honshū, SW Japan
145 S16 **Tatti** *var.* Tatty. Zhambyl, S Kazakhstan
Tatty *see* Tatti
60 L10 **Tatuí** São Paulo, S Brazil
37 V14 **Tatum** New Mexico, SW USA
25 X7 **Tatum** Texas, SW USA
Ta-t'ung/Tatung *see* Datong
Tatuno *see* Tatsuno
137 R14 **Tatvan** Bitlis, SE Turkey
95 C16 **Tau** Rogaland, S Norway
192 L17 **Ta'ū** *var.* Tau. *island* Manua Islands, E American Samoa
193 W15 **Tau** *island* Tongatapu Group, N Tonga
59 O14 **Tauá** Ceará, E Brazil
60 N10 **Taubaté** São Paulo, S Brazil
101 I19 **Tauber** ≈ SW Germany
101 I19 **Tauberbischofsheim** Baden-Württemberg, C Germany
144 E14 **Tauchik** *Kaz.* Taūshyq. Mangistau, SW Kazakhstan
191 W10 **Tauere** *atoll* Îles Tuamotu, C French Polynesia
101 H17 **Taufstein** ▲ C Germany
190 I17 **Taukoka** *island* SE Cook Islands
145 T15 **Taukum, Peski** *desert* SE Kazakhstan
184 L10 **Taumarunui** Manawatu-Wanganui, North Island, NZ
59 A15 **Taumaturgo** Acre, W Brazil
27 X6 **Taum Sauk Mountain** ▲ Missouri, C USA
83 H22 **Taung** North-West, N South Africa
166 L6 **Taungdwingyi** Magwe, C Burma
166 M6 **Taunggyi** Shan State, C Burma
166 L5 **Taungtha** Mandalay, C Burma
166 K7 **Taungup** Arakan State, W Burma
149 S9 **Taunsa** Punjab, E Pakistan
97 K23 **Taunton** SW England, UK
19 O12 **Taunton** Massachusetts, NE USA
101 F18 **Taunus** ⛰ W Germany
101 G18 **Taunusstein** Hessen, W Germany
184 N9 **Taupo** Waikato, North Island, NZ
184 M9 **Taupo, Lake** ◎ North Island, NZ
109 R8 **Taurach** *var.* Taurachbach. ≈ E Austria
Taurachbach *see* Taurach
118 D12 **Tauragė** *Ger.* Tauroggen. Tauragė, SW Lithuania
118 D13 **Tauragė** ⬖ *province* SW Lithuania
54 G10 **Tauramena** Casanare, C Colombia
184 N7 **Tauranga** Bay of Plenty, North Island, NZ
15 O10 **Taureau, Réservoir** ⊞ Québec, SE Canada
107 N22 **Taurianova** Calabria, SW Italy
Tauris *see* Tabrīz
184 I2 **Tauroa Point** *headland* North Island, NZ
Tauroggen *see* Tauragė
Tauromenium *see* Taormina
Taurus Mountains *see* Toros Dağları
Taus *see* Domažlice
Taūshyq *see* Tauchik
105 R5 **Tauste** Aragón, NE Spain
191 V16 **Tautara, Motu** *island* Easter Island, Chile, E Pacific Ocean
191 R8 **Tautira** Tahiti, W French Polynesia
Tauz *see* Tovuz
Tavālesh, Kūhhā-ye *see* Talish Mountains
136 D15 **Tavas** Denizli, SW Turkey
Tavastehus *see* Hämeenlinna
Tavau *see* Davos
122 G10 **Tavda** Sverdlovskaya Oblast', C Russian Federation
122 G10 **Tavda** ≈ C Russian Federation
105 T11 **Tavernes de la Valldigna** País Valenciano, E Spain
81 I20 **Taveta** Coast, S Kenya
187 Y14 **Taveuni** *island* N Fiji
147 R13 **Tavildara** *Rus.* Tavil'dara, Tovil'-Dora. C Tajikistan
162 L8 **Tavin** Dundgovĭ, C Mongolia
104 H14 **Tavira** Faro, S Portugal
97 I24 **Tavistock** SW England, UK
167 N10 **Tavoy** *var.* Dawei. Tenasserim, S Burma
Tavoy Island *see* Mali Kyun
115 E16 **Tavropoú, Techniti Límni** ⊞ C Greece
136 E13 **Tavşanlı** Kütahya, NW Turkey
187 X14 **Tavua** Viti Levu, W Fiji
97 J23 **Taw** ≈ SW England, UK
185 L14 **Tawa** Wellington, North Island, NZ
25 V6 **Tawakoni, Lake** ⊞ Texas, SW USA
153 V11 **Tawang** Arunāchal Pradesh, NE India
169 R17 **Tawang, Teluk** *bay* Jawa, S Indonesia
31 R7 **Tawas Bay** ◎ Michigan, N USA
31 R7 **Tawas City** Michigan, N USA
169 V8 **Tawau** Sabah, East Malaysia
141 U10 **Ṭawīl, Qalamat aṭ** *well* SE Saudi Arabia
171 N9 **Tawitawi** *island* SW Philippines
Ṭawkar *see* Tokar
Tāwūq *see* Dāqūq
Tawzar *see* Tozeur
41 O15 **Taxco** *var.* Taxco de Alarcón. Guerrero, S Mexico
Taxco de Alarcón *see* Taxco
146 H8 **Taxiatosh** *Rus.* Takhiatash. Qoraqalpog'iston Respublikasi, W Uzbekistan
158 D9 **Taxkorgan** *var.* Taxkorgan Tajik Zizhixian. Xinjiang Uygur Zizhiqu, NW China
Taxkorgan Tajik Zizhixian *see* Taxkorgan
146 H7 **Taxtako'pir** *Rus.* Takhtakupyr. Qoraqalpog'iston Respublikasi, NW Uzbekistan
96 J10 **Tay** ≈ C Scotland, UK
143 V6 **Tāybād** *var.* Taibad, Tāyybād, Tayyebāt. Khorāsān, NE Iran
Taybert at Turkz *see* Ṭayyibat at Turkī
124 J3 **Taybola** Murmanskaya Oblast', NW Russian Federation
81 M16 **Tayeeglow** Bakool, C Somalia
96 K11 **Tay, Firth of** *inlet* E Scotland, UK
122 J12 **Tayga** Kemerovskaya Oblast', S Russian Federation
162 G8 **Taygan** Govĭ-Altay, C Mongolia
123 T9 **Taygonos, Mys** *headland* E Russian Federation
96 I11 **Tay, Loch** ◎ C Scotland, UK
11 N12 **Taylor** British Columbia, W Canada
29 O14 **Taylor** Nebraska, C USA
18 I13 **Taylor** Pennsylvania, NE USA
25 T10 **Taylor** Texas, SW USA
37 Q11 **Taylor, Mount** ▲ New Mexico, SW USA
37 R5 **Taylor Park Reservoir** ⊞ Colorado, C USA
37 R6 **Taylor River** ≈ Colorado, C USA
21 P11 **Taylors** South Carolina, SE USA
20 L5 **Taylorsville** Kentucky, S USA
21 R6 **Taylorsville** North Carolina, SE USA
30 L14 **Taylorville** Illinois, N USA
140 K5 **Taymā'** Tabūk, NW Saudi Arabia
122 M10 **Taymura** ≈ C Russian Federation
123 O7 **Taymylyr** Respublika Sakha (Yakutiya), NE Russian Federation
122 L7 **Taymyr, Ozero** ◎ N Russian Federation
122 M6 **Taymyr, Poluostrov** *peninsula* N Russian Federation
122 L8 **Taymyrskiy (Dolgano-Nenetskiy) Avtonomnyy Okrug** *var.* Taymyrskiy Avtonomnyy Okrug. ⬖ *autonomous district* N Russian Federation
167 S13 **Tây Ninh** Tây Ninh, S Vietnam
122 L12 **Tayshet** Irkutskaya Oblast', S Russian Federation
171 N5 **Taytay** Palawan, W Philippines
169 Q16 **Tayu** *prev.* Tajoe. Jawa, C Indonesia
Tāyybād/Tayyebāt *see* Tāybād
138 L5 **Ṭayyibah** *var.* At Taybé. Ḥimş, C Syria
138 I4 **Ṭayyibat at Turkī** *var.* Taybert at Turkz. Ḥamāh, W Syria
145 P7 **Tayynsha** *prev.* Krasnoarmeysk. Severnyy Kazakhstan, N Kazakhstan
122 J10 **Taz** ≈ N Russian Federation
74 G6 **Taza** NE Morocco
139 T4 **Tāza Khurmātū** E Iraq
165 Q8 **Tazawa-ko** ◎ Honshū, C Japan
Taz, Bay of *see* Tazovskaya Guba
21 N8 **Tazewell** Tennessee, S USA
21 Q7 **Tazewell** Virginia, NE USA
75 S11 **Tāzirbū** SE Libya
39 S11 **Tazlina Lake** ◎ Alaska, USA
122 J8 **Tazovskiy** Yamalo-Nenetskiy Avtonomnyy Okrug, N Russian Federation
137 U10 **T'bilisi** *Eng.* Tiflis. ● (Georgia) SE Georgia
137 T10 **T'bilisi** × S Georgia
79 E14 **Tchabal Mbabo** ▲ NW Cameroon
Tchad *see* Chad
Tchad, Lac *see* Chad, Lake
77 S15 **Tchaourou** E Benin
79 E20 **Tchibanga** Nyanga, S Gabon
Tchien *see* Zwedru
77 Z6 **Tchigaï, Plateau du** ▲ NE Niger
77 V9 **Tchighozérine** Agadez, C Niger
77 T10 **Tchin-Tabaradene** Tahoua, W Niger
78 G13 **Tcholliré** Nord, NE Cameroon
Tchongking *see* Chongqing
22 K4 **Tchula** Mississippi, S USA
110 I7 **Tczew** *Ger.* Dirschau. Pomorskie, N Poland
116 I10 **Teaca** *Ger.* Tekendorf, *Hung.* Teke; *prev. Ger.* Teckendorf. Bistriţa-Năsăud, N Romania
40 J11 **Teacapán** Sinaloa, C Mexico
190 A10 **Teafuafou** *island* Funafuti Atoll, C Tuvalu
25 U8 **Teague** Texas, SW USA
191 R9 **Teahupoo** Tahiti, W French Polynesia
190 H15 **Te Aiti Point** *headland* Rarotonga, S Cook Islands
65 D24 **Teal Inlet** East Falkland, Falkland Islands
185 B22 **Te Anau** Southland, South Island, NZ
185 B22 **Te Anau, Lake** ◎ South Island, NZ
41 U15 **Teapa** Tabasco, SE Mexico
184 Q7 **Te Araroa** Gisborne, North Island, NZ
184 M7 **Te Aroha** Waikato, North Island, NZ
Teate *see* Chieti
190 A9 **Te Ava Fuagea** *channel* Funafuti Atoll, SE Tuvalu
190 B8 **Te Ava I Te Lape** *channel* Funafuti Atoll, SE Tuvalu
190 B9 **Te Ava Pua Pua** *channel* Funafuti Atoll, SE Tuvalu
184 M8 **Te Awamutu** Waikato, North Island, NZ
171 X12 **Teba** Papua, E Indonesia
104 L15 **Teba** Andalucía, S Spain
126 M15 **Teberda** Karachayevo-Cherkesskaya Respublika, SW Russian Federation
74 M6 **Tébessa** NE Algeria
62 O7 **Tebicuary, Río** ≈ S Paraguay
168 L13 **Tebingtinggi** Sumatera, W Indonesia
168 I8 **Tebingtinggi** Sumatera, N Indonesia
Tebingtinggi, Pulau *see* Rantau, Pulau
Tebriz *see* Tabrīz
137 U9 **Tebulos Mt'a** *Rus.* Gora Tebulosmta. ▲ Georgia/Russian Federation
Tebulosmta, Gora *see* Tebulos Mt'a
41 Q14 **Tecamachalco** Puebla, S Mexico
40 B1 **Tecate** Baja California, NW Mexico
136 M13 **Tecer Dağları** ⛰ C Turkey
103 O17 **Tech** ≈ S France
77 P16 **Techiman** W Ghana
117 N15 **Techirghiol** Constanţa, SE Romania
74 A12 **Techla** *var.* Techlé. SW Western Sahara
Techlé *see* Techla
63 H18 **Tecka, Sierra de** ⛰ SW Argentina
Teckendorf *see* Teaca
40 K13 **Tecolotlán** Jalisco, SW Mexico
40 K14 **Tecomán** Colima, SW Mexico
35 V12 **Tecopa** California, W USA
40 G5 **Tecoripa** Sonora, NW Mexico
41 N16 **Tecpan** *var.* Tecpan de Galeana. Guerrero, S Mexico
Tecpan de Galeana *see* Tecpan
40 J11 **Tecuala** Nayarit, C Mexico
116 L12 **Tecuci** Galaţi, E Romania
31 R10 **Tecumseh** Michigan, N USA
29 S16 **Tecumseh** Nebraska, C USA
27 O11 **Tecumseh** Oklahoma, C USA
Tedzhen *see* Harīrūd/Tejen
146 H15 **Tedzhenstroy** *Turkm.* Tejenstroy. Ahal Welaýaty, S Turkmenistan
162 I7 **Teel** Arhangay, C Mongolia
97 L15 **Tees** ≈ N England, UK
14 E15 **Teeswater** Ontario, S Canada
190 A10 **Tefala** *island* Funafuti Atoll, C Tuvalu
58 D13 **Tefé** Amazonas, N Brazil
74 K11 **Tefedest** ▲ S Algeria
136 E16 **Tefenni** Burdur, SW Turkey
58 D13 **Tefé, Rio** ≈ NW Brazil
169 P16 **Tegal** Jawa, C Indonesia
100 O12 **Tegel** × (Berlin) Berlin, NE Germany
99 M15 **Tegelen** Limburg, SE Netherlands
101 L24 **Tegernsee** ◎ SE Germany
107 M18 **Teggiano** Campania, S Italy
77 U14 **Tegina** Niger, C Nigeria
42 I7 **Tegucigalpa** ● (Honduras) Francisco Morazán, SW Honduras
42 H7 **Tegucigalpa** × Central District, C Honduras
Tegucigalpa *see* Central District, Honduras
Tegucigalpa *see* Francisco Morazán, Honduras
77 U9 **Teguidda-n-Tessoumt** Agadez, C Niger
64 Q11 **Teguise** Lanzarote, Islas Canarias, Spain, NE Atlantic Ocean
122 K12 **Tegul'det** Tomskaya Oblast', C Russian Federation
35 S13 **Tehachapi** California, W USA
35 S13 **Tehachapi Mountains** ⛰ California, W USA
Teheran *see* Tehrān
77 O14 **Téhini** NE Ivory Coast
143 N5 **Tehrān** *var.* Teheran. ● (Iran) Tehrān, N Iran
143 N6 **Tehrān** *off.* Ostān-e Tehrān, *var.* Tehran. ⬖ *province* N Iran
152 K9 **Tehri** Uttaranchal, N India
Tehri *see* Tikamgarh
41 Q15 **Tehuacán** Puebla, S Mexico
41 S17 **Tehuantepec** *var.* Santo Domingo Tehuantepec. Oaxaca, SE Mexico
41 S17 **Tehuantepec, Golfo de** *var.* Gulf of Tehuantepec. *gulf* S Mexico
Tehuantepec, Gulf of *see* Tehuantepec, Golfo de
Tehuantepec, Isthmus of *see* Tehuantepec, Istmo de
41 T16 **Tehuantepec, Istmo de** *var.* Isthmus of Tehuantepec. *isthmus* SE Mexico
41 S16 **Tehuantepec, Río** ≈ SE Mexico
191 W10 **Tehuata** *atoll* Îles Tuamotu, C French Polynesia
64 O11 **Teide, Pico de** ▲ Gran Canaria, Islas Canarias, Spain, NE Atlantic Ocean
97 I21 **Teifi** ≈ SW Wales, UK
80 B9 **Teiga Plateau** *plateau* W Sudan
97 J24 **Teignmouth** SW England, UK
Teisen *see* Chech'ŏn
116 H11 **Teiuş** *Ger.* Dreikirchen, *Hung.* Tövis. Alba, C Romania
169 U17 **Tejakula** Bali, C Indonesia
146 H14 **Tejen** *Rus.* Tedzhen. Ahal Welaýaty, S Turkmenistan
146 I15 **Tejen** *Per.* Harīrūd, *Rus.* Tedzhen. ≈ Afghanistan/Iran *see also* Harīrūd
Tejenstroy *see* Tedzhenstroy
35 S14 **Tejon Pass** *pass* California, W USA
Tejo, Rio *see* Tagus
41 O14 **Tejupilco** *var.* Tejupilco de Hidalgo. México, S Mexico
Tejupilco de Hidalgo *see* Tejupilco
184 P7 **Te Kaha** Bay of Plenty, North Island, NZ
29 S14 **Tekamah** Nebraska, C USA
184 I1 **Te Kao** Northland, North Island, NZ
185 F20 **Tekapo** ≈ South Island, NZ
185 F19 **Tekapo, Lake** ◎ South Island, NZ
184 P9 **Te Karaka** Gisborne, North Island, NZ
184 L7 **Te Kauwhata** Waikato, North Island, NZ
41 X12 **Tekax** *var.* Tekax de Álvaro Obregón. Yucatán, SE Mexico
Tekax de Álvaro Obregón *see* Tekax
Teke/Tekendorf *see* Teaca
136 A14 **Teke Burnu** *headland* W Turkey
114 M12 **Teke Deresi** ≈ NW Turkey
146 D10 **Tekedzhik, Gory** *hill range* NW Turkmenistan
145 V14 **Tekeli** Almaty, SE Kazakhstan
145 R7 **Teke, Ozero** ◎ N Kazakhstan
158 I5 **Tekes** Xinjiang Uygur Zizhiqu, NW China
145 W16 **Tekes** Almaty, SE Kazakhstan
Tekes *see* Tekes He
158 H5 **Tekes He** *Rus.* Tekes. ≈ China/Kazakhstan
80 I10 **Tekezē** *var.* Takkaze. ≈ Eritrea/Ethiopia
Tekhtin *see* Tsyakhtsin
136 C10 **Tekirdağ** *It.* Rodosto; *anc.* Bisanthe, Raidestos, Rhaedestus. Tekirdağ, NW Turkey
136 C10 **Tekirdağ** ⬖ *province* NW Turkey
155 N14 **Tekkali** Andhra Pradesh, E India
115 K15 **Tekke Burnu** *Turk.* İlyasbaba Burnu. *headland* NW Turkey
137 Q13 **Tekman** Erzurum, NE Turkey
32 M9 **Tekoa** Washington, NW USA
190 H16 **Te Kou** ▲ Rarotonga, S Cook Islands
Tekrit *see* Tikrīt
171 P12 **Teku** Sulawesi, N Indonesia
184 L9 **Te Kuiti** Waikato, North Island, NZ
42 H4 **Tela** Atlántida, NW Honduras
138 F12 **Telalim** Southern, S Israel
Telanaipura *see* Jambi
137 U10 **T'elavi** E Georgia
138 F10 **Tel Aviv** ⬖ *district* W Israel
Tel Aviv-Jaffa *see* Tel Aviv-Yafo
138 F10 **Tel Aviv-Yafo** *var.* Tel Aviv-Jaffa. Tel Aviv, C Israel
138 F10 **Tel Aviv-Yafo** × Tel Aviv, C Israel
111 E18 **Telč** *Ger.* Teltsch. Vysočina, C Czech Republic
186 B6 **Telefomin** Sandaun, NW PNG
10 J10 **Telegraph Creek** British Columbia, W Canada
190 B10 **Telele** *island* Funafuti Atoll, C Tuvalu
60 J11 **Telêmaco Borba** Paraná, S Brazil
95 E15 **Telemark** ⬖ *county* S Norway
62 J13 **Telén** La Pampa, C Argentina
Teleneshty *see* Teleneşti
116 M9 **Teleneşti** *Rus.* Teleneshty. C Moldova
104 J4 **Teleno, El** ▲ NW Spain
116 I15 **Teleorman** ⬖ *county* S Romania
116 I14 **Teleorman** ≈ S Romania
25 V5 **Telephone** Texas, SW USA
35 U11 **Telescope Peak** ▲ California, W USA
Teles Pirés *see* São Manuel, Rio
97 L19 **Telford** C England, UK
108 L7 **Telfs** Tirol, W Austria
42 I9 **Telica** León, NW Nicaragua
42 J6 **Telica, Río** ≈ C Honduras
76 I13 **Télimélé** Guinée-Maritime, W Guinea
43 O14 **Telire, Río** ≈ Costa Rica/Panama
114 I8 **Telish** *prev.* Azizie. Pleven, N Bulgaria
41 R16 **Telixtlahuaca** *var.* San Francisco Telixtlahuaca. Oaxaca, SE Mexico
10 K13 **Telkwa** British Columbia, SW Canada
25 P4 **Tell** Texas, SW USA
Tell Abiad *see* Tall Abyaḍ
Tell Abiad/Tell Abyad *see* At Tall al Abyaḍ
31 O16 **Tell City** Indiana, N USA
38 M9 **Teller** Alaska, USA
Tell Huqnah *see* Tall Ḥuqnah
155 F20 **Tellicherry** *var.* Thalassery. Kerala, SW India
20 M10 **Tellico Plains** Tennessee, S USA
Tell Kalakh *see* Tall Kalakh
Tell Mardīkh *see* Ebla
54 E11 **Tello** Huila, C Colombia
Tell Shedadi *see* Ash Shadādah
37 Q7 **Telluride** Colorado, C USA
Tel'man/Tel'mansk *see* Gubadag
117 X9 **Tel'manove** Donets'ka Oblast', E Ukraine
162 H6 **Telmen Nuur** ◎ NW Mongolia
Teloekbetoeng *see* Bandarlampung
41 O15 **Teloloapán** Guerrero, S Mexico
Telo Martius *see* Toulon
127 V8 **Telposiz, Gora** ▲ NW Russian Federation
Telschen *see* Telšiai
63 J17 **Telsen** Chubut, S Argentina
118 D11 **Telšiai** *Ger.* Telschen. Telšiai, NW Lithuania
118 D11 **Telšiai** ⬖ *province* NW Lithuania
Teltsch *see* Telč
Telukbetung *see* Bandarlampung
168 H10 **Telukdalam** Pulau Nias, W Indonesia
14 H9 **Temagami** Ontario, S Canada
14 G9 **Temagami, Lake** ◎ Ontario, S Canada

190 H16 **Te Manga** ▲ Rarotonga, S Cook Islands
191 W12 **Tematangi** *atoll* Îles Tuamotu, S French Polynesia
41 X11 **Temax** Yucatán, SE Mexico
171 E14 **Tembagapura** Papua, E Indonesia
122 L9 **Tembenchi** ≈ N Russian Federation
55 P6 **Temblador** Monagas, NE Venezuela
105 N9 **Tembleque** Castilla-La Mancha, C Spain
Temboni *see* Mitemele, Río
35 U16 **Temecula** California, W USA
168 K7 **Temengor, Tasik** ◎ Peninsular Malaysia
112 L9 **Temerin** Serbia, N Serbia and Montenegro (Yugo.)
Temes/Temesch *see* Tamiš
Temeschburg/Temeschwar *see* Timişoara
Temes-Kubin *see* Kovin
Temesvár/Temeswar *see* Timişoara
Teminaboean *see* Teminabuan
171 U12 **Teminabuan** *prev.* Teminaboean. Papua, E Indonesia
145 P17 **Temirlanovka** Yuzhnyy Kazakhstan, S Kazakhstan
145 R10 **Temirtau** *prev.* Samarkandski, Samarkandskoye. Karaganda, C Kazakhstan
14 H10 **Témiscaming** Québec, SE Canada
Témiscamingue, Lac *see* Timiskaming, Lake
15 T8 **Témiscouata, Lac** ◎ Québec, SE Canada
127 N5 **Temnikov** Respublika Mordoviya, W Russian Federation
191 Y13 **Temoe** *island* Îles Gambier, E French Polynesia
183 Q9 **Temora** New South Wales, SE Australia
40 H7 **Témoris** Chihuahua, W Mexico
40 I5 **Temósachic** Chihuahua, N Mexico
187 Q10 **Temotu** *off.* Temotu Province. ⬖ *province* E Solomon Islands
36 L14 **Tempe** Arizona, SW USA
Tempelburg *see* Czaplinek
107 C17 **Tempio Pausania** Sardegna, Italy, C Mediterranean Sea
42 K12 **Tempisque, Río** ≈ NW Costa Rica
25 T9 **Temple** Texas, SW USA
100 O12 **Templehof** × (Berlin) Berlin, NE Germany
97 D19 **Templemore** *Ir.* An Teampall Mór. C Ireland
100 O11 **Templin** Brandenburg, NE Germany
41 P12 **Tempoal** *var.* Tempoal de Sánchez. Veracruz-Llave, E Mexico
Tempoal de Sánchez *see* Tempoal
41 P13 **Tempoal, Río** ≈ C Mexico
83 E14 **Tempué** Moxico, C Angola
126 J14 **Temryuk** Krasnodarskiy Kray, SW Russian Federation
99 G17 **Temse** Oost-Vlaanderen, N Belgium
63 F15 **Temuco** Araucanía, C Chile
185 G20 **Temuka** Canterbury, South Island, NZ
189 P13 **Temwen Island** *island* E Micronesia
56 C6 **Tena** Napo, C Ecuador
41 W13 **Tenabo** Campeche, E Mexico
Tenaghau *see* Aola
25 X7 **Tenaha** Texas, SW USA
39 X13 **Tenake** Chichagof Island, Alaska, USA
155 K16 **Tenāli** Andhra Pradesh, E India
Tenan *see* Ch'ŏnan
41 O14 **Tenancingo** *var.* Tenencingo de Degollado. México, S Mexico
191 X12 **Tenararo** *island* Groupe Actéon, SE French Polynesia
167 N12 **Tenasserim** Tenasserim, S Burma
167 N11 **Tenasserim** *var.* Tanintharyi. ⬖ *division* S Burma
98 O5 **Ten Boer** Groningen, NE Netherlands
97 I21 **Tenby** SW Wales, UK
80 K11 **Tendaho** Afar, NE Ethiopia
103 V14 **Tende** Alpes Maritimes, SE France
151 Q20 **Ten Degree Channel** *strait* Andaman and Nicobar Islands, India, E Indian Ocean
80 F11 **Tendelti** White Nile, E Sudan
76 G8 **Te-n-Dghâmcha, Sebkhet** *var.* Sebkha de Ndrhamcha, Sebkra de Ndaghamcha. *salt lake* W Mauritania
165 P10 **Tendō** Yamagata, Honshū, C Japan
74 H7 **Tendrara** NE Morocco
117 Q11 **Tendrivs'ka Kosa** *spit* S Ukraine
117 Q11 **Tendrivs'ka Zatoka** *gulf* S Ukraine
Tenencingo de Degollado *see* Tenancingo
77 N11 **Ténenkou** Mopti, C Mali
77 W9 **Ténéré** *physical region* C Niger
77 W9 **Ténére, Erg du** *desert* C Niger
64 O11 **Tenerife** *island* Islas Canarias, Spain, NE Atlantic Ocean
74 J5 **Ténès** NW Algeria
170 M15 **Tengah, Kepulauan** *island group* C Indonesia
169 V11 **Tenggarong** Borneo, C Indonesia
162 J15 **Tengger Shamo** *desert* N China
158 L8 **Tenggul, Pulau** *island* Peninsular Malaysia
Tengiz Köl *see* Tengiz, Ozero
145 P9 **Tengiz, Ozero** *Kaz.* Tengiz Köl. *salt lake* C Kazakhstan
76 M14 **Tengréla** *var.* Tingréla. N Ivory Coast
160 M14 **Tengxian** *var.* Teng Xian. Guangxi Zhuangzu Zizhiqu, S China
194 H2 **Teniente Rodolfo Marsh** *Chilean research station* South Shetland Islands, Antarctica
32 G9 **Tenino** Washington, NW USA
112 I9 **Tenja** Osijek-Baranja, E Croatia
188 B16 **Tenjo, Mount** ▲ W Guam
155 H23 **Tenkāsi** Tamil Nādu, SE India
79 N24 **Tenke** Katanga, SE Dem. Rep. Congo
Tenke *see* Tinca
123 Q7 **Tenkeli** Respublika Sakha (Yakutiya), NE Russian Federation
27 R10 **Tenkiller Ferry Lake** ▣ Oklahoma, C USA
77 Q13 **Tenkodogo** S Burkina
181 Q5 **Tennant Creek** Northern Territory, C Australia
20 G9 **Tennessee** *off.* State of Tennessee; also known as The Volunteer State. ⬖ *state* SE USA
37 R5 **Tennessee Pass** *pass* Colorado, C USA
20 H10 **Tennessee River** ≈ S USA
23 N2 **Tennessee Tombigbee Waterway** *canal* Alabama/Mississippi, S USA
99 K22 **Tenneville** Luxembourg, SE Belgium
92 M11 **Tenniöjoki** ≈ NE Finland
92 L9 **Tenojoki** *Lapp.* Deatnu, *Nor.* Tana. ≈ Finland/Norway **see also** Deatnu
169 U7 **Tenom** Sabah, East Malaysia
Tenos *see* Tínos
41 V15 **Tenosique** *var.* Tenosique de Pino Suárez. Tabasco, SE Mexico
Tenosique de Pino Suárez *see* Tenosique
22 I6 **Tensas River** ≈ Louisiana, S USA
23 O8 **Tensaw River** ≈ Alabama, S USA
74 E7 **Tensift** *seasonal river* W Morocco
171 O12 **Tentena** *var.* Tenteno. Sulawesi, C Indonesia
Tenteno *see* Tentena
183 U4 **Tenterfield** New South Wales, SE Australia
23 X16 **Ten Thousand Islands** *island group* Florida, SE USA
60 H9 **Teodoro Sampaio** São Paulo, S Brazil
59 N19 **Teófilo Otoni** *var.* Theophilo Ottoni. Minas Gerais, NE Brazil
116 K5 **Teofipol'** Khmel'nyts'ka Oblast', W Ukraine
191 Q8 **Teohatu** Tahiti, W French Polynesia
41 P14 **Teotihuacán** *ruins* México, S Mexico
Teotilán *see* Teotitlán del Camino
41 Q15 **Teotitlán del Camino** *var.* Teotilán. Oaxaca, S Mexico
190 G12 **Tepa** Île Uvea, E Wallis and Futuna
191 P8 **Tepaee, Récif** *reef* Tahiti, W French Polynesia
40 L14 **Tepalcatepec** Michoacán de Ocampo, SW Mexico
190 A16 **Tepa Point** *headland* SW Niue
40 L13 **Tepatitlán** *var.* Tepatitlán de Morelos. Jalisco, SW Mexico
Tepatitlán de Morelos *see* Tepatitlán
40 J9 **Tepehuanes** *var.* Santa Catarina de Tepehuanes. Durango, C Mexico
Tepelena *see* Tepelenë
113 L22 **Tepelenë** *var.* Tepelena, *It.* Tepeleni. Gjirokastër, S Albania
Tepeleni *see* Tepelenë
40 K12 **Tepic** Nayarit, C Mexico
111 C15 **Teplice** *Ger.* Teplitz; *prev.* Teplice-Šanov, Teplitz-Schönau. Ústecký Kraj, NW Czech Republic
Teplice-Šanov/Teplitz/Teplitz-Schönau *see* Teplice
117 O7 **Teplyk** Vinnyts'ka Oblast', C Ukraine
123 R10 **Teplyy Klyuch** Respublika Sakha (Yakutiya), NE Russian Federation
40 E5 **Tepoca, Cabo** *headland* NW Mexico
191 W9 **Tepoto** *island* Îles du Désappointement, C French Polynesia
92 L11 **Tepsa** Lappi, N Finland
190 B8 **Tepuka** *atoll* Funafuti Atoll, C Tuvalu
184 N7 **Te Puke** Bay of Plenty, North Island, NZ
40 L13 **Tequila** Jalisco, SW Mexico
41 O13 **Tequisquiapan** Querétaro de Arteaga, C Mexico
104 J5 **Tera** ≈ NW Spain
77 Q12 **Téra** Tillabéri, W Niger
191 V1 **Teraina** *prev.* Washington Island. *atoll* Line Islands, E Kiribati
81 F15 **Terakeka** Bahr el Gabel, S Sudan
107 J14 **Teramo** *anc.* Interamna. Abruzzo, C Italy
98 P7 **Ter Apel** Groningen, NE Netherlands
104 H11 **Tera, Ribeira de** ≈ S Portugal
185 K14 **Terawhiti, Cape** *headland* North Island, NZ
98 N12 **Terborg** Gelderland, E Netherlands
137 P13 **Tercan** Erzincan, NE Turkey
64 O2 **Terceira** × Terceira, Azores, Portugal, NE Atlantic Ocean
64 O2 **Terceira** *var.* Ilha Terceira. *island* Azores, Portugal, NE Atlantic Ocean
Terceira, Ilha *see* Terceira
116 K6 **Terebovlya** Ternopil's'ka Oblast', W Ukraine
127 O15 **Terek** ≈ SW Russian Federation
Terekhovka *see* Tsyerakhowka
147 R9 **Terek-Say** Dzhalal-Abadskaya Oblast', W Kyrgyzstan
145 Z10 **Terekty** *prev.* Alekseevka, Alekseyevka. Vostochnyy Kazakhstan, E Kazakhstan
168 L7 **Terengganu** *var.* Trengganu. ⬖ *state* Peninsular Malaysia
127 X7 **Terensay** Orenburgskaya Oblast', W Russian Federation
58 N13 **Teresina** *var.* Therezina. *state capital* Piauí, NE Brazil
60 P9 **Teresópolis** Rio de Janeiro, SE Brazil
110 P12 **Terespol** Lubelskie, E Poland
191 V16 **Terevaka, Maunga** ☒ Easter Island, Chile, E Pacific Ocean
103 P3 **Tergnier** Aisne, N France
43 O14 **Teribe, Río** ≈ NW Panama
124 K3 **Teriberka** Murmanskaya Oblast', NW Russian Federation
Terijoki *see* Zelenogorsk
Terinkot *see* Tarīn Kowt
145 O10 **Terisakkan** *Kaz.* Terisaqqan. ≈ C Kazakhstan
Terisaqqan *see* Terisakkan
24 K12 **Terlingua** Texas, SW USA
24 K11 **Terlingua Creek** ≈ Texas, SW USA
62 K7 **Termas de Río Hondo** Santiago del Estero, N Argentina
136 M11 **Terme** Samsun, N Turkey
Termez *see* Termiz
Termia *see* Kýthnos
107 J23 **Termini Imerese** *anc.* Thermae Himerenses. Sicilia, Italy, C Mediterranean Sea
41 V14 **Términos, Laguna de** *lagoon* SE Mexico
77 X10 **Termit-Kaoboul** Zinder, C Niger
147 O14 **Termiz** *Rus.* Termez. Surxondaryo Viloyati, S Uzbekistan
107 L15 **Termoli** Molise, C Italy
Termonde *see* Dendermonde
98 P5 **Termunten** Groningen, NE Netherlands
171 R11 **Ternate** Pulau Ternate, E Indonesia
109 T5 **Ternberg** Oberösterreich, N Austria
99 E15 **Terneuzen** *var.* Neuzen. Zeeland, SW Netherlands
123 T14 **Terney** Primorskiy Kray, SE Russian Federation
107 I14 **Terni** *anc.* Interamna Nahars. Umbria, C Italy
109 X6 **Ternitz** Niederösterreich, E Austria
117 V7 **Ternivka** Dnipropetrovs'ka Oblast', E Ukraine
116 K6 **Ternopil'** *Pol.* Tarnopol, *Rus.* Ternopol'. Ternopil's'ka Oblast', W Ukraine
Ternopil' *see* Ternopil's'ka Oblast'
116 I6 **Ternopil's'ka Oblast'** *var.* Ternopil', *Rus.* Ternopol'skaya Oblast'. ⬖ *province* NW Ukraine
Ternopol' *see* Ternopil'
Ternopol'skaya Oblast' *see* Ternopil's'ka Oblast'
123 U13 **Terpeniya, Mys** *headland* Ostrov Sakhalin, SE Russian Federation
Térraba, Río *see* Grande de Térraba, Río
10 J13 **Terrace** British Columbia, W Canada
12 D12 **Terrace Bay** Ontario, S Canada
107 I16 **Terracina** Lazio, C Italy
93 F14 **Terråk** Troms, N Norway
26 M13 **Terral** Oklahoma, C USA
107 B19 **Terralba** Sardegna, Italy, C Mediterranean Sea
Terranova di Sicilia *see* Gela
Terranova Pausania *see* Olbia
105 W5 **Terrassa** *Cast.* Tarrasa. Cataluña, E Spain
15 O12 **Terrebonne** Québec, SE Canada
22 J11 **Terrebonne Bay** *bay* Louisiana, SE USA
31 N14 **Terre Haute** Indiana, N USA
25 U6 **Terrell** Texas, SW USA
Terre Neuve *see* Newfoundland and Labrador
33 Q14 **Terreton** Idaho, NW USA
103 T7 **Territoire-de-Belfort** ⬖ *department* E France
33 X9 **Terry** Montana, NW USA
28 I9 **Terry Peak** ▲ South Dakota, N USA
136 H14 **Tersakan Gölü** ◎ C Turkey
98 J4 **Terschelling** *Fris.* Skylge. *island* Waddeneilanden, N Netherlands
78 H10 **Tersef** Chari-Baguirmi, C Chad
147 X8 **Terskey Ala-Too, Khrebet** ⛰ Kazakhstan/Kyrgyzstan
Terter *see* Tärtär
105 R8 **Teruel** *anc.* Turba. Aragón, E Spain
105 R7 **Teruel** ⬖ *province* Aragón, E Spain
114 M7 **Tervel** *prev.* Kurtbunar, *Rom.* Curtbunar. Dobrich, NE Bulgaria
93 M16 **Tervo** Itä-Suomi, C Finland
92 L13 **Tervola** Lappi, NW Finland
Tervueren *see* Tervuren
99 H18 **Tervuren** *var.* Tervueren. Vlaams Brabant, C Belgium
112 H11 **Tešanj** Federacija Bosna I Hercegovina, N Bosnia and Herzegovina
Teschen *see* Cieszyn
83 M19 **Tesenane** Inhambane, S Mozambique
80 I9 **Teseney** *var.* Tessenei. W Eritrea
39 P5 **Teshekpuk Lake** ◎ Alaska, USA
162 K6 **Teshig** Bulgan, N Mongolia
165 T2 **Teshio** Hokkaidō, NE Japan
165 T2 **Teshio-sanchi** ⛰ Hokkaidō, NE Japan
Těšín *see* Cieszyn
Tesio Gawa *see* Teshio-gawa
112 H11 **Teslić** Republika Srpska, N Bosnia and Herzegovina
10 I9 **Teslin** Yukon Territory, W Canada
10 I8 **Teslin** ≈ British Columbia/Yukon Territory, W Canada
77 Q8 **Tessalit** Kidal, NE Mali
77 V12 **Tessaoua** Maradi, S Niger
99 J17 **Tessenderlo** Limburg, NE Belgium
Tessenei *see* Teseney
14 L7 **Tessier, Lac** ◎ Québec, SE Canada
Tessin *see* Ticino
97 M23 **Test** ≈ S England, UK
Testama *see* Tõstamaa
55 P4 **Testigos, Islas los** *island group* N Venezuela
37 S10 **Tesuque** New Mexico, SW USA
103 O17 **Têt** *var.* Tet. ≈ S France
54 G5 **Tetas, Cerro de las** ▲ NW Venezuela
83 M15 **Tete** Tete, NW Mozambique
83 M15 **Tete** *off.* Província de Tete. ⬖ *province* NW Mozambique
11 N15 **Tête Jaune Cache** British Columbia, SW Canada
184 O8 **Te Teko** Bay of Plenty, North Island, NZ
186 K9 **Tetepare** *island* New Georgia Islands, NW Solomon Islands
Teterev *see* Teteriv
116 M5 **Teteriv** *Rus.* Teterev. ≈ N Ukraine
100 M9 **Teterow** Mecklenburg-Vorpommern, NE Germany
114 I9 **Teteven** Lovech, N Bulgaria
191 T10 **Tetiaroa** *atoll* Îles du Vent, W French Polynesia
105 P14 **Tetica de Bacares** ▲ S Spain
Tetiyev *see* Tetiyiv
117 O6 **Tetiyiv** *Rus.* Tetiyev. Kyyivs'ka Oblast', N Ukraine
39 T10 **Tetlin** Alaska, USA
33 R8 **Teton River** ≈ Montana, NW USA
74 G5 **Tétouan** *var.* Tetouan, Tetuán. N Morocco
Tetova/Tetovë *see* Tetovo
114 L7 **Tetovo** Razgrad, N Bulgaria
113 N18 **Tetovo** *Alb.* Tetova, Tetovë, *Turk.* Kalkandelen. NW FYR Macedonia
115 E20 **Tetrázio** ⛰ S Greece
Tetschen *see* Děčín
Tetuán *see* Tétouan
191 Q8 **Tetufera, Mont** ▲ Tahiti, W French Polynesia
127 R4 **Tetyushi** Respublika Tatarstan, W Russian Federation
108 I7 **Teufen** Sankt Gallen, NE Switzerland
40 L12 **Teul** *var.* Teul de Gonzáles Ortega. Zacatecas, C Mexico
107 B21 **Teulada** Sardegna, Italy, C Mediterranean Sea
Teul de Gonzáles Ortega *see* Teul
11 X16 **Teulon** Manitoba, S Canada
42 I7 **Teupasenti** El Paraíso, S Honduras
165 S2 **Teuri-tō** *island* NE Japan
100 G13 **Teutoburger Wald** *Eng.* Teutoburg Forest. *hill range* NW Germany
Teutoburg Forest *see* Teutoburger Wald
93 K17 **Teuva** *Swe.* Östermark. Länsi-Suomi, W Finland
107 H15 **Tevere** *Eng.* Tiber. ≈ C Italy
138 G9 **Teverya** *var.* Tiberias, Tverya. Northern, N Israel
96 K13 **Teviot** ≈ SE Scotland, UK
Tevli *see* Tewli
122 H11 **Tevriz** Omskaya Oblast', C Russian Federation
185 B24 **Te Waewae Bay** *bay* South Island, NZ
97 L21 **Tewkesbury** C England, UK
119 F19 **Tewli** *Rus.* Tevli. Brestskaya Voblasts', SW Belarus
159 U12 **Têwo** *var.* Dêngkagoin. Gansu, C China
25 U12 **Texana, Lake** ◎ Texas, SW USA
27 S14 **Texarkana** Arkansas, C USA
25 X5 **Texarkana** Texas, SW USA
25 N9 **Texas** *off.* State of Texas; also known as The Lone Star State. ⬖ *state* S USA
25 W12 **Texas City** Texas, SW USA
41 P14 **Texcoco** México, C Mexico
98 I6 **Texel** *island* Waddeneilanden, NW Netherlands
26 H8 **Texhoma** Oklahoma, C USA
25 N1 **Texhoma** Texas, SW USA
37 W12 **Texico** New Mexico, SW USA
24 L1 **Texline** Texas, SW USA
41 P14 **Texmelucan** *var.* San Martín Texmelucan. Puebla, S Mexico
27 O13 **Texoma, Lake** ◎ Oklahoma/Texas, C USA
25 N9 **Texon** Texas, SW USA
83 J23 **Teyateyaneng** NW Lesotho
124 M16 **Teykovo** Ivanovskaya Oblast', W Russian Federation
126 M16 **Teza** ≈ W Russian Federation
41 Q13 **Teziutlán** Puebla, S Mexico
153 W12 **Tezpur** Assam, NE India
9 N10 **Tha-Anne** ≈ Nunavut, NE Canada
83 K23 **Thabana Ntlenyana** *var.* Thabantshonyana, Mount Ntlenyana. ▲ E Lesotho
Thabantshonyana *see* Thabana Ntlenyana
83 J23 **Thaba Putsoa** ▲ C Lesotho
167 Q8 **Tha Bo** Nong Khai, E Thailand
103 T12 **Thabor, Pic du** ▲ E France
Tha Chin *see* Samut Sakhon
166 M7 **Thagaya** Pegu, C Burma
Thai, Ao *see* Thailand, Gulf of
167 T6 **Thai Binh** Thai Binh, N Vietnam
167 S7 **Thai Hoa** Nghê An, N Vietnam
167 P9 **Thailand** *off.* Kingdom of Thailand, *Th.* Prathet Thai; *prev.* Siam. ◆ *monarchy* SE Asia
167 P13 **Thailand, Gulf of** *var.* Gulf of Siam, *Th.* Ao Thai, *Vtn.* Vinh Thai Lan. *gulf* SE Asia
Thai Lan, Vinh *see* Thailand, Gulf of
167 T6 **Thai Nguyên** Bac Thai, N Vietnam
167 S8 **Thakhèk** *prev.* Muang Khammouan. Khammouan, C Laos
153 S13 **Thakurgaon** Rajshahi, NW Bangladesh
149 S6 **Thal** North-West Frontier Province, NW Pakistan
166 M15 **Thalang** Phuket, SW Thailand
Thalassery *see* Tellicherry
167 Q10 **Thalat Khae** Nakhon Ratchasima, C Thailand
109 Q5 **Thalgau** Salzburg, NW Austria
108 G7 **Thalwil** Zürich, NW Switzerland
83 I20 **Thamaga** Kweneng, SE Botswana
Thamarīd *see* Thamarīt
141 V13 **Thamarīt** *var.* Thamarīd, Thumrayt. SW Oman
141 P16 **Thamar, Jabal** ▲ SW Yemen
184 M6 **Thames** Waikato, North Island, NZ
14 D17 **Thames** ≈ Ontario, S Canada
97 O22 **Thames** ≈ S England, UK
184 M6 **Thames, Firth of** *gulf* North Island, NZ
14 D17 **Thamesville** Ontario, S Canada
141 U13 **Thamūd** N Yemen
167 N9 **Thanbyuzayat** Mon State, S Burma
152 I9 **Thānesar** Haryāna, NW India
167 T7 **Thanh Hoa** Thanh Hoa, N Vietnam
Thanintari Taungdan *see* Bilauktaung Range
155 I21 **Thanjāvūr** *prev.* Tanjore. Tamil Nādu, SE India
Thanlwin *see* Salween
103 U7 **Thann** Haut-Rhin, NE France
167 O16 **Tha Nong Phrom** Phatthalung, SW Thailand
167 N13 **Thap Sakae** *var.* Thap Sakau. Prachuap Khiri Khan, SW Thailand
Thap Sakau *see* Thap Sakae
98 L10 **'t Harde** Gelderland, E Netherlands
152 D11 **Thar Desert** *var.* Great Indian Desert, Indian Desert. *desert* India/Pakistan
181 V10 **Thargomindah** Queensland, C Australia
150 D11 **Thar Pārkar** *desert* SE Pakistan
139 S7 **Tharthār al Furāt, Qanāt ath** *canal* C Iraq
139 R7 **Tharthār, Buḩayrat ath** ◎ C Iraq
139 R5 **Tharthār, Wādī ath** *dry watercourse* N Iraq
167 N13 **Tha Sae** Chumphon, SW Thailand
167 N15 **Tha Sala** Nakhon Si Thammarat, SW Thailand
114 I13 **Thásos** Thásos, E Greece
115 I14 **Thásos** *island* E Greece
37 N14 **Thatcher** Arizona, SW USA
167 T5 **Thất Khê** *var.* Trâng Dinh. Lang Sơn, N Vietnam
166 M8 **Thaton** Mon State, S Burma
167 S9 **That Phanom** Nakhon Phanom, E Thailand
167 R10 **Tha Tum** Surin, E Thailand
103 P16 **Thau, Bassin de** *var.* Étang de Thau. ◎ S France
Thau, Étang de *see* Thau, Bassin de
166 L3 **Thaungdut** Sagaing, N Burma
167 O8 **Thaungyin** *Th.* Mae Nam Moei. ≈ Burma/Thailand
167 R8 **Tha Uthen** Nakhon Phanom, E Thailand
109 W2 **Thaya** *var.* Dyje. ≈ Austria/Czech Republic **see also** Dyje
27 V8 **Thayer** Missouri, C USA
166 L6 **Thayetmyo** Magwe, C Burma
33 S15 **Thayne** Wyoming, C USA
166 M5 **Thazi** Mandalay, C Burma
Thebes *see* Thíva
44 L5 **The Carlton** *var.* Abraham Bay. Mayaguana, SE Bahamas
45 O14 **The Crane** *var.* Crane. S Barbados
32 I11 **The Dalles** Oregon, NW USA
28 M14 **Thedford** Nebraska, C USA
The Hague *see* 's-Gravenhage
Theiss *see* Tisa/Tisza
8 M9 **Thelon** ≈ Northwest Territories/Nunavut, N Canada
11 V15 **Theodore** Saskatchewan, S Canada
23 N8 **Theodore** Alabama, S USA
36 L13 **Theodore Roosevelt Lake** ▣ Arizona, SW USA
Theodosia *see* Feodosiya
Theophilo Ottoni *see* Teófilo Otoni
11 V13 **The Pas** Manitoba, C Canada
31 T14 **The Plains** Ohio, N USA
Thera *see* Thíra
172 H17 **Thérèse, Île** *island* Inner Islands, NE Seychelles
Therezina *see* Teresina
115 L20 **Thérma** Ikaría, Dodekánisos, Greece, Aegean Sea
Thermae Himerenses *see* Termini Imerese
Thermae Pannonicae *see* Baden
Thermaic Gulf/Thermaicus Sinus *see* Thermaïkós Kólpos
121 Q8 **Thermaïkós Kólpos** *Eng.* Thermaic Gulf; *anc.* Thermaicus Sinus. *gulf* N Greece
Thermiá *see* Kýthnos
115 L17 **Thermí** Lésvos, E Greece
115 E18 **Thérmo** Dytikí Ellás, C Greece
33 V14 **Thermopolis** Wyoming, C USA
183 P10 **The Rock** New South Wales, SE Australia
195 O5 **Theron Mountains** ⛰ Antarctica
115 G18 **Thespiés** Stereá Ellás, C Greece
115 E16 **Thessalía** *Eng.* Thessaly. ⬖ *region* C Greece
14 C10 **Thessalon** Ontario, S Canada
115 G14 **Thessaloníki** *Eng.* Salonica, Salonika, *SCr.* Solun, *Turk.* Selânik. Kentrikí Makedonía, N Greece
115 G14 **Thessaloníki** × Kentrikí Makedonía, N Greece
Thessaly *see* Thessalía
97 P20 **Thetford** E England, UK
15 R11 **Thetford-Mines** Québec, SE Canada
113 K17 **Theth** *var.* Thethi. Shkodër, N Albania
Thethi *see* Theth
99 L20 **Theux** Liège, E Belgium
45 V9 **The Valley** ○ (Anguilla) E Anguilla
27 N10 **The Village** Oklahoma, C USA
25 W10 **The Woodlands** Texas, SW USA
Thiamis *see* Thýamis
Thian Shan *see* Tien Shan
22 J9 **Thibodaux** Louisiana, S USA
29 S3 **Thief Lake** ◎ Minnesota, N USA
29 S3 **Thief River** ≈ Minnesota, N USA
29 S3 **Thief River Falls** Minnesota, N USA
Thièle *see* La Thielle
32 G14 **Thielsen, Mount** ▲ Oregon, NW USA
Thielt *see* Tielt
106 G7 **Thiene** Veneto, NE Italy
Thienen *see* Tienen
103 P11 **Thiers** Puy-de-Dôme, C France
76 F11 **Thiès** W Senegal
81 I19 **Thika** Central, S Kenya
Thikombia *see* Cikobia
151 K18 **Thiladhunmathi Atoll** *var.* Tiladummati Atoll. *atoll* N Maldives
Thimbu *see* Thimphu
153 T11 **Thimphu** *var.* Thimbu; *prev.* Tashi Chho Dzong. ● (Bhutan) W Bhutan
92 H2 **Thingeyri** Vestfirdhir, NW Iceland
92 I3 **Thingvellir** Sudhurland, SW Iceland
187 Q17 **Thio** Province Sud, C New Caledonia
103 T4 **Thionville** *Ger.* Diedenhofen. Moselle, NE France
115 K22 **Thíra** Thíra, Kykládes, Greece, Aegean Sea
115 K22 **Thíra** *prev.* Santorin, Santoríni, *anc.* Thera. *island* Kykládes, Greece, Aegean Sea
115 J22 **Thirasía** *island* Kykládes, Greece, Aegean Sea
97 M16 **Thirsk** N England, UK
14 F12 **Thirty Thousand Islands** *island group* Ontario, S Canada
Thiruvanathapuram *see* Trivandrum
95 F20 **Thisted** Viborg, NW Denmark
Thistil Fjord *see* Thistilfjördhur
92 L1 **Thistilfjördhur** *var.* Thistil Fjord. *fjord* NE Iceland
182 G9 **Thistle Island** *island* South Australia
Thithia *see* Cicia
Thiukhaoluang Phrahang *see* Luang Prabang Range
115 G18 **Thíva** *Eng.* Thebes; *prev.* Thívai. Stereá Ellás, C Greece
Thívai *see* Thíva
102 M12 **Thiviers** Dordogne, SW France
92 J4 **Thjórsá** ≈ C Iceland
9 N10 **Thlewiaza** ≈ Nunavut, NE Canada
8 L10 **Thoa** ≈ Northwest Territories, NW Canada
99 G14 **Tholen** Zeeland, SW Netherlands
99 F14 **Tholen** *island* SW Netherlands
26 L10 **Thomas** Oklahoma, C USA
21 T3 **Thomas** West Virginia, NE USA
27 U3 **Thomas Hill Reservoir** ▣ Missouri, C USA
23 S5 **Thomaston** Georgia, SE USA
19 R7 **Thomaston** Maine, NE USA
25 T12 **Thomaston** Texas, SW USA
23 O6 **Thomasville** Alabama, S USA
23 T8 **Thomasville** Georgia, SE USA
21 S9 **Thomasville** North Carolina, SE USA
35 N5 **Thomes Creek** ≈ California, W USA
11 W12 **Thompson** Manitoba, C Canada
29 R4 **Thompson** North Dakota, N USA
33 O8 **Thompson Falls** Montana, NW USA
29 Q10 **Thompson, Lake** ◎ South Dakota, N USA
34 M3 **Thompson Peak** ▲ California, W USA
27 S2 **Thompson River** ≈ Missouri, C USA
185 A22 **Thompson Sound** *sound* South Island, NZ
8 J5 **Thomsen** ≈ Banks Island, Northwest Territories, NW Canada
23 V4 **Thomson** Georgia, SE USA
103 T10 **Thonon-les-Bains** Haute-Savoie, E France
103 O15 **Thoré** *var.* Thore. ≈ S France
37 P11 **Thoreau** New Mexico, SW USA
Thorenburg *see* Turda
92 J3 **Thórisvatn** ◎ C Iceland
92 P4 **Thor, Kapp** *headland* S Svalbard
92 I4 **Thorlákshöfn** Sudhurland, SW Iceland
Thorn *see* Toruń
25 T10 **Thorndale** Texas, SW USA
14 H10 **Thorne** Ontario, S Canada
97 J14 **Thornhill** S Scotland, UK
25 U8 **Thornton** Texas, SW USA
Thornton Island *see* Millennium Island
14 H16 **Thorold** Ontario, S Canada
32 I9 **Thorp** Washington, NW USA
195 S3 **Thorshavnheiane** *physical region* Antarctica
92 L1 **Thórshöfn** Nordhurland Eystra, NE Iceland
Thospitis *see* Van Gölü
167 S14 **Thôt Nôt** Cân Thơ, S Vietnam
102 K8 **Thouars** Deux-Sèvres, W France
153 X14 **Thoubal** Manipur, NE India
102 K9 **Thouet** ≈ W France
Thoune *see* Thun
18 H7 **Thousand Islands** *island* Canada/USA
35 S15 **Thousand Oaks** California, W USA
114 L12 **Thrace** *cultural region* SE Europe
114 J13 **Thracian Sea** *Gk.* Thrakikó Pélagos; *anc.* Thracium Mare. *sea* Greece/Turkey
Thracium Mare/Thrakikó Pélagos *see* Thracian Sea
Thrá Lí, Bá *see* Tralee Bay
33 R11 **Three Forks** Montana, NW USA

◆ Country ● Country Capital ◇ Dependent Territory ○ Dependent Territory Capital ⬖ Administrative Region × International Airport ▲ Mountain ⛰ Mountain Range ☒ Volcano ≈ River ◎ Lake ▣ Reservoir

160 M8 **Three Gorges Dam** *dam* Hubei, C China
11 Q16 **Three Hills** Alberta, SW Canada
183 N15 **Three Hummock Island** *island* Tasmania, SE Australia
184 H1 **Three Kings Islands** *island group* N NZ
192 K10 **Three Kings Rise** *undersea feature* W Pacific Ocean
77 O18 **Three Points, Cape** *headland* S Ghana
31 P10 **Three Rivers** Michigan, N USA
25 S13 **Three Rivers** Texas, SW USA
83 G24 **Three Sisters** Northern Cape, SW South Africa
32 H13 **Three Sisters** ▲ Oregon, NW USA
187 N10 **Three Sisters Islands** *island group* SE Solomon Islands
Thrissur *see* Trichūr
25 Q6 **Throckmorton** Texas, SW USA
180 M10 **Throssell, Lake** *salt lake* Western Australia
115 K25 **Thrýptis** ▲ Kríti, Greece, E Mediterranean Sea
167 T13 **Thu Dâu Môt** *var.* Phu Cuong. Sông Be, S Vietnam
167 S6 **Thu Do** ✕ (Ha Nôi) Ha Nôi, N Vietnam
99 G21 **Thuin** Hainaut, S Belgium
149 Q12 **Thul** Sind, SE Pakistan
Thule *see* Qaanaaq
83 J18 **Thuli** *var.* Tuli. ≈ S Zimbabwe
Thumrayt *see* Thamarīt
108 D9 **Thun** *Fr.* Thoune. Bern, W Switzerland
12 C12 **Thunder Bay** Ontario, S Canada
30 M1 **Thunder Bay** *lake bay* S Canada
31 R6 **Thunder Bay** *lake bay* Michigan, N USA
31 R6 **Thunder Bay River** ≈ Michigan, N USA
27 N11 **Thunderbird, Lake** ▣ Oklahoma, C USA
28 L8 **Thunder Butte Creek** ≈ South Dakota, N USA
108 E9 **Thuner See** ◎ C Switzerland
167 N15 **Thung Song** *var.* Cha Mai. Nakhon Si Thammarat, SW Thailand
108 H7 **Thur** ≈ N Switzerland
108 G6 **Thurgau** *Fr.* Thurgovie. ⬖ *canton* NE Switzerland
Thurgovie *see* Thurgau
Thuringe *see* Thüringen
108 J7 **Thüringen** Vorarlberg, W Austria
101 J17 **Thüringen** *Eng.* Thuringia, *Fr.* Thuringe. ⬖ *state* C Germany
101 J17 **Thüringer Wald** *Eng.* Thuringian Forest. ▲▲ C Germany
Thuringia *see* Thüringen
Thuringian Forest *see* Thüringer Wald
97 D19 **Thurles** *Ir.* Durlas. S Ireland
21 W2 **Thurmont** Maryland, NE USA
Thurø *see* Thurø By
95 H24 **Thurø By** *var.* Thurø. Fyn, C Denmark
14 M12 **Thurso** Québec, SE Canada
96 J6 **Thurso** N Scotland, UK
194 I10 **Thurston Island** *island* Antarctica
108 I9 **Thusis** Graubünden, S Switzerland
115 C15 **Thýamis** *var.* Thiamis. ≈ W Greece
95 E21 **Thyborøn** *var.* Tyborøn. Ringkøbing, W Denmark
195 U3 **Thyer Glacier** *glacier* Antarctica
115 L20 **Thýmaina** *island* Dodekánisos, Greece, Aegean Sea
83 N15 **Thyolo** *var.* Cholo. Southern, S Malawi
183 U6 **Tia** New South Wales, SE Australia
54 H5 **Tía Juana** Zulia, NW Venezuela
Tiancheng *see* Chongyang
160 J14 **Tiandong** *var.* Pingma. Guangxi Zhuangzu Zizhiqu, S China
161 O3 **Tianjin** *var.* Tientsin. Tianjin Shi, E China
Tianjin *see* Tianjin Shi
161 P3 **Tianjin Shi** *var.* Jin, Tianjin, T'ien-ching, Tientsin. ⬖ *municipality* E China
159 S10 **Tianjun** *var.* Xinyuan. Qinghai, C China
160 J13 **Tianlin** *var.* Leli. Guangxi Zhuangzu Zizhiqu, S China
Tian Shan *see* Tien Shan
159 W11 **Tianshui** Gansu, C China
150 I7 **Tianshuihai** Xinjiang Uygur Zizhiqu, W China
161 S10 **Tiantai** Zhejiang, SE China
160 J14 **Tianyang** *var.* Tianzhou. Guangxi Zhuangzu Zizhiqu, S China
Tianzhou *see* Tianyang
159 U9 **Tianzhu** *var.* Huazangsi, Tianzhu Zangzu Zizhixian. Gansu, C China
Tianzhu Zangzu Zizhixian *see* Tianzhu
191 Q7 **Tiarei** Tahiti, W French Polynesia
74 J6 **Tiaret** *var.* Tihert. NW Algeria
77 N17 **Tiassalé** S Ivory Coast
192 I16 **Ti'avea** Upolu, SE Samoa
Tiba *see* Chiba
60 J11 **Tibagi** *var.* Tibaji. Paraná, S Brazil
60 J10 **Tibagi, Rio** *var.* Rio Tibají. ≈ S Brazil
Tibaji *see* Tibagi
Tibají, Rio *see* Tibagi, Rio
139 Q9 **Tibal, Wādī** *dry watercourse* S Iraq
54 G9 **Tibaná** Boyacá, C Colombia
79 F14 **Tibati** Adamaoua, N Cameroon
76 K15 **Tibé, Pic de** ▲ SE Guinea
Tiber *see* Tevere, Italy
Tiber *see* Tivoli, Italy
Tiberias *see* Teverya
138 G8 **Tiberias, Lake** *var.* Chinnereth, Sea of Bahr Tabariya, Sea of Galilee, *Ar.* Bahrat Tabariya, *Heb.* Yam Kinneret. ◎ N Israel
75 R12 **Tibesti** *var.* Tibesti Massif, *Ar.* Tibistī. ▲▲ N Africa
Tibesti Massif *see* Tibesti
Tibetan Autonomous Region *see* Xizang Zizhiqu
Tibet, Plateau of *see* Qingzang Gaoyuan
Tibistī *see* Tibesti
14 K7 **Tiblemont, Lac** ◎ Québec, SE Canada
139 X9 **Ṭīb, Nahr aṭ** ≈ S Iraq
Tibnī *see* At Tibnī
182 L4 **Tibooburra** New South Wales, SE Australia
95 L18 **Tibro** Västra Götaland, S Sweden
40 E5 **Tiburón, Isla** *var.* Isla del Tiburón. *island* NW Mexico
Tiburón, Isla del *see* Tiburón, Isla
23 W14 **Tice** Florida, SE USA
Tichau *see* Tychy
114 L8 **Ticha, Yazovir** ◎ NE Bulgaria
76 K9 **Tichit** *var.* Tichitt. Tagant, C Mauritania
Tichitt *see* Tichit
108 G11 **Ticino** *Fr./Ger.* Tessin. ⬖ *canton* S Switzerland
106 D8 **Ticino** ≈ Italy/Switzerland
108 H11 **Ticino** *Ger.* Tessin. ≈ SW Switzerland
Ticinum *see* Pavia
41 X12 **Ticul** Yucatán, SE Mexico
95 K18 **Tidaholm** Västra Götaland, S Sweden
Tidjikdja *see* Tidjikja
76 J8 **Tidjikja** *var.* Tidjikdja; *prev.* Fort-Cappolani. Tagant, C Mauritania
Tidore *see* Soasiu
171 R11 **Tidore, Pulau** *island* E Indonesia
Tîdra, Île *see* Et Tîdra
77 N16 **Tiébissou** *var.* Tiebissou. C Ivory Coast
Tiefa *see* Diaobingshan
108 I9 **Tiefencastel** Graubünden, S Switzerland
Tiegenhof *see* Nowy Dwór Gdański
T'ieh-ling *see* Tieling
98 K13 **Tiel** Gelderland, C Netherlands
163 W7 **Tieli** Heilongjiang, NE China
163 V11 **Tieling** *var.* T'ieh-ling. Liaoning, NE China
152 L4 **Tielongtan** China/India
99 D17 **Tielt** *var.* Thielt. West-Vlaanderen, W Belgium
T'ien-ching *see* Tianjin Shi
99 I18 **Tienen** *var.* Thienen, *Fr.* Tirlemont. Vlaams Brabant, C Belgium
Tiên Giang, Sông *see* Mekong
147 X9 **Tien Shan** *Chin.* Thian Shan, Tian Shan, T'ien Shan, *Rus.* Tyan'-Shan'. ▲▲ C Asia
Tientsin *see* Tianjin
Tientsin *see* Tianjin Shi
167 U6 **Tiên Yên** Quang Ninh, N Vietnam
95 O14 **Tierp** Uppsala, C Sweden
62 H7 **Tierra Amarilla** Atacama, N Chile
37 R9 **Tierra Amarilla** New Mexico, SW USA
41 R15 **Tierra Blanca** Veracruz-Llave, E Mexico
41 O16 **Tierra Colorada** Guerrero, S Mexico
63 J17 **Tierra Colorada, Bajo de la** *basin* SE Argentina
63 I25 **Tierra del Fuego** *off.* Provincia de la Tierra del Fuego. ⬖ *province* S Argentina
63 J24 **Tierra del Fuego** *island* Argentina/Chile
54 D7 **Tierralta** Córdoba, NW Colombia
104 K9 **Tiétar** ≈ W Spain
60 L10 **Tietê** São Paulo, S Brazil
60 J8 **Tietê, Rio** ≈ S Brazil
32 I9 **Tieton** Washington, NW USA
32 J6 **Tiffany Mountain** ▲ Washington, NW USA
31 S12 **Tiffin** Ohio, N USA
31 Q11 **Tiffin River** ≈ Ohio, N USA
Tiflis *see* T'bilisi
23 U7 **Tifton** Georgia, SE USA
171 R13 **Tifu** Pulau Buru, E Indonesia
38 L17 **Tigalda Island** *island* Aleutian Islands, Alaska, USA
115 I15 **Tigáni, Akrotírio** *headland* Límnos, E Greece
169 V6 **Tiga Tarok** Sabah, East Malaysia
117 O10 **Tighina** *Rus.* Bendery; *prev.* Bender. E Moldova
145 X9 **Tigiretskiy Khrebet** ▲▲ E Kazakhstan
79 F14 **Tignère** Adamaoua, N Cameroon
13 P14 **Tignish** Prince Edward Island, SE Canada
Tigranocerta *see* Siirt
80 I11 **Tigray** ⬖ *province* N Ethiopia
41 O11 **Tigre, Cerro del** ▲ C Mexico
56 F8 **Tigre, Río** ≈ N Peru
139 X10 **Tigris** *Ar.* Dijlah, *Turk.* Dicle. ≈ Iraq/Turkey
76 G9 **Tiguent** Trarza, SW Mauritania
74 M10 **Tiguentourine** E Algeria
77 V10 **Tiguidit, Falaise de** *ridge* C Niger
141 N13 **Tihāmah** *var.* Tehama. *plain* Saudi Arabia/Yemen
Tihert *see* Tiaret
Ti-hua/Tihwa *see* Ürümqi
41 Q13 **Tihuatlán** Veracruz-Llave, E Mexico
40 B1 **Tijuana** Baja California, NW Mexico
42 E2 **Tikal** Petén, N Guatemala
154 I9 **Tīkamgarh** *prev.* Tehri. Madhya Pradesh, C India
158 L7 **Tikanlik** Xinjiang Uygur Zizhiqu, NW China
77 P12 **Tikaré** N Burkina
39 O12 **Tikchik Lakes** *lakes* Alaska, USA
191 T9 **Tikehau** *atoll* Îles Tuamotu, C French Polynesia
191 V9 **Tikei** *island* Îles Tuamotu, C French Polynesia
126 L13 **Tikhoretsk** Krasnodarskiy Kray, SW Russian Federation
124 I13 **Tikhvin** Leningradskaya Oblast', NW Russian Federation
193 P9 **Tiki Basin** *undersea feature* S Pacific Ocean
76 K13 **Tikinsso** ≈ NE Guinea
184 Q8 **Tikitiki** Gisborne, North Island, NZ
79 D16 **Tiko** Sud-Ouest, SW Cameroon
187 R11 **Tikopia** *island*, E Soloman Islands
139 S6 **Tikrīt** *var.* Tekrit. N Iraq
124 I8 **Tiksha** Respublika Kareliya, NW Russian Federation
126 I6 **Tikshozero, Ozero** ◎ NW Russian Federation
123 P7 **Tiksi** Respublika Sakha (Yakutiya), NE Russian Federation
42 A6 **Tilapa** San Marcos, SW Guatemala
42 L13 **Tilarán** Guanacaste, NW Costa Rica
99 J14 **Tilburg** Noord-Brabant, S Netherlands
14 D17 **Tilbury** Ontario, S Canada
182 K4 **Tilcha** South Australia
Tilcha Creek *see* Callabonna Creek
29 Q14 **Tilden** Nebraska, C USA
25 R13 **Tilden** Texas, SW USA
14 H10 **Tilden Lake** Ontario, S Canada
116 G9 **Tileagd** *Hung.* Mezőtelegd. Bihor, W Romania
77 Q8 **Tilemsi, Vallée de** ≈ C Mali
123 V8 **Tilichiki** Koryakskiy Avtonomnyy Okrug, E Russian Federation
Tiligul *see* Tilihul
Tiligul'skiy Liman *see* Tilihul's'kyy Lyman
117 P9 **Tilihul** *Rus.* Tiligul. ≈ SW Ukraine
117 P10 **Tilihul's'kyy Lyman** *Rus.* Tiligul'skiy Liman. ◎ S Ukraine
Tilimsen *see* Tlemcen
Tilio Martius *see* Toulon
77 R11 **Tillabéri** *var.* Tillabéry. Tillabéri, W Niger
77 R11 **Tillabéri** ⬖ *department* SW Niger
Tillabéry *see* Tillabéri
32 F11 **Tillamook** Oregon, NW USA
32 E11 **Tillamook Bay** *inlet* Oregon, NW USA
151 Q22 **Tillanchāng Dwīp** *island* Nicobar Islands, India, NE Indian Ocean
95 N15 **Tillberga** Västmanland, C Sweden
Tillenberg *see* Dyleń
21 S10 **Tillery, Lake** ▣ North Carolina, SE USA
77 T10 **Tillia** Tahoua, W Niger
23 N8 **Tillmans Corner** Alabama, S USA
14 F17 **Tillsonburg** Ontario, S Canada
115 N22 **Tílos** *island* Dodekánisos, Greece, Aegean Sea
183 N5 **Tilpa** New South Wales, SE Australia
Tilsit *see* Sovetsk
31 N13 **Tilton** Illinois, N USA
126 K7 **Tim** Kurskaya Oblast', W Russian Federation
54 D12 **Timaná** Huila, S Colombia
Timan Ridge *see* Timanskiy Kryazh
127 Q6 **Timanskiy Kryazh** *Eng.* Timan Ridge. *ridge* NW Russian Federation
185 G20 **Timaru** Canterbury, South Island, NZ
127 S6 **Timashevo** Samarskaya Oblast', W Russian Federation
126 K13 **Timashevsk** Krasnodarskiy Kray, SW Russian Federation
Timbaki/Timbákion *see* Tympáki
22 K10 **Timbalier Bay** *bay* Louisiana, S USA
22 K11 **Timbalier Island** *island* Louisiana, S USA
76 L10 **Timbedgha** *var.* Timbédra. Hodh ech Chargui, SE Mauritania
Timbédra *see* Timbedgha
32 G10 **Timber** Oregon, NW USA
181 O3 **Timber Creek** Northern Territory, N Australia
28 M8 **Timber Lake** South Dakota, N USA
54 D12 **Timbío** Cauca, SW Colombia
54 C12 **Timbiquí** Cauca, SW Colombia
83 O17 **Timbue, Ponta** *headland* C Mozambique
Timbuktu *see* Tombouctou
169 W8 **Timbun Mata, Pulau** *island* E Malaysia
77 P8 **Timétrine** *var.* Ti-n-Kâr. *oasis* C Mali
Timfi *see* Týmfi
Timfristos *see* Tymfristós
77 V9 **Timia** Agadez, C Niger
171 X14 **Timika** Papua, E Indonesia
74 I9 **Timimoun** C Algeria
Timiris, Cap *see* Timirist, Râs
76 F8 **Timirist, Râs** *var.* Cap Timiris. *headland* NW Mauritania
145 O7 **Timiryazevo** Severnyy Kazakhstan, N Kazakhstan
116 E11 **Timiș** ⬖ *county* SW Romania
14 H9 **Timiskaming, Lake** *Fr.* Lac Témiscamingue. ◎ Ontario/Québec, SE Canada
116 E11 **Timișoara** *Ger.* Temeschwar, Temeswar, *Hung.* Temesvár; *prev.* Temeschburg. Timiș, W Romania
116 E11 **Timișoara** ✕ Timiș, W Romania
Timkovichi *see* Tsimkavichy
77 U8 **Ti-m-Meghsoï** ≈ NW Niger
100 K8 **Timmendorfer Strand** Schleswig-Holstein, N Germany
14 F7 **Timmins** Ontario, S Canada
21 S12 **Timmonsville** South Carolina, SE USA
30 K5 **Timms Hill** ▲ Wisconsin, N USA
112 P12 **Timok** ≈ E Serbia and Montenegro (Yugo.)
58 N13 **Timon** Maranhão, E Brazil
171 Q16 **Timor** *island* East Timor/Indonesia
171 Q17 **Timor Sea** *sea* E Indian Ocean
Timor Timur *see* East Timor
Timor Trench *see* Timor Trough
192 G8 **Timor Trough** *var.* Timor Trench. *undersea feature* NE Timor Sea
61 A21 **Timote** Buenos Aires, E Argentina
54 I6 **Timotes** Mérida, NW Venezuela
25 X8 **Timpson** Texas, SW USA
123 Q11 **Timpton** ≈ NE Russian Federation
93 H17 **Timrå** Västernorrland, C Sweden
20 J10 **Tims Ford Lake** ▣ Tennessee, S USA
168 L7 **Timur, Banjaran** ▲▲ Peninsular Malaysia
171 Q8 **Tinaca Point** *headland* Mindanao, S Philippines
54 K5 **Tinaco** Cojedes, N Venezuela
64 Q11 **Tinajo** Lanzarote, Islas Canarias, Spain , NE Atlantic Ocean
187 P10 **Tinakula** *island* Santa Cruz Islands, E Solomon Islands
54 K5 **Tinaquillo** Cojedes, N Venezuela
116 F10 **Tinca** *Hung.* Tenke. Bihor, W Romania
155 J20 **Tindivanam** Tamil Nādu, SE India
74 E9 **Tindouf** W Algeria
74 E9 **Tindouf, Sebkha de** *salt lake* W Algeria
104 J2 **Tineo** Asturias, N Spain
77 R9 **Ti-n-Essako** Kidal, E Mali
183 T5 **Tingha** New South Wales, SE Australia
Tingis *see* Tanger
Tinglett *see* Tinglev
95 F24 **Tinglev** *Ger.* Tinglett. Sønderjylland, SW Denmark
56 E12 **Tingo María** Huánuco, C Peru
Tingréla *see* Tengréla
158 K16 **Tingri** *var.* Xêgar. Xizang Zizhiqu, W China
95 M21 **Tingsryd** Kronoberg, S Sweden
95 P19 **Tingstäde** Gotland, SE Sweden
62 H12 **Tinguiririca, Volcán** ⛰ C Chile
94 F9 **Tingvoll** Møre og Romsdal, S Norway
188 K8 **Tinian** *island* S Northern Mariana Islands
Ti-n-Kâr *see* Timétrine
Tinnevelly *see* Tirunelveli
95 G15 **Tinnoset** Telemark, S Norway
95 F15 **Tinnsjø** ◎ S Norway
Tino *see* Chino
115 J20 **Tínos** Tínos, Kykládes, Greece, Aegean Sea
115 J20 **Tínos** *anc.* Tenos. *island* Kykládes, Greece, Aegean Sea
153 R14 **Tinpahar** Jhārkhand, NE India
153 X11 **Tinsukia** Assam, NE India
76 K10 **Tintâne** Hodh el Gharbi, S Mauritania
62 L7 **Tintina** Santiago del Estero, N Argentina
182 K10 **Tintinara** South Australia
104 I14 **Tinto** ≈ SW Spain
77 S8 **Ti-n-Zaouâtene** Kidal, NE Mali
Tiobraid Árann *see* Tipperary
28 K3 **Tioga** North Dakota, N USA
18 G12 **Tioga** Pennsylvania, NE USA
25 T5 **Tioga** Texas, SW USA
35 Q8 **Tioga Pass** *pass* California, W USA
18 G12 **Tioga River** ≈ New York/Pennsylvania, NE USA
Tioman Island *see* Tioman, Pulau
168 M9 **Tioman, Pulau** *var.* Tioman Island. *island* Peninsular Malaysia
18 C12 **Tionesta** Pennsylvania, NE USA
18 D12 **Tionesta Creek** ≈ Pennsylvania, NE USA
168 J13 **Tiop** Pulau Pagai Selatan, W Indonesia
77 O12 **Tiou** NW Burkina
18 H11 **Tioughnioga River** ≈ New York, NE USA
74 J5 **Tipasa** *var.* Tipaza. N Algeria
Tipaza *see* Tipasa
42 J10 **Tipitapa** Managua, W Nicaragua
31 R13 **Tipp City** Ohio, N USA
31 O12 **Tippecanoe River** ≈ Indiana, N USA
97 D20 **Tipperary** *Ir.* Tiobraid Árann. S Ireland
97 D19 **Tipperary** *Ir.* Tiobraid Árann. *cultural region* S Ireland
35 R12 **Tipton** California, W USA
31 P13 **Tipton** Indiana, N USA
29 Y14 **Tipton** Iowa, C USA
27 U5 **Tipton** Missouri, C USA
36 I10 **Tipton, Mount** ▲ Arizona, SW USA
20 F8 **Tiptonville** Tennessee, S USA
12 E12 **Tip Top Mountain** ▲ Ontario, S Canada
155 G19 **Tiptūr** Karnātaka, W India
Tiquisate *see* Pueblo Nuevo Tiquisate
58 L13 **Tiracambu, Serra do** ▲▲ E Brazil
Tirana *see* Tiranë
113 K19 **Tirana Rinas** ✕ Durrës, W Albania
113 L20 **Tiranë** *var.* Tirana. ● (Albania) Tiranë, C Albania
113 K20 **Tiranë** ⬖ *district* W Albania
140 I5 **Tīrān, Jazīrat** *island* Egypt/Saudi Arabia
106 F6 **Tirano** Lombardia, N Italy
182 I2 **Tirari Desert** *desert* South Australia
117 O10 **Tiraspol** *Rus.* Tiraspol'. E Moldova
184 M8 **Tirau** Waikato, North Island, NZ
136 C14 **Tire** İzmir, SW Turkey
137 O11 **Tirebolu** Giresun, N Turkey
96 F11 **Tiree** *island* W Scotland, UK
Tîrgovişte *see* Târgovişte
Tîrgu *see* Târgu Cărbuneşti
Tîrgu Bujor *see* Târgu Bujor
Tîrgu Frumos *see* Târgu Frumos
Tîrgu Jiu *see* Târgu Jui
Tîrgu Lăpuş *see* Târgu Lăpuş
Tîrgu Mures *see* Târgu Mureş
Tîrgu-Neamţ *see* Târgu-Neamţ
Tîrgu Ocna *see* Târgu Ocna
Tîrgu Secuiesc *see* Târgu Secuiesc
149 T3 **Tirich Mīr** ▲ NW Pakistan
76 J5 **Tiris Zemmour** ⬖ *region* N Mauritania
Tirlemont *see* Tienen
127 W5 **Tirlyanskiy** Respublika Bashkortostan, W Russian Federation
Tîrnava Mare *see* Târnava Mare
Tîrnava Mică *see* Târnava Mică
Tîrnăveni *see* Târnăveni
Tírnavos *see* Týrnavos
Tirnovo *see* Veliko Tŭrnovo
154 J11 **Tirodi** Madhya Pradesh, C India
108 K8 **Tirol** *off.* Land Tirol, *var.* Tyrol, *It.* Tirolo. ⬖ *state* W Austria
Tirolo *see* Tirol
Tirreno, Mare *see* Tyrrhenian Sea
107 B19 **Tirso** ≈ Sardegna, Italy, C Mediterranean Sea
95 H22 **Tirstrup** ✕ (Århus) Århus, C Denmark
155 I21 **Tiruchchirāppalli** *prev.* Trichinopoly. Tamil Nādu, SE India
155 H23 **Tirunelveli** *var.* Tinnevelly. Tamil Nādu, SE India
155 J19 **Tirupati** Andhra Pradesh, E India
155 I20 **Tiruppattūr** Tamil Nādu, SE India
155 H21 **Tiruppūr** Tamil Nādu, SW India
155 I20 **Tiruvannāmalai** Tamil Nādu, SE India
112 L10 **Tisa** *Ger.* Theiss, *Hung.* Tisza, *Rus.* Tissa, *Ukr.* Tysa. ≈ SE Europe *see also* Tisza
Tischnowitz *see* Tišnov
11 U14 **Tisdale** Saskatchewan, S Canada
27 O13 **Tishomingo** Oklahoma, C USA
95 M17 **Tisnaren** ◎ S Sweden
111 F18 **Tišnov** *Ger.* Tischnowitz. Jihomoravský Kraj, SE Czech Republic
Tissa *see* Tisa/Tisza
74 J6 **Tissemsilt** N Algeria
153 S12 **Tista** ≈ NE India
112 L8 **Tisza** *Ger.* Theiss. *Rom./Slvn./SCr.* Tisa, *Rus.* Tissa, *Ukr.* Tysa. ≈ SE Europe *see also* Tisa
111 L23 **Tiszaföldvár** Jász-Nagykun-Szolnok, E Hungary
111 M22 **Tiszafüred** Jász-Nagykun-Szolnok, E Hungary
111 L23 **Tiszakécske** Bács-Kiskun, C Hungary
111 M21 **Tiszaújváros** *prev.* Leninváros. Borsod-Abaúj-Zemplén, NE Hungary
111 N21 **Tiszavasvári** Szabolcs-Szatmár-Bereg, NE Hungary
Titibu *see* Chichibu
57 I17 **Titicaca, Lake** ◎ Bolivia/Peru
190 H17 **Titikaveka** Rarotonga, S Cook Islands
154 M13 **Titilāgarh** Orissa, E India
168 K8 **Titiwangsa, Banjaran** ▲▲ Peninsular Malaysia
Titograd *see* Podgorica
Titose *see* Chitose
Titova Mitrovica *see* Kosovska Mitrovica
Titovo Užice *see* Užice
113 M18 **Titov Vrv** ▲ NW FYR Macedonia
94 F7 **Titran** Sør-Trøndelag, S Norway
31 Q8 **Tittabawassee River** ≈ Michigan, N USA
116 J13 **Titu** Dâmboviţa, S Romania
79 M16 **Titule** Orientale, N Dem. Rep. Congo
23 X11 **Titusville** Florida, SE USA
18 C12 **Titusville** Pennsylvania, NE USA
76 G11 **Tivaouane** W Senegal
113 I17 **Tivat** Montenegro, SW Serbia and Montenegro (Yugo.)
14 E14 **Tiverton** Ontario, S Canada
97 J23 **Tiverton** SW England, UK
19 O12 **Tiverton** Rhode Island, NE USA
107 I15 **Tivoli** *anc.* Tiber. Lazio, C Italy
25 U13 **Tivoli** Texas, SW USA
141 Z8 **Ṭīwī** NE Oman
Tiworo *see* Tioro, Selat
41 Y11 **Tizimín** Yucatán, SE Mexico
74 K5 **Tizi Ouzou** *var.* Tizi-Ouzou. N Algeria
74 D8 **Tiznit** SW Morocco
113 I14 **Tjentište** Republika Srpska, SE Bosnia and Herzegovina
Tjepoe/Tjepu *see* Cepu
98 L7 **Tjeukemeer** ◎ N Netherlands
Tjiamis *see* Ciamis
Tjiandjoer *see* Cianjur
Tjilatjap *see* Cilacap
Tjiledoeg *see* Ciledug
95 F23 **Tjæreborg** Ribe, W Denmark
95 I18 **Tjörn** *island* S Sweden
92 O3 **Tjuvfjorden** *fjord* S Svalbard
Tkvarcheli *see* Tqvarch'eli
40 L8 **Tlahualilo** Durango, N Mexico
41 P14 **Tlalnepantla** México, C Mexico
41 Q13 **Tlapacoyán** Veracruz-Llave, E Mexico
41 P16 **Tlapa de Comonfort** Guerrero, S Mexico
40 L13 **Tlaquepaque** Jalisco, C Mexico
Tlascala *see* Tlaxcala
41 P14 **Tlaxcala** *var.* Tlascala, Tlaxcala de Xicohténcatl. Tlaxcala, C Mexico
41 P14 **Tlaxcala** ⬖ *state* S Mexico
Tlaxcala de Xicohténcatl *see* Tlaxcala
41 P14 **Tlaxco** *var.* Tlaxco de Morelos. Tlaxcala, S Mexico
Tlaxco de Morelos *see* Tlaxco
41 Q16 **Tlaxiaco** *var.* Santa María Asunción Tlaxiaco. Oaxaca, S Mexico
74 I6 **Tlemcen** *var.* Tilimsen, Tlemsen. NW Algeria
Tlemsen *see* Tlemcen
138 L4 **Tlété Ouâte Rharbi, Jebel** ▲ N Syria
116 J7 **Tlumach** Ivano-Frankivs'ka Oblast', W Ukraine
127 P17 **Tlyarata** Respublika Dagestan, SW Russian Federation
116 K10 **Toaca, Vârful** *prev.* Vîrful Toaca. ▲ NE Romania
Toaca, Vîrful *see* Toaca, Vârful
187 R13 **Toak** Ambrym, C Vanuatu
172 J4 **Toamasina** *var.* Tamatave. Toamasina, E Madagascar
172 J4 **Toamasina** ⬖ *province* E Madagascar
172 J4 **Toamasina** ✕ Toamasina, E Madagascar
21 X6 **Toano** Virginia, NE USA
191 U10 **Toau** *atoll* Îles Tuamotu, C French Polynesia
45 T6 **Toa Vaca, Embalse** ▣ C Puerto Rico
62 K13 **Toay** La Pampa, C Argentina
159 R14 **Toba** Xizang Zizhiqu, W China
164 K14 **Toba** Mie, Honshū, SW Japan
168 I9 **Toba, Danau** ◎ Sumatera, W Indonesia
45 Y16 **Tobago** *island* NE Trinidad and Tobago
149 Q9 **Toba Kākar Range** ▲▲ NW Pakistan
105 Q12 **Tobarra** Castilla-La Mancha, C Spain
149 U9 **Toba Tek Singh** Punjab, E Pakistan
171 R11 **Tobelo** Pulau Halmahera, E Indonesia
14 E12 **Tobermory** Ontario, S Canada
96 G10 **Tobermory** W Scotland, UK
165 S4 **Tōbetsu** Hokkaidō, NE Japan
180 M6 **Tobin Lake** ◎ Western Australia
11 U14 **Tobin Lake** ◎ Saskatchewan, C Canada
35 T4 **Tobin, Mount** ▲ Nevada, W USA
165 O9 **Tobi-shima** *island* C Japan
169 N13 **Toboali** Pulau Bangka, W Indonesia
144 M8 **Tobol** *Kaz.* Tobyl. Kostanay, N Kazakhstan
144 L8 **Tobol** *Kaz.* Tobyl. ≈ Kazakhstan/Russian Federation
122 H11 **Tobol'sk** Tyumenskaya Oblast', C Russian Federation
Tobruch/Tobruk *see* Ṭubruq
125 R3 **Tobseda** Nenetskiy Avtonomnyy Okrug, NW Russian Federation
Tobyl *see* Tobol
127 Q6 **Tobysh** ≈ NW Russian Federation
54 F10 **Tocaima** Cundinamarca, C Colombia
59 K16 **Tocantins** *off.* Estado do Tocantins. ⬖ *state* C Brazil
59 K15 **Tocantins, Rio** ≈ N Brazil
23 T2 **Toccoa** Georgia, SE USA
165 O12 **Tochigi** *off.* Tochigi-ken, *var.* Totigi. ⬖ *prefecture* Honshū, S Japan
165 O11 **Tochio** *var.* Totio. Niigata, Honshū, C Japan
95 I15 **Töcksfors** Värmland, C Sweden
42 J5 **Tocoa** Colón, N Honduras
62 H4 **Tocopilla** Antofagasta, N Chile
62 I4 **Tocorpuri, Cerro de** ▲ Bolivia/Chile
183 O10 **Tocumwal** New South Wales, SE Australia
54 K4 **Tocuyo de La Costa** Falcón, NW Venezuela
152 H13 **Toda Rāisingh** Rājasthān, N India
106 H13 **Todi** Umbria, C Italy
108 G9 **Tödi** ▲ NE Switzerland
171 T12 **Todlo** Papua, E Indonesia
165 S9 **Todoga-saki** *headland* Honshū, C Japan
59 P17 **Todos os Santos, Baía de** *bay* E Brazil
40 F10 **Todos Santos** Baja California Sur, W Mexico
40 B2 **Todos Santos, Bahía de** *bay* NW Mexico
Toeban *see* Tuban
Toekang Besi Eilanden *see* Tukangbesi, Kepulauan
Tōen *see* T'aoyüan
185 D25 **Toetoes Bay** *bay* South Island, NZ
11 Q14 **Tofield** Alberta, SW Canada
10 K17 **Tofino** Vancouver Island, British Columbia, SW Canada
189 X17 **Tofol** Kosrae, E Micronesia
95 J20 **Tofta** Halland, S Sweden
95 H15 **Tofte** Buskerud, S Norway
95 F24 **Toftlund** Sønderjylland, SW Denmark
193 X15 **Tofua** *island* Ha'apai Group, C Tonga
187 Q12 **Toga** *island* Torres Islands, N Vanuatu
80 N13 **Togdheer** *off.* Gobolka Togdheer. ⬖ *region* NW Somalia
Toghyzaq *see* Toguzak
164 L11 **Togi** Ishikawa, Honshū, SW Japan
39 N13 **Togiak** Alaska, USA
171 O11 **Togian, Kepulauan** *island group* C Indonesia
77 Q15 **Togo** *off.* Togolese Republic; *prev.* French Togoland. ◆ *republic* W Africa
162 F8 **Tögrög** Govĭ-Altay, SW Mongolia
162 E7 **Tögrög** Hovd, W Mongolia
159 N12 **Togton He** *var.* Tuotuo He. ≈ C China
Togton Heyan *see* Tanggulashan
144 L7 **Toguzak** *Kaz.* Toghyzaq. ≈ Kazakhstan/Russian Federation
37 P10 **Tohatchi** New Mexico, SW USA
191 O7 **Tohiea, Mont** ⛰ Moorea, W French Polynesia
93 O17 **Tohmajärvi** Itä-Suomi, E Finland
137 N14 **Tohma Çayı** ≈ C Turkey
93 L16 **Toholampi** Länsi-Suomi, W Finland
162 M10 **Töhöm** Dornogovĭ, SE Mongolia
23 X12 **Tohopekaliga, Lake** ◎ Florida, SE USA
164 M14 **Toi** Shizuoka, Honshū, S Japan
190 B15 **Toi** N Niue
93 L19 **Toijala** Länsi-Suomi, W Finland

◆ Country ● Country Capital ◇ Dependent Territory ○ Dependent Territory Capital ⬖ Administrative Region ✕ International Airport ▲ Mountain ▲▲ Mountain Range ⛰ Volcano ≈ River ◎ Lake ▣ Reservoir

171 P12 **Toima** Sulawesi, N Indonesia
164 D17 **Toi-misaki** headland Kyūshū, SW Japan
171 Q17 **Toineke** Timor, S Indonesia
Toirc, Inis see Inishturk
35 U6 **Toiyabe Range** ▲ Nevada, W USA
Tojikiston, Jumhurii see Tajikistan
147 R12 **Tojikobod** Rus. Tadzhikabad. C Tajikistan
164 G12 **Tōjō** Hiroshima, Honshū, SW Japan
39 T10 **Tok** Alaska, USA
164 K13 **Tōkai** Aichi, Honshū, SW Japan
111 N21 **Tokaj** Borsod-Abaúj-Zemplén, NE Hungary
165 N11 **Tōkamachi** Niigata, Honshū, C Japan
185 D25 **Tokanui** Southland, South Island, NZ
80 I7 **Tokar** var. Ṭawkar. Red Sea, NE Sudan
136 L12 **Tokat** Tokat, N Turkey
136 L12 **Tokat** ◆ province N Turkey
Tokati Gawa see Tokachi-gawa
163 X15 **Tŏkchŏk-gundo** island group NW South Korea
Tŏke see Taka Atoll
190 J9 **Tokelau** ◇ NZ overseas territory W Polynesia
Tőketerebes see Trebišov
Tokhtamyshbek see Tŭkhtamish
24 M6 **Tokio** Texas, SW USA
Tokio see Tōkyō
189 W11 **Toki Point** point NW Wake Island
Tokkuztara see Gongliu
147 V7 **Tokmak** Kir. Tokmok. Chuyskaya Oblast', N Kyrgyzstan
117 V9 **Tokmak** var. Velykyy Tokmak. Zaporiz'ka Oblast', SE Ukraine
Tokmok see Tokmak
184 Q8 **Tokomaru Bay** Gisborne, North Island, NZ
165 V3 **Tokoro** Hokkaidō, NE Japan
184 M8 **Tokoroa** Waikato, North Island, NZ
76 K14 **Tokounou** Haute-Guinée, C Guinea
38 M12 **Toksook Bay** Alaska, USA
Toksu see Xinhe
Toksum see Toksun
158 L6 **Toksun** var. Toksum. Xinjiang Uygur Zizhiqu, NW China
147 T8 **Toktogul** Talasskaya Oblast', NW Kyrgyzstan
147 T9 **Toktogul'skoye Vodokhranilishche** ⊞ W Kyrgyzstan
Toktomush see Tŭkhtamish
193 Y14 **Toku** island Vava'u Group, N Tonga
165 U16 **Tokunoshima** Kagoshima, Tokuno-shima, SW Japan
165 U16 **Tokuno-shima** island Nansei-shotō, SW Japan
164 I14 **Tokushima** var. Tokusima. Tokushima, Shikoku, SW Japan
164 H14 **Tokushima** off. Tokushima-ken, var. Tokusima. ◆ prefecture Shikoku, SW Japan
Tokusima see Tokushima
164 E13 **Tokuyama** Yamaguchi, Honshū, SW Japan
165 N13 **Tōkyō** var. Tokio. ● (Japan) Tōkyō, Honshū, S Japan
165 O13 **Tōkyō** off. Tōkyō-to. ◆ capital district Honshū, S Japan
145 T12 **Tokyrau** ∽ C Kazakhstan
149 O3 **Tokzār** Pash. Tukzār. Sar-e Pol, N Afghanistan
145 X13 **Tokzhaylau** prev. Dzerzhinskoye. Almaty, E Kazakhstan
189 U12 **Tol** atoll Chuuk Islands, C Micronesia
184 Q9 **Tolaga Bay** Gisborne, North Island, NZ
172 I7 **Tôlañaro** prev. Faradofay, Fort-Dauphin. Toliara, SE Madagascar
162 D6 **Tolbo** Bayan-Ölgiy, W Mongolia
Tolbukhin see Dobrich
60 G11 **Toledo** Paraná, S Brazil
54 G8 **Toledo** Norte de Santander, N Colombia
105 N9 **Toledo** anc. Toletum. Castilla-La Mancha, C Spain
30 M14 **Toledo** Illinois, N USA
29 W13 **Toledo** Iowa, C USA
31 R11 **Toledo** Ohio, N USA
32 F12 **Toledo** Oregon, NW USA
32 G9 **Toledo** Washington, NW USA
42 F3 **Toledo** ◆ district S Belize
104 M9 **Toledo** ◆ province Castilla-La Mancha, C Spain
25 Y7 **Toledo Bend Reservoir** ⊞ Louisiana/Texas, SW USA
104 M10 **Toledo, Montes de** ▲ C Spain
106 J12 **Tolentino** Marche, C Italy
Toletum see Toledo
94 H10 **Tolga** Hedmark, S Norway
158 J3 **Toli** Xinjiang Uygur Zizhiqu, NW China
172 H7 **Toliara** var. Toliary; prev. Tuléar. Toliara, SW Madagascar
172 H7 **Toliara** ◆ province SW Madagascar
Toliary see Toliara
54 D11 **Tolima** off. Departamento del Tolima. ◆ province C Colombia
171 N11 **Tolitoli** Sulawesi, C Indonesia
95 K22 **Tollarp** Skåne, S Sweden
100 N9 **Tollense** ∽ NE Germany
100 N10 **Tollensesee** ⊚ NE Germany
36 K13 **Tolleson** Arizona, SW USA
146 M13 **Tollimarjon** Rus. Talimardzhan. Qashqadaryo Viloyati, S Uzbekistan
Tolmein see Tolmin
106 J6 **Tolmezzo** Friuli-Venezia Giulia, NE Italy
109 S11 **Tolmin** Ger. Tolmein, It. Tolmino. W Slovenia
Tolmino see Tolmin
111 J25 **Tolna** Ger. Tolnau. Tolna, S Hungary
111 I24 **Tolna** off. Tolna Megye. ◆ county SW Hungary
Tolnau see Tolna
79 I20 **Tolo** Bandundu, W Dem. Rep. Congo
Tolochin see Talachyn
190 D12 **Toloke** Île Futuna, W Wallis and Futuna
30 M13 **Tolono** Illinois, N USA
105 Q3 **Tolosa** País Vasco, N Spain
Tolosa see Toulouse
171 O13 **Tolo, Teluk** bay Sulawesi, C Indonesia
39 R9 **Tolovana River** ∽ Alaska, USA
123 U10 **Tolstoy, Mys** headland E Russian Federation
63 G15 **Toltén** Araucanía, C Chile
63 G15 **Toltén, Río** ∽ S Chile
54 E6 **Tolú** Sucre, NW Colombia
41 O14 **Toluca** var. Toluca de Lerdo. México, S Mexico
Toluca de Lerdo see Toluca
41 O14 **Toluca, Nevado de** ※ C Mexico
127 R6 **Tol'yatti** prev. Stavropol'. Samarskaya Oblast', W Russian Federation
77 O12 **Toma** NW Burkina
30 K7 **Tomah** Wisconsin, N USA
30 L5 **Tomahawk** Wisconsin, N USA
117 T8 **Tomakivka** Dnipropetrovs'ka Oblast', E Ukraine
165 S4 **Tomakomai** Hokkaidō, NE Japan
165 S2 **Tomamae** Hokkaidō, NE Japan
104 G9 **Tomar** Santarém, W Portugal
123 T13 **Tomari** Ostrov Sakhalin, Sakhalinskaya Oblast', SE Russian Federation
115 C16 **Tómaros** ▲ W Greece
Tomaschow see Tomaszów Lubelski, Poland
Tomaschow see Tomaszów Mazowiecki, Poland
61 E16 **Tomás Gomensoro** Artigas, N Uruguay
117 N7 **Tomashpil'** Vinnyts'ka Oblast', C Ukraine
Tomaszów see Tomaszów Mazowiecki
111 P15 **Tomaszów Lubelski** Ger. Tomaschow. Lubelskie, E Poland
Tomaszów Mazowiecka see Tomaszów Mazowiecki
110 L13 **Tomaszów Mazowiecki** var. Tomaszów Mazowiecka; prev. Tomaszów, Ger. Tomaschow. Łodzkie, C Poland
40 J13 **Tomatlán** Jalisco, C Mexico
81 F15 **Tombe** Jonglei, S Sudan
23 N4 **Tombigbee River** ∽ Alabama/Mississippi, S USA
82 A10 **Tomboco** Zaire, NW Angola
77 O10 **Tombouctou** Eng. Timbuktu. Tombouctou, N Mali
77 N9 **Tombouctou** ◆ region W Mali
37 N16 **Tombstone** Arizona, SW USA
83 A15 **Tombua** Port. Porto Alexandre. Namibe, SW Angola
83 J19 **Tom Burke** Limpopo, NE South Africa
146 L9 **Tomdibuloq** Rus. Tamdybulak. Navoiy Viloyati, N Uzbekistan
146 L9 **Tomditow-Tog'lari** ▲ N Uzbekistan
62 G13 **Tomé** Bío Bío, C Chile
58 L12 **Tomé-Açu** Pará, NE Brazil
95 L23 **Tomelilla** Skåne, S Sweden
105 O10 **Tomelloso** Castilla-La Mancha, C Spain
14 H10 **Tomiko Lake** ⊚ Ontario, S Canada
77 N12 **Tominian** Ségou, C Mali
171 N12 **Tomini, Gulf of** var. Teluk Tomini; prev. Teluk Gorontalo. bay Sulawesi, C Indonesia
Tomini, Teluk see Tomini, Gulf of
165 Q11 **Tomioka** Fukushima, Honshū, C Japan
113 G14 **Tomislavgrad** Federacija Bosna I Hercegovina, SW Bosnia and Herzegovina
181 O9 **Tomkinson Ranges** ▲ South Australia/Western Australia
123 Q11 **Tommot** Respublika Sakha (Yakutiya), NE Russian Federation
171 Q11 **Tomohon** Sulawesi, N Indonesia
54 K9 **Tomo, Río** ∽ E Colombia
113 L21 **Tomorrit, Mali i** ▲ S Albania
11 S17 **Tompkins** Saskatchewan, S Canada
20 K8 **Tompkinsville** Kentucky, S USA
171 N11 **Tompo** Sulawesi, N Indonesia
180 I8 **Tom Price** Western Australia
122 J12 **Tomsk** Tomskaya Oblast', C Russian Federation
122 I11 **Tomskaya Oblast'** ◆ province C Russian Federation
18 K16 **Toms River** New Jersey, NE USA
Tom Steed Lake see Tom Steed Reservoir
26 L12 **Tom Steed Reservoir** var. Tom Steed Lake. ⊞ Oklahoma, C USA
171 U13 **Tomu** Papua, E Indonesia
158 H6 **Tomür Feng** var. Pobeda Peak, Rus. Pik Pobedy. ▲ China/Kyrgyzstan see also Pobedy, Pik
189 N13 **Tomworoahlang** Pohnpei, E Micronesia
41 U17 **Tonalá** Chiapas, SE Mexico
106 F6 **Tonale, Passo del** pass N Italy
164 I11 **Tonami** Toyama, Honshū, SW Japan
58 C12 **Tonantins** Amazonas, W Brazil
32 K6 **Tonasket** Washington, NW USA
55 Y9 **Tonate** var. Macouria. N French Guiana
18 D10 **Tonawanda** New York, NE USA
171 Q11 **Tondano** Sulawesi, C Indonesia
104 H7 **Tondela** Viseu, N Portugal
95 F24 **Tønder** Ger. Tondern. Sønderjylland, SW Denmark
Tondern see Tønder
143 N4 **Tonekābon** var. Shahsawar, Tonkābon; prev. Shahsavār. Māzandarān, N Iran
Tonezh see Tonyezh
193 Y14 **Tonga** off. Kingdom of Tonga, var. Friendly Islands. ◆ monarchy SW Pacific Ocean
83 K23 **Tongaat** KwaZulu/Natal, E South Africa
161 Q13 **Tong'an** var. Datong, Tong an. Fujian, SE China
27 Q4 **Tonganoxie** Kansas, C USA
39 Y13 **Tongass National Forest** reserve Alaska, USA
193 Y16 **Tongatapu** ✕ Tongatapu, S Tonga
193 Y16 **Tongatapu** island Tongatapu Group, S Tonga
193 Y16 **Tongatapu Group** island group S Tonga
192 L9 **Tonga Trench** undersea feature S Pacific Ocean
161 N8 **Tongbai Shan** ▲ C China
161 P8 **Tongcheng** Anhui, E China
160 L6 **Tongchuan** Shaanxi, C China
160 L12 **Tongdao** var. Tongdao Dongzu Zizhixian; prev. Shuangjiang. Hunan, S China
159 T11 **Tongde** var. Gabasumdo. Qinghai, C China
99 K19 **Tongeren** Fr. Tongres. Limburg, NE Belgium
163 Y14 **Tonghae** NE South Korea
160 G13 **Tonghai** var. Xiushan. Yunnan, SW China
163 X8 **Tonghe** Heilongjiang, NE China
163 W11 **Tonghua** Jilin, NE China
163 Z6 **Tongjiang** Heilongjiang, NE China
163 Y13 **Tongjosŏn-man** prev. Broughton Bay. bay E North Korea
163 V7 **Tongken He** ∽ NE China
167 T7 **Tongking, Gulf of** Chin. Beibu Wan, Vtn. Vinh Bắc Bộ. gulf China/Vietnam
163 U10 **Tongliao** Nei Mongol Zizhiqu, N China
161 Q9 **Tongling** Anhui, E China
161 R9 **Tonglu** Zhejiang, SE China
187 R14 **Tongoa** island Shepherd Islands, S Vanuatu
62 G9 **Tongoy** Coquimbo, C Chile
160 L11 **Tongren** Guizhou, S China
159 T11 **Tongren** var. Rongwo. Qinghai, C China
Tongres see Tongeren
153 U11 **Tongsa** var. Tongsa Dzong. C Bhutan
Tongsa Dzong see Tongsa
Tongshan see Xuzhou
Tongshi see Wuzhishan
159 P12 **Tongtian He** ∽ C China
96 I6 **Tongue** N Scotland, UK
44 H3 **Tongue of the Ocean** strait C Bahamas
33 X10 **Tongue River** ∽ Montana, NW USA
33 W11 **Tongue River Reservoir** ⊞ Montana, NW USA
159 V11 **Tongwei** Gansu, C China
159 W9 **Tongxin** Ningxia, N China
163 U9 **Tongyu** var. Kaitong. Jilin, NE China
160 J11 **Tongzi** Guizhou, S China
40 G5 **Tónichi** Sonora, NW Mexico
81 D14 **Tonj** Warab, SW Sudan
152 H13 **Tonk** Rājasthān, N India
Tonkābon see Tonekābon
27 N8 **Tonkawa** Oklahoma, C USA
167 Q12 **Tônlé Sap** Eng. Great Lake. ⊚ W Cambodia
102 L14 **Tonneins** Lot-et-Garonne, SW France
103 Q7 **Tonnerre** Yonne, C France
Tonoas see Dublon
35 U8 **Tonopah** Nevada, W USA
164 H13 **Tonoshō** Okayama, Shōdo-shima, SW Japan
43 S17 **Tonosí** Los Santos, S Panama
95 H16 **Tønsberg** Vestfold, S Norway
39 T11 **Tonsina** Alaska, USA
95 D17 **Tonstad** Vest-Agder, S Norway
193 X15 **Tonumea** island Nomuka Group, W Tonga
137 O11 **Tonya** Trabzon, NE Turkey
119 K20 **Tonyezh** Rus. Tonezh. Homyel'skaya Voblasts', SE Belarus
36 L3 **Tooele** Utah, W USA
122 L13 **Toora-Khem** Respublika Tyva, S Russian Federation
183 O5 **Toorale East** New South Wales, SE Australia
83 H25 **Toorberg** ▲ S South Africa
118 G5 **Tootsi** Pärnumaa, SW Estonia
183 U3 **Toowoomba** Queensland, E Australia
27 Q4 **Topeka** state capital Kansas, C USA
111 M18 **Topľa** Hung. Toplya. ∽ NE Slovakia
122 J12 **Topki** Kemerovskaya Oblast', S Russian Federation
Toplicza see Toplița
116 J10 **Toplița** Ger. Töplitz, Hung. Maroshévíz; prev. Toplița Română, Hung. Oláh-Toplicza, Toplicza. Harghita, C Romania
Toplița Română/Töplitz see Toplița
Toplya see Topľa
111 I20 **Topoľčany** Hung. Nagytapolcsány. Nitriansky Kraj, SW Slovakia
40 G8 **Topolobampo** Sinaloa, C Mexico
116 I13 **Topoloveni** Argeș, S Romania
114 L11 **Topolovgrad** prev. Kavakli. Khaskovo, S Bulgaria
Topolya see Bačka Topola
126 I6 **Topozero, Ozero** ⊚ NW Russian Federation
32 J10 **Toppenish** Washington, NW USA
181 P4 **Top Springs Roadhouse** Northern Territory, N Australia
189 U11 **Tora** island Chuuk, C Micronesia
Toraigh see Tory Island
189 U11 **Tora Island Pass** passage Chuuk Islands, C Micronesia
143 U5 **Torbat-e Ḩeydarīyeh** var. Turbat-i-Haidari. Khorāsān, NE Iran
143 V5 **Torbat-e Jām** var. Turbat-i-Jam. Khorāsān, NE Iran
39 Q11 **Torbert, Mount** ▲ Alaska, USA
31 P6 **Torch Lake** ⊚ Michigan, N USA
Törcsvár see Bran
Torda see Turda
104 L6 **Tordesillas** Castilla-León, N Spain
92 K13 **Töre** Norrbotten, N Sweden
95 L17 **Töreboda** Västra Götaland, S Sweden
95 J21 **Torekov** Skåne, S Sweden
92 O3 **Torell Land** physical region SW Svalbard
117 Y8 **Torez** Donets'ka Oblast', SE Ukraine
101 N14 **Torgau** Sachsen, E Germany
Torgay Üstirti see Turgayskaya Stolovaya Strana
Torghay see Turgay
95 N22 **Torhamn** Blekinge, S Sweden
99 C17 **Torhout** West-Vlaanderen, W Belgium
106 B8 **Torino** Eng. Turin. Piemonte, NW Italy
165 U15 **Tori-shima** island Izu-shotō, SE Japan
81 F16 **Torit** Eastern Equatoria, S Sudan
186 H6 **Toriu** New Britain, E PNG
148 M4 **Torkestān, Selseleh-ye Band-e** var. Bandi-i Turkistan. ▲ NW Afghanistan
104 L7 **Tormes** ∽ W Spain
Tornacum see Tournai
Torneå see Tornio
92 K12 **Torneälven** var.Torniojoki, Fin. Tornionjoki. ∽ Finland/Sweden
92 I11 **Torneträsk** ⊚ N Sweden
13 O4 **Torngat Mountains** ▲ Newfoundland and Labrador, NE Canada
24 H8 **Tornillo** Texas, SW USA
92 K13 **Tornio** Swe. Torneå. Lappi, NW Finland
Torniojoki/Tornionjoki see Torneälven
61 B23 **Tornquist** Buenos Aires, E Argentina
104 L6 **Toro** Castilla-León, N Spain
62 H9 **Toro, Cerro del** ▲ N Chile
77 R12 **Torodi** Tillabéri, SW Niger
Törökbecse see Novi Bečej
186 J7 **Torokina** Bougainville Island, NE PNG
111 L23 **Törökszentmiklós** Jász-Nagykun-Szolnok, E Hungary
42 G7 **Torola, Río** ∽ El Salvador/Honduras
Toronaíos, Kólpos see Kassándras, Kólpos
14 H15 **Toronto** Ontario, S Canada
31 V12 **Toronto** Ohio, N USA
Toronto see Lester B.Pearson
27 P6 **Toronto Lake** ⊞ Kansas, C USA
35 V16 **Toro Peak** ▲ California, W USA
124 H16 **Toropets** Tverskaya Oblast', W Russian Federation
81 G18 **Tororo** E Uganda
136 H16 **Toros Dağları** Eng. Taurus Mountains. ▲ S Turkey
183 N13 **Torquay** Victoria, SE Australia
97 J24 **Torquay** SW England, UK
104 M5 **Torquemada** Castilla-León, N Spain
35 S16 **Torrance** California, W USA
104 G12 **Torrão** Setúbal, S Portugal
104 H8 **Torre, Alto da** ▲ C Portugal
107 K18 **Torre Annunziata** Campania, S Italy
105 T8 **Torreblanca** País Valenciano, E Spain
104 L15 **Torrecilla** ▲ S Spain
105 P4 **Torrecilla en Cameros** La Rioja, N Spain
105 N13 **Torredelcampo** Andalucía, S Spain
107 K17 **Torre del Greco** Campania, S Italy
104 I6 **Torre de Moncorvo** var. Moncorvo, Tôrre de Moncorvo. Bragança, N Portugal
104 J9 **Torrejoncillo** Extremadura, W Spain
105 O8 **Torrejón de Ardoz** Madrid, C Spain
105 N7 **Torrelaguna** Madrid, C Spain
105 N2 **Torrelavega** Cantabria, N Spain
107 M16 **Torremaggiore** Puglia, SE Italy
104 M15 **Torremolinos** Andalucía, S Spain
182 I6 **Torrens, Lake** salt lake South Australia
105 S10 **Torrent** Cas. Torrente var. Torrent de l'Horta. País Valenciano, E Spain
Torrent de l'Horta/Torrente see Torrent
40 L8 **Torreón** Coahuila de Zaragoza, NE Mexico
105 R13 **Torre Pacheco** Murcia, SE Spain
106 A8 **Torre Pellice** Piemonte, NE Italy
105 O13 **Torreperogil** Andalucía, S Spain
61 J15 **Torres** Rio Grande do Sul, S Brazil
Torrès, Îles see Torres Islands
187 Q11 **Torres Islands** Fr. Îles Torrès. island group N Vanuatu
104 G9 **Torres Novas** Santarém, C Portugal
181 V1 **Torres Strait** strait Australia/PNG
104 F10 **Torres Vedras** Lisboa, C Portugal
105 S13 **Torrevieja** País Valenciano, E Spain
186 B6 **Torricelli Mountains** ▲ NW PNG
96 G8 **Torridon, Loch** inlet NW Scotland, UK
106 D9 **Torriglia** Liguria, NW Italy
104 M9 **Torrijos** Castilla-La Mancha, C Spain
18 L12 **Torrington** Connecticut, NE USA
33 Z15 **Torrington** Wyoming, C USA
94 P16 **Torröjen** see Torrön
Torrön prev. Torröjen. ⊚ C Sweden
105 N15 **Torrox** Andalucía, S Spain
94 N13 **Torsåker** Gävleborg, C Sweden
95 N21 **Torsås** Kalmar, S Sweden
95 J14 **Torsby** Värmland, C Sweden
95 N16 **Torshälla** Södermanland, C Sweden
95 B19 **Tórshavn** Dan. Thorshavn. Dependent territory capital Faeroe Islands
Torshiz see Kāshmar
146 I9 **To'rtkok'l** Rus. Turtkul'; prev. Petroaleksandrovsk. Qoraqalpog'iston Respublikasi, W Uzbekistan
45 T9 **Tortola** island C British Virgin Islands
106 D9 **Tortona** anc. Dertona. Piemonte, NW Italy
107 L23 **Tortorici** Sicilia, Italy, C Mediterranean Sea
105 U7 **Tortosa** anc. Dertosa. Cataluña, E Spain
Tortosa see Ṭarṭūs
105 U7 **Tortosa, Cap** headland E Spain
44 L8 **Tortue, Île de la** var. Tortuga Island. island N Haiti
55 Y10 **Tortue, Montagne** ▲ C French Guiana
Tortuga, Isla see La Tortuga, Isla
Tortuga Island see Tortue, Île de la
54 C11 **Tortugas, Golfo** gulf W Colombia
45 T5 **Tortuguero, Laguna** lagoon N Puerto Rico
137 Q12 **Tortum** Erzurum, NE Turkey
Torugart, Pereval see Turugart Shankou
137 O12 **Torul** Gümüşhane, NE Turkey
110 J10 **Toruń** Ger. Thorn. Toruń, Kujawsko-pomorskie, C Poland
95 K20 **Torup** Halland, S Sweden
118 I6 **Tõrva** Ger. Törwa. Valgamaa, S Estonia
Törwa see Tõrva
96 D13 **Tory Island** Ir. Toraigh. island NW Ireland
111 N19 **Torysa** Hung. Tarca. ∽ NE Slovakia
Törzburg see Bran
124 J16 **Torzhok** Tverskaya Oblast', W Russian Federation
164 F15 **Tosa-Shimizu** var. Tosasimizu. Kōchi, Shikoku, SW Japan
Tosasimizu see Tosa-Shimizu
164 G15 **Tosa-wan** bay SW Japan
83 H21 **Tosca** North-West, N South Africa
106 F12 **Toscana** Eng. Tuscany. ◆ region C Italy
107 E14 **Toscano, Archipelago** Eng. Tuscan Archipelago. island group C Italy
106 G10 **Tosco-Emiliano, Appennino** Eng. Tuscan-Emilian Mountains. ▲ C Italy
Tōsei see Tungshih
165 N15 **To-shima** island Izu-shotō, SE Japan
147 Q9 **Toshkent** Eng./Rus. Tashkent. ● (Uzbekistan) Toshkent Viloyati, E Uzbekistan
147 Q9 **Toshkent** ✕ Toshkent Viloyati, E Uzbekistan
147 P9 **Toshkent Viloyati** Rus. Tashkentskaya Oblast'. ◆ province E Uzbekistan
124 H13 **Tosno** Leningradskaya Oblast', NW Russian Federation
159 O10 **Toson Hu** ⊚ C China
162 H6 **Tosontsengel** Dzavhan, NW Mongolia
146 I8 **Tosquduq Qumlari** Rus. Peski Taskuduk. desert W Uzbekistan
105 U4 **Tossal de l'Orri** var. Llorri. ▲ NE Spain
61 A15 **Tostado** Santa Fe, C Argentina
118 F6 **Tõstamaa** Ger. Testama. Pärnumaa, SW Estonia
100 I10 **Tostedt** Niedersachsen, NW Germany
136 J11 **Tosya** Kastamonu, N Turkey
95 F15 **Totak** ⊚ S Norway
105 R13 **Totana** Murcia, SE Spain
94 H13 **Toten** physical region S Norway
83 G18 **Toteng** Ngamiland, C Botswana
102 M3 **Tôtes** Seine-Maritime, N France
Totigi see Tochigi
Totio see Tochio
Totis see Tata
189 U13 **Totiw** island Chuuk, C Micronesia
125 N13 **Tot'ma** var. Totma. Vologodskaya Oblast', NW Russian Federation
Tot'ma see Sukhona
55 V9 **Totness** Coronie, N Surinam
42 C5 **Totonicapán** Totonicapán, W Guatemala
42 A2 **Totonicapán** off. Departamento de Totonicapán. ◆ department W Guatemala
61 B18 **Totoras** Santa Fe, C Argentina
187 Y15 **Totoya** island S Fiji
183 Q7 **Tottenham** New South Wales, SE Australia
164 I12 **Tottori** Tottori, Honshū, SW Japan
164 H12 **Tottori** off. Tottori-ken. ◆ prefecture Honshū, SW Japan
76 I6 **Touâjil** Tiris Zemmour, N Mauritania
76 L15 **Touba** W Ivory Coast
76 G11 **Touba** W Senegal
74 E7 **Toubkal, Jbel** ▲ W Morocco
32 K10 **Touchet** Washington, NW USA
103 P7 **Toucy** Yonne, C France
77 O12 **Tougan** W Burkina
74 L7 **Touggourt** NE Algeria
77 Q12 **Tougouri** N Burkina
76 J13 **Tougué** Moyenne-Guinée, NW Guinea
76 K12 **Toukoto** Kayes, W Mali
103 S5 **Toul** Meurthe-et-Moselle, NE France
76 L16 **Toulépleu** var. Toulobli. W Ivory Coast
161 S14 **Touliu** C Taiwan
15 U3 **Toulnustouc** ∽ Québec, SE Canada
Toulobli see Toulépleu
103 T16 **Toulon** anc. Telo Martius, Tilio Martius. Var, SE France
30 K12 **Toulon** Illinois, N USA
102 M15 **Toulouse** anc. Tolosa. Haute-Garonne, S France
102 M15 **Toulouse** ✕ Haute-Garonne, S France
77 N16 **Toumodi** C Ivory Coast
74 G9 **Tounassine, Hamada** hill range W Algeria
166 M7 **Toungoo** Pegu, C Burma
102 L8 **Touraine** cultural region C France
Tourane see Đa Nẵng
103 P1 **Tourcoing** Nord, N France
104 F2 **Touriñán, Cabo** headland NW Spain
76 J6 **Tourine** Tiris Zemmour, N Mauritania
102 J3 **Tourlaville** Manche, N France
99 D19 **Tournai** var. Tournay, Dut. Doornik; anc. Tornacum. Hainaut, SW Belgium
102 L16 **Tournay** Hautes-Pyrénées, S France
Tournay see Tournai
103 R12 **Tournon** Ardèche, E France
103 R9 **Tournus** Saône-et-Loire, C France
59 Q14 **Touros** Rio Grande do Norte, E Brazil
102 L8 **Tours** anc. Caesarodunum, Turoni. Indre-et-Loire, C France
183 Q17 **Tourville, Cape** headland Tasmania, SE Australia
162 L8 **Töv** ◆ province C Mongolia
54 H7 **Tovar** Mérida, NW Venezuela
126 L5 **Tovarkovskiy** Tul'skaya Oblast', W Russian Federation
Tovil'-Dora see Tavildara
Tövis see Teiuș
137 V11 **Tovuz** Rus. Tauz. W Azerbaijan
165 R7 **Towada** Aomori, Honshū, C Japan
184 K3 **Towai** Northland, North Island, NZ
18 H12 **Towanda** Pennsylvania, NE USA
29 W4 **Tower** Minnesota, N USA
171 N12 **Towera** Sulawesi, N Indonesia
Tower Island see Genovesa, Isla
180 M13 **Tower Peak** ▲ Western Australia
35 U11 **Towne Pass** pass California, W USA
29 N3 **Towner** North Dakota, N USA
33 R10 **Townsend** Montana, NW USA
181 X6 **Townsville** Queensland, NE Australia
Towoeti Meer see Towuti, Danau
148 K4 **Towraghoudi** Herāt, NW Afghanistan
21 X3 **Towson** Maryland, NE USA
171 O13 **Towuti, Danau** Dut. Towoeti Meer. ⊚ Sulawesi, C Indonesia
Toxkan He see Ak-say
24 K9 **Toyah** Texas, SW USA
165 R4 **Tōya-ko** ⊚ Hokkaidō, NE Japan
164 L11 **Toyama** Toyama, Honshū, SW Japan
164 L11 **Toyama** off. Toyama-ken. ◆ prefecture Honshū, SW Japan
164 L11 **Toyama-wan** bay W Japan
164 H15 **Tōyō** Kōchi, Shikoku, SW Japan
Toyohara see Yuzhno-Sakhalinsk
164 L14 **Toyohashi** var. Toyohasi. Aichi, Honshū, SW Japan
Toyohasi see Toyohashi
164 L14 **Toyokawa** Aichi, Honshū, SW Japan
164 I14 **Toyooka** Hyōgo, Honshū, SW Japan
164 L13 **Toyota** Aichi, Honshū, SW Japan
165 T1 **Toyotomi** Hokkaidō, NE Japan
Toytepa see To'ytepa
147 Q10 **To'ytepa** Rus. Toytepa. Toshkent Viloyati, E Uzbekistan
74 M6 **Tozeur** var. Tawzar. W Tunisia
39 Q8 **Tozi, Mount** ▲ Alaska, USA
137 Q9 **Tqvarch'eli** Rus. Tkvarcheli. NW Georgia
Trâblous see Tripoli
137 O11 **Trabzon** Eng. Trebizond; anc. Trapezus. Trabzon, NE Turkey
137 O11 **Trabzon** Eng. Trebizond. ◆ province NE Turkey
13 P13 **Tracadie** New Brunswick, SE Canada
Trachenberg see Żmigród
15 O11 **Tracy** Québec, SE Canada
35 O8 **Tracy** California, W USA
29 S10 **Tracy** Minnesota, N USA
20 K10 **Tracy City** Tennessee, S USA
106 D7 **Tradate** Lombardia, N Italy
29 W13 **Traer** Iowa, C USA
104 J16 **Trafalgar, Cabo de** headland SW Spain
Traiectum ad Mosam/Traiectum Tungorum see Maastricht
Tráigh Mhór see Tramore
11 O17 **Trail** British Columbia, SW Canada
58 B11 **Traíra, Serra do** ▲ NW Brazil
109 V5 **Traisen** Niederösterreich, NE Austria
109 W4 **Traisen** ∽ NE Austria
109 X4 **Traiskirchen** Niederösterreich, NE Austria
Trajani Portus see Civitavecchia
Trajectum ad Rhenum see Utrecht
119 H14 **Trakai** Ger. Traken, Pol. Troki. Vilnius, SE Lithuania
Traken see Trakai
97 B20 **Tralee** Ir. Trá Lí. SW Ireland
97 A20 **Tralee Bay** Ir. Bá Thrá Lí. bay SW Ireland
Trá Lí see Tralee
Trälleborg see Trelleborg
Tralles see Aydın
61 J16 **Tramandaí** Rio Grande do Sul, S Brazil
108 C7 **Tramelan** Bern, W Switzerland
Trá Mhór see Tramore
97 E20 **Tramore** Ir. Tráigh Mhór, Trá Mhór. S Ireland
95 L18 **Tranås** Jönköping, S Sweden

62 *J7* **Trancas** Tucumán, N Argentina
104 *I7* **Trancoso** Guarda, N Portugal
95 *H22* **Tranebjerg** Århus, C Denmark
95 *K19* **Tranemo** Västra Götaland, S Sweden
167 *N16* **Trang** Trang, S Thailand
171 *V15* **Trangan, Pulau** *island* Kepulauan Aru, E Indonesia
Trâng Dinh *see* Thât Khê
183 *Q7* **Trangie** New South Wales, SE Australia
94 *K12* **Trängslet** Dalarna, C Sweden
107 *N16* **Trani** Puglia, SE Italy
61 *F17* **Tranqueras** Rivera, NE Uruguay
63 *G17* **Tranqui, Isla** *island* S Chile
39 *V6* **Trans-Alaska pipeline** *oil pipeline* Alaska, USA
195 *Q10* **Transantarctic Mountains** ▲ Antarctica
Transcarpathian Oblast *see* Zakarpats'ka Oblast'
Transilvania *see* Transylvania
Transilvaniei, Alpi *see* Carpații Meridionali
Transjordan *see* Jordan
172 *L11* **Transkei Basin** *undersea feature* SW Indian Ocean
117 *O10* **Transnistria** *cultural region* E Moldova
122 *E9* **Trans-Siberian Railway** *Railroad* Russian Federation
Transsylvanische Alpen/Transylvanian Alps *see* Carpații Meridionali
94 *K12* **Transtrand** Dalarna, C Sweden
116 *G10* **Transylvania** *Eng.* Ardeal, Transilvania, *Ger.* Siebenbürgen, *Hung.* Erdély. *cultural region* NW Romania
167 *S14* **Tra Ôn** Vinh Long, S Vietnam
107 *H23* **Trapani** *anc.* Drepanum. Sicilia, Italy, C Mediterranean Sea
167 *S12* **Trâpeăng Vêng** Kâmpóng Thum, C Cambodia
Trapezus *see* Trabzon
114 *L9* **Trapoklovo** Sliven, C Bulgaria
183 *P13* **Traralgon** Victoria, SE Australia
76 *H9* **Trarza** ◆ *region* SW Mauritania
Trasimenischersee *see* Trasimeno, Lago
106 *H12* **Trasimeno, Lago** *Eng.* Lake of Perugia, *Ger.* Trasimenischersee. ◎ C Italy
95 *J20* **Träslövsläge** Halland, S Sweden
Trás-os-Montes *see* Cucumbi
104 *I6* **Trás-os-Montes e Alto Douro** *former province* N Portugal
167 *Q12* **Trat** *var.* Bang Phra. Trat, S Thailand
Trá Tholl, Inis *see* Inishtrahull
Traù *see* Trogir
109 *T4* **Traun** Oberösterreich, N Austria
109 *S5* **Traun** ⁓ N Austria
Traun, Lake *see* Traunsee
101 *N23* **Traunreut** Bayern, SE Germany
109 *S5* **Traunsee** *var.* Gmundner See, *Eng.* Lake Traun. ◎ N Austria
Trautenau *see* Trutnov
21 *P11* **Travelers Rest** South Carolina, SE USA
182 *L8* **Travellers Lake** *seasonal lake* New South Wales, SE Australia
31 *P6* **Traverse City** Michigan, N USA
29 *R7* **Traverse, Lake** ◎ Minnesota/South Dakota, N USA
185 *I16* **Travers, Mount** ▲ South Island, NZ
11 *P17* **Travers Reservoir** ⊠ Alberta, SW Canada
167 *T14* **Tra Vinh** *var.* Phu Vinh. Tra Vinh, S Vietnam
25 *S10* **Travis, Lake** ⊠ Texas, SW USA
112 *H12* **Travnik** Federacija Bosna I Hercegovina, C Bosnia and Herzegovina
109 *V11* **Trbovlje** *Ger.* Trifail. C Slovenia
23 *V13* **Treasure Island** Florida, SE USA
Treasure State *see* Montana
186 *I8* **Treasury Islands** *island group* NW Solomon Islands
106 *D9* **Trebbia** *anc.* Trebia. ⁓ NW Italy
100 *N8* **Trebel** ⁓ NE Germany
103 *O16* **Trèbes** Aude, S France
Trebia *see* Trebbia
111 *F18* **Třebíč** *Ger.* Trebitsch. Vysočina, S Czech Republic
113 *I16* **Trebinje** Republika Srpska, S Bosnia and Herzegovina
111 *N20* **Trebišov** *Hung.* Tőketerebes. Košický Kraj, E Slovakia
Trebitsch *see* Třebíč
Trebizond *see* Trabzon
Trebnitz *see* Trzebnica
109 *V12* **Trebnje** SE Slovenia
111 *D19* **Třeboň** *Ger.* Wittingau. Jihočeský Kraj, S Czech Republic
104 *J15* **Trebujena** Andalucía, S Spain
100 *I7* **Treene** ⁓ N Germany
Tree Planters State *see* Nebraska
109 *S9* **Treffen** Kärnten, S Austria
Trefynwy *see* Monmouth
102 *G5* **Tréguier** Côtes d'Armor, NW France
61 *G18* **Treinta y Tres** Treinta y Tres, E Uruguay
61 *F18* **Treinta y Tres** ◆ *department* E Uruguay
122 *F11* **Trëkhgornyy** Chelyabinskaya, C Russian Federation
114 *F9* **Treklyanska Reka** ⁓ W Bulgaria
102 *K8* **Trélazé** Maine-et-Loire, NW France
63 *K17* **Trelew** Chubut, SE Argentina
95 *K23* **Trelleborg** *var.* Trälleborg. Skåne, S Sweden
113 *P15* **Trem** ▲ SE Serbia and Montenegro (Yugo.)
15 *N11* **Tremblant, Mont** ▲ Québec, SE Canada
99 *H17* **Tremelo** Vlaams Brabant, C Belgium
107 *M15* **Tremiti, Isole** *island group* SE Italy
30 *K12* **Tremont** Illinois, N USA
36 *L1* **Tremonton** Utah, W USA
105 *U4* **Tremp** Cataluña, NE Spain
30 *J7* **Trempealeau** Wisconsin, N USA
15 *P8* **Trenche** ⁓ Québec, SE Canada
15 *O7* **Trenche, Lac** ◎ Québec, SE Canada
111 *I20* **Trenčiansky Kraj** ◆ *region* W Slovakia
111 *I19* **Trenčín** *Ger.* Trentschin, *Hung.* Trencsén. Trenčiansky Kraj, W Slovakia
Trencsén *see* Trenčín
Trengganu *see* Terengganu
61 *A21* **Trenque Lauquen** Buenos Aires, E Argentina
14 *J14* **Trent** ⁓ Ontario, SE Canada
97 *N18* **Trent** ⁓ C England, UK
Trent *see* Trento
106 *F5* **Trentino-Alto Adige** *prev.* Venezia Tridentina. ◆ *region* N Italy
106 *G6* **Trento** *Eng.* Trent, *Ger.* Trient; *anc.* Tridentum. Trentino-Alto Adige, N Italy
14 *J15* **Trenton** Ontario, SE Canada
23 *V10* **Trenton** Florida, SE USA
23 *R1* **Trenton** Georgia, SE USA
31 *S10* **Trenton** Michigan, N USA
27 *S2* **Trenton** Missouri, C USA
28 *M17* **Trenton** Nebraska, C USA
18 *J15* **Trenton** *state capital* New Jersey, NE USA
21 *W10* **Trenton** North Carolina, SE USA
20 *G9* **Trenton** Tennessee, S USA
36 *L1* **Trenton** Utah, W USA
Trentschin *see* Trenčín
Treptow an der Rega *see* Trzebiatów
61 *C23* **Tres Arroyos** Buenos Aires, E Argentina
61 *J15* **Três Cachoeiras** Rio Grande do Sul, S Brazil
106 *E7* **Trescore Balneario** Lombardia, N Italy
41 *V17* **Tres Cruces, Cerro** ▲ SE Mexico
57 *K18* **Tres Cruces, Cordillera** ▲ W Bolivia
113 *N18* **Treska** ⁓ NW FYR Macedonia
113 *I14* **Treskavica** ▲ SE Bosnia and Herzegovina
59 *J20* **Três Lagoas** Mato Grosso do Sul, SW Brazil
40 *H12* **Tres Marías, Islas** *island group* C Mexico
59 *M19* **Três Marias, Represa** ⊠ SE Brazil
63 *F20* **Tres Montes, Península** *headland* S Chile
105 *O3* **Trespaderne** Castilla-León, N Spain
60 *G13* **Três Passos** Rio Grande do Sul, S Brazil
61 *A23* **Tres Picos, Cerro** ▲ E Argentina
63 *G17* **Tres Picos, Cerro** ▲ SW Argentina
60 *I12* **Três Pinheiros** Paraná, S Brazil
59 *M21* **Três Pontas** Minas Gerais, SE Brazil
Tres Puntas, Cabo *see* Manabique, Punta
60 *P9* **Três Rios** Rio de Janeiro, SE Brazil
Tres Tabernae *see* Saverne
Trestenberg/Trestendorf *see* Tăşnad
61 *R15* **Tres Valles** Veracruz-Llave, SE Mexico
94 *H12* **Tretten** Oppland, S Norway
Treuburg *see* Olecko
101 *K21* **Treuchtlingen** Bayern, S Germany
100 *N13* **Treuenbrietzen** Brandenburg, E Germany
95 *F16* **Treungen** Telemark, S Norway
63 *H17* **Trevelín** Chubut, SW Argentina
Treves/Trèves *see* Trier
106 *I13* **Trevi** Umbria, C Italy
106 *E7* **Treviglio** Lombardia, N Italy
104 *J4* **Trevinca, Peña** ▲ NW Spain
105 *P3* **Treviño** Castilla-León, N Spain
106 *I7* **Treviso** *anc.* Tarvisium. Veneto, NE Italy
97 *G24* **Trevose Head** *headland* SW England, UK
Trg *see* Feldkirchen in Kärnten
183 *P17* **Triabunna** Tasmania, SE Australia
21 *W4* **Triangle** Virginia, NE USA
83 *L18* **Triangle** Masvingo, SE Zimbabwe
115 *L23* **Tría Nisía** *island* Kykládes, Greece, Aegean Sea
Triberg *see* Triberg im Schwarzwald
101 *G23* **Triberg im Schwarzwald** *var.* Triberg. Baden-Württemberg, SW Germany
153 *P11* **Tribhuvan** ✕ (Kathmandu) Central, C Nepal
54 *C9* **Tribugá, Golfo de** *gulf* W Colombia
181 *W4* **Tribulation, Cape** *headland* Queensland, NE Australia
108 *M8* **Tribulaun** ▲ SW Austria
11 *U17* **Tribune** Saskatchewan, S Canada
26 *H5* **Tribune** Kansas, C USA
107 *N18* **Tricarico** Basilicata, S Italy
107 *Q19* **Tricase** Puglia, SE Italy
Trichinopoly *see* Tiruchchirāppalli
115 *D18* **Trichonída, Límni** ◎ C Greece
155 *G22* **Trichūr** *var.* Thrissur. Kerala, SW India
Tricorno *see* Triglav
183 *O8* **Trida** New South Wales, SE Australia
35 *S1* **Trident Peak** ▲ Nevada, W USA
Tridentum/Trient *see* Trento
109 *T6* **Trieben** Steiermark, SE Austria
101 *D19* **Trier** *Eng.* Treves, *Fr.* Trèves; *anc.* Augusta Treverorum. Rheinland-Pfalz, SW Germany
106 *K7* **Trieste** *Slvn.* Trst. Friuli-Venezia Giulia, NE Italy
Trieste, Golfo di/Triest, Golf von *see* Trieste, Gulf of
106 *J8* **Trieste, Gulf of** *Cro.* Tršćanski Zaljev, *Ger.* Golf von Triest, *It.* Golfo di Trieste, *Slvn.* Tržaški Zaliv. *gulf* S Europe
109 *W4* **Triesting** ⁓ W Austria
Trifail *see* Trbovlje
116 *L9* **Trifeşti** Iaşi, NE Romania
109 *S10* **Triglav** *It.* Tricorno. ▲ NW Slovenia
104 *I14* **Trigueros** Andalucía, S Spain
115 *E16* **Tríkala** *prev.* Trikkala. Thessalía, C Greece
115 *E17* **Trikeriótis** ⁓ C Greece
Trikkala *see* Tríkala
Trikomo/Tríkomon *see* İskele
97 *F17* **Trim** *Ir.* Baile Átha Troim. E Ireland
108 *E7* **Trimbach** Solothurn, NW Switzerland
109 *Q5* **Trimmelkam** Oberösterreich, N Austria
29 *U11* **Trimont** Minnesota, N USA
Trimontium *see* Plovdiv
Trinacria *see* Sicilia
155 *K24* **Trincomalee** *var.* Trinkomali. Eastern Province, NE Sri Lanka
65 *K16* **Trindade, Ilha da** *island* Brazil, W Atlantic Ocean
111 *J17* **Třinec** *Ger.* Trzynietz. Moravskoslezský Kraj, E Czech Republic
57 *M16* **Trinidad** Beni, N Bolivia
54 *H9* **Trinidad** Casanare, E Colombia
44 *E6* **Trinidad** Sancti Spíritus, C Cuba
37 *U8* **Trinidad** Colorado, C USA
61 *E19* **Trinidad** Flores, S Uruguay
45 *Y17* **Trinidad** *island* C Trinidad and Tobago
Trinidad *see* Jose Abad Santos
45 *Y16* **Trinidad and Tobago** *off.* Republic of Trinidad and Tobago. ◆ *republic* SE West Indies
63 *F22* **Trinidad, Golfo** *gulf* S Chile
61 *B24* **Trinidad, Isla** *island* E Argentina
107 *N16* **Trinitapoli** Puglia, SE Italy
55 *X10* **Trinité, Montagnes de la** ▲ C French Guiana
25 *W9* **Trinity** Texas, SW USA
13 *U12* **Trinity Bay** *inlet* Newfoundland and Labrador, E Canada
39 *P15* **Trinity Islands** *island group* Alaska, USA
35 *N2* **Trinity Mountains** ▲ California, W USA
35 *S4* **Trinity Peak** ▲ Nevada, W USA
35 *S5* **Trinity Range** ▲ Nevada, W USA
35 *N2* **Trinity River** ⁓ California, W USA
25 *V8* **Trinity River** ⁓ Texas, SW USA
Trinkomali *see* Trincomalee
173 *Y15* **Triolet** NW Mauritius
107 *O20* **Trionto, Capo** *headland* S Italy
115 *J16* **Tripití, Akrotírio** *headland* Ágios Efstrátios, E Greece
138 *G6* **Tripoli** *var.* Tarābulus, Ţarābulus ash Shām, Trâblous; *anc.* Tripolis. N Lebanon
29 *X12* **Tripoli** Iowa, C USA
Tripoli *see* Ţarābulus
115 *F20* **Trípoli** *prev.* Trípolis. Pelopónnisos, S Greece
Tripolis *see* Tripoli, Lebanon
Trípolis *see* Trípoli, Greece
29 *Q12* **Tripp** South Dakota, N USA
153 *V15* **Tripura** *var.* Hill Tippera. ◆ *state* NE India
108 *K8* **Trisanna** ⁓ W Austria
100 *H8* **Trischen** *island* NW Germany
65 *M24* **Tristan da Cunha** ◇ *dependency of Saint Helena* SE Atlantic Ocean
65 *L18* **Tristan da Cunha Fracture Zone** *tectonic feature* S Atlantic Ocean
167 *S14* **Tri Tôn** An Giang, S Vietnam
167 *W10* **Triton Island** *island* S Paracel Islands
155 *G24* **Trivandrum** *var.* Thiruvanathapuram. Kerala, SW India
111 *H20* **Trnava** *Ger.* Tyrnau, *Hung.* Nagyszombat. Trnavský Kraj, W Slovakia
111 *H20* **Trnavský Kraj** ◆ *region* W Slovakia
Trnovo *see* Veliko Tŭrnovo
Trobriand Island *see* Kiriwina Island
Trobriand Islands *see* Kiriwina Islands
11 *Q16* **Trochu** Alberta, SW Canada
109 *U7* **Trofaiach** Steiermark, SE Austria
93 *F14* **Trofors** Troms, N Norway
113 *E14* **Trogir** *It.* Traù. Split-Dalmacija, S Croatia
112 *F13* **Troglav** ▲ Bosnia and Herzegovina/Croatia
107 *M16* **Troia** Puglia, SE Italy
107 *K24* **Troina** Sicilia, Italy, C Mediterranean Sea
173 *O16* **Trois-Bassins** W Réunion
101 *E17* **Troisdorf** Nordrhein-Westfalen, W Germany
74 *H5* **Trois Fourches, Cap des** *headland* NE Morocco
15 *T8* **Trois-Pistoles** Québec, SE Canada
99 *L21* **Trois-Ponts** Liège, E Belgium
15 *P11* **Trois-Rivières** Québec, SE Canada
55 *Y12* **Trois Sauts** S French Guiana
99 *M22* **Troisvierges** Diekirch, N Luxembourg
122 *F11* **Troitsk** Chelyabinskaya Oblast', S Russian Federation
125 *T9* **Troitsko-Pechorsk** Respublika Komi, NW Russian Federation
127 *V7* **Troitskoye** Orenburgskaya Oblast', W Russian Federation
Troki *see* Trakai
94 *F9* **Trolla** ▲ S Norway
95 *J18* **Trollhättan** Västra Götaland, S Sweden
94 *G9* **Trollheimen** ▲ S Norway
94 *E9* **Trolltindan** ▲ S Norway
58 *H11* **Trombetas, Rio** ⁓ NE Brazil
92 *I9* **Troms** ◆ *county* N Norway
92 *I9* **Tromsø** *Fin.* Tromssa. Troms, N Norway
Tromssa *see* Tromsø
94 *H10* **Tron** ▲ S Norway
35 *U12* **Trona** California, W USA
63 *G16* **Tronador, Cerro** ▲ S Chile
94 *H8* **Trondheim** *Ger.* Drontheim; *prev.* Nidaros, Trondhjem. Sør-Trøndelag, S Norway
94 *H7* **Trondheimsfjorden** *fjord* S Norway
Trondhjem *see* Trondheim
107 *J14* **Tronto** ⁓ C Italy
Troodos *see* Ólympos
121 *P3* **Troódos** *var.* Troodos Mountains. ▲ C Cyprus
Troodos Mountains *see* Troódos
96 *I13* **Troon** W Scotland, UK
107 *M22* **Tropea** Calabria, SW Italy
36 *L7* **Tropic** Utah, W USA
64 *L10* **Tropic Seamount** *var.* Banc du Tropique. *undersea feature* E Atlantic Ocean
Tropique, Banc du *see* Tropic Seamount
Tropoja *see* Tropojë
113 *L17* **Tropojë** *var.* Tropoja. Kukës, N Albania
Troppau *see* Opava
95 *O16* **Trosa** Södermanland, C Sweden
118 *H12* **Troškūnai** Utena, E Lithuania
101 *G23* **Trossingen** Baden-Württemberg, SW Germany
117 *T4* **Trostyanets'** *Rus.* Trostyanets. Sums'ka Oblast', NE Ukraine
117 *N7* **Trostyanets'** *Rus.* Trostyanets. Vinnyts'ka Oblast', C Ukraine
116 *L11* **Trotuş** ⁓ E Romania
44 *M8* **Trou-du-Nord** N Haiti
25 *W7* **Troup** Texas, SW USA
8 *I10* **Trout** ⁓ Northwest Territories, NW Canada
33 *N8* **Trout Creek** Montana, NW USA
32 *H10* **Trout Lake** Washington, NW USA
12 *B9* **Trout Lake** ◎ Ontario, S Canada
33 *T12* **Trout Peak** ▲ Wyoming, C USA
102 *L4* **Trouville** Calvados, N France
97 *L22* **Trowbridge** S England, UK
23 *Q6* **Troy** Alabama, S USA
27 *Q3* **Troy** Kansas, C USA
27 *W4* **Troy** Missouri, C USA
18 *L10* **Troy** New York, NE USA
21 *S10* **Troy** North Carolina, SE USA
31 *R13* **Troy** Ohio, N USA
25 *T9* **Troy** Texas, SW USA
114 *I9* **Troyan** Lovech, N Bulgaria
114 *I9* **Troyanski Prokhod** *pass* N Bulgaria
145 *N6* **Troyebratskiy** Severnyy Kazakhstan, N Kazakhstan
103 *Q6* **Troyes** *anc.* Augustobona Tricassium. Aube, N France
117 *X5* **Troyits'ke** Luhans'ka Oblast', E Ukraine
35 *W7* **Troy Peak** ▲ Nevada, W USA
113 *G15* **Trpanj** Dubrovnik-Neretva, S Croatia
Tršćanski Zaljev *see* Trieste, Gulf of
Trst *see* Trieste
113 *N14* **Trstenik** Serbia, C Serbia and Montenegro (Yugo.)
126 *I6* **Trubchevsk** Bryanskaya Oblast', W Russian Federation
Trubchular *see* Orlyak
37 *S10* **Truchas Peak** ▲ New Mexico, SW USA
143 *P16* **Trucial Coast** *physical region* C UAE
Trucial States *see* United Arab Emirates
35 *Q6* **Truckee** California, W USA
35 *R5* **Truckee River** ⁓ Nevada, W USA
127 *Q13* **Trudfront** Astrakhanskaya Oblast', SW Russian Federation
14 *I9* **Truite, Lac à la** ◎ Québec, SE Canada
42 *K4* **Trujillo** Colón, NE Honduras
56 *C12* **Trujillo** La Libertad, NW Peru
104 *K10* **Trujillo** Extremadura, W Spain
54 *I6* **Trujillo** Trujillo, NW Venezuela
54 *I6* **Trujillo** *off.* Estado Trujillo. ◆ *state* W Venezuela
Truk *see* Chuuk
Truk Islands *see* Chuuk Islands
29 *U10* **Truman** Minnesota, N USA
27 *X10* **Trumann** Arkansas, C USA
36 *J9* **Trumbull, Mount** ▲ Arizona, SW USA
114 *F9* **Trŭn** Pernik, W Bulgaria
183 *Q8* **Trundle** New South Wales, SE Australia
Trupcilar *see* Orlyak
13 *Q15* **Truro** Nova Scotia, SE Canada
97 *H25* **Truro** SW England, UK
25 *P5* **Truscott** Texas, SW USA
116 *K9* **Truşeşti** Botoşani, NE Romania
116 *H6* **Truskavets'** L'vivs'ka Oblast', W Ukraine
95 *H22* **Trustrup** Århus, C Denmark
10 *M11* **Trutch** British Columbia, W Canada
37 *Q14* **Truth Or Consequences** New Mexico, SW USA
111 *F15* **Trutnov** *Ger.* Trautenau. Královéhradecký Kraj, NE Czech Republic
103 *P13* **Truyère** ⁓ C France
114 *K9* **Tryavna** Lovech, N Bulgaria
28 *M14* **Tryon** Nebraska, C USA
94 *I11* **Trysilelva** ⁓ S Norway
112 *D10* **Tržac** Federacija Bosna I Hercegovina, NW Bosnia and Herzegovina
Tržaški Zaliv *see* Trieste, Gulf of
110 *G10* **Trzcianka** *Ger.* Schönlanke. Piła, Wielkopolskie, C Poland
110 *E7* **Trzebiatów** *Ger.* Treptow an der Rega. Zachodnio-pomorskie, NW Poland
111 *G14* **Trzebnica** *Ger.* Trebnitz. Dolnośląskie, SW Poland
109 *T10* **Tržič** *Ger.* Neumarktl. NW Slovenia
Trzynietz *see* Třinec
Tsabong *see* Tshabong
162 *G7* **Tsagaanchuluut** Dzavhan, C Mongolia
163 *P7* **Tsagaandorvoo** Dornod, NE Mongolia
163 *S8* **Tsagaannuur** Dornod, E Mongolia
162 *G8* **Tsagaan-Olom** Govĭ-Altay, C Mongolia
162 *J8* **Tsagaan-Ovoo** Övörhangay, C Mongolia
162 *D5* **Tsagaantüngi** Bayan-Ölgiy, NW Mongolia
127 *P12* **Tsagan Aman** Respublika Kalmykiya, SW Russian Federation
23 *V11* **Tsala Apopka Lake** ◎ Florida, SE USA
Tsamkong *see* Zhanjiang
Tsangpo *see* Brahmaputra
162 *L9* **Tsant** Dundgovĭ, C Mongolia
83 *G17* **Tsao** Ngamiland, NW Botswana
172 *I4* **Tsaratanana** Mahajanga, C Madagascar
114 *N10* **Tsarevo** *prev.* Michurin. Burgas, E Bulgaria
Tsarigrad *see* İstanbul
Tsaritsyn *see* Volgograd
124 *G13* **Tsarskoye Selo** *prev.* Pushkin. Leningradskaya Oblast', NW Russian Federation
117 *T7* **Tsarychanka** Dnipropetrovs'ka Oblast', E Ukraine
83 *H21* **Tsatsu** Southern, S Botswana
81 *J20* **Tsavo** Coast, S Kenya
83 *E21* **Tsawisis** Karas, S Namibia
Tschakathurn *see* Čakovec
Tschaslau *see* Čáslav
Tschenstochau *see* Częstochowa
Tschernembl *see* Črnomelj
28 *K6* **Tschida, Lake** ⊠ North Dakota, N USA
Tschorna *see* Mustvee
83 *I17* **Tsebanana** Central, NE Botswana
Tsefat *see* Ẕefat
162 *G8* **Tseel** Govĭ-Altay, SW Mongolia
126 *M13* **Tselina** Rostovskaya Oblast', SW Russian Federation
Tselinograd *see* Astana
Tselinogradskaya Oblast' *see* Akmola
162 *J6* **Tsengel** Hövsgöl, N Mongolia
162 *E7* **Tsenher** Hovd, W Mongolia
Tsentral'nyye Nizmennyye Garagumy *see* Merkezi Garagumy
83 *E21* **Tses** Karas, S Namibia
Tseshevlya *see* Tsyeshawlya
162 *E7* **Tsetsegnuur** Hovd, W Mongolia
Tsetsen Khan *see* Öndörhaan
162 *J7* **Tsetserleg** Arhangay, C Mongolia
77 *R16* **Tsévié** S Togo
83 *G21* **Tshabong** *var.* Tsabong. Kgalagadi, SW Botswana
83 *G20* **Tshane** Kgalagadi, SW Botswana
Tshangalele, Lac *see* Lufira, Lac de Retenue de la
83 *H17* **Tshauxaba** Central, C Botswana
79 *F21* **Tshela** Bas-Congo, W Dem. Rep. Congo
79 *K22* **Tshibala** Kasai Occidental, S Dem. Rep. Congo
79 *J22* **Tshikapa** Kasai Occidental, SW Dem. Rep. Congo
79 *L22* **Tshilenge** Kasai Oriental, S Dem. Rep. Congo
79 *L24* **Tshimbalanga** Katanga, S Dem. Rep. Congo
79 *L22* **Tshimbulu** Kasai Occidental, S Dem. Rep. Congo
Tshiumbe *see* Chiumbe
79 *M21* **Tshofa** Kasai Oriental, C Dem. Rep. Congo
79 *K18* **Tshuapa** ⁓ C Dem. Rep. Congo
Tshwane *see* Pretoria
114 *G7* **Tsibritsa** ⁓ NW Bulgaria
Tsien Tang *see* Puyang Jiang
114 *I12* **Tsigansko Gradishte** ▲ Bulgaria/Greece
8 *H7* **Tsiigehtchic** *prev.* Arctic Red River. Northwest Territories, NW Canada
127 *Q7* **Tsil'ma** ⁓ NW Russian Federation
119 *J17* **Tsimkavichy** *Rus.* Timkovichi. Minskaya Voblasts', C Belarus
126 *M11* **Tsimlyansk** Rostovskaya Oblast', SW Russian Federation
127 *N11* **Tsimlyanskoye Vodokhranilishche** *var.* Tsimlyansk Vodoskhovshche, *Eng.* Tsimlyansk Reservoir ⊠ SW Russian Federation
Tsimlyansk Reservoir *see* Tsimlyanskoye Vodokhranilishche
Tsimlyansk Vodoskhovshche *see* Tsimlyanskoye Vodokhranilishche
Tsinan *see* Jinan
Tsing Hai *see* Qinghai Hu, China
Tsinghai *see* Qinghai, China
Tsingtao/Tsingtau *see* Qingdao
Tsingyuan *see* Baoding
Tsinkiang *see* Quanzhou
Tsintao *see* Qingdao
83 *D17* **Tsintsabis** Otjikoto, N Namibia
172 *H8* **Tsiombe** *var.* Tsihombe. Toliara, S Madagascar
123 *O13* **Tsipa** ⁓ S Russian Federation
172 *H5* **Tsiribihina** ⁓ W Madagascar
172 *I5* **Tsiroanomandidy** Antananarivo, C Madagascar
189 *U13* **Tsis** *island* Chuuk, C Micronesia
Tsitsihar *see* Qiqihar
127 *Q3* **Tsivil'sk** Chuvashskaya Respublika, W Russian Federation
137 *T9* **Ts'khinvali** *prev.* Staliniri. C Georgia
119 *J19* **Tsna** ⁓ SW Belarus
126 *I15* **Tsna** *var.* Zna. ⁓ W Russian Federation
162 *K11* **Tsoohor** Ömnögovĭ, S Mongolia
164 *K14* **Tsu** *var.* Tu. Mie, Honshū, SW Japan
165 *O10* **Tsubame** *var.* Tubame. Niigata, Honshū, C Japan
165 *V3* **Tsubetsu** Hokkaidō, NE Japan
165 *O13* **Tsuchiura** *var.* Tutiura. Ibaraki, Honshū, S Japan
165 *Q6* **Tsugaru-kaikyō** *strait* N Japan
164 *E14* **Tsukumi** *var.* Tukumi. Ōita, Kyūshū, SW Japan
162 *E5* **Tsul-Ulaan** Bayan-Ölgiy, W Mongolia
83 *D17* **Tsumeb** Otjikoto, N Namibia
83 *F17* **Tsumkwe** Otjozondjupa, NE Namibia
164 *D15* **Tsuno** Miyazaki, Kyūshū, SW Japan
164 *D12* **Tsuno-shima** *island* SW Japan
164 *K12* **Tsuruga** *var.* Turuga. Fukui, Honshū, SW Japan
164 *H12* **Tsurugi-san** ▲ Shikoku, SW Japan
165 *P9* **Tsuruoka** *var.* Turuoka. Yamagata, Honshū, C Japan
164 *C12* **Tsushima** *var.* Tsushima-tō, Tusima. *island group* SW Japan
Tsushima-tō *see* Tsushima
164 *H12* **Tsuyama** *var.* Tuyama. Okayama, Honshū, SW Japan
83 *G19* **Tswaane** Ghanzi, W Botswana
119 *N16* **Tsyakhtsin** *Rus.* Tekhtin. Mahilyowskaya Voblasts', E Belarus
119 *P19* **Tsyerakhowka** *Rus.* Terekhovka. Homyel'skaya Voblasts', SE Belarus
119 *I17* **Tsyeshawlya** *Rus.* Cheshevlya, Tseshevlya. Brestskaya Voblasts', SW Belarus
Tsyurupinsk *see* Tsyurupyns'k
117 *R10* **Tsyurupyns'k** *Rus.* Tsyurupinsk. Khersons'ka Oblast', S Ukraine
Tu *see* Tsu
186 *C7* **Tua** ⁓ C PNG
Tuaim *see* Tuam
184 *L6* **Tuakau** Waikato, North Island, NZ
97 *C17* **Tuam** *Ir.* Tuaim. W Ireland
185 *K14* **Tuamarina** Marlborough, South Island, NZ
Tuamotu, Archipel des *see* Tuamotu, Îles
193 *Q9* **Tuamotu Fracture Zone** *tectonic feature* E Pacific Ocean
191 *W9* **Tuamotu, Îles** *var.* Archipel des Tuamotu, Dangerous Archipelago, Tuamotu Islands. *island group* N French Polynesia
Tuamotu Islands *see* Tuamotu, Îles
167 *R5* **Tuân Giao** Lai Châu, N Vietnam
171 *O2* **Tuao** Luzon, N Philippines
190 *B15* **Tuapa** NW Niue
43 *N7* **Tuapí** Región Autónoma Atlántico Norte, NE Nicaragua
126 *K15* **Tuapse** Krasnodarskiy Kray, SW Russian Federation
169 *U6* **Tuaran** Sabah, East Malaysia
104 *I6* **Tua, Rio** ⁓ N Portugal
192 *H15* **Tuasivi** Savai'i, C Samoa
185 *B24* **Tuatapere** Southland, South Island, NZ
36 *M9* **Tuba City** Arizona, SW USA
138 *H11* **Ţūbah, Qaşr aţ** *castle* Ma'ān, C Jordan
Tubame *see* Tsubame
169 *R16* **Tuban** *prev.* Toeban. Jawa, C Indonesia
141 *O16* **Tuban, Wādī** *dry watercourse* SW Yemen
61 *K14* **Tubarão** Santa Catarina, S Brazil
98 *O10* **Tubbergen** Overijssel, E Netherlands
Tubeke *see* Tubize
101 *H22* **Tübingen** *var.* Tuebingen. Baden-Württemberg, SW Germany
127 *W6* **Tubinskiy** Respublika Bashkortostan, W Russian Federation
99 *G19* **Tubize** *Dut.* Tubeke. Walloon Brabant, C Belgium
76 *J16* **Tubmanburg** NW Liberia
75 *T7* **Ţubruq** *Eng.* Tobruk, *It.* Tobruch. NE Libya
191 *T13* **Tubuai** *island* Îles Australes, SW French Polynesia
Tubuai, Îles/Tubuai Islands *see* Australes, Îles
40 *F3* **Tubutama** Sonora, NW Mexico
54 *K4* **Tucacas** Falcón, N Venezuela
59 *P16* **Tucano** Bahia, E Brazil
57 *P19* **Tucavaca, Río** ⁓ E Bolivia
110 *H8* **Tuchola** Kujawsko-pomorskie, C Poland
111 *M17* **Tuchów** Małopolskie, SE Poland
23 *S3* **Tucker** Georgia, SE USA
27 *W10* **Tuckerman** Arkansas, C USA
64 *B12* **Tucker's Town** E Bermuda
Tuckum *see* Tukums
36 *M15* **Tucson** Arizona, SW USA
62 *J7* **Tucumán** *off.* Provincia de Tucumán. ◆ *province* N Argentina
Tucumán *see* San Miguel de Tucumán
37 *V11* **Tucumcari** New Mexico, SW USA
58 *H13* **Tucunaré** Pará, N Brazil
55 *Q6* **Tucupita** Delta Amacuro, NE Venezuela

◆ Country • Country Capital ◇ Dependent Territory ○ Dependent Territory Capital ◆ Administrative Region ✕ International Airport ▲ Mountain ▲ Mountain Range ⚠ Volcano ⁓ River ◎ Lake ⊠ Reservoir

58 K13 **Tucuruí, Represa de** ⊞ NE Brazil
110 F9 **Tuczno** Zachodnio-pomorskie, NW Poland
Tuddo see Tudu
105 Q5 **Tudela** *Basq.* Tutera; *anc.* Tutela. Navarra, N Spain
104 M6 **Tudela de Duero** Castilla-León, N Spain
138 K6 **Tudmur** *var.* Tadmur, Tamar, *Gk.* Palmyra; *Bibl.* Tadmor. Ḥimṣ, C Syria
118 J4 **Tudu** *Ger.* Tuddo. Lääne-Virumaa, NE Estonia
Tuebingen see Tübingen
122 J14 **Tuekta** Respublika Altay, S Russian Federation
104 I5 **Tuela, Rio** ≈ N Portugal
153 X12 **Tuensang** Nāgāland, NE India
136 L15 **Tufanbeyli** Adana, C Turkey
Tüffer see Laško
186 F9 **Tufi** Northern, S PNG
193 O3 **Tufts Plain** *undersea feature* N Pacific Ocean
Tugalan see Kolkhozobod
21 P6 **Tug Fork** ≈ S USA
39 P15 **Tugidak Island** *island* Trinity Islands, Alaska, USA
171 O2 **Tuguegarao** Luzon, N Philippines
123 S12 **Tugur** Khabarovskiy Kray, SE Russian Federation
161 P4 **Tuhai He** ≈ E China
104 G4 **Tui** Galicia, NW Spain
77 O13 **Tui** *var.* Grand Balé. ≈ W Burkina
57 J16 **Tuichi, Río** ≈ W Bolivia
64 Q11 **Tuineje** Fuerteventura, Islas Canarias, Spain, NE Atlantic Ocean
43 X16 **Tuira, Río** ≈ SE Panama
Tuisarkan see Tūysarkān
Tujiabu see Yongxiu
127 W5 **Tukan** Respublika Bashkortostan, W Russian Federation
171 P14 **Tukangbesi, Kepulauan** *Dut.* Toekang Besi Eilanden. *island group* C Indonesia
147 V13 **Tŭkhtamish** *Rus.* Toktomush, *prev.* Tokhtamyshbek. SE Tajikistan
184 O12 **Tukituki** ≈ North Island, NZ
Tu-k'ou see Panzhihua
121 P12 **Tūkrah** NE Libya
8 H6 **Tuktoyaktuk** Northwest Territories, NW Canada
168 I9 **Tuktuk** Pulau Samosir, W Indonesia
Tukumi see Tsukumi
118 E9 **Tukums** *Ger.* Tuckum. Tukums, W Latvia
81 G24 **Tukuyu** *prev.* Neu-Langenburg. Mbeya, S Tanzania
Tukzār see Tokzār
41 O13 **Tula** *var.* Tula de Allende. Hidalgo, C Mexico
41 O11 **Tula** Tamaulipas, C Mexico
126 K5 **Tula** Tul'skaya Oblast', W Russian Federation
Tulach Mhór see Tullamore
Tula de Allende see Tula
159 N10 **Tulage Ar Gol** ≈ W China
186 M9 **Tulaghi** *var.* Tulagi. Florida Islands, C Solomon Islands
Tulagi see Tulaghi
41 P13 **Tulancingo** Hidalgo, C Mexico
35 R11 **Tulare** California, W USA
29 P9 **Tulare** South Dakota, N USA
35 Q12 **Tulare Lake Bed** *salt flat* California, W USA
37 S14 **Tularosa** New Mexico, SW USA
37 P13 **Tularosa Mountains** ▲ New Mexico, SW USA
37 S15 **Tularosa Valley** *basin* New Mexico, SW USA
83 E25 **Tulbagh** Western Cape, SW South Africa
56 C5 **Tulcán** Carchi, N Ecuador
117 N13 **Tulcea** Tulcea, E Romania
117 N13 **Tulcea** ◐ *county* SE Romania
Tul'chin see Tul'chyn
117 N7 **Tul'chyn** *Rus.* Tul'chin. Vinnyts'ka Oblast', C Ukraine
Tuléar see Toliara
35 O1 **Tulelake** California, W USA
116 J10 **Tulgheş** *Hung.* Gyergyótölgyes. Harghita, C Romania
Tul'govichi see Tul'havichy
119 N20 **Tul'havichy** *Rus.* Tul'govichi. Homyel'skaya Voblasts', SE Belarus
Tuli see Thuli
25 N4 **Tulia** Texas, SW USA
8 I9 **Tulita** *prev.* Fort Norman, Norman. Northwest Territories, NW Canada
20 J10 **Tullahoma** Tennessee, S USA
183 N12 **Tullamarine** ✕ (Melbourne) Victoria, SE Australia
183 Q7 **Tullamore** New South Wales, SE Australia
97 E18 **Tullamore** *Ir.* Tulach Mhór. C Ireland
103 N12 **Tulle** *anc.* Tutela. Corrèze, C France
109 X3 **Tulln** *var.* Oberhollabrunn. Niederösterreich, NE Austria
109 W4 **Tulln** ≈ NE Austria
22 H6 **Tullos** Louisiana, S USA
97 F19 **Tullow** *Ir.* An Tullach. SE Ireland
181 W5 **Tully** Queensland, NE Australia
126 J3 **Tuloma** ≈ NW Russian Federation
114 K10 **Tulovo** Stara Zagora, C Bulgaria
27 P9 **Tulsa** Oklahoma, C USA
153 N11 **Tulsipur** Mid Western, W Nepal
126 K6 **Tul'skaya Oblast'** ◐ *province* W Russian Federation
126 L14 **Tul'skiy** Respublika Adygeya, SW Russian Federation
186 E5 **Tulu** Manus Island, N PNG
54 D10 **Tuluá** Valle del Cauca, W Colombia
116 M12 **Tuluceşti** Galați, E Romania
39 N12 **Tuluksak** Alaska, USA
41 Z12 **Tulum, Ruinas de** *ruins* Quintana Roo, SE Mexico
122 M13 **Tulun** Irkutskaya Oblast', S Russian Federation
169 R17 **Tulungagung** *prev.* Toeloengagoeng. Jawa, C Indonesia
186 J6 **Tulun Islands** *var.* Kilinailau Islands; *prev.* Carteret Islands. *island group* NE PNG
126 M4 **Tuma** Ryazanskaya Oblast', W Russian Federation
54 B12 **Tumaco** Nariño, SW Colombia
54 B12 **Tumaco, Bahía de** *bay* SW Colombia
Tuman-gang see Tumen
42 L8 **Tuma, Río** ≈ N Nicaragua
95 O16 **Tumba** Stockholm, C Sweden
Tumba, Lac see Ntomba, Lac
169 S12 **Tumbangsenamang** Borneo, C Indonesia
183 Q10 **Tumbarumba** New South Wales, SE Australia
56 A8 **Tumbes** Tumbes, NW Peru
56 A9 **Tumbes** *off.* Departamento de Tumbes. ◐ *department* NW Peru
19 P5 **Tumbledown Mountain** ▲ Maine, NE USA
11 N13 **Tumbler Ridge** British Columbia, W Canada
167 Q12 **Tumbŏt, Phnum** ▲ W Cambodia
182 G9 **Tumby Bay** South Australia
163 Y10 **Tumen** Jilin, NE China
163 Y11 **Tumen** *Chin.* Tumen Jiang, *Kor.* Tuman-gang, *Rus.* Tumyn'tszyan. ≈ E Asia
Tumen Jiang see Tumen
55 Q8 **Tumeremo** Bolívar, E Venezuela
155 G19 **Tumkūr** Karnātaka, W India
96 I10 **Tummel** ≈ C Scotland, UK
188 B15 **Tumon Bay** *bay* W Guam
77 P14 **Tumu** NW Ghana
58 I10 **Tumuc Humac Mountains** *var.* Serra Tumucumaque. ▲ N South America
Tumucumaque, Serra see Tumuc Humac Mountains
183 Q10 **Tumut** New South Wales, SE Australia
Tumyn'tszyan see Tumen
Tün see Ferdows
45 U14 **Tunapuna** Trinidad, Trinidad and Tobago
60 K11 **Tunas** Paraná, S Brazil
Tunbridge Wells see Royal Tunbridge Wells
114 L11 **Tunca Nehri** *Bul.* Tundzha. ≈ Bulgaria/Turkey *see also* Tundzha
137 O14 **Tunceli** *var.* Kalan. Tunceli, E Turkey
137 O14 **Tunceli** ◐ *province* C Turkey
152 J12 **Tūndla** Uttar Pradesh, N India
81 I25 **Tunduru** Ruvuma, S Tanzania
114 L10 **Tundzha** *Turk.* Tunca Nehri. ≈ Bulgaria/Turkey *see also* Tunca Nehri
155 H17 **Tungabhadra** ≈ S India
155 F17 **Tungabhadra Reservoir** ⊞ S India
191 P2 **Tungaru** *prev.* Gilbert Islands. *island group* W Kiribati
171 P7 **Tungawan** Mindanao, S Philippines
Tungdor see Mainling
T'ung-shan see Xuzhou
161 Q16 **Tungsha Tao** *Chin.* Dongsha Qundao, *Eng.* Pratas Island. *island* S Taiwan
161 S13 **Tungshih** *Jap.* Tōsei. N Taiwan
8 H9 **Tungsten** Northwest Territories, W Canada
Tung-t'ing Hu see Dongting Hu
56 A13 **Tungurahua** ◐ *province* C Ecuador
95 F14 **Tunhovdfjorden** ⊞ S Norway
22 K2 **Tunica** Mississippi, S USA
75 N5 **Tunis** *var.* Tūnis. ● (Tunisia) NE Tunisia
75 N5 **Tunis, Golfe de** *Ar.* Khalīj Tūnis. *gulf* NE Tunisia
75 N6 **Tunisia** *off.* Republic of Tunisia, *Ar.* Al Jumhūrīyah at Tūnisīyah, *Fr.* République Tunisienne. ◆ *republic* N Africa
Tūnisīyah, Al Jumhūrīyah at see Tunisia
Tūnis, Khalīj see Tunis, Golfe de
54 G9 **Tunja** Boyacá, C Colombia
93 F14 **Tunnsjøen** *Lapp.* Dåtnejaevrie. ◎ C Norway
39 N12 **Tuntutuliak** Alaska, USA
147 U8 **Tunuk** Chuyskaya Oblast', C Kyrgyzstan
13 Q6 **Tunungayualok Island** *island* Newfoundland and Labrador, E Canada
62 H11 **Tunuyán** Mendoza, W Argentina
197 P14 **Tunu** ◐ *province* E Greenland
62 I11 **Tunuyán, Río** ≈ W Argentina
Tunxi see Huangshan
Tuodian see Shuangbai
Tuoji see Zhongba
35 P9 **Tuolumne River** ≈ California, W USA
Tuong Buong see Tương Đương
167 R7 **Tương Đương** *var.* Tuong Buong. Nghê An, N Vietnam
160 I13 **Tuoniang Jiang** ≈ S China
Tuotuo He see Togton He
Tuotuoheyan see Tanggulashan
Tüp see Tyup
60 J9 **Tupã** São Paulo, S Brazil
191 S10 **Tupai** *var.* Motu Iti. *atoll* Îles Sous le Vent, W French Polynesia
61 G15 **Tupanciretã** Rio Grande do Sul, S Brazil
22 M2 **Tupelo** Mississippi, S USA
59 K18 **Tupiraçaba** Goiás, S Brazil
57 L21 **Tupiza** Potosí, S Bolivia
11 N13 **Tupper** British Columbia, W Canada
18 J8 **Tupper Lake** ◎ New York, NE USA
146 J10 **Tuproqqal'a** *Rus.* Turpakkla. Xorazm Viloyati, W Uzbekistan
62 H11 **Tupungato, Volcán** ※ W Argentina
163 T9 **Tuquan** Nei Mongol Zizhiqu, N China
54 C13 **Túquerres** Nariño, SW Colombia
153 U13 **Tura** Meghālaya, NE India
122 M10 **Tura** Evenkiyskiy Avtonomnyy Okrug, N Russian Federation
122 G10 **Tura** ≈ C Russian Federation
140 M10 **Turabah** Makkah, W Saudi Arabia
55 O8 **Turagua, Cerro** ▲ C Venezuela
184 L12 **Turakina** Manawatu-Wanganui, North Island, NZ
185 K15 **Turakirae Head** *headland* North Island, NZ
186 B8 **Turama** ≈ S PNG
122 K13 **Turan** Respublika Tyva, S Russian Federation
184 M10 **Turangi** Waikato, North Island, NZ
146 F11 **Turan Lowland** *var.* Turan Plain, *Kaz.* Turan Oypaty, *Rus.* Turanskaya Nizmennost', *Turk.* Turan Pesligi, *Uzb.* Turon Pasttekisligi. *plain* C Asia
Turan Oypaty/Turan Pesligi/Turan Plain/Turanskaya Nizmennost' see Turan Lowland
138 K7 **Ţurāq al 'Ilab** *hill range* S Syria
119 K20 **Turaw** *Rus.* Turov. Homyel'skaya Voblasts', SE Belarus
140 L2 **Ţurayf** Al Ḥudūd ash Shamālīyah, NW Saudi Arabia
Turba see Teruel
54 E5 **Turbaco** Bolívar, N Colombia
148 K15 **Turbat** Baluchistān, SW Pakistan
Turbat-i-Haidari see Torbat-e Ḥeydarīyeh
Turbat-i-Jam see Torbat-e Jām
54 D7 **Turbo** Antioquia, NW Colombia
Turčiansky Svätý Martin see Martin
116 H10 **Turda** *Ger.* Thorenburg, *Hung.* Torda. Cluj, NW Romania
142 M7 **Ţūreh** Markazī, W Iran
191 X12 **Tureia** *atoll* Îles Tuamotu, SE French Polynesia
110 I12 **Turek** Wielkopolskie, C Poland
93 L19 **Turenki** Etelä-Suomi, S Finland
Turfan see Turpan
145 R8 **Turgay** *Kaz.* Torghay. Akmola, W Kazakhstan
145 N10 **Turgay** *Kaz.* Torgay. ≈ C Kazakhstan
144 M8 **Turgayskaya Stolovaya Strana** *Kaz.* Torgay Üstirti. *plateau* Kazakhstan/Russian Federation
Turgel see Türi
114 L8 **Tŭrgovishte** *prev.* Eski Dzhumaya. Tŭrgovishte, N Bulgaria
114 L8 **Tŭrgovishte** ◐ *province* N Bulgaria
136 C14 **Turgutlu** Manisa, W Turkey
136 L12 **Turhal** Tokat, N Turkey
118 H4 **Türi** *Ger.* Turgel. Järvamaa, N Estonia
105 S9 **Turia** ≈ E Spain
58 M12 **Turiaçu** Maranhão, E Brazil
Turin see Torino
116 I3 **Turiys'k** Volyns'ka Oblast', NW Ukraine
Turja see Tur"ya
116 H6 **Turka** L'vivs'ka Oblast', W Ukraine
81 H16 **Turkana, Lake** *var.* Lake Rudolf. ◎ N Kenya
145 P16 **Turkestan** *Kaz.* Türkistan. Yuzhnyy Kazakhstan, S Kazakhstan
147 Q12 **Turkestan Range** *Rus.* Turkestanskiy Khrebet. ▲ C Asia
Turkestanskiy Khrebet see Turkestan Range
111 M23 **Túrkeve** Jász-Nagykun-Szolnok, E Hungary
25 O4 **Turkey** Texas, SW USA
136 H14 **Turkey** *off.* Republic of Turkey, *Turk.* Türkiye Cumhuriyeti. ◆ *republic* SW Asia
181 N4 **Turkey Creek** Western Australia
26 M9 **Turkey Creek** ≈ Oklahoma, C USA
37 T9 **Turkey Mountains** ▲ New Mexico, SW USA
29 X11 **Turkey River** ≈ Iowa, C USA
127 N7 **Turki** Saratovskaya Oblast', W Russian Federation
121 O1 **Turkish Republic of Northern Cyprus** ◇ *disputed territory* Cyprus
Türkistan see Turkestan
Turkistan, Bandi-i see Torkestān, Selseleh-ye Band-e
Türkiye Cumhuriyeti see Turkey
146 K12 **Türkmenabat** *prev. Rus.* Chardzhev, Chardzhou, Chardzhui, Lenin-Turkmenski, *Turkm.* Chärjew. Lebap Welaýaty, E Turkmenistan
146 A11 **Türkmen Aylagy** *Rus.* Turkmenskiy Zaliv. *lake gulf* W Turkmenistan
Turkmenbashi see Türkmenbaşy
146 A10 **Türkmenbaşy** *Rus.* Turkmenbashi; *prev.* Krasnovodsk. Balkan Welaýaty, W Turkmenistan
146 A10 **Türkmenbaşy Aylagy** *prev. Rus.* Krasnovodskiy Zaliv, *Turkm.* Krasnowodsk Aylagy. *lake gulf* W Turkmenistan
146 J14 **Türkmengala** *Rus.* Turkmen-kala; *prev.* Turkmen-Kala. Mary Welaýaty, S Turkmenistan
146 G13 **Turkmenistan** *off.* Turkmenistan; *prev.* Turkmenskaya Soviet Socialist Republic. ◆ *republic* C Asia
Turkmen-kala/Turkmen-Kala see Türkmengala
Turkmenskaya Soviet Socialist Republic see Turkmenistan
Turkmenskiy Zaliv see Türkmen Aylagy
136 L16 **Türkoğlu** Kahramanmaraş, S Turkey
44 L6 **Turks and Caicos Islands** ◇ *UK dependent territory* N West Indies
64 G10 **Turks and Caicos Islands** *island group* N West Indies
45 N6 **Turks Islands** *island group* SE Turks and Caicos Islands
93 K19 **Turku** *Swe.* Åbo. Länsi-Suomi, W Finland
81 H17 **Turkwel** *seasonal river* NW Kenya
27 P9 **Turley** Oklahoma, C USA
35 P9 **Turlock** California, W USA
118 I12 **Turmantas** Utena, NE Lithuania
54 L5 **Turmero** Aragua, N Venezuela
Turmberg see Wieżyca
184 N13 **Turnagain, Cape** *headland* North Island, NZ
Turnau see Turnov
42 H2 **Turneffe Islands** *island group* E Belize
18 M11 **Turners Falls** Massachusetts, NE USA
11 P16 **Turner Valley** Alberta, SW Canada
99 I16 **Turnhout** Antwerpen, N Belgium
109 V5 **Turnitz** Niederösterreich, E Austria
11 S12 **Turnor Lake** ◎ Saskatchewan, C Canada
111 E15 **Turnov** *Ger.* Turnau. Liberecký Kraj, N Czech Republic
Tŭrnovo see Veliko Tŭrnovo
116 I15 **Turnu Măgurele** *var.* Turnu-Măgurele. Teleorman, S Romania
Turnu Severin see Drobeta-Turnu Severin
Turócszentmárton see Martin
Turoni see Tours
Turan Pasttekisligi see Turan Lowland
Turov see Turaw
Turpakkla see Tuproqqal'a
158 M6 **Turpan** *var.* Turfan. Xinjiang Uygur Zizhiqu, NW China
Turpan Depression see Turpan Pendi
158 M6 **Turpan Pendi** *Eng.* Turpan Depression. *depression* NW China
158 M5 **Turpan Zhan** Xinjiang Uygur Zizhiqu, W China
Turpentine State see North Carolina
44 H8 **Turquino, Pico** ▲ E Cuba
27 Y10 **Turrell** Arkansas, C USA
43 N14 **Turrialba** Cartago, E Costa Rica
96 K8 **Turriff** NE Scotland, UK
139 V7 **Tursāq** E Iraq
Turshiz see Kāshmar
Tursunzade see Tursunzoda
147 P13 **Tursunzoda** *Rus.* Tursunzade; *prev.* Regar. W Tajikistan
162 J4 **Turt** Hövsgöl, N Mongolia
Turtkul' see To'rtko'l
29 O9 **Turtle Creek** ≈ South Dakota, N USA
30 K4 **Turtle Flambeau Flowage** ⊞ Wisconsin, N USA
11 S14 **Turtleford** Saskatchewan, S Canada
28 M4 **Turtle Lake** North Dakota, N USA
92 K12 **Turtola** Lappi, NW Finland
122 M10 **Turu** ≈ N Russian Federation
Turuga see Tsuruga
147 V10 **Turugart Pass** *pass* China/Kyrgyzstan
158 E7 **Turugart Shankou** *var.* Pereval Torugart. *pass* China/Kyrgyzstan
122 K9 **Turukhan** ≈ N Russian Federation
122 K9 **Turukhansk** Krasnoyarskiy Kray, N Russian Federation
139 N3 **Ţurumbah** *well* NE Syria
Turuoka see Tsuruoka
144 H14 **Turush** Mangistau, SW Kazakhstan
60 K7 **Turvo, Rio** ≈ S Brazil
116 J2 **Tur"ya** *Pol.* Turja, *Rus.* Tur'ya. ≈ NW Ukraine
23 O4 **Tuscaloosa** Alabama, S USA
23 O4 **Tuscaloosa, Lake** ◎ Alabama, S USA
Tuscan Archipelago see Toscano, Archipelago
Tuscan-Emilian Mountains see Tosco-Emiliano, Appennino
Tuscany see Toscana
35 V2 **Tuscarora** Nevada, W USA
18 F15 **Tuscarora Mountain** *ridge* Pennsylvania, NE USA
30 M14 **Tuscola** Illinois, N USA
25 P7 **Tuscola** Texas, SW USA
23 O2 **Tuscumbia** Alabama, S USA
92 O4 **Tusenøyane** *island group* S Svalbard
144 K13 **Tushchybas, Zaliv** *prev.* Zaliv Paskevicha. *lake gulf* SW Kazakhstan
171 Y15 **Tusirah** Papua, E Indonesia
23 Q5 **Tuskegee** Alabama, S USA
94 E8 **Tustna** *island* S Norway
39 R12 **Tustumena Lake** ◎ Alaska, USA
110 K13 **Tuszyn** Łodzkie, C Poland
137 S13 **Tutak** Ağrı, E Turkey
185 C20 **Tutamoe Range** ▲ North Island, NZ
Tutasev see Tutayev
124 L15 **Tutayev** *var.* Tutasev. Yaroslavskaya Oblast', W Russian Federation
Tutela see Tulle, France
Tutela see Tudela, Spain
Tutera see Tudela
155 H23 **Tuticorin** Tamil Nādu, SE India
113 L15 **Tutin** Serbia, S Serbia and Montenegro (Yugo.)
184 O10 **Tutira** Hawke's Bay, North Island, NZ
Tutiura see Tsuchiura
122 K10 **Tutonchany** Evenkiyskiy Avtonomnyy Okrug, N Russian Federation
114 L6 **Tutrakan** Silistra, NE Bulgaria
29 N5 **Tuttle** North Dakota, N USA
26 M11 **Tuttle** Oklahoma, C USA
27 O3 **Tuttle Creek Lake** ⊞ Kansas, C USA
101 H23 **Tuttlingen** Baden-Württemberg, S Germany
171 R16 **Tutuala** W East Timor
192 K17 **Tutuila** *island* W American Samoa
83 I18 **Tutume** Central, E Botswana
39 N7 **Tututalak Mountain** ▲ Alaska, USA
22 K3 **Tutwiler** Mississippi, S USA
162 L8 **Tuul Gol** ≈ N Mongolia
93 O16 **Tuupovaara** Itä-Suomi, E Finland
Tuva see Tyva, Respublika
190 E7 **Tuvalu** *prev.* Ellice Islands. ◆ *commonwealth republic* SW Pacific Ocean
Tuvana-i-Tholo see Tuvana-i-Colo
Tuvinskaya ASSR see Tyva, Respublika
Tuvutha see Tuvuca
141 P9 **Ţuwayq, Jabal** ▲ C Saudi Arabia
138 H13 **Ţuwayyil ash Shihāq** *desert* S Jordan
11 U16 **Tuxford** Saskatchewan, S Canada
167 U12 **Tu Xoay** Đắc Lắc, S Vietnam
40 L14 **Tuxpan** Jalisco, C Mexico
40 J12 **Tuxpan** Nayarit, C Mexico
41 Q12 **Tuxpán** *var.* Tuxpán de Rodríguez Cano. Veracruz-Llave, E Mexico
Tuxpán de Rodríguez Cano see Tuxpán
41 R15 **Tuxtepec** *var.* San Juan Bautista Tuxtepec. Oaxaca, S Mexico
41 U16 **Tuxtla** *var.* Tuxtla Gutiérrez. Chiapas, SE Mexico
Tuxtla see San Andrés Tuxtla
Tuxtla Gutiérrez see Tuxtla
Tuyama see Tsuyama
167 T5 **Tuyên Quang** Tuyên Quang, N Vietnam
167 U13 **Tuy Hoa** Bình Thuân, S Vietnam
167 V12 **Tuy Hoa** Phu Yên, S Vietnam
127 U5 **Tuymazy** Respublika Bashkortostan, W Russian Federation
142 L6 **Tūysarkān** *var.* Tuisarkan, Tuyserkān. Hamadān, W Iran
Tuyserkān see Tūysarkān
145 W16 **Tuyuk** *Kaz.* Tuyyq. Almaty, SE Kazakhstan
Tuyyq see Tuyuk
136 I14 **Tuz Gölü** ◎ C Turkey
125 Q15 **Tuzha** Kirovskaya Oblast', NW Russian Federation
113 K17 **Tuzi** Montenegro, SW Serbia and Montenegro (Yugo.)
139 T5 **Ṭūz Khurmātū** N Iraq
112 I11 **Tuzla** Federacija Bosna I Hercegovina, NE Bosnia and Herzegovina
117 N15 **Tuzla** Constanța, SE Romania
137 T12 **Tuzluca** Iğdır, NE Turkey
95 J20 **Tvååker** Halland, S Sweden
95 F17 **Tvedestrand** Aust-Agder, S Norway
124 J16 **Tver'** *prev.* Kalinin. Tverskaya Oblast', W Russian Federation
Tverya see Teverya
124 I15 **Tverskaya Oblast'** ◐ *province* W Russian Federation
126 I15 **Tvertsa** ≈ W Russian Federation
110 H13 **Twardogóra** *Ger.* Festenberg. Dolnośląskie, SW Poland
14 J14 **Tweed** Ontario, SE Canada
96 K13 **Tweed** ≈ England/Scotland, UK
98 O7 **Tweede-Exloërmond** Drenthe, NE Netherlands
183 V3 **Tweed Heads** New South Wales, SE Australia
98 M11 **Twello** Gelderland, E Netherlands
35 W15 **Twentynine Palms** California, W USA
25 P9 **Twin Buttes Reservoir** ⊞ Texas, SW USA
33 O15 **Twin Falls** Idaho, NW USA
39 N13 **Twin Hills** Alaska, USA
11 O11 **Twin Lakes** Alberta, W Canada
33 O12 **Twin Peaks** ▲ Idaho, NW USA
185 I14 **Twins, The** ▲ South Island, NZ
29 S5 **Twin Valley** Minnesota, N USA
100 G11 **Twistringen** Niedersachsen, NW Germany
185 E20 **Twizel** Canterbury, South Island, NZ
29 X5 **Two Harbors** Minnesota, N USA
11 R14 **Two Hills** Alberta, SW Canada
31 N7 **Two Rivers** Wisconsin, N USA
116 H8 **Tyachiv** Zakarpats'ka Oblast', W Ukraine
Tyan'-Shan' see Tien Shan
166 L3 **Tyao** ≈ Burma/India
117 R6 **Tyas'myn** ≈ N Ukraine
23 X6 **Tybee Island** Georgia, SE USA
Tyborøn see Thyborøn
111 J16 **Tychy** *Ger.* Tichau. Śląskie, S Poland
111 O16 **Tyczyn** Podkarpackie, SE Poland
94 I8 **Tydal** Sør-Trøndelag, S Norway
115 H24 **Tyflós** ≈ Kríti, Greece, E Mediterranean Sea
21 S3 **Tygart Lake** ⊞ West Virginia, NE USA
123 Q13 **Tygda** Amurskaya Oblast', SE Russian Federation
21 Q11 **Tyger River** ≈ South Carolina, SE USA
32 I11 **Tygh Valley** Oregon, NW USA
94 F12 **Tyin** ◎ S Norway
29 S10 **Tyler** Minnesota, N USA
25 W7 **Tyler** Texas, SW USA
25 W7 **Tyler, Lake** ⊞ Texas, SW USA
22 K7 **Tylertown** Mississippi, S USA
22 K7 **Tylihul's'kyy Lyman** ◎ SW Ukraine
Tylos see Bahrain
115 C15 **Týmfi** *var.* Tímfi. ▲ W Greece
115 E17 **Tymfristós** *var.* Timfristos. ▲ C Greece
115 J25 **Tympáki** *var.* Timbaki; *prev.* Timbákion. Kríti, Greece, E Mediterranean Sea
123 Q12 **Tynda** Amurskaya Oblast', SE Russian Federation
29 Q12 **Tyndall** South Dakota, N USA
97 L14 **Tyne** ≈ N England, UK
97 M14 **Tynemouth** NE England, UK
97 L14 **Tyneside** *cultural region* NE England, UK
94 H10 **Tynset** Hedmark, S Norway
39 Q12 **Tyonek** Alaska, USA
Tyôsi see Chōshi
Tyras see Dniester, Moldova/Ukraine
Tyras see Bilhorod-Dnistrovs'kyy, Ukraine
Tyre see Soûr
95 G14 **Tyrifjorden** ◎ S Norway
95 K22 **Tyringe** Skåne, S Sweden
123 R13 **Tyrma** Khabarovskiy Kray, SE Russian Federation
Tyrnau see Trnava
115 F15 **Týrnavos** *var.* Tírnavos. Thessalía, C Greece
127 N16 **Tyrnyauz** Kabardino-Balkarskaya Respublika, SW Russian Federation
Tyrol see Tirol
18 E14 **Tyrone** Pennsylvania, NE USA
97 E15 **Tyrone** *cultural region* W Northern Ireland, UK
93 F19 **Tyrsil** Hedmark, S Norway
182 M10 **Tyrrell, Lake** *salt lake* Victoria, SE Australia
120 L9 **Tyrrhenian Basin** *undersea feature* Tyrrhenian Sea, C Mediterranean Sea
120 L8 **Tyrrhenian Sea** *It.* Mare Tirreno. *sea* N Mediterranean Sea
Tysa see Tisa/Tisza
116 J7 **Tysmenytsya** Ivano-Frankivs'ka Oblast', W Ukraine
95 C14 **Tysnesøya** *island* S Norway
95 C14 **Tysse** Hordaland, S Norway
95 D14 **Tyssedal** Hordaland, S Norway
95 O17 **Tystberga** Södermanland, C Sweden
118 E12 **Tytuvėnai** Šiauliai, C Lithuania
144 D14 **Tyub-Karagan, Mys** *headland* SW Kazakhstan
147 V8 **Tyugel'-Say** Narynskaya Oblast', C Kyrgyzstan
122 H11 **Tyukalinsk** Omskaya Oblast', C Russian Federation
127 V7 **Tyul'gan** Orenburgskaya Oblast', W Russian Federation
122 G11 **Tyumen'** Tyumenskaya Oblast', C Russian Federation
122 H11 **Tyumenskaya Oblast'** ◐ *province* C Russian Federation
147 Y7 **Tyup** *Kir.* Tüp. Issyk-Kul'skaya Oblast', NE Kyrgyzstan
122 L14 **Tyva, Respublika** *prev.* Tannu-Tuva, Tuva, Tuvinskaya ASSR. ◐ *autonomous republic* C Russian Federation
117 N7 **Tyvriv** Vinnyts'ka Oblast', C Ukraine
97 J21 **Tywi** ≈ S Wales, UK
97 I19 **Tywyn** W Wales, UK
83 K20 **Tzaneen** Limpopo, NE South Africa
Tzekung see Zigong
41 X12 **Tzucacab** Yucatán, SE Mexico

U

82 B12 **Uaco Cungo** *var.* Waku Kungo, *Port.* Santa Comba. Cuanza Sul, C Angola
UAE see United Arab Emirates
191 X7 **Ua Huka** *island* Îles Marquises, NE French Polynesia
58 E10 **Uaiacás** Roraima, N Brazil
Uamba see Wamba
Uanle Uen see Wanlaweyn
191 W7 **Ua Pu** *island* Îles Marquises, NE French Polynesia
81 L17 **Uar Garas** *spring/well* SW Somalia
58 G12 **Uatumã, Rio** ≈ C Brazil
Ua Uíbh Fhailí see Offaly
58 C11 **Uaupés, Rio** *var.* Río Vaupés. ≈ Brazil/Colombia *see also* Vaupés, Río
145 X9 **Uba** ≈ E Kazakhstan
145 N6 **Ubagan** *Kaz.* Obagan. ≈ Kazakhstan/Russian Federation
186 G7 **Ubai** New Britain, E PNG
79 J15 **Ubangi** *Fr.* Oubangui. ≈ C Africa
Ubangi-Shari see Central African Republic
116 M3 **Ubarts'** *Ukr.* Ubort'. ≈ Belarus/Ukraine *see also* Ubort'
54 F9 **Ubaté** Cundinamarca, C Colombia
60 N10 **Ubatuba** São Paulo, S Brazil
149 R12 **Ubauro** Sind, SE Pakistan
171 Q6 **Ubay** Bohol, C Philippines
103 U14 **Ubaye** ≈ SE France
Ubayid, Wadi al see Ubayyiḍ, Wādī al
139 N8 **Ubaylah** W Iraq
139 O10 **Ubayyiḍ, Wādī al** *var.* Wadi al Ubayid. *dry watercourse* SW Iraq
98 L13 **Ubbergen** Gelderland, E Netherlands
164 E13 **Ube** Yamaguchi, Honshū, SW Japan
105 O13 **Úbeda** Andalucía, S Spain
109 V7 **Übelbach** *var.* Markt-Übelbach. Steiermark, SE Austria
59 L20 **Uberaba** Minas Gerais, SE Brazil
57 Q19 **Uberaba, Laguna** ◎ E Bolivia
59 K19 **Uberlândia** Minas Gerais, SE Brazil
101 H24 **Überlingen** Baden-Württemberg, S Germany
77 U16 **Ubiaja** Edo, S Nigeria
104 K3 **Ubiña, Peña** ▲ NW Spain
57 H17 **Ubinas, Volcán** ※ S Peru
Ubol Rajadhani/Ubol Ratchathani see Ubon Ratchathani
167 P9 **Ubolratna Reservoir** ⊞ C Thailand

◆ Country ● Country Capital ◇ Dependent Territory ○ Dependent Territory Capital ◐ Administrative Region ✕ International Airport ▲ Mountain ▲ Mountain Range ※ Volcano ≈ River ◎ Lake ⊞ Reservoir

167 S10 Ubon Ratchathani var. Muang Ubon, Ubol Rajadhani, Ubol Ratchathani, Udon Ratchathani. Ubon Ratchathani, E Thailand
119 L20 Ubort' Bel. Ubarts'. ≈ Belarus/Ukraine see also Ubarts'
104 K15 Ubrique Andalucía, S Spain
Ubsu-Nur, Ozero see Uvs Nuur
79 M18 Ubundu Orientale, C Dem. Rep. Congo
146 J13 Uçajy var. Üchajy, Rus. Uch-Adzhi. Mary Welaýaty, C Turkmenistan
137 X11 Ucar Rus. Udzhary. C Azerbaijan
56 G13 Ucayali off. Departamento de Ucayali. ◈ department E Peru
56 F10 Ucayali, Río ≈ C Peru
Uccle see Ukkel
Uch-Adzhi/Üchajy see Uçajy
127 X4 Uchaly Respublika Bashkortostan, W Russian Federation
145 W13 Ucharal Kaz. Üsharal. Almaty, E Kazakhstan
164 C17 Uchinoura Kagoshima, Kyūshū, SW Japan
165 R5 Uchiura-wan bay NW Pacific Ocean
Uchkuduk see Uchquduq
Uchkurghan see Uchqo'rg'on
146 K8 Uchquduq Rus. Uchkuduk. Navoiy Viloyati, N Uzbekistan
147 S9 Uchqo'rg'on Rus. Uchkurghan. Namangan Viloyati, E Uzbekistan
Uchsay see Uchsoy
146 G6 Uchsoy Rus. Uchsay. Qoraqalpog'iston Respublikasi, NW Uzbekistan
Uchtagan Gumy/Uchtagan, Peski see Uçtagan Gumy
123 R11 Uchur ≈ E Russian Federation
100 O10 Uckermark cultural region E Germany
10 K17 Ucluelet Vancouver Island, British Columbia, SW Canada
146 D10 Uçtagan Gumy var. Uchtagan Gumy, Rus. Peski Uchtagan. desert NW Turkmenistan
122 M13 Uda ≈ S Russian Federation
123 R12 Uda ≈ E Russian Federation
123 N6 Udachnyy Respublika Sakha (Yakutiya), NE Russian Federation
155 G21 Udagamandalam var. Udhagamandalam; prev. Ootacamund. Tamil Nādu, SW India
152 F14 Udaipur prev. Oodeypore. Rājasthān, N India
Udayadhani see Uthai Thani
143 N16 'Udayd, Khawr al var. Khor al Udeid. inlet Qatar/Saudi Arabia
112 D11 Udbina Lika-Senj, W Croatia
95 I18 Uddevalla Västra Götaland, S Sweden
Uddjaur see Uddjaure
92 H13 Uddjaure var. Uddjaur. ⊚ N Sweden
Udeid, Khor al see 'Udayd, Khawr al
99 K14 Uden Noord-Brabant, SE Netherlands
Uden see Udenhout
99 J14 Udenhout var. Uden. Noord-Brabant, S Netherlands
155 H14 Udgīr Mahārāshtra, C India
Udhagamandalam see Udagamandalam
152 H6 Udhampur Jammu and Kashmir, NW India
139 X14 'Udhaybah, 'Uqlat al well S Iraq
106 J7 Udine anc. Utina. Friuli-Venezia Giulia, NE Italy
193 O13 Udintsev Fracture Zone tectonic feature S Pacific Ocean
Udipi see Udupi
Udmurtia see Udmurtskaya Respublika
127 S2 Udmurtskaya Respublika Eng. Udmurtia. ◈ autonomous republic NW Russian Federation
124 J15 Udomlya Tverskaya Oblast', W Russian Federation
Udon Ratchathani see Ubon Ratchathani
167 Q8 Udon Thani var. Ban Mak Khaeng, Udorndhani. Udon Thani, N Thailand
Udorndhani see Udon Thani
189 U12 Udot atoll Chuuk Islands, C Micronesia
123 S12 Udskaya Guba bay E Russian Federation
155 E19 Udupi var. Udipi. Karnātaka, SW India
Udzhary see Ucar
100 O9 Uecker ≈ NE Germany
100 P9 Ueckermünde Mecklenburg-Vorpommern, NE Germany
164 M12 Ueda var. Uyeda. Nagano, Honshū, S Japan
79 L16 Uele var. Welle. ≈ NE Dem. Rep. Congo
Uele (upper course) see Uolo, Río, Equatorial Guinea/Gabon
Uele (upper course) see Kibali, Dem. Rep. Congo
123 W5 Uelen Chukotskiy Avtonomnyy Okrug, NE Russian Federation
100 J11 Uelzen Niedersachsen, N Germany
164 J14 Ueno Mie, Honshū, SW Japan
127 V4 Ufa Respublika Bashkortostan, W Russian Federation
127 V4 Ufa ≈ W Russian Federation
Ufra see Kenar
83 C18 Ugab ≈ C Namibia
118 D8 Ugāle Ventspils, NW Latvia
81 F17 Uganda off. Republic of Uganda. ◆ republic E Africa
138 G4 Ugarit Ar. Ra's Shamrah. site of ancient city Al Lādhiqīyah, NW Syria
39 O14 Ugashik Alaska, USA
107 Q19 Ugento Puglia, SE Italy
105 O15 Ugíjar Andalucía, S Spain
103 T11 Ugine Savoie, E France
123 R13 Uglegorsk Amurskaya Oblast', SE Russian Federation
125 V13 Ugleural'sk Permskaya Oblast', S Russian Federation
124 L15 Uglich Yaroslavskaya Oblast', W Russian Federation
124 I14 Uglovka var. Okulovka. Novgorodskaya Oblast', W Russian Federation
126 I4 Ugra ≈ W Russian Federation
147 V9 Ugyut Narynskaya Oblast', C Kyrgyzstan
111 H19 Uherské Hradiště Ger. Ungarisch-Hradisch. Zlínský kraj, E Czech Republic
111 H19 Uherský Brod Ger. Ungarisch-Brod. Zlínský kraj, E Czech Republic
111 B17 Úhlava Ger. Angel. ≈ W Czech Republic
Uhorshchyna see Hungary
31 T13 Uhrichsville Ohio, N USA
Uhuru Peak see Kilimanjaro
96 G8 Uig N Scotland, UK
82 B10 Uíge Port. Carmona, Vila Marechal Carmona. Uíge, NW Angola
82 B10 Uíge ◈ province N Angola
193 Y15 Uiha island Ha'apai Group, C Tonga
189 U13 Uijec island Chuuk, C Micronesia
163 X14 Ŭijŏngbu Jap. Giseifu. NW South Korea
144 H10 Uil Kaz. Oyyl. Aktyubinsk, W Kazakhstan
144 H10 Uil Kaz. Oyyl. ≈ W Kazakhstan
36 M3 Uinta Mountains ▲ Utah, W USA
83 C18 Uis Erongo, NW Namibia
83 I25 Uitenhage Eastern Cape, S South Africa
98 H9 Uitgeest Noord-Holland, W Netherlands
98 I11 Uithoorn Noord-Holland, C Netherlands
98 O4 Uithuizen Groningen, NE Netherlands
98 O4 Uithuizermeeden Groningen, NE Netherlands
189 R6 Ujae Atoll var. Wūjae. atoll Ralik Chain, W Marshall Islands
Ujain see Ujjain
111 I16 Ujazd Opolskie, S Poland
Új-Becse see Novi Bečej
Ujda see Oujda
189 N5 Ujelang Atoll var. Wujlān. atoll Ralik Chain, W Marshall Islands
111 N21 Újfehértó Szabolcs-Szatmár-Bereg, E Hungary
Újgradiska see Nova Gradiška
164 J13 Uji var. Uzi. Kyōto, Honshū, SW Japan
81 E21 Ujiji Kigoma, W Tanzania
154 G10 Ujjain prev. Ujain. Madhya Pradesh, C India
Újlak see Ilok
'Ujmān see 'Ajmān
Újmoldova see Moldova Nouă
Újszentanna see Sântana
Ujungpandang see Makassar
Ujung Salang see Phuket
Újvidék see Novi Sad
154 E11 Ukāi Reservoir ⊞ W India
81 G19 Ukara Island island N Tanzania
'Ukash, Wādī see 'Akāsh, Wādī
81 F19 Ukerewe Island island N Tanzania
139 S9 Ukhaydhir C Iraq
153 X13 Ukhrul Manipur, NE India
125 S9 Ukhta Respublika Komi, NW Russian Federation
34 L6 Ukiah California, W USA
32 K12 Ukiah Oregon, NW USA
99 G18 Ukkel Fr. Uccle. Brussels, C Belgium
118 G13 Ukmergė Pol. Wiłkomierz. Vilnius, C Lithuania
Ukraina see Ukraine
116 L6 Ukraine off. Ukraine, Rus. Ukraina, Ukr. Ukrayina; prev. Ukrainian Soviet Socialist Republic, Ukrainskaya S.S.R. ◆ republic SE Europe
Ukrainskay S.S.R/Ukrayina see Ukraine
82 B13 Uku Cuanza Sul, NW Angola
164 B13 Uku-jima island Gotō-rettō, SW Japan
83 F20 Ukwi Kgalagadi, SW Botswana
118 M13 Ula Rus. Ulla. Vitsyebskaya Voblasts', N Belarus
136 C16 Ula Muğla, SW Turkey
118 M13 Ula Rus. Ulla. ≈ N Belarus
162 L7 Ulaanbaatar Eng. Ulan Bator; prev. Urga. ● (Mongolia) Töv, C Mongolia
163 N8 Ulaan-Ereg Hentiy, E Mongolia
162 E5 Ulaangom Uvs, NW Mongolia
162 E7 Ulaantolgoy Hovd, W Mongolia
162 I8 Ulaan-Uul Bayanhongor, C Mongolia
163 O10 Ulaan-Uul Dornogovĭ, SE Mongolia
162 M14 Ulan var. Otog Qi. Nei Mongol Zizhiqu, N China
159 R10 Ulan var. Xireg; prev. Xiligou. Qinghai, C China
Ulan Bator see Ulaanbaatar
162 L13 Ulan Buh Shamo desert N China
Ulanhad see Chifeng
163 T8 Ulanhot Nei Mongol Zizhiqu, N China
127 Q14 Ulan Khol Respublika Kalmykiya, SW Russian Federation
162 M13 Ulansuhai Nur ⊚ N China
123 N14 Ulan-Ude prev. Verkhneudinsk. Respublika Buryatiya, S Russian Federation
159 N12 Ulan Ul Hu ⊚ C China
187 N9 Ulawa Island island SE Solomon Islands
138 J7 'Ulayyānīyah, Bi'r al var. Al Hilbeh. well S Syria
123 S12 Ul'banskiy Zaliv strait E Russian Federation
Ulbo see Olib
113 J18 Ulcinj Montenegro, SW Serbia and Montenegro (Yugo.)
163 O7 Uldz Hentiy, NE Mongolia
Uleåborg see Oulu
Uleälv see Oulujoki
95 G16 Ulefoss Telemark, S Norway
Uleträsk see Oulujärvi
113 L19 Ulëz var. Ulëza. Dibër, C Albania
Ulëza see Ulëz
95 F22 Ulfborg Ringkøbing, W Denmark
98 N13 Ulft Gelderland, E Netherlands
162 G7 Uliastay prev. Jibhalanta. Dzavhan, W Mongolia
188 F8 Ulimang Babeldaob, N Palau
188 H14 Ulithi Atoll atoll Caroline Islands, W Micronesia
112 N10 Uljma Serbia, NE Serbia and Montenegro (Yugo.)
144 L11 Ul'kayak Kaz. Ölkeyek. ≈ C Kazakhstan
145 Q7 Ul'ken-Karoy, Ozero ⊚ N Kazakhstan
Ülkenözen see Bol'shoy Uzen'
Ülkenqobda see Bol'shaya Khobda
104 G3 Ulla ≈ NW Spain
Ulla see Ula
183 S10 Ulladulla New South Wales, SE Australia
153 T14 Ullapara Rajshahi, W Bangladesh
96 H7 Ullapool N Scotland, UK
95 J20 Ullared Halland, S Sweden
105 T7 Ulldecona Cataluña, NE Spain
92 I9 Ullsfjorden fjord N Norway
97 K15 Ullswater ⊚ NW England, UK
101 I22 Ulm Baden-Württemberg, S Germany
33 R8 Ulm Montana, NW USA
183 V5 Ulmarra New South Wales, SE Australia
116 K13 Ulmeni Buzău, C Romania
116 K14 Ulmeni Călărași, S Romania
42 L7 Ulmukhuás Región Autónoma Atlántico Norte, NE Nicaragua
188 C8 Ulong var. Aulong. island Palau Islands, N Palau
83 N14 Ulonguè var. Ulongwé. Tete, NW Mozambique
Ulongwé see Ulonguè
95 K19 Ulricehamn Västra Götaland, S Sweden
98 N5 Ulrum Groningen, NE Netherlands
163 Z16 Ulsan Jap. Urusan. SE South Korea
94 D10 Ulsteinvik Møre og Romsdal, S Norway
97 D15 Ulster ◈ province Northern Ireland, UK/Ireland
171 Q10 Ulu Pulau Siau, N Indonesia
123 Q11 Ulu Respublika Sakha (Yakutiya), NE Russian Federation
42 H5 Ulúa, Río ≈ NW Honduras
136 D12 Ulubat Gölü ⊚ NW Turkey
136 E12 Uludağ ▲ NW Turkey
158 D7 Ulugqat Xinjiang Uygur Zizhiqu, W China
136 J16 Ulukışla Niğde, S Turkey
189 O15 Ulul island Caroline Islands, C Micronesia
83 L22 Ulundi KwaZulu/Natal, E South Africa
158 M3 Ulungur He ≈ NW China
158 K2 Ulungur Hu ⊚ NW China
181 P8 Uluru var. Ayers Rock. rocky outcrop Northern Territory, C Australia
97 K16 Ulverston NW England, UK
183 O16 Ulverstone Tasmania, SE Australia
94 D13 Ulvik Hordaland, S Norway
93 J18 Ulvila Länsi-Suomi, W Finland
117 O8 Ulyanivka Rus. Ul'yanovka. Kirovohrads'ka Oblast', C Ukraine
Ul'yanovka see Ulyanivka
127 Q5 Ul'yanovsk prev. Simbirsk. Ul'yanovskaya Oblast', W Russian Federation
127 Q5 Ul'yanovskaya Oblast' ◈ province W Russian Federation
145 S10 Ul'yanovskiy Karaganda, C Kazakhstan
Ul'yanovskiy Kanal see Ul'yanow Kanali
146 M13 Ul'yanow Kanali Rus. Ul'yanovskiy Kanal. canal Turkmenistan/Uzbekistan
Ulyshylanshyq see Uly-Zhylanshyk
26 H6 Ulysses Kansas, C USA
145 O12 Ulytau, Gory ▲ C Kazakhstan
145 N11 Uly-Zhylanshyk Kaz. Ulyshylanshyq. ≈ C Kazakhstan
112 A9 Umag It. Umago. Istra, NW Croatia
Umago see Umag
189 V13 Uman atoll Chuuk Islands, C Micronesia
117 O7 Uman' Rus. Uman. Cherkas'ka Oblast', C Ukraine
41 W12 Umán Yucatán, SE Mexico
Umanak/Umanaq see Uummannaq
'Umān, Khalīj see Oman, Gulf of
'Umān, Salṭanat see Oman
154 K10 Umaria Madhya Pradesh, C India
149 R16 Umar Kot Sind, SE Pakistan
188 B17 Umatac SW Guam
188 A17 Umatac Bay bay SW Guam
139 S6 Umayqah C Iraq
124 J5 Umba Murmanskaya Oblast', NW Russian Federation
138 I8 Umbāshi, Khirbat al ruins As Suwaydā', S Syria
80 A12 Umbelasha ≈ W Sudan
106 H12 Umbertide Umbria, C Italy
61 B17 Umberto var. Humberto. Santa Fe, C Argentina
186 E7 Umboi Island var. Rooke Island. island C PNG
126 J4 Umbozero, Ozero ⊚ NW Russian Federation
106 H13 Umbria ◈ region C Italy
Umbrian-Machigian Mountains see Umbro-Marchigiano, Appennino
106 I12 Umbro-Marchigiano, Appennino Eng. Umbrian-Machigian Mountains. ▲ C Italy
93 J16 Umeå Västerbotten, N Sweden
93 H14 Umeälven ≈ N Sweden
39 Q5 Umiat Alaska, USA
83 K23 Umlazi KwaZulu/Natal, E South Africa
139 X10 Umm al Baqar, Hawr var. Birkat ad Dawaymah. spring S Iraq
141 U12 Umm al Ḥayt, Wādī var. Wādī Amilḥayt. seasonal river SW Oman
Umm al Qaiwain see Umm al Qaywayn
143 R15 Umm al Qaywayn var. Umm al Qaiwain. Umm al Qaywayn, NE UAE
139 Q5 Umm al Tūz C Iraq
138 J3 Umm 'Āmūd Ḥalab, N Syria
141 Y10 Umm ar Ruṣāṣ var. Umm Ruṣayṣ. W Oman
141 X9 Ummas Samīn salt flat C Oman
141 V9 Umm az Zumūl oasis E Saudi Arabia
80 A9 Umm Buru Western Darfur, W Sudan
80 A12 Umm Dafag Southern Darfur, W Sudan
Umm Durmān see Omdurman
138 F9 Umm el Fahm Haifa, N Israel
80 F9 Umm Inderab Northern Kordofan, C Sudan
80 C10 Umm Keddada Northern Darfur, W Sudan
140 J7 Umm Lajj Tabūk, W Saudi Arabia
138 L10 Umm Maḥfur ≈ N Jordan
139 Y13 Umm Qaṣr SE Iraq
Umm Ruṣayṣ see Umm ar Ruṣāṣ
80 F11 Umm Ruwaba var. Umm Ruwābah, Um Ruwāba. Northern Kordofan, C Sudan
Umm Ruwābah see Umm Ruwaba
143 N16 Umm Sa'īd var. Musay'īd. S Qatar
138 K10 Umm Ṭuways, Wādī dry watercourse N Jordan
38 J17 Umnak Island island Aleutian Islands, Alaska, USA
32 F13 Umpqua River ≈ Oregon, NW USA
82 D13 Umpulo Bié, C Angola
154 I12 Umred Mahārāshtra, C India
139 Y10 Umr Sawān, Hawr ⊚ S Iraq
Um Ruwāba see Umm Ruwaba
Umtali see Mutare
83 J24 Umtata Eastern Cape, SE South Africa
77 V17 Umuahia Abia, SW Nigeria
60 H10 Umuarama Paraná, S Brazil
Umvuma see Mvuma
83 K18 Umzingwani ≈ S Zimbabwe
112 D11 Una ≈ Bosnia and Herzegovina/Croatia
112 E12 Unac ≈ W Bosnia and Herzegovina
23 T6 Unadilla Georgia, SE USA
18 I10 Unadilla River ≈ New York, NE USA
59 L18 Unaí Minas Gerais, SE Brazil
39 N10 Unalakleet Alaska, USA
38 K17 Unalaska Island island Aleutian Islands, Alaska, USA
185 I16 Una, Mount ▲ South Island, NZ
82 N13 Unango Niassa, N Mozambique
Unao see Unnāo
92 L12 Unari Lappi, N Finland
141 O6 'Unayzah var. Anaiza. Al Qaṣīm, C Saudi Arabia
138 L10 'Unayzah, Jabal ▲ Jordan/Saudi Arabia
Unci see Almería
57 K19 Uncía Potosí, C Bolivia
37 Q7 Uncompahgre Peak ▲ Colorado, C USA
37 P6 Uncompahgre Plateau plain Colorado, C USA
95 J17 Unden ⊚ S Sweden
28 M4 Underwood North Dakota, N USA
171 T13 Undur Pulau Seram, E Indonesia
Undur Khan see Öndörhaan
126 H6 Unecha Bryanskaya Oblast', W Russian Federation
39 N16 Unga Unga Island, Alaska, USA
Ungaria see Hungary
183 P8 Ungarie New South Wales, SE Australia
Ungarisch-Brod see Uherský Brod
Ungarisches Erzgebirge see Slovenské rudohorie
Ungarisch-Hradisch see Uherské Hradiště
Ungarn see Hungary
12 M4 Ungava Bay bay Québec, E Canada
12 J2 Ungava, Péninsule d' peninsula Québec, SE Canada
Ungeny see Ungheni
116 M9 Ungheni Rus. Ungeny. W Moldova
Unguja see Zanzibar
146 G10 Üngüz Angyrsyndaky Garagum Rus. Zaunguzskiye Garagumy. desert N Turkmenistan
146 H11 Unguz, Solonchakovyye Vpadiny salt marsh C Turkmenistan
Ungvár see Uzhhorod
60 I12 União da Vitória Paraná, S Brazil
111 G17 Uničov Ger. Mährisch-Neustadt. Olomoucký Kraj, E Czech Republic
110 J12 Uniejów Łódzkie, C Poland
112 A11 Unije island W Croatia
38 L16 Unimak Island island Aleutian Islands, Alaska, USA
38 L16 Unimak Pass strait Aleutian Islands, Alaska, USA
27 W5 Union Missouri, C USA
32 L12 Union Oregon, NW USA
21 Q11 Union South Carolina, SE USA
21 R6 Union West Virginia, NE USA
62 J12 Unión San Luis, C Argentina
61 B25 Unión, Bahía bay E Argentina
31 Q13 Union City Indiana, N USA
31 Q10 Union City Michigan, N USA
18 C12 Union City Pennsylvania, NE USA
20 G8 Union City Tennessee, S USA
32 G14 Union Creek Oregon, NW USA
83 G25 Uniondale Western Cape, SW South Africa
40 K13 Unión de Tula Jalisco, SW Mexico
30 M9 Union Grove Wisconsin, N USA
45 Y15 Union Island island S Saint Vincent and the Grenadines
23 Q6 Union Springs Alabama, S USA
20 H6 Uniontown Kentucky, S USA
18 C16 Uniontown Pennsylvania, NE USA
27 T1 Unionville Missouri, C USA
141 V8 United Arab Emirates Ar. Al Imārāt al 'Arabīyah al Muttaḥidah, abbrev. UAE; prev. Trucial States. ◆ federation SW Asia
United Arab Republic see Egypt
97 H14 United Kingdom off. UK of Great Britain and Northern Ireland, abbrev. UK. ◆ monarchy NW Europe
United Mexican States see Mexico
United Provinces see Uttar Pradesh
16 L10 United States of America off. United States of America, var. America, The States, abbrev. U.S., USA. ◆ federal republic
124 J10 Unitsa Respublika Kareliya, NW Russian Federation
11 S15 Unity Saskatchewan, S Canada
Unity State see Wahda
105 Q8 Universales, Montes ▲ C Spain
27 X4 University City Missouri, C USA
187 Q13 Unmet Malekula, C Vanuatu
101 F15 Unna Nordrhein-Westfalen, W Germany
152 L12 Unnāo prev. Unao. Uttar Pradesh, N India
187 R15 Unpongkor Erromango, S Vanuatu
Unruhstadt see Kargowa
96 M1 Unst island NE Scotland, UK
101 K16 Unstrut ≈ C Germany
Unterdrauburg see Dravograd
Unterlimbach see Lendava
101 L23 Unterschleissheim Bayern, SE Germany
101 H24 Untersee ⊚ Germany/Switzerland
100 O10 Unterueckersee ⊚ NE Germany
108 F9 Unterwalden ◈ canton C Switzerland
55 N12 Unturán, Sierra de ▲ Brazil/Venezuela
159 N11 Unuli Horog Qinghai, W China
136 M11 Ünye Ordu, W Turkey
Unza see Unzha
127 O14 Unzha var. Unza. ≈ NW Russian Federation
79 E17 Uolo, Río var. Eyo (lower course), Mbini, Uele (upper course), Woleu; prev. Benito. ≈ Equatorial Guinea/Gabon
55 Q10 Uonán Bolívar, SE Venezuela
161 T12 Uotsuri-shima island China/Japan/Taiwan
165 M11 Uozu Toyama, Honshū, SW Japan
42 L12 Upala Alajuela, NW Costa Rica
55 P7 Upata Bolívar, E Venezuela
79 M23 Upemba, Lac ⊚ SE Dem. Rep. Congo
197 O12 Upernavik var. Upernivik. Kitaa, C Greenland
Upernivik see Upernavik
83 F22 Upington Northern Cape, W South Africa
Uplands see Ottawa
192 I16 Upolu island SE Samoa
38 G11 'Upolu Point var. Upolu Point headland Hawai'i, USA, C Pacific Ocean
Upper Austria see Oberösterreich
Upper Bann see Bann
14 M13 Upper Canada Village tourist site Ontario, SE Canada
18 I16 Upper Darby Pennsylvania, NE USA
28 L2 Upper Des Lacs Lake ⊞ North Dakota, N USA
185 L14 Upper Hutt Wellington, North Island, NZ
29 X11 Upper Iowa River ≈ Iowa, C USA
32 H15 Upper Klamath Lake ⊚ Oregon, NW USA
34 M6 Upper Lake California, W USA
35 Q1 Upper Lake ⊚ California, W USA
10 K9 Upper Liard Yukon Territory, W Canada
97 E16 Upper Lough Erne ⊚ SW Northern Ireland, UK
80 F12 Upper Nile ◈ state E Sudan
29 T3 Upper Red Lake ⊚ Minnesota, N USA
31 S12 Upper Sandusky Ohio, N USA
Upper Volta see Burkina
95 O15 Upplandsväsby var. Upplands Väsby. Stockholm, C Sweden
95 O15 Uppsala Uppsala, C Sweden
95 O14 Uppsala ◈ county C Sweden
38 J12 Upright Cape headland Saint Matthew Island, Alaska, USA
20 K6 Upton Kentucky, S USA
33 Y13 Upton Wyoming, C USA
141 N7 'Uqlat aş Şuqūr Al Qaṣīm, W Saudi Arabia
Uqturpan see Wushi
54 C7 Urabá, Golfo de gulf NW Colombia
Uracas see Farallon de Pajaros
Uradar'ya see O'radaryo
Urad Qianqi see Xishanzui
165 U5 Urahoro Hokkaidō, NE Japan
165 T5 Urakawa Hokkaidō, NE Japan
127 X6 Ural Kaz. Zayyq. ≈ Kazakhstan/Russian Federation
183 T6 Uralla New South Wales, SE Australia
Ural Mountains see Ural'skiye Gory
144 F8 Ural'sk Kaz. Oral. Zapadnyy Kazakhstan, NW Kazakhstan
Ural'skaya Oblast' see Zapadnyy Kazakhstan
127 W5 Ural'skiye Gory var. Ural'skiy Khrebet, Eng. Ural Mountains. ▲ Kazakhstan/Russian Federation
Ural'skiy Khrebet see Ural'skiye Gory
138 I3 Urām aş Şughrá Ḥalab, N Syria
183 P10 Urana New South Wales, SE Australia
11 S10 Uranium City Saskatchewan, C Canada
58 F10 Uraricoera Roraima, N Brazil
Ura-Tyube see Üroteppa
165 O13 Urawa Saitama, Honshū, S Japan
122 H10 Uray Khanty-Mansiyskiy Avtonomnyy Okrug, C Russian Federation
141 R7 'Uray'irah Ash Sharqīyah, E Saudi Arabia
30 M13 Urbana Illinois, N USA
31 R13 Urbana Ohio, N USA
29 V14 Urbandale Iowa, C USA
106 I11 Urbania Marche, C Italy
106 I11 Urbino Marche, C Italy
57 H16 Urcos Cusco, S Peru
144 D10 Urda Zapadnyy Kazakhstan, W Kazakhstan
105 N10 Urda Castilla-La Mancha, C Spain
162 E7 Urdgol Hovd, W Mongolia
Urdunn see Jordan
145 X12 Urdzhar Kaz. Ürzhar. Vostochnyy Kazakhstan, E Kazakhstan
97 L16 Ure ≈ N England, UK
119 K18 Urechcha Rus. Urech'ye. Minskaya Voblasts', S Belarus
Urech'ye see Urechcha
127 P2 Uren' Nizhegorodskaya Oblast', W Russian Federation
122 J9 Urengoy Yamalo-Nenetskiy Avtonomnyy Okrug, N Russian Federation
184 K10 Urenui Taranaki, North Island, NZ
187 Q12 Ureparapara island Banks Islands, N Vanuatu
40 G5 Ures Sonora, NW Mexico
Urfa see Şanlıurfa
Urga see Ulaanbaatar
146 H9 Urganch Rus. Urgench; prev. Novo-Urgench. Xorazm Viloyati, W Uzbekistan
Urgench see Urganch
136 J14 Ürgüp Nevşehir, C Turkey
147 O12 Urgut Samarqand Viloyati, C Uzbekistan
158 K3 Urho Xinjiang Uygur Zizhiqu, W China
152 G5 Uri Jammu and Kashmir, NW India
108 G9 Uri ◈ canton C Switzerland
54 F11 Uribe Meta, C Colombia
54 H4 Uribia La Guajira, N Colombia
116 G12 Uricani Hung. Hobicaurikány. Hunedoara, SW Romania
57 M21 Uriondo Tarija, S Bolivia
40 I7 Urique Chihuahua, N Mexico
40 I7 Urique, Río ≈ N Mexico
56 E9 Uritiyacu, Río ≈ N Peru
Uritskiy see Sarykol'
98 K8 Urk Flevoland, N Netherlands
136 B14 Urla İzmir, W Turkey
116 K13 Urlați Prahova, SE Romania
127 V4 Urman Respublika Bashkortostan, W Russian Federation
147 P12 Urmetan W Tajikistan
Urmia see Orūmīyeh
Urmia, Lake see Orūmīyeh, Daryācheh-ye
Urmiyeh see Orūmīyeh
113 N17 Uroševac Alb. Ferizaj. Serbia, S Serbia and Montenegro (Yugo.)
147 P11 Üroteppa Rus. Ura-Tyube. NW Tajikistan
54 D8 Urrao Antioquia, W Colombia
Ursat'yevskaya see Xovos
162 I11 Urt Ömnögovĭ, S Mongolia
127 X7 Urtazym Orenburgskaya Oblast', W Russian Federation
59 K18 Uruaçu Goiás, C Brazil
40 M14 Uruapan var. Uruapan del Progreso. Michoacán de Ocampo, SW Mexico
Uruapan del Progreso see Uruapan
57 G15 Urubamba, Cordillera ▲ C Peru
57 G14 Urubamba, Río ≈ C Peru
58 G12 Urucará Amazonas, N Brazil
61 E16 Uruguaiana Rio Grande do Sul, S Brazil
Uruguai, Rio see Uruguay
61 E18 Uruguay off. Oriental Republic of Uruguay; prev. La Banda Oriental. ◆ republic E South America
61 E15 Uruguay var. Rio Uruguai, Río Uruguay. ≈ E South America
Uruguay, Río see Uruguay
Urumchi see Ürümqi
158 L5 Ürümqi var. Tihwa, Urumchi, Urumqi, Urumtsi, Wu-lu-k'o-mu-shi, Wu-lu-mu-ch'i; prev. Ti-hua. autonomous region capital Xinjiang Uygur Zizhiqu, NW China
Urumtsi see Ürümqi
Urundi see Burundi
183 V6 Urunga New South Wales, SE Australia
188 C15 Uruno Point headland NW Guam

◆ Country ● Country Capital ◇ Dependent Territory ○ Dependent Territory Capital ◈ Administrative Region ✕ International Airport ▲ Mountain ▲ Mountain Range Volcano ≈ River ⊚ Lake ⊞ Reservoir

123 U13 **Urup, Ostrov** *island* Kuril'skiye Ostrova, SE Russian Federation
141 P11 **'Urūq al Mawārid** *desert* S Saudi Arabia
Urusan *see* Ulsan
127 T5 **Urussu** Respublika Tatarstan, W Russian Federation
184 K10 **Uruti** Taranaki, North Island, NZ
57 K19 **Uru Uru, Lago** ◎ W Bolivia
55 P9 **Uruyén** Bolívar, SE Venezuela
149 O7 **Urūzgān** *var.* Oruzgān, Orūzgān. Urūzgān, C Afghanistan
149 N6 **Urūzgān** *Per.* Orūzgān. ◆ *province* C Afghanistan
165 T3 **Uryū-gawa** ↝ Hokkaidō, NE Japan
165 T2 **Uryū-ko** ◎ Hokkaidō, NE Japan
127 N8 **Uryupinsk** Volgogradskaya Oblast', SW Russian Federation
Ürzhar *see* Urdzhar
125 R16 **Urzhum** Kirovskaya Oblast', NW Russian Federation
116 K13 **Urziceni** Ialomiţa, SE Romania
U.S./USA *see* United States of America
164 E14 **Usa** Ōita, Kyūshū, SW Japan
119 L16 **Usa** *Rus.* Usa. ↝ C Belarus
127 T6 **Usa** ↝ NW Russian Federation
136 E14 **Uşak** *prev.* Ushak. Uşak, W Turkey
136 D14 **Uşak** *var.* Ushak. ◆ *province* W Turkey
83 C19 **Usakos** Erongo, W Namibia
81 J21 **Usambara Mountains** ▲ NE Tanzania
81 G23 **Usangu Flats** *wetland* SW Tanzania
65 D24 **Usborne, Mount** ▲ East Falkland, Falkland Islands
100 O8 **Usedom** *island* NE Germany
99 M24 **Useldange** Diekirch, C Luxembourg
118 L12 **Ushacha** *Rus.* Ushacha. Vitsyebskaya Voblasts', N Belarus
Ushachi *see* Ushachy
118 L13 **Ushachy** *Rus.* Ushachi. Vitsyebskaya Voblasts', N Belarus
Ushak *see* Uşak
122 L4 **Ushakova, Ostrov** *island* Severnaya Zemlya, N Russian Federation
Ushant *see* Ouessant, Île d'
Üsharal *see* Ucharal
164 B15 **Ushibuka** *var.* Usibuka. Kumamoto, Shimo-jima, SW Japan
Ushi Point *see* Sabaneta, Puntan
145 V14 **Ushtobe** *Kaz.* Üshtöbe. Almaty, SE Kazakhstan
63 I25 **Ushuaia** Tierra del Fuego, S Argentina
39 R10 **Usibelli** Alaska, USA
Usibuka *see* Ushibuka
186 D7 **Usino** Madang, N PNG
125 U6 **Usinsk** Respublika Komi, NW Russian Federation
97 K22 **Usk** *Wel.* Wysg. ↝ SE Wales, UK
Uskočke Planine/ Uskokengebirge *see* Gorjanci/Žumberačko Gorje
Uskoplje *see* Gornji Vakuf
Üsküb *see* Skopje
114 M11 **Üsküpdere** Kırklareli, NW Turkey
126 L7 **Usman'** Lipetskaya Oblast', W Russian Federation
118 D8 **Usmas Ezers** ◎ NW Latvia
125 U13 **Usol'ye** Permskaya Oblast', NW Russian Federation
41 T16 **Uspanapa, Río** ↝ SE Mexico
145 R11 **Uspenskiy** Karaganda, C Kazakhstan
103 O11 **Ussel** Corrèze, C France
163 Z6 **Ussuri** *var.* Usuri, Wusuri, *Chin.* Wusuli Jiang. ↝ China/Russian Federation
123 S15 **Ussuriysk** *prev.* Nikol'sk, Nikol'sk-Ussuriyskiy, Voroshilov. Primorskiy Kray, SE Russian Federation
136 J10 **Usta Burnu** *headland* N Turkey
149 P13 **Usta Muhammad** Baluchistān, SW Pakistan
123 V11 **Ust'-Bol'sheretsk** Kamchatskaya Oblast', E Russian Federation
127 N9 **Ust'-Buzulukskaya** Volgogradskaya Oblast', SW Russian Federation
111 C16 **Ústecký Kraj** ◆ *region* NW Czech Republic
108 G7 **Uster** Zürich, NE Switzerland
107 I22 **Ustica, Isola d'** *island* S Italy
122 M11 **Ust'-Ilimsk** Irkutskaya Oblast', C Russian Federation
111 C15 **Ústí nad Labem** *Ger.* Aussig. Ústecký Kraj, NW Czech Republic
111 F17 **Ústí nad Orlicí** *Ger.* Wildenschwert. Pardubický Kraj, E Czech Republic
Ustinov *see* Izhevsk
113 J14 **Ustiprača** Republika Srpska, SE Bosnia and Herzegovina
122 H11 **Ust'-Ishim** Omskaya Oblast', C Russian Federation
110 G6 **Ustka** *Ger.* Stolpmünde. Pomorskie, N Poland
123 V9 **Ust'-Kamchatsk** Kamchatskaya Oblast', E Russian Federation
145 X9 **Ust'-Kamenogorsk** *Kaz.* Öskemen. Vostochnyy Kazakhstan, E Kazakhstan
125 T10 **Ust'-Khayryuzovo** Koryakskiy Avtonomnyy Okrug, E Russian Federation
122 I14 **Ust'-Koksa** Respublika Altay, S Russian Federation
125 S11 **Ust'-Kulom** Respublika Komi, NW Russian Federation
123 Q8 **Ust'-Kuyga** Respublika Sakha (Yakutiya), NE Russian Federation
126 L14 **Ust'-Labinsk** Krasnodarskiy Kray, SW Russian Federation
123 R10 **Ust'-Maya** Respublika Sakha (Yakutiya), NE Russian Federation
123 R9 **Ust'-Nera** Respublika Sakha (Yakutiya), NE Russian Federation
123 P12 **Ust'-Nyukzha** Amurskaya Oblast', S Russian Federation
123 O7 **Ust'-Olenëk** Respublika Sakha (Yakutiya), NE Russian Federation
123 T9 **Ust'-Omchug** Magadanskaya Oblast', E Russian Federation
122 M13 **Ust'-Ordynskiy** Ust'-Ordynskiy Buryatskiy Avtonomnyy Okrug, S Russian Federation
122 M13 **Ust'-Ordynskiy Buryatskiy Avtonomnyy Okrug** ◆ *autonomous district* S Russian Federation
125 N8 **Ust'-Pinega** Arkhangel'skaya Oblast', NW Russian Federation
122 K8 **Ust'-Port** Taymyrskiy (Dolgano-Nenetskiy) Avtonomnyy Okrug, N Russian Federation
114 L11 **Ustrem** *prev.* Vakav. Yambol, E Bulgaria
111 O18 **Ustrzyki Dolne** Podkarpackie, SE Poland
Ust'-Sysol'sk *see* Syktyvkar
125 R7 **Ust'-Tsil'ma** Respublika Komi, NW Russian Federation
Ust Urt *see* Ustyurt Plateau
127 O11 **Ust'ya** ↝ NW Russian Federation
123 V10 **Ust'yevoye** *prev.* Kirovskiy. Kamchatskaya Oblast', E Russian Federation
117 R8 **Ustynivka** Kirovohrads'ka Oblast', C Ukraine
144 H15 **Ustyurt Plateau** *var.* Ust Urt, *Uzb.* Ustyurt Platosi. *plateau* Kazakhstan/Uzbekistan
Ustyurt Platosi *see* Ustyurt Plateau
124 K14 **Ustyuzhna** Vologodskaya Oblast', NW Russian Federation
158 J4 **Usu** Xinjiang Uygur Zizhiqu, NW China
171 O13 **Usu** Sulawesi, C Indonesia
164 E14 **Usuki** Ōita, Kyūshū, SW Japan
42 G8 **Usulután** Usulután, SE El Salvador
42 B9 **Usulután** ◆ *department* SE El Salvador
41 W16 **Usumacinta, Río** ↝ Guatemala/Mexico
Usumbura *see* Bujumbura
Usuri *see* Ussuri
171 W14 **Uta** Papua, E Indonesia
36 K5 **Utah** *off.* State of Utah; *also known as* Beehive State, Mormon State. ◆ *state* W USA
36 L3 **Utah Lake** ◎ Utah, W USA
Utaidhani *see* Uthai Thani
93 M14 **Utajärvi** Oulu, C Finland
Utamboni *see* Mitemele, Río
Utaradit *see* Uttaradit
165 T3 **Utashinai** *var.* Utasinai. Hokkaidō, NE Japan
Utasinai *see* Utashinai
193 Y14 **'Uta Vava'u** *island* Vava'u Group, N Tonga
37 V9 **Ute Creek** ↝ New Mexico, SW USA
118 H12 **Utena** Utena, E Lithuania
118 H12 **Utena** ◆ *province* E Lithuania
37 V10 **Ute Reservoir** ⊠ New Mexico, SW USA
167 O10 **Uthai Thani** *var.* Muang Uthai Thani, Udayadhani, Utaidhani. Uthai Thani, W Thailand
149 O15 **Uthal** Baluchistān, SW Pakistan
18 I10 **Utica** New York, NE USA
105 R10 **Utiel** País Valenciano, E Spain
11 O13 **Utikuma Lake** ◎ Alberta, W Canada
42 J4 **Utila, Isla de** *island* Islas de la Bahía, N Honduras
Utina *see* Udine
59 O17 **Utinga** Bahia, E Brazil
Utirik *see* Utrik Atoll
95 M22 **Utlängan** *island* S Sweden
117 U11 **Utlyuts'kyy Lyman** *bay* S Ukraine
95 P16 **Utö** Stockholm, C Sweden
25 Q12 **Utopia** Texas, SW USA
98 J11 **Utrecht** *Lat.* Trajectum ad Rhenum. Utrecht, C Netherlands
83 K22 **Utrecht** KwaZulu/Natal, E South Africa
98 I11 **Utrecht** ◆ *province* C Netherlands
104 K14 **Utrera** Andalucía, S Spain
189 V4 **Utrik Atoll** *var.* Utirik, Utrōk, Utrōnk. *atoll* Ratak Chain, N Marshall Islands
Utrōk/Utrōnk *see* Utrik Atoll
95 B16 **Utsira** *island* SW Norway
92 L8 **Utsjoki** *var.* Ohcejohka. Lappi, N Finland
165 O12 **Utsunomiya** *var.* Utunomiya. Tochigi, Honshū, S Japan
127 P13 **Utta** Respublika Kalmykiya, SW Russian Federation
167 O8 **Uttaradit** *var.* Utaradit. Uttaradit, N Thailand
152 J8 **Uttaranchal** ◆ *state* N India
152 J9 **Uttarkāshi** Uttaranchal, N India
152 K11 **Uttar Pradesh** *prev.* United Provinces, United Provinces of Agra and Oudh. ◆ *state* N India
45 T5 **Utuado** C Puerto Rico
158 K3 **Utubulak** Xinjiang Uygur Zizhiqu, W China
39 N5 **Utukok River** ↝ Alaska, USA
Utunomiya *see* Utsunomiya
187 P10 **Utupua** *island* Santa Cruz Islands, E Solomon Islands
144 G9 **Utva** ↝ NW Kazakhstan
189 Y15 **Utwe** Kosrae, E Micronesia
189 X15 **Utwe Harbor** *harbour* Kosrae, E Micronesia
162 J7 **Uubulan** Arhangay, C Mongolia
118 G6 **Uulu** Pärnumaa, SW Estonia
197 N13 **Uummannaq** *var.* Umanak, Umanaq. Kitaa, C Greenland
Uummannarsuaq *see* Nunap Isua
162 E4 **Üüreg Nuur** ◎ NW Mongolia
Uusikaarlepyy *see* Nykarleby
93 J19 **Uusikaupunki** *Swe.* Nystad. Länsi-Suomi, W Finland
127 S2 **Uva** Udmurtskaya Respublika, NW Russian Federation
113 L14 **Uvac** ↝ W Serbia and Montenegro (Yugo.)
25 Q12 **Uvalde** Texas, SW USA
155 K25 **Uva Province** ◆ *province* SE Sri Lanka
119 O18 **Uvaravichy** *Rus.* Uvarovichi. Homyel'skaya Voblasts', SE Belarus
54 J11 **Uvá, Río** ↝ E Colombia
Uvarovichi *see* Uvaravichy
127 N7 **Uvarovo** Tambovskaya Oblast', W Russian Federation
122 H10 **Uvat** Tyumenskaya Oblast', C Russian Federation
190 G12 **Uvea, Île** *island* N Wallis and Futuna
81 E21 **Uvinza** Kigoma, W Tanzania
79 O20 **Uvira** Sud Kivu, E Dem. Rep. Congo
162 E5 **Uvs** ◆ *province* NW Mongolia
162 F5 **Uvs Nuur** *var.* Ozero Ubsu-Nur. ◎ Mongolia/Russian Federation
164 F14 **Uwa** Ehime, Shikoku, SW Japan
164 F14 **Uwajima** *var.* Uwazima. Ehime, Shikoku, SW Japan
80 B5 **'Uwaynāt, Jabal al** *var.* Jebel Uweinat. ▲ Libya/Sudan
Uwazima *see* Uwajima
Uweinat, Jebel *see* 'Uwaynāt, Jabal al
14 H14 **Uxbridge** Ontario, S Canada
Uxellodunum *see* Issoudun
Uxin Qi *see* Dabqig
41 X12 **Uxmal, Ruinas** *ruins* Yucatán, SE Mexico
144 K15 **Uyaly** Kzylorda, S Kazakhstan
123 R8 **Uyandina** ↝ NE Russian Federation
122 L12 **Uyar** Krasnoyarskiy Kray, S Russian Federation
162 L10 **Üydzen** Ömnögovĭ, S Mongolia
Uyeda *see* Ueda
122 K5 **Uyedineniya, Ostrov** *island* N Russian Federation
77 V17 **Uyo** Akwa Ibom, S Nigeria
162 D8 **Üyönch** Hovd, W Mongolia
145 Q15 **Uyuk** Zhambyl, S Kazakhstan
141 V13 **'Uyūn** SW Oman
57 K20 **Uyuni** Potosí, W Bolivia
57 J20 **Uyuni, Salar de** *wetland* SW Bolivia
146 I9 **Uzbekistan** *off.* Republic of Uzbekistan. ◆ *republic* C Asia
158 D8 **Uzbel Shankou** *Rus.* Pereval Kyzyl-Dzhiik. *pass* China/Tajikistan
146 B11 **Uzboý** *prev. Rus.* Imeni 26 Bakinskikh Komissarov, *Turkm.* 26 Baku Komissarlary Adyndaky. Balkan Welaýaty, W Turkmenistan
119 J17 **Uzda** *Rus.* Uzda. Minskaya Voblasts', C Belarus
103 N12 **Uzerche** Corrèze, C France
103 R14 **Uzès** Gard, S France
147 T10 **Uzgen** *Kir.* Özgön. Oshskaya Oblast', SW Kyrgyzstan
117 O3 **Uzh** ↝ N Ukraine
Uzhgorod *see* Uzhhorod
116 G7 **Uzhhorod** *Rus.* Uzhgorod; *prev.* Ungvár. Zakarpats'ka Oblast', W Ukraine
Uzi *see* Uji
112 K13 **Užice** *prev.* Titovo Užice. Serbia, W Serbia and Montenegro (Yugo.)
Uzin *see* Uzyn
126 L5 **Uzlovaya** Tul'skaya Oblast', W Russian Federation
108 H7 **Uznach** Sankt Gallen, NE Switzerland
145 U16 **Uzunagach** Almaty, SE Kazakhstan
136 B10 **Uzunköprü** Edirne, NW Turkey
118 D11 **Užventis** Šiauliai, C Lithuania
117 P5 **Uzyn** *Rus.* Uzin. Kyyivs'ka Oblast', N Ukraine
145 N7 **Uzynkol'** *prev.* Lenin, Leninskoye. Kostanay, N Kazakhstan

V

Vääksy *see* Asikkala
83 H23 **Vaal** ↝ C South Africa
93 M14 **Vaala** Oulu, C Finland
93 N19 **Vaalimaa** Etelä-Suomi, SE Finland
99 M19 **Vaals** Limburg, SE Netherlands
93 J16 **Vaasa** *Swe.* Vasa; *prev.* Nikolainkaupunki. Vaasa, W Finland
98 L10 **Vaassen** Gelderland, E Netherlands
118 G11 **Vabalninkas** Panevėžys, NE Lithuania
Vabkent *see* Vobkent
111 J22 **Vác** *Ger.* Waitzen. Pest, N Hungary
61 I14 **Vacaria** Rio Grande do Sul, S Brazil
35 N7 **Vacaville** California, W USA
103 R15 **Vaccarès, Étang de** ◎ SE France
44 L10 **Vache, Île à** *island* SW Haiti
173 Y16 **Vacoas** W Mauritius
32 G10 **Vader** Washington, NW USA
94 D12 **Vadheim** Sogn og Fjordane, S Norway
154 D11 **Vadodara** *prev.* Baroda. Gujarāt, W India
92 M8 **Vadsø** *Fin.* Vesisaari. Finnmark, N Norway
95 L17 **Vadstena** Östergötland, S Sweden
108 I8 **Vaduz** ● (Liechtenstein) W Liechtenstein
Vág *see* Váh
127 N12 **Vaga** ↝ NW Russian Federation
94 G11 **Vågåmo** Oppland, S Norway
112 D12 **Vaganski Vrh** ▲ W Croatia
95 A19 **Vágar** *Dan.* Vågø *Island* Faeroe Islands
Vágbeszterce *see* Považská Bystrica
95 L19 **Vaggeryd** Jönköping, S Sweden
95 O16 **Vagnhärad** Södermanland, C Sweden
104 G7 **Vagos** Aveiro, N Portugal
Vágsellye *see* Sal'a
92 H10 **Vågsfjorden** *fjord* N Norway
94 C10 **Vågsøy** *island* S Norway
Vágújhely *see* Nové Mesto nad Váhom
111 I21 **Váh** *Ger.* Waag, *Hung.* Vág. ↝ W Slovakia
93 K16 **Vähäkyrö** Länsi-Suomi, W Finland
191 X11 **Vahitahi** *atoll* Îles Tuamotu, E French Polynesia
Váhtjer *see* Gällivare
Vaidei *see* Vulcan
22 L4 **Vaiden** Mississippi, S USA
155 I23 **Vaigai** ↝ SE India
191 V16 **Vaihu** Easter Island, Chile, E Pacific Ocean
118 I6 **Väike Emajõgi** ↝ S Estonia
118 I4 **Väike-Maarja** *Ger.* Klein-Marien. Lääne-Virumaa, NE Estonia
Väike-Salatsi *see* Mazsalaca
37 R4 **Vail** Colorado, C USA
193 V15 **Vaina** Tongatapu, S Tonga
118 E5 **Väinameri** *prev.* Muhu Väin, *Ger.* Moon-Sund. *sea* E Baltic Sea
93 N18 **Vainikkala** Etelä-Suomi, SE Finland
118 D10 **Vaiņode** Liepāja, SW Latvia
155 H23 **Vaippār** ↝ SE India
191 W11 **Vairaatea** *atoll* Îles Tuamotu, C French Polynesia
191 R8 **Vairao** Tahiti, W French Polynesia
103 R14 **Vaison-la-Romaine** Vaucluse, SE France
190 G11 **Vaitupu** Île Uvea, E Wallis and Futuna
190 F7 **Vaitupu** *atoll* C Tuvalu
Vajdahunyad *see* Hunedoara
Vajdej *see* Vulcan
78 K12 **Vakaga** ◆ *prefecture* NE Central African Republic
114 H10 **Vakarel** Sofiya, W Bulgaria
Vakav *see* Ustrem
137 O11 **Vakfıkebir** Trabzon, NE Turkey
122 J10 **Vakh** ↝ C Russian Federation
Vakhon, Qatorkŭhi *see* Nicholas Range
147 P14 **Vakhsh** SW Tajikistan
147 Q12 **Vakhsh** ↝ SW Tajikistan
127 P1 **Vakhtan** Nizhegorodskaya Oblast', W Russian Federation
94 C13 **Vaksdal** Hordaland, S Norway
127 O8 **Vashka** ↝ NW Russian Federation
Valachia *see* Wallachia
108 D11 **Valais** *Ger.* Wallis. ◆ *canton* SW Switzerland
113 M21 **Valamarës, Mali i** ▲ SE Albania
127 S2 **Valamaz** Udmurtskaya Respublika, NW Russian Federation
113 Q19 **Valandovo** SE FYR Macedonia
111 I18 **Valašské Meziříčí** *Ger.* Wallachisch-Meseritsch, *Pol.* Wałeckie Międzyrzecze. Zlínský Kraj, E Czech Republic
115 I17 **Valáxa** *island* Vóreioi Sporádes, Greece, Aegean Sea
95 K16 **Vålberg** Värmland, C Sweden
116 H12 **Vâlcea** *prev.* Vîlcea. ◆ *county* SW Romania
63 J16 **Valcheta** Río Negro, E Argentina
15 P12 **Valcourt** Québec, SE Canada
Valdai Hills *see* Valdayskaya Vozvyshennost'
104 M3 **Valdavia** ↝ N Spain
124 I15 **Valday** Novgorodskaya Oblast', W Russian Federation
126 I15 **Valdayskaya Vozvyshennost'** *var.* Valdai Hills. *hill range* W Russian Federation
104 L9 **Valdecañas, Embalse de** ⊠ W Spain
118 E8 **Valdemārpils** *Ger.* Sassmacken. Talsi, NW Latvia
95 N18 **Valdemarsvik** Östergötland, S Sweden
105 N8 **Valdemoro** Madrid, C Spain
105 O11 **Valdepeñas** Castilla-La Mancha, C Spain
104 L5 **Valderaduey** ↝ NE Spain
104 L5 **Valderas** Castilla-León, N Spain
105 T7 **Valderrobres** *var.* Vall-de-roures. Aragón, NE Spain
63 K17 **Valdés, Península** *peninsula* SE Argentina
39 S11 **Valdez** Alaska, USA
56 C5 **Valdéz** *var.* Limones. Esmeraldas, NW Ecuador
Valdia *see* Weldiya
103 U11 **Val d'Isère** Savoie, E France
63 G15 **Valdivia** Los Lagos, C Chile
Valdivia Bank *see* Valdivia Seamount
65 P17 **Valdivia Seamount** *var.* Valdivia Bank. *undersea feature* E Atlantic Ocean
103 N4 **Val-d'Oise** ◆ *department* N France
14 J8 **Val-d'Or** Québec, SE Canada
23 U8 **Valdosta** Georgia, SE USA
94 G13 **Valdres** *physical region* S Norway
32 L13 **Vale** Oregon, NW USA
116 F9 **Valea lui Mihai** *Hung.* Érmihályfalva. Bihor, NW Romania
11 N15 **Valemount** British Columbia, SW Canada
59 O17 **Valença** Bahia, E Brazil
104 F4 **Valença do Minho** Viana do Castelo, N Portugal
59 N14 **Valença do Piauí** Piauí, E Brazil
103 N8 **Valençay** Indre, C France
103 R13 **Valence** *anc.* Valentia, Valentia Julia, Ventia. Drôme, E France
105 S10 **Valencia** País Valenciano, E Spain
54 K5 **Valencia** Carabobo, N Venezuela
105 R10 **Valencia** *Cat.* València. ◆ *province* País Valenciano, E Spain
105 S10 **Valencia** × Valencia, E Spain
València/Valencia *see* País Valenciano
104 I10 **Valencia de Alcántara** Extremadura, W Spain
104 L4 **Valencia de Don Juan** Castilla-León, N Spain
105 U9 **Valencia, Golfo de** *var.* Gulf of Valencia. *gulf* E Spain
Valencia, Gulf of *see* Valencia, Golfo de
97 A21 **Valencia Island** *Ir.* Dairbhre. *island* SW Ireland
103 P2 **Valenciennes** Nord, N France
116 K13 **Vălenii de Munte** Prahova, SE Romania
Valentia *see* Valence, France
Valentia *see* País Valenciano
Valentia Julia *see* Valence
103 T8 **Valentigney** Doubs, E France
28 M12 **Valentine** Nebraska, C USA
24 J10 **Valentine** Texas, SW USA
Valentine State *see* Oregon
106 C8 **Valenza** Piemonte, NW Italy
94 I13 **Våler** Hedmark, S Norway
54 I6 **Valera** Trujillo, NW Venezuela
192 M11 **Valerie Guyot** *undersea feature* S Pacific Ocean
Valetta *see* Valletta
118 I7 **Valga** *Ger.* Walk, *Latv.* Valka. Valgamaa, S Estonia
118 I7 **Valgamaa** *off.* Valga Maakond. ◆ *province* S Estonia
43 Q15 **Valiente, Península** *peninsula* NW Panama
103 X16 **Valinco, Golfe de** *gulf* Corse, France, C Mediterranean Sea
112 L12 **Valjevo** Serbia, W Serbia and Montenegro (Yugo.)
Valjok *see* Válljohka
118 I7 **Valka** *Ger.* Walk. Valka, N Latvia
Valka *see* Valga
93 L18 **Valkeakoski** Länsi-Suomi, W Finland
93 M19 **Valkeala** Etelä-Suomi, S Finland
99 L18 **Valkenburg** Limburg, SE Netherlands
99 K15 **Valkenswaard** Noord-Brabant, S Netherlands
119 G15 **Valkininkai** Alytus, S Lithuania
117 U5 **Valky** Kharkivs'ka Oblast', E Ukraine
41 Y12 **Valladolid** Yucatán, SE Mexico
104 M5 **Valladolid** Castilla-León, NW Spain
104 L5 **Valladolid** ◆ *province* Castilla-León, N Spain
103 U15 **Vallauris** Alpes-Maritimes, SE France
Vall-de-roures *see* Valderrobres
105 S9 **Vall d'Uxó** País Valenciano, E Spain
95 E16 **Valle** Aust-Agder, S Norway
105 N2 **Valle** Cantabria, N Spain
42 H8 **Valle** ◆ *department* S Honduras
105 N8 **Vallecas** Madrid, C Spain
37 Q8 **Vallecito Reservoir** ⊠ Colorado, C USA
106 A7 **Valle d'Aosta** ◆ *region* NW Italy
41 O14 **Valle de Bravo** México, S Mexico
55 N5 **Valle de Guanape** Anzoátegui, N Venezuela
54 M6 **Valle de La Pascua** Guárico, N Venezuela
54 B11 **Valle del Cauca** *off.* Departamento del Valle del Cauca. ◆ *province* W Colombia
41 N13 **Valle de Santiago** Guanajuato, C Mexico
40 J7 **Valle de Zaragoza** Chihuahua, N Mexico
54 G5 **Valledupar** Cesar, N Colombia
76 G10 **Vallée de Ferlo** ↝ NW Senegal
57 M19 **Vallegrande** Santa Cruz, C Bolivia
41 P8 **Valle Hermoso** Tamaulipas, C Mexico
35 N8 **Vallejo** California, W USA
62 G8 **Vallenar** Atacama, N Chile
95 O15 **Vallentuna** Stockholm, C Sweden
121 P16 **Valletta** *prev.* Valetta. ● (Malta) E Malta
27 N6 **Valley Center** Kansas, C USA
29 Q5 **Valley City** North Dakota, N USA
32 I15 **Valley Falls** Oregon, NW USA
Valleyfield *see* Salaberry-de-Valleyfield
21 S4 **Valley Head** West Virginia, NE USA
25 T8 **Valley Mills** Texas, SW USA
75 W10 **Valley of the Kings** *ancient monument* E Egypt
29 R11 **Valley Springs** South Dakota, N USA
20 K5 **Valley Station** Kentucky, S USA
11 O13 **Valleyview** Alberta, W Canada
25 T5 **Valley View** Texas, SW USA
61 C21 **Vallimanca, Arroyo** ↝ E Argentina
92 L9 **Válljohka** *var.* Valjok. Finnmark, N Norway
107 M19 **Vallo della Lucania** Campania, S Italy
108 B9 **Vallorbe** Vaud, W Switzerland
105 V6 **Valls** Cataluña, NE Spain
94 N11 **Vallsta** Gävleborg, C Sweden
94 N12 **Vallvik** Gävleborg, C Sweden
11 T17 **Val Marie** Saskatchewan, S Canada
118 H7 **Valmiera** *Est.* Volmari, *Ger.* Wolmar. Valmiera, N Latvia
105 N3 **Valnera** ▲ N Spain
102 J3 **Valognes** Manche, N France
Valona *see* Vlorë
Valona Bay *see* Vlorës, Gjiri i
104 G6 **Valongo** *var.* Valongo de Gaia. Porto, N Portugal
Valongo de Gaia *see* Valongo
104 M5 **Valoria la Buena** Castilla-León, N Spain
119 J15 **Valozhyn** *Pol.* Wołożyn, *Rus.* Volozhin. Minskaya Voblasts', C Belarus
104 I5 **Valpaços** Vila Real, N Portugal
23 P8 **Valparaiso** Florida, SE USA
31 N11 **Valparaiso** Indiana, N USA
62 G11 **Valparaíso** Valparaíso, C Chile
40 L11 **Valparaíso** Zacatecas, C Mexico
62 G11 **Valparaíso** *off.* Región de Valparaíso. ◆ *region* C Chile
Valpo *see* Valpovo
112 I9 **Valpovo** *Hung.* Valpo. Osijek-Baranja, E Croatia
103 R14 **Valréas** Vaucluse, SE France
Vals *see* Vals-Platz
154 D12 **Valsād** *prev.* Bulsar. Gujarāt, W India
Valsbaai *see* False Bay
171 T12 **Valse Pisang, Kepulauan** *island group* E Indonesia
108 H9 **Vals-Platz** *var.* Vals. Graubünden, S Switzerland
171 X16 **Vals, Tanjung** *headland* Papua, SE Indonesia
93 N15 **Valtimo** Itä-Suomi, E Finland
115 D17 **Váltou** ▲ C Greece
127 O12 **Valuyevka** Rostovskaya Oblast', SW Russian Federation
126 K9 **Valuyki** Belgorodskaya Oblast', W Russian Federation
36 L2 **Val Verda** Utah, W USA
64 N12 **Valverde** Hierro, Islas Canarias, Spain, NE Atlantic Ocean
104 I13 **Valverde del Camino** Andalucía, S Spain
95 G23 **Vamdrup** Vejle, C Denmark
94 L12 **Våmhus** Dalarna, C Sweden
93 K18 **Vammala** Länsi-Suomi, W Finland
Vámosudvarhely *see* Odorheiu Secuiesc
137 S14 **Van** Van, E Turkey
25 V7 **Van** Texas, SW USA
137 T14 **Van** ◆ *province* E Turkey
137 T11 **Vanadzor** *prev.* Kirovakan. N Armenia
25 U5 **Van Alstyne** Texas, SW USA
33 W10 **Vananda** Montana, NW USA
116 I11 **Vânători** *Hung.* Héjjasfalva; *prev.* Vînători. Mureş, C Romania
191 W12 **Vanavana** *atoll* Îles Tuamotu, SE French Polynesia
Vana-Vändra *see* Vändra
122 M11 **Vanavara** Evenkiyskiy Avtonomnyy Okrug, C Russian Federation
15 Q8 **Van Bruyssel** Québec, SE Canada
27 R10 **Van Buren** Arkansas, C USA
19 S1 **Van Buren** Maine, NE USA
27 W7 **Van Buren** Missouri, C USA
19 T5 **Vanceboro** Maine, NE USA
21 W10 **Vanceboro** North Carolina, SE USA
21 O4 **Vanceburg** Kentucky, S USA
Vanch *see* Vanj
10 L17 **Vancouver** British Columbia, SW Canada
32 G11 **Vancouver** Washington, NW USA
10 L17 **Vancouver** × British Columbia, SW Canada
10 K16 **Vancouver Island** *island* British Columbia, SW Canada
Vanda *see* Vantaa
171 X13 **Van Daalen** ↝ Papua, E Indonesia
30 L15 **Vandalia** Illinois, N USA
27 V3 **Vandalia** Missouri, C USA
31 R13 **Vandalia** Ohio, N USA
25 U13 **Vanderbilt** Texas, SW USA
31 Q10 **Vandercook Lake** Michigan, N USA
10 L14 **Vanderhoof** British Columbia, SW Canada
18 K8 **Vanderwhacker Mountain** ▲ New York, NE USA
181 P1 **Van Diemen Gulf** *gulf* Northern Territory, N Australia
Van Diemen's Land *see* Tasmania
118 H5 **Vändra** *Ger.* Fennern; *prev.* Vana-Vändra. Pärnumaa, SW Estonia
Vandsburg *see* Więcbork
34 L4 **Van Duzen River** ↝ California, W USA
118 F13 **Vandžiogala** Kaunas, C Lithuania
41 N10 **Vanegas** San Luis Potosí, C Mexico
Vaner, Lake *see* Vänern
95 K17 **Vänern** *Eng.* Lake Vaner; *prev.* Lake Vener. ◎ S Sweden
95 J18 **Vänersborg** Västra Götaland, S Sweden
94 F12 **Vang** Oppland, S Norway
172 I7 **Vangaindrano** Fianarantsoa, SE Madagascar
137 S14 **Van Gölü** *Eng.* Lake Van; *anc.* Thospitis. *salt lake* E Turkey
186 L9 **Vangunu** *island* New Georgia Islands, NW Solomon Islands
24 J9 **Van Horn** Texas, SW USA
187 Q11 **Vanikolo** *var.* Vanikoro. *island* Santa Cruz Islands, E Solomon Islands
Vanikoro *see* Vanikolo
186 A5 **Vanimo** Sandaun, NW PNG
123 T13 **Vanino** Khabarovskiy Kray, SE Russian Federation
155 G19 **Vānīvilāsa Sāgara** ◎ SW India
147 S13 **Vanj** *Rus.* Vanch. S Tajikistan
116 G14 **Vânju Mare** *prev.* Vînju Mare. Mehedinţi, SW Romania
15 N12 **Vankleek Hill** Ontario, SE Canada
Van, Lake *see* Van Gölü
93 I16 **Vännäs** Västerbotten, N Sweden
93 I15 **Vännäsby** Västerbotten, N Sweden
102 H7 **Vannes** *anc.* Dariorigum. Morbihan, NW France
92 I8 **Vannøya** *island* N Norway
103 T12 **Vanoise, Massif de la** ▲ E France
83 E24 **Vanrhynsdorp** Western Cape, SW South Africa
21 P7 **Vansant** Virginia, NE USA
94 L13 **Vansbro** Dalarna, C Sweden
95 D18 **Vanse** Vest-Agder, S Norway
9 P7 **Vansittart Island** *island* Nunavut, NE Canada
93 M20 **Vantaa** *Swe.* Vanda. Etelä-Suomi, S Finland

◆ Country ● Country Capital ◇ Dependent Territory ○ Dependent Territory Capital ◆ Administrative Region × International Airport ▲ Mountain ▲ Mountain Range Volcano ↝ River ◎ Lake ⊠ Reservoir

93 L19 **Vantaa** ✕ (Helsinki) Etelä-Suomi, S Finland
32 J9 **Vantage** Washington, NW USA
187 Z14 **Vanua Balavu** ***prev.*** Vanua Mbalavu. *island* Lau Group, E Fiji
187 R12 **Vanua Lava** *island* Banks Islands, N Vanuatu
187 Y13 **Vanua Levu** *island* N Fiji
Vanua Mbalavu *see* Vanua Balavu
187 R12 **Vanuatu** ***off.*** Republic of Vanuatu; ***prev.*** New Hebrides. ◆ *republic* SW Pacific Ocean
31 Q12 **Van Wert** Ohio, N USA
187 Q17 **Vao** Province Sud, S New Caledonia
Vapincum *see* Gap
117 N7 **Vapnyarka** Vinnyts'ka Oblast', C Ukraine
103 T15 **Var** ◈ *department* SE France
103 U14 **Var** ≈ SE France
95 J18 **Vara** Västra Götaland, S Sweden
Varadinska Županija *see* Varaždin
118 J10 **Varakļani** Madona, C Latvia
106 C7 **Varallo** Piemonte, NE Italy
143 O5 **Varāmīn** ***var.*** Veramin. Tehrān, N Iran
153 N14 **Vārānasi** ***prev.*** Banaras, Benares, ***hist.*** Kasi. Uttar Pradesh, N India
125 T3 **Varandey** Nenetskiy Avtonomnyy Okrug, NW Russian Federation
92 M8 **Varangerbotn** Finnmark, N Norway
92 M8 **Varangerfjorden** ***Lapp.*** Várjjatvuotna. *fjord* N Norway
92 M8 **Varangerhalvøya** ***Lapp.*** Várnjárga. *peninsula* N Norway
Varannó *see* Vranov nad Topľou
107 M15 **Varano, Lago di** ⊚ SE Italy
118 J13 **Varapayeva** ***Rus.*** Voropayevo. Vitsyebskaya Voblasts', NW Belarus
Varasd *see* Varaždin
112 E7 **Varaždin** ***Ger.*** Warasdin, ***Hung.*** Varasd. Varaždin, N Croatia
112 E7 **Varaždin** ***off.*** Varadinska Županija. ◈ *province* N Croatia
106 C10 **Varazze** Liguria, NW Italy
95 J20 **Varberg** Halland, S Sweden
Vardak *see* Wardag
113 Q19 **Vardar** ***Gk.*** Axiós. ≈ FYR Macedonia/Greece ***see also*** Axiós
95 F23 **Varde** Ribe, W Denmark
137 V12 **Vardenis** E Armenia
92 N8 **Vardø** ***Fin.*** Vuoreija. Finnmark, N Norway
115 E18 **Vardoúsia** ⛰ C Greece
Vareia *see* Logroño
100 G10 **Varel** Niedersachsen, NW Germany
119 G15 **Varėna** ***Pol.*** Orany. Alytus, S Lithuania
15 O12 **Varennes** Québec, SE Canada
103 P10 **Varennes-sur-Allier** Allier, C France
112 I12 **Vareš** Federacija Bosna I Hercegovina, E Bosnia and Herzegovina
106 D7 **Varese** Lombardia, N Italy
116 J12 **Vârful Moldoveanu** ***var.*** Moldoveanul; ***prev.*** Vîrful Moldoveanu. ▲ C Romania
Varganzi *see* Warganza
95 J18 **Vårgårda** Västra Götaland, S Sweden
95 J18 **Vargön** Västra Götaland, S Sweden
95 C17 **Varhaug** Rogaland, S Norway
Várjjatvuotna *see* Varangerfjorden
93 N17 **Varkaus** Itä-Suomi, C Finland
92 J2 **Varmahlidh** Nordhurland Vestra, N Iceland
95 J15 **Värmland** ◈ *county* C Sweden
95 K16 **Värmlandsnäs** *peninsula* S Sweden
114 N8 **Varna** ***prev.*** Stalin, ***anc.*** Odessus. Varna, E Bulgaria
114 N8 **Varna** ✕ Varna, E Bulgaria
114 N8 **Varna** ◈ *province* E Bulgaria
95 L20 **Värnamo** Jönköping, S Sweden
114 N8 **Varnenski Zaliv** ***prev.*** Stalinski Zaliv. *bay* E Bulgaria
114 N8 **Varnensko Ezero** *estuary* E Bulgaria
118 D11 **Varniai** Telšiai, W Lithuania
Várnjárga *see* Varangerhalvøya
Varnoús *see* Baba
111 D14 **Varnsdorf** ***Ger.*** Warnsdorf. Ústecký Kraj, N Czech Republic
111 I23 **Várpalota** Veszprém, W Hungary
Varshava *see* Warszawa
118 K6 **Värska** Põlvamaa, SE Estonia
98 N12 **Varsseveld** Gelderland, E Netherlands
115 D19 **Vartholomió** ***prev.*** Vartholomión. Dytikí Ellás, S Greece
Vartholomión *see* Vartholomió
137 Q14 **Varto** Muş, E Turkey
95 K18 **Vartofta** Västra Götaland, S Sweden
93 O17 **Värtsilä** Itä-Suomi, E Finland
Värtsilä *see* Vyartsilya
117 R4 **Varva** Chernihivs'ka Oblast', NE Ukraine
59 H18 **Várzea Grande** Mato Grosso, SW Brazil
106 D9 **Varzi** Lombardia, N Italy
Varzimanor Ayni *see* Ayní
126 K5 **Varzuga** ≈ NW Russian Federation
103 P8 **Varzy** Nièvre, C France
111 G23 **Vas** ***off.*** Vas Megye. ◈ *county* W Hungary
Vasa *see* Vaasa
190 A9 **Vasafua** *island* Funafuti Atoll, C Tuvalu
111 O21 **Vásárosnamény** Szabolcs-Szatmár-Bereg, E Hungary
104 H13 **Vascão, Ribeira de** ≈ S Portugal
116 G10 **Vaşcău** ***Hung.*** Vaskoh. Bihor, NE Romania
Vascongadas, Provincias *see* País Vasco
Vashess Bay *see* Vaskess Bay
Väsht *see* Khāsh
Vasilevichi *see* Vasilyevichy
115 G14 **Vasiliká** Kentrikí Makedonía, NE Greece
115 C18 **Vasilikí** Lefkáda, Iónioi Nísoi, Greece, C Mediterranean Sea
115 K25 **Vasilikí** Kríti, Greece, E Mediterranean Sea
119 G16 **Vasilishki** ***Pol.*** Wasiliszki, ***Rus.*** Vasilishki. Hrodzyenskaya Voblasts', W Belarus
Vasil Kolarov *see* Pamporovo
Vasil'kov *see* Vasyl'kiv
119 N19 **Vasilyevichy** ***Rus.*** Vasilevichi. Homyel'skaya Voblasts', SE Belarus
191 Y3 **Vaskess Bay** ***var.*** Vashess Bay. *bay* Kiritimati, E Kiribati
Vaskoh *see* Vaşcău
Vaskohsziklás *see* Ştei
116 M10 **Vaslui** Vaslui, C Romania
116 L11 **Vaslui** ◈ *county* NE Romania
31 R8 **Vassar** Michigan, N USA
95 E15 **Vassdalsegga** ▲ S Norway
60 P9 **Vassouras** Rio de Janeiro, SE Brazil
95 N15 **Västerås** Västmanland, C Sweden
93 G15 **Västerbotten** ◈ *county* N Sweden
94 K12 **Västerdalälven** ≈ C Sweden
95 O16 **Västerhaninge** Stockholm, C Sweden
94 M10 **Västernorrland** ◈ *county* C Sweden
95 N19 **Västervik** Kalmar, S Sweden
95 M15 **Västmanand** ◈ *county* C Sweden
107 L15 **Vasto** ***anc.*** Histonium. Abruzzo, C Italy
95 J19 **Västra Götaland** ◈ *county* S Sweden
95 J16 **Västra Silen** ⊚ S Sweden
111 G23 **Vasvár** ***Ger.*** Eisenburg. Vas, W Hungary
117 U9 **Vasylivka** Zaporiz'ka Oblast', SE Ukraine
117 O5 **Vasyl'kiv** ***Rus.*** Vasil'kov. Kyyivs'ka Oblast', N Ukraine
122 I11 **Vasyugan** ≈ C Russian Federation
103 N8 **Vatan** Indre, C France
Vaté *see* Efate
107 G15 **Vatican City** ***off.*** Vatican City State. ◆ *papal state* S Europe
107 M22 **Vaticano, Capo** *headland* S Italy
92 K3 **Vatnajökull** *glacier* SE Iceland
95 P15 **Vätö** Stockholm, C Sweden
187 Z16 **Vatoa** *island* Lau Group, SE Fiji
172 J5 **Vatomandry** Toamasina, E Madagascar
116 J9 **Vatra Dornei** ***Ger.*** Dorna Watra. Suceava, NE Romania
116 J9 **Vatra Moldoviţei** Suceava, NE Romania
Vatter, Lake *see* Vättern
95 L18 **Vättern** ***Eng.*** Lake Vatter; ***prev.*** Lake Vetter. ⊚ S Sweden
187 X5 **Vatulele** *island* SW Fiji
117 P7 **Vatutine** Cherkas'ka Oblast', C Ukraine
187 W15 **Vatu Vara** *island* Lau Group, E Fiji
103 R14 **Vaucluse** ◈ *department* SE France
103 S5 **Vaucouleurs** Meuse, NE France
108 B9 **Vaud** ***Ger.*** Waadt. ◈ *canton* SW Switzerland
15 N12 **Vaudreuil** Québec, SE Canada
37 T12 **Vaughn** New Mexico, SW USA
54 I14 **Vaupés** ***off.*** Comisaría del Vaupés. ◈ *province* SE Colombia
54 J13 **Vaupés, Río** ***var.*** Rio Uaupés. ≈ Brazil/Colombia ***see also*** Uaupés, Rio
103 Q15 **Vauvert** Gard, S France
11 R17 **Vauxhall** Alberta, SW Canada
99 K23 **Vaux-sur-Sûre** Luxembourg, SE Belgium
172 J4 **Vavatenina** Toamasina, E Madagascar
193 Y14 **Vava'u Group** *island group* N Tonga
76 M16 **Vavoua** W Ivory Coast
127 S2 **Vavozh** Udmurtskaya Respublika, NW Russian Federation
155 K23 **Vavuniya** Northern Province, N Sri Lanka
119 G17 **Vawkavysk** ***Pol.*** Wołkowysk, ***Rus.*** Volkovysk. Hrodzyenskaya Voblasts', W Belarus
119 F17 **Vawkavyskaye Wzvyshsha** ***Rus.*** Volkovyskiye Vysoty. *hill range* W Belarus
95 P15 **Vaxholm** Stockholm, C Sweden
95 L21 **Växjö** ***var.*** Vexiö. Kronoberg, S Sweden
127 T1 **Vaygach, Ostrov** *island* NW Russian Federation
137 V13 **Vayk'** ***prev.*** Azizbekov. SE Armenia
Vazáš *see* Vittangi
125 P8 **Vazhgort** ***prev.*** Chasovo. Respublika Komi, NW Russian Federation
45 V10 **V.C.Bird** ✕ (St John's) Antigua, Antigua and Barbuda
95 C16 **Veavågen** Rogaland, S Norway
29 Q7 **Veblen** South Dakota, N USA
98 N9 **Vecht** ***Ger.*** Vechte. ≈ Germany/Netherlands ***see also*** Vechte
100 G12 **Vechta** Niedersachsen, NW Germany
100 E12 **Vechte** ***Dut.*** Vecht. ≈ Germany/Netherlands ***see also*** Vecht
118 I8 **Vecpiebalga** Cēsis, C Latvia
118 G9 **Vecumnieki** Bauska, C Latvia
Vedāvati *see* Hagari
95 J20 **Veddige** Halland, S Sweden
116 J15 **Vedea** ≈ S Romania
127 P16 **Vedeno** Chechenskaya Respublika, SW Russian Federation
98 O6 **Veendam** Groningen, NE Netherlands
98 K12 **Veenendaal** Utrecht, C Netherlands
99 E14 **Veere** Zeeland, SW Netherlands
24 M2 **Vega** Texas, SW USA
92 E13 **Vega** *island* C Norway
45 T5 **Vega Baja** C Puerto Rico
38 D17 **Vega Point** *headland* Kiska Island, Alaska, USA
95 F17 **Vegår** ⊚ S Norway
99 K14 **Veghel** Noord-Brabant, S Netherlands
Veglia *see* Krk
114 E13 **Vegorítis, Límni** ⊚ N Greece
11 Q14 **Vegreville** Alberta, SW Canada
95 K21 **Veinge** Halland, S Sweden
61 B21 **Veinticinco de Mayo** ***var.*** 25 de Mayo. Buenos Aires, E Argentina
63 I14 **Veinticinco de Mayo** La Pampa, C Argentina
119 F15 **Veisiejai** Alytus, S Lithuania
95 F23 **Vejen** Ribe, W Denmark
104 K16 **Vejer de la Frontera** Andalucía, S Spain
95 G23 **Vejle** Vejle, C Denmark
95 F23 **Vejle** ***off.*** Vejle Amt. ◈ *county* C Denmark
114 M7 **Vekilski** Shumen, NE Bulgaria
54 G3 **Vela, Cabo de la** *headland* NE Colombia
Vela Goa *see* Goa
113 F15 **Vela Luka** Dubrovnik-Neretva, S Croatia
61 G19 **Velázquez** Rocha, E Uruguay
101 E15 **Velbert** Nordrhein-Westfalen, W Germany
109 S9 **Velden** Kärnten, S Austria
Veldes *see* Bled
99 K15 **Veldhoven** Noord-Brabant, S Netherlands
112 C11 **Velebit** ⛰ C Croatia
114 N11 **Veleka** ≈ SE Bulgaria
109 V10 **Velenje** ***Ger.*** Wöllan. N Slovenia
190 E12 **Vele, Pointe** *headland* Île Futuna, S Wallis and Futuna
113 O18 **Veles** ***Turk.*** Köprülü. C FYR Macedonia
113 M20 **Velešta** SW FYR Macedonia
115 F16 **Velestíno** ***prev.*** Velestínon. Thessalía, C Greece
Velestínon *see* Velestíno
Velevshchina *see* Vyelyewshchyna
54 F9 **Vélez** Santander, C Colombia
105 Q13 **Vélez Blanco** Andalucía, S Spain
104 M17 **Vélez de la Gomera, Peñon de** *island group* S Spain
105 N15 **Vélez-Málaga** Andalucía, S Spain
105 Q13 **Vélez Rubio** Andalucía, S Spain
Velha Goa *see* Goa
Velho *see* Porto Velho
112 E8 **Velika Gorica** Zagreb, N Croatia
112 C9 **Velika Kapela** ⛰ NW Croatia
Velika Kikinda *see* Kikinda
112 D10 **Velika Kladuša** Federacija Bosna I Hercegovina, NW Bosnia and Herzegovina
112 N11 **Velika Morava** ***var.*** Glavn'a Morava, Morava, ***Ger.*** Grosse Morava. ≈ C Serbia and Montenegro (Yugo.)
112 N12 **Velika Plana** Serbia, C Serbia and Montenegro (Yugo.)
109 U10 **Velika Raduha** ▲ N Slovenia
123 V7 **Velikaya** ≈ NE Russian Federation
126 F15 **Velikaya** ≈ W Russian Federation
Velikaya Berestovitsa *see* Vyalikaya Byerastavitsa
Velikaya Lepetikha *see* Velyka Lepetykha
Veliki Bečkerek *see* Zrenjanin
112 P12 **Veliki Krš** ***var.*** Stol. ▲ E Serbia and Montenegro (Yugo.)
114 L8 **Veliki Preslav** ***prev.*** Preslav. Shumen, NE Bulgaria
112 B9 **Veliki Risnjak** ▲ NW Croatia
109 T13 **Veliki Snežnik** ***Ger.*** Schneeberg, ***It.*** Monte Nevoso. ▲ SW Slovenia
112 J13 **Veliki Stolac** ▲ E Bosnia and Herzegovina
Velikiy Bor *see* Vyaliki Bor
124 G16 **Velikiye Luki** Pskovskaya Oblast', W Russian Federation
124 H14 **Velikiy Novgorod** ***prev.*** Novgorod. Novgorodskaya Oblast', W Russian Federation
125 P12 **Velikiy Ustyug** Vologodskaya Oblast', NW Russian Federation
112 N11 **Veliko Gradište** Serbia, NE Serbia and Montenegro (Yugo.)
155 I18 **Velikonda Range** ⛰ SE India
114 K9 **Veliko Tŭrnovo** ***prev.*** Tirnovo, Trnovo, Tŭrnovo. Veliko Tŭrnovo, N Bulgaria
114 K8 **Veliko Tŭrnovo** ◈ *province* N Bulgaria
Velikovec *see* Völkermarkt
125 R5 **Velikovisochnoye** Nenetskiy Avtonomnyy Okrug, NW Russian Federation
76 H12 **Vélingara** C Senegal
76 H11 **Vélingara** S Senegal
114 H11 **Velingrad** Pazardzhik, C Bulgaria
126 H3 **Velizh** Smolenskaya Oblast', W Russian Federation
111 F16 **Velká Deštná** ***var.*** Deštná, Grosskoppe, ***Ger.*** Deschnaer Koppe. ▲ NE Czech Republic
111 F18 **Velké Meziříčí** ***Ger.*** Grossmeseritsch. Vysočina, C Czech Republic
92 N1 **Velkomstpynten** *headland* NW Svalbard
111 K21 **Veľký Krtíš** Banskobystrický Kraj, C Slovakia
186 J8 **Vella Lavella** ***var.*** Mbilua. *island* New Georgia Islands, NW Solomon Islands
107 I15 **Velletri** Lazio, C Italy
95 K23 **Vellinge** Skåne, S Sweden
155 I19 **Vellore** Tamil Nādu, SE India
Velobriga *see* Viana do Castelo
115 G21 **Velopoúla** *island* S Greece
98 M12 **Velp** Gelderland, SE Netherlands
Velsen *see* Velsen-Noord
98 H9 **Velsen-Noord** ***var.*** Velsen. Noord-Holland, W Netherlands
125 N12 **Vel'sk** ***var.*** Velsk. Arkhangel'skaya Oblast', NW Russian Federation
Velsuna *see* Orvieto
98 K10 **Veluwemeer** *lake channel* C Netherlands
28 M3 **Velva** North Dakota, N USA
115 E14 **Velvendós** ***var.*** Velvendos. Dytikí Makedonía, N Greece
117 S5 **Velyka Bahachka** Poltavs'ka Oblast', C Ukraine
117 S9 **Velyka Lepetykha** ***Rus.*** Velikaya Lepetikha. Khersons'ka Oblast', S Ukraine
117 O10 **Velyka Mykhaylivka** Odes'ka Oblast', SW Ukraine
117 W8 **Velyka Novosilka** Donets'ka Oblast', E Ukraine
117 S9 **Velyka Oleksandrivka** Khersons'ka Oblast', S Ukraine
117 T4 **Velyka Pysanivka** Sums'ka Oblast', NE Ukraine
116 G6 **Velykyy Bereznyy** Zakarpats'ka Oblast', W Ukraine
117 W4 **Velykyy Burluk** Kharkivs'ka Oblast', E Ukraine
Velykyy Tokmak *see* Tokmak
173 P7 **Vema Fracture Zone** *tectonic feature* W Indian Ocean
65 P18 **Vema Seamount** *undersea feature* SW Indian Ocean
93 F17 **Vemdalen** Jämtland, C Sweden
95 N19 **Vena** Kalmar, S Sweden
41 N11 **Venado** San Luis Potosí, C Mexico
62 L11 **Venado Tuerto** Entre Ríos, E Argentina
61 A19 **Venado Tuerto** Santa Fe, C Argentina
107 K16 **Venafro** Molise, C Italy
55 Q9 **Venamo, Cerro** ▲ E Venezuela
106 B8 **Venaria** Piemonte, NW Italy
103 U15 **Vence** Alpes-Maritimes, SE France
104 H5 **Venda Nova** Vila Real, N Portugal
104 G11 **Vendas Novas** Évora, S Portugal
102 J9 **Vendée** ◈ *department* NW France
103 Q6 **Vendeuvre-sur-Barse** Aube, NE France
102 M7 **Vendôme** Loir-et-Cher, C France
Venedig *see* Venezia
Vener, Lake *see* Vänern
106 I8 **Veneta, Laguna** *lagoon* NE Italy
Venetia *see* Venezia
39 S7 **Venetie** Alaska, USA
106 H8 **Veneto** ***var.*** Venezia Euganea. ◈ *region* NE Italy
114 M7 **Venets** Shumen, NE Bulgaria
126 L5 **Venev** Tul'skaya Oblast', W Russian Federation
106 I8 **Venezia** ***Eng.*** Venice, ***Fr.*** Venise, ***Ger.*** Venedig; anc.Venetia. Veneto, NE Italy
Venezia Euganea *see* Veneto
Venezia, Golfo di *see* Venice, Gulf of
Venezia Tridentina *see* Trentino-Alto Adige
54 K8 **Venezuela** ***off.*** Republic of Venezuela; ***prev.*** Estados Unidos de Venezuela, United States of Venezuela. ◆ *republic* N South America
54 I4 **Venezuela, Golfo de** ***Eng.*** Gulf of Maracaibo, Gulf of Venezuela. *gulf* NW Venezuela
Venezuela, Gulf of *see* Venezuela, Golfo de
64 F11 **Venezuelan Basin** *undersea feature* E Caribbean Sea
155 D16 **Vengurla** Mahārāshtra, W India
39 O15 **Veniaminof, Mount** ▲ Alaska, USA
23 V14 **Venice** Florida, SE USA
22 L10 **Venice** Louisiana, S USA
Venice *see* Venezia
106 J8 **Venice, Gulf of** ***It.*** Golfo di Venezia, ***Slvn.*** Beneški Zaliv. *gulf* N Adriatic Sea
Venise *see* Venezia
94 K13 **Venjan** Dalarna, C Sweden
94 K13 **Venjansjön** ⊚ C Sweden
155 J18 **Venkatagiri** Andhra Pradesh, E India
99 M15 **Venlo** ***prev.*** Venloo. Limburg, SE Netherlands
Venloo *see* Venlo
95 E18 **Vennesla** Vest-Agder, S Norway
107 M17 **Venosa** ***anc.*** Venusia. Basilicata, S Italy
Venoste, Alpi *see* Ötztaler Alpen
Venraij *see* Venray
99 M14 **Venray** ***var.*** Venraij. Limburg, SE Netherlands
118 C8 **Venta** ***Ger.*** Windau. ≈ Latvia/Lithuania
Venta Belgarum *see* Winchester
40 G9 **Ventana, Punta Arena de la** ***var.*** Punta de la Ventana. *headland* W Mexico
Ventana, Punta de la *see* Ventana, Punta Arena de la
61 B23 **Ventana, Sierra de la** *hill range* E Argentina
Ventia *see* Valence
191 S11 **Vent, Îles du** ***var.*** Windward Islands. *island group* Archipel de la Société, W French Polynesia
191 R10 **Vent, Îles Sous le** ***var.*** Leeward Islands. *island group* Archipel de la Société, W French Polynesia
106 B11 **Ventimiglia** Liguria, NW Italy
97 M24 **Ventnor** S England, UK
18 J17 **Ventnor City** New Jersey, NE USA
103 S14 **Ventoux, Mont** ▲ SE France
118 C8 **Ventspils** ***Ger.*** Windau. Ventspils, NW Latvia
54 M10 **Ventuari, Río** ≈ S Venezuela
35 R15 **Ventura** California, W USA
182 F8 **Venus Bay** South Australia
Venusia *see* Venosa
191 P7 **Vénus, Pointe** ***var.*** Pointe Tataaihoa. *headland* Tahiti, W French Polynesia
41 V16 **Venustiano Carranza** Chiapas, SE Mexico
41 N7 **Venustiano Carranza, Presa** ⊠ NE Mexico
61 B15 **Vera** Santa Fe, C Argentina
105 Q14 **Vera** Andalucía, S Spain
63 K18 **Vera, Bahía** *bay* E Argentina
41 R14 **Veracruz** ***var.*** Veracruz Llave. Veracruz-Llave, E Mexico
41 Q13 **Veracruz-Llave** ***var.*** Veracruz. ◈ *state* E Mexico
43 Q16 **Veraguas** ***off.*** Provincia de Veraguas. ◈ *province* W Panama
Veramin *see* Varāmīn
154 B12 **Verāval** Gujarāt, W India
106 C6 **Verbania** Piemonte, NW Italy
107 N20 **Verbicaro** Calabria, SW Italy
108 D11 **Verbier** Valais, SW Switzerland
Vercellae *see* Vercelli
106 C8 **Vercelli** ***anc.*** Vercellae. Piemonte, NW Italy
103 S13 **Vercors** *physical region* E France
Verdal *see* Verdalsøra
93 E16 **Verdalsøra** ***var.*** Verdal. Nord-Trøndelag, C Norway
Verde, Cabo *see* Cape Verde
44 J5 **Verde, Cape** *headland* Long Island, C Bahamas
104 M2 **Verde, Costa** *coastal region* N Spain
Verde Grande, Río/Verde Grande y de Belem, Río *see* Verde, Río
100 H11 **Verden** Niedersachsen, NW Germany
59 J19 **Verde, Rio** ≈ SE Brazil
57 P16 **Verde, Río** ≈ Bolivia/Brazil
40 M12 **Verde, Río** ***var.*** Río Verde Grande, Río Verde Grande y de Belem. ≈ C Mexico
41 Q16 **Verde, Río** ≈ SE Mexico
36 L13 **Verde River** ≈ Arizona, SW USA
Verdhikoúsa/Verdhikoússa *see* Verdikoússa
27 Q8 **Verdigris River** ≈ Kansas/Oklahoma, C USA
115 E15 **Verdikoússa** ***var.*** Verdhikoúsa, Verdhikoússa. Thessalía, C Greece
103 S15 **Verdon** ≈ SE France
15 O12 **Verdun** Québec, SE Canada
103 S4 **Verdun** ***var.*** Verdun-sur-Meuse; ***anc.*** Verodunum. Meuse, NE France
Verdun-sur-Meuse *see* Verdun
83 J21 **Vereeniging** Gauteng, NE South Africa
Veremeyki *see* Vyeramyeyki
125 T14 **Vereshchagino** Permskaya Oblast', NW Russian Federation
76 G14 **Verga, Cap** *headland* W Guinea
61 G18 **Vergara** Treinta y Tres, E Uruguay
108 G11 **Vergeletto** Ticino, S Switzerland
18 L8 **Vergennes** Vermont, NE USA
Veria *see* Véroia
104 I5 **Verín** Galicia, NW Spain
Verin T'alin *see* T'alin
118 K6 **Veriora** Põlvamaa, SE Estonia
117 T7 **Verkhivtseve** Dnipropetrovs'ka Oblast', E Ukraine
127 W3 **Verkhniye Kigi** Respublika Bashkortostan, W Russian Federation
Verkhnedvinsk *see* Vyerkhnyadzvinsk
122 K10 **Verkhneimbatsk** Krasnoyarskiy Kray, N Russian Federation
124 I3 **Verkhnetulomskiy** Murmanskaya Oblast', NW Russian Federation
126 I3 **Verkhnetulomskoye Vodokhranilishche** ⊠ NW Russian Federation
Verkhneudinsk *see* Ulan-Ude
123 P10 **Verkhnevilyuysk** Respublika Sakha (Yakutiya), NE Russian Federation
127 W5 **Verkhniy Avzyan** Respublika Bashkortostan, W Russian Federation
127 Q11 **Verkhniy Baskunchak** Astrakhanskaya Oblast', SW Russian Federation
117 T9 **Verkhniy Rohachyk** Khersons'ka Oblast', S Ukraine
123 Q11 **Verkhnyaya Amga** Respublika Sakha (Yakutiya), NE Russian Federation
125 V6 **Verkhnyaya Inta** Respublika Komi, NW Russian Federation
125 O10 **Verkhnyaya Toyma** Arkhangel'skaya Oblast', NW Russian Federation
126 K6 **Verkhov'ye** Orlovskaya Oblast', W Russian Federation
116 I8 **Verkhovyna** Ivano-Frankivs'ka Oblast', W Ukraine
123 P8 **Verkhoyanskiy Khrebet** ⛰ NE Russian Federation
117 T7 **Verkhn'odniprovs'k** Dnipropetrovs'ka Oblast', E Ukraine
101 G14 **Verl** Nordrhein-Westfalen, NW Germany
92 N1 **Verlegenhuken** *headland* N Svalbard
82 A9 **Vermelha, Ponta** *headland* NW Angola
103 P7 **Vermenton** Yonne, C France
11 R14 **Vermilion** Alberta, SW Canada
31 T11 **Vermilion** Ohio, N USA
22 I10 **Vermilion Bay** *bay* Louisiana, S USA
29 V4 **Vermilion Lake** ⊚ Minnesota, N USA
14 F9 **Vermilion River** ≈ Ontario, S Canada
30 L12 **Vermilion River** ≈ Illinois, N USA
29 R12 **Vermillion** South Dakota, N USA
29 R12 **Vermillion River** ≈ South Dakota, N USA
15 O9 **Vermillon, Rivière** ≈ Québec, SE Canada
115 E14 **Vérmio** ⛰ N Greece
18 L8 **Vermont** ***off.*** State of Vermont; also known as The Green Mountain State. ◈ *state* NE USA
113 K16 **Vermosh** ***var.*** Vermoshi. Shkodër, N Albania
Vermoshi *see* Vermosh
37 O3 **Vernal** Utah, W USA
14 G11 **Verner** Ontario, S Canada
102 M5 **Verneuil-sur-Avre** Eure, N France
114 D13 **Vérno** ⛰ N Greece
11 N17 **Vernon** British Columbia, SW Canada
102 M4 **Vernon** Eure, N France
23 N3 **Vernon** Alabama, S USA
31 P15 **Vernon** Indiana, N USA
25 Q4 **Vernon** Texas, SW USA
32 G10 **Vernonia** Oregon, NW USA
14 G12 **Vernon, Lake** ⊚ Ontario, S Canada
22 G7 **Vernon Lake** ⊠ Louisiana, S USA
23 Y13 **Vero Beach** Florida, SE USA
Verőcze *see* Virovitica
Verodunum *see* Verdun
115 E14 **Véroia** ***var.*** Veria, Vérroia, ***Turk.*** Karaferiye. Kentrikí Makedonía, N Greece
106 E8 **Verolanuova** Lombardia, N Italy
14 K14 **Verona** Ontario, SE Canada
106 G8 **Verona** Veneto, NE Italy
29 P6 **Verona** North Dakota, N USA
30 L9 **Verona** Wisconsin, N USA
61 E20 **Verónica** Buenos Aires, E Argentina
22 J9 **Verret, Lake** ⊚ Louisiana, S USA
Vérroia *see* Véroia
103 N5 **Versailles** Yvelines, N France
31 P15 **Versailles** Indiana, N USA
20 M5 **Versailles** Kentucky, S USA
27 U5 **Versailles** Missouri, C USA
31 Q13 **Versailles** Ohio, N USA
Versecz *see* Vršac
108 A10 **Versoix** Genève, SW Switzerland
15 Z6 **Verte, Pointe** *headland* Québec, SE Canada
111 I22 **Vértes** ⛰ NW Hungary
44 G6 **Vertientes** Camagüey, C Cuba
114 G13 **Vertískos** ⛰ N Greece
102 I8 **Vertou** Loire-Atlantique, NW France
Verulamium *see* St Albans
99 L19 **Verviers** Liège, E Belgium
103 Y14 **Vescovato** Corse, France, C Mediterranean Sea
99 L20 **Vesdre** ≈ E Belgium
117 U10 **Vesele** ***Rus.*** Veseloye. Zaporiz'ka Oblast', S Ukraine
111 D18 **Veselí nad Lužnicí** ***var.*** Weseli an der Lainsitz, ***Ger.*** Frohenbruck. Jihočeský Kraj, S Czech Republic
114 M9 **Veselinovo** Shumen, E Bulgaria
126 L12 **Veselovskoye Vodokhranilishche** ⊠ SW Russian Federation
Veseloye *see* Vesele
117 Q9 **Veselynove** Mykolayivs'ka Oblast', S Ukraine
Veseya *see* Vyasyeya
126 M10 **Veshenskaya** Rostovskaya Oblast', SW Russian Federation
127 Q5 **Veshkayma** Ul'yanovskaya Oblast', W Russian Federation
Vesisaari *see* Vadsø
Vesontio *see* Besançon
103 T7 **Vesoul** ***anc.*** Vesulium, Vesulum. Haute-Saône, E France
95 J20 **Vessigebro** Halland, S Sweden
95 D17 **Vest-Agder** ◈ *county* S Norway
23 P4 **Vestavia Hills** Alabama, S USA
92 G10 **Vesterålen** *island group* N Norway
92 H2 **Vestfirdhir** ◈ *region* NW Iceland
92 G11 **Vestfjorden** *fjord* C Norway
95 G16 **Vestfold** ◈ *county* S Norway
95 B18 **Vestmanna** ***Dan.*** Vestmanhavn Faeroe Islands
92 I4 **Vestmannaeyjar** Sudhurland, S Iceland
94 E9 **Vestnes** Møre og Romsdal, S Norway
95 I23 **Vestsjælland** ***off.*** Vestsjællands Amt. ◈ *county* E Denmark
92 H3 **Vesturland** ◈ *region* W Iceland
92 G11 **Vestvågøya** *island* C Norway
Vesulium/Vesulum *see* Vesoul
Vesuna *see* Périgueux
107 K17 **Vesuvio** ***Eng.*** Vesuvius. ☒ S Italy
Vesuvius *see* Vesuvio
124 K14 **Ves'yegonsk** Tverskaya Oblast', W Russian Federation
111 I23 **Veszprém** ***Ger.*** Veszprim. Veszprém, W Hungary
111 H23 **Veszprém** ***off.*** Veszprém Megye. ◈ *county* W Hungary
Veszprim *see* Veszprém
Vetka *see* Vyetka
95 M19 **Vetlanda** Jönköping, S Sweden
127 P1 **Vetluga** Nizhegorodskaya Oblast', W Russian Federation
127 P14 **Vetluga** ≈ NW Russian Federation
125 O14 **Vetluzhskiy** Kostromskaya Oblast', NW Russian Federation
127 P2 **Vetluzhskiy** Nizhegorodskaya Oblast', W Russian Federation
107 H14 **Vetralla** Lazio, C Italy
114 M9 **Vetren** ***prev.*** Zhitarovo. Burgas, E Bulgaria
114 M8 **Vetrino** Varna, E Bulgaria
Vetrino *see* Vyetryna
122 L7 **Vetrovaya, Gora** ▲ N Russian Federation
Vetter, Lake *see* Vättern

◆ Country
● Country Capital
◇ Dependent Territory
○ Dependent Territory Capital
◈ Administrative Region
✕ International Airport
▲ Mountain
⛰ Mountain Range
☒ Volcano
≈ River
⊚ Lake
⊠ Reservoir

…an Oklahoma, C USA
Viana de Castelo see Viana do Castelo
104 H12 Viana do Alentejo Évora, S Portugal
104 I4 Viana do Bolo Galicia, NW Spain
104 G5 Viana do Castelo var. Viana de Castelo; anc. Velobriga. Viana do Castelo, NW Portugal
104 G5 Viana do Castelo var. Viana de Castelo. ◆ district N Portugal
98 J12 Vianen Zuid-Holland, C Netherlands
167 Q8 Viangchan Eng./Fr. Vientiane. ● (Laos) C Laos
167 P6 Viangphoukha var. Vieng Pou Kha. Louang Namtha, N Laos
104 K13 Viar ≈ SW Spain
106 E11 Viareggio Toscana, C Italy
103 O14 Viaur ≈ S France
Vibiscum see Vevey
95 G21 Viborg Viborg, NW Denmark
29 R12 Viborg South Dakota, N USA
95 F21 Viborg off. Viborg Amt. ◆ county NW Denmark
107 N22 Vibo Valentia prev. Monteleone di Calabria; anc. Hipponium. Calabria, SW Italy
105 W5 Vic var. Vich; anc. Ausa, Vicus Ausonensis. Cataluña, NE Spain
102 K16 Vic-en-Bigorre Hautes-Pyrénées, S France
40 K10 Vicente Guerrero Durango, C Mexico
41 P10 Vicente Guerrero, Presa var. Presa de las Adjuntas. ⊡ NE Mexico
Vicentia see Vicenza
106 G8 Vicenza anc. Vicentia. Veneto, NE Italy
Vich see Vic
54 J10 Vichada off. Comisaría del Vichada. ◆ province E Colombia
54 K10 Vichada, Río ≈ E Colombia
61 G17 Vichadero Rivera, NE Uruguay
Vichegda see Vychegda
124 M16 Vichuga Ivanovskaya Oblast', W Russian Federation
103 P10 Vichy Allier, C France
26 K9 Vici Oklahoma, C USA
31 P10 Vicksburg Michigan, N USA
22 J5 Vicksburg Mississippi, S USA
103 O12 Vic-sur-Cère Cantal, C France
29 X14 Victor Iowa, C USA
59 I21 Victor Mato Grosso do Sul, SW Brazil
182 I10 Victor Harbor South Australia
61 C18 Victoria Entre Ríos, E Argentina
10 L17 Victoria Vancouver Island, British Columbia, SW Canada
45 R14 Victoria NW Grenada
42 H6 Victoria Yoro, NW Honduras
121 O15 Victoria var. Rabat. Gozo, NW Malta
116 I12 Victoria Ger. Viktoriastadt. Brașov, C Romania
172 H17 Victoria ● (Seychelles) Mahé, SW Seychelles
25 U13 Victoria Texas, SW USA
183 N12 Victoria ◆ state SE Australia
181 O3 Victoria ≈ Northern Territory, Australia
Victoria see Labuan, East Malaysia
Victoria see Masvingo, Zimbabwe
Victoria Bank see Vitória Seamount
11 Y15 Victoria Beach Manitoba, S Canada
Victoria de Durango see Durango
Victoria de las Tunas see Las Tunas
83 I16 Victoria Falls Matabeleland North, W Zimbabwe
83 I16 Victoria Falls ✕ Matabeleland North, W Zimbabwe
83 I16 Victoria Falls waterfall Zambia/Zimbabwe
Victoria Falls see Iguaçu, Salto do
63 F19 Victoria, Isla island Archipiélago de los Chonos, S Chile
8 K6 Victoria Island island Northwest Territories/Nunavut, NW Canada
182 L8 Victoria, Lake ◎ New South Wales, SE Australia
…merset
…a see
…Lake
…ria Peak ▲ SE Belize
…6 Victoria Range ▲ South Island, NZ
181 O3 Victoria River ≈ Northern Territory, N Australia
181 P3 Victoria River Roadhouse Northern Territory, N Australia
15 Q11 Victoriaville Québec, SE Canada
Victoria-Wes see Victoria West
83 G24 Victoria West Afr. Victoria-Wes. Northern Cape, W South Africa
62 J13 Victorica La Pampa, C Argentina
195 T3 Victor, Mount ▲ Antarctica
35 U14 Victorville California, W USA
62 G9 Vicuña Coquimbo, N Chile
62 K11 Vicuña Mackenna Córdoba, C Argentina
Vicus Ausonensis see Vic
Vicus Elbii see Viterbo
33 X7 Vida Montana, NW USA
23 V6 Vidalia Georgia, SE USA
22 J7 Vidalia Louisiana, S USA
95 F22 Videbæk Ringkøbing, C Denmark
60 I13 Videira Santa Catarina, S Brazil
116 J14 Videle Teleorman, S Romania
Videm-Krško see Krško
Víden̆ see Wien
104 H12 Vidigueira Beja, S Portugal
114 J9 Vidima ≈ N Bulgaria
114 G7 Vidin anc. Bononia. Vidin, NW Bulgaria
114 F8 Vidin ◆ province NW Bulgaria
154 H10 Vidisha Madhya Pradesh, C India
25 Y10 Vidor Texas, SW USA
95 L20 Vidöstern ◎ S Sweden
92 J13 Vidsel Norrbotten, N Sweden
118 H9 Vidzemes Augstiene ▲ C Latvia
118 J12 Vidzy Rus. Vidzy. Vitsyebskaya Voblasts', NW Belarus
63 L16 Viedma Río Negro, E Argentina
63 H22 Viedma, Lago ◎ S Argentina
45 O11 Vieille Case var. Itassi. N Dominica
104 M2 Vieja, Peña ▲ N Spain
40 E4 Viejo, Cerro ▲ NW Mexico
56 B9 Viejo, Cerro ▲ N Peru
118 E10 Viekšniai Telšiai, NW Lithuania
105 U3 Vielha var. Viella. Cataluña, NE Spain
Viella see Vielha
99 L21 Vielsalm Luxembourg, E Belgium
Vieng Pou Kha see Viangphoukha
23 T6 Vienna Georgia, SE USA
30 L17 Vienna Illinois, N USA
27 V5 Vienna Missouri, C USA
21 Q3 Vienna West Virginia, NE USA
Vienna see Wien, Austria
Vienna see Vienne, France
103 R11 Vienne anc. Vienna. Isère, E France
102 L10 Vienne ◆ department W France
102 L9 Vienne ≈ W France
Vientiane see Viangchan
Vientos, Paso de los see Windward Passage
45 V6 Vieques var. Isabel Segunda. E Puerto Rico
45 V6 Vieques, Isla de island E Puerto Rico
45 V6 Vieques, Pasaje de passage E Puerto Rico
45 V5 Vieques, Sonda de sound E Puerto Rico
Vierdörfer see Săcele
93 M15 Vieremä Itä-Suomi, C Finland
99 M14 Vierlingsbeek Noord-Brabant, SE Netherlands
101 G20 Viernheim Hessen, W Germany
101 D15 Viersen Nordrhein-Westfalen, W Germany
108 G8 Vierwaldstätter See Eng. Lake of Lucerne. ◎ C Switzerland
103 N8 Vierzon Cher, C France
40 L8 Viesca Coahuila de Zaragoza, NE Mexico
118 H10 Viesīte Ger. Eckengraf. Jēkabpils, S Latvia
107 N15 Vieste Puglia, SE Italy
167 T8 Vietnam off. Socialist Republic of Vietnam, Vtn. Công Hoa Xa Hôi Chu Nghia Việt Nam. ◆ republic SE Asia
167 S5 Việt Quang Ha Giang, N Vietnam
Vietri see Việt Tri
167 S6 Việt Tri var. Vietri. Vinh Phu, N Vietnam
30 L4 Vieux Desert, Lac ◎ Michigan/Wisconsin, N USA
45 Y13 Vieux Fort S Saint Lucia
…K6 Vieux-Habitants Basse Terre, SW Guadeloupe
…9 G14 Vievis Vilnius, S Lithuania
71 N2 Vigan Luzon, N Philippines
106 D8 Vigevano Lombardia, N Italy
107 N18 Viggiano Basilicata, S Italy
58 L12 Vigia Pará, NE Brazil
41 Y12 Vigía Chico Quintana Roo, SE Mexico
Vigie see George FL Charles
102 K17 Vignemale var. Pic de Vignemale. ▲ France/Spain
Vignemale, Pic de see Vignemale
106 G10 Vignola Emilia-Romagna, C Italy
104 G4 Vigo Galicia, NW Spain
104 G4 Vigo, Ría de estuary NW Spain
94 D9 Vigra island S Norway
95 C17 Vigrestad Rogaland, S Norway
93 L15 Vihanti Oulu, C Finland
149 U10 Vihāri Punjab, E Pakistan
102 K8 Vihiers Maine-et-Loire, NW France
111 O19 Vihorlat ▲ E Slovakia
93 L19 Vihti Etelä-Suomi, S Finland
Viipuri see Vyborg
93 M16 Viitasaari Länsi-Suomi, W Finland
118 K3 Viivikonna Ida-Virumaa, NE Estonia
155 K16 Vijayawāda prev. Bezwada. Andhra Pradesh, SE India
Vijosa/Vijosë see Aóos, Albania/Greece
Vijosa/Vijosë see Vjosës, Lumi i, Albania/Greece
Vik see Vikøyri
92 J4 Vík Sudhurland, S Iceland
94 L13 Vika Dalarna, C Sweden
92 L12 Vikajärvi Lappi, N Finland
94 L13 Vikarbyn Dalarna, C Sweden
95 J22 Viken Skåne, S Sweden
95 L17 Viken ◎ C Sweden
95 G15 Vikersund Buskerud, S Norway
114 G11 Vikhren ▲ SW Bulgaria
11 R15 Viking Alberta, SW Canada
95 M14 Vikmanshyttan Dalarna, C Sweden
94 D12 Vikøyri var. Vik. Sogn og Fjordane, S Norway
93 H17 Viksjö Västernorrland, C Sweden
Viktoriastadt see Victoria
Vila see Port-Vila
Vila Arriaga see Bibala
Vila Artur de Paiva see Cubango
Vila Bela da Santissima Trindade see Mato Grosso
58 B12 Vila Bittencourt Amazonas, NW Brazil
Vila da Ponte see Cubango
64 O2 Vila da Praia da Vitória Terceira, Azores, Portugal, NE Atlantic Ocean
Vila de Aljustrel see Cangamba
Vila de Almoster see Chiange
Vila de João Belo see Xai-Xai
Vila de Macia see Macia
Vila de Manhiça see Manhiça
Vila de Manica see Manica
Vila de Mocímboa da Praia see Mocímboa da Praia
83 N16 Vila de Sena var. Sena. Sofala, C Mozambique
104 F14 Vila do Bispo Faro, S Portugal
104 G6 Vila do Conde Porto, NW Portugal
Vila do Maio see Maio
64 P3 Vila do Porto Santa Maria, Azores, Portugal, NE Atlantic Ocean
83 K15 Vila do Zumbo prev. Vila do Zumbu, Zumbo. Tete, NW Mozambique
Vila do Zumbu see Vila do Zumbo
104 I6 Vila Flor var. Vila Flôr. Bragança, N Portugal
105 V6 Vilafranca del Penedès var. Villafranca del Panadés. Cataluña, NE Spain
104 F10 Vila Franca de Xira var. Vilafranca de Xira. Lisboa, C Portugal
Vila Gago Coutinho see Lumbala N'Guimbo
104 G3 Vilagarcía de Arousa var. Villagarcía de Arosa. Galicia, NW Spain
Vila General Machado see Camacupa
Vila Henrique de Carvalho see Saurimo
102 I7 Vilaine ≈ NW France
Vila João de Almeida see Chibia
118 K8 Viļaka Ger. Marienhausen. Balvi, NE Latvia
104 I2 Vilalba Galicia, NW Spain
Vila Marechal Carmona see Uíge
Vila Mariano Machado see Ganda
172 G3 Vilanandro, Tanjona headland W Madagascar
Vilanculos see Vilankulo
118 J10 Viļāni Rēzekne, E Latvia
83 N19 Vilankulo var. Vilanculos. Inhambane, E Mozambique
Vila Norton de Matos see Balombo
104 G6 Vila Nova de Famalicão var. Vila Nova de Famalicao. Braga, N Portugal
104 I6 Vila Nova de Foz Côa var. Vila Nova de Fozcôa. Guarda, N Portugal
104 F6 Vila Nova de Gaia Porto, NW Portugal
Vila Nova de Portimão see Portimão
105 V6 Vilanova i La Geltrú Cataluña, NE Spain
Vila Pereira de Eça see N'Giva
104 H6 Vila Pouca de Aguiar Vila Real, N Portugal
104 H6 Vila Real var. Vila Rial. Vila Real, N Portugal
104 H6 Vila Real ◆ district N Portugal
105 T9 Vila-real de los Infantes var. Villarreal. País Valenciano, E Spain
104 H14 Vila Real de Santo António Faro, S Portugal
104 J7 Vilar Formoso Guarda, N Portugal
Vila Rial see Vila Real
59 J15 Vila Rica Mato Grosso, W Brazil
Vila Robert Williams see Caála
Vila Salazar see N'Dalatando
Vila Serpa Pinto see Menongue
Vila Teixeira da Silva see Bailundo
Vila Teixeira de Sousa see Luau
104 H9 Vila Velha de Ródão Castelo Branco, C Portugal
104 G5 Vila Verde Braga, N Portugal
104 H11 Vila Viçosa Évora, S Portugal
57 G15 Vilcabamba, Cordillera de ▲ C Peru
Vîlcea see Vâlcea
122 J4 Vil'cheka, Zemlya Eng. Wilczek Land. island Zemlya Frantsa-Iosifa, NW Russian Federation
95 F22 Vildbjerg Ringkøbing, C Denmark
Vileyka see Vilyeyka
93 H15 Vilhelmina Västerbotten, N Sweden
59 F17 Vilhena Rondônia, W Brazil
115 G19 Vília Attikí, C Greece
Viliya see Viliya
119 I14 Viliya Lith. Neris, Rus. Viliya. ≈ W Belarus
Viliya see Neris
118 H5 Viljandi Ger. Fellin. Viljandimaa, S Estonia
118 H5 Viljandimaa off. Viljandi Maakond. ◆ province SW Estonia
119 E14 Vilkaviškis Pol. Wyłkowyszki. Marijampolė, SW Lithuania
118 F13 Vilkija Kaunas, C Lithuania
197 V9 Vil'kitskogo, Proliv strait N Russian Federation
Vilkovo see Vylkove
57 L21 Villa Abecia Chuquisaca, S Bolivia
41 N5 Villa Acuña var. Ciudad Acuña. Coahuila de Zaragoza, NE Mexico
40 J4 Villa Ahumada Chihuahua, N Mexico
45 O9 Villa Altagracia C Dominican Republic
56 L13 Villa Bella Beni, N Bolivia
104 J3 Villablino Castilla-León, N Spain
54 K6 Villa Bruzual Portuguesa, N Venezuela
105 O9 Villacañas Castilla-La Mancha, C Spain
105 O12 Villacarrillo Andalucía, S Spain
104 M7 Villacastín Castilla-León, N Spain
Villa Cecilia see Ciudad Madero
109 S9 Villach Slvn. Beljak. Kärnten, S Austria
107 B20 Villacidro Sardegna, Italy, C Mediterranean Sea
Villa Concepción see Concepción
104 L4 Villada Castilla-León, N Spain
40 M10 Villa de Cos Zacatecas, C Mexico
54 L5 Villa de Cura var. Cura. Aragua, N Venezuela
Villa del Nevoso see Ilirska Bistrica
Villa del Pilar see Pilar
104 M13 Villa del Río Andalucía, S Spain
Villa de Méndez see Méndez
42 H6 Villa de San Antonio Comayagua, W Honduras
105 N4 Villadiego Castilla-León, N Spain
105 T8 Villafames País Valenciano, E Spain
41 U16 Villa Flores Chiapas, SE Mexico
104 J3 Villafranca del Bierzo Castilla-León, N Spain
105 S8 Villafranca del Cid País Valenciano, E Spain
104 J11 Villafranca de los Barros Extremadura, W Spain
105 N10 Villafranca de los Caballeros Castilla-La Mancha, C Spain
Villafranca del Panadés see Vilafranca del Penedès
106 F8 Villafranca di Verona Veneto, NE Italy
107 J23 Villafrati Sicilia, Italy, C Mediterranean Sea
Villagarcía de Arosa see Vilagarcía de Arousa
41 O9 Villagrán Tamaulipas, C Mexico
61 C17 Villaguay Entre Ríos, E Argentina
62 O6 Villa Hayes Presidente Hayes, S Paraguay
41 U15 Villahermosa prev. San Juan Bautista. Tabasco, SE Mexico
105 O11 Villahermosa Castilla-La Mancha, C Spain
64 O11 Villahermoso Gomera, Islas Canarias, Spain, NE Atlantic Ocean
Villa Hidalgo see Hidalgo
105 T12 Villajoyosa Cat. La Vila Joíosa. País Valenciano, E Spain
Villa Juárez see Juárez
Villalba see Collado Villalba
41 N8 Villaldama Nuevo León, NE Mexico
104 L5 Villalón de Campos Castilla-León, N Spain
61 A25 Villalonga Buenos Aires, E Argentina
104 L5 Villalpando Castilla-León, N Spain
40 K9 Villa Madero var. Francisco I.Madero. Durango, C Mexico
41 O9 Villa Mainero Tamaulipas, C Mexico
Villamaña see Villamañán
104 L4 Villamañán var. Villamaña. Castilla-León, N Spain
62 L10 Villa María Córdoba, C Argentina
61 C17 Villa María Grande Entre Ríos, E Argentina
57 K21 Villa Martín Potosí, SW Bolivia
104 K15 Villamartín Andalucía, S Spain
62 J8 Villa Mazán La Rioja, NW Argentina
Villa Mercedes see Mercedes
Villamil see Puerto Villamil
Villa Nador see Nador
54 G5 Villanueva La Guajira, N Colombia
42 H5 Villanueva Cortés, NW Honduras
40 L11 Villanueva Zacatecas, C Mexico
42 I9 Villa Nueva Chinandega, NW Nicaragua
37 T11 Villanueva New Mexico, SW USA
104 M12 Villanueva de Córdoba Andalucía, S Spain
105 O12 Villanueva del Arzobispo Andalucía, S Spain
104 K11 Villanueva de la Serena Extremadura, W Spain
104 L5 Villanueva del Campo Castilla-León, N Spain
105 O11 Villanueva de los Infantes Castilla-La Mancha, C Spain
61 C14 Villa Ocampo Santa Fe, C Argentina
40 J8 Villa Ocampo Durango, C Mexico
40 J7 Villa Orestes Pereyra Durango, C Mexico
105 N3 Villarcayo Castilla-León, N Spain
104 L5 Villardefrades Castilla-León, N Spain
105 S9 Villar del Arzobispo País Valenciano, E Spain
105 Q6 Villaroya de la Sierra Aragón, NE Spain
Villarreal see Vila-real de los Infantes
62 P6 Villarrica Guairá, SE Paraguay
63 G15 Villarrica, Volcán ⛰ S Chile
105 P10 Villarrobledo Castilla-La Mancha, C Spain
105 N10 Villarrubia de los Ojos Castilla-La Mancha, C Spain
18 J17 Villas New Jersey, NE USA
105 O3 Villasana de Mena Castilla-León, N Spain
107 M23 Villa San Giovanni Calabria, S Italy
61 D18 Villa San José Entre Ríos, E Argentina
Villa Sanjurjo see Al-Hoceïma
105 P6 Villasayas Castilla-León, N Spain
107 C20 Villasimius Sardegna, Italy, C Mediterranean Sea
41 N6 Villa Unión Coahuila de Zaragoza, NE Mexico
40 K10 Villa Unión Durango, C Mexico
40 J10 Villa Unión Sinaloa, C Mexico
62 K12 Villa Valeria Córdoba, C Argentina
105 N8 Villaverde Madrid, C Spain
54 F10 Villavicencio Meta, C Colombia
104 L2 Villaviciosa Asturias, N Spain
104 L12 Villaviciosa de Córdoba Andalucía, S Spain
57 L22 Villazón Potosí, S Bolivia
14 J8 Villebon, Lac ◎ Québec, SE Canada
Ville de Kinshasa see Kinshasa
102 J5 Villedieu-les-Poêles Manche, N France
Villefranche see Villefranche-sur-Saône
103 N16 Villefranche-de-Lauragais Haute-Garonne, S France
103 N14 Villefranche-de-Rouergue Aveyron, S France
103 R10 Villefranche-sur-Saône var. Villefranche. Rhône, E France
14 H9 Ville-Marie Québec, SE Canada
102 M15 Villemur-sur-Tarn Haute-Garonne, S France
105 S11 Villena País Valenciano, E Spain
Villeneuve-d'Agen see Villeneuve-sur-Lot
102 L13 Villeneuve-sur-Lot var. Villeneuve-d'Agen; hist. Gajac. Lot-et-Garonne, SW France
103 P6 Villeneuve-sur-Yonne Yonne, C France
22 H8 Ville Platte Louisiana, S USA
103 R11 Villeurbanne Rhône, E France
101 G23 Villingen-Schwenningen Baden-Württemberg, S Germany
29 T15 Villisca Iowa, C USA
Villmanstrand see Lappeenranta
Vilna see Vilnius
119 H14 Vilnius Pol. Wilno, Ger. Wilna; prev. Rus. Vilna. ● (Lithuania) Vilnius, SE Lithuania
119 H15 Vilnius ◆ province SE Lithuania
119 H14 Vilnius ✕ Vilnius, SE Lithuania
117 S7 Vil'nohirs'k Dnipropetrovs'ka Oblast', E Ukraine
117 U8 Vil'nyans'k Zaporiz'ka Oblast', SE Ukraine
93 L17 Vilppula Länsi-Suomi, W Finland
101 M20 Vils ≈ SE Germany
118 C5 Vilsandi Saar island W Estonia
117 P8 Vil'shanka Rus. Olshanka. Kirovohrads'ka Oblast', C Ukraine
101 O22 Vilshofen Bayern, SE Germany
155 J20 Viluppuram Tamil Nādu, SE India
113 I16 Vilusi Montenegro, SW Serbia and Montenegro (Yugo.)
99 G18 Vilvoorde Fr. Vilvorde. Vlaams Brabant, C Belgium
Vilvorde see Vilvoorde
119 J14 Vilyeyka Pol. Wilejka, Rus. Vileyka. Minskaya Voblasts', NW Belarus
123 V11 Vilyuchinsk Kamchatskaya, Oblast', E Russian Federation
123 P10 Vilyuy ≈ NE Russian Federation
123 P10 Vilyuysk Respublika Sakha (Yakutiya), NE Russian Federation
123 N10 Vilyuyskoye Vodokhranilishche ⊡ NE Russian Federation
104 G2 Vimianzo Galicia, NW Spain
95 M19 Vimmerby Kalmar, S Sweden
102 L5 Vimoutiers Orne, N France
93 L16 Vimpeli Länsi-Suomi, W Finland
79 G14 Vina ≈ Cameroon/Chad
62 G11 Viña del Mar Valparaíso, C Chile
19 R8 Vinalhaven Island island Maine, NE USA
105 T8 Vinaròs País Valenciano, E Spain
Vînători see Vânători
31 N15 Vincennes Indiana, N USA
195 Y12 Vincennes Bay bay Antarctica
25 O7 Vincent Texas, SW USA
95 H24 Vindeby Fyn, C Denmark
93 I15 Vindeln Västerbotten, N Sweden
95 F21 Vinderup Ringkøbing, C Denmark
Vindhya Mountains see Vindhya Range
153 N14 Vindhya Range var. Vindhya Mountains. ▲ N India
Vindobona see Wien
20 K6 Vine Grove Kentucky, S USA
18 J17 Vineland New Jersey, NE USA
116 E11 Vinga Arad, W Romania
95 M16 Vingåker Södermanland, C Sweden
167 S8 Vinh Nghê An, N Vietnam
104 I5 Vinhais Bragança, N Portugal
167 T9 Vinh Linh Quang Tri, C Vietnam
Vinh Loi see Bac Liêu
167 S14 Vinh Long var. Vinhlong. Vinh Long, S Vietnam
113 Q18 Vinica NE FYR Macedonia
109 V13 Vinica SE Slovenia
114 G8 Vinishte Montana, NW Bulgaria
27 Q8 Vinita Oklahoma, C USA
Vinju Mare see Vânju Mare
98 I11 Vinkeveen Utrecht, C Netherlands
116 L6 Vin'kivtsi Khmel'nyts'ka Oblast', W Ukraine
112 I10 Vinkovci Ger. Winkowitz, Hung. Vinkovcze. Vukovar-Srijem, E Croatia
Vinkovcze see Vinkovci
Vinnitsa see Vinnytsya
Vinnitskaya Oblast'/Vinnytsya see Vinnyts'ka Oblast'
116 M7 Vinnyts'ka Oblast' var. Vinnytsya, Rus. Vinnitskaya Oblast'. ◆ province C Ukraine
117 N6 Vinnytsya Rus. Vinnitsa. Vinnyts'ka Oblast', C Ukraine
117 N6 Vinnytsya ✕ Vinnyts'ka Oblast', N Ukraine
Vinogradov see Vynohradiv
194 L8 Vinson Massif ▲ Antarctica
94 G11 Vinstra Oppland, S Norway
116 K12 Vintilă Vodă Buzău, SE Romania
29 X13 Vinton Iowa, C USA
22 F9 Vinton Louisiana, S USA
155 J17 Vinukonda Andhra Pradesh, E India
Vioara see Ocnele Mari
83 E23 Vioolsdrif Northern Cape, SW South Africa
109 S12 Vipava ≈ SW Slovenia
82 M13 Viphya Mountains ▲ C Malawi
171 Q4 Virac Catanduanes Island, N Philippines
124 K8 Virandozero Respublika Kareliya, NW Russian Federation
137 P16 Viranşehir Şanlıurfa, SE Turkey
154 D13 Virār Mahārāshtra, W India
11 W16 Virden Manitoba, S Canada
30 K14 Virden Illinois, N USA
Virdois see Virrat
102 J5 Vire Calvados, N France
102 J4 Vire ≈ N France
83 A15 Virei Namibe, SW Angola
Vîrful Moldoveanu see Vârful Moldoveanu
35 R5 Virgina Peak ▲ Nevada, W USA
45 U9 Virgin Gorda island C British Virgin Islands
83 I22 Virginia Free State, C South Africa
30 K13 Virginia Illinois, N USA
29 W4 Virginia Minnesota, N USA
21 T6 Virginia off. Commonwealth of Virginia; also known as Mother of Presidents, Mother of States, Old Dominion. ◆ state NE USA
21 Y7 Virginia Beach Virginia, NE USA
33 R11 Virginia City Montana, NW USA
35 Q6 Virginia City Nevada, W USA
14 H8 Virginiatown Ontario, S Canada
Virgin Islands see British Virgin Islands
45 T9 Virgin Islands (US) var. Virgin Islands of the United States; prev. Danish West Indies. ◇ US unincorporated territory E West Indies
45 T9 Virgin Passage passage Puerto Rico/Virgin Islands (US)
35 Y10 Virgin River ≈ Nevada/Utah, W USA
Virihaur see Virihaure
92 H12 Virihaure var. Virihaur. ◎ N Sweden
167 T11 Virôchey Rôtânôkiri, NE Cambodia
93 N19 Virolahti Etelä-Suomi, S Finland
30 J8 Viroqua Wisconsin, N USA
112 G8 Virovitica Ger. Virovititz, Hung. Verőcze; prev. Ger. Werowitz. Virovitica-Podravina, NE Croatia
112 G8 Virovitica-Podravina off. Virovitičko-Podravska Županija. ◆ province NE Croatia
Virovititz see Virovitica
113 J17 Virpazar Montenegro, SW Serbia and Montenegro (Yugo.)
93 L17 Virrat Swe. Virdois. Länsi-Suomi, SW Finland
95 M20 Virserum Kalmar, S Sweden
99 K25 Virton Luxembourg, SE Belgium
118 F5 Virtsu Ger. Werder. Läänemaa, W Estonia
56 C12 Virú La Libertad, C Peru
Virudhunagar see Virudunagar
155 H23 Virudunagar var. Virudhunagar. Tamil Nādu, SE India
118 I3 Viru-Jaagupi Ger. Sankt-Jakobi. Lääne-Virumaa, NE Estonia
57 N19 Viru-Viru var. Santa Cruz. ✕ (Santa Cruz) Santa Cruz, C Bolivia
113 E15 Vis It. Lissa; anc. Issa. island S Croatia
Vis see Fish
118 I12 Visaginas prev. Sniečkus. Utena, E Lithuania
155 M15 Visākhapatnam Andhra Pradesh, SE India
35 R11 Visalia California, W USA
Vişău see Vişeu
95 P19 Visby Ger. Wisby. Gotland, SE Sweden
197 N9 Viscount Melville Sound prev. Melville Sound. sound Northwest Territories/Nunavut, N Canada
99 L19 Visé Liège, E Belgium
112 K13 Višegrad Republika Srpska, E Bosnia and Herzegovina
58 L12 Viseu Pará, NE Brazil
104 H7 Viseu prev. Vizeu. Viseu, N Portugal

◆ Country ● Country Capital ◇ Dependent Territory ○ Dependent Territory Capital ◆ Administrative Region ✕ International Airport ▲ Mountain ▲ Mountain Range ⛰ Volcano ≈ River ◎ Lake ⊡ Reservoir

104 H7 **Viseu** var. Vizeu. ◈ district N Portugal
116 I8 **Vişeu** Hung. Visó; prev. Vişău. ≈ NW Romania
116 I8 **Vişeu de Sus** var. Vişeul de Sus, Ger. Oberwischau, Hung. Felsővisó. Maramureş, N Romania
Vişeul de Sus see Vişeu de Sus
127 R10 **Vishera** ≈ NW Russian Federation
95 J19 **Viskafors** Västra Götaland, S Sweden
95 J20 **Viskan** ≈ S Sweden
95 L21 **Vislanda** Kronoberg, S Sweden
Vislinskiy Zaliv see Vistula Lagoon
Visó see Vişeu
112 H13 **Visoko** Federacija Bosna I Hercegovina, C Bosnia and Herzegovina
106 A9 **Viso, Monte** ▲ NW Italy
108 E10 **Visp** Valais, SW Switzerland
108 E10 **Vispa** ≈ S Switzerland
95 M21 **Vissefjärda** Kalmar, S Sweden
100 I11 **Visselhövede** Niedersachsen, NW Germany
95 G23 **Vissenbjerg** Fyn, C Denmark
35 U17 **Vista** California, W USA
58 C11 **Vista Alegre** Amazonas, NW Brazil
114 J13 **Vistonída, Límni** ◎ NE Greece
92 K12 **Vittasjohka** ≈ N Sweden
Vistula see Wisła
119 A14 **Vistula Lagoon** Ger. Frisches Haff, Pol. Zalew Wiślany, Rus. Vislinskiy Zaliv. lagoon Poland/Russian Federation
114 I8 **Vit** ≈ NW Bulgaria
Vitebsk see Vitsyebsk
Vitebskaya Oblast' see Vitsyebskaya Voblasts'
107 H14 **Viterbo** anc. Vicus Elbii. Lazio, C Italy
112 H12 **Vitez** Federacija Bosna I Hercegovina, C Bosnia and Herzegovina
167 S14 **Vi Thanh** Cân Thơ, S Vietnam
Viti see Fiji
186 E7 **Vitiaz Strait** strait NE PNG
104 J7 **Vitigudino** Castilla-León, N Spain
187 W15 **Viti Levu** island W Fiji
123 O11 **Vitim** ≈ C Russian Federation
123 O12 **Vitimskiy** Irkutskaya Oblast', C Russian Federation
109 V2 **Vitis** Niederösterreich, N Austria
Vitoria see Vitoria-Gasteiz
59 O20 **Vitória** Espírito Santo, SE Brazil
Vitoria Bank see Vitória Seamount
59 N18 **Vitória da Conquista** Bahia, E Brazil
105 P3 **Vitoria-Gasteiz** var. Vitoria, Eng. Vittoria. País Vasco, N Spain
65 J16 **Vitória Seamount** var. Victoria Bank, Vitoria Bank. undersea feature C Atlantic Ocean
112 F13 **Vitorog** ▲ SW Bosnia and Herzegovina
102 J6 **Vitré** Ille-et-Vilaine, NW France
103 R5 **Vitry-le-François** Marne, N France
114 D13 **Vítsoi** ▲ N Greece
118 N13 **Vitsyebsk** Rus. Vitebsk. Vitsyebskaya Voblasts', NE Belarus
118 K13 **Vitsyebskaya Voblasts'** prev. Rus. Vitebskaya Oblast'. ◈ province N Belarus
92 J11 **Vittangi** Lapp. Vazáš. Norrbotten, N Sweden
103 R8 **Vitteaux** Côte d'Or, C France
103 S6 **Vittel** Vosges, NE France
95 N15 **Vittinge** Västmanland, C Sweden
107 K25 **Vittoria** Sicilia, Italy, C Mediterranean Sea
Vittoria see Vitoria-Gasteiz
106 I7 **Vittorio Veneto** Veneto, NE Italy
187 W15 **Vitu Levu** island W Fiji
192 L6 **Vityaz Seamount** undersea feature C Pacific Ocean
192 K8 **Vityaz Trench** undersea feature W Pacific Ocean
108 G8 **Vitznau** Luzern, W Switzerland
104 I1 **Viveiro** Galicia, NW Spain
105 S9 **Viver** País Valenciano, E Spain
103 Q13 **Viverais, Monts du** ▲▲ C France
122 L9 **Vivi** ≈ N Russian Federation
22 F4 **Vivian** Louisiana, S USA
29 N10 **Vivian** South Dakota, N USA
103 R13 **Viviers** Ardèche, E France
Vivis see Vevey
83 K19 **Vivo** Limpopo, NE South Africa
102 L10 **Vivonne** Vienne, W France
Vizakna see Ocna Sibiului
105 O2 **Vizcaya** Basq. Bizkaia. ◈ province País Vasco, N Spain
Vizcaya, Golfo de see Biscay, Bay of
136 C10 **Vize** Kırklareli, NW Turkey
122 K4 **Vize, Ostrov** island Severnaya Zemlya, N Russian Federation
Vizeu see Viseu
155 M15 **Vizianagaram** var. Vizianagram. Andhra Pradesh, E India
Vizianagram see Vizianagaram
103 S12 **Vizille** Isère, E France
125 R11 **Vizinga** Respublika Komi, NW Russian Federation
116 M13 **Viziru** Brăila, SE Romania
113 K21 **Vjosës, Lumi i** var. Vijosa, Vijosë, Gk. Aóos. ≈ Albania/Greece see also Aóos
99 H18 **Vlaams Brabant** ◈ province C Belgium
Vlaanderen see Flanders
98 G12 **Vlaardingen** Zuid-Holland, SW Netherlands
116 F10 **Vlădeasa, Vârful** prev. Vîrful Vlădeasa. ▲ NW Romania
Vlădeasa, Vîrful see Vlădeasa, Vârful
113 P16 **Vladičin Han** Serbia, SE Serbia and Montenegro (Yugo.)
127 O16 **Vladikavkaz** prev. Dzaudzhikau, Ordzhonikidze. Respublika Severnaya Osetiya, SW Russian Federation
126 M3 **Vladimir** Vladimirskaya Oblast', W Russian Federation
144 M7 **Vladimirovka** Kostanay, N Kazakhstan
Vladimirovka see Yuzhno-Sakhalinsk
126 L3 **Vladimirskaya Oblast'** ◈ province W Russian Federation
126 I3 **Vladimirskiy Tupik** Smolenskaya Oblast', W Russian Federation
Vladimir-Volynskiy see Volodymyr-Volyns'kyy
123 Q7 **Vladivostok** Primorskiy Kray, SE Russian Federation
117 U13 **Vladyslavivka** Respublika Krym, S Ukraine
98 P6 **Vlagtwedde** Groningen, NE Netherlands
Vlajna see Kukavica
112 J12 **Vlasenica** Republika Srpska, E Bosnia and Herzegovina
112 G12 **Vlašić** ▲ C Bosnia and Herzegovina
111 D17 **Vlašim** Ger. Wlaschim. Středočeský Kraj, C Czech Republic
113 P15 **Vlasotince** Serbia, SE Serbia and Montenegro (Yugo.)
123 Q7 **Vlasovo** Respublika Sakha (Yakutiya), NE Russian Federation
98 I11 **Vleuten** Utrecht, C Netherlands
98 I5 **Vlieland** Fris. Flylân. island Waddeneilanden, N Netherlands
98 I5 **Vliestroom** strait NW Netherlands
99 J14 **Vlijmen** Noord-Brabant, S Netherlands
99 E15 **Vlissingen** Eng. Flushing, Fr. Flessingue. Zeeland, SW Netherlands
Vlodava see Włodawa
Vlonë/Vlora see Vlorë
113 K22 **Vlorë** prev. Vlonë, It. Valona, Vlora. Vlorë, SW Albania
113 K22 **Vlorë** ◈ district SW Albania
113 K22 **Vlorës, Gjiri i** var. Valona Bay. bay SW Albania
Vlotslavsk see Włocławek
111 C16 **Vltava** Ger. Moldau. ≈ W Czech Republic
126 K3 **Vnukovo** ✕ (Moskva) Gorod Moskva, W Russian Federation
146 L11 **Vobkent** Rus. Vabkent. Buxoro Viloyati, C Uzbekistan
25 Q9 **Voca** Texas, SW USA
109 R5 **Vöcklabruck** Oberösterreich, NW Austria
112 D13 **Vodice** Šibenik-Knin, S Croatia
126 K10 **Vodlozero, Ozero** ◎ NW Russian Federation
112 A10 **Vodnjan** It. Dignano d'Istria. Istra, NW Croatia
125 S9 **Vodnyy** Respublika Komi, NW Russian Federation
95 G20 **Vodskov** Nordjylland, N Denmark
92 H4 **Vogar** Sudhurland, SW Iceland
Vogelkop see Doberai, Jazirah
77 X15 **Vogel Peak** prev. Dim lang. ▲ E Nigeria
101 H17 **Vogelsberg** ▲ C Germany
106 D8 **Voghera** Lombardia, N Italy
112 I13 **Vogošća** Federacija Bosna I Hercegovina, SE Bosnia and Herzegovina
101 M17 **Vogtland** historical region E Germany
127 V12 **Vogul'skiy Kamen', Gora** ▲ NW Russian Federation
187 P16 **Voh** Province Nord, C New Caledonia
Vohémar see Iharaña
172 H8 **Vohimena, Tanjona** Fr. Cap Sainte Marie. headland S Madagascar
172 J6 **Vohipeno** Fianarantsoa, SE Madagascar
118 H5 **Võhma** Ger. Wõchma. Viljandimaa, S Estonia
81 J20 **Voi** Coast, S Kenya
76 K15 **Voinjama** N Liberia
103 S12 **Voiron** Isère, E France
109 V8 **Voitsberg** Steiermark, SE Austria
95 F24 **Vojens** Ger. Woyens. Sønderjylland, SW Denmark
112 K9 **Vojvodina** Ger. Wojwodina. Region N Serbia and Montenegro (Yugo.)
15 S6 **Volant** ≈ Québec, SE Canada
Volaterrae see Volterra
43 P15 **Volcán** var. Hato del Volcán. Chiriquí, W Panama
Volchansk see Vovchans'k
Volchya see Vovcha
94 D10 **Volda** Møre og Romsdal, S Norway
98 J9 **Volendam** Noord-Holland, C Netherlands
124 L15 **Volga** Yaroslavskaya Oblast', W Russian Federation
29 R10 **Volga** South Dakota, N USA
122 C11 **Volga** ≈ NW Russian Federation
Volga-Baltic Waterway see Volgo-Baltiyskiy Kanal
Volga Hills/Volga Uplands see Privolzhskaya Vozvyshennost'
126 L13 **Volgo-Baltiyskiy Kanal** Eng. Volga-Baltic Waterway. canal NW Russian Federation
126 M12 **Volgodonsk** Rostovskaya Oblast', SW Russian Federation
127 O10 **Volgograd** prev. Stalingrad, Tsaritsyn. Volgogradskaya Oblast', SW Russian Federation
127 N9 **Volgogradskaya Oblast'** ◈ province SW Russian Federation
127 P10 **Volgogradskoye Vodokhranilishche** ⊠ SW Russian Federation
101 J19 **Volkach** Bayern, C Germany
109 U9 **Völkermarkt** Slvn. Velikovec. Kärnten, S Austria
124 I12 **Volkhov** Leningradskaya Oblast', NW Russian Federation
101 D20 **Völklingen** Saarland, SW Germany
Volkovysk see Vawkavysk
Volkovyskiye Vysoty see Vawkavyskaye Wzvyshsha
83 K22 **Volksrust** Mpumalanga, E South Africa
98 L8 **Vollenhove** Overijssel, N Netherlands
119 L16 **Vol'ma** Rus. Volma. ≈ C Belarus
Volmari see Valmiera
117 W9 **Volnovakha** Donets'ka Oblast', SE Ukraine
116 K6 **Volochys'k** Khmel'nyts'ka Oblast', W Ukraine
117 O6 **Volodarka** Kyyivs'ka Oblast', N Ukraine
117 W9 **Volodars'ke** Donets'ka Oblast', E Ukraine
127 R13 **Volodarskiy** Astrakhanskaya Oblast', SW Russian Federation
Volodarskoye see Saumalkol'
117 N8 **Volodars'k-Volyns'kyy** Zhytomyrs'ka Oblast', N Ukraine
116 K3 **Volodymerets'** Rivnens'ka Oblast', NW Ukraine
116 I3 **Volodymyr-Volyns'kyy** Pol. Włodzimierz, Rus. Vladimir-Volynskiy. Volyns'ka Oblast', NW Ukraine
124 L14 **Vologda** Vologodskaya Oblast', W Russian Federation
124 L12 **Vologodskaya Oblast'** ◈ province NW Russian Federation
126 K3 **Volokolamsk** Moskovskaya Oblast', W Russian Federation
126 K9 **Volokonovka** Belgorodskaya Oblast', W Russian Federation
115 G16 **Vólos** Thessalía, C Greece
124 M11 **Voloshka** Arkhangel'skaya Oblast', NW Russian Federation
Vološinovo see Novi Bečej
116 H7 **Volovets'** Zakarpats'ka Oblast', W Ukraine
114 K7 **Volovo** Ruse, N Bulgaria
Volozhin see Valozhyn
127 Q7 **Vol'sk** Saratovskaya Oblast', W Russian Federation
77 Q17 **Volta** ≈ SE Ghana
Volta Blanche see White Volta
77 P16 **Volta, Lake** ⊠ SE Ghana
Volta Noire see Black Volta
60 O9 **Volta Redonda** Rio de Janeiro, SE Brazil
Volta Rouge see Red Volta
106 F12 **Volterra** anc. Volaterrae. Toscana, C Italy
107 K17 **Volturno** ≈ S Italy
113 I15 **Volujak** ▲ SW Serbia and Montenegro (Yugo.)
Volunteer Island see Starbuck Island
65 F24 **Volunteer Point** headland East Falkland, Falkland Islands
Volunteer State see Tennessee
114 H13 **Vólvi, Límni** ◎ N Greece
Volyn see Volyns'ka Oblast'
116 I3 **Volyns'ka Oblast'** var. Volyn, Rus. Volynskaya Oblast'. ◈ province NW Ukraine
Volynskaya Oblast' see Volyns'ka Oblast'
127 Q3 **Volzhsk** Respublika Mariy El, W Russian Federation
127 O10 **Volzhskiy** Volgogradskaya Oblast', SW Russian Federation
172 I7 **Vondrozo** Fianarantsoa, SE Madagascar
114 K9 **Voneshta Voda** Veliko Tŭrnovo, N Bulgaria
39 P10 **Von Frank Mountain** ▲ Alaska, USA
115 C17 **Vónitsa** Dytikí Ellás, W Greece
118 J6 **Võnnu** Ger. Wendau. Tartumaa, SE Estonia
98 G12 **Voorburg** Zuid-Holland, W Netherlands
98 H11 **Voorschoten** Zuid-Holland, W Netherlands
98 M11 **Voorst** Gelderland, E Netherlands
98 K11 **Voorthuizen** Gelderland, C Netherlands
92 L2 **Vopnafjördhur** Austurland, E Iceland
92 L2 **Vopnafjördhur** bay E Iceland
Vora see Vorë
119 H15 **Voranava** Pol. Werenów, Rus. Voronovo. Hrodzyenskaya Voblasts', W Belarus
108 I8 **Vorarlberg** off. Land Vorarlberg. ◈ state W Austria
109 X7 **Vorau** Steiermark, E Austria
98 N11 **Vorden** Gelderland, E Netherlands
108 H9 **Vorderrhein** ≈ SE Switzerland
92 J2 **Vordhufell** ▲ N Iceland
95 I24 **Vordingborg** Storstrøm, SE Denmark
113 K19 **Vorë** var. Vora. Tiranë, W Albania
115 H17 **Vóreioi Sporádes** var. Vórioi Sporádhes, Eng. Northern Sporades. island group E Greece
115 J17 **Vóreion Aigaíon** Eng. Aegean North. ◈ region SE Greece
115 G18 **Voreiós Evvoïkós Kólpos** gulf E Greece
197 S16 **Voring Plateau** undersea feature N Norwegian Sea
Vórioi Sporádhes see Vóreioi Sporádes
125 W4 **Vorkuta** Respublika Komi, NW Russian Federation
95 I14 **Vorma** ≈ S Norway
118 E4 **Vormsi** var. Vormsi Saar, Ger. Worms, Swed. Ormsö. island W Estonia
Vormsi Saar see Vormsi
127 N7 **Vorona** ≈ W Russian Federation
126 L7 **Voronezh** Voronezhskaya Oblast', W Russian Federation
126 L7 **Voronezh** ≈ W Russian Federation
126 K8 **Voronezhskaya Oblast'** ◈ province W Russian Federation
Voronovitsya see Voronovytsya
Voronovo see Voranava
117 N6 **Voronovytsya** Rus. Voronovitsya. Vinnyts'ka Oblast', C Ukraine
122 K7 **Vorontsovo** Taymyrskiy (Dolgano-Nenetskiy) Avtonomnyy Okrug, N Russian Federation
126 K3 **Voron'ya** ≈ NW Russian Federation
Voropayevo see Varapayeva
Voroshilov see Ussuriysk
Voroshilovgrad see Luhans'k, Ukraine
Voroshilovgrad see Luhans'ka Oblast', Ukraine
Voroshilovgradskaya Oblast' see Luhans'ka Oblast'
Voroshilovsk see Stavropol', Russian Federation
Voroshilovsk see Alchevs'k, Ukraine
137 V13 **Vorotan** Az. Bärgușad. ≈ Armenia/Azerbaijan
127 P3 **Vorotynets** Nizhegorodskaya Oblast', W Russian Federation
117 S3 **Vorozhba** Sums'ka Oblast', NE Ukraine
117 T5 **Vorskla** ≈ Russian Federation/Ukraine
99 I17 **Vorst** Antwerpen, N Belgium
83 G21 **Vorstershoop** North-West, N South Africa
118 H6 **Võrtsjärv** Ger. Wirz-See. ◎ SE Estonia
118 J7 **Võru** Ger. Werro. Võrumaa, SE Estonia
147 R11 **Vorukh** N Tajikistan
118 I7 **Võrumaa** off. Võru Maakond. ◈ province SE Estonia
83 G24 **Vosburg** Northern Cape, W South Africa
147 Q14 **Vose'** Rus. Vose; prev. Aral. SW Tajikistan
103 S6 **Vosges** ◈ department NE France
103 U6 **Vosges** ▲▲ NE France
126 L4 **Voskresensk** Moskovskaya Oblast', W Russian Federation
127 P2 **Voskresenskoye** Nizhegorodskaya Oblast', W Russian Federation
127 V6 **Voskresenskoye** Respublika Bashkortostan, W Russian Federation
124 K13 **Voskresenskoye** Vologodskaya Oblast', NW Russian Federation
94 D13 **Voss** Hordaland, S Norway
94 D13 **Voss** physical region S Norway
99 I16 **Vosselaar** Antwerpen, N Belgium
94 D13 **Vosso** ≈ S Norway
Vostochno-Kazakhstanskaya Oblast' see Shygys Konyrat
145 T12 **Vostochno-Kounradskiy** Kaz. Shyghys Qongyrat. Zhezkazgan, C Kazakhstan
123 S5 **Vostochno-Sibirskoye More** Eng. East Siberian Sea. sea Arctic Ocean
145 X10 **Vostochnyy Kazakhstan** off. Vostochno-Kazakhstanskaya Oblast', var. East Kazakhstan, Kaz. Shyghys Qazagastan Oblysy. ◈ province E Kazakhstan
Vostochnyy Sayan see Eastern Sayans
Vostock Island see Vostok Island
195 U10 **Vostok** Russian research station Antarctica
191 X5 **Vostok Island** var. Vostock Island; prev. Stavers Island. island Line Islands, SE Kiribati
127 T2 **Votkinsk** Udmurtskaya Respublika, NW Russian Federation
127 U15 **Votkinskoye Vodokhranilishche** var. Votkinsk Reservoir. ⊠ NW Russian Federation
Votkinsk Reservoir see Votkinskoye Vodokhranilishche
60 J7 **Votuporanga** São Paulo, S Brazil
104 H7 **Vouga, Rio** ≈ N Portugal
115 E14 **Voúrinos** ▲ N Greece
115 G24 **Voúxa, Akrotírio** headland Kríti, Greece, E Mediterranean Sea
103 R4 **Vouziers** Ardennes, N France
117 V7 **Vovcha** Rus. Volchya. ≈ E Ukraine
117 V4 **Vovchans'k** Rus. Volchansk. Kharkivs'ka Oblast', E Ukraine
103 N6 **Voves** Eure-et-Loir, C France
79 M14 **Vovodo** ≈ S Central Africa Republic
94 M12 **Voxna** Gävleborg, C Sweden
94 L11 **Voxnan** ≈ C Sweden
114 F7 **Voynishka Reka** ≈ NW Bulgaria
125 T9 **Voyvozh** Respublika Komi, NW Russian Federation
124 M12 **Vozhega** Vologodskaya Oblast', NW Russian Federation
126 L12 **Vozhe, Ozero** ◎ NW Russian Federation
117 Q9 **Voznesens'k** Rus. Voznesensk. Mykolayivs'ka Oblast', S Ukraine
124 J12 **Voznesen'ye** Leningradskaya Oblast', NW Russian Federation
144 J14 **Vozrozhdeniya, Ostrov** Uzb. Wozrojdeniye Oroli. island Kazakhstan/Uzbekistan
Vpadina Mynbulak see Mingbuloq Botig'l
95 G20 **Vrå** var. Vraa. Nordjylland, N Denmark
Vraa see Vrå
114 H9 **Vrachesh** Sofiya, NW Bulgaria
115 C19 **Vrachíonas** ▲ Zákynthos, Iónioi Nísoi, Greece, C Mediterranean Sea
117 P8 **Vradiyivka** Mykolayivs'ka Oblast', S Ukraine
113 G14 **Vran** ▲ SW Bosnia and Herzegovina
116 K12 **Vrancea** ◈ county E Romania
147 T14 **Vrang** SE Tajikistan
123 T4 **Vrangelya, Ostrov** Eng. Wrangel Island. island NE Russian Federation
112 H13 **Vranica** ▲ C Bosnia and Herzegovina
113 O16 **Vranje** Serbia, SE Serbia and Montenegro (Yugo.)
Vranov see Vranov nad Topl'ou
111 N19 **Vranov nad Topl'ou** var. Vranov, Hung. Varannó. Prešovský Kraj, E Slovakia
114 H8 **Vratsa** Vratsa, NW Bulgaria
114 H8 **Vratsa** ◈ province NW Bulgaria
114 F10 **Vrattsa** prev. Mirovo. Kyustendil, W Bulgaria
112 G11 **Vrbanja** ≈ NW Bosnia and Herzegovina
112 K9 **Vrbas** Serbia, NW Serbia and Montenegro (Yugo.)
112 G13 **Vrbas** ≈ N Bosnia and Herzegovina
112 E8 **Vrbovec** Zagreb, N Croatia
112 C9 **Vrbovsko** Primorje-Gorski Kotar, NW Croatia
111 E15 **Vrchlabí** Ger. Hohenelbe. Královéhradecký Kraj, NE Czech Republic
83 J22 **Vrede** Free State, E South Africa
100 E13 **Vreden** Nordrhein-Westfalen, NW Germany
83 E25 **Vredenburg** Western Cape, SW South Africa
99 I23 **Vresse-sur-Semois** Namur, SE Belgium
95 L16 **Vretstorp** Örebro, C Sweden
113 G15 **Vrgorac** prev. Vrhgorac. Split-Dalmacija, SE Croatia
Vrhgorac see Vrgorac
109 T12 **Vrhnika** Ger. Oberlaibach. W Slovenia
9[illegible]
98 [illegible]
95 L[illegible]
108 H9 [illegible] S Switzer[illegible]
112 E13 **Vrlika** Split-Dalmacija, S Croatia
113 M14 **Vrnjačka Banja** Serbia, C Serbia and Montenegro (Yugo.)
Vrondádhes/Vrondados see Vrontádos
115 L18 **Vrontádos** var. Vrondados; prev. Vrondádhes. Chíos, E Greece
98 N9 **Vroomshoop** Overijssel, E Netherlands
112 N10 **Vršac** Ger. Werschetz, Hung. Versecz. Serbia, NE Serbia and Montenegro (Yugo.)
112 M10 **Vršački Kanal** canal N Serbia and Montenegro (Yugo.)
83 H21 **Vryburg** North-West, N South Africa
83 K22 **Vryheid** KwaZulu/Natal, E South Africa
111 I18 **Vsetín** Ger. Wsetin. Zlínský Kraj, E Czech Republic
111 J20 **Vtáčnik** Hung. Madaras, Ptacsnik; prev. Ptačník. ▲ W Slovakia
Vuadil' see Wodil
Vuanggava see Vuaqava
114 I11 **Vŭcha** ≈ SW Bulgaria
113 N16 **Vučitrn** Serbia, S Serbia and Montenegro (Yugo.)
99 J14 **Vught** Noord-Brabant, S Netherlands
117 W8 **Vuhledar** Donets'ka Oblast', E Ukraine
112 I9 **Vuka** ≈ E Croatia
113 K17 **Vukël** var. Vukli. Shkodër, N Albania
Vukli see Vukël
112 J9 **Vukovar** Hung. Vukovár. Vukovar-Srijem, E Croatia
112 I10 **Vukovar-Srijem** off. Vukovarsko-Srijemska Županija. ◈ province E Croatia
125 U8 **Vuktyl** Respublika Komi, NW Russian Federation
11 Q17 **Vulcan** Alberta, SW Canada
116 G12 **Vulcan** Ger. Wulkan, Hung. Zsilyvajdevulkán; prev. Crivadia Vulcanului, Vaidei, Hung. Sily-Vajdej, Vajdej. Hunedoara, W Romania
116 M12 **Vulcăneşti** Rus. Vulkaneshty. S Moldova
107 L22 **Vulcano, Isola** island Isole Eolie, S Italy
114 G7 **Vŭlchedrŭm** Montana, NW Bulgaria
114 N8 **Vŭlchidol** prev. Kurt-Dere. Varna, NE Bulgaria
Vulkaneshty see Vulcăneşti
123 V11 **Vulkannyy** Kamchatskaya Oblast', E Russian Federation
36 J13 **Vulture Mountains** ▲▲ Arizona, SW USA
167 T14 **Vung Tau** prev. Fr. Cape Saint Jacques, Cap Saint-Jacques. Ba Ria-Vung Tau, S Vietnam
187 X15 **Vunisea** Kadavu, SE Fiji
Vuohčču see Vuotso
93 N15 **Vuokatti** Oulu, C Finland
93 M15 **Vuolijoki** Oulu, C Finland
Vuolleriebme see Vuollerim
92 J13 **Vuollerim** Lapp. Vuolleriebme. Norrbotten, N Sweden
Vuoreija see Vardø
92 L10 **Vuotso** Lapp. Vuohčču. Lappi, N Finland
114 J11 **Vŭrbitsa** prev. Filevo. Khaskovo, S Bulgaria
114 J12 **Vŭrbitsa** ≈ S Bulgaria
127 Q4 **Vurnary** Chuvashskaya Respublika, W Russian Federation
114 G8 **Vŭrshets** Montana, NW Bulgaria
119 F17 **Vyalikaya Byerastavitsa** Pol. Brzostowica Wielka, Rus. Bol'shaya Berëstovitsa; prev. Velikaya Berestovitsa. Hrodzyenskaya Voblasts', SW Belarus
119 N20 **Vyaliki Bor** Rus. Velikiy Bor. Homyel'skaya Voblasts', SE Belarus
119 J18 **Vyaliki Rozhan** Rus. Bol'shoy Rozhan. Minskaya Voblasts', S Belarus
124 H10 **Vyartsilya** Fin. Värtsilä. Respublika Kareliya, NW Russian Federation
119 K17 **Vyasyeya** Rus. Veseya. Minskaya Voblasts', C Belarus
127 R15 **Vyatka** ≈ NW Russian Federation
Vyatka see Kirov
125 S16 **Vyatskiye Polyany** Kirovskaya Oblast', NW Russian Federation
123 S14 **Vyazemskiy** Khabarovskiy Kray, SE Russian Federation
126 I4 **Vyaz'ma** Smolenskaya Oblast', W Russian Federation
127 N3 **Vyazniki** Vladimirskaya Oblast', W Russian Federation
127 O8 **Vyazovka** Volgogradskaya Oblast', SW Russian Federation
[illegible] Voblasts', E Belarus
118 K11 **Vyerkhnyadzvinsk** Rus. Verkhnedvinsk. Vitsyebskaya Voblasts', N Belarus
119 P18 **Vyetka** Rus. Vetka. Homyel'skaya Voblasts', SE Belarus
118 L12 **Vyetryna** Rus. Vetrino. Vitsyebskaya Voblasts', N Belarus
Vygonovskoye, Ozero see Vyhanawskaye, Vozyera
126 J9 **Vygozero, Ozero** ◎ NW Russian Federation
Vyhanashchanskaye Vozyera see Vyhanawskaye, Vozyera
119 I18 **Vyhanawskaye, Vozyera** var. Vyhanashchanskaye Vozyera, Rus. Ozero Vygonovskoye. ◎ SW Belarus
127 N4 **Vyksa** Nizhegorodskaya Oblast', W Russian Federation
117 O12 **Vylkove** Rus. Vilkovo. Odes'ka Oblast', SW Ukraine
127 R9 **Vym'** ≈ NW Russian Federation
116 H8 **Vynohradiv** Cz. Sevluš, Hung. Nagyszöllös, Rus. Vinogradov; prev. Sevlyush. Zakarpats'ka Oblast', W Ukraine
124 G13 **Vyritsa** Leningradskaya Oblast', NW Russian Federation
97 J19 **Vyrnwy** Wel. Afon Efyrnwy. ≈ E Wales, UK
145 X9 **Vysheivanovskiy Belak, Gora** ▲ E Kazakhstan
117 P4 **Vyshhorod** Kyyivs'ka Oblast', N Ukraine
124 I15 **Vyshniy Volochek** Tverskaya Oblast', W Russian Federation
111 G18 **Vyškov** Ger. Wischau. Jihomoravský Kraj, SE Czech Republic
111 F17 **Vysoké Mýto** Ger. Hohenmauth. Pardubický Kraj, C Czech Republic
117 S9 **Vysokopillya** Khersons'ka Oblast', S Ukraine
126 K3 **Vysokovsk** Moskovskaya Oblast', W Russian Federation
124 K12 **Vytegra** Vologodskaya Oblast', NW Russian Federation
116 J8 **Vyzhnytsya** Chernivets'ka Oblast', W Ukraine

W

77 O14 **Wa** NW Ghana
Waadt see Vaud
Waag see Váh
Waagbistritz see Považská Bystrica
Waagneustadtl see Nové Mesto nad Váhom
81 M16 **Waajid** Gedo, SW Somalia
98 L13 **Waal** ≈ S Netherlands
187 O16 **Waala** Province Nord, W New Caledonia
99 I14 **Waalwijk** Noord-Brabant, S Netherlands
99 E16 **Waarschoot** Oost-Vlaanderen, NW Belgium
186 C7 **Wabag** Enga, W PNG
15 N7 **Wabano** ≈ Québec, SE Canada
11 P11 **Wabasca** ≈ Alberta, SW Canada
31 P12 **Wabash** Indiana, N USA
29 X9 **Wabasha** Minnesota, N USA
31 N13 **Wabash River** ≈ N USA
14 C7 **Wabatongushi Lake** ◎ Ontario, S Canada
81 L15 **Wabē Gestro Wenz** ≈ SE Ethiopia
14 B9 **Wabos** Ontario, S Canada
11 W13 **Wabowden** Manitoba, C Canada
110 J9 **Wąbrzeźno** Kujawsko-pomorskie, N Poland
21 U12 **Waccamaw River** ≈ South Carolina, SE USA
23 U11 **Waccasassa Bay** bay Florida, SE USA
99 F16 **Wachtebeke** Oost-Vlaanderen, NW Belgium
25 T8 **Waco** Texas, SW USA
26 M3 **Waconda Lake** var. Great Elder Reservoir. ⊠ Kansas, C USA
Wadai see Ouaddaï
Wad Al-Hajarah see Guadalajara
164 I12 **Wadayama** Hyōgo, Honshū, SW Japan
80 D10 **Wad Banda** Western Kordofan, C Sudan
75 P9 **Waddān** NW Libya
98 J4 **Waddeneilanden** Eng. West Frisian Islands. island group N Netherlands
98 J6 **Waddenzee** var. Wadden Zee. sea SE North Sea

◆ Country ● Country Capital ◇ Dependent Territory ○ Dependent Territory Capital ◈ Administrative Region ✕ International Airport ▲ Mountain ▲▲ Mountain Range Volcano ≈ River ◎ Lake ⊠ Reservoir

10 L16 **Waddington, Mount** ▲ British Columbia, SW Canada
98 H12 **Waddinxveen** Zuid-Holland, C Netherlands
11 U15 **Wadena** Saskatchewan, S Canada
29 T6 **Wadena** Minnesota, N USA
108 G7 **Wädenswil** Zürich, N Switzerland
21 S11 **Wadesboro** North Carolina, SE USA
155 G16 **Wādi** Karnātaka, C India
138 G10 **Wādī as Sīr** *var.* Wadi es Sir. 'Al 'Ammān, NW Jordan
Wadi es Sir *see* Wādī as Sīr
80 F5 **Wadi Halfa** *var.* Wādī Ḥalfā'. Northern, N Sudan
138 G13 **Wādī Mūsā** *var.* Petra. Ma'ān, S Jordan
23 V4 **Wadley** Georgia, SE USA
Wad Madanī *see* Wad Medani
80 G10 **Wad Medani** *var.* Wad Madanī. Gezira, C Sudan
80 F10 **Wad Nimr** White Nile, C Sudan
165 U16 **Wadomari** Kagoshima, Okinoerabu-jima, SW Japan
111 K17 **Wadowice** Małopolskie, S Poland
35 R5 **Wadsworth** Nevada, W USA
31 T12 **Wadsworth** Ohio, N USA
25 T11 **Waelder** Texas, SW USA
Waereghem *see* Waregem
163 U13 **Wafangdian** *var.* Fuxian, Fu Xian. Liaoning, NE China
171 R13 **Waflia** Pulau Buru, E Indonesia
Wagadugu *see* Ouagadougou
98 K12 **Wageningen** Gelderland, SE Netherlands
55 V9 **Wageningen** Nickerie, NW Surinam
9 O8 **Wager Bay** *inlet* Nunavut, N Canada
183 P10 **Wagga Wagga** New South Wales, SE Australia
180 J13 **Wagin** Western Australia
108 H8 **Wägitaler See** ⊚ SW Switzerland
29 P12 **Wagner** South Dakota, N USA
27 Q9 **Wagoner** Oklahoma, C USA
37 U10 **Wagon Mound** New Mexico, SW USA
32 J14 **Wagontire** Oregon, NW USA
110 H10 **Wągrowiec** Wielkopolskie, NW Poland
149 U6 **Wāh** Punjab, NE Pakistan
171 S13 **Wahai** Pulau Seram, E Indonesia
169 V10 **Wahau, Sungai** ≈ Borneo, C Indonesia
Wahaybah, Ramlat Al *see* Wahībah, Ramlat Āl
80 D13 **Wahda** *var.* Unity State. ◈ *state* S Sudan
38 D9 **Wahiawā** *var.* Wahiawa. O'ahu, Hawai'i, USA, C Pacific Ocean
Wahībah, Ramlat Ahl *see* Wahībah, Ramlat Āl
141 Y9 **Wahībah, Ramlat Āl** *var.* Ramlat Ahl Wahībah, Ramlat Al Wahaybah, *Eng.* Wahibah Sands. *desert* N Oman
Wahibah Sands *see* Wahībah, Ramlat Āl
101 E16 **Wahn** ✕ (Köln) Nordrhein-Westfalen, W Germany
29 R15 **Wahoo** Nebraska, C USA
29 R6 **Wahpeton** North Dakota, N USA
Wahran *see* Oran
36 J6 **Wah Wah Mountains** ▲ Utah, W USA
38 D9 **Waialua** O'ahu, Hawai'i, USA, C Pacific Ocean
38 D9 **Wai'anae** *var.* Waianae. O'ahu, Hawai'i, USA, C Pacific Ocean
184 Q8 **Waiapu** ≈ North Island, NZ
185 I17 **Waiau** Canterbury, South Island, NZ
185 I17 **Waiau** ≈ South Island, NZ
185 B23 **Waiau** ≈ South Island, NZ
101 H21 **Waiblingen** Baden-Württemberg, S Germany
Waidhofen *see* Waidhofen an der Ybbs, Niederösterreich, Austria
Waidhofen *see* Waidhofen an der Thaya, Niederösterreich, Austria
109 V2 **Waidhofen an der Thaya** *var.* Waidhofen. Niederösterreich, NE Austria
109 U5 **Waidhofen an der Ybbs** *var.* Waidhofen. Niederösterreich, E Austria
171 T11 **Waigeo, Pulau** *island* Maluku, E Indonesia
184 L5 **Waiheke Island** *island* N NZ
184 M7 **Waihi** Waikato, North Island, NZ
185 C20 **Waihou** ≈ North Island, NZ
Waikaboebak *see* Waikabubak
170 M17 **Waikabubak** *prev.* Waikaboebak. Pulau Sumba, C Indonesia
185 D23 **Waikaia** ≈ South Island, NZ
185 D23 **Waikaka** Southland, South Island, NZ
184 L13 **Waikanae** Wellington, North Island, NZ
184 M7 **Waikare, Lake** ⊚ North Island, NZ
184 O9 **Waikaremoana, Lake** ⊚ North Island, NZ
185 I17 **Waikari** Canterbury, South Island, NZ
184 L8 **Waikato** *off.* Waikato Region. ◈ *region* North Island, NZ
184 M8 **Waikato** ≈ North Island, NZ
182 J9 **Waikerie** South Australia
185 F23 **Waikouaiti** Otago, South Island, NZ
38 H11 **Wailea** Hawai'i, USA, C Pacific Ocean
38 F10 **Wailuku** Maui, Hawai'i, USA, C Pacific Ocean
185 H18 **Waimakariri** ≈ South Island, NZ
38 D9 **Waimānalo Beach** *var.* Waimanalo Beach. O'ahu, Hawai'i, USA, C Pacific Ocean
185 G15 **Waimangaroa** West Coast, South Island, NZ
185 G21 **Waimate** Canterbury, South Island, NZ
38 G11 **Waimea** *var.* Kamuela. Hawai'i, USA, C Pacific Ocean
38 D9 **Waimea** *var.* Maunawai. O'ahu, Hawai'i, USA, C Pacific Ocean
38 B8 **Waimea** Kaua'i, Hawai'i, USA, C Pacific Ocean
99 M20 **Waimes** Liège, E Belgium
154 J11 **Wainganga** *var.* Wain River. ≈ C India
Waingapoe *see* Waingapu
171 N17 **Waingapu** *prev.* Waingapoe. Pulau Sumba, C Indonesia
55 S7 **Waini** ≈ N Guyana
55 S7 **Waini Point** *headland* NW Guyana
Wain River *see* Wainganga
11 R15 **Wainwright** Alberta, SW Canada
39 O5 **Wainwright** Alaska, USA
184 K4 **Waiotira** Northland, North Island, NZ
184 M11 **Waiouru** Manawatu-Wanganui, North Island, NZ
171 W14 **Waipa** Papua, E Indonesia
184 L8 **Waipa** ≈ North Island, NZ
184 P9 **Waipaoa** ≈ North Island, NZ
185 D25 **Waipapa Point** *headland* South Island, NZ
185 I18 **Waipara** Canterbury, South Island, NZ
184 N12 **Waipawa** Hawke's Bay, North Island, NZ
184 K4 **Waipu** Northland, North Island, NZ
184 N12 **Waipukurau** Hawke's Bay, North Island, NZ
171 U14 **Wair** Pulau Kai Besar, E Indonesia
Wairakai *see* Wairakei
184 N9 **Wairakei** *var.* Wairakai. Waikato, North Island, NZ
185 M14 **Wairarapa, Lake** ⊚ North Island, NZ
185 J15 **Wairau** ≈ South Island, NZ
184 P10 **Wairoa** Hawke's Bay, North Island, NZ
184 P10 **Wairoa** ≈ North Island, NZ
184 J4 **Wairoa** ≈ North Island, NZ
184 N9 **Waitahanui** Waikato, North Island, NZ
184 M6 **Waitakaruru** Waikato, North Island, NZ
185 F21 **Waitaki** ≈ South Island, NZ
184 K10 **Waitara** Taranaki, North Island, NZ
184 M7 **Waitoa** Waikato, North Island, NZ
184 L8 **Waitomo Caves** Waikato, North Island, NZ
184 L11 **Waitotara** Taranaki, North Island, NZ
184 L11 **Waitotara** ≈ North Island, NZ
32 L10 **Waitsburg** Washington, NW USA
Waitzen *see* Vác
184 L6 **Waiuku** Auckland, North Island, NZ
164 L10 **Wajima** *var.* Wazima. Ishikawa, Honshū, SW Japan
81 K17 **Wajir** North Eastern, NE Kenya
81 I14 **Waka** Southern, SW Ethiopia
79 J17 **Waka** Equateur, NW Dem. Rep. Congo
14 D9 **Wakami Lake** ⊚ Ontario, S Canada
164 I12 **Wakasa** Tottori, Honshū, SW Japan
164 J12 **Wakasa-wan** *bay* C Japan
185 C22 **Wakatipu, Lake** ⊚ South Island, NZ
11 T15 **Wakaw** Saskatchewan, S Canada
164 I14 **Wakayama** Wakayama, Honshū, SW Japan
164 I15 **Wakayama** *off.* Wakayama-ken. ◈ *prefecture* Honshū, SW Japan
26 K4 **Wa Keeney** Kansas, C USA
185 I14 **Wakefield** Tasman, South Island, NZ
97 M17 **Wakefield** N England, UK
27 O4 **Wakefield** Kansas, C USA
30 L4 **Wakefield** Michigan, N USA
21 U9 **Wake Forest** North Carolina, SE USA
Wakeham Bay *see* Kangiqsujuaq
189 Y11 **Wake Island** ◇ *US unincorporated territory* NW Pacific Ocean
189 Y12 **Wake Island** ✕ NW Pacific Ocean
189 Y12 **Wake Island** *atoll* NW Pacific Ocean
189 X12 **Wake Lagoon** *lagoon* Wake Island, NW Pacific Ocean
166 L8 **Wakema** Irrawaddy, SW Burma
Wakhan *see* Khandūd
164 H14 **Waki** Tokushima, Shikoku, SW Japan
165 T1 **Wakkanai** Hokkaidō, NE Japan
83 K22 **Wakkerstroom** Mpumalanga, E South Africa
14 C10 **Wakomata Lake** ⊚ Ontario, S Canada
183 N10 **Wakool** New South Wales, SE Australia
Wakra *see* Al Wakrah
Waku Kungo *see* Uaco Cungo
186 J7 **Wakunai** Bougainville Island, NE PNG
Walachei/Walachia *see* Wallachia
155 K26 **Walawe Ganga** ≈ S Sri Lanka
111 F15 **Wałbrzych** *Ger.* Waldenburg, Waldenburg in Schlesien. Dolnośląskie, SW Poland
183 T6 **Walcha** New South Wales, SE Australia
101 K24 **Walchensee** ⊚ SE Germany
99 D14 **Walcheren** *island* SW Netherlands
29 Z14 **Walcott** Iowa, C USA
33 W16 **Walcott** Wyoming, C USA
99 G21 **Walcourt** Namur, S Belgium
110 G9 **Wałcz** *Ger.* Deutsch Krone. Zachodnio-pomorskie, NW Poland
108 H7 **Wald** Zürich, N Switzerland
109 U3 **Waldaist** ≈ N Austria
180 I9 **Waldburg Range** ▲ Western Australia
37 R3 **Walden** Colorado, C USA
18 K13 **Walden** New York, NE USA
Waldenburg/Waldenburg in Schlesien *see* Wałbrzych
11 T15 **Waldheim** Saskatchewan, S Canada
Waldia *see* Weldiya
101 M23 **Waldkraiburg** Bayern, SE Germany
27 T14 **Waldo** Arkansas, C USA
23 V9 **Waldo** Florida, SE USA
19 R7 **Waldoboro** Maine, NE USA
21 W4 **Waldorf** Maryland, NE USA
32 F12 **Waldport** Oregon, NW USA
27 S11 **Waldron** Arkansas, C USA
195 Y13 **Waldron, Cape** *headland* Antarctica
101 F24 **Waldshut-Tiengen** Baden-Württemberg, S Germany
171 P12 **Walea, Selat** *strait* Sulawesi, C Indonesia
Wałeckie Międzyrzecze *see* Valašské Meziříčí
108 H8 **Walensee** ⊚ NW Switzerland
38 L8 **Wales** Alaska, USA
97 J20 **Wales** *Wel.* Cymru. *national region* UK
9 O7 **Wales Island** *island* Nunavut, NE Canada
77 P14 **Walewale** N Ghana
99 M24 **Walferdange** Luxembourg, C Luxembourg
183 Q5 **Walgett** New South Wales, SE Australia
194 K10 **Walgreen Coast** *physical region* Antarctica
29 Q2 **Walhalla** North Dakota, N USA
21 O11 **Walhalla** South Carolina, SE USA
79 O19 **Walikale** Nord Kivu, E Dem. Rep. Congo
Walk *see* Valga, Estonia
Walk *see* Valka, Latvia
29 U5 **Walker** Minnesota, N USA
15 V4 **Walker, Lac** ⊚ Québec, SE Canada
35 S7 **Walker Lake** ⊚ Nevada, W USA
35 R6 **Walker River** ≈ Nevada, W USA
28 K10 **Wall** South Dakota, N USA
173 U9 **Wallaby Plateau** *undersea feature* E Indian Ocean
33 N8 **Wallace** Idaho, NW USA
21 V11 **Wallace** North Carolina, SE USA
14 D17 **Wallaceburg** Ontario, S Canada
22 F5 **Wallace Lake** ⊡ Louisiana, S USA
11 P13 **Wallace Mountain** ▲ Alberta, W Canada
116 J14 **Wallachia** *var.* Walachia, *Ger.* Walachei, *Rom.* Valachia. *cultural region* S Romania
Wallachisch-Meseritsch *see* Valašské Meziříčí
183 U4 **Wallangarra** New South Wales, SE Australia
182 I8 **Wallaroo** South Australia
32 L10 **Walla Walla** Washington, NW USA
45 V9 **Wallblake** ✕ (The Valley) C Anguilla
101 H19 **Walldürn** Baden-Württemberg, SW Germany
100 F12 **Wallenhorst** Niedersachsen, NW Germany
Wallenthal *see* Haţeg
109 S4 **Wallern** Oberösterreich, N Austria
Wallern *see* Wallern im Burgenland
109 Z5 **Wallern im Burgenland** *var.* Wallern. Burgenland, E Austria
18 M9 **Wallingford** Vermont, NE USA
25 V11 **Wallis** Texas, SW USA
Wallis *see* Valais
192 K9 **Wallis and Futuna** *Fr.* Territoire de Wallis et Futuna. ◇ *French overseas territory* C Pacific Ocean
108 G7 **Wallisellen** Zürich, N Switzerland
190 H11 **Wallis, Îles** *island group* N Wallis and Futuna
99 H19 **Wallon Brabant** ◈ *province* C Belgium
31 Q5 **Walloon Lake** ⊚ Michigan, N USA
32 K10 **Wallula** Washington, NW USA
32 K10 **Wallula, Lake** ⊚ Washington, NW USA
21 S8 **Walnut Cove** North Carolina, SE USA
35 N8 **Walnut Creek** California, W USA
26 K5 **Walnut Creek** ≈ Kansas, C USA
27 W9 **Walnut Ridge** Arkansas, C USA
25 S7 **Walnut Springs** Texas, SW USA
182 L10 **Walpeup** Victoria, SE Australia
187 R17 **Walpole, Île** *island* SE New Caledonia
39 N13 **Walrus Islands** *island group* Alaska, USA
97 L19 **Walsall** C England, UK
37 T7 **Walsenburg** Colorado, C USA
11 S17 **Walsh** Alberta, SW Canada
37 W7 **Walsh** Colorado, C USA
100 I11 **Walsrode** Niedersachsen, NW Germany
Waltenberg *see* Zalău
21 R14 **Walterboro** South Carolina, SE USA
Walter F. George Lake *see* Walter F. George Reservoir
23 R6 **Walter F. George Reservoir** *var.* Walter F. George Lake. ⊡ Alabama/Georgia, SE USA
26 M12 **Walters** Oklahoma, C USA
101 J16 **Waltershausen** Thüringen, C Germany
173 N10 **Walters Shoal** *var.* Walters Shoals. *reef* S Madagascar
Walters Shoals *see* Walters Shoal
22 M3 **Walthall** Mississippi, S USA
20 M4 **Walton** Kentucky, S USA
18 J11 **Walton** New York, NE USA
79 O20 **Walungu** Sud Kivu, E Dem. Rep. Congo
Walvisbaai *see* Walvis Bay
83 C19 **Walvis Bay** *Afr.* Walvisbaai. Erongo, NW Namibia
83 B19 **Walvis Bay** *bay* NW Namibia
Walvish Ridge *see* Walvis Ridge
65 O17 **Walvis Ridge** *var.* Walvish Ridge. *undersea feature* E Atlantic Ocean
171 X16 **Wamal** Papua, E Indonesia
171 U15 **Wamar, Pulau** *island* Kepulauan Aru, E Indonesia
77 V15 **Wamba** Nassarawa, C Nigeria
79 O17 **Wamba** Orientale, NE Dem. Rep. Congo
79 H22 **Wamba** *var.* Uamba. ≈ Angola/Dem. Rep. Congo
27 P4 **Wamego** Kansas, C USA
18 I10 **Wampsville** New York, NE USA
42 K6 **Wampú, Río** ≈ E Honduras
171 X16 **Wan** Papua, E Indonesia
Wan *see* Anhui
183 N4 **Wanaaring** New South Wales, SE Australia
185 D21 **Wanaka** Otago, South Island, NZ
185 D20 **Wanaka, Lake** ⊚ South Island, NZ
171 W14 **Wanapiri** Papua, E Indonesia
14 F9 **Wanapitei** ≈ Ontario, S Canada
14 F10 **Wanapitei Lake** ⊚ Ontario, S Canada
18 K14 **Wanaque** New Jersey, NE USA
171 U12 **Wanau** Papua, E Indonesia
185 F22 **Wanbrow, Cape** *headland* South Island, NZ
Wanchuan *see* Zhangjiakou
171 W13 **Wandai** *var.* Komeyo. Papua, E Indonesia
163 Z8 **Wanda Shan** ▲ NE China
197 R11 **Wandel Sea** *sea* Arctic Ocean
160 D13 **Wanding** *var.* Wandingzhen. Yunnan, SW China
Wandingzhen *see* Wanding
99 H20 **Wanfercée-Baulet** Hainaut, S Belgium
184 L12 **Wanganui** Manawatu-Wanganui, North Island, NZ
184 L11 **Wanganui** ≈ North Island, NZ
183 P11 **Wangaratta** Victoria, SE Australia
160 J8 **Wangcang** *var.* Hongjiang; *prev.* Fengjiaba. Sichuan, C China
Wangda *see* Zogang
101 I24 **Wangen im Allgäu** Baden-Württemberg, S Germany
Wangerin *see* Węgorzyno
100 F9 **Wangerooge** *island* NW Germany
171 W13 **Wanggar** Papua, E Indonesia
160 J13 **Wangmo** *var.* Fuxing. Guizhou, S China
Wangolodougou *see* Ouangolodougou
161 S9 **Wangpan Yang** *sea* E China
163 Y10 **Wangqing** Jilin, NE China
167 P8 **Wang Saphung** Loei, C Thailand
167 O6 **Wan Hsa-la** Shan State, E Burma
55 W9 **Wanica** ◈ *district* N Surinam
79 M18 **Wanie-Rukula** Orientale, C Dem. Rep. Congo
Wankie *see* Hwange
Wanki, Río *see* Coco, Río
81 N17 **Wanlaweyn** *var.* Wanle Weyn, *It.* Uanle Uen. Shabeellaha Hoose, SW Somalia
Wanle Weyn *see* Wanlaweyn
180 I12 **Wanneroo** Western Australia
160 L17 **Wanning** Hainan, S China
167 Q8 **Wanon Niwat** Sakon Nakhon, E Thailand
155 H16 **Wanparti** Andhra Pradesh, C India
Wansen *see* Wiązów
160 L11 **Wanshan** Guizhou, S China
99 M14 **Wanssum** Limburg, SE Netherlands
184 N12 **Wanstead** Hawke's Bay, North Island, NZ
Wanxian *see* Wanzhou
188 F16 **Wanyaan** Yap, Micronesia
160 K8 **Wanyuan** Sichuan, C China
161 O11 **Wanzai** *var.* Kangle. Jiangxi, S China
99 J20 **Wanze** Liège, E Belgium
160 K9 **Wanzhou** *var.* Wanxian. Chongqing Shi, C China
31 R12 **Wapakoneta** Ohio, N USA
12 D7 **Wapaseese** ≈ Ontario, C Canada
32 I10 **Wapato** Washington, NW USA
29 Y15 **Wapello** Iowa, C USA
11 N13 **Wapiti** ≈ Alberta/British Columbia, SW Canada
27 X7 **Wappapello Lake** ⊡ Missouri, C USA
18 K13 **Wappingers Falls** New York, NE USA
29 X13 **Wapsipinicon River** ≈ Iowa, C USA
14 L9 **Wapus** ≈ Québec, SE Canada
160 H7 **Waqên** Sichuan, C China
21 Q7 **War** West Virginia, NE USA
80 D13 **Warab** Warab, SW Sudan
81 D14 **Warab** ◈ *state* SW Sudan
155 J15 **Warangal** Andhra Pradesh, C India
Warasdin *see* Varaždin
183 O16 **Waratah** Tasmania, SE Australia
183 O14 **Waratah Bay** *bay* Victoria, SE Australia
101 H15 **Warburg** Nordrhein-Westfalen, W Germany
182 I1 **Warburton Creek** *seasonal river* South Australia
180 M9 **Warbuton** Western Australia
99 M20 **Warche** ≈ E Belgium
149 P5 **Wardag** *var.* Wardak, *Per.* Vardak. ◈ *province* E Afghanistan
Wardak *see* Wardag
32 K9 **Warden** Washington, NW USA
154 I12 **Wardha** Mahārāshtra, W India
121 N15 **Wardija, Ras il-** *var.* Wardija Point. *headland* Gozo, NW Malta
139 P3 **Wardīyah** N Iraq
185 E19 **Ward, Mount** ▲ South Island, NZ
10 L11 **Ware** British Columbia, W Canada
99 D18 **Waregem** *var.* Waereghem. West-Vlaanderen, W Belgium
99 J19 **Waremme** Liège, E Belgium
100 N10 **Waren** Mecklenburg-Vorpommern, NE Germany
171 W13 **Waren** Papua, E Indonesia
101 F14 **Warendorf** Nordrhein-Westfalen, W Germany
21 P12 **Ware Shoals** South Carolina, SE USA
98 N4 **Warffum** Groningen, NE Netherlands
81 O15 **Wargalo** Mudug, E Somalia
146 M12 **Warganza** *Rus.* Varganzi. Qashqadaryo Viloyati, S Uzbekistan
Wargla *see* Ouargla
183 T4 **Warialda** New South Wales, SE Australia
154 F13 **Wāri Godri** Mahārāshtra, C India
167 R10 **Warin Chamrap** Ubon Ratchathani, E Thailand
25 R11 **Waring** Texas, SW USA
39 O8 **Waring Mountains** ▲ Alaska, USA
110 M12 **Warka** Mazowieckie, E Poland
184 L5 **Warkworth** Auckland, North Island, NZ
171 U12 **Warmandi** Papua, E Indonesia
83 E22 **Warmbad** Karas, S Namibia
98 H8 **Warmenhuizen** Noord-Holland, NW Netherlands
110 L8 **Warmińsko-Mazurskie** ◈ *province* NE Poland
97 L22 **Warminster** S England, UK
18 I15 **Warminster** Pennsylvania, NE USA
35 V8 **Warm Springs** Nevada, W USA
32 H12 **Warm Springs** Oregon, NW USA
21 S5 **Warm Springs** Virginia, NE USA
100 M8 **Warnemünde** Mecklenburg-Vorpommern, NE Germany
27 Q10 **Warner** Oklahoma, C USA
35 Q2 **Warner Mountains** ▲ California, W USA
23 T5 **Warner Robins** Georgia, SE USA
57 N18 **Warnes** Santa Cruz, C Bolivia
100 M9 **Warnow** ≈ NE Germany
Warnsdorf *see* Varnsdorf
98 M11 **Warnsveld** Gelderland, E Netherlands
154 I13 **Warora** Mahārāshtra, C India
182 L11 **Warracknabeal** Victoria, SE Australia
183 O13 **Warragul** Victoria, SE Australia
183 O4 **Warrego River** *seasonal river* New South Wales/Queensland, E Australia
183 Q6 **Warren** New South Wales, SE Australia
11 X16 **Warren** Manitoba, S Canada
27 V14 **Warren** Arkansas, C USA
31 S10 **Warren** Michigan, N USA
29 R3 **Warren** Minnesota, N USA
31 U11 **Warren** Ohio, N USA
18 D12 **Warren** Pennsylvania, NE USA
25 X10 **Warren** Texas, SW USA
97 G16 **Warrenpoint** *Ir.* An Pointe. SE Northern Ireland, UK
27 S4 **Warrensburg** Missouri, C USA
83 H22 **Warrenton** Northern Cape, N South Africa
23 U4 **Warrenton** Georgia, SE USA
27 W4 **Warrenton** Missouri, C USA
21 V8 **Warrenton** North Carolina, SE USA
21 V4 **Warrenton** Virginia, NE USA
77 U17 **Warri** Delta, S Nigeria
97 L18 **Warrington** C England, UK
23 O9 **Warrington** Florida, SE USA
23 P3 **Warrior** Alabama, S USA
182 L13 **Warrnambool** Victoria, SE Australia
29 T2 **Warroad** Minnesota, N USA
183 S6 **Warrumbungle Range** ▲ New South Wales, SE Australia
154 J12 **Wārsa** Mahārāshtra, C India
31 P11 **Warsaw** Indiana, N USA
20 L4 **Warsaw** Kentucky, S USA
27 T5 **Warsaw** Missouri, C USA
18 E10 **Warsaw** New York, NE USA
21 V10 **Warsaw** North Carolina, SE USA
21 X5 **Warsaw** Virginia, NE USA
Warsaw/Warschau *see* Warszawa
81 N17 **Warshiikh** Shabeellaha Dhexe, C Somalia
101 G15 **Warstein** Nordrhein-Westfalen, W Germany
110 M11 **Warszawa** *Eng.* Warsaw, *Ger.* Warschau, *Rus.* Varshava. ● (Poland) Mazowieckie, C Poland
110 J13 **Warta** Sieradz, C Poland
110 D11 **Warta** *Ger.* Warthe. ≈ W Poland
Wartberg *see* Senec
20 M9 **Wartburg** Tennessee, S USA
108 J7 **Warth** Vorarlberg, NW Austria
Warthe *see* Warta
169 U12 **Waru** Borneo, C Indonesia
171 T13 **Waru** Pulau Seram, E Indonesia
139 N6 **Wa'r, Wādī al** *dry watercourse* E Syria
183 U3 **Warwick** Queensland, E Australia
15 Q11 **Warwick** Québec, SE Canada
97 M20 **Warwick** C England, UK
18 K13 **Warwick** New York, NE USA
29 P4 **Warwick** North Dakota, N USA
19 O12 **Warwick** Rhode Island, NE USA
97 L20 **Warwickshire** *cultural region* C England, UK
14 G14 **Wasaga Beach** Ontario, S Canada
77 U13 **Wasagu** Kebbi, NW Nigeria
36 M2 **Wasatch Range** ▲ W USA
35 R12 **Wasco** California, W USA
29 V10 **Waseca** Minnesota, N USA
14 H13 **Washago** Ontario, S Canada
19 S2 **Washburn** Maine, NE USA
28 M5 **Washburn** North Dakota, N USA
30 K3 **Washburn** Wisconsin, N USA
31 S14 **Washburn Hill** *hill* Ohio, N USA
154 H13 **Wāshīm** Mahārāshtra, C India
97 M14 **Washington** NE England, UK
23 U3 **Washington** Georgia, SE USA
30 L12 **Washington** Illinois, N USA
31 N15 **Washington** Indiana, N USA
29 X15 **Washington** Iowa, C USA
27 O3 **Washington** Kansas, C USA
27 W5 **Washington** Missouri, C USA
21 X9 **Washington** North Carolina, SE USA
18 B15 **Washington** Pennsylvania, NE USA
25 V10 **Washington** Texas, SW USA
36 J8 **Washington** Utah, W USA
21 V4 **Washington** Virginia, NE USA
32 I9 **Washington** *off.* State of Washington; also known as Chinook State, Evergreen State. ◈ *state* NW USA
Washington *see* Washington Court House
31 S14 **Washington Court House** *var.* Washington. Ohio, NE USA
21 W4 **Washington DC** ● (USA) District of Columbia, NE USA
31 O5 **Washington Island** *island* Wisconsin, N USA
Washington Island *see* Teraina
19 O7 **Washington, Mount** ▲ New Hampshire, NE USA
26 M11 **Washita River** ≈ Oklahoma/Texas, C USA
97 O18 **Wash, The** *inlet* E England, UK
32 L9 **Washtucna** Washington, NW USA
Wasiliszki *see* Vasilishki
110 P9 **Wasilków** Podlaskie, NE Poland
39 R11 **Wasilla** Alaska, USA
55 U9 **Wasjabo** Sipaliwini, NW Surinam
11 X11 **Waskaiowaka Lake** ⊚ Manitoba, C Canada
11 T14 **Waskesiu Lake** Saskatchewan, C Canada
25 X7 **Waskom** Texas, SW USA
110 G13 **Wąsosz** Dolnośląskie, SW Poland
42 M6 **Waspam** *var.* Waspán. Región Autónoma Atlántico Norte, NE Nicaragua
Waspán *see* Waspam
165 T3 **Wassamu** Hokkaidō, NE Japan
108 G9 **Wassen** Uri, C Switzerland
98 G11 **Wassenaar** Zuid-Holland, W Netherlands
99 N24 **Wasserbillig** Grevenmacher, E Luxembourg
Wasserburg *see* Wasserburg am Inn
101 M23 **Wasserburg am Inn** *var.* Wasserburg. Bayern, SE Germany
101 I17 **Wasserkuppe** ▲ C Germany
103 R5 **Wassy** Haute-Marne, N France
171 N14 **Watampone** *var.* Bone. Sulawesi, C Indonesia
171 R13 **Watawa** Pulau Buru, E Indonesia
Watenstedt-Salzgitter *see* Salzgitter
18 M13 **Waterbury** Connecticut, NE USA
21 R11 **Wateree Lake** ⊡ South Carolina, SE USA
21 R12 **Wateree River** ≈ South Carolina, SE USA
97 E20 **Waterford** *Ir.* Port Láirge. S Ireland
31 S9 **Waterford** Michigan, N USA
97 E20 **Waterford** *Ir.* Port Láirge. *cultural region* S Ireland
97 E21 **Waterford Harbour** *Ir.* Cuan Phort Láirge. *inlet* S Ireland
98 G12 **Wateringen** Zuid-Holland, W Netherlands
99 G19 **Waterloo** Walloon Brabant, C Belgium
14 F16 **Waterloo** Ontario, S Canada
15 P12 **Waterloo** Québec, SE Canada
30 K16 **Waterloo** Illinois, N USA
29 X13 **Waterloo** Iowa, C USA
18 G10 **Waterloo** New York, NE USA
30 L4 **Watersmeet** Michigan, N USA
23 V9 **Watertown** Florida, SE USA
18 I8 **Watertown** New York, NE USA
29 R9 **Watertown** South Dakota, N USA
30 M8 **Watertown** Wisconsin, N USA
22 L3 **Water Valley** Mississippi, S USA
27 O3 **Waterville** Kansas, C USA
17 V6 **Waterville** Maine, NE USA
29 V10 **Waterville** Minnesota, N USA
18 I10 **Waterville** New York, NE USA
14 E16 **Watford** Ontario, S Canada
97 N21 **Watford** SE England, UK
28 K4 **Watford City** North Dakota, N USA
141 X12 **Wāṭif** S Oman
18 G11 **Watkins Glen** New York, NE USA
Watlings Island *see* San Salvador
171 U15 **Watnil** Pulau Kai Kecil, E Indonesia
26 M10 **Watonga** Oklahoma, C USA
11 T16 **Watrous** Saskatchewan, S Canada
37 T10 **Watrous** New Mexico, SW USA
79 P16 **Watsa** Orientale, NE Dem. Rep. Congo
31 N12 **Watseka** Illinois, N USA
79 J19 **Watsikengo** Equateur, C Dem. Rep. Congo
182 C5 **Watson** South Australia
11 U15 **Watson** Saskatchewan, S Canada
195 O10 **Watson Escarpment** ▲ Antarctica
10 K9 **Watson Lake** Yukon Territory, W Canada
35 N10 **Watsonville** California, W USA
167 Q8 **Wattay** ✕ (Viangchan) Viangchan, C Laos

◆ Country ● Country Capital ◇ Dependent Territory ○ Dependent Territory Capital ◈ Administrative Region ✕ International Airport ▲ Mountain ▲ Mountain Range ⩚ Volcano ≈ River ⊚ Lake ⊡ Reservoir

109 N7 **Wattens** Tirol, W Austria
20 M9 **Watts Bar Lake** ⊠ Tennessee, S USA
108 H7 **Wattwil** Sankt Gallen, NE Switzerland
171 T14 **Watubela, Kepulauan** *island group* E Indonesia
101 N24 **Watzmann** ▲ SE Germany
186 E8 **Wau** Morobe, C PNG
81 D14 **Wau** *var.* Wāw. Western Bahr el Ghazal, S Sudan
29 Q8 **Waubay** South Dakota, N USA
29 Q8 **Waubay Lake** ⊚ South Dakota, N USA
183 U7 **Wauchope** New South Wales, SE Australia
23 W13 **Wauchula** Florida, SE USA
30 M10 **Wauconda** Illinois, N USA
182 J7 **Waukaringa** South Australia
31 N10 **Waukegan** Illinois, N USA
30 M9 **Waukesha** Wisconsin, N USA
29 X11 **Waukon** Iowa, C USA
30 L8 **Waunakee** Wisconsin, N USA
30 L7 **Waupaca** Wisconsin, N USA
30 M8 **Waupun** Wisconsin, N USA
26 M13 **Waurika** Oklahoma, C USA
26 M12 **Waurika Lake** ⊠ Oklahoma, C USA
30 L6 **Wausau** Wisconsin, N USA
31 R11 **Wauseon** Ohio, N USA
30 L7 **Wautoma** Wisconsin, N USA
30 M9 **Wauwatosa** Wisconsin, N USA
22 L9 **Waveland** Mississippi, S USA
97 Q20 **Waveney** ≈ E England, UK
184 L11 **Waverley** Taranaki, North Island, NZ
29 W12 **Waverly** Iowa, C USA
27 T4 **Waverly** Missouri, C USA
29 R15 **Waverly** Nebraska, C USA
18 G12 **Waverly** New York, NE USA
20 H8 **Waverly** Tennessee, S USA
21 W7 **Waverly** Virginia, NE USA
99 H19 **Wavre** Wallon Brabant, C Belgium
166 M8 **Waw** Pegu, SW Burma
Wāw *see* Wau
14 B7 **Wawa** Ontario, S Canada
77 T14 **Wawa** Niger, W Nigeria
75 Q11 **Wāw al Kabīr** S Libya
43 N7 **Wawa, Río** *var.* Rio Huahua. ≈ NE Nicaragua
186 B8 **Wawoi** ≈ SW PNG
25 T7 **Waxahachie** Texas, SW USA
158 L9 **Waxxari** Xinjiang Uygur Zizhiqu, NW China
23 V7 **Waycross** Georgia, SE USA
180 K10 **Way, Lake** ⊚ Western Australia
31 P9 **Wayland** Michigan, N USA
29 R13 **Wayne** Nebraska, C USA
18 K14 **Wayne** New Jersey, NE USA
21 P5 **Wayne** West Virginia, NE USA
23 V4 **Waynesboro** Georgia, SE USA
22 M7 **Waynesboro** Mississippi, S USA
20 H10 **Waynesboro** Tennessee, S USA
21 U5 **Waynesboro** Virginia, NE USA
18 B16 **Waynesburg** Pennsylvania, NE USA
27 U6 **Waynesville** Missouri, C USA
21 O10 **Waynesville** North Carolina, SE USA
26 L8 **Waynoka** Oklahoma, C USA
Wazan *see* Ouazzane
Wazima *see* Wajima
149 V7 **Wazīrābād** Punjab, NE Pakistan
Wazzan *see* Ouazzane
110 I8 **Wda** *var.* Czarna Woda, *Ger.* Schwarzwasser. ≈ N Poland
187 Q16 **Wé** Province des Îles Loyauté, E New Caledonia
97 O23 **Weald, The** *lowlands* SE England, UK
186 A9 **Weam** Western, SW PNG
97 L15 **Wear** ≈ N England, UK
Wearmouth *see* Sunderland
26 L10 **Weatherford** Oklahoma, C USA
25 S6 **Weatherford** Texas, SW USA
34 M3 **Weaverville** California, W USA
27 R7 **Webb City** Missouri, C USA
192 G8 **Weber Basin** *undersea feature* S Ceram Sea
Webfoot State *see* Oregon
18 F9 **Webster** New York, NE USA
29 Q8 **Webster** South Dakota, N USA
29 V13 **Webster City** Iowa, C USA
27 X5 **Webster Groves** Missouri, C USA
21 S4 **Webster Springs** *var.* Addison. West Virginia, NE USA
171 S11 **Weda, Teluk** *bay* Pulau Halmahera, E Indonesia
65 B25 **Weddell Island** *var.* Isla San Jose. *Island* W Falkland Islands
65 K22 **Weddell Plain** *undersea feature* SW Atlantic Ocean
65 K23 **Weddell Sea** *sea* SW Atlantic Ocean
65 B25 **Weddell Settlement** Weddell Island, W Falkland Islands
182 M11 **Wedderburn** Victoria, SE Australia
100 I9 **Wedel** Schleswig-Holstein, N Germany
92 N3 **Wedel Jarlsberg Land** *physical region* SW Svalbard
100 I12 **Wedemark** Niedersachsen, NW Germany
10 M17 **Wedge Mountain** ▲ British Columbia, SW Canada
23 R4 **Wedowee** Alabama, S USA
171 U15 **Weduar** Pulau Kai Besar, E Indonesia
35 N2 **Weed** California, W USA
15 Q12 **Weedon Centre** Québec, SE Canada
18 E13 **Weedville** Pennsylvania, NE USA
100 F10 **Weener** Niedersachsen, NW Germany
29 S16 **Weeping Water** Nebraska, C USA
99 L16 **Weert** Limburg, SE Netherlands
98 I10 **Weesp** Noord-Holland, C Netherlands
183 S5 **Wee Waa** New South Wales, SE Australia
110 N7 **Węgorzewo** *Ger.* Angerburg. Warmińsko-Mazurskie, NE Poland
110 E9 **Węgorzyno** *Ger.* Wangerin. Zachodnio-pomorskie, NW Poland
110 N11 **Węgrów** *Ger.* Bingerau. Mazowieckie, E Poland
98 N5 **Wehe-Den Hoorn** Groningen, NE Netherlands
98 M12 **Wehl** Gelderland, E Netherlands
Wehlau *see* Znamensk
168 F7 **Weh, Pulau** *island* NW Indonesia
Wei *see* Weifang
161 P1 **Weichang** *prev.* Zhuizishan. Hebei, E China
Weichsel *see* Wisła
101 M16 **Weida** Thüringen, C Germany
Weiden *see* Weiden in der Oberpfalz
101 M19 **Weiden in der Oberpfalz** *var.* Weiden. Bayern, SE Germany
161 Q4 **Weifang** *var.* Wei, Wei-fang; *prev.* Weihsien. Shandong, E China
161 S4 **Weihai** Shandong, E China
160 K6 **Wei He** ≈ C China
Weihsien *see* Weifang
101 G17 **Weilburg** Hessen, W Germany
101 K24 **Weilheim in Oberbayern** Bayern, SE Germany
183 P4 **Weilmoringle** New South Wales, SE Australia
101 L16 **Weimar** Thüringen, C Germany
25 U11 **Weimar** Texas, SW USA
160 L6 **Weinan** Shaanxi, C China
108 H6 **Weinfelden** Thurgau, NE Switzerland
101 I24 **Weingarten** Baden-Württemberg, S Germany
101 G20 **Weinheim** Baden-Württemberg, SW Germany
160 H11 **Weining** *var.* Weining Yizu Huizu Miaozu Zizhixian. Guizhou, S China
Weining Yizu Huizu Miaozu Zizhixian *see* Weining
181 V2 **Weipa** Queensland, NE Australia
11 Y11 **Weir River** Manitoba, C Canada
21 R1 **Weirton** West Virginia, NE USA
32 M13 **Weiser** Idaho, NW USA
160 F12 **Weishan** Yunnan, SW China
161 P6 **Weishan Hu** ⊚ E China
101 M15 **Weisse Elster** *Eng.* White Elster. ≈ Czech Republic/Germany
Weisse Körös/Weisse Kreisch *see* Crişul Alb
108 L7 **Weissenbach am Lech** Tirol, W Austria
101 K21 **Weissenburg in Bayern** Bayern, SE Germany
Weissenburg *see* Wissembourg, France
Weissenburg *see* Alba Iulia, Romania
101 M15 **Weissenfels** *var.* Weißenfels. Sachsen-Anhalt, C Germany
109 R9 **Weissensee** ⊚ S Austria
Weissenstein *see* Paide
108 E11 **Weisshorn** *var.* Flüela Wisshorn. ▲ SW Switzerland
Weisskirchen *see* Bela Crkva
23 R3 **Weiss Lake** ⊠ Alabama, S USA
101 Q14 **Weisswasser** *Lus.* Běla Woda. Sachsen, E Germany
99 M22 **Weiswampach** Diekirch, N Luxembourg
109 U2 **Weitra** Niederösterreich, N Austria
161 O4 **Weixian** *var.* Wei Xian. Hebei, E China
159 V11 **Weiyuan** Gansu, C China
Weiyuan *see* Shuangjiang
160 F14 **Weiyuan Jiang** ≈ SW China
109 W7 **Weiz** Steiermark, SE Austria
Weizhou *see* Wenchuan
160 K16 **Weizhou Dao** *island* S China
110 I6 **Wejherowo** Pomorskie, NW Poland
27 Q8 **Welch** Oklahoma, C USA
24 M6 **Welch** Texas, SW USA
21 Q6 **Welch** West Virginia, NE USA
45 O14 **Welchman Hall** C Barbados
80 J11 **Weldiya** *var.* Waldia, *It.* Valdia. Amhara, N Ethiopia
21 W8 **Weldon** North Carolina, SE USA
25 V9 **Weldon** Texas, SW USA
99 M19 **Welkenraedt** Liège, E Belgium
193 O2 **Welker Seamount** *undersea feature* N Pacific Ocean
83 I22 **Welkom** Free State, C South Africa
14 H16 **Welland** Ontario, S Canada
14 G16 **Welland** ≈ Ontario, S Canada
97 O19 **Welland** ≈ C England, UK
14 H17 **Welland Canal** *canal* Ontario, S Canada
155 K25 **Wellawaya** Uva Province, SE Sri Lanka
Welle *see* Uele
181 T4 **Wellesley Islands** *island group* Queensland, N Australia
99 J22 **Wellin** Luxembourg, SE Belgium
97 N20 **Wellingborough** C England, UK
183 R7 **Wellington** New South Wales, SE Australia
14 J15 **Wellington** Ontario, SE Canada
185 L14 **Wellington** ● (NZ) Wellington, North Island, NZ
83 E26 **Wellington** Western Cape, SW South Africa
37 T2 **Wellington** Colorado, C USA
27 N7 **Wellington** Kansas, C USA
35 R7 **Wellington** Nevada, W USA
31 T11 **Wellington** Ohio, N USA
25 P3 **Wellington** Texas, SW USA
36 M4 **Wellington** Utah, W USA
185 M14 **Wellington** *off.* Wellington Region. ⬖ *region* North Island, NZ
185 L14 **Wellington** × Wellington, North Island, NZ
Wellington *see* Wellington, Isla
63 F22 **Wellington, Isla** *var.* Wellington. *island* S Chile
183 P12 **Wellington, Lake** ⊚ Victoria, SE Australia
29 X14 **Wellman** Iowa, C USA
24 M6 **Wellman** Texas, SW USA
97 K22 **Wells** SW England, UK
29 V11 **Wells** Minnesota, N USA
35 X2 **Wells** Nevada, W USA
25 W8 **Wells** Texas, SW USA
18 F12 **Wellsboro** Pennsylvania, NE USA
21 R1 **Wellsburg** West Virginia, NE USA
184 K4 **Wellsford** Auckland, North Island, NZ
180 L9 **Wells, Lake** ⊚ Western Australia
181 N4 **Wells, Mount** ▲ Western Australia
97 P18 **Wells-next-the-Sea** E England, UK
31 T15 **Wellston** Ohio, N USA
27 O10 **Wellston** Oklahoma, C USA
18 E11 **Wellsville** New York, NE USA
31 V12 **Wellsville** Ohio, N USA
36 L1 **Wellsville** Utah, W USA
36 I14 **Wellton** Arizona, SW USA
109 S4 **Wels** *anc.* Ovilava. Oberösterreich, N Austria
99 K15 **Welschap** × (Eindhoven) Noord-Brabant, S Netherlands
100 P10 **Welse** ≈ NE Germany
22 H9 **Welsh** Louisiana, S USA
97 K19 **Welshpool** *Wel.* Y Trallwng. E Wales, UK
97 O21 **Welwyn Garden City** SE England, UK
79 K18 **Wema** Equateur, NW Dem. Rep. Congo
81 G21 **Wembere** ≈ C Tanzania
11 N13 **Wembley** Alberta, W Canada
12 I9 **Wemindji** *prev.* Nouveau-Comptoir, Paint Hills. Québec, C Canada
99 G18 **Wemmel** Vlaams Brabant, C Belgium
32 J8 **Wenatchee** Washington, NW USA
160 M17 **Wenchang** Hainan, S China
161 R11 **Wencheng** *var.* Daxue. Zhejiang, SE China
77 P16 **Wenchi** W Ghana
Wen-chou/Wenchow *see* Wenzhou
160 H8 **Wenchuan** *var.* Weizhou. Sichuan, C China
Wendau *see* Võnnu
Wenden *see* Cēsis
161 S4 **Wendeng** Shandong, E China
81 J14 **Wendo** Southern, S Ethiopia
36 J2 **Wendover** Utah, W USA
14 D9 **Wenebegon** ≈ Ontario, S Canada
14 D8 **Wenebegon Lake** ⊚ Ontario, S Canada
108 E9 **Wengen** Bern, W Switzerland
161 O13 **Wengyuan** *var.* Longxian. Guangdong, S China
189 P15 **Weno** *prev.* Moen. Chuuk, C Micronesia
189 V12 **Weno** *prev.* Moen. *atoll* Chuuk Islands, C Micronesia
158 N13 **Wenquan** Qinghai, C China
159 H4 **Wenquan** *var.* Arixang. Xinjiang Uygur Zizhiqu, NW China
Wenquan *see* Yingshan
160 H14 **Wenshan** *var.* Kaihua. Yunnan, SW China
158 H6 **Wensu** Xinjiang Uygur Zizhiqu, W China
182 L8 **Wentworth** New South Wales, SE Australia
27 W4 **Wentzville** Missouri, C USA
159 V12 **Wenxian** *var.* Wen Xian. Gansu, C China
161 S10 **Wenzhou** *var.* Wen-chou, Wenchow. Zhejiang, SE China
34 L4 **Weott** California, W USA
99 I20 **Wépion** Namur, SE Belgium
100 O11 **Werbellinsee** ⊚ NE Germany
99 L21 **Werbomont** Liège, E Belgium
83 G20 **Werda** Kgalagadi, S Botswana
Werder *see* Virtsu
81 N14 **Werder** Somali, E Ethiopia
Werenów *see* Voranava
171 U13 **Weri** Papua, E Indonesia
98 I13 **Werkendam** Noord-Brabant, S Netherlands
101 M20 **Wernberg-Köblitz** Bayern, SE Germany
101 J18 **Werneck** Bayern, C Germany
101 K14 **Wernigerode** Sachsen-Anhalt, C Germany
Werowitz *see* Virovitica
101 J16 **Werra** ≈ C Germany
183 N12 **Werribee** Victoria, SE Australia
183 T6 **Werris Creek** New South Wales, SE Australia
Werro *see* Võru
Werschetz *see* Vršac
101 K23 **Wertach** ≈ S Germany
101 I19 **Wertheim** Baden-Württemberg, SW Germany
98 J8 **Wervershoof** Noord-Holland, NW Netherlands
Wervicq *see* Wervik
99 C18 **Wervik** *var.* Wervicq, Werwick. West-Vlaanderen, W Belgium
Werwick *see* Wervik
101 D14 **Wesel** Nordrhein-Westfalen, W Germany
Weseli an der Lainsitz *see* Veselí nad Lužnicí
Wesenberg *see* Rakvere
100 H12 **Weser** ≈ NW Germany
Wes-Kaap *see* Western Cape
25 S17 **Weslaco** Texas, SW USA
14 J13 **Weslemkoon Lake** ⊚ Ontario, SE Canada
181 R1 **Wessel Islands** *island group* Northern Territory, N Australia
29 P9 **Wessington** South Dakota, N USA
29 P10 **Wessington Springs** South Dakota, N USA
25 T8 **West** Texas, SW USA
West *see* Ouest
30 M9 **West Allis** Wisconsin, N USA
182 E8 **Westall, Point** *headland* South Australia
West Antarctica *see* Lesser Antarctica
14 G11 **West Arm** Ontario, S Canada
West Azerbaijan *see* Āzarbāyjān-e Gharbī
138 F10 **West Bank** *disputed region* SW Asia
11 N17 **Westbank** British Columbia, SW Canada
14 E11 **West Bay** Manitoulin Island, Ontario, S Canada
22 L11 **West Bay** *bay* Louisiana, S USA
30 M8 **West Bend** Wisconsin, N USA
153 R16 **West Bengal** ⬖ *state* NE India
West Borneo *see* Kalimantan Barat
29 Y14 **West Branch** Iowa, C USA
31 R7 **West Branch** Michigan, N USA
18 F13 **West Branch Susquehanna River** ≈ Pennsylvania, NE USA
97 L20 **West Bromwich** C England, UK
19 P8 **Westbrook** Maine, NE USA
29 T10 **Westbrook** Minnesota, N USA
29 Y15 **West Burlington** Iowa, C USA
96 L2 **West Burra** *island* NE Scotland, UK
30 J8 **Westby** Wisconsin, N USA
44 L6 **West Caicos** *island* W Turks and Caicos Islands
185 A24 **West Cape** *headland* South Island, NZ
18 I16 **West Chester** Pennsylvania, NE USA
185 E18 **West Coast** *off.* West Coast Region. ⬖ *region* South Island, NZ
25 V12 **West Columbia** Texas, SW USA
29 W10 **West Concord** Minnesota, N USA
29 V14 **West Des Moines** Iowa, C USA
37 Q6 **West Elk Peak** ▲ Colorado, C USA
44 F1 **West End** Grand Bahama Island, N Bahamas
44 F1 **West End Point** *headland* Grand Bahama Island, N Bahamas
98 O7 **Westerbork** Drenthe, NE Netherlands
98 N3 **Westereems** *strait* Germany/Netherlands
98 O9 **Westerhaar-Vriezenveensewijk** Overijssel, E Netherlands
100 G6 **Westerland** Schleswig-Holstein, N Germany
99 I17 **Westerlo** Antwerpen, N Belgium
19 N13 **Westerly** Rhode Island, NE USA
81 G18 **Western** ⬖ *province* W Kenya
153 N11 **Western** ⬖ *zone* C Nepal
186 A8 **Western** ⬖ *province* SW PNG
186 J8 **Western** *off.* Western Province. ⬖ *province* NW Solomon Islands
83 G15 **Western** ⬖ *province* SW Zambia
180 K8 **Western Australia** ⬖ *state* W Australia
80 A13 **Western Bahr el Ghazal** ⬖ *state* SW Sudan
Western Bug *see* Bug
83 F25 **Western Cape** *off.* Western Cape Province, *Afr.* Wes-Kaap. ⬖ *province* SW South Africa
80 A11 **Western Darfur** ⬖ *state* W Sudan
Western Desert *see* Sahara el Gharbîya
118 G9 **Western Dvina** *Bel.* Dzvina, *Ger.* Düna, *Latv.* Daugava, *Rus.* Zapadnaya Dvina. ≈ W Europe
81 D15 **Western Equatoria** ⬖ *state* SW Sudan
155 E16 **Western Ghats** ▲ SW India
186 C7 **Western Highlands** ⬖ *province* C PNG
Western Isles *see* Outer Hebrides
80 C12 **Western Kordofan** ⬖ *state* C Sudan
21 T3 **Westernport** Maryland, NE USA
155 J26 **Western Province** ⬖ *province* SW Sri Lanka
74 B10 **Western Sahara** ◇ *disputed territory* N Africa
Western Samoa *see* Samoa
Western Sayans *see* Zapadnyy Sayan
Western Scheldt *see* Westerschelde
Western Sierra Madre *see* Madre Occidental, Sierra
99 E15 **Westerschelde** *Eng.* Western Scheldt; *prev.* Honte. *inlet* S North Sea
31 S13 **Westerville** Ohio, N USA
101 F17 **Westerwald** ▲ W Germany
65 C25 **West Falkland** *var.* Gran Malvina, Isla Gran Malvina. *island* W Falkland Islands
29 R5 **West Fargo** North Dakota, N USA
188 M15 **West Fayu Atoll** *atoll* Caroline Islands, C Micronesia
18 C11 **Westfield** New York, NE USA
30 L7 **Westfield** Wisconsin, N USA
West Flanders *see* West-Vlaanderen
27 S10 **West Fork** Arkansas, C USA
29 P16 **West Fork Big Blue River** ≈ Nebraska, C USA
29 U12 **West Fork Des Moines River** ≈ Iowa/Minnesota, C USA
25 S5 **West Fork Trinity River** ≈ Texas, SW USA
30 L16 **West Frankfort** Illinois, N USA
98 I8 **West-Friesland** *physical region* NW Netherlands
West Frisian Islands *see* Waddeneilanden
19 T5 **West Grand Lake** ⊚ Maine, NE USA
18 M12 **West Hartford** Connecticut, NE USA
18 M13 **West Haven** Connecticut, NE USA
27 X12 **West Helena** Arkansas, C USA
28 M2 **Westhope** North Dakota, N USA
195 Y8 **West Ice Shelf** *ice shelf* Antarctica
West Irian *see* Papua
West Java *see* Jawa Barat
36 L3 **West Jordan** Utah, W USA
West Kalimantan *see* Kalimantan Barat
99 D14 **Westkapelle** Zeeland, SW Netherlands
31 O13 **West Lafayette** Indiana, N USA
31 T13 **West Lafayette** Ohio, N USA
West Lake *see* Kagera
29 Y14 **West Liberty** Iowa, C USA
21 O5 **West Liberty** Kentucky, S USA
Westliche Morava *see* Zapadna Morava
10 J13 **Westlock** Alberta, SW Canada
14 E17 **West Lorne** Ontario, S Canada
96 J12 **West Lothian** *cultural region* S Scotland, UK
99 H16 **Westmalle** Antwerpen, N Belgium
192 G6 **West Mariana Basin** *var.* Perece Vela Basin. *undersea feature* W Pacific Ocean
97 E17 **Westmeath** *Ir.* An Iarmhí, Na h-Iarmhidhe. *cultural region* C Ireland
27 Y11 **West Memphis** Arkansas, C USA
21 W2 **Westminster** Maryland, NE USA
21 O11 **Westminster** South Carolina, SE USA
22 I5 **West Monroe** Louisiana, S USA
18 D15 **Westmont** Pennsylvania, NE USA
27 O3 **Westmoreland** Kansas, C USA
35 W17 **Westmorland** California, W USA
186 E6 **West New Britain** ⬖ *province* E PNG
West New Guinea *see* Papua
83 K18 **West Nicholson** Matabeleland South, S Zimbabwe
29 T14 **West Nishnabotna River** ≈ Iowa, C USA
192 K11 **West Norfolk Ridge** *undersea feature* W Pacific Ocean
25 P12 **West Nueces River** ≈ Texas, SW USA
West Nusa Tenggara *see* Nusa Tenggara Barat
29 T11 **West Okoboji Lake** ⊚ Iowa, C USA
33 R16 **Weston** Idaho, NW USA
21 R4 **Weston** West Virginia, NE USA
97 J22 **Weston-super-Mare** SW England, UK
23 Z14 **West Palm Beach** Florida, SE USA
West Papua *see* Papua
188 E9 **West Passage** *passage* Babeldaob, N Palau
23 O9 **West Pensacola** Florida, SE USA
27 V8 **West Plains** Missouri, C USA
35 P7 **West Point** California, W USA
23 R5 **West Point** Georgia, SE USA
22 M3 **West Point** Mississippi, S USA
29 R14 **West Point** Nebraska, C USA
21 X6 **West Point** Virginia, NE USA
182 G10 **West Point** *headland* South Australia
65 B24 **Westpoint Island Settlement** Westpoint Island, NW Falkland Islands
23 R4 **West Point Lake** ⊠ Alabama/Georgia, SE USA
97 B16 **Westport** *Ir.* Cathair na Mart. W Ireland
185 G15 **Westport** West Coast, South Island, NZ
32 F10 **Westport** Oregon, NW USA
32 F9 **Westport** Washington, NW USA
31 S15 **West Portsmouth** Ohio, N USA
West Punjab *see* Punjab
11 V14 **Westray** Manitoba, C Canada
96 J4 **Westray** *island* NE Scotland, UK
14 F9 **Westree** Ontario, S Canada
97 L16 **West Riding** *cultural region* N England, UK
West River *see* Xi Jiang
30 J7 **West Salem** Wisconsin, N USA
65 H21 **West Scotia Ridge** *undersea feature* W Scotia Sea
West Sepik *see* Sandaun
173 N4 **West Sheba Ridge** *undersea feature* W Indian Ocean
West Siberian Plain *see* Zapadno-Sibirskaya Ravnina
31 S11 **West Sister Island** *island* Ohio, N USA
West-Skylge *see* West-Terschelling
West Sumatra *see* Sumatera Barat
98 J5 **West-Terschelling** *Fris.* West-Skylge. Friesland, N Netherlands
64 J7 **West Thulean Rise** *undersea feature* N Atlantic Ocean
29 X12 **West Union** Iowa, C USA
31 R15 **West Union** Ohio, N USA
21 R3 **West Union** West Virginia, NE USA
31 N13 **Westville** Illinois, N USA
21 R3 **West Virginia** *off.* State of West Virginia; also known as The Mountain State. ⬖ *state* NE USA
99 A17 **West-Vlaanderen** *Eng.* West Flanders. ⬖ *province* W Belgium
35 R7 **West Walker River** ≈ California/Nevada, W USA
35 P4 **Westwood** California, W USA
183 P9 **West Wyalong** New South Wales, SE Australia
171 Q16 **Wetar, Pulau** *island* Kepulauan Damar, E Indonesia
171 R16 **Wetar, Selat** *var.* Wetar Strait. *strait* Nusa Tenggara, S Indonesia
Wetar Strait *see* Wetar, Selat
11 Q15 **Wetaskiwin** Alberta, SW Canada
81 K21 **Wete** Pemba, E Tanzania
166 M4 **Wetlet** Sagaing, C Burma
37 T6 **Wet Mountains** ▲ Colorado, C USA
101 E15 **Wetter** Nordrhein-Westfalen, W Germany
101 H17 **Wetter** ≈ W Germany
99 F17 **Wetteren** Oost-Vlaanderen, NW Belgium
108 F7 **Wettingen** Aargau, N Switzerland
27 P11 **Wetumka** Oklahoma, C USA
23 Q5 **Wetumpka** Alabama, S USA
108 G7 **Wetzikon** Zürich, N Switzerland
101 G17 **Wetzlar** Hessen, W Germany
99 C18 **Wevelgem** West-Vlaanderen, W Belgium
38 M6 **Wevok** *var.* Wewuk. Alaska, USA
23 R9 **Wewahitchka** Florida, SE USA
186 C6 **Wewak** East Sepik, NW PNG
27 O11 **Wewoka** Oklahoma, C USA
Wewuk *see* Wevok
97 F20 **Wexford** *Ir.* Loch Garman. SE Ireland
97 F20 **Wexford** *Ir.* Loch Garman. *cultural region* SE Ireland
30 L7 **Weyauwega** Wisconsin, N USA
11 U17 **Weyburn** Saskatchewan, S Canada
Weyer *see* Weyer Markt
109 U5 **Weyer Markt** *var.* Weyer. Oberösterreich, N Austria
100 H11 **Weyhe** Niedersachsen, NW Germany
97 L24 **Weymouth** S England, UK
19 P11 **Weymouth** Massachusetts, NE USA
99 H18 **Wezembeek-Oppem** Vlaams Brabant, C Belgium
98 M9 **Wezep** Gelderland, E Netherlands
184 M9 **Whakamaru** Waikato, North Island, NZ
184 O8 **Whakatane** Bay of Plenty, North Island, NZ
184 O8 **Whakatane** ≈ North Island, NZ
9 O9 **Whale Cove** Nunavut, C Canada
96 M2 **Whalsay** *island* NE Scotland, UK
184 L11 **Whangaehu** ≈ North Island, NZ
184 M6 **Whangamata** Waikato, North Island, NZ
184 Q9 **Whangara** Gisborne, North Island, NZ
184 K3 **Whangarei** Northland, North Island, NZ
184 K3 **Whangaruru Harbour** *inlet* North Island, NZ
25 V12 **Wharton** Texas, SW USA
173 U8 **Wharton Basin** *var.* West Australian Basin. *undersea feature* E Indian Ocean
185 E18 **Whataroa** West Coast, South Island, NZ
8 K10 **Wha Ti** *prev.* Lac La Martre. Northwest Territories, W Canada
184 K6 **Whatipu** Auckland, North Island, NZ
33 Y16 **Wheatland** Wyoming, C USA
14 D18 **Wheatley** Ontario, S Canada
30 M10 **Wheaton** Illinois, N USA
29 R7 **Wheaton** Minnesota, N USA
37 T4 **Wheat Ridge** Colorado, C USA
25 P2 **Wheeler** Texas, SW USA
23 O2 **Wheeler Lake** ⊠ Alabama, S USA
35 Y6 **Wheeler Peak** ▲ Nevada, W USA
37 T9 **Wheeler Peak** ▲ New Mexico, SW USA
31 S15 **Wheelersburg** Ohio, N USA
21 R2 **Wheeling** West Virginia, NE USA
97 L16 **Whernside** ▲ N England, UK
182 F9 **Whidbey, Point** *headland* South Australia
180 I7 **Whim Creek** Western Australia
10 L17 **Whistler** British Columbia, SW Canada
21 W8 **Whitakers** North Carolina, SE USA
14 H15 **Whitby** Ontario, S Canada
97 N15 **Whitby** N England, UK
10 G6 **White** ≈ Yukon Territory, W Canada
13 T11 **White Bay** *bay* Newfoundland and Labrador, E Canada
20 I8 **White Bluff** Tennessee, S USA
28 J6 **White Butte** ▲ North Dakota, N USA
19 R5 **White Cap Mountain** ▲ Maine, NE USA
22 J9 **White Castle** Louisiana, S USA
182 M5 **White Cliffs** New South Wales, SE Australia
31 P8 **White Cloud** Michigan, N USA
11 P14 **Whitecourt** Alberta, SW Canada
25 O2 **White Deer** Texas, SW USA
White Elster *see* Weisse Elster
24 M5 **Whiteface** Texas, SW USA
18 K7 **Whiteface Mountain** ▲ New York, NE USA
29 W5 **Whiteface Reservoir** ⊠ Minnesota, N USA
33 O7 **Whitefish** Montana, NW USA
31 N9 **Whitefish Bay** Wisconsin, N USA
31 Q3 **Whitefish Bay** *lake bay* Canada/USA
14 E11 **Whitefish Falls** Ontario, S Canada
14 B7 **Whitefish Lake** ⊚ Ontario, S Canada
29 U6 **Whitefish Lake** ⊚ Minnesota, C USA
31 Q3 **Whitefish Point** *headland* Michigan, N USA

◆ Country ● Country Capital ◇ Dependent Territory ○ Dependent Territory Capital ⬖ Administrative Region × International Airport ▲ Mountain ▲ Mountain Range 𝕏 Volcano ≈ River ⊚ Lake ⊠ Reservoir

31 O4 **Whitefish River** ≈ Michigan, N USA
25 O4 **Whiteflat** Texas, SW USA
27 V12 **White Hall** Arkansas, C USA
30 K14 **White Hall** Illinois, N USA
31 O8 **Whitehall** Michigan, N USA
18 L9 **Whitehall** New York, NE USA
31 S13 **Whitehall** Ohio, N USA
30 J7 **Whitehall** Wisconsin, N USA
97 J15 **Whitehaven** NW England, UK
10 I8 **Whitehorse** *territory capital* Yukon Territory, W Canada
184 O7 **White Island** *island* NE NZ
14 K13 **White Lake** ◎ Ontario, SE Canada
22 H10 **White Lake** ◎ Louisiana, S USA
186 G7 **Whiteman Range** ⛰ New Britain, E PNG
183 Q15 **Whitemark** Tasmania, SE Australia
35 S9 **White Mountains** ⛰ California/Nevada, W USA
19 N7 **White Mountains** ⛰ Maine/New Hampshire, NE USA
80 F11 **White Nile** ◈ *state* C Sudan
81 E14 **White Nile** *Ar.* Al Baḩr al Abyaḑ, An Nīl al Abyaḑ, Bahr el Jebel. ≈ SE Sudan
25 W5 **White Oak Creek** ≈ Texas, SW USA
10 H9 **White Pass** *pass* Canada/USA
32 I9 **White Pass** *pass* Washington, NW USA
21 O9 **White Pine** Tennessee, S USA
18 K14 **White Plains** New York, NE USA
25 O5 **White River** ≈ Texas, SW USA
28 M11 **White River** South Dakota, N USA
27 W12 **White River** ≈ Arkansas, SE USA
37 P3 **White River** ≈ Colorado/Utah, C USA
31 N15 **White River** ≈ Indiana, N USA
31 O8 **White River** ≈ Michigan, N USA
28 K11 **White River** ≈ South Dakota, N USA
18 M8 **White River** ≈ Vermont, NE USA
37 N13 **Whiteriver** Arizona, SW USA
25 O5 **White River Lake** ⊞ Texas, SW USA
32 H11 **White Salmon** Washington, NW USA
18 I10 **Whitesboro** New York, NE USA
25 T5 **Whitesboro** Texas, SW USA
21 O7 **Whitesburg** Kentucky, S USA
White Sea *see* Beloye More
White Sea-Baltic Canal/White Sea Canal *see* Belomorsko-Baltiyskiy Kanal
63 I25 **Whiteside, Canal** *channel* S Chile
33 S10 **White Sulphur Springs** Montana, NW USA
21 R6 **White Sulphur Springs** West Virginia, NE USA
20 J6 **Whitesville** Kentucky, S USA
32 I10 **White Swan** Washington, NW USA
21 U12 **Whiteville** North Carolina, SE USA
20 F10 **Whiteville** Tennessee, S USA
77 Q13 **White Volta** *var.* Nakambé, *Fr.* Volta Blanche. ≈ Burkina/Ghana
30 M9 **Whitewater** Wisconsin, N USA
37 P14 **Whitewater Baldy** ▲ New Mexico, SW USA
23 X17 **Whitewater Bay** *bay* Florida, SE USA
31 Q14 **Whitewater River** ≈ Indiana/Ohio, N USA
11 V16 **Whitewood** Saskatchewan, S Canada
28 J9 **Whitewood** South Dakota, N USA
25 U5 **Whitewright** Texas, SW USA
97 I15 **Whithorn** S Scotland, UK
184 M6 **Whitianga** Waikato, North Island, NZ
19 N11 **Whitinsville** Massachusetts, NE USA
20 M8 **Whitley City** Kentucky, S USA
21 Q11 **Whitmire** South Carolina, SE USA
31 R10 **Whitmore Lake** Michigan, N USA
195 N9 **Whitmore Mountains** ⛰ Antarctica
14 I12 **Whitney** Ontario, SE Canada
25 T8 **Whitney** Texas, SW USA
25 S8 **Whitney, Lake** ⊞ Texas, SW USA
35 S11 **Whitney, Mount** ▲ California, W USA
181 Y6 **Whitsunday Group** *island group* Queensland, E Australia
25 S6 **Whitt** Texas, SW USA
29 U12 **Whittemore** Iowa, C USA
39 R12 **Whittier** Alaska, USA
35 T15 **Whittier** California, W USA
83 I25 **Whittlesea** Eastern Cape, S South Africa
20 K10 **Whitwell** Tennessee, S USA
8 L10 **Wholdaia Lake** ◎ Northwest Territories, NW Canada
182 H7 **Whyalla** South Australia
Whydah *see* Ouidah
14 F13 **Wiarton** Ontario, S Canada
171 O13 **Wiau** Sulawesi, C Indonesia
111 H15 **Wiązów** *Ger.* Wansen. Dolnośląskie, SW Poland
33 Y8 **Wibaux** Montana, NW USA
27 N6 **Wichita** Kansas, C USA
25 R5 **Wichita Falls** Texas, SW USA
26 L11 **Wichita Mountains** ⛰ Oklahoma, C USA
25 R5 **Wichita River** ≈ Texas, SW USA
96 K6 **Wick** N Scotland, UK
36 K13 **Wickenburg** Arizona, SW USA
24 L8 **Wickett** Texas, SW USA
180 I7 **Wickham** Western Australia
182 M14 **Wickham, Cape** *headland* Tasmania, SE Australia
20 G7 **Wickliffe** Kentucky, S USA
97 G19 **Wicklow** *Ir.* Cill Mhantáin. E Ireland
97 F19 **Wicklow** *Ir.* Cill Mhantáin. *cultural region* E Ireland
97 G19 **Wicklow Head** *Ir.* Ceann Chill Mhantáin. *headland* E Ireland
97 F18 **Wicklow Mountains** *Ir.* Sléibhte Chill Mhantáin. ⛰ E Ireland
14 H10 **Wicksteed Lake** ◎ Ontario, S Canada
Wida *see* Ouidah
65 G15 **Wideawake Airfield** × (Georgetown) SW Ascension Island
97 K18 **Widnes** C England, UK
110 H9 **Więcbork** *Ger.* Vandsburg. Kujawsko-pomorskie, C Poland
101 E17 **Wied** ≈ W Germany
101 F16 **Wiehl** Nordrhein-Westfalen, W Germany
111 L17 **Wieliczka** Małopolskie, S Poland
110 G12 **Wielkopolskie** ◈ *province* C Poland
111 J14 **Wieluń** Sieradz, C Poland
109 X4 **Wien** *Eng.* Vienna, *Hung.* Bécs, *Slvk.* Vídeň, *Slvn.* Dunaj; *anc.* Vindobona. ● (Austria) Wien, NE Austria
109 X4 **Wien** *off.* Land Wien, *Eng.* Vienna. ◈ *state* NE Austria
109 X5 **Wiener Neustadt** Niederösterreich, E Austria
110 G7 **Wieprza** *Ger.* Wipper. ≈ NW Poland
98 O10 **Wierden** Overijssel, E Netherlands
98 I7 **Wieringerwerf** Noord-Holland, NW Netherlands
Wieruschow *see* Wieruszów
111 I14 **Wieruszów** *Ger.* Wieruschow. Łódzkie, C Poland
109 V9 **Wies** Steiermark, SE Austria
Wiesbachhorn *see* Grosses Wiesbachhorn
101 G18 **Wiesbaden** Hessen, W Germany
Wieselburg and Ungarisch-Altenburg/Wieselburg-Ungarisch-Altenburg *see* Mosonmagyaróvár
Wiesenhof *see* Ostrołęka
101 G20 **Wiesloch** Baden-Württemberg, SW Germany
100 F10 **Wiesmoor** Niedersachsen, NW Germany
110 I7 **Wieżyca** *Ger.* Turmberg. *hill* Pomorskie, N Poland
97 L17 **Wigan** NW England, UK
37 U3 **Wiggins** Colorado, C USA
22 M8 **Wiggins** Mississippi, S USA
Wigorna Ceaster *see* Worcester
97 I14 **Wigtown** S Scotland, UK
97 H14 **Wigtown** *cultural region* SW Scotland, UK
97 I15 **Wigtown Bay** *bay* SW Scotland, UK
98 L13 **Wijchen** Gelderland, SE Netherlands
92 N1 **Wijdefjorden** *fjord* NW Svalbard
98 M10 **Wijhe** Overijssel, E Netherlands
98 J12 **Wijk bij Duurstede** Utrecht, C Netherlands
98 J13 **Wijk en Aalburg** Noord-Brabant, S Netherlands
99 H16 **Wijnegem** Antwerpen, N Belgium
14 E11 **Wikwemikong** Manitoulin Island, Ontario, S Canada
108 H7 **Wil** Sankt Gallen, NE Switzerland
29 R16 **Wilber** Nebraska, C USA
32 K8 **Wilbur** Washington, NW USA
27 Q11 **Wilburton** Oklahoma, C USA
182 M6 **Wilcannia** New South Wales, SE Australia
18 D12 **Wilcox** Pennsylvania, NE USA
Wilczek Land *see* Vil'cheka, Zemlya
109 U6 **Wildalpen** Steiermark, E Austria
31 O13 **Wildcat Creek** ≈ Indiana, N USA
108 L9 **Wilde Kreuzspitze** *It.* Picco di Croce. ▲ Austria/Italy
Wildenschwert *see* Ústí nad Orlicí
98 O6 **Wildervank** Groningen, NE Netherlands
100 G11 **Wildeshausen** Niedersachsen, NW Germany
108 D10 **Wildhorn** ▲ SW Switzerland
11 R17 **Wild Horse** Alberta, SW Canada
27 N12 **Wildhorse Creek** ≈ Oklahoma, C USA
28 L14 **Wild Horse Hill** ▲ Nebraska, C USA
109 W8 **Wildon** Steiermark, SE Austria
24 M2 **Wildorado** Texas, SW USA
29 R6 **Wild Rice River** ≈ Minnesota/North Dakota, N USA
Wilejka *see* Vilyeyka
195 Y9 **Wilhelm II Coast** *physical region* Antarctica
195 X9 **Wilhelm II Land** *physical region* Antarctica
55 U11 **Wilhelmina Gebergte** ⛰ C Surinam
18 B13 **Wilhelm, Lake** ⊞ Pennsylvania, NE USA
92 O2 **Wilhelmøya** *island* C Svalbard
Wilhelm-Pieck-Stadt *see* Guben
109 W4 **Wilhelmsburg** Niederösterreich, E Austria
100 G10 **Wilhelmshaven** Niedersachsen, NW Germany
Wilia/Wilja *see* Neris
18 H13 **Wilkes Barre** Pennsylvania, NE USA
21 R9 **Wilkesboro** North Carolina, SE USA
195 W15 **Wilkes Coast** *physical region* Antarctica
189 W12 **Wilkes Island** *island* N Wake Island
195 X12 **Wilkes Land** *physical region* Antarctica
11 S15 **Wilkie** Saskatchewan, S Canada
194 I6 **Wilkins Ice Shelf** *ice shelf* Antarctica
182 D4 **Wilkinsons Lakes** *salt lake* South Australia
Wiłkomierz *see* Ukmergė
182 K11 **Willalooka** South Australia
32 G11 **Willamette River** ≈ Oregon, NW USA
133 O8 **Willandra Billabong Creek** *seasonal river* New South Wales, SE Australia
32 F9 **Willapa Bay** *inlet* Washington, NW USA
27 T7 **Willard** Missouri, C USA
37 S12 **Willard** New Mexico, SW USA
31 S12 **Willard** Ohio, N USA
36 L1 **Willard** Utah, W USA
186 G6 **Willaumez Peninsula** *headland* New Britain, E PNG
37 N15 **Willcox** Arizona, SW USA
37 N16 **Willcox Playa** *salt flat* Arizona, SW USA
99 G17 **Willebroek** Antwerpen, C Belgium
45 P16 **Willemstad** ○ (Netherlands Antilles) Curaçao, Netherlands Antilles
99 G14 **Willemstad** Noord-Brabant, S Netherlands
11 S11 **William** ≈ Saskatchewan, C Canada
23 O6 **William "Bill" Dannelly Reservoir** ⊞ Alabama, S USA
182 G3 **William Creek** South Australia
181 T15 **William, Mount** ▲ South Australia
36 K11 **Williams** Arizona, SW USA
29 X14 **Williamsburg** Iowa, C USA
20 M8 **Williamsburg** Kentucky, S USA
31 R15 **Williamsburg** Ohio, N USA
21 X6 **Williamsburg** Virginia, NE USA
10 M15 **Williams Lake** British Columbia, SW Canada
21 P6 **Williamson** West Virginia, NE USA
31 N13 **Williamsport** Indiana, N USA
18 G13 **Williamsport** Pennsylvania, NE USA
21 W9 **Williamston** North Carolina, SE USA
21 P11 **Williamston** South Carolina, SE USA
20 M4 **Williamstown** Kentucky, S USA
18 L10 **Williamstown** Massachusetts, NE USA
18 J16 **Willingboro** New Jersey, NE USA
11 Q14 **Willingdon** Alberta, SW Canada
25 W10 **Willis** Texas, SW USA
108 F8 **Willisau** Luzern, W Switzerland
83 F24 **Williston** Northern Cape, W South Africa
23 V10 **Williston** Florida, SE USA
28 J3 **Williston** North Dakota, N USA
21 Q13 **Williston** South Carolina, SE USA
10 L12 **Williston Lake** ⊞ British Columbia, W Canada
34 L5 **Willits** California, W USA
29 T8 **Willmar** Minnesota, N USA
10 K11 **Will, Mount** ▲ British Columbia, W Canada
31 T11 **Willoughby** Ohio, N USA
11 U17 **Willow Bunch** Saskatchewan, S Canada
32 J11 **Willow Creek** ≈ Oregon, NW USA
39 R11 **Willow Lake** Alaska, USA
8 I9 **Willowlake** ≈ Northwest Territories, NW Canada
83 H25 **Willowmore** Eastern Cape, S South Africa
30 L5 **Willow Reservoir** ⊞ Wisconsin, N USA
35 N5 **Willows** California, W USA
27 V7 **Willow Springs** Missouri, C USA
182 I7 **Wilmington** South Australia
21 Y2 **Wilmington** Delaware, NE USA
21 V12 **Wilmington** North Carolina, SE USA
31 R14 **Wilmington** Ohio, N USA
20 M6 **Wilmore** Kentucky, S USA
29 R8 **Wilmot** South Dakota, N USA
Wilna/Wilno *see* Vilnius
101 G16 **Wilnsdorf** Nordrhein-Westfalen, W Germany
99 G16 **Wilrijk** Antwerpen, N Belgium
100 I10 **Wilseder Berg** *hill* NW Germany
21 V9 **Wilson** North Carolina, SE USA
25 N5 **Wilson** Texas, SW USA
182 A7 **Wilson Bluff** *headland* South Australia/Western Australia
35 Y7 **Wilson Creek Range** ⛰ Nevada, W USA
23 O1 **Wilson Lake** ⊞ Alabama, S USA
26 M4 **Wilson Lake** ⊞ Kansas, SE USA
37 P7 **Wilson, Mount** ▲ Colorado, C USA
183 P13 **Wilsons Promontory** *peninsula* Victoria, SE Australia
29 Y14 **Wilton** Iowa, C USA
19 P7 **Wilton** Maine, NE USA
28 M5 **Wilton** North Dakota, N USA
97 L22 **Wiltshire** *cultural region* S England, UK
99 M23 **Wiltz** Diekirch, NW Luxembourg
180 K9 **Wiluna** Western Australia
99 M23 **Wilwerwiltz** Diekirch, NE Luxembourg
29 P5 **Wimbledon** North Dakota, N USA
42 K7 **Wina** *var.* Güina. Jinotega, N Nicaragua
31 O12 **Winamac** Indiana, N USA
81 G19 **Winam Gulf** *var.* Kavirondo Gulf. *gulf* SW Kenya
83 I22 **Winburg** Free State, C South Africa
19 N10 **Winchendon** Massachusetts, NE USA
14 M13 **Winchester** Ontario, SE Canada
97 M23 **Winchester** *hist.* Wintanceaster, *Lat.* Venta Belgarum. S England, UK
32 M10 **Winchester** Idaho, NW USA
30 J14 **Winchester** Illinois, N USA
31 Q13 **Winchester** Indiana, N USA
20 M5 **Winchester** Kentucky, S USA
18 M10 **Winchester** New Hampshire, NE USA
20 K10 **Winchester** Tennessee, S USA
21 V3 **Winchester** Virginia, NE USA
99 L22 **Wincrange** Diekirch, NW Luxembourg
10 I5 **Wind** ≈ Yukon Territory, NW Canada
183 S8 **Windamere, Lake** ◎ New South Wales, SE Australia
Windau *see* Ventspils, Latvia
Windau *see* Venta, Latvia/Lithuania
18 D15 **Windber** Pennsylvania, NE USA
23 T3 **Winder** Georgia, SE USA
97 K15 **Windermere** NW England, UK
14 C7 **Windermere Lake** ◎ Ontario, S Canada
31 U11 **Windham** Ohio, N USA
83 D19 **Windhoek** *Ger.* Windhuk. ● (Namibia) Khomas, C Namibia
83 D20 **Windhoek** × Khomas, C Namibia
Windhuk *see* Windhoek
15 O8 **Windigo** Québec, SE Canada
15 O8 **Windigo** ≈ Québec, SE Canada
Windischfeistritz *see* Slovenska Bistrica
109 T6 **Windischgarsten** Oberösterreich, W Austria
Windischgraz *see* Slovenj Gradec
37 T16 **Wind Mountain** ▲ New Mexico, SW USA
29 T10 **Windom** Minnesota, N USA
37 Q7 **Windom Peak** ▲ Colorado, C USA
181 U9 **Windorah** Queensland, C Australia
37 O10 **Window Rock** Arizona, SW USA
31 N9 **Wind Point** *headland* Wisconsin, N USA
33 U14 **Wind River** ≈ Wyoming, C USA
13 P15 **Windsor** Nova Scotia, SE Canada
14 C17 **Windsor** Ontario, S Canada
15 Q12 **Windsor** Québec, SE Canada
97 N22 **Windsor** S England, UK
37 T3 **Windsor** Colorado, C USA
18 M12 **Windsor** Connecticut, NE USA
27 T5 **Windsor** Missouri, C USA
21 X9 **Windsor** North Carolina, SE USA
18 M12 **Windsor Locks** Connecticut, NE USA
25 R5 **Windthorst** Texas, SW USA
45 Z14 **Windward Islands** *island group* E West Indies
Windward Islands *see* Vent, Îles du, Archipel de la Société, French Polynesia
Windward Islands *see* Barlavento, Ilhas de, Cape Verde
44 K8 **Windward Passage** *Sp.* Paso de los Vientos. *channel* Cuba/Haiti
55 T9 **Wineperu** C Guyana
23 O3 **Winfield** Alabama, S USA
29 Y15 **Winfield** Iowa, C USA
27 O7 **Winfield** Kansas, C USA
25 W6 **Winfield** Texas, SW USA
21 Q4 **Winfield** West Virginia, NE USA
29 N5 **Wing** North Dakota, N USA
183 U7 **Wingham** New South Wales, SE Australia
12 G16 **Wingham** Ontario, S Canada
33 T8 **Winifred** Montana, NW USA
12 E8 **Winisk** ≈ Ontario, S Canada
12 E9 **Winisk Lake** ◎ Ontario, C Canada
24 L8 **Wink** Texas, SW USA
36 M14 **Winkelman** Arizona, SW USA
11 X17 **Winkler** Manitoba, S Canada
109 Q9 **Winklern** Tirol, W Austria
Winkowitz *see* Vinkovci
32 G9 **Winlock** Washington, NW USA
77 P17 **Winneba** SE Ghana
29 U11 **Winnebago** Minnesota, N USA
29 R13 **Winnebago** Nebraska, C USA
30 M7 **Winnebago, Lake** ◎ Wisconsin, N USA
30 M7 **Winneconne** Wisconsin, N USA
35 T3 **Winnemucca** Nevada, W USA
35 R4 **Winnemucca Lake** ◎ Nevada, W USA
101 H21 **Winnenden** Baden-Württemberg, SW Germany
29 N11 **Winner** South Dakota, N USA
33 U9 **Winnett** Montana, NW USA
14 I9 **Winneway** Québec, SE Canada
22 H6 **Winnfield** Louisiana, S USA
29 U4 **Winnibigoshish, Lake** ◎ Minnesota, N USA
25 X11 **Winnie** Texas, SW USA
11 Y16 **Winnipeg** Manitoba, S Canada
11 X16 **Winnipeg** × Manitoba, S Canada
11 X16 **Winnipeg Beach** Manitoba, S Canada
11 W14 **Winnipeg, Lake** ◎ Manitoba, C Canada
11 W15 **Winnipegosis** Manitoba, S Canada
11 W15 **Winnipegosis, Lake** ◎ Manitoba, C Canada
19 O8 **Winnipesaukee, Lake** ◎ New Hampshire, NE USA
22 I6 **Winnsboro** Louisiana, S USA
21 R12 **Winnsboro** South Carolina, SE USA
25 W6 **Winnsboro** Texas, SW USA
29 X10 **Winona** Minnesota, N USA
22 L4 **Winona** Mississippi, S USA
27 W7 **Winona** Missouri, C USA
25 W6 **Winona** Texas, SW USA
18 M7 **Winooski River** ≈ Vermont, NE USA
98 P6 **Winschoten** Groningen, NE Netherlands
100 J10 **Winsen** Niedersachsen, N Germany
36 M11 **Winslow** Arizona, SW USA
19 Q7 **Winslow** Maine, NE USA
18 M12 **Winsted** Connecticut, NE USA
32 F14 **Winston** Oregon, NW USA
21 S9 **Winston Salem** North Carolina, SE USA
98 N5 **Winsum** Groningen, NE Netherlands
Wintanceaster *see* Winchester
23 W11 **Winter Garden** Florida, SE USA
10 J16 **Winter Harbour** Vancouver Island, British Columbia, SW Canada
23 W12 **Winter Haven** Florida, SE USA
23 X11 **Winter Park** Florida, SE USA
25 P8 **Winters** Texas, SW USA
29 U15 **Winterset** Iowa, C USA
98 O12 **Winterswijk** Gelderland, E Netherlands
108 G6 **Winterthur** Zürich, NE Switzerland
29 U9 **Winthrop** Minnesota, N USA
32 J7 **Winthrop** Washington, NW USA
181 V7 **Winton** Queensland, E Australia
185 C24 **Winton** Southland, South Island, NZ
21 X8 **Winton** North Carolina, SE USA
101 K15 **Wipper** ≈ C Germany
101 K14 **Wipper** ≈ C Germany
Wipper *see* Wieprza
182 G6 **Wirraminna** South Australia
182 F4 **Wirrida** South Australia
182 F7 **Wirrulla** South Australia
Wirsitz *see* Wyrzysk
Wirz-See *see* Võrtsjärv
97 O19 **Wisbech** E England, UK
Wisby *see* Visby
19 Q8 **Wiscasset** Maine, NE USA
Wischau *see* Vyškov
30 J5 **Wisconsin** *off.* State of Wisconsin; *also known as* The Badger State. ◈ *state* N USA
30 L8 **Wisconsin Dells** Wisconsin, N USA
30 L8 **Wisconsin, Lake** ⊞ Wisconsin, N USA
30 L7 **Wisconsin Rapids** Wisconsin, N USA
30 L7 **Wisconsin River** ≈ Wisconsin, N USA
33 P11 **Wisdom** Montana, NW USA
21 P7 **Wise** Virginia, NE USA
39 Q7 **Wiseman** Alaska, USA
96 J12 **Wishaw** W Scotland, UK
29 O6 **Wishek** North Dakota, N USA
32 I11 **Wishram** Washington, NW USA
111 J17 **Wisła** Śląskie, S Poland
110 K11 **Wisła** *Eng.* Vistula, *Ger.* Weichsel. ≈ C Poland
Wiślany, Zalew *see* Vistula Lagoon
111 M16 **Wisłoka** ≈ SE Poland
100 L9 **Wismar** Mecklenburg-Vorpommern, N Germany
29 R14 **Wisner** Nebraska, C USA
103 V4 **Wissembourg** *var.* Weissenburg. Bas-Rhin, NE France
30 J6 **Wissota, Lake** ⊞ Wisconsin, N USA
97 O18 **Witham** ≈ E England, UK
97 O17 **Withernsea** E England, UK
37 Q13 **Withington, Mount** ▲ New Mexico, SW USA
23 U8 **Withlacoochee River** ≈ Florida/Georgia, SE USA
110 H11 **Witkowo** Wielkopolskie, C Poland
97 M21 **Witney** S England, UK
101 E15 **Witten** Nordrhein-Westfalen, W Germany
101 N14 **Wittenberg** Sachsen-Anhalt, E Germany
30 L6 **Wittenberg** Wisconsin, N USA
100 L11 **Wittenberge** Brandenburg, N Germany
103 U7 **Wittenheim** Haut-Rhin, NE France
180 I7 **Wittenoom** Western Australia
Wittingau *see* Třeboň
100 K12 **Wittingen** Niedersachsen, C Germany
101 E18 **Wittlich** Rheinland-Pfalz, SW Germany
100 F9 **Wittmund** Niedersachsen, NW Germany
100 M10 **Wittstock** Brandenburg, NE Germany
186 F6 **Witu Islands** *island group* E PNG
110 O7 **Wiżajny** Podlaskie, NE Poland
55 W10 **W.J. van Blommesteinmeer** ⊞ E Surinam
110 L11 **Wkra** *Ger.* Soldau. ≈ C Poland
110 I6 **Władysławowo** Pomorskie, N Poland
Wlaschim *see* Vlašim
111 E14 **Wleń** *Ger.* Lähn. Dolnośląskie, SW Poland
110 J11 **Włocławek** *Ger./Rus.* Vlotslavsk. Kujawsko-pomorskie, C Poland
110 P13 **Włodawa** *Rus.* Vlodava. Lubelskie, SE Poland
Włodzimierz *see* Volodymyr-Volyns'kyy
111 K15 **Włoszczowa** Świętokrzyskie, C Poland
83 C19 **Wlotzkasbaken** Erongo, W Namibia
15 R12 **Woburn** Québec, SE Canada
19 O11 **Woburn** Massachusetts, NE USA
Wocheiner Feistritz *see* Bohinjska Bistrica
Wöchma *see* Võhma
147 S11 **Wodil** *var.* Vuadil'. Farg'ona Viloyati, E Uzbekistan
181 V14 **Wodonga** Victoria, SE Australia
111 I17 **Wodzisław Śląski** *Ger.* Loslau. Śląskie, S Poland
98 I11 **Woerden** Zuid-Holland, C Netherlands
98 I8 **Wognum** Noord-Holland, NW Netherlands
Wohlau *see* Wołów
108 F7 **Wohlen** Aargau, NW Switzerland
195 R2 **Wohlthat Mountains** ⛰ Antarctica
Wojerecy *see* Hoyerswerda
Wōjjā *see* Wotje Atoll
Wojwodina *see* Vojvodina
171 V15 **Wokam, Pulau** *island* Kepulauan Aru, E Indonesia
97 N22 **Woking** SE England, UK
Woldenberg Neumark *see* Dobiegniew
188 K15 **Woleai Atoll** *atoll* Caroline Islands, W Micronesia
Woleu *see* Uolo, Río
79 E17 **Woleu-Ntem** *off.* Province du Woleu-Ntem, *var.* Le Woleu-Ntem. ◈ *province* W Gabon
32 F15 **Wolf Creek** Oregon, NW USA
26 K9 **Wolf Creek** ≈ Oklahoma/Texas, SW USA
37 R7 **Wolf Creek Pass** *pass* Colorado, C USA
19 O9 **Wolfeboro** New Hampshire, NE USA
25 U5 **Wolfe City** Texas, SW USA
14 L15 **Wolfe Island** *island* Ontario, SE Canada
101 M14 **Wolfen** Sachsen-Anhalt, E Germany
100 J13 **Wolfenbüttel** Niedersachsen, C Germany
109 T4 **Wolfern** Oberösterreich, N Austria
109 Q6 **Wolfgangsee** *var.* Abersee, St Wolfgangsee. ◎ N Austria
39 P9 **Wolf Mountain** ▲ Alaska, USA
33 X7 **Wolf Point** Montana, NW USA
22 L8 **Wolf River** ≈ Mississippi, S USA
30 M7 **Wolf River** ≈ Wisconsin, N USA
109 U9 **Wolfsberg** Kärnten, SE Austria
100 K12 **Wolfsburg** Niedersachsen, N Germany
57 B17 **Wolf, Volcán** ※ Galapagos Islands, Ecuador, E Pacific Ocean
100 O8 **Wolgast** Mecklenburg-Vorpommern, NE Germany
108 F8 **Wolhusen** Luzern, W Switzerland
110 D8 **Wolin** *Ger.* Wollin. Zachodnio-pomorskie, NW Poland
109 Y3 **Wolkersdorf** Niederösterreich, NE Austria
Wołkowysk *see* Vawkavysk
Wöllan *see* Velenje
8 J6 **Wollaston, Cape** *headland* Victoria Island, Northwest Territories, NW Canada
63 J25 **Wollaston, Isla** *island* S Chile
11 U11 **Wollaston Lake** Saskatchewan, C Canada
11 T10 **Wollaston Lake** ◎ Saskatchewan, C Canada
8 J6 **Wollaston Peninsula** *peninsula* Victoria Island, Northwest Territories/Nunavut, NW Canada
Wollin *see* Wolin
183 S9 **Wollongong** New South Wales, SE Australia
Wolmar *see* Valmiera
100 L13 **Wolmirstedt** Sachsen-Anhalt, C Germany
110 M11 **Wołomin** Mazowieckie, C Poland
110 G3 **Wołów** *Ger.* Wohlau. Dolnośląskie, SW Poland
Wołożyn *see* Valozhyn
14 G11 **Wolseley Bay** Ontario, S Canada
29 P10 **Wolsey** South Dakota, N USA
110 F12 **Wolsztyn** Wielkopolskie, W Poland
98 M7 **Wolvega** *Fris.* Wolvegea. Friesland, N Netherlands
Wolvegea *see* Wolvega
97 K19 **Wolverhampton** C England, UK
Wolverine State *see* Michigan
99 G18 **Wolvertem** Vlaams Brabant, C Belgium
99 H16 **Wommelgem** Antwerpen, N Belgium
186 D7 **Wonenara** *var.* Wonerara. Eastern Highlands, C PNG
Wonerara *see* Wonenara
Wongalara Lake *see* Wongalarroo Lake
183 N6 **Wongalarroo Lake** *var.* Wongalara Lake. *seasonal lake* New South Wales, SE Australia
163 Y15 **Wŏnju** *Jap.* Genshū. N South Korea
10 M12 **Wonowon** British Columbia, W Canada
163 X13 **Wŏnsan** SE North Korea
183 O13 **Wonthaggi** Victoria, SE Australia
23 N2 **Woodall Mountain** ▲ Mississippi, S USA
23 W7 **Woodbine** Georgia, SE USA
29 S14 **Woodbine** Iowa, C USA
18 J17 **Woodbine** New Jersey, NE USA
21 W4 **Woodbridge** Virginia, NE USA
183 V4 **Woodburn** New South Wales, SE Australia
32 G11 **Woodburn** Oregon, NW USA
20 K9 **Woodbury** Tennessee, S USA
183 V5 **Wooded Bluff** *headland* New South Wales, SE Australia
183 V3 **Woodenbong** New South Wales, SE Australia
35 R11 **Woodlake** California, W USA
35 N7 **Woodland** California, W USA
19 T5 **Woodland** Maine, NE USA

◆ COUNTRY ◇ DEPENDENT TERRITORY ◈ ADMINISTRATIVE REGION ▲ MOUNTAIN ※ VOLCANO ◎ LAKE
● COUNTRY CAPITAL ○ DEPENDENT TERRITORY CAPITAL × INTERNATIONAL AIRPORT ⛰ MOUNTAIN RANGE ≈ RIVER ⊞ RESERVOIR

32 G10 **Woodland** Washington, NW USA
37 T5 **Woodland Park** Colorado, C USA
186 I9 **Woodlark Island** *var.* Murua Island. *island* SE PNG
Woodle Island *see* Kuria
11 T17 **Wood Mountain** ⛰ Saskatchewan, S Canada
30 K15 **Wood River** Illinois, N USA
29 P16 **Wood River** Nebraska, C USA
39 R9 **Wood River** ≈ Alaska, USA
39 O13 **Wood River Lakes** *lakes* Alaska, USA
182 C1 **Woodroffe, Mount** ▲ South Australia
21 P11 **Woodruff** South Carolina, SE USA
30 K4 **Woodruff** Wisconsin, N USA
25 T14 **Woodsboro** Texas, SW USA
31 U13 **Woodsfield** Ohio, N USA
181 P4 **Woods, Lake** ◎ Northern Territory, N Australia
11 Z16 **Woods, Lake of the** *Fr.* Lac des Bois. ◎ Canada/USA
25 Q6 **Woodson** Texas, SW USA
13 N14 **Woodstock** New Brunswick, SE Canada
14 F16 **Woodstock** Ontario, S Canada
30 M10 **Woodstock** Illinois, N USA
18 M9 **Woodstock** Vermont, NE USA
21 U4 **Woodstock** Virginia, NE USA
19 N8 **Woodsville** New Hampshire, NE USA
184 M12 **Woodville** Manawatu-Wanganui, North Island, NZ
22 J7 **Woodville** Mississippi, S USA
25 X9 **Woodville** Texas, SW USA
26 K9 **Woodward** Oklahoma, C USA
29 O5 **Woodworth** North Dakota, N USA
171 W12 **Wool** Papua, E Indonesia
183 V5 **Woolgoolga** New South Wales, E Australia
182 H6 **Woomera** South Australia
19 O12 **Woonsocket** Rhode Island, NE USA
29 P10 **Woonsocket** South Dakota, N USA
31 T12 **Wooster** Ohio, N USA
80 L12 **Woqooyi Galbeed** *off.* Gobolka Woqooyi Galbeed. ◈ *region* NW Somalia
108 E8 **Worb** Bern, C Switzerland
83 F26 **Worcester** Western Cape, SW South Africa
97 L20 **Worcester** *hist.* Wigorna Ceaster. W England, UK
19 N11 **Worcester** Massachusetts, NE USA
97 L20 **Worcestershire** *cultural region* C England, UK
32 H16 **Worden** Oregon, NW USA
109 O6 **Wörgl** Tirol, W Austria
171 V15 **Workai, Pulau** *island* Kepulauan Aru, E Indonesia
97 J15 **Workington** NW England, UK
98 K7 **Workum** Friesland, N Netherlands
33 V13 **Worland** Wyoming, C USA
Wormatia *see* Worms
99 N25 **Wormeldange** Grevenmacher, E Luxembourg
98 I9 **Wormer** Noord-Holland, C Netherlands
101 G19 **Worms** *anc.* Augusta Vangionum, Borbetomagus, Wormatia. Rheinland-Pfalz, SW Germany
Worms *see* Vormsi
101 K21 **Wörnitz** ≈ S Germany
101 G21 **Wörth am Rhein** Rheinland-Pfalz, SW Germany
25 U8 **Wortham** Texas, SW USA
109 S9 **Worther See** ◎ S Austria
97 O23 **Worthing** SE England, UK
29 S11 **Worthington** Minnesota, N USA
31 S13 **Worthington** Ohio, N USA
35 W8 **Worthington Peak** ▲ Nevada, W USA
171 Y13 **Wosi** Papua, E Indonesia
171 V13 **Wosimi** Papua, E Indonesia
189 R5 **Wotho Atoll** *var.* Wōtto. *atoll* Ralik Chain, W Marshall Islands
189 V5 **Wotje Atoll** *var.* Wōjjā. *atoll* Ratak Chain, E Marshall Islands
Wotoe *see* Wotu
Wottawa *see* Otava
Wōtto *see* Wotho Atoll
171 O13 **Wotu** *prev.* Wotoe. Sulawesi, C Indonesia
98 K11 **Woudenberg** Utrecht, C Netherlands
98 I13 **Woudrichem** Noord-Brabant, S Netherlands
43 N8 **Wounta** *var.* Huaunta. Región Autónoma Atlántico Norte, NE Nicaragua
171 P14 **Wowoni, Pulau** *island* C Indonesia
81 J17 **Woyamdero Plain** *plain* E Kenya
Woyens *see* Vojens
Wozrojdeniye Oroli *see* Vozrozhdeniya, Ostrov
Wrangel Island *see* Vrangelya, Ostrov
39 Y13 **Wrangell** Wrangell Island, Alaska, USA
38 C15 **Wrangell, Cape** *headland* Attu Island, Alaska, USA
39 S11 **Wrangell, Mount** ▲ Alaska, USA
39 T11 **Wrangell Mountains** ⛰ Alaska, USA
197 S7 **Wrangel Plain** *undersea feature* Arctic Ocean
96 H6 **Wrath, Cape** *headland* N Scotland, UK
37 W3 **Wray** Colorado, C USA
44 K13 **Wreck Point** *headland* C Jamaica
83 C23 **Wreck Point** *headland* W South Africa
23 V4 **Wrens** Georgia, SE USA
97 K18 **Wrexham** NE Wales, UK
27 R13 **Wright City** Oklahoma, C USA
194 J12 **Wright Island** *island* Antarctica
13 N9 **Wright, Mont** ▲ Québec, E Canada
25 X5 **Wright Patman Lake** ⊟ Texas, SW USA
36 M16 **Wrightson, Mount** ▲ Arizona, SW USA
23 U5 **Wrightsville** Georgia, SE USA
21 W12 **Wrightsville Beach** North Carolina, SE USA
35 T15 **Wrightwood** California, W USA
8 H9 **Wrigley** Northwest Territories, W Canada
111 G14 **Wrocław** *Eng./Ger.* Breslau. Dolnośląskie, SW Poland
110 F10 **Wronki** *Ger.* Fronicken. Wielkopolskie, NW Poland
110 H11 **Września** Wielkolpolskie, C Poland
110 F12 **Wschowa** Lubuskie, W Poland
Wsetin *see* Vsetín
161 O5 **Wu'an** Hebei, E China
180 I12 **Wubin** Western Australia
163 W9 **Wuchang** Heilongjiang, NE China
Wuchang *see* Wuhan
Wu-chou/Wuchow *see* Wuzhou
160 M16 **Wuchuan** *var.* Meilu. Guangdong, S China
160 K10 **Wuchuan** *var.* Duru, Gelaozu Miaozu Zizhixian. Guizhou, S China
163 O13 **Wuchuan** Nei Mongol Zizhiqu, N China
163 V6 **Wudalianchi** Heilongjiang, NE China
163 V6 **Wudalianchi** *prev.* Dedu, Qingshan. Heilongjiang, NE China
159 O11 **Wudaoliang** Qinghai, C China
141 Q13 **Wuday'ah** *spring/well* S Saudi Arabia
77 V13 **Wudil** Kano, N Nigeria
160 G12 **Wuding** *var.* Jincheng. Yunnan, SW China
182 G8 **Wudinna** South Australia
157 P10 **Wudu** Gansu, C China
160 L9 **Wufeng** Hubei, C China
161 O11 **Wugong Shan** ⛰ S China
157 P7 **Wuhai** *var.* Haibowan. Nei Mongol Zizhiqu, N China
161 O9 **Wuhan** *var.* Han-kou, Han-k'ou, Hanyang, Wuchang, Wu-han; *prev.* Hankow. Hubei, C China
161 Q7 **Wuhe** Anhui, E China
Wuhsi/Wu-hsi *see* Wuxi
Wuhsien *see* Suzhou
161 Q8 **Wuhu** *var.* Wu-na-mu. Anhui, E China
Wūjae *see* Ujae Atoll
160 K11 **Wu Jiang** ≈ C China
Wūjlān *see* Ujelang Atoll
77 W15 **Wukari** Taraba, E Nigeria
160 H11 **Wulian Feng** ⛰ SW China
160 F13 **Wuliang Shan** ⛰ SW China
160 K11 **Wuling Shan** ⛰ S China
109 Y5 **Wulka** ≈ E Austria
Wulkan *see* Vulcan
109 T3 **Wullowitz** Oberösterreich, N Austria
Wu-lu-k'o-mu-shi/ Wu-lu-mu-ch'i *see* Ürümqi
79 D14 **Wum** Nord-Ouest, NE Cameroon
160 H12 **Wumeng Shan** ⛰ SW China
160 K14 **Wuming** Guangxi Zhuangzu Zizhiqu, S China
100 I10 **Wümme** ≈ NW Germany
Wu-na-mu *see* Wuhu
171 X13 **Wunen** Papua, E Indonesia
12 D9 **Wunnummin Lake** ◎ Ontario, C Canada
80 D13 **Wun Rog** Warab, S Sudan
101 M18 **Wunsiedel** Bayern, E Germany
100 I12 **Wunstorf** Niedersachsen, NW Germany
166 M3 **Wuntho** Sagaing, N Burma
101 F15 **Wupper** ≈ W Germany
101 E15 **Wuppertal** *prev.* Barmen-Elberfeld. Nordrhein-Westfalen, W Germany
160 K5 **Wuqi** Shaanxi, C China
161 P4 **Wuqiao** *var.* Sangyuan. Hebei, E China
101 L23 **Würm** ≈ SE Germany
77 T12 **Wurno** Sokoto, NW Nigeria
101 I19 **Würzburg** Bayern, SW Germany
101 N15 **Wurzen** Sachsen, E Germany
160 L9 **Wu Shan** ⛰ C China
158 G7 **Wushi** *var.* Uqturpan. Xinjiang Uygur Zizhiqu, NW China
Wusih *see* Wuxi
65 N18 **Wüst Seamount** *undersea feature* S Atlantic Ocean
Wusuli Jiang/Wusuri *see* Ussuri
161 N3 **Wutai Shan** *var.* Beitai Ding. ▲ C China
160 H10 **Wutongqiao** Sichuan, C China
159 P6 **Wutongwozi Quan** *spring* NW China
99 H15 **Wuustwezel** Antwerpen, N Belgium
186 B4 **Wuvulu Island** *island* NW PNG
159 U9 **Wuwei** *var.* Liangzhou. Gansu, C China
161 R8 **Wuxi** *var.* Wuhsi, Wu-hsi, Wusih. Jiangsu, E China
Wuxing *see* Huzhou
160 L14 **Wuxuan** Guangxi Zhuangzu Zizhiqu, S China
Wuyang *see* Zhenyuan
160 K11 **Wuyang He** ≈ S China
163 X6 **Wuyiling** Heilongjiang, NE China
157 T12 **Wuyi Shan** ⛰ SE China
161 Q11 **Wuyishan** *prev.* Chong'an. Fujian, SE China
162 M13 **Wuyuan** Nei Mongol Zizhiqu, N China
160 L17 **Wuzhi Shan** ▲ S China
160 L17 **Wuzhishan** *prev.* Tongshi. Hainan, S China
159 W8 **Wuzhong** Ningxia, N China
160 M14 **Wuzhou** *var.* Wu-chou, Wuchow. Guangxi Zhuangzu Zizhiqu, S China
18 H12 **Wyalusing** Pennsylvania, NE USA
182 M10 **Wycheproof** Victoria, SE Australia
97 K21 **Wye** *Wel.* Gwy. ≈ England/Wales, UK
Wyłkowyszki *see* Vilkaviškis
97 P19 **Wymondham** E England, UK
29 R17 **Wymore** Nebraska, C USA
182 E5 **Wynbring** South Australia
181 N3 **Wyndham** Western Australia
29 R6 **Wyndmere** North Dakota, N USA
27 X11 **Wynne** Arkansas, C USA
27 N12 **Wynnewood** Oklahoma, C USA
183 O15 **Wynyard** Tasmania, SE Australia
11 U15 **Wynyard** Saskatchewan, S Canada
33 V11 **Wyola** Montana, NW USA
182 A4 **Wyola Lake** *salt lake* South Australia
31 P9 **Wyoming** Michigan, N USA
33 V14 **Wyoming** *off.* State of Wyoming, also known as The Equality State. ◈ *state* C USA
33 S15 **Wyoming Range** ⛰ Wyoming, C USA
183 T8 **Wyong** New South Wales, SE Australia
110 G9 **Wyrzysk** *Ger.* Wirsitz. Wielkopolskie, C Poland
Wysg *see* Usk
110 O10 **Wysokie Mazowieckie** Łomża, E Poland
110 M11 **Wyszków** *Ger.* Probstberg. Mazowieckie, C Poland
110 L11 **Wyszogród** Mazowieckie, C Poland
21 R7 **Wytheville** Virginia, NE USA

X

80 Q12 **Xaafuun** *It.* Hafun. Bari, NE Somalia
80 Q12 **Xaafuun, Raas** *var.* Ras Hafun. *headland* NE Somalia
Xàbia *see* Jávea
42 C4 **Xacbal, Río** *var.* Xalbal. ≈ Guatemala/Mexico
137 Y10 **Xaçmaz** *Rus.* Khachmas. N Azerbaijan
80 O12 **Xadeed** *var.* Haded. *physical region* N Somalia
159 O14 **Xagquka** Xizang Zizhiqu, W China
167 Q6 **Xai** *var.* Muang Xay, Muong Sai. Oudômxai, N Laos
158 F10 **Xaidulla** Xinjiang Uygur Zizhiqu, W China
167 Q7 **Xaignabouli** *prev.* Muang Xaignabouri, *Fr.* Sayaboury. Xaignabouli, N Laos
167 R7 **Xai Lai Leng, Phou** ▲ Laos/Vietnam
158 L15 **Xainza** Xizang Zizhiqu, W China
158 L16 **Xaitongmoin** Xizang Zizhiqu, W China
83 M20 **Xai-Xai** *prev.* João Belo, Vila de João *Bel.* Gaza, S Mozambique
Xalbal *see* Xacbal, Río
80 P13 **Xalin** Nugaal, N Somalia
146 H7 **Xalqobod** *Rus.* Khalkabad. Qoraqalpog'iston Respublikasi, W Uzbekistan
167 R6 **Xam Nua** *var.* Sam Neua. Houaphan, N Laos
82 D11 **Xá-Muteba** *Port.* Cinco de Outubro. Lunda Norte, NE Angola
Xangda *see* Nangqên
83 C16 **Xangongo** *Port.* Rocadas. Cunene, SW Angola
137 W12 **Xankändi** *Rus.* Khankendi; *prev.* Stepanakert. SW Azerbaijan
137 V11 **Xanlar** *Rus.* Khanlar. NW Azerbaijan
114 J13 **Xánthi** Anatolikí Makedonía kai Thráki, NE Greece
60 H13 **Xanxerê** Santa Catarina, S Brazil
81 O15 **Xarardheere** Mudug, E Somalia
137 Z11 **Xärä Zirä Adası** *Rus.* Ostrov Bulla. *island* E Azerbaijan
162 K13 **Xar Burd** *prev.* Bayan Nuru. Nei Mongol Zizhiqu, N China
163 T11 **Xar Moron** ≈ NE China
Xarra *see* Xarrë
113 L23 **Xarrë** *var.* Xarra. Vlorë, S Albania
82 D12 **Xassengue** Lunda Sul, NW Angola
105 S11 **Xátiva** *var.* Jativa; *anc.* Setabis. País Valenciano, E Spain
Xauen *see* Chefchaouen
60 K10 **Xavantes, Represa de** *var.* Represa de Chavantes. ⊟ S Brazil
158 I7 **Xayar** Xinjiang Uygur Zizhiqu, W China
Xäzär Dänizi *see* Caspian Sea
167 S8 **Xé Bangfai** ≈ C Laos
167 T9 **Xé Banghiang** *var.* Bang Hieng. ≈ S Laos
Xêgar *see* Tingri
31 R14 **Xenia** Ohio, N USA
Xeres *see* Jeréz de la Frontera
115 E15 **Xeriás** ≈ C Greece
115 G17 **Xeró** ▲ Évvoia, C Greece
83 H18 **Xhumo** Central, C Botswana
161 N15 **Xiachuan Dao** *island* S China
Xiacun *see* Rushan
Xiaguan *see* Dali
159 U11 **Xiahe** *var.* Labrang. Gansu, C China
161 Q13 **Xiamen** *var.* Hsia-men; *prev.* Amoy. Fujian, SE China
160 L6 **Xi'an** *var.* Changan, Sian, Signan, Siking, Singan, Xian. Shaanxi, C China
160 L10 **Xianfeng** *var.* Gaoleshan. Hubei, C China
Xiang *see* Hunan
161 N7 **Xiangcheng** Henan, C China
160 F10 **Xiangcheng** *var.* Sampê, *Tib.* Qagcheng. Sichuan, C China
160 M8 **Xiangfan** *var.* Xiangyang. Hubei, C China
161 N10 **Xiang Jiang** ≈ S China
Xiangkhoang *see* Pèk
167 Q7 **Xiangkhoang, Plateau de** *var.* Plain of Jars. *plateau* N Laos
161 N11 **Xiangtan** *var.* Hsiang-t'an, Siangtan. Hunan, S China
161 N11 **Xiangxiang** Hunan, S China
Xiangyang *see* Xiangfan
161 S10 **Xianju** Zhejiang, SE China
Xianshui *see* Dawu
160 F8 **Xianshui He** ≈ C China
161 N9 **Xiantao** *var.* Mianyang. Hubei, C China
161 R10 **Xianxia Ling** ⛰ SE China
160 K6 **Xianyang** Shaanxi, C China
158 L5 **Xiaocaohu** Xinjiang Uygur Zizhiqu, W China
161 O9 **Xiaogan** Hubei, C China
Xiaogang *see* Dongxiang
163 W6 **Xiao Hinggan Ling** *Eng.* Lesser Khingan Range. ⛰ NE China
160 M6 **Xiao Shan** ⛰ C China
160 M12 **Xiao Shui** ≈ S China
Xiaoxi *see* Pinghe
161 P6 **Xiaoxian** *var.* Longcheng, Xiao Xian. Anhui, E China
160 G11 **Xichang** Sichuan, C China
41 P11 **Xicoténcatl** Tamaulipas, C Mexico
Xieng Khouang *see* Pèk
Xieng Ngeun *see* Muong Xiang Ngeun
160 J11 **Xifeng** *var.* Yongjing. Guizhou, S China
Xifeng *see* Qingyang
Xigang *see* Helan
158 L16 **Xigazê** *var.* Jih-k'a-tse, Shigatse, Xigaze. Xizang Zizhiqu, W China
160 I8 **Xi He** ≈ C China
159 W11 **Xihe** *var.* Hanyuan. Gansu, C China
Xihuachi *see* Heshui
159 W10 **Xiji** Ningxia, N China
160 M14 **Xi Jiang** *var.* Hsi Chiang, *Eng.* West River. ≈ S China
159 Q7 **Xijian Quan** *spring* NW China
160 K15 **Xijin Shuiku** ⊟ S China
Xilaganí *see* Xylaganí
Xiligou *see* Ulan
160 I13 **Xilin** *var.* Bada. Guangxi Zhuangzu Zizhiqu, S China
163 Q10 **Xilinhot** *var.* Silinhot. Nei Mongol Zizhiqu, N China
Xilinji *see* Mohe
Xilokastro *see* Xylókastro
Xin *see* Xinjiang Uygur Zizhiqu
161 R10 **Xin'anjiang Shuiku** ⊟ SE China
Xin'anzhen *see* Xinyi
Xin Barag Youqi *see* Altan Emel
Xin Barag Zuoqi *see* Amgalang
163 W12 **Xinbin** *var.* Xinbin Manzu Zizhixian. Liaoning, NE China
Xinbin Manzu Zizhixian *see* Xinbin
161 O7 **Xincai** Henan, C China
Xincheng *see* Zhaojue
Xindu *see* Luhuo
161 O13 **Xinfeng** *var.* Jiading. Jiangxi, S China
161 O14 **Xinfengjiang Shuiku** ⊟ S China
Xingba *see* Lhünzê
163 T13 **Xingcheng** Liaoning, NE China
82 E11 **Xinge** Lunda Norte, NE Angola
161 P12 **Xingguo** *var.* Lianjiang. Jiangxi, S China
159 S11 **Xinghai** *var.* Ziketan. Qinghai, C China
161 R7 **Xinghua** Jiangsu, E China
Xingkai Hu *see* Khanka, Lake
161 P13 **Xingning** Guangdong, S China
160 I13 **Xingren** Guizhou, S China
161 O4 **Xingtai** Hebei, E China
59 J14 **Xingu, Rio** ≈ C Brazil
159 P6 **Xingxingxia** Xinjiang Uygur Zizhiqu, NW China
160 I13 **Xingyi** Guizhou, S China
158 I6 **Xinhe** *var.* Toksu. Xinjiang Uygur Zizhiqu, NW China
161 Q10 **Xin Hot** *var.* Abag Qi. Nei Mongol Zizhiqu, N China
Xinhua *see* Funing
163 T12 **Xinhui** *var.* Aohan Qi. Nei Mongol Zizhiqu, N China
159 T10 **Xining** *var.* Hsining, Hsi-ning, Sining. *province capital* Qinghai, C China
161 O4 **Xinji** *prev.* Shulu. Hebei, E China
161 P10 **Xinjiang** Jiangxi, S China
Xinjiang *see* Xinjiang Uygur Zizhiqu
162 D8 **Xinjiang Uygur Zizhiqu** *var.* Sinkiang, Sinkiang Uighur Autonomous Region, Xin, Xinjiang. ◈ *autonomous region* NW China
160 H9 **Xinjin** *var.* Meixing, *Tib.* Zainlha. Sichuan, C China
Xinjin *see* Pulandian
Xinjing *see* Jingxi
163 U12 **Xinmin** Liaoning, NE China
160 M12 **Xinning** *var.* Jinshi. Hunan, S China
Xinpu *see* Lianyungang
Xinshan *see* Anyuan
161 P5 **Xintai** Shandong, E China
Xinwen *see* Suncun
Xin Xian *see* Xinzhou
161 N6 **Xinxiang** Henan, C China
161 O8 **Xinyang** *var.* Hsin-yang, Sinyang. Henan, C China
161 Q6 **Xinyi** *var.* Xin'anzhen. Jiangsu, E China
161 Q6 **Xinyi He** ≈ E China
161 O11 **Xinyu** Jiangxi, S China
158 I5 **Xinyuan** *var.* Künes. Xinjiang Uygur Zizhiqu, NW China
Xinyuan *see* Tianjun
161 N3 **Xinzhou** *var.* Xin Xian. Shanxi, C China
Xinzhou *see* Longlin
104 H4 **Xinzo de Limia** Galicia, NW Spain
Xions *see* Książ Wielkopolski
161 O7 **Xiping** Henan, C China
Xiping *see* Songyang
159 T11 **Xiqing Shan** ⛰ C China
59 N16 **Xique-Xique** Bahia, E Brazil
Xireg *see* Ulan
115 E14 **Xirovoúni** ▲ N Greece
162 M13 **Xishanzui** *var.* Urad Qianqi. Nei Mongol Zizhiqu, N China
160 J11 **Xishui** Guizhou, S China
Xi Ujimqin Qi *see* Bayan Ul
160 K11 **Xiushan** *var.* Zhonghe. Chongqing Shi, C China
Xiushan *see* Tonghai
161 O10 **Xiu Shui** ≈ S China
146 H9 **Xiva** *Rus.* Khiva. Xorazm Viloyati, W Uzbekistan
158 J16 **Xixabangma Feng** ▲ W China
160 M7 **Xixia** Henan, C China
Xixón *see* Gijón
Xixona *see* Jijona
Xizang *see* Xizang Zizhiqu
Xizang Gaoyuan *see* Qingzang Gaoyuan
160 E9 **Xizang Zizhiqu** *var.* Thibet, Tibetan Autonomous Region, Xizang, *Eng.* Tibet. ◈ *autonomous region* W China
163 U14 **Xizhong Dao** *island* N China
Xoi *see* Qüxü
146 H8 **Xo'jayli** *Rus.* Khodzheyli. Qoraqalpog'iston Respublikasi, W Uzbekistan
Xolotlán *see* Managua, Lago de
146 I9 **Xonqa** *Rus.* Khanka. Xorazm Viloyati, W Uzbekistan
146 H9 **Xorazm Viloyati** *Rus.* Khorezmskaya Oblast'. ◈ *province* W Uzbekistan
159 N9 **Xorkol** Xinjiang Uygur Zizhiqu, NW China
147 P11 **Xovos** *var.* Ursat'yevskaya, *Rus.* Khavast. Sirdaryo Viloyati, E Uzbekistan
41 X14 **Xpujil** Quintana Roo, E Mexico
161 Q8 **Xuancheng** *var.* Xuanzhou. Anhui, E China
167 T9 **Xuân Đuc** Quang Binh, C Vietnam
160 L9 **Xuan'en** *var.* Zhushan. Hubei, C China
160 K8 **Xuanhan** Sichuan, C China
161 O2 **Xuanhua** Hebei, E China
161 P4 **Xuanhui He** ≈ E China
Xuanzhou *see* Xuancheng
161 N7 **Xuchang** Henan, C China
137 X10 **Xudat** *Rus.* Khudat. NE Azerbaijan
81 M16 **Xuddur** *var.* Hudur, *It.* Oddur. Bakool, SW Somalia
80 O13 **Xudun** Nugaal, N Somalia
160 L11 **Xuefeng Shan** ⛰ S China
Xulun Hobot Qagan *see* Qagan Nur
42 F2 **Xunantunich** *ruins* Cayo, W Belize
163 W6 **Xun He** ≈ NE China
160 L7 **Xun He** ≈ C China
160 L14 **Xun Jiang** ≈ S China
163 W5 **Xunke** *var.* Qike. Heilongjiang, NE China
161 P13 **Xunwu** *var.* Changning. Jiangxi, S China
161 O3 **Xushui** Hebei, E China
160 L16 **Xuwen** Guangdong, S China
160 I11 **Xuyong** *var.* Yongning. Sichuan, C China
161 P6 **Xuzhou** *var.* Hsu-chou, Suchow, Tongshan; *prev.* T'ung-shan. Jiangsu, E China
114 K13 **Xylaganí** *var.* Xilaganí. Anatolikí Makedonía kai Thráki, NE Greece
115 F19 **Xylókastro** *var.* Xilokastro. Pelopónnisos, S Greece

Y

160 H9 **Ya'an** *var.* Yaan. Sichuan, C China
182 L10 **Yaapeet** Victoria, SE Australia
79 D15 **Yabassi** Littoral, W Cameroon
81 J15 **Yabēlo** Oromo, C Ethiopia
114 H9 **Yablanitsa** Lovech Oblast, W Bulgaria
43 N7 **Yablis** Región Autónoma Atlántico Norte, NE Nicaragua
123 O14 **Yablonovyy Khrebet** ⛰ S Russian Federation
162 J14 **Yabrai Shan** ⛰ NE China
45 U6 **Yabucoa** E Puerto Rico
160 J11 **Yachi He** ≈ S China
32 H10 **Yacolt** Washington, NW USA
54 M10 **Yacuaray** Amazonas, S Venezuela
57 M22 **Yacuiba** Tarija, S Bolivia
57 K16 **Yacuma, Río** ≈ C Bolivia
155 H16 **Yādgīr** Karnātaka, C India
21 R8 **Yadkin River** ≈ North Carolina, SE USA
21 R9 **Yadkinville** North Carolina, SE USA
127 P3 **Yadrin** Chuvashskaya Respublika, W Russian Federation
165 O16 **Yaeyama-shotō** *var.* Yaegama-shotō. *island group* SW Japan
75 O8 **Yafran** NW Libya
165 S2 **Yagashiri-tō** *island* NE Japan
65 H21 **Yaghan Basin** *undersea feature* SE Pacific Ocean
123 S9 **Yagodnoye** Magadanskaya Oblast', E Russian Federation
Yagotin *see* Yahotyn
78 G12 **Yagoua** Extrême-Nord, NE Cameroon
159 Q11 **Yagradagzê Shan** ▲ C China
Yaguachi *see* Yaguachi Nuevo
56 B7 **Yaguachi Nuevo** *var.* Yaguachi. Guayas, W Ecuador
Yaguarón, Río *see* Jaguarão, Rio
117 Q11 **Yahorlyts'kyy Lyman** *bay* S Ukraine
117 Q5 **Yahotyn** *Rus.* Yagotin. Kyyivs'ka Oblast', N Ukraine
40 L12 **Yahualica** Jalisco, SW Mexico
79 L17 **Yahuma** Orientale, N Dem. Rep. Congo
136 K15 **Yahyalı** Kayseri, C Turkey
167 N15 **Yai, Khao** ▲ SW Thailand
164 M14 **Yaizu** Shizuoka, Honshū, S Japan
160 G9 **Yajiang** *var.* Hekou, *Tib.* Nyagquka. Sichuan, C China
119 O14 **Yakawlyevichi** *Rus.* Yakovlevichi. Vitsyebskaya Voblasts', NE Belarus
163 S6 **Yakeshi** Nei Mongol Zizhiqu, N China
32 I9 **Yakima** Washington, NW USA
32 J10 **Yakima River** ≈ Washington, NW USA
114 G7 **Yakimovo** Montana, NW Bulgaria
Yakkabag *see* Yakkabog'
147 N12 **Yakkabog'** *Rus.* Yakkabag. Qashqadaryo Viloyati, S Uzbekistan
148 L12 **Yakmach** Baluchistān, SW Pakistan
77 O12 **Yako** W Burkina
39 W13 **Yakobi Island** *island* Alexander Archipelago, Alaska, USA
79 K16 **Yakoma** Equateur, N Dem. Rep. Congo
114 H11 **Yakoruda** Blagoevgrad, SW Bulgaria
Yakovlevichi *see* Yakawlyevichi
127 T2 **Yakshur-Bod'ya** Udmurtskaya Respublika, NW Russian Federation
165 Q5 **Yakumo** Hokkaidō, NE Japan
164 B17 **Yaku-shima** *island* Nansei-shotō, SW Japan
39 V12 **Yakutat** Alaska, USA
39 U12 **Yakutat Bay** *inlet* Alaska, USA
Yakutia/Yakutiya/Yakutiya, Respublika *see* Sakha (Yakutiya), Respublika
123 Q10 **Yakutsk** Respublika Sakha (Yakutiya), NE Russian Federation
167 O17 **Yala** Yala, SW Thailand
182 D6 **Yalata** South Australia
31 S9 **Yale** Michigan, N USA
180 I11 **Yalgoo** Western Australia
114 O12 **Yalıköy** İstanbul, NW Turkey
79 L14 **Yalinga** Haute-Kotto, C Central African Republic
119 M17 **Yalizava** *Rus.* Yelizovo. Mahilyowskaya Voblasts', E Belarus
44 L13 **Yallahs Hill** ▲ E Jamaica
22 L3 **Yalobusha River** ≈ Mississippi, S USA
79 H15 **Yaloké** Ombella-Mpoko, W Central African Republic
160 E7 **Yalong Jiang** ≈ C China
136 E11 **Yalova** Yalova, NW Turkey
136 E11 **Yalova** ◈ *province* NW Turkey
Yaloveny *see* Ialoveni
Yalpug *see* Ialpug
Yalpug, Ozero *see* Yalpuh, Ozero
117 N12 **Yalpuh, Ozero** *Rus.* Ozero Yalpug. ◎ SW Ukraine
117 T14 **Yalta** Respublika Krym, S Ukraine
163 W12 **Yalu** *Chin.* Yalu Jiang, *Jap.* Oryokko, *Kor.* Amnok-kang. ≈ China/North Korea
Yalu Jiang *see* Yalu
136 F14 **Yalvaç** Isparta, SW Turkey
165 R9 **Yamada** Iwate, Honshū, C Japan
165 D14 **Yamaga** Kumamoto, Kyūshū, SW Japan
165 P10 **Yamagata** Yamagata, Honshū, C Japan
165 P9 **Yamagata** *off.* Yamagata-ken. ◈ *prefecture* Honshū, C Japan
164 C16 **Yamagawa** Kagoshima, Kyūshū, SW Japan
164 E13 **Yamaguchi** *var.* Yamaguti. Yamaguchi, Honshū, SW Japan
164 E13 **Yamaguchi** *off.* Yamaguchi-ken, *var.* Yamaguti. ◈ *prefecture* Honshū, SW Japan
Yamaguti *see* Yamaguchi
123 X5 **Yamalo-Nenetskiy Avtonomnyy Okrug** ◈ *autonomous district* N Russian Federation
122 J7 **Yamal, Poluostrov** *peninsula* N Russian Federation
165 N13 **Yamanashi** *off.* Yamanashi-ken, *var.* Yamanasi. ◈ *prefecture* Honshū, S Japan
Yamanasi *see* Yamanashi
Yamaniyah, Al Jumhūrīyah al *see* Yemen
127 W5 **Yamantau** ▲ W Russian Federation
Yamasaki *see* Yamazaki
15 P12 **Yamaska** ≈ Québec, SE Canada
192 G4 **Yamato Ridge** *undersea feature* S Sea of Japan
164 I13 **Yamazaki** *var.* Yamasaki. Hyōgo, Honshū, SW Japan
183 V5 **Yamba** New South Wales, SE Australia
81 D16 **Yambio** *var.* Yambiyo. Western Equatoria, S Sudan
Yambiyo *see* Yambio
114 L10 **Yambol** *Turk.* Yanboli. Yambol, E Bulgaria
114 M11 **Yambol** ◈ *province* E Bulgaria
79 M17 **Yambuya** Orientale, N Dem. Rep. Congo
171 T15 **Yamdena, Pulau** *prev.* Jamdena. *island* Kepulauan Tanimbar, E Indonesia
165 O14 **Yame** Fukuoka, Kyūshū, SW Japan
166 M6 **Yamethin** Mandalay, C Burma
186 C6 **Yaminbot** East Sepik, NW PNG
181 U9 **Yamma Yamma, Lake** ◎ Queensland, C Australia
76 M16 **Yamoussoukro** ● (Ivory Coast) C Ivory Coast
37 P3 **Yampa River** ≈ Colorado, C USA
117 S2 **Yampil'** Sums'ka Oblast', NE Ukraine
116 M8 **Yampil'** Vinnyts'ka Oblast', C Ukraine
123 T9 **Yamsk** Magadanskaya Oblast', E Russian Federation
152 J8 **Yamuna** *prev.* Jumna. ≈ N India
152 I9 **Yamunānagar** Haryāna, N India
Yamundá *see* Nhamundá, Rio
145 U8 **Yamyshevo** Pavlodar, NE Kazakhstan
159 N16 **Yamzho Yumco** ◎ W China
123 Q8 **Yana** ≈ NE Russian Federation
186 H9 **Yanaba Island** *island* SE PNG
155 L16 **Yanam** *var.* Yanaon. Pondicherry, E India
160 L5 **Yan'an** *var.* Yanan. Shaanxi, C China
Yanaon *see* Yanam
127 U3 **Yanaul** Respublika Bashkortostan, W Russian Federation
118 O12 **Yanavichy** *Rus.* Yanovichi. Vitsyebskaya Voblasts', NE Belarus
Yanboli *see* Yambol
140 K8 **Yanbu' al Baḥr** Al Madīnah, W Saudi Arabia
21 T8 **Yanceyville** North Carolina, SE USA
161 R7 **Yancheng** Jiangsu, E China
159 W8 **Yanchi** Ningxia, N China
160 L5 **Yanchuan** Shaanxi, C China
183 O10 **Yanco Creek** *seasonal river* New South Wales, SE Australia
183 O6 **Yanda Creek** *seasonal river* New South Wales, SE Australia

◆ COUNTRY ● COUNTRY CAPITAL ◇ DEPENDENT TERRITORY ○ DEPENDENT TERRITORY CAPITAL ◈ ADMINISTRATIVE REGION ✕ INTERNATIONAL AIRPORT ▲ MOUNTAIN ⛰ MOUNTAIN RANGE ⩰ VOLCANO ≈ RIVER ◎ LAKE ⊟ RESERVOIR

182 K4 **Yandama Creek** *seasonal river* New South Wales/South Australia
161 S11 **Yandang Shan** ▲ SE China
Yandua see Yadua
159 O6 **Yandun** Xinjiang Uygur Zizhiqu, W China
76 L13 **Yanfolila** Sikasso, SW Mali
79 M18 **Yangambi** Orientale, N Dem. Rep. Congo
158 M15 **Yangbajain** Xizang Zizhiqu, W China
Yangchow see Yangzhou
160 M15 **Yangchun** Guangdong, S China
161 N2 **Yanggao** Shanxi, C China
Yanggeta see Yaqeta
Yangiabad see Yangiobod
Yangibazar see Dzhany-Bazar, Kyrgyzstan
Yangi-Bazar see Kofarnihon, Tajikistan
Yangiklshak see Yangiqishloq
146 M13 **Yangi-Nishon** *Rus.* Yang-Nishan. Qashqadaryo Viloyati, S Uzbekistan
147 Q9 **Yangiobod** *Rus.* Yangiabad. Toshkent Viloyati, E Uzbekistan
147 O10 **Yangiqishloq** *Rus.* Yangiklshak. Jizzax Viloyati, C Uzbekistan
147 P11 **Yangiyer** Sirdaryo Viloyati, E Uzbekistan
147 P9 **Yangiyo'l** *Rus.* Yangiyul'. Toshkent Viloyati, E Uzbekistan
160 M15 **Yangjiang** Guangdong, S China
Yangku see Taiyuan
Yang-Nishan see Yangi-Nishon
166 L8 **Yangon** *Eng.* Rangoon. ● (Burma) Yangon, S Burma
166 M8 **Yangon** *Eng.* Rangoon. ◈ *division* SW Burma
160 K17 **Yangpu Gang** *harbour* Hainan, S China
161 N4 **Yangquan** Shanxi, C China
161 N13 **Yangshan** Guangdong, S China
167 U12 **Yang Sin, Chu** ▲ S Vietnam
Yangtze see Chang Jiang/Jinsha Jiang
Yangtze Kiang see Chang Jiang
161 R7 **Yangzhou** *var.* Yangchow. Jiangsu, E China
160 L5 **Yan He** ⇝ C China
163 Y10 **Yanji** Jilin, NE China
Yanji see Longjing
Yanjing see Yanyuan
29 Q12 **Yankton** South Dakota, N USA
161 O12 **Yanling** *prev.* Lingxian, Ling Xian. Hunan, S China
Yannina see Ioánnina
123 Q7 **Yano-Indigirskaya Nizmennost'** *plain* NE Russian Federation
Yanovichi see Yanavichy
155 K24 **Yan Oya** ⇝ N Sri Lanka
158 K6 **Yanqi** *var.* Yanqi Huizu Zizhixian. Xinjiang Uygur Zizhiqu, NW China
Yanqi Huizu Zizhixian see Yanqi
161 Q10 **Yanshan** *var.* Hekou. Jiangxi, S China
160 H14 **Yanshan** *var.* Jiangna. Yunnan, SW China
161 P2 **Yan Shan** ▲ E China
163 X8 **Yanshou** Heilongjiang, NE China
123 Q7 **Yanskiy Zaliv** *bay* N Russian Federation
183 O4 **Yantabulla** New South Wales, SE Australia
161 R4 **Yantai** *var.* Yan-t'ai; *prev.* Chefoo, Chih-fu. Shandong, E China
118 A13 **Yantarnyy** *Ger.* Palmnicken. Kaliningradskaya Oblast', W Russian Federation
114 J9 **Yantra** Gabrovo, N Bulgaria
114 K9 **Yantra** ⇝ N Bulgaria
160 G11 **Yanyuan** *var.* Yanjing. Sichuan, C China
161 P5 **Yanzhou** Shandong, E China
79 E16 **Yaoundé** *var.* Yaunde. ● (Cameroon) Centre, S Cameroon
188 I14 **Yap** ◈ *state* W Micronesia
188 F16 **Yap** *island* Caroline Islands, W Micronesia
57 M18 **Yapacani, Rio** ⇝ C Bolivia
171 W14 **Yapa Kopra** Papua, E Indonesia
Yapan see Yapen, Selat
Yapanskoye More see East Sea/Japan, Sea of
77 P15 **Yapei** N Ghana
12 M10 **Yapeitso, Mont** ▲ Québec, E Canada
171 W12 **Yapen, Pulau** *prev.* Japen. *island* E Indonesia
171 W12 **Yapen, Selat** *var.* Yapan. *strait* Papua, E Indonesia
61 E15 **Yapeyú** Corrientes, NE Argentina
136 I11 **Yapraklı** Çankırı, N Turkey
192 H7 **Yap Trench** *var.* Yap Trough. *undersea feature* SE Philippine Sea
Yap Trough see Yap Trench
Yapurá see Caquetá, Rio, Brazil/Colombia
Yapurá see Japurá, Rio, Brazil/Colombia
197 I12 **Yaqaga** *island* N Fiji
197 H12 **Yaqeta** *prev.* Yanggeta. *island* Yasawa Group, NW Fiji
40 G6 **Yaqui** Sonora, NW Mexico
32 E12 **Yaquina Bay** *bay* Oregon, NW USA
40 G6 **Yaqui, Río** ⇝ NW Mexico
54 K5 **Yaracuy** *off.* Estado Yaracuy. ◈ *state* NW Venezuela
Yaradzhi see Yarajy
146 E13 **Yarajy** *Rus.* Yaradzhi. Ahal Welaýaty, C Turkmenistan
125 Q15 **Yaransk** Kirovskaya Oblast', NW Russian Federation
136 F17 **Yardımcı Burnu** *headland* SW Turkey
97 Q19 **Yare** ⇝ E England, UK
125 S9 **Yarega** Respublika Komi, NW Russian Federation
116 I7 **Yaremcha** Ivano-Frankivs'ka Oblast', W Ukraine
189 Q9 **Yaren** SW Nauru
125 Q10 **Yarensk** Arkhangel'skaya Oblast', NW Russian Federation
155 F16 **Yargatti** Karnātaka, W India
164 M12 **Yariga-take** ▲ Honshū, S Japan
141 O15 **Yarīm** W Yemen
54 F14 **Yarí, Río** ⇝ SW Colombia
54 K5 **Yaritagua** Yaracuy, N Venezuela
Yarkand see Yarkant He
Yarkant see Shache
158 E9 **Yarkant He** *var.* Yarkand. ⇝ NW China
149 U3 **Yarkhūn** ⇝ NW Pakistan
Yarlung Zangbo Jiang see Brahmaputra
116 L6 **Yarmolyntsi** Khmel'nyts'ka Oblast', W Ukraine
13 O16 **Yarmouth** Nova Scotia, SE Canada
Yarmouth see Great Yarmouth
Yaroslav see Jarosław
124 L15 **Yaroslavl'** Yaroslavskaya Oblast', W Russian Federation
124 K14 **Yaroslavskaya Oblast'** ◈ *province* W Russian Federation
123 N11 **Yaroslavskiy** Respublika Sakha (Yakutiya), NE Russian Federation
183 P13 **Yarram** Victoria, SE Australia
183 O11 **Yarrawonga** Victoria, SE Australia
182 L4 **Yarriarraburra Swamp** *wetland* New South Wales, SE Australia
122 I8 **Yar-Sale** Yamalo-Nenetskiy Avtonomnyy Okrug, N Russian Federation
122 K11 **Yartsevo** Krasnoyarskiy Kray, C Russian Federation
126 I4 **Yartsevo** Smolenskaya Oblast', W Russian Federation
54 E8 **Yarumal** Antioquia, NW Colombia
187 W14 **Yasawa Group** *island group* NW Fiji
77 V12 **Yashi** Katsina, N Nigeria
77 S14 **Yashikera** Kwara, W Nigeria
147 T14 **Yashilkŭl** *Rus.* Ozero Yashil'kul'. ⊚ SE Tajikistan
Yashil'kul', Ozero see Yashilkŭl
165 P9 **Yashima** Akita, Honshū, C Japan
127 P13 **Yashkul'** Respublika Kalmykiya, SW Russian Federation
146 F13 **Yashlyk** Ahal Welaýaty, C Turkmenistan
Yasinovataya see Yasynuvata
114 N10 **Yasna Polyana** Burgas, SE Bulgaria
167 R10 **Yasothon** Yasothon, E Thailand
183 R10 **Yass** New South Wales, SE Australia
Yassy see Iasi
164 H12 **Yasugi** Shimane, Honshū, SW Japan
143 N10 **Yāsūj** *var.* Yesuj; *prev.* Tal-e Khosravī. Kohgīlūyeh va Būyer Aḩmad, C Iran
136 M11 **Yasun Burnu** *headland* N Turkey
117 X8 **Yasynuvata** *Rus.* Yasinovataya. Donets'ka Oblast', SE Ukraine
136 C15 **Yatağan** Muğla, SW Turkey
165 Q7 **Yatate-tōge** *pass* Honshū, C Japan
187 Q17 **Yaté** Province Sud, S New Caledonia
27 P6 **Yates Center** Kansas, C USA
185 B21 **Yates Point** *headland* South Island, NZ
9 N9 **Yathkyed Lake** ⊚ Nunavut, NE Canada
171 T16 **Yatoke** Pulau Babar, E Indonesia
79 M18 **Yatolema** Orientale, N Dem. Rep. Congo
164 C15 **Yatsushiro** *var.* Yatusiro. Kumamoto, Kyūshū, SW Japan
164 C15 **Yatsushiro-kai** *bay* SW Japan
138 F11 **Yatta** *var.* Yuta. S West Bank
81 J20 **Yatta Plateau** *plateau* SE Kenya
Yatusiro see Yatsushiro
57 F17 **Yauca, Río** ⇝ SW Peru
45 S6 **Yauco** W Puerto Rico
Yaunde see Yaoundé
Yavan see Yovon
Yavarí see Javari, Rio
56 G9 **Yavari Mirim, Río** ⇝ NE Peru
40 G7 **Yavaros** Sonora, NW Mexico
154 I13 **Yavatmāl** Mahārāshtra, C India
54 M9 **Yaví, Cerro** ▲ C Venezuela
43 W16 **Yaviza** Darién, SE Panama
138 F10 **Yavne** Central, W Israel
116 H5 **Yavoriv** *Pol.* Jaworów, *Rus.* Yavorov. L'vivs'ka Oblast', NW Ukraine
Yavorov see Yavoriv
164 F14 **Yawatahama** Ehime, Shikoku, SW Japan
Ya Xian see Sanya
136 L17 **Yayladağı** Hatay, S Turkey
125 V13 **Yayva** Permskaya Oblast', NW Russian Federation
127 V12 **Yayva** ⇝ NW Russian Federation
143 Q9 **Yazd** *var.* Yezd. Yazd, C Iran
143 Q8 **Yazd** *off.* Ostān-e Yazd, *var.* Yezd. ◈ *province* C Iran
Yazgulemskiy Khrebet see Yazgulom, Qatorkŭhi
147 S13 **Yazgulom, Qatorkŭhi** *Rus.* Yazgulemskiy Khrebet. ▲ S Tajikistan
22 K5 **Yazoo City** Mississippi, S USA
22 K5 **Yazoo River** ⇝ Mississippi, S USA
127 Q5 **Yazykovo** Ul'yanovskaya Oblast', W Russian Federation
109 U4 **Ybbs** Niederösterreich, NE Austria
109 U4 **Ybbs** ⇝ C Austria
95 G22 **Yding Skovhøj** *hill* C Denmark
115 G20 **Ýdra** *var.* Ídhra, Idra. Ýdra, S Greece
115 G21 **Ýdra** *var.* Ídhra. *island* S Greece
115 G20 **Ýdras, Kólpos** *strait* S Greece
167 N10 **Ye** Mon State, S Burma
183 O12 **Yea** Victoria, SE Australia
Yebaishou see Jianping
78 I5 **Yebbi-Bou** Borkou-Ennedi-Tibesti, N Chad
158 F9 **Yecheng** *var.* Kargilik. Xinjiang Uygur Zizhiqu, NW China
105 R11 **Yecla** Murcia, SE Spain
40 H5 **Yécora** Sonora, NW Mexico
Yedintsy see Edineț
124 J13 **Yefimovskiy** Leningradskaya Oblast', NW Russian Federation
126 K6 **Yefremov** Tul'skaya Oblast', W Russian Federation
Yêgainnyin see Henan
137 U12 **Yeghegis** *Rus.* Yekhegis. ⇝ C Armenia
145 T10 **Yegindybulak** *Kaz.* Egindibulaq. Karaganda, C Kazakhstan
126 L4 **Yegor'yevsk** Moskovskaya Oblast', W Russian Federation
Yehuda, Haré see Judaean Hills
81 E15 **Yei** ⇝ S Sudan
161 P8 **Yeji** *var.* Yejiaji. Anhui, E China
Yejiaji see Yeji
122 G10 **Yekaterinburg** *prev.* Sverdlovsk. Sverdlovskaya Oblast', C Russian Federation
Yekaterinodar see Krasnodar
Yekaterinoslav see Dnipropetrovs'k
123 R13 **Yekaterinoslavka** Amurskaya Oblast', SE Russian Federation
127 O7 **Yekaterinovka** Saratovskaya Oblast', W Russian Federation
76 K16 **Yekepa** NE Liberia
127 T3 **Yelabuga** Respublika Tatarstan, W Russian Federation
Yela Island see Rossel Island
127 O8 **Yelan'** Volgogradskaya Oblast', SW Russian Federation
117 Q9 **Yelanets'** *Rus.* Yelanets. Mykolayivs'ka Oblast', S Ukraine
126 L7 **Yelets** Lipetskaya Oblast', W Russian Federation
125 W4 **Yeletskiy** Respublika Komi, NW Russian Federation
76 J11 **Yélimané** Kayes, W Mali
Yelisavetpol see Gäncä
Yelizavetgrad see Kirovohrad
123 T12 **Yelizavety, Mys** *headland* SE Russian Federation
Yelizovo see Yalizava
127 S5 **Yelkhovka** Samarskaya Oblast', W Russian Federation
96 M1 **Yell** *island* NE Scotland, UK
155 E17 **Yellāpur** Karnātaka, W India
11 U17 **Yellow Grass** Saskatchewan, S Canada
Yellowhammer State see Alabama
11 O15 **Yellowhead Pass** *pass* Alberta/British Columbia, SW Canada
8 K10 **Yellowknife** *territory capital* Northwest Territories, W Canada
8 K9 **Yellowknife** ⇝ Northwest Territories, NW Canada
23 P8 **Yellow River** ⇝ Alabama/Florida, S USA
30 I4 **Yellow River** ⇝ Wisconsin, N USA
30 J6 **Yellow River** ⇝ Wisconsin, N USA
30 K7 **Yellow River** ⇝ Wisconsin, N USA
Yellow River see Huang He
157 V8 **Yellow Sea** *Chin.* Huang Hai, *Kor.* Hwang-Hae. *sea* E Asia
33 S13 **Yellowstone Lake** ⊚ Wyoming, C USA
33 T13 **Yellowstone National Park** *national park* Wyoming, NW USA
33 Y8 **Yellowstone River** ⇝ Montana/Wyoming, NW USA
96 L1 **Yell Sound** *strait* N Scotland, UK
27 U9 **Yellville** Arkansas, C USA
122 K10 **Yeloguy** ⇝ C Russian Federation
Yëloten see Ýolöten
119 M20 **Yel'sk** *Rus.* Yel'sk. Homyel'skaya Voblasts', SE Belarus
77 T13 **Yelwa** Kebbi, W Nigeria
21 R15 **Yemassee** South Carolina, SE USA
141 O15 **Yemen** *off.* Republic of Yemen, *Ar.* Al Jumhūrīyah al Yamanīyah, Al Yaman. ◆ *republic* SW Asia
116 M4 **Yemil'chyne** Zhytomyrs'ka Oblast', N Ukraine
124 M10 **Yemtsa** Arkhangel'skaya Oblast', NW Russian Federation
126 M10 **Yemtsa** ⇝ NW Russian Federation
125 R10 **Yemva** *prev.* Zheleznodorozhnyy. Respublika Komi, NW Russian Federation
77 U17 **Yenagoa** Bayelsa, S Nigeria
117 X7 **Yenakiyeve** *Rus.* Yenakiyevo; *prev.* Ordzhonikidze, Rykovo. Donets'ka Oblast', E Ukraine
Yenakiyevo see Yenakiyeve
166 L6 **Yenangyaung** Magwe, W Burma
167 S5 **Yên Bai** Yên Bai, N Vietnam
183 P9 **Yenda** New South Wales, SE Australia
77 Q14 **Yendi** NE Ghana
Yêndum see Zhag'yab
158 E8 **Yengisar** Xinjiang Uygur Zizhiqu, NW China
121 R1 **Yenierenköy** *var.* Yialousa, *Gk.* Agialoúsa. NE Cyprus
Yenipazar see Novi Pazar
136 E12 **Yenişehir** Bursa, NW Turkey
Yenisei Bay see Yeniseyskiy Zaliv
122 K12 **Yeniseysk** Krasnoyarskiy Kray, C Russian Federation
197 W10 **Yeniseyskiy Zaliv** *var.* Yenisei Bay. *bay* N Russian Federation
127 Q12 **Yenotayevka** Astrakhanskaya Oblast', SW Russian Federation
124 L4 **Yenozero, Ozero** ⊚ NW Russian Federation
Yenping see Nanping
39 Q11 **Yentna River** ⇝ Alaska, USA
180 M10 **Yeo, Lake** *salt lake* Western Australia
183 R7 **Yeoval** New South Wales, SE Australia
97 K23 **Yeovil** SW England, UK
40 H6 **Yepachic** Chihuahua, N Mexico
181 Y8 **Yeppoon** Queensland, E Australia
126 M5 **Yerakhtur** Ryazanskaya Oblast', W Russian Federation
Yeraliyev see Kuryk
146 F12 **Yerbent** Ahal Welaýaty, C Turkmenistan
123 N11 **Yerbogachen** Irkutskaya Oblast', C Russian Federation
137 T12 **Yerevan** *Eng.* Erivan. ● (Armenia) C Armenia
137 U12 **Yerevan** ✕ C Armenia
145 R9 **Yereymentau** *var.* Jermentau, Yermentau, *Kaz.* Ereymentaū. Akmola, C Kazakhstan
127 O12 **Yergeni** *hill range* SW Russian Federation
Yeriho see Jericho
35 R6 **Yerington** Nevada, W USA
136 J13 **Yerköy** Yozgat, C Turkey
114 L13 **Yerlisu** Edirne, NW Turkey
Yermak see Aksu
145 R9 **Yermentau** *Kaz.* Ereymentaū, Jermentau. Akmola, C Kazakhstan
145 R9 **Yermentau, Gory** ▲ C Kazakhstan
125 R5 **Yermitsa** Respublika Komi, NW Russian Federation
35 V14 **Yermo** California, W USA
123 P13 **Yerofey Pavlovich** Amurskaya Oblast', SE Russian Federation
99 F15 **Yerseke** Zeeland, SW Netherlands
127 Q8 **Yershov** Saratovskaya Oblast', W Russian Federation
125 P9 **Yërtom** Respublika Komi, NW Russian Federation
56 D13 **Yerupaja, Nevado** ▲ C Peru
Yerushalayim see Jerusalem
105 R4 **Yesa, Embalse de** ⊞ NE Spain
144 F9 **Yesensay** Zapadnyy Kazakhstan, NW Kazakhstan
145 V15 **Yesik** *Kaz.* Esik; *prev.* Issyk. Almaty, SE Kazakhstan
145 O8 **Yesil'** *Kaz.* Esil. Akmola, C Kazakhstan
136 K15 **Yeşilhisar** Kayseri, C Turkey
136 L11 **Yeşilırmak** *anc.* Iris. ⇝ N Turkey
37 U12 **Yeso** New Mexico, SW USA
Yeso see Hokkaidō
127 N15 **Yessentuki** Stavropol'skiy Kray, SW Russian Federation
122 M9 **Yessey** Evenkiyskiy Avtonomnyy Okrug, N Russian Federation
105 P12 **Yeste** Castilla-La Mancha, C Spain
Yesuj see Yāsūj
183 T4 **Yetman** New South Wales, SE Australia
76 L4 **Yetti** *physical region* N Mauritania
166 M4 **Ye-u** Sagaing, C Burma
102 H9 **Yeu, Île d'** *island* NW France
Yevlakh see Yevlax
137 W11 **Yevlax** *Rus.* Yevlakh. C Azerbaijan
117 S13 **Yevpatoriya** Respublika Krym, S Ukraine
126 K12 **Yeya** ⇝ SW Russian Federation
158 I10 **Yeyik** Xinjiang Uygur Zizhiqu, W China
126 K12 **Yeysk** Krasnodarskiy Kray, SW Russian Federation
Yezd see Yazd
Yezerishche see Yezyaryshcha
Yezhou see Jianshi
Yezo see Hokkaidō
118 N11 **Yezyaryshcha** *Rus.* Yezerishche. Vitsyebskaya Voblasts', NE Belarus
Yialí see Gyalí
Yialousa see Yenierenköy
163 V7 **Yi'an** Heilongjiang, NE China
Yiannitsá see Giannitsá
160 I10 **Yibin** Sichuan, C China
158 K13 **Yibug Caka** ⊚ W China
160 M9 **Yichang** Hubei, C China
160 L5 **Yichuan** Shaanxi, C China
157 W3 **Yichun** Heilongjiang, NE China
163 X6 **Yichun** *var.* I-ch'un. Heilongjiang, NE China
161 O11 **Yichun** Jiangxi, S China
160 M9 **Yidu** *prev.* Zhicheng. Hubei, C China
Yidu see Qingzhou
188 C15 **Yigo** NE Guam
161 Q5 **Yi He** ⇝ E China
163 X8 **Yilan** Heilongjiang, NE China
136 C9 **Yıldız Dağları** ▲ NW Turkey
136 L13 **Yıldızeli** Sivas, N Turkey
163 U4 **Yilehuli Shan** ▲ NE China
163 S7 **Yimin He** ⇝ NE China
159 W8 **Yinchuan** *var.* Yinch'uan, Yin-ch'uan, Yinchwan. Ningxia, N China
Yinchwan see Yinchuan
Yindu He see Indus
161 N14 **Yingde** Guangdong, S China
161 O7 **Ying He** ⇝ C China
163 U13 **Yingkou** *var.* Ying-k'ou, Yingkow; *prev.* Newchwang, Niuchwang. Liaoning, NE China
Yingkow see Yingkou
161 P9 **Yingshan** *var.* Wenquan. Hubei, C China
Yingshan see Guangshui
161 Q10 **Yingtan** Jiangxi, S China
Yin-hsien see Ningbo
158 H5 **Yining** *var.* I-ning, *Uigh.* Gulja, Kuldja. Xinjiang Uygur Zizhiqu, NW China
160 K11 **Yinjiang** *var.* Yinjiang Tujiazu Miaozu Zizhixian. Guizhou, S China
Yinjiang Tujiazu Miaozu Zizhixian see Yinjiang
166 L4 **Yinmabin** Sagaing, C Burma
163 N13 **Yin Shan** ▲ N China
Yin-tu Ho see Indus
159 P15 **Yi'ong Zangbo** ⇝ W China
Yioúra see Gyáros
81 J14 **Yirga 'Alem** *It.* Irgalem. Southern, S Ethiopia
61 E19 **Yí, Río** ⇝ C Uruguay
81 E14 **Yirol** El Buhayrat, S Sudan
163 S8 **Yirshi** *var.* Yirxie. Nei Mongol Zizhiqu, N China
Yirxie see Yirshi
161 Q5 **Yishui** Shandong, E China
Yisrael/Yisra'el see Israel
Yíthion see Gýtheio
Yitiaoshan see Jingtai
163 W10 **Yitong** *var.* Yitong Manzu Zizhixian. Jilin, NE China
Yitong Manzu Zizhixian see Yitong
159 P5 **Yiwu** *var.* Aratürük. Xinjiang Uygur Zizhiqu, NW China
163 U12 **Yiwulü Shan** ▲ N China
163 T12 **Yixian** *var.* Yizhou. Liaoning, NE China
161 N10 **Yiyang** Hunan, S China
161 Q10 **Yiyang** Jiangxi, S China
161 N13 **Yizhang** Hunan, S China
Yizhou see Yixian
93 K19 **Yläne** Länsi-Suomi, W Finland
93 L14 **Yli-Ii** Oulu, C Finland
93 L14 **Ylikiiminki** Oulu, C Finland
92 N13 **Yli-Kitka** ⊚ NE Finland
93 K17 **Ylistaro** Länsi-Suomi, W Finland
92 K13 **Ylitornio** Lappi, NW Finland
93 L15 **Ylivieska** Oulu, W Finland
93 L18 **Ylöjärvi** Länsi-Suomi, W Finland
95 N17 **Yngaren** ⊚ C Sweden
25 T12 **Yoakum** Texas, SW USA
77 X13 **Yobe** ◈ *state* NE Nigeria
165 R3 **Yobetsu-dake** ✱ Hokkaidō, NE Japan
80 L11 **Yoboki** C Djibouti
22 M4 **Yockanookany River** ⇝ Mississippi, S USA
22 L2 **Yocona River** ⇝ Mississippi, S USA
171 Y15 **Yodom** Papua, E Indonesia
169 Q16 **Yogyakarta** *prev.* Djokjakarta, Jogjakarta, Jokyakarta. Jawa, C Indonesia
169 P17 **Yogyakarta** *off.* Daerah Istimewa Yogyakarta, *var.* Djokjakarta, Jogjakarta, Jokyakarta. ◈ *autonomous district* S Indonesia
165 Q3 **Yoichi** Hokkaidō, NE Japan
42 G6 **Yojoa, Lago de** ⊚ NW Honduras
79 G16 **Yokadouma** Est, SE Cameroon
Yokaiti see Yōkaichi
164 K13 **Yōkaichi** *var.* Yokaiti. Mie, Honshū, SW Japan
Yokkaiti see Yokkaichi
79 E15 **Yoko** Centre, C Cameroon
165 V15 **Yokoate-jima** *island* Nansei-shotō, SW Japan
165 R6 **Yokohama** Aomori, Honshū, C Japan
165 O14 **Yokosuka** Kanagawa, Honshū, S Japan
164 G12 **Yokota** Shimane, Honshū, SW Japan
165 Q9 **Yokote** Akita, Honshū, C Japan
77 Y14 **Yola** Adamawa, E Nigeria
79 L19 **Yolombo** Equateur, C Dem. Rep. Congo
146 J14 **Ýolöten** *Rus.* Yëloten, *prev.* Iolotan'. Mary Welaýaty, S Turkmenistan
165 Y15 **Yome-jima** *island* Ogasawara-shotō, SE Japan
76 K16 **Yomou** Guinée-Forestière, SE Guinea
171 Y15 **Yomuka** Papua, E Indonesia
188 C16 **Yona** E Guam
164 H12 **Yonago** Tottori, Honshū, SW Japan
165 N16 **Yonaguni** Okinawa, SW Japan
165 N16 **Yonaguni-jima** *island* Nansei-shotō, SW Japan
165 T16 **Yonaha-dake** ▲ Okinawa, SW Japan
163 X14 **Yonan** SW North Korea
165 P10 **Yonezawa** Yamagata, Honshū, C Japan
161 Q12 **Yong'an** *var.* Yongan. Fujian, SE China
Yong'an see Fengjie
159 T9 **Yongchang** Gansu, N China
161 P7 **Yongcheng** Henan, C China
163 Z15 **Yŏngch'ŏn** *Jap.* Eisen. SE South Korea
160 J10 **Yongchuan** Chongqing Shi, C China
159 U10 **Yongdeng** Gansu, C China
Yongding see Yongren
161 P11 **Yongfeng** *var.* Enjiang. Jiangxi, S China
158 L5 **Yongfengqu** Xinjiang Uygur Zizhiqu, W China
160 L13 **Yongfu** Guangxi Zhuangzu Zizhiqu, S China 24.57
163 X13 **Yŏnghŭng** E North Korea
159 U10 **Yongjing** Gansu, C China
Yongjing see Xifeng
163 Y15 **Yŏngju** *Jap.* Eishū. C South Korea
Yongning see Xuyong
160 E12 **Yongping** Yunnan, SW China
160 G12 **Yongren** *var.* Yongding. Yunnan, SW China
160 L10 **Yongshun** *var.* Lingxi. Hunan, S China
161 P10 **Yongxiu** *var.* Tujiabu. Jiangxi, S China
160 M12 **Yongzhou** Hunan, S China
18 K14 **Yonkers** New York, NE USA
103 Q7 **Yonne** ◈ *department* C France
103 P6 **Yonne** ⇝ C France
54 H9 **Yopal** *var.* El Yopal. Casanare, C Colombia
158 E8 **Yopurga** *var.* Yukuriawat. Xinjiang Uygur Zizhiqu, NW China
147 S11 **Yordon** *var.* Iordan, *Rus.* Jardan. Farg'ona Viloyati, E Uzbekistan
180 J12 **York** Western Australia
97 M16 **York** *anc.* Eboracum, Eburacum. N England, UK
23 N5 **York** Alabama, S USA
29 Q15 **York** Nebraska, C USA
18 G16 **York** Pennsylvania, NE USA
21 R11 **York** South Carolina, SE USA
14 J13 **York** ⇝ Ontario, SE Canada
15 X6 **York** ⇝ Québec, SE Canada
181 V1 **York, Cape** *headland* Queensland, NE Australia
182 I9 **Yorke Peninsula** *peninsula* South Australia
182 I9 **Yorketown** South Australia
19 P9 **York Harbor** Maine, NE USA
21 X6 **York River** ⇝ Virginia, NE USA
97 M16 **Yorkshire** *cultural region* N England, UK
97 L16 **Yorkshire Dales** *physical region* N England, UK
11 V16 **Yorkton** Saskatchewan, S Canada
25 T12 **Yorktown** Texas, SW USA
21 X6 **Yorktown** Virginia, NE USA
30 M11 **Yorkville** Illinois, N USA
42 I5 **Yoro** Yoro, C Honduras
42 H5 **Yoro** ◈ *department* N Honduras
165 T16 **Yoron-jima** *island* Nansei-shotō, SW Japan
77 N13 **Yorosso** Sikasso, S Mali
35 R8 **Yosemite National Park** *national park* California, W USA
127 Q3 **Yoshkar-Ola** Respublika Mariy El, W Russian Federation
Yosino Gawa see Yoshino-gawa
Yösönbulag see Altay
171 Y16 **Yos Sudarso, Pulau** *var.* Pulau Dolak, Pulau Kolepom; *prev.* Jos Sudarso. *island* E Indonesia
163 Y17 **Yŏsu** *Jap.* Reisui. S South Korea
165 R4 **Yotei-zan** ▲ Hokkaidō, NE Japan
97 D21 **Youghal** *Ir.* Eochaill. S Ireland
97 D21 **Youghal Bay** *Ir.* Cuan Eochaille. *inlet* S Ireland
18 C15 **Youghiogheny River** ⇝ Pennsylvania, NE USA
160 K14 **You Jiang** ⇝ S China
183 Q9 **Young** New South Wales, SE Australia
11 T15 **Young** Saskatchewan, S Canada
61 E18 **Young** Río Negro, W Uruguay
182 G5 **Younghusband, Lake** *salt lake* South Australia
182 J10 **Younghusband Peninsula** *peninsula* South Australia
184 Q10 **Young Nicks Head** *headland* North Island, NZ
185 D20 **Young Range** ▲ South Island, NZ
191 Q15 **Young's Rock** *island* Pitcairn Island, Pitcairn Islands
11 R16 **Youngstown** Alberta, SW Canada
31 V12 **Youngstown** Ohio, N USA
159 N9 **Youshashan** Qinghai, C China
Youth, Isle of see Juventud, Isla de la
77 N11 **Youvarou** Mopti, C Mali
160 K10 **Youyang** *var.* Zhongduo. Chongqing Shi, C China
163 Y7 **Youyi** Heilongjiang, NE China
147 P13 **Yovon** *Rus.* Yavan. SW Tajikistan
136 J13 **Yozgat** Yozgat, C Turkey
136 K13 **Yozgat** ◈ *province* C Turkey
62 O6 **Ypacaraí** *var.* Ypacaray. Central, S Paraguay
Ypacaray see Ypacaraí
62 P5 **Ypané, Río** ⇝ C Paraguay
Ypres see Ieper
114 I13 **Ypsário** *var.* Ipsario. ▲ Thásos, E Greece
31 R10 **Ypsilanti** Michigan, N USA
34 M1 **Yreka** California, W USA
Yrendagüé see General Eugenio A. Garay
186 G5 **Ysabel Channel** *channel* N PNG
14 K8 **Yser, Lac** ⊚ Québec, SE Canada
147 Y8 **Yshtyk** Issyk-Kul'skaya Oblast', E Kyrgyzstan
Yssel see IJssel
103 Q12 **Yssingeaux** Haute-Loire, C France
95 K23 **Ystad** Skåne, S Sweden
Ysyk-Köl see Balykchy, Kyrgyzstan
Ysyk-Köl see Issyk-Kul', Ozero, Kyrgyzstan
Ysyk-Köl Oblasty see Issyk-Kul'skaya Oblast'
96 L8 **Ythan** ⇝ NE Scotland, UK
Y Trallwng see Welshpool
94 C13 **Ytre Arna** Hordaland, S Norway
94 B12 **Ytre Sula** *island* S Norway
93 G17 **Ytterhogdal** Jämtland, C Sweden
Yu see Henan
Yuan Jiang see Red River
161 S13 **Yüanlin** *Jap.* Inrin. C Taiwan
161 N3 **Yuanping** Shanxi, C China
Yuanquan see Anxi
Yuanshan see Lianping
161 O11 **Yuan Shui** ⇝ S China
35 O6 **Yuba City** California, W USA
35 O6 **Yuba River** ⇝ California, W USA
80 H13 **Yubdo** Oromo, C Ethiopia
165 U3 **Yūbetsu** Hokkaidō, NE Japan
Yūbetsu-gawa see Yabetsu-gawa
126 L3 **Yubileynyy** Moskovskaya Oblast', SW Russian Federation
41 X12 **Yucatán** ◈ *state* SE Mexico
Yucatán, Canal de see Yucatan Channel
41 Y10 **Yucatan Channel** *Sp.* Canal de Yucatán. *channel* Cuba/Mexico
Yucatan Peninsula see Yucatán, Península de
41 X13 **Yucatán, Península de** *Eng.* Yucatan Peninsula. *peninsula* Guatemala/Mexico
36 I11 **Yucca** Arizona, SW USA
35 V15 **Yucca Valley** California, W USA
161 P4 **Yucheng** Shandong, E China
Yuci see Jinzhong
161 P12 **Yudu** *var.* Gongjiang. Jiangxi, C China
Yue see Guangdong
Yuecheng see Yuexi
160 M12 **Yuecheng Ling** ▲ S China
Yuegaitan see Qumarlêb
181 P7 **Yuendumu** Northern Territory, N Australia
160 H10 **Yuexi** *var.* Yuecheng. Sichuan, C China

◆ Country ● Country Capital ◇ Dependent Territory ○ Dependent Territory Capital ◈ Administrative Region ✕ International Airport ▲ Mountain ▲ Mountain Range ✱ Volcano ⇝ River ⊚ Lake ⊞ Reservoir

161 N10 **Yueyang** Hunan, S China
125 U14 **Yug** Permskaya Oblast', NW Russian Federation
127 P13 **Yug** ≈ NW Russian Federation
123 R10 **Yugorenok** Respublika Sakha (Yakutiya), NE Russian Federation
122 H9 **Yugorsk** Khanty-Mansiyskiy Avtonomnyy Okrug, C Russian Federation
122 H7 **Yugorskiy Poluostrov** *peninsula* NW Russian Federation
Yugoslavia *see* Serbia and Montenegro (Yugo.)
146 K14 **Yugo-Vostochnyye Garagumy** *prev.* Yugo-Vostochnyye Karakumy. *desert* E Turkmenistan
Yugo-Vostochnyye Karakumy *see* Yugo-Vostochnyye Garagumy
Yuhu *see* Eryuan
161 S10 **Yuhuan Dao** *island* SE China
160 L14 **Yu Jiang** ≈ S China
Yujin *see* Qianwei
123 S7 **Yukagirskoye Ploskogor'ye** *plateau* NE Russian Federation
118 L11 **Yukhavichy** *Rus.* Yukhovichi. Vitsyebskaya Voblasts', N Belarus
126 J4 **Yukhnov** Kaluzhskaya Oblast', W Russian Federation
Yukhovichi *see* Yukhavichy
79 J20 **Yuki** *var.* Yuki Kengunda. Bandundu, W Dem. Rep. Congo
Yuki Kengunda *see* Yuki
26 M10 **Yukon** Oklahoma, C USA
39 Q8 **Yukon** ≈ Canada/USA
Yukon *see* Yukon Territory
39 S7 **Yukon Flats** *salt flat* Alaska, USA
10 I5 **Yukon Territory** *var.* Yukon, *Fr.* Territoire du Yukon. ◆ *territory* NW Canada
137 T16 **Yüksekova** Hakkâri, SE Turkey
123 N10 **Yukta** Evenkiyskiy Avtonomnyy Okrug, C Russian Federation
165 O13 **Yukuhashi** *var.* Yukuhasi. Fukuoka, Kyūshū, SW Japan
Yukuhasi *see* Yukuhashi
Yukuriawat *see* Yopurga
127 O9 **Yula** ≈ NW Russian Federation
181 P8 **Yulara** Northern Territory, N Australia
127 W6 **Yuldybayevo** Respublika Bashkortostan, W Russian Federation
23 W8 **Yulee** Florida, SE USA
158 K7 **Yuli** *var.* Lopnur. Xinjiang Uygur Zizhiqu, NW China
161 T14 **Yüli** C Taiwan
160 L15 **Yulin** Guangxi Zhuangzu Zizhiqu, S China
160 L4 **Yulin** Shaanxi, C China
161 T14 **Yüli Shan** ▲ E Taiwan
160 F11 **Yulong Xueshan** ▲ SW China
36 H14 **Yuma** Arizona, SW USA
37 W3 **Yuma** Colorado, C USA
54 K5 **Yumare** Yaracuy, N Venezuela
63 G14 **Yumbel** Bío Bío, C Chile
79 N19 **Yumbi** Maniema, E Dem. Rep. Congo
159 R8 **Yumen** *var.* Laojunmiao, Yümen. Gansu, N China
159 Q7 **Yumenzhen** Gansu, N China
158 J3 **Yumin** Xinjiang Uygur Zizhiqu, NW China
Yun *see* Yunnan
136 G14 **Yunak** Konya, W Turkey
45 O8 **Yuna, Río** ≈ E Dominican Republic
38 I17 **Yunaska Island** *island* Aleutian Islands, Alaska, USA
160 M6 **Yuncheng** Shanxi, C China
161 N14 **Yunfu** Guangdong, S China
57 L18 **Yungas** *physical region* E Bolivia
Yungki *see* Jilin
Yung-ning *see* Nanning
160 I12 **Yungui Gaoyuan** *plateau* SW China
Yunjinghong *see* Jinghong
160 M15 **Yunkai Dashan** ▲ S China
Yunki *see* Jilin
160 E11 **Yun Ling** ▲ SW China
161 N9 **Yunmeng** Hubei, C China
157 N14 **Yunnan** *var.* Yun, Yunnan Sheng, Yünnan, Yun-nan. ◆ *province* SW China
Yunnan *see* Kunming
Yunnan Sheng *see* Yunnan
165 P15 **Yunomae** Kumamoto, Kyūshū, SW Japan
161 N8 **Yun Shui** ≈ C China
182 J7 **Yunta** South Australia
161 Q14 **Yunxiao** Fujian, SE China
160 K9 **Yunyang** Sichuan, C China
193 S9 **Yupanqui Basin** *undersea feature* E Pacific Ocean
Yuping Guizhou, China *see* Libo
Yuping Yunnan, China *see* Pingbian
Yuratishki *see* Yuratsishki
119 I15 **Yuratsishki** *Pol.* Juraciszki, *Rus.* Yuratishki. Hrodzyenskaya Voblasts', W Belarus
Yurev *see* Tartu
122 J12 **Yurga** Kemerovskaya Oblast', S Russian Federation
56 E10 **Yurimaguas** Loreto, N Peru
127 P3 **Yurino** Respublika Mariy El, W Russian Federation
41 N13 **Yuriria** Guanajuato, C Mexico
125 T13 **Yurla** Komi-Permyatskiy Avtonomnyy Okrug, NW Russian Federation
Yuruá, Río *see* Juruá, Rio
114 M13 **Yürük** Tekirdağ, NW Turkey
158 G10 **Yurungkax He** ≈ W China
125 Q14 **Yur'ya** *var.* Jarja. Kirovskaya Oblast', NW Russian Federation
Yur'yev *see* Tartu
125 N16 **Yur'yevets** Ivanovskaya Oblast', W Russian Federation
126 M3 **Yur'yev-Pol'skiy** Vladimirskaya Oblast', W Russian Federation
117 V7 **Yur"yivka** Dnipropetrovs'ka Oblast', E Ukraine
42 I7 **Yuscarán** El Paraíso, S Honduras
161 P12 **Yu Shan** ▲ S China
159 R13 **Yushu** *var.* Gyêgu. Qinghai, C China
127 P12 **Yusta** Respublika Kalmykiya, SW Russian Federation
124 I10 **Yustozero** Respublika Kareliya, NW Russian Federation
137 Q11 **Yusufeli** Artvin, NE Turkey
164 F14 **Yusuhara** Kōchi, Shikoku, SW Japan
125 T14 **Yus'va** Permskaya Oblast', NW Russian Federation
Yuta *see* Yatta
161 P2 **Yutian** Hebei, E China
158 H10 **Yutian** *var.* Keriya. Xinjiang Uygur Zizhiqu, NW China
62 K5 **Yuto** Jujuy, NW Argentina
62 P7 **Yuty** Caazapá, S Paraguay
160 G13 **Yuxi** Yunnan, SW China
161 O2 **Yuxian** *prev.* Yu Xian. Hebei, E China
165 Q9 **Yuzawa** Akita, Honshū, C Japan
125 N16 **Yuzha** Ivanovskaya Oblast', W Russian Federation
Yuzhno-Alichurskiy Khrebet *see* Alichuri Janubí, Qatorkŭhi
Yuzhno-Kazakhstanskaya Oblast' *see* Yuzhnyy Kazakhstan
123 T13 **Yuzhno-Sakhalinsk** *Jap.* Toyohara; *prev.* Vladimirovka. Ostrov Sakhalin, Sakhalinskaya Oblast', SE Russian Federation
127 P14 **Yuzhno-Sukhokumsk** Respublika Dagestan, SW Russian Federation
145 Z10 **Yuzhnyy Altay, Khrebet** ▲ E Kazakhstan
Yuzhnyy Bug *see* Pivdennyy Buh
145 O15 **Yuzhnyy Kazakhstan** *off.* Yuzhno-Kazakhstanskaya Oblast', *Eng.* South Kazakhstan, *Kaz.* Ongtüstik Qazaqstan Oblysy; *prev.* Chimkentskaya Oblast'. ◆ *province* S Kazakhstan
123 U10 **Yuzhnyy, Mys** *headland* E Russian Federation
127 W6 **Yuzhnyy Ural** *var.* Southern Urals. ▲ W Russian Federation
159 V10 **Yuzhong** Gansu, C China
Yuzhou *see* Chongqing
103 N5 **Yvelines** ◆ *department* N France
108 B9 **Yverdon** *var.* Yverdon-les-Bains, *Ger.* Iferten; *anc.* Eborodunum. Vaud, W Switzerland
Yverdon-les-Bains *see* Yverdon
102 M3 **Yvetot** Seine-Maritime, N France
146 H8 **Ýylanly** *Rus.* Il'yaly. Daşoguz Welaýaty, N Turkmenistan

Z

147 T12 **Zaalayskiy Khrebet** *Taj.* Qatorkŭhi Pasi Oloy. ▲ Kyrgyzstan/Tajikistan
Zaamin *see* Zomin
Zaandam *see* Zaanstad
98 I10 **Zaanstad** *prev.* Zaandam. Noord-Holland, C Netherlands
Zabadani *see* Az Zabdānī
119 L18 **Zabalatstsye** *Rus.* Zabolot'ye. Homyel'skaya Voblasts', SE Belarus
112 L9 **Žabalj** *Ger.* Josefsdorf, *Hung.* Zsablya; *prev.* Józseffalva;. Serbia, N Serbia and Montenegro (Yugo.)
Zāb aş Şaghīr, Nahraz *see* Little Zab
123 P14 **Zabaykal'sk** Chitinskaya Oblast', S Russian Federation
Zāb-e Kūchek, Rūdkhāneh-ye *see* Little Zab
Zabeln *see* Sabile
Zabéré *see* Zabré
Zabern *see* Saverne
141 O16 **Zabīd** W Yemen
141 N16 **Zabīd, Wādī** *dry watercourse* SW Yemen
Żabinka *see* Zhabinka
Ząbkowice *see* Ząbkowice Śląskie
111 G15 **Ząbkowice Śląskie** *var.* Ząbkowice, *Ger.* Frankenstein, Frankenstein in Schlesien. Dolnośląskie, SW Poland
110 P10 **Zabłudów** Podlaskie, NE Poland
112 D8 **Zabok** Krapina-Zagorje, N Croatia
143 W9 **Zābol** *var.* Shahr-i-Zabul, Zabul; *prev.* Nasratabad. Sīstān va Balūchestān, E Iran
Zābol *see* Zābul
143 W13 **Zābolī** Sīstān va Balūchestān, SE Iran
Zabolot'ye *see* Zabalatstsye
77 Q13 **Zabré** *var.* Zabéré. S Burkina
111 G17 **Zábřeh** *Ger.* Hohenstadt. Olomoucký Kraj, E Czech Republic
111 J16 **Zabrze** *Ger.* Hindenburg, Hindenburg in Oberschlesien. Śląskie, S Poland
149 O7 **Zābul** *Per.* Zābol. ◆ *province* SE Afghanistan
Zabul *see* Zābol
42 E6 **Zacapa** Zacapa, E Guatemala
42 A3 **Zacapa** *off.* Departamento de Zacapa. ◆ *department* E Guatemala
40 M14 **Zacapú** Michoacán de Ocampo, SW Mexico
41 V14 **Zacatal** Campeche, SE Mexico
40 M11 **Zacatecas** Zacatecas, C Mexico
40 L10 **Zacatecas** ◆ *state* C Mexico
42 F8 **Zacatecoluca** La Paz, S El Salvador
41 P15 **Zacatepec** Morelos, S Mexico
41 Q13 **Zacatlán** Puebla, S Mexico
144 F8 **Zachagansk** Zapadnyy Kazakhstan, NW Kazakhstan
115 D20 **Zacháro** *var.* Zaharo, Zakháro. Dytikí Ellás, S Greece
22 J8 **Zachary** Louisiana, S USA
117 U6 **Zachepylivka** Kharkivs'ka Oblast', E Ukraine
Zachist'ye *see* Zachystsye
110 E9 **Zachodnio-pomorskie** ◆ *province* NW Poland
119 L14 **Zachystsye** *Rus.* Zachist'ye. Minskaya Voblasts', NW Belarus
40 L13 **Zacoalco** *var.* Zacoalco de Torres. Jalisco, SW Mexico
Zacoalco de Torres *see* Zacoalco
41 P13 **Zacualtipán** Hidalgo, C Mexico
112 C12 **Zadar** *It.* Zara; *anc.* Iader. Zadar, W Croatia
112 C12 **Zadar** *off.* Zadarsko-Kninska Županija *prev.* Zadar-Knin. ◆ *province* SW Croatia
Zadar-Knin *see* Zadar
166 M14 **Zadetkyi Kyun** *var.* St. Matthew's Island. *island* Mergui Archipelago, S Burma
159 Q13 **Zadoi** *var.* Qapugtang. Qinghai, C China
126 L7 **Zadonsk** Lipetskaya Oblast', W Russian Federation
75 X8 **Za'farâna** E Egypt
149 W7 **Zafarwāl** Punjab, E Pakistan
121 Q1 **Zafer Burnu** *var.* Cape Andreas, Cape Apostolas Andreas, *Gk.* Akrotíri Apostólou Andréa. *headland* NE Cyprus
107 J23 **Zafferano, Capo** *headland* Sicilia, Italy, C Mediterranean Sea
114 M7 **Zafirovo** Silistra, NE Bulgaria
115 L23 **Zaforá** *island* Kykládes, Greece, Aegean Sea
104 J12 **Zafra** Extremadura, W Spain
110 E13 **Żagań** *var.* Zagań, Żegań, *Ger.* Sagan. Lubuskie, W Poland
118 F10 **Žagarė** *Pol.* Żagory. Šiauliai, N Lithuania
75 W7 **Zagazig** *var.* Az Zaqāzīq. N Egypt
74 M5 **Zaghouan** *var.* Zaghwān. NE Tunisia
Zaghwān *see* Zaghouan
115 G16 **Zagorá** Thessalía, C Greece
Zagorod'ye *see* Zaharoddzye
Żagory *see* Žagarė
Zágráb *see* Zagreb
112 E8 **Zagreb** *Ger.* Agram, *Hung.* Zágráb. ● (Croatia) Zagreb, N Croatia
112 E8 **Zagreb** *prev.* Grad Zagreb. ◆ *province* NC Croatia
142 L7 **Zāgros, Kūhhā-ye** *Eng.* Zagros Mountains. ▲ W Iran
Zagros Mountains *see* Zāgros, Kūhhā-ye
112 O12 **Žagubica** Serbia, E Serbia and Montenegro (Yugo.)
Zagunao *see* Lixian
111 L22 **Zagyva** ≈ N Hungary
Zaharo *see* Zacháro
119 G19 **Zaharoddzye** *Rus.* Zagorod'ye. *physical region* SW Belarus
143 W11 **Zāhedān** *var.* Zahidan; *prev.* Duzdab. Sīstān va Balūchestān, SE Iran
Zahidan *see* Zāhedān
Zahlah *see* Zahlé
138 H7 **Zahlé** *var.* Zaḩlah. C Lebanon
146 J14 **Zähmet** *Rus.* Zakhmet. Mary Welaýaty, C Turkmenistan
111 O20 **Záhony** Szabolcs-Szatmár-Bereg, NE Hungary
141 N13 **Zahrān** 'Asīr, S Saudi Arabia
139 R12 **Zahrat al Baṭn** *hill range* S Iraq
120 H11 **Zahrez Chergui** *var.* Zahrez Chergúi. *marsh* N Algeria
Zainhla *see* Xinjin
127 S4 **Zainsk** Respublika Tatarstan, W Russian Federation
82 A10 **Zaire** *prev.* Congo. ◆ *province* NW Angola
Zaire *see* Congo (Democratic Republic of)
Zaire *see* Congo (river)
112 P13 **Zaječar** Serbia, E Serbia and Montenegro (Yugo.)
83 L18 **Zaka** Masvingo, E Zimbabwe
122 M14 **Zakamensk** Respublika Buryatiya, S Russian Federation
116 G7 **Zakarpats'ka Oblast'** *Eng.* Transcarpathian Oblast, *Rus.* Zakarpatskaya Oblast'. ◆ *province* W Ukraine
Zakarpatskaya Oblast' *see* Zakarpats'ka Oblast'
Zakataly *see* Zaqatala
Zakháro *see* Zacháro
Zakhidnyy Buh/Zakhodni Buh *see* Bug
Zakhmet *see* Zähmet
139 Q1 **Zākhō** *var.* Zākhū. N Iraq
Zākhū *see* Zākhō
Zákinthos *see* Zákynthos
111 L18 **Zakopane** Małopolskie, S Poland
78 J12 **Zakouma** Salamat, S Chad
115 L25 **Zákros** Kríti, Greece, E Mediterranean Sea
115 C19 **Zákynthos** *var.* Zákinthos. Zákynthos, W Greece
115 C20 **Zákynthos** *var.* Zákinthos, *It.* Zante. *island* Iónioi Nísoi, Greece, C Mediterranean Sea
115 C19 **Zakýnthou, Porthmós** *strait* SW Greece
111 G24 **Zala** *off.* Zala Megye. ◆ *county* W Hungary
111 G24 **Zala** ≈ W Hungary
138 M4 **Zalābiyah** Dayr az Zawr, C Syria
111 G24 **Zalaegerszeg** Zala, W Hungary
104 K11 **Zalamea de la Serena** Extremadura, W Spain
104 J13 **Zalamea la Real** Andalucía, S Spain
163 U7 **Zalantun** *var.* Butha Qi. Nei Mongol Zizhiqu, N China
111 G23 **Zalaszentgrót** Zala, SW Hungary
Zalatna *see* Zlatna
116 G9 **Zalău** *Ger.* Waltenberg, *Hung.* Zilah; *prev. Ger.* Zillenmarkt. Sălaj, NW Romania
109 V10 **Žalec** *Ger.* Sachsenfeld. C Slovenia
117 S9 **Zalenodol's'k** Dnipropetrovs'ka Oblast', E Ukraine
110 K8 **Zalewo** *Ger.* Saalfeld. Warmińsko-Mazurskie, NE Poland
141 N9 **Ẓalim** Makkah, W Saudi Arabia
80 A11 **Zalingei** *var.* Zalinje. Western Darfur, W Sudan
Zalinje *see* Zalingei
116 K7 **Zalishchyky** Ternopil's'ka Oblast', W Ukraine
Zallah *see* Zillah
98 J13 **Zaltbommel** Gelderland, C Netherlands
124 H15 **Zaluch'ye** Novgorodskaya Oblast', NW Russian Federation
Zamak *see* Zamakh
141 Q14 **Zamakh** *var.* Zamak. N Yemen
136 K15 **Zamantı Irmağı** ≈ C Turkey
Zambesi/Zambeze *see* Zambezi
83 G14 **Zambezi** North Western, W Zambia
83 K15 **Zambezi** *var.* Zambesi, *Port.* Zambeze. ≈ S Africa
83 O15 **Zambézia** *off.* Província da Zambézia. ◆ *province* C Mozambique
83 I14 **Zambia** *off.* Republic of Zambia; *prev.* Northern Rhodesia. ♦ *republic* S Africa
171 O8 **Zamboanga** *off.* Zamboanga City. Mindanao, S Philippines
54 E5 **Zambrano** Bolívar, N Colombia
110 N10 **Zambrów** Łomża, E Poland
83 L14 **Zambué** Tete, NW Mozambique
77 T13 **Zamfara** ≈ NW Nigeria
Zamkog *see* Zamtang
56 C9 **Zamora** Zamora Chinchipe, S Ecuador
104 K6 **Zamora** Castilla-León, NW Spain
104 K5 **Zamora** ◆ *province* Castilla-León, NW Spain
Zamora *see* Barinas
56 A13 **Zamora Chinchipe** ◆ *province* S Ecuador
40 M13 **Zamora de Hidalgo** Michoacán de Ocampo, SW Mexico
111 P15 **Zamość** *Rus.* Zamoste. Lubelskie, E Poland
Zamoste *see* Zamość
160 G7 **Zamtang** *var.* Zamkog; *prev.* Gamba. Sichuan, C China
75 O8 **Zamzam, Wādī** *dry watercourse* NW Libya
79 F20 **Zanaga** La Lékoumou, S Congo
41 T16 **Zanatepec** Oaxaca, SE Mexico
105 P9 **Záncara** ≈ C Spain
Zancle *see* Messina
158 G14 **Zanda** Xizang Zizhiqu, W China
98 H10 **Zandvoort** Noord-Holland, W Netherlands
39 P8 **Zane Hills** *hill range* Alaska, USA
31 T13 **Zanesville** Ohio, N USA
Zanga *see* Hrazdan
142 L4 **Zanjān** *var.* Zenjan, Zinjan. Zanjān, NW Iran
142 L4 **Zanjān** *off.* Ostān-e Zanjān, *var.* Zenjan, Zinjan. ◆ *province* NW Iran
Zante *see* Zákynthos
81 J22 **Zanzibar** Zanzibar, E Tanzania
81 J22 **Zanzibar** ◆ *region* E Tanzania
81 J22 **Zanzibar** *Swa.* Unguja. *island* E Tanzania
81 J22 **Zanzibar Channel** *channel* E Tanzania
165 P10 **Zaō-san** ▲ Honshū, C Japan
161 N8 **Zaoyang** Hubei, C China
124 J2 **Zaozërsk** Murmanskaya Oblast', NW Russian Federation
161 Q6 **Zaozhuang** Shandong, E China
28 L4 **Zap** North Dakota, N USA
112 L13 **Zapadna Morava** *Ger.* Westliche Morava. ≈ C Serbia and Montenegro (Yugo.)
124 H16 **Zapadnaya Dvina** Tverskaya Oblast', W Russian Federation
Zapadnaya Dvina *see* Western Dvina
122 I9 **Zapadno-Sibirskaya Ravnina** *Eng.* West Siberian Plain. *plain* C Russian Federation
Zapadnyy Bug *see* Bug
144 E9 **Zapadnyy Kazakhstan** *off.* Zapadno-Kazakhstanskaya Oblast', *Eng.* West Kazakhstan, *Kaz.* Batys Qazaqstan Oblysy; *prev.* Ural'skaya Oblast'. ◆ *province* NW Kazakhstan
122 K13 **Zapadnyy Sayan** *Eng.* Western Sayans. ▲ S Russian Federation
63 H15 **Zapala** Neuquén, W Argentina
62 I4 **Zapaleri, Cerro** *var.* Cerro Sapaleri. ▲ N Chile
25 Q16 **Zapata** Texas, SW USA
44 D5 **Zapata, Península de** *peninsula* W Cuba
61 G19 **Zapicán** Lavalleja, S Uruguay
65 J19 **Zapiola Ridge** *undersea feature* SW Atlantic Ocean
65 L19 **Zapiola Seamount** *undersea feature* S Atlantic Ocean
124 I2 **Zapolyarnyy** Murmanskaya Oblast', NW Russian Federation
117 U8 **Zaporizhzhya** *Rus.* Zaporozh'ye; *prev.* Aleksandrovsk. Zaporiz'ka Oblast', SE Ukraine
Zaporizhzhya *see* Zaporiz'ka Oblast'
117 U9 **Zaporiz'ka Oblast'** *var.* Zaporizhzhya, *Rus.* Zaporozhskaya Oblast'. ◆ *province* SE Ukraine
Zaporozhskaya Oblast' *see* Zaporiz'ka Oblast'
Zaporozh'ye *see* Zaporizhzhya
40 L14 **Zapotiltic** Jalisco, SW Mexico
158 G13 **Zapug** Xizang Zizhiqu, W China
137 V10 **Zaqatala** *Rus.* Zakataly. NW Azerbaijan
159 P13 **Zaqên** Qinghai, W China
159 Q13 **Za Qu** ≈ C China
136 M13 **Zara** Sivas, C Turkey
Zara *see* Zadar
Zarafshan *see* Zarafshon
147 P12 **Zarafshon** *Rus.* Zeravshan. W Tajikistan
146 L9 **Zarafshon** *Rus.* Zarafshan. Navoiy Viloyati, N Uzbekistan
Zarafshon *see* Zeravshan
147 O12 **Zarafshon, Qatorkŭhi** *Rus.* Zeravshanskiy Khrebet, *Uzb.* Zarafshon Tizmasi. ▲ Tajikistan/Uzbekistan
Zarafshon Tizmasi *see* Zarafshon, Qatorkŭhi
54 E7 **Zaragoza** Antioquia, N Colombia
40 I5 **Zaragoza** Chihuahua, N Mexico
41 N6 **Zaragoza** Coahuila de Zaragoza, NE Mexico
41 O10 **Zaragoza** Nuevo León, NE Mexico
105 R5 **Zaragoza** *Eng.* Saragossa; *anc.* Caesaraugusta, Salduba. Aragón, NE Spain
105 R6 **Zaragoza** ◆ *province* Aragón, NE Spain
105 R5 **Zaragoza** ✕ Aragón, NE Spain
143 S10 **Zarand** Kermān, C Iran
148 J9 **Zaranj** Nīmrūz, SW Afghanistan
118 I11 **Zarasai** Utena, E Lithuania
62 N12 **Zárate** *prev.* General José F.Uriburu. Buenos Aires, E Argentina
105 Q2 **Zarautz** *var.* Zarauz. País Vasco, N Spain
Zarauz *see* Zarautz
Zaravecchia *see* Biograd na Moru
Zarāyīn *see* Zarēn
126 L4 **Zaraysk** Moskovskaya Oblast', W Russian Federation
55 N6 **Zaraza** Guárico, N Venezuela
Zarbdar *see* Zarbdor
147 P11 **Zarbdor** *Rus.* Zarbdar. Jizzax Viloyati, C Uzbekistan
142 M8 **Zard Kūh** ▲ SW Iran
124 I5 **Zarechensk** Murmanskaya Oblast', NW Russian Federation
127 P6 **Zarechnyy** Penzenskaya Oblast', W Russian Federation
149 Q7 **Zareh Sharan** Paktīkā, E Afghanistan
39 Y14 **Zarembo Island** *island* Alexander Archipelago, Alaska, USA
139 V4 **Zarēn** *var.* Zarāyīn. E Iraq
149 Q7 **Zarghūn Shahr** *var.* Katawaz. Paktīkā, SE Afghanistan
77 V13 **Zaria** Kaduna, C Nigeria
116 K2 **Zarichne** Rivnens'ka Oblast', NW Ukraine
122 J13 **Zarinsk** Altayskiy Kray, S Russian Federation
116 J12 **Zărnești** *Hung.* Zernest. Brașov, C Romania
115 J25 **Zarós** Kríti, Greece, E Mediterranean Sea
100 O9 **Zarow** ≈ NE Germany
Zarqa/Zarqā', Muḩāfaẓat az *see* Az Zarqā'
111 G20 **Záruby** ▲ W Slovakia
56 B8 **Zaruma** El Oro, SW Ecuador
110 E13 **Żary** *Ger.* Sorau, Sorau in der Niederlausitz. Lubuskie, W Poland
54 D10 **Zarzal** Valle del Cauca, W Colombia
42 I7 **Zarzalar, Cerro** ▲ S Honduras
152 I5 **Zāskār** ≈ NE India
152 I5 **Zāskār Range** ▲ NE India
119 K15 **Zaslawye** Minskaya Voblasts', C Belarus
116 K7 **Zastavna** Chernivets'ka Oblast', W Ukraine
111 B16 **Žatec** *Ger.* Saaz. Ústecký Kraj, NW Czech Republic
Zaumgarten *see* Chrzanów
Zaunguzkiye Garagumy *see* Üngüz Angyrsyndaky Garagum
25 X9 **Zavalla** Texas, SW USA
99 H18 **Zaventem** Vlaams Brabant, C Belgium
99 H18 **Zaventem** ✕ (Brussel/Bruxelles) Vlaams Brabant, C Belgium
Zavertse *see* Zawiercie
114 L7 **Zavet** Razgrad, NE Bulgaria
127 O12 **Zavetnoye** Rostovskaya Oblast', SW Russian Federation
156 M3 **Zavhan Gol** ≈ W Mongolia
112 H12 **Zavidovići** Federacija Bosna I Hercegovina, N Bosnia and Herzegovina
123 R13 **Zavitinsk** Amurskaya Oblast', SE Russian Federation
Zawia *see* Az Zāwiyah
111 K15 **Zawiercie** *Rus.* Zavertse. Śląskie, S Poland
75 P11 **Zawīlah** *var.* Zuwaylah, *It.* Zueila. C Libya
138 I4 **Zāwīyah, Jabal az** ▲ NW Syria
109 Y3 **Zaya** ≈ NE Austria
166 M8 **Zayatkyi** Pegu, C Burma
145 Y11 **Zaysan** Vostochnyy Kazakhstan, E Kazakhstan
Zaysan Köl *see* Zaysan, Ozero
145 Y11 **Zaysan, Ozero** *Kaz.* Zaysan Köl. ◎ E Kazakhstan
159 R16 **Zayü** *var.* Gyigang. Xizang Zizhiqu, W China
Zayyq *see* Ural
44 F6 **Zaza** ≈ C Cuba
116 K5 **Zbarazh** Ternopil's'ka Oblast', W Ukraine
116 J5 **Zboriv** Ternopil's'ka Oblast', W Ukraine
111 F18 **Zbraslav** Jihomoravský Kraj, SE Czech Republic
116 K6 **Zbruch** ≈ W Ukraine
Žďár *see* Žďár nad Sázavou
111 F17 **Žďár nad Sázavou** *Ger.* Saar in Mähren; *prev.* Žďár. Vysočina, C Czech Republic
116 K4 **Zdolbuniv** *Pol.* Zdolbunów, *Rus.* Zdolbunov. Rivnens'ka Oblast', NW Ukraine
Zdolbunov/Zdolbunów *see* Zdolbuniv
110 J13 **Zduńska Wola** Sieradz, C Poland
117 O4 **Zdvizh** ≈ N Ukraine
Zdzięciół *see* Dzyatlava
111 I16 **Zdzieszowice** *Ger.* Odertal. Opolskie, S Poland
Zealand *see* Sjælland
188 K6 **Zealandia Bank** *undersea feature* C Pacific Ocean
63 H20 **Zeballos, Monte** ▲ S Argentina
83 K20 **Zebediela** Limpopo, NE South Africa
113 L18 **Zebë, Mal** *var.* Mali i Zebës. ▲ NE Albania
Zebës, Mali i *see* Zebë, Mal
21 V9 **Zebulon** North Carolina, SE USA
112 K8 **Žednik** *Hung.* Bácsjózseffalva. Serbia, N Serbia and Montenegro (Yugo.)
99 C15 **Zeebrugge** West-Vlaanderen, NW Belgium
183 N16 **Zeehan** Tasmania, SE Australia
99 L14 **Zeeland** Noord-Brabant, SE Netherlands
29 N7 **Zeeland** North Dakota, N USA
99 E14 **Zeeland** ◆ *province* SW Netherlands
83 I21 **Zeerust** North-West, N South Africa
98 K10 **Zeewolde** Flevoland, C Netherlands
138 G8 **Ẕefat** *var.* Safed, Tsefat, *Ar.* Safad. Northern, N Israel
Żegań *see* Żagań
Zehden *see* Cedynia
100 O11 **Zehdenick** Brandenburg, NE Germany
Zē-i Bādīnān *see* Great Zab
Zeiden *see* Codlea
146 M14 **Zeidskoye Vodokhranilishche** ⊞ E Turkmenistan
Zē-i Kōya *see* Little Zab
181 P7 **Zeil, Mount** ▲ Northern Territory, C Australia
98 J12 **Zeist** Utrecht, C Netherlands
101 M16 **Zeitz** Sachsen-Anhalt, E Germany
159 T11 **Zêkog** *var.* Sonag. Qinghai, C China
Zelaya Norte *see* Atlántico Norte, Región Autónoma
Zelaya Sur *see* Atlántico Sur, Región Autónoma
99 F17 **Zele** Oost-Vlaanderen, NW Belgium
110 N12 **Żelechów** Lubelskie, E Poland
113 H14 **Zelena Glava** ▲ SE Bosnia and Herzegovina
113 I14 **Zelengora** ▲ S Bosnia and Herzegovina
124 I5 **Zelenoborskiy** Murmanskaya Oblast', NW Russian Federation
127 R3 **Zelenodol'sk** Respublika Tatarstan, W Russian Federation
122 L12 **Zelenogorsk** Krasnoyarskiy Kray, C Russian Federation
124 G12 **Zelenogorsk** *Fin.* Terijoki. Leningradskaya Oblast', NW Russian Federation
126 K3 **Zelenograd** Moskovskaya Oblast', W Russian Federation
118 B13 **Zelenogradsk** *Ger.* Cranz, Kranz. Kaliningradskaya Oblast', W Russian Federation
127 O15 **Zelenokumsk** Stavropol'skiy Kray, SW Russian Federation
165 X4 **Zelënyy, Ostrov** *var.* Shibotsu-jima. *island* NE Russian Federation
Železna Kapela *see* Eisenkappel
Železna Vrata *see* Demir Kapija
112 L11 **Železniki** Serbia, N Serbia and Montenegro (Yugo.)
98 N12 **Zelhem** Gelderland, E Netherlands
113 N18 **Želino** NW FYR Macedonia
113 M14 **Željin** ▲ C Serbia and Montenegro (Yugo.)
101 K17 **Zella-Mehlis** Thüringen, C Germany
109 P7 **Zell am See** *var.* Zell-am-See. Salzburg, S Austria
109 N7 **Zell am Ziller** Tirol, W Austria
Zelle *see* Celle
109 W2 **Zellerndorf** Niederösterreich, NE Austria
109 U7 **Zeltweg** Steiermark, S Austria
119 G17 **Zel'va** *Pol.* Zelwa. Hrodzyenskaya Voblasts', W Belarus
118 H13 **Želva** Vilnius, C Lithuania
Zelwa *see* Zel'va
99 E16 **Zelzate** *var.* Selzaete. Oost-Vlaanderen, NW Belgium
118 E11 **Žemaičių Aukštumas** *physical region* W Lithuania
118 C12 **Žemaičių Naumiestis** Klaipėda, SW Lithuania
Zembin *see* Zyembin
127 N6 **Zemetchino** Penzenskaya Oblast', W Russian Federation
79 M15 **Zémio** Haut-Mbomou, E Central African Republic
41 R16 **Zempoaltepec, Cerro** ▲ SE Mexico
99 G17 **Zemst** Vlaams Brabant, C Belgium
112 L11 **Zemun** Serbia, N Serbia and Montenegro (Yugo.)
Zendajan *see* Zendeh Jan
148 J5 **Zendeh Jan** *var.* Zendajan, Zindajān. Herāt, NW Afghanistan
Zengg *see* Senj
112 H12 **Zenica** Federacija Bosna I Hercegovina, C Bosnia and Herzegovina
Zenjan *see* Zanjān
Zen'kov *see* Zin'kiv
Zenshū *see* Chŏnju
Zenta *see* Senta
Zentūzi *see* Zentsūji
82 B11 **Zenza do Itombe** Cuanza Norte, NW Angola
112 H12 **Žepče** Federacija Bosna I Hercegovina, N Bosnia and Herzegovina

♦ Country ● Country Capital ◇ Dependent Territory ○ Dependent Territory Capital ◆ Administrative Region ✕ International Airport ▲ Mountain ▲ Mountain Range Volcano ≈ River ◎ Lake ⊞ Reservoir

23 W12 **Zephyrhills** Florida, SE USA
192 L9 **Zephyr Reef** *reef* Pacific Ocean
158 F9 **Zepu** *var.* Poskam. Xinjiang Uygur Zizhiqu, NW China
147 Q12 **Zeravshan** *Taj./Uzb.* Zarafshon. ≈ Tajikistan/Uzbekistan
Zeravshan *see* Zarafshon
Zeravshanskiy Khrebet *see* Zarafshon, Qatorkŭhi
101 M14 **Zerbst** Sachsen-Anhalt, E Germany
145 P8 **Zerenda** Akmola, N Kazakhstan
110 H12 **Żerków** Wielkopolskie, C Poland
108 E11 **Zermatt** Valais, SW Switzerland
Zernest *see* Zărneşti
108 J9 **Zernez** Graubünden, SE Switzerland
126 L12 **Zernograd** Rostovskaya Oblast', SW Russian Federation
Zestafoni *see* Zestap'oni
137 S9 **Zestap'oni** *Rus.* Zestafoni. C Georgia
98 H12 **Zestienhoven** ✕ (Rotterdam) Zuid-Holland, SW Netherlands
113 J16 **Zeta** ≈ SW Serbia and Montenegro (Yugo.)
8 L6 **Zeta Lake** ⊚ Victoria Island, Nunavut, N Canada
98 L12 **Zetten** Gelderland, SE Netherlands
101 M17 **Zeulenroda** Thüringen, C Germany
100 H10 **Zeven** Niedersachsen, NW Germany
98 M12 **Zevenaar** Gelderland, SE Netherlands
99 H14 **Zevenbergen** Noord-Brabant, S Netherlands
123 R13 **Zeya** ≈ SE Russian Federation
Zeya Reservoir *see* Zeyskoye Vodokhranilishche
143 T11 **Zeynalābād** Kermān, C Iran
123 R12 **Zeyskoye Vodokhranilishche** *Eng.* Zeya Reservoir. ⊡ SE Russian Federation
104 H8 **Zêzere, Rio** ≈ C Portugal
Zgerzh *see* Zgierz
138 H6 **Zgharta** N Lebanon
110 K12 **Zgierz** *Ger.* Neuhof, *Rus.* Zgerzh. Łódź, C Poland
111 E14 **Zgorzelec** *Ger.* Görlitz. Dolnośląskie, SW Poland
158 I15 **Zhabdün** Xizang Zizhiqu, W China
119 F19 **Zhabinka** *Pol.* Żabinka, *Rus.* Zhabinka. Brestskaya Voblasts', SW Belarus
Zhaggo *see* Luhuo
159 R15 **Zhag'yab** *var.* Yêndum. Xizang Zizhiqu, W China
144 L9 **Zhailma** *Kaz.* Zhayylma. Kostanay, N Kazakhstan
145 V16 **Zhalanash** Almaty, SE Kazakhstan
Zhalashash *see* Dzhalagash
145 S7 **Zhalauly, Ozero** ⊚ NE Kazakhstan
144 E9 **Zhalpaktal** *prev.* Furmanovo. Zapadnyy Kazakhstan, W Kazakhstan
119 G16 **Zhaludok** *Rus.* Zheludok. Hrodzyenskaya Voblasts', W Belarus
Zhaman-Akkol', Ozero *see* Akkol', Ozero
Zhambyl *see* Taraz
145 Q14 **Zhambyl** *off.* Zhambylskaya Oblast', *Kaz.* Zhambyl Oblysy; *prev.* Dzhambulskaya Oblast'. ◈ *province* S Kazakhstan
Zhambyl Oblysy/Zhambylskaya Oblast' *see* Zhambyl
Zhamo *see* Bomi
145 S12 **Zhamshy** ≈ C Kazakhstan
144 M15 **Zhanadar'ya** Kzylorda, S Kazakhstan
145 O15 **Zhanakorgan** *Kaz.* Zhangaqorghan. Kzylorda, S Kazakhstan
159 N16 **Zhanang** *var.* Chatang. Xizang Zizhiqu, W China
145 T12 **Zhanaortalyk** Karaganda, C Kazakhstan
144 F15 **Zhanaozen** *Kaz.* Zhangaözen, *prev.* Novyy Uzen'. Mangistau, W Kazakhstan
145 Q16 **Zhanatas** Zhambyl, S Kazakhstan
Zhangaözen *see* Zhanaozen
Zhangaqazaly *see* Ayteke Bi
Zhangaqorghan *see* Zhanakorgan
161 O2 **Zhangbei** Hebei, E China
Zhangdian *see* Zibo
Zhanggu *see* Danba
163 X9 **Zhangguangcai Ling** ▲▲ NE China
145 W10 **Zhangiztobe** Vostochnyy Kazakhstan, E Kazakhstan
159 W11 **Zhangjiachuan** Gansu, N China
160 L10 **Zhangjiajie** *var.* Dayong. Hunan, S China
161 O2 **Zhangjiakou** *var.* Changkiakow, Zhang-chia-k'ou, *Eng.* Kalgan; *prev.* Wanchuan. Hebei, E China
161 Q13 **Zhangping** Fujian, SE China
161 Q13 **Zhangpu** *var.* Sui'an. Fujian, SE China
163 U11 **Zhangwu** Liaoning, NE China
159 S8 **Zhangye** *var.* Ganzhou. Gansu, N China
161 Q13 **Zhangzhou** Fujian, SE China
163 W6 **Zhan He** ≈ NE China
Zhanibek/Zhänibek *see* Dzhanibek
160 L16 **Zhanjiang** *var.* Chanchiang, Chan-chiang, *Cant.* Tsamkong, *Fr.* Fort-Bayard. Guangdong, S China
Zhansügirov *see* Dzhansugurov
163 V8 **Zhaodong** Heilongjiang, NE China
Zhaoge *see* Qixian
160 H11 **Zhaojue** *var.* Xincheng. Sichuan, C China
161 N14 **Zhaoqing** Guangdong, S China
Zhaoren *see* Changwu
158 H5 **Zhaosu** *var.* Mongolküre. Xinjiang Uygur Zizhiqu, NW China
160 H11 **Zhaotong** Yunnan, SW China
163 V9 **Zhaoyuan** Heilongjiang, NE China
163 V9 **Zhaozhou** Heilongjiang, NE China
145 X13 **Zharbulak** Vostochnyy Kazakhstan, E Kazakhstan
158 J15 **Zhari Namco** ⊚ W China
144 I12 **Zharkamys** *Kaz.* Zharqamys. Aktyubinsk, W Kazakhstan
145 W15 **Zharkent** *prev.* Panfilov. Almaty, SE Kazakhstan
124 H17 **Zharkovskiy** Tverskaya Oblast', W Russian Federation
145 W11 **Zharma** Vostochnyy Kazakhstan, E Kazakhstan
144 F14 **Zharmysh** Mangistau, SW Kazakhstan
Zharqamys *see* Zharkamys
118 L13 **Zhary** *Rus.* Zhary. Vitsyebskaya Voblasts', N Belarus
Zhaslyk *see* Jasliq
158 J14 **Zhaxi Co** ⊚ W China
Zhayylma *see* Zhailma
Zhdanov *see* Beylǝqan, Azerbaijan
Zhdanov *see* Mariupol', Ukraine
Zhe *see* Zhejiang
161 R10 **Zhejiang** *var.* Che-chiang, Chekiang, Zhe, Zhejiang Sheng. ◈ *province* SE China
Zhejiang Sheng *see* Zhejiang
145 S7 **Zhelezinka** Pavlodar, N Kazakhstan
119 C14 **Zheleznodorozhnyy** *Ger.* Gerdauen. Kaliningradskaya Oblast', W Russian Federation
Zheleznodorozhnyy *see* Yemva
122 K12 **Zheleznogorsk** Krasnoyarskiy Kray, C Russian Federation
126 J7 **Zheleznogorsk** Kurskaya Oblast', W Russian Federation
127 N15 **Zheleznovodsk** Stavropol'skiy Kray, SW Russian Federation
Zhëltyye Vody *see* Zhovti Vody
Zheludok *see* Zhaludok
Zhem *see* Emba
160 K7 **Zhenba** Shaanxi, C China
160 I13 **Zhenfeng** Guizhou, S China
Zhengjiatun *see* Shuangliao
159 X10 **Zhengning** Gansu, N China
Zhengxiangbai Qi *see* Qagan Nur
161 N6 **Zhengzhou** *var.* Ch'eng-chou, Chengchow; *prev.* Chenghsien. Henan, C China
161 R8 **Zhenjiang** *var.* Chenkiang. Jiangsu, E China
163 U9 **Zhenlai** Jilin, NE China
160 I11 **Zhenxiong** Yunnan, SW China
160 K11 **Zhenyuan** *var.* Wuyang. Guizhou, S China
161 R11 **Zherong** *var.* Shuangcheng. Fujian, SE China
145 U15 **Zhetigen** *prev.* Nikolayevka. Almaty, SE Kazakhstan
Zhetiqara *see* Zhitikara
144 F15 **Zhetybay** Mangistau, SW Kazakhstan
145 P17 **Zhetysay** *var.* Dzhetysay. Yuzhnyy Kazakhstan, S Kazakhstan
160 M11 **Zhexi Shuiku** ⊡ C China
145 O12 **Zhezdy** Karaganda, C Kazakhstan
145 O12 **Zhezkazgan** *Kaz.* Zhezqazghan; *prev.* Dzhezkazgan. Karaganda, C Kazakhstan
Zhezqazghan *see* Zhezkazgan
Zhicheng *see* Yidu
Zhidachov *see* Zhydachiv
159 Q12 **Zhidoi** *var.* Gyaijêpozhanggê. Qinghai, C China
122 M13 **Zhigalovo** Irkutskaya Oblast', S Russian Federation
127 R6 **Zhigulevsk** Samarskaya Oblast', W Russian Federation
118 D13 **Zhilino** *Ger.* Schillen. Kaliningradskaya Oblast', W Russian Federation
Zhiloy, Ostrov *see* Çiloy Adası
127 O8 **Zhirnovsk** Volgogradskaya Oblast', SW Russian Federation
Zhitarovo *see* Vetren
144 L8 **Zhitikara** *Kaz.* Zhetiqara. *prev.* Dzhetygara, NW Kazakhstan
Zhitkovichi *see* Zhytkavichy
127 P10 **Zhitkur** Volgogradskaya Oblast', SW Russian Federation
Zhitomir *see* Zhytomyr
Zhitomirskaya Oblast' *see* Zhytomyrs'ka Oblast'
126 J5 **Zhizdra** Kaluzhskaya Oblast', W Russian Federation
119 N18 **Zhlobin** Homyel'skaya Voblasts', SE Belarus
Zhmerinka *see* Zhmerynka
116 M7 **Zhmerynka** *Rus.* Zhmerinka. Vinnyts'ka Oblast', C Ukraine
149 R9 **Zhob** *var.* Fort Sandeman. Baluchistān, SW Pakistan
149 R8 **Zhob** ≈ C Pakistan
Zhodino *see* Zhodzina
119 L15 **Zhodzina** *Rus.* Zhodino. Minskaya Voblasts', C Belarus
123 Q5 **Zhokhova, Ostrov** *island* Novosibirskiye Ostrova, NE Russian Federation
Zholkev/Zholkva *see* Zhovkva
Zholsaly *see* Dzhusaly
Zhondor *see* Jondor
158 I15 **Zhongba** *var.* Tuoji. Xizang Zizhiqu, W China
160 F11 **Zhongdian** Yunnan, SW China
Zhongduo *see* Youyang
Zhonghe *see* Xiushan
Zhonghua Renmin Gongheguo *see* China
159 V9 **Zhongning** Ningxia, N China
Zhongping *see* Huize
161 N15 **Zhongshan** Guangdong, S China
195 X7 **Zhongshan** *Chinese research station* Antarctica
160 M6 **Zhongtiao Shan** ▲▲ C China
159 V9 **Zhongwei** Ningxia, N China
160 K9 **Zhongxian** *var.* Zhong Xian, Zhongzhou. Chongqing Shi, C China
161 N9 **Zhongxiang** Hubei, C China
Zhongzhou *see* Zhongxian
161 O7 **Zhoukou** *var.* Zhoukouzhen. Henan, C China
Zhoukouzhen *see* Zhoukou
161 S9 **Zhoushan** Zhejiang, S China
161 S9 **Zhoushan Qundao** *Eng.* Zhoushan Islands. *island group* SE China
116 I5 **Zhovkva** *Pol.* Żółkiew, *Rus.* Zholkev, Zholkva; *prev.* Nesterov. L'vivs'ka Oblast', NW Ukraine
117 S7 **Zhovti Vody** *Rus.* Zhëltyye Vody. Dnipropetrovs'ka Oblast', E Ukraine
117 Q10 **Zhovtneve** *Rus.* Zhovtnevoye. Mykolayivs'ka Oblast', S Ukraine
Zhovtnevoye *see* Zhovtneve
114 K9 **Zhrebchevo, Yazovir** ⊡ C Bulgaria
163 V13 **Zhuanghe** Liaoning, NE China
159 W11 **Zhuanglang** *var.* Shuiluocheng. Gansu, C China
145 P15 **Zhuantobe** *Kaz.* Zhūantöbe. Yuzhnyy Kazakhstan, S Kazakhstan
161 Q5 **Zhucheng** Shandong, E China
159 V12 **Zhugqu** Gansu, C China
161 N15 **Zhuhai** Guangdong, S China
Zhuizishan *see* Weichang
Zhuji *see* Shangqiu
125 I5 **Zhukovka** Bryanskaya Oblast', W Russian Federation
161 N7 **Zhumadian** Henan, C China
161 O3 **Zhuozhou** *prev.* Zhuo Xian. Hebei, E China
152 L14 **Zhuozi Shan** ▲ N China
Zhuravichi *see* Zhuravichy
119 O17 **Zhuravichy** *Rus.* Zhuravichi. Homyel'skaya Voblasts', SE Belarus
145 Q8 **Zhuravlevka** Akmola, N Kazakhstan
117 Q4 **Zhurivka** Kyyivs'ka Oblast', N Ukraine
144 J11 **Zhuryn** Aktyubinsk, W Kazakhstan
145 T15 **Zhusandala, Step'** *grassland* SE Kazakhstan
160 L8 **Zhushan** Hubei, C China
Zhushan *see* Xuan'en
Zhuyang *see* Dazhu
161 N11 **Zhuzhou** Hunan, S China
116 I6 **Zhydachiv** *Pol.* Żydaczów, *Rus.* Zhidachov. L'vivs'ka Oblast', NW Ukraine
144 G9 **Zhympity** *prev.* Dzhambeyty. Zapadnyy Kazakhstan, W Kazakhstan
119 K19 **Zhytkavichy** *Rus.* Zhitkovichi. Homyel'skaya Voblasts', SE Belarus
117 N4 **Zhytomyr** *Rus.* Zhitomir. Zhytomyrs'ka Oblast', NW Ukraine
Zhytomyr *see* Zhytomyrs'ka Oblast'
116 M4 **Zhytomyrs'ka Oblast'** *var.* Zhytomyr, *Rus.* Zhitomirskaya Oblast'. ◈ *province* N Ukraine
153 U15 **Zia** ✕ (Dhaka) Dhaka, C Bangladesh
111 J20 **Žiar nad Hronom** *var.* Svätý Kríž nad Hronom, *Ger.* Heiligenkreuz, *Hung.* Garamszentkereszt. Banskobystrický Kraj, C Slovakia
161 Q4 **Zibo** *var.* Zhangdian. Shandong, E China
160 L4 **Zichang** *prev.* Wayaobu. Shaanxi, C China
Zichenau *see* Ciechanów
111 G15 **Ziębice** *Ger.* Münsterberg in Schlesien. Dolnośląskie, SW Poland
Ziebingen *see* Cybinka
Ziegenhais *see* Głuchołazy
110 E12 **Zielona Góra** *Ger.* Grünberg, Grünberg in Schlesien, Grüneberg. Lubuskie, W Poland
99 F14 **Zierikzee** Zeeland, SW Netherlands
160 I10 **Zigong** *var.* Tzekung. Sichuan, C China
76 G12 **Ziguinchor** SW Senegal
41 N16 **Zihuatanejo** Guerrero, S Mexico
Ziketan *see* Xinghai
Zilah *see* Zalău
127 W7 **Zilair** Respublika Bashkortostan, W Russian Federation
136 L12 **Zile** Tokat, N Turkey
111 J18 **Žilina** *Ger.* Sillein, *Hung.* Zsolna. Žilinský Kraj, N Slovakia
111 J19 **Žilinský Kraj** ◈ *region* N Slovakia
75 Q9 **Zillah** *var.* Zallah. C Libya
Zillenmarkt *see* Zalău
109 N7 **Ziller** ≈ W Austria
Zillertal Alps *see* Zillertaler Alpen
109 N8 **Zillertaler Alpen** *Eng.* Zillertal Alps, *It.* Alpi Aurine. ▲▲ Austria/Italy
118 K10 **Zilupe** *Ger.* Rosenhof. Ludza, E Latvia
41 O13 **Zimapán** Hidalgo, C Mexico
83 I16 **Zimba** Southern, S Zambia
83 J17 **Zimbabwe** *off.* Republic of Zimbabwe; *prev.* Rhodesia. ◆ *republic* S Africa
116 H10 **Zimbor** *Hung.* Magyarzsombor. Sălaj, NW Romania
Zimmerbude *see* Svetlyy
116 J15 **Zimnicea** Teleorman, S Romania
114 L9 **Zimnitsa** Yambol, E Bulgaria
127 N12 **Zimovniki** Rostovskaya Oblast', SW Russian Federation
Zindajān *see* Zendeh Jan
77 V12 **Zinder** Zinder, S Niger
77 W11 **Zinder** ◈ *department* S Niger
77 P12 **Ziniaré** C Burkina
Zinjan *see* Zanjān
141 P16 **Zinjibār** SW Yemen
117 T4 **Zin'kiv** *var.* Zen'kov. Poltavs'ka Oblast', NE Ukraine
Zinov'yevsk *see* Kirovohrad
Zintenhof *see* Sindi
31 N10 **Zion** Illinois, N USA
54 F10 **Zipaquirá** Cundinamarca, C Colombia
Zipser Neudorf *see* Spišská Nová Ves
111 H23 **Zirc** Veszprém, W Hungary
113 D14 **Žirje** *It.* Zuri. *island* S Croatia
Zirknitz *see* Cerknica
108 M7 **Zirl** Tirol, W Austria
101 K20 **Zirndorf** Bayern, SE Germany
160 M11 **Zi Shui** ≈ C China
109 Y3 **Zistersdorf** Niederösterreich, NE Austria
41 O14 **Zitácuaro** Michoacán de Ocampo, SW Mexico
Zito *see* Lhorong
101 Q16 **Zittau** Sachsen, E Germany
112 I12 **Živinice** Federacija Bosna I Hercegovina, E Bosnia and Herzegovina
Ziwa Magharibi *see* Kagera
81 J14 **Ziway Hāyk'** ⊚ C Ethiopia
161 N12 **Zixing** Hunan, S China
127 W7 **Ziyanchurino** Orenburgskaya Oblast', W Russian Federation
160 K8 **Ziyang** Shaanxi, C China
Zizhixian *see* Taxkorgan
111 I20 **Zlaté Moravce** *Hung.* Aranyosmarót. Nitriansky Kraj, SW Slovakia
112 K13 **Zlatibor** ▲▲ W Serbia and Montenegro (Yugo.)
114 L9 **Zlati Voyvoda** Sliven, E Bulgaria
116 G11 **Zlatna** *Ger.* Kleinschlatten, *Hung.* Zalatna; *prev. Ger.* Goldmarkt. Alba, C Romania
114 I8 **Zlatna Panega** Lovech, N Bulgaria
114 N8 **Zlatni Pyasŭtsi** Dobrich, NE Bulgaria
122 F11 **Zlatoust** Chelyabinskaya Oblast', C Russian Federation
111 M19 **Zlatý Stôl** *Ger.* Goldener Tisch, *Hung.* Aranyosasztal. ▲ C Slovakia
113 P18 **Zletovo** NE FYR Macedonia
111 H18 **Zlín** *prev.* Gottwaldov. Zlínský Kraj, SE Czech Republic
113 H19 **Zlínský Kraj** ◈ *region* E Czech Republic
75 O7 **Zlīṭan** W Libya
110 F9 **Złocieniec** *Ger.* Falkenburg in Pommern. Zachodnio-pomorskie, NW Poland
110 J13 **Złoczew** Sieradz, S Poland
Złoczów *see* Zolochiv
111 F14 **Złotoryja** *Ger.* Goldberg. Dolnośląskie, W Poland
110 G9 **Złotów** Wielkopolskie, NW Poland
110 G13 **Żmigród** *Ger.* Trachenberg. Dolnośląskie, SW Poland
126 J6 **Zmiyevka** Orlovskaya Oblast', W Russian Federation
117 V5 **Zmiyiv** Kharkivs'ka Oblast', E Ukraine
Zna *see* Tsna
Znaim *see* Znojmo
126 M7 **Znamenka** Tambovskaya Oblast', W Russian Federation
Znamenka *see* Znam"yanka
127 P11 **Znamensk** Astrakhanskaya Oblast', SW Russian Federation
119 C14 **Znamensk** *Ger.* Wehlau. Kaliningradskaya Oblast', W Russian Federation
117 R7 **Znam"yanka** *Rus.* Znamenka. Kirovohrads'ka Oblast', C Ukraine
110 H10 **Żnin** Kujawsko-pomorskie, C Poland
111 F19 **Znojmo** *Ger.* Znaim. Jihomoravský Kraj, S Czech Republic
79 N16 **Zobia** Orientale, N Dem. Rep. Congo
83 N15 **Zóbuè** Tete, NW Mozambique
98 G12 **Zoetermeer** Zuid-Holland, W Netherlands
108 E7 **Zofingen** Aargau, N Switzerland
159 R15 **Zogang** *var.* Wangda. Xizang Zizhiqu, W China
106 E7 **Zogno** Lombardia, N Italy
142 M10 **Zohreh, Rūd-e** ≈ SW Iran
160 H7 **Zoigê** *var.* Dagcagoin. Sichuan, C China
Żółkiew *see* Zhovkva
108 D8 **Zollikofen** Bern, W Switzerland
Zolochev *see* Zolochiv
117 U4 **Zolochiv** *Rus.* Zolochev. Kharkivs'ka Oblast', E Ukraine
116 J5 **Zolochiv** *Pol.* Złoczów, *Rus.* Zolochev. L'vivs'ka Oblast', W Ukraine
117 X7 **Zolote** *Rus.* Zolotoye. Luhans'ka Oblast', E Ukraine
117 Q6 **Zolotonosha** Cherkas'ka Oblast', C Ukraine
Zolotoye *see* Zolote
Zólyom *see* Zvolen
83 N15 **Zomba** Southern, S Malawi
Zombor *see* Sombor
99 D17 **Zomergem** Oost-Vlaanderen, NW Belgium
147 P11 **Zomin** *Rus.* Zaamin. Jizzax Viloyati, C Uzbekistan
79 I15 **Zongo** Equateur, N Dem. Rep. Congo
136 G10 **Zonguldak** Zonguldak, NW Turkey
136 H10 **Zonguldak** ◈ *province* NW Turkey
99 K17 **Zonhoven** Limburg, NE Belgium
142 J2 **Zonūz** Āzarbāyjān-e Khāvarī, NW Iran
103 Y16 **Zonza** Corse, France, C Mediterranean Sea
Zoppot *see* Sopot
Zorgho *see* Zorgo
77 Q13 **Zorgo** *var.* Zorgho. C Burkina
104 K10 **Zorita** Extremadura, W Spain
147 U14 **Zorkŭl** *Rus.* Ozero Zorkul'. ⊚ SE Tajikistan
Zorkul', Ozero *see* Zorkŭl
56 A8 **Zorritos** Tumbes, N Peru
111 J16 **Żory** *var.* Zory, *Ger.* Sohrau. Śląskie, S Poland
76 K15 **Zorzor** N Liberia
99 E18 **Zottegem** Oost-Vlaanderen, NW Belgium
77 R15 **Zou** ≈ S Benin
78 H6 **Zouar** Borkou-Ennedi-Tibesti, N Chad
76 J6 **Zouérat** *var.* Zouérate, Zouîrât. Tiris Zemmour, N Mauritania
Zouérate *see* Zouérat
Zoug *see* Zug
Zouîrât *see* Zouérat
76 M16 **Zoukougbeu** C Ivory Coast
98 M5 **Zoutkamp** Groningen, NE Netherlands
99 J18 **Zoutleeuw** *Fr.* Léau. Vlaams Brabant, C Belgium
112 L9 **Zrenjanin** *prev.* Petrovgrad, Veliki Bečkerek, *Ger.* Grossbetschkerek, *Hung.* Nagybecskerek. Serbia, N Serbia and Montenegro (Yugo.)
112 E10 **Zrinska Gora** ▲▲ C Croatia
Zsablya *see* Žabalj
101 N16 **Zschopau** ≈ E Germany
Zsebely *see* Jebel
Zsibó *see* Jibou
Zsil/Zsily *see* Jiu
Zsilyvajdevulkán *see* Vulcan
Zsolna *see* Žilina
Zsombolya *see* Jimbolia
Zsupanya *see* Županja
55 N7 **Zuata** Anzoátegui, NE Venezuela
105 N14 **Zubia** Andalucía, S Spain
65 P16 **Zubov Seamount** *undersea feature* E Atlantic Ocean
124 I16 **Zubtsov** Tverskaya Oblast', W Russian Federation
108 M8 **Zuckerhütl** ▲ SW Austria
Zueila *see* Zawīlah
76 M16 **Zuénoula** C Ivory Coast
105 S5 **Zuera** Aragón, NE Spain
141 V13 **Zufār** *Eng.* Dhofar. *physical region* SW Oman
108 G8 **Zug** *Fr.* Zoug. Zug, C Switzerland
108 G8 **Zug** *Fr.* Zoug. ◈ *canton* C Switzerland
137 R9 **Zugdidi** W Georgia
108 G8 **Zuger See** ⊚ NW Switzerland
101 K25 **Zugspitze** ▲ S Germany
99 E15 **Zuid-Beveland** *var.* South Beveland. *island* SW Netherlands
98 K10 **Zuidelijk-Flevoland** *polder* C Netherlands
Zuider Zee *see* IJsselmeer
98 G12 **Zuid-Holland** *Eng.* South Holland. ◈ *province* W Netherlands
98 N5 **Zuidhorn** Groningen, NE Netherlands
98 O6 **Zuidlaardermeer** ⊚ NE Netherlands
98 O6 **Zuidlaren** Drenthe, NE Netherlands
99 K14 **Zuid-Willemsvaart Kanaal** *canal* S Netherlands
98 N8 **Zuidwolde** Drenthe, NE Netherlands
Zuitai/Zuitaizi *see* Kangxian
105 O14 **Zújar** Andalucía, S Spain
104 L11 **Zújar** ≈ W Spain
104 L11 **Zújar, Embalse del** ⊡ W Spain
80 J9 **Zula** E Eritrea
54 G6 **Zulia** *off.* Estado Zulia. ◈ *state* NW Venezuela
Zullapara *see* Sinchaingbyin
Züllichau *see* Sulechów
105 P3 **Zumárraga** País Vasco, N Spain
112 D8 **Žumberačko Gorje** *var.* Gorjanči, Uskocke Planine, Žumberak, *Ger.* Uskokengebirge; *prev.* Sichelburger Gebirge. ▲ Croatia/Slovenia *see also* Gorjanci
Žumberak *see* Gorjanci/Žumberačko Gorje
194 K7 **Zumberge Coast** *coastal feature* Antarctica
Zumbo *see* Vila do Zumbo
29 W10 **Zumbro Falls** Minnesota, N USA
29 W10 **Zumbro River** ≈ Minnesota, N USA
29 W10 **Zumbrota** Minnesota, N USA
99 H15 **Zundert** Noord-Brabant, S Netherlands
77 U14 **Zungeru** Niger, C Nigeria
161 P2 **Zunhua** Hebei, E China
37 O11 **Zuni** New Mexico, SW USA
37 P11 **Zuni Mountains** ▲▲ New Mexico, SW USA
160 J11 **Zunyi** Guizhou, S China
160 J15 **Zuo Jiang** ≈ China/Vietnam
108 J9 **Zuoz** Graubünden, SE Switzerland
112 I10 **Županja** *Hung.* Zsupanya. Vukovar-Srijem, E Croatia
113 M17 **Žur** Serbia, S Serbia and Montenegro (Yugo.)
127 T2 **Zura** Udmurtskaya Respublika, NW Russian Federation
139 V8 **Zurbāṭīyah** E Iraq
Zuri *see* Žirje
108 F7 **Zürich** *Eng./Fr.* Zurich, *It.* Zurigo. Zürich, N Switzerland
108 G6 **Zürich** *Eng./Fr.* Zurich. ◈ *canton* N Switzerland
Zurich, Lake *see* Zürichsee
108 G7 **Zürichsee** *Eng.* Lake Zurich. ⊚ NE Switzerland
Zurigo *see* Zürich
149 V1 **Zūrkūl** *Pash.* Sarī Qūl, *Rus.* Ozero Zurkul'. ⊚ Afghanistan/Tajikistan *see also* Sarī Qūl
Zurkul', Ozero *see* Sarī Qūl/Zūrkūl
110 K10 **Żuromin** Mazowieckie, C Poland
108 J8 **Zürs** Vorarlberg, W Austria
77 T13 **Zuru** Kebbi, W Nigeria
108 F6 **Zurzach** Aargau, N Switzerland
101 J22 **Zusam** ≈ S Germany
98 M11 **Zutphen** Gelderland, E Netherlands
75 N7 **Zuwārah** NW Libya
Zuwaylah *see* Zawīlah
125 R14 **Zuyevka** Kirovskaya Oblast', NW Russian Federation
161 N10 **Zuzhou** Hunan, S China
Zvenigorodka *see* Zvenyhorodka
117 P6 **Zvenyhorodka** *Rus.* Zvenigorodka. Cherkas'ka Oblast', C Ukraine
123 N12 **Zvezdnyy** Irkutskaya Oblast', C Russian Federation
125 U14 **Zvëzdnyy** Permskaya Oblast', NW Russian Federation
83 K18 **Zvishavane** *prev.* Shabani. Matabeleland South, S Zimbabwe
111 J20 **Zvolen** *Ger.* Altsohl, *Hung.* Zólyom. Banskobystrický Kraj, C Slovakia
112 J12 **Zvornik** E Bosnia and Herzegovina
98 M5 **Zwaagwesteinde** *Fris.* De Westerein. Friesland, N Netherlands
98 H10 **Zwanenburg** Noord-Holland, C Netherlands
98 L8 **Zwarte Meer** ⊚ N Netherlands
98 M9 **Zwarte Water** ≈ N Netherlands
98 M8 **Zwartsluis** Overijssel, E Netherlands
76 L17 **Zwedru** *var.* Tchien. E Liberia
98 O8 **Zweeloo** Drenthe, NE Netherlands
101 E20 **Zweibrücken** *Fr.* Deux-Ponts; *Lat.* Bipontium. Rheinland-Pfalz, SW Germany
108 D9 **Zweisimmen** Fribourg, W Switzerland
101 M15 **Zwenkau** Sachsen, E Germany
109 V3 **Zwettl** Wien, NE Austria
109 T3 **Zwettl an der Rodl** Oberösterreich, N Austria
99 D18 **Zwevegem** West-Vlaanderen, W Belgium
101 M17 **Zwickau** Sachsen, E Germany
101 O21 **Zwiesel** Bayern, SE Germany
98 H13 **Zwijndrecht** Zuid-Holland, SW Netherlands
101 N16 **Zwikauer Mulde** ≈ E Germany
Zwischenwässern *see* Medvode
Zwittau *see* Svitavy
110 N13 **Zwoleń** Mazowieckie, SE Poland
98 M9 **Zwolle** Overijssel, E Netherlands
22 G6 **Zwolle** Louisiana, S USA
110 K12 **Żychlin** Łodzkie, C Poland
Żydaczów *see* Zhydachiv
119 L14 **Zyembin** *Rus.* Zembin. Minskaya Voblasts', C Belarus
Zyōetu *see* Jōetsu
110 L12 **Żyrardów** Mazowieckie, C Poland
123 S8 **Zyryanka** Respublika Sakha (Yakutiya), NE Russian Federation
145 Y9 **Zyryanovsk** Vostochnyy Kazakhstan, E Kazakhstan
111 J17 **Żywiec** *Ger.* Bäckermühle Schulzenmühle. Śląskie, S Poland

◆ Country ● Country Capital ◇ Dependent Territory ○ Dependent Territory Capital ◈ Administrative Region ✕ International Airport ▲ Mountain ▲▲ Mountain Range Volcano ≈ River ⊚ Lake ⊡ Reservoir

Picture Credits

PICTURE CREDITS
Dorling Kindersley would like to thank Georgina Garner for help with picture research.

Key:
t=top; b=bottom; c=centre; l=left; r=right; A=above; B=below.

i DK Images: Christopher & Sally Gable.
ii–iii Getty Images: Jeff Spielman.
xviii–1 Getty Images: Simon Wilkinson.
2–3 Corbis: Jim Craigmyle br; Jim Reed cAr; **DK Images:** Andy Holligan cBl, tcl; Francesca Yorke bl.
4–5 Alamy Images: Bryan & Cherry Alexander Photography cr; **DK Images:** Francesca Yorke cBr; Kim Sayer cl.
6–7 Corbis: Richard Berenholtz cAl; Richard Cummins br; Royalty-Free bl; **DK Images:** Topbar (8); Dave King Topbar (10); David Lyons Topbar (7); Demetrio Carrasco cAr, Topbar (3), Topbar (5); Gunter Marx Topbar (4); Linda Whitwam Topbar (6), Topbar (9); Peter Wilson Topbar (1); Scott Pitts Topbar (2).
8–9 DK Images: Barnabas Kindersley tcr; Francesca Yorke bl; Gunter Marx tl.
10–11 DK Images: Gunter Marx cl; Peter Wilson cr, tcr.
12–13 DK Images: Alan Keohane bcr, tcr; Francesca Yorke cr.
14–15 DK Images: Alan Keohane tr, tcr; Francesca Yorke tcl.
16–17 DK Images: Andy Holligan bl; Dave King tr; Demetrio Carrasco br.
18–19 Alamy Images: Pegaz tcl; DK Images: Alan Briere tr; Michael Moran cr.
20–21 DK Images: Jon Spaull bl; Kim Sayer br; Kit Houghton tcl.
22–23 DK Images: Linda Whitwam bcl, cBr; Peter Wilson cl.
24–25 Corbis: Danny Lehman tr; DK Images: Peter Wilson cl, tcl.
26–27 DK Images: Jon Spaull cl, bcl; Peter Wilson bcr.
28–29 DK Images: Jon Spaull cl, bl, tcl.
30–31 DK Images: Andrew Leyerle cl; Jon Spaull tr, bl.
32–33 DK Images: Andy Holligan tcl; Bruce Forster cl; Scott Pitts tr.
34–35 DK Images: Andrew McKinney cl; Andy Keohane bcl; Demetrio Carrasco tcl.
36–37 DK Images: Andy Keohane clB; Demetrio Carrasco crB, bl.
38–39 DK Images: tcr; Andy Holligan cr; Rob Reichenfeld cAl.
40–41 DK Images: Demetrio Carrasco cr, bcl; Linda Whitwam tr.
42–43 Corbis: Macduff Everton tcr; ML Sinibaldi bcl; Stephen Frink cr.
44–45 Corbis: Carl & Ann Purcell tr; Macduff Everton bcl; **DK Images:** Lucio Rossi tc.
46–47 Getty Images: Andy Caulfield.
48–49 Alamy Images: Sue Cunningham Photographic cr; **Corbis:** bcl; Layne Kennedy tcl; **DK Images:** Barnabas Kindersley clB; **JPG Photo:** Chris Jagger br.
50–51 Alamy Images: Eye Ubiquitous / David Cumming bcl; **Corbis:** Jeffrey L. Rotman cl; **JPG Photo:** Chris Jagger tcl.
52–53 Alamy Images: Apex News and Pictures Agency / Tim Cuff Topbar (5); ImageState / Frank Chmura br; Stock Connection / Jacques Jangoux Topbar (1); **Corbis:** Charles & Josette Lenars Topbar (4); Charles O'Rear Topbar (6); Eduardo Longoni Topbar (2); Galen Rowell Topbar (8); Jeremy Horner clA; Kevin Schafer bcl; Reuters / Bruno Domingos Topbar (9); Reuters / David Mercado Topbar (7); Reuters / Jorge Silva Topbar (10); **JPG Photo:** Chris Jagger crA, Topbar (3).
54–55 Alamy Images: Edward Parker bl; Tom Till cr; **Corbis:** Eye Ubiquitous / Laurence Fordyce tcr.
56–57 Corbis: Craig Lovell bl; Tiziana and Gianni Baldizzone crA.; **JPG Photo:** Chris Jagger br.
58–59 Corbis: Ricardo Azoury tcl; Richard T. Nowitz clB; Tom Brakefield crA.
60–61 Alamy Images: PCL bc; Stock Connection / James May clA; **JPG Photo:** Ian Powell tc.
62–63 Alamy Images: blickwinkel crB; **Corbis:** Ludovic Maisant clA; **JPG Photo:** Laurence Postgate bl.
64–65 DK Images: cl; Linda Whitwam tc.
66–67 Getty Images: Stan Osolinski.
68–69 Alamy Images: Gary Cook bl; Nature Picture Library / Bernard Castelein cl; **DK Images:** Max Alexander br; Shaen Adey tcl; **JPG Photo:** Carolyn Postgate cr.
70–71 DK Images: c, br; Cecile Treal & Jean-Michel Ruiz cl.
72–73 Corbis: Christine Osbourne Topbar (9); Dave G. Houser Topbar (8); Inge Yspeert bl; Joe McDonald crA; Jonathan Blair cl; Martin Harvey / Gallo Images Topbar (6); Patrick Ward br; Peter Johnson Topbar (10); **DK Images:** Peter Wilson Topbar (5); Angus Beare Topbar (4); Cecile Treal & Jean-Michel Ruiz Topbar (7); Christopher & Sally Gable Topbar (1); Irv Beckman Topbar (2); Shaen Adey Topbar (3).
74–75 DK Images: Alistair Duncan br; Cecile Treal & Jean-Michel Ruiz bl; Peter Wilson tcl.
76–77 Alamy Images: Adrian Arbib tr; **DK Images:** Christopher & Sally Gable tcl, tcr.
78–79 Alamy Images: Gary Cook clA; **DK Images:** Christopher & Sally Gable crA; Irv Beckman bcl.
80–81 Alamy Images: Robert Preston br; **Corbis:** Tim Davis crA; **DK Images:** Irv Beckman bl.
82–83 DK Images: br; Christopher & Sally Gable bl; Shaen Adey cA.
84–85 Alamy Images: Oliver Benn.
86–87 Alamy Images: Andre Jenny cAr; Karsten Wrobel clA; Worldwide Picture Library / John Cleare tcl; **DK Images:** Erik Svensson & Jeppe Wilkstrom bcl; Paul Harris bcr.
88–89 Alamy Images: Michelle Chaplow tcr; Pat Behnke bcr; **DK Images:** John Hesteltine tcl.
90–91 Corbis: Ashley Cooper Topbar (2); Barry Lewis cl; Bob Krist Topbar (4); Craig Aurness Topbar (10); Gideon Mendel Topbar (9); Jose Fusle Raga crA; Kevin Schafer clB; **DK Images:** Topbar (8); Barnabas Kindersley Topbar (7); Demetrio Carrasco Topbar (3); Linda Whitwam Topbar (6); Max Alexander Topbar (1); Nigel Hicks br; Rupert Horrox Topbar (5).
92–93 Alamy Images: Imagebroker / Harald Theissen cAl; **DK Images:** Demetrio Carrasco crA; Linda Whitwam bcr.
94–95 DK Images: Demetrio Carrasco br; Erik Svensson crA; Linda Whitwam tc.
96–97 DK Images: Joe Cornish bl; Paul Harris tc; Rob Reichenfeld cr.
98–99 DK Images: tc; Demetrio Carrasco br; Paul Kenward bl.
100–101 DK Images: Dorota and Marius Jarymowicz clA, crB; Pawel Wojcik tc.
102–103 DK Images: John Parker tr; Kim Sayer cl; Max Alexander tcl.
104–105 DK Images: Ella Milroy / Departure Lounge bcr; Linda Whitwam bl; Neil Lukas tr.
106–107 DK Images: Demetrio Carrasco cr; John Heseltine tr; Kim Sayer cBl.
108–109 DK Images: Kim Sayer bcr; Peter Wilson bcl; **JPG Photo:** Chris Jagger tc.
110–111 DK Images: Kit Houghton br; Peter Wilson clA; Stanislaw Michta tc.
112–113 Corbis: Otto Lang crA; Setboun bl; **DK Images:** Lucio Rossi tr.
114–115 DK Images: Peter Wilson bl; Rob Reichenfeld crB; Rupert Horrox clA.
116–117 Corbis: Catherine Karnow br; Lawrence Manning tr; Tiziana and Gianni Baldizzone cl.
118–119 DK Images: Demetrio Carrasco tr, bc; **JPG Photo:** Chris Jagger clB.
120–121 DK Images: Joe Cornish bcl; Peter Wilson bcr; Rob Reichenfeld tc.
122–123 Corbis: Joe McDonald bcl; **DK Images:** Demetrio Carrasco tcr, cr.
124–125 Corbis: Demetrio Carrasco br; Diego Lezama Orezzoli bl; **DK Images:** John Heseltine tcr.
126–127 Corbis: Dean Conger bl; **DK Images:** Demetrio Carrasco cl, br.
128–129 Alamy Images: ViewStock.
130–131 Alamy Images: Jamie Marshall cAr; Louise Murray bl; Worldwide Picture Libray / Colin Monteath tcl; **DK Images:** Barnabas Kindersley clA; Philip Blenkinsop br.
132–133 DK Images: Demetrio Carrasco cr; M. Balan cAr.
134–135 Corbis: Benjamin Rondel cl; Catherine Karnow Topbar (8); Dean Conger bcr; Free Agents Limited bcl; Galen Rowell Topbar (4); Sygma / Jacques Langevin Topbar (10); **DK Images:** Chris Stowers Topbar (3); Christopher & Sally Gable Topbar (5), Topbar (9); Dinesh Khanna Topbar (1); Kate Clow, Terry Richardson, Dominic Whiting Topbar (7); Stuart Isett cr, Topbar (2); Tim Stuart Topbar (6).
136–137 DK Images: cAl; Christopher & Sally Gable br; Francesca Yorke tcr.
138–139 DK Images: Alastair Duncan tr, br; Magnus Rew bcl.
140–141 Alamy Images: Robert Harding Picture Library tr; **JPG Photo:** Chris Jagger cl, br.
142–143 Alamy Images: Robert Harding Picture Library bcl; **Corbis:** Carl & Ann Purcell cl; **DK Images:** Christopher & Sally Gable tr.
144–145 Alamy Images: Jon Arnold Images / Gavin Hellier tcl; Michael Grant tcr; Robert Harding Picture Library bl.
146–147 Alamy Images: TNT Magazine tr; **Corbis:** David Samuel Robbins br; Janet Wishnetsky bl.
148–149 Alamy Images: Robert Harding Picture Library / Sybil Sassoon crB; **DK Images:** Christopher & Sally Gable cl, bl.
150–151 Alamy Images: Jon Arnold Images br; **DK Images:** Barnabas Kindersley bl; B.P.S. Walia crA.
152–153 DK Images: Amit Pashricha tr; Christopher & Sally Gable bl, cAr.
154–155 DK Images: Christopher & Sally Gable crA, cl, br.
156–157 Alamy Images: View Stock China br; **Corbis:** Free Agents Limited bcl; Liu Ligun cl.
158–159 Alamy Images: Marco Brivio bl; **Corbis:** Galen Rowell tr; **DK Images:** Ken Robertson br.
160–161 Alamy Images: View Stock China tcl; **Corbis:** Reuters / Bobby Yip br; **DK Images:** Chris Stowers bl.
162–163 Corbis: Jose Fuste Raga tr; Setboun bcr; **DK Images:** Barnabas Kindersley tcr.
164–165 Alamy Images: Chad Ehlers cl; **DK Images:** Demetrio Carrasco tc, cr.
166–167 DK Images: Ken Roberston tr; Michael Spencer bcl; Philip Blenkinsop cl.
168–169 Alamy Images: Bildagentur Franz Waldhaeusl / Cromorange bcl; Bruce Coleman / Tom Brakefield tcl; **DK Images:** Koes Karnadi tr.
170–171 Corbis: Paul Almasy bcl; Wolfgang Kaehler tcl; **DK Images:** Tim Stuart tr.
172–173 Alamy Images: ImageState / Pictor International bl; **Corbis:** Wolfgang Kaehler cl.
174–175 Alamy Images: SCPhotos / Dallas & John Heaton.
176–177 Alamy Images: Penny Tweedie tcr; **DK Images:** Max Alexander tcl; Ron Redfern bl.
178–179 Corbis: Adam Woolfitt bl; Craig Lovell cAr; Jack Fields Topbar (1); Massimo Mastrorillo clA; Peter Guttman Topbar (8); Theo Allofs Topbar (4); **DK Images:** Topbar (5); Alan Keohane Topbar (9); Lloyd Park br, Topbar (6); Max Alexander Topbar (7); Peter Bush Topbar (10), Topbar (3); Rob Reichenfeld Topbar (2).
180–181 DK Images: Alan Keohane bl, bcr; Max Alexander tcl.
182–183 DK Images: tcr; Max Alexander bcl, bcr.
184–185 DK Images: Gerald Lopez cAl; Lloyd Park crB; Ron Redfern cl.
186–187 Alamy Images: David Wall cr; **Corbis:** Bob Krist bcl; **DK Images:** Mark O'Shea tcr.
188–189 Alamy Images: David Fleetham bcl; Greg Vaughn cBr; Sylvia Cordaiy Photo Library Ltd / Matt Harris crA.
190–191 Alamy Images: Jan Stromme br; Mark Lewis bl; **Corbis:** Free Agents Limited tcl; Jim Zuckerman cBr.
192–193 Alamy Images: Stephen Frink Collection / James D. Watt bcr; **Corbis:** Anders Ryman tr.
194–195 Corbis: Kevin Schafer cl; Ralph A. Clevenger bcl; Wolfgang Kaehler br.
196–197 Alamy Images: Alaska Stock LLC tcl; **Corbis:** Frank Lane Picture Agency / Christiana Carvalho cl; Hubert Stadler bcl.